South Asia
2009

40°
80°
120°
160°
ARCTIC OCEAN
ARCTIC OCEAN
SVALBARD (NORWAY)
Barents Sea
Laptev Sea
East Siberian Sea
Bering Strait
SWEDEN
FINLAND
ALAND ISLANDS (FINLAND)
Helsinki
Stockholm
Tallinn
ESTONIA
Riga
LATVIA
Baltic Sea
LITHUANIA
Vilnius
Minsk
BELARUS
Moscow
RUSSIAN FEDERATION
Sea of Okhotsk
Bering Sea
Warsaw
POLAND
Prague
SLOVAKIA
Bratislava
Budapest
HUNGARY
Zagreb
ROMANIA
Bucharest
Kyiv
UKRAINE
MOLDOVA
Chişinău
SERBIA
BULGARIA
Sofia
Skopje
Tirana
ALBANIA
GREECE
Athens
MALTA
Black Sea
Astana
KAZAKHSTAN
Ulan Bator
MONGOLIA
DEMOCRATIC PEOPLE'S REPUBLIC OF KOREA
Sea of Japan
JAPAN
Tokyo
Pyongyang
Seoul
REPUBLIC OF KOREA
Beijing
GEORGIA
Tbilisi
ARMENIA
Yerevan
AZERBAIJAN
Baku
UZBEKISTAN
Tashkent
Bishkek
KYRGYZSTAN
Almaty
TURKMENISTAN
Asgabat
Dushanbe
TAJIKISTAN
Ankara
TURKEY
Nicosia
CYPRUS
SYRIA
Damascus
Beirut
LEBANON
ISRAEL
Amman
JORDAN
Baghdad
IRAQ
Tehran
IRAN
AFGHANISTAN
Kabul
Islamabad
PAKISTAN
PEOPLE'S REPUBLIC OF CHINA
East China Sea
Mediterranean Sea
Sirte
LIBYA
Cairo
EGYPT
PALESTINIAN AUTONOMOUS AREAS
Kuwait City
KUWAIT
BAHRAIN
Manama
QATAR
Doha
Riyadh
SAUDI ARABIA
UAE
Abu Dhabi
Muscat
OMAN
Red Sea
New Delhi
NEPAL
Kathmandu
Thimphu
BHUTAN
BANGLADESH
Dhaka
INDIA
Taipei
TAIWAN
Tropic of Cancer
MACAO (CHINA)
HONG KONG (CHINA)
MYANMAR
Pyinmana
Yangon
Vientiane
Hanoi
LAOS
THAILAND
VIET NAM
Bangkok
CAMBODIA
Phnom-Penh
South China Sea
Manila
PHILIPPINES
Philippine Sea
NORTHERN MARIANA ISLANDS (USA)
GUAM (USA)
PACIFIC OCEAN
CHAD
ERITREA
Asmara
Khartoum
SUDAN
San'a
YEMEN
N'Djamena
DJIBOUTI
Addis Ababa
ETHIOPIA
SOMALIA
CENTRAL AFRICAN REPUBLIC
Bay of Bengal
SRI LANKA
Colombo
Sri Jayawardenepura
MALDIVES
PALAU
MARSHALL ISLANDS
FEDERATED STATES OF MICRONESIA
NAURU
BRUNEI
Bandar Seri Begawan
MALAYSIA
Kuala Lumpur
Putrajaya
SINGAPORE
KIRIBATI
DEMOCRATIC REPUBLIC OF THE CONGO
KENYA
UGANDA
Kampala
Nairobi
RWANDA
Kigali
BURUNDI
Bujumbura
Kinshasa
Mogadishu
Victoria
SEYCHELLES
Dodoma
TANZANIA
Dar es Salaam
BRITISH INDIAN OCEAN TERRITORY (UNITED KINGDOM)
Jakarta
INDONESIA
PAPUA NEW GUINEA
Dili
TIMOR-LESTE
Port Moresby
Honiara
SOLOMON ISLANDS
TUVALU
TOKELAU (NEW ZEALAND)
CHRISTMAS ISLAND (AUSTRALIA)
ANGOLA
Lubumbashi
ZAMBIA
Lusaka
Lilongwe
MALAWI
Harare
COMOROS
Moroni
MAYOTTE (FRANCE)
INDIAN OCEAN
COCOS ISLANDS (AUSTRALIA)
Coral Sea
WALLIS AND FUTUNA ISLANDS (FRANCE)
SAMOA
VANUATU
Port Vila
FIJI
Suva
AMERICAN SAMOA (USA)
NAMIBIA
BOTSWANA
ZIMBABWE
MOZAMBIQUE
Mozambique Channel
MADAGASCAR
Antananarivo
MAURITIUS
Port Louis
RÉUNION (FRANCE)
Gaborone
Pretoria
Maputo
Mbabane
SWAZILAND
LESOTHO
Maseru
SOUTH AFRICA
AUSTRALIA
NIUE (NZ)
NEW CALEDONIA (FRANCE)
TONGA
NORFOLK ISLAND (AUSTRALIA)
Canberra
Tasman Sea
NEW ZEALAND
Wellington

# South Asia 2009

6th Edition

LONDON AND NEW YORK

**First published 2003**
**Sixth Edition 2009**


Albert House, 1–4 Singer Street, London EC2A 4BQ, United Kingdom
(Routledge is an imprint of the Taylor & Francis Group, an Informa business)



ISBN13: 978-1-85743-476-7
ISBN10: 1-85743-476-5
ISSN 1740-0147

Editor: Jillian O'Brien

Associate Editor: Meena Khan

Regional Organizations Editors: Catriona Appeatu Holman, Helen Canton

Statistics Editor: Philip McIntyre

Assistant Editors: Kim Chamberlain, Laura Davis, Adrian Reynolds, Gareth Vaughan

Contributing Editor (States and Territories of India): Gareth Wyn Jones

Contributing Editor (Commodities): Simon Chapman

Contributing Editor (Who's Who of South Asia): Robert Elster

Associate Editor, Directory Research: James Middleton

Series Editor: Joanne Maher

Typeset in New Century Schoolbook

Typeset by Data Standards Limited, Frome, Somerset

Printed and bound in Great Britain by Polestar Wheatons, Exeter

# FOREWORD

The sixth edition of SOUTH ASIA provides a unique perspective of this increasingly important region.

During 2007–08 South Asia remained one of the world's most eventful regions, and developments, particularly those within a turbulent Pakistan and Afghanistan, had global repercussions in terms of politics and international security. Frequent clashes between Islamist insurgents and Pakistani government troops in the volatile border regions between Afghanistan and Pakistan added to the political unrest in Pakistan. This upheaval, which culminated in the assassination of Benazir Bhutto in December 2007, was followed by the resignation of Pervez Musharraf from the presidency in August 2008, and the parliamentary election of Asif Ali Zardari as his successor in early September. The processes of democratization continued apace in Bhutan, Nepal and the Maldives. A general election was held in a relatively organized and peaceful fashion in Bhutan in March 2008; the Maoists won the largest number of seats in a new Constituent Assembly in Nepal in April, and the country was formally declared a federal democratic republic; and in August President Gayoom of the Maldives ratified the country's new Constitution. Following a period of political inertia in Bangladesh, it was finally announced that the long-delayed general election would be held in late December 2008. In July 2008 opposition to the controversial Indo-US Nuclear Agreement almost led to the downfall of the Indian Government when it narrowly survived a parliamentary vote of no confidence amid allegations of rampant bribery. Meanwhile, the situation in Sri Lanka appeared increasingly bleak with the official acknowledgement of the collapse of the cease-fire agreement in January 2008 and the continuing violence between Tamil separatists and government troops. A Calendar of Political Events between September 2007 and August 2008 provides a convenient reference guide to the major developments of the year under review, complementing the narrative and analysis within this edition.

Part One contains specially commissioned articles on various topics relating to the region as a whole. These articles encompass the subjects of security issues, the rise of India as a superpower, globalization and human development, corruption and governance, population and environment, forced migration and gender issues. An essay on the religions of South Asia is also included.

Part Two provides a detailed survey of each country. All essays are updated annually by specialist authors and researchers. The statistical surveys, directories and bibliographies are also revised on a regular basis. Extensive information on the states and territories of India is included in the volume.

Further insights may be gained from the Who's Who of South Asia, which is presented in Part Three of the volume. This section provides biographical profiles of around 400 individuals prominent within the region.

Detailed coverage of international organizations and their recent activities in South Asia is given in Part Four, along with a section on the major commodities of South Asia, a comprehensive directory of research institutes, and a general bibliography listing titles of particular relevance.

The editors are grateful to all the contributors for their articles and advice, and to the numerous organizations that have provided statistical material and other information.

September 2008

# ACKNOWLEDGEMENTS

The editors gratefully acknowledge the co-operation, interest and advice of all the authors who have contributed to this volume. We are also greatly indebted to innumerable organizations connected with the South Asia region, especially the national statistical and information offices, whose valued co-operation in providing information is greatly appreciated.

We are particularly grateful for the use of material from the following sources: the UN's statistical databases, *Statistical Yearbook, Statistical Yearbook for Asia and the Pacific, Demographic Yearbook, Industrial Commodity Statistics Yearbook* and *International Trade Statistics Yearbook*; the World Tourism Organization's *Compendium* and *Yearbook of Tourism Statistics*; the *UNESCO Statistical Yearbook* and Institute for Statistics database; FAO's statistical database; the *Human Development Report* of the United Nations Development Programme; the US Geological Survey; the International Telecommunication Union; the statistical databases of the World Health Organization; the ILO's statistical database and *Yearbook of Labour Statistics*; the IMF's statistical database, *Government Finance Statistics Yearbook* and monthly *International Financial Statistics*; the World Bank's *World Bank Atlas, Global Development Finance, World Development Report* and *World Development Indicators*; and the Asian Development Bank's *Asian Development Outlook* and *Key Indicators of Developing Asian and Pacific Countries*. We are also grateful to the International Institute for Strategic Studies, Arundel House, 13–15 Arundel Street, London, WC2R 3DX, United Kingdom, for the use of defence statistics from *The Military Balance 2008*.

The following publications and related internet sites have been of special value in providing regular coverage of the affairs of the South Asia region: *IMF Survey*, Washington, DC, USA; and *Keesing's Record of World Events*, Cambridge, United Kingdom.

# HEALTH AND WELFARE STATISTICS: SOURCES AND DEFINITIONS

**Total fertility rate** Source: WHO Statistical Information System. The number of children that would be born per woman, assuming no female mortality at child-bearing ages and the age-specific fertility rates of a specified country and reference period.

**Under-5 mortality rate** Source: WHO Statistical Information System. Defined by WHO as the probability of a child born in a specific year or period dying before reaching the age of five, if subject to the age-specific mortality rates of that year or period.

**HIV/AIDS** Source: UNAIDS. Estimated percentage of adults aged 15 to 49 years living with HIV/AIDS. < indicates 'fewer than'.

**Health expenditure** Source: WHO Statistical Information System.

*US $ per head (PPP)*

International dollar estimates, derived by dividing local currency units by an estimate of their purchasing-power parity (PPP) compared with the US dollar. PPPs are the rates of currency conversion that equalize the purchasing power of different currencies by eliminating the differences in price levels between countries.

*% of GDP*

GDP levels for OECD countries follow the most recent UN System of National Accounts. For non-OECD countries a value was estimated by utilizing existing UN, IMF and World Bank data.

*Public expenditure*

Government health-related outlays plus expenditure by social schemes compulsorily affiliated with a sizeable share of the population, and extrabudgetary funds allocated to health services. Figures include grants or loans provided by international agencies, other national authorities, and sometimes commercial banks.

**Access to water and sanitation** Source: WHO/UNICEF Joint Monitoring Programme on Water Supply and Sanitation (JMP) (Mid-Term Assessment, 2004). Defined in terms of the percentage of the population using improved facilities in terms of type of technology and levels of service afforded. For water, this includes house connections, public standpipes, boreholes with handpumps, protected dug wells, protected spring and rainwater collection; allowance is also made for other locally defined technologies. Sanitation is defined to include connection to a sewer or septic tank system, pour-flush latrine, simple pit or ventilated improved pit latrine, again with allowance for acceptable local technologies. Access to water and sanitation does not imply that the level of service or quality of water is 'adequate' or 'safe'.

**Human Development Index (HDI)** Source: UNDP, *Human Development Report* (2007/08). A summary of human development measured by three basic dimensions: prospects for a long and healthy life, measured by life expectancy at birth; knowledge, measured by adult literacy rate (two-thirds' weight) and the combined gross enrolment ratio in primary, secondary and tertiary education (one-third weight); and standard of living, measured by GDP per head (PPP US $). The index value obtained lies between zero and one. A value above 0.8 indicates high human development, between 0.5 and 0.8 medium human development, and below 0.5 low human development. A centralized data source for all three dimensions was not available for all countries. In some cases other data sources were used to calculate a substitute value; however, this was excluded from the ranking. Other countries, including non-UNDP members, were excluded from the HDI altogether. In total, 177 countries were ranked for 2005.

# CONTENTS

## PAKISTAN



## SRI LANKA



PART THREE

## Who's Who of South Asia



PART FOUR

## Regional Information

## REGIONAL ORGANIZATIONS

# THE CONTRIBUTORS

**Lok Raj Baral.** Former Professor, Department of Political Science, Tribhuvan University, Kathmandu, Nepal.

**Sanjaya Baru.** Former Chief Editor, The Financial Express, New Delhi, India.

**T. Louise Brown.** Former Lecturer in Asian Studies, The Japan Centre, University of Birmingham, United Kingdom.

**Gouranga Lal Dasvarma.** Senior Lecturer and Director, Graduate Program in Applied Population Studies, School of Geography, Population and Environmental Management, Flinders University, Adelaide, Australia.

**Sir Martin Ewans.** Former Head of Chancery, British Embassy, Afghanistan, writer on Afghanistan affairs, London, United Kingdom.

**B. H. Farmer.** Late former Director, Centre of South Asian Studies, University of Cambridge, United Kingdom.

**W. B. Fisher.** Late Professor of Geography, University of Durham, United Kingdom.

**Rajat Ganguly.** Senior Lecturer, Politics and International Studies, School of Social Sciences and Humanities, Murdoch University, Australia.

**Michael Gillan.** Lecturer, School of Economics and Commerce, UWA Business School, University of Western Australia, Australia.

**Santosh Jatrana.** Research Fellow, Department of Public Health, Wellington School of Medicine and Health Sciences, University of Otago, Wellington, New Zealand.

**A. R. Kemal.** Late former Professor of Economics, Fatima Jinnah Women University, Rawalpindi, Pakistan.

**Mushtaq H. Khan.** Professor of Economics, Department of Economics, Faculty of Law and Social Sciences, School of Oriental and African Studies, University of London, United Kingdom.

**Peter Lehr.** Lecturer in Terrorism Studies, Centre for the Study of Terrorism and Political Violence, University of St Andrews, United Kingdom.

**Peter Marsden.** Special Adviser, British Agencies Afghanistan Group, and writer on Afghanistan, London, United Kingdom.

**Matthew McCartney.** Lecturer in Economics (South Asia), Department of Economics, Faculty of Law and Social Sciences, School of Oriental and African Studies, University of London, United Kingdom.

**Allister McGregor.** Senior Lecturer in International Development, University of Bath, United Kingdom.

**John McGuire.** Adjunct Professor, Faculty of Media, Society and Culture, Curtin University of Technology, Perth, Australia.

**Kenneth McPherson.** Fellow, South Asia Institute, University of Heidelberg, Germany, Adjunct Professor, La Trobe University, Melbourne, Australia, and Research Associate, Asia Research Centre, Murdoch University, Perth, Australia.

**Geoffrey Parrinder.** Late Emeritus Professor of the Comparative Study of Religions, University of London, United Kingdom.

**G. H. Peiris.** Former Senior Professor, Department of Geography, University of Peradeniya, Sri Lanka.

**David Rampton.** Visiting Lecturer and Course Convenor, Department of Development Studies, School of Oriental and African Studies, University of London, United Kingdom.

**C. Rammanohar Reddy.** Editor, Economic and Political Weekly, Mumbai, India.

**Peter Robb.** Professor and Pro-Director, Department of History, South Asia, School of Oriental and African Studies, University of London, United Kingdom.

**S. W. R. de A. Samarasinghe.** Chairman and Executive Director, Global Vision, Kandy, Sri Lanka, and Visiting Associate Professor, Payson Center for International Development, Tulane University of Louisiana, New Orleans, USA.

**Brian Shaw.** Honorary Research Fellow, Centre of Asian Studies, The University of Hong Kong, Hong Kong.

**Kingsley M. de Silva.** Chairman, International Centre for Ethnic Studies, Kandy, Sri Lanka.

**Clemens Spiess.** Lecturer, Department of Political Science, South Asia Institute, University of Heidelberg, Germany.

**David Taylor.** Former Vice Provost (Academic Development and Special Projects), Aga Khan University, Karachi, Pakistan.

**Achin Vanaik.** Professor of International Relations and Global Politics, Department of Political Science, and Dean, Faculty of Social Sciences, University of Delhi, India.

**Marika Vicziany.** Director, Monash Asia Institute and National Centre for South Asian Studies, Monash University, Clayton, Victoria, Australia.

# ABBREVIATIONS

Acad. Academician; Academy
AD Anno Domini
ADB Asian Development Bank
Adm. Admiral
Admin. Administration, Administrative, Administrator
AFTA ASEAN Free Trade Area
AG Aktiengesellschaft (limited company)
agric. agriculture
a.i. ad interim
AIDS acquired immunodeficiency syndrome
Alt. Alternate
AM Amplitude Modulation
Amb. Ambassador
Apdo Apartado (Post Box)
apptd appointed
APEC Asia-Pacific Economic Co-operation
approx. approximately
Apt Apartment
AR Autonomous Region
ARF ASEAN Regional Forum
ASEAN Association of South East Asian Nations
Ass. Assembly
Asscn Association
Assoc. Associate
Asst Assistant
Aug. August
auth. authorized
Ave Avenue

BC Before Christ
Bd Board
b/d barrels per day
BIS Bank for International Settlements
Bldg(s) Building(s)
Blk Block
Blvd Boulevard
BOOT build-own-operate-transfer
BOT build-operate-transfer
BPO business process outsourcing
br.(s) branch(es)
Brig. Brigadier

C Centigrade
c. circa; child(ren)
cand. candidate
cap. capital
Capt. Captain
Cdre Commodore
Cen. Central
CEO Chief Executive Officer
cf. confer (compare)
CFA cease-fire agreement
CFC chlorofluorocarbon
Chair. Chairman/Chairwoman
CIA (US) Central Intelligence Agency
c.i.f. cost, insurance and freight
C-in-C Commander-in-Chief
circ. circulation
CIS Commonwealth of Independent States
cm centimetre(s)
CMEA Council for Mutual Economic Assistance (COMECON)
cnr corner
c/o care of
Co Company
Col Colonel
Coll. College
Comm. Commission
Commdr Commander
Commdt Commandant
Commr Commissioner
Conf. Conference
Confed. Confederation
Corpn Corporation
CPO Central Post Office
Cttee Committee
cu cubic
cwt hundredweight

d. daughter(s)
Dec. December
del. delegate
Dem. Democratic
Dep. Deputy
dep. deposit(s)
Dept Department
Devt Development
Dir Director
Dist. District
Div. Division
DNA deoxyribonucleic acid
DPRK Democratic People's Republic of Korea
Dr Doctor
Dr. Drive
DRAM dynamic random access memory
dwt dead weight tons

E East, Eastern
EAEC East Asia Economic Caucus
EC European Community
Econ. Economic
ECU European Currency Unit(s)
Ed.(s) Editor(s)
Edif. Edifício (Building)
edn edition
Educ. Education
e.g. exempli gratia (for example)
Eng. Engineer; Engineering
EPZ Export Processing Zone
ESCAP Economic and Social Commission for Asia and the Pacific
est. established; estimate, estimated
etc. et cetera
EU European Union
excl. excluding
Exec. Executive
exhbn(s) exhibition(s)
Ext. Extension

f. founded
FAO Food and Agriculture Organization
FATA Federally Administered Tribal Areas
FDI foreign direct investment
Feb. February
Fed. Federal, Federation
feds federations
Flt Flight
FM Frequency Modulation
fmr(ly) former(ly)
f.o.b. free on board
Fr Father
FRG Federal Republic of Germany
Fri. Friday
FTA free trade agreement/area
ft foot (feet)

g gram(s)
GATT General Agreement on Tariffs and Trade
GDP gross domestic product
Gen. General
GNI gross national income
GNP gross national product
Gov. Governor
Govt Government
GPO General Post Office
grt gross registered tons
GSM Global System for Mobile Communications
GSP gross state product
GWh gigawatt hour(s)

ha hectare(s)
HDI human development index
HE His (or Her) Excellency; His Eminence
HEP hydroelectric power
HH His (or Her) Highness; His Holiness
HIV human immunodeficiency virus
hl hectolitre(s)
HM His (or Her) Majesty
HMS His (or Her) Majesty's Ship
HMSO Her Majesty's Stationery Office
Hon. Honorary
Hosp. Hospital
hp horsepower
HPAI highly pathogenic avian influenza
HQ Headquarters
hr(s) hour(s)
HRH His (or Her) Royal Highness
HYV high-yielding variety

ibid. ibidem (from the same source)
IBRD International Bank for Reconstruction and Development (World Bank)
ICT information and communication technology
IDPs Internally Displaced Persons
i.e. id est (that is to say)
ILO International Labour Organization
IMF International Monetary Fund
in inch(es)
Inc Incorporated
incl. including
Ind. Independent
Inst. Institute
Int. International

| | |
|---|---|
| IPCC | Intergovernmental Panel on Climate Change |
| IRF | International Road Federation |
| Is | Islands |
| ISIC | International Standard Industrial Classification |
| IT | information technology |
| ITUC | International Trade Union Confederation |
| Jan. | January |
| Jr | Junior |
| Jt | Joint |
| Jtly | Jointly |
| kg | kilogram(s) |
| kHz | kilohertz |
| km | kilometre(s) |
| kW | kilowatt(s) |
| kWh | kilowatt hour(s) |
| lb | pound(s) |
| LDC | least developed country |
| LNG | liquefied natural gas |
| LPG | liquefied petroleum gas |
| Lt | Lieutenant |
| Ltd | Limited |
| m | metre(s) |
| m. | million; married/marriage |
| Maj. | Major |
| Man. | Manager, Managing |
| MDG | Millennium Development Goal |
| MDRI | Multilateral Debt Relief Initiative |
| mem. | member |
| mfg | manufacturing |
| mfr(s) | manufacturer(s) |
| mg | milligram |
| Mgr | Monseigneur, Monsignor |
| MHz | megahertz |
| Mil. | Military |
| Mlle | Mademoiselle |
| mm | millimetre(s) |
| Mme | Madame |
| Mon. | Monday |
| MP | Member of Parliament |
| Mt | Mount |
| MV | Motor Vessel |
| MW | megawatt(s) |
| MWh | megawatt hour(s) |
| N | North, Northern |
| n.a. | not available |
| NAFTA | North American Free Trade Agreement |
| Nat. | National |
| NCO | Non-Commissioned Officer |
| n.e.s. | not elsewhere specified |
| NGO | non-governmental organization |
| NIC | newly industrializing country |
| NIE | newly industrializing economy |
| No. | number |
| Nov. | November |
| NPL | non-performing loan(s) |
| NR | Nepalese Rupee(s) |
| nr | near |
| nrt | net registered tons |
| NWFP | North-West Frontier Province |
| Oct. | October |
| OECD | Organisation for Economic Co-operation and Development |
| OER | official exchange rate |
| OHCHR | Office of the United Nations High Commissioner for Human Rights |
| OPEC | Organization of the Petroleum Exporting Countries |
| opp. | opposite |
| Ord. | ordinary |
| Org.(s) | Organization(s) |
| oz | ounce(s) |
| p(p). | page(s) |
| p.a. | per annum |
| Parl. | Parliament(ary) |
| PB | Private Bag |
| Perm. | Permanent |
| Pl. | Place |
| PLC | Public Limited Company |
| PMB | Private Mail Bag |
| PO | Post Office |
| POB | Post Office Box |
| PPP | purchasing power parity |
| Pres. | President |
| Prin. | Principal |
| Prof. | Professor |
| Propr | Proprietor |
| Prov. | Province, Provincial |
| P-TOMS | Post-Tsunami Operational Management Structure |
| Pt | Point |
| Pte | Private |
| PTWC | Pacific Tsunami Warning Centre |
| Pty | Proprietary |

| | |
|---|---|
| p.u. | paid up |
| publ.(s) | publication(s); published |
| Publr | Publisher |
| Pvt | Private |
| QIP | Quick Impact Project |
| q.v. | quod vide (to which refer) |
| R(s) | Rupee(s) |
| R & D | research and development |
| Rd | Road |
| regd | registered |
| Regt | Regiment |
| Rep. | Representative |
| Repub. | Republic |
| res | reserves |
| resgnd | resigned |
| retd | retired |
| Rev. | Reverend |
| Rm | Room |
| ro-ro | roll-on roll-off |
| Rt | Right |
| s | son(s) |
| S | South, Southern |
| SA | Société anonyme, Sociedad Anónima (limited company) |
| SAARC | South Asian Association for Regional Co-operation |
| SAFTA | South Asian Free Trade Area |
| SAR | Special Administrative Region |
| SARS | Severe Acute Respiratory Syndrome |
| SARL | Sociedade Anônima de Responsibilidade Limitada (limited company) |
| Sat. | Saturday |
| SDR | Special Drawing Right(s) |
| Sec. | Secretary; Section |
| Secr. | Secretariat |
| Sept. | September |
| SEZ | Special Economic Zone |
| SITC | Standard International Trade Classification |
| SMEs | small and medium-sized enterprises |
| Soc. | Society |
| SOE | State-Owned Enterprise |
| Sq. | Square |
| sq | square (in measurements) |
| Sr | Senior |
| St | Street; Saint, San, Santo |
| STI(s) | sexually transmitted infection(s) |
| subs. | subscribed |
| Sun. | Sunday |
| Supt | Superintendent |
| tech. | technical/technology |
| tel. | telephone |
| TEU | 20-foot equivalent unit |
| Thur. | Thursday |
| trans. | translator, translated |
| Treas. | Treasurer |
| Tue. | Tuesday |
| TV | television |
| UHF | ultra-high frequency |
| UK | United Kingdom |
| UN | United Nations |
| UNAMA | United Nations Assistance Mission in Afghanistan |
| UNCTAD | United Nations Conference on Trade and Development |
| UNDP | United Nations Development Programme |
| UNEP | United Nations Environment Programme |
| UNESCO | United Nations Educational, Scientific and Cultural Organization |
| UNFPA | United Nations Population Fund |
| UNHCHR | United Nations High Commissioner for Human Rights |
| UNHCR | United Nations High Commissioner for Refugees |
| UNIDO | United Nations Industrial Development Organization |
| UNMOGIP | United Nations Military Observer Group in India and Pakistan |
| UNWTO | World Tourism Organization |
| US | United States |
| USA | United States of America |
| USAID | United States Agency for International Development |
| USSR | Union of Soviet Socialist Republics |
| VAT | value-added tax |
| Ven. | Venerable |
| VHF | very high frequency |
| viz. | videlicet (namely) |
| Vol(s) | Volume(s) |
| W | West, Western |
| Wed. | Wednesday |
| WHO | World Health Organization |
| WIPO | World Intellectual Property Organization |
| WSSD | World Summit on Sustainable Development |
| WTO | World Trade Organization |
| yr(s) | year(s) |

# INTERNATIONAL TELEPHONE CODES

To make international calls to telephone and fax numbers listed in *South Asia*, dial the international code of the country from which you are calling, followed by the appropriate country code for the organization you wish to call (listed below), followed by the area code (if applicable) and telephone or fax number listed in the entry.

| | Country code | + or − GMT* |
|---|---|---|
| Afghanistan | 93 | +4½ |
| Bangladesh | 880 | +6 |
| Bhutan | 975 | +6 |
| India | 91 | +5½ |
| The Maldives | 960 | +5 |
| Nepal | 977 | +5¾ |
| Pakistan | 92 | +5 |
| Sri Lanka | 94 | +5½ |

*Time difference in hours + or − Greenwich Mean Time (GMT). The times listed compare the standard (winter) times. Some countries may adopt Summer (Daylight Saving) Times—i.e. + 1 hour—for part of the year.

# EXPLANATORY NOTE ON THE DIRECTORY SECTION

The Directory section of each chapter is arranged under the following headings, where they apply:

THE CONSTITUTION

THE GOVERNMENT
- HEAD OF STATE
- CABINET/COUNCIL OF MINISTERS
- MINISTRIES

LEGISLATURE

PROVINCIAL GOVERNMENTS

ELECTION COMMISSION

POLITICAL ORGANIZATIONS

DIPLOMATIC REPRESENTATION

JUDICIAL SYSTEM

RELIGION

THE PRESS

PUBLISHERS

BROADCASTING AND COMMUNICATIONS
- TELECOMMUNICATIONS
- RADIO
- TELEVISION

FINANCE
- CENTRAL BANK
- STATE BANKS
- COMMERCIAL BANKS
- DEVELOPMENT BANKS
- INVESTMENT BANKS
- SAVINGS BANKS
- FOREIGN BANKS
- STOCK EXCHANGE
- INSURANCE

TRADE AND INDUSTRY
- GOVERNMENT AGENCIES
- DEVELOPMENT ORGANIZATIONS
- CHAMBERS OF COMMERCE AND INDUSTRY
- INDUSTRIAL AND TRADE ASSOCIATIONS
- EMPLOYERS' ASSOCIATIONS
- UTILITIES
- MAJOR COMPANIES
- CO-OPERATIVES
- TRADE UNIONS

TRANSPORT
- RAILWAYS
- ROADS
- INLAND WATERWAYS
- SHIPPING
- CIVIL AVIATION

TOURISM

DEFENCE

EDUCATION

# CALENDAR OF POLITICAL EVENTS IN SOUTH ASIA, SEPTEMBER 2007–AUGUST 2008

### SEPTEMBER 2007

4 **Bangladesh:** it was announced that Iajuddin Ahmed's term as President, which was due to expire on the following day, would be extended in light of the delayed legislative elections.

18 **Afghanistan:** Sher Mohammad Etebari was nominated to the position of Minister of Refugees and Repatriation.

29 **Maldives:** a bomb explosion in the capital, Malé, injured 12 foreign tourists; it was the first recorded terrorist attack to take place in the country.

### OCTOBER 2007

6 **Pakistan:** Pervez Musharraf was re-elected as President by the incumbent national and provincial legislatures.

8 **India:** the Chief Minister of Karnataka, H. D. Kumaraswamy, resigned and, in response to political instability in the state, direct presidential rule was imposed on the following day.

11 **Pakistan:** Shamsul Mulk was sworn in as Chief Minister of the North-West Frontier Province.

31 **Maldives:** Aishath Azima Shakoor was sworn in as Attorney-General, following the resignation of Hassan Saeed from the position in August; Mohamed Nasheed formally assumed the role of Minister of Legal Reform, Information and Arts.

### NOVEMBER 2007

2 **Sri Lanka:** S. P. Thamilselvan, the head of the political wing of the Liberation Tigers of Tamil Eelam, was killed in an aerial bombardment by the country's military.

3 **Pakistan:** President Pervez Musharraf declared a state of emergency and suspended the Constitution; the Chief Justice of the Supreme Court, Iftikhar Mohammad Chaudhry, was dismissed and replaced by Abdul Hameed Dogar.

12 **India:** B. S. Yeddyurappa was sworn in as Chief Minister of Karnataka, but resigned on 19 November; direct presidential rule was once again imposed in the state.

15 **Pakistan:** the National Assembly was dissolved and the Chairman of the Senate, Mohammad Mian Soomro, was sworn in to lead an interim government on the following day.

19 **Pakistan:** acting Chief Ministers were appointed in three provinces: Sheikh Ejaz Nisar in Punjab, Abdul Qadir Halepota in Sindh, and Sardar Mohammad Saleh Bhootani in Balochistan.

22 **Pakistan:** the Commonwealth Ministerial Action Group on the Harare Declaration suspended Pakistan from the Councils of the Commonwealth.

28 **Pakistan:** Gen. Musharraf resigned as Chief of Army Staff; his inauguration as civilian head of state took place on the following day.

### DECEMBER 2007

10 **Nepal:** the Minister of Environment, Science and Technology, Mahantha Thakur, resigned, together with several ethnic Madhesi members of the Interim Parliament, citing the Government's unwillingness to address the ongoing unrest in the Terai.

11–16 **India:** the Bharatiya Janata Party secured an overwhelming victory in legislative elections held in Gujarat; Narendra Damodardas Modi was once more sworn in as Chief Minister on 25 December.

12 **Sri Lanka:** the Minister of Posts and Telecommunication, Abdul Rauf Hakeem, resigned after the Sri Lanka Muslim Congress, of which he was leader, withdrew its support for the governing coalition.

14 **Sri Lanka:** Anura Bandaranaike resigned as Minister of National Heritage.

15 **Pakistan:** President Musharraf revoked the state of emergency declared in the previous month.

26 **Bangladesh:** Ayub Quadri resigned as Adviser in charge of Education, of Primary and Mass Education, and of Cultural Affairs.

27 **Pakistan:** Benazir Bhutto, leader of the Pakistan People's Party, was killed during an attack on a rally in Rawalpindi; on 30 December Bilawal Bhutto Zardari was named to succeed his mother as leader of the party following the completion of his university studies, with Asif Ali Zardari, Benazir Bhutto's widower, assuming the role in an interim capacity.

28 **Nepal:** the Government signed an agreement with the United Democratic Madhesi Front, allowing for increased autonomy and representation for the Madhesi people; the agreement brought to an end a blockade organized by the United Democratic Madhesi Front, which had led to fuel shortages.

30 **India:** Prem Kumar Dhumal was sworn in as Chief Minister of Himachal Pradesh after the Bharatiya Janata Party prevailed in legislative elections in the state, held during November and December; the representation of Congress in the Assembly was significantly reduced.

31 **Bhutan:** the country's first election was held, to the National Council (Upper House); a second stage of voting in a further five electoral districts was conducted on 29 January 2008.

### JANUARY 2008

3 **India:** Nagaland was brought under direct presidential rule, owing to political uncertainty following the successful passage of a vote of no confidence against the state government.

8 **Maldives:** President Maumoon Abdul Gayoom escaped unhurt after an attempted knife attack by a Maldivian man, while visiting an atoll in the north of the island chain.

**Sri Lanka:** Minister of Nation Building D. M. Dassanayake was killed in a bomb attack.

9 **Bangladesh:** four advisers resigned from the interim Government, citing personal reasons; their replacements included former Attorney-General A. F. Hassan Ariff and Hossain Zillur Rahman.

10 **Nepal:** a ministerial reorganization took place, in which Pharmullah Mansur became Minister of Environment, Science and Technology.

16 **Sri Lanka:** the Government formally withdrew from its cease-fire agreement with the Liberation Tigers of Tamil Eelam.

20 **Bhutan:** four bomb explosions occurred in different locations, including one in the capital Thimphu; an apparent link to the Bhutan Tiger Force, the armed wing of the Bhutan Communist Party (Marxist-Leninist-Maoist), led to widespread assumption that the party wanted to disrupt preparations for the upcoming general election.

### FEBRUARY 2008

6 **Bangladesh:** the High Court ruled that most of the charges against Sheikh Hasina Wajed, the leader of the Bangladesh Awami League, were invalid as the emergency laws could not be employed in the case of events that took place before their imposition; however, she remained incarcerated.

18 **Pakistan:** at a general election the Pakistan People's Party Parliamentarians (established by the Pakistan People's Party in 2002 in order to meet electoral requirements) secured the largest number of general and reserved seats in the National Assembly, while the Pakistan Muslim League, which supported Musharraf, was resoundingly defeated; the Pakistan Muslim League (Nawaz) became the second biggest party in the Assembly.

23 **India:** the Communist Party of India—Marxist won a fourth term in office in Tripura after the ruling Left Front coalition secured a victory in legislative elections in the state; Manik Sarkar was sworn in as Chief Minister on 10 March.

### MARCH 2008

3 **India:** following legislative elections in the state, Congress remained the single largest party in the coalition government in Meghalaya, albeit without a majority; consequently the Chief Minister resigned on 19 March and his replacement, Donkupar Roy of the United Democratic Party, was sworn in on the same day.

5 **India:** an election in Nagaland saw the Nagaland People's Front remain as the largest party in the Legislative Assembly, despite the increased representation of Congress; direct presidential rule in the state was revoked on 12 March, when Neiphiu Rio was sworn in as Chief Minister.

9 **Pakistan:** the Pakistan People's Party and the Pakistan Muslim League (Nawaz) announced a coalition agreement.

24 **Bhutan:** a general election was held to the National Assembly (Lower House); the Druk Phuensum Tshogpa secured 45 legislative seats, while the People's Democratic Party won the remaining two seats.

25 **Pakistan:** Yousaf Raza Gillani of the Pakistan People's Party was sworn in as Prime Minister; the new Cabinet, installed on 31 March, included Pakistan People's Party members Chaudhry Ahmed Mukhtar and Shah Mehmud Qureshi as Minister of Defence and of Foreign Affairs respectively, and Muhammad Ishaq Dar of the Pakistan Muslim League (Nawaz) as Minister of Finance.

### APRIL 2008

1 **Pakistan:** Amir Haider Khan Hoti was sworn in as Chief Minister of the North-West Frontier Province after being elected unopposed to the position.

6 **India:** Prime Minister Manmohan Singh effected a government reorganization, which included the introduction of seven new ministers, following the resignations of six members of the Council of Ministers; among those appointed was former Chief Election Commissioner Dr M. S. Gill, as Minister of State for Youth Affairs and Sports.

7 **Pakistan:** Syed Qaim Ali Shah was elected as Chief Minister of Sindh, and sworn in on the following day.

8 **Pakistan:** Nawab Mohammad Aslam Raisani was elected unopposed as Chief Minister of Balochistan, and formally assumed the position on the following day.

9 **Bhutan:** Lyonpo Jigmi Yozer Thinley's nomination as Prime Minister was endorsed by the King; on the same day the composition of the Council of Ministers was announced, including former Prime Ministers Khandu Wangchuck and Wangdi Norbu as Minister of Economic Affairs and Minister of Finance, respectively.

10 **Nepal:** at an election to the Constituent Assembly, the Communist Party of Nepal (Maoist) won 220 out of a total of 575 elected seats, twice as many as the second largest party, the Nepali Congress Party; the Madhesi People's Rights Forum won 52 seats.

12 **Pakistan:** Sardar Dost Muhammad Khosa was sworn in as Chief Minister of Punjab, having been elected unopposed.

17 **Maldives:** Abdulla Hameed, Dr Mohamed Zahir Hussain, Umar Zahir, Fathulla Jameel and Ali Umar Maniku were appointed as Senior Ministers.

27 **Afghanistan:** President Hamid Karzai was the target of an assassination attempt when Taliban militants launched an attack on a military parade; Karzai escaped unharmed.

### MAY 2008

8 **Bhutan:** the first session of the first Parliament of Bhutan commenced.

10–22 **India:** at legislative elections to the Karnataka Assembly, which were held in three phases, the Bharatiya Janata Party won an overwhelming victory, just short of an absolute majority with 110 of the 224 elected seats; B. S. Yeddyurappa was once again sworn in as Chief Minister, and direct presidential rule was revoked.

12 **Bangladesh:** Chief Adviser Dr Fakhruddin Ahmed announced that legislative elections would be held in the third week in December.

13 **India:** 63 people were killed and a further 216 were injured as a result of a series of bomb explosions in Jaipur, Rajasthan.
**Pakistan:** the nine cabinet ministers of the Pakistan Muslim League (Nawaz) resigned from their positions due to disagreements between the party and the Pakistan People's Party regarding the reinstatement of judges dismissed by President Musharraf in November 2007.

28 **Nepal:** in its first session the Constituent Assembly formally declared Nepal a federal democratic republic, thus revoking the royal status of King Gyanendra and his family.

## JUNE 2008

2 **Bhutan:** the National Council and the National Assembly approved the country's draft constitution.

7 **Pakistan:** Muhammad Shahbaz Sharif was sworn in as Chief Minister of Punjab, replacing Sardar Dost Muhammad Khosa.

26 **Nepal:** Prime Minister Girija Prasad Koirala submitted his resignation in order to allow the formation of a new Government following the election in April.

## JULY 2008

7 **Afghanistan:** a suicide bomb attack at the Indian embassy in Kabul killed 58 people and injured a further 150; no group claimed responsibility for the incident.

**Bhutan:** Rinzin Penjor was appointed as Attorney-General.

**India:** Ghulam Nabi Azad resigned as Chief Minister of Jammu and Kashmir; the Governor, Narendra Nath Vohra, assumed direct administration on 10 July.

15 **Maldives:** Abdulla Jihad was sworn in as Minister of Finance and Treasury, and Abdulla Mausoom as Minister of Tourism and Civil Aviation, following the resignations of the previous incumbents.

16 **Bangladesh:** Attorney-General Fida Kamal resigned.

**Maldives:** Mohamed Jaleel resigned as Minister of Economic Development and Trade.

17 **Afghanistan:** Attorney-General Abdul Jabar Sabit was dismissed by President Karzai after Sabit announced his intention to stand in the next presidential elections, contravening the code of conduct associated with his position.

18 **Bhutan:** the country adopted its first formal Constitution.

19 **Nepal:** in an election to select the country's first president no candidate secured the 298 votes necessary to win the poll, although legislature members did elect Paramananda Jha, supported by the Madhesi People's Rights Forum, to the position of Vice-President.

21 **Nepal:** in a second round of voting in the presidential election, Dr Ram Baran Yadav was successful, having secured the votes of 308 of the 590 Constituent Assembly members who took part in the ballot; Yadav's nomination was supported by the Nepali Congress Party (of which he was General Secretary), the Communist Party of Nepal (Unified Marxist-Leninist) and the Madhesi People's Rights Forum.

26 **India:** a series of 21 bomb explosions in Ahmedabad, Gujarat, killed at least 55 people and injured more than 200.

## AUGUST 2008

7 **Maldives:** President Gayoom ratified the country's new Constitution: major points included the direct election of the President and the restriction of presidential terms of office to two; the election, rather than presidential appointment, of the Speaker and Deputy Speaker of the People's Majlis; the establishment of a Supreme Court as the highest judicial authority; and the granting to citizens of the right to hold peaceful demonstrations.

15 **Nepal:** Pushpa Kamal Dahal ('Prachanda'), the leader of the Communist Party of Nepal (Maoist), was elected as Prime Minister by the Constituent Assembly, formally assuming his duties on 18 August; a new Council of Ministers was sworn in on 22 August, comprising members of the Communist Party of Nepal (Maoist) and the Madhesi People's Rights Forum; members of the Communist Party of Nepal (Unified Marxist-Leninist), the Communist Party of Nepal (United), People's Front Nepal (Janamorcha Nepal) and the Sadbhavana Party joined the Council on 1 September.

18 **Maldives:** in a cabinet reorganization, Dr Aishath Shiham was appointed Minister of Youth and Sports and Dr Ibrahim Hassan Minister of Higher Education, Employment and Social Security.

**Pakistan:** Pervez Musharraf announced his resignation as President after the Pakistan People's Party and the Pakistan Muslim League (Nawaz) announced they were seeking impeachment proceedings against him; the Chairman of the Senate, Mohammad Mian Soomro, was appointed President in an acting capacity, pending the parliamentary election of a successor.

25 **Pakistan:** the Pakistan Muslim League (Nawaz) announced its withdrawal from the coalition Government.

27 **India:** Shibu Soren was sworn in as Chief Minister of Jharkhand, following the resignation of Madhu Kora on 23 August.

28 **India:** N. Rangasamy resigned as Chief Minister of Puducherry; V. Vaithilingam was chosen to replace him.

# PART ONE
# General Survey

# THE SOUTH ASIAN SECURITY SCENARIO IN 2008–09

RAJAT GANGULY

## INTRODUCTION

Conflict and violence continue to be endemic in South Asia, a region comprising India, Pakistan, Sri Lanka, Bangladesh, Nepal, Bhutan, Afghanistan and the Maldives, leading to many expert commentators terming the region as 'the most dangerous place on Earth'. This essay will attempt to identify and analyse the major threats to security in South Asia at the present moment and will discuss their implications. It will argue that insecurity in South Asia stems from five main sources: continued hostility between India and Pakistan and the unresolved nature of the Kashmir dispute; continued instability in Afghanistan, with spill-over effects in Pakistan and to a lesser extent in India; internal divisions and schisms in South Asian states leading to various types of intra-state 'identity conflicts'; the enormous spread of transnational terror networks in the region; and the failure of the South Asian Association of Regional Co-operation (SAARC) to promote regional integration, co-operation and peace.

The trauma of partition, communal violence and mass-scale population migration that accompanied the birth of India and Pakistan in 1947 was a portent of things to come. From that date, India and Pakistan became locked into a highly antagonistic relationship, which produced four wars (all but one over Kashmir) and several near misses over the following six decades. Aside from generating devastating damage and human suffering, Indo-Pakistani hostility has contributed significantly to the undermining of regional peace and prosperity by creating an escalating arms race (including weapons of mass destruction) in the subcontinent and preventing the emergence of a common market and trading regime in the region.

For the past four decades Afghanistan has been a 'problem state' not just for South Asian but also for global security. The overthrow of the Afghan monarchy in the early 1970s at the hands of the communists opened the door for the Soviet military to march into the country in December 1979. Over the next decade, the violent conflict that was fought between the Soviet forces and the Afghan resistance took a heavy toll. Following the Soviet withdrawal in 1989, all-out civil war ensued until the Taliban captured power in the mid-1990s. The Taliban rule, which lasted for around five years, was one of the most brutal and repressive periods in the country's history. The Taliban regime also formed strong links with the world's most notorious terrorist leader and his organization, namely Osama bin Laden and al-Qa'ida. In the immediate aftermath of the terrorist strikes against the USA in September 2001, Afghanistan was faced with further conflict when the Taliban refused to hand over bin Laden and his followers to the USA The consequent US-led incursion into Afghanistan resulted in the overthrow of the Taliban regime and the installation of a new democratic political system. The Government of President Hamid Karzai that assumed power enjoyed the support of the US Administration and the United Nations, but was soon faced with problems in its attempts to subdue a whole host of recalcitrant war-lords and a resurgent Taliban in the southern regions of the country. With the Karzai Government unable to control the rising tide of violence in the country, US and NATO military involvement, rather than gradually declining, actually steadily increased. At mid-2008 the US and NATO forces faced fierce resistance from a regrouped and rearmed Taliban, who, according to many analysts, continue to receive staunch support from Pakistan's border-straddling tribal population as well as from factions within the Pakistani military. As the fighting has intensified in Afghanistan, the national and regional security scenario has drastically deteriorated.

All the states of South Asia suffer from various degrees of internal schisms and divisions, which have often led to violence and conflict within their own societies and contributed to the creation of situations of insecurity and complex humanitarian emergencies. The internal schisms in South Asian states are usually the result of competing ethno-national, religious, tribal and class identities (and in the case of India also caste identity). Ethno-national mobilizations have typically generated political and insurgency movements for autonomy and secession, leading to fierce resistance on the part of the authorities. Many of these insurgency movements continue today (such as in Kashmir and the Indian north-east, in northern Sri Lanka and in western Pakistan), putting thousands of lives at risk. Clashes between and within religious communities have also chronically generated major violence and insecurity in South Asia. In the recent past, India has witnessed major communal riots in Gujarat and Maharashtra, in which thousands of people died or were seriously injured along with massive destruction to private property, businesses and public infrastructure. Communal clashes between mostly Hindu Tamils and Buddhist Sinhalese and between Tamils and Muslims have also occurred with regular frequency in Sri Lanka, which has further complicated the ethno-national and secessionist conflict that has been raging in the island nation for the past three decades or so. In addition, ethnic and sectarian clashes have been a major source of insecurity in Pakistan, especially in urban centres such as Karachi, Hyderabad and Lahore. The rapidly spreading Maoist insurgency in India and the recently concluded Maoist armed struggle in Nepal further demonstrate vividly that class identity and conflict continue to be a potent source of insecurity in South Asia, particularly in regions of extreme poverty and deprivation. In both countries, caste identity is often subsumed within class identity and conflict.

The tentacles of transnational terrorism have spread rapidly in South Asia, thus adding a new source of conflict and insecurity in the region. Some of the world's most notorious terrorist groups, such as the Lashkar-e-Taiba, the Hizbul Mujahidin, the Jamiat-i-Islami, the Taliban, the Hizb-ul Jehadi Islami, the Students' Islamic Movement of India, the Liberation Tigers of Tamil Eelam (LTTE), the Babbar Khalsa and the United Liberation Front of Assam, are all located in South Asian states. Most of these groups have links with each other; almost all of the major Islamic fundamentalist groups have links with and receive assistance from al-Qa'ida. The growing strength of Islamic fundamentalist forces and ideology has further worsened the internal security environment in Pakistan, and through its ties with al-Qa'ida and the concomitant network of transnational terrorism, Islamic fundamentalism in Pakistan has also become a source of regional and global insecurity. The existence of criminal networks that traffic narcotics and weapons has significantly boosted the capabilities of insurgent and terrorist organizations operating in the region, particularly in fragile states such as Pakistan, Bangladesh, Nepal and Sri Lanka. The relative ease with which insurgent and terrorist groups can procure weapons from the underground market and finance their activities through illegal drugs-trafficking affords them a degree of freedom and fighting capability that they never had before—the Taliban in Pakistan/Afghanistan, the LTTE in Sri Lanka, and a host of insurgent groups in north-east India all prove this point vividly. The threat to security from such groups has, therefore, never been higher.

When it was established in 1985 amid much fanfare, the SAARC raised the expectations of the people of South Asia that, much like similar regional arrangements in Europe, North America and South-East Asia, this new regional body would help to stop the endemic disagreements between the various South Asian states and usher the region towards economic integration, co-operation and peace. Over the following two decades or so, however, SAARC has failed to live up to these initial expectations. The basic failure of SAARC to promote the rapid economic integration of the region means that with regard to security issues it lacks the requisite clout and credibility to play any meaningful role. Therefore, SAARC's impact on bilateral disputes (such as that between India and Pakistan over Kashmir), the 'war on terrorism' and internal conflicts in South Asia has been minimal or frankly non-existent.

## THE INDO-PAK IMBROGLIO

The roots of Indo-Pakistani hostility can be traced back to the Indian freedom movement, which represented a struggle between two rival ideologies. One vision, championed by the Indian National Congress, believed that India's diverse religious, linguistic, and ethnic groups could co-exist together in a single secular and democratic state. In contrast, the Indian Muslim League regarded Hindus and Muslims as forming two separate nations with distinct social customs and practices, philosophies and ways of life, which precluded peaceful co-existence between the two communities in an undivided India. When a Congress/League compromise proved elusive, a complex formula was devised to partition the subcontinent into two states—India and Pakistan. Under the partition plan, contiguous Muslim majority provinces of British India were to become Pakistan, with the border provinces of Bengal and Punjab (with nearly equal number of Hindus/Sikhs and Muslims) to be divided.

The partition of the subcontinent resulted in a massive population migration accompanied by severe communal violence and rioting. Millions died as a result of communal slaughter, dislocation, hunger, hardship and disease. In this highly polarized and vitriolic environment, Congress and Muslim League leaders also argued bitterly over the division of public assets between the two new states. A further arena of fierce competition between the two states was regarding the status of the 565 princely states, which were hitherto controlled by the British according to the doctrine of paramountcy. (During the British rule of India, two categories of states existed. In the first category were states of British India that were ruled directly from London. The second category of states, known as the 'princely states', was not ruled directly by the British and thus was nominally independent. However, the rulers of such princely states recognized the British Crown as the 'paramount' power in India.) British disengagement from the subcontinent meant that the doctrine of paramountcy was to lapse and, hence, the princely states could technically become independent. This was vehemently opposed by both the Congress and the Muslim League and intense political pressure was exerted on the princes to join either India or Pakistan, bearing in mind the issues of geographical contiguity and the communal allegiance of the population of the princely state. All the princely states, with the exceptions of Hyderabad, Junagadh, and Jammu and Kashmir (hereafter referred to as Kashmir), had joined either India or Pakistan by the time the British transferred power. While Junagadh and Hyderabad, which were located deep within Indian territory but nevertheless wanted to join Pakistan, were forcibly annexed by New Delhi, Kashmir posed a problem. The state had a Hindu ruler but an overwhelming majority of its population was Muslim; it was also contiguous to both India and Pakistan. Kashmir was, accordingly, claimed by both sides on the basis of ideology.

The ideological conflict soon turned into military conflict when pro-Pakistan groups in Kashmir established contact with Pathan tribes in Pakistan and laid the foundation for an armed invasion and forcible seizure of power in the state. The Hindu ruler of Kashmir, Maharaja Hari Singh, had calculated that by not joining either India or Pakistan during the transfer of power he would emerge as the ruler of an independent Kashmir state.Faced with a Pathan tribal invasion in October 1947, however, the Maharaja was forced to appeal to the Indian Government for help. Prime Minister Jawaharlal Nehru agreed to provide military assistance in return for Hari Singh's acceptance of Kashmir's legal accession to India, a move that was supported by Sheikh Muhammad Abdullah, the leader of a popular, secular and democratic political movement in Kashmir. Once the Instrument of Accession had been signed, Indian troops were airlifted into Kashmir Valley. By early 1948 the battle had been joined by the regular Pakistan army. A UN-sponsored cease-fire agreement, which came into effect on 1 January 1949, finally brought the first Indo-Pakistani war to an end. At that time India occupied roughly two-thirds of Kashmir, with Pakistan controlling the remaining third. The Indian portion of Kashmir consisted of three main regions: the Valley, Jammu and Ladakh; while the Pakistani part consisted of Azad (Free) Kashmir and the Northern Areas. Over the next 20 years, both India and Pakistan sought to absorb their respective portions of Kashmir and the 1949 Cease-fire Line (CFL) gradually became the *de facto* border between the two states.

Based on the assumptions that India was militarily vulnerable after the Sino-Indian war of 1962 and that widespread popular discontent existed in Indian Kashmir against New Delhi, Pakistan launched another military offensive in 1965 to seize Indian Kashmir by force. Pakistan's confidence in its military strength also stemmed from the massive weapons procurement programme that it had undertaken since joining the Central Treaty Organization (CENTO), a US-led military alliance, as a founder member in 1955. The offensive was to take place in two phases: during the first phase, regular Pakistani troops were to cross the CFL disguised as local tribesmen and foment an insurgency in the border areas; then, in the second phase, regular units of the Pakistan army were to take advantage of the prevailing chaos and suddenly invade and seize Indian Kashmir. The plan failed when the people in Indian Kashmir chose not to rise up in revolt when provoked by the Pakistani infiltrators and the Indian military mounted a strong counterattack (belying Pakistan's expectations). A cease-fire was eventually drawn up by the UN on 22 September 1965. Thereafter, under Soviet Prime Minister Alexei Kosygin's initiative, both sides met at Tashkent in the USSR to formulate a peace agreement, which was finally signed in January 1966. Under this agreement, which restored the status quo ante, India and Pakistan renounced the resort to war between their countries and withdrew their respective forces behind the CFL in Kashmir and the international boundaries in the Punjab.

A third Indo-Pakistani war broke out in 1971, but not directly over the situation in Kashmir. Instead, the Pakistani military's crackdown on Bengali secessionists in East Pakistan precipitated the conflict by creating an enormous refugee burden for India. As the Pakistani military's offensive continued in East Pakistan, New Delhi calculated that it was cheaper to go to war against Pakistan on behalf of the Bengali secessionists than to absorb the 6m. Bengali refugees who had taken shelter in the province of West Bengal. East Pakistan, separated from West Pakistan by nearly 2,000 km of Indian territory, was militarily indefensible for the Pakistani military; therefore, when the Indian army attacked East Pakistan, the regime of Gen. Agha Muhammad Yahya Khan in Pakistan countered by attacking Indian Kashmir. The war in the Kashmir sector proved to be of short duration, however, since the Indian military offensive in East Pakistan lasted only two weeks and led to the creation of the independent state of Bangladesh. In addition, the war in the Kashmir sector did not change the military status quo (although the CFL was slightly modified and renamed as the line-of-control or LOC). India, however, won a significant diplomatic victory with regard to the Kashmir issue in the post-war peace agreement that was signed between Prime Ministers Indira Gandhi and Zulfikar Ali Bhutto at Simla in 1972. The second paragraph of the Simla Agreement stated that India and Pakistan were 'resolved to settle their differences by peaceful means through bilateral negotiations or by any other peaceful means mutually agreed upon between them'. In the years since the signing of the Simla Agreement, New Delhi has steadfastly insisted on a strict interpretation of this paragraph—that India and Pakistan have agreed to settle the Kashmir dispute bilaterally without outside intervention—in order to deny any international involvement in the dispute, thereby scuttling Pakistan's persistent efforts to focus international attention on Kashmir.

During the 1980s Indo-Pakistani relations were taut with tension. Following the USSR invasion of Afghanistan in December 1979, the USA (as well as Saudi Arabia) used the services of Pakistan's military and intelligence agencies to channel millions of dollars and large quantities of weapons and ammunition to the Afghan *mujahidin* (traditionalist Islamist rebel tribesmen). Military training was also provided to these self-styled 'freedom fighters' by US and Pakistani military personnel in camps based in north-west Pakistan. Being elevated to the status of a frontline ally of the USA suited Pakistan well since it allowed the latter access to millions of dollars in US aid and sophisticated weapons. In addition, the US Administration turned a blind eye towards Pakistan's covert nuclear weapons and missiles programmes, which were being developed with assistance from China and the Democratic People's Republic of Korea. Some of the weapons that Pakistan received from the USA that were intended to be passed onto Afghan *mujahidin* were reportedly diverted by Pakistan military intelligence services to insurgent groups operating in India's Punjab province. India responded to Pakistan's massive military expenditure by undertaking its own military modernization programme. A destructive and destabilizing arms race thus developed in the region and tensions remained high. New Delhi also proclaimed the 'Indian Doctrine of Regional Security', which pointedly warned India's neighbours and extra-regional powers not to indulge in any anti-Indian activities, and started holding massive military exercises in an apparent show of strength and resolve. India's assertiveness and warnings further damaged Indo-Pakistani relations and even appeared threatening to India's smaller neighbours like Sri Lanka, Bangladesh and Nepal. India's relations with a number of these smaller states became fractious and strained throughout this period, which greater undermined regional co-operation, stability and security.

In the 1990s Kashmir once again became the focal point of tensions between India and Pakistan. The main reason for this was the outbreak of a widely popular secessionist insurgency in Indian Kashmir (mainly in the Valley) in the late 1980s, which, it was alleged, was actively encouraged and supported by Pakistan. From its inception, the secessionist insurgency in Indian Kashmir split into two factions based upon ideology and objective. One faction, represented by the nationalist Jammu and Kashmir Liberation Front (JKLF), advocated the formation of an independent and secular Kashmir state comprising the five main regions of the former princely state; this was to be achieved by the secession of the Indian and Pakistani parts of Kashmir followed by a merger of these two areas. A second and more dominant faction within the secessionist movement, represented by Pakistan-based and -supported fundamentalist groups such as the Hizbul Mujahidin, the Lashkar-e-Taiba and the Jaish-i-Mohammad, advocated Indian Kashmir's secession from India followed by either a merger with Pakistan or, at the very least, the creation of an independent Islamic state with close ties to Pakistan. These groups endorsed the 'ethnic cleansing' of the minority Hindu Pandit community from the Valley and the Tibetan Buddhist community from Ladakh. Massacres of Hindu and Sikh families were also carried out in the Jammu region. Pakistan-supported Islamic militants even perpetrated terrorist attacks in other parts of India, often with the aid of international terrorist organizations like al-Qa'ida, disgruntled domestic groups such as the Students Islamic Movement of India and the criminal underworld.

The diffusion and encouragement of the secessionist insurgency in Indian Kashmir offered Pakistan a relatively inexpensive and effective way to tie India down in costly and unpopular counterinsurgency operations, to discredit its secular and liberal ideological tenets and slowly to undermine New Delhi's hold over the region. Most of the training centres for Kashmiri insurgents were located either in Pakistani Kashmir or in north-west Pakistan along the border with Afghanistan and were allegedly operated by the Pakistan military's Inter Services Intelligence (ISI) directorate. It was also reported that the ISI, which is allegedly Pakistan's premier espionage agency, encouraged veteran guerrillas of the Afghan war, left aimless after the Soviet withdrawal from Afghanistan, to infiltrate Kashmir in order to conduct a *jihad* or holy war against India. To facilitate the infiltration of insurgents across the LOC, the Pakistani military periodically fired upon and shelled Indian forward positions and border villages. The Pakistan Government also lost no opportunity to internationalize the Kashmiri dispute by highlighting in international forums New Delhi's alleged corrupt rule in Indian Kashmir and the human rights abuses reportedly committed by the Indian counterinsurgency forces against the Kashmiri people. Islamabad also consistently demanded international mediation in the Kashmir dispute and called for the holding of a UN-sponsored plebiscite to ascertain the wishes of the Kashmiri people regarding the state's future political status.

While keeping the door open for political negotiations, the Indian Government mainly responded to the secessionist insurgency in Indian Kashmir by force. In the early 1990s personnel from the Central Police Organizations (CPOs) and the army were deployed in the Valley to launch counter-insurgency operations together with the Jammu and Kashmir Police (JKP). These operations had two main objectives: to destroy local insurgent organizations and their support networks within Indian Kashmir and to prevent the infiltration of armed insurgents from across the LOC. To accomplish the first objective, the security forces created and maintained secure zones, launched combing (cordon and search) operations and administered both judicial and extrajudicial punishments. Border sealing and counter-infiltration operations were undertaken to fulfil the second objective. The security forces also created a network of informers and established an anti-insurgency body composed of former insurgents. In addition, New Delhi imposed president's rule (direct rule by the centre) in Indian Kashmir.

The insurgency in Indian Kashmir took a heavy toll on Indo-Pakistani relations and contributed greatly to insecurity in South Asia. In the immediate aftermath of the outbreak of the insurgency, bilateral relations plummeted to an all-time low and both countries appeared to be on the verge of full-scale war. Although war was avoided during the 1990 crisis, tempers flared up again in mid-1998 in the immediate aftermath of controversial nuclear weapons testing by India and Pakistan. In this charged atmosphere, the prospect of a real nuclear exchange (no matter how limited) between the two countries seemed fairly high given the long history of animosity between them, their zero-sum mentality regarding Kashmir and the hardening of emotions on both sides of the LOC following the tests. The immediate crisis was diffused by US diplomacy; however, an undeclared border war broke out in May 1999 when local insurgents and foreign volunteers, supported by regular Pakistani soldiers in civilian garb, crossed the LOC in the Kargil sector in Kashmir and occupied large tracts of land and several unmanned peaks and ridges on the Indian side. Though initially stunned by the suddenness and scope of the border incursion, New Delhi responded militarily with vigour and determination. The real question during this war was whether it would escalate into a bigger showdown, perhaps even involving nuclear weapons. Thankfully, in July 1999 the status quo ante was restored after Pakistan was forced, by a massive Indian counteroffensive and intense US diplomatic pressure, to withdraw its own troops and the insurgent forces under its control from the Indian side of the LOC.

The Kargil war was followed by a military coup in Pakistan in October 1999. The military Government under Gen. Pervez Musharraf that took power in Islamabad attempted to overcome the frustrations of the Kargil fiasco by referring to the possibility of a real catastrophic nuclear war in South Asia if the Kashmir dispute was not resolved quickly. In the aftermath of the terrorist attacks in the USA on 11 September 2001, when Pakistan was elevated to the status of a frontline ally by the Administration of President George W. Bush in return for backing the subsequent US-led 'war on terror', the Musharraf regime reportedly increased its support to terrorist organizations operating against India. In late 2001/early 2002 a series of spectacular terrorist attacks were carried out by the Lashkar-e-Taiba in different parts of India, including an attack on the Indian Parliament in New Delhi. Public opinion in India was outraged and opinion polls revealed that an overwhelming majority of the population favoured launching a decisive war against Pakistan. The Indian Government reacted by mobilizing and deploying the Indian military on the Indo-Pakistani border and by placing the forces on the highest state of alert; Pakistan responded in similar fashion. New Delhi also recalled its ambassador from Islamabad and revoked Pakistan's 'over flight' permission. With two of the world's largest armies squaring up to each other, war in South Asia appeared imminent.

Sensing trouble, the Bush Administration's crisis managers, including Secretary of State Colin Powell, Assistant Secretary of State Richard Armitage and Secretary of Defense Donald Rumsfeld, made several trips to New Delhi and Islamabad during 2002 and 2003. The US officials followed a dual track in their attempts to diffuse the Indo-Pakistani crisis. On one hand they impressed on Pakistan that in the post-Kargil and post-September 11 scenario Islamabad was required to take specific steps, such as clamping down on terrorist groups and their training camps in Pakistan and halting the infiltration of terrorists into Indian Kashmir and India, in order to create political space for New Delhi to agree to bilateral peace talks. On the other hand they firmly indicated to India that the USA did not consider New Delhi's decision to suspend bilateral talks with Pakistan until Islamabad stopped all cross-border terrorism as realistic.

Although it remained unconvinced that the Musharraf regime stood against terrorism and was doing its best to crack down on terrorist outfits operating out of Pakistan, acquiescing to intense US pressure the Indian Government grudgingly agreed to demobilize its military forces and initiate a composite dialogue with Islamabad with the aim of resolving all outstanding disputes between the two states, including Kashmir. Several rounds of official bilateral meetings were held and a number of confidence-building measures were initiated, including the setting up of a Srinagar–Muzaffarabad bus service linking Indian and Pakistani parts of Kashmir. The two countries' cricket teams and large contingents of supporters also visited each other, and for the first time ever the atmosphere at the cricket matches was very cordial. While these gains were noteworthy, not much progress was made regarding the vexatious issue of Kashmir. Terrorist attacks in Indian Kashmir and in other parts of India (most recently in Varanasi, Hyderabad and Mumbai) also continued to be carried out by Pakistan-based terrorist organizations such as the Lashkar-e-Taiba, vitiating the positive atmosphere that had been created. In addition, there was no halt to the infiltration of militants across the LOC, putting a further damper on the bilateral negotiations and undermining prospects for peace.

Following the assumption of power by a popularly elected civilian government in Pakistan in February 2008, there was widespread optimism that bilateral ties between India and Pakistan would improve and that a resolution to the Kashmir dispute would finally be reached. Within a short span of time, however, serious doubts were raised in India regarding the new Pakistani Government's ability and determination to crack down on Pakistan-based terrorist groups that intended to strike against India itself and against Indian assets and personnel in other countries such as Afghanistan. The allegation made by the US Administration that the Pakistani military was implicated in the suicide terrorist attack against the Indian embassy in Kabul in July 2008, which killed several Indian diplomatic and security personnel, aggravated the situation and heightened tension. In addition, the exchange of fire between Indian and Pakistani troops across the frontier in Kashmir in mid-2008 provided further indication of the deterioration in Indo-Pakistani relations. For the sake of the millions of people in both countries who have no real control over the situation, one can only hope that the recent rapid decline in bilateral relations does not lead to the outbreak of a fifth major war in the subcontinent.

## THE AFGHANISTAN CONUNDRUM

Afghanistan, a landlocked state that acts as a bridge between South Asia and the Middle East, has been wracked by instability and civil war since the forcible overthrow of its last monarch, Mohammed Zahir Shah, at the hands of Gen. Sardar Mohammad Daoud Khan in 1973. Daoud's leadership style quickly alienated the people, particularly the left-wing factions, which joined together to oust him from power in 1978. Communist rule rapidly led to factional infighting, which prompted the Soviet Union to invade Afghanistan in December 1979. Over the next decade the country experienced fully-fledged war between the Soviet occupying forces and a non-communist multi-ethnic Afghan resistance force collectively known as the *mujahidin*, which was funded, trained and equipped by the USA, Saudi Arabia and Pakistan. After the Soviet withdrawal in 1988, the communist regime of Najibullah stood no chance against the *mujahidin* forces and collapsed within a short span of time. With the fall of communism in Afghanistan, serious fighting broke out among the various ethnic factions within the victorious *mujahidin*. The Pashtun tribes, who collectively form Afghanistan's largest ethnic group and comprise approximately 40% of the total population, wanted to reassert their historic dominance over other ethnic groups by making an exclusive claim to power. The smaller ethnic minorities, notably the Tajiks and the Uzbeks, were resentful of the historic Pashtun domination in the country and saw an ideal opportunity to reverse that trend. The Tajiks and the Uzbeks, therefore, formed an alliance (known as the Northern Alliance) to oppose the various Pashtun war-lords hankering for power. The civil war that ensued lasted for almost five years. It is against this backdrop that the Taliban came to power in Kabul in 1996.

Comprised in the main of fundamentalist Pashtun students from the hundreds of *madrassas* (Islamic seminaries) that had been established in the tribal areas of Pakistan during the decades-long Afghan war, the Taliban became a fighting force under the alleged guidance of Pakistan's ISI directorate in the mid-1990s. After suppressing the forces of the various Pashtun war-lords clamouring for power in Kabul, the Taliban turned its attention to the Northern Alliance. The Northern Alliance-supported fledgling government, which was headed by the elderly Tajik statesman Burhanuddin Rabbani, soon fled the capital and the Taliban captured the city in September 1996. Fierce fighting subsequently erupted in the Panjshir Valley in the north of the country, where the Northern Alliance forces under the Tajik war-lord Ahmed Shah Masoud had retreated. In western Afghanistan, the forces of the Uzbek war-lord Gen. Abdul Rashid Dostam also clashed with the advancing Taliban troops. By the late 1990s the Taliban had taken control of most of the country (except for pockets of resistance in the north and the west) and had implemented a harsh and puritanical Islamic rule.

The association of the Pashtun Taliban leaders with Osama bin Laden and al-Qa'ida stretched back to the days of the anti-Soviet resistance in Afghanistan. During the 1980s, when droves of Arab jihadists poured into Afghanistan to fight the Soviet occupiers, Pashtun leaders welcomed their help for tactical reasons. During the early 1990s, when the Taliban launched its military campaign and attempted to sweep through Afghanistan, it welcomed the active support of Arab and other foreign volunteers, as well as the help that it received from the Pakistani and Saudi intelligence communities. The Arab volunteers were greatly inspired by the ideology of *jihad* (holy war), which found resonance among the fundamentalist Taliban and led to the establishment of close personal and political ties between the supreme Taliban leader Mullah Mohammad Omar and bin Laden. The Taliban regime provided a safe sanctuary for bin Laden and his associates and allowed al-Qa'ida to operate a number of terrorist training camps in Afghanistan.

Following the terrorist attacks in September 2001 the USA was determined to capture bin Laden. The Taliban, however, refused to hand him over and the Bush Administration undertook a full-scale military offensive against Afghanistan and the Taliban regime. The key US objective was to launch air and ground attacks from aircraft carriers located in the Persian (Arabian) Gulf and also from bases in Pakistan and Tajikistan. The USA also secured the services of the Northern Alliance, whose leaders (such as Masoud and Dostam) had a large following and knew the harsh, mountainous terrain well. By the end of 2001 the Northern Alliance, with massive support from US Special Forces and fighter jets, had recaptured most of the country, including the capital city of Kabul and the northern city of Mazar-i-Sharif.

Although the Taliban was ousted from power relatively easily, the high-ranking leaders of the former regime, such as Mullah Mohammad Omar, together with Osama bin Laden and his deputy, Ayman al-Zawahiri, evaded capture by the US Special Forces and the Northern Alliance troops. It is widely believed that they initially hid in mountain caves in the rugged

Tora Bora region of Afghanistan, thus escaping the relentless bombing campaign inflicted on the region by the US forces. Thereafter, with the help of Pashtun war-lords and tribal leaders, the fugitive leaders were reported to have crossed the Durand Line (the border between Afghanistan and Pakistan) and to have found shelter among Pashtun tribes in Pakistan's quasi-autonomous Federally Administered Tribal Areas (FATA).

With the leading figures of the Taliban and al-Qa'ida reportedly in hiding in Pakistan, the US forces turned their attention to state-building in Afghanistan, thus effectively leaving the main responsibility for 'neutralizing' these groups with President Musharraf and the Pakistani military. In December 2001 the Bonn Agreement was signed, under which the various ethnic groups of Afghanistan agreed to form a multi-ethnic interim government. In April 2002 an emergency Loya Jirga (Grand National Council) was convened in order to allow tribal leaders from various parts of the country to endorse the formation of the new Government, which was headed by Hamid Karzai, a Pashtun leader supported by the USA, as President. However, Pashtun opinion regarding Karzai remained divided, with many regarding him with suspicion and mistrust.

The formation of the interim Government did not, however, solve Afghanistan's security predicament. The country was, to all intents and purposes, divided into various enclaves that were controlled by different ethnic and tribal war-lords. Hence, the writ of Karzai's Government did not extend much beyond the immediate surroundings of Kabul. In addition, Afghanistan was awash with weapons and criminal and illegal drugs-trafficking networks operated at will. The economy was in utter disarray and the infrastructure was completely destroyed. The black market flourished openly and food production was severely curtailed as farmers opted for the more lucrative cultivation of opium poppies.

Realising that the security situation in Afghanistan was dire and would require the long-term military presence of Western forces in the country, the USA persuaded its NATO allies to establish the International Security Assistance Force (ISAF) in January 2002. ISAF was initially composed of 10,000 soldiers drawn from more than 30 NATO countries. Its mission in Afghanistan was the first time that NATO had conducted military operations outside of Europe. ISAF's mandate was at first restricted to security operations within the Kabul region alone, while a large contingent of US-led coalition forces conducted military operations in the south and east of the country. Despite these measures, the security situation in Afghanistan continued to decline steadily throughout 2004 and 2005. By early 2006 there were clear signs that the power wielded by key regional war-lords and the Taliban was on the ascendancy, largely owing to the fact the Afghan Government and the coalition forces were powerless to halt the flow of money and weapons to these groups from their foreign patrons (mostly, it was alleged, Afghanistan's neighbours). The USA's policy of using war-lords to fight the Taliban also meant that Karzai's Government could exercise little control over these mercenaries.

In political and economic terms, however, certain positive developments took place in Afghanistan between 2004 and 2006. Another Loya Jirga was held in January 2004 in order to ratify a new Constitution for the 'Islamic Republic of Afghanistan' and in October 2004 a presidential election was held, which was won by Hamid Karzai under controversial circumstances. This was followed in September 2005 by the first parliamentary and provincial elections to be held in Afghanistan in more than 30 years; in December the new Parliament convened for the first time. In addition, the economic situation showed signs of improvement. In February 2006 an international donors' meeting in London pledged more than US $10,000m. in reconstruction aid over five years. Afghanistan also began to register improved economic growth rates and foreign private-sector investment began to increase, particularly in Kabul and the surrounding areas.

From mid-2006, however, the security situation deteriorated. In May violent anti-US protests erupted in Kabul after a road accident involving a US military vehicle resulted in the deaths of many bystanders. In May–June there were reports of serious gun battles between Taliban fighters and Afghan and coalition forces in the south. The severity of the clashes demonstrated that the Taliban had recovered and gained in strength following the set-backs that it had suffered in 2001. The resurgence of the Taliban prompted ISAF to assume the leadership of military operations in the south of Afghanistan in July 2006. Over the next three months heavy fighting took place in the south and east, where the Taliban had once again established bases. In October ISAF took over the responsibility of providing security across the whole of Afghanistan, taking command in the east from a US-led coalition force. However, despite concerted efforts on the part of ISAF (which numbered some 30,000 troops at October 2006), the Taliban continued to grow in strength and its leaders remained at large.

In March 2007 heavy fighting erupted in the southern province of Helmand after the Afghan and ISAF forces launched 'Operation Achilles' against the Taliban. Although the Taliban's most senior military commander, Mullah Dadullah, was killed during the fighting, the military operation failed to curb the Taliban's rapidly growing military and political clout. In July a resurgent Taliban kidnapped a group of Christian charity workers from the Republic of Korea; two were killed by their captors, but the rest were eventually released. In October the Taliban kidnapped and executed several other foreign workers, and in the following month members of the organization carried out a devastating suicide attack on a parliamentary delegation in the northern town of Baghlan, which killed at least 41 people.

The US and NATO commanders blamed Pakistan (particularly the ISI) for the resurgence of the Taliban, claiming that the organization's senior leaders (together with high-ranking officials of al-Qa'ida) were hiding in the quasi-independent tribal areas of Pakistan where they were being protected by fiercely loyal Pashtun tribesmen. The USA accused President Musharraf and his military of not doing enough to flush out the insurgents from their tribal hideouts. A number of commanders even voiced their suspicions that elements within the Pakistani authorities, particularly within the ISI, were sympathetic to the Taliban and al-Qa'ida and were actually helping these groups to revive and strengthen. Religious fundamentalist groups in Pakistan were also suspected of providing support to the Taliban and al-Qa'ida, and the Musharraf regime appeared to be doing nothing to prevent this. As US and NATO frustration mounted, the commanders even discussed taking direct military action in the tribal areas of Pakistan in order to attempt to neutralize the Taliban and al-Qa'ida. The Pakistan Government expressed its firm opposition to this proposal and vehemently argued that such a move would be direct violation of Pakistan's sovereignty and would be interpreted as an act of war. Islamabad further counter-argued that Pakistan itself was a victim of terrorist acts carried out by the Taliban and al-Qa'ida and that its troops were involved in heavy fighting with members and sympathizers of these organizations in the tribal areas.

Be that as it may, the fact remains that by mid-2008 both the Taliban and al-Qa'ida had probably regained the strength that they had enjoyed in 2001 just before the 9/11 attacks. Both organizations have also become much more emboldened in recent times, mainly as a result of their successes in the battlefield. For instance, in June 2008 the Taliban organized a massive jail break from Qandahar prison, freeing at least 350 of their supporters and sympathizers. This was followed in July by a suicide bomb attack on the Indian embassy in Kabul, which killed more than 40 people. Consequently, NATO leaders have had no option but to pledge their unwavering long-term commitment to fighting the Taliban and al-Qa'ida in Afghanistan.

## IDENTITY CONFLICTS IN SOUTH ASIA

A major threat to the security of South Asian states and peoples stems from violent intra-state conflicts mostly over competing notions of 'identity'. The majority of these identity conflicts have long and chequered histories and some are legacies of European colonization and decolonization. A striking feature of these conflicts is the massive challenge that they pose for human security and for national integration. Many of these conflicts have involved gross and deliberate abuse of human rights, produced large numbers of refugees and internally displaced persons and shackled the states' security apparatus in protracted counterinsurgency operations. If allowed to fester, many of these conflicts have the potential to cause major breakdown in the states of this region. In a broad sense, three distinct types of identity conflicts are found in South Asia: i) ethno-nationalist conflicts, which often take the form of secessionist–anti-secessionist warfare; ii) communal and sectarian violence; and iii) class struggle, which often subsumes within it caste and tribal identities.

**Ethno-nationalist Conflicts**

India's ethnic diversity is simply of staggering proportions and starting from the immediate post-independence years the country has had to deal with the nationalist aspirations of many constituent ethnic groups. The initial challenges came in the form of the Naga and Mizo insurgencies in north-east India, which were eventually managed through political accommodation and the creation of the new states of Nagaland and Mizoram. However, strong feelings of deprivation, neglect, economic and social marginalization and lack of empowerment continued to create resentment among many ethno-tribal groups in this region towards the Indian State. Such resentment often generated nationalist/separatist sentiments and political movements leading to violent clashes between competing ethnic groups and between various ethnic groups and the Indian State. Of the various active insurgent groups in north-east India today, the United Liberation Front of Assam (ULFA) is by far the most powerful and dangerous. Apart from the north-east, India has also had to deal with secessionist ethno-nationalist movements in the Punjab and in Indian Kashmir. The Sikh revolt in the Punjab occurred during the early 1980s and eventually led to an invasion of the Golden Temple in Amritsar (the holiest Sikh religious shrine) by the Indian army (in an operation codenamed Operation Blue Star) in June 1984 to flush out religious fanatics and militants who had taken shelter there. The Golden Temple was severely damaged in the fighting, which further inflamed the anger felt by the Sikhs. In an act of retribution, two Sikh bodyguards assassinated Prime Minister Indira Gandhi in October 1984, which, in turn, led to anti-Sikh riots encouraged by some senior leaders of Indira Gandhi's Congress (I) party. In May 1988 Indian security forces were once again forced to enter the Golden Temple to evict militants who had moved back there and were using it as a shelter and a base of operations. In the early 1990s the Punjab police force launched a harsh counter-insurgency operation against Sikh insurgent groups such as the Babbar Khalsa International, the Khalistan Zindabad Force, the Khalistan Commando Force and the Khalistan Liberation Army, which gradually weakened the potency of Sikh militancy in Punjab. During the 1990s the focus of attention shifted to the Kashmir Valley, where student demonstrations in 1987 had rapidly escalated into a full-blown secessionist insurgency. The uprising in Indian Kashmir was allegedly supported by Pakistan and was also reported to have the backing of Osama bin Laden's al-Qa'ida organization. Confronted with such a grave challenge to its authority, the Indian Government resorted to harsh counter-insurgency measures through the Indian army, paramilitary forces and Kashmir state police. Throughout the 1990s the violence in Indian Kashmir continued to escalate and led to extremely tense relations between India and Pakistan. Although some positive developments have taken place in Indian Kashmir and in Indo-Pakistani bilateral relations in recent years, the dispute is far from being resolved. Hence, the potential of the Kashmir situation to destabilize India and endanger regional security in the near future remains very high. In mid-2008 there was a marked resurgence in sectarian violence in Kashmir (more than 20 Muslim protestors were shot dead by police in August alone) and the outlook for the troubled state appeared increasingly bleak.

In Pakistan ethno-nationalist and secessionist movements have occurred with regular frequency, posing serious political and security problems for the State. In the immediate aftermath of Pakistan's foundation in 1947, the State had to use force to crush the secessionist aspirations of the Baloch and Pashtun ethno-tribal groups. During the 1950s and 1960s nationalist and secessionist sentiments continued to grow amongst the Bengalis in East Pakistan. When the Pakistani military attempted to suppress the Bengalis, it led to a complex humanitarian emergency and a fully-fledged war of liberation. Eventually, the new state of Bangladesh was created after the third Indo-Pakistani war of 1971. In the 1980s and 1990s the major ethnic conflict in Pakistan was between the Sindhis and Mohajirs in the province of Sindh. Due to this conflict, the port city of Karachi, which is Pakistan's commercial capital, witnessed almost daily murders, shootings and bomb blasts. The neighbouring province of Balochistan also became restive during the 1990s. By the time the military had resumed power in Islamabad in 1999, a Baloch insurgency, spearheaded by the Baloch Liberation Army (BLA), was under way in the province. In recent years the Pakistani military has had to launch major counter-insurgency operations in Balochistan. The political climate in the North-West Frontier Province (NWFP) and the tribal areas bordering Afghanistan also became volatile following the terrorist attacks in the USA in September 2001 owing to the subsequent US military operations in Afghanistan (and later Iraq) and President Musharraf's decision to support the US-led 'war on terror'. After the Taliban was ousted from power in Kabul in December 2001, a number of high-ranking leaders of the former regime (such as Mullah Mohammad Omar) and al-Qa'ida (including Osama bin Laden and his deputy Ayman al-Zawahiri) were reported to be hiding in the tribal areas protected by the fiercely independent and radical Pashtun tribes. The Musharraf regime's relations with the Pashtun tribes thus became strained and the Pakistani military, under intense US pressure, mounted repeated offensives in the tribal areas in an attempt to capture or kill bin Laden and the other al-Qa'ida and Taliban leaders. The situation remains extremely volatile and could potentially have serious implications for the future territorial integrity and political stability of Pakistan.

As in India and Pakistan, Sri Lanka has also suffered from secessionist ethnic conflict over the past 30 years or so, which has resulted in thousands of deaths from war and terrorist attacks, caused widespread damage and injury to civilian populations, and severely undermined the unity and integrity of the country. The ethnic civil war took a particularly ugly turn during the 1990s as the Sri Lankan Government and the LTTE favoured a decisive military showdown. This militaristic approach effectively sidelined moderate voices on both sides but resulted in a military stalemate on the ground. With neither side able to break the deadlock, a fragile peace process initiated by Norway seemed to hold some promise. A cease-fire agreement was signed in April 2002 and the two sides agreed to meet face-to-face for talks. Six rounds of direct peace talks were held between the representatives of the LTTE and the Sri Lankan Government but ultimately failed to produce an agreement acceptable to all parties. Serious fighting resumed in 2005, indicating that both sides had used the cease-fire to regroup and reaffirm their faith in a conclusive military showdown.

**Communal and Sectarian Violence**

Communal and sectarian conflicts have been a major source of insecurity in South Asia. In India relations between Hindus and Muslims have proved tense and conflictual since independence. However, during the past two decades or so communal relations have deteriorated as both Hindu and Muslim fundamentalist forces have gained ground and Indian politics entered an era of weak central governments. In December 1992 Hindu fanatics destroyed a 16th-century mosque called the Babri Masjid in the city of Ayodhya in Uttar Pradesh, disregarding orders against such an action from the Supreme Court and warnings from the Indian Government. This incident sparked major communal rioting across the country; Muslim criminal gangs also orchestrated a series of bomb blasts in Mumbai, India's commercial and financial capital, in January 1993 in which around 250 people were killed. To avenge the bomb attacks, Hindu mobs in Mumbai, allegedly supported by the ruling Hindu fundamentalist Shiv Sena (Army of Shiv) party and segments of the state security forces, carried out a nine-day massacre of Muslims in the city. In

February 2002 further communal carnage took place in Gujarat when several compartments of a train (the Sabarmati Express) carrying Hindu workers and pilgrims returning from Ayodhya caught fire just as it pulled out of Godhra station, killing 58 people. Rumours quickly spread that the train had been attacked by Muslim mobs (Godhra station was located in a predominantly Muslim area of the town), although no conclusive evidence regarding how the fire started and whether the incident was a pre-planned attack has as yet emerged. The Godhra fire led to one of the worst cases of anti-Muslim riots in Indian history. In this campaign of terror and massacre, which many commentators viewed as deliberately planned, the Gujarat state government, which was led by the Hindu fundamentalist Bharatiya Janata Party (BJP or Indian People's Party), and the state's police and security forces were thoroughly implicated.

Communal violence has also plagued Sri Lanka. In July 1983 an anti-Tamil riot was organized by the Sinhalese Buddhist community in the capital city of Colombo. According to some commentators, during the rioting state machinery and resources were used by senior government personnel in a concerted effort directed against the lives and properties of the Hindu Tamils. This set the stage for the outbreak of the fully-fledged secessionist war by the LTTE and other Sri Lankan Tamil insurgent groups. As the war gained ground in the north and east of the country, clashes between Hindu Tamils and Muslim also became frequent. Over the years the LTTE expelled about 1m. Muslims from the Jaffna Peninsula and repeatedly attacked and massacred Muslim civilians in the east, mainly because the Muslims, along with the Sinhalese settlers, refused to accept the merger of the northern and eastern provinces and rejected LTTE rule in the areas that it controlled. The Muslims also suffered constant harassment and extortion from the LTTE. In recent years, as clashes between members of the Tamil and Muslim communities intensified in the eastern region, Muslim youth were reported to be forming anti-LTTE 'Osama suicide squads' in order to retaliate against their attackers. Communal clashes between the Sinhalese and Tamil communities have also recently worsened. Sinhalese soldiers have been accused by several prominent human rights groups of deliberately killing innocent Tamil civilians in the north and east of the country. The Sinhalese Government has also been charged with forcibly expelling Tamil families from Colombo. In retaliation, the LTTE has carried out massacres of captured Sinhalese soldiers and stepped up attacks on innocent Sinhalese villagers.

Sectarian clashes are not new to Pakistan. Although tensions between majority Sunni and minority Shi'a communities have been apparent since the immediate post-independence years, sectarian conflict has intensified since the mid-1980s. In 1985 the Sipah-e-Sahaba Pakistan (SSP), a militant Sunni Islamist organization belonging to the Deobandi school of thought, was established. The SSP was formed partly in response to the Iranian Revolution and to curb the growing influence of Shi'as in Pakistan, especially in Punjab where Shi'a feudal landlords were reported to be oppressing (in socio-economic terms) the Sunni peasantry. The alleged policy of the military Government of Gen. Mohammad Zia ul-Haq actively to support fanatical religious groups (with financial backing from Saudi Arabia) and encourage the creation of a large number of *madrassas* (seminaries) within Pakistan was also partly responsible for the increased assertiveness and aggressiveness of the Sunnis. The Afghan war and the influx of millions of Afghan refugees further contributed to the creation of a volatile situation and the rise in sectarian tensions and clashes. Throughout the late 1980s and 1990s the SSP carried out a series of terrorist attacks on the Shi'a community, some of which were directed at prominent religious leaders and popular mosques. The SSP also attacked Iranian interests and personnel in Pakistan; for example, in December 1990 Sadegh Ganji, a prominent Iranian diplomat, was killed in Lahore by the SSP. In 1996 there was a split within the SSP, which led to the creation of the Lashkar-e-Jhangvi (LEJ). The LEJ became known as the armed wing of the SSP and carried out most of the subsequent attacks on the Shi'a community. Although most of the SSP/LEJ attacks have been directed at the Shi'a community, on occasion the very small Christian and Hindu communities in Pakistan have been targeted as well. President Musharraf outlawed the LEJ in August 2001 and the SSP in January 2002.

### Class Warfare

Class warfare in the form of popular insurgency or Maoist insurgency has become a major source of insecurity in South Asia today, with Nepal and India bearing the main brunt of the violence. In April 1990 a popular movement for the restoration of democracy (MRD) succeeded in reintroducing multi-party democracy in Nepal after almost 30 years of absolute rule by the monarchy. Within a short period, however, Nepal was confronted with the outbreak of a violent Maoist insurgency that rapidly spread and gained in popularity. By the turn of the century, the Maoists controlled almost 80% of the country, with rural areas completely under their domination.

In November 1990 a new Constitution was introduced in Nepal and in May 1991 the country held its first democratic general election for 32 years. The Nepali Congress Party (NCP) won the election and formed a new government under Prime Minister Girija Prasad Koirala. However, problems of governance emerged straightaway. The Prime Minister was reputed to be the most outspoken critic of the communists within the NCP and it was not surprising therefore that the main opposition party, the Communist Party of Nepal (Unified Marxist-Leninist—UML), along with other communist parties adopted an unco-operative attitude towards the Koirala Government. The Government was further hampered by a stagnant economy, which soon increased public frustration at the poor performance of the NCP in power and led to an outbreak of serious factional infighting. The Koirala Government eventually collapsed in June 1994. Fresh elections held in November of that year resulted in a 'hung' parliament. The King therefore invited Man Mohan Adhikari, the leader of the single largest party, the UML, to form a minority government. The minority Adhikari Government lasted for only nine months. In September 1995 the King appointed Sher Bahadur Deuba as the new Prime Minister at the head of a coalition government comprising the NCP, the Rashtriya Prajatantra Party (RPP) and the Nepali Sadbhavana Party (NSP). Although the Deuba Government lasted against all odds until March 1997, it expended most of its time and energy on fending off concerted efforts by the opposition UML to bring down the coalition; in the process, the basic needs of the people were largely ignored and living standards remained dismal.

As political shenanigans were taking place in Kathmandu, important developments were happening within the ranks of the communist movement in Nepal. In 1983 the Communist Party of Nepal (CPN) had split when Mohan Bikram and Baburam Bhattarai left the party to form the CPN-Masal. In 1985 the CPN-Masal itself split when a group headed by Pushpa Kamal Dahal (better known as Prachanda) broke away to form the CPN-Mashal. During the struggle for the restoration of democracy in Nepal, four left-wing parties, including the Fourth Convention, CPN-Masal and CPN-Mashal, had joined forces to form the Communist Party of Nepal (Unity Centre) and demanded that a new constituent assembly be established to draft a new popular constitution. A political wing of the Unity Centre, the United People's Front (UPF), was subsequently created to contest the 1991 parliamentary elections,in which it won nine seats. By the time the 1994 parliamentary elections took place, however, the Unity Centre had suffered a major split. One faction, led by Nirmal Lama, was officially recognized in Parliament and by the Election Commission, while the other faction, led by Baburam Bhattarai, was denied recognition and decided to change its name to the Communist Party of Nepal (Maoist). This faction announced that henceforward it would resort to armed struggle in the form of a 'people's war' (as developed by the Chinese leader Mao Zedong) in order to capture power and usher in a genuine democratic revolution. On 4 February 1996 Bhattarai presented the Deuba Government with a list containing 40 specific demands, including the abrogation of the 1950 Peace and Friendship Treaty and new Mahakali Treaty with India, the divestment of the monarchy of all powers and privileges, the drafting of a new constitution by a popularly elected constituent assembly, the introduction of work permits for foreign nationals working in Nepal, the nationalization of the property and assets of capitalists, the declaration of Nepal as a secular nation, a halt to all foreign aid, and the initiation of a large number of social reforms and development projects, such as the building of roads and the provision of electricity and drinking water to rural areas. Bhattarai warned that if the Government failed to act on these demands by 17 February, the CPN (Maoist) would be compelled to launch an armed struggle against the Nepali State. Four days before the deadline was due to expire, the Maoists struck simultaneously in six districts. A number of police outposts were attacked and weapons and ammunition stolen. Foreign-owned factories and businesses were also attacked.

Pervasive poverty and underdevelopment were key structural reasons for the outbreak of the Maoist insurgency. This was reflected in the overwhelming strength and popularity of the Maoists in some of the poorest districts of Nepal. By 2001 the Maoist insurgency had spread to 68 of Nepal's 75 districts; of these 68, 32 districts were under the close control of the insurgents and in these areas the Maoist guerrillas could roam around freely and organize mass meetings at will. The insurgency was also more pronounced in the mid-western region, which comprised the most backward and least accessible districts of Nepal. The Maoists enjoyed widespread popularity (especially in rural areas), a trend that increased as a series of political crises gripped Kathmandu and discredited both the mainstream political parties as well as the institution of the monarchy (particularly under the unpopular King Gyanendra, who succeeded to the throne following the assassination of King Birendra by his own son, Crown Prince Dipendra, in June 2001). Another notable feature of the Maoist movement was the large part played by women in the uprising. In the past, female participation in the communist movement has been mostly confined to the electoral arena. Under the Maoists in Nepal, however, it was estimated that almost 30% of the armed guerrillas were women. The Maoists were also mindful of the factors of ethnicity and caste in Nepal. For example, the Maoists spoke up for oppressed minority ethnic groups such as the Magars of western Nepal; similarly, unlike previous communist politics, which remained confined within Nepal's upper castes, such as the Brahmins, Chhetris and Newars, the Maoist movement encouraged broader participation, especially from people belonging to 'untouchable' castes such as the Kami, Sarki and Damai.

If economic and social underdevelopment provided the key structural reasons for the emergence of the Maoist movement, then malgovernance and growing public frustration with the political system were the immediate causes of the outbreak and widespread popularity of the insurgency. In particular, the insurgency was a direct result of the complete inability of Nepal's multiparty political system to govern effectively and to deliver equitable economic development and social justice to the impoverished, marginalized and disempowered masses in rural areas who had suffered greatly under monarchical rule for 30 years. The deep unpopularity of King Gyanendra and his alleged scheming ways further undermined public confidence in the monarchy and contributed massively to the growing popularity and strength of the Maoists. The complete failure of the security forces to suppress the Maoist uprising undermined morale within the forces and contributed to the aura, prestige and image of invincibility enjoyed by the guerrillas. Eventually, in 2006 a massive popular uprising against the King and the institution of the monarchy led to a victory for parliamentary democracy. A multiparty interim Government headed by G. P. Koirala of the NCP assumed power in May and accepted the Maoists' demands that the power of the monarchy be curtailed and a popularly elected constituent assembly be formed to draft a new constitution for Nepal. The interim Government abrogated most of the powers of the monarchy and virtually confined the King to the royal palace. In early 2007 the Maoists agreed to join the interim Government, proclaiming that their rebellion was over. In April 2008 elections were held to a constituent assembly that was to draft Nepal's new constitution and in August the Maoist leader Prachanda was appointed as the country's new Prime Minister.

While the Maoist rebellion has ended in Nepal, in neighbouring India it is growing in strength. The Maoist insurgency in India is currently manifested in parts of Andhra Pradesh, Bihar, Jharkhand, Karnataka, Maharashtra, Uttar Pradesh, Chhattisgarh, Orissa and West Bengal. About 12 Maoist groups are known to be active across these nine states. Of these groups, the Peoples' War Group and Maoist Co-ordination Committee are the best organized and most active. These groups are known to be in possession of large quantities of weapons and ammunition (many of which have been forcibly seized from the police) and conduct periodic military training that includes jungle warfare and ambush skills. The Maoist groups are also believed to have links with foreign left-wing insurgent groups such as the People's Liberation Army of Peru, the Kurdistan Workers Party and the Sri Lankan LTTE. In July 2001 several Maoist groups in India joined forces with the Maoist insurgents in Nepal and smaller Maoist groups in Bangladesh and Sri Lanka to form an umbrella organization entitled the Coordination Committee of Maoist Parties and Organisations of South Asia.

The Indian Maoists typically attack those they regard as class enemies, for example the rural landed élite, representatives of the bourgeois state such as police and security personnel, government officials, bureaucrats and politicians, and anyone that they suspect to be working as agents and informers for the State. Over the years, public buildings and railway property have also come under attack from the Maoists in India.

The Maoist insurgency in India is the latest manifestation of peasant struggles that have periodically emerged owing to conditions of grinding poverty, exploitation and inequality prevalent in the countryside for centuries. Historically, abysmal levels of poverty, widespread hunger and abject caste-based exploitation and discrimination have been rampant in rural society and have set the stage for widespread discontent among poor farmers. Following independence, the inability of the Indian State to deliver on its promises of agrarian reform—promises on which the hopes of millions of rural families were pinned—led many poor farmers completely to lose faith in the State and to brand it (in the words of S. Banerjee) as 'the state of big landlords and comprador-bureaucrat capitalists'. Although the Indian Government implemented a number of poverty alleviation and rural development programmes, most of these measures further marginalized the small farmers, the landless peasantry and the tribal populations. As the bourgeois leanings of the Indian State became apparent, the rural masses felt betrayed and disillusioned, and believed that their hopes of achieving a more equitable social order through peaceful means had been dashed. Accordingly, a number of peasant leaders started drawing inspiration from Mao Zedong's ideas of 'guerrilla warfare', 'protracted armed struggle' and 'the forcible seizure of state power'.

The original aim of the 1967 Naxalbari uprising (hence the name Naxalite for Maoists), which marked the beginning of peasant armed struggle against the Indian State per se, was to capture state power by encircling cities. This aim was not realized, however, and the uprising was ruthlessly suppressed by the security forces. Nevertheless the Maoist movement in India survived (mostly underground) and from the early 1980s began to spread. Their ability to procure sophisticated weapons and training meant that gradually the Maoists were able to take control of a large area consisting of parts of Andhra Pradesh, Bihar, Jharkhand, Karnataka, Maharashtra, Uttar Pradesh, Chhattisgarh, Orissa and West Bengal. In the densely forested areas that incorporate some of the remotest tribal districts of the country and where the State's administrative machinery is either totally absent or rudimentary at best, the Maoists run a 'parallel state'. Cases of theft, robbery, rape, prostitution and the exploitation of lower castes by upper castes are decided promptly in people's courts; punishment can range from maiming to death sentences, with the decision of the 'kangaroo court' being final and binding. Besides enforcing law and order, the Maoist groups are also reported to have assumed responsibility for education, irrigation reservoirs, community kitchens, mobile medical units and the enforcement of minimum wages for labourers. Furthermore, the Maoists often play the role of Robin Hood in the areas they control—collecting money from forest contractors, traders and landlords and distributing it to the poor and needy; halting the extortion of tolls by local goons from poor tribal women; forcing wealthy farmers to raise their employees' wages; and enforcing social reforms such as bans on alcohol and on extravagant expenditure at weddings, a custom that usually sends poor families deep into debt.

Counter-insurgency operations launched by the security forces against the Maoists in India have so far achieved little success and it is this reality that poses the gravest security threat to the Indian State. The Maoist groups have the ability to disrupt elections, target police and paramilitary installations at will, and to hold the law and order machinery to ransom by sporadic attacks on public property. They have forged links with insurgent groups in other countries, from whom they have obtained ideological, financial and military support. The Maoist presence has already reached disturbing proportions in nine states and has further expanded into new areas such as north Bihar, north Orissa, central Chhattisgarh and eastern Uttar Pradesh. As Maoist attacks grow in frequency and intensity, the State's law and order apparatus is becoming increasingly overstretched. The political threat posed by the Maoists is also substantial. In most of the backward tribal districts of the country the Maoists provide the only beacon of hope for impoverished and exploited people. From building and maintaining basic infrastructure in villages, restoring the rights of tribal people over their ancestral lands, effecting land distribution among the landless poor, to ensuring law and order, the Maoists have taken responsibility for and carried out tasks that ideally should have been the State's responsibility. In performing these tasks the Maoists are providing a perfect replacement for the State in areas where development means little to many. By effectively replacing the State in the areas under its control, the Maoist movement has begun to challenge the State's very legitimacy.

## TRANSNATIONAL TERRORISM

The proliferation of terrorist groups across much of South Asia poses a grave risk to security in the region. Events in Afghanistan, the apparent growing appeal of religious fundamentalism and radical ideology, the presence of disgruntled domestic groups, state rivalry and the weakness of regional arrangements have all contributed to the steady growth of terrorism in the South Asian region. The political turmoil in Afghanistan since the Soviet military invasion in December 1979 was a principal reason for the growth and consolidation of Islamic fundamentalism in West Asia, which has now spread to parts of South Asia as well. During the Soviet occupation of Afghanistan in 1979–89, the USA, with support from Saudi Arabia and Pakistan, organized, funded, trained and armed an anti-Soviet resistance force—the *mujahidin* —which was composed of members belonging to various Afghan ethnic groups (such as the Pashtuns, Tajiks and Uzbeks) as well as volunteers from many other Muslim countries. The *mujahidin* was mainly motivated by the ideology of *jihad* ('holy war'). Although not a widely known fact at the time, a key player in the creation of this *jihadi* resistance force was the now notorious terrorist Osama bin Laden and his al-Qa'ida ('Base') organization.

Throughout the 1980s, as the conflict in Afghanistan dragged on, the strength of Islamic forces in Pakistan continued to rise rapidly. There had been a military coup in Pakistan in July 1977 and the country's new ruler, Gen. Muhammad Zia-ul Haq, deliberately set about to increase the power and influence of the Islamic parties such as the Jamaat-e-Islami Pakistan in an attempt to legitimize his rule and to create a bulwark against the so-called democratic parties. Consequently, large sums of money reportedly started to flow into the coffers of the Islamic parties (much of it from the Middle East), *madrassas* (Islamic seminaries) began to proliferate, and Islamic groups began to wield more influence over the foreign and security policies of the country. The presence of millions of Afghan refugees in Pakistan also provided a fertile recruiting ground for the radical Islamic parties and clerics. Many of these parties and clerics established links with the various factions of the Afghan *mujahidin* and with al-Qa'ida; connections were also made with Islamic fundamentalist groups in India and Bangladesh.

In the aftermath of the Soviet withdrawal from Afghanistan in 1989, which was followed by US demobilization in the region, a power struggle amongst the various Afghan ethnic groups and factions erupted and escalated into a fully-fledged civil war. During this war the Pakistani military intelligence agencies initially supported a few Pashtun warlords, such as the fundamentalist Gulbuddin Hekmatyar and his Hizb-i Islami party; they subsequently changed tactics, however, and helped to create (with the assistance of a number of Islamic parties and organizations in Pakistan) a fighting force called the Taliban (composed mainly of Afghan students from *madrassas* in Pakistan). With such backing, the Taliban took power in Kabul in 1996. Osama bin Laden's relations with the Taliban leaders were strong from the outset and Taliban-controlled Afghanistan therefore became al-Qa'ida's main base of operations. Along with the 'talibanization' of Afghanistan, religious extremism in Pakistan also became more widespread during the second half of the 1990s. By the time Musharraf came to power in 2001, Islamic extremist groups that advocated using terrorism as a means of *jihad*, such as the Sipah-e-Sahaba Pakistan, Lashkar-e-Jhangvi, Lashkar-e-Taiba and Jaish-e-Mohammed, operated openly within Pakistan. Moreover, in the October 2002 elections an alliance of six Islamic parties called the Muttahida Majlis-e-Amal secured 58 seats in the National Assembly, an absolute majority in the North-West Frontier Province and second position in Balochistan.

The 'talibanization' of Afghanistan and the rise of Islamic fundamentalism in Pakistan greatly magnified the threat of terrorism in South Asia. India in particular became a major victim when religious extremist groups in Afghanistan and Pakistan made common cause with Kashmiri insurgents fighting a secessionist war in Indian Kashmir. As mentioned above, during the initial years of the insurgency Kashmiri groups such as the JKLF reportedly received support and training in Pakistan. Following the termination of the Afghan war in 1989, however, more hardline *jihadi* groups, such as the Lashkar-e-Taiba, the Jaish-e-Mohammed and the Hizbul Mujahidin, became operational in Indian Kashmir. These groups were less interested in Kashmiri nationalism and more concerned with waging *jihad* with the aim of wresting Indian Kashmir from India's control and converting it into an independent Islamic state or merging it with Pakistan. They were therefore often as brutal in their attacks on local Kashmiri Muslims as they were on other ethno-religious groups. These groups also incorporated a large number of foreign volunteers (many of them veterans of the Afghan war) and were readily inclined to use terrorism indiscriminately as a means of warfare. Most of the terrorist attacks in Indian Kashmir were perpetrated by these groups. Over time and with the alleged encouragement of the military intelligence agencies of Pakistan and al-Qa'ida, groups such as the Lashkar-e-Taiba forged links with disgruntled groups and organizations within India (e.g. the outlawed Students Islamic Movement of India) and expanded their terrorist campaigns to include targets outside of Indian Kashmir. For example, in 2002 Lashkar-e-Taiba operatives carried out a spectacular attack against the Indian Parliament in New Delhi, which brought India and Pakistan to the brink of war. In recent years, the bomb blasts that killed hundreds of innocent civilians on suburban trains in Mumbai and in mosques in Malegaon and Hyderabad were allegedly the handiwork of Lashkar-e-Taiba agents.

The tentacles of Islamic terrorism also spread rapidly into Bangladesh. Because of its parliamentary dependency on the support of Islamic parties such as the Jamaat-e-Islami Bangladesh and the Islami Jatiya Oikya Jote, the Bangladesh National Party, which was in power in 2001–06, turned a blind eye to the activism of domestic Islamic groups and the spread of Islamic fundamentalist ideology in the country. This allowed hardline Islamic groups such as the Jamaat-ul-Mujahideen Bangladesh, the Jagrata Muslim Janata Bangladesh and the Harakat-ul-Jihad-i-Islami Bangladesh openly to launch attacks on the opposition Awami League party leaders and activists, to intimidate journalists and civil servants, to harass and threaten religious minorities, and to coerce men to grow beards and wear skull caps and women to wear veils. A key challenge for the army-supported current caretaker administration in Bangladesh (which assumed power in November 2006) would be to curb the activities of the various fundamentalist and terrorist groups that have links with and receive support from similar groups in Pakistan and Afghanistan.

The Islamization of Pakistan also came back to haunt the Musharraf regime after its decision to succumb to US pressure following the terrorist attacks in the USA in September 2001 and to support the US-led invasion of Afghanistan and global 'war on terror'. As part of the deal, the Pakistani military was asked to provide the US special forces with the use of military airports and bases in Balochistan, from where they could launch raids into southern and eastern Afghanistan, to share intelligence regarding the Taliban, al-Qa'ida and bin Laden, and to capture or eliminate suspected Taliban and al-Qa'ida personnel who had fled Afghanistan and were sheltering in the FATA under the protection of the fiercely independent and fundamentalist Pashtun tribes. The decision by the Musharraf regime to co-operate with the USA and to take military action against the Pashtun tribes and the Taliban/al-Qa'ida fighters led to fierce conflict in the tribal areas. It also resulted in an increase in clashes between the Government and hardline Islamic clerics and their supporters. In July 2007 these clashes culminated in the siege and invasion of Islamabad's Lal Masjid (Red Mosque) by Pakistani government forces after Abdul Rashid Ghazi, a radical cleric, and his supporters had barricaded themselves inside the complex along with many women and children hostages. The military operation, which resulted in the deaths of Ghazi and about 70 of his supporters, provoked retaliatory suicide bomb attacks against the Pakistani military and government personnel in the North-West Frontier Province and in the tribal areas; by the end of July around 100 soldiers had been killed in these attacks. Radical Islamic groups elsewhere in Pakistan also vowed to avenge the 'martyrdom' of Ghazi by carrying out more terrorist attacks against the regime and the security forces. In addition, Osama bin Laden's deputy, Ayman al-Zawahiri, called upon Pakistanis to revolt against President Musharraf in order to avenge the invasion of the Red Mosque. The threat of domestic terrorism and civil war has therefore been greatly heightened in Pakistan in recent times. This threat was compounded by the assassination of the opposition leader Benazir Bhutto in December 2007, the imposition of the state of emergency in the following month and by the prospect of political upheaval arising from the resignation of President Musharraf in August 2008.

Sri Lanka, too, has been affected by severe terrorist violence. Following the devastating tsunami that brought havoc and destruction to the island in December 2004, the bad blood that developed between the LTTE and the Sri Lankan Government over the perceived lack of adequate relief and reconstruction work in the Tamil areas contributed to an increase in terrorist violence and the eventual resumption of full-scale war. To avenge the poor treatment reportedly being meted out to the Tamils by the Government in the aftermath of the tsunami, the LTTE assassinated the Sri Lankan foreign minister, Lakshman Kadirgamar, in August 2005. This was followed in December by the killing of 11 government soldiers and a policeman in the northern Jaffna peninsula. The Government's response was to launch a full-scale invasion in an attempt to drive the LTTE out of the Eastern Province. In early 2006 major battles took place off the east coast between the Sea Tigers (the LTTE's naval wing) and the Sri Lankan navy. The Sri Lankan air force also resorted to the aerial bombardment of Tamil areas. The LTTE retaliated by carrying out suicide attacks against the Sri Lankan army headquarters in Colombo, killing several people and seriously wounding the head of the army, Lt-Gen. Sarath Fonseka. By late 2006/early 2007 the war had intensified in the east and gross human rights abuses were committed by both sides. Eventually the Sri Lankan military succeeded in recapturing the Eastern Province and driving the LTTE back into the northern Jaffna peninsula. The LTTE responded to the Sri Lankan air raids by carrying out a series of daring air strikes of their own on two Sri Lankan air force bases and two oil storage facilities located in Colombo airport. They further vowed to avenge their recent military set-back in the east by resorting to guerrilla tactics and carrying out terrorist attacks against the Sri Lankan military and the Government.

## SAARC AND THE FUTILE SEARCH FOR REGIONAL INTEGRATION AND PEACE

On its establishment in December 1985, the South Asian Association for Regional Co-operation (SAARC) was widely expected to follow in the footsteps of the European Union (EU), the North American Free Trade Agreement (NAFTA) and the Association of South East Asian Nations (ASEAN) in promoting regional economic integration, co-operation and peace. But after nearly 23 years of existence and 15 summits, most critics would agree that, while SAARC has been very successful in providing a regional forum where member states are able to meet and talk, in reality it has achieved very little.

For example, in 2005 intra-regional trade in South Asia accounted for only 5% of total trade, compared with 62% for the EU and 55% for NAFTA. In 1995 the South Asian Preferential Trading Arrangement (SAPTA) was launched, but its impact was severely limited as it only allowed for commodity-by-commodity negotiations aimed at reducing tariffs. After a decade of SAPTA, the South Asian Free Trade Agreement (SAFTA) was instigated in 2004. However, some critics have already claimed this to be a flawed agreement, the short-term impact of which will be minimal. A key goal of SAFTA is to reduce tariffs to the range of 0%–5%, but this was to be realized over a long-term period (by 2013–16); by that time these targets may have become irrelevant as a result of multilateral negotiations (under World Trade Organization) and/or bilateral trade agreements. According to the commentator Muchkund Dubey, SAFTA has also avoided making commitments to lower non-tariff barriers to promote intra-regional trade and lacks any special provision that would allow 'for the adoption of measures of deeper integration, such as granting of transit facilities, cooperation for development of transport and other forms of infrastructure, liberalization of investment and trade in services, co-operation in the financial and monetary fields, and co-ordination, if not harmonization, of macroeconomic policies'. Moreover, Pakistan has refused to apply the provisions of SAFTA to Indo-Pakistani trade, the largest component of intra-regional trade in South Asia.

If SAARC's record in promoting regional economic integration is rather dismal, its performance and achievement in the areas of security and peace are even worse. At the Islamabad summit in 2004, the member states drew up an agreement known as the SAARC Regional Convention on the Suppression of Terrorism, which contained a list of provisions aimed at promoting regional co-operation in dealing with the threat of terrorism in the South Asian region. A key provision concerns the extradition of persons suspected of committing terrorist acts in another state within the region. If implemented properly, this provision could potentially act as a powerful deterrent against terrorist attacks. However, the agreement does not create an obligation for the contracting states to extradite suspected terrorists and any co-operation in this regard is entirely up to the discretion of the state concerned. SAARC member states have seldom co-operated regarding extradition, thereby making a mockery of the agreement. Indeed, SAARC member states have often provided support and encouragement (sometimes overtly but most of the time covertly) to insurgent and terrorist groups in neighbouring states; at times SAARC member states have even allowed their own territory to be used by such groups to launch attacks on a neighbouring state. Interference in the internal affairs of neighbouring states and state sponsorship of terrorism has thus been a prominent and consistent feature of the South Asian political landscape. The worst culprits in this regard are allegedly the two largest states in South Asia, India and Pakistan.

## CONCLUSION

To sum up, this essay has essentially argued that insecurity in South Asia stems from five main sources: Indo-Pakistani hostility and conflict; the deteriorating security situation in Afghanistan; various types of internal identity conflicts within South Asian states; the threat of domestic and international terrorism; and SAARC's failure to promote regional integration, co-operation and peace. None of these sources of insecurity seem likely to disappear at present, which means that South Asia is expected to remain a highly dangerous, divided and volatile region for the foreseeable future.

## BIBLIOGRAPHY


Bajpai, Kanti. 'Diversity, Democracy, and Devolution in India', in Brown, Michael E., and Ganguly, Sumit (Eds), *Government Policies and Ethnic Relations in Asia and the Pacific*. Cambridge, MA, The MIT Press, 1997.

Banerjee, S. *India's Simmering Revolution: The Naxalite Uprising*. London, Zed Books, 1984.

Burrows, William E., and Windrem, Robert. *Critical Mass: The Dangerous Race for Superweapons in a Fragmenting World*. New York, Simon and Schuster, 1994.

Chadda, Maya. *Ethnicity, Security and Separatism in India*. New York, Columbia University Press, 1997.

Chandran, S., and Joseph, M. 'India: The Naxalite Movement', in Mekenkamp, Monique, van Tongeren, Paul, and van de Veen, Hans (Eds), *Searching for Peace in Central and South Asia*. Boulder, CO, Lynne Reinner, 2002.

Dash, Kishore C. 'The Political Economy of Regional Cooperation in South Asia', *Pacific Affairs*, Vol. 69, No. 2, Summer 1996.

Dubey, Muchkund. 'SAARC and South Asian Economic Integration', *Economic and Political Weekly*, 7 April 2007.

Ganguly, Sumit. 'A New Challenge for Bangladesh', *Yale Global* (Online), 30 March 2006.

*Conflict Unending: India-Pakistan Tensions Since 1947*. New York, Columbia University Press, and Washington, DC, Woodrow Wilson Centre Press, 2001.

*The Origins of War in South Asia: Indo-Pakistani Conflicts Since 1947*. Boulder, CO, Westview Press, 1994.

Ganguly, Sumit, and Hagerty, Devin T. *Fearful Symmetry: India-Pakistan Crises in the Shadow of Nuclear Weapons*. New Delhi, Oxford University Press, 2005.

Hachhethu, Krishna. 'Nepal in 1996: Experimenting With a Coalition Government', *Asian Survey*, Vol. 37, No. 2, February 1997.

Jaffrelot, Christophe. *The Hindu Nationalist Movement in India*. New York, Columbia University Press, 1996.

Kearney, Robert N. 'Ethnic Conflict and the Tamil Separatist Movement in Sri Lanka', *Asian Survey*, Vol. 25, No. 9, September 1985.

Khadka, Narayan. 'Democracy and Development in Nepal: Prospects and Challenges', *Pacific Affairs*, Vol. 66, No. 1, Spring 1993.

Krishna, Sankaran. *Postcolonial Insecurities: India, Sri Lanka, and the Question of Nationhood*. Minneapolis, MN, University of Minnesota Press, 1999.

Manor, James. 'Sri Lanka: Explaining the Disaster', *The World Today*, November 1983.

Mehra, A. K. 'Naxalism in India: Revolution or Terror?' *Terrorism and Political Violence*, Vol. 12, No. 2, 2000.

Misra, Ashutosh. 'Rise of Religious Parties in Pakistan: Causes and Prospects', *Strategic Analysis*, Vol. 27, No. 2, April–June 2003.

Nayak, N. 'The Lull Before the Storm', *Outlook* (Online Edition), 23 June 2004.

'Osama Squads to Fight the LTTE', *The Times of India* (Online), 19 August 2003.

Phadnis, Urmila, and Ganguly, Rajat. *Ethnicity and Nation Building in South Asia*. New Delhi, London, Thousand Oaks, CA, Sage Publications, revised edn, 2001.

Poudyal, Ananta Raj. 'Nepal in 1994: The Hung Parliament', *Asian Survey*, Vol. 35, No. 2, February 1995.

Rajan, K. V. 'Renewing SAARC', paper presented at the Regional Conference on 'New Life within SAARC' organized by the Institute of Foreign Affairs, Kathmandu, Nepal, 15–16 July 2005.

Roul, Animesh. 'Sipah-e-Sahaba: Fomenting Sectarian Violence in Pakistan', *Terrorism Monitor*, Vol. 3, No. 2, 27 January 2005, pp. 6–8.

Taras, Raymond C. 'Rising Insurgency, Faltering Democratisation in Nepal', *Journal of South Asian Development*, Vol. 1, No. 1, January–June 2006.

Thomas, Raju G. C. 'Reflections on the Kashmir Problem', in Thomas, Raju G. C. (Ed.), *Perspectives on Kashmir: The Roots of Conflict in South Asia*, Boulder, CO Westview Press, 1992.

Wirsing, Robert G. *India, Pakistan, and the Kashmir Dispute: On Regional Conflict and Its Resolution*. New York, St Martin's Press, 1994.

# INDIA: THE EMERGING POWER

ACHIN VANAIK

## INTRODUCTION: THE NEW IMAGE

Before the collapse of the Soviet Union and the end of the Cold War, India was viewed as a somewhat stagnant 'Middle Power'. Its enduring democratic system was widely admired and it was seen as South Asia's 'natural hegemon', given that it had helped to dismember its regional rival Pakistan in 1971 during the Bangladesh war of national liberation. The persistence of mass poverty in India, however, did little to boost the country's credentials, especially when contrasted with the rapidly developing countries of East Asia. The People's Republic of China was clearly a future world power and was flanked by other East Asian 'miracle' economies that were destined eventually to make the region (including Japan) the epicentre of the world economy. Three factors helped to change this image of India.

First, the collapse of the USSR automatically raised the relative status of other 'significant' powers such as Japan, Germany, China, India and Brazil. Second, an Indian shift, in economical and political terms, towards what was widely considered admirable in the West resulted in an altogether more favourable and sympathetic attitude towards India in circles of influence—governments, élites, high-ranking academia and leading media outlets. The new economic policy (NEP), which was introduced by the Indian Government in 1991, represented an ideological shift towards acceptance and endorsement of the post- and anti-Keynesianism that from the beginning of the 1980s had started reshaping the economies of the advanced capitalist countries. Suddenly, the high and steady average annual growth rates of the Indian economy—consistently reaching just under 6% from the early 1980s right up to 2003, after which the average growth rate increased to around 8% per year—were recognized and lauded. India was now perceived as a new economic giant. Moreover, India had abandoned its strategic tilt towards Russia, increasingly giving only lip service to the Non-Aligned Movement (NAM) of which it had been a leader, and was now seeking to establish and consolidate a strategic friendship, even partnership, with the USA. Third, in 1998 India became, in effect, a nuclear power following its overt conduct of a number of controversial underground nuclear tests. The USA and other Western nations and Japan initially opposed but eventually accepted this new status. In becoming a nuclear power, India effectively defied the rest of the world, including its dominant powers, and paid no serious or lasting price in doing so. Leaving aside the merits/demerits or dangers/consequences of what it had carried out, India's successful defiance enhanced its status as a major power—a power that could set new global rules of behaviour that others would eventually follow.

So how significant a power is India going to be? That depends on the criteria used for making such a judgement. Conventional understandings of international relations which view this as, above all, an inter-state system in which key states basically shape the world order—hence the notions of unipolarity, bipolarity and multipolarity (more than two but still only a few states)—will naturally afford very considerable weight to India's 'rise'. Here, economic strength is not so much seen as a function of per caput output or of egalitarian distribution, but of overall output and proportionate weight in the world economy. India is destined, by this standard, eventually to become one of the top three global economies alongside the USA and China. If current growth rates, of 8%–10%, are maintained (which is what the Indian Government's economic policy is primarily aimed at achieving), by 2030 India will have a per caput income of US $20,000, placing it among the world's advanced countries. In military terms, India's nuclear arsenal will increase in size and sophistication. Its armed forces are among the world's largest and it is one of the most prolific purchasers of weaponry. India aims to build a 'blue-water' navy eventually to rival the top five—namely the navies of the USA, China, Russia, Japan and the United Kingdom. In socio-political terms India has enjoyed remarkable macro-stability largely owing to its democratic system, which has, in the final analysis, enabled it to manage all the periodic tensions that have surfaced as a result of cleavages created by the country's incredible and unrivalled diversity, be these of language, race, religion, climate, topography, ideology, political parties (some 28 are represented in Parliament), income, wealth, caste, class, gender, literacy or skill levels. So where does the problem lie? Is India's destiny not assured?

There is another view of the world order that does not give quite as much weight to the inter-state system and is more sceptical of what major states can achieve either on their own or even in alliance structures. This viewpoint is also more questioning of the relationship between élites and masses (even in democracies) and is more critical of the intentions and ambitions of the leading states and of the outcomes of their behaviour. In addition, such a general perspective tends to be more cautious and critical in its judgements about where India is heading, domestically and internationally. This is the approach that will be taken here.

## ECONOMY AND POLITY

It is undeniable that India's average annual growth rate over the last 25 years puts it firmly in the top 10 performing countries in economic terms. Over the last 15 years only China and Viet Nam have performed better. But whereas the 'boom' in those two countries has been led by the manufacturing sector, in India it has been led by the services sector, which currently accounts for 58.1% of gross domestic product (GDP), compared with industry's share of 24.5% and only 17.4% for agriculture. Within the services sector, the four 'leaders' have been business services such as IT and IT-enabled services (ITES) including 'back-office' outsourcing; communications (especially telecommunications); trade, hotels and restaurants; and transport (with the exception of the railways).

The first two of these leaders together accounted for one-fifth of total incremental value-added in the services sector between 1991/92 and 2006/07. However, whereas growth in the communications sector has been domestically driven (for example, India has the fastest growing internal market for mobile telephones), growth in business services has been export driven. Before 1991 the government policy was to promote computer hardware as well as software production. The reduction in tariffs, however, which was implemented as part of the NEP, gravely weakened the domestic hardware industry, while low-cost engineering skills (nurtured by government-subsidized technical education over the previous decades) helped software exports to boom, especially as the spread of fibre optics greatly reduced communication costs. The Indian IT industry saw extremely rapid growth, being worth US $1,100m. in 1993/94 and rising to an impressive $37,300m. in 2005/06. IT workers are the highest paid professionals in India and the sector is therefore a great attraction to educated youth. About 1m. people are now directly employed in the IT sector with a further 3m. benefiting from indirect employment. The number of people employed by ITES totals 4.2m. Although women account for less than one-fifth of this work-force, their numbers are growing. The 'typical' Indian software worker will be an urban Hindu, upper class and upper caste male in his mid- to late twenties who, compared to other educated youth, will earn more, work longer hours, get promoted more quickly and have more opportunities to travel abroad.

While rising productivity is partly the cause of these high growth rates, the major reason is simply the rise in domestic savings and investments. The savings rate in India currently stands at almost 35% of GDP and investment at 36%. In 2006/07 foreign direct investment totalled US$16,400m., inflows from foreign institutional investors reached $9,180m., external commercial borrowing by 812 companies was $20,240m., and the country's foreign exchange reserves were more than $225,000m. Although at a slower rate than China and a number of South-East Asian countries, India is nevertheless being steadily integrated into global channels of production, trade, investment and financial speculation. The National Stock Exchange of India is the third fastest growing in the world and the Bombay Stock Exchange has the largest number of listed companies in the world. Additionally, since the services sector has the highest sectoral growth rate in India, its influence over the economy will continue to increase, just as the importance of the business services, communications, wholesale and retail trade, hotels and restaurants, transport, real estate and construction will also grow relatively faster than other sub-sectors. Looking at their respective production and export profiles, it is not surprising that China is being touted as the 'world's factory' and India as the 'world's office'.

Yet it is precisely because this 'boom' is services-led that its positive impact on most Indians has been much weaker than in the case of China (around 60% of the population of India still depends on agriculture/agriculture-related activities for its livelihood). Overall rates of employment generation and poverty reduction have been much slower than in China, while the three major forms of inequality in income and wealth have all worsened. These three types of inequality are that between the rural and urban populations; that of class, as measured by the shift in the distribution of income between profits (proportionately greater) and wages; and that between regions, as measured by the widening gap between average per caput incomes in backward states compared with more advanced ones. In China the proportion of poor decreased from 63.8% of the total population in 1981 to 9.9% in 2004; however, two-thirds of this decline took place before 1987 when the focus of reforms was on the agricultural sector, including land leasing (the household responsibility system), a spurt in agricultural output and growth rates, readjustment of farm procurement prices, and the promotion of town and village enterprises to make consumer goods.

In 1983 India's level of poverty stood at 44% of the total population, but, unlike the case in China, there were higher rates of malnourishment and no provision of basic healthcare and education. The level of poverty had fallen to 27% by 2004/05, with the rate of decline faster in the 1980s than in the 1990s but accelerating again after 2003. According to the current international standard of poverty (below purchasing power parity—PPP—of US $2 a day), approximately 77% of Indians (about 836m. people) fall short. Of these, 70m. are classified as being extremely poor, 167m. as poor, 207m. as marginal and 392m. as vulnerable. These data are consistent with the World Development Report for 2006, which stated that in that year 35% of Indians lived below the level of PPP of $1 a day. This group included 88% of the country's Dalits ('Untouchables') and tribals, 85% of Muslims, and 80% of 'middle castes' (also called 'Other Backward Classes' or OBCs), who are themselves divided into higher and lower ranks. In terms of occupation, the poor are overwhelmingly the unorganized workers of rural and urban India. Despite its impressive growth performance, India's ranking, according to the UNDP human development index for countries, has hovered between 120 and 130 since 1990.

However, these figures, which starkly illustrate the continuing high level of poverty in India, still leave some 200m. in the lower middle, middle and upper income groups. Some 100m. people fall in the middle income group, earning between Rs 200,000 and Rs 1m. a year (according to figures for 2006). India is the fastest growing country in terms of numbers of millionaires (some 126,000 high net worth individuals have more than US $1m. in assets, not counting their residences) and has the highest number of US dollar billionaires in Asia—these 36 individuals enjoy accumulated wealth equal to around 25% of India's total GDP. As India's population increases (it is estimated that it will overtake China as the most populous country within the next two or three decades) and as upward mobility takes place through faster rising incomes for some social layers, in due course what is referred to as the 'Great Indian Middle Class' (GIMC) will easily outnumber the total population of the USA, itself the third most populous country in the world. This GIMC has been the biggest beneficiary of the still disturbingly dualist pattern of Indian economic performance. It is the social layer that most strongly identifies with concepts such as 'Shining India' and the 'Emerging Giant'. Like its counterparts elsewhere, the GIMC identifies its own interests with that of the State, and its own sense of self-worth and self-respect with the power and authority of the State and whether the Indian nation is 'respected' or not by other powers.

This 'middle class', unlike its counterparts in the West, is not a median category but incorporates only the top 20% of the population and thus does not serve as a social buffer between, for example, the top 10%–15% and the approximately 40% working poor and underclass, as would be the case in the West. It is also internally differentiated in that its lower end, overlapping with a significant section of the 'vulnerables', fears slippage downwards. Furthermore, Indian democracy has one important feature that sets it apart from the democracies in the advanced countries—people in India are more electorally active the lower down the social and economic scale you go. Indeed, voter participation, which is already comparatively high at national level, becomes progressively greater as you descend through the election levels of state, municipal and village panchayat. This means that, although the GIMC has disproportionate influence in academia, the national and provincial media, the civilian and military bureaucracies, the professions, the corporate sector, and over government policy-making and shaping, it does not control the political process. India is not like the 'two-thirds society' of today's advanced democracies where two-thirds prosper and enjoy the benefits of affluence while the remaining third merely copes and remains locked in poverty or near-poverty. Rather, it is more like a 'one-quarter society' where as yet only the top 25% prospers. Consequently, pressures from below—electoral and otherwise—do at times result in the introduction of policy measures that upset the GIMC.

What are these other pressures? There is increasing Muslim ferment as disillusionment with the traditional clerical leadership has grown. The latter has neither been able to provide protection to ordinary Muslims at a time when anti-Muslim prejudices have risen and have been accompanied by an increase in communal violence against Muslims, nor has it been able to address the crucial secular needs for more and better education and jobs. Indian Muslims are increasingly aware of the disadvantages faced by them as a community and are disturbed and angered as a consequence. In addition, the Hindu OBCs (who constitute around 52% of the total population) and the Dalits are becoming more and more assertive. These two sources of caste pressure have ensured the consolidation of reservation policies (and the growing demand for their further extension to the private non-governmental and corporate sectors) in job allocations and in tertiary-level educational access. This has created a substantial and growing 'middle class' among lower castes, much as the history of affirmative action in the USA has led to a four- or five-fold increase in the proportion of middle-class blacks, while leaving the majority of the black population in the lower social ranks.

On balance this process has provided a social safety-valve of sorts, creating a lower-caste leadership that is much keener on reformist policies of potential benefit to its own aspiring upper echelons than on radical measures in support of its most deprived. However, this type of self-improvement within the lower castes, when added to the unease created by growing Muslim ferment, leads to new tensions within the GIMC that makes the forward castes and Brahmins more attracted by the appeal of Hindu upper-caste assertion. The Bharatiya Janata Party (BJP) and its politics of Hindu nationalism embodies this appeal and has benefited most from the growing angst of the upper-caste Hindu 'middle class'. The BJP is one part of a whole cohort of organizations that espouses a politics of militarized Hindu unity and which has functioned for several decades in the very heart of Indian civil society. In 1984 the BJP could garner only two seats out of the total of 543 in India's parliamentary lower house. In the succeeding two and a half decades, however, the party's rise has been nothing short of spectacular, to the point where it is now accepted as the alternative (to the Congress Party) leading player of a national coalition government. From its origins as a party representing the interests and values of urban upper caste Hindu traders and non-professional 'petit-bourgeoisie', the BJP has seen its social and electoral base expand to include substantial sections of the upper echelons of the intermediate castes and, most importantly, the professionals and upper classes of India.

Furthermore, the business world in general approves of the BJP because of its pro-liberalization economic stance. In addition, the party is strongly committed to a strategic alliance with Israel and the USA, even more so than the Congress, among the ranks of which exist some dissenting and more cautious voices and which suffers from the 'ideological shackles' of its past. It was the BJP that authorized the 1998 nuclear tests and the party has long been obsessed with the creation of a 'strong India' whose cultural foundations would be based on a more militaristic interpretation of Hinduism that would forge a Hindu unity to take on the 'Muslim Other'. The various organizations of Hindu nationalism in India were responsible for the horrendous Gujarat pogrom of February 2002 (the worst such event since the partition of India at independence), in which more than 2,000 Muslims were massacred and well over 100,000 Muslims brutally displaced from their homes and places of work. The Chief Minister of Gujarat, Narendra Modi, who presided over this pogrom and openly attempted to justify it, has not been called to task for his actions. Despite this—and perhaps even partly because of this—the BJP is now the most favoured single party among the GIMC. In Gujarat the BJP achieved an unprecedented third consecutive election victory in the state assembly elections of 2007, while Narendra Modi is widely tipped to be a future leader of the BJP and hence a likely prime ministerial candidate in any future coalition government headed by the party.

Given this overall context it is hardly surprising that all kinds of insecurities, resentments and frustrations are shaping the world view and self-assertion of the GIMC. Its general political instincts are to maintain and deepen social exclusions—i.e. to sustain and strengthen the divide separating them from those below and to do so at various levels. Consequently, the GIMC seeks geographic/urban exclusion through beautification and 'enclosure' programmes that create gated communities and keep the 'lower classes' (outside of necessary functional relationships) at a safe distance. Such exclusion is also carried out through various caste, religious and gender practices. It is achieved through making the promotion and protection of consumer rights, rather than producer or citizenship rights, the touchstone of what Indian democracy should increasingly be about. This is a GMIC that is more self-righteous, belligerent, communal and insensitive to the poor and disadvantaged than ever before, and the 'official nationalism' of the Indian state substantially reflects the values and beliefs of this social layer.

In truth, India's unusual combination of economic change led from above and political pressures from below (exercised in and expressed through the peculiarities of India's democratic system) creates a social amalgam that threatens dangerous instability in the future. One way out of this dilemma would be the achievement of a significantly more egalitarian distribution of income and wealth, accompanied by a successful redressal of a host of other cultural and political grievances which have their own distinctive sources and origins. In regard to the former requirement, the dominant wisdom in India (and abroad) is that high levels of economic growth remain the key. This, it is widely believed, will in time not only eliminate mass poverty but will also result in much greater middle-class convergence of incomes and wealth even as the rich and super-rich flourish. Even if this view is accepted (and there are many observers, both within India as well as outside, who do not hold anywhere near so sanguine a view of the strengths of the market mechanism), it still means that exceptionally high growth rates must be sustained for very long periods. In the increasingly integrated world economy of today even the continental-sized economies of India and China cannot remain unaffected by major adverse developments elsewhere, especially when global financial activity has become both so much more influential and uncontrollable. Placing one's hopes on such continuous high growth rates remains a gamble of sorts on which history will give a definitive verdict.

With regard to the latter requirement (the ability to handle myriad cultural and political grievances), there is in India both a centralizing and authoritarian thrust and a growing regionalization of the Indian polity most obviously expressed in the emergence of coalitional rule at the Centre. At a macro-level Indian democratic institutions have proved to be remarkably durable, yet at the meso- and micro-level India is in so many ways a very undemocratic and violent society. There is not only a very high frequency of episodic violence related to ethno-national (secessionist) and religious tensions, but there is also deep and widespread institutionalized violence relating to caste, class and gender. The rise of Hindu nationalist forces (with their many Fascistic characteristics) currently poses the single biggest threat to liberal democracy in India. The Hindu nationalists' programme for forging a 'Great India' through the construction of a Hindu Rashtra or 'Hindu Nation' (inconceivable without there being a Hindu state) is a recipe for disaster. A secular state is the necessary (although not alone sufficient) condition for preserving a democratic India. One of the largest obstacles to the country's centralizing and authoritarian thrust is the emergence of a more federalized entity where successfully negotiated compromises of all kinds between national and regional political forces, and among these forces themselves, become one of the key avenues to securing social stability and political cohesion.

So far the overall result has been mixed. To use a metaphor, the 'train' of Hindu nationalism—in reality it is several trains on multiple tracks—has covered much ground and continues to move forward, albeit at different velocities and with stops, occasional reverses and restarts. The brutalities of everyday life remain. Anti-democratic pieces of legislation are introduced at national and provincial levels and are sought to be justified by reference to left-wing extremism (Maoism remains a significant armed force, strongly embedded among the poorest tribals and landless labourers, and Dalits in central India who are fighting for their rights) and to 'Muslim terrorism', both internal and external (Pakistan). However, as newer social and regional groups are empowered by the persistence of the democratic system, this only reinforces the popular commitment to its preservation. As always, vigilance (rather than complacency) is demanded, and it is the actual play of living politics in the future that will determine the health, sustainability and content of India's democracy.

## INDIA IN THE WORLD

For India the two crucial and related events of 1991 were the collapse of the Soviet Union and the inauguration of the NEP by the recently elected Congress Government. Although there was considerable continuity with earlier liberalizing policies, the NEP did represent a decisive shift in ideological terms towards neoliberalism, with very significant policy implications. It was from that time on that both New Delhi and Washington began to talk of forging a new post-Cold War relationship with each other.

In abstract theoretical terms, supposedly sovereign independent governments can pursue any of five possible diplomatic strategies in relation to a dominant or hegemonizing power like the USA. A country such as India can a.) bandwagon, b.) balance, c.) hide, (i.e. practice neutrality), d.) transcend (i.e. appeal to international law to justify its postures), or e.) co-bind (i.e. eliminate a potential threat by tying that country tightly to its own political and economic structures). This fifth option does not really exist for India vis-à-vis the USA, although it is what France did to Germany after the Second World War, and what India could do with Pakistan if both countries had a mind to (which they do not). It is also what Japan and China could consider doing if so minded (which they are not) and providing that the USA would not strive at all costs to prevent it (which it would).

The fact that India has bandwagoned with the USA is obvious. However, this situation was not reached all at once, but rather in three distinct phases: 1991–98, 1998–2004, 2004 onwards.

### Phase I: 1991–98

Shortly after the collapse of the Soviet Union both India and the USA began to discuss forging a 'strategic friendship', if not a 'strategic partnership'. India's NEP had won plaudits from the USA and the West, but the asymmetry of power meant that the terms of any such strategic relationship would be determined by the USA. Since the latter would not contemplate a shift away from its close relations with Pakistan, the establishment of such a strategic friendship was not initially that attractive to India. The history of India's foreign policy reorientation since 1991 is basically that of the country accommodating itself to US strategic perspectives, regardless of the nuclear issue (where it was the USA that moved from its initial stance of opposition to one of acceptance). Thus, between 1991 and 1998 the Indo-US diplomatic and military relationship moved forward, albeit slowly, half-heartedly and haltingly.

### Phase II: 1998–2004

This phase saw the accession of a BJP-led Government and was marked above all by the nuclear issue following the tests of May 1998 and their impact on the triangle of US-Indo-Pakistani relations. All countries that openly declare themselves to be nuclear powers claim that this development has been necessitated by some external threat. In some cases, however, it is changing self-perception rather than a change in the perception of threat that constitutes the main motivating factor. Accordingly, in 1945 the USA was not fearful of some other military power, but wanted to show (especially to the communist USSR) that it was the predominant military global power. Similarly, the decisions by France and the United Kingdom to 'go nuclear' had more to do with wanting to remain at the 'high table' of global powers even as their colonial empires were progressively dismantled. In contrast, the Soviets felt the need to develop a nuclear bomb because the USA had done so and, likewise, China became a nuclear power because both the USA and the USSR had done so. Pakistan openly declared itself a nuclear power in 1998 owing to the threat that India was seen as posing in its new role as a nuclear power. However, India's decision to carry out the tests had little to do with the perception of looming threats. In fact, Indo-Chinese relations had improved considerably following the disintegration of the USSR (China no longer had to worry about confronting the possibility of a Soviet-Indian alliance). Thus, in the early 1990s India and China signed two major treaties that were consciously aimed at reducing tensions and promoting better bilateral relations between the two countries.

India's decision to go openly nuclear through the tests in 1998 was status-driven not threat-driven and was made by the only party in India that, in an earlier incarnation (the BJP was formerly known as the Jan Sangh), had from the 1950s onwards (before either China or Pakistan had the bomb) repeatedly declared that India must possess nuclear weapons. One of the founding fathers of Hindu nationalism, Veer Savarkar, had long ago provided the necessary rationale for this: if India was to be strong and respected then it had to 'unite Hindus and militarize Hinduism'! The initial explanation for the conduct of the tests given by the BJP-led Government of 1998 (the controversial decision was kept secret from all of the BJP's coalition partners, but not, of course, from the unelected Hindu nationalist organization, the Rashtriya Swayamsevak Sangh, which was central to making the decision) was that it was motivated by concerns about threats from Pakistan and China. China's negative reaction quickly made it apparent that this declaration had been a wholly avoidable and quite unhelpful diplomatic provocation. Within a month the Indian Government had retracted this explanation and officially declared that the tests were 'not country-specific'. Furthermore, within a year the Government had officially announced that the tests were 'not threat-specific' either.

Far from the dual nuclearization of India and Pakistan effecting greater regional stability (as was initially claimed by both sides), Pakistan, with its newly acquired 'nuclear shield', launched the Kargil border war of early 1999 and both countries prepared their nuclear arsenals for possible use 'just in case'. Under intense pressure from the USA, Pakistan was forced to withdraw its troops, thus creating the basis for a much stronger rapport between Washington and New Delhi. The post-Kargil phase witnessed the most sustained rounds of high-level diplomatic-strategic discussions ever between the USA and India. The BJP-led Government sought to convince the US Administration that it should accept Indian nuclearization since India was, in strategic terms, on the same side as the USA. Bill Clinton's Government readily accepted this and the US President made an official visit to India in 2000. None the less, the US Administration demanded that India clarify what its nuclear ambitions and preparations were and would be—the unspoken message was that the US wanted India to remain a small nuclear power (SNP).

The period 1998–2004 was also when a strategic triad was being forged between India, Israel and the USA. In addition, following the terrorist attacks in the USA in September 2001, India came around to accepting the USA's refusal to sacrifice its alliance with Pakistan at the altar of its growing strategic relationship with India. This readjustment on India's part from 'pre-9/11' hopes has been rationalized as follows: the Indo-US alliance is a first-tier relationship, compared with the second-tier US-Pakistani relationship. Moreover, the relationship between the USA and Pakistan is, in the long term, an aberration, which the USA will eventually abandon. Consequently, it is in India's best interest to put most of its strategic eggs into the US basket.

### Phase III: 2004 Onwards

The accession of a Congress-led Government in 2004 witnessed further consolidation of the NEP, creating strong economic and media lobbies that were committed to maintaining a strategic alliance between India and the USA. Perceived economic needs are believed to necessitate a close strategic partnership in geopolitical terms. Prime Minister Manmohan Singh has gone on record as declaring that his historic contribution was to introduce the NEP in 1991 as India's way of decisively integrating with the world economy—a process for which close and enduring Indo-US relations are, he believes, a must. While it was expected that the economic direction of the new Congress-led Government would remain the same as that of the previous administration, what was not expected was that the foreign policy trajectory laid out by the previous Government would be accelerated. This bandwagoning on the part of India has been rationalized as the best way to promote a more 'multipolar' world order, while the USA views such regional alliances as the optimum mode of sustaining its 'unipolarity' and global hegemony. The push for this acceleration, moreover, originated from the American side. In contrast to the Clinton Administration, which had favoured a gradualist approach, the Administration of George W. Bush, who was inaugurated as US President in January 2001, decided dramatically to accelerate this process by signalling its willingness in the mid-2000s to enter an Indo-US nuclear deal that would effectively rewrite both US domestic and international (in terms of its membership of the Nuclear Suppliers Group) rules and norms to reward a rule-breaker (India) in nuclear proliferation matters, in return for that country's long-term strategic realignment with the USA.

The bargain inherent in this deal is perfectly understood by both Governments. For the USA the purpose of the deal is fundamentally strategic—paying the price for eliminating intra-élite reservations among Indians. Side benefits include greater sales of civilian nuclear materials and equipment and, in due course, an increase in sales of conventional military equipment with the result that the USA and Israel will eventually emerge as the top suppliers of military hardware to India, replacing Russia. In India the dominant public response to the nuclear deal, barring the parties of the Left, has been very supportive. If concluded, it would amount to a de facto recognition and acceptance by the USA, NATO, Russia and possibly China of India's nuclear status. It would also enable India to import uranium and expand simultaneously and significantly its military and civilian nuclear programmes. Consequently, India's strategic partnership with the USA is considered necessary and desirable.

What would happen if the nuclear deal with the USA fell through? It would prove a set-back to the forging of closer ties between the two countries, but its potential negative impact should not be exaggerated. The socio-political-ideological foundations for a long-term alliance between India and the USA are robust and do not preclude a degree of flexibility in India's foreign policy. However, India's manœuvring room would be increased not so much by the collapse of the deal but by the wider consequences of what would happen to the USA in geopolitical terms should its current state of impasse in the

Middle East (above all in the quagmire of Iraq) turn into a decisive defeat, i.e. if the USA is unable fully to 'Iraqi-ize' its control and simultaneously retain the major military bases currently being constructed to house its troops for the longer term. The USA views Iran as a key obstacle to its ambitions in Western Asia and has sought to isolate and squeeze it politically, to the extent of even holding out a threat of future military assault. The Indian vote in September 2006 in support of transferring the Iran dossier from the International Atomic Energy Agency to the UN Security Council revealed that India will not place serious obstacles in the way of US efforts in this regard even as it attempts to retain 'friendly' ties with Iran.

### Key Triangles

A closer look at certain triangles is imperative. The USA aims to be the key balancer in South Asia in the US-Indo-Pakistani triangle and in East Asia in the US-Chinese-Japanese triangle. The USA also aims to link the two regions via South-East Asia by promoting closer relations between India and Japan. Additionally, in the US-Chinese-Indian triangle, it is the evolution of the US-Chinese relationship (the future trajectory of which will essentially be determined by US behaviour) that will determine the Indo-Chinese relationship. Not only is the Indo-Chinese relationship linked to each country's relationship with the USA, but it is these respective bilateral relationships with the strongest global power that will determine the direction taken by their own bilateral relationship. For example, even a resolution of the longstanding border dispute between India and China would not guarantee enduringly friendly relations between the two countries.

Regarding the US-Chinese-Japanese triangle, the USA currently has every interest in promoting (within limits) a more nationalist and ambitious Japan. The USA also wants to promote a more geopolitically ambitious India. Official US strategy documents talk of helping to make India a major power while calling on Japan to shed its political-military inhibitions of the past to play a greater role both within and outside the Far East (i.e. urging it to behave like the major power that it already is). The USA needs both to promote a more aggressive Japan to unsettle China and also to highlight the case to China that it would be in its interest to accept the US-Japan security pact that allows the former to control the latter. The US stance towards China currently incorporates two seemingly contradictory postures, but is probably the most effective way for it to pursue its longer-term project of nullifying any future Chinese geopolitical challenge, either through its incorporation in a framework of accepted US leadership and hegemony, or by isolating it sufficiently so that the costs of a Chinese challenge are viewed in Beijing as being too high. Thus, the USA treats today's China both as a potential opponent and as a potential friend and makes its preparations—military, economic, cultural and political—accordingly. China, on its part, has every wish to avoid making the USA consider it as a strategic opponent and therefore to be left to pursue its programme of modernization over the next two decades or more without undue external pressure.

In South Asia the USA's relationship with India is set to become increasingly important and will thus be of concern to many Pakistanis. After all, US (and Western) economic interests in India are general and diverse but only specific and limited for the other countries of South Asia. Nevertheless, barring the unforeseen, such as the ascendance of an anti-US regime, Islamist or otherwise, in Pakistan, the USA will continue to act as a balance between India and Pakistan since each country is vital in serving American interests. Pakistan serves US geopolitical interests westwards (West Asia) and northwards (Central Asia), while India serves US geopolitical interests southwards and eastwards, above all as a junior naval partner to control the Indian Ocean. This requires developing India's military relationships not just with South-East Asian countries such as the Philippines, Singapore and Indonesia, but also with more distant ones such as Australia and Japan. The US idea is to construct an Asian equivalent of NATO and, for this to happen, India needs to become, in political and military terms, more regionally and globally ambitious. Since 2003 serious discussions have taken place between the USA and India regarding the possibility of the establishment of an Asian NATO, in which India, Japan, Viet Nam, the Republic of Korea, the Philippines, Indonesia, Malaysia and Singapore could play important roles (linking up with Australia) in the overall project of containing China. The Indian attitude towards an Asian NATO can be gleaned from official statements made by the former Indian foreign secretary Shyam Saran and reported in *The Times of India* in November 2005. Saran was quoted as saying that 'In the context of Asia, there is no doubt that a major realignment of forces is taking place' and that China was emerging as a 'global economic power'. He went on to say that the USA and India could 'contribute to creating a greater balance in Asia' and that to manage the uncertain security situation in the area, it would be necessary to bring in 'more and more countries within the discipline of a security paradigm for this region'.

## CONCLUSION: TWO UNCERTAINTIES

The emergence for the first time in human history of truly global capitalism and of increasingly globalized élites has raised a distinctive problem. The continued economic prosperity and social dominance of these élites requires the establishment of enduring and effective mechanisms of global co-operation and management. However, for the long-term future it is still only the system of national states that can hope to provide this global co-ordination and stability. It is national states that provide the legal, regulatory, institutional and infrastructural framework for market economies based on increasingly unfettered capitalist competition. The national states police capital-labour relations in favour of the former; they manage the macro-economy; and they are the medium (especially if they are electoral democracies) that provides popular legitimacy for élite rule. However, how is this system of states to be co-ordinated, managed and stabilized given that inter-state tensions are capable of being far more disruptive and destructive than the tensions created by competition between corporations and other economic actors?

Can a 'global hegemonic stability' be provided? Is this even desirable, or is the goal itself a shorthand for simply justifying the domination of and exploitation at the hands of the strong and the rich (whether classes or nations) over the weak and the poor? The dominant Indian discourse entertains no such qualms. Rather, it holds that such global hegemonic stability is both necessary and desirable. Great powers, after all, also have great 'collective responsibilities' besides their own 'national interests'. Since the USA is an indispensable component of any such 'hegemonic order', this discourse declares that one has to work with it and not—contra Indian leftists—work against it. In such a perspective, the challenge is to effect just such a collective organizing mechanism through existing international bodies ranging from the UN to the World Trade Organization via changes within these institutions (e.g. assigning India a permanent seat in the UN Security Council) as well as through external developments. This then is the overarching vision that is likely to guide India's external behaviour over the coming years.

However, there is one huge problem area in the generally optimistic vision that Indian élites have of their country's future prospects, and it is a problem area that remains poorly and insufficiently addressed. What about ecological sustainability, nationally and globally? The official and popular Indian stance is that since the developed countries are the principal culprits in causing the environmental problems they must accordingly pay the biggest price in resolving them. Even if, in absolute terms, India's and China's high-energy intensive path of development is a huge contributor to ecological despoliation, in per caput terms the 'responsibility' becomes much less and this is the preferred line of defence in reponse to all accusations of ecological insensitivity. The growth obsession remains paramount. A world without constant growth is inconceivable and hence solutions to the ecological crisis must revolve around two approaches—using the market itself to deal with the problem through the utilization of carbon credit mechanisms and through faith in technological advances and solutions (such as promoting 'cleaner' as well as renewable energy sources). China currently obtains 17% of its electricity from renewable sources and India around a mere 4%, but the aim in both countries is to come as close as possible to emulating the prosperity levels in the advanced nations of the world. In short, both India and China, along with a host of other large developed countries such as the USA, are still more part of the problem rather than part of the solution.

It is all the more ironic that the official 'father of the Indian nation', Mahatma Gandhi, should have warned long ago that, while there is enough for everyone's need there is never enough for everyone's greed! Moreover, Gandhi was also an advocate of democracy and an apostle of non-violence who was horrified by nuclear weapons. What would he have made of today's India? It is a safe bet that, although he would have been pleased by certain aspects, such as the endurance of Indian democracy, Gandhi would also have been disturbed and alarmed by many other developments as India marches into a future that is more uncertain than most would like to believe.

## BIBLIOGRAPHY

Alternative Economic Survey 2005–06: Disempowering Masses.

Alternative Economic Survey 2006–07: Pampering Corporates/Pauperizing Masses.

Bardhan, P. 'Poverty and Inequality in China and India: Elusive Link with Globalization', *Economic and Political Weekly*, 22–28 September. Mumbai, 2007.

Basu, Amrita, and Roy, Srirupa (Eds). *Violence and Democracy in India*. Kolkata, Seagull Books, 2007.

Basu, K. 'The Political Economy of Policy-Making in a Globalising World', *Economic and Political Weekly*, 2–8 February. Mumbai, 2008.

Blank, Stephen. *Natural Allies? Regional Security in Asia and Prospects for Indo-American Strategic Cooperation*. Strategic Studies Institute of the US Army War College, 2005.

Fernandes, Leela. *India's New Middle Class*. New Delhi, Oxford University Press, 2006.

Foreign Service Institute. *Indian Foreign Policy: Agenda for the 21st Century*. New Delhi, Konark Publishers, 1997 and 1998.

Jaffrelot, Christophe. *The Sangh Parivar: A Reader*. New Delhi, Oxford University Press, 2005.

Kar, S., and Sakhtivel, S. 'Reforms and Regional Inequality in India', *Economic and Political Weekly*, 24–30 November. Mumbai, 2007.

Mahendra Dev, S., and Ravi, C. 'Revising Estimates of Poverty', *Economic and Political Weekly*, 8–14 March. Mumbai, 2008.

Mohan, R. 'Growth Record of the Indian Economy 1950–2008: A Study of Sustained Savings and Investment', *Economic and Political Weekly*, 10–16 May. Mumbai, 2008.

Nagaraj, R. 'India's Recent Economic Growth: A Closer Look', *Economic and Political Weekly*, 12–18 April. Mumbai, 2008.

Pai, Sudha. *Dalit Assertion and the Unfinished Democratic Revolution*. New Delhi, Sage Publications, 2002.

Ray, R. 'Diversity in Calorie Sources and Undernourishment During Rapid Economic Growth', *Economic and Political Weekly*, 23–29 February. Mumbai, 2008.

Sen, K. 'Why Did the Elephant Start to Trot? India's Growth Acceleration Re-examined', *Economic and Political Weekly*, 27 October–2 November. Mumbai, 2007.

Sengupta, A., Kannan, K. P., and Raveendran, G. 'India's Common People: Who Are They, How Many Are They and How Do They Live? *Economic and Political Weekly*, 15–21 March. Mumbai, 2008.

Tellis, Ashley. *India as a New Global Power: An Action Agenda for the United States*. Carnegie Endowment for International Peace, 2005.

US Department of Defense. *The Indo-US Military Relationship: Expectations and Perceptions*. 2002.

Virmani, A. 'Growth and Poverty: Policy Implications for Lagging States', *Economic and Political Weekly*, 12–18 January. Mumbai, 2008.

# GLOBALIZATION AND HUMAN DEVELOPMENT IN SOUTH ASIA

C. RAMMANOHAR REDDY

## INTRODUCTION

South Asia, comprising Afghanistan, Bangladesh, Bhutan, India, the Maldives, Nepal, Pakistan and Sri Lanka, is one of the fastest growing regions in the world. The gross domestic product (GDP) of South Asia grew at an average annual rate of 7.0% in 2000–06, more than double the average for the global economy (3.0%) over the same period. This pace of growth dates back to the 1990s: GDP in South Asia increased by an average of 5.5% per year in 1990–2000, which was again considerably greater than the average rate for the overall world economy (2.9% per year). Growth has fluctuated from year to year, varied from country to country and has been affected by conflict in the region and also by natural disasters. However, there is little doubt that South Asia is no longer caught in the 3%–5% growth path that it was on until the 1970s. According to the World Bank, the only region of low- and middle-income countries that registered a faster GDP growth rate than South Asia in the 1990s and the early years of the first decade of the 2000s was East Asia and the Pacific, largely owing to the rapid pace of expansion in the People's Republic of China. South Asia's good record of overall growth extends back to the early 1980s, with an average annual growth rate in 1980–90 of 5.5%, compared with 4.4% for all low-income countries in the same period. (Low-income countries, according to a World Bank classification, are those with a 2006 gross national income—GNI—per head of less than US $905; middle-income countries are those with a GNI per head of between $905 and $11,116.)

The averages for the South Asian region conceal large variations, both from year to year and between country to country. In recent years, the Indian pace of growth has dominated the region. Since 2003, following a period of low rates of growth, Pakistan too has recorded very high rates of economic expansion. Bangladesh and the Maldives have also performed reasonably well. At the other extreme, growth has been erratic in Sri Lanka; the economy in Nepal has been performing poorly; and Afghanistan, which continues to be plagued by violence, remains in a devastated state. It is significant that the three economies that recorded a poor performance in the initial years of the 21st century had experienced a substantial measure of internal strife and war over a prolonged period. Yet, the brief revival of economic growth in 2003–05 in Sri Lanka following the 2002 cease-fire (which finally collapsed in 2006) demonstrated how much could be gained by an end to conflict in the region.

South Asia's overall impressive economic performance since the early 1990s gives hope of a rapid solution to the region's problem of immense poverty and poor human development. Furthermore, the growth acceleration in South Asia during a decade in which the region embraced globalization suggests that close interaction with the world market could contribute to a faster pace of human development.

During the 1990s and first half of the first decade of the 21st century human development, whether formally measured by the UN Development Programme's (UNDP) Human Development Index (HDI) or by indicators of certain levels of social development, did improve in South Asia. For example, adult female illiteracy (for those aged 15 and above) in South Asia decreased from 66% to 46% of the region's population between 1990 and 2006. The infant mortality rate (per 1,000 live births) declined from 86 to 62 between 1990 and 2006, and life expectancy at birth for women improved from 59 to 66 years over the same period. (Unless otherwise indicated, the South Asian averages presented here do not include Afghanistan. This is because most international organizations that collate data for the region exclude Afghanistan and because decades of war and conflict have destroyed much of the country's statistical collection system. It was only in the middle years of the first decade of the 2000s that some economic statistics began to be collected and published for Afghanistan.) The principal questions that arise from these trends are: whether this rate of improvement is rapid enough, considering the size of the challenges confronting South Asia; whether the improvement can be attributed to faster growth during the era of globalization; and whether it accelerated after South Asia embraced globalization.

## HUMAN DEVELOPMENT IN SOUTH ASIA

In spite of the impressive GDP growth rate in South Asia during the 1990s, some of the lowest levels of human development in the world continue to be found in the region. South Asia compares poorly with most other regions in the world in terms of GNI per caput, nutrition, education and health levels.

Table 1 provides averages of some indicators of human development in terms of income, education and health in the low- and middle-income countries of various regions. Income, education and health levels are far lower in South Asia than in most other regions. South Asia compares well only in contrast to sub-Saharan Africa, the region commonly associated with extreme deprivation in all economic and social areas. However, although GNI per caput and life expectancy at birth are higher in South Asia than in sub-Saharan Africa, the countries of South Asia contain the largest number of people living in extreme poverty. Furthermore, the status of women, in terms of education levels, is better in sub-Saharan Africa than in South Asia and the rate of infant mortality, too, is lower in sub-Saharan Africa. New World Bank estimates published in mid-2008 revealed that, while South Asia is home to 23% of the world's population, as much as 40% of the world's poor, where the poor are defined as those whose local purchasing power is equivalent to less than US $1 a day. In 2005 around 350m. people in South Asia (about 23.7% of the population) continued

**Table 1. Basic Indicators of Human Development**

| Low- and Middle-Income Countries by Region | GNI per caput, 2006* | Population (in millions) living in poverty, 2005† | Life expectancy (years at birth), 2006 | Infant mortality (per 1,000 live births), 2006 | Youth female literacy (15–24 years, %), 2005 | Adult female literacy (15 years and above, %), 2005 |
|---|---|---|---|---|---|---|
| East Asia and the Pacific | 4,539 | 180 (9.5%) | 71 | 24 | 98 | 87 |
| Europe and Central Asia | 9,791 | 16 (3.4%) | 69 | 22 | 98 | 96 |
| Latin America and the Caribbean | 8,682 | 28 (5.0%) | 73 | 22 | 96 | 89 |
| Middle East and North Africa | 6,710 | 6 (2.0%) | 70 | 34 | 84 | 63 |
| South Asia | 2,289 | 350 (23.7%) | 64 | 62 | 65 | 46 |
| Sub-Saharan Africa | 1,681 | 299 (39.2%) | 50 | 94 | 64 | 50 |
| **All Low- and Middle-Income Countries** | 4,436 | 879 (16.0%) | 66 | 54 | 82 | 73 |

* Purchasing-power parity (PPP) in US $ at current international prices.

† Those living on less than US $1 per day.

Sources: World Bank, *World Development Indicators 2008* and *World Development Indicators* database.

**Table 2. Basic Indicators of Human Development in South Asia (2004)**

| | GDP per caput (constant, US $, 2006) | GDP per caput (purchasing-power parity, US $, 2006) | Life expectancy (years at birth, 2006) | Adult literacy (%, 15 years and over, 1995–2005) | Infant mortality (per 1,000 live births, 2006) |
|---|---|---|---|---|---|
| Afghanistan | n.a. | n.a. | 43 | 28 | n.a. |
| Bangladesh | 419 | 1,155 | 64 | 47 | 52 |
| Bhutan | 1,086 | 4,010 | 65 | n.a. | 63 |
| India | 634 | 2,469 | 64 | 61 | 57 |
| Maldives | 3,251 | 5,008 | 68 | 96 | 26 |
| Nepal | 242 | 999 | 63 | 49 | 46 |
| Pakistan | 635 | 2,361 | 65 | 50 | 78 |
| Sri Lanka | 1,070 | 3,747 | 75 | 91 | 11 |

Sources: World Bank, *World Development Indicators 2008*, *World Development Indicators* database; UNDP, *Human Development Report 2007/08*.

to live in extreme poverty, with the largest number (266.5m. or 24.3% of the population) resident in India.

South Asia, however, is not a homogeneous region. Averages of indicators of human development conceal country-to-country variations and reflect, in large part, the dominance of the population of India in the region (75%) and, to a lesser extent, that of Bangladesh and Pakistan. Country-wise indicators of certain criteria of human development, shown in Table 2, reveal these variations. The Maldives and Sri Lanka have considerably higher levels of human development and are at the more prosperous end of the scale in South Asia. The Maldives, the smallest country in the region, benefits from a GDP per head that is closer to that of middle-income countries. In terms of basic education and health standards as well, the Maldives belongs closer to the group of middle-income countries than the rest of South Asia. Sri Lanka's GDP per caput is substantially lower than that of the Maldives, but many of its social indicators are of the order found in middle-income countries. At the less prosperous end of the scale are Bangladesh, Bhutan, Nepal and Pakistan, where both income and social indicators reflect poor development. India appears in the middle in terms of both GDP per caput and social indicators of education and health. The little information that is available for Afghanistan suggests an extremely poor level of human development and grossly inadequate public services. For instance, World Bank estimates for 2004 indicated that the rate of adult literacy in Afghanistan was as low as 29% and only 13% of the population had access to protected drinking water.

The differing levels of human development in the countries of South Asia are reflected in the UNDP's HDI rankings. The HDI is a composite index using GDP per head (in purchasing-power parity—PPP—terms), life expectancy at birth and indicators of education (school enrolment and literacy rates). According to the HDI rankings for 2007 (based largely on data for 2005), Sri Lanka (99th in a list of 177 countries), the Maldives (100th), India (128th), Bhutan (133rd), Pakistan (136th), Bangladesh (140th) and Nepal (142nd) were classified as belonging to the second or 'medium human development' group of countries. No country in South Asia belongs to the category of 'high human development'. Over the years there has been a slow rise in the HDI value for each of the countries in South Asia. Thus, Bangladesh, Bhutan, India, Nepal and Pakistan, which all earlier belonged to the group of 'low human development' countries, have now moved up to the second category. The improvement has been very slow—most countries in the region continue to record poor levels of human development in individual areas. Pakistan, which on the basis of 2002 data was classified as a 'low human development' country, is now placed in the 'medium human development' category.

One distressing feature of recent trends in human development in two of the largest countries in the region—India and Pakistan—is that they have been doing less than what is actually possible at their current levels of income to promote social advancement. This was indicated by the fact that in 2005 India and Pakistan occupied lower positions when ranked by HDI than by GDP per caput. For India the difference was as much as 11 ranks, and for Pakistan eight. The gap in India has been increasing in recent years and was accorded special mention as a cause for concern in the 2005 edition of UNDP's Human Development Report as, despite its rapid economic growth in recent years, the country had, in relative terms, slipped in terms of human development. On the other hand, surprisingly, war-torn Sri Lanka and Nepal occupied far higher rankings in HDI than GDP per caput, suggesting that they performed much better than other countries at similar levels of income. The ranking differences were seven and eight, respectively.

The development of the social sector in Sri Lanka occupies a significant place in the global evolution of the approach to human development. Sri Lanka was one of the few developing countries in the 1960s to place an emphasis on social sectors, such as education and health. By the 1970s Sri Lanka had become well known for achieving standards in life expectancy, education, and rates of infant and maternal mortality that were comparable to levels attained in high-income countries. This was attributed to an active state policy of allocating funds to education and health services, as well as providing food subsidies for the malnourished. Eventually, Sri Lanka (along with the south-western Indian state of Kerala) began to be considered as a model for human development. The lessons derived from the Sri Lankan experiment were that considerable levels of human development could be achieved even at low levels of GDP per head, provided that the state gave priority to the social sectors. The implication was that economic growth as such was not an end in itself; rather, the use to which that growth was put for advancing human development was important. Significant as this insight was for policy, the levelling of human development in Sri Lanka and Kerala since the 1980s (which has been coterminous with a moderation in GDP growth) has demonstrated that an acceleration in economic growth is necessary for a steady improvement in social indicators. In other words, the consensus now is that human development and economic growth (as traditionally understood) are inextricably linked.

## ECONOMIC GLOBALIZATION IN SOUTH ASIA

### Changes in Policy Regimes during the 1990s

The regulated, closed and public-sector orientated policies in the South Asian countries of Bangladesh, India, Pakistan and Sri Lanka began to be dismantled from the 1980s onwards. South Asia, in some respects, was the last region in the world to embrace globalization in trade and investment. The transition to an economy with closer links with the global market was a slow and uneven process.

Deregulation was encouraged partly by external pressure from multilateral funding agencies, partly by the collapse of socialism in Eastern Europe, and partly by development outcomes in East Asia. As late as 1970, GNI per head in South Asia (US $222 in constant 1995 prices) was higher than in East Asia and the Pacific (excluding Japan, at $190). By 1980 the position had been reversed: per caput income in East Asia and the Pacific had grown to $290, but had risen in South Asia to only $237. The gap in income widened thereafter. Since the successful development outcomes in East Asia were perceived to be the result of export-orientated policies fuelled by foreign investment and domestic private enterprise, as opposed to the policies that emphasized import substitution, domestic capital and the public sector in India and, to a slightly lesser extent, in Bangladesh, Pakistan and Sri Lanka, strong pressures were placed on South Asian governments to change their economic approach.

From the 1980s onwards (the process began in Sri Lanka in the late 1970s) the larger South Asian economies gradually became more closely integrated with the global economy. By the early 1990s, Bangladesh, India, Pakistan and Sri Lanka had in large measure embraced trade and capital globalization. The Maldives had always depended on exports (mainly of fish) for its economic success, and in the 1990s tourism became an important revenue earner. The economies of Bhutan and Nepal remained, at different levels, tied to India. In Afghanistan the rural economy continued to be disrupted by years of external and domestic conflict; in 1996–2001 the Taliban regime went as far as to proscribe female education and ban much of modern technology. In the larger countries of South Asia, the implementation measures to integrate the domestic economy with the global had been essentially completed by the early years of the first decade of the 21st century. Foreign investment was permitted without much regulation in most sectors of the economy. The South Asian governments had lifted controls on imports and introduced a tariff-based import regime on all commodities (apart from a few banned commodities, generally narcotics and armaments). Average and peak import tariffs declined considerably during the 1990s. Furthermore, exchange-control regulations were relaxed and currencies were made convertible on the current account of the balance of payments, even if full or capital convertibility was not yet in operation. There were still many policies and regulations that protected the domestic economy from the global market—import tariffs, for instance, were among the highest in the world in the early 21st century—but, compared with the situation before the early 1990s, South Asia has become far more open to the international economy.

Table 3 illustrates some of the changes that have taken place in the economies of South Asia since the early 1990s. They are all connected to the globalization process. The external trade orientation of four countries (Bangladesh, India, Nepal and Sri Lanka) increased substantially during the 1990s. In Bhutan a very gradual lowering of its self-imposed economic isolation began to take place only after 2000. In Afghanistan the destruction of the economy during the 1990s meant that, after the war in 2001, the country became significantly dependent on the external world.

Particular sectors witnessed considerable growth in each country. In Bangladesh, and to a lesser extent in Sri Lanka, the garment industry expanded. In India the computer software industry and, more recently, the business process outsourcing (BPO) industry emerged as dynamic sectors, and in the Maldives the tourism industry grew.

Foreign capital flows into the South Asian countries, as a percentage of the GDP of each economy in the early years of the first decade of the 2000s, appear insignificant. However, considering that even in China, the largest recipient of foreign capital in the world, the percentage of foreign capital to GDP was only 2.8% in 2004, it would be fair to say that the inflows into some of the countries in South Asia are, in fact, not of an inconsequential magnitude. What is important is the change over a period of time; in this respect, India and Sri Lanka are noticeable for the sharp increases in the inflow of foreign capital since the early 1990s. While net foreign direct investment (FDI) inflows are still relatively small in South Asia, the receipt of other forms of capital—particularly of portfolio investment by India—has been substantial from the late 1990s onwards. In 2007/08, however, net FDI inflows into India rose by a massive 83.3% to reach US $15,545m., compared with the previous year's total of $8,479m., with the increase in 2007/08 following on a 79.5% rise in 2006/07.

Although the transformation from inward to outward economic orientation was dramatic for South Asia, the region's integration with the world economy is still not as deep as that experienced by other developing country regions. For example, trade in goods as a percentage of GDP was 34% in South Asia in 2006, significantly lower than the world low- and middle-income average of 59% in the same year. In East Asia and the Pacific the proportion was 76%, and even sub-Saharan Africa registered a much higher 61%. The gradual approach to structural shift was also reflected in the reduction in import tariffs. Consequently, despite the reductions made during the 1990s, average import tariffs in South Asia—other than in Sri Lanka—remained among the highest in the world in the early years of the first decade of the 21st century.

International tourism, another facet of globalization, expanded rapidly during the 1990s. In South Asia it was more important for some of the smaller countries in the region. In 2006 the Maldives attracted 602,000 foreign visitors, the largest number in South Asia after India and Pakistan. (Tourism in the Maldives was showing strong recovery following the devastation caused by the tsunami in late 2004—in that year the country had 617,000 visitors.) Tourist receipts as a percentage of export income in the Maldives increased sharply during the 1990s, from 50% in 1990 to 70% in 2001, thereby becoming the country's biggest source of foreign-exchange income. (In 2006 tourism was equivalent to 63% of the Maldives' total income from exports.) Other countries that hoped to reap the benefits of the growth in tourism suffered because internal conflicts deterred tourists. Nepal and Sri Lanka witnessed a decline in the late 1990s in the number of tourist arrivals, with the internal strife discouraging visitors. Sri Lanka had hoped to rebuild its tourism sector after reaching a peace accord with the Tamil separatists in early 2002, but the tsunami disaster of December 2004 destroyed a considerable proportion of its infrastructure and a resurgence of internal tensions in 2005 once again severely hampered recovery in the tourism sector. In 2006 tourism receipts in Sri Lanka were equivalent to only 8.6% of total export income, down from 11.1% in 2004. Nepal is more dependent on tourist income than Sri Lanka, but a decade of internal strife affected the flow of international tourists to that country as well. The declaration of a truce in 2006 and the agreement made between the mainstream political parties and the Maoist insurgents to work together offered hope for the return of peace to Nepal and consequently for an increase in tourist arrivals. In 2006 revenue from tourism provided the equivalent of 12.7% of Nepal's total export income (down from 21% in 2004). None the less, one country in South Asia experienced a steady rise in income from international tourism, despite attempting to

**Table 3. Trends in Indicators of Economic Globalization**

| | Exports (goods and services) as % of GDP | | Total value of trade (exports plus imports) as % of GDP | | Net foreign direct investment as % of GDP | | % of average (weighted) import tariffs | |
|---|---|---|---|---|---|---|---|---|
| | 1990 | 2006 | 1990 | 2006 | 1990 | 2006 | — | — |
| Afghanistan | n.a. | 12 | n.a. | n.a. | n.a. | n.a. | n.a. | n.a. |
| Bangladesh | 11 | 19 | 20 | 44 | 0.1 | 1.1 | 88 (1989) | 56 (2005) |
| Bhutan | 27 | 32 | 58 | 77 | 0.5 | 0.6 | n.a. | n.a. |
| India | 11 | 23 | 16 | 49 | 0.1 | 1.9 | 56 (1990) | 15 (2005) |
| Maldives | n.a. | n.a. | n.a. | n.a. | 2.6 | 1.5 | n.a. | n.a. |
| Nepal | 25 | 14 | 32 | 45 | 0.2 | (–)0.1 | 18 (1993) | 14 (2005) |
| Pakistan | 17 | 15 | 39 | 39 | 0.6 | 3.4 | 44 (1995) | 12 (2005) |
| Sri Lanka | 36 | 32 | 67 | 75 | 0.5 | 1.8 | 27 (1990) | 8 (2005) |

Where data for a particular year are not available, data for the closest available year are provided.

Sources: World Bank, *World Development Indicators* database and *World Development Indicators 2008*.

discourage a large influx of visitors: Bhutan. Seeking to protect its natural and cultural heritage from the destructive effect of tourism, Bhutan imposed a fee on all foreign tourists. This measure did not prevent a rise in the number of tourists from 6,000 in 2003 to 17,000 in 2006.

As a result of South Asia's closer integration with the global economy and, in particular, the gradual lifting of earlier travel restrictions (imposed to conserve foreign exchange), in some countries outbound tourism increased just as rapidly as inbound tourism. This is most evident in India, where the number of outbound tourists has grown to exceed the number of visitors from abroad. In 2006 8.3m. Indians travelled abroad, almost double the 4.4m. tourists who visited the country. Indians travelling abroad had more than doubled in a decade; in 1995 they numbered only 3m. Outbound tourists in 2005 exceeded the number of inbound visitors in Bangladesh and Sri Lanka as well, although the difference was not as large as that in India.

### A Movement to the South Asian Free-Trade Area

South Asia has been a latecomer to the global trend of creating regional economic groups. In early 2004 the governments in the region took the important decision of outlining a plan for the formation of a South Asian Free Trade Area (SAFTA) in 2016. Such a development would represent a milestone on the path to creating a South Asian Customs Union (SACU) and, ultimately, a South Asian Economic Union (SAEU)—similar to the European Union (EU)—which would have a common currency.

In 2006 intra-South Asian exports amounted to a mere 5.5% of the region's total exports. The percentage share of intra-regional exports was higher for the smaller economies in the region and lower for the large economies of India and Pakistan. Although various independent estimates suggest that the value of informal trade (generated from smuggling and shipments routed through third countries in West Asia) is equivalent to the formal component, the combined value of informal and formal trade within South Asia would still be much lower than that within other regional economic zones in Asia. In 2006 merchandise exports between members of the South Asian Association for Regional Co-operation (SAARC) totalled US $9,109m., accounting for a mere 1.3% of world exports, compared with the $194,321m. generated by the Association of South East Asian Nations (ASEAN), which was equivalent to 6.5% of global exports. The low volume of regional trade in South Asia is a legacy of decades of tension between its two largest economies (India and Pakistan) and suspicion on the part of the smaller ones that India would dominate any regional trade bloc.

SAARC was created only in 1985 and comprises all the South Asian countries (in April 2007 Afghanistan joined the seven founding members to become the eighth full member). The first measure to promote greater regional trade was introduced in 1993, when members of the group drew up the South Asian Preferential Trade Arrangement (SAPTA). The agreement came into force in 1995. Since the emergence of SAARC and the implementation of SAPTA were both practically coterminous with a rapid deterioration in political relations between India and Pakistan, the preferential tariffs were introduced on goods that were largely of insignificant trading interest in the region. Pakistan is yet to provide India with Most Favoured Nation (MFN) status—the principle of non-discrimination which is the cornerstone of the multilateral trading system—because of fears that its economy would be inundated with imports from India. In a scenario marked by hostile political and economic relations between India and Pakistan, there was little opportunity for SAPTA to grow. Nevertheless, there is some evidence that SAPTA did boost exports and that the economies of the smaller members of SAARC, which were also in the forefront of demands for a movement to a free-trade bloc, have benefited from the preferential agreement.

In 2004 South Asia finally decided to create a free-trade bloc. The original date for the emergence of SAFTA was 2008; it will now only be fully realized in 2016. The slow development of SAPTA does not hold out much hope for a smooth transition to regional free trade. There are also concerns that the 2004 accord did not pay sufficient attention to important details such as the removal of non-tariff barriers and clarification of the rules regarding origin of exports. Another major shortcoming of the proposed free-trade zone is that it covers only goods. Services will not be covered by the free-trade treaty and, for now, a free movement of people between the countries is not on the agenda.

SAFTA came into force on 1 January 2006, but while all of the SAARC member countries ratified the agreement, the regional grouping continues to be plagued by the lack of a greater opening of trade between India and Pakistan.

### The Importance of Migration and Remittances

South Asia's integration with the global economy, particularly with regard to the trade in goods and cross-border movement of capital, might have been late and hesitant, but the region remains one of the world's major sources of economic migrants. Movement—temporary and permanent—of labour for economic reasons would be even higher if certain visa restrictions were not in force in developed countries. Labour migration from the region is a historical phenomenon that extends back to the 19th century. By the early years of the first decade of the 2000s well-developed intra-South Asian migration networks were in operation. Legal labour immigration into India from Nepal was substantial. Conversely, a different kind of emigration, involving low-wage, unskilled migrants from very poor households in Bangladesh moving to India, has developed since the 1980s. This movement has become the subject of political controversy within India and between India and Bangladesh.

There are also large emigration flows—temporary and permanent—to countries outside South Asia. The departure of semi-skilled and skilled migrants from India and Pakistan to West Asia has been occurring since the 1970s. From the 1980s onwards highly skilled personnel have been moving from India to North America and Western Europe. Conversely, acute economic deprivation has forced the emigration (legal and illegal) of unskilled and semi-skilled workers from Bangladesh to West Asia and Western Europe since the 1990s. Emigration from Sri Lanka has been of two kinds: the movement of people for humanitarian reasons (refugees generated by the civil war in the 1980s and 1990s were mainly from north-east and east Sri Lanka); and migration for economic reasons, largely by female domestic workers. Indeed, Sri Lanka has joined the Philippines as a major source of domestic workers for the homes of West Asia.

An illegal migrant from South Asia may have to travel in life-threatening conditions to reach Western Europe. Occasionally illegal migrants are given inhuman work; children from Bangladesh, for example, are smuggled into West Asia to serve as 'camel jockeys'.

Remittances from South Asian migrants (legal and illegal) working in West Asia, North America and Western Europe and also within the South Asian region itself make a very large contribution to the domestic economies. According to World Bank estimates, the remittances to South Asia reached a total of US $39,800m. in 2006. According to IMF and World Bank statistics, India is now the recipient of the largest amount of remittances in the world, receiving as much as $25,426m. in 2006. With the exception of Afghanistan (for which no information is available), Bhutan and the Maldives, remittances are very important for all the countries in the South Asian region and their role in supporting the domestic economies and in helping workers to compensate for the lack of employment opportunities at home has increased substantially. In Nepal remittances and workers' compensation from abroad were equivalent to 16.3% of GDP in 2006; the corresponding figure in 2000 was as low as 2.0%. The sharp rise was, to a large extent, the result of an increase in the number of Nepalis emigrating to seek a better livelihood abroad, mainly in India. In Bangladesh and Sri Lanka as well, the relative contribution of remittances to the domestic economies was large—8.8% and 8.7% of GDP respectively in 2006. Given the size of the Indian economy, remittances accounted for a relatively smaller proportion (2.8% of GDP in 2006). In both India and Pakistan, however, income from remittances has risen very rapidly in absolute terms: between 2000 and 2006, remittances in India increased from $12,890m. to $25,426m. and in Pakistan from

$1,075m. to $5,121m. A significant reason for India's healthy balance-of-payments situation from the mid-1990s onwards was not faster growth of merchandise exports, but the rise in remittances. The importance of remittances to the economies of South Asia persuaded the governments of these countries to raise the issue of 'labour mobility' in global trade negotiations. They argued that the process of globalization would be incomplete if it was restricted to freedom of movement of goods and capital, and that labour, the other factor of production, should be given a similar freedom of movement across national borders. South Asian governments increasingly consider their large reserve of unskilled, semi-skilled and highly skilled personnel as their 'competitive strength' in the global economy.

### War, Internal Strife, Terrorism, Natural Disasters and Human Development

In assessing the impact of 'gradual' globalization on human development in the region, the effect of external and internal wars, and terrorism must be taken into account. South Asia also suffers significant human and economic losses as a result of natural disasters. The high population density in most of the countries in the region means that, when disasters strike, a much larger number of people are affected than in other parts of the world. In addition, a limited capacity for disaster preparedness and management magnifies the impact, while increasing environmental degradation contributes to the regularity of the occurrence of disasters such as floods. In recent years a series of major disasters has affected South Asia, the most prominent being the earthquake in the state of Gujarat, India, in 2002; nation-wide floods in Bangladesh in July–August 2004; the tsunami of December 2004, which wreaked havoc in Sri Lanka, the Maldives, south India and India's littoral Andaman and Nicobar Islands, on the eastern fringes of the Bay of Bengal; the major earthquake that struck the Pakistan-controlled area of Kashmir (and, to a lesser extent, Indian Kashmir) in October 2005; and a major cyclone that devastated southern Bangladesh in late 2007.

South Asia has suffered from widespread armed conflict. Only Bhutan and the Maldives have not been affected by domestic and international conflict and/or terrorist activity. Afghanistan suffered from a protracted civil war, which was followed by the emergence of the fundamentalist Islamist Taliban regime in the latter half of the 1990s. The regime was then overthrown by a US-led military coalition in late 2001. The administration that replaced the Taliban remained fragile and unable to ensure governance, despite the holding of elections and the formation of a democratically elected government. In 2007 there was a resurgence in Taliban activity and a concomitant weakening of the Afghan Government's hold on power. In Sri Lanka a civil war that continued throughout the 1990s and into the 2000s suppressed GDP growth, depleted considerable resources, deterred tourists and, as expected, had an adverse impact on human development in the east and north-eastern provinces, where the civil war lasted the longest and was the most intense. Unusually, however, while the civil war ravaged the eastern and north-eastern regions, the average national HDI continued to improve. Despite this, the World Bank estimated that the infant mortality rate in the north-east was double the national average and the maternal mortality rate three times the national figure in the early years of the first decade of the 21st century.

In India militancy in the state of Jammu and Kashmir (as well as simmering tensions in the north-east) caused governance in the state virtually to collapse during a great part of the 1990s, although the formation of an elected state government in 2003 with considerable electoral participation, held out hope for a revival of local-level administration. In Pakistan human development was hindered by internal strife in Sindh and Balochistan provinces, the increase in terrorist violence in 2007, and the secondary effects of the conflict in Afghanistan.

During the 1990s, the first decade of integration by South Asia with the global economy, the domestic political and social situation in the countries of that region was not very conducive to accelerated human development. In the first decade of the 21st century the countries of South Asia made attempts to end cross-border and internal tensions so that the environment for human development could be improved and more resources deployed for the social sector. The signing of a peace accord in Sri Lanka in early 2002 held out the promise of an end to two decades of civil war; the accord collapsed, however, in 2006 and violence erupted thereafter. On their part, India and Pakistan, after nearly going to war against each other in 2002, made major advances in bettering bilateral relations. Internally, Pakistan saw the holding of elections in 2008 and the formation of a new government, but terrorism began to strike with renewed force from 2007 onwards. The domestic situation in India was better, but violence continued in the north-east, and in parts of central India left-wing groups controlled much of the administration. Nepal offered a refreshing contrast. The restoration of democracy in Nepal in mid-2006, as a result of a people's movement against the monarchy, was followed by a cease-fire between the insurgent Maoists and the Government and the holding of elections to a constituent assembly in 2008, in which the Maoists emerged as the single largest bloc. It was widely hoped that Nepal, which had suffered the effects of around 10 years of civil war, could now look forward to an era of peace, during which the country's abysmal human development standards could be addressed by a democratic government.

Two natural disasters that caused immense suffering in the first half of the first decade of the 2000s were the tsunami of December 2004 that struck Sri Lanka and the southern parts of India, and the earthquake in Kashmir in October 2005. The devastation caused by the tsunami was, after Indonesia, most extensive in South Asia. The northern, eastern, southern and, to some extent, western coasts of Sri Lanka suffered the worst human and economic losses. In India the eastern coast of the state of Tamil Nadu and the Andaman and Nicobar Islands were badly affected. More than 30,000 people died in Sri Lanka and 10,000 in India. In Sri Lanka an estimated 1m. people—5% of the population—were affected. Beyond the immediate loss of life and property, the principal challenge for the two countries was to rebuild their economic and social fabrics.

An unusual aspect of the impact of the tsunami was that, while it caused colossal human suffering, the impact on economic growth was marginal. In 2005/06, the fiscal year immediately following the tsunami, GDP growth in Sri Lanka was provisionally estimated to be 6%. Similarly, in Pakistan, in spite of the destruction caused by the earthquake of 2005, economic growth in 2005/06 reached an estimated 6.6%, although this represented a deceleration compared with the 8.4% growth registered in 2004/05. Yet, despite these levels of growth, there was no question of the scale of devastation and human suffering inflicted on the two countries by the natural disasters.

## THE OUTCOMES OF GLOBALIZATION

### Opportunities and Pitfalls

South Asia's closer integration with the world economy has benefited certain sectors and some population groups. The region has also had to accept that there are no certainties in the global market. Two examples are the garment industry in Bangladesh and the outsourcing, or BPO, sector in India. Bangladesh's exports of textiles have grown more than five-fold since the early 1990s. Three-quarters of Bangladesh's export earnings are provided by exports of textiles—mainly ready-made garments, such as shirts, sweaters and trousers, at the lower end of the market. More than 95% of the ready-made garment exports go to the USA and the EU. Most significantly for Bangladesh itself, this labour-intensive industry provides employment to around 2m. workers, almost all of whom are women.

The female employees in the garment units are largely migrants to the cities, and the phenomenal increase in garment exports has presented them with an opportunity to earn a livelihood and aspire to a life that would not be possible in the villages. However, Bangladesh's textile exports faced a major threat in the middle years of the first decade of the 21st century with the dismantling of the global quota regime that facilitated the growth of the country's garment industry. Bangladesh does not grow any cotton itself, and its success with textile exports has been based hitherto on preferential access to, and quotas in, the US and EU markets. Since 2005 a global agreement on textile quotas that assured preferential access to Bangladesh's exports has not been operative, and Bangladesh's export industry now competes with textile exporters from China, India and Pakistan, which are much larger exporting countries. While it was initially feared that Bangladesh would experience difficulties in the world textile market, thereby jeopardizing the jobs of the many hundreds of thousands of women who have benefited so far from globalization, this was not the immediate experience. In fact, textile exports grew by more than 40% between 2004/05 and 2006/07 from US $6,400m. to $9,200m.

The young and educated work-force in India's thriving BPO industry is confronted with a different kind of challenge in the global market. Building on its success in computer software exports, India has capitalized on its pool of low-cost and English-speaking personnel to make an impact on the global market with its outsourcing industry. The most visible forms of such activity are the business call centre and back-office operations that US and British companies transfer to India. In 2007/08 this industry registered an income of US $12,500m., employed an estimated 704,000 people, and has recorded annual growth rates of more than 35% since 2000. The BPO sector has become a sign of what India could achieve in the world market and as a precursor to the country's emergence as the global supplier of services. For the young and educated Indian, a relatively highly paid job with a BPO company is the preferred option. However, this dynamic sector is currently confronted with two different kinds of problems from those faced by the Bangladeshi garment industry. Resentment in the USA and the United Kingdom over the movement of call centre and back-office operations to India and other low-wage countries has given rise to a new protectionist sentiment against what is seen as the transfer of white-collar (non-production) jobs to other countries, even though all evidence suggests that in the long term more jobs will be created than lost in the home countries. The second source of anxiety is the fear of what would happen if global economic growth were to slow, as widely expected, in the wake of the financial crisis and rising petroleum prices. There is widespread concern that the first impact of an economic slowdown in the USA and EU would hit South Asia in the form of reductions in outsourcing contracts. The garment industry in Bangladesh and the BPO sector in India are only two examples of a larger phenomenon that South Asia is experiencing with globalization.

### Fluctuations in Economic Growth

Although it is possible to identify specific examples of considerable success in terms of integration of the regional economy into the world economy, the overall effects of economic globalization on human development in South Asia are not unambiguously positive. In the first instance, it is as yet premature to say that globalization has had a positive impact on GDP growth in the region over a longer period. Given the very high growth rates recorded between 2003/04 and 2007/08 in both India and Pakistan—the two largest economies in the region—such an observation may seem erroneous. But globalization as a process took root in the early 1990s in the region and it is only since the early/middle years of the first decade of the 2000s that growth has shown any marked acceleration in these two countries. While India was heralded as the new rival to China in the growth league, the change in Pakistan from a very poor macro-economic performance in the late 1990s was no less remarkable. However, taking a longer view there is as yet no clear acceleration in the South Asian region as a whole: if there is one clear trend, it is of volatility.

The GDP growth rate in the region was high in the 1990s, compared with that of other regions, but the pace of annual economic growth actually slowed down after the mid-1990s, before accelerating once again after 2002. Growth for South Asia as a whole during the 1990s was more or less the same as in the 1980s. According to World Bank estimates, the average annual GDP growth rate was 5.5% in 1990–2000, exactly the same as the growth rate in 1980–90. In other words, in the first decade of closer integration with the global market the more rapid rates of growth that were expected as a result of integration with the world market did not take place. Of course, World Bank estimates also point to a definite acceleration in the period 2000–06, driven and dominated by the economic performances of India and Pakistan. But this acceleration, concentrated as it was over just six years, took place over too short a period to give any degree of confidence that South Asia (including all the countries in the region and not just India and Pakistan) had permanently broken through a growth barrier. The first test for South Asia will come in 2008/09 when all the countries in the region will have to cope with a multitude of challenges such as increasing petroleum prices, a slowing global economy, rising inflation and a general end to the overall positive external environment that predominated during the first half of the first decade of the 21st century.

**Table 4. Growth Rates in South Asia**

| | Average annual GDP growth (%) | | |
|---|---|---|---|
| | 1980–90 | 1990–2000 | 2000–06 |
| Afghanistan | n.a. | n.a. | 10.7 |
| Bangladesh | 3.7 | 4.8 | 5.6 |
| Bhutan | n.a. | n.a. | 7.0* |
| India | 5.7 | 5.9 | 7.4 |
| Maldives | n.a. | 6.9 | 4.6 |
| Nepal | 4.6 | 4.9 | 3.3 |
| Pakistan | 6.3 | 3.8 | 5.5 |
| Sri Lanka | 4.0 | 5.3 | 4.8 |
| South Asia | 5.5 | 5.5 | 7.0 |

* Figure for 2000–05.

Sources: World Bank, *World Development Indicators 2008* and *World Development Indicators* database.

### Employment Generation and Economic Inequalities

On the ground the larger disappointment with globalization in South Asia has been caused by the general absence of an acceleration in employment generation. The situation has varied from country to country, and the employment statistics have been subject to a great deal of analysis. However, the general opinion appears to be that, during the 1990s, only in Nepal was employment growth faster than the expansion of the labour force. In India, Pakistan and Bangladesh the rate of job creation was not adequate to absorb the new entrants to the labour force. This has been ascribed to the relative neglect of agriculture during the decade of globalization. Although a few dynamic areas in the industrial and service sectors might have benefited from integration with the global economy, this has made little difference to the comparatively larger pool of labour, since the overwhelming majority of the labour force in South Asia continues to earn its livelihood in the rural sector. Indeed, the disappointing performance in employment generation has been the biggest source of resentment against globalization in the region.

The other issue of concern is economic inequality. Extreme differences in income and wealth are not a new phenomenon to South Asia. However, disparities have apparently worsened owing to the uneven growth generated by globalization. The average GDP growth rates in South Asia since the early 1990s do not reveal the vastly different performances between regions. In India high economic growth was concentrated in the southern and western regions and parts of the northern states. These states attracted considerable amounts of industrial investment and became major centres of financial and export activity, as well as the sites of the burgeoning software industry. Conversely, much of northern and eastern India, which has the larger share of the country's population and is also home to most of the poor, has experienced low or negative growth. As a result, regional income disparities have widened; in some areas human development has even regressed. Research has also suggested growing inequalities at different levels: between geographic regions; between rural and urban India; and within urban India. Such widening disparities have evoked an undercurrent of hostility to globalization, much like the disappointing performance in job creation. Disparities in the globalization process have not been unique to India. In Pakistan economic growth has been concentrated in the province of Punjab and the Federal Capital Territory of Islamabad, leaving Balochistan province and the North-West Frontier Province relatively deprived and static.

### Gradual Improvements in Basic Education and Health Standards

Although there has been some indication of an acceleration in growth rates in the middle years of the first decade of the 2000s, the era of globalization has not, thus far, led to a dramatic improvement in human development indicators, such as malnutrition, health and illiteracy. The indicators shown in Table 5 (which do not cover Afghanistan) suggest that, in general, there was an improvement in basic education and health levels in South Asia during the 1990s, but the progress was at much the same rate as before and in some areas perhaps slower. Data for individual countries show a very poor record in some important areas. For example, in India, the fastest growing economy in the region, progress in reducing rates of child malnutrition has been dismal. National surveys revealed that in 2005/06 as many as 46% of children under the age of five were underweight; this figure had barely changed since the previous survey conducted in 1998/99 when the relevant percentage was 47%. (In 1992/93 it stood at 52%.)

**Table 5. Trends in Social Indicators in South Asia**

| | 1980 | 1990 | 2006 |
|---|---|---|---|
| Youth literacy (% of population, 15–24 years) | n.a. | 60 | 73* |
| Life expectancy (males, years at birth) | 54† | 58 | 63 |
| Life expectancy (females, years at birth) | 55† | 59 | 66 |
| Infant mortality rate (per 1,000 births) | n.a. | 86 | 62 |
| Prevalence of malnutrition (weight for age) in under-5s (%) | 71‡ | 64 | 41§ |

* Figure for 2005.

† Figure for 1982.

‡ Figure for 1979.

§ Figure for 2000–06.

Sources: World Bank, *World Development Indicators* database and *World Development Indicators 2008*.

Human development is often measured in the first instance by the trend in income poverty, in other words the number and proportion of the population living below a certain level of income. In this regard, some progress was achieved in South Asia as a whole during the 1990s, although no more rapidly than in the decade before globalization took root. A sharp reverse also appeared to have taken place in Pakistan and Sri Lanka during part of the decade. According to new estimates published in mid-2008, the proportion of the population living below the World Bank's international poverty line (less than US $1 a day) in South Asia declined from 34% to 24% between 1990 and 2005, and the number of people living in such extreme poverty decreased from 378m. to 350m. over the same period. (The incidence of poverty had been lowered from 42% to 34% between 1981 and 1990, and the absolute number of people living in poverty had also fallen from 394m. to 378m.)

According to the estimates based on national poverty lines in Pakistan, the proportion of the total population living below the national poverty line increased from 29% to 33% between 1993 and 1998/99 (there is no information for the subsequent period). In Sri Lanka the income poverty ratio rose from 20% to 25% between 1990/91 and 1995/96. Conversely, in Bangladesh and Nepal the poverty ratio according to the national poverty line declined. In Bangladesh the fall was marginal (from a very high 51% in 1995/96 to 50% in 2000). In Nepal, the setting for a violent civil war from the mid-1990s, the incidence of poverty declined quite sharply, from 42% in 1995/96 to 31% in 2003/04.

The biggest ambiguity regarding trends in poverty has been in India. Survey information collated in the late 1990s (and used by the World Bank) indicated a sharp fall in poverty, but changes in survey methodology raised a question mark over the reliability of the 1999/2000 data. Subsequent survey information from 2004/05 (based on comparable methodology) revealed some troubling trends. The incidence of poverty had in fact declined between 1993/94 and 2004/05, from 36% to 28%. However, this actually indicated a speed of decline which was slower than the rate of decline in the 1980s (i.e. before India embraced the globalization process).

In terms of the progress in meeting the UN's Millennium Development Goals, South Asia is set to achieve the goal of reducing by 50% the proportion of people living in extreme poverty between 1990 and 2015. South Asia is the only region other than East Asia and the Pacific that is expected to realize this target. However, although income poverty in general steadily declined in South Asia during the 1990s, the survival indicators in other critical areas continue to be among the worst in the world. According to UN agencies, the rate of child malnutrition (percentage of children under five who are underweight) in South Asia stood at 41% in 2000–06, the highest level in the world, and far higher than the low-income global average of 24.5%. The situation does differ from country to country. Sri Lanka is one country where the national indicators are better than the South Asian average. It is evident, therefore, that during the process of globalization GDP growth did not lead to an improvement in the food security of South Asia's children, although this should have been one of the first priorities in human development.

In general, South Asia's progress in meeting the Millennium Development Goals has been mixed. The region as a whole has succeeded in reducing income poverty, but Afghanistan, Bangladesh and India have failed to achieve the required rate of decrease in levels of hunger (under-nourishment). Similarly, Pakistan's progress in reducing child mortality rates has been poor and access to sanitation in Bangladesh, India and Nepal has not improved sufficiently. A particular cause for concern is that in 2004 only 37% of the population in South Asia had access to improved sanitation facilities.

In summary, while the economies of South Asia initially grew from the early 1990s at more or less the same rate as in the preceding decade of inward-orientated policies, and have in India and Pakistan shown an acceleration since the middle years of the first decade of the 21st century, human development (particularly in the areas of education and health) has improved no more quickly than before. The basic indicators of literacy, life expectancy and infant and under-five mortality in South Asia generally improved during the 1990s and thereafter; however, the rates of improvement were measured no faster than those recorded during the 1980s and, considering the scale of the challenges in education and health, were considerably slower than necessary for ending basic deprivation in these areas. In some countries and in some areas, progress in fact slowed down from the early 1990s. One example of this was the deceleration in the reduction in infant mortality levels in India. Such trends in social indicators, where progress is dependent on government provision of services, has been attributed to the deterioration in public services. This, in turn, has been in part a consequence of cuts in funding, a common feature in the decade of globalization. From the late 1990s onwards, governments sought to reverse this trend by increasing allocations for social services. This attempt to improve public services is yet to show itself in any sustained improvement in the important areas of health, education, malnutrition, availability of water and sanitation. Economic growth, after the fluctuations of the 1990s and slowdown in the late 1990s and early years of the first decade of the 2000s, has shown a marked acceleration since 2003, especially in India and Pakistan. However, this has yet to have a definite impact on human development indicators among the poorer social strata and in more backward regions.

The UNDP's HDI reflects the moderate improvement in South Asia during the 1990s. The UNDP's Human Poverty Index (HPI), on the other hand, indicates the limited progress in human development in South Asia during the 1990s. The HPI is a composite index, which assesses the extent of deprivation in income, education and health. The HPI is the obverse of the HDI, which measures achievements in the same areas. In the 2000–06 HPI rankings for 108 developing countries, India was placed 62nd, Pakistan 77th, Nepal 84th and Bangladesh 93rd. Only the Maldives (42nd) and Sri Lanka (44th) were classified in the top half of the HPI ranks.

There have been some notable successes in raising human development standards in the region. In Bangladesh, for example, there has been a dramatic reduction in the rate of infant mortality, from 129 deaths per 1,000 live births in 1980 to 100 deaths in 1990. The rate declined again to a significantly lower 52 deaths in 2006. The level was lower than in India and Pakistan, where the rates in the same year were 57 and 78, respectively. This was a reversal of the situation in the early 1980s. Another of Bangladesh's noteworthy achievements was the attainment by 2002 of gender equality in school enrolment, ahead of India and Pakistan.

There have also been, however, catastrophic developments in South Asia. War and a complete breakdown of governance in Afghanistan took human development to abysmally low levels that have not yet shown signs of recovery since the end of war in late 2001. However, the Afghan official (non-drug) economy was estimated to have grown by more than 15% per annum between 2001 and 2003 and there have been some signs of an improvement in human development in a few areas (notably a rise in the level of primary-school enrolment).

## CONCLUSIONS

Human development improved in South Asia after the economies of the region began to develop closer links with the global economy during the 1990s. However, only a modest rise in the basic standards of human development occurred, the pace of change being no greater than during the era of regulated and inward-orientated economic policies. Globalization, which was forecast to engender a dramatic improvement in the well-being of the people of the region, has yet to yield results in this respect.

There are two contesting views pertaining to why globalization has not led to a faster rise in basic human development standards in South Asia. One is that a rapid improvement in human development requires a much closer integration with the global economy than the governments of South Asia have managed to develop so far. The opposing view is that, while there was a need to dismantle the old system of close regulation, the governments in the region have been reckless in their pursuit of economic globalization. East Asia succeeded in the export-orientation of its economies because it first created the necessary preconditions (a literate, well-educated labour force; a population that enjoyed basic standards of health) for a successful engagement with the world market. It is therefore argued that, unless the core elements of human development (such as food security, full literacy, universal elementary education, higher life expectancy, and lower maternal and child mortality rates) become the norm rather than the exception in the South Asian countries, there cannot be a successful engagement with globalization. Correspondingly, greater attention has to be paid to directing the profits of economic growth to human development. In this respect, the two biggest countries in the region, India and Pakistan, cause the greatest concern. During 2000–06 the two countries were placed considerably lower in the world ranking of countries by HDI than by GDP per head. This implies that the two nations were not taking full advantage of their rising income levels to promote human development. This trend reflects a disturbing widening between human development and GDP per caput at even low levels of income. That this was happening in spite of a substantial acceleration in economic growth in the middle years of the first decade of the 2000s highlighted the limited distribution of the gains from faster growth and partly explained why globalization continues to receive very limited support in these two countries.

Most governments in South Asia since the 1990s, irrespective of the political formation or the military alliance in power, have been committed to economic globalization. The exceptions have been Bhutan, which started late and chose its own pace of integration, and Afghanistan, where war and the rise of fundamentalist Islamism caused Afghan society to retreat. Yet, mass support for globalization in the region is absent. The lack of support, which at times is reflected in a strong opposition to globalization, is due to the slow pace of improvement in human development that took place during the 1990s. Globalization and deregulation in South Asia were expected to make available state capacity and resources which would be directed towards the provision of basic education and health services. Incomes were predicted to rise with private initiative and globalization, while governments were expected to pay close attention to the challenges of extreme malnourishment, illiteracy and ill health. Incomes did rise and particular groups and individual regions (especially urban centres) in each country showed a remarkable transformation in economic well-being. New sectors such as information technology in India generated jobs and helped Indian firms make an impact in the global market. However, such examples were few and far between. Moreover, there was no sign of greater government involvement in raising human development standards. Governments continued to address the problems of food insecurity, ill health and illiteracy, but generally with no greater urgency than previously. In many cases governmental services have even deteriorated, especially in the poorer regions within a country. Such neglect of government responsibility towards aspects of human development has influenced, and will continue to influence, the pace of economic globalization in South Asia.

## BIBLIOGRAPHY

### General


Bhagwati, Jagdish. *In Defense of Globalization*. New York, Oxford University Press, 2004.

Bhattacharya, Mita, Smyth, Russell, and Vicziany, Marika (Eds). *South Asia in the Era of Globalization: Trade, Industrialization and Welfare*. Hauppauge, NY, Nova Science Publishers, 2004.

Chari, P. R., and Gupta, Sonika (Eds). *Human Security in South Asia: Energy, Gender, Migration and Globalisation*. New Delhi, Social Science Press, 2003.

Hoque, Serajul. *Global Trade Liberalization*. Oxford, Peter Lang, 2004.

Khan, Abdur Rob (Ed.). *Globalization and Non-Traditional Security in South Asia*. Dhaka, Academic Press and Publisher, 2001.

Kinnvall, Catarina, and Jonsson, Kristina. *Globalization and Democratization in Asia*. London, RoutledgeCurzon, 2002.

Mahbub-ul-Haq Human Development Centre. *Human Development in South Asia 2001: Globalisation and Human Development*. Karachi, Oxford University Press, 2002.

*Human Development in South Asia 2002: Agriculture and Rural Development*. Karachi, Oxford University Press, 2003.

*Human Development in South Asia 2003: The Employment Challenge*. Lahore, Oxford University Press, 2004.

Mandle, Jay R. *Globalization and the Poor*. Cambridge, Cambridge University Press, 2003.

Meuleman, Johan (Ed.). *Islam in the Era of Globalization: Muslim Attitudes towards Modernity and Identity*. London, RoutledgeCurzon, 2002.

Mohammadi, Ali (Ed.). *Islam Encountering Globalization*. London, RoutledgeCurzon, 2002.

Moore, Mike. *A World Without Walls: Freedom, Development, Free Trade and Global Governance*. Cambridge, Cambridge University Press, 2003.

Ramaswamy, K. V. *Globalization and Industrial Labor Markets in South Asia: Some Aspects of Adjustment in a Less Integrated Region*. Honolulu, HI, East-West Center, University of Hawaii Press, 2003.

RIS (Research and Information System) for the Non-Aligned and Other Developing Countries. *South Asia Development and Cooperation Report 2004*. New Delhi, 2004.

Sarkar, Sonita, and De, Esha Niyogi (Eds). *Trans-Status Subjects: Gender in the Globalization of South and Southeast Asia*. Durham, NC, Duke University Press, 2002.

Sharma, Kishor (Ed.). *Trade Policy, Growth and Poverty in Asian Developing Countries*. London, Routledge, 2003.

Sharma, Usha. *Women in South Asia: Employment, Empowerment and Human Development*. Delhi, Authors Press, 2003.

UN Development Programme. *Human Development Report*. New Delhi, Oxford University Press, annually.

Vainak, Achin (Ed.). *Globalization and South Asia: Multidimensional Perspectives*. New Delhi, Manohar Publishers and Distributors, 2004.

World Bank. *Global Development Finance*. Washington, DC, annually.

*World Development Indicators*. Washington, DC, annually.

**Afghanistan**

World Bank. *Country Brief: South Asia Region Afghanistan*. Washington, DC, 2002.

**Bangladesh**

Centre for Policy Dialogue. *Changes and Challenges: A Review of Bangladesh's Development*. Dhaka, University Press, 2001.

*Bangladesh: Facing the Challenges of Globalisation*. Dhaka, University Press, 2002.

Muqtada, M. A. Singh, and Rashid, M. A. *Bangladesh: Economic and Social Challenges of Globalisation*. Dhaka, University Press, 2002.

**India**

Assayag, J., and Fuller, C. (Eds). *Globalizing India: Perspectives from Below*. New Delhi, Anthem Press, 2005.

Banerjee, Parthasarathi, and Richter, Frank-Jürgen (Eds). *Economic Institutions in India: Sustainability under Liberalization and Globalization*. Basingstoke, Palgrave Macmillan, 2003.

Deaton, Angus, and Dreze, Jean. 'Poverty and Inequality in India: A Re-examination', *Economic and Political Weekly*. Mumbai, 7 September 2002.

Dreze, Jean, and Sen, Amartya. *India: Development and Participation*. New Delhi, Oxford University Press, 2002.

Greenspan, Anna. *India and the IT Revolution: Networks of Global Culture*. Basingstoke, Palgrave Macmillan, 2004.

Nayar, Baldev Raj. *Globalization and Nationalism: The Changing Balance in India's Economic Policy, 1950–2000*. New Delhi, Sage, 2001.

Planning Commission, Government of India. *National Human Development Report 2001*. New Delhi, 2002.

Prabhu, K. S. *Economic Reform and Social Sector Development: A Study of Two Indian States*. New Delhi, Sage, 2001.

Ray, Pradeep, *et al. FDI and Industrial Organisation in Developing Countries: The Challenge of Globalisation in India*. Aldershot, Ashgate Publishing, 2005.

Srinivasan, T. N., and Tendulkar, Suresh. *Reintegrating India with the World Economy*. Washington, DC, Institute for International Economics, 2002.

**The Maldives**

Poverty Reduction and Economic Management Unit, South Asia Region, World Bank. *Maldives: Policies for Sustaining Economic Growth*. Washington, DC, 1999.

**Nepal**

Prennushi, Giovanna. *Nepal: Poverty at the Turn of the Twenty-First Century*. May 1999, World Bank; internet poverty.worldbank.org/library/view/11002.

World Bank. *Country Brief: South Asia Region Nepal*. Washington, DC, 2002.

**Pakistan**

Asian Development Bank. *Poverty in Pakistan: Issues, Causes and Institutional Responses*. Manila, 2002.

Easterly, William. 'The Political Economy of Growth without Development: A Case Study for Pakistan'. *Paper for the Analytical Narratives of Growth Project*, Kennedy School of Government, Harvard University, Cambridge, MA, 2002. Reprinted in Rodrik, Dani (Ed.), *In Search for Prosperity*. Princeton, NJ, Princeton University Press, 2003.

Hasan, P. *Pakistan's Economy at the Crossroads*. Karachi, Oxford University Press, 1998.

Zaidi, Akbar. *Issues in Pakistan's Economy*. Karachi, Oxford University Press, 1999.

**Sri Lanka**

Institute of Policy Studies of Sri Lanka. *State of the Economy 2002*. Colombo, 2003.

# CORRUPTION AND GOVERNANCE IN SOUTH ASIA

MUSHTAQ H. KHAN

Since the early 1980s the problem of corruption and issues of governance have come to the fore in all South Asian countries. Internal public concern over corruption, and pressure from international agencies, such as the World Bank and the IMF, and from bilateral agencies alarmed by the misuse of aid, has been growing. Closely linked to the issue of corruption is a wider set of concerns regarding governance, including the operation of the judicial system, the stability of property rights, and the functioning of democracy. Corruption has been foremost on the agenda, out of all these issues, as it is widely perceived to be not just a problem in itself but also an indicator of other failures of governance. In response to internal and external pressures, political parties in South Asia have adopted anti-corruption programmes, although usually only as populist slogans or to attack their opponents. Furthermore, citizens' groups and local and international non-governmental organizations (NGOs) have led intense campaigns and, significantly, a mainstreaming of anti-corruption policies by the World Bank and other international agencies has occurred. However, the problem of corruption persists in South Asia, as measured by the intense public debate on and media coverage of corruption, the ongoing concern of international agencies and investors, as well as the poor showing of these countries in international rankings of corruption indices constructed by the NGO Transparency International and other such agencies. On the other hand, the debate on governance in South Asia has also been very narrowly defined, with insufficient attention being paid to many important aspects of growth-enhancing governance capabilities.

Since the early 1980s prime ministers and presidents in Bangladesh, India and Pakistan have been legally implicated in, and sometimes even convicted of, corruption, and in Nepal and Sri Lanka prime ministers have been regularly accused of corruption by their political rivals and the media. Provincial, state and local governments in all South Asian countries have also been accused of being equally corrupt, with a number of flamboyant chief ministers in India acquiring an international reputation for corruption. The form of government also seems to have had little effect on the magnitude of corruption, with both democracies and authoritarian regimes displaying equally high levels of corruption. Public disclosures of large-scale corruption in Bangladesh, India and Pakistan have often been dominated by major irregularities in government procurements. While in the past public-sector industries attracted the most attention for nepotism and clientelism, recently a number of spectacular corruption-related scandals and crises in privatization deals and the regulation of financial markets have been exposed. At a lower level, government functionaries of all types are widely engaged in corruption; police, customs, land registration and irrigation officials receive frequent negative attention in the media. In public opinion surveys, police forces throughout the Indian subcontinent are often accused of being the most corrupt agencies, not necessarily because they appropriate the greatest amount in bribes but because for most people their corruption is the most visible and irksome on a daily basis. This qualitative and journalistic evidence of widespread corruption in South Asia is supported by surveys of public perceptions of corruption that are collated by the World Bank to provide indices for the 'control of corruption' in different countries. These indices are constructed in such a way that they range from –2.5 (the highest level of corruption) to +2.5 (the lowest level of corruption), with the average of all countries' indices being 0.0. Below each index listed in the following table appears the standard error, which shows the degree of confidence given the variation in the indices available for each country.

These indices should be interpreted carefully as they are based on subjective perceptions; however, they do suggest that official policies and pressure from NGOs and civil society had minimal effect on reducing corruption between 1996 and 2007. There have been small improvements in the index over this period in Pakistan, Sri Lanka, Afghanistan and Bhutan, but even in these cases the improvements were not significant, given the standard error in the indices. In the other South Asian countries the corruption measure worsened. There is some concern, particularly in Bangladesh, about whether the decline in these subjective indicators in recent years reveals the changing sensitivities of respondents rather than real changes in the degree of corruption. Nevertheless, while subjective perception indices may not reflect true changes in the degree of corruption, they do reveal growing public disquiet with the slow progress in dealing with the problem. Sri Lanka, which is considered a much more developed nation, with a per caput gross national income two to three times higher than its neighbours, registered a correspondingly lower corruption index. However, even in Sri Lanka, corruption has become one of the main issues to dominate accusations and counter-accusations made by government and opposition parties. The Maldives and Bhutan had the lowest recorded levels of corruption in the Indian subcontinent, and were the only South Asian countries with corruption indicators that were positive in 1998, which means that they had corruption rankings better than the global average. By 2007, however, the Maldives had reverted to the South Asian pattern, suggesting that the early

**Table 1. Control of Corruption Index for South Asia**

| | Control of Corruption Index for South Asia* | | | | | | | | |
|---|---|---|---|---|---|---|---|---|---|
| Country | 1996 | 1998 | 2000 | 2002 | 2003 | 2004 | 2005 | 2006 | 2007 |
| Afghanistan | n.a. | –1.92 | –1.91 | –1.54 | –1.62 | –1.49 | –1.47 | –1.46 | –1.53 |
| | n.a. | (0.37) | (0.30) | (0.31) | (0.29) | (0.19) | (0.20) | (0.20) | (0.23) |
| Bangladesh | –0.49 | –0.72 | –0.94 | –1.02 | –1.17 | –1.32 | –1.23 | –1.26 | –1.05 |
| | (0.26) | (0.20) | (0.16) | (0.15) | (0.15) | (0.15) | (0.15) | (0.14) | (0.13) |
| Bhutan | n.a. | 0.66 | 0.56 | 0.55 | 0.89 | 0.81 | 0.87 | 0.89 | 0.92 |
| | n.a. | (0.31) | (0.24) | (0.23) | (0.23) | (0.26) | (0.25) | (0.25) | (0.19) |
| India | –0.36 | –0.29 | –0.38 | –0.41 | –0.34 | –0.34 | –0.31 | –0.25 | –0.39 |
| | (0.17) | (0.15) | (0.14) | (0.14) | (0.13) | (0.12) | (0.12) | (0.12) | (0.12) |
| Maldives | n.a. | 0.11 | –0.14 | –0.13 | 0.06 | –0.15 | –0.32 | –0.52 | –0.78 |
| | n.a. | (0.31) | (0.24) | (0.23) | (0.24) | (0.28) | (0.27) | (0.28) | (0.28) |
| Nepal | –0.31 | –0.35 | –0.43 | –0.33 | –0.23 | –0.61 | –0.75 | –0.67 | –0.66 |
| | (0.53) | (0.25) | (0.20) | (0.19) | (0.19) | (0.179) | (0.16) | (0.16) | (0.15) |
| Pakistan | –1.04 | –0.89 | –0.76 | –0.83 | –0.74 | –1.03 | –0.99 | –0.78 | –0.83 |
| | (0.25) | (0.20) | (0.17) | (0.15) | (0.15) | (0.14) | (0.14) | (0.13) | (0.13) |
| Sri Lanka | –0.27 | –0.17 | –0.18 | –0.21 | –0.21 | –0.14 | –0.26 | –0.13 | –0.13 |
| | (0.26) | (0.20) | (0.16) | (0.15) | (0.15) | (0.15) | (0.15) | (0.14) | (0.13) |

* Range: –2.5 to +2.5; standard error shown in parentheses.

Source: Kaufmann, Daniel, Kraay, Aart, and Mastruzzi, Massimo. *Governance Matters VII: Aggregate and Individual Governance Indicators 1996–2007*; internet www.govindicators.org.

results could have been the result of lower public awareness of corruption as a problem in the islands, rather than a significant real change in the degree of corruption in less than a decade. Indeed, the standard errors again suggest that there may have been little real change in corruption in this country. Afghanistan has consistently had the highest corruption indicator in South Asia, reflecting the continuing role of warlords and criminality in its economy. Here the corruption is largely of a different type and magnitude, compared with its neighbours, since a nation-wide state structure does not yet exist.

The extent of corruption in South Asia has led to wider concern regarding poor governance, which in turn is responsible for poor economic performance, persistent poverty, the subversion of democracy and the inability to attract sufficient foreign investment. However, in assessing corruption in South Asia, it is desirable to remember that corruption is rife in all developing countries, regardless of their economic growth rates; indeed, the level of corruption is strongly connected to the country's level of development. Generally, the poorer and less developed a country is, the more it suffers from corruption. This is even true of high-growth developing countries such as the Republic of Korea in the 1960s or the People's Republic of China in the first decade of the 2000s. This cross-country evidence suggests that studying the aggregate evidence of corruption is likely to be misleading, since even rapidly growing economies experience relatively high levels of corruption in their nascent stages. Clearly, it is necessary to distinguish between different types of corruption and to identify why the more damaging types predominate in less dynamic economies such as those found in South Asia. This will also help to assess the likelihood of success for specific anti-corruption strategies.

## A TYPOLOGY OF SOUTH ASIAN CORRUPTION

Corruption can be defined in various ways, but it is typically understood to mean a violation of law by public officials for private gain. The violation of law may result in the provision of a proscribed service and/or the subversion of state policies in a way advantageous for the bribe-payer. At a general level, all corruption is damaging: time and resources are wasted in the paying of bribes, in identifying the officials to bribe and determining the amounts to pay, and all these resources could evidently have been better used in productive investments. Moreover, unlike taxes, the payment of a bribe is not guaranteed, and there is often little redress if the public official taking bribes does not deliver the promised services or decisions. In addition, corruption can have important indirect effects on business confidence and thus on investments. For instance, corruption could potentially result in sudden changes in government policy or in the reallocation of property rights, thereby adversely affecting the investment climate and increasing the overall costs of corruption. However, while bribery always imposes a cost on society, the net economic effect of corruption also depends on the type of intervention or subversion of policy that is achieved as a result of the bribe. Violations of useful and necessary laws are clearly damaging for the economy, and examples of such corruption are not difficult to find in South Asia. In these cases corruption is unquestionably damaging for the economy. However, there are also many legal violations in developing countries that may be necessary. For instance, emerging capitalists might have to navigate around politically necessary but restrictive laws, or necessary interventions might exist that have not yet been legally sanctioned. In some cases these interventions cannot be legally sanctioned for political reasons even though they are essential for maintaining political stability or economic growth. In these cases, the economic effects of corruption are anomalous; accordingly, corruption could be associated with either stagnation or growth. These types of corruption can also be found in the South Asian countries. The distinction between types of corruption is important in order to understand both the economic and political effects of corruption and the appropriateness of different anti-corruption strategies. It is possible to distinguish between at least four types of corruption in South Asia, based on whether the underlying interventions are potentially necessary for economic or political reasons, and whether the law allows these interventions. This classification is shown below.

i) *Interventions that are required for economic development or political stability and are legally permitted:* the corruption associated with these interventions may be associated with growth or stagnation depending on the extent to which necessary interventions (market regulation, promotion of industries, subsidies for political stabilization) are subverted. Anti-corruption policy in these areas should seek to improve implementation and reduce corruption, but not to remove the interventions.

ii) *Interventions that are required for economic development or political stability but are legally prohibited:* all these interventions are likely to be associated with corruption. These types of corruption may again be associated with growth or stagnation depending on the nature and extent of these interventions (discriminatory benefits for powerful groups to maintain stability, preferential access to resources for emerging capitalists). Policy in these areas should focus on gradually legalizing necessary interventions so that these can be transparently regulated and on reducing damaging interventions.

iii) *Interventions that are not required for economic development or political stability and are legally permitted:* the types of corruption associated with dysfunctional interventions (unnecessary paperwork and permissions, protection of inefficient industries) always have negative effects. Policy should seek to remove these state 'functions' (through liberalization and privatization). This has been the focus of mainstream anti-corruption strategies, but they actually cover only a small part of the range of corrupt activities.

iv) *Interventions that are not required for economic development or political stability and are legally prohibited:* the corruption associated with these types of 'interventions' are primarily predatory extortions. While some instances of predatory corruption can be found in all South Asian states, this type of corruption only begins to predominate in failed or failing states where armed groups can extort from society regardless of their effects on political stability or economic performance. In order to tackle this type of corruption, effective policy has to focus on strengthening the centralized coercive power of the State.

The first type of corruption explained above is associated with interventions that are potentially necessary for the economy or polity, and are allowed and regulated by law. Examples of these interventions are subsidies to maintain political stability, different types of schemes to help domestic industry catch up with foreign competitors, and the regulation of financial markets. Although economic liberalization has been taking place in all the major South Asian countries since the 1980s, a wide range of interventions remains important and necessary for economic growth and political stability. Individuals and groups might become involved in corrupt activity to subvert the implementation of these interventions. However, here the problem is not the interventions themselves, but the State's lack of capacity to implement them. Here, anti-corruption policies should concentrate on strengthening the capacity of the State to enforce the necessary policies and development strategies. There are a number of critical governance capabilities that need to be strengthened in this area to enhance or sustain the growth prospects of these economies, but this is one area of governance that has received far less attention than it deserves.

The second type of corruption, concerning necessary interventions that are not—or cannot be—regulated by law, is much more problematic. In South Asia, much of the widespread political corruption that involves allocating resources in partisan ways to maintain political stability is an example of this type of corruption. Similarly, interventions to accelerate and promote emerging capitalism in countries where domestic capitalism is weak often have to be partisan and cannot be recognized in law. These interventions are very likely to result in corruption, since they cannot be explicitly recognized in law for political reasons. Attempts to target this form of corruption directly have proved futile, since such action threatens to damage the fundamental interests of the State and is therefore never effectively implemented. A more feasible, albeit limited, policy would be damage-limitation in the short term and, in the longer term, ensuring the country's rapid progress to a position where it would be possible to legalize some of these interventions, or achieving political and economic development so that these interventions are no longer essential. Unfortunately, this is the area in which feasible anti-corruption strategies in South Asia are most lacking.

The third type of corruption has received more attention than the other types. It comprises corrupt acts associated with laws that enable interventions in contexts where the interventions themselves are not required. Typical examples of these are tariff protection for industries that do not have the potential to achieve the productivity of their competitors; or excessive regulation and requirements of permissions that have no purpose except to enable bureaucrats to extract bribes from businessmen. South Asian countries have been well known for these types of regulations. These dysfunctional interventions not only cause direct economic damage, but also create secondary damage, as entrepreneurs use corrupt means in an attempt to gain monopoly profits or to circumvent futile restrictions. In these circumstances the liberal prescription of liberalization and privatization is most appropriate, combined with direct anti-corruption measures. However, this is not the most important type of corruption in South Asia, and an excessive focus on this type hitherto has hindered, rather than aided, the development of feasible anti-corruption strategies.

Finally, the worst type of corruption is the fourth one, which is most prevalent in areas where the enforcement of social order by the State has broken down completely. Illegal interventions take place that do not serve any economic or political purposes for any groups apart from the avaricious 'officials' involved in this form of corruption. Thus, this type of corruption is based solely on the coercive power of small groups to extort from the public. While there are aspects of such extortions in every South Asian society, it is only in Afghanistan that it takes on significant proportions.

## POLITICAL CORRUPTION

Political corruption refers to the corruption operated by politicians. Political players can be involved in all types of corruption, but political calculations are particularly important for the second type of corruption where corruption is directly involved in the political process. In all South Asian countries, political corruption can be traced from the highest levels of the political establishment, down to the lowest. Unsurprisingly, it has proved difficult for the political system to engage credibly in anti-corruption activities lower down the hierarchy. In democratic Bangladesh, India, Nepal and Sri Lanka, prime ministers have been frequently accused of corruption, and have sometimes been convicted of criminal offences, as have their authoritarian counterparts in Bangladesh and Pakistan during military or authoritarian regimes. In the latter countries, where there have been cycles of democracy and dictatorship, no significant long-term difference is observed in the extent of corruption under either type of regime. This evidence compels us to question the widespread belief that corruption is caused by the lack of accountability of public officials. In fact the evidence from South Asia shows that electors are very aware of the corruption and even criminality of their political representatives but still vote for corrupt politicians, often at the expense of 'clean' campaigners who occasionally stand against them.

In 1997 the Indian Election Commission conservatively estimated that 40 members of parliament and 700 state assembly representatives in India, altogether equal to 10% of all legislators, had been convicted of serious criminal offences or faced serious criminal charges, ranging from extortion to murder. In the 2002 Indian state elections as many as 20% of the candidates in certain states were convicted criminals or had been charged with crimes. The true number of legislators involved in crime is likely to be considerably higher than these figures, which account for legislators who have already been convicted or whose cases are being processed in the courts. It is fairly certain that many other legislators in the first decade of the 2000s are engaged in criminal activities without being indicted. It is also widely perceived in the Indian press and in opinion surveys that the proportion of criminals involved in politics is increasing. The visibility of political corruption reached a new level in India in July 2008 when the ruling Congress-led coalition Government achieved a narrow victory in the parliamentary vote of confidence precipitated by the Indo-US nuclear deal. Three opposition MPs of the Bharatiya Janata Party carried bags of money into the Lok Sabha and accused the ruling coalition of attempting to bribe them with Rs 10m. to boycott the vote. Whatever the findings of the inquiry that was subsequently instituted, the incident was unprecedented and will be remembered as a particularly low point in the history of the Lok Sabha. In November 2006 an interim Government took power in Bangladesh and declared a state of emergency in January 2007. More than 200 politicians, including the heads of two previous governments, were arrested on charges of corruption. Several prominent politicians were convicted, but in the majority of cases sufficient evidence was not available and many of the cases were dropped. By mid-2008 one of the arrested former prime ministers had been acquitted and the release of the second was imminent, marking the end of the anti-corruption drive. However, while the frontal attack on political corruption in Bangladesh was badly conceived, it may yet prove to have some lasting impact on the operation of political parties in the future if a smooth transition through democratic elections is achieved in December 2008. Despite all this, the freedom of the media in reporting political corruption in India is comparable to advanced countries, and even in Bangladesh, Pakistan and other South Asian countries, the evidence of corrupt activity by leading politicians is well known and freely available.

When asked to explain their voting decisions, South Asian voters frequently report that they vote for 'mafia-style' politicians because they have proved able to deliver resources and security to powerful local constituents, who in turn provide the organizational weight to ensure electoral victories and enforce political order. The logic driving this pattern of politics can be better understood once the constraints facing the delivery of services and the provision of security are studied. As is the case in other developing countries, South Asian states generally lack the fiscal resources to perform these functions effectively because their central budgets are in structural deficit; funds are not available to provide even the most essential services adequately. In these circumstances conflicts over resources are intense; 'intermediate-class' groups often organize themselves around factional symbols, based on ethnicity, religion or caste in competing for these resources. Politicians subsequently find that they can only be successful if they offer selective benefits to at least some of these effectively organized factions. Since providing preferential benefits to some but not others is not legal, the legitimacy of the politician is not of great concern to his or her most critical supporters. Indeed, a truly honest politician would find it impossible to secure any organized support from these critical factional groups, and without their support, power cannot be attained. The growing malaise of criminality in politics and the rise of factional politics in South Asia is at least partly due to the 'prisoner's dilemma problem', where credible politicians are excluded by the competition from less scrupulous political entrepreneurs who can offer more to factions that are in search of a patron. Thus, while democracy is desirable in itself, it has anomalous effects on the extent of corruption. A long-term change in this pattern of politics is unlikely before economic development has proceeded to the point where the central budget can provide sufficient resources for honest politicians to stay in power through providing widespread service-delivery and redistribution. Meanwhile, in the first decade of the 2000s a symbiotic relationship between politicians who use political power for personal enrichment and the enrichment of their close allies, and the powerful social factions, which require access to resources, jobs and contracts (all services that honest politicians cannot possibly provide) remains a dominant characteristic in South Asian politics. This would explain why all major political parties regularly accuse each other of corruption while eagerly recruiting criminals who can offer resources and secure the support of powerful factions. It also explains why ordinary citizens criticize their politicians for being involved in corruption while simultaneously voting for corrupt leaders who they think are most likely to protect their constituency and provide their own faction with disproportionate benefits.

South Asian political corruption is largely of the second type (see above), since the current strategies of maintaining political power cannot be legalized, and the approach of legitimately maintaining power through the provision of generalized benefits is not viable given the level of economic development. This type of political corruption may eventually result in sufficient political stability for rapid economic growth to take place, as did happen in some South-East Asian countries, such as Thailand. This would, subsequently, permit the growth of formal budgetary redistributions and service-delivery to take place, thereby allowing more honest politics and politicians to emerge in the future. However, in South Asia the continual emergence of new groups and factions has meant that, over time, politics has become more factional, fragmented and crime-driven. As this continues to happen, the risk is always present that more and more political corruption will convert into the fourth type, where the criminal activities of politicians enrich only themselves, using the coercive force of private mafias to extort from the rest of society. In Afghanistan in the first decade of the 2000s an extreme version of this fragmentation exists, where regional military commanders can extort from society and engage in crime and the central State continues to find it difficult to constrain their activities. However, this degree of social fragmentation and the use of coercive force should be distinguished from the clientelist politics of other South Asian countries, where local mafias have had to engage in a political process of suborning powerful groups and forming political coalitions that, however imperfectly, has maintained some form of social stability. But in all these cases, where political corruption is driven by the demands of politically powerful groups, greater transparency, democracy or civil society participation would be unlikely on their own to have a significant impact on reducing this type of corruption in South Asia. There is no reason to suggest that democracy or transparency would reduce the political requests of powerful groups. Indeed, the focus on greater democracy and transparency as a method of countering corruption in Bangladesh and Pakistan has yielded very disappointing results. In Bangladesh a decade of democracy witnessed a rapid rise in political corruption. The extreme measures adopted by the military-supported emergency Government in 2007–08 in Bangladesh, including the arrest of leading politicians from all major political parties on corruption charges, reflects frustration with this democratic process. These measures were initially widely supported by the general public. However, precisely because political leaders do deliver to critical constituencies, it is not credible that they can be incarcerated for long. As a result, the emergency Government found that it was not possible to obtain significant testimonies and evidence in court from individuals who held this information, possibly because those who could provide convincing testimony were hedging their bets. Consequently, the majority of corruption cases collapsed, and it remains unclear whether the few individuals who were convicted will remain in prison once an elected government assumes power. This experience shows that a sound analysis of the drivers of political corruption is required before undertaking large scale anti-corruption campaigns. A much more narrowly focused attack on a small number of high-ranking politicians may have proved more successful in signalling that there are limits to the extent of political corruption that would be tolerated by other social constituencies such as the army. The only significant immediate result of the Bangladeshi anti-corruption drive was a decrease in business confidence, since many businessmen were charged with tax evasion and the bribery of politicians. The sole positive note is the possibility that this experience will set some limits to the types and extent of corruption that subsequent governments will engage in. The irony is that the real problem that led to the imposition of the state of emergency in January 2007 was not directly due to political corruption but was caused by a political impasse between the major political parties where the ruling party was engaging in activities that the opposition considered would compromise its ability to win the forthcoming election. In Pakistan the return of military rule in 1999 appeared to reduce corruption, although the sustainability of this development proved questionable once it became necessary for the Government to begin constructing wider political support bases to remain in power.

The greater fiscal capacity necessary for governments to provide legally the demands of its constituents will be generated only once the region undergoes longer-term economic development. In the mean time, the rapid growth and negative effects of political corruption could conceivably be reduced through the development of large, inclusive political parties that aim to impose social discipline in order to achieve long-term development goals. Such parties would not entirely curb political corruption, but might succeed in countering the growing fragmentation and factionalization of politics across South Asia. It is not surprising that the Indian states that perform relatively better than others are those that are run by disciplined and centralized parties; however, such parties are not visible at the national level in India. Even in the much smaller countries of South Asia, national parties have become loose coalitions of factions, with each faction demanding ever greater rewards for not defecting to the opposition. This explains the escalating cost of politics in these countries and the escalating cost of political corruption.

Further, albeit limited, progress towards mitigating the extent of political corruption would also be possible through the legalization of large donations to political parties. Allowing political parties to pay legally for some of their expenses during and after election campaigns would not remove the problem entirely, since political organizers demand much more than the cost of organizing elections in exchange for their support; nevertheless, it would reduce the need for political parties to engage in corrupt or criminal activities simply to raise funds for election campaigns. In Bangladesh and India politics is increasingly funded by so-called 'black money' (money generated by crime or from 'grey' activities that are not declared to avoid paying tax). It has been estimated that the black economy has burgeoned to approximately one-third of the size of the official economies in these countries. However, attempts to regularize election funding have been blocked by other political considerations. In India the proposed Election and Other Related Laws Bill was introduced in Parliament in 2001–02 to provide, among other measures, income tax exemptions for private and corporate donations to political parties. This legislation was stalled in Parliament, partly because it challenged the dominant political ideology shared by all major parties that rejects any 'disproportionate' political influence for the rich. Aside from ideology, in an emerging economy it is also problematic to legalize donations from such sources when much of the wealth of this emerging rich élite is tainted by association with 'sharp practices' (a large proportion of the 'new rich' has engaged in corrupt activity, such as illegally obtaining land, or using political connections to gain lucrative contracts). However, although there are problems surrounding political fund-raising reform, the current system is far worse. Thus, when the Indian Election Commission attempted to prohibit criminals from contesting elections, the Government also delayed this proposal. The Indian Election Commission has imposed limits on election spending by candidates, but these restrictions have proved difficult to enforce; in any case, the limits currently apply only to spending by individual candidates and not to expenditure by their political parties. Indeed, rather than showing any signs of being constrained by these attempts, it is widely perceived that election expenditure is increasing. However, under a new law enacted in 2003, all candidates for election now have to submit details of any criminal case pending against them, a record of their assets and liabilities, and their educational qualifications. These measures may help to encourage political parties not to field questionable candidates, but it is not clear how reported assets and liabilities can be cross-checked to confirm their accuracy. Indeed, it has proved difficult to make any progress on taking action against the more than 700 incumbent legislators who actually have criminal cases pending against them.

Similar tendencies of entrenched political corruption are observed in Bangladesh, Pakistan, and other South Asian countries. In 2002 the Pakistani President, Gen. Pervez Musharraf, enforced a strict electoral rule barring politicians convicted of criminal offences from contesting elections. However, critics argued that the real intention behind the enforcement of this rule was to exclude the two prominent civilian political leaders of the country from standing against the military regime in elections held later that year. The possibility of enforcing such a rule under a future civilian administration is arguable, given the pressures outlined above. Even the National Accountability Bureau (NAB) in Pakistan, which has achieved considerable success in recent years in prosecuting public officials and retrieving their misappropriated funds, is considered to be an agency of the armed forces rather than an independent authority. It is significant that the military (and the judiciary) are excluded from its mandate. Although President Musharraf came to power ostensibly to save the country from the corruption of the political élites, the centralization of power in the executive arguably created greater instability in Pakistan. In mid-2007 the Pakistan judiciary achieved a significant victory over the executive headed by President Musharraf when it succeeded in reinstating the Chief Justice, Iftikhar Mohammad Chaudhry, who had been suspended from his post by the President. This case was expected to have an impact on broader questions of governance in Pakistan and may even be considered to have marked the onset of the transition to civilian rule and greater checks on executive power. Following a period of serious political unrest, a democratically elected Government came to power in Pakistan in February 2008 and, under threat of impeachment, President Musharraf resigned from the presidency in August. In Bangladesh an Independent Anti-Corruption Commission (IACC) was established in 2004 with the power to investigate allegations of corruption against any public official without first having to seek government permission, as was previously the case; in practice, however, the IACC proved to be fairly ineffectual. The emergency Government that took power in 2007 reconstituted the Anti-Corruption Commission in Bangladesh and acceded to the United Nations Convention against Corruption; however, the effectiveness of these measures will take some time to assess. In November 2007, in a move that was intended to strengthen the power of the judiciary to put on trial and convict corrupt politicians and bureaucrats, the emergency Government also implemented an eight-year-old ruling of the Supreme Court that demanded the formal separation of the judiciary from the executive. Again, whether the implementation of this measure will actually enable the judiciary to prosecute the most serious cases of political and administrative corruption remains to be seen. In India the Central Vigilance Commission is regarded as autonomous, but its remit covers only state employees and not politicians. Most importantly though, if it is accepted that much political corruption in these countries is entrenched and 'society-driven', the task of any anti-corruption commission would at best be partial in the short term, and this would make it difficult for it to defend itself convincingly as non-partisan. India's great advantage over its smaller neighbours is that paradoxically its very size and complexity make it impossible for any one faction to monopolize power for too long, and electoral competition imposes natural checks on the degree of appropriation that factions in power can get away with. Citizen activism in India, in the form of civil society 'election watches' which publicize the affidavits on criminal cases, assets and liabilities submitted by candidates, has played a role in this context.

## BUREAUCRATIC CORRUPTION

Corruption committed by bureaucratic officials in South Asia ranges from the petty corruption of police officers collecting nominal bribes for minor traffic offences, to multi-million dollar bribes collected by senior army officers and defence officials in major military contracts. Once again, bureaucrats are likely to be involved in all types of corruption. Bureaucratic corruption is intimately connected with political corruption; at the highest levels politicians and bureaucrats have to collude in large-scale corrupt activity. Moreover, the persistence of low-level bureaucratic corruption cannot be understood without taking into account the absence of political will to combat corruption on the part of high-level political office-holders who are themselves vulnerable to attack for their own corruption. For example, newspapers in South Asian countries frequently report stories of police forces being prevented from prosecuting heads of criminal organizations or of crime cartels protected by powerful politicians.

A common argument in South Asia is that low bureaucratic pay contributes to high levels of bureaucratic corruption. This is undoubtedly true, but it is not clear that raising bureaucratic salaries would necessarily reduce corruption. Higher-paid bureaucrats would only consider refraining from corrupt activity if it were possible to identify the perpetrators and dismiss those who were occasionally caught. However, if the political capacity to attack bureaucratic corruption is absent, higher salaries may have little effect. Furthermore, bureaucratic corruption takes many different forms in South Asian countries, and there are instances of each of the four types identified above. First, the misappropriation of funds by bureaucrats engaged in the operation of legally recognized regulatory structures that have necessary or useful economic or political functions is common. These include structures established to regulate markets, promote industry and agriculture, and manage subsidies and redistributions that aim to maintain political stability. Although these systems of state intervention or regulation are beneficial for society, they inevitably confer benefits on some and costs on others and are therefore susceptible to either the attempts of bureaucrats to extract a share of the benefit by demanding bribes from intended beneficiaries, or attempts by non-eligible recipients to obtain some of these benefits by offering bribes, or both. The degree to which state policy is subverted and the magnitude of the bribes determines whether the act of corruption has encouraged or discouraged reasonable economic performance or not. If bureaucrats were to implement what was intended by policy and then extract bribes, the result would be much more favourable than if they were to accept a bribe to subvert what was intended.

Unfortunately, in many parts of South Asia bureaucratic corruption has seriously subverted numerous critical state functions, including regulatory functions and the protection of property rights. For instance, corrupt activity has subverted the operation of welfare subsidies and of policies to encourage industrialization or regional development. Factories that never produce anything continue to receive production subsidies or are permitted to roll over their debt to publicly owned banks, for example. A further problem is the absence of a functioning judicial system. In South Asia many civil cases take more than a decade to resolve. The judicial process is susceptible to manipulation: those who want to prevent a judgment can pay relatively small bribes on a regular basis to delay a case or force an adjournment. Some attempts have been made to address these problems through state withdrawal in the form of liberalization and privatization. However, progress has been slow and in the case of effective state functions, interventions and regulations, state withdrawal is not a solution.

Nevertheless, strategies of liberalization and privatization were introduced in the major South Asian countries from the 1980s onwards; an acceleration of liberalization occurred in the 1990s. In India the average tariff rate was reduced from 87% in 1990 to 25% by 1998. Licensing of industries and controls over imports were almost entirely removed. In Bangladesh and Pakistan the nationalization process that took place in the 1970s was reversed through extensive privatization programmes. Some of the restrictions that were removed had no potentially positive function, and little was lost as a result. However, other parts of the regulatory structure had been intended to accelerate the development of local entrepreneurial capacity through industrial policy and protection, or to maintain internal regional and social balance, and here state withdrawal was potentially damaging. Even the privatization of large enterprises in Bangladesh and Pakistan, in the absence of effective regulatory structures and safeguards, often resulted in inefficiency and subsidy appropriation in the private sector replacing the inefficiency and deficits of the public sector. In India liberalization of financial markets resulted in dramatic allegations in 2001 of widespread share price manipulation in the stock market and multi-million dollar irregularities in India's largest investment fund, the Unit Trust of India. Moreover, the withdrawal of the State from traditional redistributive and regulatory functions has resulted in the development of illegal redistributive mechanisms governed by the type of criminal organizations described in the section on political corruption. Finally, in the case of the police force and judiciary, state withdrawal is not even possible. In fact, the appropriate response in all cases of corruption associated with the subversion of essential state functions is to strengthen state capacities. Progress on this front has been limited across South Asia. If the State had the capacity to enforce decisions that were beneficial for society, bribery committed by public servants would be undesirable but would not subvert development goals completely. However, where corruption undermines the enforcement of necessary regulations, the results are much more detrimental. This is an important aspect in the difference between corruption in high-growth and low-growth economies.

The second type of bureaucratic corruption that emerges because a legal framework to enforce a large number of necessary state actions or decisions does not exist is more prevalent and causes greater problems for government anti-corruption policy. In the same way that political stability in South Asia is partially dependent on powerful factional groups receiving disproportionate benefits, rationing scarce resources often requires disproportionate amounts of resources being allocated to the rich, or to emerging capitalists. Although developing countries are often legally committed to granting equal access to public resources to all citizens, if public resources become very scarce, not only will the rich be willing to pay a high price to gain privileged access, but it may also be desirable to give emerging capitalists privileged access to *some* resources to accelerate growth. However, state agencies involved in the allocation of public resources, such as land rights, credit, and other scarce resources, or indeed any aspect of regulation or service-delivery, are legally bound to operate according to rules that are far removed from the reality of stark differences in the purchasing power, economic potential, social status or political influence of claimants. In all these cases, alternative rationing devices are used in practice, based either on willingness to pay or political power. This kind of corruption is ubiquitous, ranging from the illegal sale of formally free hospital services, to the allocation of government land for new developments in exchange for bribes. These types of corruption are difficult to deal with because state capacity alone is not the issue. The real obstacle is that, for political reasons, realistic criteria for resource allocation cannot be legally recognized. Some legal changes could be enforced to improve the situation, for instance introducing a nominal fee for some services that would be sufficient to achieve rationing. In most cases, however, charging would not solve the problem because the market price that would balance demand and supply would not be politically acceptable. In any case, it is not desirable that all public resources should be allocated through the market; however, where resources are publicly allocated on the basis of need or any other criteria, sufficient resources have to be available to meet the demands from all those who satisfy these criteria. Since this requirement is generally not met in developing countries, there may be no alternative but to endure some of this corrupt activity until the economy is developed enough to provide the State with sufficient funds to allocate resources in the way expected by law. In the mean time, the only policy response would be to strengthen state capacities and prevent egregious violations, although these actions alone would clearly not remove this type of corruption.

Much of the anti-corruption strategy advocated by international agencies is dominated by the assumption that the third type of corruption is the dominant force in South Asia. This is the corruption associated with unnecessary legislation that hampers the operation of markets and creates opportunities for corruption among relatively poorly paid public officials. This type of corruption is associated with entirely unnecessary and damaging state interventions in the form of legislation, and could easily be dealt with by removing such restrictions. It is not hard to find many examples of excessively restrictive and apparently superfluous regulations in all South Asian countries. These include requirements to fill in many different forms for all kinds of permissions, which are then subject to inordinate delays. Whether it is an application for a passport or even an attempt to pay the correct amount of tax on time, the ordinary citizen faces endless delays and frustration. However, while this type of corruption is tiresome, it is only a part, and perhaps a small part, of the overall problem. The conventional policies of liberalization, privatization and greater accountability would appear to be the most relevant solutions to this type of corruption, but they may have little overall effect in either reducing corruption or mitigating its negative effects when we consider all types of corruption together. Moreover, many of the procedures of bureaucratic record-keeping, on which this type of corruption is based, are very difficult to change rapidly even with liberalization and privatization. After more than a decade of liberalization in a number of South Asian countries, the daily procedures of the bureaucracy have undergone some simplification, but a great deal more progress needs to be achieved. Furthermore, liberalization has added new regulatory burdens on the State with respect to financial markets and the corporate sector. Liberalized markets require strong and effective regulatory frameworks to operate properly, and the absence of adequate state capacity in these areas has created a paradox whereby corruption of the first type has increased in the aftermath of liberalization. This explains why, when all types of corruption are studied together, journalistic reports or corruption perception indices record rapidly worsening corruption in South Asia in the 1980s, precisely when liberalization began to be introduced.

Finally, South Asian countries suffer to varying extents from corruption linked to extortion and other forms of crime. By definition, extortion offers no economic or political benefits to anyone other than the extortionists. There are many low-level examples of this type of extortion in all South Asian countries, particularly involving the police force, customs officials and, increasingly, criminal organizations associated with the political élite. Individuals without political connections and patrons, for example, are regularly forced to pay police officers bribes in exchange for a (temporary) end to harassment. Also, political mafias seize land from the weak, encouraged by the knowledge that the criminal justice system repeatedly fails the aggrieved. However, only in Afghanistan has the central state apparatus collapsed to the point where this type of corruption plays a significant role in the operation of the economy as a whole. In other South Asian countries there are pockets of extortion, but the State still retains enough centralized coercive capacity to limit its extent and is able and willing occasionally to use this capacity for the simple reason that extortion is a threat to the survival of the dominant élites and the State itself. It is not enough to expect democratic pressure to limit this type of corruption because unarmed citizens are not likely to be able to stop extortion through a democratic process. The coercive capacity of the central State is the critical determinant of the extent to which this type of corruption can grow. So far, at least, most South Asian countries still have central States that have been able to limit the uncontrolled growth of extortion.

## PROSPECTS

A large number of mechanisms have contributed to the entrenchment of corruption and the associated problems of governance in South Asian countries. Foremost among these has been the deep-rooted phenomenon of political corruption, and its growth over time, closely connected to the growing fragmentation of politics in South Asia. Since political corruption has become embedded in the democratic process, its removal is likely to be a long-term effort. Significant progress is likely to depend on economic development, which will allow the State to enhance tax collection and redistribute more resources legally in order to achieve political stability. As well as being an important issue in itself, the reduction of political corruption would also allow the diminution of different types of bureaucratic corruption. Bureaucratic corruption persists and thrives largely because the political élite is dependent on corruption for its survival. An examination of the significance of different types of bureaucratic corruption in South Asia shows why moves towards liberalization and privatization have had anomalous effects on corruption; in the short term, at least, the economic developments have appeared to contribute to an increase in corruption. The public concern with corruption and the role of the media and of NGOs have so far also had limited effects on reducing corruption even in the more democratic countries of South Asia. The more prevalent types of corruption in South Asia have particularly damaging effects on economic performance for a number of reasons. First, political fragmentation has always been prevalent in these countries and appears to be increasing. Greater fragmentation is likely to lead to more extensive political corruption and reduce the ability of central States to control the predatory tendencies of competing factions. Second, bureaucratic corruption has been particularly damaging in South Asia because state capacities have not been strong enough to prevent the subversion of essential state functions and interventions. Enhancing state capacities across the entire range of state functions is a particularly important task in all South Asian countries. Expanding state capacity is not likely to reduce all levels of corruption in the short term, but is expected to enhance governance by ensuring that economic development and political stability are achieved to a greater extent. Finally, the problem of military factionalism (although it is prominent only in Afghanistan) has emerged in the milder form of mafia-dominated politics in all the major South Asian countries, drawing attention once again to the importance of enhancing central state capacities in all these countries.

## BIBLIOGRAPHY

Beg, Mirza Arshad Ali. *Democracy Displaced in Pakistan: Case History of Disasters of Social Pollution*. Karachi, Research and Development Publications, 1998.

Bhargava, B. S. *Hawala Scam: Politics of Corruption*. New Delhi, Arnold Associates, 1996.

Corbridge, Stuart, Williams, Glyn, Srivastava, Manoj, and Veron, Rene. *Seeing the State: Governance and Governmentality in India*. Cambridge, Cambridge University Press, 2005.

Heidenheimer, Arnold J., and Johnston, Michael (Eds). *Political Corruption: Concepts and Contexts*. 3rd Edn, New Brunswick, Transaction Publishers, 2002.

Jalal, Ayesha. *Democracy and Authoritarianism in South Asia: A Comparative and Historical Perspective*. Cambridge, Cambridge University Press, 1995.

Karmakar, Madhusudan. *Bubble: A Study of Scam, Scandal and Corruption in Indian Stock Market*. New Delhi, Regency Publications, 1999.

Kashyap, Subhash C. *Institutions of Governance in South Asia*. Delhi, Konark, 2000.

Khan, Mushtaq, and Sundaram, Jomo Kwame (Eds). *Rents, Rent-seeking and Economic Development: Theory and Evidence in Asia*. Cambridge, Cambridge University Press, 2000.

Kidd, John B., and Richter, Frank-Jürgen (Eds). *Corruption and Governance in South Asia*. Basingstoke, Palgrave Macmillan, 2003.

Kumar, Arun. *The Black Economy in India*. New Delhi, Penguin Books, 1999.

Lal, Bhure. *Corruption: Functional Anarchy in Governance*. New Delhi, Siddharth Publications, 2002.

Lewis, David J. *Corruption in Bangladesh: Discourse, Judgements and Moralities*. Bath, Centre for Development Studies, University of Bath, 1996.

Mahbub-ul-Haq Human Development Centre. *Human Development in South Asia 1999: The Crisis of Governance*. Oxford, Oxford University Press, 1999.

Mitra, Chandan. *The Corrupt Society: The Criminalization of India from Independence to the 1990s*. New Delhi, Penguin Books, 1998.

Mitra, Subrata K. *The Puzzle of India's Governance: Culture, Context and Comparative Theory*. Abingdon, Routledge, 2005.

Oza, B. M. *Bofors: The Ambassador's Evidence*. Delhi, Konark, 1997.

Pai Panandiker, V. A. *Problems of Governance in South Asia*. Delhi, Konark, 2000.

Ray, Binayak. *India: Sustainable Development and Good Governance Issues: A Case for Radical Reassessment*. New Delhi, Atlantic Publishers and Distributors, 1999.

Transparency International. *South Asia, Global Corruption Report 2004*. London, Profile Books, 2004.

Vittal, N., and Mahalingham, S. *Fighting Corruption and Restructuring Government*. New Delhi, Manas Publishers, 2000.

Williams, Robert (Ed.). *Explaining Corruption*. Cheltenham, Edward Elgar, 2000.

Williams, Robert, and Theobald, Robin (Eds). *Corruption in the Developing World*. Cheltenham, Edward Elgar, 2000.

# POPULATION AND ENVIRONMENTAL ISSUES IN SOUTH ASIA

GOURANGA LAL DASVARMA

## POPULATION, DEVELOPMENT AND THE ENVIRONMENT

South Asia, comprising Afghanistan, Bangladesh, Bhutan, India, the Maldives, Nepal, Pakistan and Sri Lanka, contains some of the poorest nations of the world. Large sections of the region's population lack the most basic human needs such as sufficient food and nutrition, clean water, adequate shelter and access to education and health care. The region is quite diverse in terms of population, size, growth and density. According to World Bank classifications, all countries of the South Asian region may be considered to be in the medium level of economic development, as indicated by gross domestic product (GDP) per caput (measured in terms of purchasing-power parity (PPP) in US dollars), with the Maldives and Sri Lanka in the upper medium level of development and the remaining countries in the lower medium level of development. The level of development in India falls just short of being in the upper medium level. Further, diversity among these countries in terms of GDP per head is not so stark. At mid-2006 the region contained an estimated population of 1,531.2m, spread between the world's second most populous country, India, and one of the least populous countries, the Maldives. The population growth rate of India has declined appreciably in recent years, but those of all the other countries of the region have remained virtually unchanged. Thus, with the exception of Bhutan, India, Maldives, Sri Lanka and, to a lesser extent, Bangladesh, the populations of these countries are growing quite rapidly and will double in less than 40 years if current rates of population growth continue. The populations of Afghanistan and Pakistan are growing especially fast, with the potential to double in 30 years or less at current rates of population growth (see Table 1).

Rapid population growth can be detrimental to the environment, first by causing the increased use of the earth's natural resources and, subsequently, by placing greater stress on the earth's ecosystem through the production of more waste that is released back to the air, land and water. One indicator of the impact of development and consumption on the environment is the emission of carbon dioxide. Compared with more affluent countries, the per caput emission of carbon dioxide in each of the countries of South Asia was still very low as of 2004 (less than 1 metric ton in each of Bangladesh, Bhutan, Nepal, Pakistan and Sri Lanka, around 1 metric ton in India and 2.5 metric tons in Maldives). India, one of the world's top 30 total emitters of $CO_2$ in 2004, accounted for only 1.2 metric tons of emission per caput. Between 1990 and 2004 the total emission of $CO_2$ for the region (excluding Afghanistan) increased by around 7 % per year. In terms of total emission of $CO_2$, most countries in the region contribute negligible proportions to the world-wide emission of carbon dioxide, except India, which contributes 4.6%, and Pakistan, which contributes 0.4% (see Table 2). However, unless these countries gain access to improved energy-producing technologies, the rapid growth of South Asia's already large population has the potential to cause considerable environmental damage, particularly since the level of resource consumption is likely to increase with economic development. It should be noted, however, that a small number of affluent countries with much slower rates of population growth can create a more significant impact on the environment because they have much higher levels of consumption. According to Table 24 of the Human Development Report 2007/2008, published by UNDP, the emission of carbon dioxide per caput in 2004 was 13.3 metric tons in the high-income countries, 4.0 metric tons in the middle-income countries and 0.9 metric tons in the low-income countries. The share of the world's total carbon dioxide emission in 2004 was 44.8%, 42.0% and 7.2% in the high-income, middle-income and low-income countries, respectively. It should be noted that, according to the report, the world total includes $CO_2$ emissions not incorporated in national totals, such as those from bunker fuels, the oxidation of non-fuel hydrocarbon products and emissions by countries not listed in the main indicators tables. Consequently, the emissions by region do not add up to 100%.

The region contains two of the world's most densely populated countries, the Maldives and Bangladesh, with population densities of 1,020 and 1,035 persons per sq km, respectively, in mid-2007. At the other end of the scale, Bhutan, with a population density of 19 persons per sq km, is one of the more sparsely populated countries of the world. With the exception of Sri Lanka and, to some extent, Pakistan, the countries of South Asia have the highest prevalence of extreme poverty as shown by the percentage of population living below the income poverty line. Nor do these countries rank well in the world community in terms of human development or gender-related development. Although all those South Asian countries for which data are available have achieved small improvements in their human development index (HDI) values in recent years, some of these countries (India, Maldives and Sri Lanka) have experienced a deterioration in their ranking (see Table 1). The South Asian region also has some of the most pressing environmental issues of the world such as land

**Table 1. Demographic, Economic and Gender Indicators of South Asian Countries**

| Countries | Population (million, mid-2007) | Annual rate of natural growth (%)* | Population doubling time at current growth rate (years) | Density (persons per sq km, mid-2007) | GDP per caput (PPP US $) 2004 | % of total population living below poverty line† (1990–2005) | Human Development Index (HDI) ranking 2000 | HDI ranking 2005 | Trend in HDI value 2000 | Trend in HDI value 2005 | Gender Related Development Index (GDI) ranking (2005) | HDI rank minus GDI rank (2005) |
|---|---|---|---|---|---|---|---|---|---|---|---|---|
| Afghanistan | 31.9 | 2.6 | 26.7 | 49 | n.a. | n.a. | n.a. | n.a. | n.a. | n.a. | n.a. | n.a. |
| Bangladesh | 149.0 | 1.9 | 36.5 | 1,035 | 2,053 | 41.3 | 145 | 140 | 0.510 | 0.547 | 121 | 1 |
| Bhutan | 0.9 | 1.3 | 53.3 | 19 | 1,969 (2004) | n.a. | 140 | 133 | n.a. | 0.579 | n.a. | n.a. |
| India | 1,131.9 | 1.6 | 43.3 | 344 | 3,452 | 34.3 | 124 | 128 | 0.578 | 0.619 | 113 | 0 |
| Maldives | 0.3 | 1.6 | 43.3 | 1,020 | 5,261 | n.a. | 84 | 100 | n.a. | 0.741 | 85 | 4 |
| Nepal | 27.8 | 1.9 | 36.5 | 189 | 1,550 | 24.1 | 142 | 142 | 0.502 | 0.534 | 128 | –4 |
| Pakistan | 169.3 | 2.3 | 30.1 | 213 | 2,370 | 17.0 | 138 | 136 | 0.516 | 0.551 | 125 | –7 |
| Sri Lanka | 20.1 | 1.2 | 57.8 | 306 | 4,595 | 5.6 | 89 | 99 | 0.731 | 0.743 | 89 | –1 |

* Annual rate of natural growth is given by the birth rate minus death rate, expressed as a percentage.

† Percentage of population living on less than US $1.08 per day on a 1993 purchasing-power parity (PPP) basis.

Sources: Population data from Population Reference Bureau (www.prb.org/Datafinder/Geography/Summary.aspx?); other data from UNDP, *Human Development Report 2007/2008*; World Bank, *World Development Indicators* database; HDI 2000 rank from Human Development Report 2002.

degradation, deforestation, loss of biodiversity, indoor and outdoor air pollution, water scarcity and water pollution, all of which have an impact on human life.

**Table 2. Carbon Dioxide ($CO_2$) Emissions in South Asia**

| | Total emissions (million metric tons)† | | % annual increase | Metric tons per caput | | Share of world total (%)† |
|---|---|---|---|---|---|---|
| | 1990 | 2004 | (1990–2004) | 1990 | 2004 | 2004 |
| Afghanistan | n.a. | n.a. | n.a. | n.a. | n.a. | n.a. |
| Bangladesh | 15.4 | 37.1 | 10.1 | 0.1 | 0.3 | 0.1 |
| Bhutan | 0.1 | 0.4 | 15.9 | 0.1 | 0.2 | (.)‡ |
| India | 682.0 | 1,342.0 | 6.9 | 0.8 | 1.2 | 4.6 |
| Maldives | 0.2 | 0.7 | 26.5 | 0.7 | 2.5 | (.) |
| Nepal | 0.6 | 3.0 | 27.3 | (.) | 0.1 | (.) |
| Pakistan | 68.0 | 125.6 | 6.0 | 0.6 | 0.8 | 0.4 |
| Sri Lanka | 3.8 | 11.5 | 14.8 | 0.2 | 0.6 | (.) |
| Total excluding Afghanistan | 770.1 | 1,520.3 | 6.9 | | | |

* 1 million metric tons are equivalent to 1 mega metric ton (Mt). 1 metric ton is equal to 1,000 kg.

† According to *Human Development Report 2007/2008*, the world total includes $CO_2$ emissions not included in national totals, such as those from bunker fuels, the oxidation of non-fuel hydrocarbon products and emissions by countries not listed in the main indicators tables. Such emissions amount to about 5.0% of the world total.

‡ (.) = less than 0.1%.

Source: UNDP, *Human Development Report 2007/2008*.

The region provides ample proof that environmental issues are inextricably linked to issues of population, and economic and human resources development. Prominent among these issues are those dealing with poverty and gender. The three components of development, namely population growth, increasing affluence and technology, provide an indication of the level of environmental impact. In order to minimize the environmental impact of the increasing affluence that results from development in rapidly growing populations, developing nations need massive transfers of ecologically appropriate technology from the developed nations. Unfortunately, however, many previous attempts at rapid industrialization in the countries of the region have utilized outmoded 'dirty' technologies, which have only exacerbated environmental damage.

Another way of examining the environmental impact of a population's lifestyle and consumption habits is the 'ecological footprint' approach. Through this approach it can be ascertained whether nature provides enough resources to secure good living conditions for the people. Resources in this context comprise the supply of food, energy and fibre, the absorption of waste products and other life-support services. This approach requires that, in order to continue enjoying good living conditions, nature's productivity is not used more quickly than it can be renewed, and that waste is not discharged more quickly than nature can absorb it.

The ecological footprint is an accounting tool for ecological resources that consists of translating the categories of human consumption into areas of productive land required to provide the resources and to assimilate the waste products; it also measures how sustainable our lifestyles are. According to data obtained from the *Living Planet Report 2004*, published by the international organization, the World Wildlife Fund (WWF), in partnership with the UN Environment Programme (UNEP) World Conservation Monitoring Centre, the countries of South Asia produce only a small ecological footprint, ranging from 0.3 ha per person in Afghanistan to 1.1 ha per person in Sri Lanka. The footprints produced by India (0.8 ha per person), Pakistan (0.7 ha per person) and Bangladesh and Nepal (both 0.6 ha per person) are on the higher side of the range for the South Asia region. All countries of the region except Afghanistan have a small 'ecological deficit', ranging from 0.2 ha per person in Nepal to 0.7 ha per person in Sri Lanka. However, India and Pakistan may actually have a small surplus (or 'ecological remainder'), if their relatively low use of sea space and below-average fish consumption are considered. Despite this, it is not difficult to imagine that their potential ecological surplus will not last long in view of their rapidly growing populations and their fast increasing per caput consumption of natural resources. There are no data available concerning the ecological footprints of Bhutan and the Maldives.

Allowing for the preservation of biodiversity, only 1.7 ha per caput is available for human use world-wide. Assuming no further environmental degradation, the average available biologically productive space will be reduced to 1 ha per caput once the world's population reaches the predicted 10,000m. in the mid-2030s. Since South Asia contains some of the fastest growing populations of the world, the ecological benchmark for this region may well be smaller than 1.7 ha per caput at present and less than 1 ha per caput in the 2030s.

In 1992 Daniel Joseph Hogan argued that attention must be directed to localized empirical studies of the relationship between population growth and the physical environment, and further that the key to understanding such relationships lies in the studies of migration and settlements patterns and their relationship to the physical environment. In South Asia, and in particular in India, Pakistan and Bangladesh, significant population movements take place, especially from rural to urban areas and their impact on the physical environment in terms of resource depletion and degradation.

In addition, in 1992 Richard E. Billsborrow demonstrated that rural population growth and internal migration are associated with increases in arable land area and deforestation. His study included countries of Asia, including India, and while detailed data are not available for the South Asian countries considered in this essay, it is not difficult to comprehend what environmental degradation the relatively high population growth rate in these countries (particularly taking into account the higher rates of growth in the rural areas) is causing.

## MAJOR ENVIRONMENTAL ISSUES

The South Asian region exhibits a great variety of environmental problems, such as deforestation, loss of biodiversity, degradation of agricultural land, air and water pollution, global warming and rising sea levels. At the same time, there are urban environmental problems such as urban air pollution and solid waste disposal and an overall water supply problem. Some countries in the region, particularly Bangladesh and India, are experiencing the rather severe problem of arsenic poisoning of ground water.

A brief review of environmental concerns that have national, as well as cross-national, implications in South Asia has listed land degradation, water scarcity, water quality, air pollution, urbanization, the marine environment and deforestation as the principal environmental concerns of South Asian economies. These concerns warrant regional, rather than exclusively national, action to address them.

### Air Pollution

The region's heavy dependence on coal (particularly in India) to meet the substantial expansion in energy demand has resulted in large increases in airborne pollution. This is more apparent in the deterioration of urban air quality caused by the growth in industrial activity, transport needs and energy production. Estimates show that every year in India 30m.–40m. metric tons of fly ash are produced by thermal power plants, of which only 2%–3% is recycled. Excessive loads of acid level are found in parts of northern India and Bangladesh. Atmospheric studies of the Indian Ocean show the presence of high concentrations of aerosol particles suspended over the northern part of the Indian Ocean, including the Arabian Sea and the Bay of Bengal. There are several other issues of air pollution in this region (see The Asian Brown Cloud, below).

### Water Shortages and Water Pollution

The rapid growth of agriculture and of urbanization has placed increasing pressure on the quantity and quality of the region's water resources. With the increasing needs of a rapidly growing population, per caput availability of fresh water has been gradually declining in the region. For example, in India it decreased from 6,000 cu m in 1947 to 2,300 cu m in 1998 and is predicted to decline further, to 1,600 cu m. Much of this decline can be attributed to India's population increase. Owing to the uneven distribution of water resources, some regions of India already suffer from severe water stress, with per caput availability as low as 400 cu m in the east, between the Kanyakumari and Pennar rivers. There have been unprecedented increases in the number of privately owned shallow tube wells in response to the 'Green Revolution' and its emphasis on the production of high-yielding varieties of cereal crops. An arid country such as Afghanistan suffers from chronic water shortages. Overexploitation of ground water for irrigation purposes has exceeded the critical limits in many parts of northern and western India, such as the states of the Punjab, Haryana, Gujarat and Rajasthan. Estimates show that 36% of the blocks in India will have been overexploited by 2015, and overexploitation of ground water in Bangladesh has led to salinity and land subsidence in the capital city of Dhaka.

Groundwater pollution has been manifested in another form, namely by the presence of arsenic in Bangladesh and India (mainly in the state of West Bengal as well as some other parts of the country). Arsenic poisoning can lead to skin lesions and cause the degeneration of parts of the body, cancer or serious damage of the liver. Arsenic, one of the oldest poisons known to humankind, commonly occurs as a chemical element in the earth's crust. As a result of the human exploitation of nature, such as the extraction of ground water for irrigation, mining operations or geothermal power plants, arsenic rises to the surface of the earth and contaminates ground water. According to WHO, nearly 85m. people living in Bangladesh are faced with the threat of arsenicosis. However, ironically, in Bangladesh at least, the arsenic poisoning of ground water was the 'result of an initiative to provide Bangladeshis with fresh water that went terribly wrong', according to the journalist Bob Forsberg. In the 1970s international agencies spent millions of US dollars in aid in Bangladesh on the construction of deep tube wells to provide 'clean' drinking water, in order to reduce the risk of chronic water-borne diseases. However, according to WHO, the result of this initiative has been the 'biggest outbreak of mass poisoning in history', because, prior to boring the tube wells, no one tested for the naturally occurring arsenic, which is widely found in underground water.

Although the presence of arsenic in ground water in Bangladesh has received wide publicity, the problem is also widespread in the adjoining state of West Bengal in India, where it was first noticed in 1983, 12 years before it was detected in Bangladesh. In the early years of the first decade of the 2000s estimates indicated that more than 3,000 villages in West Bengal and more than 2,000 villages in Bangladesh were affected by groundwater arsenic poisoning, and new villages were being identified almost every year. The risk of arsenic poisoning, however, is not confined to Bangladesh or West Bengal, and is believed to be present in the entire Gangetic plain. Areas of arsenic-contaminated ground water have been identified further west in the Bhojpur district of the Indian state of Bihar, as far north as the Indian city of Chandigarh, and in the Terai region of Nepal. Despite the fact that arsenic poisoning in West Bengal has been a matter of public concern for more than 20 years, large-scale substantial plans to solve the problem have yet to be implemented. The scale of disaster in Bangladesh and West Bengal is regarded as larger than that of the 1984 gas leak at a chemical plant in Bhopal (India) and the accident at the Chornobyl (Chernobyl) nuclear power station in Ukraine in 1986.

However, there are some signs of hope in the fight against this threat. An arsenic crisis information centre, established in January 1998, provides information about the problem of arsenic poisoning in Bangladesh and West Bengal. Professor Arup SenGupta of the Department of Civil and Environmental Engineering at Lehigh University in the USA reports a simple and indigenous method that reduces dangerously high levels of arsenic content in drinking water to safe levels. This is achieved by the use of arsenic removal columns, which are simple to operate manually (no electricity is required) and can be attached to the existing tube wells with hand pumps. The primary absorbent used in the column is activated alumina, which selectively removes dissolved arsenic from ground water without changing its composition. The column is expected to last for 10–15 years without the requirement of any maintenance, apart from the regeneration of the unit with caustic soda once every four months. A pilot project has been introduced in the 24 Paraganas and Nadia districts of West Bengal through collaboration between the Bengal Engineering College and Water For People, an affiliate of the American Water Works Association (AWWA) located in Denver, Colorado. It is claimed that, regardless of the extent of contamination in well water, the arsenic concentration in treated water will be less than 20 parts per 1,000m.—the standard set by WHO for drinking water. Each unit costs approximately US $1,250 and has the capacity to serve 200–300 households. This innovation, if implemented properly, could very well result in a success story in the fight against ground water pollution.

Deteriorating water quality owing to contamination from untreated sewage and industrial effluents is common in parts of India and Pakistan. In India, for example, an average of less than three-quarters of the municipal solid waste is collected, while the rest is deposited into sewers or burnt in the open. Some of the major Indian rivers now contain water that is unfit for drinking or bathing, even though they may be able to support aquatic life. Causes of declining water quality are common to all countries of the region; therefore, opportunities exist for regional co-operation aimed at the introduction of remedial measures.

However, according to UNEP estimates, access to safe drinking water was reported to have increased in all South Asian countries during 1990–2000, although water availability per caput had decreased in most countries except Nepal and Sri Lanka. According to the Intergovernmental Panel on Climate Change (IPCC), the availability of fresh water in Central, South, East and South-East Asia, particularly in the large river basins, is projected to decrease as a result of climate change. This shortfall is expected to be exacerbated by population growth and by increasing demands for water caused by rising standards of living. In 2007 the IPCC estimated that freshwater shortages could ultimately affect more than 1,000m. people by the 2050s.

### Land Degradation

Dictated by the needs to provide food for the teeming millions of the region, soils suffer from varying degrees of degradation owing to rapid deforestation, poor irrigation, inadequate drainage and overgrazing. Desertification and the loss of nutrient-rich top soil through wind and flood erosion are causing rapid depletion of land resources, which in turn threaten the livelihood of millions of people of the region. About 27% of the soil in India is badly eroded. Areas worst affected include the Thar desert region of India and Pakistan and selected watersheds of the Himalayan region of India and Nepal. Indiscriminate and unscientific mining, devoid of any environmental management or land reclamation plans, is another cause of land degradation in the South Asian region. Such mining practices in the dolomite-mining areas of Bhutan have caused increasing landslides and soil erosion in the adjoining state of West Bengal in India. Poor mining practices are also likely to have considerable impact on groundwater pollution of aquifers.

Land degradation is a major problem in all South Asian countries, where diverse ecosystems exist and different kinds of forests can be found from the Himalayas to the mangroves. One of the contributory factors to land degradation has been the modern methods of agriculture, such as excessive use of fertilizers and pesticides and over-irrigation of saline lands together with shifting cultivation. Almost all countries of South Asia have suffered land degradation, with India topping the list.

## DEFORESTATION

Population pressure and the clearing of forests for agriculture and human settlement are liable to deplete the forest cover. However, it is believed that due to well-organized conservation programmes carried out in Bangladesh, India and Pakistan forest cover in these countries increased during the decade 1990–2000. Bhutan and the Maldives maintained a stable forest cover during this period, while Nepal and Sri Lanka both reported losses of forest cover.

In general, levels of deforestation are high in South Asia, with Bangladesh and Pakistan exhibiting the highest rates in the region. Nepal is also badly affected by deforestation; more than three-quarters of the population are dependent on fuel wood to meet their energy needs. Bangladesh and India once had large areas of forest, but most of it has now been converted into agricultural land. Much of the remaining forest is badly degraded, with declining forest cover caused by logging, firewood collection and heavy grazing. Although initially a concern of ecologists, deforestation is now receiving greater attention from the common people of the region. They are increasingly becoming aware of the significance of natural forests in preventing soil erosion and flooding, maintaining soil productivity and providing a rich resource for timber. Deforestation affects the environment through the loss of biodiversity and also through its effects on soils and hydrology.

In Bangladesh and the adjoining Indian state of West Bengal, the famous Royal Bengal Tiger has been reduced in number because of poaching and encroachment on its habitat in the Sunderbans, a stretch of mangrove forest that crosses the border between the two countries. The Sunderbans comprises a part of the world's largest delta, formed from sediments deposited by several major rivers, including the Ganges and the Brahmaputra. At the last count in 2002, the Indian side of the Sunderbans had 271 tigers. The numbers of tigers in Bangladesh are not known with any certainty, but they have been reduced in the past few years, despite reports that some of the tigers may have migrated from the Indian side into Bangladesh during this period.

Forests such as the Sunderbans are very important for a large number of other species as well as the endangered tigers. Harmful effluents enter the Sunderbans from nearby areas that may be responsible for polluting the water which, according to some sources, could be affecting tiger behaviour. However, there appears to be new hope for the Royal Bengal Tigers through a joint biodiversity project between Bangladesh and India. Increasing salinity of the water in the Sunderbans could also be affecting tiger behaviour and causing the loss of certain types of trees in the area. Poaching is another cause of the loss of biodiversity in the area, and the joint project mentioned above includes education of the local people in order to minimize poaching. Most people living in the Sunderbans depend on fishing for their livelihood, but fishing is proving difficult to sustain because of falling water levels.

A nation-wide campaign, known as 'Project Tiger', was launched in 1973 in an attempt to reverse a massive trend of decline in India's tiger population. The number of tiger reserves under this project grew from nine in the mid-1970s to 23 in mid-2005. A success story at a tiger reserve in another part of India, in the state of Madhya Pradesh, could provide inspiration to save other wild tigers. The number of tigers has doubled at the Panna Tiger Reserve in the state of Madhya Pradesh, after a successful move to stop illegal logging and grazing. The tigers in this area had radio devices attached to their collars to monitor their daily movements and discourage poaching. The Government was persuaded to close sandstone mines around the reserve and to improve conditions at state-owned diamond mines that were polluting local water supplies. By 2001 the vulnerable population of two–three tigers per 100 sq km had increased to seven–eight tigers per 100 sq km, a healthy number for breeding. On average, one tiger dies a day in India from poaching or habitat loss.

However, despite the efforts of the Government and NGOs, the drive to save the tiger has not always been successful. Recent revelations, mainly from the northern Indian states, do not augur well for the survival of this magnificent animal in India. One such report pertains to the Sariska National Park, which, with its area of 800 sq km, is part of 'Project Tiger'. According to a March 2005 report issued by India's Central Bureau of Investigation (CBI), not a single tiger had been seen in Sariska since January of that year. The report contended that Sariska, which was supposed to have at least 15 tigers, according to a census taken in June 2004, would now be left with neel gai (blue bulls), spotted deer, and wild boars, but no tigers. According to disputed official estimates, there are between 3,500 and 3,700 tigers left in India, compared with an estimated 40,000 tigers prior to India's independence in 1947.

However, even the figures of 3,500–3,700 tigers are doubtful, and it is feared that many more tiger reserves in India may be destined for the fate of Sariska for various reasons, such as poaching, tourism, insurgent activities from a neighbouring country and general encroachment by the local population and cattle. Some other estimates by NGOs put the number of tigers in India in 2005 at fewer than 2,000.

According to a report published in the newspaper *The Times of India*, the Indian Prime Minister has agreed to consider creating a separate wildlife secretariat to facilitate the conservation of wildlife, including the tiger. However, according to the director of a New Delhi-based independent 'think tank', the tiger problem needs to be addressed using a commercial approach, rather than a conservationist or environmental approach, because the conservationist strategy of 'stopping the supply' has made the trade in tigers highly profitable and alienated the local population. The suggested commercial approach calls for the creation of tiger farms to ease the pressure on tigers, lower the price of dead tigers and reduce the incentive for smugglers to kill wild tigers. This suggestion is based on the success of crocodile and buffalo farms in the USA, which have helped these species to make a comeback on the basis of commerce. However, according to others, this suggestion is impractical because tigers raised on farms cannot survive in their natural habitat, the forest, as they cannot learn natural hunting skills on a farm.

According to the preliminary results of a tiger census undertaken by the Wildlife Institute of India in 2007, it appeared that urbanization and poaching had both taken their toll on the tiger population, with numbers being substantially lower than earlier assumed. Experts from the Institute claimed that most of the tiger disappearances had taken place in Maharashtra and Madhya Pradesh, both of which states previously had the largest numbers of tigers. It was estimated that the number of tigers in Madhya Pradesh had decreased to only 255 head, compared with the 710 counted in the previous census of 2001–02, while the tiger population in Maharashtra had declined from 238 to a mere 95. According to an article published in *The Times of India* in mid-2007, the total number of tigers worldwide has fallen from an estimated 100,000 a century ago to less than a few thousand at present. On a more optimistic note, however, in June 2007 the member countries of the Convention on International Trade in Endangered Species (CITES) passed a resolution rejecting a plan proposed by the People's Republic of China to raise captive tigers for trade in their parts, which would have undone a 14-year-old ban on tiger trade.

### Urban Environmental Problems

No less important than these 'green issues' are the emerging 'brown issues' of the South Asian region. Because rural areas still contain the majority of the populations of South Asia, rural environmental problems have so far been of the most significance in terms of their global impact and the sheer number of people affected by them. However, the 'brown' environmental issues of the urban areas, especially the major cities of South Asia, will be of greater significance in the coming years, as the number and the proportion of urban populations in the region are expected to have increased very substantially by 2030.

According to the 'medium variant' population projections of the UN (which were revised in 2007), the number of urban inhabitants in South Asia is forecast to grow from 432.3m. in 2005 to 856.3m. in 2030, giving an urban growth rate of 2.7% per year. In the same period the total population is projected to grow from 1,518.0m. to 2,080.5m., giving an annual population growth rate of 1.3%. The estimated proportion of urban population in South Asia in 2005 was 28.5%, varying from 15.1% in Sri Lanka and 15.8% in Nepal to 34.9% in Pakistan. This proportion is projected to increase to 41.2% in 2030, ranging from 21.4% in Sri Lanka to 60.7% in Maldives. By 2030 Pakistan, Maldives and Bhutan were projected to have 50% or more of their respective populations living in urban areas, while India and Bangladesh were forecast to have 41% living in urban areas. It was also expected that even Afghanistan and Nepal would have around one-third of their populations living in urban areas. Sri Lanka was forcast to be the least urbanized country in South Asia at 2030, with just over one-fifth of its population living in urban areas. The proportion of the urban population in the region's largest populated country, India, was projected to grow from 28.7% in 2005 to 40.6% in

**Table 3. Total Population, Urban Population and Percentage of Urban Population of the South Asian Region (2005–30)**

| Country | 2005 population ('000) | | | 2020 population ('000) | | | 2030 population ('000) | | |
|---|---|---|---|---|---|---|---|---|---|
| | Total | Urban | % urban | Total | Urban | % urban | Total | Urban | % urban |
| Afghanistan | 25,067 | 5,740 | 22.9 | 40,993 | 12,175 | 29.7 | 53,252 | 19,330 | 36.3 |
| Bangladesh | 153,281 | 39,351 | 25.7 | 193,333 | 65,523 | 33.9 | 217,932 | 89,448 | 41.0 |
| Bhutan | 637 | 197 | 31.0 | 780 | 372 | 47.7 | 851 | 478 | 56.2 |
| India | 1,134,403 | 325,574 | 28.7 | 1,379,198 | 472,561 | 34.3 | 1,505,748 | 611,407 | 40.6 |
| Maldives | 295 | 100 | 33.9 | 383 | 200 | 52.1 | 434 | 264 | 60.7 |
| Nepal | 27,094 | 4,269 | 15.8 | 35,868 | 8,582 | 23.9 | 41,742 | 12,776 | 30.6 |
| Pakistan | 158,081 | 55,135 | 34.9 | 208,315 | 89,070 | 42.8 | 240,276 | 119,652 | 49.8 |
| Sri Lanka | 19,121 | 2,895 | 15.1 | 20,229 | 3,419 | 16.9 | 20,249 | 4,333 | 21.4 |
| **Total** | 1,517,979 | 433,261 | 28.5 | 1,879,099 | 651,902 | 34.7 | 2,080,484 | 857,689 | 41.2 |

Source: UN, *World Population Prospects: The 2007 Revision Population Database*.

2030 (see Table 3). It should be noted that Bhutan and Maldives were previously reported to have much smaller proportions of urban populations, but Table 3 shows the statistics as of the latest revision of 2007.

Another data source—UN Population Division, *World Urbanization Prospects: The 2007 Revision Population Database*—which spans the period 1950–2025, shows that the Indian cities of Kolkata (Calcutta) and Mumbai (Bombay) were the only two megacities of South Asia in 1980, each having populations of 8m. or more. In 1990 another Indian city, Delhi, was added to the list of megacities. Dhaka (Bangladesh) and Karachi (Pakistan) joined the list in 1995. At 1995 the combined population of these five megacities was more than 52.9m. These five cities continued to be the only megacities in the South Asian region as of 2007, although their combined population had increased to 75.3m., implying an average annual rate of growth of nearly 3%. Projections show that these would remain as the five megacities of South Asia until 2010, but by 2020 four more megacities, namely Bangalore, Chennai (formerly Madras) and Hyderabad in India and Lahore in Pakistan, would appear on the list. Needless to say, during these periods, the megacities (as indeed other cities) have been growing, or would be growing, at a rapid rate.

Even more notable are the potential environmental implications posed by the sheer size of some of the megacities of the region. For example, in 1980 Kolkata had a population of just over 9m. and Mumbai 8.7m. In 1995 Mumbai had a population of 14.1m., Kolkata 11.9m., Delhi 10m., Dhaka 8.3m. and Karachi 8.5m. By 2020, according to the international network City Mayors, Mumbai is projected to have 24.1m., people, making it the second largest urban agglomeration in the world after the Japanese capital city of Tokyo (with a forecast population of 37.3m. by 2020). According to the same source, Delhi would be in third place with 25.8m. and Dhaka in fourth place with 22m. Karachi and Kolkata would be in the 10th and 11th places respectively, each with more than 18.5m.people. Lahore, Chennai, Bangalore and Hyderabad would have between 8.2m. and 9.3m. people each. Thus, of the top 10 urban agglomerations of 8m. people or more in the world in 2020, four (Mumbai, Delhi, Dhaka and Karachi) are expected to be in South Asia, and of the top 30 urban agglomerations, seven are forecast to be in South Asia.

As noted earlier, the urban population of the region is projected to grow at an average annual rate of 2.7% between 2005 and 2030. This rate of growth is more than double that of the total population (growth rate 1.3% per year) for the same period. Thus, a very high proportion of the economic growth of South Asia would be generated by the rapidly increasing urban populations of the region. The environmental sustainability of this economic growth, therefore, would depend very much on the urban areas of South Asia, particularly the mega cities of the region. It can also be argued that, since most of the major cities of the region are situated near rivers or estuaries, any serious environmental pollution in these cities could damage fertile agricultural land, aquaculture in surrounding areas or the marine environment. Such problems may not be of immediate concern to the fast-growing middle classes of these urban areas, who may be more worried about the environmental health problems such as air pollution, water supplies, traffic accidents and inadequate waste disposal.

The dynamics of environmental health risks in the cities of developing countries constitute a major issue. Environmental risk factors for health can be classified into traditional risk factors and modern environmental/technological risk factors. The traditional risk factors, which operate at the early stages of economic development, affect the health of people through parasitic and infectious diseases associated with urban poverty, poor nutrition, inferior sanitation and unclean water supply. With the progress of economic development, these conditions of infectious and parasitic diseases recede, but new conditions emerge such as pesticide runoff, inadequate toxic waste disposal, air pollution, motor vehicle accidents and the stresses of modern living and working. All these conditions are associated with 'diseases of civilization', such as heart disease, strokes, cancers and accidents. Economic development leads to a transition from a condition of high health risks from the many traditional environmental factors associated with low development to a condition of low overall health risks from environmental conditions under more developed conditions. In the latter case, the causal factors are modern and post-industrial in nature. The transition in environmental health risk begins at a level of economic development when there is equal risk to health from both traditional and modern factors. It may be argued that the overall risk to health in the urban areas of South Asia during the transition point may be greater than the low point predicted in the risk transition model. This is because there may be a considerable degree of overlap of traditional and modern environmental risk factors, which will also have synergistic effects.

The environmental risk transition hypothesis states that the health risks of a city resident may be predicted by the level of economic development of that city. In the poorest cities of South Asia, such as Dhaka and Kolkata, and in their slums, traditional problems such as poor sanitation, inadequate access to clean drinking water, pollution of water by human waste and the incidence of water-borne diseases have increased. In Dhaka, more than 80% of hospital admissions have been said to be due to water-borne diseases. Kolkata also has the problem of heavy smog, particularly in the winter months of December and January. This is the time when the vast majority of city residents, particularly those living in the city's countless slums, who do not have the means to use clean cooking fuel such as electricity or gas and who are unable to protect themselves from cold, use highly inefficient cooking fuel such as hard coal and burn spent rubber tyres in the open, and sit around the fires to warm themselves. The resulting black smoke remains suspended in the atmosphere owing to a thermal inversion. To this may be added the unclean emissions from poorly maintained engines of motor vehicles. The result is an increase in the incidence of respiratory diseases. Thus, a city such as Kolkata is an example where traditional risk factors (water-borne diseases) and modern risk factors (air pollution) exist side by side.

In the middle-income cities, such as Delhi and Mumbai, more modern problems, for example air pollution, are major concerns. This is caused by a rapid increase in the number of motor vehicles, inadequate road systems and the growth of industries in and around these cities. However, recent measures adopted by the authorities in Delhi requiring public transport vehicles, such as buses, taxis and three-wheeled auto rickshaws, to use liquefied natural gas (LNG) instead of petrol or diesel have significantly reduced air pollution in the city from motorized vehicle emissions. It is widely hoped that other cities of the South Asian region where motorized transport is increasing at a rapid pace will emulate Delhi's example and do likewise. Rising living standards have increased the production of both domestic and industrial solid wastes in middle-income cities, the safe disposal of which is a major problem. The poorer neighbourhoods of these cities are at the same time exposed to high traditional health risks, owing to inadequate sanitation and poor water quality, which lead to a high incidence of water-borne diseases. The overlap of traditional and modern health risk factors, and a possible synergism between the two, makes the overall health risk in the middle-income cities greater than that in the poorer cities. A study of 10 Asian cities, conducted by UNEP and WHO, found that the air quality of these cities was seriously affected by suspended particulate matter. Serious to moderate sulphur dioxide pollution was prevalent in the Chinese cities of Beijing and Shanghai, and also in the South Korean capital city of Seoul; a moderate lead problem was prevalent in Bangkok, Jakarta and Manila (the capital cities of Thailand, Indonesia and the Philippines, respectively); carbon monoxide was moderately present in the atmosphere of Jakarta; and there was a moderate ozone problem in Beijing and Jakarta. However, none of the cities had excessive nitrogen dioxide in their atmosphere. The study also found that almost all the major cities of India (and China), as well as Bangkok and Jakarta, experienced more than 100 days in a year when the concentration of particulate matter exceeded the WHO standard of 230 micrograms per cu m. In Mumbai, where there is a large concentration of heavy industry, the population residing near the congested industrial areas suffered from much higher levels of chronic bronchitis, tuberculosis, skin allergies, anaemia and eye irritation than the population living in cleaner suburbs. The above-mentioned environmental health problems are generally attributable to problems of governance, in some cases exacerbated by weak national economies.

### The Asian Brown Cloud

An important study, the Indian Ocean Experiment (INDOEX), commissioned by UNEP and conducted by the Center for Clouds, Chemistry and Climate (C4) during January–April 1999, concludes that the most visible impact of air pollution is the haze, a brownish layer of pollutants and particles from biomass and fossil fuel burning and industrial emissions that extends over South, South-East and East Asia. These are the most densely populated areas of the world, characterized by monsoon climates, high pollution levels, and increasing problems of water stress, of agricultural productivity and of health. The haze is transported far beyond the source region, particularly during the dry season from December to April. The preliminary conclusions of the study are that biomass burning is a major cause of gaseous pollution such as carbon monoxide, while both fossil fuel and biomass burning contribute to produce particulate (aerosol) pollution.

The above study has documented two types of effects of the Asian Brown Cloud or the haze, namely direct effects and indirect effects. Although the study does not include the effects of increases in greenhouse gases, it illustrates the potential effects of the haze on the region's climate, water budget, agriculture and health.

In its most direct effect the haze produces a significant reduction in solar radiation reaching the surface and a 50%–100% increase in solar heating of the lower atmosphere. Other possible direct effects include a reduction in precipitation efficiency by obstructing the formation of larger raindrop particles, reduction in agricultural productivity and adverse health effects. Indirectly, the haze can cause a cooling of the land surface; an increase in the frequency and strength of thermal inversion, thereby trapping more pollution; perturbation of the winter rainfall patterns; and a reduction in the average tropical evaporation and precipitation. The effects of these pollutants on the hydrological cycles of the tropics and sub-tropics have serious implications for water availability and water quality, the major environmental concerns of the time.

More specifically, the haze has a direct impact upon agricultural productivity through a reduction in photosynthesis, as a result of a decrease in total solar radiation; obstruction of the exposure of plant leaves to solar radiation by depositing on them aerosol particles (fly ash, black carbon and dust); and by an increase of plant acidity (leading to plant damage), owing to aerosol deposition on the leaves. The haze can also indirectly affect agricultural productivity through changes in surface temperatures leading either to lengthening of the growing season (owing to surface cooling resulting from aerosols) or shortening of the growing season (as a result of greenhouse gas warming); and through changes in rainfall or surface evaporation.

The adverse effects of the haze are linked with short- and long-term impacts on human health. The occurrences of respiratory diseases from both indoor and outdoor pollution in South Asia are quite substantial. A WHO study, cited in the INDOEX report, reveals that, in each of the 23 cities of India with 1m. or more inhabitants, air pollution levels exceed WHO standards. One expert, cited in the INDOEX report, has estimated that about 500,000 premature deaths occur among mothers and children under five in India as a result of indoor pollution. Both indoor and outdoor pollution are considered to be responsible for serious respiratory problems in the large Indian cities of Ahmedabad, Delhi, Kolkata, Lucknow and Mumbai.

However, India's capital city, New Delhi, has made some progress towards improving its air quality by converting its entire fleet of public transport buses to compressed natural gas (see above).

## THE IMPACT OF MEGAPROJECTS

The Narmada Valley Project in India is a megaproject that could have environmental implications for a large number of people. The project is aimed at producing hydroelectricity and increasing water storage, but it has attracted world-wide attention from environmentalists and humanitarian groups. The prize-winning writer Arundhati Roy has been at the forefront of protests against this project. Until 2003 work on the largest component of this project, the Sardar Sarovar Dam, had remained far from being implemented, owing to frequent protests, legal stoppages and the withdrawal of funding from major sources. The movement appeared to have gained momentum in June 2004, with the raising of the dam height to 110 m.

The project was originally envisaged in 1947. The central Government approved the scheme in 1980, but funds were released only in 1988, nearly four decades after the initial planning had started. The advanced plans for the project envisaged the construction of 30 large dams, 135 medium and 3,000 small dams on the Narmada River. The Sardar Sarovar Dam in central Gujarat is one of the most important of the large dams; it has been at the centre of the controversy because of the displacement of a large number of people that will be caused by the construction of its reservoir and by the laying of canals to carry its water for irrigation in Gujarat and Rajasthan. The dam is expected to irrigate 1.8m. ha in Gujarat, 75,000 ha in Rajasthan and 37,500 ha in Maharashtra. It is expected to generate 1,450 MW of electricity, to be distributed among Madhya Pradesh (27%), Maharashtra (57%) and Gujarat (16%). However, on the negative side, the implications are enormous. When completed, the reservoir would submerge about 37,000 ha, including 11,000 ha of forest. This would displace about 100,000 persons in 248 villages in Madhya Pradesh, Maharashtra and Gujarat, of which three villages in Gujarat would be completely submerged and the remaining 245 partially submerged. According to project sources, the population to be affected by the project would comprise 0.33% of that which would benefit from the project, compared with an average of 4% in similar projects in the country. The Gujarat Government has offered to compensate the project-affected persons (PAPs) through a resettlement and rehabilitation programme, which was once acclaimed by the World Bank. It was reported that thousands of PAPs had accepted the resettlement and rehabilitation proposals, but thousands of others were reported to prefer submergence to the programme offered. The World Bank and Overseas Economic Cooperation Fund (OECF) of Japan eventually withdrew from the project, owing to the controversy over the environmental damage that would be caused by the dam. Thus, by 2003 work on the dam had been beset by numerous protests, court cases, disputes among the states about the dam height and the inability of some of the states to provide enough land to resettle the PAPs if the dam height were to be raised.

In March 2004 the Narmada Control Authority (NCA), which was established to monitor the construction, resettlement and rehabilitation of the project-affected families, gave the Gujarat Government permission to raise the height of the dam to 110.64 m, after assurances were given by the latter that the resettlement of the dispossessed population would be carried out simultaneously with work on raising the dam height. By 30 June the Sardar Sarovar Narmada Nigam Ltd (SSNNL), which was implementing the ambitious Sardar Sarovar Dam project, was successful in raising the height of the dam from 100 m to 110.64 m. Meanwhile, in May the NCA began to consider further raising the dam height, to 121.92 m by June 2005, and asked the participating states of Gujarat, Madhya Pradesh, Maharashtra and Rajasthan to estimate how many more people would be affected if the height were raised to this level. This discussion occurred at a time when the rehabilitation and resettlement of the people affected by the increase in dam height to 110 m had not yet been completed. With the approaching monsoon and the imminent threat of the dam-related submergence of their land in mid-2004, the Narmada tribals were faced with the prospect of having to occupy denuded forest land in the Nandurbar district of Maharashtra. Whatever the fate of this megaproject, environmentalists and human rights activists will continue to argue about and protest against the potential or actual environmental impact of this project, while the supporters of the project will continue to argue about its potential or actual contribution to development.

Similar arguments about the environmental, social and demographic effects, and the benefits, of dams have been voiced in neighbouring Pakistan, where two megaprojects have been at the centre of great controversy. One is the proposed construction of the large Kalabagh dam on the River Indus, about 160 km south-west of the Pakistani capital, Islamabad. The project was devised in 1953 and a technical and economic feasibility study of the dam was carried out in 1984. In August 2003 the President of Pakistan approved the construction of the large dam, which would produce 3,600 MW of electricity and conserve almost 21,000m. cu m of water per year that currently flows into the sea. However, the announcement provoked strong criticism from politicians and activists in the provinces of Sindh, the North-West Frontier Province (NWFP) and Balochistan. Politicians drew attention to the adverse effect the construction of the dam might have on the water supply from the River Indus to the three provinces. However, a very significant part of the criticism, voiced mainly by activists, focused on the environmental impact of the large dam. For example, activists warned that the dam would submerge towns such as Mardan, Charsada and Nowshehra in the NWFP and the town of Makkad, the site of an ancient Buddhist civilization. Furthermore, it would displace 250,000 people and severely affect the livelihood of about 0.5m. other people. The other controversial megaproject is the Greater Thal Canal, envisaged to extend to 1,965 km, including its tributaries, and estimated to be completed within seven years at a cost of US $610m. There is strong opposition in Sindh and the NWFP to both the Greater Thal Canal and the Kalabagh dam projects.

The construction of several dams and canals upstream of the River Indus over the years has left the river with very little fresh water downstream, in Sindh. As a result, salt water from the Arabian Sea is absorbed into the once fertile soil, to the detriment of farmers and fishermen. An estimated 0.5m. ha of farmland have been covered by the advancing seawater and large areas are turning into desert, destroying vital mangrove swamps.

## NATURAL DISASTERS

Large parts of South Asia are regularly subjected to natural disasters, such as floods and heatwaves, which result in the deaths of hundreds of people. The end of 2004 brought a gigantic natural disaster hitherto uncommon in the South Asian region, namely the Asian tsunami, which killed thousands of people and rendered millions homeless, particularly in Sri Lanka and the southern part of India.

### The Asian Tsunami

On 26 December 2004 a huge earthquake, with a magnitude of 8.9 on the Richter Scale, struck the seabed off the coast of Aceh province in northern Sumatra, Indonesia. This was followed by another severe earthquake several hours later. These earthquakes generated a tsunami of unprecedented scale and magnitude, resulting in one of the deadliest disasters in modern history. Besides the massive damage to life and property suffered in Aceh province, the location closest to the epicentre of the earthquakes, the rapidly advancing gigantic waves of the tsunami caused death and destruction in Bangladesh, India, Malaysia, the Maldives, Myanmar, Sri Lanka and Thailand in Asia and Kenya, Somalia and Tanzania in Africa. Indonesia bore the brunt of the damage caused by the tsunami; however, in South Asia the extent of the damage was much more severe in Sri Lanka and India than in other countries of the region.

The word 'tsunami' comes from two Japanese words: 'tsu', meaning harbour, and 'nami', meaning wave. It is not a tidal wave, but a series of giant sea waves caused by an underwater earthquake, landslide, or volcanic eruption. Very rarely, it can be caused by a giant meteor hitting the earth's oceans. When a tectonic earthquake takes place beneath the sea, causing large areas of the sea floor to elevate or subside abruptly, it displaces the water above it from its equilibrium position and, as gravity forces the water to regain equilibrium, giant waves are formed. There can be large vertical movements of the earth's crust at the boundaries of the earth's plates or faults. When denser oceanic plates slip under continental plates they create subduction earthquakes, which are one of the major causes of tsunamis. The Asian tsunami was caused by a subduction earthquake, when the Indo-Australia plate slipped under the Burma plate. As the sea water swells, it rushes towards the coast, assuming its highest proportions upon impact with the land.

In the minutes before a tsunami strikes an area, the sea often recedes temporarily from the coast. Residents of the Pacific region recognize this phenomenon as a warning sign of a tsunami and run for higher ground. However, around the Indian Ocean region, where tsunamis are relatively rare, people might have been tempted to visit the coast and collect stranded fish from more than 2 km of exposed beach, before being drowned in the returning waves of an oncoming tsunami.

At February 2005 the estimated number of deaths as a result of the tsunami was: 242,300 in Indonesia, 31,000 in Sri Lanka, 16,400 in India, 5,400 in Thailand, 300 in Somalia, 82 in the Maldives, 68 in Malaysia, 61 in Myanmar, 10 in Tanzania, two in Bangladesh and one in Kenya, a total of just over 295,600 deaths.

In Sri Lanka more than 1m. people were reported to have been directly affected by the tsunami, and infrastructure was destroyed up to 2 km inland. In the Maldives approximately 100,000 people were affected. In India, the waves hit the coastal states of Tamil Nadu, Andhra Pradesh, Orissa and Kerala, and the Union Territories of Pondicherry (or Puducherry as it was later renamed) and the Andaman and Nicobar Islands. Of these, the worst affected were Tamil Nadu, Car Nicobar island and the Greater Nicobar islands. About 26m. people lived in these areas. It was estimated that the cost of rebuilding the affected areas would be US $4,500m. in Sri Lanka, $1,500m. in India and $500m. in the Maldives.

Besides the immediate loss of life and damage to property, there are several long-term impacts of the Asian tsunami disaster. In Sri Lanka, for example, about two-thirds of the fishing fleet and industrial infrastructure in coastal regions were destroyed, with adverse effects at both the local and national levels. In general, the tsunami has had an enormous environmental impact, which will affect the region for many years to come. There has been severe damage to ecosystems such as mangroves, coral reefs, forests, coastal wetlands, vegetation, sand dunes and rock formations, animal and plant biodiversity and ground water. The spread of solid and liquid waste and industrial chemicals, water pollution and the destruction of sewage collection and treatment plants pose long-term threats to the environment. Both freshwater supplies and soil have been poisoned by saltwater filtration and the deposit of salt layers on arable land. There have also been reports of widespread psychological trauma among those affected.

Human interference in the ecological system appears to have exacerbated the extent of the death and destruction caused by the tsunami. For example, the human destruction of coral reefs that had previously protected some coastal areas significantly added to the loss of lives in those areas. Similarly, the removal of coastal mangrove trees and coastal dunes that had protected the coast, to make way for residences or hotels, is believed to have added to the damage caused. The noted environmental and development activist, Dr Vandana Shiva, stresses that the destruction of coastal mangrove trees, sand dunes or coral reefs in the interests of development projects (e.g. shrimp farms, oil refineries) or recreational projects (e.g. holiday resorts, hotels) in coastal areas can only lead to inconceivable destruction. She warns further that the Asian tsunami may serve as an example of the possible effects of other future environmental disasters, including climate change. The waves that submerged the islands of the Maldives, for instance, could be perceived as a grim harbinger of the consequences of a continued rise in sea levels as a result of climate change.

The Asian tsunami took the world by surprise. There was no warning of the impending disaster and hundreds of thousands of family members of the victims have demanded to know why this was so. In the tsunami bulletin that it issued in the immediate aftermath of the first earthquake, the Pacific Tsunami Warning Centre (PTWC) had concluded that there was no threat to the Pacific nations under its jurisdiction, but did not extend its warning to South and South-East Asia. It became clear after the event that Indian Ocean nations should have requested coverage from the PTWC, or that there should be a separate tsunami warning centre for the Indian Ocean region. The Tsunami Warning System in the Pacific, established by UNESCO, is located in Hawaii, USA, at the International Tsunami Information Centre and the PTWC. It serves 26 member states in the region, including the People's Republic of China, Indonesia and Thailand. It locates earthquakes throughout the Pacific region and issues a Pacific-wide warning of any potentially destructive long-range tsunamis. The tragic losses in the Indian Ocean area would almost certainly have been less if a similar monitoring system had been in place.

There are plans to set up a tsunami warning system for the Indian Ocean region and, eventually, for the whole world. India has announced that it is to establish such a system of its own by 2007 and has offered to issue tsunami warnings for the whole region. However, according to some observers, all such efforts should be co-ordinated, so that information can be effectively shared between countries.

### Unusual Floods

Floods are not uncommon in Bangladesh and parts of India, but they do not occur with such regularity in Pakistan. In mid-2005 flash floods displaced more than 7,000 people and inundated 87 villages in Pakistan's NWFP. These floods were precipitated by the unusually rapid melting of snow in the Hindu Kush mountain range, when an abnormal heatwave gripped the entire South Asian region in June of that year. In the populous Pakistani province of Punjab, a week-long flooding of the Indus and Chenab rivers killed at least 17 people and affected some 400,000 others. As there had not been a significant amount of water in the Indus river since 1992, people had started cultivating land on the riverbed and had settled there. Although many had heeded government warnings and evacuated the area before the floods, their crops were destroyed. The floods in Punjab, like those in the NWFP, were caused by extremes of environmental conditions, which produced an intense heatwave, causing above average snowmelt in the northern mountain ranges, which finally flooded the rivers.

As in Pakistan, floods are not common in the northern Indian state of Rajasthan, parts of which usually have to contend with drought every summer. In 2006, however, Rajasthan experienced unprecedented floods following abnormal and torrential rains. Hundreds died, hundreds were made homeless and there was extensive damage to property, infrastructure, livestock and crops.

In mid-2007 heavy rainfall and severe flooding occurred in Balochistan, Pakistan, and in the states of Gujarat, Maharashtra and elsewhere in India, resulting in the deaths of around 240 people in Pakistan and about 190 in India. In April 2007 the IPCC predicted that glacier melt in the Himalayas would lead to an increase in incidences of flooding and rock avalanches (from destabilized slopes) over the next 20–30 years, to be followed by decreased river flows as the glaciers receded. The panel also forecast that the heavily populated mega-delta regions of South, East and South-East Asia would be at greatest risk of increased flooding from both the sea and from the rivers.

### Heatwaves

At least 375 people were reported to have died in 2005 as a result of sunstroke and dehydration during a scorching heatwave extending over Bangladesh, India, Nepal and Pakistan, in one of the hottest summers experienced in South Asia in recent years. In some parts of the region, temperatures soared to 50°C (122°F), emptying dams, drying out riverbeds and resulting in parched fields. India's Orissa state was the worst affected area, with 100 people killed as a result of the intense temperatures. Meanwhile, in the Indian states of Uttar Pradesh and Madhya Pradesh, villagers were forced to travel for miles to fetch water from deep wells as ponds and lakes had dried up. According to Reuters news agency, more than 100 people died in Bangladesh and over 65 in Pakistan, while Nepal suffered at least 11 casualties as a result of the heatwave.

## POVERTY-ENVIRONMENT AND GENDER-ENVIRONMENT LINKAGES

The links between poverty and environmental degradation and between gender and environmental degradation are well established. Eradication of poverty has been recognized as an indispensable requirement for the achievement of sustainable development. The empowerment of the world's poor, the majority of whom are women, particularly rural women, must therefore be seen as a necessary part of any environmental conservation strategy. Recognizing this crucial link, a number of countries have incorporated economic activities into their environmental conservation strategies.

### Poverty and Environment

The linkages between poverty and environmental degradation are multi-dimensional and complex. The key linkages between poverty and the environment operate through the absence or denial of the basic environmental services to the poor. In addition to their exclusion from access to basic resources, the poor are also likely to be subjected to the polluting and degrading impacts of the consumption patterns of others. Although the poor supply their share of resources for the benefit of others, they are forced to move towards environmentally vulnerable areas as a result of their disempowerment by society.

According to some authors, poverty, population growth and environmental change may not have a causative link, but their interaction varies under different socio-cultural compositions of the population, comprising local institutions, cultural norms, social hierarchies, entitlements, social stability, use of technology and land tenure systems. The direction and strength of their interaction vary over time and space. Other factors, such as trade, debt, donor policies, governmental policies, consumption patterns and migration, also influence the whole process of socio-cultural interaction among poverty, population and environmental change.

The World Summit on Sustainable Development (WSSD), held in Johannesburg, South Africa, in 2002, recognized poverty reduction as a central principle of achieving sustainable development. Prior to this summit meeting, in 1992 heads of government of seven South Asian countries had signed the

South Asian Poverty Commission Report, asserting that poverty would be eliminated from South Asia by 2002. However, by 2002 poverty in South Asia appeared to have stabilized, if not to have increased.

Table 1 shows the percentage of population living in extreme poverty (that is, with income of less than $1.08 per day on the basis of 1993 PPP to the US dollar). This varies between 41% in Bangladesh and 6% in Sri Lanka. Data on poverty are not available for Afghanistan, Bhutan and the Maldives, but for countries for which data are available, it seemed that at least 446.6m. people in South Asia were living in extreme poverty in 1990–2002. The prevalence of poverty is higher in rural areas than in urban areas. The socio-cultural characteristics of the populations and external forces such as globalization put pressure on the poor, more particularly the rural poor, to be driven to more and more vulnerable areas, where they would be subjects of environmental forces that would affect their health and well-being. The poor, both in urban and rural areas, use cheap and available means of household fuel in the form of biomass and other combustible material, which contribute to indoor and outdoor air pollution.

### Gender and Environment

Since the early 1980s considerable attention has been given to the relationship between women and the environment. As the world's food producers, both women and men have an interest in the preservation of the environment and in environmentally sustainable development. In this context, the proper use of land and water resources is vital to sustained food production. Women have an important part to play in preserving the environment and natural resources such as land and water, and in promoting sustainable development. For example, women still have the main responsibility for meeting household needs and are therefore a major force in determining consumption trends. Water is present at various levels in women's lives. They collect water and manage its use in the household. In many parts of the world they farm irrigated and rain-fed crops. They are familiar with the sources of water, they manage its storage, they are the first to know about its scarcity and whether it is safe for family consumption. Similarly, women farmers are very much involved in the use of land; they tend to use traditional methods of cropping and cultivation and, as such, they play an important role in preserving soil fertility.

Women are also responsible for producing food in the household; they gather fuel for cooking. Their access to cooking fuel and its proper use determines to a large extent the conservation of the sources of cooking fuel and the effects of the use of the fuel on household health (particularly their own and their children's health).

Poverty is inextricably linked to environmental degradation in the developing world, and the majority of poor people are women. Women are also much less educated than men in most of the developing world. Thus, they tend to employ less efficient and environmentally less sustainable methods in using the three most important resources: water, land and cooking fuel.

Women's participation in the formulation, planning and execution of environmental policy continues to be low. At the same time, the international community has recognized that sustainable development cannot be achieved without women's full participation. The Platform for Action, adopted by the Fourth World Conference on Women in Beijing in 1995, identified the need actively to involve women in environmental decision-making at all levels, and to incorporate a gender perspective in all strategies for sustainable development, as one of the 12 critical areas of concern requiring action by states, the international community and civil society.

The UN Commission on the Status of Women took up the issue of women and the environment for discussion during its 41st session in 1997. The Commission proposed further action be taken to promote women's active involvement in environmental management at all levels, including the 'mainstreaming' of a gender perspective into all environmental policies and programmes. Among the agreed conclusions of the session were measures to encourage gender-sensitive research on the impact of environmental pollutants and other harmful substances, including their impact on the reproductive health of men and women, and the active involvement of women in the development and implementation of policies aimed at promoting and protecting the environmental aspects of human health, such as setting standards for drinking water.

Table 1 provides data on the human development index (HDI) and the gender-related development index (GDI) for those countries of South Asia for which data are available. The HDI is a summary measure of overall human development in terms of average achievement in three basic dimensions of human life: a long and healthy life, as measured by life expectancy at birth; knowledge, as measured by the adult literacy rate (with two-thirds' weight) and the combined primary, secondary and tertiary gross education enrolment ratio (with one-third weight); and a decent standard of living, as measured by GDP per caput at PPP in US dollars. The GDI adjusts the average achievement to reflect the inequalities between men and women in the three components of the HDI.

For the 177 countries for which HDI values are available, the countries of South Asia do not perform well in terms of overall human development. The best-ranked countries are Sri Lanka, with an HDI rank of 99, and the Maldives, with an HDI rank of 100. All the South Asian countries fall into the lower 50% of countries in terms of HDI ranking. Data on GDI are available for 140 countries. In terms of HDI ranking, all the South Asian countries that also have GDI data fall into the lower half, except for Sri Lanka. However, all countries in the region (except Bhutan and Afghanistan, for which data are not available) show positive trends in HDI values. Furthermore, even though the percentage of poor people in the region remains high (with Bangladesh having the highest percentage and Sri Lanka the lowest), these percentages declined over the period 1990–2005, with India showing a particularly significant reduction in levels of poverty.

The performance of countries on gender-related development compared with overall human development can be measured by a calculation of HDI rank minus GDI rank. This value is calculated only for those countries for which data on both HDI and GDI are available. To do this, the HDI ranks are recalculated for those countries for which GDI values are also available. A positive value of this figure indicates that the GDI rank is higher than the HDI rank, that is, gender-related development has been better than overall human development. A negative value indicates the opposite. These figures are not available for Afghanistan and Bhutan. For those countries where the data are available, it can be seen from the HDI minus GDI values published in the *Human Development Report 2007/2008* that Maldives (with a value of 4) is the only countries in the region that has achieved better in terms of gender-related development in comparison with overall human development. India, with a value of zero, has registered an equally low rate of achievement in both gender-related and overall human development. In Nepal, Pakistan and Sri Lanka (with HDI rank minus GDI rank values of −4, −7 and −1, respectively) gender-related development has been worse than the overall human development. Thus, most of the countries of South Asia exhibit not only low levels of overall human development but also show equally low or lower levels of gender-related development.

These human development and gender-related development dimensions of environmental degradation in South Asia, though implicitly understood, need to be brought into a more explicit focus for a proper environmental management of the region.

## THE AGEING POPULATION

An ageing of the population occurs when the proportion of the elderly increases. In demographic terms the elderly are defined as those who are aged 65 years and over (60 years and over in developing countries), and if the proportion of such persons in a population becomes 10% or more, then that population is considered to be an ageing population. Alternatively, if the median age of a population becomes 30 years or more—i.e. if one-half of the population is aged below 30 years and the other half is aged above 30 years, then that population is also considered to be an ageing population. These are the two most commonly used measures of population ageing, and in this essay the former gauge is employed (the proportion of those aged 60 years and over). Ageing of a population occurs if the fertility rate declines over an extended period, thus reducing the proportion of young persons; if the mortality rate decreases over an extended period, thus increasing the proportion of the elderly (as well as persons of other ages); or if significant numbers of young people emigrate from or large numbers of elderly persons migrate into the population, again producing an increased proportion of the elderly. Of the three demographic determinants of population ageing, fertility and mortality are usually the most common, as migration between countries (especially between developing countries) is not usually on such a scale as to affect the age-composition of a population. It may also be mentioned that both fertility and mortality, apart from being synergistic to changes in each other, also respond to improvements in a set of common socio-economic and health variables. By 2005 Sri Lanka was experiencing the early effects of an ageing population, with nearly 11% of its people aged 60+, while India, with around 7.5% of its population in this age bracket, was nearing classification as an ageing population (see Table 4). Projections made by the International Data Base of the US Census Bureau in mid-2007 show that all the South Asian countries, with the exception of Afghanistan, would be categorized as having ageing populations by 2050, and, in particular, well over one-quarter of the Sri Lankan population and more than one-fifth of the Indian population would be aged 60+.

In 2005 the sex ratios among the elderly revealed that Bangladesh, Bhutan and the Maldives had an excess of males over females, perhaps indicating a higher mortality rate among elderly females compared with their male counterparts. By 2030, however, all the South Asian countries were projected to have fewer males than females in the 60+ age category, reflecting the universally observed phenomenon of higher rates of mortality amongst males as compared to females. More specifically, Indian men aged 35 years or more have significantly shorter life expectancies than women of the same age, and the age-specific death rates are about twice those for women above 35. The higher rate of male mortality is partly caused by tuberculosis and by unhealthy lifestyle factors, such as tobacco smoking and alcohol consumption, the latter also contributing to increased levels of cardiovascular disease among men. However, elderly Indian women suffer from increasing rates of cervical and breast cancer and they develop osteoporosis, often leading to hip fractures and premature death, some 10–15 years earlier than women of similar ages in other countries.

The rates of growth given in Table 4 illustrate that the elderly population is projected to rise at a much faster rate than the overall population of each South Asian country. The growth rate of the elderly is especially rapid for Sri Lanka where the elderly population is forecast to increase at a rate more than six times faster than the total population, while for India and Pakistan the rate of growth of the elderly population is projected to grow at around three times faster than the total population. The data also show that by 2050 India is expected to have to care for 394m. elderly persons, while Bangladesh and Pakistan will have to look after around 45m. elderly people. Such large numbers of elderly people in countries that do not yet have well developed social security systems to cater for their specific needs will inevitably pose enormous problems for the various governments and welfare organizations concerned. Even if the social security systems in these countries see improvements over the next 40 years or so, the immediate problems confronting a country such as India, where in 2005 there were an estimated 82m. elderly people, are really huge.

In most South Asian countries only small sections of the population work on regular salaries and these tend to be predominantly urban and male. Accordingly very small proportions of the elderly have access to pensions and social security benefits following their retirement. Further, although in many cases widows are eligible to receive the pensions of their deceased husbands, most women, particularly those in rural areas are not aware of their entitlements or of the rules and regulations with regard to drawing such pensions. The majority of the elderly population depends on family support or personal savings, or continues to work for as long as possible. In South Asia labour force participation among the elderly is high, ranging from nearly one-third to about one-half, and is projected to decline very little by 2050. Health care systems in most South Asian countries are still orientated towards dealing with infectious and parasitic diseases and maternal and child health problems that are typical of younger populations in developing countries. As such, they are not adequately equipped effectively to manage the growing burden of chronic and degenerative diseases that are typical of ageing populations. In South Asia the concept of 'healthy ageing' has not yet gained wide acceptance, and there is a definite lack of preventive and palliative care for chronic conditions among the elderly. Chronic and degenerative diseases are viewed as natural consequences of getting old, both by the elderly themselves and by the health providers. This attitude leads to little support or action for preventing or treating such diseases.

Most elderly people in South Asia live with family members as this continues to be the tradition and the social norm in the region. Facilities for extrafamilial residence are very few in number. As the various countries of South Asia have different family systems, co-residence with family members has different implications for elderly men and women according to which system they live in. Under the patrilineal/patrilocal systems, elderly men, in their role as the senior male members of the household, can expect lifelong residential support and care from their married sons, although such support varies according to socio-economic status, whether they own land, whether a spouse is present, and the number of surviving sons. Elderly women, particularly widows with no son, are more vulnerable under patrilineal/patrilocal systems, and even though women have varying inheritance and property rights, in practice such rights largely depend upon the goodwill of the male kin. On the other hand, elderly women belonging to groups that practise matrilineal inheritance/matrilocal residence usually enjoy considerable security in their old age owing to the fact that they reside with their married daughters and property is inherited following the female line. Social and legal changes during the 20th century, however, have more and more frequently led to a breakdown in such traditional arrangements and have introduced patrilineal inheritance and nuclear residence patterns. This is illustrated by the previously unknown phenomenon of destitute elderly women in the state of Kerala in India, which was traditionally noted for the high status accorded to its female population.

Throughout the region declining rates of fertility and mortality mean that fewer siblings are required to care for larger numbers of the elderly, who are, in addition, living longer. The geographical mobility of the working-age population, increasing numbers of women working outside the household, and a more pronounced shift towards the nuclear family, with an emphasis on providing for the nurture, education and careers of children, are the other important factors that influence the living conditions of the elderly. While the migration of working-age children to seek employment may on the one hand reduce the financial hardships of the elderly, it may on the other hand also result in increasing loneliness and isolation on the part of the elderly.

The low male to female ratio among the elderly observed in Table 4 is a reflection of the greater prevalence of widowhood among South Asian women compared with men. Moreover, while widowed men may not find it difficult to remarry, widowed women face a number of restrictions to remarriage based on region, religion and caste. Many widowed women are forced to live alone or at the head of households and are at a great risk of poverty.

## EMERGING CONCERNS

Two emerging concerns for environmental security in South Asia are the trans-boundary movement of hazardous wastes and climate change.

### Trans-boundary Movement of Hazardous Wastes

In the South Asian region in general, recycling is emerging as a lucrative economic activity. This is certainly true of Bhutan, where recycling is becoming a major economic activity because

**Table 4. Trends in Population Ageing in the South Asia Region (2005–50)**

| | 2005 | | 2020 | | 2030 | | 2050 | |
|---|---|---|---|---|---|---|---|---|
| Country | % aged 60+, both sexes | Sex ratio aged 60+* | % aged 60+, both sexes | Sex ratio aged 60+* | % aged 60+, both sexes | Sex ratio aged 60+* | % aged 60+, both sexes | Sex ratio aged 60+* |
| Afghanistan | 4.1 | 96.3 | 4.3 | 93.8 | 4.7 | 94.3 | 6.7 | 96.1 |
| Bangladesh | 5.4 | 116.3 | 7.3 | 105.9 | 9.1 | 98.7 | 16.2 | 94.8 |
| Bhutan | 6.2 | 102.3 | 6.9 | 96.0 | 8.0 | 95.2 | 11.3 | 97.3 |
| India | 7.5 | 95.0 | 10.6 | 90.8 | 14.1 | 88.8 | 21.8 | 87.5 |
| Maldives | 4.8 | 101.8 | 5.0 | 88.3 | 7.0 | 87.5 | 12.0 | 89.1 |
| Nepal | 5.8 | 95.4 | 6.7 | 94.1 | 8.0 | 95.3 | 13.9 | 97.3 |
| Pakistan | 6.1 | 93.1 | 7.1 | 87.5 | 9.2 | 90.3 | 16.0 | 92.1 |
| Sri Lanka | 10.7 | 89.9 | 16.6 | 81.0 | 21.2 | 79.1 | 28.7 | 78.8 |

| | Population aged 60+ (millions) | | | | Annual rates of growth, 2005–50 | |
|---|---|---|---|---|---|---|
| Country | 2005 | 2020 | 2030 | 2050 | Elderly population | Total population |
| Afghanistan | 1.23 | 1.92 | 2.65 | 5.49 | 3.3 | 2.2 |
| Bangladesh | 7.79 | 13.86 | 19.99 | 45.35 | 3.9 | 1.5 |
| Bhutan | 0.14 | 0.21 | 0.29 | 0.53 | 3.0 | 1.6 |
| India | 82.02 | 144.38 | 216.10 | 394.12 | 3.5 | 1.1 |
| Maldives | 0.02 | 0.03 | 0.04 | 0.10 | 3.9 | 1.9 |
| Nepal | 1.61 | 2.47 | 3.43 | 7.41 | 3.4 | 1.5 |
| Pakistan | 9.69 | 14.49 | 21.37 | 44.41 | 3.4 | 1.2 |
| Sri Lanka | 2.19 | 3.84 | 5.13 | 7.15 | 2.6 | 0.4 |

* Sex ratio denotes the number of males per 100 females.

Source: Computed from International Database, www.census.gov/cgi-bin/ipc/idbagg, 11 July 2007.

power is available as well as cheap labour. Large-scale recycling, such as ship-breaking, has become a major industry in the coastal regions of India and Pakistan. Without a common approach among South Asian countries to regulate the movement of hazardous wastes across national boundaries, which such recycling projects entail, the environmental impact of the trans-boundary movement of hazardous wastes could be enormous and far-reaching.

## Climate Change

It is projected that the extent of climate changes in tropical South Asia will be such that they will have significant impacts on both land and water ecosystems, water resources and agriculture. They will also have major implications for human health. Compared with the 1980s, the annual mean maximum and minimum surface air temperatures in the land regions of the Indian subcontinent are projected to rise by 0.7°C and 1.0°C, respectively, by 2040. This projected warming is expected to be lower than that over the adjoining ocean, which could lead to a decline of mean summer monsoon rainfall of about 0.5 mm per day over the region.

Climate change is projected adversely to affect the sustainable development efforts of most developing countries in Asia, since it will increase the pressure on natural resources and the environment associated with rapid urbanization and economic development. It is feared that crop yields could decrease by up to 30% in Central and South Asia by the mid-21st century, exacerbating the already very high risk of hunger in several developing countries in the context of rapid population growth and urbanization. Owing to the projected changes in the hydrological cycle associated with global warming, the rates of endemic morbidity and mortality from diarrhoeal diseases, mainly associated with floods and droughts, are projected to increase in East, South and South-East Asia and the rises in coastal water temperatures are expected to lead to an intensification in the incidence and toxicity of cholera in South Asia.

## Worsening Gender Balance

In most populations of the world, there are more females than males overall. In other words, most countries have a sex ratio that is favourable to females, which may partly be attributed to the overall lower mortality rate among females compared with males. However, the sex ratio of the Indian population (as well as in some other Asian populations such as the People's Republic of China) has not been favourable to females. What is worse about this situation is that the sex ratio (measured in India by the number of females per 1,000 males) has been on a downward trend since 1901. This is due to higher female mortality rate and female selective abortion as a result of strong preference for the male child. The continuing worsening of the sex ratio in India has been a matter for concern and renders the females of India a vulnerable population. The unfavourable sex ratio reflects the much weaker position of women in South Asia in general and therefore their limited capacity to play an important role in the preservation of the environment in the region.

## Biofuels

The production and use of biofuels are still in their early stages, not only in South Asia but throughout the world. With increasing awareness of greenhouse gas emissions from the burning of fossil fuels and the increasing costs of fossil fuels such as petroleum and diesel, biofuels are being given greater consideration as potentially more environmentally friendy and cheaper alternatives to fossil fuels. There are, however, significant pros and cons involved in the production and use of biofuels, depending on which perspective one uses to view them.

In general, biofuels can be defined as any solid, liquid or gas fuel that is derived from biomass and can be produced from any renewable carbon source such as plants. In the South Asian context, biofuels are renewable liquid fuels that can substitute for petroleum. For commercial feasibility, three liquid biofuels could be considered for South Asia—namely vegetable oil, biodiesel and bioethanol.

In theory, biofuels are supposed to be carbon neutral and to reduce greenhouse gas emissions when compared with conventional fuels. However, in practice, biofuels are not really carbon neutral since energy is required to produce the crops and to convert them into fuel. None the less, the main advantage of the use of biofuels appears to be a reduction in carbon emissions. It is estimated that, in the long term, the use of biofuels would reduce carbon emissions by about 50%–60%. In addition, the use of biofuels may be financially advantageous for drivers of cars in countries that give tax reductions as incentives for using environmentally friendly vehicles. It can also be argued that the use of biofuels could help to reduce poverty through wider economic growth and increased employment opportunities brought about by the positive effects of biofuel production on energy prices.

On the other hand, there are a number of potential disadvantages inherent in the use of biofuels. These include a decrease in biodiversity through the loss of habitat for animals and wild plants and a reduction in the extent of the rain forests owing to the need for more land for the production of biofuel crops; a reduction in food production caused by farmers converting to lucrative biofuel production, thereby increasing food prices (an effect that would have particularly adverse repercussions in developing countries); no guarantee of a reduction in greenhouse gas emissions, as it has been reported that the burning of rapeseed or corn could produce nitrous oxide emissions that could outweigh the decrease in greenhouse gas emissions through not burning fossil fuels; and the fact that the production of biofuels (at least the first-generation biofuels) is not sustainable in that it would affect food prices and might not be free itself of environmental problems.

From the above, it may be inferred that, in the short term, the disadvantages of the production of biofuels by developing countries could outweigh the advantages, but, in the long term, with more efficient production of biofuels, the advantages could prevail over the disadvantages.

There is divided opinion on biofuel production in South Asia and most of the debate over the issue pertains to India. On the one hand, a number of economists and specialists argue that the implementation of a well-conceived biofuel programme with effective co-operation among the countries of the region could lead South Asia to attaining high levels of sustainable energy production. On the other hand, farmers, people's movements, NGOs and concerned individuals from various different regions of India have expressed their opposition to the promotion and production of biofuels and a whole range of allied issues. The Indian Minister of Finance, P. Chidambaram, is reported strongly to oppose biofuels for the reason that he considers that the diversion of the production of food to the production of biofuels in a number of countries was having an adverse affect on the developing countries, which were already suffering the effects of continually rising basic food prices.

In the last year or so there have been record increases in food prices all over the world, especially in countries such as India, Pakistan, China, Russia and in the countries of Latin America. According to the Food and Agriculture Organization (FAO) these price rises are due to a number of factors, but are mainly owing to record oil prices, US farmers switching from the cultivation of cereals to biofuel crops, extreme weather and increasing demand from rapidly developing countries such as India and China. According to the IMF, the shift by agro-industries to the more profitable production of biofuels could further worsen the situation and have grave implications for the growing demand for food. Measures adopted by countries switching to biofuel production over the next few years could force millions of people off the land. The other factors exacerbating the problem of rising food prices are continuing population growth, extreme weather and ecological stress. There may, however, be grounds for some optimism regarding food supply as it is hoped that the introduction of new varieties and technologies could help crops to adapt to changing climatic conditions, a change in eating habits and the imposition of controls on population growth could ease pressure on the food market, and the cultivation of hitherto unproductive land could also help supply. However, the cultivation of greater areas of land would have implications for biodiversity loss.The High-Level Conference on World Food Security: The Challenges of Climate Change and Bioenergy, which was convened by the FAO in Rome, Italy, in June 2008 expressed its reservations regarding biofuels and considered it 'essential to address the challenges and opportunities posed by biofuels, in view of the world's food security, energy and sustainable development needs'. The conference declaration added that it was necessary to conduct in-depth studies for ensuring the sustainable production and use of biofuels in accordance with the three pillars of sustainable development (social, environmental and economic) and that the production and use of biofuels should take into account the need to achieve and maintain global food security. The declaration considered it desirable that countries exchanged experiences on biofuels technologies, norms and regulations and called upon the relevant intergovernmental organisations, including the FAO, 'to foster a coherent, effective and results-oriented international dialogue on biofuels in the context of food security and sustainable development needs'.

## CONCLUSION

This essay has highlighted the environmental issues of South Asia and their links with the demographic, economic and gender characteristics of the region. The population-poverty/gender-environment linkages will be shaped by the future demographic, socio-economic and political situations of each country and by external factors such as globalization in trade and commerce, external financial aid and technical co-operation. An emerging demographic trend in South Asia is the growing rate of increase in the size of the ageing population, which by the middle of the century is expected to result in a worrying situation where there are huge numbers of the elderly to care for without the necessary support systems in place adequately to address the concomitant issues of health care, economic support and suitable living arrangements. Another emerging issue is the production and use of biofuels in South Asia. Since this is still in its early stages, time will only tell whether, in the interests of a reduction in the emissions of greenhouse gases by motor vehicles, the production and use of biofuels will outweigh the inherent disadvantages in terms of food security and loss of biodiversity. As the countries of the region aspire to and work towards economic development, their access to affordable and appropriate technologies will determine to a large extent the potential environmental impact of development projects.

This essay has also brought into focus some of the natural calamities that have caused, in the short-term, loss of human life and damage to property and housing and, in the long-term, have had significant effects on the economy, human health and the environment. The most severe of these natural disasters, the Asian tsunami, made its most significant impact upon Indonesia, Thailand, Sri Lanka, southern India and the Maldives in Asia and Somalia in Africa. It is probable that human interference in the ecosystem in the form of destruction of coral reefs and the removal of coastal mangroves and coastal dunes exacerbated the losses caused by the tsunami.

## BIBLIOGRAPHY

Alauddin, Mohammad, and Tisdell, Clement Allan. *The Environment and Economic Development in South Asia: An Overview Concentrating on Bangladesh*. Basingstoke, Macmillan, 1998.

Arnold, David, and Guha, Ramachandra (Eds). *Nature, Culture, Imperialism: Essays on the Environmental History of South Asia*. Delhi, Oxford University Press, 1995.

Arsenic Crisis Information Centre—West Bengal and Bangladesh; internet www.bicn.com/aic.

Asheville Global Report. *Water Wars: Pakistani Provinces Clash Over Mega Dam*; internet www.agrnews.org/issues/267/environment.html, 26 February–3 March 2004.

BBC News. *India's Tiger Success Story*; internet news.bbc.co.uk/1/hi/sci/tech/1565437.stm, 27 September 2001.

BBC News. *Indian Minister Attacks Biofuels.*; internet news.bbc.co.uk.go/pr/fr/-/2/hi/south_asia/7315308.stm, 26 March 2008.

*New Hope for Bengal Tigers*; internet news.bbc.co.uk/2/hi/south_asia/1716056.stm, 17 December 2001.

*Bengal Tiger Census Plan*; internet news.bbc.co.uk/2/hi/south_asia/3112391.stm, 31 July 2003.

Billsborrow, Richard. E. 'Population Growth, Internal Migration, and Environmental Degradation in Rural Areas of Developing Countries.' *European Journal of Population*, Vol. 8 (2), pp.125–148, 1992.

Business Standard. *Narmada Height Raised to 110.64 metres*. New Delhi, 30 June 2004.

Campbell, Philip (Ed.). *Nature*, Vol. 433, No. 7024, Nature Publishing Group, 27 January 2005.

Center of Excellence in Disaster Management and Human Assistance. *Asia-Pacific Daily Report*; internet pdmin.coe-dmha.org/apdr.

Chakraborti, Dipankar, *et al*. 'Arsenic Groundwater Contamination in Middle Ganga Plain, Bihar, India: A Future Danger?' *Environmental Health Perspectives*, Vol. 111, No. 9, pp. 1,194–1,201.

Chatterjee, Romir, Mehra, Meeta, and Banerjee, Shilpi. *Environmental Security in South Asia*; internet www.teriin.org/energy/envsec.htm, 2000.

City Mayors. *World's Largest Urban Areas in 2020"*; internet www.citymayors.com/statistics/urban_2020_1.html ", 2008.

Das Gupta, Monica, Chen, L. C., and Krishnan, T. N. (Eds). *Women's Health in India: Risk and Vulnerability*. Mumbai, Oxford University Press, 1995.

Dasvarma, Gouranga. 'Vulnerable Females: The Case of the Declining Femininity Ratio in India's Population'. Paper presented at the Population Vulnerability Session of the International Geographical Union Conference, Brisbane, Australia, July 2006.

Deccan Herald. *India, Pakistan Suffer High Food Price Inflation*. 4 November 2007.

Deutsche Presse Agentur. *Flash Floods Displace Over 7,000 People in Pakistan*; internet www.reliefweb.int/rw/RWB.NSF/db900SID/EVIU-6DYL23?, 4 July 2005.

The Earth Council. *Ranking the Ecological Impact of Nations*; internet www.ecouncil.ac.cr, 23 August 2003.

*The Ecological Benchmark: How Much Nature is there per Global Citizen?*; internet www.ecouncil.ac.cr.

Eckholm, Erik. 'A Province is Dying of Thirst, and Cries Robbery', *The New York Times*. New York, 17 March 2003.

Food and Agriculture Organization. 'Declaration of the High-Level Conference on World Food Security: The Challenges of Climate Change and Bioenergy'. Rome, June 2008.

Forest Conservation Archives, Forest Conservation Portal. *Pakistan's Mega-Dam Plan Hits Opposition Barrage*; internet forests.org/articles/reader.asp?linkid=25379, 3 September 2003.

Forsberg, Bob. *Arsenic Threat in Bangladesh*; internet www.rnw.nl/development/html/030506arsenic.html, 6 May 2003.

Gender Unit, Food and Agriculture Organization; internet www.gdrc.org/gender/1pager004.html.

TheGreenCarWebsite; internet www.thegreencarwebsite.co.uk

Greenough, Paul R., and Tsing, Anna Lowenhaupt (Eds). *Nature in the Global South: Environmental Projects in South and Southeast Asia*. Durham, NC, Duke University Press, 2003.

Guest, Philip. 'The Impact of Population Change on the Growth of Mega-cities', *Asia-Pacific Population Journal*, Vol. 9, No. 1, pp. 37–56.

Gupta, A. 'Osteoporosis in India: the Nutritional Hypothesis', *National Medicine Journal of India*, Vol. 9 (6), pp. 268–274, 1996.

Harrison, P. *The Third Revolution: Population, Environment and a Sustainable World*. London, Penguin Books, 1992.

*The Hindu*. 'Gujarat Given Permission to Raise Narmada Dam Height'. New Delhi, 17 March 2004.

'Narmada Control Authority Discusses Hiking Dam Height Further'. New Delhi, 13 May 2004.

Hogan, Daniel Joseph. 'The Impact of Population Growth on the Physical Environment', *European Journal of Population*, Vol. 8 (2), pp.109–123, 1992.

Intergovernmental Panel on Climate Change (IPCC). *Climate Change 2007: Impacts, Adaptation and Vulnerability*. Working Group II Contribution to the IPCC. Fourth Assessment Report. Summary for Policymakers. IPCC Secretariat, Geneva.; internet www.ipcc.ch.

International Data Base; internet www.census.gov/cgi-bin/ipc/idbagg, 11 July 2007.

International Human Dimensions Programme. *Newsletter of the International Human Dimensions Programme on Global Environmental Change, No. 4/2002*; internet www.ihdp.uni-bonn.de/html/publications/publications.html, Bonn.

International Monetary Fund. *Finance and Development*. Vol. 42, March 2005.

Kumar, Linoj, Prabha Dhavala, N. V., Goswami, Anandajit and Maithel, Sameer.'Liquid Biofuels in South Asia—Resources and Technologies'. *Asian Biotechnology and Development Review*.Vol. 8, No. 2. pp.31-49, 2006.

Madsen, Stig Toft. *State, Society and the Environment in South Asia*. Richmond, Curzon Press, 1999.

Mallik, Pradeep. *Narmada Project: Most-Debated but Least-Implemented*; internet newsarchives.indiainfo.com/spotlight/narmada/20dam.html, 2000.

Pearce, Fred. 'Bangladesh's Arsenic Poisoning: Who is to Blame?' *The UNESCO Courier*; internet www.unesco.org/2001_01/uk/planet.htm, January 2001.

Raju, K.V. 'Biofuels in South Asia: An Overview—Editorial Introduction'. *Asian Biotechnology and Development Review*.-Vol. 8, No. 2. pp.1-9, 2006.

SenGupta, Arup K. *Arsenic Content in the Indian Subcontinent: An Indigenous Solution*; internet www.lehigh.edu/~aks0/arsenic.html, 2004.

Shiva, Vandana. 'The Lessons of the Tsunami', *The Ecologist*, Vol. 35, Issue 2, pp. 21–24, March 2005.

Smith, K. R., and Lee, Y. F. 'Urbanisation and the Environmental Risk Transition' in Kasarda, J. D., and Parnell, A. M. (Eds), *Third World Cities: Problems, Policies and Prospects*. London, Sage Publications, pp. 161–179, 1993.

The South Asian. *'Biofuels: A Boon or A Curse"*. 16 December 2007.

Steele, Ross. 'Environmental Issues of Asia and the Pacific' in *The Far East and Australasia 2003*. London, Europa Publications, 2002.

Sudha, S., and Rajan, S. Irudaya. 'South Asia—Trends in population aging, living arrangements, economic status and retirement patterns, sex ratios in the elderly population'. *Aging Healthy* Vol. 4; internet //medicine.jrank.org/pages/1630/South-Asia.html, 11 July 2007.

Synolakis, Costas. 'Why There Was No Warning', *The Wall Street Journal*. New York; internet www.opinionjournal.com/editorial/feature.html?id=110006084, 29 December 2004.

Tsunamis.com; internet www.tsunamis.com/tsunami-deaths.html.

*Tsunamis–Tidal Waves–Flooding*; internet www.crystalinks.com/tsunami.html

UN Department of Public Information. *Review and Appraisal of the Implementation of the Beijing Platform for Action: Report of the Secretary-General*. UN Department of Public Information DPI/2035/K. New York, May 2000.

UN Development Programme. *Human Development Report*, annually. New York.

*Regional Human Development Report: HIV/AIDS and Development in South Asia 2003*. Bangkok.

UN Environment Programme. *Forest and Poverty Mapping in South Asia*. Forest Programme, UNEP World Conservation Monitoring Centre; internet www.wcmc.org.uk/forest/poverty/pep%20nexus.htm.

*Environmental Indicators for South Asia*. UNEP Regional Resource Centre for Asia and the Pacific, Asian Institute of Technology, Thailand, 2004.

UN Environment Programme and C4. *National Geographic News*; internet http://news.nationalgeographic.com/news/2004/12/1228_041228_tsunami.html

*The Asian Brown Cloud: Climate and Other Environmental Impacts.* Bangkok, 2002.

UNESCO Media Services; internet portal.unesco.org/en/ev.php-URL_ID=24341=DO_TOPIC=201.html, 4 July 2005.

UN Population Division. *World Population Prospects: The 2004 Revision Population Database*; internet esa.un.org/unpp/p2k0data.asp

World Health Organization. *Health Action in Crises Situation Report 2*; internet www.who.int/hac/en/.

# FORCED MIGRATION ISSUES IN SOUTH ASIA

DAVID RAMPTON

## INTRODUCTION

South Asia's post-colonial history has been inextricably bound up with forced migration issues. Indeed, two of the subcontinent's most significant regional players (namely India and Pakistan) won their independence in the midst of the paroxysms of Partition in 1947, when violence erupted and spread outwards from the Punjab in a conflagration that led to around 600,000 deaths and the displacement of some 14m. people between 1947 and 1951. Again, in 1971, the birth of a new nation, Bangladesh, resulted in the mass flight of about 10m. refugees from East Pakistan and formed the backdrop for India's intervention and war against Pakistan over the fledgling state. Such events epitomized on a colossal, yet tragic, scale the deep correlation between forced migration and South Asian social, economic and political processes.

Some scholars have characterized such South Asian forced migration patterns as archetypes of the classic 20th-century refugee paradigm (e.g. Prof. Aristide Zolberg *et al*), as they have paralleled the population exchanges of minorities that afflicted interwar Europe after the dissolution of the Ottoman, Tsarist and Austro-Habsburg Empires. Such analyses have emphasized that the dynamics of conflict, displacement and refugeehood are intimately related to the imagining of community around the legacy of the administrative, territorial and identity structures consequent upon colonial and imperial intervention. Obviously, South Asia was composed of a myriad of ethnic, religious, linguistic, cultural, regional and caste-based forms of cleavage, identification and consciousness. It has been argued that as a result of the transmutations and rigidity that colonialism imposed upon these facets of identity, these cleavages formed the nuclei around which political, socio-economic and cultural power operated, including domination over post-colonial states and administrative structures. Consequently, large-scale displacement has frequently resulted from conflicts over admission to citizenship and other resources revolving around just such reinvented facets of identity and their relation to the power structures inherited from colonial rule.

Furthermore, it is also clear that many of the nationalist, secessionist and ethnic conflicts and tensions that have impacted upon forced migration patterns in South Asia, including the long-running insurgency of the Liberation Tigers of Tamil Eelam (LTTE) against the Government of Sri Lanka and a host of smaller insurgent-led struggles in the north-east of India and in Pakistan, have been nurtured by similar nationalist and identity-related movements and struggles launched in search of separate states or regional autonomy. In addition to this, one can include in this paradigm of state formation and exclusion the situation of minority groups that have been discriminated against, expelled and/or denied citizenship, despite the fact that the depressed and marginalized status of such groups has thus far precluded their capacity for mounting counter-state or separatist struggles. This has been the experience of Bihari Muslims and Rohingyas in Bangladesh, as well as of the Bhutanese Lhotshampa refugees in Nepal, all groups rendered stateless by both their states of origin and exile.

However, despite the prominence of these dynamics in the subcontinent, forced migration in South Asia cannot be reduced solely to this 'classic' model. Whilst this must also be linked to the shifting scope of forced migration studies, which has considerably widened its focus as a sub-discipline over the last 20 years, it is, none the less, clear that South Asia has experienced the full gamut of 'forced migration' dynamics. So, beyond the aforementioned processes of displacement that have resulted from nationalist and identity-related conflict-induced struggles or the dispossession, marginalization and dislocation of persecuted minority groups, the subcontinent has also borne witness to forced migration as a consequence of ongoing revolutionary projects (e.g. Maoist insurgency and counter-insurgency in Nepal), development projects (for instance, the construction of large dams), and, very recently, as a result of large-scale 'natural' disasters such as the Indian Ocean tsunami and the 2005 South Asian earthquake, events which, in the scale of displacement, cannot be gauged without consideration of the style and character of the 'human' responses proceeding from them. It is, therefore, clear that although 'classic' persecutory dynamics relating to nationalism, state formation, identity construction and domination figure prominently in the South Asian region, other forms of forced migration, which frequently overlap with, but are not reducible to, such dynamics have also been significant. However, before studying the details of this diversity in the currents of South Asian displacement, any survey must also address the ongoing problem of the lack of either an international or regional framework for addressing many of the existing forced migration issues in the subcontinent, as this continues to play a role in the nature of the aid and assistance received by the displaced in the region.

## ADDRESSING SOUTH ASIAN FORCED MIGRATION IN A GLOBAL CONTEXT

Despite the tragic, yet fertile, history of the diverse and increasingly complex currents of forced migration in the subcontinent, the fact remains that until August 2005, when Afghanistan signed the 1951 UN Convention relating to the Status of Refugees and the 1967 Protocol, no state within the region had signed either of these documents. Nor has there been the type of anti-colonial historical context or shared geopolitical consensus for the development of a regional convention or protocol such as the Organization of African Unity (OAU) Convention of 1967 and the Organization of American States (OAS) Cartagena Declaration of 1984. The reasons for this historical absence of international or regional instruments are manifold, but can be reduced to some central operating factors following the implementation of the 1951 UN Convention. First, there was an overriding suspicion of the eurocentric and Cold War foundations and contexts of the Convention (as in Africa, for example, which none the less did develop alternative regional instruments out of the context of anti-colonial nationalist and pan-African currents). Second, there was also considerable wariness, from different angles and in shifting historical contexts, concerning the political motivations of international intervention in both Cold War and post-Cold War contexts. This wariness also extended to mutual suspicions and fears amongst the vying interests of the South Asian regional states in exploiting the dynamics of exile for geopolitical purposes. These historical fissures precluded the formation of a consensus or political will to assume the obligations that might arise from either an international or regional instrument.

Third, it has also become clear that the present global context is one in which the dominant 'Donor States' have increasingly disregarded, undermined or even stripped away aspects of the 1951 UN Convention since the demise of both the bipolar structures of the Cold War and the need for mass immigrant labour in the more developed states. In a context where the displaced have therefore become increasingly 'warehoused' or 'contained' in their countries or regions of 'origin', both the authorities and some scholars concerned with the region have stressed the inadvisability of becoming signatories to an international instrument under siege, because of the unsustainable burdens and obligations that this would place upon South Asian states in such a context. Finally, South Asian states have always argued that the pragmatic, crisis-by-crisis approach has adequately served the needs of refugees within the region.

This has resulted, however, in an ad hoc approach to refugee movements, so that each state in the region, whilst they have by no means always relinquished protection for refugees, have none the less reacted in very selective ways to different refugee movements according to their political interests. This has also led to ad hoc, inconsistent and varying approaches to the UN High Commissioner for Refugees (UNHCR) and international non-governmental organizations (NGOs) amongst South Asian states, either warding off or requesting their assistance as it has suited the interests of particular regimes. While a defence of this approach might argue that it is far better fitting with the contemporary condition of both the global context of the dominant norms for refugee assistance (what is sometimes described as the 'International Refugee Regime') and the *realpolitik* that has always been present in the selectivity of assistance and aid afforded to refugee movements, this does not address the needs of the refugees themselves. It should also be noted that both the nature of conflict and the pressure for regional containment and repatriation as a 'durable solution' for refugees have added to the increasing significance of internal displacement over and against refugeehood as a pressing human rights issue that currently lacks any effective international legal protocol. Although there exists the Guiding Principles on Internal Displacement, which was presented to the Office of the UN High Commissioner for Human Rights (OHCHR) in 1998, this is a set of voluntary guidelines rather than a binding legal framework. Furthermore it has been noted by observers that, just as South Asian states have been reluctant to sign up to the 1951 UN Convention, internal displacement has also frequently been considered an internal matter over which the state has sovereign prerogative. This attitude has led to a similar reluctance to abide by the 'Guiding Principles' and a continuing tendency to view internal displacement assistance in terms of welfare rather than rights and protection—a facet of displacement in South Asia that is more than borne out by recent examples of forced return and resettlement in Sri Lanka (see below). Consequently, the examples highlighted in the following sections illustrate these ongoing institutional and legal problems, which impact upon the form and type of assistance offered to the displaced in the region, whether in the case of 'refugees' or the internally displaced.

## CONFLICT-INDUCED DISPLACEMENT IN SOUTH ASIA

It has become clear that forms of 'environmental' and development-induced internal displacement produce displacement flows of massive proportions, far outstripping either conflict-related internal displacement or refugee figures. For instance, in India the number of conflict-induced internally displaced persons (IDPs) has been estimated at 600,000, while development-induced dynamics had rendered more than 21m. internally displaced at February 2006. Yet, the prioritization of the targeted refugee exile or conflict-induced displaced within the 'traditional' international refugee regime and the sustained 'political' impact and objectives often associated with such conflict dynamics both account for the high profile still afforded to conflict-related forced migration by state authorities, international NGOs and forced migration scholarship.

However, these dynamics are not monolithic, but arise from multiple forms of conflict, including both revolutionary insurgent movements operating to overturn the existing framework of the State and those nationalist or separatist struggles that seek autonomy, self-determination or secession from South Asian states on the basis of identity-related factors. As almost every South Asian country has experienced one or other of these displacement factors, this overview will not seek to be exhaustive but to illustrate these dynamics with reference to examples.

### Revolution, Regime Change, Insurgency and Displacement

South Asia as a whole is no stranger to revolutionary upheaval and its historical centre in both the colonial and post-colonial period has been India, owing to the potency of the Marxist tradition in the country and the interconnections forged between Indian nationalism and the Marxist parties. Following independence, radical Marxist parties continued to thrive and in 1967 the Maoist-aligned radical revolutionary force launched an insurgency movement in West Bengal and Bihar, targeting 'class enemies' in the form of landlords, policemen and governmental officers; these actions led to a brutal government counter-insurgency. Over time, many commentators presumed that the radicals and dynamics behind the so-called 'Naxalite' movement had been eradicated. However, in the course of India's economic liberalization in the 1990s, the revival of Naxalite movements and 'People's War Groups' in India's poorer states, including Andhra Pradesh, Bihar, Madhya Pradesh and Uttar Pradesh, signified a revival of revolutionary Marxism in response to the deleterious impact of liberalization amongst poor rural and low-caste groups. Conflicts arising from these movements continue to cause displacement in those Indian states. Yet, more recently, the place where the impact of revolutionary secular Marxism has been most keenly felt within the region has been Nepal, where the Communist Party of Nepal (Maoist) (CPN (M)) led intermittent but escalating insurgency campaigns (in classic Naxalite style) against the Royal Nepalese Army (RNA) and any 'enemies' of the 'People's War' who were perceived to be aligned with the Government of Nepal. From 1996 this set in motion cycles of violent insurgency and counter-insurgency, which led to internal displacement and 'refugee' flows on a large scale.

The 'causative' factors underlying the insurgency and the subsequent displacements must be understood in the context of the beleaguered economy and politics of Nepal, a country that had seen an autocratic and semi-feudal monarchy resisting parliamentary reform and perpetuating forms of ethnic, regional, caste and other status and class inequalities since 1962. These inequalities found expression in the far- and mid-western regions, particularly in Rolpa and Rukum, where the CPN (M) developed its traditional power bases. Nepal is one of the poorest countries in the world and it is clear that liberalization policies and aid and development strategies have not improved the distribution of wealth, but have, rather, served to increase inequality in the income structure, particularly for rural areas, where up to 80% of the population depend on agriculture for a living. The Nepalese State has promoted development in urban areas, particularly in the tourism and textile sectors. As a result, urban–rural inequalities and inadequate public investment in infrastructure and social sectors have increased, rather than lessened, disparities and it is no surprise that the Maoist-led insurgency had its origins in those regions where human and infrastructural development levels were extremely low and poverty was widespread. Additionally, the introduction of democratic politics and a new Constitution in 1990 failed to bring about a challenge to the traditional dominance of the élites, who simply reasserted their control through the appropriation of the existing, but narrow, democratic institutions.

It was in this context that the Maoist insurgency was launched in 1996. Conflict between the Nepalese Government and the Maoists escalated sharply in mid-2001, when King Gyanendra acceded to the throne in the aftermath of the palace massacre, in which Crown Prince Dipendra allegedly murdered King Birendra and Queen Aishwarya (together with six other members of the royal family) before killing himself. Despite a short-lived cease-fire in 2003, the cycle of insurgency, counter-insurgency and repressive measures to combat insecurity on the part of the King remained the norm. King Gyanendra suspended Parliament in 2002 and declared a repressive state of emergency from February 2005 to April 2005, introducing restrictions on freedom of movement, assembly and political expression, whilst assuming full executive powers. Under overwhelming pressure after a widely observed general strike and the failing legitimacy of the King following the 2005 royal coup, the King reinstated Parliament and the premiership in April 2006. In May a cease-fire agreement was reached between the new Government and the Maoist rebels, on the basis of a prior peace plan that had been agreed in November 2005 between the opposition seven-party alliance and the Maoists.

The 10-year long Maoist insurgency led to forced migration and de facto urbanization on a large scale, as the CPN (M) rebels, in a classic Maoist strategy, increasingly assumed control of the countryside and the Government retained the urban centres. Forced migration flows therefore arose in three main areas. First, during the initial years of the insurgency the wealthier sections of the rural populace, including landlords, members of the security forces, party officials, teachers and

Village Development Committee members, fled the impact of Maoist control of the rural areas to escape the violent targeting of pro-Government and élite forces and representatives branded as 'enemies of the People's War'. This led to tens of thousands of the displaced seeking refuge in urban centres, such as Kathmandu, Biratnagar and Nepalgunj.

Second, a significant proportion of the displaced were youths and children fleeing recruitment by the rebels, who deliberately targeted schools for this purpose. It has been estimated that about 40,000 children were displaced between 1996 and 2005. Third, considerable displacement resulted from the violent counter-insurgency practices of the Nepalese security services and of the Village Defence Committees (VDCs), which were encouraged after November 2003 by the Nepalese Government in an effort to secure some control in the rural areas. The VDCs were effectively vigilante militias supported and supplied by the RNA, often drawn from local élites and landlords, which, if anything, increased the level of conflict. For example, in February 2005 in Kapilvastu district it was estimated that 708 houses were burned down and 31 suspected 'Maoists' brutally executed or lynched, events in which the VDCs were heavily implicated. These events led to the displacement of between 20,000 and 30,000 people. This is just one example of the atrocities (and consequent displacements) committed in the conflict, not only by the Maoists, but in greater numbers by the RNA, which deliberately targeted civilians suspected of aiding and abetting the rebels.

In terms of numbers of the displaced, it is clear that the scale over the 10 years of conflict was massive, but precise figures are difficult to calculate. This is due to a number of factors. First, as regards refugee numbers, exiles from Nepal are free to establish residence, employment and property relations across the border in India, as are Indian citizens in Nepal, according to the India-Nepal Treaty of 1950. As a result of this and India's ad hoc legal approach to the granting of refugee status (which is partly sub-contracted to UNHCR in Delhi), Nepalese 'refugees' are, on the whole, undifferentiated from 'economic' and other migrants who cross the border. Second, there has been an absence of co-ordinated registration of the internally displaced by the State, rebels and international organizations. Third, until at least the signing of the Comprehensive Peace Agreement (CPA) between the CPN (M) and the Government of Nepal in November 2006, those who were displaced as a result of counter-insurgent activity were reluctant to declare this to the Nepalese authorities for obvious reasons, opting instead to seek assistance from relatives, often in urban areas. Furthermore, the new national IDP policy issued by the Nepalese Government in March 2006 continued to discriminate between those displaced by Maoist and those displaced by state action. As a result, the available figures for displacement related primarily to those internally displaced by the Maoist insurgency rather than providing an overall figure of IDPs, including those displaced by the retaliatory attacks of the RNA. Nevertheless, according to the estimates of a number of human rights organizations, by the time the CPA was declared in November 2006, some 200,000 Nepalese nationals had been displaced by a decade-long conflict that had claimed approximately 14,000 lives. Recent estimates as to the IDP population in Nepal range from between as high as 50,000–70,000 by the UN in mid-2007 and as low as 25,000 as of January 2008 according to the Government.

The recall of Parliament in April 2006, the establishment of the CPA, the interim government and the UN Mission in Nepal (UNMIN), the elections to and functioning of the new Constituent Assembly, the abolition of the monarchy and declaration of a republic, and the election of the leader of the CPN (M), Prachanda, as Prime Minister in August 2008 have all helped to create an environment in which the dynamics of displacement have been partially ameliorated. Accordingly, the processes of return and reintegration of both exiles and IDPs commenced in May 2006, albeit on a very small and gradual scale. In March 2007 the Norwegian Refugee Council (NRC) launched an 'Information, Counselling and Legal Assistance' programme (ICLA) in Nepalgunj, Biratnagar and Kathmandu in order to dispense legal advice and impart information to returning IDPs, whilst at the same time also collecting data on the statistics and conditions of displacement. In this respect, the NRC, UNHCR, the Office for the Co-ordination of Humanitarian Affairs (OCHA) and the OHCHR have all co-operated with the Nepalese Government and the National Human Rights Commission (NHRC) of Nepal (which was founded in 2000) in an effort to disseminate the Guiding Principles on Internal Displacement at national, regional and local levels.

Nevertheless, continuing tensions between a number of political actors in Nepal have impeded the processes of return, reconstruction and reintegration of the displaced. Amongst the problems reported in 2007 were failures to re-establish police posts in rural areas where the CPN (M) remained dominant and accusations that the Maoists were continuing to develop parallel local government institutions and authorities, that they had interfered with the reclamation of land by titleholders and that they had blocked the activities of Village Development Committees (VDCs) and District Development Committees (DDCs). There have also been claims that a number of political bodies, including the Madhesi People's Rights Forum (MPRF) and Tarai Janatantrik Mukti Morcha (TJMM), have harassed humanitarian workers and NGOs through abductions, threats and tax demands. Yet the recognition of the CPN(M)-led administration and the democratic election of Prachanda also led to reiterated pledges by the Government that land seized by rebels during the years of insurgency would be returned and that the implementation of local governance and the rule of law would be implemented under a less fractious and more unified regime. However, renewed dynamics of displacement also occurred between September 2007 and mid-2008 in relation to ethnic conflict between hill-country Pahadis and the plains-dwelling Madhesis in the Terai district. This conflict was triggered by Madhesi-led protests and strikes at the ongoing failure of political and social integration suffered by this community and the slowness of the peace process and the political framework to respond to these demands. In this forced migration flow as many as 8,000 (predominantly Pahadi) individuals were displaced. So, although the contemporary context in Nepal is one in which the conflict dynamics relating to the Maoist-led insurgency appear to have diminished, the potential for future forced migration dynamics emerging in relation to other sources of discontent will depend on the pace and evenness of reforms of governance, development and the rule of law in the context of what is still a highly aid-dependent, agriculture-based society which is still affected by poverty and by the effects of more than a decade of conflict.

The impact of revolutionary insurgency and regime change in South Asia has not only been restricted to radical Marxist insurgency in Nepal. It has also deeply affected Afghanistan, which has undergone numerous regime changes (including Marxist, Islamic and Liberal governments) over the last 30 years or so and subsequent forced migration flows of massive proportions; at the height of the crisis in the 1980s there were around 6.3m. Afghan refugees exiled in Pakistan and Iran. Over the long term what the Afghanistan conflicts illustrate, in stark contrast with the case of rural but secular insurrection in Nepal, is the way in which parallel rural–urban, mass–élite and centre–periphery disparities have translated themselves into movements from the rural periphery that have been dynamized by religious and 'traditional' forms of identification against a secular centre.

It was the emergence of these tensions that initiated Afghanistan's recurrent patterns of conflict-induced displacement in 1978, when the People's Democratic Party of Afghanistan (PDPA) regime assumed power through a military coup over a country with one of the lowest per caput rates of gross national income (GNI) and one of the highest infant mortality rates in the world. Afghanistan was also agriculturally dependent, despite having a cultivable area of only 13% of the total land area at that time. The PDPA was a narrowly secular, urban and élite-based Marxist-Leninist political movement with a very weak party machinery and few ties in the rural periphery. As a result of its attempts to dismantle the traditional order, the regime faced immediate resentment and rebellion from the rural population, amongst whom power had traditionally been based on a mixture of ethnic and clan-based power blocks with Islam acting as a significant ideological 'cement' underlying village life. The PDPA's actions provoked a violent counter-insurgency, which set in motion the intensification of the international and geo-political dimensions of the phases of conflict and the increasing displacement of millions of Afghanis, to the extent that up to one-third of the population were refugees by the late 1980s. With the collapse of the PDPA regime imminent, the USSR intervened in December 1979.

Consequently, Afghanistan was drawn into the Cold War and the regional geo-political dynamics that fuelled the conflict, with the USA funding the bulk of the massive refugee aid programme to Pakistan's North-West Frontier Province (NWFP), where more than 300 refugee 'villages' were located. The distribution of the aid was channelled through Pakistani authorities, which acted as a conduit for between US $4,000m. and $5,000m. in US financial and military assistance distributed to the USA's *mujahidin* militant proxies, in order to achieve its regional political objectives. This impacted both on the host areas and on the country of origin, to the extent that many refugee-affected areas became indivisible from combatants' camps, a classic instance of the so-called 'refugee warrior' syndrome, in which humanitarian assistance became implicated in military objectives. The politics of aid were also clearly apparent in the disparity between international aid and assistance given to refugees in Iran when compared with the situation in Pakistan.

After the withdrawal of the USSR from Afghanistan (completed in February 1989), the Najibullah regime that remained collapsed in 1992 and the return of 900,000 refugees was assisted by UNHCR—the largest and swiftest repatriation scheme it had hitherto organized. Much of the reason for the rapidity of repatriation was pressure from the host state and a lack of donor funding, political and strategic interests in the area having receded. Inducements for the refugees themselves came in the form of the encashment of refugee ration cards, which were removed altogether in 1995. However, the dynamics that had resulted in the *mujahidin* victory in Afghanistan also sowed the seeds of further rounds of conflict and displacement, as civil war between the diverse *mujahidin* factions erupted. The civil war itself emerged from the failure to secure a political alliance among the *mujahidin* forces, particularly between northern political leaders, such as the Tajik commander Ahmad Shah Masoud, and the Pashtun forces which had traditionally dominated Afghanistan's political centre, forces that the Pakistani State was eager to restore to power in order to secure a friendly ally in the buffer state of Afghanistan. It was thus with the backing of the Pakistani State and Islamist elements in Pakistani society that the Taliban rose to power, out of a movement built upon refugees socialized into Islamic extremism at the Saudi and Pashtun-dominated refugee *madrassas* (mosque schools) in Pakistan. With this support, the Taliban first secured control of their base in Qandahar and of southern and western Afghanistan as a whole and, by 1998, they had finally captured the Northern Alliance capital of Mazar-i-Sharif.

Taliban control, based on a mixture of rigid Islamic ideology and a puritanical reinvention of the social code of Pashtunwali, which stresses the importance of tribal honour and strict religious observance, also placed onerous restrictions on female agency *vis-à-vis* education, employment and health care through the obligatory observance of purdah. Taliban rule instigated new waves of displacement as many of Kabul's educated strata, including teachers, government officials and health workers fled to Pakistan. At the same time, many of the minorities in the north also fled, fearing the spectre of Taliban control and Pashtun dominance, as well as the effects of ongoing conflict between the Iranian- and US-funded Northern Alliance and the Taliban. For instance, in 2000 alone an estimated 172,000 Afghan refugees were believed to have entered Pakistan. Taliban control also rendered the dynamics of emergency, development and refugee aid all the more complex, as NGOs and international NGOs struggled to work within the gender-restrictive and anti-Western Taliban-dominated context. The struggle was considerably exacerbated by the imposition of UN sanctions against the Taliban regime in 1999 and again in December 2000, actions of which many development and aid practitioners disapproved because of the deleterious impact that they had upon their relations with the Taliban and, consequently, their ability to distribute aid.

At the same time, aid and assistance to refugees during 1999–2001 were also hindered by Pakistan's decision intermittently to close its borders to refugees and to seek the large-scale repatriation of both 'new' refugees and of 'long-stay' refugee communities dating back to the Cold War period. Between March and September 2002 more than 1.5m. refugees were repatriated from Afghanistan and 220,000 from Iran. The repatriation programme was again rapid, and some critics have argued that it placed a heavy burden on limited reconstruction resources against a background of ongoing conflict, further contributing to the overall figure of 1m. IDPs in Afghanistan at this time.

None the less, the pressure for further refugee returns also led, in March 2003, to a tripartite agreement being signed between Afghanistan, Pakistan and UNHCR regarding the return of long-stay exiled populations. As part of this agreement, a three-year plan was drawn up for the 'gradual and sustainable' repatriation of the remaining Afghan refugees in Pakistan. By 2005, however, the number of Afghan refugees still residing in Pakistan was estimated to total around 3m. according to the results of a census conducted in that year. The end of Pakistan's hospitality and its willingness to close borders at times of vulnerability for the displaced are both illustrative of the country's ad hoc and politically motivated attitude towards refugee rights, as well as a reflection of the shifting geo-political strategy of the dominant donor states, in which Afghan refugees were no longer viewed as the valuable political resource they had once been. Following the withdrawal of aid, the welcome for Afghan refugees in Pakistan was no longer forthcoming and the policy increasingly shifted towards a push for repatriation on a mass scale.

Since the overthrow of the Taliban by a US-led coalition in 2001, and the election of the President, Hamid Karzai, in October 2004 and the legislature in September 2005, a modicum of relative stability in Afghanistan has allowed for the aforementioned return and resettlement of some 5.5m refugees from both Iran and Pakistan. In addition, around 950,000 IDPs have returned to their homes—some 500,000 with UNHCR assistance and a further 450,000 of their own accord. During the period between October 2006 and February 2007 the Pakistan Government and UNHCR, with funding from the European Commission, the USA and the United Kingdom, engaged in a 15-week biometric registration exercise, providing Afghan refugees and migrants in Pakistan with Proof of Registration cards (PoRs), which recognized them as Afghan refugees temporarily resident in Pakistan and which were valid until December 2009. During the process 2,153,000 Afghans were registered, of whom 976,605 were in official refugee settlements. It was also confirmed that the majority of the Afghan population in Pakistan were resident in the NWFP (64%) and in Balochistan (21%). The registration process was both an attempt to draw up a statistical profile of the Afghan population in Pakistan and, in so doing, to demarcate between the previous blurring of distinctions regarding Pakistan and Afghanistan citizens and refugees and 'economic migrants', and also an attempt to facilitate the implementation of future return and repatriation programmes. While UNHCR has been keen to insist that all returns must be effected 'voluntarily and in safety and dignity' and that return and temporary residence must be part of a two-pronged approach to assisting Afghan refugees, it is clear from the extensive schedule for the closure of camps in 2007, together with the financial inducements of assisted return, that the durable solution for the refugees is repatriation (although this was expected, in turn, to lead to another cycle of internal displacement owing to renewed conflict within Afghanistan).

Consequently, it is clear that obstacles to such returns remain. Problems of security and failures of governmental legitimacy continue to afflict the state and much of rural Afghanistan remains at the mercy of powerful regional leaders and warlords. The Taliban are engaged in an ongoing insurgency, which has intensified since the legislative elections in the latter half of 2005 and which spread in mid-2008 beyond the Helmand, Qandahar and Uruzgan provinces of southern Afghanistan, which had been the chief sites of conflict between

NATO troops and the resurgent Taliban in 2006–07, to areas in the immediate south-west vicinity of Kabul such as Wardak province, igniting fears that the recapture of the capital by the Taliban insurgents was not inconceivable. These conflicts have inevitably resulted in renewed and expanding cycles of displacement. For instance, in late 2006 around 90,000 people were internally displaced in the provinces of Helmand, Qandahar and Uruzgan, adding to the 115,000 already resident in IDP camps in the three provinces (the actual number of IDPs in the country as a whole at this time was unclear). It is also evident that the dynamics of conflict have not been purely internal but have been affected by the porous boundary between Pakistan and Afghanistan. The Pashtun/Taliban nexus has been demonstrated by ongoing cycles of conflict and displacement in South, and to a lesser extent, North Waziristan, where the Pakistan Government, under pressure from the US Administration, has engaged in battles with pro-Taliban militants leading to significant displacement. Many commentators have attributed the gradual resurgence of Taliban-led resistance to the weak legitimacy of an Afghan Government that is highly dependent on both international aid and foreign security forces, combined with the slow rate of reconstruction and reintegration consequent upon limited aid resources. In other words, the Taliban are successfully spearheading a now globally expanding resistance to what was once a hegemonic but now flagging combination of the 'war on terror' and the 'liberal peace'.

Whatever the dynamics of renewed conflict, the current highly precarious situation in Afghanistan poses major concerns for ongoing repatriation efforts from either Iran or Pakistan despite the pressure applied by both states to that effect in the current context. Indeed, the unstable situation in Afghanistan led to a major rethink on the part of the UNHCR in 2008 regarding the possibility of further repatriations taking place in a context of heightened insecurity, conflict, internal displacement and logistical difficulties vis-à-vis the provision of aid and efforts for integration. In addition, the already existing problems of landlessness, the after-effects of recent droughts in a country dependent on foreign aid and a fragile agricultural economy subject to restrictions on poppy production have all imposed limits on the absorptive and reconstructive capacity of the return programme in Afghanistan. Moreover, it has been voiced by UNHCR that the repatriation of those refugees with the necessary ties to Afghanistan to facilitate return has already taken place and that any further pressure on the part of Pakistan and Iran to effect further returns will endanger the principle of 'voluntary return' for populations that have few connections to Afghanistan and even less desire to return to a place that has never really been 'home'. As a result, it remains to be seen how soon the significant numbers of both IDPs and refugees estimated to remain within and without Afghanistan will be resettled, or if resumed hostilities in Afghanistan will create renewed cycles of conflict-induced displacement related to the difficulties of regime change and state formation in an increasingly internationalized context. The internationalized merger of security on the one hand and development and humanitarianism on the other has not altered the past tendencies for insurrection but has itself contributed to the delegitimizing of the new Afghan regime, to renewed Taliban insurgency and, increasingly, to the killing of NGO staff, who since 2006 have been more and more frequently targeted in the course of their humanitarian activities because of their association with Western occupation.

### Movements for Autonomy, Nationalist Conflict, Ethnic Violence and Displacement

In many ways separatist conflict has been a mainstay of South Asian conflict-related displacement. Since independence was achieved for South Asian states there have been movements for secession, autonomy or self-determination for Bangladesh, for Tamils in Sri Lanka, for Balochis in Pakistan, Sikhs in the Punjab, Muslim groups in Kashmir, amongst numerous tribal groups in north-east India and Bangladesh, and, most recently, for the Madhesi population in the Terai region of Nepal. Unlike the revolutionary dynamics outlined in the previous section, separatist movements, often constructed around ethno-nationalist identity, seek to challenge the geopolitical contours and framework of the post-colonial state. Accordingly, such movements frequently emerge as a centrifugal reaction to pre-existing ethno-nationalist domination, revealing the fragility of 'the national order of things' in a plural environment such as South Asia and in an increasingly mobile and globalizing world. However, paradoxically, such movements have also served to reinforce the 'national order' as they battle for a 'homeland' state, yet frequently set in motion new fissures and fragmentary dynamics if and when they gain autonomy and self-determination. It is also notable that diaspora, refugeehood and exile often play a major role in funding and sustaining such movements. So, while exile frequently serves as a dynamic behind many conflicts, including those in Afghanistan (see above), in separatist conflicts, unlike in Afghanistan, the role of long-distance transnationalist national identification amongst the diaspora has frequently played a major role in the provision of funding and ideological support. It did so in the now diminished Khalistan Sikh nationalist movement of the 1980s and 1990s, in Kashmiri separatism and continues to do so in the case of LTTE-led Tamil nationalism in Sri Lanka, an example to be explored in further detail, owing to the powerful relationship between separatist conflict and displacement evident in this case.

Since July 1983, when riots and pogroms against the Tamil minorities erupted, leading to the killing of 2,000–3,000 Tamils and the immediate displacement of between 100,000 and 200,000 people, Sri Lanka has been beset by a violent civil war between the Sinhala-dominated Government and Tamil nationalist militant groups, who have been fighting for a separate Tamil homeland (*Eelam* or *Eezham*) for the Tamil minority in the northern and eastern areas of the country. Although the conflict is most readily described as an 'ethnic' conflict, it is also clear that it has its roots in the colonial legacy of an overly centralized State in a polity that has been subject to the arithmetical dominance of Sinhala majoritarianism. It is in this context that Tamil nationalism has been described as a predominantly minoritarian 'reactive' nationalism, which shifted politically from peacefully articulating demands for autonomous governance and representation within a federal Sri Lanka until the 1970s to the growth of a separatist claim over the north-east of the island. The Vaddukoddai Resolution of 1976 demanded self-determination for the Tamil-speaking people owing to the mounting Sinhalization of the Sri Lankan State, in which economic and political forms of discrimination increasingly interlocked to produce discriminatory dynamics which disadvantaged the Tamil community in terms of equitable access to political, socio-cultural and economic resources and rights in the form of, for example, citizenship, development, freedom of movement, education, employment and language. Whilst, for the most part, the Muslim minority (numbering around 8% of the total population), at least one-third of which reside in the north-east of the country and of which the majority are Tamil-speaking, have resisted allying themselves with the Tamil nationalist cause and have instead established Muslim parties that have opted to co-operate with the Sinhala-dominated mainstream parties, these political actors have also begun to articulate the right to autonomy for Muslim communities. With regard to the development and reproduction of both Tamil and Muslim political movements, it should also be noted that 24 years of ongoing conflict have left stark developmental disparities between the north-east of Sri Lanka and the south, in a country with a highly Colombo-centric economy that has disproportionately benefited the south-western littoral of the island.

The conflict between the Government of Sri Lanka and the LTTE has undergone a series of phases varying in intensity, location and in the form of conflict, shifting from more conventional forms of territorial warfare in which the Sri Lankan army and Tamil separatists have fought for possession of geographical areas (e.g. Jaffna or the Eastern Province), to the de facto division between government-held areas and rebel-held 'uncleared' areas. The Tamil separatists have also engaged in guerrilla and terrorist tactics, which have varied from assaults and ambushes on security-force objectives and personnel, to the targeting of civilian populations and commercial properties (e.g. attacks on buses, trains, Colombo hotels, banks and, in July 2001, on Katunayake Airport) and the assassination of both government politicians and political rivals by guerrillas and suicide bombers.

In this process, the LTTE have assumed a potent political prominence and influence in both Sri Lanka, especially in the north-east, and globally through the Tamil diaspora, a significant proportion of which is composed of past waves of refugees, who have sought exile in Canada, Europe, India, the USA and Australia. In 2001 UNHCR estimated the total number of internationally displaced Tamils to be 817,000 (the majority holding refugee or asylum-related status), while the estimate for those internally displaced in Sri Lanka due to the conflict (as opposed to the impact of the Indian Ocean tsunami of December 2004) was 455,000 as of May 2008, the majority being Tamils and Muslims. Of this total, 182,000 of the IDPs had recently been displaced in the course of renewed hostilities in 2006–07, while 272,000 had suffered long-term displacement dating back to pre-2002. Between May and August 2008, as the Government sought to recapture territory in the Vanni region and to eradicate the LTTE strongholds in Mannar, Killinochchi, and Mullaitivu, this led to further displacement, with up to 75,000 people moving into the LTTE-held areas of Killinochchi to escape the advance of government troops.

Accordingly, the cycles of conflict have led to refugee flows and internal displacement on a large scale, as civilians seek to escape zones of conflict, a process which has led to renewed identification with Tamil nationalism both locally and transnationally. A point that should also be noted, but one that is often neglected in research, is that, although the majority of the displaced are Tamils, a significant number of Muslims have also suffered from displacement in the north and east of the country owing both to the generalized violence of the conflict but also to deliberate targeting by the LTTE and, more recently, by state security forces and allied paramilitary groups such as the Tamil Makkal Viduthalai Pulikal (TMVP). For example, in 1990 it was reported that the LTTE forcibly expelled an estimated 75,000 Muslims from the districts of Jaffna and Mannar to the Vavuniya, Anuradhapura and Puttalam districts, despite the fact that prior to this Muslim-Tamil relations had been accommodating and interdependent. In 2007 some 65,000 'northern' Muslims continued to reside in camps, huts and more permanent structures in the Puttalam district, many of whom still wished to return to homes that had been occupied by formerly displaced Tamils in the north. Muslims have also suffered as a consequence of the escalating conflict in the east where they form a significant demographic presence. Their problems have arisen not only from the renewed military activity by government troops, but also from the expropriation of their land and property by Tamil militants, particularly the TMVP (see below), who have turned areas of Batticaloa, Trincomalee and Amaparai into their local power bases. In addition, there have been allegations of Sinhalese encroachment on and colonization of Muslim property sponsored by certain elements of the business sector and government officials.This has led to a re-emergence of claims that the current regime is intent on renewing colonization of eastern areas, a tactic that has already led to major demographic changes, with Sinhala settlements being vigorously pursued as part of government development strategy from independence until the 1980s.

The conflict has also experienced shifting geo-political, international and regional dynamics, which have, at times, interlocked with refugee cycles. For instance, after 1983, when Tamils began leaving the island in their thousands, 125,000 refugees were being supported in South India by the Congress-led federal Government of India, the state government of Tamil Nadu and its two leading political parties, the Dravida Munnetra Kazhagam (DMK) and the All-India Anna Dravida Munnetra Kazhagam (AIADMK). This produced similar but more regionalized 'refugee warrior' dynamics to that noted in the case of Afghanistan, as the Research and Analysis Wing (the Indian intelligence agency), the Indian Government and the Chief Minister of Tamil Nadu all provided training and weaponry, as well as humanitarian assistance, to the refugee community, leading to the emergence of a highly effective array of armed Tamil militant groups (including the LTTE). It has been argued that the Indian Government's interest in maintaining some control and influence over the militant operations mainly stemmed from its desire to ward off the perceived threat of US intervention in the region and to contain the threat of separatism spreading to Tamil Nadu. This led to India's disastrous direct intervention after the signing of the 1987 Indo-Lanka Accord, with the installation of the Indian Peace-Keeping Force on the island, a policy that failed, resulting in LTTE–Indian conflict (with Sri Lankan President Ranasinghe Premadasa supporting the LTTE), the ending of Indian support to the militants and, in 1991, the assassination of Indian Prime Minister Rajiv Gandhi by a Tamil suicide bomber. However, by that time the nexus between exile and Tamil nationalism had been firmly consolidated and the LTTE had developed a sophisticated diaspora-based transnational counter-state organization of truly global dimensions.

After a period of military stalemate had developed between the Sri Lankan armed forces and the LTTE in the north, a cease-fire agreement (CFA) between the LTTE and the Government was signed in February 2002, resulting in a significant reduction in large-scale conflict and the commencement of a co-ordinated programme leading to the return of 385,400 IDPs between 2002 and 2005 and of several thousand refugees from India. Nevertheless, significant obstacles to the 'normalization' of life in the north-east persisted, even during the more peaceful years of the CFA. A major concern was security, particularly the frequent violations of the CFA (4,181 by the end of April 2007), the vast majority of which (3,830) were attributable to the LTTE. Although the CFA brought the benefit of peace to vast swathes of the civilian populace in Sri Lanka between 2002 and 2005, low-intensity conflict, recruitment, abductions of adults and children as well as harassment, beatings and political killings were still regular occurrences in the north and east. Indeed, it is widely accepted that the duration of the CFA was used by the LTTE for the consolidation of military and political control and infiltration, including increasing drives for child and adult recruitment and the elimination of political rivals. At the same time, the Sri Lankan Government used the 'no-peace-no-war' context of the CFA years not as an opportunity for political reform of the centralized State but rather as an opportunity for rearming the military and for bringing international and regional donors and actors together into an international security net or 'peace trap, through which to bring the LTTE to heel via the use of European, Australian, Canadian and US bans on the organization and the 'freezing' of LTTE assets. The peace process, therefore, produced little in the way of tangible progress on the reform of the state but instead became a method of defeating the LTTE through other means. Indeed, government forces became inextricably involved in the fomenting of a split between the eastern faction of the LTTE, now known as the TMVP, which was headed by Colonel 'Karuna' Amman (also known as Vinayagamoorthi Muralitharan) and 'Pillaiyan' (Sivanesathurai Chandrakanthan), and the main body of the LTTE (the Vanni—'North'—faction led by Velupillai Prabhakaran) in March 2004. Both this split within the LTTE, the failures of the peace process and the political resurgence of Sinhala nationalism, in the form of an alliance between the United People's Freedom Alliance (UPFA), headed by the current President, Mahinda Rajapakse, and the Sinhala nationalist Janatha Vimukthi Peramuna and the Jathika Hela Urumaya, all combined to bring about the electoral victory and consolidation of a political regime that was hostile to any kind of devolutionary solution to the ethnic conflict. This uncompromising attitude signalled a further deterioration in the peace process and a return to high-intensity conflict centring on a government strategy of eradicating the LTTE from firstly the Eastern Province between 2006 and August 2007 and currently from the North where its quasi-state structures are located. In this return to a military solution the Government's security forces have forged a potent alliance with the TMVP, a nexus that has been accompanied by a breakdown in the rule of law, the collapse or undermining of constitutional safeguards for human rights, and mounting human rights abuses, abductions and extrajudicial killings committed predominantly against Sri Lanka's minority Tamil and Muslim communities not only in the conflict-affected areas of the north-east but also in the south, including the capital, Colombo.

The worsening situation in the north-east has also resulted in gradual, growing waves of refugees and IDPs from that area, with 21,000 refugees reported to have crossed the Palk Straits to India between January 2006 and May 2008, joining the 72,000 refugees already resident in camps in Tamil Nadu and the 22,000 registered refugees living outside the camps. In addition, an estimated 223,000 people were internally displaced owing to the conflict in the north-east between April 2006 and March 2007 alone. During January–February 2007 the military assault by government troops on Vaharai on the east coast also led to the displacement of at least 20,000 people, and in February–March approximately 40,000 civilians fled rebel areas in the eastern district of Batticaloa to escape a fresh government offensive against LTTE strongholds in the Thoppigala area. Between September 2006 and June 2007 official attempts to impose more rapid cycles of return upon those displaced by conflict in areas of the east retaken by the Sri Lankan military caused intermittent tensions between the Government and the displaced population and advocates of IDP rights, with the latter accusing the Government of failing adequately to respect the Guiding Principles on Internal Displacement by forcibly returning and resettling the internally displaced or preventing their return through the declaration of high security zones (highlighting, once again, the widespread concern that the attitude of a number of South Asian states towards those suffering displacement lacks sufficient focus on rights). It was also asserted that the TMVP was being given *carte blanche* for access to IDP camps and to the screening of returnees.

Nevertheless, by June 2007 the Government was engaged in the large-scale resettlement of IDPs in the east under what were generally accepted to be more satisfactory conditions by the majority of humanitarian organizations, despite continuing restrictions on humanitarian access. However, the Government came under renewed criticism in June for expelling and deporting 376 Tamils from lodging houses and hostels in Colombo, citing security fears. This act prompted immediate world-wide condemnation for its violation of the most basic tenets of human rights law and was subsequently reversed. None the less, such actions are symptomatic of the general breakdown in the rule of law and discrimination against the minority community has remained consistently characteristic of the current Rajapakse regime.

After the 'liberation' of the Eastern Province in August 2007, the Government sought to consolidate political control there through local and provincial elections held in 2008, in which the UPFA and the TMVP formed a potent alliance leading to the appointment of Pillaiyan as Chief Minister of the province. Although this was held up by the Government as a sign of its commitment to representative democracy and of its intention to free the east of conflict dynamics through development, the fact that the TMVP has been implicated in a number of human rights abuses, including extrajudicial killings, abductions, the expropriation of land from Muslim villagers and electoral intimidation and vote-rigging does not bode well for the prospects of conflict dynamics and therefore future cycles of displacement in the Eastern Province.

These conflict-displacement dynamics have, since the end of 2007, shifted to the Northern region where government military advances and aerial and artillery bombardment of areas in Mannar, Kilinochchi and Mullaitivu have resulted in large-scale displacement. It was estimated that up to 75,000 people were newly displaced by conflict in these areas between May and August 2008 alone. Many of the IDPs chose to flee to LTTE-held areas in the Killinochchi District and therefore moved into areas that were under attack by the Sri Lankan military in the course of their advance on the LTTE stronghold of Killinochchi Town. Consequently, the displaced were vulnerable to renewed exposure to bombardment and to repeat cycles of displacement, with allegations being made that both the Government and the LTTE were restricting their movement out of the conflict zone owing to fears of LTTE infiltration on the part of the Government and claims that the LTTE were using those displaced as a 'human shield' to slow the advance of the military on Killinochchi Town. What is clear, however, is that problems of humanitarian access and a lack of supplies have turned the situation into a humanitarian catastrophe for the thousands of families caught in the crossfire.

Consequently, the period 2006–08 witnessed a serious reversal of the relative stability provided by the CFA between 2002 and 2005, as new waves of internal displacement and refugee exile from the north and east of the island occurred, signifying an escalation in the violence and a return to the conflict-displacement dynamics that had taken place prior to the imposition of the CFA. Whilst 170,000 IDPs returned between August 2006 and throughout 2007 and 2008 as the Government secured control of eastern areas, the shifting of the scenario of war resulted in renewed dynamics of displacement in the North. It remains to be seen whether a military solution, in the absence of significant political state reform, will prove secure enough to prevent renewed cycles of displacement in the near future. As in so many conflict-induced displacement scenarios, the case of Tamil separatist nationalism in Sri Lanka has demonstrated a potent nexus between conflict and displacement in a double sense. Conflict has led to substantial forced migration flows both of IDPs within the island and of refugees intermingled with 'economic migrants' abroad, including substantial numbers to destinations in the developing world. This has led to the development of both regional and long-distance diaspora-related nationalist identification and organization, as well as local populations of the displaced within the island itself, who form a well of discontent feeding into LTTE recruitment channels. In that sense, the experience of displacement recycles the conflict. In the long term, it is extremely doubtful if this nexus will be broken unless some means of addressing the framework of the overly centralized State inherited from colonial rule can be found.

While the case of Tamil separatism in Sri Lanka has been perceived by some commentators as an example of the struggles of an 'advanced group from a backward region', because of a long history of the disproportionate success of Tamils in educational and employment terms, Balochis in Pakistan have suffered in terms of the lack of social, economic and human development available to them within a Punjabi-élite dominated State. As a result, Balochistan is one of the most socially and economically impoverished provinces in Pakistan, despite possessing almost 20% of the country's mineral and energy resources (including gas, oil, coal and valuable metal deposits) and having both military and commercial strategic importance because of the location of the two ports of Gwadar and Ormara on the Balochistan coast. The Balochis, who constitute 55% of the provincial population whilst Pashtuns make up 29%, are therefore marginalized from the developmental resources of their own region. The province has the lowest female literacy rate in Pakistan (16%), high maternal mortality rates (600 in every 100,000) and the majority of the population remains dependent on rural agriculture.

The Balochs have long resisted the encroachment of the Punjabi élite and the centralized State, and conflicts centred upon autonomy for Balochistan surfaced in 1948, 1958 and, more aggressively, from 1973–77, when the Baloch People's Liberation Front (BPLF), led by Sher Mohammed Marri, led an insurrection of 55,000 guerrillas against 70,000 Pakistan army troops. This was triggered by Pakistan's deployment of troops in the region after attempts by the National Awami Party to oust Punjabi, Pathan and Sindhi bureaucrats had met with resistance. This led to the overwhelming defeat of the Balochs and the imprisonment, exile or death of the Baloch nationalist leadership. The insurrection also resulted in the internal displacement of 250,000 Balochs, the exile of 4,700 Balochs in Afghanistan, including many of the nationalist leadership, the exile of 5,000 other cadres in the Gulf states and the imprisonment of 30,000 suspected insurgents.

While the Zia-ul-Haq regime increased expenditure on infrastructural development in Balochistan after the insurrection, Baloch nationalists themselves have claimed that development was not focused upon their needs but was directed towards communications, transport and security; in other words, an intensification of the Punjabi colonization of Balochistan. As a result, although the State suppressed the nationalist movement, the seeds of its re-emergence remained and have been exacerbated by the intensification of extraction of resources by the State and Pakistan's élites without addressing the ongoing marginalization of the Balochi tribes, who receive a meagre return on valuable gas resources in the form of royalties from the State. Since 2005 there has been a marked revival of the insurgency, led predominantly but not exclusively by the Bugti, Marri and Mengal tribes, resulting in widespread sabotage of gas pipelines, gas fields, electrical and railway infrastructure, and rocket and land-mine attacks against an enlarged Pakistan military presence intended to combat the insurrection—in other words, attacks against the material and symbolic infrastructure of colonization. There are claims that internecine fighting between tribal groups has also impacted upon the conflict, notably within the Bugti tribe, elements of which the federal Government is using to divide the Baloch nationalist camp. In early to mid-2006 this internal conflict resulted in thousands of people being internally displaced, particularly around the town of Dera Bugti (where the largest gas fields in Pakistan are located), with reports in April suggesting that 90% of the populace in that area had fled their homes. The violence further escalated in mid-2006 with the death of the rebel leader Akbar Khan Bugti; a series of riots erupted in the wake of his killing at the hands of government troops. Between 2007 and 2008, owing to the potency of the counter-insurgency and the killing and disappearances of tribal leaders and rebel cadres, including Nawabzada Balach Marri, the head of the Balochistan Liberation Army (BLA), the insurgency has declined in ferocity, although guerrilla strikes against commercial, government and military infrastructure continue to occur on a routine basis, indicating that the insurrection is far from over and is still fuelled by the same deprivations that first sparked the conflict.

As assistance has been lacklustre to say the least, largely owing to the reluctance of the State to intervene or to allow humanitarian access, the displaced in Balochistan have suffered intense hardships, including a lack of adequate water, shelter, food and sanitation. These problems of humanitarian access and response have also led to difficulties in assessing the numbers of those displaced. In May 2007 President Pervez Musharaff claimed that only 25,000 IDPs remained with the vast majority having returned home, whilst various NGOs and press sources claimed that anywhere between 50,000 and 200,000 people were estimated to be still seeking assistance in the region and in other provinces such as Sindh and Punjab.

Thus, although Balochi nationalists have not shared the long history of transnationalist linkages that have sustained the dynamics of the ongoing conflict between the LTTE and the Government in Sri Lanka, it is, none the less, clear that a major insurgency, fuelled by the marginalization of the Balochis, has led to displacement dynamics that have spread beyond the tribal areas of the province. However, it remains to be seen whether the nationalist movement can overcome the tribal fissures that have also served to preclude its emergence as a sustained guerrilla force. Nevertheless, at mid-2008 it represented the most potent source for displacement within Pakistan, with the exception of the NWFP where conflicts between government troops and the pro-Taliban insurgent movements led to the displacement of hundreds of thousands of people in 2007–08. The first of these insurrections was led by a movement called Tehrik Nifhaz-e-Sheriat-e-Muhammadi (TNSM) or the Movement for the Enforcement of Shari'a Law, which sought the establishment of an Islamic state and occupied more than 60 towns and villages in the Swat Valley, leading to the temporary displacement of 500,000–900,000 people, the majority of whom returned home after counter-insurgency operations banished the rebels to the hills. In mid-2008, however, various other pro-Taliban militants continued to wage insurgency against the Pakistan Government in the NWFP and in the Federally Administered Tribal Areas (FATA), leading to the renewed displacement of hundreds of thousands of people, highlighting the porous nature of Pakistan's border with Afghanistan and the extent to which the same dynamics that have afflicted centre-periphery, rural-urban and mass-élite relations in Afghanistan are also at work in areas of Pakistan that have served as the strongholds of Taliban recruitment and militancy.

Although levels of displacement within Pakistani-administered Kashmir have fallen dramatically since a November 2003 cease-fire, the situation in Indian-administered Jammu and Kashmir, resulting from militant Kashmiri separatists seeking either a separate state or accession to Pakistan, as well as the militarization of the area by Indian security forces, has continued to fuel the conflict dynamics that have plagued the subcontinent since 1947, leaving the legacy of Partition frozen in time. While there has been some reduction in the scale of the conflict, due to the diplomatic pledges undertaken by both Pakistan and India, which have lessened the magnitude of the cycles of displacement that have occurred during the Indo-Pakistani conflict in the region—including the 2003 Kargil episode, when 60,000 to 100,000 people were displaced—this *rapprochement* has not eradicated attacks launched against the Indian military and the Hindu Pandit community in the state. For example, in May 2006 Islamist militants massacred 35 civilians in two incidents in Indian-controlled Jammu and Kashmir. These attacks have prevented the implementation of any durable solution for India's largest group of IDPs, the 300,000 Hindu Kashmiri Pandits who have fled the area since 1989. Indeed, the context is such that 160 of the 700 Pandit families that remained in the area as of 2004 have since fled because of ongoing threats and violence, despite attempts to implement a return programme for exiled Pandits. The conflict dynamics deteriorated in 2008 after massive protests and riots demanding Kashmiri independence from India were sparked by a local government decision to erect prefabricated houses upon a 99-acre site that serves Hindu pilgrims to the Himalayan shrine of Amarnath. The revoking of this decision also led to massive counter-demonstrations and violence by Hindus in Jammu. That these events have occurred in the context of political turmoil in Pakistan, the resignation of Musharraf and recent exchanges of fire between the Pakistan and Indian military across the Line of Control does not bode well for a conflict that had subsided in recent years as Pakistan and India sought to overcome the anatagonisms that had resulted in the Kargil confrontation in 1999. Yet the current situation in Kashmir is also indicative of the way in which simmering and unresolved tensions can be reignited by individual events and the extent to which the troubled area remains a thorn in the side of regional South Asian relations.

Elsewhere in India, and also in Bangladesh, there are also other sizeable minority communities displaced as a result of violence at the hands of both Hindu nationalists and extremist Islamists, respectively. In India there were outbreaks of communal violence in Gujarat in February 2002, after the state's Muslim population became the target of reprisals for an attack on a train carrying Hindu nationalists returning from the disputed religious site at Ayodhya. This led to a spate of frenzied violence and there have been allegations that the former ruling Bharatiya Janata Party (BJP) was involved in instigating the killing sprees, in looting and in ensuring the silent and inactive acquiescence of the police. The violence, which continued sporadically until early 2003, led to the killing of 2,000 and the wounding of at least 2,500 predominantly Muslim victims and the displacement of a further 100,000, who had to contend with both the inadequate assistance provided by the Gujarat state government and India's refusal to allow international assistance. In early 2007 it was reported that 4,182 families (or 21,547 persons) remained displaced in 72 colonies and 19 scattered clusters and houses in the state of Gujarat as a result of the conflict and that many of those formerly displaced had been forcibly urbanized, partly as a result of the failure of the Government to extend its assistance beyond relief to reparation, rehabilitation and reintegration. Only in May 2008 did the Indian Government finally announce its intention to grant compensation to those families who had suffered death, injury and property loss.

Meanwhile, in Bangladesh mounting violence occurred against the country's religious minority groups, particularly Hindus, who faced increasing human rights abuses following the election in 2001 of the Bangladesh National Party (BNP) as part of a coalition including the Jamaat-i-Islami and the Islami Oikya Jote, two Islamist parties. Post-election violence led to the displacement of up to 200,000 Hindus, either internally or to India. Bangladeshi Hindus have long experienced forms of discrimination, typified by the passing of the pre-Independence Enemy Property Act of 1965 and the post-Independence

Vested Property Act of 1974, which enabled the State to seize the assets and property of those considered to be an 'enemy of the state', but which was basically used as a means of acquiring land owned by minorities. Although the Act was repealed in 2001 by the Awami League Government, rather than decreasing, the appropriation of land (held by owners who were either still resident or already exiled) by the ruling élite accelerated in the aftermath of the BNP victory in late 2001. These seizures of land were accompanied by mounting violence against minorities in the form of killings, assaults, the destruction of religious sites, abductions, torture and rape. Although the military caretaker Government that assumed power in January 2007 pledged to eradicate corruption, no steps were taken to implement the 2001 reversal of these Property Acts, and, furthermore, it has been claimed that the new regime has extended land-grabbing to tribal areas.

In this respect, both India and Bangladesh have produced cycles of violence and displacement due to ongoing conflicts in tribal areas. In the Indian context there have been a series of low-intensity conflicts in almost every north-eastern state: in Arunachal Pradesh, Assam, Manipur, Meghalaya, Mizoram, Nagaland, Sikkim and Tripura inter-tribal, counter-state and tribal versus non-tribal violence have continued to lead to the displacement of tens of thousands of people. Much of this conflict relates to the lingering impact of tribal autonomist movements, as well as new fissures and conflicts created in the aftermath of the establishment of these new north-eastern states, especially between fresh stratifications of citizenship and denizenship formed by these new entities, demonstrating that while federal solutions can contain or appease existing social antagonisms, these political solutions will also create new forms of conflict and displacement.

Similar dynamics are also evident in the Chittagong Hill Tracts of Bangladesh, where the tensions between tribal and non-tribal groups have been exacerbated by state-sponsored colonization of these areas by landless Bengalis. As a result, since independence in 1971, conflict and tensions, particularly over land rights and the threat to tribal identity, led to the exile of 65,000 refugees in the Indian state of Tripura and the internal displacement of even greater numbers. The cycles of exile and displacement across the borders between India and Bangladesh also mean that the conflicts in tribal areas of each country impact upon one another. In Bangladesh, a peace accord between the state and the Jumma Refugee Welfare Association (JRWA), representing refugees drawn from the 13 Chittagong Hill Tract tribes, was signed in 1997, leading to the repatriation of the refugees. However, many of these refugees have now joined the multitudes of IDPs within Bangladesh's border areas, so that as of 2000 there were 128,364 IDPs in the Chittagong Hill Tracts. Efforts to resolve the IDP problem have been hampered by Jumma hostility to the inclusion of non-tribal Bengalis within the enumeration of IDPs in the area and within the task force appointed to resolve displacement and to implement autonomy for the area through a regional council. It therefore remains to be seen whether these problems and the central issue of land rights can be resolved. Without this and the political support of a reluctant Bangladeshi Government, as well as much-needed co-ordination between international actors, donors and the State, it remains to be seen whether the US $50m. UN Development Programme (UNDP) project for the area can contribute to solving a problem which has thus far only been addressed in a very ad hoc manner. Since the imposition of the state of emergency and military-backed caretaker rule in January 2007, however, the army and police forces have engaged in widespread human rights abuses against Jumma activists and civil society organizations as well as forcibly evicting indigenous people from their land. The army is also heavily involved in colonization projects, including the recent settlement of Bengalis in the Sajek area of the Chittagong Hill Tracts. These settlements have resulted in conflict between colonists and the tribal inhabitants, with claims that the army has also been involved in attacks on Jumma settlements. The most recent example of these abuses occurred in April 2008 when Bengali settlers, with the support of the Bangladesh Army, attacked and razed seven Jumma villages. These actions have exacerbated the scale of displacement and have undermined the potential for developing a durable solution to the sufferings experienced by the displaced, whether tribal or non-tribal.

To conclude, although environmental and development-induced displacement form a more quantitatively significant share of the total numbers of those displaced in South Asia (see below), it is clear that the challenges represented by revolutionary, secessionist or autonomist movements remain a far greater threat to the frameworks, contours and structures of dominance of South Asian states, as well as to social conflicts between identities in the region. Thus, the significance of conflict-induced displacement cannot be denied. It is also clear that the trauma and memory of displacement, as well as the actuality of exile and displacement for succeeding generations of forced migrants and refugees, frequently fuels further cycles of violence. In this sense, it would be true to say that, while much of the conflict and displacement reveals the difficulties of state-building and the impossibility of nation-building in such a plural world as South Asia, it is also clear that the vast number of minority-based movements within South Asia, which are the mainstay of displaced communities, seldom have any other recourse but to work inside the frameworks that proliferate within this 'national order'. Yet, having said this, we should also be aware that the divide between development-induced displacement and, for instance, the displacement caused by secessionist or ethno-nationalist conflict is not as wide as might initially appear. Almost all of the latter conflicts are a reaction to the way in which states have introduced an ethnic, majoritarian or hegemonic logic into, for example, settlement or infrastructural development projects in terms of the demographic changes that ensue and/or the raw materials that are developed within any region or the resources that are made available to given groups. In this sense the logical borders established between development-induced displacement and ethno-nationalist conflict immediately break down, indicating that conflict and forced migration in relation to identity is always about development and vice versa, provoking an interrogation of the rationality and dominating knowledge that always underlies development and the conflict that ensues from its processes.

## MARGINALIZATION AND STATELESSNESS

At the outset of this essay, the crucial role tensions and conflicts revolving around inclusion and exclusion from citizenship continue to play in most aspects of forced migration in South Asia was hinted at. Although the previous section on conflict-induced displacement elucidated this relationship, an understanding of 'statelessness' in the South Asia region clarifies the outer limits of the 'national order', in so far as it will focus on populations who have become radically excluded from access to durable solutions due to their often protracted experiences of displacement from citizenship structures. Such has been the impact of displacement on these communities that they have not immediately had the resources to challenge their own marginalization that have characterized many of the insurgent movements previously described (although, as shown below, this is also subject to historical change). The theme can be illustrated through two case studies: the Myanmar Rohingyas in Bangladesh and the Bhutanese Lhotshampas in Nepal.

The Rohingyas are a Muslim minority group within colonial and majority Buddhist Myanmar (formerly Burma), who were excluded from citizenship by the Myanmar state after independence in 1948, as it claimed that they had recently migrated from the subcontinent and did not, therefore, qualify for citizenship. This effectively rendered the Rohingya people stateless within the borders of Myanmar. In 1978 the Burmese Government began systematically to exclude those whom the State had taxonomically defined as foreigners or non-citizens, as part of its operations in border areas against groups such as the Rohingyas. This led to a mass exile of between 200,000 and 250,000 Rohingyas into Bangladesh, placing a severe burden upon the capacity of a poor state and society. After Bangladesh placed the issue before the UN, UNHCR became involved in co-ordinating relief and refugee camps for the Rohingyas. In July 1978 a bilateral agreement (in which UNHCR was not involved) between Myanmar and Bangladesh was signed, leading to the repatriation of 180,000 Rohingyas in 1979, but not without conflict erupting between reluctant returnees and the Bangladeshi authorities. Indeed, it is questionable as to whether the repatriation can be defined as voluntary in a context of arrests of Rohingya leaders, conflict with the host state authorities, the turning off of the 'aid tap' within Bangladesh and the commencement of UNHCR-led reintegration aid within Myanmar. However, the repatriation of the Rohingyas did not resolve their stateless condition or questions of expropriation from, or access to, land. Consequently, this pattern of exile and bilateral agreement leading to repatriation was repeated in the early 1990s and again between 1996 and 1999, revealing Myanmar's continued discrimination against the Rohingyas and Bangladesh's reluctance to allow for local integration or settlement within its borders. Although substantial numbers of the registered Rohingya refugees have returned and there are now only between 20,000 and 30,000 Rohingyas still residing in refugee camps within Bangladesh's borders, predominantly in the Cox's Bazaar area, there are estimated to be between 100,000 and 200,000 unregistered self-settled Rohingyas in Bangladesh's border areas. Additionally, recent reports indicate that Rohingya refugees are experiencing mistreatment and abuse at the hands of the Bangladeshi authorities, including the destruction of the 'Tal' refugee camp (which had housed 6,000 refugees), sexual assault by members of the security forces, restrictions on movement outside the camps, and significant deficiencies in humanitarian assistance, including meagre health and educational provision, partly owing to the State's imposition of limits on the level and scale of humanitarian access which hampers the efforts of UNHCR and Médecins Sans Frontières to improve conditions in the camps. However, UNHCR reports indicate that some improvements were made in 2007 in respect of better shelter, and the provision of longer-term shelter and improved health facilities (with European Commission funding) in Kutupalong camp. In 2008 individual refugee identity cards were also announced, as opposed to the family ration books that had existed previously. However, it remains to be seen whether these changes will have any impact upon the generally negative representation and treatment that this community have suffered in Bangladesh. Consequently, the generally dire conditions suffered by the Rohingyas and the protracted nature of their displacement have led many to seek exile further afield, for example through secondary migration by boat to South-East Asia. In October 2006 40 boats carrying 2,000 Rohingya refugees arrived in Thailand, where their treatment at the hands of the Thai authorities was unfortunately little better than that meted out by the authorities in Bangladesh, with reports of the 'refoulement' or forcible return of many refugees across the border into Myanmar. As a result, although some returns and limited third-country resettlement to Canada, the United Kingdom and New Zealand have taken place, the limbo of statelessness remains the norm for significant numbers of Rohingya exiles.

The Bhutanese Lhotshampa refugees in Nepal, a Nepali-origin Hindu community who moved to Bhutan in the 19th century, have suffered a similar process of marginalization within Bhutan's Druk Buddhist-dominated social, political and cultural structure. Inspired by fears of a demographic shift which threatened the hegemony of the Druk Buddhist national order, in 1985 the Bhutanese State redefined Bhutanese citizenship and disenfranchised many ethnic Nepalis in the process, while also restricting access to schooling for ethnic Nepalis and restricting public and educational use of the Nepali language. This disenfranchisement was followed by a repressive crackdown on democratic activists in Bhutan and on Lhotshampa political mobilization, attacks on Lhotshampa-owned property and finally, in 1990, the expulsion of all Lhotshampas unable to prove pre-1958 residency. Consequently, Nepal, the poorest country in South Asia, currently hosts a Lhotshampa refugee population of 107,000 housed within refugee camps in the east of the country. UNHCR has co-ordinated care and maintenance aid to the camps in the absence of any political will from the Nepalese Government to accept integration of the Lhotshampas as a durable solution to the problem. Bilateral talks between Nepal and Bhutan after 1993 to resolve the issue excluded UNHCR and failed to use any other mediator. As a result, no progress was made, with the Bhutanese Government claiming that the Lhotshampa exiles were voluntary migrants, due to declarations that 70% of the refugees claim they were forced to sign under duress when expelled. It is also clear that, in the interest of maintaining good relations with Bhutan and the lack of political interest within India for the Lhotshampa cause (including Ghorka hostility to Nepalese migrants in India), Bhutan's most powerful regional neighbour, India, has chosen to remain silent on one of the most blatant forms of ethnic cleansing witnessed in South Asia. Nevertheless, recent progress has been made in developing third-country resettlement as a durable solution for the Lhotshampa refugee population, with offers by the USA, Canada, Denmark, Norway, Australia, New Zealand and the Netherlands to resettle at least 65,000 refugees. These resettlements commenced in March 2008 with USA taking the first 100 resettlers. However, the resettlement progamme has not been without controversy, as it continues to cause tension and conflict between those refugees who wish to pursue resettlement and those who see this as an abandonment of their just claim of their right to return. In July 2007 two refugees were killed by Nepalese police officers in violent internecine clashes that were only quelled witth the imposition of a curfew by the Nepalese authorities. In July 2008 the simmering discontent also resulted in attacks on an office of the International Organization for Migration office in Damak, in eastern Nepal, which was being used for the orchestration of ongoing resettlement. These events illustrate not only the heterogeneous desires and aspirations of different refugee communities and individuals in their quest for durable solutions to their problem but also the fact that, notwithstanding the constant referral to this stateless community as being helpless, elements within the refugee community are in fact becoming increasingly politicized and organized, despite 17 years of statelessness and the refusal of the Bhutanese Government to recognize their right to return.

## DEVELOPMENT-INDUCED DISPLACEMENT

Until only recently, development-induced displacement was considered marginal to the study of forced migration because of orthodox perceptions of state sovereignty and the perceived utilitarian right of states to engage in displacement for the 'greater common good' of the nation's long-term development goals. However, as the scope of forced migration studies has expanded from its narrow focus on the exilic 'refugee' towards an understanding of the rising global population of conflict-induced IDPs, which in 2004 stood at 24m. people world-wide, far outstripping the 9.2m. refugees for the same period, it is clear that internal displacement has become a pressing and unavoidable concern. Additionally, international and domestic NGOs, 'civil society' actors, social movements and human rights advocates have placed increasing focus on areas of forced migration hitherto neglected, including a wider focus on human rights abuses resulting from the developmental actions of states, international financial institutions and corporations. As a result, the focus on development-induced displacement has become pressing and it is clear that many of the issues that have been discussed in relation to conflict-induced displacement overlap with or recur in research and literature studying the impact of infrastructural development, especially of settlement and colonization as well as large dam and/or irrigation projects. Estimates of development-induced displacement in India alone for 2005 indicate that up to 21m. people were affected. Although this is repeated elsewhere historically, both regionally and globally, if the Indian case is considered it is minority groups that have been most severely impacted upon by large development projects. As both the commentators Sanjay Sangvai and Courtland Robinson have argued in the context of the Narmada Valley Dam Project (NVDP) in the states of Gujarat and Madhya Pradesh, it is members of the Scheduled Tribes, or Adivasis, in the region who constitute the highest proportion of India's development-induced displaced (40%), although they constitute only 8% of the national population. The impact of this project upon the region has already been considerable, with 114,000 people displaced from 162 villages by the Bargi Dam, which was completed in 1990, and claims that the Sardar Sarovar section of the project will eventually displace between 200,000 and 500,000 people.

It is not only the fact that minority ethnic and tribal and subaltern groups were deliberately targeted for such displacement, but also the manner in which the displacement has been conducted and the impact that it has had upon these groups that is significant in forced migration terms. The study of the Sardar Sarovar section and wider NVDP (which planned 3,165 dams in total) by numerous scholars and writers has revealed a catalogue of human rights abuses and traumatic effects imposed en masse on such populations. These have included: the effective loss of land, community and livelihoods; failures of resettlement; the absence of compensation; forced urbanization; and impoverishment, as well as the ongoing conflicts and traumas that result from resistance to these projects. Critics of such projects have also argued that it is precisely the populations that are displaced through development projects such as this who are least likely to reap the benefits accruing from them. In a sense, it is clear that many of these groups are in as bad, if not worse, a position than many refugees, as there is frequently no national or international institutional or legal recourse of formalized protection. Although the World Bank claimed that it had strict guidelines for resettlement and reintegration in place, the NVDP uncovered flaws in the World Bank's evaluation and monitoring of the impact of the project; these discoveries led to the Bank's withdrawal from the project in 1993. Such controversial projects have also produced vocal social resistance movements—in the case of the NVDP, the Narmada Bachao Andolan (Movement to Save Narmada), which has engaged in grass-roots resistance and legal battles in the Supreme Court of India over the construction of the dams and the rights of those displaced to proper compensation and reintegration.

To conclude, what the study of development-induced displacement in South Asia, as elsewhere, demonstrates is that forced migration cycles in this area reveal similar disparities in access to citizenship, rights and protection as are found amongst studies of the conflict-induced displaced. Indeed, it is only because the framework has remained trapped within the 'nation state' paradigm that privileges states the right to 'development' that the parallels in terms of human rights and citizenship issues have been missed up to now.

## 'ENVIRONMENTAL' DISPLACEMENT

Just as development-induced displacement for some time remained peripheral to forced migration studies because of the traditional refugee-focused and state-centric approach to the sub-discipline, the study of 'environmental' displacement is a relatively recent focus, which has proved contentious. Many critics, while not rejecting a focus on environmental factors per se, have argued that a reductive focus on the environment and the use of terms like 'environmental refugee' miss the concatenation of other human-related and political factors, including the aid and assistance response, which either serve to mitigate or exacerbate displacement dynamics. They also point out that as there is no international legal protocol that recognizes a need for protection ensuing from 'environmental' displacement, states and international actors may be tempted to disqualify claims for protection on those grounds. Thus, while environmental factors often form the self-evident trigger for displacement, it is clear that it is the nature and quality of the aid response by national, international and civil society actors that will determine the situation and outcome for the displaced, including access to durable and dignified solutions. Although the South Asian states have long suffered the effects of environment-related displacement, including droughts and floods, both the Indian Ocean tsunami of December 2004 and the earthquake of October 2005 resulted in massive death tolls and internal displacement. However, what a brief study of both these events reveals is that problems in the provision of assistance to the displaced caused by diverse factors in differing contexts, including ongoing conflict, discrimination against marginalized groups, alleged corruption, patronage politics and state failures have all contributed to the duration of displacement, the degree of trauma, loss and adaptation experienced in the process of displacement and the relative failures or success of assistance and reconstruction efforts.

### The Indian Ocean Tsunami

The Indian Ocean tsunami that struck on 26 December 2004 led to more than 280,000 deaths world-wide and resulted in the displacement of 1.8m. people within Asia alone. Within South Asia the tsunami waves devastated coastal villages and towns and an even greater number of livelihoods through the destruction of buildings, fishing vessels, crops and the salination of fields and wells. The greatest impact within the region was felt on the east coast of India, the Andaman and Nicobar Islands, Sri Lanka and the Maldives. The sheer scale of the disaster demanded an unprecedented emergency response at international, national and local levels. The international response mobilized 18 teams from the International Federation of Red Cross and Red Crescent Societies (IFRC), 16 UN agencies and at least 160 international NGOs in the initial phase. Thirty-five different military forces, both foreign and national, were also mobilized to provide logistical support for the emergency and relief effort. The first phase of the response comprised rescue and relief, including the clearing of debris, the cremation and burial of bodies, the provision of temporary shelter and camps, medical aid and emergency food and water provision. The second phase was that of rehabilitation, geared towards the construction of permanent, as opposed to transitional, housing and towards economic and ecological reconstruction. The third and final phase, which is scheduled for completion in 2010, is, in theory, a 'build-back-better' approach towards sustainable livelihoods and the reconstruction of rural and coastal productivity.

Different countries responded in different ways to the management of the relief and reconstruction effort. For instance, in India, where 10,273 people were killed (with a further 5,823 missing in the Andaman and Nicobar islands) and 647,556 were displaced, the Government refused some international offers of relief assistance and instead dispatched assistance to Sri Lanka, the Maldives and Indonesia. India's rehabilitation effort was also highly state-driven, limiting the number of international agencies involved and placing supervision of reconstruction and rehabilitation in the hands of state governments. The federal Government also established the National Crisis Manangement Committee and a Core Group on Reconstruction, Management and Monitoring in the Planning Commission in order to oversee relief and reconstruction efforts at a national level. In Sri Lanka, which suffered a high toll of 31,000 deaths and 1m. IDPs, the reverse was the case, with the Government of Sri Lanka allowing the involvement of foreign military actors in the relief effort and effectively contracting out rehabilitation and reconstruction efforts to international NGOs under the co-ordinating governmental umbrella of the Task Force for Rebuilding the Nation (TAFREN) and its successor, the Reconstruction and Development Agency (RADA). Whilst Sri Lanka's relief and rehabilitation effort was fairly effective and rapidly deployed and funded, there have still been criticisms of its outcomes. With regard to the relief effort, the sheer scale and proliferation of the NGO response contributed to heightened competition and evident lack of co-ordination between NGOs of varying capacities and sizes; the smaller NGOs often lacked experience in relief efforts; many NGOs had little or no knowledge of the Sri Lankan context; there were failures of consultation, participation and representation for civil societal, NGO and displaced groups; and the delivery of assistance was highly uneven between recipient groups and individuals in a geographic, ethnic and, at times, socio-economic sense. The rehabilitation phase has also suffered similar problems and has moreover faced additional obstacles, including a lack of development expertise within the TAFREN and criticisms that relief-orientated NGOs were ill-suited to development tasks, lacked experience in both housing construction and local knowledge, and had begun to use the 'build-back-better' motto as an excuse for delays. In addition, there were also cases where, owing to vulnerability caused by lack of local knowledge and experience, the control of rehabilitation programmes was taken over by local politicians. In India, on the other hand, co-ordination was seen as effective, although there were criticisms, mainly from the evaluations of international NGOs, of 'top-down' and anti-participatory planning and of strictly enforced but onerous deadlines emanating from the Indian authorities.

In the aftermath of the tsunami, it was also hoped in Sri Lanka that the tragedy might serve to revive a dangerously flagging peace process and act to bring the Tamil, Muslim and Sinhalese communities estranged by conflict together. In the immediate post-tsunami context there were many examples of bridges built across ethnic divides. However, political polarization rapidly occurred between the Government and the LTTE over disparities in the distribution of aid to the north and east, where Tamil and Muslim communities had suffered the worst of the tsunami's impact, along with the legacy of 21 years of war. Indeed, the Sri Lankan peace process, development in the island and post-conflict and post-tsunami reconstruction have all suffered from the failure to implement a joint mechanism for aid distribution. The Joint Task Force and the Sub-Committee on Immediate Humanitarian and Rehabilitation Needs in the North-East (SIHRN, which was also tasked with addressing the urgent need to facilitate IDP and refugee returns) agreement of 2003 and the P-TOMS agreement of 2005 between the Government and the LTTE have either been undone by political forces, or the political will to implement them has been lacking. In this regard, there are serious inequalities in aid distribution regionally and ethnically in Sri Lanka. In addition, new tensions have arisen among communities in certain areas, particularly in the north-east of the island between those displaced by the conflict and those receiving post-tsunami assistance, the former feeling aggrieved at their relative neglect in comparison to the relief, rehabilitation and development efforts undertaken on behalf of the latter. The Sri Lankan aid effort has also been accused of being deeply non-participatory and insensitive to the needs and voices of those displaced by the tsunami. For instance, the 100 m–200 m buffer zone (which was later reduced and often, in practice, completely ignored), restricting reconstruction along the seashore, was accused by critics of being a business-orientated strategy for effecting a 'slum clearance' of poor and vulnerable coastal dwellers, particularly fishing communities. Buffer zoning was also clearly discriminatory, being applied differently between southern and north-eastern areas, revealing, if anything, the logic of securitization in the context of ongoing tensions between the LTTE and the Government rather than the needs of the displaced themselves. While the Government introduced regional reductions in the buffer zones in late 2005, the aid and assistance process was plagued by bureaucratic inertia, slowness, political patronage in the unequal distribution of aid and accusations of corruption against high-profile politicians. This has acted to worsen the marginalization of already vulnerable groups. The Indian aid effort has also been criticized for failing to address the needs of the vulnerable, including a lack of attention to gender, especially in the use of aid personnel and the distribution of aid. This may have been more sensitively and effectively addressed had UNHCR guidelines been followed. There were also criticisms of the lack of access to aid experienced by Dalits, sharecroppers, tenants, landless labourers and artisans and discrimination against Dalits and lower castes in aid distribution on the part of higher-caste fishing groups. In addition, there have been some reports that relocation of coastal dwellers displaced inland has been operative as a result of tourist and real-estate business interests, despite the state of Tamil Nadu's assertion of the coastal communities' right to the coast.

Consequently, it must be recognized that, in both the Indian and Sri Lankan contexts, the experiences of displacement, its duration, the level of access to and quality of aid and rehabilitation have all involved social and political factors that cannot be understood through the depiction of this form of displacement as merely 'environmental'. The tsunami also reveals the very political nature of aid and assistance and the inequalities that can be operative in relief and rehabilitation processes, to the extent that the same kinds of rights' issues apparent behind conflict-induced displacement are paralleled in this case.

### The South Asian Earthquake

In October 2005 an earthquake measuring 7.6 on the Richter scale, with its epicentre close to Balakot on the border of Azad Kashmir and the NWFP in Pakistan resulted in more than 73,000 deaths and displaced more than 3m. people. The shock waves were also felt in India, where 1,400 people were killed and 140,000 displaced, mainly in Indian-controlled Kashmir and the Punjab. The earthquake destroyed 600,000 rural homes and much infrastructure, including schools and health facilities. Although UNHCR was quick to react because of its long-standing presence in the area, at the outset the aid response suffered from severe access problems due to the nature of the terrain and the damage caused by the earthquake, leaving hundreds of thousands without assistance. There were also considerable fears that malnutrition and the cold winter would lead to further fatalities among the 300,000 displaced who were sheltered in tents. However, the relatively mild winter and close monitoring in the aid effort prevented the outbreak of epidemics or malnutrition. Between April and August 2006 140,000 of the displaced returned home and by the end of March 2007 there were 'only' 30,000 displaced remaining in 45 relief camps in Pakistan. In April the authorities decided to attempt to close the camps by the end of June, despite the fact that a significant number of refugees remained effectively landless or in danger from landslides if they returned to their homes. Returnees were consequently encouraged to relocate tents and camp facilities to their home areas.

A major concern with the humanitarian assistance effort is that many aid agencies were overly eager to focus the reconstruction effort on the home areas of the earthquake zone; this approach led to the relative neglect of those displaced remaining in camps. The camps and humanitarian relief efforts consequently suffered from a range of problems, including gaps in the supply of water and food, with heavy rains at times destroying sanitation facilities and tented shelters. There has also been concern expressed that for some areas the process of return and reconstruction has been implemented too rapidly without proper assessment of the safety of home areas with regard to the danger of landslides or the adequate reconstruction of infrastructure. Moreover, in mid-2006 there was renewed displacement into the camps owing to further seismic activity in the earthquake-affected area. To sum up, although the relief response has been rapid as has the shift into the reconstruction phase, criticisms persist that the varying needs of those displaced have not been adequately addressed, including those whose capacity for swift progress into the return and reconstruction phase may be problematic, such as those displaced from areas more vulnerable to landslides, the landless and the large number of single-parent households. These criticisms bear testament to the tendency for humanitarian assistance offered to both refugees and IDPs to impose a 'one-size-fits-all' approach to resolving forced migration experiences.

## CONCLUSION

South Asia is subject to a myriad of different forms of forced migration dynamics. Even when one surveys the conflicts in the region that have resulted in displacement cycles, it is clear that these cover forms of ethno-nationalist, secessionist, revolutionary and autonomy-based struggles led by political movements. However, there are also outbreaks of social violence that overlap with such political projects, including recently, for example, the aforementioned anti-Muslim riots in Gujarat. All these forms of conflict impact upon forced migration, creating waves of both internal displacement and refugeehood of varying magnitude. It is also clear that the experience of displacement itself, whether internally or in exile, can form the space for the recycling of conflict dynamics, even forging transnational political and socio-economic linkages over long distances, as can be seen in Tamil nationalism *vis-à-vis* Sri Lanka.

However, South Asia's spectrum of forced migration issues cannot be reduced to conflict alone, as both development-induced and environment-related displacement have created massive displacement populations. The trend both regionally and globally seems to be for internal displacement numbers related to these issues to rise and to challenge the traditional focus on refugees in forced migration studies, a focus that, until very recently, has reflected a state-centric 'common sense' framework reinforcing the 'national order' of things, with its accompanying stress on exile, state-led political persecution etc. Yet, it is clear when we analyse the forced migration experiences of those who have suffered from development-induced displacement, for example, that human rights issues in terms of equitable access to citizenship resources, to development and to aid are all replicated in areas that were once peripheral to forced migration studies and that the divide between development and environmental displacement and conflict-induced displacement are tenuous to say the least. The implications of this for forced migration studies, a recent sub-discipline of the social sciences, are only just becoming apparent but indicate clear parallels between areas that have hitherto been kept apart in all but more searching fields of political philosophy.

In terms of South Asian states' attitudes towards displacement in the region it could be argued that the lack of signatories to the 1951 UN Convention in the area has had negative consequences for refugees, in so far as the lack of a formal framework has at times also precluded the development of national forms of protection to refugees and has certainly left the region open to very ad hoc and selective approaches to different refugee flows. That this has happened in a global context where the 1951 Convention is being eroded by the dominant donor states should, however, also be understood. The reluctance of states to sign the Convention could be explained by their quite justified disillusionment with and suspicion of the general objectives and repercussions of becoming signatory to areas of universal jurisdiction. As Afghanistan has recently signed the 1951 Convention and the 1967 protocol, it will be interesting to see if this impacts upon its own approach to the issue and upon the region more widely.

## BIBLIOGRAPHY


Abrar, Chowdury R. 'Legal Protection of Refugees in South Asia', *Forced Migration Review*, No. 10, pp. 21–23, 2001.

Ahmed, Imtiaz, *et al. State, Society, and Displaced People in South Asia.* Dhaka, Dhaka University Press, 2004.

Banerjee, Paula, Chaudhury, Sabyasachi Basu Ray, and Das, Samir Kumar (Eds). *Internal Displacement in South Asia: The Relevance of the UN's Guiding Principles.* New Delhi, Sage Publications, 2005.

Baruah, S. 'Citizens and Denizens: Ethnicity, Homelands and the Crisis of Displacement in Northeast India', *Journal of Refugee Studies*, Vol. 16, No. 1, pp. 44–66. Oxford University Press, 2003.

Batt, C., and Mukta, P. 'Hindutva in the West: Mapping the Antinomies of Diaspora Nationalism', *Ethnic and Racial Studies*, Vol. 22, No. 2, 1999.

Black, R., and Koser, K. (Eds). *The End of the Refugee Cycle?* Berghahn, 1999.

Black, R. *Refugees, Environment and Development*. Longman, 1998.

Bose, Tapan. 'Protection of Refugees in South Asia: Need for a Legal Framework', *SAFHR Paper Series*, No. 6, South Asia Forum for Human Rights, 2000.

Centilivres, P., and Centilivres, M. 'The Afghan Refugees in Pakistan: An Ambiguous Identity', *Journal of Refugee Studies*, Vol. 1, No.2, pp. 141–52, 1988.

Cernea, M. M. 'Internal Refugee Flows and Development-induced Population Displacement', *Journal of Refugee Studies* Vol. 3, No. 4, pp. 298–319, 1990.

Chari, P. R., Joseph, Mallika, and Chandran, Suba (Eds). *Missing Boundaries: Refugees, Migrants, Stateless and Internally Displaced Persons in South Asia*. Manohar, 2004.

Chimni, B. S. (Ed.). *International Refugee Law: A Reader*. Sage Publications, 2000.

Chimni, B. S. 'The Law and Politics of Regional Solution of the Refugee Problem: The Case of South Asia', *RCSS Policy Studies*, Vol. 4, Colombo, 1998.

Deranityagala, S. 'The Political Economy of Civil Conflict in Nepal', *Oxford Development Studies*, Vol. 33, No. 1, pp. 47–62, March 2005.

Drèze, J., Samson, M., and Singh, S. *The Dam and the Nation: Displacement and Resettlement in the Narmada Valley*. Delhi, Oxford University Press, 1997.

Emmott, S. 'Dislocation, Shelter and Crisis: Afghanistan's Refugees and Notions of Home', *Gender and Development*, Vol. 4, No. 1, pp. 31–38, 1996.

Frerks, G., and Klem, B. 'Tsunami Response in Sri Lanka', *Disaster Studies* Series, Clingndael Institute, Wageningen University, March 2005.

Fuglerud, Oivind. *Life on the Outside: The Tamil Diaspora and Long-Distance Nationalism*. Pluto, 1999.

Garikipati, Supriya. 'Consulting the Development-Displaced Regarding their Resettlement: Is there a Way?', *Journal of Refugee Studies*, No. 18, pp. 340–361. Oxford University Press, 2005.

Ghosh, Partha S. *Unwanted and Uprooted: A Political Study of Migrants, Refugees, Stateless and Displaced of South Asia*. Sankriti, 2004.

Grare, Frédéric. 'Pakistan: The Resurgence of Baluch Nationalism', *Carnegie Papers*, No. 65, January 2006.

'The Geopolitics of Afghan Refugees in Pakistan' in Stedman, S. J., and Tanner, F. (Eds), *Refugee Manipulation: War, Politics, and the Abuse of Human Suffering.* New York, NY, Brookings Institute, 2003.

Haddad, E. 'The Refugee: The Individual between Sovereigns', *Global Society*, Vol. 17, No. 3, pp. 297–322, 2003.

Hampton, J. *Internally Displaced People: A Global Survey*. Earthscan Books, 2002.

Harris, Simon. 'Disaster Response, Peace and Conflict in Post-Tsunami Sri Lanka', University of Bradford Centre of Conflict Resolution, *Working Papers*, Vol. 16, February 2006.

Hasbullah, S. H. *Muslim Refugees: The Forgotten People in Sri Lanka's Ethnic Conflict.* RASFD, 2001.

Human Rights Watch. 'After the Deluge: India's Reconstruction after the 2004 Tsunami', *Human Rights Watch*, Vol. 17, No. 3, May 2005.

'The Human Cost: The Consequences of Insurgent Attacks in Afghanistan', *Human Rights Watch*, Vol. 19, No. 6 (C), April 2007.

*Rohingya Refugees from Burma Mistreated in Bangladesh.*- Human Rights Watch Press Release, March 2007.

'Return to War: Human Rights Under Siege', *Human Rights Watch*, Vol.19, No. 11 (C), August 2007.

Hutt, M. *Unbecoming Citizens: Culture, Nationhood, and the Flight of Refugees from Bhutan*, New Delhi, Oxford University Press, 2005.

Hutt, M. (Ed.). *Himalayan People's War: Nepal's Maoist Rebellion*. Hurst & Co, 2004.

Hyndman, J. 'The Securitization Of Fear In Post-Tsunami Sri Lanka', *Annals of the Association of American Geographers*, Vol. 97, Issue 2, pp. 335–37, June 2007.

International Crisis Group. 'Central Asian Perspectives on 11 September and the Afghan Crisis'. Geneva, 2001.

'Nepal's Constitutional Process', *Asia Report* No. 128, February 2007.

'Pakistan's Tribal Areas: Appeasing the Militants', *Asia Report*, No. 125, December 2006.

'Sri Lanka's Muslims: Caught in the Crossfire', *Asia Report*, No. 134, May 2007.

'Restoring Democracy in Bangladesh', *Asia Report*, No. 151, April 2008.

*Afghanistan's Endangered Compact*. Asia Briefing No. 59, January 2007.

'Sri Lanka: Sinhala Nationalism and the Elusive Southern Consensus', *Asia Report* No. 141, November 2007.

'Nepal's New Political Landscape', *Asia Report* No. 156, July 2008.

Kenyon Lischer, S. *Dangerous Sanctuaries: Refugee Camps, Civil War, and the Dilemmas Of Humanitarian Aid*. Cornell University Press, 2005.

Kohli, A. 'Can Democracies Accommodate Ethnic Nationalism? Rise and Decline of Self-Determination Movements in India', *Journal of Asian Studies*, Vol. 56, No. 2, pp. 325–344, 1997.

Kudaisya Gyanesh, Tai, and Yong Tan (Eds). *The Aftermath of Partition in South Asia*. London, Routledge, 2000.

Marsden, Peter. 'Repatriation and Reconstruction: The Case of Afghanistan' in Black, R., and Koser, K. (Eds), *The End of the Refugee Cycle?* pp. 56–84. Berghahn, 1999.

'Afghanistan: Minorities, Conflict and the Search for Peace', Minority Rights Group, 2001.

McCully, P. *Silenced Rivers: The Ecology and Politics of Large Dams*. Zed, 2001.

Mishra, Omprakash (Ed.). *Forced Migration in the South Asian Region: Displacement, Human Rights and Conflict Resolution*. Kolkata, 2004.

Mishra, Pankaj. 'The People's War', *London Review of Books*, Vol. 27, No. 12, June 2005.

Muggah, Robert. 'Distinguishing Means and Ends: The Counterintuitive Effects of UNHCR's Community Development Approach in Nepal', *Journal of Refugee Studies*, Vol. 18, pp. 151–164. Oxford University Press, 2005.

Norwegian Refugee Council, Internal Displacement Monitoring Centre (Asia Pacific Region); internet www .internal-displacement.org.

Oberoi, P. *Exile and Belonging: Refugees and State Policy in South Asia*. New Delhi, Oxford University Press, 2006.

Osella, F., and Gardner, K. (Eds). *Migration, Modernity and Social Transformation in South Asia*. New Delhi, Sage Publications, 2004.

Pandey, G., *et al*. *Remembering Partition: Violence, Nationalism and History in India*. Cambridge University Press, 2001.

Pierpaoli, Y. *Rohingya Refugees in Bangladesh*. Refugees International, 1994.

Rajasingham Senanayake, D. 'Humanitarian Assistance and The International Aid. Architecture After the Tsunami: Lessons from Sri Lanka and India' (draft manuscript). 2005.

'Sri Lanka and the Violence of Reconstruction', *Development*, Vol. 48, pp.111–20, 2005.

Rampton, D., and Welikala, A.*The Politics of the South*. Asia Foundation, 2005.

Robinson, C. 'Risks and Rights, Consequences and Challenges of Development-induced Displacement', *Brookings Institute Occasional Papers*, SAIS, May 2003.

Roy, A. 'The Greater Common Good' in *The Cost of Living*. Flamingo, 1999.

Ruiz, Hiram A. 'Afghanistan, Conflict and Displacement', *Forced Migration Review*, Vol. 13, pp. 8–10, June 2002.

Samaddar, Ranabir. *Refugees and the State: Practices of Asylum and Care in India, 1947–2000*. New Delhi, Sage Publications, 2003.

Sangvai, S. *The River and Life: People's Struggle on the Narmada Valley*. Earthcare, 2000.

Shahrani, M. N. 'Afghanistan's Muhajirin: Politics of Mistrust and Distrust of Politics' in Valentine, Daniel E., and Knudsen, J. (Eds), *Mistrusting Refugees*. University of California Press, 1996.

Sriskandarajah, D. 'The Migration-Development Nexus: Sri Lanka Case Study', *International Migration*, Vol. 40, No. 5, pp. 283–306, 2002.

Stirrat, Jock. 'Competitive Humanitarianism: Relief and the Tsunami in Sri Lanka', *Anthropology Today*, Vol. 22, No. 5, pp.11–16, October 2006.

Turton, D. 'Refugees, Forced Resettlers and Other Forced Migrants: Towards a Unitary Study of Forced Migration'. *UNHCR: New Issues in Refugee Research*, Working Paper No. 94, September 2003.

Turton, D., and Marsden, P. 'Taking Refugees for a Ride? The Politics of Refugee Return to Afghanistan', *AREU Issues Paper* Series, AREU, 2002.

UNHCR. *The State of the World's Refugees: 50 Years of Humanitarian Action*. Oxford University Press, 2000.

*The State of the World's Refugees: Human Displacement in the New Millennium*. Oxford University Press, 2006.

UNHCR website: www.unhcr.org

Valentine, Daniel E. *Charred Lullabies: Chapters in an Anthropography of Violence*. Princeton University Press, 1996.

Valentine, Daniel E., and Knudsen, J. (Eds). *Mistrusting Refugees*. University of California Press, 1996.

Van Beek, Martijn. 'Tibetans in Nepal: The Dynamics of International Assistance Among a Community in Exile', *Journal of Refugee Studies*, No. 17, pp. 136–137. Oxford University Press, March 2004.

Van Der Veer, P. *Nation and Migration: The Politics of Space in the South Asian Diaspora*. University of Pennsylvania Press, 1995.

Weiner, M. 'The Clash of Norms: Dilemmas in Refugee Policies', *Journal of Refugee Studies*, Vol. 11, No. 4, pp. 433–53, 1998.

Wilson, Antony Jeyaratnam. *Sri Lankan Tamil Nationalism: Its Origins And Development In The Nineteenth And Twentieth Centuries*. London, Hurst & Co, 2000.

Zolberg, A., and Benda, P. (Eds). *Global Migrants, Global Refugees*. Berghahn, 2001.

Zolberg, A., Suhrke, A., and Aguayo, S. *Escape from Violence: Conflict and the Refugee Crisis in the Developing World*. Oxford University Press, 1989.

# GENDER ISSUES IN SOUTH ASIA

SANTOSH JATRANA

## BACKGROUND

South Asia, comprising Afghanistan, Bangladesh, Bhutan, India, the Maldives, Nepal, Pakistan and Sri Lanka, is a diverse region which accounts for about 40% of the Asian population. Gender as a subject of enquiry in South Asia raises the issue of commonality and diversity. Women across the region face amazing commonalities in conditions, despite the economic, demographic, religious, cultural and political diversities among the countries of the region. Within these diversities, the South Asian region stands together on a number of conditions facing its women. Given that gender roles are at least in part culturally constructed, this can place a variety of expectations and constraints on women, and can result in adverse outcomes. For example, in a South Asian context, gender roles can influence the health of women by putting emphasis on women's reproductive role, resulting in early and excessive childbearing; the preference for male infants can manifest itself in discrimination against female children in the areas of health, nutrition and general care, causing severe repercussions on health and self-respect. Women in South Asia are still typically at a social and economic disadvantage compared with men. In patriarchal South Asian societies, women often occupy lower status roles than men; they lack autonomy, leading to lack of decision-making power and independent income. They are less likely ever to have worked, and, if in employment, are typically in unpaid or lower-paid jobs than men. This translates into women having fewer economic resources in old age. As a result, the outcomes in various fields are less favourable to girls than boys in South Asia.

South Asia is characterized by one of the lowest gender indices in the world. Gender disparity, narrowly defined as different outcomes between males and females, exists between and within the countries of South Asia. In fact, the level of gender disparity in certain outcomes such as health and education for girls at the national level in South Asia is the largest in the world. Equality refers to equal opportunities in terms of access to sources of livelihood, health, and education, as well as to social, economic and political participation without discrimination. Gender inequalities stem from relations of power and authority, class-religion-caste-ethnic hierarchies and socio-cultural traditions, customs and norms. Empowerment is the process of transforming these structures and institutions, thereby ensuring equality. Gender inequalities in the allocation of such resources as education, health care, nutrition and political voice matter both at micro and macro level. These inequalities matter at the individual level because of the strong association with well-being, productivity, and economic growth. At national level, a country cannot flourish if half of the population is left out of the development process.

Gender equality is an over-arching concern that can enhance the performance of every indicator of human development. Over the years there has been marked progress within the region towards gender equity. As a result women in South Asia are better off than they were a decade ago, according to a number of well-being indicators. They have higher and improving life expectancy; higher rates of participation in education and in the labour force; many of them have entered politics at least at the local governance level; and there is an increasing recognition of and work towards gender equality and empowerment of women. However, despite these improvements, much more effort is needed to eliminate gender inequality in the region. The Human Development Reports of the various years of the UN Development Programme (UNDP) note this region as one of the worst in the world as regards gender-related development levels.

## DEMOGRAPHIC IMBALANCE IN SEX RATIO

The sex ratio, defined as the number of males per 100 females, is an important social indicator for measuring the extent of prevailing equity between males and females in a society at a given point of time. It is mainly the outcome of the interplay of sex differentials in mortality, sex-selective migration, sex ratio at birth and, at times, the sex differentials in population enumeration. When there is no human intervention, slightly more boys are born, but this small surplus of boys is offset by a slightly higher male mortality disadvantage at each stage of life. However, discrimination against females has affected this demographic balance in some South Asian countries, leading to fewer female births, more female deaths, and hence a disproportionate number of men to women. South Asia is one of the few regions (other than the People's Republic of China and parts of the Arab world) where the proportion of men to women is higher than the global sex ratio of 94 men per 100 women, at 106 men per 100 women in the population.

Evidence of demographic diversity and similarity in South Asia can be seen in the sex ratio as well. Relatively balanced sex ratios are recorded for Sri Lanka, Bhutan and Nepal, while Pakistan, India, Bangladesh and the Maldives have a higher proportion of males to females (Table 1). The situation in India has long been unfavourable to females. According to the 2001 census, the sex ratio for India's population was 107 males per

**Table 1. Gender Disparity in Health in South Asian Countries**

| | Sex ratio[1] | Life expectancy (years at birth, 2006) | | Under-five mortality (2006) | | Child mortality rate (1997–2004)[1] | | Infant mortality rate (2006)[1] | | Maternal/reproductive health | | | GDI ranking | HDI rank minus GDI rank |
|---|---|---|---|---|---|---|---|---|---|---|---|---|---|---|
| Country | | Male | Female | Male | Female | Male | Female | Male | Female | Mortality, 2000[2] | Prenatal care (%, 2000–05)[3] | Skilled health staff at birth (%, 2000–05)[4] | | |
| Afghanistan | n.a. | 42 | 43 | 260 | 254 | n.a. | n.a. | 176 | 154 | 1,900 | 16 | 14 | n.a. | n.a. |
| Bangladesh | 105 | 63 | 63 | 73 | 65 | 24 | 29 | 57 | 46 | 380 | 49 | 13 | 121 | 1 |
| Bhutan | 102 | 62 | 67 | 75 | 65 | n.a. | n.a. | 68 | 58 | n.a. | n.a. | n.a. | n.a. | n.a. |
| India | 106 | 62 | 64 | 72 | 81 | 25 | 37 | 57 | 58 | 540 | n.a. | 43 | 113 | 0 |
| Maldives | 107 | 72 | 73 | 34 | 27 | n.a. | n.a. | 24 | 17 | n.a. | n.a. | n.a. | 85 | 4 |
| Nepal | 100 | 62 | 63 | 60 | 59 | 28 | 40 | 46 | 46 | 740 | 28 | 15 | 128 | –4 |
| Pakistan | 108 | 62 | 63 | 98 | 96 | n.a. | n.a. | 85 | 71 | 500 | 36 | 31 | 125 | –7 |
| Sri Lanka | 102 | 69 | 76 | 15 | 11 | n.a. | n.a. | 14 | 9 | 92 | 100 | 96 | 89 | –1 |

Note: Gender-related development index = GDI; Human development index = HDI.

[1] Latest available year.

[2] Maternal mortality ratio (modelled estimates per 100,000 live births).

[3] Percentage of pregnant women receiving prenatal care; latest available year.

[4] Percentage of total births attended by skilled health staff; latest available year.

Sources: UNDP, *Human Development Report 2005*, UNFPA, *State of the World Population*, World Bank, *World Development Indicators* and WHO, *World Health Statistics*.

100 females. There are, however, phenomenal differences in sex ratio across states in India. According to the 2001 census, the sex ratio among the major states ranged from 94 in Kerala to 113 in Haryana. Of the 10 districts with the lowest sex ratios in India, however, four were in Haryana state alone. One of the interesting trends that is emerging is that the child sex ratio for the 0–6-year age group is growing; it increased to 117 in 2001, compared with 115 in 1991. The sharpest decline in the child sex ratio has been observed in prosperous states such as Punjab, Haryana and Maharashtra. In certain parts of India where the sex ratios have been increasing, the practices of female infanticide and foeticide to prevent the birth of girls have been noted.

This imbalance in sex ratio may be the result of neglect of girl children, resulting in their higher mortality at younger ages, higher maternal mortality, sex-selective female abortions, selective emigration of females, and infanticide. All these reasons are indicative of discrimination against girls and women, a widespread preference for boys, and the low status of women in South Asia. The low status of women in most of the countries of South Asia is confirmed by the Human Development Report of the UNDP, which places these countries in the bottom quartile of all countries on both of its measures of the status of women. There is evidence that with the reduction in fertility, combined with a traditional preference for sons and the development and increased availability of ultrasound scanning and amniocentesis testing, as many as 50m. women are 'missing' in South Asia alone. Availability of pre-birth sex determination techniques means that parents can now detect the sex of their child and abort the unwanted foetuses. As a result of sex-selective abortion of female foetuses, the birth ratio of boys to girls is now 6% above normal levels in India. In Bangladesh and Pakistan, where women still have many more children than in India, the sex of a baby is rarely known before birth, but discrimination against girls and women is severe due to son preference.

Why do men in certain South Asian societies have an advantage over women and why are women mistreated and neglected? Asian societies affected by this trend share a strong preference for sons, a situation exacerbated by an overall decline in the birth rate. In India, for example, the average number of children per woman has fallen from nearly five 20 years ago to less than three today. With the reduction in fertility and smaller family sizes becoming desirable, together with the growing cost of raising children, parents have started opting for aborting female foetuses. Since women are held responsible for childbirth and their status depends on giving birth to a boy, the pressure to bear a son is immense in the context of falling birth rates, which further results in the worsening health and status of women. In fact, in some cases failure to produce a male child becomes a cause for violence, abuse and torture against them. Even when girls are born, they are then discriminated against in the allocation of resources. The governments of South Asian countries have made political attempts at solutions to these problems. For example, in 1994 the Indian Government passed the Prenatal Diagnosis Techniques Act, which made it illegal to reveal the sex of an unborn child. Despite the threat of imprisonment and fines, the practice is still widespread, however, because the law is not an adequate deterrent. What is needed? A change in attitude?

## POSSIBLE EXPLANATIONS FOR SON PREFERENCE IN SOUTH ASIA

Son preference in South Asia is the direct result of women's inferior social status, attributable to patriarchal systems, patrilineal families, arranged marriages and a socializing process that encourages women to be submissive to their husbands and in-laws. In most parts of South Asian society where marriage is exogamous, the residence pattern is patrilocal, and the family system is patrilineal: the man's role is central to the family and society. In such societies, women's status is low and autonomy is negligible; therefore, women cannot participate as equals in decision-making processes. A son is necessary to provide for the family, perpetuate its name and ensure its social and biological continuity.

The economic basis of gender preference in South Asia is the prevalence of a patrilineal system of inheritance, which severely restricts women from providing economic and other support to their parents; therefore, boys provide economic security to their parents in old age. Since the society is patrilineal, the boys perpetuate the line of descent, and family status depends on leaving a surviving son. The authority of the head of the household is passed from father to son. A girl, on the other hand, is always a financial liability. She requires an extensive dowry at the time of marriage, and she is committed to making gifts to her husband's household when she visits her parents, for at least the first few years of their marriage. In South Asian countries where there are no universal old-age pension systems, raising a son acts as old-age security. According to an Indian saying, to raise a daughter is 'to water a neighbour's garden'.

There are also psychological and religious reasons for son preference; men prefer sons because they regard having sons as a sign of masculinity, and sons are believed to provide men with greater companionship than daughters. In some cases, parents think that boys are easier to raise than girls. Since boys carry the family name, the lack of a male heir means the extinction of the family lineage. In Hinduism, the souls of parents without sons are condemned to eternal wandering, since a son is necessary for the performance of certain death rites at the pyre of his father.

## GENDER AND HEALTH ISSUES

Life expectancy of women is usually greater than that of men by six or seven years for many reasons: genetic, social, cultural and behavioural. However, many South Asian countries are exceptions to this overall rule. Except for Sri Lanka and Bhutan, the difference in life expectancy between the genders is much smaller in South Asian countries—about one to two years or no difference at all (Table 1). In Bangladesh, for example, males and females have the same life expectancy, of 63 years. In Afghanistan, the Maldives, Nepal and Pakistan the difference in life expectancy between the genders is only one year; in India, women outlive men by two years. In Sri Lanka, which has the highest life expectancy for females in the region, women live on average until they are 76, seven years longer than men; in the Maldives, which has the highest life expectancy for males in the region, women live on average until the age of 73, only one year longer than men. On the other hand, in Afghanistan, which has the shortest life expectancy in the region, the life expectancies are 42 and 43 years respectively for men and women. In Bhutan, the life expectancies for males and females are 62 and 67 years respectively. In other countries of the region the life expectancy for men and women varies between 62 and 64. The fact that the typical female advantage in life expectancy is not seen in many South Asian countries suggests that there are systematic problems with women's health.

In most populations, female mortality rates are lower than those for males at all ages, apparently owing to the males' higher degree of biologically-based susceptibility to disease and to the greater prevalence of poor health habits and risky behaviour, especially among adolescent and adult men. However, in most parts of South Asia with strong son preference attitudes, the situation is different, with either a smaller gap between male and female infant and child mortality, or higher mortality rates for females, particularly during childhood. Sex differentials in infant mortality (0–1 year age group), under-five (0–5 year age group) and child mortality (1–5 year age group) are evident from Table 1. In India female infant and under-five mortality rates are higher than male infant and under-five mortality rates, implying an excess of female mortality in these age groups. However, the gap between male and female mortality is even more pronounced in child mortality in Bangladesh, India and Pakistan—the countries for which the data are available. These findings clearly indicate that behavioural factors raise the mortality rates of female children. By far the best performance, both in terms of total survival and the gap between males and females, is witnessed in the case of Sri Lanka. The under-five mortality and child mortality rates are highest in Afghanistan, both for males and females.

The gender difference in child mortality rates is a good indicator of female social disadvantage because the outcome is less likely to be affected by the children themselves, and environmental and care-related factors (such as nutrition and medical interventions) that are susceptible to societal manipulation come into play at this stage of the life cycle. The evidence of an excess of female deaths in childhood is usually interpreted as the result of parental discrimination against daughters in the allocation of food and health care, neglect or even abuse of girls, relative medical and nutritional neglect of the girl child within the household, and the inferior social status of females.

The impact of discrimination also contributes to poor reproductive health outcomes for women in South Asia. Early age at marriage leads to early and unintended pregnancies, which are associated with greater risks of complications and of death. South Asia has one of the highest maternal mortality rates in the world. For every 100,000 live births in Afghanistan and Nepal respectively, 1,900 and 740 mothers die—a sharp contrast to Sri Lanka, where the number is 92. The comparatively low maternal mortality rate in Sri Lanka seems very high, however, when compared with Japan, where it is only 10 women per 100,000 births. Most maternal deaths result from preventable causes, and good and timely prenatal care can help in recognizing, diagnosing and promptly treating the complications and thus saving women from dying. Lack of access to health care is one of the leading contributors to high maternal mortality rates in some South Asian countries. As is clear from Table 1, with the exception of Sri Lanka and to some extent Bangladesh, the proportion of women receiving prenatal care is very low. The utilization of prenatal care varies by education level and place of residence of women (rural or urban). Literate women and women in urban areas are more likely to visit antenatal clinics than their illiterate and rural counterparts. For the health of the child and the mother, it is advantageous for the birth of the baby to take place with the assistance of a trained medical practitioner. With the exception of Sri Lanka and to some extent India, all countries in the region show a poor performance as far as the number of births attended by skilled health staff is concerned. Apart from health care, the mother's age at her first pregnancy, the large total number of pregnancies and the prevalence of anemia also influence maternal mortality and health. Anemia, which can be treated with inexpensive iron tablets, accounts for nearly 20% of all maternal deaths in India.

## GENDER AND EDUCATION ISSUES

Women's participation and achievement in the formal education system is a key indicator of their condition and social status in society. Because of deep-rooted gender inequalities and because the populations of South Asia are large, the region has the highest number of out-of-school girls in the world. UNESCO estimates that nearly 24m. girls of primary school age are not receiving education in South Asia. Although most countries in the region have shown an improvement over the past 10 years and are significantly ahead of other developing countries, gender equity in education remains a major issue throughout the region. The gains being made, however, have major implications for the demographic dynamics of the region. Women have greater exposure to 'modernization', which has been crucial for the acceptance of family-planning and hence future population control.

Some countries in the region, such as the Maldives and Sri Lanka, have achieved remarkable levels of adult literacy and youth literacy among females (Table 2). There is no gender gap in adult literacy and youth literacy in the Maldives and in the case of adult literacy the gap is very low in Sri Lanka. Youth literacy is higher among females than males in Sri Lanka. Such advances, however, have not been uniform throughout the region, and gender gaps in adult literacy as well as in youth literacy are high in Afghanistan, Bangladesh, India, Nepal and Pakistan. However, Bangladesh has made very good progress in primary-level enrolment for girls, with girls outnumbering boys in primary enrolment rates. There is no gender gap in primary enrolment rates in the Maldives and Sri Lanka, and in these two countries girls outnumber boys in tertiary-level enrolment. In all other countries of the region boys outnumber girls at each level of education enrolment from primary to tertiary. Overall, Sri Lanka and the Maldives are among the best performing countries in the region. For Afghanistan no reliable data are available for tertiary-level enrolment.

**Table 2. Gender Disparity in Education in South Asian Countries**

| Country | Adult literacy, 2006* | Youth literacy, 2006† | Net primary enrolment, 2005‡ | Gross tertiary enrolment, 2005‡ |
|---|---|---|---|---|
| Afghanistan | 30 | 35 | 0.39 | n.a. |
| Bangladesh | 76 | 90 | 1.03§ | 0.53 |
| Bhutan | n.a. | n.a. | n.a. | 0.77 |
| India | 65 | 81 | 0.93 | 0.70 |
| Maldives | 100 | 100 | 1.00§ | 2.37 |
| Nepal | 56 | 74 | 0.87§ | 0.40 |
| Pakistan | 57 | 72 | 0.76 | 0.88 |
| Sri Lanka | 97 | 101 | 1.00§ | n.a. |

* Ages 15 years and above, female rate as percentage of male rate.
† Ages 15 to 24, female rate as percentage of male rate.
‡ Ratio of female to male.
§ Data refer to an earlier period than specified.

Sources: UNDP, *Human Development Report* and World Bank, *World Development Indicators*.

In many South Asian societies that are lagging behind in girls' education, societal traditions and financial incentives exert pressure on parents to invest in the long-term economic viability of sons over daughters. Given the resource constraints and social ordering along patrilineal-patrilocal families, investment in long-term contributors to the household economy (i.e. sons) is more easily justified than investment in short-term ones (i.e. daughters). The balance of household decision making is further tipped in favour of educating sons because of important considerations surrounding marriage. Although some level of education for girls is required to enhance their value on the marriage market, too much education could result in reduced marital opportunities for them. Other factors accounting for the unequal access to education for girls include a general lack of girls' schools and availability of female teachers, a requirement that girls stay at home to perform needed tasks (for example, housekeeping, care of younger siblings and income-earning activities), and a conflict between the process of education and the desire of parents to prevent girls from having unsanctioned contact with boys, particularly as girls approach marriageable age.

Attempts have been made in almost all countries to close large gender gaps by introducing free and compulsory primary education, as well as encouraging the enrolment and retention of girls in schools. Various incentive schemes, such as scholarships for girls, free school meals, and separate schools for girls, have been instigated. Efforts have also been made to increase the numbers of female teachers in schools. However, there is still a long way to go to achieve universal literacy goals and eliminate gender discrimination in these societies.

## GENDER AND ECONOMIC ACTIVITY

Women's wage work is important for economic growth and the well-being of families. However, a lower level of education and vocational skills and training, heavy workloads at home and in non-paid domestic and market activities, and labour market discrimination often constrain women's participation in paid economic activity, lower their productivity, and reduce their wages. None the less, many women in South Asia do participate in economic activity and actively contribute their labour. Women make up 53% of the labour force in Bangladesh (the highest proportion in South Asia), followed by 50% in Nepal, 49% in the Maldives, 47% in Bhutan and 35% in Sri Lanka. However, women in South Asia continue to undertake all the major domestic duties, which consume a tremendous portion of their time. Numerous studies in India and in other countries of the region show that women, both in rural and urban areas, spend substantial time on household activities, which include cooking, cleaning up and washing. In rural areas, women perform other domestic duties in addition to these tasks; they collect fuel from nearby forests, fetch water from the

**Table 3. Gender Inequality in Economic Activity in South Asian Countries**

| Country | Female labour force participation rate (% ages 15 and older) | | Unpaid family worker (% employment, 2000–05*) | | Women in non-agric. sector (% of total, 2004) | Employment in agriculture (% of employment, 1995–2005*) | | Employment in industry (% of employment, 1995–2005*) | | Employment in services (% of employment, 1995–2005*) | |
|---|---|---|---|---|---|---|---|---|---|---|---|
| | % of labour force, 2005 | % of male rate, 2005 | Male | Female | | Male | Female | Male | Female | Male | Female |
| Afghanistan | n.a. | n.a. | n.a. | n.a. | n.a. | n.a. | n.a. | n.a. | n.a. | n.a. | n.a. |
| Bangladesh | 52.7 | 61 | 9.9 | 48.0 | 23.1 | 50 | 59 | 12 | 18 | 38 | 23 |
| Bhutan | 46.7 | 58 | n.a. | n.a. | n.a. | n.a. | n.a. | n.a. | n.a. | n.a. | n.a. |
| India | 34.0 | 42 | n.a. | n.a. | 17.3 | 58 | 78 | 17 | 11 | 25 | 11 |
| Maldives | 48.5 | 67 | n.a. | n.a. | n.a. | 18 | 5 | 16 | 24 | 56 | 39 |
| Nepal | 49.9 | 64 | n.a. | n.a. | n.a. | 79 | 94 | 5 | 1 | 13 | 5 |
| Pakistan | 32.7 | 39 | 16.4 | 46.9 | 8.6 | 38 | 65 | 22 | 16 | 40 | 20 |
| Sri Lanka | 34.9 | 45 | 4.2 | 20.9 | 43.2 | 32 | 40 | 40 | 35 | 29 | 25 |

* Latest available year.

Sources: HDSA, *Human Development in South Asia*, UNDP, *Human Development Report* and World Bank, *World Development Indicators*.

village well or public tap, carry clothes to the village well for laundering, make cowdung cakes, clean grain and feed the animals, and fill the manure pits. These activities are rarely considered economic, either by the national accounts system or by the women themselves, thus making them statistically invisible as far as their economic participation is concerned. Although such activities are highly productive, they are usually called 'marginal economic activity' or 'expenditure-saving activity'. Since the majority of activities performed by women are statistically not counted as economic and hence not monetarily valued, women's roles and their contribution are assigned a lower status. Moreover, a significant proportion of women in South Asia mix work and family activities during the day by working without pay on a farm or in some other family enterprise, or working in or near home. Countries differ in the criteria used to determine the extent to which such workers are to be counted as part of the labour force. This reflects the fact that, for women, demographic, social, legal, and cultural trends and norms determine whether their activities are regarded as economic.

Despite the methodological, conceptual and definitional flaws, statistics on women's work reveal that, in general, estimates for women in the labour force are lower than those for men. In most countries, however, the gap between male and female labour force participation rates has been narrowing since 1980. This stems from both falling rates for men and rising rates for women. The largest gap between men and women in labour force participation is observed in Pakistan and India, where the low rate of participation of women in the work force also brings down the overall labour force participation rate. The smallest gap between men and women in labour force participation is observed in the Maldives, Nepal and Bangladesh, where the share of women in the labour force is higher than that of other countries in the region; this raises the overall labour force participation rate (Table 3).

When women are in salaried employment, they tend to be concentrated in the non-agricultural sector. By and large, however, women's share in the non-agricultural sector is low. Sri Lanka and Bangladesh have a higher share of women's employment in the non-agricultural sector, with 43% and 23% respectively, whereas Pakistan and India have a lower share, with 9% and 17% respectively. However, in many countries of South Asia women work as unpaid family workers. Among people who are unsalaried, women are more likely than men to be unpaid family workers, while men are more likely than women to be working in industry and the service sector. The largest gender gap in unpaid family work is found in Bangladesh, where 10% of men and 48% of women work as unpaid family workers. The narrowest gender gap and lowest proportion of women working as unpaid family workers are found in Sri Lanka, where 4% of men and 21% of women are unpaid family workers. However, the higher proportion of women working as unpaid family labour may also be due to misclassification biases.

The distribution of sectoral employment by gender reveals some clear patterns. Industry accounts for a larger share of male than female employment in South Asia, as in other parts of the world, whereas a higher proportion of women work in the agricultural sector in South Asia. However, unlike other parts of the world where service jobs are increasingly important for women and the service sector is female-dominated, in South Asia employment in the service sector is male-dominated. Sri Lanka has the highest share of women's employment in the industry and service sector sector—35% and 25% respectively, whereas Nepal has the lowest share of women's employment in the industry and service sectors—1% and 5% respectively (Table 3).

Despite an increase in women's economic participation over the years, they endure sexual harassment, poor working conditions and pregnancy-based discrimination. Women in South Asia often receive less pay than men for equal work. The ratio of estimated female to male earned income is less than 1 in all the countries of South Asia for which data are available. While women earn half of what men earn in Bangladesh, Nepal and Sri Lanka, the proportion of female earnings is much lower in India and Pakistan. Some South Asian countries have introduced policies of reservation in government jobs to encourage women's participation in economic activity. For example, in Bangladesh and Pakistan 15% and 20% respectively of government jobs are reserved for women. However, the extension of women's work into the paid market without a change in gender relations would cause them a double burden. Gender roles need to be renegotiated in order that women's work has a positive impact on women's well-being and the well-being of their families. Unless gender roles and gender relations are renegotiated, any attempt to increase women's participation in economic activity is likely only to add stress for women and to have a harmful effect on their health and well-being, as well as on the well-being of their children and families.

## GENDER AND POLITICAL PARTICIPATION

**Table 4. Female Political Participation in South Asian Countries**

| Country | Parliament* | Government† |
|---|---|---|
| Afghanistan | 27 | 10 |
| Bangladesh | 15 | 8.3 |
| Bhutan | n.a. | 0 |
| India | 8 | 3.4 |
| Maldives | n.a. | 11.8 |
| Nepal | 6 | 7.4 |
| Pakistan | 21 | 5.6 |
| Sri Lanka | 5 | 10.3 |

* Women in parliament; % of total seats, 2006.

† Women in government; % of total positions at ministerial level, 2005.

Sources: UNDP, *Human Development Report 2005* and World Bank, *World Development Indicators* database 2006.

Gender parity in parliamentary representation in South Asia is far from being realized (Table 4). This is despite the fact that this region has had the largest number of women leaders who have been heads of state or government (Sirimavo Bandaranaike, Benazir Bhutto, Indira Gandhi, Sheikh Hasina, Chandrika Kumaratunga and Khaleda Zia). The first female head of any country in the world, as early as 1960, was from South Asia (Sirimavo Bandaranaike). The highest percentage of women's parliamentary representation in 2006 in the region was 27% in Afghanistan. This was followed by Pakistan (21%), Bangladesh (15%) and India (8%). Thus, in spite of the visibility of South Asian women at the higher level of government, the overall level of political participation remains very low. Without representation in decision-making positions in government, it is difficult for women to influence policy. However, parliamentary representation by women and other indicators of gender equality display certain discrepancies in the ordering of countries. For example, Pakistan had one of the highest number of women parliamentarians in 2006, but has one of the lowest gender indices in the region.

As a result of proactive women's movements in many South Asian countries, the demand for positive intervention in the form of reservation of seats for women in the governance structures has been met to some extent. In India, as a result of the 73rd and 74th constitutional amendments introduced in 1992, one-third of seats in its local government structures are reserved for women. Other countries of the region have also followed suit. In 1997 both Nepal and Bangladesh introduced women's reservation in their local bodies. The proportion reserved in Nepal was 20%, but in Bangladesh it was one-third of the seats in all four tiers of local government. In Pakistan, also, one-third of seats are reserved in local bodies, which is visible in the current figures for women's political participation. This policy has clearly assisted women's participation, which would otherwise have been denied, given the deep-rooted traditional attitudes towards women, patriarchy and male domination in politics.

## MARRIAGE, DOWRY AND 'HONOUR-KILLING'

With the exception of Sri Lanka, most South Asian marriages are arranged, at a young age, for both men and women. Marriage patterns have changed less radically in South Asia (with the exception of Sri Lanka) than in East and South-East Asia. This marriage pattern cuts across religious boundaries. Since, according to tradition, wives should be younger than their husbands, the age at marriage for girls is lower than for the boys. Historically, women in South Asia, with the exception of Sri Lanka, married around or before menarche. The countries have laws specifying the age at which girls may be married, but they are often ignored. For example, the Child Marriage Restraint Act was passed in 1929 in India, making it a criminal offence to marry a girl under the age of 15 years. This law was modified in 1978, raising the legal age for marriage to 18 years for girls and 21 for boys. Under this act, parents of underage spouses and the marriage officials performing the ceremonies are subject to criminal prosecution. Despite this, however, more than 50% of girls still marry before the age of 18 (some even without giving their consent) in Nepal, Bangladesh, India, Pakistan and Afghanistan. It is widely believed that early marriage for girls makes them more malleable and accepting of their new family circumstances, and in particular of the authority of their husbands and in-laws. The pressure for early marriage for girls also emerges from the notion of conforming to tradition, and to preserve the chastity of daughters. For Hindus, this may derive from ancient teaching whereby a girl should be married before she attains puberty and not later than after the first menstruation. Parents are concerned about their daughters' 'sexual purity' and 'honour' and marry them off early in order to safeguard them from sexual exploitation. Early marriage is also encouraged by there being no respected role for unmarried adult women. In fact, a daughter is considered a debt of honour and there is hardly a more shameful failure for a man than the inability to marry off his daughter.

A customary practice that is associated with marriage in South Asia is the practice of paying dowry to the groom's family and this also cuts across religious boundaries. Historically, dowry played an important role in supporting a married woman in times of difficulty. The traditional Hindu law of inheritance excluded women from inheriting ancestral property. Hence, dowry was justified as a necessary custom to give women some sense of inheritance or security. In present times, however, dowry has assumed a wide-ranging and different meaning. Dowry is not merely confined to the presents to the bride in terms of jewellery, clothing, household gifts, luxury and modern electronic items such as television, fridges and valuable immovable property made to the husband, but also includes other offerings made to the bridegroom or members of his family as a token of gratitude for accepting their daughter as a daughter-in-law and for giving kind treatment to their daughter.

The traditional custom of dowry may take a potentially ruinous, and at times cruel, form. Families of prospective grooms have started asking for exorbitant dowries, and failure to give an agreed amount has sometimes resulted in bride-burning. Dowry-related deaths among South Asian women have been on the increase in recent years. In particular, the practice of bride-burning reached its height in the 1990s. Women in India, Pakistan and Bangladesh often suffer violence and torture in the event of disagreement over dowry payments. Most of these cases remain unreported. A Dowry Prohibition Act was passed in India in 1961, declaring both the giving and receiving of dowry a punishable act under law. However, this code is rarely followed, and infractions against it are almost never prosecuted. The custom of large dowries has further devalued the already low status of women in South Asia.

There is evidence that this practice may have delayed female marriage in India while parents save for dowry, but it can also act to hasten marriage for older brides who may require higher dowries. Moreover, dowry is central to the arrangement of marriage, and may act to perpetuate or, alternatively, to undermine the family's role in marriage, thereby indirectly affecting marriage patterns.

Another South Asian customary practice that has received great international attention has been the practice of 'honour killing'. In many parts of South Asia (in particular Pakistan and Bangladesh), women may be killed by a family member if they commit adultery, if they are the victims of rape, if they fall in love with the wrong person, or if they seek to divorce an abusive husband—in short, if their sexual and emotional behaviour is considered to bring dishonour or shame to their family. The problem of 'honour killing' is not one of morality; rather it is seen as a disturbing illustration of male power hierarchy in the family. This acceptance of the male patriarch's right to kill the women in his family to protect the family honour is a deep-rooted tradition, which according to reports often has the full endorsement of women in the family. Every year hundreds of women are known to die as a result of 'honour killings'. In Pakistan alone in 2005 more than 260 'honour killings' were documented by the Human Rights Commission, mostly from media reports. Many more cases go unreported and almost all go unpunished. As a result, it is a practice that remains strong, and such 'honour killings' are seldom prosecuted. The failure by the state to prevent and to investigate the practice of 'honour killing' is the result of government indifference and gender bias in law and within the police force.

## GENDER-RELATED DEVELOPMENT INDEX (GDI)

The Gender-related Development Index (GDI), published in the Human Development Report 2005, notes the inequalities between men and women according to the same variables that constitute the Human Development Index (HDI) and which are related to overall achievement in a particular society. These are the variables of education (adult literacy rate and the combined primary, secondary and tertiary gross education enrolment ratio), health (life expectancy at birth) and income (gross domestic product—GDP—per caput at purchasing power parity—PPP—in US dollars). Although the GDI has been criticized on the grounds that, by considering only three variables, it fails to take into account important dimensions which are particularly salient for women (such as safety and security), it nevertheless serves as an important tool for the analysis of gender inequality.

With the exception of the Maldives, no other South Asian country for which data are available performs well in terms of the GDI (Table 1). Among the 140 countries for which the GDI is available, the Maldives ranks 85, Sri Lanka 89, India 113, Bangladesh 121, Nepal 125 and Pakistan 128. The Human Development Report 2005 also publishes HDI minus GDI values to measure the performance of countries on gender-related development against overall human development. This value is calculated only for those countries for which data on both the HDI and GDI are available. A positive value for this figure indicates that the GDI rank is higher than the HDI rank; that is, gender-related development has been better than overall human development. A negative value indicates the opposite. The Maldives and Bangladesh, with values of 4 and 1 respectively, are the only countries in the region that have performed better in terms of gender-related development in comparison with overall human development. India, with a value of zero, has achieved a low level of achievement, equally low both in gender-related development and human development. In Pakistan, Nepal and Sri Lanka, with values of –7, –4 and –1 respectively, gender-related development has been worse than overall human development. Thus, most of the countries of South Asia demonstrate a low level of gender-related development.

## IMPLICATIONS OF GENDER DISPARITY

Sex discrimination in South Asia has immense demographic implications because of the size of the populations involved. A high level of son preference, accompanied by falling fertility, has already resulted in a skewed sex ratio at birth in some states of India because women have access to methods of identifying the sex of foetuses and to induced abortions. A skewed sex ratio, in turn, has worrisome implications for future population structure, the marriage and labour market, and personality development. This imbalance will result in a huge number of men reaching marriageable age unable to find a wife. In this regard, population policy needs to pay special attention to the possible consequences of high son preference that go beyond the retardation of fertility decline. This is particularly important in places like the Indian state of Haryana, where the practice of sex-selective abortion is most widespread.

Sex discrimination in nutrition has implications for reproductive health. Some women have difficulties in carrying a pregnancy successfully to term because of childhood discrimination. Failure to nourish girl children can limit their capacity for healthy motherhood through, for example, stunting and a small pelvis, and a reluctance to provide medical care may compound these problems. If a pregnancy goes wrong, lack of obstetric care may be fatal, yet millions of women continue to face such risks every year.

## CONCLUDING REMARKS

Despite much economic progress in recent years, gender inequalities in many dimensions of life remain pervasive in many countries of South Asia. While gender disparities exist in most of South Asia, they are most prevalent in a band across north-west India, Pakistan and Bangladesh. Sri Lanka stands out as an outlier in the subcontinent. In most of the other countries of South Asia discrimination against girl children begins immediately after birth, with boys routinely receiving a larger share of education and health expenditure, for example, than girls. Although the neglect of girl children within various parameters can be conscious or unconscious, this neglect is a response to the prevalent and deep-rooted gender ideologies that operate at all institutional levels, and is resistant to change. Many factors contribute to this preference: the presence of the dowry system; a culture in which sons inherit family land and are responsible for taking care of elderly parents and continuing the family line; and the lesser economic worth of women, who are less educated and less likely than men to work outside the home. Patriarchal values are so deeply rooted that, even though many women realize that girls often remain closer to their mothers than sons and often take better care of their parents in old age, they still prefer sons. It may take several generations, as well as an improvement in the status of women, before couples become indifferent to their children's gender. If the practice of female discrimination continues at the present rate, several million women will go 'missing' every decade and the repercussions will be enormous. Fewer women means fewer children, and still fewer girls for future generations.

## BIBLIOGRAPHY

Agarwal, B. 'Gender, resistance and land: interlinked struggles over resources and meanings in South Asia', *Journal of Peasant Studies* , Vol. 22 (1), pp. 81–125, Oct. 1994.

Agnihotri, S. B. *Sex Ratio Patterns in the Indian Population—A Fresh Exploration*. New Delhi, Sage Publications, 2000.

Amin, S. 'The effect of women's status on sex differentials in infant and child mortality in South Asia', *Genus*, Vol. 46, pp. 3–4, 55–69, 1990.

Arnold, F. 'Gender preferences for children: findings from the demographic and health surveys'. International Population Conference, Beijing, IUSSP, 1997.

Arnold, F., Choe, M. K., and Roy, T. K. 'Son preference, family building process and child mortality in India'. *East-West Centre Working Paper*, Vol. 85, pp. 1–34, 1996.

Bairagi, R. 'Gender preference of children and its consequences'. XXII IUSSP General Conference, Beijing, 1997.

Bardhan, P. K. 'On life and death question', *Economic and Political Weekly*, Vol. 9, pp. 1293–1304, 1974.

Basu, A. K. 'How pervasive are sex differentials in childhood nutritional levels in South Asia?', *Social Biology*, Vol. 40, pp.1–2, 25–37.

*Culture, the Status of Women, and Demographic Behaviour*. Oxford, Clarendon Press, 1992.

Bentley, M. E., and Griffiths, P. L. 'The burden of anemia among women in India', *European Journal of Clinical Nutrition* , Vol. 57 (1), pp. 52–60, 2003.

Bhat, M. P. N. and Halli, S. S. 'Demography of brideprice and dowry: Causes and consequences of the Indian marriage squeeze', *Population Studies*, Vol. 53, pp. 129–148, 1999.

Bhuta, Z. A. 'Why has so little changed in maternal and child health in South Asia?', *British Medical Journal*, Vol. 321, pp. 809–812, 2000.

Bhuta, Z. A., Gupta, In., de'Silva, H., Manandhar, D., Awasthi, S., Hossain, S. M., and Salam, M. A. 'Maternal and child health: Is South Asia ready for change?', *British Medical Journal*, Vol. 328, pp. 816–819, 2004.

Booth, B. E. 'Decreased access to medical care for girls in Punjab, India: the role of age, religion, and distance', *American Journal of Public Health*, Vol. 82 (8), pp. 1155–1157, 1992.

Bose, A. 'Gender issues and population change: tradition, technology and social turbulence', *International Social Science Journal*, Vol. 46 (3), pp. 387–395, 1994.

Bourne, K., and Walker, G. M. 'The differential effect of mother's education on mortality of boys and girls in India', *Population Studies*, Vol. 45 (2), pp. 203–19, 1991.

Caldwell, P., and Caldwell, J. C. 'Gender implications for survival in South Asia', *Health Transition Working Paper No. 7*. Canberra, National Centre for Epidemiology and Population Health, Australian National University, 1990.

Coale, A. J. 'Excess female mortality and the balance of the sexes in the population: an estimate of the number of missing females', *Population and Development Review*, Vol. 17 (3), pp. 517–523, 1991.

Daniel, G. 'On substituting sex preference strategies in East Asia', *Population and Development Review*, Vol. 22 (1), pp. 111–125, 1996.

Das Gupta, M. 'Explaining Asia's "missing women": a new look at the data', *Population and Development Review,* Vol. 31 (3), pp. 529–535, 2005.

Das Gupta, M., and Mari Bhat, P. N. 'Fertility decline and increased manifestation of sex bias in India', *Population Studies*, Vol. 51, pp. 307–315, 1997.

Das Gupta, M., and Shuzhuo, Li. 'Gender bias in China, South Korea and India 1920-1990: effects of war, famine and fertility decline', *Development and Change*, Vol. 30, pp. 619–652, 1999.

Fikree. F. F. and Pasha, O. 'Role of gender in health disparity: the South Asian context', *British Medical Journal*, Vol. 328 (7443), pp. 823–826, 2004.

George, S., Abel, R., and Miller, B. 'Female infanticide in rural South India', *Economic and Political Weekly*, Vol. 27 (22), pp. 1153–1156, 1992.

HDSA. *Human Development in South Asia*. Mahbub-ul-Haq Human Development Centre, Karachi, Oxford University Press, 2003.

Hossain, M. B., Phillips, J. F., and Pence, B. 'The effect of women's status on infant and child mortality in four rural areas of Bangladesh', *Journal of Biosocial Science* , Vol. 39 (3), pp. 355–366, May 2007.

Huda S. 'Sex trafficking in South Asia', *International Journal of Gynaecology & Obstetrics*, Vol. 94 (3), pp. 374–381, Sept. 2006.

Hussain, R., Fikree, F. F., and Berendes, H. W. 'The role of son preference in reproductive behaviour in Pakistan', *Bulletin of the World Health Organization,* Vol. 78 (3), pp. 379–388, 2000.

Kanitkar, S. D. 'Gender discrimination in the family: views and experiences of teenage girls', *Journal of Family Welfare*, Vol. 42 (4), pp. 32–38, 1996.

Karkal, M. 'Invisibility of the girl child in India', *Indian Journal of Social Work*, Vol. 52 (1), pp. 5–12, 1991.

Kaur, M. 'Female foeticide—a sociological perspective', *Journal of Family Welfare*, Vol. 39 (1), pp. 40–43, 1993.

Kaur, R. 'Across region marriages—poverty, female migration and the sex ratio', *Economic and Political Weekly*, Vol. 25, pp. 2595–2603, 2004.

'Dispensable daughters and bachelor sons: sex discrimination in North India', *Economic and Political Weekly*, Vol. 43, pp. 109–114, 2008.

Kishor, S. '"May God give sons to all": gender and child mortality in India', *American Sociological Review*, Vol. 58, pp. 247–265, 1993.

Klasen, S., and Wink, C. 'Missing women: revisiting the debate', *Feminist Economics,* Vol. 9 (2–3), pp. 263–299, 2003.

Kusum, L. 'The use of pre-natal diagnostic techniques for sex selection: the Indian scene', *Bioethics*, Vol. 7, pp. 149–165, 1993.

Leone, T., Matthews, Z., and Dalla Zuanna, G. 'Impact and determinants of sex preference in Nepal', *International Family Planning Perspectives*, Vol. 29 (2), pp. 69–75, June 2003.

Mahalingam, R., Haritatos, J., and Jackson, B. 'Essentialism and the cultural psychology of gender in extreme son preference communities in India', *American Journal of Orthopsychiatry*, Vol. 77 (4), pp. 598–609, 2007.

Mazumdar, V., and Krishnaji, N. (Eds). *Enduring Conundrum: India's Sex Ratio*. Delhi, Rainbow Publishers, 2001.

Miller, B. D. 'Social class, gender and intrahousehold food allocations to children in South Asia', *Social Science & Medicine*, Vol. 44 (11), pp. 1685–1695, June 1997.

Mishra, V., Roy, T. K., and Retherford, T. K. 'Sex differentials in childhood feeding, health care, and nutritional status in India', *Population and Development Review*, Vol. 30 (2), pp. 269–295, 2004.

Mumtaz, Z., and Salway, S. M. 'Gender, pregnancy and the uptake of antenatal care services in Pakistan', *Sociology of Health & Illness*, Vol. 29 (1), pp. 1–26, Jan. 2007.

Mumtaz, Z., Salway, S., Waseem, M., and Umer, N. 'Gender-based barriers to primary health care provision in Pakistan: the experience of female providers', *Health Policy and Planning*, Vol. 18 (3), pp. 261–269, Sept. 2003.

Murthi, M., Guio, A. C., and Dreze, J. 'Mortality, fertility, and gender bias in India: a district level analysis', *Population and Development Review*, Vol. 21 (4), pp. 745–782, 1995.

Murthy, R.K. 'Fighting female infanticide by working with midwives: an Indian case study', *Gender and Development*, Vol. 4 (2), pp. 20–27, 1996.

Mutharayappa, R., Choe, M. K., Arnold, F., and Roy, T. K. 'Is son preference slowing down India's transition to low fertility?', *NFHS Bulletin*, IIPS, Bombay and East-West Centre Program on Population, Honolulu.

Nath, D. C., and Land, K. C. 'Sex preference and third birth intervals in a traditional Indian society', *Journal of Biosocial Sciences*, Vol. 26 (3), pp. 377–388, 1994.

Park, C. B., and Cho, N. H. 'Consequences of son preference in low fertility countries in East Asia: rising imbalance of sex ratio at birth', *Population and Development Review*, Vol. 21, pp. 59–84, 1995.

Pebley, A. R., and Amin, S. 'The impact of a public-health intervention on sex differentials in childhood mortality in rural Punjab, India', *Health Transition Review*, Vol. 1 (2), pp. 143–169, 1991.

Premi, M. K., and Raju, S. 'Born to die: female infanticide in Madhya Pradesh', *Search Bulletin*, Vol. 13 (3), 1998.

Rahman, L., and Rao, V. 'The determinants of gender equity in India: examining Dyson and Moore's thesis with new data', *Population and Development Review*, Vol. 30 (2), pp. 239–268, 2004.

Rahman, M. 'Gender preference, fertility behaviour, and excess female child mortality in Matlab, Bangladesh', *Johns Hopkins University*, Baltimore, Maryland, 1990.

Rajaretnam, T., and Deshpande, R. V. 'The effect of sex preference on contraceptive use and fertility in rural south India', *International Family Planning Perspectives*, Vol. 20 (3), pp. 88–95, 1994.

Silverman, J. G., Decker, M. R., Gupta, J., Maheshwari, A., Brian, M., and Raj, A. 'HIV prevalence and predictors of infection in sex-trafficked Nepalese girls and women', *JAMA,* Vol. 298, pp. 536–542, 2007.

Thaddeus, S., and Maine, D. *Too Far to Walk: Maternal Mortality in Context*. New York, Centre for Population and Family Health, Faculty of Medicine, Columbia University, 1991.

van Balen, F., and Inhorn, M. C. 'Son preference, sex selection, and the "new" new reproductive technologies', *International Journal of Health Services*, Vol. 33 (2), pp. 235–252, 2003.

World Health Organization. *Gender and Health: Technical Paper*. Geneva, World Health Organization, Women's Health and Development, 1998.

World Health Organization. *World Health Statistics*. Geneva, World Health Organization, 2008.

# THE RELIGIONS OF SOUTH ASIA

GEOFFREY PARRINDER

Revised for this edition by the editorial staff

## HINDUISM

Hinduism, with an estimated 1,071m. adherents in 2000, is the name given by Europeans to the major religion of India.

### Historical Background

The name is derived from India and the River Indus in the north-west. Here flourished an extensive city culture from about 2500 to 1500 BC, contemporary with ancient Mesopotamia and Egypt. These cities were destroyed by invading Aryans, but remains indicate that Indus Valley religion included worship of a Mother Goddess and of a Lord of Yogis and animals, like Shiva, a great god today. A caste system arose from conquest and colour, at the head of which were the Brahmin priests who imposed their religion.

The Brahmins compiled the most ancient religious texts, the *Vedas* ('knowledge'), in four collections. These were not written down for many centuries but passed on orally. The early history of Hinduism is scanty, with no historical founder and no organized church, but development can be traced in religious texts. The Vedas are hymns to many gods of heaven and earth, and they portray a relatively simple religion in some ways like that of the Homeric Greeks, who were also Aryans. The Vedic hymns were probably compiled between 1500 and 800 BC, but their use was restricted to the upper castes. Today they are used only by priests and at marriage and funeral ceremonies. They were followed by the *Upanishads* ('sitting-down-near', teaching sessions), dialogues of which the principal were compiled between 800 and 300 BC. The Upanishads are called *Vedanta* ('end of the Vedas'), although this term is also used for some later philosophies. They discuss philosophical questions: the origins of the world and man, the nature of divinity and the human soul, death and immortality, self-discipline and devotion.

From this time onwards arose masses of religious works, which became the chief inspiration of most Hindus. Two great epic poems, the *Mahabharata*, 'great India' story, and the *Ramayana*, 'the story of Rama', include myth, history, theology and ethics. The personal gods of the Vedas reappear but with many others, no doubt from the Indus Valley and indigenous sources. A creating deity, Brahma, plays a small part, but Shiva, Vishnu and the Goddess come from now on to be the major deities of Hinduism. Vishnu, a minor Vedic god, became important through his *Avatars* ('descents'), visible embodiments on earth in animal and human form. The two chief human Avatars were Rama and Krishna, the latter a dark god of herdsmen, a warrior king, and a lover of the soul. A small section of the Great Epic is the *Bhagavad-Gita*, 'the Song of the Lord' Krishna, the best known of all Indian scriptures, which gives the teachings of the god Krishna on reincarnation, salvation, deity and devotion. Stories of Krishna and other gods continued in the *Puranas*, 'ancient tales', composed down to the Middle Ages. Many medieval Indian poets also produced popular songs in praise of Krishna, Rama, Shiva and the Goddess, and devotional groups flourished, especially in Bengal and southern India.

In modern times external influences and internal pressures brought reforms of Hinduism. Muslim invasions began in the eighth century AD, but became most potent under the rule of the Mughals from the 16th to the 19th centuries. Christian missions and European trade developed especially in the 19th and 20th centuries. Both Islam and Christianity criticized Hinduism for polytheism, idolatry and practices such as *suttee* (*satī*, widow-burning). Modern Hinduism is presented as 'eternal truth', including all that is best from other faiths, but with its special emphasis either in pantheism or devotion.

### Beliefs

Belief in the indestructibility of the soul is basic to Hinduism; it is both pre-existence and post-existence. Transmigration from one life to another, or reincarnation, is universally held, but the endless births and deaths are a harsh cycle from which ways of salvation are offered, through knowledge, works or devotion. The next life is conditioned by *Karma*, 'works' or the entail of works. This explains the inequalities and sufferings of life, to those who accept it in faith, but it does not necessarily lead to fatalism. Karma can be improved by good actions, and the next rebirth may be to a higher level. Yet those who do wrong may descend to the animal level or even lower; hence there is a great respect for animal life and many Hindus are vegetarians.

From early times Indians have practised self-discipline, and there are many holy men, sadhus, swamis and the like. *Yoga* is a general name for both discipline and union, related to the English 'yoke'. It may consist in forms of physical exercise and control, in Hatha ('force') Yoga. Some adepts claim supernatural powers, like levitation. Most practitioners engage in breath-control and sit in cross-legged postures. Raja ('royal') Yoga proceeds to mastery of mind, concentration or emptying of thought, and attainment of supreme knowledge or bliss.

### *The Caste System*

The caste system greatly developed over the centuries. There are four basic castes: Brahmin priests, Raja or Kshatriya rulers and warriors, Vaishya artisan merchants and Shudra servants. The first three are 'twice born' through initiation with sacred threads at adolescence. However, the castes have been expanded with many local and occupational castes, said to number over 3,000, with further sub-castes, and below these are millions of outcastes who perform the most menial tasks. Caste distinctions are rigid in theory, and Brahmins in particular are offended by any contact with low castes; eating between castes is prohibited. Many occupational and guild distinctions remain, but modern conditions, liberal laws and closer communications are breaking down exclusiveness. Communal quarrels arise between castes and religions, particularly in anything that touches the sacredness of the cow.

### Temples and Worship

India is a land of magnificent architectural monuments, most of them religious. The temples have small inner sanctuaries surrounded by large open paved courtyards, tanks for ritual washing, and walls with stone gates and towers. Temple worship is performed by priests without much lay assistance, but people visit the courtyards for quiet prayer and meditation.

Modern temples are less impressive, but there are countless little shrines by the wayside or in the middle of streets, at which people stop to place gifts and pray. Hindu homes have rooms or corners for images and devotion, where flowers are placed and incense burns. Worship is performed at home. There is no sabbath or regular obligation to visit temples, but for festivals and annual events great crowds assemble there, when images are carried in procession in chariots or on elephants.

There are countless holy places, from the Himalayas in the north to the extreme southern capes, and pilgrimages are made to seven chief sites. The holiest place of all is Varanasi (Benares) on the middle Ganges (Ganga), where steps (*ghats*) lead down from temples into the sacred river in which people wash and pray. 'Burning ghats' are reserved for cremation, the normal lot of the Hindu dead. Varanasi is full of holy men, dressed in yellow robes or smeared with ashes, begging and awaiting death in the sacred city. Great assemblies are held here and at other places every few years, at which millions of people gather to bathe in the river.

There are many Hindu festivals and all deities have sacred days. *Holi* in the spring is an ancient fertility feast when coloured water is sprinkled on participants and the praises of Krishna and his loves are chanted. *Dashara* or *Dassehra* in the autumn is marked by carnival figures of the hero Rama and his demon enemy, Ravana, the latter being packed with crackers which are set alight at the end. *Divali* in November is a feast of lights for the gracious goddess, Lakshmi, consort of Vishnu, when lamps welcome the patroness of wealth, business and learning. In other popular feasts the god of fortune, Ganesha, son of Shiva, is carried in the form of images of pink elephants, or Shiva, the lord both of Yoga and the dance, is depicted as the dancing god within a flaming circle, often represented in bronze images.

**Organization and Distribution**

There is little widespread organization in Hindu religion. The followers of Shiva, Vishnu and the Mother are joined in their own cult sympathy, and sometimes divided between cults in antagonism. There are centres of learning and worship, but many local differences of practice. Monasteries and retreat houses (*ashrams*) cater for cults and societies, but no large-scale monastic organization compares with those of Buddhism and Christianity. Many Hindu holy men are solitaries, and may be seen sitting alone or living in secluded places with a few disciples.

In modern times the Brahmo and Arya Samaj have organized themselves, and also significant is the Ramakrishna Mission. Taking its name from a 19th-century holy man of Bengal, Shri Ramakrishna, and directed by his disciple Swami Vivekananda, the Mission initiated religious, educational and social works and undertakes much literary propaganda. The Vishwa Hindu Parishad (World Hindu Council) takes religious and political action to promote the role of Hinduism as the religion of India, and it inspired action against the Muslim Babri mosque at Ayodhya (see Recent History of India). From Puducherry (Pondicherry), south of Chennai (Madras), the Aurobindo Ashram engages in meditation, education, industrial work and literary propaganda, and there are many smaller similar agencies.

Hinduism is virtually confined to the peoples of the Indian subcontinent, although it is practised also by peoples of Indian origin in Sri Lanka. It has commonly been said that a Hindu is one born into a caste and who accepts the Vedic scriptures, and therefore it is an ethnic and not a missionary religion; but in past centuries Hinduism spread as far away as Bali and Cambodia, and today some of its missionaries choose Europe and North America as their fields.

## ISLAM

Islam means 'submission' or surrender to God, and a Muslim, from the same root, is a surrendered person. This faith was taught by Muhammad, but Muslims object to being called Muhammadan or Mahometan because they do not worship the founder of their religion. Although a late entrant among the world's great religions, Islam is a universal faith, with an estimated 1,200m. followers in the year 2000.

**Historical Background**

Muhammad lived from AD 570 to 632 in Arabia, which was largely pagan and polytheistic, with small communities of Jews and Christians. The town of Mecca was already a sacred place, and it was part of the religious genius of Muhammad to purge some of its holy sites of idolatrous associations and incorporate them into the new religion, particularly the Ka'ba shrine, a cube-like sanctuary in the middle of Mecca. Jewish and Christian figures were also honoured by Muhammad, especially Abraham, Moses and Jesus, and many of their stories occur in the sacred book, the Koran. Yet the central themes of Muhammad's teaching came in his own experience: the unity of God, his word to man, the judgement of unbelievers and paradise for the righteous. From AD 610 onwards Muhammad received divine visions and messages and preached a monotheistic faith. Most of the leaders of Mecca, however, rejected it, and in AD 622 Muhammad migrated to Medina 320 km to the north. This 'migration' (*Hijra* or *Hegira*) was later taken as the beginning of the Muslim era from which its calendar is dated. In Medina, Muhammad became leader of a community, and after successful battles against the Meccans he eventually ruled over much of Arabia. He returned to Mecca in triumph in AD 630, cleansing the Ka'ba of idols, but going back to Medina where he died two years later.

Muhammad was followed by Caliphs (*Khalifas*, 'successors') who greatly extended the rule of Islam. Under Abu Bakr the Arab armies conquered Babylon, and under 'Umar (Omar) Syria, Palestine and Egypt fell to their rule. Jerusalem and Alexandria surrendered, led by their Christian patriarchs who were glad to be rid of Eastern Roman (Byzantine) Greek overlords. Arab rule was not unduly oppressive, allowing the survival of Christian communities to this day in Syrian, Coptic, Greek and other churches. Arab armies slowly pressed on into North Africa, crossed into Spain in AD 711, and were only repelled from central France in AD 732. To the east the second Persian empire fell to the Arabs, who entered northern India in AD 705 and sent embassies as far as China. As the Arab empire consolidated, it absorbed Eastern and Western cultures and produced its own contributions; Greek philosophy, mathematics and medicine were preserved by the Arabs during the Dark Ages of Europe.

The Arab empire dominated the Near and Middle East, from Spain to central Asia, and the caliphate came to be located in Baghdad until its fall to the Mongols in 1258. After the capture of Constantinople (İstanbul) in 1453 the Caliph lived there until his office was abolished by the Turkish Government in 1924. The Turkish (Ottoman) empire broke up into independent polities, and Turkey itself became Westernized and secularized, a tendency that has prevailed in varying degrees in other Islamic countries.

**Beliefs and Practice**

There are Five Pillars of practical religion in Islam:

(i) The first is the Witness that 'there is no god but God' (*Allah*) and that 'Muhammad is the Apostle of God'. This confession is called from the minaret or a mosque by a *muezzin* ('crier') at the times of daily prayer. It stresses the unity and omnipotence of God, but it does not necessarily make Muslims into fatalists, an attitude that may derive as much from social as from theological reasons;

(ii) The second Pillar is Prayer, which is to be said five times a day, turning towards the Ka'ba shrine in Mecca. Muslims unroll prayer mats and pray in a *mosque* (a 'place of prostration'), at home, or wherever they are, bowing and prostrating to God and reciting set verses from the Koran in Arabic. On Fridays there is congregational worship in central mosques attended by men but not normally by women, in which worship includes the formal prayers and usually a short sermon;

(iii) No collection of money is made in the mosque, but the third Pillar is Almsgiving, which provides for the sick and poor in lands where there are few social services;

(iv) The fourth Pillar is Fasting from food and drink, which is obligatory on all healthy adults during the hours of daylight for the whole of the ninth month, Ramadan. The sick, pregnant women, travellers and children are exempt, but adults should fast when restored to normal life. Some modern states extend exemption to students, soldiers and factory workers, and it is said that the true fast is from sin. Since the Islamic year is lunar, the date of Ramadan falls a little earlier each year compared with the solar calendar (see section on Calendars and Weights and Measures), and in northern countries fasting in summer is a considerable trial. The fast ends with one of the two great Muslim festivals, *Id al Fitr* (festival of breaking the fast) or *Little Bairam*;

(v) The fifth Pillar is Pilgrimage (*hajj*) to Mecca, which is incumbent at least once in a lifetime on every Muslim, who may then take the title *Hajji*. About 1m. pilgrims go every year to Mecca, which is the holy city forbidden to all but Muslims, and some take months or years to perform the ambition of a lifetime, travelling by air, sea, lorry or on foot. The pilgrimage is in the 12th month and must be performed in simple dress donned at a distance of 16 km from Mecca, women's heads covered, faces usually unveiled. The central ritual entails going round the Ka'ba seven times, kissing a Black Stone in its walls, and visiting hills outside Mecca where sheep and other animals are sacrificed. At the same time Muslims all over the world sacrifice sheep, and this constitutes the principal festival, *Id al Kabir, Qurban* or *Bairam*. This ceremony unites all Muslims and is popularly linked with Abraham's sacrifice of a sheep in place of his son. *Mouloud* (*Maulid*), the birthday of the Prophet, is another popular modern anniversary.

The Holy War (*Jihad*) was one means of the unparalleled spread of Islam in the first centuries, but despite pressures it has not been elevated into a Pillar of religion. Today theologians interpret the *Jihad* as war against sin in the soul.

The Koran (*Qur'ān*, 'recitation' or 'reading') is regarded as the very Word of God and not to be subjected to criticism. The Koran is about as long as the New Testament, in 114 chapters (*suras*) of uneven length, the longest ones coming first after the opening chapter. The Opening (*Fatiha*) is repeated twice at least at all times of daily prayer, preceded by the ascription 'in the name of God, the Merciful, the Compassionate'. Two short chapters at the end are also used in prayers, and instructed and pious Muslims may repeat other chapters, always in Arabic. Modern translations of the Koran are now allowed for private use and there have always been many commentaries. The chief message of the Koran is the majesty of God, his oneness, demand for human obedience and coming judgement. The later and longer chapters include much family and social legislation, for marriage, divorce, personal and communal behaviour.

The Koran is not the only authority for Muslims, but it is supplemented by numerous Traditions (*Hadith*), which include sayings attributed to the Prophet and his companions. Doctrine and morals are further interpreted by Comparison and Consent. Four law schools arose, which apply Islamic law (*Shari'a*) to all activities of life. In Asia the two principal law schools are the *Hanafi* in central Asia and the Indian subcontinent, and the *Shafi'i* in the East Indies. In modern times interpretation of law ranges between conservative rigorism and modernism; many of the Traditions are debated but the Koran remains sacrosanct.

The Islamic community (*umma*) is the basis of the brotherhood of Islam, which from the early centuries aimed at making this religion international and above tribal rivalries. This is still the ideal, though the rise of nationalism has brought divisive interests into the Muslim world.

### Sects and Mystics

The great majority, probably over 80%, of Muslims are *Sunni*, followers of 'the path', custom or tradition. They accept the first four Caliphs (Abu Bakr, 'Umar, 'Uthman, 'Ali) as 'rightly guided', receive six authentic books of Traditions, and belong to one of the four schools of law. Other Muslims claim to follow true tradition but differ on its interpretation.

#### *Shi'a Muslims*

The major division came early. The Shi'a or 'followers' of 'Ali believed that as cousin and son-in-law of Muhammad, 'Ali should have been his first successor and they reject the first three Caliphs of Sunni Islam. When at last his turn came, there was a division and another Caliph was set up in Damascus. The Shi'a became linked with patriotism in Iraq, which objected to rule from Syria. Husain, a son of 'Ali, went to found a kingdom in Iraq, but was intercepted by rival troops and slain at Karbala. Husain became the great Shi'a martyr, the anniversary of whose death in Muharram, the first month of the Islamic calendar, is the occasion for days of mourning and long Passion Plays in Shi'a towns. At the climax of the play Husain receives the key of intercession from the Angel Gabriel and promises paradise to all who call upon him.

The basic Shi'a beliefs are the same as those of the Sunni, but 'Ali is added after Muhammad in the confession of faith. Their most distinctive doctrine is that of the *Imam*, spiritual 'leader', which was used in preference to caliph for the head of state. Most Shi'a are 'Twelvers', recognizing 12 Imams, of whom the last disappeared in AD 878, but it is believed that he will return again as the *Mahdi* ('guided one') to put down evil and restore righteousness on earth. In 1502 Shi'ism became the established religion of Iran, and it is strongest there and in Iraq and north India. *Ayatollahs* ('signs of God') are conservative religious leaders in Iran.

#### *Isma'ilis*

Some of the Shi'a are Isma'ilis, believing that it was the seventh Imam, Isma'il, who was the last when he disappeared in AD 765, hence they are also called 'Seveners'. There were political as well as religious reasons for the schism. There are mystical beliefs in the 'light' of the Imam, eternal and ever-present, and various grades of initiation into mysteries. There are small groups of Isma'ilis in Afghanistan and Central Asia, and larger ones in Pakistan, Bangladesh and India. Offshoots are most of the Khojas whose leader is the Aga Khan. These Isma'ili Khojas are found in Mumbai (Bombay), Gujarat, Sindh, other Indian and neighbouring towns and in East Africa. They number over 200,000, in active and educated communities, noted for social works.

#### *Ahmadiyya Movement*

At Qadian in India and Lahore in Pakistan there are centres of a modern movement called Ahmadiyya, after Ghulam Ahmad of the Punjab who, from 1890, was set forth as the expected Mahdi, Messiah and Avatar. After struggles and divisions the Ahmadiyya have published many books in English, sent missionaries to Africa, and propounded teachings, most of which are orthodox Islam but with some modern polemics.

#### *Sufis*

Sufi mystics have been found in all branches of Islam from the early days, so called from the woollen (*suf*) robes that they wore, like Christian monks. In the face of orthodox formalism and deism, the Sufis taught the love of God, and sometimes this verged on pantheism or identity with God. The Sufis came to be accepted, partly through the efforts of the Persian philosopher, Ghazali, himself a mystic. Many popular shrines are tombs of holy men or sheikhs.

### Distribution

Most of the population of Afghanistan are Sunni Muslims. In Pakistan Islam is the state religion, about 97% of the population being Muslim. By 2000 the number of Muslims in Bangladesh was estimated at 127m. and, according to the 2001 census results in India, the number of Muslims in that country totalled 138.2m. (13.4% of the population). There are Muslim minorities in Sri Lanka.

## ZOROASTRIANISM

This ancient religion, which in origins was akin to that of the Aryan Indians, was practised by related peoples in Iran, but it survives today mainly in small communities in India. The Parsis (Persians) migrated to India from the ninth century onwards under pressure from Muslim invaders. They settled mainly in the region of Mumbai, although there are groups elsewhere in India and East Africa, numbering in all about 218,000. The prophetic reformer of the religion was Zoroaster (Zarathushtra), generally dated 630–553 BC. He taught faith in one God, Ahura Mazda ('Lord Wisdom'), who was goodness opposed to the spirit of evil, Ahriman. In hymns, *Gathas*, attributed to him, Zoroaster told of visions of the heavenly court to which he was summoned, and received the doctrines and duties that would reform his country's religion. Following set-backs in its first decade, the movement attracted support in Bactria to the east of Persia, and after years of preaching, Zoroaster was killed in a struggle with opposing priests. His religion slowly developed, led by priests called *Magi*, and in the early Christian centuries it became the state religion of Iran (Persia) until the Muslim conquest in the seventh century AD. There are now some 28,000 Zoroastrians in Iran.

### Beliefs and Practice

The basic Parsi scriptures are the *Avesta*, which include hymns and ritual and practical regulations and are still recited in ancient Persian. Belief in the opposition of the good and evil spirits has caused this religion to be called dualistic, but Parsis believe that the dualism is temporary since Ahura Mazda (Ohrmazd) will triumph. There is a strong moral emphasis, and its followers call it the Religion of the Good Life; by virtuous conduct and moderation men help God to overcome evil. Ahura Mazda is the supreme God, but there are other angelic and demonic spirits. Especially important is Mithra or Meher, a god of the old Iranian religion, who now becomes the judge at death. Belief in life after death is strong in Zoroastrianism and probably influenced Judaism and Christianity with its ideas of angels and demons, the end of the world, judgement and eternal life. It is believed that departed souls have their deeds weighed in scales and then cross a narrow bridge to paradise; the evil fall into a purgatory but eventually all are saved.

Parsi temples contain no images, but sacred fire always burns there, fed by sandalwood. Thus, they are called 'fire temples' by other Indians. The dead are disposed of in 'towers of silence' where vultures destroy the flesh, which must not defile the earth or fire. Some of these towers are outside Mumbai, though closed to the public. A decline in vulture numbers owing to disease, however, in 2001 prompted the Parsi community of Mumbai to install a solar reflector at the site in order to accelerate the process of decomposition, pending the implementation of a vulture-breeding programme. Elsewhere Parsi dead are buried in lead coffins. There have been reforms in modern times, and religious instruction is given in new expositions of the faith. Parsi priests wear white robes, while old Parsis have traditional dress with hard hats and robes, but many Parsis wear modern European or Indian dress. As a small ingrown community, the Parsis are highly educated, and in trade and public service they play a disproportionately large role. Women are emancipated, enter temples equally with men, and take part in educational and public affairs.

## JAINISM

The Jains are an Indian religious community, numbering around 4.2m., according to census results, in 2001. It is possible that the religion existed in India before the arrival of the Aryan invaders in about 1500 BC, since its beliefs in reincarnation and types of asceticism seem to have been non-Aryan. The Jains say that their religion is eternal and is renewed in successive ages by *Jinas* ('conquerors'), of whom there have been 24 at long intervals in the present world aeon. The last Jina was given the title of Mahavira ('great man') and lived in the sixth century BC, a little before Gautama Buddha, whose life was similar in some ways. After the death of his parents, Mahavira left his wife and family (though one sect says he was celibate) and went about naked begging alms and seeking enlightenment. He achieved this after 13 years, and became a *Jina* and omniscient. He is said to have had great success, with a community of 50,000 monks and nuns and many lay followers. Mahavira died in the lower Ganges valley in 527 BC, entering *Nirvana* or *Moksha*, the 'blowing out' of desire and life.

### Beliefs and Practice

Jains do not believe in a creator God, since the world is eternal, and they have been called atheistic. The 24 *Jinas*, however, are objects of worship, and some Hindu gods also figure in their temple imagery. Jains believe in the eternity of countless souls, which are immersed in matter and evil, but by renunciation of desire they can rise to Nirvana at the ceiling of the universe. Monks are the nearest to salvation, and sectarian differences divide the 'white-clad' monks in robes from the 'sky-clad' who are naked. The best known Jain doctrine is 'non-violence' or harmlessness (*ahimsa*). All life is sacred; this involves vegetarianism and abstention from taking any life by hunting, farming or fishing. Monks sweep the ground in their path to avoid treading on insects, filter their drink, and wear cloths before their mouths to keep out insects. In modern times Jain stress on non-violence has inspired reformers, like the Hindu Mahatma Gandhi.

Despite ascetic practices and absence of deity, the Jains have built some of the most splendid temples in India through the patronage of rich followers. The main anniversary is at the end of August when wrongs are confessed, fasting practised and the birthday of Mahavira is celebrated. *Divali* is also important, which, for Jains, marks the anniversary of the attainment of Nirvana by Mahavira. Being excluded from many occupations that involve taking or endangering life, the Jains have prospered in commerce and are influential in public affairs. Some modern Jains try to adapt asceticism to current conditions, but monks continue on the hard way to Nirvana.

## SIKHISM

The Sikhs are one of the largest Indian religious minorities; according to census results, the number of followers totalled 19.2m. in 2001 (the majority of whom lived in the Punjab). The men are easily recognizable by turbans and beards. The Sikh religion is relatively modern and developed, like Hindu devotional movements, with some influence from Islam.

Medieval Hindu poets sang the praises of Krishna and Rama, the Avatars of Vishnu, and in the 15th century Kabir concentrated on Rama as the sole deity. Kabir was a Muslim weaver of Varanasi, but was trained by a Hindu teacher. He taught that there is one God behind the many names of Allah, Rama and Krishna. Kabir composed and sang poems denouncing priests and scriptures. He suffered persecution, but at his death both Hindus and Muslims claimed him for their own and established rival shrines. The followers of the path of Kabir, *Kabir-panthis*, number about 1m., chiefly in north-central India.

A little later in the Punjab lived Nanak (1469–1538) who founded the Sikhs. He was a Hindu who also sought the unity of God and had a vision in which he was told to teach faith in God as the True Name. He travelled widely, but was most successful in the Punjab where groups of *Sikhs* ('disciples') followed him. Nanak was the great *Guru* ('teacher'), and though he was followed by nine other Gurus they were regarded as essentially identical to Guru Nanak. The Sikhs suffered persecution from the Muslims. The 10th Guru, Gobind Singh, founded an inner militant society, Khalsa ('the pure'), with initiation by a sword and adding the name Singh ('lion') to all initiates. Members of the Khalsa have five marks: beard and hair uncut (hence the turban), wearing shorts, steel comb in hair, steel bangle on the right wrist and steel dagger at the side. With this militant force the Sikhs won independence in the Punjab until British rule intervened. At the partition of India in 1947 the line between India and Pakistan ran across the Punjab, and the Sikhs rose to assert their independence. They were subsequently expelled from Pakistan and placed within the Indian state, although constant moves have been made towards fuller autonomy.

### Beliefs and Practice

Sikhs believe in one God, with Guru Nanak his perfect teacher, and their temples have no images. Their scriptures, the *Adi Granth* ('first book'), contain poems by Kabir and by Hindu and Muslim composers, as well as by Guru Nanak and other Gurus. It is an anthology of lofty religious verse, which is chanted daily, in the Punjabi language, by Sikhs in public and private devotion.

Sikh temples are usually white buildings with golden domes, and alongside is a tank or small lake for ritual washing. The Adi Granth scriptures are carried into the temple at dawn and chanted by relays of readers until nightfall, when the book is returned to a treasury. The principal shrine is the Golden Temple at Amritsar, the most sacred Sikh town and centre of administration. Sikhs are found in many Indian cities, as well as in Africa, Europe and North America, but their strength remains in the Punjab.

## BUDDHISM

Buddhism arose in India and spread to other parts of South Asia. The number of Buddhists in India has significantly decreased; according to census results, there were only 8m. Buddhists in India in 2001, representing 0.8% of the population.

### Historical Background

The founder was named Siddhartha, but is more generally known by the family name of Gautama (the Sanskrit form; Gotama in Pali), or from his clan Shakyamuni, 'the sage of the Shakyas'. The dates commonly accepted for Gautama by Western scholars are 563–483 BC, though Chinese Buddhists put them hundreds of years earlier. Primary evidence is scanty, and begins with inscriptions made by the Emperor Ashoka from about 260 BC, some of which still remain.

Gautama was born in Lumbini, in Nepal (the place being marked by a stone), of a local king and into the warrior caste rather than the priestly Brahmin. From many legends it is clear that his parents were married, the birth was not virginal, and the boy grew up in relative seclusion but was married and had a son. Riding outside the palace at the age of 29, Gautama saw four signs: an old man, a sick man, a corpse and an ascetic. These showed him the suffering of the world, and the calm of leaving it, and led to his great renunciation. He left his wife and child by night, and for years tried various teachers and ways towards enlightenment but without success. Finally, near Gaya on a tributary of the Ganges, Gautama sat under a tree called the Bo or Bodhi-tree, the 'tree of enlightenment', and waited for light to come. After a day and a night knowledge came; he understood the rising and passing away of beings, the cause of suffering, the end of rebirth and the way to Nirvana. Now he was a Buddha, an 'enlightened one', and went to preach his doctrine in a park to the north of the holy city of Varanasi.

The Buddha was followed at first by small groups of monks and laymen but soon became successful, especially in middle India, where the town of Rajagriha (modern Rajgir) was a centre for the religion. For some 40 years the Buddha went about teaching. The monastic order (*Sangha*) was the centre of activity, and, after some hesitation, orders of nuns were formed as well. Finally, the Buddha died after eating tainted food and was cremated, tradition saying that his relics were divided among eight regions.

At the Buddha's death, 500 monks met in a cave and the chief disciple, Ananda, recited the *Vinaya*, the monkish rules that form the first part of the Buddhist scriptures. The Buddha and his followers came into conflict with Brahmin priests, Jains, Yoga teachers and others, and taught that the way of the Buddha was best. They rejected the Hindu scriptures and were regarded as heretics. There was also some caste rivalry, and possibly Buddhism inherited both some of the communal differences and the religious beliefs of the ancient Indus Valley cultures.

A great impulse to the spread of Buddhism was given by Ashoka in the third century BC, who turned from martial conquests to the peaceful way of Buddhism, inscribing decrees ordering faith and morality, restoring Buddhist sacred sites and sending missionaries to Sri Lanka and elsewhere. In the land of its origin Buddhism flourished for over 1,000 years, but finally almost died out in India under pressure from reviving Hindu devotional cults and destruction of temples and monasteries by invading Muslims. Recently there has been some Buddhist success among the Indian outcastes, claiming 5m. converts.

### Beliefs

The Buddha taught *Dharma* (or *Dhamma*) which is law, virtue, right, religion or truth, and this is expounded as the Middle Way between the extremes of sensuality and asceticism. At his enlightenment Gautama saw the solution of the suffering that had troubled him and enunciated it in the Four Noble Truths. These are: the universal fact of suffering; the cause of suffering, which is craving or desire; the cessation of suffering by ending craving; and the method of cessation by the Noble Eightfold Path. This Path is a way of discipline in eight steps, each of which is called Right. They fall into three groups, the first beginning the path in Right View and Resolve. Then come practical activity in Right Speech, Action and Livelihood. Finally, there are higher spiritual states: Right Effort, Concentration and Contemplation.

This is a scheme of moral and spiritual improvement without reference to the Hindu gods. Some of them appear in Buddhist legend, but always subservient to the Buddha. The Hindu teaching of the impersonal divine Brahman seems to have been unknown to the Buddha and his system has been called atheistic or agnostic; but in fact the Buddha himself is the supreme and omniscient teacher and object of adoration. A Buddhist does not save himself, but he relies on the teaching of experts and the celestial Buddha.

The Buddha also criticized the Hindu doctrine of the soul, which he declared could not be identified with any of the bodily elements. At death the five constituents of the body dissolved and were not passed on to another life. Yet Buddhism held firmly to the Indian belief in rebirth, and the cycle of existence was caused by desire from which one could escape only by following the path of the Buddha. The link between one life and another was *Karma*, the entail of deeds that determined a higher or lower destiny in the next life. To become free from this round of existence was the supreme goal, the indescribable *Nirvana* (*Nibbana*), the 'blowing out' of desire and life.

### Northern Buddhism

The above are the basic beliefs of southern Buddhists, but in the north further doctrines developed in which multitudes of celestial beings offered gracious help to mankind. Southern Buddhists believe that there have been several Buddhas in the past and there will be some in the future, the next one, Maitreya, being a fat jolly figure bringing fortune. In the present long world aeon, however, there is only one Buddha, the supreme Gautama. In northern Buddhism not only are thousands of Buddhas accepted now but there are countless *Bodhisattvas* ('beings of enlightenment'), who have deferred their own salvation until all beings are saved. This led to a universalism and a religion of faith and grace, which was able to absorb many Chinese and other deities in the guise of Bodhisattvas. The Chinese Kwanyin (Japanese Kwannon) is the 'lady of compassion', not a goddess but a Bodhisattva, a kindly giver of children and a saviour who immediately hears the cries of all suppliants. In Tibet (Xizang, People's Republic of China) the Dalai Lama is the incarnation of this Bodhisattva, not of Gautama.

More abstruse philosophical doctrines were also taught in northern Buddhism: the three bodies of the Buddha, and an idealistic doctrine of the Void in which Buddhas and believers are merged in a neutral monism somewhat like the Hindu Brahman. On the popular level, *Pure Land* Buddhism offered the hope of a Western paradise, presided over by another Buddha, Amida.

### Schools

The southern Buddhists call themselves *Theravada*, followers of the 'tradition of the elders'. In South Asia they are concentrated in Sri Lanka, where their graceful buildings decorate towns and countryside. Here relics are enshrined, innumerable Buddha images sit in various postures, and worshippers go to meditate. Traditional education was in the monasteries, which are still strong. Yellow-robed monks go on begging rounds every morning, and scholars study the scriptures, the *Tripitaka* ('three baskets'). There are minor sects, but general uniformity of belief and practice.

The northern Buddhists are *Mahayana*, followers of the 'great Vehicle' to salvation, as against the others whom they call *Hinayana*, of the 'small Vehicle'. In Bhutan the Tantric form of Mahayana Buddhism has traditionally been the state religion.

### Organization

The different Buddhist schools have loose organization. Traditionally, monasteries have been the centres of doctrine and discipline, and their chief abbots are the religious authorities. Monks and nuns are, of course, celibate, but where there are large numbers of priests they are usually married. Since the days of Ashoka, laymen have been encouraged to attend the monasteries at weekly or fortnightly special days, and many go there also for meditation during the rainy season.

## CHRISTIANITY IN SOUTH ASIA

Christianity began as an Asian religion and, although its principal expansion was to the West, it has spread in missions to most Asian countries. The Syrian Orthodox Church in India claims to have been founded by the Apostle Thomas, and there is evidence of its existence at least from the fifth century. The rites and traditions are derived from the Jacobite Church of Syria, which separated from other Orthodox churches after the Council of Chalcedon in AD 451. These Indian churches are divided into Orthodox Syrian and Mar Thoma Syrian, and a further section has been in communion with Rome since the 17th century as one of its Uniate churches. These Syrian Christians are found almost exclusively in Malabar, Travancore and Cochin, and number over 2m. Other Christian communities all over India are the result of modern Western missions and have 45m. adherents, of whom more than one-half are Roman Catholics. In Pakistan there are 2m. Christians. Sri Lanka has 1.7m. Christians, the majority of whom are Roman Catholic and found in Sinhalese, Tamil and mixed communities.

## OTHER RELIGIONS AND SECTS

The small Jewish community in South Asia is found mainly in India. Tradition claims Jewish settlements at the Indian city of Cochin from the first century; one branch is now clearly Semitic and the other more typically Indian. There are around 17,000 Jews in India.

In many countries there are members of the modern missionary Bahá'í faith, founded in Iran by Bahá'u'llah in 1863, with a synthesis of religion claimed as scientific and evolutionary.

Various types of syncretistic religions have flourished, including the Transcendental Meditation and Hare Krishna societies, which mingle Indian and Western ideas and practices.

## BIBLIOGRAPHY

### General

Babb, Lawrence A., and Wadley, Susan S. (Eds). *Media and the Transformation of Religion in South Asia*. Philadelphia, PA, University of Pennsylvania Press, 1995.

Baird, Robert D. (Ed.). *Religion in Modern India*. New Delhi, Manohar Publications, 2nd edn, 1989.

Barth, A. *The Religions of India*. London, Routledge, 2000.

Bayly, Susan. *Saints, Goddesses and Kings: Muslims and Christians in South Indian Society, 1700–1900*. Cambridge, Cambridge University Press, 1990.

Beckerlegge, Gwilym (Ed.). *The World Religions Reader*. London, Routledge, 2000.

Bowker, John (Ed.). *The Oxford Dictionary of World Religions*. Oxford, Oxford University Press, 1999.

*The Cambridge Illustrated History of Religions*. Cambridge, Cambridge University Press, 2002.

Brown, A. (Ed.). *Festivals in World Religions*. London and New York, Longman, 1986.

Cady, Linell E., Simon, Sheldon W. (Eds). *Religion and Conflict in South and Southeast Asia: Disrupting Violence*. Abingdon, Routledge, 2006.

Carr, Brian, and Mahalingam, Indira (Eds). *Companion Encyclopedia of Asian Philosophy*. London, Routledge, 2000.

Chilson, Clark, and Knecht, Peter. *Shamans in Asia*. London, RoutledgeCurzon, 2003.

Eliade, Mircea (Ed.). *Encyclopedia of Religion*. New York, Macmillan, 1987.

Fischer-Schreiber, Ingrid, *et al*. *The Encyclopedia of Eastern Philosophy and Religion: Buddhism, Hinduism, Taoism, Zen*. Boston, MA, Shambhala Publications, 1994.

Fisher, Mary Pat. *Religion in the Twenty-First Century*. London, Routledge, 1999.

*Religions Today*. London, Routledge, 2001.

Fletcher, Richard. *The Cross and the Crescent: Christianity and Islam from Muhammad to the Reformation*. Allen Lane, 2003.

Fowler, Jeaneane, *et al*. *World Religions*. Brighton, Sussex Academic Press, 1997.

Hardy, Friedhelm (Ed.). *The World's Religions: The Religions of Asia*. London, Routledge, 1990.

Hinnells, John R. (Ed.). *The Penguin Dictionary of Religions*. Harmondsworth, Penguin Books, 1997.

*The New Penguin Handbook of Living Religions*. Harmondsworth, Penguin Books, 2000.

Hinnells, John R., and King, Richard (Eds). *Religion and Violence in South Asia: Theory and Practice*. Abingdon, Routledge, 2006.

Joshi, A. P., Srinivas, M. D., and Bajaj, J. K. *Religious Demography of India*. Chennai, Centre for Policy Studies, 2003.

Keene, Michael. *World Religions*. Oxford, Lion Publishing, 2002.

King, Ursula (Ed.). *Turning Points in Religious Studies*. Edinburgh, T. & T. Clark, 1990.

Kitagawa, Joseph M. (Ed.). *The Religious Traditions of Asia—Religion, History and Culture*. London, RoutledgeCurzon, 2002.

Knappert, Jan. *Indian Mythology: An Encyclopedia of Myth and Legend*. London, Aquarian Press, 1991.

Leaman, Oliver (Ed.). *Encyclopedia of Asian Philosophy*. London, Routledge, 2001.

Liebert, Gosta. *Iconographic Dictionary of the Indian Religions: Hinduism, Buddhism, Jainism*. Leiden, E. J. Brill, 1976.

Lopez, Donald S., Jr (Ed.). *Religions of India in Practice*. Princeton, NJ, Princeton University Press, 1995.

Lorenzen, David N. (Ed.). *Religious Movements in South Asia 600–1800 (Debates in Indian History and Society)*. New Delhi, Oxford University Press, 2004.

Madan, T. N. (Ed.). *Religion in India*. New Delhi, Oxford University Press, 1992.

*India's Religions: Perspectives from Sociology and History*. New Delhi, Oxford University Press, 2005.

Mittal, Sushil, and Thursby, Gene (Eds). *Religions of South Asia: An Introduction*. Abingdon, Routledge, 2006.

Oddie, Geoffrey A. (Ed.). *Religion in South Asia: Religious Conversion and Revival Movements in South Asia in Medieval and Modern Times*. New Delhi, Manohar Publications, 2nd edn, 1991.

Palmer, Martin. *'The Times' World Religions*. London, Times Books, 2002.

Parrinder, E. G. *A Dictionary of Non-Christian Religions*. London and Philadelphia, PA, Hulton, 2nd edn, 1981.

*Sexual Morality in the World's Religions*. Oxford, Oneworld Publications, 1996.

Ridgeon, Lloyd (Ed.). *Major World Religions*. London, RoutledgeCurzon, 2003.

Rogers, Kirsteen, and Hickman, Clare. *The Usborne Internet-linked Encyclopedia of World Religions*. London, Usborne Publishing, 2001.

Smart, Ninian. *The World's Religions*. Cambridge, Cambridge University Press, 1989.

*Reasons and Faiths*. London, Routledge, 2000.

*World Philosophies*. London, Routledge, 2000.

Smith, Jonathan Z. (Ed.). *The HarperCollins Dictionary of Religion*. London, Fount, 1996.

Woodhead, Linda, *et al* (Eds). *Religions in the Modern World—Traditions and Transformations*. London, Routledge, 2001.

Zaehner, R. C. *The Hutchison Encyclopedia of Living Faiths*. Oxford, Helicon, 1997.

### Hinduism

Bhatt, Chetan. *Hindu Nationalism*. Oxford, Berg Publishers, 2001.

Chaudhuri, Nirad C. *Hinduism: A Religion to Live by*. London, Chatto and Windus, 1979.

Chinmoy, Sri. *Commentaries on the Vedas, Upanishads and Bhagavad Gita*. Oxford, Blue Beyond Books, 1996.

Cross, Stephen. *Way of Hinduism*. London, HarperCollins, 2002.

Cush, Denise, Robinson, Catherine, York, Michael (Eds). *Encyclopedia of Hinduism*. Abingdon, Routledge, 2007.

Dallapiccola, Anna L. *Dictionary of Hindu Lore and Legend*. London, Thames and Hudson, 2004.

De Bary, W. T. (Ed.). *Sources of Indian Tradition*. New York, Columbia University Press, and London, Oxford University Press, 1958.

Deshpande, P. Y. *The Authentic Yoga*. London, Rider & Co, 1978.

Dubois, Abbé J. A. *Hindu Manners, Customs and Ceremonies*. London, Kegan Paul, 2004.

Easwaran, Eknath. *The Bhagavad Gita—Translated for the Modern Reader*. Vintage Books, 2000.

Flood, Gavin. *An Introduction to Hinduism*. Cambridge, Cambridge University Press, 1996.

Flood, Gavin (Ed.). *The Blackwell Companion to Hinduism*. Oxford, Blackwell, 2003.

Fowler, Jeaneane. *Hinduism—Beliefs and Practices*. Brighton, Sussex Academic Press, 1997.

Fuller, C. J. *The Camphor Flame: Popular Hinduism and Society in India*. Princeton, NJ, Princeton University Press, 2004.

Gelberg, S. J. (Ed.). *Hare Krishna*. New York, 1983.

Klostermaier, Klaus K. *A Concise Encyclopedia of Hinduism*. Oxford, Oneworld Publications, 1998.

*Hinduism: A Short History*. Oxford, Oneworld Publications, 2000.

Knott, Kim. *Hinduism: A Very Short Introduction*. Oxford, Oxford Paperbacks, 2000.

Lipner, Julius J. *Hindus—Their Religious Beliefs and Practices*. London, Routledge, 1998.

Michell, George. *The Hindu Temple: An Introduction to its Meaning and Form*. London, Elek, 1977.

O'Flaherty, W. D. *Hindu Myths*. Harmondsworth, Penguin Books, 1975.

*The Rig Veda, An Anthology*. Harmondsworth, Penguin Books, 1981.

Parrinder, E. G. *The Bhagavad Gita, A Verse Translation*. Oxford, Oneworld Publications, 1996.

*Avator and Incarnation*. Oxford, Oneworld Publications, 1997.

Radice, William (Ed.). *Swami Vivekananda and the Modernization of Hinduism*. Delhi, Oxford University Press, 1998.

Rao, S. R. *Worship of Shiva*. London, Sangam Books, 1998.

Richards, Glyn. *A Source-Book of Modern Hinduism*. London, Curzon, 1996.

Rodrigues, Hillary. *Introducing Hinduism*. Abingdon, Routledge, 2006.

Ross, Floyd H. *The Meaning of Life in Hinduism and Buddhism*. Abingdon, Routledge, 2008.

Sastri, S. M. Natesa. *Hindu Feasts, Fasts and Ceremonies*. New Delhi, Vedams Books, revised edn, 2003.

Savarkar, Vinayak Damodar. *Hindutva: Who is a Hindu?* New Delhi, Bharti Sahitya Sadan, 1989.

Sen, K. M. *Hinduism*. Harmondsworth, Penguin Books, 1991.

Sharma, Arvind (Ed.). *The Study of Hinduism*. Columbia, SC, University of South Carolina Press, 2002.

Sharma, Jyotirmaya. *Hindutva: Exploring the Idea of Hindu Nationalism*. New Delhi, Viking, 2003.

Shattuck, Cybelle. *Hinduism*. London, Routledge, 1999.

Singh, D. N. *A Study of Hinduism*. Sangam Books, 2000.

Singh, Khushwant. *Gurus, Godmen and Good People*. Delhi, 1975.

Sondhi, M. L., and Sondhi, Madhuri Santanam (Eds). *The Making of Modern Hinduism*. New Delhi, Har-Anand, 1999.

Srinivasan, Ramakrishnan. *Vedic Tradition in the New Millennium*. Mumbai, Bharatiya Vidya Bhavan, 2000.

Stutley, Margaret and James. *A Dictionary of Hinduism*. London, Routledge and Kegan Paul, 1977.

Walker, Benjamin. *Hindu World: An Encyclopedic Survey of Hinduism*. London, Allen & Unwin, 1968.

Warrier, Maya. *Hindu Selves in a Modern World*. London, RoutledgeCurzon, 2004.

Werner, Karel. *A Popular Dictionary of Hinduism*. Richmond, Surrey, Curzon, 1994.

Whicher, Ian, and Carpenter, David. *Yoga—The Indian Tradition*. London, RoutledgeCurzon, 2003.

Zaehner, R. C. *Hindu Scriptures*. London and New York, Dent, 1965.

**Islam**

Ahmed, Akbar S. *Islam Today*. London, I. B. Tauris, 1998.

Armstrong, Karen. *Islam: A Short History*. London, Weidenfeld & Nicolson, 2000.

Asani, Ali S. *Ecstasy and Enlightenment: The Ismaili Devotional Literature of South Asia*. London, I. B. Tauris, 2002

Baldick, Julian. *Mystical Islam: An Introduction to Sufism*. London, I. B. Tauris, 1989.

Bloom, Jonathan, and Blair, Sheila. *Islam—Empire of Faith*. London, BBC Consumer Publishing (Books), 2001.

Boivin, Michel. *La Rénovation du Shi'isme Ismaelien en Inde et au Pakistan*. London, RoutledgeCurzon, 2003.

Cole, Juan. *Sacred Space and Holy War: The Politics, Culture and History of Shi'ite Islam*. London, I. B. Tauris, 2002.

Cook, Michael. *The Koran: A Very Short Introduction*. Oxford, Oxford Paperbacks, 2000.

Cragg, Kenneth. *Counsels in Contemporary Islam*. Edinburgh and Chicago, IL, Edinburgh University Press, 1965.

*The Wisdom of the Sufis*. London, Sheldon Press, 1976.

*Muhammad and the Christian: A Question of Response*. Oxford, Oneworld Publications, 1999.

*Jesus and the Muslim: An Exploration*. Oxford, Oneworld Publications, 1999.

*The Call of the Minaret*. Oxford, Oneworld Publications, 2000.

Daniel, Norman. *Islam and the West: The Making of an Image*. Oxford, Oneworld Publications, 1995.

Dawood, N. J. (Trans.). *The Koran*. Harmondsworth, Penguin Books, 1997.

Denny, Frederick M. *An Introduction to Islam*. New York, Macmillan, 2nd edn, 1994.

Doonan, Hastings (Ed.). *Interpreting Islam*. London, Sage Publications, 2002.

Elias, Jamal J. *Islam*. London, Routledge, 1999.

Engineer, Asghar Ali. *Status of Women in Islam*. Delhi, Ajanta Publications, 1987.

Esposito, John L. (Ed.). *The Oxford History of Islam*. Oxford, Oxford University Press, 2000.

*The Oxford Dictionary of Islam*. Oxford, Oxford University Press, 2003.

Esposito, John L., and Voll, John. *Makers of Contemporary Islam*. New York, Oxford University Press, 2001.

Fisher, H. J. *Ahmadiyya*. London, Oxford University Press, 1963.

Friedmann, Yohanan. *Prophecy Continues: Aspects of Ahmadi Religious Thought and its Medieval Background*. New Delhi, Oxford University Press, 2003.

Glassé, Cyril. *New Encyclopedia of Islam: A Revised Edition of the Concise Encyclopedia of Islam*. Lanham, MD, Rowman and Littlefield Publishing, 2001.

Goodman, Lenn E. *Islamic Humanism*. New York, Oxford University Press, 2003.

Green, Nile. *Indian Sufism since the Seventeenth Century: Saints, Books and Empires in the Muslim Deccan*. Abingdon, Routledge, 2006.

Hardy, Paul (Ed.). *Traditions of Islam: Understanding the Hadith*. London, I. B. Tauris, 2002.

Hassan, Riaz. *Faithliness: Muslim Conceptions of Islam and Society*. Oxford, Oxford University Press, 2002.

Is'harc, Istafiah. *Islam and its Festivals*. London, Ta-Ha Publishers, 1997.

Jones, Alan (Ed.). *The Koran*. London, Phoenix Press, 2001.

Jordan, Michael. *Islam*. London, Carlton Books, 2002.

Kaltner, John. *Islam*. Nashville, TN, Abingdon Press, 2003.

Khan, Masood Ali, and Ram, S. (Eds). *Encyclopaedia of Sufism*. New Delhi, Anmol Publications, 2003.

Khan, M. Z. *Muhammad, Seal of the Prophets*. London, Routledge, 1980.

Lewis, Bernard. *The Crisis of Islam*. London, Weidenfeld & Nicolson, 2003.

Metcalf, Barbara Daly (Ed.). *Moral Conduct and Authority: The Place of Adab in South Asian Islam*. Berkeley, CA, University of California Press, 1992.

Mutalib, Hussin, and Hashmi, Taj ul-Islam (Eds). *Islam, Muslims and the Modern State*. New York, St Martin's Press, 1994.

Nasr, S. H. *Living Sufism*. London, 1972.

Parrinder, E. G. *Jesus in the Qur'ān*. Oxford, Oneworld Publications, 3rd edn, 1995.

Peters, F. E. *Muhammad: A Life and a Guide*. New York, Seven Bridges Press, 2003.

Rahman, Fazlur. *Islam*. Lahore, Kazi Publications, 1979.

*Major Themes of the Qur'ān*. Minneapolis, MN, Bibliotheca Islamica, 2nd edn, 1989.

Robinson, Francis (Ed.), and Lapidus, Ira M. *The Cambridge Illustrated History of the Islamic World*. Cambridge, Cambridge University Press, 1999.

Robinson, Francis. *Islam and Muslim History in South Asia*. New Delhi and Oxford, Oxford University Press, 2000.

Robinson, Neal. *The Sayings of Muhammad*. London, Duckworth, 1991.

*Islam: A Concise Introduction*. Richmond, Surrey, Curzon, 1998.

Rogerson, Barnaby. *The Prophet Muhammad: A Biography*. Boston, MA, Little Brown & Co, 2003.

Ruthven, Malise. *Islam: A Very Short Introduction*. Oxford, Oxford Paperbacks, 2000.

*Islam in the World*. Harmondsworth, Penguin Books, 2000.

Shah, Idries. *The Sufis*. London, Octagon Press, 1999.

Shomali, Mohammed A. *Shi'i Islam: Origins, Faiths and Practices*. London, Islamic College for Advanced Studies, 2003.

Smith, M. *The Way of the Mystics*. London, Sheldon Press, 1976.

Sonn, Tamara. *A Brief History of Islam*. Malden, MA, Blackwell, 2004.

Suvorova, Anna. *Muslim Saints of South Asia: The Eleventh to Fifteenth Centuries*. London, RoutledgeCurzon, 2004.

Tayob, Abdulkader. *Islam: A Short Introduction*. Oxford, Oneworld Publications, 1999.

Trimingham, J. S. *The Sufi Orders in Islam*. Oxford, Clarendon Press, 1971.

Watt, W. M. *Muhammad, Prophet and Statesman*. London and New York, Oxford University Press, 1961.

*Islamic Fundamentalism and Modernity*. London and New York, 1988.

Zebiri, Kate. *Muslims and Christians Face to Face*. Oxford, Oneworld Publications, 1996.

**Zoroastrianism**

Boyce, Mary. *Zoroastrians: Their Religious Beliefs and Practices*. London, Routledge, revised edn, 2000.

Choksy, Jamsheed K. *Purity and Pollution in Zoroastrianism: Triumph Over Evil*. Austin, TX, University of Texas Press, 1989.

Clark, Peter. *Zoroastrianism—An Introduction to an Ancient Faith*. Brighton, Sussex Academic Press, 1998.

Godrej, Pheroza J., and Mistree, Firoza Punkathey (Eds). *A Zoroastrian Tapestry: Art, Religion and Culture*. Ahmedabad, Mapin Publishing, 2002.

Hinnells, John. *Persian Mythology*. London, Newnes, 2nd edn, 1985.

*Zoroastrianism and Parsi Studies*. Aldershot, Ashgate Publishing, 2000.

Kapadia, S. A. *Teachings of Zoroaster and the Philosophy of the Parsi Religion (1908)*. Belle Fourche, SD, R. A. Kessinger Publishing, 1998.

Kreyenbroek, Philip G., and Munshi, Shehnaz N. *Living Zoroastrianism*. Richmond, Surrey, Curzon, 2000.

Kriwaczek, Paul. *In Search of Zarathustra: The First Prophet and the Ideas that Changed the World*. London, Weidenfeld & Nicolson, 2002.

Nigosian, S. A. *The Zoroastrian Faith*. Montréal, McGill-Queen's University Press, 1993.

Williams, Ron G. *Ritual Art and Knowledge: Aesthetic Theory and Zoroastrian Ritual*. Columbia, SC, University of South Carolina Press, 1993.

Zaehner, R. C. *The Teachings of the Magi*. London and New York, Dent, 1975.

*Dawn and Twilight of Zoroastrianism*. London, Phoenix Press, 2002.

**Jainism**

Cort, John E. *Jains in the World*. New York, Oxford University Press, 2001.

Dundas, Paul. *The Jains*. London, Routledge, 2nd edn, 2002.

Jacobi H., and Oldenberg, H. *The Jaina Sutras (Sacred Books of the East)*. Delhi, Motilal Banarsidass Publishers, 1989.

Jain, J. P. *Religion and Culture of the Jains*. New Delhi, Bharatiya Jnanpith, 1975.

Jain, K. C. *Lord Mahavira and his Times*. Delhi, Motilal Banarsidass Publishers, revised edn, 1991.

Jaini, P. S. *The Jaina Path of Perfection*. Berkeley, CA, University of California Press, 1979.

*Collected Papers on Jaina Studies*. Delhi, Motilal Banarsidass Publishers, 2000.

Kapashi, V. J. *In Search of the Ultimate*. London, V. K. Publications, 1984.

Mardia, K. V. *The Scientific Foundations of Jainism*. Delhi, Motilal Banarsidass Publishers, 2002.

Mookerjee, S. *The Jaina Philosophy of Non-absolutism*. Delhi, 2nd edn, 1978.

Quarnstrom, Olle. *The Yogasastra of Hemacandra: A Twelfth Century Handbook of Svetambara Jainism (Harvard Oriental Series)*. Cambridge, MA, Harvard University Press, 2002.

Raynade, B. B. *Jaina Philosophy: Religion and Ethics*. Delhi, Bharatiya Vidya Prakashan, 1998.

Roy, A. K. *History of the Jains*. New Delhi, Gitanjali Publishing House, 1984.

Schubring, W. *The Doctrine of the Jains*. Varanasi, Motilal, 1962.

Shah, Natubhai. *Jainism—The World of Conquerors*. Brighton, Sussex Academic Press, 1998.

Sharma, Arvind. *A Jaina Perspective on the Philosophy of Religion*. Delhi, Motilal Banarsidass Publishers, 2001.

Sinclair Stevenson, M. *Heart of Jainism*. New Delhi, Munshiram Manoharlal Publishers, 1995.

Sogani, K. C. *Ethical Doctrines in Jainism*. Sholapur, Jaina Samskriti Samrakshaka Sangha, 1967.

Talib, G. S. (Ed.). *Jainism*. Patiala, Punjab University, 1975.

Upadhye, A. N., *et al*. *Lord Mahavira and his Teachings*. Mumbai, Shree Vallabhsuri Smarak Nidhi, 2nd edn, 1983.

Von Glasenapp, Helmuth, and Shrotri, Shridar B. (Trans.). *Jainism*. Delhi, Motilal Banarsidass Publishers, 1999.

Warren, Herbert, and Gandhi, Virchand R. (Eds). *Jainism*. Crest Publishing House, 1999.

Wiley, Kristi L. *Aghatiya Karmas: Agents of Embodiment in Jainism*. Berkeley, CA, University of California Press, 2000.

**Sikhism**

Chranjit, Ajitsingh. *Wisdom of Sikhism*. Oxford, Oneworld Publications, 2001.

Cole, W. Owen, and Singh Sambhi, Piara. *The Sikhs—Their Religious Beliefs and Practices*. Brighton, Sussex Academic Press, 1995.

Daljeet. *The Sikh Heritage*. London, Mercury Books, 2005.

Dogra, Ramesh Chandra, and Mansukhani, Gobind Singh. *Encyclopaedia of Sikh Religion and Culture*. New Delhi, Vikas Publishing House, 1995.

Fenech, Louis E. *Martyrdom in the Sikh Tradition—Playing the 'Game of Love'*. New Delhi, Oxford University Press, 2001.

Kaur, Gurnam. *Khalsa: A Thematic Perspective*. Patiala, Punjabi University Press, 2001.

Kohli, Surindar Singh. *A Conceptual Encyclopaedia of Guru Granth Sahib*. New Delhi, Manohar Publications, 1992.

McLeod, W. H. *Gurū Nānak and the Sikh Religion*. Oxford, Clarendon Press, 1968.

*Historical Dictionary of Sikhism*. Lanham, MD, Scarecrow Press, 1995.

*Exploring Sikhism*. New York, Oxford University Press, 2000.

Shackle, Christopher, Mandair, Arvind-pal, and Singh, Gurharpal (Eds). *Sikh Religion, Culture and Ethnicity*. Richmond, Surrey, Curzon, 2001.

Singh, D. *Indian Bhakti Tradition and the Sikh Gurus*. Chandigarh, Panjab Publishers, 1968.

Singh, Daljeet, and Singh, Kharak. *Sikhism: Its Philosophy and History*. Chandigarh, Institute of Sikh Studies, 1997.

Singh Kalsi, Sewa. *The Simple Guide to Sikhism*. Folkestone, Global Books, 1999.

Singh, Kharak (Ed.). *Current Thoughts on Sikhism*. Chandigarh, Institute of Sikh Studies, 1996.

Singh, Khushwant. *History of the Sikhs: 1469–1839*. Vol. 1, New Delhi, Oxford University Press, 2nd edn, 2005.

*History of the Sikhs: 1839–2004*. Vol. 2, New Delhi, Oxford University Press, 2nd edn, 2005.

Singh Mann, Gurinder. *Sikhism*. London, Routledge, 2002.

Singh, Patwant. *The Sikhs*. London, John Murray, 1999.

Singh, Paushara. *The Guru Granth Sahib—Canon, Meaning and Authority*. New Delhi, Oxford University Press, 2000.

Singh, T. (Ed.). *Selections from the Sacred Writings of the Sikhs*. London, Allen & Unwin, 1960.

Sondhi, S. P. *Grace of God and Guru in Sikh Philosophy*. Delhi, Global Vision, 2002.

Vaudeville, C. *Kabīr*. Oxford, Clarendon Press, 1974.

**Buddhism**

Allen, Charles. *The Buddha and the Sahibs: The Men Who Discovered India's Lost Religion*. London, John Murray, 2002.

Anderson, Carol S. *Pain and Its Ending: The Four Noble Truths in the Theravada Buddhist Canon*. Richmond, Surrey, Curzon, 1999.

Armstrong, Karen. *Buddha*. London, Orion, 2002.

Bechert, Heinz, and Gombrich, Richard. *The World of Buddhism*. London, Thames & Hudson, 1991.

Bhajracharya, Naresh Man. *Buddhism in Nepal: 465* BC *to 1199* AD. Delhi, Eastern Book Linkers, 1998.

Carrithers, Michael. *Buddha: A Very Short Introduction*. Oxford, Oxford Paperbacks, 2001.

Conze, Edward. *A Short History of Buddhism*. Oxford, Oneworld Publications, 1996.

Conze, Edward (Ed.). *Buddhist Texts through the Ages*. Oxford, Oneworld Publications, 1995.

Corless, R. *The Vision of Buddhism*. New York, Paragon House, 1989.

Duerlinger, James. *Indian Buddhist Theories of Person*. London, RoutledgeCurzon, 2003.

Eckel, Malcolm David. *Buddhism: Origins, Beliefs, Practices, Holy Texts, Sacred Places*. Oxford, Oxford University Press, 2002.

Fowler, Merv. *Buddhism—Beliefs and Practices*. Brighton, Sussex Academic Press, 1999.

Gethin, Rupert. *The Foundations of Buddhism*. Oxford, Oxford Paperbacks, 1998.

*The Buddhist Path to Awakening: A Study of the Bodhi-Pakkhiya Dhamma*. Oxford, Oneworld Publications, 2nd edn, 2001.

Gombrich, Richard. *Theravada Buddhism: A Social History from Ancient Benares to Modern Colombo*. London, Routledge, 1988.

Gombrich, Richard, and Obeyesekere, Gananath. *Buddhism Transformed: Religious Change in Sri Lanka*. Delhi, Motilal Banarsidass Publishers, 1999.

Harvey, Peter. *An Introduction to Buddhism*. Cambridge, Cambridge University Press, 1990.

Hawkins, Bradley K. *Buddhism*. London, Routledge, 1999.

Holt, John Clifford, Kinnard, Jacob N., and Walters, Jonathan S. (Eds). *Constituting Communities: Theravada Buddhism and the Religious Cultures of South and Southeast Asia*. Albany, NY, State University of New York Press, 2003.

Humphreys, Christmas. *Buddhism*. Harmondsworth, Penguin Books, 1990.

Keown, Damien. *Buddhism: A Very Short Introduction*. Oxford, Oxford Paperbacks, 2000.

Ling, T. O. *The Buddha: Buddhist Civilization in India and Ceylon*. London, Temple Smith, 1973.

*Buddhist Revival in India*. 1975.

*The Buddha's Philosophy of Man; Early Indian Buddhist Dialogues*. London, Dent, 1981.

Olschak, Blanche Christine. *Ancient Bhutan: A Study on Early Buddhism in the Himalayas*. Zurich, Swiss Foundation for Alpine Research, 1979.

Parrinder, E. G. *The Sayings of the Buddha*. London, Duckworth, 1991.

Pye, M. *The Buddha*. London, 1979.

Rahula, Walpola. *History of Buddhism in Ceylon*. Colombo, M. D. Gunasena & Co, 1956.

Regmi, Jagadish Chandra. *A Glossary of Himalayan Buddhism*. Jaipur, Nirmala Publications, 1994.

Skilton, Andrew. *A Concise History of Buddhism*. Birmingham, Windhorse Publications, 1997.

Strong, John S. *Relics of the Buddha*. Princeton, NJ, Princeton University Press, 2004.

Upasak, C. S. *History of Buddhism in Afghanistan*. Sarnath and Varanasi, Central Institute of Higher Tibetan Studies, 1990.

Waldron, William S. *The Buddhist Unconscious—The Alaya-vijnana in the Context of Indian Buddhist Thought*. London, RoutledgeCurzon, 2003.

Williams, Paul. *Buddhist Thought—A Complete Introduction to the Indian Tradition*. London, Routledge, 2000.

*Mahayana Buddhism—The Doctrinal Foundations*. London, Routledge, 1989.

**Christianity**

Barraclough, G. (Ed.). *The Christian World*. London, 1981.

Barrett, D. B. (Ed.). *World Christian Encyclopedia*. Nairobi, Oxford University Press, 1982.

Chidester, David. *Christianity—A Global History*. London, Allen Lane, 2000.

Cross, F. L. (Ed.). *The Oxford Dictionary of the Christian Church*. London, Oxford University Press, 3rd edn, 1997.

Downs, Frederick S. *Essays on Christianity in North-East India*. New Delhi, Indus Publishing Co, 1994.

Hastings, Adrian (Ed.). *A World History of Christianity*. London, Cassell, 1999.

Hastings, Adrian, Mason, Alistair, and Pyper, Hugh (Eds). *The Oxford Companion to Christian Thought*. Oxford, Oxford University Press, 2000.

Neill, S. *A History of Christianity in India: The Beginnings to* AD *1707*. Cambridge, Cambridge University Press, 1984.

*A History of Christianity: 1707–1858*. Cambridge, Cambridge University Press, 1985.

*A History of Christian Missions*. Harmondsworth, Penguin Books, 2nd edn, 1990.

Parrinder, E. G. *A Concise Encyclopedia of Christianity*. Oxford, Oneworld Publications, 1998.

Rooney, John. *The Hesitant Dawn: Christianity in Pakistan, 1579–1760*. Rawalpindi, Christian Study Centre, 1984.

Schimmel, A., and Falaturi, A. *We Believe in One God: The Experience of God in Christianity and Islam*. London, 1979.

Sunquist, Scott W. (Ed.), *et al*. *A Dictionary of Asian Christianity*. Grand Rapids, MI, Eerdmans, 2001.

Visvanathan, Susan. *The Christians of Kerala: History, Belief and Ritual among the Yakoba*. Chennai, Oxford University Press, 1993.

Walbridge, Linda. *The Christians of Pakistan: The Passion of Bishop John Joseph*. London, RoutledgeCurzon, 2002.

Wilson, Brian. *Christianity*. London, Routledge, 1999.

**Other Religions**

Barker, E. (Ed.). *New Religious Movements*. New York, Mellen Press, 1982.

*Becoming a Moonie*. Oxford, 1985.

Cohn-Sherbok, Dan. *Judaism and other Faiths*. London, Macmillan, 1994.

*A Short History of Judaism*. Oxford, Oneworld Publications, 1996.

*A Concise Encyclopedia of Judaism*. Oxford, Oneworld Publications, 1998.

Goldberg, D. J., and Rayner, J. D. *The Jewish People*. Harmondsworth, Penguin Books, 1987.

Israel, Rachael Rukmini. *The Jews of India: Their Story*. New Delhi, Mosaic Books, 2002.

Momen, Moojan. *The Bahá'í Faith: A Short Introduction*. Oxford, Oneworld Publications, 1999.

Perkins, M., and Hainsworth, P. *The Bahá'í Faith*. London, 1980.

Smith, Peter. *The Bahá'í Faith: A Short History*. Oxford, Oneworld Publications, 1999.

*A Concise Encyclopedia of the Bahá'í Faith*. Oxford, Oneworld Publications, 1999.

Timberg, Thomas A. (Ed.). *Jews in India*. New Delhi, Vikas Publishing House, 1986.

# PART TWO

# Country Surveys

# AFGHANISTAN

## Physical and Social Geography

W. B. FISHER

Occupying an area of 652,225 sq km (according to official figures; other estimates are in the range 620,000 sq km–700,000 sq km), Afghanistan has the shape of a very irregular oval, with its major axis running from north-east to south-west and extending over roughly 1,125 km, and the minor axis at right angles to this, covering about 560 km. The country is, in the main, a highland mass lying mostly at an altitude of 1,200 m or more, but it presents a very variable pattern of extremely high and irregular mountain ridges, some of which exceed 6,000 m, ravines and broader valleys, parts of which are very fertile, and an outer expanse of undulating plateau, wide river basins, and lake sumps.

Politically, Afghanistan has two frontiers of major length: one on the north with Turkmenistan, Uzbekistan and Tajikistan, the other on the south and east with Pakistan. The latter frontier follows what was once termed the Durand Line (after the representative of British India, Sir Mortimer Durand, who negotiated it in 1893 with the ruler of Afghanistan). So long as the British occupied India, it was generally accepted as forming the Indo-Afghan frontier, but in 1947, with the recognition of Pakistan as a successor to the British, the Afghan Government recalled that, for much of the 18th century, Peshawar and other parts of the Indus Valley had formed part of a larger Afghan state and were, moreover, occupied largely by Pashtuns, who are of closely similar ethnic character to many Afghans. Accordingly, the Durand Line frontier was denounced by Afghanistan, and claims were made that the territories as far as the line of the Indus, including Chitral, Swat and Peshawar, and continuing as far as the Pashtun areas of the North-West Frontier Province and Balochistan, ought to be recognized as an autonomous state, 'Pashtunistan'. This remains a subject of dispute between Afghanistan and Pakistan.

There are shorter but no less significant frontiers on the west with Iran and on the north-east with the People's Republic of China. This last was fully agreed only in 1963, and the precise location of others in the south and west has not been completely delimited—an indication of the extreme difficulties of terrain, and an explanation of the uncertainty regarding the actual area of Afghanistan. It is noteworthy that, in order to erect a 'buffer' between the then competing empires of Russia and India, under the Durand Treaty of 1893 the Wakhan district, a narrow strip of land 320 km long and under 16 km wide in its narrowest part, was attached to Afghanistan. The allocation of this strip, which controls the Baroghil Pass over the Pamir, avoided the existence of a Soviet-Indian frontier.

### PHYSICAL FEATURES

The main topographical feature of Afghanistan is a complex of irregular highlands, which is relatively broad and low in the west and very much higher and narrower towards the east. In this eastern part the mountains form a group of well-defined chains, which are known by the general name of the Hindu Kush ('Hindu destroyer'), and are linked further eastward first to the Pamirs and then to the main Himalayan system. The Eastern Hindu Kush ranges form the southern defining limit of the Wakhan strip while, a short distance to the north and east, a small but high ridge, the Little Pamir, forms the topographic link between the Hindu Kush and the main Pamir. From maximum heights of 6,000 m–7,000 m the peaks decline in altitude westwards, attaining 4,500 m–6,000 m in the zone close to Kabul. Further west still, the ridges are no more than 3,500 m–4,500 m and in the extreme west they open out rather like the digits of a hand, with much lower Parapamisus ridges (proto-Pamir) forming the last member of the mountain complex. The various ridges are distinguished by separate names. The Hindu Kush, which has a general altitude of about 4,500 m, with peaks 2,000 m–3,000 m higher still, is, however, narrow and crossable by quite a number of passes, some of which are indirect and snow-bound for much of the year.

Afghanistan forms a major watershed from which rivers flow outward. The Amu-Dar'ya (Oxus) rises on the north side of the Hindu Kush and flows north-westward into Turkmenistan. Here, away from the mountains, the presence of small pockets of loess (a yellowish soil of high fertility) offers scope for agriculture. The Hari Rud rises a short distance only from the Amu-Dar'ya, but flows westward through Herat to terminate in a salt, closed basin on the Iranian frontier. From the south and west of the Hindu Kush flow a number of streams that become tributaries of the Indus; and in the extreme south-west the Helmand river flows through arid country to end, like the Hari Rud, in a closed basin that is partly within Iranian territory. The Helmand basin is of interest in that, because of a curious balance in water-level at its lowest part, the river here reverses its flow seasonally, and remains for much of its length non-brackish instead of becoming progressively more saline, as is normal when there is no outlet to the sea. The Helmand basin thus offers distinct potential for agricultural improvement, including the development of irrigation schemes; but political difficulties (part of the lower basin is Iranian territory) and remoteness have been inhibiting factors.

The lower-lying areas, which are in the main more densely peopled, occur either as a series of peripheral zones to north and south, or as a series of interior valleys and basins between the main mountain ridges of the centre. Largest of these areas is the piedmont lying on the northern flanks of the mountains and dropping northward in altitude to merge into the steppe-lands of former Soviet Central Asia. This is Bactria (Balkh), a region of, in places, light yellowish, loessic soils. An interior situation, shut off from the sea by mountains, means that rainfall is deficient and falls mainly over the mountains. Streams fed partly by mountain snowmelt straggle across the plain, to lose themselves in the sand, feed salt swamps or, in a few cases, join others to form larger rivers such as the Hari Rud. Much of Bactria thus consists of semi- or full desert with sheets of sand and gravel in many places, with, nearer the mountains, outwash of larger, coarser scree. Given stable political conditions, this region with its areas of highly fertile loess soils and moderate water supplies offers much scope for economic development. For long inhabited by pastoral nomads, and disputed politically by various claimants (Afghanistan, Iran and the former USSR), this northern zone was developed rapidly with irrigated cotton-growing as a main element. Links with the former USSR were considerable, and the two chief towns of Herat in the west and Mazar-i-Sharif in the north have grown considerably in size over recent years, mainly for political (rather than economic) reasons.

In the south, towards the east, is the Kabul basin, which is a relatively flat zone hemmed in closely by steep mountain ridges. Some distance away to the north-west, and reachable through two major passes, is the narrower Vale of Bamian, whilst south-east of Kabul lies another fertile lowland zone around Jalalabad. Here lower elevation and southerly situation produce warmer conditions, especially in winter, as compared with most of the rest of Afghanistan.

In the south-west, extending through Ghazni as far as Qandahar, there is another series of cultivated zones, but the extent of this piedmont area is much smaller than the corresponding one described above as Bactria. To the west, aridity, the price of declining altitude, increases, so the lowland passes into the desert areas of Registan and the Dasht-i-Mayo. Registan has seasonal flushes of grass, which support relatively large numbers of pastoral nomads, who, however, are becoming increasingly settled following irrigation development on the Helmand and Arghandab rivers.

Two other regional units may be mentioned. South of the Parapamisus and Kuh-i-Baba mountain ranges are a number of parallel but lower massifs, with narrow valleys between. Here because of altitude there is a relatively abundant rainfall, but owing to topography, the region is one of remoteness and difficulty. This is the Hazarajat, so called from the name of the Hazara inhabitants, and it still remains, despite a central position, one of the least known and visited parts of the country. Another equally remote highland, this time located north-east of Kabul, is Nuristan, again high and mountainous, but well-wooded in places, and supporting a small population of cultivators and pastoralists who use the summer pastures of the high hills and move to lower levels in winter.

### CLIMATE

Climatically, Afghanistan demonstrates a very clear relationship with Iran and the Middle East, rather than with Monsoon Asia, in that it has an almost arid summer, a small amount of rainfall, which is largely confined to the winter season, and considerable seasonal variation in temperature. The monsoonal condition of heavy summer rainfall does not occur, despite Afghanistan's proximity to India. Annual rainfall ranges from 100 mm–150 mm in the drier, lower areas of the west and north, to 250 mm–400 mm in the east; on the highest mountains there is more still. Kabul, with an average of 330 mm per annum, is typical of conditions in the east, and Herat with 125 mm typical of the west. Almost all this falls in the period December to April, though there can be a very occasional downpour at other times, even in summer, when a rare damp monsoonal current penetrates from the Indian lowlands. Temperatures are best described as extreme. In July the lowlands experience temperatures of 43°C, with 49°C not uncommon—this is true of Jalalabad on the edge of the Indus lowlands. Yet the effects of altitude are important, and Kabul, at an elevation of 1,800 m, does not often experience temperatures of over 38°C. Winter cold can be bitter, with minima of −22°C to −26°C on the higher plateau areas, and, as a result, there are heavy blizzards in many mountain areas. The January mean in Kabul is −4°C. A further difficulty is the prevalence of strong winds, especially in the west, where a persistent and regular wind blows almost daily from June to September and affects especially the Sistan area of the lower Helmand basin, where it is known as the 'Wind of 120 Days'.

### POPULATION

The considerable variation in the types of terrain, and the substantial obstacles imposed by high mountains and deserts, have given rise to marked ethnic and cultural differences, so that heterogeneity in human populations is most characteristic. The Pashtuns live mainly in the centre, south and east of the country, and are probably numerically the largest group. The Ghilzai, also of the areas adjacent to Pakistan, are thought to be of Turkish origin, like the Uzbeks who live in the north, mainly in the Amu-Dar'ya lowlands. Another important element comprises the Tajiks or Farsiwan who are of Persian origin, and in the opinion of some represent the earliest inhabitants of the country. Other groups, such as the Hazara (who are reputed to have come in as followers of Genghis Khan) and the Chahar Aimaq, may have Mongol ancestry, but they now speak Farsi (Persian) and the Hazara are Shi'a Muslims. In the north-east, the presence of fair-haired groups has suggested historic connections with Europe. Another possibly indigenous group of long standing is the Nuristani or Kafirs, now small in number. Most Afghans (the Hazara and Qizilbash of Kabul excepted) are Muslims of the Sunni sect. Pashto (Pakhto), one of the eastern group of Iranian languages, is spoken by about 30% of the total population (numerous other Pashto-speakers live across the frontier in Pakistan). Since 1936 Pashto and Dari (a dialect of Farsi) have been the official languages of the country, using an augmented Arabic script.

Economic progress has been inhibited by a difficult topography, an extreme climate with a generally deficient rainfall and political instability. Traditionally, small communities lived by cultivation where water and soil were available, and there were relatively numerous pastoralists, mostly nomads, who formed an important section of the community. Even today, it is estimated that about 15% of the population is nomadic, and tribal organization is strong. In 2003/04, according to the IMF, only 15% of Afghanistan's total area was classified as arable land.

# History

MARTIN EWANS

### SOCIETY AND EARLY HISTORY

Afghanistan, with a population of perhaps 20m.–25m., is a country of unusual ethnic diversity—a result of the many migrations and invasions it has experienced over millennia. Roughly 20 main ethnic groups coexist with more than 30 minor ones. In addition to the two principal languages, Pashto (Pakhto) and Dari (a dialect of Farsi—Persian), there are many others, some 30 in all. Almost 50% of the population are Pashtuns (or Pakhtoons or Pathans), most of whom inhabit the south and east of the country. They comprise two large tribal confederations, the Durranis and the Ghilzai, along with a number of so-called 'hill tribes', settled to the east of the country and across the border in Pakistan. Between 1747 and 1978, the year in which the communist *coup d'état* took place, central power lay with the Durranis, who came to form the ruling dynasty. The great majority of Pashtuns are Sunni Muslims, but their society is also regulated by a code of honour (*pashtunwali*), which is dominated by principles of revenge, hospitality and asylum. The basic social unit is the *qawm*, a flexible term defining a community which is bound by interacting obligations of protection, co-operation and support, and which normally overrides all other social linkages. The *qawm* combines elements of leadership, practised by *khans*, and democracy, exercised through the jirga (council or assembly of adult men). Throughout Pashtun history, the *qawm* has been the focal point of allegiance. Pashtuns have always considered the state to be something external, and often hostile, to their interests.

Afghanistan's other ethnic groups are less influential, although the Tajiks, constituting around 25% of the population, have played an important role in the country's administration. As well as the Tajiks, the Turkmen and Uzbeks in Afghanistan have ethnic links with the populations of the Central Asian republics to the north, while the Hazaras, who, from their features, appear to be of Mongol descent, live mainly in the centre of the country. Among other groups are the Balochis and Brahui, who live largely in the south of the country; the Aimaq and Farsiwan in the west; and the Nuristani in the east.

Islam is almost universal among Afghans. The majority are Sunni Muslims and perhaps one-fifth are Shi'a. The main Shi'a community, the Hazaras, have consequently encountered much religious hatred and oppression. Throughout the country, the main religious focus is the village or community mosque, served by a Mullah, although *ulema* (religious scholars) are also influential. Several Sufi orders, which emphasize the personal and spiritual life within Islam, have attracted numbers of adherents. In recent decades, an Islamist movement has developed, aiming to adapt a religious ethos to the challenges of modern life and create a progressive Islamic state. Its founding nucleus was the Faculty of Theology at Kabul University, headed by Prof. Burhanuddin Rabbani.

Both the Sufis and the Islamists were prominent in the resistance organizations that were formed in response to the Soviet occupation of the 1980s. Although Islam has been a unifying force in countering external threats to the country, it has failed to bring Afghanistan's peoples together in a spirit of national unity. The country remains divided along cultural, tribal, ethnic and religious lines.

Afghanistan first appeared in recorded history in the 6th century BC as part of the Achaemenid Empire. It was subsequently invaded by a succession of conquerors, including Alexander III ('the Great') of Macedon, the Mauryan dynasty, the Bactrians, the Kushans and the White Huns. Islam reached Afghanistan in the 7th century and spread slowly across the country. Towards the end of the first millennium AD, a substantial Afghan empire developed, based in Ghazni, which extended its influence well into India. However, disaster occurred in the 13th and 14th centuries, when first the Mongol Genghis Khan and then the Turko-Mongol Tamerlane the Great conquered Afghanistan, amid much bloodshed and destruction. In the 15th century, there followed something of a 'golden age', the Timurid Renaissance, which was based in Herat and became renowned for its architectural, literary, graphic and musical achievements. Early in the 16th century, Babur the Great, an adventurer from Central Asia, seized control of Kabul and went on to found the Mughal dynasty in India.

### The Emergence of the Afghan Kingdom

From the 16th century onwards, the Persian Safavid dynasty and the Mughal Empire vied for supremacy in Afghanistan. The Mughals exercised a somewhat uncertain rule over Kabul and Peshawar (now in Pakistan), while the Safavids held Herat and the lands to the west. Qandahar changed hands several times, while to the north a number of Uzbek khanates maintained their independence from both parties. At the beginning of the 18th century, however, Mir Wais Hotaki, a chief of the Ghilzai tribe, led an uprising against the Safavids and captured Qandahar. His son, Mir Mahmud, proceeded to invade Persia, and to seize and plunder the capital, Isfahan. Mir Mahmud was, however, deposed and succeeded by his cousin, Ashraf, in 1725. In 1729 the latter was defeated by a resurgent Persian army under a former camel driver and bandit, Nadir Shah, who succeeded in capturing Herat in 1732. In doing so, he also defeated the Afghan Abdali tribe and then recruited a number of Abdalis and Ghilzais to serve as his personal bodyguard during his advance on India in 1738–39. Following his capture of Delhi, he returned to Persia, laden with booty, and conducted further campaigns into Central Asia, until he was finally assassinated in 1747.

Nadir Shah's death created a crisis for his Abdali bodyguard; however, under the leadership of a young Abdali officer, Ahmed Khan, they managed to fight their way out and return to Qandahar. There, Ahmed Khan was elected Shah by a tribal jirga and changed his name to Ahmed Shah Durrani. His election was probably due to the fact that he belonged to a small clan—the Saddozai branch of the Popalzai sub-tribe—and was perceived to be easily influenced. Nevertheless, he proved to be an effective and charismatic leader, and founded an empire which covered the whole of present Afghanistan, as well as Kashmir and Sindh (the latter now in Pakistan), and stretched from Meshed in the west to Delhi in the east. He captured and plundered Delhi in 1749 and returned to sack it again in 1756. In 1761 he fought a major battle against the Marathas of India at Panipat, which he won, following a large-scale massacre. This battle was particularly significant because it ended the supremacy of the Marathas, who might otherwise have been a major impediment to the British, as they advanced to Delhi and the Punjab later in the century.

Ahmed Shah eventually wearied of campaigning, and died in 1772, still only in his fifties. Although noteworthy as a leader and a warrior, he and his unruly followers were incapable of establishing a permanent empire. Nevertheless, the dynasty that he founded lasted until 1818 and continued under a different sub-tribe up to 1978. He is therefore respected by Afghans as the 'Father of the Nation', although he was more the leader of a tribal confederation than of anything approaching a nation state.

Ahmed Shah was succeeded by his second son, Taimur, who moved his capital to Kabul in 1775. He managed to keep his empire largely intact until his death in 1793. However, following his demise, internecine strife among his sons (23 of whom were by his 36 official wives) caused the empire to disintegrate. The fifth son, Zaman Mirza, managed to secure the succession, with the help of a prominent Durrani chief from the Mohammadzai clan, Painda Khan. However, Zaman Shah proved a largely ineffectual ruler. His empire gradually disintegrated and, as revenues from his Indian possessions declined, he was increasingly constrained by lack of funds. His tribal chiefs became correspondingly more powerful, and he was eventually blinded and deposed following a rebellion headed by his half-brother, Mahmud, and Painda Khan's son, Fateh Khan. Mahmud assumed control but a struggle with Zaman's brother, Shah Shuja, ensued, in which the latter eventually prevailed. It was during Shah Shuja's reign that the British envoy Mountstuart Elphinstone arrived in Peshawar in 1809 to negotiate a treaty of mutual defence against the threat to British India that was seen to be developing from the direction of Persia; this visit marked the first official contact with the British.

## PAWN IN THE 'GREAT GAME'

A few weeks after Elphinstone's visit, Shah Shuja was defeated in battle and deposed, and eventually became, along with the blind Zaman Shah, a pensioner in British India. Meanwhile, fratricide and treachery prevailed in Afghanistan, with a succession of rivals holding Kabul for varying lengths of time. Peshawar was captured in 1819 by the Sikh ruler of the Punjab, Ranjit Singh, and eventually, in 1826, Fateh Khan's young brother, Dost Mohammad Khan, managed to gain power in Kabul and the neighbouring districts. Qandahar was held by another branch of the Mohammadzai clan, known as the 'Qandahar Sirdars', and Peshawar by a third branch, the 'Peshawar Sirdars'. Herat, meanwhile, was controlled by Mahmud's son, Kamran Mirza.

British concerns about the security of their north-west India frontier began to emerge towards the end of the 18th century, when the Governor-General, Lord Wellesley, was engaged in extending British rule towards the Punjab. Zaman soon proved not to present a threat, but apprehensions revived shortly afterwards, when the French leader Napoleon Bonaparte sailed for Egypt and was believed to be intending to invade India. British Admiral Horatio Nelson's victory at the Battle of the Nile temporarily thwarted French ambitions, but concerns arose again in 1807, when Napoleon sent a mission to Persia and negotiated a treaty that envisaged a joint Franco-Persian invasion. It was in response to this apparent threat that Elphinstone was sent to Peshawar and treaties were concluded with other chiefs. However, Napoleon then signed the Treaty of Tilsit with the Russians, a development that not only antagonized the Persians, but caused concern in Britain and India over the possibility of a joint Franco-Russian invasion. This never occurred, but the prospect did cause the British to believe subsequently that Russia's aim was to incorporate India into its successfully expanding empire in Asia.

This was the situation until the late 1820s when, following a successful war, the Russians succeeded in gaining preponderant influence over the Persian Shah and encouraged him to besiege Herat, in the British view the precursor to another attempt to acquire India. The siege eventually took place in late 1837, when a Persian force led by a new Shah, Mohammad Mirza, arrived before the city. Mohammad Shah was accompanied by the Russian envoy Count Simonich, a number of seconded Russian officers and a regiment of Russian 'deserters'. However, despite the presence of the Russians, the siege was conducted with total incompetence and was raised in late 1838, when the Shah was threatened with British invasion. The Shah's decision to end the siege caused the Russians to suffer a diplomatic, as well as a military, reverse.

That should have been the end of the affair, but events in India had by then assumed a momentum of their own. There, the British Governor-General, Lord Auckland, had sent a young army officer, Alexander Burnes, to the court of Dost Mohammad in an effort to counter Russia's attempts to extend its influence in the region. There is some uncertainty over precisely what happened at Kabul, but the probability is that Burnes exceeded his instructions and led Dost Mohammad to understand that he would receive more in return for an alliance than Auckland was prepared to concede. The main issue was Peshawar, which Dost Mohammad wished to recover. Auckland, however, was not prepared to challenge the ruler of the area, Ranjit Singh, his ally of almost 30 years. Burnes' mission therefore failed, and Dost Mohammad turned to a Russian envoy, Captain Vitkevich, who had meanwhile arrived in Kabul with proposals for a relationship with Russia. Auckland concluded that Dost Mohammad was an unreliable neighbour and, despite the raising of the siege of Herat, pressed ahead with preparations for an invasion of Afghanistan. The aim was, in alliance with Ranjit Singh, to replace Dost Mohammad with Shah Shuja, who was still living in pensionable exile in India. The fate of the British 'Army of the Indus' is well known. Kabul was captured without much difficulty and Shah Shuja was restored to his throne. The Afghans, however, were never reconciled to the presence of 'infidels' on their land, and eventually the British position became untenable. Hampered by overconfident political advice and incompetent military leadership, some 5,000 British troops and 12,000 camp followers retreated from Kabul during the winter of 1841/42 and were almost totally annihilated. An 'Army of Retribution' duly arrived in Kabul the following year, destroyed its bazaar and wreaked havoc in surrounding villages; nevertheless, the damage to British prestige was long-lasting.

Having recovered his throne, Dost Mohammad proceeded to reign for a further 20 years, during which time he maintained good relations with the British. The British meanwhile occupied Sindh and the Punjab, while the Russians made some limited advances in Central Asia. However, it was not until the 1860s that the seizure by the Russians of several Central Asian khanates, including Samarkand and Bukhara, and the establishment of a Russian province of Turkestan with its capital at Tashkent, caused renewed concern in British India over Russian intentions. There were two schools of thought: one that it was best to await any Russian advance at the Indian frontier (the 'stationary policy', or the 'policy of masterly inactivity'); the other (the 'forward policy') that the Russians should be met on a 'scientific frontier' as far away from India as possible. The advocates of a 'stationary policy' were at first in the ascendancy; however, when the new British Prime Minister, Benjamin Disraeli, assumed office in 1876, and Dost Mohammad's successor, Sher Ali, was seen to be receiving a Russian mission in Kabul, the policies advocated by the 'forward' school prevailed. In 1879 the British Viceroy, Lord Lytton, ordered an invasion of Afghanistan. Three columns were dispatched: up the Khyber Pass, towards Qandahar, and through the Kurram Valley. The British military campaign was successful and Sher Ali, after the Russians had rejected his appeal for assistance, retired to Mazar-i-Sharif, where he died shortly afterwards. In May a treaty was concluded with his son, Yakub Khan, in which he ceded areas west of the Indus, including Kurram, Pishin, Sibi and the Khyber and Michni Pass and relinquished control of his foreign affairs to the British. A British representative, Louis Cavignari, was installed in Kabul. The British forces then withdrew, congratulating themselves on a successful campaign. However, within a few weeks, Cavignari was murdered and Gen. Frederick 'Frank' Roberts (later to be Lord Roberts of Kandahar) was sent back to Afghanistan with an avenging force. He managed to reach Kabul and proceeded to institute a 'reign of terror', hanging many Afghans who had played no part in Cavignari's murder. Following Yakub Khan's abdication, Roberts assumed total authority. He occupied Sher Ali's military cantonment, where he repulsed a large tribal onslaught, but his position remained precarious. Some 15,000 men had to be deployed merely to keep his lines of communication open.

It was soon clear that the British would have to extricate themselves, particularly after the British army suffered an ignominious defeat at the Battle of Maiwand, in the south; however, it was less evident how they might ensure that the kingdom would be strong enough to resist Russian encroachments following their departure. By good luck rather than judgement, in 1880 they were able to conclude a satisfactory arrangement with Sher Ali's nephew, Abdul Rahman, who had just returned to Afghanistan. Although, or perhaps because, he had spent some years in exile in Turkestan, he kept his distance from the Russians and, while he was often a difficult neighbour, he remained loyal to the British.

This was not, however, the end of the 'Great Game'. The Russians continued to expand their influence in Central Asia, subduing the Tekke Turkmen in 1881 and occupying Merv (now Mari, Turkmenistan) in 1884. In 1886 they advanced to Panjdeh, an oasis situated between Merv and Herat. In response, the British mobilized their troops and warned of war if the advance continued. Fortunately, however, conflict was averted. In 1887 the British and Russians demarcated the frontier between Turkestan and northern Afghanistan. In 1895–96 they established the Wakhan Corridor, which acted as a 'buffer' between British and Russian territories and gave Afghanistan a short frontier with China in the far north-east. In 1907 they concluded the Anglo-Russian Convention, which, without any consultation with the Afghans, stipulated that Afghanistan should stay outside the Russians' sphere of influence, while Britain agreed that it would not occupy or annex that country, nor interfere in its internal affairs.

It is doubtful if the Russians ever had any serious intention of invading India, although it was certainly something that they would have liked to achieve, if given the chance. To any competent soldier, the difficulties of campaigning far from their bases and across Afghanistan, and the likely prospect of their encountering fierce resistance from the Afghans in the process, would have been considered as a decisive deterrent. However, this was the perception in British India, while the Russians, for their part, believed that Britain had imperial and commercial designs in Central Asia. More often, however, political and military manoeuvres in that part of the world were a function of the 'Eastern Question'—the contest for supremacy in South-East Europe, Turkey and the Dardanelles (a Turkish waterway). When the Russians saw their opportunity, they tried to exert pressure in Central Asia in order to further their designs in the Black Sea and the Mediterranean Sea, while Britain was determined to resist these efforts in order to protect its sea route to India. The 1907 Convention marked the impasse that ended the 'Game'.

## INDEPENDENCE AND ISOLATION

It is not surprising that Abdul Rahman became known as the 'Iron Amir'. His 20-year reign was brutal and tyrannical: he relied upon British subsidies to maintain an army, which he had to use repeatedly to keep his rebellious subjects in order. He had to cope with some 40 tribal revolts, several of them of major consequence, and did so in extremely ruthless ways, including the use of mass executions. Claiming that he ruled with divine sanction, he did his utmost to break the power of the Mullahs, destroying their economic independence by taking over their religious trusts. He also established a state administration, and eventually managed to exercise a reasonably firm control over the whole country. Under pressure from the British, in 1893 he was forced to acquiesce in the demarcation of his eastern and southern frontier, separating a large number of Pashtun and Baloch subjects from his rule. However, he managed to keep the rest of the world at a distance by adopting policies of extreme isolation. He refused to allow the extension of the railway or telegraph into Afghanistan; allowed very few foreigners to work in the country; and almost entirely restricted the British representative's contact with local society. He died in 1901 and the throne passed peacefully to his son Habibullah.

It was during the reign of Habibullah that the first stirrings of nationalism and independence began to appear in Afghanistan. Inspired by a distant cousin, Mohammad Beg Tarzi, whom he recalled from exile, a 'Young Turk' movement emerged at his court, with leanings towards pan-Islamism, anti-imperialism and self-determination, and the modernization and liberalization of society. During the First World War (1914–18), the 'Young Turks' formed the nucleus of a 'war party'. Despite encountering pressure from the movement and a Turko-German mission to declare war against British India, Habibullah remained neutral. However, when the war ended, he received no reply to his request to be accorded independent status as a reward for his neutral position. He was assassinated whilst on a hunting trip in 1919, probably at the instigation of one of the 'war party'.

Immediately after Amanullah succeeded his father as Amir, he proclaimed Afghan independence and declared war on the British. Amanullah chose his moment well: Britain had become war-weary and much of the Indian army was still overseas; furthermore, demobilization of the British army in India was fully under way. There was also much latent unrest in British India. The British managed to avert a full-scale tribal uprising, but were unable to achieve more than an impasse on the ground. The decisive factor in the conflict was air power. British aircraft succeeded in bombing Jalalabad and Kabul, where they struck the royal palace and Abdul Rahman's tomb. One month into the war, Amanullah sued for peace, and in 1921 a treaty between the British and the Afghan leader was signed, granting Afghanistan full independence. The Government in Britain disapproved; however, there was no desire in India for a prolonged war, not least because the outcome of a conflict would be uncertain.

Amanullah then turned his attention to modernization within Afghanistan. Many of his proposals were regarded as sensible and enlightened, but he took no account of the conservatism of tribal society. Eventually, he was denounced as an infidel, the tribes revolted and in 1929 he was forced to flee the country. Some nine months of anarchy followed, under a Tajik by the name of Baccha-i-Saqao ('Son of the Water Carrier'). His rule was ended when the 'Musahiban' brothers, from the line of the 'Peshawar Sirdars', raised a tribal force and invaded the country from British India. The eldest brother, Nadir Shah, took the throne and managed to establish his rule through a combination of conciliation and brute repression. Although he introduced a new Constitution, which was to last until the 1960s, in practice Nadir Shah and his brothers governed the country more or less as a family concern. He received a subsidy and a gift of weapons from the British and was careful not to support tribal unrest along the frontier. Internally, he managed to restore stability and began to encourage commerce and some limited industry.

Nadir Shah was assassinated in 1933, apparently in an act of personal revenge, and the remaining Musahiban brothers united in support of his son, Mohammad Zahir Shah. The latter reigned until 1973, although for much of the time the country continued to be ruled by his uncles. The Musahiban family adopted a cautious and conservative style: while some modest economic progress was made, Afghanistan remained a predominantly agricultural and pastoral nation. In Kabul, meanwhile, an educated élite gradually emerged. Four high schools functioned and, in 1932, the University of Kabul was established. Afghans also went abroad for education. A rift thus gradually emerged between an increasingly sophisticated urban society and the traditional countryside. Externally, the regime turned mainly to Italy, Germany and Japan for assistance; some Afghans became pro-German and even pro-Nazi. During the Second World War (1939–45), however, Afghans were careful to remain neutral and to avoid provoking the British and the Russians. Indeed, in response to British and Russian demands, in 1941 the Afghan Government expelled German and Italian citizens from the country.

## WIDENING HORIZONS

Following the Second World War, Afghanistan found itself facing new challenges. When the British left India in 1947, the Afghans were surprised to discover that they could bring no influence to bear on the shape of the newly independent subcontinent. Their demands that the Pashtuns living east of the Durand Line should be given the option of self-determination were ignored: instead, these Pashtuns were incorporated into Pakistan (the latter having recently been created by the Partition of India). This gave rise to the 'Pashtunistan' issue, which for many years was to blight relations between Afghanistan and Pakistan. In response to Afghan propaganda and tribal incursions, the Pakistanis engineered delays in the transit trade and in 1950 imposed a blockade on petroleum products destined for Afghanistan. As a result, the Afghans turned to Russia, thereby giving the latter its first opportunity to make its presence felt in the country. Trade between the two countries soon doubled and the Russians began to prospect for oil in northern Afghanistan.

At the same time, the Afghan authorities were, like other governments in the post-war era, anxious to achieve some worthwhile development. They approached the US Government, but the latter was not interested. Instead, the US firm Morrison Knudsen was engaged to help construct two dams and associated irrigation projects on the Helmand River. However, the scheme achieved very little, despite the substantial investment involved. Afghanistan was also keen to modernize its armed forces, but again the USA was reluctant to assist. The US Government suspected that any weapons were to be used in the confrontation with Pakistan over the Pashtunistan issue. Indeed, it was Pakistan, rather than Afghanistan, that featured in US plans for military alliances designed to contain the USSR's influence in South Asia and the Middle East. The internal situation also caused concern. Under Shah Mahmud, the youngest Musahiban brother, a measure of political liberalization had been permitted in the late 1940s, leading to fears that it might destabilize the country. In 1953 the royal family took counsel among itself and decided that a fresh start was needed. The result was the appointment as Prime Minister of Lt-Gen. Sardar Mohammad Daoud Khan, the cousin and brother-in-law of the King, Zahir Shah.

Daoud was a man of considerable force of character: he was robust, dynamic and autocratic. He made one more attempt to obtain weapons from the USA, but when he was again rebuffed, he turned to Russia. With the death of the Soviet leader Stalin (Iosif V. Dzhugashvili) in 1953, the USSR was intent on strengthening its influence in the Third World and responded positively to Afghanistan's requests. As a result, Afghanistan became set on a course of military and economic dependence on the Soviet Union. As well as receiving Soviet military equipment, Afghans were also given military training, with members of the armed forces being trained in the Soviet Union. Those who travelled to the USSR were routinely indoctrinated and many became committed Marxists—an ominous development for the future. In 1955 a renewed confrontation with Pakistan over Pashtunistan, over which Daoud was an activist, occurred. Relations deteriorated as a result, and the border was closed. This incident gave the USSR the opportunity to intervene again, and commercial and economic relations between the two countries were substantially strengthened. Taking advantage of the situation, the Soviet leader Nikita Khrushchev and premier Nikolai Bulganin visited Kabul in the same year and offered a large programme of developmental assistance, which included the construction of an all-weather road from Kabul to the Soviet border, through the Hindu Kush. Tardily, the USA decided that efforts should be made to prevent Afghanistan from being drawn into an exclusively Soviet sphere of influence, and thus they too offered developmental assistance. Generally, by the early 1960s, Daoud's policies seemed to be producing positive results. His *bi-tarafi* (without sides) posture was working and Afghanistan was gaining a reputation in the non-aligned group of nations. The army was becoming more effective in strengthening the regime, educational opportunities were expanding, and women were becoming emancipated. All might have been well had Daoud not tried in 1961 to force the pace over Pashtunistan, causing Pakistan to break off diplomatic relations and again close the border. Before long the effects of the border closure began to become serious and by early 1963 the economy was in crisis. At the same time, the monarchy was becoming apprehensive on several counts: Daoud's autocratic style of government was becoming increasingly resented, and the extent of dependence on the Soviet Union was causing concern. More importantly, the recent overthrow of several traditional Middle Eastern rulers had led the royal family to conclude that a constitutional monarchy and a more democratic form of government was needed if it were to survive. In March 1963 Daoud resigned and was replaced by a commoner, Dr Mohammad Yousuf.

### THE CONSTITUTIONAL PERIOD AND DAOUD'S RETURN

Action was quick to follow Daoud's resignation. Prompt efforts were made to settle the impasse with Pakistan, and normal trade and diplomatic relations were restored through the good offices of the Shah of Iran. A constitutional committee was established, which one year later produced the draft of a new, more democratic, constitution. In September 1964 a Loya Jirga (Grand National Council) was convened and the draft was extensively debated. It provided for a bicameral legislature and for the exclusion of all members of the royal family from political office. The legal system was also reformed, giving it a partly secular basis, but within an Islamic framework. At the beginning of October, the Constitution came into effect and elections were held for the lower house of parliament (Wolasi Jirga) a year later. The traditional rural and religious leadership fared well and, despite the low turn-out at the polls, the outcome was regarded as satisfactory. Trouble, however, began as soon as the Wolasi Jirga met. Since the Constitution had made no provision for political parties and the Government was appointed by the King, the relationship between the Government and the legislature was immediately confrontational. Disorder ensued a few days later, when students from Kabul University and high schools invaded the legislature and forced it to adjourn. A student demonstration the following day was fired upon by the army and two students were killed. Dr Yousuf resigned as a result of the crisis. Although his successor, Hashim Maiwandwal, managed to relieve the tensions, the precedents for an unruly legislature and student unrest had been set.

Although political parties were not strictly legal, several were formed during the constitutional period and were, to an extent, tolerated. In addition to the Islamist movement centred on the University, left-wing parties were also formed: two of them were 'Maoist' in character, and one—the People's Democratic Party of Afghanistan (PDPA)—had links with the Soviet Union. The founder of the PDPA was Nur Mohammad Taraki, a Ghilzai Pashtun who had earlier worked in Bombay, India, and, on returning to Afghanistan, had embarked on an administrative and journalistic career. He later became a Soviet agent. Babrak Karmal, the son of an army general and thus with an establishment background, was also instrumental in establishing the PDPA. Karmal was imprisoned for his left-wing views between 1953 and 1956 and later worked as a civil servant. A flexible, outgoing man and an accomplished orator, he represented a complete contrast to the retiring, doctrinaire Taraki. Nevertheless, in early 1965 the two joined forces and formed the PDPA, which was in all but name the Communist Party of Afghanistan. In 1967, however, the PDPA split into their original two factions: the Marxist *Khalq* (People) under Taraki and the Marxist *Parcham* (Banner) formed by Karmal. A third founder member of the PDPA, Hafizullah Amin, a thrusting, energetic man and an excellent administrator, supported Taraki.

By the early 1970s the King's constitutional experiment was experiencing serious problems. Unwilling to legalize political parties, which he feared would be extremist in nature, the King continued to leave his governments without political support. The governments were mostly ineffective. This became particularly evident in 1971–73 when, owing to corruption and incompetence, the authorities failed to deal with a serious famine, in which many died. This encouraged Daoud, who had been awaiting his opportunity, to take advantage of the King's absence abroad in July 1973 to mount a virtually bloodless coup. He acted with the support of disaffected military officers and Karmal's Parcham faction. It was this move, more than any other, that broke the mould of Afghan society and set the country on the path to disaster.

Daoud received no support from the USSR for the coup, although the latter initially welcomed it. It was Daoud who had earlier sought the Soviet Union's involvement in Afghanistan, and the inclusion of Parchamis in his Government was welcome. As he was now an elderly man, the USSR no doubt expected that Daoud would not survive long and that he would be succeeded by a well-disposed government in which Parcham would play a significant role. The USSR, however, was soon to be disappointed. The reasons for Daoud's change of course are unclear, but by 1975 he had removed the Parchamis from their positions of power, was restoring relations with Pakistan and was establishing close links with Iran. Soviet influence in the armed forces was being reduced and Daoud was turning to Egypt, India and even the USA for military training. In 1976 he introduced a new Constitution, which provided for a one-party state, thereby outlawing both Parcham and Khalq. Consequently, the Soviet Union withdrew its support for Daoud and directed its efforts towards reuniting Parcham and Khalq. By 1977 it had succeeded, although the union was tenuous and the underlying tensions remained.

#### The Khalq Regime

Although the reunited PDPA had plans for a coup and the Soviet Union was undoubtedly hoping that Daoud would be replaced by a more progressive, friendly regime, the *coup d'état* that took place on 27 April 1978 was the result of accident rather than design. A few days earlier, a Parcham activist, Mir Akbar Khyber, was assassinated by unknown gunmen. The large demonstrations that accompanied his funeral prompted Daoud to arrest a number of the PDPA leaders, including Taraki, Karmal and Amin. Amin subsequently claimed that before his arrest he had managed to issue instructions for a coup to the PDPA's supporters in the military, but there is little doubt that the relevant military leaders, Col Abdul Qadir of the air force and Maj. Aslam Watanjar, a tank commander, had realized that they too were at risk and needed no prompting. On the day of the coup Watanjar's tanks, with support later in the day from Qadir's aircraft, attacked the presidential palace, where Daoud was holding a cabinet meeting to decide the fate of those arrested. Despite a desperate resistance on the part of the presidential guard, which lasted until the early hours of the next morning, the palace was seized and Daoud, his family and associates were killed. The majority of the army stationed around Kabul failed to come to Daoud's assistance. The division that did attempt to help was attacked from the air and dispersed before it could reach the capital.

Essentially, therefore, this was a military coup, carried out while the civilian PDPA leaders were under detention, and for several days the Russian news agency TASS referred to it as such. While Soviet military advisers must have played some part in it, the initial Soviet reaction was one of concern, fearing that the coup, known (from the month) as the 'Saur Revolution', might have been the work of 'forces of reaction'. It was certainly not a pre-planned communist revolution undertaken at the USSR's instigation. However, the 'Military Council' that was initially set up, for whatever reasons deferred to the PDPA civilians and a Revolutionary Council was formed. Taraki was named its Chairman and Prime Minister; Karmal and Watanjar were designated Deputy Prime Ministers. Seats in the Council were equally divided between Khalq and Parcham members. During a meeting two days after the coup, Taraki assured the Soviet ambassador, Aleksandr Puzanov, that Afghanistan would 'belong to the Socialist camp'. However, with Soviet encouragement, the PDPA at first concealed its communist, pro-Soviet leanings and presented itself merely as progressive and non-aligned, while the USA and other countries chose a policy of 'wait and see' before deciding what policies to adopt towards the new Government.

Almost immediately, the PDPA once again split into Khalq and Parcham factions and a period described by the Soviet Committee for State Security (KGB) Residency as a 'real terror' began. At the end of June 1978 Karmal and other leading Parchamis were exiled as ambassadors. Extensive purges followed: Qadir and others were accused of plotting against the regime and imprisoned. Having thus settled its internal differences, the regime began to demonstrate its true nature. Several decrees were promulgated: the first cancelled most land mortgages and indebtedness and reduced payments on the remainder. A land decree was also introduced, which placed strict limits on landholdings and ordered the redistribution of land. As a result, any surplus land was seized without compensation and distributed to landless peasants. Although, ostensibly, these decrees introduced a degree of justice that had previously been lacking in rural relationships, they also provoked widespread opposition. Without credit, farmers were unable to obtain the materials, seed, fertilizer and tools that they needed; furthermore, rural communities were united in believing that it was un-Islamic to accept property that had been seized from another. When attempts were made to introduce the decrees by force, strong resistance developed. Much hardship ensued and possibly one-third of agricultural land went out of cultivation. At the same time, a further decree was introduced to regulate marriage and abolish bride-price; efforts were also made to reform educational curricula and introduce universal literacy. Again, these measures were designed to remedy patent social ills, but they were similarly bitterly resisted. The marriage decree struck at the roots of traditional familial relationships and there was strong resentment at the educational reforms, particularly where they affected women and girls and enforced co-education. In terms of presentation, too, the regime began to display its true intentions. The traditional flag was replaced by a red banner, virtually indistinguishable from those of other communist states; a treaty of friendship was concluded with the Soviet Union; communist-style mass rallies were held; and a cult of personality was created around Taraki, the 'Great Teacher'. All these measures, both substantive and presentational, pushed the country into revolt. Opposition to the Government began to assume alarming dimensions once the 1978 harvest had been gathered and the traditional fighting season began. Insurrections were soon under way across the country and the Government retaliated in force, attacking villages by air with bombs and napalm. A 'reign of terror' ensued, in which possibly 50,000–100,000 people were killed. The resistance began to organize itself, and training camps for militants were established in Pakistan. A strong attack on Asadabad, in Kunar province, was mounted in January 1979. However, it was in March that the first significant uprising took place, when rebels were joined by part of the city's military garrison in a revolt in the city of Herat. Government officials were murdered, as well as a number of Soviet advisers and their families.

In the Soviet capital of Moscow members of the Politburo met on three consecutive days to consider what action to take. They were clear that 'in no circumstances can Afghanistan be lost', but were equally aware that Soviet military intervention could not be allowed. Taraki, whose request for tanks and armoured cars manned by Russians was rejected, was summoned to Moscow and lectured by the Soviet leader, Leonid Brezhnev, on the need to adopt more conciliatory policies. The Soviet Union also promised to donate additional military and economic assistance and to provide more civilian and military experts. Eventually, the Herat uprising was suppressed by the Afghans themselves, at the reported cost of as many as 25,000 civilian casualties.

As the resistance strengthened in subsequent months, infighting intensified within the regime. In July 1979 antagonism between Taraki and Amin reached its peak, with Amin accusing Taraki of incompetence and Taraki accusing Amin of nepotism. By August Amin's grip on power was almost comprehensive and Taraki was reduced to little more than a figurehead. The Soviet Union made a series of attempts to achieve a reconciliation, but without success. A senior diplomat, Vasilii Safronchuk, was posted to Kabul for this specific purpose and the Director of the International Department of the Communist Party of the Soviet Union, Boris Ponomarev, paid a number of visits, but both had to report a lack of results. Meanwhile, the resistance grew throughout the country and several major towns—Jalalabad, Faizabad and Bamian among them—were attacked. Increased numbers of Soviet advisers had little impact on the situation. Several Afghan army units mutinied or simply defected, including an armoured unit in Kabul itself. In early September the KGB Residency advised Moscow that the regime was in danger of total collapse and attributed the blame to Amin. Their recommendation was that he should be removed from power and that a broad-based government be established. Brezhnev agreed with the advice and gave Taraki, when the latter was transiting Moscow on his return from a non-aligned conference in Cuba, a 'direct and open instruction to get rid of Amin'. Unfortunately for the USSR, the plan did not turn out as expected. Amin was apparently warned about the Moscow meeting and forced a confrontation when Taraki returned. Too weak to prevail openly, Taraki resorted to a plot to have Amin assassinated while he was *en route* to a meeting at the presidential palace. A shoot-out ensued, in which Amin's bodyguard was killed, but Amin himself survived. Amin summoned troops and besieged the palace and had Taraki deposed and himself appointed as President and General Secretary of the PDPA. Taraki was murdered a few days later.

The Soviet Union was thus confronted with the worst possible outcome. Amin, whose atrocities and hardline policies had been largely responsible for the deteriorating situation, was now firmly in charge, supported by relatives and adherents. He suspected, with reason, that Moscow had been responsible for the attempt to remove him and he sought to expand his options. He tried to establish relations with the Pakistani Government, and made overtures to the USA and to conservative elements within the country. The main Soviet concern was not so much that the military situation was critical, although it was certainly continuing to deteriorate (the view of the US Embassy was that the Afghan army was not in danger of military defeat); rather, the conclusion that the USSR reached was that Amin might well 'do a Sadat', in other words abandon the Soviet sphere of influence for that of the West. This, in the view of the Soviet authorities, would be inadmissible.

## THE SOVIET OCCUPATION

The responsibility for the Soviet invasion of Afghanistan at the end of 1979 lay primarily with Yurii Andropov, the head of the KGB, and Dmitrii Ustinov, the Soviet Minister of Defence. Before taking such an extreme step, however, Andropov tried first to remove Amin by means of assassination. One, or possibly two, attempts were made, and at one point Karmal—who was now in Moscow—was flown to the Bagram airbase, north of Kabul, to take over once Amin was killed. The attempts, however, failed, leaving invasion as the only option. Andropov planned to send troops by air to Kabul and to remove Amin by a *coup de main*. Ustinov, however, believed this to be too risky, and insisted on a full-scale invasion. The two then had to convince Brezhnev, but it seems that this was not too difficult. He was ailing and barely functioning, and the emotion uppermost in his mind was anger that Amin, that 'dirty fellow', had killed Taraki shortly after he had received him in Moscow. Gromyko, the veteran Minister of Foreign Affairs, would also have to agree, but was known for his willingness to acquiesce to whatever others had decided. In early December the four men discussed the issue at some length and decided that the Andropov-Ustinov proposal should be adopted. When Marshal Ogarkov, the Chief of the Soviet General Staff, was informed, he was 'surprised and outraged', argued strongly against the proposal and urged that a political solution should be found. He warned that the Afghans did not tolerate invaders and that the Soviet army would have to fight. He was, however, overruled and orders were given to prepare the invasion. On 12 December the action was endorsed by the Politburo. It is significant that the premier, Aleksei Kosygin, was ill at the time and therefore absent from the meeting. Known to have been opposed to the invasion, he never endorsed the document. It is probable that, had he been fit and present, the decision to go ahead with the invasion would not have been taken.

There has been much speculation about the Politburo's motives for the invasion. Some have considered it as strategic in character: the US Defense Intelligence Agency described it as 'a move to bring long-standing strategic goals closer within reach. Control of Afghanistan would be a major step towards overland access to the Indian Ocean and the domination of the Asian sub-continent'. However, now that much of the relevant Soviet documentation and other evidence is available, it is clear that the motive was essentially defensive in nature. The overriding consideration was the one that had been decisive at the time of the Herat uprising: that 'in no circumstances can Afghanistan be lost'. Such an outcome was ideologically inadmissible since, under the Brezhnev Doctrine, enunciated at the time of the Soviet invasion of Czechoslovakia in 1968, no retreat from the 'onward march of socialism' could be allowed. Moreover, Soviet prestige would be gravely damaged by the loss of Afghanistan and unrest might well spread to other Soviet satellite states and non-Russian republics within the Soviet Union. The Soviet leadership was also concerned by the revolution in Iran and was fearful that Islamist extremism might unsettle the Central Asian republics were it to spread along the USSR's southern borders. The prospect of US influence growing in an area that had always been one of some sensitivity was also unacceptable. In any event, even without an invasion, it seemed unlikely that the USA would ratify the Strategic Arms Limitation Treaty (SALT II). *Détente* was, according to the Soviet leadership, 'for most purposes, already dead'. The USA was also demoralized by its military experience in Viet Nam and was occupied with the hostage crisis in Iran. Furthermore, neither the USA nor the rest of the international community seemed to be in a position to impose any effective sanctions. In any case, Moscow hoped to be able to bring about Amin's replacement and present the invasion as a response to a request from a new Afghan government.

On 24 December 1979 a succession of flights started to land at Kabul airport and troops began to mass. A final attempt was made to incapacitate Amin, by arranging for his Russian cooks to tamper with his lunch. However, this also failed, leaving assassination as the only available option. Some three days later, 5,000 troops had arrived and assaults began on key points in the capital and on Amin's headquarters, which were situated a short distance outside Kabul. Amin was killed and the city was rapidly secured. Two motorized infantry divisions meanwhile crossed the frontier and drove to Herat and Kabul; two more arrived several days later. Within a few weeks, some 85,000 troops had been deployed and the whole operation appeared to have been a virtually unopposed success. Less successful, however, were Moscow's attempts to minimize the damage to public relations. Late on 27 December, before the Kabul radio station had been captured, a statement by Karmal was broadcast on its frequency, announcing that Amin had been overthrown. It transpired, however, that the broadcast had come from Central Asia and Karmal was not seen in Kabul until 1 January 1980. Although the Soviet authorities tried vainly to maintain that they had invaded in response to a request from a legitimate Afghan government, the questions immediately raised were: if the request was from Karmal, he was not in Afghanistan; and if Amin had sought Soviet intervention, why had they killed him. In any case, the invasion had started before the dates variously given for the requests. The inconsistencies were such that the truth was inescapable: that the Soviet Union had unilaterally invaded an independent, non-aligned, Islamic, developing country, killed its President and installed a 'puppet' regime.

US President Jimmy Carter led the international condemnation. Describing what had happened as 'one of the most serious threats to peace since the Second World War', he announced a range of measures designed to penalize the Soviet Union and declared that any attempt by it to gain control of the Persian (Arabian) Gulf would be regarded as an attack on US vital interests. In the UN General Assembly, the Non-aligned Movement and the Organization of the Islamic Conference, resolutions condemning the invasion were passed by overwhelming majorities. However, the widespread feeling was that the statements were merely 'for the record'. The universal conclusion was that the Soviets would stay in Afghanistan for as long as was necessary and there was no way in which they could be forced to withdraw.

The Soviet plan was that the occupation would be only temporary. The Soviet forces would maintain control of strategic bases and support the Afghan army as it dealt with the rebels. As soon as the Afghan army was strong enough, the 'Limited Contingent of Soviet Forces in Afghanistan' (LCSFA) would be withdrawn. The assumptions on which this scenario was based were soon to be proved false. The Afghan army was unable to overcome the resistance. It suffered from mass desertions and mutinies and became severely weakened. Consequently, the LCSFA was itself compelled to fight. It found that both its experience of conventional warfare and the heavy equipment it had brought with it were wholly unsuited to the conduct of a guerrilla war in Afghanistan's remote and difficult terrain. The centralization of command and control and lack of scope for initiative at lower command levels was also a major disadvantage, one which the LCSFA was never entirely to overcome. Meanwhile, hundreds of thousands of Afghan refugees began to flee to Pakistan and Iran, where increasing numbers joined resistance organizations in order to take up arms as *mujahidin* ('holy warriors') and fight a *jihad* (holy war) against the infidel invader. In Pakistan, weapons supplies, funded mainly by the USA and Saudi Arabia, were distributed by the Pakistan Inter-Services Intelligence (ISI) agency to the seven organizations that it allowed to operate on its territory. These organizations, in turn, supplied the commanders who were affiliated to them and were involved in the fighting within Afghanistan. The nature of the resistance movements varied. The one most favoured by the Pakistanis was Hizb-i Islami, led by Gulbuddin Hekmatyar, an Islamist whose views were the most compatible with those of the Pakistan regime but who was more interested in enhancing his long-term position than in seriously engaging the Soviets. Of the other six, two—including Burhanuddin Rabbani's Jamiat-i Islami—were also of an Islamist character. The remainder were more 'traditional', some favouring the return of King Zahir (who had been in exile in Italy since 1973). Some Shi'a resistance organizations were also established, with support from Iran.

The resistance groups fighting in the country were of varying sizes and effectiveness, and many of the *mujahidin* fought part time, returning to their farms and families between operations. Their strengths were hardiness, a willingness to die if necessary, knowledge of the terrain, skill with weaponry, and the possession of safe havens outside the country. Their main weakness was lack of unity. However, this was not too important in the type of war that was developing, and it also meant that there was no central focus of command and control that could be targeted.

In due course, the LCSFA repatriated most of its heavy weaponry, brought in more aircraft and helicopters, and tried to adapt its tactics to guerrilla warfare. However, it possessed insufficient personnel to seal the borders with Pakistan and Iran, let alone to establish a permanent presence outside the cities and key locations. Indeed, the LCSFA had to spend much of its time and resources guarding convoys along the main routes, particularly the one between Kabul and the Salang Pass, leading to the Soviet Union, where frequent ambushes took place. One of the more successful commanders, Ahmad Shah Masoud, posed a particular threat to the Salang Pass route from his base in the Panjshir Valley. The LCSFA mounted a succession of major operations designed to counteract him, but had little success. Since they were unable to control the countryside, the Soviets adopted a 'scorched earth' policy, bombing valleys, destroying villages, animals and crops, and trying to drive the rural populations into exile. However, these policies of 'migratory genocide' also had only limited effect in reducing the effectiveness of the *mujahidin*, and earned widespread international condemnation.

In Kabul, meanwhile, Karmal tried to present his Government as moderate and broadly-based. He attempted to mitigate the communist ideology, but failed to persuade the great majority of Afghans that his Government was not a Soviet 'puppet' regime. Indeed, some 6,000–8,000 Soviet experts controlled the military and civilian establishments, while the regime itself continued to be divided by factionalism. Although at the outset Karmal released numbers of prisoners, the gaols filled up again. A security organization, KhAD (Government Intelligence Agency), modelled on and controlled by the KGB, was established under a tough Parcham activist, Dr Najibullah. The agency's methods were ruthless in the extreme and had some success in maintaining control over the cities and generating dissension among the resistance organizations.

As the war progressed, international support for the *mujahidin* grew. The long-standing period of hostility between the USA and the Soviet Union known as the Cold War led the USA to become involved in the conflict. Using secret funds, matched dollar for dollar by Saudi Arabia, the US Central Intelligence Agency (CIA) started to supply the resistance groups with Soviet-style weapons, some of which were manufactured in Egypt and the People's Republic of China, while others were acquired from Israel and even Poland. These weapons were delivered by sea or air to the Pakistani cities of Karachi and Islamabad, where the ISI took them over for onward distribution. Meanwhile, all training was carried out by Pakistani instructors, and at no point did any US representative meet the *mujahidin*. The aim throughout was to achieve 'plausible deniability'; however, as the USA's role in the Afghan conflict increased—in response to pressure from the US Congress—this proved increasingly hard to maintain. By 1987 the programme had cost US $700m.; the total eventually rose to $300,000m. On the civilian front, the USA established a Cross Border Humanitarian Aid Programme, partly to assist the Afghan refugees, and partly to help those still in Afghanistan to remain in their homes. The USA throughout relied on the support of Pakistan. In return for Pakistani President Mohammad Zia ul-Haq's co-operation, the country's human rights record and nuclear aid programme were ignored and a substantial military and civilian aid programme was devised. In 1986, with the policy of 'plausible deniability' losing credibility, the CIA began to supply highly effective *Stinger* anti-aircraft missiles. These had a marked effect in reducing the threat to the *mujahidin* from aircraft and helicopter gunships. By that time, however, the Soviet Union had become weary of the conflict, and Soviet President Mikhail Gorbachev publicly condemned it as a 'bleeding wound'.

**The Soviet Withdrawal**

The Politburo realized at an early stage that the USSR had somehow to extricate itself from Afghanistan. At first, however, the loss of prestige that this would entail, coupled with continuing fears over the destabilization and loss of Afghanistan, prevented it from taking any realistic steps in this direction. Its insistence on direct negotiations between the Afghan and Pakistani Governments, and the cessation of 'external interference' by the USA before the USSR's withdrawal were both unacceptable preconditions. The Politburo did, however, prompt Karmal to establish some conditions, which became part of the later negotiations: non-interference in Afghanistan's internal affairs, supported by Soviet and US guarantees; the return of refugees; and the withdrawal of Soviet troops 'in the context of a political settlement'.

In November 1980 the UN General Assembly coupled its condemnation of the invasion with an expression of hope that the Secretary-General would appoint a representative to pursue the possibility of a settlement. As a result, Javier Pérez de Cuéllar was appointed as the Secretary-General's 'Personal Representative on the situation relating to Afghanistan'. He was succeeded by Diego Córdovez in 1982. In June 'proximity talks' were arranged in Geneva, Switzerland. The Afghan and Pakistani delegations met in separate rooms, with Córdovez shuttling between them. Neither Iran nor the *mujahidin* were involved. In late 1982, when Andropov became the General Secretary of the Communist Party of the Soviet Union and adopted a more forthcoming attitude, progress was made: by April 1983 Córdovez was able to report that '95% of the text of a draft comprehensive settlement' had been agreed. At that point, however, for various reasons the negotiations stalled: both the *mujahidin* and the Pakistanis saw advantage in continuing the conflict, while in the USA the increasingly influential 'hawks'—in particular President Ronald Reagan's Director of the CIA, William Casey—were insisting that the 'Soviet wound' should be kept bleeding. In Moscow, meanwhile, Andropov's hospitalization in August 1983 and his succession by Konstantin Chernenko in 1984 led to a lapse in the sense of urgency. The points that continued to prevent resolution were: the USSR's insistence that outside interference should cease before Soviet troops could be withdrawn; and Pakistan's assertion that a timetable for withdrawal should be agreed before the question of outside interference could be addressed.

It was not until March 1985, when Gorbachev succeeded Chernenko as party leader, that a way out of the impasse began to be found. Gorbachev realized from the outset that a settlement had to be reached if he were to achieve an improvement in relations with the USA, an essential development if he were to be able to address the deteriorating economic and social situation which was threatening to overwhelm the country. Initially, however, his grip on power was not strong enough to enable him to overcome the resistance of those in the KGB, the Communist Party of the Soviet Union, the foreign policy hierarchy and the industrial/military complex, whose interests and prestige were bound up in the war in Afghanistan. Consequently, he allowed the military one year in which to settle the issue, with the result that the fighting in 1985–86 was the bloodiest of the conflict. At the same time, Gorbachev relaxed the restrictions on the reporting of the war, so that the Soviet people became aware, for the first time, of what was happening in Afghanistan. In November 1986 a decisive debate in the Politburo resulted in the conclusion that the USSR had 'lost the battle for the Afghan people' and that withdrawal should take place within two years. Dr Najibullah, whom Moscow had appointed to succeed the failing Karmal, was informed of the decision; in May 1987 the Afghan delegation at the ongoing Geneva talks for the first time offered a deadline for the withdrawal of troops. For some time, the issue was stalled by the USA because of its reluctance to consider guaranteeing a settlement or to cease aid to the resistance once the Soviet Union had started to withdraw. In February 1988, therefore, Gorbachev announced unilaterally that, provided an agreement was quickly reached, the LCSFA would leave Afghanistan by February 1989. In response, the USA reluctantly altered its position on the cessation of external interference by proposing a policy of 'symmetry'. US assistance to the *mujahidin* would cease once the Soviet Union stopped supporting the Afghan Government. Otherwise, there would be 'positive symmetry', with US assistance matching that supplied by the USSR. No agreement was reached on the composition of a post-settlement government, which Gorbachev dismissed as an issue for the Afghans themselves to settle. What were known as the Geneva accords were signed in April 1988 and the Soviet withdrawal began. The *mujahidin*, however, who at no point had any part in the negotiations, refused to accept the agreement, and external intervention from Pakistan continued. Gorbachev pressured a reluctant Najibullah into accepting the settlement, on the apparent understanding that he would be provided with lavish military and economic aid. The Soviet timetable was adhered to and the withdrawal was complete by February 1989. The Soviet Union was thus able to extricate itself with some semblance of respectability; however, 'all else was window dressing'. No political settlement was achieved; the war continued, with external assistance to both sides; and the refugees were unable to return.

The consequences of the war for the Soviet Union were severe. While the direct costs were not insurmountable and only a small proportion of the Soviet army was serving in Afghanistan at any one time, the critical result was that Gorbachev's plans to alleviate the USSR's social problems and to revitalize its economy were delayed. The war itself had exacerbated the Soviet Union's social difficulties, through neglect of the *Afghantsi*, the war veterans whose interests had been almost totally discounted in the attempt to conceal the events in Afghanistan. The Soviet army had also been discredited and the Brehznev Doctrine had been shown to exist only on paper. The Soviet satellites in Eastern Europe and the non-Russian republics within the USSR, as a result, were given hope that their state of subservience to Russia might not be permanent. Afghanistan was not itself the cause of the dissolution of the Soviet Union: this was due to the corruption and systemic failures of the Soviet economy and society. However, the Afghan war could be considered to have been the catalyst that led to the collapse that followed.

The consequences for the Afghans themselves were, proportionately, much more dire. Some 1.25m. people were killed and many more injured in the conflict. The cities and the countryside were covered with land-mines, making Afghanistan reportedly the most mined country in the world. The limited industry the country had possessed was destroyed, and agriculture and its accompanying infrastructure severely damaged. Thousands of villages had been devastated or destroyed. Afghan society had also been thoroughly disrupted: some 3.0m.–3.5m. refugees had fled to Pakistan and some 2.0m.–2.5m. to Iran, while a further 2m. had fled to the cities to escape the fighting and famine in the countryside. Almost 50% of the pre-war population, therefore, had been forced to abandon their homes. If peace had followed and the international community had been even slightly concerned for post-war Afghanistan, recovery might have begun. Instead, civil war was now to ensue.

## CIVIL WAR

Contrary to all expectations, the Najibullah regime survived the Soviet departure. There were several reasons for this. Najibullah was able to assert that the *jihad* was over and that the time had come for national reconciliation. He tried his utmost to present his regime as democratic and Islamist. Throughout the country, the *qawms* reasserted themselves, but more often under regional military commanders than traditional *khans*. Many received financial incentives from the regime, but others associated themselves with the *mujahidin* or remained distant from both parties. Substantial Soviet aid was extended to the regime, including *Scud* missiles and MiG-27 fighter bombers. Owing to the lack of security on the road between Kabul and the Soviet frontier, massive airlifts brought supplies to the capital. The Afghan army had also been considerably reorganized and had practically returned to its pre-war strength, while the unwillingness of the *mujahidin* to take prisoners reinforced its will to fight. There were also considerable apprehensions over the prospect of a *mujahidin* government led by such Islamist fundamentalists as Hekmatyar. The continued inability of the *mujahidin* to abandon their differences and form a combined front also helped to ensure the survival of the Najibullah Government. A *shura* (council) was convened in Peshawar in February 1989 and, under much Saudi and Pakistani pressure and bribery, a 'government-in-exile' was assembled. However, it continued to sit in Peshawar, and few governments were willing to recognize it as the legitimate government until it had established itself in Afghanistan and was seen to enjoy popular support. The ISI therefore organized an assault on Jalalabad in an attempt to gain territory, but this encountered fierce resistance. After four months of fighting, in which some 4,000 *mujahidin* were killed or injured, the deployment of guerrillas to participate in a conventional assault on a defended town was recognized to have been a mistake and the assault was abandoned. Khost was later captured, but the *mujahidin* commanders were unable to take advantage of this success to capture Gardez. An impasse thus developed, while efforts on the part of the UN and the Soviet Union to broker a cease-fire and the formation of a coalition government proved fruitless. Divisions persisted both within the regime and among the *mujahidin*. In 1989 Hekmatyar's fighters ambushed and killed 36 of Masoud's commanders. Masoud retaliated by trying and hanging four of the men suspected of carrying out the assassinations. Meanwhile, in 1990 Najibullah survived an attempted coup.

Once again, it was a unilateral decision by the Soviet leadership that broke the impasse. Following the failure of the coup against Gorbachev in August 1991, the Soviet Government decided that it could no longer afford to support Najibullah. It negotiated an agreement on 'negative symmetry' with the USA and all Soviet aid—both military and economic—ceased. This development brought about the demise of the Najibullah regime. Masoud joined forces with an Uzbek militia under Gen. Abdul Rashid Dostam and advanced on Kabul from the north, while Hekmatyar marched on the city from the south. Najibullah fled to the UN compound and, after a sharp battle with Hekmatyar's forces, Masoud and Dostum occupied the city. In Peshawar the *mujahidin* leaders agreed, under strong pressure, to form a transitional government, the Islamic Jihad Council, and this finally reached Kabul at the end of April 1992. Hekmatyar, however, refused to join. The Government of the newly proclaimed Islamic State of Afghanistan achieved almost universal diplomatic recognition. The interim Council of Ministers was headed by the moderate Prof. Sighatullah Mojaddedi, but he was replaced by Burhanuddin Rabbani within one month.

For a further three years, the *mujahidin* parties argued and fought among themselves for control of Kabul. Alliances were formed and then broken. Hekmatyar, who was not prepared to join the Government except on his own terms, spent most of his time bombarding the capital with rockets from the neighbouring countryside. Civilian casualties mounted and the city itself, which had escaped mostly intact during the Soviet occupation, was gradually reduced to ruins. UN mediators made repeated attempts to construct a political settlement, but to no avail. Elsewhere, military commanders fought for supremacy or maintained control over their own areas. In the post-Cold War era, Afghanistan was no longer of any consequence to the rest of the world and little effort was made to help it recover, either politically or economically. Change came only in 1994 when Pakistan switched its support to a new player in the game, the Taliban.

## THE TALIBAN ERA

Pakistan's ambitions over Afghanistan remained constant both during and after the Soviet occupation. The Pakistani Government went as far as possible to exclude others from gaining influence in Afghanistan, in particular the Soviet Union and India, and to eradicate Afghan irredentist activity along the Pakistani–Afghan border. It was also keen for a like-minded Islamist government to be installed in Kabul, and wished to secure through Afghanistan a trade route with Central Asia. A pipeline across Afghanistan to deliver Central Asian petroleum and gas to Pakistan was also an objective. Until 1994 Pakistan consistently supported Hekmatyar, considering this to be the best means of achieving these ends, and consequently gave him a large proportion of its financial and military assistance, despite the comparative ineffectiveness of his campaigning. By 1994, however, it had become clear that this policy had failed, and the Pakistani Government decided to look elsewhere.

Talib (Taliban being the plural) means 'student' or 'seeker of religious knowledge'. The origins of the Taliban movement were to be found in the network of *madrassas* (religious schools) that had flourished over the years in Pakistan, mainly in Balochistan and the North-West Frontier Province, and the Pashtun areas of Afghanistan. Extensively funded by Saudi Arabia, and similar in outlook to the Wahhabi movement there, the teaching at these *madrassas* was derived from the religious college at Deoband in India, where many Afghan *ulema* were trained. Unlike the Islamists, who wished to create an Islamic state in a modern context, the Deobandis advocated a 'traditional' Islamic society, free from the corrupting influences of modernism. The Taliban attracted numbers of Pashtun students from the refugee camps in Pakistan, to whom they gave a renewed sense of purpose, and had strong support both from conservative and religious groups in Pakistan. The Taliban were also supported by drugs-traffickers and the 'trucking mafia', who equally wished for Central Asia to be made more accessible. From the outset, the Taliban forces used tanks, artillery and even aircraft. Their sophisticated range of equipment left no doubt that they were reliant on extensive Pakistani military and logistic support (although Pakistan denied this). Within a few months, they were able to deploy as many as 20,000 fighters. Much of the funding for the Taliban almost certainly came from Saudi Arabia and, while not directly involved, the USA initially regarded them favourably—not least because the US oil company, UNOCAL, was in the market for a contract for a pipeline between Turkmenistan and Pakistan.

In late 1994, with the use of both force and bribery, the Taliban captured the city of Qandahar, under the leadership of a local Mullah, Mohammad Omar. From there they gathered strength and by early 1995 had advanced as far as Shindand, where they were halted by the Herati military commander, Ismail Khan. At the same time, they advanced on Kabul, causing Hekmatyar's forces to flee. After some fierce fighting, the Taliban were repulsed by Masoud, but continued to launch rocket attacks on the city from their positions nearby. In the south, they were forced to retreat from Shindand, but were able to regroup and launch a counter-offensive. In early September they recaptured Shindand and seized control of the north-western city of Herat. The fight for control over Kabul continued until mid-1996. In September the Taliban managed to advance through eastern Afghanistan and capture Jalalabad. At the end of the month they went on to seize control of the capital, the defenders of which fled northwards with the deposed Government. On assuming power, the Taliban declared Afghanistan a 'complete' Islamic state and appointed an interim Council of Ministers.

Under the leadership of Mullah Mohammad Omar and a *shura* based in Qandahar, the Taliban proceeded to impose on Kabul and other cities their particular interpretation of Islamic law (*Shari'a)* and practice. Women were banned from employment and education, and made to observe strict purdah. Sentences imposed on criminals in accordance with the principles of *Shari'a* were often carried out publicly and in horrific fashion. Beards had to be grown and strict religious practice was enforced. Films, television, taped music and various sports were also banned. Among their more notorious deeds was the destruction of the world's tallest standing statues of Buddha at Bamian and many priceless artefacts at Kabul Museum. Initially, the Taliban were welcomed, at least in the areas where they brought a degree of peace and stability that had been unknown for many years. They were not, however, able to impose their rule over the whole country. In May 1997, when the Taliban briefly took control of Mazar-i-Sharif, it was thought that they had achieved this; however, they were quickly driven out. In October, nevertheless, the Taliban decided to change the country's name to the 'Islamic Emirate of Afghanistan' and altered the state flag. The northern alliance, which was formed in 1996 by Masoud, Gen. Dostam and the Hazara leader, Gen. Karim Khalili, under the presidency of Burhanuddin Rabbani, continued to fight against the Taliban, although the proportion of Afghanistan that it held, mainly in the north-east, was small. The alliance, which was known as the Supreme Council for the Defence of Afghanistan in late 1996, was expanded and strengthened in June 1997 and restyled as the United National Islamic Front for the Salvation of Afghanistan (commonly known as the Northern Alliance or United Front). The support for the Northern Alliance came from Iran, Russia and the Central Asian republics, which were all alarmed at the emergence of a new radical force on or near their borders. The Pakistani objectives were therefore never attained, and Afghanistan's civil war continued. Then came the events of 11 September 2001.

### US Intervention

During the Soviet occupation, numbers of young Muslims arrived in Afghanistan to join the resistance. Known generally as 'Arab Afghans', they were mostly, but by no means exclusively, from Arab countries—principally Algeria, Saudi Arabia and Yemen. They were funded mainly by the Saudis and were trained and equipped by the ISI. Reliable estimates of their numbers are hard to obtain, but the accepted figure is between 15,000 and 35,000. Many were motivated not merely to fight in the *jihad*, but to acquire military skills which they could put to use in their own countries. They were not always welcome by their Afghan hosts, who often disliked their fanaticism and found them disruptive. Initially, they were mostly recruited by a Palestinian lawyer and academic, Abdullah Azzam, who in the early 1980s set up a 'Services Office' in Peshawar for the purpose. In 1984 he was joined by a charismatic young Saudi-born millionaire, Osama bin Laden, who also established himself in Peshawar and started to support and finance the volunteers. Much of his activity was directed towards building bases and training camps close to the border in Afghanistan, his family having made its fortune in the construction business. In 1989 he founded his own organization, al-Qa'ida (Base), but returned to Saudi Arabia after the Soviet withdrawal. The USA did not fund the Arab Afghans directly. However, since its policy, at Pakistan's insistence, was to allow the ISI complete control over the distribution of its military and financial assistance, there can be no doubt that the Arab Afghans benefited, through the ISI and the resistance organizations, from the CIA's supply of weapons, funding, training and general support. While it was probably sensible, in the early stages of the war, for the CIA to rely on the ISI's judgement, the US agency's failure to control the way in which its military and financial assistance was being employed led not only to its indirect support of such groups as Hekmatyar's Hizb-i Islami, which was rabidly anti-Western, but to the development of the Arab Afghan contingent. At the time, focus was placed solely on the aim of bringing about the Soviet Union's defeat, and no thought was given to the possible longer-term consequences.

After his return to Saudi Arabia, bin Laden became estranged from the Saudi Government, which he had condemned for having, in the context of the Gulf War of 1990–91, allowed US forces into the 'Land of the Two Holy Places'. The Saudi Government restricted bin Laden's movements, but in 1991 he managed to leave the country and established himself in Sudan. There he built up a flourishing group of companies and constructed a number of training camps for his al-Qa'ida adherents. It is uncertain to what extent he was personally involved in the various terrorist attacks of the early 1990s, but in 1996 pressure was brought to bear on the Sudanese Government by Saudi Arabia and the USA for him to be deported. He consequently returned to Afghanistan, where al-Qa'ida was still in existence and his training camps remained in use. It is unclear how welcome he was by the Taliban; nevertheless, they allowed him to settle and he continued to plot his *jihad*. There is no doubt that he supplied the Taliban with funds and that numbers of his Arab Afghan supporters had fought with them from the outset of their Afghan campaign. In 1998 he joined forces with Ayman al-Zawahiri, an Egyptian who had earlier been active in the militant Islamic Jihad. Together, they formed an 'International Islamic Front'. Evidence of their involvement in terrorist activities emerged at a trial of four of those responsible for the bombing of the US embassies in Kenya and Tanzania in August 1998. The USA retaliated against the attacks by launching air-strikes against al-Qa'ida camps in Afghanistan. Some occupants were killed, but bin Laden and his senior associates were elsewhere at the time and were therefore unharmed. The result was to expose the attack as a futile exercise and to turn bin Laden from 'a marginal figure in the Muslim world to a global celebrity'.

The USA then attempted to have bin Laden extradited for trial. Not surprisingly, the Taliban were evasive. In 1999 and 2000 the UN Security Council imposed sanctions on the Afghan regime as a result of the latter's continuing refusal to surrender the suspected terrorist leader. These were equally futile and had little effect on a regime which was, in any case, largely isolated from the outside world. Despite its ongoing campaign for international recognition, only Pakistan, Saudi Arabia and the United Arab Emirates formally recognized the Taliban Government; the UN continually rejected Taliban requests to represent Afghanistan and the seat at the UN remained under the control of President Burhanuddin Rabbani, the leader of the 'Islamic State of Afghanistan'. The Taliban also believed that relinquishing bin Laden, who as a fellow Muslim had fought with them against the Russians and had helped them in their own conflict, would have violated the Pashtun code of asylum and would in any case have been demeaning. The CIA also made some attempt to search for bin Laden, but its efforts received little support from the US Government, and nothing effective was done. The USA also failed to support either the Northern Alliance or other Afghans who, with assistance, might have been able to mount an effective challenge to the Taliban regime.

Following the devastating suicide attacks on the USA on 11 September 2001, the US Government decided that it was 'at war' and began to formulate a plan of action. It soon became clear that al-Qa'ida was involved: in a pre-recorded videotape, bin Laden himself boasted of his foreknowledge and complicity. However, there were no military plans available and the CIA lacked the contacts within Afghanistan which might have made a covert operation feasible. Eventually, therefore, it was decided to strengthen and assist the anti-Taliban Northern Alliance. This was not an attractive option, since it risked alienating both the Pakistanis and the majority Pashtun population within Afghanistan, particularly if the Northern Alliance were to capture Kabul. (The Northern Alliance, comprising mainly Tajiks, Uzbeks and Hazaras, had, meanwhile, suffered a set-back when Masoud was killed by suicide bombers days before the terrorist attacks on the USA. Evidence that emerged from deserted al-Qa'ida camps a few months later indicated that the Arab suicide bombers were linked to bin Laden.) Since air power would have to be used, a preliminary bombing campaign would also be necessary, primarily to destroy the Taliban's aircraft and air defence capability.

On 7 October 2001, therefore, the USA, with the support of the United Kingdom, began the aerial bombardment of suspected al-Qa'ida camps and strategic Taliban positions. The US-led coalition, however, quickly ran out of targets and the operation incurred failures: villages and warehouses used by the International Committee of the Red Cross were struck, resulting in civilian casualties and the interruption of much-needed food supplies. Soon there was talk of a 'quagmire' and no early solution to the issue was expected. By early November, however, US teams had arrived in northern Afghanistan with lavish supplies of money; arms and military equipment had also been obtained for the Northern Alliance, mostly from Russia. Special operations forces were then flown in, with equipment to enable them to direct precision air-strikes on Taliban positions. Results were quick to appear: on 9 November the Northern Alliance captured Mazar-i-Sharif; two days later it had seized Taloqan. The following day the Taliban evacuated Kabul and on 13 November the Alliance took over the capital, amid scenes of jubilation. Herat, Kunduz and Jalalabad also fell and, although the Taliban insisted that they would defend their headquarters to the end, Qandahar too was occupied by Pashtun militia by December.

Everything thus pointed to a decisive military success, but it was to be spoilt in the aftermath. Because the US-led coalition had been slow to exercise the 'southern option'—troops were not sent into southern Afghanistan until late November 2001—a great number of Taliban members, possibly as many as 18,000, were able to flee to Pakistan, where they could find refuge among the frontier tribes. Many Qa'ida members also escaped. Two major operations against al-Qa'ida—in the Tora Bora mountains south of Jalalabad in December and in the Shah-i-Kot mountains east of Gardez in March 2002—achieved meagre results.

## THE PRESENT AND THE FUTURE

Following the defeat of the Taliban, there were two urgent requirements. One was that Kabul should be protected from any repetition of the infighting between the *mujahidin* groups that had devastated the capital prior to the Taliban occupation. The other was to fill the dangerous political vacuum that had been created by the Northern Alliance's seizure of the capital. A 5,000-strong International Security Assistance Force (ISAF) was accordingly deployed, under UN authorization, in Kabul and at Bagram airbase to help maintain security in the area. To deal with the political exigencies, a conference of representatives of various Afghan groups assembled in Bonn, Germany, at the end of November 2001. After several days of intense negotiations, and after former President Burhanuddin Rabbani had been quietly sidelined by his own Tajik associates, an agreement was reached on the composition of a 30-member, broadly based, multi-ethnic interim government under a Pashtun chief, Hamid Karzai. The Interim Authority was inaugurated on 22 December and comprised 11 Pashtuns, eight Tajiks, five Hazaras, three Uzbeks and three members of smaller tribal and religious groups. Preparations were also launched for the convening of a Loya Jirga, to meet within six months and carry the process forward, and this duly met in May–June 2002. Showing considerable courage, the aged former King, Zahir Shah, returned to Afghanistan for the convention, but disclaimed a political role for himself. At the Jirga, Karzai was re-elected President and an agreement was reached on the formation of a transitional administration, which was charged with carrying forward the government, drafting a new constitution and preparing the country for elections. The Transitional Authority cabinet retained most of the incumbent members of the Interim Authority. In April 2003 a Constitutional Drafting Commission, which had been meeting since late 2002, presented its draft of a new constitution to a newly established Constitutional Commission. The latter then reviewed it, and submitted it to a Constitutional Loya Jirga, which met in December 2003. After three weeks of intense negotiations, the 502 delegates at the Loya Jirga reached an agreement on a new constitution, which provided for a strong presidential system of government, but with an elected bicameral legislature holding significant powers. The divisions in the Loya Jirga lay principally between the Pashtun delegates, who wanted strong central rule, and the ethnic minorities, who wanted greater regional autonomy. It was significant that the Islamist factions were unable to dominate the proceedings: with Rabbani's eclipse, this appeared to mark the end of their ambitions to recreate Afghanistan in an Islamist mould. However, the compromises reached by the delegates succeeded only minimally in abating the continuing ethnic tensions within the country. In March 2004 the presidential election was postponed, owing partly to delays in voter registration and partly to security concerns. In July, however, the UN-sponsored Afghan Election Commission announced that the presidential election would be held in early October 2004 and the parliamentary elections in April–May 2005.

There were serious doubts in the run-up to the presidential election as to its feasibility, in the face of considerable logistical problems, continuing high levels of violence, and the seemingly preponderant power of regional warlords, whose fiefdoms covered much of the country, whose human rights abuses were notorious and who had some 100,000 armed men at their disposal. These warlords may indeed have been strengthened as a result of the policies adopted by the USA following the removal of the Taliban, several military commanders being employed and paid to assist the US-led forces which remained deployed to deal with the remnants of al-Qa'ida and the Taliban in the south and east of the country. In response to President Karzai's appeals to the international community for a stronger military presence to oversee the election, ISAF, which had come under NATO control in August 2003, increased its numbers to some 8,000, although this was still considerably less than appeared necessary. Many areas of the south and east were considered too dangerous for UN election officials to visit, and only 200 observers were available to monitor a total of some 5,000 polling stations. President Karzai himself was forced to abandon an election rally when his helicopter was fired on as it approached Gardez.

In the event, however, the presidential election, held on 9 October 2004, proceeded unexpectedly well. Of an estimated 11m. electorate, 8.7m., of whom 41% were women, succeeded in registering. At the election itself, there was a 70% turnout, and President Karzai received 55.4% of the vote, thus avoiding the need for a run-off contest. Of his rivals, the former Northern Alliance leader and Minister of Education, Younis Qanooni, received 16%, the Hazara leader Haji Mohammed Mohaqqeq 12%, and the Uzbek warlord Abdul Rashid Dostam 10%. None of the other 14 candidates polled more than 2%. During the election process there were threats of a boycott in protest at alleged irregularities, but the issue was not pressed and the election was conceded by all the candidates, an international panel of observers declaring that there was insufficient evidence of irregularities to affect materially the overall result. With enhanced prestige and clear legitimacy for a five-year term, Karzai was sworn in on 7 December, and formed an ethnically balanced Cabinet, a notable feature of which was a preponderance of technocrats and the almost total absence of warlords. The former Minister of Defence, Marshal Muhammad Fahim, was omitted from the new administration, and no post was allotted to Dostam, although both retained their militias. However, the former governor of Herat, Ismail Khan, who had earlier been dismissed by Karzai, was appointed Minister of Water and Energy, while a new Ministry of Counter Narcotics was founded under Habibullah Qaderi.

On 18 September 2005 elections were held for the 249-member Wolasi Jirga (House of Representatives) and for the provincial councils, which, in turn, elect members to the 102-member Meshrano Jirga (House of Elders). On this occasion, 12.5m. voters were registered, but the turnout, at 6.4m., was much less than in the presidential election. This was partly because so many candidates were standing—some 2,700 for the Wolasi Jirga, together with a further 3,200 for the provincial councils—and it was difficult to determine what they stood for. Of particular note, however, was the fact that women were elected to just under 30% of the seats in the Wolasi Jirga. The main problem was that, although the Electoral Law prohibited any commander or member of an illegal armed group from standing for parliament, it was estimated, none the less, that some 80 warlords, 'drug barons' and members of illegal militias were elected. The Electoral Complaints Commission had neither the staff nor the time to investigate the thousands of complaints about individual candidates that they received, which meant that only a few disqualifications were carried out. Another possible contributing factor was the commission's concern that too many disqualifications might have affected the security of the elections, and so there was a reluctance to be overly stringent.

In December 2005 the Meli Shura (National Assembly) held its first session, signalling the conclusion of the so-called Bonn Process. Following President Karzai's extensive cabinet reorganization in March 2006, 20 of the 25 ministerial nominees were approved by the Meli Shura in April; the remaining five positions were filled in August. Of especial note in the cabinet reshuffle was the replacement of Dr Abdullah Abdullah as Minister of Foreign Affairs by Dr Rangin Dadfar Spanta, and the allocation of the interior affairs portfolio to Zarar Ahmad Moqbel on a permanent basis (he had previously held the position in an acting capacity). In May 2007 the Wolasi Jirga conducted votes of no confidence against Spanta and the Minister of Refugees, Mohammad Akbar, over their alleged mishandling of Iran's deportation of Afghan refugees. Akbar was immediately dismissed, and, although Spanta survived the initial vote, the Wolasi Jirga gained a sufficient majority in a second round of voting to remove him from his position. The Supreme Court, however, subsequently ruled that Spanta's dismissal was unconstitutional and reversed the Wolasi Jirga's decision, a move that was supported by Karzai and his Cabinet. In July Mohammad Zahir Shah, the 92-year-old former King of Afghanistan, died in Kabul following a long illness. President Karzai declared three days of national mourning and attended the state funeral in the capital.

Drugs production and trafficking remains one of Afghanistan's principal internal problems and a serious cause for international concern. Before September 2001 the Taliban had imposed an effective ban on opium production, probably to enable them to sell their substantial stocks at advantageous prices. Following their defeat in late 2001, poppy cultivation quickly revived. Despite President Karzai's introduction in January 2002 of a ban on poppy cultivation and the processing, trafficking and abuse of opiates, in 2003 production rose to 3,600 metric tons and cultivation was taking place in 28 of Afghanistan's 32 provinces. Although, on account of drought and disease, yields fell in 2004, the resulting crop rose to 4,475 tons, valued at US $2,800m., equivalent to around 60% of Afghanistan's gross domestic product (GDP) in 2003. Production in 2005 was 4% lower than in 2004, but was still well over 4,000 tons, and in 2006 it rose to more than 6,000 tons. In 2007, with favourable weather conditions, opium production increased by another third to an extraordinary 8,200 tons, with a value of $4,000m., equivalent to around one-half of the country's licit GDP. The area under poppy cultivation in 2008 was reported to be even larger than that of the previous year. While production in 2007 decreased in central and northern Afghanistan, with six of the 13 provinces opium-free, in southern Afghanistan output soared, with 50% of the total originating from a single province, Helmand, and a further 30% from the five provinces bordering Pakistan. Two conclusions can be drawn from these facts: first, that opium production is not linked to poverty, since the main opium-producing provinces in the south are the richest and most fertile; second, that production is closely linked to insurgency, the proceeds of opium production being a major source of funding for the Taliban. Some 93% of the world's opium is currently produced in Afghanistan, and the production of heroin in laboratories within the country itself is increasing. As always, a vast share of the proceeds has gone to traffickers and dealers, but the modest cash income that otherwise near-destitute farmers receive for growing opium has remained a major incentive to continuing cultivation. For the peasant farmer, poppies are a more hardy and profitable crop than any other; in a climate afflicted by periodic drought, a crop that does not require much water is particularly attractive. Polls suggest that most Afghans would prefer not to grow the crop, but see no viable alternative.

Efforts to curb production have continued to have little success. Although a British-led eradication programme costing some £70m. a year over three years was put in place in 2006, concentrating mainly on compensating farmers for growing less profitable crops, it has achieved only negligible results. With some 1.7m. farmers dependent on opium production, an effective solution can only be achieved through a long-term campaign on several fronts, including building popular support for the counter-narcotics effort through public awareness campaigns; creating substantial alternative income sources in rural areas; increasing the capacity of the law enforcement and judicial systems; dealing with the associated corruption; destroying drug laboratories; dismantling the trafficking networks; and eradicating crops. All this will require continued foreign assistance both with the specific problem and with closely associated issues, including more general economic development, the elimination of private militias and 'warlordism', and the development of the Afghan National Army (ANA) and police force which together are able to establish and assert the central Government's authority over the country as a whole. A joint report issued in February 2008 by the British Government and the World Bank estimated that it would take up to 20 years and require investment of at least £1,000m. to eliminate the Afghan opium economy.

A further problem still affecting Afghanistan is that of landmine contamination. While about 60% of contaminated areas has been cleared, including many of the most crucial, some 4,000 areas remain in all but one of the country's provinces that are suspected of being contaminated. The aim is to have cleared all but the least critical areas by 2013. Meanwhile, by mid-2008 casualties from landmines and abandoned ordnance had decreased from some 500–600 per month to around 50–60.

The problem of security also persists and, indeed, deteriorated during 2006 and 2007, particularly in the south and east of the country, with the Taliban insurgency, largely emanating from Pakistan, becoming increasingly dangerous. In mid-2006 some 600 Taliban were killed by Afghan and coalition forces, but by August it was estimated that as many as 6,000 could be operating, in groups as large as 400. Apparent new tactics on the part of the insurgents included the intimidation of civilians, the killing of officials and tribal leaders, and the burning down of schools. Some 200 schools were forced to close in southern Afghanistan in the first half of 2006. Senior government officers were also targeted and several killed. However, the insurgency movement has itself suffered losses, mainly through targeted assassinations, with reports of the deaths of a number of senior Taliban leaders (including Mullah Dadullah, who was believed to have been its highest ranking military commander) in coalition raids in 2007. In 2007 and into 2008, the Taliban's tactics shifted again, with less emphasis on ambushes and firefights, in the course of which they tended to suffer heavy casualties, and more on roadside bombings and suicide attacks, no doubt inspired by similar activity in Iraq. In 2007 232 coalition soldiers died in Afghanistan, and this worrying trend showed no sign of improving in the first half of 2008. Some 8,000 Afghans were also killed in 2007, more than 1,500 of them civilians. A rise in the rate of civilian casualties prompted demands from President Karzai and other quarters for further investigation and greater care, with the UN estimating that many of the civilian fatalities were as a result of coalition action. In the south and east of the country, sizeable areas of land remain under Taliban control and it has been growing increasingly difficult to undertake development work, or even to carry on normal commercial activities. Commerce in Qandahar has declined sharply, and villagers have begun to urge aid workers to stay away, for fear of Taliban reprisals. The problem is one that has been observed in emergency situations elsewhere. The villagers are caught between two opposing sides: the insurgents who pressurize and intimidate them, and the Government, which inflicts reprisals should they do anything to help the insurgents, or even fail to inform on them.

The main problem in the security field is that the NATO-led ISAF, which comprised some 53,000 troops in mid-2008, is, in the words of its outgoing Commander, Gen. Dan McNeill, 'seriously under-resourced', while the ANA, although now 50,000 strong and improving in capacity, is still a long way from being able to function as an independent, effective fighting force. The available military strength is neither sufficient to take territory from the Taliban nor to hold it permanently, with the result that large areas in the Pashtun belt are currently under insurgent control. The United Kingdom, Canada and the Netherlands, which, next to the USA, are principally involved in the critical southern and eastern provinces, are becoming increasingly dissatisfied with the perceived lack of commitment of other major NATO members such as France, Germany, Italy and Spain. Canada has gone so far as to threaten to withdraw its contingent unless its partners make more of an effort. In the face of the apparent inevitability of a long haul in Afghanistan, the staying power of the coalition appears to be in doubt.

The ability of the Taliban to recruit and enjoy safe havens in Pakistan is also a continuing hindrance to progress in dealing with the Afghan conflict. In the first half of 2008, however, there were signs that, under the new Pakistan leadership, co-operation between Afghanistan and Pakistan, whose past relationships have often been acrimonious, might be improving.

Owing partly to the lack of security, progress regarding reconstruction and development, which are crucial factors to the success of the political process, has also been less than satisfactory. There has been a succession of international donors' conferences, the first being held in Tokyo in January 2002, at which US $4,500m. was pledged over a five-year period, against an estimated requirement of $15,000m. over the next decade. Cash disbursements were slow to arrive and much funding had to be applied to relief activity, following the return of large numbers of refugees from Pakistan and Iran. A further conference was held in Berlin, Germany, in March 2004, at which pledges of $4,400m. were made for that year and $8,200m. for the following three years. Due mainly to the continuing violence, however, disbursements remained tardy. From 31 January–1 February 2006 a conference was held in London to mark the end of the Bonn Process and to look to the future for Afghanistan. In the course of the conference three documents were approved: namely the 'Afghanistan Compact', the 'Afghanistan National Development Strategy' (ANDS), and the 'National Drugs Control Strategy'. The Afghanistan Compact set out a series of targets and aspirations which Afghanistan and its international partners hoped to achieve over the following four to five years. Renewed aid pledges were tabled at the conference, totalling around $10,500m. over five years, although some $2,500m. of this represented pledges made earlier. The Afghan Government, however, stated that it needed about double this amount of aid—i.e. $4,000m. a year.

In June 2008, at the International Conference in Support of Afghanistan, which was held in Paris, the Afghan Government submitted a National Development Strategy requiring US $43,000m. over the following five years. In response, donors pledged a total of $20,000m. in new funds, perhaps exceeding the Afghan Government's expectations. To date, development has been hindered partly by the insurgency, partly by the failure of the many donor countries and agencies to co-ordinate their efforts, and partly by the weakness and alleged corruption of the Afghan Government. The UN does not have executive powers in Afghanistan, and efforts to bring some coherence and direction to development activities, notably the proposed appointment of Lord (Paddy) Ashdown in a co-ordinating role, have been thwarted by the Afghan Government. To put the issue in context, Afghanistan is currently receiving some $67 in aid per caput per year, while the comparable figure for post-conflict Bosnia and Herzegovina was $249. One problem is Iraq, which, as one commentator has put it, is 'sucking the oxygen' out of aid efforts elsewhere. The problem of finance applies equally to ANDS and the National Drugs Control Strategy. The Afghan Government's own domestic revenue is sufficient to cover about only 8% of its total expenditure, and the fiscal deficit is almost entirely financed by external aid. There is virtually no income tax, and, while the customs system may work to some extent at the periphery, it fails to generate any substantial funds at the centre. The key questions are whether the Government will succeed in generating tax revenue at a faster rate than spending, whether there will be sufficient external aid, and whether external aid providers will stay the course.

The exercise of so-called 'transitional justice' also continues to pose a problem in Afghanistan. There is no real doubt what the vast majority of Afghans want. The Afghanistan Independent Human Rights Commission (AIHRC), which conducted a survey published in early 2005, reported a near unanimous demand for justice and accountability. Against that background, the parliamentary elections in September 2005 constituted a clear set-back, and there remains considerable discontent at the continuing power of the warlords. A Peace, Reconciliation and Justice Action Plan produced by the AIHRC was approved both by the Government and by an official conference convened in December 2005. The issue of war crimes resurfaced in early 2007 with a protracted debate on proposed amnesty legislation to protect alleged war criminals of the previous 30 years from prosecution. In March, following President Karzai's intervention, a revised version of the amnesty bill that allowed for individual prosecution while retaining a state amnesty was approved by the Wolasi Jirga and subsequently signed into law. In April 2007 the Afghanistan Development Forum highlighted the growing need to tackle corruption, and received a progress report on the activities of the Government's Anti-Corruption Commission. In July of that year, the Rome Conference on Justice and the Rule of Law in Afghanistan concluded that 'without justice and the rule of law no sustainable security, stabilization, economic development and human rights can be achieved'. The co-participants in the conference, namely the UN and the Governments of Afghanistan and Italy, agreed to establish a National Justice Programme which would be committed to implementing judicial reform.

Despite these various initiatives, practical measures have been lacking, and there is little prospect of nation-wide stability as long as warlords and drug barons possess the means to corrupt or coerce the legitimate authorities, and the Afghan Government fails to take action against alleged war criminals. The continuing weakness of the country's judicial and law-enforcement agencies, resulting in a persistent 'culture of impunity', remains a major hindrance to the emergence of good government and effective development.

After nearly three decades of invasion, conflict and civil war, Afghanistan remains one of the five least developed countries in the world. Average life expectancy is just 46 years, while possibly one in three Afghan children die before their fifth birthday and one in two is malnourished. The population is increasing in what is naturally a poorly endowed country, and the environment has become highly degraded. The lack of a trustworthy and effective administration and countrywide security remain the critical issues, although the picture is not wholly bleak. About 2m. girls now attend school, and 82% of the population enjoy basic health care. According to estimates published by the International Monetary Fund (IMF), the Afghan economy grew, in real terms, by 15.7% in 2003/04, by 8.0% in 2004/05, by 14.0% in 2005/06, by 7.5% in 2006/07 and by 11.6% in 2007/08. A certain amount of financial and economic discipline has been imposed and the IMF seems, on the whole, to be satisfied. Afghans who were polled at the end of 2007 said that they were mostly content with their lives; few wanted to see the return of the Taliban and a majority wished foreign forces to remain. The signs are, however, that confidence is gradually eroding, and that Afghans are dissatisfied both with their own Government and with the lack of progress in dealing with the insurgency. With elections due in 2009, the omens are not good. A vicious circle exists in today's Afghanistan: without security, economic recovery and development will not be possible, while, without visible recovery and progress, the underlying causes of the insecurity will not be addressed. Unless these issues are finally tackled, there remains the real prospect that Afghanistan will revert to 'warlordism' and anarchy. The key lies in continued international involvement and assistance. The worst thing that could happen—and this is what concerns the Afghans the most—is that the international community may once again lose interest.

# Economy

PETER MARSDEN

## INTRODUCTION

The Afghan economy is predominantly a product of the country's geographical characteristics. With a largely mountainous and desert terrain, Afghanistan offers only limited opportunities for agricultural production, confined to scattered valleys and isolated oases. The population has, therefore, had to survive on subsistence agriculture, based on the production of irrigated and rain-fed wheat, together with barley, vegetables and fruits. Livestock has provided an important source of supplementary sustenance and a significant source of income during periods of hardship.

The industrial base has always been minimal and has been largely associated with agricultural processing, carpet manufacturing and the production of dried fruits. Cement factories were established in a number of locations before the outbreak of hostilities. The extraction of natural gas became an important element in the economy in the time when the USSR wielded significant influence in Afghanistan, but has declined to almost nothing since the late 1980s.

Since the early 1970s, and particularly since the 1978 coup which brought to power a Soviet-supported Government, families have sought to diversify their incomes by dispatching some family members to undertake intermittent daily labouring work in Pakistan, Iran and, to a lesser extent, the Arabian Gulf. This trend was greatly heightened by the exodus of 3m. refugees to Pakistan in the early 1980s and by a similar number seeking exile in Iran.

The land-locked nature of the country has meant that it is largely dependent on its neighbours for trade and inward investment. As a result, distinct micro-economies have emerged, with outputs that are inextricably linked with those across the Afghan border. A characteristic of some micro-economies is an involvement in activities broadly defined as illegal—smuggling, opium production and the opium and heroin trades.

The official population of Afghanistan was, according to the first national census conducted in June 1979, a total of 15,551,358, of whom 2.5m. were nomads. In 2004 the UN Development Programme (UNDP) estimated the population to be 23.85m., of whom 28.8% were living in urban areas and 71.2% in rural regions. Other estimates range between 20m. and 25m.

### Data

Before studying the nature of the economy in recent decades, it is important to mention the difficulties inherent in seeking to quantify any economic activity that has taken place in Afghanistan and, therefore, to assess the economy. Even before the 1978 coup and Soviet invasion of December 1979, the collection of data for the purpose of economic measurement was never sufficient to provide more than intelligent approximate estimates of the likely reality and to indicate broad trends. During the Soviet occupation, statistics tended to reflect their propaganda value rather than an accurate picture. Their scope was also limited because the Government had no control beyond the boundaries of the urban centres. Following the collapse of the Soviet-supported Government in April 1992, the collection of official national data ceased altogether. Since then, the UN has sought to extrapolate data from micro-studies carried out by non-governmental organizations (NGOs) and UN consultants, in which systems of measurement have varied, often resulting in contradictory sets of statistics. The Afghan Interim Authority, which was established in December 2001 under the Bonn Agreement, did not embark on a comprehensive data collection process, nor did the Afghan Transitional Administration, which succeeded it in June 2002. Its successor, the Islamic Republic of Afghanistan, is far from having the capacity to undertake the task. Thus, while every effort has been made here to obtain data from various potential sources such as the UN, the Afghan Government, the Asian Development Bank (ADB) and the World Bank, there is no set of data that comprehensively describes the nature of the present economy.

The rapid pace of change and the very different fortunes of the various micro-economies within Afghanistan also need to be taken into account in any assessment of the economy. For this reason, it might be more useful to take an historical view of the economy as the best means of examining it rather than seek to quantify a situation that defies quantification.

## THE PRE-WAR ECONOMY

Prior to the 1950s, there was little investment to strengthen the infrastructure. Entrepreneurial activity during the early years of the 20th century included trading in the skins and wool of karakul (a breed of sheep), together with the establishment of textile and sugar companies. A growing *rapprochement* with the USSR after 1953 led to the first of a series of Five-Year Plans in 1957. The first Plan focused on communications, including the construction of a major highway system and the creation of internal and international air links. By the mid-1960s Kabul was linked with Herat, Mazar and Qandahar by a high-quality road, built with support from both the USSR and the USA. By the end of the third Five-Year Plan, in 1972, the country had 2,780 km of paved roads and two international and 29 local airports. Dams and bridges had been constructed. The Plan also sought to expand the industrial base. By 1972 the production of cotton cloth had quadrupled, cement making and shoe manufacturing had begun and the output of the soap, sugar and coal industries had grown by up to 300%. Fertilizer and artificial silk were other important products. Electricity production had increased nine-fold. Natural gas production reached 2,635m. cu m annually following the construction of a pipeline by the USSR in 1967 to transport gas from northern Afghanistan to its own territories. Industrial employment rose from 18,000 in 1962 to nearly 27,000 in 1971. The education service was also expanded: the number of schools increased from 804 to almost 4,000, teachers from 4,000 to 20,000, and pupils from 125,000 to 700,000. It is useful to compare the latter figure with the current school population of more than 6m. to demonstrate that, in spite of 30 years of conflict, the situation is better in the late-2000s, in some respects, than it was pre-war, although the quality of education is not yet up to pre-war standards. The State became increasingly involved in the economy from the 1950s onwards. The banks were nationalized, along with heavy industry and mining.

The economy grew steadily in 1960–80, roughly at the same level as the least developed countries overall. During 1970–78 international reserves increased at a rate of 27% per annum. Gross domestic investment rose from 5.5% of gross domestic product (GDP) in 1970 to 14% in 1978. Domestic savings grew from 3.3% to 10.8% of GDP over the same period. According to the UN Conference on Trade and Development (UNCTAD), manufacturing output increased by 4.6% per year during the 1970s and provided 9% of GDP in 1980. (The Economist Intelligence Unit had placed it at 4% of GDP in 1974–75.) Exports expanded significantly during the 1970s and the trade deficit was relatively low. Cereal production yields increased to the level where, by 1974, it was no longer necessary to import cereals. During the 1970s, however, revenues were lower than anticipated, causing the budget deficit to rise steadily. About one-half of the total revenue was derived from indirect taxes and only 10% from direct taxes. Natural gas provided 21% of total revenue in 1979 and 34% in 1980.

## THE ECONOMY DURING 1978–92

The rural economy in 1978–92 was seriously weakened by the ongoing conflict between the *mujahidin* ('holy warriors') and the Soviet and Afghan armed forces. As a result of the exodus of 6m. refugees to Pakistan and Iran, primarily from the rural areas, the irrigation systems and flood protection structures, upon which agricultural production depended, were seriously neglected. In 1978–90 cereal production declined by 50% while the area under cultivation decreased by 30%. Many livestock were killed as a direct result of the conflict or by stepping on land-mines. UNDP reported in 1983 that 'most manufacturing enterprises ... have now ceased to operate or are producing well below capacity because of war damage and shortages of raw materials and spare parts'. By 1990 the trade deficit was US $649m., compared with $69m. in 1980. According to UNCTAD, GDP declined by 20% between 1980 and 1990.

In the mean time, the condition of the road network, both the major highway system and the subsidiary roads, deteriorated significantly; military vehicles compounded the situation. Land-mines were routinely laid on either side of the major roads. Other elements of the infrastructure also suffered from neglect or damage—in particular, water supply, telecommunications and, most of all, the housing stock. The urban economy depended heavily on Soviet subsidies, which were sufficient to maintain livelihoods and basic services for government employees at an adequate level while others struggled to survive. There was also active trade with the rural areas to ensure that food was available in the local markets. However, prices were steep and inflation over this period was also relatively high. The population of urban areas increased as people from the surrounding rural areas took refuge from the ongoing fighting with the *mujahidin*. The collapse of the USSR in 1991 brought an end to subsidies and led to the fall of the Soviet-supported Government in April 1992.

## THE ECONOMY SINCE 1992

The installation of a *mujahidin* administration in April 1992 encouraged the return of 1.8m. refugees from Pakistan during that year; however, the pace of return decelerated dramatically over the next few years once it became clear that the new Government was not in a position to provide security. A gradual improvement in the agricultural economy was, nevertheless, witnessed, as returning refugees repaired irrigation systems, flood protection structures, local roads and their property. Humanitarian agencies, such as NGOs, the Food and Agriculture Organization (FAO) and the World Food Programme (WFP), gave an important boost to the efforts of farmers by providing engineering expertise, construction materials, improved wheat seed, veterinary support and food assistance. Thus, according to UNCTAD, agricultural production improved in certain areas between 1992 and 1996.

However, the situation in the urban areas in the early 1990s was more complex. Kabul suffered from three years of intense conflict between the various *mujahidin* groups competing for power, and much of the west and south of the city was extensively damaged. This led to an inevitable outflow of civilians, including a significant proportion of the professionals and business community on whom the effective functioning of the government and the economy depended. Qandahar descended deeper into anarchy. Herat, in the north-west, and Mazar-i-Sharif, in the north, fared better under strong local leadership and were able to achieve gradual economic growth, helped by links with Iran, in the case of Herat, and Uzbekistan and Russia, in the case of Mazar-i-Sharif.

By early 1995 the conflict in Kabul was easing and normal economic activity was able to resume. By this stage a new political movement had emerged, known as the Taliban. With a radical Islamist philosophy and a strong focus on law and order, the Taliban had captured Qandahar in October 1994 and seized large areas of the south, thereby creating a secure environment more conducive to economic activity. Their occupation of Herat, in September 1995, resulted in an exodus of thousands of professionals to Iran, but the damage to economic growth was only temporary. Herat became an important trading centre, along with Qandahar, owing to a significant increase in trade between Pakistan and Central Asia. However, Kabul suffered economic damage when it was captured in September 1996. This was due to conflict to the north of the capital, where the Taliban encountered resistance from one of the *mujahidin* groups in the Shomali Valley. This area remained a battleground until 2001, during which time the agricultural economy lost one of the largest concentrations of fertile land in the country. The valley was seriously damaged by the Taliban 'scorched earth' policy (the removing or destroying of everything that might be useful to an invading enemy, especially by fire). As a direct consequence of the ongoing conflict, the important trading route that linked Kabul with Mazar-i-Sharif and Uzbekistan was closed. Both Kabul and Mazar-i-Sharif became, effectively, 'dead' economies, particularly after Uzbekistan closed its border with Afghanistan following the Taliban seizure of Mazar-i-Sharif in August 1998. The dire economic situation was compounded by the failure of the Taliban to maintain regular salary payments to government staff. As a consequence, both cities came to depend very heavily on food assistance from WFP. Thus, while Herat and Qandahar thrived owing to the expansion of one trade route, the economies of Kabul and Mazar-i-Sharif collapsed from the blocking of another.

A severe drought during 1999–2002 damaged the economy further. The rain-fed areas in the north-west of the country and the grazing areas of the Registan desert to the west of Qandahar were particularly seriously affected. As a result, the nomadic Kuchi population in the Registan desert lost most of its livestock and had to seek support in temporary camps in Qandahar and on the Pakistani border. The absence of crucial snowmelt also led to a significant decline in water tables throughout the country. Wheat production decreased to 1.9m. metric tons, a level comparable to that reached during the drought of 1971. However, unlike the earlier drought, it was possible for the aid community to provide food assistance to the people worst affected by the disaster. The mass starvation of the 1971 drought was, therefore, avoided but the more recent drought, which lasted until 2004 in the south of the country, rendered large numbers of people vulnerable, owing to a depletion of their assets (including livestock) and the need to borrow money to survive. The lowering of the water table also took many shallow wells out of use and forced the population of large numbers of villages to travel some distance to collect water from rivers and other sources used by animals, thus increasing the risk of contamination. An added complexity was an increasing resort to opium cultivation by impoverished communities. Although the drought had eased and water tables had begun to rise by mid-2003, full recovery was expected to take longer to occur, not least because it had become necessary again to repair neglected irrigation and flood protection structures. It was hoped that the significant snowfall of early 2005, combined with heavy rains, would bring the water tables to a sufficiently high level substantially to address the crisis. In July 2006, however, the Afghan Government and the UN were forced to launch an appeal to raise US $76.4m. to support the 2.5m. people affected by the renewed drought conditions caused by the failure of the spring rains and an anticipated shortfall in the rain-fed wheat harvest. It was reported in August that, while overall wheat production had declined by 13% compared with 2005, production in rain-fed areas had decreased to 50% of its 2005 level. In some localities farmers experienced a total, or near total, loss of their crop. The north-western and southern provinces were affected particularly badly. Wheat production in 2007 reached the relatively high level of 5.6m. tons, compared with 4.4m. tons in 2006, but the country remained dependent on wheat imports to supplement domestic production. In the first half of 2008 the rise in global wheat prices caused significant hardship.

The UN *Statistical Yearbook* indicated that GDP declined at an average rate of 7.4% per year between 1990 and 1995, but increased by 26% in 1995, when the security situation showed a dramatic improvement. According to the ADB, the economy subsequently contracted owing to the drought, a reduction in unofficial trade, the deterioration of infrastructure, macroeconomic imbalance and the absence of effective government. The ADB also estimated that gross national income (GNI) in 1997/98 reached US $6,738m., providing a per caput GNI of $280. It was estimated that at May 2002 GNI had decreased by at least 30%–40%, producing a per caput GNI of between $155 and $180, on a par with Eritrea and Somalia.

The launch of the US-led military campaign in Afghanistan in October 2001 occurred when the drought was at its most severe and had the effect of disrupting aid supplies to drought-stricken villages until early January 2002. Fortunately, the impact of this was not as serious as it might have been. The intervention also led to the fall of the Taliban regime and the creation of an Interim Authority based on the Bonn Agreement of December 2001. The significant involvement of the USA and the United Kingdom, in particular, in the establishment of this Authority ensured an immediate investment in advisers to assist the new Government in its formative stages. The World Bank and the ADB were also important participants in the reconstruction process. The UN agencies expanded massively to assume new responsibilities arising from the process and the NGO community also grew significantly following public appeals for assistance with regard to the drought. The diplomatic community similarly arrived in force. As a consequence, the international presence in Kabul increased from fewer than 50 personnel to several thousand. This had the effect of creating an artificial economy based on the demand for residential and office accommodation, builders to refurbish premises, and transport. Rents for extremely poor quality accommodation reached the levels found in Western capitals, which subsequently led to escalating inflation rates in the housing market. This was compounded by the return of several hundred thousand refugees to Kabul under heavy pressure from the Pakistani and Iranian Governments. Refugees had also been encouraged by media coverage suggesting that there would be major international investment in Afghanistan. Inflationary pressures as a result of the rapid return of refugees had an adverse effect on rents for basic accommodation which, in turn, led to increasing overcrowding: a UN report published in April 2003 mentioned densities reaching 10–15 people per room in many houses in the city. Those who could not secure accommodation were forced to eke out an existence in the ruins of southern and western Kabul. Prices were fuelled further by the growing trade in opium and heroin and the decision of many of those involved in it to invest in property.

The impact of the international presence, combined with the arrival of thousands of taxis from Pakistan, with their Afghan refugee owners, has given Kabul an illusion of prosperity. However, this economic 'bubble' is not sustainable, and the general population has failed to experience the benefits on any scale. The lack of anticipated reconstruction activity has caused disillusionment, which has begun to generate growing public anger against the Afghan Government and the aid community.

In part, the low level of reconstruction activity can be attributed to the severity of the humanitarian crisis and the fact that a high proportion of the initial assistance provided by the donor community, following a conference held in Tokyo, Japan, in January 2002, was used on relief programmes to address the effects of the drought. The international community's delay in committing funds for major infrastructure projects is also to blame. The US-led military intervention in Iraq from March 2003 has further affected reconstruction. This has led to a targeted campaign of terrorism aimed at undermining what is seen by radical elements as a US-led state-building process. The victims of the attacks have included members of the aid community and contractors working on reconstruction projects, such as the repair of the main highway system. As a result, mounting concern over falling levels of security has impeded operations of aid and reconstruction programmes, particularly in the south and south-east.

A further major obstacle to the reconstruction process is the influence of regional militia commanders, who took advantage of the power vacuum created by the US-led military campaign in Afghanistan in late 2001. Thus, although an internationally recognized Government is in existence, further legitimized by the legislative elections that took place in September 2005, it exercises limited power, even in Kabul. Consequently, customs revenues, which could be an important source of income for the central Government, are being diverted to a significant degree because of corrupt practices.

The economy is also under threat owing to the ongoing repatriation of refugees from neighbouring countries eager to send them back at the earliest opportunity. Despite the return of a reported 3,918,000 refugees from Pakistan and Iran during 2002–06, Pakistan still has 2.1m. Afghans living within its borders and Iran a further 915,000. This suggests that both countries continue to receive large numbers of economic migrants from Afghanistan. However, there are growing pressures on Afghans in both countries to return to their homeland and there are indications that it will become increasingly difficult for Afghans to enter employment in either Pakistan or Iran in the future. This could have potentially serious consequences for household incomes in Afghanistan, as wage remittances constitute a sizeable proportion of overall earnings and many families depend upon sending one or more family members to seek work in Pakistan or Iran. In addition, European countries are actively seeking to repatriate several hundred thousand more Afghan refugees. The Afghan Government and UNHCR continue to seek sustainable solutions for the 120,000 people displaced within the country. A high proportion of these are nomads, who have been dispossessed by the drought and who have been unable to re-establish their livestock herds. There also remains a significant number who fled ethnic persecution in the north of the country in the aftermath of the fall of the Taliban regime. Some limited progress has since been made in their relocation, but the underlying causes of their displacement represent a major obstacle. People have also been displaced in their tens of thousands by the military offensives launched by the international forces in southern Afghanistan. In addition to coping with the return of refugees and displaced people, the Government also needs to create the economic conditions to achieve sustainable livelihoods for the tens of thousands who are currently fighting for militia groups, ensuring their disarmament, demobilization and reintegration into society. The fact that the economy has not grown sufficiently to provide an alternative source of income is a contributory factor to the extremely slow pace of disarmament, along with the reluctance of the major power holders to see a reduction in the arms at their disposal while the situation in the country remains so volatile and their hold on power so tenuous.

### The National Development Framework

In recognition of the importance of international donor support, the Interim Authority, which held power for the first six months following the Bonn Agreement, gave early priority to the production of a blueprint defining how it might achieve progress in the development of the country. This National Development Framework (NDF) was initiated by Ashraf Ghani, a former Afghan exile with World Bank experience, and incumbent Minister of Finance. The NDF stressed the importance of creating an environment that would facilitate the private sector's role as the primary engine of Afghanistan's recovery: 'the market and the private sector is a more effective instrument of delivering sustained growth than the State'. The role of the State in this context is to create a regulatory framework to support the activities of the private sector. The NDF also advocated streamlined government as an alternative to the centralized and over-bureaucratic structure inherited from the Soviet period. Thus, the Transitional Administration, and later the elected government, would determine overall policy, but depend on the national and international private sector, and on communities and NGOs, to implement programmes.

While the NDF is an impressive document, its application is hindered by the absence of broad-based commitment within the Government to its objectives. In particular, its aim to reduce the number of civil servants in order to increase the effectiveness of the civil service runs counter to the tradition of patronage, which continues to prevail within the various ministries and which, in turn, gives power to the respective ministers. Furthermore, the dismissal of civil servants increases the number of people who need to be found a sustainable income within the economy; the retrenchment process is already leading to unrest. It is also far from evident that all ministers are in favour of the Government not having a major role in the implementation of services. The Government may, in addition, encounter difficulty finding a sufficient number of private-sector operators and NGOs to carry out programmes, given the adverse security environment, which is inhibiting inward investment and also reducing the proportion of the country in which NGOs can operate. Certainly, the indications are that the international private sector does not regard the prevailing conditions as conducive to any significant level of investment. None the less, the Afghan Government is drafting legislation to reduce the bureaucratic and tax disincentives to investment which are, at present, particularly onerous.

It is, however, worth noting the broad contents of the NDF. The objectives are divided into three sections: 'Humanitarian and Human and Social Capital', incorporating refugee return, education and vocational training, livelihood and social protection, and cultural heritage, media and sports; 'Physical Reconstruction and Natural Resources', encompassing transport and communications, water and sanitation, energy, urban development and natural resource management; and 'Private Sector Development, Governance and Security', incorporating trade and investment, governance and public administration, and security and rule of law. Within the NDF, six National Development Programmes were drawn up for 2003–04. Five of these programmes sought to secure improvements in education, urban development, water, governance and transport. The sixth project covered two new programmes: the National Solidarity Programme, which aimed to provide resources direct to villages based on priorities identified through participatory rural appraisal methodologies; and a National Emergency Employment Programme, which focused on the establishment of large-scale job creation programmes intended to reduce poverty.

Under the present Afghan Government, therefore, large-scale infrastructure programmes, such as the restoration of the national highway system, are of primary importance, both in giving a boost to the economy and in theoretically providing an important source of employment for returning refugees, demobilized fighters and retrenched civil servants. However, to achieve these aims, a secure environment, which is conducive to the necessary inward investment and implementation of these programmes, is essential. It is important to note, in this regard, that the US contractor engaged to repair the Kabul–Qandahar highway opted for capital- rather than labour-intensive methods because of the highly insecure operating conditions. Furthermore, a significant proportion of the workforce, for this and other highway projects, has been brought in from Pakistan, Turkey, India, the Republic of Korea and the People's Republic of China.

The Interim Authority, and the Transitional Administration which succeeded it, produced three budgets based on the NDF. In March 2002 expenditures were budgeted at US $460m., with an additional $23m. to clear wage arrears accumulated prior to the Interim Authority's tenure. The budget was primarily allocated to the wages and salaries of government employees and other expenses. Some $83m. was to be financed by domestic revenue and $400m. by external sources. The subsequent budget, published in March 2003, included two main elements: an ordinary budget of $550m. and a national development budget of $1,700m. The Government committed itself to raise $200m. towards the ordinary budget, while international donors agreed to fund almost 90% of the national development budget.

The 2004 budget was set out in a document entitled *Securing Afghanistan's Future: Accomplishments and the Strategic Path Forward*, which was presented to international donors at a conference held in Berlin, Germany, in March 2004. This document stated that 'Afghanistan is aiming for a small yet effective government whose role will, as far as possible, be limited to ensuring the security and safety of citizens, creating an enabling but properly regulated environment for the private sector and ensuring that all citizens have access to basic services'. In the same manner as the NDF, there thus remains a strong emphasis on the role of the government as providing a regulatory framework for a robust private sector. The report made it clear that there will be no state-owned enterprises, but did envisage some investment by the State to lay the foundations for future private-sector activity.

The programme anticipated annual growth of 9% in the legal economy, based on agriculture, mining, industry (including construction, transport, telecommunications and manufacturing) and services. It recognized that this growth rate would still leave a vulnerable population of around 4m., who would need support through social welfare initiatives. Meanwhile, a stated aim of the Afghan Government was to raise the per caput annual income from less than US $200 to $500.

The document further envisaged that the Government would seek to finance the wage portion of its recurrent expenditure in five years and the entire recurrent budget in nine years. Some US $13,500m. of the $27,500m. nine-year budget has been allocated to improvements to the physical infrastructure, while $2,700m. has been assigned to education, $2,600m. to security measures, $2,300m. to livelihoods and social protection, $1,400m. to health care, and $400m. to culture, media and sport. Of the $27,500m., $7,200m. will be needed to fund the Government's recurrent expenditure. The balance will be designated to specific projects, including major capital schemes. Primary among these will be the reconstruction of the major highway system, referred to as the ring road, linking the major cities.

The report noted that, apart from agriculture, the economy depended very heavily on small-scale enterprises, primarily at the household level. It identified potential for expansion through the development of hydropower and the exploitation of gas reserves in northern Afghanistan, which were estimated at 120,000m. cu m. Private investment opportunities were also to be sought further to develop telecommunications and to explore and extract new oil reserves, together with substantial mineral reserves, including coal, iron ore, salt, copper, quarry materials, marble, industrial minerals and gemstones. The report none the less noted that 'investor perception of the difficulties of doing business in Afghanistan constrains funding from international markets for exploration and development'. The opening of several international banks in Afghanistan from 2003 onwards was considered significant in facilitating both international trade and inward investment.

In identifying the constraints to economic progress, the report stated that 'until key concerns around the security situation and the extent to which rule of law is followed are addressed, the level of private investment will be limited'. The document stressed that the low level of general education, the shortage of specific professional skills and poor health indicators are undermining the capacity of the country to achieve significant growth in the short term. It added that 'investments in human and social capital will not be productive if citizens do not enjoy basic protections and guarantees' and emphasized that 'an integrated strategy must address core structural issues of human rights, human security and the rule of law'. Concern was expressed about the 'increasingly heavy demands . . . being placed on national resources and capacities, not least by large numbers of returnees and ex-combatants seeking to reintegrate, and by the rapid growth of urban centres'. In this context, 'pressures by asylum countries to accelerate the rate of return' were said to exacerbate the 'significant pressure on already fragile national resources'. It also commented that there 'are currently strong and concentrated interests in Afghanistan who are angling for a weak central government which will allow them to undertake narcotic production and illegal natural resource exploitation'.

In focusing on capacity considerations, the document presented a key dilemma that confronted the Government as a result of, for example, its heavy dependence on NGOs to provide education and health services: the need for an ongoing international presence constrained the Government in its quest to build up its institutional base because it was unable to offer terms and conditions of employment that were competitive with those provided by international organizations and the diplomatic sector.

It is interesting to relate this document to a report on the Afghan economy, which was published by the International Monetary Fund (IMF) in September 2003, entitled *Islamic State of Afghanistan: Rebuilding a Macroeconomic Framework for Reconstruction and Growth*. This paper presented many interesting perspectives on the characteristics and state of the Afghan economy and on the reconstruction process. It is, therefore, worth highlighting some of the key points.

According to the IMF report, economic growth, excluding opium production, was estimated to have reached almost 30% in 2002/03 and was forecast to register a rate of about 20% in 2003/04. The growth was most evident in agriculture, with an ending of the drought, and in the construction and service sectors, which were fuelled by donor assistance. Cereal production had risen from a low of 1.8m. metric tons in 2000 to

5.4m. tons in 2003. The production of fruit and vegetables as well as livestock-related products, such as dairy items, meat, wool and hides, had also increased. In addition, the retail trade had expanded significantly. Per caput GDP was estimated at US $180–$190 in 2002/03, which placed it at one of the lowest levels in the world. The paper noted that the value of opium exports in 2002 was estimated by the UN Office on Drugs and Crime (UNODC) to be about $2,500m., which made it the largest source of export earnings. It commented that, if opium production were to be included in the formal economy, it would represent between 40% and 60% of the value. The paper added that two decades of expanding Afghan production had contributed to the dramatic decline in the street price of heroin (in real terms) in Western Europe, which fell from the equivalent of about $300 per gram (after adjusting for inflation) in 1987 to $70 per gram in 2000.

Investment, apart from donor-funded projects such as road construction, was said to have been largely small-scale, focusing on rebuilding damaged stores, repairs on farms, or importing taxis. Large-scale private investment had been limited to telecommunications and the construction or rebuilding of hotels.

The IMF document reported that the level of aid provided for Afghanistan had been relatively low compared with other recent post-conflict countries, adding that pledges may also have been low relative to actual needs. The paper thus noted that during January 2002–March 2003 Afghanistan received a total of US $67 per caput per year. This compared with $249 per caput per year for Bosnia and Herzegovina between 1995 and 1997; $256 per caput for Timor-Leste in 1999–2001; $219 per caput for the Palestinian (National) Authority (PA) in the West Bank and Gaza Strip between 1994 and 2001; and $98 per caput for Rwanda in 1994–2001. It stressed that, although some costs would be lower in Afghanistan, expenditure on expatriate salaries, transport and security would be equally high, if not higher. The IMF also judged that sizeable international assistance would be required for several years in order to revive the country, and this would need to be overwhelmingly in the form of grants to avoid possible future debt-servicing difficulties. The paper, none the less, stressed that, of the $2,100m. pledged at the January 2002 donor conference in Tokyo for the first 15 months, more than $1,800m. had been disbursed. Having said this, the IMF urged that pledged assistance should materialize in a timely manner and noted that, as of early September 2003, existing pledges were still below the requirements of both the operating and development budgets.

The IMF called for the establishment of an adequate level of security in the provinces to permit the implementation of reforms and projects, the resumption of private-sector economic activity and the provision of basic public services in all rural areas. It expressed the view that 'a dangerous potential exists for Afghanistan to progressively slide into a narco-state where all legitimate institutions become penetrated by the power and wealth of traffickers'. Furthermore, the paper drew attention to the risk that external assistance might cease before the required target was reached. It commented that the experience of post-conflict countries in the past showed that assistance typically started to decline after a few years, just when the recipient country's capacity to absorb aid and use it effectively was increasing. The IMF, therefore, expressed concern that, in the case of Afghanistan, the decline in donor attention might happen even sooner, as other post-conflict cases compete for funds. The international financial institution also drew on global experience to comment that early attention to critical elements of infrastructure (primary roads and telecommunication) and capacity building within the Government was essential to ensure progress in the reconstruction process. In addition, the report noted that, with a high proportion of returning refugees settling in urban areas, facilities and services—already under severe pressure to serve existing residents—were being stretched beyond capacity. The urban population was estimated to have reached 30% of the total population.

In September 2004 the World Bank produced its first economic report on Afghanistan for 25 years. The report commented that 'daily life is still shaped by the consequences of almost a quarter century of conflict. One of these is 'informality'—most economic activities do not follow, and are not protected by, official and legal rules and some of them, such as cultivating opium poppy and the arms trade, are criminal'. It thus noted that 90% of the economy was based on the informal sector, and commented that this seriously constrained the potential tax revenue. It added that donor funding was not sufficient to cover the cost of crucial government administrative functions. The report concluded that Afghanistan's future prospects depended on whether 'the political leadership can free it from a vicious cycle in which a largely informal economy, the opium trade and violence reinforce each other'.

In looking at some of the detailed findings of the World Bank report, it is interesting to note that the economy grew by 29% in 2002, albeit from a very low base, and by 16% in 2003. However, the factors generating this growth were seen as 'to a considerable extent, temporary and recovery-related (e.g. the boost in grain output)'. The opium economy in 2003, valued at US $2,300m., was said to comprise one-third of total, drug-inclusive, GDP, estimated at around $7,000m. It was, therefore, equivalent to one-half of GDP, if one excludes the drug economy. Agriculture, accounting for 32% of GDP, was the next largest sector. Manufacturing represented only 9%—most of it small-scale agricultural processing and other small-scale activities—followed by transport, telecommunications and power (8%), trade (6%) and construction (3%). Smuggling generated an estimated $1,000m. per year for those involved. Trade in illegally exploited natural resources was cited as another important sector of the economy and included the trafficking of illegally harvested timber and of emeralds from the Panjshir Valley. Among more obviously illegal activities, the report noted the appropriation of customs duties; illegal taxation; human trafficking; land seizures; and real estate speculation based on armed force or corruptly obtained contracts.

In examining economic prospects, the report concluded that 'some of the drivers behind the economic recovery will diminish in coming years'. By way of example, it stated that 'Afghan cereal yields are approaching those in neighbouring countries' after two years of sharp increases and added that, although there was 'scope for substantial further yield increases by moving toward best practice levels', this 'will require good agricultural policies, institutions and investments'. In noting that raisins were a major export crop before 1978, it commented that processed agricultural products had export potential.

The report stressed that Afghanistan remains a very poor country, with extremely low social indicators (e.g. an infant mortality rate of 115 and under-five mortality rate of 172 per 1,000 live births and maternal mortality of 1,600 per 100,000 live births, equivalent to one in 62.5). One-fifth of rural households are estimated, in the report, to be extremely poor, manifested in food insecurity throughout the year. They are often landless and depend heavily on wage employment or share-cropping. Between 50% and 60% of rural households are deemed to be 'doing a little better', while remaining poor and vulnerable to falling deeper into poverty. These tend to be engaged in half a dozen or more activities through the employment of different household members in agriculture, non-farm wage employment and labour migration. These households are thought to maintain adequate calorific intake but chronic malnutrition is common due to 'poor dietary diversity, high incidence of water-borne disease and improper feeding practices of young children'. The welfare indicators of this population are said to be 'better than for the extreme poor, but not by a large margin'. Non-farm earnings are said to represent 'a more significant form of employment than farm management' for the remaining 20%–30%, even though most are landowners. The profile of the urban population is thought to be broadly similar.

A further assessment of the Afghan economy was given on 27 January 2005, when the IMF issued a Public Information Notice in response to its Article IV Consultation with the Islamic State of Afghanistan. This concluded that GDP (excluding opium) was estimated at US $2,463m. in 2001/02, at $4,084m. in 2002/03, at $4,585m. in 2003/04 and was projected to reach $5,392m. in 2004/05. It estimated real GDP growth to have been 29% in 2002/03 and 16% in 2003/04, and projected that GDP would increase by 8% in 2004/05.

GDP per caput was estimated at $123 in 2001/02, $182 in 2002/03, $199 in 2003/04 and was projected to rise to $228 in 2004/05.

The Notice commented, however, that 'while there was some improvement in social indicators, including in school enrolment and food security, the social challenges remain daunting', adding that 'poverty is widespread'. It thus noted that agricultural production had been negatively affected by adverse weather conditions, while growth had 'remained strong in other sectors, especially in construction and services, which continued to benefit from a buoyant aid-related, and possibly opium-related, demand'. In adding that there had been 'sharp increases in rents and petroleum products prices', it made it clear that economic conditions remained extremely difficult. This reinforces the picture given by other sources of growing polarization within the economy, with a small élite benefiting from property speculation and other trading interests while those without property are pushed further into poverty by rising rents. Recent studies indicate that speculation in the property market is also leading to growing displacement as people are forced to look elsewhere for accommodation when rents increase.

The IMF reports, in addition, that the level of government expenditure has 'significantly lagged behind budget projections because of weak implementation capacity', arising from the 'widespread shortages of skilled civil servants'. It expressed concern 'about under spending on social programmes'. The Notice perceived current policies as 'building a solid foundation for a possible transition to a Fund program that could be supported by the Poverty Reduction and Growth Facility' and noted that the Government planned to draw up an Interim Poverty Reduction Strategy Paper. It stated that safeguards should be established 'to alleviate any significant adverse economic impact of opium eradication, particularly for the most vulnerable'. A further concern expressed related to 'widespread corruption, the rise in drug activities and the lack of transparency in many areas'. The Notice therefore reinforces the view given by the World Bank in its 2004 report on the Afghan economy that the prospects for economic growth remain quite limited and that a high percentage of the population are vulnerable to falling deeper into poverty.

The French news agency Agence France-Presse (AFP) reported on 15 March 2005 that the Afghan Government's budget for 2005 had increased by 15%, to US $678m. Of this, $333m. was projected to come from domestic taxes, with the balance from international donor funding. GDP was reported to have increased by 7.5% in 2004, compared with growth of 18% in 2003 and 29% in 2002.

Towards the end of 2005 a review of the state of the economy was presented with the publication of the conclusions of an IMF mission which visited Afghanistan during 8–22 November 2005 under its Staff-Monitored Program and 2005 Article IV Consultation. This concluded that agricultural output had increased on the basis of good rainfall and that growth had also been evident in construction, trade, transportation and telecommunications. It noted that increases in rents had slowed markedly, while there had been a sharp rise in petroleum product prices. Inflation was expected to be around 10% at year end. The review commented that lower than expected development spending reflected 'longstanding capacity constraints, unrealistic expectations on the pace of implementation, weaknesses in budget formulation and security concerns'. In a similar vein, it stated that 'lingering insecurity, illicit drug industry activities, the poor state of infrastructure and weak institutions remained the key constraints to investment, sustainable growth and improvements in social welfare'. Growth in 2005 was estimated to be 14%, but this was expected to decline to an average annual rate of around 10% during 2006–08, based on agricultural growth and 'sustained, albeit decelerating, activity in construction and services'.

In January 2006 the Afghan Government outlined its development plans for the following five years through its Interim Afghanistan National Development Strategy (IANDS). The key priority areas are security, governance and the rule of law, human rights, sustainable economic and social development, and counter narcotics. The document reaffirms the underlying principle of the 2002 NDF—namely that the Afghan State will seek to create an environment in which the private sector can flourish and that it will also seek to minimize its own role as a service delivery entity by contracting out to private-sector organizations and NGOs.

The agricultural economy is seen as the principal vehicle for economic growth, although this growth is expected to be relatively slow. To maximize its productivity, the strategy includes mechanisms to improve access to markets, provide sources of power and support the creation of cold-storage facilities. The Government plans to take initiatives to strengthen non-farm economic opportunities within the rural areas, in the hope of reducing migration to the major cities. It will also increase the availability of credit to rural communities, address water resource management and develop irrigation.

In recognition of the heavy dependence of the Afghan economy on the ability of the population to seek work in Pakistan, Iran and elsewhere, the strategy notes that, by 2010, the Government will reach agreements with its neighbours 'to enable Afghans to seek work in the region and send remittances home'.

The strategy does not anticipate significant private-sector investment in the manufacturing sector and looks to small and medium-sized enterprises as the primary elements in the non-farm economy. The creation of access to electricity for a majority of these is seen as an important objective, whether through arrangements with Afghanistan's neighbours or through hydro-power generated within the country. Hope is none the less expressed that international investment can be attracted into the extraction and processing of Afghanistan's mineral (iron, copper, coal, hydrocarbons and quarry materials) and gemstone deposits, as well as into a trans-Afghanistan pipeline to bring gas from Turkmenistan to Pakistan and, possibly, India. Important potential is also seen in Afghanistan's role as a transit country for goods travelling between the Central Asian Republics and the Indian sub-continent. To facilitate this, the Government envisaged that a major highway system would be completed by the end of 2008.

Significant emphasis is placed on the need to address the very high level of poverty, the ramifications of health indicators and the limited access to clean water and sanitation. The rapid urbanization process is seen as of particular concern in this context. The strategy recognizes that economic growth will not automatically benefit the poorest in society; it therefore proposes specific initiatives to provide a safety net for such people.

The strategy outlines all the many constraints to progress, including insecurity, the opium trade, corruption, the low revenue base, the very limited capacity of the government bureaucracy, the severe shortage of skills and 'a pervasive culture of impunity ... due to the lack of an independent judiciary and professional law enforcement'. It thus notes that: 'the legal and regulatory framework necessary for Government to function effectively, ensure the rule of law and protect our citizens is still nascent or absent. While the Government has passed new laws designed to protect the rights of citizens, our ability to enforce these laws is compromised. Our different government branch members lack legislative, oversight and representational experience. Our sub-national administrative structure is especially weak, which inhibits coordination across Government at the provincial and district levels and lowers our accountability to the vast majority of our population, who live in rural areas. Too many of these sub-national governance structures remain under the influence of illicit power holders.' The document comments that 'control over arms and money enables power holders to seize land, levy tributes and control access to credit and markets' and adds that 'the poor have no effective rights to land or other assets'. It further states that 'in the justice sector, the sale of judicial access and favourable decisions to the highest bidder fundamentally undermines the security and basic rights of citizens, especially the poor, women and children' and adds that 'state and non-state actors who violate the law are emboldened by this state of impunity'. In recognition of the enormous difficulties that returning refugees have faced in recovering their land, the strategy identifies the registration of entitlement to land as a major objective in both rural and urban areas, together with measures to ensure that the judicial system can handle disputes fairly.

To address competence and corruption in the government service, the strategy envisages that 'a clear and transparent national appointments mechanism will be established ... for all senior level appointments' and that 'merit-based appointments, vetting procedures and performance-based reviews will be undertaken for the civil services at all levels of government'. To improve the skills of civil servants, the strategy anticipates that the Government will offer on-the-job training, special courses and intensive study abroad.

To improve skills within the wider economy, the strategy includes plans to 'provide the less educated with vocational skills to fill demands for construction, infrastructure building and maintenance of assets' and to orientate the higher education system towards managerial and professional skills. Literacy and numeracy are also seen as key targets.

On counter-narcotics, the document stresses the continuing use of simultaneous strategies, including law enforcement, the use of eradication 'as appropriate', regional co-operation and the provision of alternative livelihoods.

The strategy anticipates that the current Consultative Groups, which bring together the Government and other key actors, will be reformed to align with the structure of the IANDS. The groups will co-ordinate the implementation of the strategy and assist in the preparation of the national budget. Information and analysis in support of the strategy will be sought from 'sub-national monitoring and coordination mechanisms, including Community and Provincial Development Councils, NGOs, Provincial Reconstruction Teams, the private sector, civil society and research units'. Progress will be reviewed through the annual Afghanistan Development Forum.

In preparation for the full Afghanistan National Development Strategy, the Government planned to consult with a wide range of actors, including 'line ministries, the National Assembly, sub-national administrative units, UN agencies, NGOs, civil society representatives, communities and the private sector'. Through this process, the Government will seek to gain 'a much better understanding of demographic, economic, political and security-related realities at the sub-national level'. The Government estimated that the implementation of the IANDS would cost US $19,829m. over the following five years.

The ADB produced an assessment of the Afghan economy in March 2007 in its annual publication the *Asian Development Outlook*. This noted that overall growth in GDP for the financial year ending 20 March 2007 was expected to reach only 8%, compared with the 12% projected in the IMF Poverty Reduction and Growth Facility Programme. The report predicted, however, that the growth rate would again reach double figures in 2007/08 and 2008/09 if the agriculture sector continued to recover from the most recent drought. It commented that growth prospects for the medium term were dependent on the security situation. According to the ADB, the rate of inflation in 2006/07 was reported to have declined to a little less than 4%, benefiting from a decline in energy prices and renting costs in Kabul. Export levels continued to rise slowly; the trade deficit in 2005/06 reached US $2,600m. By 2006/07 the generation of revenue by the Government itself had increased by 500% compared with revenue generation in 2003; the level of government revenue was expected to rise by 15%–20% in 2007/08. However, a reduction in customs revenues during the second half of 2006/07 was only partly offset by higher revenues from taxes on income, profits and business receipts. The Government's capacity to implement the development budget increased from 43% in 2005/06 to 55%–60% in 2006/07. The ADB's assessment also noted that an estimated 80%–90% of economic activity remained in the private sector owing to 'political uncertainty, the lack of the rule of law, inefficient business registration procedures and the tax regime'. In conclusion, the report stated that 'Despite impressive growth and a solid track record of macroeconomic policy and structural reforms, the country still faces substantial challenges. The currect reconstruction-related drivers of growth will neither sustain growth, create employment nor reduce poverty over the medium term'.

In April 2007 the Afghan Minister of Finance, Prof. Anwar-ul-Haq Ahadi, forecast that the Afghan economy would grow by 11%–12% during 2007/08. He also predicted that tax receipts would increase by 30%, to more than US $715m. At the same time the Senior Economic Adviser to President Karzai noted that annual income per head now stood at around $380, compared with $182 in 2001. The ordinary (operating) budget agreed by the Afghan Parliament for 2006/07 totalled more than $831m., while $1,370m. was allocated to development projects.

The ADB's *Asian Development Outlook* published in April 2008 noted that GDP growth in the licit economy was estimated to have reached 13.9% in 2007/08, reflecting a significant improvement in agricultural production. Growth in the industry and services sectors was reported to be 13.3% and 12.4% respectively. The construction sector, which achieved growth of 20% in 2007/08, was the main driver of expansion in industry. However, the rate of growth of overall GDP growth was forecast to decrease to around 9.0% in 2008/09 and 2009/10. In addition, the annual rate inflation had increased to 9.8% in 2007/08. Further, the ratio of domestic revenues to the core operating budget showed very little improvement, indicating that the Government's goal of fully financing operating expenditures by 2013/14 might remain elusive. The external budget, which is directly executed by donors, continued to account for nearly one-half of total public expenditure in 2007/08 and was projected to increase by about 75% in 2008/09. Recent estimates indicated that 40% of the labour force was unemployed, partly owing to the inability of the agricultural sector and the still-limited formal economy to absorb fully the rapidly expanding supply of labour. The ADB concluded that the performance of the Afghan economy over the medium term would depend heavily on government success in combating corruption, overcoming infrastructure 'bottlenecks' such as transport and electricity, and implementing further structural reforms aimed at stimulating private-sector investment.

### The Role of International Donors

International donors pledged a total of US $4,300m. to Afghanistan at the 2002 Tokyo conference. However, cash disbursements arising from these pledges were slow to arrive and in the early months the Government had almost no funds of its own and no material evidence of the widely publicized offers of international support to show the population. In retrospect, it would have made a considerable difference to the economy, and to the credibility of the Transitional Administration, if international donors had embarked immediately and noticeably on major infrastructure programmes.

The Berlin conference of March 2004 brought together international donors to review funding over the next seven years based on a projected budget, presented by the Afghan Government, of US $27,500m. The conference was successful in that pledges of $4,500m. were secured for the first year, which slightly exceeded the budgeted figure. Pledges for the initial three years were also encouraging, reaching more than two-thirds of the budget. Based on the pledges made hitherto, the USA was clearly the largest donor, having allocated a total of $5,036m. It was followed by the European Union (EU), which allocated $1,421m. Among the other major donors were Japan ($900m.), the United Kingdom ($850m.), Germany ($729m.), the World Bank ($553m.), Canada ($440m.), India ($400m.), the Netherlands ($285m.), Italy ($263m.), Iran ($254m.), Norway ($253m.), Saudi Arabia ($230m.), Spain ($147m.), Sweden ($144m.), Denmark ($130m.), the ADB ($115m.) and Pakistan ($105m.). It is noteworthy that the combined allocation from the EU and individual European governments totalled $4,525m. It is equally significant that contributions from Afghanistan's immediate and near neighbours (including Pakistan, Iran, China, Russia, India, Saudi Arabia, Turkey and the Arab Gulf states) amounted to $1,240m. Caution should be exercised in drawing conclusions from these figures, in that governments vary in their willingness or capacity actually to disburse funds promptly and on the basis of pledges made.

The Afghan Transitional Administration brought together representatives of donor governments and international organizations on 20–21 April 2004 at the Afghanistan Development

Forum to discuss development priorities, which were to be funded, in part, by the assistance pledged at the recent donor conference in Berlin. Among the programmes announced were the National Agriculture Programme, the National Accountability and Rule of Law Programme, the National Private Sector Support Programme and the National Skills Development Programme. After the meeting, the Afghan Minister of Finance stated that all major reconstruction projects for the country should receive full funding.

The Afghanistan Development Forum brought the Afghan Government and donors together again during 4–6 April 2005. The Forum drew attention to the accelerating urbanization process and the need to strengthen the urban infrastructure through the provision of additional housing, electricity, water supply and sewerage. It also noted the need for rural communities to have access to off-farm economic opportunities, including the processing of agricultural produce, notably fruit and vegetables, for the wider market. Among the more difficult issues addressed was that of the balance to be achieved between initiatives targeted at the alleviation of rural poverty and those seeking to address urban deprivation. Much stress was placed on the desirability of building an infrastructure that would strengthen the overall economy. This included the creation of conditions that would enable the private sector to generate more employment opportunities. It was also emphasized that economic growth which was not broad-based, pro-poor and gender-sensitive would undermine efforts to build democracy, stability and the rule of law and would be unsustainable. Repeated reference was made to the slow progress in building the capacity of the government administration and to the persistent corruption that had undermined efforts to strengthen the public sector. Priority was also given to judicial reform, both to address the continuing absence of a rule of law and to resolve land disputes and underpin investment by the private sector. It was noted that progress in this regard had been extremely limited. Concern was expressed at the large number of illegal militia in existence and the need to address this problem to ensure the success of the disarmament programme. The reform of the police force was seen to represent a greater challenge than the task of building up the national army. The level and quality of training to date was viewed as far from adequate.

International donors met representatives of the Afghan Government in London on 31 January and 1 February 2006. The donors committed themselves to supporting the reconstruction process in Afghanistan for a further five years on the basis of an agreed plan of action. This agreement, known as the Afghanistan Compact, sets out the expectations of both parties with regard to their respective contributions to the process. The document, which is supported by the IANDS, incorporates pledges totalling US $10,500m.; however, this figure may include the costs of deploying international forces. A total of 26 countries made pledges, including 13 European countries and seven of Afghanistan's immediate or near neighbours (Pakistan, Iran, China, India, the United Arab Emirates (UAE), Saudi Arabia and Turkey). In addition, pledges were made by the USA, Canada, Japan, the Republic of Korea, Australia and New Zealand. The non-state donors comprised the World Bank, the ADB, the Islamic Development Bank, the European Commission, UN agencies and the Aga Khan Development Fund. The major donors were the USA, the World Bank, the ADB, the United Kingdom, Germany, Japan and the European Commission. However, a total of 16 countries pledged more than $100m. each, five of which are among Afghanistan's neighbours. The Afghanistan Compact commits the Islamic Republic of Afghanistan and the international community to 'work toward a stable and prosperous Afghanistan, with good governance and human rights protection for all under the rule of law and to maintain and strengthen that commitment over the term of this Compact and beyond'. The Compact notes that both parties are 'mindful that Afghanistan's transition to peace and stability is not yet assured, and that strong international engagement will continue to be required to address remaining challenges'. It further notes that both are 'resolved to overcome the legacy of conflict in Afghanistan by setting conditions for sustainable economic growth and development; strengthening state institutions and civil society; removing remaining terrorist threats; meeting the challenge of counter-narcotics; rebuilding capacity and infrastructure; reducing poverty; and meeting basic human needs'. The agreement identifies three critical areas of activity for the five years from the adoption of the Compact: security; governance, rule of law and human rights; and economic and social development. Counter-narcotics is noted as a further vital area of work.

Through the Compact, the Government of Afghanistan commits itself to the realization of a shared vision and the international community reciprocally commits itself to providing resources and support to that end. Both parties also commit themselves to improving the effectiveness and accountability of international assistance. The Compact further envisages that both parties will work towards building Afghan capacity at state, civil society and individual levels, with due regard for gender equality; that they will seek to ensure a balanced and fair allocation of resources; that policies and programmes will recognize that men and women have equal rights and responsibilities; and that corruption will be combated, and public transparency and accountability will be ensured. With regard to economic and social development, the parties agree to give priority to infrastructure and natural resources, education, health, agriculture and rural development, social protection, and economic governance and private-sector development. With regard to counter-narcotics, the Compact envisages that economic alternatives to the cultivation of opium poppies will be provided 'in the context of comprehensive rural development' and that crop eradication will be pursued 'as appropriate'.

Through the Compact, the Afghan Government and the international community commit themselves to certain benchmarks and deadlines. These include the following, to be achieved by the end of 2010: electricity will be provided to at least 65% of households and 90% of non-residential establishments in major urban areas and to at least 25% of households in rural areas; net enrolment in primary school for girls and boys will be at least 60% and 75%, respectively; the rate of maternal mortality will be reduced by 15% and under-5 mortality by 20%.

The Compact includes specific measures to improve the effectiveness of aid, including:

a) a recognition on the part of the leadership of the Afghan Government in setting its development priorities;

b) transparency and accountability on the part of both the Government and the donors of the international assistance being provided to Afghanistan;

c) agreement by the Government to draw up an Afghanistan National Development Strategy, to improve its revenue base, to agree benchmarks for the channelling of aid through the Government's core budget, and to provide regular reports to the National Assembly, the donor community and the public at large on the use of donor assistance and on performance against benchmarks;

d) agreement by the donors to provide assistance within the framework of the Afghanistan National Development Strategy; to agree all programmes and projects with the Government in order to focus on priorities; to eliminate duplication and rationalize donor activities; to provide more predictable and multi-annual funding commitments; to provide untied aid where possible; to increase the proportion of donor assistance channelled directly through the Afghan core budget or the various trust funds; to provide assistance for the development of public expenditure management systems with the aim of improving transparency and accountability; to design programmes aimed at building capacity within the Government; to ensure that development policies, including salary policies, strengthen national institutions; to harmonize the delivery of technical assistance in accordance with government needs; to promote the use of the Afghan private sector; to use a greater number of Afghan nationals as implementers; and to increase the procurement of supplies within Afghanistan itself for both civilian and military purposes;

e) agreement by the donors to, within the principles of international competitive bidding, promote the participation in the bidding process of the Afghan private sector and South-South co-operation in order to overcome capacity constraints and to lower costs of delivery;

f) agreement by donors to provide timely, transparent and comprehensive information on foreign aid flows, including levels of pledges, commitments and disbursements in a format that will enable the Afghan Government to plan its own activities and present comprehensive budget reports to the National Assembly. This will cover the nature and amount of assistance being provided to Afghanistan through the core and external budgets;

g) agreement by donors to report to the Government on the utilization of funds and on the efficiency, quality and effectiveness of external budgetary assistance. Implementation of the Compact will be overseen by a joint Co-ordination and Monitoring Board, which will be supported by a small secretariat and co-chaired by the Afghan Government and the UN.

Although the US Government has been Afghanistan's largest donor, it is difficult to map its allocations or its policies. It has not produced a country strategy for Afghanistan and appears to be operating in an *ad hoc* manner with regard to the reconstruction process. In July 2003, however, the US authorities announced that they would be allocating US $1,000m. towards the reconstruction of Afghanistan, to be spent before the Afghan elections, then planned for June 2004. It was not clear, however, whether this was new money or how it would be spent. In the mean time, the USA had committed itself to providing the major part of the funding for the construction of the highway linking Kabul with Qandahar and Herat. In addition, the US Senate, in November 2002, passed the Afghanistan Freedom Support Act, authorizing expenditure of $3,300m., to include allocations of $1,700m. for economic, humanitarian and development assistance, $300m. to establish an enterprise fund to encourage private-sector development and $300m. in 'drawdown authority' for military and other security assistance. However, owing to the complex and relatively non-transparent financial systems in operation, it is unclear what progress has been made in allocating and disbursing these funds. The US President, George W. Bush, was reported in September 2003 to have asked the US Congress for an additional $1,200m. for Afghanistan, of which $400m. would need to be made available immediately and $800m. would be taken from the allocation for 2004. The stated purposes of the funding included: reconstruction of the Qandahar–Herat road; provision of support to the Disarmament, Demobilization and Reintegration Programme; payment of civil servants; development of communications between Kabul and provincial capitals; provision of support to the electoral process; financial assistance for 'technical experts' in Afghan ministries; rehabilitation or construction of schools; teacher training; construction of clinics; provision of support for the reform of property laws; creation of a land registry; completion of a natural resources assessment to promote private-sector investment; creation of a venture-capital fund; and assistance for a short-term power generation project to improve electricity supply to Kabul.

Construction of the highway linking Kabul with Qandahar has proved to be problematic. The decision to embark on this project was a direct reaction to an assassination attempt on President Hamid Karzai in September 2002. The implementation process had barely started before the conflict in Iraq led to a deterioration in the security environment in Afghanistan, which considerably hampered progress. The US Agency for International Development (USAID) contracted The Louis Berger Group, of the USA, to manage the programme and it, in turn, subcontracted the work to one Afghan–US firm, three Turkish firms and one Indian firm. However, there was strong political pressure from the US Administration to complete the work by the end of 2003 and this meant that only one layer of tarmac was laid. It also transpired that work to the foundations and camber had been poorly carried out and the surface soon began to break up under the pressure of heavy usage, provoking widespread public concern and cynicism. Work has since been carried out to bring the road up to a reasonable standard, but travel carries a high degree of risk owing to the adverse security situation.

It was announced in November 2003 by the US embassy in Dushanbe, Tajikistan, that US military engineers had begun preliminary work on building a road bridge over the Amu-Dar'ya (Oxus) river, which separates Afghanistan and Tajikistan. US engineers also started work, in September 2004, on a new road to link Qandahar to Terin Kowt, the provincial capital of Uruzgan. This was being financed from an additional US $1,760m. in reconstruction funds allocated in 2004, and was scheduled to be completed by the end of 2006. This initiative clearly had important security benefits in an area that had seen a high level of Taliban activity. Similar considerations may have influenced the decision of the USA to support the resurfacing of the road from Shiberghan to Sar-e Pol, in northern Afghanistan. In recent years Sar-e Pol has been an area of particular tension, arising from local power struggles. The US military announced in April 2005 that it had awarded a contract for the construction of a bridge connecting Tajikistan with Afghanistan at Sher Khan Bandar in Kunduz province. This bridge is not thought to be the same as that reported on in September 2004.

On 1 December 2005 the US and Afghan Governments signed a memorandum of understanding on US assistance to Afghanistan over the next five years, covering support for programmes in education and health care, and in economic and democratic governance. It was unclear how much of the budget of US $5,500m. was to be spent on US contractors. There has been much recent debate within Afghanistan and the international press about the high cost of contracts issued by USAID to US companies. This has included concern over the poor quality of many programmes, arising, in part, from the extreme difficulties that US personnel face in monitoring projects as a consequence of the adverse security situation. One notable example of a contract granted by USAID to US companies was that awarded in September 2006 as a joint venture to Black & Veatch and the Louis Berger Group, which was valued at $1,400m. over five years. This contract was to include, during the initial period, the rehabilitation of power transmission networks and power generation capacity as well as the rehabilitation and extension of roads. Subsequent work was expected to focus on urban development and water and sanitation systems as well as improvements to public buildings. Another recent example was the contract awarded by USAID to Bearing Point of McLean, Virginia, in March 2007. This contract, valued at $218.6m., was to provide training to government officials in budget preparation and disbursement, inter-agency co-ordination and human resources. Bearing Point began working in Afghanistan in 2002 to help develop the banking system and create capacity within a number of ministries. The new project was expected to extend this process to a wider group of ministries.

The European Commission published its *Country Strategy Paper for Afghanistan: 2003–06* in February 2003. The Commission focused on four main areas in its paper: building the capacity of principal government ministries; rural development and food security; economic infrastructure (particularly the Kabul–Jalalabad road); and the provision of a basic health-care programme aimed at reducing rates of infant and maternal mortality. In October 2004 the Commission announced a new budget of €34m., known as the Sixth Reconstruction Programme, out of its €400m. allocation for 2003–04. This budget was to be used to strengthen an ongoing rural recovery programme, help re-establish a public animal health system, support the public administration reform process, support the emergence of a professional journalistic community and address the problem of domestic violence, with the balance used for audits, evaluation and information purposes. The reconstruction of the Kabul–Jalalabad highway, with funding from the European Commission, has been completed, using a Swedish engineering consultancy and a Chinese construction company. In January 2007 the European Commission announced an allocation of €600m. over the following four years, with a particular focus on strengthening the judiciary and the police force. Additional priority areas identified were rural development, including identifying and promoting alternatives to opium production, and health.

In May 2003 the British Government's Department for International Development (DFID) published a consultation draft of its Transitional Country Assistance Plan for Afghanistan for 2003–04. DFID, concerned with ensuring that the Transitional Administration had the capacity to implement the NDF, agreed to allocate a relatively high level of resources to the provision of direct support to the Government. It also strongly encouraged reform of the civil service in order to increase the effectiveness of the state apparatus. In addition, it gave priority to reform of the security sector, which aims to create a functioning army, police force and judiciary. It remained mindful, none the less, of the continuing very high levels of poverty in the country and the vulnerability of the population to any future disasters or adverse economic or security conditions. Funding would therefore be made available for programmes that help create sustainable livelihoods and alleviate poverty in the short term. The DFID strategy thus envisaged that priority would be given to the following areas: financial support for the NDF; political and technical support for the political transition process, including reform of the security sector; technical support for state-building, economic and financial management and public administration development; support for the development of sustainable livelihoods for poor Afghans, by working with both the Government and the private sector; and humanitarian assistance.

DFID subsequently produced the *DFID Interim Strategy for Afghanistan: 2005/6*, pending the publication of a final strategy to take account of the Afghan Government's National Development Strategy. The DFID strategy identified certain key priorities: the need to tackle terrorism and extremism, address poverty and injustice and make progress on counter-narcotics; the creation of the requisite conditions for sustainable poverty reduction in the medium to long term; the stabilization of the country; the strengthening of government capacity to deliver services; and the establishment of the rule of law within a democratic political system that safeguarded human rights. The programme had three focal areas: livelihoods; economic management and effectiveness; and state-building. DFID sought to support the Afghan leadership by channelling more than 70% of its funds through the national budget and national programmes. Around one-half of the total budget of £90m. allocated for 2005–06 was to be spent on alternative livelihoods. DFID was also to explore how it could support the United Kingdom's increasing focus on the southern province of Helmand in 2006. In June 2006 the British Government announced that it had allocated £38m. to Helmand for the financial year 2006/07. More than one-half of this was to be allocated to rural development programmes (including the Afghan Government's National Solidarity Programme) through DFID.

In August 2003 Italy announced that it would donate €36m. towards the construction of a road linking Kabul with Herat via Bamian. Work on the road, which was to be carried out by a Chinese construction company, commenced in September 2006 and was scheduled for completion within four years. Japan has been providing particular support to the Disarmament, Demobilization and Reintegration Programme, which aims to achieve a disbandment of the many militias operating in the country and the reintegration into normal economic activity of those combatants who do not join the national army or police force. This programme faces many challenges and is not likely to be effective unless the economy grows sufficiently to provide ample employment. As noted above, demobilized fighters will be competing for income-earning opportunities with returning refugees, those without land, and civil servants made redundant as a consequence of efforts to streamline the government bureaucracy. Japan has also been supporting the Disbandment of Illegal Armed Groups programme, which aims to reduce the number of arms in circulation amongst the many informal militias in operation throughout the country. In July 2006 the Japanese Government announced that it had allocated a further $60m. to strengthen the Afghan National Police and support efforts to combat illegal drugs production and trafficking. Owing to the greatly limited capacity of the government service to manage funds on any scale, international donors have opted to provide funding to the Transitional Administration through the Afghanistan Reconstruction Trust Fund. This is administered by a committee, which includes representatives of UNDP and the World Bank. International donors have also invested a significant amount of effort into helping the Afghan Government to build financial and other systems to strengthen its capacity to function effectively. Good progress has been made in building the capacity of the Ministries of Finance, Public Health, Rural Rehabilitation and Development, and Agriculture, Irrigation and Livestock, but the movement to increase capacity in other ministries has been severely undermined by the patronage system, among other factors. In an effort to create incentives for staff who were deemed to be working effectively, it was announced in November 2003 that the Afghan Government had agreed to increase the salaries of government staff by up to seven times. About 40% of the 450,000 employees were believed to have benefited.

It was reported in April 2007 that the World Bank and the IMF had decided that Afghanistan was eligible for assistance under the enhanced Heavily Indebted Poor Countries (HIPC) initiative, subject to certain conditions being met. The HIPC initiative seeks 'to create a framework in which all creditors, including multilateral creditors, can provide debt relief to the world's poorest and most heavily indebted countries, and thereby reduce the constraints on economic growth and poverty reduction imposed by the debt-service burdens in these countries'.

In July 2006 it was announced that, following mediation by the Paris Club, Afghanistan's major creditors—Russia, the USA and Germany—had written off US $1,400m. in debt, representing 92% of Afghanistan's outstanding debt to the three creditors (most of which had come from the former USSR).

**The Role of the International Financial Institutions**

Both the World Bank and the ADB took more than one year to begin implementing reconstruction efforts on any scale, although a significant amount of preparatory work was undertaken from late 2001. In December 2002 both banks announced the resumption of loans to Afghanistan after the British and other Governments decided to settle Afghanistan's outstanding arrears.

In March 2003 the World Bank approved a US $108m. interest-free credit for an Emergency Transport Rehabilitation Project. The funds were to be used to achieve improvements to the highway from Kabul to Faizabad in north-eastern Afghanistan via Kunduz. By April 2006 the World Bank had completed reconstruction of the section of this highway between Kabul and Kunduz, including the Salang Tunnel, and had almost finished work on the road from Kunduz to the border at Sher Khan Bandahar. Work on the road from Kunduz to Taloqan and Kishem in north-east Afghanistan was originally scheduled for completion by mid-2007. Final work on the stretch of road between Taloqan and Kishem was rescheduled for completion in June 2008. The loan was also earmarked for the reconstruction of the runway at Kabul's international airport, which was completed in 2005, and the provision of equipment to support safe air travel. In July 2005 it was announced that a new air traffic control system had been installed at Kabul airport which would facilitate communication with high-altitude aircraft. This would service commercial airlines overflying Afghanistan and thus add to the revenue base. An instrument landing system has also been installed at the airport. In addition, the World Bank planned to provide grants to help develop the health and banking sectors.

The World Bank announced in June 2003 that it had approved a grant of US $18.8m. and a credit of $20.4m. to fund labour-intensive public-works programmes to improve rural access roads. This project was part of the Government's National Emergency Employment Programme, which was being implemented by the Ministries of Public Works and Rural Rehabilitation and Development.

The World Bank approved additional funding for Afghanistan in December 2003. This included a grant of US $95m. for the National Solidarity Programme, which supported reconstruction at the village level and benefited 3,082 villages in mid-2004. In addition, interest-free loans of $40m. and $31m., respectively, were issued to rehabilitate the agricultural irrigation system and upgrade customs. The latter project aimed to increase government revenue from trade, to reduce corruption and to prevent smuggling by developing checkpoints at border crossings and customs facilities at Kabul airport. The World Bank announced in June 2004 that it had approved a

$105m. credit to the Afghan Government to restore and expand the electricity distribution network in Kabul and rehabilitate the Naglu hydropower station. In July it also announced that it was lending $5m. to the Afghan Government to finance political risk insurance to encourage foreign investment in the country.

The World Bank has played a major role in building the institutional capacity of the Afghan Government to manage the economy, which was, as noted above, extremely limited at the time of the Bonn Agreement. The World Bank, thus, has joined the IMF, the US Treasury, the British Government and others to provide technical support in the following areas: budget preparation; currency reform; central banking and a payments system; an exchange rate regime; financial sector reform; and the articulation of monetary, fiscal and trade policies to ensure macroeconomic stability. It also announced, in January 2005, that it had approved a US $27m. grant to strengthen government administration, public procurement and financial and accountability systems.

Among the challenges faced by the Transitional Administration that required World Bank and other international support was the need to replace the two currencies in circulation by a single currency and to revalue the national currency, the afghani, by creating a new afghani equivalent to 1,000 of the old currency. This process began in October 2002 and continued for several months without undue incident but with some inflationary pressures occurring as a result.

In an effort to attract inward investment, the Afghan Government decided in July 2003 to join the World Bank's Multilateral Investment Guarantee Agency (MIGA) by subscribing to its capital base. This provides coverage against the risks of transfer restriction, expropriation, breach of contract, and war and civil disturbance (including terrorism). The Afghan Minister of Finance stated that investment priorities were primarily in the power, roads, telecommunications, agriculture, industry and tourism sectors. The Executive Vice-President of MIGA noted there was a 'healthy pipeline' of investors interested in doing business in Afghanistan who were concerned about the safety of their investments.

In April 2008 the World Bank reported that, since April 2002, it had financed 36 development and emergency reconstruction projects and three budget support operations in Afghanistan at a total cost of US $1,650m. Of this, more than $1,200m. had been in grant form and $436.4m. in interest-free loans.

The ADB announced its Initial Country Strategy and Program for Afghanistan in May 2002. This focused on the reconstruction of national and district roads, basic education and the rehabilitation of irrigation systems and agriculture. Additional support was allocated to health, energy (power transmission and the gas sub-sector), finance and trade, environment and community development. Grants and concessional loans totalling US $500m. were offered over a two-year period.

The ADB revealed in August 2003 that it would provide loan assistance to restore road links to Uzbekistan and to rehabilitate electricity transmission lines in the northern provinces as well as the power distribution system in Kabul. The loan would also be used to repair damaged gas production, transmission and distribution facilities in Shiberghan. Kuwait, meanwhile, agreed to provide a grant of US $15m. to support reconstruction of the Qandahar–Spin Boldak road, which would be administered by the ADB. Work on this road was partly completed in October 2005. In November 2003 the ADB agreed to fund a preparatory study of the road linking Herat to Andkhoy, in Faryab province. This part of the circular ring road that connects Kabul, Qandahar, Herat and Mazar-i-Sharif covers relatively difficult terrain and has, historically, suffered from underinvestment. Improvement of this road was expected significantly to increase trade with the Central Asian republics as well as facilitate internal communications. In December 2004 the ADB approved a concessionary loan of $80m. to reconstruct the 210-km section of this road between Qaisar and Andkhoy. The loan was also to be used to install toll facilities in order to increase customs revenue. The loan had a 40-year term, including a grace period of 10 years, based on an interest rate of 1% per annum. In July 2005 the ADB approved a $55m. grant to fund reconstruction of the 90-km section of this road between Qaisar and Bala Murghab. The completion date for both projects was June 2008.

In the mean time, in January 2003 the ADB had approved a grant of US $3m. from its Japan Fund for Poverty Reduction to support integrated community development programmes in northern Afghanistan. These programmes were to be undertaken along the road being repaired under the ADB's Emergency Infrastructure Rehabilitation and Reconstruction Project. Projects supported under this programme were to be implemented by NGOs.

At the Berlin Donors' Conference at the end of March 2004, the ADB announced that it would provide the Afghan Government with approximately US $800m. in highly concessional Asian Development Fund loans and grants for 2005–08. In addition, it had identified loan and equity investments of up to $100m. in partnership with local and foreign investors, as well as guarantees of about $100m. to encourage private-sector investments in Afghanistan.

In September 2004 the ADB published its Country Strategy and Program Update for 2004–06. This envisaged an allocation of US $570m. over three years for 12 programmes and projects; 50% of this allocation was to be provided in the form of grants. An additional $30m. in grant aid was to come from a special fund earmarked for technical assistance.

The planned areas of focus, which involved a considerable input of institutional support and technical assistance, included:

i) support for agricultural development, including rehabilitation of irrigation systems;

ii) rehabilitation of the electric power infrastructure, with particular attention given to the repair of power transmission and distribution lines and sub-stations;

iii) support for gas production, transmission and distribution;

iv) rehabilitation of national roads;

v) rehabilitation of regional airports;

vi) support for the development of the cellular telephone communications system;

vii) support for the governance process through public-service delivery reform;

viii) support for financial institutions, including the Afghanistan International Bank;

ix) programme support for financial market and private-sector development;

x) the provision of political risk guarantees to potential investors;

xi) support for an edible-oil processing venture in Mazar-i-Sharif;

xii) support for programmes aimed at improving air quality in Kabul.

In November 2004 the ADB approved a US $30m. concessional loan to help repair the airports at Bamian, Chaghcharan, Faizabad, Farah, Maymana, Qaleh-ye-Now and Zaranj. This aimed to increase access to some of the more remote areas of the country. In December 2004 the ADB approved a further loan, of $10m., to improve irrigation networks and water resource management in the Balkh river basin, to the west of Mazar-i-Sharif. In February 2005 the ADB announced that it had provided $500m. in grants and soft loans to Afghanistan during 2004. Annual assistance for 2005 and 2006 was projected to be $200m., at least one-half of which would be in the form of grants. In January 2005 the ADB stated that it had approved a technical assistance grant of $750,000 to help Afghanistan develop solar energy in remote rural areas. In April of that year it made a further allocation of $50m., part loan and part grant, to provide electricity supply in 11 rural areas: Breshna Kot, Imam Sahib, Jalalabad, Khan Abad, Mehter Lam, Muhammad Agha, Pul-i-Alam, Qarghayi, Sar-e Pol, Sarobi and Taloqan. Work was scheduled to be completed by June 2008. In December 2005 the ADB announced that it had approved the first part of a projected $105m. programme to reform Afghanistan's fiscal management and public administration systems. In January 2006 it announced the allocation of $75m. for the rehabilitation and upgrading of 55,000–65,000 traditional irrigation systems in the Hari Rud river basin, which includes part of Herat province, and the Murghab river basin, which is located in Badghis, Ghor and Herat provinces.

The project will also seek to strengthen the capacity of the Ministry of Water and Energy and of the *mirabs*, who are the traditional community-based managers of irrigation systems. Including this project, the ADB provided $235m. in loans and grants to Afghanistan during 2005. A total of $100m. of this figure was in the form of grants and the remainder in the form of highly concessional loans. In September 2006 the ADB advised that it had allocated $138.2m. for the rehabilitation of a 140.3-km section of the Mazar-e-Sharif to Dara-e-Suf road, in northern Afghanistan, and also for a 98.9-km section of the Bamian to Yakawlang road in central Afghanistan. Reconstruction work on these roads was scheduled to be completed by 2008. The ADB further advised, in 2008, that the ring road was scheduled for completion in 2010.

In December 2006 the ADB announced that it would be providing loans of US $35m. and $21.5m., respectively, to Afghanistan and Tajikistan to fund the construction of a 220-kilovolt double circuit transmission line, to connect the hydroelectric power stations on Tajikistan's Vakhsh River to the Afghan border town of Sherkan Bandar from where linkages to Kunduz, Baghlan, Pul-e-Khomri and Kabul would be developed. Other financiers of the project, which was expected to cost some $109.5m., are the OPEC Fund for International Development, the Islamic Development Bank, the Afghanistan Reconstruction Trust Fund and the Governments of Afghanistan and Tajikistan. Work was scheduled for completion in March 2009.

In June 2006 the IMF announced that it had approved a loan arrangement of around US $119m., under the Poverty Reduction and Growth Facility, to support Afghanistan's economic programme up to March 2009.

### The Role of Afghanistan's Neighbours

Iran has demonstrated a particular interest in developing strong political and economic links with Herat and, to this end, has completed reconstruction of the road between Herat and the Iranian border. In January 2005 President Karzai participated in the official opening of this road, together with the inauguration of a new power transmission line between Iran and Herat, also funded by Iran. The latter will complement another transmission line created in March 2004 and will further increase the potential for an expansion of manufacturing in the area. Among several joint projects under discussion, Iran plans to construct a cement factory in the country.

In November 2004 Iran inaugurated a new bridge and road linking the south-eastern town of Zaranj, in Nimroz province, to Iranian road networks and the Iranian port of Chabahar. This will link with a road that India is constructing from Zaranj to the main Herat–Qandahar highway at Delaram. However, Iran has halted work on a road from Herat to Badghis after completing only part of it.

In June 2005 Iran's commercial attaché to Afghanistan announced that 50 Iranian trade and service companies were active in Afghanistan. These companies produced potable water, medicine, polyethylene pipe, electrical switches, concrete, computers and liquid gas cylinder filling devices. He added that, out of the 35 countries investing in Afghanistan, Iran was the fourth largest. The Afghan Minister of Foreign Affairs attended a meeting of the Economic Co-operation Organization (ECO) in Tehran on 1 October 2005. Among the issues that he discussed with his Iranian counterpart was the role of the Iranian private sector in Afghanistan. Afghan businessmen in Herat were reported to have demanded that the Afghan Government erect tariff barriers against Iranian goods, stating that they were unable to compete in a situation in which the Iranian Government was providing subsidies for Iranian manufacturers.

It was reported in December 2005 that Iran planned to resurface roads in and around the city of Farah in western Afghanistan and also in Nimroz province. In addition, it intended to undertake further road improvement work in Herat province. President Karzai visited Iran in late May 2006, accompanied by nine cabinet ministers as well as by the Governors of the three provinces that border Iran (Herat, Farah and Nimroz). During this official visit, seven agreements were signed on Iranian participation in the reconstruction process (including railway construction), investment in Afghanistan, and cultural and scientific co-operation. The Iranian Government expressed its concerns regarding the flow of narcotics across the border and the quantity of water that reaches Iran's Sistan and Baluchestan province from Afghanistan's Helmand river. President Karzai noted that the volume of Iran's annual exports to Afghanistan had increased from US $50m. to $500m. over the previous four years, while Afghanistan exported only around $2m. worth of goods per annum to Iran. President Mahmoud Ahmadinejad of Iran commented that his country was seeking to develop co-operation with Afghanistan in the fields of agriculture, telecommunications, science and technology, transport, information technology, education and culture. At the same time, the head of the Iran-Afghanistan Chamber of Commerce demanded the implementation of specific measures to facilitate Iranian investment in industrial units in Afghanistan, including the improved processing of materials and machinery by customs offices and the introduction of a single policy on customs tariffs. It was also announced that a 150-km fibre-optic link had been put into operation between the Iranian town of Taibad and Herat. The project, which was financed by Iran, aimed further to strengthen links between Herat and international telecommunications networks.

In April 2007 the Iranian Government announced plans to construct a gas pipeline from Razavi Khorasan province in Iran to Herat province in Afghanistan. It also pledged to create a rail link from Sangan Khaf, where Iran has an iron-ore processing facility, to Herat, where an estimated 1,200m. metric tons of iron ore reserves are believed to exist. To date, Iran is estimated to have donated about US $600m. in aid to Afghanistan.

Agreement was reached with Turkmenistan in October 2003 for the latter to supply electricity to Torghundi and Herat in the north-west and Andkhoy in Faryab. This will complement the contribution that Iran has made to Herat's electricity supply. The Presidents of Afghanistan and Tajikistan laid the foundation stone, on 18 June 2005, for a US-funded bridge to be built over the Pyandzh river to connect Tajikistan to Kunduz province. It was planned that the bridge, which would take two years to complete, would carry electricity supplies from Tajikistan to Afghanistan. The energy ministers of Tajikistan, Iran and Afghanistan met in Dushanbe in February 2006 to discuss a project to build a high-voltage electricity transmission line from Tajikistan's Sangtuda hydroelectric power plant to Kunduz and Herat in Afghanistan and to Mashhad in Iran. This was scheduled for completion within five years.

India has sought to capitalize on the antipathy of many in the Afghan Government towards Pakistan (arising from Pakistan's former support for the Taliban) to build stronger political and economic ties. One example of its investment in Afghanistan is the provision of a number of, relatively aged, planes to Ariana Afghan Airlines. India has also taken the opportunity to negotiate a sea and road link to Central Asia, circumventing Pakistan, and in doing so has come to an agreement with Iran to transport goods to Chabahar in south-eastern Iran. To this end, Iran is strengthening transport links from Chabahar to the Afghan border. As noted above, India is constructing a new, 219-km road from this border crossing to connect with the major highway between Herat and Qandahar. Construction was originally expected to take two years. However, this road passes through unstable areas and construction has been impeded by poor security, including the killing of several Indian workers, and by harsh climatic conditions. By May 2008 80% of the new road had been completed and India's Border Roads Organisation announced that it hoped to finish the project by July. India is currently not allowed to transit goods across Pakistan to Afghanistan, and the indications are that Pakistan will not readily agree to such a concession. However, conversely, goods are permitted to transit Pakistan en route to India from Afghanistan.

India's Prime Minister, Dr Manmohan Singh, visited Kabul in late August 2005. A sum of US $50m. was pledged during the visit to supplement the more than $500m. that had already been allocated by India to projects relating to education, health care, power, transportation, aviation and telecommunications. It was also announced that Power Grid Corporation of India Ltd had been commissioned to construct a 220-km electricity transmission line from Pul-e-Khomri to Kabul and to erect a new electricity sub-station in the Afghan capital. The project was to be funded by the Indian Government and would enable Kabul to access power from Uzbekistan. Work was scheduled to be completed by February 2009.

In May 2008 it was estimated that, in addition to the Indian personnel engaged on the construction of the Zaranj to Delaram highway, about 3,300 Indian nationals were working on reconstruction projects in Afghanistan. Water and Power Consultancy Services (India) Ltd announced in January 2006 that Indian engineers had started work on the construction of the Salma Dam on the Hari Rud river. This was to transmit power to Herat, and so supplement the electricity that it already drew from Iran and Turkmenistan. The project was scheduled to be completed in four years.

During a five-day visit to New Delhi in April 2006, President Karzai signed agreements on Indian assistance to Afghanistan together with memoranda of understanding on rural development and education exchange programmes. He also attended meetings with India's leading industrial bodies, including the major IT companies, with a view to attracting further investment. In doing so, Karzai may have been hoping to build on the fact that many young Afghans have undertaken IT training in private institutes to compensate for the curtailment of their formal education. An additional US $50m. was pledged by the Indian Government during the visit, bringing the cumulative total committed to Afghanistan since 2001 to $600m. (by May 2008 this figure had risen to $850m.).

In April 2008 it was announced that the Afghan Ministry of Mines and Industries had signed a contract with two private-sector Indian companies to construct a metal-smelting factory in Mazar-i-Sharif. The factory, which would smelt scrap metal to produce girders, was expected to employ around 300 people.

In August 2006 Pakistan completed work on the 75-km road between Jalalabad and the Pakistan border. The Pakistan Government subsequently announced that it would provide the necessary capital to upgrade the road into a dual carriageway. The Pakistani Government has taken active steps to address its loss of political and economic influence in Afghanistan and has achieved a measure of success. According to IMF figures, the value of Pakistan's exports to Afghanistan increased significantly between 2003/04 and 2004/05, from US $181m. to $326m. The principal products exported were wheat, flour, rice, ghee, sugar, cement, paints, varnishes, mild steel products, sanitary wares, construction materials, electrical goods, medicines, other grains and pulses. In 2004/05 the IMF estimated that exports from Afghanistan to Pakistan were worth $258m. These included fresh fruit, dry fruit, spices, timber, scrap and plant-based medicines. In October 2006 the United States Institute of Peace reported that Pakistan's exports to Afghanistan totalled $1,200m. in 2005/06, while Afghanistan's exports to Pakistan had risen to $700m.

The Pakistani and Afghan Governments discussed a range of issues at a meeting of the Pakistan-Afghanistan Joint Economic Commission held in July 2005 in Kabul. Agreement was reached to establish a joint customs committee to streamline the procedures that continue considerably to hamper bilateral trade. Pakistan is currently creating a network of roads to connect Karachi Port, Port Qasim and Port Gwadar to Afghanistan. At the meeting, Pakistan announced a further grant of US $100m. for reconstruction efforts in Afghanistan. The projects supported by Pakistan include rehabilitation of the Torkham to Jalalabad road and the Ghulam Khan to Khost road. Additional assistance has been provided to specific projects aimed at strengthening the transport, education and health sectors. It was also announced in July 2005 that Pakistan and Afghanistan had signed a memorandum of understanding for Pakistan to supply electricity to Khost in south-eastern Afghanistan. It was further reported that Pakistan had agreed to allow an additional three items—namely, tyres and tubes, televisions and telephones—to enter Afghanistan without the imposition of tariffs. The three remaining items on which duty would continue to be levied were cigarettes, cooking oil and automobile parts. In May 2006 Pakistan's Minister of Railways advised that Afghan traders transporting their goods by rail from Karachi to Peshawar could now benefit from a 50% fare reduction. This decision was believed to be in response to a growing trend by traders to import goods through the port of Bandar Abbas in Iran owing to delays in the transfer of goods from Karachi.

In March 2004 it was announced that the Chinese Government had agreed to rebuild a major irrigation project 50 km to the north of Kabul. This was originally completed, with funding from China, in the 1970s, but had since fallen into disrepair, exacerbated by war damage. The project, which will benefit 24,800 ha, was expected to cost US $10m. Work was due to start at the end of that month and was expected to last two years. In July 2005 the Afghan Minister of Communications stated that the digital wireless network currently operating in Kabul would be extended to the provinces by the end of the year to facilitate internet access across the country. Two Chinese telecommunications companies—ZPE and Huaway—had been contracted to build the network. In November 2007 the Afghan Government awarded rights to operate the Aynak copper mine to the state-owned China Metallurgical Group Corporation.

President Karzai addressed a conference in Kabul in early May 2006 aimed at encouraging investment in the economy. He cited as potential areas of investment agri-business, communications, mines and industry. In connection with the conference, the Vice-President of the Government's Afghanistan Investment Support Agency noted that most of the investors registering over the previous two years were from Turkey, China, Pakistan and Iran. During a visit to Abu Dhabi in late May President Karzai invited UAE investors to participate in the proposed construction project of a gas pipeline from Turkmenistan to Afghanistan, Pakistan and India. He also invited UAE businessmen to invest in other sectors, including building, communications and banking. An announcement was made simultaneously that the Abu Dhabi company Etisalat had been granted a licence to operate Afghanistan's fourth GSM mobile network.

It is important to note that Afghanistan has not been invited to participate in the Shanghai Co-operation Organization (SCO), which was created in June 2001 and is composed of representatives from Russia, China, Kazakhstan, Kyrgyzstan, Tajikistan and Uzbekistan. Observer status has been granted to Iran, India, Pakistan and Mongolia. Although this body represents largely a defensive arrangement, aimed to counter US influence in the region, it also provides its members with economic benefits, Thus, for example, Iran is currently in active discussions with Pakistan and India to export natural gas via a pipeline through Pakistan and with China to supply gas from the Yadavaran oilfield. There is therefore considerable economic and political activity between Afghanistan's immediate neighbours while it remains, in many respects, an economic backwater. However, an SCO-Afghanistan Contact Group was established in November 2005, and serves as a mechanism for SCO member states to contribute jointly to reconstruction and the restoration of stability in Afghanistan.

### Strategies to Address Poverty

For the duration of the conflict, Afghanistan was, on the basis of the normal poverty indicators, one of the poorest countries in the world. The 2004 report *Securing Afghanistan's Future* (see above) placed emphasis on the low socio-economic base from which progress has to be made. Among the indicators noted were the average maternal mortality rate of 1,600 deaths per 100,000 live births (increasing to 6,500 deaths in Badakhshan) and the rate of chronic malnutrition (moderate and severe stunting) of around 50%. According to WHO, life expectancy at birth was 41 years for males and 42 for females in 2003. The UN Children's Fund (UNICEF) estimated illiteracy levels in 1996 to be 52.8% for males and 85.0% for females. In February 2005 UNDP published its National Human Development Report on Afghanistan for 2004. This ranked Afghanistan 173rd out of 178 countries assessed. The level of diarrhoeal disease remains extremely high, as does the incidence of respiratory infections, including tuberculosis, together with malaria, measles and leishmaniasis. Women have been heavily burdened by early marriage and multiple pregnancies, which have adversely affected their health. Tuberculosis is a particular problem for women because they spend long hours in confined spaces. Societal taboos on women leaving the home without the permission of the husband's family, combined with restrictions placed on mobility under the Taliban regime, have meant that women have not benefited from equal access to health care. As expected, the drought of 1999–2002 weakened resistance to disease while it was at its worst. In addition, land-mine injuries occur at an alarming level and would have an even more damaging impact on economic activity if it were not for the surgical and prosthetic services provided by the International Committee of the Red Cross (ICRC) and a number of NGOs. In August 2006 the United Nations Assistance Mission in Afghanistan (UNAMA) reported that more than 1,000m. sq m of land had been cleared of mines since 1989, leaving a total of 720m. sq m still to be cleared. It added that, on average, 60 Afghans were killed or injured each month by mines or unexploded ordnance, compared with 140 in 2001. In January 2008 the UN reported that, according to statistics from the UN Mine Action Centre for Afghanistan, a total of 143 people were killed and 438 wounded by mines and unexploded ordnance in 2007. UN agencies, the ICRC and NGOs have largely been responsible for addressing food insecurity, the relative absence of clean water and constraints on access to health care and education both during and after the conflict.

The impact of the conflict would have been even more serious if the population had not been able to retreat into subsistence agriculture, the informal economy and take advantage of employment options in neighbouring countries. The ability of the aid community to provide relief commodities to vulnerable districts and households has also been an important element in averting famine and destitution during the periods of greatest economic misfortune, such as the drought.

WFP has worked with NGOs to distribute free food and to support programmes for public works through Food for Work or FOODAC (Food for Asset Creation). WFP reported that during 2005 about 4,000 km of roads and 500 km of canals were constructed or repaired through food-for-work programmes aimed at vulnerable households. UNICEF and WHO have similarly worked with NGOs to organize vaccination programmes and support networks of primary health care clinics, and to tackle diseases such as cholera, tuberculosis, measles, polio and leishmaniasis. UN Habitat has worked in the urban areas to improve waste disposal. In December 2003 the ICRC handed over to the local authorities a reconstructed water-supply system that served 150,000 people in north-west Kabul. The Danish NGO DACAAR has created a nation-wide network of covered shallow wells to provide access to clean water. The work undertaken by NGOs and UN agencies over the years to improve wells, piped water systems, sanitation and drainage will hopefully have mitigated the effects of the drought, but long-term solutions need to be found for effective water harvesting and management.

In March 2003 the Afghan Ministry of Public Health introduced the Basic Package of Health Services, which aimed to provide services that have the greatest impact on the major health problems, are cost-effective in addressing these and provide equal access to both rural and urban populations. The key areas of focus were maternal and newborn health, child health and immunization, public nutrition, communicable diseases and the supply of essential drugs. Mental health and disability were identified as second-tier priorities to be addressed when resources allowed. Delivery was through outreach by community health workers, outpatient care at basic health centres and inpatient care at comprehensive health centres and district hospitals. Implementation was by a combination of Ministry of Public Health personnel, NGOs and private-sector organizations, with the latter working under contract to the Ministry to provide the services in designated areas.

As a consequence of these programmes, the health status of the population is probably better now than it was before the 1978 coup. The refugee populations in Iran and Pakistan will also have had easy access to (relatively high quality, in the case of Iran) clinics in the urban areas and camps. The role of the British Broadcasting Corporation's Pashto and Persian Services in transmitting health messages through radio programmes and other means has been enormously important. Vaccination campaigns against measles, polio and tetanus have regularly been organized. Efforts to address the high incidence of tetanus during childbirth were expected to have been augmented by the opening, in 2003, of two new centres for maternal health in Kabul and Jalalabad. A salt iodination plant was opened in January 2004 in Shiberghan, in northern Afghanistan, to help reduce the incidence of iodine-deficiency disorders, which include still births, goitre, cretinism and severe hearing problems. In March 2007 WHO reported that the number of people being treated for tuberculosis had increased from 9,500 in 2001 to 25,443 (16,538 of whom were women) in 2006. The organization claimed that this increase could possibly be explained by the dramatic improvement in the detection and diagnoses of the illness. The number of polio cases decreased from 137 in 1997, when the annual immunization campaign was launched, to five in 2004. The number of cases increased to nine in 2005, however, and by August 2006 a total of 26 cases had already been reported since the beginning of that year. These cases were localized to the southern provinces where the ongoing insurgency had seriously constrained aid operations. In April 2007 UNICEF announced that nearly 7.3m. children had been vaccinated against polio during a nation-wide campaign carried out in the same month. In August 2006 the Ministry of Public Health reported that more than 11,000 people had died during the previous year from hepatitis B, which was alleged to be spreading rapidly. Measures were being taken to vaccinate children against the illness.

In April 2007 UNAMA announced that, according to the preliminary findings of a survey conducted by the Johns Hopkins University (JHU) of Maryland, USA, infant mortality rates in Afghanistan had declined from an estimated 165 per 1,000 live births in 2001 to about 135 per 1,000 in 2006. The survey also found that the proportion of women receiving antenatal care increased from 5% in 2003 to 30% in 2006, and that the proportion of couples using a modern form of family planning had risen from 5% to 15% over the same period. Similarly, the proportion of pregnant women who had been attended by a skilled health worker increased by 5% to nearly 19%. An assessment by the JHU of more than 600 Afghan health facilities each year since 2004 had indicated a 25% improvement in the overall quality of health services.

In April 2006 FAO announced that the H5N1 strain of bird flu had been detected in two provinces in the vicinity of Kabul. In November the Afghan Government advised that the country was free of bird flu. However, in February and March 2007 new outbreaks of the disease were reported in Kabul and in the eastern provinces of Nangarhar and Kunar. The Government responded by culling poultry, disinfecting and quarantining affected areas, undertaking vaccination campaigns and placing a ban on imports of poultry from Pakistan.

NGOs have worked over many years to provide support for primary education. The Afghan Government has been able to assume increasing responsibility for this provision since the beginning of 2002. A report published by Oxfam in November 2006 found that the number of children attending school had increased from 1m. in 2001 to 5m. in 2006. However, 7m. children were still not attending school. The report added that only one in every five girls was attending primary school and that only one in 20 was attending secondary school. In March 2007 UNICEF estimated that 6m. children had enrolled at the start of the new academic year. Notably, around 2m. of these pupils were girls; female attendance at school, however, varied significantly throughout the country. Enrolment rates for girls were as high as 50% in Kabul and Herat, but in the southern provinces of Uruzgan and Zabul, the rates were estimated to be less than 10%.

It should be stressed that the various strategies that continue to be adopted to address poverty will not help people reach more than a minimal level of survival without a sustainable improvement in the wider economy. It should also be noted that the ability of NGOs and the UN to provide the various services outlined above has been increasingly constrained by the orchestrated campaign of terrorism in Afghanistan that followed the US-led military intervention in Iraq of March 2003. More than 80 aid workers have been killed and large areas of the country are considered too dangerous to operate in.

### Agricultural Trends

Agriculture represented 60% of GDP before 1978, while rural trade and handicrafts accounted for a further 25%. Wheat represented 40% of crop production. The other major crops were barley, corn, rice, vegetables and fruit. In 1989 the UN reported agriculture to be the primary source of income for 85% of the population. According to the UN Environment Programme (UNEP), in the early 2000s the agricultural population had decreased to 78% of the total, owing to the continuing process of migration to the urban areas as well as the desertification process. The urban population continues to grow. In 2004 it was estimated to be 30% and was projected to double by 2015. Calculation of the rural population is, however, complicated by the fact that families are diversifying their income sources so that some family members work on the land while others seek work in the cities or in one of the neighbouring countries.

As mentioned above, livestock provides an important source of income and is a significant asset. The drought of 1999–2002 had a devastating effect on livestock numbers, but evidence in mid-2003 indicated that the stock was replenishing itself more quickly than anticipated. However, following the publication in December 2003 of preliminary results of the first livestock census ever conducted in Afghanistan, FAO commented that it could take up to 10 years for the animal herds in Afghanistan to regenerate naturally following the recent drought. The main livestock types are sheep, goats and cattle. Pastureland covers 45% of the total land area.

A significant proportion of the population does not own land; many people own land that is not sufficient for their survival. These members of the community, therefore, have to enter into sharecropping or tenancy arrangements or provide their labour to others. Moreover, a survey undertaken in 2002 found that 2.2% of the population owned 19% of the total land area. Landlord–tenant and sharecropping arrangements are most common in the fertile plains around Qandahar, while farmers in the mountainous east and north-east are more likely to possess their own land. The exodus of more than 6m. refugees and the internal displacement of further millions at one point in the conflict or another, have complicated land entitlement issues and have led to land disputes as refugees and displaced people return. Many farmers have, however, retained access to their land, particularly those in areas relatively close to the borders with Pakistan and Iran. The drought, though, forced many to sell or mortgage their land, creating increased vulnerability and growing debt.

The 1.9m. metric tons of cereal produced in 2000, at the height of the drought of 1999–2002, can usefully be compared with the 3.85m. tons produced in 1998, following six years of sustained agricultural improvement. WFP estimated in September 2002 that cereal production in that year was to reach 3.59m. tons, only marginally lower than the 1998 level. The food assessment mission undertaken by WFP and FAO in July 2003 concluded that the total harvest was likely to be 5.37m. tons in 2003, the best for 25 years. Sustained and good rainfall since September 2002 had allowed farmers to plant a much larger area than before, and the use of new, high-yielding varieties of grain and the widespread use of fertilizer had also contributed to the rise in production. However, a continuation of the drought in some southern provinces meant that, while northern Afghanistan would have a large surplus of crops, the south of the country might still experience some deficit. It was forecast that the bumper crop would include 4.36m. tons of wheat, 410,000 tons of barley, 310,000 tons of maize and 291,000 tons of milled rice. The FAO/WFP assessment team stressed that there remained pockets of malnutrition in the country and that the benefits of the improved economic and agricultural situation were not reaching all households. Relief assistance would still, therefore, be needed for a considerable number of Afghans who faced food shortages. It stated that the demand for this would be gauged through the National Risk and Vulnerability Assessment (NRVA) that was being undertaken by the Afghan Government.

The preliminary findings of the NRVA for 2003 were published in December and indicated that, out of an estimated 16m. rural Afghans, 3.2m. would not be able to meet 80% of their minimum food requirements. The highest proportion of these were located in the south and east of the country, primarily in districts affected by insecurity, adverse climatic conditions and limited employment opportunities. This population was to be targeted by the National Emergency Employment Programme and WFP's food assistance interventions. The assessment found that the major priorities for rural households were water, access to health facilities, roads and access to education. The increased cost of fuel and electricity during the winter months was also a major concern. The NRVA was carried out by the Ministry of Rural Rehabilitation and Development, the Ministry of Agriculture, Irrigation and Livestock, the Ministry of Public Health and the Ministry of Women's Affairs, with support from the UN, the World Bank, the Afghanistan Research and Evaluation Unit, DFID and the NGO partners of the National Surveillance System.

FAO announced in July 2003 that, in conjunction with the Ministry of Agriculture, Irrigation and Livestock and the NGO GOAL (from Ireland), it had been able to minimize damage to the wheat crop caused by a locust plague which it described as the most severe in living memory. The FAO/WFP Crop and Food Supply Assessment Mission to Afghanistan undertaken in 2004 found that agricultural production had suffered a sharp decline, owing to reduced precipitation in some areas and drought in others. The aggregate cereal harvest for 2004 was estimated at 3.06m. metric tons, which represented a reduction of 43% compared with the 2003 harvest. Early indications suggested that the situation would be much improved in 2005, due to the significant level of snowfall and heavy rains in the early part of that year.

The NRVA for 2005 found that 5.5m. Afghans were extremely poor and chronically food insecure. A further 8.5m. were seasonally food insecure. In addition, around 400,000 people each year were seriously affected by natural disasters such as droughts, floods, earthquakes and extreme weather conditions. WFP estimated that the cereal harvest in 2005 was 4.36m. metric tons and that agricultural production in that year was equivalent to 47.2% of GDP.

In October 2006 FAO reported that wheat production for 2006, estimated at 3.71m. metric tons, was 13% lower than that achieved in 2005. This decrease was attributed to lower than average rainfall and higher temperatures. The areas exhibiting the greatest potential for growth in the agricultural sector were reported to be: horticulture, intensive livestock rearing, the production of cotton, sugar beet and cereals, forestry and rangeland livestock. It was hoped that the introduction of high-value crops—such as perfume, medicinal and aromatic plants—would stimulate the further growth and diversification of agricultural activities. On the negative side, however, the expanding forestry sector was reported to have caused rapid deforestation, with only 2% of the land remaining covered by forest.

In November 2007 the online publication *New Agriculturist* reported that wheat production in Afghanistan decreased to 3.11m. metric tons in 2007. In June 2008 UNAMA projected that the output of wheat and other cereals would fall significantly in 2008 owing to low levels of rainfall and prevailing drought conditions.

### Industrial Potential

According to the UN, the industrial sector (including mining, manufacturing, power and construction) provided 20% of GDP in 1993. Manufacturing has continued to be dominated by relatively small-scale enterprises linked to the agricultural sector. Many such industries are engaged in the processing of food products, such as flour, sugar and vegetable oil. Other branches in the manufacturing industry include textiles, carpets, leather products and handicrafts. Woodwork shops, motor workshops and construction-related activity have also been very much in evidence, subject to fluctuations in the economy.

An important area of potential for industrial expansion would appear to lie in the manufacture of carpets for export. About 500,000 Afghans were reported to be involved in the carpet business in Pakistan prior to 2002, under arrangements with department stores in Western capitals; the NDF expressed its intention to re-link Afghan producers with a number of large department stores. Meanwhile, a number of countries, including the USA and the members of the EU, have removed barriers to imports from Afghanistan. The Deputy Special Representative of the UN Secretary-General in Afghanistan, Nigel Fisher, announced in July 2003 that 400 production units for Afghan carpets had returned in the previous 18 months from Pakistan and were operating in Afghanistan and exporting the goods world-wide. The production of raisins and other dried fruits for export had also recommenced. The Afghan Minister of Finance announced in February 2004 that 'textile parks' would be established in Jalalabad and Qandahar to produce textile items under special quotas for export to the USA. The parks would also be used to facilitate the transport of cotton from the Commonwealth of Independent States to Pakistan. It was reported in December 2004 that, with funding from the German Government, FAO planned to rehabilitate the country's only sugar factory, in Baghlan, which ceased operations in the late 1970s. In December 2006 it was announced that the factory had begun production and was employing 120 people.

In August 2003 it was announced that a contract had been signed between the Afghan Government and two of China's major telecommunications equipment manufacturers to improve and enlarge fixed-line telephone networks in Kabul and in eight provincial cities. The two companies had already started work on the networks in Kabul and Qandahar during the Taliban's period in power.

Initiatives to create a cellular telephone network commenced from the beginning of 2002. The US newspaper *Investor's Business Daily* reported, in March 2005, that Afghanistan's largest mobile supplier, Roshan, had 450,000 subscribers. In second place was the Afghan Wireless Communication Company (AWCC), with about 260,000 subscribers. In April 2006 Roshan reported that the number of its subscribers had increased to 750,000, almost double that of AWCC. Its operations covered 27 of the 34 provinces and 150 urban and district centres. The company noted that it employed 700 people and estimated that it provided work to an additional 14,000 people through contractual and commercial arrangements. Roshan stated that it was also the largest tax payer, providing US $25m. in 2005, equivalent to 5% of the national budget. Roshan is 51% owned by the Aga Khan Development Network, with 36.75% held by Monaco Telecom International and 12.25% by the Afghan-US group, MCT. AWCC is 80% owned by US-based Telephone Systems International, Inc, while the Afghan Government's Ministry of Communications owns the remaining 20%. At a conference on information and communications technology held in Kabul in late April 2006, UNDP reported that by the end of 2006 fixed wireless telephone lines would reach 285,000 users in Afghanistan to allow both voice and data exchange. In July 2006 it was announced that a third cell-phone company, Areeba, had commenced operations, while another company, Etisalat (of the UAE), was due to start shortly. In February 2007 the Afghan Government advised that licences had been issued to two new telecommunications companies, Shaheen and Irtibat, which were to provide services in the provinces of Herat, Loghar, Khost and Paktia. A third company, Wasil Telecom, was given a licence to operate in Kunduz.

An initiative to establish a national fibreoptic cable network was formally inaugurated in April 2007. The 3,131-km network was to be constructed by a Chinese communications company, the Zhong Xing Telecommunication Equipment Company Limited (ZTE), and was to connect most provinces as well as linking with Pakistan, Iran, Uzbekistan and Turkmenistan. The network, when completed, will have the potential to provide audio, video and data transfer services and will greatly strengthen telephone communications and access to the internet. Work on the project was scheduled to take 26 months.

In July 2005 UNDP announced that a factory was being established in Kabul to produce generic medicines. The factory, which was scheduled to commence production by the end of that year, would be Afghan-owned. Support has been given by the Business Humanitarian Forum, the Brussels-based European Generic Medicines Association and UNDP. Funding has been provided by the German Government and a German finance institute.

A new asphalt-producing plant was inaugurated by the Mayor of Kabul in July 2005. Equipment for the plant was made in India and donated by USAID. In April 2006 the Afghan Government announced that it was encouraging increased investment in the production of cement, in the wake of Pakistan's recent ban on cement exports, to meet local demand and control prices. Afghanistan already had a number of cement factories the capacity of which could be enhanced through greater investment. Pakistan was encountering unprecedented domestic demand owing to the devastating earthquake of October 2005. In July 2006 the Government further advised that licences had been issued for the construction of four new private-sector cement factories, the combined production of which was projected to provide around one-half of Afghanistan's total requirements. One of the factories was to be located in Pul-e-Khomri, which already has a small cement factory, and another in Herat. In February 2007 Pajhwok Afghan News reported that foreign investment in Herat had increased by US $15m., compared with the previous year. It noted that this investment, which was mainly focused on the industrial, construction and public-service sectors, had primarily originated from businesses and individuals in Iran, Germany, Turkey and the USA. The Herat industrial zone was reported to have more than 200 factories, employing 13,000 people and producing motorcycles, tractors, electrical instruments, food products and fruit juices. A $25m. Coca Cola bottling plant, which was financed by a Dubai-based Afghan family, was formally opened in Kabul in September 2006.

In January 2007 the Afghan Government announced that it planned to sell off 54 of the 63 remaining state-owned enterprises over the following three years. These businesses included firms in the dried fruit, wool, machinery and fertilizer sectors. Enterprises that were to be retained within the state-sector were involved in transport, power, water, accommodation, prisons and agricultural plants.

**Mining and Energy**

Afghanistan has extensive resources of coal, salt, chromium, iron ore, silver, gold, fluorite, talc, mica, copper and lapis lazuli, but the costs of extraction have obstructed any significant commercial investment. Even the mining of lapis lazuli, which has provided an important source of income for particular regional commanders in north-east Afghanistan, would benefit from more sophisticated techniques. The NDF envisaged that the Transitional Administration would carry out a full geological survey of Afghanistan to provide information on the use and development of precious stones. In March 2007 the British Geological Survey (BGS) reported on work that it had undertaken, alongside the Afghanistan Geological Survey, to scan, digitize and reinterpret data produced by Russian geologists during the late 1970s and 1980s on the Aynak copper deposit, (located 35 km south of Kabul). The total reserves of copper were estimated at 4.7m. metric tons and international firms were invited to tender for investment in the deposit. Companies from Australia, Canada, China, India, Kazakhstan, Russia and the USA all expressed interest in the venture. The BGS also helped the Afghan Ministry of Mines and Industries to draft a new Mining Law in 2005, to enable better regulation of the mining industry. In November 2007 the Afghan Government awarded the rights to work the Aynak copper mine to the China Metallurgical Group Corporation, which announced plans to invest about US $3,000m. in the mining project.

The most successful find has been of natural gas in northern Afghanistan. In 1980 a new complex for the extraction and purification of gas became operational at Jarquduq, with an annual capacity of 2,000m. cu m. During the 1980s and early 1990s natural gas was Afghanistan's major export commodity, and, according to the IMF, accounted for about 24% of total export income in 1988/89. Up until 1991 90% of the output was transported by pipeline to the USSR. Production halted for an extended period, although it is not clear whether it ceased immediately after the collapse of the Soviet-supported Government in April 1992 or continued until the first Taliban attack on Mazar-i-Sharif in May 1997 set in motion a period of instability. Gas reserves were estimated at 150,000m. cu m in 2002, whereas petroleum reserves from six oilfields were thought to amount to only 12m. metric tons. Gas production has resumed since the Bonn Agreement of December 2001, but only at a minimal level.

However, following the completion of a four-year assessment, the US Geological Survey and the Afghan Ministry of Mines and Industries reported in mid-March 2006 that two geological basins in northern Afghanistan held 18 times the petroleum and triple the natural gas resources previously believed. They thus estimated that almost 1.6m. barrels of petroleum, mainly in the Afghan-Tajik Basin but also in Herat, Helmand and Paktika, together with about 4,000m. cu m of natural gas, primarily in the Amu-Dar'ya Basin, could be tapped. The assessment, which was funded by the independent US Trade and Development Agency, covered only one-sixth of the 518,000 sq km of the two basins that lie within Afghanistan. Further work remains to be undertaken to assess petroleum reserves, conduct seismic exploration and rehabilitate wells. Afghanistan's ambassador to the USA stated, in an interview, that companies could start developing the oil and gas fields within two to three years. In October 2006 the Afghan Minister of Mines and Industries stated that he had met US officials and investors to discuss investment and technical support in the oil and gas fields and added that the process of privatization of the Jowzjan field would commence in the near future. In December it was announced that a US company, Professional Construction Services Network, had agreed to join forces with a Russian company, RUMO, 'to help the Government of Afghanistan reopen and redevelop its oil and gas fields'. Two Afghan companies were also scheduled to participate in the venture.

Hard coal production, centred at Pul-e-Khomri in northern Afghanistan, reached 167,000 metric tons in 1987, aided by considerable investment in coal-mining equipment, supplied by Czechoslovakia. However, one year later, production decreased by 17.4% and by 1996 annual production had plummeted to only 4,000 tons. An estimated 1,700m. tons of high-grade iron ore are to be found at Hajigak in Bamian province; however, much of it is located at heights of 3,500 m or more. In August 2006 the Afghan Minister of Mines and Industries noted that Turkey was already investing in Afghan mines and that the United Kingdom was about to commence a mining project in Afghanistan. In October the minister announced that contracts had been agreed with the private sector regarding the Karkar-e-Dodkash coal mine in Baghlan, a fluoride mine in Uruzgan, a gold mine in Herat and a precious stones mine in Nuristan.

Hydroelectricity constituted 80% of Afghanistan's energy resources under the Soviet-supported regime. The first hydroelectric power station began operating at Asadabad, in eastern Afghanistan, in 1983. The construction of the large Sarobi hydroelectric dam on the Kabul River was still under way in 1991 when the USSR collapsed. It has since provided the primary source of power for Kabul, albeit on the basis of an extremely curtailed and erratic supply compounded by war damage and heavily constrained access to spare parts. In August 2006 the Afghan Minister of Water and Energy claimed that Afghanistan was only able to produce 240 MW of electrical energy per year against a requirement of 1,000 MW. He added that the country had the untapped potential to produce 3,000 MW of hydroelectric power and 1,000 MW of thermoelectric power every year. In November an agreement was reached with Uzbekistan for the latter to supply electricity to Afghanistan; the electricity was to be transmitted to Kabul. In May 2007 USAID announced that it had allocated US $180m. to rehabilitate the Kajaki Dam in the southern province of Helmand, as well as the power lines that supplied electricity to Lashkar Gah and Qandahar. Work on the project was delayed, however, by counter-insurgency operations in the area.

The ADB has played a leading role in investigating the possibility of constructing pipelines across Afghanistan to transport gas from the Dauletabad gas fields in south-east Turkmenistan to markets in Afghanistan, Pakistan and, possibly, India. This project had been under consideration since 1996, but interest has fluctuated owing to complex political, security and market-related developments. However, the Governments of Afghanistan, Pakistan and Turkmenistan signed a framework agreement for development of the project in December 2002, and the ADB, thereafter, invited interested parties to submit, by 29 May 2003, expressions of interest for participation in the project. The invitation to bid noted that the pipeline would be 'designed, constructed, owned, operated and maintained by a consortium led by an internationally reputed oil and gas company, or an association of companies, that has the technical and financial capacity, and the experience, to undertake this work'. It added that an independent pipeline company would be established, the shares of which would be held by the selected international oil and gas company or a consortium, the three Governments, developmental financial institutions, commercial financial institutions and other interested parties. The ADB would assist interested consortium members to mobilize financial resources. The ADB estimated the final cost of the project to be between US $2,000m. and $2,500m.

The ADB outlined proposals received from potential sponsors and international financial institutions to a meeting of representatives of Afghanistan, Pakistan and Turkmenistan in the Turkmen capital, Aşgabat, on 26 June 2003. It also presented a preliminary feasibility study on the gas pipeline. The meeting discussed draft agreements on the sale and purchase of gas, transport and the partner countries' obligations. However, in July the ADB announced that the prequalification process had been postponed to assess the viability of an alternative route through southern Afghanistan, which would transit Herat, Qandahar and the Pakistani cities of Quetta and Multan. The Steering Committee for the proposed project, comprising oil and gas ministers from the three countries, had hitherto been focusing on a route through the north, travelling past Mazar-i-Sharif, Kabul and Jalalabad to the Pakistani border, from where it would transit Peshawar, Islamabad and Lahore. The Steering Committee also asked for an estimate of reserves in the Daulatabad gas fields in Turkmenistan, as the latter had recently signed a 25-year gas supply agreement with Russia which gave Russia effective control of Turkmen gas and of its transportation and marketing. India, which had come under pressure from Turkmenistan, Afghanistan and Pakistan to join the project in order to increase its financial viability, announced at the end of July 2003 that it had rejected a proposal by the ADB to extend the pipeline into its own territory, citing security concerns. A spokesman stated that it was considering importing natural gas from Iran, which would involve the construction of an offshore pipeline.

Interest in the pipeline project subsequently appeared to wane. A considerable period of time passed before the ADB announced, in September 2005, that the gas reserves in Turkmenistan had proved to be smaller than expected and that the delivery of gas from Turkmenistan's Daulatabad field to Pakistan and India, through a trans-Afghanistan pipeline, might not be possible. The ADB stated that Turkmenistan would be able to meet the proposed target of 30,000m. cu m of gas exports to South Asia for the first few years, after construction of a pipeline, but that production was predicted subsequently to decline.

In mid-January 2006 Pakistan and Afghanistan held ministerial-level talks in Islamabad on the pipeline. These were followed by a visit, in mid-February, by energy officials from Afghanistan, Pakistan and India to Aşgabat, Turkmenistan, to discuss related options. India, at this point, appeared to be shifting its position in favour of full participation. This may have been due, in part, to US concerns over the alternative pipeline route from Iran that India had been actively exploring. The USA is believed to be supporting the trans-Afghanistan pipeline, but the nature of its involvement is not clear.

At the meeting in Aşgabat, a memorandum of understanding was signed according to which Turkmenistan undertook to supply 90.5m. cu m of gas per day to Pakistan for a 30-year period. In June 2006 the Indian Government was set to consider a proposal by the Indian Ministry of Petroleum and Natural Gas that it should participate in the pipeline project. However, in September the President of Turkmenistan expressed doubt about the proposed pipeline across Afghanistan, and stated that priority would be given to the supply of gas to Russia, which in May 2007 was reportedly drafting an agreement that would guarantee its purchase of 85% of

Turkmenistan's gas exports until 2028. Iran was expected to maintain its position as a residual market for Turkmenistan's gas exports and the trans-Afghanistan pipeline proposal appeared likely to be abandoned.

In the light of these developments, it is difficult to know what weight to give to an agreement signed on 24 April 2008 between the oil ministers of Turkmenistan, Afghanistan, Pakistan and India to commence construction work on the trans-Afghanistan pipeline in 2010. Concerns remain regarding the ability of the Turkmen Government to guarantee a sufficient quantity of gas to justify the investment that would be required in the construction of the pipeline. The volatile security situation in Afghanistan also continues to dominate the talks between the four governments. In addition, discussions are ongoing regarding the installation of an alternative pipeline to bring gas from Iran to Pakistan and India. Even if the pipeline across Afghanistan were constructed, additional supplies of natural gas would be required from other sources.

### Trade, Balance of Payments and Finance

Throughout the 1970s, the balance of payments showed a surplus, owing to tourism and remittances from Afghans working abroad. The principal export items at that time were fresh fruit and vegetables, natural gas, karakul skins and wool, carpets and rugs, raw cotton, dried fruit and nuts. Imports included machinery, petroleum, pharmaceuticals, textiles and other consumer goods. Heavy dependence on the USSR as a trading partner in 1978–92 caused the total value of exports to decline sharply, from US $284m. in 1991 to $60m. in 1992. Similarly, the cost of imports decreased from $765m. in 1991 to $237m. in 1992. The increase in trade generated by the Taliban caused the value of exports to increase, by 1996/97, to $125m. and imports to $496m. The major export commodities at that time included fruits and nuts, hand-woven carpets, wool, hides and pelts, and precious and semi-precious gems. The most important export markets were Pakistan, Western Europe and the USA. The major import commodities were food, petroleum products and other consumer goods. The principal sources of imports were Singapore, Japan and Western Europe.

In November 2005 the Afghan Minister of Commerce announced that Afghanistan had launched its accession process to the World Trade Organization. It currently has observer status. In April 2004 and November 2005 Afghanistan hosted meetings of the ECO, aimed at strengthening trade and economic co-operation in the region. President Karzai attended a meeting of ECO in Baku, Azerbaijan, in May 2006. The 10 members of ECO are Afghanistan, Azerbaijan, Iran, Kazakhstan, Kyrgyzstan, Pakistan, Tajikistan, Turkey, Turkmenistan and Uzbekistan. ECO was established by Iran, Pakistan and Turkey in 1985. It was announced in November 2005 that Afghanistan had joined the Central Asia Regional Economic Cooperation (CAREC) programme. CAREC now brings together Azerbaijan, Afghanistan, China, Kazakhstan, Kyrgyzstan, Mongolia, Tajikistan and Uzbekistan. The programme was set up in 1997, with the support of the ADB, with the aim of strengthening regional economic co-operation through improvements in transport links (especially by road), energy, trade policy and trade facilitation (particularly customs co-operation). Afghanistan was also admitted to the South Asian Association for Regional Co-operation (SAARC) in April 2007. This organization comprises representatives of India, Bangladesh, Pakistan, Sri Lanka, Maldives, Nepal and Bhutan and seeks to strengthen economic integration within the region.

The Afghan and British Governments co-chaired a regional economic conference held in Kabul in early December 2006. The conference was attended by representatives of Tajikistan, Uzbekistan, Turkmenistan, Iran, Pakistan, China, India, Turkey, the UAE, Kazakhstan and Kyrgyzstan and was aimed at encouraging an increased level of trade. Following the conference, the delegates jointly agreed to co-operate in a number of areas, including the supply of electricity to Afghanistan, trade, water resource management and counter-narcotics.

In January 2007 the ADB announced a grant of US $1.2m. to help the Afghan Government to facilitate trade, through a harmonization of customs procedures and laws with its neighbours, a concerted campaign against corruption, the promotion of private-sector involvement and the improvement of transit arrangements.

In mid-2003 the Transitional Administration was endeavouring to raise US $200m. in internal revenues. A major part of this sum was to be derived from customs revenues, subject to the various regional commanders handing over receipts to the central Government. Income was also secured through overflight rights. The Transitional Administration announced in April 2004 that it was planning to introduce personal income tax, together with road tolls and agricultural land tax. These would supplement the taxes already introduced on money changing, rents above $300 per month, snuff and tobacco. In September 2005 it was announced that the Afghan Government had adopted a law on income tax which required that all Afghans, as well as foreign nationals working in Afghanistan, were liable to pay tax on their earnings above a specified level.

In 1975 the Afghan Government nationalized all banks; however, the banking system effectively ceased to function following the collapse of the Soviet-supported Government in April 1992. Since then, financial transfers have been largely carried out through the 'hawala' system, using informal networks, and through the informal money market for foreign-exchange transfers. However, a number of international banks have established branches in Afghanistan since late 2003. These include the National Bank of Pakistan and the Standard Chartered Bank. The National Bank of Pakistan announced in February 2004 that it would open new branches in Jalalabad and Qandahar in the first half of the year to supplement the branch already operating in Kabul. Authority was given by the Afghan Transitional Administration in August 2003 for two Iranian banks—the Central Bank of Iran and Bank Saderat Iran—to open branches in Afghanistan. Iran's Aryan Bank opened a branch in Kabul in December 2004.

The NDF provides for the re-establishment of a functioning central bank, a competitive commercial banking sector and non-banking financial services including micro-finance, credit unions, insurance and pensions.

### The Environment

In January 2003 UNEP published a 'Post-Conflict Environmental Assessment' on Afghanistan, which considered pollution, surface and ground water resources, deforestation, waste and sanitation, air quality and desertification. UNEP found that the conifer forests in the provinces of Nangarhar, Kunar and Nuristan in eastern Afghanistan had been reduced by an average of 50% since 1978. The pistachio forests in Badghis and Takhar in the north of Afghanistan were found to have declined even further, by 50%–70%. The report expressed concern about the desertification process caused by shortages of fuel and the consequent need to collect brushwood wherever possible. It noted that the reduction in stabilizing vegetation had led to increased sand dune movement in some areas. Furthermore, flood risks were reported to have increased owing to the erosion of river banks. Concern was expressed over the drilling of deep wells with insufficient regard to the impact on shallow wells, springs and traditional sources of underground water such as *karezes* (hillside tunnels). The report also commented on the very poor regard for staff health and safety, the emission of fumes and the disposal of waste in the few industrial units that exist. Particular concern was expressed about the employment of children in these environments.

### The Economic Position of Women

Traditionally, women and men have had complementary economic roles in the agricultural sector: women, for example, carry out sowing, weeding and livestock care, while men plough and take care of the major share of harvesting. A minority of women were able to benefit, over a limited period corresponding roughly with the 1970s and 1980s, from access to education at secondary and tertiary levels and to enter professions such as teaching, medicine and office work. However, the exodus of professionals from Afghanistan since 1992 has included a high proportion of these women and the educated female population is now extremely small.

### The Illegal Economy

The illegal economy, based on smuggling and the opium, heroin and timber trades, has represented a very significant source of income, although the profits generated from these practices outside the country are likely to have been much greater than those generated within. The smuggling trade has as its foundation the Afghan Transit Trade Agreement, through which Afghanistan is permitted to transport goods across Pakistan from Karachi duty-free for use in Afghanistan. This agreement has been abused so that goods have been smuggled back into Pakistan, having barely entered Afghanistan, and have then been sold in what are termed *bara* markets near the border and elsewhere in Pakistan, thus benefiting from the absence of duty. The Government of Pakistan estimated in 1991 that cross-border smuggling was resulting in an annual loss of more than US $5,000m. to its economy. The Pakistani Government sought to clamp down progressively on this smuggling through a combination of measures, including further restrictions on the goods that could be imported duty-free, the imposition of sales tax on goods sold in the *bara* markets and the introduction of greater border controls. However, in an effort to generate goodwill with the new Afghan Government, it agreed to reduce the number of items (which had decreased to four by April 2007, compared with 12 in June 2004) on which it levied tax.

Opium production in Afghanistan reached its highest ever level (at that stage) in 1999, at 4,600 metric tons. However, production declined by 29% in 2000, to an estimated 3,275 tons, largely owing to the prevailing drought. In 2001 the ban on opium production, announced by the Taliban in July 2000, took effect in Taliban-controlled areas. Although this decision might have been taken on religious grounds and out of concern over possible opium and heroin addiction within Afghanistan, the international community responded with caution to the visible evidence that production had effectively ceased. In part, this caution could be seen as a response to the very strong financial arguments for the imposition of a ban, including the fact that high production in previous years risked leading to a saturation of the international market and thus creating a substantial decline in opium prices. The international community was also mindful of the fact that significant stockpiles, sufficient to meet global demand for many years to come, reportedly remained within Afghanistan. This scepticism was further enhanced by reports that the ban had resulted in a 10-fold increase in the price of opium in Afghanistan over the previous year. The collapse of the Taliban regime in late 2001 created an immediate opportunity for opium cultivation to resume and, in spite of efforts by the Interim Authority to clamp down on production and offer compensation to farmers, production reached 3,400 tons in 2002. Production rose by a further 6% in 2003, to 3,600 tons, according to the annual survey produced by UNODC in October 2003. Opium was cultivated on 80,000 ha in 2003, an increase of 8% compared with 2002. This represented about 3% of Afghanistan's irrigated arable land. However, the price of fresh opium declined by 19%.

The number of provinces where poppy was grown had increased from 18 out of 32 in 1999 to 28 in 2003, an increase of four provinces compared with 2002. This was due to the fact that poppy cultivation had been introduced to 31 districts for the first time. Conversely, production had declined by 49% in Helmand, which used to provide 50% of the crop, and by 23% in Qandahar. Nangarhar, which formerly produced 25% of the output, had become the largest producer, supplying 23% of the total. Badakhshan, which used to produce a very small proportion of the total, had experienced an increase of 55% in production in 2003, compared with the previous year, raising its share of the output to 16%. It is of interest to note that production in the non-traditional growing areas in 2003 represented 24% of total production and had grown by 301%. Some of these areas had suffered particularly badly from the drought. It was also likely that the relatively high price of opium and the depressed price of wheat in 2003, resulting from the effect of high quantities of food aid on the market, created a strong incentive to grow poppy crops.

UNODC estimated that 264,000 families, cultivating an average of 0.3 ha of opium poppy, were producing opium in 2003. On this basis, about 7% of the total population of Afghanistan was deriving a direct income from poppy cultivation in that year. This was estimated to equate to an average of US $3,900 per opium-growing family, which was more than three times the national average GDP per caput. However, there were significant regional discrepancies in income per family from opium, ranging from $1,700 in the north to $6,800 in the south.

In November 2004 UNODC issued its annual survey of opium production for 2004. This indicated that the area on which opium was cultivated expanded from 80,000 ha in 2003 to 131,000 ha in 2004, representing an increase of 64%. However, yields were lower than in 2003, due to bad weather, drought and crop disease, and this meant that the increase in actual opium production was only 17%. Production was, none the less, relatively high, with the 4,200 metric tons produced in 2004 only being surpassed, since 1980, by the 4,600 tons of 1999. This increase in opium production had clearly been at the expense of cereal production, although drought and other factors had meant that the decline in cereal production had been much greater than the increase in opium production.

Opium production had now extended to all 32 provinces of Afghanistan on the basis of a trend that has been evident for some years. However, production was concentrated in six provinces, namely Helmand (with 23% of the national area under opium cultivation), Nangarhar (22%), Badakshan (12%), Uruzgan (8%), Ghor (4%) and Qandahar (4%); 73% of the total cultivated area was, thus, in these provinces. Within each province, there were further geographical concentrations of production.

A particular trend that was evident in 2004 was a substantial growth in poppy cultivation in northern Afghanistan (an increase of 156% compared with the previous year), although the combined output of the northern provinces accounted for only 13% of total opium production. Even more striking was the increase in cultivation on rain-fed land (growth of 294% compared with the previous year) across the country. The pattern that was evident during the 1990s of Helmand province, in southern Afghanistan, accounting for 50% of the opium output, followed by Nangarhar, with 25%, and with Badakshan a long way behind, had now shifted in favour of the latter two provinces. In 2004 Nangarhar was responsible for 23% of opium production, while Helmand and Badakshan produced 20% and 18%, respectively. Opium yields were much higher in Badakshan than in Helmand, but this was compensated for by significantly higher prices for opium in Helmand.

In 2004 an estimated 356,000 families were involved directly in opium production, representing 10% of the total population. In addition, at least 480,000 people were believed to have worked as itinerant workers in the opium harvest. The price of opium paid to farmers in 2004, while demonstrating substantial variations from one area to another, manifested an average overall decline of 67% for fresh opium and 69% for dry opium since 2003. However, the value of opium and its derivatives at the border actually increased by 22%. This relative price stability was thought by UNODC to be due, in part, to law enforcement measures taken in 2003 and 2004, which resulted in the destruction of many heroin laboratories and also hindered smuggling efforts. However, opium production, valued at US $2,800m., was estimated to represent 37.8% of GDP, if this element of the economy was included, and to be equivalent to about 60% of licit GDP.

It is useful to look at the UNODC report alongside the section on the drug economy in the World Bank study of the Afghan economy published in September 2004, *Afghanistan: State Building, Sustaining Growth and Reducing Poverty: A Country Economic Report*. This report stressed that the poorest farmers were severely disadvantaged, in drawing economic benefit from opium production, by punitive credit arrangements, which often meant that they needed to continue to produce in order to pay off debts to opium traders.

Thus, while the World Bank report argued strongly that success in addressing opium production was dependent on the availability of competitive economic alternatives to the population at large, combined with an effective law and order infrastructure, it made it clear that specific measures to reduce indebtedness, including alternative forms of rural credit, needed to be identified. It commented that 'what is really needed is generalized economic growth and rural development—alternative livelihoods for Afghanistan as a whole ... which can only be accomplished through reforms, policies and substantial programs implemented nationwide'.

The report thus drew attention to the inter-relationship between normal agricultural production, opium production and off-farm economic opportunities, including labour migration. On this basis, it may be anticipated that labour migration opportunities, either within Afghanistan or in one of the neighbouring countries, which have the potential to bring the poorest families out of their indebtedness, are as important as programmes to encourage the use of alternative crops to opium. Conversely, measures by Pakistan and Iran that reduce labour migration possibilities are likely to increase impoverishment, which could have an impact on opium production.

The report commented that the eradication initiatives taken in 2003 and 2004, aimed to destroy crops in specific areas, tended to hit the poorest households hardest and noted that the corruption involved undermined the credibility of the Government. It urged caution in relation to future eradication measures, stressing that experience elsewhere in the world had indicated that these were not effective unless preceded by patient steps to rebuild the economy and provide viable alternatives. It thus stated that 'a key lesson is that eradication alone will not work and is likely to be counterproductive, resulting in perverse incentives for farmers to grow more drugs (e.g. in Colombia), displacement of production to more remote areas, and fuelling of violence and insecurity'. It added that 'abrupt shrinkage of the opium economy or falling opium prices without new means of livelihood would significantly worsen rural poverty' and that 'without alternative livelihoods already in place, premature eradication damages the environment for rural development'. It also drew lessons from successful campaigns to eliminate opium production in Thailand and Pakistan in noting that the drug industry moved to neighbouring countries rather than shutting down. In spite of this evidence, it observed that 'there is pressure on the Government to vigorously pursue eradication quickly'. The report also noted that demand for heroin was growing slowly in Western European markets but very rapidly in Asia and the former USSR. It added that 'although the rate of addiction to opiates in Afghanistan is relatively low, it appears to be rising, facilitated by the increasing trend of refining opium into heroin in-country'.

In February 2005 the Afghan Government published its counter-narcotics strategy in a new document entitled *The 2005 Narcotics Implementation Plan*. The strategy included a public information campaign, which highlighted the fact that poppy cultivation was undermining national security, Afghanistan's international reputation, the security of local communities and the growth of the legal economy. It also noted that it was leading to a substantial increase in addiction to opium and heroin within Afghanistan and, at the same time, supplying millions of addicts in neighbouring Islamic countries. Representatives of the Government were to visit local communities to inform them of plans to create alternative livelihood opportunities and also to eradicate poppy cultivation.

Programmes to provide alternative livelihoods were given the highest priority. These were to be implemented on the basis of priorities identified in Provincial Development Plans. Input to these were to come from District Development Councils and Provincial Development Shuras. During 2005 there was to be a particular focus on the provision of alternative livelihoods in seven key provinces, with Helmand, Qandahar, Nangarhar and Badakshan being targeted in the first instance. Initiatives were to be taken to test possible mechanisms for improving income generation and food security, both agricultural and off-farm. The need to address the punitive debt arrangements which cripple many of the poorest producers would also be given special attention.

The Afghan Government was to lead the eradication campaign. However, the strategy made clear the Government's opposition to aerial spraying. Implementation of the eradication programme was to be through the Central Poppy Eradication Force, in combination with governors and chiefs of police.

Action was also to be taken through the Afghan Special Narcotics Force to destroy opium and precursor chemicals stockpiles, together with drug laboratories. In addition, this Force was to close opium bazaars and arrest drugs traffickers. Drug addiction treatment centres were to be established in Herat, Qandahar, Mazar-i-Sharif and Nangarhar.

UNODC's 2005 Opium Survey indicated that the area cultivated declined by 21%, from 131,000 ha in 2004 to 104,000 ha in 2005 (equivalent to 2.3% of Afghanistan's total cultivable area). However, owing to favourable weather conditions, the overall yield increased by 22%, resulting in a fall of only 2.4% in the total production of opium. Production in 2005 was estimated at 4,100 metric tons, compared with 4,200 tons in 2004. At this level, Afghanistan produced 87% of the world's opium. Based on an increase in GDP from US $4,700m. in 2004 to $5,200m. in 2005, the drug economy was reported to represent 52% of Afghanistan's GDP in 2005, compared with 61% of GDP in 2004. In 2005 the drug economy was valued at $2,700m., including both production and trafficking. The UNODC report also estimated that in Afghanistan itself 50,000 people were using heroin, 15% of whom were injecting. The highest level of drug use was reported to be found in Kabul, followed by the provinces bordering Turkmenistan and Uzbekistan in the north-west and north of the country.

The decline in the area cultivated in 2005 masked a significant change in the distribution of opium production. Thus, while Nangarhar reduced the area cultivated with opium by 96% and Badakhshan by 53%, the area cultivated in Farah increased by 348%, that in Balkh by 334% and the area in Qandahar by 162%. Significant increases were also registered in Nuristan, Takhar, Badghis, Sar-e Pol, Samangan and Nimroz. This resulted in a regional shift, with the major producing areas now in the southern provinces (an increase of 30% in the combined total opium production in the provinces of Helmand, Qandahar, Uruzgan and Zabul), the northern provinces (an increase of 106% in the combined total in the provinces of Balkh, Badghis, Fariab, Baghlan, Jawzjan, Sar-e Pol, Samangan, Kunduz and Bamian) and western Afghanistan (an increase of 98% in the combined total in the provinces of Herat, Farah, Ghor and Nimroz).

Helmand produced the largest amounts of opium, having a cultivated area allocated to opium equivalent to 25% of the area cultivated nationally. The three south-western provinces of Helmand, Qandahar and Farah between them represented 47.8% of the area cultivated. The northern provinces listed above contained 27% of the cultivated area, with a particularly large concentration to the immediate north-west of Mazar-i-Sharif. What is particularly significant is that, whereas Helmand has traditionally been the largest producer of opium, the northern provinces only started producing in about the year 2000 and Qandahar and Farah had only recently started to grow opium on any scale. It is also significant that Nangarhar and Badakhshan, which are traditional opium-producing areas, had reduced production levels, massively in the case of Nangarhar.

The UNODC Opium Survey for 2006 found that the area cultivated had increased to 165,000 ha, resulting in a production level of 6,100 metric tons. The major part of this rise resulted from an increase of 162% in the area cultivated in Helmand, which now accounted for 42% of the total area cultivated with opium poppy. Elsewhere, there was a mixed picture, with cultivation increasing in 19 provinces and declining in 10.

The UNODC Opium Survey for 2007 recorded a further dramatic rise in both the area cultivated, to 193,000 ha, and in the quantity of opium produced, to a record 8,200 metric tons. Five southern provinces produced 70% of this output, with Helmand alone accounting for 50% of total Afghan production. In contrast, in the centre and north of the country the number of opium-free provinces increased from six in 2006 to 13 in 2007.

In April 2008 the World Bank, in combination with the UK DFID, published 'Afghanistan: Economic Incentives and Development Intitiatives to Reduce Opium Production'. This paper recommended:

i) accelerating rural development through better community-based programmes;

ii) expanding arable agricultural land through irrigation;

iii) increasing livestock to provide more livelihoods and assets for the poor;

iv) creating opportunities for rural enterprise and business development;

v) encouraging international partners involved in protecting and rebuilding Afghanistan to buy and hire locally;

vi) exploiting potential opportunities for the production and marketing of suitable industrial crops;

Meanwhile, the large-scale illegal timber trade has continued for some years, based on arrangements between Pakistani entrepreneurs and regional commanders in certain eastern provinces, and has had a major impact on the scarce timber reserves of the country. The Pakistan daily newspaper *Dawn* reported in September 2003 that the scale of the illegal smuggling of timber from Afghanistan to Pakistan had shown a 'quantum leap' from July to mid-September, owing to the better quality and competitive price of the imported timber. The newspaper reported that most of the timber originated from the forests of Kunar, which are controlled by the Governor of Nangarhar and his security chief.

**Security**

As noted above, work on the major highway system has been significantly constrained by a deterioration in the security environment following the war in Iraq. It is noteworthy that the cost of transportation has increased markedly, both as a consequence of the rising levels of insecurity and also because of the bribes imposed by the police on truck drivers. Recent protests by the hauliers suggest that the bribery situation is reaching serious proportions. The worsening security situation is also a consequence of a growing insurgency movement, organized by the Taliban and other radical elements, against the international forces in Afghanistan. Elsewhere in Afghanistan, growing fragmentation of power-holding arrangements has led to greater lawlessness as local militia groups seek to extract benefit. Negotiations with the major regional power holders, combined with the removal of heavy weapons through the disarmament programme, have reduced the scale of inter-factional clashes. However, engagement with the radical elements is much more complex, because these have an active interest in stopping reconstruction activity in order to reduce the credibility of the Afghan Government.

# Statistical Survey

Sources (unless otherwise stated): Central Statistics Authority, Block 4, Microrayon, Kabul; tel. (93) 24883; Central Statistics Office, Ansari Wat, Kabul; e-mail info@cso.gov.af; internet www.cso.gov.af.

## Area and Population

**AREA, POPULATION AND DENSITY**

| | |
|---|---|
| Area (sq km) | 652,225* |
| Population (census results) | |
| 23 June 1979† | |
| Males | 6,712,377 |
| Females | 6,338,981 |
| Total | 13,051,358 |
| Population (official estimates) | |
| 2002‡ | 21,800,000 |
| 2006§ | 22,575,900 |
| Density (per sq km) at 2006 | 34.6 |

* 251,773 sq miles.

† Figures exclude nomadic population, estimated to total 2,500,000. The census data also exclude an adjustment for underenumeration, estimated to have been 5% for the urban population and 10% for the rural population.

‡ This figure includes an estimate for nomadic population (1.5m. in 2002), but takes no account of emigration by refugees. At the end of 2007 UNHCR estimated that the total Afghan refugee population numbered 1.9m., of whom 900,000 were located in Pakistan and a similar number in Iran.

§ Males 11,545,800, females 11,030,100; estimate for settled population only.

**PROVINCES**

(2006, excluding nomad population, estimates)

| | Area (sq km) | Population ('000) | Density (per sq km) | Capital |
|---|---|---|---|---|
| Kabul | 4,462 | 3,138 | 703.3 | Kabul |
| Kapisa | 1,842 | 383 | 207.9 | Mahmud-e-Iraqi |
| Parvan (Parwan)§ | n.a. | 573 | n.a. | Charikar |
| Wardak* | 8,938 | 517 | 57.8 | Maidanshahr |
| Loghar (Logar)* | 3,880 | 340 | 87.6 | Pul-i-Alam |
| Ghazni | 22,915 | 1,063 | 46.4 | Ghazni |
| Paktika | 19,482 | 377 | 19.4 | Sharan |
| Paktia (Paktya) | 6,432 | 478 | 74.3 | Gardez |
| Khost† | 4,152 | 498 | 119.9 | Khost |
| Nangarhar | 7,727 | 1,289 | 166.8 | Jalalabad |
| Kunar (Kunarha) | 4,942 | 390 | 78.9 | Asadabad |
| Laghman | 3,843 | 386 | 100.4 | Mehter Lam |
| Nuristan (Nooristan)† | 9,225 | 128 | 13.9 | Nuristan |
| Badakhshan | 44,059 | 823 | 18.7 | Faizabad |
| Takhar | 12,333 | 845 | 68.5 | Taloqan |
| Baghlan* | 21,118 | 779 | 36.9 | Baghlan |
| Kunduz | 8,040 | 851 | 105.8 | Kunduz |
| Samangan | 11,262 | 335 | 29.7 | Aybak |
| Balkh | 17,249 | 1,096 | 63.5 | Mazar-i-Sharif |
| Jawzjan (Juzjan) | 11,798 | 462 | 39.2 | Shiberghan |
| Sar-e Pol (Sar-e-Pul)‡ | 15,999 | 483 | 30.2 | Sar-e Pol |
| Faryab | 20,293 | 859 | 42.3 | Maymana |
| Badghis | 20,591 | 430 | 20.9 | Qaleh-ye-Now |
| Herat | 54,778 | 1,578 | 28.8 | Herat |
| Farah | 48,471 | 438 | 9.0 | Farah |
| Nimroz | 41,005 | 141 | 3.4 | Zaranj |
| Helmand | 58,584 | 799 | 13.6 | Lashkar Gah |
| Qandahar (Kandahar) | 54,022 | 1,012 | 18.7 | Qandahar |
| Zabul | 17,343 | 263 | 15.2 | Qalat |
| Uruzgan (Urizan)§ | n.a. | 304 | n.a. | Terin Kowt |
| Ghor | 36,479 | 599 | 16.4 | Chaghcharan |
| Bamian (Bamyan) | 14,175 | 387 | 27.3 | Bamian |
| Panjshir§ | n.a. | 133 | n.a. | Bazarat |
| Daikundi§ | n.a. | 400 | n.a. | Neli |
| **Total** | 652,225 | 22,575,900 | 34.6 | |

* By 1996 the capital of Loghar province had changed to Pul-i-Alam from Baraki Barak and the capital of Wardak province had moved to Maidanshahr from Kowt-i-Ashrow; it was reported that the capital of Baghlan province had moved to Pul-e-Khomri: this was yet to be confirmed.

† Nuristan province (formerly part of Kunar and Laghman provinces) and Khost province (formerly part of Paktia province) had been created by 1991 and 1995, respectively.

‡ Sar-e Pol province (formerly part of Balkh, Jawzjan and Samangan provinces) had been created by 1990.

§ Panjshir province (formerly part of Parvan province) and Daikundi province (formerly part of Uruzgan province) were created in 2004.

**PRINCIPAL TOWNS**

(estimated settled population at 2006)

| | | | |
|---|---|---|---|
| Kabul (capital) | 2,536,300 | Pul-e-Khomri | 180,800 |
| Qandahar | 450,300 | Jalalabad | 168,600 |
| Herat | 349,000 | Baghlan | 149,300 |
| Mazar-i-Sharif | 300,600 | Ghazni | 141,000 |
| Kunduz | 264,100 | Maymana | 67,800 |

**BIRTHS AND DEATHS**
(annual averages, UN estimates)

| | 1990–95 | 1995–2000 | 2000–05 |
|---|---|---|---|
| Birth rate (per 1,000) | 51.7 | 51.5 | 49.3 |
| Death rate (per 1,000) | 20.5 | 20.3 | 19.6 |

Source: UN, *World Population Prospects: The 2006 Revision*.

**Expectation of life** (years at birth, WHO estimates): 42.1 (males 41.7; females 42.6) in 2006 (Source: WHO, *World Health Statistics*).

**ECONOMICALLY ACTIVE POPULATION***
(ISIC major divisions, '000 persons aged 15–59 years, year ending 20 March, estimates)

| | 2000/01 | 2001/02 | 2002/03 |
|---|---|---|---|
| Agriculture, hunting, forestry and fishing | 4,986.1 | 5,082.6 | 5,181.4 |
| Mining, quarrying, manufacturing and utilities | 348.6 | 355.3 | 362.2 |
| Construction | 94.9 | 96.7 | 98.6 |
| Wholesale and retail trade | 490.4 | 499.9 | 509.6 |
| Transport, storage and communications | 163.1 | 166.3 | 169.5 |
| Other services | 1,083.6 | 1,104.5 | 1,126.0 |
| **Total** | 7,166.6 | 7,305.4 | 7,447.3 |

* Figures refer to settled population only.

**Mid-2005** ('000, FAO estimates): Agriculture, etc. 7,529; Total labour force 11,527 (Source: FAO).

# Health and Welfare

**KEY INDICATORS**

| | |
|---|---|
| Total fertility rate (children per woman, 2006) | 7.2 |
| Under-5 mortality rate (per 1,000 live births, 2006) | 257 |
| HIV/AIDS (% of persons aged 15–49, 2005) | <0.01 |
| Physicians (per 1,000 head, 2005) | 0.2 |
| Hospital beds (per 1,000 head, 2003) | 0.4 |
| Health expenditure (2005): US $ per head (PPP) | 26 |
| Health expenditure (2005): % of GDP | 5.2 |
| Health expenditure (2005): public (% of total) | 20.0 |
| Access to water (% of persons, 2004) | 39 |
| Access to sanitation (% of persons, 2004) | 34 |

For sources and definitions, see explanatory note on p. vi.

# Agriculture

**PRINCIPAL CROPS**
('000 metric tons)

| | 2003 | 2004 | 2005 |
|---|---|---|---|
| Wheat | 3,480 | 2,293* | 4,265* |
| Rice (paddy) | 260 | 465 | 470* |
| Barley | 240 | 220* | 337* |
| Maize | 210 | 234* | 315* |
| Millet | 17 | 20* | 20* |
| Potatoes* | 240 | 241 | 242 |
| Sesame seed | 23† | 23† | 22* |
| Cottonseed | 37† | 40* | 41* |
| Watermelons* | 95 | 92 | 92 |
| Cantaloupes and other melons* | 28 | 28 | 28 |
| Grapes* | 350 | 349 | 346 |
| Sugar cane* | 38 | 36 | 35 |
| Plums* | 35 | 35 | 35 |
| Apricots* | 38 | 38 | 38 |

* FAO estimate(s).
† Unofficial figure.

**2006** ('000 metric tons, FAO estimates): Wheat 320; Rice 540; Barley 220; Maize 240; Millet 20.

**Aggregate production** ('000 metric tons, may include official, semi-official or estimated data): Total cereals 4,207 in 2003, 3,232 in 2004, 5,407 in 2005, 4,220 in 2006; Total roots and tubers 240 in 2003, 241 in 2004, 242 in 2005, 242 in 2006; Total pulses 42 in 2003, 42 in 2004, 42 in 2005, 42 in 2006; Total vegetables (incl. melons) 663 in 2003, 660 in 2004, 660 in 2005, 660 in 2006; Total fruits (excl. melons) 705 in 2003, 706 in 2004, 704 in 2005, 704 in 2006.

Source: FAO.

**LIVESTOCK**
('000 head, year ending 20 March)

| | 2004/05 | 2005/06 | 2006/07 |
|---|---|---|---|
| Horses | 155 | 149 | 146 |
| Asses and mules | 1,641 | 1,420 | 1,238 |
| Cattle | 3,494 | 3,723 | 4,110 |
| Camels | 190 | 188 | 174 |
| Sheep | 10,136 | 10,773 | 9,259 |
| Goats | 7,648 | 6,977 | 6,746 |
| Chickens | 13,022 | 14,414 | 10,880 |

Source: IMF, *Islamic Republic of Afghanistan: Statistical Appendix* (February 2008).

**LIVESTOCK PRODUCTS**
('000 metric tons, FAO estimates)

| | 2003 | 2004 | 2005 |
|---|---|---|---|
| Cattle meat | 144 | 157 | 165 |
| Sheep meat | 72 | 72 | 72 |
| Goat meat | 33 | 33 | 33 |
| Chicken meat | 16 | 16 | 16 |
| Other meat | 12 | 12 | 12 |
| Cows' milk | 2,035 | 2,035 | 2,035 |
| Sheep's milk | 132 | 132 | 132 |
| Goats' milk | 110 | 110 | 110 |
| Hen eggs | 18 | 19 | 20 |
| Wool: greasy | 11 | 11 | 11 |

Source: FAO.

# Forestry

### ROUNDWOOD REMOVALS

('000 cubic metres, excl. bark, FAO estimates)

| | 2004 | 2005 | 2006 |
|---|---|---|---|
| Sawlogs, veneer logs and logs for sleepers* | 856 | 856 | 856 |
| Other industrial wood† | 904 | 904 | 904 |
| Fuel wood | 1,427 | 1,467 | 1,498 |
| **Total** | 3,187 | 3,227 | 3,258 |

* Assumed to be unchanged from 1976.
† Assumed to be unchanged from 1999.

Source: FAO.

### SAWNWOOD PRODUCTION

('000 cubic metres, incl. railway sleepers, FAO estimates)

| | 1974 | 1975 | 1976 |
|---|---|---|---|
| Coniferous (softwood) | 360 | 310 | 380 |
| Broadleaved (hardwood) | 50 | 20 | 20 |
| **Total** | 410 | 330 | 400 |

**1977–2006:** Annual production as in 1976 (FAO estimates).

Source: FAO.

# Fishing

(metric tons, live weight, FAO estimates)

| | 2003 | 2004 | 2005 |
|---|---|---|---|
| Total catch (freshwater fishes) | 900 | 1,000 | 1,000 |

**2006:** Catch assumed to be unchanged from 2005 (FAO estimate).

Source: FAO.

# Mining

('000 metric tons, unless otherwise indicated, estimates)

| | 2001 | 2002 | 2003 |
|---|---|---|---|
| Hard coal | 190 | 185 | 185 |
| Natural gas (million cu metres)* | 3,000 | 3,000 | 3,000 |
| Copper ore† | 5 | 5 | 5 |
| Salt (unrefined) | 13 | 13 | 13 |
| Gypsum (crude) | 3 | 3 | 3 |

* Figures refer to gross output. Estimated marketed production was 2,500 million cubic metres per year in 2001–03.
† Figures refer to metal content.

Source: US Geological Survey.

# Industry

### SELECTED PRODUCTS

(year ending 20 March, '000 metric tons, unless otherwise indicated)

| | 1986/87 | 1987/88 | 1988/89 |
|---|---|---|---|
| Margarine | 3.5 | 3.3 | 1.8 |
| Vegetable oil | 4 | n.a. | n.a. |
| Wheat flour* | 187 | 203 | 166 |
| Wine ('000 hectolitres)* | 289 | 304 | 194 |
| Soft drinks ('000 hectolitres) | 8,500 | 10,300 | 4,700 |
| Woven cotton fabrics (million sq metres) | 58.1 | 52.6 | 32.1 |
| Woven woollen fabrics (million sq metres) | 0.4 | 0.3 | 0.3 |
| Footwear—excl. rubber ('000 pairs)* | 613 | 701 | 607 |
| Rubber footwear ('000 pairs)* | 2,200 | 3,200 | 2,200 |
| Nitrogenous fertilizers† | 56 | 57 | 55 |
| Cement | 103 | 104 | 70 |
| Electric energy (million kWh)*‡ | 1,171 | 1,257 | 1,109 |

* Production in calendar years 1986, 1987 and 1988.
† Production in year ending 30 June.
‡ Provisional.

**Wheat flour** ('000 metric tons): 1,832 in 1994; 2,029 in 1995; 2,145 in 1996.

**Nitrogenous fertilizers** (provisional, year ending 30 June, '000 metric tons): 49 in 1994/95; 50 in 1995/96; 50 in 1996/97; 5 in 1997/98; 5 in 1998/99; 5 in 1999/2000.

**Cement** (year ending 20 March, '000 metric tons): 15.2 in 2004/05; 29.8 in 2005/06; 29.3 in 2006/07.

**Electric energy** (year ending 20 March, million kWh): 782.7 in 2004/05; 907.3 in 2005/06; 916.9 in 2006/07.

Sources: UN, *Industrial Commodity Statistics Yearbook* and *Statistical Yearbook for Asia and the Pacific*, FAO, US Geological Survey and IMF, *Islamic Republic of Afghanistan: Statistical Appendix* (February 2008).

# Finance

### CURRENCY AND EXCHANGE RATES

**Monetary Units**

100 puls (puli) = 2 krans = 1 afghani (Af).

**Sterling, Dollar and Euro Equivalents** (30 April 2008)

£1 sterling = 98.340 afghanis;
US $1 = 50.000 afghanis;
€1 = 77.700 afghanis;
1,000 afghanis = £10.17 = $20.00 = €12.87.

**Exchange Rate:**The foregoing information refers to the official exchange rate. The official rate was maintained at US $1 = 1,000 afghanis between 1 May 1995 and 30 April 1996. From 1 May 1996 a rate of US $1 = 3,000 afghanis was in operation. However, this rate was applicable to only a limited range of transactions. There was also a market-determined rate, which was US $1 = 34,000 afghanis in March 2002. A new afghani, equivalent to 1,000 of the old currency, was introduced in October 2002.

### OPERATING BUDGET

(million afghanis, year ending 20 March)

| Revenue* | 2004/05 | 2005/06 | 2006/07† |
|---|---|---|---|
| Tax revenue | 9,546 | 14,035 | 21,893 |
| Taxes on income, profits and capital gains | 995 | 2,621 | 3,850 |
| Taxes on international trade and transactions | 7,247 | 9,446 | 11,980 |
| Other taxes | 1,304 | 1,968 | 6,063 |
| Non-tax revenue | 3,254 | 6,624 | 6,896 |
| **Total** | 12,800 | 20,660 | 28,789 |

| Expenditure‡ | 2004/05 | 2005/06 | 2006/07† |
|---|---|---|---|
| Wages and salaries | 18,902 | 20,430 | 26,454 |
| Purchase of goods and services | 4,182 | 6,679 | 10,200 |
| Transfers and subsidies | 764 | 495 | 2,176 |
| Pensions | 889 | 1,540 | 2,461 |
| Capital expenditure | 1,979 | 3,054 | 1,987 |
| Interest | — | 150 | 169 |
| **Total** | 26,716 | 32,348 | 43,448 |

* Excluding donor assistance grants and loans (million afghanis): 14,984 in 2004/05; 16,732 in 2005/06; 19,214 in 2006/07 (estimate), and development assistance grants and loans: 8,250 in 2004/05; 19,251 in 2005/06; 16,625 in 2006/07 (estimate).

† Estimates.

‡ Excluding development spending (million afghanis): 12,834 in 2004/05; 21,089 in 2005/06; 32,254 in 2006/07 (estimate).

Source: IMF, *Islamic Republic of Afghanistan: Statistical Appendix* (February 2008).

## FOREIGN EXCHANGE RESERVES

(million afghanis at 20 March)

| | 2005/06 | 2006/07* | 2007/08† |
|---|---|---|---|
| Gold‡ | 19,230 | 23,006 | 23,006 |
| Other | 63,765 | 80,370 | 96,087 |
| **Total** | 82,995 | 103,376 | 119,093 |

* Estimates.

† Projections.

‡ Excluding gold held in palace vaults.

Source: IMF, *Islamic Republic of Afghanistan: Statistical Appendix* (February 2008).

## MONEY SUPPLY

(million afghanis at 20 March)

| | 2005/06 | 2006/07* | 2007/08† |
|---|---|---|---|
| Reserve money | 46,111 | 57,277 | 57,281 |
| Currency in circulation | 44,441 | 48,884 | 53,021 |
| Bank deposits with central bank | 1,670 | 7,392 | 4,260 |

* Estimates.

† Projections.

Source: IMF, *Islamic Republic of Afghanistan: Statistical Appendix* (February 2008).

## COST OF LIVING

(Consumer Price Index for Kabul; base: 2002 = 100)

| | 2004 | 2005 | 2006 |
|---|---|---|---|
| Food | 109.3 | 113.7 | 119.0 |
| Non-food | 115.6 | 126.1 | 139.4 |
| **All items** | 111.8 | 118.4 | 126.9 |

Source: Asian Development Bank, *Key Indicators of Developing Asian and Pacific Countries*.

## NATIONAL ACCOUNTS

(million afghanis at current prices, year ending 20 March)

### Expenditure on the Gross Domestic Product

| | 2004/05 | 2005/06 | 2006/07* |
|---|---|---|---|
| Public consumption expenditure | 80,139 | 121,199 | 139,975 |
| Private consumption expenditure | 271,836 | 316,617 | 342,067 |
| Gross domestic investment | 119,214 | 143,627 | 161,778 |
| **Total domestic expenditures** | 471,189 | 581,443 | 643,820 |
| Exports of goods and services | 82,317 | 94,183 | 96,440 |
| *Less* Imports of goods and services | 269,001 | 337,086 | 368,816 |
| **Gross domestic product at market prices** | 284,504 | 338,540 | 371,445 |

### Gross Domestic Product by Economic Activity

| | 2004/05 | 2005/06 | 2006/07* |
|---|---|---|---|
| Agriculture, hunting, forestry and fishing | 103,674 | 129,309 | 117,277 |
| Mining and quarrying | 624 | 788 | 876 |
| Manufacturing | 43,879 | 51,401 | 62,618 |
| Electricity, gas and water | 1,683 | 461 | 593 |
| Construction | 21,872 | 30,135 | 37,412 |
| Trade | 29,698 | 28,347 | 33,139 |
| Transport, storage and communications | 42,877 | 31,384 | 45,535 |
| Public administration | 14,224 | 21,860 | 27,543 |
| Other services, incl. finance | 19,966 | 33,841 | 33,874 |
| Statistical discrepancy | — | — | 999 |
| **Gross domestic product (GDP) at factor cost** | 278,496 | 327,526 | 359,866 |
| Indirect taxes, less subsidies | 6,008 | 11,014 | 11,579 |
| **GDP at market prices** | 284,504 | 338,540 | 371,445 |

* Estimates.

Source: IMF, *Islamic Republic of Afghanistan: Statistical Appendix* (February 2008).

## BALANCE OF PAYMENTS

(US $ million, year ending 20 March)

| | 2005/06* | 2006/07† | 2007/08‡ |
|---|---|---|---|
| Exports of goods§ | 1,794.8 | 1,923.8 | 2,074.8 |
| Imports of goods | –4,317.0 | –5,095.5 | –5,584.0 |
| **Trade balance** | –2,522.2 | –3,171.7 | –3,509.2 |
| Services and other income (net) | –538.3 | –505.9 | –438.4 |
| **Balance on goods, services and income** | –3,060.5 | –3,677.6 | –3,947.6 |
| Current transfers (net) | 3,103.6 | 3,580.5 | 3,703.0 |
| **Current balance** | 43.1 | –97.0 | –244.6 |
| Capital and financial account (net) | 360.8 | 391.2 | 443.2 |
| Net errors and omissions | –42.9 | 46.4 | –64.0 |
| **Overall balance** | 360.9 | 340.5 | 134.6 |

* Estimates.

† Preliminary estimate.

‡ Projected.

§ Excludes opium exports and flows associated with US Army and International Security Assistance Force activities.

Source: IMF, *Islamic Republic of Afghanistan: Second Review Under the Three-Year Arrangement Under the Poverty Reduction and Growth Facility - Staff Report; Press Release on the Executive Board Discussion; and Statement by the Executive Director for the Islamic Republic of Afghanistan* (July 2007).

## OFFICIAL DEVELOPMENT ASSISTANCE

(US $ million)

| | 1998 | 1999 | 2000 |
|---|---|---|---|
| Bilateral | 88.5 | 104.2 | 88.2 |
| Multilateral | 65.7 | 38.3 | 52.7 |
| Total | 154.2 | 142.5 | 140.9 |
| Grants | 154.3 | 140.9 | 140.9 |
| Loans | −0.1 | 1.6 | — |
| Per caput assistance (US $) | 7.4 | 6.7 | 6.5 |

Source: UN, *Statistical Yearbook for Asia and the Pacific*.

**2002/03** (US $ million, excl. grants used for clearing debt arrears): Bilateral grants 26.4; Multilateral grants 157.1 (Source: IMF, *Islamic State of Afghanistan: 2003 Article IV Consultation—Staff Report; Public Information Notice on the Executive Board Discussion; and Statement by the Executive Director for the Islamic State of Afghanistan*).

# External Trade

**PRINCIPAL COMMODITIES**
(US $ million, year ending 20 March)

| Imports c.i.f.* | 2004/05 | 2005/06 | 2006/07 |
|---|---|---|---|
| Machinery and equipment | 528 | 599 | 532 |
| Petroleum and petroleum products | 77 | 653 | 254 |
| Metals | 85 | 268 | 274 |
| Chemical materials | 3 | 23 | 14 |
| Food | 404 | 333 | 328 |
| Fabrics, clothing and footwear | 330 | 150 | 225 |
| Household items and medicine | 241 | 279 | 330 |
| **Total** (incl. others) | 2,177 | 2,678 | 2,744 |

| Exports f.o.b.* | 2004/05 | 2005/06 | 2006/07 |
|---|---|---|---|
| Fresh fruits | 13 | 17 | 39 |
| Dried fruit | 81 | 87 | 126 |
| Medicinal plants | 14 | 5 | 10 |
| Animal skins | 22 | 31 | 23 |
| Wool | 8 | 5 | 4 |
| Carpets and handicrafts | 156 | 207 | 187 |
| **Total** (incl. others) | 305 | 384 | 416 |

* Official recorded only; excluding re-exports.

Source: IMF, *Islamic Republic of Afghanistan: Statistical Appendix* (February 2008).

**PRINCIPAL TRADING PARTNERS**
(US $ million, year ending 20 March)

| Imports* | 2004/05 | 2005/06 | 2006/07 |
|---|---|---|---|
| China, People's Republic | 385 | 317 | 475 |
| Germany | 182 | 21 | 48 |
| India | 83 | 68 | 125 |
| Japan | 353 | 414 | 418 |
| Kenya | 22 | 34 | n.a. |
| Korea, Republic of | 79 | 64 | n.a. |
| Pakistan | 326 | 394 | 419 |
| Turkmenistan | 26 | 30 | n.a. |
| **Total** (incl. others) | 2,177 | 2,471 | 2,744 |

| Exports† | 2004/05 | 2005/06 | 2006/07 |
|---|---|---|---|
| Finland | — | 5 | n.a. |
| Germany | 1 | 7 | 4 |
| India | 20 | 23 | 79 |
| Pakistan | 258 | 298 | 265 |
| Russia | 4 | 13 | n.a. |
| **Total** (incl. others) | 305 | 384 | 416 |

* Figures refer to official recorded imports only and include re-exports.
† Excluding re-exports.

Source: IMF, *Islamic Republic of Afghanistan: Statistical Appendix* (February 2008).

# Transport

**ROAD TRAFFIC**
(year ending 20 March, motor vehicles in use)

| | 2004/05 | 2005/06 | 2006/07 |
|---|---|---|---|
| Passenger cars | 197,449 | 262,700 | 314,165 |
| Taxicabs | 49,414 | 55,412 | 62,376 |
| Lorries | 83,347 | 100,883 | 117,460 |
| Buses | 40,590 | 41,731 | 48,513 |
| Motorcycles | 62,417 | 64,817 | 108,282 |
| Rickshaws | 6,355 | 3,342 | 5,228 |
| Foreign vehicles | 12,237 | 12,668 | 13,296 |

Source: IMF, *Islamic Republic of Afghanistan: Statistical Appendix* (February 2008).

**CIVIL AVIATION**
('000)

| | 2004/05 | 2005/06 | 2006/07 |
|---|---|---|---|
| Kilometres flown | 12,898 | 12,887 | 5,407 |
| Passengers carried | 333 | 353 | 235 |
| Freight ton-km | 20,624 | n.a. | 15,032 |

* Provisional figures.

Source: IMF, *Islamic Republic of Afghanistan: Statistical Appendix* (February 2008).

# Tourism

| | 1996 | 1997 | 1998 |
|---|---|---|---|
| Tourist arrivals ('000) | 4 | 4 | 4 |
| Tourism receipts (US $ million) | 1 | 1 | 1 |

Source: World Tourism Organization, *Yearbook of Tourism Statistics*.

# Communications Media

| | 2004 | 2005 | 2006 |
|---|---|---|---|
| Telephones ('000 main lines in use) | 50.0 | 100.0 | 165.0 |
| Mobile cellular telephones ('000 subscribers) | 600.0 | 1,200.0 | 2,520.4 |
| Personal computers ('000 in use) | 25.0 | 30.0 | n.a. |
| Internet users ('000) | 25.0 | 300.0 | 535.0 |
| Broadband subscribers | 200.0 | 200.0 | 500.0 |

**Radio receivers** ('000 in use): 2,400 in 1995; 2,550 in 1996; 2,750 in 1997.

**Television receivers** ('000 in use): 290 in 1998; 300 in 1999.

Sources: mainly UNESCO, *Statistical Yearbook* and UN, *Statistical Yearbook*.

**Daily newspapers:** *Number*: 15 in 1995, 12 in 1996; *Average circulation* ('000 copies): 200 in 1995 (estimate), 113 in 1996.

# Education

(2002)

| | Institutions | Teachers | Pupils |
|---|---|---|---|
| Pre-primary | 147 | 3,286 | 9,367 |
| Primary | 4,876 | 58,312 | 3,083,434 |
| Secondary* | 1,994 | 34,271 | 621,801 |
| Higher | n.a. | 1,449 | 22,717 |

* Figures refer to general secondary education only, excluding vocational and teacher training.

Sources: Ministries of Education, of Higher Education and of Social and Labour Affairs, Kabul, and UNICEF.

**Teachers** (2003/04, unless otherwise indicated): Pre-primary 3,510; Primary 51,802 (2004/05); Secondary vocational 674 (2004/05); Tertiary 1,781 (Source: UNESCO Institute for Statistics).

**Adult literacy rate** (UNESCO estimates): 28.0% (males 43.1%; females 12.6%) in 2000 (Source: UNESCO Institute for Statistics).

# Directory

## The Constitution

On 5 December 2001 28 Afghan leaders signed the Agreement on Provisional Arrangements in Afghanistan Pending the Re-establishment of Permanent Government Institutions (also known as the Bonn Agreement), stipulating a timetable for the creation of a permanent constitution and the holding of free national elections. In accordance with the agreement, Afghanistan temporarily reverted to the Constitution of 1964. On 11–19 June 2002 an Emergency Loya Jirga (Grand National Council), comprising approximately 1,650 delegates, convened. The Loya Jirga appointed a broad-based, gender-sensitive Transitional Authority and a Head of State. The Transitional Authority, with the assistance of the UN, established a Constitutional Drafting Commission in November to draw up a new constitution. A new charter providing for a presidential system of government and a bicameral legislature following eventual elections by universal suffrage was approved by a Constitutional Loya Jirga in early January 2004. A democratic presidential election, based on the principles of the new Constitution, took place on 9 October, following which the President appointed a new Government. Legislative elections were held on 18 September 2005, to determine the composition of the Meli Shura (National Assembly). The first meeting of the Meli Shura in December signified the end of the transitional period of government that had been initiated with the holding of the Emergency Loya Jirga in 2002.

## The Government

### HEAD OF STATE

**President:** HAMID KARZAI (inaugurated as Chairman of Interim Authority 22 December 2001; elected as President of Transitional Authority by Loya Jirga 13 June 2002 and as President of the Islamic Republic of Afghanistan by direct popular vote 9 October 2004).

**Vice-Presidents:** AHMAD ZIA MASOUD, KARIM KHALILI.

### CABINET
(August 2008)

**Senior Minister in the Cabinet:** HEDAYAT AMIN ARSALA.

**Minister of Commerce and Industry:** Dr MOHAMMAD AMIN FARHANG.

**Minister of Defence:** Gen. ABDUL RAHIM WARDAK.

**Minister of Foreign Affairs:** Dr RANGIN DADFAR SPANTA.

**Minister of Finance:** Prof. Dr ANWAR-UL-HAQ AHADI.

**Minister of Interior Affairs:** ZARAR AHMAD MOQBEL.

**Minister of Economy:** Dr MOHAMMAD JALIL SHAMS.

**Minister of Communications and Information Technology:** AMIRZAI SANGIN.

**Minister of Border and Tribal Affairs:** ABDUL KARIM BARAHAWI.

**Minister of Refugees and Repatriation:** SHER MOHAMMAD ETEBARI.

**Minister of Mines and Industries:** IBRAHIM ADIL.

**Minister of Water and Energy:** MOHAMMED ISMAIL KHAN.

**Minister of Public Health:** Dr MOHAMMAD AMIN FATEMI.

**Minister of Agriculture, Irrigation and Livestock:** OBAIDOLLAH RAMIN.

**Minister of Justice:** MOHAMMAD SARWAR DANESH.

**Minister of Culture and Youth Affairs:** ABDUL KARIM KHORAM.

**Minister of Hajj and Islamic Affairs:** NEMATULLAH SHAHRANI.

**Minister of Urban Development:** MOHAMMAD YOUSEF PASHTUN.

**Minister of Public Welfare:** SUHRAB ALI SAFARI.

**Minister of Work, Social Affairs, the Martyred and the Disabled:** NOOR MOHAMMAD KARKIN.

**Minister of Higher Education:** Dr MOHAMMAD AZAM DADFAR.

**Minister of Transport and Aviation:** HAMIDULLAH QADERI.

**Minister of Education:** Dr MOHAMMED HANIF ATMAR.

**Minister of Rural Rehabilitation and Development:** EHSAN ZIA.

**Minister of Women's Affairs:** HOSNA BANU GHAZANFAR.

**Minister of Counter Narcotics:** Gen. KHODAIDAD.

**National Security Adviser:** Dr ZALMAI RASSOUL.

### MINISTRIES

**Office of the President:** Gul Khana Palace, Presidential Palace, Kabul; e-mail president@afghanistangov.org; internet www.president.gov.af.

**Ministry of Agriculture** (Irrigation and Livestock): Jamal Mena, Kart-i-Sakhi, Kabul; tel. (20) 2500315; e-mail info@agriculture.gov.af; internet www.agriculture.gov.af.

**Ministry of Border and Tribal Affairs:** Shah Mahmud Ghazi Wat, Kabul; tel. (20) 2101365.

**Ministry of Commerce:** Darulaman Wat, Kabul; tel. (20) 2290090; fax (20) 2500356; e-mail info@commerce.gov.af; internet www.commerce.gov.af.

**Ministry of Communications and Information Technology:** Mohammad Jan Khan Wat, Kabul; tel. (20) 2101107; fax (20) 2101708; e-mail khalid.saleem@moc.gov.af; internet www.moc.gov.af.

**Ministry of Counter Narcotics:** Kabul-Jalalabad Rd, Banaiey, Macroyan, Kabul; tel. (79) 9871886; e-mail info@mcn.gov.af; internet www.mcn.gov.af.

**Ministry of Culture and Youth Affairs:** Mohammad Jan Khan Wat, Kabul; tel. and fax (20) 2101301; fax (20) 2290088; e-mail aziza_ahmadyar@hotmail.com.

**Ministry of Defence:** Shash Darak, Kabul; tel. (20) 2100451; fax (20) 2104172.

**Ministry of Economy:** Kabul; tel. (20) 2100394; internet www.moec.gov.af.

**Ministry of Education:** Mohammad Jan Khan Wat, Kabul; tel. (79) 9332015; e-mail awassay.arian@moe.gov.af; internet www.moe.gov.af.

**Ministry of Finance:** Pashtunistan Wat, Kabul; tel. (20) 2004199; fax (20) 2103439; e-mail info@mof.gov.af; internet www.mof.gov.af.

**Ministry of Foreign Affairs:** Malak Azghar Rd, Kabul; tel. (70) 104024; fax (20) 2100360; e-mail contact@mfa.gov.af; internet mfa.gov.af.

**Ministry of Hajj and Islamic Affairs:** nr District 10, Shir Pur, Shar-i-Nau, Kabul; tel. (20) 2201338.

**Ministry of Higher Education:** Karte Char, Kabul; tel. (20) 2500324; e-mail afmohe@hotmail.com; internet www.mohe.gov.af.

**Ministry of Interior Affairs:** Shar-i-Nau, Kabul; tel. (20) 32441.

**Ministry of Justice:** Pashtunistan Wat, Kabul; tel. (20) 2101325; e-mail info@moj.gov.af; internet www.moj.gov.af.

**Ministry of Mines and Industries:** Pashtunistan Wat, Kabul; tel. (20) 2100309; e-mail info@mom.gov.af; internet www.mom.gov.af.

**Ministry of Public Health:** Wazir Akbar Khan, Sub-district 9, Kabul; tel. (20) 2301377; e-mail info@moph.gov.af; internet www.moph.gov.af.

**Ministry of Public Welfare:** Microrayon 1, Kabul; tel. (20) 2301363; fax (20) 2301362.

**Ministry of Refugees and Repatriation:** Jungaluk, off Darlaman Rd, Kabul; e-mail afgmorr@afgmorr.com.

**Ministry of Rural Rehabilitation and Development:** Shah Mahmud Ghazi Wat, Kabul; tel. (70) 222118; e-mail info@mrrd.gov.af; internet www.mrrd.gov.af.

**Ministry of Transport and Aviation:** Ansari Wat, Kabul; tel. (20) 2103064; e-mail arasikh@motca.gov.af; internet motca.gov.af.

**Ministry of Urban Development:** Microrayon 3, Kabul.

**Ministry of Water and Energy:** Kabul.

**Ministry of Women's Affairs:** beside Cinema Zainab, Shar-i-Nau, Kabul; tel. and fax (20) 2201378; e-mail info@mowa.gov.af; internet www.mowa.gov.af.

**Ministry of Work, Social Affairs, the Martyred and the Disabled:** Old Microrayon, Kabul; tel. (20) 2300369.

## President and Legislature

### PRESIDENT

**Presidential Election, 9 October 2004**

| Candidates | Votes | % of votes |
|---|---|---|
| Hamid Karzai | 4,443,029 | 55.37 |
| Younis Qanooni | 1,306,503 | 16.28 |
| Haji Mohammad Mohaqqeq | 935,325 | 11.66 |
| Abdul Rashid Dostam | 804,861 | 10.03 |
| Abdul Latif Pedram | 110,160 | 1.37 |
| Masooda Jalal | 91,415 | 1.14 |
| Sayed Ishaq Gailani | 80,081 | 1.00 |
| Others | 253,162 | 3.15 |
| **Total** | 8,024,536 | 100.00 |

### MELI SHURA
(National Assembly)

**Meshrano Jirga**
(House of Elders)

The Meshrano Jirga, the upper house of the Meli Shura, comprises 102 members (three times the number of provinces in Afghanistan). One-third are elected by provincial councils (for a four-year term), one-third by district councils (for a three-year term) and the remaining members are nominated by the President (for a five-year term). The Constitution requires that one-half of the members nominated by the President must be women.

**Speaker:** Prof. SIBGHATULLAH MOJADDEDI.

**Wolasi Jirga**
(House of Representatives)

The Wolasi Jirga, the lower house of the Meli Shura, comprises 249 directly elected members, all of whom serve a five-year term. Sixty-eight seats are reserved for women. The most recent election was held on 18 September 2005.

**Speaker:** YOUNIS QANOONI.

## Election Commission

**Independent Election Commission of Afghanistan (IEC):** IEC Compound, Jalalabad Rd, Paktia Kot, POB 979, Kabul; tel. (75) 2035203; e-mail info@iec.org.af; internet iec.org.af; established by 2004 Constitution; appointed by the President; functions performed by Joint Electoral Management Body (JEMB) during transitional period of govt; following elections to the Wolasi Jirga and Provincial Councils in 2005, the JEMB was dissolved and the IEC assumed regulation and supervision of all election activities from 2006; Pres. Dr AZIZULLAH LODIN; Chief Electoral Officer Dr DAOUD ALI NAJAFI.

## Political Organizations

In September 2003 a new law allowing the formation of political parties was passed. By July 2007 more than 80 parties were registered with the Ministry of Justice, including the following:

**Afghan Mellat** (Afghan Social Democratic Party): National Bank Club, 3rd Floor, Nader Pashtoon Jadah, Kabul; tel. (70) 224793; e-mail afghanmellat@afghanmellat.org; internet www.afghanmellat.org; Pres. Prof. Dr ANWAR-UL-HAQ AHADI.

**Da Afghanistan Da Solay Ghorzang Gond** (Afghanistan Peace Movement): Kolola Poshta (adjacent to Dost Hotel), Kabul; tel. (79) 9311523; Leader SHAHNAWAZ TANAI.

**Harakat-i Islami i Afghanistan** (Islamic Movement of Afghanistan): Street 4, Qala-i Fathullah, Shar-e-Nau, Kabul; tel. (79) 9343998; Leader SAYYED MOHAMMAD ALI JAWED.

**Hizb-i Adalat-i Islami Afghanistan** (Islamic Justice Party of Afghanistan): nr Aryub Cinema, Bagh-e-Bala, District 4, Kabul; tel. (79) 9312641; f. 2004; Leader MOHAMMAD KABIR MARZBAN.

**Hizb-i Afghanistan-i Nawin** (New Afghanistan Party): 1st Rd Khair Khana Phase One, Parwan Hotel Rd, District 11, Kabul; tel. (79) 9342942; f. 2005; Leader YOUNIS QANOONI.

**Hizb-i Afghanistan-i-Wahid** (United Afghanistan Party): 53–54, Block 11, Qasiba-e-Khana Sazi, Kabul; tel. (70) 7803738; e-mail xl_branch_afg@yahoo.com; f. 1999; Leader MOHAMMAD WASEL RAHIMY.

**Hizb-i Hambastagi Afghanistan** (Solidarity Party of Afghanistan): Spare Parts St, Parwan 3, Kabul; tel. (70) 231590; Leader ABDUL KHALEQ NE'MAT.

**Hizb-i Hambastagi-yi Melli-yi Jawanan-i Afghanistan** (National Youth Solidarity Party of Afghanistan): House No. 2, St 3, Haji Yaqub Sq., towards Shaheed, Kabul; tel. (79) 9424290; f. 2004; Leader MOHAMMAD JAMIL KARZAI.

**Hizb-i Harakat-i-Islami Mardum-i Afghanistan** (Islamic Movement Party of the People of Afghanistan): Rd 2–3, Qala-i-Fatullah, Kabul; tel. (79) 9183484; f. 2004; Leader Al-Hajj SYED HUSSAIN ANWARI.

**Hizb-i Harakat-i-Melli Wahdat-i-Afghanistan** (National Movement for the Unity of Afghanistan): Jamia Mosque, 6th Floor, Karte 4, District 3, Kabul; tel. (70) 204847; f. 2004; Chair. MOHAMMAD NADIR ATASH.

**Hizb-i Islami Afghanistan** (Islamic Party of Afghanistan): Area A, Khushal Mena, Kabul; tel. (79) 9421474; Pashtun/Turkmen/Tajik; Leader KHALED FAROOQI; c. 50,000 supporters; based in Iran in 1998–99.

**Hizb-i Isteqlal-i Afghanistan** (Independence Party of Afghanistan): Khair Khana, nr Al-Farooq Healthcare Clinic, Kabul; f. 2004; Leader Dr GHULAM FAROOQ NAJRABI.

**Hizb-i Jumhuri-i Khwahan-i Afghanistan** (Republican Party of Afghanistan): Zainaba St, 6th Rd, Qala-i-Fathullal, Kabul; tel. (70) 275107; f. 2003; supporter of presidential system of government; Leader SEBGHATULLAH SANGAR; c. 35,000 mems.

**Hizb-i Junbesh-i Melli-i Islami** (National Islamic Movement): St 4, Rd 15, Wazir Akbar Khan, Kabul; tel. (70) 511511; f. 1992; formed mainly from troops of fmr Northern Command of the Afghan army; predominantly Uzbek/Tajik/Turkmen/Ismaili and Hazara Shi'a; Leader SAYED NOORULLAH; 65,000–150,000 supporters.

**Hizb-i Kar wa Tawse'ah Afghanistan** (Labour and Progress of Afghanistan Party): Karte 4, Rd 2, Kabul; f. 1999 in Pakistan; previously known as the National Reconciliation Party; Leader ZULFIQAR OMID.

**Hizb-i Melli Afghanistan** (National Party of Afghanistan): Apt 4, Block 12, Microrayon 1, Kabul; tel. (70) 298392; Leader ABDUL RASHID ARYAN.

**Hizb-i-Melli Wahdat-i-Aqwam-i-Islami-i-Afghanistan** (Party of National Unity of Muslim Tribes of Afghanistan): Bahadur Ulya, Khugiana, Nangarhar; Leader MOHAMMAD SHAH KHOGIANI.

**Hizb-i Nizat-i Azady Wa Demokrasi-ye Afghanistan** (Movement for Democracy and Freedom in Afghanistan): Karte 4, adjacent to Suraya Lycee, Kabul; tel. (70) 281953; f. 2004; Leader ABDUL RAQIB JAVED KOHISTANI.

**Hizb-i Rastakhaiz-i Mardum-i Afghanistan** (Renaissance Party of the People of Afghanistan): Apt 4, 1st Floor, Block 15, Tahya Maskan, Kabul; tel. (79) 9372310; f. 2003; Chair. SAYED ZAHER QAID OMULBELADI.

**Hizb-i Rifah-i Mardum-i Afghanistan** (Party of Welfare of the People of Afghanistan): Khwaja Musafir Bazaar, Paghman, Kabul; tel. (79) 9215852; f. 2004; Leader MIAGUL WASIQ.

**Hizb-i Sahadat-i Mardum-i-Afghanistan** (Welfare Popular Party of Afghanistan): Apt 1, Block 13, Air Force Blocks, Kabul; tel. (70) 204847; Leader MOHAMMAD ZUBAIR PAYROZ.

**Hizb-i-Wahdat-i Islami Afghanistan** (Islamic Unity Party of Afghanistan): Mokhabirat, Karte 4, Kabul; tel. (70) 2501413; Leader MOHAMMAD KARIM KHALILI.

**Hizb-i Wahdat-i Islami Mardum-i Afghanistan** (People's Islamic Unity Party of Afghanistan): House 3, Mohammadia St, Tapa-i-Salaam, Karte Sakhi, Kabul; tel. (70) 278276; represents Hazaras; advocate of equal rights, freedom and social justice; Leader Haji MOHAMMAD MOHAQQEQ.

**Hizb-i Wahdat Melli Afghanistan** (National Unity Party of Afghanistan): Qaisar Market, 2nd Floor, adjacent to Gul-i-Surkh Hotel, Old Kolola Poshta Sq., Kabul; tel. (79) 9210998; Leader ABDUL RASHID JALILI.

**Jamiat-i Islami** (Islamic Society): Karte Parwan, Phase 2, Badaam Bagh; tel. (70) 278950; Turkmen/Uzbek/Tajik; Leaders Prof. BURHANUDDIN RABBANI, Marshal MUHAMMAD FAHIM; Sec.-Gen. ENAYATOLLAH SHADAB; c. 60,000 supporters.

**Kangra-i Melli Afghanistan** (National Congress of Afghanistan): Kabul; e-mail mcnafghan@hotmail.com; internet mouv.national.afghan.free.fr; f. 2004; Leader ABDUL LATIF PEDRAM.

**Mahaz-i-Melli-i-Islami** (National Islamic Front): Malalai Wat, Interior Ministry Rd, Kabul; tel. (70) 231345; Pashtun; Leader SAYED AHMAD GAILANI; Dep. Leader HAMED GAILANI; c. 15,000 supporters.

**Nizat-i Hambastagi Melli** (National Solidarity Movement): St 6, Taimani, Kabul; tel. (79) 9486558; Chair. Pir SAYED ISHAQ GAILANI.

**Nizat-i Melli-i Afghanistan** (National Movement of Afghanistan): Taimani, St 1, Kabul; tel. (70) 277938; f. 2002; Leader AHMAD WALI MASOUD.

**Tanzim-i Dawat-i Islami** (Organization for Invitation to Islam): Ansari Sq., Rd 1, District 4, Kabul; tel. (70) 277007; Pashtun; fmrly

Ittihad-i Islami; name changed as above 2005; Leader Prof. ABDUL RASUL SAYEF.

The following are unregistered political organizations:

**Hizb-i Islami Khalis** (Islamic Party Khalis): Pashtun; promotes establishment of an Islamic state in accordance with Qu'ran, Sunnah and Shari'a doctrines; Leader Maulvi MOHAMMAD YUNUS KHALIS; c. 40,000 supporters.

**Jabhe-ye-Motahed-e-Milli** (United National Front—UNF): f. 2007; informal political grouping incl. fmr mems of United Front; advocates parliamentary system of govt rather than presidential system; mems incl. Younis Qanooni, Ahmad Zia Masoud, Gen. Abdul Rashid Dostam and Marshal Muhammed Qassim Fahim; Chair. Prof. BURHANUDDIN RABBANI.

**Taliban:** emerged in 1994; Islamist fundamentalist; mainly Sunni Pashtuns; in power 1996–2001; also active in the Federally Administered Tribal Areas of Pakistan; Leader Mullah MOHAMMAD OMAR; c. 12,000 supporters.

# Diplomatic Representation

## EMBASSIES IN AFGHANISTAN

**Australia:** c/o Serena Hotel, Froshgah St, Kabul; tel. (79) 9654840; Ambassador MARTIN QUINN.

**Belgium:** House 1–3, St 1, Taimani Wat, Qala-i-Fathullah, Kabul; tel. (70) 294149; e-mail kabul@diplobel.org; internet www.diplomatie.be/kabul; Ambassador PIETER LEENKNEGT.

**Bulgaria:** St 15, Shirpur St, Wazir Akbar Khan, Kabul; tel. (20) 2103257; fax (20) 2101089; e-mail bgembkabul@yahoo.com; Ambassador KRASIMIR TULECHKI.

**Canada:** House 256, St 15, Wazir Akbar Khan, POB 2052, Kabul; tel. (79) 9742800; fax (79) 9742805; e-mail kabul@international.gc.ca; internet www.international.gc.ca/afghanistan; Ambassador ARIF LALANI.

**China, People's Republic:** Sardar Shah Mahmoud Ghazi Wat, Kabul; tel. (20) 2102545; fax (20) 2102728; e-mail chinaemb_af@mfa.gov.cn; Ambassador YANG HOULAN.

**Denmark:** House 35–36, Road 13, Lane 1, Wazir Akbar Khan, Kabul; tel. and fax (20) 2300968; e-mail kblamb@um.dk; internet www.ambkabul.um.dk; Head of Mission JENS HAARLOV.

**Egypt:** Road 15, Wazir Akbar Khan, Kabul; tel. (20) 2021901; fax (20) 2104064; e-mail egypt_kabul@mfa.gov.eg; Ambassador MOHAMMAD SHARIF HASSAN RAYHAN.

**Finland:** House 39, Street 10, Lane 1, Wazir Akbar Khan, Kabul; tel. (20) 2103051; fax (60) 581504; e-mail sanomat.kab@formin.fi; internet www.finland.org.af; Ambassador TIMO OULA.

**France:** Cherpour Ave, Shar-i-Nau, POB 62, Kabul; tel. (70) 284032; e-mail chancellerie.kaboul-amba@diplomatie.gouv.fr; internet www.ambafrance-af.org; Ambassador RÉGIS KOETSCHET.

**Germany:** Wazir Akbar Khan, Mena 6, POB 83, Kabul; tel. (20) 2101512; fax (30) 50007518; e-mail zreg@kabu.auswaertiges-amt.de; internet www.kabul.diplo.de; Ambassador Dr HANS-ULRICH SEIDT.

**Hungary:** c/o Embassy of the Federal Republic of Germany, Zanbaq Sq., Wazir Akbar Khan, Mena 6, POB 83, Kabul; tel. (79) 7035375; e-mail huembkbl@gmail.com; Chargé d'affaires a.i. SANDOR MATYUS.

**India:** Malalai Wat, Shar-i-Nau, Kabul; tel. (873) 763095560; fax (873) 763095561; e-mail embassy@indembassy-kabul.com; internet meakabul.nic.in; Ambassador JAYANT PRASAD.

**Indonesia:** Interior Ministry St, Shar-i-Nau, POB 532, Kabul; tel. and fax (20) 2201066; e-mail kabul.kbri@deplu.go.id; internet www.kbri-kabul.go.id; Chargé d'affaires Brig.-Gen. ERMAN HIDAYAT.

**Iran:** Charahi Shir Pur, Kabul; tel. (20) 2101393; Ambassador FADA-HOSSEIN MALEKI.

**Italy:** Great Masoud Rd, Kabul; tel. and fax (20) 2103144; e-mail ambasciata.kabul@esteri.it; internet www.ambkabul.esteri.it; Ambassador ETTORE FRANCESCO SEQUI.

**Japan:** House 83, St 15, Wazir Akbar Khan, Kabul; tel. (873) 762853777; fax (873) 761218272; e-mail ejafgl@web-sat.com; Ambassador JUNICHI KASUGE.

**Kazakhstan:** House 1, St 10, Wazir Akbar Khan, Kabul; tel. (70) 284296; e-mail sher60@mail.ru; Ambassador AGYBAY SMAGULOV.

**Korea, Republic:** Wazir Akbar Khan, St 10, House 34, Kabul; tel. (932) 02102481; fax (873) 762728481; e-mail kabul@mofat.go.kr; Ambassador SUNG-ZU KANG.

**Libya:** Charahi Zanbaq, Wazir Akbar Khan, Kabul; tel. (20) 2101084; fax (20) 290160; Chargé d'affaires MOHAMMAD AMER ALZAIDY.

**Lithuania:** House 2, St 1, Wazir Akbar Khan, Kabul; tel. (79) 9740521; e-mail biruteatiene@yahoo.com; Head of Mission and Chargé d'affaires BIRUTĖ ABRAITIENĖ.

**Netherlands:** Houses 2 and 3, St 4, Ansari and Ghiassudin Wat, Shar-i-Nau, Kabul; tel. (70) 286847; e-mail kab@minbuza.nl; internet www.mfa.nl/kab-en; Ambassador HANS BLANKENBERG.

**Norway:** St 15, Lane 4, Wazir Akbar Khan, Kabul; tel. (20) 2300899; e-mail emb.kabul@mfa.no; internet www.norway.org.af; Ambassador JAN ERIK LEIKVANG.

**Pakistan:** 10 Nijat Watt Rd, Wazir Akbar Khan, Kabul; tel. (20) 2300911; fax (20) 2300912; e-mail embassy@pakembassykbl.com; Ambassador TARIQ AZIZ-UD-DIN KHAN.

**Russia:** House 63, Lane 5, St 15, Wazir Akbar Khan, Kabul; tel. (20) 2300500; e-mail rusembafg@neda.af; Ambassador ZAMIR N. KABULOV.

**Saudi Arabia:** Shash Darak (behind Eyes Office), Kabul; tel. (20) 2102064; e-mail ksa_kemb@hotmail.com; Ambassador GHURAM BIN SAID BIN MALHAN.

**Spain:** House 274, 4R, St 15, Wazir Akbar Khan, Kabul; tel. (79) 9816349; e-mail embespaf@mail.mae.es; Ambassador JOSÉ TURPÍN.

**Tajikistan:** House 41, St 10, Wazir Akbar Khan, Kabul; tel. (20) 2101080; fax (20) 2300392; e-mail kabultj@tojikistan.com; Ambassador FARKHOD MAHKAMOV.

**Turkey:** House 134, Shah Mahmoud Ghazi Khan St, Kabul; tel. (20) 2101581; fax (20) 2101579; e-mail etokdemir@mfa.gov.tr; Ambassador İSMAIL ETHEM TOKDEMIR.

**Turkmenistan:** House 280, St 13, Lane 3, Wazir Akbar Khan, Kabul; tel. (20) 2300541; e-mail kabulemb@neda.af; Ambassador ATAJAN MOVLAMOV.

**United Arab Emirates:** Charahi Zambak, Wazir Akbar Khan, Kabul; tel. (20) 2101578; Ambassador ALI MUHAMMAD AL-SHAMSI.

**United Kingdom:** St 15, Roundabout Wazir Akbar Khan, POB 334, Kabul; tel. (70) 102000; fax (70) 102250; e-mail britishembassy.kabul@fco.gov.uk; internet www.britishembassy.gov.uk/afghanistan; Ambassador Sir SHERARD LOUIS COWPER-COLES.

**USA:** Great Masoud Rd, Kabul; tel. (20) 2300436; fax (20) 2301364; e-mail usambassadorkabul@state.gov; internet kabul.usembassy.gov; Ambassador WILLIAM BRAUCHER WOOD.

**Uzbekistan:** House 14, St 13, Wazir Akbar Khan, Kabul; tel. (20) 2300124; Ambassador PARVEZ MIRIYEVICH ALIYEV.

# Judicial System

In December 2001, following more than 20 years of civil conflict, there no longer existed a functioning national judicial system in Afghanistan. In accordance with the Bonn Agreement signed in that month, Afghanistan temporarily reverted to the Constitution of 1964, which combined *Shari'a* with Western concepts of justice. A new Constitution was introduced in early 2004, which made no specific reference to the role of *Shari'a* but stated that Afghan laws should not contravene the main tenets of Islam. The Constitution made provision for the creation of a Supreme Court (Stera Mahkama) as the highest judicial organ in Afghanistan. Until the inauguration of the Court, which took place shortly after the Meli Shura (National Assembly) was officially opened on 19 December 2005, an interim Supreme Court, established in January 2005, functioned in the country.

The Supreme Court comprises nine members, including the Chief Justice, who are appointed by the President, subject to the approval of the Wolasi Jirga (House of Representatives).

**Chief Justice:** ABDUL SALAM AZIMI.

**Attorney-General:** (vacant).

# Religion

The official religion of Afghanistan is Islam. Muslims comprise 99% of the population, approximately 84% of them of the Sunni sect and the remainder of the Shi'ite sect. There are small minority groups of Hindus, Sikhs and Jews.

## ISLAM

**The High Council of Ulema and Clergy of Afghanistan:** Kabul; f. 1980; 7,000 mems; Chair. Mawlawi ABDOL GHAFUR SENANI.

# The Press

Many newspapers and periodicals stopped appearing on a regular basis or, in a large number of cases, ceased publication during the civil war. Following the defeat of the Taliban in late 2001, a number of newspapers and periodicals resumed publication or were established for the first time. In February 2002 the Media Law was amended, removing most restrictions on independent media. Newspapers and periodicals were required to obtain a licence under the legislation. By early 2005 more than 250 publications had been registered with the then Ministry of Information and Culture.

### PRINCIPAL DAILIES

**Anis** (Friendship): Ministry of Communications and Information Technology, Mohammad Jan Khan Wat, Kabul; f. 1927; evening; Dari, Uzbek and Pashto; state-owned; news and literary articles; Editor-in-Chief Prof. GHOLAM SAKHI MONIR; circ. 5,000.

**Arman-e Melli** (Hope of the Nation): 4 Muslim St, Shar-i-Nau, Kabul; f. 2002 by the Afghan Interim Authority; now independent; Dari and Pashto; Editor-in-Chief MIR HAYDAR MOTAHAR; circ. 4,200.

**Cheragh** (Light): 112 Shar-i-Nau, Kabul; e-mail cheragh_daily@hotmail.com; Dari, Pashto and English; independent; Editor-in-Chief KATHERINE WEDA; circ. 17,000.

**Erada** (Intention): Parwan Mina, Cinema Baharistan, House 95, Hajji Mir Ahmad St, Kabul; tel. (70) 224787; e-mail eradadaily@hotmail.com; f. 2000 as weekly in Pakistan; relaunched as daily in Afghanistan 2002; independent; Dari and Pashto; Editor-in-Chief Haji SYED DAUD.

**Eslah** (Reform): Azadi Printing Press, 4th Floor, Microrayon Part II, Kabul; e-mail islahdaily@yahoo.com; f. 1921; Dari and Pashto; state-owned; Editor-in-Chief SHAMSOLHAQ ARIANFAR.

**Hewad** (Homeland): Azadi Press Centre, Microrayon, Kabul; tel. (20) 22279; f. 1949; Pashto and Dari; state-owned; Editor-in-Chief SHAH MAHMUD ZIARMAL; circ. 5,000.

**Ittefaq-e Islam:** Herat; f. 1920; Dari; Editor-in-Chief NAQIB AROIN; circ. 2,000.

**Jahan-i-Naw** (New World): Mazar-i-Sharif; Editor QAYOUM BAABAK.

**Kabul Times:** Azady Press Centre, Microrayon, POB 1560, Kabul; tel. (20) 61847; e-mail thekabultimes@yahoo.com; f. 1962 as Kabul Times, renamed Kabul New Times in 1980; ceased publication in 2001; revived in 2002 under new management; English; state-owned; Editor-in-Chief (vacant).

**Rah-e Nejat:** Kabul; e-mail info@rahenejat.com; internet www.rahenejatdaily.com; fmrly weekly, daily from 2005; Dari and Pashto; independent; Editor-in-Chief SAYED MOHAMMAD ALEMI.

**Sahar** (Dawn): Mazar-i-Sharif; f. 2005; circ. 2,000.

**Shari'at:** Kabul.

### PERIODICALS

**Aamu:** Aria Press, Kabul; quarterly; research; circ. 1,000.

**Afghan Scene:** e-mail info@afghanscene.com; internet www.afghanscene.com; monthly; free magazine; Editor SAAD MOHSENI.

**Amanat:** House 3, Moslem St, Shar-i-Nau, POB 1158, Kabul; tel. (70) 280988; weekly; organ of Hindukosh News Agency; Editor-in-Chief SYED SHABIR ABIR.

**Ambastagi:** Aria Press, Kabul; weekly; circ. 1,000.

**Anees:** Kabul; weekly; govt-supported; Editor AHMAD ZIA SYAMAK.

**Awa-e Naw:** Herat; fortnightly; independent; circ. 2,000.

**Ayina-e Zan** (Women's Mirror): House 186, St 12, Wazir Akbar Khan, Kabul; tel. (70) 0281864; e-mail womensmirror@hotmail.com; f. 2002; weekly; women's; Dari, Pashto and English; Chief Editor SHUKRIA BAREKZAI; circ. 3,000.

**Cinema:** Kabul; f. 2003; monthly; entertainment and culture; Editor-in-Chief SIDDIQ BARMAK.

**Eqtedar-e Melli:** POB 4024, Kartai Char, University Rd, Kabul; tel. (70) 283554; e-mail eqtedaremelli@yahoo.com; weekly; Dari and Pashto.

**Farda** (Tomorrow): POB 1758, Kabul; tel. (20) 2100199; fax (20) 2100699; e-mail farda-news@yahoo.com; weekly; Publr ABDUL GHAFUR AITEQAD; circ. 4,000.

**Kabul Weekly:** Afghan Visual Communication Institute, Malik Ashgar Crossroads, POB 1831, Kabul; tel. (20) 2101589; e-mail kabulweekly@lycos.com; internet www.ainaworld.org; f. 1993; banned in 1997, revived in 2002; Dari, Pashto and English; weekly; independent; political, social and cultural issues; Editor-in-Chief FAHIM DASHTY; Sec. ABDUL AKBAR; circ. 8,000.

**Killid** (The Key): The Killid Group Main Office, Kolola Pushta, Kabul; tel. (20) 2200573; fax (20) 2200574; e-mail killidweekly@thekillidgroup.com; internet www.thekillidgroup.com/c/divisions/killidweekly.htm; weekly; current affairs; Editor SEDIQULLAH BADR; circ. 25,000.

**Malalai:** Afghan Visual Communication Institute, Malik Ashgar Crossroads, Kabul; internet www.ainaworld.org; f. 2002; monthly; women's; Dari, Pashto and English; publ. of Aïna humanitarian org.; Chief Editor JAMILA MUJAHID; circ. 3,000.

**Mojahed:** POB 226, Kabul; e-mail mujahidweekly@yahoo.com; weekly; Dari and Pashto; Editor WAQIF HAKIMI.

**Mursal:** The Killid Group Main Office, Kolola Pushta, Kabul; tel. (20) 2200573; fax (20) 2200574; e-mail mursal@thekillidgroup.com; internet www.thekillidgroup.com/c/divisions/mursal.htm; f. 2003; weekly; Pashto and Dari; circ. 15,000.

**Les Nouvelles de Kaboul** (Kabul News): Afghan Visual Communication Institute, Malik Ashgar Crossroads, Kabul; tel. (70) 286215; e-mail dimitri.beck@ainaworld.org; internet www.ainaworld.org; f. 2002; quarterly; English and French; publ. of Aïna humanitarian org.; Chief Editor DIMITRI BECK; Propr and Dir SHAFIQA HABIBI.

**Parvaz** (Flight): Afghan Visual Communication Institute, Malik Ashgar Crossroads, Kabul; e-mail roshanak@ainaworld.org; internet www.ainaworld.org; f. 2002; Dari and Pashto; every two months; children's; Editor MIRHASAMADEEN BRUMAND; circ. 25,000.

**Payam-e-Mujahid** (Holy Warrior's Message): POB 5051, Kabul; e-mail payamemojahed@hotmail.com; internet www.payamemojahed.com; f. 1996; weekly; Dari and Pashto; sponsored by the Northern Alliance; Editor HAFIZ MANSOOR.

**Roz** (The Day): Kabul; f. 2002; monthly; women's; Dari, Pashto, French and English; Editor-in-Chief LAILOMA AHMADI.

**Rozgaran:** POB 2018, Clola Pushta, Kabul; tel. (70) 207933; e-mail rozgaran@yahoo.com; internet www.geocities.com/rozgaran2; f. 2004; Dari and Pashto.

**Takhassos** (Experts): Jadai Baghi Azadi, Herat; tel. (70) 280258; monthly; Dari; published by Council of Professionals; Editor MOHAMMAD RAFIQ SHAHIR.

**Tolo-e Afghan:** Qandahar; several times a week; Pashto; Editor-in-Chief ABDUL QODUS BAES.

**Zanbil-e-Gham:** Afghan Visual Communication Institute, Malik Ashgar Crossroads, Kabul; f. 1997; monthly; satirical; Editor OSMAN AKRAM; circ. 2,000.

### NEWS AGENCIES

**Afghan Islamic Press:** POB 520, GPO, Peshawar, North-West Frontier Province, Pakistan; tel. (91) 5701100 (Peshawar); fax (91) 5842544 (Peshawar); e-mail info@afghanislamicpress.com; internet www.afghanislamicpress.com.

**Ariana Press Agency:** Kabul; f. 1987 in Dushanbe, Tajikistan; independent; publishes three newsletters.

**Bakhtar News Agency (BNA):** Ministry of Communications and Information Technology, Mohammad Jan Khan Wat, Kabul; tel. and fax (20) 2101304; e-mail meenawee13@yahoo.com; internet www.bakhtarnews.com.af; f. 1939; govt news agency; correspondents in 32 provinces; Dir-Gen. SULTAN AHMAD BAHEEN.

**Hindukosh News Agency (HNA):** House 3, Moslem St, Shar-i-Nau, POB 1158, Kabul; f. 2002; independent; offices in Herat, Qandahar and Mazar-i-Sharif; Dir SYED NAJIBULLAH HASHIMI.

**Pajhwok Afghan News:** Interior Ministry Rd, Shahr-e-Kabul, Kabul; tel. (20) 2201814; fax (20) 2201813; e-mail feedback@pajhwok.com; internet www.pajhwok.com; f. 2004; independent; regional bureaux in Mazar-i-Sharif, Qandahar, Herat and Jalalabad; news service provided in English, Pashto and Dari; Dir and Editor-in-Chief DANISH KAROKHEL.

### PRESS ASSOCIATIONS

**Afghanistan Independent Journalists' Association (AIJA):** Maiwand Press Club, Alam Ganj, Kabul; fax (20) 70285515; f. 2003; Chair. ABDULHAMID HAAMI.

**Afghanistan Women in Media Network:** Afghan Media and Cultural Centre, Malik Ashgar Crossroads, Kabul; e-mail najibamaram@hotmail.com; f. 2002; association of female media staff; Pres. JAMILA MUJAHID; Vice-Pres. NAJIBA MARAM.

## Publishers

Some of the following publishers were forced to close down during the Taliban regime. Since the Taliban's fall from power in December 2001, publishers have been slowly reopening, with the help of the UN and other international aid agencies and foreign publishing houses.

**Afghan Book:** POB 206, Kabul; f. 1969; books on various subjects, translations of foreign works on Afghanistan, books in English on Afghanistan and Dari language textbooks for foreigners; Man. Dir JAMILA AHANG.

**Afghanistan Today Publishers:** c/o The Kabul Times, Ansari Wat, POB 983, Kabul; tel. (20) 61847; publicity materials; answers enquiries about Afghanistan.

**Ariana Press:** Poli Jarkhi, Kabul; under the supervision of the Ministry of Culture and Youth Affairs; Dir ABDUL KADER.

**Azady (Freedom) Press:** Ministry of Culture and Youth Affairs, Mohammad Jan Khan Wat, Kabul; tel. (20) 2100113; under supervision of the Ministry of Culture and Youth Affairs; Dir JAHAN YAR.

**Balhaqi Book Publishing and Importing Institute:** POB 2025, Kabul; tel. (20) 26818; f. 1971 by co-operation of the Government Printing House, Bakhtar News Agency and leading newspapers; publishers and importers of books; Pres. MUHAMMAD ANWAR NUMYALAI.

**Beihagi Publishers:** Azady Press Centre, Microrayon, Kabul; tel. (20) 63623; books on Afghan culture; also prints information related to the Govt and its plans; Dir SADIQ AYAR.

**Book Publishing Institute:** Herat; f. 1970 by co-operation of Government Printing House and citizens of Herat; books on literature, history and religion.

**Book Publishing Institute:** Qandahar; f. 1970; supervised by Government Printing House; mainly books in Pashto language.

**Educational Publications:** Ministry of Education, Mohammad Jan Khan Wat, Kabul; tel. and fax (20) 200000; textbooks for primary and secondary schools in the Pashto and Dari languages; also three monthly magazines in Pashto and in Dari.

**Historical Society of Afghanistan:** Kabul; tel. (20) 30370; f. 1931; mainly historical and cultural works and two quarterly magazines: *Afghanistan* (English and French), *Aryana* (Dari and Pashto); Pres. AHMAD ALI MOTAMEDI.

**Institute of Geography:** Kabul University, Kabul; geographical and related works.

**International Center for Pashto Studies:** Kabul; f. 1975 by the Afghan Govt with the assistance of UNESCO; research work on the Pashto language and literature and on the history and culture of the Pashtun people; Pres. and Assoc. Chief Researcher J. K. HEKMATY; publs *Pashto* (quarterly).

**Kabul University Press:** Kabul; tel. (20) 42433; f. 1950; textbooks; two quarterly scientific journals in Dari and in English, etc.

**Research Center for Linguistics and Literary Studies:** Afghanistan Academy of Sciences, Akbar Khan Mena, Kabul; tel. (20) 26912; f. 1978; research on Afghan languages (incl. Pashto, Dari, Balochi and Uzbek) and Afghan folklore; publs *Kabul* (Pashto), *Zeray* (Pashto weekly) and *Khurasan* (Dari); Pres. Prof. MOHAMMED R. ELHAM.

### GOVERNMENT PUBLISHING HOUSE

**Government Printing House:** Kabul; tel. (93) 26851; f. 1870; under supervision of the Ministry of Communications and Information Technology; Dir SAID AHMAD RAHAA.

### PUBLISHERS' ASSOCIATION

**Afghan Libraries' and Publishers' Association:** Chari Ansari, between Ansari Crossroads and Popo Lano Restaurant, Kabul.

## Broadcasting and Communications

### TELECOMMUNICATIONS

**Afghanistan Telecom Regulatory Authority (ATRA):** Ministry of Communications and Information Technology, MOC Headquarters Tower, 10th Floor, Mohammad Jan Khan Wat, Kabul; tel. (20) 2101179; e-mail z.hamidy@atra.gov.af; internet atra.gov.af; succeeded Telecom Regulatory Board.

**Afghan Telecom** (AfghanTel): Post Parcel Bldg, 4th Floor, Mohammad Jan Khan Wat, Kabul; tel. (75) 2033333; fax (75) 2033344; e-mail info@afghantelecom.af; internet www.afghantelecom.af; f. 2004; state-owned; provides wireless and digital fixed-line services; 80% of shares offered for sale in March 2008; Dir AMIRZAI SANGIN.

**Afghan Wireless Communication Company (AWCC):** Agricultural Bank, 3rd Floor, Maiwand Wat, Kabul; tel. and fax (70) 803803; e-mail info@afghanwireless.com; internet www.afghan-wireless.com; f. 1999; jt venture between the Ministry of Communications and Information Technology (20% ownership) and Telephone Systems International, Inc of the USA (80% ownership); reconstruction of Afghanistan's national and international telecommunications network; by June 2002 mobile and fixed-line telecommunications services covered Herat, Jalalabad, Kabul, Mazar-i-Sharif and Qandahar; the first centre providing internet services was opened in Kabul in July of that year; 1.3m. subscribers (July 2007); Chair. EHSAN BAYAT.

**Etisalat Afghanistan** (UAE): POB 800, Kabul; e-mail info@etisalat.af; internet www.etisalat.af; commenced operations in Afghanistan in 2007; GSM operator; CEO SALEM AL KENDI.

**Telecom Development Co Afghanistan Ltd** (Roshan): Roshan Shop, St 13, off Main St, Wazir Akbar Khan, Kabul; tel. (79) 9977755; fax (79) 9978800; e-mail roshanca@roshan.af; internet www.roshan.af; f. 2002 by an international consortium comprising the Aga Khan Fund for Economic Development (AKFED), French cos Monaco Telecom International (MTI) and Alcatel, and US co MCT Corpn; 51% owned by AKFED, 36.75% by MTI and 12.25% by MCT Corpn; provides mobile telecommunications services; CEO KARIM KHOJA.

### BROADCASTING

The media were severely restricted by the militant Taliban regime (1996–2001): television was banned and Radio Afghanistan was renamed Radio Voice of Shari'a. The overthrow of the Taliban in November–December 2001 led to the liberation of the media. On 13 November Radio Afghanistan was revived in Kabul; music was broadcast for the first time in five years. A few days later Kabul TV was resurrected, and a woman was employed as its newsreader. By early 2005 there were 42 radio stations and eight private television stations broadcasting in Afghanistan.

#### Radio

**Radio-Television Afghanistan:** St 10, Lane 2, Wazir Akbar Khan, POB 544, Kabul; tel. (20) 2101086; e-mail rtakabul@hotmail.com; revived in 2001; programmes in Dari, Pashto, Turkmen and Uzbek; Dir-Gen. MOHAMMAD ESHAQ; Head of Radio GHULAM HASSAN HAZRATI.

**Balkh Radio and TV:** Mazar-i-Sharif; Pashto and Dari; Chair. ABDORRAB JAHED.

**Radio Herat:** Herat.

**Radio Kabul:** Ansari Wat, Kabul; tel. (20) 2101087; Dir GHULAM HASSAN HAZRATI.

**Voice of Freedom:** Kabul; f. 2002; broadcasts one hour a day in Dari and Pashto; German-funded.

Independent

**Arman FM:** POB 1045, Central Post Office, Kabul; tel. (79) 9321010; e-mail info@arman.fm; internet www.arman.fm; f. 2003; Afghanistan's first privately owned independent FM radio station; broadcasts in Kabul, Mazar, Herat, Qandahar and Jalalabad; broadcasts popular music and culture 24 hours a day; Dir SAAD MOHSENI.

**Radio Azad Afghan:** Qandahar; f. 2004; broadcasts five hours daily; Dir ISMAIL TIMUR.

**Radio Bamian:** Bamian; f. 2003.

**Radio Killid:** The Killid Group Main Office, Kolola Pushta, Kabul; tel. (20) 2200573; fax (20) 2200574; e-mail info@thekillidgroup.com; internet www.thekillidgroup.com/c/divisions/radio.htm; f. 2003 by Development and Humanitarian Services for Afghanistan; broadcasts 24 hours daily; stations in Kabul and Herat; Man. NAJIBA AYUBI.

**Radio Sahar:** Herat; f. 2003; Dari; women's; broadcasts 12 hours daily; Dir HULAN KHATIBI; Station Man. HUMAIRA HABIB.

**Radio Sharq:** Jalalabad; f. 2003; broadcasts 12 hours daily.

**Radio Tiraj Mir:** Pol-e-Khomri; f. 2003; broadcasts 16 hours daily.

**Voice of Afghan Women:** Kabul; f. 2003; relaunched in 2005 following closure owing to lack of funds; dedicated to interests of women; Dir JAMILA MUJAHID.

#### Television

**Radio-Television Afghanistan:** see Radio.

**Balkh Radio and TV:** see Radio.

**Herat TV:** Herat; state-owned.

**Kabul TV:** Kabul; revived in 2001; broadcasts four hours daily; Dir HUMAYUN RAWI.

**TV Badakhshan:** Faizabad; f. 1987 as Faizabad TV, name changed in 2000; Pashto and Dari.

Independent

**Afghan TV:** Kabul; f. 2004; broadcasts 24 hours daily; Man. AHMED SHAH AFGHANZAI.

**Aina** (Mirror): Shebarghan; f. 2003; broadcasts to Jawzjan, Sar-e Pol and Balkh provinces and to the bordering areas of Turkmenistan and Uzbekistan; Dir SYED ANWAR SADAT.

**Ariana Radio and Television Network:** 318 Darulaman Wat, Kabul; tel. (70) 0111000; e-mail feedback@arianatelevision.com; internet www.arianatelevision.com; broadcasts to 34 provinces in Afghanistan, as well as Europe, the USA, Canada and the Middle East; f. 2005; Chair. EHSANULLAH BAYAT.

**Tolo TV:** POB 225, Central Post Office, Kabul; tel. (79) 9321010; e-mail info@tolo.tv; internet www.tolo.tv; f. 2004; commercial station; broadcasts news, current affairs, entertainment, lifestyle and culture programmes; Dir SAAD MOHSENI.

# Finance

(cap. = capital; brs = branches)

### BANKING

The banking sector was under reconstruction from 2002, following the collapse of the Taliban regime in late 2001. In September 2003 the President approved a law allowing foreign banks to open branches in Afghanistan. By the end of 2004 11 foreign banks had begun operations in the country.

#### Central Bank

**Da Afghanistan Bank** (Central Bank of Afghanistan): Ibne Sina Wat, Kabul; tel. (20) 2100301; fax (20) 2100305; e-mail info@centralbank.gov.af; internet www.centralbank.gov.af; f. 1939; cap. and res 9,423m. afghanis, dep. 40,864m. afghanis (March 2006); main functions: banknote issue, modernize the banking system, re-establish banking relations with international banks, create a financial market system, foreign exchange regulation, govt and private depository; granted complete independence in September 2003; Gov. ABDUL QADEER FITRAT; 76 brs.

#### Other Banks

**Afghanistan International Bank:** House 1608, behind Amani High School, Wazir Akbar Khan, POB 2074, Kabul; tel. (79) 9089898; fax (79) 9798989; e-mail info@aib.af; internet www.aib.af; f. 2004; established and managed by the ING Institutional and Government Advisory Group (Netherlands) on behalf of a consortium of Afghan and US investors; 75% owned by Afghan nationals, 25% owned by Asian Development Bank; cap. US $10m. (March 2004); CEO KHALIL SEDIQ; seven brs.

**Azizi Bank:** Malik Asghar Sq., POB 221, Kabul; tel. (20) 2104470; fax (20) 21044701; e-mail info@azizibank.com; internet www.azizibank.af; f. 2006; Pres. and CEO DEEPAK SHRIVASTAVA.

**Banke Millie Afghan** (Afghan National Bank): Jade Ibne Sina, POB 522, Kabul; tel. (20) 21003311; fax (20) 2101801; e-mail info@bma.com.af; internet www.bma.com.af; f. 1933 as private bank, nationalized in 1976; Chair. and CEO MOHAMMAD NAIM DINDAR; Pres. Prof. Dr ABDUL QAYOUM ARIF; 20 brs in Afghanistan, six brs overseas.

**BRAC Afghanistan Bank:** Charai Torabaz Khan Zarghona Midan, Shar-i-Nau, Kabul; tel. (70) 7275703; e-mail info@bracafbank.com; internet www.bracafbank.com; f. 2006; business with retail sector and small and medium-sized enterprises; managed by a Bangladeshi team; CEO M. EHSANUL HAQUE.

**Development Bank of Afghanistan:** Shah Mahmod Ghazi Rd, opposite Chinese Embassy, Kabul; tel. (20) 2104660; e-mail info@bankdba.com; internet www.bankdba.com; f. 2006; Chair. of Supervisory Bd SERGEY M. TSOY; CEO TATYANA B. KIM (acting); 13 brs.

**Export Promotion Bank of Afghanistan:** Park-e-Timor Shahi, Kabul; tel. (20) 2100284; fax (20) 2103947; e-mail epbafghan@yahoo.com; f. 1976; provides financing for exports and export-orientated investments; state-owned; operations suspended under Taliban rule in 1996–2001; CEO ABDUL HAMID MOHEBBI; three brs.

**First MicroFinance Bank (FMFB):** 2nd Floor, Park Plaza, Torabaz Khan Rd, Shar-i-Nau, Kabul; tel. (79) 9322765; e-mail info@fmfb.com.af; f. 2004; 51% owned by Aga Khan Agency for Microfinance, 32% by Kreditanstalt fur Wiederaufbau, 17% by International Finance Corpn; provides sustainable financial services to the poor in order to contribute to poverty alleviation and economic development; CEO MUSLIM UL-HAQ.

**Kabul Bank:** 10–42 Turabaz Khan, Shar-i-Nau, Kabul; tel. (20) 222666; fax (216) 84400171; e-mail info@kabulbank.af; internet www.kabulbank.af; f. 2004; cap. 761.3m. afghanis, res 939.9m. afghanis, dep. 18,194.3m. afghanis (March 2007); Chair. SHERIN KHAN; CEO SHERKHAN FARNOOD; four brs.

**Pashtany Bank:** Mohammad Jan Khan Watt, Kabul; tel. (20) 2100306; fax (20) 2102905; e-mail info@pashtanybank.com; internet www.pashtanybank.com; f. 1955 to provide short-term credits, forwarding facilities, opening letters of credit, purchase and sale of foreign exchange; nationalized in 1975; Chair. ABDUL TAWAB; CEO HAYAT ULLAH DAYANI; 14 brs in Afghanistan, three brs in Pakistan.

### INSURANCE

**Afghan National Insurance Co:** Second Ave, Kartai Parwan, nr fmr British Embassy, POB 329, Kabul; tel. and fax (20) 2200189; e-mail insuranceafghan@yahoo.com; f. 1964; mem. of Asian Reinsurance Corpn; marine, aviation, fire, motor and accident insurance; Pres. Eng. AHMAD SHAH ALIZAI; Claims Man. S. OMAR.

# Trade and Industry

### GOVERNMENT AGENCIES

**Afghanistan Investment Support Agency** (AISA): opposite Ministry of Foreign Affairs, Kabul; tel. (20) 2103404; fax (20) 2103402; e-mail invest@aisa.org.af; internet www.aisa.org.af; f. 2003; promotes and regulates domestic and foreign investment in the private sector; Pres. and CEO OMAR ZAKHILWAL.

**Export Promotion Agency of Afghanistan** (EPAA): off Karte Char 2nd St, Kabul; tel. (798) 300333; e-mail info@epaa.org.af; internet www.epaa.org.af; f. 2006; provides guidance for traders, collects and disseminates trade information; CEO SULEMAN FATIMIE.

### CHAMBERS OF COMMERCE AND INDUSTRY

**Afghan Chamber of Commerce and Industry (ACCI):** Chaman-e-Huzuri, next to Kabul Nendari, Kabul; tel. (75) 2025854; fax (20) 2290089; e-mail info@acci.org.af; internet www.acci.org.af; scheduled to merge with Afghanistan International Chamber of Commerce; Pres. Dr GHULAM MUHAMMAD YAYLAQI.

**Afghanistan International Chamber of Commerce:** House 92, St 2, Shash Darak, Kabul; e-mail admin@aicc-online.org.af; f. 2004; scheduled to merge with Afghan Chamber of Commerce and Industry; Chair. AZARAKHSH HAFIZI; CEO HAMIDULLAH FAROOQI.

**Federation of Afghan Chambers of Commerce and Industry:** Darulaman Wat, Kabul; f. 1923; includes chambers of commerce and industry in Ghazni, Qandahar, Kabul, Herat, Mazar-i-Sharif, Fariab, Jawzjan, Kunduz, Jalalabad and Andkhoy.

### INDUSTRIAL AND TRADE ASSOCIATIONS

**Afghan Carpet Exporters' Guild:** Darulaman Wat, POB 3159, Kabul; tel. (70) 224575; f. 1967; non-profit, independent organization of carpet manufacturers and exporters; Pres. ZIAUDDIN ZIA; c. 1,000 mems.

**Afghan Raisin and Other Dried Fruits Institute:** Sharara Wat, POB 3034, Kabul; tel. (20) 30463; exporters of dried fruits and nuts; Pres. NAJMUDDIN MUSLEH.

**Afghanistan Karakul Institute:** Puli Charkhi, POB 506, Kabul; tel. (20) 61852; f. 1967; exporters of furs; Pres. G. M. BAHEER.

**Animal Products Trading and Industrial Association:** Ayub Khan Mina, South of Habibia High School, 2nd St, Darulaman Wat, Kabul; tel. and fax (75) 2023490; e-mail mohsin_ataie@yahoo.com; f. 1979; promotes and exports animal products, incl. wool and animal skins; Chief Officer M. MOHSIN ATAIE.

**Handicraft Promotion Centre Joint Venture:** POB 3089, Kabul; tel. (20) 2101329; owned by Ministry of Commerce; Pres. ALHAJ GHULAM HASSAN ROSHAN.

### MAJOR COMPANIES

**Afghan Cart Company:** Zerghona Maidan, Kabul; tel. (20) 2201309; fax (20) 290238; e-mail do_ik@yahoo.com; f. 1988; imports electrical goods, machinery, metal, cars, etc.; exports raisins, medical herbs, wood, animal hides, etc.; Pres. KABIR IMAQ.

**Afghanistan Finance Co (AFC):** House No. 53, St 10, Wazir Akbar Khan, Kabul; tel. (20) 2104069; e-mail info@afc.af; internet www.afc.af; f. 2004; owned by Afghanistan Reconstruction Co; leasing services, incl. industrial and agricultural equipment.

**Afghanistan Management Group (AMG):** 173 Flower St, Shar-i-Nau, Kabul; e-mail services@amg.com.af; internet amg.com.af; consulting, investment and other activities.

**Anaar Group:** opp. Indian Embassy, Interior Ministry Rd, Shar-i-Nau, Kabul; tel. (79) 308303; e-mail sam@anaartravels.com; group of businesses incl. Anaar Travels, Anaar Consulting and Maxhealth-care Facilitation Centre.

**Bashiri Co Ltd:** Shahr Ara, Nasir Market, Kabul; tel. (20) 2200714; e-mail kabul@bashiri.ae; internet www.bashiri.ae; f. 1965; suppliers of agricultural machinery and construction equipment; six brs in Afghanistan.

**Dawi Oil:** Kabul International Airport, Kabul; tel. (79) 6700999; e-mail fuel@dawioil.af; internet www.dawioil.af; aviation fuel distributor; Pres. ABDUL GHAFAR DAWI.

**Digistan:** House No. 13, St 3, Taimany, Qualai-Fatahullah, Kabul; tel. (75) 2001708; e-mail info@digistan.com; internet www.digistan.com; information technology; Pres. TAMIM SAMEE.

**Faizan Masood Filter Co Ltd:** Juma Mohammad Mohammady Industrial Park, Baghrami; tel. (70) 274822; e-mail faizan_filter@yahoo.com; internet kabulfilter.com; heavy and light machinery filter mfr.

**Mohib Group:** e-mail mohib_marcopolo@hotmail.com; businesses incl. Mohib Ltd; commodity trading and other activities; Pres. IBRAHIM MOHIB.

**New Afghan Itifaq Sports:** Apt 34, Block 50, Microrayon 1, Kabul; tel. (75) 2010015; e-mail info@itifaqsports.com; internet www.itifaqsports.com; mfr of sports products; Gen. Man. MOHAMMAD ARIF.

**Niazi Road and Building Construction Co:** 2nd Floor, Khorasan Hotel, Taimany, Kabul; tel. (70) 292908; e-mail NRBC@hotmail.com; Pres. SHAH MOHAMMAD DADMANISH.

### TRADE UNIONS

**Afghanistan Lawyers' Union:** Shar-i-Nau, Shaheed Charahi, Kabul; tel. (75) 2004342; e-mail lawyers_union@yahoo.com; Chair. Prof. QAZI.

**Afghanistan National Union of Journalists:** f. 2006; formed through merger of Afghanistan Gen. Union of Journalists, Free Journalist Union of Afghanistan and Nat. Union of Afghan Journalists; Pres. SAYYID HUSSAIN FAZIL SANCHARAKI.

**All Afghanistan Federation of Trade Unions:** Karte Nau, First St, Kabul; tel. (79) 9340196; Chair. Dr LIAQUAT ADIL.

**National Union of Afghanistan Employees (NUAE):** POB 756, Kabul; tel. (20) 23040; f. 1978 as Central Council of Afghanistan Trade Unions, to establish and develop the trade union movement, including the formation of councils and organizational cttees in the provinces; name changed in 1990; composed of seven vocational unions; 300,000 mems; Pres. of Cen. Council MOHAMMAD QASIM EHSAS; Vice-Pres. ASAD KHAN NACEIRY.

## Transport

### RAILWAYS

There is no railway system currently operating in Afghanistan. Plans to build a rail line linking Pakistan, Afghanistan and Turkmenistan were under discussion in the mid-2000s. In February 2007 construction began on a 202-km railway line, funded by the Iranian Government, from Torbat Heidarieh, Iran, to Herat, with completion of the project anticipated by 2008. In July 2007 the Government of Turkmenistan commenced reconstruction of the retired Kushka—Torgondi railway line linking Afghanistan to the rail networks of Iran and Russia at an estimated cost of US $550,000.

### ROADS

In 2001 there were an estimated 23,500 km of roads, of which more than 18,000 km were unpaved. All-weather highways link Kabul with Qandahar and Herat in the south and west, Jalalabad in the east and Mazar-i-Sharif and the Amu-Dar'ya (Oxus) river in the north. A massive reconstruction programme of the road system in Afghanistan began in early 2002. The Salang Highway was rehabilitated, thus reconnecting Kabul with the north. In November the first of five bridges across the River Pyanj on the Tajik–Afghan border was reopened for use. By late 2004 the reconstruction of the important 482-km highway linking Kabul and Qandahar had been completed. Meanwhile, reconstruction of the 566-km highway linking Qandahar and Herat began in mid-2004 and was initially expected to be completed by the end of 2006. In January 2007, however, there were reports by USAID that, owing to concerns over security on one section of the highway, the projected completion date of the reconstruction work had been postponed until 2008. In late 2005 work began on a bridge across the Amu-Dar'ya river, linking Sher Khan Bandar in Kunduz province with Tajikistan.

In early 2005 Afghanistan, Iran and Uzbekistan signed an agreement concerning construction of a trans-Afghan transportation corridor, a 2,400-km road that would link the Uzbek city of Termez and the Iranian port of Bandar Abbas with Mazar-i-Sharif and Herat.

**Afghan Container Transport Company Ltd (ACTCO):** House 43, St 2, Shar-i-Nau, POB 3165, Kabul; tel. and fax (20) 2201392; e-mail kabul@afghancontainers.com; internet www.afghancontainers.com; f. 1974; Vice-Pres. ALI DAD BEIGH ZAD.

**Afghan Transit Company:** Ghousy Market, Mohammad Jan Khan Wat, POB 530, Kabul; tel. (20) 2101733; fax (20) 2101734; e-mail aftrans14@hotmail.com; Chair M. AZAM KARGAR.

**AFSOTR:** Kabul; tel. (20) 2102358; e-mail afsotr@svt.ru; founded as Afghan Soviet Transportation Company; resumed operations in 1998; transport co; 90 vehicles.

**Land Transport Company:** Khoshal Mena, Kabul; tel. (20) 20345; f. 1943; commercial transport within Afghanistan.

**Milli Bus Enterprise:** Ministry of Transport and Aviation, Ansari Wat, Kabul; tel. (20) 2101032; state-owned and -administered; 900 buses; Pres. Eng. AZIZ NAGHABAN.

### INLAND WATERWAYS

There are 1,200 km of navigable inland waterways, including the Amu-Dar'ya (Oxus) river, which is capable of handling vessels of up to about 500 dwt. River ports on the Amu-Dar'ya are linked by road to Kabul.

### CIVIL AVIATION

In 2005 there were 22 airports in Afghanistan, including international airports at Kabul, Qandahar, Bagram and Kunduz. Plans were under way to relocate and upgrade the airport at Kabul and to upgrade the airports at Herat, Mazar-i-Sharif and Jalalabad to international standards.

**Ariana Afghan Airlines:** POB 76, Kabul; tel. (20) 2100351; fax (873) 762523846; e-mail info@flyariana.com; internet www.flyariana.com; f. 1955; merged with Bakhtar Afghan Airlines Co Ltd in 1985; 75% state-owned; flights to India, Pakistan, Germany, the Middle East and Russia; Dir ZABIULLAH ESMATI.

**KamAir:** POB 62, Kabul; tel. and fax (20) 2200108; e-mail info@flykamair.com; internet www.flykamair.com; f. 2003; privately owned; domestic and regional flights; Pres. ZAMARIA KAMGAR.

## Tourism

Afghanistan's potential tourism attractions include: Bamian, with its thousands of painted caves; Bandi Amir, with its suspended lakes; the Blue Mosque of Mazar; Herat, with its Grand Mosque and minarets; the towns of Qandahar and Girishk; Balkh (ancient Bactria), 'Mother of Cities', in the north; Bagram, Hadda and Surkh Kotal (of interest to archaeologists); and the high mountains of the Hindu Kush. Furthermore, ruins of a Buddhist city (known locally as Kaffir Got—'Fortress of the Infidels') dating from the second century were discovered in July 2002 in a remote valley in southern Afghanistan. The restoration of cultural heritage, sponsored by UNESCO, began in 2002. In 1998 an estimated 4,000 tourists visited Afghanistan and receipts from tourism amounted to around US $1m.

**Afghan Tourist Organization (ATO):** Ansari Wat, Shar-i-Nau, Kabul; tel. (20) 30323; f. 1958; Pres. Dr HESSAMUDDIN HAMRAH.

## Defence

Following the defeat of the Taliban in late 2001, an International Security Assistance Force (ISAF) was deployed in Kabul and Bagram airbase to help maintain security in the area. In August 2003 the North Atlantic Treaty Organization (NATO) assumed command of the force and in December NATO began to expand its presence in the country by assuming command of a number of Provincial Reconstruction Teams (PRTs) in the north and west of Afghanistan. In late 2005 ISAF consisted of approximately 12,400 members from 35 countries. (This figure included about 2,000 troops deployed temporarily as Election Support Forces for the legislative elections that took place on 18 September 2005.) By August 2006 NATO troops numbered 18,500 and were positioned in every region. ISAF was also responsible for the training of the first battalion of the Afghan National Guard, which was operational in April 2003. US and French forces began training the first set of recruits for a new multi-ethnic Afghan National Army (ANA) in May 2003. It was intended that by 2008 the ANA would comprise a force of some 70,000, supported by an air force of 8,000. Four committees were established in January 2003 to accelerate the disarmament of private armies and the army-building process. By June 2005 the disarmament of the 60,000 militia fighters who had been identified and targeted for demobilization was believed to have been virtually completed; by mid-2006 the ANA comprised approximately 38,000 soldiers.It was envisaged that the ANA would be supported by a border guard of 12,000. The Afghan National Police and Border Police were to be recruited and trained, with a target membership of 62,000. In January 2008 the Joint Coordination and Monitoring Board, composed of representatives of the Afghan Government and various international bodies, agreed to increase the size of the ANA to 86,000. The Afghan Ministry of Defence expected this target to be achieved by mid-2009, and in May 2008 it announced that the ANA numbered more than 76,000 personnel. The Afghan Minister of Defence suggested that more than US $1,700m. had already been invested by the US Administration towards equipping and retraining the ANA, and that further expenditure of some $5,700m. had been allocated to the advancement of the ANA's capabilities, the majority of which was to be funded by the USA.

**Chief of Staff of the Afghan National Army:** Gen. BESMELLAH KHAN.

## Education

The prolonged war resulted in a large-scale exodus of teachers, and some 3,600 school buildings were damaged or destroyed.

Before the Taliban rose to power, primary education began at seven years of age and lasted for six years. Secondary education, beginning at 13 years of age, lasted for a further six years. As a proportion of the school-age population, the total enrolment at primary and secondary schools was equivalent to 36% (males 49%; females 22%) in 1995. Primary enrolment in that year was equivalent to an estimated 49% of children in the relevant age-group (boys 64%; girls 32%), while the enrolment ratio at general secondary schools in 1996 was equivalent to 22% (boys 32%; girls 11%).

Higher education was disrupted by the departure of many teaching staff from Afghanistan during more than 20 years of civil war. In 1991 there were six institutions of higher education (including Kabul University, which was founded in 1932) in Afghanistan; a total of 17,000 students were enrolled in these institutions in that year.

Following their seizure of power in September 1996, the Taliban banned education for girls over the age of eight, closed all the women's institutes of higher education and drew up a new Islamic curriculum for boys' schools. Education in areas under the control of the United Front continued to operate. Even in areas controlled by the Taliban, Afghans attempted to continue to educate girls. In mid-1998 the UN was angered by the Taliban's decision to close more than 100 private schools and numerous small, home-based vocational courses in Kabul, many of which were educating girls. UNICEF reported that by December 1998 about 90% of girls and 66% of boys were not enrolled in school. According to Taliban figures, in September 1999 1,586,026 pupils were being educated by 59,792 teachers in 3,836 *madrassas* (mosque schools).

After the Taliban regime was defeated in late 2001, the Afghan Interim Administration (later the Afghan Transitional Authority), with the help of foreign governments, UNICEF and humanitarian organizations, began to rehabilitate the education system. The World Food Programme (WFP) embarked on a food-for-education programme; organizations world-wide supplied educational material and tents were provided as temporary classrooms. In March 2003 4.2m. boys and girls commenced a new academic year at some 7,000 schools around the country. The number of girls attending school increased by some 37% compared with the previous year, to approximately 1.2m. The boy-girl ratio in education in 2003/04 had returned to pre-Taliban levels. However, the attendance of girls at schools in parts of southern and eastern Afghanistan remained very low. In March 2004 almost 5.5m. children reportedly sought enrolment. Primary enrolment in 2004/05 was equivalent to an estimated 86.2% of children in the relevant age-group, while enrolment in secondary schools was equivalent to 16.2% of children in the relevant age-group. In 2004 UNICEF aimed to provide 4m. primary school children with access to high-quality education, especially girls and those living in remote areas. The organization also planned to provide basic training to at least 40,000 primary school teachers and to install a safe water point in every primary school in the country. The Afghan Ministry of Education, assisted by UNICEF, was also leading an initiative to establish community-based education, initially in six provinces, in order to provide basic educational opportunities for those with no access to formal schools. In March 2005 a nation-wide campaign promoting the value of education for girls was launched, in an attempt to encourage more girls to enrol in school; according to UNICEF, more than 1m. girls of primary school age were still not attending classes. By April of that year 1,108 community-based schools had been created, attended by approximately 55,000 children. According to statistics issued by the Afghan Ministry of Education, in 2005 there were some 5.2m. children enrolled in primary and secondary levels of education. A report published by Human Rights Watch in July 2006, however, indicated that a climate of insecurity, poverty, negative attitudes towards education, and the active (and often violent) targeting of the education system and its staff and attendees, had effected a serious deterioration in the condition of, and access to, schooling in the country.

Kabul University opened for men and women in March 2002. Some 24,000 students enrolled at the higher education level. Foreign universities as well as governments and non-governmental organizations donated books and teaching materials. Universities in at least five other provinces were being rehabilitated.

In January 2003 UNESCO and the Afghan Transitional Administration launched a major project to boost literacy rates throughout Afghanistan.

# Bibliography

### General


Ahmadi, Wali. *Modern Persian Literature in Afghanistan: Anomalous Visions of History and Form*. Abingdon, Routledge, 2008.

Ahmed, Akbar S. *Mataloona: Pukhto Proverbs*. Karachi, Oxford University Press, 1975.

*Millennium and Charisma among Pathans: A Critical Essay in Social Anthropology*. London, Routledge and Kegan Paul, 1976.

*Social and Economic Change in the Tribal Areas*. Karachi, Oxford University Press, 1977.

*A Bibliography of the North-West Frontier Province*. Peshawar, Home and Tribal Affairs Department, 1979.

'Religious Presence and Symbolism in Pukhtun Society' in Ahmed, Akbar S., and Hart David M. (Eds), *Islam in Tribal Studies: From the Atlas to the Indus*. London, Routledge and Kegan Paul, 1988.

*Discovering Islam: Making Sense of Muslim History and Society*. London and New York, Routledge and Kegan Paul, 1988.

*Postmodernism and Islam: Predicament and Promise*. London and New York, Routledge, 1992.

Amnesty International. *Afghanistan: The Human Rights of Minorities*. London, Amnesty International, 1999.

Anderson, Ewan W., and Dupree, Nancy H. (Eds). *The Cultural Basis of Afghan Nationalism*. London and New York, Pinter Publishers Ltd, 1990.

Ataye, M. Ibrahim. *A Dictionary of the Terminology of Pashtun's Tribal Customary Law and Usages*. Kabul, Academy of Sciences of Afghanistan, International Centre for Pashto Studies, 1979.

Azoy, G. Whitney. *Buzkashi: Game and Power in Afghanistan*. Philadelphia, PA, University of Pennsylvania Press, 1982.

Barakat, Sultan. *After the Conflict: Reconstructions and Redevelopment in the Aftermath of War*. London, I. B. Tauris, 2005.

Barfield, Thomas J. *The Central Asian Arabs of Afghanistan: Pastoral Nomadism in Transition*. Austin, TX, University of Texas Press, 1981.

Barth, Fredrik. 'Segmentary Opposition and the Theory of Games: A Study of Pathan Organization', *Journal of the Royal Anthropological Institute*, Vol. 89, No. 5, pp. 5–21, 1959.

'Pathan Identity and Its Maintenance' in Barth, Fredrik (Ed.), *Ethnic Groups and Boundaries*. Boston, MA, Little, Brown and Co, 1969.

Bellew, H. W. *An Inquiry into the Ethnography of Afghanistan*. Karachi, Indus Publications, 1977.

Boesen, Inger W. 'Women, Honour and Love: Some Aspects of the Pashtun Woman's Life in Eastern Afghanistan', *Afghanistan Journal*, Vol. 7, No. 2, pp. 50–59, 1980.

'Conflicts of Solidarity in Pakhtun Women's Lives' in Bo Utas (Ed.), *Women in Islamic Societies: Social Attitudes and Historical Perspectives*. London, Curzon Press, 1983.

Brodsky, Anne E. *With All Our Strength: The Revolutionary Association of the Women of Afghanistan*. London, RoutledgeCurzon, 2004.

Byrd, William A. *Afghanistan: State Building, Sustaining Growth, and Reducing Poverty*. World Bank, 2005.

Caroe, Olaf. *The Pathans: 550 BC–AD 1957*. Oxford, Oxford University Press, 1976.

Centlivres, Pierre. 'Le Mouvement Taliban et la Condition Féminine', *Afghanistan Info*, March 1999.

*Les Bouddhas d'Afghanistan*. Lausanne, Editions Favre, 2001.

Chayes, Sarah. *The Punishment of Virtue: Inside Afghanistan after the Taliban*. New York, The Penguin Press, 2006.

Christensen, Asgar. 'The Pashtuns of Kunar: Tribe, Class and Community Organization', *Afghanistan Journal*, Vol. 7, pp. 79–92, 1980.

'When Muslim Identity has Different Meanings: Religion and Politics in Contemporary Afghanistan' in Ferdinand, Klaus, and Mozaffari, Mehdi (Eds), *Islam: State and Society*. London, Curzon Press, 1988.

Doubleday, Veronica. *Three Women of Herat*. London, Jonathan Cape, 1988.

Edwards, David B. 'Marginality and Migration: Cultural Dimensions of the Afghan Refugee Problem', *International Migration*, 20, pp. 313–328, 1986.

'Frontiers, Boundaries and Frames: The Marginal Identity of Afghan Refugees' in Ahmed, Akbar S. (Ed.), *Pakistan: The Social Science Perspective*. Karachi, Oxford University Press, 1990.

Emadi, Hafizullah. *Culture and Customs of Afghanistan*. London, Greenwood Publishing Group, 2005.

Evans, Anne, *et al*. *Subnational Administration in Afghanistan: Assessment and Recommendations for Action*. World Bank, 2004.

*A Guide to Government in Afghanistan*. World Bank, 2004.

Gall, Sandy. *Afghanistan: Agony of a Nation*. London, The Bodley Head, 1988.

Ghani, Ashraf. 'Islam and State-Building in a Tribal Society, Afghanistan: 1880–1901', *Modern Asian Studies*, Vol. 12, No. 2, pp. 269–284, 1978.

'Disputes on a Court of *Shari'a*, Kunar Valley, Afghanistan, 1885–90,' *International Journal of Middle East Studies*, Vol. 15, pp. 353–367, 1983.

'Islam and Counter-revolutionary Movements' in Esposito, John L. (Ed.), *Islam in Asia*. Oxford, Oxford University Press, 1987.

Griffiths, John C. *Afghanistan*. London, Pall Mall Press, 1967.

*Afghanistan: Key to a Continent*. London, André Deutsch, 1981.

Halliday, Fred. *Islam and the Myth of Confrontation*. London, I. B. Tauris, 1995.

Hiebert, Fredrik, and Cambon, Pierre (Eds). *Afghanistan: Hidden Treasures from the National Museum, Kabul*. National Geographic, 2008.

Klimburg, M. *Afghanistan*. Vienna, Austrian UNESCO Commission, 1966.

Lamb, Christina. *The Sewing Circles of Herat: My Afghan Years*. London, HarperCollins, 2002.

Latifa, and Hachemi, Shekeba. *My Forbidden Face: Growing Up Under the Taliban: A Young Woman's Story*. Talk Miramax Books, 2002.

Lessing, Doris. *The Wind Blows Away Our Words*. London, Picador, 1988.

MacDonald, David. *Drugs in Afghanistan: Opium, Outlaws and Scorpion Tales*. London, Pluto Press, 2007.

Mousavi, Sayed Askar. *The Hazaras of Afghanistan: An Historical, Cultural, Economic and Political Study*. New York, St Martin's Press, 1997.

Orywal, Erwin (Ed.). *Die ethnischen Gruppen Afghanistans: Fallstudien zu Gruppenidentität und Intergruppenbeziehungen*. Wiesbaden, Dr Ludwig Reichert Verlag, 1986.

Singer, André. *Lords of the Khyber*. London, Faber, 1984.

Skaine, Rosemarie. *The Women of Afghanistan Under the Taliban*. Jefferson, NC, McFarland & Company, Inc, 2001.

Spain, James W. *The Way of the Pathan*. Karachi, Oxford University Press, 2nd edn, 1972.

*The Pathan Borderland*. Karachi, Indus Publications, 1985.

Szabo, Albert, and Borfield, Thomas J. *Afghanistan: An Atlas of Indigenous Domestic Architecture*. Austin, TX, University of Texas Press, 1991.

Tapper, Nancy. *Bartered Brides: Politics, Gender and Marriage in an Afghan Tribal Society*. Cambridge, Cambridge University Press, 1991.

Van Dyk, Jere. *In Afghanistan. An American Odyssey*. New York, Coward-McCann, 1983.

Vogelsang, Willem. *The Afghans (People of Asia)*. Oxford, Blackwell Publishers, 2001.

Wilber, Donald N. *Afghanistan*. New Haven, CT, 1956.

*Annotated Bibliography of Afghanistan*. New Haven, CT, 1962.

### Geography and Travels

Burnes, Sir Alexander. *Cabool*. London, John Murray, 1842, reprinted Lahore 1961.

Byron, Robert. *The Road to Oxiana*. London, Jonathan Cape, 1937.

Curzon, George. *Tales of Travel*. New York, George H. Doran, 1923.

Elliot, Jason. *An Unexpected Light—Travels in Afghanistan*. London, Picador, 1999.

Elphinstone, M. *An Account of the Kingdom of Caubul and its Dependencies in Persia, Tartary and India*. London, John Murray, 1815, reprinted Oxford University Press, 1972.

Hahn, H. *Die Stadt Kabul und ihr Umland*. 2 vols. Bonn, 1964–65.

Hamilton, Angus. *Afghanistan*. London, Heinemann, 1966.

Hodson, Peregrine, *Under a Sickle Moon: A Journey through Afghanistan*. London, Hutchinson, 1986.

Humlum, J. *La Géographie de l'Afghanistan*. Copenhagen, Gyldendal, 1959.

Levi, Peter. *Journeys in Afghanistan*. London, Penguin, 1984.

Stewart, Rory. *The Places in Between*. London, Picador, 2004.

Wolfe, N. H. *Herat*. Kabul, Afghan Tourist Organization, 1966.

Wood, John. *A Personal Narrative of a Journey to the Source of the River Oxus by the Route of Indus, Kabul and Badakshan*. London, John Murray, 1841, reprinted Oxford University Press, 1976.

### History and Politics

Adamec, Ludwig W. *Afghanistan 1900–1923*. Berkeley, CA, University of California, 1967.

*Afghanistan's Foreign Affairs to the Mid-Twentieth Century*. Tucson, AZ, University of Arizona Press, 1974.

*Historical and Political Who's Who of Afghanistan*. Graz, Akademische Druk-und Verlagsanstalt, 1975.

*Historical Dictionary of Afghanistan*. London, Scarecrow Press Inc., 1991.

'Greater Afghanistan—a missed Chance?', *Afghanistan Info*, March 1998.

*Historical Dictionary of Afghan Wars, Revolutions and Insurgencies*. London, Scarecrow Press Inc., 2005.

Adamec, Ludwig W., and Clements, Frank A. *Conflict in Afghanistan: An Encyclopedia*. Santa Barbara, CA, ABC-CLIO Ltd, 2003.

Akhramovich, R. T. *Outline History of Afghanistan after the Second World War*. Moscow, 1966.

Akram, Assem. *Histoire de la guerre d'Afghanistan*. Paris, Editions Balland, 1996.

Alder, G. J. *British India's Northern Frontier, 1865–1895*. London, Longman, 1963.

Alexander, Yonah, and Swetnam, Michael. *Usama bin Laden's Al-Qaida: Profile of a Terrorist Network*. New York, Transnational Publishing, 2001.

Alexievich, Svetlana. *The Zinky Boys*. London, Chatto and Windus, 1991.

Ali-Shah, Sirdar Ikbal. *Modern Afghanistan*. Lahore, Sang-e-Meel Publications, 2004.

Anwar, Raja. *The Tragedy of Afghanistan: A First-hand Account*. London, Verso, 1988.

Arney, George. *Afghanistan's Two-Party Communism: Parchem and Khalq*. Stanford, CA, Stanford University Press, 1983.

*Afghanistan*. London, Mandarin Books, 1990.

Arnold, Anthony. *Afghanistan's Two-Party Communism: Parcham and Khalq*. Stanford University, CA, Hoover Institution Press, 1984.

Baha, L. *NWFP Administration under British Rule 1901–19*. Islamabad, National Commission on Historical and Cultural Research, 1978.

Banerjee, Mukulika. *The Pathan Unarmed: Opposition and Memory in the North West Frontier*. Karachi, Oxford University Press, 2000.

Bergen, Peter L. *Holy War, Inc.: Inside the Secret World of Osama bin Laden*. London, Weidenfeld & Nicolson, 2001.

Bhatia, Michael Vinay, and Sedra, Mark. *Afghanistan, Arms and Conflict: Armed Groups, Disarmament and Security in a Post-War Society*. Abingdon, Routledge, 2008.

Bindeman, Rolf. 'Der Politische Aufsteig und der Fall der Hazara', *Afghanistan Info*, March 1999.

Blanc, Florent. *Ben Laden et l'Amérique*. Paris, Bayard Editions, 2001.

Bocharov, Gennady. *Russian Roulette: The Afghanistan War through Russian Eyes*. London, Hamish Hamilton, 1991.

Borer, Douglas A. *Superpowers Defeated: Vietnam and Afghanistan Compared*. London, Frank Cass, 1999.

Borovik, Artyom. *The Hidden War: A Russian Journalist's Account of the Soviet War in Afghanistan*. New York, Atlantic Monthly Press, 1991.

Bosworth, C. E. *The Ghaznavids*. Edinburgh University Press, 1963.

Bradsher, Henry S. *Afghanistan and the Soviet Union*. Durham, NC, Duke University Press, 1984.

*Afghan Communism and Soviet Intervention*. Karachi, Oxford University Press, 1999.

Burke, S. M., and Ziring, Lawrence. *Pakistan's Foreign Policy: An Historical Analysis*. Oxford, Oxford University Press, 2nd edn, 1990.

Carew, Tom. *Jihad: The Secret War in Afghanistan*. Edinburgh, Mainstream Publishing Co, 2001.

Chadda, Maya. 'Talibanisation and Pakistan's Transitional Democracy', *World Affairs*, Vol. 3, No. 3, July–September 1999.

Churchill, Winston. *Frontiers and Wars*. London, Eyre and Spottiswoode, 1962.

Coll, Steve. *Ghost Wars: The Secret History of the CIA, Afghanistan and Bin Laden, from the Soviet Invasion to September 10, 2001.* London, Penguin, 2005.

Cooley, John K. *Unholy Wars: Afghanistan, America and International Terrorism.* London, Pluto Publishing Ltd, 1999.

Córdovez, Diego, and Harrison, Selig. *Out of Afghanistan: The Inside Story of the Soviet Withdrawal.* Oxford, Oxford University Press, 1995.

Crews, Robert D., and Tarzi, Amin (Eds). *The Taliban and the Crisis of Afghanistan.* Cambridge, MA, Harvard University Press, 2008.

Crile, George. *Charlie Wilson's War: The Extraordinary Story of the Largest Covert Operation in History—The Arming of the Mujahideen.* New York, Atlantic Monthly Press, 2003.

Dobbins, Amb. James F. *After the Taliban: Nation-Building in Afghanistan.* Dulles, VA, Potomac Books Inc., 2008.

Dollot, René. *Afghanistan.* Paris, Payot, 1937.

Dorronsoro, Gilles. 'Afghanistan. Du 'Djihad' à la Guerre Civile' in *Islamisme Paris: Les Dossiers de l'Etat du Monde*, 1994.

'Les Talibans: Dynamique Révolutionnaire et Environnement Régional', *Afghanistan Info*, March 1999.

*La Révolution Afghane, des Communistes aux Tâlebân.* Paris, Karthala Editions, 2000.

*Revolution Unending: Afghanistan 1979 to the Present.* New York, Columbia University Press, 2005.

Dupree, Louis. 'Tribal Warfare in Afghanistan and Pakistan: A Reflection of the Segmentary Lineage System' in Akbar S. Ahmed and David M. Hart (Eds), *Islam in Tribal Societies: From the Atlas to the Indus.* London, Routledge and Kegan Paul, 1984.

*Afghanistan.* Karachi, Oxford University Press, 1997.

Dupree, Louis, and Linnet, Albert (Eds). *Afghanistan in the 1970s.* New York, Praeger, 1974, and London, Pall Mall Press, 1975.

Dupree, Nancy Hatch. *An Historical Guide to Afghanistan.* Kabul, Afghan Tourist Organisation, 1970.

Durand, Col Algernon. *The Making of a Frontier.* Karachi, Indus Publications, 1977.

Edwards, David B. 'Charismatic Leadership and Political Process in Afghanistan', *Central Asian Surveys*, Vol. 5, pp. 273–299, 1986.

'Origins of the Anti-Soviet Jihad', in Grant M. Farr and John G. Merriam (Eds), *Afghan Resistance: The Politics of Survival.* Boulder, CO, Westview Press, 1987.

*Heroes of the Age: Moral Fault Lines on the Afghan Frontier.* Berkeley and Los Angeles, CA, University of California Press, 1996.

*Before Taliban: Genealogies of the Afghan Jihad.* Berkeley and Los Angeles, CA, University of California Press, 2002.

Ellis, Deborah. *Women of the Afghan War.* London, Greenwood Publishing Group, 2000.

Elphinstone, Mountstuart. *An Account of the Kingdom of Cabaul.* London, 1815, reprinted Karachi, Indus Publications, 1992.

Emadi, Hafizullah. *State, Revolution and Superpowers in Afghanistan.* New York, Praeger Publishers, 1990.

Esposito, John L. (Ed.). *Political Islam: Revolution, Radicalism or Reforms?* London, Lynne Rienner Publishers, 1997.

Ewans, Martin. *Afghanistan—A New History.* London, RoutledgeCurzon, 2nd edn, 2002.

*Afghanistan: A Short History of its People and Politics.* London, HarperCollins, 2002.

*Conflict in Afghanistan: Studies in Asymmetric Warfare.* Abingdon, Routledge, 2005.

Fletcher, Arnold. *Afghanistan, Highway of Conquest.* Cornell and Oxford University Presses, 1965.

Fraser-Tytler, Sir W. Kerr. *Afghanistan.* Oxford University Press, 1950, 3rd edn, 1967.

Fullerton, John. *The Soviet Occupation of Afghanistan.* London, Methuen, 1984.

Gannon, Kathy. *I is for Infidel: From Holy War to Holy Terror in Afghanistan.* New York, PublicAffairs, 2005.

Ghaus, Abdul Samad. *The Fall of Afghanistan: An Insider's Account.* Oxford, Pergamon Press, 1988.

Girardet, Edward R. *Afghanistan: The Soviet War.* London, Croom Helm, 1985.

Giustozzi, Antonio. *War, Politics and Society in Afghanistan, 1978–1992.* London, C. Hurst & Co (Publishers) Ltd, 2000.

Gohari, M. J. *Taliban: Ascent to Power.* Oxford, Oxford University Press, 2001.

Goodson, Larry P. *Afghanistan's Endless War: State Failure, Regional Politics, and the Rise of the Taliban.* Washington, DC, University of Washington Press, 2001.

Greenwood, John. *The Campaign in Afghanistan.* Dublin, Nonsuch Publishing, 2005.

Gregorian, Vartan. *The Emergence of Modern Afghanistan.* Stanford, CA, Stanford University Press, 1969.

Griffin, Michael. *Reaping the Whirlwind: The Taliban Movement in Afghanistan.* London, Pluto Publishing Ltd, 2001.

Griffiths, John C. *Afghanistan: A History of Conflict.* London, André Deutsch, 2001.

Haider, Ejaz. 'Pakistan's Afghan Policy and its Fallout', *Central Asia Monitor*, No. 5, 1998.

Harrison, Selig S. 'Inside the Afghan Talks', *Foreign Policy*, No. 72, 1988.

Heathcote, Tony. *The Afghan Wars 1839–1919.* Staplehurst, Spellmount Publishers, 2003.

Hensman, Howard. *The Afghan War of 1879–80.* Lahore, Sang-e-Meel Publications, 1978.

Hilali, A. Z. *US–Pakistan Relationship: Soviet Invasion of Afghanistan.* Aldershot, Ashgate Publishing Ltd, 2005.

Hodes, Cyrus, and Sedra, Mark. *The Search for Security in Post-Taliban Afghanistan.* Abingdon, Routledge, 2007.

Hoge, James F., and Gideon, Rose (Eds). *How Did This Happen? Terrorism and the New War.* New York, PublicAffairs, 2001.

Holt, Frank L. *Into the Land of Bones: Alexander the Great in Afghanistan.* Berkeley, CA, University of California Press, 2005.

Hopkirk, Peter. *The Great Game.* London, John Murray, 1990.

Hussain, Rizwan. *Pakistan and the Emergence of Islamic Militancy in Afghanistan.* Aldershot, Ashgate Publishing Ltd, 2005.

Hyman, Anthony. *Afghanistan under Soviet Domination: 1964–81.* New York, St Martin's Press, 1982.

Inderfurth, Karl F. 'Afghanistan at a Crossroads', Washington, DC, US Senate Foreign Relations Committee Statement, 14 April 1999.

Jalalzai, Musa Khan. *The US War on Terrorism in Afghanistan.* Lahore, Sang-e-Meel Publications, 2003.

Johnson, Chris. *Afghanistan: A Land in Shadow.* Oxford, Oxfam, 1998.

Johnson, Chris, and Leslie, Jolyon. *Afghanistan: The Mirage of Peace.* London, Zed Books Ltd, 2004.

Kakar, Hasan, *Afghanistan: A Study in International Political Developments, 1880–1896.* Lahore, Punjab Educational Press, 1971.

*Government and Society in Afghanistan.* Tucson, AZ, University of Arizona Press, 1979.

Khan, M. M. S. M. (Ed.). *The Life of Abdur Rahman, Amir of Afghanistan.* London, John Murray, 1900, reprinted Karachi, Oxford University Press, 1980.

Khan, Muhammad Fahim. 'The Life and Times of Hajji Sahib of Turangzai', *Islamic Studies*, Vol. 16, No. 1, pp. 329–341, 1977.

Khan, Riaz M. *Untying the Afghan Knot: Negotiating Soviet Withdrawal.* Durham, NC, Duke University Press, 1991.

Klass, Rosanne (Ed.). *Afghanistan: The Great Game Revisited.* New York, Freedom House, 1988.

Kleveman, Lutz. *The New Great Game: Blood and Oil in Central Asia.* Boston, MA, Atlantic Monthly Press, 2004.

Kolhatkar, Sonali, and Ingalls, James. *Bleeding Afghanistan: Washington, Warlords and the Propaganda of Silence.* New York, Seven Stories Press, 2006.

Labrousse, Alain. 'Les Drogues et les Conflits en Afghanistan', *Afghanistan Info*, March 1996.

Lee, Jonathan L. *The 'Ancient Supremacy': Bukhara, Afghanistan and the Battle for Balkh, 1731–1901.* Leiden, E. J. Brill, 1996.

Mackey, Chris, and Miller, Greg. *The Interrogator's War: Breaking Al-Qaeda in Afghanistan.* London, John Murray, 2005.

Macrory, Patrick. *Signal Catastrophe.* London, Hodder and Stoughton, 1966.

Magnus, Ralph. H., and Naby, Eden. *Afghanistan: Marx, Mullah and Mujahid.* Boulder, CO, Westview Press, 1997.

Maley, William. *Rescuing Afghanistan.* Sydney, UNSW Press, 2006.

Maley, William (Ed.). *The Foreign Policy of the Taliban.* New York, Council on Foreign Relations, 2000.

*Fundamentalism Reborn? Afghanistan and the Taliban.* London, C. Hurst & Co (Publishers) Ltd, 2001.

Maley, William, and Saikal, Fazel Haq. *Political Order in Post-Communist Afghanistan.* London, Lynne Rienner Publishers, 1992.

Maloney, Sean M. *Enduring the Freedom: A Rogue Historian in Afghanistan.* Dulles, VA, Potomac Books Inc., 2005.

Marozzi, Justin. *Tamerlane: Sword of Islam, Conqueror of the World.* London, HarperCollins, 2004.

Marsden, Peter. *The Taliban: War, Religion and the New Order in Afghanistan*. London, Zed Books Ltd, 1998.

Martin, Frank A. *Under the Absolute Amir*. London, Harper and Brothers, reprinted New Delhi, Bhavana Books, 2000.

Masson, V. M., and Romodin, V. A. *Istoriya Afghanistana*. Moscow, Academy of Sciences of the USSR, 1964–65.

Matinuddin, Kamal. *Power Struggle in the Hindu Kush*. Lahore, Wajidalis, 1991.

*The Taliban Phenomenon: Afghanistan 1994–97*. Karachi, Oxford University Press, 2000.

McChesney, Robert D. *Kabul Under Siege: Fayz Muhammad's Account of the 1929 Uprising*. Princeton, NJ, Markus Wiener Publishers, 1999.

Meyer, Karl E. *The Dust of Empire: The Race for Mastery in the Asian Heartland*. New York, PublicAffairs, 2003.

Misdaq, Nabi. *Afghanistan: Political Frailty and External Interference*. Abingdon, Routledge, 2006.

Misra, Amalendu. *Afghanistan: The Labyrinth of Violence*. Cambridge, Polity Press, 2004.

Mohun, Lal. *Life of the Amir Dost Mohammed Khan of Kabul*. London, Longman, 1846, reprinted Oxford University Press, 1978.

Moorehouse, Geoffrey. *To the Frontier*. London, Hodder and Stoughton, 1984.

Mottahedeh, Roy P. *Loyalty and Leadership in an Early Islamic Society*. Princeton, NJ, Princeton University Press, 1980.

Nevell, Capt. H. L. *Campaigns on the North-West Frontier*. Lahore, Sang-e-Meel Publishers, 1977.

Newell, Richard S. *The Politics of Afghanistan*. Ithaca, NY, Cornell University Press, 1972.

Noelle, Christine. *State and Tribe in Nineteenth-Century Afghanistan: The Reign of Amir Dost Muhammad Khan (1826–1863)*. Richmond, Curzon Press, 1998.

Nojumi, Neamotollah. *The Rise of the Taliban in Afghanistan: Mass Mobilization, Civil War and the Future of the Region*. London, Palgrave Macmillan, 2002.

Olsen, Asta. 'Afghanistan: The Development of a Modern State,' in Ferdinand, Klaus, and Mozaffari, Mehdi (Eds), *Islam: State and Society*. London, Curzon Press, 1988.

*Islam and Politics in Afghanistan*. Scandinavian Institute of Asian Studies—Monograph Series, No. 67, 1996.

Pennell, T. L. *Among the Wild Tribes of the Afghan Frontier*. London, Seeley & Co, 1909.

Peters, Rudolph. *Islam and Colonialism: The Doctrine of Jihad in Modern History*. The Hague, Mouton, 1979.

Poullada, Leon B. *Reform and Rebellion in Afghanistan, 1919–1929*. Ithaca, NY, Cornell University Press, 1972.

Rahman, Fatuhur, and Bashir, A. Qureshi. *Afghans Meet Soviet Challenge*. Peshawar, Institute of Regional Studies, 1981.

Rasanayagam, Angelo. 'Taliban Fundamentalism: Afghan Turmoils', *World Affairs*, Vol. 3, No. 3, June 1999.

*Afghanistan: A Modern History*. London, I. B. Tauris, 2003.

*Utopia Revisited*. London, I. B. Tauris, 2004.

Rashid, Ahmed. *The Resurgence of Central Asia: Islam or Nationalism?* London, Zed Books Ltd, 1994.

*Taliban: The Story of the Afghan Warlords*. London, Pan Macmillan, 2001.

*Descent into Chaos: The United States and the Failure of Nation Building in Pakistan, Afghanistan and Central Asia*. New York, Viking, 2008.

Reeve, Simon. *The New Jackals: Ramzi Yousef, Osama bin Laden and the Future of Terrorism*. Boston, MA, Northeastern University Press, 1999.

Rondinelli, Dennis, and Montgomery, John (Eds). *Beyond Reconstruction in Afghanistan*. London, Palgrave Macmillan, 2004.

Rotberg, Robert I. (Ed.) *Building a New Afghanistan*. Washington, DC, Brookings Institution, 2006.

Roy, Olivier. *L'Afghanistan: Islam et modernité politique*. Paris, Seuil, 1985.

*Islam and Resistance in Afghanistan*. Cambridge, Cambridge University Press, 1987.

(trans. Volk, Catherine). *The Failure of Political Islam*, London, I. B. Tauris, 1994.

Rubin, Barnett. *Afghanistan: Persistent Crisis Challenges the UN System*. London, Writenet, 1998.

*Testimony on the Situation in Afghanistan*. Washington, DC, US Senate, Council on Foreign Relations, 8 October 1998.

*The Fragmentation of Afghanistan: State Formation and Collapse in the International System*. London, Yale University Press, 2nd edn, 2002.

Sabir, Mohammad Shah. *Story of Khyber*. Peshawar, University Book Agency, 1964.

Saikal, Amin. 'The UN and Afghanistan: A Case of Failed Peacekeeping Intervention', *International Peacekeeping*, Vol. 3, No. 1, Spring 1996.

*Modern Afghanistan: A History of Struggle and Survival*. London, I. B. Tauris, 2004.

Saikal, Amin, and Maley, William (Eds). *The Soviet Withdrawal from Afghanistan*. Cambridge, Cambridge University Press, 1989.

Saikal, Amin, and Maley, William. *Regime Change in Afghanistan: Foreign Intervention and the Politics of Legitimacy*. Boulder, CO, Westview Press, 1991.

Schroen, Gary C. *First in: How Seven CIA Officers Opened the War on Terror in Afghanistan*. London, Presidio Press, 2005.

Shahrani, M. Nazif. 'State Building and Social Fragmentation in Afghanistan: A Historical Perspective', in Banuazizi, Ali, and Weiner, Myron (Eds), *The State, Religion and Ethnic Politics: Afghanistan, Iran and Pakistan*. Syracuse, NY, Syracuse University Press, 1986.

Sreedar (Ed.). *Taliban and the Afghan Turmoil*. New Delhi, Himalayan Books, 1997.

Sreedar, and Ved, Mahendra. *The Afghan Turmoil: Changing Equations*. New Delhi, Himalayan Books, 1998.

Stewart, Jules. *The Khyber Rifles: From the British Raj to Al Qaeda*. Stroud, Sutton Publishing, 2004.

Surke, Ami, and Woodward, Susan L. 'Make Haste Slowly in Assistance for Afghanistan', *International Herald Tribune*, 21 January 2002.

Sykes, Sir Percy. *A History of Afghanistan*. London, Macmillan, 1940.

Talbott, Strobe, and Chanda, Nayan (Eds). *The Age of Terror: America and the World after September 11*. New York, Basic Books, 2001.

Tanner, Stephen. *Afghanistan: A Military History from Alexander the Great to the Present*. Cambridge, MA, Da Capo Press, 2003.

Tapper, Richard (Ed.). *The Conflict of Tribe and State in Iran and Afghanistan*. New York, St Martin's Press, 1983.

Tate, G. P. *The Kingdom of Afghanistan: A Historical Sketch*. Bombay, Times Press, 1911, reprinted Karachi, Indus Publications, 1973.

UN High Commissioner for Refugees. *Refugees: Focus on Afghanistan*. UNHCR, Vol. 108, II, 1997.

Urban, Mark. *War in Afghanistan*. London, Macmillan Press, 1988.

Victor, Jean-Christophe. *La cité des murmures: L'enjeu afghan*. Paris, Editions J. C. Lattès, 1985.

Wahab, Shaista, and Youngerman, Barry. *A Brief History of Afghanistan*. New York, Facts on File Inc., 2007.

Waller, John H. *Beyond the Khyber Pass: Road to British Disaster in the First Afghan War*. New York, Random House, 1990.

Warburton, Sir Robert. *Eighteen Years in the Khyber, 1879–98*. London, John Murray, 1900, reprinted Karachi, Oxford University Press, 1970.

Whitlock, Monica. *Land Beyond the River: The Untold Story of Central Asia*. New York, Thomas Dunne Books, 2004.

Yousaf, Mohammed. *Silent Soldier: The Man behind the Afghan Jihad*. Lahore, Jhang Publishers, 1991.

Yousaf, Mohammed, and Adkin, Mark. *The Bear Trap: Afghanistan's Untold Story*. London, Leo Cooper, 1992.


### Economy


Ahmed, Akbar S. *Pukhtun Economy and Society: Traditional Structure and Economic Development in a Tribal Society*. London, Routledge and Kegan Paul, 1980.

Bennett, Adam (Ed.). *Reconstructing Afghanistan*. International Monetary Fund, 2005.

Carnahan, Michael, *et al* (Eds). *Reforming Fiscal and Economic Management in Afghanistan*. World Bank, 2004.

Fry, Maxwell J. *The Afghan Economy*. Leiden, 1974.

Jalalzai, Musa Khan. *The Political Economy of Afghanistan*. Lahore, Sang-e-Meel Publications, 2003.

Malekyar, Abdul Wahed. *Die Verkehrsentwicklung in Afghanistan*. Cologne, 1966.

Marsden, Peter, and Samman, Emma. 'Afghanistan: The Economic and Social Impact of Conflict' in Francis Steward and Valpy Fitzgerald, *et al.* (Eds), *War and Underdevelopment Volume 2: Country Experiences.* Oxford, Oxford University Press, 2001.

Monsutti, Alessandro. *War and Migration: Social Networks and Economic Strategies of the Hazaras of Afghanistan.* Abingdon, Routledge, 2005.

Nägler, Horst. *Privatinitiative beim Industrieaufbau in Afghanistan.* Düsseldorf, Bertelsmann Universitätsverlag, 1971.

Pain, Adam, and Sutton, Jackie (Eds). *Reconstructing Agriculture in Afghanistan.* Rugby, Practical Action Publishing, 2007.

Rhein, E., and Ghaussy, A. Ghanie. *Die wirtschaftliche Entwicklung Afghanistans, 1880–1965.* Hamburg, C. W. Leske Verlag, 1966.

# BANGLADESH

## Physical and Social Geography

B. H. FARMER

With additions by the editorial staff

The People's Republic of Bangladesh covers an area of 143,998 sq km (55,598 sq miles). It straddles the Tropic of Cancer, extending between 20° 30′ and 26° 45′ N, and between 88° 0′ and 92° 40′ E. It is wholly enclosed by Indian territory, except for a short south-eastern frontier with Myanmar (formerly Burma) and a southern, deltaic coast fronting the Bay of Bengal. From the conclusion of British rule in August 1947 until the end of the Indo-Pakistan war of December 1971, Bangladesh constituted the eastern wing of Pakistan: that is, East Pakistan or East Bengal. Bangladesh became formally independent following the capitulation of Pakistani military and civilian authorities on 16 December 1971. The capital is Dhaka.

### PHYSICAL FEATURES AND SOILS

Most of Bangladesh consists of an alluvial plain, largely made up of the still-growing, annually flooded Ganges-Brahmaputra delta, together with a tongue of similar wet plain running up the Surma river between the Assam plateau and the Lushai hills (both in India; though Bangladesh includes a very small portion of lower foothills country, on the Assam boundary, which contains some tea plantations). As in West Bengal (India), belts of older and less fertile deposits lend some little diversity to the plains, notably in the regions known as Barind and the Madhupur jungle tract. To the east of the delta lie the Chittagong Hill Tracts, an area of steep, roughly parallel ranges largely covered with jungle, much of it bamboo.

For the most part, however, Bangladesh is deltaic, and its rural people have evolved a remarkable semi-aquatic life style adapted to deep flooding in the monsoon: for instance, by constructing earthen plinths 4 m or more high to raise their houses above flood level (or so they hope) and by sowing varieties of rice that will grow in deep water.

Much of Bangladesh has relatively fertile alluvial soils, many of them benefiting from renewal by flooding. There is considerable local variation: for example, areas of sandy soils on the one hand, and of swamp soils on the other (alluvium varying with the rivers that brought it), in addition to Barind and the Madhupur jungle tract. The Chittagong hills have poor skeletal soils.

### CLIMATE

The climate of Bangladesh is tropical and is dominated by the seasonally reversing monsoons. There is no real cool season. In the capital, Dhaka, for example, the average January temperature is 19°C, and the average July temperature 29°C. The 'summer', if it can be called such, is remarkably equable: the average monthly temperature is 29°C from May right through to September. The 'winter' is dry, and crops (in the absence of irrigation or of water-holding depressions, where winter rice can be grown) have to depend on moisture remaining in the soil from the monsoon. There are pre-monsoon rains in April and May, but it is the south-west monsoon that brings heavy rain in earnest: 75% of Dhaka's annual average total of 1,880 mm falls between June and September. Bangladesh has, in fact, a typical humid tropical monsoon climate; but it is a climate subject to violence from time to time, for example when a tropical cyclone, charged with energy and with water vapour and accompanied by high winds, sweeps in and devastates low-lying areas in the coastal parts of the delta. Such 'extreme natural events' tend also to bring high seas and flooding with salt water, so that there is damage to the soil as well as severe loss of life and of crops.

### NATURAL RESOURCES

Bangladesh has small reserves of petroleum and coal, and potentially vast resources of natural gas. Gas production began in 1960, and a significant breakthrough occurred in 1995 with the discovery of Sangu, Bangladesh's first offshore field. In 1999/2000 there were approximately 20 gas fields, of which one-half were active. Natural gas provided 87.5% of Bangladesh's total electricity output in 2004. At the end of 2006 the country's proven natural gas reserves were estimated at 440,000m. cu m. Bangladesh has the potential to become a major gas producer and supplier to domestic and external markets. However, many Bangladeshis believe that gas resources should be used for domestic purposes first; both major political parties will consider gas exports only if Bangladesh has sufficient proven reserves to meet 50 years of domestic demand. Bangladesh's petroleum reserves amount to an estimated 56.9m. barrels, with production at about 1,600 barrels per day.

### POPULATION

According to the adjusted results of the census of January 2001, Bangladesh had a population of 130,522,598, giving an average density of 906.4 per sq km. Apart from territories comprising less than 1,200 sq km in area, Bangladesh is the most densely populated country in the world, despite its overwhelmingly rural and agricultural nature. Even then, average densities are misleading: the density of population is lower than the average in such areas as Barind and the Madhupur jungle tract, and higher than the very high average in other areas, notably those along the lower Padma and Meghna rivers. Bangladesh has one rapidly growing conurbation, that around the capital, Dhaka, with a population of 3,612,850 (excluding suburbs) at the March 1991 census. Chittagong, the principal seaport, had a population of 1,392,860 in 1991.

Bangla (Bengali) is the principal language in Bangladesh (as it is in Indian West Bengal), but English is widely used. Some tribal peoples retain their own languages.

# History

DAVID TAYLOR

Based on an earlier article by PETER ROBB

Bangladesh has its roots in the medieval past, when the regional differences between Bengal and other parts of South Asia were consolidated, and in the distinctions between Bengali Muslims and Hindus, which probably date from the activities of Muslim saints in the 13th century and from subsequent non-Bengali Muslim rulers. By the 20th century Muslims constituted just over one-half of the population of Bengal, being more heavily concentrated in the eastern districts which are now Bangladesh. The majority were poor, rural and, in many ways, still strongly influenced by the Hinduism from which they had converted. They had initially been relatively little affected by British rule after 1765, which had most impact on the service and landed élites of the region, but in the late 19th century and in the 20th century the distinctions between ordinary Hindus and Muslims were seen to have been strengthened and made politically relevant by legal, administrative and economic changes. Even so, Indian Muslim support for the political partition of the subcontinent was drawn particularly not from Bengal but from areas where Muslims were in the minority, and as late as 1937 the Muslim League (ML) was electorally ineffective in Bengal in comparison with the local Krishak Proja Samiti of Fazlul Huq.

Nevertheless, Bengali Muslims, too, were drawn into electoral politics and agitation by religious motivation, and many of them came to be persuaded in the 1940s of the advantages to them of the Pakistan idea. In 1943 an ML ministry was formed in Bengal, marking the advance of its propaganda and its alliance with prominent Bengalis.*

## EAST PAKISTAN, 1947–71

East Bengal duly became part of Pakistan in 1947, but its people soon came to distrust their partners in the West. East Bengal experienced an influx of officials and merchants, and was at a disadvantage nationally because of the establishment of Urdu as the national language and because of low representation in the army, which was to be the major organ of the Pakistani state. A rising Bengali middle class fostered agitation, which led to concessions that were mainly too few and too late, or undermined by the hard line that was adopted by some of Pakistan's military rulers. An early expression of this regional sentiment was the language movement in 1952 to demand equal rights for Bengali. This led to clashes with the police, in which a number of students were killed on 21 February, the anniversary of which has assumed enormous symbolic significance for Bangladesh.

Bangladeshi nationalism came to be led by Sheikh Mujibur Rahman (Mujib), one of the leaders of the language movement, and his Awami League (AL), which advocated the limitation of the central authority to defence and foreign affairs and the retention by each wing of its own economic resources. Mujib was imprisoned in 1966, but released in 1969 with the fall of the President, Field-Marshal Muhammad Ayub Khan. Elections were held in December 1970. The AL was assisted in its campaign by the devastation of the East by flooding, the West being blamed for negligence in sending relief; the AL won all but two of the East's seats in both provincial and national assemblies. President Yahya Khan refused to allow Mujib to become Prime Minister on the basis of the AL's manifesto of complete regional autonomy for East Pakistan, and insisted that he share power with Zulfikar Ali Bhutto, whose party had won the majority of the seats in West Pakistan. Subsequent talks regarding the impasse proved fruitless. The deadlock was broken by a general strike, the AL's seizure of power (10 March 1971), and its declaration of Bangladeshi independence (26 March). This last event was in direct response to a fierce army crackdown the previous day. Large numbers of Bengalis were massacred in the days that followed. Mujib himself was arrested and taken to West Pakistan, but many of his colleagues fled to India where they established a government-in-exile. Millions of refugees also flooded into India, which, on 4 December, invaded in support of the Mukti Bahini ('freedom fighters') and other irregular Bengali groups operating inside East Pakistan. The campaign was brief and successful, and Pakistan's military and civilian authorities capitulated on 16 December. Bangladesh's independence thus became a reality. While the Indian army had played the decisive role at the end of the civil war, the Bengali guerrilla groups and those Bengali troops based in East Pakistan who had deserted *en masse* to join the liberation struggle had also been instrumental in harassing and hindering the Pakistani forces.

## INDEPENDENT BANGLADESH

The new country gained prompt international recognition, but was beset by enormous difficulties. There were delicate diplomatic issues to be resolved, and a pressing need for international aid. The loss of professionals through the murder of Bengalis and the removal of Punjabis and other West Pakistanis led to serious staffing problems in commerce and the public services. A law and order problem was exacerbated by the failure of the so-called guerrilla groups to disband completely, and by campaigns against the Bihari Muslim minority, who had been arriving in East Pakistan since 1947, mostly from the Indian state of Bihar: as Urdu-speakers, the Biharis' loyalty was held to be suspect. The change of regime made no contribution to the region's economic problems, and the participation of India raised the spectre of another colonialism to replace those of the past.

Sheikh Mujib, released from prison in Pakistan following the end of the civil war, returned to Bangladesh as its first President and was popularly acclaimed as *Bangabandhu* ('Friend of Bengal'). A new, secular and parliamentary Constitution was rapidly promulgated (under which Mujib became Prime Minister) and fresh legislative elections were held in March 1973; these gave the AL a massive majority of 292 out of a total of 300 seats. On 22 February 1974 Pakistan formally recognized Bangladesh's existence and diplomatic relations were established between the two countries. Domestic political stability was not easily maintained, however. Opposition groups of both extremes resorted to terrorism, including Islamist fundamentalists opposed to secession and secularism, and Maoist groups co-operating with Indian Naxalites. In October 1973 the AL formed an alliance with the Communist Party and the pro-Soviet wing of the National Awami Party, with a joint policy of suppressing terrorism. A militia, the Rakkhi Bahini, was formed to assist the police, but was perceived by most people as serving the interests of the ruling party. Economic problems also mounted. In July and August 1974 disastrous floods exacerbated an already desperate situation and led to widespread famine. In some areas prices rose by 400%, and there was talk of official corruption, even close to the still-popular Mujib. At the end of December the Government declared a state of emergency and all fundamental rights guaranteed by the Constitution were suspended. Four weeks later the Jatiya Sangsad (Parliament) adopted a Constitution Bill, which replaced the parliamentary with a presidential form of government and provided for the introduction of a one-party system. Mujib became President, assuming absolute powers, and created the Bangladesh Krishak Sramik (Peasants and Workers) Awami League, excluding all other parties from government.

### Coup and Counter-coup

If nothing else, Bangladesh's independence struggle had created a local military power-base, elements of which were bound

* For earlier history, see also the chapter on India.

to play a political role. They began to do so on 15 August 1975, when a group of discontented young army officers staged a military coup, assassinated Mujib and almost all of his family, and installed Khandakar Mushtaq Ahmed, the former Minister of Commerce, in power. The coup was interpreted by many as the work of pro-West elements disturbed by Mujib's policies, but the young officers who carried out the murders were also driven by personal grievances. The new regime was patently weak, and on 3 November the expected counter-coup took place. In a period of confusion Brig. Khalid Musharaf, a pro-Mujib figure, came briefly to power, and the leaders of the August coup were exiled. However, a former Prime Minister, Tajuddin Ahmed, and other former associates of Mujib, who had been imprisoned after the August coup, were murdered in gaol in Dhaka. On 6 November serious fighting broke out in the Dhaka cantonment between Brig. Musharaf's supporters and left-wing soldiers who suspected his alleged pro-India leanings, in which Musharaf and many others were killed.

Musharaf had forced Mushtaq Ahmed to resign as President in favour of the Chief Justice, Abu Sadat Mohammad Sayem, who was sworn in on 6 November 1975 itself. On the next day, following Musharaf's death, President Sayem became Chief Martial Law Administrator, but real power was exercised by the Chief of Army Staff, Maj.-Gen. Ziaur Rahman (Gen. Zia). One of the most famous leaders of the liberation struggle, Gen. Zia, had been imprisoned by Brig. Musharaf, but had been freed by the left-wing soldiers on 6 November. Once in power, however, he moved swiftly to consolidate his position. One of the most important of the radicals who had brought him to power, Lt-Col (retd) Abu Taher, was put on trial and subsequently executed.

### The Zia Regime

Gen. Zia initially promised an early return to representative government. From August 1976 political parties were permitted to operate, providing that their manifesto had been approved by the Government. District council elections were held in February 1977, but the general election initially planned for that date was postponed indefinitely in November 1976. Gen. Zia's dominance was consolidated by the arrest of Mushtaq Ahmed and other possible opponents in November 1976, and by his assumption first of the powers of Chief Martial Law Administrator, and then of the presidency in April 1977, following the resignation of President Sayem.

In May 1977 a national referendum resulted in a claimed 99% vote in favour of the President and his martial rule policies. A presidential election in June 1978 confirmed Gen. Zia's position, and in July the Council of Advisers was replaced by a 28-member Council of Ministers. In September the President formed a new party, the Bangladesh Jatiyatabadi Dal (Bangladesh Nationalist Party—BNP), after a failed attempt to create a 'grand coalition'. In December the President's 'undemocratic' powers were abolished, and in January 1979 a number of political prisoners were released. In February the delayed elections to the Jatiya Sangsad were finally held. Major opposition parties had agreed to take part, after prolonged manoeuvring. A 40% poll produced a two-thirds' majority for the President's allies. In March Azizur Rahman took over as Prime Minister. A new Government was formed, and at the beginning of April martial law was lifted.

Zia's political position was strengthened by the inability of the opposition to present a united front. Several groups broke away from the AL, and an attempt by the opposition to boycott the Jatiya Sangsad in 1980 failed. (However, the BNP itself was not immune to such factional quarrels.) Zia also benefited from his efforts to give the country a more specifically Islamic tone, in contrast to the secular approach of the AL. In April 1977 the Constitution had been amended so as to delete a mention of secularism and to make specific reference to Islam, although there were few immediate consequences. As part both of his political and of his economic strategies, Zia gave considerable attention to rural development. He made a number of highly publicized visits to rural areas to take part in local development projects. In an effort to galvanize the rural areas, where the pre-1947 system of government remained in place with few alterations, he introduced a new system of local self-government based on *gram sarkars* or village governments. Despite these initiatives, which reflected considerable dynamism and vision, Zia failed to change the culture of Bangladeshi politics. Indeed, with his largely personal and non-ideological style of rule he remained very much part of it. The most serious problem he faced was that of asserting his power over the army, which had been his initial vehicle of power. He had quickly distanced himself from the radical left in the army (see above), but he had had to deal with at least six mutinies in the armed forces, and showed no hesitation in suppressing them with considerable force. In the end, however, personal rivalries among the senior officers led to the murder of Gen. Zia in Chittagong on 30 May 1981. The details are uncertain: if a coup was planned, it was poorly carried out, and its leader, Maj.-Gen. Mohammad Abdul Manzur (an army divisional commander only recently sent to Chittagong), was soon captured and then killed in confused circumstances. However, the country drew back from civil war and the constitutional provisions were allowed to operate.

Zia's Vice-President, Abdus Sattar, became acting Head of State pending a presidential election, which he won in November 1981. He was elected mainly in the interests of continuity and for the memory of Zia, but he was elderly and in poor health, and was soon embroiled in a struggle with the military under the Chief of Army Staff, Lt-Gen. Hossain Mohammad Ershad. Ershad denied personal ambition, but in January 1982 persuaded Sattar to establish a National Security Council, formally involving the military chiefs in the Government. The civilians were divided among themselves and Sattar was beginning to lose control when, on 24 March 1982, the expected coup took place. As a result, Gen. Ershad succeeded to supreme power as Chief Martial Law Administrator (in December 1983 he also proclaimed himself President).

### Consolidation of Gen. Ershad's Rule

Ershad enjoyed less immediate support than had Zia, but his strategies of political rule were quite similar. The rural areas were seen as the key to his survival, and a new system of local government was introduced to replace the *gram sarkars*. This system was based on the introduction of elected councils at the *upazilla* or sub-district level. The hope was that the distribution of development funds through this mechanism would create a class of political intermediaries tied to the regime through patronage. Regular elections were indeed held, and attracted ambitious local politicians. Ershad also attempted, unsuccessfully, to give the army an institutional role in politics. At the national level, however, and on the streets of Dhaka and the other major cities it proved harder for Ershad to consolidate his position, even though he eventually created his own party, the Jana Dal (reorganized as the Jatiya Dal—National Party—in 1986), to attract those keen to advance towards power. Resentment of Ershad's blatant seizure of power and his subsequent corrupt behaviour meant that the existing opposition parties mostly sank their differences to present a united front. Political unrest in the form of strikes and demonstrations became endemic from an early stage, and Ershad's attempts to hold elections were blocked. In 1985 he responded by holding a referendum on his position as President, which allegedly produced a 94% vote in his favour. The year 1987 witnessed particularly widespread protests, organized jointly by almost all the opposition parties, and on 27 November a state of emergency was declared. Demonstrations continued, however, and many people were killed or injured in clashes with the police. A fresh general election was held in March 1988, but the opposition boycott was largely successful. The state of emergency was repealed in the following month. The elections produced, in effect, a political stalemate. The opposition continued its agitation, but could not dislodge Ershad from power. In April 1990 Ershad declared that he would present himself as a candidate in the presidential election scheduled to be held in mid-1991. Demonstrations against the Government began again in October 1990. As often before, the epicentre of the unrest was the campus of Dhaka University. To maintain their popular credibility, both Sheikh Hasina Wajed (daughter of Sheikh Mujib and leader of an alliance of eight parties around the AL—hereafter referred to as simply Sheikh Hasina) and Begum Khaleda Zia (Zia's widow and the leader of another opposition group, of seven parties, headed by the BNP—hereafter referred to as simply Begum Zia) lent their support to the students. In late November Ershad was forced to impose a new state of emergency, but this action did not succeed in preventing a massive wave of strikes and violent demonstrations throughout the country. Consequently, Ershad resigned a few days later, on 4 December, and the state of emergency was lifted. The Chief Justice, Shahabuddin Ahmed, assumed the post of acting President (in his capacity as Vice-President) and was put at the head of a neutral caretaker Government pending fresh parliamentary elections. Ershad was placed under house arrest (he was later sentenced to 20 years' imprisonment for illegal possession of firearms and other offences). Apart from the unity and determination of the opposition, notably among the students, the key factor in Ershad's downfall was the attitude of the army. Lt-Gen. Muhammad Atiqur Rahman, who held the post of Chief of Army Staff from the time that Ershad relinquished the position in 1986 until his retirement in August 1990, was an Ershad loyalist. His successor, Lt-Gen. Nooruddin Khan, by contrast, adopted a detached stance and refused to allow the army to be used for political purposes. Yet for 10 years Ershad, himself a professional soldier, had been able to retain the support of the army and, in return, had ensured that its material interests were catered to. No civilian regime, of whatever political hue, could hope to survive in Bangladesh if the army were not in some way accommodated.

### Democracy Restored

With the new acting President installed, moves were quickly implemented to hold fresh parliamentary elections. The two main participants were the AL alliance and the BNP alliance. After a vigorous campaign, the elections were held on 27 February 1991. Slightly counter to pre-election estimates, the BNP won 138 of the 294 seats for which results were declared. A few days after the elections, the BNP was ensured a small working majority in the Jatiya Sangsad, following discussions with the Islamist party Jamaat-e-Islami, and was thus enabled to appoint deputies to 28 of the 30 parliamentary seats reserved for women. Begum Zia assumed office as Prime Minister on 19 March at the head of a new Government, which included many of her late husband's colleagues, as well as several senior bureaucrats. On 1 May, only two months after its accession to power, the Government had to contend with the immense difficulties resulting from a devastating cyclone, which killed up to 250,000 people and caused huge economic damage. Criticism of the apparent lack of alacrity with which the administrative machinery responded to the crisis was widespread.

In August 1991 the Jatiya Sangsad approved a constitutional amendment ending 16 years of presidential rule and restoring the Prime Minister as executive leader (under the previous system, both the Prime Minister and the Council of Ministers had been answerable to the President). The amendment, which was formally enforced when it was approved by national referendum in the following month, reduced the role of the President, who was now to be elected by the Jatiya Sangsad for a five-year term, to that of a titular Head of State. Accordingly, a new President was elected by the Jatiya Sangsad on 8 October. The successful candidate was the BNP nominee, the erstwhile Speaker of the Jatiya Sangsad, Abdur Rahman Biswas, who received 172 of the 264 votes cast. In September the BNP had gained an absolute majority in the Jatiya Sangsad, following the party's victory in five of the 11 by-elections.

As elsewhere in South Asia, the new Government decided to pursue a policy of economic restructuring, with the help of aid donors, in an attempt to achieve more sustained growth. This entailed the transfer to private ownership of public-sector industries and the imposition of curbs on labour activism. The Government also moved to dismantle a number of the institutions established under Ershad's regime, in particular the *upazilla* system of local administration, which had been introduced in 1982. These measures evoked some resistance from those immediately affected, but this alone does not explain the fierce and sustained opposition campaign, which was launched by the AL and other parties almost as soon as the new Government had been installed. Deep personal antipathy between Sheikh Hasina and Begum Zia, which had only barely been concealed during the anti-Ershad movement, was one factor, while no political party appeared willing to trust the democratic credentials of its opponents. In April 1992, in an apparent attempt to destabilize the Government, accusations were made against the leader of the Jamaat-e-Islami, Ghulam Azam, of complicity in Pakistani war crimes in 1971 and of having remained a Pakistani citizen while participating in Bangladeshi politics. The AL MPs boycotted the Jatiya Sangsad over the issue and demanded Azam's immediate trial before a special tribunal; in late June, however, the matter was resolved when a compromise was reached.

In the latter half of 1992 the opposition parties launched a series of campaigns against the Government in the hope of rekindling the spirit of the anti-Ershad movements. In mid-August the Government survived an AL-sponsored parliamentary motion of no confidence by 168 votes to 122. The opposition accused the Government of failing to curb the increasing lawlessness in the country, notably among university students. The stringent anti-terrorism measures introduced by the Government in November, however, were widely criticized as being excessively harsh and undemocratic. Subsequently, the opposition parties sank their differences in pursuit of a common demand that the general election due in 1996 be held under the auspices of a neutral, caretaker government. This requisition was based on claims that the Government would misuse its powers in order to engage in electoral malpractice (the AL persistently accused the Government of vote-rigging in the 1991 general election and subsequent by-elections). Many large-scale demonstrations and strikes were organized by the opposition from November 1993 onwards, including, for example, a two-week-long agitation in the second half of March 1995. Some of these events primarily affected the capital, Dhaka, but others were nation-wide. Force had to be used to quell the disturbances, and there were regular fatalities. At the end of 1994 all the opposition members of the Jatiya Sangsad, who had for the preceding nine months boycotted parliamentary sessions, submitted their resignations in an attempt to precipitate a constitutional crisis, but without success. A couple of months earlier, an envoy sent by the Commonwealth Secretariat, Sir Ninian Stephen, had attempted to mediate a solution by which an all-party government under BNP leadership would assume power to oversee the forthcoming elections. However, this proposal was rejected by the opposition parties.

Despite the strength and extent of the street protests, the occasional tests of electoral opinion produced mixed results. In January 1994 the AL won the mayoralties of Dhaka and Chittagong, the country's two largest cities, but in March a by-election success revealed the continuing strength of the BNP elsewhere. Begum Zia seemed able during the protests to maintain control of her own party. Wherever possible, however, she took steps to appease sections of the opposition. In September 1994 she cancelled a visit to the UN-sponsored International Conference on Population and Development in Cairo as a gesture to Islamic elements. In response to a severe shortage of fertilizer in late 1994, a situation that threatened to embarrass the Government, the Prime Minister dismissed the minister immediately responsible. In June 1995 former President Ershad was acquitted of illegally possessing arms; his sentence was thus reduced to 10 years. In the following month, however, Ershad was sentenced to a further three years' imprisonment for criminal misconduct.

A significant development in 1993 and 1994 demonstrated that there were forces beyond the immediate control of the Government—namely, the campaign against the feminist writer and publicist Taslima Nasreen. This had been launched in September 1993, following the publication of Nasreen's novel dealing with the hostility to the Hindu minority in Bangladesh that had manifested itself after the demolition in December 1992 of the Babri Masjid mosque at Ayodhya in Uttar Pradesh, India (see the chapter on India). The campaign was renewed in May 1994 after the controversial author had given an interview to an Indian newspaper in which she was reported as having said that the Koran needed to be revised to take account of women's issues. Despite her claim that she had been misquoted, there were outraged demands from Islamist groups in Bangladesh that Nasreen should be executed. The

Government issued a warrant for her arrest on blasphemy-related charges, although she had gone into hiding before it could be implemented. Islamist fundamentalists were also accused of instigating attacks on women who were considered to have broken traditional norms of behaviour, and of attempting to obstruct the work of non-governmental organizations (NGOs) involved in areas such as female literacy. In August, with the apparent help of government officials, Nasreen secretly fled Bangladesh and was granted refuge in Sweden. In response, the fundamentalists, led by the Jamaat-e-Islami (which had now abandoned its parliamentary support for the BNP), vowed to attack the Government for seemingly permitting the author's departure.

Despite an escalation in opposition agitation, which frequently brought the country's economy to a near halt, the Government refused to make concessions regarding the key issue of allowing the forthcoming general election to be held under neutral auspices; consequently, all of the main opposition parties boycotted the election, which was held on 15 February 1996. Independent monitors estimated the turn-out at only about 10%–15% of the electorate. The BNP, as virtually the only serious participant in the polls, won an overwhelming victory and claimed that it had thus achieved a mandate for a further term in power. Of the 207 legislative seats declared by the end of February, the BNP had won 205 (a partial repoll had been ordered in most of the 93 remaining constituencies where violence had disrupted the electoral process). The opposition refused to recognize the legitimacy of the polls and announced the launch of a 'non-co-operation' movement against the Government. Renewed street protests made the country practically ungovernable, and pressure from the army and other sources eventually forced Begum Zia to agree to the holding of fresh elections under neutral auspices, as the opposition had demanded all along. The Prime Minister and her Government duly resigned from their posts on 30 March and the Jatiya Sangsad was dissolved. President Biswas appointed the former Chief Justice, Muhammad Habibur Rahman, as acting Prime Minister and asked that a fresh general election be held, under the auspices of an interim neutral government, within three months. A new election commissioner was also appointed, who was considered to be both effective and impartial.

The fresh general election was held on 12 June 1996, with the participation of all of the country's major political parties. The turn-out was high, at an estimated 73%, and three separate teams of international observers reported that, in their view, the polls had been free and fair. There existed only minor policy differences between the main parties, and those were over economic issues; consequently, the electoral contest centred on general perceptions of the parties and their leaders. In the event, the AL won 146 of the 300 elective seats in the Jatiya Sangsad, the BNP 116, the Jatiya Dal 32 and the Jamaat-e-Islami three. An understanding was quickly reached between the AL and the Jatiya Dal, whose main interest was the release of Ershad, who had gained a legislative seat from within prison. Sheikh Hasina was sworn in as the new Prime Minister on 23 June. Her Council of Ministers incorporated one member from the Jatiya Dal; it also included a number of retired officials and army officers.

During the electoral campaign an abortive military coup attempt took place. The Chief of Army Staff, Lt-Gen. Abu Saleh Mohammed Nasim, who had objected to the action of the President (who retained direct control of the armed forces during the caretaker period prior to the general election) in dismissing some senior officers for political activity, endeavoured to seize power, but was unable to mobilize sufficient support to achieve his aim. Lt-Gen. Nasim was immediately dismissed, and a new Chief of Army Staff was appointed. The fact that the attempted coup was rapidly and bloodlessly suppressed indicated the reluctance of the army and the country alike, despite the fragility of political institutions, to return to military rule, even though the army continued to enjoy some political influence. This influence had been demonstrated when the BNP Government had agreed to hold fresh elections, partly as a result of military pressure.

The AL was quickly able to establish a reasonably firm political base for itself. On 23 July 1996 the AL's presidential nominee, retired Chief Justice and former acting President, Shahabuddin Ahmed, was elected unopposed as Bangladesh's new Head of State. Of the 30 parliamentary seats reserved for women, the AL won 27 and the Jatiya Dal three, thus giving the AL an absolute majority in the Jatiya Sangsad. Ershad was released from prison at the beginning of 1997, thereby fulfilling the terms of the AL's election agreement with the Jatiya Dal (although he continued to face legal action and spent periods in prison in 2000 and 2002). The AL Government continued to pursue the policies of economic restructuring adopted by its predecessor, while a great deal of effort was also invested in reopening the case against the assassins of Sheikh Mujib. In November 1996 the Jatiya Sangsad voted unanimously to repeal the indemnity law that had been enacted in 1975 to protect the perpetrators of the military coup in that year; the BNP and the Jamaat-e-Islami, however, boycotted the vote. In November 1998 a Dhaka court sentenced to death 15 of the 19 people accused of Mujib's assassination; four of the defendants were acquitted. Efforts to complete the judicial process were, however, hindered by the reluctance of judges to hear appeals in what was inevitably seen as a politically motivated case. Only four of those convicted were actually in custody in Bangladesh; the 11 others remained fugitives abroad. In April 2000 the Chief Justice established a two-judge bench to review the sentences. By April 2001 the High Court had upheld 12 of the sentences and acquitted three of those originally convicted. In May Bangladesh signed an extradition treaty with the USA to increase the prospects of the transfer of three defendants, reportedly living in the USA, to the Bangladeshi authorities.

### Democracy Under Stress

The opposition parties, the BNP in particular, continued to view agitational politics as the optimum mode of effecting the downfall of the Government. Claims were made that the AL was rigging by-elections, and from mid-November 1996 these assertions were used by the BNP as a reason to boycott parliamentary proceedings. From 1997 the opposition organized a continuous programme of strikes and demonstrations, citing grievances such as tax and price increases and general shortages, as well as claims that the Government was betraying national interests over issues such as the water-sharing agreement with India and the Chittagong Hill Tracts (see below). On occasion, these demonstrations turned violent and resulted in substantial loss of life (as in February and April 1999). The BNP's foremost demand was for the holding of fresh elections, echoing the AL's earlier campaign. The AL, however, strengthened its electoral and parliamentary position through a series of by-election victories. The departure of the Jatiya Dal from the coalition in March 1998 therefore had little effect on the ruling party's hold on power. In June and August Begum Zia, along with others associated with her Government, was indicted on charges of corruption and abuse of power, allegedly perpetrated during her tenure of the premiership. In December the opposition was strengthened by a decision by the BNP and the Jamaat-e-Islami to accept Ershad and the Jatiya Dal into the anti-Government movement without any conditions.

In early 1999 political instability and violence escalated. The pace of agitation increased, and in mid-1999 the BNP and other opposition parties began a boycott of parliamentary proceedings. Opposition-led strikes took place in October and December, leading to substantial economic disruption. Following a further strike at the beginning of January 2000, prominent business leaders attempted to negotiate a deal between the Prime Minister and the opposition parties, but the leader of the BNP, Begum Zia declined to take part. Strikes continued to disrupt the economy.

Discontent with the Government continued to increase. In early July 2000 an attempt to assassinate Sheikh Hasina was foiled. Bomb explosions also became a regular occurrence; the worst incident took place in mid-June 2001, when 22 people were killed at a local office of the AL. No one claimed responsibility, although it was alleged by some that militant Islamist groups were involved. Also in June 2001 the trial began of 15 people accused of involvement in the alleged attempt to assassinate the Prime Minister one year previously. In the same month the Jatiya Sangsad approved a new law under which Sheikh Hasina and her sister would receive lifelong state security.

At the end of June 2001 the Prime Minister announced that national elections would be held, as scheduled, in September. In mid-July Sheikh Hasina and her Government duly resigned from their posts, and the Jatiya Sangsad was dissolved. The former Chief Justice, Latifur Rehman, was appointed as acting Prime Minister, heading an interim neutral Government, which was responsible for the holding of elections within three months. The general election was held on 1 October. Despite the considerable violence during the election period, international monitors declared the poll to be free and fair. The BNP-led alliance won a convincing majority (214 of the 300 seats), the AL secured 62 seats and the Jatiya Dal, weakened by the legal problems of its leader, won 14 seats. Begum Zia was appointed Prime Minister. The Jamaat-e-Islami won only 16 seats (of the alliance's 214), but was able to participate in the Government through its alliance with the BNP. Following the elections a series of attacks took place on members of the country's Hindu minority, generally considered to be supporters of the AL. Subsequently, many Bangladeshi Hindus fled as refugees to India. In November the BNP Minister of Foreign Affairs, A. Q. M. Badruddoza Chowdhury, was declared elected unopposed as the country's largely ceremonial President.

The AL's immediate and predictable response to its election defeat was to launch a campaign of boycott and agitation. Newly elected members of the legislature effectively refused to take part in parliamentary proceedings until June 2002, and the party as a whole boycotted civic elections in Dhaka and elsewhere in April; a series of strikes was organized to protest against popular grievances, for example the state of law and order in major cities. Begum Zia reacted to the disruption by filing major corruption charges against Sheikh Hasina and other AL members in December 2001, with regard to an arms contract with Russia signed in 1999. Several AL leaders were arrested and kept in prison for some time. Meanwhile, a corruption case against Begum Zia, which had been filed under Sheikh Hasina's Government in 1998, was quashed. In the last few months of 2002 the army was enlisted to lead a campaign against criminal elements, although it was criticized for its heavy-handedness. Occasional bomb explosions, for which no one claimed responsibility, added to the sense of popular unease. The worst outrages occurred in the city of Mymensingh in December 2002, when around 20 people died after a series of explosions in four cinema halls.

A number of retirements and resignations took place in mid-2002. The most significant were the early retirement of the Chief of Army Staff and the resignation of the President, both in June. The President's departure was attributed to BNP claims that he had failed to attend a ceremony in honour of the anniversary of Gen. Zia's assassination. In early September the BNP candidate, Prof. Iajuddin Ahmed, was declared President by the Election Commission after it was determined that his were the only valid nomination papers for the post. In May 2003 Begum Zia effected a government reshuffle, which prompted the resignations of three ministers and four ministers of state. In March 2004 the Minister of Commerce resigned. In April Badruddoza Chowdhury (the former President) formed his own party—Bikalpa Dhara Bangladesh—and in June his son, who had also resigned as a BNP legislator, contested his seat as a candidate of the new party, winning a convincing victory against his BNP opponent. The AL boycotted the Jatiya Sangsad for more than a year, from December 2004 to February 2006.

Throughout the tenure of the BNP Government the AL continued to organize regular strikes and demonstrations, during which the whole country often came to a standstill. These episodes were often accompanied by violent clashes with the police. At the same time, members of the AL were themselves the targets of attacks: in August and September 2003 several local leaders of the party in Khulna were killed; senior AL leaders were assassinated in May 2004 and again in January 2005, when the principal victim was a former Minister of Finance. In August 2004 a grenade attack on an AL rally being addressed by Sheikh Hasina in Dhaka killed 21 people and injured hundreds more. Violent clashes between opposition supporters and the police followed, and one person died when protesters set fire to a train near the capital. As the general elections scheduled for early 2007 approached, so did the frequency of strikes and demonstrations. In April 2006, for example, two general strikes called by the AL and its allies to demand reforms to the electoral system brought the country to a virtual halt. While the strikes led by political parties generally appeared to be focused on political objectives, poverty and deprivation were important background factors in generating discontent. The pro-liberalization policies of successive governments, although successful in sustaining economic growth, did not necessarily improve individual standards of living, and particular groups of workers, for example those employed in public-sector units scheduled for privatization, felt themselves to be under pressure. In May 2006 violent clashes took place between police and private-sector garment workers striking for higher wages.

### Democracy Suspended

In accordance with the Constitution, the BNP Government resigned in October 2006 to permit the formation of a caretaker government in advance of the elections scheduled for January 2007. The first nominee for the position of Chief Adviser (the head of the caretaker government that was to oversee the election process), K. M. Hasan, a retired Chief Justice, declined the post following the AL's assertion that it would not contest the elections should he take office, in view of his alleged support of the BNP; President Iajuddin Ahmed then nominated himself as Chief Adviser. Viewing this as blatant political manipulation, the AL immediately intensified its protest campaign, with the aim of producing an acceptable alternative.

Following a series of transport blockades, demonstrations and intermittent outbreaks of violence, on 11 January 2007 the President imposed a state of emergency under which political activity was banned, and also announced the indefinite postponement of the elections; he appointed Dr Fakhruddin Ahmed, a former World Bank official, as Chief Adviser. A full team of advisers was appointed shortly afterwards, with Dr A. B. Mirza Azizul Islam assuming responsibility for the finance portfolio, Dr Iftekhar Ahmed Chowdhury the foreign affairs portfolio, and Dr Ahmed himself taking charge of the home affairs and Election Commission Secretariat portfolios, among others. Although Lt-Gen. Moeen Uddin Ahmed, the Chief of Army Staff, denied that he harboured any political ambitions, it was widely believed that the decision to suspend the electoral process was encouraged by the army, and Lt-Gen. Moeen later made public comments suggesting that democracy needed to be balanced by security. Measures were taken by the new caretaker Government to put pressure on the two rival political leaders, Begum Zia and Sheikh Hasina, by allowing charges of corruption or abuse of power to be levelled against them. Begum Zia was initially placed under virtual house arrest for some time, and in March her son Tarique Rahman was arrested on corruption charges. In April efforts were made to prevent Sheikh Hasina from returning to Bangladesh after a visit to London, although this decision was eventually reversed. In July Sheikh Hasina was arrested on extortion charges and in September Begum Zia was arrested on corruption charges. In February 2008 the High Court ruled that most of the charges against Sheikh Hasina were invalid as the emergency laws could not be employed in the case of events that took place before their imposition, but both leaders remained in custody and trial proceedings were continuing, albeit haltingly and amid further legal challenges, in mid-2008. Large numbers of prominent politicians and businessmen, including several former ministers from both parties, were also arrested on charges of corruption and related charges. In May 2007 special courts began work on the hearing process, and in the following month the Minister of State for Labour and Employment of the previous Government, Amanullah Aman, was the first to be convicted, receiving a 13-year prison sentence for corruption.

The initial public response to the postponement of the elections was generally quite favourable, although the attempt to force the two party leaders into exile had appeared to enjoy less support. In July 2007 the Election Commission stated that legislative elections would be held between October and December 2008 and work began on the preparation of new voters' lists, although no steps were taken to lift the state of emergency. The continuing lack of a democratically elected government and legislature prompted the Commonwealth Parliamentary Association to suspend Bangladesh from membership in May 2007. In August there were significant student riots in Dhaka in protest against the political situation, and several senior professors who were accused of inciting them were arrested and released only in January 2008. The Government announced a partial suspension of its ban on political activity in September 2007, while upholding restrictions on outdoor rallies and functions. Iajuddin Ahmed's term as President, which duly expired earlier that month, was extended in light of the delayed elections. In November the lengthy process of transferring power over the judiciary away from the executive arm of government appeared to be complete, with the announcement that judges and magistrates would henceforth be selected by the Supreme Court. In May 2008 Dr Fakhruddin Ahmed announced that legislative elections would be held in the third week in December, subsequent to which the police made a large number of arrests in an attempt to improve security ahead of the polls. According to the Government, almost 25,000 people (including a number of prominent party activists) were arrested over a two-week period in June, prompting criticism from leaders of various political parties that the arrests were politically motivated.

Although the Jamaat-e-Islami remained in coalition with the BNP, militant Islamist groups have exerted increasing political pressure. Aside from their continuing concern over the activities of the author Taslima Nasreen, who in 2002 was sentenced *in absentia* to one year's imprisonment, the minority Ahmadi community, who consider themselves Muslims but who are regarded by the mainstream Muslim community as heretics, has become a target of attack. In January 2004 the Government itself placed a ban on the publishing of materials by the Ahmadi community in a move to placate Islamist groups, although the ban was suspended in December of that year following a legal challenge by human rights organizations. During 2004 and 2005 several unexplained bomb explosions were attributed to militant Islamists, a number of whom were arrested and put on trial. In August 2005 more than 400 small bombs exploded virtually simultaneously in locations across Bangladesh. The militant Islamist group Jamatul Mujahideen, which had been banned in February 2005, subsequently claimed responsibility for the attacks. In November two local judges were assassinated, crimes for which two of the principal leaders of Jamatul Mujahideen were sentenced to death in May 2006. The two condemned men, who were also accused of having been involved in the August 2005 bombings, and four other militants belonging to the Islamist group were eventually executed at the end of March 2007. Two weeks later, one of the legal team who had prosecuted them was assassinated. In early May a co-ordinated series of explosions occurred at three major railway stations. In April 2008 there were reports of clashes in Dhaka between police and Islamist groups; the latter were protesting against a draft law that would give greater inheritance rights to women.

### The Chittagong Hill Tracts

Apart from the difficulties of maintaining political control of the country, successive leaders of Bangladesh from Sheikh Mujib onwards have had to confront an insurgency in the Chittagong Hill Tracts. Minority tribal groups, mostly Buddhist Chakmas, have long demanded autonomy in this region, and have attempted to prevent the continuing settlement in the area of Bengali peasants from the plains, a process which has, in fact, been going on since the 19th century (when Bengalis were settled in the Hill Tracts as plantation workers and clerks by the British administration). Initially, guerrilla activity by the Shanti Bahini ('Peace Force'), which had been waging guerrilla warfare against the Bangladeshi security forces and the Bengali settlers since the early 1970s, was met by retaliatory army action. In 1989, however, the Government took measures to achieve a political solution in the Chittagong Hill Tracts, by introducing concessions providing limited autonomy to the region in the form of three new semi-autonomous hill districts—Rangamati, Bandarban and Khagrachari. In June polls to elect councils for these new districts took place reasonably peacefully, despite attempts at disruption by the Shanti Bahini, who continued to demand total autonomy for the Chakma tribals. The powers vested in the councils were designed to give the tribals sufficient authority to regulate any further influx of Bengali settlers to the districts. By mid-1990, however, it had become increasingly apparent that the Government's peace scheme had failed. The violence had not abated and Buddhist Chakma refugees continued to flood across the border into India (the number of refugees living in camps in Tripura reached about 56,000). A series of efforts was made from 1992 to achieve a lasting solution. India became involved in the negotiations, as it was anxious to be relieved of the burden of caring for the refugees, but this also meant that the problem became embroiled in the broader issue of Indo-Bangladeshi relations. An initial agreement in 1992 failed to generate confidence among the refugees that it would be implemented; they feared persecution by the Bangladesh security forces. A fresh effort in 1994 led to only a very limited number of refugees returning. In December 1996, however, the settlement of the Farakka issue between Bangladesh and India (see below) opened the way to a new initiative. In December 1997 the Bangladeshi Government signed a peace agreement with the political wing of the Shanti Bahini, ending the insurgency in the Chittagong Hill Tracts. The treaty offered the rebels a general amnesty in return for the surrender of their arms and gave the tribal people greater powers of self-governance through the establishment of three new elected district councils (to control the area's land management and policing) and a regional council (the chairman of which was to enjoy the rank of a state minister). The peace agreement, which was strongly criticized by the opposition for representing a 'sell-out' of the area to India and a threat to Bangladesh's sovereignty, was expected to accelerate the process of repatriating the remaining refugees from Tripura (who totalled about 31,000 at the end of December 1997). According to official Indian sources, only about 5,500 refugees remained in Tripura by early February 1998. By the end of 2000 most of the Chakma refugees had been repatriated, district and regional councils were in operation and a land commission had been established. The transitional period, following the signing of the treaty, was to end with the withdrawal of the Bangladesh Army from the region by the beginning of 2001, when the army was to be replaced by the Bangladesh Rifles.

In mid-February 2001 gunmen abducted three engineers, two Danes and one Briton, working on a road-building project in the Chittagong Hill Tracts. The kidnappers demanded a ransom from the Bangladeshi Government in return for the hostages' release. It was believed that the kidnappers belonged to the separatist United People's Democratic Front, which opposed the 1997 peace agreement. In mid-March 2001 the hostages were released. The Government claimed that the army had rescued the men; other sources reported that the Government had agreed to a secret financial arrangement with the kidnappers. At the end of 2003 a strike led by the political wing of the Shanti Bahini, the Parbattya Chattagram Jana Sanghati Samity, appeared to be evidence of some local sentiment that the 1997 agreement had not been fully implemented. In December 2005 the Bangladeshi Government, in partnership with the United Nations Development Programme (UNDP), announced the launch of a US $50m. project in the south-east of the Hill Tracts in order to support local development and thereby promote stability.

### Developmental and Environmental Issues

Over many years East Bengal has been one of the poorest parts of South Asia. The colonial period was one of neglect and stagnation, and during 1947–71 East Pakistan's resources were diverted to the development of West Pakistan. While Bangladesh still lags behind many other parts of the subcontinent, it has made some progress since independence (see Economy). In fact, it has taken a number of initiatives that have been admired and copied elsewhere. Under Gen. Zia, for example, a new pharmaceuticals policy was introduced which restricted the use of expensive proprietary formulations in favour of generic and locally produced drugs. The Grameen Bank, which was established in 1976, pioneered innovative approaches to rural credit provision, and is only one example of the massive role played in Bangladesh by NGOs. These operate very often as partnerships between local organizations and local aid donors. The best of the NGOs allow for local initiatives to express themselves unfettered by government bureaucracy, although others have been criticized for the comparatively lavish lifestyles enjoyed by their employees and for too rigid a following of outside models. In February 2005 offices belonging to two of the country's leading NGOs, including the Grameen Bank, were attacked, apparently by Islamist groups. The founder of the Grameen Bank, Professor Muhammad Yunus, was awarded the 2006 Nobel Peace Prize for his work.

One of the most serious recurrent problems in Bangladesh, and one which often has political and international implications, has been the official handling of natural disasters such as cyclones and floods. The two most serious natural disasters in recent years have been the cyclone in 1991 (see above), which exceeded in intensity even the 1970 cyclone, and the monsoon floods of September 1988. During these floods, which were the most severe in the region's recorded history, three-quarters of the country, including large parts of the capital, were flooded, vast areas of arable land were submerged and as many as 30m. people were left homeless. Famine was avoided by the prompt action of the Government, but, nevertheless, the adverse impact on the economy was substantial. Such economic problems undoubtedly compound the political unrest in Bangladesh. In late 1988 the Government established a National Disaster Prevention Council and urged the use of regional co-operation (specifically with India and possibly with Nepal) to evolve a comprehensive solution to the problem of flooding. In recent years there have been major floods and cyclones in 1998, 2004 and 2007. Each episode led to the deaths of thousands of people and the displacement of many more, as well as hundreds of millions of dollars worth of damage. In the long term, Bangladesh is likely to be one of the countries worst affected by any rise in sea levels owing to global warming. In such an event, nothing less than a world-wide effort could be of any help.

## INTERNATIONAL RELATIONS

Bangladesh's most important bilateral relationship is with India. Despite (although some might say because of) India's role in Bangladesh's liberation struggle, there has always been the fear that it would use its vastly superior strength to intimidate Bangladesh, especially over economic matters. While relations between the two countries have never been overtly hostile, they have been marked by suspicion and ambiguity. The most troublesome issue to resolve has been the allocation of the Ganges waters, following India's construction of the Farakka barrage, which was completed in 1975. This major civil engineering project was undertaken in order to divert some of the river's flow through the Hooghly river and thus to alleviate the siltation problem at Calcutta (Kolkata). However, this inevitably resulted in a lesser flow of water through the part of the Ganges delta that is situated in Bangladesh, and it has been claimed that this has led to serious consequences for agricultural production, owing to greater salination in the coastal areas. Bilateral negotiations began soon after 1971, but produced only limited results, and in effect India was able to impose its own solution. However, in December 1996 there was a breakthrough. The then Indian Minister of External Affairs (shortly to be Prime Minister), I. K. Gujral, had, as soon as he assumed office, made a point of trying to improve relations with India's neighbours, and with the help of the Chief Minister of West Bengal—whose approval was vital to the political acceptability of the plan in India—presented a formula for the division of the water. The resulting 30-year agreement also allowed for India to have transit rights over Bangladesh territory in order to reach parts of its remote north-eastern states more easily. In addition, negotiations began with regard to Bangladesh selling surplus power to neighbouring parts of India.

Unresolved issues remained, however. In 1992 the demolition of the Babri Masjid mosque at Ayodhya (see the chapter on India) led to widespread protests on the streets of Bangladesh and to attacks on Hindu temples. On the Indian side, right-wing parties have regularly made a major issue of the alleged presence of large numbers of illegal Bangladeshi migrants in Delhi and elsewhere, while the long-term movement of Bengali settlers across the border into Assam, which has been going on since before 1947, is an important factor in that state's internal politics. At the same time, opposition parties in Bangladesh have often claimed that the Government is 'selling out' the country's interests to India, using as an example potential plans, supported by donor agencies such as the World Bank, for Bangladesh to supply India with natural gas.

Disputes over territorial rights to pockets of land or enclaves along the irregular border have been a further source of tension between India and Bangladesh, and armed clashes between border troops have taken place on a number of occasions. In April 2001, on the Bangladeshi border with the Indian state of Meghalaya, clashes led to the deaths of 16 Indian border troops and three members of the Bangladesh Rifles. Indian sentiments were outraged by the alleged maltreatment of Indian soldiers by Bangladeshi troops. The situation was brought under control, and both sides agreed to enter negotiations, which were under way in June and July. As a result, two joint working groups were created to review the undemarcated section of the border and the exchange of enclaves. The return to power of the BNP, traditionally seen as anti-India, further delayed the process, and in 2004, 2005 and 2008 further violent incidents occurred, leading on occasion to loss of life. In March 2006 Begum Zia paid an official visit to India for the first time since becoming Prime Minister in 2001, although no major diplomatic breakthroughs were achieved during this visit. In the mean time, India began erecting a fence along its border with Bangladesh in an effort to exclude illegal immigrants. A further area of dispute centred on regular claims made by the Indian authorities that Bangladesh was harbouring Assamese (Asomese) militants from the United Liberation Front of Asosam (ULFA). On a more positive note, in May 2007 Bangladesh agreed to enter into negotiations with India and Myanmar regarding the proposed construction of a gas pipeline traversing the three countries, and in April 2008 a Bangladesh-India train service that had been inactive for more than 40 years recommenced operations.

The question of settlers has also been the major issue in Bangladesh's relations with its eastern neighbour Myanmar (formerly Burma). While the border itself was finally demarcated in 1985, in accordance with a 1979 agreement, during 1991 more than 50,000 Rohingya Muslims, a Myanma ethnic minority who live in the western Arakan region, crossed into Bangladesh, claiming persecution by the Myanma authorities. By the end of June 1992 it was officially estimated that the number of Rohingya refugees in Bangladesh had risen to about 270,000. In that year an agreement was signed between the Governments of Bangladesh and Myanmar to allow for repatriation. By early September 1994 about 65,000 refugees had reportedly been voluntarily repatriated, but many others refused to return. Meanwhile, in December 1993 Bangladesh and Myanmar had signed an agreement to instigate border trade between the two countries. By the end of May 1995, according to government figures, more than 216,000 Rohingyas had been repatriated. Despite the expiry of the official deadline for their repatriation in August 1997, many remained, however, and in late 2006 their number was put at 26,000, according to estimates made by the UN High Commissioner for Refugees, the rate of repatriation having slowed considerably. Tension along the joint border increased in November 1999, following reports that Myanmar was laying land-mines and that Myanma troops had been deployed in the border area. Bangladeshi security forces were placed on alert. In January 2001 border guards exchanged fire amid rising tension over a controversial dam project on the River Naaf, which Bangladesh claimed would cause flooding on its territory. Border negotiations took place, but collapsed following the Myanma Government's refusal to sign the minutes. Finally, in early February Myanmar agreed permanently to cease construction of the dam. In December 2002 Myanmar's ruler, Gen. Than Shwe, paid an official visit to Bangladesh, which seemed to herald a significant improvement in relations, despite the persistence of the Rohingya issue.

Bangladesh's relations with Pakistan have been surprisingly cordial, given the circumstances of the 1971 war. Diplomatic relations between the two countries resumed in 1974. One outstanding issue is the position of the so-called Biharis, the Urdu-speaking group of some 250,000 Bihari Muslims who came to what was then East Pakistan in the wake of partition in 1947. Perceived as collaborators by the rest of the Bangladeshi population (they openly supported Pakistan in Bangladesh's war of liberation in 1971), many of them have languished in refugee camps ever since, waiting for repatriation. However, successive Pakistani Governments have been reluctant to accept them for fear of exacerbating the ethnic crisis in Karachi (see the chapter on Pakistan). In 1991 an agreement was reached between Bangladesh and Pakistan, which provided for a phased repatriation of the Bihari refugees, but implementation has been very slow. At the end of 2000 a diplomatic dispute between the two countries over claims and counter-claims on responsibility for the events of 1971 indicated that sensitivities remained. At the end of July 2002 Pakistani President Musharraf paid a successful visit to Bangladesh, during which he expressed regret for what had occurred during the 1971 war. No progress was made on the Bihari issue at this point in time, but in May 2008 a ruling by the High Court awarded Bangladeshi citizenship and voting rights to those refugees who had been minors in 1971 or who had been born in the intervening years—a decision that affected approximately 150,000 of the Biharis. In February 2006 Prime Minister Zia visited Pakistan to hold talks with her Pakistani counterpart, Shaukat Aziz; the latter hailed the visit, during which the two sides signed four memorandums of understanding on trade, agriculture, tourism, and standardization and quality control, as a turning-point in bilateral relations.

As part of its policy to attain a stable position within South Asia, Bangladesh took the initiative in establishing the South Asian Association for Regional Co-operation (SAARC). First mooted by Gen. Zia in 1980, SAARC was formally created in 1985, with a Bangladeshi official as its first Secretary-General. The first, seventh and 13th summit meetings of the organization were held in Dhaka. Included in SAARC's charter are pledges of non-interference by members in each other's internal affairs and a joint effort to avoid 'contentious' issues whenever the association meets. The SAARC Preferential Trading Arrangement (SAPTA) was signed in April 1993 and came into effect in December 1995; the Arrangement was superseded by the establishment of the South Asia Free-Trade Area (SAFTA) in January 2006 (SAFTA was not, however, due to come fully into force until 2016 and actual implementation has been slow). Tensions between India and Pakistan have often impeded progress within SAARC, with summit meetings being postponed for various reasons. In February 2005 the scheduled summit meeting in Dhaka was postponed at India's request, owing, in part, to an allegedly deteriorating security situation in the city; the meeting eventually took place in November.

Although South Asia has been Bangladesh's main area of concern with regard to foreign affairs, its relations with the major world powers have also been important. It remains heavily dependent on bilateral and multilateral aid, and holds annual meetings with a consortium of its major donors to discuss development issues. In March 2000 the US President, Bill Clinton, visited Bangladesh as part of a tour of South Asia. This momentous state visit was the first ever by a US President to Bangladesh. As a result of discussions between the two countries' leaders, who focused on development issues, Clinton announced several aid programmes. In October Sheikh Hasina visited the USA, where the two leaders discussed environmental matters and investment issues. Domestically, many groups feel that Bangladesh should not be so dependent on the West, and on the USA in particular, but, as yet, no government has attempted to find an alternative path. In June 1997 eight of the world's major Muslim states, including Bangladesh, established a new group, known as the Developing Eight, or D-8, to further economic and political co-operation among the member countries. The 1999 summit meeting was held in Dhaka. D-8, which represents 65% of the world's Muslim population, was widely viewed as an Islamic counterweight to the G-7 group of industrialized nations. In September 2001 the interim administration agreed, with the support of the AL and BNP, to offer the USA use of Bangladeshi airspace and ports in the event of military action against Afghanistan. Following the US-led military campaign to oust the regime of Saddam Hussain in Iraq in 2003, efforts appear to have been made to persuade Bangladesh to contribute peace-keeping troops to the coalition forces there, with a visit by the US Secretary of Defense, Donald Rumsfeld, in June 2004. However, the Bangladeshi Government, mindful of popular feelings, declined to commit itself. Bangladesh has been a regular contributor of troops to UN peace-keeping operations throughout the world.

# Economy

MUSHTAQ H. KHAN

Based on an earlier article by ALLISTER MCGREGOR

## RECENT TRENDS

Economic developments in 2007–08 were dominated by the uncertainty of the attempts by the interim Government to fight corruption and create new political realities in Bangladesh. These attempts had, by and large, fizzled out by mid-2008 and the old established parties had begun to engage in discussions about the forthcoming elections scheduled for December. One effect of the campaign against corruption was to dampen business confidence as a result of uncertainty about who would be targeted by the anti-corruption drive. Investment in industry was sluggish throughout 2007/08, but showed signs of recovery in the second half of the year. Exports of garments (particularly of knitwear) revived in the second half of 2007/08, as higher prices in the People's Republic of China and India resulted in a significant number of orders shifting to Bangladesh. Agriculture was severely affected by two floods and a cyclone, but, as often happens in Bangladesh, the winter rice crop benefited from the flooding in the summer and the rate of growth in the agricultural sector only fell to 2.4% from 3.2% in the previous year. Overall, the growth of gross domestic product (GDP) decreased to around 6% in 2007/08, compared with 6.5% in the previous year. As in many other developing countries, Bangladesh was seriously hit by the rising prices of petroleum and food. As a net food importer, this situation proved particularly troublesome for Bangladesh in a year of agricultural difficulties. The official rate of inflation stood at 10% in March 2008, compared with 7.2% in June 2007, but over the same period prices of rice and wheat had risen by at least 50%. In these circumstances, therefore, economic hardship increased for the urban poor and net food purchasing households.

The removal, as part of the extension of World Trade Organization (WTO) rules, at the end of 2006 of country quotas for garment imports that had previously favoured Bangladesh was not expected to have an immediately negative effect. Indeed, exports of garments, and particularly knitted garments, continued to grow. However, Bangladesh was still benefiting from temporary safeguard quotas imposed on China, and these were to be phased out in 2008. The garments sector will have to continue to adjust to greater competitive pressures. Government capacity to develop infrastructure will also prove crucial, particularly in improving ports and transportation infrastructure, and the supply of electricity, which suffers from regular loadshedding. The interim Government that came to power in January 2007 transferred the container operations at Chittagong port to the private sector; this resulted in some immediate improvements in productivity. The country has also been relatively successful in terms of progress in improving health and education, population control and food security, by allocating a major part of the budget to the social sector. Its challenge is to maintain and even increase its growth rate by attracting more investment and by developing the capacity of the State to increase investment in infrastructure and to discipline and regulate the corporate sector. Like many other developing countries, Bangladesh faces serious challenges with regard to enhancing the State's governance capacity. Important governance issues for the State range from such basic areas as maintaining law and order to regulating markets and assisting the private sector in its technology acquisition.

The manufacturing sector continued to be an engine of growth in 2007/08 despite the collapse of business confidence resulting from the emergency Government's drive against corruption in 2007, which threatened to implicate a potentially very large number of businessmen in charges of corruption and tax evasion. Manufacturing was also affected by the global economic slowdown, and the absence of a politically recognized government discouraged foreign investors to such an extent that foreign direct investment (FDI) almost entirely stopped during this period. Nevertheless, the rising value of the Indian and Chinese currencies allowed the Bangladeshi garments sector to recover in the second half of 2007/08 and exports increased substantially. The construction sector performed less well than in previous years as rising prices of raw materials and depressed demand from new investors took their toll. The service sector was buoyed by strong growth in transport and aviation, as the number of Bangladeshi migrant workers continued to rise, and in telecommunications.

Gross investment in the Bangladeshi economy was equivalent to 24.0% of GDP in 2006/07, compared with 24.7% recorded in 2005/06. Although the decline was marginal, it none the less represented a deviation from a five-year trend of gradual expansion and probably reflected widespread political uncertainty as well as the concerns of domestic investors regarding the scope of the government anti-corruption campaign. The investment share needs to rise substantially over the next few years if growth rates are to increase let alone be sustained. Public investments, particularly in the Annual Development Programme (ADP), have been constrained by the inability to raise tax revenues at the necessary rate. The implementation of the ADP fell year on year between 2005 and 2008, indicating slow progress in infrastructure improvements. Inflows of FDI have been rising considerably, but would increase even faster if there was more confidence in the political climate. The fiscal deficit has not been as great a problem as in neighbouring India, with the deficit in 2007/08 projected to be equivalent to around 4.8% of GDP, up from 3.2% in the preceding year. The widening of the deficit was largely owing to flood and cyclone rehabilitation. The Government is also ultimately liable for the accumulated losses of the Bangladesh Petroleum Corporation (BPC) whose losses have recently significantly increased as a result of the implicit subsidy with which it sells imported fuel on the domestic market at a time of rising global prices. Total losses incurred by the BPC in 2007/08 were estimated at US $1,100m. Rapidly increasing import costs and a slowdown in the rate of growth of exports caused by faltering business confidence in 2007 led to a widening trade deficit in 2007/08; concurrently, however, a sharp rise in workers' remittances resulted in a surplus on the current account and a growth in foreign exchange reserves.

Bangladesh remains a poor country, with per caput GDP of around US $480 in 2008. Despite this, the country has made remarkable progress in human development, with increases in life expectancy, reductions in population growth and in infant mortality rates, and improved access to essential drugs, sanitation and safe water. In terms of some human development goals, such as infant mortality, Bangladesh scores higher than India or Pakistan. With an average GDP growth rate of 5.0%–6.5% a year from the early 1990s, Bangladesh is also one of the world's rapidly growing developing countries. The international services and accountancy company PricewaterhouseCoopers includes Bangladesh as one of the 13 second-tier emerging economies (apart from the major emerging economies) that have the potential of growing significantly faster than the OECD countries over the next few decades. Continued improvements in living standards require sustained or even higher economic growth rates, and this requires more savings and investment. Savings rates are low because of inadequate financial institutions and political instability. The commercial banking sector is not utilizing private savings sufficiently; savings through bank deposits amount to less than 2% of GDP. The financial sector remains vulnerable, owing to the bad debts of the commercial banks. The state of the banking sector has shown some improvement in recent years. Gross non-performing loans declined from 21.5% of total loans in June 2004 to 15.8% in June 2005 and to 13.2% in 2006; this percentage remained constant in 2008.

Controlling population growth has been one of the success stories in Bangladesh. From an annual growth rate of around 3.1% in 1971, the rate has fallen to its current level of 1.6%. The fertility rate has declined from an average of seven children per mother in the 1960s to 3.5 per woman in 2002. The present population of around 130m., however, is not projected to stabilize until the second half of the 21st century, at about 250m. Average life expectancy for both men and women is approximately 63 years. The rate of literacy improved from around 26% in 1974 to 41% in 2002. Primary school enrolment rates have increased from 61% in 1980 to 100% in 2001, with a female primary enrolment rate of 101%. In recent years, the role of the non-governmental sector has proved important in education, with 40% of new schools since 1990 being established by non-governmental organizations (NGOs), usually with external assistance. However, further improvements in literacy and the quality of education are likely to require a substantial increase in the capacity of the state sector, which remains the basic provider of primary education. This, in turn, depends on the ability of the State to raise tax revenues. The role of foreign aid has been declining and is likely to decrease further in years to come. In 1999, in a break with the past, the World Bank announced that figures for aid would not be pledged at the forthcoming meeting of the Bangladesh Development Forum in Paris, France. Total aid, which includes grants and low-interest loans, has continued to decline sharply. Aid, defined as net concessional external financing, declined from 4.8% of GDP in 1990 to only 2% of GDP in 2001. To some extent, this reflects the growing ability of Bangladesh to avert disasters such as famines, so that food aid and commodity aid have declined. However, it also reflects Bangladesh's weak capacity to absorb project aid, largely because the Government often lacks the local currency counterpart funding to finance its share of development projects. The Government has increasingly been forced to borrow from domestic sources, which in turn has increased the interest component of budgetary expenditure. However, interest payments on government debt amounted to only about 16.6% of government revenues (excluding grants) in 2005 and this was projected to decline to 15.4% in 2006, which is still low in comparison with other developing countries. The projected widening of the budget deficit in 2007/08 was expected to raise the share of interest payments to 20.5% of estimated government revenue. Administrative and political problems account for a large part of the country's economic difficulties. Interest groups, such as politically connected businessmen, trade unions and public-sector employees, have extracted explicit and hidden subsidies from the Government, and have been successful in preventing changes in governance institutions and in government policies that would have potentially adversely affected them.

## AGRICULTURE

Agriculture contributed 26% of GDP and employed 63% of the labour force in the late 1990s. By 2003/04 the share of agriculture (including forestry and fishing) had decreased to 20.5% of GDP; in mid-2000 the sector employed 60.1% of the labour force. The climate allows for three crops per year. Recent agricultural growth has been based on the increase in area under the third (winter) crop, known as the boro crop, and the substitution of traditional varieties by high-yielding varieties (HYV). The average annual growth rate in agricultural output was a vigorous 3% during 1986–90, but over the next five years the rate of growth decelerated, averaging less than 0.5% per year during the period 1990–95. Thereafter, growth recovered to its prior levels, averaging around 3% per year. The volatility of Bangladeshi agriculture is strongly correlated with the effects of flooding; this is clearly illustrated by the events of 1998/99 when Bangladesh suffered the most severe flooding in recent history—68% of the country was flooded, affecting 30m. people. However, while the flood waters destroyed the summer crops, they led to bumper winter crops. The net effect was that agricultural production increased by 3.9% in 1998/99. In 2000/01 Bangladesh produced 27m. metric tons of food grains—around 2m. tons more than domestic requirements. Despite the floods in September 2000, rice production was good enough to make Bangladesh self-sufficient in food for the first time. The 3.1% growth in foodgrain production achieved in 2000/01 was not sustained in 2001/02—instead, output stagnated; none the less, self-sufficiency in food grains was maintained. In 2002/03 agricultural output grew by a robust 3.1%, and in 2003/04 by 4.1%. The floods in July–September 2004 had significant negative effects on the two summer crops, with production of each declining by around 15%, but once again the winter crop harvest increased, by around 10%. The net effect was an overall agricultural growth rate of 0.3%. In 2005/06 the agricultural sector recovered rapidly from these floods, showing a growth rate of 5.2% as levels of output rose again. The subsequent decline in growth (to just under 3% in 2006/07) was therefore partly a return to trend. In 2007/08 the agricultural sector was profoundly affected once again, by the occurence of two floods and a cyclone. These natural disasters had a devastating effect, primarily on the second rice crop, the aman, output of which fell by around 10%, compared with the previous year, as well as on poultry and fish farming. However, the third rice crop, the boro, enjoyed a bumper harvest owing to the siltation brought down by the floods as well as the greater incentives created by rising rice prices. The boro crop was 17% larger than that recorded the previous year, and this resulted in overall agricultural growth of around 2.4% in 2007/08, despite the disasters.

If high growth rates in agriculture can be sustained, Bangladesh will make good progress in combating poverty. The land-ownership pattern is characterized by considerable inequality in landholding and also by a high degree of fragmentation of individual farms. The top 10% of landowners hold 49% of the total land area, while the bottom 10% own a mere 2%. One-half of the rural population is effectively landless. The average farm size is small, about 0.8 ha, with more than 70% of all farms classified as small (below 1 ha) and only 5% as large (above 3 ha), while agricultural census figures suggest that the majority of farms consist of at least six, and often considerably more, separate plots of land. Several authors have argued that it is this agrarian structure that has represented the major obstacle to the launching of the 'Green Revolution' in Bangladesh. The fact that individual farms are highly fragmented imposes extra costs on the implementation of some of the new technology, such as irrigation and tractors, making their introduction that much more difficult. Problems of under-utilization of irrigation equipment are also common because of the pattern of land ownership and because of water distribution difficulties. There are frequent complaints about water shortages during critical periods in the crop cycle, which, because HYV yields are relatively sensitive to the timing of irrigation, can be very costly for small-scale farmers. These disruptions can usually be attributed either to political factors in the management of the distribution of water at a local level, or to wider difficulties with the maintenance of equipment or the supply of diesel fuel or electricity. It is estimated that currently only 32% of net cultivated area is under irrigation, although a recent survey suggests that this could be expanded to around 60% of the cultivable area. Such an expansion could result in almost a doubling of foodgrain production in Bangladesh. Most of the existing irrigation (around 75%) is based on small-scale tube wells and lift pumps operated by individual farmers or collectives. The lifting of huge quantities of ground water has, in recent years, resulted in concentrations of natural arsenic and widespread arsenic poisoning in rural Bangladesh. Attention to this problem raises an immediate challenge for the Government. Another factor constraining further growth in the agricultural sector is that risk aversion prevents small-scale farmers from increasing fertilizer use at the same rate as larger-scale farmers. Consequently, the growth in fertilizer use has been slowing down.

Much of the growth in agricultural output in the early 1980s was due to an expansion of the land area under the boro crop and under wheat. During 1975–80 80% of foodgrain production was provided by the rain-fed aus and aman rice crops (the two main summer/monsoon crops), 16% by the boro crop, and around 3% by wheat. By the period covering 1985–88, the contribution made by the aus and aman crops to foodgrain output had fallen to 67%, whereas the contribution made by the winter crop, boro, had increased to 26% and wheat to 7%. The expansion of land area under both the boro rice crop and wheat depended on the extension of irrigation, and these two crops largely accounted for the growth in foodgrain output in the late 1980s. At present, 40% of the total land area is double-cropped (i.e. aus and aman crops) and only 10% is triple-cropped (aus, aman and boro crops). Agricultural growth in recent years has been largely driven by an expansion of the area under the third, or boro, crop. In 2005/06 and again in 2006/07 the area under boro cultivation increased by 7%. Because it is cultivated during the dry season, the size of the boro crop depends on the availability of diesel for irrigation purposes. As more of the potential land is brought under boro, further growth will depend even more crucially on yield increases. Apart from the growth in cropping intensity, there has also been an increase in the share of land cultivated with HYV crops, and this too has contributed to the growth in agricultural output. Yields from HYV crops are about twice those from traditional varieties of rice. However, here too, investment in water systems is essential for future growth. Although optimists believe that HYV crops can be extended to the bulk of the flood plains growing aus and aman, HYV yields at present account for only 20% of the aus and aman crops. It is likely that the introduction of HYV crops in the flood plains is too risky and their extension in these areas will only happen on a large scale if floodwaters can be controlled. Investment in flood control is not only likely to be beyond the limited means of Bangladesh's hard-pressed economy, it would also probably require the involvement of neighbouring countries. The utilization of HYV yields has been most dramatic for the boro crop. However, the deceleration in the rate of growth of rice production in the first half of the 1990s was largely due to a significant decline in the rate of expansion of the area under boro HYV.

The severity of the floods in 1987 and 1988, following a number of serious floods earlier in the decade, prompted much discussion between international donors and the Government of Bangladesh, regarding the quest for long-term solutions to the country's flood problem. The UN Development Programme (UNDP), USAID (the US development assistance agency), France and Japan all embarked upon pre-feasibility studies for major flood-control programmes, and each made different proposals as to what course of action should be taken. Of the four, all except that of USAID envisaged the erection of flood-control embankments, both on the rivers and as protection around major towns. The USAID proposal did not involve an embankment solution, because of prior experiences in the USA and China, and instead raised the possibility of a regional solution to the problem, based on co-operation with both India and Nepal. In mid-1989, in order to avoid the difficulty of having to carry out four separate sets of negotiations, the Government of Bangladesh approached the World Bank and asked it to assume the role of co-ordinator of all donor efforts with respect to flood control. A Flood Action Plan (FAP) was finalized by the World Bank in November 1989, entailing an initial five-year research phase (1990–95) that would inform the development of a long-term comprehensive strategy for flood prevention and disaster preparedness in Bangladesh. It has been envisaged that a comprehensive flood-control programme might require up to US $10,000m. of assistance over a 20-year period. Implementation of the FAP research phase was, however, beset by delays and organizational failures, and little progress was achieved towards the objective of formulating and effecting a flood-control programme: severe floods affected Bangladesh once again in 2004. Of greater practical relevance was the agreement signed by Bangladesh and India in December 1996 regarding the sharing of the Ganga (Ganges) waters during the low season from March to May. India's controversial construction of the Farakka barrage in 1975 had adversely affected the livelihood of 30m. downstream farmers in Bangladesh. The new agreement gives each country a guaranteed flow of 34,000 cu ft per second of water in alternating 10-day periods during the entire lean season. The implementation of this agreement is expected to bring tremendous potential benefits to farmers in north-western Bangladesh.

For the most part, the 1990s were a period of agrarian success for Bangladesh. Total agricultural output increased by 33% in 1990–2000. Food grains were not the only area to experience growth: between 1991/92 and 2000 per caput consumption of fish increased by 9%, potatoes by 25%, meat by 48%, poultry by 120% and milk by 55%. At the same time, per caput consumption of wheat and rice declined marginally and consumption of pulses declined by 13%, reflecting a shift towards higher-value sources of protein. These changes were associated with better nutritional standards experienced by the population, such as improvements in life expectancy, a decline in infant mortality, and lower instances of stunting and wasting in children. However, despite the large share of the agricultural sector in the economy, Bangladesh does not have a global comparative advantage in agriculture because of the very small size of its farms and its vulnerable ecology. If agricultural subsidies in Western countries are slowly removed, Bangladesh is unlikely to benefit from rising global food prices. As a net food importer, it is likely to suffer. Thus, while agricultural growth has been encouraging and has contributed to a decline in poverty, in the long term poverty reduction in Bangladesh has to be led by growth in the manufacturing sector.

### Jute

Jute has traditionally occupied a pivotal position in the Bangladesh economy, in that it represents the major linkage between agriculture and industry. Despite being the country's major cash crop, the area under jute cultivation is very sensitive to relative prices, ranging, for instance, from more than 1m. ha in 1985/86 to around 500,000 ha in 1990/91. Annual jute production varies from 4m. to 4.5m. bales, of which 3m.–3.5m. bales are used to manufacture jute goods, mainly for export; the remaining 1m. bales are exported as raw jute. More than one-half of the capacity in jute-manufacturing remains within the public sector, despite very substantial denationalization (particularly of small units). The jute industry, however, has recently been in decline. In 1981/82 exports of jute (both raw and manufactured) accounted for around 65% of Bangladesh's total export earnings, but by 2001 its share of export earnings had fallen to around 4.6%, with the new export leaders, ready-made garments and knitwear, accounting for 76% of export revenue. This decline can be traced to instability on both the demand and supply sides of the market for jute, which has resulted in volatile prices, but with a general downward trend. In 2006/07 exports of raw jute and manufactured jute products declined once again.

Since 1982 the Government has denationalized about one-half of the country's jute mills, amounting to around one-third of production capacity. Privatization, however, does not appear to have directly increased efficiency, measured by profitability, and the jute mill sector is the country's largest loss-maker. Despite significant reductions in the number of employees working in the privatized jute mills, profitability does not appear to have improved. By 2001 all but six of the 35 private mills had suspended production, as their failure to service debt on time led to banks withholding vital credit lines. A number of these closed mills have subsequently resumed production, but on an irregular basis. The industry requires new investment and a small but predetermined subsidy to remain viable. Such a subsidy could be justified because the jute sector directly or indirectly employs millions of people whose next best employment option may be very unfavourable in the medium term. The World Bank offered Bangladesh a Jute Sector Adjustment Credit worth US $250m. and simultaneously insisted that nine public-sector mills be closed down or privatized by June 1997. The adjustment proposed by the World Bank was not satisfactory, however, to either the public or the private sector, and the adjustment credit was, in the end, not fully taken up. The private-sector jute mills protested strongly at the way in which the World Bank implemented the adjustment, as it led to a number of private mills having to close down while the public sector continued to receive subsidies. In the long term, with growing investment in the production of new types of 'environmentally friendly' jute-based packaging and products, the industry may well prove profitable without a subsidy. The present system of hidden subsidies to the public-sector mills and non-performing loans in the private sector appears to be the poorest solution. Some progress towards restructuring took place when the Government finally closed down the biggest loss-making jute mill in the public sector in June 2002. The huge Adamjee Jute Mills was the world's largest jute mill, employing some 17,000 workers, but it had accumulated losses of more than $200m. since it was nationalized in 1972. The emergency interim Government that took power in early 2007 announced a radical plan to restructure further the public-sector jute mills. Under this plan, another four of the 22 jute mills left in the public sector were to be closed down, and around 14,000 (or 50% of the total) employees in the remaining 18 mills were to be made redundant in an attempt to achieve profitability.

There are potential alternative uses of jute that could be promising. These include using jute to make cushion and curtain fabrics, mixing jute with other fibres to make yarn suitable for knitwear, or using jute in unconventional ways, such as making compressed jute blocks, which can be used as building insulation material in Europe and North America. The long-term future of jute as a cash crop in Bangladesh will also depend on the success of such ventures. In recent years, the manufacture of jute yarn and twine, rather than of sacking and hessian, has proved very successful. Exports of jute manufactured goods also depend on the prices of synthetics in global markets, which, in turn, are strongly linked to the price of petroleum.

## INDUSTRY, MANUFACTURING AND MINING

The industrial sector as a whole, including both formal and informal manufacturing, mining, power and construction, accounted for 26.7% of GDP in 2003/04 and employed around 10% of the work-force in 2000/01. By 2008 the industrial sector provided about 30% of GDP, reflecting the rapid growth of manufacturing, particularly export-orientated manufacturing. The manufacturing sector alone accounted for around 16% of GDP. Manufacturing includes a relatively modern 'formal' sector that consists of larger firms that are formally registered, and an 'informal' sector, comprising many micro-scale unregistered firms. Approximately 70% of manufacturing output in Bangladesh is provided by relatively large-scale manufacturing industries in the formal sector. The manufacturing sector employs about 7.5% of Bangladesh's labour force, but more than 80% of these workers are employed in micro-scale manufacturing in the informal sector, which accounts for only 30% of manufacturing output. Wage rates and working conditions are significantly worse in the informal sector and labour demand is often seasonal. These micro-scale informal sector industries include handloom weaving, bamboo-working and metal-working. The jute manufacturing industry and other large-scale industries dominated the formal sector in the past. In contrast, in the 1980s and 1990s the bulk of the growth in the formal sector was led by ready-made garments, knitwear and other smaller-scale export-based industries. Traditional heavy industries fared badly: the jute industry had particular problems (see above), but even the cotton textiles sector experienced difficulties. Many of the cotton textile units were closed down or were operating at a fraction of their capacity by the late 1990s. Power cuts and unfair competition from smuggled products, which avoided the payment of customs duties and excise taxes, were blamed. Nevertheless, largely owing to the newer industries, industrial output in general increased by a substantial 86% in 1990–

2000, ensuring Bangladesh's emergence as one of the rapidly growing and globalizing economies in the developing world.

Industrial growth in 2004/05 reached 8.6%, higher than the robust 7.6% achieved in the previous year. Manufacturing grew by 8.4%, power, water and gas by 9.0%, and construction by 8.7%. The growth of manufacturing was driven by a number of sectors: garments, jute yarn and twine, pharmaceuticals, tobacco manufacturing, printing and publishing, beverages and cement. In recent years Bangladesh has also commenced shipbuilding, with a number of international orders for Bangladeshi-constructed vessels having being placed. It had been feared that the removal of global quotas on garments exports, which had favoured Bangladesh in the past, would have damaging effects on such exports from 2005. In fact, this did not happen, although there may be consequences in the future as China, India and other competitors begin to encroach on Bangladeshi markets. More efficient and larger Bangladeshi garment factories are, however, already taking advantage of global opportunities. The knitwear sector has been registering strong growth as it operates in a niche with technologies and wages that are below the Chinese threshold, and may not be very seriously affected by the removal of quotas. Knitwear and woven garments accounted for around 75% of the country's export earnings in the middle years of the first decade of the 2000s. Other items recording high export growth included jute goods, chemical products and leather. Growth in the manufacturing sector rose to 10.8% in 2005/06 and 11.2% in 2006/07. However, the rate of growth in 2007/08 was expected to decrease owing to the political unrest and the consequent imposition of a state of emergency. In addition, the anti-corruption/anti-tax evasion campaign launched by the interim Government resulted in many investors lying low for a while. The international markets also began to tighten, but this had a limited effect on Bangladesh since it enjoyed a competitive advantage in its primary markets of garments, particularly knitwear, because of the rising currencies of its major competitors in China and India.

A number of other successes in large-scale industry in the recent past need to be acknowledged. Increased production of domestic gas has been successfully substituted for oil in the production of electricity and as the primary source of energy in industry. Gas-based fertilizer production has also increased. At present the country's five urea-fertilizer factories produce about 1.5m. metric tons per year, and there is one factory that produces triple super-phosphate (TSP) fertilizer. Domestic demand for fertilizer grew dramatically, from 210,000 tons in 1969/70 to 2.3m. tons in 1993/94. Two new fertilizer plants, at Jamuna and Karnaphuli, have recently commenced operating. The gas-fired Karnaphuli plant, Kafco—a US $510m. joint venture between the Government and an international consortium of companies—became operational in December 1994, and Bangladesh began to export liquid ammonia for the first time. In 2003/04 the output of electricity grew by 8.1% and that of gas by 8.5%. Independent Power Producers (IPPs) have grown rapidly and accounted for around 38% of electricity generation in the early years of the first decade of the 2000s. Savings in foreign exchange have also resulted from import-substitution in steel (mainly through ship-breaking) and in pharmaceuticals.

The shift to the private sector began in the 1980s, when policy changed radically to encourage exports and an increased participation of the private sector. Measures were introduced in an attempt to reduce bureaucratic obstacles both to private investment and to trade. The Industrial Policy of 1991 identified 42 large enterprises for denationalization as the first stage in the new policy of privatization. In the economy as a whole, the private sector accounts for 80% of GDP, 90% of total employment and 70% of investment. Between 1991 and 2003 the private sector accounted for 88% of GDP growth and 87% of investment growth.

The 1980s and the first half of the 1990s witnessed the dramatic growth of the ready-made garments industry, with garments becoming the foremost source of export revenue. By the end of the 1990s the industry employed about 1.5m. skilled workers, most of them women. According to the Bangladesh Bank, exports of ready-made garments in 2006/07 reached US $4,658m., amounting to 38.2% of total export earnings. (In the same year exports of knitwear and hosiery products rose to $4,554m., equivalent to 37.4% of total export revenue.) Although some domestic fabric and yarn production has commenced in Bangladesh, the majority of fabric and yarns required by the ready-made garment sector is imported. This means that the net export earnings of the sector are considerably lower. There are obviously great opportunities for developing domestic fabric and yarn production, but foreign investments or partnerships are needed to transfer the requisite technology. The incentives to develop these industries are even stronger because of the tax exemptions for exports to the European Union (EU) of garments that are manufactured within Bangladesh using Bangladeshi yarn and fabrics. In mid-2000 the EU changed its rules to allow tax-free imports from Bangladesh of garments made with yarn or fabrics from any of the member countries of the South Asian Association for Regional Co-operation (SAARC). This move was expected to help Bangladesh's garments industry, but although Bangladeshi manufacturers have established fabric import links with East Asian countries, transport links within SAARC are not yet well-developed. Paradoxically, Bangladesh is a beneficiary of the Multi-fibre Arrangement (MFA) quotas, which limit exports of garments to developed countries, since the arrangement favours very poor countries. As a result of international agreements made under the WTO, the MFA was due to be phased out by 1 January 2005. Bangladesh argued that this did not allow it sufficient time to develop the necessary yarn and fabric industries that it would require to compete with more advanced developing countries, such as China and India, which already had established domestic yarn and fabric industries. By mid-2007 the phaseout was virtually complete and Bangladesh was faced with the challenge of improving its productivity and product range to compete with India, China and other producers.

Further growth of the industrial sector requires a major commitment by the State to improve infrastructure and to provide political stability, both essential for attracting long-term investments by the private sector. Investments to improve the performance of the ports at Chittagong and Khulna are particularly important, as port delays are the cause of huge losses for Bangladeshi exporters. Chittagong port handles 85% of seaborne traffic. It suffers from poor infrastructure, low labour productivity, multiple labour unions and restrictive labour practices. Average container dwell time is 18 days, compared with 10–12 days at comparable ports in the region. However, attempts to overcome delays at the ports have been repeatedly thwarted by political resistance from powerful vested-interest groups. An opportunity for an overhaul of the ports arose with the assumption of power by the emergency interim Government in early 2007, and one of the administration's first acts was to privatize container operations at Chittagong port; this resulted in some immediate productivity gains. A further constraint to private-sector development is the availability and reliability of power. Reforms of the power sector are currently on the agenda of international financial institutions and the Government. Although the boom in private-sector investment during the 1980s was helped by some government moves to liberalize the economy, the budgetary constraints limiting public investment had an adverse effect on private-sector investment. Moreover, privatization had a limited effect on enhancing private investment. After the initial privatizations of the 1980s, the Privatization Board was established in 1993 to sell off the 270 remaining state-owned enterprises. By mid-2001 the Privatization Board had succeeded in transferring to the private sector only 28 of these enterprises, of which 12 were privatized during 1993–96, and a further 16 during 1996–2001. In fact, the growth of the private sector in the 1980s and 1990s happened quite independently of these government attempts at privatization. It was driven by new investments in niche export markets which did not require government assistance in technology acquisition. These new, mainly small-scale, enterprises included garments, shrimps and leather-product exporters, and more recently included larger enterprises in power generation and telecommunications. The mobile telephone industry has registered remarkable and exponential growth. The number of mobile telephone subscribers increased from 2.8m. in 2004 to 19.1m. in 2006. Grameen is the largest provider, with roughly one-half of the market. Other providers include Aktel, BanglaLink, CityCell and Teletalk, with others, such as Warid Telecom of the United Arab Emirates, entering the market. Competition among providers has led to a decline in prices and mobile telephone charges, making mobile telephones accessible to wider sections of the population. In 2008 the mobile network covered 85% of the country's geographic area and 97% of the population. The number of mobile telephone subscribers reached 36.4m. in 2008, amounting to a teledensity of 26.8%. There was a 100% growth in subscribers registered in 2006 and a 65% increase in 2007. The mobile telephone sector has been the largest recipient of FDI in recent years.

Despite the growth in the private sector, FDI in Bangladesh was initially disappointingly low. Foreign investment amounted to only US $180m. in 1998/99, increased to $280m. in 1999/2000, and then significantly declined to $78m. in 2000/01. Furthermore, FDI was mostly in the power and gas sectors, where foreign investors were protected by sovereign guarantees, at the cost of increasing the contingent liabilities of the Bangladeshi Government. However, from 2003 there was a significant upturn in FDI, and growth has been sustained in recent years. FDI flows in 2005 amounted to $776m., and were expected to enjoy steady growth over the next few years. Political uncertainty, though, led to a decline in FDI in the first eight months of 2006/07 to $325m., compared with the inflow of $489m. during the same period in 2005/06.

The discovery of vast reserves of natural gas in Bangladesh has opened up the possibility of a quicker path towards further development. By 1989 14 gas fields, with a total of 22 gas production wells, had been discovered (including one offshore field). The breakthrough occurred in 1995, when a British company, Cairn Energy, discovered the Sangu field, which is situated 50 km off the coast of southern Bangladesh in the Bay of Bengal. The official estimate of reserves in Sangu is 1,030,000m. cu ft, but Cairn Energy executives believe that the field could hold up to 2,000,000m. cu ft. Other large gas fields include Titas (4,100,000m. cu ft), Kailashtila (3,650,000m. cu ft), Rashidpur (2,240,000m. cu ft), Habiganj (3,670,000m. cu ft) and Jalalabad (1,500,000m. cu ft). The Bibiyana gas field could have reserves of around 5,000,000m. cu ft or more. In 2001/02 annual production of natural gas was an estimated 387,630m. cu ft, providing 70% of the country's commercial energy. There is thus the potential for the gas discoveries to contribute significantly to Bangladesh's growth rate. On the other hand, large-scale political conflicts may arise if the benefits are not widely and fairly distributed. An additional problem has been political opposition to allowing gas exports to India, the most obvious large market for the product. In the meantime, a national committee established to report on gas reserves concluded in June 2002 that proven reserves of gas range from 12,000,000m. to 15,500,000m. cu ft, suggesting that reserves are lower than previously envisaged. From an economic perspective, the decision to export gas has little to do with the size of the reserves and more to do with the price of gas abroad compared with its value in domestic use. The reluctance of many economists in Bangladesh to countenance major gas exports is probably based on fears that the Government would waste the foreign revenues earned. If this is the case, it may be rational to leave the gas unexplored until governance capacities improve. Thus, the political acceptance of gas exports may be contingent on the State improving its capacity to promote development. In June 2006 the ADB and the Bangladeshi Government signed agreements for US $230m. in loans to help expand the country's natural gas infrastructure and delivery system.

## TRADE

Bangladesh's trade balance improved during the 1980s. The trade deficit decreased from an average of more than 10% of GDP in the early 1980s to 5%–6% by 2000. This was assisted by a significant increase in exports, from 7% of GDP in 1990/91 to 15% of GDP in 1999/2000. Exports grew by 21.1% in the first eight months of 2006/07, compared with the same period the previous year, with imports increasing by 21%. The rising level of remittances from overseas Bangladeshi workers from the 1980s onwards has played an important role in easing the import constraint. It permitted Bangladesh to develop a secondary market for foreign exchange as early as the 1980s. The buoyant supply of foreign exchange from remittances helped Bangladesh to float the taka fully on 31 May 2003. In 2000/01 remittances declined by around 3% compared with the previous year, as a result of declining demand for Bangladeshi labour overseas, owing to the global slowdown. This adversely affected the balance of payments, which was already weakened by a growing trade deficit. From 2001 onwards, remittances have steadily increased, with a 10% rise in 2003/04 and a further 14.8% increase in 2004/05. In 2005/06 remittances grew by 23.8%, reflecting higher incomes in the Middle East as a result of rising petroleum prices and improved money transfer facilities (to counter the informal 'hundi' system of money transfers). As a result, despite deficits in the trade balance, the current account has normally been in surplus. Foreign-currency reserves have remained relatively stable, increasing to US $3,126m. in April 2005, and to more than $4,000m. in February 2007. A rise in the level of remittances resulted in an increase in foreign-currency reserves to $5,800m. at the end of April 2008.

The Government has sought to promote exports by establishing a series of export processing zones (EPZs). Companies establishing operations in these zones are exempt from taxes for a period of 10 years. In addition, imports for re-export are exempt from all import duties and indirect taxes, and trade union activities are restricted. The combined exports of the Chittagong, Dhaka and Mongla EPZs exceeded US $1,000m. for the first time in 2000/01, to reach $1,065m. By 2001/02 the EPZs had a total of 172 industrial units in operation, employing 117,000 workers altogether. Total investment reached more than $500m.

The Government has also liberalized its regulations concerning imports, by simplifying import procedures and removing quantitative restrictions on industrial raw materials. In addition, under the Trade and Industrial Policy Reform Programme, which was introduced in 1983, there have been attempts made to standardize the structure of tariffs and to reduce their level in an effort to improve the potential for export growth. The most radical change has been to free most imports from quantitative restrictions. The unweighted average tariff was reduced from 89% in 1990/91 to 20% in 1998/99. It had stabilized at around 17% in 2000/01. In recent years India has come under pressure from Bangladesh to allow tariff-free access to Bangladeshi exports, particularly jute products. In 2001/02 the trade imbalance with India amounted to US $1,600m. Prior to 1999 India had agreed to a tariff-free status for a list of products that Bangladesh did not really benefit from. In 1999, however, India consented to let Bangladesh itself suggest a list of 25 specific items. Bangladesh was expected to benefit substantially from such a scheme, should it be implemented.

External debt is mostly limited to the public sector and totalled US $17,300m. in 2002. This amounted to 34.9% of GDP, but, because most of the debt was in the form of soft loans at concessional interest rates, the debt service was equivalent to only 7.2% of export earnings. According to figures from the Asian Development Bank (ADB), Bangladesh's total external debt was $18,934.5m. at the end of 2005, of which $17,937.7m. was long-term public debt. In that year the cost of debt-servicing was equivalent to 5.3% of total revenue from exports of goods and services.

## FISCAL AND MONETARY POLICIES

Bangladesh enjoys a relatively stable fiscal and monetary regime, although there are concerns that the budget deficit may be worsening. In 2004/05 the overall budgetary deficit was equivalent to approximately 3.5% of GDP; however, the consolidated fiscal deficit, which includes the heavy losses incurred by state-owned enterprises that are not all included in the central government budget, was higher by at least 1%. In 2006/07, according to Bangladesh Bank figures, the overall budgetary deficit (excluding grants) was projected to amount to the equivalent of 3.7% of GDP and in 2007/08 expenditure on disaster relief and the cost of subsidizing fuel raised the deficit to around 4.8% of GDP. In 2007 radical steps were taken to limit the losses incurred by state-owned enterprises and their potential impact on public finances. In April the price of petroleum and related products was raised by 15%–21% in an attempt to minimize the losses of the Bangladesh Petroleum Corporation, which sold imported fuel at below world market prices. In March urban electricity tariffs were also raised by between 5% and 10% to reduce the losses incurred by the Bangladesh Power Development Board and to establish parity between rural and urban consumers. Government revenue was equivalent to 10.3% of GDP in 2005, significantly less than the 20% or so collected by India or the 15% collected by Pakistan. The Bangladeshi Government plans to increase revenue collection by 0.5% of GDP every year. The cost of financing the budget deficit has been increasing, owing to the decline in cheap foreign credit in the form of development aid. This has forced the Government to seek domestic assistance to finance the deficit at a much higher cost. Interest payments accounted for 11%–12% of the budget in the early years of the first decade of the 2000s, although, at around 1% of GDP, interest payments are still much lower than in many other developing countries. The revenue demands on the Government have been increasing because of a rapidly expanding civil service, which is growing at roughly twice the rate of growth of the population. Pay awards have to be implemented rapidly, as a political necessity, but reorganization of the administration as a whole is subject to delay and obstruction.

Bangladesh has been very successful in allocating a relatively high portion of the budget to the social sector: almost 35% of its total budgetary expenditure was spent on education, health, social security and disaster management in the late 1990s. Education and technology received the highest sectoral budgetary allocation in the 2008/09 budget, being allotted nearly 13% of total projected expenditure. The female stipend programme, through which female primary school students are given a stipend to attend school, has been extended. A new programme of monthly scholarships for female students pursuing graduate studies in specialized subjects was introduced. Health was allocated an estimated 5.0% of the 2008/09 budget. Compared with the levels of defence expenditure in India and Pakistan, spending on defence in Bangladesh is traditionally relatively low. For example, in 1998 defence expenditure was only 1.4% of GDP, compared with 2.3% in India and 4.3% in Pakistan. This has meant that, despite relatively low budgetary expenditures in aggregate, Bangladesh has been able to make progress in health and education.

## DEVELOPMENT OUTLOOK

In recent years Bangladesh has improved its developmental performance by encouraging the growth of small export-orientated industries. At the same time, various credit programmes are being operated by the Government and NGOs, specifically to support income-generating activities undertaken by the poorest social groups, as well as special programmes for women. The inaccessibility of the banking system for the majority of the people, particularly the poor, has, if anything, increased since the early 1980s and is a major obstacle to development. This can only be partially offset by the success of the micro-credit programmes of NGOs, such as the Grameen Bank, BRAC (formerly the Bangladesh Rural Advancement Committee, now known only by its acronym) and Proshika. The lending programmes of these organizations have been targeted at the landless and, in many cases, have focused particularly on women. In sharp contrast to the poor performances in the formal banking sector (especially regarding urban-industrial lending), the recovery rate in the credit programmes of the NGOs has been excellent. However, the small-scale lending activities of the NGOs are no substitute for a reform of the mainstream banking sector.

The resilience of the Bangladesh economy is demonstrated by its ability to grow steadily despite the disruptive impact of mighty floods and cyclones. Even though the FAP based on embankment construction (see Agriculture) has its critics, the way forward for Bangladesh must be to discover appropriate flood-control strategies and to invest in constructing infrastructure. The country's largest infrastructural project, the construction of the 4.8-km, US $700m. Jamuna Bridge, was approved by the World Bank in early 1992, and completed in June 1998. Financed largely by Japan, the ADB and the World Bank, the bridge is a sterling example of an economically viable large-scale infrastructure project. It is the longest bridge in South Asia, and has transformed the economy of northern Bangladesh. In 1999 the daily traffic across the bridge, of 2,480 vehicles, was greater than the expected 1,750 vehicles per day, and the daily toll collection was 2% higher than projected.

Ultimately, sustained development in Bangladesh will depend primarily on improvements in political stability and on the capacity of the State to boost development by effectively regulating markets, collecting taxes, investing in infrastructure and assisting in technology acquisition by the private sector. This is particularly important given the low technological base of much of Bangladesh's current exports and therefore the need for rapid technological advancement in response to growing competition from other developing countries. In addition, Bangladesh needs to make substantial investments in irrigation and flood control, which requires regional co-operation and international support.

# Statistical Survey

Source (unless otherwise stated): Bangladesh Bureau of Statistics, Statistics Division, Ministry of Planning, E-27/A, Agargaon, Sher-e-bangla Nagar, Dhaka 1207; tel. (2) 9118045; fax (2) 9111064; e-mail ndbp@bangla.net; internet www.bbs.gov.bd.

## Area and Population

### AREA, POPULATION AND DENSITY

| | |
|---|---|
| Area (sq km) | 143,998* |
| Population (census results)† | |
| 11 March 1991 | 111,455,185 |
| 22 January 2001 | |
| Males | 67,731,320 |
| Females | 62,791,278 |
| Total | 130,522,598 |
| Population (official estimates at mid-year)‡ | |
| 2005 | 138,600,000 |
| 2006 | 141,800,000§ |
| 2007 | 143,910,000§ |
| Density (per sq km) at mid-2007 | 999.4 |

* 55,598 sq miles.

† Including adjustment for underenumeration, estimated to have been 3.08% in 1991 and 4.95% in 2001.

‡ Based on sample vital registration system (SVRS).

§ Projected estimate.

### ADMINISTRATIVE DIVISIONS

(2001 census, preliminary figures)

| Division | Area (sq km) | Population ('000)* | Density (per sq km) |
|---|---|---|---|
| Barisal | 13,297 | 8,514 | 640.3 |
| Chittagong | 33,771 | 25,187 | 745.8 |
| Dhaka | 31,119 | 40,592 | 1,304.4 |
| Khulna | 22,274 | 15,185 | 681.7 |
| Rajshahi | 34,513 | 31,478 | 912.1 |
| Sylhet | 12,596 | 8,291 | 658.2 |
| **Total** | 147,570 | 129,247 | 875.8 |

* Including adjustments for net underenumeration.

### PRINCIPAL TOWNS

(population at 1991 census)*

| | | | |
|---|---|---|---|
| Dhaka (capital) | 3,612,850 | Comilla | 135,313 |
| Chittagong | 1,392,860 | Nawabganj | 130,577 |
| Khulna | 663,340 | Dinajpur | 127,815 |
| Rajshahi | 294,056 | Bogra | 120,170 |
| Narayanganj | 276,549 | Sylhet | 114,300 |
| Sitakunda | 274,903 | Brahmanbaria | 109,032 |
| Rangpur | 191,398 | Tangail | 106,004 |
| Mymensingh (Nasirabad) | 188,713 | Jamalpur | 103,556 |
| Barisal (Bakerganj) | 170,232 | Pabna | 103,277 |
| Tongi (Tungi) | 168,702 | Naogaon | 101,266 |
| Jessore | 139,710 | Sirajganj | 99,669 |

* Figures in each case refer to the city proper. The population of the largest urban agglomerations at the 1991 census was: Dhaka 6,487,459 (including Narayanganj and Tongi); Chittagong 2,079,968 (including Sitakunda); Khulna 921,365; Rajshahi 507,435; Mymensingh 273,350; Sylhet 225,541; Comilla 225,259; Rangpur 208,294; Barisal 202,746; Jessore 169,349; Bogra 161,155.

**2001** (urban agglomerations, preliminary census figures): Dhaka 9,912,908 (including Narayanganj 230,294 and Tongi 281,928); Chittagong 3,202,710 (including Patiya 47,625); Khulna 1,227,239; Rajshahi 646,716.

**Mid-2007** ('000, incl. suburbs, UN estimate): Dhaka 13,485; Chittagong 4,529 (Source: UN, *World Urbanization Prospects: The 2007 Revision*).

### BIRTHS, MARRIAGES AND DEATHS*

(crude rates per 1,000 persons)

| | Live births | Marriages | Deaths |
|---|---|---|---|
| 2000 | 19.0 | 9.0 | 4.9 |
| 2001 | 18.9 | 8.9 | 4.8 |
| 2002 | 20.1 | 9.5 | 5.1 |
| 2003 | 20.9 | 10.4 | 5.9 |
| 2004 | 20.8 | 12.4 | 5.8 |

* Estimates based on sample vital registration system (SVRS). According to UN estimates, the average annual rates per 1,000 for births and deaths were: Births 33.6 in 1990–95, 29.4 in 1995–2000, 27.8 in 2000–05; Deaths 11.1 in 1990–95, 9.2 in 1995–2000, 8.2 in 2000–05 (Source: UN, *World Population Prospects: The 2006 Revision*).

**1997** (provisional): Registered live births 3,057,000 (birth rate 24.6 per 1,000); Registered deaths 958,000 (death rate 7.7 per 1,000) (Source: UN, *Population and Vital Statistics Report*).

**Marriages:** 1,181,000 in 1997 (Source: UN, *Demographic Yearbook*).

**Expectation of life** (years at birth, WHO estimates): 62.9 (males 62.5; females 63.3) in 2006 (Source: WHO, *World Health Statistics*).

### ECONOMICALLY ACTIVE POPULATION*

(sample survey, '000 persons aged 15 years and over, year ending June 2000)

| | Males | Females | Total |
|---|---|---|---|
| Agriculture, hunting, forestry and fishing | 17,256 | 14,914 | 32,171 |
| Mining and quarrying | 107 | 188 | 295 |
| Manufacturing | 2,346 | 1,436 | 3,783 |
| Electricity, gas and water | 116 | 18 | 134 |
| Construction | 999 | 100 | 1,099 |
| Trade, restaurants and hotels | 5,769 | 506 | 6,275 |
| Transport, storage and communications | 2,432 | 77 | 2,509 |
| Financing, insurance, real estate and business services | 357 | 46 | 403 |
| Community, social and personal services | 1,243 | 1,726 | 2,969 |
| Activities not adequately defined | 1,744 | 384 | 2,126 |
| **Total employed** | 32,369 | 19,395 | 51,764 |
| Unemployed | 1,083 | 666 | 1,750 |
| **Total labour force** | 33,452 | 20,061 | 53,514 |

* Figures exclude members of the armed forces.

Note: Totals may not be equal to sum of components, owing to rounding.

Source: ILO.

**Mid-2005** (official estimates in '000): Agriculture, etc. 37,874; Total labour force 74,574 (Source: FAO).

## Health and Welfare

### KEY INDICATORS

| | |
|---|---|
| Total fertility rate (children per woman, 2006) | 2.9 |
| Under-five mortality rate (per 1,000 live births, 2006) | 69 |
| HIV/AIDS (% of persons aged 15–49, 2005) | <0.1 |
| Physicians (per 1,000 head, 2005) | 0.3 |
| Hospital beds (per 1,000 head, 2001) | 0.30 |
| Health expenditure (2005): US $ per head (PPP) | 57 |
| Health expenditure (2005): % of GDP | 3.1 |
| Health expenditure (2005): public (% of total) | 29.1 |
| Access to water (% of persons, 2004) | 74 |
| Access to sanitation (% of persons, 2004) | 39 |
| Human Development Index (2005): ranking | 140 |
| Human Development Index (2005): value | 0.547 |

For sources and definitions, see explanatory note on p. vi.

# Agriculture

**PRINCIPAL CROPS**
('000 metric tons, year ending 30 June)

| | 2003/04 | 2004/05 | 2005/06 |
|---|---|---|---|
| Wheat | 1,253 | 976 | 772 |
| Rice (paddy) | 36,236 | 39,796 | 43,729* |
| Millet | 26 | 25* | 25† |
| Potatoes | 3,907 | 4,855 | 4,161 |
| Sweet potatoes | 320 | 311 | 327† |
| Sugar cane | 6,484 | 6,423 | 6,423† |
| Other sugar crops | 317 | 342 | 342† |
| Beans (dry) | 144 | 49† | 50† |
| Lentils | 122 | 118 | 120† |
| Other pulses | 163 | 168 | 136† |
| Groundnuts (in shell) | 34 | 39 | 34* |
| Areca nuts (betel) | 55 | 57† | 55† |
| Coconuts | 133 | 88† | 88† |
| Rapeseed | 211 | 191 | 235* |
| Sesame seed* | 49 | 50 | 50 |
| Linseed* | 50 | 50 | 50 |
| Cottonseed† | 27 | 26 | 26 |
| Cabbages | 129 | 142 | 142† |
| Lettuce | 32 | 32 | 32† |
| Spinach | 29 | 29 | 29† |
| Tomatoes | 120 | 122 | 122† |
| Cauliflowers and broccoli | 101 | 109 | 109† |
| Pumpkins, squash and gourds | 226 | 228† | 228† |
| Dry onions | 272 | 589 | 589† |
| Garlic | 73 | 90 | 90† |
| Beans (green) | 59 | 61 | 61† |
| Cantaloupes and other melons | 89† | 82 | 82 |
| Guavas, mangoes and mangosteens | 243 | 228† | 228† |
| Pineapples | 213 | 235 | 235† |
| Bananas | 707 | 899 | 899† |
| Papayas | 51 | 51† | 51† |
| Tea (made) | 58 | 58 | 58† |
| Tobacco (leaves) | 39 | 39† | 39† |
| Ginger | 48 | 49 | 49† |
| Jute† | 801 | 801 | 801 |

* Unofficial figure(s).
† FAO estimate(s).

**Aggregate production** ('000 metric tons, may include official, semi-official or estimated data): Total cereals 37,759 in 2004, 41,156 in 2005, 45,010 in 2006; Total roots and tubers 4,228 in 2004, 5,167 in 2005, 4,488 in 2006; Total vegetables (incl. melons) 2,097 in 2004, 2,451 in 2005, 2,451 in 2006; Total spices 235 in 2004, 283 in 2005, 283 in 2006; Total fruits (excl. melons) 1,690 in 2004, 1,889 in 2005, 1889 in 2006.

Source: FAO.

**LIVESTOCK**
('000 head, year ending September, FAO estimates)

| | 2001 | 2002 | 2003 |
|---|---|---|---|
| Cattle | 24,100 | 24,300 | 24,500 |
| Buffaloes | 850 | 850 | 850 |
| Sheep | 1,143 | 1,194 | 1,260 |
| Goats | 34,400 | 36,900 | 36,900 |
| Chickens | 140 | 140 | 142 |
| Ducks | 12 | 11 | 12 |

**2004–06:** Figures assumed to be unchanged from 2003 (FAO estimates).

Source: FAO.

**LIVESTOCK PRODUCTS**
('000 metric tons, FAO estimates)

| | 2003 | 2004 | 2005 |
|---|---|---|---|
| Cattle meat | 180.0 | 180.0 | 180.0 |
| Buffalo meat | 3.6 | 3.6 | 3.6 |
| Sheep meat | 3.0 | 3.0 | 3.0 |
| Goat meat | 137 | 137 | 137 |
| Chicken meat | 102.0 | 109.6 | 114.2 |
| Duck meat | 14.0 | 13.7 | 14.0 |
| Cows' milk | 797 | 800 | 800 |
| Buffalo milk | 22.8 | 22.8 | 22.8 |
| Sheep's milk | 25.1 | 25.1 | 25.1 |
| Goats' milk | 1,416 | 1,416 | 1,416 |
| Hen eggs | 135 | 135 | 135 |
| Other poultry eggs | 26 | 26 | 26 |

**2006:** Figures assumed to be unchanged from 2005 (FAO estimates).

Source: FAO.

# Forestry

**ROUNDWOOD REMOVALS**
('000 cubic metres, excl. bark)

| | 2004 | 2005 | 2006 |
|---|---|---|---|
| Sawlogs, veneer logs and logs for sleepers* | 174 | 174 | 174 |
| Pulpwood† | 18 | 18 | 18 |
| Other industrial wood† | 90 | 90 | 90 |
| Fuel wood† | 27,694 | 27,662 | 27,584 |
| **Total** | 27,976 | 27,944 | 27,866 |

* Annual output assumed to be unchanged since 1996.
† FAO estimates.

Source: FAO.

**SAWNWOOD PRODUCTION**
('000 cubic metres, incl. railway sleepers)

| | 2001 | 2002 | 2003 |
|---|---|---|---|
| **Total** (all broadleaved) | 79* | 255 | 388 |

* FAO estimate.

**2004–06:** Production assumed to be unchanged from 2003 (FAO estimates).

Source: FAO.

# Fishing

('000 metric tons, live weight)

| | 2004 | 2005 | 2006 |
|---|---|---|---|
| Capture | 1,187.3 | 1,333.9 | 1,436.5 |
| Freshwater fishes | 661.1 | 781.8 | 878.4 |
| Hilsa shad | 255.8 | 275.9 | 277.1 |
| Marine fishes | 233.8 | 231.9 | 232.8 |
| Aquaculture | 914.8 | 882.1 | 892.0 |
| Roho labeo | 166.3 | 164.2 | 173.3 |
| Catla | 140.6 | 138.5 | 151.4 |
| Silver carp | 156.7 | 159.7 | 167.8 |
| Penaeus shrimps | 58.0 | 63.1 | 64.7 |
| **Total catch** | 2,102.0 | 2,216.0 | 2,328.5 |

Source: FAO.

# Mining

(million cubic metres, year ending 30 June)

| | 2003/04 | 2004/05 | 2005/06 |
|---|---|---|---|
| Natural gas | 13,000 | 14,000 | 15,000 |

Source: US Geological Survey.

# Industry

### SELECTED PRODUCTS

('000 metric tons, unless otherwise indicated; year ending 30 June)

| | 2003/04 | 2004/05 | 2005/06 |
|---|---|---|---|
| Cement | 1,850.2 | 365.4 | 2,195.6 |
| Refined sugar | 119.1 | 108.7 | 129.4 |
| Cigarettes (million) | 22,499 | 23,860 | 24,597 |
| Cotton yarn ('000 bales)* | 470 | 573 | 671 |
| Woven cotton fabrics ('000 metres) | 26,296 | 32,585 | 38,050 |
| Jute fabrics† | 282.3 | n.a. | n.a. |
| Paper | 28.9 | 24.3 | 25.7 |
| Fertilizers | 2,198.2 | 2,102.3 | 1,926.6 |
| Electric energy (million kWh) | n.a. | 21,165 | 22,741 |

* 1 bale = 180 kg.

† Production of jute mills.

Source: mainly Bangladesh Bank.

# Finance

### CURRENCY AND EXCHANGE RATES

**Monetary Units**

100 poisha = 1 taka.

**Sterling, Dollar and Euro Equivalents** (30 May 2008)

£1 sterling = 135.283 taka;
US $1 = 68.550 taka;
€1 = 106.307 taka;
1,000 taka = £7.39 = $14.59 = €9.41.

**Average Exchange Rate** (taka per US $)

2005 64.328
2006 68.933
2007 68.875

### BUDGET

(million taka, year ending 30 June)

| Revenue* | 2006/07† | 2007/08† | 2008/09‡ |
|---|---|---|---|
| Taxation | 392,470 | 480,120 | 567,890 |
| Import duties | 82,790 | 93,000 | 108,620 |
| Income and profit taxes | 89,240 | 110,050 | 130,540 |
| Excise duties | 1,850 | 2,130 | 2,510 |
| Value-added tax | 136,830 | 170,130 | 202,490 |
| Other revenue | 102,250 | 125,270 | 125,930 |
| **Total** | 494,720 | 605,390 | 693,820 |

| Expenditure§ | 2006/07† | 2007/08† | 2008/09‡ |
|---|---|---|---|
| General public services | 50,400 | 73,580 | 135,020 |
| Local government and rural development | 14,340 | 13,990 | 14,890 |
| Defence | 52,820 | 57,760 | 62,410 |
| Public order and safety | 41,310 | 47,550 | 50,490 |
| Education and technology | 80,200 | 86,580 | 87,640 |
| Health | 26,820 | 28,980 | 34,230 |
| Social security and welfare | 24,200 | 35,570 | 60,060 |
| Housing | 5,450 | 6,200 | 6,310 |
| Recreation, culture and religious affairs | 5,050 | 5,610 | 4,830 |
| Fuel and energy | 270 | 290 | 300 |
| Agriculture, forestry and fishing | 35,970 | 67,110 | 68,100 |
| Industrial and economic services | 2,010 | 3,330 | 3,380 |
| Transport and communications | 23,720 | 32,970 | 25,840 |
| Interest payments | 91,540 | 119,670 | 125,650 |
| **Gross current expenditure** | 454,120 | 579,220 | 679,180 |

* Excluding grants, loans and food account transactions.

† Revised figures.

‡ Forecasts.

§ Non-development expenditure, excluding loans and advances, domestic and foreign debt, food account operations and structural adjustment.

Note: Totals may not be equivalent to the sum of components, owing to rounding.

Source: Ministry of Finance (Finance Division).

### PUBLIC SECTOR DEVELOPMENT EXPENDITURE

(departmental allocation, million taka, year ending 30 June)

| | 2007/08 | 2008/09* |
|---|---|---|
| Agriculture | 19,760 | 23,160 |
| Local government and rural development | 55,460 | 57,950 |
| Industrial and economic services | 3,290 | 6,110 |
| Fuel and energy | 35,560 | 43,100 |
| Transport and communications | 27,450 | 34,860 |
| Housing | 1,840 | 3,040 |
| Education and technology | 29,960 | 34,950 |
| Health | 23,630 | 24,390 |
| Social security and welfare | 10,690 | 22,020 |
| Public order and safety | 3,930 | 5,380 |
| Defence | 1,750 | 1,630 |
| Recreation, culture and religious affairs | 2,760 | 3,970 |
| Public services | 16,950 | 13,230 |
| **Total development expenditure**† | 233,040 | 273,780 |

* Forecasts.

† Including transfers (million taka): 8,040 in 2007/08; 17,780 in 2008/09.

Note: Totals may not be equal to the sum of components, owing to rounding.

Source: Ministry of Finance (Economic Relations Division).

### INTERNATIONAL RESERVES

(US $ million at 31 December)

| | 2005 | 2006 | 2007 |
|---|---|---|---|
| Gold* | 58.1 | 71.4 | 94.6 |
| IMF special drawing rights | 0.9 | 1.3 | 0.8 |
| Reserve position in IMF | 0.3 | 0.4 | 0.4 |
| Foreign exchange | 2,766.0 | 3,803.9 | 5,182.2 |
| **Total** | 2,825.3 | 3,877.0 | 5,278.0 |

* Valued at market-related prices.

Source: IMF, *International Financial Statistics*.

### MONEY SUPPLY
(million taka at 31 December)

| | 2005 | 2006 | 2007 |
|---|---|---|---|
| Currency outside banks | 201,415 | 295,418 | 318,740 |
| Demand deposits at deposit money banks* | 173,896 | 200,237 | 260,326 |
| **Total money** (incl. others) | 375,311 | 495,655 | 579,066 |

* Comprises the scheduled banks plus the agricultural and industrial development banks.

Source: IMF, *International Financial Statistics*.

### COST OF LIVING
(Consumer Price Index, year ending 30 June; base: 1995/96 = 100)

| | 2004/05 | 2005/06 | 2006/07 |
|---|---|---|---|
| Food, beverages and tobacco | 158.1 | 170.4 | 184.2 |
| Rent, fuel and lighting | 141.4 | 152.0 | 162.3 |
| Household requisites | 143.2 | 151.2 | 162.6 |
| Clothing and footwear | 142.2 | 148.4 | 156.8 |
| Transport and communications | 179.9 | 191.7 | 201.2 |
| **All items** (incl. others) | 153.2 | 164.2 | 176.0 |

Source: Bangladesh Bank.

### NATIONAL ACCOUNTS
(million taka at current prices, year ending 30 June)

**Expenditure on the Gross Domestic Product**

| | 2004/05 | 2005/06 | 2006/07* |
|---|---|---|---|
| Government final consumption expenditure | 205,303 | 230,324 | 259,481 |
| Private final consumption expenditure | 2,759,817 | 3,085,199 | 3,458,817 |
| Gross capital formation | 909,241 | 1,024,795 | 1,137,307 |
| Statistical discrepancy | 72,351 | 77,664 | 141,802 |
| **Total domestic expenditure** | 3,946,712 | 4,417,982 | 4,997,407 |
| Exports of goods and services | 614,681 | 788,788 | 1,027,002 |
| *Less* Imports of goods and services | 854,323 | 1,049,491 | 1,349,436 |
| **GDP in purchasers' values** | 3,707,070 | 4,157,279 | 4,674,973 |
| **GDP at constant 1995/96 prices** | 2,669,740 | 2,846,726 | 3,032,068 |

* Provisional figures.

**Gross Domestic Product by Economic Activity**

| | 2004/05 | 2005/06 | 2006/07* |
|---|---|---|---|
| Agriculture and forestry | 561,674 | 622,233 | 678,296 |
| Fishing | 154,564 | 163,168 | 173,335 |
| Mining and quarrying | 40,411 | 46,431 | 53,005 |
| Manufacturing | 587,952 | 689,227 | 810,066 |
| Electricity, gas and water | 49,090 | 53,915 | 57,680 |
| Construction | 290,608 | 327,970 | 367,701 |
| Wholesale and retail trade | 502,782 | 569,842 | 656,826 |
| Hotels and restaurants | 25,117 | 28,532 | 32,749 |
| Transport, storage and communications | 382,890 | 432,056 | 484,287 |
| Finance and insurance | 59,343 | 66,839 | 73,873 |
| Real estate, renting and business services | 297,443 | 321,569 | 349,151 |
| Public administration and defence | 96,374 | 110,355 | 126,846 |
| Education | 87,882 | 99,345 | 114,251 |
| Health and social work | 81,043 | 90,220 | 100,175 |
| Other community, social and personal services | 338,763 | 382,832 | 435,372 |
| **Sub-total** | 3,555,936 | 4,004,534 | 4,513,613 |
| Import duties | 151,134 | 152,745 | 161,360 |
| **GDP in purchasers' values** | 3,707,070 | 4,157,279 | 4,674,973 |

* Provisional figures.

Source: Bangladesh Bank.

### BALANCE OF PAYMENTS
(US $ million)

| | 2005 | 2006 | 2007 |
|---|---|---|---|
| Exports of goods f.o.b. | 9,302.5 | 11,553.7 | 12,449.1 |
| Imports of goods f.o.b. | −12,501.6 | −14,443.4 | −16,665.3 |
| **Trade balance** | −3,199.1 | −2,889.7 | −4,216.2 |
| Exports of services | 1,249.0 | 1,333.8 | 1,623.2 |
| Imports of services | −2,206.7 | −2,340.5 | −2,853.3 |
| **Balance on goods and services** | −4,156.8 | −3,896.3 | −5,446.3 |
| Other income received | 116.6 | 177.4 | 244.1 |
| Other income paid | −910.2 | −1,018.1 | −1,243.1 |
| **Balance on goods, services and income** | −4,950.4 | −4,737.0 | −6,445.3 |
| Current transfers received | 4,785.0 | 5,941.3 | 7,259.8 |
| Current transfers paid | −10.8 | −8.2 | −9.8 |
| **Current balance** | −176.2 | 1,196.1 | 804.8 |
| Capital account (net) | 261.7 | 152.5 | 571.4 |
| Direct investment abroad | −1.9 | — | — |
| Direct investment from abroad | 813.3 | 697.2 | 765.7 |
| Portfolio investment assets | −0.1 | −2.6 | −22.9 |
| Portfolio investment liabilities | 19.5 | 30.8 | 195.3 |
| Other investment assets | −865.3 | −1,352.8 | −942.5 |
| Other investment liabilities | 176.8 | 747.6 | 893.1 |
| Net errors and omissions | −643.9 | −603.5 | −892.1 |
| **Overall balance** | −416.1 | 865.3 | 1,372.8 |

Source: IMF, *International Financial Statistics*.

### FOREIGN AID DISBURSEMENTS
(US $ million, year ending 30 June)

| | 2003/04 | 2004/05 | 2005/06 |
|---|---|---|---|
| Bilateral donors | 495 | 440 | 406 |
| Canada | 21 | 8 | 62 |
| China, People's Republic | — | 19 | 33 |
| Denmark | 20 | 5 | 14 |
| France | 7 | — | — |
| Germany | 26 | 24 | 15 |
| Japan | 79 | 45 | 31 |
| Kuwait | 7 | 5 | 9 |
| Netherlands | 41 | 5 | 13 |
| Norway | 6 | 4 | 11 |
| Sweden | 11 | — | — |
| United Kingdom | 94 | 85 | 157 |
| USA | 12 | 8 | 4 |
| Multilateral donors | 538 | 1,049 | 1,162 |
| Asian Development Bank | 172 | 208 | 265 |
| International Development Association | 225 | 696 | 635 |
| European Union | 21 | 8 | 73 |
| International Fund for Agricultural Development | 15 | 9 | 14 |
| UN Development Programme | 36 | — | 111 |
| UNICEF | 30 | 26 | 18 |
| Islamic Development Bank | 17 | 70 | 25 |
| **Total aid disbursements** | 1,033 | 1,488 | 1,568 |

Source: IMF, *Bangladesh: Statistical Appendix* (July 2007).

# External Trade

### PRINCIPAL COMMODITIES
(US $ million, year ending 30 June)

| Imports c.i.f. | 2004/05 | 2005/06 | 2006/07 |
|---|---|---|---|
| Food grains | 574 | 418 | 581 |
| Edible oil | 440 | 473 | 583 |
| Petroleum products | 1,253 | 1,400 | 1,709 |
| Chemicals | 509 | 580 | 668 |
| Plastics, rubber and articles thereof | 477 | 523 | 643 |
| Cotton | 666 | 742 | 858 |
| Yarn | 393 | 501 | 582 |
| Textiles | 1,571 | 1,728 | 1,892 |
| Iron and steel | 680 | 980 | 985 |
| Machinery | 1,211 | 1,539 | 1,929 |
| **Total** (incl. others) | 13,147 | 14,746 | 16,013 |

| Exports f.o.b. | 2004/05 | 2005/06 | 2006/07 |
|---|---|---|---|
| Raw jute | 96 | 148 | 147 |
| Jute goods (excl. carpets) | 307 | 361 | 321 |
| Leather and leather products | 221 | 257 | 266 |
| Frozen shrimp and fish | 421 | 460 | 515 |
| Ready-made garments | 3,598 | 4,084 | 4,658 |
| Knitwear and hosiery products | 2,820 | 3,817 | 4,554 |
| **Total** (incl. others) | 8,655 | 10,526 | 12,178 |

Source: Bangladesh Bank.

### PRINCIPAL TRADING PARTNERS
(US $ million)

| Imports c.i.f. | 2004 | 2005 | 2006 |
|---|---|---|---|
| China, People's Republic | 1,446 | 1,870 | 3,165 |
| Hong Kong | 518 | 567 | 739 |
| India | 1,745 | 1,951 | 2,145 |
| Japan | 614 | 571 | 660 |
| Korea, Republic | 419 | 446 | 515 |
| Singapore | 873 | 852 | 989 |
| Thailand | 324 | 316 | 484 |
| United Kingdom | 283 | 323 | 192 |
| USA | 268 | 327 | 361 |
| **Total** (incl. others) | 11,590 | 14,291 | 17,350 |

| Exports f.o.b. | 2004 | 2005 | 2006 |
|---|---|---|---|
| Belgium | 253 | 269 | 493 |
| Canada | 247 | 275 | 470 |
| France | 526 | 545 | 628 |
| Germany | 1,102 | 1,144 | 1,610 |
| Italy | 305 | 326 | 486 |
| Netherlands | 247 | 275 | 470 |
| Spain | 240 | 299 | 454 |
| Sweden | 148 | 131 | 168 |
| United Kingdom | 849 | 795 | 1,249 |
| USA | 1,698 | 2,003 | 3,179 |
| **Total** (incl. others) | 7,586 | 8,494 | 12,495 |

Source: Asian Development Bank, *Key Indicators of Developing Asian and Pacific Countries*.

# Transport

### RAILWAYS
(traffic, year ending 30 June)

| | 1995/96 | 1996/97 | 1997/98 |
|---|---|---|---|
| Passenger-km (million) | 3,333 | 3,754 | 3,855 |
| Freight ton-km (million) | 689 | 782 | 804 |

Source: UN, *Statistical Yearbook*.

**2005:** Passengers (million) 42.2; Passenger-km (million) 4,160; Freight (million metric tons) 3.2; Freight ton-km (million) 817 (Source: Bangladesh Railway).

### ROAD TRAFFIC
(motor vehicles in use at 31 December)

| | 1997 | 1998 | 1999* |
|---|---|---|---|
| Passenger cars | 54,784 | 57,068 | 60,846 |
| Buses and coaches | 29,310 | 30,361 | 32,371 |
| Lorries and vans | 40,084 | 42,425 | 45,234 |
| Road tractors | 2,769 | 2,813 | 2,999 |
| Motorcycles and mopeds | 125,259 | 145,259 | 147,205 |
| **Total** | 252,206 | 277,926 | 288,655 |

* Estimates.

Source: International Road Federation, *World Road Statistics*.

### SHIPPING

**Merchant Fleet**
(registered at 31 December)

| | 2005 | 2006 | 2007 |
|---|---|---|---|
| Number of vessels | 331 | 328 | 320 |
| Total displacement ('000 grt) | 474.9 | 444.4 | 440.5 |

Source: Lloyd's Register-Fairplay, *World Fleet Statistics*.

**International Sea-borne Freight Traffic**
('000 metric tons, year ending 30 June)

| | 2001/02 | 2002/03 | 2003/04 |
|---|---|---|---|
| Total goods loaded | 900 | 1,000 | 8,000 |
| Total goods unloaded | 14,800 | 13,600 | 15,7000 |

Source: UN, *Monthly Bulletin of Statistics*.

### CIVIL AVIATION
(traffic on scheduled services)

| | 2001 | 2002 | 2003 |
|---|---|---|---|
| Kilometres flown (million) | 26 | 26 | 27 |
| Passengers carried ('000) | 1,110 | 1,172 | 1,205 |
| Passenger-km (million) | 4,323 | 4,503 | 4,583 |
| Total ton-km (million) | 593 | 677 | 697 |

Source: UN, *Statistical Yearbook*.

# Tourism

### TOURIST ARRIVALS BY COUNTRY OF NATIONALITY

| | 2003 | 2004 | 2005 |
|---|---|---|---|
| Canada | 5,847 | 8,964 | 4,519 |
| China, People's Republic | 7,021 | 9,238 | 6,892 |
| India | 84,704 | 80,469 | 86,231 |
| Japan | 6,523 | 7,857 | 6,269 |
| Korea, Republic | 7,465 | 6,575 | 5,332 |
| Malaysia | 3,689 | 4,750 | 1,045 |
| Nepal | 3,904 | 3,144 | 3,378 |
| Pakistan | 9,238 | 11,997 | 5,671 |
| United Kingdom | 42,138 | 52,410 | 27,292 |
| USA | 24,458 | 27,895 | 13,422 |
| **Total** (incl. others) | 244,509 | 271,270 | 207,662 |

**Tourism receipts** (US $ million, incl. passenger transport): 59 in 2003; 76 in 2004; n.a. in 2005.

Source: World Tourism Organization.

## Communications Media

| | 2004 | 2005 | 2006 |
|---|---|---|---|
| Telephones ('000 main lines in use) | 831.0 | 1,070.0 | 1,134.0 |
| Mobile cellular telephones ('000 subscribers) | 2,781.6 | 9,000.0 | 19,131.0 |
| Personal computers ('000 in use) | 1,650 | 1,650 | n.a. |
| Internet users ('000) | 300 | 300 | 450 |

**Radio receivers** ('000 in use): 6,150 in 1997.

**Television receivers** ('000 in use): 2,200 in 2001.

**Facsimile machines** (number in use, year ending 30 June 1998, provisional): 75,000.

**Newspapers** (provisional, 1998): *Daily:* 233 titles with average circulation of 6,658,000. *Non-daily incl. periodicals:* 509 titles with average circulation of 9,256,000.

**Books published:** 483 titles in 1998.

Sources: mainly UNESCO, *Statistical Yearbook*; UN, *Statistical Yearbook*; International Telecommunication Union.

## Education

(2004/05)

| | Institutions | Teachers | Students |
|---|---|---|---|
| Primary schools | 80,397 | 344,789 | 16,225,658 |
| Secondary schools | 18,500 | 232,929 | 7,398,552 |
| Universities (government) | 24 | 6,852 | 115,929 |

**Technical and vocational institutes** (2004/05): 2,728 institutions, 18,185 teachers, 241,336 students.

Source: Ministry of Education.

**Adult literacy rate** (UNESCO estimates): 53.5% (males 58.7%; females 48.0%) in 2007 (Source: UNESCO Institute for Statistics).

# Directory

## The Constitution

The members who were returned from East Pakistan (now Bangladesh) for the Pakistan National Assembly and the Provincial Assembly in the December 1970 elections formed the Bangladesh Constituent Assembly. A new Constitution for the People's Republic of Bangladesh was approved by this Assembly on 4 November 1972 and came into effect on 16 December 1972. Following the military coup of 24 March 1982, the Constitution was suspended, and the country was placed under martial law. On 10 November 1986 martial law was repealed and the suspended Constitution was revived. The main provisions of the Constitution, including amendments, are listed below.

### SUMMARY

#### Fundamental Principles of State Policy

The Constitution was initially based on the fundamental principles of nationalism, socialism, democracy and secularism, but in 1977 an amendment replaced secularism with Islam. The amendment states that the country shall be guided by 'the principles of absolute trust and faith in the Almighty Allah, nationalism, democracy and socialism'. A further amendment in 1988 established Islam as the state religion. The Constitution aims to establish a society free from exploitation in which the rule of law, fundamental human rights and freedoms, justice and equality are to be secured for all citizens. A socialist economic system is to be established to ensure the attainment of a just and egalitarian society through state and co-operative ownership as well as private ownership within limits prescribed by law. A universal, free and compulsory system of education shall be established. In foreign policy the State shall endeavour to consolidate, preserve, and strengthen fraternal relations among Muslim countries based on Islamic solidarity.

#### Fundamental Rights

All citizens are equal before the law and have a right to its protection. Arbitrary arrest or detention, discrimination based on race, age, sex, birth, caste or religion, and forced labour are prohibited. Subject to law, public order and morality, every citizen has freedom of movement, of assembly and of association. Freedom of conscience, of speech, of the press and of religious worship are guaranteed.

### GOVERNMENT

#### The President

The President is the constitutional Head of State and is elected by Parliament (Jatiya Sangsad) for a term of five years. He is eligible for re-election. The supreme control of the armed forces is vested in the President. He appoints the Prime Minister and other Ministers as well as the Chief Justice and other judges.

#### The Executive

Executive authority shall rest in the Prime Minister and shall be exercised by him either directly or through officers subordinate to him in accordance with the Constitution.

There shall be a Council of Ministers to aid and advise the Prime Minister.

#### The Legislature

Parliament (Jatiya Sangsad) is a unicameral legislature. It comprises 345 members, including 45 women members elected by the other members on the basis of proportional representation. Members of Parliament, other than the 45 women members, are directly elected on the basis of universal adult franchise from single territorial constituencies. Persons aged 18 years and over are entitled to vote. The parliamentary term lasts for five years. War can be declared only with the assent of Parliament. In the case of actual or imminent invasion, the President may take whatever action he considers appropriate.

### THE JUDICIARY

The Judiciary comprises a Supreme Court with High Court and an Appellate Division. The Supreme Court consists of a Chief Justice and such other judges as may be appointed by the President. The High Court division has such original appellate and other jurisdiction and powers as are conferred on it by the Constitution and by other law. The Appellate Division has jurisdiction to determine appeals from decisions of the High Court division. Subordinate courts, in addition to the Supreme Court, have been established by law.

### ELECTIONS

An Election Commission supervises elections, delimits constituencies and prepares electoral rolls. It consists of a Chief Election Commissioner and other Commissioners as may be appointed by the President. The Election Commission is independent in the exercise of its functions. Subject to the Constitution, Parliament may make provision as to elections where necessary.

## The Government

### HEAD OF STATE

**President:** Prof. IAJUDDIN AHMED (took office 6 September 2002).

### LIST OF ADVISERS

(August 2008)

Prime Minister Khaleda Zia and the Council of Ministers stepped down in October 2006, having completed a five-year term in office; national elections were scheduled for January 2007. In early November 2006 a team of advisers was sworn in to act as an interim government, to manage key portfolios and to supervise the election process. President Iajuddin Ahmed assumed the role of Chief

Adviser. In January 2007, following widespread protests and demands for electoral reform, President Ahmed resigned as Chief Adviser, postponed the elections and declared a state of emergency. Dr Fakhruddin Ahmed was subsequently appointed as his successor in the role of Chief Adviser.

**Chief Adviser in charge of the Cabinet Division, of Establishment, and of Information:** Dr FAKHRUDDIN AHMED.

**Adviser in charge of Law, Justice and Parliament Affairs, of Religious Affairs, and of Land:** A. F. HASSAN ARIFF.

**Adviser in charge of Finance and of Planning:** Dr A. B. MIRZA AZIZUL ISLAM.

**Adviser in charge of Home Affairs, of Shipping, and of Liberation War Affairs:** Maj.-Gen. (retd) M. A. MATIN.

**Adviser in charge of Health and Family Welfare, and of Food and Disaster Management:** Dr A. M. M. SHAWKAT ALI.

**Adviser in charge of Primary and Mass Education, of Women and Children's Affairs, and of Cultural Affairs:** RASHEDA K. CHOWDHURY.

**Adviser in charge of Commerce and of Education:** Dr HOSSAIN ZILLUR RAHMAN.

**Adviser in charge of Communications and of Housing and Public Works:** Maj.-Gen. (retd) GHULAM QUADER.

**Adviser in charge of Local Government, Rural Development and Co-operatives, of Textiles and Jute, and of Labour and Employment:** MUHAMMAD ANWARUL IQBAL.

**Adviser in charge of Foreign Affairs, and of Expatriates' Welfare and Overseas Employment:** Dr IFTEKHAR AHMED CHOWDHURY.

**Adviser in charge of Agriculture and of Water Resources:** Dr CHOWDHURY SAJJADUL KARIM.

### MINISTRIES

**Chief Adviser's Office:** Old Sangsad Bhaban, Tejgaon, Dhaka 1215; tel. (2) 8151159; fax (2) 8113244; e-mail info@pmo.gov.bd; internet www.cao.gov.bd.

**Ministry of Agriculture:** Bangladesh Secretariat, Bhaban 4, 2nd 9-Storey Bldg, Dhaka; tel. (2) 832137; internet www.moa.gov.bd.

**Ministry of Chittagong Hill Tracts Affairs:** Dhaka; tel. (2) 7161774; e-mail nazma@mochta.gov.bd; internet www.mochta.gov.bd.

**Ministry of Civil Aviation and Tourism:** Bangladesh Secretariat, Bhaban 6, 19th Floor, Dhaka 1000; tel. (2) 866485.

**Ministry of Commerce:** Bangladesh Secretariat, Bhaban 3, Dhaka 1000; tel. (2) 716009; e-mail mincom@intechworld.net; internet www.mincom.gov.bd.

**Ministry of Communications:** Bangladesh Secretariat, Bhaban 7, 1st 9-Storey Bldg, 8th Floor, Dhaka 1000; tel. (2) 868752; fax (2) 866636; internet www.moc.gov.bd.

**Ministry of Cultural Affairs:** Bangladesh Secretariat, Dhaka 1000; tel. (2) 9570667; fax (2) 7169008; e-mail sas-moca@mailcity.com; internet www.moca.gov.bd.

**Ministry of Defence:** Gonobhaban Complex, Sher-i-Bangla Nagar, Dhaka; tel. (2) 8116955; e-mail modgob@bttb.net.bd; internet www.mod.gov.bd.

**Ministry of Education:** Bangladesh Secretariat, Bhaban 6, 17th–18th Floors, Dhaka 1000; tel. (2) 7168711; fax (2) 7167577; e-mail info@moedu.gov.bd; internet www.moedu.gov.bd.

**Ministry of Environment and Forests:** Bangladesh Secretariat, Bhaban 6, 13th Floor, Chamber 1314, Dhaka; tel. (2) 7163373; fax (2) 7169210; e-mail dsadmin@moef.gov.bd; internet www.moef.gov.bd.

**Ministry of Establishment:** Dhaka; e-mail estabsec@moestab.gov.bd; internet www.moestab.gov.bd.

**Ministry of Expatriates' Welfare and Overseas Employment:** Bangladesh Secretariat, Bhaban 7, 4th Floor, Dhaka 1000; tel. (2) 9570086; fax (2) 9570087; internet probashi.gov.bd.

**Ministry of Finance:** Bangladesh Secretariat, Bhaban 7, 1st 9-Storey Bldg, 3rd Floor, Dhaka 1000; tel. (2) 8690202; fax (2) 865581; internet www.mof.gov.bd.

**Ministry of Fisheries and Livestock:** Bangladesh Secretariat, Bhaban 6, 5th and 14th Floors, Dhaka 1000; tel. (2) 7164700; fax (2) 7161117; e-mail jslmofl@accesstel.net; internet www.mofl.gov.bd.

**Ministry of Food and Disaster Management:** Bangladesh Secretariat, Dhaka; tel. (2) 7165405; e-mail info@mofdm.gov.bd; internet www.mofdm.gov.bd.

**Ministry of Foreign Affairs:** Segunbagicha, Dhaka 1000; tel. (2) 9562862; fax (2) 9555283; e-mail info@mofabd.org; internet www.mofa.gov.bd.

**Ministry of Health and Family Welfare:** Bangladesh Secretariat, Main Bldg, 3rd Floor, Dhaka; tel. (2) 832079; internet www.mohfw.gov.bd.

**Ministry of Home Affairs:** Bangladesh Secretariat, School Bldg, 2nd and 3rd Floors, Dhaka; tel. (2) 7169076; fax (2) 7164788; e-mail info@mha.gov.bd; internet www.mha.gov.bd.

**Ministry of Housing and Public Works:** Bangladesh Secretariat, Bhaban 5, Dhaka 1000; tel. (2) 7163639; fax (2) 7167125; e-mail jsamohpw@bangla.net; internet www.mohpw.gov.bd.

**Ministry of Industries:** Shilpa Bhaban, 91 Motijheel C/A, Dhaka 1000; tel. (2) 9567024; fax (2) 860588; e-mail indsecy@bttb.net.bd; internet www.moind.gov.bd.

**Ministry of Information:** Bangladesh Secretariat, 2nd 9-Storey Bldg, 8th Floor, Dhaka; tel. (2) 7168555; fax (2) 7167236; e-mail moisecretary@yahoo.com; internet www.moi.gov.bd.

**Ministry of Labour and Employment:** Bangladesh Secretariat, Bldg 7, 5th Floor, Dhaka; tel. (2) 7169215; fax (2) 7168660; internet www.mole.gov.bd.

**Ministry of Land:** Bangladesh Secretariat, Bhaban 4, 2nd 9-Storey Bldg, 3rd Floor, Dhaka; tel. (2) 7164131.

**Ministry of Law, Justice and Parliamentary Affairs:** Bangladesh Secretariat, Bhaban 4, 7th Floor, Dhaka 1000; tel. (2) 7164693; e-mail info@minlaw.gov.bd; internet www.minlaw.gov.bd.

**Ministry of Liberation War Affairs:** Dhaka; internet www.mlwa.gov.bd.

**Ministry of Local Government, Rural Development and Co-operatives:** LGED Bhaban, 4th Floor, Agargaon, Dhaka 1207; tel. (2) 8119138; fax (2) 8113144; e-mail zmsajjad@lged.org.

**Ministry of Planning:** Block No. 7, Sher-e-Bangla Nagar, Dhaka; tel. (2) 815142; fax (2) 822210.

**Ministry of Post and Telecommunications:** Bangladesh Secretariat, Bhaban 7, 6th Floor, Dhaka 1000; tel. (2) 864800; fax (2) 865775.

**Ministry of Power, Energy and Mineral Resources:** Bangladesh Secretariat, Bhaban 6, 1st Floor, Dhaka 1000; tel. (2) 865918; fax (2) 861110; internet www.powerdivision.gov.bd.

**Ministry of Religious Affairs:** Bangladesh Secretariat, Dhaka; tel. (2) 7165800; fax (2) 7165040.

**Ministry of Science and Information and Communication Technology:** Bangladesh Secretariat, Bhaban 6, 9th Floor, Ramna, Dhaka 1000; tel. (2) 7163639; fax (2) 7169606; e-mail most@bangla.net; internet www.mosict.gov.bd.

**Ministry of Shipping:** Bangladesh Secretariat, Bhaban 6, 8th Floor, Dhaka 1000; tel. (2) 7165774; internet www.mos.gov.bd.

**Ministry of Social Welfare:** Bangladesh Secretariat, Bhaban 6, New Bldg, Dhaka 1000; tel. (2) 7160452; fax (2) 7168969; e-mail secsw@bttb.net.bd; internet www.msw.gov.bd.

**Ministry of Textiles and Jute:** Bangladesh Secretariat, Bhaban 6, 7th Floor, Dhaka 1000; tel. (2) 8612250; fax (2) 8618766; e-mail jutebd@bangla.net; internet www.motj.gov.bd.

**Ministry of Water Resources:** Bangladesh Secretariat, Dhaka 1000; tel. (2) 7168688; internet www.mowr.gov.bd.

**Ministry of Women and Children's Affairs:** Bangladesh Secretariat, Bhaban 6, 3rd Floor, Osman Goni Rd, Dhaka 1000; tel. (2) 7163943; fax (2) 7162892; internet www.mwca.gov.bd.

**Ministry of Youth and Sports:** 62/3, Purana Paltan, Dhaka 1000; tel. (2) 7167053; fax (2) 7162344; e-mail secmys@bttb.net.bd; internet www.moysports.gov.bd.

## President and Legislature

### PRESIDENT

On 5 September 2002 the Bangladesh Nationalist Party's presidential candidate, Prof. IAJUDDIN AHMED, was declared elected unopposed by the Election Commission as Bangladesh's new Head of State.

### JATIYA SANGSAD
(Parliament)

**Speaker:** JAMIRUDDIN SIRCAR.

**General Election, 1 and 9 October 2001**

| | Seats* |
|---|---|
| Bangladesh Jatiyatabadi Dal (Bangladesh Nationalist Party—BNP) | 199† |
| Awami League (AL) | 62 |
| Jamaat-e-Islami Bangladesh | 17 |
| Jatiya Dal | 14‡ |
| Jatiya Dal (Manju) | 1 |
| Bangladesh Krishak Sramik Party | 1 |
| Independents | 6 |
| **Total** | 300 |

* In addition to the 300 directly elected members, a further 45 seats are reserved for women members.

† Includes six seats won by the Jatiya Dal (Naziur-Firoz) and the Islami Jatiya Oikya Jote.

‡ Includes several seats won by the Islami Jatiya Oikya Front.

# Election Commission

**Bangladesh Election Commission:** Block 5/6, Election Commission Secretariat, Sher-e-Bangla Nagar, Dhaka 1207; tel. (2) 8113601; fax (2) 8117834; e-mail ecs@bol-online.com; internet www.ecs.gov.bd; f. 1972; independent; commrs appointed by the President; Chief Election Commr Dr A. T. M. SHAMSUL HUDA.

# Political Organizations

**Bangladesh Awami League (AL):** 23 Bangabandhu Ave, Dhaka; e-mail info@albd.org; internet www.albd.org; f. 1949; supports parliamentary democracy; advocates socialist economy, but with a private sector, and a secular state; pro-Indian; 28-member central executive committee, 15-member central advisory committee and a 13-member presidium; Pres. Sheikh HASINA WAJED; Acting Pres. ZILLUR RAHMAN; Gen. Sec. SYED ASHRAFUL ISLAM (acting); c. 1,025,000 mems.

**Bangladesh Jatiya League:** Dhaka; f. 1970 as Pakistan National League, renamed in 1972; supports parliamentary democracy; Leader ATAUR RAHMAN KHAN; c. 50,000 mems.

**Bangladesh Jatiyatabadi Dal** (Bangladesh Nationalist Party—BNP): Banani Office, House 23, Rd 13, Dhaka; tel. (2) 8819525; fax (2) 8813063; e-mail bnpbd@e-fsbd.net; internet www.bnpbd.com; f. 1978 by merger of groups supporting Ziaur Rahman, including Jatiyatabadi Gonotantrik Dal (Jagodal—Nationalist Democratic Party); right of centre; favours multi-party democracy and parliamentary system of govt; Chair. Begum KHALEDA ZIA; Sec.-Gen. KHANDAKER DELWAR HOSSAIN.

**Bangladesh Kalyan Dal** (Bangladesh Welfare Party): Siddiq Mansion, 4th Floor, Purana Paltan, Dhaka 1000; tel. (2) 9555864; e-mail info@bkp-bd.org; internet www.bkp-bd.org; f. 2007; Chair. Maj.-Gen. (retd) SYED MUHAMMAD IBRAHIM.

**Bangladesh Khelafat Andolon** (Bangladesh Caliphate Movement): 314/2 Lalbagh Kellar Morr, Dhaka 1211; tel. (2) 8612465; fax (2) 9881436; e-mail khelafat@cimabd.com; Supreme Leader SHAH AHMADULLAH ASHRAF IBN HAFEZZEE; Sec.-Gen. Maulana MUHAMMAD ZAFRULLAH KHAN.

**Bangladesh Krishak Sramik Party** (Peasants' and Workers' Party): Sonargaon Bhavan, 99 South Kamalapur, Dhaka 1217; tel. (2) 834512; f. 1914; renamed 1953; supports parliamentary democracy, non-aligned foreign policy, welfare state, guarantee of fundamental rights for all religions and races, free market economy and non-proliferation of nuclear weapons; 15-mem. exec. council; Pres. A. S. M. SULAIMAN; Sec.-Gen. RASHEED KHAN MEMON; c. 125,000 mems.

**Bangladesh Muslim League:** Dhaka; Pres. A. H. M. KAMRUZZAMAN; Sec.-Gen. Alhaj MOHAMMAD ZAMIR ALI.

**Communist Party of Bangladesh:** 'Mukti Bhaban', 21/1, Purana Paltan, Dhaka 1000; tel. (2) 9558612; fax (2) 9552333; e-mail info@cpbdhaka.com; internet www.cpbdhaka.org; f. 1968 following split from Communist Party of Pakistan; Pres. MANZURUL AHASAN KHAN; Gen. Sec. MUJAHIDUL ISLAM SELIM; c. 22,000 mems.

**Freedom Party:** f. 1987; Islamic; Co-Chairs Lt-Col (retd) SAID FARUQ RAHMAN, Lt-Col (retd) KHANDAKAR ABDUR RASHID.

**Gonoazadi League:** 30 Banagran Lane, Dhaka.

**Gonotantrik Jatiya Party:** Leader SHAFIUL ALAM PRADHAN.

**Islami Jatiya Oikya Front** (Islamic National Unity Front): Dhaka; coalition of parties, including Jatiya Dal.

**Islami Oikya Jote** (Islamic Unity Front): Dhaka; mem. of the BNP-led alliance; Leader Mufti SHAHIDUL ISLAM; Sec.-Gen. Mufti FAZLUL HAQ AMINI.

**Islamic Solidarity Movement:** 84 East Tejturi Bazar, Tejgaon, Dhaka 1215; tel. (2) 8121017; fmrly known as Islamic Democratic League; renamed as above in 1984; Pres. ANOWEAR ULLAH; Sec.-Gen. Maulana MUHAMMAD AZIZ UL-HOQ MURAD.

**Jamaat-e-Islami Bangladesh:** 505 Elephant Rd, Bara Maghbazar, Dhaka 1217; tel. (2) 9331581; fax (2) 9556626; e-mail info@jamaat-e-islami.org; internet www.jamaat-e-islami.org; f. 1941; Islamist party striving to establish an Islamic state through the democratic process; mem. of the BNP-led alliance; Chair. MOTIUR RAHMAN NIZAMI; Sec.-Gen. ALI AHSAN MOHAMMAD MUJAHID.

**Jatiya Dal** (National Party): c/o Jatiya Sangsad, Dhaka; e-mail ershad@dhaka.agni.com; internet www.jatiyaparty.org; f. 1983 as Jana Dal; reorg. 1986, when the National Front (f. 1985), a five-party alliance of the Jana Dal, the United People's Party, the Gonotantrik Dal, the Bangladesh Muslim League and a breakaway section of the Bangladesh Nationalist Party, formally converted itself into a single pro-Ershad grouping; advocates nationalism, democracy, Islamic ideals and progress; Chair. Lt-Gen. HOSSAIN MOHAMMAD ERSHAD; Sec.-Gen. A. B. M. RUHUL AMIN HAWLADER; in April 1999 a group of dissidents, led by MIZANUR RAHMAN CHOWDHURY and ANWAR HUSSAIN MANJU, formed a rival faction; another rival faction, led by KAZI FIROZ RASHID, was also formed.

**Jatiya Samajtantrik Dal (Inu):** f. 2002; breakaway faction of JSD; Pres. HASANUL HAQUE INU; Gen. Sec. SYED JAFAR SAZZAD.

**Jatiya Samajtantrik Dal (JSD—S)** (National Socialist Party): 23 DIT Ave, Malibagh Choudhury Para, Dhaka; f. 1972; left-wing; Leader SHAJAHAN SIRAJ; c. 5,000 mems.

**Jatiya Samajtantrik Dal (Rab):** breakaway faction of JSD; Pres. A. S. M. ABDUR RAB.

**Jatiyo Janata Party:** Janata Bhaban, 47A Toyenbee Circular Rd, Dhaka 1000; tel. (2) 7167423; f. 1976; social democratic; Chair. NURUL ISLAM KHAN; Gen. Sec. MUJIBUR RAHMAN HERO; c. 40,000 mems.

**Liberal Democratic Party:** Dhaka; f. 2006; comprises several former members of BNP; reported to have split into two factions June 2007; Exec. Chair. Col (retd) OLI AHMAD; Pres. A. Q. M. BADRUDDOZA CHOWDHURY.

**National Awami Party—Bhashani–Mustaq (NAP):** Dhaka; f. 1957; Maoist; Leader MUSTAQ AHMED; Gen. Sec. ABDUS SUBHANI.

**National Awami Party—Muzaffar (NAP—M):** 21 Dhanmandi Hawkers' Market, 1st Floor, Dhaka; f. 1957; reorg. 1967; Pres. MUZAFFAR AHMED; Sec.-Gen. PANKAJ BHATTACHARYA; c. 500,000 mems.

**National People's Party (NPP):** Dhaka; f. 2007; Chair. SHAWKAT HOSSAIN NILU.

**Parbattya Chattagram Jana Sanghati Samity** (Chittagong Hill Tracts United Peoples' Party): Central Office, Kalyanpur, Rangamati 4500, Chittagong Hill Tracts; tel. (351) 61248; e-mail pcjss.org@gmail.com; internet www.pcjss.org; f. 1972; political wing of the Shanti Bahini; represents interests of Buddhist tribals in Chittagong Hill Tracts; Leader JATINDRA BODDHIPRIYA ('SHANTU') LARMA.

**Samyabadi Dal:** Dhaka; Marxist-Leninist; Leader DILIP BARUA.

**Zaker Party:** f. 1989; supports sovereignty and the introduction of an Islamic state system; Leader SYED HASMATULLAH; Mem. of the Presidium MUSTAFA AMIR FAISAL.

# Diplomatic Representation

## EMBASSIES AND HIGH COMMISSIONS IN BANGLADESH

**Afghanistan:** House CWN(C) 2A, 24 Gulshan Ave, Gulshan Model Town, Dhaka 1212; tel. (2) 9895994; fax (2) 9884767; e-mail afghanembassydhaka@yahoo.com; Ambassador AHMAD KARIM NAWABI.

**Australia:** 184 Gulshan Ave, Gulshan 2, Dhaka 1212; tel. (2) 8813101; fax (2) 8811125; e-mail ahc.dhaka@dfat.gov.au; internet www.bangladesh.embassy.gov.au; High Commissioner DOUGLAS FOSKETT.

**Bhutan:** House 12, Rd 107, Gulshan 2, Dhaka 1212; tel. (2) 8826863; fax (2) 8823939; e-mail bhtemb@bdmail.net; Ambassador Dasho TSHERING DORJI.

**Brunei:** House 26, Rd 6, Baridhara, Dhaka; tel. (2) 8819552; fax (2) 8819551; e-mail bruhcomm@citechco.net; High Commissioner Dato' Haji ABDUL RAHMAN BIN ABDUL HAMID.

**Canada:** House 16A, Rd 48, Gulshan 2, Dhaka 1212; tel. (2) 9887091; fax (2) 8823043; e-mail dhaka@international.gc.ca; internet www.international.gc.ca/bangladesh; High Commissioner BARBARA RICHARDSON.

**China, People's Republic:** Plots 2 and 4, Rd 3, Block 1, Baridhara, Dhaka; tel. (2) 8824862; fax (2) 8823004; e-mail chinaemb@bdmail .net; internet bd.china-embassy.org; Ambassador ZHENG QINGDIAN.

**Denmark:** House (NW) H 1, Rd 51, Gulshan Model Town, POB 2056, Dhaka 1212; tel. (2) 8811799; fax (2) 8813638; e-mail dacamb@um .dk; internet www.ambdhaka.um.dk; Ambassador EINAR H. JENSEN.

**Egypt:** House NE (N) 9, Rd 90, Gulshan Model Town, Dhaka 1212; tel. (2) 8858737; fax (2) 8858747; e-mail egypt_embassy_dhaka@ themail.com; Ambassador FAYEZ MUSTAFA NOSEIR.

**France:** House 18, Rd 108, Gulshan Model Town, POB 22, Dhaka 1212; tel. (2) 8813811; fax (2) 8813812; internet www.ambafrance-bd .org; Ambassador CHARLEY CAUSERET.

**Germany:** 178 Gulshan Ave, Gulshan 2, Dhaka 1212; tel. (2) 8853521; fax (2) 8853528; e-mail aadhaka@optimaxbd.net; internet www.dhaka.diplo.de; Ambassador FRANK MEYKE.

**Holy See:** United Nations Rd 2, Diplomatic Enclave, Baridhara Model Town, POB 6003, Dhaka 1212; tel. (2) 8822018; fax (2) 8823574; e-mail nuntius@dhaka.net; Apostolic Nuncio JOSEPH MARINO.

**India:** House 2, Rd 142, Gulshan-I, Dhaka; tel. (2) 9889339; fax (2) 8817487; e-mail hc@hcidhaka.org; internet www.hcidhaka.org; High Commissioner PINAK RANJAN CHAKRAVARTY.

**Indonesia:** Plot No. 14, Rd 53, Gulshan 2, Dhaka 1212; tel. (2) 9881640; fax (2) 8810993; e-mail indhaka@bangla.net; internet www .jakarta-dhaka.com; Ambassador WARMAS HASAN SAPUTRA.

**Iran:** House No. 7, Rd 6, Baridhara Model Town, Dhaka; tel. (2) 8825896; fax (2) 8828780; e-mail dacembiran@yahoo.com; Ambassador HASSAN FARAZANDEH.

**Italy:** Plots 2 and 3, Rd 74/79, Gulshan Model Town, POB 6062, Dhaka 1212; tel. (2) 8822781; fax (2) 8822578; e-mail ambdhaka@ dominox.com; internet dominox.com/italydhaka; Ambassador ITALA MARIA MARTA OCCHI.

**Japan:** 5 and 7, Dutabash Rd, Baridhara, Dhaka 1212; tel. (2) 8810087; fax (2) 8826737; e-mail information@embjp.accesstel.net; internet www.bd.emb-japan.go.jp; Ambassador MASAYUKI INOUE.

**Korea, Democratic People's Republic:** House 6, Rd 7, Baridhara Model Town, Dhaka; tel. (2) 601250; Ambassador MUN SONG MO.

**Korea, Republic:** 4 Madani Ave, Diplomatic Enclave, Baridhara, Dhaka; tel. (2) 8812088; fax (2) 8823871; e-mail embdhaka@ embdhaka.org; internet bgd.mofat.go.kr; Ambassador SUK BUM PARK.

**Kuwait:** Plot 39, Rd 23, Block J, Banani, Dhaka 13; tel. (2) 8822700; fax (2) 8823753; e-mail dhaka@mofa.gov.kw; Ambassador ABDULLATIF AL-MAWASH.

**Libya:** NE(D), 3A Gulshan Ave (N), Gulshan Model Town, Dhaka 1212; tel. (2) 600141; Chargé d'affaires LUTFI ALAMIN M. MUGHRABI.

**Malaysia:** House 19, Rd 6, Baridhara, Dhaka 1212; tel. (2) 8827759; fax (2) 8823115; e-mail mwdhaka@citech-bd.net; internet www.kln .gov.my/perwakilan/dhaka; High Commissioner ABDUL MALEK ABDUL AZIZ.

**Maldives:** Dhaka; High Commissioner Dr ABDUL SAMAD ABDULLAH (designate).

**Morocco:** House 44, United Nations Rd, POB 6112, Baridhara, Dhaka; tel. (2) 8823176; fax (2) 8810028; e-mail sifmadac@citechco .net; internet www.morocco-dhaka.com; Ambassador MOHAMED HOURORO.

**Myanmar:** NE(L) 3, Rd 84, Gulshan 2, Dhaka 1212; tel. (2) 600988; fax (2) 8823740; e-mail mofa.aung@mptmail.net.mm; Ambassador U NYAN LYNN.

**Nepal:** United Nations Rd, Rd 2, Diplomatic Enclave, Baridhara, Dhaka; tel. (2) 601790; fax (2) 8826401; e-mail rnedhaka@bdmail .net; Ambassador PRADEEP KHATIWADA.

**Netherlands:** House 49, Rd 90, Gulshan Model Town, POB 166, Dhaka 1212; tel. (2) 8822715; fax (2) 8823326; e-mail dha@minbuza .nl; internet www.netherlandsembassydhaka.org; Ambassador BERENDINA MARIA (BEA) TEN TUSSCHER.

**Nigeria:** House 9, Rd 1, Baridhara, Dhaka; tel. (2) 8817944; fax (2) 8817989; High Commissioner (vacant).

**Norway:** House 9, Rd 111, Gulshan, Dhaka 1212; tel. (2) 8816276; fax (2) 8823661; e-mail emb.dhaka@mfa.no; internet www.norway .org.bd/info/embassy.htm; Ambassador INGEBJØRG STØFRING.

**Pakistan:** House NE(C) 2, Rd 71, Gulshan Model Town, Dhaka 1212; tel. (2) 8825388; fax (2) 8850673; e-mail parepdka@citech-bd .com; High Commissioner ALAMGIR BABUR.

**Philippines:** House 6, Rd 101, Gulshan 2, Dhaka 1212; tel. (2) 9881590; fax (2) 8823686; e-mail philemb1@citechco.net; Ambassador ZENAIDA TACORDA-RABAGO.

**Qatar:** House 1, Rd 79/81, Gulshan 2, Dhaka 1212; tel. (2) 9887429; fax (2) 9896071; e-mail dhaka@mofa.gov.qa; Ambassador IBRAHIM MOHAMMAD A. AL-ABDULLA.

**Russia:** NE(J) 9, Rd 79, Gulshan 2, Dhaka 1212; tel. (2) 8828147; fax (2) 8823735; e-mail info@rusdhaka.org; internet www.bangladesh .mid.ru; Ambassador GENNADII P. TROTSENKO.

**Saudi Arabia:** House 12, Rd 92, Gulshan (North), Dhaka 1212; tel. (2) 889124; fax (2) 883616; Ambassador ABDULLAH MOHAMMAD AL-OBAID AL-NAMLA.

**Sri Lanka:** House 4A, Rd 113, Gulshan Model Town, Dhaka 1212; tel. (2) 9896353; fax (2) 8823971; High Commissioner V. KRISHNAMOORTHY.

**Sweden:** House 1, Rd 51, Gulshan 2, Dhaka 1212; tel. (2) 8833144; fax (2) 8823948; e-mail berth.abrahamsson@foreign.ministry.se; internet www.swedenabroad.com/dhaka; Ambassador BRITT FALKMAN HAGSTRÖM.

**Switzerland:** House 31B, Rd 18, Banani, Dhaka 1213; tel. (2) 8812874; fax (2) 8823872; Ambassador Dr DORA RAPOLD.

**Thailand:** 18 & 20, Madani Ave, Baridhara, Dhaka 1212; tel. (2) 8812795; fax (2) 8854280; e-mail thaidac@mfa.go.th; internet www .thaidac.com; Ambassador CHALERMPOL THANCHITT.

**Turkey:** House 14A, Rd 62, Gulshan 2, Dhaka 1212; tel. (2) 8823536; fax (2) 8823873; e-mail dakkabe@citech-bd.com; Ambassador FERIT ERGIN.

**United Arab Emirates:** POB 6014, Dhaka 1212; tel. (2) 9882244; fax (2) 8823225; e-mail info@uaeembassydhaka.com; Ambassador KHALFAN BATTAL AL MANSOURI.

**United Kingdom:** United Nations Rd, Baridhara, POB 6079, Dhaka 1212; tel. (2) 8822705; fax (2) 8826181; e-mail Dhaka .Chancery@fco.gov.uk; internet www.ukinbangladesh.org; High Commissioner STEPHEN EVANS.

**USA:** Madani Ave, Baridhara, POB 323, Dhaka 1212; tel. (2) 8824700; fax (2) 8823744; e-mail ustc@bangla.net; internet dhaka .usembassy.gov; Ambassador JAMES F. MORIARTY.

**Viet Nam:** House 8, Rd 51, Gulshan 2, Dhaka 1212; tel. and fax (2) 8854051; e-mail vietnam@citech-bd.com; internet www .vietnamembassy-bangladesh.org; Ambassador NGUYEN VAN THAT.

# Judicial System

A judiciary, comprising a Supreme Court with High Court and Appellate Divisions, is in operation (see under Constitution). On 1 November 2007 the Government announced the formal separation of the judiciary from the executive.

### Supreme Court

Dhaka 2; tel. (2) 433585.

**Chief Justice:** M. M. RUHUL AMIN.

**Attorney-General:** SALAHUDDIN AHMED.

**Deputy Attorney-General:** A. M. FAROOQ.

# Religion

The results of the 2001 census classified 89.7% of the population as Muslims (the majority of whom were of the Sunni sect), 9.2% as caste Hindus and scheduled castes, and the remainder as Buddhists, Christians, animists and others.

Freedom of religious worship is guaranteed under the Constitution but, under the 1977 amendment to the Constitution, Islam was declared to be one of the nation's guiding principles and, under the 1988 amendment, Islam was established as the state religion.

### ISLAM

**Islamic Foundation Bangladesh:** Agargaon, Sher-e-Bangla Nagar, Dhaka 1207; tel. (2) 9115010; fax (2) 9144235; e-mail islamicfoundationbd@yahoo.com; internet www.islamicfoundation .org.bd; f. 1975; under supervision of Ministry of Religious Affairs; Dir-Gen. MUHAMMAD FAZLUR RAHMAN.

### BUDDHISM

**World Fellowship of Buddhists Regional Centre:** Dharmarajik Buddhist Monastery, Atish Dipanker Sarak, Basabo, Dhaka 1214; tel. (2) 7205665; fax (2) 7202503; e-mail mahathero@dhammarajika .com; internet www.dhammarajika.com; f. 1962; Pres. Ven. SUDDHANANDA MAHATHERO; Sec.-Gen. P. K. BARUYA.

### CHRISTIANITY

**Jatiyo Church Parishad** (National Council of Churches): POB 220, Dhaka 1000; tel. (2) 9332869; fax (2) 8312996; e-mail nccb@ bangla.net; f. 1949 as East Pakistan Christian Council; four mem. churches; Pres. Dr SAJAL DEWAN; Gen. Sec. SUBODH ADHIKARY.

### Church of Bangladesh—United Church

After Bangladesh achieved independence, the Diocese of Dacca (Dhaka) of the Church of Pakistan (f. 1970 by the union of Anglicans, Methodists, Presbyterians and Lutherans) became the autonomous Church of Bangladesh. In 2001 the Church had an estimated 14,000 members. In 1990 a second diocese, the Diocese of Kushtia, was established.

**Bishop of Dhaka:** Rt Rev. MICHAEL S. BAROI, St Thomas's Church, 54 Johnson Rd, Dhaka 1100; tel. (2) 7116546; fax (2) 7118218; e-mail cbdacdio@bangla.net.

**Bishop of Kushtia:** Rt Rev. PAUL SHISHIR SARKAR, Church of Bangladesh, 94 N. S. Rd, Thanapara, Kushtia; tel. (71) 54618; fax (71) 54618.

### The Roman Catholic Church

For ecclesiastical purposes, Bangladesh comprises one archdiocese and five dioceses. At 31 December 2006 there were an estimated 312,003 adherents in the country.

**Catholic Bishops' Conference:** Archbishop's House, 1 Kakrail Rd, Ramna, POB 3, Dhaka 1000; tel. (2) 9358247; fax (2) 9127339; e-mail archbp@bangla.net; f. 1978; Pres. Most Rev. PAULINUS COSTA (Archbishop of Dhaka).

**Secretariat:** CBCB Centre, 24C Asad Ave, Mohammadpur, Dhaka 1207; tel. and fax (2) 9127339; e-mail cbcbsg@bdonline.com; Sec.-Gen. Rt Rev. THEOTONIUS GOMES (Titular Bishop of Zucchabar).

**Archbishop of Dhaka:** Most Rev. PAULINUS COSTA, Archbishop's House, 1 Kakrail Rd, Ramna, POB 3, Dhaka 1000; tel. (2) 8314384; e-mail archbp@bangla.net.

### Other Christian Churches

**Bangladesh Baptist Sangha:** 33 Senpara Parbatta, Mirpur 10, Dhaka 1216; tel. (2) 8012967; fax (2) 9005842; e-mail bbsangha@bdmail.net; f. 1922; 35,150 mems (2004); Pres. Dr S. M. CHOWDHURY; Gen. Sec. Rev. ROBERT SARKAR.

In early 2002 there were about 51 denominational churches active in the country, including the Bogra Christian Church, the Evangelical Christian Church, the Garo Baptist Union, the Reformed Church of Bangladesh and the Sylhet Presbyterian Synod. The Baptist Sangha was the largest Protestant Church.

## The Press

### PRINCIPAL DAILIES

#### Bengali

**Banglar Bani:** 81 Motijheel C/A, Dhaka 1000; tel. (2) 9551173; e-mail bani@bangla.net; f. 1972; Editor Sheikh FAZLUL KARIM SALIM; circ. 20,000.

**Daily Azadi:** 9 C.D.A. C/A, Momin Rd, Chittagong; tel. (31) 612380; e-mail azadi@globalctg.net; f. 1960; Editor M. A. MALEK; circ. 13,000.

**Daily Jugantor:** 12/7, North Kamalpur, Dhaka 1217; tel. (2) 7102701; fax (2) 7101917; e-mail jugantor@gononet.com; internet www.jugantor.com; Editor GOLAM SARWAR.

**Daily Sangbad:** 36 Purana Paltan, Dhaka 1000; tel. (9) 9558147; fax (2) 9562882; e-mail sangbad@gononet.com; internet www.thedailysangbad.com; Editor BAZLUR RAHMAN; circ. 77,109.

**Dainik Arthaneeti:** Bangladesh Media Services Ltd, Biman Bhaban, 5th Floor, 100 Motijheel C/A, Dhaka 1000; tel. (2) 9667789; fax (2) 9555707; e-mail dartho@citecho.net; Editor ZAHIDUZZAMAN FARUQUE.

**Dainik Bhorer Kagoj:** Rahat Tower, 14 Link Rd, Banglamotor, Dhaka; tel. (2) 9666545; fax (2) 8618801; e-mail bkagoj@yahoo.com; internet www.bhorerkagoj.net; Editor SHYAMAL DUTTA (acting); circ. 50,000.

**Dainik Birol:** Dhaka; tel. (2) 7121620; fax (2) 8013721; Chair. of Editorial Bd ABDULLAH AL-NASER.

**Dainik Inqilab:** 2/1 Ramkrishna Mission Rd, Dhaka 1203; tel. (2) 9563162; fax (2) 9552881; e-mail inqilab@bttb.net; internet www.dailyinqilab.com; Editor A. M. M. BAHAUDDIN; circ. 180,025.

**Dainik Ittefaq:** 1 Ramkrishna Mission Rd, Dhaka 1203; tel. (2) 7122660; e-mail info@ittefaq.com; internet www.ittefaq.com; f. 1953; Editor RAHAT KHAN; circ. 200,000.

**Dainik Jahan:** 3/B Shehra Rd, Mymensingh; tel. (91) 5677; f. 1980; Editor MUHAMMAD HABIBUR RAHMAN SHEIKH; circ. 4,000.

**Dainik Janakantha** (Daily People's Voice): Globe Janakantha Shilpa Paribar, Janakantha Bhaban, Dhaka 1000; tel. (2) 9347780; fax (2) 9351317; e-mail janakantha@bttb.net.bd; internet www.dailyjanakantha.com; f. 1993; Man. Editor TOAB KHAN; Exec. Editor BORHAN AHMED; circ. 100,000.

**Dainik Janata:** 24 Aminbagh, Shanti Nagar, Dhaka 1217; tel. (2) 400498; e-mail djanata@dhaka.net; internet www.dailyjanata.com; Editor Dr M. ASADUR RAHMAN.

**Dainik Janmabhumi:** 110/2 Islampur Rd, Khulna; tel. (41) 721280; fax (41) 724324; e-mail janmo@khulna.bangla.net; f. 1982; Editor WADUDUR RAHMAN PANNA (acting); circ. 30,000.

**Dainik Karatoa:** Chalkjadu Rd, Bogra 5800; tel. (51) 63660; fax (51) 73057; e-mail abas@bttb.net.bd; internet www.karatoa.com; f. 1976; Editor MOZAMMEL HAQUE LALU; circ. 44,000.

**Dainik Khabar:** 137 Shanti Nagar, Dhaka 1217; tel. (2) 406601; f. 1985; Editor PATRA GIAS KAMAL CHOWDHURY; circ. 18,000.

**Dainik Millat:** Dhaka; tel. (2) 9560026; Editor CHOWDHURY MOHAMMAD FAROOQ.

**Dainik Patrika:** 85 Elephant Rd, Maghbazar, Dhaka 1217; tel. (2) 415057; fax (2) 841575; e-mail patrika@citechco.net; Publr and Chief Editor MIA MUSA HOSSAIN; Editor M. FAISAL HASSAN HASSAN (acting).

**Dainik Purbanchal:** Purbanchal House, 38 Iqbal Nagar Mosque Lane, Khulna 9100; tel. (41) 722251; fax (41) 721013; e-mail liakat@purbanchal.com; internet www.purbanchal.com; f. 1974; Editor LIAKAT ALI; circ. 46,000.

**Dainik Rupashi Bangla:** Abdur Rashid Rd, Natun Chowdhury Para, Bagicha Gaon, Comilla 3500; tel. (81) 76689; f. 1972; a weekly until 1979; Editor Prof. HASINA WAHAB; Publr and Printer ASHIK AMITAV; circ. 10,000.

**Dainik Sangram:** 423 Elephant Rd, Baramaghbazar, Dhaka 1217; tel. (2) 9346448; fax (2) 9330579; e-mail dsangram@gmail.com; internet www.dailysangram.com; f. 1970; Chair. ALI AHSAN MUHAMMAD MUJAHID; Editor ABUL ASAD; circ. 50,000.

**Dainik Sphulinga:** Amin Villa, P-5 Housing Estate, Jessore 7401; tel. (421) 6433; f. 1971; Editor Mia ABDUS SATTAR; circ. 14,000.

**Jaijaidin:** Jaijaidin Mediaplex, Love Rd, Tejgaon Industrial Area, Dhaka 1000; tel. (2) 8832222; fax (2) 8832233; e-mail jajadi@aitlbd.net; internet www.jaijaidin.com; f. 1984; Editor SHAFIK REHMAN; circ. 100,000.

**Janabarta:** 5 Babu Khan Rd, Khulna; tel. (41) 21075; f. 1974; Editor SYED SOHRAB ALI; circ. 4,000.

**Jugabheri:** Sylhet; tel. (821) 715461; f. 1931; Editor FAHMEEDA RASHEED CHOWDHURY; circ. 6,000.

**Manav Jamin** (Human Land): 21 Kazi Nazrul Islam Ave, Dhaka 1000; tel. (2) 9669193; fax (2) 8618130; e-mail manabzamin@yahoo.com; internet www.manabzamin.ne; f. 1998; tabloid; Editor MATIUR RAHMAN CHOUDHURY.

**Naya Bangla:** 101 Momin Rd, Chittagong; tel. (31) 206247; f. 1978; Editor ABDULLAH AL-SAGIR; circ. 12,000.

**Prothom Alo:** C. A. Bhaban, 100 Kazi Nazrul Islam Ave, Karwan Bazar, Dhaka 1215; tel. (2) 8110081; fax (2) 9130496; e-mail info@prothom-alo.com; internet www.prothom-alo.com; f. 1998; publ. by MediaStar Ltd; Editors MATIUR RAHMAN, ABDUL QUAYUM.

**Protidin:** Ganeshtola, Dinajpur; tel. (531) 4555; f. 1980; Editor KHAIRUL ANAM; circ. 3,000.

**Sangbad:** 36 Purana Paltan, Dhaka 1000; tel. (2) 9558147; fax (2) 9562882; e-mail sangbad@bangla.net; f. 1952; Editor AHMADUL KABIR; circ. 71,050.

**Shamokal:** 136 Tejgaon Industrial Area, Dhaka 1208; tel. (2) 9889821; fax (2) 8855981; e-mail info@shamokalbd.com; internet www.shamokal.com; Editor GOLAM SARWAR.

**Swadhinata:** Chittagong; tel. (31) 209644; f. 1972; Editor ABDULLAH AL-HARUN; circ. 4,000.

#### English

**Bangladesh Observer:** Observer House, 33 Toyenbee Circular Rd, Motijheel C/A, Dhaka 1000; tel. (2) 9555105; fax (2) 9562243; e-mail observer@dhaka.net; internet www.bangladeshobserveronline.com; f. 1949; morning; Editor IQBAL SOBHAN CHOWDHURY; circ. 75,000.

**The Bangladesh Today:** 9 Motijheel C/A, Dhaka 1000; tel. (2) 9556254; fax (2) 9565257; e-mail editor@thebangladeshtoday.com; internet www.thebangladeshtoday.com; Editor Col (retd) MAHMUDUR RAHMAN CHOUDHURY (acting).

**Daily Evening News:** Dhaka; tel. (2) 7121619; fax (2) 8013721; Chair. of Editorial Bd ABDULLAH AL-NASER.

**Daily Rupali:** 28/A/3 Toyenbee Circular Rd, Dhaka 1000; tel. (2) 235542; fax (2) 9565558; e-mail network@bangla.net; Editor MAFUZUR RAHMAN MITA.

**Daily Star:** 19 Karwan Bazar, Dhaka 1215; tel. (2) 8124944; fax (2) 8125155; e-mail editor@thedailystar.net; internet www.thedailystar.net; f. 1991; Publr and Editor MAHFUZ ANAM; circ. 40,000 (weekdays), 60,000 (weekends).

**Daily Tribune:** 38 Iqbal Nagar Mosque Lane, Khulna 9100; tel. (41) 721944; fax (41) 721013; e-mail ferdousi@purbanchal.com; f. 1978; morning; Editor FERDOUSI ALI; circ. 24,000.

**Financial Express:** Tropicana Tower, 4th Floor, 45 Topkhana Road, POB 2526, Dhaka 1000; tel. (2) 9568154; fax (2) 9567049; e-mail tfe@bangla.net; internet www.financialexpress-bd.com; f. 1994; Editor MOAZZEM HOSSAIN.

**The Independent:** Beximco Media Complex, 32 Kazi Nazrul Islam Ave, Karwan Bazar, Dhaka 1215; tel. (2) 9129938; fax (2) 9127722; e-mail ind@bol-online.com; internet www.theindependent-bd.com; f. 1995; Editor MAHBUBUL ALAM.

**New Age:** Holiday Bldg, 30 Tejgaon Industrial Area, Dhaka 1208; tel. (2) 8153034; fax (2) 8112247; e-mail newagebd@global-bd.net; internet www.newagebd.com; f. 2003; Editor NURUL KABIR.

**New Nation:** 1 Ramkrishna Mission Rd, Dhaka 1203; tel. (2) 7122654; fax (2) 7122650; e-mail n_editor@bangla.net; internet nation.ittefaq.com; f. 1981; Editor MOSTAFA KAMAL MAJUMDER; circ. 15,000.

**The News Today:** 2 Outer Circular Rd, Mogh Bazar, Dhaka; tel. (2) 9355567; fax (2) 9355569; e-mail today@gononet.com; internet www.newstoday-bd.com; Editor REAZUDDIN AHMED.

**People's View:** 102 Siraj-ud-Daulla Rd, Chittagong; tel. (31) 227403; f. 1969; Editor SABBIR ISLAM; circ. 3,000.

## PERIODICALS

### Bengali

**Aachal:** Dhaka; weekly; Editor FERDOUSI BEGUM.

**Adhuna:** 1/3 Block F, Lalmatia, Dhaka 1207; tel. (2) 812353; fax (2) 813095; e-mail adab@bdonline.com; f. 1974; quarterly; publ. by the Asscn of Devt Agencies in Bangladesh (ADAB); Exec. Editor MINAR MONSUR; circ. 10,000.

**Ahmadi:** 4 Bakshi Bazar Rd, Dhaka 1211; tel. (2) 7300808; fax (2) 7300925; e-mail amgb@bol-online.com; f. 1925; fortnightly; Editor-in-Chief M. A. S. MAHMOOD; Exec. Editor MOHAMMAD M. RAHMAN.

**Alokpat:** 166 Arambagh, Dhaka 1000; tel. (2) 413361; fax (2) 863060; fortnightly; Editor RABBANI JABBAR.

**Amod:** Chowdhury Para, Comilla 3500; tel. (81) 65193; e-mail info@weeklyamod.com; internet www.weeklyamod.com; f. 1955; weekly; Editor SHAMSUN NAHAR RABBI; circ. 6,000.

**Begum:** 66 Loyal St, Dhaka 1; tel. (2) 233789; f. 1947; women's illustrated weekly; Editor NURJAHAN BEGUM; circ. 25,000.

**Chakra:** 242A Nakhalpara, POB 2682, Dhaka 1215; tel. (2) 604568; social welfare weekly; Editor HUSNEARA AZIZ.

**Chitra Desh:** 24 Ramkrishna Mission Rd, Dhaka 1203; weekly; Editor HENA AKHTAR CHOWDHURY.

**Chitrali:** Observer House, 33 Toyenbee Circular Rd, Motijheel C/A, Dhaka 1000; tel. (2) 9550938; fax (2) 9562243; f. 1953; film weekly; Editor PRODIP KUMAR DEY; circ. 25,000.

**Ekota:** 15 Larmini St, Wari, Dhaka; tel. (2) 257854; f. 1970; weekly; Editor AFROZA NAHAR; circ. 25,000.

**Fashal:** 28J Toyenbee Circular Rd, Motijheel C/A, Dhaka 1000; tel. (2) 233099; f. 1965; agricultural weekly; Chief Editor ERSHAD MAZUMDAR; circ. 8,000.

**Ispat:** Majampur, Kushtia; tel. (71) 3676; f. 1976; weekly; Editor WALIUR BARI CHOUDHURY; circ. 3,000.

**Jhorna:** 4/13 Block A, Lalmatia, Dhaka; tel. (2) 415239; Editor MUHAMMAD JAMIR ALI.

**Kalantar:** 87 Khanjahan Ali Rd, Khulna; tel. (41) 61424; f. 1971; weekly; Editor NOOR MOHAMMAD; circ. 12,000.

**Kankan:** Nawab Bari Rd, Bogra; tel. (51) 6424; f. 1974; weekly; Editor SUFIA KHATUN; circ. 6,000.

**Kirajagat:** National Sports Council, 62/63 Purana Paltan, Dhaka 1000; f. 1977; fortnightly; Editor MAHMUD HOSSAIN KHAN DULAL; circ. 10,000.

**Kishore Bangla:** Observer House, Motijheel C/A, Dhaka 1000; juvenile weekly; f. 1976; Editor RAFIQUL HAQUE; circ. 5,000.

**Moha Nagar:** 4 Dilkusha C/A, Dhaka 1000; tel. (2) 255282; Editor SYED MOTIUR RAHMAN.

**Moshal:** 4 Dilkusha C/A, Dhaka 1000; tel. (2) 231092; Editor MUHAMMAD ABUL HASNAT; circ. 3,000.

**Muktibani:** Toyenbee Circular Rd, Motijheel C/A, Dhaka 1000; tel. (2) 253712; f. 1972; weekly; Editor NIZAM UDDIN AHMED; circ. 35,000.

**Natun Bangla:** 44/2 Free School St Bylane, Hatirpool, Dhaka 1205; tel. (2) 866121; fax (2) 863794; e-mail mujib@bangla.net; f. 1971; weekly; Editor MUJIBUR RAHMAN.

**Natun Katha:** 31E Topkhana Rd, Dhaka; weekly; Editor HAJERA SULTANA; circ. 4,000.

**Nipun:** 520 Peyarabag, Magbazar, Dhaka 11007; tel. (2) 312156; monthly; Editor SHAJAHAN CHOWDHURY.

**Parikrama:** 65 Shanti Nagar, Dhaka; tel. (2) 415640; Editor MOMTAZ SULTANA.

**Prohar:** 35 Siddeswari Rd, Dhaka 1217; tel. (2) 404206; Editor MUJIBUL HUQ.

**Protirodh:** Dept of Answar and V.D.P. Khilgoan, Ministry of Home Affairs, School Bldg, 2nd and 3rd Floors, Bangladesh Secretariat, Dhaka; tel. (2) 405971; f. 1977; fortnightly; Editor ZAHANGIR HABIBULLAH; circ. 20,000.

**Purbani:** 1 Ramkrishna Mission Rd, Dhaka 1203; tel. (2) 256503; f. 1951; film weekly; Editor KHONDKER SHAHADAT HOSSAIN; circ. 22,000.

**Robbar:** 1 Ramkrishna Mission Rd, Dhaka; tel. (2) 256071; e-mail robbar@nation-online.com; internet www.robbar.com; f. 1978; weekly; Editor SYED TOSHARRAF ALI; circ. 20,000.

**Rokshena:** 13B Avoy Das Lane, Tiktuli, Dhaka; tel. (2) 255117; Editor SYEDA AFSANA.

**Sachitra Bangladesh:** 112 Circuit House Rd, Dhaka 1000; tel. (2) 402129; f. 1979; fortnightly; Editor A. B. M. ABDUL MATIN; circ. 8,000.

**Sachitra Sandhani:** 68/2 Purana Paltan, Dhaka; tel. (2) 409680; f. 1978; weekly; Editor GAZI SHAHABUDDIN MAHMUD; circ. 13,000.

**Sandip Bhabhan:** 28/A/3 Toyenbee Circular Rd, Dhaka; tel. (2) 235542; fax (2) 9565558; e-mail network@bangla.net; weekly; Editor MAFUZUR RAHMAN MITA.

**Shaptahik Ekhon:** Dhaka; internet www.weeklyekhon.com; weekly; Editor ALTAUS SAMAD.

**Shishu:** Bangladesh Shishu Academy, Old High Court Compound, Dhaka 1000; tel. (2) 230317; f. 1977; children's monthly; Editor GOLAM KIBRIA; circ. 5,000.

**Sonar Bangla:** 423 Elephant Rd, Mogh Bazar, Dhaka 1217; tel. (2) 8319065; fax (2) 8315571; e-mail news@weeklysonarbanglabd.com; internet www.weeklysonarbangla.com; f. 1961; Editor MUHAMMED QAMARUZZAMAN; circ. 25,000.

**Swadesh:** 19 B.B. Ave, Dhaka; tel. (2) 256946; weekly; Editor ZAKIUDDIN AHMED; circ. 8,000.

**Tarokalok:** Tarokalok Complex, 25/3 Green Rd, Dhaka 1205; tel. (2) 506583; fax (2) 864330; weekly; Editor AREFIN BADAL.

**Tilotwoma:** 14 Bangla Bazar, Dhaka; Editor ABDUL MANNAN.

### English

**ADAB News:** 1/3, Block F, Lalmatia, Dhaka 1207; tel. (2) 327424; f. 1974; 6 a year; publ. by the Asscn of Devt Agencies in Bangladesh (ADAB); Editor-in-Chief AZFAR HUSSAIN; circ. 10,000.

**Bangladesh:** 112 Circuit House Rd, Dhaka 1000; tel. (2) 402013; fortnightly; Editor A. B. M. ABDUL MATIN.

**Bangladesh Gazette:** Bangladesh Government Press, Tejgaon, Dhaka; f. 1947; name changed 1972; weekly; official notices; Editor M. HUDA.

**Bangladesh Illustrated Weekly:** Dhaka; tel. (2) 23358; Editor ATIQUZZAMAN KHAN; circ. 3,000.

**Cinema:** 81 Motijheel C/A, Dhaka 1000; Editor Sheikh FAZLUR RAHMAN MARUF; circ. 11,000.

**Detective:** Polwell Bhaban, Naya Paltan, Dhaka 1000; tel. (2) 9357451; e-mail detective.bd@gmail.com; f. 1960; monthly; also publ. in Bengali; Editor-in-Chief N. B. K. TRIPURA; circ. 5,000.

**Dhaka Courier:** Cosmos Centre, 69/1 New Circular Rd, Malibagh, Dhaka 1217; tel. (2) 408420; fax (2) 831942; e-mail dhakacourier@dhakacourier.net; internet www.dhakacourier.net; weekly; Exec. Editor ROUSHAN ZAMAN; circ. 18,000.

**Holiday:** Holiday Bldg, 30 Tejgaon Industrial Area, Dhaka 1208; tel. (2) 9122950; fax (2) 9127927; e-mail holiday@bangla.net; internet www.weeklyholiday.net; f. 1965; weekly; independent; Editor SAYED KAMALUDDIN; circ. 18,000.

**Motherland:** Khanjahan Ali Rd, Khulna; tel. (41) 61685; f. 1974; weekly; Editor M. N. KHAN.

**Tide:** 56/57 Motijheel C/A, Dhaka; tel. (2) 259421; Editor ENAYET KARIM.

**Voice from the North:** Dinajpur Town, Dinajpur; tel. (531) 3256; f. 1981; weekly; Editor Prof. MUHAMMAD MOHSIN; circ. 5,000.

**Weekly Blitz:** Skylark Point, 8th Floor, 24/A Bijoy Nagar, Dhaka 1000; tel. (19) 326232; e-mail ediblitz@yahoo.com; internet www.weeklyblitz.net; f. 2003; weekly (Wednesdays); Publr and Editor SALAH UDDIN SHOAIB CHOUDHURY; circ. 9,000.

## NEWS AGENCIES

**Bangladesh Sangbad Sangstha (BSS)** (Bangladesh News Agency): 68/2 Purana Paltan, Dhaka 1000; tel. (2) 9555036; fax (2) 9568970; e-mail bssadmin@bssnews.org; internet www.bssnews.net; f. 1972; Man. Dir and Chief Editor GAZIUL HASAN KHAN.

**Islamic News Society (INS):** 24 R. K. Mission Rd, Motijheel C/A, Dhaka 1203; tel. (2) 7121619; fax (2) 8013721; Editor ABDULLAH AL-NASER.

**United News of Bangladesh (UNB):** Cosmos Centre, 69/1 New Circular Rd, Malibagh, Dhaka 1217; tel. (2) 9345543; fax (2) 9344556; e-mail unbnews@dhaka.net; internet www.unbnews.org; f. 1988; independent; Chair. AMANULLAH KHAN.

### PRESS ASSOCIATIONS

**Bangladesh Press Council:** 2nd Floor, House 497, Rd 33, Mohakhali, Dhaka 1206; tel. (2) 9862426; e-mail info@presscouncilbd.com; internet www.presscouncilbd.com; f. 1974; established under an act of Parliament to preserve the freedom of the press and maintain and develop standards of newspapers and news agencies; Chair. Justice ABU SAYEED AHAMMED.

**Bangladesh Sangbadpatra Karmachari Federation** (Newspaper Employees' Fed.): Dhaka; tel. (2) 235065; f. 1972; Pres. MATIUR RAHMAN TALUKDER; Sec.-Gen. MIR MOZAMMEL HOSSAIN.

**Bangladesh Sangbadpatra Press Sramik Federation** (Newspaper Press Workers' Federation): 1 Ramkrishna Mission Rd, Dhaka 1203; f. 1960; Pres. M. ABDUL KARIM; Sec.-Gen. BOZLUR RAHMAN MILON.

**Dhaka Union of Journalists:** National Press Club, Dhaka; f. 1947.

**Newspaper Owners' Association of Bangladesh:** c/o The Independent, Beximco Media Complex, 32 Kazi Nazrul Islam Ave, Karwan Bazar, Dhaka 1215; f. 2002; promotes interests of the newspaper industry; Pres. MAHBUBUL ALAM.

**Overseas Correspondents' Association of Bangladesh (OCAB):** 18 Topkhana Rd, Dhaka 1000; e-mail naweed@bdonline.com; f. 1979; Pres. ZAHIDUZZMAN. FARUQUE; Gen. Sec. SHAMIM AHMED; 60 mems.

**Press Institute of Bangladesh:** 3 Circuit House Rd, Dhaka 1000; tel. (2) 9330081; fax (2) 8317458; e-mail pib@bdonline.com; internet www.pib.gov.bd; f. 1976; trains journalists, conducts research, operates a newspaper library and data bank; Dir-Gen. HAIDAR ALI (acting).

## Publishers

**Academic Publishers:** 35 Syed Awlad Hossain Lane, Dhaka 1100; tel. (2) 507355; fax (2) 863060; f. 1982; social sciences and sociology; Jt Man. Dir HABIBUR RAHMAN.

**Agamee Prakashani:** 36 Bangla Bazar, Dhaka 1100; tel. (2) 7111332; fax (2) 7123945; e-mail agamee@bdonline.com; f. 1986; fiction and academic; Chief Exec. OSMAN GANI.

**Ahmed Publishing House:** 7 Zindabahar 1st Lane, Dhaka; tel. (2) 36492; f. 1942; literature, history, science, religion, children's, maps and charts; Man. Dir KAMALUDDIN AHMED; Man. MESBAHUDDIN AHMED.

**Ankur Prakashani:** 40/1 Purana Paltan, Dhaka 1000; tel. (2) 9564799; fax (2) 9553635; e-mail ankur@agnionline.net; internet www.ankur-prakashani.com; f. 1986; academic and general; Dir MESBAHUDDIN AHMED.

**Ashrafia Library:** 4 Hakim Habibur Rahman Rd, Chawk Bazar, Dhaka 1000; Islamic religious books, texts, and reference works of Islamic institutions.

**Asiatic Society of Bangladesh:** 5 Old Secretariat Rd, Ramna, Dhaka; tel. (2) 9560500; fax (2) 7168853; e-mail asb@bangla.net; internet www.asiaticsociety.org.bd/journals.htm; f. 1952; periodicals on science, Bangla and humanities.

**Bangla Academy (National Academy of Arts and Letters of Bangladesh):** Burdwan House, 3 Kazi Nazrul Islam Ave, Dhaka 1000; tel. (2) 8619577; fax (2) 8612352; e-mail bacademy@citechco.net; internet www.banglaacademy.org.bd; f. 1955; higher education textbooks in Bengali, books on language, literature and culture, language planning, popular science, drama, encyclopaedias, translations of world classics, dictionaries; Dir-Gen. Dr ABUL KALAM MANZUR MORSHED; Pres. A. NISUZZAMAN.

**Bangladesh Books International Ltd:** Ittefaq Bhaban, 1 Ramkrishna Mission Rd, POB 377, Dhaka; tel. (2) 256071; f. 1975; reference, academic, research, literary, children's in Bengali and English; Chair. MOINUL HOSSEIN; Man. Dir ABDUL HAFIZ.

**Bangladesh Publishers:** 45 Patuatully Rd, Dhaka 1100; tel. (2) 233135; f. 1952; textbooks for schools, colleges and universities, cultural books, journals, etc.; Dir MAYA RANI GHOSAL.

**Gatidhara:** 38/2-Ka Bangla Bazar, POB 2723, Dhaka 1000; tel. (2) 7117515; fax (2) 7123472; e-mail gatidara@bdonline.com; f. 1988; academic, general and fiction; Publr and Chief Exec. SIKDER ABUL BASHAR.

**Gono Prakashani:** House 14/E, Rd 6, Dhanmondhi R/A, Dhaka 1205; tel. (2) 8617208; fax (2) 8613567; e-mail gk@citechco.net; f. 1978; science and medicine; Man. Dir SHAFIQ KHAN; Editor BAZLUR RAHIM.

**Muktadhara:** 22 Payridas Rd, Banglabazar, Dhaka 1100; tel. (2) 7111374; e-mail muktadhara1971@yahoo.com; f. 1971; educational and literary; Bengali and English; Dir JAHAR LAL SAHA; Man. Dir C. R. SAHA.

**Mullick Brothers:** 160–161, Dhaka New Market, Dhaka; tel. (2) 8619125; fax (2) 8610562; educational; Man. Dir KAMRUL HASAN MULLICK.

**Osmania Book Depot:** 30/32 North Brook Hall Rd, Dhaka 1100.

**Rahman Brothers:** 5/1 Gopinath Datta, Kabiraj St, Babu Bazar, Dhaka; tel. (2) 282633; educational.

**Royal Library:** Ispahani Bldg, 31/32 P. K. Roy Rd, Bangla Bazar, Dhaka; tel. (2) 250863.

**Shahitya Prakash:** 42 Topkhana Road, Dhaka 1000; tel. (2) 281327; fax (2) 863797; f. 1970; Prin. Officer MOFIDUL HOQUE.

**University Press Ltd:** Red Crescent House, 61 Motijheel C/A, POB 2611, Dhaka 1000; tel. (2) 9565444; fax (2) 9565443; e-mail upl@bttb.net.bd; internet www.uplbooks.com; f. 1975; educational, academic and general; Man. Dir MOHIUDDIN AHMED.

### GOVERNMENT PUBLISHING HOUSES

**Bangladesh Bureau of Statistics:** Parishankhan Bhaban, E-27/A, Agargaon, Sher-e-Bangla Nagar, Dhaka 1207; tel. (2) 9118045; fax (2) 9111064; e-mail ndbp@bangla.net; internet www.bbs.gov.bd; f. 1971; statistical year book and pocket book, censuses, surveys, agricultural year book, special reports, etc.; Dir-Gen. A. Y. M. EKRAMUL HOQUE; Sec. BADIUR RAHMAN.

**Bangladesh Government Press:** Tejgaon, Dhaka 1209; tel. (2) 606316; f. 1972.

**Department of Films and Publications:** 112 Circuit House Rd, Dhaka 1000; tel. (2) 8331034; fax (2) 8331030; e-mail dfp_bd@yahoo.com; internet www.dfpbd.com; Dir-Gen. MIR MOSHARRAF HOSSAIN.

**Press Information Department:** Bhaban 6, Bangladesh Secretariat, Dhaka 1000; tel. (2) 7163639; fax (2) 7165942; e-mail pid_1@bangla.net; internet www.bdpressinform.org/activities.htm.

### PUBLISHERS' ASSOCIATIONS

**Bangladesh Publishers' and Booksellers' Association:** 3 Liaquat Ave, 3rd Floor, Dhaka 1100; tel. (2) 7111666; e-mail info@publisher-bookseller.org; internet www.publisher-bookseller.org; f. 1972; Pres. ABU TAHER; 2,500 mems.

**National Book Centre of Bangladesh:** 5C Bangabandhu Ave, Dhaka 1000; f. 1963; to promote the cause of 'more, better and cheaper books'; organizes book fairs, publs a monthly journal; Dir FAZLE RABBI.

## Broadcasting and Communications

### TELECOMMUNICATIONS

**Bangladesh Telecommunication Regulatory Commission (BTRC):** Setu Bhaban, 4th Floor, New Airport Rd, Banani, Dhaka 1212; tel. (2) 9893917; fax (2) 9890029; e-mail info@btrc.org.bd; internet www.btrc.gov.bd; f. 2002; regulates the telecommunications sector; Chair. Maj.-Gen. (retd) MANZURUL ALAM; Vice-Chair. A. M. M. REZA-E-RABBI.

**Bangladesh Telecommunications Co Ltd (BTCL):** Central Office, Telejogajog Bhaban, 37/E Eskaton Garden, Dhaka 1000; tel. (2) 8322661; fax (2) 832577; e-mail md@btcl.net.bd; internet www.bttb.net; formed through division of Bangladesh Telegraph and Telephone Board in 2008; Chair. IQBAL MAHMUD; Man. Dir ASHRAFUL ALIM.

**Aktel:** 1st Floor, Silver Tower, 52 South Gulshan C/A, Gulshan 1, Dhaka 1212; e-mail 123@aktel.com; internet www.aktel.com; f. 1996; jt venture between Telekom Malaysia Bhd and A. K. Khan & Co Ltd; provides mobile cellular telephone services; Man. Dir and CEO JEFRI AHMAD TAMBI.

**BanglaLink:** FM Center (Tiger House), Level 1, House SW(H)04, Gulshan Ave, Gulshan Model Town, Dhaka 1212; tel. (2) 9885770; fax (2) 8827265; e-mail info@banglalinkgsm.com; internet www.banglalinkgsm.com; f. 1998; owned by Orascom Telecom; provides mobile cellular telephone services; Man. Dir and CEO RASHID KHAN.

**GrameenPhone Ltd:** Celebration Pt, Plots 3 & 5, Rd 113A, Gulshan 2, Dhaka 1212; tel. (2) 9882990; fax (2) 9882970; e-mail info@grameenphone.com; internet www.grameenphone.com; f. 1996 by Grameen Bank to expand cellular telephone service in rural areas; CEO ANDERS JENSEN.

**Pacific Bangladesh Telecom Ltd:** Pacific Centre, 14 Mohakhali C/A, Dhaka 1212; tel. (2) 8822186; fax (2) 8823575; e-mail customerservice@citycell.com; internet www.citycell.com; Man. Dir FAISAL MORSHED KHAN; CEO CHYE HOON PIN.

**Teletalk Bangladesh Ltd:** House 41, Rd 27, Block A, Banani, Dhaka 1213; tel. (2) 8851060; fax (2) 9882828; e-mail info@teletalk.com.bd; internet www.teletalk.com.bd; f. 2004; govt-owned; controls mobile cellular telephone operations of Bangladesh Telegraph and Telephone Board; Man. Dir MUHAMMAD AMINUL HASSAN.

**Warid Telecom International:** POB 3016, Dhaka; fax (2) 8951786; internet www.waridtel.com.bd; f. 2005; owned by Abu Dhabi Group of United Arab Emirates; operates mobile cellular telephone services; CEO MUNEER FAROOQUI.

### BROADCASTING

#### Radio

**Bangladesh Betar:** NBA House, 121 Kazi Nazrul Islam Ave, Shahabag, Dhaka 1000; tel. (2) 8615294; e-mail dgbetar@bd.drik.net; internet www.betar.org.bd; f. 1971; govt-controlled; regional stations at Dhaka, Chittagong, Khulna, Rajshahi, Rangpur, Sylhet, Rangamati and Thakurgaon broadcast a total of approximately 160 hours daily; transmitting centres at Lalmai and Rangamati; external service broadcasts 8 transmissions daily in Arabic, Bengali, English, Hindi, Nepalese and Urdu; Dir-Gen. MAHBUBUL ALAM.

#### Television

**ATN Bangla:** WASA Bhaban, 1st Floor, 98 Kazi Nazrul Islam Ave, Kawran Bazar, Dhaka 1215; tel. (2) 8111207; fax (2) 8111876; e-mail info@atnbangla.tv; internet www.atnbangla.tv; f. 1997; private satellite channel; broadcasts in Bengali; Chair. MAHFUZUR RAHMAN.

**Bangladesh Television (BTV):** Television House, Rampura, Dhaka 1219; tel. (2) 9330131; fax (2) 8621839; e-mail info@btv.gov.bd; internet www.btv.gov.bd; f. 1964; govt-controlled; daily broadcasts on one channel from Dhaka station for 12 hours; transmissions also from nation-wide network of 15 relay stations; Dir-Gen. KAMAL U AHMED; Gen. Man. Sheikh REAZ UDDIN BAADSHA.

**Channel-i:** Impress Telefilm Ltd, 62/A, Shiddeshwari Rd, Dhaka 1217; tel. (2) 9332444; fax (2) 9338285; e-mail info@channel-i-tv.com; internet www.channel-i-tv.com; f. 1999; Dir SHYKH SERAJ.

**NTV Bangladesh:** BSEC Bhaban, 6th Floor, 102 Kazi Nazrul Islam Ave, Karwan Bazar, Dhaka 1215; tel. (2) 9143381; fax (2) 9143386; e-mail info@ntvbd.com; internet www.ntvbd.com; f. 2003; private satellite channel; Chair. M. ENAYETUR RAHMAN.

## Finance

(cap. = capital; res = reserves; dep. = deposits; m. = million; brs = branches; amounts in taka)

### BANKING

#### Central Bank

**Bangladesh Bank:** Motijheel C/A, POB 325, Dhaka 1000; tel. (2) 7126101; fax (2) 9566212; e-mail banglabank@bangla.net; internet www.bangladesh-bank.org; f. 1971; cap. 30m., res 59,503.5m., dep. 201,800.9m. (June 2006); Gov. SALEHUDDIN AHMED; 9 brs.

#### Nationalized Commercial Banks

**Agrani Bank:** 9D Dilkusha C/A, POB 531, Dhaka 1000; tel. (2) 9566160; fax (2) 9563662; e-mail enquiry@agranibank.org; internet www.agranibank.org; f. 1972; 100% state-owned; cap. 2,484.2m., res 292.2m., dep. 128,920.7m. (Dec. 2006); Chair. SIDDIQUR RAHMAN CHOWDHURY; Man. Dir SYED ABU NASER BUKHTEAR AHMED; 866 brs.

**Janata Bank:** 110 Motijheel C/A, POB 468, Dhaka 1000; tel. (2) 9565041; fax (2) 9564644; e-mail id-obd@janatabank-bd.com; internet www.janatabank-bd.com; f. 1972; 100% state-owned; cap. 2,593.9m., res 1,726.5m., dep. 182,946.5m. (Dec. 2006); Chair. SUHEL AHMED CHOUDHURY; Man. Dir MUHAMMAD MUKTER HUSSAIN; 847 brs in Bangladesh, 4 brs in the UAE.

**Rupali Bank Ltd:** Rupali Bhaban, 34 Dilkusha C/A, POB 719, Dhaka 1000; tel. (2) 9554122; fax (2) 9564148; e-mail rblhocom@bdcom.com; internet www.rupali-bank.com; f. 1972; cap. 1,250m., res 855.8m., dep. 59,967.9m. (Dec. 2003); Chair. Dr MOHAMMAD TAREQUE; Man. Dir ABDUL HAMID MIAH; 508 brs in Bangladesh, 1 br. in Pakistan.

**Sonali Bank:** 35–44 Motijheel C/A, POB 3130, Dhaka 1000; tel. (2) 9550426; fax (2) 9561410; e-mail sbhoitd@bttb.net; internet www.sonalibank.com.bd; f. 1972; 100% state-owned; cap. 3,272.2m., res 3,034.0m., dep. 290,140.1m. (Dec. 2005); Chair. Prof. MAHBUB ULLAH; Man. Dir TAHMILAR RAHMAN; 1,186 brs incl. 2 overseas brs.

#### Private Commercial Banks

**Al-Arafah Islami Bank Ltd:** Rahman Mansion, 161 Motijheel C/A, Dhaka; tel. (2) 9568007; fax (2) 9569351; e-mail alarafah@bangla.net; internet www.al-arafah.com; f. 1995; 100% owned by 23 sponsors; cap. 720m., res 10m., dep. 852.0m. (Feb. 2004); Chair. MUHAMMAD ANOWER HOSSAIN; Man. Dir MUHAMMAD ABDUS SAMAD SHEIKH.

**Arab Bangladesh Bank Ltd:** Head Office, BCIC Bhaban, 30–31 Dilkusha C/A, POB 3522, Dhaka 1000; tel. (2) 9560312; fax (2) 9564122; e-mail abbank@abbank.org; internet www.abbank.org; f. 1981; 99.3% owned by Bangladesh nationals and 0.7% by Bangladesh Govt; cap. 571.7m., res 1,456.5m., dep. 43,374.4m. (Dec. 2006); Chair. FAISAL MORSHED KHAN; Pres. and Man. Dir KAISER A. CHOWDHURY; 66 brs, 1 br. in India.

**The City Bank Ltd:** Jiban Bima Tower, 10 Dilkusha C/A, POB 3381, Dhaka 1000; tel. (2) 9565925; fax (2) 9562347; e-mail mail@thecitybank.com; internet www.thecitybank.com; f. 1983; 50% owned by sponsors and 50% by public; cap. 720.0m., res 1,205.2m., dep. 30,647.8m. (Dec. 2005); Chair. AZIZ AL-KAISER; Man. Dir K. MAHMOOD SATTAR; 82 brs.

**Dhaka Bank Ltd:** Biman Bhaban, 100 Motijheel C/A, Dhaka 1000; tel. (2) 9554514; fax (2) 9556584; e-mail dhakabank@bdonline.com; internet www.dhakabankltd.com; f. 1995; cap. 1,289.5m., res 871.0m., dep. 41,553.6m. (Dec. 2006); Chair. JASMINE SULTANA; Man. Dir SHAHED NOMAN; 20 brs.

**Dutch-Bangla Bank Ltd:** 3rd, 4th, 5th and 10th Floors, Sena Kalyan Bhaban, 195 Motijheel C/A, Dhaka 1000; tel. (2) 7176390; fax (2) 9561889; e-mail id@dutchbanglabank.com; internet www.dutchbanglabank.com; f. 1996; cap. 202.1m., res 724.7m., dep. 40,111.5m. (Dec. 2006); Chair. ABUL HASNAT MOHAMMAD RASHIDUL ISLAM; Man. Dir MOHAMMED YEASIN ALI; 39 brs.

**Eastern Bank Ltd:** Jiban Bima Bhaban, 2nd Floor, 10 Dilkusha C/A, POB 896, Dhaka 1000; tel. (2) 9556360; fax (2) 9562364; e-mail info@ebl-bd.com; internet www.ebl-bd.com; f. 1992; appropriated assets and liabilities of fmr Bank of Credit and Commerce International (Overseas) Ltd; 83% owned by public, 17% owned by govt and private commercial banks; cap. 828.0m., res 2,293.9m., dep. 30,139.7m. (Dec. 2006); Chair. AHMED QUAMRUL ISLAM CHOWDHURY; Man. Dir and CEO ALI REZA IFTEKHAR; 22 brs.

**International Finance Investment and Commerce Bank Ltd (IFICB):** BSB Bldg, 8th, 10th & 16th–19th Floors, 8 Rajuk Ave, POB 2229, Dhaka 1000; tel. (2) 9563020; fax (2) 9562015; e-mail info@ificbankbd.com; internet www.ificbankbd.com; f. 1983; 35.5% state-owned; cap. 406.4m., res 964.4m., dep. 28,620.9m. (Dec. 2006); Chair. Al-haj MOHAMMAD MOSADDAK ALI; Man. Dir MASHIUR RAHMAN; 65 brs in Bangladesh.

**Islami Bank Bangladesh Ltd (IBBL):** Head Office, Islami Bank Tower, 40 Dilkusha C/A, POB 233, Dhaka 1000; tel. (2) 9563040; fax (2) 9564532; e-mail info@islamibankbd.com; internet www.islamibankbd.com; f. 1983 on Islamic banking principles; cap. 3,801.6m., res 8,039.7m., dep. 166,325.3m. (Dec. 2007); Chair. Prof. ABU NASSER MUHAMMED ABDUZ ZAHER; Man. Dir and CEO FARIDUDDIN AHMED; 196 brs.

**Mercantile Bank Ltd:** 61 Dilkusha C/A, Dhaka 1000; tel. (2) 9559333; fax (2) 9561213; e-mail mbl@bol-online.com; internet www.mblbd.com; f. 1999; cap. 1,199.1m., res 751.6m., dep. 32,462.5m. (Dec. 2006); Chair. MOHAMMED ABDUL JALIL; Man. Dir and CEO SHAH MOHAMMAD NURAL ALAM; 25 brs.

**National Bank Ltd:** 18 Dilkusha C/A, POB 3424, Dhaka 1000; tel. (2) 9563081; fax (2) 9563953; e-mail nblho@citechco.net; internet www.nblbd.com; f. 1983; 50% owned by sponsors and 50% by general public; cap. 805.5m., res 2,059.3m., dep. 40,350.9m. (Dec. 2006); Chair. PARVEEN HAQUE SIKDER; Man. Dir M. AMINUZZAMAN; 91 brs.

**National Credit and Commerce Bank Ltd:** 7–8 Motijheel C/A, GPOB 2920, Dhaka 1000; tel. (2) 9561902; fax (2) 9566290; e-mail nccbl@bdmail.net; internet www.nccbank-bd.com; f. 1993; 50% owned by sponsors, 50% by general public; cap. 1,201.8m., res 925.2m., dep. 28,147.3m. (Dec. 2006); Chair. TOFAZZAL HOSSAIN; Man. Dir MUHAMMAD NURUL AMIN; 49 brs.

**ONE Bank Ltd:** HRC Bhaban, 46 Kawaran Bazar C/A, Dhaka; tel. (2) 8122046; fax (2) 9134794; e-mail obl@onebankbd.com; internet www.onebankbd.com; f. 1999; cap. 888.0m., res 627.2m., dep. 20,253.3m. (Dec. 2006); Chair. SAYEED HOSSAIN CHOWDHURY; Man. Dir FARMAN R. CHOWDHURY.

**Oriental Bank Ltd:** T. K. Bhaban, 14th–16th Floors, 13 Karwan Bazar, Dhaka 1215; tel. (2) 9143361; fax (2) 9562768; internet www.oriental-bank.com; f. 1987 on Islamic banking principles; fmrly Al-Baraka Bank Bangladesh Ltd; name changed as above 2003; 34.68% owned by Al-Baraka Group, Saudi Arabia, 5.78% by Islamic Development Bank, Jeddah, 45.91% by local sponsors, 5.75% by Bangladesh Govt, 7.8% by general public; Chair. Dr MASUM AHMED CHOWDHURY; Man. Dir C. M. KOYES SAMI; 33 brs.

**Prime Bank Ltd:** Adamjee Court, Annex Bldg No. 2, 119–120 Motijheel C/A, Dhaka 1000; tel. (2) 9567265; fax (2) 9567230; e-mail info@primebank.com; internet www.prime-bank.com; f. 1995; cap. 1,750.0m., res 1,404.1m., dep. 54,724.1m. (Dec. 2006); Chair. AZAM J. CHOWDHURY; Man. Dir M. EHSANUL HAQUE; 65 brs.

**Pubali Bank Ltd:** Pubali Bank Bhaban, 26 Dilkusha C/A, POB 853, Dhaka 1000; tel. (2) 9551614; fax (2) 9564009; e-mail pubali@bdmail .net; internet www.pubalibangla.com; f. 1959 as Eastern Mercantile Bank Ltd; name changed to Pubali Bank in 1972; 98.5% privately owned, 1.5% state-owned; cap. 1,200.0m., res 2,395.8m., dep. 48,676.0m. (Dec. 2006); Chair. HAFIZ AHMED MAZUMDAR; Man. Dir HELAL AHMED CHOWDHURY; 350 brs.

**Social Investment Bank:** 15 Dilkusha C/A, Dhaka 1000; tel. (2) 9559014; fax (2) 9559013; e-mail sibl@bdonline.com; internet www .siblbd.com; f. 1995; cap. 585.0m., res 395.7m., dep. 17,940.5m. (Dec. 2006); Chair. Maj. (retd) Dr REZAUL HAQUE; Man. Dir K. M. ASHADUZ ZAMAN; 5 brs.

**Southeast Bank Ltd:** 1 Dilkusha C/A, 3rd Floor, Dhaka 1000; tel. (2) 9550081; fax (2) 9550093; e-mail seastbk@citechco.net; internet www.sebankbd.com; f. 1995; cap. 2,112.7m., res 2,344.8m., dep. 46,056.2m. (Dec. 2006); Chair. ALAMGIR KABIR; Pres. and Man. Dir NEAZ AHMED; 32 brs.

**United Commercial Bank Ltd:** Federation Bhaban, 4th–6th Floors, 60 Motijheel C/A, Dhaka 1000; tel. (2) 9568690; fax (2) 9560587; e-mail info@ucbl.com; internet www.ucbl.com; f. 1983; 50% owned by sponsors, 45% by general public and 5% by Govt; Chair. MD JAHANGIR ALAM KHAN; Man. Dir and CEO M. SHAJAHAN BHUIYAN; 84 brs.

**Uttara Bank Ltd:** 90 Motijheel C/A, POB 818, Dhaka 1000; tel. (2) 9551162; fax (2) 7168376; e-mail ublid@citecho.net; internet www .uttarabank-bd.com; f. 1965 as Eastern Banking Corpn Ltd; name changed to Uttara Bank in 1972 and to Uttara Bank Ltd in 1983; cap. 199.7m., res 1,881.8m., dep. 39,360.2m. (Dec. 2006); Chair. AZHARUL ISLAM; Man. Dir and CEO SHAMSUDDIN AHMED; 203 brs.

### Development Finance Organizations

**Bangladesh House Building Finance Corpn (BHBFC):** HBFC Bldg, 22 Purana Paltan, POB 2167, Dhaka 1000; tel. (2) 9562767; fax (2) 9561324; e-mail bhbfc@bangla.net; internet bhbfc.gov.bd; f. 1952; provides low-interest credit for residential house-building; 100% state-owned; cap. 972.9m. (Dec. 2003); Chair. A. S. ABDUL QADIR MAHMUD; Man. Dir Dr JADAB CHANDRA SAHA; 9 zonal offices, 13 regional offices and 2 camp offices.

**Bangladesh Krishi Bank (BKB):** 83–85 Motijheel C/A, POB 357, Dhaka 1000; tel. (2) 9560021; fax (2) 9561211; e-mail bkb@citechco .net; internet www.krishibank.org.bd; f. 1961; as the Agricultural Development Bank of Pakistan, name changed as above in 1973; provides credit for agricultural and rural devt; also performs all kinds of banking; 100% state-owned; cap. 1,400m., res 820.4m., dep. 44,611m. (June 2002); Chair. KHONDKAR IBRAHIM KHALED; Man. Dir MUKTER HUSSAIN; 938 brs.

**Bangladesh Samabaya Bank Ltd (BSBL):** 'Samabaya Sadan', 9D Motijheel C/A, POB 505, Dhaka 1000; tel. (2) 9564628; f. 1948; provides credit for agricultural co-operatives; Chair. Dr ABDUL MOYEEN KHAN; Gen. Man. MUHAMMAD ABDUL WAHED.

**Bangladesh Shilpa Bank (BSB)** (Industrial Development Bank): Shilpa Bank Bhaban, 8 Rajuk Ave, POB 975, Dhaka; tel. (2) 9556786; fax (2) 9562061; e-mail misd@shilpabank.gov.bd; internet www .shilpabank.gov.bd; f. 1972; fmrly Industrial Devt Bank; provides long- and short-term financing for industrial devt in the private and public sectors; also provides underwriting facilities and equity support; 51% state-owned; cap. 2,000.0m., res 957.5m., dep. 710.4m. (June 2005); Chair. Dr MUHAMMAD AMINUL ISLAM BHUIYAN; Man. Dir MIZANUR RAHMAN; 15 brs.

**Bangladesh Shilpa Rin Sangstha (BSRS)** (Industrial Loan Agency): BSRS Bhaban 12, Karwan Bazar Commercial Area, Dhaka 1215; tel. (2) 9137265; fax (2) 9111274; e-mail info@bsrs.org.bd; internet www.bsrs.org.bd; f. 1972; 100% state-owned; Chair. NAZEM A. CHOUDHURY; Man. Dir HAFIZ UL ISLAM; 4 brs.

**Bank of Small Industries and Commerce Bangladesh Ltd (BASIC Bank):** Suite 601–602, Sena Kalyan Bhaban, 6th Floor, 195 Motijheel C/A, Dhaka 1000; tel. (2) 9564830; fax (2) 9564829; e-mail basicho@citechco.net; internet www.basicbanklimited.com; f. 1988; 100% state-owned; cap. 300m., res 713m., dep. 10,698m. (Dec. 2002); Chair. MOHAMMAD NURUL AMIN; Man. Dir A. H. EKBAL HOSSAIN; 19 brs.

**Export-Import Bank of Bangladesh Ltd:** Printers' Bldg, 5 Rajuk Ave, Motijheel C/A, Dhaka 1000; tel. (2) 9561604; fax (2) 7162379; e-mail itd@eximbankbd.com; internet www.eximbankbd.com; f. 1999; cap. 3,3467.4m., res 810.9m., dep. 35,032.0m. (Dec. 2006); Chair. NAZRUL ISLAM MAZUMDER; Man. Dir KAZI MASIHUR RAHMAN; 32 brs.

**Grameen Bank:** Grameen Bank Bhavan, Mirpur 1, Dhaka 1216; tel. (2) 9005257-68; fax (2) 803559; internet www.grameen.com; f. 1976; provides credit for the landless rural poor; 6.97% owned by Govt; Chair. REHMAN SOBHAN; Man. Dir Dr MUHAMMAD YUNUS; 2,515 brs.

**Infrastructure Development Co Ltd (IDCOL):** UTC Bldg, 16th Floor, 8 Panthapath, Kawran Bazar, Dhaka 1215; tel. (2) 9114385; fax (2) 8116663; e-mail contact@idcol.org; internet www.idcol.org; f. 1999; state-owned; Chair. MUHAMMAD AMINUL ISLAM BHUIYAN; Exec. Dir and CEO MUHAMMAD SHAHEEDUL HAQUE.

**Investment Corpn of Bangladesh (ICB):** BSB Bldg, 12th–15th Floors, 8 DIT Ave, POB 2058, Dhaka 1000; tel. (2) 9563455; fax (2) 9563313; e-mail icb@agni.com; internet www.icb.gov.bd; f. 1976; provides investment banking services; 27% owned by Govt; cap. 500.0m., res 691.1m. (June 2004); Chair. FEROZ AHMED; Man. Dir MUHAMMAD ZIAUL HAQUE KHONDKER; 7 brs.

**Rajshahi Krishi Unnayan Bank:** Sadharan Bima Bhaban, Kazihata, Greater Rd, Rajshahi 6000; tel. (721) 775008; fax (721) 775947; e-mail info@rakub.org.bd; internet www.rakub.org.bd; f. 1987; 100% state-owned; Chair. MUHAMMAD YAHIA MOLLA; Man. Dir M. FAZLUL HOQUE; 357 brs.

### Banking Association

**Bangladesh Association of Banks:** Iqbal Centre, 12th Floor, 42 Kamal Atatürk Ave, Banani C/A, Dhaka 1213; tel. and fax (2) 8851015; e-mail bab@citechco.net; Chair. SYED MANZUR ELAHI.

## STOCK EXCHANGES

**Chittagong Stock Exchange:** CSE Bldg, 1080 Sheikh Mujib Rd, Agrabad, Chittagong; tel. (31) 714632; fax (31) 714101; e-mail info@ cse.com.bd; internet www.cse.com.bd; Chair. M. K. M. MOHIUDDIN; CEO A. B. SIDDIQUE.

**Dhaka Stock Exchange Ltd:** 9F Motijheel C/A, Dhaka 1000; tel. (2) 9564601; fax (2) 9564727; e-mail dse@bol-online.com; internet www .dsebd.org; f. 1954; 278 listed cos; Pres. ABDULLAH BOKHARI; CEO SALAHUDDIN AHMED KHAN.

### Regulatory Authority

**Bangladesh Securities and Exchange Commission:** Jiban Bima Tower, 15th, 16th and 20th Floors, 10 Dilkusha C/A, Dhaka 1000; tel. (2) 9568101; fax (2) 9563721; e-mail secbd@bdmail.net; internet www.secbd.org; f. 1993; Chair. FARUQ AHMAD SIDDIQI; CEO Dr MIRZA AZIZUL ISLAM.

## INSURANCE

**Department of Insurance:** Sadharan Bima Bhaban, 2nd Floor, 139 Motijheel C/A, Dhaka 1000; e-mail di@bdonline.com; attached to Ministry of Commerce; supervises activities of domestic and foreign insurers; Chief Controller of Insurance Dr MAHFUZUL HAQUE.

**Bangladesh Insurance Association:** Rupali Bima Bhaban, 7th Floor, 7 Rajuk Ave, Dhaka 1000; tel. (2) 9557330; fax (2) 9562345; e-mail bia@bdcom.com; Chair. NASIR A. CHOWDHURY.

**Bangladesh General Insurance Co Ltd:** 42 Dilkusha C/A, Dhaka 1000; tel. (2) 9555073; fax (2) 9564212; e-mail bgic@citechco.net; Chair. and Man. Dir M. A. SAMAD.

**Eastern Insurance Co Ltd:** 44 Dilkusha C/A, Dhaka 1000; tel. (2) 9563033; fax (2) 9569735; e-mail eicl@dhaka.net; Chair. MOHAMMED MOHSIN; Man. Dir A. K. M. IFTKEKHAR AHMAD.

**Jiban Bima Corpn:** 24 Motijheel C/A, POB 346, Dhaka 1000; tel. (2) 9552047; fax (2) 868112; state-owned; comprises 37 national life insurance cos; life insurance; Man. Dir A. K. M. MOSTAFIZUR RAHMAN.

**Pioneer Insurance Co Ltd:** 6th Floor, Jiban Bima Bhaban, 10 Dilkusha C/A, Dhaka 1000; tel. (2) 9557674; fax (2) 9557676; e-mail piclho@msnbd.net; internet www.pioneerinsurancebd.com; f. 1996; Man. Dir Q. A. F. M. SERAJUL ISLAM.

**Pragati Insurance Ltd:** Pragati Bhaban, 12th Floor, 20–21 Kawran Bazar, Dhaka 1215; tel. (2) 8117996; fax (2) 8122980; e-mail pilbima@bangla.net; Man. Dir A. K. M. RAFIQUL ISLAM.

**Reliance Insurance Ltd:** BSB Bldg, 8 Rajuk Ave, Dhaka 1000; tel. (2) 9560105; fax (2) 9562005; e-mail info@reliance-bd.com; f. 1988; Man. Dir AKHTAR AHMED.

**Sadharan Bima Corpn:** 33 Dilkusha C/A, Dhaka 1000; tel. (2) 9552070; fax (2) 9564197; e-mail head-office@sbc.org.bd; internet www.sbc.gov.bd; state-owned; general insurance; Chair. SIDDIQUR RAHMAN CHOUDHURY; Man. Dir ELIAS AHMED.

# Trade and Industry

## GOVERNMENT AGENCIES

**Board of Investment:** Jiban Bima Tower, 19th Floor, 10 Dilkusha C/A, Dhaka 1000; tel. (2) 9563570; fax (2) 9562312; e-mail ecboi@ bdmail.net; internet www.boi.gov.bd; f. 1989; Exec. Chair. KAMALUDDIN AHMED.

**Export Promotion Bureau:** TCB Bhaban, 1st Floor, 1 Kawran Bazar, Dhaka 1215; tel. (2) 9144821; fax (2) 9119531; e-mail info@epb.gov.bd; internet www.epb.gov.bd; f. 1972; attached to Ministry of Commerce; regional offices in Chittagong, Khulna, Rajshahi, Narayanganj, Comilla and Sylhet; Dir-Gen. KHALILUR RAHMAN; Vice-Chair. MUHAMMAD SHAHAB ULLAH.

**Petrobangla** (Bangladesh Oil, Gas and Mineral Corpn): Petrocenter Bhaban, 3 Kawran Bazar C/A, POB 849, Dhaka 1215; tel. (2) 8114972; fax (2) 9120224; e-mail petchair@petrobangla.org; internet www.petrobangla.org.bd; f. 1972; explores and develops gas, petroleum and mineral resources, manages Bangladesh Petroleum Exploration Co Ltd and Sylhet Gas Fields Ltd; Chair. Dr Sheikh ABDUR RASHID.

**Planning Commission:** Planning Commission Secretariat, G.O. Hostel, Sher-e-Bangla Nagar, Dhaka 1207; e-mail mohammadalibd@hotmail.com; internet www.plancomm.gov.bd; f. 1972; govt agency responsible for all aspects of economic planning and development including the preparation of the five-year plans and annual development programmes (in conjunction with appropriate govt ministries), promotion of savings and investment, compilation of statistics and evaluation of development schemes and projects; Planning Division Sec. JAFAR AHMAD CHOWDHURY.

**Privatization Commission:** Jiban Bima Tower, 14th Floor, 10 Dilkusha C/A, Dhaka 1000; tel. (2) 9551986; fax (2) 9556433; e-mail pb@bdonline.com; internet www.bangladeshonline.com/pb; f. 1993; Chair. KAZI ZAFRULLAH; Sec. ABDUL MAZID.

**Trading Corpn of Bangladesh:** 2nd Floor, TCB Bhaban, 1 Kawran Bazar, Dhaka 1215; tel. (2) 8111521; fax (2) 8113582; e-mail tcb@bdonline.com; internet www.tcb.gov.bd; f. 1972; national trade org. of the Ministry of Commerce; imports, exports and markets goods through appointed dealers and agents; Chair. MOHAMMAD ZIAUL ISLAM; Dir MOHAMMAD MUKHLESUR RAHMAN.

## DEVELOPMENT ORGANIZATIONS

**Bangladesh Chemical Industries Corpn:** BCIC Bhaban, 30–31 Dilkusha C/A, Dhaka; tel. (2) 955280; fax (2) 9564120; e-mail bciccomp@bangla.net; internet www.bcic.gov.bd; Chair. Maj.-Gen. (retd) IMAMUZ-ZAMAN.

**Bangladesh Export Processing Zones Authority (BEPZA):** BEPZA Complex, House 19/D, Rd 6, Dhaka 1000; tel. (2) 9670530; fax (2) 8650060; e-mail chairman@epzbangladesh.org.bd; internet www.epzbangladesh.org.bd; f. 1983 to plan, develop, operate and manage export processing zones (EPZs) in Bangladesh; Exec. Chair. Brig.-Gen. ASHRAF ABDULLAH YUSUF.

**Bangladesh Fisheries Development Corpn:** 24–25 Dilkusha C/A, Dhaka 1000; tel. (2) 9552689; fax (2) 9563990; e-mail bfdc@citechco.net; f. 1964; under Ministry of Fisheries and Livestock; development and commercial activities; Chair. Brig.-Gen. (retd) CHOWDHURY KHALEQUZZAMAN; Sec. A. K. M. SHAHIDUL ISLAM.

**Bangladesh Forest Industries Development Corpn:** 73 Motijheel C/A, Dhaka; tel. (2) 9552010; fax (2) 9563990; Chair. M. ATIKULLAH.

**Bangladesh Jute Mills Corpn:** Adamjee Court, 115–120 Motijheel C/A, Dhaka 1000; tel. (2) 9558182; fax (2) 9567508; e-mail info@bjmc.gov.bd; internet www.bjmc.gov.bd; f. 1972; operates 32 jute mills; bags, carpet backing cloth, yarn, twine, tape, felt, floor covering, etc.; Chair. ATHARUL ISLAM.

**Bangladesh Small and Cottage Industries Corpn (BSCIC):** 137/138 Motijheel C/A, Dhaka 1000; tel. (2) 9565612; fax (2) 9550704; e-mail cbscic@aitlbd.net; f. 1957; Chair. MUHAMMAD SIRAJUDDIN.

**Bangladesh Steel and Engineering Corpn (BSEC):** BSEC Bhaban, 102 Kazi Nazrul Islam Ave, Dhaka 1215; tel. (2) 9115144; fax (2) 8112846; e-mail bsec@bdcom.com; internet www.bsec.gov.bd; 16 industrial units; Chair. S. M. A. MANNAN; Gen. Man. (Marketing) ASHRAFUL HAQ; 2,826 employees.

**Bangladesh Sugar and Food Industries Corpn:** Adamjee Court 115–120, Motijheel C/A, Dhaka; tel. (2) 9565869; fax (2) 9550481; e-mail chinikal@bttb.net.bd; f. 1972; Chair. MOMTAJUL ISLAM.

## CHAMBERS OF COMMERCE

**Federation of Bangladesh Chambers of Commerce and Industry (FBCCI):** Federation Bhaban, 60 Motijheel C/A, Dhaka 1000; tel. (2) 9560598; fax (2) 9560588; e-mail fbcci@bol-online.com; internet www.fbcci-bd.org; f. 1973; comprises 221 trade asscns and 77 chambers of commerce and industry; Pres. ANNISUL HUQ; Sec.-Gen. SYED JAMALUDDIN.

**Barisal Chamber of Commerce and Industry:** Chamber Bhabab, Nasir Pool, Shaw Rd, POB 30, Barisal; tel. (431) 61876; fax (51) 66257; Pres. EBADUL HAQUE CHAN.

**Bogra Chamber of Commerce and Industry:** Chamber Bhaban, 2nd Floor, Kabi Nazrul Islam Rd, Jhawtola, Bogra 5800; tel. (51) 64138; fax (51) 66257; e-mail bccibgr@btcl.net.bd; f. 1963; Pres. Alhaj MOHAMMAD FAZLUR RAHMAN PAIKER.

**Chittagong Chamber of Commerce and Industry:** Chamber House, 38 Agrabad C/A, POB 481, Agrabad, Chittagong; tel. (31) 713366; fax (31) 710183; e-mail ccci@globalctg.net; internet www.chittagongchamber.com; f. 1959; more than 5,000 mems; Pres. SAIFUZZAMAN CHOWDHURY; Sec. OSMAN GANI CHOWDHURY.

**Comilla Chamber of Commerce and Industry:** Rammala Rd, Ranir Bazar, Comilla; tel. (81) 68075; Pres. AFZAL KHAN.

**Dhaka Chamber of Commerce and Industry:** Dhaka Chamber Bldg, 1st Floor, 65–66 Motijheel C/A, POB 2641, Dhaka 1000; tel. (2) 9552562; fax (2) 9560830; e-mail dcci@bangla.net; internet www.dhakachamber.com; f. 1958; 5,000 mems; Pres. MATIUR RAHMAN; Sr Vice-Pres. AM MUBASH-SHAR.

**Dinajpur Chamber of Commerce and Industry:** Chamber Bhaban, Maldhapatty, Dinajpur 5200; tel. (531) 63189; Pres. KHAIRUL ANAM.

**Faridpur Chamber of Commerce and Industry:** Chamber House, Niltuly, Faridpur; tel. (631) 63530; fax (631) 61070; Pres. KHANDOKER MOHSIN ALI.

**Foreign Investors' Chamber of Commerce and Industry:** 'Prime View', 7 Gulshan Ave, Gulshan 1, Dhaka 1212; tel. (2) 9892913; fax (2) 9893058; e-mail ficci@bangla.net; internet www.ficci.org.bd; f. 1963 as Agrabad Chamber of Commerce and Industry, name changed as above in 1987; Pres. MASIH AL-KARIM; Sec. M. A. MATIN.

**Khulna Chamber of Commerce and Industry:** 5 KDA C/A, Khulna; tel. (41) 721695; fax (41) 417937; e-mail kcci@bttb.net.bd; f. 1934; Pres. S. M. NAZRUL ISLAM.

**Kushtia Chamber of Commerce and Industry:** 15, S Rd, Kushtia; tel. (71) 54068; e-mail kushcham@kushtia.com; Pres. MOHAMMAD MOZIBAR RAHMAN.

**Metropolitan Chamber of Commerce and Industry:** Chamber Bldg, 4th Floor, 122–124 Motijheel C/A, Dhaka 1000; tel. (2) 7161028-30; fax (2) 9565211; e-mail sg@citechco.net; internet www.mccibd.org; f. 1904; 310 mems; Sec.-Gen. C. K. HYDER.

**Noakhali Chamber of Commerce and Industry:** Noakhali Pourshara Bhaban, 2nd Floor, Maiydee Court, Noakhali; tel. (321) 5229; Pres. MOHAMMAD NAZIBUR RAHMAN.

**Rajshahi Chamber of Commerce and Industry:** Chamber Bhaban, Station Rd, PO Ghoramara, Rajshahi 6100; tel. (721) 772115; fax (721) 772412; f. 1960; 800 mems; Pres. MOHAMMAD LUTFAR RAHMAN.

**Sylhet Chamber of Commerce and Industry:** Chamber Bldg, Jail Rd, POB 97, Sylhet 3100; tel. (821) 714403; fax (821) 715210; e-mail scci@btsnet.net; Pres. MOHD MOHIUDDIN.

## INDUSTRIAL AND TRADE ASSOCIATIONS

**Bangladesh Frozen Foods Exporters' Association:** 50/1 Inner Circular Rd, 2nd Floor, Shantinagar, Dhaka; tel. (2) 418720; fax (2) 837531; e-mail bffea@drik.dgd.toolnet.org; Pres. MAKSUDUR RAHMAN.

**Bangladesh Garment Manufacturers' and Exporters' Association:** 7–9 Karwanbazar, BTMC Bhaban, Dhaka 1215; tel. (2) 8115597; fax (2) 8113951; e-mail info@bgmea.com; internet www.bgmea.com; Pres. ANNISUL HUQ; Vice-Pres. NURUL HAQ SIKDAR.

**Bangladesh Jute Association:** BJA Bldg, 77 Motijheel C/A, Dhaka; tel. (2) 9552916; fax (2) 9560137; e-mail beejay@bangla.net; internet www.juteministry.org/html/bja.html; Chair. FARHAND AHMED AKHAND; Sec. S. H. PRODHAN.

**Bangladesh Jute Exporters' Association:** Nahar Mansion, 2nd Floor, 150 Motijheel C/A, Dhaka 1000; tel. (2) 9561102.

**Bangladesh Jute Goods Association:** Nahar Mansion, 2nd Floor, 150 Motijheel C/A, Dhaka 1000; tel. (2) 253640; f. 1979; 17 mems; Chair. M. A. KASHEM; Sec. Haji MOHAMMAD ALI.

**Bangladesh Jute Mills Association:** Adamjee Court, 4th Floor, 115–120 Motijheel C/A, Dhaka 1000; tel. (2) 9560071; fax (2) 9566472; e-mail bjmajutegood@agnionline.com; Chair. KAMRAN T. RAHMAN.

**Bangladesh Jute Spinners' Association:** 55 Purana Paltan, 3rd Floor, Dhaka 1000; tel. (2) 9551317; fax (2) 9562772; internet www.bjsa.org; f. 1979; 44 mems; Chair. SHABBIR YOUSUF; Sec. SHAHIDUL KARIM.

**Bangladesh Knitwear Manufacturers' and Exporters' Association (BKMEA):** National Plaza, 4th Floor, 1/G Free School St, Sonagargaon Rd, Dhaka; tel. (2) 8620377; fax (2) 9673337; e-mail info@bangla.net; internet www.bkmea.com; f. 1996; Pres. FAZLUL HOQUE.

**Bangladesh Tea Board:** 171–172 Baizid Bostami Rd, Nasirabad, Chittagong; tel. (31) 682903; fax (31) 682863; e-mail btb@spnetctg.com; internet www.teaboard.gov.bd; f. 1951; regulates, controls and promotes the cultivation and marketing of tea, both in Bangladesh and abroad; Chair. Brig.-Gen. MOSHARRAF HOSSAIN.

**Bangladesh Textile Mills Association:** Moon Mansion, 6th Floor, Block M, 12 Dilkusha C/A, Dhaka 1000; tel. (2) 9552799; fax (2) 9563320; e-mail btma@citechco.net; internet www.btmadhk.com; Chair. M. A. AWAL.

**Bangladeshiyo Cha Sangsad** (Tea Association of Bangladesh): 'Progressive Tower', 4th Floor, 1837 Sheikh Mujib Rd (Badamtali), Agrabad, Chittagong 4100; tel. (31) 716407; f. 1952; Chair. M. SALMAN ISPAHANI; Sec. G. S. DHAR.

## UTILITIES

### Electricity

**Bangladesh Atomic Energy Commission (BAEC):** 4 Kazi Nazrul Islam Ave, POB 158, Dhaka 1000; tel. (2) 5021600; fax (2) 8613051; e-mail baec@agni.com; f. 1964 as Atomic Energy Centre of the fmr Pakistan Atomic Energy Comm. in East Pakistan; reorg. 1973; operates an atomic energy research establishment and a 3-MW research nuclear reactor (inaugurated in January 1987) at Savar, an atomic energy centre at Dhaka, etc.; Chair. M. A. QUAIYUM; Sec. RAFIQUL ALAM.

**Bangladesh Energy Regulatory Commission:** Anchor Tower, Level 7, 1/1B Sonargaon Rd, Dhaka 1205; tel. (2) 9669925; internet www.berc.org.bd; f. 2004; regulates activities of power sector; Sec. ABDUL BARI.

**Bangladesh Power Development Board:** WAPDA Bldg, Motijheel C/A, Dhaka; tel. (2) 9562154; fax (2) 9564765; e-mail chbpdb@bol-online.com; internet www.bpdb.gov.bd; f. 1972; under Ministry of Power, Energy and Mineral Resources; generation, transmission and distribution of electricity; installed capacity 4,710 MW (2002); Chair. A. N. M. RIZWAN.

**Dhaka Electric Supply Co Ltd (DESCO):** House 3, Rd 24, Block K, Banani Model Town, Dhaka 1213; tel. (2) 8859642; fax (2) 823140; internet www.desco.org.bd; f. 1997; Chair. Brig.-Gen. NAZRUL HASAN; Man. Dir Eng. SALEH AHMED.

**Dhaka Power Distribution Co Ltd (DPDC):** SCADA Bhaboon, Kataboon, Sonargaon Rd, Dhaka 1000; f. 2008 to replace Dhaka Electric Supply Authority; under Ministry of Power, Energy and Mineral Resources; Man. Dir ATAUL MASUD.

**Power Grid Company of Bangladesh Ltd (PGCB):** Red Crescent Concord Tower, 6th Floor, 17 Mohakhali C/A, Dhaka 1212; tel. and fax (2) 9888589; e-mail info@pgcb.org.bd; internet www.pgcb.org.bd; f. 1996; responsible for power transmission throughout Bangladesh; Chair. A. N. M. RIZWAN; Sec. MOHAMMAD SALIM.

**Rural Electrification Board:** House 3, Rd 12, Nikanja-2, Khilkhet, Dhaka 1229; tel. (2) 8924035; fax (2) 8916400; e-mail seict@reb.gov.bd; internet www.reb.gov.bd; under Ministry of Power, Energy and Mineral Resources; Chair. HABIB ULLAH MAJUMDER.

### Water

**Chittagong Water Supply and Sewerage Authority:** Dampara, Chittagong; tel. (31) 621606; fax (31) 610465; f. 1963; govt corpn; Chair. SULTAN MAHMUD CHOWDHURY.

**Dhaka Water Supply and Sewerage Authority:** 98 Kazi Nazrul Islam Ave, Kawran Bazar, Dhaka 1215; tel. (2) 8116792; fax (2) 8112109; e-mail secretary@dwasa.org.bd; internet www.dwasa.org.bd; f. 1963; govt corpn; Man. Dir RAIHANUL ABEDIN.

## MAJOR COMPANIES

### Automobile Industry

**Navana Ltd/Aftab Automobiles Ltd:** 125A Motijheel C/A, Dhaka 1000; tel. (2) 9552212; fax (2) 9566324; e-mail navana@bangla.net; internet www.navana.com; f. 1964; distributor of vehicles and tyres; Chair. and Man. Dir SHAFIUL ISLAM KAMAL.

### Chemicals

**ACI Ltd:** ACI Centre, 245 Tejgaon Industrial Area, Dhaka 1212; tel. (2) 9885694; fax (2) 9884784; e-mail info@aci-bd.com; internet www.aci-bd.com; f. 1992; mfr of pharmaceuticals, personal care, food and animal health products and agrochemicals; also operates a salt refining plant at Rupganj under ACI Salt Ltd co; entered into jt venture with Godrej meat-packing business of India to establish a poultry processing co under ACI Godrej Agrovet Pvt Ltd; sales 3,413.1m. taka (2005); Chair. M. ANIS UD DOWLA; Group Man. Dir ARIF DOWLA; 2,000 employees.

**The ACME Laboratories Ltd:** Court de la ACME 1/4, Mirpur Rd, Kallayanpur, Dhaka 1207; tel. (2) 9004194; fax (2) 9016872; e-mail headoffice@acmeglobal.com; internet acmeglobal.com/acme_laboratories.htm; f. 1954; mfr and exporter of pharmaceuticals; Chair. NASIR-UR RAHMAN SINHA; Man. Dir MIZANUR RAHMAN SINHA.

**Ambee Pharmaceuticals Ltd:** 1, Rd 71, Gulshan 2, Dhaka 1212; tel. (2) 8813991; fax (2) 8827777; e-mail info@ambeepharma.com; internet www.ambeepharma.com; f. 1976; Chair. and Man. Dir AZIZ MOHAMMAD BHAI.

**Amico Laboratories Ltd:** 12/3, Tajmahal Rd, Mohammadpur, Dhaka 1207; tel. (2) 8125656; fax (2) 8118346; e-mail info@amicolab.com; internet www.amicolab.com; f. 1976; relaunched under new ownership in 1994; manufacturing, marketing and distribution of pharmaceutical products; Chair. Al-haj MOCKBUL HOSSAIN; Man. Dir MOJIBUL ISLAM.

**Aristopharma Ltd:** 7 Purana Paltan Line, Dhaka 1000; tel. (2) 9351691; fax (2) 8317005; e-mail aplhc@bangla.net; internet www.aristopharma.com; f. 1986; manufacturing, marketing and exporting of finished pharmaceutical formulations; Chair. and Man. Dir M. A. HASSAN; 2,600 employees.

**Aventis Ltd:** 6/2/A, Segun Bagicha, Dhaka 1000; tel. (2) 9562893; fax (2) 9550009; e-mail info.bd@sanofi-aventis.com; internet www.sanofi-aventis.com.bd; Bangladesh subsidiary of Sanofi-Aventis group; pharmaceuticals; Man. Dir IFTEKHARUL ISLAM.

**Beximco Pharmaceuticals:** 19 Dhanmondi R/A, Rd 7, Dhaka 1205; tel. (2) 8619151; fax (2) 8613888; e-mail info@bpl.net; internet www.beximco-pharma.com; f. 1976; largest producer of drugs and medicines in Bangladesh; member of Beximco Group; commenced export of pharmaceutical products to Central America in March 2007; annual turnover US $50m. (2006); Chair. SOHAIL RAHMAN; CEO NAZMUL HASSAN; 2,043 employees.

**General Pharmaceuticals Ltd:** 48/A, Rd 11/A, Dhanmondi R/A, Dhaka 1209; tel. (2) 9132594; fax (2) 9120657; e-mail info@generalpharma.com; internet www.generalpharma.com; f. 1984; nationwide distribution of pharmaceutical products; Man. Dir Dr MOMENUL HAQ; 2,000 employees.

**Incepta Pharmaceuticals Ltd:** 40 Shahid Tajuddin Ahmed Sarani, Tejgaon I/A, Dhaka 1208; tel. (2) 8837811; fax (2) 8837952; e-mail incepta@inceptapharma.com; internet www.inceptapharma.com; f. 1999; mfr and marketer of pharmaceuticals; Man. Dir ABDUL MUKTADIR.

**Karnaphuli Fertilizer Co Ltd (KAFCO):** IDB Bhaban, 13th Floor, E/8–A, Rokeya Sharani, Sher-e-Bangla Nagar, Dhaka 1207; tel. (2) 8125377; fax (2) 8124490; e-mail kafco@kafcobd.com; internet www.kafcobd.com; f. 1981; cap. and res US $125m., sales US $200m. (2004/05); Bangladesh's largest multinational joint-venture project; 100% export-orientated fully integrated fertilizer complex in Chittagong; exports of 671,000 metric tons of granular urea and 160,000 tons of ammonia (2004/05); Man. Dir PETER A. MAY; Chair. MUHAMMAD NURUL AMIN; 611 employees.

**Pharmadesh Laboratories Ltd:** 334, Segun Bagicha, Dhaka 1000; tel. (2) 9330048; e-mail pharmadesh_bd@yahoo.com; internet www.pharmadesh.com; f. 1961; pharmaceuticals; cap. 100m. taka; Chair. AZIZUR RAHMAN; Man. Dir HABIBUR RAHMAN; 400 employees.

**Square Pharmaceuticals Ltd:** Square Centre, 48 Mohakhali C/A, Dhaka 1212; tel. (2) 8859007; fax (2) 8834941; e-mail pmdmail@squaregroup.com; internet www.squarepharma.com.bd; f. 1958; part of Square Group of cos; cap. and res 7,333.3m. taka, sales 8,711.0m. taka (2006/07); Chair. SAMSON H. CHOWDHURY; 3,001 employees.

**Zia Fertilizer Co Ltd:** Ashuganj, Brahmanbaria 3403; tel. (2) 9352055; fax (2) 9351847; f. 1974; urea and ammonia fertilizer producers; sales 1,826.8m. taka (2001); Man. Dir MOSTAFIZUR RAHMAN; Gen. Man. ROKONUDDIN AHMED; 1,210 employees.

### Cotton Textiles, Jute, Man-Made Fibres

**Abir International:** 75 Saleh Sadan, 4th Floor, 145 Motijheel C/A, Dhaka 1000; tel. and fax (2) 7166368; e-mail abirint@bdcom.com; f. 1990; exporter of jute goods, ready-made garments, leather goods and household textiles; Pres. ASLAM HOSSAIN.

**Ahad Jute Mills Ltd:** 3rd Floor, 55 Purana Paltam Azad Centre, Dhaka 1000; tel. (2) 9567533; fax (2) 9553439; Man. Dir Dr S. M. ASHIQUZZAMAN.

**Amin Brothers Textile Mills Ltd:** 3rd Floor, 108 Islampur Rd, Dhaka 1000; tel. (2) 852842; fax (2) 9564676; mfr and wholesaler of fabrics; Man. Dir ABDUL RAZZAK AMIN.

**Apex Spinning and Knitting Mills Ltd:** Biman Bhaban, 5th Floor, 100 Motijheel C/A, Dhaka 1000; tel. (2) 9562383; fax (2) 9562213; e-mail info@apexknitting.com; internet www.apexknitting.com; f. 1990; mfr and exporter of garments; cap. and res 191m. taka, sales 1,010m. taka (2003/04); Chair. ZAFAR AHMED; Man. Dir Dr ZAHUR AHMED; 3,017 employees.

**Bangladesh Jute Mills Corporation (BJMC):** Adamjee Court (Annexe 1), 115–120 Motijheel C/A, Dhaka 1000; tel. (2) 9558182; fax (2) 9567508; e-mail info@bjmc.gov.bd; internet www.bjmc.gov.bd; f. 1972; operates 32 jute mills; manufacturing, marketing and exporting of all kinds of jute goods; Chair. ATHARUL ISLAM.

**Bangladesh Textile Mills Corporation (BTMC):** Bastra Bhaban, 7–9 Kawran Bazar C/A, Dhaka 1215; tel. (2) 9115051; fax (2)

8114600; e-mail btmc@citecho.net; internet www.btmc.gov.bd; f. 1972; mfr of cotton and wool items; Chair. Brig.-Gen. (retd) ANWAR HUSAIN CHOWDHURY; Man. Dir MAHMOUD E. ALAM.

**Dacca Dyeing and Manufacturing Co Ltd:** Sharif Mansion, 4th Floor, 56–57 Motijheel C/A, Dhaka 1000; tel. (2) 9558131; fax (2) 9560666; e-mail info@dd.qc-group.com; internet www.dacca-dyeing.com; f. 1963; mfr and exporter of household linen and garment fabrics; cap. and res 323.5m. taka, sales 65.5m. taka (2000); Chair. SAIFUDDIN QUADER CHOWDHURY; Man. Dir GIASUDDIN QUADER CHOWDHURY; 350 employees.

**Islam Jute Mills Ltd:** 727 Satmasjid Rd, Dhanmondi R/A, Dhaka 1205; tel. (2) 9118791; fax (2) 813228; Man. Dir RAHIMA BEGUM.

**Karim Jute Mills Ltd:** Karim Chambers, 99 Motijheel C/A, Dhaka 1000; tel. (2) 9555729; f. 1957; mfr of jute products; Dir ABDUL GHANI AHMED; 3,200 employees.

**Prime Textile Spinning Mills Ltd:** Sena Kalyan Bhaban, 8th Floor, 195 Motijheel C/A, Dhaka 1000; tel. (2) 9564851; fax (2) 9564857; e-mail prime@bangla.net; f. 1989; producer of export-quality yarn; cap. and res 1,027.2m. taka, sales 707.0m. taka (1998/99); Chair. and Man. Dir M. A. AWAL; 1,497 employees.

**Reaz Garments Ltd:** BTMC Bhaban, 3rd Floor, 7–9 Kawran Bazar C/A, Dhaka 1215; tel. (2) 9120785; fax (2) 9123010; mfrs and exporters of ready-made garments; Contact SALAUDDIN SAGAR MOHD.

**Square Textiles Ltd:** Square Centre, 48 Mohakhali C/A, Dhaka 1212; tel. (2) 8827729; fax (2) 8828768; f. 1997; mfr and exporter of textiles; cap. and res 1,349m. taka (2004); Man. Dir TAPAN CHOWDHURY.

### Gas and Petroleum

**Bangladesh Petroleum Corporation (BPC):** BSC Bhaban, Saltgola Rd, Chittagong 4100; tel. (31) 716336; fax (31) 720147; e-mail info@bpc.gov.bd; internet bpc.gov.bd; f. 1976; state-owned; producer, importer and exporter of petroleum products, manages Jamuna Oil Co Ltd and Padma Oil Co Ltd; Chair. ANWARUL KARIM.

**Bangladesh Petroleum Exploration Co Ltd:** Shah Jalal Tower 80/A-B, 4th Floor, Shiddeshwari Circular Rd, Dhaka 1217; tel. and fax (2) 9360119; fax (2) 9355704; e-mail gmplanning@bapex.com.bd; internet www.bapex.com.bd; explores and develops gas, petroleum and mineral resources; state-owned; Chair. MOHAMMAD MOHSIN.

**BOC Bangladesh Ltd:** 285 Tejgaon I/A, Dhaka 1208; tel. (2) 8821240; fax (2) 8823771; e-mail corporate@bocbangladesh.com; Man. Dir WALIUR RAHMAN BHUIYAN.

**Padma Oil Co Ltd:** Padma Bhaban, Strand Rd, POB 4, Chittagong 4000; tel. (31) 614235; fax (31) 618312; e-mail padma@spnetctg.com; f. 1965; produces and markets pesticides and markets petroleum products; cap. and res 666.1m. taka, sales 24,930m. taka (2001/02); Chair. MOHAMMAD RAFIQUL ISLAM; CEO A. JAMAL KHAN CHOWDHURY; 1,048 employees.

**Petrobangla** (Bangladesh Oil, Gas and Mineral Corpn): Petrocenter Bhaban, 3 Kawran Bazar C/A, Dhaka 1215; tel. (2) 8117116; fax (2) 9120224; e-mail admn@petrobangla.org.bd; internet www.petrobangla.org.bd; f. 1972; state-owned; explores and develops gas, petroleum and mineral resources, manages Bangladesh Petroleum Exploration Co Ltd and Sylhet Gas Fields Ltd; Chair. JALAL AHMED; 8,312 employees.

### Paper

**Bangladesh Monospool Paper Manufacturing Co Ltd:** 3rd Floor, BCIC Bhabhan, 30–31 Dillkusha C/A, Dhaka 1000; tel. (2) 9560600; fax (2) 9564192; internet monospool.com.

**Bangladesh Paper Products Ltd:** 12 Abedin Colony, Love Lane, Chittagong; tel. (31) 206327; fax (31) 223172; f. 1963; Chair. and Man. Dir MOHAMMED SHAFIQUR RAHAMAN; Exec. Dir M. S. ISLAM; 362 employees.

**Eagle Box and Carton Group:** Postagola, Dhaka 1204; tel. (2) 7411119; fax (2) 7410641; e-mail eaglebox@bol-online.com; f. 1961; mfr of packaging goods; Man. Dir SHAMSUL ARAFIN.

### Miscellaneous

**A. K. Khan Group:** Batali Hills, Chittagong 4000; tel. (31) 611050; fax (31) 610596; e-mail akkhan@spnetctg.com; internet akkhangroup.com; interests in textiles, telecommunications, manufacturing, distribution and trading; Chair. A. K. SHAMSUDDIN KHAN; Man. Dir SALAHUDDIN KASEM KHAN.

**Akij Group:** Akij Chamber, 73 Dilkusha C/A, Dhaka 1000; tel. (2) 9563008; fax (2) 9564519; e-mail info@akij.net; internet www.akij.net; interests incl. tobacco, textiles, printing and packaging, and real estate.

**Alpha Tobacco Manufacturing Co Ltd:** Jatiya Scout Bhaban 70/1, Purana Paltan, Line Kakrail, Dhaka 1000; tel. (2) 9332342; fax (2) 9332968; e-mail erba@bdmail.net; Chair. A. AHMED YUSUF.

**Apex Foods Ltd:** Biman Bhaban, 5th Floor, 100 Motijheel C/A, Dhaka 1000; tel. (2) 9562383; fax (2) 9562213; e-mail apex@apexfoods.com; internet www.apexfoods.com; f. 1980; mfr and exporter of frozen seafood; cap. and res 360.8m. taka, sales 837.1m. taka (2000/01); Man. Dir ZAFAR AHMED; 506 employees.

**Apex Tannery Ltd:** DCCI Bldg, 2nd Floor, 65–66 Motijheel C/A, Dhaka 1000; tel. (2) 9566182; fax (2) 9562386; e-mail mandal@bdcom.com; mfr of leather and leather goods; Chair. SYED MANZUR ELAHI.

**Bata Bangladesh:** Tongi Industrial Area, Tongi, Gazipur; tel. (2) 9800501; fax (2) 9800511; e-mail contact@batabd.com; internet www.batabd.com; f. 1962; subsidiary co of Bata Shoe Organization; mfr of footwear and leather; Man. Dir DOUGLAS HEARNS.

**Bengal Fine Ceramics Ltd:** H. H. Bhaban, 2nd–3rd Floors, 52/1 New Eskaton Rd, Dhaka 1000; tel. (2) 9345174; fax (2) 8314933; e-mail bfc@bdmail.net; internet www.bfcl.net; Man. Dir R. MOWDUD KHAN.

**Bengal Glass Works Ltd:** 2, Sadharan Bima Bhaban, 10th Floor, 139 Motijheel C/A, Dhaka 1000; tel. (2) 9565524; fax (2) 9565523; e-mail bglass@citech.net; f. 1967; glass bottle and electric bulb mfr; sales US $10.0m. (2005); Chair. and Man. Dir HISHAMUDDIN SALEH; 350 employees.

**China-Bangla Ceramic Industries Ltd:** National Plaza, 5th Floor, 1/G Free School St, Sonargaon Rd, Dhaka 1205; tel. (2) 9668278; fax (2) 9674076; e-mail info@cbctiles.com; internet www.cbctiles.com; f. 2001; jt venture public ltd co between Bangladesh and People's Republic of China; mfrs ceramics and homogenous tiles; Chair. QU BO; Man. Dir MUHAMMAD SHIRAJUL ISLAM MOLLAH.

**Meghna Group of Industries:** Fresh Villa, House 15, Rd 34, Gulshan 1, Dhaka 1212; tel. (2) 9887545; fax (2) 9884896; internet www.meghnagroup.biz; products incl. food and cement; Chair. and Man. Dir MOSTAFA KAMAL.

**Meher Industries (Bangladesh) Ltd:** Airport Rd, Dhaka 1000; electronics.

**People's Ceramic Industries Ltd:** Amin Court, 3rd Floor, 62–63 Motijheel C/A, Dhaka 1000; tel. (2) 9561947; fax (2) 9561946; e-mail pepcer@bol-online.com; internet www.peoplesceramic.com; f. 1962; mfr of fine porcelain tableware; associates in the United Kingdom, Greece, Belgium and France; Man. Dir LUTFUR RAHMAN.

**PRAN Group:** Property Heights, 12 R. K. Mission Rd, Dhaka 1203; tel. (2) 9563126; fax (2) 9556415; e-mail amcl@prangroup.com; internet www.pranfoods.net; f. 1980; fruit and vegetable processing, dairy products; Group CEO Maj.-Gen. (retd) AMJAD KHAN CHOWDHURY.

**Rahimafrooz Batteries Ltd:** 705 West Nakhalpara, Tejgaon, Dhaka 1215; tel. (2) 9893442; fax (2) 8827780; e-mail raco@rahimafrooz.com; internet www.rahimafrooz.com; f. 1960; mfr of batteries; cap. and res 215m. taka, sales 400m. taka; Man. Dir FEROZ RAHIM; Gen. Man. K. M. ALI; 504 employees.

**Standard Ceramic Industries Ltd:** Amin Court, 3rd Floor, 62–63 Motijheel C/A, Dhaka 1000; tel. (2) 9561947; fax (2) 9561950; e-mail info@standardceramic.net; internet standardceramic.net; f. 1993; mfr of stoneware products; Chair. and Man. Dir ANSARUDDIN AHMED; 600 employees.

## TRADE UNIONS

In 2001 only 4.3% of the non-agricultural labour force was unionized. There were about 4,200 registered unions, organized mainly on a sectoral or occupational basis. There were 23 national trade unions to represent workers at the national level.

**Bangladesh Free Trade Union Congress (BFTUC):** 6A 1–19 Mirpur, Dhaka 1216; tel. (2) 8017001; fax (2) 8015919; e-mail bftuc@agni.com; Gen. Sec. M. R. CHOWDHURY; 115,000 mems.

**Bangladesh Jatio Sramik League (BJSL):** POB 2730, Dhaka; tel. (2) 282063; fax (2) 863470; 62,000 mems.

# Transport

## RAILWAYS

In July 2000 Bangladesh Railway and the Indian Railway Board signed an agreement to resume rail services on the Benapole–Petrapole route. The service opened fully in January 2001. In December regular rail services between Bangabandhu and Kolkata (Calcutta, India) resumed, as did those between Dhaka and Kolkata in April 2008.

**Bangladesh Railway:** Rail Bhaban, 16 Abdul Ghani Rd, Dhaka 1000; tel. (2) 9561200; fax (2) 9563413; e-mail dg_rail@bangla.net; internet www.railway.gov.bd; f. 1862; supervised by the Ministry of Communications; divided into East and West Zones, with East Zone HQ at Chittagong (tel. (31) 843200; fax (31) 843215) and West Zone HQ at Rajshahi (tel. (721) 761576; fax (721) 761982); total length of 2,855 route km; 459 stations; Dir-Gen. BELAYET HOSSAIN; Gen. Man.

(East Zone) HALIM F. M. ABDUL MEAH; Gen. Man. (West Zone) MUHAMMAD AKHTARUZ ZAMAN.

### ROADS

In 1999 the total length of roads in use was 207,486 km (19,775 km of highways, 17,297 km of secondary roads and 170,413 km of other roads), of which 9.5% were paved. In 1992 the World Bank approved Bangladesh's US $700m. Jamuna Bridge Project. The construction of the 4.8-km bridge, which was, for the first time, to link the east and the west of the country with a railway and road network, was begun in early 1994. The bridge, which was renamed the Bangabandhu Jamuna Multipurpose Bridge, was officially opened in June 1998.

In June 1999 the first direct passenger bus service between Bangladesh (Dhaka) and India (Kolkata) was inaugurated.

**Bangladesh Road Transport Corpn:** Paribahan Bhaban, 21 Rajuk Ave, Dhaka; tel. (2) 9555786; fax (2) 9555788; e-mail info@brtc.gov.bd; internet www.brtc.gov.bd; f. 1961; state-owned; operates transport services, incl. truck division; transports govt food grain; Chair. HEDAYETULLAH AL MAMUN.

### INLAND WATERWAYS

In Bangladesh there are some 8,433 km of navigable waterways, which transport 70% of total domestic and foreign cargo traffic and on which are located the main river ports of Dhaka, Narayanganj, Chandpur, Barisal and Khulna. A river steamer service connects these ports several times a week. Vessels of up to 175 m overall length can be navigated on the Karnaphuli river.

**Bangladesh Inland Water Transport Corpn:** 5 Dilkusha C/A, Dhaka 1000; tel. (2) 9552561; internet www.mos.gov.bd/biwtc.htm; f. 1972; 608 vessels.

### SHIPPING

The chief ports are Chittagong, where the construction of a second dry-dock is planned, and Mongla, where a modern seaport is being developed.

**Atlas Shipping Lines Ltd:** 142 Sir Iqbal Rd, 3rd Floor, Khulna; tel. and fax (4) 1732669; e-mail atlas@khulna.bangla.net; Man. Dir S. U. CHOWDHURY; Gen. Man. M. KAMAL HAYAT.

**Bangladesh Shipping Corpn:** BSC Bhaban, Saltgola Rd, POB 641, Chittagong 4100; tel. (31) 724479; fax (31) 710506; e-mail bsc-ctg@spnetctg.com; internet www.mos.gov.bd/bsc.htm; f. 1972; maritime shipping; 13 vessels; Chair. MOFAZZAL HOSSAIN CHOWDHURY MAYA; Man. Dir JAMIL OSMAN.

**Bengal Shipping Line Ltd:** Palm View, 100A Agrabad C/A, Chittagong 4100; tel. (31) 714800; fax (31) 710362; e-mail bsl@mkrgroup.com; Chair. MOHAMMED ABDUL AWWAL; Man. Dir MOHAMMED ABDUL MALEK.

**Broadway Shipping Line:** 39 Dilkusha C/A, Dhaka 1223; tel. (2) 404598; fax (2) 412254.

**Chittagong Port Authority:** POB 2013, Chittagong 4100; tel. (31) 812200; fax (31) 710593; e-mail info@cpa.gov.bd; internet www.cpa.gov.bd; f. 1887; provides bunkering, ship repair, towage and lighterage facilities as well as provisions and drinking water supplies; Chair. MUHAMMAD FARUQUE.

**Continental Liner Agencies:** Facy Bldg, 3rd Floor, 87 Agrabad C/A, Chittagong; tel. (31) 721572; fax (31) 710965; Man. SAIFUL AHMED; Dir (Technical and Operations) Capt. MAHFUZUL ISLAM.

**Nishan Shipping Lines Ltd:** Monzoor Bldg, 1st Floor, 67 Agrabad C/A, Chittagong; tel. (31) 710855; fax (31) 710044; Dir Capt. A. K. M. ALAMGIR.

### CIVIL AVIATION

There is an international airport at Dhaka (Zia International Airport), situated at Kurmitola, with the capacity to handle 5m. passengers annually. There are also airports at all major towns. In 1997 the civil aviation industry was deregulated to permit domestic competition to Biman Bangladesh Airlines.

**Best Air:** House 43, Rd 1/A, Block J, Baridhara Diplomatic Area, Dhaka 1212; tel. (2) 8855254; fax (2) 8860248; e-mail info@bestairbd.com; internet www.bestairbd.com; f. 1999; est. as helicopter operator, later freight airline; currently operates international and domestic passenger services; Chair. M. HAIDER UZZAMAN.

**Biman Bangladesh Airlines:** Head Office, Balaka, Kurmitola, Dhaka 1229; tel. (2) 8917400; fax (2) 8913005; e-mail dgmcmis@bdbiman.com; internet www.bimanair.com; f. 1972; fmrly state-owned; transferred to private ownership in 2007; domestic services to seven major towns; international services to 19 destinations in the Middle East, the Far East, Europe, and North America; CEO and Man. Dir Dr M. A. MOMEN.

**GMG Airlines:** ABC House, 9th Floor, 8 Kamal Atatürk Ave, Banani, Dhaka 1213; tel. (2) 8825845; fax (2) 8826115; e-mail gmgair@gmggroup.com; internet www.gmgairlines.com; f. 1997; private, domestic airline; Dir (Flight Operations) Capt. HABIBUR RAHMAN; Man. Dir HAFIZUR RAHMAN BHUIYAN.

**Royal Bengal:** House 56C, Rd 132, Gulshan 1, Dhaka 1212; internet www.royalbengalairline.com; owned by Royal Bengal Group; operates domestic services as well as flights to India; Group Chair. ABDUL KADIR CHOWDHURY.

**United Airways (BD) Ltd:** tel. (2) 8931712; fax (2) 8955959; e-mail info@uabdl.com; internet www.uabdl.com; private domestic airline; gained permit for international flights 2008; Chair. and Man. Dir Capt. TASBIRUL AHMED CHOUDHURY.

## Tourism

Tourist attractions include the cities of Dhaka and Chittagong, Cox's Bazar—which has the world's longest beach (120 km)—on the Bay of Bengal, and Teknaf, at the southernmost point of Bangladesh. Tourist arrivals decreased from 271,270 in 2004 to 207,662 in 2005. Earnings from tourism reached US $76m. in 2004. The majority of visitors are from India, Pakistan, the People's Republic of China, the United Kingdom and the USA.

**Bangladesh Parjatan Corpn** (National Tourism Organization): 233 Biruttam Ziaur Rahman Rd, Tejgaon, Dhaka 1215; tel. (2) 8117855; fax (2) 8126501; e-mail bpcho@bangla.net; internet www.bangladeshtourism.gov.bd; f. 1973; there are four tourist information centres in Dhaka, and one each in Bogra, Chittagong, Cox's Bazar, Dinajpur, Khulna, Kuakata, Rangamati, Rangpur, Rajshahi and Sylhet; Chair. Dr MAHFUZUL HAQUE.

## Defence

As assessed at November 2007, the total active armed forces numbered 150,000: the army had a total strength of 120,000, the navy 16,000 and the air force 14,000. The paramilitary forces, which totalled 63,910, included an armed police reserve of 5,000, a 20,000-strong security guard and the Bangladesh Rifles (border guard), numbering 38,000. Military service is voluntary.

**Defence Budget:** Estimated at 52,830m. taka for 2007/08.

**Chief of Army Staff:** Lt-Gen. MOEEN U. AHMED.

**Chief of Naval Staff:** Vice-Adm. SARWAR JAHAN NIZAM.

**Chief of Air Staff:** Air Marshal SHAH MOHAMMAD ZIAUR RAHMAN.

**Dir-Gen. of Bangladesh Rifles:** Maj.-Gen. SHAKIL AHMED.

## Education

The Government provides free schooling for children of both sexes for eight years. Primary education, which is compulsory, begins at six years of age and lasts for five years. Secondary education, beginning at the age of 11, lasts for up to seven years, comprising a first cycle of three years, a second cycle of two years and a third cycle of two further years. In 2000/01 an estimated 100% of children (100% of boys; 101% of girls) in the relevant age group attended primary schools, while the comparable enrolment ratio at secondary schools was 46% (45% of boys; 47% of girls). In the late 1980s the Government laid great emphasis on the improvement of the primary education system in an attempt to raise the rate of literacy. A scheme was, therefore, undertaken to establish one primary school for every 2,000 people in Bangladesh. Secondary schools and colleges in the private sector vastly outnumber government institutions. In 2004/05 there were 26 state universities, including one for agriculture and one for engineering and technology, and an Islamic university. The Government launched an Open University Project in 1992 at an estimated cost of US $34.3m. In 2003/04 there were 79,833 primary schools and 17,386 secondary schools. In 1999 the Indigenous People's Association, representing the Santal minority, opened Bangladesh's first school teaching the national curriculum in the Santal language. The school is funded by the Grameen Trust. In 2003/04 there were 2,317 technical colleges, vocational institutes and colleges offering general education. Educational reform is designed to assist in satisfying the manpower needs of the country, and the greatest importance is given to primary, technical and vocational education. The 2007/08 budget allocated 86,590m. taka to education and technology (equivalent to 16.1% of total government expenditure).

# Bibliography

See also India and Pakistan


### History and General

Ahamed, Emajuddin. *Military Rule and the Myth of Democracy*. Dhaka, University Press Ltd, 1988.

Ahmad, Aziz. *Studies in Islamic Culture in the Indian Environment*. Oxford University Press, 1964.

*Islamic Modernism in India and Pakistan 1857–1964*. London and New York, Oxford University Press, 1967.

Ahmed, Moudud. *Bangladesh: Constitutional Quest for Autonomy*. Germany, 1976, later Dhaka.

*Bangladesh: Era of Sheikh Mujibur Rahman*. Dhaka, University Press Ltd, 1983.

*Democracy and the Challenge of Development: A Study of Politics and Military Interventions in Bangladesh*. Dhaka, University Press Ltd, 1995.

Ahmed, Nizam. *The Parliament of Bangladesh*. Aldershot, Hampshire, Ashgate, 2002.

Ahmed, Rafiuddin. *The Bengal Muslims 1871–1906*. Delhi, Oxford University Press, 1981.

*Religion, Nationalism and Politics in Bangladesh*. New Delhi, South Asia Publishers, 1990.

Ahmed, Sufia. *Muslim Community in Bengal 1884–1912*. Dhaka, 1974.

Alam, M. M., *et al*. *Development through Decentralization*. Dhaka, University Press Ltd, 1994.

Alauddin, Mohammad, *et al*. *Development, Governance and the Environment in South Asia: The Case of Bangladesh*. New York, St Martin's Press, 1999.

Asian Development Bank. *Women in Bangladesh: Country Briefing Paper*. Asian Development Bank, 2002.

Baxter, Craig, and Rahman, Syedur. *Historical Dictionary of Bangladesh*. Lanham, MD, Scarecrow Press, 2003.

Bhattacharjee, G. P. *Renaissance and Freedom Movement in Bangladesh*. Kolkata, 1973.

Brauns, Claus-Dieter, and Loeffler, Lorenz G. *Mru: Hill People on the Border of Bangladesh*. Basel, Birkhauser Verlag, 1990.

Chakravarty, S. R. *Bangladesh under Mujib, Zia and Ershad*. New Delhi, Har-Anand Publications, 1995.

Chatterji, Joya. *Bengal Divided: Hindu Communalism and Partition, 1932–1947*. Cambridge, Cambridge University Press, 1994.

Chittagong Hill Tracts Commission. *Life is Not Ours: Land and Human Rights in the Chittagong Hill Tracts*. Copenhagen and Amsterdam, 1991.

Choudhury, G. W. *The Last Days of United Pakistan*. London, C. Hurst, 1974.

Gardner, Katy. *Songs at the River's Edge: Stories from a Bangladeshi Village*. London, Virago Press, 1991.

Gordon, Leonard A. *Bengal: The Nationalist Movement*. Delhi, 1974.

Haroon, Asif. *Roots of 1971 Tragedy*. Lahore, Sang-e-Meel Publications, 2005.

Harun-or-Rashid. *The Foreshadowing of Bangladesh: Bengal Muslim League and Muslim Politics 1936–47*. Dhaka, Asiatic Society of Bangladesh, 1987.

Hasan, Perween. *Sultans and Mosques: The Early Muslim Architecture of Bangladesh*. London, I. B. Tauris and Co Ltd, 2007.

Hashmi, Taj-ul-Islam. *Pakistan as a Peasant Utopia: The Communalization of Class Politics in East Bengal, 1920–1947*. Boulder, CO, Westview Press, 1992.

*Women and Islam in Bangladesh: Beyond Subjection and Tyranny*. New York, St Martin's Press, 2000.

Hussain, T. *Land Rights in Bangladesh: Problems of Management*. Dhaka, University Press Ltd, 1995.

Islam, Sirajul (Ed.). *History of Bangladesh*. 3 vols, Dhaka, Asiatic Society of Bangladesh, 1992.

Jacques, Kathryn. *Bangladesh, India and Pakistan: International Relations and Regional Tensions in South Asia*. New York, St Martin's Press, 2000.

Jahan, Rounaq. *Pakistan: Failure in National Integration*. New York, Columbia University Press, 1972.

*Bangladesh Politics: Problems and Issues*. Dhaka, 1980.

Kabir, Bhuian Mohammad Monoar. *Politics of Military Rule and the Dilemmas of Democratization in Bangladesh*. New Delhi, South Asian Publishers, 1999.

Karim, Abdul. *Social History of the Muslims in Bengal*. Dhaka, 1959.

Karlekar, Hiranmay. *Bangladesh: The Next Afghanistan?* New Delhi, Sage Publications, 2005.

Khan, Mohammad Mohabbat, and Thorp, John (Eds). *Bangladesh: Society, Politics and Bureaucracy*. Dhaka, 1984.

Khan, Muin-Ud-Din Ahmad. *History of the Fara'idi Movement in Bengal 1818–1906*. Karachi, 1965.

Khan, Zillur Rahman. *Leadership in the Least Developed Nations: Bangladesh*. Syracuse, New York, 1983.

Kochanek, Stanley. *Patron—Client Politics and Business in Bangladesh*. New Delhi, Sage Publications, 1993.

Lifschultz, Lawrence. *Bangladesh: The Unfinished Revolution*. London, Zed Press, 1979.

Majumdar, R. C., and Sarkar, Sir Jadunath (Eds). *The History of Bengal*. University of Dhaka, 2 vols, 1942 and 1948.

Maniruzzaman, Talukder. *The Bangladesh Revolution and its Aftermath*. Dhaka, Bangladesh Books International, 1980.

Marshall, P. J. *East Indian Fortunes*. Oxford, Clarendon Press, 1976.

Mascarenhas, Anthony. *Bangladesh: A Legacy of Blood*. London, Hodder and Stoughton, 1986.

Mastaller, Michael, Montgomery, Roger D., and Weinstock, Joseph A. *Bangladesh: Towards an Environment Strategy*. Asian Development Bank, 2001.

Mohsin, Amena. *The Chittagong Hill Tracts, Bangladesh: On the Difficult Road to Peace*. Boulder, CO, Lynne Rienner Publishers, 2003.

Mujeeb, M. *The Indian Muslims*. London, Allen and Unwin, 1967.

Mukherjee, Ramkrishna. *Six Villages of Bengal*. Mumbai, 1971.

Murshid, Tazeen. *The Sacred and the Secular: Bengal Muslim Discourses, 1871–1977*. Kolkata, Oxford University Press, 1995.

Novak, James J. *Bangladesh: Reflections on the Water*. Bloomington and Indianapolis, IN, Indiana University Press, 1993.

Rahman, Aminur. *Women and Microcredit in Rural Bangladesh: An Anthropological Study of Grameen Bank Lending*. Boulder, CO, Westview Press, 1999.

Rahman, Pk. Md. Motiur, Matsui, Noriatsu, and Ikemoto, Yukio. *The Chronically Poor in Rural Bangladesh: Livelihood Constraints and Capabilities*. Abingdon, Routledge, 2008.

Rahman, Mujibur. *Bangladesh, My Bangladesh*. New Delhi and Dhaka, 1972.

Riaz, Ali. *God Willing: The Politics of Islamism in Bangladesh*. Lanham, MD, Rowman & Littlefield, 2004.

*Unfolding State: The Transformation of Bangladesh*. Whitby, Ontario, De Sitter Publications, 2005.

*Islamist Militancy in Bangladesh: A Complex Web*. Abingdon, Routledge, 2007.

Rolt, Francis. *On the Brink in Bengal*. London, John Murray, 1991.

Roy, Rajkumari Chandra. *Land Rights of the Indigenous Peoples of the Chittagong Hill Tracts, Bangladesh*. Copenhagen, International Work Group for Indigenous Affairs, 2000.

Saigal, Lt Col J. R. *Pakistan Splits: The Birth of Bangladesh*. New Delhi, Manas Publications, 2008.

Saikia, Jaideep (Ed.). *Bangladesh: Treading the Taliban Trail*. New Delhi, Vision Books, 2006.

Salahuddin, Ahmed. *Bangladesh: Past and Present*. New Delhi, APH Publishing, 2004.

Sarkar, Sumit. *The Swadeshi Movement in Bengal 1903–1908*. New Delhi, 1973.

Seabrook, Jeremy. *Freedom Unfinished: Fundamentalism and Popular Resistance in Bangladesh Today*. London, Zed Books, 2002.

Sharma, S. *US—Bangladesh Relations: A Critique*. London, Sangam Books, 2002.

Shelley, Mizanur Rahman (Ed.). *The Chittagong Hill Tracts of Bangladesh: The Untold Story*. Dhaka, Centre for Development Research, 1993.

Siddiqi, Abdul Rehman. *East Pakistan: The Endgame—An Onlooker's Journal 1969–1971*. Karachi, Oxford University Press, 2004.

Siddiqui, Kalim. *Conflict, Crisis and War in Pakistan*. London, Macmillan, 1972.

Siddiqui, Khaleda Akter. *Urban Working Women in the Formal Sector in Bangladesh*. Frankfurt, Peter Lang, 2000.

Singh, Nagendra Kr. *Bangladesh: Land and People*. New Delhi, Anmol Publications, 2003.

Sisson, Richard, and Rose, Leo E. *War and Secession: Pakistan, India and the Creation of Bangladesh.* Berkeley, CA, University of California Press, 1990.

Timm, R. W. *The Adivasis of Bangladesh*. London, Minority Rights Group, 1991.

Uddin, Sufia M. *Constructing Bangladesh: Religion, Ethnicity, and Language in an Islamic Nation*. Chapel Hill, NC, University of North Carolina Press, 2006.

Umar, Badruddin. *The Emergence of Bangladesh: Class Struggles in East Pakistan, 1947–58*. Karachi, Oxford University Press, 2004.

Wilcox, W. *The Emergence of Bangladesh: Problems and Opportunities for a Redefined American Policy in South Asia*. A Foreign Affairs Study, 1973.

Wright, Denis. *Bangladesh: Origins and Indian Ocean Relations (1971–1975)*. New Delhi, Sterling Publishers, 1988.

Zafarullah, Habib, and Khan, Mohammad Mohabbat. *The Bureaucratic Ascendancy: Public Administration in Bangladesh*. New Delhi, South Asian Publishers and A. H. Development Publishing House, 2005.

Zafarullah, Habib (Ed.). *The Zia Episode in Bangladesh Politics*. New Delhi, South Asian Publications, 1996.

Zaheer, Hasan. *The Separation of East Pakistan: The Rise and Realisation of Bengali Muslim Nationalism.* Karachi, Oxford University Press, 1994.

Zene, Cosimo. *The Rishi of Bangladesh*. London, RoutledgeCurzon, 2002.

Ziring, Lawrence. *Bangladesh from Mujib to Ershad: An Interpretive Study*. Karachi, Oxford University Press, 1992.

**Economy**

Abdullah, Abu (Ed.). *Modernisation at Bay: Structure and Change in Bangladesh.* Dhaka, University Press Ltd, 1991.

Ahmad, N. A. *New Economic Geography of Bangladesh.* New Delhi, 1976.

Ahmed, M. Farid. *Capital Markets and Institutions in Bangladesh.* Burlington, VT, Ashgate Publishing, 1997.

Alamgir, Mohiuddin. *Bangladesh: A Case of Below Poverty Level Equilibrium Trap.* Dhaka, Bangladesh Institute of Development Studies, 1978.

Alauddin, Mohammad, and Hossain, Mosharaff. *Environment and Agriculture in a Developing Economy: Problems and Prospects for Bangladesh*. Northampton, MA, Edward Elgar, 2001.

Arens, J., and Beurden, J. V. *Jhagrapur: Poor Peasants and Women in a Village in Bangladesh.* Birmingham, Third World Publications, 1977.

Asian Development Bank. *Commercialization of Microfinance: Bangladesh Country Study*. Manila, Asian Development Bank, 2003.

Bornstein, David. *The Story of the Grameen Bank*. Chicago, IL, University of Chicago Press, 1996.

Boyce, James. *Agrarian Impasse in Bengal.* Oxford University Press, 1987.

Chen, L. C. *Disaster in Bangladesh*. London, Oxford University Press, 1973.

Crow, Ben. *Sharing the Ganges: The Politics and Technology of River Development.* New Delhi, Sage Publications, 1995.

Datta, Anjan Kumar. *Land and Labor Relations in South-West Bangladesh: Resources, Power and Conflict.* New York, St Martin's Press, 1998.

de Bruyn, Tom, and Kuddus, Umbareen. *Dynamics of Remittance Utilization in Bangladesh*. Geneva, International Organization for Migration, 2005.

Duyne, Jennifer E. *Local Initiatives: Collective Water Management in Rural Bangladesh*. New Delhi, DK Print World Pvt Ltd, 2004.

Faaland, J., and Parkinson, J. R. *Bangladesh, The Test Case for Development*. London, Hurst, 1976.

Grieve, Roy H., and Huq, M. Mozammel (Eds). *Bangladesh: Strategies for Development.* Dhaka, University Press Ltd, 1995.

Hartmann, Betsy, and Boyce, James. *A Quiet Violence: View from a Bangladesh Village.* London, Zed Press, 1983.

Hoque, Serajul. *Global Trade Liberalization: Impact on the Readymade Garments Industry in Bangladesh*. New York, Peter Lang, 2004.

Humphrey, C. E. *Privatization in Bangladesh: Economic Transition in a Poor Country*. Dhaka, University Press Ltd, 1992.

Islam, Nazrul (Ed.). *Addressing the Urban Poverty Agenda in Bangladesh: Critical Issues and the 1995 Survey Findings.* Manila, Asian Development Bank Publications, 1997.

Islam, Rizwanul, and Muqtada, M. *Bangladesh: Selected Issues in Employment and Development.* New Delhi, ILO, 1986.

Jannuzi, F. T., and Peach, J. T. *The Agrarian Structure of Bangladesh.* Boulder, CO, Westview Press, 1980.

Jansen, Eirik G. *Rural Bangladesh: Competition for Scarce Resources.* Oxford and Oslo, Oxford University Press (for Norwegian University Press), 1986.

Johnson, B. L. C. *Bangladesh.* London, Heinemann, 1975.

Kabeer, Naila. *Power to Choose: Bangladeshi Women and Labour Market Decisions in London and Dhaka.* London, Verso, 2000.

Khan, Azizur Rahman, and Hossain, Mahabub. *The Strategy of Development in Bangladesh.* London, Macmillan, 1990.

Khan, Shakeeb Adnan. *The State and Village Society.* Dhaka, University Press Ltd, 1989.

Mintoo, Abdul Awal. *Bangladesh: Anatomy of Change*. London, Athena Press, 2006.

Norbye, O. D. K. (Ed.). *Bangladesh Faces the Future.* Dhaka, University Press Ltd, 1990.

Rahman, Atiur. *Peasants and Classes: A Study in Differentiation in Bangladesh*. London, Zed Press, 1986.

*Education for Development: Lessons from East Asia for Bangladesh*. Singapore, Institute of Southeast Asian Studies, 2002.

Rashid, S. (Ed.). *Bangladesh Economy: Evaluation and a Research Agenda*. Dhaka, University Press Ltd, 1995.

Robinson, E. A., and Griffin, K. *The Economic Development of Bangladesh within a Socialist Framework: Proceedings of a Conference held by the IEA at Dhaka*. 1974.

Schreiner, Mark. *Performance of Subsidized Microfinance Organizations—BancoSol of Bolivia and the Grameen Bank of Bangladesh*. New York, Edwin Mellen Press, 2003.

Singh, Inderjit. *The Great Ascent: The Rural Poor in South Asia.* London, Johns Hopkins University Press, 1990.

Sobhan, Rehman. *Public Enterprise and the Nature of the State in South Asia.* Dhaka, Centre for Social Studies, 1983.

(Ed.). *The Decade of Stagnation: The State of the Bangladesh Economy in the 1980s.* Dhaka, University Press Ltd, 1991.

(Ed.). *Debt Default to the Development Finance Institutions: The Crisis of State Sponsored Entrepreneurship in Bangladesh.* Dhaka, University Press Ltd, 1991.

Stepanek, J. F. *Bangladesh: Equitable Growth*. Oxford, Pergamon Press, 1979.

Stevens, R., *et al*. *Rural Development in Bangladesh and Pakistan.* Honolulu, HI, University of Hawaii Press, 1976.

Sultana, Shamima. *Foreign Aid and Rural Development in Bangladesh*. 3 vols, Peacock Trust United Kingdom, 2005.

Westergaard, K. *State and Rural Society in Bangladesh.* London, Curzon Press, 1985.

Wood, Geoff D. *Bangladesh: Whose Ideas, Whose Interests?* London, Intermediate Technology Publications, 1994.

Younis, Talib A., and Mostafa, Iqbal M. D. *Accountability in Public Management and Administration in Bangladesh*. Aldershot, Hampshire, Ashgate Publishing, 2000.

Yunus, Mohammad. *Banker to the Poor: Micro-Lending and the Battle Against World Poverty*. New York, PublicAffairs, 2003.

# BHUTAN

## Physical and Social Geography

BRIAN SHAW

The Kingdom of Bhutan is a small, land-locked country. To the north and north-west, it adjoins Tibet (the Xizang Autonomous Region) in China. To the south, Bhutan is bordered (west to east) by the present-day Indian states of Sikkim, West Bengal, Assam (Asom) and Arunachal Pradesh. The country's total area is some 38,364 sq km (14,812 sq miles). It extends approximately from 26° 45′ to 28° 20′ N, and from 88° 50′ to 92° 05′ E. The borders are mostly natural ones; that with Tibet is traditional, following the watershed of the Chumbi valley in the north-west, and the crest of the Himalaya mountain range in the north. The border with India was established by treaty with the United Kingdom in the 19th century. However, it was not until many years later, between 1973 and 1984, that the border's detailed delineation and demarcation were agreed in principle and completed, apart from some portions in southern Bhutan and the area of the Sino–Indian–Bhutanese border in eastern Bhutan, which generally follows the line separating the foothills from the plains. It was announced in mid-2004 that the demarcation of the Bhutan–India boundary (along the Indian states of Arunachal Pradesh and West Bengal) had been finalized in February, and that the construction of 'boundary pillars' was being implemented. The Government also stated that work on the demarcation of the border between Bhutan and the Indian state of Sikkim was under way. In June 2005 the National Assembly resolved that the Bhutan–India border should be finalized by the end of 2006; by December 2006 all 62 'strip maps' had been signed by both sides, except the two eastern and western tri-junctions with China (see History). Bhutan's area, meanwhile, was officially adjusted in the late 1990s, following more accurate technical measurements of the Sino–Bhutanese border. The capital is Thimphu.

### PHYSICAL FEATURES

Bhutan is almost entirely mountainous, and its terrain is among the most rugged in the world. The elevation above sea-level may increase from 160 m to more than 7,000 m in less than 100 km of distance. Bhutan's physiography is similar to that of Nepal, with the Churia hill belt being known here, as in nearby Bengal and Assam, as the Duars. From the level plains areas of the Duars in the south, the hills rise steadily to the Great Himalayas. Flat land is limited to the lower reaches of the broader (generally north–south) river valleys, and in small sections of the Duars. Bhutan's highest peak is Gangkar Punsum, whose summit is 7,561 m above sea-level. Chomo Lhari, overlooking the Chumbi valley, is 7,352 m high, Jitchu Drake is 6,789 m, and there are many other peaks over 5,000 m. The country's relatively remote location and the terrain have acted as strong barriers between Bhutan and its neighbours, and between the peoples of different valleys within the country.

### CLIMATE

The country can be divided vertically into three distinct climatic zones, corresponding broadly to the three main geographical divisions (southern foothills, rising from the plains of India; 'inner' Himalayas; and high Himalayas). The southern belt, rising to about 1,500 m above sea-level, has a hot, humid climate, with temperatures remaining fairly even throughout the year (between 15°C and 30°C) and with annual rainfall ranging between 2,500 mm and 5,000 mm in some areas. The middle inner Himalayas, from 1,500 m up to about 3,000 m, have a cool, temperate climate, with annual precipitation averaging some 1,000 mm but with more rain in the west. The high northern region, above 3,000 m, has a severe alpine climate, with annual precipitation of around 400 mm. Much of the rain is concentrated in the summer months (from mid-June to September), with the south-west monsoon accounting for 60%–90% of the total annual rainfall. The monsoon is particularly strong in the west. Within these broad ranges, however, there is substantial variation. The climate and rainfall characteristics change dramatically from one valley to the next, with consequent sharp changes in the possibilities for agricultural and pastoral production.

### SOILS AND NATURAL RESOURCES

There is little reliable information on soils. In general, the more fertile soils are confined to the valley floors and the Duars. The Geological Survey of Bhutan was established in 1982 to develop preliminary work carried out by the Geological Survey of India, which has shown that Bhutan is comparatively well endowed with natural resources. Deposits of limestone, dolomite, coal, gypsum, tungsten, graphite, copper, lead, zinc, marble, slate and talc have been indicated. Limestone (processed into cement) and dolomite are the principal minerals currently being exploited. Coal reserves are of moderate size and quality. Slate quarrying is operating on a small scale: in 1975 the Bonsegoema deposit, near Wangdiphodrang, was described by feasibility consultants as 'one of the best slate deposits so far known in the world'.

The deep gorges of fast-flowing rivers, fed by the snowmelt of the Himalayas, provide enormous hydroelectric power potential, although the cost of harnessing this energy is also enormous. Forests, covering 74% of the land area, are another major natural resource, although exploitation is at present unbalanced: remote forests are over-mature, while accessible areas (especially in the south) are becoming degraded.

### POPULATION AND ETHNIC GROUPS

In December 2004 the King, in his National Day address, publicized a population figure for Bhutan of just over 500,000. This figure was significantly lower than the previously published 'official overall' population of Bhutan, given in late 1996 as 600,000. The latter figure, first given endorsement in 1990, was to remain an approximation pending the long-delayed completion of a nation-wide census, which took place on 31 May 2005 (see below). Bhutan's first census, held in 1969, had reported a total population of 931,514. A 1980 census reported a total of 1,165,000, and the mid-1988 projection, based on this, was for a total of 1,375,400. At that time, according to official figures, the annual growth rate of the population was 2.5%, which, on the basis of an estimated population of 638,000 in 2000, suggested a total of about 688,062 in 2004. However, in January 2005 the National Statistical Bureau presented a revised current growth rate for 2003/04 of 1.3%, and revised its own estimate for 2002/03 to 2.4%. These latest revised figures remain approximate. Whereas the notional population density at mid-1988 was therefore more than 35 per sq km, that for 2005 (using the census figures that exclude the floating population) was 16.55 per sq km. The population is unevenly distributed: the southern Duar valleys and the eastern region, around Trashigang, are the most heavily populated areas. According to an address made by Bhutan's Minister of Planning at a World Population Day function in July 1997, the then very high rate of population growth of 3.1% would—if unchecked—double the population in 24 years, with major economic and social consequences. At the same time, the Secretary for Health reported that it was hoped, through education, to lower the annual growth rate of the population to 2.56% by 2002. He stated that, of Bhutan's 20 districts, population growth was already lower than 2% in 10 and stood at 2% in six; only four districts currently showed a growth rate of more than 2%. A formal population policy was to be finalized before the end of the Eighth Plan period (1997–2002). The 2000 edition of the five-yearly *National Health Survey* (published in early 2001) reported that the growth rate within a sample section of the population had declined from 3.1% in 1994 to 2.5% in 2000, while the average (sample) household size was reported to be 5.42 persons; the 2005 census (see below) reported an average household size of 4.6 persons based on the figure of 126,115 'regular' households.

A preliminary report on selected tables of the May 2005 population and housing census was made to the 84th session of the National Assembly, indicating that Bhutan had a total population of 553,000; there were, in addition, more than 125,000 non-nationals working in the country. Of the 553,000, some 44% (243,320) were between the ages of 15 and 50 years (the target group for adult non-formal education); and, of this section of the population, about 47% (114,360) were illiterate. The target date for full adult literacy (one of several 'millennium development goals') was therefore extended from 2012 to 2015. The final report issued in April 2006 clarified that the total population of Bhutan on 31 May 2005 was 672,425 persons (364,482 males and 307,943 females); of this total, 37,443 were members of the 'floating population', who had entered the country 'to work and visit' and who were excluded from detailed questionnaires. Of the total 'resident' population of 634,982 (including foreign nationals), some 333,595 were males and 301,387 females (giving a sex ratio of 111:100). Of the 634,982, some 30.9% resided in urban areas and 69.1% in rural areas. The actual population of Bhutanese citizens on census day was 552,996. In the 12 months prior to the census date, there were 12,538 live births and 4,498 deaths recorded, giving a natural growth rate of 1.3%; during the same period, 5,509 persons emigrated and 18,109 persons immigrated to Bhutan, giving a net migration of 2.0%. The National Statistical Bureau currently continues to publicize a net population increase rate of 1.3% per year; this rate is also being used in official documents. The most populated districts at 31 May 2005 were Thimphu (98,676 persons), Chhukha (74,387), and Samtse (60,100); the least populated were Gasa (3,116), Ha (11,648) and Pemagatshel (13,864). Of the whole population, some 56% were below 24 years of age.

The main western valleys are peopled by Ngalong (showing some similarities with Central Tibetans). The Sharchops of the east are most numerous, and are considered by some to be among the earliest (although not aboriginal) inhabitants. The people of central Bhutan, around Bumthang, speak an old and separate language. Nepalese settlers came to work in the southern foothills of Bhutan in the early 20th century, and others migrated until such movement was banned by Bhutan in 1959. Unofficial migration of Nepalese settlers continued, both from Nepal and Assam (following their expulsion from the Indian state in the 1970s), until the 1988–89 southern district censuses, when the recently known illegal migrants were obliged to leave the country. The descendants of these settlers, mostly Hindus, dominate southern Bhutan, and are today referred to as southern Bhutanese. They are thought to comprise 20%–35% of the country's total population, although no reliable figures are available. The Government encourages social integration, and the major religious festivals of Hindus, as well as those of Buddhists, are celebrated. Intermarriage between northern and southern Bhutanese was until 1990 encouraged with gifts of land and money.

# History

BRIAN SHAW

## EARLY HISTORY

Little is known of the pre-history of Bhutan, although stone artefacts and some remaining megaliths suggest that it was already inhabited by about 2000–1500 BC. No comprehensive archaeological survey has yet been carried out within Bhutan. Buddhism was introduced in the seventh century AD by the Tibetan Buddhist King Srongtsen Gampo, who is recorded as having ordered the building of the first lhakhangs (temples) in old Bhutan: Jampe, in Bumthang (central Bhutan), and Kyichu, in the Paro valley. Since this time, Buddhism has played a large part in shaping the country's institutions, in developing a native artistic spirit and in moulding a national sentiment transcending the localism of particular valleys or regions.

At the end of the eighth century the Indian Buddhist Saint Padmasambhava (revered in Bhutan as Guru Rimpoche, protector-saint of the kingdom) came from Tibet to Bumthang, and arranged for the construction of rock monasteries in various places, including Taktsang (Tiger's Nest) lhakhang in the Paro valley, thus founding the Nyingmapa school of Mahayana Buddhism. The subsequent history of Bhutan is obscure until the end of the 11th century, but by the end of the 12th century a Lhapa school of the Kagyupa sect was established at Paro.

The Drukpa sub-sect was introduced in the first decades of the 13th century by the Tibetan Phajo Drugom Shigpo. He confronted, and finally prevailed over, the Lhapa school, which nevertheless continued to propagate its rival teachings until the 17th century. Phajo Drugom Shigpo founded the first Drukpa monasteries at Phajoding and Tango, in the Thimphu valley.

Other sages of various sects came south to Bhutan from Tibet between the 12th and 17th centuries, and constructed other monasteries. In the 15th century the 'divine madman', Drukpa Kinley, came to western Bhutan, and the accounts of his itinerant and Rabelaisian lifestyle continue to be recited with great sympathy and affection by all Bhutanese. Also at this time, the scholar Pema Lingpa was born in Bumthang; he later founded temples there, and created religious and secular dances, based on his vision of Zandog Pelri (the 'copper-coloured mountain'), the heavenly abode of Guru Rimpoche.

The independent theocracy of Druk-yul ('land of the thunder-dragon'), and thus of historical Bhutan, emerges from the early 17th century. A prominent Tibetan lama of the Drukpa sub-sect, Ngawang Namgyal, fled from Tibet to Bhutan in 1616, after the Gelugpa sect, headed by the Dalai Lama, had come to achieve an intolerant dominance at Lhasa, the Tibetan capital. In due course, he took the title Shabdrung ('at whose feet one submits'), and it is as the first Shabdrung that he is widely venerated today, as unifier of the disparate powerful families, as promulgator of a code of law, and as builder of most of the remarkable administrative-temple-fortress complexes known as dzongs (the first of which was started at Simtokha in 1629). After his arrival, successive armies from Tibet, variously at the invitation of opponents of the Shabdrung and at the instigation of the Mongols (who by the late 1630s had overrun the Tsang province of Tibet), attacked western Bhutan, but were always successfully repelled.

The Shabdrung established himself as both temporal and religious ruler of Bhutan, and he created an administrative structure which still finds echoes in present-day arrangements. He founded a state monastic body under an elected spiritual leader, the Je Khenpo (head abbot), and a theocracy under the Desi, or Deb. The Desi was to deal with civil matters, although the Shabdrung retained ultimate authority. A State Council (lhengye tshokdu) was also created, and was the forerunner of today's organs of government.

The first Shabdrung's death, some time after 1651, was kept secret for half a century in a successful attempt to prevent the disintegration of the newly unified state. During the first decades of the 18th century, a theory of triple reincarnations of the Shabdrung was established. These were said to take the form of physical, oral and mental aspects, and the persons manifesting the latter were to be considered as successors to the Shabdrung as head of state. Between the recognition of successive Shabdrungs (only six 'mental incarnations' were recognized in the period up to the founding of the monarchy), the Je Khenpo and the Desi sought to maintain a dual system of government; the membership of the State Council, however, became increasingly secular in orientation. This was true also for the successive Desi and the leaders of the regional administrations. The latter were called dzongpöns, and the three most important—at Daga, Trongsa and Paro—were styled penlops. In due course, rivalry between penlops led to continuing internal disorder; this, together with the developing British hegemony in Assam (Asom), brought new challenges to the Bhutanese state from the late 18th century.

## BRITISH INTERVENTION

The British had no relations with Bhutan prior to 1772. Bhutan had developed political influence over Cooch Bihar in 1730 and succeeding years, but, by an agreement made in 1773 between one of the claimants to the throne of this principality and the East India Co, Cooch Bihar became virtually a company dependency. A British expeditionary force drove a Bhutanese garrison from Cooch Bihar and, in hot pursuit, captured the Bhutanese forts of Pasakha and Damimkot. The then Desi thereupon appealed for assistance to the Panchen Lama at Lhasa, acting as regent; the latter responded with an appeasing letter to Warren Hastings (then Governor-General of India). Hastings grasped this opportunity to seek trading relations with both Tibet and Bhutan. Following a peace treaty between the British and the Bhutanese (25 April 1774), in which both sides agreed, in effect, to restore the status quo, he dispatched George Bogle on a political mission to Lhasa, via Thimphu. Further missions by Hamilton (1776, 1777), and by Turner and Davis (1783), were also well received in Bhutan. In the 19th century, however, southern boundary disputes became increasingly troublesome, leading to further British missions, led by Bose in 1815 and by Pemberton and Griffiths in 1838. A draft treaty which was presented by the latter mission, primarily designed to establish commercial intercourse between British India and Bhutan, was rejected by the Bhutanese.

At this time, Bhutan fell into increasing civil disorder; further Bhutanese incursions into the Assam Duars were made, and in 1841 the Assam Duars were annexed, with compensation of Rs 10,000 annually to be paid by the British to Bhutan. Continuing Bhutanese raids into Sikkim and Cooch Bihar in 1862 led to the mission of Ashley Eden (1863–64), which was disastrous in its manner and execution. Following Eden's return, a proclamation of war was issued against Bhutan in November 1864. The south-eastern area of Bhutan, around Dewangiri (present-day Samdrup Jongkhar), was lost to the British forces, and the Duar War came to an end with the signing of the Treaty of Sinchula in November 1865. By this instrument, Bhutan ceded the seven Assam Duars and the 11 Bengal Duars to the United Kingdom, and also lost hill territory on the left bank of the river Teesta (including Kalimpong and Pedong), in return for an annual compensation of Rs 50,000.

Towards the end of the 19th century, the weakening of the powers of the central Government in Bhutan was paralleled by the emergence to power of provincial governors, especially the penlops of Paro and of Trongsa (who, in practice, controlled western and central Bhutan, respectively), who were fiercely competitive, and who sought to increase their powers. The external situation of Bhutan came to play a part in the settlement of these tendencies. By this time, Bhutan had enjoyed a millennium of trade and religious ties with northern Tibet. While the United Kingdom and Tibet remained on amicable terms, Bhutan could maintain good relations with both neighbours. However, the extension of British power to the south of Bhutan, together with Tibetan border violations against Sikkim and the subsequent growing tension between the British and Tibetans, led Bhutanese leaders to recognize that they should choose which authority of their neighbours they would prefer.

A British mission, led by Younghusband, to Lhasa in 1903–04, ostensibly to open Tibet to trade and to forestall Russian dominance at Lhasa, gave the then Trongsa penlop, Ugyen Wangchuck, his opportunity. Advised by Kazi Ugyen Dorji, and in opposition to the Paro penlop (who preferred to side with the Tibetans), Ugyen Wangchuck accompanied the expedition and was a valuable intermediary between the British and the authorities at Lhasa. He was knighted by the British, and emerged with enhanced prestige within Bhutan.

Although British imperial policy came to repudiate the treaty with Lhasa and to recognize Chinese claims to suzerainty over Tibet, the Younghusband expedition alarmed the Chinese Government into attempting, once again, to assert the long-desired *de facto* political authority over Tibet. In 1910 the Dalai Lama fled to the refuge of India when Chinese forces occupied Lhasa, and the Chinese Government laid claim to Bhutan, Nepal and Sikkim. British and Bhutanese interests coincided at this point. The last Shabdrung had died in 1903, and the Desi had died in 1904. No reincarnation of the Shabdrung had appeared by 1906. The management of Bhutan's civil affairs had come into the hands of Sir Ugyen Wangchuck, and in November 1907 an assembly of the leading members of the clergy, officials and important families agreed to create a hereditary monarchy. Sir Ugyen Wangchuck was unanimously elected first King of Bhutan, thereby ending the dual system of government that had lasted for nearly 300 years.

In 1910 Bhutan signed the Treaty of Punakha with the United Kingdom, amending two articles of the Treaty of Sinchula to increase the allowance payable to Rs 100,000 per year, and to provide a British undertaking 'to exercise no interference in the internal administration of Bhutan' in return for a Bhutanese agreement 'to be guided by the advice of the British Government in regard to its external relations'. These agreements provided the defence that was desired by both parties against Chinese imperial claims. Successive Chinese Governments, up to the present time, seem to have accepted that, by this treaty, Bhutan came within the Indian sphere of influence, whatever the theoretical options may have been prior to 1910. British India seemed to be content to have declared a northern interest where Chinese interests should not encroach.

For a further half-century, Bhutan remained isolated from the outside world. British India maintained sporadic contact with the Bhutanese Government through its political agent at Gangtok, in Sikkim, and the Bhutan trade agent at Kalimpong. In 1949 independent India renewed the provisions of the 1910 treaty with Bhutan, increased the annual payment to Rs 500,000, and restored Dewangiri.

## MODERN BHUTAN

The era of the contemporary Bhutanese state dates from 1907. Acceptance of the principle of an hereditary monarchy was the base from which evolved the modified form of what might be described as a proto-constitutional monarchy. Sir Ugyen Wangchuck ruled as Druk Gyalpo ('Precious Ruler of the Dragon People' or 'Dragon King') until 1926, when he was succeeded by his son, Jigme Wangchuck, who ruled until 1952. The third monarch, Jigme Dorji Wangchuck, ruled until his early death in 1972, at the age of 43. Major developments occurred during his reign, including the decision to modernize Bhutan, and he is today venerated as the 'father of modern Bhutan'. His son, the former King Jigme Singye Wangchuck, had been appointed Trongsa penlop in May 1972, at the age of 16; he became King in July 1972, on the demise of his father, and formally accepted the Raven Crown, on the Golden Throne of Bhutan, in June 1974. In December 2006 the King formally transferred his responsibilities to his 26-year-old son, Jigme Khesar Namgyel Wangchuck, who was to oversee the country's moves towards the promulgation of a new constitution and elections to the first democratically elected government.

During his first visit to Bhutan in 1958, the Indian Prime Minister, Jawaharlal Nehru, had stated clearly that 'our only wish is that you remain an independent country, choosing your own way of life and taking the path of progress according to your will'. This premise has been acted upon by successive Indian Prime Ministers. In the wake of events in Tibet from 1959, Bhutan aligned itself with India, closed its borders with

Tibet in 1960, and began a massive process of modernization (mostly funded by India) to escape Tibet's fate of subjugation. The first, enormous task was to build roads from the Indian plains to central Bhutan, and from west to east; Indian engineers laboured from 1959 to 1962 to complete the all-weather road between Phuentsholing and Thimphu, with Bhutanese providing the labour as national service, and subsequent development efforts have evolved from this.

Bhutan joined the Colombo Plan in 1962, the UN in 1971, the UN Economic and Social Commission for Asia and the Pacific in 1972, the IMF and the World Bank in 1981 and the Asian Development Bank in 1982. Bhutan is also a committed member of the Non-aligned Movement. Regionally, Bhutan was an enthusiastic founder member of the South Asian Regional Co-operation (SARC) organization (inaugurated in August 1983), consisting of Bangladesh, Bhutan, India, the Maldives, Nepal, Pakistan and Sri Lanka. In May 1985 Bhutan was host to the first meeting of Ministers of Foreign Affairs from SARC member countries, which later agreed to give their grouping the formal title of South Asian Association for Regional Co-operation (SAARC).

After 1959 Bhutan accepted more than 6,000 refugees from Tibet. The involvement of some of these in the domestic affairs of Bhutan (in 1964 and again in 1974), and an unwillingness by many to accept proffered Bhutan citizenship, forced the Bhutanese Government by 1979 to decide to expel those who declined to accept its authority. India initially refused to accept any further refugees, but in January 1980 it was agreed that India would absorb some 1,500 of them. By September 1985 some 1,633 refugees had been accepted by India, and 4,206 had requested and received Bhutanese citizenship, while 1,461 had not yet accepted the offer. A revised Citizenship Act, adopted by the tshogdu chenmo (National Assembly) in 1985, confirmed residence in Bhutan in 1958 as a fundamental basis for automatic citizenship (as provided for by the 1958 Nationality Act), but this was to be flexibly interpreted. Provision was also made for citizenship by registration for Nepalese immigrants who had resided in the country for at least 20 years (15 years if employed by the Government) and who could meet linguistic and other tests of commitment to the Bhutanese community.

The violent ethnic Nepalese agitation in India for a 'Gurkha homeland' in the Darjeeling-Kalimpong region during the late 1980s and the populist movement in Nepal in 1988–90 (see the chapters on India and Nepal, respectively) spilled over into Bhutan in 1990. Ethnic unrest became apparent in that year when a campaign of intimidation and violence, directed by militant Nepalese against the authority of the Government in Thimphu, was initiated. In September thousands of southern Bhutanese villagers, and Nepalese who marched in from across the Indian border, demonstrated in at least nine border towns in southern Bhutan to protest against domination by the indigenous Buddhist Drukpa. The 'anti-nationals' or 'terrorists', as they are called by the Bhutanese authorities, demand a greater role in the country's political and economic life and are bitterly opposed to official attempts to strengthen the Bhutanese sense of national identity through an increased emphasis on Tibetan-derived, rather than Nepalese, culture and religion (including a formal dress code, Dzongkha as the sole official language, etc.). Bhutanese officials, on the other hand, view the southerners as recent arrivals who abuse the hospitality of their hosts through acts of violence and the destruction of development infrastructure.

Most southern villagers are relatively recent arrivals from Nepal and many of them have made substantial contributions to the development of the southern hills. The provision of free education and health care by the Bhutanese Government acted for many years as a magnet for Nepalese who were struggling to survive in their own country and who came to settle illegally in Bhutan. This population movement was largely ignored by local administrative officials, many of whom accepted incentives to disregard the illegal nature of the influx. The Government's policy of encouraging a sense of national identity, together with rigorous new procedures (introduced in 1988) to check citizenship registration, revealed thousands of illegal residents in southern Bhutan, many of whom had lived there for a decade or more, married local people and raised families. During the ethnic unrest in September 1990, the majority of southern villagers were coerced into participating in the demonstrations by groups of armed and uniformed young men (including many of Nepalese origin who were born in Bhutan). Many of these dissidents, including a large number of secondary school students and former members of the Royal Bhutan Army (RBA) and of the police force, had fled Bhutan in 1989 and early 1990. In 1988–90 a large number of the dissidents resided in the tea gardens and villages adjoining southern Bhutan. Following the demonstrations that took place in Bhutan in September–October 1990, other ethnic Nepalese left Bhutan. In January 1991 some 234 persons, who claimed to be Bhutanese refugees, reportedly arrived in Maidhar and Tinmai in the Jhapa district of eastern Nepal. In September, at the request of the Nepalese Government, the office of the UN High Commissioner for Refugees (UNHCR) inaugurated a relief programme providing food and shelter for more than 300 people in the *ad hoc* camps. By December the number of people staying in the camps had risen to about 6,000.

The sizes of these camps have been substantially augmented by landless and unemployed Nepalese, who have been expelled from Assam and other eastern states of India. The small and faction-ridden ethnic Nepalese Bhutan People's Party (BPP), which was founded in Kathmandu, Nepal, in 1990 (as a successor to the People's Forum on Democratic Rights, an organization established in 1989), purports to lead the agitation for 'democracy', but has, as yet, presented no clear or convincing set of objectives and has attracted no significant support from within Bhutan itself. Schools and bridges became principal targets for arson and looting during 1990–92, and families known to be loyal to the Bhutanese Government were robbed of their valuables. Most of the schools in southern Bhutan were closed indefinitely from the end of September 1990, in response to threats to the lives of teachers and students' families, but the majority of pupils affected by these closures were provided with temporary places in schools in northern Bhutan. By mid-1995, despite the continuing security problems, some 74 schools and 89 health facilities had been reopened in the five southern districts.

From 1988 King Jigme personally authorized the release of more than 1,700 militants captured by the authorities. He stated that, while he had an open mind regarding the question of the pace and extent of political reform (including a willingness to hold discussions with any minority group that had grievances), his Government could not tolerate pressures for change that were based on intimidation and violence. Although several important leaders of the dissident movement remained in custody, the King said that they would be released when conditions of law and order returned to normal. Some leaders of the BPP stated that they had no quarrel with the King, but with 'corrupt officials'; on the other hand, certain militants strongly condemned the King as their 'main enemy'. A number of southern Bhutanese officials (including the then Director-General of Power, Bhim Subba, and the Managing Director of the State Trading Corporation, R. B. Basnet) absconded in June 1991 (on the eve of the publication of departmental audits) and went directly to Nepal, where they reportedly sought political asylum on the grounds of repression and atrocities against southern Bhutanese. These accusations were refuted in detail by the Government in Thimphu. The former Secretary-General of the BPP, D. K. Rai, was tried by the High Court in Thimphu in May 1992 and was sentenced to life imprisonment for terrorist acts; a further 35 defendants received lesser sentences and five were acquitted. The alleged mastermind behind the ethnic unrest, Teknath Rizal, came to trial, and was sentenced to life imprisonment in November 1993 after having been found guilty on four of nine charges of offences against the Tsawa Sum ('the country, the King, and the people'); one decision was deferred in the absence of key witnesses. King Jigme subsequently decreed that Rizal would be released from prison 'once the Governments of Bhutan and Nepal resolve the problems of the people living in the refugee camps in eastern Nepal'; he was released in December 1999 (see below). About 130 detainees, who were accused of criminal and terrorist acts, were tried during 1995.

Violence continued in the disturbed areas of Samtse, Chhukha, Tsirang, Sarpang and Gelephu throughout 1991–97, and companies of trained militia volunteers were posted to these areas to relieve the forces of the regular army. The state government of West Bengal in India, the territory of which abuts much of the western part of southern Bhutan, reaffirmed in 1991 and 1992 that its land would not be used as a base for any agitation against Bhutan.

In late 1991 and throughout 1992 several thousand legally settled villagers left southern Bhutan for the newly established refugee camps in eastern Nepal. The Bhutanese Government alleged that the villagers were being enticed or threatened to leave their homes by militants based outside Bhutan, in order to augment the population of the camps and gain international attention; the dissidents, on the other hand, claimed that the Bhutanese Government was forcing the villagers to leave. The formation of the Bhutan National Democratic Party (BNDP), including members drawn from supporters of the BPP and with the leading dissident, R. B. Basnet, as its President, was announced in Kathmandu in February 1992. Incidents of ethnic violence, almost all of which involved infiltration from across the border by ethnic Nepalese who had been trained and dispatched from the camps in Nepal, reportedly diminished substantially in the first half of 1993 as talks continued between Bhutanese and Nepalese government officials regarding proposals to resolve the issues at stake. The Nepalese Government steadfastly refused to consider any solution that did not include the resettlement in Bhutan of all ethnic Nepalese 'refugees' living in the camps (by November 1993 the number of alleged ethnic Nepalese refugees from Bhutan totalled about 85,000). This proposal was rejected by the Bhutanese Government, which claimed that the majority of the camp population merely professed to be from Bhutan, had absconded from Bhutan (and thus forfeited their citizenship, according to Bhutan's citizenship laws), or had voluntarily departed after selling their properties and surrendering their citizenship papers and rights.

The apparent deadlock was broken, however, when a joint statement was signed by the Ministers of Home Affairs of Bhutan and Nepal on 18 July 1993, which committed each side to establishing a 'high-level committee' to work towards a settlement and, in particular, to fulfilling the following mandate prior to undertaking any other related activity: to determine the different categories of people claiming to have come from Bhutan in the refugee camps in eastern Nepal (which now numbered eight); and to specify the positions of the two Governments on each of these categories, which would provide the basis for the resolution of the problem. The two countries held their first ministerial-level meeting regarding the issue in Kathmandu in October, at which it was agreed that four categories would be established among the people in the refugee camps—'(i) bona fide Bhutanese who have been evicted forcefully; (ii) Bhutanese who emigrated; (iii) non-Bhutanese; and (iv) Bhutanese who have committed criminal acts'. (These categories are henceforth referred to as Category I, II, III and IV.) Further meetings were held in 1994. Following the election of a new Government in Nepal in November of that year, however, little progress was made at joint ministerial meetings held in the first half of 1995. Nepal's communist Government demanded that all persons in the camps be accepted by Bhutan; the Bhutanese authorities, on the other hand, were prepared to accept only the unconditional return of any bona fide Bhutanese citizens who had left the country involuntarily. The Nepalese Government seemed reluctant to enquire too closely into the national status of the ethnic Nepalis in the camps. Nevertheless, diplomatic exchanges continued in the latter half of the year, despite serious political instability in Nepal.

In January 1996 the new Nepalese Prime Minister, Sher Bahadur Deuba, proposed a resumption of intergovernmental talks, this time at foreign minister level. King Jigme welcomed this proposal, but the seventh round of talks, which was held in early April, resulted in demands by Nepal that went beyond the mandate drawn up by the joint ministerial committee in mid-1993. It was widely understood that the Nepalese Government had again reverted to a requirement that all persons in the camps be accepted by Bhutan, regardless of status. This demand remained unacceptable to the Bhutanese Government, which stated that the problem of the people in the camps would not have arisen in the first place if conditions (such as prospects of free food, shelter, health and education, and 'moral support' by the Nepalese authorities for all persons claiming to be Bhutanese refugees) had not been created when there were only 234 persons in Jhapa making such claims. In addition, the Bhutanese Government stated that even with such conditions attracting people to the refugee camps, a well-organized screening process would have prevented the sheer scale of ethnic Nepalese claiming to be Bhutanese refugees. (Until June 1993 no screening of claimants to refugee status had been enforced on the Indo-Nepalese border.) In August 1996 a UNHCR delegation visited Bhutan at the invitation of the authorities and received detailed information from the Bhutanese Government regarding the issue of the camps. Talks at official level were held in March and July 1997 without any public communiqué. Following informal meetings during the SAARC summit in Colombo, Sri Lanka, in July 1998, the new Chairman of the Council of Ministers and Head of Government in Bhutan, Lyonpo Jigmi Yozer Thinley, held talks with the Nepalese Prime Minister, G. P. Koirala; both leaders stated that their meeting had been 'very positive'. Thinley and Koirala agreed that bilateral negotiations would continue through their respective Ministers of Foreign Affairs on the issue of persons claiming refugee status in Nepal (who now numbered about 100,000); talks were held in Kathmandu in September 1999. The 77th National Assembly session, which took place in June–August 1999, unanimously reiterated that the Bhutanese Government accepted full responsibility for any Bhutanese found to have been forcefully evicted (Category I—see above): such persons would be recognized and accepted as genuine refugees, while those responsible for their eviction would be punished. Category II people who had voluntarily emigrated from the country would be dealt with according to the respective immigration and citizenship laws of Bhutan and Nepal; Category III people 'must return to their own country'; and the repatriation of those in Category IV was to be conducted in accordance with the laws of the two countries.

According to the Bhutanese authorities, following the expulsion of illegal ethnic Nepalese from 1988, the goal of ethnic Nepalese dissidents has been clear and is supported by various political leaders in Kathmandu. In this view, the dissidents wish to obstruct, and if possible reverse, Bhutan's determination to control and restrict the illegal entry of aliens into the country. Ethnic Nepalese view this restriction as 'unfair' and 'against their human rights', especially in the context of continuing unrestricted access into India for Nepalese persons. The Bhutanese Government counters that immigration controls, based on national legislation, are a precondition of Bhutan's sovereignty and security, and also of its cultural survival.

While senior Nepalese government officials now better understand the concerns of the Bhutanese Government, the media of Kathmandu continue to make statements that, at best, uncritically reflect the viewpoint of the anti-Thimphu organizations. During 1994–98 the US State Department and a prominent human rights organization, Amnesty International, issued reports on human rights in Bhutan which were based on acceptance of the claims of persons in the camps, but which did not appear to balance such assertions against the realities of sanctioned policy and practice within Bhutan.

Following an initial invitation by the Government (in 1991) and subsequent formal agreements between the parties, representatives of the International Committee of the Red Cross (ICRC) make regular visits to Bhutan to speak with detainees and to inspect prison facilities. After several visits (the first of which took place in January 1992), an ICRC delegation leader stated in May 1994 that the ICRC had 'an excellent working relationship' with the Government. The 1993 memorandum of understanding between the ICRC and the Government was renewed in 1998, and in October 1999 the ICRC stated that it had benefited from the 'good co-operation' of the authorities. In July 1994 the newly appointed UN High Commissioner for Human Rights (UNHCHR) was invited to Thimphu and on departure claimed that he had received 'very important information' on the matter of refugees in Nepal. In October the Office of the UN High Commissioner for Human Rights (OHCHR) working group on arbitrary detention visited Bhutan at the invitation of the authorities. In March 1995 the working group reported to the OHCHR plenum that the arrest and detention of Teknath Rizal (see above) had been 'not arbitrary', and—at the request of the Bhutanese Government—made 15 recommendations concerning problems in the administration of justice. The Government subsequently invited the working group to return to verify the implementation of these recommendations, which it did in April–May 1996. In its report to the OHCHR, the working group concluded that the recommendations had generally been implemented, and urged the speedy adoption of a revised Code of Criminal Procedure (then being drafted). In addition, the group proposed that technical training for judges and jabmis (publicly certificated advocates or defenders) should be augmented with assistance, as already agreed between Bhutan and the OHCHR. (An Act regulating jabmis was passed by the 81st session of the National Assembly in mid-2003.) In May 1997 Bhutan was re-elected, for a second three-year term, as one of the six Asian representatives to the UN Commission on Human Rights. An Amnesty International delegation visited eastern Bhutan and Sarpang by invitation in late November 1998. On 17 December 1999 (Bhutan's National Day) King Jigme announced the pardon of 200 common-law and other prisoners, including 40 who had been convicted for 'anti-national' acts since 1988. Teknath Rizal was among those pardoned. King Jigme noted that Rizal had already served 10 years in prison, but that he 'had not physically carried out acts of violence and terrorism'. The BPP, however, claimed that the Government had released Rizal only to discredit him, and that he was effectively prohibited from participating in political activity.

In southern Bhutan in 1994 pro-Government southern villagers seized a number of armed terrorists who had allegedly attacked their villages. Those arrested in 1993 and 1994 confirmed that the majority of them were absconders from Bhutan who had been induced by dissident leaders to go to the refugee camps in Nepal, where they subsequently received rudimentary military training before reportedly being ordered to return to Bhutan to commit robbery, arson and other terrorist activities. From December 1995, however, terrorist incidents were fewer, coinciding with the adoption of the 'peace march' tactic by persons claiming to be Bhutanese and seeking to travel from Nepal into Bhutan. These marches continued throughout 1996; a small group of marchers actually reached Phuentsholing in mid-August and again in December, before being forced to return to India. The Bhutanese Minister of Home Affairs asserted that those participating in the marches were not Bhutanese, but were non-nationals and emigrants who were attempting to enter the country illegally. A number of isolated bombing incidents occurred throughout Bhutan during 1998–99, most notably in Thimphu's main stadium in early November 1998. In June 1999 it was reported that the Bhutanese police had arrested 80 alleged Bhutanese refugees who were conducting a peaceful demonstration (organized by the Bhutan Gurkha National Liberation Front) in Phuentsholing; the demonstrators claimed to be genuine Bhutanese citizens who were seeking to travel from the camps in Nepal back into Bhutan.

In 1991 'Rongthong' Kinley Dorji (also styled Kuenley or Kunley), a former Bhutanese businessman accused of failing to repay loans and of acts against the State, had absconded to Nepal and joined the anti-Government movement. In 1992 he established and became President of a 'Druk National Congress' claiming human rights violations in Bhutan. The 74th session of the National Assembly, held in July 1996, discussed Kinley Dorji's case at length, and unanimously demanded his extradition from Nepal in conjunction with the Bhutan-Nepal talks. Following the signing of an extradition treaty between India and Bhutan in December, Kinley was arrested by the Indian authorities during a visit to Delhi in April 1997, and remained in detention until June 1998, when he was released on bail while his case was being examined by the Indian courts; the bail remained in force in August 1999. The extradition treaty was read to the 75th session of the National Assembly in July 1997, when Kinley Dorji's case was again discussed at length and demands for his return to Bhutan for trial were unanimously supported (as they were also at the 76th session in mid-1998 and the 77th session in 1999). At the same time the Assembly unanimously resolved that all relatives of 'ngolops' (anti-national militants) in government service should 'be compulsorily retired with post-service benefits', and that the Royal Civil Service Commission should implement this decision 'without undue delay'. By the end of January 1998 some 219 civil servants had been compulsorily retired with full post-service benefits. In July the Minister of Home Affairs reported that the main civil service still retained 2,900 Lhotshampas (Bhutanese of Nepalese origin), constituting some 24% of the total civil service, excluding those in the armed forces and corporations. The 75th Assembly also discussed the intrusions into Bhutan's south-eastern border forests by Bodo and Maoist extremists from the neighbouring Indian state of Assam. The Bhutanese people (especially those from the east of the country) have traditionally enjoyed good relations with the Bodos of Assam.

During 1997 anti-Government activities (culminating in rallies in south-eastern Bhutan in October) were alleged to have been organized in eastern Bhutan by several lay-preacher (Gomchen) students of Lam Dodrup in Sikkim; a number of arrests were subsequently made. Part of the famous historic retreat of Taktsang Monastery, which was visited by Prince Charles of the United Kingdom in February 1998, was badly damaged by fire under suspicious circumstances in April. Reconstruction work, which had cost some Nu 94m. by mid-2003, was completed in 2005. The main chapel was re-consecrated in March 2006.

Important institutional changes were introduced in mid-1998, whereby King Jigme relinquished his role as Head of Government (while remaining Head of State) in favour of a smaller elected Council of Ministers (lhengye zhungtshog), which was to consist of six ministers and all nine members of the Royal Advisory Council (lodoi tsokde) and which was to enjoy full executive power under the leadership of a Chairman (elected by ministers, on a rotational basis, for a one-year term in office) who would be Head of Government. On 16 June the King informed the members of the existing Council of Ministers that it was to be dissolved on 26 June, and stated that he had issued a kasho (royal decree) to the Speaker of the National Assembly, which was to be discussed at the pending 76th session. In the decree the King stressed the necessity to promote greater popular participation in the decision-making process, to strengthen the Government's mandate from the people, and to enhance the administration's transparency and efficiency with integral checks and balances 'to safeguard our national interest and security'. He said that the Council of Ministers should now be restructured as an elected body 'vested with full executive powers', and he put forward three key points—(i) all government ministers should henceforth be elected by the National Assembly, with the first election to take place during the 76th session; (ii) a decision should be taken on the exact role and responsibilities of the Council of Ministers; and (iii) the National Assembly should have a mechanism to move a vote of confidence in the King. In elaboration, King Jigme advised that the Council of Ministers should henceforth consist of elected ministers and the members of the Royal Advisory Council, ministers should be elected by secret ballot, candidates should be selected from those who have held senior government posts at the rank of Secretary or above, and a candidate must secure a majority of the votes cast to be considered elected. The portfolios for the elected ministers were to be awarded by the King. A minister's term in office was to be five years, after which he would undergo a vote of confidence in the National Assembly (previously there was no time limit on the tenure of ministerial posts). All decisions adopted by the Council of Ministers were to be based on consensus, and, while the Council 'shall govern Bhutan with full executive powers', it must also keep the King fully informed 'on all matters that concern the security and sovereignty' of the country. The procedures of the Council of Ministers were to be supervised by a Cabinet Secretary appointed by the Council. The 76th session of the National Assembly voted by secret ballot on six new ministerial nominees; all were successful, but all received some negative votes.

An act to regulate the Council of Ministers, which was framed by a committee comprising members of the Government, clergy and people's representatives of the 20 districts, was presented to the 77th session of the National Assembly in mid-1999 and was subjected to extensive discussion and amendment. The rules, as finally endorsed, explicitly specified that the King had full power to dissolve the Council of Ministers, although King Jigme observed that this meant that the monarch could exercise this mandate for purely personal reasons, even if the Council was discharging its duties in a responsible manner. Procedures for a confidence vote (with regard to the King) were also drafted by the aforementioned committee and presented to the 77th session of the National Assembly, where members unanimously expressed regret over (and opposition to) the draft and repeatedly requested that King Jigme withdraw the proposal. Following a further earnest plea by the King, however, a key draft provision that a confidence vote regarding the monarch should only be placed on the agenda of an assembly session if a minimum of 50% of the districts requested it, was amended to allow the initiative if supported by at least one-third of the assembly members. The 77th session also agreed that ministers should serve a maximum of two consecutive five-year terms.

King Jigme told the Council of Ministers at a special sitting in mid-August 1999 (held for the formal change of Chairman) that it should streamline the Government and create mobility in the higher levels of the civil service when staffing ministries and other organizations, and that it must be responsive to the needs of the people. He also stressed that, while governance was the responsibility of the Council of Ministers, the Royal Advisory Council was empowered to ensure that all the policies, laws and resolutions passed by the National Assembly were implemented by the Government. The outgoing Chairman of the Council, Lyonpo Jigmi Y. Thinley, stated that all the elements were now in place for a democratic system of decision-making, while government was being institutionalized and made more accountable and transparent. At the ceremony held for the formal rotation of Chairman of the Council of Ministers in August 2001, King Jigme expressed satisfaction at the progress of political reform since July 1998, and advised that changes in the fields of national security, the development of the Ninth Plan, and youth employment should be the Council's priorities. At the 11th SAARC summit, held in Kathmandu in January 2002, the incumbent Chairman of the Council, Lyonpo Khandu Wangchuck, was referred to as 'Prime Minister' of Bhutan, a title that subsequently became accepted usage. In accordance with a decree issued by King Jigme in September 2001, a committee to draft a written constitution for Bhutan was inaugurated in late November and began functioning at the end of the year. The 39-member committee was chaired by the Chief Justice and included the Chairman and members of the Royal Advisory Council, five government representatives, the Speaker of the National Assembly, representatives from each of the 20 districts, a nominee of the King, and two lawyers from the High Court. It was initially agreed that the first draft, to be completed by October 2002, would be subjected to extensive public comment and review before being presented to the Assembly for formal approval; however, by mid-2003 two further drafts had only been studied by the committee, King and Council of Ministers, and it appeared likely that a final draft would not be agreed upon until some time in 2005 or even 2006. Further evolution of the role of the National Assembly and the Royal Advisory Council was expected to continue alongside constitutional discussions. At the ceremony held for the formal rotation of Chairman of the Council of Ministers in August 2002, King Jigme reiterated his satisfaction at the achievements of the previous year, but emphasized the importance of closely guiding the process of devolution of authority at the district and geog (village block) level. The Government was also responsible for strengthening the private sector in order to accommodate the growing number of school-leavers. The King also recommended that investigations into a site for a second international airport be reviewed.

The creation of four new ministerial positions was announced in June 2003, bringing the total number of ministers to 10. The former Ministry of Health and Education was bifurcated into two ministries and the erstwhile Ministry of Communications was converted into the Ministry of Information and Communications and the Ministry of Works and Human Settlements. The Ministry of Labour and Human Resources was also created, incorporating the Central Statistical Office, the National Technical Training Authority and, amongst others, the Department of Employment and Labour. Under the government reorganization, the Ministry of Finance was to incorporate the Planning Commission Secretariat; the Ministry of Agriculture was instructed to take over the land records and survey departments; and the Ministry of Education was to incorporate the UNESCO national commission and Dzongkha Development Commission. The Ministry of Home Affairs absorbed the National Commission of Cultural Affairs to become the Ministry of Home and Cultural Affairs. In late August Lyonpo Jigmi Y. Thinley, the Minister of Home and Cultural Affairs, was appointed Chairman of the Council of Ministers; a new Cabinet Secretary was also appointed.

The activities of the militant 'anti-nationals' were unanimously condemned at the 76th session of the National Assembly in July 1998, but the most pressing security issue was judged to be the perceived threat from the presence of Assamese tribal (Bodo) and communist (United Liberation Front of Assam—ULFA) militants, who had established military training bases in the jungle border regions of south-eastern Bhutan. Particular concern was expressed regarding the Indian military incursions into Bhutanese territory in an attempt to drive the militants out. A serious incident that had taken place in May in Sarpang, reportedly involving 165 armed Indian soldiers, was discussed during the session, and was to be investigated by the Bhutanese and Indian authorities. The Indian authorities subsequently apologized for the incident. In mid-1999 the Minister of Home Affairs, addressing the 77th session of the National Assembly, reported that talks with ULFA second-tier and senior leadership (in November 1998 and May 1999, respectively) had elicited the response that members of the ULFA had been forced to enter Bhutanese territory in 1992, but that they were not ready to leave Bhutanese territory for at least another 18 months. They asserted that they were determined to fight until independence for Assam was achieved, but offered to reduce their military presence in Bhutan. The Bhutanese Government reiterated to the ULFA leaders that its concern was at the very presence of any number of armed militants on Bhutanese soil. After detailed discussion, assembly members decided that all supplies of food and other essentials to the ULFA and Bodo militants must be stopped, that any Bhutanese who assisted the militants should be punished according to the National Security Act, and that discussions should continue with the ULFA to seek a peaceful withdrawal of these foreign forces from Bhutan. The ULFA agreed to be represented at 'the highest level' at future talks.

The 78th session of the National Assembly, held in June–July 2000, thoroughly reviewed the problem of the presence of the armed ULFA and Bodo militants. It was eventually decided that negotiations with the militants' leaders should be further pursued, but that, if talks were not successful, Bhutan's armed forces should be used to expel the tribal insurgents from Bhutanese territory. Following two rounds of negotiations, held in November 1998 and May 1999, the ULFA subsequently failed to respond to a proposed third session of talks. In April 2000 the ULFA's Commander-in-Chief, Paresh Barua, expressed disappointment that details of the previous negotiations had been announced to the National Assembly in 1999, and stated that he and the ULFA Chairman now had to consider the 'very serious security risks' involved in entering Bhutan. He suggested sending one of the ULFA's senior advisers and the organization's financial secretary instead, but this level of involvement was not acceptable to the Bhutanese Government, which again insisted that the highest leadership should attend by 15 June 2000 (i.e. immediately prior to the Assembly's 78th session). Barua later confirmed the inability of the senior leadership to attend. The Bodo militants, specifically the National Democratic Front of Bodoland (NDFB), were to be engaged in parallel talks by 15 June, but in early June Ranjan Daimary, the Chairman of the NDFB, advised that he was unable to visit Bhutan for security reasons.

In mid-2001 the Minister of Home Affairs, addressing the 79th session of the National Assembly, reported that negotiations had been held with leaders of the NDFB in October 2000 and May 2001. During the talks, NDFB leaders had responded to a demand for the removal of their camps by declaring their intention to leave Bhutan, but would not commit themselves to a deadline. Following three days of discussions in June, representatives of the ULFA agreed to seven points, including the removal of four of the nine military camps in Bhutan by December 2001, and the reduction in strength of the cadres in the remaining camps. Further meetings were planned in order to find a solution to the issue of the remaining five camps. Members of the National Assembly were informed of the Government's preparations in the event of armed conflict with the militants: security had been strengthened, funds had been reserved for fuel supplies and medical support services, and contingency plans had been made to ensure the continued operation of the communications and transport systems. In addition, essential food supplies, such as grains, sufficient to last for three to six months, were stored in towns throughout Bhutan. Disappointment and concern were expressed at the low level of volunteer recruitment; of the 880 men recruited to the army in 2000/01, 27 had deserted and 131 had requested special leave. Districts were asked to send lists of volunteers to army headquarters immediately after the Assembly session. It was subsequently reported at the 80th session of the National Assembly in mid-2002 that, of the 2,581 men who volunteered for militia training, only 1,410 reported for training, and, of those, 380 were medically unfit and 198 sought to leave because of domestic problems. Only 24 volunteers from the 20 districts wished to join as militia. The remaining 808 volunteers wished to join the army permanently as soldiers. The training of volunteers for the militia, therefore, was rendered unviable. Nevertheless, in mid-2003 it was reported to the 81st session of the National Assembly that some 4,558 persons had since volunteered and, of these, some 667 volunteers (including 15 women) had been selected for a two-month training programme from mid-July.

In December 2001 the army visited the four designated ULFA training camps and, confirming that these had been abandoned, began to disable and destroy the training and accommodation facilities. Initially, the whereabouts of the ULFA militants was unknown. It was not possible immediately to ascertain whether the ULFA units had managed to leave Bhutan and, evading Indian military forces in Assam, reach their presumed goals of Bangladesh and Myanmar. At the same time there were concerns that the militants had relocated their camps elsewhere in Bhutan. At the 80th session of the National Assembly in mid-2002 the Minister of Home Affairs confirmed that the ULFA had closed down its military training centre in Martshala geog and camps at Gobarkonda, Nangri and Deori. The ULFA, however, had opened a new camp on a mountain ridge above the main Samdrup Jongkhar–Trashigang highway, raising the total number of camps remaining in Bhutan to six. In the mean time, the NDFB had three main camps and four mobile camps between Lhamoizingkha and Daifam. The Minister of Home Affairs also reported that the Government had only recently become aware that the Indian militant Kamtapur Liberation Organization (KLO) had established camps in Bhangtar dungkhag and near Piping in Lhamoizingkha dungkhag. The KLO armed militants were Rajbansi tribals of North Bengal, bordering Chhukha and Samtse dzongkhags, who were campaigning for separate statehood for the Kamtapuris.

The Minister of Home Affairs stressed that the presence of armed militants in Bhutan remained a grave threat. It appeared that no more negotiations could be held with the NDFB. The issue was further complicated by the presence of KLO militants in Bhutan. Assembly members vigorously debated the developments; some questioned how such events could have arisen, suggesting that Bhutan could not depend on India and should instead look to 'our neighbour in the north'. The Minister of Foreign Affairs countered these views by asserting that there was 'only one path' for India and Bhutan—'the path of goodwill and friendship'. The Assembly endorsed three decisions proposed by the Council of Ministers: first, to hold joint negotiations with the Chairman and the military commander of the ULFA, since in previous meetings no decisions could be taken on the pretext of the absence of one of these leaders; second, the Government would not agree to participate in any more meetings on the reduction of ULFA camps, but was prepared to discuss only the closure of the militants' main training camp and headquarters: 'the headquarters of the ULFA must be moved out of Bhutan'. Finally, if ULFA leaders refused to relocate their headquarters, there would be no option but to evict them physically. King Jigme informed the National Assembly that it was important to hold talks with the ULFA and NDFB separately. Although the KLO was a new, relatively unknown, group—the Government did not even know the identity of its leaders—the King warned that the authorities, if they had to resort to military action, would have to deal with all three organizations. Little progress was made during the following year, and the 81st session of the National Assembly in mid-2003 reaffirmed the previous resolutions: the new 10-member Government of Bhutan should make a last attempt to persuade the senior ULFA leaders to enter negotiations and to close down their main camp; if negotiations were unsuccessful, Bhutan would resort to military action to compel the militants to leave the country. Addressing the National Assembly, the Minister of Home Affairs reported that the ULFA had increased the total number of camps inside Bhutan to eight, with an estimated 1,560 militants. The NDFB had eight camps, with about 740 militants. The KLO from West Bengal had three camps in Bhutan, with an estimated 430 militants in mid-2003. Following talks held in March with mid-level KLO leaders, the Government proposed entering dialogue with the Chairman of the organization in Thimphu before the 81st session of the Assembly commenced; the KLO, however, did not respond. At the Assembly session the Minister of Home Affairs stressed that military action would cause unimaginable suffering to the people, directly affecting more than 66,000 people in 304 villages in 10 districts. The Council of Ministers approved a contingency budget of up to Nu 2,000m. in the event of military action. In addition, two refugee camps and 12 transit camps were being prepared to accommodate the Bhutanese population that might be displaced. Many chimis (National Assembly members) proposed immediate military action. King Jigme informed the Assembly that India had given its assurance that the Indian army would not enter Bhutan without the permission of the Council of Ministers and the National Assembly. However, he observed, with reference to newspaper reports in India, that, as the Assembly had been holding similar discussions and passing similar resolutions every year since 1997 on the issue, it was natural that people in India would consider this discussion process as a ploy to avoid taking actions against the militants. He again stressed that, if the ULFA agreed to remove their central headquarters, other camps would subsequently close, and that, if the negotiations failed, military action would be aimed at all three militant groups.

King Jigme visited India in mid-September 2003 to discuss mainly economic and defence issues. The Bhutanese Government subsequently made further efforts to seek a peaceful resolution of the issue of foreign militants, by directly addressing the three armed Indian groups that had encampments in Bhutan. An ULFA delegation attended negotiations in October, but insisted that its executive council would need to discuss the closure of the group's chief camp (without which the others would not be viable), and that ULFA leaders would visit in early December to convey their decision. According to a government statement in mid-December, however, the leaders had failed to appear. At a meeting with the NDFB delegation in late November, the NDFB representatives stated that even if they left now, they would have to return and establish camps in other parts of Bhutan. The Ministry of Home Affairs thus concluded that 'given such an attitude, there is no scope for resolving the problem through dialogue'. Meanwhile, the KLO continued not to respond to any initiatives taken by the Bhutanese Government. The government statement of 13 December, published the same day in the *Kuensel* newspaper, stated that Bhutan might have to implement the decision of the 81st session of the National Assembly. Two days later the RBA simultaneously attacked most of the 30 training camps, concentrating on the elimination of the general headquarters camp of the ULFA. By the end of the month the Government was able to report that all camps of the militants had been seized and burnt down—the ULFA had 14 camps (10 in Samdrup Jongkhar, three in Sarpang, one in lower Zhemgang), the NDFB had 11 camps (four in Sarpang and seven in Samdrup Jongkhar), and the KLO had five camps (one in Samdrup Jongkhar, one in Kalikhola, and three in Samtse). Large quantities of armaments and equipment were seized, including an anti-aircraft gun. No casualty figures were released by the militants, but King Jigme told an Indian journalist in May 2004 that Bhutan had suffered 13 dead and 36 wounded. Responding to a demand by the National Assembly at the 82nd session, the Minister of Home Affairs stated that 142 people suspected of aiding and abetting the militants were being tried in the district courts; several additional cases had been abandoned owing to lack of evidence. Those charged included eight civil servants, 36 business people and 94 farmers.

The Chief of Operations of the RBA visited Delhi in August 2006 for discussions with his Indian counterparts; according to Indian media reports (citing 'official sources'), the ULFA was attempting to re-establish its presence in Bhutan and had set up 'at least three camps' in Samdrup Jongkhar district, despite India's deployment of the 'Shashtra Seema Bal' military units along the Assam-Bhutan border; the cadres were reportedly led by Hira Sarania,who was believed to be a close associate of Barua.

The 78th and 79th sessions of the National Assembly also reviewed the progress of negotiations with the Government of Nepal concerning people in camps in Nepal. Two meetings, in November 1999 and in March 2000, resulted in an agreement on measures to strengthen the mechanism for verifying the national status of these people; although 'much progress' had been made, there was still 'no conclusive agreement' on a number of issues. The verification process could not yet begin, owing to disagreement over one issue: the Bhutanese Government wanted verification of all adults aged 18 years and above, whereas Nepal required verification only on the basis of head of family. According to the Minister of Foreign Affairs at the 78th session, Bhutan found the latter proposal unacceptable, because the head of a family would include as members of the family those who were not legally members; the problem in conducting a census in southern Bhutan was created by (among other factors) the inclusion of non-family members into the registered families. Although many Assembly members argued strongly that no persons who had left Bhutan should be allowed to return, the Minister of Home Affairs reiterated that the Bhutanese Government would take full responsibility for any Bhutanese national found to have been forcibly expelled from Bhutan, while those found to have evicted any genuine Bhutanese would be liable for punishment under Bhutanese law.

Nepal and Bhutan finally achieved a breakthrough at the 10th round of joint ministerial negotiations in December 2000. Both countries agreed that nationality would be verified on the basis of the head of the refugee family for those over 25 years of age. Refugees under 25 would be verified on an individual basis. By the end of January 2001 a Joint Verification Team (JVT), consisting of five officials each from the Nepalese and Bhutanese Governments, had concluded the inspection of the refugee camps. Verification of the nationality of 98,897 people (including 13,000 children born in the camps) claiming refugee status began at the end of March 2001, commencing with the Khudanabari camp. The Minister of Foreign Affairs informed the National Assembly of the progress of the JVT, which had, by early July, verified the status of 4,128 individuals. Despite criticisms in the Nepalese press that the pace was too slow, the Minister argued that it was essential for both parties to maintain a credible verification process. He planned to meet his Nepalese counterpart immediately after the Assembly to review how harmonization could conclude simultaneously with verification, as anticipated in the December 2000 bilateral agreement. The Assembly endorsed the ongoing verification process, and decided that any ensuing problems should be resolved first at the secretary level of the two Governments, or, if necessary, at the ministerial level. At a meeting in early November the Ministers of Foreign Affairs of Bhutan and Nepal were unable to harmonize the positions of their respective governments with regard to the four categories for the people in the camps. The Nepalese Minister of Foreign Affairs proposed the reduction of the categories to two—Bhutanese and non-Bhutanese—a suggestion rejected by his Bhutanese counterpart. The Nepalese Minister of Foreign Affairs requested a meeting at the ministerial level (the 12th of its kind) to be convened in early 2002. In late 2001 the verification of individuals in the Khudanabari camp was completed; however, with the recent disagreements over harmonization, the process reached a standstill. Although unofficial discussions with various parties took place in early 2002, the Bhutanese Minister of Foreign Affairs, at the 80th session of the National Assembly, warned that 'the unstable political situation in Nepal might affect the ongoing dialogue and delay a solution'. King Jigme further informed the Assembly that the Government of Nepal's refusal to abide by the agreements reached and signed by previous ministerial joint committees was hindering progress in resolving the problems and delaying the convening of the 12th ministerial level meeting. The Assembly agreed that the Government should continue discussions with the Nepalese Government to seek a lasting solution to the problem. In January 2003 Bhutan hosted the 12th ministerial joint committee (MJC), at which the two Governments finally harmonized their positions on each of the four categories. The 14th MJC in May resolved all the remaining issues in order to finalize the categorization process. Details of the results of the verification process at Khudanabari were published on 18 June: 74 families (293 people) were in Category I (forcefully evicted Bhutanese people); 2,182 families (8,595 people) were in Category II (Bhutanese who had emigrated); 817 families (2,948 people) were in Category III (non-Bhutanese people); and 85 families (347 people) were in Category IV (Bhutanese who had committed criminal acts). The JVT allowed 14 days for appeals (which were to be rejected if not based on documentation), and was to submit its recommendation on the appeals to the 15th meeting of the MJC, scheduled to meet in Thimphu later that year. The 15th MJC was also required to select the next camp to undergo verification. However, a new Government in Nepal from late May criticized the agreements made by its predecessor; several political parties in Nepal also called for the Nepalese Government to repudiate the arrangements. None the less, arrangements were being made to conduct the repatriation to Bhutan of most of the families in Category I by the end of 2003. Those in Category II might choose to return to Bhutan and reapply for citizenship in accordance with Bhutanese laws, or they might wish to apply for Nepalese citizenship. The Minister of Home Affairs informed the 81st session of the National Assembly that there were more than 55,000 non-national workers in Bhutan in 2003, all of whom would also like to claim Bhutanese citizenship, and stated that it was imperative that any persons returning to the country should be dealt with strictly according to the citizenship and immigration laws. He also claimed that the ultimate agenda of those who had left Bhutan and now resided in camps in Nepal was to bring into Bhutan a large number of non-Bhutanese people of Nepalese origin, take over the country's political power and government machinery, and provide themselves and other people of Nepalese origin with land and Bhutanese citizenship.

The 15th meeting of the MJC, charged with providing strategic direction for the detailed work of the JVT, was held in Thimphu in October 2003 and was hailed as very successful by the leader of Nepal's team, Dr B. B. Thapa. The JVT was to return to Jhapa at the end of November to review the remaining appeals from persons in the Khudanabari camp and then start work in the Sanischare camp. It was agreed that Bhutan would be fully responsible for any Category I persons, while Category II people could apply for either Bhutanese or Nepalese citizenship, in accordance with the respective laws. Appeals by Category III people were to be resolved by the end of January 2004. However, in December 2003 an attack was made on the Bhutanese members of the JVT by a crowd of several thousand, who had gathered near to where the JVT was explaining the remaining procedures to members of the Khudanabari camp. The JVT members were withdrawn to Thimphu and the planned initial repatriation of some of the Category I persons could not take place by mid-February 2004. The attack, described by a Nepalese government spokesperson as regrettable, was discussed by the two Governments at the SAARC summit meeting in early January, and further talks were to be held by the Ministers of Foreign Affairs in an effort to avoid a recurrence. A report of the investigation into the incident by the Nepalese Government, received in May by the Bhutanese counterpart, was described by the latter as 'falling far short' of its request for a full investigation, and reportedly contained several factual inaccuracies. However, by early August there appeared to be an agreement that the verification process could continue in a second camp in Nepal. The Bhutanese Ministry of Foreign Affairs informed the 82nd session of the National Assembly of related developments, which it stated could have serious implications for the security of the country: first, a Bhutan Gorkha Liberation Front and a Bhutan Communist Party (Marxist-Leninist-Maoist) (BCP—MLM) had been formed, with the latter reportedly having links with the Maoists in Nepal; and second, the Maoists had been recruiting people in the camps—some of these people had even participated in Maoist attacks in Nepal. The Ministry declared that if such camp members were to enter Bhutan, the country would be 'infested with communists and Maoists'. Nevertheless, the Ministry asserted that the Government would abide by all the agreements reached with the Nepalese Government in order to find a 'lasting and durable solution to the issue of the people in the camps'. Little concrete progress on this issue was possible during 2005–06, particularly because of the political disturbances in Nepal, but the two sides continued to exchange views at international meetings. At the 15th SAARC summit held in Colombo in early August 2008, Bhutan's Prime Minister, Jigmi Yozer Thinley, met with his Nepalese counterpart, G. P. Koirala; the two leaders agreed that their respective Governments would resume the stalled talks.

Reflecting the increasing complexities of contemporary administration, the 77th Assembly passed an unprecedented number of acts in mid-1999 to enhance the prevailing legal framework relating to telecommunications (providing for the creation of a state-owned public corporation, Bhutan Telecom, from the existing Telecommunications Division), the postal sector (enabling Bhutan Post to become an autonomous public sector corporation), bankruptcy (giving a contemporary context for the rights and duties of borrowers and lenders), movable and immovable property (setting a legal framework for the management of loans, mortgages and related securities and financial services), legal deposit (copies of all 'documentary material' published in Bhutan 'or related to Bhutan' are to be deposited with the National Library in Thimphu), municipalities (establishing legal authority for municipalities to enforce rules relating to urban development), and road safety (strengthening the legal basis for administration of passenger safety and vehicle management). Further indications of the modernization of Bhutan were the inauguration of (limited) television and internet services in June and July, respectively, and the election of nine women to attend the 1999 session of the National Assembly (this number had increased to 11 and 16 by 2000 and 2001, respectively). In the mid-2001 Assembly session, a female councillor was for the first time elected to the Royal Advisory Council. At the end of 1999 a government-endorsed report proposed the rationalization of government under 10 ministries; the proposals were to be fully implemented by 2002. In addition, two new government agencies—the Department of Legal Affairs (subsequently renamed as the Office of Legal Affairs) and the National Employment Board—were established, and a new Department of Aid and Debt Management was created. In mid-2001 the Council of Ministers decided to reduce the number of skilled expatriate (principally Indian) workers from 50,000 to 25,000 with immediate effect, and aimed further to decrease the foreign work-force to 12,500 by the end of 2002. The Bhutan Chamber of Commerce and Industries protested against the decision, regarding it as too hasty and arguing that Bhutan's labour force was seasonal, owing to rural harvesting, and that the Bhutanese generally disparage manual labour. In October 2001 the Council of Ministers permitted the mining industry more time to reduce imported labour, but insisted that all firms and industries would have similar obligations from 2004. Revised rules for geog and district development committees to create a legal basis for local autonomy in development matters (a fundamental issue under the Ninth Plan) were approved by the National Assembly at its 80th session in mid-2002. This was considered an important development in the devolution of political authority. New elections for gups (heads of geogs) took place in October 2002. Meanwhile, in accordance with the 1999 Municipal Act, residents of Thimphu elected members of the municipal council in late December 2001. At the 81st session of the Assembly, a number of international treaties and conventions (including SAARC conventions) were ratified. The Royal Civil Service Commission (RCSC) was formally established as an autonomous body by the 81st National Assembly; the heads of the three branches of Government (the judiciary, with 271 employees; the legislature, with 39 employees; and the executive branch, with 13,151 employees) would propose the members, functions, and responsibilities of the commission members, while appointment of the RCSC Chairman would be on the advice of the King.

During the 82nd session of the National Assembly, held in June–August 2004, a controversial Speaker's Act was adopted (to be confirmed in mid-2005), providing that the Speaker must be fluent in both Dzongkha and English, would have the status of a cabinet minister, and would be elected for a five-year term (extendable for a second term) only by and from the elected members of the Assembly (i.e. excluding appointed government officials). The 82nd session also approved a reduction in the personal income tax 'ceiling' from 25% to 15%, endorsed a number of important acts further to consolidate the administrative infrastructure, and ratified various international agreements (including the WHO Framework Convention on Tobacco Control, the Berne Convention for the Protection of Literary and Artistic Works, and the Vienna Convention for the Protection of the Ozone Layer). Also, importantly, the Assembly resolved that henceforth tobacco smoking should be banned in Bhutan. The policy was formally implemented in December 2004.

In October 2004 the US Assistant Secretary of State for Population, Refugees and Migration, Arthur Dewey, visited Bhutan in order to hold discussions on how to end the deadlock regarding the ongoing problem of those in refugee camps in Nepal. At the end of his visit he stated that he was reassured by the commitment of the Bhutanese Government to finding a solution to the problem. However, by early 2005 it appeared that the absence of a strong administration in Nepal would preclude any early resumption of the registration process in the camps.

Meanwhile, in March 2004 the death penalty was formally abolished in a decree issued by King Jigme. In September, following eight months of trials in district courts, 111 people (including seven women) were sentenced to prison terms ranging from four years to life, having been convicted of aiding and abetting Indian militants while the latter had been camped on Bhutanese territory. With effect from the same month visas were waived for Bhutanese and Thai holders of diplomatic or official passports visiting the country for up to 90 days. In order to ensure better security, new Bhutanese passports were to be issued from late 2005.

On 31 October 2004 the Crown Prince, Dasho Jigme Khesar Namgyel Wangchuck, was formally installed at Trongsa as Chhoetse penlop (heir to the throne). After accompanying the King to India in January 2005 (see below), he entered a one-year course at India's National Defence College.

In November 2004 Bhutan hosted its first World Trade Organization (WTO)-related working party meeting in Geneva, Switzerland, to discuss its Memorandum on the Foreign Trade Regime (MFTR) with WTO members. (The MFTR, circulated in February 2003, describes the financial, economic and trade policies in effect in Bhutan and serves as the basis for discussions moving towards a formal request for admission to the WTO.) Bhutan, one of 31 countries seeking WTO membership at mid-2005, submitted its formal application in September 1999.

King Jigme visited India in late November 2004. During his visit, the Indian Prime Minister, Manmohan Singh, made observations pertaining to the close and co-operative nature of Indo-Bhutan relations. Subsequently, the Indian Government agreed to a request made by the King for a revision of the Chhukha electricity tariff from Nu 1.50 to Nu 2 per unit, effective from January 2005. The Bhutanese Government made clear its appreciation of the Indian gesture, noting that it would contribute a net additional Nu 734m. in annual revenue. At the same time, the Bhutanese Government announced its concern regarding the sustainability of its ambitious budget for the Ninth Plan, and noted that many planned activities and expenditures were, in consequence, being scaled down.

King Jigme visited India again (accompanied by the Crown Prince) in January 2005, having been invited as chief guest for the celebration of Republic Day. The visit, according to a subsequent joint declaration, greatly contributed to 'further enhancing the mutual understanding, trust and friendship between the governments, leaders and peoples of the two countries'; and the visit (and agreements signed during it) was widely regarded as indicative of India's appreciation of the December 2003 military operation that had removed Indian militants from Bhutan. (Several Bhutanese soldiers were killed in the operation.) The two countries agreed to address cross-border security concerns, and India agreed to increase its assistance for the Ninth Plan from Rs 4,300m. to Rs 7,100m. In addition, three memoranda of understanding were signed, agreeing to: (i) the preparation of detailed project feasibility reports on an additional two hydroelectric projects (the 1,000 MW Punatsangchhu I, and 1,500 MW Punatsangchhu II with Mangdechhu); (ii) the preparation of feasibility studies on the establishment of railway links between India's West Bengal and Assam states to southern Bhutan towns—from Hashimara (West Bengal) to Phuentsholing with bifurcation to Pasakha (18 km), from Kokrajkar (Assam) to Gelephu (70 km), from Pathsala (Assam) to Nanglam (40 km), from Rangia (Assam) to Samdrup Jongkhar via Darranga (60 km), and between Banarhat (West Bengal) and Samtse (16 km); (iii) co-operation in the field of agriculture and allied sectors.

From 17 December 2004 (National Day) all tobacco sales were banned, making Bhutan the first sovereign state to declare such a policy. Imports of tobacco were permitted for private consumption, although these attracted either a 100% sales tax (when originating from India) or a 200% sales tax (when originating from other countries, comprising a 100% sales tax and 100% customs duty). A ban on smoking in public places was also under discussion. As decided by the 82nd Assembly, personal income tax rates were reduced from January 2005.

In late November 2004 the fourth draft of the Constitution, comprising 34 articles, was presented by King Jigme to the lhengye zhungtshog; formally receiving the document, the Prime Minister, Lyonpo Yeshey Zimba, observed that the biggest challenge lay in the interim period, 'when the people were not fully educated and prepared'. In his National Day speech, King Jigme stated that the highest importance was attached to the establishment of parliamentary democracy and a system of government that would provide good governance. The draft would be distributed to districts in 2005 for public consultation, following which he would personally visit every district to meet with the people and hold discussions on all issues regarding the document. Only after the consultation had been completed would adoption of the Constitution take place. In early January 2005 the Secretary-General of India's Lok Sabha (the lower house of parliament) visited Bhutan by invitation, stating on his departure that Bhutan was set to have an 'excellent' constitution that would 'serve the welfare of the people'. In the same month the Government approved a 45% increase in salary for all civil servants, general service cadres, and royal advisory councillors. In March the draft Constitution was released to the public. A second draft of the document, with several simplified clauses, was distributed for public review in September of that year. In the same month Lyonpo Sangay Ngedup Dorji assumed the office of Prime Minister.

The issue of new citizenship identity cards, valid for 10 years, had been completed in Thimphu by early 2005, and the registration for these cards continued from eastern Bhutan. In late May a nation-wide population and housing census took place, and final results were published in April 2006 (see Physical and Social Geography—Population and Ethnic Groups).

In September 2005, on the occasion of the annual handover of prime ministerial authority within the Council of Ministers, King Jigme informed the ministers that work on the Constitution should be completed before the two-year lona (inauspicious years) commenced on 2 January 2006 (the lona was to conclude on the winter solstice day in January 2008). He observed that long-delayed plans for a new Supreme Court building were ready, and that a new building for the National Council had to be constructed adjacent to the existing National Assembly building (preliminary construction work on each of these projects began in mid-October 2005). An Electoral Act was being prepared and an Election Commission was to be established, to (among other tasks) 'educate and prepare the people in the 202 geogs' during 2006–07 for elections in 2008. King Jigme also emphasized the importance of further professionalization of the media, commenting that the (government-owned) Kuensel Corporation should divest its shares, and that the establishment of one or two private newspapers should be encouraged. In view of the lona, the celebrations for the centenary of the monarchy (nominally from 17 December 2007) were to take place in 2008, and were to be combined with celebrations for the inauguration of the Constitution and the holding of general elections; separate celebrations for each of these events would prove too costly. The King also stated that the principal concern of the Government should be the achievement of a 'better quality of life' for the people of Bhutan, and that its 'highest priority' was to provide for the employment of youth.

The 84th session of the National Assembly in November 2005 adopted acts relating to narcotics (as a basis further to combat the increasing incidence of drugs abuse), moveable cultural property (to provide stronger protection to cultural properties that were more than 100 years old), food (to establish quality standards and rules for food safety, and to counter the dumping of sub-standard foodstuffs in Bhutan), and evidence. A National Narcotics Control Board, with 11 members and chaired by the Minister of Health, was commissioned in mid-2006.

In his national day speech on 17 December 2005, King Jigme observed that in 2007 Bhutan would no longer be categorized as a least-developed country. Regarding constitutional change, he stated that during 2006 and 2007 the Election Commission 'will educate our people in the process of parliamentary democracy, and electoral practice sessions will be conducted . . . The first national election to elect a government under a system of parliamentary democracy will take place in 2008'. He also announced (almost as an aside) his forthcoming abdication: 'I would also like our people to know that the Chhoetse penlop will be enthroned as the fifth Druk Gyalpo in 2008 . . . I will be delegating my responsibilities to [him] before 2008'.

Appointments to the first foreshadowed constitutional posts were announced at the end of December 2005: the incumbent Auditor-General became Chief Election Commissioner; the Secretary of the Ministry of Foreign Affairs became the Chairperson of the Anti-Corruption Commission; and the former Director of the National Pension and Provident Fund was appointed to the post of Auditor-General. Legislation for these, and for evolving the Office of Legal Affairs into an office of the Attorney-General, was adopted at the 85th session of the National Assembly in June 2006. Five new judges were appointed to the High Court in January 2006, increasing membership of the Full Bench to nine.

The report *Good Governance Plus*, which was published in November 2005, reviewed the performance of government over the past several years and proposed 231 points for action or reform by the Government, demanding both more professionalism in the civil service and the development of a strategy to make the private sector 'the engine of economic growth'. Alleviation of corruption was also given high priority, reflecting a comment made by the Crown Prince in late 2005 to graduate students that the 'biggest challenges' facing Bhutan were complacency and corruption.

Members of the 85th session of the Assembly in June 2006 strongly advocated the construction of a new internal southern highway from Phuentsholing to Dewathang, which would mean that travelling through India's West Bengal and Assam would no longer be necessary. The Minister of Works and Human Settlement responded that the estimated cost of such a project, approximately Nu 3,065m., currently made it unviable; however, some 200 km of this east–west highway were projected to be built during the 10th Plan, with possible completion scheduled by the end of the 11th Plan (in 2018).

The 85th session also adopted enabling legislation for the new constitutional posts: the Anti-Corruption Commission Act, giving the legal basis for preventive measures, awareness education, and investigative authority; and the Audit Act, providing full autonomy for the Royal Audit Authority.

By August 2006 the Election Commission had prepared (and circulated to districts for confirmation) a draft list of some 400,000 potential voters (all persons who were older than 16 years in January 2006 were listed). This was to constitute the basis for a formal electoral roll of those who would be 18 years (the minimum voting age) or older at the time of voting in 2008; additionally, voters were required to be 'authentic Bhutan citizens', of sound mind and with no criminal record. It was widely expected that two trial elections would be held, the first in early 2007 and the second towards the end of the year. Additional election rules and enabling legislation (e.g. the Election Bill, a Public Election Fund Bill, and a National Referendum Bill) were being prepared for discussion at the 86th and subsequent sessions of the National Assembly. In September 2006 the Chief Election Commissioner, Kunzang Wangdi, confirmed that all political parties registered with the Election Commission would be permitted to enter the first round of the 2008 general elections; the two parties with the highest number of votes would then contest the second and final round to gain parliamentary seats.

In his address to the Council of Ministers on 7 September 2006 at the handover of the rotating prime ministership, King Jigme advised that the Ninth Plan programme should be completed by the end of 2007, and the 10th Plan budget should be mobilized before the 2008 elections. He also stated that the Government should attempt to identify and eradicate the underlying causes of unemployment and 'not merely seek to reduce' the level of unemployment. The King proposed the establishment of a Trust Fund for Employment with proposed initial funding of US $100m., advising that the establishment of trust funds made it more difficult for future governments to exhaust hard currency resources. He recommended that projected building expenditure for government offices, a new National Council building, and a residential complex for new members of Parliament in 2008 be put on hold, placing the onus on the new king to usher in the new system and ensure the success of parliamentary democracy in Bhutan.

On 9 December 2006 King Jigme Singye Wangchuck issued a kasho transferring his responsibilities as head of state to the Crown Prince, Dasho Jigme Khesar Namgyel Wangchuck (henceforth referred to as King Jigme Khesar). The retiring King envisaged a 'very bright future' for Bhutan, with the 'leadership of a new King and a domestic system of government that is best suited for our country as enshrined under the Constitution'. The kasho was formally announced at an enlarged meeting of the Council of Ministers on 14 December, at which the Chief Justice expressed the deep gratitude of the Bhutanese people to the King 'for giving them the identity that they were so proud of'. King Jigme advised the meeting that political parties should be established at least six months before the elections, so that they could obtain political experience prior to the holding of the polls; that there should be at least three, and ideally four or five, parties contesting the polls to give credibility to the electoral process; and that ministers, civil servants and private-sector businessmen should have no reservations about forming parties if they so wished. According to the outgoing King, the establishment of parliamentary democracy was not a goal in itself, and he expressed his hopes that the process of democratization would enhance good government and also enable Bhutan to interact further with the global community.

The 86th session of the National Assembly, which was held in December 2006/January 2007, reviewed the status of people in the camps in Nepal. The Minister of Foreign Affairs reported that Bhutan had offered to take back from Khudanabari camp all Category I (forcefully evicted) persons, together with those Category IV people (those who had undertaken criminal acts) who chose to return to Bhutan. In November 2005 he had proposed that the JVT members of both countries visit the camp to explain procedures and collect applications from those opting to return, but his Nepalese counterpart refused to allow the 'incorporation in any written form (in a joint communiqué or otherwise)' of the terms and procedures previously agreed. In 2006 the Nepalese Government introduced a new element to the refugee issue, stating that the problem was between Bhutan and the camp people, that a direct dialogue between these two sides should be established, and that the ultimate aim was the repatriation of all the camp people. Bhutan refused to accept Nepal's new position in light of its view that most of the people in the camps were not Bhutanese; moreover, Bhutan asserted that the involvement of the Nepalese Government in the bilateral process was necessary as there was clear agreement that people under Category II who did not wish to return to Bhutan would be given the option to apply for Nepalese citizenship. A meeting between the two Governments scheduled to be held in late November 2006 was postponed at the request of the Nepalese authorities. The Bhutanese Minister of Foreign Affairs also expressed concern at the 'growing nexus' between militant elements in the camps and Indian Maoists and Naxalites and insurgent groups evicted from Bhutan in December 2003.

Legislation adopted by the 86th session included bills relating to judicial services (enhancing the functional and institutional independence of the judiciary over court personnel, particularly through the establishment of a Judicial Services Council), immigration (consolidating existing immigration laws and enhancing procedures), and labour and employment (outlining rules governing employer-employee relations and permitting workers to establish associations). The session also reviewed drafts of election-related bills scheduled to be adopted by the new government in 2008: an election bill, a national referendum bill and a public election fund bill. A number of national assembly members expressed strong opposition to a proposal in the election bill that only those with a formal first university degree would be eligible to stand as members of Parliament in the 2008 elections, but the Election Commissioner counter-argued that it was extremely important to ensure quality of governance under the new parliamentary regime.

Nation-wide 'mock' elections were held in April and May 2007, with a reasonable turn-out from the electorate. In May–June Bhutan police arrested 30 persons (including three students) in Samtse, who were alleged to have joined the BCP—MLM based in Jhapa, Nepal, and who were reportedly attempting to enlist members for training in arms and explosives and to establish a base for armed rebellion within Bhutan. The BCP—MLM's armed wing, the Bhutan Tiger Force, was also reported to have distributed pamphlets in the camps in Nepal advising residents to refuse an offer by the US Administration of 60,000 resettlement places (offering also the possibilities of permanent residency after one year and citizenship after five years). Nevertheless, in February 2008 Nepal began issuing exit permits to those people in the Nepalese camps who had opted for resettlement, and in March the first group of refugees left for the USA and New Zealand.

The 87th session, held in June 2007, was the final meeting of the National Assembly as it had developed from its foundation in 1953 (its role was to be assumed by the new Parliament that would assemble in mid-2008 after the holding of the national elections a few months earlier). Political considerations relating to the pending organization of the various political parties and elections overshadowed much of the business of the meeting. The session's work was principally to receive and discuss the report on the work of the outgoing government and the annual budget report, as well as to discuss and enact additional draft legislation relating to the organization of both religious and civil societies (regulating non-profit groups for transparency and accountability under a legal committee of authority—both types of body were banned from involvement in public elections and political affairs), local government (clarifying and limiting the mandate of local government officers), thromde (towns) (providing for the establishment of various types and sizes of towns and townships, and granting various levels of planning and service authority), public finance (confirming ministerial responsibility for any oversights), and national environment protection. A long-awaited revision of the land act was adopted, which provided for the establishment of a National Land Commission, retained a 25-acre (around 10 ha) limit for personal land-holding, but exempted 'industrial land' from this limit. A final ruling on a civil service bill was postponed for decision by the new Parliament in 2008, in part owing to inconsistencies in its drafting. The session also received the first annual report of the Anti-Corruption Commission. Support was expressed for the training of militia, and concern voiced regarding the poor performance of the education sector.

In June 2007 King Jigme Khesar instructed the Chief Election Commissioner to conduct elections for the National Council in December of that year, a primary round for the National Assembly in February 2008, and general elections for the Assembly in March 2008. The Election Commission declared itself open to receive party nominations from the beginning of July 2007, but the initial response was slow. An informal party associated with Lyonpo Sangay Ngedup Dorji, the People's Democratic Party (PDP), had begun drawing up lists of members and potential electoral candidates well in advance of the 87th Assembly; two other groups—the Bhutan National Party (BNP) and the Bhutan United People Party (BUPP)—initially merged (the former to the latter) shortly after the announcement of the formation of another body, the All People's Party (APP), with which several ministers were believed to be associated. By mid-July, however, although no formal party registration applications had been made, the announcement of the establishment of yet another party, the Druk Phuensum Tshogpa (DPT), which was composed of members of both the BUPP and the APP (which thus ceased to exist as separate groups) as well as five ministers, suggested that the field of contestants had been reduced to two parties: the DPT (which, in August 2007, elected Lyonpo Jigmi Yozer Thinley, the former Minister of Home and Cultural Affairs, as its President) and the PDP (led by former Minister of Agriculture Lyonpo Sangye Ngedup). Pending formal registration and further direction from the Election Commission, there was speculation that, if this remained the case, only one round of national elections would be necessary in early 2008, as one of the two parties would certainly form the government and the other would constitute the parliamentary opposition.

In July 2007 the Prime Minister and Minister of Foreign Affairs, Lyonpo Khandu Wangchuck, tendered the resignation of himself and six other ministers prior to joining the political process. In his subsequent address to the local media the erstwhile Prime Minister highlighted the importance of the democratization process and its potential benefits to the people. Lyonpo Kinzang Dorji, hitherto Minister of Works and Human Settlement, assumed the role of Prime Minister at the head of a greatly diminished Council of Ministers, which was to regulate government affairs pending the formation of an interim administration at the end of the year. The Royal Advisory Council was dissolved in early August.

By January 2008 only two parties had successfully registered with the Election Commission ahead of elections to the National Assembly—the DPT, led by former Prime Minister and Minister of Home and Cultural Affairs Lyonpo Jigmi Yozer Thinley, and the PDP, headed by former Minister of Agriculture Lyonpo Sangye Ngedup. A third party, the recently formed Bhutan National Party, had its application for registration cancelled, while the application of the Bhutan People's United Party (established by a breakaway faction of the DPT) was rejected by the Election Commission in November 2007. Consequently, the Commission announced that elections to the new National Assembly would be completed in one day (rather than in two rounds as originally envisaged) and the election date was set as 24 March. An indication of the authorities' optimism regarding the future prospects of Bhutan was their decision to rename the Planning Commission the Gross National Happiness (GNH) Commission in January.

Candidates in the National Council elections campaigned without party affiliation and the Election Commission ruled that only university graduates from approved institutions were eligible to stand. The latter restriction meant that the requisite minimum of two candidates was not available in five electoral districts before the date of the election, 31 December 2007. Consequently, a second stage of voting was held in these districts on 29 January 2008. Overall, some 53% of registered voters participated in the ballot. The 20 successful candidates, four of whom were women, were to serve five-year terms. An additional five members of the National Council were to be appointed by the King.

Four bomb blasts occurred in mid-January 2008 at Samtse, Thimphu, Chhukha and Dagapela, and another at Samtse in February. Persons identified as members of the Bhutan Tiger Force were apprehended by security forces in Dagana, Tsirang and Samdrup Jongkhar shortly afterwards, and under interrogation they reportedly identified training camps in Tsirang and within the forests of Samdrup Jongkhar district. The bombs were improvised devices, but there was widespread assumption that the BCP—MLM wanted to disrupt preparations for the general election.

The elections to the National Assembly took place without incident on 24 March 2008. The DPT candidates won 45 of the 47 legislative seats and 67.0% of valid votes cast, with the PDP, as the only other party contesting the ballot, winning the remaining two seats, despite almost universal expectation that representation might be rather evenly split. Of a total of 318,465 registered voters, some 79.4% cast their votes, mostly using electronic voting machines. There were in addition some 17,000 postal votes. Lyonpo Jigmi Yozer Thinley was subsequently nominated as Prime Minister by the DPT and his premiership was endorsed by the King on 9 April. The new Council of Ministers was installed two days later and included key appointments for a number of former ministers, including the former Prime Ministers Khandu Wangchuck and Wangdi Norbu, who were appointed Minister of Economic Affairs and Minister of Finance, respectively.

The first session of the first Parliament of Bhutan was inaugurated as a joint session of the National Assembly and the National Council on 8 May 2008 and it concluded on 29 July. The draft Constitution was debated throughout May, and was formally signed on the astrologically auspicious date of 18 July. After agreement on the Constitution, the bicameral Parliament discussed separately (and then jointly, to resolve differences) six bills, which were eventually adopted as the National Council Act, the National Assembly Act, the Election Act, the Election Fund Act, the Parliamentary Entitlements Act, and the National Referendum Act. The Parliament also approved the 2008/09 national budget, as well as agreements for the establishment of a SAARC food bank and a South Asia University. In addition, the Government was instructed to review legislation on the sale of meat and the ban on the sale of tobacco and plastic bags to ensure that they were being enforced.

Indian Prime Minister Manmohan Singh visited Bhutan on 16–17 May 2008 (exactly 50 years after Indian Premier Jawaharlal Nehru visited, and the fifth Indian Prime Minister to do so) and addressed the joint session of the Bhutanese Parliament. In his address he pledged Rs 100,000m. to be provided by the Government of India for the next five years of Bhutan's development; the financial support would be available primarily for the development of hydroelectric power, to support the Indian railway project from Hashimara to Phuentsholing, and other new projects. He also inaugurated the Tala hydroelectricity project and unveiled a foundation stone for the 1,095 MW Punatsangchhu I project, which is now under construction. The Indian Foreign Secretary, who was accompanying the Prime Minister, stated that the two countries were not just satisfied 'but convinced that their relations had made major contributions' to what both governments described as 'our shared prosperity, [. . .] shared security and [. . .] shared destiny'. During the visit officials from both sides agreed to investigate the possibility of doubling the target for hydroelectricity generation in Bhutan by 2020 from 5,000 MW to 10,000 MW.

In July 2008 proposals put forward by the DPT for some Nu 15m. to be paid to each of the two parties who had stood for election to the National Assembly, to sustain the parties and to defray outstanding expenses, were opposed by the National Council and by the Chief Election Commissioner as unconstitutional. The leader of the opposition, Tshering Tobgay, also came to oppose the proposal after earlier supporting it and it was subsequently withdrawn; discussion of a related proposal on constituency development funding was postponed until the November parliamentary session.

In July 2008 it was announced that the formal coronation of Jigme Khesar Namgyel Wangchuck was to take place on 6 November, with two days of celebrations to follow.

## FOREIGN RELATIONS AND BORDER ISSUES

Following the relaxation of many policies in the People's Republic of China since 1978, and looking forward to improved relations between India and China, Bhutan has moved cautiously to assert positions on regional and world affairs that take account of those of India but are not necessarily identical to them.

### The Bhutan–India Border

In June 2005, during the 83rd session of the National Assembly, following requests from chimis that permanent demarcation of the Bhutan–India border be completed, Bhutan's Secretary for International Boundaries observed that the demarcation was initiated as a result of the 1865 Duar War, when the British had defined the boundary between Bhutan and West Bengal, Assam, Arunachal Pradesh and Sikkim—unilaterally at first, but later in consultation with Gongzim Ugyen Dorji. After 1947, it was agreed that the boundary should be resurveyed, agreed 'strip maps' exchanged, and new 'boundary pillars' erected. Joint formal demarcation of the boundary—started in 1963—had been completed, with 60 strip maps and 358 main pillars, excluding Sikkim and the eastern tri-junction. By June 2005 29 of these strip maps had been signed. Of the remaining 31 strip maps, 18 were signed in February 2003, while at mid-2005 the remaining 15 (including two strips with Sikkim, five in the Arunachal Pradesh area, and eight in the south) were still being processed. Officials from both sides meeting in June 2003 had recommended relay surveying and pillar maintenance along the entire Indo-Bhutan border (based on the previously agreed base maps of 1971 and 1972), and proposed that the Bhutan–Sikkim boundary should also be demarcated, based on B. J. Gould's award, already agreed between the two Governments. (Gould was the British Political Officer for Sikkim, Bhutan and Tibet between 1935 and 1945. He had adjudicated between Bhutan and Sikkim with regard to boundary issues during his tenure.) In December 2003 Bhutan's Council of Ministers had approved these recommendations. Following the June 2003 officials' meeting, five further technical review meetings had been held. The Secretary for International Boundaries informed the National Assembly that it was intended that the remaining 15 strip maps would be signed by 2007, although King Jigme intervened to state that it was hoped this would in fact be completed by 2006, as most of the border had already been demarcated in the reign of his father, King Jigme Dorji Wangchuk. During discussions regarding Bhutan's borders at the 84th session of the National Assembly in June 2006, the Secretary for International Boundaries reaffirmed that the border with India (excluding the eastern and western tri-junctions) should be agreed by the end of that year. He also clarified that the entire boundary between Bhutan and India was covered by 62 strip maps. As regards the boundary with the Sikkim sector, seven main pillars and 239 subsidiary pillars were to be established, with work having already been commenced in January 2006. In addition, the Secretary informed the session that, of the 15 strip maps remaining in mid-2005, seven were in fact signed in December 2005—five relating to the Bhutan–Arunachal Pradesh border, and two relating to the Assam sector. He added that 'we are working with India to complete the last eight strip maps (two with Sikkim and six in the south) by November 2006', and that the construction of main and subsidiary boundary pillars was proceeding. The Assembly (somewhat ambiguously) resolved that the work 'must be completed by 2006–07'. Some 62 strip maps covering the entire Bhutan–India boundary (excluding the two eastern and western tri-junctions) were signed in December 2006, bringing to a close a process begun more than four decades ago. The Indian Ambassador to Bhutan commented that the boundary was a 'marker of friendship' rather than a border.

### The Bhutan–China Border

Discussions with China regarding the formal delineation and demarcation of the northern border opened in April 1984, and substantive negotiations began in April 1986. The 12th round of talks was held in Beijing in December 1998. Following negotiations, Bhutan and China signed an official interim agreement (the first agreement ever to be signed between the two countries), based on the five principles of peaceful coexistence, to maintain peace and tranquillity in the Bhutan–China border area and, importantly, to observe the status quo of the border as it was prior to May 1959, pending a formal agreement on the border alignment. The disputed area, which was 1,128 sq km during the early rounds of bilateral talks, has since been reduced to 269 sq km in three areas in the north-west of Bhutan. Demarcation of the southern border has been agreed with India, except for small sectors in the middle zone (between Sarpang and Gelephu) and in the eastern zone of Arunachal Pradesh and the *de facto* Sino-Indian border. Following further bilateral discussions in Thimphu in September 1999, the 14th round of negotiations took place in Beijing in November 2000, at which Bhutan extended the area of its claim beyond the boundary offered by the Chinese Government, somewhat to the surprise of the latter. The four sectors under discussion were in the Doklam (a disputed area of about 89 sq km), Sinchulumpba and Gieu (an area of about 180 sq km) and Dramana areas, and the Pasamlum area in the middle sector. The negotiations continued in Thimphu in November 2001, following which the Chinese Deputy Minister of Foreign Affairs stated that the boundary question generally had been resolved, although relatively minor issues remained outstanding. Bhutan's Minister of Home Affairs led a delegation of experts to Beijing in mid-June 2002 to assert Bhutan's area of claim, where it was agreed that the boundaries claimed by both sides would, henceforth, be depicted on one map to facilitate negotiations. The 80th session of the National Assembly determined that the issue of the northern boundary should be resolved as soon as possible. The 16th round of bilateral talks took place in Beijing in October 2002. In 2001 two delegations from Bhutan (a cultural group, led by the Dorji Lopon, and an officials group, led by the Foreign Secretary) also visited China, in April and July, respectively. The 17th round of talks in Thimphu in April 2004 had 'laid a solid foundation for the final settlement of the boundary issue', according to the Chinese Vice-Minister of Foreign Affairs, Wang Yi. The two sides agreed to form a technical expert group to verify the boundary, as drawn by the respective sides, at the earliest opportunity.

During the 83rd session of the National Assembly in mid-2005, the chimis from Haa district noted that the mule track constructed by the Chinese towards the RBA outpost in Shakhatoey area a few years ago had been converted into a motor road, and another motor road had been built from the Langmarpo Chhu to Dolepchen in 2004. The construction was a serious development, raising fears that the Chinese intention was to claim the area, the members said, observing that according to the 1998 Sino-Bhutan agreement, peace and tranquillity were to be maintained along the border and neither country would engage in any controversial activities until the boundary was finalized.

The Secretary for International Boundaries reported that the Bhutanese Government had raised the issue of the construction of six motor roads in the northern border areas several times with the Chinese Embassy in New Delhi, India, since August 2004. Bhutan's Ambassador in New Delhi had also conveyed the Government's concern that the road constructions were not in keeping with either the letter or the spirit of Article III of the 1998 Agreement. In addition, the Bhutanese Minister of Foreign Affairs had raised the matter with his Chinese counterpart during their meeting in New York, USA, in September 2004 and had been assured that the road construction work would be stopped. The Chinese Government had also conveyed its commitment to the amicable settlement of the issue. Assembly members subsequently sought clarification as to whether the motor roads were being constructed on the Chinese side of the border or inside Bhutanese territory, as it was important to know whether the Chinese Government was directly involved in the activities.

King Jigme stated that Assembly members should consider that, of the six motor roads constructed by the Chinese in the northern border areas in the previous year, two had extended to the border between Bhutan and China, while the other four roads had crossed into Bhutanese territory. The roads had not been constructed secretly, but had been built in areas where RBA outposts were located. He said that the RBA conducted daily patrols from these outposts and regularly met Tibetan workers and Chinese soldiers involved in road construction works. The officers leading the patrols always spoke to the Chinese soldiers and pointed out to them that the roads were being constructed inside Bhutanese territory and that these activities were not in keeping with the agreement signed between Bhutan and China. In response, the Chinese soldiers had always claimed that, first, they were constructing the roads in their own territory and not on Bhutanese land, second, they were building roads for the benefit of the local Tibetans, and finally, the construction works were being carried out on the instructions of their Government.

The Minister of Foreign Affairs confirmed that he had conveyed to his Chinese counterpart at their September 2004 meeting that, despite the cordial relations between Bhutan and China, the construction of six motor roads in the bordering areas had caused deep concern to the Royal Government and the people of Bhutan. He had requested that China cease the road construction activities immediately. In response, the Chinese Minister of Foreign Affairs had insisted that the roads were being constructed in Chinese territory but that, in view of the good relations between the two countries, the road construction would be stopped.

During a meeting in January 2005, the Chinese Embassy in New Delhi conveyed that China greatly valued and cherished its relations with Bhutan, and confirmed that no road construction activities had taken place since November 2004. The Chinese Government had conducted an investigation and found that the construction activities in the border areas were within the Chinese boundary, but gave its assurance that, based on the cordial relations between Bhutan and China and the past agreements signed between the two countries, no further construction activities would be taken up in the border areas. The Minister of Foreign Affairs assured the National Assembly that concrete steps would be taken to find a way of finalizing the Bhutan–China boundary issue as quickly as possible. A second 'intensive' meeting of the expert group to discuss the boundary issue was held in mid-July 2005 (the Chinese delegation was led by the Deputy Director-General of the Asia Department of China's Ministry of Foreign Affairs). Concerns expressed the previous month at the 83rd session of the National Assembly had been conveyed orally and in writing. The Chinese response was that 'the Bhutanese were overreacting', as the roads were being 'legitimately constructed for the economic development of the western part of China including Tibet' and would 'not affect Bhutan in any way'; nevertheless, in view of Bhutan's concerns, the work had been halted. The Secretary informed the Assembly that the RBA reported that, while roads were being constructed in six different areas near the border in 2004, construction work was being carried out in only two areas in 2005. 'Some maintenance and clearing work was carried out on the existing motor road, measuring 600 metres, between Asm Jakphu and Delepchen in August 2005', maintenance work was also carried out on the existing road in the Shakhateo area, and 700 m of mule track had been broadened to form a motor road in September. The Secretary reported that, during the 'open and frank' discussions at the experts' meeting, the two sides found major differences on their respective maps at 1:500,000 scale, which would need to be narrowed before formal exchange of maps. The Secretary also reported that the Chinese contingent had expressed its willingness to consider some adjustments in the demarcation of the border; any adjustments would be limited, however, since the Chinese stated that Bhutan was claiming large areas that did not actually belong to Bhutan. Nevertheless, the Secretary confirmed that the meeting had been 'very fruitful' and that the two sides had agreed to change the claim line. The two contingents of experts agreed to meet as often as possible in the future, in order to reach a solution regarding an acceptable common boundary line. At the 84th session of the National Assembly in June 2006, the chimis urged that 'a clear solution' must be in place before the political changes planned for 2008; in response, the Secretary stressed that no new road construction had been carried out since 2005, although maintenance work was continuing. The 18th round of the Bhutan–China boundary discussions was held in Beijing in mid-August 2006, and the Chinese expert group was to come to Thimphu at a convenient date in 2007 to discuss and seek to narrow the differences between the two claim lines. The Bhutanese secretary for International Boundaries stated in December 2006 that talks regarding the tri-junction boundary were progressing well, with only about 269 sq km remaining to be discussed with the Chinese Government, but the issue remained unresolved in early 2008 following reports of further Chinese border incursions in late 2007.

**Other Foreign Relations**

The Bhutanese Minister of Foreign Affairs visited Thailand in mid-May 2001, observing that 'Bhutan considered Thailand as the most suitable point' for the conduct of its diplomacy in the region. The Thai Prime Minister, Thaksin Shinawatra, visited Bhutan in June 2005 and announced 180 scholarships for Bhutanese taking up university and technical studies in Thailand; the two Governments also signed a memorandum of understanding on cultural co-operation. In addition, an agreement regarding co-operation between the Bhutan Chamber of Commerce and Industry and its Thai counterpart were discussed.

In July 1989 a four-day state visit to India by King Jigme Singye Wangchuck reaffirmed the good relations (both political and economic) that exist between Bhutan and India. During a visit to Bhutan in August 1993, the Indian Prime Minister, P. V. Narasimha Rao, stated that he was 'absolutely certain' that these relations would grow stronger. The Crown Prince, Dasho Jigme Khesar Namgyal Wangchuck, made his first official visit to India in early 2002. King Jigme, accompanied by the Crown Prince, led a delegation to Delhi in late July 2006. During the visit several important agreements were signed between Bhutan and India relating to co-operation in the field of hydroelectric power, a protocol specifying the commercial arrangements for the purchase of Tala hydroelectric power by India was drawn up, and a new Agreement on Trade, Commerce and Transit (the draft of which had been finalized in September 2005) was formalized.

As Crown Prince, Jigme Khesar Namgyel Wangchuck visited Thailand for a second time in November 2006 to attend a horticultural exposition in Chiang Mai and to receive an honorary doctorate from Rangsit University. As the fifth King, he also visited India from 7–12 February 2007; a revised India-Bhutan Friendship Treaty was signed between the two countries on 8 February 2007. (Instruments of ratification were exchanged in Thimphu on 2 March 2007 between Lyonpo Khandu Wangchuck, the Minister of Foreign Affairs of Bhutan, on behalf of the Royal Government, and Sudhir Vyas, the Ambassador of India to Bhutan, and the treaty came into force on that date.) The document was described as 'an update' of the treaty signed between Bhutan and India in 1949, 'reflecting the contemporary and expanded nature of the relationship between the two countries'.

Bhutan's Prime Minister visited Kuwait in May 2006 at the invitation of his counterpart, and there received an assurance of Kuwaiti technical assistance grants for feasibility studies on the development of industrial estates in Bhutan. In August the Kuwaiti Minister of Energy visited Bhutan and observed that Bhutan could 'look to Kuwait for assistance through the Kuwait fund, to finance projects'.

Although Bhutan continues to have few resident diplomatic representatives (namely, in Bangladesh, India, Kuwait and Thailand), it has established formal relations with 22 countries (including, from 2003, Australia, Canada and Singapore) and with the European Union (EU). It also maintains missions to the UN in New York, USA, and Geneva, Switzerland, and several honorary consulates.

# Economy

## BRIAN SHAW

Until recently, the pattern of economic activity in Bhutan was determined by the country's natural and self-imposed isolation. Subsistence agriculture was supplemented by livestock rearing and by cottage industries based on traditional handicrafts. In the northern region, migrant pasturing of yak and sheep was virtually the sole economic activity. There were few marketable surpluses, limited to what could be carried on a man's back or on a pack-horse, and disposed of by means of barter, mainly in Tibet. Bhutan traded rice in return for wool, salt, tea and precious metals.

In terms of average income, Bhutan is one of the poorest countries in the world, although the statistics should be considered in the context of a self-sufficient, barter economy. According to estimates by the World Bank, Bhutan's gross national income (GNI) per head averaged US $80 in 1980, $90 in 1983 and $140 in 1984. In 2003, according to estimates by the same source, the kingdom's GNI, measured at average 2001–03 prices, was $584m., equivalent to about $660 per head. In 1990–98 GNI per head increased, in real terms, at an average annual rate of 2.1%. During 1990–2003, it was estimated, gross domestic product (GDP) increased, in real terms, by an average of 6.5% per year. Over the same period, according to the World Bank, GDP per head rose at an average annual rate of 2.6%. Total GDP was projected to increase from Nu 18,760.8m. in 1999 to Nu 21,261.3m. in 2000. Compared with the previous year, real GDP growth was estimated at 7.7% in 2002 and at 6.7% in 2003. It must be noted, however, that, in the absence of definitive population data prior to the national census of May 2005, all of these figures are purely notional (on the basis of the current smaller population estimate, GNI per head in the late 1990s was reckoned to be much higher). In June 2007 Bhutan's Minister of Finance stated that total GDP in 2005 had reached $1,513.7m. In June 2008 the Minister noted that Bhutan's economy had expanded by some 14% in 2006/07, compared with 7.8% in 2005/06, mainly owing to the commissioning of the Tala hydroelectric project (see below); the rate of growth was expected to fall to about 12% in 2007/08, and return to a 'normal trend' in 2008/09. However, in the medium term, the undertaking of new major projects is expected to lead to real growth of some 9% per year.

During 1990–2003 the average annual rate of inflation was 7.6%. The rise in consumer prices reached 12.1% in 1998, before declining to 4.5%, 4.4% and 3.3% in 1999, 2000 and 2001, respectively. According to the National Statistics Bureau (previously the Central Statistical Office), the inflation rate stood at 5.3% in December 2006, compared with 1.3% in December 2003. According to the 2007/08 budget report, inflation had risen to 6.0%, compared with 4.3% in 2006/07, and was expected to grow further with continuing increases in the prices of diesel, petroleum and cooking gas (all of which were imported from India). In his June 2008 report to the first session of the first democratically elected Parliament, the Minister of Finance stated that key future challenges included the maintenance of the overall fiscal balance at sustainable levels in view of the rising recurrent costs and increasing demand for infrastructure developments, which, with Bhutan's narrow revenue base and limited grant assistance, could lead to unsustainable levels of debt from borrowings. The rising inflation rate posed further challenges, as did the goal of providing gainful employment to the rapidly increasing pool of educated youth. The Minister stated that the current unemployment rate of 3.7% was expected to be reduced during the 10th Plan (2008–13).

The Minister also reported that, following the introduction of the Public Finance Act in 2007, the Government had established a budgetary policy and a fiscal framework: the budgetary policy set out broad strategies to manage public finances in a prudent and efficient manner (for example, the Government would aim to avoid current operating deficits and to limit overall fiscal deficits to a maximum of 5% of GDP), while the fiscal framework would take structural account of variables (e.g. growth, debt and inflation) and project resources and expenditures for the two consecutive following years as well as for the next fiscal year, in part 'to sensitize the Government to the fiscal challenges ahead'. Thus, while total revenue and grants for 2008/09 were estimated at Nu 15,081m., the projected figures for 2009/10 and 2010/11 were Nu 15,348m. and Nu 15,526m., respectively. Similarly, total expenditures for these three years were estimated at Nu 23,072m., Nu 24,516m. and Nu 25,287m., respectively. External debt for 2009/10 and 2010/11 was expected to grow to around 59.4% and 65.0%, respectively, of estimated GDP (compared with an estimate of 58.5% for 2008/09). Debt service ratio was projected to decline from 10.5% (2008/09) to 9.5% (2009/10) and to 8.7% (2010/11), with no large loan-servicing required other than that for the loan for the Tala hydroelectric plant (which would be repaid primarily from revenues provided by the project itself).

### AGRICULTURE

The economy of Bhutan is essentially agrarian, with an estimated 94% of the economically active population engaged in agriculture and livestock raising, with 9% of the land under cultivation or permanent pasture, and with agriculture contributing an estimated 25.6% of GDP in 2004.

Under the Fifth Plan (1981–87), only a small expansion of cropped area was proposed, with increases in the output of paddy rice, maize, wheat, barley, buckwheat and millet to come mainly from an increase in yields. Total cereal production was about 196,900 metric tons in 1988. The total land area under paddy cultivation in that year was 34,000 ha; total production of rice was 33,800 tons, and the shortfall in requirements was imported. Maize, the staple diet in eastern and south-central Bhutan, is grown on about 59,000 ha and yielded 86,100 tons in 1988. Output of wheat and barley, cultivated on 16,000 ha, totalled 17,800 tons in 1988. Buckwheat and millet occupy approximately 20,800 ha, cultivated mostly by the swidden (shifting) method, with an annual output of some 16,600 tons. According to FAO, Bhutan's rice crop reached an estimated 45,000 tons in 2004 and output of maize totalled an estimated 70,000 tons. Emphasis continues to be placed on improving stock, soil fertility, plant protection and farm mechanization.

In early 1988 the newly established Bhutan Development Finance Corporation (BDFC) took over the administration of rural credit schemes, which had been operated by the Royal Monetary Authority of Bhutan since 1982, for loans of up to Nu 20,000 for land improvements and livestock, and for smaller loans, of up to Nu 5,000, for seasonal requirements. The BDFC also extends longer-term development loans. In December 1988 the Asian Development Bank (ADB) granted a US $2.5m. concessional loan to the BDFC, to aid the expansion of small- and medium-scale industrial enterprises in the private sector. By early 1989, about Nu 20m. had been disbursed by the BDFC to more than 20,000 beneficiaries, and in 1999, together with the Synovus Financial Corporation (SNV) and Rabobank of the Netherlands, it started a rural microfinance project. The UN Capital Development Fund (UNCDF) has assisted BDFC's supply of rural credit since the 1980s. The Bank of Bhutan finances larger loans. Major irrigation schemes were inaugurated in south-central Bhutan, where shortage of water and insanitary sources are major problems. By mid-1996, however, it had become generally accepted that the size of the national economy was too limited for domestic demand-based industries and that small-scale industries (particularly in the service sector) better suited the local market. Therefore, the Government's main industrial development strategy in the future needs to be export-orientated. According to the Ministry of Agriculture, its objective of achieving food security by balancing import costs with earnings from exports of cash crops had been achieved by 1999. Increased self-sufficiency remained its aim.

Forests represent one of the most important potential sources of wealth in Bhutan, and it was recognized early that preservation of the forest cover was essential in order to conserve the ecological balance. In the Fifth Plan, detailed surveying, demarcation and management plans for harvesting the forests, and for conservation, were drawn up and implemented. The Forestry Services Division (under the Ministry of Agriculture) has responsibility for maintaining the mature forest, with good tree cover at a minimum of 60% of total land area. (This latter requirement was enshrined in Article Five of the country's Constitution, which was adopted in mid-2008.) In early 1996 a major forest industry complex, the Gedu Wood Manufacturing Corporation, was closed down and all of the failed enterprise's debts were taken up by a Danish aid organization. However, the Bhutan Board Products Ltd (BBPL) factory at nearby Tala continued to operate for some years; although near bankruptcy in 1999 (with a loss of Nu 37m. and an unpaid loan of Nu 166m.), under new management, BBPL improved sales in 2004 by 20% (compared with 2003), to Nu 302.5m., brought profits after tax up by 110% (to Nu 19.82m., compared with Nu 9.32m.) and transferred about one-third of those profits to reserves. Wildlife sanctuaries have been maintained and extended. Since late 1990 many plantations in southern Bhutan (especially of teak and sal), which were planted in the 1950s and 1960s, have been indiscriminately felled or destroyed by anti-Government militants and by opportunistic smugglers.

## INDUSTRY AND COMMUNICATIONS

The proposed expenditure on trade and industry in the Seventh Plan (1992–97) was Nu 1,402.4m. (9% of the total), and was based on exploitation of mineral and forest resources, agricultural produce, and inexpensive power. Private enterprise is mainly small-scale industries, partly reflecting the limited development of entrepreneurial skills in Bhutan. In the Seventh Plan, however, considerable emphasis was to be placed on the formulation of a strategy for the rapid expansion of export-orientated industries. The production of low-cost electricity by the Chhukha hydroelectric power (HEP) project (see below) was expected to help to stimulate growth in the industrial sector. The Penden cement factory in southern Bhutan began operating in 1981, and in 2000 produced 263,234 metric tons of cement and 246,140 tons of clinker, earning after-tax profits of Nu 170m. A second cement plant, at Nganglam, with a potential output of 1,500–2,500 tons per day, was to be completed by 1991. Initial access tracks to the site were constructed, but in November 1989 the National Assembly confirmed the Council of Ministers' decision to postpone further development because of doubts concerning the venture's economic viability; work was resumed, however, in 1992. In March 1996 Bhutan signed an agreement with India regarding the construction of a cement plant (which was to have an annual capacity of 500,000 tons) at Dungsam. The project, which was due to be completed by 2002, was then estimated to cost Nu 3,000m. (as a grant from India), with an additional Nu 1,000m. required for the necessary infrastructure (roads, power lines, railway sidings, etc.). It was decided in late 1999 that, because of the security situation on the Bhutan–Assam border, the Dungsam project would once again be suspended; in November 2001 it was officially closed and the access road from Patshala in India to Nganglam was formally sealed. However, it was agreed that the project would be re-established as soon as the security situation improved. Vast limestone deposits in Nganglam and a favourable potential market in north-east India rendered the project economically viable. In mid-2006 it was decided to revive the project, as it would provide employment and assist in the opening up of a part of the country—as a growth centre for the south-east—that has remained poor for a long time. Construction of a 37-km double-lane road within India to the Bhutanese border was scheduled to commence by September 2006; this new road would link with a 13-km road within Bhutan, and a road connecting Kuruchhu (Gyelpoishing) to Nganglam is also currently under construction, with completion due in mid-2009. The 2006 re-costing of the Dungsam project set a figure of Nu 5,260m., with a projected daily production total of 3,000 tons of cement; the construction of the plant was scheduled to be completed by 2009 or 2010. Yangsom Cement Industries (a private undertaking) produces about 30 tons per day. In May 1985 the World Bank announced a 50-year interest-free loan of US $9m. to assist in the establishment of a plant to produce calcium carbide at Pasakha, near Phuentsholing. Commercial production began in June 1988, and output reached about 10,000 tons (valued at around Nu 85m.) in the six months to January 1989. By 2000 annual production was 19,827 tons, with a value of Nu 474.6m.; sales in 2005 increased to Nu 760.2m. Bhutan Ferro Alloys Ltd, which is also based in Pasakha, commenced production in April 1995 and has an installed annual capacity of 15,000 tons of ferro-silicon and micro-silicon; sales in 2006 (exported almost wholly to India) totalled Nu 658.3m. The production of both these facilities, however, decreased in 2000 compared with 1999, owing to heavy floods in August–October 2000. Sales increased in 2001 to reach Nu 579.0m. In 2001 Bhutan Fruit Products Ltd produced goods (mainly canned fruits and juices) valued at Nu 111.6m. In addition, small industrial estates have been established at Phuentsholing, Gelephu and Samdrup Jongkhar, producing a variety of raw materials for consumer goods and industrial products.

In 1984 the Indian Government financed the Indo-Bhutan microwave link, connecting Thimphu with Hashimara. At present the link provides 60 channels out of a total capacity of 300. Thimphu subscribers can now communicate directly, through operator trunk dialling, with Kolkata (Calcutta) and New Delhi and thence to third countries. A Thimphu–Kolkata teleprinter circuit was incorporated in the link. The international service began operating in January 1987, with the Delhi 'gateway' exchange being used for access to third countries. A Japanese company was awarded a contract in 1988 to construct a satellite earth station at Thimphu. This facility, which was inaugurated at the end of March 1990, provides direct high-quality telecommunications access (e.g. by fax) to third countries via London, United Kingdom. Agreements have been reached with many countries for two-way access. In July 1991 a public high-speed fax facility for domestic and international services was commissioned at the new GPO building in Thimphu, with technical assistance from India's Department of Telecommunications. Similar facilities are now available in all major towns in Bhutan. Since 1991 the Government of Japan has funded a fully digital domestic telecommunications network linking all districts with Thimphu. The four-phase plan, using microwave repeaters, was completed in May 1999 at a cost of more than 5,800m. yen, with the capability to transmit video signals. With the establishment of an internet service, DrukNet, in July 1999, three 'points of presence' were set up in Thimphu, Trashigang and Phuentsholing to enable direct-dial access from any part of the country. Mobile satellite telephones were made available to the public by Bhutan Telecom from August 2001. A mobile cellular network (B-Mobile), using the Global System for Mobile Telephony (GSM) standard, has operated since late 2003, initially along the Paro–Thimphu highway and in Phuentsholing. By mid-2007 services had been extended to the main centres in all districts; more remote areas, such as Laya, Lunana, Merak and Shingkhar Lauri, were connected by satellite voice services. Global bidders have been invited to offer their own services, in a bid to liberalize the country's telecommunications industry, as local operators do not have adequate funds to provide services in the mountainous regions on their own. In any joint telecommunications venture, the foreign partner was to be permitted a maximum 49% equity stake. In mid-2006 there were about 50,000 cellular telephone subscribers (some 20,000 in Thimphu) in Bhutan and more than 40,000 fixed-line customers. State-owned Bhutan Telecom Ltd, the sole start-up operator, was expected to compete with foreign operators from late 2006. By 2008 B-Mobile (a subsidiary of Bhutan Telecom Ltd) had more than 167,000 subscribers. All districts had B-Mobile services by early 2008. In a competitive auction for a 15-year licence to provide cellular services, Bhutan's Tashi Group successfully bid Nu 777m. and commenced its service in April 2008; 25% of the bid price had been paid by mid-2008, while the remaining 75% was to be paid in equal instalments over the next 15 years. Bhutan Telecom Ltd has been requested to pay a similar amount for operating B-Mobile.

## TRADE

Free trade between India and Bhutan was traditional, but mainly by those in the southern region of Bhutan, and the total amount was small compared with the trade between Tibet and Bhutan. From 1960 trade ties were completely reorientated towards India, which in 2003/04 accounted for an estimated 94.6% of Bhutan's exports and 87.8% of imports. A 10-year agreement on trade and transit arrangements between Bhutan and India, signed in 1972, provided for the continuation of free trade. This pact was revised by a 1983 agreement (operative from April 1984), with terms substantially more favourable to Bhutan. In March 1990 the two countries signed a third agreement, which provided for the continuation of Bhutan's free trade with India. This agreement expired in March 2005 but was renewed in July of that year, to last 'until a new agreement was reached'; the current arrangement also includes the uncomplicated movement of forestry goods (principally timber) from one part of Bhutan to another, or to export destinations, via Assam and West Bengal (these had previously been restricted from travelling on Indian roads). Additional entry and exit points in India for Bhutan's trade with third countries was also discussed, with agreement in principle given to using Mumbai and Chennai for this purpose. India remains Bhutan's largest trading partner, and transit procedures for 13 transhipment points were made simpler. The current trade agreement, which was signed in July 2006 and is valid for 10 years, extends the previous agreement on trade and commerce and provides for continued free trade arrangements between India and Bhutan with simplified procedures for imports and exports. The protocol to the new agreement specifies additional facilities and four additional exit/entry points (two road routes at Phulbari in West Bengal and Dawki in Meghalaya, and two sea and air routes confirmed at Mumbai and Chennai—supplementing the 12 existing exit/entry points that were agreed by protocol to the 1995 agreement) for Bhutan's transit trade with third countries. Movement of goods from one part of Bhutan to another through Indian territory has now been made simpler through a transit declaration. Excise duties will continue to be refunded. Third-country exports and imports will be free from customs duties and trade restrictions. In 1987 Bhutan earned US $500,000 from trade with third countries, but by 2003/04 the annual total had risen to $8.56m. The main exports from Bhutan to India are electricity, wood and wood products, and cement and agricultural products; liquor and canned fruits are also exported. An agreement on trade was also signed with Bangladesh in 1980 and renewed for a further 10 years in 1990; it was extended in May 2003 for a further five years. In March a memorandum of understanding was signed between the Bhutan Chamber of Commerce and Industry and its Nepalese counterpart to foster business links between the two communities; at the signing ceremony, Bhutan's Minister of Trade and Industry spoke of Bhutan and Nepal signing a trade agreement in the near future.

The BIST-EC (Bangladesh-India-Sri Lanka-Thailand Economic Co-operation) met first in Bangkok, Thailand, in June 1997; after Myanmar joined in December 1997, Nepal and Bhutan were granted full membership status in 2003. The organization agreed to change its name to BIMST-EC (Bay of Bengal Initiative for Multi-Sectoral Technical and Economic Co-operation) at the first summit meeting of member heads of state in Bangkok in July 2004. In February of that year six of the member states (excepting initially Bangladesh, which finally subscribed in June) signed a Framework Agreement on the BIMST-EC Free Trade Area, which, amongst other matters, looked to intra-regional assistance on a wide front, and especially to the gradual reduction or elimination by members of trade tariffs on goods by 2017. This agreement was expected to become effective in mid-2006. In addition to the above arrangements, the agreement regarding the South Asia Free Trade Area (SAFTA), drawn up by members of the South Asian Association for Regional Co-operation (SAARC), envisaged that phased tariff liberalization would come into force from 1 January 2006. Under SAFTA, which was in many ways complementary to the BIMST-EC Free Trade Area, by the end of 2007 the Least Developed Contracting States (LDCSs—Bhutan, Bangladesh, the Maldives and Nepal) would reduce tariffs to 30%; non-LDCSs would then bring down tariffs from 20% to 0%–5% in five years, while LDCSs would do so in eight years. SAFTA was expected to be in effect fully by 2016, although the existing bilateral trade agreement that India has with Nepal and Bhutan would continue to be in force even after the implementation of SAFTA.

After the inauguration of the postal system in 1972, Bhutan's postage stamps became, for a time, the country's main source of foreign exchange earnings. Since 1976, however, tourism has become an important source of convertible currency (grossing US $24 m. in 2006). Bhutan joined the World Tourism Organization in 2003. Tourist numbers were at their highest ever in 2006, having reached 17,365, with gross receipts of US $24m. Foreign direct investment (FDI) in tourism facilities continued, although these cater mainly for the luxury end of the market (at the lower end, some 11,000 mainly self-catering Indian tourists visit each year). A joint venture between the Bhutanese Government and Aman Resorts had completed construction of the AmanKora tourist resort in Paro by June 2004; projects in Thimphu and Punakha were completed in 2005, and in Bumthang, Gangtey Gompa and Trongsa in 2006, creating a total of 72 new hotel rooms. Another joint venture funded by FDI planned to construct 'exotic' resort hotels in Paro (the Paro Uma hotel, completed in October 2004) and subsequently in Haa and Punakha. The Indian Hotels Company (Taj Group) agreed in early 2005 to build a new 'five-star' hotel in central Thimphu, which opened in late 2007. A hotel and tourism management institute was to be established fully by 2009, offering in-service training courses, and one- to two-year diploma courses for new entrants, with the aim of professionalizing the quality of service in the tourism industry. Druk Air's two new 114-passenger Airbus A-319s arrived in late 2004. Gaya was officially added to the list of ports in India to be served by the airline, and Chennai, Guwahati and Mumbai were to follow, together with Singapore; by mid-2008, however, only Gaya was being served by Druk Air.

## DEVELOPMENT PLANNING

Planning for economic development began in 1961. The formation of capital had to be achieved almost entirely through external grants, and, to begin with, little revenue could be generated internally. Rising expectations among the people have come to provide a strong impetus to further expansion of development activity. Both the First Plan (1961–66) and the Second Plan (1966–71) were largely financial budgeting exercises. A development secretariat was formed, and sectoral directorates were established. The highest priority was given to ending Bhutan's isolation through constructing transportation links, and 66% of the total outlay in the First Plan was for roads, mainly in the Phuentsholing–Thimphu and Samdrup Jongkhar–Trashigang sectors. In the Second Plan, the outlay on roads dropped to 42% of total allocations, while education received 18%. In the Third Plan (1971–76) 20% of expenditure was allocated to roads, and 19% to education. District development committees (Dzongkhag Yargye Tshogchungs, or DYTs) were established in the Fourth Plan (1976–81), and were asked to submit development proposals of direct concern to their respective districts. Total expenditures under the provisions of the first four Plans were Nu 107.2m., 202.2m., 475.2m., and 1,106.2m. respectively; the contribution from India was 100%, 98.9%, 89.9%, and 77.1% respectively. Domestic resources provided 1%, 7% and 5.5% for the Second, Third and Fourth Plans respectively. Assistance from the UN system was received for the first time under the Third Plan, providing 3% of total outlay; the proportion increased to 17.5% in the Fourth Plan.

The Fifth Plan (1981–87) was generally regarded as a crucial phase in Bhutan's socio-economic development. The first four Plans had established a minimal infrastructure, and the Fifth Plan provided the occasion for an intensive and continuing review of actual and desired achievements. In outline, this Plan envisaged an outlay of Nu 4,338m. (the actual total of Nu 4,711m., excluding separate provision for the Chhukha HEP project of Nu 1,800m., reflected the imposition of stringent fiscal controls by the Government), of which 30.9% was to be financed by India, and 21.7% from internal revenue. The average annual increase of GDP, in real terms, was estimated at 6.4% during the Fifth Plan period.

In addition to international aid under UN auspices, Helvetas (the Swiss Association for Technical Assistance), a non-profit organization, has maintained a formal and important presence in Bhutan since 1975. Working with Bhutanese counterparts, its experts have advised on a wide range of projects, involving an actual expenditure (1975–83) of 11,335m. Swiss francs, funded both by the voluntary contributions of its members and by the Swiss Development Corporation of the Swiss Federal Department of Political (Foreign) Affairs. Since 1985, Helvetas has been the co-ordinator for all of the Swiss Government's multilateral assistance to Bhutan.

King Jigme Singye Wangchuck had already, in his 1974 coronation speech, stressed the need to avoid excessive dependence on external assistance, and, instead, to seek to achieve economic self-reliance. To achieve these goals, he proposed five major strategies, to be pursued in the Fifth Plan: self-reliance in each of the country's dzongkhags (districts); decentralization of development administration; increasing popular participation in development decisions; control of maintenance expenditure; and optimum mobilization of internal resources.

Decentralization is a principal current goal, partly to counter a tendency towards a lack of realism that had begun to appear in the central planning process. It is intended to relate policy to the locally perceived needs of the districts, although at present only 30% of projects are implemented at that level. During the first four Plans, there developed a habit of reliance on the central Government's provision of new services; the traditional contribution of free labour was much reduced. The King has clearly expressed the view, during his extensive travels throughout the country, that central assistance towards local projects will depend very much on the willingness of the local people to make their own contributions, especially of labour, to public works.

During an important meeting of officials at the end of 1984, in preparation for drafting the Sixth Plan, the strategies for the Fifth Plan were critically reviewed. In general, it was considered that the concept of dzongkhag self-reliance had been introduced prematurely, and that it needed refinement; that decentralization had come to mean the transfer, rather than the devolution, of power; and that people's participation had been encouraging but needed further strengthening. On the other hand, internal revenue had been increased to the equivalent of 85% of total government maintenance expenditure.

The Sixth Plan (1987–92), which was finally approved by the Tshogdu in July 1987 (but was revised in late 1989), envisaged a total outlay of Nu 9,559.2m., which represented an increase of more than 100%, compared with total expenditure (excluding expenditure on the Chhukha HEP project) in the Fifth Plan. Nine major policy objectives were declared in the Sixth Plan: the strengthening of government administration (including the continued campaign against corruption and nepotism); the preservation and promotion of national identity (particularly through the strengthening of the newly formed Special (now National) Commission for Cultural Affairs and of traditional institutions); the mobilization of internal resources; the enhancement of rural incomes; the improvement of rural housing and resettlement; the consolidation and improvement of services; the development of human resources; the promotion of popular participation in the formulation and execution of development plans and strategies; and the promotion of national self-reliance. The Plan also took into account the increasing international debt burden that would develop as a result of loan repayments due in the early 1990s, and some capital-intensive projects were postponed until the next Plan. By the end of the Plan period (June 1992), total outlay had reached Nu 9,559.2m., but resources were under considerable strain as a result of the destruction of much of the social services infrastructure in southern Bhutan, combined with a commitment by the Government to continue development work in the disturbed areas.

The Seventh Plan (1992–97) asserted seven main objectives: self-reliance, with emphasis on internal resource mobilization; sustainability, with emphasis on environmental protection; private sector development; decentralization and popular participation; human resources' development; balanced development in all districts; and national security. The proposed outlay was Nu 15,590.7m., principally within the Ministry of Social Services, the Ministry of Communications and the Ministry of Agriculture. By mid-1997 expenditure on the Seventh Plan was already estimated at Nu 21,603.6m.

The Eighth Plan (1997–2002) further refined the seven objectives of the Seventh Plan and explicitly added another: 'the preservation and promotion of cultural and traditional values', relating to literature, art, architecture and religious institutions. During these five years, GDP was forecast to expand at an average annual rate of 6.7%, while the population growth rate was projected to decline to 2.56%. The agriculture sector was projected to grow by 2.5% per year over the plan period through productivity gains and horticultural development. Exports to India and third countries were expected to increase by 15% and 10%, respectively, by 2002. The guiding goal was declared as the establishment of sustainability in development, while balancing achievements with the popular sense of contentment. Core areas were to be the further development of HEP (long-term potential generating capacity was assessed at 20,000 MW) and further industrialization (including project reports on the Mangdechhu and Punatsangchhu power sites—see below, and the implementation of a silicon carbide project). The Dungsam cement project and the Basochhu and Kurichhu HEP projects were to be completed during the Plan period, as was 50% of the Tala project. The reconstruction work on the damaged Taktsang Monastery, which commenced in May 2000, was expected to cost Nu 45.88m. The Plan also provided for further development of the infrastructure and social services, human resources' development, and renewable natural resources. Development partners, meeting in Geneva, Switzerland, in January 1997, pledged US $450m. (about 50% of the projected plan outlay). By 2000 the Government had made satisfactory progress in reaching its targets. The mid-term review of the Eighth Plan, carried out in February 2000, showed fund utilization was around 40% of the original planned outlay of Nu 30,000m. This review served as the basis for the Ninth Plan (2002–07). In June 2002 the Minister of Finance reported that actual expenditure on the Eighth Plan was around Nu 40,000m., some 33% more than the original planned outlay, with equal increases in both current and capital expenditure. Nevertheless, the overall resource deficit was limited to Nu 307.8m., owing to a significant increase of Nu 7,580m. in domestic revenues to Nu 20,580m. International concessional loans financed about 5% of the plan.

The Ninth Plan, presented to and approved by the National Assembly in June 2002, consisted (unlike previous plans) of separate programmes and budget allocations for individual sectors and dzongkhags. The main priorities included the development of rural infrastructure, qualitative improvement in health and education services, greater decentralization and private sector development. The main Plan document devoted a chapter to expounding the view that 'Gross National Happiness (GNH) is the overarching development philosophy of Bhutan'; indeed, King Jigme stated that GNH was 'more important than Gross National Product'. The document asserted that the King's statement regarding GNH had 'been the guiding principle of the country's development efforts for the last two decades' and that 'the maximization of [GNH] is a philosophy and objective of the country's development'. The four main pillars of GNH were: economic growth and development; the preservation and promotion of cultural heritage; the preservation and sustainable use of the environment; and good governance.

These 'pillars' were reflected in five overall goals: improving quality of life and income (especially of the poor); ensuring good governance; promoting private sector growth and employment generation; preserving and promoting cultural heritage and environmental conservation; and achieving rapid economic growth and transformation. GDP was forecast to grow at a higher average annual rate, of 7%–8%, in 2002–07; this level was deemed necessary in order to maintain momentum in development and to create jobs for new school-leavers. A dynamic private sector was also required for the latter. The major HEP projects at Tala, Kurichhu and Basochhu (see below) were scheduled for completion during the Plan period (although outside the Plan's financial framework). The first 170-MW turbine of the Tala project was commissioned in July 2006. It was hoped that the projects would earn sufficient revenue for Bhutan to achieve economic self-reliance. Expenditure during the Plan was expected to reach Nu 70,000m., of which Nu 31,700m. was allocated to current expenditures, Nu 34,900m. was directed to capital investment, and Nu 3,400m. was for debt-servicing. Domestic revenue, which was forecast to reach Nu 32,000m., and external resources, amounting to an estimated Nu 35,000m., were expected to cover the proposed outlay (the former covering current expenditure). India would continue to be Bhutan's largest development partner, contributing about 30% of the total plan outlay. Inflation was forecast to reach an average annual rate of 7% in 2002–07. The dzongkhag plans were geog-based, with special focus on the potential, needs and priorities of the individual geogs or lowest level of administrative units. By mid-2006 the completion date for the Ninth Five-Year Plan had been extended for a further year (to mid-2008). This was partly because it was considered appropriate for the new government, which would be in power by that date, to consider and agree on the immediately subsequent 10th Five-Year Plan, but 'mainly' because 'external assistance could not be finalized' for all planned projects.

The 10th Five-Year Plan (2008–13) was to introduce three-year 'rolling' plans (essentially one-year plans with a two-year projection, restated annually). According to the Planning Commission guidelines, 'although the Tenth Plan will witness momentous socio-political change, our development philosophy of maximizing Gross National Happiness will still hold true and its four pillars will continue to form the core values for the 10th Plan. In view of the significant proportion of people living below the national poverty line and the incompatibility of such a situation with the principles of GNH, the government has decided that poverty reduction will be the main development goal for the 10th Plan. Given this focus, all sectors should formulate programmes and projects that target the poor, the vulnerable and the unreached'. According to a UN Development Programme report published in 2007, some 23.2% of the country's population were classed as poor. In addition, the development of 'cultural industries' was to be encouraged, while the promotion of the tourism sector was to achieve three main aims: to raise the sector's contribution to GDP to 9%; to increase annual tourist arrivals to 100,000; and to increase the rate of employment growth within the industry to 5%. The Government was also seeking to implement an installed hydropower capacity of 10,000 MW by 2020, while the draft 10th Plan proposed to achieve a target of 2,705 MW by 2013. In early 2008 the draft 10th Plan outlay was estimated at Nu 141,692m., of which current expenditure accounted for Nu 62,060m. and capital expenditure Nu 79,630m. Grants and loans were expected to fund Nu 66,400m. of capital expenditure, leaving a resource deficit of some Nu 13,200m. The Government was expected to discuss and approve the 10th Plan at the first session of the country's first democratically elected Parliament in May–July 2008; however, although its provisions were officially effective from 1 July, formal adoption was postponed until the second session of Parliament in November to allow for further revision. The Minister of Finance, Lyonpo Wangdi Norbu, explained that the Government was reassessing the importance and scale of some of the Plan's projects following the Indian Government's recent commitment of Rs 100,000m.

The Budget and Appropriation Bill 2008/09, prepared in accordance with the Public Finance Act 2007 and presented with the budget in June 2008, set expenditure limits (with any deviation to be reported to the Parliament): total current expenditure was set at Nu 11,501.4m. and total capital expenditure at Nu 11,571.0m.

In 2002 Chhukha power sales to India brought in receipts of Nu 1,983.1m. India's agreement to double the Chhukha power tariff (to Nu 1 per unit) from April 1997 earned an extra Nu 124m. in the last quarter of 1996/97. King Jigme announced in June 1999, during ceremonies celebrating his 25 years as monarch, that India had agreed to pay an additional tariff on electricity purchased from Bhutan of 50 chetrum per unit (to Nu 1.50 per unit, compared with Nu 1 previously), thereby making it feasible temporarily to postpone the introduction of personal income tax (PIT). The tariff increase generated additional revenue of Nu 669.5m., which, for the most part, counterbalanced the increases in salary and travel allowances for civil servants implemented in July 1999. Revised PIT, which was due to be levied from July 1999 and which was to include rental income (previously exempt), was deferred, owing to widespread misunderstanding and opposition by the business community, in addition to the absence of the requisite legislation. At the 78th session of the National Assembly, however, a draft PIT act was circulated, for further public discussion; this was debated and adopted at the 79th session. Consequently, Bhutanese earning more than Nu 100,000 annually were to pay tax from January 2002 at rates commencing at 10%. (In 2000, meanwhile, taxes paid by the rural population—85% of citizens—remained at less than 1% of the Government's total revenue.) In addition, new legislation regarding a sales, customs and excise tax was passed; about Nu 110m. was expected to be raised from PIT in 2002 alone, with a 9% annual increase thereafter. PIT revenue in 2007/08 was Nu 237m.

A national pension plan (National Pension and Provident Fund Plan—NPPF—and the Armed Forces Pension and Provident Fund Scheme—AFPPFS) was implemented in 2000; monthly payment of pension entitlements commenced in July 2002. By mid-June 2006 the NPPF had become the third largest financial institution in Bhutan, after the Bank of Bhutan and the Bhutan National Bank. Since its inception the NPPF has continued to increase its membership. At the end of 2003/04 NPPF and the AFPPFS had witnessed membership growth of approximately 7.8%, with 34,574 members on 30 June 2004 (compared with 32,079 members in June 2003); by 30 June 2006 there were 36,114 members. The NPPF was able to declare a return of 5.00% per annum to the members' accounts during 2003/04 and 6.75% during 2005/06. In 2003/04 the NPPF launched housing and education loan schemes for members, and made provision for contingencies against loan defaults of Nu 5.25m. (1.5% of standard assets). There were no loan defaults during 2003/04. In mid-2005 the NPPF and the Armed Forces Pension and Provident Fund Scheme covered civil servants, employees of the government corporations and members of the Armed Forces, who constitute only about 5% of the total population. The plans provide multi-tiered benefits, with some lump sum payment and a series of monthly payments for life on retirement. Besides, the Royal Insurance Corporation of Bhutan continues to manage the provident fund operations of the employees of non-governmental organizations (NGOs) and the private sector. The Bank of Bhutan and the Army Welfare Project also manage their own provident fund plans, paying benefits to the members in the form of a lump sum on retirement as they only manage provident fund plans. In June 2005 a total of 520 members were reportedly receiving benefits from the pension scheme. During 2005/06 the NPPF serviced 1,088 beneficiaries and signed an understanding with Bhutan Post to use its services to improve the disbursement of the pension to recipients. It also increased its investment in government aircraft funding (see below) in the form of a 10-year loan of Nu 1,060m. to the Government. Income from housing rental and education loans grew significantly (the latter increasing from Nu 264.6m. in 2004/05 to Nu 385.0m. in 2005/06). NPPF also currently holds 7.35% (Nu 3.68m.) of the share capital of Kuensel Corporation. At 30 June 2006 the NPPF had granted outstanding loans totalling Nu 1,742.62m.; non-performing loans (defaults) amounted to 1.5% of loans outstanding.

In his comments on the 2002/03 budget, the Minister of Finance noted that tax revenues would surpass non-tax revenues for the first time. Reporting on the 2003/04 budget in July 2003, he also stated that GDP grew by about 7% and the average rate of inflation declined to 2.7% in 2002/03. Bhutan's accumulated foreign reserves were equivalent to US $335m. (sufficient to cover 19 months of imports) and convertible-currency reserves were $259.4m.; Indian rupee reserves amounted to Rs 4,617m. At the end of 2002 total outstanding convertible-currency foreign debt was about $147.9m., while outstanding Indian rupee loans stood at $183.7m.—in total about $331.7m., or 58% of GDP. The debt-service ratio was

3.5% of the value of exports of goods and services. In his June 2005 budget report, the Minister of Finance estimated real GDP growth at December 2004 to be 8.4%. External debt increased by 27% in 2004 compared with the previous year, to $598m., but of this amount some 61% was in the form of Indian rupee loans for power projects and thus self-liquidated as the projects came on stream. The total debt-service ratio at the end of 2004 was less than 5%. The current-account deficit increased to Nu 8,400m. in 2004/05, mainly owing to a huge widening of the trade deficit, from Nu 4,000m. in 2003/04 to Nu 10,000m. (The purchase of two aircraft by the Druk Air Corporation Limited was partly responsible for the huge rise in the cost of imports in 2004/05.) In addition, the winding down of the construction phase of the Tala project led to decreased flows in the capital and financial account in the form of grants and loans, resulting in a negative overall balance of Nu 918.5m. for 2004/05.

External debt outstanding at December 2006 amounted to US $679.4m., equivalent to about 75.7% of estimated GNP. During the 87th session of the National Assembly, which was held in December 2006/January 2007, the Minister of Finance acknowledged that this was 'fairly high by international standards' and could pose a burden on future generations. He claimed that the Government had consequently exercised 'extreme caution' in seeking further loans, and then only for essential activities. Nevertheless, the Minister also reported that the Government had been able to repay all external loans 'without fail' when due. By the end of March 2007 the total debt had risen to $715.1m. (of which $294.7m., or 41.2% of total debt, was in the form of outstanding convertible currency debt), and Rs 18,300m. (58.8%) in Indian rupee debt. Debt-servicing (interest plus capital repaid) for the three months ending March 2007 amounted to $ 4.27m. on the convertible currency debt and the equivalent of $11.07m. on the Indian rupee debt. According to the Minister of Finance, outstanding external debt at 30 June 2008 was estimated to be Nu 33,254m., equivalent to about 58.5% of estimated GDP; of this, the Indian rupee component was expected to be about Nu 16,720.4m. (50.2% of the total). Debt-servicing of interest for 2008/09 was estimated at Nu 1,734.6m., of which Nu 1,497.6m. was to be paid to the Government of India in respect of loans for the Tala project (Nu 1296m.) and the road-building at Kuruchhu (Nu 201.6m.). Debt-servicing for principal repayments for 2008/09 was estimated at Nu 2,110.8m., with Nu 1,935.5m. for external repayments and Nu 175.3m. for internal repayments.

The 87th Assembly also approved provisions for the costs of preparing and holding the 2008 national parliamentary elections: actual (2005/06) and revised (2006/07) expenditure totalled Nu 272.4m., while estimates for 2007/08 were put at Nu 390.1m.—giving a total of Nu 662.5m. The figures included Nu 110.6m. for the Public Election Fund, as provided by Article 16 of the draft constitution, to fund registered political parties and their candidates during elections to the National Assembly, as well as the election campaigns of candidates to the National Council.

Druk Air, Bhutan's only national airline, was established in 1981 and commenced flying in January 1983 with an 18-seat Dornier aircraft. A second Dornier joined the fleet in October 1983. Two larger, 82-seat British Aerospace BAe-146-100s were purchased in 1988 and 1992, and in 1991 both Dorniers were sold in India. The first BAe-146 aircraft arrived in October 1988 against a cash deposit of 20% of the purchase price (made by the Bhutanese Government), with 80% taken in the form of a commercial 10-year loan from a consortium of British banks at an interest rate of 7.5%. The second BAe-146 arrived in December 1992, financed by a government loan from the Bank of Bhutan. Growing tourist numbers, and the decision of British Aerospace to cancel development of the 82-seat RJX aircraft (two of which had already been ordered in January 2000 by Druk Air, and which were due for delivery in November 2001 and January 2002 respectively) forced delays and a search for alternative transport. Contracts for two larger (114-seat) Airbus A-319 aircraft with a range of 6,800 km were signed in October 2003, and these arrived in October and December 2004, at a cost of approximately US $39m. Ten-year Druk Air bonds offering a rate of 7.5% interest were issued during 2003 and 2004, and, at the end of June 2004 Bhutan's two major banks (Bank of Bhutan and Bhutan National Bank) held Nu 760.73m. of bonds and the NPPF Nu 531m. (Efforts to sell the two BAe-146s that remained in Druk Air's fleet were successful only in early 2007, when both aircraft were sold to a European buyer for $3.3m. They were scheduled to leave Bhutan by September 2007.) One of the A-319 aircraft was to remain as the Bhutanese Government's equity holding in the airline, while the other was to be bought by Druk Air, with government loans. As a result, Druk Air would be able to implement new routes: from Paro to Dubai, in the United Arab Emirates, via Delhi, and to Singapore via Kolkata, for example. The national carrier suspended flights to the Bangladeshi capital of Dhaka from mid-December 2003 for security reasons, as leaders of the militant United Liberation Front of Assam (ULFA) were resident in the country; twice-weekly flights were resumed, however, in March 2006. In February 2004 the airline signed a memorandum of understanding with Nepal to increase its flights to Kathmandu from the existing two to seven times a week; the memorandum also allowed Druk Air to commence flights to the Indian towns of Gaya, Chennai and Mumbai via Kathmandu. However, the right to operate flights to new destinations via Kathmandu is subject to a code-sharing arrangement between the national flag carriers. Bhutan planned to conduct similar bilateral air service agreement meetings with India and Bangladesh. In addition, an air service agreement was signed with Myanmar (formerly Burma) in August 2002; air services were introduced on a thrice-weekly basis to and from Myanmar, but were in abeyance during 2005 and were definitively abandoned in early 2006 as they were not commercially viable.

From 1983 Druk Air's aircraft have not been commercially viable when depreciation is taken into account, but operation does not take place on a strictly commercial basis. SAARC nationals (including Bhutanese) were charged well below actual costs for fares, while third-party foreigners paid an excessive amount by global standards. At 2008 all now pay the same nominal fares, but tickets are heavily discounted in SAARC countries. Nevertheless, air transport capability since 1983 has greatly assisted the development of tourism, as well as official travel to a rapidly growing number of international conferences (consequent upon Bhutan's greater involvement in the international community), and also postal and cargo services. In his budget report to the National Assembly in June 2005, the Minister of Finance observed that, 'Druk Air plays an indispensable role in the communications structure of our landlocked kingdom, and so (members) will appreciate that given the limited avenues for profitable operations of the airline, the Government will have to continue to subsidize its operations'. Nu 142m. was budgeted in 2005/06 for a subsidy to the Druk Air Corporation to cover interest payments on its bonds, and on its previous loans; the interest subsidy allocated for 2008/09 was Nu 86.1m.

Preparations for the introduction of a domestic helicopter service were discussed in 2003—initially, five heliports had been surveyed and found acceptable for use—but details of operations could not be resolved. A detailed report on a site for an all-weather international airport at Khotokha showed that this location—the only feasible site near the capital—was not practicable; in late 2005 an Indian team was scheduled to investigate three possible further sites for an alternative international airport near Gelephu. In addition, Swedish experts were to examine and report on the feasibility of constructing an airstrip in the eastern dzongkhags. Phuentsholing, Bumthang and Yonphula were identified as possible locations, while Bartsham (strongly argued for by parliamentary members from the east of the country at the 86th session of the Assembly) also appeared suitable. The experts were to report after their visit in the latter part of 2007.

For 2000/01, grants from the Government of India provided an estimated 17.1% of total budgetary revenue, and direct grants from international agencies amounted to 17.0%. Following the terrorist attacks on the USA in September 2001, several hundred foreign tourists cancelled their visits to Bhutan. The downturn in the tourist industry was exacerbated in 2003 by the outbreak of Severe Acute Respiratory Syndrome (SARS) in East Asia. Druk Air replaced its discriminatory fare structure, which favoured nationals from SAARC countries, from early 2006 with a one-price-for-all service. From late 2005 and during 2006 the airline offered (US dollar) fares at a small discount during the off-peak season (December–February, and June–August). From mid-October 2005 it provided a helicopter service on 'wet lease' from Air Dynasty (Nepal), which by the end of the year had been operated for 30 paying hours. In 2005 the number of tourist arrivals increased by 48%, compared with the 2004 total, to 13,645 persons. By 2007 this figure had risen to 21,094 persons. Foreign-exchange earnings from the tourism sector totalled US $18.5m. in 2005, compared with $12.45m. in 2004, and increased to $24m. in 2007. A revised tourism master plan was adopted in 2006. A new tourism pricing policy for 2007 (giving US $100 per night as government royalty against the existing US $65 per night) was adopted (only the July and August wet seasons would now qualify for 'low season' reductions); consideration was being given to increasing tourism daily fees further from January 2008, but by mid-2007 it had been decided to postpone any decision on possible further increases until after the 2008 celebrations.

In June 1999 the Minister of Finance told the National Assembly that Bhutan needed to promote exports and narrow the current-account deficit. During 1999/2000 the current-account deficit grew marginally, but the overall balance of payments was positive, owing to large inflows of aid and concessional loans. Non-performing assets decreased in 1998/99 to about 10% (compared with 20% in 1994/95), but increased to less than 15% in 2001/02. Efforts were under way in 2002/03 to reduce this to less than 10%. A major domestic problem in 2000 was rising unemployment (up to 50,000 school-leavers were expected to join the work-force over the next five years; this figure was, however, expected to rise to 70,000 over 2002–07).

The Minister of Finance announced several tax initiatives in June 2002, notably tax 'holidays' (ranging from three to seven years for new industries and institutes, particularly those established in the interior dzongkhags), abolition of export tax on oranges, apples and cardamom, a reinvestment allowance of 20% for incorporated companies as an incentive to expand, and education and life insurance premium deductions for PIT. The Minister reiterated that the Government would consider military action if peaceful means to persuade ULFA and Bodo militants to leave Bhutan failed, despite the fact that armed conflict would seriously hinder the country's development. In June 2003 the Minister added that an emergency fund of Nu 1,000m. had already been created (with plans to increase it to Nu 2,000m. if necessary) to ensure that the welfare of internally displaced people would be well protected in case of military action, and that the Government was prepared to devote all resources necessary to resolve the problem. Referring to PIT at the same time, the Minister of Finance observed that more than 23,000 people had registered their tax returns, and that collections to date amounted to Nu 91m. The 81st National Assembly resolved at the end of July 2004 to reduce the maximum limit for PIT from 25% to 15%, but the 86th National Assembly in December 2006 agreed to revert PIT rates to the level pertaining prior to that reduction.

The National Technical Training Authority was established to co-ordinate vocational and technical education, and thereby increase employment prospects and promote traditional arts and crafts; private sector participation in education was also being explored. Bhutan National Bank extended loans totalling Nu 738.8m. in 1998 and declared a 50% dividend on post-tax profits of Nu 47.8m. in that year. However, the excess liquidity that had accumulated in Bhutan's banks was another problem in 2000, requiring prudent fiscal management.

The innovative Bhutan Trust Fund for Environmental Conservation (BTF), which was formally established in 1992 with the help of major contributions from donor countries and agencies, totalled an estimated US $32.7m. at the end of December 2006. By mid-2001 some 40 similar trust funds had been established throughout the world, modelled on the BTF. Income from the Fund is used to finance projects that are deemed to be productively useful for Bhutan's environment. Management of the Fund was passed to Bhutan in March 2001. Following efforts to mobilize finance for the Health Trust Fund, contributions (including interest) totalled around $22m. by December 2007. Bhutan also established a Cultural Heritage Trust Fund (totalling Nu 40.8m.—about $900,000 at December 2007) and a Youth Development Fund (totalling Nu 77.2m.—including a one-time government seed grant of Nu 45m.—at the end of 2002). In April 2000 the Bhutanese Government, the World Bank and a Dutch international development organization initiated the Rural Access Project, designed to provide financial and technical assistance for the construction of roads without damaging the environment. The 78th session of the National Assembly approved new legislation regarding environmental protection, augmented by further legislation introduced during the 87th session.

Guidelines for the participation of foreign investors in Bhutan's further development were approved in December 2002. This framework was to be followed by a foreign investment act in 2004, which would clearly define the legal parameters within which foreign investment would be made. In the mean time, the Bhutanese stock exchange (the Royal Securities Exchange of Bhutan Ltd) remained closed to external investors. A credit guarantee scheme was launched in 2003, to provide access to capital, particularly for small self-employed businesses. The scheme, especially devised with the intention of benefiting the poorer business people, did not require any equity or collateral from those who qualified for funds. Approval was granted in 2001 for two Singapore-based foreign hotel operators, one of which was to work in partnership with the Bhutan Tourism Corporation, to invest in hotel infrastructure catering to high-income visitors to Bhutan. A third Indian-based hotel chain was granted approval in September 2001 to construct a joint-venture luxury resort in Thimphu from 2002. In 2001 the Bhutanese Government continued to divest its shares in state-owned corporations, to encourage further private sector participation: 20% of government shares in the Royal Insurance Corporation of Bhutan were sold, reducing government shareholding to less than 40%. In September 2001 the Council of Ministers approved the establishment of a soft drinks bottling and preform manufacturing industry at Pasakha, near Phuentsholing, but the facility ceased operations in early 2007.

In mid-2001 the Government was formulating a Memorandum on Foreign Trade Regime in preparation for membership of the World Trade Organization, with which Bhutan held observer status. At its consultation with Bhutan in late 2002 the IMF commended the Government's financial management. In its subsequent consultation report of July 2005, the IMF assessed Bhutan's medium-term growth prospects as favourable, but stated that: 'the main challenge will be to spur private sector development and economic diversification' to generate jobs for the growing projected output of educated school-leavers; the education sector could be better aligned to 'market needs', and the high level of the minimum wage 'could result in higher unemployment'; also, the tax base should be broadened; the exchange-rate peg to the Indian rupee should be continued, but excess liquidity could fuel excessive credit growth, 'especially to the construction sector'. The IMF directors also reiterated that 'considerable work remains to be done to upgrade statistical systems', especially in fiscal and external sections. Bhutan acceded to the World Customs Organization in February 2003. In December 2003 the Government joined the International Finance Corporation (IFC), a World Bank subsidiary, as its 176th member, in the hope that this would bring enormous potential benefits for the Bhutanese business community, both through technical assistance and through access to large international financing based solely on the economic viability of a project. By mid-2007 the IFC had one investment in Bhutan of US $10m. (of which $9.4m. had been committed), which was in the tourism sector in the form of a loan supporting the construction of six luxury guest-houses under the Bhutan Hotels Corporation Limited. While IFC views its role as the promotion of growth in the domestic private sector, it will also support sustainable foreign investment, especially in tourism. The IFC subsidiary SouthAsia Enterprise Development Facility (SEDF), in partnership with the Bhutan Chamber of Commerce and Industry, has established a knowledge centre offering business information and training skills in Thimphu, has assisted the National Women's

Association of Bhutan, and has assisted in financial and agricultural management training. The Minister of Finance reported in June 2003 that the country's financial institutions continued to have excess liquidity, although private sector credit had grown by 29% in 2002/03. He stressed that excess liquidity was not caused by the financial sector, rather it was the symptom of larger problems within the economy which tend to constrain investments. Furthermore, there was concern that the issue of excess liquidity could easily turn into a large non-performing loans problem if the financial sector became too aggressive. Therefore, efforts to improve access to finances would be matched by the implementation of revised prudential guidelines by the monetary authority. The Minister also observed that the percentage of non-performing loans had decreased from 16.5% in 1999 to 9.7% in 2002.

In mid-2003 Denmark committed Nu 1,920m. (about US $42.7m.) to support the health sector (Nu 492m.), the good governance programme (Nu 267m.) and the education sector. Danish financial assistance to the environment sector was to be gradually phased out. In August 2003 the World Bank announced a 40-year low-interest credit worth $31m. for the education sector. Some 10,000 primary and secondary school places (mostly in rural areas) are to be created in order to expand access to schooling, and education quality at all levels is to be improved. The education project will also extend and upgrade 25 existing schools and build four new ones; the curriculum is to be improved and information technology introduced into secondary schools. Also, a permanent secretariat was established for the Royal University of Bhutan (formally established in June 2003). (The university comprised 10 institutes, including Sherubtse College, the Centre for Bhutan Studies, the National Institutes of Education in Paro and Samtse, and the Royal Institute of Management.) Project-tied assistance from India for the Ninth Plan was, by agreement in January 2005, extended to 11 new projects, with a value of Nu 1,300m. This brought the number of Indian-assisted Ninth Plan projects to 70, with an approved ceiling of Nu 7,338.2m. Emphasis was being placed particularly on agriculture (produce marketing systems) and on strengthening the livestock base. The new projects included: computerized tomography (CT)-scan and magnetic resonance imaging (MRI) diagnostic equipment for the national referral hospital in Thimphu (Nu 120m.); double-laning of the highway between Chunzom and Paro; information technology (IT) support (mainly computers) for 100 primary schools (Nu 20m.); study of an east-east optical fibre broadband system (Nu 20m.); renovation of Semtokha dzong (Nu 108m.); Bhutan Broadcasting Service (BBS) support (Nu 224m.); establishment of a Youth Development Centre at Thimphu (Nu 75m.); and the development of tourism facilities at Haa (Nu 71m.). A 43-km road between Gomphu and Panbang has also been agreed, and India was to consider constructing part of the road during the Ninth Plan period.

A wholly owned government company, Druk Holding and Investments Ltd (DHI) was established in November 2007 to hold and manage government interest in seven major corporations and seven 'DHI-linked companies' (the latter with partial government ownership), for 'the long-term benefit of the country'.

## ENERGY

The Chhukha HEP project was launched in 1975 and the first turbine was test-turned in April 1986 and synchronized to the neighbouring Indian grid in September. The additional turbines came into operation by mid-1988, and the project was formally inaugurated by the President of India in October 1988. Most of western Bhutan, up to Punakha, is now able to receive electricity from this source. Under the existing arrangements, India bore 60% of all costs of the Chhukha project, with the remaining 40% of costs constituting a long-term, low-interest loan to Bhutan; and the Government of India purchases, at a low price, all power not consumed by Bhutan. Bhutan reimports some power through the Indian grid at the same low price (plus costs for transmission) to serve several southern districts. In 2001 the Chhukha project provided Bhutan with a gross income of Nu 2,175.1m. (Nu 2,034.9m. in power sales to India; Nu 140.2m. in domestic power sales). It is hoped that this relatively cheap power will give a substantial impetus to industrial development in the private sector. By the end of June 1998 electricity was being supplied to 39 of the principal towns of Bhutan and 363 villages, and in mid-1996 total installed capacity under the Department of Power (including the Chhukha project) was 342 MW (of which the Chhukha project provided 325 MW and diesel plants 12 MW), with maximum generation potential of 1,632.9m. units. Maximum domestic demand, however, remained low at 20 MW. Total domestic energy requirement rose from 186.7m. units in 1991/92 to 195.3m. units in 1992/93. The installed capacity of generators within Bhutan includes 35 diesel stations (12 at industrial sites), eight HEP stations and 14 micro-hydroelectric stations.

In November 1990 India and Bhutan signed a memorandum of understanding to permit the execution of detailed reports on the proposed Tala HEP project and the Wangchu reservoir scheme (Chhukha II and Chhukha III, respectively). In March 1996 Bhutan and India agreed to proceed with the Tala project, at an estimated cost of Nu 14,080m. (of which 60% was to be in the form of grants from India and 40% was to be in the form of a loan repayable over 12 years). The water diversion channel was completed in May 1999, and the supply of generating plant contracts (worth Nu 4,210m.) was awarded in October of that year. In 2003, with 66% of the works completed, the project completion date of September 2005 was agreed upon. In late 2001 the total cost of the project was expected to reach some Nu 36,000m. When completed, the Tala project will have an installed capacity of 1,020 MW. India and Bhutan also agreed in late 1992 to co-operate to examine the power potential of the Sunkosh river in south-central Bhutan. The detailed Sunkosh Multipurpose Project report presented at the end of 1996, which the Government is still considering, foresees power capacity of 4,060 MW and a construction cost of Nu 77,930m. The project would be based at Kerabari village (Kalikhola); it would take a decade to complete, and could supply power to India's northern and eastern grids. In February 1994 Bhutan and India signed an agreement regarding the construction of the 45-MW Kurichhu HEP project at Gyelpoishing, near Mongar in eastern Bhutan. The first turbine was commissioned in early 2001; a fourth 15-MW unit will bring total capacity to 60 MW on completion. Costs had reached Nu 5,685m. by mid-2001. The first two units of power from the Kurichhu project were connected to the Indian grid in Salakati (Assam) in August 2001, and by mid-2002 three generating units were fully commissioned, with the fourth nearing completion. The project was expected to supply consistent and sufficient electricity to the 10 districts of eastern and central Bhutan, which would eventually lead to social and economic benefits. A 198-km, 132-kilovolt feeder power line from Kurichhu to Gelephu (via Pemagatshel, Nganglam, Panbang and Tingtibi) was completed in less than one year. In November 2001 Samdrup Jongkhar received power from Kurichhu for the first time via a substation at Deothang. The Basochhu project (66 MW) was completed in late 2004 at a revised cost of Nu 1,659m.; the first (upper) 25-MW phase was inaugurated in mid-January 2002, thereby boosting national electricity capacity to 440 MW, and the second (lower) 40-MW phase became operational in September 2004. Power was initially distributed to the five western districts, and was subsequently extended to the southern districts of Dagana, Tsirang and Sarpang. Eventually, the Basochhu project will be linked with the Kurichhu project at Gelephu to form an integrated national power transmission grid. The Bunakha project (180 MW) is currently being assessed; and the Rangjung project (2.2 MW), which was commissioned in April 1996, supplies electricity to more than 3,000 households in the districts of Trashigang and Trashi Yangtse. Bilateral aid donated by the Austrian Government has also assisted the energy sector (including rural electrification) and the provision of renewable natural resources.

Bhutan and India signed important agreements in New Delhi in July 2006 concerning co-operation in the field of hydroelectric power (laying down the framework for future bilateral co-operation), and a protocol to the inter-governmental Agreement signed in March 1996 on the establishment of the Tala hydroelectric project (specifying the commercial arrangements for the purchase of Tala power by India); an

Agreement on Trade, Commerce and Transit was also signed (see above). The hydropower co-operation agreement (which was to be valid for 60 years, with a review every 10 years) provides that India will facilitate funds and manpower for the construction of power projects in Bhutan. A joint group was to be formed to 'facilitate identification of projects, preparation of detailed project reports, and to select agencies' to implement the projects to be undertaken by the public sector. The private sector was also to be involved in future projects. The power co-operation agreement also allows Bhutan to use India's carbon emission baseline within the Kyoto Protocol, thus making Bhutan eligible for carbon trading and so able to receive compensation for its contribution to the reduction of emissions. The then Bhutanese Minister of Trade and Industry, commenting on the agreement on power co-operation, pointed out that it provided a systematic framework for co-operation in the development of hydropower projects; the ad hoc system of the past had worked because of the close friendship and trust between the two countries, but the new understandings would ensure the long-term success of this capital-intensive industry. In addition, the minister said that Bhutan would rationalize the use of hydropower, which was closely linked not only to the water flow and forests but also to the preservation of the environment and ecological balance. The Government would continue with watershed management, control the growth of industries (even those that were profitable), and adopt other conservation measures to ensure the production of competitive, reliable, and clean power for the benefit of the two countries. The minister added that 'all industries are linked to power' and remarked that 'power, which is an industry in itself, is the most important export commodity and source of revenue for Bhutan'.

In late July 2007 India and Bhutan signed an agreement to establish the 1,095-MW Punatsangchhu-I hydel plant, at an estimated cost of Nu 35,000m. This project was expected to be completed in around eight years and was hailed as a 'key pillar' in future Indo-Bhutanese relations. Under an agreement drawn up by the two countries in 2006, India was committed to purchasing 5,000 MW of power from Bhutan by 2020. Two further hydel projects (Punatsangchhu-II and Manaduchhu) are the subjects of current detailed project reports.

## HEALTH SERVICES

Modern medical facilities were established in 1962, at a time when low nutritional intake and poor sanitation, along with a high level of parasitic infections and contagious diseases, continued to debilitate the population. By 2001 services provided by the then Department of Health covered about 90% of the total population, although it was acknowledged that there was still insufficient reliable data available on a number of important issues, including infant mortality. Life expectancy at birth reached about 61 years in 2002, according to WHO. The infant mortality rate stood at about 94 per 1,000 live births in the same year. Health institutions were, at first, concentrated in the urban areas, but by the beginning of the 21st century the emphasis had shifted to rural areas. National, regional and district hospitals serve as referral centres; basic health units (BHUs), the core of Bhutan's public health system, serve remote communities.

Health assistants, auxiliary-nurse midwives and basic health workers who are employed by the BHUs are given paramedical training at Thimphu's Royal Institute of Health Sciences (RIHS, established as a health school in January 1974 and upgraded in September 1989). In addition, during the Fifth Plan (1981–87), 193 village volunteer health workers were trained in basic health care. At the end of 2006 there were 29 hospitals (as well as one indigenous hospital, 21 indigenous units and five leprosy hospitals, providing general health services also), 176 BHUs, 32 dispensaries, 485 outreach clinics, 19 malaria centres and three training institutes in 205 gewogs. The total number of hospital beds was 1,078 (one for every 623 inhabitants, on the basis of the 2005 census population figure), and there were 145 doctors (including expatriates; about one for every 4,637 inhabitants). The ratio of doctors to hospital beds was 1:7. In April 2006 there were 1,200 village health workers. The Government has placed considerable importance on the development of indigenous medicine, along with the development of modern medical practices. Indigenous medical units are attached to district hospitals (21 in 2005), each attended by a *drungtsho* (physician) and a *menpa* (compounder) trained by the National Institute of Traditional Medicine Services (NITMS). In addition to this training, the NITMS provides alternative medical services for outpatients, and researches, collects and manufactures indigenous medicines. In 2005 there were 30 physicians and 36 compounders working in 21 indigenous medical service units. The RIHS (under the Royal University of Bhutan from June 2003) has collaborated with LaTrobe University (Melbourne, Australia) in offering BSc nursing degrees to selected staff nurses.

The Government's principal recent health-care objective was to eliminate, by the year 2000, the most common diseases—waterborne parasites, diarrhoea and dysentery, malaria, tuberculosis, pneumonia and goitre. Extensive publicity is being given, in the rural areas, to the preparation of oral rehydration fluid. Access to safe drinking water increased from 31% of the population in 1987 to 78.2% in 2005. In the same year, 89.0% of villages had access to health services within three hours of walking. An immunization programme against six diseases, for infants aged up to 10 months, has been operating since 1979. In 1990 WHO declared that universal child immunization had been achieved in Bhutan. In 2000 12,686 children were vaccinated against tuberculosis, 10,757 against measles, and 12,228 against both diphtheria and poliomyelitis. Coverage is currently being sustained at more than 80% of infants over the age of one. The number of leprosy patients is decreasing each year (36 at the end of 2005—of whom 15 were new cases—compared with 3,764 in 1979), and the leprosy hospitals, which were previously operated by the Norwegian Mission, have been nationalized (although the Mission retains a presence in Bhutan). The district hospital at Gidakom functions as the national referral centre for leprosy and for tuberculosis. An iodizing plant came into operation in 1984, and all sales of non-iodized salt are now banned. This constituted a major step towards the eventual elimination of hypothyroidism and cretinism. Malaria is still an endemic disease in southern Bhutan; in 1999 51% of 79,589 blood tests for malaria were positive. Malaria cases peaked in 1994 (38,901 cases) and have been declining since (there were only 1,825 cases in 2005, including five deaths). The malaria control programme launched in 1964 (now the vector-borne disease control programme) includes surveillance of Japanese encephalitis and dengue fever, as well as malaria—all of which are endemic in five southern districts. DDT (an insecticide) spraying technique was replaced in 1995 by use of synthetic pyrethroid; from 1985, insecticide-treated bed-nets have been deployed with success.

By June 2003 42 HIV/AIDS cases had been reported in Bhutan. In August 2004 King Jigme took the strong measure of issuing a kasho (royal directive) reminding the country that the number of HIV/AIDS cases continued to increase and that there was 'a grave risk that the socio-economic development of Bhutan would be seriously affected' if the disease were to spread among the small and vulnerable population. By April 2006 83 HIV/AIDS cases had been detected in sample screenings; of these, 19 persons died (17 as a result of AIDS-related illnesses). The total of HIV/AIDS cases had reached 90 by July and 105 by the end of 2006. Sexually-transmitted diseases are a substantial problem; a 1989 study reported about 7% prevalence in the general population, most frequently among males of the 15–49 years age group and involving the police (14%), lay monks and military (7%), and students (4%). Most infections appear to be acquired by travellers to border towns. The rising trend of HIV/AIDS cases is exacerbated by the greater external mobility of persons, an increase in prostitution, and lighter restrictions on sexual relations in Bhutan compared with other countries in the region.

In 2005 the six main diseases requiring hospital treatment were the common cold (25%), skin infections (8%), diarrhoea (7%), peptic ulcer syndrome (5%), conjunctivitis (5%), and dysentery (3%). The main cause of death (in hospital facilities) during 2003–05 was alcohol-related liver diseases. The budget for the financial year 2001/02 allocated an estimated Nu 1,000.2m. (10.2% of total projected expenditure) to health;

this sum was increased to Nu 1,550.2m. (11% of projected expenditure) for 2004/05, and to Nu 2,280.3m. (about 12% of total expenditure for all sectors) in the 2006/07 budget. In 2005 Nu 82m. was spent on the procurement of essential drugs. Priorities in the health sector for 2006/07 were the intensification of training programmes, continuing support for reproductive health, and HIV/AIDS programmes.

An indefinite ban on the import of poultry and related products was imposed from February 2006 because of fears of H5N1 viral infection.

In mid-2006 a 16-slice CT-scan (costing Nu 100m.) and MRI equipment were installed at the Thimphu referral hospital (funded by the Government of India). This equipment was expected both to speed up medical treatment and to reduce greatly diagnostic referrals outside Bhutan (in 2005 Nu 80m. was spent on referral costs to treat some 500 patients, mainly in India). In practice, it is expected that Bhutanese patients will bring their CT or MRI scan records with them when they attend hospitals in Thailand or India for further treatment.

# Statistical Survey

Source (unless otherwise stated): National Statistics Bureau, POB 338, Thimphu; tel. (2) 322753; fax (2) 323069; internet www.nsb.gov.bt.

## Area and Population

**AREA, POPULATION AND DENSITY**

| | |
|---|---|
| Area (sq km) | 38,364* |
| Population (census results) | |
| 30–31 May 2005† | |
| Males | 364,482 |
| Females | 307,943 |
| Total | 672,425 |
| Population (official projected estimates) | |
| 2006 | 646,851 |
| 2007 | 658,888 |
| 2008 | 671,083 |
| Density (per sq km) at 2008 | 17.5 |

* 14,812 sq miles; figure corresponds to official adjustment recorded in Ninth Plan.

† Including adjustment for estimated 37,443 persons with no permanent residence; the enumerated total was 634,982. The number of Bhutanese nationals was 552,996.

**DISTRICTS**
(population by dzongkhag at 2005 census)

| | |
|---|---|
| Bumthang | 16,116 |
| Chhukha | 74,387 |
| Dagana | 18,222 |
| Gasa | 3,116 |
| Haa | 11,648 |
| Lhuentse | 15,395 |
| Mongar | 37,069 |
| Paro | 36,433 |
| Pemagatshel | 13,864 |
| Punakha | 17,715 |
| Samdrup Jongkhar | 39,961 |
| Samtse | 60,100 |
| Sarpang | 41,549 |
| Thimphu | 98,676 |
| Trashigang | 51,134 |
| Trashiyangtse | 17,740 |
| Trongsa | 13,419 |
| Tsirang | 18,667 |
| Wangdue Phodrang | 31,135 |
| Zhemgang | 18,636 |
| **Total dzongkhags** | 634,982 |
| No permanent residence | 37,443 |
| **Total** | 672,425 |

**PRINCIPAL TOWNS**
(2005 census )

| | | | |
|---|---|---|---|
| Thimphu (capital) | 79,185 | Gelephu | 9,199 |
| Phuentsholing | 20,537 | Wangdue | 6,714 |

Source: Thomas Brinkhoff, *City Population* (internet www.citypopulation.de).

**2007** (official estimate at 1 January): Thimphu 95,000.

**BIRTHS AND DEATHS**
(annual averages, UN estimates)

| | 1990–95 | 1995–2000 | 2000–05 |
|---|---|---|---|
| Birth rate (per 1,000) | 35.7 | 29.3 | 22.4 |
| Death rate (per 1,000) | 12.6 | 10.0 | 7.8 |

Source: UN, *World Population Prospects: The 2006 Revision*.

**2005 census** (year ending 31 May 2005): Live births 12,538 (birth rate 20 per 1,000); Deaths 4,498 (death rate 7 per 1,000).

**Expectation of life** (years at birth, WHO estimates): 64.3 (males 62.4; females 66.7) in 2006 (Source: WHO, *World Health Statistics*).

**EMPLOYMENT**
('000 persons)

| | 2003 | 2004 | 2005 |
|---|---|---|---|
| Agriculture and forestry | 167.2 | 132.8 | 108.6 |
| Mining and quarrying | 0.4 | 0.1 | 2.8 |
| Manufacturing | 4.5 | 12.6 | 4.9 |
| Electricity, gas and water supply | 1.0 | 1.0 | 4.1 |
| Construction | 2.9 | 6.9 | 30.9 |
| Wholesale and retail trade; repairs of motor vehicles and personal and household goods | 6.9 | 4.8 | 6.7 |
| Hotels and restaurants | 1.3 | 1.4 | 4.0 |
| Transport, storage and communications | 0.2 | 2.6 | 8.1 |
| Financial intermediation | 0.3 | 2.5 | 2.3 |
| Public administration and defence; compulsory social security | 19.5 | 10.0 | 17.5 |
| Education | 3.5 | 3.9 | 7.8 |
| Health and social work | 2.7 | 2.4 | 2.5 |
| Other community, social and personal service activities | 11.4 | 29.1 | 48.7 |
| **Total** | 221.8 | 210.1 | 249.0 |

Source: Royal Monetary Authority of Bhutan, *Annual Report*.

**2005 census:** Total employed 308,998; Unemployed 7,236; Total labour force 316,234.

# Health and Welfare

### KEY INDICATORS

| | |
|---|---|
| Total fertility rate (children per woman, 2006) | 2.3 |
| Under-5 mortality rate (per 1,000 live births, 2006) | 70 |
| HIV/AIDS (% of persons aged 15–49, 2005) | <0.1 |
| Physicians (per 1,000 head, 2004) | 0.05 |
| Hospital beds (per 1,000 head, 2001) | 1.6 |
| Health expenditure (2005): US $ per head (PPP) | 85 |
| Health expenditure (2005): % of GDP | 4.0 |
| Health expenditure (2005): public (% of total) | 71 |
| Access to water (% of persons, 2004) | 62 |
| Access to sanitation (% of persons, 2004) | 70 |
| Human Development Index (2005): ranking | 133 |
| Human Development Index (2005): value | 0.579 |

For sources and definitions, see explanatory note on p. vi.

# Agriculture

### PRINCIPAL CROPS

('000 metric tons)

| | 2004 | 2005 | 2006* |
|---|---|---|---|
| Rice (paddy) | 54.4 | 67.6 | 68.0 |
| Maize | 90.6 | 94.0 | 94.0 |
| Potatoes | 47.4 | 53.6 | 55.0 |
| Sugar cane* | 12.8 | 12.8 | 13.0 |
| Oranges* | 36.0 | 36.0 | 36.0 |
| Apples | 5.9 | 10.4 | 10.5 |
| Nutmeg, mace and cardamom* | 5.8 | 5.8 | 5.8 |

* FAO estimate(s).

**Aggregate production** ('000 metric tons, may include official, semi-official or estimated data): Total cereals 157.6 in 2004, 193.1 in 2005, 193.5 in 2006; Total roots and tubers 69.2 in 2004, 75.4 in 2005, 77.0 in 2006; Total vegetables (incl. melons) 9.6 in 2004;, 24.4 in 2005, 24.8 in 2006; Total fruits (excl. melons) 82.2 in 2004, 87.5 in 2005, 77.5 in 2006.

Source: FAO.

### LIVESTOCK

('000 head, year ending September)

| | 2004* | 2005 | 2006 |
|---|---|---|---|
| Horses | 28* | 25 | 26* |
| Asses, mules or hinnies* | 28 | 27 | n.a. |
| Cattle | 372* | 381 | 385* |
| Buffaloes* | 2 | 2 | n.a. |
| Pigs | 41* | 28 | 35* |
| Sheep | 20* | 18 | 18* |
| Goats* | 30 | 30 | 30 |
| Chickens* | 230 | 230 | 230 |

* FAO estimate(s).

Source: FAO.

### LIVESTOCK PRODUCTS

('000 metric tons, FAO estimates)

| | 2004 | 2005 | 2006 |
|---|---|---|---|
| Cattle meat | 5.1 | 5.1 | 5.1 |
| Pig meat | 1.1 | 0.8 | 0.9 |
| Cows' milk | 41.1 | 41.1 | 41.1 |
| Buffaloes' milk | 0.3 | 0.3 | 0.3 |
| Hen eggs | 0.2 | 0.2 | 0.2 |

Source: FAO.

# Forestry

### ROUNDWOOD REMOVALS

('000 cubic metres, excl. bark, FAO estimates)

| | 2003 | 2004 | 2005 |
|---|---|---|---|
| Sawlogs, veneer logs and logs for sleepers | 63 | 63 | 63 |
| Other industrial wood | 70 | 70 | 70 |
| Fuel wood | 4,413 | 4,479 | 4,546 |
| **Total** | 4,546 | 4,612 | 4,679 |

**2006:** Figures assumed to be unchanged from 2005 (FAO estimates).

Source: FAO.

### SAWNWOOD PRODUCTION

('000 cubic metres, incl. railway sleepers, FAO estimates)

| | 1998 | 1999 | 2000 |
|---|---|---|---|
| Coniferous (softwood) | 12 | 15 | 21 |
| Broadleaved (hardwood) | 6 | 7 | 10 |
| **Total** | 18 | 22 | 31 |

**2001–06:** Annual production as in 2000 (FAO estimates).

Source: FAO.

# Fishing

(metric tons, live weight, FAO estimates)

| | 1999 | 2000 | 2001 |
|---|---|---|---|
| Capture (Freshwater fishes) | 300 | 300 | 300 |
| Aquaculture (Freshwater fishes) | 30 | 30 | 30 |
| **Total catch** | 330 | 330 | 330 |

**2002–06:** Capture 300 (FAO estimates).

Source: FAO.

# Mining

('000 metric tons, unless otherwise indicated, estimates)

| | 2004 | 2005 | 2006* |
|---|---|---|---|
| Dolomite | 452 | 389 | 410 |
| Limestone | 561 | 536 | 550 |
| Gypsum | 131 | 151 | 160 |
| Coal | 30 | 85 | 82 |
| Marble chips ('000 sq m) | 3 | 4 | n.a. |
| Slate ('000 sq m) | 12 | 0 | 1 |
| Quartzite | 43 | 53 | 50 |
| Talc | 40 | 43 | 45 |

* Estimates.

**Iron ore** ('000 metric tons, estimate): 5 in 2006.

Source: US Geological Survey.

# Industry

**GROSS SALES AND OUTPUT OF SELECTED INDUSTRIES**
(million ngultrum)

| | 2004 | 2005 | 2006 |
|---|---|---|---|
| Penden Cement Authority | 851.8 | 807.0 | 1,041.8 |
| Bhutan Ferro Alloys | 748.3 | 651.2 | 678.3 |
| Bhutan Fruit Products | 174.1 | 69.4 | 134.7 |
| Army Welfare Project* | 233.8 | 240.0 | 279.4 |
| Bhutan Carbide and Chemicals | 731.6 | 760.2 | — |
| Bhutan Board Products | 546.2 | 158.3 | 251.8 |
| Eastern Bhutan Coal Company | 26.0 | 180.0 | 203.0 |
| Druk Satair Corporation Ltd | 140.4 | 172.9 | 258.4 |

* Manufacturer of alcoholic beverages.

Source: Royal Monetary Authority of Bhutan.

**Electric energy** (million kWh, year ending 30 June): 1,972.2 in 1995/96; 1,838.4 in 1996/97; 1,800.0 in 1997/98 (Source: Department of Power, Royal Government of Bhutan).

**Revenue from the Chhukha, Basochhu and Kurichhu Hydroelectric Projects*** (million ngultrum): 2,875.0 (Internal consumption 271.4; Exports 2,603.5) in 2003; 3,077.4 (Internal consumption 365.7; Exports 2,711.7) in 2004; 3,780.5 (Internal consumption 586.5, Exports 3,194.0) in 2005; 1,100.8 (Internal consumption 603.0, Exports 497.8) in 2006; 10,908.6 (Internal consumption 960.0, Exports 9,948.6) in 2007.

* From 2006 figures also include revenue from the Tala hydroelectric project.

Source: Department of Power, Royal Government of Bhutan.

# Finance

**CURRENCY AND EXCHANGE RATES**

**Monetary Units**

100 chetrum (Ch) = 1 ngultrum (Nu).

**Sterling, Dollar and Euro Equivalents** (30 May 2008)

£1 sterling = 84.051 ngultrum;
US $1 = 42.590 ngultrum;
€1 = 66.049 ngultrum;
1,000 ngultrum = £11.90 = $23.48 = €15.14.

**Average Exchange Rate** (ngultrum per US $)

2005 44.101
2006 45.307
2007 41.389

Note: The ngultrum is at par with the Indian rupee, which also circulates freely within Bhutan. The foregoing figures relate to the official rate of exchange, which is applicable to government-related transactions alone. Since April 1992 there has also been a market rate of exchange, which values foreign currencies approximately 20% higher than the official rate of exchange.

**GOVERNMENT FINANCE**
(general government transactions, cash basis, million ngultrum, year ending 30 June)

**Summary of Balances**

| | 2001/02 | 2002/03 | 2003/04 |
|---|---|---|---|
| Revenue | 8,792.0 | 7,015.3 | 10,371.5 |
| *Less* Expense | 4,827.1 | 5,373.2 | 5,409.2 |
| **Net cash inflow from operating activities** | 3,965.0 | 1,642.1 | 4,962.2 |
| *Less* Purchase of non-financial assets | 4,953.4 | 4,517.2 | 4,393.0 |
| Sales of non-financial assets | 34.7 | 25.0 | 73.5 |
| **Cash surplus/deficit** | –953.7 | –2,850.1 | 642.7 |

**Revenue**

| | 2001/02 | 2002/03 | 2003/04 |
|---|---|---|---|
| Taxes | 2,414.6 | 2,713.6 | 2,446.6 |
| Taxes on income, profit and capital gains | 1,305.0 | 1,272.7 | 1,419.4 |
| Taxes on goods and services | 915.0 | 1,219.5 | 750.1 |
| Grants | 3,748.5 | 2,269.1 | 5,367.4 |
| Other revenue | 2,628.9 | 2,032.7 | 2,557.5 |
| **Total** | 8,792.0 | 7,015.3 | 10,371.5 |

**Expense/Outlays**

| | 2001/02 | 2002/03 | 2003/04 |
|---|---|---|---|
| Compensation of employees | 1,897.1 | 1,947.0 | 2,086.8 |
| Use of goods and services | 2,161.2 | 2,093.2 | 2,386.6 |
| Interest | 115.8 | 168.9 | 220.3 |
| Subsidies | 65.1 | 143.9 | 114.3 |
| Grants | — | 24.0 | 61.7 |
| Social benefits | 228.7 | 203.9 | 279.6 |
| Other expense | 359.2 | 792.3 | 260.0 |
| **Total** | 4,827.1 | 5,373.2 | 5,409.2 |

| Outlays by function of government* | 2001/02 | 2002/03 | 2003/04 |
|---|---|---|---|
| General public services | 2,320.3 | 3,202.8 | 3,571.6 |
| Public order and safety | 482.4 | 519.8 | 552.7 |
| Economic affairs | 3,876.6 | 3,291.9 | 2,925.4 |
| Agriculture, forestry, fishing and hunting | 883.2 | 1,115.3 | 989.1 |
| Fuel and energy | 1,835.1 | 1,015.6 | 789.5 |
| Transport | 979.5 | 946.8 | 1,042.7 |
| Housing and community amenities | 340.8 | 411.1 | 501.7 |
| Health | 1,142.8 | 848.7 | 831.8 |
| Recreation, culture and religion | 183.6 | 139.6 | 155.7 |
| Education | 1,434.0 | 1,476.5 | 1,303.3 |
| Statistical discrepancy | — | — | –40.0 |
| **Total** | 9,780.4 | 9,890.5 | 9,802.3 |

* Including purchases of non-financial assets.

Source: IMF, *Government Finance Statistics Yearbook*.

**2004/05** (million ngultrum, year ending 30 June): *Revenue:* Total revenue 6,128.0 (Tax 3,382.4, Non-tax 2,683.7, Other 61.9); Grants 4,373.1 (India 2,625.0, Other 1,748.1); Total revenue and grants 10,501.1. *Expenditure (incl. net lending):* Total 12,893.7 (Current 6,170.6, Capital 6,723.0) (Source: Royal Monetary Authority of Bhutan, *Annual Report*).

**2005/06** (million ngultrum, year ending 30 June): *Revenue:* Total revenue 7,027.4 (Tax 4,124.7, Non-tax 2,778.2, Other 124.5); Grants 6,424.7 (India 3,417.2, Other 3,007.5); Total revenue and grants 13,452.2. *Expenditure (incl. net lending):* Total 13,770.9 (Current 7,098.5, Capital 6,672.4) (Source: Royal Monetary Authority of Bhutan, *Annual Report*).

**2006/07** (million ngultrum, year ending 30 June, preliminary): *Revenue:* Total revenue 9,951.0 (Tax 4,073.7, Non-tax 5,545.2, Other 332.1); Grants 6,718.5 (India 3,791.2, Other 2,927.3); Total revenue and grants 16,669.5. *Expenditure (incl. net lending):* Total 18,316.2 (Current 8,185.7, Capital 10,130.5) (Source: Royal Monetary Authority of Bhutan, *Annual Report*).

**2007/08** (million ngultrum, year ending 30 June, preliminary): *Revenue:* Total revenue 11,932.6 (Tax 5,486.0, Non-tax 6,446.6); Grants 3,147.9 (India 0.0, Other 3,147.9); Total revenue and grants 15,080.5. *Expenditure (incl. net lending):* Total 23,072.5 (Current 11,501.4, Capital 11,571.0) (Source: Royal Monetary Authority of Bhutan, *Annual Report*).

**FOREIGN EXCHANGE RESERVES**
(at 30 June)

| | 2004 | 2005 | 2006 |
|---|---|---|---|
| Indian rupee reserves (million Indian rupees) | 4,362.8 | 4,737.3 | 3,768.5 |
| Royal Monetary Authority | 1,822.4 | 2,539.7 | 200.8 |
| Bank of Bhutan | 1,988.3 | 1,833.6 | 3,120.5 |
| Bhutan National Bank | 552.1 | 364.0 | 447.2 |
| Convertible currency reserves (US $ million) | 287.4 | 354.3 | 453.1 |
| Royal Monetary Authority* | 249.0 | 316.0 | 399.0 |
| Bank of Bhutan | 31.3 | 24.9 | 26.4 |
| Bhutan National Bank | 7.0 | 13.4 | 27.7 |

* Includes tranche position in the IMF.

Source: Royal Monetary Authority of Bhutan.

**MONEY SUPPLY**
(million ngultrum at 31 December)

| | 2004 | 2005 | 2006 |
|---|---|---|---|
| Currency outside banks* | 2,070.7 | 2,404.4 | 2,762.5 |
| Demand deposits at the Bank of Bhutan | 5,983.1 | 6,565.2 | 9,790.9 |
| **Total money** (incl. others)† | 23,045.4 | 26,772.2 | 33,537.5 |

* Including an estimate for Indian rupees.
† Including non-monetary deposits with the Royal Monetary Authority by financial institutions.

Source: Royal Monetary Authority of Bhutan.

**COST OF LIVING**
(Consumer Price Index at 31 December, excluding rent; base: 30 September 2003 = 100 )

| | 2005 | 2006 | 2007 |
|---|---|---|---|
| Food | 108.4 | 113.8 | 123.0 |
| Non-food items | 110.8 | 116.4 | 120.8 |
| **All items** | 110.0 | 115.5 | 121.5 |

**NATIONAL ACCOUNTS**
(million ngultrum at current prices)

**Expenditure on the Gross Domestic Product**

| | 2004 | 2005 | 2006 |
|---|---|---|---|
| Government final consumption expenditure | 6,649.7 | 7,911.5 | 8,737.9 |
| Private final consumption expenditure | 13,806.7 | 14,586.2 | 15,553.7 |
| Changes in stocks | –77.8 | 103.0 | 107.2 |
| Gross fixed capital formation | 20,078.2 | 18,574.4 | 18,720.1 |
| **Total domestic expenditure** | 40,456.8 | 41,175.1 | 43,118.9 |
| Exports of goods and services | 10,053.2 | 14,105.7 | 21,206.9 |
| *Less* Imports of goods and services | 18,407.0 | 22,662.0 | 24,555.0 |
| Statistical discrepancy | 217.0 | 3,962.1 | 1,672.2 |
| **GDP in purchasers' values** | 32,320.0 | 36,581.2 | 41,443.3 |

**Gross Domestic Product by Economic Activity**

| | 2004 | 2005 | 2006 |
|---|---|---|---|
| Agriculture, forestry and livestock | 7,864 | 8,256 | 8,859 |
| Mining and quarrying | 440 | 550 | 960 |
| Manufacturing | 2,361 | 2,560 | 2,924 |
| Electricity and water | 3,085 | 3,661 | 5,127 |
| Construction | 5,741 | 6,219 | 6,020 |
| Wholesale and retail trade | 1,726 | 2,089 | 2,374 |
| Restaurants and hotels | 169 | 212 | 301 |
| Transport, storage and communications | 3,295 | 3,891 | 4,496 |
| Finance, insurance, real estate | 2,280 | 2,873 | 3,400 |
| Community and social services | 3,823 | 4,472 | 4,989 |
| Personal service, business and recreational activities | 144 | 172 | 213 |
| **Sub-total** | 30,928 | 34,955 | 39,663 |
| Taxes, less subsidies, on products | 1,393 | 1,628 | 1,781 |
| **GDP at current prices** | 32,320 | 36,581 | 41,444 |
| **GDP at constant 2000 factor cost** | 27,269 | 29,201 | 31,673 |

Source: Royal Monetary Authority of Bhutan, *Annual Report*.

**BALANCE OF PAYMENTS**
(million ngultrum, year ending 30 June, estimates)

| | 2004/05 | 2005/06 | 2006/07* |
|---|---|---|---|
| Merchandise exports f.o.b. | 9,457.1 | 13,959.8 | 22,674.3 |
| Merchandise imports c.i.f. | –20,556.0 | –19,456.5 | –22,119.2 |
| **Trade balance** | –11,099.0 | –5,496.7 | 555.1 |
| Exports of services | 1,894.9 | 2,313.8 | 2,661.2 |
| Imports of services | –3,647.9 | –2,886.8 | –2,519.2 |
| **Balance on goods and services** | –12,852.0 | –6,069.7 | 697.1 |
| Other income received | 537.2 | 813.3 | 1,159.5 |
| Other income paid | –1,244.9 | –1,125.8 | –1,036.0 |
| **Balance on goods, services and income** | –13,559.7 | –6,382.2 | 820.6 |
| Current transfers received | 5,492.8 | 7,313.7 | 6,737.7 |
| Current transfers paid | –2,420.5 | –2,627.2 | –2,500.4 |
| **Current balance** | –10,487.4 | –1,695.7 | 5,057.8 |
| Capital transfers | 4,586.4 | 1,751.5 | 1,111.8 |
| Direct investment from abroad | 401.5 | 273.9 | 3,238.1 |
| Foreign aid (net of loans) | 2,939.4 | 3,474.7 | 881.0 |
| Other loans | 89.2 | 347.0 | –37.8 |
| Other investment | 1,456.9 | — | — |
| Net errors and omissions | 95.5 | 1,057.7 | –5,066.6 |
| **Overall balance** | –918.6 | 5,209.1 | 5,184.4 |

* Provisional.

Source: Royal Monetary Authority of Bhutan, *Annual Report*.

**OFFICIAL DEVELOPMENT ASSISTANCE**
(US $ million)

| | 2000 | 2001 | 2002 |
|---|---|---|---|
| Bilateral donors | 33.7 | 42.5 | 42.9 |
| Multilateral donors | 19.6 | 18.0 | 30.6 |
| **Total** | 53.3 | 60.5 | 73.5 |
| Grants | 42.5 | 47.1 | 52.0 |
| Loans | 10.8 | 13.4 | 21.5 |
| Per caput assistance (US $) | 25.9 | 28.3 | 33.4 |

Source: UN, *Statistical Yearbook for Asia and the Pacific*.

# External Trade

**PRINCIPAL COMMODITIES**
(million ngultrum)

| Imports | 2004 | 2005 | 2006 |
|---|---|---|---|
| Animal products | 436.8 | 570.2 | 631.4 |
| Fruit, vegetables and cereal crops (incl. tea, coffee and spices) | 646.3 | 773.7 | 846.6 |
| Vegetable fats and oils | 312.9 | 323.4 | 1,597.2 |
| Processed foods and beverages (incl. alcohol) | 779.0 | 903.1 | 919.0 |
| Mineral products (incl. fuels) | 2,226.2 | 2,748.8 | 3,259.2 |
| Chemical products (incl. medicines and pharmaceuticals) | 743.6 | 732.2 | 793.8 |
| Plastics and rubber products | 606.8 | 609.9 | 735.0 |
| Wood and products thereof | 132.4 | 133.3 | 141.8 |
| Woodpulp and products thereof | 271.9 | 277.6 | 287.7 |
| Textiles, clothing and footwear | 802.3 | 781.7 | 689.7 |
| Machinery, mechanical appliances, base metals and products thereof, and electronic equipment | 10,597.3 | 5,245.4 | 7,367.2 |
| Transport vehicles and equipment* | 570.9 | 548.7 | 903.3 |
| **Total** (incl. others) | 18,639.5 | 17,035.1 | 18,998.6 |

* Trade with India only.

| Exports | 2004 | 2005 | 2006 |
|---|---|---|---|
| Fruit, vegetables and cereal crops (incl. tea, coffee and spices) | 585.2 | 601.4 | 560.8 |
| Processed foods and beverages (incl. alcohol) | 417.3 | 619.0 | 418.5 |
| Mineral products (incl. fuels) | 816.4 | 1,244.4 | 1,836.1 |
| Chemical products (including medicines and pharmaceuticals)* | 712.5 | 714.0 | 587.0 |
| Plastics and rubber products | 291.8 | 298.0 | 262.1 |
| Woodpulp and products thereof | 281.6 | 314.7 | 257.7 |
| Textiles, clothing and footwear | 537.6 | 787.4 | 485.4 |
| Machinery, mechanical appliances, base metals and products thereof, and electronic equipment | 1,827.8 | 3,144.4 | 4,163.2 |
| Electricity* | 2,711.7 | 3,439.9 | 4,982.0 |
| **Total** (incl. others) | 8,271.2 | 11,386.1 | 18,771.8 |

* Trade with India only; figures for 2003 refer to sales of electricity from Chhukha and Kurichhu hydroelectric projects only.

Source: Royal Monetary Authority of Bhutan, *Annual Report*.

**PRINCIPAL TRADING PARTNERS**
(million ngultrum)

| Imports c.i.f. | 2004 | 2005 | 2006 |
|---|---|---|---|
| China, People's Rep. | 205.3 | 182.2 | 281.7 |
| Germany | 4,248.4 | 200.4 | 200.3 |
| India | 10,193.9 | 12,795.1 | 13,053.9 |
| Indonesia | 65.3 | 240.0 | 1,331.3 |
| Japan | 598.2 | 648.2 | 395.9 |
| Korea, Republic | 501.8 | 247.5 | 459.4 |
| Malaysia | 80.3 | 174.9 | 351.8 |
| Russia | 1.8 | 162.1 | 874.8 |
| Singapore | 420.1 | 447.2 | 515.1 |
| Thailand | 349.6 | 275.5 | 257.8 |
| **Total** (incl. others) | 18,639.5 | 17,035.1 | 19,012.0 |

| Exports f.o.b. | 2004 | 2005 | 2006 |
|---|---|---|---|
| Bangladesh | 410.7 | 561.8 | 470.1 |
| India | 7,761.6 | 9,969.8 | 14,488.0 |
| **Total** (incl. others) | 8,271.1 | 11,386.2 | 18,771.9 |

Source: Royal Monetary Authority of Bhutan, *Annual Report*.

# Transport

**Road traffic:** At April 2003 there were 25,046 registered, roadworthy vehicles—10,574 light four-wheeled vehicles, 8,373 two-wheeled vehicles (motorcycles and scooters), 2,062 heavy vehicles (trucks, buses, bulldozers, etc.), 1,517 taxis and 730 others (Source: National Statistical Bureau, Ministry of Planning, Royal Government of Bhutan).

**CIVIL AVIATION**
(traffic on scheduled services)

| | 2001 | 2002 | 2003 |
|---|---|---|---|
| Kilometres flown (million) | 1 | 2 | 2 |
| Passengers carried ('000) | 35 | 41 | 36 |
| Passenger-km (million) | 47 | 61 | 56 |
| Total ton-km (million) | 4 | 6 | 5 |

Source: UN, *Statistical Yearbook*.

# Tourism

**FOREIGN VISITORS BY COUNTRY OF ORIGIN***

| | 2004 | 2005 | 2006 |
|---|---|---|---|
| Australia | 315 | 458 | 774 |
| Austria | 223 | 319 | 484 |
| Canada | 257 | 292 | 375 |
| France | 434 | 532 | 708 |
| Germany | 671 | 1,042 | 1,074 |
| Italy | 462 | 529 | 648 |
| Japan | 1,087 | 1,554 | 1,815 |
| Netherlands | 163 | 329 | 389 |
| Spain | 198 | 185 | 281 |
| Switzerland | 173 | 363 | 427 |
| United Kingdom | 954 | 1,462 | 5,018 |
| USA | 3,243 | 4,681 | 5,018 |
| **Total** (incl. others) | 9,249 | 13,626 | 17,358 |

* Figures relate to tourists paying in convertible currency.

**2007:** Total arrivals 21,094.

**Tourism receipts** (US $ million): 18.5 in 2005; 24 in 2006; 24 in 2007.

Source: Royal Monetary Authority of Bhutan, *Annual Report*.

# Communications Media

| | 2004 | 2005 | 2006 |
|---|---|---|---|
| Telephones ('000 main lines in use) | 30.3 | 32.7 | 31.5 |
| Mobile cellular telephones ('000 subscribers) | 19.1 | 37.8 | 82.1 |
| Personal computers ('000 in use) | 11 | n.a. | n.a. |
| Internet users ('000) | 20 | 25 | 25 |

**Radio receivers** ('000 in use): 37 in 1997.

**Television receivers** ('000 in use): 13.5 in 2000.

**Facsimile machines** ('000 in use): 1.5 in 1998.

Sources: International Telecommunication Union; UNESCO, *Statistical Yearbook*.

# Education

(2007 unless otherwise indicated)

| | Institutions | Teachers | Students |
|---|---|---|---|
| Community primary schools | 249 | 896 | 28,953 |
| Primary schools | 99 | 904 | 25,760 |
| Lower secondary schools | 88 | 1,627 | 48,966 |
| Middle secondary schools | 37 | 1,093 | 29,829 |
| Higher secondary schools | 29 | 852 | 18,686 |
| Private schools* | 23 | 334 | 5,421 |
| Institutes | 19 | 457 | 4,467 |
| Non-formal education (NFE) centres | 777 | 762 | 14,436 |

* Data for 2006.

Source: Ministry of Education, Thimphu.

**Adult literacy rate** (UNESCO estimates): 55.6% (males 67.1%; females 42.2%) in 2007 (Source: UNESCO Institute for Statistics).

# Directory

## The Constitution

Prior to 2008 the Kingdom of Bhutan had no formal constitution. However, the state system was a modified form of constitutional monarchy. Written rules, which were changed periodically, governed procedures for the election of members of the Council of Ministers, the Royal Advisory Council and the Legislature, and defined the duties and powers of those bodies.

A special committee was convened in late 2001 to prepare a draft written constitution (Tsa-Thrim). A completed first draft was formally presented to King Jigme Singye Wangchuck in December 2002, who then passed the draft to the Prime Minister. Another draft was submitted to King Jigme in mid-2003 for further revisions. In November 2004 King Jigme submitted a 34-article fourth draft to the Council of Ministers; the document was made public for review and comment in March 2005.

The fourth draft of the Constitution provided for, amongst other things: the establishment of a democratic constitutional monarchy in accordance with the principle of hereditary succession, with an age limit of 65 years to be imposed for both the monarch and public officials; the establishment of a parliament consisting of the monarch, the National Council and the National Assembly, with members of the National Assembly to be elected by universal secret ballot from constituencies with approximately equivalent populations; and for two political parties to be represented in the National Assembly, the election campaigns of which would be funded by the State. An additional draft (called the 'second draft' but in fact the fifth) was published in August 2005; the wording of this version was considerably simplified for easier comprehension. A further, final, version of the draft constitution was adopted by the new legislature in July 2008.

The first round of elections to the National Council (Upper House) were held on 31 December 2007 and a second round (for the remaining five districts) took place on 29 January 2008. Under the new legislative structure, the Council would comprise 25 members (20 elected members, and five 'eminent members' nominated by the King), and would function as a house of review on security and national issues; Council members are required to be independent of any political party affiliation. (Registration of political parties was permitted from 1 July 2007.) A general election to the 47-member National Assembly (Lower House) was held on 24 March 2008, ahead of the convening of the new bicameral legislature, which took place in early May.

The Preamble of the Constitution declares that the people of Bhutan solemnly resolve to strengthen the sovereignty of Bhutan and to ensure for all its citizens justice, tranquillity, unity, happiness and well-being. There are 35 articles and four schedules, which form a comprehensive document.

### FUNDAMENTAL RIGHTS, DUTIES AND FREEDOMS

The main freedoms accorded to citizens of Bhutan are freedom of speech, opinion and expression, of thought, conscience and religion, of movement and residence within Bhutan, and of peaceful assembly and association. There shall be freedom of information.

All persons are equal before the law and shall not be discriminated against on the grounds of race, sex, language, religion, politics or other status.

In criminal matters, a person charged with a penal offence has the right to be presumed innocent until proven guilty in accordance with the law. Torture and capital punishment are not permitted under law.

The Constitution contains a proviso that the State may enact reasonable restriction by law when the sovereignty, security, unity or integrity of Bhutan is threatened, or its peace, stability or well-being.

Citizens of Bhutan are expected to preserve, protect and defend the sovereignty, territorial integrity, security and unity of Bhutan, and to render national service when called upon to do so by Parliament.

### THE CROWN

The King (Druk Gyalpo) is the Head of State and the symbol of unity of the Kingdom and of its people. The title to the Golden Throne of Bhutan shall be passed on by hereditary succession in order of seniority when the King reaches the age of 65, with precedence given to sons of the King, providing that the heir has reached the age of 21. The King, in exercise of his royal perogatives, may:

award titles and decorations in accordance with tradition and custom;

grant citizenship, land kidu and other kidus;

grant amnesty, pardon and reduction of sentences;

command bills and other measures to be introduced in Parliament;

exercise powers relating to matters which are not provided for under the Constitution or other laws.

The King shall also appoint key members of the Judiciary, the Election Commission, the Royal Civil Service Commission, the Anti-Corruption Commission, the defence forces, the Governor of the Central Bank, the Chairperson of the Pay Commission, the Cabinet Secretary, the Secretary-Generals of the National Council and the National Assembly, Ambassadors and Consuls, Secretaries to the Government, and District Administrators, on the advice of government officials where appropriate.

### THE PARLIAMENT

The Parliament of Bhutan consists of the King, the National Council and the National Assembly. Members of each House are elected for a five-year term. The National Council consists of 25 elected members and five eminent members nominated by the King. The National Assembly has a maximum of 55 members, elected by adult franchise from each district in proportion to its population.

The Constitution provides that bills, other than money bills, can be introduced in either House. A bill adopted by Parliament may only come into force upon assent of the King.

### THE JUDICIARY

The Supreme Court consists of the Chief Justice and four Judges, appointed by the King, and is the highest appellate authority to entertain appeals against the judgments, orders or decisions of the High Court.

## The Government

### HEAD OF STATE

**Druk Gyalpo ('Dragon King'):** HM JIGME KHESAR NAMGYEL WANGCHUCK (succeeded to the throne on 21 December 2006).

### LHENGYE ZHUNGTSHOG

(Council of Ministers)
(August 2008)

**Prime Minister and Chairman:** Lyonchhen JIGMI YOZER THINLEY.

**Minister of Agriculture:** Lyonpo PEMA GYAMTSHO.

**Minister of Economic Affairs:** Lyonpo KHANDU WANGCHUCK.

**Minister of Education:** Lyonpo THAKUR SINGH POWDYEL.

**Minister of Finance:** Lyonpo WANGDI NORBU.

**Minister of Foreign Affairs:** Lyonpo UGYEN TSHERING.

**Minister of Health:** Lyonpo ZANGLEY DUKPA.

**Minister of Home and Cultural Affairs:** Lyonpo MINJUR DORJI.

**Minister of Information and Communications:** Lyonpo NANDALAL RAI.

**Minister of Labour and Human Resources:** Lyonpo DORJI WANGDI.

**Minister of Works and Human Settlements:** Lyonpo YESHEY ZIMBA.

**Cabinet Secretary, Spokesperson for the Government:** Dasho SHERUB TENZIN.

### MINISTRIES AND OTHER MAJOR GOVERNMENT BODIES

**Ministry of Agriculture:** POB 252, Thimphu; tel. (2) 323765; fax (2) 323153; e-mail s_thinley@moa.gov.bt; internet www.moa.gov.bt.

**Ministry of Economic Affairs:** Tashichhodzong, POB 141, Thimphu; tel. (2) 322211; fax (2) 323617; e-mail kdorjee@druknet.bt; internet www.mti.gov.bt; internet www.tourism.gov.bt (Department of Tourism).

**Ministry of Education:** POB 112, Thimphu; tel. (2) 325325; fax (2) 325183; e-mail p_thinley@hotmail.com; internet www.education.gov.bt.

**Ministry of Finance:** Tashichhodzong, POB 117, Thimphu; tel. (2) 322223; fax (2) 323154; e-mail yanki@mof.gov.bt.

**Ministry of Foreign Affairs:** Convention Centre, POB 103, Thimphu; tel. (2) 322781; internet www.mfa.gov.bt.

**Ministry of Health:** Kawangsa, POB 108, Thimphu; tel. (2) 322602; fax (2) 323113; e-mail dr.gado@health.gov.bt; internet www.health.gov.bt.

**Ministry of Home and Cultural Affairs:** Tashichhodzong, POB 133, Thimphu; tel. (2) 322301; fax (2) 324320; internet www.mohca

.gov.bt; internet www.ctf.gov.bt (Cultural Trust Fund); internet www.library.gov.bt (National Library).

**Ministry of Information and Communications:** POB 278, Thimphu; tel. (2) 322144; fax (2) 324860; e-mail info@moic.gov.bt; internet www.moic.gov.bt; overall responsibility for various corpns (Bhutan Post, Bhutan Telecom, BBS, Kuensel, Druk Air); Dept of Information and Media; Bhutan Information, Communication and Media Authority (fmrly Bhutan Communications Authority); Dept of Civil Aviation; Road Safety and Transport Authority; Dept of Information Technology.

**Ministry of Labour and Human Resources:** Thongsel Lam, Lower Motithang, POB 1036, Thimphu; tel. (2) 333867; fax (2) 326731; e-mail doe@molhr.gov.bt; internet www.molhr.gov.bt.

**Ministry of Works and Human Settlements:** POB 791, Thimphu; tel. (2) 327998; fax (2) 323122; e-mail mowhs@mowhs.gov.bt; internet www.mowhs.gov.bt.

**Anti-Corruption Commission:** POB 1113, Thimphu; tel. (2) 334863; fax (2) 334865; e-mail anticorruption@druknet.bt; internet www.anti-corruption.org.bt; f. 2006; Chair. Aum NETEN ZANGMO; Commrs THINLAY WANGDI, KEZANG JAMTSHO.

**National Environment Commission:** POB 466, Thimphu; tel. (2) 323384; fax (2) 323385; e-mail rnrec@druknet.bt; internet www.nec.gov.bt; Hon. Dep. Minister Dasho NADO RINCHEN; Dir SONAM YANGLEY.

**Pay Commission:** Thimphu; f. 2008; Chair. Dasho SONAM TSHERING.

**Royal Audit Authority:** POB 191, Kawajangsa, Thimphu; tel. (2) 322111; fax (2) 323491; e-mail bhutanaudit@bhutanaudit.gov.bt; internet www.raa.gov.bt; f. 1985; Auditor-Gen. UGYEN TSHEWANG.

**Royal Civil Service Commission:** POB 163, Thimphu; tel. (2) 322491; fax (2) 323086; internet www.rcsc.gov.bt; f. June 1982 under Royal Charter; successor to Dept of Manpower; restructured four times, most recently in October 2003; Chair. Dasho TASHI PHUNTSOG; Sec. Dasho BAP KESANG.

**Cabinet Secretariat:** Tashichhodzong, Thimphu; tel. (2) 321437; fax (2) 321438; e-mail cabinet@druknet.bt.

# Legislature

The National Assembly (tshogdu chenmo—which was established in 1953) was dissolved on 31 July 2007. The following month the Royal Advisory Council was similarly disbanded, in preparation for the inauguration of a new governmental structure: a bicameral legislature, comprising a 25-member National Council and a newly configured 47-member National Assembly.

## NATIONAL COUNCIL (UPPER HOUSE)

Within the National Council, 20 members—one representing each of the 20 electoral districts—were directly elected by a national vote, with the remaining five 'eminent persons' selected by royal appointment. The first round of elections to the National Council was held on 31 December 2007 in 15 districts, and a second round, held on 29 January 2008 in the five remaining districts, completed the voting process.

**Chairperson:** NAMGAY PENJOR.

**Vice-Chairperson:** Dasho KARMA URA.

**Elected Members:** TSHEWANG JURMI (Bumthang), TSHEWANG LHAMO (Chhukha), SONAM DORJI (Dagana), SANGAY KHANDU (Gasa), TSHERING DORJI (Haa), RINZIN (Lhuentse), NAICHU (Mongar), UGYEN TSHERING (Paro), JIGME RINZIN (Pemagatshel), NAMGAY PENJOR (Punakha), JIGME WANGCHUK (Samdrup Jongkhar), Dr MANI KUMAR RAI (Samtse), KARMA DONNEN WANGDI (Sarpang), SANGAY ZAM (Thimphu), SONAM KUENGA (Trashigang), Dr JAGAR DORJI (Trongsa), JUTSIN GURUNG (Tsirang), KESANG NAMGYEL (Trashiyangtse), SONAM YANGCHEN (Wangdue Phodrang), PEMA LHAMO (Zhemgang).

**Appointed Members:** Dasho KARMA URA, Drangpon KUENLEY TSHERING, KARMA YEZER RAYDI, KARMA DAMCHO NIDUP, TASHI WANGMO.

## NATIONAL ASSEMBLY (LOWER HOUSE)

**Speaker:** Dasho JIGME TSHULTIM.

**Deputy Speaker:** YANGKHU TSHERING.

**General Election, 24 March 2008**

| Party | % of votes | Seats |
|---|---|---|
| Druk Phuensum Tshogpa (DPT) | 67 | 45 |
| People's Democratic Party (PDP) | 33 | 2 |
| **Total** | 100 | 47 |

# Election Commission

In mid-April 2006 there were reported to be a total of 400,626 eligible voters in Bhutan.

A draft Election Bill 2008 was published in March 2007, featuring the proposed delimitation of 47 electoral constituencies to embrace all 205 geogs (blocks of several villages) of Bhutan: five were allocated to Trashigang, four to Samtse, three to Monggar and Pemagatshel respectively and two each for the remaining 16 districts. The allocation of constituencies to the 20 electoral districts, ensuring representation of no less than two and no more than seven representatives to Parliament from each, was enacted in the same month. Delimitation of constituencies was subject to review by the Election Commission at 10-year intervals. Registration of political parties was permitted from 1 July 2007.

**Election Commission of Bhutan:** Thimphu; tel. (2) 334761; fax (2) 334763; e-mail kwangdi@druknet.bt; internet www.election-bhutan.org.bt; f. 2006; appointed by the King; Chief Election Commr Dasho KUNZANG WANGDI; Election Commrs Dasho CHOGYAL DAGO RIGDZIN, Aum DEKI PEMA.

# Political Organizations

Although previously banned in accordance with long-standing legislation, all political parties registered with the Election Commission were to be permitted to contest the first round of the 2008 legislative elections. Formal registration commenced in July 2007, although by March 2008 only two parties—the People's Democratic Party (PDP) and the Druk Phuensum Tshogpa (DPT)—had successfully registered with the Election Commission.

There are a number of anti-Government organizations, composed principally of Nepali-speaking former residents of Bhutan, based in Kathmandu, Nepal and New Delhi, India.

**Bhutan Communist Party (Marxist-Leninist-Maoist) (BCP—MLM):** Nepal; f. 2003; advocates complete revolution in Bhutan; Gen. Sec. VIKALPA.

**Bhutan Gorkha Liberation Front:** f. 2003; based in southern Bhutan; Chair. TARA MUKARUNG.

**Bhutan Gurkha National Liberation Front (BGNLF):** Nepal; f. 1994; Vice-Pres. D. R. KATEL; Gen. Sec. LALIT PRADHAN.

**Bhutan National Democratic Party (BNDP):** POB 3334, Kathmandu, Nepal; tel. (1) 525682; f. 1992; also has offices in Delhi and Varanasi, India, and in Thapa, Nepal; Pres. (vacant); Vice-Pres. D. N. S. DHAKAL; Gen. Sec. Dr HARI P. ADHIKARI.

**Bhutan People's Party (BPP):** POB 13, Anarmani-4, Bhadrapur Rd, Birtamode, Jhapa, Nepal; tel. and fax (23) 542561; e-mail bpparty@ntc.net.np; internet www.bhutanpeoplesparty.org; f. 1990 as a successor to the People's Forum on Democratic Rights (f. 1989); advocates unconditional release of all political prisoners, judicial reform, freedom of religious practices, linguistic freedom, freedom of press, speech and expression, and equal rights for all ethnic groups; Pres. BALA RAM POUDYAL; Gen. Sec. DURGA GIRI.

**Druk National Congress (DNC):** B-125, 1st Floor, Dayanand Colony, Lajpat Nagar IV, New Delhi 110 024, India; tel. (11) 65641453; fax (11) 26472636; e-mail dnc@bhutandnc.com; internet www.bhutandnc.com; f. 1994; advocates democracy and human rights in Bhutan; Pres. 'RONGTHONG' KUNLEY DORJI; Gen. Sec. RINZIN DORJI.

**Druk Phuensum Tshogpa (DPT):** Chang Lam, Thimphu; tel. (2) 336336; fax (2) 335845; e-mail dpt@druknet.bt; internet www.dpt.bt; f. 2007 in asscn with five ministers of the outgoing Govt; Pres. Lyonpo JIGMI YOZER THINLEY; Gen. Sec. THINLEY JAMTSHO.

**Human Rights Organization of Bhutan (HUROB):** Patan Dhoka, POB 172, Lalitpur, Kathmandu, Nepal; tel. (1) 525046; fax (1) 526038; f. 1991; documents alleged human rights violations in Bhutan and co-ordinates welfare activities in eight refugee camps in Nepal for ethnic Nepalese claiming to be from Bhutan; Chair. S. B. SUBBA; Gen. Sec. OM DHUNGEL.

**People's Democratic Party (PDP):** Drizang Lam, Lower Motithang, Thimphu; tel. (2) 335557; fax (2) 335757; e-mail info@pdp.bt; internet www.pdp.bt; f. 2007 in asscn with a minister of the outgoing Govt; Pres. SANGYE NGEDUP; Sec.-Gen. Lyonpo LAM KESANG.

## Diplomatic Representation

### EMBASSIES IN BHUTAN

**Bangladesh:** POB 178, Upper Choubachu, Thimphu; tel. (2) 322539; fax (2) 322629; e-mail bdoot@druknet.bt; Ambassador A. K. M. ATIQUR RAHMAN.

**India:** India House, Jungshina, Thimphu; tel. (2) 322162; fax (2) 323195; e-mail hocbht@druknet.bt; Ambassador SUDHIR VYAS.

## Judicial System

Bhutan has Civil and Criminal Codes, which are based on those laid down by the Shabdrung Ngawang Namgyal in the 17th century. An independent judicial authority was established in 1961, but law was mostly administered at the district level until 1968, when the High Court was set up. Existing laws were consolidated in 1982, although annual or biennial conferences of Drangpons (previously styled Thrimpons) are held to keep abreast of changing circumstances and to recommend (in the first instance, to the King) amendments to existing laws. Most legislation is sent by the Council of Ministers to the National Assembly for approval and enactment. A substantially revised Civil and Criminal Procedure Code was endorsed by the 79th National Assembly session in July 2001. In accordance with the law, a National Judicial Commission was established in September 2003. The principal role of the judicial board was to professionalize further the appointment and tenure of judges in the court system; the Chief Justice was to preside over the Commission. A revised Penal Code was adopted by the National Assembly in mid-2004. The historic Judicial Services Act, which was enacted by the National Assembly in January 2007, provided for the complete administrative independence of the judiciary with regard to personnel (excepting judges of the Supreme Court and High Court) through the establishment of a Judicial Services Council. Following the promulgation of the new Constitution in July 2008, the Supreme Court of Bhutan (which was to consist of the Chief Justice and four Drangpons) was to be the highest appellate authority in the country.

### High Court (Thrimkhang Gongma)

Thimphu; tel. (2) 322344; fax (2) 322921; internet www.judiciary.gov.bt.

Established in 1968 to review appeals from Lower Courts, although some cases are heard at the first instance. The Full Bench is presided over by the Chief Justice. There are normally eight other judges (Drangpons), who are appointed by the King on the recommendation of the National Judicial Commission and who serve until their superannuation. Three judges form a quorum. Assistance to defendants is available through jabmis (certificated pleaders), whose responsibilities were formalized by the Jabmi Act in mid-2003. The operation of the legal system and proposed amendments are considered by regular meetings of all the judges and Drangpons (usually annually, or at least once every two years). Following the mid-1998 grant of governance to an elected Council of Ministers, major changes to the structure, administration and personnel of the High Court were implemented from mid-2001.

**Chief Justice:** Lyonpo SONAM TOBGYE.

**Judges (Drangpons) of the High Court:** Dasho THINLEY YOEZER, Dasho PASANG TOBGAY, Dasho KARMA D. SHERPA, Dasho K. B. GHALLEY, Dasho JIGME ZANGPO, Dasho SHERUB GYELTSHEN, Dasho SITHER NAMGYEL, Dasho KUENLEY TSHERING, Dasho TSHERING WANGCHUCK.

**District Courts** (Dzongkhag Thrimkhang): Each district has a court, headed by the drangpon (magistrate), which tries most cases. Appeals are made to the High Court, and less serious civil disputes may be settled by a gup or mandal (village headman) through written undertakings (genja) by the parties concerned.

All citizens have the right to make informal appeal for redress of grievances directly to the King, through the office of the gyalpoi zimpon (court chamberlain).

**Office of the Attorney-General:** POB 1045, Thori Lam, Lower Motithang, Thimphu; tel. (2) 326889; fax (2) 324606; e-mail oag@oag.gov.bt; internet www.oag.gov.bt; f. 2006; fmrly Office of Legal Affairs; Attorney-Gen. RINZIN PENJOR.

## Religion

The state religion is Mahayana Buddhism, but the southern Bhutanese are predominantly followers of Hinduism. Buddhism was introduced into Bhutan in the eighth century AD by the Indian saint Padmasambhava, known in Bhutan as Guru Rimpoche. In the 13th century Phajo Drugom Shigpo made the Drukpa school of Kagyupa Buddhism pre-eminent in Bhutan, and this sect is still supported by the dominant ethnic group, the Drukpas. The main monastic group, the Central Monastic Body (comprising about 1,600 monks in Thimphu and Punakha), led by an elected Head Abbot (Je Khenpo), is directly supported by the State and spends six months of the year at Tashichhodzong and at Punakha, respectively. A further 2,120 monks, who are members of the District Monastic Bodies, are sustained by the lay population. The Council for Ecclesiastical Affairs oversees all religious bodies. Monasteries (Gompas) and shrines (Lhakhangs) are numerous. Religious proselytizing, in any form, is illegal.

**Council for Ecclesiastical Affairs** (Dratshang Lhentshog): POB 254, Thimphu; tel. (2) 322754; fax (2) 323867; e-mail dratshang@druknet.bt; f. 1984, replacing the Central Board for Monastic Studies, to oversee the national memorial chorten and all Buddhist meditational centres and schools of Buddhist studies, as well as the Central and District Monastic Bodies; daily affairs of the Council are run by the Central Monastic Secretariat; Chair. His Holiness the 70th Je Khenpo Trulku JIGME CHOEDRA; Sec. Dasho SANGAY WANGCHUCK; Dep. Sec. NGAWANG PHUNTSHO.

## The Press

**The Bhutan Review:** Patan Dhoka, POB 172, Lalitpur, Kathmandu, Nepal; tel. 525046; fax 523819; f. 1993; monthly organ of the Human Rights Organization of Bhutan (HUROB); opposed to existing government policies.

**Kuensel Corporation:** POB 204, Thimphu; tel. (2) 322483; fax (2) 322975; e-mail editor@kuensel.com.bt; internet www.kuenselonline.com; f. 1965 as a weekly govt bulletin; reorg. as a national weekly newspaper in 1986; became autonomous corporation in 1992 (previously under Dept of Information), incorporating former Royal Government Press; also published weekly from Kanglung from Dec. 2005; in English and Dzongkha; offered 49% of shares to public in 2006, while Government retained controlling 51%; Man. Dir and Editor-in-Chief KINLEY DORJI; Editors TIKA RAM SHARMA (Nepali), PHUNTSO WANGDI (English), CHOKI DHENDUP (Dzongkha); 12,875 (English), 4,280 (Dzongkha).

**Bhutan Times:** POB 1365, Norzim Lam, Thimphu; tel. (2) 328450; fax (2) 328451; e-mail editor@bhutantimes.bt; internet www.bhutantimes.bt; f. 2006; weekly newspaper; publ. by Bhutan Times Ltd; initially in English edn only; publ. *Bhutan NOW* magazine; CEO TENZIN RIGDEN; Editor GOPILAL ACHARYA.

**Bhutan Observer:** POB 1112, Norzin Lam, Thimphu; tel. (2) 334890; fax (2) 327981; e-mail editor@bhutanobserver.com.bt; internet www.bhutanobserver.bt; f. 2006; weekly newspaper; publ. in English and Dzongkha, by KMT Printing Press Pvt Ltd; Man. Dir MANI DORJI; Man. Editor K. B. LAMA; Dir TENZIN WANGDI.

## Broadcasting and Communications

### TELECOMMUNICATIONS

**Bhutan Infocomm and Media Authority (BICMA):** Kawajangia, POB 1072, Thimphu; tel. (2) 321506; fax (2) 326909; internet www.bicma.gov.bt; f. 2000 as Bhutan Telecommunications Authority under Bhutan Telecommunications Act; telecommunications and media regulatory body; regulatory remit extended to include Information and Communication Technology and media services in 2005; began operations as autonomous authority, independent of Ministry of Information and Communications, from 1 January 2007; Dir KINLEY T. WANGCHUK.

**Bhutan Telecom Ltd:** POB 134, Thimphu; tel. (2) 322678; fax (2) 324312; e-mail info@telecom.net.bt; internet www.telecom.net.bt; f. 2000; state-owned public corpn; regulation authority; agency for satellite telephones; Chair. LAM DORJI; Exec. Dir Dasho SANGEY TENZING; Man. Dir THINLEY DORJI.

**B-Mobile:** c/o Bhutan Telecom, Drophenlam, POB 134, Drophenlam, Thimphu; tel. (2) 320194; fax (2) 320193; e-mail mkto@telecom.net.bt; internet www.telecom.net.bt; f. 2002; offered mobile cellular telephone services from Nov. 2003; covered Thimphu and most of Paro by mid-2004; coverage extended to all 20 districts by early 2008; more than 167,000 subscribers (2008); subsidiary of Bhutan Telecom Ltd; Gen. Man. TANDI WANGCHUK.

**DrukNet:** Bhutan Telecom, 2/28 Drophenlam, POB 134, Thimphu; tel. (2) 326998; fax (2) 328160; e-mail info@druknet.bt; internet www.druknet.bt; f. 1999; internet service provider; Head GANGA SHARMA; Gen. Man. JICHEN THINLEY.

**Tashi InfoComm Ltd** (TashiCell): POB 176, Norzim Lam, Thimphu; tel. (2) 335476; fax (2) 336318; f. 2008; first privately owned mobile cellular telephone company in Bhutan; initially covered six western districts; more than 13,000 subscribers (2008); Chair. Lyonpo NANDALAL RAI; Exec. Dir TASHI TSHERING.

## BROADCASTING

### Radio

In 1994 there were 52 radio stations for administrative communications. Of these, 34 were for internal communications (to which the public had access), and three were external stations serving Bhutan House at Kalimpong and the Bhutanese diplomatic missions in India and Bangladesh. Following the passage of an Information, Communications and Media Act in June 2006, the country's first two private radio stations, *Radio Valley* and *Kuzoo FM*, were granted FM operating licences.

**Bhutan Broadcasting Services Corporation (BBSC):** POB 101, Thimphu; tel. (2) 323071; fax (2) 323073; e-mail bbs@bbs.com.bt; internet www.bbs.com.bt; f. 1973 as Radio National Youth Association of Bhutan (NYAB); became autonomous corporation in 1992 (previously under Dept of Information); short-wave radio station broadcasting daily in Dzongkha, Sharchopkha, Nepali (Lhotsamkha) and English; a daily FM programme (for Thimphu only) began in 1987; simultaneous broadcasting on FM for western Bhutan and parts of central and southern Bhutan began in 2000; a one-hour daily television service for Thimphu was introduced in mid-1999 and later increased to five hours in the morning and five in the evening; the nationwide television service expanded onto satellite in February 2007, allowing BBSC to broadcast to almost 40 countries; Chair. Dasho TASHI PHUNTSHOG; Man. Dir Aum PEMA CHHODEN.

**Centennial Radio 101 FM:** Ground Floor, Karma Tshongkhang Bldg, Thimphu; internet centennialradio.net; f. 2008; news, current affairs, music and entertainment programmes; CEO DORJI WANGCHUK.

**Kuzoo FM:** POB 419, Thimphu; tel. (2) 335984; fax (2) 335263; e-mail fm@kuzoo.net; internet www.kuzoo.net; f. 2006; broadcasts 24 hours a day on FM in Dzongkha and English; news, information and entertainment programmes.

**Radio Valley:** Rabten Lam, Thimphu; tel. (2) 323390; e-mail the_soundweaver@hotmail.com; internet www.radiovalley.bt; f. 2007; broadcasts 12 hours a day on FM; music, entertainment and information programmes to be broadcast upon commencement of full operations; Founder KINLEY CHOZOM.

### Television

In June 1999 the BBSC started operating a television service (in Dzongkha and English) in Thimphu; the service was gradually to be expanded throughout the country. Broadcasts are limited to a few hours a day and consist principally of national news and documentaries about Bhutan. By March 2002, according to official figures, each of the two cable television operators was providing 45 channels. In mid-2006 television broadcasts were for five hours each evening (three hours in Dzongkha, two hours in English). Satellite broadcasting was introduced in February 2007.

# Finance

(cap. = capital; auth. = authorized; p.u. = paid up; res = reserves; dep. = deposits; m. = million; brs = branches; amounts in ngultrum)

## BANKING

### Central Bank

**Royal Monetary Authority (RMA):** POB 154, Thimphu; tel. (2) 323111; fax (2) 322847; e-mail rma@rma.org.bt; internet www.rma.org.bt; f. 1982; bank of issue; frames and implements official monetary policy, co-ordinates the activities of financial institutions and holds foreign-exchange deposits on behalf of the Govt; cap. 4.4m., res 1,443.0m., dep. 11,017.3m. (June 2006); Chair. Lyonpo KINZANG DORJI; Man. Dir DAW TENZIN.

### Commercial Banks

**Bank of Bhutan Ltd:** Samdrup Lam, POB 75, Phuentsholing; tel. (5) 252225; fax (5) 252641; e-mail bobho_hrd@druknet.bt; internet www.bobltd.com.bt; f. 1968; 20% owned by the State Bank of India and 80% by the Govt of Bhutan; wholly managed by Govt of Bhutan from 1997; cap. 100.0m., res 1,160.3m., dep. 15,174.5m. (Dec. 2006); Dirs nominated by the Bhutan Govt: Chair. KARMA Y. RAYDI; Dirs KARMA PENJOR, PEMA NADIK; Dirs nominated by the State Bank of India RAKESH SHARMA, P. S. PRAKESH RAO; 26 brs and 3 extension counters.

**Bhutan National Bank (BNB):** POB 439, Thimphu; tel. (2) 328577; fax (2) 328839; e-mail bnbpling@druknet.bt; internet www.bhutannationalbank.com; f. 1996; Bhutan's second commercial bank; partially privatized in 1998; 27.2% owned by Govt and 20.1% by Asian Development Bank; cap. 119.0m., res 705.6m., dep. 8,622.9m. (2006); Chair. Lyonpo YESHEY ZIMBA; Man. Dir KIPCHU TSHERING; 7 brs.

### Development Bank

**Bhutan Development Finance Corporation (BDFC):** POB 256, Thimphu; tel. (2) 322579; fax (2) 323428; e-mail bdfc@druknet.bt; internet www.bdfcl.com.bt; f. 1988; provides industrial loans and short- and medium-term agricultural loans; cap. p.u. 100m., loans 1,114m. (2003); Chair. Dasho WANGDI NORBU; Man. Dir KARMA RANGDOL.

## STOCK EXCHANGE

**Royal Securities Exchange of Bhutan Ltd (RSEB):** POB 742, Thimphu; tel. (2) 323995; fax (2) 323849; e-mail rseb@druknet.bt; f. 1993; supervised by the Royal Monetary Authority; open to Bhutanese nationals only; 16 listed cos (2006); Chair. DAW TENZIN; CEO TASHI YEZER.

## INSURANCE

**Royal Insurance Corporation of Bhutan:** POB 77, Phuentsholing; tel. (5) 252453; fax (5) 252640; e-mail ricbho@druknet.bt; internet www.ricb.com.bt; f. 1975; provides general and life insurance and credit investment services; Chair. Lyonpo YESHEY ZIMBA; Man. Dir NAMGAY LHENDUP; 10 brs and development centres.

# Trade and Industry

## GOVERNMENT AGENCIES

**Druk Holding and Investments Ltd (DHI):** POB 1127, Motithang, Thimpu; tel. and fax (2) 335794; e-mail info@dhi.bt; internet www.dhi.bt; f. 2007 to manage the existing and future investments of the Govt; managed an initial grouping of 14 companies in sectors including hydropower, banking, minerals and natural resources; Chair. Lyonpo OM PRADHAN; CEO KARMA YONTEN.

**Food Corporation of Bhutan (FCB):** POB 80, Phuentsholing; tel. (5) 252241; fax (5) 252289; e-mail drukfood@druknet.bt; f. 1974; activities include procurement and distribution of food grains and other essential commodities through appointed Fair Price Shop Agents; marketing of surplus agricultural and horticultural produce through FCB-regulated market outlets; logistics concerning World Food Programme food aid; maintenance of buffer stocks to offset any emergency food shortages; maintenance of SAARC Food Security Reserve Stock; importing consumer goods from major Indian enterprises; exporting oranges and apples; Man. Dir KUNZANG NAMGYEL; 19 outlets and 66 Fair Price Shops.

**Gross National Happiness Commission:** Convention Centre, POB 127, Thimphu; tel. (2) 323176; fax (2) 325402; e-mail ldorji@pc.gov.bt; internet www.gnhc.gov.bt; f. 1971 as Planning Commission; headed by the King until 1991; reconstituted 1999 as department under Ministry of Finance; re-established as separate 11-mem. commission from Jan. 2006; renamed as above in Jan. 2008; proposes socio-economic policy guide-lines, issues directives for the formulation of development plans, ensures efficient and judicious allocation of resources, directs socio-economic research, studies and surveys, and appraises the Govt on the progress of development plans and programmes; Chair. Lyonpo KINZANG DORJI; Sec. KARMA TSHITEEM.

**Natural Resources Development Corporation:** Thimphu; tel. (2) 323834; fax (2) 325585; fmrly Forestry Development Corporation; renamed as above in 2007; fixes price of sand and timber; oversees quarrying and mining of sand; Chair. KARMA DUKPA; Man. Dir SANGAY GYALTSHEN.

**State Trading Corpn of Bhutan Ltd (STCB):** POB 76, Phuentsholing; tel. (5) 252745; fax (5) 252619; e-mail stcbl@druknet.bt; internet www.stcb.com.bt; f. 1969; manages imports and exports of vehicles, IT and construction materials on behalf of the Govt; Chair. Dasho KARMA DORJI; Man. Dir SAMDRUP K. THINLEY; brs in Thimphu (POB 272; tel. (2) 324785; fax (2) 322953; e-mail stcbthim@druknet.bt) and Kolkata (Calcutta), India (e-mail stcbkol@vsnl.net).

## CHAMBER OF COMMERCE

**Bhutan Chamber of Commerce and Industry (BCCI):** Doebum Lam, POB 147, Thimphu; tel. (2) 322742; fax (2) 323936; e-mail bsdbcci@druknet.bt; internet www.bcci.com.bt; f. 1980; reorg. 1988; promotion of trade and industry and privatization, information dissemination, private-sector human resource development; 14 exec. mems; 20-mem. district executive committee; Pres. Dasho UGEN DORJI; Vice-Pres. and CEO Dasho BAP KINGA.

## UTILITIES

### Electricity

**Bhutan Electricity Authority** (BEA): Thimphu; e-mail ceo@bea.gov.bt; internet www.bea.gov.bt; f. 1991; regulates the electricity supply industry; CEO (vacant); Exec. Eng. PEM DORJEE.

**Department of Energy:** c/o Ministry of Economic Affairs, Tashichhodzong, POB 141, Thimphu; tel. (2) 322279; fax (2) 328278.

**Basochhu Hydropower Corporation:** Basochhu; tel. (2) 471021; fax (2) 471020; e-mail bhpc@druknet.bt; co-ordinates construction of dam and hydroelectric power-generating facilities; operates and maintains two power stations with a total installed capacity of 64MW; became part of Druk Green Power Corpn in 2008; Sr Plant Eng. OM BHANDARI.

**Bhutan Power Corporation:** POB 580, Thimphu; tel. (2) 325095; fax (2) 322279; e-mail hr@bpc.com.bt; internet www.bpc.com.bt; f. 2002; responsible for ensuring electricity supply for the whole country at an affordable cost by 2020 and for providing uninterrupted transmission access for export of surplus power; operations in 19 districts; Chair. YESHEY WANGDI; Man. Dir BHARAT TAMANG.

**Chhukha Hydropower Corporation:** Phuentsholing; tel. (5) 252575; fax (5) 252582; f. 1991; state-owned; 70% of power generated by the project is exported to India; became part of Druk Green Power Corpn in 2008; Chair. Lyonpo YESHEY ZIMBA; Man. Dir YESHEY WANGDI.

**Kurichhu Project Authority:** Gyelpozhing (Monggar); tel. (4) 744113; fax (4) 744130; e-mail kpa@druknet.bt; operates and maintains a 60-MW hydroelectric power-generating facility at Gyelpozhing; became part of Druk Green Power Corpn in 2008; Chair. Lyonpo KHANDU WANGCHUCK; Man. Dir TSHEWANG RINZIN.

**Tala Hydroelectric Project Authority:** THPA Office Complex, Gedu; tel. (5) 282001; fax (5) 282010; e-mail mdthpa@druknet.bt; co-ordinates construction of dam and hydroelectric power-generating facilities; Man. Dir R. N. KHAZANCHI.

### Water

**Thimphu City Corporation (Water Supply Unit):** POB 215, Thimphu; tel. (2) 324710; fax (2) 324315; e-mail tda@druknet.bt; f. 1982; under Ministry of Home and Cultural Affairs from mid-2003; responsible for water supply of Thimphu municipality; Head BHIMLAL DHUNGEL.

## MAJOR COMPANIES

**Army Welfare Project:** POB 92, Phuentsholing; tel. (5) 252503; fax (5) 252386; e-mail awppledp@druknet.bt; govt undertaking; mfr of alcoholic beverages; Gen. Man. PHUCHU DORJI.

**Bhutan Agro Industries Ltd:** POB 329, Thimphu; tel. (2) 351069; fax (2) 351089; e-mail btnagro@druknet.net.bt; f. 1993; govt undertaking; mfr of high quality fruits and vegetables, fruit juices and natural spring water; cap. US $3m., sales US $1m. (2004); Man. Dir GYEM DORJI; 77 employees.

**Bhutan Board Products Ltd (BBPL):** POB 91, Phuentsholing; tel. (5) 252130; fax (5) 252676; e-mail bbplmd@druknet.bt; internet bbplbhutan.tripod.com; f. 1983; govt undertaking; mfr of plain and prelaminated graded wood-particle board and ready-to-assemble furniture; Chair. Lyonpo LEKI DORJI; Man. Dir NAMGEY NIDUP.

**Bhutan Carbide and Chemicals Ltd:** 1st Floor, TCC Complex Bldg, POB 103, Phuentsholing; tel. (5) 252105; fax (5) 252112; e-mail bccl@druknet.bt; f. 1987; 52% owned by Tashi Group and 48% by financial institutions and public shareholders; production of calcium carbide and charcoal; mines chemical-grade limestone; provides reafforestation; located at Pasakha; Chair. Dasho U. DORJI; Man. Dir. P. K. RAO.

**Bhutan Dairy Ltd:** POB 196, Phuentsholing; tel. (5) 252351; e-mail bdairy@druknet.bt; f. 1990 by Ministry of Agriculture; transferred to private ownership in 1994; milk-processing plant at Phuentsholing; produces pasteurized milk, butter, ghee and yoghurt; auth. cap. Nu 30m., cap. p.u. Nu 5.10m.; Man. Dir UGEN WANGDI.

**Bhutan Engineering Co (Pvt) Ltd:** Tenzin and Wangmo Bldg, Chubachu, POB 378, Thimphu; tel. (2) 324524; fax (2) 323475; e-mail becplth@druknet.bt; f. 1990; sales US $75.8m. (2002); civil engineering and architectural consultants, major road and bridge construction works, sewerage works and hydropower project works; Man. Dir Dasho DORJI NORBU; 98 employees.

**Bhutan Ferro Alloys Ltd:** TCC Complex Bldg, 1st Floor, POB 211, Phuentsholing; tel. (5) 252246; fax (5) 252282; e-mail contact@bhutanferroalloys.com; internet www.bhutanferroalloys.com; f. 1990; 25% owned by Govt, 28.5% by Tashi Commercial Corpn, 14% by financial institutions and corporate bodies, 12.5% by private shareholders, 12% by Marubeni Corpn and 8% by Japan International Development Organization Ltd; manufactures and sells ferro-silicon, micro-silica and magnesium ferro-silica; Chair. Lyonpo KHANDU WANGCHUK; Man. Dir Dasho TOPGYAL DORJI.

**Bhutan Fruit Products Pvt Ltd:** POB 317, Samtse; tel. (5) 365369; fax (5) 365287; e-mail bfpl@druknet.bt; mfr of processed canned fruits and vegetables; CEO K. N. MALHOTRA.

**Bhutan Marble and Minerals Ltd:** Hotel Taktsang, RICB Bldg, Doibom Lam, POB 199, Thimphu; tel. (5) 252973; fax (5) 252248; Man. Dir THINLEY PALDEN DORJI.

**Bhutan Polythene Co Ltd:** POB 152, Phuentsholing; tel. (5) 252407; fax (5) 252653; e-mail drukpipe@druknet.bt; f. 1989; 100%-owned by private investors; sales US $3.3m. (2004); mfrs of high- and medium-density polyethylene pipes; Man. Dir and CEO K. S. DHENDUP; 30 employees.

**Bhutan Resorts Corporation Ltd:** POB 831, Thimphu; tel. (2) 322298; construction and management of resort hotels.

**Chhundu Enterprises:** POB 131, Phuentsholing; tel. (5) 252386; fax (5) 252786; operates Bhutan Dolomite Mine, Pagli, and Khagrakhola Dolomite Mine, Gomtu; Propr and Chair. Dasho LHENDUP DORJI; Gen. Man. P. THOMAS OOMMEN.

**Dhendup Group:** POB 188, Phuentsholing; tel. (5) 252802; fax (5) 252440; e-mail ajaybtn@druknet.bt; conglomerate consisting of:

**Dhendup Construction:** POB 188, Thimphu; tel. (2) 323051; fax (2) 324753.

**Dhendup Enterprises:** POB 182, Thimphu; tel. (2) 323133; fax (2) 323779; e-mail dilinfo@druknet.bt.

**Dhendup Home Industries:** Phuentsholing; tel. (5) 252621; mfrs and suppliers of RCC spun pipes and electrical poles.

**Dhendup Informatics:** POB 182, Thimphu; tel. (2) 323133; e-mail dilinfo@druknet.bt.

**Dhendup Travel Service:** Phuentsholing; tel. (5) 252437; deluxe minibus service between Thimphu and Phuentsholing.

**Dhendup Tshongkhang:** Phuentsholing; tel. (5) 252580; general order suppliers, hardware, electrical goods, paint, office equipment, pipe fittings, etc.

**Dragon Wood Products:** Thimphu; tel. (2) 323051; fax (2) 323130; plywood, block boards, flush doors, door/window frames; Chair. Gup LHENKEY GYALTSHEN.

**Dralha Group of Industries:** POB 105, Phuentsholing; tel. (5) 252284; conglomerate consisting of: Bhutan Biscuits, Drahla Flour Mill and Druk Wood Industries; Man. Dir HRH Ashi Pema C. WANGCHUK.

**Druk Penden Group of Companies:** Head Office, POB 226, Phuentsholing; tel. and fax (5) 252607; e-mail drukpen@druknet.bt; conglomerate consisting of Penden Cement Authority, Druk Penden Hardware Agency, Druk Penden Transport Corporation and Druk Penden Engineering.

**Druk Petroleum Corpn Ltd:** Phuentsholing; tel. (5) 252861; Man. Dir SANGAY DORJI.

**Druk Satair Corpn Ltd:** POB 129, Samdrup Jongkhar; tel. (7) 251106; fax (7) 251226; e-mail dsatair@druknet.bt; f. 1993; mining and sale of gypsum; auth. cap. Nu 100m.; annual capacity of 120,000 metric tons; CEO YADUNATH SHARMA.

**Druk Plaster and Chemicals Ltd:** POB 129, Samdrup Jongkhar; tel. (7) 251106; fax (7) 251226; mfr of plaster of Paris.

**Druk Sherig Group of Companies:** POB 188, Wogzin Lam, Thimphu; tel. (2) 323911; fax (2) 322714; e-mail travelbt@druknet.bt; conglomerate consisting of Druk Sherig Construction, Druk Sherig Press, Druk Sherig Uppayla Hotel, Druk Sherig Norzang Enterprises and Travel Bhutan Tours and Treks.

**Eastern Bhutan Coal Co:** POB 107, Samdrup Jongkhar; tel. (7) 251111; fax (7) 251159; e-mail ebcc@druknet.bt; mining and supplier of non-coking coal to cement plants and heavy industries.

**Handicrafts Development Corpn:** POB 771, Thimphu; tel. (2) 322810; fax (2) 323732; e-mail hdc@druknet.bt; f. 1971 as Handicrafts Emporium; taken over by Bhutan Women's Assen in 1991; Man. Dir LUNGTEN WANGDE.

**Karma Group Organisation:** POB 57, Phuentsholing; tel. (5) 252304; fax (5) 252391; incorporates Karma Feeds (tel. (5) 252602), Karma Steel Furniture Factory (tel. (5) 252303), Karma Steel Works (Gomtu), Karma Tshongkhang (tel. (5) 253761), Druk Carpets (tel. (5) 252004), Druk Dolomite Corpn (Gomtu) and Slates and Granite Mines (tel. (5) 252890); exports boulders, dolomite and woollen carpets; contractors for road and building construction; contractors for supply of charcoal; mfrs of animal feed and steel furniture; Man. Dir KARMA DORJI.

**Lhaki Group of Companies:** Lhaki Shopping Complex, Blocks 3 and 4, POB 179, Thimphu; tel. (2) 322570; fax (2) 323916; e-mail info@lhakigroup.com; internet www.lhakigroup.com; trading conglomerate; Chair. Dasho UGEN DORJI.

**Jigme Industries Pvt Ltd:** Pagli; tel. (5) 240158; fax (5) 240164; e-mail jipl@lhakigroup.com; mfr and supplier of dolomite products.

**Jigme Mining Corporation Ltd:** Pagli; tel. (5) 240158; fax (5) 240164; e-mail dolomite@lhakigroup.com; extractor of high-grade low silica dolomite.

**Jigme Polytex Pvt Ltd:** Gomtu; tel. (5) 371230; fax (5) 371227; e-mail polytex@lhakigroup.com; mfr of polyester textured yarn.

**Lhaki Cement Pvt Ltd:** Gomtu; tel. (5) 371042; fax (5) 371020; e-mail cement@lhakigroup.com.

**Lhaki Steel and Rolling Pvt Ltd:** Phuentsholing; tel. and fax (5) 252909; e-mail steel@lhakigroup.com; mfr of rolled products, bars and structural steel.

**Peljorkhang Enterprise:** N-18 Bldg, Ground Floor, Zhenphen Lam, Upper Chubachu, POB 187, Thimphu; tel. (2) 323386; fax (2) 322716; e-mail sales@peljorkhang.com.bt; internet www.peljorkhang.com.bt; computer services; CEO Nirpa Raj Rai.

**Rabten Wood Industries:** POB 72, Industrial Estate, Phuentsholing; tel. (5) 252213; fax (5) 252908; f. 1988; manufactures and exports (to Europe) wood products; Man. Dir Lt Yenzing Dhendup.

**Singye Group of Companies:** Singye Agencies, POB 336, Phuentsholing; tel. (5) 252188; fax (5) 253002; e-mail sagencies@druknet.bt; incorporates Singye Industries Pvt Ltd (POB 289, Thimphu; tel. (2) 322585; fax (2) 324152); consultancy services in engineering, management and finance; authorized dealers for motor vehicles and lubricants; Vice-Chair. Dasho K. Ugyen T. Dorji.

**Tashi Group of Companies:** TCC Complex Bldg, POB 78, Phuentsholing; tel. (5) 252246; fax (5) 252110; e-mail tashi@druknet.bt; f. 1959; Bhutan's major privately owned commercial group active in wholesale and retail trade, insurance, telecommunications, real estate, tourism, agriculture, hotels, mining, construction and manufacturing; turnover Nu 3,000m. (1997); Chair. Dasho Ugen Dorji; Man. Dir P. K. Rao.

**Ugen Trading House:** POB 231, Thimphu; tel. (2) 321019; fax (2) 321071; e-mail ugen@druknet.bt; supplier of automobiles, computer software, telecom consumer goods, electrical goods and consultancy.

**Yangzome Cement Pvt Ltd:** POB 331, Tashi Jong, Samtse; tel. (5) 365341; producer of portland cement; Man. Dir Dasho U. D. Tangbi.

### TRADE UNIONS

Under long-standing legislation, trade union activity is illegal in Bhutan. During the 86th session of the National Assembly, which was held in December 2006/January 2007, the Labour Act was passed, permitting (among other things) the formation of 'workers' associations'.

## Transport

### ROADS AND TRACKS

In June 2005 there were 4,392.5 km of roads in Bhutan, of which 2,461.3 km were black-topped and included 1,579 km designated national highways. Surfaced roads link the important border towns of Phuentsholing, Gelephu, Sarpang and Samdrup Jongkhar in southern Bhutan to towns in West Bengal and Assam (Asom) in India. There is a shortage of road transport. Yaks, ponies and mules are still the chief means of transport on the rough mountain tracks. By 1990 most of the previously government-operated transport facilities (mainly buses and minibuses) on major and subsidiary routes had been transferred to private operators on the basis of seven-year contracts. Construction work was continuing in 2008 on a 64-km highway connecting Samtse and Phuentsholing. A Roads Sector Master Plan (2007–27) envisaged the construction of 2,587.4 km of feeder roads throughout Bhutan, a second East–West Highway (794 km) stretching from Sipsu to Jomotshankha, and 410 km of highways to improve inter-connectivity between districts. It was hoped that 75% of the country's rural population would live within half a day's walk of the nearest road by the end of the 10th Five-Year Plan in 2012.

**Road Safety and Transport Authority:** Thimphu; tel. (2) 321282; fax (2) 321281; e-mail director_rsta@druknet.bt; f. 1995; under Ministry of Information and Communications; regulates all motor vehicle activities and surface transport services; Dir Nima Wangdi.

**Transport Corpn of Bhutan:** Phuentsholing; tel. (5) 252476; f. 1982; subsidiary of Royal Insurance Corpn of Bhutan; operates direct coach service between Phuentsholing and Kolkata via Siliguri.

Other operators are **Barma Travels** (f. 1990), **Dawa Transport** (Propr Sherub Wangchuck), **Dhendup Travel Service** (Phuentsholing; tel (5) 252437), **Gyamtsho Transport**, **Gurung Transport Service**, **Namgay Transport**, **Nima Travels** (Phuentsholing; tel. (5) 252384), and **Rimpung Travels** (Phuentsholing; tel. (5) 252354).

Lorries for transporting goods are operated by the private sector.

### CIVIL AVIATION

There is an international airport at Paro, and a runway strip at Trashigang. There are also some 30 helicopter landing pads, which are used, by arrangement with the Indian military and aviation authorities, solely by government officials. The Council of Ministers approved the operation of a domestic helicopter service to improve mobility and to promote tourism; by mid-2003 five domestic heliports had been surveyed and found acceptable. The national carrier, Druk Air Corporation Limited, began operating helicopter services in 2005.

**Department of Civil Aviation:** c/o Ministry of Information and Communications, Woochu, Paro; tel. (8) 271347; fax (8) 271909; e-mail aviation@druknet.bt; state-owned; f. 1986; Dir Phala Dorji.

**Druk Air Corpn Ltd** (Royal Bhutan Airlines): Head Office, Nemizampa, PO Paro; tel. (8) 271856; fax (8) 271861; e-mail drukair@druknet.bt; internet www.drukair.com.bt; national airline; f. 1981; became fully operational in 1983; services from Paro to Delhi and Gaya (winter only) in India, Bangladesh, Nepal and Thailand; additional services planned to increase utilization of aircraft; charter services available; helicopter services introduced in 2005; Chair. Lyonpo Jigmi Y. Thinley; Man. Dir Tandin Jamtsho (acting).

## Tourism

Bhutan was opened to tourism in 1975. In 2007 the total number of foreign visitors was 21,094, compared with 17,365 in 2006. Receipts from tourism in 2007 remained at their 2006 level of $24m. Tourists travel in organized 'package', cultural or trekking tours, or individually, accompanied by trained guides; independent, unaccompanied travel is not permitted within the kingdom. Hotels have been constructed at Phuentsholing, Paro, Bumthang, Wangduephodrang and Thimphu, with lodges at Trongsa, Trashigang and Monggar. In addition, there are many small privately operated hotels and guesthouses. Plans for several foreign-managed commercial hotels, in the style of resorts, were under way in the mid-2000s. The Government exercises close control over the development of tourism. In 1987 the National Assembly resolved that all monasteries, mountains and other holy places should be inaccessible to tourists from 1988 (this resolution is flexibly interpreted, however—e.g. Japanese Buddhist tour groups are permitted to visit 'closed' monasteries). In 1991 the Government began transferring the tourism industry to the private sector and licences were issued to new private tourism operators. Rules were introduced in 1995 asserting more stringent controls over private operators through the Tourism Authority of Bhutan (TAB). In 1998 the Government's tourism policy was liberalized further. In 2001 the TAB was reorganized as the Department of Tourism, under the Ministry of Trade and Industry (renamed the Ministry of Economic Affairs in 2007). The Government has identified and encouraged the industry's potential to grow and to provide significant employment opportunities. A levy of $10 per visitor contributed to a Tourist Development Fund, which by the end of 2002 amounted to more than Nu 10m. The Association of Bhutan Travel Operators (ABTO) was established in 1998 to act as a forum for co-ordinating tourism issues among the travel agencies. ABTO also surveyed new trekking routes in Haa, following the opening of the district to tourists from mid-2001. By the end of 2007 there were 349 registered tour operators in the country, but only 200 of these were actually functioning during that year. In 2008 the Tourism Council of Bhutan was established as an autonomous inter-governmental agency, replacing the Department of Tourism, to optimize the role of the industry.

**Tourism Council of Bhutan (TCB):** POB 126, Thimpu; tel. (2) 323251; fax (2) 323695; e-mail dot@tourism.gov.bt; internet www.tourism.gov.bt; f. 2008 to replace the Department of Tourism; autonomous inter-governmental agency; manages and develops the tourism industry; aims to promote Bhutan as an 'exclusive tourist destination'; Chair. Kinzang Dorji; Dir-Gen. Kesang Wangdi.

**(ABTO):** POB 938, Thimphu; tel. (2) 322862; fax (2) 325286; e-mail abto@druknet.bt; internet www.abto.org.bt; f. 1998 to provide forum for members' views and to unite, supervise and co-ordinate activities of members; Chair. Dasho Ugen Tsechup Dorji; 238 mem. tour operators (March 2008).

## Defence

The strength of the Royal Bhutan Army, which is under the direct command of the King, is officially said to number just over 9,000 and is based on voluntary recruitment augmented by a form of conscription. Part-time militia training for senior school pupils, graduates and civil servants was in operation in 1989–91; subsequently, this training was held in abeyance. However, three months' militia training was held in mid-2003 for militia volunteers, as part of the preparations for later military action against Indian militants encamped on Bhutanese territory (see History). Regular army training facilities are provided, on a functional basis, by an Indian military training team (IMTRAT), whose main personnel are stationed at Haa. In addition, the Royal Bhutan Army's Wing 5 is stationed at the Shaba training facility, and a number of militia training camps have been established throughout the country. The Royal Bhutan Army, the Royal Bhutan Guards and the Royal Bhutan Police were significantly strengthened from 2000 owing to the growing numbers of armed Indian militants who had established military camps on southern Bhutanese territory.

No reference is made in the Indo-Bhutan Treaty to any aid by India for the defence of Bhutan. In November 1958, however, the Prime Minister of India declared that any act of aggression against Bhutan would be regarded as an act of aggression against India.

In October 2005 King Jigme stated that the strength of the armed forces was 10,000, and alluded to the possible creation of a militia force similar to the traditional *pazap* system. In December the Crown Prince elaborated on this, asserting that the goal was to reduce the size of the standing army. The Chief of Army Operations subsequently advised, in June 2007, that the country's standing army numbered 9,021 and proposed a reduction in military personnel to 8,000 by 2008. The National Assembly resolved that recruitment and training of militia should be renewed by 2008, with the age limit, numbers and training centres to be determined by the Royal Bhutan Army.

**Chief of Operations, Royal Bhutan Army:** Goongloen Wogma Batoo Tshering.

# Education

Traditionally, education in Bhutan was purely monastic, and the establishment of the contemporary state education system, with English as the medium of instruction, was the result of the reforming zeal of the third King, Jigme Dorji Wangchuck. The proposed outlay on education under the Ninth Plan (2002–07) was about 3.7% of total expenditure. The 2007/08 budget allocated an estimated Nu 3,385m. (14% of total projected expenditure) to education, of which Nu 1,465m. was capital expenditure (12% of total capital expenditure) and Nu 1,920m. was current expenditure (13% of total current expenditure). Emphasis has increasingly been placed on the development of human resources and the expansion of educational infrastructure as demand for places continues to grow. In 2005/06 a further 10 schools were to be constructed. Education is not compulsory, but virtually free education (nominal fees are demanded), including degree courses, is provided by the State. There are no mission schools in Bhutan. By July 2007 30 privately operated schools had been established (the majority in Thimphu), under the supervision of the Ministry of Education. A few Tibetan-language schools operate autonomously. English is the medium of instruction, and Dzongkha is a compulsory subject.

The total number of enrolled students in Bhutan was 14,000 in 1974. By July 2007, however, the total had risen to 171,912. In the mid-1980s several hundred primary students had to be denied admission to schools in Thimphu because of a lack of places. In order to accommodate additional children, especially those living outside urban areas, community schools (established in 1989 as 'extended classrooms', and later renamed 'community primary schools') were set up as essentially one-teacher schools for basic primary classes, whence children were to be 'streamed' to other schools. Each community primary school caters to either a single village or cluster of villages; all of the households in a particular school community contribute towards the construction and maintenance of the school, while the Government supplies teachers, stationery and textbooks. In June 2008 the Government announced plans to construct 104 new primary and community schools over the following five years to increase the total number of schools to 615, increasing access for students in remote areas.

All schools are co-educational and follow a syllabus that initially reflected British and Indian practices, but has become increasingly localized, in order to take into account national needs. The objective of primary education is to educate students in basic literacy and numeracy skills, knowledge of Bhutan's history, geography, culture and traditions, and elements of practical functional skills (the fundamentals of agriculture, health and hygiene, and population issues). The secondary curriculum has also become mainly localized in nature. Primary education begins with a pre-primary year (the minimum entry age being six years) and lasts for seven years. Secondary education lasts a further six years, with two years spent at each of three levels, following a 2002 reclassification of secondary schools into lower, middle and higher secondary schools. Tertiary education includes various first degree courses offered by institutes under the supervision of the Royal University of Bhutan (RUB), which was established in 2003. Most RUB courses are full-time, although the Royal Institute of Management (RIM) offers several that operate on a part-time basis. (The RIM was established in Thimphu in 1986, incorporating two existing commercial schools.) At the RUB, post-secondary diplomas are normally granted after two years of successful full-time study and degrees are usually awarded after three years, with provision for a specialized fourth-year 'Honours' degree. Distance learning is also offered under the auspices of the RUB.

Enrolment at primary schools (excluding community primary schools) increased from 9,039 (including only 456 girls) in 1970 to 25,760 (including 12,518 girls) in 2007. Between 1970 and 2007, enrolment at secondary schools increased from 714 (boys 690; girls 24) to 97,481 (boys 49,691; girls 47,790). In 2007 there were 28,953 pupils in community primary schools—14,978 boys and 13,975 girls. In 2007 girls' enrolment was nearing that of boys at all levels, averaging around 49% of total enrolment at all levels of secondary education. At the basic educational level (from primary to the end of middle secondary school), however, girls accounted for 43% of all students enrolled.

The total number of teachers in Bhutan increased from 461 in 1970 to 6,610 in 2007; of these, 457 were employed in tertiary, special and vocational institutions, and 896 in community primary schools. To compensate, in part, for a shortage of qualified teachers, instruction is provided by contract teachers from India (mainly Kerala) and by young volunteers from New Zealand and, previously, the United Kingdom, as well as through the UN Volunteers scheme.

A National Board of Secondary Education and Training was established in 1984, with the aim of revising existing curricula to give a stronger national content. In the same year, the existing teacher-training college at Samtse was upgraded to a National Institute of Education (NIE) for secondary teachers. Primary teachers are also trained at the NIE in Samtse as well as at the second NIE established at Paro (formerly designated a teacher-training college). A second teacher-training college was to be established at Kanglung. From 2001, board examinations at the end of middle secondary school were delinked fully from the former arrangement with the Council for Indian School Certificate Examination (CISCE), and the first national board examinations conducted by the Bhutan Board of Examinations were held in December of that year.

In addition to the schools and training institutes in Bhutan, regular courses are organized by different government departments in agriculture, computer programming, health, secretarial work, etc. A number of students are receiving higher education and training in various technical fields in Australia, Bangladesh, India, Japan, New Zealand, Singapore, Switzerland, the United Kingdom and the USA. Returning graduates must complete a one-year induction course, during which they must perform practical work, arranged by the RIM, before becoming eligible to sit the competitive examination for entrance into the civil service. Students from one part of the country are encouraged by the Government to seek admission to schools and educational institutions in other regions, as part of its policy to increase integration of people throughout the country.

Adult literacy and non-formal education (NFE) programmes began in Bhutan in 1992, with the establishment of 10 pilot NFE centres targeting those who had left school before completing the curriculum and those without a formal education. By the end of 2001 more than 15,000 learners had completed the basic literacy couse in 243 NFE centres. By 2005 about 5,000 adults were enrolling in the NFE programme each year. The programme offered a one-year basic literacy programme together with a nine-month post-literacy course in Dzongkha covering practical issues such as agriculture, health and sanitation. By early 2006 about 24,000 persons had completed the courses, and there were 777 NFEs with some 14,694 adults enrolled (of whom some 68% were women).

By late 2005 doubts had arisen concerning aspects of the quality of education being offered. In part to address these concerns, a new English curriculum was introduced to senior classes from the beginning of 2006. Including all students abroad and in the monk body classes, there were some 190,000 enrolled in March 2006.

There are five main linguistic groups in Bhutan but Dzongkha, spoken in western Bhutan, has been designated the official language (with English the medium of school instruction). No formal literacy survey has been conducted in Bhutan. According to UNESCO, the literacy rate in 1991 was believed to be around 35%–50%, with the most recent estimate putting the adult literacy rate at 54%. (This concurs with the figure published by the Bhutanese Government in the years 2003–05, although UNESCO has speculated that women's formal literacy may be as low as 20%.) UNESCO has estimated that Bhutan's illiterate adult population may total 150,000–180,000, most of whom live in remote rural areas.

# Indo-Bhutan Treaty

The Treaty of Friendship with India was signed on 8 August 1949.

## TREATY OF FRIENDSHIP BETWEEN THE GOVERNMENT OF INDIA AND THE GOVERNMENT OF BHUTAN

Article 1. There shall be perpetual peace and friendship between the Government of India and the Government of Bhutan.

Article 2. The Government of India undertakes to exercise no interference in the internal administration of Bhutan. On its part, the Government of Bhutan agrees to be guided by the advice of the Government of India in regard to its external relations.

Article 3. In place of the compensation granted to the Government of Bhutan under Article 4 of the Treaty of Sinchula and enhanced by the treaty of the eighth day of January 1910 and the temporary subsidy of Rupees one lakh per annum granted in 1942, the Government of India agrees to make an annual payment of Rupees five lakhs to the Government of Bhutan. And it is further hereby agreed that the said annual payment shall be made on the 10th day of January every year, the first payment being made on the 10th day of January 1950. This payment shall continue so long as this treaty remains in force and its terms are duly observed.

Article 4. Further to mark the friendship existing and continuing between the said governments, the Government of India shall, within one year from the date of signature of this treaty, return to the Government of Bhutan about 32 square miles of territory in the area known as Dewangiri. The Government of India shall appoint a competent officer or officers to mark out the area so returned to the Government of Bhutan.

Article 5. There shall, as heretofore, be free trade and commerce between the territories of the Government of India and of the Government of Bhutan; and the Government of India agrees to grant to the Government of Bhutan every facility for the carriage, by land and water, of its produce throughout the territory of the Government of India, including the right to use such forest roads as may be specified by mutual agreement from time to time.

Article 6. The Government of India agrees that the Government of Bhutan shall be free to import with the assistance and approval of the Government of India, from or through India into Bhutan, whatever arms, ammunition, machinery, warlike materials or stores may be required or desired for the strength and welfare of Bhutan and that this arrangement shall hold good for all time as long as the Government of India is satisfied that the intentions of the Government of Bhutan are friendly and that there is no danger to India from such importations. The Government of Bhutan, on the other hand, agrees that there shall be no export of such arms, ammunition, etc., across the frontier of Bhutan either by the Government of Bhutan or by private individuals.

Article 7. The Government of India and the Government of Bhutan agree that Bhutanese subjects residing in Indian territories shall have equal justice with Indian subjects, and that Indian subjects residing in Bhutan shall have equal justice with the subjects of the Government of Bhutan.

Article 8.*† (1) The Government of India shall, on demand being duly made in writing by the Government of Bhutan, take proceedings in accordance with the provisions of Indian Extradition Act, 1903 (of which a copy shall be furnished to the Government of Bhutan), for the surrender of all Bhutanese subjects accused of any of the crimes specified in the first schedule of the said Act who may take refuge in Indian territory.

(2) The Government of Bhutan shall, on requisition being duly made by the Government of India, or by any officer authorized by the Government of India in this behalf, surrender any Indian subjects, or subjects of a foreign power, whose extradition may be required in pursuance of any agreement or arrangements made by the Government of India with the said power, accused of any of the crimes specified in the first schedule of Act XV of 1903, who may take refuge in the territory under the jurisdiction of the Government of Bhutan and also any Bhutanese subjects who, after committing any of the crimes referred to in Indian territory shall flee into Bhutan, on such evidence of their guilt being produced as that satisfy the local court of the district in which the offence may have been committed.

Article 9. Any differences and disputes arising in the application or interpretation of this treaty shall in the first instance be settled by negotiation. If within three months of the start of negotiations no settlement is arrived at, then the matter shall be referred to the Arbitration of three arbitrators, who shall be nationals of either India or Bhutan, chosen on the following basis:

(i) one person nominated by the Government of India;

(ii) one person nominated by the Government of Bhutan; and

(iii) a Judge of the Federal court or of a High Court of India, to be chosen by the Government of Bhutan, who shall be Chairman.

The judgment of this tribunal shall be final and executed without delay by either party.

Article 10. This treaty shall continue in force in perpetuity unless terminated or modified by mutual consent.

* Article 8 was revised by an exchange of letters between the Bhutanese and Indian Governments in 1969 to read as follows: (1) The Government of India shall, on demand being duly made in writing by the Government of Bhutan, take proceedings in accordance with the provisions of the Indian Extraction Act, 1962 (of which a copy shall be furnished to the Government of Bhutan), for the surrender of all Bhutanese subjects accused of any of the crimes specified in the first schedule of the said Act who may take refuge in Indian territory. (2) The Government of Bhutan shall, on requisition being duly made by the Government of India, or by any officer authorized by the Government of India in this behalf, surrender any Indian subjects, or subjects of a foreign power, whose extradition may be required in pursuance of any agreement or arrangements made by the Government of India with the said power, accused of any of the crimes specified in the second schedule of Indian Extraction Act 1962, who may take refuge in the territory under the jurisdiction of the Government of Bhutan and also any Bhutanese subjects who, after committing any of the crimes referred to in Indian territory shall flee into Bhutan, on such evidence of their guilt being produced as that satisfy the local court of the district in which the offence may have been committed.

† An extradition agreement signed on 28 December 1996 (terminable on six months notice and effective from 21 May 1997) makes no reference to either this Treaty (and in particular Article 8) or to the amendment described herewith. The preamble states that the parties have agreed to enter into a new extradition agreement whereby each side agrees to extradite any person accused of, charged with or convicted of an extraditable offence who is found in the territory of the other party, whether or not such offence was committed before or after the coming into force of the agreement. Extraditable offences include: those punishable by law by deprivation of liberty for a period of one year or more; those acts committed in a third state which, under the law of the requesting state, are deemed to be an offence liable to prosecution; and an attempt or a conspiracy to commit, aiding or abetting, counselling, or procuring the commission of, or being an accessory before or after the fact to, any extraditable offence.

## INDO-BHUTAN FRIENDSHIP TREATY

An updated version of the Treaty of Friendship (1949), amending and revising the existing document, was signed in New Delhi on 8 February 2007 and became effective on 2 March of the same year.

### India-Bhutan Friendship Treaty

The Government of the Republic of India and the Government of the Kingdom of Bhutan: Reaffirming their respect for each other's independence, sovereignty and territorial integrity; recalling the historical relations that have existed between our two countries; recognizing with deep satisfaction the manner in which these relations have evolved and matured over the years into a model of good neighbourly relations; being fully committed to further strengthening this enduring and mutually beneficial relationship based on genuine goodwill and friendship, shared interests, and close understanding and co-operation; desiring to clearly reflect this exemplary relationship as it stands today; and having decided, through mutual consent, to update the 1949 Treaty relating to the promotion of, and fostering the relations of friendship and neighbourliness between India and Bhutan; have agreed as follows:

Article 1. There shall be perpetual peace and friendship between India and Bhutan.

Article 2. In keeping with the abiding ties of close friendship and co-operation between Bhutan and India, the Government of the Kingdom of Bhutan and the Government of the Republic of India shall co-operate closely with each other on issues relating to their national interests. Neither Government shall allow the use of its territory for activities harmful to the national security and interest of the other.

Article 3. There shall, as heretofore, be free trade and commerce between the territories of the Government of Bhutan and the Government of India. Both the Governments shall provide full co-operation and assistance to each other in the matter of trade and commerce.

Article 4. The Government of India agrees that the Government of Bhutan shall be free to import, from or through India into Bhutan, whatever arms, ammunition, machinery, warlike material or stores as may be required or desired for the strength and welfare of Bhutan, and that this arrangement shall hold good for all time as long as the Government of India is satisfied that the intentions of the Government of Bhutan are friendly and that there is no danger to India from such importations. The Government of Bhutan agrees that there shall be no export of such arms, ammunition and materials outside Bhutan either by the Government of Bhutan or by private individuals.

Article 5. The Government of Bhutan and the Government of India agree that Bhutanese subjects residing in Indian territories shall have equal justice with Indian subjects, and that Indian subjects residing in Bhutan shall have equal justice with the subjects of the Government of Bhutan.

Article 6. The extradition of persons wanted by either state for crimes and for unlawful activities affecting their security shall be in keeping with the extradition agreements between the two countries.

Article 7. The Government of Bhutan and the Government of India agree to promote cultural exchanges and co-operation between the two countries. These shall be extended to such areas as education, health, sports, science and technology.

Article 8. The Government of Bhutan and the Government of India agree to continue to consolidate and expand their economic co-operation for mutual and longterm benefit.

Article 9. Any differences and disputes arising in the interpretation and application of this Treaty shall be settled bilaterally by negotiations in a spirit of trust and understanding in consonance with the historically close ties of friendship and mutually beneficial co-operation that form the bedrock of Bhutan-India relations.

Article 10. This Treaty shall come into force upon the exchange of Instruments of Ratification by the two Governments which shall take place in Thimphu within one month of the signing of this Treaty. The Treaty shall continue in force in perpetuity unless terminated or modified by mutual consent.

# Bibliography

Aris, Michael. *Bhutan: The Early History of a Himalayan Kingdom*. Warminster, Aris and Phillips, 1979.

*The Raven Crown: The Origins of Buddhist Monarchy in Bhutan*. London, Serindia Publications, 1994.

Aris, Michael, and Hutt, Michael (Eds). *Bhutan: Aspects of Culture and Development*. Gartmore, Kiscadale, 1994.

Armington, Stan. *Lonely Planet Bhutan*. Hawthorn, Vic., Lonely Planet Publications, 2nd edn, 2002.

Aung San Suu Kyi. *Let's Visit Bhutan*. London, Burke Publishing Co Ltd, 1985.

Basu, Gautam Kumar. *Bhutan: The Political Economy of Development*. Denver, CO, Academic Books, 2000.

Bartholomew, Teresa Tse and Johnston, John (Eds). *The Dragon's Gift: The Sacred Arts of Bhutan*. Chicago, Serindia Publications, 2008.

Berthold, John. *Bhutan: Land of the Thunder Dragon*. Boston, MA, Wisdom Publications, 2005.

Brown, Linsay, and Mayhew, Bradley (with contributing authors Armington, Stan, and Whitecross, Richard W.). *Bhutan* (3rd ed.). Footscray, Lonely Planet Publications Pty. Ltd, 2007

Carpenter, Russ, and Carpenter, Blyth. *The Blessings of Bhutan*. Honolulu, HI, University of Hawaii Press, 2002.

Collister, Peter. *Bhutan and the British*. London, Serindia Publications, 1987.

Cooper, Robert. *Bhutan*. New York, Marshall Cavendish, 2001.

Crossette, Barbara. *So Close to Heaven: The Vanishing Buddhist Kingdoms of the Himalayas*. New York, Alfred A. Knopf, Inc., 1995.

Dago Tshering (Ed.). *Bhutan: Himalayan Kingdom*. New York, Royal Government of the Kingdom of Bhutan, 1979.

Das, Britta. *Buttertea at Sunrise: A Year in the Bhutan Himalaya*. New Delhi, Rupa & Co., 2006.

Das, Smriti. *Assam–Bhutan Trade Relations 1865–1949: A Socio-Economic Study*. New Delhi, Anshah Publishing House, 2005.

Dhakal, D. N. S., and Strawn, Christopher. *Bhutan: A Movement in Exile*. New Delhi, Nirala Publications, 1994.

Dimri, Jaiwanti. *The Drukpa Mystique: Bhutan in 21st Century*. Delhi, Authors Press, 2004.

Dogra, Ramesh C. (compiler). *Bhutan* (bibliography). London, Clio, 1991.

Dompnier, Robert. *Bhutan: Kingdom of the Dragon*. Boston, MA, Shambala Publications, 1999.

Dorji Wangmo Wangchuk (HM Ashi). *Of Rainbows and Clouds: The Life of Yab Ugyen Dorji as told to his Daughter*. London, Serindia Publications, 1999.

*Treasures of the Thunder Dragon: A Portrait of Bhutan*. New Delhi, Penguin Books, 2006.

Dowman, Keith (Trans.). *The Divine Madman: The Sublime Life and Songs of Drukpa Kinley*. London, Rider, 1980.

Edmunds, Tom Owen. *Bhutan: Land of the Thunder Dragon*. London, Elm Tree Books, 1989.

Gregson, Jonathan. *Kingdoms Beyond the Clouds: Journeys in Search of the Himalayan Kings*. London, Pan Macmillan, 2001.

Grover, Verinder (Ed.). *Encyclopaedia of SAARC Nations: Vol. 6, Bhutan*. New Delhi, Deep and Deep Publications, 1997.

*Bhutan: Government and Politics*. New Delhi, Deep and Deep Publications, 2000.

Gulati, M. N. *Tibetan Wars Through Sikkim, Bhutan and Nepal*. Delhi, Manas Publications, 2002.

*Rediscovering Bhutan*. Delhi, Manas Publications, 2003.

Gupta, Bhabani Sen. *Bhutan: Towards a Grass-root Participatory Polity*. Delhi, Konark Publishers Pvt Ltd, 1999.

Gyurme Dorji. *Footprint Bhutan*. Bath, Footprint, 1st edn, 2004.

Hawley, Michael. *Bhutan: A Visual Odyssey Across the Last Himalayan Kingdom*. Boston, MA, Friendly Planet, 2003.

Hickman, Katie. *Dreams of the Peaceful Dragon: A Journey through Bhutan*. London, Gollancz, 1987.

Hutt, Michael (Ed.). *Bhutan: Perspectives on Conflict and Dissent*. Gartmore, Kiscadale, 1994.

*Unbecoming Citizens: Culture, Nationhood and the Flight of Refugees from Bhutan*. Oxford, Oxford University Press, 2003.

International Bank for Reconstruction and Development (World Bank). *Bhutan: Development Planning in a Unique Environment*. Washington, DC, World Bank, 1989.

Jordan, Bart. *Bhutan: A Trekker's Guide*. Milnthorpe, Cicerone Press, 2006.

Karan, P. P. *Bhutan: A Physical and Cultural Geography*. Lexington, KY, University of Kentucky Press, 1967.

*Bhutan: Development amid Environmental and Cultural Preservation*. Tokyo, Institute for the Study of Languages and Cultures of Asia and Africa, 1987.

Karma Ura. *The Hero with a Thousand Eyes: A Historical Novel*. Thimphu, 1995.

*The Ballad of Pemi Tshewang Tashi: A Wind-borne Feather*. Thimphu, 1996.

*Bureaucracy and Peasantry in Decentralization in Bhutan* (discussion paper). Chiba-shih, Chiba, Institute of Developing Economies, 2005.

Kharat, Rajesh C. *Bhutan in SAARC: Role of a Small State in a Regional Alliance*. New Delhi, South Asian Publishers, 1999.

*Foreign Policy of Bhutan*. New Delhi, Manak Publications, 2005.

Kohli, Capt. M. S. *Bhutan: A Kingdom in the Sky*. New Delhi, Vikas Publishing House, 2004.

Kuhn, Delia, and Kuhn, Ferdinand. *Borderlands*. New York, Knopf, 1962.

Kunzang Choden. *Folktales of Bhutan*. Bangkok, White Lotus Press, 1993.

*Bhutanese Tales of the Yeti*. Bangkok, White Lotus Press, 1997.

Lamb, Alastair. *The China-India Border: The Origins of the Disputed Boundaries*. London, Chatham House Essays, Oxford University Press, 1964.

*Asian Frontiers: Studies in a Continuing Problem*. London, Pall Mall Press, 1968.

Leifer, M. *Himalaya: Mountains of Destiny*. London, Galley Press, 1962.

Mathew, Joseph C. *Ethnic Conflict in Bhutan*. New Delhi, Nirala Publications, 1999.

Mehra, G. N. *Bhutan: Land of the Peaceful Dragon*. New Delhi, Vikas Publishing House, 1974.

Mehra, Parshotam. *The Younghusband Expedition. An Interpretation*. Asia Publishing House, 1968.

Misra, H. N. *Bhutan: Problems and Policies*. New Delhi, Heritage Publishers, 1988.

Misra, R. C. *Emergence of Bhutan*. Jaipur, Sandarbh Prakashan, 1989.

Olschak, Blanche C. *Ancient Bhutan: A Study on Early Buddhism in the Himalayas*. Zürich, Swiss Foundation for Alpine Research, 1979.

Olsen, Gunnar (Ed.). *The Case of Bhutan: Development in a Himalayan Kingdom*. Copenhagen, Danish UN Asscn, 1985.

Parmanand. *The Politics of Bhutan: Retrospect and Prospect*. Delhi, Pragati Publications, 1992.

Pitiot, Michael. *Bhoutan: Voyage au Pays de Bouddha*. Paris, Presses de la Renaissance, 2005.

Pommaret, Françoise. *Bhutan*. Hong Kong, Odyssey Passport, 5th edn, 2005.

Rahul, Ram. *Royal Bhutan*. Delhi, ABC Publishing House, 1983.

Ramakant, M. A., and Misra, R. C. (Eds). *Bhutan: Society and Polity*. New Delhi, Indus Publishing Co, 1996.

Rizal, Dhurba P. *Administrative System in Bhutan: Retrospect and Prospect*. Delhi, Adroit Publishers, 2002.

Robinson, Francis (Ed.). *The Cambridge Encyclopaedia of India, Pakistan, Bangladesh, Sri Lanka, Nepal, Bhutan and the Maldives*. Cambridge, Cambridge University Press, 1989.

Rose, Leo E. *The Politics of Bhutan*. Ithaca, NY, Cornell University Press, 1977.

Rustomji, N. K. *Enchanted Frontiers: Sikkim, Bhutan and India's North-Eastern Borderlands*. Calcutta, Oxford University Press, 1973.

*Bhutan: The Dragon Kingdom in Crisis*. New Delhi, Oxford University Press, 1978.

Sangay Wangchuk. *Seeing with the Third Eye: Growing up with Angay in Rural Bhutan*. Thimphu, T. Sangay Wangchuk, 2006.

Savada, Andrea Matles (Ed.). *Nepal and Bhutan: Country Studies*. Washington, DC, Library of Congress for the Department of the Army, 1993.

Schicklgruber, Christian, and Pommaret, Françoise (Eds). *Bhutan: Mountain Fortress of the Gods*. London, Serindia Publications, 1997.

Sharma, S. K., and Sharma, Usha (Eds). *Encyclopaedia of Sikkim and Bhutan* (3 vols). New Delhi, Anmol Publications Pvt Ltd, 1997.

Singh, Amar Kaur Jasbir. *Himalayan Triangle*. London, British Library, 1988.

Singh, Nagendra. *Bhutan, a Kingdom in the Himalayas*. New Delhi, Thomson Press, 1980 (revised edn 1985).

Sinha, A. C. *Bhutan: Ethnic Identity and National Dilemma*. New Delhi, Reliance Publishing House, 1991.

*Himalayan Kingdom Bhutan: Tradition, Transition and Transformation*. New Delhi, Indus Publishing Co, 2001.

Slocum, Thomas. *In His Majesty's Civil Service: and Other Contemporary Tales of the Kingdom of Bhutan*. New York, Rivercross Publications, 1998.

Snellgrove, David L. *Himalayan Pilgrimage*. Oxford, Bruno Cassirer, 1961.

Solverson, Howard. *The Jesuit and the Dragon: The Life of Father William Mackey in the Himalayan Kingdom of Bhutan*. Montréal, Robert Davies Publishing, 1995.

Sonam Kinga. *Speaking Names, Flying Rocks*. Thimphu, DSB Publications, 2005.

Spierenburg, Peter. *Birds in Bhutan: Status and Distribution*. Bedford, Oriental Bird Club, 2005.

Ueeda, Akiko. *Culture and Modernisation: From the Perspectives of Young People in Bhutan*. Thimphu, Centre for Bhutan Studies, 2003.

Upadhyay, B. N. *From Mountain Kingdom to Public Sector*. New Delhi, Devika Publications, 2000.

Upreti, B. C. *Bhutan: Dilemma of Change in a Himalayan Kingdom*. Delhi, Kalinga Publications, 2004.

van Strydonck, Guy, Pommaret-Imaeda, F., and Imaeda, Yoshiro. *Bhutan: A Kingdom of the Eastern Himalayas*. London, Serindia, 1984.

Vas, E. A. *The Dragon Kingdom: Journeys through Bhutan*. New Delhi, Lancer International, 1986.

Verma, Ravi. *India's Role in the Emergence of Contemporary Bhutan*. Delhi, Capital Publishing House, 1988.

von Nebesky-Wojkowitz, René. *Where the Mountains are Gods*. London, Weidenfeld and Nicolson, 1956.

Wehrheim, John.*Bhutan's Hidden Lands of Happiness*. Chicago, Serindia Publications, 2008.

White, John Claude. *Sikkim and Bhutan: Twenty-One Years on the North-East Frontier, 1887–1908*. London, Arnold, 1909.

Williamson, Margaret D. *Memoirs of a Political Officer's Wife in Tibet, Sikkim and Bhutan*. London, Wisdom Publications, 1988.

Woodman, Dorothy. *Himalayan Frontiers: A Political Review of British, Chinese, Indian and Russian Rivalries*. London, Barrie and Jenkins, 1969.

Yongten Dargye. *History of the Drukpa Kagyud School in Bhutan (12th to 17th Century AD)*. Thimphu, Yongten Dargye, 2001.

Zeppa, Jamie. *Beyond the Earth and Sky: A Journey into Bhutan*. New York, Riverhead Books, 1999.

Zhu Zaiming, Mingchao Tang. *Budan*. Beijing, She Huike Xue Wen Xian Chu Ban She, 2004.

Zurcher, Dieter, and Kunzang Choden. *Bhutan: Land of Spirituality and Modernization—Role of Water in Daily Life*. New Delhi, New Dawn Press, 2004.

# INDIA

## Physical and Social Geography

B. H. FARMER

The Republic of India is one of the largest countries in the world, with an area of 3,166,414 sq km (1,222,559 sq miles), including the Indian-held part of Jammu and Kashmir (the territory is divided between India and Pakistan). India stretches from 8° to 33° 15′ N, and from 68° 5′ to 97° 25′ E. Its northern frontiers are with Tibet (the Xizang Autonomous Region of the People's Republic of China), Nepal and Bhutan. On the north-west it bounds Pakistan; on the north-east it borders Myanmar (formerly Burma); and in the east Bangladesh. India's great southern peninsula stretches far down into the tropical waters of the Indian Ocean, where its territorial boundaries extend to the Andaman and Nicobar Islands, in the Bay of Bengal, and the Lakshadweep archipelago, in the Arabian Sea.

### PHYSICAL FEATURES

India has three well-marked and, indeed, obvious relief regions: the Himalayan system in the north, the plateaux of the peninsula and, in between, the great plains of the Indus and Ganga (Ganges) basins.

The Himalayan system, between the Tibet plateau and the Indo-Gangetic plains, is made up of complex ranges arranged more or less in parallel, but in places combining and then dividing again, in others taking on the apparent form of a series of peaks divided by deep gorges rather than that of a range. The Great Himalaya is, in general, just such an array of giant peaks, mostly over 6,100 m in height, covered by perpetual snows, and nurturing great glaciers, which in turn feed the rivers flowing to the Indus, Ganga and Brahmaputra. The southernmost range of the system, the Shivaliks, presents a wall-like margin to the plains; while in the extreme north-east the whole system bends very sharply on crossing the Brahmaputra and forms the wild, forest-clad country of the Naga and other hills on the marches of Myanmar.

Peninsular India, the Deccan or South Country, begins at another but more broken wall that fringes the plains to the south, and stretches away to Kanyakumari (Cape Comorin), the southernmost extremity of India. The whole peninsula is built, fundamentally, of ancient and largely crystalline rocks which have been worn down through long geological ages and now form a series of plateaux, mostly sloping eastward and drained by great rivers, like the Mahanadi, Krishna and Godavari, flowing to the Bay of Bengal. Where plateaux end abruptly their edges present, from the lower plains or plateaux below, the appearance of mountain ranges. This feature is most evident in the Western Ghats, the great scarp overlooking the narrow western coastal plain. Two major rivers, the Narmada and Tapti (Tapi), flow east. Between them, and on east into the jungle country of Chotanagpur, lies wild hilly territory that has done much to isolate the southern Deccan from the plains through long periods of Indian history. The Garo and Khasi Hills of Meghalaya form a detached piece of plateau country. In places there are variants on the ancient crystalline-rock plateau theme. Thus, in the north-eastern Deccan narrow, down-faulted basins preserve the most important of India's coal measures; while inland of Mumbai (formerly Bombay), and covering most of the state of Maharashtra, great basalt flows have given rise to distinctive countryside with broad open valleys floored by fertile, though difficult, *regur* (black cotton soils) separated by flat-topped hills. The west coast is fringed by a narrow alluvial plain. The plain on the east coast is generally wide, especially where it broadens out into the highly productive deltas of the great east-flowing rivers.

The Indo-Gangetic plain, between the Shivaliks and the northernmost plateau-edges of the Deccan, is one of the really great plains of the world. Consisting entirely of alluvium, it presents an appearance of monotonous flatness from the air or, indeed, to the uninitiated traveller on land. In fact, however, its general flatness conceals a great deal of variety. The fine muds and clays of the Ganga-Brahmaputra delta contrast, for instance, with the sands of the Rajasthan desert at the western extremity of the Indian portion of the plains. Almost everywhere, too, there is a contrast of floodplains (along the rivers) and naturally dry belts, often of older alluvium, well above the reach of even the highest floods.

### CLIMATE

In northern India there are three seasons. A 'cool season' lasts from December to February, and brings average temperatures of 10°–15°C to Delhi and the Punjab, but with a high diurnal range (from as high as 26°C by day to freezing point or below at night) and, although this is the season of the 'dry' north-east monsoon, depressions from the north-west may bring rain to the Punjab and, indeed, further down the plains to the east. In the 'hot season' of the north temperatures rise until, in May, the average is 32°–35°C (as high as 48°C by day), and rain is very rare. With the 'burst' of the monsoon in June and July, temperatures fall and the rains begin, to last until September or October.

In the Ganga delta, to take another regional example, the cool season is less cool than in Delhi (19°C average for January in Kolkata—formerly Calcutta), the hot season less hot (30°C May average), and the rains much heavier—there is hardly a year in which Kolkata's streets do not suffer serious flooding at least once. The hot season is, moreover, punctuated by 'mango showers', which are even more significant in Assam (Asom).

In the peninsula, the coolness of the cool season tends to be diminished as one goes south, as does the striking heat of the hot season, partly because in places such as Mumbai temperatures are never as high as in, say, Delhi, and partly because in the far south it is always hot, except where temperatures are mitigated by altitude. In Tamil Nadu, for example, average monthly temperatures vary only from 24°C in January to 32°C in May and June. In the peninsula, too, the south-west monsoon brings particularly heavy rains to the westward-facing scarps of the Western Ghats, which receive 2,000–2,500 mm in four months. The dry season also decreases southward till in Kerala, in the far south-west, it lasts for only a month or two. In Tamil Nadu, there is an almost complete reversal of the normal monsoonal rainfall regime: the heaviest rains fall in October to January (inclusive) and the south-west monsoon period is relatively dry.

The theme of contrast in Indian climate is best expressed by drawing attention to the tremendous difference between, on the one hand, the deserts of Rajasthan and the rather less dry sands of Ramanathapuram, in south-eastern Tamil Nadu, and, on the other, the verdant landscapes of the north-eastern Deccan and of Kerala.

### SOILS AND VEGETATION

The soils of the Himalayan mountains and plateaux are generally thin, skeletal and infertile, except in intermontane basins or in areas of artificial terracing, and therefore of artificial depth and fertility. The soils of the peninsula are also generally poor, though for a different reason—that in general they have been derived from long years of weathering from unpromising crystalline rocks. There are, however, noteworthy exceptions—particularly the rich alluvia, with a generally high potential for improvement by means of fertilizers, to be found in the east coast deltas of the Mahanadi, Godavari, Krishna and Kaveri (Cauvery), and the *regur* of the basalt areas of Maharashtra. The latter are naturally of quite high fertility and retain moisture (an important property in a monsoon climate, especially in the axis of semi-aridity that runs east of the Ghats through Pune) but are sticky, erodible and hard to cultivate when wet, and also difficult to irrigate satisfactorily. The soils of the plains are, by nature, generally much more fertile than those of the Himalayas or of the Deccan, though this does not apply to the sandier soils that are to be found (for example) in the Rajasthan desert, or to the leached soils of old alluvial terraces like those on the western margins of the Bengal delta. Yet infertility has tended to creep in as a result of human occupancy. This is partly, and very widely, a matter of long continued cultivation without adequate manuring, partly a matter of salinity and alkalinity induced by a causal chain that stretches from canal irrigation through rising water-tables to the capillary ascent of salts to the surface. The problem of salinity particularly afflicts the fields of Uttar Pradesh.

The tremendous variations in rainfall, not to say temperature and relief, to be met in India mean that there must have been, far back in time, very wide variations in natural vegetation. These probably ranged from near-desert or even complete desert (in Rajasthan); through thorn scrub (in semi-arid regions like the western Maharashtran Deccan) and tropical dry deciduous forest (in slightly wetter areas lying along a broad crescentic belt from the middle Ganga plains to Hyderabad and Chennai—formerly Madras—in the south-east) and moist tropical deciduous forest (in the north-east Deccan); to tropical wet evergreen forest, approaching rain forest (along the Western Ghats and in Kerala). There must also have been a complete altitudinal gradation from plains vegetation through deciduous and coniferous forests to montane vegetation in the Himalayas. Little natural vegetation of any sort survives in the plains or in the east and west coast deltas and coastal strips, except in rare groves; or, for that matter, over much of Tamil Nadu or the plateau areas of Maharashtra (apart from the still-forested eastern districts of the latter state). In all these regions, and many more, the landscape is dominated not by natural vegetation but by arable cultivation. Even in apparently uncultivated areas the natural vegetation has been modified out of all recognition. It may well be that part of the Rajasthan desert is man-made or, at any rate, degraded by man. The savannah-like jungles of parts of central India have developed from denser forest formations, by the action of man and his animals. Even the surviving forests of the north-east Deccan, dominated by sal (*Shorea robusta*, a useful timber tree), are often, if not generally, derived from more heterogeneous forests by the action of fire. Not surprisingly, India's forest resources, although not by any means inconsiderable, do not match its needs.

## MINERALS

India possesses some of the largest and richest reserves of iron ore in the world. These occur particularly in the north-east Deccan, in the states of Jharkhand, Orissa and in the western part of West Bengal. Other deposits occur farther afield—for example, around Salem, in Tamil Nadu; in Karnataka; and in Goa. Altogether it has been estimated that India has reserves of no less than 22,000m. metric tons of iron ore. This is ample to supply the country's present industrial needs and to allow for exports. There are perhaps resources of 80,000m. tons of poor and medium coals, but only 2,500m. tons of coking coals. Some 95% of Indian production, and nearly all of the coking coal, comes from seams in the down-faulted basins in the north-east Deccan. It will be appreciated that the bulk of the iron-ore reserves are in the same region. Elsewhere, there is a little coal in Assam and lignite (brown coal) in Rajasthan and Tamil Nadu.

India is rich in the non-ferrous minerals used in alloys, notably in manganese (of which India in most years is the second or third largest producer in the world; ores are found widely distributed in the Deccan). About 75% of the world's mica comes from India, notably from Jharkhand, Tamil Nadu and Rajasthan. The known reserves of various minerals in December 1976 were: haematite 9,000m. metric tons; magnetite 2,800m. tons; lignite 2,000m. tons; limestone 50,000m. tons; dolomite 1,800m. tons; china clay 365m. tons; fire clay 300m. tons; copper 333m. tons; kyanite 143m. tons; lead 120m. tons; zinc 101m. tons; manganese 98m. tons; nickel 78m. tons; and phosphorite 78m. tons. Onshore deposits of petroleum have been found in Assam, Gujarat and Nagaland, and offshore oilfields have been discovered in the western continental shelf off the Maharashtra coast, notably in the Mumbai High. Estimates of recoverable reserves vary but are officially put at about 1,500m. tons. There is no shortage of building-stone or of the raw materials for the cement industry.

## POPULATION AND ETHNIC GROUPS

With a population at the March 2001 census of 1,028,610,328 (including the Indian-held part of Jammu and Kashmir), India is the world's second most populous country. The population officially reached 1,000m. on 11 May 2000 and had increased to an estimated 1,148m. by 1 March 2008. The annual exponential rate of growth of population was about 2.2% in 1971–81, declining to 2.1% in 1981–91. The annual rate of growth declined again in 1991–2001, to 1.93%. At March 2001 the population density was 325 persons per sq km. By any standards, large areas of India are now overpopulated; economic development is a constant race against population increase, and the control of future growth has become a major issue.

There are great variations in population density in the Indian countryside. There are very high densities of rural population in the rice-growing areas of the lower Ganga plain and in the Bengal delta; in parts of Assam; in parts of the eastern peninsular deltas and around Chennai; in Kerala; and in the coastal plains stretching from south of Mumbai north into Gujarat. Less spectacular, but still high densities are to be found in the upper Ganga plains and in the Punjab and Haryana, in Assam, and in Tamil Nadu generally. At the other extreme, low densities occur in the Himalayas and the Rajasthan desert (not surprisingly); in the jungle-covered hills and plateaux of the north-eastern Deccan (though these have been invaded by mining, by the iron and steel industry, and by agricultural colonists, refugees from Bangladesh); in inland Gujarat and Saurashtra; and in the marchland-hills that stretch from west to east in the region of the Narmada and Tapti. India also has its great and growing urban concentrations, especially in and around Mumbai, Delhi, Kolkata and Chennai.

The peoples of India are extremely varied in composition. It is not particularly profitable to attempt to divide them into 'racial' groups distinguished by physical characteristics. It is more useful to consider the linguistic divisions of the Indian people, particularly since these in large measure form the basis for the current division of the federal Union into states. The languages of north India are of the Indo-Aryan family, the most important member of which is Hindi, the language particularly of Uttar Pradesh and Haryana (the latter now separated by an inter-state boundary from the Punjabi-speaking area to the west). Other members of the family (the corresponding linguistic states of which will be readily identified) are Rajasthani, Bihari, Bengali, Oriya and Marathi. In south India the languages are of a quite different family, the Dravidian, and include Tamil (in Tamil Nadu), Malayalam (in Kerala), Telugu (in Andhra Pradesh) and Kannada (in Karnataka). There are also many tribal languages in the jungle areas and Tibetan languages in the Himalayas.

As is well known, Indian society is also divided into castes, each of which is endogamous and into one of which a man or woman enters irrevocably at birth. Status and, to some extent, occupation are still largely determined by caste, and caste considerations enter significantly into politics; although the scene is a complex and rapidly shifting one in many regions.

Religion is in India both a divisive and a cohesive force. Communal friction and disharmony are often largely a matter of religion, especially as between Hindus and Muslims in north India. Most of India's peoples, however, are, apart from certain tribal groups, united to a greater or lesser extent by cultural traits and the consciousness of a common heritage, and these derive in very large measure from age-old Hinduism.

# History

## DAVID TAYLOR

Based on an earlier article by PETER ROBB

### INDIA BEFORE COLONIAL RULE

Ever since the third millennium BC, the South Asian region has been home to settled agricultural and urban populations. Despite the many political changes that have taken place, there have remained important elements of continuity embodied in religious and social institutions. Internal and external challenges have been absorbed in ways that have usually enriched rather than destroyed existing practices.

The earliest South Asian archaeological records go back to the Neolithic period. By the middle of the third millennium BC the region saw the emergence of one of the ancient world's most striking civilizations. Parallel with Mesopotamia, with which it was in regular contact, the Indus Valley or Harappan civilization witnessed the appearance of sophisticated urban settlements across not only the Indus Valley itself (the two most famous sites—Harappa and Mohenjo-daro—are both in present-day Pakistan) but other parts of northern and western India. The evidence, for example the careful town planning, suggests that these bronze age settlements were engaged in regular trade with their neighbours to the West, and that there were clear social and political hierarchies. The Indus Valley civilization possessed a written language, but it has yet to be deciphered.

While earlier historians believed that the Indus Valley civilization came to a sudden end as a result of the eruption into the region of nomadic invaders from outside, the current orthodoxy suggests a more gradual decline, possibly as a result of climate change. At the same time, tribal groups from Central Asia migrated to the richer lands of South Asia. These people came to be known as the Aryans by later generations. The newcomers gradually merged with the existing population from the Harappan period and spread southwards and eastwards across the region, encompassing other scattered groups that had already settled there.

By about 1000 BC, by which time iron smelting had become established, a new phase began in Indian history with the emergence of centres of activity across northern India. At about this time, the first sacred books of Hinduism, the four *Vedas*, were composed. New urban centres were established, and gradually political dynasties established control over large areas of the country. The social order associated with Hinduism and based on distinctions between different caste groups also emerged in this period. The most successful of the dynasties was the Mauryan. The two most important of the Mauryan emperors were the dynasty's founder, Chandragupta Maurya (321–297 BC), and his grandson, Ashoka (272–235 BC). During the latter's reign the Mauryan empire reached its greatest extent. Ashoka is most famous, however, for his patronage of Buddhism, which had been founded in India several centuries before, as a reaction to some of the more regressive features of early Hinduism.

In 327 BC, contemporaneously with the emergence of the Mauryan empire, Alexander III ('the Great') of Macedon made his famous incursion into South Asia. He was unable to establish a permanent presence, however, and was forced to retreat. Nevertheless, Greek influence remained important in the north-west of India (as well as in parts of Central Asia) for some centuries, and Indo-Greek kingdoms produced a distinctive style of art and culture.

With the decline of the Mauryan dynasty, other dynasties arose across India. Some were content to confine themselves to one particular region, or, like the Kushans, controlled empires that overlapped with Central Asia; others, such as the Guptas in the 4th century AD, ruled across a large part of northern India.

Buddhism continued to flourish alongside Hinduism for some centuries until political changes led to its gradual decline. Hinduism itself evolved both philosophically and in terms of devotional patterns, where the rich mythological and epic traditions associated with the gods of the Hindu pantheon developed. Different regional traditions emerged, interacting with each other but developing their own distinctive cultural patterns. Gradually, distinct regional languages evolved, which have remained recognizably the same in modern-day India. South India in particular developed its own cultural and, to some extent, religious traditions, based on the Tamil language and a distinctive philosophical system.

The first Muslim contacts with India were established in the early eighth century, when Arab invaders established a kingdom in what is now the Sindh province of Pakistan. From the 12th century onwards nomadic groups from Central Asia began to move into the subcontinent through the mountain passes in the north-west. Relying on superior military tactics, successive dynasties from Central Asia took control of state power across the north of the country, basing themselves especially at Delhi. Taimur (Tamerlane), the great Turko-Mongol leader, made a brief but devastating raid on north India in 1398, during which Delhi was sacked. Muslim by faith, the new rulers made little effort to convert by force the populations they governed, although Muslims from elsewhere came and settled at the new courts. However, in some parts of the country—for example the deltaic region of Bengal—the presence of Muslim holy men (*pirs* or Sufis) led many from the lower strata of society to adopt elements of an Islamic identity, while often keeping intact many of their original beliefs and practices.

At the beginning of the 16th century one final incursion from Central Asia, by a group that became known as the Mughals, led to the establishment of the largest empire that had been seen since Mauryan rule. Founded by the emperor Babur, the Mughal dynasty reached its political peak under Akbar (1556–1605), and its cultural peak under his son Jahangir (1605–27) and grandson Shah Jahan (1627–58), the builder of the Taj Mahal. The Mughals brought almost the whole of the subcontinent, with the exception of parts of the south, under their control, and developed new and effective methods of military, political and administrative control.

While by the early centuries of the second millennium AD the different schools of Hindu thought had achieved more or less their final pre-modern form—for example the *Advaita Vedanta* system of ideas, which was formalized by the great philosopher Shankara at the end of the eighth century AD—there was a constant renewal of popular belief through devotional sects. Known collectively as *bhakti* (devotional) movements, such sects brought people together across caste and even religious boundaries.

The Mughal dynasty gradually declined during the course of the 18th century. Outlying parts of the Empire were seized by force, for example by the Marathas in western India, while the core lost its capacity for self-renewal. The most important factor in the 18th century was, however, the rapidly increasing penetration by the European powers. Contact between India and Europe had, of course, existed since the earliest times; however, from the 16th century onwards the rise of the European trading empires changed the terms of the engagement. The first trading posts were established by the Portuguese. The London-based (British) East India Company began its operations in the early 17th century and by the end of the century was well established at several points along the coast, most importantly in the three port cities of Calcutta, Madras and Bombay (now known as Kolkata, Chennai and Mumbai, respectively). During the 18th century a combination of factors—competition between French and British interests, increasing opportunities for penetration of local Indian states, and greater economic pressures from Europe—led to the assertion of military power and the eventual defeat both of the French and of any potential Indian rival, most importantly the Marathas. By the beginning of the 19th century India was effectively under British control, although it was not until 1858 and the defeat of the large-scale rebellion that had started the previous year (once known as the Indian Mutiny) that British power was complete. It was in that year that the nominal role of the East India Company was replaced by direct British rule.

## THE BRITISH IN INDIA

During their period in power the British generally preferred to rule with a relatively light hand, except where direct economic interests were involved, and often used Indian intermediaries and allies, but they inevitably changed the institutional structure of the society they dominated. They introduced Western laws in regard to property, and a succession of Western concepts of the role and character of government. They allowed, if they did not positively encourage, the spread of ideas of equality, social justice, nationalism and representative democracy. Their land revenue settlements, the building of telegraph lines, railways and canals, and the development of commercial agriculture subtly distorted the shape of rural society. In the towns, new classes appeared from among those whom the British had educated in English (mainly to serve in the administration, in minor roles) or those who had benefited from the British system and the functions that it called upon Indians to perform—there were merchants, landlords, officials, lawyers, doctors and teachers who had common interests which, to some extent, superseded caste, communal and regional differences. Some people in these categories came together after 1885 in an annual conference called the Indian National Congress.

In the 19th century the Government listened most to those whom they believed to head traditional social and political networks, but they also responded to English-educated Indians who were needed to run the administration and whose spokesmen carried weight in some quarters in the United Kingdom. These Indians stood out because of their class and education, and the constitutional concessions that the British made to them encouraged them to seek wider support. Controversies arose in the early 20th century about how best to persuade the British to relinquish their power; those who advocated more active agitation and more permanent, popular organizations inevitably came into contact with religious movements. The rise of Mahatma Gandhi after 1920 represented a fusion of these forces, a rethinking of the approach of the Indian National Congress (widely referred to simply as Congress) and the incorporation of a wider range of people into the nationalist movement—changes, in fact, encouraged by the political reforms that Gandhi wished to boycott.

In the 1880s the British introduced a degree of local self-government (with powers to raise local revenue); in 1892, indirectly, and again in 1909, they conceded the elective principle in choosing who were to advise, though not control, the executive through the legislative councils. Finally, between 1915 and 1919, in an even more important breakthrough, they admitted publicly that they would eventually have to introduce responsible government, and in 1919 an Act of Parliament began this process by introducing shared control at the provincial level (diarchy). In 1935 this was extended to full control of provincial affairs under normal circumstances. Congress insisted, however, that without sovereignty political power would be meaningless, and persisted with its campaigns until independence was finally achieved in 1947. The timing of the transfer of power depended on the interaction of many factors, including changes in the United Kingdom following the Second World War, but the leading one was the mobilization of much of the population by Gandhi and Congress. This was a continuous process after 1919, but was marked by peaks of activity in 1919–22 (the Non-Co-operation Movement), 1930–32 (the Civil Disobedience Movement) and 1942–43 (the Quit India Movement).

As Congress came to occupy the pre-eminent position in Indian politics, so it had to address the question of India's cultural and social diversity. Most urgently, this meant the question of Hindu–Muslim relations, where the earlier ambiguity had been replaced by an elaborated categorization, influenced by British policies of classification and enumeration, for example through the introduction of decennial censuses. Although Congress leaders insisted that Congress was a movement for every Indian, Muslims were alarmed by what they perceived as the priority given to Hindu symbols and were themselves often caught up by the pan-Islamic movement of the time. Muslim élites, who had been favoured by the introduction of separate electorates in 1909, became increasingly concerned about their future as majority rule came closer. This anxiety was transmitted from the political classes, who hoped to inherit British power, through the *ulema* (the religious leadership) to the population at large. It was not helped by Congress insistence that it was an alternative government to the British, and thus superior in status to other political associations; the fact that the dangers were real, at least at street level, was demonstrated in many savage communal riots, which though due to faults on both sides were obviously more alarming for the minority community. In the 1940s Muslim demands hardened, after the resignation of Congress ministries and the movement's subsequent outlawing because of Gandhi's 'Quit India' campaign. The British began to treat the Muslim League, which had at last consolidated its all-India status, as an equal with Congress. After the Second World War the British believed they could hold India only by force, and they had lost the will for this. Thus, after 1945, the British wished to leave, and when the Muslim League under Muhammad Ali Jinnah stood in their way, the British Prime Minister, Clement Attlee, and the last Viceroy, Lord Louis Mountbatten of Burma, cut the knot and partitioned the country. The majority Muslim areas in the east and north-west, never wholeheartedly behind the League (which had been led by men from the Muslim minority areas), found themselves yoked, for a time, as a new country: Pakistan.

## INDEPENDENT INDIA AND THE NEHRUVIAN PERIOD

India became an independent dominion on 15 August 1947. The new Prime Minister, Jawaharlal Nehru, promised that it now would 'awake to life and freedom'. His administration, however, was marked by continuity as well as change. The immediate task was to restore the authority of the Government following a rising tide of panic and massacre as refugees fled from one part to the other of the divided Punjab. Millions were uprooted and hundreds of thousands killed as the boundary force set up by Mountbatten proved wholly inadequate. Both the migration and the enormous death toll left permanent scars on India and Pakistan, but in the short term order was restored relatively quickly. Its accomplishment, however, claimed the life of Gandhi, who had rushed to Delhi to try to stop the communal violence, and was assassinated in January 1948 by a Hindu extremist who seems to have considered him too conciliatory to the Muslims. Nehru told the nation 'the light has gone out'; but the shock of Gandhi's death restored order, at least for a time, by discrediting communalists.

It was necessary also to address the problem of the princely states, which numbered about 560, comprised two-fifths of the area of the subcontinent, and which varied enormously in size and population. Although in theory a state could opt for independence or for union with either India or Pakistan, in practice the withdrawal of British suzerainty made the first option difficult (if not impossible). By Independence Day all but four had acceded to one country or the other; and during 1948 the home minister, Vallabhbhai Patel, coerced and cajoled those that had joined India into being absorbed into the new Indian federation.

Two of the princely states that held aloof from the Indian Union were Junagadh (on the coast of Gujarat) and Hyderabad, the largest of them all. Both states had Muslim rulers (that of Hyderabad being known as the Nizam), but predominantly Hindu populations. Junagadh was occupied by Indian troops after its prince opted for union with Pakistan, while Hyderabad was also occupied following the assumption of power by a local extremist group. Both states were subsequently taken into the Indian Union. (At the same time Kalat, situated in a remote desert area of Balochistan, was absorbed by Pakistan.) The remaining French colonial outposts on the subcontinent were later incorporated into India: Chandernagore in 1951, followed by Pondicherry (or Puducherry as it was later renamed), Karaikal (Karikal), Mahe (Mahé) and Yanam in 1954. The Portuguese territories were all annexed by 1961 (see below).

The state of Jammu and Kashmir, with its predominantly Muslim population and Hindu ruler, had also remained undecided, until October 1947 when Pathan tribesmen from the Pakistani North-West Frontier Province, organized by elements within Pakistan, invaded in support of an internal rising. The Maharajah was promptly persuaded to opt for India (in circumstances which remain deeply contested by historians inside and outside South Asia). India's troops subsequently retained for him Jammu (with its Hindu-Sikh majority), Ladakh (with a substantial Tibetan-speaking Buddhist element) and the Vale of Kashmir, but only after extensive fighting with Pakistani troops. A 'popular' government was installed under Sheikh Muhammad Abdullah, with a promise, embodied in the UN resolution that brought about a cease-fire between India and Pakistan, of a plebiscite to follow.

Unity was maintained within India at one level through the Constitution, which established the Indian Union as a secular parliamentary democracy on the Western model, with a federal structure but a strong centre. On 26 January 1950 India became a republic with a President as its constitutional head, but recognizing the British sovereign as head of the Commonwealth.

Indian unity was potentially threatened by the divisive element of language. Two issues were at stake. One was whether the state (previously provincial) boundaries should follow linguistic divisions. At least 14 language areas could be so demarcated, although inevitably there were inconsistencies and ambiguities. Although Gandhi had been an advocate of linguistic provinces, Nehru's initial stance after 1947 was to reject the redrawing of boundaries on the grounds that it would encourage local at the expense of national loyalties. However, it became clear that demands for linguistic states enjoyed widespread support, and in 1956 an extensive state reorganization, using language as the most important criterion, was carried out, which also allowed the distinction between former British and former princely areas to be abolished. In 1960 the erstwhile Bombay presidency was divided into Gujarat and Maharashtra, and in 1966 Haryana was created out of the Hindi-speaking but also predominantly Hindu areas of the Punjab, ostensibly on linguistic grounds, but, in fact, to form a Sikh-majority state in the new Punjab. On the north-east borders of the country, where predominantly tribal groups had been isolated during the colonial period, a number of local insurgencies, notably among the Naga and Mizo tribes, challenged the Government's authority. In 1963 the state of Nagaland was created out of what had been part of the state of Assam (Asom), in the hope of placating some sections of the rebels.

The other linguistic issue was that of the national language. While the British had used English as the language of administration at the all-India level, Congress had become increasingly committed to the use of Hindi (sometimes referred to, for example by Gandhi, as Hindustani to avoid any Hindu overtone), the language spoken widely in northern and parts of central India but not elsewhere. At independence it was decided to allow English to be used alongside Hindi as the country's official language for a limited period until 1965. As this date approached, however, it became clear that many non-Hindi speakers, especially in Tamil Nadu, wanted the use of English as an official language to continue, so as to counterbalance a possible dominance at the national level by Hindi speakers. Nehru had already taken a conciliatory line on the issue and his successors have continued to postpone the phasing out of English. At the same time, Hindi has become widely spoken as a second language throughout India, especially in the urban areas.

The supremacy of Congress in India's political life was ensured by the resolution of internal struggles in favour of Nehru, and from 1951 until the Chinese invasion in 1962 his influence was paramount. The assassination of Gandhi provided the occasion for an outright attack on communalist parties (as well as communalists within Congress) who had been encouraged by the war with Pakistan and the influx of Hindu refugees. The latter issue was further defused by the Nehru-Liaquat pact in 1950, temporarily settling relations between India and Pakistan. At the first general election in 1951–52 Congress scored an overwhelming victory. Some breakaway groups from the left wing of Congress and the Communist Party of India managed to win a scattering of seats, but posed no significant threat to Congress. Communalist parties such as the Hindu nationalist Jana Sangh, founded just before the elections, performed especially poorly.

The very success of Nehru's Congress posed a problem, however. In so far as Congress became the inevitable party of government after independence, it was bound to attract the ambitious and thus to find it difficult to evolve a consistent ideology: a compendium of more or less diverse interests could not also be a unified force for, say, socialism. There did not evolve after independence, any more than before, a credible alternative party or parties of government. This lack resulted partly from deliberate Congress policy, partly from the wide slice of the political sphere encompassed by Congress as a result of its history as the central nationalist movement, and partly from the divisions among opposition groups. Potential or long-standing opposition leaders were ready to take office at times under Congress while permanent opposition groupings of any size proved elusive. The various opposition leaders, R. M. Lohia, Jayaprakash Narayan, Asok Mehta, J. B. Kripalani and so on, tended to be individualists rather than organization-men. Thus, under Nehru, the pre-eminence of Congress during the independence struggle was modified and preserved.

The initial Congress victory in the 1951–52 elections was followed by further victories in 1957 and 1962. Although Congress never quite succeeded in gaining an absolute majority of the popular vote, it far surpassed any other party, and, under India's 'first past the post' electoral system, easily won a majority of seats both at the national level and in almost all of the states, although the southern state of Kerala witnessed the world's first ever election of a communist government in 1957 (it was dismissed in controversial circumstances two years later).

There was broad continuity too, under Nehru, in the social composition of the political leadership. In spite of a certain shift in legislative and party membership towards agricultural classes and peasant castes, the beneficiaries tended to be those already dominant socially or economically; individuals whose ability and resources brought them to the top proved mostly to be members of dominant landholding castes. The monopoly of politics by an English-speaking professional élite, whose talents fitted them to negotiate with the British, may have continued slowly to be weakened, as it had begun to be with the advent of popular agitation in the 1920s; but independence and democracy have also further emphasized the resilience of customary power structures, particularly the caste system, which had operated all along beside the British-inspired politicians.

Neither did change spread to the bureaucracy. Nehru opted for continuity among the administrators, partly through necessity, for the Congress cadres could not replace the bureaucracy the British had built. At the highest levels, it is true, political leaders displaced the administrator-rulers, but they worked closely with their senior civil service advisers, many of whom shared their ambitions for economic and social development. At middle levels, however, the executive functions of the higher civil servant remained, as for example in the district officer as the fount of authority in the locality. At the local level, government officials and police officers continued to be widely regarded as corrupt and inefficient.

Independence did nevertheless change the priorities of government, even when policies continued existing trends. Thus, Nehru continued the social reforming tendencies which resulted from Western influence in British days, but with a determination impossible for alien rulers. He insisted on the secular nature of India's Government, on equality before the law (untouchability, as a status, was formally abolished under the Constitution) and on the passage of legislation providing, among other things, for divorce, monogamy and equal rights of inheritance for Hindu women (although the Constitution called for the introduction of a common civil code, this did not have the force of law and the question of the status of Muslim family law, for instance, was left unresolved). Under Nehru too, education was greatly expanded, but (repeating the mistake of the British) most notably at university and higher technical levels, and in towns; in the countryside the literacy rate has remained low, although it is gradually improving.

During the 1950s Nehru conducted foreign affairs with little interference. He began by supporting nationalist forces in Indonesia, mainland South-East Asia and elsewhere. Acutely aware of East–West tension, and of the dangers of a nuclear war in the post-1945 years, he declared the policy of non-involvement, and strove to build up a third force of uncommitted or non-aligned nations. This led him to welcome the communist rise to power in the People's Republic of China in 1949 and brought him to the Bandung conference of Afro-Asian states in 1955.

This was the zenith of Nehru's international influence and from this moment his star seemed to decline. He was forthright in condemning the United Kingdom and France over Suez in 1956, but equivocated on the issue of Soviet intervention in Hungary. In 1959 the Chinese decision to rule, instead of control, Tibet (Xizang), followed by the Dalai Lama's flight to India, put him under further pressure from right-wing opinion and embroiled him with China itself. It gradually became clear that China did not regard its border with India as settled, and, partly under pressure from public opinion and the army, Nehru agreed to a policy of asserting Indian presence up to the border it claimed. The dispute became serious with the discovery of a Chinese road across the desolate Aksai Chin plateau, to the north of Ladakh. Nehru made some bellicose speeches, and the Indians engaged in minor skirmishes. Suddenly, in 1962, the Chinese advanced in full force against apparently unprepared Indian positions, overran them, continued rapidly on into India across the eastern section of the border (into what is now the state of Arunachal Pradesh), and then withdrew to their earlier positions. Thus, Nehru's plan for an unaligned bloc, to be led by India in close friendship with China, was finally destroyed, and the way was open for even closer ties with the USSR. In December 1961 India's remaining credit as a peacemaker was undermined with the occupation of the Portuguese enclaves of Goa, Daman and Diu (the last remaining colonial footholds in the country), when Nehru finally abandoned, under heavy internal pressure, the unpromising negotiations with Portugal to have these territories accede to India without force.

## INDIRA GANDHI'S RULE

### The First Period, 1966–77

Although in the last 18 months of his life Nehru was much criticized, there were serious concerns about what would happen after his death. In the event, in May 1964, the transition was smooth and the succession passed to Lal Bahadur Shastri, not the most able nor the closest to Nehru among the members of the outgoing Government, but something of a consensus figure. Shastri soon found himself faced with three national crises; first, over the proclamation of Hindi as the sole official language in January 1965, followed by the Rann of Kutch incident with Pakistan in April and, finally, the three-week war with Pakistan in September. His stature grew with this last event, in which India resisted Pakistan's efforts to seize Kashmir by force. He died, however, in January 1966, after going to Tashkent (Uzbekistan—then part of the USSR) to meet the Pakistani President, Ayub Khan, and the Soviet premier, Aleksei Kosygin. His successor was Nehru's daughter, Indira Gandhi, with the kingmaker, K. Kamaraj, in the background and the existing Congress team in office, except for Morarji Desai, who left because he would be Prime Minister or nothing.

In 1967 the general election ended the nearly general domination of Congress in the states, and returned it to power in Delhi with a much reduced majority. Indira Gandhi continued as Prime Minister, but was now strengthened by a deal with Morarji Desai who became deputy premier and Minister of Finance. In Madras state (subsequently renamed Tamil Nadu) the strongly regionalist Dravida Munnetra Kazhagam (DMK) took power, and in Kerala communist rule was restored. Anti-Congress ministries were set up in several other states, but proved so unstable that mid-term elections were held from Haryana to West Bengal. The chief beneficiaries of the Congress losses were the left-wing, pro-communist groups and the Jana Sangh.

The Congress managers had supported Indira Gandhi as another consensus figure, and had no intention of reducing their influence in her favour, or condoning any substantial change in the Congress programme. The election results of 1967, however, had shaken their credibility, and shown to many, including Indira Gandhi, that Congress needed a new image and revitalized organization if it was to remain in power. It was not in Indira Gandhi's personal style, either, to leave the initiative in the hands of others. The crisis was precipitated by the death of the respected President Zakir Husain in May 1969. The presidency possesses considerable reserve powers, which would have placed it in a key position in the event, as then seemed quite possible, of the next general election failing to give Congress an overall majority. The right wing adopted N. S. Reddy as the Congress candidate. Indira Gandhi retorted by implementing the long-standing Congress promise to nationalize the banks, by dismissing Desai from the finance ministry and by supporting the Vice-President, V. V. Giri, a left-wing Congress politician and labour leader, as an independent candidate for the presidency. His subsequent success in winning the post greatly strengthened her hand.

In November 1969 Congress openly split. Although in the legislature Indira Gandhi retained the support of a majority of the party's members, reflecting the support she commanded in the country as a whole, she was obliged to depend, in the first instance, on left-wing groups outside Congress to maintain a majority in the Lok Sabha (House of the People, the lower parliamentary chamber). In 1970 Congress success with communist allies in the Kerala elections encouraged the Prime Minister to dissolve the Lok Sabha. The elections of February–March 1971 proved a notable success, both for Indira Gandhi herself and for her wing of Congress, which was initially known as Congress (R). The success of the campaign *garibi hatao* (abolish poverty) showed the extent of the desire for social and economic change. Once again an effective opposition failed to emerge, largely because Congress (R) occupied the centre and left-of-centre ground ideologically and, by being in power, attracted recruits as the party of government. The rival Congress (O) was left with little positive policy; and the degree to which Indira Gandhi had commandeered the territory of the socialists was marked by their evident confusion about how to react to her.

Hard on the election results came a fresh crisis with Pakistan: its army's intervention in East Pakistan (now Bangladesh). India was faced with an immense refugee problem: about 7m. by August 1971, nearly all in West Bengal. First, India publicized the problem and asked for help. Next, it concluded in August a treaty with the USSR: 'non-alignment' was safeguarded, but the two countries promised mutual support, short of actual military involvement, in the event of either being attacked by a third. Finally, thus assured of non-interference, India first sheltered, then trained and armed, and finally gave support to Bangladeshi guerrilla forces along and across the border. These actions eventually resulted in open warfare between India and Pakistan. In December, after 11 days of fighting, India won a comprehensive victory in East Pakistan (eastern Bengal, independent under the name of Bangladesh), while maintaining its position in the west. In July 1972 Indira Gandhi and the President of Pakistan, Zulfikar Ali Bhutto, signed the Simla (later renamed Shimla) Agreement, in which both countries renounced the use of force and agreed to respect the cease-fire line in Kashmir and international borders elsewhere. They also agreed to discuss outstanding issues on a bilateral basis rather than taking them to international fora such as the UN.

Indira Gandhi's personal prestige domestically and abroad had been hugely enhanced by the victory over Pakistan, and was further strengthened by victories in state elections in 1972. With Congress ministries in almost all states, she was able to secure chief ministers who would carry out her policies. Nevertheless, discontent grew as India was severely affected by drought in 1973 and 1974, while the world-wide petroleum crisis pushed up inflation and lowered the standard of living among many sections of Indian society. Unrest developed in a number of states, while in Gujarat and Bihar the veteran socialist, Jayaprakash Narayan, headed popular campaigns against the local Congress governments, alleging corruption. During 1974 he sought allies more widely and began to attack the central Government. His coalition lacked ideological coherence, including, as it did, parties both to the right and left of Congress, but in June 1975, as the Janata Front, it won control of the state government in Gujarat.

Also in June 1975 the Allahabad High Court in Uttar Pradesh found Indira Gandhi guilty of electoral malpractices in her own constituency in the 1971 election (although most observers considered them to have been rather trivial). Indira Gandhi then proclaimed a state of emergency and arrested large numbers of her opponents. Parliament was recalled and, in the absence of non-Government members (other than the Communist Party of India), rapidly approved constitutional amendments to strengthen the executive and legislature, and to protect the Prime Minister through retrospective legislation.

The emergency saw some gains in administrative efficiency, an apparently successful attack on the 'black market' and some reduction in the predicted rate of inflation. Opponents were silenced where they were not imprisoned, news censorship was imposed and non-Congress state governments in Tamil Nadu and Gujarat were removed. In January 1977 Indira Gandhi unexpectedly announced that the general election, hitherto postponed, would be held in March, when the state of emergency would also be terminated. A number of its restrictions were immediately lifted. Three explanations for this manoeuvre seem plausible: that Indira Gandhi was misinformed about her popularity or, being informed, saw this as her last chance to gain a popular mandate; that she wished to allow the political advance of her second son, Sanjay, and members of his Youth Congress; and that, once again, she needed to outflank opponents within her own party, an idea supported by the resignation of Jagjivan Ram, a senior Congress leader, after the elections were announced.

### The Janata Interlude, 1977–80

Congress faced a large number of straight contests, as the opposition groups had either come together formally in the Janata Party or had entered into electoral agreements, as was the case with Jagjivan Ram's new Congress for Democracy. The results must rank among the most extraordinary in recent times. Indira Gandhi lost her own seat in the Lok Sabha and Congress was defeated throughout north India, winning no seats at all in areas where they had always seemed invincible. Indira Gandhi had alienated local political machines through her assertions of central power and her encouragement of Sanjay, the middle classes through the attacks on the courts, the press and freedom of expression, the farmers through the development tax, the workers through the freezing of wages and the ban on strike action, and the poor through real or imagined excesses in slum clearance and sterilization. However, in the south, Congress and its allies maintained or improved their position: there, emergency measures were less effective and fewer leaders were imprisoned, Jagjivan Ram was less well known and the Janata Party unimportant, the government-controlled radio was still the main source of outside information, and the major opposition party, Tamil Nadu's DMK, had been discredited by charges of corruption.

The first tasks for the Janata Government, under the leadership of Morarji Desai, were to dismantle the machinery of the state of emergency and to repair the Constitution. It had its successes. It transformed an electoral alliance into a ruling party, helped by the reluctant agreement of Jagjivan Ram and his supporters to merge with the majority. It secured its candidate, N. S. Reddy, as President in July 1977.

However, serious rifts soon appeared, especially between the Jana Sangh element in the party and the others: they widened or narrowed in tandem with Indira Gandhi's fortunes. Politically unsuccessful in 1978, strongly criticized by the Shah Commission on the state of emergency and even subject to criminal charges, Indira Gandhi none the less won a Lok Sabha by-election in the southern state of Karnataka in November 1978; by then her supporters had overall majorities in state assemblies in Karnataka and Andhra Pradesh, had formed a brief coalition in Maharashtra, and had become the major parliamentary opposition at the Centre. Over the same period, the Janata Government threatened to disintegrate. The party rallied a little in 1979, however, while Indira Gandhi's supporters were themselves broken into factions by her quarrels with Devaraj Urs, the architect of the Congress victory in Karnataka. At this point the Congress faction led by Indira Gandhi became known as Congress (I).

Gradually, however, the Janata Party's huge majority disappeared, and the withdrawal of communist and socialist support forced Morarji Desai's resignation in July 1979. President Reddy, in an unprecedented situation, first called on Y. B. Chavan, leader of the then official opposition, and later asked Charan Singh, former Minister of Finance and of Home Affairs in the Janata Government and now head of the Lok Dal, to form a government. Singh was dependent on the tacit support of Indira Gandhi, which was withdrawn as soon as he took office. Finally, ignoring the claims of Jagjivan Ram, who eventually succeeded Desai as Janata leader, the President dissolved Parliament in August. Elections to the Lok Sabha were held in January 1980.

### The Final Phase, 1980–84

Indira Gandhi won an overwhelming victory, though still without a majority of the total vote. Sanjay Gandhi entered the Lok Sabha for the first time. Sanjay had come to have the support of men and women of his own generation and, because of his influence on the selection of candidates, many were elected with him. He was, of course, himself influential by virtue of being the heir apparent and, when he met his death in an air crash in June 1980, this need continued to be felt. By 1981 some people spoke of the inevitable succession of his elder brother, Rajiv, and in June 1981 Rajiv won, by a large majority, Sanjay's former seat. In February 1983 he became General Secretary of the All-India Congress Committee.

Indira Gandhi's second term in office was overshadowed by the violent regional or religious separatism that was expressed in some communities, including those that had enjoyed economic advantages. In Assam and north-eastern India, feelings against Bengali residents, especially those who had migrated recently from Bangladesh, were expressed in murders, bomb outrages, strikes and a campaign of non-co-operation; in 1982 and 1983 many hundreds of lives were lost in this region. The most serious outbreaks of violence occurred, however, in the Punjab, where a militant Sikh secessionist movement had emerged, and had, it is widely believed, been encouraged by Congress (I) in order to outflank the moderate wing of its local opponents, the Shiromani Akali Dal, a Sikh-based political party which had held power between 1977 and 1980.

Certainly, Indira Gandhi succeeded in ousting the Shiromani Akali Dal from office in the Punjab, but with tragic consequences. At first her Government faced demands from a small minority for a separate Sikh state ('Khalistan') and, more generally, for a settlement of grievances about land and water rights, communal recognition and the state capital at Chandigarh, which was shared with Haryana. By 1984, however, there was a growing polarization of Hindus and Sikhs, advanced chiefly by the killing of hundreds of people by terrorists. Reluctant to act, the Government came under severe pressure from Hindus. With considerable financial resources and discipline, Sikh followers of the extremist leader, Jarnail Singh Bhindranwale, transformed the Golden Temple at Amritsar into a terrorist stronghold. Communal polarization was completed in June by the storming of the Temple complex by the Indian army, the death of Bhindranwale and hundreds of his supporters, damage to sacred buildings and an army blockade and curfew in the Punjab. Serious negotiations seemed to be impossible, and foreign as well as communal relations worsened, with officially supported claims of Pakistani involvement and criticism of British failure to silence Sikhs in exile. The climax came, without breaking the impasse: Indira Gandhi was assassinated in October 1984 by Sikh members of her personal guard. Her death was followed by riots, especially in Delhi, in which many hundreds of Sikhs were massacred.

## FROM INDIRA GANDHI TO NARASIMHA RAO

### Rajiv Gandhi's Succession

In contrast to her father, Indira Gandhi had centralized and personalized power, weakening the judiciary, Parliament and the party. Her attempts to control state as well as central politics had strained the Union and often brought no more than pyrrhic victories to her cause. The succession of her son, Rajiv, to lead the party and the Government—when he had so recently been regarded as unready for such responsibilities—was a comment not only on Indira Gandhi's dynastic ambitions but on her political legacy. The assassination, none the less, brought genuine feelings of outrage, especially among Hindus in north India, and a readiness to accept Rajiv as a true leader. His early command of events won respect, too, though also criticism of his failure to prevent the violence against Sikhs in the immediate aftermath of his mother's murder, and to eschew appeals to Hindu chauvinism during the campaigning for the Lok Sabha elections in December 1984. The results of the elections were an unprecedented triumph for Congress (I) in seats, and a solid gesture of support in terms of votes. National opposition was reduced to 44 seats among five parties out of the 508 seats contested. State elections in many areas in 1985 confirmed the strength of Rajiv Gandhi's position in most of the country.

The new Prime Minister's initial moves were conciliatory and progressive. He consulted with opposition leaders, promised to avoid interfering with the judiciary and embarked upon reforms to increase efficiency and reduce corruption. He soon became seen as representative of a new breed of technocrats, with an appeal to the younger generation. In particular, the 1985 budget, drawn up by the Minister of Finance, Vishwanath Pratap (V. P.) Singh, initiated a process of liberalization and restructuring which continues to the present and which, in some respects, marked the end of the Nehruvian approach to economic planning. Rajiv Gandhi also, in the face of opposition from some of his advisers, attempted to revitalize Congress (I) by promising internal party elections for the first time since the split of 1969.

In the short term, however, Rajiv Gandhi's most significant achievement was to reverse his mother's fiercely power-orientated centralizing approach and to talk seriously to the leaders of various regional movements. In August 1985 he signed an agreement in Assam limiting the voting rights of immigrants (mainly Bangladeshis), a move which led to the holding of state elections in December of the same year. These were won by the Asom Gana Parishad (AGP), which represented militant Assamese sentiment.

Rajiv Gandhi's new conciliatory approach achieved what appeared to be its greatest success in July 1985, when he came to an agreement with the principal leader of the Shiromani Akali Dal, Harchand Singh Longowal, under which fresh elections were to be held in the Punjab and some concessions were to be made to Sikh demands. The agreement seemed to have the potential to defuse separatist demands and bypass the militants. Although Longowal himself was assassinated by terrorists, the promised elections, which were held in September 1985, gave victory to the Shiromani Akali Dal, and its leader, S. S. Barnala, became Chief Minister.

In June 1986 Laldenga, the leader of the Mizo National Front (MNF), signed a peace agreement with Rajiv Gandhi, thus ending 25 years of rebellion. The accord granted Mizoram limited autonomy in the drafting of local laws, independent trade with neighbouring foreign countries and a general amnesty for all Mizo rebels. Laldenga led an interim coalition government, formed by the MNF and Congress (I), until February 1987, when the MNF won an absolute majority at elections to the state assembly. In the same month, Mizoram and Arunachal Pradesh were officially admitted as the 23rd and 24th states of India, respectively, and in May the Union Territory of Goa (without Daman and Diu) became India's 25th state.

From the beginning of 1986, however, it became apparent that the 'honeymoon' period was over, and gradually problems began to accumulate which eventually overwhelmed the still-inexperienced Prime Minister. It was, in fact, in the Punjab where the situation first began to show signs of deterioration. The agreement with Longowal had left a number of issues unresolved. Protracted negotiations led to an increase in Sikh extremism and encouraged a temporary recapture of the Golden Temple by Sikh militants in early 1986. Measures to combat violence by the police and paramilitary forces, who were often accused of brutality and arbitrary executions of suspects, jeopardized the standing of the popular state government, and the ruling Shiromani Akali Dal began to be plagued by internal dissent. At the same time, the proposed concessions to the Sikhs, which were regarded as inadequate in the Punjab, gave rise to a strong reaction elsewhere, especially in the neighbouring state of Haryana. State elections were due to be held in Haryana in mid-1987 and, in an attempt to improve Congress (I)'s chances, Rajiv Gandhi dismissed the Barnala Government in the Punjab in May of that year and introduced President's Rule (a constitutional provision that allowed the central government to dismiss state governments). However, not only did this move fail to prevent the defeat of Congress (I) in Haryana, it also ended any prospect of co-operation with moderate Sikhs in the Punjab. In addition, as Barnala had predicted, it also worsened the security situation, and in the late 1980s and into the early 1990s, thousands of people on all sides of the conflict died in the ensuing disturbances.

Other regional demands came to the fore in the late 1980s and created difficulties not only for Rajiv Gandhi's Government but also for state government leaders. In the hill areas of West Bengal in 1987, for example, a regional movement, led by the Gorkha (Gurkha) National Liberation Front under Subhas Ghising, emerged in Darjiling (Darjeeling) to demand a separate state for the Nepali speakers of the area. It was claimed by the communist state government of West Bengal that the regionalist agitation had been supported by Congress (I) in an attempt to destabilize it. At all events, an agreement was drawn up by the Minister of Home Affairs in July 1988, which attempted to reach a compromise. Under the agreement, a semi-autonomous Hill Development Council was established, which remained, however, within the framework of West Bengal. In Assam and other north-eastern states, there continued to be localized tribal insurgencies. In Tripura the Tripura National Volunteers were responsible for the deaths of several hundred people in the 1980s, but in August 1988 they were persuaded by the central Government to come to an agreement by which they ceased hostilities and abandoned their demands for a separate state in return for a number of specific concessions. In Assam the Bodo tribal group increased its pressure for an independent state in early 1989, but, again, a potentially explosive situation was defused by the opening up of peaceful negotiations between the separatists and government officials.

While the Punjab remained the most serious problem facing Rajiv Gandhi, he lost political momentum and credibility in other areas as well. Tension between rival castes and communities (particularly between Hindus and Muslims) grew, and there were several major outbreaks of violence. Within his own party, Rajiv Gandhi's leadership came increasingly into question, as he failed to reconcile the various factions. In 1987, following a number of major electoral set-backs for Congress (I) (e.g. in Kerala and Haryana), several ministers resigned, notably V. P. Singh, who had been moved from the Ministry of Finance to the Ministry of Defence, allegedly because of pressure from businessmen who resented his efforts to eradicate malpractice and tax evasion. In July Singh and some other senior figures were expelled from Congress (I) for 'anti-party activities' and in October established their own Jan Morcha (People's Front), advocating more radical social change. It was against this background that allegations of financial corruption in the upper echelons of Congress (I) began to be made, especially regarding the 'Bofors affair', in which large payments appeared to have been made to Indian agents by a Swedish company in connection with its sales of artillery to the Indian Government. Rajiv Gandhi's response to the mounting pressure was to fall back on the style of politics that had been identified with his mother. Several of her advisers, who had been moved aside, were brought back into favour and there was, again, a marked centralization of party authority. A more confrontational style appeared to be adopted by the central administration towards non-Congress (I) state governments.

After the death in December 1987 of the popular Chief Minister of Tamil Nadu, M. G. Ramachandran, Congress (I) attempted to take advantage of a rift within his party, the All-India Anna Dravida Munnetra Kazhagam (AIADMK) to re-establish itself as a political force in the state. President's Rule was imposed in January 1988 and AIADMK activists were arrested.

The opposition parties responded by seeking a common position from which to resist Congress (I). A new anti-Government alliance was formed at the end of 1987 and was strengthened in mid-1988 with the creation of the National Front (Rashtriya Morcha): a coalition of the four major centrist parties (the Indian National Congress—S, the Jan Morcha, the Janata Party and the Lok Dal—A) and three major regional parties (the Asom Gana Parishad, the DMK and Andhra Pradesh's Telugu Desam). In October the Jan Morcha, Janata Party and Lok Dal merged to form the Janata Dal (People's Party), which was to work in collaboration with the National Front. V. P. Singh, who in July had achieved a major parliamentary by-election victory in the Gandhi home territory of Allahabad, was elected President of the Janata Dal. Further opposition to Rajiv Gandhi's Government was incited by serious drought and social conflict that occurred in a number of different areas of the country.

In January 1989 Congress (I) was decisively defeated by the DMK in the elections to the state assembly in Tamil Nadu, following the period of presidential rule, but gained outright majorities over the regional parties in elections in the less significant states of Nagaland and Mizoram, where local factors operated. During the remainder of 1989 both Congress (I) and the opposition fronts clearly began to prepare for the general election that was due to be held by the end of the year. While the opposition continued its campaign against alleged government corruption and inefficiency, it had difficulty in overcoming its own very marked internal quarrels. Apart from doing its utmost to exploit the internecine differences within the opposition, Congress (I) took steps to increase its popularity and political control. For example, in mid-1989 the Government proposed to consolidate the Panchayat Raj scheme (see Directory—The Constitution) so as to standardize and democratize local government on the basis of more regular elections and to strengthen its link with district-level planning.

As 1989 progressed, however, the political calculations of all the parties were affected by a continuing increase in Hindu militancy, orchestrated by the so-called Sangh Parivar, a grouping of organizations headed by the Rashtriya Swayamsevak Sangh (RSS—National Volunteer Organization). The RSS originated prior to 1947, when it articulated communal Hindu unease with Congress policies. It was, indeed, banned in the early years of independence. Operating through organizations such as the Vishwa Hindu Parishad (VHP—World Hindu Council), and closely associated first with the Jana Sangh and then with the Bharatiya Janata Party (BJP—Indian People's Party), which had replaced the Jana Sangh in 1980, it had begun to make an impact in the early 1980s by exploiting citizens' uncertainties about their place in a rapidly changing environment, both in India and world-wide. Indira Gandhi had herself understood this sentiment and had taken advantage of it in her Punjab strategy. An episode in 1986, when for short-term political reasons Rajiv Gandhi's Government had introduced special legislation restricting the rights of divorced Muslim women, gave the RSS and its allies new opportunities. In 1984 a campaign was launched over the status of a disputed religious site in the town of Ayodhya in northern India. It was claimed that a disused 16th-century mosque (the Babri Masjid) stood on the site of the birthplace of the god Ram (Ram Janambhoomi) and that an ancient Hindu temple had been demolished to allow its construction. During 1989 those who advocated the building of a new temple on the site, including the BJP, organized a high-profile foundation ceremony at Ayodhya. Congress (I) was faced with the dilemma as to which attitude to adopt. In the end, it chose to appear accommodating towards the temple protagonists, thus, in effect, losing Muslim support while failing to curtail the BJP's strength. The Janata Dal, although it had an electoral understanding with the BJP, maintained a broadly secular posture.

### The 1989 Elections and Coalition Government

Finally, Rajiv Gandhi called the general election a few weeks ahead of schedule and polling took place on 22–26 November 1989 for 525 of the 545 seats in the Lok Sabha, as well as for assemblies in a number of states. Assam did not take part in the elections, owing to tribal unrest and to the incomplete state of the electoral rolls. Congress (I) had clearly been damaged by the corruption charges and by the public perception that it had reverted to the patterns of the Indira Gandhi period, and won only 193 seats, which constituted a massive decline compared with its result in the general election of 1984. The party also lost control of the large northern states of Uttar Pradesh and Bihar in the concurrent state assembly elections. The Janata Dal won 141 seats in the Lok Sabha. The BJP had been the main beneficiary of the recent surge in Hindu communal feeling and was able to secure 88 seats, mainly in the Hindi-speaking areas of northern and central India. The Communist Party of India—Marxist (CPI—M, which is well established in West Bengal and Tripura but enjoys only limited support elsewhere), together with the Communist Party of India, won 51 seats. Once all the votes had been counted, the balance of forces was such that almost any combination of parties was theoretically possible, but, in the end, the National Front was able to form a minority Government with support from both the BJP and the communist parties. V. P. Singh was elected leader of the Janata Dal parliamentary party and thus became Prime Minister in early December, but only after performing complex and calculating manoeuvres to outflank his rival, Chandra Shekhar. To maintain a political balance, V. P. Singh appointed Devi Lal, the populist Chief Minister of Haryana, as Deputy Prime Minister.

Domestic events in India during V. P. Singh's period in office were dominated by a series of interrelated crises, which eventually overwhelmed the National Front Government, while confirming the new agenda of Indian politics. Factional conflict within the Government led eventually to Devi Lal's dismissal. Partly to counter Devi Lal and partly in an attempt to increase and strengthen his longer-term support, V. P. Singh made the dramatic announcement in 1990 that his Government planned to implement the recommendations of the Mandal Commission. This had been established by the Morarji Desai Government in the late 1970s to consider how best to improve the welfare of the more deprived sections of society. It was, in particular, concerned with the so-called 'other backward classes' (OBCs), who had not been eligible at the national level for the range of benefits in education and employment that had been given after independence to the former untouchables (Harijans) or 'Scheduled Castes'. The OBCs had become increasingly powerful in political terms, as they utilized their electoral strength. The Commission had proposed, in the absence of any better criterion, that jobs and other benefits within the central government sector should be allocated on the basis of caste. This recommendation, in fact, only reflected what was already being practised at state government level in much of the country, but was regarded, nevertheless, as a symbolic attack on the position of the urban middle class, which is drawn disproportionately from the upper castes. V. P. Singh's announcement provoked widespread unrest in northern Indian cities, and by early October 1990 about 40 students had, as a form of protest, committed suicide by self-immolation. Thereafter, attention shifted to the renewed BJP campaign over the disputed religious site at Ayodhya. The campaign, at a time of political uncertainty, was designed to publicize the BJP's *Hindutva* (Hinduness) slogan and its claim that it represented the interests of India's majority. The means employed to convey this message was a *rath yatra* (procession) across India to Ayodhya led by L. K. Advani, the BJP President. The procession itself was halted by government action before it reached Ayodhya, but there was a major confrontation between security forces and demonstrators at the disputed shrine on 30 October, and a number of people were killed. Many arrests were made elsewhere, in an attempt to contain the disturbances. As a consequence of the confrontation, there were riots in many northern Indian cities, in which Muslims were the principal victims.

It was against this highly charged background that the BJP withdrew its support for the National Front Government.

Following a series of complicated political manoeuvres behind the scenes and the defeat of V. P. Singh in a vote of 'no confidence', a new Government was formed in November 1990 by Chandra Shekhar, the erstwhile President of the Janata Dal, who had defected from the party with a small group of supporters to form the Janata Dal (S) (which merged with the Janata Party in April 1991 to become the Samajwadi Party). The new Government was totally dependent, however, on the support of Congress (I). This was withdrawn in March 1991, and consequently there was no alternative other than to hold fresh elections, which were scheduled to take place over three days in late May. Unlike the situation in 1989, there was no co-operation on a nation-wide scale between the various political parties, except between the Janata Dal and the communist parties. Congress (I), the BJP and the Janata Dal each sought to exploit its particular appeal, on the basis of stability and experience, *Hindutva* and caste-based social justice, respectively, while other parties, particularly the Samajwadi Party, tried to strengthen their position in particular states.

As the elections approached, it seemed likely that no party would win an outright majority, and that the political stalemate would continue. On 21 May 1991, however, after the first day's polling had taken place, Rajiv Gandhi was assassinated while campaigning in the southern state of Tamil Nadu. The assassination was almost certainly carried out by members of the Liberation Tigers of Tamil Eelam (LTTE), which had suffered most as a result of India's intervention in Sri Lanka in 1987–90 (see below). The remaining elections were postponed while the funeral of the former Prime Minister took place, and were held in mid-June. The final results gave Congress (I) 227 of the 511 seats contested (its ally, the AIADMK, also regained control of Tamil Nadu with a convincing majority). This was a significant increase on the predicted figure and undoubtedly represented the effect of a 'sympathy wave'. More remarkable, however, was the success of the BJP, which increased its number of seats in the Lok Sabha from 88 to 119 and almost doubled its share of the vote.

The death of Rajiv Gandhi had left his party without any immediately obvious successor. In the end, P. V. Narasimha Rao, a long-standing Gandhi family loyalist who, at the same time, enjoyed wide respect within Congress (which was gradually shedding its 'I' suffix), was chosen as interim party President and assumed the premiership. Narasimha Rao's Council of Ministers represented a careful balance between existing factions and groups within Congress. In the early weeks of Narasimha Rao's Government, which lacked a majority in the Lok Sabha, it became clear that the other parties did not want yet another political upheaval and were prepared to allow the new Government, initially at least, an easy passage. With the exception of the BJP, the main parties abstained on a vote of confidence in July 1991, and the choice of Speaker was reached by consensus. At around the same time, the Congress candidate, Dr Shankar Dayal Sharma, was elected, without any serious opposition, to the country's presidency.

## INDIA IN TRANSITION

### The Narasimha Rao Government

While it was clear from the beginning of his premiership that Narasimha Rao would need to utilize all his political skills to face the multifarious challenges of Hindu nationalism, lower-caste unrest and regional autonomist movements, he used the initial 'honeymoon' period of office to inaugurate a new and much more far-reaching phase of economic restructuring than any previously undertaken. The economy in 1991 was in a parlous state, and simultaneous foreign-exchange and fiscal crises meant that the country was on the verge of bankruptcy. In a bold move, Narasimha Rao appointed an economist and former Governor of the Reserve Bank of India, Dr Manmohan Singh, to the post of Minister of Finance. Dr Singh immediately carried out a number of emergency measures, including a substantial devaluation of the rupee and stringent curbs on imports. At the same time, help was sought from the IMF, and gradually the economic situation stabilized. It was widely felt that, in the longer term, a new departure in economic policy was necessary, and this was implemented in the July 1991 and February 1992 budgets. During this period, almost the whole of the apparatus of economic regulation was dismantled, the rupee was made partially convertible, the banking system overhauled and foreign investment encouraged. Some of these measures were unpopular with the opposition and with certain sections of Congress, and progress in some areas was impeded; for example, the removal of subsidies on fertilizer directly affected many farmers and therefore had to be modified. The rapid removal of controls also created the climate for a massive bank fraud in May 1992 linked to stock-exchange speculation. The most prominent figure in these events, Harshad Mehta, was arrested, but the ramifications were much wider and led, among other things, to the resignation of the Minister of Commerce. Nevertheless, the rapidly expanding Indian middle class responded favourably to the new policies, and among left-wing circles it was also accepted that some of the new economic initiatives were long overdue.

The generally positive news on the economic front, however, was overshadowed by the return, with redoubled strength, of the Ayodhya question. The BJP had been buoyed by its success in the 1991 elections, and had also to satisfy the expectations of its many supporters who thought that the mosque would now be demolished and a temple constructed. In January 1992 an attempt on the part of the BJP to exploit the Kashmir issue (see below) went awry, but by the middle of the year it had begun to set deadlines for work to begin on the temple, and was able to use its control of the state government in Uttar Pradesh to good effect. Narasimha Rao's response was cautious and aimed at exhausting the BJP through discussion and legal manoeuvre. In November, however, the BJP launched yet another mass campaign. This culminated on 6 December with the demolition of the mosque at Ayodhya and the creation of a makeshift temple on the site. Claims and counterclaims were immediately made about who was responsible for these events. It was clear that neither the central Government nor the state government had been able to take the necessary swift action that might have averted the demolition, but whether this reflected incompetence or deliberate intent is unclear. Whatever the position adopted by the party leaders, the demolition of the mosque was clearly regarded as a great victory by many of the BJP's supporters. One consequence was an outbreak of rioting in many cities in which hundreds of lives (the majority Muslim) were lost. The worst-affected city was Mumbai (then still known as Bombay), and in January 1993 renewed violence broke out there, resulting in more than 500 deaths, again mainly Muslim. On 12 March there were a number of bomb explosions in Mumbai, which caused about 250 casualties. The Government claimed that these last incidents were linked to Pakistani intelligence agencies.

The Government's immediate response to the demolition of the mosque was to arrest the senior leadership of the BJP (although they were later released), ban the RSS and dismiss the BJP state governments in Uttar Pradesh and three other states. It was also announced that the mosque would be rebuilt. This did not in fact happen and much of the rest of 1993 appeared to be characterized by political drift. In July a vote of 'no confidence' was moved in the Lok Sabha by virtually all the opposition parties; Narasimha Rao survived by a narrow margin of 14 votes, composed, for the most part, of defectors from another party who had been attracted by promises of reward. However, in the polls that were held in November in the states where the BJP governments had been dismissed, the BJP advance was very clearly halted. In Uttar Pradesh the BJP lost control, not to Congress, whose credibility had been unable to recover from the events at Ayodhya, but to a coalition of parties representing the interests of the OBCs, the Scheduled Castes and Muslims. In the remaining three states, the BJP held one and lost two to Congress; it also gained control of the newly established legislative assembly in the capital, Delhi. With hindsight, it appeared to many observers that the Prime Minister had followed a successful strategy of defusing confrontation, although some critics argued that his actions had given the BJP added respectability.

The following year, 1994, was again a period of consolidation. The economic reforms were allowed to stand, and continued to show results, but there were few fresh initiatives and the Government went out of its way to emphasize its commitment to social welfare. Rao's administration was, however, vulnerable to opposition charges that it was too willing to accept external interference in economic management. This issue came to a head in the early part of the year with the launch by the opposition of a campaign against India signing the new General Agreement of Tariffs and Trade (GATT) accord, the so-called Dunkel draft. Other areas where the Congress Government was challenged included the question of corruption. In July and August there was a three-week boycott of Parliament by the opposition over what it regarded as lack of effective action following a parliamentary inquiry into the 1992 bank scandal (see above) in order to downplay the involvement of Congress ministers.

Numerous state elections were held in two rounds in late 1994 and early 1995. These seemed to indicate that the political manoeuvring that had maintained the Prime Minister in power and had avoided renewed confrontation with the forces of Hindu nationalism had not succeeded in recruiting new support for Congress. Ten states went to the polls, six of which were among the largest in the country. Of these six, Congress succeeded only in winning in Orissa, where it defeated a fading Janata Dal Government. In the other states regional parties won in some and the BJP and its allies in others, notably in Maharashta where the BJP and the extremist and fiercely anti-Muslim Shiv Sena formed a coalition Government.

A direct consequence of the defeats suffered in the first set of state elections was the emergence in late 1994 of a personal challenge to the Prime Minister from within the ruling party. Arjun Singh, who had been closely associated with Indira Gandhi claimed that the new strategies of economic liberalization were harming the poor, and that Narasimha Rao had been too accommodating to the *Hindutva* forces. Arjun Singh resigned from the Council of Ministers in late December and subsequently from Congress, and in conjunction with N. D. Tewari, a former Congress Chief Minister of Uttar Pradesh, he eventually forced a formal split in the party in May 1995. The newly established All India Indira Congress (Tewari) was able to recruit dissident members of Congress in many states, but Singh himself was not an uncontroversial figure and consequently his appeal was limited.

As the 1996 elections approached, each party began to establish its agenda. Each had to balance an appeal to the electorate in terms of social justice and greater welfare for all with an awareness of the requirements of the new economic policies. Congress was able to accentuate the significant results that the new economic programmes were beginning to deliver, while claiming to remain a party that cared for the poor. Low inflation rates and good harvests seemed to favour its cause. The BJP emphasized that economic development could be achieved without allowing indiscriminate entry to foreign capital. It was able to dramatize this belief through its involvement in the struggle over the Dabhol power project, which constituted the first major foreign investment in India's electricity sector. When the BJP came to power in Maharashtra in 1995, almost its first action had been to cancel the project (although it was later renegotiated). This controversial move bolstered the party's image at the local level but may have lost it credibility in some quarters. The BJP continued to project itself as a strongly nationalist party, although with less stress on the Hindu component of national identity. The parties on the left and centre offered variations on the themes of social and economic justice, although the force of the job reservation issue diminished as the other main parties adopted versions of the same policy. At the same time, regional issues and demands for increased powers for state governments began to assume greater significance. Wherever a party was in power, either at the national or at the state level, it introduced welfare programmes, for example the provision of subsidized meals, which were designed to benefit as many of the electorate as possible. In several states opposition parties made the introduction of prohibition (of alcohol) a major electoral issue.

Despite the efforts of the parties to establish distinct identities in terms of policy, the more important questions revolved around image and personality. In January 1996 Prime Minister Rao attempted a bold gamble to outflank his rivals inside Congress and to discredit the opposition. He did this by allowing the disclosure of the names (often identified only by initials) in a diary kept by a Delhi-based industrialist and political intermediary, Surendra K. Jain. These names appeared to be connected to payments of large amounts of money for political favours. While a number of Congress ministers were listed, so too were opposition leaders, including L. K. Advani of the BJP and prominent Janata Dal figures. The Prime Minister's own name was subsequently implicated in the so-called Hawala (illegal money transfer) scandal, but he was also by then faced with more serious and potentially more damaging difficulties concerning the prosecution, on charges of cheating and criminal conspiracy, of a flamboyant faith healer and 'godman', Chandraswami, who had been consulted by generations of political leaders, including Rao himself.

### The 1996 Elections and the United Front Government

As the 1996 elections approached, political alliances emerged and solidified. The BJP campaigned alongside the Shiv Sena, and arrived at understandings with the Shiromani Akali Dal in the Punjab and two smaller local parties. Congress was faced with the choice of which of the two major regional parties to ally itself with in Tamil Nadu; its decision to support the AIADMK, the ruling party, the leader of which, the former film actress, Jayalalitha Jayaram, had alienated many groups in the state, proved to be a serious error of judgement, both in terms of popular support and because it impelled a number of important local members of Congress to leave and establish a rival party, the Tamil Maanila Congress. The Janata Dal and its allies continued to work together as the National Front, and had an electoral understanding with the Left Front, which represented the two major communist parties.

The general election itself, which was held over three days at the end of April and early May 1996, was relatively muted, largely owing to the Election Commission's stringent enforcement of limits on expenditure, although the turn-out was no lower than in the past. The results, as had been widely predicted, gave no party or group an overall majority. The largest party in terms of seats was the BJP, which won 160 seats, and with the support of the Shiv Sena and other smaller allies could count on an overall legislative strength of 194 seats. Congress gained 136 seats. Neither the BJP nor Congress, however, performed as well or as badly, respectively, as certain observers had predicted. The National Front and the Left Front together obtained 179 seats, with the remainder won by minor parties and independents. State elections held concurrently in a number of states generally confirmed the national trend. Congress lost power in the states of Assam, Haryana and Kerala, while the AIADMK was defeated in Tamil Nadu. In West Bengal the Left Front, which had ruled the state since 1977, was again returned to power, but with a reduced majority. On 15 May 1996, as soon as the electoral position was clear, the President asked the BJP under its new parliamentary leader, Atal Bihari Vajpayee, to form the new Government and to prove its majority within two weeks. Given the antagonism felt towards the BJP by the majority of other political parties, this proved impossible, and Vajpayee resigned on 28 May in anticipation of his Government's inevitable defeat in a parliamentary vote of confidence. In the mean time, the National and Left Fronts had merged to form an informal coalition known as the United Front (UF), which comprised a total of 13 parties, with the Janata Dal, the Samajwadi Party, the two communist parties and the regional DMK and Telugu Desam as its major components. With Congress prepared to lend external support, the UF was able to form a Government at the end of May. With no overwhelmingly powerful individual leader within the UF, several names had been put forward to head the coalition and therefore to assume the premiership. Eventually H. D. Deve Gowda was selected to lead the UF and the new Government. Although with only limited experience at national level, Deve Gowda had formerly held the position of Chief Minister of the state of Karnataka and was widely identified as a pragmatic political figure with an interest in further economic change and development. To hold the key finance portfolio the new Prime Minister chose Palaniappan Chidambaram, who had been Minister of State for Commerce under Narasimha Rao and a committed liberalizer. The other major portfolios were distributed on political grounds. The home affairs ministry was assigned to Indrajit Gupta, a member of the Communist Party of India, while a well-respected politician, diplomat and intellectual, Inder Kumar Gujral, who was affiliated with the Janata Dal, was appointed Minister of External Affairs.

On assuming power, the UF drew up a 'common minimum programme', which committed it to a combination of pragmatic economic reform and anti-poverty policies. An early effort by P. Chidambaram to raise the prices of petroleum products achieved only partial success in the face of opposition not only from the BJP but also from the Minister's own supporters and allies. Other early signals of potential problems were: the expulsion from the Janata Dal of another Karnataka politician and erstwhile aspirant for the prime ministership, Ramakrishna Hegde; the ongoing conflict between the two UF-ruled states of Karnataka and Tamil Nadu over the allocation of water resources; and a major corruption inquiry in Bihar, a bastion of UF support.

In September 1996 Narasimha Rao resigned from the leadership of Congress after he was ordered to stand trial for his alleged involvement in the Chandraswami case; the party presidency was assumed, on an acting basis, by the veteran politician, Sitaram Kesri. Later that month separate charges of forgery and criminal conspiracy (dating back to the former Prime Minister's tenure of the external affairs ministry in the 1980s) were made against the beleaguered Rao (the cases led eventually to guilty verdicts and a jail sentence in 2000, but an appeal led to the judgment being overturned and Rao never went to prison—he died in December 2004). Kesri moved quickly to establish his position. He succeeded in bringing back many former dissidents, such as Arjun Singh and Congress (Tewari), into the ranks of Congress and he also benefited, at least in the short term, from the decision by Sonia Gandhi, Rajiv's widow, to join the party in March 1997. While Narasimha Rao had established an understanding with Deve Gowda, this was not shared by Kesri, and strains soon began to develop between the opposition and the ruling power. In March 1997 Kesri finally launched his attack by threatening to withdraw Congress's support for the Government unless Deve Gowda resigned as Prime Minister. Although in some respects this threat might have been a bluff, since Congress would not necessarily have won any subsequent election, it nevertheless achieved its goal by forcing Deve Gowda's resignation in mid-April (following his defeat in a parliamentary vote of confidence). After considerable uncertainty, Inder Kumar Gujral, who had enjoyed a number of successes as Minister of External Affairs, was selected to be the new Prime Minister. While Gujral had a considerable reputation as an intellectual, his major problem was lack of any substantial political base outside Delhi; this meant that he would always be required to balance carefully the divergent elements in his coalition. The price of Congress support for the UF administration was regular consultation by the latter with Kesri and the playing down of inquiries that had been launched into Congress finances. More generally, the political climate made it very difficult for the Government to advance its economic programme, and important but potentially problematic decisions over matters such as domestic petroleum prices and the future of the insurance sector were postponed or evaded.

While the UF Government had managed to survive the resignation of Deve Gowda, it was confronted with other major problems that dominated the political scene for the rest of 1997, as every political party and individual leader manoeuvred for power and influence. Chief among these was the forced resignation in July followed by the arrest of Lalu Prasad Yadav, the Chief Minister of Bihar and President of the Janata Dal. The reason for these events was an allegation that Yadav had been involved in a major corruption scandal based on the supply of fodder for non-existent animals. Despite his resignation, Yadav continued to dominate the politics of his home state by contriving that his wife be appointed as Chief Minister in his place, and by forming a breakaway faction of his party, known as the Rashtriya Janata Dal (RJD). The RJD proceeded to play a prominent role in the national coalition, despite reservations being expressed by some other members, especially among the left-wing parties. Towards the end of the year Congress finally withdrew its support for the UF Government over issues concerning an inquiry into Rajiv Gandhi's assassination, and Prime Minister Gujral was consequently forced to resign on 28 November. This constituted the third government collapse in less than two years. In early December the President dissolved the Lok Sabha following the inability of both Congress and the BJP to form an alternative coalition government. It was announced that Gujral would retain the premiership in an acting capacity pending the holding of a fresh general election in February–March 1998.

One consequence of the series of high-level corruption cases was the increased sensitivity of positions such as the Director of the Central Bureau of Investigation. Joginder Singh, who had overseen some of the most important cases and had gained a reputation as an independent if controversial figure, was moved from this post in June 1997, allegedly as a result of political pressure exerted on the Prime Minister from various quarters, including Congress. A lively debate also developed over the question of whether the appointment of senior judges should be made by the Government or by the Chief Justice. The President, however, continued to be regarded as above the political fray, and, as so often in the past, was widely seen as a key figure in maintaining Indian political stability. In July 1997 the widely respected Kocheril Raman Narayanan was elected President almost unanimously by members of both Houses of Parliament and the state assemblies. Narayanan was notable both for his distinguished diplomatic career and for being the first President of India to come from a Scheduled Caste (or 'untouchable') background.

### The 1998 and 1999 Elections and the BJP in Power

Three main groupings contested the 1998 elections: the UF, Congress, and the BJP in alliance with a number of small local parties (most significantly the AIADMK in Tamil Nadu). The campaign, as in 1996, was relatively low-key, with all parties aiming to minimize areas of conflict and emphasize their commitment both to further economic liberalization and to programmes of social investment. There occurred, however, a series of fatal bomb explosions in Tamil Nadu, allegedly perpetrated by Islamist militants. The results gave each of the groupings some strength, but none of them achieved an overall majority. Congress won 142 seats in the Lok Sabha, which represented a mediocre but not disastrous performance. While the party's role in bringing down the UF Government was held against it, Congress's fortunes were helped considerably by Sonia Gandhi's decision to campaign actively for the first time (shortly after the elections she replaced Sitaram Kesri as the party's President). The various components of the UF enjoyed mixed results, depending on the strength of their respective regional bases and on the appeal of their leaders. While the Janata Dal performed badly, other elements of the grouping, for example the Telugu Desam in Andhra Pradesh and the CPI (M) in West Bengal, retained all or most of their strength. The biggest gainer overall, however, was the BJP, which increased its tally of legislative seats from 160 to 182. With the support of its pre-election allies, especially the AIADMK, which won 18 of the seats in Tamil Nadu, the BJP could count on approximately 250 seats, the largest bloc in the legislature but considerably fewer than the 273 seats needed to form a government. Although the constitutional position was not entirely clear, the President decided to ask Vajpayee as leader of the BJP to form a government, and the latter assumed the premiership on 19 March. As in 1996, Vajpayee was given two weeks to garner sufficient support to win a parliamentary vote of confidence. This he did (by 274 votes to 261) on 28 March, principally on the basis of the support of the Telugu Desam, which eventually left the UF. Nevertheless, it was clear from the very outset that Vajpayee's Government had only a tenuous hold on power, and that the Prime Minister would need to exercise both tact and skill to retain his position. Within his own party he would have to face pressure for demonstrative action to fulfil the Hindu nationalist agenda of the more extremist members, while many of the Prime Minister's allies had very specific demands which they insisted be met. Although the partners in the coalition Government produced a National Agenda for Governance to guide their actions, it was clear that government matters would not always proceed smoothly.

After a seemingly lacklustre few weeks in power, the new Government startled India and the rest of the world by exploding a series of underground nuclear test devices on 11 and 13 May 1998 (see below). This provocative action was initially greeted with huge popular enthusiasm, but Pakistan's tests in response, and an awareness of the negative international consequences (particularly the imposition of economic sanctions by the USA) soon led to a more measured domestic assessment. The budget, which was introduced in June by the Minister of Finance, Yashwant Sinha (an experienced former bureaucrat as well as BJP politician), was widely considered to be uninspired, and the almost immediate decision to rescind some of the measures, notably an increase in petrol prices, further eroded the Government's image. In early July, in the face of strong opposition from various groups, the Government was forced to defer a parliamentary bill proposing the reservation of one-third of seats in the Lok Sabha and in state legislatures for women (male deputies subsequently continued to prevent the introduction of the Women's Reservation Bill).

Shortly after its accession to power, the demands of the smaller parties in the governing coalition created problems for the BJP. The most difficult partner was the AIADMK, the leader of which, Jayalalitha, faced ongoing investigations into corruption allegations relating to her earlier period as Chief Minister of Tamil Nadu. In the mean time, however, Congress, which was by now firmly under the control of Sonia Gandhi and her immediate colleagues, began to explore ways of destabilizing the Government by exploiting its internal divisions. In late November Congress performed well in state elections in Rajasthan, Delhi and Madhya Pradesh, defeating incumbent BJP Governments in the first two. The dilemma facing Congress, however, was how to engineer the downfall of the BJP coalition in such a way as to enhance rather than damage its own position with the electorate. In April 1999 Sonia Gandhi thought that an opportune moment had arrived, and, with the help of the AIADMK, which withdrew from the ruling coalition (allegedly in protest at the earlier dismissal of the Chief of Staff of the Navy), was able to create a political stalemate, which the President resolved by forcing the Prime Minister to seek a vote of confidence. This was held on 17 April and resulted in the Government's defeat, although by the margin of only a single vote. The President then gave Sonia Gandhi the opportunity to assemble a new coalition. Her political skills were unequal to the task, however; putting together a coalition for the purpose of ousting a common enemy was very different from sharing the fruits of office among many different partners, as the BJP had earlier found to its cost. On 27 April, therefore, the Lok Sabha was dissolved, and fresh elections were called. Vajpayee and his Government remained in power in an acting capacity pending the holding of the polls.

Immediately after the elections were called, it was difficult to see exactly who or which party was likely to be the main beneficiary. Indeed, all political groups suffered to some extent from popular annoyance at the failure of the Vajpayee administration to survive. Sonia Gandhi had staked her reputation on being able to form a new government and her failure to do so damaged her standing both within the ranks of Congress as well as at a national level. Her foreign origins were used against her, and in May 1999 Sharad Pawar, the leader of Congress in the Lok Sabha until its dissolution and the most powerful of the old-guard party heads, was expelled from Congress for voicing public criticism on this point. The following month Pawar announced the establishment of a new party, the Nationalist Congress Party. Among the non-Congress parties apart from the BJP, new alliances emerged but without the capacity to dominate national politics. All the opposition parties tried to capitalize on the anti-incumbency factor and on economic issues such as the soaring prices of basic commodities (notably onions, India's most basic staple after rice and wheat).

While the BJP seemed less well placed immediately after the dissolution of the Lok Sabha in April 1999, the subsequent hostilities with Pakistan (see below) had a very positive effect on the nationalist party's standing and in particular on that of the Prime Minister. The widely held perception that Vajpayee had responded with dignity and firmness to Pakistani provocation, and that India had, in effect, won the war had a major impact on public opinion.

In the general election, which was staggered over five weekends during September and early October 1999, the 24-member BJP-led alliance, known as the National Democratic Alliance (NDA) and comprising numerous minor regional parties with little shared ideology, won an outright majority in the Lok Sabha, with 299 of the 545 seats, while Congress and its allies obtained 134 seats. Although Sonia Gandhi won both of the seats that she contested herself in Karnataka and Uttar Pradesh, her lack of political experience, her relatively weak grasp of Hindi and her foreign birth all contributed to Congress's worst electoral defeat since independence. Vajpayee was sworn in as Prime Minister for a third time, at the head of a large coalition Government, on 13 October.

State elections, both those that coincided with the general election and those held in February 2000, demonstrated that, while the BJP was still the most successful political party in the country, it was far from unchallenged. In Maharashtra, which includes Mumbai, the BJP-Shiv Sena coalition was replaced in October 1999 by a Congress-led partnership with the Nationalist Congress Party. In February 2000 the BJP was successfully challenged in Bihar, where Lalu Prasad Yadav's RJD suffered defeat in the general election, but performed unexpectedly well at the expense of the BJP in the February state elections, and after a few weeks formed a coalition with the support of Congress. By contrast, in Haryana the BJP and its allies retained power, and in Orissa they ousted the Congress Government. In addition to these electoral problems, the Prime Minister faced difficulties in managing the NDA coalition partners. In July 2000 events surrounding attempts to arrest and prosecute the founder of the Shiv Sena, Balashaheb (Bal) Thackeray, in connection with the riots of 1992–93, led to the resignation of Ram Jethmalani, the Minister of Law, Justice and Company Affairs. Even within the BJP there were critics who felt that Vajpayee was moving away from his party's core values. Claims that he was neglecting the demands of the RSS for greater stress on Hindu nationalism were reinforced in March 2000 when he conceded to pressure from Congress and some of the BJP allies to force the Government of Gujarat to rescind its decision to remove the ban on civil servants becoming members of the RSS.

It was against this political background that Vajpayee and his colleagues had to struggle to implement their policies. Continued moves to restructure the economy provoked resistance from those who would be disadvantaged by the changes and, as in the past, measures announced in the budget had to be withdrawn. Large-scale projects such as the Sardar Sarovar dam on the Narmada River in Gujarat, seen as integral to economic development, encountered resistance from environmentalist activists representing the many thousands of people who would be displaced. Pledges made during election campaigns to create new states for various ethnic groups were not easy to implement. In May 2000, however, the Government introduced legislation to establish the states of Chhattisgarh, Jharkhand and Uttaranchal, and amended versions were finally passed by the Lok Sabha and Rajya Sabha in August. Meanwhile, natural disasters severely tested all levels of government. In October 1999, for example, shortly after the elections, a major cyclone ravaged the Congress-held state of Orissa and killed at least 10,000 people. The drought in Andhra Pradesh, Gujarat and Rajasthan in 2000 was another large-scale tragedy emphasizing the magnitude of the task facing all authorities. Worst of all, in January 2001 a devastating earthquake occurred in Gujarat, the epicentre being near the western town of Bhuj. It severely affected the surrounding area of Kachch (Kutch) and caused serious damage as far away as Ahmedabad. More than 30,000 were killed and over 1m. were made homeless.

In 2001 the problems facing the NDA coalition further increased. A scandal involving senior government officials over bribe-taking for a defence contract, exposed by an internet news service, tehelka.com, in March, demonstrated the extent of corruption in the senior ranks of the Government. The President of the BJP, Bangaru Laxman, resigned. The Minister of Defence, George Fernandes, also resigned (but was reinstated in October); he was implicated by association after evidence showed the President of his Samata Party, Jaya Jaitley, accepting bribes at his official residence. Jaitley also resigned as leader of the party. The leader of the All India Trinamool Congress and Minister of Railways, Mamata Banerjee, used this opportunity to resign from the coalition and to gain some political capital. During 2001 a major state-owned financial institution, the Unit Trust of India, encountered serious difficulties. The Chairman, P. Subramanyam, resigned in early July and was later arrested on charges of conspiracy, abuse of public office and corruption. Vajpayee himself faced health problems and appeared tired and listless. The results of the state elections in May demonstrated the extent of the disquiet. The BJP performed badly in all four states. In Tamil Nadu the AIADMK returned to power, despite the conviction in October 2000 of Jayalalitha on corruption charges, for which she was sentenced to three years' imprisonment. She was sworn in as Chief Minister (an office she had previously held in 1991–96) but in order to remain in office she was instructed to win appeals against her convictions within six months. In June 2001 she ordered the arrest of her predecessor, M. Karunanidhi, in circumstances that were widely considered as retaliation for her own earlier arrest. The incident provoked extensive condemnation, prompting the central Government to force the Governor of Tamil Nadu, Fathima Beevi, to resign. In September the Supreme Court overturned Jayalalitha's appointment as Chief Minister. Congress fared well in the May state elections in Assam and Kerala. In West Bengal neither Congress nor the All India Trinamool Congress was able to displace the Left Front, which won its sixth successive victory and its first under Buddhadev Bhattacharya, the CPI (M) leader who had replaced Jyoti Basu on the latter's retirement. Congress attempted to exploit the situation, although Sonia Gandhi, who had been re-elected party leader in September 2000, had to deal with the continuing allegations surrounding the Bofors case. (See above—at the beginning of 2001 charges were brought against the three Hinduja brothers, members of a hugely wealthy business family based in the United Kingdom, for allegedly accepting bribes in the Bofors affair. The case was eventually dismissed by the High Court in Delhi in May 2005, by which time a Congress Government had returned to power.) Vajpayee also faced some unrest within his own party, especially after the failure of the summit meeting with Pakistan (see below). In August he tendered his resignation to his party, amid continuing disputes within the NDA and within the BJP, but was persuaded to withdraw his offer. At the end of the month the All India Trinamool Congress and the Pattali Makkal Katchi (which left in February) rejoined the NDA.

The Prime Minister also faced difficulties posed by the continuing demands from Hindu communal elements, significantly represented among the members of the BJP, for the construction of the Ram Janmabhoomi, the Hindu temple, on the site at Ayodhya where the Babri Masjid (mosque) had stood before its demolition in 1992 (see above). Vajpayee needed simultaneously to keep his own party support intact and to maintain an image of a national, non-partisan leader. At the end of 2000 he declared that the construction of the temple was an expression of 'national sentiment that had yet to be realized' and part of the Government's agenda. Although he later attempted to diminish the significance of his remarks, declaring that he did not support the destruction of the old mosque, the opposition demanded an immediate apology and forced the abrupt adjournment of the Lok Sabha and Rajya Sabha. Opposition members also demanded the resignation of three ministers, including L. K. Advani, who were charge-sheeted by the Central Bureau of Investigation in a case relating to the demolition of the Babri Masjid. Vajpayee rejected the demand; however, he confirmed that the Government would abide by the judgment of the Supreme Court. In January 2001 plans for a negotiated settlement over the site suffered a set-back when the All India Babri Masjid Action Committee ruled out negotiations with the VHP. VHP leaders convened a religious parliament, the Dharma Sansad, at the Maha Kumbh Mela (the largest ever Hindu gathering, centring on Allahabad, Uttar Pradesh) in January–February. The Dharma Sansad stated that all obstacles impeding the construction of the temple should be removed by the relevant organizations by mid-March 2002. In February 2001 an Indian high court ruled that nearly 40 people could be brought to trial in connection with the destruction of the mosque in Ayodhya, but that, on technical grounds, senior BJP leaders would not be among the defendants. In view of this verdict, in May a special Central Bureau of Investigation court hearing also discontinued criminal proceedings against the ministers. However, a separate criminal case was registered against the BJP and VHP leaders. In the mean time, a commission of inquiry into the events in Ayodhya took place.

As the deadline set by the Dharma Sansad to begin building the temple in mid-March 2002 approached, hundreds of Hindu activists, in an echo of events a decade before, assembled in Ayodhya to take part in the illegal construction. This led to a major outbreak of communal violence in the BJP-held state of Gujarat in late February, after a train carrying Hindu activists returning from a rally at Ayodhya was allegedly attacked by a group of Muslims (although subsequent inquiries cast doubt on this version of events). Some 60 Hindu activists were killed when the train caught fire. In the days and weeks that followed, up to 2,000 people, mainly Muslims, were killed in horrific circumstances in towns and cities across the state, including the commercial capital, Ahmedabad. The BJP Chief Minister of Gujarat, Narendra Modi, was heavily criticized for his inaction during the riots and it was widely reported that the local police did little to protect those under attack. Eventually, after considerable criticism from opposition parties, Modi resigned in July and the state assembly was dissolved.

In February 2002 state elections took place in four states, including the country's largest—Uttar Pradesh. The results demonstrated clearly the decline in the BJP's fortunes. In Uttar Pradesh the party lost almost one-half of its seats. No evident winner emerged from the election, although the Samajwadi Party, a representative of various less-privileged sections of the population, secured the largest number of seats. Eventually, Mayawati, the General Secretary of the Bahujan Samaj Party (BSP)—also representing the poorer sections of society—formed a coalition government with the BJP (similar coalitions had been made before), and she was appointed the state's Chief Minister. Congress enjoyed victory and formed governments in the Punjab, Uttaranchal and Manipur, giving a welcome boost to the party. In the same month Jayalalitha, who had succeeded in having her convictions overturned in December 2001, returned to the Tamil Nadu state assembly and immediately took over again as Chief Minister.

The BJP appeared to founder somewhat after its poor performance at the state elections. Its tough stance towards Pakistan (see below) was generally popular but did not deliver a great deal of additional political support, and was counterbalanced by the appearance of indecision over the Ayodhya issue. In July 2002 a government reorganization took place in which Jaswant Singh and Yashwant Sinha, the Ministers of Foreign Affairs and Finance, respectively, exchanged portfolios, while L. K. Advani, the Minister of Home Affairs, was given the additional title of Deputy Prime Minister. In May a member of the Shiv Sena, Manohar Joshi, was chosen as the new Speaker of the Lok Sabha, in a perceived attempt to strengthen the right-wing element within the Government. However, the Government's candidate for the presidential election, held in July, was Aavul Pakkiri Jainulabidin Abdul Kalam, a Muslim from south India who was closely associated over many years with the development of the country's missile and nuclear programmes. He won an overwhelming majority in the election. In the following month a more orthodox figure, Bhairon Singh Shekhawat (a former BJP Chief Minister of Rajasthan), was elected Vice-President.

As the national elections scheduled for 2004 began to approach, the question of how the BJP should present itself became ever more acute. The victory of Narendra Modi in Gujarat in mid-term state elections in December 2002 appeared to demonstrate the appeal of a campaign based on blatant communalism; however, a victory for Congress in the small but important hill state of Himachal Pradesh, where the BJP had usually enjoyed significant support, pointed in the opposite direction, as did the collapse of the BJP-supported Government in Uttar Pradesh in August 2003 and its replacement by a coalition led by the left-of-centre Samajwadi Party. A widely observed strike in May 2003 against the Union Government's privatization policies was also noted. In the end, however, Vajpayee decided to stand on his record as an economic modernizer who had, through all the successes and tribulations of his period in power, brought prosperity to a growing urban middle class and given India a more clearly defined place in the world. His decision to take the initiative in improving relations with Pakistan (see below) was also evidence of his attempt to present himself as an inclusive leader. In the run-up to the elections, the Government launched a major publicity campaign around the theme of 'India Shining', highlighting the 'feel-good' factor that it was hoped would produce victory. Against the advice of some of his colleagues, Vajpayee decided in January 2004 to bring the election date forward by a few months, and the polls actually took place in April and May of that year. While the BJP projected its achievements in the economic field, Congress emphasized the failure of the Government to address issues of wealth distribution and the growing gap between the rich and the poor. Sonia Gandhi and her now adult children, Rahul (who stood for election in the family's traditional constituency of Amethi in Utttar Pradesh) and Priyanka, took leading roles in the campaign and attracted huge crowds. Compared with her earlier interventions in Indian politics, Sonia Gandhi now seemed fully to be accepted. Equally important as the efforts of the two main parties were the alliances that were made, and the performance of their respective partners. The Telugu Desam party in Andhra Pradesh, the leader of which, N. Chandrababu Naidu, had done so well in previous elections, came under increasing pressure as a result of acute distress among the state's agricultural population. The BJP decided to maintain its alliance with the AIADMK, despite its leader's growing unpopularity.

## A NEW BALANCE OF POWER

### The Manmohan Singh Government

The national elections were held over a period of several weeks, with the results finally being announced on 13 May 2004. To general surprise, Congress alone won 145 of the 543 elective seats and with its immediate allies a further 72. The BJP secured only 138, while its allies also performed poorly, especially the Telugu Desam party. Although not part of the Congress coalition, the left-wing parties in general scored notable successes: the CPI (M) alone won 43 seats, including several outside West Bengal. Another success was recorded by the Samajwadi Party, which won 36 of the seats in Uttar Pradesh. While Congress and its allies did not have an overall majority, they were substantially ahead of the BJP alliance and could depend on the support of the Left Front and other parties. The results were widely interpreted as a rejection of the BJP's economic policies, which had been seen as favouring the relatively wealthy at the expense of the poor. However, while this was clearly a factor, regional issues were undoubtedly important, as were the quirks of India's first-past-the-post electoral system. In fact, both Congress and the BJP won slightly smaller shares of the popular vote than they had in 1999.

Most people had assumed that Sonia Gandhi, as leader of Congress, would become the Prime Minister, but she announced on 18 May 2004 that she had decided not to put herself forward, perhaps to avoid her Italian origins becoming an issue, as they had in the past. Instead, Dr Manmohan Singh, who as Minister of Finance in the early 1990s was widely credited with introducing India's programme of economic liberalization, became the party's choice and took office on 22 May with her full support. Other key appointments were: K. Natwar Singh, a former diplomat and Nehru family loyalist, as Minister of External Affairs; P. Chidambaram, like the Prime Minister associated with the earlier programme of economic reform, as Minister of Finance; and Shivraj Patil, a veteran party leader from western India, as Minister of Home Affairs.

In December 2005 11 MPs from several different parties, including both Congress and the BJP, were expelled from the Indian Parliament after having been filmed accepting bribes. Although similar 'sting' operations had led to ministerial resignations in the 1990s, this was the first time that action had been taken against such a large group. In the same month K. Natwar Singh, was forced to resign after being implicated in the Iraq 'oil-for-food' scandal. The Prime Minister, following the practice of many of his predecessors, subsequently assumed the external affairs portfolio himself for almost a year, before transferring it to Congress veteran Pranab Mukherjee in October 2006; A. K. Antony, a former Chief Minister of Kerala, replaced Mukherjee as Minister of Defence. In July 2007 Pratibha Devisingh Patil, the Congress candidate and former Governor of Rajasthan, was elected to succeed A. P. J. Abdul Kalam as President of India, thus becoming the first woman to hold this position. Mohammad Hamid Ansari replaced Bhairon Singh Shekhawat as Vice-President in the following month.

As usual, changes in state politics accompanied those in the national political arena, although the regular pattern of swings against incumbent governments sometimes transgressed national trends. State elections that were held in parallel with the general election in April 2004 led to a Congress victory in Andhra Pradesh, while in neighbouring Karnataka the BJP emerged as the largest party (although Congress was able to put together a coalition government that lasted until February 2006). In the key state of Maharashtra, where elections took place in October 2004, the Congress government fought off a determined challenge from the BJP-Shiv Sena coalition, but only by allowing a faction of dissident Congress members, the Nationalist Congress Party, to take the lead. In February 2005 the state of Bihar, which had been ruled by the left-of-centre RJD, led by Rabri Devi, wife of Lalu Prasad Yadav, went to the polls. The RJD won only 75 seats and Rabri Devi was forced to tender her resignation. However, no other party was able to form a government in the state, and direct rule from the Centre was imposed. In May the state legislative assembly was dissolved, leading to street protests organized by the BJP and its allies, who believed that they had been close to forming a government. Elections were eventually held in November, and led to a victory by a coalition of the Janata Dal—United and the BJP. The new Chief Minister, Nitish Kumar, was another prominent spokesman for the rights of the lower castes.

Given the status of Congress as a coalition leader, Manmohan Singh had to allow his allies some room for manoeuvre, even though some had poor reputations. For example, he had to appoint Lalu Prasad Yadav as Minister of Railways, despite his reputation for corruption. Part of Manmohan Singh's pitch to his coalition partners was to reopen the issue of reservations for lower caste groups. Although the issue had been allowed to fade after the emotionalism aroused by the Mandal report in the early 1990s (see above), its potential was again revealed in May 2006 when the Government announced that it was to create a new set of reservations in India's élite professional colleges, especially in the field of medicine. This predictably led to widespread protests from the urban middle class who believed that the introduction of such a measure would restrict their own opportunities. In March 2007 the Supreme Court put the plans on hold, but in April 2008 they were finally allowed to be implemented. In May and June 2007 protests by tribal peoples in Rajasthan, demanding greater inclusion in affirmative action schemes, erupted into violence and resulted in some 23 deaths. Protests were repeated a year later until in June 2008 a compromise agreement was reached.

Meanwhile, Singh's position within Congress itself appeared reasonably secure, despite his lack of an independent political base, and he maintained good relations with the Gandhi family. His economic policies were firmly directed towards sustaining India's growth path through broadly market-friendly policies, and he was able to ensure the country's impressive economic performance, while at the same time avoiding the implementation of measures that bore too harshly upon the rural and urban poor. Southern India was badly affected by the Asian tsunami of 26 December 2004, but the Government was able to manage the aftermath of the disaster using its own resources, as it was also able in October 2005 when Jammu and Kashmir were hit by a major earthquake. In June 2006 Singh announced a major aid programme for farmers in drought-affected areas of western India. Despite this, the Government remained open to criticism from both the opposition and its own ranks and allies that it was too zealously pursuing globalization policies, for example in the area of privatization of government-owned industries. As a result of pressure exerted by the DMK in Tamil Nadu, the Government announced in July 2006 that it was suspending further privatization in the state sector for the foreseeable future. The budget introduced in February 2007 was notable for its emphasis on health and education, paid for in part by higher taxes levied on the corporate sector.

Several state elections were held in May 2006. In West Bengal the CPI—M recorded its seventh successive win, and the coalition of left-wing parties that it led in Kerala was able to displace the incumbent Congress administration. Congress performed better in Assam, however, where it emerged as the leader of a coalition government, and in Tamil Nadu, where its coalition partner, the DMK, defeated the AIADMK. In addition, Sonia Gandhi won, by a comfortable margin, a parliamentary by-election that had been necessitated by her resignation in March in a technical dispute over her chairmanship of the National Advisory Council. Both her children, Rahul and Priyanka, played major roles in organizing her electoral campaign.

In February 2007 elections were held in the Punjab, Manipur and the small state of Uttarakhand (formerly known as Uttaranchal). In the Punjab, a Shiromani Akali Dal-BJP coalition displaced the Congress government, and in Uttarakhand the BJP succeeded in doing likewise; a Congress-led coalition did, however, secure victory in Manipur. In April and May elections were held in Uttar Pradesh. The BSP under Mayawati performed even better than had been predicted, and gained an overall majority. As well as general support from its base constituency among the poor and excluded, the party gained support from some sections of the Brahmin community who believed that the former Samajwadi Party government had achieved nothing on their behalf. Congress, the BJP and the Samajwadi Party all performed poorly in the Uttar Pradesh state elections—the BJP despite success in local elections in 2006 and Congress despite the popular appeal of the Gandhi family. The BSP did, however, commit its support to Congress at national level, although it withdrew it in May 2008, at a time when Mayawati herself was clearly beginning to harbour ambitions in New Delhi. Meanwhile, in December 2007 the BJP's Narendra Modi scored a fourth successive victory in state elections in Gujarat, where his popularity was based both on the state's strong economic performance and on his own reputation as a Hindu chauvinist who had presided over the massacres of 2002 (see above). In May 2008 elections in Karnataka, which followed a period of political impasse, brought the BJP to power in the state for the first time.

The poor showings by Congress in these elections reflected the difficulties being faced by the Manmohan Singh Government in maintaining economic policies that promoted rapid growth without benefiting the interests of the poorer sections of society. As the next general election, which was scheduled to be held by May 2009 at the latest, began to loom, the Government, to counteract rising oil and food prices, introduced a tax-cutting budget in February 2008 as well as writing off the bank loans of many small farmers. The CPI—M administration in West Bengal faced similar dilemmas, when an attempt to create a special economic zone (SEZ) in the vicinity of Nandigram, for a chemical plant situated on land that been acquired from local farmers, led to clashes with the police in March 2007 in which at least 14 people were killed; plans to establish the SEZ were subsequently abandoned. Unrest, however, continued.

Shortly after the 2004 general election results were declared, Vajpayee relinquished his role as parliamentary leader of the BJP and was replaced by L. K. Advani, widely recognized to be the party's most powerful figure, despite being in his late seventies. Advani also succeeded Venkaiah Naidu as President of the party later that year, following Naidu's resignation as a result of the defeat in the October state elections in Maharashtra (see above). Advani, himself well known for his hard-line stance on communal issues, had to maintain the fine balance between satisfying the party and ensuring its acceptability to a wide enough range of public opinion to make it a serious political force. In June 2005 he visited Pakistan and made statements that supported the credentials of the founder of Pakistan, Muhammad Ali Jinnah, as a secular political leader. This duly provoked strong criticism from some sections of the BJP. Advani announced that he would resign, but was persuaded to change his mind shortly afterwards. At the end of the year, however, he handed over charge of the party to Rajnath Singh, a former Chief Minister of Uttar Pradesh. The BJP's coalition partner in Maharashtra, the often rabidly communal Shiv Sena, split into two factions in March 2006.

In 2006–08 India suffered from a number of major terrorist attacks. In March 2006 a number of bombs were detonated in the religious centre of Varanasi, killing at least 15 people. The police subsequently arrested a Muslim cleric who, they claimed, had masterminded the attacks. On 11 July a highly co-ordinated series of bomb blasts took place on the Mumbai suburban rail system, killing more than 180 people. No one claimed responsibility for this attack, but it seemed plausible that it was the work of extreme separatist groups in Kashmir (although the most high-profile of such groups specifically denied any involvement). Several suspects were arrested in connection with the explosions. In September a bomb explosion in the city of Malegaon, in Maharashtra, claimed some 37 lives. Members of a militant Islamist group were subsequently arrested, although it was suggested that a militant Hindu group might have been responsible for the attack. In February 2007 incendiary bombs were detonated on the Samjhauta Express train service between India and Pakistan, with the loss of at least 67 lives. Again, Islamist extremists were widely suspected of having perpetrated the attack, but there was no clear proof of their culpability. In May a bomb explosion at a mosque in the southern city of Hyderabad resulted in nine fatalities, followed by another round of bombings in the city in August which killed more than 40 people. In May 2008 there was a co-ordinated series of bomb blasts in the major tourist centre of Jaipur, leading to at least 63 deaths. Further explosions occurred in Bangalore and Ahmedabad in July, the latter resulting in more than 60 deaths. All three incidents in 2008 took place in states under BJP rule.

Meanwhile, in 2007 the civilian nuclear agreement between India and the USA (see below) met with opposition not only from the BJP, but from the UPA coalition's allies, the left-wing parties comprising the Left Front, which feared the possibility of US intervention in India's foreign policy and other areas. As the dispute intensified, the future of the agreement appeared increasingly uncertain, while the UPA parliamentary majority itself seemed to be under threat. By early 2008 progress on the implementation of the agreement had almost slowed to a halt. In July the threat of a withdrawal of support from the left-wing parties became a reality after the Government indicated that it intended to proceed with the agreement. The Government was forced to seek a parliamentary vote of confidence, amid speculation about the possibility of early elections. However, on 22 July the Government won enough votes to ensure it remained in power, securing a majority with the help of minor parties and independents.

## REGIONAL PROBLEMS

Even before independence the unity of India was a major concern of the country's political leaders. The partition of 1947, in which large areas in the north-west and north-east (West Pakistan and East Pakistan) were detached in the name of religion, heightened anxiety over other apparently divisive political movements claiming autonomy or separation. The linguistic reorganization of the states of the Indian Union (see above) provided a framework in which the conflicts over language were reduced to a minimum, although occasionally, as in the city of Bangalore in south India, the rights of linguistic minorities have led to local problems. The tensions were exploited at the end of the 1990s by a flamboyant outlaw in the region, Veerappan, who resorted to kidnappings of prominent politicians (one of whom died in captivity at the end of 2002) and a major film actor until he was killed by police in October 2004. There have also been regular differences both between individual states and between states and the Centre over the allocation of financial and other resources. Some of the most intractable problems in south India have arisen over the sharing of water resources. However, although these disputes have often created severe political pressure, they have never taken the form of direct challenges to the integrity of India.

In other parts of the country, however, where for one reason or another a major group has felt marginalized, separatist and autonomist movements have emerged, placing great strain on the Indian Government, both in the past and at present. In the Punjab, the crisis that had begun in the late 1970s (see above) continued until the early 1990s, when a combination of severe police repression (leading to widespread allegations of human rights abuses) and political overtures led to a tacit settlement between the Government and the mainstream Sikh political parties. Although there was a brief resurgence of violence in 1995, when the Congress Chief Minister, Beant Singh, was killed by a car-bomb, it proved to be an isolated incident. Since the 1996 national elections, the Shiromani Akali Dal has been the dominant political force in the state. In state elections in February 1997 and again in the 1998 and 1999 parliamentary elections, the Shiromani Akali Dal established an electoral alliance with the BJP, thus demonstrating the Indian political system's capacity to bring together parties with divergent views. The Shiromani Akali Dal was also represented in the Vajpayee Government, which was formed in March 1998. The 2002 state elections returned Congress to power in the Punjab under Capt. Amarinder Singh, whose ancestors had been the rulers of the state of Patiala, a major Sikh centre, but in 2007 the state reverted to Shiromani Akali Dal-BJP control (see above).

Separatist or autonomist movements continue to operate throughout north-eastern India, notably in Tripura, Manipur, Nagaland and Assam. Most of them are based around particular tribal groupings, which use violence against those perceived as outsiders as well as against the security forces. Substantial numbers of people have been killed in ambushes and other acts of violence. In May 2003, for example, a number of Bengali settlers were massacred in Tripura. The longstanding policy of the national Government aims to achieve political settlements with the separatist groups where possible, as in the 1993 agreement with leaders of the Bodo tribal group in Assam, which provided for the establishment of a local council, and in agreements with two separate Naga groups in 1997 and 2000. When this has not been possible, however, the Government has tended to resort to the use of military force in an attempt to repress the movements. As a result, there is regular alternation between repression and accommodation. Bodo insurgency, for example, was renewed in the late 1990s, but a cease-fire was negotiated in March 2000, and a pact providing enhanced autonomy was signed with one of the principal guerrilla groups in February 2003. Further agreements were reached in May 2005. In mid-June 2001 the Government agreed to a cease-fire with separatist groups in Manipur. In the same month the Government also extended the scope of its existing cease-fire in Nagaland to include the National Socialist Council of Nagaland (Khaplang)—NSCN (K), along with all underground organizations in north-east India, and offered to involve the NSCN (K) and the NSCN (Issak-Muivah—IM) in peace negotiations. The decision to extend the cease-fire to Naga groups in the neighbouring states of Assam, Manipur and Arunachal Pradesh, as well as Nagaland, gave rise to fears of the creation of a 'Greater Nagaland' as part of an eventual settlement at the expense of the other states. Strikes and violent protests took place in Manipur. In an effort to curb the violence, the Prime Minister consulted the leaders of the seven north-eastern states of India in July and subsequently announced the Government's decision to limit the cease-fire to the state of Nagaland. However, further negotiations with Naga militants in January 2003 led to renewed violence and casualties in Manipur. In February 2007, at India's request, Myanma troops took action against NSCN (K) bases inside Myanma territory.

One of the most prominent of the separatist groups in the region, which operates within a somewhat broader context than the others, is the United Liberation Front of Assam (ULFA), a militant Maoist group that emerged in the 1980s and seeks the outright secession of the state of Assam from India. The ULFA was outlawed by the central Government in 1990, but continued its armed activity against the state. In late 2000 there was a sharp upsurge in the ULFA's terrorist activities, and increased security activity merely forced the armed groups to shift their bases into remote areas both within neighbouring Indian states and in other countries such as Bhutan and Bangladesh. There have been a number of attacks on migrant workers from northern India in Assam which have been attributed to ULFA; in January 2007 some 62 workers were killed in a series of such attacks, and other such incidents have since taken place.

Although the situations in the Punjab and north-eastern India remained major security issues throughout the 1980s, the most protracted and, in many ways, most serious of the regional problems confronting India was the Kashmir crisis. Following the initial conflict in 1947–48, the cease-fire line (the Line of Control—LoC—as it was renamed in 1972) effectively defined the division of the state between Indian- and Pakistani-controlled sections, and the wars with Pakistan in 1965 and 1971 made little change to this. India eventually renounced its commitment to a plebiscite under UN auspices, arguing that Pakistan had never acted in good faith.

Sheikh Abdullah, who had initially supported accession to India and had emerged as the dominant political figure in Kashmir after 1947, but who then began to talk of independence, was imprisoned, without trial, for many years. Meanwhile, Jammu and Kashmir was dominated by politicians who toed the official line and relied on Indian support. In 1954 the state assembly proclaimed that it had joined the Indian Union. Sheikh Abdullah eventually accepted Kashmir's position in India and returned to the state as Chief Minister from 1975 until his death in 1982. He was succeeded by his son, Dr Farooq Abdullah. Although Farooq Abdullah and his party, the Jammu and Kashmir National Conference (JKNC), in alliance with Congress (I), succeeded in winning state elections in 1987 (which many observers believed were rigged), he failed to establish a rapport with the people of Kashmir. It was against this background that political forces in the state that wanted either accession to Pakistan or, increasingly, independence became more prominent and more militant, particularly the outlawed Jammu and Kashmir Liberation Front (JKLF). They were able to enforce an effective boycott of the national elections in November 1989 and, thenceforth, the violence escalated, with fierce clashes between militants and security forces. The entire Srinagar area was placed under an indefinite curfew, and many more troops were sent in. Dr Farooq Abdullah's Government resigned in January 1990, and the state was placed under direct rule from the Centre, with power in the state shared between bureaucrats and military leaders. In May the principal Muslim religious leader in Kashmir, Mirwaiz Maulvi Muhammad Farooq, was murdered (by whom was not clear) and his funeral was the occasion for another major clash in which many people died.

Over the next few years the level of violence escalated, with both sides accusing the other of atrocities. In October 1993 there was a major incident in the town of Bijbehara, in which nearly 40 protesters were killed by the security forces. In the same month militants seized the revered Hazrat Bal mosque in Srinagar, in an effort to provoke the Government into action that would further alienate the population. In the face of a deliberate policy of restraint on the part of the Government, however, the militants were eventually forced into a negotiated surrender. In May 1995, however, a similar episode in the town of Charar-e-Sharief ended less agreeably, with the total destruction of a 15th-century shrine and with each side blaming the other. Another negative development in this year was the taking by a previously unknown Islamist separatist group called Al-Faran of foreign tourists as hostages (a Norwegian hostage was executed by his captors in August 1995; others remain missing and are believed to be dead).

In addition to attempting to gain the ascendancy militarily, from 1994 the Government tried to initiate a political dialogue with the Kashmiri separatists. Selected militant leaders were released, the JKLF declared a cease-fire and in 1996 elections were held to Jammu and Kashmir's Lok Sabha seats, although it was widely believed that the security forces had coerced many people into voting in the face of a boycott declared by the main pro-militant political grouping. State elections were then held in September, and attracted a substantially higher turnout, despite continuing calls for a boycott. Dr Farooq Abdullah and the JKNC returned to power on the basis of a pledge to find a negotiated solution within the framework of the Indian

Union. Although Dr Abdullah began by promising to talk to the militant leaders and also established a committee to consider the vexed question of regional divisions within the state (notably between the Muslim-majority areas and the Hindu and Buddhist regions in the south and in the east), the political impetus inspired by the elections soon began to wane. Although at a lesser level than in the early 1990s, militant activity continued to be a major problem, increasingly perpetrated by Islamist groups from outside of Kashmir, for example from Pakistan and Afghanistan, and on occasion, as in June 1998 and March 2000, members of the Hindu and Sikh minorities were massacred for purely sectarian reasons. The accession to power of the BJP Government in March 1998 led to no immediate change in policy with regard to the situation in Jammu and Kashmir. Although he had earlier been associated with the UF, Dr Abdullah made a point of keeping on good terms with the new central administration, in which his son became a minister. He failed to extend his own political base, however, and often appeared vulnerable to charges of ineffectiveness.

At the beginning of 2000 the situation in Kashmir deteriorated, but in early April there were indications that the Indian Government was willing to re-establish dialogue. Leaders of the All-Party Hurriyat Conference (APHC), who had been arrested during the 1999 general election campaign, were released in April and May. The APHC represented a wide range of separatist and autonomist political opinion. In July one of the main militant groups, the Hizbul Mujahideen, declared a three-month cease-fire. The gesture obtained a quick and positive response from the Indian Government: the Indian Army suspended all offensive operations against the Kashmiri militants for the first time in 11 years, and in November, although the cease-fire by the Hizbul Mujahideen had ended, the army maintained the suspension of its operations. Despite the changes in the security situation, which were generally welcomed, both domestically and internationally, initial attempts to develop a meaningful political dialogue faltered, with Pakistan and India still far apart on questions such as participation in the dialogue by Kashmiri leaders. The cease-fire ended in May 2001, and during Indo-Pakistani negotiations in July violence in the region escalated. From December 2001 the situation within Kashmir precipitated a major crisis between India and Pakistan (see below). In May 2002 a prominent moderate separatist, Abdul Ghani Lone was assassinated; the perpetrators, however, remained unidentified. As a result of the crisis and the associated militant activity within Kashmir, the Indian authorities adopted a less conciliatory approach towards politicians associated with the APHC. In early August it was announced that state elections in Jammu and Kashmir were to take place in four phases, from mid-September to early October. Islamist militant groups declared their intention to disrupt the campaign and the voting. Although the campaign was marked by considerable violence, including the assassination of one of Dr Farooq Abdullah's ministerial colleagues, the conduct of the polls and the level of participation (estimated at just below 50% of the electorate) was regarded by outside observers as a considerable improvement on previous elections, despite the fact that the APHC ultimately boycotted the polls. The JKNC and Dr Farooq Abdullah personally suffered a major defeat, although the JKNC remained the largest single party. No single party won an outright majority and a coalition government was eventually formed between Congress and the People's Democratic Party. The coalition was led initially by a veteran political figure, Mufti Mohammad Sayeed, and after three years, by mutual agreement, a Congress leader, Ghulam Nabi Azad, assumed power. Although Sayeed made it clear that he was prepared to enter dialogue with the central Government, and the latter in turn made a positive gesture in November by releasing Yasin Malik, one of the most prominent APHC leaders who had been arrested earlier in the year, progress depended critically on the levels of militant violence, a factor beyond the control of the state government, and on the state of Indo-Pakistani relations. The latter concern appeared to enter a new phase from April 2003 onwards (see below), following a speech by Vajpayee in Srinagar itself. Preliminary talks were held in January 2004 between government officials and one of the factions of the APHC, led by Mirwaiz Umer Farooq. Immediately after the elections in May 2004, an attack by militants on a bus carrying soldiers and their relatives killed at least 33 people, but this did not appear to derail the peace process.

A meeting between the Indian Prime Minister, Manmohan Singh, and the Pakistani President, Gen. Pervez Musharraf, in New York, USA, in September 2004 signalled that the two sides were willing to explore new ideas. While substantive negotiations had yet to begin, a number of major symbolic events occurred in 2005–06. In particular, a bus service was initiated in 2005 between the two sides of the LoC (with a second launched in 2006), to enable divided Kashmiri families to visit each other without the need for passports, thus underlining the possibility of a long-term solution based in some way on 'soft borders'. A group of APHC leaders took advantage of the bus service to make a two-week visit to Pakistan in June, during which they held extensive talks with Pakistani and Kashmiri leaders. At the same time, the more moderate elements within the APHC began a series of informal talks with the Indian Government, including, on one occasion, with the Prime Minister. As the pace of Indo-Pakistani dialogue accelerated (see below) so did the frequency of these interactions. While clashes between security forces and militants continued, as did allegations of human rights abuses, the level declined somewhat. A further visit to Pakistan by APHC leaders, headed by Mirwaiz Umar Farooq, took place in January 2007, during which the delegation lent support to President Musharraf's proposals for a long-term solution to the Kashmiri problem. However, one important section of the APHC, led by Syed Ali Shah Geelani, remained firmly opposed to any discussions with the Indian Government.

The earthquake of October 2005 affected both sides of the LoC, although it had a much greater impact on the Pakistani section. Indo-Pakistani co-operation in the relief effort was relatively limited. In May 2006 Manmohan Singh visited Srinagar to meet local leaders, although on this occasion separatist groups refused to meet him.

It is clear that a solution to the Kashmir problem requires that a more general settlement be reached between India and Pakistan. While India perceives Kashmir to be one of a number of issues, including economic relations, within a 'composite dialogue', Pakistan insists that, without real progress on Kashmir, nothing else can move ahead. However, the leaders of both countries have made statements indicating a willingness to consider new ideas. Besides settling the dispute between India and Pakistan, a lasting solution to the problem will require the implementation of measures that adequately address local feelings within Kashmir. The Muslims of the Kashmir Valley are only one of several different groups within the region, with religion, language and geography as important factors.

### Revolutionary Movements

Besides the violence associated with some of the regional movements mentioned above, some of which have also identified themselves as being socialist in terms of their ideology, India has faced revolutionary guerrilla movements from time to time. Shortly after independence, the Communist Party itself launched an uprising in the Telangana region of what is now Andhra Pradesh. It was defeated after the Indian army intervened, and thereafter the Communist Party of India (which itself split into two factions in 1964, to some extent in line with the divide between Russia and the People's Republic of China at that time) followed a predominantly parliamentary route. However, in 1967 a breakaway group popularly known as the Naxalites, which eventually established the Communist Party of India (Marxist-Leninist), launched an insurgency that had some success in West Bengal and Bihar. Repressive action by the security forces led to its virtual demise in the early 1970s. However, radical movements continue to exercise some influence in small pockets of the country, notably parts of Andhra Pradesh and Bihar, although by the early 2000s it was feared that the area affected by Naxalite activity was increasing. In 2004 two major Naxalite groups united as the Communist Party of India (Maoist), an indication of increased co-operation among the insurgent groups. In early 2007 there were fears of an escalation in violence amid reports of shootings and offensives allegedly carried out by Maoist activists, including an attack in the state of Chhattisgarh in March 2007, which resulted in the deaths of 55 trainee security personnel. Isolated attacks and clashes took place in several other states in 2008.

## FOREIGN RELATIONS

India's relations with its neighbours have been fraught with difficulties. While India considers itself as the natural leader of the region, this attitude has often been resented by the smaller countries, especially when, under the leadership of Indira Gandhi, India began to assert its superior power more directly. India was also concerned that domestic problems on its borders might have negative consequences for itself.

In the case of Sri Lanka, India initially maintained stable and friendly relations, but in the 1980s found itself drawn into the civil war between the Sinhalese-dominated Government and the Tamil minority, led by the LTTE, which enjoyed considerable support among India's own Tamil people. India was also concerned that external powers, the USA in particular, might begin to play a part. As the Sri Lankan army appeared, in 1987, to be gaining the advantage, but at a high cost in terms of civilian casualties in the Tamil areas of Sri Lanka, the Indian Government put considerable pressure on Sri Lanka to accept an India-mediated agreement with the LTTE and to invite an Indian Peace-Keeping Force (IPKF) to oversee the agreement. An accord was signed between Rajiv Gandhi and the Sri Lankan President, J. R. Jayewardene, in July 1987 and Indian troops were immediately dispatched to Tamil areas in Sri Lanka. Although, initially, the Indo-Sri Lankan accord brought Rajiv Gandhi considerable domestic dividends, the situation rapidly turned against him as the Indian troops, which, by February 1988, numbered about 50,000, struggled to persuade the Tamil guerrillas to surrender their arms and to abide by the terms of the agreement. The IPKF encountered considerable resistance from the Tamil militants, especially during the siege of the Tamil stronghold in Jaffna in October 1987. Following the gradual implementation of the peace accord, however, several thousand IPKF troops were withdrawn from Sri Lanka in the latter half of 1988 and early 1989. In August 1989 an agreement between India and Sri Lanka was signed in Colombo, the Sri Lankan capital, in which India stated that it would immediately cease hostilities against the Tamil guerrillas and that it would make 'all efforts' to withdraw its 43,000 troops from Sri Lanka by 31 December. For its part, the Sri Lankan Government agreed to strengthen the civil administration as early as possible to ensure peace and normality in the Tamil-dominated northern and eastern provinces, and to establish a peace committee to coincide with the start of the cease-fire. The complete withdrawal of Indian troops from Sri Lanka was, in fact, accomplished by the end of March 1990, although violent conflict in the island flared up again very shortly afterwards. The flow of Sri Lankan refugees into Tamil Nadu increased considerably. By late 1991 the number of Sri Lankans in refugee camps in Tamil Nadu was estimated at more than 200,000. The assassination of the former Indian Prime Minister, Rajiv Gandhi, almost certainly by members of the LTTE, completed India's disenchantment with that organization. Measures were subsequently taken by the state government in Tamil Nadu to suppress LTTE activity within the state, and also to begin the process of repatriating refugees. This proved a slow and difficult process. In May 1992 the LTTE was officially banned in India. India has subsequently been supportive of the Sri Lankan Government's efforts to defeat the LTTE and to achieve a negotiated settlement within a Sri Lankan framework, but has avoided playing any direct diplomatic role. Where necessary, it has also taken action against local south Indian politicians who have had links with the LTTE. In June 2006 one of the senior LTTE leaders implicitly admitted the organization's responsibility for Rajiv Gandhi's assassination and apologized for it, apparently in an attempt to rekindle Indian concern over the conflict in Sri Lanka, where the cease-fire that had been negotiated in 2002 had broken down in early 2006.

India inherited the colonial view of Nepal as an important buffer state (between itself and China) and played a significant role in the country's internal politics. Relations between the two deteriorated in early 1989, when India decided not to renew the two treaties determining trade and transit, insisting that a common treaty covering both issues be negotiated. Nepal refused, stressing the importance of keeping the treaties separate on the grounds that Indo-Nepalese trade issues are negotiable, whereas the right of transit is a recognized right of land-locked countries. India responded by closing many of the transit points through which most of Nepal's trade is conducted. It was widely believed that another matter aggravating the dispute was Nepal's recent acquisition of Chinese-made military equipment, which, according to India, violated the Treaty of Peace and Friendship of 1950. Following several rounds of high-level talks, a joint agreement was signed by the two countries in June 1990, restoring trade relations and reopening the transit points. Chandra Shekhar visited Kathmandu in February 1991 (the first official visit to Nepal by an Indian Prime Minister since 1977), shortly after it was announced that the first free elections there were to be held in May. Following these elections a generally pro-Congress Government took office in Nepal, and Indo-Nepalese relations were more or less restored to their earlier state. The Nepalese Prime Minister, G. P. Koirala, visited India in December 1991. Although Koirala was defeated in elections in 1994, his left-wing successor (who himself lost his post after only a few months) was reluctant to alienate India, although his election campaign had included a great deal of anti-India rhetoric. In June 1997 the new Indian Prime Minister, Inder Kumar Gujral, made a visit to Nepal and announced the opening of a transit route through north-east India between Nepal and Bangladesh. Gujral and the Nepalese Prime Minister, Lokendra Bahadur Chand, also agreed that there should be a review of the 1950 treaty between the two countries. However, an outbreak of anti-India violence in December 2000 over a minor incident demonstrated the extent of popular suspicion. The escalation of a Maoist insurrection in Nepal was a matter of great concern to India. However, it also expressed its displeasure at the assertion of royal power in the country in February 2005, when the elected Government was dismissed by the King, and played a discreet role in encouraging the popular movement that restored elected institutions in early 2006. The new Prime Minister of Nepal, G. P. Koirala, a politician with strong links to India, made an official visit to Delhi in June.

India's relations with Bhutan have also been based on a colonial model, with the 1949 Indo-Bhutan Treaty of Friendship effectively asserting Indian suzerainty over Bhutan's international relations. The treaty was renegotiated in 2007 during an official visit to India by the new King of Bhutan, giving Bhutan greater scope for independent action.

Relations with Bangladesh obviously started on a high note, given India's role in the 1971 conflict, but, particularly after the assassination of the Bangladesh Prime Minister, Sheikh Mujibur Rahman, in August 1975 (see chapter on Bangladesh), successive Bangladeshi leaders have been wary of what they view as India's 'big brother' approach. The most important bilateral issue for a long period of time was the distribution of the Ganga (Ganges) waters following the controversial construction of a barrage on the Indian side of the border. Fruitless negotiations regarding this question extended over many years, but finally in December 1996 Gujral concluded an agreement with Bangladesh that seemed to be fair and acceptable to both countries. Unresolved issues remained, including the dispute over territorial rights to pockets of land or enclaves along the irregular border, despite intermittent efforts to resolve these problems. Local border disputes therefore occurred over the years, leading to occasional clashes. In April 2001 the worst fighting since 1976 took place, on the border between the Indian state of Meghalaya and Bangladesh. Some 16 Indian border troops and three members of the Bangladesh Rifles were killed. Indians were outraged by the alleged maltreatment of Indian soldiers before their deaths. The situation was brought under control, and both sides agreed to take part in negotiations. Subsequently, two joint working groups were established to review the undemarcated section of the border and the exchange of enclaves, although further clashes took place from time to time; for example, in March and April 2005 along the border with the Indian state of Tripura, where India had been attempting to control smuggling and illegal immigration. Another issue was Bangladesh's concern over the treatment of Bangladeshi migrants in India. Some sections of the BJP called for their expulsion, claiming that there were many millions of illegal immigrants in the country; efforts were made at the beginning of 2003 to deport some of the alleged illegal immigrants. Occasional clashes on the border continued under the Congress Government. In March 2006, however, the Bangladesh Prime Minister, Begum Khaleda Zia, made an official visit to India (her first since assuming office in 2001), and in April 2008 the railway service between the two countries, which had been suspended in 1965, reopened. One of India's principal concerns has been the alleged use of Bangladesh territory by members of ULFA and by extremist Islamist groups.

Relations with the People's Republic of China remained very restricted for many years after the 1962 war, not least because of China's links with Pakistan. India's long-standing friendship with Viet Nam was also an obstacle to an improvement in Indo-Chinese relations, especially around 1980. Regular official-level meetings were held during the 1980s but little progress was made. A visit to China by Rajiv Gandhi in December 1988, however, proved a turning point. Trade links were gradually improved and talks were held on the border question. In 1993 Narasimha Rao visited the Chinese capital, Beijing (returning a visit by the Chinese Premier, Li Peng, in 1991), and signed an agreement allowing for a reduction in military confrontation along the disputed border. This process was taken further when the Chinese President, Jiang Zemin, visited New Delhi in November 1996. Yet despite the gradual improvement in relations, India signalled on many occasions that it was unhappy with the nuclear asymmetry between the two countries and with what it perceived as China's willingness to transfer missiles and missile technology to Pakistan. India's relations with China suffered badly following the 1998 nuclear tests, in part because of China's belief that India was using a fabricated threat from China to justify its actions. However, in June of the following year the Indian Minister of External Affairs visited Beijing to reinstigate dialogue. During border negotiations in November 2000, India and China exchanged detailed maps of the middle sector of the so-called Line of Actual Control, a significant step towards resolving differences. In January 2001 Li Peng, Chairman of the National People's Congress, visited India. The focus of his successor's visit one year later was economic issues. Prime Minister Atal Bihari Vajpayee made a state visit to China in June 2003, during which a number of agreements were signed, the most important being India's recognition of Chinese sovereignty over Tibet. The two countries agreed to appoint special representatives to discuss the border disputes that had led to the 1962 war. The Chinese Minister of National Defence visited India in March 2004 for talks with his counterpart. In April 2005 the Chinese Premier, Wen Jiabao, paid a very successful visit to India, which confirmed the steady improvement in bilateral relations in both the political and economic spheres. India (together with Pakistan) was given 'observer status' in 2006 by the Shanghai Co-operation Organization (SCO), the regional security body established by China and Russia, and attended the fifth summit meeting of the SCO held in Shanghai in June 2006. Chinese President Hu Jintao paid an official visit to India in November 2006, during which talks focused primarily on economic relations, as was also the case when Prime Minister Manmohan Singh made a return visit to China in January 2008. The Indian authorities have continued to be supportive of China's position over Tibet (the Xizang Autonomous Region—in June 2003 India signed an agreement giving official recognition to China's sovereignty of the region), and did nothing to exacerbate China's difficulties arising from the pro-Tibet protests that took place in many Western countries in the run-up to the holding of the Olympics in Beijing in 2008. At the same time, however, India and China continue to regard each other as strategic rivals for the unofficial leadership of Asia, and this rivalry surfaces from time to time in various forms.

Relations between India and Pakistan have been tense since 1947 and have been marked by three wars and numerous lesser clashes. The fate of Jammu and Kashmir (see above) has been the most important issue, serving also as a symbol for the broader conflicts and rivalries between the two countries. The nuclear and missile capabilities of both sides have added a new dimension to the conflict, while domestic political factors have had a major impact on decisions at various times. Following the 1971 conflict and the Shimla Agreement (see above), relations very gradually improved, but without any further breakthrough. In 1987 army manoeuvres close to the Pakistan border seemed to presage new conflict, but in December 1988 Rajiv Gandhi visited Islamabad, the Pakistani capital, for discussions with Pakistan's new Prime Minister, Benazir Bhutto. At this meeting, which constituted the first official visit of an Indian Prime Minister to Pakistan for nearly 25 years, the two leaders signed three agreements, including a formal pledge not to attack each other's nuclear installations. In June 1989 India and Pakistan moved one step closer to defusing the tension created by the confrontation over the Siachen Glacier in the sensitive Kashmir LoC area, when high-level talks were held in Islamabad, at which the two countries agreed to attempt to find a formula to bring about the eventual complete withdrawal of their troops from the area. From the end of 1989, however, the renewed crisis in Kashmir meant that relations were largely frozen, although the agreement not to attack each other's nuclear installations came into effect in January 1991. India gained a notable diplomatic victory in February 1994 when it was able to force the withdrawal, at the UN Commission on Human Rights, of a hostile resolution put forward by Pakistan condemning alleged human rights abuses by Indian security forces in Jammu and Kashmir. In June 1994 the Indian army had begun to deploy a new missile, named the Prithvi, which has the capacity to reach most of Pakistan.

The nuclear tests of May 1998 (see below) marked a low point in Indo-Pakistani relations, but talks resumed towards the end of that year and in February 1999, in an unprecedented gesture, Prime Minister Vajpayee crossed the land border between the two countries (inaugurating the first passenger bus service between India and Pakistan) and visited Lahore, the capital of the Pakistani province of Punjab and the home city of the Pakistani Prime Minister, Nawaz Sharif. Vajpayee and Sharif signed the Lahore Declaration on 21 February, which, with its pledges regarding peace and nuclear security, was patently designed to allay world-wide fears of a nuclear 'flashpoint' in South Asia, and committed the two sides to working towards better relations and to implementing a range of confidence-building measures. In March the two foreign ministers agreed a timetable for further talks.

At the very time that the Lahore Declaration was signed, however, preparations had been under way in Pakistan for an audacious move along the LoC in Kashmir. In early May 1999 it became clear to the Indian army that guerrilla groups, probably reinforced by regular Pakistani troops, had occupied positions on the Indian side of the cease-fire line, near the town of Kargil, thus posing a threat to a vital communication line to the Ladakh region. Air-strikes launched by the Indian air force at the end of the month failed to dislodge the infiltrators, and the army was forced into a lengthy and costly campaign in which at least 400 Indian soldiers died and two Indian military aircraft were shot down. By mid-July, however, the Indian forces had gained the upper hand in the conflict, and the Indian military dominance combined with diplomatic pressure applied by the USA eventually led to a Pakistani withdrawal. Despite some demands from various sectors of the population, the Indian Government refused to allow its troops to cross the LoC into Pakistani-held territory, and thereby strengthened its position internationally. World opinion was generally very supportive of India, and the presumed Pakistani attempt to force the 'internationalization' of the Kashmir issue was thwarted. On 10 August there was renewed tension when India shot down a Pakistani naval patrol aircraft near Pakistan's border with Gujarat, killing all 16 people on board; Pakistan retaliated the following day by firing at Indian military helicopters in the same area. Skirmishing continued along the LoC, and in December 1999 tension was further heightened following the hijack of an Indian

Airlines plane by militants with strong Pakistani connections. India was forced to release several prominent Islamist militants from Indian prisons in exchange for the safe return of the captive passengers and crew. Following unsuccessful attempts to enter negotiations with local Kashmiri groups (see above), in May 2001 Vajpayee issued an unexpected invitation to Gen. Pervez Musharraf to visit India for discussions. The Pakistani leader, who had recently named himself President, duly attended the negotiations in Agra in mid-July. Despite hopes of a dramatic breakthrough, the discussions broke down after both leaders failed to agree on a concluding joint communiqué. Pakistan remained insistent that the two sides agree that Kashmir was the principal issue, while India was resolute that Kashmir be discussed only in the context of cross-border terrorism. Meanwhile, both sides continued to develop their missile programmes. In April 1999 and January 2001 India tested its Agni II missile, which was capable of carrying nuclear warheads; this was matched by Pakistan's comparable test of its Ghauri II missile.

The conflict reached a new stage at the end of 2001 when on 13 December militants gained access to the grounds of the parliament building in New Delhi and attempted to launch an apparent suicide attack. Although no political leaders died, nine people (including a number of policemen, some security officials and a groundsman) were killed and some 25 were injured in the assault; the five assailants were also killed. The attack was seen as an assault on democracy, and was blamed by India on Pakistani intelligence agencies; no proof was produced, however, to support this allegation. By the end of the month positions on both sides of the LoC were reinforced; eventually, up to 1m. troops were mobilized on both sides of the border on a high state of alert, exchanging gunfire daily. President Musharraf's speech in mid-January 2002, in which he promised to combat Pakistan-based militant groups, and subsequent arrests of some of the most prominent militant leaders, combined with international pressure to defuse the tension between the neighbouring countries, had a positive effect in the short term. However, following a further militant attack on an Indian army camp in Jammu in mid-May, in which a number of civilians, including women and children, were killed, the two countries appeared to be on the brink of war again, with the attendant risk of a nuclear exchange. Many politicians and publicists, supporting the argument that India would be doing no more in dealing with terrorism than the USA after the September 2001 attacks on New York and Washington, DC, demanded decisive action against militant bases in Pakistan, while Pakistan made it clear that, under certain circumstances, it would not rule out first use of nuclear weapons. Intense diplomatic efforts, most notably by the US Government, which sent the Deputy Secretary of State to visit both countries in early June and the Secretary of Defense, Donald Rumsfeld, later in the month, appeared to have played a major role in defusing the immediate crisis, although troops on both sides remained in position and diplomatic relations between the two countries were downgraded. Visits in July by the British Foreign Secretary, Jack Straw, and by the US Secretary of State, Gen. Colin Powell, were attempts to encourage further dialogue but produced no immediate result.

While it was assumed that in private there was considerable pressure from the USA and other countries for India and Pakistan to exercise restraint, the situation remained extremely tense for the rest of 2002 and the first few months of 2003. In April 2003, however, Vajpayee made a speech, symbolically in Srinagar, in which he called for negotiations to be resumed. This was followed by the restoration of full diplomatic relations by both India and Pakistan, and by other moves such as the reinstatement of the Delhi–Lahore bus service and of direct air links in early 2004. In late 2003 a cease-fire was implemented along the LoC in Kashmir and in January 2004 Vajpayee and Musharraf held major direct negotiations at the regional summit meeting in Islamabad. In March–April India's first cricket tour of Pakistan in 15 years took place. The change of government in India placed control of foreign relations in the hands of two individuals, K. Natwar Singh as Minister of Foreign Affairs and J. N. Dixit as National Security Adviser, who had been associated with the power projection policies of former premier Indira Gandhi. However, there seemed to be a desire to continue the dialogue, and in early June official-level talks regarding the nuclear issue took place, which led to an agreement on technical measures to reduce the risk of accidental conflict. In September a major meeting took place between new Prime Minister Manmohan Singh and Musharraf when both were attending the UN General Assembly in New York. From then on, the pace of meetings at both official- and ministerial-level accelerated, with topics including not only Kashmir but also other bilateral issues.

In April 2005 Musharraf made a high-profile visit to India. Although no major breakthrough was achieved, the general atmosphere of the talks was regarded as very positive. As well as the Kashmir issue, there was discussion of issues surrounding water sharing between the two countries, which connected with the Kashmir question as certain disputed construction projects by India were actually located in Indian-controlled Kashmir. Fruitless talks over the design of the Baglihar dam led in May 2005 to Pakistan invoking the arbitration clauses of the Indus Waters Treaty (an agreement signed by India and Pakistan in 1960 to control the sharing and management of the waters of the Indus basin). The eventual arbitration, announced in 2007, was a compromise between the two positions, although slightly favouring Pakistan. Other meetings since the Musharraf visit have been principally at the official level and have produced little real progress, although there have been symbolic moves such as the opening of bus services across the LoC (see above). The Mumbai bomb attacks on 11 July 2006 (see above) renewed tensions between the two countries, following the Indian Prime Minister's claim that the perpetrators must have had Pakistani links, and an immediate and forthright rebuttal of this by the Pakistan Government. In September, however, Prime Minister Singh and President Musharraf met on the sidelines of the Havana summit meeting of the Non-Aligned Movement and were able to restart the dialogue. Regular meetings at foreign minister level resumed, as well as diplomatic manoeuvring behind the scenes. These meetings continued after the Pakistan general election of February 2008 brought in a new civilian government.

In December 2006, during an interview with Indian television, President Musharraf stated that, under certain circumstances, Pakistan would relinquish its claim to potential sovereignty over Kashmir. These conditions were based on a porous border, substantial powers of self-government within the various component parts of Kashmir on both sides of the border, and some form of joint management of the territory between India and Pakistan. The argument put forward by Musharraf was that in the course of time borders would become irrelevant. India seemed reluctant to accept these ideas, although it was willing to consider allowing Pakistan a consultative role as part of an eventual settlement.

Indo-US relations had begun to improve during the late 1980s, despite the feeling in India that the USA was always more favourably disposed to Pakistan and China and unwilling to afford India its rightful standing in world affairs. India's recently introduced programme of economic reform was widely welcomed by the USA, and Indian policy-makers recognized the importance of US goodwill to its future investment and trade opportunities. Nevertheless, US efforts to persuade India to reverse its nuclear and rocket programmes through discussions and negotiations with Pakistan, together with concerns in some quarters about the long-term consequences for India's freedom of action if what was seen as a US-inspired economic reform programme were fully implemented, meant that the path has not been an easy one. In 1992 an agreement between India and Russia regarding the supply of rocket engines from the latter provoked a threat of sanctions from the USA and the suspension of the arrangement. During a visit to India by the US Secretary of Defense in January 1995 a 'landmark' agreement on defence and security co-operation was signed by the two countries. India's nuclear tests in May 1998 were a set-back to its relations with the USA; although sanctions were imposed, they were generally regarded as primarily symbolic. In March 2000 US President Bill Clinton made a six-day visit to India, which was widely regarded as initiating a new era in bilateral relations. Abandoning any effort to give India and Pakistan equal weight, the US President seemed to endorse India's position that the Kashmir question was a local matter and of no direct concern to the international community. India reciprocated by indicating that it would maintain a de facto halt to further nuclear tests. In September 2000 the Indian Prime Minister visited the USA and was accorded the honour of addressing a joint session of Congress. In response to the terrorist attacks on US mainland targets on 11 September 2001, India offered full support to the USA and its counter-terrorism initiatives. In late September US President George W. Bush announced an end to the military and economic sanctions imposed against India and Pakistan in 1998. During the US-led military campaign to remove the regime of Saddam Hussain in Iraq in March–April 2003 India deliberately maintained a low-key position, which appeared designed not to embarrass or impede US actions. However, it was not prepared to agree to a US request to contribute peace-keeping troops. India was clearly hoping for a wide range of benefits in return for its stance in both these crises. Although its long-term relationship with the USA, increasingly based on economic ties, was undoubtedly strengthened, India also had to accept that the USA was anxious about the risk of nuclear conflict in South Asia, and would therefore put pressure on it and Pakistan to come to a settlement over the Kashmir issue that would require substantial concessions from both sides. The new Indian Minister of External Affairs, K. Natwar Singh, made a visit to Washington, DC, in June 2004, soon after assuming office, but again made no commitment to sending Indian troops to Iraq.

In June 2005 the Indian Minister of Defence, Pranab Mukherjee, visited Washington in order to sign a major agreement on joint weapons production and related issues. This indicated clearly the increasing depth of India's relationship with the USA, based both on economic ties and on strategic convergence. Following on from the success of that meeting, President Bush visited India in March 2006 and signed a landmark agreement on nuclear co-operation, which, in effect, condoned India's nuclear weapons programme and facilitated potential civilian collaboration. In June the agreement cleared its first hurdle in the US Congress, although there was some significant opposition to an accord which some viewed as rewarding India for its refusal to sign the Nuclear Non-Proliferation Treaty. In December 2006 the US-India Civilian Nuclear Agreement was finally signed by President Bush; however, US opponents to the agreement were subsequently able to stall its implementation and the Indian Government also faced considerable internal political opposition from the communist parties to making any concessions. The sticking points were India's insistence on the one hand that the arrangement to supply US nuclear fuel for civilian reactors would not be affected by any future Indian nuclear test explosion and on the other that it could utilize recycled US nuclear fuel for military purposes. India also refused to succumb to US pressure to terminate discussions with Iran regarding the proposed construction of a natural gas pipeline between the two countries. In June 2007 a senior US official, Nicholas Burns, visited India but was not able to resolve the outstanding issues. In the following month, however, it was announced that negotiations on the implementation of the agreement had been completed, but it had yet to be approved by the US Congress and the Nuclear Suppliers Group.

To some extent in parallel with the development of its relations with the USA, India has from the 1980s onwards steadily improved its relations with Israel, from which it has purchased major weapons systems.

Although the context of the Indo-Russian relationship has changed drastically since the end of the Cold War, it remains important to both sides. A visit by the Indian Prime Minister to the USA in May 1994 was closely followed at the end of June by a trip to Moscow, the Russian capital. The following month it was announced that Russian rocket engines would be supplied to India, despite US concerns (see above), albeit without any transfer of technology. In October 1996 India and Russia signed a defence co-operation agreement (later extended to 2010), and in December India signed a US $1,800m. contract to purchase 40 fighter aircraft from Russia. In June 1998 Russia defied a G-8 ban on exporting nuclear technology to India by agreeing to supply the latter with two nuclear reactors, and in December the Russian Prime Minister visited Delhi, in part to demonstrate diplomatic support for India in the face of Western criticism of the nuclear tests earlier in the year. During Russian President Vladimir Putin's visit to India in October 2000, the two countries signed a declaration of 'strategic partnership', which involved co-operation on defence, economic matters and international terrorism issues. India signed a contract to purchase 50 Sukhoi-30 fighter aircraft from Russia, with a licence to manufacture 150 more. The deal, reportedly worth more than $3,000m., was finalized in December. In February 2001 India agreed to buy 310 Russian T-90 tanks, at an estimated cost of $700m. In June the two countries successfully conducted a joint test of a new supersonic cruise missile. At the Conference on Interaction and Confidence-Building Measures in Asia in June 2002 at Almaty, Kazakhstan, Putin attempted to act as a mediator between India and Pakistan, without success. Putin also paid a visit to India in December 2004, during which an attempt was made to reactivate old linkages, although these ties were clearly less important to India than its relations with the USA. In January 2007 Putin was the chief guest at India's Republic Day celebrations; during his visit an agreement was reached regarding the proposed construction by Russian investors of a number of nuclear power stations in India.

India's nuclear ambitions, as indicated above, have always been an issue in its international relations, both with Pakistan and China, and with the West. Although the 1974 test did not lead to any immediate development, it was clear that India was steadily acquiring the technological capacity to move ahead, if it so wished. Its long-standing refusal to sign the Nuclear Non-Proliferation Treaty (NPT) was repeated at the 1995 conference at which the treaty was renewed. In mid-1996, in a move that provoked widespread international condemnation, India decided not to be party to the Comprehensive Test Ban Treaty (CTBT), which it had earlier supported, so long as the existing nuclear powers were unwilling to commit themselves to a strict timetable for full nuclear disarmament. In early April 1998 Pakistan provoked stern condemnation from the new right-wing Government in India following its successful test-firing of a new intermediate-range missile (capable of reaching deep into Indian territory). In the following month the arms race escalated dramatically and to potentially dangerous proportions when India took a momentous decision to explode five nuclear test devices and to claim thereby that it was now a nuclear-weapons state. This action should also be considered in the light of India's progress in developing missiles capable of carrying nuclear warheads. At least three reasons can be proffered as to why the new BJP Government carried out the nuclear tests. First, according to an official announcement, the Government was concerned at the growing power of China, and felt it necessary to take long-term measures to maintain a measure of equality between the two most prominent countries in Asia. Second, there was concern over Pakistan's nuclear programme, and the possibility that, with help from China, it might have moved ahead of India in certain respects. Third, India's future position as a major world power, entitled, for example, to a permanent seat on the UN Security Council, was believed to depend on its ability to match the existing nuclear powers. India's controversial decision led to two immediate consequences—Pakistan responded with its own series of nuclear tests, and the USA, with limited support from other countries, subsequently imposed economic sanctions on both India and Pakistan until such time as they had signed the NPT and the CTBT and taken steps to reverse their nuclear programmes. Having made its point in no uncertain terms, Indian policy seemed to be to attempt to negotiate a deal with the USA. Immediately after the tests a self-imposed moratorium on further testing was announced, followed by intense diplomatic activity. By mid-2001, however, no further substantive progress had been made. India's substantive nuclear plans remained closely intertwined with its relations with the USA (see above). With regard to Pakistan, India stated that it was prepared to hold bilateral talks aimed at a 'no-first-use' agreement. However, both countries seemed more concerned about gaining the diplomatic initiative than holding serious discussions. The Indo-Pakistani hostilities of 1999 and the crisis of 2002 raised the possibility of an actual nuclear conflict between the two sides. However, subsequent improvements in relations and specific dialogues on nuclear issues (see above) reduced the risks considerably. In April 2007 and again in May 2008 India successfully tested its most advanced nuclear-capable missile, Agni-III, which has a range of more than 3,000 km.

# Economy

## SANJAYA BARU

### Revised by C. RAMMANOHAR REDDY

In 2000 India became a nation of more than 1,000m. people. Its population at 1 March 2008 was estimated at around 1,147.7m. Size and diversity are the two most distinctive features of the Indian economy. India is a vast country, in terms both of its area and its population. It has a total area of about 3.3m. sq km, making it the third largest among the developing countries, exceeded only by the People's Republic of China and Brazil. In terms of population, however, India is second only to China, the one other nation in the world with a population exceeding 1,000m. India's diversity is both regional and structural, and, consequently, any average statistic for India conceals both this diversity and the disparity in levels of development. Regionally, India extends from the subtropical deltaic regions of the east and the south, to the semi-arid plains and plateaux of central India; from the areas of heavy, seasonal monsoon rains to the desert lands of Rajasthan. There are, on the one hand, relatively prosperous states, such as Gujarat, Maharashtra, Haryana and the Punjab, where the levels of income per caput are much higher than the national average, and are growing rapidly. There are, on the other hand, underdeveloped, poverty-ridden states, such as Bihar, Madhya Pradesh and parts of eastern and north-eastern India, where the standard of living is abysmal. To sum up, wide inter-regional inequalities in almost all indicators of development are an important defining feature of the Indian subcontinent.

In terms of its overall economic structure, when measured by the structure of output, India is no longer an economy dependent on agriculture. In the fiscal year 2007/08 (April–March) only 20% of gross domestic product (GDP) originated in the primary sector (agriculture, forestry, fishing and mining), the secondary sector (manufacturing, construction and power) contributed 25% of GDP, and the tertiary, or services, sector accounted for as much as 55% of GDP. Agriculture itself accounted for a mere 18% of GDP. Over the decades agriculture's share in GDP has declined sharply, while its share in employment has fallen only marginally. The agricultural sector still sustains an overwhelming majority of the working population: according to official national sample surveys conducted in 2004/05, agriculture provided 56% of total employment in India, industry 18% and services the remaining 26%. The major challenge, therefore, has always been to generate high-productivity work outside agriculture so that the working population in the low-productivity farming sector can move out. Indian agriculture itself is diverse, including small-scale peasant farmers, who cultivate subsistence holdings under traditional practices, as well as relatively large-scale farmers who practise high-productivity, commercial agriculture. Similarly, at one extreme, India's manufacturing sector produces basic industrial inputs such as steel, cement and chemicals, as well as very sophisticated high technology equipment, while, at the other, there is a very large and dynamic 'informal' sector, producing a wide range of products by means of 'back-yard' technologies. A new phenomenon that has become established in the first decade of the 2000s is the emergence of high-quality and precision industries of global standards, although this sub-sector remains a small component of the manufacturing sector. India's services are just as heterogeneous as agriculture and industry. The sector includes dynamic and high-productivity areas such as the computer software and business process outsourcing (BPO) industries, which can compete with the best in the world, and modern financial enterprises that deal in complex financial products and services. It also comprises a mass of small-scale and low-productivity services such as single-person retail outlets, pavement repair stalls, restaurants offering basic foods, and a variety of activities where those in search of work are compelled to find low-skilled and low-paying self-employment.

#### INDIA AT INDEPENDENCE

Almost two centuries of British colonial rule ended on 15 August 1947, when India became independent. Colonial policy during the inter-war period (1918–39) sought to foster some industrial and agricultural development by investing in the required infrastructure, but at independence the Indian economy had not fully recovered from the ravages wreaked by the 19th-century processes of enforced commercialization in agriculture and deindustrialization, coupled with the drain of economic surpluses through the levy of 'home charges'. The first half of the 20th century witnessed a decline in levels of industrial productivity and in the rates of growth of agricultural output in some parts of India, thus accentuating inter-regional inequalities and constricting the home market in manufactured goods. The more reliable estimates of economic activity during this period indicate that the output of major food crops expanded at a rate lower than the rate of increase of population, thus depressing the standard of living. In turn, this acted as a constraint on the growth of industrial activity. This resulted from the adverse ratio of population to agricultural land, the effects of which on crop productivity were not offset by any significant changes in technology or investment in infrastructure. The output of commercial non-food crops expanded at a faster rate than that of food crops, partly in response to the export demand, for example in jute, and partly in response to growing domestic demand for sugar and oilseeds. Indian industry, the growth of which can be directly attributed to the policy of 'discriminating protection' that was pursued after the mid-1920s, was restricted largely to consumer goods, such as cotton textiles, sugar, paper and a few chemicals and engineering goods, and was mostly confined to a small number of urban centres. Up until the 1950s Indian industry was dependent on imports for all its requirements of capital goods and machinery. While the United Kingdom was the major source of all such imports, the proportion has declined over the years, as both domestic production and imports from other advanced industrial economies have increased.

India had a stable and efficient administration, both fiscal and legal, and fairly well-developed means of communication, especially railway transport and shipping. There was an uneven educational system, which neglected primary education and literacy for the masses, but produced an adequate supply of people with higher education for recruitment into the lower levels of administration and the professions. A very small industrial labour force, and an even smaller number of industrialists, provided a base that could be built upon for the future.

#### ECONOMIC RESOURCES

India has a rich base of natural resources, many of which remain inadequately exploited. This potential, together with a large number of underemployed people and underutilized assets, makes it possible for India to aim for a much higher rate of economic growth, if productivity and efficiency are improved.

The most recent decennial census was conducted in February 2001, when India's population was placed at 1,028,610,328.

According to the latest official projections, India's population is expected to reach 1,269m. in 2016 and 1,400m. in 2026. The proportion of the population in the working age group (15–59 years) stood at 57.7% in 2001; this was projected to rise to 64.3% by 2026. It is this large and rising percentage of the economically active population—commonly referred to as India's 'demographic dividend'—which will work to the country's advantage.

According to the 2001 census, 743m. Indians live in rural areas and 285m. in urban areas. The net increase in population in rural areas between 1991 and 2001 was 113m., while in urban areas it was 69m. The percentage decadal growth of population in rural and urban areas during the same period was estimated to be 17.9% and 31.2%, respectively. The percentage of urban population in relation to total population had increased by 2.1% compared with 1991, to reach 27.8% in 2001. The annual rate of growth of total population in 1991–2001 was 2.76%, compared with 2.88% in 1981–91. Based on the 2001 census, the annual exponential rate of growth of population was estimated at 1.93%, lower than the annual rate recorded in 1981–91 (2.14%).

The country-wide average population growth rate was a sum of wide regional variations. Southern India recorded much lower average annual rates of growth of population, with the lowest rate, of 0.90%, being recorded by the southern state of Kerala. The highest annual rate of growth of population, 4.97%, was recorded by the north-eastern state of Nagaland. The density of the population increased from 142 per sq km in 1961 to 324 in 2001, with the highest density of 904 per sq km being recorded in West Bengal and the lowest, 13, recorded by Arunachal Pradesh, in the north-east. Among urban centres, Kolkata (formerly Calcutta) has the highest density, with 23,783 per sq km recorded in 1999. In 2005 India's crude birth rate (per 1,000) was estimated to be 23.8, compared with 45 in 1965, and the crude death rate (per 1,000) was placed at 7.6, in comparison with 20 in 1965. The total fertility rate, which was 6.2 births per woman in 1965, had declined to 3.0 by 2004. In 1998–99 48.2% of the population in the relevant age-group was estimated to be using contraceptives. The infant mortality rate, which is a useful guide to the level of social welfare, declined from 150 per 1,000 live births in 1965 to 58 per 1,000 in 2005. Although lower than the average (of 80 per 1,000) for low-income countries, this compares poorly with China's rate of 32. Life expectancy at birth for men rose from 37.2 years in 1951, to 59.7 years in 1991 and to 61.8 years in 2002/03. For women, the respective figures were 36.2, 60.9 and 63.5 years.

The population is still largely rural, with about 72% of the total residing in approximately 600,000 villages. India's population is, however, gradually becoming more urbanized, with the process of change varying from state to state. Official projections forecast that the urban population as a percentage of the total population would increase from 27.9% in 2001 to 30.1% in 2011, 31.2% in 2016 and 33.5% in 2026. It was estimated that by 2026 in two of the larger states—namely Tamil Nadu and Maharashtra—more than 50% of the population would be living in towns and cities.

While the overall urban proportion of the population is small, total numbers are large: in 1981 there were about 160m. inhabitants in urban areas, of whom about 60% or more resided in the larger cities, i.e. those with a population of 100,000 or more. According to the 2001 census, the urban population was an estimated 285m. The four largest urban agglomerations, Mumbai (formerly Bombay), Kolkata, Delhi and Chennai (formerly Madras), had a combined population of about 49m. Since the late 1970s cities such as Bangalore, Ahmedabad and Hyderabad have also expanded rapidly as new industrial centres. Of the larger states, Tamil Nadu is the most urbanized, with 44.0% of its population living in urban areas in 2001, followed by Maharashtra (42.4%) and Gujarat (37.4%); Bihar is the least urbanized, with just 10.5% of its population living in urban areas. Including the smaller states, Goa (49.8%) and Mizoram (49.6%) are more urbanized and Himachal Pradesh (10.0%) less so.

Of India's total area of around 3.3m. sq km, about 55% is available for cultivation. The remainder consists of forests, deserts, land in urban use, meadows and pasture, or fallow land. Of the cultivable land, only about 33% is under assured irrigation, despite a substantial expansion of irrigation facilities since the 1960s. The rest is dependent upon rain-fed agriculture. The pattern of rainfall, under the south-west and the north-east monsoons, is highly seasonal and variable. Except in the extreme south, most of the rain falls in the summer months of June to September, and is critical for prosperity and survival. A small but essential amount of rain falls in the winter, allowing some areas to grow winter food crops in addition to summer crops. The monsoon rains are highly unreliable from year to year, in terms of both their timing and the amount of rain that they bring. An additional problem is that the amount of rainfall varies widely across the country, diminishing rapidly from east to west; areas where average rainfall is low also suffer from the high variability.

As agriculture is critically dependent on the monsoon, the fear that inadequate rainfall in every third or fifth year is likely to produce unfavourable conditions affects the populace and government planners. Although agriculture now accounts for less than one-fifth of India's GDP, the economy remains vulnerable to the vagaries of the monsoon because lower farm incomes affect the demand for industrial products and services. Since a poor monsoon reduces agricultural output, prices of foodstuffs and, therefore, inflation then threaten to rise sharply. The impact of both these sets of effects has weakened in recent years. The growing importance of exports means that the economy has become less dependent on the nature of the monsoon to maintain domestic demand. Since India is no longer constrained by limited foreign-exchange reserves, imports of agricultural commodities can be used to dampen inflation whenever farm production is affected by less than average rainfall. However, with a majority of the working population still dependent on agriculture, a drought does continue to have an adverse effect on rural incomes. Much of India's farmland is of poor natural fertility, being subject to erosion, salinity or leaching: the result of years of population pressure on a poor agricultural economy. In addition, the land that is available for cultivation is distributed very unequally among the farming population. The land itself is being subjected to environmental pressures, the long-term effects of which may be catastrophic but are, as yet, incalculable. The growing demand for fuelwood, for energy needs, is leading to large-scale deforestation and soil erosion which, if not halted or reversed, may have serious effects on agricultural productivity and the social environment.

## NATIONAL INCOME AND STRUCTURE OF PRODUCTION

Estimates of India's gross national income (GNI), and consequently of national income per head, may be derived from two main sources. These are official Indian sources, which provide estimates in terms of Indian rupees, which can be converted into US dollar values for international comparison. There are also estimates in US dollars, calculated by international institutions such as the World Bank. These two types of estimates often differ from each other and there are a number of reasons for this being so. In addition, US dollar values provide only an approximation to levels of real income in India. This is chiefly because relative price ratios differ between countries, and a typical Indian 'basket' of commodities would cost less to buy in India than in the USA. While the actual rupee and US dollar values of levels of GNI or incomes may not be exactly the same (after conversion at market exchange rates), however, the overall trends in rates of growth are similar.

India's GDP at current factor cost was estimated by the country's official statistical agencies to be the equivalent of US $1,049,670m. in 2007/08, based on an average exchange rate of Rs 41 per US dollar. GDP per caput was approximately $922. (World Bank estimates, as reported in *World Development Indicators 2008*, placed India's GNI per head at $820 in 2008.)

India experienced a steady acceleration of its national income growth in the latter half of the 20th century. Following near-zero growth between 1900 and 1950, India's GDP grew, in real terms, at an average annual rate of about 3.5% between 1950 and 1980, and at an average annual rate of approximately 5.6% in the period 1980–2000. The 1990s witnessed a fluctuation in growth: GDP recorded a yearly growth of 6.7% between 1992/93 and 1996/97 before declining to 5.5% per year in the late 1990s. The early years of the 21st century saw a further deceleration in growth: the Indian economy grew by an average of a mere 4.6% a year between 2000/01 and 2002/03.

Since then, however, the economy has shown a sustained period of very high growth. In the five-year period between 2003/04 and 2007/08 GDP expanded by an average of as much as 8.8% a year: 8.5% in 2003/04, 7.5% in 2004/05, 9.4% in 2005/06, 9.6% in 2006/07 and 9.0% in 2007/08. The industrial sector recorded annual growth of 7.4%–10.0% and services grew by between 8.5% and 11.2% per year. The only blip during this exceptional period of economic growth occurred in 2004/05, when the primary sector recorded zero growth. During the preceding half century the Indian economy had never before registered annual GDP growth rates of more than 8% over a five-year period nor had it ever registered 9% and more for three years in succession. The performance of the economy in the middle years of the first decade of the 2000s has given room for optimism that the period of moderate growth is now behind India.

On a purchasing-power parity (PPP) basis—as estimated by the World Bank—India's GNI per caput was reckoned to be US $2,460 in 2006. On this basis India was the fifth largest economy in the world in that year, with a GNI of $2,726,300m., after the USA, China, Japan and Germany. Based on the argument that market exchange rates do not reflect their PPP equivalents, owing to differences in the relative value of traded versus non-traded output, the IMF has adopted the view that PPP estimates of income per caput represent more accurately the distribution of real income across the world. (In 2007 the World Bank, citing methodological revisions, lowered the PPP estimates of China, India and a number of other developing countries by between 25% and 30%.)

In US dollar terms, and at market exchange rates, in 2005 the GNI of the Indian economy, according to the World Bank, was $909,100m. When output is measured according to market exchange rates the Indian economy is the 10th largest in the world.

Compared with the near-zero growth in output in British India during the first half of the 20th century, and the long-term average annual growth rate of 3.5% during 1950–80, real GDP increased by an average of about 5.0% per year in 1980–90 and an estimated 5.8% in 1992–2003. As discussed above, growth since 2003 has been even higher: averaging 8.8% per year between 2003/04 and 2007/08.

Estimates of India's per caput income, low as it is by international standards, give a misleading picture of the standard of living that most Indians enjoy for two major reasons. First, valuations in terms of the market exchange rate do not accurately portray the real purchasing power of income for reasons discussed above. Second, the averages conceal wide disparities in income across both social groups and regions. For example, some parts of western and southern India are as prosperous as the majority of South-East Asian economies, just as the top 5% of the Indian population enjoys a standard of living comparable to most upper-middle to upper income economies. However, according to official estimates, 28% of the population lives below the government-defined 'poverty line'. There are varying estimates of the incidence of poverty in India. Alternative sources of data, as well as varying definitions of poverty, have contributed to a continued controversy among academic economists and policy-makers on the actual incidence of poverty in India as well as on the trend of change. What is largely undisputed is that as a percentage of the population, the proportion of people living below the poverty line has declined from more than 50% in the 1960s to 28% in the middle years of the first decade of the 2000s. There has also been discussion of the impact of the recent acceleration of growth in the 1990s, and the policies of trade liberalization, on poverty. Critics claim that higher growth has not 'trickled down' to the poor and that, consequently, there has been no improvement in their status. Economists in the Planning Commission claim that the statistics are not comprehensive and do not capture structural changes under way in the economy. It is clear that some regions of the country have succeeded in lowering the incidence of poverty, while others (many of which are home to a larger number of the poor), have experienced a very slow pace of poverty reduction. On the whole, peninsular India has made greater progress than the plains of north India.

Not surprisingly, the structure of production has changed during the process of economic growth in India. In 1950/51 agriculture and allied activities (primary sector) contributed 58% of total national income, while manufacturing, construction and mining (industrial sector) together accounted for 17%, and the services sector (including defence and public administration) contributed the remaining 25%. More than half a century later, the share of the primary sector has more than halved, that of services has doubled, while the industrial sector has increased its share only modestly: the primary sector accounted for 20% of GDP in 2007/08, the industrial sector for 25% and services for 55%. The trajectory shown by the Indian economy has differed substantially from the present-day advanced economies in that it has not moved first from an agricultural to an industrial economy and then subsequently to a services-dominated economy, but has instead seen services grow at the expense of agriculture in terms of GDP without the industrial sector growing in any major fashion. The phenomenal increase in the size of the services sector is in part a reflection of the deceleration of industrial production in the latter half of the 1990s and in part represents the growth of the financial, government, hotel and tourism and trade sectors. Although the economy has been undergoing a process of structural change, this change has not been of a kind associated with the growth of modern, large-scale industry, and the small-scale (non-factory) sector continues to account for a very large share of total manufacturing output. In terms of the structure of employment, the economy has undergone little change. As mentioned above, agriculture still accounts for an overwhelmingly large percentage of the total labour force, employing 56% of the total, industry 18% and services 26%. These figures indicate the limited ability of the modern industrial sector to absorb the growing labour force, partly compounded by its relatively low weight in total output and partly by the dominance of a capital-intensive technology, which creates few job opportunities per unit of capital invested. As a rough estimate, the capital cost of each job being created is perhaps 20 times as much in organized industry as in agriculture. While much of the recent expansion in industrial activity has been in the private sector, it is the public sector that has, throughout the past few decades, provided greater employment, with its share in total industrial employment estimated at nearly 70% in 1996.

Although employment in the organized large-scale manufacturing sector has not increased in recent years, there is evidence to suggest that overall employment growth in the economy kept pace with population growth until the mid-1990s and decelerated thereafter. Employment increased in the rural non-farm and urban informal sectors. However, while the growth rate of employment in 1987/88 to 1993/94 was estimated to be 2.43%, compared with a lower rate in the preceding two decades, between 1993/94 and 1999/2000 overall employment was estimated to have grown by only 1.0%. Analysts believe that the deceleration in employment growth was mainly due to the decline in employment generation in the public sector and a slower growth in agricultural employment. The positive growth in employment in the services sector and in non-farm businesses has not compensated for the loss in on-farm and organized industrial sector employment.

There has been a very encouraging trend in savings and investment in recent years. As a proportion of GDP, gross domestic savings more than doubled, from around 12% in the early 1960s to 25% in 1995/96. Although the savings rate subsequently slumped to around 23% during much of the second half of the 1990s, it has since recovered and has risen very strongly since 2002/03. Gross savings as a proportion of GDP reached 34.8% in 2006/07. The overwhelming contribution came from household savings (23.8%), followed by private corporate savings (7.8%) and the public sector (3.2%).

The rate of investment has grown in tandem with the rate of savings, with the difference being covered by inflows of foreign aid until the 1990s. In addition, more diverse forms of foreign capital have been supplementing domestic investment in recent years. Investment or gross domestic capital formation reached 35.6% in 2006/07, a record high for the Indian economy. The recent upturn in the rate of investment have been attributed to the private corporate sector rather than the household sector, which had traditionally supplied India with the greatest amount of investment. In 2006/07 investment as a percentage of GDP in the corporate sector was 14.5%, compared with 12.5% in the household sector. The public sector no longer drives investment as it did until the 1980s and managed an investment rate of just 7.8% in 2006/07. India altered its strategy of resource mobilization in the 1990s, moving in favour of increased foreign direct investment (FDI) and reducing its dependence on external debt. Consequently, the external debt-to-GDP ratio decreased from 38.7% in 1991/92 to 15.8% in 2005/06. India's external debt in absolute terms remains large. At the end of March 2008 foreign debt was US $221,200m. This represented a sizeable increase by as much as $51,500m. from March 2007 and was largely owing to substantial borrowings by Indian companies and short-term debt. Despite this large debt burden, India had a low debt service ratio of 5.4% in 2007/08. One worrying factor is the rise in the level of short-term borrowings as a proportion of total external debt: the percentage increased five-fold from 4% in 2003/04 to 20% in 2007/08.

While aiming to achieve a lower debt-to-GDP ratio, India pursued increased capital flows through FDI and portfolio investment. In the early 21st century India continued to attract less FDI than East and South-East Asia; however, the Government remained committed to a more open external economic policy, welcoming portfolio investment as well as FDI.

By developing-country standards, India's inflation rate is not very high. The long-term average annual rate of inflation (measured by the wholesale price index) for 1960–90 reached about 8%. The 1990s began with a much higher rate of inflation, with an average of 10.6% per year in 1991–96. However, inflation declined after the mid-1990s. In 1996–2001 the average annual rate of inflation was 5.1%, falling further, to 4.7%, in 2001–06. The economy remains susceptible, none the less, to sudden surges in the rate of inflation. In 2006/07 a combination of factors (high petroleum prices and price rises in a select group of agricultural commodities) meant that inflation became a major issue again. Wholesale price inflation crossed 5.5% in 2006/07 and consumer price inflation was more than 7% in the same year. The era of low inflation of the early years of the first decade of the 2000s appeared to have ended, at least temporarily, with inflation reaching the 10% mark in mid-2008. The surge in global prices for petroleum, food and commodities in general was communicated to the Indian economy, which also showed the effects of overheating after three years of growth of 9% plus.

## AGRICULTURE

Until the fourth quarter of the 20th century, the fortunes of the Indian economy depended largely on how well the agricultural sector performed. With agriculture now contributing less than one-fifth of GDP, this is no longer so. Yet, in other respects agriculture remains a vital constituent of the economy. Close to three-fifths of the labour force is still dependent on agriculture for its livelihood. Moreover, India's food security depends on the steady domestic production of cereals and pulses, as well as on stable inflation. The volume of agricultural output is highly sensitive to the nature of the monsoon, and can fluctuate widely and unpredictably from year to year. One of the important features of the Indian economy in recent years has been the relative 'drought-proofing' of the industrial sector, with the result that the impact of poor agricultural harvests is not felt with the same intensity as in the past in the urban and industrial sectors.

Since the mid-1990s Indian agriculture has registered an erratic record, raising concerns about the quality of life of the rural population and about the ability of the Indian economy to grow consistently by more than 7%–8% per year.

The GDP of the agricultural sector as a whole experienced a healthy average annual growth rate of 4.4% in the 1980s, before decelerating sharply in the 1990s. In the five-year period between 1997/98 and 2002/03 growth slowed to as little as an average of 0.9% per year. Subsequently, however, agricultural GDP recovered to reach an average annual rate of 4.6% between 2003/04 and 2007/08. None the less, this recovery has been too short-lived and has been too marked by sharp fluctuations to give confidence that the years of slow growth are behind India. With a few exceptions, the slowdown in the 1990s affected both food and commercial crops. Per caput food availability (measured in terms of cereals and pulses) declined to levels not seen since the mid-1970s. Further; the deceleration was more acute in the rain-fed areas where the protection of irrigation was not yet available. A notable aspect of the recent volatility in the agricultural sector has been fluctuations in the output of grain, as illustrated by the production data: 196.8m. metric tons (2000/01), 212.9m. tons (2001/02), 174.8m. tons (2002/03), 213.2m. tons (2003/04), 198.4m. tons (2004/05), 208.6m. tons (2005/06), 217.3m. tons (2006/07) and 227.3m. tons (2007/08).

India is a major producer of a number of agricultural commodities, including rice, wheat, cotton, groundnuts, sugar cane (of which it is the region's leading producer) and tea, although its share of world trade in these commodities is generally low. Domestic production is dominated by food grains (cereals and pulses), which constitute roughly two-thirds of total agricultural output. The bulk of India's production of food grains consists of cereals, principally rice, wheat, sorghum (jowar), maize and various forms of millet, mainly cattail millet (bajra). Less than 8% of the production of food grains is provided by pulses, which are a useful source of vegetable protein for consumers. Productivity is low, yet, in absolute terms, India is a leading global producer in a number of commodities and products: for example, it is the world's largest producer of milk and the second largest producer of fruits and vegetables.

There are two important growing seasons in India: the *kharif*, or the summer season, especially important for rice; and the *rabi*, or the winter season, during which most of the wheat is grown. The *kharif* crop is particularly dependent on the monsoon rains, although failure of the winter rains can damage the *rabi* crops also. However, the latter is becoming increasingly reliant on irrigation and, to that extent, a little more protected from the vagaries of the climate. Compared with an irrigation potential of 22.6m. ha at the time of India's independence, 2005 estimates by the Planning Commission place the irrigation area at 82.6m. ha (equivalent to 43% of the total cropped area of 192m. ha). The country's 'Ultimate Irrigation Potential' is estimated to be 139.9m. ha. During the 1950s and the early 1960s the bulk of the increase in India's output of food grains resulted from an expansion of the area sown. However, the supply of cultivable land has practically reached its limit, with increasing competition for land between food grains and non-food crops. Recent increases in output have resulted chiefly from improvements in yields, especially for wheat, but also for rice and bajra, particularly on irrigated land planted with new high-yielding varieties (HYV). By international standards, however, yields are still very low, and practices such as multiple cropping affect only a small proportion of the total cultivable area.

There is naturally some doubt as to whether India can succeed in producing enough food for its growing population. This was a major concern in the mid-1960s when widespread droughts and stagnant grain production compelled the Government to seek large amounts of food aid from abroad. Subsequent success with the 'Green Revolution' meant that India could increasingly do without large-scale imports. The evidence over the long-term is rather contradictory, however, and future prospects are not easy to determine. On the one hand, the rate of increase in the country's total production of food grains has barely kept pace with the rate of population growth. On the other hand, net imports of food have declined significantly in recent years, especially as a proportion of total availability. Net imports of food were less than 2% of total supply in the 1990s, compared with an estimated 8%–10% in the 1960s and 5%–8% in the 1970s. The view that India is achieving self-sufficiency in food has to be qualified, without denying the very substantial progress that the country has made towards this objective. The effective economic demand for food depends not on population growth, but on increases in purchasing power. The persistence of large-scale poverty in India reflects the limited growth in purchasing power of potential consumers of food grains. In 2006 India returned to the global grain market as a buyer for the first time in a decade when it decided to import 330,000 metric tons of wheat to replenish government food stocks in order to meet emergency requirements. Slow growth in wheat production, together with falling procurement by official agencies, had brought government holdings down to minimum buffer stock norms, leaving the Government with limited room to manoeuvre in an emergency. In 2008, however, a record purchase by procurement agencies from a record wheat harvest gave the Government the confidence that it would not have to buy wheat from the global market. In early 2008 the Government banned rice exports in an attempt to dampen domestic rice prices.

Non-food crops have expanded less rapidly in terms of output and yield, particularly those that are not plantation crops, as are tea and coffee. Owing to an increase in the profitability of producing food crops, there has been little increase in the area under non-food crops, and there has been no comparable development of HYV for these crops. An exception, to some extent, is sugar cane, production of which reached a peak of 355.5m. metric tons in 2006/07. Production of sugar cane has always fluctuated, and, with that, output of sugar. The result has been that, with domestic demand having the first claim on sugar production, India has been only a very hesitant participant in the global sugar market. Government policy also favours the satisfaction of domestic demand for tea (India is the world's leading consumer), as with many other consumer goods, and treats export supplies, to some extent, as a residual item, partly to ward off inflationary pressures.

An important feature of Indian agriculture in recent years has been the widening of inter-regional disparities in agricultural production, productivity and standards of living. While regions serviced by assured irrigation (particularly north-western India and the deltaic regions of peninsular India) have prospered, dry land and semi-arid regions have not done so well. The inability to transfer the success of the 'Green Revolution' to dry-land farming has widened the divide, in terms of standards of living, between dry and wet regions. Consequently, food consumption levels are also uneven and the incidence of poverty and malnourishment varies widely across the country.

Policy-makers believe that to sustain overall economic growth of 7.0% to 8.0%, Indian agriculture will have to expand by at least 4.0% per year, a target that was met in the early 1990s, but has not since been ensured. Higher agricultural growth is contingent upon increased public investment in irrigation, rural roads, agricultural research and extension services and soil conservation. New public investment will, however, require the reduction of input subsidies, especially subsidies for fertilizer use, irrigation water and power. These subsidies have contributed to environmental damage and wastage of natural resources. As a result of this degradation of natural resources, ecological pressures have emerged as a new constraint on agriculture. According to government estimates, in ecological terms, only one-third of Indian farmland is in good health, with the remaining two-thirds suffering from various types of ecological damage. Increased public investment in agriculture also requires the removal of restrictions on trade, particularly the movement of agricultural produce within the country. A decline in capital formation in the agricultural sector has emerged as a major concern for policy-makers and agricultural planners. Although some state governments have been investing funds in rural infrastructure, particularly in irrigation and road-building, widespread neglect in productivity improvement and inadequate investment in new technology continue. India will have to increase land productivity and rural incomes in order to accelerate the rate of economic growth.

More recently, a breakdown in the institutional credit system has been held responsible for the slowdown in agricultural production. An important element of the production strategy of the 1970s and 1980s was the easy availability of bank credit to farmers at very low rates of interest. Banks, which faced a less regulated regime in the 1990s, slowed the flow of credit to agriculture and also raised interest rates. The resultant increase in dependence on informal sources—e.g. high-cost loans from money-lenders—was perceived to have been one important contributory factor to a wave of suicides by farmers in many parts of the country in the late 1990s and the early years of the 21st century. The United Progressive Alliance (UPA) Government has made agricultural credit a priority area of policy. One of its goals is to double the flow of institutional credit to the agricultural sector.

Recognizing that a turnaround in the sector was essential to protect rural livelihoods, ensure food security and realize a 7%–8% overall annual economic growth rate, the Government unveiled a new agricultural strategy in mid-2007. This was based on increasing crop productivity by closing the gap between farm and research yields and facilitating substantial investments to increase crop productivity. The Government announced that its ultimate goal was to bring about a 'second' Green Revolution.

As mentioned above, a symptom of the crisis in agriculture is the growing phenomenon of suicides among the farming population, mainly in peninsular India but also in the north-western state of the Punjab. According to official statistics, as many as 8,900 farmers took their lives between 2001 and 2006 in the states of Andhra Pradesh, Karnataka, Kerala and Maharashtra. Independent studies attribute the high number of suicides to rising input costs, fluctuating output and reductions in the price of crops such as cotton. In February 2008, in response to concerns that high levels of debt were causing extreme distress, the UPA Government announced a one-time waiver for bank loans taken out by farmers operating small and medium-sized holdings. The waiver, which was to be lifted the same year, would total Rs 700,000m. (approximately US $17,000m.).

## INDUSTRY AND INFRASTRUCTURE

In 2000–05 the acceleration in India's economic growth rate, manufacturing growth rates of more than 9% per year and the emergence of globally competitive industrial companies in the fields of pharmaceuticals, engineering, chemicals, automobiles and even in high technology generated expectations that the transformation of India's industrial sector was finally taking place. Simultaneously, the major overseas expansion drive of Indian companies in select sectors—mainly in the form of acquisitions—heralded the arrival of Indian companies as manufacturing units in North America and Western Europe. However, major constraints in infrastructure, especially in the power and transport sectors, remain, and mass manufacturing on the scale that is currently being witnessed in China has yet to emerge in India. The breakthrough in industrial growth in India in the first half of the first decade of the 21st century also took place in the midst of a boom in the global economy. The big challenge for the manufacturing sector in particular is whether this growth can be sustained in the context of the financial turmoil and surging petroleum prices that affected the world from 2007.

At independence in 1947 India was producing a limited range of industrial products. These consisted of cotton textiles, jute, some iron and steel, a few consumer goods, but very little machinery. Most of the demand for manufactured goods was met through imports. Thus, in the 1950s more than one-third of total steel supplies were imported, as was 70% of textile machinery, almost 100% of sugar-mill machinery and about 90% of metal-working machinery. By the late 1960s imports of these industrial products had declined significantly: to less than 15% of the total iron and steel supply, a little over one-half of metal-working and textile machinery, and hardly any sugar-milling equipment. These circumstances coincided with a period during which the absolute level of demand for almost all of these commodities had increased substantially. Other figures provide further evidence of the rapid growth and diversification of industrial production in India, to such an extent that India in the 1980s could reasonably be included as one of the so-called newly industrialized countries (NICs). While this rapidly diminishing dependence on imports was achieved, Indian industry was at that time characterized by a relatively low level of productivity and a lack of competitiveness in international markets, which hampered India's export efforts.

Much of the development and diversification of India's industrial base in the 1950s and 1960s can be attributed to the system of planning and large-scale investment in the public sector. The effects of the delicensing and liberalization of industry in the early 1990s posed questions regarding the older industrial policies (especially the pessimism about exports); however; it is accepted that without public-sector intervention and state-directed investment in a diverse set of industries, India would not have developed such a diversified industrial structure.

In recent years the structure of industrial production has undergone significant change, with chemical-based industries increasing their share of industrial production at the expense of agro-based industries. A new vibrant industry that grew rapidly in the mid-1990s was the automobile and auto ancillary segment. The former was based largely on the assembly of imported components, but the latter was characterized by a considerable degree of sophisticated production. Three characteristics of the pattern of industrial growth may be noted. First, statistics are most readily available for the organized sector of industry, which is defined in terms of units consisting of 10 or more workers using power or of 20 or more without power. Much of the industrial activity, however, is carried out by smaller units. The structure of this unorganized sector has changed in recent years. The older 'small-scale' sector, supported by bank finance and state subsidies, has found itself in difficulties as the protection offered by a closed economy and government aid has gradually been dismantled. At the same time, an informal sector in industry that supplies export houses (as in textiles and jewellery) has thrived and in services a variety of small enterprises have emerged to feed the growing organized firms in the tertiary sector. Second, within the organized sector, the distribution of employment and output is extremely unbalanced. In the early 1980s only 6.3% of factories had capital of more than Rs 2m. However, these provided 60.6% of total employment in the organized sector, and produced 80% of the value added. By contrast, 38.2% of the factories had capital of less than Rs 100,000; they provided 11.5% of employment and only 4.1% of value added. Third, the growth of industrial production has been uneven, with fluctuations between different years and between regions. Following India's independence in 1947, industrial growth was rapid in the period up to the mid-1960s. The rate of growth of industrial production slowed thereafter as Indian industry entered a phase of relative stagnation, but it recovered in the early 1980s. Compared with an average annual rate of growth of industrial production of 4.1% for the period 1965–80, output increased at an average rate of 7.3% per year during 1981–91. This coincided with a decade of modest deregulation and large investments by public-sector companies.

Following the second wave of deregulation and liberalization in the early 1990s, there was a marked acceleration in industrial production, with the index of industrial production (IIP) recording a peak growth rate of 12.8% in 1995/96. This boom was short-lived, however, and there was a decline in industrial output for the rest of the decade and into the early 2000s. After reaching a low of 2.6% growth in 2001/02, the IIP recorded a sustained recovery. Gradually picking up momentum from 2002/03 onwards, the industrial sector experienced an upswing for five consecutive years, with the IIP registering double-digit growth (11.6%) in 2006/07. This revival was mainly led by the manufacturing sector, which grew by more than 9% in both 2004/05 and 2005/06 and by an impressive 12.5% in 2006/07. The growth rates of the industrial sector as a whole (including mining and electricity generation) in 2006/07 were the highest recorded in a decade.

The sustained high growth rate in industry from 2002/03 raised hopes that the Indian economy had finally broken through the constraints that had caused such fluctuations during the 1990s. There were more immediate and more fundamental reasons for the upturn in fortunes. First, a series of normal to excellent monsoons maintained domestic demand for industrial goods. Second, a buoyant world economy bolstered demand for exports of Indian manufactures. Third, the introduction of a low interest rate regime from the late 1990s onwards facilitated corporate investment, which, in turn, contributed to rapid industrial growth. Fourth, a high level of liquidity in the economy and a reorientation in bank lending fuelled credit expansion, which boosted domestic demand for manufactured products. Fifth, increased investment in industry led to a rise in demand for infrastructural services (power, telecommunications, roads, ports, etc.), which catalysed major private and public investment programmes (which, in turn, further boosted industrial growth). Sixth, a substantial amount of FDI entered the country in the form of 'greenfield' investment to take advantage of low wages and skilled labour.

The first signs that the exceptional times for the Indian economy may have passed were witnessed in 2007/08. Industrial growth in that year dipped to 8.3% and manufacturing growth to 8.7%, as the Indian industrial sector began to feel the effect of rising interest rates, the slowdown in the world economy and the surge in global petroleum prices. Nevertheless, growth rates of 8% and more remained a formidable achievement.

While Indian industry has performed on the whole exceptionally well in the first decade of the 21st century, the sector is yet to provide jobs on a mass scale to low and medium-skilled labour as China has. The industrial boom has also largely bypassed the small enterprises that in 2004/05 were estimated to contribute close to two-fifths of manufacturing output. And with a regional concentration of investment and growth in industry—in the southern and western states and around New Delhi—much of central and eastern India, home to high levels of poverty and under-employment, has been overlooked.

A number of industries stand out for their contribution to the new found confidence in Indian industry, the most notable of which is the automobile industry. Since the mid-1990s a number of major international automobile manufacturers have established branches in India and, while individual volumes remain small in the majority of cases, the country's total output has increased so dramatically that India has joined the Republic of Korea, China and Brazil as a developing country member among the world's 15 largest automobile producers. Equally important has been the concomitant development of an automobile ancillary industry network of both Indian and foreign companies, which has supplied the manufacturers. The boom in the automobile industry has been led by domestic demand, which has grown rapidly since the mid-1990s. The emergence of Indian exports of both automobiles and automobile parts is no less important, with exports in 2005/06 contributing to more than 15% of total turnover in both sectors.

Another notable success has been in pharmaceuticals, where a foundation was laid during the 1980s, before restrictions under global intellectual property regimes began to be imposed. The Indian pharmaceutical industry, with its reputation for producing generic drugs at low cost, continues to report strong export growth. Other industries that have performed very well have been engineering goods and gems and jewellery (the latter entirely on the world market). In addition, of course, there was the success in computer-software services and the BPO sector, which continued into the middle years of the first decade of the 2000s but belongs more to the services sector.

India is a major coal-mining country, with total coal production (excluding lignite) of an estimated 407.2m. metric tons in 2005/06, compared with a mere 32m. tons in 1950/51. However, low levels of productivity in underground mines, high ash content and low calorific value are some of the shortcomings of India's coal industry. In recent years the Government has liberalized coal-mining policies, permitting private investment in mining and deregulating coal prices and retail trade.

In the 1950s the average annual per caput consumption of electricity in India was about 4.5 kWh. In 2005/06 this figure was estimated to have risen to 90.6 kWh. Power is generated by hydro-, thermal-, nuclear- and gas-based installations. In 1950/51 total energy generated by the utilities was 6,600m. kWh, of which 2,500m. kWh was generated by hydroelectric power (HEP) and 2,600m. kWh by thermal power. In 2006/07 total energy generated by the utilities was 667,500m. kWh, of which hydroelectric and wind power accounted for 101,500m. kWh, thermal and non-conventional energy sources for

506,000m. kWh and nuclear power for 17,300m. kWh. The policy of permitting private investment in power generation for captive use contributed to an increase in the share of non-utilities in energy generation. In 2006/07 non-utilities generated 76,800m. kWh, compared with 25,100m. kWh in 1990/91.

A major constraint on India's economic growth is inadequate and poor-quality electric power. Capacity addition in the power sector has been slow, resulting in the emergence of power shortages (a major hindrance in the infrastructure sector). A number of policy changes at both central and state government level to encourage greater public- and private-sector investment have not had the desired results. The major constraint has been in distribution, with large transmission losses, subsidies and theft making companies in this sector financially crippled. The target for generating capacity addition during the 10th Plan (2002/03–2006/07) was 41,110 MW, but the addition actually achieved was only 23,250 MW. For the 11th Plan (2007/08–2011/12) the target for new generating capacity was raised even higher, to 78,577 MW, comprising hydro (21%), thermal (75%) and nuclear (4%).

India's nuclear power generating capacity currently accounts for only 3% of total capacity. Following initial help from Canada and the USA, India's nuclear industry has largely been developed locally following the imposition of an international embargo in the mid-1970s and India's refusal to sign the international Nuclear Non-Proliferation Treaty. Since 2005 the Government has been working towards signing a civilian nuclear power agreement with the USA, which would lead to a lifting of the global embargo and give a boost to the country's nuclear power generating capacity. In the event of the international embargo being lifted, India has set the ambitious target of achieving nuclear power generating capacity of 20,000 MW by 2050, compared with the 3,900 MW at present. Even if this target were reached, however, nuclear power would still account for just 10% of India's total power generating capacity.

Indian crude petroleum production did not keep pace with increased demand in the 1990s, and India's dependence on imported energy is projected to increase further. Petroleum imports currently constitute more than 30% of the cost of total imports. Between 1990 and 2020 oil demand is expected to quadruple, while oil imports are expected to increase eightfold. In 1990 indigenous oil accounted for 60% of total consumption, while imported oil accounted for 40%. However, by 2000 this ratio had been reversed, with imported oil accounting for more than 60% of consumption. In 2007/08 oil imports constituted 75% of total consumption. Although India remains self-sufficient in coal, and coal will continue to be the country's most important source of energy, imported petroleum and natural gas are expected to become significant alternative sources. Hence, ensuring reliable supplies of imported petroleum and gas will be a major security concern for India. India imports most of its petroleum requirements from West Asia, but is exploring the possibility of tapping the petroleum and natural gas resources of Bangladesh, Iran, Oman and the Central Asian republics. In recent years, Indian state-owned oil companies have ventured to acquire stakes in petroleum ventures in Africa, Central Asia and South-East Asia. From 2004 onwards, India also explored various options to secure gas from West Asia and South-East Asia. These included the construction of a gas pipeline linking Myanmar with India and, more controversially, a pipeline between Iran and India. The recent thaw in India–Pakistan relations removed many of India's fears about the security of gas supplies routed from Iran through Pakistan, but a new obstacle emerged in the form of US opposition to the Iran–India pipeline.

From the mid-1990s onwards, infrastructure was a key area of reform and privatization. While public investment was traditionally the main source of funding for new projects in the infrastructure sector, including power, roads, ports, communication, transportation, etc., the Government now permits private investors, both domestic and foreign, to invest in these areas. A major undertaking, involving public and private investment under various types of management contract, is the National Highway Development Project, which is to criss-cross the country, linking the four largest cities: Delhi, Mumbai (Bombay), Kolkata (Calcutta) and Chennai (Madras). Another highway project aims to connect north to south and east to west.

The major consumers of energy in India are the industrial and the transport sectors, which together account for about 70% of consumption. Industry remains a heavy consumer of coal-based energy and of electricity, while in transport there has been a substantial change-over from coal to petroleum, owing partly to the expansion of road transport, and partly to the increasing use of diesel-powered, rather than coal-based, locomotives on India's railways.

In the transport sector, railways and highways have been the focus of infrastructure modernization in the early 21st century. The government-owned railways showed strong improvement in efficiency indicators in the middle years of the first decade of the 2000s, facilitating substantial new investment. With regard to roads, away from the national highways, quality and all-weather availability declines, and rural roads are poorly developed and inadequately maintained, thus adding considerably to the problems of marketing agricultural products. However, these facilities also vary from one state to another. In the more developed states like Andhra Pradesh, Maharashtra and Tamil Nadu, even rural roads are being renewed.

India's shipping sector is the second largest in Asia, and there are substantial shipbuilding facilities. At the end of 2007 the total registered merchant fleet comprised 1,417 vessels, with a total displacement of 9.2m. grt. India has several well-established seaports, notably Mumbai and Kolkata, and has invested in the establishment and development of a number of new ones, such as Visakhapatnam, Mormugao and Paradip (Paradeep). The modernization of shipping and port-handling has been another area of increased activity in the early 21st century.

A very significant change has taken place in the aviation sector, especially with regard to domestic travel. Passenger aviation was first opened to the private sector in the early 1990s. The initial wave of new entrants faded away in the mid-1990s as a result of over-investment and poor planning. A fresh wave of investment in the middle years of the first decade of the 2000s witnessed an explosion in the number of new airlines, fleet expansion and passenger movement. Between 2004 and 2007 the number of domestic air passengers almost doubled, from 1m. passengers a year to just under 2m. passengers. The main factor driving this expansion was the low fares offered by the airlines, both established and new, to capture market share. An inevitable consequence of this at a time when fuel prices were high was the accumulation of losses, resulting in a number of mergers and acquisitions in 2007. There was a slowdown in growth in the aviation sector in that year as airlines were constrained to increase passenger fares to keep pace with the sharp rise in cost of aviation turbine fuel. In the fiscal year 2007/08 all of the Indian airlines reported losses, raising concerns about the future of the domestic aviation sector. In 2006 the Government privatized the two major airports, at Mumbai and Delhi, and proposed major expansion in several others. 'Greenfield' airports were opened in Bangalore and Hyderabad in 2008, and new ones were planned for Mumbai and Chennai.

From the 1950s enterprises in the public sector were designed to play a strategic role in India's industrial development. A large part of total industrial output originates in the public sector. In the early 1980s public-sector industries, which consisted mainly of modern large-scale enterprises, provided about 26% of total factory employment and 70% of fixed industrial capital. Joint-sector enterprises provided an additional 5%–6% of both output and employment. Enterprises in the public sector may be divided into two categories: manufacturing enterprises and service enterprises. Among the former is the Steel Authority of India, which is the largest industrial public-sector body in terms of investment (Rs 46,000m. in the early 1980s). Other important operations include the Fertilizer Corporation of India Ltd, Bharat Heavy Electricals Ltd and Hindustan Machine Tools (HMT) Ltd. Among the service enterprises are a number of major trading companies, such as the Food Corporation of India and the Minerals and Metals Trading Corporation.

India has developed a substantial volume of industrial production, which is able to satisfy the bulk of domestic demand for manufactured commodities. Indian industry produces a wide variety of products, ranging from consumer goods to fairly advanced forms of capital equipment. The country has developed a substantial domestic defence potential, and is now moving into the assembly, production and, more recently, the export of fairly advanced military equipment, under collaboration agreements. India is one of the very few developing countries that has an indigenously created potential for using nuclear power. It has been involved in establishing fertilizer factories and other production facilities under 'turn-key' arrangements in other developing countries. Indian multinational corporations now operate in a number of East African, West Asian and South-East Asian countries. In the past the productivity of Indian industries was well below international levels, making it difficult for India to maintain or advance its share in world trade in a number of traditional and new commodities. Indian industry was also regarded as being slow to adopt new technologies or improved designs, and as being technologically backward. However, much of this has changed since the mid/late 1990s. Although the transformation of Indian industry has been nowhere as complete as that in China and the changes have been more noticeable in specialized high-technology industries, a considerable number of Indian companies in diverse areas—ranging from engineering goods to pharmaceuticals—have emerged as the best in their fields and have begun to expand overseas.

While the public sector remains an important feature of Indian industry, since 1991 successive governments have initiated policies to reduce public ownership, end public monopolies, expose public enterprises to market competition at home and abroad and, eventually, to privatize the public sector. The National Democratic Alliance (NDA) Government, which was in office between 1999 and 2004, placed privatization of the public sector at the centre of its policy agenda. Private investment, including FDI, is now permitted in all infrastructure industries, including power, telecommunications, coal and civil aviation, and in the financial sector, including insurance. Independent regulatory authorities have been established in the spheres of power, telecommunications and insurance, to ensure equal treatment for public- and private-sector companies. Only the railways remain entirely in the public sector. However, in this area too, the Government began permitting private companies to offer services ranging from manufacture of wagons to catering. In the early years of the first decade of the 2000s, the Government privatized several major public enterprises across a range of industries, including a bread-making firm, an aluminium company, a telecommunications firm, an oil company and several hotels. By the middle of the decade, this process had come to a standstill in the face of opposition and criticism of privatization procedures.

Throughout the 1990s the policy of opening India up to FDI continued. Whereas in the 1980s India witnessed a minimal inflow of FDI and no foreign portfolio investment in the capital market, net foreign investment of all kinds grew in the first half of the 1990s, reaching US $6,133m. in 1996/97. It fluctuated thereafter, even declining to $2,401m. in 1998/99. The major spurt in net capital inflows took place really from 2003/04 onwards, with annual receipts even doubling from 2005/06. Net capital inflows in 2007/08 reached as much as $108,000m. (equivalent to 9.2% of GDP), compared with $25,500m. (3.1% of GDP) in 2005/06. An important aspect of the surge in capital inflows in the middle of the first decade of the 2000s was that, unlike the situation in China, the growth in India was often largely in funds for the stock markets—foreign institutional investment (FII)—or loans mobilized abroad by Indian companies. For instance, in 2007/08 net FDI was $15,545m., while portfolio investment totalled $29,261m. and external commercial borrowings by Indian firms $22,165m. There have been annual fluctuations in FII flows, but they have become a major force in the Indian stock markets and comprise significant amounts of holdings in many of India's most profitable and best-known companies. The stock of FII investment in Indian companies stood at $68,007m.at the end of March 2008.

Three aspects of the changing face of Indian industry deserve mention. The first is what can be described as the 'internationalization of Indian business'. The increasing outward orientation of Indian business means that, besides exporting a larger share of their output, Indian companies have also been aggressively seeking a foothold in foreign markets. Whereas in the past Indian companies established ventures or acquired firms only in smaller markets such as Africa and South-East Asia, they now seek to acquire firms in the major markets of the USA and Western Europe. No precise estimates are currently available and the individual size of acquisitions remains small, but what is noteworthy is that Indian purchases are in a number of areas—all reflecting sectors where Indian industry seeks to hold an edge in international competition. A spate of acquisitions in the middle of the first decade of the 2000s took place in pharmaceuticals, food products (tea and coffee), transport equipment (trucks) and industrial products. The number of these purchases exceeded the numerous acquisitions by Indian companies in the software industry. A high point in 2006/07 was the acquisition by the Tata Iron and Steel Co Ltd of the European steel-maker Corus. This was followed in 2007/08 by another high-profile acquisition by a company in the Tata group, Tata Motors, which bought, at a cost of US $2,300m., the renowned British automobile brands of Jaguar and Land Rover from Ford of the USA. Investment abroad by Indian companies has steadily risen, from US $2,800m. in 2004/05 to $7,950m. in 2006/07. The acquisitions have been financed by the availability of substantial internal reserves and the ease of obtaining inexpensive finance.

Even as Indian companies continue to make acquisitions abroad, there have also been a number of major high-value sales in the reverse direction. In 2008 India's largest pharmaceutical company, Ranbaxy, sold a majority stake to the Japanese company Daiichi Sankyo for US $6,400m. This was widely viewed as a new sign that in cases where Indian companies realised that they were not able to expand further on their own they would prefer to sell their assets to a larger foreign company with the capacity to do so.

The second feature of the recent transformation is the emphasis on low-cost manufacturing, resulting in the ability to offer products at very low prices. Partly as a result of competition and partly because of the demands of the Indian market where low purchasing power demands products at a low price, Indian manufacturers have been relentlessly searching for ways to reduce costs. This is exemplified in the development of the world's cheapest car, the Nano, by Tata Motors; the car was expected to go on sale in late 2008/early 2009 at a price of just US $3,000.

The third notable transformation in Indian industry during the late 1990s and early years of the first decade of the 2000s has been the fact that, while labour-intensive industry has not developed on the same large scale as in China, numerous Indian companies have made their mark on the global market. This has occurred in the fields of precision engineering, automobile components, pharmaceuticals and steel. Some of India's manufacturing companies are the world's lowest-cost producers in steel and rank among the largest in terms of production of select industrial goods. However, this development has not made a material difference to job creation in India since there has not been a similar expansion in production in the labour-intensive areas of manufacturing, such as textiles, leather goods and agricultural products.

## THE SERVICES SECTOR

In 2002/03 the services sector for the first time contributed more than 50% of India's GDP. Since the early 1980s an extraordinary growth in India's services has taken place. The meaning and contribution of this phenomenon to long-term growth have not yet been fully understood. In India, this sector comprises a very heterogeneous set of activities. There are the unorganized and small-scale services such as one-room retailing, household services and informal pavement repair activities. At the other end of the scale are the highly organized, modern and capital-intensive services such as computer software, modern banking and supermarket retailing. There are government services such as public administration (with large numbers of staff) and defence, private services such as trade and transport, and community services provided by non-governmental organizations. While some services have grown more rapidly than others, there is no disputing that the sector as a whole has grown much faster than either industry or agriculture, and has progressively made a larger contribution to economic growth. Services are conventionally categorized by India's national account statistics into three broad groups: trade, transport, storage and communication; finance, insurance, real estate and business services; and public administration, defence and other services. The average rate of growth during the 1970s was 4.5% per year; in the 1980s it accelerated to 6.6% per year; and in the 1990s to 7.6% per year. There are some questions about the accuracy of the statistics underlying the growth of India's service economy, but it is very apparent that the services sector has become extremely dynamic. The major categories showing rapid growth are hotels, trade, finance and telecommunications. The services sector accounted for 68% of total employment in urban India in 1999/2000. Retail trade was the single largest service (providing 33% of employment in the sector), with road transport accounting for a further 14% of sectoral employment.

Two examples of sub-sectors that show dynamism are computer software and telecommunications. The Indian success in the area of software exports is well known. Since the early 1990s the industry has been registering export growth of more than 30% per year—in some years growth exceeded 50%—to emerge as a remarkably successful facet of the Indian economy. Although the domestic software sector remains smaller than the export sector, it too has been growing by more than 25% per year. In 2007/08 industry estimates placed the (domestic and export) revenues of the entire software and outsourcing industry at US $52,000m., an increase of more than 33% over the previous year. Industry estimates placed total employment in the software sector at more than 2,000m. men and women in that year (an increase of nearly 375,000 on the previous year), most of whom were young and university-educated. Of total revenues, $40,300m. came from exports of software and related services. India has become the preferred service provider for many global businesses. Indian companies, however, continue to struggle to gain a foothold in the market of branded software products. In the initial years of the 21st century a new business segment emerged. Defined as 'Information Technology-Enabled Services-Business Process Outsourcing' (ITES-BPO), normally referred to as 'outsourcing', Indian companies and subsidiaries of foreign firms began to make their presence in the global market more noticeable by offering low-cost alternatives to services that could be performed anywhere in the world. In 2007/08 the ITES-BPO sector's business was worth $12,500m. and it employed 704,000 people. The ITES-BPO sector has been the most dynamic in terms of performance since 2000. While many large information technology firms began to consider ITES-BPO as a profitable business opportunity, the industry was very quickly confronted with protectionism in the US and British markets. Unions and workers employed in call centres and software companies from where business was being outsourced had begun lobbying governments to prevent what they described as an exporting of jobs. The real extent of job loss was very small but, because of the emotive value of the campaign, it was apparent that the Indian industry's drive to establish India as the 'service capital' of the world would not proceed smoothly. In addition to global firms outsourcing some of their activities to Indian companies, a major development has been the decision of many of the world's leading companies in IT and finance to establish subsidiaries in India to perform some of their service and even their research functions. For example, the international computer services giant IBM has its largest pool of workers outside the USA based in India.

Telecommunications is another area in the Indian services sector where remarkable changes have taken place. For decades India was known for an extremely low level of 'teledensity' (usually defined as the number of phones for every 100 people), high tariffs and poor quality of service. In the mid-1990s the sector was opened to competition, and at the same time mobile cellular services were introduced in the country. Changes in the regulatory framework, declining costs in technology and intense competition led to a huge increase in the number of new connections in the early years of the first decade of the 2000s. Teledensity rose from 2.86 in 1999/2000 to 7.02 in 2003/04 and touched 23.9 at the end of 2007. In that year the total number of connections increased by 44%, compared with the previous year, to reach 272.9m. by December. As many as 7m. new connections were provided every month in 2007. Despite the rapid growth of recent years, however, the spread of the telecommunications network remains less developed than in other large countries. India's teledensity remains far lower than Brazil and China, both of which have a teledensity of 42. What is significant is the change in teledensity, which has been driven by many new companies, almost all of which have foreign collaboration. Two aspects of the development in telecommunications need to be stressed. First, the growth has been the result more of an expansion in mobile cellular service connections than in fixed-line telephones. In 2004/05 (just one decade after mobile telephones first came into use in India) the number of mobile telephone connections surpassed that of fixed-line connections. By the end of 2007 there were nearly six times as many mobile connections as fixed-line phones: 233.6m. against 39.2m., with the number of fixed-line connections in fact declining. Second, growth has been uneven. The addition of new lines has been concentrated in the cities and towns; the rural areas continue to have very few telephones. The rapid overall increase in urban teledensity conceals the fact that in rural India in 2007 there were still only 7.9 telephones for every 100 people, compared with as many as 60 per 100 people in urban India.

Finance has been another extremely rapidly growing area in the services sector. Since the early 1990s the financial sector has recorded net output growth in excess of 7% a year. The pace of growth has accelerated since the late 1990s to between 9% and 10% per year. This rapid growth is the reflection of a number of trends. The establishment of new institutions and changes in government policies have facilitated growth. The entry of private banks into India's financial sector in the mid-1990s was one such factor. The creation of a new regulatory body for the stock exchanges (the Securities and Exchange Board of India) and the establishment of a second stock exchange (the National Stock Exchange) led to an improvement in settlement practices, which in turn resulted in a growth in trading and market capitalization. The liberalization of the financial sector—life insurance being the most prominent example—also contributed to the growth of the financial sector. The introduction of a market exchange rate mechanism for the rupee in 1992, followed by current account convertibility in 1994, was the catalyst for the growth of the foreign exchange market. Policy changes in the money market enabled a rapid increase in the value of trading. The low interest rate regime from the early years of the first decade of the 2000s onwards coincided with a new emphasis on retail lending by banks, which was responsible for the emergence of consumer finance as a dynamic area. All told, the financial markets have been exhibiting a substantial amount of both widening and deepening, although there are concerns that the very rapid growth of the first 10 years of the 2000s may have placed the economy at some risk.

Accompanying the growth of the services sector in the domestic economy has been the emergence of a dynamic export business. India's exports of services grew by an estimated average annual rate of 17.3% during the 1990s, compared with a world average annual growth of 5.6%. India's export growth was the fastest in the world during that period, exceeding that of other major service suppliers in the global market such as China and the Republic of Korea. India's presence in the global services market was much greater than in the field of merchandise trade: the country had a 2.7% share in global services exports in 2006, while its share in world exports of goods was only 1.0%. In individual sectors, too, the Indian profile was well marked: the Indian industry had a 17% share in the global software-services market in 2001, while in the textiles trade India's share was only 3.2%. Software services are the most renowned of India's service exports, but other areas are also emerging as important sources of economic dynamism. These include business services which broadly cover trade-related services, consultancy, architectural services, engineering and office maintenance services. In 2007/08 exports of software services were valued at US $40,300, or 28% of gross receipts of invisibles in the balance of payments. In the same year business services totalled $16,624m., or 11% of gross receipts of invisibles.

## TRADE AND BALANCE OF PAYMENTS

There has been a fundamental reorientation in India's external economic policies since the early 1990s. After independence in 1947 India pursued a strategy of import-substituting industrialization. While India's share in world merchandise exports in 1950 was 1.8%, it declined over the ensuing 40 years of inward-orientated industrial development to a low of 0.4% in the mid-1980s. A steady rise, following a more outward orientation, led to India's share crossing the 1% mark once again in 2006. In the mean time, the share of exports in GDP rose from 5.8% in 1991/92 to 14.0% in 2006/07. Furthermore, the share of trade in GDP grew from 13.3% in 1991/92 to 34.9% in 2006/07, indicating the country's increased trade openness.

Although India has pursued a more outward-orientated economic policy since the early 1980s, the decisive shift in policy occurred in 1991, when the Government responded to a balance-of-payments crisis by radically altering its industrial and trade policies. Since the introduction of reforms in 1991, India's import-weighted average tariff rate for all products had been reduced from 87% to 30% by 1998/99. The maximum tariff rate was gradually reduced from over 200% in 1990/91 to 45% by 1998/99. In early 2004 the peak tariff rate on non-agricultural products was reduced from 25% to 20%. In mid-2005 the lowest average tariff rate of 16% was on agricultural products and the highest (39%) on consumer goods; capital goods and intermediate goods attracted a customs duty rate of around 30%. In any case, actual customs duty collected on imports was far lower than the published tariffs. The collection rate for import tariffs was only 10% in 2007/08, compared with as much as 47% in 1990/91 on the eve of the reform process.

India's exports (in US dollar terms) increased at an average annual rate of 10% between 1992/93 and 1999/2000, compared with 7.6% between 1980/81 and 1991/92. Import growth, which averaged 8.5% per year (in US dollar terms) between 1980/81 and 1991/92, increased to an average annual rate of 13.4% in 1992/93–1999/2000. Thereafter, there was an acceleration in export growth. Between 2002/03 and 2007/08 India's merchandise exports grew at an average annual rate of more than 20%, in US dollar terms, a record performance for what was until the early 1990s an inward-looking economy. Exports grew by more than 23% in 2007/08 despite an appreciation of the rupee during much of the year. The main sources of export growth were engineering goods, chemicals, gems and jewellery, textiles, pharmaceuticals, automobile parts, iron ore (the latter being a recent addition to high-performing exports) and refined petroleum. This reflected a continuing move away from an export basket dominated by agricultural commodities or agricultural processed products (India's exports in the 1950s and 1960s were mainly tea, tobacco, plantation crops and suchlike). The emergence by 2007/08 of petroleum products as one of the main export items reflects the establishment of substantial refining capacity; India remains largely dependent on imports for its requirement of crude oil. The USA and the European Union (EU) have traditionally been India's main trading partners. In the early years of the first decade of the 2000s China—as a source of both imports and as a destination of exports—also emerged as a major trading partner. By 2007/08 China had become India's second largest trading partner and was poised to replace the USA as the main trading partner. Another group of countries that has emerged as important trading nations are the economies of South-East Asia.

In 2005 the Government initiated a new policy to promote exports which has since caused considerable controversy and provoked widespread protests. A new piece of legislation enacted in that year facilitated the establishment of special economic zones (SEZs), which were to enjoy large tax and other fiscal incentives from the central and state governments. This bill led to a flood of proposals and by mid-2008 as many as 222 such zones were already functional (notified). The Government claimed that the SEZs had already attracted large investments and had boosted exports. However, the establishment of these SEZs necessitated the acquisition of land; this inevitably meant the displacement of people, a fact that led to violent protests in rural and semi-urban areas, at times with loss of life.

While exports have been growing rapidly, imports have always been larger and have continued to increase. In 2007/08 India's merchandise exports were valued at US $158,461m. and imports at $248,521m., resulting in a trade deficit of $90,060m., which was 45% larger than the deficit recorded in 2006/07. Rising petroleum prices in the global market were mainly responsible for the large cost of imports, although purchases of machinery and inputs from the global market were also contributing factors. India recorded a merchandise trade deficit throughout the 1990s and thereafter, but this did not cause a problem for its management of the current account of the balance of payments owing to the emergence of large earnings from 'invisibles'. These exports, comprising mainly software exports, remittances from Indians working abroad and a number of new services, have been able to finance the greater part of the merchandise trade deficit since the early 1990s. In 1990/91 gross earnings from the invisibles trade were a modest $7,464m. and net receipts were a negative $242m. Earnings steadily increased throughout the decade and into the early years of the 2000s. In 2007/08 India's net earnings from invisibles reached $72,657m. Software exports have made an important contribution to this transformation, but just as significant (if not more so) has been the impact of remittances. There was no dramatic growth in temporary migration from India from the early 1990s. Instead, the use of organized banking (as opposed to illegal channels) to transfer wages from abroad resulted in the emergence of remittances as one of the biggest 'export earners' for India. Throughout the 1990s and early years of the first decade of the 2000s remittances exceeded the value of income from software exports. In 2006/07 this trend was reversed for the first time: income from software exports totalled $31,300m. against $28,223m. from remittances. The following year, however, gross remittances ($43,343m.) once again exceeded earnings from software exports ($40,300m.). In recent years, the larger area of service exports—construction, consultancy, accountancy and a heterogeneous group of services—has grown in importance and is now increasing as rapidly as software and outsourcing. The expansion of invisibles has meant that the widening of the trade deficit during the middle years of the first decade of the 2000s has not posed a major problem to the Indian economy. In 2007/08, as in the previous year, the earnings from invisibles helped to keep the current-account deficit under control, at $17,403m., or 1.7% of GDP.

An improvement in India's external trade profile was also accompanied by an accumulation of foreign-exchange reserves. At the time of the balance-of-payments crisis in early 1991, India's foreign-exchange reserves declined to less than US $1,000m. The policy of external trade and investment liberalization and of opening up the Indian stock market to investment by foreign institutional investors led to a rapid accumulation of foreign-exchange reserves. From the very low level of reserves in 1991, India's reserves reached a huge $309,700m. in March 2008, the fourth largest in the world. Reserves in early 1991 were sufficient to pay for only three weeks of imports of goods and services, but by mid-2008 they were extensive enough to finance 15 months of imports.

Steadily rising foreign-exchange reserves, a stable, if appreciating, exchange rate (maintained by the Reserve Bank of India's policy of 'managed float' until early 2007 when the rupee was allowed a modest degree of appreciation) and a healthy current-account position constitute the three major strengths of India's external economic profile. India has also managed to stabilize its external debt and to insulate the domestic economy from the inflationary consequences of rising foreign-exchange reserves. A potential risk in the middle of the first decade of the 2000s was the widening of the current-account deficit. The availability of large reserves and continued inflows of capital, however, implied that this deficit would remain manageable.

Concern has been expressed with regard to the impact of huge inflows of external capital (other than FDI) on domestic liquidity, inflation, the exchange rate and the stock markets. The accretion in foreign reserves from the late 1990s onwards was the result not of large inflows in the current account, but of substantial receipts of external capital. In 2007/08 net capital inflows reached US $108,031m. As discussed above, capital inflows were composed more of portfolio investment rather than FDI. In 2007/08 net portfolio investment was as much as $29,261m., almost double the net FDI receipts of $15,545m. Indeed, even external commercial borrowings (by Indian companies), at $22,165m., were larger than FDI. The surge in portfolio investment and the tendency of Indian companies to borrow heavily from abroad (because of lower international interest rates) posed immense challenges to the Reserve Bank of India (RBI) in containing domestic liquidity. The RBI, which is the country's central bank, has been worried about the dangers of excessive dependence on FII capital. In early 2005 the RBI publicized its concerns and even suggested that it might be necessary to explore ways of controlling FII inflows.

## ECONOMIC POLICY AND RECENT PERFORMANCE

For the first three decades following independence, India consciously sought to build a mixed economy. One of the main objectives of economic policy was to redress the weaknesses inherent in a developing economy with a poor capital and infrastructural base. State intervention and investment were justified on the grounds of 'private investment failure'. The Second Five-Year Plan (1955–60) witnessed heavy public investment in the core industrial sector as well as in transport and communications. While this was politically advertised as being the basis for the building of a 'socialistic pattern of society', in reality, public investment, both in industry and agriculture, was supplemented by private investment, which laid the foundations for the growth of indigenous business enterprise.

India's protected industrial sector thrived during the first half of the 1960s. However, a series of poor monsoons, two wars with Pakistan (in 1965 and 1971) and rising social and political discontent curbed productive investment, leading to a deceleration in the rate of growth of industrial production throughout the 1970s. In order to adjust to this low-growth phase and in response to pressures from new business groups (both domestic and non-resident Indians), a series of policy changes were carried out, liberalizing the highly regulated economy and making production for exports, rather than for the internal market, relatively profitable. The first phase of this new liberal economic policy was introduced in 1978–80. The rise in the cost of petroleum on the world market in 1979, however, forced the Government to revert to a more regulated economy. The second phase of economic liberalization was implemented during the early months of Rajiv Gandhi's premiership (1985–1989).

Compared with the low economic growth rate of the 1970s (with an average annual GDP growth rate of 3.5%), the 1980s witnessed moderate to high growth, with an average annual GDP growth rate of 5.5%. This increase was largely due to a steep rise in public expenditure and investment. The modest liberalization of the import regime facilitated access to new technologies, which, in turn, encouraged expansion in the consumer durables, electronics and petrochemicals industries. The Government had not, however, protected itself against an excessive level of borrowing, both domestically and internationally. India's excellent sovereign credit rating allowed it easy access to global financial markets in the late 1980s, and both long- and short-term debts were rapidly accumulated.

Given the high accumulation of debt and the concomitant burden of debt servicing, and in the absence of an adequate growth in exports, India found itself unable to withstand the adverse effects of the Gulf crisis in mid-1990. Partly on account of this and partly on account of the poor political assessments of credit-rating agencies, which believed that a minority Government would be unable to pursue policies that would stabilize the Indian economy, India's credit rating began to slip in the latter half of 1990. Faced with the risk of default, the Government imposed draconian import control measures, borrowed extensively from the IMF and, in July 1991, devalued the rupee by 20%.

The balance-of-payments crisis of mid-1991 coincided with the arrival in office of a new Congress Party Government led by Prime Minister P. V. Narasimha Rao, with the highly regarded economist and former Governor of the Reserve Bank of India, Dr Manmohan Singh, as Minister of Finance. The Rao-Singh team utilized the opportunity opened by the payments crisis to make the Indian economy more accessible to foreign trade and investment flows. Implementing a traditional structural adjustment programme designed with the assistance of the World Bank and the IMF, India liberalized its trade and investment policies, announced a programme of fiscal stabilization aimed at reducing the fiscal deficit from more than 8.5% of GDP to 5.0%, instigated a policy for phasing out short-term external debt exposure and reduced the current-account deficit from more than 3.0% of GDP to less than 2.0% within a year. Along with this medium-term adjustment and stabilization programme, the Government gradually introduced extensive changes in industrial and tax policies.

The policies to transform the Indian economy from an inward-orientated, import-substituting model of industrial development to an outward-orientated model were further developed by successive governments throughout the 1990s. As a result, the policies not only prevented external default, but also helped to increase India's foreign-exchange assets several-fold within a short period of time. There was a sharp decrease in both fiscal and current-account deficits and an improvement in the external debt profile. The rise in reserves in the mid-1990s coincided with India's opening of its stock market to investment by foreign institutional investors, such as pension and mutual funds. India's recovery from a balance-of-payments crisis is regarded as one of the fastest achieved under an IMF-World Bank adjustment and stabilization programme. In part, the success of the Indian strategy lay in the ability of the authorities to ensure relative freedom from the IMF-World Bank orthodoxy, in order to pursue an unorthodox and unconventional approach to fiscal and balance-of-payments correction. As well as stabilizing the economy, these policies also helped to accelerate the rate of growth of the Indian economy. Compared with the long-term annual rate of growth of around 4.0% during 1950–90, the Indian economy was able to register an average rate of growth of more than 5.5% per year in the period 1992–2006. This acceleration of growth was accompanied by a decline in the rate of inflation. Yet growth in the period 1998–2003 decelerated in relative terms, owing to low levels of domestic investment and the inability of agriculture to cope with erratic monsoons. In the middle of the first decade of the 21st century GDP growth picked up momentum and recorded an average annual growth rate of 8.8% in the five years between 2003/04 and 2007/08.

The strong acceleration in growth and the new international profile of India has also been reflected in the surge in equity share prices. The Bombay Stock Exchange index of shares—one of the main indices of equity prices—doubled in value in just two years, between 2003/04 and 2005/06, and was as much as four times higher by the end of 2007. At the same time, equity funds mobilized by Indian companies from the capital market tripled in amount between 2003/04 and 2005/06. Much of this surge in the stock market was driven by foreign portfolio investors and therefore made the capital market vulnerable to a shift in international perceptions about India. However, there was no denying that the overall mood of optimism about India's economic prospects had filtered into the stock markets—at least, that is, until early 2008 (the market had lost nearly 40% of its value by June 2008).

According to the UN Development Programme's *Human Development Report 2007*, India's human development indicators showed an improvement in the 1990s. India, once considered a country with 'low' human development, has advanced to the category of 'medium' human development. According to the report's estimates of the Human Development Index (HDI), India ranked 128 in a list of 177 countries. These estimates of HDI, however, were based on the profile in 2005. While India's HDI did rise during the 1990s, the increasingly widening gap between the country's HDI and per caput GDP ranking in the 'negative direction' has been a worrying phenomenon. According to the *Human Development Report 2007*, India's position in terms of per caput GDP was 11 places higher than its ranking in terms of HDI, indicating that the country could do much better in distributing the benefits of its GDP growth. Until the late 1990s there was little difference between India's HDI and per caput GDP rank.

India's success in software exports and, more recently, in attracting a significant share of the outsourcing business, has raised expectations within and outside the country that the economy has moved onto a path of high growth. The remarkable performance of the economy in the middle years of the first decade of the 2000s attracted much international attention, but in comparison with its East and South-East Asian neighbours, India remains underdeveloped. Clearly, the challenge facing India today is to grow faster, increase its share of world trade and improve its human development indicators.

## OLD AND NEW CHALLENGES

The rapid acceleration in Indian economic growth in the early years of the 21st century has changed global impressions of India. Indian companies have made their mark in the world marketplace in a number of fields, from consumer products to sophisticated engineering and IT; Indian professionals are much sought after in numerable services, of which computer software is only one; Indian exports have been growing at a rate of more than 20% per year; and the country has emerged as the preferred global location for the provision of low-cost services. India is no longer seen as a poor economy that has consistently under-fulfilled its potential. Instead, it is now seen as a new driving force in the global economy, one that rivals China in the changing international balance of economic power.

The Indian economy has grown by more than 5% per year since the early 1980s. However, the acceleration to an 8% or more growth rate took place only during the first decade of the 21st century—an average of 8.8% growth per year between 2003/04 and 2007/08, and 9% or higher between 2005/06 and 2007/08. This acceleration prompted the Planning Commission of the Indian Government to set a target of average annual growth of 9% during the 11th Five-Year Plan (2007/08–2011/12).

The first major test for the Indian economy came during 2008 when a combination of factors made it clear that growth in 2008/09 would slow considerably. The global financial crisis did not affect India—in fact, if anything, it increased capital flows to India in early 2008. The major challenge that emerged in that year was food and fuel price inflation. The increases in global food prices hit India first, although, with the help of a record grain harvest in 2007/08, the economy was able to place some check on cereals. The doubling of international crude oil prices in 2007/08 meant that the Indian Government was finally forced to increase petroleum prices. Inflation almost tripled between January and June 2008, with the annual wholesale price inflation shooting up from less than 4% to more than 11%. A tightening of interest rates by the RBI was expected to affect growth. By mid-2008 industrial growth had slowed down marginally and exports too were beginning to falter. The stock market index lost more than 40% off its peak between January and June 2008 and the general prediction was that the rate of growth of the Indian economy would decelerate to less than 8% in 2008/09. Given the adverse circumstances, such a level of growth would still be no mean achievement, but much depended on how India performed as the global economy experienced a slowdown.

The description of India as having arrived on the global scene is as incomplete as the earlier characterization of the country as an underdeveloped and backward economy. The acceleration in GDP growth in 2003–07 to more than 8% per year is, of course, a continuation of a two-decade old process of improvement. The increase in India's rate of economic growth began in the early 1980s, although it was only in the early years of the first decade of the 2000s that the economy appeared ready to climb to new heights of growth. While there is little denying the acceleration in the rate of growth, a number of issues are regularly posed within India on various aspects of the new momentum, all of which relate to its quality and sustainability. Of especial concern in the midst of the acceleration in economic growth are the sharp divisions in the economy which have been accentuated since the 1990s. There are many facets to these divisions. There are the increasing regional disparities: growth in southern, western and parts of northern India has accelerated, but it has slowed down in many states in central, eastern and other parts of northern India. The latter group of regions contain the bulk of the population and a predominant majority of the country's poor, implying that inequalities have grown and economic benefits have been distributed unequally. There are also the sectoral disparities. The service sector and, to a lesser extent, the manufacturing sector have performed well since the 1990s, but the agricultural sector, which still employs nearly three-fifths of the work-force, has seen a deceleration in its growth rate and widespread discontent among the farming community. This is reflected in the rural-urban divide, with the cities and towns showing an economic dynamism and rural India experiencing considerable economic difficulties. Yet another divide is apparent within the cities themselves, with the poor and marginalized (many of them migrants from the rural areas) being pushed to the outer fringes of the urban centres and being denied basic facilities, while the city centres and suburbs begin to mirror the more prosperous urban locations elsewhere in the world. All these disparities are expressed in a general unease that rapid growth has not been broadly based. There is an awareness across the political spectrum that uneven economic expansion is not sustainable.

In mid-2006 the Planning Commission published estimates that showed only a very modest reduction in the incidence of poverty between 1993/94 and 2004/05, which was when economic liberalization became established and growth accelerated. The official estimate of the percentage of Indians who were poor (according to a government-defined nutritional norm) declined from 36% in 1993/94 to 28% in 2004/05. This was a pace of reduction in the incidence of poverty of only 0.8% per year—a rate of decline which was actually slower than the reduction of 1% per year recorded during 1987/88 to 1993/94. In other words, economic liberalization and more rapid growth have as yet far resulted in a faster rate of decline in the incidence of poverty. Other indicators that reflect an inequitable accrual of the benefits of faster growth include a slowdown in the rate of decline in infant mortality, a stagnation in maternal mortality rates and a general deterioration in the quality of government services in health, education and a number of other social sectors.

In the light of such an uneven spread of the gains from rapid growth it has become apparent, at least internally, that focusing only on some areas of success and transformation does not provide a complete picture of the Indian economy today. The IT sector is growing in leaps and bounds, but, although it employs more than 2m. young men and women, this still constitutes just a small fraction of the Indian labour force of 400m. A true transformation of the Indian economy will take place only when the manufacturing and agricultural sectors enjoy the same degree of success as the IT sector.

# Statistical Survey

Source (unless otherwise stated): Central Statistical Organization, Ministry of Statistics and Programme Implementation, Sardar Patel Bhavan, Patel Chowk, New Delhi 110 001; tel. (11) 23742150; fax (11) 23344689; e-mail moscc@bol.net.in; internet mospi.nic.in.

## Area and Population

### AREA, POPULATION AND DENSITY*

| | |
|---|---|
| Area (sq km) | 3,166,414† |
| Population (census results) | |
| 1 March 1991‡§ | 846,302,688 |
| 1 March 2001‖ | |
| Males | 532,156,772 |
| Females | 496,453,556 |
| Total | 1,028,610,328 |
| Population (official projected estimates at 1 March)¶ | |
| 2006 | 1,114,202,000 |
| 2007 | 1,131,043,000 |
| 2008 | 1,147,677,000 |
| Density (per sq km) at 1 March 2008 | 362.5 |

* Including the Indian-held part of Jammu and Kashmir.
† 1,222,559 sq miles.
‡ Excluding adjustment for underenumeration, estimated at 1.5%.
§ Including estimate for the Indian-held part of Jammu and Kashmir.
‖ Including estimates for certain areas in the states of Gujarat and Himachal Pradesh where the census could not be conducted, owing to recent natural disasters.
¶ Source: Office of the Registrar General and Census Commissioner, *Census of India* (2001).

Source: unless otherwise indicated, Registrar General of India.

### STATES AND TERRITORIES
(population at 2001 census)

| | Area (sq km) | Population | Density (per sq km) | Capital |
|---|---|---|---|---|
| *States* | | | | |
| Andhra Pradesh | 275,069 | 76,210,007 | 277 | Hyderabad |
| Arunachal Pradesh* | 83,743 | 1,097,968 | 13 | Itanagar |
| Assam | 78,438 | 26,655,528 | 340 | Dispur |
| Bihar† | 94,163 | 82,998,509 | 881 | Patna |
| Chhattisgarh | 135,191 | 20,833,803 | 154 | Raipur |
| Goa‡ | 3,702 | 1,347,668 | 364 | Panaji |
| Gujarat | 196,022 | 50,671,017 | 258 | Gandhinagar |
| Haryana | 44,212 | 21,144,564 | 478 | Chandigarh§ |
| Himachal Pradesh | 55,673 | 6,077,900 | 109 | Shimla |
| Jammu and Kashmir‖ | 101,387 | 10,143,700 | 100 | Srinagar |
| Jharkhand | 79,714 | 26,945,829 | 338 | Ranchi |
| Karnataka | 191,791 | 52,850,562 | 276 | Bangalore |
| Kerala | 38,863 | 31,841,374 | 819 | Thiruvananthapuram (Trivandrum) |
| Madhya Pradesh† | 308,245 | 60,348,023 | 196 | Bhopal |
| Maharashtra | 307,713 | 96,878,627 | 314 | Mumbai (Bombay) |
| Manipur | 22,327 | 2,166,788 | 97 | Imphal |
| Meghalaya | 22,429 | 2,318,822 | 103 | Shillong |
| Mizoram¶ | 21,081 | 888,573 | 42 | Aizawl |
| Nagaland | 16,579 | 1,990,036 | 120 | Kohima |
| Orissa | 155,707 | 36,804,660 | 236 | Bhubaneswar |
| Punjab | 50,362 | 24,358,999 | 483 | Chandigarh§ |
| Rajasthan | 342,239 | 56,507,188 | 165 | Jaipur |
| Sikkim | 7,096 | 540,851 | 76 | Gangtok |
| Tamil Nadu | 130,058 | 62,405,679 | 479 | Chennai (Madras) |
| Tripura | 10,486 | 3,199,203 | 305 | Agartala |
| Uttaranchal† | 53,483 | 8,489,349 | 159 | Dehradun |
| Uttar Pradesh† | 240,928 | 166,197,921 | 690 | Lucknow |
| West Bengal | 88,752 | 80,176,197 | 903 | Kolkata (Calcutta) |
| *Territories* | | | | |
| Andaman and Nicobar Islands | 8,249 | 356,152 | 43 | Port Blair |
| Chandigarh§ | 114 | 900,635 | 7,900 | Chandigarh |
| Dadra and Nagar Haveli | 491 | 220,490 | 449 | Silvassa |
| Daman and Diu‡ | 112 | 158,204 | 1,411 | Daman |
| Delhi | 1,483 | 13,850,507 | 9,340 | Delhi |
| Lakshadweep | 32 | 60,650 | 1,895 | Kavaratti |
| Puducherry (Pondicherry) | 480 | 974,345 | 2,029 | Puducherry (Pondicherry) |

* Arunachal Pradesh was granted statehood in February 1987.
† Chhattisgarh, Jharkhand and Uttaranchal (formerly parts of Madhya Pradesh, Bihar and Uttar Pradesh, respectively) were granted statehood in November 2000; Uttaranchal was renamed Uttarakhand in 2006.
‡ Goa was granted statehood in May 1987. Daman and Diu remain a Union Territory.
§ Chandigarh forms a separate Union Territory, not within Haryana or the Punjab. As part of a scheme for a transfer of territory between the two states, Chandigarh was due to be incorporated into the Punjab on 26 January 1986, but the transfer was postponed.
‖ Figures refer only to the Indian-held part of the territory.
¶ Mizoram was granted statehood in February 1987.

Source: *Census of India* (2001).

### PRINCIPAL TOWNS
(population at 2001 census*)

| | | | |
|---|---|---|---|
| Greater Mumbai (Bombay) | 11,978,450 | Hubli-Dharwad | 786,195 |
| Delhi | 10,181,535 | Mysore | 755,379 |
| Kolkata (Calcutta) | 4,572,876 | Tiruchirapalli | 752,066 |
| Chennai (Madras) | 4,343,645 | Thiruvananthapuram (Trivandrum) | 744,983 |
| Bangalore | 4,301,326 | Bareilly | 718,395 |
| Hyderabad | 3,612,427 | Jalandhar | 706,043 |
| Ahmedabad | 3,520,085 | Navi Mumbai | 704,002 |
| Kanpur (Cawnpore) | 2,551,337 | Salem | 696,760 |
| Pune (Poona) | 2,538,473 | Kota | 694,316 |
| Surat | 2,433,835 | Aligarh | 669,087 |
| Lucknow | 2,185,927 | Bhubaneswar | 648,032 |
| Nagpur | 2,052,066 | Moradabad | 641,583 |
| Jaipur (Jeypore) | 1,870,771 | Gorakhpur | 622,701 |
| Indore | 1,474,968 | Raipur | 605,747 |
| Bhopal | 1,437,354 | Bhiwandi | 598,741 |
| Ludhiana | 1,398,467 | Jamshedpur | 573,096 |
| Patna | 1,366,444 | Bhilai Nagar | 556,366 |
| Vadodara (Baroda) | 1,306,227 | Amravati | 549,510 |
| Agra | 1,275,134 | Cuttack | 534,654 |
| Thane (Thana) | 1,262,551 | Warangal | 530,636 |
| Kalyan-Dombivli | 1,193,512 | Bikaner | 529,690 |
| Varanasi (Banares) | 1,091,918 | Mira-Bhayandar | 520,388 |
| Nashik | 1,077,236 | Guntur | 514,461 |
| Meerut | 1,068,772 | Bhavnagar | 511,085 |
| Faridabad Complex | 1,055,938 | Kochi (Cochin) | 504,550 |
| Pimpri-Chinchwad | 1,012,472 | Durgapur | 493,405 |
| Haora (Howrah) | 1,007,532 | Kolhapur | 493,167 |
| Visakhapatnam (Vizag) | 982,904 | Ajmer | 485,575 |
| Allahabad | 975,393 | Asansol | 475,439 |
| Ghaziabad | 968,256 | Ulhasnagar | 473,731 |
| Rajkot | 967,476 | Saharanpur | 455,754 |
| Amritsar | 966,862 | Jamnagar | 443,518 |
| Jabalpur (Jubbulpore) | 932,484 | Bhatpara | 442,385 |
| Coimbatore | 930,882 | Sangli-Miraj-Kupwad | 436,781 |

*—continued*

| | | | |
|---|---|---|---|
| Madurai | 928,869 | Kozhikode (Calicut) | 436,556 |
| Srinagar | 898,440 | Nanded-Waghala | 430,733 |
| Aurangabad | 873,311 | Ujjain | 430,427 |
| Solapur | 872,478 | Dehradun | 426,674 |
| Vijayawada (Vijayavada) | 851,282 | Gulbarga | 422,569 |
| Jodhpur | 851,051 | Jaipur | 419,778 |
| Ranchi | 847,093 | Tirunelveli | 411,831 |
| Gwalior | 827,026 | Malegaon | 409,403 |
| Guwahati | 809,895 | Akola | 400,520 |
| Chandigarh | 808,515 | | |

* Figures refer to the city proper in each case.

**Capital:** New Delhi, provisional population 294,783 at 2001 census.

**Population of principal urban agglomerations at 2001 census:** Greater Mumbai 16,434,386; Kolkata 13,205,697; Delhi 12,877,470; Chennai 6,560,242; Hyderabad 5,742,036; Bangalore 5,701,446; Jaipur 5,251,071; Ahmedabad 4,525,013; Pune 3,760,636; Ludhiana 3,032,831; Surat 2,811,614; Kanpur 2,715,555; Lucknow 2,245,509; Faridabad 2,194,586; Nagpur 2,129,500; Patna 1,697,976; Indore 1,516,918; Vadodara 1,491,045; Coimbatore 1,461,139; Bhopal 1,458,416; Kochi 1,355,972; Visakhapatnam 1,345,938; Agra 1,331,339; Varanasi 1,203,961; Madurai 1,203,095; Meerut 1,161,716; Nashik 1,152,326; Jamshedpur 1,104,713; Jabalpur 1,098,000; Asansol 1,067,369; Dhanbad 1,065,327; Allahabad 1,042,229; Vijayawada 1,039,518; Amritsar 1,003,917; Rajkot 1,003,015.

**Mid-2007** ('000, incl. suburbs, UN estimates): Greater Mumbai 18,978; Delhi 15,926; Kolkata 14,787; Chennai 7,163; Bangalore 6,787; Hyderabad 6,376; Ahmedabad 5,375; Pune (Poona) 4,672; Surat 3,842; Kanpur 3,162 (Source: UN, *World Urbanization Prospects: The 2007 Revision*).

### BIRTHS AND DEATHS

(estimates based on Sample Registration Scheme)

| | 2004 | 2005 | 2006 |
|---|---|---|---|
| Birth rate (per 1,000) | 24.1 | 23.8 | 23.5 |
| Death rate (per 1,000) | 7.5 | 7.6 | 7.5 |

**Expectation of life** (years at birth, WHO estimates): 62.8 (males 61.8; females 63.8) in 2006 (Source: WHO, *World Health Statistics*).

### ECONOMICALLY ACTIVE POPULATION

(persons aged five years and over, 1991 census, excluding Jammu and Kashmir)

| | Males | Females | Total |
|---|---|---|---|
| Agriculture, hunting, forestry and fishing | 139,361,719 | 51,979,110 | 191,340,829 |
| Mining and quarrying | 1,536,919 | 214,356 | 1,751,275 |
| Manufacturing | 23,969,433 | 4,702,046 | 28,671,479 |
| Construction | 5,122,468 | 420,737 | 5,543,205 |
| Trade and commerce | 19,862,725 | 1,433,612 | 21,296,337 |
| Transport, storage and communications | 7,810,126 | 207,620 | 8,017,746 |
| Other services | 23,995,194 | 5,316,428 | 29,311,622 |
| **Total employed** | 221,658,584 | 64,273,909 | 285,932,493 |
| Marginal workers | 2,705,223 | 25,493,654 | 28,198,877 |
| **Total labour force** | 224,363,807 | 89,767,563 | 314,131,370 |

**Unemployment** (work applicants at 31 December, '000 persons aged 14 years and over): 40,458 (males 29,746, females 10,712) in 2004; 39,348 (males 28,742, females 10,606) in 2005; 41,466 (males 29,685, females 11,781) in 2006 (Source: ILO).

**2001 census:** Cultivators 127,312,851 (males 85,416,498, females 41,896,353); Agricultural labourers 106,775,330 (males 57,329,100, females 49,446,230); Household industry workers 16,956,942 (males 8,744,183, females 8,212,759); Other 151,189,601 (males 123,524,695, females 27,664,906); Total employed 402,234,724 (incl. 89,229,741 marginal workers).

**Mid-2005** (official estimates in '000): Agriculture, etc. 280,716; Total labour force 489,509 (Source: FAO).

# Health and Welfare

### KEY INDICATORS

| | |
|---|---|
| Total fertility rate (children per woman, 2006) | 2.9 |
| Under-5 mortality rate (per 1,000 live births, 2006) | 76 |
| HIV/AIDS (% of persons aged 15–49, 2005) | 0.9 |
| Physicians (per 1,000 head, 2005) | 0.6 |
| Hospital beds (per 1,000 head, 2002) | 0.70 |
| Health expenditure (2005): US $ per head (PPP) | 100 |
| Health expenditure (2005): % of GDP | 5.0 |
| Health expenditure (2005): public (% of total) | 19.0 |
| Access to water (% of persons, 2004) | 86 |
| Access to sanitation (% of persons, 2004) | 33 |
| Human Development Index (2005): ranking | 128 |
| Human Development Index (2005): value | 0.619 |

For sources and definitions, see explanatory note on p. vi.

# Agriculture

### PRINCIPAL CROPS

('000 metric tons, year ending 30 June)

| | 2005/06 | 2006/07* | 2007/08† |
|---|---|---|---|
| Rice (milled) | 91,790 | 93,350 | 96,430 |
| Sorghum (Jowar) | 7,630 | 7,150 | 7,780 |
| Cat-tail millet (Bajra) | 7,680 | 8,420 | 9,790 |
| Maize | 14,710 | 15,100 | 19,310 |
| Finger millet (Ragi) | 2,350 | 1,440 | 2,130 |
| Small millets | 470 | 480 | 490 |
| Wheat | 69,350 | 75,810 | 78,400 |
| Barley | 1,220 | 1,330 | 1,230 |
| **Total cereals** | 195,220 | 203,080 | 215,560 |
| Chick-peas (Gram) | 5,600 | 6,330 | 5,910 |
| Pigeon-peas (Tur) | 2,740 | 2,310 | 3,090 |
| Dry beans, dry peas, lentils and other pulses | 5,050 | 5,560 | 6,110 |
| **Total food grains** | 208,600 | 217,280 | 230,670 |
| Groundnuts (in shell) | 7,993 | 4,864 | 9,363 |
| Sesame seed | 641 | 618 | 785 |
| Rapeseed and mustard | 8,131 | 7,438 | 5,803 |
| Linseed | 173 | 168 | 144 |
| Castorseed | 991 | 762 | 1,011 |
| **Total edible oilseeds** (incl. others) | 27,979 | 24,289 | 28,825 |
| Cotton lint‡ | 18,499 | 22,632 | 25,806 |
| Jute and kenaf§ | 10,840 | 11,273 | 11,176 |
| Sugar cane: production cane | 281,172 | 355,520 | 340,557 |

* Final estimates.

† Estimates at 9 July 2008.

‡ Production in '000 bales of 170 kg each.

§ Production in '000 bales of 180 kg each.

Sources: Directorate of Economics and Statistics, Ministry of Agriculture.

**Tea (made)** ('000 metric tons): 850 in 2004; 831 in 2005; 893 in 2006 (Source: FAO).

**Tobacco (leaves)** ('000 metric tons): 550 in 2003/04; 550 in 2004/05; 550 in 2005/06 (Source: FAO).

**Potatoes** ('000 metric tons): 23,060 in 2003/04; 23,631 in 2004/05; 23,910 in 2005/06 (Source: FAO).

**LIVESTOCK**
('000 head, year ending September, unrevised data)

| | 2003 | 2004 | 2005 |
|---|---|---|---|
| Cattle | 187,382 | 185,500* | 185,000* |
| Sheep | 61,789 | 62,500* | 62,500* |
| Goats | 120,097 | 120,000* | 120,000* |
| Pigs | 14,142 | 14,300* | 14,300* |
| Horses | 788 | 800* | 800* |
| Asses, mules and hinnies* | 1,050 | 1,050 | 1,050 |
| Buffaloes | 96,616 | 98,175† | 98,875† |
| Camels | 635 | 635* | 635* |
| Chickens | 409,000† | 425,000 | 430,000* |
| Ducks | 32,900† | 33,000 | 33,000* |

* FAO estimate(s).
† Unofficial figure.

**2006** ('000 head, year ending September, FAO estimates): Cattle 180,837; Sheep 62,850; Goats 124,906; Pigs 14,000; Horses 750; Asses, mules and hinnies 800; Buffaloes 98,805; Camels 630; Chickens 475,000; Ducks 30,000.

Source: FAO.

**LIVESTOCK PRODUCTS**
('000 metric tons)

| | 2004 | 2005 | 2006 |
|---|---|---|---|
| Cattle meat | n.a. | n.a. | 1,333.9* |
| Buffalo meat* | 1,483.1 | 1,487.6 | 1,487.6 |
| Sheep meat* | 238.8 | 238.8 | 238.8 |
| Goat meat | n.a. | n.a. | 475* |
| Pig meat* | 498.0 | 503.0 | 503.0 |
| Chicken meat† | 1,650 | 1,900 | 2,000 |
| Duck meat* | 65.0 | 65.0 | 65.0 |
| Cows' milk | 37,344 | 39,759 | 39,775† |
| Buffaloes' milk | 50,178 | 52,070 | 52,100 |
| Goats' milk† | 3,437 | 3,790 | 3,790* |
| Hen eggs* | 2,486.0 | 2,539.0 | 2,604 |
| Wool: greasy | 44.6 | 44.9 | 45.2 |

* FAO estimate(s).
† Unofficial figure(s).

Source: FAO.

# Forestry

**ROUNDWOOD REMOVALS**
('000 cubic metres, excl. bark)

| | 2004 | 2005 | 2006* |
|---|---|---|---|
| Sawlogs, veneer logs and logs for sleepers | 22,014 | 22,390 | 22,390 |
| Pulpwood | 621 | 624 | 624 |
| Other industrial wood | 175 | 178 | 178 |
| Fuel wood* | 303,839 | 305,485 | 306,252 |
| **Total** | 326, 649 | 328,677 | 329,444 |

* FAO estimate(s).

Source: FAO.

**SAWNWOOD PRODUCTION**
('000 cubic metres, incl. railway sleepers)

| | 2003 | 2004 | 2005 |
|---|---|---|---|
| Coniferous sawnwood | 7,990 | 9,300 | 9,900 |
| Broadleaved sawnwood | 3,890 | 4,361 | 4,889 |
| **Total** | 11,880 | 13,661 | 14,789 |

**2006:** Figures assumed to be unchanged from 2005 (FAO estimates).

Source: FAO.

# Fishing

('000 metric tons, live weight)

| | 2004 | 2005 | 2006 |
|---|---|---|---|
| Capture | 3,391.0 | 3,691.4 | 3,855.5 |
| Bombay-duck (Bummalo) | 171.5 | 188.4 | 188.2 |
| Croakers and drums | 241.2 | 235.4 | 238.9 |
| Indian oil-sardine (Sardinella) | 273.3 | 262.7 | 289.4 |
| Giant tiger prawn | 177.2 | 186.5 | 207.2 |
| Aquaculture | 2,794.6 | 2,962.0* | 3,123.1* |
| Roho labeo | 923.2 | 931.6 | 945.2 |
| Mrigal carp | 221.1 | 217.1 | 230.0 |
| Catla | 1,010.8 | 1,135.7 | 1,168.0 |
| Silver carp | 279.8 | 352.2 | 361.6 |
| **Total catch** | 6,185.6 | 6,653.3* | 6,978.6* |

* FAO estimate.

Source: FAO.

# Mining

('000 metric tons, unless otherwise indicated)

| | 2003/04 | 2004/05 | 2005/06 |
|---|---|---|---|
| Coal | 361,156 | 382,615 | 407,222 |
| Lignite | 27,958 | 30,337 | 30,049 |
| Iron ore* | 122,838 | 145,942 | 154,436 |
| Manganese ore* | 1,776 | 2,386 | 2,003 |
| Bauxite | 10,925 | 11,964 | 12,335 |
| Chalk (Fireclay) | 657 | 663 | 486 |
| Kaolin (China clay) | 897 | 934 | 1,097 |
| Dolomite | 4,051 | 4,339 | 4,428 |
| Gypsum | 2,774 | 3,685 | 3,137 |
| Limestone | 153,390 | 165,753 | 170,378 |
| Crude petroleum | 33,373 | 34,015 | 32,204 |
| Chromium ore* | 2,905 | 3,621 | 3,423 |
| Phosphorite | 1,436 | 1,723 | 1,373 |
| Kyanite | 9 | 8 | 7 |
| Magnesite | 324 | 384 | 351 |
| Steatite | 726 | 684 | 627 |
| Copper ore* | 2,903 | 2,929 | 2,643 |
| Lead concentrates* | 73 | 82 | 98 |
| Zinc concentrates* | 590 | 666 | 893 |
| Mica—crude (metric tons) | 1,076 | 1,276 | 1,259 |
| Gold (kilograms) | 3,457 | 3,526 | 3,050 |
| Diamonds (carats) | 71,260 | 78,316 | 44,170 |
| Natural gas (million cu m)† | 30,908 | 30,820 | 31,223 |

* Figures refer to gross weight. The estimated metal content is: Iron 63%; Manganese 40%; Chromium 30%; Copper 1.2%; Lead 70%; Zinc 60%.
† Figures refer to gas utilized.

Source: Indian Bureau of Mines.

# Industry

**SELECTED PRODUCTS**
('000 metric tons, unless otherwise indicated)

| | 2004/05 | 2005/06 | 2006/07 |
|---|---|---|---|
| Refined sugar* | 13,000 | 18,000 | 24,000 |
| Cotton cloth (million sq metres) | 13,193 | 14,826 | 16,663 |
| Paper and paper board | 5,793 | 5,885 | 6,129 |
| Soda ash | 2,027 | 2,327 | 2,085 |
| Fertilizers | 15,326 | 15,564 | 16,153 |
| Petroleum products (excl. gas) | 113,946 | 115,116 | 128,710 |
| Motor spirit | 11,019 | 10,501 | 12,539 |
| Cement | 125,338 | 140,512 | 154,746 |
| Pig-iron | 3,982 | 3,697 | 4,550 |
| Stainless steel | 1,795 | 2,120 | 2,320 |
| Aluminium ingots (metric tons) | 516,000 | 561,000 | 719,000 |
| Diesel engines—stationary (number) | 298,974 | 337,653 | 460,767 |
| Sewing machines (number) | 41,188 | 184 | — |
| Television receivers (number) | 5,044,000 | 6,060,000 | 5,853,000 |
| Electric fans (number) | 10,000,000 | 11,000,000 | 12,000,000 |
| Passenger cars | 965,391 | 1,047,493 | 1,238,737 |
| Commercial vehicles (number) | 350,032 | 391,078 | 520,000 |
| Motorcycles, mopeds and scooters (number) | 6,454,765 | 7,601,801 | 8,436,186 |
| Bicycles (number) | 8,030,000 | 8,268,000 | 10,599,000 |

* Figures relate to crop year (beginning November) and are in respect of cane sugar only.

# Finance

**CURRENCY AND EXCHANGE RATES**

**Monetary Units**
100 paise (singular: paisa) = 1 Indian rupee (R).

**Sterling, Dollar and Euro Equivalents** (30 May 2008)
£1 sterling = Rs 84.051;
US $1 = Rs 42.590;
€1 = Rs 66.049;
1,000 Indian rupees = £11.90 = $23.48 = €15.14.

**Average Exchange Rate** (rupees per US $)
2005 44.100
2006 45.307
2007 41.349

**UNION BUDGET**
(Rs million, rounded, year ending 31 March)

| Revenue | 2006/07 | 2007/08* | 2008/09† |
|---|---|---|---|
| Tax revenue (net) | 3,459,710 | 4,317,730 | 5,071,500 |
| Customs receipts | 818,000 | 1,007,660 | 1,189,300 |
| Union excise duties | 1,172,660 | 1,279,470 | 1,378,740 |
| Corporation tax | 1,464,970 | 1,861,250 | 2,263,610 |
| Other taxes on income | 825,100 | 1,183,200 | 1,383,140 |
| Other taxes and duties | 397,750 | 522,520 | 662,360 |
| *Less* States' share of tax revenue | 1,203,770 | 1,518,370 | 1,787,650 |
| *Less* Surcharge transferred to National Calamity Contingency Fund | 15,000 | 18,000 | 18,000 |
| Other current revenue | 773,600 | 933,250 | 957,850 |
| Interest receipts (net) | 201,307 | 174,640 | 191,350 |
| Dividends and profits | 304,383 | 361,080 | 432,040 |
| Receipts of Union Territories | 7,240 | 8,200 | 8,150 |
| External grants | 24,690 | 20,910 | 17,950 |
| Other receipts (net) | 235,980 | 368,420 | 308,360 |
| Recoveries of loans (net) | 54,500 | 44,970 | 44,970 |
| **Total** | 4,287,810 | 5,295,950 | 6,074,320 |

| Expenditure | 2006/07 | 2007/08* | 2008/09† |
|---|---|---|---|
| Central Ministries/Departments | 5,354,120 | 6,492,602 | 6,862,886 |
| Agriculture and co-operation (incl. agricultural research and education) | 73,440 | 91,105 | 102,088 |
| Atomic energy | 45,112 | 39,390 | 47,970 |
| Defence | 1,008,100 | 1,095,190 | 1,235,348 |
| Drinking water supply | 52,971 | 74,618 | 85,019 |
| Economic affairs | 1,788,298 | 1,992,335 | 2,254,174 |
| External affairs | 39,464 | 47,830 | 50,620 |
| Fertilizers | 263,264 | 305,820 | 312,000 |
| Food and public distribution | 243,599 | 320,600 | 330,950 |
| Health and family welfare | 105,679 | 145,000 | 169,683 |
| Home affairs | 183,740 | 201,155 | 240,828 |
| Education and literacy | 168,975 | 231,914 | 278,500 |
| Petroleum and natural gas | 32,960 | 28,970 | 29,380 |
| Railways | 75,542 | 81,213 | 71,000 |
| Road transport and highways | 146,615 | 151,213 | 160,582 |
| Rural development | 242,842 | 285,235 | 315,241 |
| Urban development | 29,900 | 45,240 | 41,288 |
| State plans | 436,373 | 545,809 | 587,785 |
| Union territories | 43,373 | 55,322 | 58,164 |
| **Total** | 5,833,866 | 7,093,733 | 7,508,835 |
| Current‡ | 5,146,086 | 5,885,864 | 6,581,190 |
| Capital | 687,780 | 1,207,869 | 927,645 |

* Estimates.
† Forecasts.
‡ Including interest payments (Rs million): 1,461,920 in 2006/07; 1,719,710 in 2007/08 (estimate); 1,908,070 in 2008/09 (forecast).

Source: Government of India, Union Budget 2008/09.

**INTERNATIONAL RESERVES**
(US $ million at 31 December)

| | 2005 | 2006 | 2007 |
|---|---|---|---|
| Gold (national valuation) | 4,102 | 5,367 | n.a. |
| IMF special drawing rights | 4 | 1 | 3 |
| Reserve position in IMF | 902 | 550 | 432 |
| Foreign exchange | 131,018 | 170,187 | 266,553 |
| **Total** | 136,026 | 176,105 | 266,988* |

* Excluding gold.

Source: IMF, *International Financial Statistics*.

**MONEY SUPPLY**
(Rs million, last Friday of year ending 31 March)

| | 2005/06 | 2006/07 | 2007/08 |
|---|---|---|---|
| Currency with the public | 4,131,430 | 4,829,770 | 5,676,150 |
| Demand deposits with banks | 4,102,580 | 4,789,350 | 5,761,670 |
| Other deposits with Reserve Bank | 68,690 | 74,960 | 90,690 |
| **Total money** | 8,302,700 | 9,694,080 | 11,528,510 |

Source: Reserve Bank of India.

**COST OF LIVING**
(Consumer Price Index for Industrial Workers; base: 2000 = 100)

| | 2004 | 2005 | 2006 |
|---|---|---|---|
| Food (incl. beverages) | 111.5 | 115.0 | 125.0 |
| Fuel and light | 138.6 | 136.1 | 140.0 |
| Clothing (incl. footwear) | 108.9 | 111.4 | 114.0 |
| Rent | 136.4 | 157.9 | 137.0 |
| **All items** (incl. others) | 116.6 | 121.5 | 127.7 |

**2007:** Food (incl. beverages) 137.0; All items (incl. others) 136.0.

Source: ILO.

## NATIONAL ACCOUNTS

(Rs '000 million at current prices, year ending 31 March)

### National Income and Product

| | 2004/05 | 2005/06 | 2006/07 |
|---|---|---|---|
| Domestic factor incomes | 25,487.83 | 28,968.66 | 33,555.95 |
| Consumption of fixed capital | 3,289.23 | 3,788.04 | 4,344.68 |
| **Gross domestic product at factor cost** | 28,777.06 | 32,756.70 | 37,900.63 |
| Indirect taxes | 3,639.67 | 4,238.99 | 5,198.21 |
| *Less* Subsidies | 922.61 | 1,192.25 | 1,640.74 |
| **GDP in purchasers' values** | 31,494.12 | 35,803.44 | 41,458.10 |
| Net factor income from abroad | –223.75 | –261.16 | –297.78 |
| **Gross national product** | 31,270.37 | 35,542.28 | 41,160.32 |
| *Less* Consumption of fixed capital | 3,289.23 | 3,788.04 | 4,344.68 |
| **National income in market prices** | 27,981.14 | 31,754.24 | 36,815.64 |

### Expenditure on the Gross Domestic Product

| | 2004/05 | 2005/06 | 2006/07 |
|---|---|---|---|
| Government final consumption expenditure | 3,380.52 | 3,730.76 | 4,270.07 |
| Private final consumption expenditure | 18,404.06 | 20,553.87 | 23,121.05 |
| Increase in stocks | 602.15 | 862.48 | 961.03 |
| Gross fixed capital formation | 8,946.74 | 11,091.60 | 13,465.01 |
| Acquisitions, less disposals, of valuables | 410.54 | 413.92 | 497.09 |
| **Total domestic expenditure** | 31,744.01 | 36,652.63 | 42,314.25 |
| Exports of goods and services | 5,690.51 | 7,120.87 | 9,156.74 |
| *Less* Imports of goods and services | 6,259.45 | 8,134.66 | 10,407.97 |
| Statistical discrepancy | 319.05 | 164.60 | 395.08 |
| **GDP in purchasers' values** | 31,494.12 | 35,803.44 | 41,458.10 |
| **GDP at constant 1999/2000 prices** | 26,016.30 | 28,419.67 | 31,173.71 |

### Gross Domestic Product by Economic Activity

(at current factor cost)

| | 2004/05 | 2005/06 | 2006/07 |
|---|---|---|---|
| Agriculture | 5,014.15 | 5,571.18 | 6,345.19 |
| Forestry and logging | 233.51 | 258.39 | 268.55 |
| Fishing | 276.56 | 328.88 | 340.50 |
| Mining and quarrying | 847.76 | 941.53 | 1,018.16 |
| Manufacturing | 4,536.03 | 5,193.87 | 6,179.54 |
| Electricity, gas and water supply | 598.92 | 644.06 | 705.63 |
| Construction | 2,128.12 | 2,646.16 | 3,194.97 |
| Trade, hotels and restaurants | 4,612.87 | 5,385.42 | 6,303.64 |
| Transport, storage and communications | 2,447.86 | 2,771.56 | 3,191.04 |
| Banking and insurance | 1,678.31 | 1,805.19 | 2,133.81 |
| Real estate and business services | 2,372.50 | 2,720.74 | 3,133.74 |
| Public administration and defence | 1,734.91 | 1,948.00 | 2,188.83 |
| Other services | 2,295.56 | 2,541.72 | 2,897.03 |
| **GDP at factor cost** | 28,777.06 | 32,756.70 | 37,900.63 |
| Indirect taxes | 3,639.67 | 4,238.99 | 5,198.21 |
| *Less* Subsidies | 922.61 | 1,192.25 | 1,640.74 |
| **GDP in market prices** | 31,494.12 | 35,803.44 | 41,458.10 |

## BALANCE OF PAYMENTS

(US $ million)

| | 2004/05 | 2005/06 | 2006/07* |
|---|---|---|---|
| Exports of goods f.o.b. | 85,206 | 105,152 | 127,090 |
| Imports of goods f.o.b. | –118,908 | –156,993 | –191,995 |
| **Trade balance** | –33,702 | –51,841 | –64,905 |
| Services (net) | 15,426 | 23,881 | 32,727 |
| **Balance on goods and services** | –18,276 | –27,960 | –32,178 |
| Other income (net) | –4,979 | –5,510 | –4,846 |
| **Balance on goods, services and income** | –23,255 | –33,470 | –37,024 |
| Current transfers (net) | 20,785 | 24,284 | 27,415 |
| **Current balance** | –2,470 | –9,186 | –9,609 |
| Direct investment abroad | 5,987 | 7,661 | 19,442 |
| Direct investment from abroad | –2,274 | –2,931 | –11,005 |
| Portfolio investment assets | 9,311 | 12,494 | 7,004 |
| Portfolio investment liabilities | –24 | — | 58 |
| Net loans | 10,909 | 6,113 | 21,129 |
| Banking capital (net) | 3,874 | 1,373 | 2,087 |
| Rupee debt service | –417 | –572 | –162 |
| Other capital (net) | 656 | –738 | 6,391 |
| Net errors and omissions | 607 | 838 | 1,271 |
| **Overall balance** | 26,159 | 15,052 | 36,606 |

* Preliminary figures.

Source: Reserve Bank of India.

## OFFICIAL DEVELOPMENT ASSISTANCE

(US $ million)

| | 1998 | 1999 | 2000 |
|---|---|---|---|
| Bilateral donors | 896.4 | 826.7 | 638.7 |
| Multilateral donors | 713.2 | 664.6 | 848.5 |
| **Total** | 1,609.6 | 1,491.3 | 1,487.2 |
| Grants | 802.6 | 772.2 | 775.3 |
| Loans | 807.0 | 719.1 | 711.9 |
| Per caput assistance (US $) | 1.7 | 1.5 | 1.5 |

Source: UN, *Statistical Yearbook for Asia and the Pacific*.

# External Trade

## PRINCIPAL COMMODITIES

(Rs million, year ending 31 March)

| Imports c.i.f. | 2004/05 | 2005/06 | 2006/07 |
|---|---|---|---|
| Animal and vegetable oils, fats and waxes | 113,727 | 101,517 | 102,614 |
| Mineral fuels, mineral oils and products of their distillation | 1,564,454 | 2,227,402 | 2,799,073 |
| Organic chemicals | 187,849 | 227,752 | 273,297 |
| Natural or cultured pearls, precious and semi-precious stones, precious metals and articles thereof; imitation jewellery; coin | 933,873 | 916,041 | 1,022,499 |
| Iron and steel | 150,774 | 241,133 | 277,419 |
| Nuclear reactors, boilers, machinery, mechanical appliances and parts thereof | 433,670 | 616,068 | 842,283 |
| Electrical machinery and equipment and parts thereof; sound and television apparatus | 401,933 | 526,804 | 659,248 |
| Aircraft, spacecraft, and parts thereof | 71,539 | 220,456 | 238,190 |
| **Total** (incl. others) | 5,010,646 | 6,604,089 | 8,405,063 |

| Exports f.o.b. | 2004/05 | 2005/06 | 2006/07 |
|---|---|---|---|
| Cereals | 90,226 | 72,326 | 76,705 |
| Ores, slag and ash | 167,992 | 197,133 | 220,595 |
| Mineral fuels, mineral oils and products of their distillation | 320,829 | 525,376 | 855,420 |
| Organic chemicals | 162,674 | 215,040 | 259,496 |
| Iron and steel | 189,537 | 168,836 | 253,371 |
| Articles of iron or steel | 103,798 | 124,614 | 153,842 |
| Cotton | 101,675 | 132,122 | 177,555 |
| Articles of apparel and clothing accessories, knitted or crocheted | 118,677 | 141,282 | 163,717 |
| Articles of apparel and clothing accessories, not knitted or crocheted | 176,701 | 240,649 | 239,086 |
| Natural or cultured pearls, precious and semi-precious stones, precious metals and articles thereof; imitation jewellery; coin | 648,641 | 702,087 | 727,842 |
| Nuclear reactors, boilers, machinery, mechanical appliances and parts thereof | 148,588 | 185,398 | 230,385 |
| Vehicles other than railway or tramway rolling stock, and parts and accessories thereof | 110,740 | 145,805 | 170,406 |
| **Total** (incl. others) | 3,753,395 | 4,564,179 | 5,717,793 |

Source: Ministry of Commerce and Industry.

**PRINCIPAL TRADING PARTNERS**
(Rs million, year ending 31 March)

| Imports c.i.f. | 2004/05 | 2005/06 | 2006/07 |
|---|---|---|---|
| Australia | 171,842 | 219,061 | 317,109 |
| Belgium | 206,187 | 209,198 | 187,416 |
| China, People's Republic | 318,923 | 481,167 | 790,086 |
| France | 85,105 | 182,110 | 190,593 |
| Germany | 180,416 | 266,687 | 341,468 |
| Hong Kong | 77,737 | 97,711 | 112,393 |
| Indonesia | 117,619 | 133,180 | 188,649 |
| Italy | 61,696 | 82,155 | 121,017 |
| Japan | 145,359 | 179,799 | 207,949 |
| Korea, Republic | 157,654 | 202,058 | 217,470 |
| Malaysia | 103,298 | 106,947 | 239,588 |
| Russia | 59,433 | 89,529 | 109,028 |
| Singapore | 119,131 | 148,483 | 248,400 |
| South Africa | 98,744 | 109,435 | 111,841 |
| Switzerland | 266,890 | 290,248 | 412,832 |
| United Arab Emirates | 208,532 | 192,770 | 391,749 |
| United Kingdom | 160,235 | 174,008 | 188,893 |
| USA | 314,581 | 418,595 | 531,054 |
| **Total** (incl. others) | 5,010,646 | 6,604,089 | 8,405,063 |

| Exports f.o.b. | 2004/05 | 2005/06 | 2006/07 |
|---|---|---|---|
| Bangladesh | 73,289 | 73,687 | 73,660 |
| Belgium | 112,765 | 127,120 | 157,217 |
| Brazil | 30,471 | 48,285 | 65,768 |
| Canada | 38,947 | 45,229 | 50,245 |
| China, People's Republic | 252,330 | 299,249 | 375,298 |
| France | 75,527 | 92,071 | 95,060 |
| Germany | 126,988 | 158,770 | 180,072 |
| Hong Kong | 165,879 | 197,961 | 211,794 |
| Indonesia | 59,876 | 61,106 | 91,770 |
| Iran | 55,328 | 52,612 | 65,648 |
| Israel | 45,190 | 53,194 | 59,794 |
| Italy | 102,713 | 111,527 | 162,124 |
| Japan | 95,610 | 109,854 | 129,536 |
| Korea, Republic | 46,804 | 80,897 | 113,790 |
| Malaysia | 48,708 | 51,440 | 59,019 |
| Nepal | 33,390 | 38,074 | 42,014 |
| Netherlands | 72,109 | 109,567 | 120,825 |
| Nigeria | 28,966 | 38,696 | 40,882 |
| Russia | 28,364 | 32,459 | 40,855 |
| Saudi Arabia | 63,446 | 80,125 | 117,137 |

| Exports f.o.b.—*continued* | 2004/05 | 2005/06 | 2006/07 |
|---|---|---|---|
| Singapore | 179,753 | 240,197 | 274,616 |
| South Africa | 44,214 | 67,600 | 101,653 |
| Spain | 62,426 | 71,088 | 84,970 |
| Sri Lanka | 63,496 | 89,639 | 102,064 |
| Taiwan | 27,791 | 27,850 | 41,335 |
| Thailand | 40,501 | 47,608 | 65,356 |
| United Arab Emirates | 330,151 | 380,388 | 544,450 |
| United Kingdom | 165,397 | 223,992 | 254,213 |
| USA | 618,516 | 768,281 | 853,685 |
| **Total** (incl. others) | 3,753,395 | 4,564,179 | 5,717,793 |

Source: Ministry of Commerce and Industry.

# Transport

**RAILWAYS**
(million, year ending 31 March)

| | 2004/05 | 2005/06 | 2006/07 |
|---|---|---|---|
| Passengers | 5,378 | 5,725 | 6,219 |
| Passenger-km | 575,702 | 615,614 | 694,764 |
| Freight (metric tons) | 626.2 | 682.4 | 744.6 |
| Freight (metric ton-km) | 411,280 | 441,762 | 483,422 |

Source: Railway Board, Ministry of Railways and Indian Railways.

**ROAD TRAFFIC**
('000 motor vehicles in use at 31 March)

| | 2002 | 2003 | 2004* |
|---|---|---|---|
| Private cars, jeeps and taxis | 7,613 | 8,599 | 9,451 |
| Buses and coaches | 635 | 721 | 768 |
| Goods vehicles | 2,974 | 3,492 | 3,749 |
| Motorcycles and scooters | 41,581 | 47,519 | 51,922 |
| Others | 6,121 | 6,676 | 6,828 |
| **Total** | 58,924 | 67,007 | 72,718 |

* Provisional figures.

Source: Ministry of Road Transport and Highways.

**SHIPPING**

**Merchant Fleet**
(registered at 31 December)

| | 2005 | 2006 | 2007 |
|---|---|---|---|
| Vessels | 1,096 | 1,181 | 1,417 |
| Displacement ('000 grt) | 8,056.0 | 8,381.2 | 9,168.0 |

Source: Lloyd's Register-Fairplay, *World Fleet Statistics*.

**International Sea-borne Traffic**
(year ending 31 March)

| | 2000/01 | 2001/02 | 2002/03* |
|---|---|---|---|
| Vessels ('000 nrt)†: | | | |
| entered | 55,466 | 55,981 | n.a. |
| cleared | 38,043 | 41,716 | n.a. |
| Freight ('000 metric tons)‡: | | | |
| loaded | 135,331 | n.a. | 115,534 |
| unloaded | 233,007 | n.a. | 182,229 |

* Provisional figures.
† Excluding minor and intermediate ports.
‡ Including bunkers.

Sources: Transport Research Division, Ministry of Surface Transport; Department of Shipping, Ministry of Shipping, Road Transport and Highways; Directorate General of Commercial Intelligence and Statistics.

**CIVIL AVIATION**
(all Indian carriers, traffic on scheduled services)

| | 2004/05 | 2005/06 | 2006/07 |
|---|---|---|---|
| Passengers carried ('000) | 24,771 | 31,752 | 43,354 |
| Passenger-km (million) | 40,303 | 51,567 | 63,874 |
| Freight carried (metric tons) | 328,000 | 335,000 | 368,000 |
| Freight ton-km (million) | 737 | 801 | 861 |
| Mail carried (metric tons) | 29,000 | 34,000 | 23,000 |
| Mail ton-km ('000) | 41 | 49 | 33 |

Source: Directorate General of Civil Aviation.

## Tourism

**FOREIGN VISITORS BY COUNTRY OF ORIGIN***

| | 2004 | 2005 |
|---|---|---|
| Australia | 81,608 | 96,258 |
| Canada | 135,884 | 157,643 |
| France | 131,824 | 152,258 |
| Germany | 116,679 | 120,243 |
| Italy | 65,561 | 67,642 |
| Japan | 96,851 | 103,082 |
| Malaysia | 84,390 | 96,276 |
| Nepal | 51,534 | 77,024 |
| Netherlands | 51,211 | 52,755 |
| Singapore | 60,710 | 68,666 |
| Sri Lanka | 128,711 | 136,400 |
| United Kingdom | 555,907 | 651,083 |
| USA | 526,120 | 611,165 |
| **Total** (incl. others) | 3,367,980 | 3,920,000 |

* Figures exclude nationals of Bangladesh and Pakistan.

**Receipts from tourism** (US $ million): 3,533 in 2003; 4,769 in 2004; 5,731 in 2005.

Source: Ministry of Tourism.

## Communications Media

| | 2004 | 2005 | 2006 |
|---|---|---|---|
| Telephones ('000 main lines in use) | 43,960 | 49,750 | 40,770 |
| Mobile cellular telephones ('000 subscribers) | 47,300 | 90,000 | 166,050 |
| Personal computers ('000 in use) | 13,030 | 17,000 | n.a. |
| Internet users ('000) | 35,000 | 60,000 | n.a. |
| Broadband subscribers ('000) | 180 | 1,348 | 2,300 |

**1997:** Radio receivers ('000 in use) 116,000; Facsimile machines ('000 in use, year ending 31 March) 100.

**Television receivers** ('000 in use): 79,000 in 2000; 85,000 in 2001.

**Daily newspapers:** 5,364 in 2000; 5,638 in 2001.

**Non-daily newspapers and other periodicals:** 43,781 in 2000; 46,322 in 2001.

Sources: International Telecommunication Union; UN, *Statistical Yearbook*; Register of Newspapers for India, Ministry of Information and Broadcasting.

## Education

(2002/03)

| | Institutions | Teachers | Students |
|---|---|---|---|
| Primary | 651,382 | 1,912,931 | 122,397,715 |
| Middle | 245,274 | 1,581,739 | 46,845,207 |
| Secondary (high school)<br>Higher secondary (new pattern)<br>Intermediate/pre-degree/junior college | 137,207 | 2,033,509 | 33,214,100 |

Source: Ministry of Human Resource Development.

**Adult literacy rate** (UNESCO estimates): 66.0% (males 76.9%; females 54.5%) in 2007 (Source: UNESCO Institute for Statistics).

# Directory

## The Constitution

The Constitution of India, adopted by the Constituent Assembly on 26 November 1949, was inaugurated on 26 January 1950. The Preamble declares that the People of India solemnly resolve to constitute a Sovereign Democratic Republic and to secure to all its citizens justice, liberty, equality and fraternity. There are 397 articles and nine schedules, which form a comprehensive document.

### UNION OF STATES

The Union of India comprises 28 states, six Union Territories and one National Capital Territory. There are provisions for the formation and admission of new states.

The Constitution confers citizenship on a threefold basis of birth, descent, and residence. Provisions are made for refugees who have migrated from Pakistan and for persons of Indian origin residing abroad.

### FUNDAMENTAL RIGHTS AND DIRECTIVE PRINCIPLES

The rights of the citizen contained in Part III of the Constitution are declared fundamental and enforceable in law. 'Untouchability' is abolished and its practice in any form is a punishable offence. The Directive Principles of State Policy provide a code intended to ensure promotion of the economic, social and educational welfare of the State in future legislation.

### THE PRESIDENT

The President is the head of the Union, exercising all executive powers on the advice of the Council of Ministers responsible to Parliament. He is elected by an electoral college consisting of elected members of both Houses of Parliament and the Legislatures of the States. The President holds office for a term of five years and is eligible for re-election. He may be impeached for violation of the Constitution. The Vice-President is the *ex officio* Chairman of the Rajya Sabha and is elected by a joint sitting of both Houses of Parliament.

### THE PARLIAMENT

The Parliament of the Union consists of the President and two Houses: the Rajya Sabha (Council of States) and the Lok Sabha (House of the People). The Rajya Sabha consists of 245 members, of whom a number are nominated by the President. One-third of its members retire every two years. Elections are indirect, each state's legislative quota being elected by the members of the state's legislative assembly. The Lok Sahba has up to 550 members elected by adult franchise; not more than 20 represent the Union Territories and National Capital Territory. Two members are nominated by the President to represent the Anglo-Indian community.

### GOVERNMENT OF THE STATES

The governmental machinery of states closely resembles that of the Union. Each of these states has a governor at its head appointed by the President for a term of five years to exercise executive power on the advice of a council of ministers. The states' legislatures consist of the Governor and either one house (legislative assembly) or two houses (legislative assembly and legislative council). The term of the assembly is five years, but the council is not subject to dissolution.

### LANGUAGE

The Constitution provides that the official language of the Union shall be Hindi. (The English language will continue to be an associate language for many official purposes.)

### LEGISLATION—FEDERAL SYSTEM

The Constitution provides that bills, other than money bills, can be introduced in either House. To become law, they must be passed by both Houses and receive the assent of the President. In financial affairs, the authority of the Lower House is final. The various subjects of legislation are enumerated on three lists in the seventh schedule of the Constitution: the Union List, containing nearly 100 entries, including external affairs, defence, communications and atomic energy; the State List, containing 65 entries, including local government, police, public health and education; and the Concurrent List, with more than 40 entries, including criminal law, marriage and divorce and labour welfare. The Constitution vests residuary authority in the Centre. All matters not enumerated in the Concurrent or State Lists will be deemed to be included in the Union List, and in the event of conflict between Union and State Law on any subject enumerated in the Concurrent List the Union Law will prevail. In time of emergency Parliament may even exercise powers otherwise exclusively vested in the states. Under Article 356, 'If the President on receipt of a report from the government of a state or otherwise is satisfied that a situation has arisen in which the Government of the state cannot be carried on in accordance with the provisions of this Constitution, the President may by Proclamation: (a) assume to himself all or any of the functions of the government of the state and all or any of the powers of the governor or any body or authority in the state other than the Legislature of the state; (b) declare that the powers of the Legislature of the state shall be exercisable by or under the authority of Parliament; (c) make such incidental provisions as appear to the President to be necessary': provided that none of the powers of a High Court be assumed by the President or suspended in any way. Unless such a Proclamation is approved by both Houses of Parliament, it ceases to operate after two months. A Proclamation so approved ceases to operate after six months, unless renewed by Parliament. Its renewal cannot be extended beyond a total period of three years. An independent judiciary exists to define and interpret the Constitution and to resolve constitutional disputes arising between states, or between a state and the Government of India.

### OTHER PROVISIONS

Other Provisions of the Constitution deal with the administration of tribal areas, relations between the Union and states, inter-state trade and finance.

### AMENDMENTS

The Constitution is flexible in character, and a simple process of amendment has been adopted. For amendment of provisions concerning the Supreme Courts and the High Courts, the distribution of legislative powers between the Union and the states, the representation of the states in Parliament, etc., the amendment must be passed by both Houses of Parliament and must further be ratified by the legislatures of not less than half the states. In other cases no reference to the state legislatures is necessary.

Numerous amendments were adopted in August 1975, following the declaration of a state of emergency in June. The Constitution (39th Amendment) Bill laid down that the President's reasons for proclaiming an emergency may not be challenged in any court. Under the Constitution (40th Amendment) Bill, 38 existing laws may not be challenged before any court on the ground of violation of fundamental rights. Thus detainees under the Maintenance of Internal Security Act could not be told the grounds of their detention and were forbidden bail and any claim to liberty through natural or common law. The Constitution (41st Amendment) Bill provided that the President, Prime Minister and state Governors should be immune from criminal prosecution for life and from civil prosecution during their term of office.

In November 1976 a 59-clause Constitution (42nd Amendment) Bill was approved by Parliament and came into force in January 1977. Some of the provisions of the Bill are that the Indian Democratic Republic shall be named a 'Democratic Secular and Socialist Republic'; that the President 'shall act in accordance with' the advice given to him by the Prime Minister and the Council of Ministers, and, acting at the Prime Minister's direction, shall be empowered for two years to amend the Constitution by executive order, in any way beneficial to the enforcement of the whole; that the term of the Lok Sabha and of the state assemblies shall be extended from five to six years; that there shall be no limitation on the constituent power of Parliament to amend the Constitution, and that India's Supreme Court shall be barred from hearing petitions challenging constitutional amendments; that strikes shall be forbidden in the public services and the Union Government has the power to deploy police or other forces under its own superintendence and control in any state. Directive Principles are given precedence over Fundamental Rights: 10 basic duties of citizens are listed, including the duty to 'defend the country and render national service when called upon to do so'.

The Janata Party Government, which came into power in March 1977, promised to amend the Constitution during the year, so as to 'restore the balance between the people and Parliament, Parliament and the judiciary, the judiciary and the executive, the states and the centre, and the citizen and the Government that the founding fathers of the Constitution had worked out'. The Constitution (43rd Amendment) Bill, passed by Parliament in December 1977, the Constitution (44th Amendment) Bill, passed by Parliament in December 1977 and later redesignated the 43rd Amendment, and the Constitution (45th Amendment) Bill, passed by Parliament in December 1978 and later redesignated the 44th Amendment, reversed most of the changes enacted by the Constitution (42nd Amendment) Bill. The 44th Amendment is particularly detailed on emergency provisions: an emergency may not be proclaimed unless 'the security of India or any part of its territory was threatened by war or external aggression or by armed rebellion'. Its introduction must be approved by a two-thirds' majority of Parliament within a month, and after six months the emergency may be continued only with the approval of Parliament. Among the provisions left unchanged after these Bills were a section subordinating Fundamental Rights to Directive Principles and a clause empowering the central Government to deploy armed forces under its control in any state without the state government's consent. In May 1980 the Indian Supreme Court repealed sections 4 and 55 of the 42nd Amendment Act, thus curtailing Parliament's power to enforce directive principles and to amend the Constitution. The death penalty was declared constitutionally valid.

The 53rd Amendment to the Constitution, approved by Parliament in August 1986, granted statehood to the Union Territory of Mizoram; the 55th Amendment, approved in December 1986, granted statehood to the Union Territory of Arunachal Pradesh; and the 57th Amendment, approved in May 1987, granted statehood to the Union Territory of Goa (Daman and Diu remains, however, a Union Territory). The 59th Amendment, approved in March 1988, empowered the Government to impose a state of emergency in the Punjab, on the grounds of internal disturbances. In December 1988 the minimum voting age was lowered from 21 to 18 years. The 69th Amendment, enacted in 1991, declared the Union Territory of Delhi to be the National Capital Territory, and granted it responsible government. The 71st Amendment, approved in August 1992, gave official-language status to Nepali, Konkani and Manipuri. In August 2000 legislation to permit the establishment of three new states, Chhattisgarh, Jharkhand and Uttaranchal (later renamed Uttarakhand), was approved by Parliament. The 93rd amendment, approved in May 2002, ensured free and compulsory education for children from the age of six to 14. The 91st amendment, approved in December 2003, stipulated that the size of the Council of Ministers at the centre and the states should not exceed 15% of the numbers in the Lok Sabha and state legislative assemblies, respectively. The 100th amendment, also approved in December 2003, extended official-language status to Bodo, Santhali, Maithali and Dogri, bringing the total number of official languages in the country to 22.

### THE PANCHAYAT RAJ SCHEME

This scheme is designed to decentralize the powers of the Union and state governments. It is based on the Panchayat (Village Council) and the Gram Sabha (Village Parliament) and envisages the gradual transference of local government from state to local authority. Revenue and internal security will remain state responsibilities at present. The 72nd Amendment, approved in late 1992, provided for direct elections to the Panchayats, members of which were to have a tenure of five years.

## The Government

**President:** Pratibha Devisingh Patil (sworn in 25 July 2007).

**Vice-President:** Mohammad Hamid Ansari (sworn in 12 August 2007).

### COUNCIL OF MINISTERS

(August 2008)

A coalition of the Indian National Congress (Congress), the Nationalist Congress Party (NCP), the Rashtriya Janata Dal (RJD), the Lok Jan Shakti Party (LJSP), Dravida Munnetra Kazhagam (DMK), Jharkhand Mukti Morcha (JMM), Pattali Makal Katchi (PMK), Marumalarchi Dravida Munnetra Kazhagam (MDMK), the Rashtriya Lok Dal (RLD), the Muslim League Kerala State Committee (MUL), the Republican Party of India—A (RPI—A), the All India Majlis-e-Ittehadul Muslimeen (AIMIM), the People's Democratic Party (PDP) and Kerala Congress.

**Prime Minister and Minister-in-charge of Personnel, Public Grievances and Pensions, of Planning, of Atomic Energy, of Space, of Coal and of Environment and Forests:** Dr Manmohan Singh (Congress).

**Minister of Defence:** A. K. Antony (Congress).

**Minister of External Affairs:** Pranab Mukherjee (Congress).

**Minister of Human Resource Development:** Arjun Singh (Congress).

**Minister of Agriculture and of Consumer Affairs, Food and Public Distribution:** Sharad Pawar (NCP).

**Minister of Railways:** LALU PRASAD YADAV (RJD).

**Minister of Home Affairs:** SHIVRAJ V. PATIL (Congress).

**Minister of Chemicals and Fertilizers and of Steel:** RAM VILAS PASWAN (LJSP).

**Minister of Urban Development:** S. JAIPAL REDDY (Congress).

**Minister of Mines:** SISH RAM OLA (Congress).

**Minister of Finance:** P. CHIDAMBARAM (Congress).

**Minister of Micro, Small and Medium Enterprises:** MAHAVIR PRASAD (Congress).

**Minister of Tribal Affairs:** P. R. KYNDIAH (Congress).

**Minister of Shipping, Road Transport and Highways:** T. R. BAALU (DMK).

**Minister of Textiles:** SHANKARSINH VAGHELA (Congress).

**Minister of Commerce and Industry:** KAMAL NATH (Congress).

**Minister of Law and Justice:** H. R. BHARDWAJ (Congress).

**Minister of Rural Development:** RAGHUVANSH PRASAD SINGH (RJD).

**Minister of Information and Broadcasting:** PRIYARANJAN DASMUNSI (Congress).

**Minister of Panchayati Raj and of Development of North Eastern Region:** MANI SHANKAR AIYAR (Congress).

**Minister of Social Justice and Empowerment:** MEIRA KUMAR (Congress).

**Minister of Communications and Information Technology:** A. RAJA.

**Minister of Health and Family Welfare:** Dr ANBUMANI RAMDOSS (PMK).

**Minister of Power:** SUSHIL KUMAR SHINDE (Congress).

**Minister of Minority Affairs:** A. R. ANTULAY (Congress).

**Minister of Overseas Indian Affairs and of Parliamentary Affairs:** VAYALAR RAVI (Congress).

**Minister of Petroleum and Natural Gas:** MURLI DEORA (Congress).

**Minister of Tourism and of Culture:** AMBIKA SONI (Congress).

**Minister of Water Resources:** Prof. SAIFUDDIN SOZ (Congress).

**Minister of Heavy Industries and Public Enterprises:** SANTOSH MOHAN DEV (Congress).

**Minister of Corporate Affairs:** PREM CHAND GUPTA (RJD).

**Minister of Science and Technology and of Earth Sciences:** KAPIL SIBAL (Congress).

### Ministers of State with Independent Charge

**Minister of State for Statistics and Programme Implementation:** G. K. VASAN (Congress).

**Minister of State for Labour and Employment:** OSCAR FERNANDES (Congress).

**Minister of State for Women and Child Development:** RENUKA CHOWDHURY (Congress).

**Minister of State for Food Processing Industries:** SUBODH KANT SAHAY (Congress).

**Minister of State for New and Renewable Energy:** VILAS MUTTEMWAR (Congress).

**Minister of State for Housing and Urban Poverty Alleviation:** KUMARI SELJA (Congress).

**Minister of State for Civil Aviation:** PRAFUL PATEL (NCP).

**Minister of State for Youth Affairs and Sports:** Dr M. S. GILL.

There are, in addition, 40 Ministers of State without independent charge.

## MINISTRIES

**President's Office:** Rashtrapati Bhavan, New Delhi 110 004; tel. (11) 23015321; fax (11) 23017290; e-mail presidentofindia@rb.nic.in; internet presidentofindia.nic.in.

**Vice-President's Office:** 6 Maulana Azad Rd, New Delhi 110 011; tel. (11) 23016344; fax (11) 23018124; e-mail vpindia@nic.in; internet vicepresidentofindia.nic.in.

**Prime Minister's Office:** South Block, Raisina Hill, New Delhi 110 011; tel. (11) 23012312; fax (11) 23016857; internet www.pmindia.nic.in.

**Ministry of Agriculture:** Krishi Bhavan, Dr Rajendra Prasad Rd, New Delhi 110 001; tel. (11) 23383370; fax (11) 23384555; e-mail am.krishi@nic.in.

**Department of Atomic Energy:** Anushakti Bhavan, Chatrapathi Shivaji Maharaj Marg, Mumbai 400 001; tel. (22) 22862500; fax (22) 22048476; e-mail usadmn@dae.gov.in; internet www.dae.gov.in.

**Ministry of Chemicals and Fertilizers:** Shastri Bhavan, New Delhi 110 001; tel. (11) 23388481; fax (11) 23388116; internet chemicals.gov.in; internet fert.nic.in.

**Ministry of Civil Aviation:** Rajiv Gandhi Bhavan, Safdarjung Airport, New Delhi 110 023; tel. (11) 24613050; fax (11) 24613054; e-mail web.moca@nic.in; internet www.civilaviation.nic.in.

**Ministry of Coal:** Shram Shakti Bhavan, Rafi Marg, New Delhi 110 001; tel. (11) 23384884; fax (11) 23381678; e-mail secy.moc@nic.in; internet coal.nic.in.

**Ministry of Commerce and Industry:** 45C Udyog Bhavan, New Delhi 110 011; tel. (11) 23063086; fax (11) 23019947; e-mail ikeshari@gmail.com; internet commerce.nic.in.

**Ministry of Communications and Information Technology:** Electronic Niketan, Lodhi Rd, New Delhi 110 003; tel. (11) 24369191; fax (11) 24362333; internet www.mit.gov.in.

**Ministry of Consumer Affairs, Food and Public Distribution:** Krishi Bhavan, New Delhi 110 001; tel. (11) 23382349; fax (11) 23386052; e-mail secy-food@nic.in; internet www.fcamin.nic.in.

**Ministry of Corporate Affairs:** 'A' Wing, Shastri Bhavan, Rajendra Prasad Rd, New Delhi 110 001; tel. (11) 23384660; e-mail manoj.arora@mca.gov.in; internet www.mca.gov.in.

**Ministry of Culture:** Rm 334, 'C' Wing, Shastri Bhavan, Dr Rajendra Prasad Rd, New Delhi 110 001001; tel. (11)23382331; fax (11) 23384867; e-mail js.culture@nic.in; internet indiaculture.nic.in.

**Ministry of Defence:** 104 South Block, New Delhi 110 011; tel. (11) 23019030; fax (11) 23015403; e-mail ak.antony@sansad.nic.in; internet www.mod.nic.in.

**Ministry of Development of North Eastern Region:** 233 Vigyan Bhavan Annexe, Maulana Azad Rd, New Delhi 110 011; tel. (11) 23022020; fax (11) 23022024; e-mail secydoner@nic.in; internet northeast.nic.in.

**Ministry of Earth Sciences:** Block No. 12, CGO Complex, Lodi Rd, New Delhi 110 003; tel. (11) 24360874; fax (11) 24360779; e-mail dodsec-dod@nic.in; internet dod.nic.in.

**Ministry of Environment and Forests:** Paryavaran Bhavan, CGO Complex Phase II, Lodhi Rd, New Delhi 110 003; tel. (11) 24360721; fax (11) 24362222; e-mail envisect@nic.in; internet www.envfor.nic.in.

**Ministry of External Affairs:** South Block, Room 144C, New Delhi 110 011; tel. (11) 23011849; fax (11) 23013387; e-mail asppr@mea.gov.in; internet meaindia.nic.in.

**Ministry of Finance:** North Block, Rm 166-D, 1st Floor, New Delhi 110 001; tel. (11) 23094905; fax (11) 23093422; e-mail mprasad@nic.in; internet www.finmin.nic.in.

**Ministry of Food Processing Industries:** Panchsheel Bhavan, August Kranti Marg, New Delhi 110 049; tel. (11) 26492475; fax (11) 26493228; e-mail ajitji@nic.in; internet mofpi.nic.in.

**Ministry of Health and Family Welfare:** Nirman Bhavan, Maulana Azad Rd, New Delhi 110 011; tel. (11) 23018863; fax (11) 23014252; e-mail resp-health@hub.nic.in; internet www.mohfw.nic.in.

**Ministry of Heavy Industries and Public Enterprises:** Udyog Bhavan, New Delhi 110 011; tel. (11) 23061854; fax (11) 23062633.

**Ministry of Home Affairs:** North Block, Central Secretariat, New Delhi 110 001; tel. (11) 23092011; fax (11) 23093750; e-mail mhaweb@mhant.delhi.nic.in; internet www.mha.nic.in.

**Ministry of Housing and Urban Poverty Alleviation:** Nirman Bhavan, Maulana Azad Rd, New Delhi 110 011; tel. (11) 23061444; fax (11) 23061991; e-mail secy-muepa@nic.in; internet mhupa.gov.in.

**Ministry of Human Resource Development:** Shastri Bhavan, New Delhi 110 001; tel. (11) 23782698; fax (11) 23382365; e-mail hrm@sb.nic.in; internet education.nic.in.

**Ministry of Information and Broadcasting:** 'A' Wing, Rm 552, Shastri Bhavan, New Delhi 110 001; tel. (11) 23384453; e-mail jsp.onb@nic.in; internet www.mib.nic.in.

**Ministry of Labour and Employment:** Shram Shakti Bhavan, Rafi Marg, New Delhi 110 001; tel. (11) 23710265; fax (11) 23718730; e-mail laborweb@nic.in; internet www.labour.nic.in.

**Ministry of Law and Justice:** 'A' Wing, 4th Floor, Shastri Bhavan, Dr Rajendra Prasad Rd, New Delhi 110 001; tel. (11) 23387557; fax (11) 23384241; e-mail vnathan@nic.in; internet lawmin.nic.in.

**Ministry of Micro, Small and Medium Enterprises:** Udyog Bhavan, Rafi Marg, New Delhi 110 011; tel. (11) 23062107; fax (11) 23063045; e-mail raj.pal@nic.in; internet ssi.nic.in.

**Ministry of Mines:** 'A' Wing, 3rd Floor, Shastri Bhavan, New Delhi; tel. (11) 23385173; fax (11) 23386402; e-mail secy-mines@nic.in; internet mines.nic.in.

**Ministry of Minority Affairs:** 11th Floor, Paravaran Bhavan, CGO Complex, Lodhi Rd, New Delhi 110 003; tel. (11) 24364271; e-mail sdatta@nic.in; internet minorityaffairs.gov.in.

**Ministry of New and Renewable Energy:** Block 14, CGO Complex, Lodhi Rd, New Delhi 110 003; tel. (11) 24361027; fax (11) 24367413; e-mail sunilkhatri@nic.in; internet mnes.nic.in.

**Ministry of Overseas Indian Affairs:** 9th Floor, Akbar Bhavan, Chanakya Puri, New Delhi 110 021; tel. (11) 24197900; fax (11) 24197919; e-mail info@moia.nic.in; internet moia.gov.in.

**Ministry of Panchayati Raj:** Krishi Bhavan, Dr Rajendra Prasad Rd, New Delhi 110 001; tel. (11) 23389074; fax (11) 23389028; e-mail nicmopr@nic.in; internet panchayat.nic.in.

**Ministry of Parliamentary Affairs:** 87, Parliament House, New Delhi 110 001; tel. (11) 23017663; fax (11) 23017726; e-mail secympa@nic.in; internet mpa.nic.in.

**Ministry of Personnel, Public Grievances and Pensions:** North Block, New Delhi 110 001; tel. (11) 23094848; fax (11) 23012432; e-mail secy_mop@nic.in; internet persmin.nic.in.

**Ministry of Petroleum and Natural Gas:** Shastri Bhavan, New Delhi 110 001; tel. (11) 23382889; fax (11) 23382673; e-mail jse.png@nic.in; internet petroleum.nic.in.

**Ministry of Power:** Shram Shakti Bhavan, New Delhi 110 001; tel. (11) 23710271; fax (11) 23721487; e-mail razdana@ias.nic.in; internet powermin.nic.in.

**Ministry of Railways:** Rail Bhavan, Raisina Rd, New Delhi 110 001; tel. (11) 23386645; fax (11) 23387333; e-mail secyrb@rb.railnet.gov.in; internet www.indianrailways.gov.in.

**Ministry of Rural Development:** Krishi Bhavan, Dr Rajendra Prasad Rd, New Delhi 110 001; tel. (11) 23382230; fax (11) 23382408; e-mail secyrd@nic.in; internet rural.nic.in.

**Ministry of Science and Technology:** Technology Bhavan, New Mehrauli Rd, New Delhi 110 016; tel. (11) 26567373; fax (11) 26864570; e-mail dstinfo@nic.in; internet dst.gov.in.

**Ministry of Shipping, Road Transport and Highways:** Ground Floor, Parivahan Bhavan, 1 Parliament St, New Delhi 110 001; tel. (11) 23719955; e-mail ifcmost@nic.in; internet www.morth.nic.in.

**Ministry of Social Justice and Empowerment:** Shastri Bhavan, Dr Rajendra Prasad Rd, New Delhi 110 001; tel. (11) 23717294; fax (11) 23311802; e-mail secywel@nic.in; internet socialjustice.nic.in.

**Ministry of Statistics and Programme Implementation:** Sardar Patel Bhavan, Patel Chowk, New Delhi 110 001; tel. (11) 23340884; fax (11) 23340138; e-mail gkvasan@sasnsad.nic.in; internet mospi.nic.in.

**Ministry of Steel:** Udyog Bhavan, New Delhi 110 011; tel. (11) 23793432; fax (11) 23013236; e-mail fcis@nic.in; internet steel.nic.in.

**Ministry of Textiles:** Udyog Bhavan, New Delhi 110 011; tel. (11) 23061338; fax (11) 23063711; e-mail secy-ub@nic.in; internet texmin.nic.in.

**Ministry of Tourism:** Transport Bhavan, Rm 123, 1 Parliament St, New Delhi 110 001; tel. (11) 23715084; e-mail sectour@nic.in; internet tourism.gov.in.

**Ministry of Tribal Affairs:** Rm 750A, Shastri Bhavan, New Delhi 110 001; tel. (11) 23388482; fax (11) 23381499; e-mail dirit@tribal.nic.in; internet tribal.nic.in.

**Ministry of Urban Development:** Nirman Bhavan, Maulana Azad Rd, New Delhi 110 011; tel. (11) 23062377; fax (11) 23061459; e-mail secyurban@nic.in; internet urbanindia.nic.in.

**Ministry of Water Resources:** Shram Shakti Bhavan, Rafi Marg, New Delhi 110 001; tel. and fax (11) 23710343; e-mail jsadm-mowr@nic.in; internet wrmin.nic.in.

**Ministry of Women and Child Development:** Shastri Bhavan, New Delhi; tel. (11) 23383586; fax (11) 23381495; e-mail secy.wcd@nic.in; internet wcd.nic.in.

**Ministry of Youth Affairs and Sports:** 501, 'B' Wing, Shastri Bhavan, Dr Rajendra Prasad Rd, New Delhi 110 001; tel. (11) 23383292; fax (11) 23071193; e-mail dsadmn.yas@nic.in; internet yas.nic.in.

# Legislature

## PARLIAMENT

### Rajya Sabha

(Council of States)

Most of the members of the Rajya Sabha are indirectly elected by the State Assemblies for six years, with one-third retiring every two years. The remaining members are nominated by the President.

**Chairman:** MOHAMMAD HAMID ANSARI.

**Deputy Chairman:** K. RAHMAN KHAN.

**Distribution of Seats, July 2004**

| Party | Seats |
|---|---|
| Congress* | 70 |
| Communist Party of India (Marxist) | 14 |
| Telugu Desam | 9 |
| Bharatiya Janata Party | 49† |
| Samajwadi Party | 12 |
| Rashtriya Janata Dal | 9 |
| Dravida Munnetra Kazhagam | 2 |
| Shiromani Akali Dal | 2 |
| Biju Janata Dal | 5 |
| Nationalist Congress Party | 4 |
| Samata Party | 1 |
| Muslim League | 2 |
| All-India Anna Dravida Munnetra Kazhagam | 12 |
| Communist Party of India | 2 |
| Jammu and Kashmir National Conference | 1 |
| Shiv Sena | 4 |
| Bahujan Samaj Party | 6 |
| Revolutionary Socialist Party | 3 |
| Indian National Lok Dal | 4 |
| Independents and others | 23 |
| Nominated | 9 |
| Vacant | 2 |
| **Total** | 245 |

* Formerly known as the Indian National Congress (Indira) or Congress (I); name gradually changed to the Indian National Congress or Congress Party in the early to mid-1990s.

† Including three nominated members.

### Lok Sabha

(House of the People)

**Speaker:** SOMNATH CHATTERJEE.

**General Election, 20, 22 and 25 April and 5 and 10 May 2004***

| Party | Seats |
|---|---|
| Congress and allies | 222 |
| Congress | 145 |
| Rashtriya Janata Dal | 24 |
| Dravida Munnetra Kazhagam | 16 |
| Nationalist Congress Party | 9 |
| Pattali Makkal Katchi | 6 |
| Telangana Rashtra Samithi | 5 |
| Jharkhand Mukti Morcha | 5 |
| Lok Jan Shakti Party | 4 |
| Marumalarchi Dravida Munnetra Kazhagam | 4 |
| All India Majlis-e-Ittehadul Muslimeen | 1 |
| Muslim League Kerala State Committee | 1 |
| People's Democratic Party | 1 |
| Republican Party of India (A) | 1 |
| National Democratic Alliance | 186 |
| Bharatiya Janata Party | 138 |
| Shiv Sena | 12 |
| Biju Janata Dal | 11 |
| Shiromani Akali Dal | 8 |
| Janata Dal (United) | 8 |
| Telugu Desam | 5 |
| All India Trinamool Congress | 2 |
| Mizo National Front | 1 |
| Nagaland People's Front | 1 |
| Left Front | 59 |
| Communist Party of India (Marxist) | 43 |
| Communist Party of India | 10 |
| All India Forward Bloc | 3 |
| Revolutionary Socialist Party | 3 |
| Samajwadi Party | 36 |
| Bahujan Samaj Party | 19 |
| Janata Dal (Secular) | 3 |
| Rashtriya Lok Dal | 3 |
| Jammu and Kashmir National Conference | 2 |
| Asom Gana Parishad | 2 |
| Bharatiya Navshakti Party | 1 |
| Kerala Congress | 1 |
| Sikkim Democratic Front | 1 |
| Independents and others | 8 |
| Nominated | 2† |
| **Total** | 545 |

* Includes the results of voting in several constituencies where the elections were postponed until 12–31 May, owing to irregularities and technical error.

† Nominated by the President to represent the Anglo-Indian community.

## Election Commission

**Election Commission of India:** Nirvachan Sadan, Ashoka Rd, New Delhi 110 001; tel. (11) 23717391; fax (11) 23713412; e-mail feedback@eci.gov.in; internet www.eci.gov.in; f. 1950; independent; Chief Election Commr N. GOPALASWAMI.

## Political Organizations

### MAJOR NATIONAL POLITICAL ORGANIZATIONS

**Bahujan Samaj Party** (Majority Society Party): c/o Lok Sabha, New Delhi; internet www.bahujansamajp.com; promotes the rights of the *Harijans* ('Untouchables') of India; Founder KANSHI RAM; Pres. KUMARI MAYAWATI.

**Bharatiya Janata Party (BJP)** (Indian People's Party): 11 Ashok Rd, New Delhi 110 001; tel. (11) 23382234; fax (11) 23782163; e-mail bjpco@vsnl.com; internet www.bjp.org; f. 1980 as a breakaway group from Janata Party; right-wing Hindu party; Pres. RAJNATH SINGH; Gen. Secs RAM LAL, GOPINATH MUNDE, ARUN JAITLEY, ANANTH KUMAR, THAWARCHAND GEHLOT, OM PRAKASH MATHUR, VINAY KATIYAR; 10.5m. mems.

**Communist Party of India (CPI):** 15 Ajoy Bhavan, Kotla Marg, New Delhi 110 002; tel. (11) 23235546; fax (11) 23235543; e-mail cpi@cpofindia.org; internet www.cpindia.org; f. 1925; advocates the establishment of a socialist society led by the working class, and ultimately of a communist society; nine-mem. central secretariat; Leader GURUDA DASGUPTA; Gen. Sec. ARDHENDU BHUSHAN BARDHAN; 486,578 mems (2004).

**Communist Party of India—Marxist (CPI—M):** A. K. Gopalan Bhavan, 27–29 Bhai Vir Singh Marg, New Delhi 110 001; tel. (11) 23344918; fax (11) 23747483; e-mail cpim@vsnl.com; internet www.cpim.org; f. 1964 as breakaway group from the CPI; maintained an independent position; managed by a central committee of 87 mems and a politburo of 15 mems; Leaders BUDDHADEV BHATTACHARYA, JYOTI BASU, PRAKASH KARAT, SITARAM YECHURY, SOMNATH CHATTERJEE; Gen. Sec. PRAKASH KARAT; 975,799 mems (2006).

**Indian National Congress:** 24 Akbar Rd, New Delhi 110 011; tel. (11) 23019080; fax (11) 23017047; e-mail aicc@congress.org.in; internet www.congress.org.in; f. 1969 as separate faction under Indira Gandhi; originally known as Indian National Congress (R), then as Indian National Congress (I); name of party gradually changed to Indian National Congress or Congress Party in the early to mid-1990s; Pres. SONIA GANDHI; Gen. Secs MUKUL WASNIK, JANARDAN DWIVEDI, MARGARET ALVA, DIGVIJAY SINGH, ASHOK GEHLOT, B. K. HARIPRASAD, V. NARAYANSWAMY, MOHSINA KIDWAI, RAHUL GANDHI, PRITHVIRAJ CHAVAN, V. KISHORE CHANDRA S. DEO; 35m. mems (1998).

**Nationalist Congress Party (NCP):** 10 Dr Bishambhar Das Marg, New Delhi 110001; tel. (11) 23359218; fax (11) 23352112; e-mail mail@ncp.org.in; internet www.ncp.org.in; f. 1999 as breakaway faction of Congress; split into two factions in Jan. 2004—one headed by Sharad Pawar and another by Purno Shangma; faction led by Shangma merged with the All India Trinamool Congress; Pres. SHARAD PAWAR; Gen. Secs P. A. SANGMA, TARIQ ANWAR, T. P. PEETHAMBARAN MASTER, Prof. DEVI PRASAD TRIPATHI, Dr AKHTAR HASAN RIZVI, Dr V. RAJESHWARAN.

**Rashtriya Janata Dal (RJD)** (National People's Party): 13 V. P. House, Rafi Marg, New Delhi 110 011; f. 1997 as a breakaway group from Janata Dal; Leader LALU PRASAD YADAV.

### MAJOR REGIONAL POLITICAL ORGANIZATIONS

**Akhil Bharat Hindu Mahasabha:** Hindu Mahasabha Bhavan, Mandir Marg, New Delhi 110 001; tel. (11) 23342087; e-mail chakrapani_hms@yahoo.co.in; f. 1915; seeks the establishment of a democratic Hindu state; Pres. SWAMI CHAKRAPANI; Gen. Sec. MUNNA KUMAR SHARMA; 525,000 mems.

**All-India Anna Dravida Munnetra Kazhagam (AIADMK)** (All-India Anna Dravidian Progressive Asscn): 275 Avvai Shanmugam Salai, Royapet, Chennai 600 014; tel. (44) 28132266; fax (44) 28133510; e-mail aiadmk@vsnl.net; internet aiadmkallindia.org; f. 1972; breakaway group from the DMK; Leader and Gen. Sec. JAYARAM JAYALALITHA.

**All India Forward Bloc:** 28 Gurudwara Rakabganj Rd, New Delhi 110 001; tel. and fax (11) 23714131; e-mail dbiswas@sansad.nic.in; internet www.forwardbloc.org; f. 1940 by Netaji Subhash Chandra Bose; socialist aims, including nationalization of major industries, land reform and redistribution, and the establishment of a union of socialist republics through revolution; Leader and Gen. Sec. DEBABRATA BISWAS; 900,000 mems (1999).

**All India Trinamool Congress:** 30B Harish Chatterjee St, Kolkata 700 026; tel. (33) 24540881; fax (33) 24540880; e-mail info@trinamoolcongress.com; internet www.trinamoolcongress.com; merged with the Sangma faction of the Nationalist Congress Party in 2004; Leader MAMATA BANERJEE; Gen. Secs MUKUL ROY, DINESH TRIBEDI.

**Asom Gana Parishad (AGP)** (Assam People's Council): Gopinath Bordoloi Rd, Guwahati 781 001; f. 1985; draws support from the All-Assam Gana Sangram Parishad and the All-Assam Students' Union (Leader SAMUJJAL KUMAR BHATTACHARYYA; Gen. Sec. TAPAN KUMAR GOGOI); advocates the unity of India in diversity and a united Assam; Pres. BRINDABAN GOSWAMI.

**Biju Janata Dal:** Naveen Nivas, Aerodrome Gate, Bhubaneswar 751 009; Pres. NAVEEN PATNAIK.

**Dravida Munnetra Kazhagam (DMK):** Anna Arivalayam, Anna Salai, Chennai 600 018; f. 1949; aims at full autonomy for states (primarily Tamil Nadu) within the Union; Pres. MUTHUVEL KARUNANIDHI; Gen. Sec. K. ANBAZHAGAN; more than 4m. mems.

**Indian National Lok Dal:** 18 Janpath, New Delhi 110 001; tel. (11) 23793409; fmrly mem. of the National Democratic Alliance; Leader OM PRAKASH CHAUTALA; Sec.-Gen. AJAY SINGH CHAUTALA.

**Jammu and Kashmir National Conference (JKNC):** Mujahid Manzil, Srinagar 190 002; tel. (194) 271500; fmrly All Jammu and Kashmir National Conference; f. 1931; renamed 1939, reactivated 1975; state-based party campaigning for internal autonomy and responsible self-govt; Pres. OMAR ABDULLAH; Gen. Sec. Maulana MASOODI; 1m. mems.

**Janata Dal—Secular** (People's Party—Secular): 5 Safdarjung Lane, New Delhi 110 003; f. 2000 following split of Janata Dal; Pres. H. D. DEVE GOWDA; Sec.-Gen. KUNWAR DANISH ALI.

**Janata Dal—United** (People's Party—United): 7 Jantar Mantar Rd, New Delhi 110 001; tel. (11) 23368833; fax (11) 23368138; f. 2000 following split of Janata Dal; merged with Samata Party in 2003; advocates non-alignment, the eradication of poverty, unemployment and wide disparities in wealth, and the protection of minorities; Pres. SHARAD YADAV; State Gen. Sec. OM PRAKASH KHEMKARANI.

**Jharkhand Mukti Morcha:** Bariatu Rd, Ranchi 834 008; aligned with national ruling coalition, the United Progressive Alliance; Leader SHIBU SOREN.

**Lok Jan Shakti Party (LJSP):** New Delhi; f. 2000 as breakaway faction of Janata Dal—United; left-wing; Pres. RAM VILAS PASWAN.

**Pattali Makkal Katchi:** Gounder St, Dharamapuri 636 701; tel. (4342) 263275; Leader Dr ANBUMANI RAMDOSS; Pres. G. K. MANI.

**Peasants' and Workers' Party of India:** Mahatma Phule Rd, Naigaum, Mumbai 400 014; f. 1949; Gen. Sec. DAJIBA DESAI; c. 10,000 mems.

**Republican Party of India (RPI):** Ensa Hutments, I Block, Azad Maidan, Fort, Mumbai 400 001; tel. (22) 22621888; f. 1952; by 2003 the group had split into 10 factions; the three main factions were led by PRAKASH RAO AMBEDKAR, RAMDAS ATHAVALE and R. S. GAVAI, respectively.

**Revolutionary Socialist Party:** 17 Feroz Shah Rd, New Delhi 110 001; tel. (11) 23782167; fax (11) 23782342; e-mail abani@sansad.nic.in; Leaders DEBABRATA BANDOPADHYAY, ABANI ROY; Gen. Sec. T. J. CHANDRACHOODAN.

**Samajwadi Party** (Socialist Party): 18 Copernicus Lane, New Delhi; e-mail samajwadiparty@gmail.com; f. 1991; Pres. MULAYAM SINGH YADAV; Gen. Sec. AMAR SINGH.

**Shiromani Akali Dal:** Baradan Shri Darbar Sahib, Amritsar; internet www.shiromaniakalidalbadal.com; f. 1920; Pres. (Shiromani Akali Dal—Badal) PARKASH SINGH BADAL; Sec.-Gen. SUKHDEV SINGH DHINDSA.

**Shiv Sena** (Army of Shiv): Shiv Sena Bhavan, Ram Ganesh Gadkari Chowk, Dadar, Mumbai 400 028; tel. (22) 24309128; e-mail shivalay@shivsena.org; internet www.shivsena.org; f. 1966; militant Hindu group; labour union, Bharatiya Kamgar Sena (Indian Workers' Army), affiliated to the party; Exec. Pres. BAL THACKERAY.

**Sikkim Democratic Front:** Upper Deorali, Gangtok, East Sikkim; Pres. Dr PAWAN KUMAR CHAMLING; Gen. Sec. DAWCHU LEPCHA.

**Telangana Rashtra Samithi:** Karimnagar; f. 2001; Pres. K. CHANDRASEKHAR RAO.

**Telangana Rashtra Samithi (Nationalist):** Hyderabad; f. 2008 by breakaway faction of the Telangana Rashtra Samithi; Pres. ANAND RAO.

**Telugu Desam** (Telugu Nation): NTR Bhavan, Rd 2, Banjara Hills, Hyderabad 500 034; tel. (40) 30699999; fax (40) 23542108; e-mail contact@telugudesam.com; internet www.telugudesam.com; f. 1982; state-based party (Andhra Pradesh); Pres. N. CHANDRABABU NAIDU; 8m. mems.

# Diplomatic Representation

## EMBASSIES AND HIGH COMMISSIONS IN INDIA

**Afghanistan:** 5/50F Shanti Path, Chanakyapuri, New Delhi 110 021; tel. (11) 2410331; fax (11) 26875439; e-mail afghanspirit@yahoo.com; Ambassador Dr SAYED MAKHDOOM RAHEEN.

**Algeria:** E-6/5 Vasant Vihar, New Delhi 110 057; tel. (11) 26147036; fax (11) 26147033; internet www.embalgind.com; Ambassador Dr NOUREDDINE BARDAD DAJDJ.

**Angola:** 5/50F, Nyaya Marg, Chanakyapuri, New Delhi 110 021; tel. (11) 26882680; fax (11) 24673785; e-mail xietuang@del2.vsnl.net.in; internet www.angolaembassyindia.com; Ambassador ANTONIO FWAMINY DACOSTA FERNANDES.

**Argentina:** A-2/6, Vasant Vihar, New Delhi 110 057; tel. (11) 41661982; fax (11) 41661988; Ambassador ERNESTO CARLOS ALVAREZ.

**Armenia:** E-1/20, Vasant Vihar, New Delhi 110 057; tel. (11) 24112851; fax (11) 24112853; e-mail armemb@vsnl.com; Ambassador ASHOT KOCHARYAN.

**Australia:** 1/50-G Shanti Path, Chanakyapuri, New Delhi 110 021; tel. (11) 41399900; fax (11) 41494490; e-mail austhighcom.newdelhi@dfat.gov.au; internet www.ausgovindia.com; High Commissioner JOHN MCCARTHY.

**Austria:** EP-13 Chandragupta Marg, Chanakyapuri, New Delhi 110 021; tel. (11) 26889037; fax (11) 26886929; e-mail new-delhi-ob@bmeia.gv.at; internet www.aussenministerium.at/newdelhi; Ambassador Dr FERDINAND MAULTASCHL.

**Azerbaijan:** Vasant Marg, Vasant Vihar E-70, New Delhi; tel. (11) 26152228; fax (11) 26152227; e-mail azembassy@airtelbroadband.in; Ambassador TAMERLAN GARAYEV.

**Bahrain:** 4 A-4, Palam Marg, Vasant Vihar, New Delhi 110 057; tel. (11) 26154153; fax (11) 26146731; e-mail newdelhi.mission@mofa.gov.bh; Ambassador MOHAMMED GHASSAN SHAIKHO.

**Bangladesh:** EP-39 Dr S. Radhakrishnan Marg, Chanakyapuri, New Delhi 110 021; tel. (11) 24121389; fax (11) 26878953; e-mail bhcdelhi@mantraonline.com; internet www.bhcdelhi.org; High Commissioner LIAQUAT ALI CHOUDHURY.

**Belarus:** 163 Jor Bagh, New Delhi 110 003; tel. (11) 24697025; fax (11) 24697029; e-mail india@belembassy.org; Ambassador OLEG LAPTENOK.

**Belgium:** 50N Shanti Path, Chanakyapuri, New Delhi 110 021; tel. (11) 42428000; fax (11) 42428002; e-mail newdelhi@diplobel.be; internet www.diplomatie.be/newdelhi; Ambassador JEAN M. DEBOUTTE.

**Bhutan:** Chandragupta Marg, Chanakyapuri, New Delhi 110 021; tel. (11) 26889807; fax (11) 26876710; e-mail bhutan@vsnl.com; Ambassador Lyonpo DAGO TSHERING.

**Bosnia and Herzegovina:** E-9/11 Vasant Vihar, New Delhi 110 057; tel. (11) 51662481; fax (11) 51662482; e-mail bosher@airtelbroadband.in; Ambassador KEMAL MUFTIĆ.

**Brazil:** 8 Aurangzeb Rd, New Delhi 110 011; tel. (11) 23017301; fax (11) 23793684; e-mail brasindi@vsnl.com; Ambassador JOSÉ VICENTE DE SA PIMENTEL.

**Brunei:** 4 Poorvi Marg, Vasant Vihar, New Delhi 110 057; tel. (11) 26148340; fax (11) 26142101; e-mail newdelhi.india@mfa.gov.bn; High Commissioner Haji SIDEK BIN Haji ALI.

**Bulgaria:** 16/17 Chandragupta Marg, Chanakyapuri, New Delhi 110 021; tel. (11) 26115550; fax (11) 26876190; e-mail bulemb@bulgariaembindia.com; internet bulgariaembindia.com; Ambassador DRAGOVEST GORANOV.

**Burkina Faso:** P 3/1 Vasant Vihar, New Delhi 110 057; tel. (11) 26140641; fax (11) 26140630; e-mail emburnd@bol.net.in; internet www.embassyburkinaindia.com; Chargé d'affaires OUSMAN NACAMBO.

**Cambodia:** N-14 Panchsheel Park, New Delhi 110 017; tel. (11) 26495092; fax (11) 26495093; e-mail camboemb@bol.net.in; Ambassador CHOEUNG BUNTHENG.

**Canada:** 7/8 Shanti Path, Chanakyapuri, New Delhi 110 021; tel. (11) 41782000; fax (11) 41782020; e-mail delhi@international.gc.ca; internet www.india.gc.ca; High Commissioner DAVID MALONE.

**Chile:** 146 Jorbagh, New Delhi 110 003; tel. (11) 24617123; fax (11) 24617102; e-mail embchile@airtelbroadband.in; internet www.echileindia.com; Ambassador OSCAR ALFONSO SILVA.

**China, People's Republic:** 50D Shanti Path, Chanakyapuri, New Delhi 110 021; tel. (11) 26112345; fax (11) 26885486; e-mail chinaemb_in@mfa.gov.cn; internet www.chinaembassy.org.in; Ambassador ZHANG YAN.

**Colombia:** 3 Palam Marg, Vasant Vihar, New Delhi 110 057; tel. (11) 51662106; fax (11) 51662108; e-mail edelhi@minrelext.gov.co; Ambassador JUAN ALFREDO PINTO SAAVEDRA.

**Congo, Democratic Republic:** B-2/6, Vasant Vihar, New Delhi 110 057; tel. (11) 51660976; fax (11) 51663152; e-mail congoembassy@yahoo.co.in; Ambassador BALUMUENE NKUNA FRANCOIS.

**Côte d'Ivoire:** B-9/6, Vasant Vihar, New Delhi 110 057; tel. (11) 51704234; fax (11) 51704236; e-mail embassy@amb2ci-inde.org; Ambassador GILBERT BLEU-LAINE.

**Croatia:** A-15 West End, New Delhi 110 021; tel. (11) 41663101; fax (11) 24116873; e-mail croemb.new-delhi@mvpei.hr; Ambassador (vacant).

**Cuba:** W-124A, Greater Kailash Part I, New Delhi 110 048; tel. (11) 26222467; fax (11) 26222469; e-mail embcuind@del6.vsnl.net.in; Ambassador MIGUEL ANGEL RAMIREZ RAMOS.

**Cyprus:** 106 Jor Bagh, New Delhi 110 003; tel. (11) 24697503; fax (11) 24628828; e-mail cyprus@del3.vsnl.net.in; High Commissioner ANDREAS G. ZENONOS.

**Czech Republic:** 50M Niti Marg, Chanakyapuri, New Delhi 110 021; tel. (11) 26110205; fax (11) 26886221; e-mail newdelhi@embassy.mzv.cz; internet www.mfa.cz/newdelhi; Ambassador HYNEK KMOníček.

**Denmark:** 11 Aurangzeb Rd, New Delhi 110 011; tel. (11) 42090700; fax (11) 23792019; e-mail delamb@um.dk; internet www.ambnewdelhi.um.dk; Ambassador OLE LØNSMANN-POULSEN.

**Djibouti:** c/o A 2–20 Sarfarjung Enclave, New Delhi 110 029; tel. (11) 41354491; fax (11) 41354490; e-mail info@embassyofdjibouti.org; internet embassyofdjibouti.org/EmbasyNewDelhi.htm; Ambassador YOUSSOUF OMAR DOUALEH.

**Dominican Republic:** 1st Floor, 4 Munirka Marg, Vasant Vihar, New Delhi 110 057; tel. (11) 46015000; fax (11) 46015004; e-mail info@dr-embassy-india.com; Ambassador FRANK HANS DANNENBERG.

**Ecuador:** C-156 Second Floor, Defence Colony, New Delhi 110 014; tel. (11) 51555602; fax (11) 51555604; e-mail eecuindia@mmrree.gov.ec; Chargé d'affaires CARLOS ABAD ORTIZ.

**Egypt:** 1/50M Niti Marg, Chanakyapuri, New Delhi 110 021; tel. (11) 26114096; fax (11) 26885355; e-mail egypt@del2.vsnl.net.in; Ambassador MUHAMMAD ABDUL HAMEED HIJAZI.

**Eritrea:** C-7/9, Vasant Vihar, New Delhi 110 057; tel. (11) 26146336; fax (11) 26146337; e-mail eriindia@yahoo.co.in; internet www.eritreaembindia.com; Ambassador ALEM TSEHAYE WOLDEMARIAM.

**Ethiopia:** 7/50G Satya Marg, Chanakyapuri, New Delhi 110 021; tel. (11) 26119513; fax (11) 26875731; e-mail delethem@yahoo.com; Ambassador GENET ZEWDIE.

**Fiji:** N-57, Panchsheel Park, New Delhi 110 017; tel. (11) 41751092; fax (11) 41751095; e-mail fijihighcommission@yahoo.co.in; High Commissioner SAVENACA KAUNISELA.

**Finland:** E-3 Nyaya Marg, Chanakyapuri, New Delhi 110 021; tel. (11) 41497500; fax (11) 41497555; e-mail sanomat.NDE@formin.fi; internet www.finland.org.in; Ambassador ASKO NUMMINEM.

**France:** 2/50E Shanti Path, Chanakyapuri, New Delhi 110 021; tel. (11) 24196100; fax (11) 24196119; e-mail webmaster@france-in-india.org; internet www.france-in-india.org; Ambassador JÉRÔME BONNAFONT.

**Germany:** 6 Block 50G, Shanti Path, Chanakyapuri, POB 613, New Delhi 110 021; tel. (11) 44199199; fax (11) 26873117; internet www.new-delhi.diplo.de; Ambassador BERND MÜTZELBURG.

**Ghana:** 50-N Satya Marg, Chanakyapuri, New Delhi 110 021; tel. (11) 26883298; fax (11) 26883202; High Commissioner (vacant).

**Greece:** EP–32, Dr S. Radhakrishnan Marg, Chanakyapuri, New Delhi 110 021; tel. (11) 26880700; fax (11) 26888010; e-mail gremb@bol.net.in; internet www.greeceinindia.com; Ambassador STAVROS LYKIDIS.

**Guyana:** F-8/22, Vasant Vihar, New Delhi 110 057; tel. (11) 41669717; fax (11) 41669714; e-mail hcommguy.del@gmail.com; High Commissioner J. RONALD GAJRAJ.

**Holy See:** 50C Niti Marg, Chanakyapuri, New Delhi 110 021 (Apostolic Nunciature); tel. (11) 26889184; fax (11) 26874286; e-mail nuntius@apostolicnunciatureindia.com; internet www.apostolicnunciatureindia.com; Nuncio Most Rev. PEDRO LÓPEZ QUINTANA (Titular Archbishop of Agropoli).

**Hungary:** Plot 2, 50M Niti Marg, Chanakyapuri, New Delhi 110 021; tel. (11) 26114737; fax (11) 26886742; e-mail mission.del@kum.hu; Ambassador Dr IVÁN NÉMETH.

**Iceland:** 11 Aurangzeb Rd, New Delhi 110 011; tel. (11) 43530300; fax (11) 42403001; e-mail emb.newdelhi@mfa.is; internet www.iceland.org/in; Ambassador Dr GUNNAR PÁLSSON.

**Indonesia:** 50A Kautilya Marg, Chanakyapuri, New Delhi 110 021; tel. (11) 26118642; fax (11) 26874402; e-mail iembassy@giasdl01.vsnl.net.in; internet www.indonesianembassy.org.in; Ambassador Lt-Gen. (retd) ANDI MUHAMMAD GHALIB.

**Iran:** 5 Barakhamba Road, New Delhi 110 001; tel. (11) 23329600; fax (11) 23325493; e-mail info@iran-embassy.org.in; internet www.iran-embassy.org.in; Ambassador SAYED MAHDI NABIZADEH.

**Iraq:** B-5/8, Vasant Vihar, New Delhi 110 057; tel. (11) 26149085; fax (11) 26149076; e-mail dlhemb@iraqmofamail.net; Chargé d'affaires a.i. MUAYAD HUSSAIN.

**Ireland:** 230 Jor Bagh, New Delhi 110 003; tel. (11) 24626733; fax (11) 24697053; e-mail ireland@ndf.vsnl.net.in; internet www.irelandinindia.com; Ambassador KIERAN DOWLING.

**Israel:** 3 Aurangzeb Rd, New Delhi 110 011; tel. (11) 23013238; fax (11) 23014298; e-mail info@newdelhi.mfa.gov.il; internet delhi.mfa.gov.il; Ambassador MARK SOFER.

**Italy:** 50E Chandragupta Marg, Chanakyapuri, New Delhi 110 021; tel. (11) 26114355; fax (11) 26873889; e-mail ambasciata.newdelhi@esteri.it; internet www.ambnewdelhi.esteri.it; Ambassador ANTONIO ARMELLINI.

**Japan:** Plots 4–5, 50G Shanti Path, Chanakyapuri, New Delhi 110 021; tel. (11) 26876581; fax (11) 26885587; e-mail jpembjic@bol.net.in; internet www.in.emb-japan.go.jp; Ambassador HIDEAKI DOMICHI.

**Jordan:** 30 Golf Links, New Delhi 110 003; tel. (11) 24653318; fax (11) 24653353; e-mail jordan@jordanembassyindia.org; internet www.jordanembassyindia.org; Ambassador MOHAMMAD ALI DAHER.

**Kazakhstan:** 61 Poorvi Marg, Vasant Vihar, New Delhi 110 057; tel. (11) 46007700; fax (11) 46007701; e-mail embassy@kazind.com; internet www.kazind.com; Ambassador KAIRAT UMAROV.

**Kenya:** 34 Paschimi Marg, New Delhi 110 057; tel. (11) 26146537; fax (11) 26146550; e-mail info@kenyamission-delhi.com; internet www.kenyamission-delhi.com; High Commissioner Prof. FESTUS KABERIA.

**Korea, Democratic People's Republic:** D-14 Maharani Bagh, New Delhi 110 065; tel. (11) 26829644; fax (11) 26829645; e-mail dprk194899@yahoo.com; Ambassador HAN CHANG ON.

**Korea, Republic:** 9 Chandragupta Marg, Chanakyapuri, POB 5416, New Delhi 110 021; tel. (11) 26885412; fax (11) 26884840; e-mail kobe@mail.mofat.go.kr; internet ind.mofat.go.kr; Ambassador PAEK YUNG-SUN.

**Kuwait:** 11 Olof Palme Marg, Vasant Vihar, New Delhi 110 057; tel. (11) 26150124; fax (11) 26873516; e-mail kuinfo@kuwait-info.com.com; internet www.kuwait-info.com; Ambassador KHALAF ABBAS KHALAF AL-FOUDARI.

**Kyrgyzstan:** C-93 Anand Niketan, New Delhi 110 021; tel. (11) 24108008; fax (11) 24108009; e-mail alatoo@starith.net; Ambassador IRINA A. OROLBAYEVA.

**Laos:** A-104/7 Parmanand Estate, Maharani Bagh, New Delhi 110 065; tel. (11) 26933319; fax (11) 26323048; Ambassador LY BUN KHAM.

**Lebanon:** H-1, Anand Niketan, New Delhi 110 021; tel. (11) 24111415; fax (11) 24110818; e-mail lebemb@bol.net.in; Ambassador KHALED SALMAN.

**Libya:** 22 Golf Links, New Delhi 110 003; tel. (11) 24697717; fax (11) 24633005; e-mail libya@bol.net.in; Chargé d'affaires MAHFUD R. M. RAHIAM.

**Luxembourg:** 730 Gadaipur Rd, Branch Post Office, Gadaipur, New Delhi 110 030; tel. (11) 26801966; fax (11) 26801971; e-mail vm.bharathi@mae.etat.lu; internet www.luxembourgindia.org; Ambassador MARC COURTE.

**Malaysia:** 50M Satya Marg, Chanakyapuri, New Delhi 110 021; tel. (11) 26111291; fax (11) 26881538; e-mail maldelhi@kln.gov.my; internet www.kln.gov.my/perwakilan/newdelhi; High Commissioner Datuk TAN SENG SUNG.

**Maldives:** B–2, Anand Niketan, New Delhi 110 021; tel. (11) 41435701; fax (11) 41435709; e-mail admin@maldiveshighcom.in; internet www.maldiveshighcom.in; High Commissioner Lt-Gen. (retd) ANBAREE ABDUL SATTAR ADAM.

**Malta:** D70 East of Kailash, New Delhi 110 065; tel. (11) 26439090; fax (11) 41659090; e-mail malta@kathpalia.in; High Commissioner WILFRED KENNELY.

**Mauritius:** 41 Jesus and Mary Marg, Chanakyapuri, New Delhi 110 021; tel. (11) 24102161; fax (11) 24102194; e-mail mhcnd@bol.net.in; High Commissioner M. CHOONEE.

**Mexico:** C-8 Anand Niketan, New Delhi 110 021; tel. (11) 24107182; fax (11) 24117193; e-mail embamexindia@airtelbroadband.in; internet www.sre.gob.mx/india; Ambassador ROGELIO GRANGUILLHOME MORFIN.

**Mongolia:** 34 Archbishop Makarios Marg, New Delhi 110 003; tel. (11) 24631728; fax (11) 24633240; e-mail mongemb@vsnl.net; internet www.mongemb.com; Ambassador VOROSHILOV ENKHBOLD.

**Morocco:** 33 Golf Links, New Delhi 110 003; tel. (11) 24636920; fax (11) 24636925; e-mail sifamand@giasdl01.vsnl.net.in; internet www.moroccoembindia.com; Ambassador LARBI MOUKHARIQ.

**Mozambique:** B-3/24, Vasant Vihar, New Delhi 110 057; tel. (11) 26156663; fax (11) 26156665; e-mail salvaro64@hotmail.com; High Commissioner CARLOS A. DO ROSARIO.

**Myanmar:** 3/50F Nyaya Marg, Chanakyapuri, New Delhi 110 021; tel. (11) 26889007; fax (11) 26877942; e-mail myandeli@nda.vsnl.net.in; Ambassador U KYI THEIN.

**Namibia:** B-8/9, Vasant Vihar, New Delhi 110 057; tel. (11) 26140389; fax (11) 26146120; e-mail nhcdelhi@del2.vsnl.net.in; internet www.nhcdelhi.com; High Commissioner MARTEN KAPEWASHA.

**Nepal:** Barakhamba Rd, New Delhi 110 001; tel. (11) 23329218; fax (11) 23326857; e-mail nepembassydelhi@bol.net.in; Ambassador Dr DURGESH MAN SINGH.

**Netherlands:** 6/50F Shanti Path, Chanakyapuri, New Delhi 110 021; tel. (11) 24197600; fax (11) 24197710; e-mail nde@minbuza.nl; internet www.holland-in-india.org; Ambassador BOB H. HIENSCH.

**New Zealand:** Sir Edmund Hillary Marg, Chanakyapuri, New Delhi 110 021; tel. (11) 26883170; fax (11) 26883165; e-mail nzhc@ndf.vsnl.net.in; internet www.nzembassy.com/home.cfm?c=26; High Commissioner RUPERT HOLBOROW.

**Nigeria:** Plot No. 4, Chandragupta Marg, Chanakyapuri, New Delhi 110 021; tel. (11) 24122142; fax (11) 24122138; e-mail nhcnder@vsnl.com; High Commissioner ABUBAKAR GARBA ABDULLAHI.

**Norway:** 50C Shanti Path, Chanakyapuri, New Delhi 110 021; tel. (11) 41779200; fax (11) 41680145; e-mail emb.newdelhi@mfa.no; internet www.norwayemb.org.in; Ambassador ANN OLLESTAD.

**Oman:** EP-10/11, Chandragupta Marg, Chankyapuri, New Delhi 110 021; tel. (11) 26885622; fax (11) 26885621; e-mail omandelhi@vsnl.com; Ambassador MOHAMMED BIN YOUSUF SHALWANI.

**Pakistan:** 2/50G Shanti Path, Chanakyapuri, New Delhi 110 021; tel. (11) 26110601; fax (11) 26872339; e-mail pakhc@nda.vsnl.net.in; High Commissioner SHAHID MALIK.

**Panama:** 3-D, Palam Marg, Vasant Vihar, New Delhi 110 057; tel. (11) 26148268; fax (11) 26148261; e-mail panaind@bol.net.in; Ambassador ALBERTO J. PINZÓN.

**Peru:** G-15 Maharani Bagh, New Delhi 110 065; tel. (11) 26312610; fax (11) 26312557; e-mail info@embaperuindia.com; internet www.embaperuindia.com; Ambassador MANUEL ERNESTO PICASSO BOTTO.

**Philippines:** 50N Nyaya Marg, Chanakyapuri, New Delhi 110 021; tel. (11) 26889091; fax (11) 26876401; e-mail newdelhipe@bol.net.in; Ambassador TERESITA V. BERNER.

**Poland:** 50M Shanti Path, Chanakyapuri, New Delhi 110 021; tel. (11) 41496900; fax (11) 26871914; e-mail polemb@airtelmail.in; internet www.newdelhi.polemb.net; Ambassador (vacant).

**Portugal:** 8 Olof Palme Marg, Vasant Vihar, New Delhi 110 057; tel. (11) 26142215; fax (11) 26152837; e-mail embportin@ndf.vsnl.net.in; internet www.embportindia.com; Ambassador JOAQUIM JOSÉ L. F. MARQUES CURTO.

**Qatar:** EP-31A, Chandragupta Marg, Chanakyapuri, New Delhi 110 021; tel. (11) 26117988; fax (11) 26886080; e-mail newdelhi@mofa.gov.qa; Ambassador HUSSAN MOHAMMED RAFEH ALEMADI.

**Romania:** A-47 Vasant Marg, Vasant Vihar, New Delhi 110 057; tel. (11) 26140447; fax (11) 26140611; e-mail embrom@touchtelindia.net; Ambassador VASILE SOFINETI.

**Russia:** Shanti Path, Chanakyapuri, New Delhi 110 021; tel. (11) 26873799; fax (11) 26876823; e-mail indrusem@del2.vsnl.net.in; internet www.india.mid.ru; Ambassador VYACHESLAV TRUBNIKOV.

**Rwanda:** 41 Paschimi Marg, Vasant Vihar, New Delhi 110 057; tel. (11) 51661604; fax (11) 51661605; e-mail ambadelhi@minaffet.gov.rw; Ambassador Lt-Gen. KAYUMBA NYAMWASA.

**Saudi Arabia:** 2 Paschimi Marg, Vasant Vihar, New Delhi 110 057; tel. (11) 26144102; fax (11) 26144244; Ambassador SALEH M. AL-GHAMDI.

**Senegal:** C-6/11, Vasant Vihar, New Delhi 110 057; tel. (11) 26147687; fax (11) 41662673; e-mail embassy@senindia.org; Ambassador AMADOU BOCOUM.

**Serbia:** 3/50G Niti Marg, Chanakyapuri, New Delhi 110 021; tel. (11) 26873661; fax (11) 26885535; e-mail office@embassyofserbiadelhi.net.in; internet www.embassyofserbiadelhi.net.in; Ambassador VUK ZUGIĆ.

**Singapore:** N-88 Panchsheel Park, New Delhi 110 017; tel. (11) 41019801; fax (11) 41019805; e-mail singhc_del@sgmfa.gov.sg; internet www.mfa.gov.sg/newdelhi; High Commissioner CALVIN EU MUN HOO.

**Slovakia:** 50M Niti Marg, Chanakyapuri, New Delhi 110 021; tel. (11) 26889071; fax (11) 26877941; e-mail skdelhi@giasdl01.vsnl.net.in; Ambassador ALEXANDER ILASCIK.

**Slovenia:** 46 Poorvi Marg, Vasant Vihar, New Delhi 110 057; tel. (11) 51662891; fax (11) 51662895; e-mail vnd@mzz-dkp.gov.si; Chargé d'affaires MIKLAVZ BORŠTNIK.

**Somalia:** A-7, Defence Colony, New Delhi 110 024; tel. (11) 24335026; e-mail mosman65@yahoo.com; Ambassador EBYAN MAHAMED SALAH.

**South Africa:** B-18 Vasant Marg, Vasant Vihar, New Delhi 110 057; tel. (11) 26149411; fax (11) 26143605; e-mail highcommissioner@sahc-india.com; internet www.sahc-india.com; High Commissioner SEHLOHO FRANCIS MOLOI.

**Spain:** 16 Sunder Nagar, New Delhi 110 003; tel. (11) 24359004; fax (11) 24359040; e-mail embspain@ndb.vsnl.net.in; Ambassador Don RAFAEL CONDE DE SARO.

**Sri Lanka:** 27 Kautilya Marg, Chanakyapuri, New Delhi 110 021; tel. (11) 23010201; fax (11) 23793604; e-mail lankacom@del2.vsnl.net.in; High Commissioner C. ROMESH JAYASINGHE.

**Sudan:** Plot No. 3, Shanti Path, Chanakyapuri, New Delhi 110 021; tel. (11) 26873785; fax (11) 26883758; e-mail sudandel@del3.vsnl.net.in; internet www.embassysudanindia.org; Ambassador ABDEL RAHMAN MOHAMED BAKHIET.

**Suriname:** C-15 Malcha Marg, New Delhi 110 021; tel. (11) 26888543; fax (11) 26888450; e-mail embsurnd@vsnl.net; internet www.embsurnd.com; Ambassador K. BAJNATH.

**Sweden:** Nyaya Marg, Chanakyapuri, New Delhi 110 021; tel. (11) 24197100; fax (11) 26885401; e-mail ambassaden.new-delhi@foreign.ministry.se; internet www.swedenabroad.se/pages/start_21488.asp; Ambassador LARS-OLOF LINDGREN.

**Switzerland:** Nyaya Marg, Chanakyapuri, New Delhi 110 021; tel. (11) 26878372; fax (11) 26873093; e-mail ndh.vertretung@eda.admin.ch; Ambassador DOMINIQUE DREYER.

**Syria:** D-5/8, Vasant Vihar, New Delhi 110 057; tel. (11) 26140233; fax (11) 26143107; Ambassador FAHD SALIM.

**Tajikistan:** D-1/13, Vasant Vihar, New Delhi 110 057; tel. and fax (11) 26154282; e-mail tajembindia@yahoo.com; Ambassador SALOHODDIN NASRIDDINOV.

**Tanzania:** 10/1 Sav Priya Vihar, New Delhi 110 016; tel. (11) 26153148; fax (11) 26153289; e-mail tanzrep@del1.vsnl.net.in; High Commissioner EVA LILIAN NZARO.

**Thailand:** 56N Nyaya Marg, Chanakyapuri, New Delhi 110 021; tel. (11) 26118103; fax (11) 26872029; e-mail thaidel@mfa.go.th; internet www.thaiemb.org.in; Ambassador CHIRASAK THANESNANT.

**Trinidad and Tobago:** 6/25 Shanti Niketan, New Delhi 110 021; tel. (11) 24118427; fax (11) 24118463; e-mail admin@hctt.org; High Commissioner PUNDIT MANIDEO PERSAD.

**Tunisia:** A-42 Vasant Marg, Vasant Vihar, New Delhi 110 057; tel. (11) 26145346; fax (11) 26145301; e-mail embtundelhi@dishnetdsl.net; Ambassador RAOUF CHATTI.

**Turkey:** 50N Nyaya Marg, Chanakyapuri, New Delhi 110 021; tel. (11) 26889054; fax (11) 26881409; e-mail tembdelhi@mantraonline.com; Ambassador LEVENT BILMAN.

**Turkmenistan:** C-11, West End Colony, New Delhi 110 021; tel. (11) 24676526; fax (11) 24676527; e-mail turkmind@starith.net; Ambassador PARAHAT HOMMADOVICH DURDYEV.

**Uganda:** B-3/26, Vasant Vihar, New Delhi 110 057; tel. (11) 26144413; fax (11) 26144405; e-mail ughcom@ndb.vsnl.net.in; High Commissioner NIMISHA MADHVANI.

**Ukraine:** E-1/8 Vasant Vihar, New Delhi 110 057; tel. (11) 26146041; fax (11) 26146043; e-mail embassy@bol.net.in; internet www.ukraineembassyindia.org; Chargé d'affaires a.i. MISCHUK MYKOLA.

**United Arab Emirates:** EP-12 Chandragupta Marg, New Delhi 110 021; tel. (11) 26872937; fax (11) 26873272; e-mail embassyabudhabi@bol.net.in; Chargé d'affaires ABDULLA JASSIM KASHWANI.

**United Kingdom:** Shantipath, Chanakyapuri, New Delhi 110 021; tel. (11) 26872161; fax (11) 26870065; e-mail postmaster.nedel@fco.gov.uk; internet www.ukinindia.com; High Commissioner Sir RICHARD STAGG.

**USA:** Shanti Path, Chanakyapuri, New Delhi 110 021; tel. (11) 24198000; fax (11) 241900170; e-mail ndcentral@state.gov; internet newdelhi.usembassy.gov; Ambassador DAVID CAMPBELL MULFORD.

**Uruguay:** A-16/2 Vasant Vihar, New Delhi 110 057; tel. (11) 26151991; fax (11) 26144306; e-mail uruind@del3.vsnl.net.in; Ambassador WILLIAM EHLERS.

**Uzbekistan:** EP-40 Dr S. Radhakrishnan Marg, Chanakyapuri, New Delhi 110 021; tel. (11) 24670774; fax (11) 24670773; e-mail uzembind@vsnl.com; internet www.uzbekembassy.in; Ambassador Prof. SAYDAKMAL SAYDAKHMEDOVITCH SAYDAMINOV.

**Venezuela:** E-106 Malcha Marg, Chanakyapuri, New Delhi 110 021; tel. (11) 41680218; fax (11) 41750743; e-mail embavene@del2.vsnl.net.in; Ambassador MILENA SANTANA-RAMÍREZ.

**Viet Nam:** 17 Kautilya Marg, Chanakyapuri, New Delhi 110 021; tel. (11) 23012123; fax (11) 23017714; e-mail sqdelhi@del3.vsnl.net.in; Ambassador VU QUANG DIEM.

**Yemen:** B-3/61, Safdarjung Enclave, New Delhi 110 029; tel. (11) 26179612; fax (11) 26179614; e-mail yemenembnd@yahoo.com; Ambassador MUSTAFA NUAMAN.

**Zambia:** D/54 Vasant Vihar, New Delhi 110 057; tel. (11) 26145883; fax (11) 26145764; e-mail zambiand@sify.com; High Commissioner S. K. WALUBITA.

**Zimbabwe:** E 12/7, Vasant Vihar, New Delhi 110 057; tel. (11) 26140430; fax (11) 26154316; e-mail ambassador@zimdelhi.com; internet www.zimdelhi.com; Ambassador JONATHAN WUTAWUNASHE.

# Judicial System

### THE SUPREME COURT

The Supreme Court, consisting of a Chief Justice and not more than 25 judges appointed by the President, exercises exclusive jurisdiction in any dispute between the Union and the states (although there are certain restrictions where an acceding state is involved). It has appellate jurisdiction over any judgment, decree or order of the High Court where that Court certifies that either a substantial question of law or the interpretation of the Constitution is involved. The Supreme Court can enforce fundamental rights and issue writs covering habeas corpus, mandamus, prohibition, quo warranto and certiorari. The Supreme Court is a court of record and has the power to punish for its contempt.

Provision is made for the appointment by the Chief Justice of India of judges of High Courts as ad hoc judges at sittings of the Supreme Court for specified periods, and for the attendance of retired judges at sittings of the Supreme Court. The Supreme Court has advisory jurisdiction in respect of questions which may be referred to it by the President for opinion. The Supreme Court is also empowered to hear appeals against a sentence of death passed by a State High Court in reversal of an order of acquittal by a lower court, and in a case in which a High Court has granted a certificate of fitness.

The Supreme Court also hears appeals which are certified by High Courts to be fit to be heard, subject to rules made by the Court. Parliament may, by law, confer on the Supreme Court any further powers of appeal.

The judges hold office until the age of 65 years.

**Supreme Court:** Tilak Marg, New Delhi 110 001; tel. (11) 23388942; fax (11) 23383792; e-mail supremecourt@nic.in; internet supremecourtofindia.nic.in.

**Chief Justice of India:** K. G. BALAKRISHNAN.

**Judges of the Supreme Court:** A. K. MATHUR, ASHOK BHAN, C. K. THAKKAR, HOTOI KHETOHO SEMA, BISHWANATH AGARWAL, SAROSH HOMI KAPADIA, S. B. SINHA, GOVIND PRASAD MATHUR, ARIJIT PASSAYAT, PRAKASH P. NAOLEKAR, TARUN CHATTERJEE, P. K. BALASUBRAMANYAM, ALTAMAS KABIR, RAJU VARADARAJULU RAVEENDRAN, DALVEER BHANDARI, LOKESHWAR SINGH PANTA, D. K. JAIN, MARKANDEY KATJU, H. S. BEDI, V. S. SIRPURKAR, B. SUDERSHAN REDDY, P. SATHASIVAM, G. S. SINGHVI, AFTAB ALAM, J. M. PANCHAL.

**Attorney-General:** MILON BANERJEE.

### HIGH COURTS

The High Courts are the Courts of Appeal from the lower courts, and their decisions are final except in cases where appeal lies with the Supreme Court.

### LOWER COURTS

Provision is made in the Code of Criminal Procedure for the constitution of lower criminal courts called Courts of Session and Courts of Magistrates. The Courts of Session are competent to try all persons duly committed for trial, and inflict any punishment authorized by the law. The President and the local government concerned exercise the prerogative of mercy.

The constitution of inferior civil courts is determined by regulations within each state.

# Religion

### BUDDHISM

The Buddhists in Ladakh (Jammu and Kashmir) are followers of the Dalai Lama. Head Lama of Ladakh: KAUSHAK SAKULA, Dalgate, Srinagar (Jammu and Kashmir). The Buddhists in Sikkim are also followers of Mahayana Buddhism. In 2001 there were 8.0m. Buddhists in India, representing 0.8% of the population.

**Mahabodhi Society of India:** 4-A, Bankim Chatterjee St, Kolkata 700 073; tel. and fax (33) 22415214; internet www.mahabodhiindia.com; 11 centres in India, five centres world-wide; Pres. Dr BHUPENDRA KUMAR MODI; Gen. Sec. Dr D. REWATHA THERO.

### HINDUISM

In 2001 there were 827.6m. Hindus in India, representing 80.5% of the population.

**Rashtriya Swayamsevak Sangh (RSS)** (National Volunteer Organization): Keshav Kunj, Jhandewala, D. B. Gupta Marg, New Delhi 110 055; tel. (11) 23611372; fax (11) 23611385; e-mail rss@rss.org; internet www.rss.org; f. 1925; 934,000 service centres in tribal, rural and urban slum areas; 58,000 working centres; Pres. K. S. SUDARSHAN; Gen. Sec. MOHAN BHAGWAT.

**Sarvadeshik Arya Pratinidhi Sabha:** 3/5 Asaf Ali Rd, Near Ram Lila Maidan, New Delhi 110 002; tel. (11) 23274771; e-mail sanjayyogi1@rediffmail.com; f. 1875 by Maharishi Dayanand Saraswati; the international body for Arya Samaj temples propagating reforms in all fields on the basis of Vedic principles; Pres. Capt. DEV RATNA ARYA; Sec. VIMAL WADHAWAN.

**Vishwa Hindu Parishad (VHP)** (World Hindu Council): Sankat Mochan Ashram, Ramakrishna Puram Sector 6, New Delhi 110 022; tel. (11) 26178992; fax (11) 26195527; e-mail vishwahindu@gmail.com; internet www.vhp.org; f. 1964, banned in Dec. 1992–June 1993 for its role in the destruction of the Babri mosque in Ayodhya; Pres. ASHOK SINGHAL; Sec.-Gen. Dr PRAVINBHAI TOGADIYA.

### ISLAM

Muslims are divided into two main sects, Shi'as and Sunnis. Most of the Indian Muslims are Sunnis. At the 2001 census Islam had 138.2m. adherents (13.4% of the population).

**Jamiat Ulama-i-Hind** (Assembly of Muslim Religious Leaders of India): 1 Bahadur Shah Zafar Marg, New Delhi 110 002; tel. (11) 23311455; fax (11) 23316173; e-mail jamiat@vsnl.com; internet jamiatulama.org; f. 1919; Pres. ASAD MADANI; Gen. Sec. Maulana MAHMOOD MADANI.

### SIKHISM

In 2001 there were 19.2m. Sikhs (comprising 1.9% of the population), the majority living in the Punjab.

**Shiromani Gurdwara Parbandhak Committee:** Darbar Sahab, Amritsar 143 001; tel. (183) 2553956; fax (183) 2553919; e-mail info@sgpc.net; internet www.sgpc.net; f. 1925; highest authority in Sikhism; Pres. Jathedar AVTAR SINGH; Jathedar Shri Akal Takht Saheb JOGINDER SINGH VEDANTI.

### CHRISTIANITY

According to the 2001 census, Christians represented 2.3% of the population in India.

**National Council of Churches in India:** Christian Council Lodge, Civil Lines, POB 205, Nagpur 440 001; tel. (712) 2561464; fax (712) 2520554; e-mail nccindia_ngp@sancharnet.in; internet www.nccindia.in; f. 1914; mems: 30 protestant and orthodox churches, 17 regional Christian councils, 17 All-India ecumenical orgs and seven related agencies; represents c. 13m. mems; Pres. Bishop Dr TARANATH S. SAGAR; Gen. Sec. Bishop D. K. SAHU.

#### Orthodox Churches

**Malankara Orthodox Syrian Church:** Devalokam, Kottayam 686 038; tel. (481) 2578500; fax (481) 2570569; e-mail orthodox@md4.vsnl.net.in; c. 2.5m. mems (1995); 22 bishops, 21 dioceses, 1,340 parishes; Catholicos of the East and Malankara Metropolitan HH BASELIUS MARTHOMA MATHEWS II; Asscn Sec. A. K. THOMAS.

**Mar Thoma Syrian Church of Malabar:** Mar Thoma Sabha Office, Tiruvalla 689 101; tel. (469) 2630449; fax (469) 2630327; e-mail sabhaoffice@marthoma.in; internet www.marthomasyrianchurch.org; c. 1m. mems (2001); Valia Metropolitan Most Rev. Dr JOSEPH MAR THOMA; Sec. Rev. KUTTIKATTU MAMMEN MAMMEN.

The Malankara Jacobite Syrian Orthodox Church is also represented.

#### Protestant Churches

**Church of North India (CNI):** CNI Bhavan, 16 Pandit Pant Marg, New Delhi 110 001; tel. (11) 23731079; fax (11) 23716901; e-mail gscni@ndb.vsnl.net.in; internet www.cnisynod.org; f. 1970 by merger of the Church of India (Anglican—fmrly known as the Church of India, Pakistan, Burma and Ceylon), the Council of the Baptist Churches in Northern India, the Methodist Church (British and Australasian Conferences), the United Church of Northern India (a union of Presbyterians and Congregationalists, f. 1924), the Church of the Brethren in India, and the Disciples of Christ; comprises 26 dioceses; c. 1.2m. mems (1999); Moderator Most Rev. JOEL V. MAL (Bishop of Chandigarh); Gen. Sec. Rev. Dr ENOS DAS PRADHAN.

**Church of South India (CSI):** CSI Centre, 5 Whites Rd, Chennai 600 014; tel. (44) 28521566; fax (44) 28523528; e-mail csi@vsnl.com; internet www.csisynod.com; f. 1947 by merger of the Weslyan Methodist Church in South India, the South India United Church (itself a union of churches in the Congregational and Presbyterian/Reformed traditions) and the four southern dioceses of the (Anglican) Church of India; comprises 22 dioceses (incl. one in Sri Lanka); c. 3m. mems (2003); Moderator Most Rev. Dr B. P. SUGANDHAR (Bishop of Medak); Gen. Sec. Dr PAULINE SATHIAMURTHY.

**Methodist Church in India:** Methodist Centre, 21 YMCA Rd, Mumbai 400 008; tel. (22) 23094316; fax (22) 23074137; e-mail gensecmci@vsnl.com; f. 1856 as the Methodist Church in Southern Asia; 648,000 mems (2005); Gen. Sec. Rev. Dr ELIA PRADEEP SAMUEL.

**Samavesam of Telugu Baptist Churches:** A. B. M. Compound, Kavali 524 201; tel. (8626) 241201; fax (8626) 241847; f. 1962; comprises 856 independent Baptist churches; 578,295 mems (1995); Functional Adviser Dr G. DEVADANAM.

**United Evangelical Lutheran Church in India:** Martin Luther Bhavan, 95 Purasawalkam High Rd, Kilpauk, Chennai 600 010; tel. and fax (44) 26430008; e-mail uelci@vsnl.net; internet www.uelci-india.org; f. 1975; 11 constituent denominations: Andhra Evangelical Lutheran Church, Arcot Lutheran Church, Evangelical Lutheran Church in Madhya Pradesh, Evangelical Lutheran Church in the Himalayan States, Gossner Evangelical Lutheran Church in Chotanagpur and Assam (Asom), India Evangelical Lutheran Church, Jeypore Evangelical Lutheran Church, Northern Evangelical Lutheran Church, South Andhra Lutheran Church, Good Samaritan Evangelical Lutheran Church and Tamil Evangelical Lutheran Church; more than 1.5m. mems; Pres. Rt Rev. Dr GIDEON DEVANESAN; Exec. Sec. Rev. Dr A. G. AUGUSTINE JEYAKUMAR.

Other denominations active in the country include the Assembly of the Presbyterian Church in North East India, the Bengal-Orissa-Bihar Baptist Convention (6,000 mems), the Chaldean Syrian Church of the East, the Convention of the Baptist Churches of Northern Circars, the Council of Baptist Churches of North East India, the Council of Baptist Churches of Northern India, the Hindustani Convent Church and the Mennonite Church in India.

#### The Roman Catholic Church

India comprises 30 archdioceses and 134 dioceses. These include five archdioceses and 11 dioceses of the Syro-Malabar rite, and two archdioceses and four dioceses of the Syro-Malankara rite. The archdiocese of Goa and Daman is also the seat of the Patriarch of the East Indies. The remaining archdioceses are metropolitan sees. In December 2006 there were an estimated 26.9m. adherents of the Roman Catholic faith in the country.

**Catholic Bishops' Conference of India (CBCI):** CBCI Centre, 1 Ashok Place, nr Gole Dakkhana, New Delhi 110 001; tel. (11) 23344470; fax (11) 23364615; e-mail cbci@vsnl.com; internet www.cbcisite.com; f. 1944; Pres. Cardinal TELESPHORE P. TOPPO (Archbishop of Ranchi); Sec.-Gen. Most Rev. STANISLAUS FERNANDES (Archbishop of Gandhinagar).

##### Latin Rite

**Conference of Catholic Bishops of India (CCBI):** CCBI Centre, 2nd Cross, Hutchins Rd, POB 8490, Bangalore 560 084; tel. (80) 25498282; fax (80) 25498180; e-mail ccbi@airtelbroadband.in; internet www.ccbi.in; f. 1994; Pres. Cardinal TELESPHORO P. TOPPO (Archbishop of Ranchi).

##### Syro-Malabar Rite

**Major Archbishop of Ernakulam-Angamaly:** Cardinal MAR VARKEY VITHAYATHIL, Major Archbishop's House, Thrikkakara, POB 2580, Kochi 682 031; tel. (484) 2352629; fax (484) 2355010; e-mail secretary@ernakulamarchdiocese.org; internet www.ernakulamarchdiocese.org.

**Archbishop of Kottayam:** Most Rev. MATHEW MOOLAKKATTU, Archbishop's House, POB 71, Kottayam 686 001; tel. (481) 2563527; fax (481) 2563327; e-mail cbhktym@hotmail.com; internet www.kottayamad.org.

**Archbishop of Changanasserry:** Most Rev. JOSEPH MAR POWATHIL, Archbishop's House, POB 20, Changanasserry 686 101; tel. (481) 2420040; fax (481) 2422540; e-mail abpchry@sancharnet.in; internet www.archdiocesechanganacherry.org.

**Archbishop of Tellicherry:** Most Rev. GEORGE VALIAMATTAM, Archbishop's House, POB 70, Tellicherry 670 101; tel. (490) 2341058; fax (49) 2341412; e-mail diocese@eth.net; internet www.archdioceseoftellicherry.org.

**Archbishop of Trichur:** Most Rev. MAR ANDREWS THAZHATH, Archbishop's House, Trichur 680 005; tel. (487) 2333325; fax (487) 2338204; e-mail carbit@md4.vsnl.net.in; internet www.trichurarchdiocese.org.

Syro-Malankara Rite

**Archbishop of Trivandrum:** Most Rev. Dr THOMAS MAR KOORILOS, Archbishop's House, Pattom, Thiruvananthapuram 695 004; tel. (471) 2541643; fax (471) 2541635; e-mail marcleemis@hotmail.com; internet www.malankara.net.

### BAHÁ'Í FAITH

**National Spiritual Assembly:** Bahá'í House, 6 Shrimant Madhavrao Scindia Rd, POB 19, New Delhi 110 001; tel. (11) 23389326; fax (11) 23782178; e-mail nsaindia@bahaindia.org; internet www.bahaindia.org; f. 1923; c. 2m. mems; Sec.-Gen. Dr A. K. MERCHANT.

### OTHER FAITHS

**Jainism:** 4.2m. adherents (2001 census), 0.4% of the population.

**Zoroastrianism:** In 2001 69,601 Parsis practised the Zoroastrian religion, compared with 76,382 in 1991.

## The Press

Freedom of the Press was guaranteed under the 1950 Constitution. In 1979 a Press Council was established (its predecessor was abolished in 1975), the function of which was to uphold the freedom of the press and maintain and improve journalistic standards.

The growth of a thriving press has been inhibited by cultural barriers caused by religious, social and linguistic differences. Consequently the English-language press, with its appeal to the educated middle-class urban readership throughout the states, has retained its dominance. The English-language metropolitan dailies are some of the widest circulating and most influential newspapers. The main Indian language dailies, by paying attention to rural affairs, cater for the increasingly literate non-anglophone provincial population. Most Indian-language papers have a relatively small circulation.

The majority of publications in India are under individual ownership (75% in 2002/03), and they claim a large part of the total circulation (60% in 1999). The most powerful groups, owned by joint stock companies, publish most of the large English dailies and frequently have considerable private commercial and industrial holdings. Four of the major groups are as follows:

**Times of India Group:** controlled by family of the late ASHOK JAIN; dailies: *The Times of India* (published in 11 regional centres), *Economic Times*, the Hindi *Navbharat Times* and *Sandhya Times*, the Marathi *Maharashtra Times* (Mumbai); periodicals: the English fortnightly *Femina* and monthly *Filmfare*.

**Indian Express Group:** controlled by the family of the late RAMNATH GOENKA; publishes nine dailies including the *Indian Express*, the Marathi *Lokasatta*, the Tamil *Dinamani*, the Telugu *Andhra Prabha*, the Kannada *Kannada Prabha* and the English *Financial Express*; six periodicals including the English weeklies the *Indian Express* (Sunday edition), *Screen*, the Telugu *Andhra Prabha Illustrated Weekly* and the Tamil *Dinamani Kadir* (weekly).

**Hindustan Times Group:** controlled by the K. K. BIRLA family; dailies: the *Hindustan Times* (published from 10 regional centres), *Pradeep* (Patna) and the Hindi *Hindustan* (Delhi, Lucknow, Patna and Ranchi); periodicals: the weekly *Overseas Hindustan Times* and the Hindi monthly *Nandan* and *Kadambini* (New Delhi).

**Ananda Bazar Patrika Group:** controlled by AVEEK SARKAR and family; dailies: the *Ananda Bazar Patrika* (Kolkata) and the English *The Telegraph* (Guwahati, Kolkata and Siliguri); periodicals include: *Business World*, Bengali weekly *Anandamela*, Bengali fortnightly *Desh*, Bengali monthly *Anandalok* and the Bengali monthly *Sananda*.

### PRINCIPAL DAILIES

#### Delhi (incl. New Delhi)

**The Asian Age:** S-7, Green Park, Main Market, New Delhi 110 016; tel. (11) 26530001; fax (11) 26530027; e-mail marketing@asianage.com; internet www.asianage.com; f. 1994; morning; English; also publ. from Ahmedabad, Bangalore, Kolkata, Mumbai and London; Editor-in-Chief M. J. AKBAR.

**Business Standard:** Pratap Bhavan, 5 Bahadur Shah Zafar Marg, New Delhi 110 002; tel. (11) 23720202; fax (11) 23720201; e-mail editor@business-standard.com; internet www.business-standard.com; morning; English; also publ. from Kolkata, Ahmedabad, Bangalore, Chennai, Hyderabad and Mumbai; Editor T. N. NINAN; combined circ. 61,700.

**Daily Milap:** 8A Bahadur Shah Zafar Marg, New Delhi 110 002; tel. (11) 23317651; fax (11) 23319166; e-mail info@milap.com; internet www.milap.com; f. 1923; Urdu; nationalist; Man. Editor PUNAM SURI; Chief Editor NAVIN SURI; circ. 37,057.

**Daily Pratap:** Pratap Bhawan, 5 Bahadur Shah Zafar Marg, New Delhi 110 002; tel. (11) 23317938; fax (11) 41509555; e-mail admin@dailypratap.com; internet www.dailypratap.com; f. 1919; Urdu; Chief Editor K. NARENDRA; CEO S. M. AFIF AHSEN; circ. 47,962.

**Delhi Mid Day:** World Trade Tower, Barakhamba Lane, New Delhi 110 001; tel. (11) 23414224; fax (11) 23412491; e-mail editordelhi@mid-day.com; f. 1989; Editor ANIL SHARMA (acting).

**The Economic Times:** 7 Bahadur Shah Zafar Marg, New Delhi 110 002; tel. (11) 23492234; fax (11) 23491248; internet www.economictimes.com; f. 1961; English; also publ. from Kolkata, Ahmedabad, Bangalore, Hyderabad, Chennai and Mumbai; Editor (Delhi) RAHUL JOSHI; combined circ. 461,900, circ. (Delhi) 125,800.

**Financial Express:** The Indian Express Online Media (Pvt) Ltd, B14/A Qutab Institutional Area, New Delhi 110 016; tel. (11) 23702167; fax (11) 26530114; e-mail editor@financialexpress.com; internet www.financialexpress.com; f. 1961; morning; English; also publ. from Ahmedabad (in Gujarati), Mumbai, Bangalore, Kolkata and Chennai; Editor MYTHILI BHUSNURMATH; combined circ. 50,000.

**The Hindu:** INS Bldg, Rafi Marg, New Delhi 110 001; tel. (11) 23715426; fax (11) 23718158; e-mail thehindu@vsnl.com; internet www.hinduonnet.com; f. 1878; morning; English; also publ. from 11 other regional centres; Editor-in-Chief N. RAM; combined circ. 1,180,000.

**Hindustan:** 18–20 Kasturba Gandhi Marg, New Delhi 110 001; tel. (11) 23361234; fax (11) 23704600; internet www.hindustandainik.com; f. 1936; morning; Hindi; also publ. from Lucknow, Muzaffarpur, Ranchi, Bhagalpur, Varanasi and Patna; Group Editor MRINAL PANDE; combined circ. 753,500.

**Hindustan Times:** 18–20 Kasturba Gandhi Marg, New Delhi 110 001; tel. (11) 23361254; fax (11) 23704600; e-mail feedback@hindustantimes.com; internet www.hindustantimes.com; f. 1923; morning; English; also publ. from nine regional centres; Editor-in-Chief CHAITANYA KALBAG; combined circ. 1,142,600.

**Indian Express:** Bahadur Shah Zafar Marg, New Delhi 110 002; tel. (11) 26511015; fax (11) 26511615; e-mail editor@expressindia.com; internet www.indianexpress.com; f. 1953; English; also publ. from seven other towns; Man. Editor VIVEK GOENKA; Editor-in-Chief SHEKHAR GUPTA; combined circ. 688,878, circ. 138,100 (New Delhi, Jammu and Chandigarh).

**Janasatta:** 9/10 Bahadur Shah Zafar Marg, New Delhi 110 002; tel. (11) 23702100; fax (11) 23702141; e-mail jansatta@expressindia.com; f. 1983; Hindi; also publ. from Kolkata and Raipur; Editor OM THANVI.

**National Herald:** Herald House, 5A Bahadur Shah Zafar Marg, New Delhi 110 002; tel. (11) 23313815; fax (11) 23313458; e-mail nationalheralddelhi@rediffmail.com; f. 1938; English; nationalist; Editor T. V. VENKITACHALAM; circ. 33,000.

**Navbharat Times:** 7 Bahadur Shah Zafar Marg, New Delhi 110 002; tel. (11) 23492041; fax (11) 23492168; f. 1947; Hindi; also publ. from Mumbai; Editor MADHUSUDAN ANAND; combined circ. 398,300, circ. 248,400 (Delhi).

**The Pioneer:** Link House, 3 Bahadur Shah Zafar Marg, New Delhi 110 002; tel. (11) 23755271; fax (11) 23755275; e-mail feedback@dailypioneer.com; internet www.dailypioneer.com; f. 1865; also publ. from Lucknow; Editor CHANDAN MITRA; combined circ. 154,000, circ. 78,000 (Delhi).

**Punjab Kesari:** Romesh Bhavan, 2 Printing Press Complex, nr Wazirpur DTC Depot, Ring Rd, Delhi 110 035; tel. (11) 27194459; fax (11) 27194470; e-mail ashwanik@nda.vsnl.net.in; internet www.punjabkesari.com; f. 1983; Hindi; also publ. from Jalandhar and Ambala; circulated in Haryana, Rajasthan, Uttar Pradesh, Uttarakhand, Madhya Pradesh, Punjab, Himachal Pradesh, Maharashtra, Bihar and Gujarat; Resident Editor ASHWINI KUMAR; circ. 333,031 (Delhi), Sunday circ. 448,519 (2007).

**Rashtriya Sahara:** Amba Deep, Kasturba Gandhi Marg, New Delhi 110 001; tel. (11) 23704193; fax (11) 23704113; morning; Hindi; also publ. from Lucknow and Gorakhpur; Resident Editor NISHIT JOSHI; circ. 81,900 (New Delhi), 42,300 (Lucknow), 30,600 (Gorakhpur).

**Sandhya Times:** 7 Bahadur Shah Zafar Marg, New Delhi 110 002; tel. (11) 23492162; fax (11) 23492047; f. 1979; Hindi; evening; Editor SAT SONI; circ. 44,400.

**The Statesman:** Statesman House, 148 Barakhamba Rd, New Delhi 110 001; tel. (11) 23315911; fax (11) 23315295; e-mail thestatesman@vsnl.com; internet www.thestatesman.net; f. 1875; English; also publ. from Bhubaneswar, Kolkata and Siliguri; Editor and Man. Dir RAVINDRA KUMAR; combined circ. 180,000.

**The Times of India:** 7 Bahadur Shah Zafar Marg, New Delhi 110 002; tel. (11) 23492049; fax (11) 23351606; internet www.timesofindia.com; f. 1838; English; also publ. from 10 other towns; Resident Editor ARINDAM SENGUPTA; combined circ. 2,214,700.

## Andhra Pradesh

### Hyderabad

**Deccan Chronicle:** 36 Sarojini Devi Rd, Hyderabad 500 003; tel. (40) 27803930; fax (40) 27805256; f. 1938; English; also publ. from six other regional centres; Editor-in-Chief M. J. AKBAR; Editor A. T. JAYANTI; circ. 342,100.

**Eenadu:** Somajiguda, Hyderabad 500 082; tel. (40) 23318181; fax (40) 23318555; e-mail feedback@eenadu.net; internet www.eenadu .net; f. 1974; Telugu; also publ. from 22 other towns; Chief Editor RAMOJI RAO; circ. 1,010,300 (weekdays), 1,145,000 (Sunday).

**Rahnuma-e-Deccan:** 12-2-837/A/3, Asif Nagar, Hyderabad 500 028; tel. (40) 23534943; fax (40) 23534945; e-mail rahnumadeccan@email.com; f. 1949; morning; Urdu; independent; Chief Editor SYED VICARUDDIN; circ. 25,000.

**Siasat Daily:** Jawaharlal Nehru Rd, Hyderabad 500 001; tel. (40) 24744109; fax (40) 24603188; e-mail info@siasat.com; internet www .siasat.com; f. 1949; morning; Urdu; Editor ZAHID ALI KHAN; circ. 41,600.

### Vijayawada

**Andhra Jyoti:** Andhra Jyoti Bldg, POB 712, Vijayawada 520 010; tel. (866) 2474532; f. 1960; Telugu; also publ. from 13 other regional centres; Editor K. RAMACHANDRA MURTHY; combined circ. 162,400.

**Andhra Prabha:** 16-1-28, Kolandareddy Rd, Poornanandampet, Vijayawada 520 003; tel. (866) 2571351; e-mail info@andhraprabha .com; internet www.andhraprabha.com; f. 1935; Telugu; also publ. from Bangalore, Hyderabad, Chennai and Visakhapatnam; Editor M. SATISH CHANDRA; combined circ. 24,500.

**New Indian Express:** 16-1-28, Kolandareddy Rd, Poornanandampet, Vijayawada 520 003; tel. (866) 2571351; English; also publ. from Bangalore, Belgaum, Kochi, Kozhikode, Thiruvananthapuram, Madurai, Chennai, Hyderabad, Visakhapatnam, Coimbatore and Bhubaneswar; Man. Editor MANOJ KUMAR SONTHALIA; Editor (Andhra Pradesh) P. S. SUNDARAM; combined circ. 197,400.

## Assam (Asom)

### Guwahati

**Amar Asom:** G. S. Rd, Ulubari, Guwahati 781 007; tel. (361) 2544356; fax (361) 2540664; e-mail glpl@sancharnet.in; f. 1997; Assamese; also publ. from Jorhat; Editor HOMEN BORGOHAIN; circ. 76,500.

**Asomiya Pratidin:** Maniram Dewan Rd, Guwahati 781 003; tel. (361) 2660420; fax (361) 2666377; e-mail pratidinedi@vsnl.net; morning; Assamese; also published from Dibrugarh, Lakhimpur and Bongaigaon; circ. 121,800.

**Assam Tribune:** Tribune Bldgs, Maniram Dewan Rd, Chandmari, Guwahati 781 003; tel. (361) 2661357; fax (361) 2666398; e-mail webmaster@assamtribune.com; internet www.assamtribune.com; f. 1939; English; Man. Dir and Editor P. G. BARUAH; circ. 59,200.

**Dainik Agradoot:** Agradoot Bhavan, Dispur, Guwahati 781 006; tel. (361) 2261923; fax (361) 2260655; e-mail agradoot@sify.com; internet www.dainikagradoot.com; f. 1995; Assamese; Editor K. S. DEKA; circ. 70,973.

**Dainik Assam:** Tribune Bldgs, Maniram Dewan Rd, Chandmari, Guwahati 781 003; tel. (361) 2541360; fax (361) 2516356; e-mail webmaster@assamtribune.com; internet www.assamtribune.com; f. 1965; Assamese; Editor DHIRENDRA NATH CHAKRAVARTTY; circ. 16,700.

**Dainik Jugasankha:** Jugasankha Bldg, Green Path, G. S. Rd, Guwahati 781 007; tel. (361) 2547444; fax (361) 2544971; e-mail dainikjugasankha@yahoo.com; f. 1950; Bengali; also publ. from Silchar; Editor-in-Chief BIJOY KRISHNA NATH; Editor SANTANU GHOSH; circ. 52,900.

**The North East Daily:** Maniram Dewan Rd, Chandmari, Guwahati 781 003; tel. (361) 2524594; fax (361) 2524634; e-mail protidin@gw1 .vsnl.net.in; Assamese; circ. 34,891.

**The Sentinel:** G. S. Rd, Guwahati 781 005; tel. (361) 2529237; fax (361) 2529624; e-mail sentinelghy@sancharnet.in; internet www .sentinelassam.com; f. 1983; English; Editor INDIRA RAJKHEWA; circ. 44,900.

### Jorhat

**Dainik Janmabhumi:** Tulsi Narayan Sarma Rd, Jorhat 785 001; tel. (376) 2320033; fax (376) 2321713; e-mail editordj@sify.com; f. 1972; Assamese; also published from Tinsukia, Guwahati and Tezpur; Editor HEMANTA BARMAN; Man. Partner SUBROTO SHARMA; circ. 47,879.

## Bihar

### Patna

**Aryavarta:** Mazharul Haque Path, Patna 800 001; tel. (612) 2230716; fax (612) 2222350; e-mail aryavart@dte.vsnl.net.in; morning; Hindi; Editor BHAKTISHWAR JHA.

**Hindustan Times:** Buddha Marg, Patna 800 001; tel. (612) 2223434; fax (612) 2226120; f. 1918; morning; English; also publ. from nine regional centres; Editor SHEKHAR BHATIA; combined circ. 1,142,600.

**Indian Nation:** Mazharul Haque Path, Patna 800 001; tel. (612) 2237780; fax (612) 2222350; e-mail aryavart@dte.vsnl.net.in; morning; English; Editor BHAKTISHWAR JHA.

**The Times of India:** Times House, Fraser Rd, Patna 800 001; tel. (612) 2226301; fax (612) 2233525; internet www.timesofindia.com; also publ. from New Delhi, Mumbai, Ahmedabad, Bangalore and Lucknow; Exec. Editor ARINDAM SENGUPTA; combined circ. 2,214,700.

## Chhattisgarh

### Raipur

**Dainik Bhaskar:** Press Complex, Rajbandha Mandan, G. E. Rd, Raipur 492 001; tel. (771) 2535277; fax (771) 2535255; Hindi; morning; also publ. from 18 other regional centres; Editor R. C. AGRAWAL; circ. 109,300.

**Deshbandhu:** Deshbandhu Complex, Ramsagar Para, Raipur 492 001; tel. (771) 2292011; fax (771) 2534955; e-mail deshbandhuraipur@gmail.com; internet www.deshbandhu.co.in; f. 1959; Hindi; also publ. from Jabalpur, Satna, Bilaspur and Bhopal; Chief Editor LALIT SURJAN; circ. 84,357 (Raipur), 24,289 (Satna), 46,785 (Bhopal), 50,468 (Jabalpur), 59,013 (Bilaspur).

**Highway Channel:** Deshbandhu Complex, Ramsagar Para, Raipur 492 001; tel. (771) 2292011; fax (771) 2534955; e-mail deshbandhu@ mantrafreenet.com; internet www.dailydeshbandhu.com; f. 1997; evening; Hindi; also publ. from Bilaspur and Jagdalpur; Chief Editor LALIT SURJAN; Editor PRABHAKAR CHOUBEY; combined circ. 49,468.

**Nava Bharat:** Nava Bharat Bhavan Press Complex, G. E. Rd, Raipur 492 001; tel. (771) 2535544; fax (771) 2534936; Hindi; also publ. from six other regional centres; Editor PRAKASH MAHESHWARI; circ. 177,600 (Raipur and Bilaspur).

## Goa

### Panaji

**Gomantak:** Gomantak Bhavan, St Inez, Panaji, Goa 403 001; tel. (832) 2422700; fax (832) 2422701; f. 1962; morning; Marathi and English edns; Editor LAXMAN T. JOSHI; circ. 20,700 (Marathi), 6,200 (English).

**Navhind Times:** Navhind Bhavan, Rua Ismail Gracias, POB 161, Panaji, Goa 403001; tel. (832) 6651111; fax (832) 2224258; e-mail advt@navhindtimes.com; internet www.navhindtimes.com; f. 1963; morning; English; Editor ARUN SINHA; circ. 37,204.

### Panjim

**O Heraldo:** Herald Publications Pvt Ltd, POB 160, Rua St Tome, Panjim 403 001; tel. (832) 2224202; fax (832) 2225622; e-mail editor@ herald-goa.com; internet www.oheraldo.in; f. 1900; English; Editor-in-Chief WALTER D'COSTA; Editor ASHWIN TOMBAT; circ. 47,000.

## Gujarat

### Ahmedabad

**Gujarat Samachar:** Gujarat Samachar Bhavan, Khanpur, Ahmedabad 380 001; tel. (79) 5504010; fax (79) 5502000; e-mail editor@gujaratsamachar.com; f. 1930; morning; Gujarati; also publ. from Surat, Rajkot, Vadodara, Mumbai, London and New York; Editor SHANTIBHAI SHAH; combined circ. 1,051,000.

**Indian Express:** 5th Floor, Sanidhya Bldg, Ashram Rd, Ahmedabad 380 009; tel. (79) 26583023; fax (79) 26575826; e-mail praman@ express2.indexp.co.in; f. 1968; English; also publ. in 10 other towns; Man. Editor VIVEK GOENKA; Chief Editor SHEKHAR GUPTA; circ. (Ahmedabad and Vadodara) 28,200.

**Lokasatta—Janasatta:** Mirzapur Rd, POB 188, Ahmedabad 380 001; tel. (79) 25507307; fax (79) 25507708; f. 1953; morning; Gujarati; also publ. from Rajkot and Vadodara; Man. Editor VIVEK GOENKA; circ. (Ahmedabad) 48,000.

**Sandesh:** Sandesh Bhavan, Lad Society Rd, Ahmedabad 380 054; tel. (79) 40004000; fax (79) 40004121; e-mail advt@sandesh.com; internet www.sandesh.com; f. 1923; Gujarati; also publ. from Bhavnagar, Vadodara, Rajkot and Surat; Editor FALGUNBHAI C. PATEL; combined circ. 743,200.

**The Times of India:** 139 Ashram Rd, POB 4046, Ahmedabad 380 009; tel. (79) 26553300; fax (79) 26583758; f. 1968; English; also publ.

from Mumbai, Delhi, Bangalore, Patna, Kolkata, Chandigarh, Pune, Mangalore and Lucknow; Resident Editor BHARAT DESAI; circ. (Ahmedabad) 129,100.

**Western Times:** Western House, Sudama Resort Bldg, Pritamnagar's First Slope, Ashram Rd, Ahmedabad 380 006; tel. (79) 26576738; fax (79) 26577421; e-mail westerntimes@gmail.com; internet www.westerntimes.co.in; f. 1967; English and Gujarati edns; also publ. (in Gujarati) from eight other towns; Man. Editor NIKUNJ PATEL; Editor RAMU PATEL; total circ. more than 200,000.

Bhuj

**Kutchmitra:** Kutchmitra Bhavan, nr Indirabai Park, Bhuj 370 001; tel. (2832) 252090; fax (2832) 250271; e-mail kutchmitra@yahoo.com; f. 1947; Gujarati; Propr Saurashtra Trust; Editor KIRTI J. KHATRI; circ. 41,241.

Rajkot

**Jai Hind:** Jai Hind Press Bldg, Babubhai Shah Rd, POB 59, Rajkot 360 001; tel. (281) 3048684; fax (281) 2448677; e-mail info@jaihinddaily.com; internet www.jaihinddaily.com; f. 1948; morning and evening (in Rajkot as Sanj Samachar); Gujarati; also publ. from Ahmedabad; Editor Y. N. SHAH; combined circ. 107,300.

**Phulchhab:** Phulchhab Bhavan, Phulchhab Chowk, Rajkot 360 001; tel. (281) 2444611; fax (281) 2448751; f. 1950; morning; Gujarati; Propr Saurashtra Trust; Editor DINESH RAJA; circ. 84,500.

Surat

**Gujaratmitra and Gujaratdarpan:** Gujaratmitra Bhavan, nr Old Civil Hospital, Sonifalia, Surat 395 003; tel. (261) 2599992; fax (261) 2595400; e-mail gujaratmitra@satyam.net.in; f. 1863; morning; Gujarati; Editor B. P. RESHAMWALA; circ. 91,000.

### Haryana

Rohtak

**Bharat Janani:** Sonipat Rd, Rohtak; tel. and fax (1262) 427191; f. 1971; Hindi; morning; Editor Dr R. S. SANTOSHI.

### Himachal Pradesh

Shimla

**Dainik Himachal Sewa:** Hans Kutir, Khalini, Shimla 171 002; tel. (177) 2224119; fax (177) 2260187; f. 1986; Hindi; Editor-in-Chief Dr R. S. SANTOSHI.

**Himachal Times:** Himachal Times Complex, 64–66, The Mall, Shimla 171 001; tel. (177) 2201057; f. 1949; English; Chief Editor VIJAY PANDHI.

### Jammu and Kashmir

Jammu

**Daily Excelsior:** Excelsior House, Excelsior Lane, Janipura, Jammu Tawi 180 007; tel. (191) 2537055; fax (191) 2537831; e-mail editor@dailyexcelsior.com; internet www.dailyexcelsior.com; f. 1965; English; Editor S. D. ROHMETRA.

**Kashmir Times:** Residency Rd, Jammu 180 001; tel. (191) 2543676; fax (191) 2542028; e-mail kashmirtimes@rediffmail.com; internet www.kashmirtimes.com; f. 1955; morning; English and Hindi; Editor PRABODH JAMWAL.

Srinagar

**Greater Kashmir:** 6 Pratap Park, Residency Rd, Srinagar 190 001; tel. (194) 2474339; fax (194) 2477782; e-mail editor@greaterkashmir.com; internet www.greaterkashmir.com; f. 1993; English; Chief Editor FAYAZ AHMED KALOO.

### Jharkhand

Ranchi

**Aj:** Main Rd, Ranchi 834 001; tel. (651) 2311416; fax (651) 2306224; Hindi; morning; also publ. from eight other cities; Editor SHARDUL V. GUPTA; circ. 43,800; combined circ. 930,200.

**Hindustan:** Circular Court, Circular Rd, Ranchi 834 001; tel. (651) 2205811; Hindi; morning; also publ. from Patna, Delhi, Bhagalpur, Lucknow, Varanasi and Muzaffarpur; Editor MRINAL PANDE; combined circ. 753,500.

**Prabhat Khabar:** 15-P, Kokar Industrial Area, Kokar, Ranchi 834 001; tel. (651) 2544002; fax (651) 254405; e-mail pkhabar@ushamartin.co.in; internet www.prabhatkhabar.com; f. 1984; Hindi; also publ. from Dhanbad, Kolkata, Jamshedpur and Patna; Chief Editor H. B. N. SINGH; circ. 123,100 (Ranchi).

**Ranchi Express:** 55 Baralal St, Ranchi 834 001; tel. (651) 2206320; fax (651) 2203466; e-mail rexpress@dte.vsnl.net.in; internet www.ranchiexpress.com; f. 1963; Hindi; morning; Editor AJAY MAROO; circ. 72,400.

### Karnataka

Bangalore

**Deccan Herald:** 75 Mahatma Gandhi Rd, Bangalore 560 001; tel. (80) 25588000; fax (80) 25580523; e-mail ads@deccanherald.co.in; internet www.deccanherald.com; f. 1948; morning; English; also publ. from Hubli-Dharwar, Mangalore and Gulbarga; Editor-in-Chief K. N. SHANTH KUMAR; combined circ. 154,600.

**Kannada Prabha:** Express Bldgs, 1 Queen's Rd, Bangalore 560 001; tel. (80) 22866893; fax (80) 22866617; e-mail bexpress@bgl.vsnl.net.in; internet www.kannadaprabha.com; f. 1967; morning; Kannada; also publ. from Belgaum and Shimoga; Editor Y. N. KRISHNAMURTHY; circ. 60,700.

**New Indian Express:** 1 Queen's Rd, Bangalore 560 001; tel. (80) 22256998; fax (80) 22256617; f. 1965; English; also publ. from Kochi, Hyderabad, Chennai, Madurai, Vijayawada and Vizianagaram; Man. Editor MANOJ KUMAR SONTHALIA; combined circ. 197,400.

**Prajavani:** 75 Mahatma Gandhi Rd, Bangalore 560 001; tel. (80) 25588999; fax (80) 25586443; e-mail ads@deccanherald.co.in; internet www.prajavani.net; f. 1948; morning; Kannada; also publ. from Hubli-Dharwar and Gulbarga; Editor-in-Chief K. N. SHANTH KUMAR; combined circ. 309,500.

Hubli-Dharwar

**Samyukta Karnataka:** Koppikar Rd, Hubli 580 020; tel. (836) 2364303; fax (836) 2362760; e-mail skhubli@gmail.com; internet www.samyuktakarnataka.com; f. 1933; Kannada; also publ. from Bangalore, Davangere, Gulburga and Mangalore; Editor MANOJ PATIL; combined circ. 130,823.

**Vijay Karnataka:** Giriraj Annexe, Circuit House Rd, Hubli 580 029; tel. (836) 2237556; fax (836) 2253630; e-mail hubli@vkmktg.com; f. 1999; Kannada; also publ. from Bangalore, Gangavati, Gulbarga, Mangalore, Mysore, Bagalkot, Chitradurga and Shimoga; Printer and Publr VIJAY SANKESHWAR; combined circ. 576,071.

Manipal

**Udayavani:** Udayavani Bldg, Press Corner, Manipal 576 104; tel. (820) 2570845; fax (820) 2570563; e-mail udayavani@manipalpress.com; internet www.udayavani.com; f. 1970; Kannada; also publ. from Manipal-Udupi and Mumbai; Editor T. SATISH U. PAI; Regional Editors N. GURAJ (Manipal), R. POORNIMA (Bangalore), T. SATISH (Mumbai); circ. 198,233.

### Kerala

Kottayam

**Deepika:** POB 7, Kottayam 686 001; tel. (481) 2566706; fax (481) 2567947; e-mail deepika@deepika.com; internet www.deepika.com; f. 1887; Malayalam; independent; also publ. from Kannur, Kochi, Kozhikode, Thiruvananthapuram and Thrissur; Man. Dir JOSE T. PATTARA; Chief Editor JOSE PANTHAPLAMTHOTTIYIL; combined circ. 251,000.

**Malayala Manorama:** K. K. Rd, POB 26, Kottayam 686 001; tel. (481) 2563646; fax (481) 2562479; e-mail editor@malayalamanorama.com; internet www.manoramaonline.com; f. 1890; Malayalam; also publ. from 16 other regional centres; morning; Man. Dir and Editor MAMMEN MATHEW; Chief Editor K. M. MATHEW; combined circ. 1,589,823.

Kozhikode

**Deshabhimani:** 11/127 Convent Rd, Kozhikode 673 032; tel. (495) 2365286; fax (495) 2365883; f. 1946; Malayalam; morning; publ. by the CPI—M; also publ. from Kochi, Kottayam, Thrissur and Thiruvananthapuram; Chief Editor S. RAMACHANDRAN PILLAI; combined circ. 266,400.

**Mathrubhumi:** Mathrubhumi Bldgs, K. P. Kesava Menon Rd, POB 46, Kozhikode 673 001; tel. (495) 2366655; fax (495) 2366656; e-mail mathrelt@md2.vsnl.net.in; internet www.mathrubhumi.com; f. 1923; Malayalam; also publ. from Thiruvananthapuram, Kannur, Thrissur, Kollam, Malappuram, Kottayam, Kochi, Bangalore, Chennai and Mumbai; Editor R. GOPALAKRISHNAN; combined circ. 910,000.

Thiruvananthapuram

**Kerala Kaumudi:** POB 77, Pettah, Thiruvananthapuram 695 024; tel. (471) 2461010; fax (471) 2461985; e-mail editor@kaumudi.com; internet www.keralakaumudi.com; f. 1911; Malayalam; also publ. from Kollam, Alappuzha, Kochi, Kannur, Kozhikode and Bangalore; Editor-in-Chief M. S. MANI; Man. Editor DEEPU RAVI; combined circ. 147,126.

**Vikshanam:** Thiruvananthapuram; f. 2005; Malayalam; publ. by Kerala Congress.

### Madhya Pradesh

Bhopal

**Dainik Bhaskar:** 6 Press Complex, M. P. Nagar, Bhopal; tel. (755) 39888840; fax (755) 5270333; e-mail md.office@bhaskarnet.com; internet www.bhaskar.com; f. 1958; morning; Hindi; also publ. from 18 other regional centres; Chief Editor R. C. Agarwal; combined circ. 3,715,465.

Indore

**Naidunia:** 60/1 Babu Labhchand Chhajlani Marg, Indore 452 009; tel. (731) 2763111; fax (731) 2763120; e-mail editor@naidunia.com; internet www.naidunia.com; f. 1947; morning; Hindi; Editor Abhay Chhajlani; circ. 145,600.

### Maharashtra

Kolhapur

**Pudhari:** 2318, 'C' Ward, Kolhapur 416 002; tel. (231) 222251; fax (231) 222256; internet www.pudhari.com; f. 1974; Marathi; Editor P. G. Jadhav; circ. 211,200.

Mumbai (Bombay)

**Afternoon Courier:** 6 Nanabhai Lane, Fort, Mumbai 400 001; tel. (22) 22871616; fax (22) 22870371; e-mail aftnet@bom2.vsnl.net.in; internet www.cybernoon.com; evening; English; Editor Mark Manuel Hubert; circ. 65,800.

**Bombay Samachar:** Red House, Syed Abdulla Brelvi Rd, Fort, Mumbai 400 001; tel. (22) 22045501; fax (22) 22046642; e-mail samachar@vsnl.com; f. 1822; morning and Sunday; Gujarati; political, social and commercial; Editor Pinky Dalal (acting); circ. 107,300.

**Daily News and Analysis (DNA):** Lower Parel, Mumbai; f. 2005; English; also publ. from Delhi, Chennai, Bangalore, Hyderabad and Kolkata; Chief Editor Gautam Adhikari.

**Dainik Saamana:** Sadguru Darshan, Nagu Sayaji Wadi, Dainik Saamana Marg, Prabhadevi, Mumbai 400 028; tel. (22) 24370591; fax (22) 24316590; f. 1989; Marathi; Exec. Editor Sanjay Raut; circ. 102,900.

**The Economic Times:** Times of India Bldg, Dr Dadabhai Naoroji Rd, Mumbai 400 001; tel. (22) 22733535; fax (22) 22731344; e-mail etbom@timesgroup.com; internet www.economictimes.com; f. 1961; also publ. from New Delhi, Kolkata, Ahmedabad, Hyderabad, Chennai and Bangalore; English; Editor (Mumbai) Sudeshna Sen; combined circ. 461,900, circ. (Mumbai) 140,200.

**Financial Express:** Express Towers, Nariman Point, Mumbai 400 021; tel. (22) 22022627; fax (22) 22022139; e-mail iemumbai@express .indexp.co.in; internet www.financialexpress.com; f. 1961; morning; English; also publ. from New Delhi, Bangalore, Kolkata, Coimbatore, Kochi, Ahmedabad (Gujarati) and Chennai; Man. Editor Vivek Goenka; Editor Mythili Bhusnurmath; combined circ. (English) 50,000.

**The Free Press Journal:** Free Press House, 215 Free Press Journal Rd, Nariman Point, Mumbai 400 021; tel. (22) 22874566; fax (22) 22874688; e-mail fpj@vsnl.com; f. 1930; English; also publ. from Indore; Man. Editor G. L. Lakhotia; combined circ. 87,000.

**Hindustan Times:** 220–230, Mhatre Pen Building Complex, 'B' Wing, 2nd Floor, Senapati Bapat Marg, Dadar (W), Mumbai 400 028; tel. (22) 24368012; fax (22) 24303625; e-mail feedback@ hindustantimes.com; internet www.hindustantimes.com/mumbai; f. 1923; also publ. from Delhi, Lucknow, Bhopal and Chandigarh; Editor Shekhar Bhatia; combined circ. 1,142,600.

**Indian Express:** 3/50, Lalbaug Industrial Estate, Dr B. Ambedkar Marg, Lalbaug, Mumbai 400 012; tel. (22) 24717600; fax (22) 24717636; f. 1940; English; also publ. from Pune and Nagpur; Man. Editor Vivek Goenka; Chief Editor Shekhar Gupta; combined circ. 191,900.

**Inquilab:** 156 D. J. Dadajee Rd, Tardeo, Mumbai 400 034; tel. (22) 24942586; fax (22) 24936571; e-mail azizk@mid-day.mailserve.net; internet www.inquilab.com; f. 1938; morning; Urdu; Editor Fuzail Jafferey; circ. 35,600.

**Janmabhoomi:** Janmabhoomi Bhavan, Janmabhoomi Marg, Fort, POB 62, Mumbai 400 001; tel. (22) 22870831; fax (22) 22874097; e-mail bhoomi@bom3.vsnl.net.in; f. 1934; evening; Gujarati; Propr Saurashtra Trust; Editor Kundan Vyas; circ. 55,395.

**Lokasatta:** 3/50, Lalbaug Industrial Estate, Dr B. Ambedkar, Lalbaug, Mumbai 400 012; tel. (22) 24717677; fax (22) 24717654; internet www.loksatta.com; f. 1948; morning (incl. Sunday); Marathi; also publ. from Pune, Nagpur and Ahmednagar; Editor Kumar Ketkar; combined circ. 369,400.

**Maharashtra Times:** Dr Dadabhai Naoroji Rd, POB 213, Mumbai 400 001; tel. (22) 22353535; fax (22) 22731175; f. 1962; Marathi; Editor Bharat Kumar Raut; circ. 247,100.

**Mid-Day:** 64 Sitaram Mills Compound, N. M. Joshi Marg, Lower Parel, Mumbai 400 011; tel. (22) 23054545; fax (22) 23054861; e-mail mid-day@giasbm01.vsnl.net.in; internet www.mid-day.com; f. 1979; daily and Sunday; English; Editor Akar Patel; circ. 136,000.

**Mumbai Mirror:** Mumbai; tel. (22) 26005555; e-mail mumbai .mirror@timesgroup.com; internet www.mumbaimirror.com; f. 2005; English; Editor Meenal Baghel.

**Navakal:** 13 Shenviwadi, Khadilkar Rd, Girgaun, Mumbai 400 004; tel. (22) 23860978; fax (22) 23860989; f. 1923; Marathi; Editor N. Y. Khadilkar; circ. 139,800.

**Navbharat Times:** Dr Dadabhai Naoroji Rd, Mumbai 400 001; tel. (22) 22733535; fax (22) 22731144; f. 1950; Hindi; also publ. from New Delhi, Jaipur, Patna and Lucknow; Chief Editor Vishwanath Sachdev; circ. (Mumbai) 142,100.

**Navshakti:** Free Press House, 215 Nariman Point, Mumbai 400 021; tel. (22) 22874566; fax (22) 22874688; f. 1932; Marathi; Chief Editor Prakash Kulkarni; circ. 65,000.

**Sakal:** Sakal Bhavan, Plot No. 42-B, Sector No. 11, CBD Belapur, Navi Mumbai 400 614; tel. (22) 27572916; fax (22) 27574280; e-mail sakal@vsnl.in; f. 1970; Marathi; also publ. from Pune, Aurangabad, Nasik, Kolhapur and Solapur; Chief Editor Sanjeev Latkar; combined circ. 667,500.

**The Times of India:** The Times of India Bldg, Dr Dadabhai Naoroji Rd, Mumbai 400 001; tel. (22) 56353535; fax (22) 22731444; e-mail toieditorial@timesgroup.com; internet www.timesofindia.com; f. 1838; morning; English; also publ. from 10 regional centres; Exec. Editor Arindam Sengupta; circ. (Mumbai) 545,600, combined circ. 2,214,700.

Nagpur

**The Hitavada:** Pandit Jawaharlal Nehru Marg, POB 201, Nagpur 440 012; tel. (712) 2523155; fax (712) 2535093; e-mail hitavada_ngp@ sancharnet.in; f. 1911; morning; English; also publ. from Raipur and Jabalpur; Man. Editor Banwarilal Purohit; Editor V. Phanshikar; circ. 60,700.

**Lokmat:** Lokmat Bhavan, Wardha Rd, Nagpur 440 012; tel. (712) 2523527; fax (712) 2526923; internet onlinenews.lokmat.com; also publ. from Jalgaon, Pune and Nasik; Marathi; Lokmat Samachar (Hindi) publ. from Nagpur, Akola and Aurangabad; Lokmat Times (English) publ. from Nagpur and Aurangabad; Editor Vijay Darda; combined circ. (Marathi) 436,800, (Hindi) 62,300.

**Nava Bharat:** Nava Bharat Bhavan, Cotton Market, Nagpur 440 018; tel. (712) 2726677; fax (712) 2723444; f. 1938; morning; Hindi; also publ. from 10 other cities; Editor-in-Chief R. G. Maheswari; combined circ. 640,400.

**Tarun Bharat:** 28 Farmland, Ramdaspeth, Nagpur 440 010; tel. (712) 2525052; fax (712) 2531758; e-mail ibharat_ngp@sancharnet .in; internet www.tarunbharat.net; f. 1941; Marathi; independent; also publ. from Belgaum; Man. Editor Anil Dandekar; Chief Editor Sudhir Pathak; circ. (Nagpur) 58,200.

Pune

**Kesari:** 568 Narayan Peth, Pune 411 030; tel. (20) 4459250; fax (20) 4451677; f. 1881; Marathi; also publ. from Solapur, Chiplun, Ahmednagar and Sangli; Editor Arvind Vyankatesh Gokhale; circ. (Pune) 42,600.

**Sakal:** 595 Budhawar Peth, Pune 411 002; tel. (20) 24455500; fax (20) 24450583; e-mail sakal@giaspn01.vsnl.net.in; internet www.esakal .com; f. 1932; daily; Marathi; also publ. from 10 other regional centres; Editor Yamaji Malkar (Pune); Man. Editor Pratap Pawar; combined circ. 830,654.

### Meghalaya

Shillong

**The Shillong Times:** Rilbong, Shillong 793 004; tel. (364) 2223488; fax (364) 2229488; e-mail shillongtimes@yahoo.com; f. 1945; English; Editor Manas Chaudhuri; circ. 28,700.

### Orissa

Bhubaneswar

**Dharitri:** B-26, Industrial Estate, Bhubaneswar 751 010; tel. (674) 2580101; fax (674) 2580795; e-mail advt@dharitri.com; internet www .dharitri.com; evening and morning; Oriya; Editor Tathagata Satpathy; circ. 175,100.

**Pragativadi:** 178-B, Mancheswar Industrial Estate, Bhubaneswar 751 010; tel. (674) 2588297; fax (674) 2582709; e-mail pragativadi@ yahoo.com; internet www.pragativadi.com; f. 1973; Exec. Editor Samahit Bal; circ. 182,089.

**The Samaya:** Plot No. 44 and 54, Sector A, Zone D, Mancheswar Industrial Estate, Bhubaneswar 751 017; tel. (674) 2583690; fax (674) 2582565; e-mail samayabbsr@usanet.com; internet www.thesamaya.com; f. 1966; Oriya; Editor SATAKADI HOTA; circ. 134,400.

**Sambad:** Eastern Media Ltd, A-62, Nayapalli, Bhubaneswar 751 003; tel. (674) 2561198; fax (674) 2562914; e-mail sambad00@rediffmail.com; internet www.orissasambad.com; f. 1984; Oriya; also publ. from seven other regional centres; Editor S. R. PATNAIK; combined circ. 213,600.

Cuttack

**Prajatantra:** Prajatantra Bldg, Behari Bag, Cuttack 753 002; tel. (671) 2608071; fax (671) 2607111; f. 1947; Oriya; Editor GOVINDA DAS; circ. 113,824.

**Samaja:** Gopabandhu Bhavan, Buxibazar, Cuttack 753 001; tel. (671) 2301598; fax (671) 2301384; e-mail samajactc@hotmail.com; internet www.thesamaja.com; f. 1919; Oriya; also publ. from Sambalpur, Vizag, Bhubaneswar, Rourkela and Kolkata; Editor MANORAMA MAHAPATRA; circ. 170,700.

### The Punjab

Chandigarh

**The Tribune:** Sector 29C, Chandigarh 160 020; tel. (172) 2655066; fax (172) 2651293; e-mail tribunet@ch1.dot.net.in; internet www.tribuneindia.com; f. 1881 (English edn), f. 1978 (Hindi and Punjabi edns); Editor-in-Chief H. K. DUA; Editor (Hindi edn) VIJAY SAIGHAL; Editor (Punjabi edn) G. S. BHULLAR; circ. 220,500 (English), 40,300 (Hindi), 66,200 (Punjabi).

Jalandhar

**Ajit:** Ajit Bhavan, Nehru Garden Rd, Jalandhar 144 001; tel. (181) 22800960; f. 1955; Punjabi; Man. Editor S. BARJINDER SINGH; CEO SARVINDER KAUR; circ. 369,474.

**Hind Samachar:** Civil Lines, Jalandhar 144 001; tel. (181) 2280104; fax (181) 2280113; e-mail punjabkesari@vsnl.com; f. 1948; morning; Hindi; also publ. from Ambala Cantt and Jammu; Editor-in-Chief VIJAY KUMAR CHOPRA; Jt Editor AVINASH CHOPRA; combined circ. 30,041.

**Jag Bani:** Civil Lines, Jalandhar 144 001; tel. (181) 2280104; fax (181) 2280113; e-mail punjabkesari@vsnl.com; f. 1978; morning; Punjabi; also publ. from Ludhiana; Editor-in-Chief VIJAY KUMAR CHOPRA; Jt Editor AVINASH CHOPRA; circ. 298,883.

**Punjab Kesari:** Civil Lines, Jalandhar 144 001; tel. (181) 2280104; fax (181) 2280113; e-mail punjabkesari@vsnl.com; f. 1965; morning; Hindi; also publ. from Ludhiana, Ambala, Panipat, Hisar, Palampur and Jammu; Editor-in-Chief VIJAY KUMAR CHOPRA; Jt Editor AVINASH CHOPRA; combined circ. 592,541.

### Rajasthan

Jaipur

**Rajasthan Patrika:** Kesargarh, Jawaharlal Nehru Marg, Jaipur 302 004; tel. (141) 2561582; fax (141) 2566011; e-mail info@rajasthanpatrika.com; internet www.rajasthanpatrika.com; f. 1956; Hindi edn also publ. from 17 other towns; Chief Editor GULAB KOTHARI; combined circ. 732,800 (Hindi).

**Rashtradoot:** M.I. Rd, POB 30, Jaipur 302 001; tel. (141) 2372634; fax (141) 2373513; f. 1951; Hindi; also publ. from Kota, Udaipur, Ajmer, Bikaner and Jalore; CEO SOMESH SHARMA; Chief Editor RAJESH SHARMA; circ. 200,672 (Jaipur), 90,936 (Kota), 49,402 (Bikaner), 62,375 (Udaipur), 53,851 (Ajmer), 62,547 (Jalore).

### Tamil Nadu

Chennai (Madras)

**Daily Thanthi:** 86 E.V.K. Sampath Rd, POB 467, Chennai 600 007; tel. (44) 26618661; fax (44) 26618676; f. 1942; Tamil; also publ. from 13 other regional centres; Gen. Man. R. CHANDRASEKARAN; Editor V. SUNDARESON; combined circ. 817,194.

**Dinakaran:** 229 Kutchery Rd, Mylapore, POB 358, Chennai 600 004; tel. (44) 24641006; fax (44) 24951008; e-mail murasu@dishdsl.net; internet www.dinakaran.com; f. 1977; Tamil; also publ. from Madurai, Tiruchirapalli, Vellore, Tirunelveli, Salem, Coimbatore and Puducherry (Pondicherry); Man. Dir KALANIDHI MARAN; Editor R. M. R. RAMESH; combined circ. 351,872.

**Dinamalar:** 8 Casa Major Rd, Egmore, Chennai 600 008; tel. (44) 28195000; fax (44) 28195003; e-mail demregr@dinamalar.com; internet www.dinamalar.com; f. 1951; Tamil; also publ. from 10 other towns; Editor Dr R. KRISHNAMURTHY; combined circ. 582,958.

**Dinamani:** Express Estates, Mount Rd, Chennai 600 002; tel. (44) 8520751; fax (44) 8524500; e-mail express@giasmd01.vsnl.net.in; internet www.dinamani.com; f. 1934; morning; Tamil; also publ. from Madurai, Coimbatore and Bangalore; Editor T. SAMBANDAM; combined circ. 136,300.

**Financial Express:** Vasanthi Medical Center, 30/20 Pycrofts Garden Rd, Chennai 600 006; tel. (44) 28231112; fax (44) 28231489; internet www.financialexpress.com; f. 1961; morning; English; also publ. from Mumbai, Ahmedabad (in Gujarati), Bangalore, Kochi, Kolkata and New Delhi; Man. Editor VIVEK GOENKA; combined circ. 32,594.

**The Hindu:** Kasturi Bldgs, 859/860 Anna Salai, Chennai 600 002; tel. (44) 28413344; fax (44) 28415325; e-mail wsvcs@thehindu.co.in; internet www.hinduonnet.com; f. 1878; morning; English; independent; also publ. from 11 other regional centres; Editor-in-Chief N. RAM; combined circ. 981,600.

**The Hindu Business Line:** Kasturi Bldgs, 859/860 Anna Salai, Chennai 600 002; tel. (44) 28589060; fax (44) 28545703; e-mail bleditor@thehindu.co.in; internet www.blonnet.com; f. 1994; morning; English; also publ. from 11 other regional centres; Editor-in-Chief N. RAM; combined circ. 56,100.

**Murasoli:** 93 Kodambakkam High Rd, Chennai 600 034; tel. (44) 28270044; fax (44) 28217515; f. 1960; organ of the DMK; Tamil; Editor S. SELVAM; circ. 54,000.

**New Indian Express:** Club House Rd, Chennai 600 002; tel. (44) 28461260; fax (44) 28461829; e-mail newexpress@vsnl.com; internet www.newindpress.com; f. 1932 as Indian Express; morning; English; also publ. from 11 other cities; Chair. and Man. Dir MANOJ KUMAR SONTHALIA; combined circ. 197,400.

### Tripura

Agartala

**Dainik Sambad:** 11 Jagannath Bari Rd, POB 2, Agartala 799 001; tel. (381) 2326676; fax (381) 2324845; e-mail dainik2@sanchar.net.in; f. 1966; Bengali; morning; Editor BHUPENDRA CHANDRA DATTA BHAUMIK; circ. 49,000.

### Uttarakhand

Dehradun

**Amar Ujala:** Shed 2, Patel Nagar Industrial Estate, Dehradun 248 003; tel. (135) 2720378; fax (135) 2721776; internet www.amarujala.com; Hindi; morning; also publ. from 10 other cities; Editor AJAY K. AGRAWAL; combined circ. 630,100.

### Uttar Pradesh

Agra

**Amar Ujala:** Sikandra Rd, Agra 282 007; tel. (562) 2321600; fax (562) 2322181; e-mail amarujal@nde.vsnl.net.in; internet www.amarujala.com; f. 1948; Hindi; also publ. from Bareilly, Allahabad, Jhansi, Kanpur, Moradabad, Chandigarh and Meerut; Editor AJAY K. AGARWAL; combined circ. 630,100.

Allahabad

**Amrita Prabhat:** 10 Tashkent Marg, Allahabad 211 001; tel. (532) 2600654; fax (532) 2605394; f. 1977; Hindi; CEO S. S. BAGGA; circ. 44,000.

**Northern India Patrika:** 10 Edmonstone Rd, Allahabad 211 001; tel. (532) 2600654; fax (532) 2605394; f. 1959; English; CEO S. S. BAGGA; circ. 46,000.

Kanpur

**Dainik Jagran:** Jagran Bldg, 2 Sarvodaya Nagar, Kanpur 208 005; tel. (512) 2216161; fax (512) 2216972; e-mail jpl@jagran.com; internet www.jagran.com; f. 1942; Hindi; also publ. from 25 other cities; Man. Editor MAHENDRA MOHAN GUPTA; Editor SANJAY GUPTA; combined circ. 2,600,000.

Lucknow

**National Herald:** Lucknow; f. 1938 Lucknow, 1968 Delhi; English; Editor-in-Chief D. V. VENKITACHALAM.

**The Pioneer:** Sahara Shopping Centre, Faizabad Rd, Lucknow 226 016; tel. (522) 2346444; fax (522) 2345582; f. 1865; English; also publ. from New Delhi; Editor CHANDAN MITRA; combined circ. 136,000.

**Swatantra Bharat:** 1st Floor, Suraj Deep Complex, 1 Jopling Rd, Lucknow 226 001; tel. (522) 2204306; fax (522) 2208701; e-mail sbharats@satyam.net.in; f. 1947; Hindi; also publ. from Kanpur; Editor K. K. SRIVASTAVA; circ. 80,700 (Lucknow), 65,157 (Kanpur).

Varanasi

**Aj:** Aj Bhavan, Sant Kabir Rd, Kabirchaura, Varanasi 221 001; tel. (542) 2393981; fax (542) 2393989; f. 1920; Hindi; also publ. from Gorakhpur, Patna, Allahabad, Ranchi, Agra, Bareilly, Lucknow,

Jamshedpur, Dhanbad and Kanpur; Editor SHARDUL VIKRAM GUPTA; combined circ. 930,200.

### West Bengal

Kolkata (Calcutta)

**Aajkaal:** 96 Raja Rammohan Sarani, Kolkata 700 009; tel. (33) 23509803; fax (33) 23500877; e-mail aajkaal@cal.vsnl.net.in; f. 1981; morning; Bengali; also publ. from Agartala and Siliguri; Chief Editor PRATAP K. ROY; circ. 140,100.

**Ananda Bazar Patrika:** 6 Prafulla Sarkar St, Kolkata 700 001; tel. (33) 22374880; fax (33) 22253241; internet www.anandabazar.com; f. 1922; morning; Bengali; also publ. from Baharampore and Siliguri; Editor AVEEK SARKAR; circ. 950,400.

**Bartaman:** 76A A. J. C. Bose Rd, Kolkata 700 014; tel. (33) 22443907; fax (33) 22441215; internet www.bartamanpatrika.com; f. 1984; also publ. from Barddhaman and Siliguri; Editor BARUN SENGUPTA; circ. 427,100.

**Business Standard:** 4/1 Red Cross Place, Kolkata 700 001; tel. (33) 22101314; fax (33) 22101599; f. 1975; morning; also publ. from New Delhi, Ahmedabad, Hyderabad, Bangalore, Chennai and Mumbai; English; Editor T. N. NINAN; combined circ. 60,000.

**The Economic Times:** 105/7A, S. N. Banerjee Rd, Kolkata 700 014; tel. (33) 22444243; fax (33) 22453018; English; also publ. from Ahmedabad, Delhi, Bangalore, Chennai, Hyderabad and Mumbai; circ. (Kolkata) 54,300.

**Financial Express:** 83 B. K. Pal Ave, Kolkata 700 005; morning; English; also publ. from Mumbai, Ahmedabad, Bangalore, Coimbatore, Kochi, Chennai and New Delhi; Man. Editor VIVEK GOENKA; combined circ. 30,800.

**Ganashakti:** 74A A. J. C. Bose Rd, Kolkata 700 016; tel. (33) 22278950; fax (33) 2278090; e-mail mail@ganashakti.co.in; internet www.ganashakti.com; f. 1967; owned by Communist Party of India (Marxist), West Bengal State Cttee; morning; Bengali; also publ. from Durgapur and Siliguri; Editor NARAYAN DATTA; circ. 167,320.

**Sandhya Aajkaal:** 96 Raja Rammohan Sarani, Kolkata 700 009; tel. (33) 23509803; fax (33) 23500877; evening; Bengali; Chief Editor PRATAP K. ROY; circ. 17,400.

**Sangbad Pratidin:** 20 Prafulla Sarkar St, Kolkata 700 072; tel. (33) 22128400; fax (33) 22126031; e-mail pratidin@cal2.vsnl.net.in; internet www.sangbadpratidin.com; morning; Bengali; also publ. from Ranchi and Siliguri; Editor SWAPAN SADHAN BASU; circ. 278,700.

**Sanmarg:** 160B Chittaranjan Ave, Kolkata 700 007; tel. (33) 22414800; fax (33) 22415087; e-mail sanmarg@satyam.net.in; f. 1948; Hindi; Editor RAMAWATAR GUPTA; circ. 107,700.

**The Statesman:** Statesman House, 4 Chowringhee Sq., Kolkata 700 001; tel. (33) 22127070; fax (33) 22126181; e-mail thestatesman@vsnl.com; internet www.thestatesman.net; f. 1875; morning; English; independent; also publ. from New Delhi, Siliguri and Bhubaneswar; Editor RAVINDRA KUMAR; combined circ. 174,300.

**The Telegraph:** 6 Prafulla Sarkar St, Kolkata 700 001; tel. (33) 22374880; fax (33) 22253240; e-mail thetelegraphindia@newscom.com; f. 1982; English; also publ. from Guwahati, Jamshedpur and Siliguri; Editor AVEEK SARKAR; circ. 325,100.

**Uttar Banga Sambad:** 7 Old Court House St, Kolkata 700 001; tel. (33) 22435663; fax (33) 22435618; e-mail uttarmail@sify.com; internet www.uttarbangasambad.com; f. 1980; Bengali; Editor S. C. TALUKDAR; circ. 134,209.

**Vishwamitra:** 74 Lenin Sarani, Kolkata 700 013; tel. (33) 22651139; fax (33) 22656393; e-mail vismtra@vsnl.com; f. 1915; morning; Hindi; commercial; Editor PRAKASH CHANDRA AGRAWALLA; circ. 77,727.

## SELECTED PERIODICALS

### Delhi and New Delhi

**Alive:** Delhi Press Bldg, E-3 Jhandewala Estate, Rani Jhansi Rd, New Delhi 110 055; tel. (11) 41398888; fax (11) 41540714; e-mail editorial@delhipressgroup.com; internet www.grihshobaindia.com; f. 1940 as Caravan; monthly; English; men's interests; Editor, Publr and Printer PARESH NATH; circ. 10,000.

**Bal Bharati:** Patiala House, Publications Division, Ministry of Information and Broadcasting, New Delhi; tel. (11) 2387038; f. 1948; monthly; Hindi; for children; Editor SHIV KUMAR; circ. 30,000.

**Biswin Sadi:** B-1, Nizamuddin West, New Delhi 110 013; tel. (11) 24626556; f. 1937; monthly; Urdu; Editor Z. REHMAN NAYYAR; circ. 32,000.

**Business Today:** Videocon Towers, E-1 Jhandelwalan Extn, New Delhi 110 055; tel. (11) 23684893; fax (11) 23684819; e-mail btoday@giasdl01.vsnl.net.in; internet www.business-today.com; fortnightly; English; Editor SANJAY NARAYAN; circ. 124,600.

**Catholic India:** CBCI Centre, 1 Ashok Place, Goldakkhana, New Delhi 110 001; tel. (11) 23344470; fax (11) 23364615; e-mail cbci@vsnl.com; internet www.cbcisite.com; quarterly.

**Champak:** Delhi Press Bldg, E-3 Jhandewala Estate, Rani Jhansi Rd, New Delhi 110 055; tel. (11) 41398888; fax (11) 41540714; e-mail editorial@delhipressgroup.com; internet www.grihshobaindia.com; f. 1968; fortnightly (Hindi, English, Gujarati, Tamil, Telugu, Malayalam, Marathi and Kannada edns); children's; Editor, Publr and Printer PARESH NATH; circ. 77,000 (Hindi), 32,089 (English), 17,000 (Marathi), 20,000 (Gujarati), 10,000 (Malayalam), 3,664 (Telugu), 2,153 (Tamil), 10,000 (Kannada).

**Children's World:** Nehru House, 4 Bahadur Shah Zafar Marg, New Delhi 110 002; tel. (11) 23316970; fax (11) 23721090; e-mail cbtnd@vsnl.com; internet www.childrensbooktrust.com; f. 1968; monthly; English; Editor NAVIN MENON; circ. 25,000.

**Competition Refresher:** 2767, Bright House, Daryaganj, New Delhi 110 002; tel. (11) 23282226; fax (11) 23269227; e-mail psbright@ndf.vsnl.net.in; internet www.brightcareers.com; f. 1984; monthly; English; Chief Editor, Publr and Man. Dir PRITAM SINGH BRIGHT; circ. 175,000.

**Competition Success Review:** 604 Prabhat Kiran Bldg, Rajendra Place, Delhi 110 008; tel. (11) 25712898; fax (11) 25754647; e-mail csrindia@mantraonline.com; monthly; English; f. 1964; Editor S. K. SACHDEVA; circ. 247,400.

**Computers Today:** Marina Arcade, G-59 Connaught Circus, New Delhi 110 001; tel. (11) 23736233; fax (11) 23725506; e-mail ctoday@india-today.com; f. 1984; Editor J. SRIHARI RAJU; circ. 46,300.

**Cosmopolitan:** 5th Floor, Videocon Tower, E-1 Jhandewalan Extn, New Delhi 110 055; tel. (11) 23684800; e-mail cathy.cosmo@intoday.com; monthly; English; women's lifestyle; Editor PAYAL KOHLI.

**Cricket Samrat:** L-1, Kanchan House, Najafgarh Rd, Commercial Complex, nr Milan Cinema, New Delhi 110 015; tel. (11) 25191175; fax (11) 25469581; f. 1978; monthly; Hindi; Editor ANAND DEWAN; circ. 64,000.

**Employment News:** Government of India, East Block IV, Level 5, R. K. Puram, New Delhi 110 066; tel. (11) 26174975; fax (11) 26105875; e-mail empnews@bol.net.in; f. 1976; weekly; Hindi, Urdu and English edns; Gen. Man. and Chief Editor VISHWANATH RAMESH; Editor RANJANA DEV SARMAH; combined circ. 550,000.

**Filmi Duniya:** 16 Darya Ganj, New Delhi 110 002; tel. (11) 23278087; fax (11) 23279341; f. 1958; monthly; Hindi; Chief Editor NARENDRA KUMAR; circ. 132,100.

**Filmi Kaliyan:** 4675-B/21 Ansari Rd, New Delhi 110 002; tel. (11) 23272080; f. 1969; monthly; Hindi; cinema; Editor-in-Chief V. S. DEWAN; circ. 82,400.

**Global Travel Express:** 26F Rajiv Gandhi Chowk (Connaught Place), New Delhi 110 001; tel. (11) 23312329; fax (11) 24621636; e-mail indian_observer@hotmail.com; f. 1993; monthly; English; travel and tourism; Chief Editor HARBHAJAN SINGH; Editor GURINDER SINGH; circ. 28,902.

**Grihshobha:** Delhi Press Bldg, E-3 Jhandewala Estate, Rani Jhansi Rd, New Delhi 110 055; tel. (11) 41398888; fax (11) 41540714; e-mail editorial@delhipressgroup.com; internet www.grihshobaindia.com; f. 1979; fortnightly Hindi and Bangla edns; monthly Tamil, Telugu, Kannada, Marathi, Malayalam and Gujarati edns; women's interests; Editor, Publr and Printer PARESH NATH; circ. 80,000 (Kannada), 46,355 (Gujarati), 105,096 (Marathi), 364,096 (Hindi), 28,000 (Telugu), 32,000 (Tamil), 35,000 (Malayalam), 10,000 (Bangla).

**India Perspectives:** Room 149B, 'A' Wing, Shastri Bhavan, New Delhi 110 001; tel. (11) 23389471; f. 1988; Editor BHARAT BHUSHAN.

**India Today:** F-14/15, Connaught Place, New Delhi 110 001; tel. (11) 23315801; fax (11) 23316180; e-mail ratnam@intoday.com; internet www.india-today.com; f. 1975; English, Tamil, Telugu, Malayalam and Hindi; weekly; Editor PRABHU CHAWLA; Editor-in-Chief AROON PURIE; circ. 463,800 (English), 353,700 (Hindi), 65,300 (Tamil), 42,900 (Malayalam), 56,800 (Telugu).

**Indian Railways:** 411 Rail Bhavan, Raisina Rd, New Delhi 110 001; tel. (11) 23383540; fax (11) 23383540; e-mail kalyanimr@rediffmail.com; f. 1956; monthly; English; publ. by the Ministry of Railways (Railway Board); Editor M. R. KALYANI; circ. 12,000.

**Journal of Industry and Trade:** Ministry of Commerce, Delhi 110 011; tel. (11) 23016664; f. 1952; monthly; English; Man. Dir A. C. BANERJEE; circ. 2,000.

**Junior Science Refresher:** 2769, Bright House, Daryaganj, New Delhi 110 002; tel. (11) 23282226; fax (11) 23269227; e-mail psbright@ndf.vsnl.net.in; internet www.brightcareers.com; f. 1987; monthly; English; Chief Editor, Publr and Man. Dir PRITAM SINGH BRIGHT; circ. 118,000.

**Kadambini:** Hindustan Times House, Kasturba Gandhi Marg, New Delhi 110 001; tel. and fax (11) 55561605; e-mail vnagar@hindustantimes.com; f. 1960; monthly; Hindi; Editor MRINAL PANDE; Exec. Editor VISHNU NAGAR; circ. 120,000.

**Krishak Samachar:** Bharat Krishak Samaj, Dr Panjabrao Deshmukh Krishak Bhavan, A-1 Nizamuddin West, New Delhi 110 013; tel. (11) 24619508; e-mail ffi@mantraonline.com; f. 1957; monthly; English and Hindi edns; agriculture; Editor Dr KRISHAN BIR CHAUDHARY; circ. 6,000 (English), 17,000 (Hindi).

**Kurukshetra:** Ministry of Rural Development, Room No. 655/661, 'A' Wing, Nirman Bhavan, New Delhi 110 011; tel. (11) 23015014; fax (11) 23386879; monthly; English; rural development; Editor KAPIL KUMAR; circ. 19,000.

**Mainstream:** 145/1D Shahpur Jat, 1st Floor, nr Asiad Village, New Delhi 110 049; tel. (11) 26497188; fax (11) 26569352; e-mail mnstrm@nda.vsnl.net.in; internet www.mainstreamweekly.com; English; weekly; politics and current affairs; Editor SUMIT CHAKRAVARTTY.

**Maxim India:** Media Transasia (India) Ltd, K-35, Green Park, New Delhi 110 016; tel. (11) 26862687; fax (11) 26867641; e-mail circulation@mediatransasia.com; f. 2005; monthly; English; men's lifestyle; CEO PIYUSH SHARMA; Editor SUNIL MEHRA.

**Mayapuri:** A-5, Mayapuri Phase 1, New Delhi 110 064; tel. (11) 28116120; fax (11) 25133120; e-mail mayapuri@hotmail.com; f. 1974; weekly; Hindi; cinema; Editor A. P. BAJAJ; circ. 146,144.

**Mukta:** Delhi Press Bldg, E-3 Jhandewala Estate, Rani Jhansi Rd, New Delhi 110 055; tel. (11) 41398888; fax (11) 41540714; e-mail editorial@delhipressgroup.com; internet www.grihshobhaindia.com; f. 1961; monthly; Hindi; youth; Editor, Publr and Printer PARESH NATH; circ. 13,000.

**Nandan:** Hindustan Times House, Kasturba Gandhi Marg, New Delhi 110 001; tel. (11) 23704562; fax (11) 23704600; e-mail jbharti@hindustantimes.com; f. 1963; monthly; Hindi; Editor JAI PRAKASH BHARTI; circ. 58,400.

**New Age Weekly:** Ajoy Bhavan, 15 Comrade Indrajeet Gupta Marg, Delhi 110 002; tel. (11) 23230762; fax (11) 23235543; e-mail cpindia@del2.vsnl.net.in; f. 1953; main organ of the Communist Party of India; weekly; English; Editor SHAMEEM FAIZEE; Man. N. S. NEGI; circ. 215,000.

**Organiser:** Sanskriti Bhavan, D. B. Gupta Rd, Jhandewalan, New Delhi 110 055; tel. (11) 23626977; fax (11) 23516635; e-mail editor@organiserweekly.com; internet www.organiser.org; f. 1947; weekly; English; Editor R. BALASHANKAR; circ. 44,100.

**Outlook:** AB-10 Safdarjung Enclave, New Delhi 110 029; tel. (11) 51651471; fax (11) 51651472; e-mail outlook@outlookindia.com; internet www.outlookindia.com; f. 1995; weekly; Hindi and English edns; Editor-in-Chief VINOD MEHTA; circ. 256,300.

**Panchjanya:** Sanskriti Bhavan, Deshbandhu Gupta Marg, Jhandewala, New Delhi 110 055; tel. (11) 23514244; fax (11) 23558613; e-mail panch@nde.vsnl.net.in; f. 1947; weekly; Hindi; general interest; nationalist; Chair. S. N. BANSAL; Editor TARUN VIJAY; circ. 59,300.

**Punjabi Digest:** 209 Hemkunt House, 6 Rajendra Place, POB 2549, New Delhi 110 008; tel. (11) 25715225; fax (11) 25761053; f. 1971; literary monthly; Gurmukhi; Chief Editor Sardar S. B. SINGH; circ. 48,600.

**Sainik Samachar:** Block L-1, Church Rd, New Delhi 110 001; tel. (11) 23094668; f. 1909; pictorial fortnightly for India's armed forces; English, Hindi, Urdu, Tamil, Punjabi, Telugu, Marathi, Kannada, Gorkhali, Malayalam, Bengali, Assamese and Oriya edns; Editor P. K. PATTANAYAK; circ. 20,000.

**Saras Salil:** Delhi Press Bldg, E-3 Jhandewala Estate, Rani Jhansi Rd, New Delhi 110 055; tel. (11) 41398888; fax (11) 41540714; e-mail editorial@delhipressgroup.com; internet www.grihshobhaindia.com; f. 1993; fortnightly; Hindi, Telugu, Tamil, Gujarati and Marathi edns; Editor, Publr and Printer PARESH NATH; circ. 1,051,279 (Hindi), 10,059 (Telugu), 8,223 (Tamil), 5,388 (Gujarati), 20,000 (Marathi).

**Sarita:** Delhi Press Bldg, E-3 Jhandewala Estate, Rani Jhansi Rd, New Delhi 110 055; tel. (11) 41398888; fax (11) 41540714; e-mail editorial@delhipressgroup.com; internet www.grihshobhaindia.com; f. 1945; fortnightly; Hindi; family magazine; Editor, Publr and Printer PARESH NATH; circ. 110,001.

**Shama:** 13/14 Asaf Ali Rd, New Delhi 110 002; tel. (11) 23232674; fax (11) 23235167; f. 1939; monthly; Urdu; art and literature; Editors M. YUNUS DEHLVI, IDREES DEHLVI, ILYAS DEHLVI; circ. 58,000.

**Suman Saurabh:** Delhi Press Bldg, E-3 Jhandewala Estate, Rani Jhansi Rd, New Delhi 110 055; tel. (11) 41398888; fax (11) 41540714; e-mail editorial@delhipressgroup.com; internet www.grihshobhaindia.com; f. 1983; monthly; Hindi; youth; Editor, Publr and Printer PARESH NATH; circ. 39,477.

**Sushama:** 13/14 Asaf Ali Rd, New Delhi 110 002; tel. (11) 23232674; fax (11) 23235167; f. 1959; monthly; Hindi; art and literature; Editors IDREES DEHLVI, ILYAS DEHLVI, YUNUS DEHLVI; circ. 30,000.

**Vigyan Pragati:** NISCAIR (CSIR), Dr K. S. Krishnan Marg, New Delhi 110 012; tel. (11) 25846301; fax (11) 25847062; e-mail vp@niscair.res.in; f. 1952; monthly; Hindi; popular science; Editor PRADEEP SHARMA; circ. 40,000.

**Woman's Era:** Delhi Press Bldg, E-3 Jhandewala Estate, Rani Jhansi Rd, New Delhi 110 055; tel. (11) 41398888; fax (11) 41540714; e-mail editorial@delhipressgroup.com; internet www.grihshobhaindia.com; f. 1973; fortnightly; English; women's interests; Editor, Publr and Printer PARESH NATH; circ. 83,655.

**Yojana:** Yojana Bhavan, Sansad Marg, New Delhi 110 001; tel. (11)23717910; e-mail yojana@techpilgrim.com; f. 1957; monthly; English, Tamil, Bengali, Marathi, Gujarati, Assamese, Malayalam, Telugu, Kannada, Punjabi, Urdu, Oriya and Hindi edns; Chief Editor SUBHASH SETIA; circ. 72,000.

### Andhra Pradesh

#### Hyderabad

**Andhra Prabha Illustrated Weekly:** 591 Lower Tank Bund Rd, Express Centre, Domalaguda, Hyderabad 500 029; tel. (40) 2233586; internet www.andhraprabha.com/apweekly; f. 1952; weekly; Telugu; Editor POTTURI VENKATESWARA RAO; circ. 21,800.

#### Secunderabad

**Andhra Bhoomi Sachitra Masa Patrika:** 36 Sarojini Devi Rd, Secunderabad 500 003; tel. (842) 27802346; fax (842) 27805256; f. 1977; fortnightly; Telugu; Editor T. VENKATRAM REDDY; circ. 25,600.

#### Vijayawada

**Andhra Jyoti Sachitra Vara Patrika:** Vijayawada 520 010; tel. (866) 2474532; f. 1967; weekly; Telugu; Editor PURANAM SUBRAMANYA SARMA; circ. 59,000.

**Bala Jyoti:** Labbipet, Vijayawada 520 010; tel. (866) 2474532; f. 1980; monthly; Telugu; Assoc. Editor A. SASIKANT SATAKARNI; circ. 12,500.

**Jyoti Chitra:** Andhra Jyoti Bldgs, Vijayawada 520 010; tel. (866) 2474532; f. 1977; weekly; Telugu; Editor T. KUTUMBA RAO; circ. 20,100.

**Swati Saparivara Patrika:** Anil Bldgs, Suryaraopet, POB 339, Vijayawada 520 002; tel. (866) 2431862; fax (866) 2430433; e-mail advt_swati@sify.com; f. 1984; weekly; Telugu; Editor VEMURI BALARAM; circ. 252,100.

**Vanita Jyoti:** Labbipet, POB 712, Vijayawada 520 010; tel. (866) 2474532; f. 1978; monthly; Telugu; Asst Editor J. SATYANARAYANA; circ. 13,100.

### Assam (Asom)

#### Guwahati

**Agradoot:** Agradoot Bhavan, Dispur, Guwahati 781 006; tel. (361) 2261923; fax (361) 2260655; e-mail agradoot@sify.com; f. 1971; bi-weekly; Assamese; Editor K. S. DEKA; circ. 29,463.

**Asam Bani:** Tribune Bldg, Guwahati 781 003; tel. (361) 2661356; fax (361) 2660594; e-mail dileepchandan@yahoo.com; internet www.assamtribune.com; f. 1955; weekly; Assamese; Editor DILEEP CHANDAN; circ. 14,000.

**Sadin:** Maniram Dewan Rd, Chandmari, Guwahati 781 003; tel. (361) 2524594; fax (361) 2524634; e-mail protidin@gw1.vsnl.net.in; weekly; Assamese; circ. 39,500.

### Bihar

#### Patna

**Anand Digest:** Govind Mitra Rd, Patna 800 004; tel. (612) 2656557; fax (612) 2225192; f. 1981; monthly; Hindi; family magazine; Editor Dr S. S. SINGH; circ. 44,500.

**Balak:** Govind Mitra Rd, POB 5, Patna 800 004; tel. (612) 2650341; f. 1926; monthly; Hindi; children's; Editor S. R. SARAN; circ. 32,000.

### Chhattisgarh

#### Raipur

**Krishak Jagat:** A-23, Sector 1, Shankar Nagar, Raipur 492 001; tel. (771) 2420449; e-mail krishjag@sancharnet.in; internet www.krishakjagatindia.com; weekly; Hindi; Chief Editor VIJAY KUMAR BONDRIYA; circ. 35,000.

### Gujarat

#### Ahmedabad

**Akhand Anand:** Anand Bhavan, Relief Rd, POB 123, Ahmedabad 380 001; tel. (79) 2357482; e-mail innitadi@sancharnet.in; f. 1947; monthly; Gujarati; Pres. ANAND AMIN; Editor Dr DILAVARSINH JADEJA; circ. 10,000.

**Chitralok:** Gujarat Samachar Bhavan, Khanpur, POB 254, Ahmedabad 380 001; tel. (79) 5504010; fax (79) 5502000; f. 1952; weekly; Gujarati; films; Man. Editor SHREYANS S. SHAH; circ. 20,000.

**Sakhi:** Sakhi Publications, Jai Hind Press Bldg, nr Gujarat Chamber, Ashram Rd, Navrangpura, Ahmedabad 380 009; tel. (79) 26581734; fax (79) 26587681; f. 1984; fortnightly; Gujarati; women's; Man. Editor NITA Y. SHAH; Editor Y. N. SHAH; circ. 10,000.

**Shree:** Gujarat Samachar Bhavan, Khanpur, Ahmedabad 380 001; tel. (79) 5504010; fax (79) 5502000; f. 1964; weekly; Gujarati; women's; Editor SMRUTIBEN SHAH; circ. 20,000.

**Stree:** Sandesh Bhavan, Lad Society Rd, Ahmedabad 380 054; tel. (79) 26765480; fax (79) 26753587; e-mail stree@sandesh.com; internet www.sandesh.com; f. 1962; weekly; Gujarati; Editor RITABEN PATEL; circ. 42,000.

**Zagmag:** Gujarat Samachar Bhavan, Khanpur, Ahmedabad 380 001; tel. (79) 5508001; f. 1952; weekly; Gujarati; for children; Editor BAHUBALI S. SHAH; circ. 38,000.

Rajkot

**Amruta:** Jai Hind Publications, Jai Hind Press Bldg, Babubhai Shah Marg, Rajkot 360 001; tel. (281) 2440513; fax (281) 2448677; e-mail info@jaihinddaily.com; f. 1967; weekly; Gujarati; films; Editor Y. N. SHAH; circ. 12,500.

**Parmarth:** Jai Hind Publications, Jai Hind Press Bldg, Babubhai Shah Marg, Rajkot 360 001; tel. (281) 2440511; fax (281) 2448677; e-mail info@jaihinddaily.com; monthly; Gujarati; philosophy and religion; Editor Y. N. SHAH; circ. 8,000.

**Phulwadi:** Jai Hind Publications, Jai Hind Press Bldg, Babubhai Shah Marg, Rajkot 360 001; tel. (281) 2440513; fax (281) 2448677; e-mail info@jaihinddaily.com; f. 1967; weekly; Gujarati; for children; Editor Y. N. SHAH; circ. 10,000.

### Karnataka

Bangalore

**Mayura:** 75 Mahatma Gandhi Rd, Bangalore 560 001; tel. (80) 25588999; fax (80) 25587179; e-mail ads@deccanherald.co.in; f. 1968; monthly; Kannada; Editor-in-Chief K. N. SHANTH KUMAR; circ. 28,600.

**Sudha:** 75 Mahatma Gandhi Rd, Bangalore 560 001; tel. (80) 25588999; fax (80) 25587179; e-mail ads@deccanherald.co.in; f. 1965; weekly; Kannada; Editor-in-Chief K. N. HARI KUMAR; circ. 67,400.

Manipal

**Taranga:** Udayavani Bldg, Press Corner, Manipal 576 104; tel. (820) 2570845; fax (820) 2570563; e-mail taranga@manipalpress.com; internet www.udayavani.com; f. 1983; weekly; Kannada; Editor-in-Chief SANDHYA S. PAI; circ. 85,400.

### Kerala

Kochi

**The Week:** Malayala Manorama Buildings, POB 4278, Kochi 682 036; tel. (484) 2316285; fax (484) 2315745; e-mail editor@theweek.com; internet week.manoramaonline.com; f. 1982; weekly; English; current affairs; Chief Editor MAMMEN MATHEW; Editor PHILIP MATHEW; circ. 202,000.

Kottayam

**Balarama:** MM Publications Ltd, POB 226, Kottayam 686 001; tel. (481) 2563721; fax (481) 2564393; e-mail childrensdivision@mmpublications.com; f. 1972; children's weekly; Malayalam; Chief Editor BINA MATHEW; Senior Gen. Man. V. SAJEEV GEORGE; circ. 295,288.

**Malayala Manorama:** K. K. Rd, POB 26, Kottayam 686 001; tel. (481) 2563646; fax (481) 2562479; e-mail editor@malayalamanorama.com; internet www.manoramaonline.com; f. 1937; weekly; Malayalam; also publ. from Kozhikode; Man. Dir and Editor MAMMEN MATHEW; Chief Editor K. M. MATHEW; combined circ. 1,589,823.

**Vanitha:** MM Publications Ltd, POB 226, Kottayam 686 001; tel. (481) 2563721; fax (481) 2564393; e-mail vanitha@mmp.in; f. 1975; women's fortnightly; Malayalam (monthly) and Hindi editions; Chief Editor PREMA MAMMEN MATHEW, MARIAM MAMMEN MATHEW; Gen. Man. V. SAJEEV GEORGE; circ. 479,452 (Malayalam), 145,060 (Hindi).

Kozhikode

**Arogya Masika:** Mathrubhumi Bldgs, K. P. Kesava Menon Rd, Kozhikode 673 001; tel. (495) 2765381; fax (495) 2760138; e-mail arogyamasika@mpp.co.in; owned by Mathrubhumi Printing and Publishing Co Ltd; monthly; Malayalam; health; Man. Editor P. V. CHANDRAN; circ. 198,367.

**Balabhumi:** Matrabhumi Bldgs, K. P. Kesava Menon Rd, Kozhikode 673 001; tel. (495) 2366655; fax (495) 2366656; e-mail balabhumi@mpp.co.in; internet www.mathrabhumi.com; f. 1996; weekly; Malayalam; children's; Editor K. K. SREEDHARAN NAIR; circ. 95,500.

**Chithrabhumi:** Mathrubhumi Bldgs, K. P. Kesava Menon Rd, Kozhikode 673 001; tel. (495) 2366655; fax (495) 2366656; e-mail cinema@mpp.co.in; internet www.mathrubhumi.com; f. 1982; weekly; Malayalam; films; Editor K. K. SREEDHARAN NAIR; circ. 33,241.

**Grihalakshmi:** Mathrubhumi Bldgs, K. P. Kesava Menon Rd, POB 46, Kozhikode 673 001; tel. (495) 2366655; fax (495) 2366656; e-mail mathrclt@md2.vsnl.net.in; internet www.mathrubhumi.com; f. 1979; monthly; Malayalam; women's; Editor K. K. SREEDHARAN NAIR; circ. 167,800.

**Mathrubhumi Illustrated Weekly:** Mathrubhumi Bldgs, K. P. Kesava Menon Rd, POB 46, Kozhikode 673 001; tel. (495) 2366655; fax (495) 2356656; f. 1923; weekly; Malayalam; Editor K. K. SREEDHARAN NAIR; circ. 38,300.

**Sports Masika:** Mathrubhumi Bldgs, K. P. Kesava Menon Rd, Kozhikode 673 001; tel. (495) 366655; fax (495) 366656; e-mail sports@mpp.co.in; internet www.mathrubhumi.com; monthly; Malayalam; sport; Editor K. K. SREEDHARAN NAIR; circ. 67,900.

**Thozhilvartha:** Mathrubhumi Bldgs, K. P. Kesava Menon Rd, Kozhikode 673 001; tel. (495) 2366655; fax (495) 2366656; e-mail mathrclt@md2.vsnl.net.in; internet www.mathrubhumi.com; f. 1992; weekly; Malayalam; employment; Editor K. K. SREEDHARAN NAIR; circ. 172,200.

Quilon

**Kerala Sabdam:** Thevally, Quilon 691 009; tel. (474) 2745772; fax (474) 2740710; f. 1962; weekly; Malayalam; Man. Editor B. A. RAJAKRISHNAN; circ. 66,600.

Thiruvananthapuram

**Kalakaumudi:** Kaumudi Bldgs, Pettah, Thiruvananthapuram 695 024; tel. (471) 2443531; fax (471) 2442895; e-mail kalakaumudi@vsnl.com; f. 1975; weekly; Malayalam; Chief Editor M. S. MANI; Editor N. R. S. BABU; circ. 73,000.

**Vellinakshatram:** Kaumudi Bldgs, Pettah, Thiruvananthapuram 695 024; tel. (471) 2443531; fax (471) 2442895; e-mail kalakaumudi@vsnl.com; internet www.vellinakshatram.com; f. 1987; film weekly; Malayalam; Editor PRASAD LAKSHMANAN; Man. Editor SUKUMARAN MANI; circ. 55,000.

### Madhya Pradesh

Bhopal

**Krishak Jagat:** 14 Indira Press Complex, M. P. Nagar, POB 37, Bhopal 462 011; tel. (755) 2768452; fax (755) 2760449; e-mail krishjag@sancharnet.in; internet www.krishakjagat.com; f. 1946; weekly; Hindi; agriculture; also published in Jaipur and Raipur; Chief Editor VIJAY KUMAR BONDRIYA; Editor SUNIL GANGRADE; combined circ. 150,000.

### Maharashtra

Mumbai (Bombay)

**Abhiyaan:** Sambhaav Media Ltd, 4 AB, Government Industrial Estate, Charkop, Kandivli (W), Mumbai 400 067; tel. (22) 28687515; fax (22) 28680991; e-mail rajeshpathak@sambhaav.com; f. 1986; weekly; Gujarati; Chief Man. Dir KIRAN VADODARIA; Group Editor DEEPAL TREVEDIE; circ. 99,300.

**Arogya Sanjeevani:** C-14 Royal Industrial Estate, 5-B Naigaum Cross Rd, Wadala, Mumbai 400 031; tel. (22) 24138723; fax (22) 24133610; e-mail woman17@zediffmail.com; f. 1990; quarterly; Hindi; Editor RAM KRISHNA SHUKLA; circ. 56,472.

**Auto India:** Nirmal, Nariman Point, Mumbai 400 021; tel. (22) 22883946; fax (22) 22883940; e-mail editor@auto-india.com; f. 1994; monthly; Editor RAJ WARRIOR; circ. 44,500.

**Bhavan's Journal:** Kulapati Dr K. M. Munshi Marg, Chowpatty, Mumbai 400 007; tel. (22) 23631261; fax (22) 23630058; e-mail brbhavan@bom7.vsnl.net.in; f. 1954; fortnightly; English; literary; Man. Editor J. H. DAVE; Editor V. N. NARAYANAN; circ. 25,000.

**Bombay Samachar:** Red House, Sayed Abdulla Brelvi Rd, Mumbai 400 001; tel. (22) 22045531; fax (22) 22046642; e-mail samachar@vsnl.com; f. 1822; weekly; Gujarati; Editor P. D. DALAL (acting); circ. 118,213.

**Business India:** Nirmal, 14th Floor, Nariman Point, Mumbai 400 021; tel. (22) 22883943; fax (22) 22883940; f. 1978; fortnightly; English; Publr ASHOK ADVANI; circ. 75,700.

**Business World:** 25–28 Atlanta, 2nd Floor, Nariman Point, Mumbai 400 021; tel. (22) 22851352; fax (22) 22870310; f. 1980; weekly; English; Editor TONY JOSEPH; circ. 146,500.

**Chitralekha:** 62 Vaju Kotak Marg, Fort, Mumbai 400 001; tel. (22) 22614730; fax (22) 22615895; e-mail advertise@chitralekha.com; internet www.chitralekha.com; f. 1950 (Gujarati), f. 1989 (Marathi); weekly; Gujarati and Marathi; Editors BHARAT GHELANI, GYANESH MAHARAO; circ. 240,300 (Gujarati), 95,300 (Marathi).

**Cine Blitz Film Monthly:** Rifa Publications Pvt Ltd, A/3, Sangam Bhavan, Ground Floor, Brahma Kumaris Rd, nr Strand Cinema, Colaba, Mumbai 400 005; tel. (22) 22830668; fax (22) 22830672; e-mail cbedit@sify.com; f. 1974; English; Editor NISHI PREM; circ. 184,100.

**Debonair:** Mumbai; e-mail maurya@debonairindia.com; f. 1972; monthly; English; Publr CHAITANYA PRABHU; CEO JOSEPH MASCARENHAS; circ. 110,000.

**Economic and Political Weekly:** 320–321, A to Z Industrial Estate, Ganapatrao Kadam Marg, Lower Parel, Mumbai 400 013; tel. (22) 40638282; fax (22) 24934515; e-mail epw.mumbai@gmail.com; internet www.epw.in; f. 1966; English; Editor C. RAMMANOHAR REDDY; circ. 12,500.

**Femina:** Times of India Bldg, Dr Dadabhai Naoroji Rd, Mumbai 400 001; tel. and fax (22) 22731385; e-mail femina@timesgroup.com; internet www.feminaindia.com; f. 1959; fortnightly; English; Editor AMY FERNANDES; circ. 122,200.

**Filmfare:** 4th Floor, Times of India Bldg, Dr Dadabhai Naoroji Rd, Mumbai 400 001; tel. (22) 22731187; fax (22) 22731585; e-mail shashi.baliga@wwm.co.in; internet www.filmfare.com; f. 1952; monthly; English; Exec. Editor SHASHI BALIGA; circ. 147,000.

**G:** 62 Vaju Kotak Marg, Fort, Mumbai 400 001; tel. (22) 22614730; fax (22) 22615895; e-mail advertise@chitralekha.com; internet www.gmagazine.com; f. 1989; monthly; English; Editor MAULIK KOTAK; circ. 65,000.

**Gentleman:** B-201, Teritex Business Service Centre, Saki Vihar, Mumbai 400 072; tel. (22) 28571490; fax (22) 28572447; e-mail gentleman@vsnl.com; f. 1980; monthly; English; Editor PREMNATH NAIR (acting).

**Hi Blitz:** Rifa Publications Pvt Ltd, A/3, Sangam Bhavan, Ground Floor, Brahma Kumaris Rd, nr Strand Cinema, Colaba, Mumbai 400 005; tel. (22) 22830668; fax (22) 22830672; e-mail cbedit@sify.com; f. 2002; English; lifestyle; Editor SHALINI SHARMA; 65,000.

**Indian PEN:** Theosophy Hall, 40 New Marine Lines, Mumbai 400 020; tel. (22) 22032175; e-mail ambika.sirkar@gems.vsnl.net.in; f. 1934; quarterly; organ of Indian Centre of the International PEN; Editor RANJIT HOSKOTE.

**Janmabhoomi-Pravasi:** Janmabhoomi Bhavan, Janmabhoomi Marg, Fort, POB 62, Mumbai 400 001; tel. (22) 22870831; fax (22) 22874097; e-mail bhoomi@bom3.vsnl.net.in; f. 1939; weekly; Gujarati; Propr Saurashtra Trust; Editor KUNDAN VYAS; circ. 94,100.

**JEE:** 62 Vaju Kotak Marg, Fort, Mumbai 400 001; tel. (22) 22614730; fax (22) 22615895; e-mail advertise@chitralekha.com; fortnightly; Gujarati and Marathi; Editor MADHURI KOTAK; circ. 92,160 (Gujarati), 30,150 (Marathi).

**Meri Saheli:** C-14 Royal Industrial Estate, 5-B Naigaum Cross Rd, Wadala, Mumbai 400 031; tel. (22) 24138723; fax (22) 24133610; e-mail woman17@zediffmail.com; f. 1987; monthly; Hindi; Editor HEMA MALINI; circ. 352,362.

**Movie:** Mahalaxmi Chambers, 5th Floor, 22 Bhulabhai Desai Rd, Mumbai 400 026; tel. (22) 24935636; fax (22) 24938406; f. 1981; monthly; English; Editor DINESH RAHEJA; circ. 70,700.

**New Woman:** C-14 Royal Industrial Estate, 5-B Naigaum Cross Rd, Wadala, Mumbai 400 031; tel. (22) 24138723; fax (22) 24133610; e-mail newwomanmag@gmail.com; f. 1996; monthly; English; Editor HEMA MALINI; circ. 69,023.

**Onlooker:** Free Press House, 215 Free Press Journal Marg, Nariman Point, Mumbai 400 021; tel. (22) 22874566; f. 1939; fortnightly; English; news magazine; Exec. Editor K. SRINIVASAN; circ. 61,000.

**Reader's Digest:** 45 Vaju Kotak Marg, Ballard Estate, Mumbai 400 001; tel. (22) 22617292; fax (22) 22613347; e-mail ashok.mahadevan@intoday.com; internet www.rd-india.com; f. 1954; monthly; English; Publr and Editor ASHOK MAHADEVAN; circ. 389,378.

**Savvy:** Magna Publishing Co Ltd, Magna House, 100/E Old Prabhadevi Rd, Prabhadevi, Mumbai 400 025; tel. (22) 24362270; fax (22) 24306523; e-mail savvy@magnamags.com; internet www.magnamags.com; f. 1984; monthly; English; Editor SAIRA MENEZES; circ. 99,500.

**Screen:** Express Tower, Nariman Point, Mumbai 400 021; tel. (22) 22022627; fax (22) 22022139; e-mail iemumbai@expressindia.co.in; internet www.screenindia.com; f. 1950; film weekly; English; Editor BHAVNA SOMAYA; circ. 90,000.

**Society:** Magna Publishing Co Ltd, Magna House, 100/E Old Prabhadevi Rd, Prabhadevi, Mumbai 400 025; tel. (22) 24362270; fax (22) 24306523; e-mail society@magnamags.com; internet www.magnamags.com; f. 1979; monthly; English; Editorial Dir ASHWIN VARDE; circ. 67,200.

**Stardust:** Magna Publishing Co Ltd, Magna House, 100/E Old Prabhadevi Rd, Prabhadevi, Mumbai 400 025; tel. (22) 24362270; fax (22) 24306523; e-mail magnapub@vsnl.com; internet www.stardustindia.com; f. 1985; monthly; English; Editor ASHWIN VARDE; circ. 308,000.

**Vyapar:** Janmabhoomi Bhavan, Janmabhoomi Marg, POB 62, Fort, Mumbai 400 001; tel. (22) 22870831; fax (22) 22874097; e-mail rajeshbhayani@hotmail.com; f. 1949; (Gujarati), 1987 (Hindi); Gujarati (2 a week) and Hindi (weekly); commerce; Propr Saurashtra Trust; Editor RAJESH M. BHAYANI; circ. 27,900 (Gujarati), 12,800 (Hindi).

Nagpur

**All India Reporter:** AIR Ltd, Congress Nagar, POB 209, Nagpur 440 012; tel. (712) 2534321; fax (712) 2526283; e-mail air@allindiareporter.com; internet www.allindiareporter.com; f. 1914; weekly and monthly; English; law journals; Chief Editor V. R. MANOHAR; circ. 55,500.

### Rajasthan

Jaipur

**Balhans:** Kesargarh, Jawahar Lal Nehru Marg, Jaipur 302 004; tel. (141) 2561582; fax (141) 2566011; e-mail info@rajasthanpatrika.com; internet www.rajasthanpatrika.com; fortnightly; Hindi; circ. 26,700.

**Itwari Patrika:** Kesargarh, Jawahar Lal Nehru Marg, Jaipur 302 004; tel. (141) 2561582; fax (141) 2566011; weekly; Hindi; circ. 12,000.

**Krishak Jagat:** F-47, Ghiya Marg, Bani Park, Jaipur 302 016; tel. (141) 2207680; e-mail krishjag@sancharnet.in; internet www.krishakjagatindia.com; Hindi; weekly; Chief Editor VIJAY KUMAR BONDRIYA; circ. 32,000.

**Rashtradoot Saptahik:** M.I. Rd, POB 30, Jaipur 302 001; tel. (141) 2372634; fax (141) 2373513; f. 1983; Hindi; also publ. from Kota and Bikaner; Chief Editor and Man. Editor RAJESH SHARMA; CEO SOMESH SHARMA; combined circ. 324,721.

### Tamil Nadu

Chennai (Madras)

**Ambulimama:** 82 Defence Officers Colony, Ekkatuthangal, Chennai 600 097; tel. (44) 22313637; e-mail chandamama@vsnl.com; f. 1947; children's monthly; Tamil; Editor B. VISWANATHA REDDI; circ. 65,000.

**Ambuli Ammavan:** 82 Defence Officers Colony, Ekkatuthangal, Chennai 600 097; tel. (44) 22313637; e-mail chandamama@vsnl.com; f. 1970; children's monthly; Malayalam; Editor B. VISWANATHA REDDI; circ. 12,000.

**Ananda Vikatan:** 757 Anna Salai, Chennai 600 002; tel. (44) 28524054; fax (44) 28523819; e-mail editor@vikatan.com; internet www.vikatan.com; f. 1924; weekly; Tamil; Editor and Man. Dir S. BALASUBRAMANIAN; circ. 316,000.

**Aval Vikatan:** 757 Anna Salai, Chennai 600 002; tel. (44) 28524054; fax (44) 28523819; e-mail editor@vikatan.com; internet www.vikatan.com; f. 1998; fortnightly; Tamil; Editor B. SRINIVASAN; circ. 100,000.

**Chandamama:** 82 Defence Officers Colony, Ekkatuthangal, Chennai 600 097; tel. (44) 22313637; e-mail chandamama@vsnl.com; f. 1947; children's monthly; Hindi, Gujarati, Telugu, Kannada, English, Sanskrit, Bengali, Assamese; Editor B. VISWANATHA REDDI; combined circ. 420,000.

**Chandoba:** 82 Defence Officers Colony, Ekkatuthangal, Chennai 600 097; tel. (44) 22313637; e-mail chandamama@vsnl.com; f. 1952; children's monthly; Marathi; Editor B. VISWANATHA REDDI; circ. 93,000.

**Chutti Vikatan:** 757 Anna Salai, Chennai 600 002; tel. (44) 28524054; fax (44) 28523819; e-mail editor@vikatan.com; internet www.chuttivikatan.com; f. 1999; fortnightly; children's; Tamil; Editor B. SRINIVASAN; Man. Dir S. BALASUBRAMANIAN; circ. 100,000.

**Devi:** 727 Anna Salai, Chennai 600 006; tel. (44) 28521428; f. 1979; weekly; Tamil; Editor B. RAMACHANDRA ADITYAN; circ. 64,800.

**Dinamani Kadir:** Express Estate, Mount Rd, Chennai 600 002; tel. (44) 28520751; fax (44) 28524500; weekly; Editor G. KASTURI RANGAN (acting); circ. 55,000.

**Frontline:** Kasturi Bldgs, 859/860 Anna Salai, Chennai 600 002; tel. (44) 28413344; fax (44) 28415325; e-mail subs@thehindu.co.in; internet www.flonnet.com; f. 1984; fortnightly; English; current affairs; independent; Publr S. RANGARAJAN; Editor N. RAM; circ. 62,700.

**The Hindu International Edition:** Kasturi Bldgs, 859/860 Anna Salai, Chennai 600 002; tel. (44) 28413344; fax (44) 28415325; e-mail subs@thehindu.co.in; f. 1975; weekly; English; independent; Publr S. RANGARAJAN; Editor N. RAVI; circ. 1,590.

**Jahnamamu (Oriya):** 82 Defence Officers Colony, Ekkatuthangal, Chennai 600 097; tel. (44) 22313637; e-mail chandamama@vsnl.com; f. 1972; children's monthly; Editor B. VISWANATHA REDDI; circ. 111,000.

**Junior Vikatan:** 757 Anna Salai, Chennai 600 002; tel. (44) 28524054; fax (44) 28523819; e-mail editor@vikatan.com; internet www.vikatan.com; f. 1983; twice a week; Tamil; Editor and Man. Dir S. BALASUBRAMANIAN; circ. 190,300.

**Kalai Magal:** POB 604, Chennai 600 004; tel. (44) 24983099; f. 1932; monthly; Tamil; literary and cultural; Editor R. NARAYANASWAMY; circ. 10,200.

**Kalki:** Kalki Bldgs, 47-NP Jawaharlal Nehru Rd, Ekkatuthangal, Chennai 600 097; tel. (44) 22345622; fax (44) 22345621; e-mail kalki@kalkiweekly.com; internet www.kalkionline.com; f. 1941; weekly; Tamil; literary and cultural; Editor SEETHA RAVI; circ. 42,700.

**Kumudam:** 151 Purasawalkam High Rd, Chennai 600 010; tel. (44) 26422146; fax (44) 26425041; e-mail kumudam@hotmail.com; internet www.kumudam.com; f. 1947; weekly; Tamil; Editor Dr S. A. P. JAWAHAR PALANIAPPAN; circ. 385,900.

**Kungumam:** 93A Kodambakkam High Rd, Chennai 600 034; tel. (44) 28268177; f. 1978; weekly; Tamil; Editor PARASAKTHI; circ. 63,700.

**Malaimathi:** Chennai; f. 1958; weekly; Tamil; Editor P. S. ELANGO; circ. 48,100.

**Muththaram:** 93A Kogambakkam High Rd, Chennai 600 034; tel. (44) 2476306; f. 1980; weekly; Tamil; Editor PARASAKTHI; circ. 11,800.

**Rani Muthu:** 86 Periyar E.V.R. High Rd, Chennai 600 007; tel. (44) 25324771; fax (44) 26426884; e-mail raniweekly@vsnl.net; f. 1969; fortnightly; Tamil; Editor RAGUPATHY BASKARAN; circ. 38,180.

**Rani Weekly:** 86 Periyar E.V.R. High Rd, Chennai 600 007; tel. (44) 25324771; fax (44) 26426884; e-mail raniweekly@vsnl.net; f. 1962; Tamil; Editor RAGUPATHY BASKARAN; circ. 141,911.

**Sportstar:** Kasturi Bldgs, 859/860 Anna Salai, Chennai 600 002; tel. (44) 28413344; fax (44) 28415325; e-mail wsvcs@thehindu.co.in; internet www.tssonnet.com; f. 1978; weekly; English; independent; Publr S. RANGARAJAN; Editor N. RAM; circ. 48,900.

**Thuglak:** 46 Greenways Rd, Chennai 600 028; tel. (44) 24936913; fax (44) 24936915; f. 1970; weekly; Tamil; Editor CHO S. RAMASWAMY; circ. 78,130.

### Uttar Pradesh

Allahabad

**Manohar Kahaniyan:** 1A, Tagore Town, Hashimpur Rd, Allahabad 211 002; tel. (532) 2415549; fax (532) 2415533; e-mail mayapressalld@rediffmail.com; f. 1940; monthly; Hindi; Editor ASHOK MITRA.

**Nutan Kahaniyan:** 15 Sheo Charan Lal Rd, Allahabad 211 003; tel. (532) 2400612; f. 1975; Hindi; monthly; Chief Editor K. K. BHARGAVA; circ. 167,500.

**Satya Katha:** 1A, Tagore Town, Hashimpur Rd, Allahabad 211 002; e-mail mayapressalld@rediffmail.com; f. 1974; monthly; Hindi; Editor ASHOK MITRA.

### West Bengal

Kolkata (Calcutta)

**All India Appointment Gazette:** 7 Old Court House St, Kolkata 700 001; tel. (33) 22435663; fax (33) 22435618; e-mail sambadmail@sify.com; f. 1973; weekly; English; Editor S. C. TALUKDAR; circ. 37,469.

**Anandalok:** 6 Prafulla Sarkar St, Kolkata 700 001; tel. (33) 22374880; fax (33) 22253240; f. 1975; fortnightly; Bengali; film; Editor DULENDRA BHOWMIK; circ. 98,600.

**Anandamela:** 6 Prafulla Sarkar St, Kolkata 700 001; tel. (33) 22216600; fax (33) 22253240; f. 1975; weekly; Bengali; for children; Editor DEBASHIS BANDOPADHYAY; circ. 41,800.

**Contemporary Tea Time:** c/o Contemporary Brokers Pvt Ltd, 1 Old Court House Corner, POB 14, Kolkata 700 001; tel. (33) 22307241; fax (33) 22435753; e-mail cbkol@dataone.in; internet www.ctl.co.in; f. 1988; quarterly; English; tea industry; Editor SAMAR SIRCAR; circ. 5,000.

**Desh:** 6 Prafulla Sarkar St, Kolkata 700 001; tel. (33) 22374880; fax (33) 22253240; f. 1933; fortnightly; Bengali; literary; Editor HARSHA DATTA; circ. 100,000.

**Khela:** 96 Raja Rammohan Sarani, Kolkata 700 009; tel. (33) 23509803; f. 1981; weekly; Bengali; sports; Editor ASOKE DASGUPTA; circ. 7,800.

**Naba Kallol:** 11 Jhamapookur Lane, Kolkata 700 009; tel. (33) 23504294; e-mail devsahityer@caltiger.com; f. 1960; monthly; Bengali; Editor P. K. MAZUMDAR; circ. 37,000.

**Prabuddha Bharata** (Awakened India): 5 Dehi Entally Rd, Kolkata 700 014; tel. (33) 22866450; e-mail mail@advaitaashrama.org; internet www.advaitaashrama.org; f. 1896; monthly; art, culture, religion and philosophy; Publr Swami BODHASARANANDA; Editor Swami SATYASWARUPANANDA; circ. 7,500.

**Sananda:** 6 Prafulla Sarkar St, Kolkata 700 001; tel. (33) 22374880; fax (33) 22253241; f. 1986; monthly; Bengali; Editor APARNA SEN; circ. 172,500.

**Saptahik Bartaman:** 76A J. C. Bose Rd, Kolkata 700 014; tel. (33) 22448208; fax (33) 22441215; f. 1988; weekly; Bengali; Editor BARUN SENGUPTA; circ. 111,900.

**The Statesman:** Statesman House, 4 Chowringhee Sq., Kolkata 700 001; tel. (33) 22127070; fax (33) 22126178; e-mail thestatesman@vsnl.com; internet www.thestatesman.net; f. 1875; overseas weekly; English; Editor RAVINDRA KUMAR.

**Suktara:** 11 Jhamapooker Lane, Kolkata 700 009; tel. (33) 23504294; e-mail devsahityer@caltiger.com; f. 1948; monthly; Bengali; juvenile; Editor M. MAJUMDAR; circ. 44,300.

## NEWS AGENCIES

**Press Trust of India Ltd:** PTI Bldg, 4 Parliament St, New Delhi 110 001; tel. (11) 23716621; fax (11) 23718714; e-mail trans@pti.in; internet www.ptinews.com; f. 1947; re-established 1978; Chair. Dr R. LAKSHMIPATHY; Editor-in-Chief and CEO M. K. RAZDAN.

**United News of India (UNI):** 9 Rafi Marg, New Delhi 110 001; tel. (11) 23710522; fax (11) 23355841; e-mail uninet@uniindia.com; internet www.uniindia.com; f. 1959; national and international news service in English, Hindi (UNIVARTA) and Urdu; photograph and graphics service; brs in 67 centres in India; Chair. MANOJ KUMAR SONTHALIA; Gen. Man. MAHINDER KUMAR LAUL.

## CO-ORDINATING BODIES

**Press Information Bureau:** Shastri Bhavan, Dr Rajendra Prasad Rd, New Delhi 110 001; tel. (11) 23383643; fax (11) 23383203; e-mail pib@alpha.nic.in; internet www.pib.nic.in; f. 1946 to co-ordinate press affairs for the govt; represents newspaper managements, journalists, news agencies, parliament; has power to examine journalists under oath and may censor objectionable material; Prin. Information Officer DEEPAK SANDHU.

**Registrar of Newspapers for India:** Ministry of Information and Broadcasting, West Block 8, Wing 2, Ramakrishna Puram, New Delhi 110 066; tel. (11) 26107504; fax (11) 26189801; e-mail rni.hub@nic.in; internet rni.nic.in; f. 1956 as a statutory body to collect press statistics; maintains a register of all Indian newspapers; Press Registrar AMITABHA CHAKRABARTI.

## PRESS ASSOCIATIONS

**All-India Newspaper Editors' Conference:** 36–37 Northend Complex, Rama Krishna Ashram Marg, New Delhi 110 001; tel. (11) 23364519; fax (11) 23317947; f. 1940; c. 300 mems; Pres. VISHWA BANDHU GUPTA; Sec.-Gen. UTTAM CHANDRA SHARMA.

**All India Small and Medium Newspapers' Federation:** 26-F Rajiv Gandhi Chowk (Connaught Place), New Delhi 110 001; tel. (11) 23326000; fax (11) 24621636; e-mail indian_observer@hotmail.com; c. 9,000 mems; Pres. HARBHAJAN SINGH; Gen. Secs B. C. GUPTA, B. M. SHARMA.

**The Foreign Correspondents' Club of South Asia:** AB-19 Mathura Rd, opp. Pragati Maidan Gate 3, New Delhi 110 001; tel. (11) 23385118; fax (11) 23385517; e-mail fcc@fccsouthasia.org; internet www.fccsouthasia.com; f. 1992; 450 mems; Pres. Dr WAIEL S. H. AWWAD; Man. KIRAN KAPUR.

**Indian Federation of Working Journalists:** A-4/199 Basant Lane, nr Connaught Pl., New Delhi 110 055; tel. (11) 23348871; fax (11) 23348871; e-mail ifwj.media@gmail.com; internet www.ifwj.in; f. 1950; 30,000 mems; Pres. K. VIKRAM RAO; Sec.-Gen. PARMANAND PANDEY.

**Indian Journalists' Association:** New Delhi; Pres. VIJAY DUTT; Gen. Sec. A. K. DHAR.

**Indian Languages Newspapers' Association:** Janmabhoomi Bhavan, Janmabhoomi Marg, POB 10029, Fort, Mumbai 400 001; tel. (22) 22870537; f. 1941; 320 mems; Pres. VIJAY KUMAR BONDRIYA; Hon. Gen. Secs PRADEEP G. DESHPANDE, KRISHNA SHEWDIKAR, LALIT SHRIMAL.

**Indian Newspaper Society:** INS Bldg, Rafi Marg, New Delhi 110 001; tel. (11) 23715401; fax (11) 23723800; e-mail indnews@nde.vsnl

.net.in; f. 1939; 685 mems; Pres. M. P. VEERENDRAKUMAR; Sec.-Gen. DEEPAK S. RAJA.

**National Union of Journalists (India):** 7 Jantar Mantar Rd, 2nd Floor, New Delhi 110 001; tel. (11) 23368610; e-mail nujindia@ndf.vsnl.in; internet www.education.vsnl.com/nujindia; f. 1972; 12,000 mems; Pres. A. N. MISHRA; Sec.-Gen. M. D. GANGWAR.

**Press Club of India:** 1 Raisina Rd, New Delhi 110 001; tel. (11) 23719844; fax (11) 23357048; f. 1948; 4,500 mems.

**Press Council of India:** Soochna Bhavan, 8 C. G. O. Complex, Ground Floor, Lodhi Rd, New Delhi 110 003; tel. (11) 24366746; e-mail pcids@vsnl.net; internet www.presscouncil.nic.in; established under an Act of Parliament to preserve the freedom of the press and maintain and improve the standards of newspapers and news agencies in India; 28 mems; Chair. Justice GANENDRA NARAYAN RAY; Sec. VIBHA BHARGAVA.

**Press Institute of India:** Rind Premises, Second Main Rd, Taramani, CPT Campus, Chennai 600 113; e-mail arunchacko@pressinstitute.org; internet www.pressinstitute.org; f. 1963; 32 mem. newspapers and other orgs; Chair. N. MURALI; Dir ARUN CHACKO.

# Publishers

### DELHI AND NEW DELHI

**Affiliated East-West Press (Pvt) Ltd:** G-1/16 Ansari Rd, Daryaganj, New Delhi 110 002; tel. (11) 23264180; fax (11) 23260538; e-mail affiliat@vsnl.com; internet www.aewpress.com; textbooks and reference books; also represents scientific societies; Dirs SUNNY MALIK, KAMAL MALIK.

**Allied Publishers (Pvt) Ltd:** 13–14 Asaf Ali Rd, New Delhi 110 002; tel. (11) 23239001; fax (11) 23235967; e-mail alliedpublishers@eth.net; internet alliedpublishers.com; academic and general; Man. Dir SUNIL SACHDEV.

**All India Publishers & Distributors:** 4380/4B, Ansari Rd, Kaushalya Bldg, Daryaganj, New Delhi 110 002; tel. (11) 22324429; fax (11) 22467613; e-mail aipdraj@vsnl.com; CEO ARYA RAJENDER.

**Amerind Publishing Co (Pvt) Ltd:** c/o Mohan Primlani, A-61, Mayfair Gardens, New Delhi 110 016; tel. (11) 23324578; fax (11) 23710090; e-mail mohanprimlani@hotmail.com; f. 1970; offices at Kolkata, Mumbai and New York; scientific and technical; Dirs MOHAN PRIMLANI, GULAB PRIMLANI.

**Arnold Heinman Publishers (India) Pvt Ltd:** New Delhi; f. 1969 as Arnold Publishers (India) Pvt Ltd; literature and general; Man. Dir G. A. VAZIRANI.

**Atma Ram and Sons:** 1376 Kashmere Gate, POB 1429, Delhi 110 006; tel. (11) 23946466; fax (11) 23973082; e-mail atmaram_books@hotmail.com; f. 1909; scientific, technical, humanities, medical; Man. Dir S. PURI; Dir Y. PURI.

**B. I. Publications Pvt Ltd:** B. I. House, 54 Janpath, New Delhi 110 001; tel. (11) 23325313; fax (11) 23323138; e-mail bipgroup@vsnl.com; internet www.biindia.in/publication.htm; f. 1959; academic, general and professional; Man. Dir SHASHANK BHAGAT.

**Book Circle:** 19A Ansari Rd, Daryaganj, New Delhi 110 002; tel. (11) 23264444; fax (11) 23263050; e-mail bookcircle@vsnl.net; f. 2001; social sciences, art and architecture, technical, medical, scientific; Propr and Dir HIMANSHU CHAWLA.

**S. Chand and Co Ltd:** 7361 Ram Nagar, Qutab Rd, nr New Delhi Railway Station, New Delhi 110 055; tel. (11) 23672080; fax (11) 23677446; e-mail schand@vsnl.com; internet www.schandgroup.com; f. 1917; educational and general in English and Hindi; also book exports and imports; Man. Dir RAVINDRA KUMAR GUPTA.

**Children's Book House:** A-4 Ring Rd, South Extension Part I, POB 3854, New Delhi 110 049; tel. (11) 24636030; fax (11) 24636011; e-mail info@neetaprakashan.com; internet www.neetaprakashan.com; f. 1952; educational and general; Dir R. S. GUPTA.

**Children's Book Trust:** Nehru House, 4 Bahadur Shah Zafar Marg, New Delhi 110 002; tel. (11) 23316970; fax (11) 23721090; e-mail cbtnd@vsnl.com; internet www.childrensbooktrust.com; f. 1957; children's books in English and other Indian languages; Editor C. G. R. KURUP; Gen. Man. RAVI SHANKAR.

**Concept Publishing Co:** A/15-16, Commercial Block, Mohan Garden, New Delhi 110 059; tel. (11) 25351794; fax (11) 25357103; e-mail publishing@conceptpub.com; f. 1975; agriculture and rural development, Ayurveda, health sciences, communication, mass media, journalism, education, psychology, community development, management; Man. Dir ASHOK KUMAR MITTAL; CEO NITIN MITTAL.

**Frank Bros & Co (Publishers) Ltd:** 4675A Ansari Rd, 21 Daryaganj, New Delhi 110 002; tel. (11) 23263393; fax (11) 23269032; e-mail connect@frankbros.com; f. 1930; children's, educational and management; Chair. and Man. Dir R. C. GOVIL.

**Heritage Publishers:** 19A Ansari Rd, Daryaganj, New Delhi 110 002; tel. (11) 23266633; fax (11) 23263050; e-mail heritage@nda.vsnl.net.in; internet www.meditechbooks.com; f. 1973; social sciences, art and architecture, technical, medical, scientific; Propr and Dir B. R. CHAWLA.

**Hindustan Publishing Corpn (India):** 4805/24 Bharat Ram Rd, Suite 102, Daryaganj, New Delhi 110 002; tel. (11) 43580512; e-mail hpcedu@rediffmail.com; archaeology, anthropology, business management, demography and population dynamics, economics, pure and applied sciences, geology, mathematics, physics, sociology; publ. *Demography India* and *Journal of Economic Geology and Georesource Management* ; exporter of Indian journals and periodicals, Indian and foreign books; Man. Partner B. B. JAIN.

**Kali for Women:** K-36 Hauz Khas Enclave, New Delhi 110 016; tel. (11) 26964947; fax (11) 26496597; e-mail womenunltd@vsnl.net; women's studies, social sciences, humanities, general non-fiction, fiction, etc.; Heads of Organization URVASHI BUTALIA, RITU MENON.

**Lalit Kala Akademi:** Rabindra Bhavan, New Delhi 110 001; tel. (11) 23387241; fax (11) 23782485; e-mail lka@lalitkala.org.in; internet www.lalitkala.gov.in; books on Indian art; CEO Dr SUDHAKAR SHARMA.

**Lancers Books:** POB 4236, New Delhi 110 048; tel. (11) 26241617; fax (11) 26992063; e-mail lancersbooks@hotmail.com; f. 1977; politics (with special emphasis on north-east India), defence; Propr S. KUMAR.

**Motilal Banarsidass Publishers (Pvt) Ltd:** 41 U.A. Bungalow Rd, Jawahar Nagar, Delhi 110 007; tel. (11) 23851985; fax (11) 25797221; e-mail mlbd@vsnl.com; internet www.mlbd.com; f. 1903; religion, philosophy, astrology, yoga, linguistic, history, art, architecture, literature, music and dance, alternative medicine, in English and Sanskrit; offices in Bangalore, Chennai, Kolkata, Mumbai, Patna, Pune and Varanasi; Man. Dir N. P. JAIN.

**Munshiram Manoharlal Publishers Pvt Ltd:** 54 Rani Jhansi Rd, POB 5715, New Delhi 110 055; tel. (11) 23671668; fax (11) 23612745; e-mail mrml@mrmlbooks.com; internet www.mrmlbooks.com; f. 1952; Indian art, architecture, archaeology, religion, music, law, medicine, dance, dictionaries, travel, history, politics, numismatics, Buddhism, philosophy, sociology, etc.; Man. Dir ASHOK JAIN.

**National Book Trust:** A-5 Green Park, New Delhi 110 016; tel. (11) 26518607; fax (11) 26851795; e-mail nbtindia@ndb.vsnl.net.in; internet www.nbtindia.org.in; f. 1957; autonomous organization established by the Ministry of Human Resources Development to produce and encourage the production of good literary works; Chair. Prof. BIPAN CHANDRA; Dir NUZHAT HASSAN.

**National Council of Educational Research and Training (NCERT):** Sri Aurobindo Marg, New Delhi 110 016; tel. (11) 26560620; fax (11) 26868419; e-mail directorncert@vsnl.com; internet www.ncert.nic.in; f. 1961; school textbooks, teachers' guides, research monographs, journals, etc.; Dir Prof. KRISHNA KUMAR.

**Neeta Prakashan:** A-4 Ring Rd, South Extension Part I, POB 3853, New Delhi 110 049; tel. (11) 24636010; fax (11) 24636011; e-mail neetabooks@vsnl.com; internet www.neetaprakashan.com; f. 1960; educational, children's, general; Dir RAJESH GUPTA.

**New Age International Pvt Ltd:** 4835/24 Ansari Rd, Daryaganj, New Delhi 110 002; tel. (11) 23276802; fax (11) 23267437; e-mail saumya.gupta@newagepublishers.com; internet www.newagepublishers.com; f. 1966; science, engineering, technology, management, humanities, social science; Man. Dir SAUMYA GUPTA.

**Oxford and IBH Publishing Co (Pvt) Ltd:** 66 Janpath, New Delhi 110 001; tel. (11) 23415896; fax (11) 51517599; e-mail oxford@vsnl.com; f. 1964; science, technology and reference in English; Man. Dir MOHAN PRIMLANI.

**Oxford University Press:** YMCA Library Bldg, 1st Floor, 1 Jai Singh Rd, POB 43, New Delhi 110 001; tel. (11) 23747124; fax (11) 23360897; e-mail manzar.khan@oup.com; internet www.oup.com/in; f. 1912; educational, scientific, medical, general, humanities and social science, dictionaries and reference; Man. Dir MANZAR KHAN.

**Penguin Books India (Pvt) Ltd:** 11 Community Centre, Panchsheel Park, New Delhi 110 017; tel. (11) 26494401; fax (11) 26494403; e-mail penguin@del2.vsnl.net.in; internet www.penguinbooksindia.com; f. 1987; Indian literature and general non-fiction in English; Chair. JOHN MAKINSON; Pres. THOMAS ABRAHAM.

**People's Publishing House (Pvt) Ltd:** 5E Rani Jhansi Rd, New Delhi 110 055; tel. (11) 27524701; f. 1947; Marxism, Leninism, peasant movt; Dir SHAMEEM FAIZEE.

**Pitambar Publishing Co Pvt Ltd:** 888 East Park Rd, Karol Bagh, New Delhi 110 005; tel. (11) 23676058; fax (11) 23676058; e-mail pitambar@bol.net.in; internet www.pitambarbooks.com; academic, children's books, textbooks and general; Man. Dir ANAND BHUSHAN; five brs.

**Prentice-Hall of India (Pvt) Ltd:** M-97 Connaught Circus, New Delhi 110 001; tel. (11) 22143344; fax (11) 23417179; e-mail phi@

phindia.com; internet www.phindia.com; f. 1963; university-level text and reference books; Man. Dir A. K. GHOSH.

**Pustak Mahal:** J-3/16 Daryaganj, New Delhi 110 002; tel. (11) 23272783; fax (11) 23260518; e-mail info@pustakmahal.com; internet www.pustakmahal.com; children's, general, computers, religious, encyclopaedias; Chair. R. A. GUPTA; Man. Dir ASHOK GUPTA.

**Rajkamal Prakashan (Pvt) Ltd:** 1B Netaji Subhas Marg, Daryaganj, New Delhi 110 002; tel. (11) 23274463; fax (11) 23278144; e-mail info@rajkamalprakashan.com; internet www.rajkamalprakashan.com; f. 1947; Hindi; literary; also literary journal and monthly trade journal; Man. Dir ASHOK KUMAR MAHESHWARI.

**Rajpal and Sons:** 1590 Madrasa Rd, Kashmere Gate, Delhi 110 006; tel. (11) 23865483; fax (11) 23867791; e-mail orienpbk@ndb.vsnl.net.in; f. 1891; humanities, social sciences, art, juvenile; Hindi; Chair. VISHWANATH MALHOTRA.

**Research and Information System for Developing Countries:** Zone IV-B, 4th Floor, India Habitat Centre, Lodhi Rd, New Delhi 110 003; tel. (11) 24682177; fax (11) 24682173; e-mail dgoffice@ris.org.in; internet www.ris.org.in; f. 1983; trade and development issues; Dir-Gen. Dr NAGESH KUMAR.

**Rupa & Co:** 7/16 Ansari Rd, Daryaganj, POB 7017, New Delhi 110 002; tel. (11) 23278586; fax (11) 23277294; e-mail rupa@ndb.vsnl.net.in; internet www.rupapublications.com; f. 1936; Chief Exec. R. K. MEHRA.

**Sage Publications India Pvt Ltd:** B-42, Panchsheel Enclave, POB 4109, New Delhi 110 017; tel. and fax (11) 26491290; e-mail journalsubs@indiasage.com; internet www.indiasage.com; f. 1981; social science, development studies, business and management studies; Man. Dir TEJESHWAR SINGH.

**Sahitya Akademi:** Rabindra Bhavan, 35 Ferozeshah Rd, New Delhi 110 001; tel. (11) 23386626; fax (11) 23382428; e-mail secy@ndb.vsnl.net.in; internet www.sahitya-akademi.gov.in; f. 1956; bibliographies, translations, monographs, encyclopaedias, literary classics, etc.; Pres. SUNIL GANGOPADHYAY; Sec. A. KRISHNA MURTHY.

**Scholar Publishing House (P) Ltd:** 85 Model Basti, New Delhi 110 005; tel. (11) 23541299; fax (11) 23676565; e-mail scholar@vsnl.com; internet www.scholargroup.com; f. 1968; educational; Man. Dir RAMESH RANADE.

**Shiksha Bharati:** 1590 Madrasa Rd, Kashmere Gate, Delhi 110 006; tel. (11) 23869812; fax (11) 23867791; e-mail orientpbk@vsnl.com; f. 1955; textbooks, creative literature, popular science and juvenile in Hindi and English; Editor MEERA JOHRI.

**Sterling Publishers (Pvt) Ltd:** A-59 Okhla Industrial Area, Phase II, New Delhi 110 020; tel. (11) 26387070; fax (11) 26383788; e-mail sterlingpublishers@airtelmail.in; internet www.sterlingpublishers.com; f. 1965; academic books on the humanities and social sciences, children's books, trade paperbacks; Chair. and Man. Dir S. K. GHAI; Dirs VIKAS GHAI, GAURAV GHAI.

**Tata McGraw-Hill Publishing Co Ltd:** 7 West Patel Nagar, New Delhi 110 008; tel. (11) 25882743; fax (11) 25885154; e-mail info_india@mcgraw-hill.com; internet www.tatamcgrawhill.com; f. 1970; engineering, computers, sciences, medicine, management, humanities, social sciences; Chair. Dr F. A. MEHTA; Man. Dir Dr N. SUBRAHMANYAM.

**A. H. Wheeler & Co Ltd:** 411 Surya Kiran Bldg, 19 K. G. Marg, New Delhi 110 001; tel. (11) 23312629; fax (11) 23357798; e-mail wheelerpub@mantraonline.com; f. 1958; textbooks, reference books, computer science and information technology, electronics, management, telecommunications, social sciences, etc.; Exec. Pres. ALOK BANERJEE.

### CHENNAI (MADRAS)

**Emerald Publishers:** 15A Casa Major Rd, 1st Floor, Egmore, Chennai 600 008; tel. (44) 28193206; fax (44) 28192380; e-mail emeraldpublishers@touchtelindia.net; internet www.emeraldpublishers.com; self-help and general, college and university textbooks in English; CEO G. OLIVANNAN.

**Eswar Press:** Archana Arcade, 27 Natesan St, T. Nagar, Chennai 600 017; tel. (44) 52030431; fax (44) 24339590; e-mail gempeyes@md3.vsnl.net.in; science and technology; CEO M. PERIYASAMY.

**Higginbothams Ltd:** 814 Anna Salai, POB 311, Chennai 600 002; tel. (44) 28520640; fax (44) 28528101; e-mail higginbothams@vsnl.com; f. 1844; general; Dir S. CHANDRASEKHAR.

**Minerva Publications:** 6 Pycrofts Rd, 1st Floor, Triplicane, Chennai 600 005; tel. (44) 28445674; fax (44) 28445674; e-mail minerva@hathway.com; internet www.minervaa.com; children's books and dictionaries; CEO T. NAZIBUDEEN.

**Premier Publishing (Pvt) Ltd:** 47 Noor Veerasamy St, Nungambakkam, Chennai 600 034; tel. (44) 28222566; e-mail manahabi2002@hotmail.com; internet www.sambooks.com; business and management, health, religion, culture, etc.; Man. Dir S. HABIBULLAH.

**Scitech Publications (India) (Pvt) Ltd:** 7/3-C Madley Rd, T. Nagar, Chennai 600 017; tel. (44) 24328737; e-mail scitech@md5.vsnl.net.in; internet www.scitechpublications.com; science, technology, management, reference, etc.; Man. Dir M. R. PURUSHOTHAMAN.

**Sura Books (Pvt) Ltd:** 1620 J Block, 16th Main Rd, Anna Nagar, Chennai 600 040; tel. (44) 26161099; fax (44) 26162173; e-mail surabooks@eth.net; internet www.surabooks.com; children's books, dictionaries, examinations guides, tourist guides, Indology, etc.; Man. Dir V. K. SUBBURAJ.

**T. R. Publications Pvt Ltd:** PMG Complex, 2nd Floor, 57 South Usman Rd, T. Nagar, Chennai 600 017; tel. (44) 24340765; fax (44) 24348837; e-mail trpubs@md5.vsnl.net.in; internet www.trpublications.com; Chief Exec. S. GEETHA.

### JAIPUR

**Aavishkar Publishers, Distributors:** 807 Vyas Bldg, Chaura Rasta, Jaipur 302 003; tel. (141) 2708286; fax (141) 2578159; e-mail aavishkarbooks@hotmail.com; internet www.pointerpublishers.com; f. 1984; general and reference books on humanities, arts, science, agriculture, environmental science, commerce; CEO PREM C. BAKLIWAL.

**Mangal Deep Publications:** Duggar Bldg, M. I. Rd, Jaipur 302 001; tel. (141) 2365086; fax (141) 5102022; e-mail mdpbk@sancharnet.net; humanities, social sciences, science, technology; Propr B. K. MANGAL.

**Pointer Publishers:** 807 Vyas Bldg, Chaura Rasta, Jaipur 302 003; tel. and fax (141) 2578159; e-mail pointerpub@hotmail.com; internet www.pointerpublishers.com; f. 1986; sciences, commerce, economics, education, literature, history, journalism, law, philosophy, psychology, sociology, tourism; in English and Hindi; Contact VIPIN JAIN.

**Publication Scheme:** C 12/13, 1st Floor, Ganga Mandir, Sansar Chandra Rd, Jaipur 302 001; tel. (141) 5104038; fax (141) 2376922; e-mail parampsj@datainfosys.net; internet www.pubscheme.com; social sciences, humanities, Ayurveda, Indology; Propr S. S. NATANI.

**Rajasthan Hindi Granth Akademi:** Plot No. 1, Jhalana Institutional Area, Jaipur 302 004; tel. (141) 2711129; fax (141) 2710341; e-mail hindigranth@indiatimes.com; internet www.rajhga.org; engineering, agriculture, science, social sciences, law, education, fine arts and journalism; Dir Dr R. D. SAINI.

**Shyam Prakashan:** Film Colony, Chaura Rasta, Jaipur 302 003; tel. (141) 2317659; fax (141) 2326554; Propr OM PRAKASH AGARWAL.

**University Book House (Pvt) Ltd:** 79 Chaura Rasta, Jaipur 302 003; tel. (141) 2311466; fax (141) 2313382; e-mail uni_bookhouse@yahoo.com; commerce, management, home science, history, political science, public administration; Man. Dir CHETAN K. JAIN.

### KOLKATA (CALCUTTA)

**Academic Publishers:** 12/1A Bankim Chatterjee St, POB 12341, Kolkata 700 073; tel. (33) 22414857; fax (33) 22413702; e-mail acabooks@cal.vsnl.net.in; f. 1958; textbooks, management, medical, technical; Man. Partner B. K. DHUR.

**Advaita Ashrama:** 5 Dehi Entally Rd, Kolkata 700 014; tel. (33) 22164000; e-mail mail@advaitaashrama.org; internet www.advaitaashrama.org; f. 1899; religion, philosophy, spiritualism, Vedanta; publication centre of Ramakrishna Math and Ramakrishna Mission; Publication Man. Swami BODHASARANANDA.

**Allied Book Agency:** 18A Shyama Charan De St, Kolkata 700 073; general and academic; Dir B. SARKAR.

**Ananda Publishers (Pvt) Ltd:** 45 Beniatola Lane, Kolkata 700 009; tel. (33) 22414352; fax (33) 22193856; e-mail ananda@cal3.vsnl.net.in; internet www.anandapub.com; literature, general; Man. Dir S. MITRA.

**Assam Review Publishing Co:** 27A Waterloo St, 1st Floor, Kolkata 700 069; tel. (33) 22482251; fax (33) 22482251; e-mail assamrev@yahoo.co.in; f. 1926; publrs of The Assam Review and Tea News (monthly) and The Assam Directory and Tea Areas Handbook (annually); Chief Exec. GOBINDALAL BANERJEE.

**Dev Sahitya Kutir:** 21 Jhamapukur Lane, Kolkata 700 009; tel. (33) 22417406; children's, general; Dir PRABIR KUMAR MAJUMDAR.

**Dey's Publishing:** 13 Bankim Chatterjee St, Kolkata 700 073; tel. (33) 22412330; fax (33) 22192041; e-mail deyspublishing@hotmail.com; academic books, religion, philosophy, general; Dir SUDHANGSHU KUMAR DEY.

**Eastern Law House (Pvt) Ltd:** 54 Ganesh Chunder Ave, Kolkata 700 013; tel. (33) 22151989; fax (33) 22150491; e-mail elh@cal.vsnl.net.in; internet www.easternlawhouse.com; f. 1918; legal, commercial and accountancy; Dir ASOK DE; br. in New Delhi.

**Firma KLM Private Ltd:** 257B B. B. Ganguly St, Kolkata 700 012; tel. (33) 22374391; fax (33) 22217294; e-mail fklm@satyam.net.in; f. 1950; Indology, scholarly in English, Bengali, Sanskrit and Hindi, alternative medicine; Man. Dir S. MUKHERJI.

**Indian Museum:** 27 Jawaharlal Nehru Rd, Kolkata 700 016; tel. (33) 22499902; fax (33) 22495696; e-mail imbot@cal12.vsnl.net.in; internet www.indianmuseum-calcutta; social sciences and humanities; Dir S. K. CHAKRAVARTI.

**Intertrade Publications (India) (Pvt) Ltd:** 55 Gariahat Rd, POB 10210, Kolkata 700 019; f. 1954; economics, medicine, law, history and trade directories; Man. Dir Dr K. K. ROY.

**A. Mukherjee and Co (Pvt) Ltd:** 2 Bankim Chatterjee St, Kolkata 700 073; tel. (33) 22417406; fax (33) 27448172; f. 1940; educational and general in Bengali and English; Man. Dir RAJEEV NEOGI.

**Naya Udyog:** 206 Bidhan Sarani, Kolkata 700 006; tel. (33) 22413540; e-mail navudyog@vsnl.net; f. 1992; books in English and Bengali; agriculture, horticulture, social science, history, botany; distributes Naya Prokash publications; Man. Dir PARTHA SANKAR BASU.

**New Age Publishers (Pvt) Ltd:** 12B Bankim Chatterjee St, Kolkata 700 073; tel. (33) 22418509; e-mail newagepub@vsnl.net; literature, art, philosophy, history, social and cultural studies; Propr SHILADITYA.

**Patra's Publication:** 2 Shyamacharan Dey St, Kolkata 700 073; tel. (33) 22197297; e-mail manaspatra@vsnl.net; f. 1975; fiction, general; Propr PRAFULLA KUMAR PATRA.

**Punthi Pustak:** 136/4B Bidhan Sarani, Kolkata 700 004; tel. and fax (33) 25555573; e-mail info@punthipustak.com; f. 1956; religion, history, philosophy; Propr P. K. BHATTACHARYA.

**Renaissance Publishers (Pvt) Ltd:** 15 Bankim Chatterjee St, Kolkata 700 012; f. 1949; politics, philosophy, history; Man. Dir J. C. GOSWAMI.

**Sahitya Sansad:** 32A Acharya Prafulla Chandra Rd, Kolkata 700 009; tel. (33) 23507669; fax (33) 23603508; e-mail samsad@cal3.vsnl.net.in; internet www.samsadbooks.com; children's, reference, science, literature; Man. Dir DEBAJYOTI DUTTA.

**Samya:** 16 Southern Ave, Kolkata 700 026; tel. (33) 24660812; fax (33) 24644614; e-mail stree@cal2.vsnl.net.in; internet www.samyabooks.com; f. 1996; owned by joint partnership, Bhatkal and Sen; social change, culture and Dalit issues; Dir MANDIRA SEN.

**Saraswati Library:** 206 Bidhan Sarani, Kolkata 700 006; f. 1914; history, philosophy, religion, literature; Man. Partner B. BHATTACHARJEE.

**M. C. Sarkar and Sons (Pvt) Ltd:** 14 Bankim Chatterjee St, Kolkata 700 073; f. 1910; reference; Dir SAMIT SARKAR.

**Seagull Books (Pvt) Ltd:** 26 Circus Ave, Kolkata 700 017; tel. (33) 22403636; fax (33) 22805143; e-mail seagullfoundation@vsnl.com; internet www.seagullindia.com; academic, literary, general; CEO NAVIN KISHORE.

**Stree-Samya:** 16 Southern Ave, Kolkata 700 026; tel. (33) 24660812; fax (33) 24644614; e-mail stree@cal2.vsnl.net.in; internet www.streebooks.com; f. 1990 (Stree); 1996 (Samya); imprints publ. by joint venture of Harsha Bhatkal, Popular Prakashan and Mandira Sen; women's issues and writings in English and Bengali; Dir MANDIRA SEN.

**Visva-Bharati:** 6 Acharya Jagadish Bose Rd, Kolkata 700 017; tel. (33) 22479868; f. 1923; literature; Dir Prof. KUKUM BHATTACHARYA.

### MUMBAI (BOMBAY)

**Bharatiya Vidya Bhavan:** Munshi Sadan, Kulapati K. M. Munshi Marg, Mumbai 400 007; tel. (22) 24950916; fax (22) 23630058; e-mail brbhavan@bom7.vsnl.net.in; internet www.bhavans.info; f. 1938; art, literature, culture, education, philosophy, religion, history of India; various periodicals in English, Hindi, Sanskrit and other Indian languages; Pres. PRAVINCHANDRA V. GANDHI; Dir-Gen. DHIRU MEHTA.

**Himalaya Publishing House:** Dr Bhalerao Marg (Kelewadi), Girgaon, Mumbai 400 004; tel. (22) 23860170; fax (22) 23877178; e-mail himpub@vsnl.com; internet www.himpub.com; f. 1976; textbooks and research work; Publr MEENA PANDEY.

**India Book House (Pvt) Ltd:** 412 Tulsiani Chambers, Nariman Point, Mumbai 400 021; tel. (22) 22840165; fax (22) 22835099; e-mail info@ibhworld.com; internet www.ibhworld.com; Man. Dir DEEPAK MIRCHANDANI.

**International Book House (Pvt) Ltd:** Indian Mercantile Mansions (Extension), Madame Cama Rd, Mumbai 400 039; tel. (22) 22021634; fax (22) 22851109; e-mail ibh@vsnl.com; internet www.intbh.com; f. 1941; children's, general, educational, scientific, technical, engineering, social sciences, humanities and law; Dir ROHIT GUPTA; Dir SANJEEV GUPTA.

**Jaico Publishing House:** A2, Jash Chambers, Sir P. M. Rd, Fort, Mumbai 400 001; tel. (22) 40306767; fax (22) 22656412; e-mail jaicowbd@vsnl.com; internet www.jaicobooks.com; f. 1947; general paperbacks, management, computer and engineering books, etc.; imports scientific, medical, technical and educational books; Man. Dir ASHWIN J. SHAH.

**Popular Prakashan (Pvt) Ltd:** 35C Pandit Madan Mohan Malaviya Marg, Tardeo, opp. Crossroads, Mumbai 400 034; tel. (22) 23265245; fax (22) 24945294; e-mail infor@popularprakashan.com; internet www.popularprakashan.com; f. 1968; sociology, biographies, religion, philosophy, fiction, arts, music, current affairs, medicine, history, politics and administration in English and Marathi; CEO HARSHA BHATKAL.

**Sheth Publishing House:** G-12 Suyog Industrial Estate, nr LBS Marg, Vikhroli (W), Mumbai 400 083; tel. (22) 25773707; fax (22) 25774200; e-mail no.sph@bom5.vsnl.net.in; educational, children's; Propr NILESH M. SHETH.

**Somaiya Publications (Pvt) Ltd:** 172 Mumbai Marathi Granthasangrahalaya Marg, Dadar, Mumbai 400 014; tel. (22) 24130230; fax (22) 22047297; e-mail somaiyabooks@rediffmail.com; internet www.somaiya.com; f. 1967; economics, sociology, history, politics, mathematics, sciences, language, literature, education, psychology, religion, philosophy, logic; Chair. Dr S. K. SOMAIYA.

**Taraporevala, Sons and Co (Pvt) Ltd D.B.:** 210 Dr Dadabhai Naoroji Rd, Fort, Mumbai 400 001; tel. (22) 22071433; f. 1864; Indian art, culture, history, sociology, scientific, technical and general in English; Chief Exec. R. J. TARAPOREVALA.

**N. M. Tripathi (Pvt) Ltd:** 164 Shamaldas Gandhi Marg, Mumbai 400 002; tel. (22) 22013651; e-mail mistertripathi@rediffmail.com; f. 1888; general in English and Gujarati; Chair. A. S. PANDYA; Man. Dir KARTIK R. TRIPATHI.

**K. M. Varghese Co:** Hind Rajasthan Bldg, Dada Saheb Phalke Rd, Dadar, Mumbai 400 014; tel. (22) 24149074; fax (22) 24146904; e-mail km@varghese.net; internet www.varghese.net; f. 1960; medicine, pharmacy, nursing, physiotherapy; Propr K. M. VARGHESE.

**Vora Medical Publications:** 6 Princess Bldg, E. R. Rd, Mumbai 400 003; tel. (22) 23754161; fax (22) 23704053; e-mail voramedpub@yahoo.co.in; medicine, nursing, management, spiritualism, general knowledge; Propr R. K. VORA.

### OTHER TOWNS

**Anada Prakashan (Pvt) Ltd:** 1756 Gandhi Rd, Ahmedabad 380 001; tel. (79) 2169956; fax (79) 2139900; e-mail anadaad1@sancharnet.in; internet www.anada.com; children's, educational, dictionaries; Man. Dir B. R. ANADA.

**Bharati Bhawan:** Thakurbari Rd, Kadamkuan, Patna 800 003; tel. (612) 2671356; fax (612) 2670010; e-mail bbpdpat@sancharnet.in; f. 1942; educational and juvenile; Man. Partner TARIT KUMAR BOSE.

**Bishen Singh Mahendra Pal Singh:** 23A New Connaught Place, POB 137, Dehradun 248 001; tel. (135) 2715748; fax (135) 2715107; e-mail bsmps@vsnl.com; f. 1957; botany, forestry, agriculture; Dirs GAJENDRA SINGH GAHLOT, ABHIMANYU GAHLOT.

**Books for Change:** 139 Richmond Rd, Bangalore 560 025; tel. (80) 25321747; fax (80) 25586284; e-mail shoba.ram@actionaid.org; internet www.booksforchange.net; f. 1997; operated by ActionAid Karnataka Projects; pblr and distributor of books and other media relating to social issues; Publr and Chief Editor SHOBA RAMACHANDRAN.

**Catholic Press:** Ranchi 834 001; f. 1928; books and periodicals; Dir WILLIAM TIGGA.

**DC Books:** POB 214, DC Kizhakemuri Edam, Good Shepherd St, Kottayam 686 001; tel. (481) 2563114; fax (481) 2564758; e-mail ceo@dcbooks.com; internet www.dcbooks.com; f. 1974; fiction, general and reference books in Malayalam; CEO RAVI DEECEE.

**Hind Pocket Books (Pvt) Ltd:** B-13, Sector 81, Phase II, Noida 201305; tel. (120) 3093992; fax (120) 2563983; e-mail gbp@del2.vsnl.net.in; f. 1958; fiction and non-fiction paperbacks in English, Hindi, Punjabi, Malayalam and Urdu; Chair DINA NATH MALHOTRA; Man. Dir SHEKHAR MALHOTRA.

**Indica Books:** D-40/18 Godowlia, Varanasi 221 001; tel. (542) 3094999; fax (542) 2452258; e-mail indicabooks@satyam.net.in; internet www.indicabooks.com; Indology, philosophy, religion, culture; Propr DILIP KUMAR JAISWAL.

**Jnan Bichitra:** Jogendranagar, Vidyasagar Chowmuhani, Agartala, West Tripura 799 001; tel. (381) 2323781; e-mail jnanbichitra@rediffmail.com; f. 1976; general, science; Propr DEBANANDA DAM.

**Kalyani Publishers:** 1/1 Rajinder Nagar, Civil Lines, Ludhiana 141 008; tel. (161) 2745756; fax (161) 2745872; textbooks; Dir RAJ KUMAR.

**Krishna Prakashan Media (P) Ltd:** (Unit) Goel Publishing House, 11 Shivaji Rd, Meerut 250 001; tel. (121) 2644766; fax (121) 2645855; e-mail sk_kpm@yahoo.com; textbooks; Man. Dir SATYENDRA KUMAR RASTOGI; Dir ANITA RASTOGI.

**Law Publishers:** Sardar Patel Marg, Civil Lines, POB 1004, Allahabad 211 001; tel. (532) 2622758; fax (532) 2622781; e-mail lawpub@vsnl.com; internet www.law-publishers.com; f. 1929; legal texts in English; Dir NARESH SAGAR.

**Macmillan India Ltd:** 315/316 Raheja Chambers, 12 Museum Rd, Bangalore 560 001; tel. (80) 25594120; fax (80) 25588713; e-mail rberi@bgl.vsnl.net.in; internet www.macmillanindia.com; school and university books in English; general; Pres. and Man. Dir RAJIV BERI; Dir (Technical) DEBASHISH BANERJEE.

**Madhuban Educational Books:** A-22, Sector 4, Noida 201 301; tel. (120) 4078900; fax (120) 4078999; e-mail info@madhubunbooks.com; f. 1969; school books, children's books; Dir SAJILI SHIRODKAR.

**Mapin Publishing (Pvt) Ltd:** 10B Vidyanagar Society Part I, Usmanpura, Ahmedabad 380 014; tel. (79) 27545390; fax (79) 27545392; e-mail mapin@mapinpub.com; internet www.mapinpub.com; f. 1984; illustrated books on Indian art, culture, history, architecture, photography, crafts and literature; collaborates with art book publrs and museums to provide custom packaging services; Man. Dir BIPIN SHAH.

**Navajivan Publishing House:** PO Navajivan, Ahmedabad 380 014; tel. (79) 7540635; f. 1919; Gandhiana and related social science; in English, Hindi and Gujarati; Man. Trustee JITENDRA DESAI; Sales Man. KAPIL RAWAL.

**Neelkamal Publications (Pvt) Ltd:** NN Complex, Hyderabad 500 095; tel. (40) 24757140; fax (40) 24757951; e-mail suresh@neelkamalpub.com; internet www.neelkamalpub.com; education, psychology, dictionaries, encyclopaedias; Man. Dir SURESH CHANDRA SHARMA.

**Orient Longman (Pvt) Ltd:** 3-6-752 Himayat Nagar, Hyderabad 500 029; tel. (40) 27665466; fax (40) 27645046; e-mail hyd2_orlongco@sancharnet.in; f. 1948; educational, technical, general and children's in English and almost all Indian languages; Chair. SHANTA RAMESHWAR RAO; Dirs Dr NANDINI RAO, J. KRISHNADEV RAO.

**Parikalpana Prakashan:** D-68 Nirala Nagar, Lucknow 226 010; tel. (522) 2786782; fax (11) 27296559; e-mail janchetna@rediffmail.com; f. 1996; fiction, poetry, literary criticism, history, political sciences, philosophy; Hindi and English; Pres. KATYAYANI.

**Pilgrims Publishing:** Pilgrims Book House, B27/98-A-8 Nawabganj Rd, Durga Kund, Varanasi 221 001; tel. (542) 2314060; fax (542) 2314059; e-mail pilgrims@satyam.net.in; internet www.pilgrimsbooks.com; f. 1986; first edition and reprint books on Nepal, Tibet, India and the Himalayas; also operates Pilgrims Book House; Man. Editor CHRISTOPHER N. BURCHETT.

**Publication Bureau:** Panjab University, Chandigarh 160 014; tel. (172) 2541782; f. 1948; textbooks, academic and general; CEO DARSHAN SINGH; Man. H. R. GROVER.

**Publication Bureau:** Punjabi University, Patiala 147 002; tel. (175) 3046093; fax (175) 2283073; internet www.universitypunjabi.org; f. 1966; university-level text and reference books, and other general interest books; Punjabi, English and other languages; CEO Dr B. S. MANGAT.

**Ram Prasad and Sons:** Hospital Rd, Agra 282 003; tel. (562) 2461904; fax (562) 2460920; e-mail rpsons@sancharnet.in; f. 1905; agricultural, arts, history, commerce, education, general, computing, engineering, pure and applied science, economics, sociology; Dirs R. N, B. N, Y. N, RAVI AGARWAL; Man. S. N. AGARWAL; br. in Bhopal.

**Sahitya Bhandar:** 50 Chahchand Zero Rd, Allahabad 211 001; tel. (532) 2400787; Hindi literature, children's, science, literary criticism, etc.; Propr SATISH CHANDRA AGGARWAL.

**Sahitya Bhawan Publications:** Hospital Rd, Agra 282 003; tel. (562) 2151665; fax (562) 2151568; e-mail info@sbpagra.com; internet www.sbpagra.com; social sciences, humanities; Propr RAHUL BANSAL.

**Sahitya Sangam:** New 100, Lukerganj, Allahabad 211 001; Hindi literature, communication, journalism, political science, art, history, etc.; Propr ALOK CHATURVEDI.

**Samvad Prakashan:** I-499 Shastri Nagar, Meerut 250 004; tel. (121) 2764866; e-mail samvadindia@vsnl.net; Hindi translations of world literature; biographies, autobiographies, fiction, cinema; Propr NAMITA SRIVASTAVA.

**Universities Press (India) (Pvt) Ltd:** 3-6-747/1/A & 3-6-754/1 Himayat Nagar, Hyderabad 500 029; tel. (40) 27662849; fax (40) 27645046; e-mail info@universitiespress.com; internet www.universitiespress.com; academic and educational books on science, technology, management; Man. Dir MADHU REDDY.

**Vikas Publishing House Pvt Ltd:** A-22, Sector 4, Noida 201 301; tel. (120) 4078900; fax (120) 4078999; e-mail helpline@vikaspublishing.com; internet www.vikaspublishing.com; f. 1969; computers, management, commerce, sciences, engineering textbooks; Dir PIYUSH CHAWLA.

**Vishwavidyalaya Prakashan:** Vishalakshi Bldg, POB 1149, Chowk, Varanasi 221 001, Uttar Pradesh; tel. (542) 2413741; fax (542) 2413082; e-mail vvp@vsnl.com; internet www.vvpbooks.com; f. 1950; Hindu and Sanskrit literature, Indology, history, art and culture, spiritualism, religion, philosophy, education, sociology, psychology, music, journalism, mass communication, science and social science; Partner ANURAG KUMAR.

## GOVERNMENT PUBLISHING HOUSE

**Publications Division:** Ministry of Information and Broadcasting, Govt of India, Patiala House, New Delhi 110 001; tel. and fax (11) 24366670; e-mail dpd@sb.nic.in; internet publicationsdivision.nic.in; f. 1941; culture, art, literature, planning and development, general; also 21 periodicals in English and 13 Indian languages; Dir VEENA JAIN.

## PUBLISHERS' ASSOCIATIONS

**Bombay Booksellers' and Publishers' Association:** No. 25, 6th Floor, Bldg No. 3, Navjivan Commercial Premises Co-op Society Ltd, Dr Bhadkamkar Marg, Mumbai 400 008; tel. (22) 23088691; e-mail bbpassn@yahoo.co.in; f. 1961; 400 mems; Pres. D. D. JANI; Hon. Gen. Sec. B. S. FERNANDES.

**Delhi State Booksellers' and Publishers' Association:** 3026/7-H Shiv Chowk, (South Patel Nagar) Ranjit Nagar, New Delhi 110 008; tel. (11) 25847377; fax (11) 25842605; e-mail rpnbooks@indiatimes.com; f. 1941; 400 mems; Pres. Dr S. K. BHATIA; Sec. K. K. SAXENA.

**Federation of Educational Publishers in India:** X-39, Institutional Area, Karkardoma, New Delhi 110 092; tel. (11) 22377017; f. 1987; 14 affiliated asscns; 150 life mems; 45 annual mems; Pres. R. K. GUPTA; Sec.-Gen. KAMAL ARORA.

**Federation of Indian Publishers:** Federation House, 18/1-C Institutional Area, nr JNU, New Delhi 110 067; tel. (11) 26964847; fax (11) 26864054; e-mail fipl@satyam.net.in; internet www.fiponweb.com; 18 affiliated asscns; 190 mems; Pres. ANAND BHUSHAN; Hon. Gen. Sec. SHAKTI MALIK.

**Akhil Bharatiya Hindi Prakashak Sangh:** 139, Purani Anarkali, Gali No. 4, Delhi 110 051; f. 1954; 400 mems; Pres. KRISHNAN DEV SHARMA; Gen. Sec. ARUN KUMAR SHARMA.

**Akhil Bharatiya Marathi Prakashak Sangha:** c/o Dilipraj Prakashan (Pvt) Ltd, 251-C, Shaniwar Peth, Pune 411 030; Pres. SHARAD GOGATE.

**All Assam Publishers' and Booksellers' Association:** Chancellor Bldg, H. B. Rd, Panbazar, Guwahati 781 001; tel. (361) 2634790; fax (361) 2513886; e-mail devchowdhurygp@rediffmail.com; Pres. GIRIPADA DEV CHOWDHURY; Sec. BIDYUT GUHA.

**All India Urdu Publishers' and Booksellers' Association:** 3243 Kuchatarachand, Daryaganj, New Delhi 110 002; tel. (11) 23257189; fax (11) 23265480; e-mail aakif@del3.vsnl.net.in; internet www.indiamart.com/aakifbooks; f. 1988; 175 mems; Pres. Dr KHALIQ ANJUM; Gen. Sec. S. M. ZAFAR ALI.

**All Kerala Publishers' and Booksellers' Association:** D. C. Kizhakemuri Edam, Good Shepherd St, Kottayam 686 001; tel. (481) 2563114; fax (481) 2564758; e-mail info@dcbooks.com; Pres. E. N. NANTHAKUMAR.

**Booksellers' and Publishers' Association of South India:** 8, 2nd Floor, Sun Plaza, G. N. Chetty Rd, Chennai 600 006; 251 mems; Pres. GANDHI KANNADASAN; Sec. R. S. SHANMUGAM.

**Gujarati Publishers' Association:** Navajivan Trust, PO Navajivan, Ahmedabad 380 014; tel. (79) 7540635; 125 mems; Pres. JITENDRA DESAI; Sec. K. N. MADRASI.

**Karnataka Publishers' Association:** c/o Ankita Pustaka, 53 Sham Singh Complex, Gandhi Bazar Main Rd, Bangalore 560 004; tel. (80) 26617100; Pres. Dr RAMAKANT JOSHI.

**Orissa Publishers' and Booksellers' Association:** Binodbihari, Cuttack 753 002; tel. (671) 2620637; f. 1973–74; 280 mems; Pres. PITAMBAR MISHRA; Sec. SUBHENDU SEKHAR RATHA.

**Paschimbanga Prakasak Sabha:** 206 Bidhan Sarani, Kolkata 700 006; tel. (33) 23506720; fax (33) 22413852; Pres. BIPLAB BHOWAL; Gen. Sec. SOMENATH MUKHERJEE.

**Publishers' Association of West Bengal:** 6-B, Ramanath Mazumder St, Kolkata 700 009; tel. (33) 2325580; 164 mems; Pres. MOHIT KUMAR BASU; Gen. Sec. SHANKARI BHUSAN NAYAK.

**Publishers' and Booksellers' Association of Bengal:** 93 Mahatma Gandhi Rd, Kolkata 700 007; tel. (33) 22411993; f. 1912; 4,500 mems; Pres. KHIMANGSHU BANDYOPADHYAY; Gen. Sec. CHITTA SINGHA ROY.

**Punjabi Publishers' Association:** Bazar Mai Sewan, Amritsar 143 006; tel. (183) 2545787; fax (183) 2543965; Pres. KULWANT SINGH SURI; Gen. Sec. PARAMJIT SINGH.

**Vijayawada Publishers' Association:** 27-1-68, Karl Marx Rd, Vijayawada 520 002; tel. (866) 2433353; fax (866) 2426348; 41 mems; Pres. DUPATI VIJAY KUMAR; Sec. U. N. YOGI.

**Federation of Publishers' and Booksellers' Associations in India:** 2nd Floor, 84 Daryaganj, New Delhi 110 002; tel. (11) 23272845; fax (11) 23281227; e-mail fpbai@vsnl.net; internet www.fpbai.org; f. 1955; 12 affiliated asscns; 507 mems; Pres. A. S. CHOWDHRY; Hon. Sec. BALDEV VERMA.

**Publishers' and Booksellers' Guild:** Guild House, 2B Jhamapukur Lane, Kolkata 700 009; tel. (33) 23544417; fax (33) 23604566; e-mail guild@cal2.vsnl.net.in; internet www.kolkatabookfaironline.com; f. 1975; 35 mems; organizes annual internationally recognized Kolkata Book Fair; Pres. JAYANT MANAKTALA; Hon. Gen. Sec. TRIDIB KR. CHATTERJEE.

**UP Publishers' Association:** Bharati Bhavan, Western Kutchery Rd, Meerut 250 001; Pres. RAJENDRA AGARWAL.

# Broadcasting and Communications

## TELECOMMUNICATIONS

**Telecom Regulatory Authority of India (TRAI):** Mahanagar Doorsanchar Bhavan (next to Zakir Hussain College), Jawaharlal Nehru Marg (Old Minto Rd), New Delhi 110 002; tel. (11) 23211934; fax (11) 23213294; e-mail trai@del2.vsnl.net.in; internet www.trai.gov.in; f. 1998; Chair. NRIPENDRA MISRA; Vice-Chair. BAL KRISHAN ZUTSHI.

**Bharat Sanchar Nigam Ltd (BSNL):** Statesman House, B-148, Barakhamba Rd, New Delhi 110 001; fax (11) 23765296; internet www.bsnl.co.in; f. 2000; fmrly Dept of Telecom Operations; state-owned; Chair. and Man. Dir ANIL K. SINHA.

**Bharti Airtel Ltd:** Quatab Ambience, H-5/12, Mehrauli Rd, New Delhi 110 030; tel. (11) 51666000; fax (11) 51666011; e-mail gupta_n@bhartient.com; internet www.bhartiairtel.in; f. 1998; India's first privately owned telephone network; Chair. and Man. Dir SUNIL BHARTI MITTAL.

**Ericsson India Pvt Ltd:** Ericsson Forum, DLF Cyberciti, Sector 25A, 60 Mtr. Sector Rd, Gurgaon 122 002; tel. (124) 2560808; fax (124) 2565454; e-mail marketing-int.communications@eci.ericsson.se; internet www.ericsson.co.in; Man. Dir JAN CAMPBELL.

**Hutchison Essar Ltd** (Hutch): Hutch House, Peninsula Corporate Park, Ganpatrao Kadam Marg, Lower Parel, Mumbai 400 013; tel. (22) 66645000; fax (22) 66661222; e-mail isaac.d@hutch.in; internet www.hutch.in; f. 1994; Vodafone (United Kingdom) acquired controlling 67% share from Hutchison Telecommunications International (Hong Kong) in Feb. 2007, 33 % owned by Essar Group; CEO ARUN SARIN.

**Idea Cellular:** Sharada Centre, 11/1, Erandwane, off Karve Rd, Pune 411 004; tel. (20) 24123123; fax (20) 24123999; e-mail carson.dalton@ideacellular.com; internet www.ideacellular.com; f. 2001; provides mobile telephony services in seven states; CEO VIKRAM MEHMI.

**ITI (Indian Telephone Industries) Ltd:** F29 Ground Floor, Doorvaninagar, Bangalore 560 016; tel. (80) 255660527; fax (80) 25660521; e-mail dgm_swr@itiltd.co.in; internet www.itiltd-india.com; f. 1948; mfrs of all types of telecommunication equipment, incl. telephones, automatic exchanges and long-distance transmission equipment; also produces optical fibre equipment and microwave equipment; will manufacture all ground communication equipment for the 22 earth stations of the Indian National Satellite; in conjunction with the Post and Telegraph Department, a newly designed 2,000-line exchange has been completed; Chair. and Man. Dir Y. K. PANDEY.

**Mahanagar Telephone Nigam Ltd (MTNL):** Jeevan Bharati Tower 1, 124 Connaught Circus, New Delhi 110 001; tel. (11) 23742212; fax (11) 23314243; e-mail cmd@bol.net.in; internet www.mtnl.net.in; f. 1986; 56% state-owned; owns and operates telecommunications and information technology services in Mumbai and Delhi; Chair. and Man. Dir R. S. P. SINHA.

**Reliance Infocomm Ltd:** Dhirunhai Ambani Knowledge City, Navi Mumbai 400 709; tel. (22) 30373333; e-mail customercare@relianceinfo.com; internet www.relianceinfo.com; f. 1999; provides mobile and fixed-line telephony services throughout India; Chair. and Man. Dir ANIL D. AMBANI.

**Tata Teleservices Ltd:** Ispat House, B. G. Kher Marg, Worli, Mumbai 400 018; tel. (22) 56615445; fax (22) 4605517; internet www.tataindicom.com; f. 1996; privately owned telecommunications services provider; Chair. RATAN N. TATA; CEO DARRYL GREEN.

**Videsh Sanchar Nigam Ltd (VSNL):** Lok Manya Videsh Sanchar Bhawan, Kasinath Dhuru Marg, Prabhadevi, Mumbai 400 028; tel. (22) 66578765; fax (22) 24365689; e-mail helpdesk@giaspn01.vsnl.net.in; internet www.vsnl.com; f. 1986; 26% state-owned; 45% owned by the Tata Group; Chair. SUBODH BHARGAVA.

## BROADCASTING

**Prasar Bharati** (Broadcasting Corpn of India): 2nd Floor, PTI Bldg, Sansad Marg, New Delhi 110 001; tel. (11) 23737603; fax (11) 23352549; e-mail kssarma@prasarbharati.org.in; f. 1997; autonomous body; oversees operations of state-owned radio and television services; Chair. M. V. KAMATH; CEO K. S. SARMA.

### Radio

**All India Radio (AIR):** Akashvani Bhavan, Parliament St, New Delhi 110 001; tel. (11) 23710300; fax (11) 23421956; e-mail dgair@air.org.in; internet allindiaradio.org; broadcasting is controlled by the Ministry of Information and Broadcasting and is primarily govt-financed; operates a network of 208 stations and 332 transmitters (grouped into four zones—north, south, east and west), covering almost the entire population and over 90% of the total area of the country; Dir-Gen. BRIJESHWAR SINGH.

The News Services Division of AIR, centralized in New Delhi, is one of the largest news organizations in the world. It has 45 regional news units, which broadcast 364 bulletins daily in 24 languages and 38 dialects. Eighty-four bulletins in 19 languages are broadcast in the Home Services, 187 regional bulletins in 65 languages and dialects, and 64 bulletins in 25 languages in the External Services.

### Television

**Doordarshan India** (Television India): Mandi House, Doordarshan Bhavan, Copernicus Marg, New Delhi 110 001; tel. (11) 23385958; fax (11) 23386507; e-mail webadmin@dd.nic.in; internet www.ddindia.gov.in; f. 1976; broadcasting is controlled by the Ministry of Information and Broadcasting and is govt-financed; programmes: 280 hours weekly; 5 all-India channels, 11 regional language satellite channels, 5 state networks and 1 international channel; Dir-Gen. NAVEEN KUMAR.

By March 2005 78% of the country's area and 90% of the population were covered by the television network. There were 1,314 transmitters in operation, and 56 studio centres and 23 satellite channels had been established.

# Finance

(cap. = capital; p.u. = paid up; res = reserves; dep. = deposits; m. = million; brs = branches; amounts in rupees unless otherwise stated)

## BANKING

### State Banks

**Reserve Bank of India:** Central Office Bldg, Shahid Bhagat Singh Rd, POB 10007, Mumbai 400 001; tel. (22) 22661602; fax (22) 22658269; e-mail helpprd@rbi.org.in; internet www.rbi.org.in; f. 1934; nationalized 1949; sole bank of issue; cap. 50m., res 65,000m., dep. 1,883,189m. (June 2006); Gov. D. SUBBA RAO; Dep. Govs Dr RAKESH MOHAN, V. LEELADHAR, SHYAMALA GOPINATH, USHA THORAT; 4 offices and 14 brs.

**State Bank of India:** Corporate Centre, Madame Cama Rd, POB 10121, Mumbai 400 021; tel. (22) 22022426; fax (22) 22851391; e-mail gm.gbu@sbi.co.in; internet www.statebankofindia.com; f. 1955; cap. p.u. 5,263.0m., res 307,719.2m., dep. 4,752,244.2m. (March 2007); 7 associates, 7 domestic subsidiaries/affiliates, 3 foreign subsidiaries, 4 jt ventures abroad; Chair. O. P. BHATT; Man. Dir S. K. BHATTACHARYYA; 9,593 brs (incl. 52 overseas brs and rep. offices in 34 countries).

### State-owned Commercial Banks

Fourteen of India's major commercial banks were nationalized in 1969 and a further six in 1980. They are managed by 15-member boards of directors (two directors to be appointed by the central Government, one employee director, one representing employees who are not workmen, one representing depositors, three representing farmers, workers, artisans, etc., five representing persons with special knowledge or experience, one Reserve Bank of India official and one Government of India official). The Department of Banking of the Ministry of Finance controls all banking operations.

There were 66,644 branches of public-sector and other commercial banks in June 2003.

Aggregate deposits of all scheduled commercial banks amounted to an estimated Rs 19,406,940m. in December 2005.

**Allahabad Bank:** 2 Netaji Subhas Rd, Kolkata 700 001; tel. (33) 22208668; fax (33) 22488323; e-mail cmd@allahabadbank.co.in; internet www.allahabadbank.com; f. 1865; nationalized 1969; cap. p.u. 4,467.0m., res 39,276.3m., dep. 598,008.1m. (March 2007); Chair. and Man. Dir AVINASH CHANDER MAHAJAN; Exec. Dir SUBODH KUMAR GOEL; 1,935 brs.

**Andhra Bank:** Andhra Bank Bldgs, Saifabad, 5-9-11 Secretariat Rd, Hyderabad 500 004; tel. (40) 23230001; fax (40) 23211050; e-mail customerser@andhrabank.co.in; internet www.andhrabank.in; f. 1923; nationalized 1980; cap. 4,850.0m., res 23,327.5m., dep. 346,809.1m. (March 2006); Chair. and Man. Dir Dr K. RAMAKRISHNAN; Exec. Dir KALYAN MUKHERJEE; 1,100 brs and 113 extension counters.

**Bank of Baroda:** Baroda Corporate Centre, C-26, G Block, Bandra-Kurla Complex, Bandra (East), Mumbai 400 054; tel. (22) 26985000;

fax (22) 22610341; e-mail secbob@bol.net.in; internet www.bankofbaroda.com; f. 1908; nationalized 1969; merged with Benares State Bank in 2002; cap. 3,655.3m., surplus and res 82,844.1m., dep. 1,249,159.8m. (March 2007); Chair. and Man. Dir ANIL K. KHANDELWAL; Exec. Dir A. C. MAHJAN; 2,641 brs in India, 38 brs overseas.

**Bank of India:** Star House, C-5, G Block, 3rd Floor, Bandra-Kurla Complex, Bandra (East), Mumbai 400 051; tel. (22) 66684444; fax (22) 56684558; e-mail hocsd@bankofindia.co.in; internet www.bankofindia.com; f. 1906; nationalized 1969; cap. 4,881.4m., res 48,654.7m., dep. 1,265,025.6m. (March 2007); Chair. and Man. Dir T. S. NARAYANASAMI; 2,562 brs in India, 19 brs overseas.

**Bank of Maharashtra:** 'Lokmangal', 1501 Shivajinagar, Pune 411 005; tel. (20) 25532731; fax (20) 25533246; e-mail bomcocmd@vsnl.com; internet www.maharashtrabank.com; f. 1935; nationalized 1969; cap. 4,305.2m., surplus and res 13,113.7m., dep. 339,193.4m. (March 2007); Chair. and Man. Dir S. C. BASU; 1,291brs.

**Canara Bank:** 112 Jayachamarajendra Rd, POB 6648, Bangalore 560 002; tel. (80) 22223118; fax (80) 22223168; e-mail canbank@blr.vsnl.net.in; internet www.canbankindia.com; f. 1906; nationalized 1969; cap. 4,100.0m., res and surplus 99,439.9m., dep. 1,439,558.0m. (March 2007); Chair. and Man. Dir M. B. N. RAO; Exec. Dir ALOK KUMAR MISRA; 2,512 brs.

**Central Bank of India:** Chandermukhi, Nariman Point, Mumbai 400 021; tel. (22) 66387777; fax (22) 22044336; e-mail cbicpp@b01.net.in; internet www.centralbankofindia.co.in; f. 1911; nationalized 1969; cap. 11,241.4m., res and surplus 23,178.2m., dep. 664,826.5m. (March 2006); Chair. and Man. Dir HOMAI A. DARUWALLA; 3,130 brs.

**Corporation Bank:** Mangaladevi Temple Rd, POB 88, Mangalore 575 001; tel. (824) 2426416; fax (824) 2444617; e-mail corpho@corpbank.com; internet www.corpbank.com; f. 1906; nationalized 1980; cap. 1,434.4m., res 22,267.6m., dep. 231,909.3m. (March 2004); Chair. and Man. Dir B. SAMBAMURTHY; Exec. Dir P. K. GUPTA; 617 brs.

**Dena Bank:** C-10, G Block, Bandra-Kurla Complex, Bandra (East), Mumbai 400 051; tel. (22) 26545607; fax (22) 26545605; e-mail akk@denabank.co.in; internet www.denabank.com; f. 1938 as Devkaran Nanjee Banking Co Ltd; nationalized 1969; cap. 2,868.2m., res and surplus 12,095.8m., dep. 276,899.1m. (March 2007); Chair. and Man. Dir P. L. GAIROLA; Exec. Dir U. S. KOHLI; 1,122 brs.

**Indian Bank:** 31 Rajaji Salai, POB 1866, Chennai 600 001; tel. (44) 25233231; fax (44) 25231278; e-mail indianbank@vsnl.com; internet www.indian-bank.com; f. 1907; nationalized 1969; cap. 7,438.2m., res and surplus 17,475.8m., dep. 408,055.0m. (March 2006); Chair. and Man. Dir M. S. SUNDARA RAJAN; 1,376 brs.

**Indian Overseas Bank:** 763 Anna Salai, POB 3765, Chennai 600 002; tel. (44) 28524212; fax (44) 28523595; e-mail iobmail@vsnl.com; internet www.iob.com; f. 1937; nationalized 1969; cap. 5,448.0m., res and surplus 34,455.7m., dep. 716,366.4m. (March 2007); Chair. and Man. Dir T. S. NARAYANASAMI; Exec. Dir A. V. DUGADE; 1,496 brs.

**Oriental Bank of Commerce:** Harsha Bhavan, E Block, Connaught Place, POB 329, New Delhi 110 001; tel. (11) 23323444; fax (11) 23321514; e-mail bdncmd@obcindia.com; internet www.obcindia.co.in; f. 1943; nationalized 1980; cap. 2,505.4m., res 59,493.6m., dep. 639,959.7m. (March 2007); Chair. and Man. Dir K. N. PRITHVIRAJ; Exec. Dir ALLEN C. A. PEREIRA; 1,130 brs.

**Punjab and Sind Bank:** Bank House, 21 Rajendra Place, New Delhi 110 008; tel. (11) 25768831; fax (11) 25752501; internet www.psbindia.com; f. 1908; nationalized 1980; cap. 7,430.6m., res and surplus 6,626.3m., dep. 195,238.3m. (March 2007); Chair. and Man. Dir R. P. SINGH; Exec. Dir G. S. MATTA; 866 brs.

**Punjab National Bank:** 7 Bhikaiji Cama Place, Africa Ave, New Delhi 110 066; tel. (11) 26102303; fax (11) 26196456; e-mail cmd@pnb.co.in; internet www.pnbindia.com; f. 1895; nationalized 1969; merged with New Bank of India in 1993; cap. 3,153.0m., res 101,046.4m., dep. 1,418,085.3m. (March 2007); Chair. and Man. Dir K. C. CHAKRABARTY; Exec. Dirs K. RAGHURAMAN, J. M. GARG; 4,487 brs.

**Syndicate Bank:** POB 1, Manipal 576 119; tel. (825) 2571181; fax (825) 2570266; e-mail idcb@syndicatebank.com; internet www.syndicatebank.com; f. 1925 as Canara Industrial and Banking Syndicate Ltd; name changed as above 1964; nationalized 1969; cap. 5,219.7m., res 23,116.5m., dep. 539,674.5m. (March 2006); Chair. C. P. SWARNKAR; Exec. Dir GEORGE JOSEPH; 1,963 brs.

**UCO Bank:** 10 Biplabi Trailokya Maharaj Sarani (Brabourne Rd), POB 2455, Kolkata 700 001; tel. (33) 22254120; fax (33) 22253986; e-mail ucobank@vsnl.net; internet www.ucobank.com; f. 1943 as United Commercial Bank Ltd; nationalized 1969; name changed as above 1985; cap. 7,993.6m., res 14,574.6m., dep. 673,258.7m. (March 2007); Chair. and Man. Dir S. K. GOEL; Exec. Dir V. K. DHINGRA; 1,849 brs.

**Union Bank of India:** Union Bank Bhavan, 239 Vidhan Bhavan Marg, Nariman Point, Mumbai 400 021; tel. (22) 22024647; fax (22) 22025238; e-mail ibd@unionbankofindia.com; internet www.unionbankofindia.co.in; f. 1919; nationalized 1969; cap. 5,051.2m., res 46,842.7m., dep. 893,957.5m. (March 2007); Chair. and Man. Dir M. V. NAIR; 2,023 brs.

**United Bank of India:** 16 Old Court House St, Kolkata 700 001; tel. (33) 2487471; fax (33) 2485852; e-mail homail@unitedbank.co.in; internet www.unitedbankofindia.com; f. 1950; nationalized 1969; cap. 15,324.3m., res and surplus 8,828.6m., dep. 375,663.8m. (March 2007); Chair. and Man. Dir P. K. GUPTA; Exec. Dir T. M. BHASIN; 1,354 brs.

**Vijaya Bank:** 41/2 Mahatma Gandhi Rd, Bangalore 560 001; tel. (80) 25584066; fax (80) 25598040; e-mail ibd@vijayabank.co.in; internet www.vijayabank.com; f. 1931; nationalized 1980; cap. 4,335.2m., res and surplus 12,356.3m., dep. 282,251.1m. (March 2006); Chair. and Man. Dir PRAKASH P. MALLYA; Exec. Dir T. VALLIAPPAN; 932 brs.

### Principal Private Banks

**The Bank of Rajasthan Ltd:** C-3 Sardar Patel Marg, Jaipur 302 001; tel. (141) 2381222; fax (141) 2381123; e-mail p&d@rajbank.com; internet www.bankofrajasthan.com; f. 1943; cap. 1,075.7m., res and surplus 2,550.8m., dep. 89,023.3m. (March 2006); Chair. PRAVIN KUMAR TAYAL; Man. Dir and CEO B. M. SHARMA; 430 brs.

**Bharat Overseas Bank Ltd:** Habeeb Towers, 196 Anna Salai, Chennai 600 002; tel. (44) 28522983; fax (44) 28524700; e-mail help@bharatoverseasbank.com; internet www.boblonline.com; f. 1973; cap. 157.5m., res 1,826.4m., dep. 27,492.4m. (March 2005); Chair. and CEO G. KRISHNA MURTHY; Gen. Man. G. CHANDRAN; 77 brs.

**Bombay Mercantile Co-operative Bank Ltd:** 78 Mohammed Ali Rd, Mumbai 400 003; tel. (22) 23425961; fax (22) 23433385; e-mail bmcb@bom5.vsnl.net.in; f. 1939; cap. 213.8m., res 3,365.6m., dep. 16,889.4m. (March 2006); Chair. M. RAHMAN; Man. Dir S. U. PATHAN; 52 brs.

**Catholic Syrian Bank Ltd:** St Mary's College Rd, POB 502, Trichur 680 020; tel. (487) 2333020; fax (487) 2333435; e-mail chairman@csb.co.in; internet www.csb.co.in; f. 1920; cap. 107.1m., res 2,048.6m., dep. 42,891.6m. (March 2006); Chair. and CEO R. VENKATARAMAN; Gen. Man. V. P. ISWARDAS; 297 brs.

**Centurion Bank of Punjab Ltd:** 1201 Raheja Centre, Free Press Journal Marg, Nariman Point, Mumbai 400 021; tel. (22) 22047234; fax (22) 22845860; e-mail cblho@bom3.vsnl.net.in; internet www.centurionbop.co.in; f. 1995; fmrly Centurion Bank Ltd; name changed as above following merger with Bank of Punjab in 2005; cap. 1,566.9m., res and surplus 12,149.0m., dep. 157,946.1m. (March 2007); Chair. RANA TALWAR; Man. Dir and CEO SHAILENDRA BHANDARI.

**City Union Bank Ltd:** 149 TSR (Big) St, Kumbakonam 612 001; tel. (435) 2432322; fax (435) 2431746; e-mail cubco_kmb@sancharnet.in; internet www.cityunionbank.com; f. 1904; cap. 252.0m., res 3,404.4m., dep. 47,192.2m. (March 2007); Chair. S. BALASUBRAMANIAN; Exec. Dir N. KAMAKODI; 125 brs.

**The Federal Bank Ltd:** Federal Towers, POB 103, Alwaye 683 101; tel. (484) 2623620; fax (484) 2621687; e-mail fbl@federalbank.co.in; internet www.federal-bank.com; f. 1931; cap. 856.0m., res 11,509.2m., dep. 184,892.3m. (March 2006); Chair. M. VENUGOPALAN; 520 brs.

**HDFC Bank:** HDFC Bank House, Senapati Bapat Marg, Lower Parel, Mumbai, 400 013; tel. (22) 66521185; fax (22) 24960696; internet www.hdfcbank.com; announced plans to merge with Centurion Bank of Punjab in Feb. 2008; cap. 3,193.9m., res and surplus 61,137.6m., dep. 682,979.4m. (March 2007); Man. Dir ADITYA PURI; 744 brs.

**ICICI Bank Ltd:** ICICI Towers, 4th Floor, South Tower, Bandra-Kurla Complex, Bandra (East), Mumbai 400 051; tel. (22) 26531414; fax (22) 26531167; e-mail info@icicibank.com; internet www.icicibank.com; f. 1994; cap. 12,398.3m., res 210,227.2m., dep. 1,650,831.7m. (March 2006); Man. Dir K. V. KAMATH; Chair. N. VAGHUL; 348 brs.

**IndusInd Bank Ltd:** IndusInd House, 425 Dadasaheb Bhadkamkar Marg, Lamington Rd, nr Opera House, Mumbai 400 004; tel. (22) 23859901; fax (22) 23859913; e-mail glob@indusind.com; internet www.indusind.com; f. 1994; cap. 2,905.1m., res 3,896.6m., dep. 155,412.5m. (March 2006); Chair. R. J. SAHANEY; Man. Dir BHASKAR GHOSE; 77 brs.

**ING Vysya Bank Ltd:** 22 M. G. Rd, Bangalore 560 001; tel. (80) 25005000; fax (80) 22272220; e-mail ingvysyabank@ingvysyabank.com; internet www.ingvysyabank.com; f. 1930; cap. 909.0m., res 9,939.5m., dep. 162,621.4m. (March 2007); Man. Dir and CEO VAUGHN NIGEL RICTOR; 404 brs.

**Jammu and Kashmir Bank Ltd:** Corporate Headquarters, M. A. Rd, Srinagar 190 001; tel. (194) 2481930; fax (194) 2481923; e-mail jkbcosgr@jkbmail.com; internet jkbank.net; f. 1938; cap. p.u. 484.9m., res and surplus 19,602.4m., dep. 258,144.8m. (March 2007); Chair. Dr HASEEB A. DRABU; Exec. Dir ABDUL RAUF FAZILI; 462 brs.

**Karnataka Bank Ltd:** POB 716, Kodialbail, Mangalore 575 003; tel. (824) 2228222; fax (824) 2225588; e-mail info@ktkbank.com; internet www.ktkbankltd.com; f. 1924; cap. 1,213.5m., res 11,172.5m., dep. 140,374.4m. (March 2007); Chair. and CEO ANANTHAKRISHNA; 370 brs.

**The Karur Vysya Bank Ltd:** Erode Rd, POB 21, Karur 639 002; tel. (4324) 226520; fax (4324) 225700; e-mail kvbpdd@kvbmail.com; internet www.kvb.co.in; f. 1916; cap. 539.4m., res 11,360.6m., dep. 125,499.9m. (March 2008); Man. Dir and CEO P. T. KUPPUSWAMY; Chief Gen. Man. R. SUKUMAR; 292 brs.

**Lakshmi Vilas Bank Ltd:** Kathaparai, Salem Rd, POB 2, Karur 639 006; tel. (4324) 220051; fax (4324) 220068; e-mail info@lvbank.com; internet www.lvbank.com; f. 1926; cap. 195.3m., res 2,711.5m., dep. 43,416.8m. (March 2006); Chair. and CEO R. M. NAYAK; 234 brs.

**Sangli Bank Ltd:** Rajwada Chowk, POB 158, Sangli 416 416; tel. (233) 2623611; fax (233) 2620666; e-mail san_sanbank@sancharnet.in; internet www.sangli-bank.com; f. 1916; cap. p.u. 204.1m., res 560m., dep. 16,777.6m. (March 2003); Chair. and CEO A. R. BORDE; Gen. Man. S. R. GODBOLE; 178 brs.

**South Indian Bank Ltd:** SIB House, Mission Quarters, Thrissur 680 001; tel. (487) 2420020; fax (487) 2442021; e-mail sib@vsnl.com; internet www.southindianbank.com; f. 1929; cap. 704.1m., res 5,639.7m., dep. 95,793.8m. (March 2006); Man. Dir and CEO V. S. REDDY; 450 brs.

**Tamilnad Mercantile Bank Ltd:** 57 Victoria Extension Rd, Tuticorin 628 002; tel. (461) 2321932; fax (461) 2322994; e-mail ttn_tmbankhi@sancharnet.in; internet www.tmb.in; f. 1921 as Nadar Bank; name changed as above 1962; cap. 2.8m., surplus res 6,565.0m., dep. 52,260.1m. (March 2006); Chair. M. G. M MARAN; 173 brs.

### Banking Organizations

**Indian Banks' Association:** Unit Nos 1, 2 and 4, 6th Floor, Centre I Bldg, World Trade Centre Complex, Cuffe Parade, Mumbai 400 005; tel. (22) 22844999; fax (22) 22835638; e-mail webmaster@iba.org.in; internet www.iba.org.in; 156 mems; Chair. V. P. SHETTY; Chief Exec. H. N. SINOR.

**Indian Institute of Banking and Finance:** 'The Arcade', World Trade Centre Complex, 2nd Floor, East Wing, Cuffe Parade, Mumbai 400 005; tel. (22) 22187003; fax (22) 22185147; e-mail iibgen@bom5.vsnl.net.in; internet www.iibf.org.in; f. 1928; 343,202 mems; Pres. K. CHERIAN VARGHESE; CEO R. BHASKARAN; four zonal offices.

**National Institute of Bank Management:** NIBM Post Office, Kondhwe Khurd, Pune 411 048; tel. (20) 26833080; fax (20) 26834478; e-mail director@nibmindia.org; internet www.nibmindia.org; f. 1969; Chair. Dr Y. V. REDDY; Dir Dr ASHISH SAHA.

## DEVELOPMENT FINANCE ORGANIZATIONS

**Agricultural Finance Corporation Ltd:** Dhanraj Mahal, 1st Floor, Chhatrapati Shivaji Maharaj Marg, Mumbai 400 001; tel. (22) 22028924; fax (22) 22028966; e-mail afcl@vsnl.com; internet www.afcindia.com; f. 1968 by a consortium of 45 public- and private-sector commercial banks including development finance institutions to help increase the flow of investment and credit into agriculture and rural development projects; provides project consultancy services to commercial banks, Union and state govts, public-sector corpns, the World Bank, the ADB, FAO, the International Fund for Agricultural Development and other institutions and to individuals; undertakes techno-economic and investment surveys in agriculture and agro-industries etc.; publishes quarterly journal Financing Agriculture; three regional offices and nine br. offices; cap. p.u. 150m., res and surplus 20.5m. (March 2001); Chair. Y. C. NANDA; Man. Dir A. K. GARG.

**Export-Import Bank of India:** Centre One Bldg, Floor 21, World Trade Centre Complex, Cuffe Parade, Mumbai 400 005; tel. (22) 22185272; fax (22) 22182572; e-mail eximcord@vsnl.com; internet www.eximbankindia.com; f. 1982; cap. 8,499.9m., res 16,625.0m., dep. 22,023.1m. (March 2005); Chair. and Man. Dir T. C. VENKAT SUBRAMANIAN; Exec. Dirs R. M. V. RAMAN, S. SRIDHAR; 14 offices worldwide.

**Housing Development Finance Corpn Ltd (HDFC):** Ramon House, 169 Backbay Reclamation, Churchgate, Mumbai 400 020; tel. (22) 22836255; fax (22) 22046758; e-mail info@hdfc.com; internet www.hdfc.com; f. 1977; provides loans to individuals and corporate bodies; cap. p.u. 2,466.1m., res 36,471.8m., dep. 93,376.5m. (March 2004); Chair. DEEPAK S. PAREKH; Man. Dir KEKI M. MISTRY; 173 brs (incl. one overseas br).

**IFCI Ltd:** IFCI Tower, 61 Nehru Place, New Delhi 110 019; tel. (11) 41732000; fax (11) 26488471; e-mail helpdesk@ifciltd.com; internet www.ifciltd.com; CEO and Man. Dir ATHUL K. RAI.

**Industrial Development Bank of India (IDBI):** IDBI Tower, World Trade Centre Complex, Cuffe Parade, Mumbai 400 005; tel. (22) 56553355; fax (22) 22181294; internet www.idbi.com; f. 1964; reorg. 1976; 72.1% govt-owned; merged with The United Western Bank Ltd in 2006; provides direct finance, refinance of industrial loans and bills, finance to large- and medium-sized industries, extends financial services, such as merchant banking and forex services, to the corporate sector; cap. 7,238m., res and surplus 56,744m., dep. 26,009m. (March 2006); Chair. and Man. Dir V. P. SHETTY; five zonal offices and 36 br. offices.

**Small Industries Development Bank of India:** 10/10 Madan Mohan Malviya Marg, Lucknow 226 001; tel. (522) 2209517; fax (522) 2209514; e-mail snairan@sidbi.com; internet www.sidbi.com; f. 1990; wholly owned subsidiary of Industrial Development Bank of India; promotes, finances and develops small-scale industries; cap. p.u. 4,500m., res 24,240m. (March 2000); Chair. and Man. Dir N. BALASUBRAMANIAN; 39 offices.

**Industrial Investment Bank of India:** 19 Netaji Subhas Rd, Kolkata 700 001; tel. (33) 22209941; fax (33) 22208049; e-mail iibiho@vsnl.com; internet www.iibiltd.com; Chair. and Man. Dir Dr B. SAMAL (acting).

**National Bank for Agriculture and Rural Development:** Plot no. C-24, G Block, Bandra-Kurla Complex, Bandra (East), Mumbai 400 051; tel. (22) 26539060; fax (22) 26539399; e-mail nabrmd@vsnl.net; internet www.nabard.org; f. 1982 to provide credit for agricultural and rural development through commercial, co-operative and regional rural banks; cap. p.u. 20,000m., res 52,910m. (March 2004); held 50% each by the cen. Govt and the Reserve Bank; Man. Dir Y. S. P. THORAT; Chair. RANJANA KUMAR; 28 regional offices, 10 sub-office and six training establishments.

## STOCK EXCHANGES

There are 23 stock exchanges (with a total of more than 9,985 listed companies) in India, including:

**National Stock Exchange of India Ltd:** Exchange Plaza, Bandra-Kurla Complex, Bandra (East), Mumbai 400 051; tel. (22) 26598100; fax (22) 26598120; e-mail cc_nse@nse.co.in; internet www.nseindia.com; f. 1994; New York Stock Exchange, Goldman Sachs, General Atlantic (all of the USA) and SoftBank Asian Infrastructure Fund (Hong Kong) each acquired a 5% share in Jan. 2007; Chair. S. B. MATHUR; Man. Dir RAVI NARAIN.

**Ahmedabad Stock Exchange:** Kamdhenu Complex, opp. Sahajanand College, Panjarapole, Ambawadi, Ahmedabad 380 015; tel. (79) 26307971; fax (79) 26308877; e-mail cosec@aseindia.org; internet www.aseindia.org; f. 1894; 2,000 mems; Administrator P. K. GHOSH; Exec. Dir V. V. RAO.

**Bangalore Stock Exchange Ltd:** 51 Stock Exchange Towers, 1st Cross, J. C. Rd, Bangalore 560 027; tel. (80) 22995234; fax (80) 22995242; e-mail edbgse@giasbg01.vsnl.net.in; 234 mems; Pres. JAGDISH V. AHUJA; Exec. Dir K. KAMALA.

**Bombay Stock Exchange:** Phiroze Jeejeebhoy Towers, 25th Floor, Dalal St, Fort, Mumbai 400 001; tel. (22) 22721233; fax (22) 22721919; e-mail info@bseindia.com; internet www.bseindia.com; f. 1875; 4,482 listed cos; Chair. JAGDISH CAPOOR; Man. Dir. and CEO RAJNIKANT PATEL; Sec. VISHVESH BHAGAT.

**Calcutta Stock Exchange Association Ltd:** 7 Lyons Range, Kolkata 700 001; tel. (33) 22104470; fax (33) 22104486; e-mail secretary@cse.india.com; internet www.cse-india.com; f. 1908; 917 mems; Sec. P. K. RAY.

**Delhi Stock Exchange Association Ltd:** DSE House, 3/1 Asaf Ali Rd, New Delhi 110 002; tel. (11) 23292182; fax (11) 23292174; e-mail admin@dseindia.org.in; internet www.dseindia.org.in; f. 1947; some 3,000 listed cos (March 2007); Exec. Dir P. K. SINGHAL.

**Ludhiana Stock Exchange Association Ltd:** Firoze Gandhi Market, Ludhiana 141 001; tel. (161) 2412318; fax (161) 2401645; e-mail lse@satyam.net.in; internet lse.co.in; f. 1981; 292 mems; Chair. DINA RATH SHARMA; Gen. Man. H. S. SIDHU.

**Madras Stock Exchange Ltd:** Exchange Bldg, 30 Second Line Beach, POB 183, Chennai 600 001; tel. (44) 25228951; fax (44) 25244897; e-mail mseed@vsnl.com; f. 1760; 158 mems; Exec. Dir R. K. PILLAI.

**Mangalore Stock Exchange:** Rama Bhavan Complex, 4th Floor, Kodialbail, Mangalore 575 003; tel. (824) 2440581; fax (824) 2440736; 146 mems; Pres. RAMESH RAI; Exec. Dir UMESH P. MASKERI.

**Thiruvananthapuram Stock Exchange:** Thiruvananthapuram; Dir JOSE JOHN.

**Uttar Pradesh Stock Exchange Association Ltd:** Padam Towers, 14/113 Civil Lines, Kanpur 208 001; tel. (512) 2293115; fax (512) 2293175; e-mail upse@vsnl.net.in; 540 mems; Pres. R. K. AGARWAL; Exec. Dir Dr J. N. GUPTA.

The other recognized stock exchanges are: Hyderabad, Madhya Pradesh (Indore), Kochi, Pune, Guwahati, Jaipur, Bhubaneswar (Orissa), Coimbatore, Saurashtra, Meerut, Vadodara and Magadh (Patna).

### INSURANCE

In January 1973 all Indian and foreign insurance companies were nationalized. The general insurance business in India is now transacted by only four companies, subsidiaries of the General Insurance Corpn of India, formed under the 1972 General Insurance Business Nationalisation Act. The Insurance Regulatory Development Authority Bill, approved by the legislature in December 1999, established a regulatory authority for the insurance sector and henceforth permitted up to 26% investment by foreign companies in new domestic, private-sector insurance companies.

**General Insurance Corpn of India (GIC):** 'Suraksha', 170 J. Tata Rd, Churchgate, Mumbai 400 020; tel. (22) 22833046; fax (22) 22855423; e-mail pcghosh@gicofindia.com; internet www.gicofindia.com; f. 1973 by the reorg. of 107 private non-life insurance cos (incl. brs of foreign cos operating in the country) as the four subsidiaries listed below; Chair. R. K. JOSHI; Man. Dir P. B. RAMANUJAN.

**National Insurance Co Ltd:** 3 Middleton St, Kolkata 700 071; tel. (33) 22831705; fax (33) 22831740; e-mail website.administrator@nic.co.in; internet www.nationalinsuranceindia.com; Chair. and Man. Dir V. RAMASAAMY; 19 regional offices, 254 divisional offices and 690 branch offices.

**New India Assurance Co Ltd:** New India Assurance Bldg, 87 Mahatma Gandhi Rd, Fort, Mumbai 400 001; tel. (22) 22674617; fax (22) 22652811; e-mail cmd.nia@newindia.co.in; internet www.newindia.co.in; f. 1919; 26 regional offices, 393 divisional offices, 703 branch offices and 37 overseas offices; Chair. and Man. Dir B. CHAKRABARTI.

**The Oriental Insurance Co Ltd:** Oriental House, A-25/27 Asaf Ali Rd, New Delhi 110 002; tel. (11) 23279221; fax (11) 23263175; e-mail slmohan@oriental.nic.in; internet www.orientalinsurance.nic.in; Chair. and Man. Dir RAMADASS.

**United India Insurance Co Ltd:** 24 Whites Rd, Chennai 600 014; tel. (44) 28520161; fax (44) 28525280; e-mail knb@united.nic.in; internet www.united.nic.in; Chair. and Man. Dir MAHINDER KUMAR GARG.

**Life Insurance Corpn of India (LIC):** 'Yogakshema', Jeevan Bima Marg, Mumbai 400 021; tel. (22) 22021645; fax (22) 22810680; e-mail chairman@licindia.com; internet www.licindia.com; f. 1956; controls all life insurance business; Chair. A. K. SHUKLA; Man. Dirs T. S. VIJAYAN, D. K. MEHROTRA; 100 divisional offices, 2,048 brs and three overseas offices.

## Trade and Industry

### GOVERNMENT AGENCIES AND DEVELOPMENT ORGANIZATIONS

**Coal India Ltd:** 10 Netaji Subhas Rd, Kolkata 700 001; tel. (33) 22488099; fax (33) 22435316; e-mail cil@wb.nic.in; internet www.coalindia.nic.in; cen. govt holding co with eight subsidiaries; responsible for almost total (more than 90%) exploration for, planning and production of coal mines; owns 467 coal mines throughout India; marketing of coal and its products; cap. p.u. Rs 72,205.4m., res and surplus Rs 21,324.9m. (March 2002), sales Rs 258,029m. (2004/05); Chair. PARTHA S. BHATTACHARYYA; 462,000 employees (2005).

**Cotton Corpn of India Ltd:** Plot No. 3A, Sector No. 10, CBD Belapur, Navi Mumbai 400 614; tel. (22) 27579217; fax (22) 27576030; e-mail headoffice@cotcorp.com; internet www.cotcorp.gov.in; f. 1970 as an agency in the public sector for the purchase, sale and distribution of home-produced cotton and imported cotton staple fibre; exports long staple cotton; cap. p.u. Rs 250m., res and surplus Rs 2,159.7m. (March 2002), sales Rs 14,627.7m. (2004/05); Chair. and Man. Dir SUBHASH C. GROVER.

**Export Credit Guarantee Corpn of India Ltd:** Express Towers, 10th Floor, Nariman Point, Mumbai 400 021; tel. (22) 22845471; fax (22) 22045253; e-mail webmaster@ecgcindia.com; internet www.ecgcindia.com; f. 1957 to insure for risks involved in exports on credit terms and to supplement credit facilities by issuing guarantees, etc.; cap. Rs 3,900m., res Rs 4,079.3m. (March 2002); Chair. and Man. Dir P. K. DASH; 29 brs.

**Fertilizer Corpn of India Ltd:** PDIL Bhavan, A-14, 5th Floor, Sector 1, Noida 201 301, Uttar Pradesh; tel. (120) 2530023; fax (120) 2537612; e-mail fci@fci.hub.nic.in; internet fertcorpindia.nic.in; f. 1961; fertilizer factories at Sindri (Jharkhand), Gorakhpur (Uttar Pradesh), Talcher (Orissa) and Ramagundam (Andhra Pradesh), producing nitrogenous and some industrial products; production suspended at all factories since 2002; cap. Rs 7,547.3m., sales Rs 1,262m. (March 2002); Gen. Man. K. L. RAO.

**Food Corpn of India:** DDA Complex, Ground Floor, Rajendra Pl., Rajendra Bhavan, New Delhi 110 008; tel. (11) 25710962; fax (11) 25750670; e-mail rgm@fcidelhiro.in; internet www.fciweb.nic.in; f. 1965 to undertake trading in food grains on a commercial scale but within the framework of an overall govt policy; to provide farmers an assured price for their produce; to supply food grains to the consumer at reasonable prices; also purchases, stores, distributes and sells food grains and other foodstuffs and arranges imports and handling of food grains and fertilizers at the ports; distributes sugar in a number of states and has set up rice mills; cap. p.u. Rs 23,245m., sales Rs 315,562.2m. (March 2002); Man. Dir Dr P. C. RAM; 59,800 employees (2002).

**Handicrafts and Handlooms Exports Corpn of India Ltd:** Jawahar Vyapar Bhavan Annexe, 5th Floor, 1 Tolstoy Marg, New Delhi 110 001; tel. (11) 23701086; fax (11) 23701051; e-mail hhecnd@eth.net; internet www.hhecworld.com; f. 1958; govt undertaking dealing in export of handicrafts, handloom goods, ready-to-wear clothes, carpets, jute, leather and precious jewellery, and import of bullion and raw silk; promotes exports and trade development; cap. p.u. Rs 138.2m., res and surplus Rs 91.8m., sales Rs 3,339.4m. (March 2002); Chair. and Man. Dir K. K. SINHA.

**Housing and Urban Development Corpn Ltd:** HUDCO Bhavan, India Habitat Centre, Lodhi Rd, New Delhi 110 003; tel. (11) 24649610; fax (11) 24625308; e-mail hudco@hudco.org; internet www.hudco.org; f. 1970 to finance and undertake housing and urban development programmes including the establishment of new or satellite towns and building material industries; cap. p.u. Rs 20,019.0m., res Rs 17,735.0m., sales Rs 37,359.9m. (Jan. 2007); 21 brs; Chair. and Man. Dir T. PRABAKARAN; Sec. M. K. GUPTA.

**India Trade Promotion Organisation (ITPO):** Pragati Bhavan, Pragati Maidan, Lal Bahadur Shastri Marg, New Delhi 110 001; tel. (11) 23371540; fax (11) 23371492; e-mail info@itpo-online.com; internet www.indiatradefair.com; f. 1992 following merger; promotes selective development of exports of high quality products; arranges investment in export-orientated ventures undertaken by India with foreign collaboration; organizes trade fairs; operates Trade Information Centre; cap. p.u. Rs 2.5m., res and surplus Rs 2,311.8m., sales Rs 818.4m. (March 2002); regional offices in Bangalore, Mumbai, Kolkata and Chennai, and international offices in Frankfurt, New York, Moscow, São Paulo and Tokyo; Chair. and Man. Dir N. N. KHANNA; Exec. Dir RAJIV YADAV.

**Jute Corpn of India Ltd:** 15-N, Nellie Sengupta Sarani, 7th Floor, Kolkata 700 087; tel. (33) 22166770; fax (33) 22166771; e-mail feedback@jutecorp.com; internet www.jutecorp.com; f. 1971; objects: (i) to undertake price support operations in respect of raw jute; (ii) to ensure remunerative prices to producers through efficient marketing; (iii) to operate a buffer stock to stabilize raw jute prices; (iv) to handle the import and export of raw jute; (v) to promote the export of jute goods; cap. p.u. Rs 50m., sales Rs 576.0m. (March 2002); Chair. and Man. Dir R. C. TEWARI.

**Minerals and Metals Trading Corpn of India Ltd (MMTC):** Scope Complex, Core-1, 7 Institutional Areas, Lodhi Rd, New Delhi 110 003; tel. (11) 24362200; fax (11) 24360724; e-mail cpmr@mmtclimited.com; internet www.mmtclimited.com; f. 1963; export of iron and manganese ore, ferro-manganese, finished stainless steel products, engineering, agricultural and marine products, textiles, leather items, chemicals and pharmaceuticals, mica, coal and other minor minerals; import of steel, non-ferrous metals, rough diamonds, fertilizers, etc. for supply to industrial units in the country; cap. p.u. Rs 500m., sales Rs 62,546.8m. (March 2003); res Rs 6,348.0m. (March 2004); 13 regional offices in India; foreign offices in Japan, the Republic of Korea, Jordan and Romania; Chair. and Man. Dir SANJIV BATRA; 2,378 employees (2002).

**National Co-operative Development Corpn:** 4 Siri Institutional Area, Hauz Khas, New Delhi 110 016; tel. (11) 26569246; fax (11) 26962370; e-mail editor@ncdc.stpn.soft.net; f. 1963 to plan, promote and finance country-wide programmes through co-operative societies for the production, processing, marketing, storage, export and import of agricultural produce, foodstuffs and notified commodities and minor forest produce; also programmes for the development of poultry, dairy, fish products, coir, handlooms, distribution of consumer articles in rural areas, industrial and service co-operatives, water conservation work, irrigation, micro-irrigation, animal care, health, disease prevention, agricultural insurance and credit, rural sanitation etc.; 18 regional directorates; Pres. SHARAD PAWAR; Man. Dir P. UMA SHANKAR.

**National Industrial Development Corpn Ltd:** Chanakya Bhavan, Africa Ave, New Delhi 110 021; tel. (11) 24670153; fax (11) 26876166; e-mail nidc123@del2.vsnl.net.in; f. 1954; consultative engineering, management and infrastructure services to cen. and state govts, public and private sector enterprises, the UN and overseas investors; cap. p.u. Rs 18.7m. (March 2002); Chair. and Man. Dir PRANAB GHOSH.

**National Mineral Development Corpn Ltd:** Khanij Bhavan, 10-3-311/A Castle Hills, Masab Tank, POB 1352, Hyderabad 500 028; tel. (40) 23538713; fax (40) 23538711; e-mail hois@nmdc.co.in; internet www.nmdc.co.in; f. 1958; cen. govt undertaking; to exploit minerals (excluding coal, atomic minerals, lignite, petroleum and natural gas) in public sector; may buy, take on lease or otherwise acquire mines for prospecting, development and exploitation; iron ore mines at Bailadila-11C, Bailadila-14 and Bailadila-5 in Madhya Pradesh, and at Donimalai in Karnataka State; new 5m. metric ton iron ore mine under construction at Bailadila-10/11A; diamond mines at Panna in Madhya Pradesh; research and development laboratories and consultancy services covering all aspects of mineral exploitation at Hyderabad; investigates mineral projects; cap. p.u. Rs 1,321.6m., res and surplus Rs 18,932m., sales Rs 14,536.9m. (March 2004); Chair. and Man. Dir B. RAMESH KUMAR.

**National Productivity Council:** Utpadakta Bhavan, 5–6 Institutional Area, Lodhi Rd, New Delhi 110 003; tel. (11) 24690331; fax (11) 24615002; e-mail info@npcindia.org; internet www.npcindia.org; f. 1958 to increase productivity and to improve quality by improved techniques which aim at efficient and proper utilization of available resources; autonomous body representing national orgs of employers and labour, govt ministries, professional orgs, local productivity councils, small-scale industries and other interests; 13 regional professional management groups, one training institute; 75 mems; Chair. AJAY SHANKAR; Dir-Gen. PRADEEP SINGH.

**National Research Development Corpn:** 20–22 Zamroodpur Community Centre, Kailash Colony Extension, New Delhi 110 048; tel. (11) 29240401; fax (11) 29240409; e-mail write2@nrdcindia.com; internet www.nrdcindia.com; f. 1953 to stimulate development and commercial exploitation of new inventions with financial and technical aid; finances development projects to set up demonstration units in collaboration with industry; exports technology; cap. p.u. Rs 44.2m., res and surplus Rs 47.6m. (March 2002); Chair. and Man. Dir SOMENATH GHOSH.

**National Seeds Corpn Ltd:** Beej Bhavan, Pusa, New Delhi 110 012; tel. (11) 25846292; fax (11) 25846462; e-mail nsc@vsnl.com; internet www.indiaseeds.com; f. 1963 to improve and develop the seed industry; cap. p.u. Rs 206.2m., res and surplus Rs 216.1m., sales Rs 658.5m. (March 2002); Chair. and Man. Dir R. S. PANDEY.

**National Small Industries Corpn Ltd:** NSIC Bhavan, Okhla Industrial Estate, New Delhi 110 020; tel. (11) 26926275; fax (11) 26926820; e-mail pro@nsic.co.in; internet www.nsic.co.in; f. 1955 to aid, advise, finance and promote the interests of small industries; establishes and supplies machinery for small industries in other developing countries on turn-key basis; cap. p.u. Rs 1,679.9m., res and surplus Rs 87.2m., sales Rs 1,851m. (March 2002); all shares held by the Govt; Chair. and Man. Dir H. P. KUMAR.

**PEC Ltd:** 'Hansalaya', 15 Barakhamba Rd, New Delhi 110 001; tel. (11) 23314723; fax (11) 23314797; e-mail pec@peclimited.com; internet www.peclimited.com; f. 1971; export of engineering, industrial and railway equipment; undertakes turn-key and other projects and management consultancy abroad; countertrade, trading in agrocommodities, construction materials (steel, cement, clinkers, etc.) and fertilizers; cap. p.u. Rs 15m., res and surplus Rs 245.6m., sales Rs 22,499.9m. (March 2002); sales Rs 58,500.0m. (March 2004); Chair. and Man. Dir A. K. SRIVASTAVA.

**Rehabilitation Industries Corpn Ltd:** Kolkata; tel. (33) 22441185; fax (33) 22451055; f. 1959 to create employment opportunities through multi-product industries, ranging from consumer goods to engineering products and services, for refugees from Bangladesh and migrants from Pakistan, repatriates from Myanmar and Sri Lanka, and other immigrants of Indian extraction; cap. p.u. Rs 47.6m. (March 2000); Chair. and Man. Dir ASHOK BASU.

**State Farms Corpn of India Ltd:** Farm Bhavan, 14–15 Nehru Place, New Delhi 110 019; tel. (11) 26446903; fax (11) 26226898; e-mail sfci@vsnl.net; internet sfci.nic.in; f. 1969 to administer the central state farms; activities include the production of quality seeds of high-yielding varieties of wheat, paddy, maize, bajra and jowar; advises on soil conservation, reclamation and development of waste and forest land; consultancy services on farm mechanization; auth. cap. Rs 241.9m., res and surplus Rs 371.0m., sales Rs 465.4m. (March 2002); Chair. and Man. Dir Brig. S. P. MEHLA.

**State Trading Corpn of India Ltd:** Jawahar Vyapar Bhavan, Tolstoy Marg, New Delhi 110 001; tel. (11) 23701100; fax (11) 23701123; e-mail co.stc@nic.in; internet stc.gov.in; f. 1956; govt undertaking dealing in exports and imports; cap. p.u. Rs 300m., res and surplus Rs 2,628m., sales Rs 83,487.5m. (March 2004); sales Rs 71,240.0m. (March 2006); 10 regional brs, five sub-brs and one office overseas; Chair. and Man. Dir Dr ARVIND PANDALAI; 1,069 employees (2002).

**Steel Authority of India Ltd (SAIL):** Ispat Bhavan, Lodhi Rd, POB 3049, New Delhi 110 003; tel. (11) 24367481; fax (11) 24367015; e-mail sail.co@vsnl.com; internet www.sail.co.in; f. 1973 to provide co-ordinated development of the steel industry in the public sector; integrated steel plants at Bhilai, Bokaro, Durgapur, Rourkela; stainless and alloy steel plants at Chhattisgarh, West Bengal, Orissa, Jharkhand, Tamil Nadu and Karnataka; subsidiary co Maharashtra Elektrosmelt Ltd (Maharashtra); five jt venture power and steel-related cos, with sixth proposed at mid-2007; subsidiaries: Bhilai Oxygen Ltd (Chhattisgarh), Indian Iron and Steel Co (West Bengal)86% govt-ownedMaharashtra Elektrosmelt Ltd; combined crude steel capacity is 12m. metric tons annually; equity cap. Rs 41,304m., res and surplus Rs 9,072.7m., sales Rs 248,773.1m. (March 2004); Chair. S. K. ROONGTA; 131,910 employees (March 2004).

**Tea Board of India:** 14 B. T. M. Sarani (Brabourne Rd), POB 2172, Kolkata 700 001; tel. (33) 2251411; fax (33) 2251417; provides financial assistance to tea research stations; sponsors and finances independent research projects in universities and tech. institutions to supplement the work of tea research establishments; also promotes tea production and export; Chair. N. K. DAS.

## CHAMBERS OF COMMERCE

**Associated Chambers of Commerce and Industry of India (ASSOCHAM):** 1 Community Centre, Zamrudpur Kailash Colony, New Delhi 110 048; tel. (11) 46550555; fax (11) 46536481; e-mail assocham@nic.in; internet www.assocham.org; f. 1920; central org. of 350 chambers of commerce and industry and industrial asscns representing more than 100,000 cos throughout India; five promoter chambers, 115 ordinary mems, 45 patron mems and 500 corporate associates; Pres. VENUGOPAL N. DHOOT; Sec.-Gen. D. S. RAWAT.

**Federation of Indian Chambers of Commerce and Industry (FICCI):** Federation House, Tansen Marg, New Delhi 110 001; tel. (11) 23738760; fax (11) 23320714; e-mail ficci@ficci.com; internet www.ficci.com; f. 1927; more than 1,500 corporate mems, 500 chamber of commerce and business asscn mems; Pres. HABIL KHORAKIWALA; Sec.-Gen. Dr AMIT MITRA.

**ICC India:** Federation House, Tansen Marg, New Delhi 110 001; tel. (11) 23322472; fax (11) 23320714; e-mail iccindia@iccindiaonline.org; internet www.iccindiaonline.org; f. 1929; 43 org. mems, 375 corporate mems, eight patron mems, 130 cttee mems; Pres. SAROJ KUMAR PODDAR; Exec. Dir ASHOK UMMAT.

**Associated Chambers of Commerce and Industry of Uttar Pradesh:** 2/210 Vikas Khand, Gomti Nagar, POB 17, Lucknow 226 010; tel. (522) 2301957; fax (522) 2301958; e-mail asochmup@yahoo.com; internet www.asochamup.org; 405 mems; Pres. IRSHAD MIRZA; Sec.-Gen. S. B. AGRAWAL.

**Bengal Chamber of Commerce and Industry:** 6 Netaji Subhas Rd, Kolkata 700 001; tel. (33) 22203733; fax (33) 22301289; e-mail bencham@bengalchamber.com; internet www.bengalchamber.com; f. 1853; more than 220 mems; Pres. S. RADHAKRISHNAN; Vice-Pres. SUPRIYA DAS GUPTA.

**Bengal National Chamber of Commerce and Industry:** BNCCI House, 23 Sir R. N. Mukherjee Rd, Kolkata 700 001; tel. (33) 22482951; fax (33) 22487058; e-mail bncci@bncci.com; internet www.bncci.com; f. 1887; 500 mems, 35 affiliated industrial and trading asscns; Pres. K. K. NAVADA; Sec. D. P. NAG.

**Bharat Chamber of Commerce:** 9 Park Mansions, 2nd Floor, 57-A Park Street, Kolkata, 700 016; tel. (33) 22299591; fax (33) 22294947; e-mail bcc@cal2.vsnl.net.in; internet www.bharatcham.com; f. 1900; c. 500 mems; Pres. P. R. AGARWALA; Sec. K. SARMA.

**Bihar Chamber of Commerce:** Khem Chand Chaudhary Marg, POB 71, Patna 800 001; tel. (612) 2670535; fax (612) 2689505; e-mail bcc_chamber@rediffmail.com; f. 1926; 552 ordinary mems; Pres. S. K. CHOUDHARY; Sec.-Gen. RAJA BABU GUPTA.

**Bombay Chamber of Commerce and Industry:** Mackinnon Mackenzie Bldg, 4 Shoorji Vallabhdas Rd, Ballard Estate, POB 473, Mumbai 400 001; tel. (22) 22614681; fax (22) 22621213; e-mail bcci@bombaychamber.com; internet www.bombaychamber.com; f. 1836; 935 ordinary mems, 650 assoc. mems, 75 hon. mems; Pres. ASHOK WADHWA; Exec. Dir L. A. D'SOUZA.

**Calcutta Chamber of Commerce:** 18H Park St, Stephen Court, Kolkata 700 071; tel. (33) 22298236; fax (33) 22298961; e-mail calchamb@cal3.vsnl.net.in; internet www.calcuttachamber.com; 300 mems; Pres. H. V. PATODIA; Vice-Pres. ALKA BANGUR.

**Chamber of Commerce and Industry (Regd):** OB 31, Rail Head Complex, Jammu 180 012; tel. (191) 2472266; fax (191) 2472255; 1,069 mems; Pres. RAM SAHAI; Sec.-Gen. RAJENDRA MOTIAL.

**Cochin Chamber of Commerce and Industry:** Bristow Rd, Willingdon Island, POB 503, Kochi 682 003; tel. (484) 2668349; fax (484) 2668651; e-mail cochinchamber@eth.net; internet www.cochinchamber.org; f. 1857; 206 mems; Pres. JOSE DOMINIC; Sec. EAPEN KALAPURAKAL.

**Federation of Andhra Pradesh Chambers of Commerce and Industry:** Federation House, 11-6-841, Red Hills, POB 14, Hyderabad 500 004; tel. (40) 23393658; fax (40) 23393712; e-mail info@fapcci.in; internet www.fapcci.in; f. 1917; 2,674 mems; Pres. ATLURI SUBBA RAO; Sec. G. HEMALATA.

**Federation of Karnataka Chambers of Commerce and Industry:** Federation House, Dempegowda Rd, POB 9996, Bangalore 560 009; tel. (80) 22262355; fax (80) 22251826; e-mail fkcci@blr.vsnl.net

.in; internet www.fkcci.org; f. 1916; 2,100 mems; Pres. R. C. PUROHIT; Sec. C. MANOHAR.

**Federation of Madhya Pradesh Chambers of Commerce and Industry:** Udyog Bhavan, 129A Malviya Nagar, Bhopal 462 003; tel. (755) 2573612; fax (755) 2551451; e-mail fmcci@bom6.vsnl.net.in; f. 1975; 500 ordinary mems, 58 asscn mems; Pres. PRAFULLA K. MAHESHWARI.

**Goa Chamber of Commerce and Industry:** Narayan Rajaram Bandekar Bhavan, Rua de Ormuz, POB 59, Panaji 403 001; tel. (832) 2422635; fax (832) 2425560; e-mail goachamber@gmail.com; internet www.goachamber.org; f. 1908 as Associacao Commercial da India Portuguesa; more than 500 mems; Pres. NITIN KUNKOLIENKER; Dir-Gen. Air Cmmdre (retd) P. K. PINTO.

**Gujarat Chamber of Commerce and Industry:** Shri Ambica Mills, Gujarat Chamber Bldg, Ashram Rd, POB 4045, Ahmedabad 380 009; tel. (79) 26582301; fax (79) 26587992; e-mail gujaratchamber@gmail.com; internet www.gujaratchamber.org; f. 1949; 7,713 mems; Pres. RUPESH C. SHAH; Sr Vice-Pres. SAMIR N. PATEL.

**Indian Chamber of Commerce:** ICC Towers, 4 India Exchange Place, Kolkata 700 001; tel. (33) 22203242; fax (33) 22213377; e-mail info@indianchamber.org; internet www.indianchamber.org; f. 1925; 500 corporate group mems, more than 1,200 mem. cos; Pres. S. K. BANGUR; Sec.-Gen. Dr RAJEEV SINGH.

**Indian Chamber of Commerce and Industry:** 49 Community Centre, New Friends Colony, New Delhi 110 065; tel. (11) 26836468; fax (11) 26840775; e-mail iccind@yahoo.co.in; internet www.iccinewdelhi.com; f. 1987; Pres. LALIT K. MODI; Sec.-Gen. R. P. SWAMI.

**Indian Merchants' Chamber:** IMC Bldg, IMC Marg, Churchgate, Mumbai 400 020; tel. (22) 22046633; fax (22) 22048508; e-mail imc@imcnet.org; internet www.imcnet.org; f. 1907; 185 asscn mems, 2,915 mem. firms; Pres. NIRAJ BAJAJ; Sec.-Gen. P. N. MOGRE.

**Karnataka Chamber of Commerce and Industry:** G. Mahadevappa Karnataka Chamber Bldg, Jayachamaraj Nagar, Hubli 580 020; tel. (836) 2218234; fax (836) 2360933; e-mail kccihble@sify.com; internet www.kccihubli.org; f. 1928; 2,500 mems; Pres. V. P. LINGANGOUDAR; Hon. Sec. BASAVARAJ H. BYALI.

**Madhya Pradesh Chamber of Commerce and Industry:** Chamber Bhavan, Sanatan Dharam Mandir Marg, Gwalior 474 009; tel. (751) 2332916; fax (751) 2323844; e-mail info@mpcci.com; internet www.mpcci.com; f. 1906; 1,705 mems; Pres. G. D. LADHA; Hon. Sec. VIJAY GOYAL.

**Madras Chamber of Commerce and Industry:** Karumuttu Centre, 634 Anna Salai, Chennai 600 035; tel. (44) 24349452; fax (44) 24349164; e-mail mascham@md3.vsnl.net.in; internet www.mascham.com; f. 1836; 375 mem. firms, 20 affiliated, 10 hon., three others; Pres. ARUN BEWOOR; Sec.-Gen. R. SUBRAMANIAN.

**Maharashtra Chamber of Commerce, Industry and Agriculture:** Oricon House, 6th Floor, 12 K. Dubhash Marg, Fort, Mumbai 400 001; tel. (22) 22855859; fax (22) 22855861; e-mail maharashtrachamber@vsnl.com; internet www.maccia.org.in; f. 1927; more than 3,500 mems; more than 800 affiliated trade asscns and professional bodies; Pres. HEMANT RATHI; Sec.-Gen. SHRIKANT SARDESHPANDE.

**Mahratta Chamber of Commerce, Industries and Agriculture:** MCCIA Trade Tower, 505, A-Wing, ICC Complex, 403 Senapati Pabat Rd, Pune 411 016; tel. (20) 25709000; fax (20) 25709021; e-mail info@mcciapune.com; internet www.mcciapune.com; f. 1934; more than 2,000 mems; Pres. MADHUR BAJAJ; Additional Dir-Gen. ANANT SARDESHMUKH.

**Merchants' Chamber of Commerce:** 15B Hemanta Basu Sarani, Kolkata 700 001; tel. (33) 22483123; fax (33) 22488657; e-mail mercham@cal.vsnl.net.in; internet www.mercham.org; f. 1901; 600 mems; Pres. ADITYA VARDHAN AGARWAL; Dir-Gen. R. K. SEN.

**Merchants' Chamber of Uttar Pradesh:** 14/76 Civil Lines, Kanpur 208 001; tel. and fax (512) 2530877; fax (512) 2531306; e-mail info@merchantschamber-up.com; internet www.merchantschamber-up.com; f. 1932; 200 mems; Pres. JWALA PRASAD AGRAWAL; Sec. A. K. SINHA.

**North India Chamber of Commerce and Industry:** 9 Gandhi Rd, Dehra Dun; tel. (935) 223479; f. 1967; 105 ordinary mems, 29 asscn mems, seven mem. firms, 91 assoc. mems; Pres. DEV PANDHI; Hon. Sec. ASHOK K. NARANG.

**Oriental Chamber of Commerce:** 6A Dr Rajendra Prasad Sarani (Clive Row), Kolkata 700 001; tel. (33) 22302120; fax (33) 22303609; e-mail orientchamb@vsnl.net; f. 1932; 250 ordinary mems, three assoc. mems; Pres. N. D. MEHTA; Sec. Kazi ABU ZOBER.

**PHD Chamber of Commerce and Industry (PHDCCI):** PHD House, 4/2 Siri Institutional Area, August Kranti Marg, New Delhi 110 016; tel. (11) 26863801; fax (11) 26863135; e-mail phdcci@phdcci.in; internet www.phdcci.in; f. 1905; 1,760 mems, 150 asscn mems; Pres. SANJAY BHATIA; Sec.-Gen. KRISHAN KALRA.

**Rajasthan Chamber of Commerce and Industry:** Rajasthan Chamber Bhavan, M. I. Rd, Jaipur 302 003; tel. (141) 2565163; fax (141) 2561419; e-mail info@rajchamber.com; internet www.rajchamber.com; 575 mems; Pres. MAHENDRA S. DAGA; Hon. Sec.-Gen. Dr K. L. JAIN.

**Southern India Chamber of Commerce and Industry:** Indian Chamber Bldgs, 6 Esplanade, POB 1208, Chennai 600 108; tel. (44) 25342228; fax (44) 25341876; e-mail sicci@md3.vsnl.net.in; f. 1909; 1,000 mems; Pres. R. VEERAMANI; Sec. S. RAGHAVAN.

**Upper India Chamber of Commerce:** 113/47, Swaroop Nagar, POB 63, Kanpur 208 002; tel. (512) 2543905; fax (512) 2531684; f. 1888; 52 mems; Pres. DILIP BHARGAVA; Sec. S. P. SRIVASTAVA.

**Utkal Chamber of Commerce and Industry Ltd:** N/6, IRC Village, Nayapalli, Bhubaneswar 751 015; tel. (674) 3296035; fax (674) 25575981; e-mail contact@utkalchamber.com; internet utkalchamber.com; f. 1964; 250 mems; Pres. M. V. RAO; Hon. Sec. JAYANTA KUMAR SAHOO.

**Uttar Pradesh Chamber of Commerce:** 15/197 Civil Lines, Kanpur 208 001; tel. 2211696; f. 1914; 200 mems; Pres. Dr B. K. MODI; Sec. AFTAB SAMI.

## INDUSTRIAL AND TRADE ASSOCIATIONS

**Ahmedabad Textile Mills' Association:** Ashram Rd, Navrangpura, POB 4056, Ahmedabad 380 009; tel. (79) 26582273; fax (79) 26588574; e-mail sec_gen@atmaahd.com; f. 1891; 21 mems; Pres. CHINTAN N. PARIKH; Sec.-Gen. ABHINAVA SHUKLA.

**All India Federation of Master Printers:** 605 Madhuban, 55 Nehru Place, New Delhi 110 019; tel. (11) 26451742; fax (11) 26451743; e-mail aifmp@vsnl.com; internet www.aifmp.org; f. 1953; 52 affiliates, 800 mems; Pres. R. N. DUTTA BARUAH; Hon. Gen. Sec. RITWIK MITRA.

**All India Manufacturers' Organization (AIMO):** Jeevan Sahakar, 4th Floor, Sir P.M. Rd, Fort, Mumbai 400 001; tel. (22) 22661016; fax (22) 22660838; e-mail aimoindia@mtnl.net.in; internet www.aimoindia.com; f. 1941; 800 mems; Pres. AMIT KUMAR SEN; Sr Vice-Pres. JAGDISH P. TODI.

**All India Plastics Manufacturers' Association:** AIPMA House, A-52, St No. 1, MIDC, Andheri (East), Mumbai 400 093; tel. (22) 28217324; fax (22) 28216390; e-mail aipma@bom2.vsnl.net.in; internet www.aipma.net; f. 1947; 1,800 mems; Chair. SURESH J. ATRE; Hon. Sec. AJAY DESAI.

**All India Shippers' Council:** Federation House, Tansen Marg, New Delhi 110 001; tel. (11) 23738760; fax (11) 23320714; e-mail ficci.bisnet@gems.vsnl.net.in; f. 1967; 82 mems; Chair. RAMU S. DEORA; Sec. M. Y. REDDY.

**Association of Man-made Fibre Industry of India:** Resham Bhavan, 78 Veer Nariman Rd, Mumbai 400 020; tel. (22) 22040009; fax (22) 22049172; e-mail amfiirayon@hotmail.com; internet www.viscoserayonindia.com; f. 1954; seven mems; Pres. K. K. MAHESHWARI; Sec. M. P. JOSEPH.

**Automotive Component Manufacturers' Association of India:** 6th Floor, The Capital Court, Olof Parme Marg, Munirka, New Delhi 110 067; tel. (11) 26160315; fax (11) 26160317; e-mail acma@vsnl.com; internet www.acmainfo.com; 485 mems; Pres. RAGHU MODY; Exec. Dir VISHNU MATHUR.

**Automotive Tyre Manufacturers' Association:** PHD House, opp. Asian Games Village, Siri Fort Institutional Area, New Delhi 110 016; tel. (11) 26851187; fax (11) 26864799; e-mail atma@vsnl.in; internet www.atmaindia.org; 10 mems; Chair. RAGHUPATI SINGHANIA; Dir-Gen. D. RAVINDRAN.

**Bharat Krishak Samaj** (Farmers' Forum, India): Dr Panjabrao Deshmukh Krishak Bhavan, A-1 Nizamuddin West, New Delhi 110 013; tel. (11) 24359508; fax (11) 24359509; e-mail ffi@mantraonline.com; f. 1954; national farmers' org.; 5m. ordinary mems, 75,000 life mems; Chair. Dr BAL RAM JAKHAR; Exec. Chair. and Gen. Sec. Dr KRISHAN BIR CHAUDHARY.

**Bombay Metal Exchange Ltd:** 88/90 Kika St, 1st Floor, Gulalwadi, Mumbai 400 004; tel. (22) 22421964; fax (22) 22422640; e-mail bme@bom8.vsnl.net.in; f. 1950; promotes trade and industry in non-ferrous metals; 460 mems; Pres. ROHIT V. SHAH; Sec. T. S. B. IYER.

**Bombay Shroffs Association:** 233 Sheikh Memon St, Mumbai 400 002; tel. (22) 23425588; f. 1910; 325 mems; Pres. PRANLAL R. SHETH; Hon. Secs MOHANBHAI M. PATEL, DHIRAJ S. KOTHARI.

**Calcutta Flour Mills Association:** 25/B Shakespeare Sarani, Kolkata 700 017; tel. (33) 22876723; fax (33) 22875944; e-mail swaika@vsnl.com; f. 1932; 28 mems; Chair. NAVNEET SWAIKA; Hon. Sec. RAVI BHAGAT.

**Calcutta Tea Traders' Association:** 6 Netaji Subhas Rd, Kolkata 700 001; tel. (33) 22301574; fax (33) 22301289; e-mail ctta@cal3.vsnl.net.in; internet www.cttacal.org; f. 1886; 1,300 mems; Chair. AZAM MONEM; Sec. J. KALYANA SUNDARAM.

**Cement Manufacturers' Association:** CMA Tower, A-2E, Sector 24, Noida 201 301; tel. (95120) 2411955; fax (95120) 2411956; e-mail cmand@vsnl.com; internet cmaindia.org; 54 mems; 126 major cement plants; Pres. N. SRINIVASAN; Sec.-Gen. E. N. MURPHY.

**Confederation of Indian Industry (CII):** 23 Institutional Area, Lodhi Rd, New Delhi 110 003; tel. (11) 24629994; fax (11) 24626149; e-mail cii@ciionline.org; internet www.ciionline.org; f. 1974; 3,800 mem. cos; Pres. SUNIL KANT MUNJAL; Dir-Gen. N. SRINIVASAN.

**Consumer Electronics and Appliances Manufacturers' Association (CEAMA):** J-13, 1st Floor, Jangpura Extension, New Delhi 110 014; tel. (11) 24327777; fax (11) 24321616; e-mail ceama@vsnl.net; internet www.cetmaindia.org; f. 1978; 98 mems; Pres. ANOOP KUMAR; Sec.-Gen. SURESH KHANNA.

**Cotton Association of India:** Cotton Exchange Bldg, 2nd Floor, Cotton Green, Mumbai 400 033; tel. (22) 23704401; fax (22) 23700337; e-mail eica@eica.in; internet www.eica.in; f. 1921; 400 mems; Pres. P. D. PATODIA; Exec. Dir and Sec.-Gen. OM PRAKASH AGARWAL.

**Electronic Component Industries Association (ELCINA):** ELCINA House, 422 Okhla Industrial Estate, New Delhi 110 020; tel. (11) 26928053; fax (11) 26923440; e-mail elcina@vsnl.com; internet www.elcina.com; f. 1967; 255 mems; Pres. R. G. DESHPANDE; Sec.-Gen. RAJOO GOEL.

**Federation of Automobile Dealers Associations:** 805 Surya Kiran, 19 Kasturba Gandhi Marg, New Delhi 110 001; tel. (11) 23320046; fax (11) 23320093; e-mail fadadelhi@vsnl.net; internet www.fadaweb.com; f. 1964; Pres. JAYENDRA KACHALIA; Sec.-Gen. GULSHAN AHUJA; 1,072 mems.

**Federation of Gujarat Industries:** Sidcup Tower, 4th Floor, Race Course, Vadodara 390 007; tel. (265) 2311101; fax (265) 2339054; e-mail info@fgibaroda.org; internet www.fgibaroda.org; f. 1918; 350 mems; Pres. YOGENDRA GANGWAL; Sec. Dr PARESH RAVAL.

**Federation of Hotel and Restaurant Associations of India:** B-82 Himalaya House, 23 K. G. Marg, New Delhi 110 001; tel. (11) 23322634; fax (11) 23322645; e-mail fhrai@vsnl.com; internet www.fhrai.com; f. 1955; 2,572 mems; Pres. S. K. KHULLAR; Sec.-Gen. KAMAL SHARMA.

**Federation of Indian Export Organisations:** PHD House, 3rd Floor, Siri Institutional Area, Hauz Khas, New Delhi 110 016; tel. (11) 26851310; fax (11) 26863087; e-mail fieo@nda.vsnl.net.in; internet www.fieo.org; f. 1965; 8,000 mems; Pres. O. P. GARG; Dir-Gen. G. BALACHANDHRAN.

**Federation of Indian Mineral Industries (FIMI):** B-311, Okhla Industrial Area, Phase 1, New Delhi 110 020; e-mail fimi@fedmin.com; internet www.fedmin.com; f. 1966; 350 mems; Pres. RAHUL N. BALDOTA.

**The Fertiliser Association of India:** 10 Shaheed Jit Singh Marg, New Delhi 110 067; tel. (11) 26567144; fax (11) 26960052; internet www.faidelhi.org; f. 1955; 1,414 mems; Chair. H. C. GROVER; Dir-Gen. B. K. SAHA; Sec. DEEPAK BHANDARI.

**Grain, Rice and Oilseeds Merchants' Association:** 14-C, Groma House, 2nd Floor, Sector 19, Vashi, Navi Mumbai 400 703; tel. (22) 27897454; fax (22) 27897458; e-mail groma@vsnl.com; f. 1899; 1,200 mems; Pres. SHARADKUMAR D. MARU.

**Indian Drug Manufacturers' Association:** 102B Poonam Chambers, Dr A. B. Rd, Worli, Mumbai 400 018; tel. (22) 24944624; fax (22) 24950723; e-mail idma@idmaindia.com; internet www.idma-assn.org; 600 mems; Pres. SURESH KARE; Sec.-Gen. DAARAB PATEL.

**Indian Electrical and Electronics Manufacturers' Association (IEEMA):** 501 Kakad Chambers, 132 Dr Annie Besant Rd, Worli, Mumbai 400 018; tel. (22) 24936528; fax (22) 24932705; e-mail mumbai@ieema.org; internet www.ieema.org; f. 1948; 400 mems; Pres. P. KRISHNAKUMAR; Sec.-Gen. SUNIL P. MORE.

**Indian Jute Mills Association:** Royal Exchange, 6 Netaji Subhas Rd, Kolkata 700 001; tel. (33) 22309918; fax (33) 22313836; e-mail ijma@cal2.vsnl.net.in; sponsors and operates export promotion, research and product development; regulates labour relations; 35 mems; Chair. SANJOY KAJARIA; Exec. Vice-Chair. S. K. BHATTACHARYA.

**Indian Leather Products Association:** Suite 6, Chatterjee International Centre, 14th Floor, 33-A, Jawaharlal Nehru Rd, Kolkata 700 071; tel. (33) 22267102; fax (33) 22468339; e-mail ilpa@cal2.vsnl.net.in; 135 mems; Pres. SATYABRATA MUKHOPADHYAY; Exec. Dir P. P. RAY CHAUDHURI.

**Indian Machine Tool Manufacturers' Association:** Plot 249F, Phase IV, Udyog Vihar, Sector 18, Gurgaon 122 015; tel. (124) 4014101; fax (124) 4014108; e-mail imtma@del2.vsnl.net.in; internet www.imtma.org; 400 mems; Pres. C. P. RANGACHAR; Sec. and Exec. Dir V. ANBU.

**Indian Mining Association:** 6 Netaji Subhas Rd, Kolkata 700 001; tel. (33) 22203733; f. 1892; 50 mems; Sec. K. MUKERJEE.

**Indian Motion Picture Producers' Association:** IMPPA House, Dr Ambedkar Rd, Bandra (West), Mumbai 400 050; tel. (22) 26486344; fax (22) 26480757; e-mail indiafilm@gmail.com; f. 1938; 10,200 mems; Pres. T. P. AGGARWAL; Sec. ANIL NAGRATH.

**Indian National Shipowners' Association:** 22 Maker Tower F, Cuffe Parade, Mumbai 400 005; tel. (22) 22182103; fax (22) 22182104; e-mail secygen@insa.org.in; internet www.insa.org.in; f. 1929; 35 mems; Pres. S. HAJARA; Sec.-Gen. S. S. KULKARNI.

**Indian Oilseeds & Produce Exporters' Association (IOPEA):** 78/79 Bajaj Bhavan, Nariman Point, Mumbai 400 021; tel. (22) 22023225; fax (22) 22029236; e-mail info@iopea.org; internet www.iopea.org; f. 1956; export promotion council; 350 mems; Chair. SANJIV SAWLA; Sec. A. N. SUBRAMANIAN.

**Indian Refractory Makers' Association:** 5 Lala Lajpat Rai Sarani, 4th Floor, Kolkata 700 020; tel. (33) 22810868; fax (33) 22814357; e-mail irma@vsnl.com; internet www.irmaindia.org; 85 mems; Chair. U. C. DEVESHWAR; Exec. Dir P. DAS GUPTA.

**Indian Soap and Toiletries Makers' Association:** 614 Raheja Centre, 6th Floor, Free Press Journal Marg, Nariman Point, Mumbai 400 021; tel. (22) 22824115; fax (22) 22853649; e-mail istma@bom3.vsnl.net.in; 26 mems; Pres. K. V. VAIDYANATHAN; Sec.-Gen. R. HARIHARAN.

**Indian Sugar Mills' Association:** Ansal Plaza, C-Block, 2nd Floor, Andrews Ganj, New Delhi 110 049; tel. (11) 26262294; fax (11) 26263231; e-mail sugarmil@nda.vsnl.net.in; internet www.indiansugar.com; f. 1932; 181 mems; Pres. VIVEK M. PITTIE; Dir-Gen. S. L. JAIN.

**Indian Tea Association:** Royal Exchange, 6 Netaji Subhas Rd, Kolkata 700 001; tel. (33) 22102474; fax (33) 22434301; e-mail ita@indiatea.org; internet www.indiatea.org; f. 1881; 210 mem. cos; 420 tea estates; Chair. C. K. DHANUKA; Sec.-Gen. D. CHAKRABARTI.

**Indian Woollen Mills' Federation:** Churchgate Chambers, 7th Floor, 5 New Marine Lines, Mumbai 400 020; tel. (22) 22624372; fax (22) 22624675; e-mail iwmf@vsnl.com; f. 1963; 50 mems; Chair. V. K. BHARTIA; Sec.-Gen. MAHESH N. SANIL.

**Industries and Commerce Association:** ICO Association Rd, POB 70, Dhanbad 826 001; tel. (326) 2303147; fax (326) 2303787; f. 1933; 70 mems; Pres. B. N. SINGH; Sec. PRADEEP CHATTERJEE.

**Jute Balers' Association:** 12 India Exchange Place, Kolkata 700 001; tel. (33) 22201491; f. 1909; 300 mems; Chair. NIRMAL KUMAR BHUTORIA; Sec. SUJIT CHOUDHURY.

**Maharashtra Motor Parts Dealers' Association:** 13 Kala Bhavan, 3 Mathew Rd, Mumbai 400 004; tel. (22) 23614468; 375 mems; Pres. J. C. UNADKAT; Sec. J. R. CHANDAWALLA.

**Millowners' Association, Mumbai:** Elphinstone Bldg, 10 Veer Nariman Rd, Fort, Mumbai 400 001; tel. (22) 22040411; fax (22) 22832611; f. 1875; 23 mem. cos; Chair. R. K. DALMIA; Sec.-Gen. V. Y. TAMHANE.

**Mumbai Motor Merchants' Association Ltd:** 304 Sukh Sagar, N. S. Patkar Marg, Mumbai 400 007; tel. (22) 28112769; 409 mems; Pres. S. TARLOCHAN SINGH ANAND; Gen. Sec. S. BHUPINDER SINGH SETHI.

**Mumbai Textile Merchants' Mahajan:** 250 Sheikh Memon St, Mumbai 400 002; tel. (22) 22411686; fax (22) 22400311; f. 1879; 1,900 mems; Pres. SURENDRA TULSIDAS SAVAI; Hon. Secs DHIRAJ S. KOTHARI, RAJESH B. PATEL.

**National Association of Software and Service Companies (NASSCOM):** International Youth Centre, Uma Shankar Dixit Marg, Chanakyapuri, New Delhi 110 021; tel. (11) 23010199; fax (11) 23015452; e-mail info@nasscom.in; internet www.nasscom.in; 1,200 mems; Pres. SOM MITTAL; Chair. Dr GANESH NATARAJAN.

**Organisation of Pharmaceutical Producers of India (OPPI):** Peninsular Corporate Park, Peninsular Chambers, Ground Floor, Ganpatrao Kadam Marg, Lower Parel, Mumbai 400 013; tel. (22) 24918123; fax (22) 24915168; e-mail indiaoppi@vsnl.com; internet www.indiaoppi.com; 74 mems; Pres. RANJIT SHAHANI; Dir-Gen. Dr AJIT DANGI.

**Society of Indian Automobile Manufacturers:** Core 4B, 5th Floor, India Habitat Centre, Lodhi Rd, New Delhi 110 003; tel. (11) 24647810; fax (11) 24648222; e-mail siam@vsnl.com; f. 1960; 36 mems; Pres. JAGDISH KHATTER; Dir-Gen. DILIP CHENOY.

**Southern India Mills' Association:** 41 Race Course, Coimbatore 641 018; tel. (422) 2211391; fax (422) 2217160; e-mail info@simamills.com; internet www.simamills.com; f. 1933; 360 mems; Chair. Dr K. Y. SRINIVASAN; Sec.-Gen. Dr K. SELVARAJAN.

**Surgical Manufacturers and Traders' Association:** 60 Darya Ganj, New Delhi 110 002; tel. (11) 23271027; fax (11) 23258576; e-mail raviawasthi@hotmail.com; Pres. RAVI AWASTHI; Sec. S. B. SAWHNEY.

**Synthetic and Art Silk Mills' Association Ltd:** Sasmira Bldg, 3rd Floor, Sasmira Marg, Worli, Mumbai 400 030; tel. (22) 24945372; fax (22) 24938350; e-mail sasma_100@rediffmail.com; f. 1939; 100 mems; Chair. KAVAL MEHRA; Sec.-Gen. N. T. RAO.

**Telecom Equipment Manufacturers' Association of India (TEMA):** PHD House, 4th Floor, Khel Gaon Marg, Hauz Khas, New Delhi 110 016; tel. (11) 26859621; fax (11) 26859620; e-mail tema@eth.net; internet www.tematelecom.net; Pres. P. S. RAMESH; Sec.-Gen. RAKESH MALIK.

**Travel Agents' Association of India:** 2D Lawrence and Mayo House, 276 Dr D. N. Rd, Mumbai 400 001; tel. (22) 22074022; fax (22) 22074559; e-mail taai@hathway.com; internet www.taainet.com; 1,692 mems; Pres. S. THOMAS; Hon. Sec.-Gen. BHAGWAN KANUGA.

**United Planters' Association of Southern India (UPASI):** Glenview, POB 11, Coonoor 643 101; tel. (423) 2230270; fax (423) 2232030; e-mail upasi@sancharnet.in; internet www.upasi.org; f. 1893; 850 mems; Pres. D. P. MAHESHWARI; Sec.-Gen. ULLAS MENON.

### EMPLOYERS' ORGANIZATIONS

**Council of Indian Employers:** Federation House, Tansen Marg, New Delhi 110 001; tel. (11) 23316121; fax (11) 23320714; e-mail aioe@del3.vsnl.net.in; f. 1956; comprises:

**All India Organisation of Employers (AIOE):** Federation House, Tansen Marg, New Delhi 110 001; tel. (11) 23316121; fax (11) 23320714; e-mail aioe@del3.vsnl.net.in; f. 1932; 115 mems; Pres. SAROJ KUMAR PODDAR; Sec.-Gen. Dr AMIT MITRA.

**Employers' Federation of India (EFI):** Army and Navy Bldg, 148 Mahatma Gandhi Rd, Mumbai 400 001; tel. (22) 22844232; fax (22) 22843028; e-mail efisolar@vsnl.com; f. 1933; 28 asscn mems, 182 ordinary mems, 18 hon. mems; Pres. Dr RAM S. TARNEJA; Sec.-Gen. SHARAD S. PATIL.

**Standing Conference of Public Enterprises (SCOPE):** 1st Floor, Core No. 8, SCOPE Complex, 7 Lodhi Rd, New Delhi 110 003; tel. (11) 24362604; fax (11) 24361371; e-mail scope_dg@yahoo.co.in; internet www.scopeonline.in; f. 1973; representative body of all central public enterprises in India; advises the Govt and public enterprises on matters of major policy and co-ordination; trade enquiries, regarding imports and exports of commodities, carried out on behalf of mems; 211 mems; Chair. SARTHAK BEHURIA; Vice-Chair. ARUP ROY CHOUDHURY.

**Employers' Association of Northern India:** 14/113 Civil Lines, POB 344, Kanpur 208 001; tel. (512) 2210513; f. 1937; 190 mems; Chair. RAJIV KEHR; Sec.-Gen. P. DUBEY.

**Employers' Federation of Southern India:** Karumuttu Centre, 1st Floor, 634 Anna Salai, Chennai 600 035; tel. (44) 24349452; fax (44) 24349164; e-mail efsi@vsnl.net; internet www.efsi.org.in; f. 1920; 520 mems; Pres. SHAJI VARGHESE; Sec. T. M. JAWAHARLAL.

### UTILITIES

#### Electricity

**Central Electricity Authority (CEA):** Sewa Bhavan, R. K. Puram, New Delhi 110 066; tel. (11) 26108476; fax (11) 26105619; e-mail cea-edp@hub.nic.in; internet www.cea.nic.in; responsible for technical co-ordination and supervision of electricity programmes; advises Ministry of Power on all technical, financial and economic issues; Chair. RAKESH NATH.

**Bangalore Electricity Supply Co Ltd:** K. R. Circle, 4th Floor, Bangalore 560 001; tel. (80) 22354939; internet www.bescom.org.

**Calcutta Electricity Supply Corpn Ltd (CESC):** CESC House, Chouringhee Sq., Kolkata 700 001; tel. (33) 22256040; fax (33) 22256334; internet cesc.co.in; f. 1978; generation and supply of electricity; Chair. R. P. GOENKA; Man. Dir SUMANTRA BANERJEE.

**Chattisgarh Electricity Co Ltd:** Industrial Growth Centre, Siltara, Raipur 493 111; tel. (771) 5093925; Dir P. K. JAIN.

**Damodar Valley Corpn:** DVC Towers, VIP Rd, Kolkata 700 054; tel. (33) 23551935; fax (33) 23551937; e-mail dvchq@wb.nic.in; internet www.dvcindia.org; f. 1948 to administer the first multi-purpose river valley project in India, the Damodar Valley Project, which aims at unified development of irrigation, flood control and power generation in West Bengal and Jharkhand; operates nine power stations, incl. thermal, hydel and gas turbine; power generating capacity 2,761.5 MW (1999); Chair. AJAY SHANKAR.

**Essar Power Ltd:** Essar House, 11 Keshavrao Khadye Marg, Mahalaxmi, Mumbai 400 034; tel. (22) 56601100; fax (22) 24954787; e-mail essarpower@essar.com; internet www.essar.com/power; Chair. S. N. RUIA; Man. Dir A. K. SRIVASTAVA.

**Jaipur Vidyut Vitran Nigam Ltd:** Old Power House Premises, Banipark, Jaipur 302 006; tel. (141) 2208098; fax (141) 2202025.

**National Hydroelectric Power Corporation:** Sector 33, Faridabad 121 003; tel. (129) 2278421; fax (129) 2277941; e-mail webmaster@nhpc.nic.in; internet www.nhpcindia.com; f. 1975; Chair and Man. Dir S. K. GARG.

**National Thermal Power Corporation Ltd:** Core-7, SCOPE Complex, Lodhi Rd, New Delhi 110 003; tel. (11) 24360100; fax (11) 24361018; e-mail info@ntpc.co.in; internet www.ntpc.co.in; f. 1975; operates 11 coal-fired and five gas-fired power stations throughout India; Chair. and Man. Dir T. SANKARALINGAM; 24,000 employees.

**Noida Power Co Ltd:** Commercial Complex, H Block, Alpha Sector II, Greater Noida 201 308; tel. (95120) 4326559; fax (95120) 4326448; e-mail npcl@noidapower.com; internet www.noidapower.com; f. 1922; distribution of electricity; Chair. and Man. Dir USHA CHATRATH; CEO P. NEOGI.

**Nuclear Power Corporation of India Ltd:** Commerce Center-1, World Trade Centre, Cuffe Parade, Mumbai 400 005; tel. (22) 22182171; fax (22) 22180109; e-mail cswtc@vsnl.com; internet www.npcil.org; Chair. and Man. Dir SHREYANS KUMAR JAIN.

**Power Grid Corporation of India Ltd:** Saudamani, Plot No. 2, Sector 29, Gurgaon 122 001; tel. (124) 2571700; fax (124) 2571760; internet www.powergridindia.com; f. 1989; responsible for formation of national power grid; Chair. and Man. Dir R. P. SINGH.

**Ratnagiri Gas and Power Pvt Ltd:** NTPC Bhavan, SCOPE Complex, 7 Institutional Area, Lodi Rd, New Delhi 110 003; tel. (11) 24367089; fax (11) 24361003; internet www.rgppl.com; f. 2005 to take over assets and revive operations of Dabhol Power Co; 28% owned by National Thermal Power Corpn Ltd, 28% by Gas Authority of India Ltd, 15% by the Maharashtra State Electricity Board (MSEB) and 29% by Indian banking institutions; operates plant with three units with a total combined power-generating capacity of 2,150 MW; Chair. R. K. GOEL; Man. Dir A. K. AHUJA.

**Reliance Energy:** Reliance Energy Centre, Santacruz (East), Mumbai 400 055; tel. (22) 30099999; fax (22) 30099536; e-mail rel.website@rel.co.in; internet www.rel.co.in; f. 1929 as Bombay Suburban Electric Supply Ltd, merged with the Reliance Group in Jan. 2003; generates, transmits and distributes power in Maharashtra, Goa and Andhra Pradesh; Chair. and Man. Dir ANIL AMBANI.

**Rural Electrification Corpn Ltd:** Core-4, SCOPE Complex, 7 Lodhi Rd, New Delhi 110 003; tel. (11) 24365161; fax (11) 24360644; e-mail recorp@recl.nic.in; internet www.recindia.com; Chair. and Man. Dir M. N. PRASAD.

**Tata Power Co Ltd:** Bombay House, 24 Homi Mody St, Mumbai 400 001; tel. (22) 56658282; fax (22) 56658801; internet www.tatapower.com; generation, transmission and distribution of electrical energy; Chair. RATAN N. TATA; Man. Dir FIRDOSE VANDREWALA.

**Thana Electric Supply Co Ltd:** Asian Bldg, 1st Floor, 17 Ramji Kamani Marg, Ballard Estate, Mumbai 400 001; tel. (22) 22615444; fax (22) 22611069; e-mail thanaele@bom2.vsnl.net.in; f. 1927; Man. Dir SURESH S. HEMMADY.

**Torrent Power Ltd (TPL):** Torrent House, off Ashram Road, Ahmedabad 380 009; tel. (79) 26583060; fax (79) 26589581; e-mail tpld@torrentpower.com; internet www.torrentpower.com; generation and distribution of electricity; f. 1996; Exec. Chair. SUDHIR MEHTA.

#### Gas

**Gas Authority of India Ltd:** 16 Bhikaji Cama Place, R. K. Puram, Delhi 110 066; tel. (11) 26172580; fax (11) 26185941; internet gail.nic.in; f. 1984; 80% state-owned; transports, processes and markets natural gas; constructing gas-based petrochemical complex; Chair. and Man. Dir MOHAN R. HINGNIKAR; 1,513 employees.

**Gujarat Gas Co Ltd:** 2 Shantisadan Society, Ellis Bridge, Ahmedabad 380 006; Chair. HASMUKH SHAH; Man. Dir B. S. SHANTHARAJU.

**Indraprastha Gas Ltd:** Dr Gopal Das Bhawan, 14th–15th Floors, 28 Barakhamba Rd, New Delhi 110 001.

#### Water

**Brihanmumbai Municipal Corporation (Hydraulic Engineers' Department):** Municipal Corporation Head Offices, Ground Floor, Annex Bldg, Mahapalika Marg, Mumbai 400 001; tel. (22) 22620251; fax (22) 22634329; Head Eng. R. R. HASINAME.

**Calcutta Municipal Corporation (Water Supply Department):** 5 S. N. Banerjee Rd, Kolkata 700 013; tel. (33) 22444518; fax (33) 22442578; f. 1870; Chief Municipal Eng. DIBYENDU ROY CHOWDHURY.

**Chennai Metropolitan Water Supply and Sewerage Board:** No. 1 Pumping Station Rd, Chintadripet, Chennai 600 002; tel. (44) 28525717; f. 1978; Chair. and Man. Dir SANTHA SHEELA NAIR.

**Delhi Jal Board:** Varunalaya Phase II, Karol Bagh, New Delhi 110 005; tel. and fax (11) 23678380; e-mail prodjb@bol.net.in; internet www.delhijalboard.nic.in; f. 1957 as Delhi Water Supply and Sewage Disposal Undertaking, reconstituted as above in 1998; part of the Delhi Municipal Corporation; production and distribution of potable water and treatment and disposal of waste water in Delhi; Chair. SHEILA DIXIT.

**Karnataka Rural Water Supply and Sanitation Agency:** 2nd Floor, E Block, KHB Complex, Cauvery Bhavan, K. G. Rd, Bangalore

560 009; tel. (80) 22246508; fax (80) 22240509; e-mail jalnirmal@vsnl.net; internet www.jalnirmal.org.

**Karnataka Urban Water Supply and Drainage Board:** Sir M. Visveswaraya Rd, D. C. Compound, Dharwad 580 001; tel. (836) 2447090; fax (836) 2446890; internet www.kuwsdb.org.

## MAJOR COMPANIES

### Government Industrial Undertakings

The following are some of the more important industrial and commercial undertakings in which the Government holds a controlling interest.

**Bharat Coking Coal Ltd:** Koyla Bhawan, Koyla Nagar, Dhanbad 826 005; tel. (326) 2230112; fax (326) 2230153; e-mail bcclcmd@cmpdi.co.in; internet bccl.cmpdi.co.in; f. 1972; cap. p.u. Rs 2,180m., sales Rs 20,822m. (March 2003); a subsidiary of Coal India Ltd; manages coking coal mines nationalized in 1972; Chair. and Man. Dir ASOKE KUMAR PAUL.

**Bharat Electronics Ltd:** Nagavara, Outer Ring Rd, Bangalore 560 045; tel. (80) 25039300; fax (80) 25039305; e-mail imd@bel-india.com; internet www.bel-india.com; f. 1954; cap. p.u. Rs 800m., res and surplus Rs 11,558.2m., sales Rs 27,985.9m. (March 2004); sales Rs 39,603.8m. (March 2007); mfrs of communications and radar equipment and electronic components; 9 manufacturing units; Chair. and Man. Dir V. V. R. SASTRY; 15,700 employees.

**Bharat Heavy Electricals Ltd:** BHEL House, Siri Fort, New Delhi 110 049; tel. (11) 26001010; fax (11) 26493021; e-mail query@bhel.com; internet www.bhel.com; f. 1964; cap. p.u. Rs 2,448m., res and surplus Rs 50,512m., sales Rs 86,625m. (March 2004); integrated global service in power generation, transmission and utilization equipment; plants at Bhopal, Jhansi, Haridwar, Hyderabad, Bangalore and Tiruchirappalli; overseas offices in Dubai, United Arab Emirates, and South-East Asia; Chair. and Man. Dir K. RAVI KUMAR; 42,600 employees.

**Bharat Petroleum Corpn Ltd:** Bharat Bhavan, 4 and 6 Currimbhoy Rd, Ballard Estate, POB 688, Mumbai 400 001; tel. (22) 22713000; fax (22) 22632951; e-mail infor@bharatpetroleum.com; internet www.bharatpetroleum.com; f. 1928; as Burmah-Shell Oil Storage and Distributing Co of India Ltd, nationalized 1976; cap. p.u. Rs 3,615m., res and surplus Rs 99,120m., sales Rs 1,074, 523m. (March 2007); refinery at Trombay with crude processing capacity of 6.6m. metric tons a year; mfrs of MS, superior kerosene, aviation turbine fuel, high speed diesel oil, light diesel oil, bitumen, liquefied petroleum gas (LPG), solvents, naphtha, mineral turpentine and low sulphur heavy stock; owns eight port installations, six inland installations, two bunkering installations, one lubricating oil blending plant, 11 pipeline TOPS, 67 company-operated depots, 64 commission operated/special agreement depots, 26 dispatch units, 33 LPG-bottling plants, 16 aviation service stations, 1,345 LPG distributorships and 4,489 retail outlets throughout India; Chair. and Man. Dir ASHOK SINHA; 12,494 employees (2003).

**Bongaigaon Refinery and Petrochemicals Ltd:** Dhaligaon, Chirang District, Assam 783 385; tel. (3664) 241233; fax (3664) 241027; e-mail info@brplindia.com; internet www.brplindia.com; oil refinery and petrochemical plant producing transportation and industrial fuels, DMT and PSF; a subsidiary of Indian Oil Corpn Ltd; cap. p.u. Rs 1,998.2m. (March 2005), res and surplus Rs 2,229.4m. (March 2003), sales Rs 6,426.0m. (March 2007); Chair. SARTHAK BEHURIA; Man. Dir A. K. SARMAH.

**Cement Corpn of India Ltd:** Core-V, SCOPE Complex, 7 Lodhi Rd, New Delhi 110 003; tel. (11) 24360158; fax (11) 24360464; e-mail cci_co@cementcorporation.co.in; internet www.cementcorporation.co.in; f. 1965; cap. Rs 4,283m., sales Rs 1,220m. (March 2003); establishes cement factories and sells cement in various parts of the country; surveys and prospects for limestone deposits; 10 operating factories in six states and in the Union Territory of Delhi; also offers consultancy services from concept to commissioning; Chair. and Man. Dir K. TECKCHANDANI.

**Central Coalfields Ltd:** Darbhanga House, Ranchi 834 001; tel. (651) 2301606; fax (651) 2301624; e-mail cmd_ccl@cmpdi.co.in; internet ccl.cmpdi.co.in; f. 1975; cap. p.u. Rs 9,400m., sales Rs 29,333m. (March 2003); wholly owned subsidiary of Coal India Ltd; Chair. R. P. RITOLIA.

**Chennai Petroleum Corporation Ltd:** 536 Anna Salai, Chennai 600 018; tel. (44) 24349519; fax (44) 24341753; e-mail smv@cpcl.co.in; internet www.cpcl.co.in; f. 1965 as Madras Refineries Ltd; partly govt-owned; 51.9% owned by Indian Oil Co, 15.4% by National Iranian Oil Co; a subsidiary of Indian Oil Corpn Ltd; oil refinery in Tamil Nadu; cap pu. Rs 1,490m.; res and surplus Rs 11,443.3m., sales Rs 86,299.5m. (March 2003); net profit Rs 4,810.0m. (March 2006); Chair. SARTHAK BEHURIA; Man. Dir K. K. ACHARYA.

**Coal India Ltd:** Coal Bhavan, 10 Netaji Subhas Rd, Kolkata 700 001; tel. (33) 22488099; fax (33) 22435316; e-mail cil@wb.nic.in; internet www.coalindia.nic.in; f. 1975; cap. p.u. Rs 63,164m. (March 2005), sales Rs 339,981.1m. (March 2006); coal mining, pricing and distribution; Chair. PARTHA S. BHATTACHARYYA.

**Eastern Coalfields Ltd:** Sanctoria, PO Dishergarh 713 333, Burdwin; tel. (341) 2520053; fax (341) 2523574; e-mail cmd.easterncoal@nic.in; internet www.easterncoal.nic.in; f. 1975; cap. p.u. Rs 22,184.5m., sales Rs 35,182m. (March 2007); subsidiary of Coal India Ltd; Chair. and Man. Dir SAMARJIT CHAKRABARTI.

**Engineers India Ltd:** Engineers India Bhavan, 1 Bhikaiji Cama Place, R.K. Puram, New Delhi 110 066; tel. (11) 26102121; fax (11) 26178210; e-mail eil.mktg@eil.co.in; internet www.engineersindia.com; provides engineering consultancy in India and abroad with specialization in the fields of petroleum refineries, pipelines, oil and gas processing, petrochemicals, offshore platforms, ports and terminals, metallurgy, fertilizers, power, chemicals; cap. p.u. Rs 561.6m., res and surplus Rs 6,950.7m., sales Rs 8,182.7m. (March 2003); net profit Rs 13,864.3m; Chair. and Man. Dir MUKESH ROHATGI.

**The Fertilizers and Chemicals Travancore Ltd (FACT):** POB 14, Udyogamandal, Kochi 683 501; tel. (484) 2545101; fax (484) 2545475; e-mail factcoin@factltd.com; internet www.fact.co.in; f. 1943; cap. p.u. Rs 3,547.7m., sales Rs 9,193.7m. (March 2003); major shareholdings were acquired by Govt in 1963; mfrs of fertilizers, chemicals and petrochemicals (caprolactam); Chair. and Man. Dir Dr GEORGE SLEEBA.

**Gujarat State Fertilizers and Chemicals Ltd:** PO Fertilizernagar, Vadodara 391 750; tel. (265) 2242051; fax (265) 2240966; e-mail info@gsfcltd.com; internet www.gsfclimited.com; cap. p.u. Rs 797.4m., res Rs 9,137.4m., sales Rs 27,604.1m. (March 2005); Chair. Dr MANJULA SUBRAMANIAM; Man. Dir HARIBHAI V. PATEL.

**Heavy Engineering Corpn Ltd:** Plant Plaza Rd, Dhurwa Ranchi 834 004, Jharkhand; tel. (651) 2408192; fax (651) 2408571; e-mail bkumar@hecltd.com; internet www.hecltd.com; f. 1958; cap. p.u. Rs 4,481m., res and surplus Rs 407.7m., sales Rs 1,413.8m. (March 2003); operates a heavy machine building plant, a foundry forge plant and a heavy machine tools plant; project and consultancy division; Chair. and Man. Dir G. K. PILLAI.

**Hindustan Aeronautics Ltd:** Corporate Office, 15/1 Cubbon Rd, POB 5150, Bangalore 560 001; tel. (80) 22866701; fax (80) 22867533; e-mail cmc@hal-india.com; internet www.hal-india.com; f. 1964; sales Rs 77,830m. (March 2007); mfrs of aircraft, helicopters, aero-engines, airborne electronic equipment and accessories; undertakes overhaul of aircraft, etc.; main customer is the Indian air force; 14 factories and nine design bureaux; Chair. ASHOK K. BAWEJA; 34,448 employees.

**Hindustan Cables Ltd:** 9 Elgin Rd, Kolkata 700 020; tel. (33) 22832910; fax (33) 22832986; e-mail hicabcal@cal2.vsnl.net.in; internet www.hindcables.com; cable factories at Rupnarainpur in West Bengal, Hyderabad, and Naini in Allahabad; cap. p.u. Rs 4,793.6m., res and surplus Rs 567.4m. (March 2003); Chair. and Man. Dir Shri KISHOR RUNGTA; 3,197 employees.

**Hindustan Copper Ltd:** Tamra Bhavan, 1 Ashutosh Chowdhury Ave, Kolkata 700 019; tel. (33) 22832529; fax (33) 22408884; e-mail hindcop@vsnl.com; internet www.hindustancopper.com; f. 1967; cap. p.u. Rs 9,051.5m., res. and surplus Rs 71.0m., sales Rs 4,992.8m. (March 2004); sales Rs 18,000.0m. (March 2007); responsible for the development of Indian Copper Complex, Ghatsila, in Bihar, Khetri Copper Complex, in Rajasthan, Taloja Copper Project in Maharashtra, and Malanjkhand Copper Project in Madhya Pradesh; annual capacity: 50,000 metric tons of finished copper (1994); Chair. and Man. Dir SATISH CHANDRA GUPTA; 5,995 employees (2005).

**Hindustan Fertilizer Corpn Ltd:** Madhuban, 55 Nehru Place, New Delhi 110 019; tel. (11) 26489520; fax (11) 26488652; e-mail hfcl1@vsnl.com; cap. p.u. Rs 6,865m., sales Rs 719m. (March 2003); operates Namrup fertilizer plant; Chair. and Man. Dir BALVINDER KUMAR.

**Hindustan Newsprint Ltd:** Newsprint Nagar, Kottayam District, Kerala 686 616; tel. (4829) 256211; fax (4829) 256777; e-mail hnl@hnlonline.com; internet www.hnlonline.com; f. 1982; newsprint factory in Kerala; cap. p.u. Rs 825.4m., res and surplus Rs 1,090.0m., sales Rs 2,526.8m. (2003); Man. Dir N. P. PRABHU; 1,125 employees.

**Hindustan Paper Corporation Ltd:** Ruby Bldg, 75-C, Park St, Kolkata 700 016; tel. (33) 22296931; fax (33) 22494996; e-mail rajip@hindpaper.in; internet www.hindpaper.in; operates several paper mills; cap. p.u. Rs 7,004m., sales Rs 6,397m. (March 2003); Chair. and Man. Dir RAJI PHILIP.

**Hindustan Petroleum Corpn Ltd:** Petroleum House, 17 Jamshedji Tata Rd, Churchgate, Mumbai 400 020; tel. (22) 22863900; fax (22) 22872992; e-mail corphqo@hpcl.co.in; internet www.hindustanpetroleum.com; f. 1952; as Esso Standard Refining Co of India Ltd; fully nationalized 1976; cap. Rs 3,386m., res and surplus Rs 92,597m., sales Rs 1,120,982m. (March 2008); petroleum refining, manufacture of lubricating oil base stocks and marketing of petroleum products; refinery at Mahul (capacity 5.5m. metric tons a year), producing petrol, kerosene, diesel oils, fuel oils, solvents, LPG, asphalts, etc., and at Visakhapatnam (AP) (total refining capacity of 13.8m. metric tons a year), producing liquid petroleum gas, naphtha, motor gasoline, aviation turbine fuel, mineral turpentine, kerosene, etc.; lube refinery at Mahul uses crude from fuel refinery (capacity 335,000 metric tons a year); has about 19.5% share in the Indian oil market and 40% share of lube market; Chair. and Man. Dir ARUN BALAKRISHNAN; Dir (Finance) B. MUKHERJEE; 11,213 employees (2004).

**HMT Machine Tools Ltd:** 59 Bellary Rd, Bangalore 560 032; tel. (80) 23330333; fax (80) 23339111; e-mail admin@hmtindia.com; internet www.hmtindia.com; f. 1953; cap. Rs 100.5m., sales Rs 1,982.1m. (March 2004); India's largest machine tools and watch mfr with units at Aurangabad, Bangalore, Pinjore (Haryana), Kalamassery (Kerala), Hyderabad, Ajmer, Tumkur and Srinagar; 3 subsidiaries; Chair. and Man. Dir A. V. KAMAT; 4,709 employees.

**Indian Iron and Steel Co Ltd:** 7 The Ridge, West Bengal 713 325; tel. (341) 230441; fax (341) 231605; e-mail iiscomd@dte.vsnl.net.in; internet www.iiscosteel.com; f. 1918; cap. p.u. Rs 3,876.7m., sales Rs 9,242.7m. (March 2003); a subsidiary of Steel Authority of India Ltd (SAIL); major establishments include iron and steel works at Burnpur, collieries at Chasnalla and iron ore mines and foundry at Kulti and the township of Burnpur and Kulti, West Bengal; Man. Dir G. S. GARCHA.

**Indian Oil Corporation Ltd:** Corporate Office, 3079/3, J. B. Tito Marg, Sadiq Nagar, New Delhi 110 049; tel. (11) 26260101; fax (11) 24362607; internet www.iocl.com; f. 1964; acquired petroleum product mfr, IBP Co Ltd (Kolkata), April 2007; cap. p.u. Rs 11,680.1m., res and surplus Rs 218,794m., sales Rs 1,139m. (March 2004); the Refineries and Pipelines Division in New Delhi manages six refineries; the division lays pipelines and manages the Gauhati–Siliguri, Haldia–Barauni–Kanpur, Haldia–Maurigram–Rajbandh, Salaya–Koyali–Mathura, Kandla–Bhatindaand Koyali–Ahmedabad oil pipelines; the Marketing Division in Mumbai distributes petroleum products and has about 55% share in the Indian oil market; lube blending plant at Chennai; Research and Development Centre at Faridabad; Indian Oil Blending Ltd, a wholly owned subsidiary, has blending plants at Kolkata and Mumbai; Assam Oil Division manages Digboi Refinery (Assam) and markets petroleum products in the north-east; Chair. SARTHAK BEHURIA; 30,048 employees.

**Instrumentation Ltd:** Kanjikode West, Palakkad, Kerala 678 623; tel. (491) 2566127; fax (491) 2566135; e-mail contact@ilpgt.com; internet www.ilpgt.com; f. 1964; cap. p.u. Rs 240.5m., sales Rs 1,750m. (March 2005); the largest mfrs of industrial process control instruments in India; designs, builds, erects and commissions instrumentation systems; manufactures control valves and allied items with the technical collaboration of Japan, gas analysers used in pollution control with Germany and modernized process control instruments with the United Kingdom; plants at Kota, Jaipur and Palghat; Chair. and Man. Dir K. N. MISHRA.

**National Aluminium Company Ltd:** Nalco Bhavan, P/1 Nayapalli, Bhubaneswar 751 013; tel. (674) 2301999; fax (674) 2300550; e-mail rmsdel@satyam.net.in; internet nalcoindia.com; aluminium plant in Orissa; cap. p.u. Rs 6,443.1m., res and surplus Rs 70,509.1 m., sales Rs 65,145.1m. (March 2007); Chair. and Man. Dir C. VENKETARAMANA.

**National Fertilizers Ltd:** A-11, Sector 24, Noida 201 301; internet www.nationalfertilizers.com; cap. p.u. Rs 4,906m., res and surplus Rs 5,851.5m. (March 2004), sales Rs 3,591.0m. (March 2006); approx. 16.5% share in the Indian urea production market; Chair. and Man. Dir G. S. MANGAT; Sec. A. K. MAITRA.

**National Textile Corporation Ltd:** Scope Complex, Core No. IV, 7 Lodhi Rd, New Delhi 110 003; tel. (11) 24360101; fax (11) 24361112; e-mail nntcga@vsnl.net; internet www.ntcltd.in; f. 1968; operates 52 textile mills throughout the country; nine subsidiary cos to be merged with NTC Holding Co in 2007; cap. p.u. Rs 5,121m., res Rs 952m. (March 2001), sales Rs 6,380m. (March 2005); Chair. and Man. Dir K. RAMACHANDRAN PILLAI; 22,000 employees.

**Neyveli Lignite Corpn Ltd:** Block 1, Neyveli, Cuddalore District, Tamil Nadu 607 801; tel. (4142) 252214; fax (4142) 252646; e-mail cmdnlc@nlcindia.com; internet www.nlcindia.co.in; f. 1956; cap. p.u. Rs 16,777.1m., res and surplus Rs 51,673.2m., sales Rs 28,075.4m. (March 2004); activities include lignite mining, power generation, production of urea and carbonized briquettes; Chair. and Man. Dir S. JAYAMARAN.

**Northern Coalfields Ltd:** Singrauli Colliery, Sidhi 486 889; tel. (7805) 266393; fax (7805) 266640; e-mail cmd.ncl@nclhq.nic.in; internet www.ncl.nic.in; cap. p.u. Rs 5,776.7m., res and surplus Rs 25,348.9m., sales Rs 32,442m. (March 2003); Chair. and Man. Dir V. K. SINGH; Dir (Finance) S. N. CHOUDHURY; 17,006 employees.

**Oil India Ltd:** Plot No. 19, Film City, Sector 16A, Noida 201301; tel. (120) 2488333; fax (120) 2488310; e-mail oilindia@oil.delhi.nic.in; internet www.oilindia.nic.in; f. 1959; 98.1% govt-owned; cap. p.u. Rs 2,140m., res and surplus Rs 58,483.0m., sales Rs 55,502.0m. (March 2006); formed as a result of an agreement between the Govt of India, the Burmah Oil Co Ltd and the Assam Oil Co Ltd, for the development of new oilfields in Assam; the company has mining leases for the exploration and production of crude petroleum and natural gas in Naharkatiya, Hugrijan, Moran, Doom Doma (Assam) and Ningru (Arunachal Pradesh), and petroleum exploration licences in Assam, Orissa, Rajasthan, Arunachal Pradesh, Uttar Pradesh and offshore areas of Saurashtra; it supplies crude petroleum to the refineries at Barauni, Guwahati, Bongaigaon, Digboi and Numaligarh; it supplies natural gas to the Rajasthan Electricity Board; it is also engaged in the transport of oil and the sale of gas; for this purpose the company has constructed and is operating a network of pipelines; the company also produces liquefied petroleum gas; Chair. and Man. Dir M. R. PASRIJA.

**Oil and Natural Gas Corporation Ltd (ONGC):** Jeevan Bharati, Tower II, 8th Floor, 124 Indira Chowk, New Delhi 110 001; tel. (11) 23301000; fax (11) 23316413; internet www.ongcindia.com; f. 1956; as the Oil and Natural Gas Commission, name changed as above in 1994; cap. Rs 14,259m., res and surplus Rs 383,264.9m., sales Rs 320,639.3m. (March 2004); petroleum exploration and exploitation in India and abroad; crude petroleum production 26.0m. metric tons (2003/04); Chair. and Man. Dir R. S. SHARMA; 43,700 employees.

**Projects and Development India Ltd:** A-14, Sector 1, Noida 201 301; tel. (120) 4529842; fax (120) 4541045; e-mail noida@pdilin.com; internet www.pdilin.com; cap. p.u. Rs 535.2m., sales Rs 277m. (March 2002); a design engineering and technical consultancy organization in the field of fertilizers, industrial chemicals, petroleum, gas and pollution monitoring; Chair. and Man. Dir R. J. RAJAN; brs in Vadodara, Kolkata, Mumbai and Chennai.

**Rashtriya Chemicals and Fertilizers Ltd:** Priyadarshini Bldg, Eastern Express Highway, Mumbai 400 022; tel. (22) 24045001; fax (22) 24045111; e-mail anujsharma@rcfltd.com; internet www.rcfltd .com; f. 1978; cap. p.u. Rs 5,517m., res and surplus Rs 6,334.1m. (March 2003), sales Rs 348,799.0m. (March 2007); operates Trombay and Thal Fertilizers and Industrial Chemicals plant; expansion projects and proposed new projects and jt ventures abroad; Chair. and Man. Dir U. S. JHA.

**South Eastern Coalfields Ltd:** SECL Bhavan, Seepat Rd, POB 60, Bilaspur 495 006; tel. (7752) 242674; fax (7752) 240306; e-mail cmd@ seclhq.com; internet secl.nic.in; cap. p.u. Rs 6,597m., res and surplus Rs 20,540m. (March 2003), sales Rs 53,656.6m. (March 2004); Chair. and Man. Dir M. P. DIXIT.

**Tea Trading Corpn of India Ltd:** 7 Wood St, 2nd Floor, Kolkata 700 016; tel. (33) 23701192; fax (33) 23701092; f. 1973; cap. p.u. Rs 111.4m., sales Rs 34.3m. (March 2001); promotes the export and local sale of tea; owns and manages tea estates; processes and manufactures tea in blended and packaged form; is expanding into export of seafoods and processed fruit and food products; Man. Dir P. K. GUPTA.

**Western Coalfields Ltd:** Coal Estate, Civil Lines, Nagpur 440 001; tel. (712) 2510315; fax (712) 2510500; e-mail wclcmd_ngp@ sancharnet.in; internet westerncoal.nic.in; f. 1975; cap. p.u. Rs 2,971m., res and surplus Rs 11,804.4m. (March 2003), sales Rs 55,101.8m. (March 2006); wholly owned subsidiary of Coal India Ltd; Chair. and Man. Dir DINESH CHANDRA GARG.

### Private Companies

The following are among India's major industrial enterprises in the private sector, listed by industry.

#### Automobile Industry

**Ashok Leyland Ltd:** 19 Rajaji Salai, POB 1305, Chennai 600 001; tel. (44) 25342141; fax (44) 25342493; e-mail al@webindia.com; internet www.ashokleyland.com; f. 1948; cap. Rs 1,323.9m., res and surplus Rs 17,621.8m. (2007), sales Rs 77,291m. (2007/08); mfrs of light, medium and heavy duty commercial vehicles, industrial and marine diesel engines and spare parts; six factories; Chair. R. J. SHAHANEY; Man. Dir R. SESHASAYEE; 11,860 employees (March 2003).

**Bajaj Auto Ltd:** Mumbai-Pune Rd, Akurdi, Pune 411 035; tel. (20) 27472851; fax (20) 27473399; e-mail sdkamath@bajajauto.co.in; internet www.bajajauto.com; f. 1945; cap. Rs 1,011.8m., res Rs 31,394.2m. (March 2003), sales Rs 59,271m. (March 2005); manufactures and sells scooters, motorcycles, mopeds, three-wheelers, etc.; two subsidiaries: Bajaj Auto Holdings Ltd and Bajaj Auto Finance Ltd; Chair. RAHUL BAJAJ; Man. Dir RAJIV BAJAJ; 12,338 employees (March 2003).

**Bosch Ltd:** Hosur Rd, Adugodi, POB 3000, Bangalore 560 030; tel. (80) 22220088; fax (80 22212728; internet www.boschindia.com; f. 1951; owned by Bosch of Germany; fmrly Motor Industries Co Ltd; manufactures automotive components; Chair. HUBERT ZIMMERER; Man. Dir Dr ALBERT HIERONIMUS.

**Eicher Motors Ltd:** Eicher House, 12 Commercial Complex, Greater Kailash-II (Masjid Moth), New Delhi 110 048; tel. (11) 29225521; fax (11) 29220501; e-mail reach@eicher.co.in; internet www.eicherworld.com; mfrs of commercial vehicles; cap. p.u. Rs 280.9m., res Rs 2,128.6m., sales Rs 19,825.6m. (March 2005); Chair. S. SANDILYA; Man. Dir and CEO SIDDHARTHA LAL.

**Escorts Ltd:** 15/5 Mathura Rd, Faridabad 121 003; tel. (129) 2250222; fax (129) 2250036; e-mail escortsgroup@escortscorporate.com; internet www.escortsgroup.com; f. 1942; manufactures and sells motor cycles, tractors, pistons, self-propelled mobile cranes, road construction equipment, röntgen equipment, hydraulic shock absorbers, etc.; five subsidiaries; cap. p.u. Rs 722.3m., res and surplus Rs 7,073.2m. (March 2002), net sales Rs 23,660.5m. (Sept. 2006); Chair. and Man. Dir RAJAN NANDA; Exec. Dir NIKHIL NANDA.

**Fiat India Pvt Ltd:** LBS Marg, Kurla, Mumbai 400 070; tel. (22) 25097006; fax (22) 25097571; mfrs of passenger cars; Man. Dir Dr PAOLA CASTAGNA.

**Force Motors Ltd:** Mumbai–Pune Rd, Akurdi, Pune 411 035; tel. (20) 27476381; fax (20) 27404678; internet forcemotors.com; fmrly known as Bajaj Tempo Ltd; Chair. and Man. Dir ABHAY N. FIRODIA.

**Ford India Ltd:** Via S. P. Koil Post, Chengalpattu 603 204; tel. (44) 27454375; fax (44) 2745517; e-mail custmail@ford.com; internet www.india.ford.com; mfrs of passenger cars; Pres. and Man. Dir ARVIND MATHEW.

**General Motors India Ltd:** Chandrapura Industrial Estate, Halol 389351; tel. (2676) 221000; fax (2676) 220666; e-mail gmi.cac@gm.com; internet www.gm.co.in; f. 1995; mfrs of passenger cars; Pres. and Man. Dir ADITYA VIJ.

**Hero Honda Motors Ltd:** 34 Community Centre, Basant Lok, Vasant Vihar, New Delhi 110 057; tel. (11) 26142451; fax (11) 26143321; internet www.herohonda.com; f. 1984; cap. p.u. Rs 399.4m., res and surplus Rs 10,988.7m., sales Rs 58,324.3m. (March 2004); mfrs of motor cycles; Chair. BRIJMOHAN LALL MUNJAL; Man. Dir PAWAN MUNJAL.

**Hindustan Motors Ltd:** Birla Bldg, 9/1 R. N. Mukherjee Rd, Kolkata 700 001; tel. (33) 22201680; fax (33) 22480055; internet www.hindmotor.com; f. 1942; cap. p.u. Rs 1,611.7m., res Rs 448.0m., sales Rs 7,309.5m. (March 2004); mfrs of cars, truck chassis, cranes, presses, excavators, steel structurals, steel castings and forgings at factory at Hindmotor (West Bengal); car plant at Kadambathur (Tamil Nadu); power shift transmissions and torque converters at Hosur (Tamil Nadu), engines and transmissions for cars at Pithampur (Madhya Pradesh); two subsidiaries: Hindustan Motor Finance Corpn Ltd and Hindustan Export Ltd; Chair. CHANDRA KANT BIRLA; Man. Dir R. SANTHANAM; 7,924 employees (2003).

**Honda Siel Cars India Ltd:** Plot No. A-1, Sector 40/41, Surajpur-Kasna Rd, Dist. Gautam Budh Nagar, Greater Noida Industrial Development Area, Uttar Pradesh 201 306; tel. (95120) 2341313; fax (95120) 2341261; internet www.hondacarindia.com; Pres. and CEO MASAHIRO TAKEDAGAWA.

**Hyundai Motor India Ltd:** A-30, Mohan Co-operative Industrial Estate, Mathura Rd, New Delhi 110 044; tel. (11) 41678800; fax (11) 41678811; e-mail cr@hmil.net; internet www.hyundai.co.in; wholly owned subsidiary of Hyundai Motor Co (South Korea); mfrs of passenger cars; Man. Dir LHEEM HEUNG-SOO.

**India Yamaha MotorPvt Ltd:** 19/6 Mathura Rd, Faribad 121 006; tel. (95129) 2283620; fax (95129) 2264707; internet www.yamaha-motor-india.com; mfrs of motorcycles; CEO and Man. Dir H. YANAGI.

**Kinetic Motor Company Ltd:** D-1 Block, Plot No. 18/2, Chinchwad, Pune 411 019; tel. (20) 27472715; fax (20) 27475843; internet www.kineticindia.com; cap. p.u. Rs 150.9m., res Rs 355.9m., sales Rs 1,972.8m. (March 2004); mfrs of two-wheel vehicles; Chair. A. H. FIRODIA.

**LML Ltd:** C-3, Panki Industrial Estate, Kanpur 208 022; tel. (512) 691181; fax (512) 691191; e-mail lmlknp@lml-india.com; cap. p.u. Rs 437m., res Rs 7,223.5m., sales Rs 5,750m. (March 2003); mfrs of scooters; Chair. M. R. B. PUNJA; Man. Dir D. K. SINGHANIA.

**Maharashtra Scooters Ltd:** Mumbai-Pune Rd, Akurdi, Pune 411 035; tel. (20) 27472851; fax (20) 27473398; subsidiary of Bajaj Auto; cap. p.u. Rs 114m., sales Rs 1,040m. (March 2002); Chair. RAHUL BAJAJ; Man. Dir RANJIT GUPTA.

**Mahindra and Mahindra Ltd:** Mahindra Towers, 5th Floor, G. M. Bhosale Marg, Worli, Mumbai 400 018; tel. (22) 24931441; fax (22) 24900830; e-mail corporate.communications@mahindramail.com; internet www.mahindra.com; f. 1945; flagship co of the Mahindra Group; cap. p.u. Rs 1,160m., res Rs 13,800.8m., sales Rs 37,320m. (March 2003); res Rs 33,148.8m., net sales Rs 96,277.1m. (March 2007); mfrs of 'Mahindra' range of vehicles, tractors and agricultural implements, industrial engines, industrial process and control instruments; trades in steel and machine tools, exports and imports chemicals, engineering goods, diesel engines, oilfield services, telecommunications, construction and road building, etc.; 13 subsidiaries; Chair. KESHUB MAHINDRA; Man. Dir ANAND G. MAHINDRA; 11,800 employees (2003).

**Majestic Auto Ltd:** C-48, Focal Point, Ludhiana 141 010; tel. (161) 2670233; fax (161) 2672790; e-mail info@heromajestic.com; internet www.heromajestic.com; cap. p.u. Rs 65.5m., sales Rs 1,348m. (March 2003); mfrs of motor cycles and mopeds; Chair. O. P. MUNJAL; Man. Dir PANKAJ MUNJAL.

**Maruti Udyog Ltd:** 11th Floor, Jeevan Prakash Bldg, 25 Kasturba Gandhi Marg, New Delhi 110 001; tel. (11) 23316831; fax (11) 23318754; internet www.marutiudyog.com; f. 1981; Govt sold its 18.28% stake in May 2007; controlling share owned by Suzuki Motor Co (Japan); cap. p.u. Rs 1,445m., res and surplus Rs 34,467m., sales Rs 93,456m. (March 2004); largest mfrs of passenger cars and light utility commercial vehicles in collaboration with Suzuki Motor Co of Japan; annual sales of more than 500,000 vehicles in India; Chair. SHINZO NAKANISHI; Man. Dir JAGDISH KHATTAR; 4,590 employees (2004).

**Mercedes-Benz India Pvt Ltd:** Sector 15A, Chikhali Village, Pimpri, Pune 411 018; tel. (20) 27505000; fax (20) 27505953; e-mail dccac1@daimler.com; internet www.mercedes-benz.co.in; Man. Dir and CEO HANS-MICHAEL HUBER.

**SkodaAuto India Pvt Ltd:** A-1/1, M. I. D. C., Five Star Industrial Area, Shendra, Aurangabad 431 201; tel. (240) 6631111; fax (240) 6631299; e-mail info@skoda-auto.co.in; internet www.skoda-auto.co.in; Man. Dir I. HASSAN.

**Swaraj Mazda Ltd:** SCO 204–205, Sector 34-A, Chandigarh 160 022; tel. (172) 2647700; fax (172) 2615111; e-mail yashmahajan@swarajenterprise.com; internet www.swarajenterprise.com; f. 1984 in collaboration with Mazda Motor Corpn and Sumitomo Corpn (Japan); part of the Swaraj Enterprise Ltd group, which also operates Punjab Tractors Ltd, Swaraj Engines Ltd and Swaraj Automotives Ltd; mfrs of light commercial vehicles; cap. p.u. Rs 105m., res Rs 69.4m., sales Rs 2,950m. (March 2002); sales Rs 6,126m. (March 2006); Chair. S. K. TUTEJA; Vice-Chair. and Man. Dir YASH MAHAJAN.

**Tata Motors Ltd:** Bombay House, 24 Homi Mody St, Hutatma Chowk, Mumbai 400 001; tel. (22) 56658282; fax (22) 56657799; internet www.tatamotors.com; f. 1945; cap. p.u. Rs 3,568.3m., res Rs 32,367.7m., sales Rs 132,821.2m. (March 2004); manufactures and sells Tata Diesel truck and bus chassis, light commercial vehicles, passenger cars; factories at Jamshedpur, Lucknow, Dharwar and Pune; Chair. RATAN TATA; 21,271 employees (2004).

**Toyota Kirloskar Motor Pvt Ltd:** Plot No. 1, Bidadi Industrial Area, Ramnagar Taluk, Bangalore (Rural) District 562 109; tel. (80) 66292929; internet www.toyotabharat.com; f. 1997; mfrs of utility vehicles and passenger cars; Chair. RYOICHI SASAKI; Man. Dir. ATSUSHI TOYOSHIMA; 2,275 employees.

**TVS Motor Company Ltd:** 5th Floor, Jayalakshmi Estates, 8 Haddows Rd, Chennai 600 006; tel. (44) 28272233; fax (44) 28257121; internet www.tvsmotor.co.in; cap. p.u. Rs 237m., res Rs 5,512.0m., sales Rs 28,202.1m. (March 2004); mfrs of mopeds, motor cycles and scooters; Chair. and Man. Dir VENU SRINIVASAN.

**Volvo India Pvt Ltd:** 201 Embassy Sq., 148 Infantry Rd, Bangalore 560 003; tel. (80) 27965251; fax (80) 27965280; internet www.volvo.com/group/india/en-in; Man. Dir ULF NORDQVIST.

### Biotechnology

**Avestha Gengraine Technologies Pvt Ltd:** 'Discoverer', 9th Floor, Unit 3, International Technology Park Ltd, Whitefield Rd, Bangalore 560 066; tel. (80) 28411665; fax (80) 28418780; e-mail info@avesthagen.com; internet www.avesthagen.com; f. 1998; Chair. DARIUS E. UDWADIA; 140 employees.

**Bharat Biotech International Ltd (BBIL):** Genome Valley, Shameerpet, Hyderabad 500 078; tel. (40) 23480567; fax (40) 23480560; e-mail info@bharatbiotech.com; internet www.bharatbiotech.com; f. 1996; specializes in product-orientated research and development and manufacturing of vaccines and biotherapeutics; Chair. and Man. Dir Dr KRISHNA M. ELLA.

**Biocon Ltd:** 20th K. M., Hosur Rd, Electronics City, Bangalore 560 100; tel. (80) 28082808; fax (80) 28523423; e-mail contact.us@biocon.com; internet www.biocon.com; f. 1978; cap. Rs 500m., res and surplus Rs 6,910m., sales Rs 6,470m. (March 2005); involved in the research, development and manufacture of healthcare pharmaceutical products and industrial enzymes; Chair. KIRAN MAZUMDAR-SHAW; c. 3,000 employees (2007).

**Cipla Ltd:** Mumbai Central, 289 J. B. B. Marg, Mumbai 400 008; tel. (22) 23082891; fax (22) 23070013; e-mail corporate@cipla.com; internet www.cipla.com; f. 1935; cap. p.u. Rs 599.7m., sales Rs 22,419.2m. (March 2005); research and development; manufacture and sale of drugs; Chair. and Man. Dir Dr YUSUF K. HAMIED; 2,227 employees.

**Dr Reddy's Laboratories Ltd:** Greenlands, Ameerpet, Hyderabad 500 016; tel. (40) 23731946; fax (40) 23731955; e-mail corpcom@drreddys.com; internet www.drreddys.com; f. 1984; research, development, manufacture and marketing of pharmaceutical products; research in molecular biology and infectious diseases; cap. Rs 382.6m., res Rs 20,358.2m., sales Rs 15,577.0m. (March 2005); Chair. Dr K. ANJI REDDY; Vice-Chair. and CEO G. V. PRASAD.

**Greenearth Biotechnologies Ltd:** 14A Jigani Industrial Area, Bangalore 562106; tel. (80) 8398793; fax (80) 8394936; e-mail sjn@greenearthbiotech.com; internet www.greenearthbiotech.com.

**Maharashtra Hybrid Seed Co Ltd** (Mahyco): Dawalwadi, POB 76, Jalna 431 203; tel. (2482) 262371; fax (2482) 262002; e-mail info@mahyco.com; internet www.mahyco.com; research, production and processing of cereals, oilseeds, pulses and vegetables; production of agro-based food products; research in biotechnology, biochemistry and plant-breeding; Man. Dir R. B. BARWALE.

**Ranbaxy Laboratories Ltd:** 25 Nehru Place, New Delhi 110 019; tel. (11) 26452666; fax (11) 26465748; e-mail seema.ahuja@ranbaxy.com; internet www.ranbaxy.com; f. 1961; manufactures therapeutic and pharmaceutical products; cap. Rs 23,198m., sales 34,649m. (Dec. 2003); Chair. HARPAL SINGH; CEO and Man. Dir MALVINDER MOHAN SINGH; 11,000 employees (2007).

**Shantha Biotechnics (Pvt) Ltd:** House No. 5-10-173, 3rd and 4th Floors, Vasantha Chambers, Fateh Maidan Rd, Basheerbagh, Hyderabad 500 004; tel. (40) 23234136; fax (40) 23234103; e-mail info@shanthabiotech.com; internet www.shanthabiotech.com; research, development and production of drugs and vaccines; Chair. GEORGES HIBON; Man. Dir K. V. REDDY.

### Cement Industry

**Associated Cement Companies Ltd (ACC):** Cement House, 121 Maharashi Karve Rd, POB 11025, Mumbai 400 020; tel. (22) 66654321; fax (22) 66317440; e-mail nandkumar@acccement.com; internet www.acclimited.com; f. 1936; manufacture and sale of cement (14 cement works in eight states); Subsidiaries: Bulk Cement Corpn of India Ltd, ACC Concrete Ltd; Chair. N. S. SEKHSARIA; Man. Dir SUMIT BANERJEE; some 9,000 employees (2007).

**India Cements Ltd:** Dhun Bldg, 827 Anna Salai, Chennai 600 002; tel. (44) 28521526; fax (44) 28521753; internet www.indiacements.co.in; f. 1946; cap. Rs 1,385.9m., res and surplus Rs 2,008.1m., sales Rs 12,329m. (March 2004); mfrs of cement, cement clinker, grinding media, malleable cast iron material, etc.; factories at Sankarnagar (Tirunelveli District), Sankaridrug (Salem District); 11 subsidiary cos; Chair. N. SANKAR; Vice-Chair. and Man. Dir N. SRINIVASAN; 6,000 employees.

**Mysore Cements Ltd:** Infinity Towers 'C', 9th Floor, DLF Cyber City, Phase II, Gurgaon 122 002; tel. (124) 4503700; fax (124) 4147698; internet www.mycemco.com; f. 1958; subsidiary of Cementrum I BV (Netherlands); cap. p.u. Rs 687m., sales Rs 2,980m. (March 2002); net sales Rs 4,143.8m. (Dec. 2006); Chair. S. K. BIRLA; Man. Dir ASHISH KUMAR GUHA.

**OCL India:** B-47 Connaught Place, New Delhi 110 001; tel. (11) 23321212; fax (11) 23731333; e-mail ocl@nda.vsnl.net.in; internet www.oclindialtd.in; f. 1949; fmrly Orissa Cement Ltd; manufactures cement and refractories; factory at Rajgangpur in Orissa; four subsidiaries; cap. Rs 71.8m., res Rs 1,337.3m. (March 2000), sales Rs 3,100m. (March 2003); Jt Pres R. H. DALMIA, M. H. DALMIA.

**Shree Cement Ltd:** Bangur Nagar, POB 33, Beawar 305 901; tel. (1462) 228101; e-mail sclbwr@shreecementltd.com; internet www.shreecementltd.com; f. 1979; cap. p.u. Rs 348.4m., res Rs 2,546.5m., sales Rs 5,820.8m. (March 2005); capacity of 2m. metric tons per year; Exec. Chair. B. G. BANGUR; Man. Dir H. M. BANGUR.

### Chemicals and Fertilizers

See also under Cotton Textiles

**Atul Ltd:** Dist. Valsad, Gujarat 396 020; tel. (2632) 233261; fax (2632) 233375; e-mail ho@atul.co.in; internet www.atul.co.in; f. 1947; cap. p.u. Rs 296.7m., sales Rs 6,060m. (March 2003); manufacturing and marketing of dyes, dye intermediates, chemicals, pesticides and pharmaceutical intermediates; six subsidiaries; Man. Dir and CEO SUNIL SIDDHARTH LALBHAI.

**Chambal Fertilisers and Chemicals Ltd:** International Trade Tower, F Block, 3rd Floor, Nehru Pl., New Delhi 110 019; tel. (11) 26462162; fax (11) 26465218; e-mail corpcomm@cfert.com; internet www.zuari-chambal.com; f. 1985 by Zuari Industries Ltd; subsidiary of K. K. Birla Group; diversity of interests incl. fertilizers, phosphoric acid, agri-biotechnology, textiles, information technology, food processing, shipping; operates two urea production plants (Gadepan, Rajasthan: 1.73m. metric tons); cap. p.u. Rs 4,060.0m., res and surplus Rs 2,724.6m., sales Rs 21,048.1m. (March 2004); Chair. K. K. BIRLA; Man. Dir ANIL KAPOOR; more than 1,000 employees.

**Coromandel Fertilisers Ltd:** Coromandel House, 1-2-10 Sardar Patel Rd, Secunderabad 500 003; tel. (40) 27842034; fax (40) 27844117; internet www.cflindia.com; f. 1961; manufactures and markets chemical fertilizers; cap. p.u. Rs 254.1m., res and surplus Rs 3,598.2m., sales Rs 10,750.5m. (March 2005); Chair. A. VELLAYAN; Pres. V. RAVICHANDRAN.

**Gujarat Heavy Chemicals Ltd:** B-38, Institutional Area, Sector 1, Noida 201 301; tel. (120) 2536572; fax (120) 2535209; internet www.ghclindia.com; cap. p.u. Rs 932.5m., res Rs 1,699m., sales Rs 3,620m. (March 2002); Chair. SANJAY DALMIA.

**ICI India Ltd:** DLF Plaza Tower, 10th Floor, DLF Qutab Enclave Phase 1, Gurgaon 122 002; tel. (124) 2540400; fax (124) 2540839; e-mail r_guha@ici.com; internet www.iciindia.com; f. 1954; cap. Rs 408.7m., res Rs 4,780.5m., sales Rs 8,741.8m. (March 2005); mfrs of commercial blasting explosives, nitrocellulose, paints, rubber chemicals, polythene, pharmaceuticals etc.; factories in West Bengal, Bihar, Andhra Pradesh, Maharashtra and Tamil Nadu; Chair. ADITYA NARAYAN; Man. Dir and CEO R. L. JAIN; 4,100 employees (1994).

**National Organic Chemical Industries Ltd (NOCIL):** Mafatlal House, H. T. Parekh Marg, Backbay Reclamation, Churchgate, Mumbai 400 020; tel. (22) 66364062; fax (22) 66364060; internet www.nocilrubberchemicals.com; f. 1961; merged with Polyolefins Industries Ltd in 1994; manufactures and sells petrochemicals, polymers, rubber chemicals and plastics; Chair. ARVIND N. MAFATLAL; Vice-Chair. and Man. Dir Dr N. M. DHULDHOYA.

**Reliance Industries Ltd:** Makers Chambers IV, Nariman Point, Mumbai 400 021; tel. (22) 22785000; internet www.ril.com; acquired Indian Petrochemicals Corpn Ltd 2007; Chair. MUKESH AMBANI.

**Southern Petrochemical Industries Corporation Ltd (SPIC):** 97 Mount Rd, Chennai 600 032; tel. (44) 22350245; fax (44) 22352163; e-mail spiccorp@spic.co.in; internet www.spic.co.in; f. 1969; manufactures and sells fertilizers, caustic soda, etc.; cap. p.u. Rs 880.5m., res Rs 3,129.0m., sales Rs 24,277.5m. (March 2005); manufacturing plants at Tuticorin, Cuddalore and Manali; Chair. Dr A. C. MUTHIAH; Man. Dir BABU K. VERGHESE.

**Tata Chemicals Ltd:** Bombay House, 24 Homi Mody St, Mumbai 400 001; tel. (22) 66658282; fax (22) 66658143; internet www.tatachemicals.net; f. 1939; owns and operates the largest inorganic chemical complex in India and a gas-based fertilizer project; soda ash mfr; res Rs 19,525.4m., sales Rs 35,174.8m. (March 2006); Chair. RATAN TATA; Man. Dir HOMI KHUSROKHAN.

### Computer Services

**HCL Technologies Ltd:** A 10–11, Sector 3, Noida 201 301; tel. (120) 2535071; fax (120) 2530591; e-mail investor@corp.hcltech.com; internet www.hcltech.com; f. 1991; cap. Rs 592.2m., res and surplus Rs 22,912.1m., sales Rs 25,637m. (June 2004); software consultancy, development, support, maintenance and training sevices; Chair. SHIV NADAR; CEO VINEET NAYAR; 22,034 employees (2005).

**Infosys Technologies Ltd:** Plot 44, 3rd Cross, Electronic City, Hosur Rd, Bangalore 561 229; tel. (80) 28520261; fax (80) 28520352; e-mail infosys@inf.com; internet www.infosys.com; f. 1981; cap. Rs 2,860m., res and surplus Rs 108,760m., revenue Rs 131,490m. (March 2007); developer, producer and exporter of software products; Co-Chairs NARAYANA N. R. MURTHY, NANDAN M. NILEKANI; Man. Dir and CEO S. GOPALAKRISHNAN; 39,806 employees.

**Satyam Computer Services Ltd:** 1st Floor, Mayfair Centre, Sardar Patel Rd, Secunderabad 500 003; tel. (40) 30654343; fax (40) 27840058; e-mail corporatecommunications@satyam.com; internet www.satyam.com; f. 1987; cap. p.u. Rs 632.5m., res and surplus Rs 25,175.2, sales Rs 26,232.8m. (March 2004); develops software products; Chair. B. RAMALINGA RAJU; Man. Dir B. R. RAJU.

**Tata Consultancy Services:** 11th Floor, Air India Bldg, Nariman Point, Mumbai 400 021; tel. (22) 22024827; fax (22) 22040711; e-mail indiageo.pmo@tcs.com; internet www.tcs.com; f. 1968; cap. Rs 480.1m., res and surplus Rs 32,730.4m., sales Rs 81,025.8m. (March 2005); provides computer consultancy services; more than 100 offices world-wide; Chair. RATAN N. TATA; CEO and Man. Dir S. RAMADORAI.

**Wipro Corporation:** Doddakannelli, Sarjapur Rd, Bangalore 560 035; tel. (80) 28440011; fax (80) 28440256; internet www.wipro.com; f. 1945; cap. Rs 1,407.1m., res and surplus Rs 47,517.3m., sales Rs 72,331.6m. (March 2005); develops software systems, as well as manufacturing household goods and hospital equipment; agreement to acquire consumer goods co, Unza Holdings (Singapore) formalized July 2007; Chair. AZIM HASHIM PREMJI.

### Construction

**DLF Group:** DLF Shopping Mall, 3rd Floor, Arjun Marg, DLF City Phase I, Gurgaon 122 002; tel. (124) 4334200; internet www.dlf.in; f. 1946; initial public offering of 10% shares in the group announced in June 2007; developers of commercial and residential property, real estate, hotels, infrastructure and Special Economic Zones; noteworthy devts incl. urban colonies South Extension, Greater Kailash, Kailash Colony and Hauz Khas; landmark 3,000-acre project, DLF

City, located in Gurgaon; Chair. K. P. Singh; Vice-Chair. and Man. Dir Rajiv Singh.

**Hindustan Construction Co Ltd:** Hincon House, L.B.S. Marg, Vikhroli (West), Mumbai 400 038; tel. (22) 25775959; fax (22) 25775732; e-mail corpcomm@hccindia.co.in; internet www.hccindia.com; f. 1926; cap. p.u. Rs 229.4m., res Rs 3,274.4m., sales Rs 15,781.6m. (March 2005); constructs concrete dams, railways and hydro tunnels, power houses, docks, jetties, barrages, industrial structures, environmental engineering projects, bridges, highways, etc.; major projects: Maneri Bhali, Salal, Idamalayar and Kadamparai hydroelectric works, Teesta, Mahananda barrages, tunnelling by shield method for Kolkata Metro, Narora atomic power project, Barauni, Titagarh, Farakka and Ramagundam thermal power projects, Cochin tanker terminal and fertilizer berths at Cochin port, construction at Upper Kolab dam, Tezpur bridge over the River Brahmaputra in Assam, SSSF project for Tarapur atomic power station, Expressway Mumbai Pune, etc.; brs in New Delhi, Kolkata and Chennai; civil works in Iraq, Malawi and Tanzania; subsidiary: Ganga Construction Ltd; Chair. and Man. Dir Ajit Gulabchand.

Cotton Textiles, Jute, Man-Made Fibres

**Arvind Mills Ltd:** Naroda Rd, Ahmedabad 380 025; tel. (79) 22203030; fax (79) 22201270; e-mail feedback@arvind.com; internet www.arvindmills.com; f. 1931; cap. Rs 1,953.7m., res and surplus Rs 10,197.5m., sales Rs 16,788.6m. (March 2005); manufactures and sells cotton textiles and blended fabrics; also deals in telecommunications products and electronics; two subsidiaries; Chair. and Man. Dir Sanjay S. Lalbhai.

**Birla Corpn Ltd:** Birla Bldg, 9/1 R. N. Mukherjee Rd, Kolkata 700 001; tel. (33) 22201680; fax (33) 22487988; internet www.birlacorporation.com; f. 1919; cap. p.u. Rs 770.1m., res Rs 2,263.5m., sales Rs 13,426.7m. (March 2005); manufacture and sale of jute goods, automobile trimmings, steel foundry items, PVC floor covering and wallpapers, calcium carbide, oxy-acetylene gases, staple and synthetic fibre yarn, cement, jute carpets and webbing; one subsidiary; Chair. Rajan S. Lodha; Man. Dir K. C. Mittal.

**Birla VXL Ltd:** 801 Bhikaji Cama Bhavan, Bhikaji Cama Place, New Delhi 110 066; tel. (11) 51659900; fax (11) 51659903; e-mail bvxlfin@ndf.vsnl.net.in; internet birla-vxl.com; f. 1948; fmrly VXL India Ltd; manufactures and sells wool tops, yarns, worsted and blended fabrics, carpets, electricity meters, relays, control panels and special high precision items, vegetable oils, etc.; factories at Amritsar, Faridabad, Harda, Jamnagar and Joka; cap. Rs 651m., res Rs 1,686.6m. (June 1998), sales Rs 3,351m. (2000/01); five subsidiaries; Chair. Sudarshan K. Birla; Pres. C. L. Rathi.

**Bombay Dyeing and Manufacturing Co Ltd:** Neville House, J. N. Heredia Marg, Ballard Estate, Mumbai 400 038; tel. (22) 22618071; fax (22) 22614520; internet www.bombaydyeing.com; f. 1879; cap. p.u. Rs 385.8m., res Rs 3,033.8m., sales Rs 10,256.0m. (March 2005); cap. p.u. Rs 386.1m., net sales Rs 4,985.9m. (March 2007); mfrs and exporters of cotton yarn and textiles, and blends of cotton and synthetic fibres; two mills and a processing plant in Mumbai, one mill at Jamnagar, a processing plant at Roha (Maharashtra) and a dimethyl terephthatate plant at Patalganga (Maharashtra); three subsidiaries; Chair. Nusli N. Wadia; Jt Man. Dirs P. V. Kuppuswamy, Ness N. Wadia; 10,650 employees.

**Century Enka Ltd:** Bhosari, Pune 411 026; tel. (20) 66127300; fax (20) 27120113; e-mail iymktg@centuryenka.com; internet www.centuryenka.com; f. 1965; cap. p.u. Rs 286.4m., res Rs 5,203.8m., sales Rs 9,551.3m. (March 2005); Chair. B. K. Birla.

**Century Textiles and Industries Ltd:** Century Bhavan, Dr Annie Besant Rd, Worli, Mumbai 400 025; tel. (22) 24300351; fax (22) 24309491; e-mail info@centurytext.com; internet www.centurytext.com; f. 1897; cap. p.u. Rs 930.4m., res Rs 6,590.5m., sales Rs 24,560.9m. (March 2005); mfrs of cotton textiles and yarn; cotton yarn mill at Worli (Mumbai), plants at Satrati (Madhya Pradesh) producing viscose rayon yarn, tyre yarn and caustic soda, plants at Kalyan (Maharashtra), portland cement plants at Baikunth, Sarlanagar (Madhya Pradesh) and Gadchandur (Maharashtra), minerals and chemicals plant at Jamnagar (Gujarat), and pulp and paper plants at Lalkua (Uttar Pradesh); co is also engaged in tramp shipping, the building and development of land and property, and floriculture activities; Chair. B. K. Birla.

**Futura Polyesters Ltd:** Paragon Condominium, 3rd Floor, Pandurang Budhkar Marg, Mumbai 400 013; tel. (22) 24952311; e-mail futuraho@futurapolyesters.com; internet www.futurapolyesters.com; f. 2002 by merger of Futura Ploymers Ltd and Indian Organic Chemicals Ltd; mfrs range of speciality polymers, fibres and pre-form products; sales Rs 5,170.6m. (March 2007); Pres. and Dir S. T. Kulkarni; Chair. and Man. Dir S. B. Ghia.

**Grasim Industries Ltd:** Birlagram, Nagda 456 331; tel. (7366) 246760; fax (7366) 244114; e-mail shares@adityabirla.com; internet www.grasim.com; f. 1947; cap. Rs 916.9m., res Rs 35,138.3m., sales Rs 52,332.7m. (March 2004); fmrly the Gwalior Rayon Silk Manufacturing (Weaving) Co Ltd; mem. Aditya Birla Group; mfrs of viscose staple fibre; dissolving pulp and paper; man-made fabrics; cotton textiles; also mfrs of rayon and allied chemical plant and machinery; Chair. Kumar Mangalam Birla; 15,000 employees.

**JCT Ltd:** Thapar House, 124 Janpath, New Delhi 110 001; tel. (11) 23342860; fax (11) 23368707; e-mail jctadmin@jctphg.com; internet www.jcttextiles.com; f. 1946; manufactures polyester blended and cotton fabrics and nylon/polyester filament and cotton yarn; textile mills at Phagwara and Srinagar and ginning factories at Abohar, Khanna and Jagraon; four subsidiaries; cap. Rs 859.2m., res Rs 1,034.7m., sales Rs 4,900m. (March 2002); Chair. M. M. Thapar.

**Kesoram Industries Ltd:** 9/1 R. N. Mukherjee Rd, Kolkata 700 001; tel. (33) 22429454; fax (33) 22209455; e-mail kesocorp@cal3.vsnl.net.in; internet www.kesocorp.com; f. 1919; cap. p.u. Rs 457.4m., res Rs 2,913.3m., sales Rs 15,767.3m. (March 2004); mfrs of cotton textiles and piece goods, rayon yarn, transparent paper, cellulose film, sulphuric acid, carbon disulphide, cast iron spun pipes and fittings, cement, refractories, etc.; two subsidiaries: Bharat General and Textile Industries Ltd and KICM Investment Ltd; factories in West Bengal, Andhra Pradesh and Karnataka; Chair. B. K. Birla.

**Mafatlal Industries Ltd:** Mafatlal House, 5th Floor, H. T. Parekh Marg, Backbay Reclamation, Mumbai 400 020; tel. (22) 40083636; fax (22) 56345154; e-mail gujar@mafatlals.com; internet www.mafatlals.com; f. 1913; manufactures and sells textile goods and yarn, ready-made garments, plastic processing machines, electronic professional grade connectors, flurione chemicals, and dyes and intermediates of chemicals; two subsidiaries; Chair. Arvind N. Mafatlal; Vice-Chair. and Man. Dir Hrishikesh A. Mafatlal.

**Raymond Ltd:** Mahindra Towers, 2nd Floor, B Wing, Pandurang Budhkar Marg, Worli, Mumbai 400 018; tel. (22) 56609999; e-mail webmaster@raymondindia.com; internet www.raymondindia.com; f. 1925; cap. Rs 613.8m., res Rs 10,425.5m., sales Rs 11,438.3m. (March 2005); manufactures and sells wool/blended suiting fabrics, furnishing fabrics, rugs, blankets, knitting yarn, steel files and rasps, twist drills, garments; plants in Maharashtra and Madhya Pradesh; Chair. and Man. Dir Gautam Singhania.

**Reliance Industries Ltd:** Reliance Centre, 19 Walchand Hirachand Marg, Ballard Estate, Mumbai 400 038; tel. (22) 30327000; fax (22) 22870072; internet www.ril.com; f. 1973; cap. Rs 13,959.2m., res Rs 336,216.0m., sales Rs 520,253.4m. (March 2004); mfrs and sellers of blended and synthetic yarn polyester staple fibre and of synthetic and worsted fabrics; petrochemicals; owns the country's largest refinery in Gujarat; Chair. and Man. Dir Mukesh D. Ambani; 14,255 employees.

Electrical Goods

**Blue Star Ltd:** Kasturi Bldgs, Mohan T. Advani Chowk, Jamshedji Tata Rd, Mumbai 400 020; tel. (22) 66654000; fax (22) 66654151; e-mail ccm@bluestarindia.com; internet www.bluestarindia.com; cap. p.u. Rs 179.9m., res and surplus Rs 975.4m., sales Rs 5,868.8m. (March 2003); air-conditioning, electronics, industrial and commercial equipment; Chair and Man. Dir Ashok M. Advani.

**BPL Ltd:** Dynamic House, 64 Church St, POB 5194, Bangalore 560 001; tel. (80) 25588388; fax (80) 25586971; internet www.bplworld.com; f. 1963; manufacturers consumer and domestic electrical goods; cap. p.u. Rs 277m. (March 2001) sales Rs 11,940m. (March 2002); Chair. and Man. Dir Ajit G. Nambiar; CEO K. S. Jayanth Kumar.

**Crompton Greaves Ltd:** CG House, 6th Floor, Dr Annie Besant Rd, Worli, Mumbai 400 025; tel. (22) 24237777; fax (22) 24237788; e-mail cgi@cgl.co.in; internet www.cglonline.com; f. 1937; manufactures, distributes and exports electrical and electronics equipment systems, power and industrial transformers, industrial and commercial motors; cap. p.u. Rs 523.7m., res Rs 3,509.0m., sales Rs 21,718.4m. (March 2005); sales offices and manufacturing units throughout India; Chair. Gautam Thapar; Man. Dir Sudhir Mohan Trehan.

**Eveready Industries India Ltd:** Jeevan Deep Bhavan, 1 Middleton St, Kolkata 700 071; tel. (33) 22883950; fax (33) 24864673; e-mail feedback@eveready.co.in; internet www.evereadyindustries.com; f. 1934; fmrly Union Carbide India Ltd; cap. p.u. Rs 278.9m., res and surplus Rs 2,704.8m., sales Rs 6,549.3m. (March 2005); mfrs of all types of dry cells and batteries for radio and telecommunication purposes, zinc alloys, etc.; one subsidiary: Nepal Battery Co Ltd; Chair. B. M. Khaitan; Vice-Chair. and Man. Dir Deepak Khaitan.

**Philips Electronics India Ltd:** Technopolis Knowledge Park, Mahakali Caves Rd, Charala, Andheri (E), Mumbai 400 093; tel. (22) 66912000; internet www.india.philips.com; f. 1930; cap. p.u. Rs 226m., res Rs 2,382m., sales Rs 15,292m. (Dec. 2002); mfrs of consumer electronics, lighting products, domestic appliances, industrial electronics and electronic components; factories at Kolkata, Kalwa-Thane and Pune; three subsidiaries; Chair. S. M. Datta; CEO Murali Sivaraman; 5,594 employees.

**Siemens Ltd:** 130 Pandurang Budhkar Marg, Worli, Mumbai 400 018; tel. (22) 24931350; fax (22) 24940552; internet www.siemens.co

.in; f. 1957; cap. p.u. Rs 331.4m., res and surplus Rs 6,671.1m., sales Rs 22,456.3m. (Sept. 2004); railway signalling, electrical and electronic equipment, telecommunications, etc.; Man. Dir J. SCHUBERT.

**Videocon Industries:** 14 Kms Stone, Aurangabad–Paithan Rd, Chitegaon, Tq. Paithan, Aurangabad 431 105; tel. (2431) 251501; e-mail vnd@videoconmail.com; internet www.videoconworld.com; manufactures consumer electronics; Man. Dir V. N. DHOOT.

**Voltas Ltd:** Voltas House, 'A' Block, Dr Babasaheb Ambedkar Marg, Chinchpokli (E), Mumbai 400 033; tel. (22) 66656666; fax (22) 566656311; e-mail ccd@voltas.com; internet www.voltas.com; f. 1954; cap. p.u. Rs 330.5m., res Rs 1,604.6m., sales Rs 14,414.3m. (March 2005); an integrated marketing, engineering and manufacturing company with country-wide selling and service organization; mfrs of air-conditioning and refrigeration equipment, pumps, beverages, agrochemicals, capillary tubes, thermostats, CNC machines, water coolers, mining and drilling machinery, fork-lift trucks, power capacitators and air and water pollution control equipment; Chair. ISHAAT HUSSAIN; Man. Dir ASHOK SONI; 4,000 employees (2003).

Industrial and Building Supplies

**BOC India Ltd:** Oxygen House, P-43, Taratala Rd, Kolkata 700 088; tel. (33) 24014708; fax (33) 24014974; internet www.boc-india.com; f. 1935; cap. p.u. Rs 491.0m., res Rs 1,898.9m., sales Rs 4,243.6m. (March 2005); mfrs and suppliers of industrial and medical gases, including special gases and gas mixtures of ultra high purity; medical and surgical equipment; oxygen (liquid and gaseous), acetylene and nitrous oxide plants; high-pressure industrial and medical pipelines; factories and depots all over India; mem. of the BOC Group, United Kingdom; Chair. J. N. SAPRU; Man. Dir E. R. RAJ NARAYANAN; 588 employees.

**Larsen and Toubro Ltd:** L & T House, Narottam Morarji Marg, Ballard Estate, POB 278, Mumbai 400 001; tel. (22) 22685656; fax (22) 22685607; internet www.larsentoubro.com; f. 1938; cap. p.u. Rs 2,486.7m., res Rs 29,335.5m., sales Rs 103,269m. (March 2003); construction-related equipment; plants and machinery for chemical, fertilizer, cement, food-processing, steel, paper and power industries; material handling and processing plants; civil, mechanical and electrical construction; cement; industrial electronics; computer accessories; computer software; switchgear; industrial valves; packaging; shipping; plastic and rubber-processing machinery; three subsidiaries and seven associate cos; Chair. and Man. Dir A. M. NAIK; 21,900 employees.

**Texmaco Ltd:** Birla Bldg, 9/1 R. N. Mukherjee Rd, Kolkata 700 001; tel. (33) 22489101; fax (33) 22205833; e-mail texmaco@cal.vsnl.net .in; f. 1939; mfrs of textile machinery, textiles, rolling stock, boilers of all types, sugar mill machinery, steel and cast iron castings, machine tools, heavy, medium and light structurals and other engineering goods; a cement plant is under construction and the corpn has diversified into shipping; Chair. K. K. BIRLA; Pres. RAMESH MAHESWARI.

Metals

**Bharat Aluminium Co Ltd:** Aluminium Sadan, Core 6, Scope Office Complex, Lodi Rd, New Delhi 110 003; tel. (11) 24360418; fax (11) 24320177; e-mail balconr@vsnl.net; internet www.balcoindia .com; f. 1965; partially privatized in 2001, 49% state-owned, 51% owned by Sterlite Industries; operates an integrated aluminium project at Korba (Madhya Pradesh); plans to set up alumina plants in Andhra Pradesh; Chair. ANIL AGARWAL.

**Essar Steel Ltd:** Essar House, 11 Keshavrao Khadye Marg, Mahalaxmi, Mumbai 400 034; tel. (22) 24950606; fax (22) 24928896; e-mail steel@essar.com; internet www.essarsteel.com; subsidiary co of the Essar Group; cap. p.u. Rs 5,073.1m., res and surplus Rs 6,865.4m., sales Rs 61,167.1m. (March 2005); net sales Rs 819,435.0m.; mfrs of hot briquetted iron and hot rolled steel coils; operations in 50 global locations; Chair. SHASHI RUIA; Man. Dir PRASHANT RUIA; 20,000 employees.

**GKW (Guest Keen Williams) Ltd:** 3A Shakespeare Sarani, Kolkata 700 071; tel. (33) 22822385; fax (33) 22829747; e-mail gkwbby@vsnl .com; internet www.gkwltd.com; f. 1931; mfrs of metal pressings, alloys and special steels, industrial fasteners, automotive forgings, electrical stamping and laminations, strip wound cores, railway track fasteners and accessories; factories in West Bengal, Karnataka and Maharashtra; Man. Dir J. D. CURRAVALA; Vice-Chair. K. K. BANGUR.

**Hindalco Industries Ltd:** Century Bhavan, 3rd Floor, Dr Annie Besant Rd, Worli, Mumbai 400 030; tel. (22) 66626666; fax (22) 24227586; e-mail stalukdar@adityabirla.com; internet www .hindalco.com; f. 1958; as Hindustan Aluminium Corpn Ltd; cap. p.u. Rs 928m., res and surplus Rs 75,738m., sales Rs 95,233m. (March 2005); produces aluminium, rolled products, extruded products, conductor and commercial rods; subsidiaries: Minerals and Minerals Ltd, Renuka Investments and Finance Ltd, Renukeshwar Investments and Finance Ltd, Indian Aluminium Co Ltd and Annapurna Foils Ltd; acquired rival aluminium recycling and rolled products co. Novelis (Canada) in May 2007; Chair. KUMAR MANGALAM BIRLA; Man. Dir DEBU BHATTACHARYA.

**Hindustan Zinc Ltd:** Yashad Bhavan, Yashadgarh, Udaipur 313 004; tel. (294) 2529182; e-mail puneet.jagatramka@vedanta.co.in; internet www.hzlindia.com; f. 1966; cap. p.u. Rs 4,230m., res and surplus Rs 16,550m., sales Rs 21,870m. (March 2005); sales Rs 85,600.0m. (March 2007); partially privatized in 2002; 64.9% owned by Sterlite Industries Ltd; develops mining and smelting capacities for metal, particularly zinc and lead; units: zinc smelter, Debari, Rajasthan and Vishakhapatnam, Andhra Pradesh, lead smelter, Tundoo, Bihar and zinc lead smelter, Putholi, Rajasthan; produces zinc ingots, cadmium, refined lead, refined silver, sulphuric acid, etc.; zinc production output of 283,698 metric tons and 889,007 metric tons of zinc concentrate (2005/06); Chair. AGNIVESH AGARWAL.

**Indian Aluminium Co Ltd** (Hindalco Industries Ltd): Century Bhavan, 3rd Floor, Dr Annie Besant Rd, Worli, Mumbai 400 030; tel. (22) 66626666; fax (22) 24362516; e-mail stalukdar@adityabirla.com; internet www.indal.com; f. 1938; flagship co of Aditya Birla Group; cap. p.u. Rs 712.6m., res Rs 9,580.0m., sales Rs 16,139.9m. (March 2004); owns and operates bauxite mines (Lohardaga in Jharkhand, and Chandgad and Durgmanwadi in Maharashtra); alumina plants (Muri and Lohardaga in Jharkhand: 80,000 metric tons per annum) (Belgaum in Karnataka: 260,000 tons); smelters (Alupuram in Kerala: 21,000 tons) (Hirakud in Orissa: 30,000 tons) (Belgaum: 66,000 tons); sheet mills (Belur in West Bengal: 50,000 tons) (Durgamanwadi and Taloja in Maharashtra: 40,000 tons); extrusion plant (Alupuram in Kerala: 8,000 tons); foil plant (Kalwa in Maharashtra: 6,000 tons); copper smelter (Dahej in Gujarat: 500,000 tons); Chair. KUMAR MANGALAM BIRLA; Pres. S. TALUKDAR; 6,301 employees.

**Ispat Industries Ltd:** 7th Floor, Nirmal, Nariman Pt, Mumbai 400 021; tel. (22) 56542222; fax (22) 2285519; e-mail contactus@ispatind .com; internet www.ispatind.com; cap. p.u. Rs 6,858.0m., res Rs 6,964.0m., sales Rs 61,128.9m. (March 2005); Chair. and Man. Dir P. K. MITTAL.

**Lloyds Steel Industries Ltd:** Modern Centre, 'B' Wing, 2nd Floor, Sane Guruji Marg, Mahalaxmi, Mumbai 400 011; tel. (22) 30418111; fax (22) 30418260; e-mail international@lloyds.in; internet www .lloydsgroup.com; Chair. MUKESH R. GUPTA; Man. Dir RAJESH R. GUPTA.

**Mukand Ltd:** Bajaj Bhavan, 3rd Floor, Jamnalal Bajaj Marg, 226 Nariman Point, Mumbai 400 021; tel. (22) 22021060; fax (22) 22021174; e-mail co.secretary@mukand.com; internet www .mukand.com; f. 1956; subsidiary of Baja Group of cos; manufactures high carbon steel, alloy steel, stainless steel, billets, bars, rods, EOT cranes etc.; executes turnkey and highway construction projects; cap. Rs 281m., sales Rs 7,770m. (March 2003); net sales Rs 18,104.5m. (March 2007); Chair. NIRAJ R. BAJAJ; Man. Dirs RAJESH V. SHAH, SUKETU V. SHAH.

**Sterlite Industries Ltd:** B-10/4 Waluj MIDC Industrial Area, Waluj, Aurangabad 431 133; tel. (240) 2554583; fax (240) 2554590; e-mail silho@bom3.vsnl.net.in; internet www.sterlite-industries .com; f. 1975; mfrs copper products; cap. p.u. Rs 180m., sales Rs 22,080m. (March 2003); Chair. ANIL AGRAWAL; Man. Dir KULDIP KUMAR KAURA.

**Sunflag Iron and Steel Co Ltd:** 33 Mount Rd, Sadar, Nagpur 440 001; tel. (712) 520356; fax (712) 520360; e-mail admin@sunflagsteel .com; internet www.sunflagsteel.com; manufactures iron and mild and alloy steel rolled products; cap. p.u. Rs 1,622.0m., res and surplus Rs 157.6m., sales Rs 4,230m. (March 2003); Chair. P. B. BHARDWAJ; Jt Man. Dir PRANAB BHARDWAJ.

**Tata Steel:** Bombay House, 24 Homi Mody St, Fort, Mumbai 400 023; tel. (22) 66658282; fax (22) 66658113; e-mail cosectisco@tata .com; internet tatasteel.com; f. 1907; fmrly known as Tata Iron and Steel Co Ltd; took over Indian Tube Co Ltd in 1986; cap. Rs 3,691.8m., res and surplus Rs 41,466.8m., sales Rs 107,023.9m. (March 2004); integrated iron and steel plant at Jamshedpur (Bihar) with licensed annual saleable steel capacity of 2.1m. metric tons; main steel products comprise sheets, narrow strips, plates, structurals, bars, billets, high silicon sheets, rolled rings, rails, wheels, axles and agricultural implements such as hoes, picks, beaters; by-products such as benzol, ammonium sulphate; subsidiaries: Tata Refractories Ltd, The Tata Pigments Ltd, Special Sheets Ltd, and Kalamati Investment Co Ltd; Chair. RATAN N. TATA; Man. Dir B. MUTHURAMAN; 42,511 employees.

Paper

**Andhra Pradesh Paper Mills Ltd:** 501–509, 5th Floor, Swapnalok Complex 92, 93 Sarojini Devi Rd, Secunderabad 500 003; tel. (40) 7813715; fax (40) 7813717; e-mail appmcorp@andhrapaper.com; internet www.andhrapaper.com; f. 1964; cap. p.u. Rs 118.3m., res and surplus Rs 1,863.7m., sales Rs 4,494.4m. (March 2004); manufactures pulp and paper; Chair. L. N. BANGUR; Man. Dir M. K. TARA.

**Ballarpur Industries Ltd:** First India Place, Tower C, Mehrauli, Gurgaon Rd, Gurgaon, Haryana 122 002; tel. (124) 4099484; fax (124) 2804260; e-mail corpcom@bilt.com; internet www.bilt.com; f. 1945; cap. Rs 1,624.5m., res Rs 12,541.1m., sales Rs 22,447.2m. (June 2004); manufactures and sells writing, printing, industrial and speciality papers, building materials and chemicals; mills in Maharashtra, Haryana, Karnataka, Andhra Pradesh and Orissa; five subsidiaries; Chair. GAUTAM THAPAR; Man. Dir R. R. VEDERAH.

**J. K. Paper Ltd:** Nehru House, 4 Bahadur Shah Zafar Marg, POB 7057, New Delhi 110 002; tel. (11) 23311112; fax (11) 23712680; e-mail marketing@jkmail.com; internet www.jkpaper.com; f. 1938; mfrs of writing, printing, coated and speciality papers, strawboard, greyboard and cement; factories in Orissa, Madhya Pradesh, Rajasthan; Man. Dir HARSH PATI SINGHANIA.

**Orient Paper and Industries Ltd:** 9/1 R. N. Mukherjee Rd, Kolkata 700 001; tel. (33) 22480135; fax (33) 22430490; e-mail info@orientpaperindia.com; internet www.orientpaperindia.com; f. 1936; equity cap. Rs 148m., res Rs 283.7m. (March 2000), sales Rs 5,610m. (2000/01); there are paper mills at Brajrajnagar (Orissa), with a capacity of 76,000 metric tons per year, and at Amlai (Madhya Pradesh), with a capacity of 95,000 tons per year; in addition, there is a cement plant with an annual capacity of 1.18m. tons at Devapur (Andhra Pradesh); also manufactures electric fans at plants in West Bengal and Haryana (1.7m. produced annually); Chair. C. K. BIRLA.

### Rubber

**Apollo Tyres Ltd:** Apollo House, 7 Institutional Area, Sector-32, Gurgaon 122 002; tel. (124) 2383002; fax (124) 2383020; e-mail info@apollotyres.com; internet www.apollotyres.com; f. 1972; cap. p.u. Rs 383.4m., res and surplus Rs 5,349.4m., sales Rs 22,254.9m. (March 2003); manufactures, markets and exports of automobile tyres, tubes and flaps; Chair. and Man. Dir ONKAR SINGH KANWAR; 6,000 employees.

**CEAT Ltd:** 463 Dr Annie Besant Rd, Worli, Mumbai 400 030; tel. (22) 24930621; fax (22) 24938933; e-mail response@ceatltd.com; internet www.ceatyres.com; f. 1958; manufactures automobile tyres and rubber products; cap. Rs 351.0m., res Rs 2,454.2m., sales Rs 15,279.9m. (March 2005); Chair. R. P. GOENKA.

**Dunlop India Ltd:** 57B Mirza Ghalib St, Kolkata 700 016; tel. (33) 22494502; fax (33) 22499622; f. 1926; mfrs of tyres and tubes for bicycles, automobiles, aircraft, earth-moving equipment, tractors, conveyor and transmission belting, hoses, bicycle rims and Metalastik products; factories at Sahaganj and Ambattur; part of Ruia Group; one subsidiary: India Tyre and Rubber Co (India) Ltd; Chair. P. K. RUIA; 10,394 employees.

**Goodyear India Ltd:** Godrej Bhavan, 3rd Floor, Mathura Rd, New Delhi 110 065; tel. (11) 26836567; fax (11) 26836170; internet www.goodyear.co.in; f. 1960; mfr of automobile tyres, tubes, fan belts, etc.; cap. p.u. Rs 230.7m., res and surplus Rs 632m., sales Rs 6,583.3m. (Dec. 2003); Chair. and Man. Dir ANTONIO M. CAPELLINI; 1,700 employees (1995).

**J. K. Industries Ltd:** Link House, 3 Bahadur Shah Zafar Marg, New Delhi 110 002; tel. (11) 23311112; fax (11) 23716205; internet www.jktyre.com; manufactures and sells automotive tyres and tubes; cap. Rs 374.6m., res Rs 4,141.0m., sales Rs 22,375.0m. (Sept. 2004); Chair. HARI SHANKAR SINGHANIA; Man. Dir RAGHUPATI SINGHANIA.

**MRF Ltd:** 124 Greames Rd, Chennai 600 006; tel. (44) 28252777; fax (44) 2832523; internet www.mrftyres.com; f. 1960; cap. p.u. Rs 288.0m., res and surplus Rs 7,191.7m., sales Rs 29,894.3m. (Sept. 2004); manufactures and markets automobile and bicycle tyres and tubes, tread rubber and other rubber products; two subsidiaries: Funskool (India) Ltd and Crystal Investments and Finance Co Ltd; Chair. VINOO MAMMEN; Man. Dir ARUN MAMMEN.

### Miscellaneous

**Bharti Enterprises Ltd:** Qutab Amibience, Qutab Minar, Mehrauli Rd, New Delhi 110 030; tel. (11) 41666000; fax (11) 41666011; internet www.bharti.com; group of cos incl. telecommunications (Bharti Airtel. Bharti Teletech, Telecom Seychelles, Bharti Telesoft, TeleTech Services India—jt venture with TeleTech, USA), agribusiness (FieldFresh Foods), insurance (Bharti AXA Life Insurance) and retail (Bharti Retail); jt venture with Wal-Mart (USA) to create wholesale supplier co, Bharti Wal-Mart Pvt Ltd, proposed Aug. 2007; Chair. and Group CEO SUNIL BHARTI MITTAL.

**Duncans Industries Ltd:** Duncan House, 31 Netaji Subhas Rd, Kolkata 700 001; tel. (33) 2200962; fax (33) 2486021; internet www.duncans-tea.com; manufacture and sale of tea and fertilizers, trading of tobacco, etc.; 16 subsidiaries; Chair. G. P. GOENKA; Man. Dir V. P. KAUSHIK.

**Exide Industries Ltd:** Exide House, 59E Chowringhee Rd, Kolkata 700 020; tel. (33) 22832120; fax (33) 22812195; e-mail ronojoy@cal.exide.co.in; internet www.exideindustries.com; f. 1947; fmrly Chloride Industries Ltd; cap. p.u. Rs 750m., res and surplus Rs 4,100m., sales Rs 14,820m. (March 2005); manufactures batteries; factories in West Bengal, Tamil Nadu, Haryana and Maharashtra; five subsidiaries; Chair. and CEO S. B. GANGULY; Man. Dir T. V. RAMANATHAN; 5,500 employees.

**Gujarat Co-op Milk Marketing Federation Ltd:** 10 Amul Dairy Rd, POB 10, Anand, Gujarat 388 001; tel. (2692) 258506; fax (2692) 240208; e-mail gcmmf@amul.com; internet www.amul.com; f. 1973; manufacturer of milk and dairy products; sales Rs 42,778m. (2006/07); 13 district mem. unions, 2.6m. mem. producers; Chair. Dr VERGHESE KURIEN; Man. Dir B. M. VYAS; 650 employees.

**Hindustan Unilever Ltd (HLL):** Hindustan Lever House, 165/166 Backbay Reclamation, POB 409, Mumbai 400 020; tel. (22) 22870622; fax (22) 22871970; e-mail paresh.chaudhry@unilever.com; internet www.hll.com; f. 1933; cap. p.u. Rs 2,201.2m., res and surplus Rs 18,719.2m., sales Rs 99,269.5m. (Dec. 2004); fmrly Hindustan Lever Ltd, name changed as above 2007; subsidiary of Unilever; manufacture and sale of washing products, toilet preparations, diammonium phosphate, seeds, plant growth nutrient, food, beverages, marine products, leather goods, fine chemicals and exports; 16 subsidiaries; Chair. HARISH MANWANI; 36,000 employees (2000).

**ITC Ltd:** Virginia House, 37 J. L. Nehru Rd, Kolkata 700 071; tel. (33) 22889371; fax (33) 22882257; internet www.itcportal.com; f. 1910; fmrly India Tobacco Co; cap. Rs 2,476.5m., res and surplus Rs 64,704.4m., (March 2004), sales Rs 110,248.8m. (March 2003); manufacture and sale of cigarettes and smoking tobaccos; printed and packaging material; development of tobacco and tobacco cultivation; tobacco exports; manufacture of speciality papers; financial services; hoteliering; travel and tourism; 11 major subsidiaries and group cos; Chair. YOGESH DEVESHWAR; 20,000 employees (2006).

**Shaw Wallace & Co:** 4 Bankshall St, Kolkata 700 001; tel. (33) 22201334; fax (33) 22486908; internet www.shawwallace.com; f. 1946; manufacturers and traders in agrochemicals, fertilizers, synthetic detergents, leather footwear, beer and liqueurs, tea, etc.; cap. Rs 480.1m., res Rs 219.0m. (June 2002), sales Rs 2,400m. (March 2002); Chair. VIJAY MALLYA; Man. Dir W. CHHABRIA.

**Tata Tea Ltd:** 1 Bishop Lefroy Rd, Kolkata 700 020; tel. (33) 22813891; fax (33) 22811199; e-mail ttl.ho@tatatea.co.in; internet www.tatatea.com; f. 1962; cap. p.u. Rs 562.2m., res and surplus Rs 8,971.6m., sales Rs 7,826.8m. (March 2004); cultivates, manufactures and sells tea, coffee and allied products; owns 55 tea estates and one coffee estate; four subsidiaries; acquired the Tetley tea business in March 2000; Chair. RATAN N. TATA; Man. Dir PERCY SIGANPORIA; 34,000 employees (2006).

**UB Group:** Level 12–16, UB Tower, UB City 24, Vittal Mallya Rd, Bangalore 560 001; tel. (80) 22272806; fax (80) 22274890; e-mail cmo@ubmail.com; internet www.theubgroup.com; operates in 24 countries with a diversified range of interests, including brewing, spirits, life sciences, engineering, petrochemicals, fertilizers, financial services, information technology and aviation; Chair. VIJAY MALLYA; Exec. Vice-Chair. S. R. GUPTE.

## TRADE UNIONS

**Indian National Trade Union Congress (INTUC):** 4 Bhai Veer Singh Marg, New Delhi 110 001; tel. (11) 23747767; fax (11) 23364244; e-mail info@intuc.net; internet www.intuc.net; f. 1947; 4,411 affiliated unions with a total membership of 7.93m.; affiliated to ICFTU; 32 state brs and 29 nat. feds; Pres. G. SANJEEVA REDDY; Gen. Sec. RAJENDRA PRASAD SINGH.

Major affiliated unions:

**Indian National Cement Workers' Federation:** Mazdoor Karyalaya, Congress House, Mumbai 400 004; tel. (22) 23870804; fax (22) 2622286; e-mail nanjappanintuc@dataone.in; f. 1947; 35,000 mems; 42 affiliated unions; Pres. Dr G. SANJEEVA REDDY; Gen. Sec. NACHIMUTHU NANJAPPAN.

**Indian National Chemical Workers' Federation:** Tel Rasayan Bhavan, Tilak Rd, Dadar, Mumbai 400 014; tel. (22) 24121742; fax (22) 24130950; 35,000 mems; Pres. RAJA KULKARNI; Gen. Sec. R. D. BHARADWAJ.

**Indian National Electricity Workers' Federation:** 392 Sector 21-B, 452 Kotwaliward, Jabalpur 482 002; tel. (129) 2215089; fax (129) 2215868; e-mail inef@ndf.vsnl.net.in; f. 1950; 187,641 mems; 146 affiliated unions; Pres. G. SANJEEVA REDDY; Sec.-Gen. D. P. PATHAK.

**Indian National Metal Workers' Federation:** Shramik Kendra, 4 Bhai Veer Singh Marg, New Dehli 110 001; tel. (661) 24646611; Pres. G. SANJEEVA REDDY; Gen. Sec. RAJSEKHAR MANTRI.

**Indian National Mineworkers' Federation:** CJ 49 Salt Lake, Kolkata 700 091; tel. and fax (33) 23372158; e-mail imme@vsnl

.com; f. 1949; 351,454 mems in 139 affiliated unions; Pres. RAJENDRA P. SINGH; Sec.-Gen. S. Q. ZAMA.

**Indian National Paper Mill Workers' Federation:** 6/B, LIGH, Barkatpura, Hyderabad 500 027; tel. (40) 27564706; Pres. G. SANJEEVA REDDY; Gen. Sec. R. CHANDRASEKHARAN.

**Indian National Port and Dock Workers' Federation:** 15 Coal Dock Rd, Kolkata 700 043; tel. (33) 22455929; f. 1954; 18 affiliated unions; 81,000 mems; Pres. P. K. SAMANTRAY; Gen. Sec. G. KALAN.

**Indian National Sugar Mills Workers' Federation:** A-176, Darulsafa Marg, Lucknow 226 001; tel. (522) 2282719; 100 affiliated unions; 40,000 mems; Pres. ASHOK KUMAR SINGH; Gen. Sec. P. K. SHARMA.

**Indian National Textile Workers' Federation:** 27 Burjorji Bharucha Marg, Fort, Mumbai 400 023; tel. (22) 22671577; f. 1948; 400 affiliated unions; 363,790 mems; Pres. SACHINBHAU AHIR; Gen. Sec. P. L. SUBHAIH.

**Indian National Transport Workers' Federation:** Bus Mazdoor Karyalaya, L/1, Hathital Colony, Jabalpur 482 001; tel. (761) 2429210; 365 affiliated unions; 412,275 mems; Pres. G. SANJEEVA REDDY; Gen. Sec. K. S. VERMA.

**National Federation of Petroleum Workers:** Tel Rasayan Bhavan, Tilak Rd, Dadar, Mumbai 400 014; tel. (22) 24181742; fax (22) 24130950; f. 1959; 22,340 mems; Pres. RAJA KULKARNI; Gen. Sec. N. A. KHANVILKAR.

**Bharatiya Mazdoor Sangh:** Ram Naresh Bhavan, Tilak Gali, Pahar Ganj, New Delhi 110 055; tel. (11) 23562654; fax (11) 23582648; e-mail ho@bms.org.in; internet www.bms.org.in; f. 1955; 4,700 affiliated unions with a total membership of 8.5m.; 27 state brs; 34 nat. feds; Pres. GIRISH AWASTHI; Gen. Sec. UDAY RAO PATWARDHAN.

Major affiliated unions:

**Bharatiya Jute Mazdoor Sangh:** 10 Kiran Shankar Roy Rd, Kolkata 700 001; tel. (33) 22489210; Pres. RAGHUNATH SINGH; Gen. Sec. TARUN KANTI GHOSE.

**Bharatiya Paribahan Mazdoor Mahasangh** (Transport Workers' Union): 542 Dr Munje Marg, Congress Nagar, Nagpur 440 012; tel. (712) 2534464; Pres. WAMAN RAO KHEDKAR; Gen. Sec. CHETAN KUMAR DESAI.

**Kendriya Karmachari Mahasangh:** Ram Naresh Bhawan, Tilak Gali, Paharganj, New Delhi 110 055; tel. (11) 23620654; Pres. K. K. PODDAR; Gen. Sec. CHANDRA MOHAN.

**National Organisation of Bank Workers:** 542 Dr Munje Marg, Congress Nagar, Nagpur 440 012; tel. (712) 2560808; fax (712) 2542442; Pres. V. B. INDURKAR; Gen. Sec. K. R. POONJA.

**National Organisation of Insurance Workers:** 3-AB, Hashim Bldg, 40 Veer Nariman Rd, Mumbai 400 023; tel. (22) 22040958; Pres. M. P PATWARDHAN; Gen. Sec. ATUL DESHPANDE.

**Centre of Indian Trade Unions:** BTR Bhavan, 13-A Rouse Ave, New Delhi 110 002; tel. (11) 23221288; fax (11) 23221284; e-mail citu@bol.net.in; internet www.citu.org.in; f. 1970; 3.37m. mems; 24 state and union territory brs; 4,300 affiliated unions, 12 nat. federations; Pres. M. K. PANDHE; Gen. Sec. MOHAMMED AMIN.

Major affiliated unions:

**All India Coal Workers' Federation:** Koyla Shramik Bhavan, N. S. B. Rd, Raniganj 713 347; Pres. M. K. PANDHE.

**All India Road Transport Workers' Federation:** 53 A. J. C. Bose Rd, Kolkata 700 016; Pres. SHYAMAL CHAKRABORTY.

**Steel Workers' Federation of India:** 1 Vidyasagar Ave, Durgapur 713 205; Pres. ARDHENDU DHAKI.

**Water Transport Workers' Federation of India:** 16 Birsa Munda Sarani, Kolkata 700 043; Pres. T. NARENDRA RAO.

**Assam Chah Karmachari Sangha:** POB 13, Dibrugarh 786 001; tel. 20870; 13,553 mems; 20 brs; Pres. G. C. SARMAH; Gen. Sec. A. K. BHATTACHARYA.

**All-India Trade Union Congress (AITUC):** 24 Canning Lane, New Delhi 110 001; tel. (11) 23387320; fax (11) 23386427; e-mail aitucong@bol.net.in; f. 1920; affiliated to WFTU; 4.6m. mems, 2,272 affiliated unions; 28 state brs, 21 national federations; Pres. J. CHITHARANJAN; Gen. Sec. GURUDAS DASGUPTA.

Major affiliated unions:

**Annamalai Plantation Workers' Union:** Valparai, Via Pollachi, Tamil Nadu; over 21,000 mems.

**Zilla Cha Bagan Workers' Union:** Mal, Jalpaiguri, West Bengal; 15,000 mems; Pres. NEHAR MUKHERJEE; Gen. Sec. BIMAL DAS GUPTA.

**United Trades Union Congress (UTUC):** 1st Floor, 249 Bipin Behari Ganguly St, Kolkata 700 012; tel. (33) 22259234; fax (33) 22375609; f. 1949; 1.2m. mems from 387 affiliated unions; 12 state brs and six nat. feds; Pres. SHANKARAN NAIR; Gen. Sec. ABANI ROY.

Major affiliated unions:

**Bengal Provincial Chatkal Mazdoor Union:** Kolkata; textile workers; 28,330 mems.

**Dooars Cha Bagan Union:** Jalpaiguri; tel. (3564) 255220; 94,532 mems; Pres. SURESH TALUKDAR; Gen. Sec. MANOHAR TIRKEY.

**Hind Mazdoor Sabha (HMS):** 120 Babar Rd, New Delhi 110 011; tel. (11) 23413519; fax (11) 23411037; e-mail hms@nde.vsnl.net.in; internet www.mkiindia.org; f. 1948; affiliated to ICFTU; 4.8m. mems from 2,800 affiliated unions; 25 state councils; 18 nat. industrial feds; Pres. MANOHAR KOTWAL; Gen. Sec. UMRAOMAL PUROHIT.

Major affiliated unions:

**Colliery Mazdoor Congress** (Coalminers' Union): Bengal Hotel, 2nd Md Hussain St, Asansol 713 301; tel. (341) 202342; fax (341) 201336; 45,188 mems; Pres. MADHU DANDAVATE; Gen. Sec. JAYANTA PODDER.

**Mumbai Port Trust Dock and General Employees' Union:** Port Trust Kamgar Sadan, Nawab Tank Rd, Mazgaon, Mumbai 400 010; tel. (22) 23776320; fax (22) 23754794; e-mail mbptdgeu@vsnl.net; 7,448 mems; Pres. Dr SHANTI PATEL; Gen. Sec. S. K. SHETYE.

**South Central Railway Mazdoor Union:** 7C Railway Bldg, Accounts Office Compound, Secunderabad 500 371; tel. (40) 27821351; fax (40) 27821351; e-mail scrmu@hotmail.com; internet www.scrmu.org; f. 1966; 88,900 mems; Pres. C. SANKARA RAO; Gen. Sec. C. H. SANKARRAO; 135 brs.

**Transport and Dock Workers' Union:** P. D. Mello Bhavan, P. D. Mello Rd, Carnec Bunder, Mumbai 400 038; tel. (22) 22616951; fax (22) 22659087; 25,979 mems; Pres. S. R. KULKARNI.

**West Bengal Cha Mazdoor Sabha:** Cha Shramik Bhavan, Jalpaiguri 735 101, West Bengal; tel. (3561) 231140; fax (3561) 230349; f. 1947; 55,000 mems; Pres. Prof. SUSHIL ROY; Gen. Sec. SAMIR ROY.

**Western Railway Employees' Union:** Grant Road Railway Station Bldg, Grant Rd (East), Mumbai 400 007; tel. (22) 23088102; fax (22) 23003185; 150,000 mems; Pres. UMRAOMAL PUROHIT; Gen. Sec. C. S. MENON.

**Confederation of Central Government Employees and Workers:** 4B/6 Ganga Ram Hospital Marg, New Delhi 110 060; tel. (11) 22587804; 1.2m. mems; Pres. S. MADHUSUDAN; Sec.-Gen. S. K. VYAS.

Affiliated union:

**National Federation of Postal Employees (NFPE):** D-7, North Ave Post Office Bldg, 1st Floor, New Delhi 110 001; tel. and fax (11) 23092771; e-mail nfpe_hq@hotmail.com; f. 1954 as National Federation of Post and Telegraph Employees, reconstituted as above in 1986; 400,000 mems from seven affiliated unions; Pres. R. N. CHAUDHARY; Sec.-Gen. C. CHANDRAN PILLAI.

**All India Bank Employees' Association (AIBEA):** Prabhat Nivas, Singapore Plaza, 164 Linghi Chetty St, Chennai 600 001; tel. (44) 25351522; fax (44) 25358853; e-mail aibeahq@gmail.com; internet bankunionaibea.org; 32 state units, 710 affiliated unions, 525,000 mems; Pres. RAJEN NAGAR; Gen. Sec. C. H. VENKATACHALAM.

**All India Defence Employees' Federation (AIDEF):** Survey No. 81, Elphinstone Rd, Khadki, Pune 411 003; tel. (20) 25818761; 358 affiliated unions; 200,000 mems; Pres. S. N. PATHAK; Gen. Secs S. BHATTACHARYA, C. SRIKUMAR.

**All India Port and Dock Workers' Federation:** 9 Second Line Beach, Chennai 600 001; tel. (44) 25224222; fax (44) 25225983; f. 1948; 100,000 mems in 34 affiliated unions; Pres. S. R. KULKARNI; Gen. Sec. S. C. C. ANTHONY PILLAI.

**All India Railwaymen's Federation (AIRF):** 4 State Entry Rd, New Delhi 110 055; tel. (11) 23343493; fax (11) 23363167; e-mail airf@ndb.vsnl.net.in; f. 1924; 1,034,747 mems (2005); 24 affiliated unions; Pres. UMRAOMAL PUROHIT; Gen. Sec. J. P. CHAUBEY.

**National Federation of Indian Railwaymen (NFIR):** 3 Chelmsford Rd, New Delhi 110 055; tel. (11) 23343305; fax (11) 23744013; e-mail nfir@satyam.net.in; f. 1952; 26 affiliated unions; 925,500 mems (2003); Pres. GUMAN SINGH; Gen. Sec. M. RAGHAVAIAH.

# Transport

## RAILWAYS

India's railway system is the largest in Asia and the fourth largest in the world. In March 2003 the total length of Indian railways exceeded 63,140 route-km. The network carried 14m. passengers and more than 1m. metric tons of freight traffic per day. The Government exercises direct or indirect control over all railways through the Railway Board. India's largest railway construction project of the 20th century, the 760-km Konkan railway line (which took seven years and almost US $1,000m. to build), was officially opened in January 1998.

A 16.45-km underground railway, which carries more than 1m. people daily, was completed in Kolkata in 1995. The first phase of a partially underground new metro system in New Delhi was completed in late 2004; the final phase was expected to be completed in 2010.

**Ministry of Railways (Railway Board):** Rail Bhavan, Raisina Rd, New Delhi 110 001; tel. (11) 23384010; fax (11) 23384481; e-mail crb@del2.vsnl.net.in; internet www.indianrailways.gov.in; Chair. KALYAN COOMAR JENA.

### Zonal Railways

The railways are grouped into 16 zones:

**Central Railway:** Chhatrapati Shivaji Terminus (Victoria Terminus), Mumbai 400 001; tel. (22) 22621230; fax (22) 22612354; e-mail gmcr@bom2.vsnl.net.in; internet www.centralrailwayonline.com; Gen. Man. SOWMYA RAGHAVAN.

**East Central Railway:** Hajipur 844 101; tel. (6224) 274728; fax (6224) 274738; internet www.ecr.railnet.gov.in; f. 1996; Gen. Man. R. S. VARSHNEYA.

**East Coast Railway:** Rail Vihar, Chandrasekhar Pur, Bhubaneswar 751 023; tel. (674) 230073; fax (674) 2300196; internet www.eastcoastrailway.gov.in; f. 1996; Gen. Man. A. K. GOYAL.

**Eastern Railway:** 17 Netaji Subhas Rd, Kolkata 700 001; tel. (33) 22207596; fax (33) 22480370; internet www.easternrailway.gov.in; Gen. Man. N. K. GOEL.

**North Central Railway:** Allahabad 211 001; tel. (532) 2603551; fax (532) 2603900; e-mail secyncr@hotmail.com; f. 1996; Gen Man. BUDH PRAKASH.

**North Eastern Railway:** Gorakhpur 273 012; tel. (551) 2201041; fax (551) 2201299; e-mail gm@ner.railnet.gov.in; internet www.ner.railnet.gov.in; Gen. Man. OM PRAKASH.

**North Western Railway:** Ganpati Nagar, opp. Railway Hospital, Loco Colony Rd, Jaipur 302 006; tel. (141) 2222695; fax (141) 2222936; e-mail itnwr@yahoo.com; internet www.northwesternrailway.gov.in; Gen. Man. S. S. BHATTACHARYA.

**Northeast Frontier Railway:** Maligaon, Guwahati 781 011; tel. (361) 2570422; fax (361) 2570580; e-mail gm@nfr.railnet.gov.in; internet www.nfr.railnet.gov.in; f. 1958; Gen. Man. ASHUTOSH SWAMI.

**Northern Railway:** Baroda House, Kasturba Gandhi Marg, New Delhi 110 001; tel. (11) 23747084; fax (11) 23363469; e-mail cpro@nr.railnet.gov.in; internet www.nr.indianrail.gov.in; Gen. Man. Shri PRAKASH.

**South Central Railway:** Rm 312, 3rd Floor, Rail Nilayam, Secunderabad 500 071; tel. (40) 27822874; fax (40) 27833203; internet www.scrailway.gov.in; Gen. Man. H. K. PADHEE.

**South East Central Railway:** R. E. Complex, Bilaspur 495 004; tel. (7752) 47102; e-mail webmaster@secr.railnet.gov.in; internet www.secr.gov.in; Gen. Man. PRADEEP KUMAR.

**South Eastern Railway:** 11 Garden Reach Rd, Kolkata 700 043; tel. (33) 24393532; fax (33) 24397831; e-mail gm@ser.railnet.gov.in; internet www.serailway.gov.in; Gen. Man. A. K. JAIN.

**South Western Railway:** Club Road, Keshwapur, Hubli 580 023; tel. (836) 2360888; fax (836) 2365209; e-mail gm@southwesternrailway.in; internet www.southwesternrailway.in; f. 1996; Gen. Man. PRAVEEN KUMAR.

**Southern Railway:** Park Town, Chennai 600 003; tel. (44) 25353455; fax (44) 25354950; e-mail srailway@gmail.com; internet www.southernrailway.org; Gen. Man. RAKESH CHOPRA.

**West Central Railway:** Jabalpur 482 001; tel. (761) 2627444; fax (761) 2607555; e-mail osdwcr@yahoo.com; internet www.westcentralrailway.com; f. 1996; Gen. Man. MAHEEP KAPUR.

**Western Railway:** Churchgate, Mumbai 400 020; tel. (22) 22005670; fax (22) 22068545; e-mail secygm@wr.railnet.gov.in; internet www.wr.indianrail.gov.in; Gen. Man. M. Z. ANSARI.

## ROADS

In December 2002 there were an estimated 3.3m. km of roads in India, 58,112 km of which were national highways. About 50% of the total road network was paved. In March 2004 there were an estimated 65,569 km of national highways. In January 1999 the Government launched the ambitious Rs 500,000m. National Highways Development project, which included plans to build an east–west corridor linking Silchar with Porbandar and a north–south corridor linking Kashmir with Kanyakumari, as well as a circuit of roads linking the four main cities of Mumbai, Chennai, Kolkata and New Delhi. A further phase of the project, the widening and upgrading of an estimated 65,000 km of national highways, was implemented in 2005. In May 2007 the Government pledged Rs 480,000m. for the upgrade of India's rural road network by 2009 with the stated aim of connecting 66,000 villages; the allocation represented part of a four-year initiative (at an estimated cost of Rs 1,740,000m.) to enhance infrastructure and rural incomes by increasing connectivity with roads, telecommunications and drinking water.

**Ministry of Shipping, Road Transport and Highways:** Parivahan Bhavan, 1 Sansad Marg, New Delhi 110 001; tel. (11) 23710121; fax (11) 23719023; internet morth.nic.in; responsible for the construction and maintenance of India's system of national highways, with a total length of 65,569 km in March 2004, connecting the state capitals and major ports and linking with the highway systems of neighbouring countries. This system includes 172 national highways which constitute the main trunk roads of the country.

**Border Roads Organisation:** Seema Sadak Bhavan, Ring Road Naraina, Delhi 110 010; e-mail bro-jdedp@nic.in; internet www.bro.nic.in; f. 1960 to accelerate the economic development of the north and north-eastern border areas; it has constructed 31,061 km and improved 37,077 km of roads, and built permanent bridges totalling a length of 19,544 m in the border areas.

**National Highways Authority of India:** G-5 and 6, Sector 10, Dwarka, New Delhi 110 075; tel. (11) 25074100; fax (11) 25093507; e-mail scjindal@nhai.org; internet www.nhai.org; f. 1995; planning, designing, construction and maintenance of national highways; under Ministry of Shipping, Road Transport and Highways; Chair. N. GOKULRAM.

## INLAND WATERWAYS

About 14,500 km of rivers are navigable by power-driven craft, and 3,700 km by large country boats. Services are mainly on the Ganga and Brahmaputra and their tributaries, the Godavari, the Mahanadi, the Narmada, the Tapti and the Krishna.

**Central Inland Water Transport Corpn Ltd:** 4 Fairlie Place, Kolkata 700 001; tel. (33) 22202321; fax (33) 22436164; e-mail ciwtc@cal3.vsnl.net.in; internet www.ciwtcltd.com; f. 1967; inland water transport services in Bangladesh and the east and north-east Indian states; also shipbuilding and repairing, general engineering, lightering of ships and barge services; Chair. and Man. Dir PRAFUL TAYAL.

## SHIPPING

In March 2002 India was 15th in terms of dwt and 19th in terms of gwt on the list of principal merchant fleets of the world. At December 31 2007 the total fleet had 1,417 ships, with a total displacement of 9.16m. grt. There were some 102 shipping companies operating in India in January 2000. The major ports are Chennai, Haldia, Jawaharlal Nehru (at Nhava Sheva near Mumbai), Kandla, Kochi, Kolkata, Mormugao, Mumbai, New Mangalore, Paradip (Paradeep), Tuticorin and Visakhapatnam.

### Chennai (Madras)

**South India Shipping Corpn Ltd:** Chennai; Chair. J. H. TARAPORE; Man. Dir F. G. DASTUR.

### Kolkata (Calcutta)

**India Steamship Co Ltd:** 44 Park St, Kolkata 700 016; tel. (33) 22481171; fax (33) 22488133; e-mail india.steamship@gems.vsnl.net.in; f. 1928; cargo services; Chair. K. K. BIRLA; Man. Dir ASHOK KAK; br in Delhi.

**Surrendra Overseas Ltd:** Apeejay House, 15 Park St, Kolkata 700 016; tel. (33) 22172372; fax (33) 22179596; e-mail solcal@apeejaygroup.com; internet www.apeejaygroup.com; shipowners; Chair. JIT PAUL.

### Mumbai (Bombay)

**Century Shipping Ltd:** Mumbai; tel. (22) 22022734; fax (22) 22027274; Chair. B. K. BIRLA; Pres. N. M. JAIN.

**Chowgule Brothers (Pvt) Ltd:** Malhotra House, 3rd Floor, Mumbai 400 001.; tel. (22) 22616301; fax (22) 22610659; e-mail mumbai.cb@chowgule.co.in; internet www.chowgulebros.com.

**Essar Shipping Ltd:** Essar House, 11 Keshavrao Khadye Marg, Mahalaxmi, Mumbai 400 034; tel. (22) 24950606; fax (22) 24954312; e-mail contactshipping@essar.com; internet www.essar.com/shipping.htm; f. 1975; Chair. S. N. RUIA; Man. Dir SANJAY MEHTA.

**The Great Eastern Shipping Co Ltd:** Ocean House, 134/A Dr Annie Besant Rd, Worli, Mumbai 400 018; tel. (22) 66613000; fax (22) 24925900; e-mail corp_comm@greatship.com; internet www.greatship.com; f. 1948; shipping; Exec. Chair. K. M. SHETH; Dep. Chair. and Man. Dir BHARAT SHETH; br. in New Delhi.

**Shipping Corpn of India Ltd:** Shipping House, 245 Madame Cama Rd, Mumbai 400 021; tel. (22) 22026666; fax (22) 22026905; e-mail mail@sci.co.in; internet www.shipindia.com; f. 1961 as a govt undertaking; Chair. and Man. Dir S. HAJARA; brs in Kolkata, New Delhi, Chennai and London.

**Tolani Shipping Co Ltd:** 10A Bakhtawar, Nariman Point, Mumbai 400 021; tel. (22) 56568989; fax (22) 22870697; e-mail ops@tolanigroup.com; Chair. and Man. Dir Dr N. P. TOLANI.

**Varun Shipping Co Ltd:** Laxmi Bldg, 3rd Floor, 6 Shoorji Vallabhdas Marg, Ballard Estate, Mumbai 400 001; tel. (22) 66350100; fax (22) 66350274; e-mail systems@varunship.com; internet www.varunship.com; f. 1971; Chair. DILIP D. KHATAU.

### CIVIL AVIATION

There are 11 designated international airports, 85 domestic airports and 28 civil enclaves. By 2004 10 airports (in Ahmedabad, Amritsar, Goa, Guwahati, Jaipur, Lucknow, Mangalore, Madurai, Thiruvananthapuram and Udaipur) had been identified for the second round of modernization and restructuring. The process of long-term leasing of Mumbai, Delhi, Chennai and Kolkata airports was under way in 2006.

**Airports Authority of India:** Rajiv Gandhi Bhavan, Safdarjung Airport, New Delhi 110 003; tel. (11) 24632950; fax (11) 24641088; e-mail aaichmn@vsnl.com; internet www.aai.aero; manages 124 international and domestic airports; Chair. K. RAMALINGAM; Gen. Man. PRAM NATH.

**Air Deccan:** 214/33, 7th Cross, Vasanthnagar, Bangalore 560 052; tel. (80) 51148190; fax (80) 22352645; internet www.airdeccan.net; f. 2003; unit of Deccan Aviation Pvt Ltd; low-cost domestic passenger service; Man. Dir Capt. G. R. GOPINATH.

**Air-India:** Air-India Bldg, 218 Backbay Reclamation, Nariman Point, Mumbai 400 021; tel. (22) 22024142; fax (22) 22023686; e-mail hqpsai@bom3.vsnl.net.in; internet www.airindia.com; f. 1932 as Tata Airlines; renamed Air-India in 1946; in 1953 became a state corpn responsible for international flights; merged with Indian Airlines in Aug. 2007 to form the National Aviation Company of India, operating as Air-India; services to 46 online stations (incl. two cargo stations) and 84 offline offices throughout the world; Chair. and Man. Dir RAGHU MENON.

**Air Sahara:** Dr Gopaldas Bhawan, 3rd Floor, 28 Barakhamba Rd, New Delhi 110 001; tel. (11) 23326851; fax (11) 23755510; internet www.airsahara.net; f. 1991 as Sahara India Airlines; commenced operations 1993; acquired by Jet Airways (India) Ltd in April 2007; private co; scheduled passenger and cargo services to domestic and regional destinations; Man. GARRY KINGSHOTT.

**Airline Allied Services Ltd:** Domestic Arrival Terminal, 1st Floor, Indira Gandhi International Airport, Palam, New Delhi 110 037; tel. (11) 25672729; fax (11) 25672006; e-mail aaslmd@del2.net.in; internet www.allianceair-india.com/; f. 1996; 100% owned by Indian Airlines; scheduled passenger services to regional destinations; Man. Dir MANET PAES.

**Archana Airways:** 41A Friends Colony (East), Mathura Rd, New Delhi 110 065; tel. (11) 26842001; fax (11) 26847762; f. 1991; commenced operations 1993; scheduled and charter passenger services to domestic destinations; Dir/Chair. A. K. BHARTIYA; Man. Dir N. K. BHARTIYA.

**Blue Dart Express:** 88–89 Old International Terminal, Meenambakkam Airport, Chennai 600027; tel. (44) 22334995; fax (44) 22349067; e-mail bdal@md2.vsnl.net.in; internet www.bluedart.com; f. 1983 as Blue Dart Courier Services; name changed as above in 1990; air express transport co; Chair. TUSHAR K. JANI; Chief Exec. NITEEN GUPTE.

**Go Air:** Paper Box House, off Mahakali Caves Rd, Andheri (East), Mumbai 400 093; e-mail feedback@goair.in; internet www.goair.in; f. 2005; passenger services to domestic destinations; Man. Dir JEHANGIR 'JEH' WADIA.

**Gujarat Airways Ltd:** Sapana Shopping Centre, 1st Floor, 20 Vishwas Colony, Alkapuri, Vadodara 390 005; tel. (265) 2330864; fax (265) 2339628; e-mail info@gujaratairways.com; f. 1994; commenced operations 1995; scheduled services to domestic destinations; Chair. G. N. PATEL; Man. Dir R. C. SHARMA.

**Indigo Airlines:** internet www.flyindigo.com; f. 2005; private co; passenger services to domestic destinations; Man. Dir RAHUL BHATIA; CEO BRUCE ASHBY.

**Jagson Airlines:** Vandana Bldg, 3rd Floor, 11 Tolstoy Marg, New Delhi 110 001; tel. (11) 23721594; fax (11) 23324693; e-mail jagson-id@eth.net; internet www.jagsonairline.com; f. 1991; scheduled and charter passenger services to domestic destinations; Chair. JAGDISH GUPTA.

**Jet Airways (India) Ltd:** S. M. Centre, 1st Floor, Andheri-Kurla Rd, Andheri (East), Mumbai 400 059; tel. (22) 40191000; fax (22) 29201313; internet www.jetairways.com; f. 1992; commenced operations 1993; acquired Air Sahara in April 2007; private co; scheduled passenger services to domestic and regional destinations; operates flights to 50 domestic and international destinations; Chair. and Man. Dir NARESH GOYAL; CEO WOLFGANG PROCK-SCHAUER.

**Kingfisher Airlines:** Bhagwati House, 2nd Floor, A/19, off Veera Desai Rd, Fun Republic Theatre Rd, Andheri (West), Mumbai 400 053; tel. (22) 55031091; fax (22) 55031095; e-mail info@flykingfisher.com; internet www.flykingfisher.com; f. 2005; 100% owned by UB Group; low-cost domestic passenger service; Chair. and Man. Dir VIJAY MALLYA.

**Paramount Airways:** Rajanarayan Towers, 70 Race Course, Coimbatore 641 018; fax (422) 5394441; e-mail feedback@paramountairways.com; internet www.paramountairways.com; f. 2005; scheduled flights to domestic destinations; Man. Dir M. THIAGARAJAN.

**SpiceJet:** Cargo Complex, Terminal 1-B, Indira Gandhi International Airport, Domestic Terminal, New Delhi 110 037; e-mail corpoffice@spicejet.com; internet www.spicejet.com; f. 2005; low-cost domestic passenger service; Chair. SIDDHANTA SHARMA; CEO MARK WINDERS.

**Trans Bharat Aviation Ltd:** 212–213, Somdutt Chamber I, 2nd Floor, Bhikaji Cama Place, Delhi 110 066; tel. (11) 26181824; fax (11) 26160146; e-mail qcmtba@rediffmail.com; internet www.transbharataviation.com; f. 1990; commenced operations 1991; charter services throughout India.

**UP Airways Ltd:** Roopali House, A-2 Defence Colony, New Delhi 110 024; tel. (11) 24646290; fax (11) 24646292; e-mail sgsimpex@del3.vsnl.net.in; private co; charter services to domestic destinations; Chair. and Man. Dir SUBHASH GULATI; Chief Exec. Capt. H. S. BEDI.

## Tourism

The tourist attractions of India include its scenery, its historic forts, palaces and temples, and its rich variety of wildlife. Tourist infrastructure has recently been expanded by the provision of more luxury hotels and improved means of transport. In 2006 there were about 4.4m. foreign visitors to India, and revenue from tourism totalled an estimated US $6,569.3m.

**Ministry of Tourism:** Transport Bhavan, Rm 123, 1 Parliament St, New Delhi 110 001; tel. and fax (11) 23715084; e-mail sectour@nic.in; internet tourism.gov.in; formulates and administers govt policy for promotion of tourism; plans the organization and development of tourist facilities; operates tourist information offices in India and overseas; Sec. SHILABHADRA BANERJEE.

**India Tourism Development Corpn Ltd:** SCOPE Complex, Core 8, 6th Floor, 7 Lodhi Rd, New Delhi 110 003; tel. (11) 24360182; fax (11) 24360185; e-mail cmditdc@theashokgroup.com; internet www.theashokgroup.com; f. 1966; operates Ashok Group of hotels (largest hotel chain owner), resort accommodation, tourist transport services, duty-free shops and a travel agency and provides consultancy and management services; Chair. and Man. Dir PARVEZ DEVAN.

## Defence

As assessed at November 2007, India's total armed forces numbered 1,288,000: army 1,100,000, navy 55,000 (incl. naval air force), air force 125,000. There were also 8,000 members of the coast guard. Active paramilitary forces totalled 1,155,000 members, including the 208,422-strong Border Security Force (based mainly in the troubled state of Jammu and Kashmir). Military service is voluntary, although the Constitution states that every citizen has a fundamental duty to perform national service when called upon to do so.

**Defence Budget (2007/08):** Estimated at Rs 1,123,000m.

**Chair. of Joint Chiefs of Staff Committee:** Adm. SUREESH MEHTA.

**Chief of Staff of the Army:** Gen. DEEPAK KAPOOR.

**Chief of Staff of the Navy:** Adm. SUREESH MEHTA.

**Chief of Staff of the Air Force:** Air Chief Marshal FALI HOMI MAJOR.

## Education

Under the Constitution, education in India is primarily the responsibility of the individual state governments, although the central Government has several direct responsibilities, some specified in the Constitution, as for example, responsibility for the Central Universities, all higher institutions, promotion and propagation of Hindi, co-ordination and maintenance of higher education standards, scientific and technological research and welfare of Indian students abroad.

Education in India is administered centrally by the Ministry of Human Resources Development (Department of Education). At state level, there is an Education Minister. There are facilities for free primary education (lower and upper stages) in all the states. Priority has been given to an expansion in elementary and community education as well as in education for girls. An amendment to the Constitution, approved in May 2002, ensures free and compulsory education for children from the age of six to 14. Budgetary expenditure on education for 2008/09 was forecast at Rs 344,000m. (equivalent to 4.6% of total spending).

### ELEMENTARY EDUCATION

The notable characteristic of elementary education in India is the use of what is known as basic education. There is an activity-centred curriculum which educates through socially useful, productive activities such as spinning, weaving, gardening, leather work, book craft, domestic crafts, pottery, elementary engineering, etc. The emphasis is on introducing important features of basic education in non-basic schools. Basic education is the national pattern of all elementary education and all elementary schools will ultimately be brought over to the basic system. Twenty per cent already have, and the rest are gradually being converted under an 'orientation' system for teachers.

In lower primary classes, for children between six and 11 years of age, the total number of pupils increased from 50m. in 1965 to an estimated 113.9m. in 2001/02. Enrolment in higher primary or middle schools (age-group 11–14 years) in 2001/02 was 44.8m. Similarly, the number of primary (lower and higher) schools increased from 466,862 in 1965/66 to an estimated 883,000 in 2001/02. Enrolment at primary schools in 2005/06 included 88.7% of pupils in the relevant age-group (90.4% of boys; 86.8% of girls).

### SECONDARY EDUCATION

Education at this level is provided for those between the ages of 14 and 17. Many state governments have taken steps to reorganize secondary schools, resulting in great expansion since 1965. There were approximately 133,492 secondary and higher secondary schools in 2001/02, with some 30.5m. pupils and 1.78m. teachers. In 2004/05 enrolment at secondary schools was equivalent to 54.0% of pupils in the relevant age-group (59.0% of boys; 48.6% of girls).

Most schools follow what is known as the 'three language formula' which comprises teaching of the regional dialect, Hindi and English. Much emphasis is now also being laid on physical training, which has become a compulsory subject.

### HIGHER AND ADULT EDUCATION

The universities are for the most part autonomous as regards administration. The University Grants Commission is responsible for the promotion and co-ordination of university education and has the authority to make appropriate grants and to implement development schemes.

India had a total of 394 universities and institutions with university status in 2004/05, and some 15,615 university and affiliated colleges. In that year university enrolment was equivalent to some 10.0% of students in the relevant age group.

A National Council for Higher Education in Rural Areas was established in 1953 to advise the Government on all matters relating to the development of rural higher education. In 1977 there were 10 rural institutes functioning in seven states, most of them affiliated to the state university.

Educational work is being undertaken for the eradication of illiteracy, education in citizenship, cultural and recreational activities and organization of youth and women's groups for community development. A National Board for Adult Education has been set up, but the state governments are largely responsible for adult education programmes. The main emphasis is on improving literacy rates, especially in rural areas; there are also Urban Adult Education Programmes and in 1976 a major programme of non-formal education was launched for the 15–25 age group. The rate of literacy rose from 43.6% of the adult population in 1981 to 58.0% in 2001, which is still, however, far lower than the literacy rate of most developing countries at comparable levels of economic development.

# THE STATES AND TERRITORIES OF INDIA

## States

### Andhra Pradesh

The State of Andhra Pradesh lies in southern India, on the eastern shores of the peninsula, and occupies much of the central plateau region known as the Deccan. To the south lies the state of Tamil Nadu, to the west, Karnataka, and to the north-west and north, Maharashtra. In the north-east there is a short border with the new state of Chhattisgarh (part of Madhya Pradesh until 2000) and a longer border with Orissa, where Andhra Pradesh stretches an arm north-eastwards along the coast of the Bay of Bengal. In the Godavari delta Andhra Pradesh surrounds an enclave of the Union Territory of Puducherry (Pondicherry), the small port of Yanam. The state, the 'land of the Andhras', was formed on 1 November 1956, by uniting Andhra (the northern, Telugu-speaking part of the old Madras presidency—territories which themselves can be divided into Coastal Andhra and Rayalseema) and the bulk of the former princely state of Hyderabad (the Dominions of the Nizam, which had only entered the Indian Union in 1948—this area is known as Telangana). It is the fourth largest state in India, with an area of some 275,069 sq km (106,245 sq miles).

The Eastern Ghats form a series of hill ranges inland from the coast, and the highest point is the peak of Mahendragiri (1,501 m—4,116 ft), on the border with Orissa. The western and north-western parts of the state rise into the central Indian plateau of the Deccan. Much of the state, therefore, is dry and rocky, although woodland and forest cover over one-fifth of the land area. The coastal plains are fertile, particularly in the deltas, watered by Andhra Pradesh's major rivers, the Godavari (which flows from the northern borderlands) and the Krishna (which bisects the state), both of which debouch in the north-central part of the 974-km (605-mile) coastline. The third major river basin is that of the Penner, in the south. The climate varies with altitude, but is generally hot and humid. The average annual rainfall is 925 mm (36 inches), most of it falling between June and October and on the coast.

Andhra Pradesh is the fifth most populous state of the Union, with 76,210,007, according to the results of the census of 1 March 2001. This compared with 66,508,008 in 1991, when it was the fourth most populous state, but the decade saw the population growth rate fall significantly below the national average. In 2001, therefore, Andhra Pradesh had a population density of 277 per sq km. The state was formed as a linguistic unit and over 85% of the population of Andhra Pradesh speak Telugu (based on 1991 figures), the most widely spoken Dravidian tongue, which became the official language in 1966. A vestige of Muslim rule can be seen in the 7% of the population who speak Urdu, particularly in Hyderabad, the state capital. There are also speakers of Tamil in the south and of Kanarese or Kannada in the west. Most of the population are Hindu (89.0% in 2001), but the Muslim community remains numerous (9.2%) and other faiths are represented, such as Christians (1.6%), Jains, Buddhists and Sikhs. Historically, the area was an important Buddhist centre and remains an important pilgrimage centre—in January 2006 the Kalachakra festival in Amravati, the cradle of Mahayana Buddhism, was attended by the Dalai Lama and many thousands from around the world. In 2001 the Scheduled Castes constituted 16.2% of the population and the Scheduled Tribes 6.6%.

According to the final results of the 2001 census, 27.3% of the residents of Andhra Pradesh were defined as urban. The largest city, as well as the seat of state government, is Hyderabad, the seventh largest city in India—the city proper of Hyderabad had a population of 3,612,427 in 2001, according to the census results. Other important cities are the northern port of Visakhapatnam (Vizag, 982,984), Vijayawada (Vijayavada, 851,282), on the Krishna delta, and Warangal (530,636), to the north-east of Hyderabad. The main city of the south is Tirupati. The state is divided into 23 administrative districts.

#### HISTORY

Vedic tradition has the original Andhras as an Aryan people who migrated into peninsular India and mixed with the local Dravidian population. Certainly a proto-Dravidian culture had appeared throughout southern India by the middle of the first millennium BC and a distinct 'Andhra' language, Telugu, emerged thereafter. The first recorded mention of the Andhras dates from the end of the reign of Ashoka (third century BC), when much of the territory of the modern state seems to have fallen under Mauryan sway. The original centre for the Andhra kings was probably on the Krishna delta, but their conquests were into the northern Deccan, and the early capital was in modern Maharashtra, at Prathinistapura (Paithan).

The first Andhra power was the realm of the Satavahanas, a dynasty that was based in the north-western Deccan, in Maharashtra and southern Madhya Pradesh, from the beginning of the Christian era. Over four centuries of stability allowed the development of flourishing trade relations with South-East Asia, China and even Japan and the Roman Empire. It also witnessed the emergence of the Mahayana form of Buddhism. For much of this period rule of the Telugu-speaking peoples was divided among a number of polities, and this was to be a consistent feature of the political geography of the area, with the fates of the north, the south and the coast of modern Andhra Pradesh diverging. Thus, there were a number of other dynasties contemporaneous with the Satavahanas worth noting. The Ikshvakus, from around AD 300, were prominent in the south and their capital was known as Vijayapuri, near modern Nagarjunakonda, famed as a centre of Buddhist learning. The Salankayanas were based at Vinukonda, in the Guntur district. Also, two Andhra kingdoms north of the Godavari were subdued by Samudra-Gupta in the fourth century.

In the second half of the first millennium AD most of modern Andhra Pradesh fell under the Chalukyas, a Karnatakan dynasty. An offshoot of this dynasty, known as the Eastern Chalukyas, ruled Vengi from their capital at Rajamahendrapuri (now Rajahmundry, near the coast between the Godavari and Krishna rivers) until they succumbed to dependence on the Rashtrakutas in the eighth century. This last dynasty had itself seceded from the main Chalukya realm, which was weakened by its struggles with Pallavas, who originated in the Tamil lands and frequently held sway over the southern Telugu lands. However, by the end of the millennium Vengi had become a dependency of the Cholas, who had displaced the Pallavas as the main power in southern India, and were, briefly, to challenge the normal play of power in the subcontinent by intervening in the north. Meanwhile, in the Andhran Deccan, in around 1000 a Telugu dynasty, the Kakatiyas of Warangal, established a realm known as Telangana. In 1326 they finally succumbed to the Hindu south's new enemy, Muslim invaders from the northern sultanate.

The 14th century was a crucial period for the modern history of Andhra Pradesh. The advent of Muslim influence was confirmed by the foundation of the Bahamani kingdom by Hassan Gangu in 1347, to the north and west of the Telugu heartlands. The governors of the Delhi sultanate on the coast had been driven from other Andhra lands by an alliance of nayaks or military potentates, who founded independent realms in the east in 1325, under the Reddys of Kondaivu (to 1425) and the Velamas of Nalgonda (to 1474). Later another nayak territory, under the Reddys of Rajahmundry, was established in 1403, but only lasted to 1448. Most importantly, however, in 1336 two Hindu brothers founded a city at modern Hampi in Karnataka—Vijayanagar. This became a prosperous and vibrant empire, which led southern resistance to the Muslim advance, and was a power in the region for over two centuries, under four successive dynasties, the Sangama, the Saluva, the Tuluva and the Aravidu. They were great patrons of Telugu language and literature, and built many temples and works of civic engineering. The empire reached its apogee under the Tuluva monarch, Krishna Deva Raya (1509–30), who was also known as Andhra Bhoja. The empire was defeated and the capital abandoned in January 1565, after the battle of Talikota, in which the combined forces of the successor states of the Bahamanis secured political hegemony for Islam.

The Sultanate of Golconda was the main Muslim principality to emerge in the Andhra lands of the Bahamani kingdom, which had disintegrated at the end of the 15th century. The sultanate, one of five Bahamani successors, was founded in 1518 by a Turkic officer, Quli Qutub Shah, and maintained its independence until 1686, when the Mughal emperor, Aurangzeb, annexed it. Golconda was famed for its diamond mines and held the fertile territory between the Krishna and Godavari rivers, as well as the north-west and territory right down to the Bay of Bengal. Although Golconda had joined the confederacy against Vijayanagar, the sultanate was generally tolerant and many Hindus were employed in the administration. Also, in

1591 Muhammed Quli Qutub Shah had founded a new city, Bhagyanagar, which was to become the capital of Muslim rule in the region—modern Hyderabad.

Effective Mughal power in southern India did not long persist following the death of Aurangzeb. In 1724 the Subedar of the Deccan, Nizam-ul-Mulk Asaf Jah, declared his independence. His capital was in Hyderabad. His successors, known as the Nizams, established their Dominions in the Deccan and the Andhra lands. However, meanwhile, European traders had begun to establish posts in India, mainly the Portuguese in the 16th century, but then followed by the Dutch, the French and English (the English Crown granted a charter to the East India Company in 1600—this was to become the British instrument for the acquisition of an empire in the subcontinent). By the time an independent Hyderabad was established, the European powers were increasingly becoming involved in local Indian politics, as well as their own domestic rivalries. Thus, French help in a succession struggle in the early 1750s meant that a grateful Nizam granted them the Northern Circars, the coastal districts from the Krishna delta north-eastwards into modern Orissa. However, the French lost this territory to the British in 1766. Further British gains in the region during the rest of the century were at the expense of Mysore (which, under Haider Ali from 1761, had acquired a considerable amount of territory in Rayalseema from the Marathas) and with the help of the Nizam. Although Hyderabad added to its own extent, many of these gains were sacrificed in return for a favourable financial settlement with the British. On 12 October 1800 the Nizam entered into subsidiary alliance with the British, but avoided the usual arrangement of having to pay for the presence of British troops (gaining imperial protection and saving considerable wealth for almost 150 years) by the concession of territory. Thus, over less than four decades the British had acquired the coastal and southern Andhra lands, and these Ceded Districts formed part of the Madras presidency. There were several revolts by local landed magnates, the zamindars, in the early years of the 19th century, and even in 1846 there was a significant rebellion led by Koilkuntla Narasimha Reddy. However, during the so-called Indian Mutiny or Great Revolt of 1857, southern India was relatively quiet, although there was some trouble in the Ceded Districts and in Hyderabad.

With the dissolution of the East India Company and the assumption of direct sovereignty of British possessions in the subcontinent by the Crown in 1858, the formal establishment of an Empire helped provoke a climate ready to ripen into a political awakening in the Andhra region. The social reform movement and the rise of Telugu journalism prepared for the fillip given to the independence movement by the foundation of the Indian National Congress in 1885. It was the rise of the Vandemataram and Swadeshi movements that really stimulated political awareness in the Andhra lands of the Madras presidency, with students particularly impressed by the 1907 tour of Bipin Chandra Pal. From 1913 an annual Andhra Mahasabha Conference pressed for the creation of a separate Andhra state and, in 1918, an Andhra Congress Circle was formed. Despite some British concessions to reform after the First World War, popular sentiments remained dissatisfied and the non-co-operation movement continued to gain support. Notable figures in the national-independence struggle from the Andhra region were Duggirala Gopalakrishnayya, Alluri Sitarama Raju and Tanguturi Prakasam (who was later a state premier). The civil disobedience movement led by Mahatma Gandhi enjoyed rising support in the Andhra territories, but, upon the achievement of Indian independence in 1947, local demands for an Andhra state were not met.

In the Dominions of the Nizam, meanwhile, Andhran consciousness only really began with the foundation of the Andhra Jana Sangh in 1921, which encouraged the formation of Telugu-language schools, publications and libraries. In 1931 the Andhra Jana Sangh became the Andhra Mahasabha, led by Suruvaram Prathapa Reddy. The real expression of Andhran aspirations in Telangana, the Telugu-speaking districts of Hyderabad, only became effective with the creation of the Hyderabad State Congress in 1938 (inspired by Swamy Ramananda Tirtha). In the same year students at Osmania University agitated against the ban on the Vandemataram in the nizamate, although the Muslim authorities therefore became increasingly suspicious of the Andhran movement. Moreover, the Government of the principality was automatically opposed to the leftist orientation of the Andhra Mahasabha from 1941. Indeed, in 1946, under its leader, Ravi Narayana Reddy, it launched an anti-feudal armed struggle usually known as the Telangana Movement, which, in turn, provoked activity by the 'Razakars', the paramilitary wing of the Ittehadul Muslimeen party. It was against this disturbed background that the surrounding territories of British India became independent in 1947. International pressure meant that the Nizam had been given time to consider the future of his Dominions, a decision that was complicated by the distance of Hyderabad from other Muslim territories and the fact that the majority of his subjects were Hindu. The national Government of India resolved the dilemma forcibly in the following year and sent troops into Hyderabad. The Nizam's forces surrendered on 17 September 1948 and Gen. J. N. Chaudhary, in command of the 'police action' in the former principality, became the military governor for the new state of the Union. An eminent Telugu leader, Burgula Ramakrishna Rao, became the Chief Minister of Hyderabad state after elections in 1952.

The movement for language-based states was still gathering momentum, however. Potti Sreeramulu, an Andhran living in Madras (now Chennai, in Tamil Nadu), had died while fasting ('hunger strike') in support of a distinct state for Telugu speakers. Finally, the central authorities conceded the separation of what was essentially the old Ceded Territories and Northern Circars from the Madras presidency—Andhra state came into existence on 1 October 1953, with its capital at Kurnool and Prakasam as Chief Minister. Soon after, however, a commission investigating the reorganization of the states of the Union recommended the three-way division of Hyderabad on the basis of language. Thus, Telangana, the Telugu-speaking districts of the old nizamate, was added into a greater Andhra (Visalandhra) and the State of Andhra Pradesh came into existence on 1 November 1956, with N. Sanjeeva Reddy of the Congress Party as Chief Minister.

The old political class of the original Andhra dominated the new state, although its capital was Hyderabad, and the integration of the two main Telugu-speaking regions into one entity was not effortless. There were two serious political agitations. The first was in 1969, when it was felt in Telangana that the Andhran leaders had betrayed the understanding that had formed the state. This separatist movement was led by Dr Marri Chenna Reddy of the Praja Samithi. The Jai Andhra movement, provoked by the issue of Mulki rules, was the second serious disturbance, in 1972. However, many political forces were committed to the unity of the new state and the Communist Party of India organized rallies against separatism in both Andhra and Telangana. More importantly, the election of Chenna Reddy as the state Congress leader and his becoming Chief Minister in 1978 calmed the political debate. Later developments revealed the strength of Telugu-language identity, as opposed to regional loyalties—in 1983 a new party, Telugu Desam, founded by N. T. Rama Rao less than one year previously, ended Congress rule in Andhra Pradesh.

A change in the leadership of the Telugu Desam in 1995 meant a former Congress minister in the state government, the son-in-law of Rama Rao and General-Secretary of the Telugu Desam since 1985, N. Chandrababu Naidu, became Chief Minister. He ousted his father-in-law after harnessing party discontent with the unelected influence of Rama Rao's second wife, Lakshmi Parvathi. The Naidu faction of Telugu Desam received an overwhelming popular mandate in the state elections of 5 October 1999, winning almost two-thirds of the seats in the state legislature. The Naidu administration had reformist credentials and was widely credited with encouraging bureaucratic, economic and fiscal modernization. The Chief Minister was personally connected with the state Government's encouragement of the new-technology sector, particularly focused in Hyderabad. In April 2003 Naidu became Andhra Pradesh's longest-serving chief minister. However, even for an efficient and reformist administration, poverty remained a considerable challenge, particularly in the countryside, and this contributed to the continuation of some extremist violence, mainly in the north-east, by the Naxalite movement, notably the People's War Group (PWG), originally a faction of the Communist Party of India (Marxist-Leninist) or CPI (ML).

In national politics the ruling Telugu Desam of Andhra Pradesh was a coalition partner of the Government led by the Bharatiya Janata Party (BJP), although, as a secular party, Telugu Desam was noticeable in maintaining some detachment from some of the policies and statements of the Union Government. Although the Government of Andhra Pradesh condemned the explosion of a bomb near a Hindu temple in Hyderabad in December 2002, for instance, it discouraged the presence of Hindu-chauvinist activists in the state thereafter. In the formal, electoral National Democratic Alliance formed for the 1999 general election, the Telugu Desam had been the second largest party after the BJP, winning 28 Lok Sabha seats (Telugu Desam was also the largest regional party represented in the Rajya Sabha, with 13 seats). Andhra Pradesh sends 42 members in total to the Lok Sabha, the lower house of the national parliament, and 18 to the Rajya Sabha.

Naidu experienced some opposition from his younger brother, Ramamurthy Naidu, who, in January 2003, was reported to be interested in leading a movement in favour of a separate Rayalseema state. However, the main separatist group was now the Telangana Rashtriya Samiti (TRS), which had been founded in 2001 by K. Chandrasekhar Rao, a Telugu Desam kingmaker and erstwhile ally of Naidu, who left the Government in pursuit of the campaign for a separate state of Telangana. In anticipation of the state elections, the TRS came to an electoral accommodation with Congress, led by Dr Yedugoori Sandinti Rajasekhar Reddy (popularly known as 'YSR'). The main thrust of their criticism of the Government was its neglect of the countryside, where the pressures of drought and debt had given Andhra Pradesh an unenviably high suicide rate (three-quarters of India's farmer suicides were reckoned to take place in the state in the early 2000s). The failure of the rural economy to develop in parallel with the new urban wealth also fuelled the

Naxalite insurgency, which actually attempted to assassinate the Chief Minister himself on 1 October 2003, by remotely triggering land-mines as his convoy was en route to Tirupati. Naidu and the Telugu Desam had incurred the particular enmity of the PWG by their response to the Naxalite threat, with police actions allegedly continuing against the insurgents even during talks convened between the Government and the rebels in mid-2003. Prompted by the likelihood of a sympathy vote after his narrow escape from a terrorist assault, Naidu asked for the Legislative Assembly to be dissolved in November. However, he underestimated the scale of rural discontent, as well as how long it would be before the election authorities would allow a poll, and the voting eventually took place in conjunction with the general election, in May 2004.

In 2004 the Telugu Desam suffered its worst electoral performance since its foundation, retaining only 47 of the 294 elected seats in the Andhra Pradesh legislature and five of the state's 42 seats in the Lok Sabha. Later elections to some of the Rajya Sabha seats reduced Telugu Desam representation there to nine. Nationally, anti-incumbency sentiments and rural discontent also displaced the BJP-led coalition (the BJP gained only two Assembly seats in the state). The opposition alliance (Congress, the TRS and two communist parties) in Andhra Pradesh won 226 of the Assembly seats and, although Congress alone had an absolute majority, the state's first coalition Government was formed instead. On 14 May Dr Rajasekhar Reddy was sworn in as Chief Minister, and in June the TRS formally became part of the Government, when six new ministers were appointed (two TRS members had earlier joined the national coalition Government). The new state premier, a Christian, was a veteran Congress politician, having first tried to become Chief Minister in 1985. He had then served in the Lok Sabha for a decade, until returning to his home state to head a Congress revival in 1999 (when the party won 91 seats, from a low of 26 in 1994). His active campaigning against what he described as the 'anti-people' policies of the previous administration had made him the most popular Congress politician state-wide, so he gained the premiership. The new Government soon sought to implement its promises to the disadvantaged: farmers were given free power (against the wishes of the national Government and of the World Bank); in June a cease-fire with the Naxalites was achieved and negotiating teams to treat between the Government and the PWG were appointed (a ban on People's War was lifted in July); and a 5% public-jobs quota was promised to the state's Muslims. On the issue of a separate Telangana state, Telugu Desam remained strongly against the aspirations of the TRS, and Congress and Muslim politicians carefully neutral. However, the Congress partners on the left (both locally and nationally) were strongly opposed to further disintegration of the federal units, which could create problems for the ruling coalitions. The PWG supported a separate Telangana, but its ultimate agenda was the creation of a greater 'Dandakaranya', a state formed from tribal-dominated areas of six other states and consisting of 100m. people.

If Telangana were to be made a separate state, it would consist of 10 districts comprising 42% of the total area of Andhra Pradesh and 40% of the population, including Hyderabad (although some suggested that the city might be a joint capital, like Chandigarh, and federally administered). The separation of Telangana was also likely to trigger separatist demands in Rayalseema. K. C. Rao and the TRS had promised resolution of the Telangana statehood issue by the December after the elections, but soon conceded that a decision might not be reached until one year later. With Congress effectively stalling negotiations by saying that any decision would have to be taken in the context of a second States Reorganization Committee, and no sign of one being appointed, the TRS had begun to agitate by November 2004. At the end of the month Congress established a panel to examine the issue, although the TRS maintained the pressure through December and into 2005. However, in early July five TRS ministers resigned from the state Government, the sixth and last one also resigning within two weeks (his delay was prompted by a demand that Rao and his TRS colleague in the Union Government should also resign). Such events provoked tensions not only between the TRS and its Congress ally in the national Government, but also within the TRS, which suffered splits in 2005. Certainly the party did not perform well in the local elections, in September, at which Congress recorded strong gains. Those results probably emboldened Chief Minister Reddy in his belief that additional development funds for the largely poor Telangana area would placate separatist opinion. Cross-party support for Telangana statehood remained rhetorical, and TRS frustration with this was increasingly evident. The separatist party had also incurred much criticism in September for forming a militant wing, Telangana Jagarana Sena, which some feared implied the threat of political violence. In August 2006 the TRS ratcheted up the political pressure, with the resignation of its two ministers, including party leader Rao, from the Union cabinet and the staging of a number of disruptions of proceedings in the national and state legislatures. One month later the TRS withdrew its support from the ruling coalition at the Centre, while Rao had resigned his parliamentary seat, claiming that the by-election would be a referendum on the Telangana issue, which Congress had betrayed. Such agitations certainly raised the immediacy of the issue and also provoked divisions within Congress. When Rao was re-elected with a record majority in December, discussion of a separate state of Telangana was firmly back on the political agenda. Later that month all nine ministers from Telangana and 36 of the 42 state Congress deputies elected from there petitioned the Chief Minister to lobby the Centre for a second States Reorganization Committee and, in January 2007, Reddy agreed that a commission should be set up to investigate the demand.

The Naxalites enjoyed strong support among the poor rural communities of Telangana, and were able to appear there more openly from the second half of 2004. The new cease-fire had been followed in late July by the Andhra Pradesh Government not renewing the ban on the PWG (in force for all but a year in the mid-1990s since May 1992), resulting in a large Naxalite rally in Hyderabad at the end of September. Although the Government sent representatives to the inter-state summit on the Naxalite problem in that month, it also offered negotiations to the Maoist movement. The first direct talks began on 15 October, in Hyderabad, just before the commencement of which two of the attending factions announced their merger in the previous month-the PWG and the Maoist Communist Centre of India (itself the result of a merger) united into the Communist Party of India (Maoist), with A. H. Ramakrishna as secretary. This new CPI—M was joined in the negotiations by the CPI—ML (Janasakthi), although they conceded that they too might unite, which was indicative of the growing co-operation between the Maoist groups throughout South Asia. There were rumours that an international association of insurgents was attempting to form a 'revolutionary corridor' from Nepal down to Andhra Pradesh. Arguably the respite from government offensives against them was the chief benefit to the Naxalites of the cease-fire and negotiations, although they, for their part, accused the Government of bad faith and continued actions against them. Certainly there were violent clashes in January 2005, reinforcing official demands that Naxalite disarmament was a prerequisite of peace, but the progress towards negotiations limped on, despite escalating violence in March and into April. However, on 4 April the Maoist groups declared the peace process at an end. Meanwhile, the Government had engaged in a process of land reform (the main subject of the October round of negotiations with the Naxalites), distributing some 40,000 ha of land to impoverished farmers in January. There had also been other initiatives to encourage development in the Naxalite heartlands. The second phase of the land programme took place in August 2005, just after the ban on the CPI—M and seven 'front' organizations had been reimposed. The immediate cause of the ban's reintroduction was the murder of a Congress legislator and eight others at Independence Day celebrations near Hyderabad. Although the authorities achieved a number of successes against the Naxalites and the number of incidents was lower, violence continued and the ban was extended for a further year in 2006, 2007 and 2008.

In April 2005 the alliance between the Telugu Desam and the BJP seemed to be over, in opposition, as the secular regional party objected to the latter's increased emphasis of the *Hindutva* ideology (relations had been uneasy since the previous August). The Telugu Desam was again encouraging its traditional (until 1998) links with the left-wing parties, which also opposed the separation of Telangana and the Congress desire to revive the Legislative Council or upper house of the legislature. However, there were also stirrings of discontent within the Telugu Desam, with a number of members expressing discontent with Naidu's style of leadership, increasingly so after the disappointment of the September local elections (a prominent critic was expelled from the party in late 2005). In late 2005 and early 2006 the opposition parties favoured disruption in the Assembly in order to make their point about allegations of corruption, police brutality, rural poverty and other issues, although there remained points of agreement with Congress. Most parties were united in their alarm at the fear of extremist-Muslim terrorism spreading to southern India after the deadly incident at an educational institute in neighbouring Karnataka in December 2005 (however, in May 2007 there was also a fatal bomb explosion at a mosque in Hyderabad, followed by twin blasts in August that killed 40 people). These concerns gave added piquancy to the issue of the judicial quashing of the Government's proposed Muslim reservation and the visit of the US President, George W. Bush, to Hyderabad in March 2006. With a major Congress leadership summit in the state earlier in the year, as well as an important international Buddhist meeting attended by the Dalai Lama, security was a major concern in early 2006. The failure to address rural poverty, which had contributed to Telugu Desam's eviction from power, was forcing itself further on to the political agenda as it was recognized as a root of both Naxalite violence and the radicalization of some young Muslims.

Chief Minister Reddy was widely considered to be in favour of action against poverty and was commended for his social governance policies, although the opposition parties were keen to counter his popularity by seizing on issues that would damage his reputation. Thus, there was considerable disruption in the Legislative Assembly when he and his family handed land considered surplus under state ownership-limitation legislation over to the authorities in December (the opposition protested that he had clearly been breaking the law prior to that); extended protests by deputies ensued when Reddy allegedly made personally insulting remarks about the opposition leader, Naidu, in the Assembly in July 2007. From April 2007 such protests could also be made in a second chamber of the state legislature, with the inauguration of a revived Legislative Council (abolished in 1985). Indirect elections the previous month had returned a Congress majority, although the filling of almost 30% of the seats was delayed by electoral inquiries.

The Congress Government announced its response to the August 2007 bomb attacks in Hyderabad in October, pledging 30% more police over five years and a dedicated anti-terrorist unit. The authorities also remained active against the Naxalites into 2008, while still holding out the possibility of negotiations. Relations between the Chief Minister and Telugu Desam leader Naidu remained acrimonious, as evidenced by an exchange of accusations of corruption in December 2007 or by the debate on the Telugu Desam no-confidence motion (which was defeated on 3 April 2008). Congress was also challenged by an escalation of the Telangana issue in 2008, with the TRS wanting a decision by March and the Chief Minister urging restraint, because of the complexity of the issues to be decided and their ramifications (such as borders, the question of further bifurcations and security in smaller states). On 3 March the four TRS members of the Lok Sabha resigned their seats in support of Telangana statehood, with the state deputies following suit the next day (16 from the Assembly and three from the Legislative Council). The ensuing by-elections, however, proved to be disastrous for the TRS, which lost over half its seats when the results of the 29 May poll were announced: two Lok Sabha seats went to Congress and Telugu Desam; and nine Assembly ones were taken, five by Congress and four by Telugu Desam (Congress and Telugu Desam each retained the other two seats being contested in addition to the TRS ones). K. C. Rao, who had only retained his Lok Sabha seat with a narrower majority, offered his resignation, but ended up remaining as TRS leader.

The shock to the aspirations for Telangana statehood in the defeat of the TRS was partly assuaged by the outcome of Telangana activism within the Telugu Desam. Internal dissatisfaction about Telugu Desam's opposition to Telangana statehood mounted throughout June, culminating in the departure of Tulla Devender Goud and his supporters, who eschewed a link with the TRS and set up a new movement in July, the Nava Telangana Praja Party. Telugu Desam also had to endure other defections in July and August, as members left for Congress or the new political party of the prominent film actor, Chiranjeevi. There had been credible rumours of Chiranjeevi entering politics since December 2007, with people joining his cause openly since May 2008. The former actor only announced his ambitions and a new party in mid-August.

## ECONOMY

Andhra Pradesh is a relatively prosperous state, with a productive agricultural sector and one of the leading information-technology and software centres of India clustered in and around Hyderabad (earning itself the name of 'Cyberabad'). However, drought has beleaguered agriculture in most years since 1997, severely affecting over two-thirds of the population. Estimates of state income (net domestic product), in current prices, for 1997/98 amounted to Rs 787,050m. (old series), of which the primary sector contributed 32.5%, industry 22.3% and services 45.3%. Per caput income was put at Rs 10,590. In real terms, the net domestic product had actually contracted in that year, for the first time since the recession of the early 1990s, but robust annual growth resumed thereafter. By 2004/05 the net domestic product was put at Rs 1,831,230m. (new series), in current prices, making it the fourth largest state economy in India. This was equivalent to Rs 23,153 per head (the poorest of the southern states, but 13th among all the states). Hyderabad and Visakhapatnam are the principal industrial centres, with the latter being one of India's main ports. Transport infrastructure is well developed in the state, which has some 5,055 km of railway routes and almost 195,000 km of road (2001 figures—2% of which are national highways, 4% state highways and 18% major district roads), although inland Telangana and, particularly, Rayalseema complain of lacking a fair share of investment. Installed electricity capacity in Andhra Pradesh at the end of May 2006 totalled some 11,325 MW (61% from the state sector, 22% from the Centre and the rest from the private sector). In March of the same year only 21 villages were identified as being without an electricity supply, but only 38% of rural households had electricity. The 2001 census recorded a significant increase in the literacy rate since the previous census (61.1%, compared with 44.1% in 1991), which could have been the result of the fall in the population's rate of growth, enabling investment in education to have some effect.

Agriculture contributed 24.2% of the state's gross domestic product in 2001/02. The sector remained the principal economic activity of almost 70% of the population into the beginning of the 21st century. Government plans to reduce this proportion to 40% by 2020, by encouraging large-scale farming and the use of genetically modified crops, were the cause of some controversy in the early 2000s. The activity was supported by good rainfall on the fertile coast and extensive irrigation further inland, as well as good educational and research facilities. However, all but two of the years between 1997 and 2004 were severely affected by drought, particularly in Rayalseema. Meanwhile, Andhra Pradesh remained one of India's principal producers of rice, which usually accounted for about one-half of the state's total foodgrain production, which was a record 16.0m. metric tons in 2000/01. In the following year this figure fell slightly, to 14.8m. tons, of which rice accounted for 11.4m. tons (12% of national production), coarse cereals 2.3m. tons and pulses 1.1m. tons. In 2002/03 the total foodgrain harvest fell to 10.5m. tons, which was 6.0% of the all-India production and put Andhra Pradesh fifth among the states. Other important cash crops included sugar cane (a record 18.5m. tons in 1999/2000), groundnuts (1.1m. tons), cotton (1.6m. tons), tobacco (193,000 tons) and chillies (496,000 tons—the presence of this crop has famously encouraged its use in Andhran cooking). Except for the last two, production of all these crops was estimated to have risen in 2000/01, while in the following year there were 17.6m. tons of sugar cane, 1.6m. tons of oilseeds (including groundnuts) and 1.9m. tons of cotton, as well as 667,000 tons of jute and mesta. Livestock was also important, particularly poultry, and the state was India's largest producer of eggs, with anticipated production of 16,742m. in 2003/04, following 14,862m. in the previous year, which was equivalent to 37% of the all-India total. Andhra Pradesh was an important milk producer (6.6m. tons in 2002/03), ranking fourth among the states, and also produced wool (3,731 tons). In 1997/98 23.2% of Andhra Pradesh was covered in forest and woodland. The other primary-sector activity of economic significance was mining. The state possesses the largest deposits of chrysolite asbestos in India and accounts for 93% of barytes production in the country. The Government reckons Andhra Pradesh to be the second most mineral-rich state in India, and is encouraging exploration and exploitation. Certainly, in 2002/03 the sector produced minerals worth more than Rs 55,476m., that year more than any other state in India (8.7% of the all-India total), although it only employed about 764,000 people in the previous year, which was fewer than in Tamil Nadu and Maharashtra. Forty-two industrial minerals are currently mined, including barytes, copper ore, manganese, mica, coal, bauxite, limestone, quartz and beach sands.

Major industrial sectors in Andhra Pradesh include machine tools, synthetic drugs and pharmaceuticals, heavy electrical machinery, shipbuilding, fertilizers and chemicals, electronic equipment, construction materials, glass and watches. Manufacturing is encouraged by the availability of power (the state has the third largest installed capacity in the country—7,330 MW generated in 2000) and good transport connections to the rest of India and to the outside world. Government incentives and the rise of high-technology industries, particularly in Hyderabad, fuelled the sector from the 1990s. In 2000 it was estimated that between one-fifth and one-quarter of India's software professionals were from Andhra Pradesh. In 1999 there were 2,539 large and medium-sized industries in the state, providing employment for 0.74m. people and 132,504 small enterprises employing 1.16m. people. Only two years later there were 3,208 large and medium-sized industries and 142,950 small enterprises.

The services sector has also benefited from Hyderabad's pre-eminent position in the information-technology sector, but, traditionally, the leading activity is tourism. The state has a rich and varied cultural legacy, as well as a diverse landscape. Hyderabad and nearby Golconda are rich in tourist sites, while other ancient capitals such as Warangal and Rajahmundry also attract visitors. Andhra Pradesh is rich in temples, which attract pilgrims as well as tourists, notably at Ramappa, Vemulavada, Bhadrachalam, Amaravati, Srisailam, Tirupati and Tirumala, and Simhachalam. For domestic tourists, Andhra Pradesh is the second most popular state (Uttar Pradesh is first), receiving 22.3% of all such visits in 2002.

## DIRECTORY

**Governor:** N. D. TIWARI, Office of the Governor, Raj Bhavan Rd, Hyderabad; tel. (40) 23310521; fax (40) 23312650; e-mail governor@ap.nic.in.

**Chief Minister:** Dr Y. S. RAJASEKHARA REDDY (Congress), Office of the Chief Minister, Government of Andhra Pradesh, C-Block, 4th Floor, AP Secretariat, Hyderabad; tel. (40) 23456698; fax (40) 23546886; e-mail cmap@ap.nic.in.

**Speaker of the Legislative Assembly:** K. R. SURESH REDDY, Vidhan Sabha, Hyderabad; tel. (40) 23232377; fax (40) 23210408; e-mail apla@ap.nic.in; the unicameral Legislative Assembly has 295 mems (incl. one appointed mem.): Congress 186; Telugu Desam 44; Telangana Rashtriya Samithi 26; Communist (CPI—Marxist) 9; Communist Party of India 6; All-India Majlis-e-Ittehadul Muslimeen 5; Bharatiya Janata Party 2; Bahujan Samaj Party 1; Samata Party 1; independents and others 13, vacant 1.

**Chairman of the Legislative Council:** A. CHAKRAPANI, Hyderabad; the upper house of the state legislature, which was abolished in 1985 and revived in April 2007, has 90 mems (3 vacant in July 2007): Congress 38; Telugu Desam 13; Telangana Rashtriya Samithi 3; Communist Party of India 2; Communist (CPI—Marxist) 1; All-India Majlis-e-Ittehadul Muslimeen 1; independents 17, nominated 12.

**State Resident Commissioner in New Delhi:** C. VISWANATH, Andhra Pradesh Bhavan, 1 Ashoka Rd, New Delhi 110 001; tel. (11) 23387089; fax (11) 23388175; e-mail apbnd@del2.vsnl.net.in.

# Arunachal Pradesh

The State of Arunachal Pradesh is the easternmost part of India—hence its name, the 'land of the rising sun'. A mountainous territory, only properly brought under formal administration since independence, its former name was also descriptive—the North-East Frontier Agency (NEFA). It, thus, has international borders with Bhutan in the west, the People's Republic of China in the north (the Autonomous Region of Tibet or Xizang) and Myanmar (formerly Burma) in the east and south-east. The bulk of the state's territory lies to the north of Assam (Asom), of which it formed a part until 1972, but it curves around the upper, eastern arm of that state, which stretches up the valley of the Brahmaputra, to include some territory extending south of Assam and ending in a short western border with Nagaland. The NEFA became a Union Territory in 1972 and was renamed Arunachal Pradesh, becoming the 24th state of the Union on 20 February 1987. It has an area of 83,743 sq km (32,346 sq miles), making it the largest state in the north-eastern region of India, but it is the least densely populated in the country (see below).

Lying on the south-eastern flank of the Himalayas, most of Arunachal Pradesh is mountainous, consisting of high ridges, variously aligned, separating deep valleys. It rises to the north, culminating in the crests of the Great Himalaya (this constitutes the so-called 'McMahon Line', originally proposed in the 1910s, and is recognized by the Indian Government as the northern international border, but has long been disputed by China). The highest point is the peak of Kangto (7,102 m—23,301 ft), in the west of that Chinese border. The state's main rivers are the Brahmaputra, known as the Siang in Arunachal Pradesh (or the Tsangpo higher up its course, in Tibet), and its tributaries, such as the Tirap, the Lohit (Zayü Qu), the Subansiri, the Kameng and the Bhareli. Although the heights are barren and snow-bound, there is extensive forest cover and the valleys are fertile. The climate of the foothills is subtropical, but temperatures fall rapidly with rising altitude, and this contributes to a great variety in types of flora and fauna (including the Arunachal macaque, a primate species 'discovered' only in 2004). Rainfall, although year-round, is varied: valleys opening out to the Assam plain can receive 4,000 mm (157 inches) per year; but more sheltered valleys might only receive 2,000 mm.

According to the census of March 2001, the total population of Arunachal Pradesh was 1,097,968, compared with 864,558 in the 1991 census. The population density in 2001, therefore, was 13 per sq km, the lowest of any state or territory in India. Most of the population of Arunachal Pradesh consists of tribal peoples (in 2001 64% were included among the Scheduled Tribes), related to the Tibetans and the peoples of Myanmar. There are 82 tribes and sub-tribes, of which the main ones in the west are the Nissi (Nishi or Dafla), Sulung, Sherdukpen, Aka, Monpa, Apa Tani and Hill Miri. The largest tribal group is that of the Adi, who occupy the central part of Arunachal Pradesh, while the Mishmi dominate the north-eastern hill country and the Wancho, Nocte and Tangsa are centred in the south-east of the state, around the district of Tirap (which neighbours Nagaland). Between them, the tribal peoples speak over 50 distinct languages and dialects (mostly of the Tibeto-Burmese branch of the Sino-Tibetan language family), making English (the official language of the state), Hindi, Bengali and Assamese the main means of inter-communication. Although influenced by Buddhism, most of the tribal peoples are animists, venerating natural and elemental deities or spirits and often practising ritual animal sacrifices (notably of the mithun, a semi-domesticated gaur or wild ox). Near the Chinese border some adhere to Tibetan Buddhism, while in the south-east Hinayana Buddhism, as practised in much of South-East Asia, is more common (in 2001 some 13% of the state population avowed Buddhism). Hindu beliefs have been adopted by about 35% of the population, while a slightly lower proportion still practises traditional beliefs (31%, also according to the 2001 census), especially near the Assam lowlands. Christianity (19% in 2001, up from 10% in 1991) is a more recent arrival, its growth originally limited among the tribes (relative to those in Nagaland, for instance) by long-standing restrictions on the entry of missionaries to the area.

Most of the population is rural, and towns of any size are few (only 20.8% of the population were described by the 2001 census as urban, although this represented a significant increase on the 12.8% recorded at the 1991 census). The state capital is Itanagar (Yupia), in the west, near the southern border with Assam. Some of the administrative offices and the legislature are based in Naharlagun, some 10 km (6 miles) from the capital. The main town in the east is Tezu. The state is divided into 16 districts.

## HISTORY

The earliest Sanskrit writings make mention of the area now known as Arunachal Pradesh, but otherwise its early history and the origins of the various native tribes exist only as oral tradition and myth. The extent and nature of a number of archaeological remains, most dating from around the beginning of the Christian era, indicate that Arunachal Pradesh was not completely isolated and the inhabitants had close relations with the rest of the subcontinent and other neighbouring peoples. The society was politically and culturally developed, but much of the terrain is inhospitable and, while the larger powers in India, Burma (Myanmar) and China have long disputed the region, none had seriously considered enforcing these claims. Historical references and archaeological investigations have pieced together isolated fragments about the region—thus, the ruins near the modern capital of Itanagar have been identified with Mayapur, the seat of the 11th-century Jiti dynasty. Reliable records about the area appear only from the 16th century, when the Ahom kings of Assam (Asom) annexed part of the territory. They exercised a tentative sovereignty until dissension among the royalty of the kingdom made them vulnerable to Burmese occupations by the beginning of the 19th century. The British then intervened, however, and by the Treaty of Yandaboo of February 1826 Assam (at least nominally including Arunachal Pradesh) was ceded to the British in India.

The British, now administering India as a direct possession of the Crown, did not try to bring this north-eastern fringe of their Empire properly under their authority until the 1880s, although free movement in the region had been stopped (it remains a restricted area). The first attempts to establish a firm claim to the northern part of the territory, essentially the southern flanks of the Great Himalaya, led to a border dispute with the Chinese Empire. This was exacerbated when the authorities in British India included the disputed area in the North-Eastern Frontier Tract (NEFT—the area of modern Arunachal Pradesh), which they made into an administrative district of the province of Assam. Although later that same year Tibet declared its independence, in 1913 the Chinese rejected the proposed 'McMahon Line' (settling the boundary along the crests of the Great Himalaya). Nevertheless, it became the de facto international frontier, even when the Chinese restated their claims to much of the northern NEFT after Indian independence in 1947—the claim only became a dangerous issue when Chinese rule was re-established in Tibet during the 1950s (China also had disputes over other parts of the Indian border, notably in Kashmir). Meanwhile, in 1954 the NEFT became the North-East Frontier Agency (NEFA), still constitutionally part of Assam state, but, because of its strategic significance, administered by the national Ministry of External Affairs. In 1957 the Tuensang Frontier Division was separated from the NEFA and joined in administrative union with the Naga Hills District of Assam (together they now form Nagaland).

On 26 August 1959 troops of the People's Republic of China crossed the McMahon Line and captured a nearby Indian outpost at Longju, which remained occupied until 1961. In October 1962 the Chinese military again crossed the line, but this time in force. Their first move was into the west of the NEFA, near the border with Bhutan, with a strike towards the Tanghla ridge and Tawang, but they widened the conflict along the length of the country's northern border. The dispute demonstrated the weakness of the Indian army. Only in 1963 did China agree to withdraw its forces to the environs of the McMahon Line and to return Indian prisoners of war, but the six border crossings remained closed. The Indian Government was prompted to reinforce its symbolic claims to the NEFA and, in 1965, transferred responsibility for its administration to the Ministry of Home Affairs, through the Governor of Assam. In 1972 the NEFA was separated from Assam and became a Union Territory under the name Arunachal Pradesh. Finally, in 1981 relations between India and the People's Republic of China improved sufficiently for them to agree to find an early solution to their border disputes. However, the accession of Arunachal Pradesh to full statehood in the Indian Union in 1987 provoked formal Chinese protests, and both sides accused the other of troop movements along the border. Joint working groups on border disputes and on trade were established in 1989, and in 1991 progress was made in improving relations, with the official visit to India by the Chinese premier and agreement on reopening some border posts. Military liaison also improved the situation in the region. The following year, in July, bilateral border trade resumed and Sino-Indian contacts increased thereafter. By 1995 tensions had eased sufficiently for the state to be opened to tourists; however, foreigners are still only able to travel there with a Restricted Areas Permit from the federal Ministry of Home Affairs. In April 2005 the Union Government dismissed the significance of remarks by the Chinese ambassador to the effect that Arunachal Pradesh remained a disputed territory. The situation along the border remained tranquil and at the end of May 2006 Chinese and Indian soldiers and their families met at a village in Tawang district as part of confidence-building measures along the Sino-Indian border. However, in November 2006 there was some diplomatic tension when the Chinese ambassador to India reiterated his country's claim to the whole of Arunachal Pradesh; in the following month he caused political ructions within India by stating that the negotiations on the border, ongoing since 2003, included discussion of the status of certain areas. The federal Government repeated at such times, and again in 2007, that all of Arunachal Pradesh was an integral part of India. Later that year there were allegations made in Parliament that Chinese troops had violated the so-called Line of Actual Control, but they were denied by the Government. Promises by the Prime Minister of development aid to the state early in 2008 seemed to be motivated partly by the Indian military's awareness that access and infrastructure were far more advanced on the Chinese side of the border.

A provisional legislature of the territory first met in August 1975, already dominated by Congress. In January 1980 Gegong Apang became Chief Minister, and he was to hold office for 19 years, in four Assemblies, becoming one of the longest-serving premiers in India. In 1996 he had left Congress, after disagreements with the national leadership, and formed the Arunachal Congress. However, Mukut Mithi formed a group of legislators that displaced Apang from office in January 1999 (Mithi's Congress—M eventually rejoined the mainstream Congress), and this result was confirmed by the election results of October 1999, when Congress was returned to power with 53 seats. Eventually the Mithi Government commanded the support of all 60 members of the Legislative Assembly apart from the lone voice of the Arunachal Congress (Apang). Mithi seemed firmly in control, despite some reports of dissatisfaction with his performance by the national Congress leadership, but the political situation in the state was revolutionized by developments in July–August 2003. On 27 July Apang formed a United Democratic Front with 38 defectors from Congress (including most of Mithi's ministers and the Speaker) and the Governor asked Mithi to seek the confidence of the Assembly by 2 August. Mithi alleged the connivance of the Centre, where the federal Government was led by the Bharatiya Janata Party (BJP), and of the Naga separatists in the plot against his administration. He claimed it was the result of his opposition to the loss of border areas in Tirap and Changlang to a proposed 'Greater Nagaland'. Nevertheless, Mithi had to concede defeat, and Apang returned to the premiership on 3 August. His Deputy Chief Minister was Kameng Dolo, the leader of the new Congress (D) grouping. However, further developments took place within weeks, when the BJP accepted the applications for membership of Apang of the Arunachal Congress, all the Congress (D) legislators and three others. The BJP, therefore, at the end of August finally found itself in charge of its first north-eastern state.

The parliamentary representatives of the state remained loyal to Congress—Arunachal Pradesh sends one member to the upper house of the national parliament and two members to the Lok Sabha or lower house. However, in the general election of May 2004 the BJP won both the Lok Sabha seats, only to find itself under pressure from further factionalism in the Legislative Assembly. A new national constitutional limit on the size of state cabinets saw the Government reduced from 33 members to 12, provoking the defection of nine deputies to the Mithi Congress faction in early July. As others also began to express their support for Congress (which now led the national Government), the Legislative Assembly of Arunachal Pradesh was dissolved on 7 July. Less than one week later 13 deputies were reported to be joining Congress and, in late August, Chief Minister Apang led his cabinet back into that party.

The state legislative elections were held on 7 October 2004, with three of the 60 Assembly members elected unopposed and a low turnout in the other constituencies. Congress won 34 seats and Apang was returned as Chief Minister, because the national party leadership favoured him over Mithi, as did groups among the opposition—the next largest grouping in the legislature was that of the 13 independents, most of them rebel Congress politicians. The BJP managed to win its first seats at an election, with nine deputies returned. The Nationalist Congress Party and the Arunachal Congress each won two seats. Within two years the political scene had changed dramatically. Apang was accused by his cabinet of an authoritarian style, and there was significant support among some legislative deputies for the complaints made to the Centre about his leadership. At a meeting on 9 April 2007 only five Congress legislators supported Apang; he resigned and himself nominated the rebels' favoured successor, the former power minister Dorjee Khandu, to replace him. Khandu duly became Chief Minister. A Buddhist Monpa from the disputed Tawang district, the new Chief Minister was, only one month later, denying rumours of a Chinese incursion into Indian territory. Four weeks after that, in early June, Khandu welcomed eight of the nine BJP deputies into Congress, giving him the support of 41 in the 60-seat Assembly. The following year the Government had to deal with pro-Tibetan agitation in the approach to the Beijing Olympics in the People's Republic of China, against a background of reported incursions by Chinese troops across the border. The authorities at both national and state levels denied any border tensions and, while maintaining sympathy for the human rights situation in Tibet, forbade public demonstrations against the Chinese in Arunachal Pradesh. In May the Buddhist Chief Minister formally invited the Dalai Lama, the Tibetan religious leader exiled in India, to open a hospital in Tawang, but denied that it was a provocative move. The Chief Minister continued to forbid public rallies about the status of Tibet.

## ECONOMY

Arunachal Pradesh is not a prosperous state, although its natural resources give it some potential, and central government traditionally provides a significant subsidy. In 2001/02 the net domestic product was put at Rs 16,280m., giving a per head income of Rs 14,771, at current prices. There was consistent real growth from the 1980s, until the economy faltered in 1994/95; it contracted in 1996/97 and, slightly, in 1998/99, before growth of 11.9% in the following year. Real growth contracted in 2001/02, before recovering strongly. In 2004/05 the current net domestic product reached Rs 22,660m. (one of the smallest economies in India) or Rs 19,724 per head. Industry is sufficiently small-scale to deny any settlement a claim to be an industrial centre, but there is a concentration of activity around Itanagar and industrial training institutes in Roing and Daporijo. The lack of developed infrastructure limits the economic efficiency of the state, which could claim only 330 km of national highway in 1999. There are no railways. Although the Arunachal Pradesh state authorities had an installed electricity capacity of only 44 MW (1999), this was a five-fold increase on 1981. There is a vast potential for the further development of hydroelectric power sources, which already accounted for 55% of installed capacity in 1999. Moreover, most (72% in 2005) of the state's total capacity of 162 MW comes from its share of central projects. Over 60% of the villages in the state had been electrified by 2004, but only 34% of rural households had electricity, according to the national Ministry of Power. Installed capacity increased significantly in 2005/06, to reach 179 MW, mainly from an increase of almost one-third in state provision to 60 MW. The census of 2001 recorded an increase in the literacy rate over the 10 years since the previous such survey, from 41.6% to 54.7%.

Agriculture accounted for 26.2% of the gross domestic product of Arunachal Pradesh in 2001/02. Most of the population are engaged in agriculture, often on a subsistence basis, but increasingly commercially. Many depended on *jhum* (shifting, 'slash-and-burn' cultivation) agriculture, in which trees and undergrowth are burned and cleared for planting for a few seasons, before the farmer moves to a new area. However, this has accounted for much of the deforestation in the state and other methods are becoming more prevalent. At the end of March 2000 the area under *jhum* amounted to 110,000 ha, with 90,000 ha under permanent cultivation (together only 2.4% of the total area of the state). The authorities have taken steps to diversify agriculture and to introduce some cash crops, such as potatoes, tea and fruits. Thus, by 1997/98 fruit production had increased to 89,528 metric tons, having almost doubled in about 20 years. Likewise, foodgrain production had increased from 131,026 tons in 1980 to above 200,000 tons for much of the 1990s, and had reached 217,500 tons by 2001/02. Rice is the principal crop, accounting for 134,600 tons of the foodgrain harvest in 2001/02, in which year a record 28,200 tons of oilseeds were grown. Livestock is locally important, but only 44,000 tons of milk and 8.7m. eggs were produced in 2002/03, the latter total the lowest of any state in India. Arunachal Pradesh also produced 60,000 kg of wool in the same year. In addition, the state has considerable forest resources.

The primary economic activity with the most lucrative future for the state, however, is the extractive sector. The Arunachal Pradesh Mineral Development and Trading Corporation Limited was established in 1991 to develop mineral reserves, notably in the south-east, at the Namchik-Namphuk coal mine (which has estimated reserves of almost 90m. metric tons). The state is also reckoned to have petroleum resources of some 1.5m. tons and significant reserves of natural gas, in addition to deposits including dolomite, limestone, graphite, marble, mica, iron, copper, lead and zinc. Minerals worth Rs 415.5m. were produced in 2002/03. Furthermore, the water resources combined with the mountainous landscape provide a potential reserve of hydroelectric power, although this very terrain and its lack of development make transport from Arunachal Pradesh difficult.

The rise of the mining sector and more commercial farming has encouraged the development of industry. By March 1999 there were 18 medium-sized industries and 4,546 small-scale industrial enterprises registered in Arunachal Pradesh (the latter employing 14,539, with production worth Rs 1,738m.). Apart from a cement plant, fruit-processing plant and citronella-oil distillery, activities include agro-processing such as timber, rice and oil milling, manufacturing soap and candles, sericulture and handicrafts (there were 88 craft and weaving training centres in the state).

The main contribution of the tertiary sector to the state, apart from government expenditure, is from tourism. It is not highly developed, as the state has only been open to tourists since 1995, but the scenery, flora and fauna, and historical, cultural and religious sites provide many attractions. Walking or trekking holidays are popular in places such as Arunachal Pradesh, but the first foreigners were permitted to do this in the state only in 1998. The main places to visit are: Along; Bomdila; Itanagar; Malinithan, an archaeological site; the Namdapha Wildlife Sanctuary, home to the rare Hoolock gibbon and unique in being home to four particular members of the cat family (tiger, leopard, snow leopard and clouded leopard); Parashuram Kund, a lake near Tezu, famous as a place of pilgrimage; Pasighat; the Tippi Orchid Centre; and Tawang, near which is the largest Buddhist monastery in India, the second oldest in the world (after Lhasa in Tibet) and the only Buddhist Lady Lamasery or nunnery in Asia.

### DIRECTORY

**Governor:** Gen. (retd) JOGINDER JASWANT SINGH, Raj Bhavan, Itanagar 791 111; tel. (360) 2212432; fax (360) 2212442; internet www.arunachalgovernor.gov.in.

**Chief Minister:** DORJEE KHANDU (Congress), Office of the Chief Minister, Government of Arunachal Pradesh, Itanagar 791 111; tel. (360) 2212456; fax (360) 2212439.

**Speaker of the Legislative Assembly:** SETONG SENA, Assembly House, Naharlagun 791 110; tel. (360) 2244381; fax (360) 2245248; the unicameral Legislative Assembly has 60 mems: Congress 34; Bharatiya Janata Party 9; Nationalist Congress Party 2; Arunachal Congress 2; independents 13.

**State Resident Commissioner in New Delhi:** T. BAGRA, Arunachal Bhavan, Kautilya Marg, Chanakyapuri, New Delhi 110 021; tel. (11) 23014136; fax (11) 23013956; e-mail rc_ap@vsnl.in.

## Assam (Asom)

The State of Assam (which the state Government announced on 27 February 2006 would be renamed Asom, upon approval by the central Government) is in the lowlands of north-eastern India, most of which region once formed part of the state (as it had of the pre-independence province and the old realm of the Ahom kings—who probably gave their name to the area, although it is also claimed that Assam derives its name from *asom*, the Sanskrit for 'peerless' or for 'undulating'). The state stretches nearly 800 km (500 miles) up the valley of the great Brahmaputra river, from the west to the north-east, with, midway, the Barak valley giving it a southern extension. As Assam is largely surrounded by states hewn from its original territory, this gives it international borders only in the west, with Bhutan to the north and Bangladesh to the south-west. The state touches Bangladesh in two places, in the south, with that country's north-eastern border, and in the west, with its northern border, where the Brahmaputra leaves the state and begins to turn south towards the sea. Between lies another Indian state, Meghalaya, on the Shillong plateau, which rears to the south of the Brahmaputra and to the west of the Cachar (Kachari) hill country. The rest of Assam's western border is an inter-state one with West Bengal, giving the north-eastern region access to the narrow corridor of national territory connecting it to the rest of India. The remaining north-eastern states also border Assam, with Tripura to the south-west and then, separating the state from China and Myanmar (Burma), Arunachal Pradesh (mainly to the north, but wrapping itself around the end of Assam's north-eastern arm), Nagaland (to the south-east), Manipur (east of Assam's southern arm) and Mizoram (to the south). These states, together with Assam itself and Meghalaya, are sometimes referred to as the 'Seven Sisters' of the north-east. The formation of these 'sisters' meant that the territory of Assam was steadily truncated during the 20th century—from 1972, however, its area remained constant at 78,438 sq km (30,297 sq miles).

The fertile alluvial plain, seldom more than 80 km wide, of the River Brahmaputra (known upstream, in Arunachal Pradesh, as the Siang) dominates the geography of Assam. This flat landscape (with a slope of only 12 cm per km—about seven and one-half inches per mile) is alleviated by numerous low, isolated hills and ridges dotted over the plain from which they can rise so abruptly. Southwards, up the course of the Kapili and over the saddle of the hills, the state extends an arm to include the Cachar plain, where the Barak flows out of the highlands of Manipur, through some swampy country, to form its own broad, fertile valley, from which the river then flows into Bangladesh. The dividing hill country, much of it to the east of the Kapili, constitutes the third geographical area of the state, averaging between 1,000 m (3,280 ft) and 1,200 m above sea level, and much dissected by tributaries of the two main rivers, such as the Jamuna and the Kapili. Mountains surround Assam, except to the west, but now lie outside the territory of the state: the Himalayas to the north, curving around the eastern end of the Brahmaputra valley and thrusting ranges southwards through the states of Nagaland and Manipur, and on to the Rongklangs in Myanmar; and the Shillong plateau (Meghalaya) in the south-east, which causes some rain shadow for the central Brahmaputra valley, but generally Assam lies in one of the wettest monsoon belts in the world. The valleys, though fertile, are, therefore, prone to flooding, often destructive flooding (another natural hazard of the area is earthquakes). The wettest period lies during the monsoon, in the summer months between June and September. Although the central Brahmaputra valley receives over 1,600 mm (63 inches) of rainfall per year, further east the average is more like 3,200 mm. Thus, the vegetation is lush, with the extensive forestland characterized by dense stands of bamboo in the lowlands and evergreens in the hills. The difference in flora is accounted for by the climate at different elevations, it being tropical in the valleys and sub-alpine in the hills. Temperatures in the valleys range from 6°C to 38°C (43°–100°F), averaging 29°C (84°F) in the hottest month of August and 16°C (61°F) in the coolest month, January.

The total population of Assam, according to the March 2001 census, was 26,655,528, giving a population density of 340 per sq km. Growth over the 10 years since the previous census (when the population was 22,414,322) was lower than the national average. The ethnic origins of the peoples of Assam are varied, with the original Australoid stock being submerged by successive waves of migration by Caucasoids from the west and Mongoloids out of the mountainous north or from South-East Asia. Now the ethnic division is mainly between the tribal populations, who mainly live in the hills, and the non-tribal plains people of Assam. The Bodo of the northern Brahmaputra are the largest minority group, while the remaining hill tribes of Assam include the Mikir of the Mikir Hills, and the North Cachar Hills' Dimasa-Kachari, as well as some Kuki and Naga peoples. However, as in India generally, language and religion are more potent symbols of difference than ethnicity. The official and main language of the state is Assamese (which has a distinct literary history clearly dating from the 14th century), which is closely related to Bengali, the second most widely spoken. Most of the population are Hindus (64.9%, according to the 2001 census), but there is significant Muslim adherence (30.9%—up from 28.4% in 1991), reinforced by immigration from Bangladesh. The majority of Hindus follow the pacific Vaishnava tradition, which focuses on the deity, Vishnu—an important centre is Majuli, on the upper Brahmaputra, which also enjoys the distinction of being the largest river island in the world (although currently reduced to an area of some 700 sq km). Of other religions represented in Assam, Christianity claims the next largest community, but this accounts for only 3.7% of the total population, and there also adherents of Buddhism (0.2%), as well as some even smaller groups of others, including Jains and Sikhs. Only 6.9% of the population were counted among the Scheduled Castes in 2001, and 12.4% in the Scheduled Tribes.

The people of Assam are largely rural (an urban population of only 12.9% in 2001), but there are towns of some size. The largest is Guwahati (anciently, Pragjyotishpur), on the southern banks of the central Brahmaputra, with 809,895 inhabitants according to the 2001 census. Dispur, effectively a south-eastern suburb of Guwahati, is known as the 'Capital Area' and has served as the state capital since 1972. Other major towns are: Bongaigong, nearer the western border; Silchar, in the south, in the centre of the Barak valley; and, at the eastern end of the state, to the north-east of the old Ahom capital of Sibsagar, Dibrugarh and Tinsukia. The state is divided into 23 districts.

### HISTORY

In contrast to the rest of India, Assam (Asom) was a region in which the pre-Dravidian inhabitants succumbed to invasion from the east before Aryan influence worked its way down the Ganga (Ganges). However, lower Assam was certainly known to Vedic literature as the land of the Kirats (who warred against the Pandavas in the *Mahabharata*), with their capital at Pragjyotishpur. This 'city of astrology' was located near Guwahati (the Navagrah or 'nine planets' temple there still reveals this history). Another town of the region famous in legend was Sonitpur ('city of blood'), now Tezpur, further up the Brahmaputra. Such associations are probably connected to the region's strong association with Tantric Hinduism, which was prevalent until the dawn of the modern era. More historical sources—Chinese, and even Greek and Roman, records from the period immediately before the beginning of the Christian era—attest to the existence of an Assam in which the Lords of Pragjyotishpur presided over the great kingdom of Kamrupa (variously rendered as Kamarupa, Kumara-rupa or, as in the modern-day district around Guwahati, Kamrup). The earliest epigraphic reference to the realm dates from reign of Samudra-Gupta (AD 335–75), in which it is described as a satellite state of the North Indian empire. Assam again figures in the history of imperial pretensions in northern India in the seventh century. According to the account of a visiting Chinese scholar, Kamrupa's great king, Kumar Bhaskara Varman, allied with Harsha Vardhana against his traditional enemies in Bengal, the kings of Gauda. Thereafter, although still known as a place of learning and of pilgrimage, Kamrupa suffered a decline, even briefly succumbing to the sovereignty of one of the ruling houses of 'Imperial Kanauj', the Bengali Palas, the last major Buddhist dynasty in India, in the eighth–ninth centuries. The main problem for medieval Kamrupa, the native dynasties of which included those of the Salastambas, the Brahmapalas or Palas (an offshoot of the Bengali dynasty) and, finally, the Bhuyans, was, however, the mutual hostility of the local tribes and dynasties, which left the region divided and weakened.

The lower Brahmaputra valley experienced its first Muslim incursions at the end of the 12th century, when the Koch Bihar (Cooch Behar—now Bangladesh) kingdom of Kamata successfully resisted invasion and, indeed, displaced the last Palas to form a united realm in northern Bengal and lower Assam. However, although the Kamata kings were eventually defeated by the Muslim rulers of Bengal during the 13th century, the region of modern Assam was again not to succumb to the advancing power from the west. Instead, a prince of the Shan people from upper Burma (modern Myanmar), Sukapha, who had led his followers across the north-eastern hills, descended into the upper Brahmaputra valley in 1228. He soon prevailed against the strongest local tribes, the Chutias and the Kacharis (Cachars). The Ahoms founded a new kingdom, soon known as Assam, with its heart further up the Brahmaputra valley than old Kamrupa, in and around Sibsagar. The first capital of the new kingdom was established in 1253 at Charaideo (28 km east of Sibsagar), and 28 Ahom kings were to reign after Sukapha, soon extending their power throughout Assam and the north-eastern region of modern India. Originally Buddhists in the Thai tradition, the Ahoms soon adopted Hinduism and the Assamese language of their subjects. Indeed, it is under the Ahoms that the distinct Assamese language, culture and architecture still in evidence today flourished. The Assamese language was also used to record events in a series of *buraji* or chronicles, a tradition unusual in the rest of India, while a more literary application of the language was encouraged by the spread of a Hindu 'Reformation' from the end of the 15th century. The distinct Vaishnava tradition of Assam was introduced by the great Hindu saint, Sankardeva (a descendant of a Bhuyan chieftain), who was born near Guwahati in 1449 (this date marks the start of the Assamese lunar calendar, the Sankarabda). He and his disciple, Madhavdeva (born in 1522), inspired a flourishing of Assamese literature and the establishment of many satras (monasteries), notably on Majuli, largely displacing the older Tantric tradition of Shakti worship.

The kingdom of Assam resisted 17 Mughal invasions, the most serious being in the 17th century, when Ahom incursions into northern Bengal provoked Aurungzeb's governor there, Mir Jumla. He secured Bengal and then occupied much of lower Assam. Sailing up the Brahmaputra, his forces seized and sacked the Ahom capital, Gargaon, and the king, Sutamla (more usually known by his Hindu name, Jayadwaj Singha; he reigned in 1648–63), was forced to flee to the hills. However, Mir Jumla's army was defeated by the monsoon and disease, and the Ahoms had regained control of Assam within four years, although Jayadwaj was forced to concede a tribute to the Mughals. His successor, Suphungmung or Chakradwaj Singha (1663–70), denied the tribute and he appointed Lasit, the son of a barphukan (governor), to lead his armies. This hero of Assam (who died in 1671) defeated the Muslim forces at a famous battle near Saraighat (near Guwahati and the modern bridge of that name over the Brahmaputra). The final Mughal attempt to invade Assam was defeated in 1683. Ahom power then revived, to reach its zenith under Sukhrungpha, Rudra Singha (1695–1714), who overcome the Kachari and Jaintia kings, annexing their realms, and even plotted to invade the Muslim states to the west, but died prematurely. He established the new capital at Rangpur, 5 km from modern Sibsagar. Although an adherent of Tantric Hinduism himself, Rudra Singha ended the persecution of the Vaishnava movement.

After Rudra Singha, the power of the kingdom then stagnated and the Ahom royalty themselves earned some unpopularity by reasserting Shakti worship and persecuting followers of the popular Vaishnava sect. This provoked powerful religious leaders to lead the bloody and destructive Moamaria rebellion, started in 1769 under Ragha Maran. Even the Ahom palaces around Sibsagar were threatened or damaged and, unable to reassert his authority or contain the famine, Gaurinath Singha (1780–95) appealed to the British in Bengal for assistance. In 1793 British troops re-established royal authority, but civil strife resumed following their departure. Assamese problems were compounded by court intrigue and noble dissension, with a barphukan, Badan Chandra, fatally asking for Burmese help against the king in 1817. The five-year invasion saw Assam crumble before a savage occupation still demonized in local folklore and reputedly killing about one-third of the population. However, the Burmese were now on the borders of British India and their moves into Kachari territory provoked a British response. The British defeated Burma and forced it to cede Assam by the February 1826 Treaty of Yandaboo. The Ahoms clung to power in Jorhat, as feudatory chiefs, but their realm and that of other tribal kingdoms was at the complete disposal of the British, who gradually annexed and variously organized the north-eastern region of modern India over the succeeding decade. The last Ahom prince, Purandar Singha (who had first assumed the throne in 1817, only to be displaced by events), was granted an independence of sorts in upper Assam from 1833 to 1838, but then the dynasty's time was finally over and Assam was brought into mainstream India by the British.

In 1874 an Assam province was separated from the Bengal presidency, and its capital sited at Shillong (now in Meghalaya). Lord Curzon's 1905–12 partition of Bengal saw Assam united with a predominantly Muslim East Bengal until 1919, when it again attained provincial status (then including the district of Syllhet, which later voted to become part of East Pakistan—now Bangladesh—upon independence in 1947). At the same time, however, Assam experienced a considerable influx of Muslim migrants, which increased local resentment of Bengalis, adding to the anti-immigrant feelings first provoked by the workers imported for the tea plantations. This sentiment remained a dominating feature of Assamese politics into the second half of the 20th century, and was compounded by tribal protests that led to the dismemberment of the original Assam state. Thus, in 1957 Nagaland became a separate unit, followed by Meghalaya, Mizoram and Arunachal Pradesh in January 1972 (less significantly, in 1951 the border town of Dewangiri had been ceded to Bhutan).

The sensitivity of Assam for the federal authorities, lying as it does at the heart of the strategic and isolated north-eastern region of India, was increased by political unrest in the state. The carving out of separate states from the original territory of Assam from the 1960s had placated many of the tribal insurgencies, although the 'rump' state was left with militant Bodo dissatisfaction. During the latter half of the 1980s the Bodos were appeased by negotiations with the federal Government, and, indeed, in 1993 an agreement provided for the establishment of a local council. However, Bodo militant activity resumed later in the decade, although a cease-fire in 2000 ended most terrorist incidents (the cease-fire was subsequently extended). It was hoped that the creation of a Bodo autonomous council, finally agreed to by all the parties in Assam in 2002, would resolve this remaining tribal problem; further, in February 2003 a pact was signed by the Centre, the state Government and Bodo militants formally agreeing upon the introduction of a Bodoland Territorial Council within six months (the main Bodo insurgent group disarmed in December, although another important group continues to operate). Aware of the threat of secessionist sentiment in Assam itself, there was a limit on the extent to which government could go in satisfying tribal opinion (as witnessed by Assamese fears of a 'Greater Nagaland' from 2000, when Naga groups in Assam and other states were included in cease-fire arrangements and in other negotiations). In fact, a Maoist secessionist organization, the United Liberation Front of Assam (ULFA), which emerged in the 1980s, also used armed attacks on government figures and installations. This, in turn, provoked a military response from the Government. The ULFA was outlawed in 1990, but continued its armed activity against the state, with incidents increasing significantly from 2000. It would also sometimes act in concert with other separatist groups in the north-east, as in the mid-2003 demand to ban Hindi-language films from cinemas and cable-television channels, under threat of violence. An escalation began in November, when ULFA retaliated against protests in Bihar (in which some Assamese had been attacked) not merely by repeating its demand for Hindi-speakers to leave Assam, but by murdering Bihari immigrants. However, ULFA and other armed groups active in north-east India suffered reverses in late 2003 and early 2004, when the Bhutanese military acted against their jungle bases in the country.

Meanwhile, there also remained a fear of violence between the main Assamese population and Bangladeshi immigrants. The influx of Bengali, Muslim workers into Assam had been a source of tension throughout the 20th century, but provoked violence in the 1970s and 1980s. In August 1985 Rajiv Gandhi, reversing the centralist tendencies of his mother, his predecessor as federal Prime Minister, negotiated an accord with the All Assam Students' Union, providing for a limit on the voting rights of immigrants. This removed some of the tension from the situation in Assam and allowed for state elections that saw the opposition party, Asom Gana Parishad (AGP—Assam People's Council), which had emerged during the anti-immigrant struggle, win a term in government. Congress returned to power in 1991, with Haiteswar Saikia as Chief Minister, but the party was once more ousted by the AGP under Prafulla Mahanta in May 1996. State elections in May 2001 restored the mandate to Congress, which won 70 of the 126 seats in the Legislative Assembly (gaining another one later). Tarun Gogoi (Congress leader in the state since 1996) subsequently became Assam's 16th Chief Minister. The AGP gained only 20 seats, but alleged that it and its allies in the Bharatiya Janata Party (BJP) had been disadvantaged by high levels of pre-poll violence. Nevertheless, Congress retained a firm grip on power for the duration of the Assembly's mandate, as did Gogoi, despite some reports in 2002 and 2003 that the national leadership had become disenchanted with his performance.

The Government's main problems remained with the high levels of violence within the state, despite hopes of a peace having been reached with the Bodo, be it from various terrorist organizations or between different ethnic groups, as in March–April 2003, between Hmars and Dimasas in the North Cachar Hills, compounded by the involvement of armed militants, or the massacre of Karbis by the outlawed Kuki National Army in March 2004. From late September 2005 until the end of the year there was a severe outbreak of inter-ethnic violence in Karbi Anglong district, between Dimasas and Karbis, in which nearly 100 died, hundreds fled their villages and there was much damage to property. Insurgent groups in the hill districts demanded separate states for Karbis and Dimasas, rather than independence outside India, but were generally engaged in peace talks with the Government: the United People's Democratic Solidarity (which suspended negotiations in September 2006) for the Karbis and Dima Halam Daogarh for the Dimasas. However, although continuing an official cease-fire with government forces (since 2001), in 2007 there were increasing reports of violence between, and widespread extortion by, the two groups and their 'ultra' factions.

In 2003 more than 400 were killed in insurgency violence (just over one-half were militants), and government action against the violence in the north-east absorbs 20,000 soldiers and 10,000 paramilitary personnel, as well as some 50,000 Assam police. In early October 2004 deadly explosions demonstrated that the ULFA and the National Democratic Front of Bodoland (NDFB) were still forces to be reckoned with, although the incidents prompted Chief Minister Gogoi to seek a co-ordinated drive against the armed groups across the north-east and with Bangladesh and Myanmar. However, the NDFB accepted the offer of a cease-fire from mid-October, made by the state Government (although delays to the negotiations were causing concern by 2006)—the ULFA rejected the offer, claiming that it would only deal with the Centre. In December ULFA rejected the Prime Minister's offer of talks, claiming that his statement about Assam being an integral part of India indicated that he was unwilling to discuss the issue of sovereignty. By February 2005 ULFA had expressed some interest in participating in negotiations, but at the end of May said that four of its imprisoned leaders needed to be released first. In September the organization nominated a panel of intermediaries, the People's Consultative Group, which conducted negotiations with the Centre on its behalf in October, December and June 2006. However, violence continued, as did the counter-insurgency activities of the security forces, and by August ULFA's insistence on sovereignty being on the agenda for direct discussion with the Centre was undermining the likelihood of the peace process proceeding. However, on 14 August, in an unusual move (particularly on the eve of the Independence Day celebrations, when security was normally enhanced), the Indian Government announced that it would suspend military operations against ULFA for 10 days, as a goodwill gesture, thereby satisfying one of the organisation's pre-requisites for direct talks. The cease-fire was extended by the Government several times, but expired on 20 September and announced to be over on 24 September, because ULFA violence was continuing and following the group's refusal to commit to direct talks—with a specified date and location—in writing. The insurgents countered with a number of demands, including the release of five leaders from gaol. Both the central and state governments announced that they remained committed to peace negotiations, offering ULFA access to its leaders for consultation, but the military resumed operations against the armed organization and its bases. The People's Consultative Group announced the end of its involvement in the peace process by the end of the month, criticizing the Government for adding its insistence on written assurances after June and for attempting to combine negotiation and army offensives. By December the authorities were explicit in their demands for direct negotiations with ULFA, while the 'ultras' warned of an intensification of their campaign and threatened Congress personnel. Rumours of a split in the ULFA leadership (military head Paresh Barua maintaining the demand for sovereignty, chairman Arabinda Rajkhova reportedly favouring negotiations without preconditions) were not borne out by public commitment to the sovereignty demand, nor did they seem to diminish the effectiveness of the insurgency's campaign of violence and terror. In early January 2007 ULFA embarked on a campaign of violence in upper Assam that targeted Hindi-speaking, low-income migrant workers, mainly from Bihar (some 60 died in 13 incidents over four days alone—the seminal ULFA 'anti-immigrant' campaign, and others in the years since its foundation, had been aimed at Bangladeshi and Muslim workers, so the change of policy indicated to the authorities that the insurgents were now sponsored by the Bangladeshi and Pakistani secret services). The Centre responded with reinforcements for the armed forces' drive against ULFA, achieving some success and helping to secure the safety of the National Games (which were held in Guwahati in February), but this did not prevent the violence—albeit more sporadic for a time—carried out by the militants. Anti-ULFA demonstrations and *bandhs*, as well as further reinforcements, were prompted by seven explosions in Assam during May, five of them in Guwahati. Violence from ULFA and other insurgency groups meant that 2007 reversed the five-year trend for fewer and less fatal incidents, although the Government claimed that anti-insurgency activity helped restore the trend in 2008. ULFA continued to prevaricate on the issue of direct negotiations with the Centre, but suffered a split in June, when some militants under Mrinal Hazarika declared themselves in favour of talks. In July official sources cited ULFA as still the largest of the nine active insurgent groups in Assam, with just over one-half of the estimated number of fighters.

Assam sends 21 members to the national Parliament, seven to the upper house and 14 to the lower house. In the general election of May 2004 Congress lost only one of its Lok Sabha, or lower house, seats in Assam, holding a total of nine, while the BJP failed to increase its tally from two. The AGP experienced something of a resurgence in its support, winning two seats and coming second in four. Gogoi's premiership was strengthened by the defeat of his main Congress rival, Paban Singh Ghatowar, and by the installation of a Congress-led Government at the Centre (with the Prime Minister, Dr Manmohan Singh, having represented Assam in the Rajya Sabha since October 1991). A simultaneous by-election to an Assembly seat long held by Congress, however, saw the ruling party pushed into third place by the Trinamool Congress and the BJP, emphasizing that Congress could not afford to be complacent. In June the main concern of the state was the rising flood levels, which by July had reached the highest since 1988, killing many, leaving thousands homeless and devastating infrastructure and wildlife alike. The imminence of the elections encouraged all the main parties to express concern about a campaign against illegal Bangladeshi workers in May and June 2005. Muslims accounted for about 30% of the electorate and were particularly important to Congress, although there were anxieties that the illegal immigrants were adding to this influence. Meanwhile, the factionalism within the AGP had resulted in the expulsion of the former leader, Mahanta, in July. He had been obliged to resign as party leader after his 2001 election defeat, mainly because of allegations that he had two wives, but, when he began to increase his influence again within the party in February 2005, the new leadership retaliated. In August Mahanta announced that he intended to form a new secular, regional party (he was elected to the legislature in 2006 as the sole representative of his AGP—Pragatisheel). However, in May 2008 Mahanta attended an AGP meeting about uniting against Congress; the Trinamool Gana Parishad and the Purbanchaliya Loka Parishad also agreed to the unity proposals.

The elections of 3 and 10 April 2006, the results of which were announced on 11 May, had confirmed both Congress in government and Gogoi's grip on the ruling party. Congress won 52 seats, but the AGP and the BJP only won 25 and 11 seats, respectively, so allowing Gogoi to rely on the support of the 12 seats won by Bodoland People's Progressive Front. Congress had mainly lost out to the new party of Badaruddin Ajmal, the Assam United Democratic Front, which represented a coalition of minority groups. The left also regained representation in the Assembly. In June 2008 the Government was embarrassed by the arrest of its Minister of Education for attempting to bribe an official investigating the murder of a student leader. Ripun Bora was promptly dismissed from office and suspended from Congress. Nevertheless, Congress felt it necessary to retrieve its reputation and, in July, instigated a programme of transparency about ministers' and legislators' income and assets.

## ECONOMY

Assam (Asom) has an agrarian economy, most famous for producing tea, but actually dominated by rice. The state authorities have severe financial problems (the 1999/2000 state budget deficit was some Rs 12,548m.), as well as having to deal with political unrest. In 1999/2000 real annual growth was put at 8.2%, giving a net domestic product of Rs 262,730m., in current prices, and Rs 10,080 per head—only Orissa, Uttar Pradesh and Bihar had lower per head figures (the other north-eastern states have lower population densities and receive relatively greater central subsidies). Official figures for 2004/05 put the size of the economy at Rs 386,240m., or Rs 13,633 per head—just ahead of Orissa and Jharkhand (the latter separated from Bihar in 2000), further ahead of Uttar Pradesh and well ahead of the 'rump' Bihar. Business organizations complained that it was not just the explicit terrorist violence that was curtailing economic progress, but also the excessive level of disruption from strikes and *bandhs* (a general boycott or strike), often mounted for political reasons and alleged to be costing Assam Rs 9,000m. annually. In 2001/02 there were nine state-wide *bandhs*, 13 regional *bandhs* and 36 district *bandhs*. The state can also be adversely affected by floods, with the devastating floods of 2004 washing away about 1m. ha of standing crops and putting 1.6m. people into temporary accommodation (by late July). Traditional, cottage industries remain important in the state, but the exploitation of hydrocarbons was located in the main industrial centres in upper Assam. The terrain permits a well developed infrastructure network, although the famous link over the mountains with Myanmar and China is closed beyond Arunachal Pradesh; the first stretch (470 km) of the 'Road to Mandalay' began at Ledo and was named for Gen. Joseph Stillwell—the road was the costliest and most ambitious engineering project of the Second World War. In 1995/96 the state had 33,110 km of road, of which 2,070 km was national highway and 2,177 km state highway. Total road length at the beginning of the 21st century was put at 68,418 km, of which 17% was surfaced. The railway centre of the north-east, Assam has a total track length of over 3,722 km, including both broad gauge (64%) and metre gauge. There are six civil, domestic airports. Installed electricity capacity in 2006 was 597.3 MW, with a further 509.0 MW share in national schemes and 24.6 MW from the private sector. Over 77% of Assam's villages were in receipt of an electricity supply, but the sector remained identified as a priority for development by state government (although no capacity had been added in the 2000s), as only 12% of rural households had electricity in 2005. Official policy to improve literacy levels saw the rate increase from 52.9% in 1991 to 64.3% in 2001.

Agriculture accounts for the livelihood of about three-quarters of Assam's population and provided 28.9% of the gross state domestic product in 2001/02 (the primary sector as a whole accounted for about 38% of net state domestic product). In 1991 agriculture accounted for 73.5% of main-worker activity, with cultivation alone providing over one-half of employment. The main food crop is rice, with paddy fields dominating the landscape of the valleys, and the major expansion in rice production at the end of the 1990s led the resurgence of agricultural production generally. Annual rice production was about 3.3m. metric tons for most of the 1990s, but increased to 3.9m. tons in 1999/2000 and to a record 4.0m. tons in the year after, before falling slightly to 3.9m. tons in 2001/02. In that last year production of other food grains came to only 0.3m. tons. Total foodgrain production in 2002/03 again fell, to 3.9m. tons. However, the main cash crop is tea, which is grown in hillier country, especially in upper Assam. The state provides some 15% of the world's tea production and Guwahati hosts the biggest auction centre for the CTC (crush, tear and curl) variety of tea. Although an indigenous Assam tea plant was finally recognized by the imperial authorities in the first half of the 1830s, the first tea plantation (tea garden) in the province was actually established using plants grown from Chinese seed, in 1836, near Tezpur. Over 160 years later there were reckoned to be 848 tea gardens in Assam, as well as a number of smaller producers, covering about 5% of the cultivated land and employing some 0.5m. people. Most of the tea grown is processed for black tea (oxidized by fermentation). Other cash crops include jute (0.7m. tons of jute and mesta was produced in 2001/02), sugar cane (1.0m. tons), citrus fruits, potatoes and some cotton. Horticultural production in 2003 included 0.5m. tons of bananas, 0.2m. tons of pineapples, 0.2m. tons of jackfruit, 0.1m. tons of citrus fruits and 0.1m. tons of papayas. In addition, ginger, chilli, black pepper and turmeric were produced. Sericulture is also an important activity, with Assam producing a number of varieties of silk, including a non-mulberry one known as muga, which is unique to the state (the other non-mulberry variety is known as eri, while the silk of worms fed on mulberry leaves is pat). According to the 1997 livestock census, the farmers of Assam had 8.0m. cattle, 2.7m. goats and 1.1m. pigs, as well as 12.9m. chickens and 5.0m. ducks. Livestock products included 704,000 tons of milk in 2003/04 (although a fall in production was expected to be recorded for the following year) and 515.9m. eggs. Timber is a plentiful resource, with some 26% of the total area of Assam under forest (2001), and over four-fifths of that being reserved forest—forestry revenue for 1998/99 reached Rs 9,590m. The exploitation of bamboo resources, in particular, is being encouraged.

The state's other main natural resources are the domain of the mining industries, with coal, petroleum, natural gas and, to a lesser extent, limestone, being of increasing importance. The oilfields of upper Assam were first exploited in 1879, with a refinery built at Digboi in 1900. Almost 100 years later the state's fourth refinery opened at Numaligarh, and the extraction and refining of petroleum is Assam's predominant heavy industry. Assam accounts for about 15% of the petroleum produced in India; in 2001 production of crude petroleum totalled some 5.1m. metric tons and of natural gas some 1,890m. cu m. The products of petroleum refining amounted to 2.5m. tons. Coal is also mainly found in this north-eastern end of the state, with the regional headquarters of Coal India Ltd located in Margherita, on the border with Nagaland. In 2001 some 0.7m. tons of coal were produced. Hydrocarbons are considered to have considerable potential still, although development of the sector was delayed by political troubles in the north-east during the 1990s and into the 2000s. Cement production is another activity driven by the extractive industries. Limestone production in 2001 was 487,000 tons, while cement production was 292,000 tons. In 2002/03 the value of all minerals produced in the state amounted to Rs 30,323m., extracted by almost 100,000 workers (92,474 in 2001/02).

State industrial production figures for 2001 also included 362,000 gross boxes of matches, 188,000 sq m of plywood, 12,000 metric tons of fertilizer and 5,306 tons of jute textiles. However, other industrial activity, apart from that provided by tea processing, by forestry and by mining and its 'downstream' processes, is limited and largely home-based (household industries provided almost one-quarter of manufacturing employment in 1991). Traditionally, weaving is an important activity for Assamese women, and textile manufacturing is an important industry. Government initiatives encourage such cottage industries, but also seek to develop projects such as an ethylene factory at Tengakhat or a software technology park near Guwahati. Small-scale industrial units numbered 45,193 at March 2003, employing 188,110 people. Between 1991 and 2001 the secondary sector's contribution to net domestic product in the state had increased from about 6% to 10%.

Services (including trade and commerce, and transport, etc.) provided 20.1% of employment in 1991 and accounted for about 40% of net state domestic product. By 2001 the tertiary sector provided 52% of net domestic product. Trade, tourism and government accounted for most of this. Tourism is the sector long considered to have the most potential, as Assam is rich in natural, historical and cultural advantages. The state had five national parks and 14 wildlife sanctuaries in 2000, with the Kaziranga National Park alone covering 474 sq km—the latter is home to the unique greater one-horned rhinoceros and the rare Bengali florican, as well as being the most important wintering ground of the bar-headed goose and the rare ferruginous duck. The Manas National Park, on the border with Bhutan, enjoys scenic beauty and a leading role in the preservation of the royal Bengal tiger. It is the main remaining centre of the pygmy hog, although in July 2005 it was announced that the species also seemed to have survived in the Bornodi wildlife sanctuary. There is a zoological garden in Guwahati, a city that also boasts a number of other historical and religious sites, notably the ancient Shakti temple of Kamakhya (a Tantric shrine). Not far north of the city lies Hajo, which is sacred to three religions—Hinduism, Buddhism and Islam. Other popular tourist destinations lie further up the Brahmaputra, such as Jorhat, the nearby island of Majuli and, in the heart of upper Assam, the old royal capital of Sibsagar. Domestic tourist arrivals in the state increased from 1.0m. in 2001 to 2.6m. in 2003, with foreign visits up from 6,171 to some 7,800.

### DIRECTORY

**Governor:** Charan Mathur, Raj Bhavan, Guwahati; tel. (361) 2540250; fax (361) 2540500.

**Chief Minister:** Tarun Gogoi (Congress), Office of the Chief Minister, Government of Assam, Janata Bhavan, Guwahati 781 006; tel. (361) 2266188; fax (361) 2262069; e-mail asmgovt@asm.nic.in.

**Speaker of the Legislative Assembly:** Tanka Bahadur Rai, Assembly House, Guwahati 781 006; tel. (361) 2261371; fax (361) 2260565; the unicameral Legislative Assembly has 126 mems: Congress 53; Asom Gana Parishad 24; Assam United Democratic Front 9; Bharatiya Janata Party 10; Communist (CPI—M) 2; independents and others 27; vacant 1.

**State Resident Commissioner in New Delhi:** S. Manoharan, Assam House, Sardar Patel Marg, Chanakyapuri, New Delhi 110 021; tel. (11) 26877111; fax (11) 26117059.

## Bihar

The State of Bihar lies in northern India, at the eastern end of the Gangetic plain, between the mighty Himalayas and the Chotanagpur plateau to the south. The state, the name of which is derived from *vihara* (monastery), has an international frontier with Nepal to the north. To the west of Bihar is Uttar Pradesh, further up the plains, and to the east is West Bengal, where the Ganga (Ganges) enters its delta. On higher ground to the south and south-east is Jharkhand, formerly the Vananchal or 'forest region' of Bihar—it was separated from the original state in November 2000, ending an administrative association dating back before independence (Bihar and Orissa was made a province separate from the Bengal presidency in 1911 and Orissa was separated in 1936; Bihar state also lost some border districts to West Bengal upon the linguistic reorganization of the states in 1956). Bihar now has an area of 94,163 sq km (36,370 sq miles).

The Bihar plains along the Ganga average about 53 m (173 ft) above sea level, although south of the holy river of the Hindus the land is hillier and the state extends to include the first foothills rising towards the Chotanagpur. The southern plains narrow in the east, while the northern plains generally are broader. The flat lands, watered by many rivers, are prone to flooding, particularly during the height of the monsoon (June–September) and if there is torrential rain in the Himalayas. There is a confluence of great rivers in the west, the border being indented where the Ganga and Ghaghara meet, then the Son flows in from the south-west corner of state, followed by the Gandak, flowing from the north-west. Another tributary joining the Ganga from the Himalayas is the Kosi, noted for its flooding and for the steady migration of its course westwards (at least 110 km in 130 years), part of the dynamic process of fertilizing the Gangetic plain with rich alluvial soils, but which also leaves the northern plains dotted with strings of lakes along old river courses. The climate is tropical to subtropical, with a monsoon season that confines the hottest months to March–May. The usual annual rainfall is 1,204.6 mm (47 inches), falling, on average, over 52.5 days.

According to the results of the national census taken at 1 March 2001, the total population of Bihar was 82,998,509. This was an increase of about 28% on the total at the previous census, in 1991, and rather a high rate for an already poor state. Bihar is the third most populous state in the Union, after Uttar Pradesh and Maharashtra, and it is the most densely populated after West Bengal (Bihar had 881 people per sq km in 2001). In 1991, when Bihar included what is now Jharkhand, the state was the second most populous in India. Upon the bifurcation of the state in 2000 Bihar retained 54% of the land area and 72% of the population, losing many of its natural resources and most of its tribal population. The state is overwhelmingly both Hindi-speaking and Hindu by religion, although exact figures for language in today's Bihar are not available—the 1991 census had the old Bihar state (i.e. including Jharkhand) with 81% of the population using Hindi (and its local dialects) as their main language and 10% Urdu. Apart from Bengali, the other significant minority languages spoken in the state were mainly tribal ones, most of which are now confined to the territory of Jharkhand. Likewise, many of the smaller religious communities held their own better in the mountainous south, but the numbers, if removed from consideration in the 'rump' state, remain insignificant compared with the teeming population of the plains. The 'rump' Bihar of 2001 consisted of 83.2% Hindus, long settled in this eastern end of the Aryan heartland, with 16.5% professing Islam, owing to long years of more recent Muslim rule. Christians were the largest single minority group, but barely accounted for 0.1% of the total population—most had belonged to the southern tribes and, therefore, not in the state as constituted today. Only 0.9% of the population in 2001 were counted among the Scheduled Tribes, with 15.7% among the Scheduled Castes.

Only 10.5% of the population of Bihar were defined as urban in the 2001 census and the state contained only one of India's 35 most populous cities. Patna, the state capital (the 17th largest city in the country, with 1.37m. people), is located on the south bank of the Ganga, near the confluence with the Gandak, in the west of the state. There are, in all, nine urban agglomerations counted within the borders of Bihar, of which two are Gaya, to the south of Patna, and Muzaffarpur, to the north. The state is divided into 38 districts.

## HISTORY

Bihar is part of the historic *arya varta*, the Aryan heartland, settled by the Aryans as they moved out of the Punjab and the Ganga–Yamuna Doab and hacked their way down the then jungle-choked Gangetic plains towards Bengal. This route became known as the *Uttarapatha* or Northern Route (as opposed to the Southern Route, *Daksinapatha*, whence comes the term for the Deccan), which not only served as the main conduit of Aryanization in the north, but also of Buddhism and the early north Indian empires. By the sixth–fifth centuries BC Bihar consisted notably of the territories of the Licchavi and the Videha clans (the former hailed as the first republic—both now described as being *gana-sangha*, having 'government by discussion', be this oligarchic or democratic), north of the Ganga, and the nascent kingdom of Magadha to the south. Both Nataputta (known as Mahavira or 'Great Hero'), who formulated the Jain code of conduct, and Gautama Siddhartha (known as the Buddha or 'Enlightened One'), who preached the Middle Way, expounded their philosophies in the rising power of Magadha. This kingdom had its capital in Rajagriha (Rajgir) and held sway from the area around modern Gaya to the Ganga.

The presence of the Jains and Buddhists in Magadha was to ensure that some records and stories survived to shed light on the history of the period, although there have been problems of exact dating, of matching the Buddhist chronologies with the now commonly used Christian era. The problem is that the actual date of Jesus Christ's birth may be debated, but the year as used for the calendar has long been generally accepted, whereas the actual date of the *parinirvana* (achievement of *nirvana*) of the Buddha, the starting point of the calendar, varies from tradition to tradition, giving dates ranging from 544 BC to as late as 350 BC. Hitherto scholars have favoured the 480s BC, owing to the coincidence of an Indian and of a Chinese tradition, but more, recently, have tended rather towards a later date, some time in 400–350 BC.

At this time the great Aryan clans, be they 'republics' or monarchies, were beginning to succumb to the power of Magadha. Its rajah, Bimbisara (his name is known from the accounts of the Buddha's life), reigned for some 50 years. He had access to the rich mineral resources of Jharkhand (southern Bihar until 2000) and also to the sea (through his conquest of Anga, modern Bengal), establishing the foundations of Magadhan power, as well as conditions conducive to the spread of Buddhism. As Christianity spread with Rome, so Buddhism and Jainism, which soon displaced the myriad other heterodox sects, if not the orthodox 'Great Tradition' of the brahmins, spread under the shield of the Magadhan peace. The son of Bimbisara, Ajatashatru, also met the Buddha, around the time the king was building a fort at a place called Pataligrama, on the south bank of the Ganga. This became Pataliputra, the capital of Magadha from the time of Ajatashatru's successor, on the site of the modern city of Patna. Meanwhile, the first Buddhist council was held at Rajgir. The succession following Ajatashatru is uncertain, and the domestic politics of Magadha opaque, until the 320s BC. Certainly the kingdom dominated the lower reaches of the Ganga and competed for power with Vatsya, based near Allahabad (Uttar Pradesh), and with Avanti or Malwa, based on Ujjain (Madhya Pradesh).

Equating dates becomes easier from the last decades of the fourth century BC, owing to the incursion by the Hellenic emperor, Alexander III ('the Great') of Macedon, into the north-west of the subcontinent in 326 BC. His soldiers, having already conquered one empire to come so far out of the west, were loath to continue any further into India, particularly given the tales of the mighty realm that was before them. This empire was that of Magadha, which now not only controlled the entire extent of the Gangetic plains, but also reached into central India and held sway over Kalinga (modern Orissa). Its ruler was the son of Mahapadma Nanda, himself the son of a barber and of low caste. Mahapadma had created a formidable military machine and was famous for his wealth, seemingly expanding his influence by exploiting caste rivalries and attacking the status quo. However, the Nandas reputedly lasted only two generations, to be usurped, in turn, by Chandragupta Maurya in *circa* 320 BC, aided by his brahminical chancellor, Chanakya or Kautilya (purported to be the author of a book on statecraft, the *Arthasastra*). Building on the achievements of the Nandas, Chandragupta consolidated the power of Magadha and was the first Indian emperor to hold sway from shore to shore (there is archaeological evidence that he conquered Gujarat), as well as the first to rule in both north and south. The extent to which the empire reached into southern India is indicated by a story of his retirement, in about 297 BC, to a place in southern Karnataka. His son, Bindusara, reigned until around 271 BC, to be followed by a three-year succession struggle won by the man who became the greatest of the Mauryans and an inspiration for Buddhist chroniclers and modern nationalists alike, Ashoka Piyadassi.

Ashoka (who died in about 233 BC) ruled an empire that reached from Bengal to Gujarat, and from southern Karnataka up through the Punjab and into modern Afghanistan. As a young prince his first post in the administration of the Mauryan emperor seems to have been in Taxila (Takashila, not far from modern Islamabad, Pakistan), an ancient centre of learning and Sanskrit orthodoxy, where he served sufficiently well to be then appointed governor in Ujjain. Upon the death of his father, Ashoka must have demonstrated sufficient ruthlessness to emerge victorious from the succession struggle, which was reportedly a bloody one for the imperial family. Equal vigour must have been shown in the maintenance of his empire, such as in the reconquest of Kalinga, where thousands died, in the fighting and afterwards, and thousands more were deported. These details are reported in the famous rock inscriptions dotted all over India, indicating the extent of his domains and the variety of languages used within them—there are 14 Major Rock Edicts, eight Minor Rock Edicts and Inscriptions and seven Major Pillar Edicts. The campaign in Kalinga is the only campaign of the Mauryas to be recorded, despite the hugeness of their achievement, and it is known only for provoking the horror of the emperor and his proclamation of concord and good governance through his concept of *dhamma* (loosely translated as good conduct or duty or toleration, all useful commandments in a realm of such variety in people, language, religion and social standing). He also sponsored Buddhism (the third Buddhist council is supposed to have been held under his patronage at Pataliputra), as his father had favoured the Ajivikas and his grandfather the Jains, although the various proclamations make it clear that encouragement was given to all the heterodox and orthodox groups of the time. His own state philosophy seems intent on finding a middle ground, a non-religious creed with which to govern, although maybe it was this policy that rejected violence that caused the decline of his empire. Although his descendants ruled from Pataliputra for another 50 years or so, and were displaced by other dynasts claiming imperial hegemony, Ashoka's pan-Indian empire disintegrated, not to be matched in extent until the Mughals approached it and British India exceeded it.

The Shunga, who usurped the last, sad relic of the Mauryas in what may have been a brahminical reaction to official sponsorship of the heterodox sects, and then the Kanva, reigned from Pataliputra for about another 160 years. Magadha then disappears from the scantily known history of the era, although tradition claims that it was conquered by the Kushana dynasty out of the north-west. The Kushana, the greatest king of which was Kanishka, were among a number of foreign invaders who established themselves in north India at this time, although their process of naturalization and conciliation of their subjects may have contributed to the flourishing of culture and the arts (Sanskrit was becoming the standard court language even before the advent of the Guptas). Certainly the triumphal progress of Buddhism, and of Jainism, began to falter in its Indian homeland as the 'Great Tradition' of the brahmins reasserted itself and the modern contours of what is called Hinduism began to appear (although co-existence continued to be usual for some time yet).

The revival of a kingdom of Magadha took place under the Guptas. North of the Ganga, in modern Bihar, the illustrious Licchavi still ruled much territory and may have occupied Pataliputra. The original patrimony of the Guptas probably neighboured them, under a Sri-Gupta and a Ghatotkacha, but the founder of the dynasty is considered to be the latter's son, Chandra-Gupta I, who married a princess of the Licchavi and re-established Magadha as an imperial power. He laid the foundations for an empire that dominated the north and centre of India and reached far down the eastern coast into Tamil country. However, this was not a bureaucratic empire like that of the Mauryas, but more a feudal sovereignty over a number of lesser kingdoms, maintained and expanded by the longevity and ability of a succession of five great monarchs. Chandra-Gupta I acceded to the throne in about AD 320, to be succeeded by his son, the great Samudra-Gupta, in around 335. Samudra-Gupta brought most of the ancient *arya varta* under his rule and spread his authority across the tangled wilds of the Ganga-Brahmaputra delta, exposing modern Assam (Asom) to direct Aryanizing influences for the first time. He conquered the Pallava king of northern Tamil Nadu and was paid tribute by the princes of modern Rajasthan and the ancient Punjab. Only the Kshatrapas or 'Western Satraps', based in Gujarat, resisted Gupta authority in the north. The first, unlucky and short-lived successor of Samudra-Gupta (who died around 375), his son, Rama-Gupta, was severely defeated by this originally Scythian dynasty and was soon displaced as emperor by his younger brother, Chandra-Gupta II (Vikramaditya). This monarch, who was often based at Ujjain rather than Pataliputra, continued the campaigns against the Kshatrapas and seems to have incorporated their territories by the first decade of the fourth century, enriching both the commerce and the culture of the Gupta realm. Kumara-Gupta (c. 415–55), like his two great predecessors, also reigned for some four decades. He, fortunately, did not have to engage in a rivalry with the main power of the western Deccan, as he benefited from the marriage of his half-sister, Prabhavati, to the Vakataka king. The latter died in around 390, leaving his Gupta queen in charge of a 20-year regency, ensuring that the two polities became allies. Kumara-Gupta's main problem was, first, a major revolt in Malwa by a Pushyamitra, who shook the stability of the empire. The revolt was eventually contained by one of the emperor's sons, Skanda-Gupta, who was then able to succeed his father in around 455 (until 467) and lead his troops to repulse the 'White' Huns (Ephthalites). However, the continuing depredations of the Huns, the debasing of the coinage and the rising powers of the regions undermined the credibility of the claims of Skanda-Gupta's descendents to imperial authority in north India. By 510, when Toramana of the Huns routed a Gupta army near Gwalior (Madhya Pradesh), the central authority of the king in Pataliputra was often ignored by his cousins and other governors in the regions, although the dynasty limped on in Magadha until around 540. Bihar's days as the imperial centre of India were over.

Bihar's loss of imperial prestige was confirmed in the seventh century, when Harsha established an imperial capital at Kannauj (now in Uttar Pradesh). This was to eclipse Pataliputra as the rightful centre of power in north India, although its own rulers were not always the emperors. Control of Kannauj was contested by three great dynasties and the fate of Bihar came to be increasingly associated with neighbouring powers in Bengal or from further up the Ganga. In the eighth and ninth centuries the Palas of Bengal were the eastern contestant for suzerainty over Kannauj. Their kingdom was based in Bengal and Bihar, and they were the last great native Buddhist dynasty of India, reviving the famous 'university' at Nalanda and building another on the Ganga in Bihar at somewhere called Vikramashila. By the 10th century Pala power had declined and Bihar was subjected to different overlords or local princes independent to some degree. A fundamental change came in the 13th century, however, as Muslim armies penetrated into the *arya varta* and raided as far as the eastern plains, sacking the great Buddhist monuments as well as the Hindu temples. The late medieval and early modern landscape of a Hindu populace ruled by Muslims was being formed. The first Muslim dynasty to control Bihar was that of the Khiljis (originally based in Varanasi, Uttar Pradesh), who seized the throne of the Delhi sultanate itself in 1290.

Bihar then fell variously under the influence of Delhi or, increasingly, Bengal, which, by the 15th century, held it fairly securely. When the Mughals seized power in Delhi in the 16th century Bihar came under central rule, until the regions had again massed sufficient weight to assert their independence under nominal Mughal sovereignty. However, in the early years of the dynasty, under the second Great Mughal, Humayun, Bihar came to be dominated by a member of the Afghan Sur clan, Sher Khan, who went on to defeat Humayun at Chausa in 1540 and himself reign from Delhi for 15 years (he is buried at Sasaran). In 1555 Humayun regained Delhi and Mughal authority was soon restored in Bihar. It lasted until the 18th century, when Bihar fell under the rulers of Bengal, who acquired steadily more autonomy from the declining centre in Delhi. The power of the nawabs of Bengal was, at first, maintained with British help, the East India Company being established in Calcutta (now Kolkata, West Bengal) and Patna (where Gobind Singh, the 10th and last Sikh Guru, was born in 1723 and spent his early life), among other places. In 1756, however, a new nawab, Siraj-ud-daula, assumed office and he soon alienated all the European communities, not least the British, and the escalating conflict resulted in a 'battle' at Plassey (West Bengal), when Mir Jafar betrayed Siraj to the British under Robert Clive. Mir Jafar was made Nawab of Bengal and was duly acknowledged by the Mughal court. The British soon acquired a variety of trading rights in Bengal and Bihar, while the Nawab was required to pay for their assistance in any struggle to defend his domain against incursions by the Mughal or Awadh (Oudh—in modern Uttar Pradesh) forces. Unwilling to yield the cost of such help, in 1760 Mir Jafar was replaced by his son-in-law, Mir Qasim, who ceded lower Bengal to the East India Company, but then proceeded to introduce reforms that again threatened British interests. The ageing Mir Jafar was restored in 1763, only for Mir Qasim to seek the help of the Mughal emperor and his powerful ally of Awadh, invading Bihar in 1764. At Baksar (Buxar) the outnumbered, but disciplined, Company forces, mainly Indian sepoys, triumphed against the varied and competing armies of the invaders. An independent nawabate and the last vestiges of Mughal power were destroyed at the battle, while the road to British supremacy in the subcontinent was begun. The following year the Mughal emperor, Shah Alam II, incorporated the Company into imperial government by granting it the *diwani* of Bengal, including effective sovereignty in Bihar, which was henceforth ruled from Calcutta.

As part of the presidency of Bengal, Bihar was at the heart of British India. During the Great Rebellion of 1857–58, started by the Indian Mutiny of elements of the Bengal army, the prompt arrival of British reinforcements ensured the quietude of Bihar, but in the more peaceful independence struggle of the 20th century the area was to be more active. Bihar, part of the West Bengal of 1905–12 and then a separate province (still with Orissa), had an indigo trade with severely exploited workers. It was among these indigo farmers that Mohandas Karamchand Gandhi (Mahatma Gandhi), newly arrived from working in London (United Kingdom), first utilized his policy of *satyagraha* (literally, 'truth-force', a form of passive resistance) against injustice in India, in 1917. Among Gandhi's followers in Bihar was Rajendra Prasad, later the first President of India, and Jay Prakash Narayan, later one of Indira Gandhi's leading opponents and a luminary of the Janata Party (from the Janata Party sprang the Janata Dal, which itself produced the current ruling party of Bihar—see below). Meanwhile, in 1935 Orissa was separated from Bihar, the latter's borders only to be altered once more in the 1900s, when some adjustment of the south-eastern border with West Bengal took place in 1956, to accord with the linguistic reorganization of the states. Bihar was, therefore, one of the original states of the Indian Union, but since the 1970s has added a reputation for corruption and lawlessness to widespread poverty.

Inter-caste violence and communal strife frequently occur in Bihar, while many state governments, of varying political persuasions, have been charged with maladministration or misuse of office. Congress was finally driven from office at the beginning of the 1980s, while from the 1990s Bihar was dominated by Lalu Prasad Yadav, who also had considerable influence at the Centre. He first became the state premier in 1989. Although he was forced to resign in 1997, while being charged with corruption, he was replaced as Chief Minister, by his wife, Rabri Devi. She and the Rashtriya Janata Dal (RJD), despite continuing corruption investigations of her and her husband, won the February 2000 state elections by an appeal to the disadvantaged, low-caste dalits ('untouchables') and Muslims, winning 124 seats to the 123 of the Bharatiya Janata Party (BJP). The Rabri Devi Government was supported (among others) by Congress and by the five members of the Bahujan Samaj Party, four of whom joined the RJD itself in mid-2002. Of course, by this stage the balance of power in the legislature had altered, owing to the bifurcation of the state in November 2000. An earlier cost of Congress support for the Rabri Devi administration, as well as the advocacy of the BJP, had resulted in the RJD conceding the separation of the southern region of Jharkhand into a state in its own right. This left the BJP, which dominated Jharkhand, the old southern Bihar, with considerably fewer seats in the truncated Assembly of the reduced Bihar state, but also left the RJD dependent upon coalition support. With unexpected gains for the BJP and for the RJD's Congress allies at the elections to the Legislative Council (the upper house of the

Bihar legislature) in 2002, however, the Government looked less secure, although realignments of party affiliations in the lower house had tended to favour it. Also in 2002 Yadav (who had already served a number of short prison sentences) finally resigned his state Assembly seat in order to assume a place in the national Parliament's upper house, the Rajya Sabha. In total, Bihar sends 16 members to the Rajya Sabha and 40 members to the lower house, the Lok Sabha. Further state elections were not due until 2005, but political machinations, including accusations that part of the high levels of violence experienced in the state was politically motivated, continued. Local politicians sometimes alleged that many of the state's disadvantages were attributed to a lack of support from the Centre. In 2004, however, Yadav was given the opportunity to influence central policy, when he and 20 other RJD candidates from Bihar (and two from Jharkhand) were elected to the Lok Sabha in the April–May general election. The RJD was staunch in its support for a secular Government, which Yadav joined at the invitation of Congress.

In state politics the RJD continued to be supported by Congress and the left-wing parties, while the main opposition remained the BJP and its National Democratic Alliance (NDA). However, in late 2003 the BJP had almost been displaced as the official opposition, when the Samata Party and the Janata Dal (United) formally merged. It was only the defection of a few deputies that prevented the new grouping, also known as the Janata Dal (United), from surpassing the BJP's representation in the Legislative Assembly, although the two remained associated in the NDA. As the legislative elections scheduled for February 2005 approached there was further political jockeying, but no significant changes. In January 2005 Congress, while not ending its alliance with the RJD, made an electoral pact with the Lok Jan Shakti Party (LJP) of Ramvilas Paswan, who was a bitter opponent of Lalu and the RJD (although also a member of the ruling coalition at the Centre) and had been petitioning Congress to help form an anti-RJD and anti-BJP coalition in Bihar. Paswan had particularly strong support among the Muslim vote, but Congress imperilled its existing alliance for little gain. At the state elections, held in several stages during February, Congress retained 10 seats, while the LJP became a kingmaker by winning 29. However, the RJD, with 75 seats, remained the largest single party—its unchallenged leadership was over, its support unable to resist the erosion from Lalu's mounting legal and political problems (Lalu and Rabri Devi were acquitted on corruption charges, originating 11 years before, in December 2007). The BJP performed strongly enough to win 37 seats, while the Janata Dal (United) won 55, but the NDA, while becoming the largest bloc, had not capitalized on the clear anti-incumbency sentiment sufficient to have a clear majority. Congress again declared its support for the RJD, but with Paswan refusing to support either an RJD-led or a BJP-led Government, neither faction could command a majority in the Assembly. The impasse was suspended, at the request of Governor Buta Singh, by the imposition of President's Rule on 7 March.

During April and May 2005 there were various attempts to form coalitions with sufficient support to form a Government, notably one led by the NDA candidate for premier, Nitish Kumar of the Janata Dal (United). Rabri Devi continued to claim the right of the RJD to form an administration. With the continued refusal of Paswan to co-operate, such attempts failed, but so did his own effort to form an anti-RJD coalition (even if dependent on outside BJP support). Paswan saw the ideal compromise as a Muslim Chief Minister and a Congress-led Government. Further developments in May threatened Paswan's influence, with reports that the 16 high-caste elected members of the LJP had deserted the party and were threatening to join the Janata Dal (United), which they duly did in June. By then Paswan was reportedly left in command of only seven deputies. Meanwhile, however, the Centre had taken action at this threat of the formation of an NDA Government in Bihar, as well as the threat to its own national coalition. On 23 May the Governor announced the dissolution of the state Assembly. New elections were eventually scheduled for November. President's Rule was duly extended in late July for six months, to cover this period. By this time there was some concern about the Governor's style of leadership and he was summoned to New Delhi for consultations at the beginning of August, but remained in office despite the controversy. In October the Supreme Court made a provisional judgment finding the dissolution unconstitutional, but refusing to reinstate the legislature as the electoral process had begun. The full judgment, delivered on 24 January 2006, strongly criticized Governor Singh for acting hastily, with a political agenda, and for misleading the Centre; he resigned two days later, having taken the salute at the Republic Day ceremonies.

Meanwhile, in four phases during October and November 2005, state elections had taken place, in a process that was considered remarkably non-violent and fair by the standards expected in Bihar, although there was one report that 28% of the candidates faced criminal charges. When the results were announced on 22 November, the NDA had secured an absolute majority in the Legislative Assembly (88 for the Janata Dal—United and 55 for the BJP), while the RJD retained only 54, conclusively ending the grip it had on power for so long; the LJP retained 10 seats and Congress nine. On 24 November President's Rule was revoked and Nitish Kumar became Chief Minister, backed by a secure majority (unlike in his previous, one-week premiership in March 2000). In early 2006 it was announced that he would enter the state legislature as a member of the upper house, the Legislative Council. The new Government was intent on restoring good governance to Bihar and attacking the poverty that exacerbated the caste-riven and violence-stricken politics and society of the state. Insecurity was typfied by the widespread occurrence of kidnappings and the increase in Naxalite activity (most dramatically, during the election, in mid-November forces of the Communist Party of India—Maoist attacked a jail in Jehanabad, releasing one of their leaders and murdering imprisoned members of the rival, high-caste, militant Ranvir Sena). However, after continuing Naxalite violence, the authorities conceded in mid-2007 that the Maoists were often better educated and equipped than the overstretched state police. The worst flooding in Bihar for many years in July–August also demonstrated the incapacity of the impoverished state authorities: over 100 people were killed, 75,000 homes destroyed and more than 12m. people in 6,000 villages, mainly in north Bihar, were affected. Politically, the state was relatively tranquil into 2008. A long-awaited expansion of the Cabinet (to 36 members) finally took place in April 2008, when 19 new ministers were sworn in. Earlier in the year all the main parties had condemned criticisms of Biharis from other parts of India, where the presence of many poor, but cheap, migrant workers aroused local resentment. Delhi's proposal to insist on identity cards for all residents was seen as an attack on the poor, while from the very end of January and again in March Marathi politician Raj Thackeray's dismissive remarks about north Indians provoked protests in Bihar.

## ECONOMY

Bihar is the poorest state in the Union, its division from Jharkhand in November 2000 depriving it of rich mineral reserves and important industrial assets, further leaving the state authorities without sufficient resources to alleviate the situation of its huge rural population. Moreover, Bihar is widely considered to be the state most prone to official corruption, lawlessness and communal and inter-caste violence. When Bihar's southern districts became a separate state, the north was left with 72% of the population, but only 36% of the established power capacity, 45% of state tax receipts (and 52% of the state share of centrally collected taxes) and 34% of the excise duty collected. Income per person in Bihar was reduced to 80% of the average for the original state (i.e. including what is now Jharkhand). Many general figures readily available, however, remain from the undivided state—thus, unless specifically stated, data from before 2000 refers to the old, larger Bihar. The total size of the state economy, as measured by net domestic product at current prices in 2004/05, was Rs 511,940m. This was already not a large economy relative to many of the other major states, but, given the size of Bihar's population, in per head terms this became by far the lowest state income in India, at Rs 6,015 per head (which was barely a recovery from a decline—even in current terms—in the previous year). Infrastructure is relatively well developed, although the profusion of easily flooded rivers provides obstacles, most notably at the broad Ganga. In 2001 the state had national highways amounting to 2,907 km, with state highways at 4,354 km. There are effectively parallel railway systems north and south of the Ganga, with connections between the two limited. The better-developed network is south of the great river and, at Dehri-on-Son, includes India's longest railway bridge. There are airports at Patna and Gaya, as well as landing strips throughout the state. Energy infrastructure was particularly badly affected by the division of the state—in 2001 Bihar was left with only three power stations, two thermal and one hydroelectric, with a total installed capacity of only 559.2 MW. At the end of May 2006, according to the Union power authorities, this total was 628.8 MW (after the first significant annual rise since 2001). A share in central schemes amounted to a rather more important 2,460.8 MW each year between 2001 and 2005, but in 2006 was only 999.8 MW (a rather minimal contribution from the private sector, at 0.02 MW, was constant in both years). In the same year, while about 70% of villages had been connected to the supply, only 6% of rural households had electricity (the lowest in India). Human resources are also undeveloped, with the lowest literacy rate in the Union in 2001—47.5%, although this was a respectable improvement on the 37.5% of 1991.

Agriculture is the main occupation of the vast majority of the population and provided 35.2% of gross state domestic product in 2001/02 (the second highest percentage recorded in the country, although in Bihar this was a sign of a poor and undeveloped economy, rather than a successful one like the Punjab). There is a relatively large area under irrigation. The main food grains are paddy, wheat, maize and pulses, while the main cash crop is sugar cane (the sector has its own government department). Other cash crops include potatoes, onions and other vegetables, and oilseeds, tobacco, chilli and jute. In 2001/02 the 'rump' Bihar produced 11.8m. metric tons of food grains (5.3m. tons of rice, 4.4m. tons of wheat, 1.6m. tons of coarse grains and 0.6m. tons of pulses), 125,800 tons of oilseeds, 1.1m. tons of jute and mesta, and 5.8m. tons of sugar cane. Total foodgrain production fell in 2002/03 to 10.3m. tons (5.9% of the all-India total). Harvests can be affected by flooding on the Gangetic plains, most dramatically demonstrated in 2007, when crops worth an estimated Rs 33,000m. were destroyed. Livestock is an important sector, with products including anticipated production in 2003/04 of 2.8m. tons of milk, 751m. eggs and 445,000 kg of wool. Forestry, since the division of the state, is a negligible sector in the economy of Bihar, with the total forest area only amounting to 7.1% of the total land area (2001), about one-half of which is protected. Fisheries, however, are an important primary activity, with the state being India's leading producer of freshwater fish, which flourish in the lakes and rivers of the north Gangetic plain particularly. Over one-half of the produce is destined for Kolkata (formerly Calcutta), in neighbouring West Bengal.

Most of the mineral resources of the pre-2001 Bihar, as well as many of the dependent industries, were in the southern uplands, leaving the 'rump' state with some reserves of glass sand and dolomite in the south-west, salt, some bauxite and, fairly widely spread, mica. Employment in the mining sector was only about 49,000 (2001/02), although the state still produced minerals worth a respectable Rs 9,687m. (2002/03). In terms of heavy industry, Bihar is now left with railway-wagon plants at Muzaffarpur and Mokama, some fertilizer factories and a number of agro-processing operations. There are five large spinning mills for cotton, almost 30 sugar mills (almost one-half of which are private), with a total crushing capacity of 46,000 metric tons per day, three large jute mills, as well as a number of other distilleries, tanneries and other textile and leather industries.

The tertiary sector is not a strong part of the economy of Bihar. Even tourism, which should benefit from the state's history and rich legacy of religious associations, is limited by the deterrence of extreme poverty and a turbulent civil society. Nevertheless, long being part of the *arya varta*, and the base for the ancient imperial kingdom of Magadha, as well as fundamental to the development of three religions—Buddhism, Jainism and Sikhism—the plains of Bihar hold interest to pilgrims and tourists: the ancient capitals of Rajgir and Patna (Pataliputra); the place where the Buddha gained enlightenment at Bodh Gaya; the old Buddhist university of Nalanda; and the location of arguably the world's oldest republic in Vaishali. There are also several bird and wildlife sanctuaries, notably the tiger project, which, like the one national park in the state, is located in West Champaran, in the north-west. Bihar was the ninth most popular state for Indian tourists in 2002 (with 2.5% of domestic tourist visits).

### DIRECTORY

**Governor:** Raghunandan Lal Bhatia, Office of the Governor, Raj Bhavan, Patna; tel. (612) 2221230; fax (612) 2232868; e-mail govnrhse@sancharnet.in.

**Chief Minister:** Nitish Kumar (Janata Dal—United), Office of the Chief Minister, Government of Bihar, Secretariat, Patna; tel. (612) 2223886; fax (612) 2223393; e-mail cmbihar@bih.nic.in.

**Speaker of the Legislative Assembly:** Udai Narayan Chaudhary, Assembly Secretariat, Patna 800 015; tel. (612) 2223856; fax (612) 2232212; the lower house of the bicameral legislature, the Legislative Assembly, has 243 mems: Janata Dal—United 88; Bharatiya Janata Party 55; Rashtriya Janata Dal 54; Lok Jan Shakti 10; Congress 9; Communist Party of India—Marxist-Leninist (Liberation) 5; Bahujan Samaj Party 4; Communist Party of India (CPI) 3; Samajwadi Party 2; Akhil Jan Vikas Dal 1; Communist Party of India—Marxist 1; Nationalist Congress Party (NCP) 1; independents 10.

**Presiding Official of the Legislative Council:** Jabir Hussan, Legislative Council Secretariat, Patna 800 015; tel. (612) 2223819; fax (612) 2233438; the upper house of the state legislature has had 54 nominated or indirectly elected mems since the division of Jharkhand from the rest of the state.

**State Resident Commissioner in New Delhi:** A. B. Prasad, Bihar Bhavan, 5 Kautilya Marg, Chanakyapuri, New Delhi 100 021; tel. (11) 23014945; fax (11) 23015035.

## Chhattisgarh

The State of Chhattisgarh, part of Madhya Pradesh until 1 November 2000, lies in central India, in the north-east of the peninsula, stretched between north and south. The state with which Chhattisgarh was until so recently united, Madhya Pradesh, lies to the west and north-west of the northern part of Chhattisgarh. West of southern Chhattisgarh is Maharashtra, while Andhra Pradesh is in the south-west and south. Orissa, to the south-east and east, separates the state from the eastern seaboard, while another new state, Jharkhand (part of Bihar until 2000), lies to the north-east and there is also a short northern border with Uttar Pradesh. Chhattisgarh, which is commonly taken to mean '36 forts', is a long, relatively thin, state, which lies along an axis that is more north-east to south-west than north–south. Slightly larger than Tamil Nadu, but smaller than neighbouring Orissa, the state covers 135,191 sq km (52,217 sq miles).

The north of the state lies on the Chotanagpur plateau, dominated by the western end of the Hazaribagh Range jutting into Chhattisgarh from the north-east. The central region, beneath the Maikala Range, which separates it from Madhya Pradesh, consists of the lowlands of the Korba basin, the 'rice bowl' of central India. In the south the land rises again, in the Bastar district, before falling away to the fringes of the Andhra Pradesh plainlands to the south. The highlands tend to be thickly forested. The climate is tropical monsoon, with annual average rainfall at about 2,000 mm (78 inches), although poor management of water resources has meant that the region has suffered from drought a number of times recently.

According to the census results for 2001, Chhattisgarh had a population of 20,833,803, which was only about 18% greater than at the 1991 census. The population density is also relatively low, at 154 per sq km in 2001, the lowest for any state outside the north-east or the Himalayas. Hindi is the most widely spoken of the official languages of India, although Oriya and Marathi are also used, but the main native language is Chhattisgarhi, which, like Hindi, is an Indo-Aryan tongue written in the Devangiri script. It is spoken in its purer form in the central districts, but there are also dialects (Laria, Khaltahi, Surgujia, Binjhwari) spoken throughout the state and as far afield as Jharkhand, Bihar and, possibly, Tripura. Numerous tribal tongues are spoken, from a variety of language groups. Tribes include the Gond (Koytoria), the most numerous (the main subdivisions include Marias and their own subgroup, the Abuhjmarias, and Murias and Dorlas), the agriculturalist Halbaa, the Bhatra (highest in the tribal hierarchy of the south), the Dhruvaa (Parjaa), the Baiga peoples, the Kanwar and, in the north, the Pando and the Korwa (both of which, owing to the association of the region with Hindu myth, claim to be descended from the clans of the *Mahabharata*, the Pandavas and the Kauravas, respectively). Although most belief systems among them are orientated on the Hindu traditions, the anomalous position of tribals in the caste system, as well as a significant proportion of the population coming from the historically disadvantaged Scheduled Castes, has encouraged the spread of a number of sects and socio-religious reform movements (in 2001 11.6% of the population came from the Scheduled Castes and 31.8% from the Scheduled Tribes). Officially, Hinduism is overwhelmingly the main religion (94.7% in 2001—the percentage is higher only in Orissa, just, and Himachal Pradesh), but Chhattisgarh has given rise to a number of unique sects or panths. In the 19th century a farm worker, Ghasidas, founded a hereditary line of gurus to lead the Satnam Panth, which preached a casteless society and the rejection of the Hindu pantheon. Low-caste leather workers formed the strength of the movement, which is centred on Bhandar and Girod. Satnamis also abstain from meat, alcohol, tobacco, certain vegetables and red pulses. The Kabir Panth (named for a 16th-century poet, saint and reformer) also rejects the pantheon and embraces equality; the sect was established in Chhattisgarh by a disciple of Kabir, Dharmadasa, and so it is sometimes called for him. The adherents of the Ramnani Panth especially revere the god Rama and reject the mediation of brahmins, so, again, have a following mainly among the lower castes or dalits. Another group consists of followers of Ramananda or Rae Das, a social religious reformer. (There is an association with dalits in one theory about the origin of the state's name—that the region was named for the 36 families of leather workers who settled here.) There are also small communities of Muslims (2.0%) and Christians (1.9%), and some Sikhs, Buddhists and Jains.

In 2001 only one-fifth (20.1%) of the population was classed as urbanized, although the state does possess some fairly large cities and industrial centres. The state capital is Raipur (605,747 inhabitants, according to the 2001 census), in the central region of the state, near where the border abuts south-eastwards into Orissa. There are proposals to move the capital to Nandghat, midway between Raipur and Bilaspur. The main city of Bastar and the south (Bastar was originally one of the largest districts in India, but was split into three by the new state authorities—Dantewada in the far south, Bastar itself and, to the north, the smaller Kanker) is Jagdalpur. West of Raipur are the cities of Durg, Bhilai and Raj Nandgaon. North-east of Raipur is the second city of the state and one of the main industrial centres, Bilaspur, and beyond that Korba, the so-called 'power capital'. The main city of the north (again, three districts formed from the old Surguja) is Ambikapur. There are now 16 districts in the State of Chhattisgarh.

## HISTORY

Chhattisgarh was known from the time of the great epics of the *Mahabharata* and the *Ramayana* as Dakshin Kosala (South Kosala) and, later, as Dandakaranya, after an Itsavaku Aryan king who ruled from near Raipur. More certain history begins around 1,000 years ago, when Kalingraja settled to the north of Korba. This prince was of the Kalchuri dynasty, which was based near Jabalpur (Madhya Pradesh). Their territory was known as the Chedi kingdom, giving yet another derivation of the name Chhattisgarh, a corruption of 'Chedisgarh'. Kalingraja's grandson, Ratanraja, founded Ratanpur, which became the capital of the Chhattisgarh basin. Its ruling Rajput dynasty became known as the Haihayas. One of the Haihaya kings, Ramachandra or his son, founded the city of Raipur, which became the seat of an autonomous, junior branch of the family in about the 14th century. Mughal overlordship was acknowledged in the 16th century, but this predominantly Hindu area continued to be ruled by Hindu princes. Meanwhile, in 1320 Annmdev established the Chalukyas in Bastar, claiming sovereignty over the settled area and the wild, tribal lands of the region, and becoming a separate kingdom in the 15th century. Various Gond polities also claimed authority in different areas.

In the 18th century the Haihayas came under assault from the Marathas out of the west, the local dynasty's power being broken in 1741 and the last member of the Ratanpur branch, Raghunathsinghji, was deposed in 1745. The Marathas formally annexed Chhattisgarh in 1758, and it came under the rule of the Bhonslas of Nagpur (now in Maharashtra), with only Gond resistance continuing. For most of Chhattisgarh, however, Maratha rule was an experience of lawlessness and constant plundering by Maratha forces, followed by the introduction of more organized systems of economic exploitation as the British gained influence (particularly after 1818). These new systems were particularly resented in Bastar, the princely state that occupied the south of modern Chhattisgarh, where the people frequently vocalized the particular disadvantages suffered by the tribes, notably over land rights. Even the Halbaa rebellion of 1774–79, which started off as a revolt by the governor of Chhota Dongar, but was supported by the famine-stricken Halbaa, was fuelled by resentment of outside influence in Bastar state. Ironically, it was this very rebellion that further compromised the independence of the Chalukyas, as Bastar needed expensive British and Maratha support to regain control. There was a disturbance at Bhopalpatnam in 1795, a rebellion at Paralkot in 1825 (Abuhjmarias protesting Maratha taxes) and a longer struggle at Tarapur in 1842–54 (although about taxation, this was mainly directed against the local diwan or premier). The tribes were not used to the new administrative or revenue-raising systems and this undoubtedly contributed to the great Maria revolt of 1842–63, although the principal reason was religion. The British and the wider Indian context that Bastar now existed in found the Maria practice of human sacrifice unacceptable, while the tribe was least prepared to accept outside interference in matters of faith. The region was, therefore, already restless at the time of the Mutiny in Uttar Pradesh in 1857, which was supported in the south by Dorlaon tribesmen under Dhruvarao, while the Gonds engaged in several battles with the British during 1858 and there was a further rising in 1859 against tree felling by outside contractors.

In central Chhattisgarh, which had lapsed to the British as a domain of Nagpur in 1854, support for the mutineers of 1857 was led by the zamindar of Sonakhan, Vir Narain Singh. He had been imprisoned by the British authorities in 1856 for seizing a grain trader's stocks—his defence was that it was for famine relief—but was released by sympathetic Indian soldiers. However, his revolt was crushed by the British and he was hanged in December 1857—at the end of the 1970s the anniversary was adopted by Chhattisgarhi regionalists as the celebration of a local martyr. Generally, however, discontent in central and northern Chhattisgarh tended to focus on social and economic inequities, which were not necessarily attributable to the British authorities, although the policies of imperial rule tended to favour support for local magnates and, therefore, often conflate the issues. Thus, the profusion of sects among the dalits usually favoured social justice, as did the Satnam Panth first established in the 1810s. By the 1890s Satnami solidarity was expressing itself in a precursor of the independence struggle, using equality and non-violence as principles to oppose British (and Maratha) injustice. The so-called malgujari settlement of property rights and revenue collection had given the high-caste Malgujars an advantage over the predominant population of small farmers, sharecroppers and farm labourers (the last constituted just under one-sixth of the population of the region in the 19th century), but provoked a resistance movement organized by the Satnamis. Meanwhile, Bastar too had succumbed to direct British rule after the imperial authorities had lost confidence in the Chalukya rajah. In 1867 he had appointed Gopinath Kapardas as diwan of Bastar, but had not listened to the appeals of the tribal population to remove him from office. This provoked a severe Muria revolt in 1876, and by March Jagdalpur was under siege. The king was barely saved by British forces from Orissa, but was removed from power in the 1880s, when allegations that he had tolerated human sacrifice were used as justification. By the time of the largest rebellion, therefore, most of Chhattisgarh was part of the Central Provinces under British administration. When these authorities made the forests reserves and granted timber rights to outside contractors, they put the tribes under threat of dispossession, while the introduction of education seemed to be an assault on local cultures, combining into the Bhumkal rebellion of 1910, Bastar's last major insurgency, before all of Chhattisgarh became involved in the wider struggle for independence and social justice (this association of the two was particularly significant in Chhattisgarh and contributed to the evolution of the regional identity). Later in the 20th century violent expressions of poverty and social injustice were confined to Naxalite activity, arriving in the coal-producing areas from West Bengal in the 1970s and in the south (old Bastar) from Andhra Pradesh in the 1980s.

The first demand for a separate Chhattisgarh was made in 1924, by Congress in the Raipur District. Likewise, at the time of the States Reorganization Committee in 1954–55, there were appeals for a distinct state, but the Committee favoured Chhattisgarh continuing to remain associated with the poorer areas of Madhya Bharat and the Central Provinces. Chhattisgarh, therefore, became part of the Madhya Pradesh state formed in November 1956, although separatist pressure continued into the following decades. A non-party political movement, Chhattisgarh Mukti Morcha, was active from the 1970s, but by the 1990s both the major parties (Congress and the Bharatiya Janata Party—BJP) had accepted the distinctness of the regional identity and the justice of separation, reinforced by the state-wide, multi-party political forum led by Chadulal Chakrakar, the Chhattisgarh Rajya Nirman Manch. The Congress-led Madhya Pradesh Assembly passed a unanimous resolution in favour of statehood for Chhattisgarh in 1994, and in 1998 the BJP-led Union Government (also wanting Congress support for the creation of another two states) initiated legislation to effect this. The legislation, foiled by the early dissolution of Parliament, was reintroduced and received presidential assent in August 2000. Raipur, once considered for the capital of Madhya Pradesh, was settled upon as the Chhattisgarh capital, while the other contender, Bilaspur, became the seat of the high court.

Despite the weight of the tribes and lower castes in the new state, all the contenders for the premiership were high caste. Finally, Ajit Jogi was chosen to be Chief Minister by 41 of the 48 Congress deputies in the 90-seat provisional legislature. The Government gained additional support in the first year of statehood (including being joined by a splinter group from the BJP) and, by December 2001, Congress commanded 62 seats. State elections were scheduled towards the end of 2003. Congress hopes of re-election were compromised by the defection of the veteran politician, Vidya Charan Shukla, to the Nationalist Congress Party (NCP—after the state elections he left the NCP and, in February 2004, formed his own party in Chhattisgarh, only to join the BJP before the general election and to leave it in September), and the BJP seemed determined to allude to Chief Minister Jogi's Christian faith as an issue. Moreover, in June there were allegations that the Chief Minister and his son were involved in the murder of a senior NCP party official, although no charges were brought against the premier (his son was acquitted in May 2007) and Congress, in turn, alleged that opposition groups were attempting to slander the Government. Such doubts about the Congress leadership seemed to have some effect, as in December the BJP was able to assume the government of the state. The 'saffron' party won 52 of the 90 seats in the Vidhan Sabha after legislative elections on 1 December. Congress had expected to win, particularly given recent bribery allegations against a senior BJP Union minister from the area. Jogi, however, was himself controversial and not only split the Congress party but also lost the support of the tribals and the countryside generally. He left office in disgrace (despite alleged attempts to remain in power through efforts to split the BJP group in the assembly by means of bribery). Although removed from the Congress leadership, Jogi was reconciled to the party in 2004, just before he suffered injury in a traffic accident. He went on to win the only Congress seat from Chhattisgarh in the Lok Sabha at the general election, while the BJP gained the remaining 10 seats. Chhattisgarh is also represented in Parliament by seven members of the upper Rajya Sabha.

Meanwhile, Dr Raman Singh had emerged as the BJP's candidate for the premiership, and he had formed a new state Government in December. Having consolidated electoral support at the general election in 2004, the Government pursued an attempt to negotiate an end to enduring Naxalite violence in the tribal areas of the state. Towards the end of May the home minister invited the Maoist Communist Centre and the People's War Group (which united into the Communist Party of India—Maoist in September) to negotiations in the southern city of Jagdalpur. However, one year later Naxalite violence was resurgent, as illustrated by a dramatic attack on the mining interests of a major metals company. In June 2005 officials from Chhattisgarh joined those of 12 other states and the Centre to discuss strategies against the Maoists. In the same month a statewide Salwa Judum or peace campaign began. As part of this process, in July the state authorities announced that it would supply arms to the tribals, some of whom had begun to form vigilante groups against the rebel Naxalites (although these subsequently attracted their own criticism). The Maoists had been making unpopular demands of the villagers, backed with violence. The villagers also suffered the brunt of the Naxalite retaliation against the new local activism. The Maoists even attacked some of the 17 relief camps to which many fled, although a concerted drive by the authorities against the Naxalite 'ultras' stemmed the number of incidents from May. However, an attack on a police station and relief camp in mid-July 2006 killed about 25 people and demonstrated that the threat was not over, with over 300 villagers now having died since June the previous year. Indeed, throughout that year and into 2007, although Naxalite violence registered at lower levels elsewhere in India, in Chhattisgarh the numbers of incidents and casualties increased. In March 2007 the worst ever incident in the state occurred at the Rani Bodli police outpost in eastern Bastar; a night-time attack by hundreds of armed Naxalites killed 55 security personnel. Such incidents, and terrorist damage to infrastructure which could result in power and water shortages or transport impediments, prompted the Assembly to sit in secret for the first time in July, so as to discuss freely the Maoist threat. As at the conference on Naxalites in February that year, the consensus was that more needed to be known about the insurgent movement, its motivation and capabilities, and that the Centre needed to follow up on its recent acknowledgement that Maoist activity was more of an all-India internal security problem than a state-based law-and-order issue. In December the struggle against the Maoists suffered a reverse when almost 300 prisoners, including more than 100 Naxalites, escaped from Dantewada gaol. There were also concerns about the effects on the government human rights record of the counter-insurgency programme, notably with the detention of Dr Binayak Sen in May 2007. The general secretary of the People's Union for Civil Liberties (PUCL) in Chhattisgarh, Dr Sen was a fierce opponent of the Salwa Judum movement, claiming it had an equally bad outcome for the tribal villagers as Naxalite oppression. Accused of links to the Maoists beyond his civil liberties role, Dr Sen had been detained for almost a year before the national press began to give publicity to his situation. An international campaign urged his release, and that of another PUCL activist, Ajay T. G., who was detained in May 2008. Such cases were unlikely to have much impact on the outcome of the legislative elections, however, which were scheduled to take place in September.

## ECONOMY

Chhattisgarh was divided from Madhya Pradesh (one of the poorer states of the Union, with per head net state domestic product falling between that of Tripura and of Manipur) on 1 November 2000, so figures for the separate states are often not yet available. Net state domestic product in the undivided Madhya Pradesh, in per head terms, was probably much the same in what were to become two states until the mid-1990s. By the beginning of the 21st century, and separate statehood, Chhattisgarh had edged ahead. Official figures for 2004/05 put net state domestic product in Chhattisgarh at Rs 336,140m., or Rs 15,703 per head (Rs 14,069 in Madhya Pradesh). Chhattisgarh has only one-fifth of its roads metalled, 68% of its houses without an electricity connection, 49% without drinking water and poor rates of literacy among the large tribal and lower-caste population. However, it has considerable potential mineral wealth, aspirations to become an important exporter of energy and some major industrial centres. There were only 35,389 km of roads (5% national highways, 6% state highway and 9% major district roads—2000/01 figures), although they are fairly extensive in the central lowlands. There are railway links from Jagdalpur and Dantewada with Andhra Pradesh in the south; otherwise the main network is in the central region, through Raipur and Bilaspur, though Mahendragarh in the north-west is connected through Madhya Pradesh. The Bilaspur division of Indian Railways is the most profitable rail operation in the country. Total railway length in 2000/01 was 1,053 km. There are airports at Raipur and Bilaspur. Chhattisgarh is endowed with growing electricity-generating capacity, accounting for 35.7% of the power in the old Madhya Pradesh. Korba, with easy access to large coal reserves, is touted as the 'power capital' of central India, with local generators joined by federal and other state facilities. In 2006 thermal generation accounted for 89% of the state's installed capacity. At the end of May 2006 installed capacity in Chhattisgarh totalled 1,649 MW, of which 13% came from a share in central capacity and only 28 MW from the private sector. The literacy rate, according to the census of 2001, was 65.2%, which was a strong improvement on 42.9% in 1991, although female and tribal literacy remain low—in the south, for instance, it is reckoned that about four-fifths of the population over 18 years of age are illiterate.

The primary sector accounted for 37% of net domestic product in 2000/01 (agriculture alone provided 20.1% of gross state domestic product in 2001/02). Agriculture is the most important sector of the economy to over 80% of the population. The 1991 census found that 82% of all workers and 90% of rural workers were in farm-related activities, notably cultivation. However, irrigation is limited and drought a recurring problem, while only one crop per year is grown on over three-quarters of the cultivated land, which encourages seasonal labour migration out of the state. The net area sown in Chhattisgarh in 2000/01 was 34.5% of the total area. The rich plains of the central region were known as Madhya Pradesh's 'rice bowl', producing over 70% of the old state's paddy and over one-half of the food grains in the relevant season (in general, Chhattisgarh accounted for about one-quarter of agricultural production). Maize, millets and pulses are other common food crops, but very few cash crops are grown. Owing to this and to falling paddy yields (claimed by some to be the result of neglecting the myriad local varieties of rice) the new state Government plans to encourage horticulture and make the state rather a 'fruit bowl'. A poor harvest in the first year of statehood was followed by an extremely good harvest in 2001/02, when 5.1m. metric tons of rice were produced (total food grains amounted to 5.8m. tons, with pulses at 0.4m. tons accounting for much of the balance), as well as 114,800 tons of oilseeds. The total foodgrain harvest in 2002/03 was only 3.2m. tons. Livestock numbers in the same year included 10.1m. cattle, 6.0m. poultry, 0.4m. pigs and 0.4m. sheep and goats, while their products included 790m. eggs, 836,000 tons of milk and 195,000 kg of wool (according to anticipated figures for 2003/04). Fisheries production amounted to almost 86,000 tons in 2000/01. Containing about 12% of all the forestland of India (45.7% of the total state area was under forest in 2000/01), forest industries are important, with timber (accounting for about two-fifths of forest revenue) being augmented by over 200 minor products such as medicinal plants. Of the state's total forest area, 43% was reserved forest and 40% protected forest (2000/01).

One-half of the mining revenue of the old Madhya Pradesh was accounted for by Chhattisgarh. The region earned Rs 3,761.9m. in 1999. Reserves of coal are reckoned to amount to some 35,000m. metric tons, those of iron ore (including some of the highest grade ore in the world) up to 2,350m. tons and those of gold to some 3,805,000 kg. The state is also India's only source of tin and has rich fields of bauxite, limestone, dolomite and corundum. There have been finds of diamonds and evidence to suggest that the state might contain one of the world's richest kimberlite fields, while industries based on other commonly found gemstones are also being encouraged. In 2000/01 production of coal amounted to 50.2m. tons, iron ore 20.3m. tons, limestone 13.8m. tons, dolomite 0.7m. tons, bauxite 0.6m. tons and tin (concentrate) 12,979 kg. The sector employed only about 66,000 people in 2001/02, but production was worth Rs 39,522.6m. in 2002/03 (only Andhra Pradesh, Gujarat and Jharkhand produced total minerals of greater value).

Only 7% of workers at the time of the 1991 census worked in the secondary sector of the economy. However, in 2000/01 the sector contributed 19% of net domestic product. Official policy is to maintain good governance, to develop infrastructure and, in industry specifically, to encourage very large ('mega') projects, such as those in the power industries, and small-scale activities, particularly in poorer areas. In terms of heavy industry, there is a huge steel works at Bhilai, as well as some 75 other iron-and-steel enterprises throughout the state, and a number of thermal electricity generators and an aluminium plant at Korba, for example. Textiles, wood-working and agro-processing provide the basis for other activities. In 2000/01 there were 2,706 registered working factories, with average daily employment in the previous year at 129,000. Industrial production in 2000/01 included 10.5m. metric tons of cement, 5.0m. tons of melted iron, 4.4m. tons of steel and 0.1m. tons of aluminium.

Services remain a small sector, although the tertiary sector provided employment for 11% of all workers (and 52% of urban workers) in Chhattisgarh in 1991. Nevertheless, services accounted for over two-fifths of the size of the economy (20% of total net domestic product came from transport, communications and trade, 16% from community and personal services and 8% from banking, finance and real estate—according to estimates for 2000/01). Tourism is being developed, concentrating on the attractions of the state's religious and historical sites and, above all, its natural environment. The state has three national parks and 11 wildlife and bird sanctuaries; it also boasts India's largest waterfall, deepest caves and densest jungle. In 2001 tourists amounted to some 10,000 foreigners and 1.5m. domestic visitors.

## DIRECTORY

**Governor:** E. S. L. NARASIMHAN, Office of the Governor, Raj Bhavan, Raipur 492 001; tel. (771) 2331102; fax (771) 2331104; e-mail governor@cg.nic.in.

**Chief Minister:** Dr RAMAN SINGH (Bharatiya Janata Party), Office of the Chief Minister, Government of Chhattisgarh, DKS Bhavan, Mantralaya, Raipur 492 001; tel. (771) 2331004; fax (771) 2331002; e-mail cm@cg.nic.in.

**Speaker of the Legislative Assembly (Vidhan Sabha):** PREM PRAKASH PANDEY, Assembly Secretariat, Zero Point, Baloda Bazar Rd, Raipur 492 005; tel. (771) 2283611; fax (771) 2283788; e-mail secygvs@rediffmail.com; the unicameral Legislative Assembly has 90 mems: Bharatiya Janata Party 52; Congress 34; Bahujan Samaj Party 2; Nationalist Congress Party 1; vacant 1.

**State Resident Commissioner in New Delhi:** R. D. MEENA, Chhattisgarh Bhavan, 7 Sardar Patel Marg, Chanakyapuri, New Delhi 110 021; tel. (11) 26117326; fax (11) 26373651; e-mail cgbhawan@rediffmail.com.

# Goa

The State of Goa, until 1961 the heart of the Portuguese 'State of India', lies midway along the western shore of the Indian peninsula, jutting down from its northern neighbour, Maharashtra, into Karnataka, which lies to the south and to the east. In 1987 Goa, hitherto a union territory with Daman and Diu, became the 25th state of the Union. It also became the smallest state, with an area of only 3,702 sq km (1,430 sq miles), which is only a little smaller than Rhode Island, the smallest state of the USA, but larger than Luxembourg, the smallest member nation of the European Union (except Malta).

Goa lies on the coastal plains below the Western Ghats, giving it some high ground, steeply rising in the east of the state with some more hill country in the south, where a spur of the Ghats stretches towards the Arabian Sea (the highest point in the state is in the south-east, at 1,022 m—3,354 ft). The state consists of upland areas of poor red laterite soils broken up by fertile alluvial plains and rich deltas. Central plains stretch northwards to the Zuari (a river which divides the south from the north of Goa) and Mandovi (Mahdei) estuaries, which once used to join at high tide, defining the original 'island of Goa'. The Terekhel (Tiracol) defines the northern border, except at its mouth, where the old Fort Tiracol gave Goa a foothold on the northern bank of the river. Some of the deltas still contain tracts of the old mangrove forests, while there is some dense woodland remaining in the highlands, but most of the landscape is dominated by coconut trees and rice cultivation in the valleys and thin, scrubby vegetation on the low, plateau uplands. The climate is tropical, tempered by the sea and, in the hills, by altitude. Heat and humidity increase from April and into June, when the torrential rains of the monsoon begin, the main season lasting to the end of July. The tropical winter is dry, but warm, lasting from October to March. Average annual rainfall in the state is 3,149 mm (124 inches).

Goa is the smallest state in area, but only the third smallest in population—1,347,668 at 1 March 2001 (according to the results of the national census). The population density was 364 per sq km. There is a large Goan diaspora, both internationally and in other Indian cities, notably Mumbai (formerly Bombay), to the north, in Maharashtra. Although there are many Goans of mixed-race descent, with Portuguese surnames, most of the population are still strongly connected to the neighbouring Indian cultures. Just over one-half speak Konkani (51.5%, according to the 1991 census), as in the coastal districts of Karnataka to the south, and it was declared Goa's official language in 2000. It is, however, more prevalent in the countryside and Marathi is more widely taught in government primary schools—in 1991 Marathi was the first language of 33.4% of the population. Marathi is also used for official purposes. Some people also speak Kannada (4.6%), while Portuguese survives among the older generations, and English and Hindi are increasingly used. Despite the profusion of churches, most of the population are Hindu (65.8% in 2001), although there is a significant Christian minority (26.7%) and a Muslim one (6.8%). Only 1.1% of the population were counted among the Scheduled Castes in 2001.

Goa is the most urbanized state in India (49.8% of the population in 2001) and, of the territories, only Delhi, Chandigarh and Puducherry (Pondicherry) have higher urbanization rates. The largest town and the state's industrial centre is Vasco da Gama, on the promontory marking the south of the Zuari delta, and its port of Mormugao (Marmagao) is one of the busiest in the region. The next largest town is the capital, Panaji (Panjim), while the commercial capital of the south is Margao (Madgaon), headquarters of the rich taluk of Salcete, part of the original 'Old Conquest' region, which also includes Bardez (a taluk headquartered in Mapusa), to the north of Panaji. The main town of the Hindu interior is Ponda. The state is divided into two districts.

## HISTORY

Today's State of Goa is very much defined by its experience of Portuguese rule, but its history, as part of the Konkan Coast, predates the arrival of Vasco da Gama and his fellow countrymen at the end of the 15th century. According to legend, Goa, if identified with Gomant in the *Mahabharata*, like Kerala, was another territory wrested from the sea by Parasurama, the sixth incarnation of Vishnu. Shiva, and Rama and Sita are also supposed to have stayed in the area. In other Vedic sources the low-lying land beneath the Western Ghats is called Gomant, but also Govapuri or Gove. The ancient Hindu city (Goa Velha—distinct from Velha Goa, the Old Goa of the Portuguese) of Govapuri or Gopakapattana lies in the south of the 'island of Goa' and once dominated trade along the Zuari, until silting inhibited traffic and the Bahmanis sacked it in the 15th century, some decades before the arrival of the Portuguese.

There is some mention of Goa in the famous rock edicts of the great Mauryan emperor, Ashoka (who sent the Buddhist monk, Dharmarakshita, to the region), where the local people are described as Peitinikas, Rashtrikas and Bhojas. Certainly, shortly after the Mauryan era, when the Satavahanas annexed the Konkan Coast, Bhoja was the name of the related house to administer the region on their behalf. A dynasty of this name seems to have survived into the Christian era, as archaeological evidence from the fourth to the seventh centuries reveals a Bhoja dynasty still in Chandrapura (now Chandor, just to the south-east of Margao). However, the Konkan region was under the Abhiras and their vassals, the Traikutakas, from the fourth century, then, briefly, under the Kalachuris and their vassals, another dynasty by the name of Maurya, in the middle of the sixth century. From 578 until 750 the overlords of the region were the Western Chalukyas, a dynasty of northern Karnataka, who were replaced by the Rashtrakutas until 1020. The Later Western Chalukyas (see History of Karnataka below) then became the dominant power on the Konkan Coast until the mid-12th century, installing the Kadambas as feudatories who were to outlast them (from 1163 to the beginning of the 14th century the Kadambas owed allegiance to the Yadavas or Sevunas, based in modern Maharashtra). Gopakapattana was developed as the capital city of the region by the Kadamba rajah, Jayakeshi I. One of his successors, Kavadeva, was ruling Goa and its environs when Yadava authority on the Konkan Coast collapsed at the end of the 13th century, because the Muslim armies of the Delhi Sultans had begun incursions into peninsular India. Kavadeva defended against the opportunistic advances from the south of the Hoysalas, defeating Balalla III early in 1301, but did not prevent further Yadava–Hoysala rivalries. However, the great Hoysala king soon had to deal with invasions by Muslim generals himself, while the Yadavas were gradually eliminated completely. Kavadeva's city of Gopakapattana was itself probably sacked in 1312—certainly the capital was moved to the fortifications of Chandrapura in 1318, only later to fall to the forces of Muhammed bin Tughluq (Sultan of Delhi in 1325–51). The Kadambas seem to have retained some territory in Goa, but they were now minor players in the emerging contest for the Konkan Coast between Vijayanagar and the initially dominant Bahmani sultans from the mid-14th century.

After a short period of peace between the two empires, problems within the Bahmani realm meant that the forces of Vijayanagar under Madhav Mantri re-established Hindu suzerainty along the Konkan Coast. By 1380 he had conquered the Kadamba capital of Chandrapura and occupied the Konkan capital at Gopakapattana or Govapuri. Madhav made Govapuri the seat of the viceroy of Konkan and dominated the western defences of Vijayanagar for the rest of the century. Goa flourished as a trading centre specializing in the import of horses, essential to the military of both the Deccan powers. There is a recorded succession of viceroys right up to about 1454, when one Baichanna Wodeyar held the post. The power of Vijayanagar in the region seems to have waned thereafter, perhaps a symptom of weakening central authority against powerful local nayaks, because formal Muslim conquest seems not to have taken place until 1470–72 (although Portuguese chroniclers believed it to have been as early as 1440), when ancient Govapuri was sacked and abandoned, and a new city built at what is now Old Goa. The nayaks of Konkan had included two Maratha brothers, Kanoji and Appaji, who ruled Bankapur, which took in Goa. After them it was their uncle, Sabaji (whose brother, Timoja, was an admiral of Vijayanagar), who ruled Goa itself for the Muslim governor of Konkan. The third governor attempted to make his fief the basis for a successor state of the disintegrating Bahmani kingdom in 1490, but was defeated and killed only three years later and the Konkan Coast fell to the Adil Shahis in Bijapur (now Karnataka), with Goa being developed as a second capital of the sultans.

The Portuguese navigator, Vasco da Gama, arrived off the coast of Kerala on 17 May 1498 and direct contact between Christian Europe and India was made for the first time. Pedro Alvares Cabral led the second voyage in 1500 and established a Portuguese base or factory in Kochi (Cochin, in Kerala) in 1503. By this time da Gama had set sail on his second voyage, in 1502, charged by the royal Government with replacing the Arabs as controllers of the sea trade with India, which ambition had been achieved by the Portuguese within two decades. At the foundations of this power—of which the first opponents were the naval powers of Kozhikode (Calicut, in Kerala), Egypt and Gujarat—was the first Viceroy of a 'State of India' (Estado da India) appointed in 1505, Francisco de Almeida, who developed friendly relations with another nominally anti-Muslim power, Vijayanagar (which had, so far, failed to retake Goa). In 1509 he was succeeded by Afonso de Albuquerque, who seized the 'island of Goa' (Tiswadi) in

1510 and made it the capital of a burgeoning Portuguese empire in the East Indies, with Malacca (Melaka, now in Malaysia) being taken in 1511 and Ormuz (Hormuz), the strait controlling the entrance to the Persian (Arabian) Gulf (now lying between Oman and Iran), in 1515, although an attempt to take Aden (now in Yemen), at the mouth of the Red Sea, failed. Later in 1515, on 15 December, Albuquerque died, although he had already consolidated Portuguese authority on the 'island of Goa' and mapped out the development of the administration and policy in the new territory—the population was militarized and the intermarriage of the Portuguese men with local women was permitted, in order to create a loyal population, who came to be known as Casados, with preferential entry to the lower orders of the administration and military. Although the Muslims of Goa were massacred when Albuquerque finally secured the city in 1510, a Hindu governor was initially appointed and most local customs were not interfered with until Christian proselytizing by Roman Catholic orders began in earnest. This was felt in force after the introduction of the Inquisition in 1540—the most famous missionary, Francis Xavier, a Jesuit, arrived in 1542 (he was recognized as a saint by the Roman Catholic Church in 1622)—and in 1543 Goa became the seat of an archbishop. At the same time, in 1543, the period of the so-called Old Conquest ended in Goa, leaving its name for the central territories of modern Goa—the island of Tiswadi, Bardez to the north and Salcete to the south. Bijapur had tried to retake Goa in 1516, but had failed, and then lost Bardez, Salcete and Ponda to the Portuguese in 1520, when distracted by war with Vijayanagar. Bijapur had recovered the territories, only to lose Bardez and Salcete again in 1532, when a local governor, Asad Khan, gave them to the Portuguese in return for help against the sultan. However, a change in monarch restored Asad Khan to loyalty and he seized the two territories back for Bijapur in 1536. In a subsequent dispute between Asad Khan and the sultan, the Portuguese sided with the latter and were rewarded with the final settlement of Bardez and Salcete in 1543, concluding the Old Conquest in Goa (Diu and Daman—now the two parts of a separate union territory, consisting of enclaves in Gujarat—were also added, in 1541 and 1559, respectively). Their position was confirmed by defeating a grand alliance under Bijapur in 1570, at which time the economic welfare of the territory required a relaxation of religious persecution of Hindus, in order not to drive them all away. By this time Goa was not only the seat of an archbishopric, but also a city with the same civic privileges as Lisbon (the capital of Portugal), and it was at its most prosperous and powerful between this time and the end of the century. It was to be broken not by a local threat, but by another European power, the Dutch, who were fighting for freedom from the rule of Spain (with which Portugal was in personal union between 1580 and 1640).

The Dutch blockaded Goa in 1603 and 1639, the latter time only four years after disease had ravaged the colony to such an extent that the defences had relied on criminals deported from Lisbon. By 1668 the Dutch had driven the Portuguese from most of their Indian possessions, as well as from Malacca and Ceylon (Sri Lanka). Pressure from the Dutch and from anti-Portuguese Indian rulers did not stop, with Goa saved from a sustained Maratha attack in 1683 only because they, in turn, were under assault from the Mughals. By this time it had been decided to move the capital to a more secure location, and one less prone to the ravages of disease. A fort was built at Mormugao in 1685, and the Viceroy actually moved to the new town in 1701, although Margao was soon settled upon as the new headquarters instead. In 1759 the capital finally moved to Panaji (Panjim—soon after this the viceroy was redesignated a governor, only for the previous title to reappear in the early 19th century and then, finally, to become a governor-general from 1837). During these moves Old Goa had rapidly dwindled in size, having had a population of 20,000 in 1695, but only 1,600 by the mid-19th century. Meanwhile, Dutch power was waning and the Portuguese were no threat to the new European rivalry in India between the French and the British. Thus, the period of the New Conquest began, from 1741, territory being expanded by force or by negotiation with disputatious local rulers. In 1776 the occupation of Fort Tiracol on the north bank of the river now known as the Terekhel extended Goa to its furthest north, while in the south the lands around Canacona and Karwar marked the southern limit, reached in 1791. During this time the Ranes, a Rajput tribe, which had migrated south to settle near Sanquelim and serve as mercenaries to the Portuguese, proceeded to lead a number of serious rebellions against the authorities when their privileges were compromised or their liberties threatened. The most serious were ended in 1855 by a peace treaty with Dipaji Rane, who was awarded the title of Captain, and in 1895, when troops were brought from Portugal and peace was again concluded with the leader, Dada Rane Advalikar. The last Rane revolt was in 1917 and was brutally suppressed.

Within the first quarter of the 20th century there was beginning to be the first stirrings of nationalist unrest in British India. In 1930 the National Congress (Goa) was formed to campaign for freedom in Portuguese India, and it demanded the withdrawal of the colonial power in 1942, gaining official support from the all-India movement in 1946. Civil disobedience in Goa, Daman and Diu began, but was treated harshly by the authorities, particularly as the old Indian Empire around it began to move towards Independence in 1947. This militarization of the situation in the colony elicited the formation of a movement in favour of armed struggle, Azad Gomantak Dal, in April. Meanwhile, newly independent India attempted to negotiate with Portugal (ruled by a nationalist dictator) about the incorporation of Goa. These attempts failed and India suspended diplomatic relations in 1953. All the Goan nationalist parties started *satyagraha* (non-violent demonstrations or passive resistance) in August 1954. Activists from India attempted to occupy Tiracol Fort in the same month, while others had already entered Dadra and Nagar Haveli (inland enclaves near the northern territory of Daman) to 'liberate' them from Portuguese rule. The Indian Government refused to permit Portuguese forces to reinforce the enclaves and, in 1955, organized an economic blockade of Goa, which heightened tensions but solved nothing. Eventually the National Congress (Goa) urged a dialogue with Portugal, but tensions continued. Finally, in the early hours of 18 December 1961 the Indian Army moved into the remnants of the Estado da India. 'Operation Vijay' (Victory) ended successfully one day later and a new administration under a military governor (K. P. Candeth—who died in May 2003) was introduced on 20 December, a date that the Indian Parliament was retrospectively to declare, in 1962, the date of Goa, Daman and Diu's incorporation (as a Union Territory) into the Union.

The first Legislative Assembly was elected in December 1962, with the winners, the Maharashtrawadi Gomantak Party (MGP), forming the first popular ministry. This party organized a referendum in 1967 on whether Goa should merge into Maharashtra (and Daman and Diu into Gujarat), but the people of the different parts of the territory opted to retain their existing status. The MGP continued to control territorial government until 1979, when Congress displaced them, although the issue of relations with Maharashtra and the status of Marathi continued to dominate politics. On 30 May 1987 Goa parted from Daman and Diu and became a full state of the Union. Meanwhile, regional issues were being displaced by the environment in local politics, and the Hindu vote was increasingly contested with the MGP by the rising Bharatiya Janata Party (BJP). In 1999 Congress only won 10 of the 40 seats in the Assembly, but formed a Government under Luizhnio Faleiro (the most recent victor of the party power struggles, before President's Rule had been imposed earlier in the year), who himself fell victim to a rebellion in November, to be replaced by Francisco Sardinha. A BJP-led coalition displaced Congress altogether in November under Manohar Parrikar (not long after the BJP had won both the state's Lok Sabha seats in the national general election). The coalition proved unable to last the full term of the third state Assembly, and the legislature was dissolved in February 2002, pending new elections, which took place at the end of May. The results were inconclusive, despite Congress hopes of a reaction to the communal violence in Gujarat. The BJP gained 17 of the 40 possible seats and Congress 16, and it was the incumbent premier, Parrikar, who was able to form a new coalition, with the support of the MGP and the Christian-dominated United Goans Democratic Party (UGDP), leaving Congress in opposition. Parrikar welcomed national proposals in April 2003 to amend the law on political defections by elected representatives at both the national and the state level—Goa had elected four assemblies since the 1990s, twice having had to dissolve them prematurely owing to defections, and the state had had 13 chief ministers in that time, as a result of defections on 21 occasions (involving 80 deputies). This fractiousness encouraged the new, Congress-led national Government to replace four BJP governors, including Goa's, in July 2004 (at the general election in May Congress and the BJP had each won one of the state's two Lok Sabha seats, whereas both had been won by the BJP in 1999). Although this move created some controversy, the Governor of Goa was himself considered a controversial character, not least for advocating the replacement of some Portuguese-era churches with the pre-existing Hindu temples. However, the new Governor, S. C. Jamir, the former premier of Nagaland, was soon to find himself in a far more controversial position.

The slender majority of the Government was again tested in the legislature in August 2004, but despite rumours that Sudin Dhavaliker of the MGP and Filip Neri Rodrigues, an independent, had withdrawn their support, the Parrikar ministry retained the confidence of the Assembly. The BJP seemed to consolidate its position when Isidore Fernandes (who had defected from Congress) won a by-election in October and when Francisco 'Micky' Pacheco, who had split from the UGDP to form his own UGDP (United), formally merged with the BJP towards the end of January 2005 (to avoid the provisions of the anti-defection law, which compels a resigning member to recontest the seat). Including the Speaker, the BJP-led Government commanded the support of 24 of the 40 Assembly members, whereas Congress held 15 seats and had the support of the Nationalist Congress Party (NCP) member. However, also at the end of the month, the deteriorating relationship between the Chief Minister and Atanasio 'Babush' Monserette, hitherto a BJP minister (also originally elected for the UGDP), provoked the latter's resignation. Monserette was joined by the recently elected Fernandes and by two ministers, Rodrigues, the independent, and Dhavaliker of the MGP. The remaining UGDP member, Mathany Saldhana, the Minister of Tourism, was away in Spain, but a letter of resignation was handed in on his behalf. Finally, Pacheco and Pandurang Madkaikar (who had originally been elected for the MGP, only to join the BJP soon after) resigned from the BJP. These last two, as well as Monserette and Fernandes, therefore had to seek re-election to the Assembly. The Governor duly instructed the Chief Minister to seek a confidence vote at the earliest possible time.

On 31 January 2005 Mathany Saldhana returned from Spain and defied his party instructions—Saldhana, the only UGDP deputy, announced that he would continue his support for the Government. On the eve of the confidence motion of 2 February, therefore, both the Government and the opposition claimed the support of 18 Assembly members in what had become a 36-member chamber. However, one of the BJP members was the Speaker, who could only vote in the event of a tie. There was, therefore, some controversy when, just before the vote of confidence was taken, the Speaker, Vishwas Satarkar, added to the agenda by disqualifying Rodrigues under the anti-defection law, claiming that he was not an independent, as elected, but had joined the BJP in 2002. Hence, with the deciding vote of the Speaker, the Government was assured of a majority and won the confidence motion.

Opposition legislators complained to the Governor, himself a former Congress politician, who condemned the action of the Speaker and promptly dismissed the Parrikar Government. Not long before midnight of the same day, 2 February 2005, the Governor appointed Congress leader Pratapsing Rane as Chief Minister. Rane, who had been premier for two terms from 1980, again (for only 75 days) in 1990 and between 1994 and 1999, appointed three of those seeking re-election to his Government, as well as the NCP member, Wilfred D'Souza (himself a former premier). Meanwhile, despite BJP attempts to keep its Assembly members together and isolated, Digamber Kamat, deputy leader in the former Government, resigned from the BJP and the Assembly, leaving the party with only 17 supporters in the chamber. On 28 February, just before the Rane Government was meant to secure the trust of the legislature, the Speaker again disqualified Rodrigues and then he and his deputy, also a BJP member, resigned, leaving the Assembly with no choice but to adjourn.

The Governor appointed a senior Congress member and another former premier, Francisco Sardinha, as acting (pro tem) Speaker, reducing the new Government's active support by one vote. A new test of confidence was scheduled for 4 March 2005. Just before that motion was considered, Speaker Sardinha disqualified the former Minister of Tourism, Saldhana, from participating on the ground that he had broken the anti-defection rules and supported the BJP Government against the official line of the UGDP. The new Government, therefore, won the confidence vote in the same way as the old one had done over three weeks earlier—by use of the Speaker's deciding vote. Obviously both state-wide and national controversy was reignited by these events. However, by now India was also gripped by the political controversy in Jharkhand, where gubernatorial judgement was also being questioned and Congress embarrassed. As a result, later on 4 March the Union authorities imposed President's Rule on Goa, despite the protests of the local Congress party.

By-elections to five Assembly seats were held in Goa on 4 June 2005. The BJP held only one seat (winning against Fernandes), while Congress won three (Monserette, Madkaikar and Kamat) and the NCP one (with Pacheco as the winning candidate). Meanwhile, in an unconnected case, the courts had annulled the original 2002 elections of two more BJP members of the Legislative Assembly, although implementation of the judgment was stayed, leaving the BJP with 15 supporters when the suspension of the legislature ended (the Supreme Court upheld the judgments in January 2007). President's Rule ended with the reappointment of Rane as Chief Minister on 7 June, now with the support of 21 members of what was currently a 39-member Assembly. There was one last twist to the saga, however, only a couple of days later. D'Souza refused to take up his appointment to the deputy premiership when it emerged that his NCP colleague, Pacheco, had not also been appointed to the Government. The threat of NCP withdrawal from the coalition was ended after the intervention of the national leadership. The continuing threat to the stability of the ruling coalition remained the fractiousness of Congress, which suffered two important defections in the approach to the 2007 state elections: former premier Churchill Alemao formed his own party, the Save Goa Front (SGF); and Babush Monserrete rejoined the UGDP, having resigned after widespread agitation against a development plan that was withdrawn (and after his wife was refused Congress backing as a candidate). Thus, at the polls on 2 June, Congress retained 16 seats, but lost two to the SGF; the NCP won three seats, but its leader, D'Souza, lost his. Vishwajit Rane, the son of the Chief Minister, won as an independent; he supported the Congress-led coalition, as did the other independent, Anil Salgaoncar, and the MGP's two deputies (who were brothers). However, the central Congress leadership surprised the two main contenders for the premiership, incumbent Pratapsing Rane and Ravi Naik (Chief Minister in 1991–93 and for less than a week in 1994), by selecting Digambar Kamat to head the Government. Kamat, a member of the BJP less than three years earlier, was sworn in on 8 June; Rane was later elected Speaker (the previous Speaker, Sardinha, had lost his constituency to the SGF). The BJP, which had kept 14 seats, headed the opposition. The UGDP retained only one seat.

The brittle nature of Goan political settlements doomed the Kamat Government to the same instability as earlier administrations. On the night of 25 July 2007, less than two months after the elections, the Congress-led coalition was unexpectedly rendered into a minority by the withdrawal of the MGP and the independent Salgaoncar and by the defection of the only woman deputy, Victoria Fernandes, from Congress to the BJP (she consequently resigned her seat). Congress complacency was punished when the BJP claimed the right to form the Government, with the support of the MGP, the SGF, the UGDP and Salgaoncar. The usual, unedifying spectacle of political and procedural machination followed, with the Governor eventually asking for a vote of confidence when the legislature met again on 30 June. However, Speaker Rane first disqualified the two MGP deputies from voting (Fernandes did not attend the sitting). Rane's casting vote thus saved the Kamat Government, but ensured that the opposition would seek redress in the courts. Congress won a by-election to the Lok Sabha in November, keeping its seat, but the essential instability of the coalition was demonstrated further in 2008. In mid-January dissatisfaction with the policies of the Minister of Finance, Dayanand Narvekar, particularly his furtherance of an information technology park in the state, led to a four-day revolt. The three NCP legislators and an independent sitting as a minister resigned, reducing the Government to a minority, although any immediate test of strength was avoided by the prorogation of the Assembly. The NCP members seemingly acted in defiance of their national leadership. The state NCP deputies then declared that they wished to form a Government and that they had the support of the independent who had left office with them, as well as the two MGP members and the UGDP member, who had hitherto supported the coalition externally, on an issue basis. It was unclear whether the grouping expected support from the BJP or Congress, but the rebellion then subsided, although tensions remained. There was a hint of further crisis in April, involving personal rivalries, party tensions and resentment within Congress as a result of the accommodation of coalition partners. Congress now commanded, nominally at least, 18 seats in the Assembly, following the late January readmittance of the SGF.

## ECONOMY

Goa is one of the country's premier tourist destinations and India's wealthiest state, in terms of per head wealth (it has been exceeded only by the territory of Chandigarh since 2003). The net state domestic product in 2004/05 was put at Rs 84,860m., or Rs 58,184 per head. A compact, small (India's smallest) state, Goa has relatively well developed infrastructure and 100% electrification of its rural areas, generating a surplus on its energy requirements. In 2006 installed capacity totalled 305.1 MW (down from 454.7 MW one year earlier): 84% from the Centre and 16% from the private sector, with less than 0.1 MW from the state sector. In 1998 there were 224 km of national highway in the state, 232 km of state highway and 815 km of district roads, contributing towards one of the highest road-network densities in India. The coastal Konkan Railway connects Goa to Mumbai (Maharashtra) in the north and Mangalore (Karnataka) and as far as Thiruvananthapuram (Kerala) in the south. Vasco da Gama also has a freight-rail connection into Karnataka (the two railway lines intersect at Margao), as well as the state's international airport of Dabolim. The city's port of Mormugao is by far the largest in the state and a significant sea link on India's western coast. Educational infrastructure is good, and the state recorded a high literacy rate of 82.3% at the census of 2001.

Agriculture provided 6.6% of gross state domestic product in 2001/02 (the lowest proportion of any state). Goa has always had trouble finding enough good agricultural land to feed itself; its main food crop is paddy (grown on 57,207 ha, or 141,358 acres, in 2000/01), but also pulses, millets, sugar cane and fruits. The main plantation crops are cashew nuts (53,767 ha) and coconuts (25,025 ha). Rice production increased fairly steadily from the mid-1990s, to reach a record 208,900 metric tons in 1999/2000, only to fall off thereafter to 126,500 tons by 2001/02 (when 136,000 tons of food grains in total were harvested, the balance consisting mostly of pulses). The sugar-cane harvest reached its record in 1989/90 (81,700 tons), but, after a decline in the mid-1990s, recovered to 72,800 tons in 2000/01 and 70,600 tons the year afterwards. In 1998/99 Goa produced 121m. coconuts. Livestock included 99,598 head of cattle and 44,674 of buffaloes in 1998, as well as 89,852 head of pigs and 928,985 poultry. Livestock products included eggs (115m. in 2002/03) and some milk (46,000 tons). The total area under forest in 2000/01 was 125,473 ha

(33.9% of the total area of the state), almost all of it government owned, and this can produce important revenues from timber, bamboo and barks. With about 105 km of coastline and extensive inland waterways, fishing is an important activity, engaging 30,225 people in 1998/99, according to official statistics, with a catch of 65,841 tons, earning some Rs 902.9m.

Traditionally, mining was the only industrial activity of any size in the state up to the 1960s, but others have been developed since, notably the electronics and software industries from the late 1990s. Given the state's success with tourism, the authorities have been eager to develop more environmentally friendly industries. Iron, manganese and bauxite ores are the most valuable minerals present in Goa, but iron ore, overwhelmingly, is the most important (of 13.7m. metric tons of mineral ores produced in 1996/97, 13.6m. tons were iron ore). In 1997/98 exports (from Mormugao) of iron ore totalled 18.4m. tons and earned Rs 9,060.9m. The industry employs about 11,000 people directly and 10,000 indirectly (a total of 21,255 in 2001/02). The value of total mineral production in 2002/03 was Rs 5,024m. In addition, there are 18 industrial estates in Goa. At the end of March 2001 there were 626 factories operating, employing almost 40,000 people daily. The number of small-scale registered units at that time was 6,157, employing over 42,300 people, while 138 medium and large-scale units employed almost 21,000.

A famous beach destination, imbued with a distinctive Portuguese inheritance, as well as a Hindu and even Muslim past, the state has attracted increasing numbers of visitors, reaching some 1.2m. annually by the end of the 1990s. This includes 12% of all India's foreign tourists and 75% of all direct charter flights. At the end of 2001, official figures put the number of hotels and guest houses at about 1,900, about four-fifths of them in north Goa. In turn, this has helped to encourage the development of other service-sector activities, such as banking and finance, commerce, transportation and communications.

### DIRECTORY

**Governor:** SHIVINDER SINGH SIDHU, Office of the Governor, Raj Bhavan, Cabo Raj Nivas, Panaji 403 004; tel. (832) 2453501; fax (832) 2453510; e-mail governor@rajbhavangoa.org.

**Chief Minister:** DIGAMBAR KAMAT (Congress), Office of the Chief Minister, Secretariat, Panaji 403 001; tel. (832) 2223970; fax (832) 2223648; e-mail cmgoa@goa.nic.in.

**Speaker of the Legislative Assembly:** PRATAPSING RANE, Office of the Speaker, Legislative Assembly Complex, Porvorim, Panaji 403 001; tel. (832) 2410915; fax (832) 2411066; the unicameral Legislative Assembly has 40 mems (one vacant, Aug. 2007): Congress 15, Bharatiya Janata Party 14, Nationalist Congress Party 3, Maharashtrawadi Gomantak Party 2, Save Goa Front 2, United Goans Democratic Party 1, independents 2.

**State Resident Commissioner in New Delhi:** DR VIJAY MADAN, Goa Sadan, 18 Amrita Shergil Marg, New Delhi 110 003; tel. (11) 24629967; fax (11) 24629956.

# Gujarat

The State of Gujarat lies in western India, where the peninsula forming much of India joins the Asian mainland. Further along the coast are the mouths of the Indus, in Pakistan, which lies north beyond a broad marshland, the Rann of Kachchh (Kutch). Another Indian state, Rajasthan, is to the north and north-east, and there is a short eastern border with Madhya Pradesh. Maharashtra, with which Gujarat was united as Bombay state until 1960, lies to the south-east and south. The southern border with Maharashtra, as it nears the sea, is broken by Nagar Haveli, part of the Union Territory of Dadra and Nagar Haveli. Dadra is just to the north of the larger enclave and is entirely surrounded by Gujarat. The territory was once Portuguese, administered from the nearby coastal district of Daman, which (except along the sea) is also enclosed by Gujarat. Daman forms part of another Union Territory, Daman and Diu, the second part of which is an island lying off the Kathiawar peninsula. The total area of Gujarat state is 196,022 sq km (75,713 sq miles).

The highly indented coastline of Gujarat is some 1,600 km (almost 1,000 miles) long. In the north-west of Gujarat the Great Rann of Kachchh (a 20,700-sq-km salt marsh) stretches eastwards from the coast, then extends an arm south to join with the Little Rann, which lies at the head of the Gulf of Kachchh. These seasonal swamps and the sea surround the higher ground of the Kachchh peninsula. South of the Gulf of Kachchh is the fanlike Kathiawar peninsula, defined in the west by the Gulf of Khambhat (Cambay). This region, known as Saurashtra, is centred on the Mandav Hills, with the higher Girnar Hills to the south and the low Barda Hills to the west. Inland (although no part of the state is more than 160 km—99 miles—from the sea), the north-east of Gujarat is an extension of the central ridge of Kachchh, consisting of small plains and low hills. These plains extend into the south-east, beyond the Gulf of Khambhat and over the mighty River Narmada, where they become coastal plains beneath the Western Ghats, running south to the Konkan Coast. The entire eastern border of the state is defined by a crescent of rising land, be it the Western Ghats and the edge of the Deccan or Mount Abu and the arid beginnings of Rajasthan. Rainfall in the state itself is highly variable, decreasing to the north, as Gujarat is not in the direct path of the main rain-bearing winds. Southern Saurashtra and the plains beneath the Ghats can sometimes receive annual rainfall in excess of 1,500 mm (59 inches), but for Ahmedabad on the plains north of the Gulf of Khambhat it is more like 900 mm, while Kachchh, on the edge of the deserts to the north, has often recorded less than 25 mm per year. Most rainfall is during the monsoon, between June and October, when the climate is humid but the extreme heat of the summer is moderated. In the north winter nights can be cold, occasionally even freezing, but in the south temperatures generally are more moderate.

According to the March 2001 census, the total population of Gujarat was 50,671,017—although this includes estimates for those districts in the west of the state most severely affected by the earthquake of January earlier that year. The average population density at the time was 258 per sq km. The state is home to 4.9% of India's total population, according to the census of 2001, but it includes a higher than average proportion from the Scheduled Tribes (in 2001 tribal people accounted for 14.8% of Gujarat's population) and lower than average Scheduled Castes (7.1% in 2001). Most of the population are of Indo-Aryan extraction, their language, Gujarati, being of that language family—it is derived from Sanskrit, but influenced by the Apabrahmsa spoken in north-west India in the 10th–14th centuries. Gujarati includes much vocabulary adopted from other languages, notably Persian, but also Arabic, Portuguese and, most recently, English, a feature indicative of its maritime history. English is widely spoken in the urban centres, but the main official minority tongue after Gujarati (which was the first language of an overwhelming 91.5% of the population in 1991) is Hindi (2.9%), followed by Sindhi (1.7%—the language of the neighbouring region of Pakistan), Marathi (1.4%) and Urdu (1.3%). Tribes represented in the state include the Bhil, the Bhangi, the Koli, the Dhubla, the Naikda and the Macchi-Kharwa. Most Gujaratis follow Hinduism (89.1%, according to the 2001 census), but there is also a significant Muslim community (9.1%) and the state is one of the main redoubts of the Jains. Although the Jains (mostly of the Svetembara sect) only constituted 1.0% of the population in 2001, they are influential in business (only banking and commerce were considered truly non-violent activities) and the cultural history of Gujarat. Mahatma Gandhi, who was born in the state, was greatly influenced by Jain concepts such as *ahimsa* (non-harm or non-violence). There are a small number of Christians and some Sikhs. There are still some Zoroastrian Parsis in Surat, which was their main settlement in India from the 12th century until the rise of Bombay (now Mumbai, in Maharashtra).

Gujarat is one of the more urbanized of the major states, with 37.4% of the population living in urban areas in 2001, and has some of India's largest cities. The old capital, Ahmedabad, is the state's largest city (it was also the country's sixth largest city, with a population of 3.52m. in 2001), followed by Surat (10th largest in India, with 2.43m.) and Vadodara (Baroda—18th, 1.31m.), both in the south-east, and Rajkot (31st, 967,476) in Saurashtra. The city named for Mahatma Gandhi, Gandhinagar, is located 23 km north of Ahmedabad and was built specifically as the capital in the 1960s, after Gujarat became a separate state. The main city of the west, and the major city most affected by the 2001 earthquake, is Bhuj. The state is divided into 25 districts.

### HISTORY

Gujarat has an ancient history, with evidence of some of India's earliest stone-age settlements and numerous Harappan sites from about 4,000 years ago, although the discovery in the early 2000s of sunken ruins in the Gulf of Khambhat (Cambay) had the potential to push back the flowering of civilization in the region still further. The Mauryas incorporated Gujarat into their empire, but as their power declined the region was exposed to invasions from the north-west. A pattern of foreign invaders establishing themselves in India and becoming naturalized can be seen clearly in Gujarat with the Scythian or Shaka people, who arrived in the centuries immediately preceding the Christian era. The originally Zoroastrian Shakas had a Persic empire based in Bactria (northern Afghanistan) and the Punjab. The satraps or governors of the south-western provinces survived the Shaka being displaced by the Kushana, and ruled in Gujarat, Sindh and Baluchistan (the latter two regions in modern Pakistan). These Shakas, known as the Western Satraps or Kshatrapas, adopted the Hindu pantheon and used Sanskrit as the language of government long before the Guptas ensured its revival in royal courts throughout the subcontinent. In fact, their kingdom made strong by wealth, they resisted Gupta domination into the fourth century AD.

In the late first century AD the Kshatrapas had extended their lands into Rajasthan and established a subsidiary satrapy to the north of the Narmada, in Malwa. The latter did not long survive the counter-attack of the Satavahanas, who ruled the western Deccan and had grown rich by encouraging trade with the ports on the Arabian Sea. Chashtana, the general commanded to restore Shaka prestige, founded his own satrapal dynasty and started the fight to reclaim for the Kshatrapas territory beyond Gujarat. His grandson, Rudradaman, who claimed to have completed this mission in around 150, was the greatest of the Kshatrapas. He not only reconquered Malwa, but also defeated the Satavahanas twice and gained extensive new territories in Sindh and Rajasthan, the latter mainly at the expense of the warrior-republic of the Yaudheyas. Rudradaman was also acclaimed for his personal attributes, which, apart from the standard boasts of martial and sporting prowess, seemed intent on promoting him as an ideal of Indian kingship—maybe a conscious policy for a naturalizing dynasty. Significantly, the inscription from which much of this information is taken is the earliest one of any substance to be found in classical Sanskrit. The Mauryas and Satavahanas tended to use variants of Prakrit, the devolved offshoot of Sanskrit from which many of the modern languages of common use were to spring: Gujarati, Hindi, Marathi and Punjabi, for instance. This early use of Sanskrit for official purposes, heralding its regularization under the Guptas, may be an early indication of brahminical revival after long years of Buddhist ascendancy.

Almost two centuries later the Kshatrapas came into contact with the expanding empire of the Guptas, as Samudra-Gupta forced his sovereignty into modern Rajasthan and to the borders of Malwa. Although the Shaka dynasty initially held its own against the Magadhan forces, this merely earned them the determined enmity of the great Chandra-Gupta II (who reigned *circa* 375–415), who soon conquered eastern Malwa and was often based there to direct the continuing struggle against the rulers of Gujarat. By 409 numismatic evidence suggests that Kshatrapa territory had succumbed in its entirety to Gupta rule. It has been suggested that the Guptas not only gained new lands and great wealth from the acquisition of the western ports, but also the rich influence of Gujarati culture and architecture to add to their own achievements. In the sixth century, as the Gupta empire declined and the Huns raided into northern India, devastating Buddhism in the Indus basin and sundering the overland trade route to China, Gujarat's ports gained in importance. In Saurashtra a local dynasty, the Maitrakas, established itself as independent of the ailing Guptas, although in the mid-seventh century they submitted briefly to the short-lived empire of Harsha Vardhana. A little later, the Chalukyas claimed to have established a viceroyalty in Gujarat. Meanwhile, the Arabs had entered maritime commerce, controlling the vital horse trade, and Muslim communities were present in a number of ports on India's western coast. The Maitraka capital of Vallabhi, misheard as 'Balhara', was the first Indian place name mentioned by Muslim chroniclers, and the neighbouring territory of Sindh was the first to suffer determined assault by the forces of Islam. Indeed, at the beginning of the eighth century Sindh had succumbed to Muslim rule and, although no further advance into India was to take place for some centuries, some military activity by the Arab princes finished the Maitrakas and left the Chalukyas and the Gurjaras to hold the front in Gujarat.

Probably in the wake of the Hun invasions of the sixth century, a nomadic people, the Gurjaras (whence the name Gujarat) had become established in southern Rajasthan. Generally, the Gurjaras share a similarly as obscure origin as the Rajputs, although they certainly spread their influence into the Punjab and made Saurashtra and much of the rest of modern Gujarat their own. One of their royal clans, the Pratiharas, gained the ascendancy in the late eighth century and led the Gurjaras to an empire based on Kannauj (Uttar Pradesh), contesting for supremacy with the Palas of Bengal and the Rashtrakutas of the Deccan. Central Gurjara-Pratihara power waned, but in Gujarat the Gurjaras resisted the incursions of Mahmud of Ghazni (Afghanistan) in the 11th century, although they did not prevent the bloody sack and desecration of the temple-city of Somnath, in southern Saurashtra, in 1025. However, it was not until the end of the 12th century that a serious Muslim advance from the Punjab into the rest of India took place, the first example in Gujarat being the sack of its capital Anhilwara (Patan). The ruling dynasty was a Gurjara-Rajput one, an offshoot of the Chalukyas, the Solankis. They maintained an independent Hindu kingdom for a further century, only finally succumbing to the Sultanate of Delhi in the last years of the 13th century. When Gujarat regained its independence, it was under Muslim rulers, be they native or based in Sindh (the latter ruled much of the west of the modern state in the first half of the 15th century).

Mongol invasions and the sack of Delhi at the end of the 14th century enabled the governor of Gujarat, a Rajput convert to Islam, to assume independence in the early years of the 15th century. However, it was Ahmed Shah, who became sultan in 1411, who began the consolidation of the kingdom. He also founded Ahmedabad as the new capital of the sultanate, which thrived governmentally and culturally on the co-operation between Muslims, Rajputs and even Jains. Thus, although the rulers were always Muslim, they frequently married Rajput princesses and their revenue departments were invariably operated by Jains. After some problem with Malwa aggression in the mid-15th century, Gujarat benefited from the long rule of an exceptional sultan, Mahmud Shah (1459–1511), who is usually known as Mahmud 'Bergarha' ('Two Forts' or 'the Beard'). It was he who conquered Saurashtra, thus gaining control of all the important west-coast ports serving northern India, and ensuring that by the end of the 16th century Ahmedabad was considered one of the richest cities in the world. By 1518 the Gujarat army was strong enough to take Mandu (now in Madhya Pradesh), the capital of Malwa, after the Muslim-Hindu co-operation that also underpinned that kingdom, disintegrated and the sultan appealed for help to Gujarat. Mandu fell to Gujarati forces again in 1531, although this struggle left Malwa ill-equipped to withstand the Mughals, who had recently become established to the north. Gujarat, meanwhile, was also assailed by a new threat, this one challenging its control of the sea trade upon which its wealth depended: the Portuguese. Portugal, with a secure base in Goa, sent forces against Gujarat several times from 1518, having already bested its navy, and eventually gained Diu and then Daman from the sultanate, which itself fell to the Mughals, under Humayun, in his 1534–36 campaign. However, Humayun's treacherous sibling, Askari, who had been installed over the incumbent Ahmed Shah, failed to retain Gujarat for the new empire and the sultanate survived for a few more decades, until finally conquered by Humayun's son, Akbar, in 1573.

Under the peace of the Great Mughals Gujarat prospered. This prosperity attracted other Europeans apart from the Portuguese, who soon lost their monopoly on the maritime trade across the Arabian Sea. At the beginning of the 17th century the Dutch and the British both established bases in Surat, which had replaced the more northerly Khambhat (Cambay) as the main port of north-west India. However, the British were eventually to displace the ports of Gujarat altogether by the foundation of Bombay (now Mumbai, Maharashtra), to where the East India Company moved its headquarters from Surat in 1673, and to where many of Gujarat's merchant classes also followed. Meanwhile, however, the later power of the Europeans was not a major concern in Gujarat, at least, and the future extent of the presidency of Bombay an undreamed of possibility. Instead, the province was a secure part of the Mughal Empire, experiencing upheaval only during succession crises. Thus, in the struggle to succeed Shah Jahan (1627–58), Gujarat provided a base and Surat the wealth for Murad Baksh, the youngest of the aspirant princes. He allied himself to the eventually successful Aurangzeb, the third son, only to be eliminated as a possible threat once victory seemed assured. Gujarat then became the base for another contender, the eldest brother, Dara Shikoh, to make another bid for the throne, only to be defeated and killed. Aurangzeb was secure in his imperial title of Alamgir I and was the last of the Great Mughals, extending the empire into the largest India had seen since that of the Mauryas. One of the impulses for the almost continuous Mughal campaigning in the Deccan from the 1680s until the end of Aurangzeb's reign was the threat of the Marathas, who established an independent state in the Western Ghats with their great leader, Shivaji, as king. One of his exploits to provoke the Great Mughal had been the 1664 raid on and systematic pillage of Surat, which suffered again in 1670, as Shivaji forged his kingdom.

In 1705 Aurangzeb died and the imperial edifice began to crumble, although there were Mughal emperors in Delhi for another 150 years. Until the end, in 1857, the fundamental legitimacy of Mughal sovereignty was not challenged, even by the British, much of whose early success could be attributed to their operation within the imperial hierarchy. Even the Marathas joined the powerful regional governors in seeking both independence and Mughal legitimacy, motivating the former to join in an intervention in Delhi court politics in 1719. By this time the Marathas were in control of Gujarat, having moved up the Konkan Coast and westwards from Malwa to conquer the north-eastern plains of the modern state. However, the Maratha kingdom, although fairly centralized by the first peshwas (hereditary chancellors), was already devolving into the confederacy of later in the century. Gujarat was held by Maratha clans initially opposed to the peshwas, only acknowledging the primacy of the house of Pune (the Maratha capital, in Maharashtra) at the end of the 1720s, after the defeat of their Muslim ally in the Deccan, Nizam-ul-Mulk. By then the Maratha prince who founded the dynasty of Baroda (Vadodara), Damaji Gaekwad, was pre-eminent in Gujarat, although much territory was also possessed by the Scindias of Gwalior (now in Madhya Pradesh). Moreover, the Maratha navy was preying on British shipping, as they were seen as allies of the Mughals, helping the revival of the port of Surat (at the expense of Bombay) for a time and enriching the new rajah. Maratha fortunes, generally, were high, but the increasing lack of cohesion under the peshwa was exposed by a succession dispute at the end of the century, at a time when the Maratha princes needed their strength most against the

British, who already dominated in Bengal and Bihar and in southern India.

The Company administrators in Bombay disrupted British policy in India of not provoking the Marathas by joining the intrigue surrounding the succession to the peshwa-ship. Since the north-western presidency lacked the territory, resources or manpower of Bengal or Madras (the latter named for the city now known as Chennai, in Tamil Nadu), intervention turned out to be damaging to the British reputation. As the British now had an all-India governor-general based in Calcutta (now Kolkata, West Bengal), however, the authorities felt obliged to support Bombay, while reprimanding its initiative. The crucial decision was to send troops overland from Bengal, shocking the Maratha princes in central and western India by their unexpected appearance in 1778. With the Gaekwad capital of Vadodara most under threat from the Company troops in north Gujarat, it became the first of the major Maratha principalities to acknowledge the suzerainty of the British. Although the Marathas resisted British advances on Pune, despite a defeat near Ahmedabad, this First Maratha War extended British influence into Gujarat. The Second Maratha War (1803–04), in which the Scindia ruler of Gwalior, in northern Madhya Pradesh, was the main opponent of the British, broke Maratha power, and Scindia was obliged to cede territory directly to the Company in northern Gujarat. The final conquest of the Marathas in 1818 formalized the settlement already effectively achieved in Gujarat. Some of the territories of the modern state were ruled directly from Bombay (a separate Gujarat province was created after the suppression of the Great Rebellion, the Mutiny, of 1857), others remained in the possession of the Gaekwads or the myriad princes of Saurashtra. The Kathiawar peninsula possessed one of the most varied political landscapes in India, consisting of 86 distinct units until Independence. Meanwhile, the great cities and ports of the region flourished along with imperial trade, exporting not only the produce but the people of India. It was in the service of one of Gujarat's great mercantile houses, for instance, that Mohandas Karamchand Gandhi (Mahatma Gandhi), who was born in Porbandar in 1869, went to Natal (South Africa) as a young man.

Gujarat provided other leaders of the independence struggle, as well as India's first non-Congress premier (Morarji Desai, 1977–79), and was the scene of Gandhi's 'salt march', which started the Civil Disobedience Movement of 1930–32. Given that its business community and urban classes enjoyed strong links with Bombay, India's commercial and financial capital, Gujarat was incorporated into Bombay at independence. The princely states of Kathiawar formed a Union of States of Saurashtra and duly acceded to the new nation of India, although the largest, Junagadh, provoked some controversy before its inclusion. Junagadh, in the south-central Kathiawar, was founded by the Mauryas and served as the Kshatrapa capital, but later acquired Muslim rulers. At the time of the Partition of the Empire into Hindu- and Muslim-dominated entities, the local nawab favoured incorporation into Muslim Pakistan. As with the more significant nizamate of Hyderabad (now the capital of Andhra Pradesh), the majority Hindu population objected, while the national Government of the new country could not accept the practicality of a Pakistani enclave deep within Indian territory. Forceful intervention by the Centre secured a different decision and the exile of the prince, who was noted for an obsessive devotion to his dogs, reserving 11% of state revenue for maintaining the royal kennels. Pakistan continues to claim that Junagadh is rightfully a part of its territory.

In 1956, with the linguistic reorganization of the states of India, the strong presence of Gujaratis in Bombay and the historical association (not shared by the city) of Maratha princes ruling the hinterlands of Gujarat and modern Maharashtra encouraged the creation of a bilingual State of Bombay. The Gujarati-speaking element was completed by the addition of Saurashtra and the Union Territory of Kachchh (Kutch). However, a distinct Gujarat state was separated from Marathi-speaking Maharashtra on 1 May 1960. Other territorial changes, or potential changes, to the state have come about only as a result of federal action in the international arena. Thus, in 1961 the Portuguese enclaves on the shores of the Gulf of Khambhat, Daman and Diu, were forcibly annexed to the Republic of India, although they rejected incorporation into Gujarat state in 1967. In 1965 a dispute with Pakistan over the Rann of Kachchh resulted in military confrontation, but a cease-fire on 1 July was accompanied by a decision to resolve the matter through international arbitration, which awarded some 90% of the territory in question to India (Gujarat) in 1968. Meanwhile, a new capital near the chief city, Ahmedabad, was decided upon—it was to be named for Gujarat's most famous son, Mahatma Gandhi, and, like Chandigarh, was designed by the Swiss architect, Le Corbusier (Charles Edouard Jeanneret). Construction of Gandhinagar began in 1965 and the main government buildings were completed by 1970. Throughout this period the state institutions based here were dominated by Congress. Apart from around the time of the 'Emergency' of 1977, Gujarat remained a Congress stronghold until the end of the 1980s. Thereafter, Hindu nationalism disrupted the eclectic traditions of the state (although caste and communal tensions have always been present) and the Bharatiya Janata Party (BJP) steadily increased its support, winning power in 1995. National elections that kept the BJP in power at the Centre in 1999 were unusual in Gujarat, in that there was a definite deterioration in Congress support in the state. The BJP achieved office despite the dissensions within the state party and the frequent clashes with the national leadership (notably in 1996–97), but its popularity suffered after the earthquake of January 2001, as well as a cyclone disaster. When this translated into electoral reverses, in October 2001 the national leadership insisted on the resignation of Keshubhai Patel, Chief Minister since 1998, who was succeeded by Narendra Modi.

Gujarat, which had hitherto attracted negative international interest mainly over the project to heighten a dam on the Narmada (thus threatening tribal and other homes with flooding), became the focus of much criticism in 2002 and a problem for the national Government, which was also led by the BJP. On 27 February the Sabarmati Express, a train returning Hindu pilgrims and activists from Ayodhya (the controversial site in Uttar Pradesh), was attacked at Godhra railway station. Some carriages were set alight, and 58 people were reported killed. A Muslim mob was blamed, provoking tension throughout India and riots in Gujarat that soon claimed almost 1,000 lives (reports vary—in May 2005 the Union Government reported that 254 Hindus and 790 Muslims were killed) and made about 100,000 people homeless. Communal violence continued sporadically for some months. Moreover, ministers in the state Government were accused of inciting the violence, and public officials of not only failing to prevent but even organizing actions against the Muslim community. Critics included the National Human Rights Commission and a number of foreign countries and international organizations, but the national BJP refused to disown Modi, rejected foreign interference and was forced to acknowledge some pressure from its staunchly militant-Hindu wing. The opposition and some of the BJP's secular allies in the ruling national coalition continued to demand action against the state authorities and condemned granting permission for state elections by the end of the year. Modi eventually resigned in July 2002 (although he remained Chief Minister in an interim capacity), with the declared aim of seeking a renewed mandate at the legislative elections (the Legislative Assembly was dissolved upon Modi's resignation). Controversy over Gujarat disrupted proceedings in both houses of the national Parliament, where the state is represented by 11 members in the upper chamber and 26 in the lower.

The result of the state elections in Gujarat, held in December 2002, assumed national importance, as the BJP, deprived of local victories for several years, unashamedly based its campaign on an appeal to religious chauvinism, *Hindutva* (Hinduness). Congress, meanwhile, which had been criticized for silence during the riots, avoided the religious question and based its campaign on the old and tested issue of caste. However, the party neglected to develop potential allies among the other secular parties, and, albeit unexpectedly, was soundly defeated at the polls. The BJP secured over two-thirds of the seats in the 182-seat Assembly, eventually winning 128 seats (up from 117), while Congress kept merely 50 (down from 57), although it did better in areas where governance had been an issue (as in the earthquake-hit west). Modi was sworn in as Chief Minister on 22 December, and a former state premier, Amarsinh Choudhary, became leader of the opposition (Choudhary died in August 2004). Controversy continued over the 2002 riots, however, as communalist tensions persisted, and there were complaints about compensation levels for victims of the riots and the failure to prosecute the perpetrators of any outrages. Indeed, in September 2003 the Supreme Court of India openly challenged the Government of Gujarat's competence and integrity to pursue any case against alleged rioters. Further such challenges, particularly with a new, Congress-led national Government from May 2004 (which replaced the BJP-appointed governor in July), placed the Modi administration under pressure and in August the Supreme Court ordered the cases to be reopened. Controversy continued, fuelled, for instance, by the discovery of a mass grave in December 2005 or, in February 2006, the conviction of nine people in the most prominent of the ongoing cases and the reopening under Supreme Court pressure of almost 1,600 other cases. Official inquiries were also ongoing.

Although Modi's application to replace unpopular Lok Sabha members as candidates in the 2004 general election had been refused (unwisely, it seemed later), the BJP's reversals in the national poll were largely attributed to his perceived arrogance and to his neglect of farmers. The BJP, which had won one of its first two parliamentary seats in Gujarat in 1984, had its tally of 21 seats in the 1999–2004 Lok Sabha dramatically reduced to 14 at the general election (Congress won the other 12). In the highly polarized atmosphere after 2002, Congress, despite its factionalism, had won the secular vote in May 2004 (it also won three Assembly by-elections in October), while the local BJP activists resented what they saw as the central leadership's appeasement of Muslims. Continuing inquiry into the Godhra incident seemed unlikely to harm Modi in the long run, particularly as he refused to discuss the ongoing cases. He even refused to react angrily when the USA refused him a visa in March 2005, despite outrage across the political spectrum in India (he later also cancelled his planned trip to the United Kingdom), and this silence helped him to avoid personal responsibility, at home at least. Modi certainly enjoyed a reputation for not being corrupt, and his personal publicity machine was most effective. His allegedly authoritarian style provoked opposition within his own party, notably led by former premier Keshubhai Patel. At the end of March, however, the BJP national leadership effectively dismissed the complaints of Patel and others by endorsing Modi in his position. They probably had little choice, given that Modi was probably the most popular and effective BJP leader in the country, with a strong and developing economy in his state and the strength of his personality in taking on an admittedly disorganized, but strong, Congress opposition. However, Modi remained a contentious figure in the BJP nationally—the party was not entirely at ease with its leadership—and there was further dissatisfaction expressed in the Gujarat BJP during August and September. However, Modi achieved some vindication with his party's success in local elections towards the end of 2005, with the BJP trouncing Congress in Ahmedabad in October and in five more municipal corporations in December. The party was damaged by what was perceived as a weak government response to severe flooding during the mid-year monsoon in both 2006 and 2007 and, more specifically, by two scandals in 2007.

In March 2007 the Government admitted that a man killed by police in 2005 had not had the terrorist links alleged; investigations into this and other 'fake encounter' killings continued into the second half of the year (with the first arrests of three police officers followed by several more), and even threatened to involve some senior figures in the BJP leadership. In April a BJP Lok Sabha deputy was arrested for a people-trafficking offence. In June Modi became the longest serving of the 14 chief ministers of Gujarat and, if as expected he lasted until the state elections scheduled for December, would be the first to serve a full term. However, he remained a controversial leader, and internal opposition to him re-emerged among some BJP activists in July. Five members of the legislature voiced their opposition, only to be suspended from the party for indiscipline in August, as the central leadership threatened to be strict in the approach to the state elections. The rebels also indicated what was likely to be a dominating feature of the election campaign, replacing religion: caste. The five rebel BJP deputies, as well as veteran dissident Keshubhai Patel, all belonged to the Leuva sub-caste of the Patel or Patidar community (comprising some 20% of the Gujarati population), which seemed to be less satisfied with Modi than the Kadva Patidars, who were likely to remain loyal to the BJP. The Koli community (15% of Gujaratis) had also become dissatisfied with the BJP, as they complained of official neglect of crimes against them—in May the only Koli member of the cabinet had resigned in protest at police failure to investigate properly a rape and a murder in Junagadh. The BJP had enjoyed Koli support since 1992. Other dissidents set out to woo Brahmins away from the BJP mainstream, while Kshatriyas seemed likely to follow another BJP defector back to Congress. Congress, meanwhile, was concentrating on the adivasi or tribal vote, which had been one of its traditional fiefdoms until 2002, although the Government countered with promises of development assistance and other initiatives. Congress could normally rely on the votes of the Scheduled Castes and Tribes and of minorities, such as Muslims, who tended to favour a secular party, but the party's determination to secure the Muslim vote in effect served to alienate other sectors of Gujarati society. Other opposition parties, such as the Nationalist Congress Party, indicated that they favoured a secular understanding, if not alliance, against the BJP in the forthcoming electoral contest.

Elections to the state Assembly were held in December 2007. Congress agreed to co-operate with the NCP in contesting the poll, but refused to nominate a candidate for the premiership in advance. The election, in essence, was a vote on Chief Minister Modi, a charismatic demagogue, but without anyone set against him. Although Modi was unpopular with many in his party, and particularly with farmers, a television 'sting' programme in October that implicated him in complicity in some organization of the 2002 Godhra riots seemed to bolster his support. That may have been in sympathy or because his otherwise moderate *Hindutva* credentials were enhanced. Moreover, many BJP dissidents, such as Keshubhai Patel, did not actually leave the party. Although the BJP and Congress electoral shares remained much as in the 2002 elections (marginally down, but the BJP still with some 49% of the votes cast) and, indeed, the BJP gained 10 fewer seats to Congress's eight extra, the defeat was felt deeply by the Congress leadership. The BJP had overcome the 'anti-incumbency factor', a divisive leader and a poor record on rural development to retain an overwhelming majority of 117 seats. Congress had 59 seats and the NCP three. The result galvanized BJP hopes across the country, but also set a national stage for any further ambitions Modi might have. On 25 December Modi was again sworn in as Chief Minister. He began in a conciliatory fashion, with a visit to his dissident predecessor Patel, but, tragically, a case for communal harmony was not strengthened by a series of bomb explosions in Ahmedabad in July. The eventual death toll was 55, and the perpetrators were believed to be 'home-grown' Islamist activists, a source of concern for the authorities.

## ECONOMY

At the beginning of the 21st century Gujarat, normally a relatively prosperous state, had problems with continuing drought and a devastating earthquake in January 2001 (Rs 153,080m. worth of damage was estimated to have been done to infrastructure), contributing to the contraction of the primary sector. Official figures for net state domestic product in 2004/05 put the total at Rs 1,525,160m. (making it the sixth largest state economy in India) and the per head figure at Rs 28,355 (well above the corresponding all-Indian average for income per head, making it the fourth most wealthy state). The controversial Sardar Sarovar gravity dam on the Narmada finally had its height raised from 119 m to 121.98 m in the last months of 2006, to provide 5,700 cu m of water and an installed electrical capacity of 1,450 MW (57% for Madhya Pradesh, 27% for Maharashtra and 16% for Gujarat). The total road length at 31 March 2002 was 74,031 km, of which 2,362 km were national highway and 19,180 km state highway. The total railway length at the same time was 5,312 km. The main port is Kandla, at the head of the Gulf of Kachchh, which handled about one-third of the cargo in all Gujarat's ports (32.6% in 2002/03). There are 40 other ports. The state has 11 airports, the main international airport being at Ahmedabad. Electricity capacity installed in Gujarat was 9,848 MW in May 2006 (59% state sector, 23% private sector and 18% a share from the Centre), and all possible villages were electrified. Fifty-six per cent of rural households received electricity in 2005. The number of telephone connections at the end of November 2001 was 2.6m., while at the end of March 2003 there were 1.0m. mobile or cellular telephone connections. In 2001 the literacy rate was 70.0% (compared with 61.6% in 1991).

The primary sector contributed only 16% of gross state domestic product in 2001/02 (compared with about one-quarter in the first half of the 1990s). Agriculture remains an important economic activity for the largest part of the population, although cash crops constitute a more significant part of production than in many other states. In 1999/2000 Gujarat still produced 33% of India's tobacco, 14% of its groundnuts (peanuts), 18% of its cotton and 15% of its bajra or bajara (pearl millet). In the same year the state produced 1.02m. metric tons of wheat, 985,000 tons of rice, 851,000 tons of bajra, 260,000 tons of jowar (white sorghum or great millet), together with over 0.5m. tons of other cereals and 406,000 tons of pulses. Non-foodgrain production included 718,000 tons of groundnuts, 200,000 tons of tobacco and 2.09m. tons of cotton. Rainfall in 2000/01 was less than 40% of the average, resulting in smaller harvests: total food grains produced amounted to 2.54m. tons (a little more than three-fifths of the previous year's total) and 1.16m. tons of cotton, for example. Conditions improved, often dramatically, in 2001/02 however, with foodgrain production reaching 4.90m. tons (2.34m. tons of coarse grains, 1.14m. tons of wheat, 1.03m. tons of rice and 383,100 tons of pulses), 3.36m. tons of oilseeds and 1.70m. tons of cotton (and 12.46m. tons of sugar cane). In 2002/03 food grains harvested fell to 3.62m. tons, mainly owing to drought. The state also produces fruits, vegetables and spices. The 1997 agricultural census counted 6.75m. head of cattle, 6.29m. buffaloes, 6.54m. sheep and goats, and 7.24m. poultry. Livestock products included 6.1m. tons of milk, 382m. eggs and 3,057 tons of wool in 2002/03. Gujarat has a long maritime tradition and fish production in 2000/01 amounted to 661,000 tons, worth Rs 13,741m. Forests cover only 9.61% of the total area; teak and bamboo are the principal woods produced.

The value of mineral output in 1999/2000 was Rs 31,240m. (7% of the all-Indian total), rising to Rs 47,030m. in 2000/01 and Rs 48,520m. (86% from petroleum and natural gas) in 2001/02. Output reached Rs 51,770m. in 2002/03 (8.1% of the value of all Indian mineral production), a figure exceeded only by Andhra Pradesh. Reserves being exploited include limestone (14.03m. metric tons in 2000/01), lignite (5.85m. tons), bauxite (1.40m. tons), dolomite (244,000 tons), crude petroleum (5.82m. tons) and natural gas (2,827m. cu m). Over 0.5m. people were employed in the sector in 2001/02.

The value of the secondary sector was worth 41% of the total economy in 2000/01. Gujarat is the second state in the country in terms of net added value by manufacture and attracts a lot of migrant workers. In 2001 there were 14,087 registered working factories, employing 748,000 people and producing goods worth Rs 1,289,620m. Many industrial activities are based directly on primary-sector production, such as sugar refining, dairy products, the processing of oilseeds, and textiles, or the production of salt and cement, and petroleum refining. The state also possesses chemical and pharmaceutical industries, electronics and engineering. One unusual specialization is the largest scrap yard for old ships, at Alang in Saurashtra, where the beach is reputed to have the second highest tides in the world. Handicrafts are an important village industry, particularly in an area such as Kachchh, where there remains a living tradition.

In 2000/01 the tertiary sector contributed 43% of Gujarat's gross domestic product, maintaining its position as the largest sector of the economy. Transport and communications, trade and business services are all important activities. There is also reckoned to be a sizeable unofficial sector of the economy, notably in the trade in alcohol, the sale of which is illegal in Gujarat. Tourism has considerable potential, owing to Gujarat's rich history and culture, ranging from Jain temples and princely palaces, to blended Muslim-Hindu architectural styles and the birthplace of Mahatma Gandhi. A number of important religious sites in the state include two on the Kathiawar peninsula, the temple at Somnath and also Dwarka, which is distinguished by being both one of Hinduism's four holy abodes and one of its seven holy places. The state is also rich in wildlife, containing the only remaining homes in India of the Asiatic lion (a symbol of the Mauryas adopted by modern India) and of the wild ass. There are also reserves for the blackbuck, which, as the second largest of the antelopes and the fastest long-distance runner of any animal, is favoured by hunters and is now an endangered species. There is a profusion of bird life (parrots and peacocks are common), native species augmented seasonally by migratory birds, and the Rann of Kachchh is the only nesting ground in India of the large flamingo.

### DIRECTORY

**Governor:** NAWAL KISHORE SHARMA, Office of the Governor, Raj Bhavan, Sector 20, Gandhinagar 382 020; tel. (79) 23243171; fax (79) 23224268.

**Chief Minister:** NARENDRA DAMODARDAS MODI (Bharatiya Janata Party), Office of the Chief Minister, Government of Gujarat, Secretariat, Gandhinagar 382 010; tel. (79) 23232611; fax (79) 23222101; e-mail cm@gujaratindia.com.

**Speaker of the Legislative Assembly:** ASHOK BHATT, Vittalbhai Patel Bhavan, Assembly Secretariat, Gandhinagar 382 010; tel. (79) 23220902; fax (79) 23220941; e-mail hsgujarat@hotmail.com; the unicameral Legislative Assembly has 182 mems: Bharatiya Janata Party 117; Congress 59; Nationalist Congress Party 3; Janata Dal (United) 1; independents 2.

**State Principal Resident Commissioner in New Delhi:** Dr K.S. SUGATHAN, A-6 State Emporia Bldg, Baba Kharak Singh Marg, New Delhi 110 001; tel. (11) 23343147; fax (11) 23742482; e-mail rcgujrat@del16.vsnl.net.in.

## Haryana

The State of Haryana lies in northern India, consisting of the eastern end of the historic Punjab region. The state capital, Chandigarh, constitutes a separate territory under the administration of the Union authorities and lies on the western border of Haryana's northern arm. Here also, but to the north-east, there is a short border with Himachal Pradesh, while the north-eastern tip of this arm of Haryana also touches a tip of Uttarakhand (formerly Uttaranchal). The eastern border lies along the Yamuna, an inward-curving crescent interrupted only where Delhi has carved out the National Capital Territory in the south-east of the state. Uttar Pradesh lies beyond the Yamuna. The blunt end of Haryana's southern arm is just to the south of Delhi, and the border then heads north-westwards, separating the state from Rajasthan, until, at the tip of the third arm, it meets the border of the Punjab state. The Punjab, of which Haryana was a part until 1 November 1966 (the two states still share Chandigarh as a capital), essentially lies to the north-west of Haryana; from the western tip of Haryana the border heads east, and a little south for a time, before gradually curving north-eastwards towards where the Union Territory of Chandigarh dissects the final stretch of Punjab frontier. These borders enclose an area of 44,212 sq km (17,077 sq miles), making it one of the smaller states of the Union, but still a little larger than Denmark.

Physically, Haryana (the 'heavenly abode' or 'green land') and the Punjab form part of the undulating, sometimes sandy (in the south-west), plains stretching between the Ganga–Yamuna Doab and the Indus basin, from the near-desert of Rajasthan to the edge of the Himalayan foothills. Although over 1,000 km (620 miles) from the sea, the plains are less than 275 m (903 ft) above sea level, sloping gently southwards to about 215 m. The highest area in the state is in the south, where it skirts the Rewari uplands, a north-eastern thrust of which forms the Delhi Ridge. In the south-east the land drops with the Yamuna to nearer the level of the Doab plains. There are no perennial rivers running through Haryana, the only significant natural waterway being the Ghaggar in the north. The landscape is generally agricultural. Mountains rear up beyond Chandigarh, the Shivaliks, the Outer Ranges of the Himalayas, just to the north-east of Haryana. It is mainly on these great mountains that Haryana depends for its water, a source of irrigation and because they cause the south-westerly monsoons to divert north-westwards and rain the length of the Gangetic plains and on towards Pakistan. Most rainfall is, therefore, between May and August, with Chandigarh receiving an average of over 400 mm (16 inches) in July alone. There is less average rainfall in the west of the state. Temperatures can reach over 40°C (104°F) just before the summer monsoon, in May, while winters can be cold.

The total population of Haryana, according to the results of the census of March 2001, was 21,144,564, giving an average population density of 478 per sq km. The growth in the population since the previous census was higher than the national average, mainly owing to immigration (people seeking work in Delhi and its environs) offsetting the decline in the natural growth rate. In 2001 the Scheduled Castes accounted for 19.3% of the total population. In 1991 Hindi speakers accounted for 91.0% of the total population (Punjabi 7.1% and Urdu 1.6%). In 2001 adherents of Hinduism accounted for 88.2% of the population (Muslims 5.8% and Sikhs 5.5%). The figures for language and religion can be no surprise in a state designed mainly to accommodate a (non-Sikh) Hindi-speaking population in the heartland of Vedic legend.

The historic chief cities of Haryana, the national capital of Delhi and its own capital of Chandigarh, have both had separate territories carved out of the state, leaving it with a relatively low rate of urbanization (28.9% in 2001). The largest city in the state is Faridabad, which had a population of 1.06m. in 2001. Other major centres include Gurgaon (like Faridabad, to the south of Delhi), Hisar and Sirsa in the west and, on the Great Trunk Road that crosses northern India, cities such as Panipat (as famed now for weaving as for ancient battles) and Ambala. There are 19 districts.

### HISTORY

Haryana lies at the heart of Indian history, at the eastern end of the ancient Punjab and neighbouring the Ganga (Ganges)–Yamuna Doab, central to the *arya varta* and the gateway for the traditional invasion route from the north-west. The first ascertainable invasion, therefore, was that of the Aryans, and Haryana forms much of the landscape for the early legends of Hinduism. Before that the Harappan civilization may have found a conduit into the area up the now 'lost' Sarasvati river (of which the Ghaggar may be a remnant), and there is certainly archaeological evidence for settlement even before that time. Haryana forms part of a Hindu creation myth, and is certainly the site of Kurukshetra, where the great battle of the *Mahabharata* was fought and Krishna divulged his divine revelation to Arjuna. The Kuru kingdom of the battling Pandavas and Kauravas was succeeded by Vatsya and, thereafter, the region succumbed to imperial Magadha. As the empire of the Mauryas declined, the north of India suffered from incursions by the Yavanas (Hellenic dynasties settled in Bactria, modern-day Afghanistan), the Pahlavas (Parthians) and the Shakas (Scythians). Finally, around the first century AD the Yueh-chi or Kushana extended their empire into northern India for a time, with an imperial capital in what is now Pakistani Punjab and a secondary capital to the east of modern Haryana. By the time of the rise of the Gupta empire in the fourth century, Haryana formed part of the territory of the 'republic' of the Yaudheyas, who were defeated by Samudra-Gupta and forced to cede land and pay tribute.

As the Gupta empire declined and north India suffered the savage incursions of the Ephthalites or 'White' Huns (Hiung-nu), the powerful local feudatories began to reassert their independence. The two main 'frontline' states, in the eastern Punjab and the Doab and in what is now central Uttar Pradesh, were ruled by the allied families of the Vardhanas and the Maukharis. They probably co-operated to repel the Hun invasions of the early sixth century, while later their conjoined realms would form the core of the last pre-Islamic pan-Indian empire. The Vardhanas had their capital at Thanesar in Haryana, not far from Kurukshetra, and in the third generation of the dynasty Prabhakhara Vardhana adopted an imperial title. His eldest son, Rajya, seemed to have been a successful warrior, but immediately upon his succession seems to have had to respond to an invasion by Malwa (Malava). The Malwan forces had already defeated and killed the Maukhari king, widowing Rajya's own sister. However, although Rajya defeated Malwa, its Bengali ally, Sasanka of Gauda, killed Rajya, allegedly by treachery. The younger son of Prabhakhara, Harsha Vardhana, therefore assumed the throne in around 606, at the age of some 16 years. Through his sister, Harsha was able to unite the Maukhari realm with his own, and later removed his court to the more central Maukhari capital at Kannauj (Uttar Pradesh). He also ruled Malwa, but his main enemy was in Bengal, which meant a number of other kings and princes had to submit to Vardhana rule before Harsha could challenge the king of Gauda. Harsha had the alliance of the king of Kamrupa (roughly modern Assam—Asom), but, although he extended his empire the length of the *arya varta* (as well as into Gujarat), it was only in the 620s, after Sasanka's death, that Bengal was fully incorporated into the Vardhana domain. He received tribute from princes as far apart as Orissa, Kashmir and Sindh (now in Pakistan) and reigned until about 647. Harsha Vardhana, like his brother, was Buddhist (although there is evidence of a resurgent and radicalized brahmanism by the time of his reign), and famed for his generosity and fairness, but he left no dynast to consolidate his empire, which, judging by the speed of its disintegration upon his death, was highly personal in nature.

The legacy of Harsha Vardhana was enough to make Kannauj the imperial city of the following centuries, displacing Pataliputra (now Patna, in Bihar), while Thanesar became a noted place for Hindu pilgrimage (it was sacked by Mahmud of Ghazni in 1011). The beginning of serious Muslim incursions in the 11th century put Haryana, now ruled by the Tomara Rajputs, in the direct route of invasion. They had founded a city at Delhi in the eighth century, adding a fort in the 11th century, but the city and its hinterland of Haryana had been finally conquered by the forces of Islam by the end of the following century, with the defeat of the Rajput leader, Prithviraj III Chahamana in 1193. Haryana's history then becomes an adjunct of the varied fortunes of Delhi, India's new imperial city.

Haryana remained the preserve of the Sultans of Delhi for longer than the rest of the empire, but the area remained exposed to the traditional invasion route from the north-west. Thus, Delhi was sacked by Taimur 'the Lame' (Tamerlane or Tamburlaine), a Mongol (or, in India, Mogul or Mughal) leader at the end of the 14th century. By the time a descendent of Taimur, Babur, invaded, the Sultanate was weak and had long since lost its wider suzerainty. The last ruler of the last dynasty, Ibrahim Lodi, was killed along with 20,000 others by Babur's army in a battle to the north of Delhi, at Panipat, on 21 April 1526. Panipat was also the scene of two other battles fundamental to the fortunes of the new Mughal Empire. After the interruption of Sher Shah (leader of the Afghan Sur clan, who displaced Humayun, Babur's son) and the restoration of the Mughals, Humayun's son and successor, Akbar, was forced to secure his reign against the threat of a pretender. Hemu ('Rajah Vikramaditya') was the chief minister of one of the Sur clan leaders and commander of the Afghan armies. However, Akbar's regent, Bayram Khan, met the insurgent forces at Panipat on 5 November 1556 and defeated them, securing Delhi for the Mughals. The third battle at Panipat was in the 18th century, during the decline of Mughal power, when Rajput princes contested for control of the Punjab and the now militant Sikhs were establishing their own principalities. The Marathas had also intervened in the politics of the Mughal court, reaching Delhi itself in 1737. The Mughal existed under their protection thereafter, until 1761, when, at the height of Maratha power, the combined forces of the Peshwa and the principal clans were conclusively defeated by an invading army under Ahmad Shah Abdali, another Afghan ruler. The battle was at Panipat, on 13 January 1761, and was, ultimately, to leave the imperial city exposed to British occupation in 1803.

In the early years of the 19th century, therefore, the frontier of British power was the Yamuna, although Delhi and parts of southern Haryana were also occupied. In effect, however, British influence extended as far as the Sutlej, with many of the princes in this intermediate region acknowledging the supremacy of the East India Company. Much of the eastern Punjab was known as the region of the 'Cis-Sutlej States', and that this was a region of British influence was conceded by the ruler of the Sikh kingdom of the Punjab, Ranjit Singh, the 'Maharajah of Lahore', in 1809. However, the incorporation of the Sikh kingdom into British India by the mid-century meant Haryana was no longer a border territory. In the Great Rebellion consequent upon the Mutiny of 1857, some of the local princes rose against the British when the rebellious soldiers took the Mughal at their figurehead. However, most of the Punjab remained loyal, as did the Sikhs (such as the rajah of Jind), and when the British regained control of Haryana by November, the rebellious nawabs of Jhajjar and Bahadurgarh, the rajah of Ballabgarh and Rao Tula Ram of Rewari were deprived of their estates. These territories were either taken under direct British administration or distributed to the loyal Sikh princes, not only Jind, but also Nabha and Patiala (the latter two based in the modern Punjab state). Many of these principalities survived until independence, by which time Haryana was again the hinterland of an imperial capital, as Delhi had been made the chief city of British India in 1912. However, Delhi was to serve as the capital of a truncated nation upon independence, as the Muslim provinces opted to become the separate country of Pakistan. In 1947, therefore, the Punjab was partitioned between Pakistan and India, resulting in extreme levels of communal violence, mass migrations of Hindus and Sikhs into Indian territory and of Muslims in the other direction, and human tragedy on a horrific scale.

After independence the Indian Punjab was organized as: a (from 1950) 'Part A' state called the Punjab; the former-princely ('Part B') Patiala and the East Punjab States Union (PEPSU); and the Punjab hill states, most of which were grouped in the 'Part C' Himachal Pradesh territories. This complicated arrangement was bound to be reorganized under any re-examination of the federal structure of the Union, but the secular Centre was determined it could not grant the continuing separatist aspirations of the Sikhs as such. With the linguistic reorganization of the states in 1956, PEPSU was merged into the Punjab, but Sikh agitation continued and, ultimately, the federal principles were preserved only by distinguishing Punjabi from other Hindi dialects and declaring it a separate language entitled to a separate state. Most Punjabi speakers were Sikhs, so on 1 November 1966 the 'rump' Punjab remained as the Sikh state, while the predominantly Hindu (or, rather, Hindi-speaking) areas were either grouped into a new Haryana state, in the south-east, or added to the territory of Himachal Pradesh. Chandigarh remained the capital of both states, but became a centrally administered Union Territory, pending a decision on whether it would be ceded to Haryana or the Punjab. There was a decision in favour of the Punjab, but it has remained the joint capital and a separate territory ever since.

Political Hindu chauvinism was strongly supported in Haryana state, although any extremism present in other parts of India is blunted by relative wealth. The local party attracting such support is the Indian National Lok Dal (INLD—a Haryana party despite its name) rather than the national Bharatiya Janata Party (BJP). The INLD had returned to power after the latest state elections, in March 2000, with 47 of the 90 Assembly seats. Its leader, Om Prakash Chautala, became Chief Minister for his fifth term (his first was in 1989, but none of the first four terms even reached six months). The state also sends 10 representatives to the all-India Lok Sabha (and five to the Rajya Sabha), five of which were won by the INLD and four by the BJP in 1999. However, at the 2004 general election the main opposition group, Congress, which by 2003 was attracting prominent figures to bolster its support in the state, won nine of the Lok Sabha seats. The BJP retained one, but the INLD lost its entire representation in the lower house of the national Parliament. In January the INLD had withdrawn from the ruling BJP-led national coalition, but had ruled out any co-operation with other parties. After the general election, Congress was able to reinforce its position, with the new central Government replacing Haryana's BJP-appointed governor in July. In October the small Haryana Vikas Party (the leader of which, Bansi Lal, was a former Congress premier—he died in January 2006) merged with Congress, consolidating its support in some areas. The BJP later announced that it would fight the Assembly election without any electoral pacts.

The elections to the Vidhan Sabha were held during February 2005. Congress won convincingly, gaining 67 of the 90 seats. The INLD only retained nine seats and the BJP two. Bhupinder Singh Hooda, a Lok Sabha member, was appointed Chief Minister, after he displaced, with the support of the national leadership, the former premier and state Congress leader, Bhajan Lal, as the main contender. Bhajan Lal, who had led three previous administrations, did not attend Hooda's installation, but later pledged his support, while his son joined the new Government (Bhajan Lal resigned his Congress leadership position in July 2006, however, complaining of unjust treatment by the party). In June 2005 Congress easily won three by-elections to the state legislature—one electing Hooda to the Assembly and the other two electing the widows of two ministers killed in a helicopter crash in March. The popularity of the new Government was challenged in late July, however, when there were allegations of police in Gurgaon using excessive force against striking car workers at a Honda factory. Despite that incident, or the outbreak of inter-caste violence in Gohana in September (when 500 dalit homes were set ablaze), Hooda's son, Deepinder Singh, was elected to his father's former Lok Sabha seat with an increased majority. In 2007, despite a terrorist bomb killing many on the 'peace train' between Delhi and Pakistan near the Haryana town of Panipat in February, the main communal violence in the state involved the Dera Sacha Sauda. In May civil peace was disturbed—mainly in the Punjab, but also in Haryana, where the Dera was based, in the town of Sirsa—by tensions between Sikhs and the followers of the heterodox sect. The Sacha Sauda leader, Gurmeet Ram Rahim Singh, had offended Sikhs by appearing dressed as the 10th Guru of their religion. Violence was scarcely abated by the sect leader's equivocal apologies, which were rejected by the Sikh high priests. The worst violence was confined to mid-May, but intermittent clashes occurred thereafter, as well as peaceful protests. By the end of June the arrest of the sect leader was being sought for offending the religious sensibilities of the Sikhs, although at the beginning of August more serious charges of murder and rape were laid against him. Clashes of the Dera leader's guards and followers with Sikh protesters occurred intermittently, the most serious incidents involving the deaths of two Sikhs, in Mumbai, Maharashtra, in June 2008 and around Sirsa in July. Meanwhile, Bhajan Lal resumed his criticism of the Congress leadership and left the party in December 2007, founding the Haryana Janhit Congress with another son. However, he and two fellow Assembly members had to fight by-elections in May 2008 because of their change of allegiance, and only Lal retained his seat, the other two constituencies reverting to Congress.

## ECONOMY

Haryana is the second most prosperous state in the Union, after Goa (having overtaken the neighbouring Punjab in 2002/03), with good physical infrastructure and the advantages of being near to Delhi. Official figures, in current prices, put the total net domestic product of Haryana at Rs 736,450m. and the income per head at Rs 32,712 in 2004/05. The total length of roadways in Haryana in 1999 was 23,684 km, of which 656 km were national highway and 3,135 km state highway. There is an extensive railway network, as the state lies near to the Delhi hub of so many routes, and five civil airports. In 2006 installed electrical capacity was 3,915 MW, of which 2,560 MW (almost 63% thermal, 37% hydroelectric) came from the state's own stations (only 7 MW of which was from the private sector). The rest of the installed capacity was from central projects. Haryana was the first state to achieve 100% rural electrification, in 1970, and in 2005 63% of rural households had electricity. There were almost 355,314 live telephone connections at the end of 1996/97. Literacy was reckoned at 65.4% of the population over seven years of age, according to the 2001 census, up from 52.2% in 1991, indicating the predominance of a rural population.

Some 80% of the population worked in agriculture. The primary sector of the economy, which constituted 42.5% of the gross domestic product in 1993/94, accounted for 29.6% by 2003/04 (at constant prices), with agriculture and allied activities being the main contributor. Haryana is one of the main grain-producing areas of India, providing a large surplus for sale outside the state, and is particularly noted for its basmati rice. The net area sown has amounted to just over four-fifths of the total area since the mid-1980s, so any improvement in yields depends on fertilizers, better irrigation or more productive crop varieties. Moreover, the dominant paddy–wheat rotation has not been good for the soil or the water table, while the overall increase in land cultivated since separate statehood has not stopped the two-crop dominance rising from 28% of the land sown in the early 1970s to 56% by the beginning of the 2000s. Total foodgrain production rose from 11.3m. metric tons in 1997/98 to 13.3m. tons in 2000/01 and a record of just over 13.3m. tons in 2001/02 (compared with only 4.8m. tons in 1970/71). In 2001/02 more specific figures put wheat production at 9.4m. tons (13% of the national total) and rice at 2.7m. tons, sugar cane at 9.3m. tons, oilseeds at 0.8m. tons and cotton at 0.7m. tons. Total foodgrain production in 2002/03 fell back to 12.3m. tons (7.1% of the all-India total, making the state the fourth largest producer in the country). Horticulture is now being encouraged, exploiting the proximity of the vast metropolis of Delhi, such that between 1990/91 and 2000/01 fruit production rose from 99,800 tons (planted on 12,640 ha) to 232,000 tons (on 30,715 ha) and vegetable production has reached 2.1m. tons (on 133,000 ha). Flowers have witnessed particularly rapid growth, accounting for only 50 ha at the beginning of the 1990s but 3,200 ha at the beginning of the 2000s, while the weight of mushrooms produced increased from 850 tons to an estimated 4,500 tons by 2001/02. Animal husbandry is another important agricultural sector, Haryana possessing a total of some 9.9m. head of livestock; 45% are buffaloes, which provide over 80% of milk production (4.85m. tons in 2000/01, making the state one of the leading producers in India). Production rose to 5.14m. tons by 2002/03, with 5.30m. tons anticipated for the following year. The state is famed for its Murrah buffaloes and Harriana breed of cows. Other livestock products include 1,180m. eggs and 2,972 tons of wool (2002/03). Fisheries were encouraged in the last decades of the 20th century and Haryana now has one of the most productive industries in the country—in 2000/01 the state landed 33,040 tons of fish. Forestry is negligible, as, in 2002/03, only 7.3% of the total area was classified as forest, although the state authorities are trying to increase woodland cover and tree plantings. The mining sector employs more than 217,000 people (2001/02) and produced minerals valued at Rs 1,477.6m. (2002/03).

The secondary sector's share of gross state domestic product rose from 26.2% in 1993/94 to 27.8% in 2003/04. Manufacturing alone, which was still performing well into the beginning of the 2000s, saw its share of net domestic product rise from 18.7% to 20.9%. In 1999 there were 7,813 registered factories, while in 2001 Haryana had the highest number of large and medium-sized enterprises of any state in the northern region of India (1,097—compared with only 162 in 1966), as well as 74,682 small industrial units. The state produces the largest number of motor cars in the country, and also leads in tractors, motor cycles, bicycles, gas stoves, scientific equipment, sanitary wear, etc. Other activities include food processing, textiles, television manufacture, handicrafts and loom work, and the production of machine tools and computer technology. The Panipat petroleum refinery is increasing its capacity and a petro-chemicals company is being located nearby. Finally, the state is a leader in the 'bio-tech' sector.

The tertiary sector (transport, trade, banking, public administration, education and health) increased its share of the state economy from 31.3% in 1993/94 to 42.6% by 2003/04. The most valuable contributor was trade (third in importance after agriculture and manufacturing), performing strongly in 2003/04, taking its own share to 18.4%, from 16.1%. Exports have increased dramatically. When Haryana came into existence in 1966 its export trade was worth only Rs 45m., but by 2001 the corresponding value had reached about Rs 70,000m., of which Rs 30,000m. came from Gurgaon software exports alone (making Haryana the third largest exporter of software technology after Karnataka and Andhra Pradesh). Traders, and business in general, have been helped by government reforms and economic liberalization during the 1990s. In tourism the state has advanced what it calls 'highway tourism', developing facilities along the great roads that traverse Haryana, while also developing conference centres, golf courses and other sporting centres. In 2002 Haryana received 2.4% of all domestic tourist visits within India, putting it in 10th place among the states.

### DIRECTORY

**Governor:** Dr AKLAKH-UR-RAHMAN KIDWAI, Office of the Governor of Haryana, Raj Bhavan, Chandigarh; tel. (172) 2740654; fax (172) 2740557; e-mail governor@hry.nic.in.

**Chief Minister:** BHUPINDER SINGH HOODA (Congress), Office of the Chief Minister, Government of Haryana, Civil Secretariat, Chandigarh 160 001; tel. (172) 2749396; fax (172) 2740774; e-mail cm@hry.nic.in.

**Speaker of the Vidhan Sabha (Legislative Assembly):** Dr RAGHAVIR SINGH KADIAN (Congress), Assembly Secretariat, Haryana Vidhan Sabha, Sector 1, Chandigarh 160 001; tel. (172) 2740030; fax (172) 2747075; e-mail speaker@hry.nic.in; the unicameral Legislative Assembly has 90 mems: Congress 67; Indian National Lok Dal 9; Bharatiya Janata Party 2; Bahujan Samaj Party 1; Nationalist Congress Party (NCP) 1; independents 10.

**State Resident Commissioner in New Delhi:** MADHUSUDAN PRASAD, Haryana Bhavan, Copernicus Marg, New Delhi 110 001; tel. (11) 23384354; fax (11) 23384913.

## Himachal Pradesh

The State of Himachal Pradesh, the 'Himalayan land', lies in north-western India, in the mountains above the ancient Punjab. In the east there is an international border with the People's Republic of China (Xizang—Tibet), while to the south-east is another mountain state of the Union, Uttarakhand (formerly Uttaranchal), formed from Uttar Pradesh in 2000. On the plains, west of the border that runs roughly from the south-east to the north-west, is the historic region of the Punjab (Himachal Pradesh once formed the hill country of the Punjab): there is a short border with Haryana in the south-west, while a Punjab state lies to the west. In the north the state border curves into Jammu and Kashmir. Himachal Pradesh was formed on 15 April 1948, as a union of 30 former princely states, which was joined by Bilaspur on 1 July 1954. In 1966 more territory was added in the west of Himachal Pradesh, when the old Punjab state was reorganized into Haryana and the Punjab (and Chandigarh). It was a centrally administered territory until 25 January 1971, when it became the 18th state of the Union. Sometimes known as Devbhumi, the 'home of the gods', the mountainous state covers an area of 55,673 sq km (21,504 sq miles).

Himachal Pradesh is orientated along the ranges rising towards the Great Himalaya, here running roughly from the north-west to the south-east. The innermost range is the Pir Panjal, while the outermost fence of the Lesser Himalayas, thrust further into the plains in the south, is the Shivalik Hills, and in between are ranges like the Parvati (Parbati). In the north and east are the bleak, arid plateau uplands of Lahul and Spiti, while the western parts of the state encroach onto the edge of the Punjab plains, the north consisting of the old region of Kangra and the centre Bilaspur. The highlands are complicated by the thrust of the great river valleys, with the Sutlej traversing the south of the state, exiting into the lowlands north of the Shimla Hills, while, further north, the upper Beas flows south through the Kullu valley before turning west into the Indus basin proper. In the north-west the valley of the Dhaola Dhar (Ravi), with the town of Chamba at the entrance, provided the natural setting for another of the old mountain kingdoms, while further in is the valley of the Chenab, which heads north and a little west out of the mountainous centre of Himachal Pradesh. In the south-west the Yamuna, which drains into the Ganga (Ganges) and hence into the Bay of Bengal, forms part of the state border with Uttarakhand. The highest peak in the state is Shilla, at 7,026 m (23,051 ft), while the lowest land is around 300 m. The immense altitude differences, as well as the varied effects of rain shadow, give the state a range of climatic conditions, from temperate to subtropical, and its thickly wooded terrain a range of vegetation types. The north and east tend to be very dry, but most of the state benefits from the monsoon. Average annual rainfall is 1,520 mm (59 inches), about one-half of which falls in the monsoon. Kangra, then Shimla, are the wettest places.

According to the results of the 2001 census—which in the Kinnaur District had to be based on estimates, owing to disruptions from 'natural calamity' (the state is prone to flooding and landfalls, the latter sometimes occasioned by earthquakes)—the total population of the state was 6,077,900. This gave an average population density of 109 per sq km. The main language is an obscure Hindi dialect known as Pahari, with 88.9% claiming Hindi as their main language at the 1991 census. Punjabi accounted for a further 6.3%, with the main Nepali language, Kinnauri, at only 1.2%. Kashmiri followed, with some Urdu speakers. Religious adherence follows linguistic affiliation, with Himachal Pradesh known as the most Hindu state in the Union. In 2001 95.4% of the population adhered to that religion (2.0% were Muslims, 1.3% Buddhists and 1.2% Sikhs). These figures obscure the strong influence of Buddhism on the region, however, with a particularly blended form of Hinduism among the Kinnauris, for instance. Most of the tribes have assimilated into a more mainstream Hindu culture, with less rigid caste systems—for example, the Gaddis, Gujars and Pangwalas. The Patians of Lahul and Spiti observe a more direct form of Buddhism, but the main reason for continuing Buddhist adherence in the region is that Dharamshala is the home of the Dalai Lama (the exiled spiritual leader of the Tibetans). In 2001 25% of the population were of the Scheduled Castes and 4% of the Scheduled Tribes.

With an urban population of only 10.0% of the total in 2001, Himachal Pradesh is the most rural state or territory in India. The state capital since 1966 has been Shimla (Simla), in the south-west of the state. The other main towns are, just to the south of Shimla, Solan, and over the hills to the north-west, Bilaspur. North-east of Bilaspur lie Mandi and Kullu, and north-west of it Hamirpur and Kangra, then Chamba in the far north-west. The state is divided into 12 districts.

## HISTORY

The Kols or Mundas are believed to be the first settlers in the hill country, followed by Mongoloid Bhotas or Khiratas, before the Aryans moved in here from the Punjab, even as they were spreading down into the Doab and onto the Gangetic plains. The early roots of Hinduism are here, with some in the Sangla valley still claiming direct descent from the Pandavas of the *Mahabharata*. The Kullu valley, particularly, is steeped in Hindu myth, lying as it does at the start of the great trans-Himalayan trade routes and the edge of the 'known world'. Himachal Pradesh, once the hill country of the historic Punjab, was soon very much dominated by Aryan clans, with some of the most prominent of the old 'republics' or limited monarchies being those of the Audumbras (the main tribe, with their own state in the second century BC), the Trigartas, the Kulutas and the Kulindas. The Mauryan empire subdued the tribal realms and, under Ashoka, introduced Buddhism. The precarious independence of the hill peoples regularly succumbed to the empires of the Punjab or the north-west, as well as to the imperial Guptas of Magadha, but in between the local chiefs, the thakurs and the ranas, ruled as they wished. By the end of the first millennium AD, the Rajputs were beginning to establish their domains in the hill country (notably the kingdom of Kangra or Nagerkot), although from the 10th century the states in the foothills were to be prone to Muslim incursions.

The great Hindu dynasty of the Shahis, based in Kabul (now Afghanistan), was the main bulwark India had against serious Muslim invasion, the power of their kings stretching into the Punjab and its hill country. However, they steadily lost land to the hosts of Islam, Kabul falling in 870. Although the Shahis consolidated their southern realms, with new capitals in the Punjab (latterly Lahore, now in Pakistan), Muslim kingdoms became established in the north and west. In the latter part of the 10th century the Shahis came under increasing threat from the Turkic Ghaznavid dynasty, under pressure from whom they moved their capital to Kangra. However, the greatest of the Ghaznavids, Mahmud (who had succeeded to the throne in 997), regularly defeated Anandapala Shahi (who had succeeded his defeated and humiliated father in around 1001). The most serious Shahi defeat came in 1008, when the whole of the western and northern Punjab fell, including the great treasure house of Kangra. Shahi wealth and power was fatally compromised, and Muslim raids soon reached as far as the temple cities of the eastern Punjab and the Gangetic plains. The last Shahi to offer resistance, Trilochanapala, was finally forced to seek haven in Kashmir, where a Hindu dynasty survived, probably because it had not supported the rajah who was now a refugee from the Punjab.

Kangra itself recovered some independence and power, probably ranking second after Kashmir among the Himalayan realms, with the 'Middle Kingdom' of Chamba between the two. Deeper into the mountains, in the 10th century Ladakh ruled Lahul, Spiti and Zanskar (the last now in Jammu and Kashmir, still part of Ladakh), with the emergent principality of Kullu as a tributary. In the 15th century Kullu expanded out of the upper Beas valley as far as Mandi, and Kullu actually became the capital in the 17th century. The realm also acquired Lahul and Spiti, Ladakh having been defeated by a combined Mongol-Tibetan force, and ruled eastwards as far as the Sutlej. Kullu benefited from its control of an important trade route, which, however, could attract unwelcome attention, such as that of the Sikh kingdom in the 19th century. The Sikhs had become established in the hill country mainly in the 18th century, seeking refuge from the Mughals, the first of them arriving to help Sirmaur in 1695. Meanwhile, Kangra had been captured by the future Shah Jahan, for his father, Jahangir, in 1620, reducing the territory to a Mughal province, but enriching the culture of its neighbours as many fled to Kullu and Chamba (the latter acknowledged Mughal suzerainty, but remained autonomous until the first half of the 19th century). Kangra reasserted its independence as Mughal power faded in the 18th century and, under Sansar Chand Khatok II (1775–1823), it conquered a number of other hill states, while its commerce and arts flourished. Continuing success was limited by the Gurkha threat; the aggressive Gurkha kingdom of Nepal had taken an interest in the hill states from about 1768, and the Gurkha armies had already taken Sirmaur and Shimla in the foothills before defeating Kangra in 1806 (aided by many of the hill peoples Sansar Chand had made into his enemies).

The Sikh kingdom of Ranjit Singh (Rajah of Lahore since 1799) was also rapidly expanding in the area and, by an 1809 treaty of non-aggression with another rising power, the British, was free to intervene in what is now Himachal Pradesh. He held Kangra fort against the Gurkhas (as sanctioned by the Treaty of Amritsar—signed in the Punjabi holy city), who had also earned British opposition once they began to head south, rather than west against the kingdom of Ranjit Singh. The Punjab became split between the kingdom based in Lahore and the British sphere of influence east of the Sutlej. However, the death of Ranjit Singh (1839) freed the British to intervene in the politics of the court of Lahore, and when they crossed the Sutlej in 1845 they were supported by many of the hill princes. South-eastern Himachal Pradesh had already fallen under British influence, the region's attraction as a refuge from the summer heat of the plains leading to the rise of 'hill stations' or resorts such as Shimla (1819). The British headquarters in the north-west of the modern state was to be Dharamshala (which became the seat-in-exile of the Dalai Lama after his flight from Tibet—now part of the People's Republic of China—in 1959), which became the administrative centre of Kangra, and extended its rule over Kullu in 1847. Generally, the hill rajahs were loyal to the British, their prestige enhanced by their proximity to the Empire of India's summer capital (between 1865 and 1939) at Shimla. The hill station therefore acquired buildings to house the Central Legislative Assembly for British India in the 1920s, furnishing it to be the temporary capital of the Indian Punjab after Partition (until Chandigarh was ready). Much of the freedom movement that engulfed India in the years to independence was directed against the princes—some (Chamba, Mandi and Bilaspur, for instance) had progressive reputations, but reformism tended to be the focus of activity in this area, rather than anti-British sentiment, although this was another expression of the independence struggle and Congress was active in Kangra especially.

After independence 30 of the princely states were united into a single province, known as Himachal Pradesh, which became a 'Part C' (centrally administered) state under the 1950 Constitution. On 1 July 1954 Bilaspur joined the state. Himachal Pradesh had elected its first Assembly in 1952, only to lose it in 1956, upon being redesignated a Union Territory. Himachal Pradesh regained an Assembly in 1963 and extra territory in 1966 (notably Kangra and Shimla, the latter becoming the capital), upon the reorganization of the Punjab. The territory achieved full statehood in January 1971.

At the state elections of March 1998 the Bharatiya Janata Party (BJP) just displaced the Congress Government of Virbhadra Singh (who had been premier since 1993, as well as in 1983–90). The BJP leader, Prof. Prem Kumar Dhumal, became the fifth Chief Minister on 24 March and was to be the first to complete his term. However, his party was increasingly troubled by internal criticism, notably from Shanta Kumar, a Union minister, and Dhumal himself was accused of corruption. Thus, in an unexpected blow to the BJP, Congress won the legislative elections of early 2003. It won 40 seats (and a further three in June, when polling took place in tribal constituencies that had been snowbound in February), against only 16 retained by the BJP, with the Himachal Vikas Congress, the Himloktantrik Morch and the Lok Jan Shakti winning one each and the balance accounted for by six independents. The independents were mainly former members of the two main parties, and gained many votes at the expense of those parties, both of which suffered a fall in their share of the vote. Singh returned to office as Chief Minister in early March. In October the BJP took an assembly seat from Congress at a by-election. Congress and the BJP share the state's four Lok Sabha seats, the latter having managed to retain one at the 2004 general election. However, the BJP Lok Sabha member was forced out by a bribery scandal, although the party retained the constituency in a by-election won by former premier Dhumal in June 2007. The conclusive BJP victory did not bode well for Congress in the state elections due in February 2008. The state also fills three seats in the Rajya Sabha.

State legislative elections in Himachal Pradesh were held in three stages in November–December 2007, anomalously before the dissolution of the current Assembly. This enabled Chief Minister Singh to claim that, even if Congress lost the election, he could continue in office until March, which was the legal term of the legislature. However, had he ever considered the option seriously, it was rendered untenable by the scale of Congress's defeat. Both Congress and the BJP suffered some dissension within their ranks over the election period, but Congress suffered far more from the advent of the Bahujan Samaj Party (BSP), which had demonstrated in its home state of Uttar Pradesh that it could rely on low-caste votes that Congress traditionally courted. The BSP only gained one seat in the new Assembly, but the split in the vote reduced the Congress tally to only 23; there were three independents. The BJP increased its number of seats to 41. Upon the announcement of the results, on 28 December, the cabinet recommended the immediate dissolution of the current Assembly and Singh resigned. Dhumal formally returned as premier on 30 December (the BJP retained his parliamentary seat at a by-election in May 2008).

### ECONOMY

Himachal Pradesh is not a particularly prosperous state, but it is the richest of the mountain states, helped by remittances from workers migrating to the nearby wealth of Delhi, Haryana and the Punjab. In 2004/05, according to official figures (at current prices), the net domestic product of the state was Rs 178,840m., or Rs 27,486 per head. These figures are boosted by capital expenditure in Himachal Pradesh, with the Centre and other states investing in major infrastructure projects (power and irrigation), as does the local Government, although the latter concentrates on developing roads and bridges. The mountainous terrain limits transport options, but, from a low base, Himachal Pradesh had achieved a total 27,217 km of motorable roads (including tracks negotiable by four-wheel-drive vehicles) by the end of March 2001. The three stretches of national highway amounted to 1,235 km. There are only two lengths of narrow-gauge railway track (209 km in all) and one broad-gauge track (16 km), three airstrips and 54 helipads. Waterways are unsuitable for transport, but are essential to the infrastructural development of the state, given their potential for power generation and the profusion of resource necessary for irrigation. By the Indus Waters Treaty of 1960, between India and Pakistan, the exploitation of the shared great rivers (for Himachal Pradesh, the Beas, the Sutlej and the Ravi) of the Punjab and the Indus basin was settled. Thus, the way was open for projects such as the Bhakra-Nangal Dam, one of the highest in the world at 225 m (738 ft), which provides electricity for Delhi, Haryana and the Punjab and water for the great Rajasthan (Indira Gandhi) Canal. The total hydroelectric potential of Himachal Pradesh has been put at 21,000–25,000 MW, although only 3,942.07 MW had been harnessed by 2001 (of that only 326.80 MW was directly under the state Government, the rest being for the Centre and other agencies). Himachal Pradesh's installed capacity in 2005 totalled 2,782.8 MW, of which only 12% was directly in the state sector, with 14% in the private sector and the rest in the central sector. Almost all villages had been electrified by 1988, with only about 100 still to connect (if possible) in 2005, and an extremely high 86% of rural households had electricity. The literacy rate at the time of the 2001 census was put at 77.1%, up from 63.9% in 1991.

The contribution of the primary sector overall to the economy in 2000/01 was 27.4%. Agriculture and allied activities (which directly employed 71% of the working population in 2001) alone contributed 22.5%, although this share had fallen from 57.9% in 1950/51 and 26.5% in 1990/91. Most of the available land has now been brought into use, so productivity has become the focus of agricultural policy. Total foodgrain production has risen from some 200,000 metric tons in 1951/52 to 1.4m. tons in 1999/2000. Provisional figures for 2000/01 put total foodgrain production at only 1.2m. tons (maize 683,640 tons, rice only 124,890 tons, and wheat only 350,000 tons, compared to over 640,000 three years previously), whereas actual figures gave only 1.1m. tons, before rising to a record 1.6m. tons in 2001/02 (52% coarse grains, over 90% maize, 38% wheat and 9% rice). Vegetable production rose from 25,000 tons in 1951/52 to 580,000 tons in 2000/01, while ginger (dry) production reached 370,000 tons by the latter year. However, the sector is obviously very weather dependent, particularly for crops such as fruit, which are not very robust but are very important to the Himachal Pradesh economy. Thus, fruit production of 447,680 tons in 1998/99 fell to only 89,410 tons in 1999/2000, before recovering to 428,030 tons the following year. Apples are the main fruit, usually accounting for almost 80% of total production, but the varied climatic conditions can suit both temperate and subtropical fruits. Oilseeds are also grown, and the state is attempting to replicate the success of a high-value crop like ginger by attempting to introduce tea. Livestock products in 2000/01 included 760,000 tons of milk, 81.6m. eggs and 1,582 tons of wool. Milk production declined in the next year, but recovered to reach an anticipated 787,000 tons in 2003/04, in which year there was also anticipated production of 87.1m. eggs and 1,601 tons of wool. The state also processes milk for paneer, butter and ghee.

Fisheries have been developed, with some 12,000 families now dependent, to some extent, on the industry. Expected fish production in 2001/02 was a record 1,600 metric tons. Forests form some 66.5% of the state's area and are exploited in a controlled fashion. In 2004 forestry was worth some Rs 410m. in revenue to the Government. Mineral reserves include glass sand, dolomite, sulphur, coal, limestone, gypsum and some gold near Bilaspur. Mining and quarrying employed almost 30,000 people in 2002/03, producing minerals worth Rs 835.6m.

The secondary sector in total contributed 32.5% of the value of the economy in 2000/01, industry alone 12.4% (from only 1.1% in 1950/51). In 2002 there were 191 large and medium-sized industrial enterprises and 29,200 small-scale units. The total turnover of industry has been put at some Rs 48,000m. annually, and the sector employs some 155,000 people. By 2004 there were 196 large and medium-sized enterprises (with investment of Rs 23,780m.) and 30,176 small-scale units (Rs 7,100m.). The state now concentrates on developing the processing of agricultural products, and associated activities such as packaging. Cottage industries, such as sericulture and handicrafts, are important in a largely rural environment.

The total contribution of the tertiary sector in 2000/01 was 40.1%, although almost one-half of this was accounted for by public administration and other community and personal services. In that year community and personal services contributed about one-fifth of the value of the economy (20.5%—compared with 5.9% in 1950/51), trade, communications and transport 11.9%, and finance and real estate 7.7%. Tourism attracts interest through historical and religious sites (for example, the Tabo Buddhist monastery in Spiti was founded in 996), adventure holidays and the natural endowments of the state (mountainous scenery and wildlife such as the ibex and the snow leopard). However, high-spending foreign tourists do not come in great numbers as yet; of the 4.68m. tourist arrivals in 2000, only 110,000 were foreign visitors, with many discouraged by the tales of missing travellers in the Parvati (Parbati) valley—famous for the sacred sulphur springs, reputed to be the hottest in the world. In 2005 plans to construct the world's highest ski village at Manali were announced.

### DIRECTORY

**Governor:** PRABHA RAU, Governor's Secretariat, Raj Bhavan, Shimla 171 002; tel. (177) 2624152; fax (177) 2624814.

**Chief Minister:** Prof. PREM KUMAR DHUMAL (Bharatiya Janata Party), Office of the Chief Minister, Government of Himachal Pradesh, Secretariat, Shimla; tel. (177) 2625400; fax (177) 2625011; e-mail cm@hp.nic.in.

**Speaker of the Legislative Assembly (Vidhan Sabha):** G. R. MUSSAFIR, Vidhan Sabha Secretariat, Council Chamber, Shimla 171 004; tel. (171) 2658246; fax (177) 2811151; e-mail vsabha@hp.nic.in; the unicameral Legislative Assembly has 68 mems: Bharatiya Janata Party 41; Congress 23; Bahujan Samaj Party 1; independents 3.

**State Resident Commissioner in New Delhi:** RENU SAHNI DHAR, Himachal Bhavan, 27 Sikandra Rd, New Delhi; tel. (11) 23716574; fax (11) 23715087; e-mail nchp@ren.02.nic.

## Jammu and Kashmir

The State of Jammu and Kashmir is the northernmost part of India, in the north-west, at the apex of the country. Its southern border is with the rest of India: at the western end a short border with the Punjab, while for the rest of its length Himachal Pradesh gently abuts into it. All the other frontiers are international ones, most of which are disputed, and, indeed, great swathes of territory have been occupied. India still claims an area coterminous with what the former Maharajah of Jammu and Kashmir ruled (except in the south where the princely state and Kangra—now part of Himachal Pradesh—exchanged some territories). In the north of what India claims is the *de jure* state, there is a relatively short border with a north-eastward extending tendril of Afghanistan, the bulk of which lies to the west, beyond Pakistan. The People's Republic of China lies to the north-east (Xinjiang Uygur) and east (Xizang—Tibet), but also administers the Aksai Chin plateau (the eastward-extended 'thumb' of the clenched fist of Jammu and Kashmir, part of Ladakh), as well as a length of territory to the west of there, beyond the Karakoram Pass, and another pocket to the south. Pakistan is in possession of a strip of territory in the south-west of the state, up the western border, which widens in the north to include much of the northern part of the state. The border dividing the state between the Pakistani zone and Indian-held territory is known as the Line of Control (LoC)—it starts just north of the Chenab, heading up through Punch (Poonch) to curve eastward round the mountains surrounding the Vale of Kashmir, continuing in an easterly direction just to the north of Kargil and then north-easterly, petering out at the Chulung Pass and the massive Siachen Glacier. The total area of the state is 222,236 sq km (85,839 sq miles—which would make it the sixth largest state in India), but, of this, 78,114 sq km is occupied by Pakistan and 42,685 sq km (including 5,130 sq km ceded by Pakistan) by the People's Republic of China. The figure given for the area of Indian-held Jammu and Kashmir (for statistical purposes) is 101,387 sq km, which would make it the 10th largest state of the Union.

Jammu and Kashmir is a mountainous territory, aligned along the ranges rising towards the great arc of the Himalayas, which here follow a roughly north-west to south-east direction. Ladakh, the 'land of passes', which occupies much of the central and south-western part of the state (Leh District and the smaller district of Kargil to its west—almost 44% of the total official area), is a high plateau lifting even loftier mountain ranges and scored by deep, sometimes fertile river valleys, which alleviate the Arctic-desert conditions of most of the highlands. Aksai Chin lies to the north-east of the Ladakh Range, beyond the valley of the Shyok, a tributary of the Indus. South-west of the Ladakh Range is the valley of the Indus itself and, in a side valley, the town of Leh. The next range is that of Zaskar, a region that looms above the foothills. The south-west of the state consists of the Hindu foothills, skirting the edge of the Punjab plains, and the cleft containing the Vale of Kashmir. In the far south-west are the Shivaliks, the outer fence of the Himalayas, the land then rising towards the heights of the Pir Panjal, between which and the Great Himalaya, is the fruitful bowl of the Vale of Kashmir. The north of the state, most of which is now under the control of Pakistan, continues the pattern of ranges running north-west to south-east, rising towards the Ghujerab Range of the Great Karakoram along the official north-eastern frontier. However, this harsh mountain land is alleviated by the mighty valley of the Indus, which, like many of the great rivers originating in Jammu and Kashmir, heads north-westwards, deep between the hills, before curving round and heading south, usually in Pakistan proper, to descend towards the distant Arabian Sea. This pattern is the same for the Jhelum and the Chenab (though the latter actually has its source in Himachal Pradesh). The Gilgit, which joins the Indus from the north, has carved out another valley to soften the highlands. The highest peaks are K2 (Qogir Feng—8,611 m or 28,261 ft), which is in an area disputed with the People's Republic of China, and Nanga Parbat (8,126 m), which rises just to the north of the LoC. In the south-western lowlands, by contrast, the city of Jammu is at an elevation of 305 m above sea level. This varied topography gives a range of climates, from the cold aridity of Ladakh, which is snowbound between November and June, to the temperate conditions of the Vale of Kashmir and the northern valleys, and the subtropical areas around Jammu. Rainfall, likewise, varies, the average annual amount in Leh (Ladakh) being 92.6 mm (3.6 inches—much of it falling as snow), in Srinagar (Vale of Kashmir) 650.5 mm and in Jammu 1,115.9 mm. Srinagar receives over one-half of its precipitation in November–April, from westerly depressions, rather than from the monsoons, which water Jammu, and most of the rest of India, earlier in the year.

The total population of Indian-held Jammu and Kashmir at the time of the 2001 census was 10,143,700, less than the population of the National Capital Territory of Delhi and 17 of the 28 states. The corresponding population density was 100 per sq km. The 1991 census could not be conducted properly in the state, owing to the troubles of the time, making comparisons and other figures unreliable. There were, therefore, no recent data on the numbers of people speaking particular languages or adhering to particular religions. The 2001 census, however, has produced updated for figures for religious adherence, showing that even in Indian-held Jammu and Kashmir Muslims remained a majority (67.0%). The area around Jammu is still a Hindu-dominated territory, while the Vale of Kashmir is a bastion of Islam (local Hindus are known as Pandits), and the thinly populated uplands of Ladakh are Buddhist (except for Muslim-dominated Kargil). Hindus in 2001 accounted for 29.6% of the total population, Sikhs 2.0% and Buddhists 1.1%. The region is one of great linguistic diversity, containing two main Indo-Aryan language groups (Indic and Dardic), Sino-Tibetan languages and the unclassified Burushaski. Most people, overall, speak Kashmiri, followed by Punjabi, but this conceals considerable local variation. According to the most recent figures for Indian-held territory (1981), just over one-half of the population speak Kashmiri (Dardic), with Dogri (the language of Jammu, which is now merely classified as Hindi) the second tongue. However, most Kashmiri speakers are confined to the Vale of Kashmir, and they accounted for 90% of the population of Kashmir, while Dogri was the first language of 53% of the population of Jammu, and Tibetan dialects (mainly Ladakhi and Zanskari) 90% of Ladakh. Other variants of Hindi (such as Pahari, Gujjari and Punjabi) and Urdu are also spoken. The bulk of the Punjabi-speaking population resides in Pakistani-held 'Azad Kashmir' (Free Kashmir), a strip of south-western territory wrapped around the northern end of the Vale of Kashmir, where they constitute 85% of the population. The main languages of the far north, also held by Pakistan, are assumed still to be the Dardic tongue, Shina, and then the Sino-Tibetan Balti (census requirements have not distinguished 'other' languages for some years). The ethnic origins of the peoples of Jammu and Kashmir are equally diverse and vary from south-west to south-east and in the north. In 2001 10.9% were counted among the Scheduled Tribes (7.6% Scheduled Castes).

The urban population of Jammu and Kashmir in 2001, according to where the Indian national census could be held, constituted 24.8% of the total. The largest city is Srinagar (898,440 inhabitants, according to the results of the 2001 census), the summer (May–October) capital of the state, followed by Jammu, the winter (November–April) capital. The only other towns of any size are in Pakistani-held territory—Muzaffarabad, on the original border with Pakistan, to the west and a little north of Srinagar, and Gilgit in the far north. For administrative purposes Jammu and Kashmir is divided into 14 districts (territory held by Pakistan is generally divided into Azad Kashmir, and the broad Northern Areas, including Gilgit, Hunzu and northern Ladakh or Baltistan).

## HISTORY

Historically, the territory of Jammu and Kashmir is at the confluence of competing cultural influences, be it the Indic influences from the south and south-east, Tibetan and even Chinese from the east, Afghan and Central Asian from the north, and Persic (and, at one time, Hellenic) from the west. The region has been more strongly influenced by one or the other at different times and has sometimes served as a conduit for more reaching penetrations (not that most of Kashmir is on the direct invasion routes), such as the spread of Buddhism out of India. This complicated position, which continues into the modern day with the dispute over the status of such a strategic area at the apex of India, is reflected in the three clear constituents of the state. Jammu shared most of its history with the rest of the old Punjab, on the edge of which it stands, while Kashmir (itself consisting of the Vale of Kashmir and the rougher, loftier and less integrated territories further to the north) was a hill state or states of a kind familiar to the Afghans or in the Indian Himalayas, while Ladakh is a Buddhist kingdom, similar to Tibet (now part of the People's Republic of China) or Sikkim. Outside control of territory such as that in northern Kashmir (for example, Gilgit and Hunzu in the Pakistan-controlled area) or Ladakh is relatively recent; the desire for exact borders is a modern phenomenon and has contributed to long stretches of Indian–Chinese territorial disputes. The more settled centres have been the targets of conquest, however, and, whatever their control of the wilder hinterlands, the region of Jammu and the Vale of Kashmir certainly have experienced the usual succession of imperial Indian hegemonies—the Mauryas, the Kushana, the Guptas, Harsha Vardhana, the Shahis, the Mughals and the British—as well as rule from Bactria/Afghanistan and the incursions of invading Scythians, Huns or Muslims, for instance.

In the wake of the invasions of the 'White' Huns or Ephthalites (Hiung-nu) and various other claimants to the territory, Kashmir settled under the primacy of a native Hindu dynasty, the Karkotas, from the 620s (the first rajah was Prajhaditya, from about 627). The most eminent of the Karkota kings was probably Lalitditya (*circa* 695–732), who campaigned as far afield as Bengal and Tibet in the east, the Konkan Coast to the south and Turkestan in the north. From 816, however, the succession becomes uncertain and the reign of the last Karkota, Utpalapida, ended in about 857, when he was supplanted by the first of the Utpalas, Avantivarman. The Utpala succession became increasingly disputed in the first part of the 10th century and the dynasty was eventually supplanted by that of Yadjaskara in 940. He died in 948 and, within two years and as many successors, his house was replaced by that of Parvagupta, who had five successors before a female ruler, Didda, survived for a reasonable length of reign (981–1004). There was then a more settled dynastic history in Kashmir, with one group of Loharas ruling for almost one century before being replaced by the Later Loharas from 1102, and their Hindu successors, the Vopyadevas (1171–1286) and then Simhadeva and his heir, Sahadeva, until 1320, when Muslim rule began. The first ruler of the Muslim Rinchana clan was Sadr ud-Din, but it was Shams ud-Din I (1339–43) who took the Vale and introduced Islam to the heart of Kashmir. The Rinchanas, under monarchs such as Shihab ud-Din (1354–73), Sikander the Iconoclast (1389–1413) and Zain ud-Abidin (1420–70), lasted until 1561, although the last 80 years were plagued by a rotation of deposed and restored monarchs and other disputes. The Chaks, relations of the last Rinchana rajah, lasted until 1588 and the Mughal conquest, having eight monarchs in that time, two of whom each managed two terms on the throne.

The Mughal emperors favoured the beauty of the Vale of Kashmir and their patronage helped establish Muslim settlement here. Their rule lasted until 1747, when the imperial forces were unable to defend Kashmir from annexation to the new kingdom of Ahmad Shah Abdali of Afghanistan, and the Pathans remained in control until conquered by the Sikh-led Punjab of Ranjit Singh in 1819. Jammu, meanwhile, a medieval kingdom of the northern Punjab, consisted of 22 hill principalities that were consolidated into a larger realm by a Dogra Rajput, Maldev. The Dogra (or Durgah) dynasty established in the late 17th century produced a number of strong rulers, culminating in Ranjit Deva (1725–82), was followed by weak successors and

Jammu succumbed to the Punjab Raj of Ranjit Singh (based in Lahore—now in Pakistan) in 1816. The kingdom was restored in 1822, when Ranjit Singh installed a member of the Dogra clan who had served him loyally as a feudatory rajah. This Ghulab Singh, a Hindu prince, began to assert his independence after the death of Ranjit Singh in 1839, as the Sikh empire crumbled before British pressure. He arranged the 1846 peace between the British and the Government in Lahore (now in Pakistan), involving the cession of Kashmir to the East India Company, which retained nominal sovereignty but promptly sold the vast, strategic area on to the Rajah of Jammu for some £750,000. Thus, in 1846 Ghulab Singh became the Maharajah of Jammu and Kashmir, a loyal client of British India.

By the time Jammu and Kashmir was formed, the Dogra domain also included Ladakh. This kingdom had been invaded by a Dogra general, on the orders of Ranjit Singh, in 1836, and essentially fell under the overlordship of the Punjab for a few years. Despite the disastrous attempt of Zorawar Singh, the Dogra commander, to then move against Tibet itself in 1840, Ladakh did not have a chance fully to recover its independence and it was formally annexed by Ghulab Singh, the top Dogra, in 1842, at the expense of the last Chosgyal-chen-pos (kings) of the house of Namrgyal. This had been the second dynasty of Ladakh, a line founded in about 1460, in succession to a first dynasty that had led the break from Tibet in the 10th century and ruled a kingdom that fluctuated in power over the years, suffering a period of Mongol suzerainty in the mid-12th to mid-13th centuries. Maharajah Ghulab Singh's successor, Ranbir Singh (1856–86), in 1859 ordered the subjugation of the north, Gilgit. However, before independence, owing to British fears of a Communist threat from the north, Gilgit was taken on by the British as a directly administered frontier agency—it was signed back to Jammu and Kashmir on 1 August 1947, but was one of the areas taken over by Pakistan in the following months.

In summary, under the arrangements for division of the Empire and the independence of the successor states into Muslim Pakistan and Hindu-dominated India, the strategic state of Jammu and Kashmir found itself with a largely Muslim population (certainly in Kashmir), but a Hindu ruler who had the power to make the choice between which country to join. Jammu was predominantly Hindu and Ladakh traditionally Buddhist, but the Vale of Kashmir and the vast mountain terrain to the north gave the principality a Muslim majority. There might have been a case for Partition, but the Vale of Kashmir was personally important to the Nehru family, who originally came from there, and politically important to a pro-secularist Congress. Moreover, Congress had links with the Jammu and Kashmir National Conference (JKNC), led by Sheikh Muhammad Abdullah ('the Lion of Kashmir'), who himself tended to secularism and leftist rhetoric, which was popular with the people of Kashmir, but not so welcomed by the Maharajah, Hari Singh, from whom the JKNC had been demanding greater popular representation since the 1930s. At the time of independence, however, Sheikh Abdullah was in prison, the JKNC was being challenged by an ally of the Muslim League and Hari Singh, Maharajah since 1925, was fearful of factionalism, communalism and the consequences of any decision.

On 22 October 1947, two months after Indian independence, armed Pakistani tribesmen crossed the frontier, prompting the fearful Dogra monarch to declare the accession of Jammu and Kashmir to the state of India on 26 October. The arrival of Indian troops provoked further Pakistani irregulars into action, and the two countries effectively went to war, with Pakistan securing most of the north ('the Northern Areas') and some of the west ('Azad Kashmir') beyond a cease-fire line negotiated by the UN in 1948. India retained Jammu, most of Ladakh and the Vale of Kashmir, and promptly built new roadways into Ladakh and the Vale (previously entrance had been through what was now Pakistani-controlled territory). Since then, although the two countries have gone to war, in 1965 (concluded by the Tashkent Declaration of January 1966) and in 1971 (mainly over independence for Bangladesh—followed by the Shimla Agreement of 1972), and the cease-fire 'frontier' is now known as the Line of Control (LoC—since 1972), the international situation has not really changed. India continues to claim the whole state because the sovereign signed the instruments of accession in a decision endorsed by Sheikh Muhammad, a popular representative (although he subsequently spent most of the time in gaol for advocating independence). The Pakistani Government insists that the Muslim majority should have been able to place the state with Pakistan, and this could have been confirmed by the plebiscite that the UN required in 1948. The situation is further complicated by Chinese disputes about the border. Indian complaints at finding a Chinese road crossing the Aksai Chin plateau of Ladakh soon after the flight of the Dalai Lama from Tibet (Xizang) in 1959 seemed to help provoke a massive Chinese military advance across the length of the Indian–Chinese border in 1962. Chinese troops later withdrew to their previous positions. By the end of the 20th century, however, the main problem was from the rise in Islamist fundamentalism, which had sent fanatical fighters crossing into Kashmir in order to fight Indian troops or to help organize terrorist attacks in Indian-held territories, encouraging the flight of many Pandits (notably in 1990). Pakistan has helped organize such units (such as the 1999 incursions near Kargil), to the outrage of India, although US pressure after September 2001 and the West's anti-terrorist action in Afghanistan thereafter did force Pakistan to make concessions. Tension and even shootings across the LoC continue to be a regular event. In December 2001 a terrorist attack on the Indian Parliament buildings in Delhi provoked Indian outrage and made the federal Government declare that Pakistan was not acting firmly enough. Tension between the two nuclear powers gradually increased in the first half of 2002, reaching its height in May, when, with troops massed close to the LoC following a number of skirmishes, the threat of war was imminent. This attracted anxious international interest, and foreign pressure helped abate the crisis, although communal violence remained high within India and bilateral relations remained fragile. It was unclear what degree of control Pakistan actually had over the guerrilla groups.

Internally, the politics of Jammu and Kashmir followed a not unfamiliar pattern, only distorted by the special status forced on it by circumstance. Agitation for reform by the JKNC began to be achieved after the accession of the princely state to India, with the Maharajah conceding a Constituent Assembly, Sheikh Muhammad to be Prime Minister from 1948 (until 1953) and a regency (of Karan Singh) from 1949. In 1952 the Assembly rejected a hereditary monarch and the regent, Karan Singh, became Sadr-e Riyasat ('head of state'—a title he held until 1965). The Assembly secured some guarantees from the Centre under the Delhi Agreement of the same year, eventually permitting it, in 1954, to resolve on full accession to the Union, although the process took over one decade and was accompanied by the granting of several special concessions. It was not until 30 March 1965 that Karan Singh adopted the title of Governor, and the Prime Minister, Bakshi Ghulam Muhammad Sadiqh, became known as the Chief Minister. Thereafter, Sheikh Muhammad, who had been imprisoned as a separatist for much of the time, accepted Jammu and Kashmir's status within India. He became Chief Minister himself from 1975 (that year concluding the so-called Sheikh-Indira Accord with the federal Prime Minister) until his death in 1982. He was succeeded by his son, Dr Farooq Abdullah, who held office until 1984, to return in 1986, with Congress support. However, the state elections did not satisfy popular sentiments and there was increasing militancy, some of it sponsored from outside, with demands for incorporation into Pakistan or independence. The increasing militarization of the area and the continuing allegations of atrocities by both sides have served to escalate the situation through the 1990s and into the 2000s, without any real progress on a political solution. Abdullah had resigned as premier in 1990 and President's Rule was imposed, but state elections in 1996 were again won by the JKNC, which sought a solution within the Indian Union. However, the various rounds of cease-fires and concessions to and by militant leaders have led nowhere substantive, and the Centre rejected JKNC proposals of greater autonomy for the state. Proposals to separate the state into Jammu, Ladakh (where there are still demands to achieve territory status, despite increased autonomy from 2002) and Kashmir might have more chance of success, but political options remained uncertain both before and after the 2002 elections. Separatist sentiments are split between favouring either independence or partition (the so-called 'Chenab solution'), the latter involving the incorporation of Muslim-majority areas into Pakistan (favoured by the premier of Pakistani-occupied Kashmir, Sardar Sikandar Hayat, for instance). Meanwhile, the 'rump' of Jammu and Kashmir held by India is represented in the national Parliament by six seats in the lower house and four in the upper house.

Pakistan continued to protest against the holding of further state elections, which seemed likely to be won by the JKNC again. The more moderate separatist leaders had little chance of being elected to oppose them in a democratic forum, either owing to Indian suspicions or to violence and intimidation by the militants. However, the electorate obviously found this choice unpalatable and humiliated the JKNC at the legislative elections held in four phases during September–October 2002. The party's candidate for the premiership, Omar Abdullah, the son of the incumbent Chief Minister, failed to be elected, and 11 ministers in all, as well as the Speaker and his deputy, lost their seats. The JKNC remained the largest single party, but only retained 28 seats. Its partner at the Centre, the country's ruling Bharatiya Janata Party (BJP), was also rejected by the voters, keeping only one of the eight seats it had held previously (the national Government, nevertheless, welcomed the success of democracy in Jammu and Kashmir, particularly as turn-out had been about 45%, conferring some legitimacy on the results). Congress won 21 seats, mainly in and around Jammu. The People's Democratic Party (PDP—founded by the veteran politician and mufti, Mohammed Sayeed, and his daughter, Mehbooba Mufti, the only woman elected to the new Assembly and herself a former Congress minister) gained 15 seats, mostly in the Vale of Kashmir. The popular rejection of the JKNC was explicit, and the 'secular' parties of Congress and the PDP, as well as the National Panthers' Party and, in time, the Democratic People's Forum (the two Communist Party of India—Marxist members and six independents), began negotiations to form a coalition. However, the PDP was firm that it should head the coalition and provide a premier from Kashmir (Sayeed), as part of a new process of conciliating those separatists who were not necessarily militant. Moreover, many in the state remained suspicious of the Congress record as a national party in the region. This favoured the PDP case, although the National Panthers' Party, with four seats, preferred Congress over PDP leadership. Nevertheless, the Panthers remained in the coalition (although the party's loyalty was questioned only months later) even when the PDP was finally conceded the premiership by the Congress leader, Ghulam Nabad Azad, under pressure from the national Congress leadership. However, this was not until the end of the month, and after Governor's Rule had been imposed on the night of 17 October (the date the term of the old Assembly expired), as coalition negotiations stumbled. Sayeed was finally sworn in as Chief Minister on 2 November, having agreed to share the premiership with Congress.

The new Government was anxious to distinguish between separatist sentiment and the militants, and operatives of the latter continued to make deadly attacks throughout the state, including one on a Hindu temple in November 2002. This illustrated the Government's vulnerability to accusations of being 'soft on terrorism', but the PDP and Congress emphasized the foreign nature of the militants and attributed blame to Pakistan rather than 'misguided' locals. In March 2003 there was a reverse for the policy of encouraging Hindu Pandits to return to or at least stay in Kashmir, when 24 Pandits were murdered in Nadimarg, in Pulwama district. Later in the year it was claimed by official Indian sources that almost 14,000 had died in the troubles since the late 1980s, mainly as a result of terrorist action, although Pakistan asserts the figure to be nearer 70,000, many of whom were victims of the Indian security forces. However, a visit to Srinagar by the Prime Minister, Atal Bihari Vajpayee, in April marked a renewed Indian commitment to good relations with Pakistan (which was welcomed by separatists as well as the elected politicians). This visit was followed by one from the Centre's new interlocutor on Kashmir, N. N. Vohra (appointed in February), who met with the representatives of the elected parties, but still not with the separatists (25 parties grouped in the All-Party Hurriyat Conference—APHC). The state Government was embarrassed by the Centre's August decision to provide funding for the controversial Special Operations Group, which had been established to lead the struggle against terrorism, but which the PDP had pledged to disband during the election campaign (a commitment it announced the implementation of in February 2003—as part of its 'healing touch' policy). Nevertheless, there were some signs of response from the separatist opposition, to both federal and state initiatives, and despite continuing high levels of violence there were encouraging reports of, for example, the return of Hindu pilgrims to temples in Kashmir. Some separatist leaders of the APHC and the Centre met in January 2004, then again in March. Meanwhile, the JKNC was reported to have split with its erstwhile ally, the BJP. Despite the progress of peace negotiations, the APHC continued to urge a boycott of voting in the Indian general election. This was held in April–May 2004. The JKNC retained two Lok Sabha seats in Jammu and Kashmir, while Congress also won two. The PDP secured one seat. The new Congress-led Government at the Centre committed itself to maintaining the improved relations with Pakistan fostered by the previous administration, as well as the peace negotiations with the separatists, 'within the four walls of the Constitution'—a phrase to which the APHC objected, claiming that it put sovereignty off the agenda.

The APHC, however, had itself been put under strain by the moves towards conciliation. The separatist opposition had been experiencing internal dissension for some time, with Syed Ali Shah Geelani of Jamaat-e-Islami, a former chairman of the Conference, at the heart of matters. Geelani was a fundamentalist believer in Islam and, politically, an uncompromising supporter of partition and the incorporation of Muslim territories into Pakistan. He was suspected of involvement in the assassination of another separatist leader in 2002, but also favoured punitive action by the APHC against another of its member parties, the People's Conference, which he accused of having endorsed proxy candidates in the state elections, in contradiction of an APHC boycott. In May 2003, however, Geelani was removed from the executive of the APHC, supposedly as part of the separatists' willingness to show some flexibility in reaction to improving Indian-Pakistani relations. The organization openly split in September, following the election for a replacement as chairman of the APHC (at the time, Abdul Gani Bhat of the Muslim Conference). The new leadership of Maulvi Abbas Ansari of the Itihadul Muslemeen, the first Shi'a Muslim to head the Hurriyat Conference, was challenged by a significant faction, which proceeded to elect Geelani instead, in a move that could only make peace negotiations more complex. While Ansari engaged in negotiations with the Indian Government, Geelani and his faction continued to favour tripartite discussions between India, Pakistan and the separatists. Ansari attempted to enable a reconciliation of the separatist factions by resigning from his position in July 2004 (Umer Farooq, the 12th Mirwaiz of Kashmir, returned as interim chairman), but Geelani rejected unity and, in August, formed a new party, the Tehreek-e-Hurriyat Jammu and Kashmir, to pursue his policies.

The rapprochement between India and Pakistan brought about developments in Jammu and Kashmir, where the moderate faction of the APHC continued to express willingness to negotiate with the Centre, although its leaders also wanted to visit Pakistan first (thereby maintaining a semblance of tripartite talks). The Geelani faction, which had hitherto enjoyed the support of Pakistan, from November 2004 came under increasing pressure to reunite with the rest of the APHC. Both groups remained reserved about some of the ideas for a solution that were coming out of Pakistan and gave a cautious welcome to confidence-building measures such as the proposed demilitarization and 'softening' of the LoC. India continued to reject international mediation or redrawing the borders, but agreed to reduce troop numbers. This was confirmed when the Prime Minister, Manmohan Singh, visited the state for two days from 17 November. With the leader of Pakistan, Gen. Pervez Musharraf, conceding that a plebiscite was not the only possible solution to the Kashmir question, the Prime Minister offered unconditional negotiations to groups renouncing violence. Singh also promised reconstruction aid worth Rs 240,000m. and rehabilitation for refugee Pandits. In January 2005 the Centre agreed to a request from the JKNC to establish a panel to discuss increased autonomy for Jammu and Kashmir, although the APHC rejected this as a solution. By mid-February the Centre indicated its readiness to open negotiations with the separatists, but events then came to be dominated by the preparations for a bus service between Srinagar and Muzaffarabad (in Pakistani Kashmir). March was riven by militant warnings and attacks, culminating in a fierce assault on the Srinagar tourist centre (the terminus for the bus service) just before the commencement date. Nevertheless, the bus service was duly inaugurated on 7 April, and proved to be popular, despite the danger posed by the militants. The service was 172 km in length and involved walking across the border. Special documentation, rather than international passports, was required (a vital bridge was damaged in the October earthquake—see below—but rebuilding enabled the 'peace bus' to resume a full service on 20 February 2006). Bolstered by the success of the bus link and by Indian reports that infiltration by militants across the border had declined, Musharraf's visit to Delhi further helped to improve relations. On 17 April Musharraf received delegations from the two factions of the APHC in Delhi. Then, on 2 June, although not joined by Geelani or his allies, the moderate leaders of the APHC were able to visit Pakistan—despite earlier complaints about obstruction by the Indian authorities. They returned without any clear vision from Pakistan, but were no longer completely opposed to a solution involving autonomy and talked of a 'United States of Kashmir' as a possible direction to explore. More importantly, the main grouping of Pakistan-based militants began to mention the possibility of a cease-fire. This was a useful fillip in countering the less compromising rhetoric of Geelani and his allies, particularly after the potential threat to negotiations in the aftermath of the militant attack on the controversial Ayodhya site in Uttar Pradesh in July. The meeting of APHC and exiled Pandit leaders in the same month also helped the spirit of reconciliation, although militant attacks continued to be frequent. The 'ultra' faction of the APHC appeared more isolated, suffering defections in July, August and October, while Geelani could not always muster public support from those who continued as his adherents. However, he remained subject to persistent bouts of house arrest by the authorities, and was refused permission to travel to Pakistan. The new Congress Chief Minister—see below—said in January 2006 that, unlike his predecessors, he was not opposed to Geelani going on the *haj*, the pilgrimage to Mecca, Saudi Arabia. In March 2007 Geelani, who was ailing, was granted a passport (confiscated since 1993) in order to seek medical treatment abroad, although he instead went to a hospital in Delhi.

The fatal bomb attacks in Mumbai (Maharashtra) in July 2006 proved to be a serious threat to the dialogue between India and Pakistan. Although the process had been faltering by the beginning of the year (following a meeting between Musharraf and Prime Minister Singh in New York, USA, at the UN the previous September), confidence-building measures had continued. Then, in February Singh had offered 'round table' talks in New Delhi, although the APHC said developments since the September discussions did not warrant their attendance. The militants' organization seemed more undecided about the second round-table conference, convened in Srinagar amid tight security in May, but did not attend, only offering to meet the Prime Minister separately. Pakistan (which had itself provoked debate in February by proposing demilitarization and self-rule in Kashmir) welcomed the initiative of the Indian Government, although many remained doubtful about substantive progress—the PDP and the JKNC both expressed reservations about a third conference before results from the first two were achieved. A third conference, again without the militants, was held in New Delhi in April 2007, after positive contacts had resumed between India and Pakistan when Singh and Musharraf met during an international conference in Cuba the previous September. However, the process retained its sense of déjà vu, with Pakistan urging unity on the militants, who continued their infighting, and with cease-fires and demilitarization being urged all round, but differing conditions being attached.

Democratic politics in the second half of 2004 were dominated by the rejection in the legislature of the Women's Rights Bill, which was supported by the PDP and opposed by Congress. The issue limped on into September, because both parties hoped to gain electoral advantage from it, the Bill being popular in the Vale of Kashmir, where the PDP had its strength, and opposition being popular in the Congress heartland of Jammu. The supposedly fragile coalition survived, however, and in August 2005 Sayeed confirmed that he would honour his pledge to surrender the office of Chief Minister to Congress in November. Certainly Sayeed had won a crucial by-election against the JKNC in Kashmir in September 2004, and the coalition partners had performed well in many areas at the civic polls conducted between December and February 2005 (although the JKNC was pleased with its overwhelming victory in Srinagar). The emergence of a peace process of sorts had no doubt helped the Government, although in February it was criticized for a poor response to the crisis caused by extremely heavy snowfalls in the state and in May the opposition made much of the cost of proposals to move the summer capital from Srinagar to the more rural Parihaspora (due to be completed by 2008). The Government performed better in its response to the devastating earthquake of 8 October 2005, although most of the effects were felt on the other side of the LoC (Muzaffarabad was virtually wiped out and, in all, almost 80,000 people died, whereas the death toll in Indian-controlled territory was nearer 1,400, with 150,000 made homeless). In general, Sayeed's term was considered successful, enough for him to feel entitled to press for an extension to his tenure of the premiership. Congress nevertheless remained determined to fill the Chief Minister's office with someone from Jammu. Concerted action by the Congress legislative deputies convinced the national leadership to insist that Sayeed keep to the original agreement. Therefore, on 2 November Ghulam Nabi Azad was sworn in as Chief Minister, with the support of the PDP. He gained some popularity with his anti-graft campaign and his determination to outlaw defections by elected representatives from their parties, but austerity measures and a critically poor power-supply system were counterweights. Nevertheless, Azad was elected to the state legislature at the by-elections in April 2006, as was constitutionally required for a minister.

Although the peace process continued to make some progress, by early 2006 it was faltering (see above) and the bombs in Mumbai stalled negotiations with Pakistan. With militant violence continuing, and even attacks on tourists in July (although such assaults proved unpopular with the local population), the Congress-led Government had less to offset against continuing complaints about the security forces. The PDP criticized Congress for not restraining the security forces as Sayeed had done—civilian casualties had risen since November 2005. Before the end of the year Azad was claiming that human rights violations in the state had decreased, with the lowest numbers of deaths in custody and of disappearances since the military had arrived in strength. However, a scandal about local police involvement in 'fake' terrorist killings—the disappearances and murders of citizens unconnected to political groups, often for private gain—in February 2007 undermined such claims. The main problem for the Government, though, remained relations between the main coalition partners, with the PDP seemingly anxious to regain the premiership before the state elections scheduled for 2008 or to distinguish itself from Congress without leaving power. Thus, the PDP welcomed President Musharraf of Pakistan's September 2006 proposal of greater self-rule for the state (alone among the major political parties), joined the JKNC at a May 2007 all-party conference in stymieing Congress proposals to regularize the position of refugees from Pakistan (those arriving in 1947, 1965 and 1971) and, perhaps most significantly, causing rumours of a rift in the ruling alliance by urging demilitarization of or troop reductions in Jammu and Kashmir. On the last issue, at the end of March, the PDP secured the agreement of Congress at the Centre to examine the case for gradually reducing troop numbers, although as army reports of an increase in infiltrations across the border emerged from May, any imminent demilitarization seemed more remote. Nevertheless, Sayeed secured written confirmation from the Prime Minister in July that troop numbers were being reviewed and that emergency legislation would also be re-examined. However, the coalition partners had avoided disagreement over a short-lived PDP rift, which had resulted in the replacement of the PDP deputy premier and legislative leader in September 2006 (he returned to office in December 2007), and they had reacted in concert later that month in opposing the death sentence for a Kashmiri convicted of conspiring with the terrorists who attacked the Indian Parliament building in 2001 (the execution was stayed in October, following widespread protests in the state, although the central Congress leadership distanced itself from Azad's appeal for clemency). In June 2007 the National Panthers' Party withdrew support from the Government (although the coalition's majority remained unthreatened) because of PDP support for troop reductions and because of the lack of progress in addressing Pandit issues—the Pandits had remained particularly dissatisfied since the April round-table conference. Generally, despite a difficult relationship with the PDP, Congress appeared to be set on remaining in office until the legislative elections, which were most likely to be held in November 2008. In December Congress won a by-election to a seat previously held by the JKNC. Violence in the state had been less in 2007 than in previous years. There had not been much progress in the peace negotiations between India and Pakistan, but moves towards unity of the separatists in the more moderate APHC were promising, even though in May the grouping refuted the rumour that it intended to participate in the elections. However, the relative calm was shattered in June 2008, damaging the peace process, communal relations and democratic government, with repercussions throughout India.

The annual Hindu pilgrimage to the Amarnath shrine began on 17 June 2008, with record numbers of participants expected. Such numbers invited appropriate facilities and Chief Minister Azad had taken the seemingly innocuous decision to grant some 40 ha of forest land on which the shrine board could build. There was a meeting between Mirwaiz Farooq and Geelani, at which a legal challenge to the grant was discussed, but the popular reaction to the land grant seemed to gather pace quite unprompted. The shrine board, consisting of members mainly from outside the state and headed by the centrally appointed Governor, did not fit well with the Kashmiri tradition of land not being owned by 'outsiders'. Particularly following the death of a youth in Srinagar in early demonstrations against the land grant, unrest escalated, until the *bandh* in the Vale was almost total. Opposition to the Amarnath land grant united separatists, militants and moderate politicians—or, at least, they were caught up in the spontaneous protests—and the PDP demanded the revocation of the grant. On 28 June the PDP withdrew from the Government, although Azad claimed still to command a majority in the legislature. The new Governor chaired a series of negotiations, arranging for the shrine board to refuse the land grant in favour of the Government providing the facilities itself and for Chief Minister Azad to seek the confidence of the Assembly by 7 July. Despite some protests in Jammu about the surrender of the land, the Government decided to consolidate the returning calm in Kashmir with a formal revocation of the land grant on 1 July. The uproar in Jammu did not subside, but increased, effectively wrong-footing Congress not only with the Muslim community, but also with Hindus. On 7 July Azad did not press the confidence motion to a vote in the Assembly, but instead resigned and, after some consultations across the political spectrum, Governor's Rule was imposed and the Assembly dissolved. Unfortunately, demonstrations and violence by Hindu activists continued. Congress accused the BJP and others of inciting the crisis for wider political gain in the elections and on the national stage. Certainly the issue was resonant for *Hindutva* militancy, and unrest in Jammu and its environs continued even into August. Unrest also resumed in Srinagar, following some deaths under police firing at a demonstration against the effective economic blockade of the Vale of Kashmir by Hindu activists. The consequences of the unexpected crisis were ominous for the restoration of a semblance of stability, and created uncertainty about the date of the legislative elections.

## ECONOMY

The economic potential of Jammu and Kashmir is stunted by the political trouble, which deters investment as well as costing physical damage, although military expenditure contributes to the size of the economy. In 2004/05 net state domestic product was put at Rs 180,090m. or Rs 12,781 per head (the latter figure was still about three times that of Bihar, the poorest state of the Union, and larger than that of seven other states). (Unless otherwise specified, any such economic data applies only to that part of Jammu and Kashmir held by India.) At March 1998 there was only a total road length of 13,540 km. Jammu is connected to the main Indian rail network, but there are plans to extend the line as far as Srinagar (it has, hitherto, only reached Udhampur). There are airports at Jammu, Srinagar and Leh. Security considerations have limited the development of telecommunications, with the security forces until mid-2003 not even prepared to consider allowing mobile (cellular) telephone networks to be established in the state. The mountainous terrain limits the options for transport, but it is an advantage for hydroelectric development, although in 2004 one such project on the Chenab, the Baglihar dam, provoked Pakistan into challenging the scheme under the 1960 Indus Waters Treaty. Pakistan claimed that the dam would hold more water than required for power generation, which would adversely affect farmers downstream. In January 2005 Pakistan threatened to invoke neutral arbitration through the offices of the World Bank (which was the original broker of the Treaty). Meanwhile, the Chief Minister of Jammu and Kashmir claimed that the project was still proceeding and the first phase would be completed in 2006. At May 2006 Jammu and Kashmir had achieved an installed electricity capacity of 1,455 MW (65% from central projects, the rest from the state sector, except for 0.52 MW from the private sector), and most rural villages have now been connected to the electricity supply (176, or less than 3%, remaining in 2005). However, many private electricity connections are illicit, depriving the state of valuable revenue for investment, and the Government announced a sustained effort to secure payment of bills from early 2003. The literacy rate in 2001 was 54.5%.

About four-fifths of the population depend on agriculture for their livelihoods. The main crops are paddy, wheat and maize, although barley and the hardier millets are also grown in places. Total foodgrain production reached 1.3m. metric tons in 1996/97, while fruit production reached 965,000 tons (of which 78% was exported). The fruit sector was particularly affected by the economic disruption caused by the unrest over the Amarnath land grant from June 2008. Horticulture has been encouraged and there are now almost 0.5m. families engaged directly or indirectly in this field. Some oilseeds and sugar cane are also grown. Foodgrain production reached a record harvest of 1.5m. tons in 1998/99, but had fallen to the lowest level since the late 1980s by 2000/01, only to recover in the following year to 1.3m. (41% coarse grains, 32% rice, 26% wheat and 1% pulses). Oilseeds production reached 70,800 tons in 1985/86, but fell back thereafter, reaching a nadir of 26,500 tons in 1994/95, before recovering steadily to 53,400 tons by 1999/2000, then plummeting to 28,400 tons, but rising again to 41,800 tons in 2001/02. Livestock numbers in 1992 totalled 8.71m. Of livestock products, the state is most widely known for its cashmere (Kashmir) wool. In 2002/03 7,358 tons of wool were produced (as well as 1.2m. tons of milk and 620m. eggs).

Mineral reserves of the state include coal and lignite, limestone, glass sand, graphite, gypsum and natural gas. Bauxite, chromium, manganese, copper, zinc, gold and sapphires are also found within the borders of Jammu and Kashmir. The mining sector employed 18,371 people in 2001/02 and produced minerals worth Rs 217.5m. in 2002/03. Extraction of these resources and their processing, where necessary, provide the basis for some heavy industry. Traditionally, however, the main industrial activity is based on small enterprises and consists of handicrafts and handloom products. These sectors also receive government encouragement, owing to the employment potential, and accounted for most of the 38,029 small-scale industrial units in the state in 1996/97. Handlooms produce woollen (especially cashmere) items such as blankets, shawls and fabrics, with the number of weavers at almost 50,000 by the mid-1990s. Handloom products worth Rs 230m. were woven in 1995/96. The handlooms often produce the raw material for handicraft workers, who produce shawls and embroidery, as well as wood carving and, most importantly, carpets. In 1996/97 handicrafts turnover was worth Rs 2,600m., while exports were put at Rs 2,930m. in value. Carpets alone earned Rs 132m. in foreign exchange in 1994/95.

The tertiary sector is mainly accounted for by public administration, although there are still a wide network of banks, post offices and other community services. Trade and transport are the next most important contributors to the sector. Tourism was once an important industry, the Vale of Kashmir a particularly famous resort since Mughal times, but the frequency of violent incidents and the restrictions of the military have confined tourist activity to trekking and the Buddhist sites of Ladakh. In September 2003 the Ladakh Autonomous Hill Development Council reported its best tourist season since 1974 (visitor numbers had stagnated, then fallen sharply after 1989, when agitation for Ladakh to achieve separate territory status began). There were 30,000 foreign visitors and 10,000 domestic visitors in 2003, although there were also concerns about the number of out-of-state workers (reportedly 20,000) attracted by the construction and restoration work permitted by a central government grant.

### DIRECTORY

**Governor:** Narendra Nath Vohra, Office of the Governor, Raj Bhavan, Jammu/Srinagar; tel. (191) 2546466 (Jammu); (194) 2452224 (Srinagar); fax (191) 2545649 (Jammu); (194) 2452120 (Srinagar); e-mail rajjk@jk.nic.in.

**Chief Minister:** (vacant), Office of the Chief Minister, Government of Jammu and Kashmir, Civil Secretariat, Jammu/Srinagar; tel. (191) 2546466 (Jammu); (194) 2452224 (Srinagar); fax (191) 2545649 (Jammu); (194) 2452120 (Srinagar); internet www.jammukashmir.nic.in/govt/welcome.html.

**Speaker of the Legislative Assembly:** Tara Chand, Assembly Secretariat, Jammu/Srinagar; tel. (191) 2546531 (Jammu); (194) 2478927 (Srinagar); fax (191) 2573473 (Jammu); (194) 2472783 (Srinagar); the Legislative Assembly is the lower chamber of the state legislature and has 87 elected mems: Jammu and Kashmir National Conference 28; Congress 20; People's Democratic Party 16; National Panthers' Party 4; Ladakh Union Territory Front 2; Communist (CPI—M) 2; independents and others 15.

**Chairman of the Legislative Council:** Abdul Rashid Dar, Legislative Council Secretariat, Jammu/Srinagar; fax (191) 2542031 (Jammu); (194) 2472402 (Srinagar); fax (191) 2570344 (Jammu); (194) 2479666 (Srinagar); the upper chamber of the bicameral legislature has 36 indirectly elected mems.

**State Resident Commissioner in New Delhi:** Khursheed Ahmed Ganai, Jammu and Kashmir House, 5 Prithviraj Rd, New Delhi 110 003; tel. (11) 24611506; fax (11) 24627047.

Direct federal rule administered by the Governor was imposed in Jammu and Kashmir on 10 July 2008.

## Jharkhand

The State of Jharkhand, the southern part of Bihar until 15 November 2000, lies in northern India, south of the Gangetic plain. Bihar lies to the north, West Bengal to the east, Orissa to the south and Chhattisgarh (itself a part of Madhya Pradesh until 2000) to the south-west. In the north-west there is a short western border with Uttar Pradesh. This hilly upland, the 'land of jungle and jhari (forest)', was also known as Vananchal (forest region) or, historically, Kukara. The state covers some 46% of the old territory of Bihar, amounting to some 79,714 sq km (30,789 sq miles).

Jharkhand occupies the east of the Chotanagpur plateau, the northern part of the state consisting of a rough crescent of territory above the plains of Bihar, extending into the plains where it reaches up to a short north-eastern border along the River Ganga (Ganges). The central waist of the state is dominated by hills in the west, the end of the Hazaribagh Range, while the lower lands around Ranchi, the state capital, provide a link between north and south. The rest of the state spills south in three bulges of territory, the south-eastern extension again reaching into the plains, those divided between West Bengal and Orissa. The climate is tropical, but tempered by altitude, with the average annual rainfall across the state being some 1,400 mm (56 inches).

The population of Jharkhand in 1991, when it was still part of Bihar, was 21,843,911. In 2001 the population had risen to 26,945,829, a decadal growth rate still slightly higher than the national average, but lower than on the plains of Bihar. Scheduled Tribes accounted for 26% of the population and Scheduled Castes 12%. In some districts the aboriginal tribal peoples account for over one-half of the population. The dominant group remains the Santhal, the third largest tribe in India, the people of which speak an Austro-Asiatic tongue (which can be written in its own Olchiki script). Modern Jharkhand emerged from an administrative association of Chotanagpur, populated by a variety of tribes, and in the south-east, the Santhal country (pargana). Other tribes include the Dravidian Oraon and Munda peoples and the Ho. Hindi is the main language of most people in Jharkhand, and Hinduism the principal religion (68.6% of the population in 2001). Islam, which claims the adherence of 13.9% of the population, is mainly found in the towns. There is a relatively large community of Christians (4.1%), with adherents concentrated among the tribal people (over one-half of the Kharia people and about one-quarter of the Munda and the Ho), and some Sikhs, Buddhists and Jains. There is some residual animism, but the process of 'Aryanization' or 'Hindu-ization' is noticeable. However, along the way, a number of cults and adaptations of other traditions has occurred, accounting for the 13.0% who claimed their religion as 'other' at the census.

The old summer capital of Bihar, Ranchi, is the state capital, but the largest cities and the main industrial centres are Jamshedpur, in the south-east (with 1.10m. people in its wider urban area in 2001), and Dhanbad (1.07m.), the latter being at the heart of the state's rich minerals region. Deogarh (Baidyanath Dham) is also an important centre. The urban population totalled about 22% of the total in 2001. Including the four created since division of the state, Jharkhand consists of 22 districts for administrative purposes.

### HISTORY

The early history of the heavily wooded high country that now constitutes Jharkhand is uncertain, as no major power was ever based here, although the kings of Magadha and other territories have long benefited from the exploitation of the region's mineral resources. Generally, the myriad tribes enjoyed their isolation, often slowly adopting cultural imports but usually resenting actual settlement by outsiders. The Nagvanshi dynasty exercised a tenuous sovereignty over much of the area, and its kings would sometimes submit to Mughal or other overlords. Such Muslim immigration as there was (the first mosque was not built until 1661) tended to be urban and did not much disturb the local economic and political structures. In the 18th century the north of Jharkhand came under the Patna Division (i.e. Bihar) of British Bengal and, in 1765, with the granting of a Mughal *diwan* to the East India Company, there was a determined military effort to bring the territory firmly under British authority, including the subjugation of the Santhals. However, this incorporation into the nascent British India involved the imposition of alien property and revenue concepts over traditional land rights, a tightening of administrative control (usually by outsiders, be they British or Indian) and the immigration of settlers (*diku*) from more crowded parts of British territory. This resulted in the turbulent history of revolt experienced by the Empire in this region, a history that probably helped forge the regional identity.

The frequent uprisings in Jharkhand did not always have a common cause, such as a rejection of British authority *per se*, but more usually arose from a resentment of outsider control or settlement, or from grievances over land or government and landlord levies. The Paharia revolt of the 1770s was promptly followed by another tribal revolt under Tilka Manjhi in the first half of the 1780s, while the decade around the turn of the century was occupied by two Munda uprisings and the Chaur and Bhoomij revolts. The 19th century enjoyed some periods of peace, but agitation particularly accumulated in the years up to the Great Rebellion or 'First War of Independence' (occasioned by the Sepoy Mutiny of 1857) and again in the last quarter of the century. Specific land grievances tended to be replaced by more general social and economic objections by the end of the 19th century. Another Munda revolt in 1819–20 was followed by the Kewar and Bhumij revolts of the 1830s, before some major upheavals from the mid-1850s. The most serious, a general uprising by the Santhal in 1855, was occasioned by the new land settlement of the British administration, and resulted in a war that undermined the myth of Company invincibility. The Santhal leader, Sidhu, set up a parallel government, passing his own laws and raising his own taxes in a move reminiscent of Maratha tactics against the Mughals. The conflict helped prompt the creation of a police brigade in the region, but the suppression of the revolt was complicated by the turbulence following the 1857 Mutiny. Although northern Bihar was promptly pacified by the presence of British troops diverted from elsewhere in Asia, in Jharkhand local uprisings of Hindus, Muslims and some of the tribes were led by Sahid Lal, Vishwanath Shahdeo, Sheik Bikhari, Ganptrai and Budhu Veer. It was 1860 before civil obedience was regained throughout the region, with the final extinction of the Santhal resistance. Towards the end of the century tribal unrest was made more powerful by wider protests, such as the Birsa and Kherwar movements. In around 1900 Bhagwan Birsa Munda led a futile rebellion against the Empire in favour of independence, but, thereafter, the tribal populations joined others in India in organizing more peaceful and more widespread opposition to British rule, without abandoning the struggle for social and economic justice. This was helped by the lessening of isolation from the rest of India and the growth of industry, particularly in the south-east, where in 1908 a Parsi industrialist, Jamshedji Tata, founded the first planned town in modern India, Jamshedpur, which produced its first steel ingots wrought from local resources in 1912.

Also in 1912 Bihar (including Jharkhand) was made a province separate from Bengal, although still in union with Orissa. At the time there was mention of a separate province in the Jharkhand region, but, instead, some of the old Chotanagpur area was retained by Bengal. Partly in response to this administrative severing of traditional links, a first attempt at pan-tribal organization was made by the Chotanagpur Developed Society in 1915, while the Tana Bhajgat movement (which commanded the support of more than 26,000 tribesmen) had started a rent-refusal campaign in the previous year. Pressure for a political solution, the creation of a Jharkhand province, followed much later, however, despite such a proposal to an official commission in 1929. Instead, Orissa alone was separated from Bihar, under the Government of India Act of 1935, and it was only in the 1940s that demands for administrative autonomy (statehood) achieved political organization.

In 1940 a tribal leader, Jaipal Singh, formed an assembly of autochthonous peoples, the Adibasi Mahasabha, which became the Jharkhand Party soon after independence. In the general elections of 1952 and 1957 this party became the main opposition grouping in southern Bihar, and it unsuccessfully urged the creation of Jharkhand on the States Reorganization Commission in 1955. However, Singh undermined his party as a political voice in favour of statehood by accepting a Congress ministerial appointment in 1963, and it was not until the 1970s that momentum was recovered. In March 1973 N. E. Horo of the Jharkhand Party appealed to the Prime Minister for statehood in southern Bihar, but it was really in 1978 that the movement returned to prominence. Now led by Shibu Soren, the Jharkhand Party had extended its influence into the tribal areas of neighbouring states and was demanding a 'Greater Jharkhand', including not only Bihar's Chotanagpur and Santhal Pargana, but also adjacent areas in West Bengal. It was sometimes suggested that parts of Orissa and Madhya Pradesh (in the latter, the part that now constitutes Chhattisgarh) should be included in such a state. In 1978 it was resolved by the Jharkhand Party that a commemorative 'Birsa Day' should be held on 9 June every year—by the late 1980s the separatist movement was also urging a boycott of the national Independence Day, to emphasize the strong feelings in favour of a Jharkhand state. By then the Jharkhand Party had undergone a number of splits and suffered a considerable degree of factionalization, although the leading political force, Jharkhand Mukti Morcha (JMM), was still led by Soren. The movement had also been joined by other organizations, such as the Jharkhand Co-ordinating Committee, the Jharkhand Kranti Dal and the All-Jharkhand Students Union (AJSU). It was the AJSU that first organized a one-day strike in support of statehood in September 1986, and AJSU and the JMM both organized longer economic blockades in 1989. Such radicalization of the movement, demonstrating its popular support, attracted the investigations of the Centre as well as a concession by the Government of Bihar in 1990 that a Jharkhand Area Autonomous Council should be formed, which was duly achieved in 1995. It covered the 18 districts that were to form the current state of Jharkhand, the traditional Chotanagpur and Santhal Pargana area of southern Bihar, and Soren became its Chairman. However, the premier of Bihar, Lalu Prasad Yadav, was vociferous in his opposition to the bifurcation of the state.

The Bharatiya Janata Party (BJP), which still forms the largest single group in the state legislature, was in favour of a separate state of Jharkhand, and also achieved the leadership of national government in 1998. The local Congress groups favoured statehood, while the national leadership was prepared to sanction it if Chhattisgarh was also made a separate state. There was support from the Samata Party, the Janata Dal (United) and the Communist Party of India (CPI). However, Chief Minister Yadav, who had split from the national Janata Dal to form his own Rashtriya Janata Dal (RJD), was strongly against the loss of the mineral-rich southern region to the rest of Bihar. However, in 1997 his political position weakened, following revelations of his involvement in the abstraction of government funds. He was forced to resign as state premier, to be replaced by his wife, Rabri Devi (Yadav subsequently served a number of brief prison sentences in connection with the affair, then continued his political career at the federal level). The support required for their party to continue in government was forthcoming from Soren and from Congress, and the appropriate measures to create a separate Jharkhand (originally Vananchal) state duly passed through the Bihar and national legislatures. Presidential assent on 25 August 2000 enshrined the Bihar Reorganization Act in law and in October it was gazetted that separation would occur at midnight on the night of 14–15 November. Meanwhile, Soren was anxious to become the first Chief Minister of Jharkhand, but the BJP was determined to consolidate its own position, with its nominee as premier. Thus, Babulal Marandi headed the Government of Jharkhand that came into existence on 15 November.

By 2002 the BJP-led coalition, which had 45 of the 81 seats in the Legislative Assembly, was under strain. In May the five Samata ministers (their representation had increased since statehood) resigned from the cabinet and threatened to withdraw from the coalition, after the BJP put up its own candidate for the by-election to the Rajya Sabha seat hitherto held by a Samata member (Jharkhand has six seats in the Rajya Sabha and 14 in the Lok Sabha). Samata also declared its support for Soren in his candidacy for re-election to the Lok Sabha. Towards the end of the year the Jharkhand People's Party withdrew its support for the Government (in May the following year there were reports that it, the JMM and Congress might form an alliance to contest the next legislative elections). Marandi was finally obliged to resign in March 2003, after seven ministers joined a revolt within the ruling coalition (led by the Speaker of the Assembly, Inder Singh Namdhari, a member of Janata Dal—United after he left the RJD) and defeated the Government on a finance motion. The Governor rejected Namdhari's bid to form an administration and the BJP retained its hold on power by securing the premiership for Arjun Munda, supported by 40 members of the Assembly. However, the Government was shaken by the results of the general election of April–May 2004 (which took place with a good turn-out, despite some constituencies being under the threat of Naxalite violence). The BJP (in the person of former premier Marandi) managed to win only one seat in the Lok Sabha (from 11). The opposition electoral alliance of Congress (six seats), the JMM (four), the RJD (two) and the left (one seat for the CPI) won all the other Jharkhand seats in the national Lok Sabha.

Following the victory of Congress and its allies in the 2004 general election, the JMM not only joined the national Government, but also secured the Union coal ministry for its leader, Shibu Soren. Already controversial for a number of criminal and corruption cases, Soren soon became prominent in the 'tainted ministers' scandal at the Centre. In July the question arose of reviving an arrest warrant for Soren issued in 1986. The case had resulted from his involvement in the 1975 Chirrudih massacre (10 people died in a Muslim-dominated village, allegedly after Soren incited a mob protesting against 'outsiders'). The state authorities sent police to Delhi to arrest the JMM leader. However, he went into hiding and petitioned the courts to dismiss the case (particularly as the first Government of the new state had promised to abandon all cases involving the Jharkhand movement). Eventually, the Prime Minister had to ask for Soren's resignation (which was received), and the JMM announced that, while it was still firm in its support for the new Congress-led Government, it would not seek office in it at this stage. The JMM and its allies in Jharkhand claimed that the BJP-led state Government had revived the charges against Soren for political reasons, in advance of the state elections, and was being misleading in describing him as an 'absconder' or 'fugitive' from justice and in portraying earlier demonstrations in favour of tribal rights as communalism. With the state elections scheduled for February and the Prime Minister saying that conditions were different, Soren was reappointed to the federal Cabinet in late November. Meanwhile, the ruling coalition was losing support in the Assembly, with four Janata Dal (United) deputies deserting in late October and the Speaker leaving the BJP just before the elections, to the benefit of the RJD, which was campaigning separately from the two alliances.

The elections to the state legislature took place over several stages in February 2005. Turn-out was good, apart from in some rural areas, where Naxalite threats and violence was a deterrence. Anti-incumbency opinion was mitigated by the divisions in the ranks of the opposition. Congress was mistaken to ignore the RJD and also indulged in some rivalry with its JMM ally, while the JMM itself alienated one of its senior leaders, Stephen Marandi, who stood as an independent against one of Soren's sons (Marandi won, but aligned himself with the 'secular' alliance). Such factionalism was to the benefit of the BJP-led coalition, which proceeded to win 36 seats (30 for the BJP and six for the Janata Dal—United). The JMM gained 17 and Congress only nine. The RJD won eight seats, while the remaining 11 went to various other parties or to independents. The Assembly was hung, but by the beginning of March the BJP-led group had announced that it could command the support of 41 of the 81 deputies, naming five apart from those elected for the BJP and the Janata Dal (United).

However, on 2 March 2005 Soren was invited to form a Government and given almost three weeks to seek the confidence of the Assembly. He claimed to have the support of 42 legislators. Appointed Chief Minister, Soren resigned from the Union coal ministry. There was immediate consternation in Jharkhand and controversy throughout the country. The President summoned the Governor, Syed Sibti Razi, to Delhi, but not before the BJP leadership had paraded its 41 named deputies in the national capital. The JMM-Congress group claimed that some elected members were being illegally detained and also pointed out that it could reinforce its majority by the appointment of a nominated Anglo-Indian member to the Assembly—the Supreme Court vetoed this move, and also ordered the confidence motion to be held on 11 March, four days before the new date stipulated by the Governor. Meanwhile, parliamentary business was repeatedly disrupted by opposition protests at the situation in Jharkhand and at the Union Government's failure to intervene. Indeed, the federal Government was increasingly embarrassed by the affair. On 11 March the Assembly, with only 77 members sworn in (but all the BJP grouping), was adjourned, amid further controversy, but not before the appointed acting Speaker had attempted to disbar one of the opposition deputies for not following his party commitment to Congress (the member, elected for the Nationalist Congress Party, later took the state branch of the party into the BJP). The next day the central authorities ordered Soren to resign the premiership. Arjun Munda duly returned as Chief Minister, being sworn in by the Governor on 13 March. Two days later, having lost one supporting vote with the election of a Janata Dal (United) member as Speaker (Namdhari, a former holder of the office), the Government won the confidence vote by 40 votes to 38. The narrowness of the majority indicated the potential for future trouble and the Government proceeded with the nomination of an Anglo-Indian member, although the opposition challenged the change in the name of the nominee in court. The promise of stability was also not helped by the dispute over which Janata Dal (United) members should be appointed ministers, Munda's initial choices causing some confusion.

The five independents who had supported the coalition were all appointed to the cabinet, although in August 2005 they objected to Munda's style of leadership; he remained as premier after mediation. Nevertheless, Munda's failure to secure his Government—by ignoring a BJP attempt to secure the allegiance of most of the RJD legislators and by neglecting the independents—lost him crucial party support when the next serious challenge to the administration occurred. Moreover, when Munda did attempt to bolster his majority in the Assembly, it was by seeking an understanding with the JMM and by offering Soren's son the deputy premiership, which undermined the Government's credibility. In early September 2006 three ministers sitting as independents in the Assembly, soon followed by the Nationalist Congress Party deputy, resigned and threw the majority of the Government into doubt. Speaker Namdhari began an attempt to disqualify three of the former ministers under the anti-defection regulations, but backed down on making a ruling before the confidence vote scheduled for 14 September. With a clear majority against the BJP-led Government, Munda resigned before a vote was taken (Namdhari also resigned as Speaker, being replaced for the interim by senior Congress deputy Pradeep Kumar Balmachu and later, by election, by another Congress deputy, Alamgir Alam). Before the end of the day it was confirmed that the leading candidate for the chief ministership was the leader of the rebel independents, Madhu Kora (who had been elected for the BJP in two elections, but refused a nomination in 2005, therefore winning his seat as an independent). He duly became Chief Minister on 18 September, the youngest serving premier in India and only the third independent to become a chief minister. However, the Kora regime was seen as essentially unstable, with most of the secular coalition supporting him from outside the Government. By mid-2007 there were already rumours of a more stable Government being constructed after Speaker Alam considered the disqualifications of up to 13 state legislators in August, eight of them from the BJP and the others including independents in the administration. Consideration of the cases was still pending in 2008.

The Government was in trouble in July 2007, with the JMM criticizing the Chief Minister's leadership, although the JMM itself was still suffering from the December 2006 gaoling of Soren (for conspiracy in the 1994 murder of his secretary, Sashi Nath Jha), who was therefore obliged to resign from the Union Government again—he also faced further charges, including more connected to the Chirrudih massacre (these were dismissed for lack of evidence in March 2008). The party had also lost one of its Lok Sabha members in March 2007, murdered by Naxalites for encouraging the anti-Maoist programme among villagers. Jharkhand had been much troubled by Naxalite insurgency violence and economic disruption during 2006 and 2007, hindering development and interrupting road and rail traffic in the state. In October 2007 a son of former BJP Chief Minister Marandi was killed in a Naxalite attack. The security forces claimed some progress in their struggle against the Maoists into 2008, but the problem was far from contained. There were also doubts about the consequences of the Salwa Judum programme of arming villagers against the Naxalites. Meanwhile, Congress had also expressed doubts about its outside support for the Kora Government, warning the Chief Minister to get a grip on corruption and development issues in October and issuing a set of conditions for continued support in November (that support was confirmed in January 2008). The main problem for the Government remained Soren and the JMM. In February 2008 Soren courted controversy by echoing the Maharashtra 'sons of the soil' furore, when he declared that Jharkhand was a state intended to favour the development of the tribal peoples, the adivasis and moolvasis (original settlers). In July he became evasive about his support for the Congress-led Government at the Centre, which was being challenged by a confidence vote over the nuclear energy agreement with the USA. In the event, Soren and the JMM supported the national Government, but he subsequently claimed Congress support for him becoming Chief Minister of Jharkhand. August was dominated by Soren urging Kora to resign the premiership and, in the middle of the month, withdrawing JMM support for the state Government. The RJD tended to prefer a continuation of the Kora ministry, but did not rule out Soren's leadership. Following Kora's resignation, Soren was sworn in as Chief Minister in late August.

## ECONOMY

Jharkhand, although long wealthier than the rest of Bihar and with considerable potential in natural resources and industrial development, remains one of the poorer states in India. In the year of bifurcation Jharkhand's per head income measured just over one-half as much again as the average level in the 'rump' Bihar state. By 2004/05 official figures put the total net domestic product of Jharkhand at Rs 371,610m. (just over 70% the size of Bihar's economy) or Rs 13,013 per head (Bihar's income per head was 44% of this level). Apart from Bihar, in all India only Uttar Pradesh was poorer than Jharkhand. However, the new state had fared better from the division of the old Bihar, gaining the best part of the energy infrastructure of the former state (64% of established power capacity), as well as much of the taxable wealth (55% of state tax collection and 66% of excise-duty collection). The length of national highways in Jharkhand in 2001 totalled 1,660 km and state highways some 4,200 km. There are fairly good railway connections and airports in Ranchi and Jamshedpur, but only 45% of villages are electrified (only 6% of rural households, in Jharkhand and Bihar together, had electricity). The total installed capacity of the state in 2006 was 2,017 MW (1,394 MW from the state sector, 263 MW from the Centre and 360 MW from the private sector). The literacy rate improved from 41.4% in 1991 to 54.1% in 2001.

Most of the population is rural and agriculture remains the most important sector of the economy for the vast majority. About one-half of the land area is cultivable and about one-quarter is currently sown. The main food crops are rice and millet, while chillies, groundnuts (peanuts) and vegetables are also grown. In 2001/02 the total foodgrain harvest was 2.0m. metric tons (rice 1.6m. tons) and the oilseeds harvest (including groundnut) 144,900 tons. Foodgrain production rose to 2.7m. tons in the following year. In horticulture, fruit is grown widely in the north-eastern hills, while the cultivation of flowers is also being encouraged. The dairy and meat industries are significant developments of primary production. Milk production increased to 1.3m. tons in 2002/03, before falling back slightly in 2003/04. Other anticipated results for the latter year included 622.7m. eggs and 308,000 kg of wool. For the 'land of jungle', forest industries are still important and the total forest area in Jharkhand at 2001 was 2,605 sq km, or 29.6% of the total area, over four-fifths of which is protected and much of the rest reserved. Bamboo is the main forest product, although minor ones include edible, aromatic and medicinal plants, such as mahua and sal seeds, lac, kendu leaf, harre and bahera. Denuded forest areas are sometimes planted with mulberry and other trees suitable for sericulture (the state produces some 60% of the country's non-mulberry tasar—tussore or tusser—silk).

Extractive industry, as well as being the basis of the state's industrial potential and existing strength, is the most lucrative primary activity. Jharkhand is the leading producer of mineral wealth in the country, claiming to produce up to two-fifths of the country's minerals. Within India Jharkhand is usually first in production of iron and copper ores, mica, kyanite and asbestos. It is also India's only producer of uranium (apart from a small mine that was due to begin production in Meghalaya in 2001), of cooking coal and of pyrite (the commonest sulphide, sometimes known as iron pyrites or fool's gold). In 2000 Jharkhand was second in India in the volume produced of chromite and of isemenite, and third in coal, bauxite and thorium. The state also produces gold (sixth in India) and graphite (eighth), clays, limestone, manganese and silver. Production volumes in 2000 included 59.92m. metric tons of coal, 8.66m. tons of iron ore, 1.24m. tons of limestone, 1.19m. tons of copper ore, 1.03m. tons of bauxite, 23,256 tons of china clay and 49,970 tons of fire clay, 18,718 tons of manganese, 7,267 tons of graphite, 4,922 tons of kyanite, 1,082 tons of mica, 13,648 kg of silver and 254 kg of gold. The total value of mineral production amounted to Rs 30,000m. in 2000, but this figure had reached Rs 46,823.1m. by 2002/03 (although in that year production in Andhra Pradesh and Gujarat was worth more). Jharkhand is an efficient producer, the mining sector employing only some 134,300 in 2001/02

Apart from the processing and exploitation of mineral resources, industry includes agro-processing (animal feed, tea, jute, sisal, hemp and other textiles, paper) and food processing, but, considering Jharkhand has an overwhelmingly rural population, the secondary sector is lacking in small-scale industrial activity. The Government is encouraging village-based handicrafts and other local manufacturing enterprises. Heavy industry includes iron-and-steel activities, engineering and automobile parts, chemicals, power generation and associated activities, electronic, computer and information-technology businesses, textiles and leather, pharmaceuticals, ceramics and metallurgical industries. Steel manufacturers in the state, for example, had a total established annual capacity of some 7.2m. metric tons in 1998, while at Chandi is India's largest coal-based sponge iron plant. Tata Industries, which founded Jamshedpur, the first planned town in modern India, remains dominant in the steel industry and other heavy industries, such as India's largest heavy-vehicles plant or largest diesel-engine plant. A truly unique installation is the uranium-processing complex at Jadugora.

The presence of important industries has helped the development of the tertiary sector in Jharkhand, although many activities were based to the north, in the 'rump' Bihar. Business services and transport services are strong, although securing investment in tourism has proved more difficult. Attractions include natural features, such as the myriad waterfalls and scenic hill country around Ranchi. There is the forested Netarhat plateau, a national park in the Hazaribagh mountains, where some tigers, panthers, nilgai and sloth bears can be found. In addition, Jharkhand has 10 wildlife sanctuaries, one biological park and two other small reserves, with projects designed to safeguard tigers and elephants. There are also a number of temples, such as the pilgrimage centre of Deoghar, and the state has associations with the famous Bengali Tagore family, which can attract visitors.

### DIRECTORY

**Governor:** Syed Sibtey Razi, Office of the Governor, Raj Bhavan, Ranchi; tel. (651) 2283469; fax (651) 2201101; e-mail vedmarwah@hotmail.com.

**Chief Minister:** Shibu Soren (Jharkhand Mukti Morcha), Office of the Chief Minister, Government of Jharkhand, Secretariat, Ranchi 834 001; tel. (651) 2403233; fax (651) 2440061.

**Speaker of the Legislative Assembly:** Inder Singh Namdhari, Legislative Assembly Secretariat, Vidhan Sabha, Ranchi 834 004; tel. (651) 2440075; fax (651) 2441712; the unicameral Legislative Assembly has one nominated (Anglo-Indian) mem., and 81 elected mems: Bharatiya Janata Party 29; Jharkhand Mukti Morcha 17; Congress 9; Rashtriya Janata Dal 7; Janata Dal (United) 4; independents and others 14; vacant 1.

**State Resident Commissioner in New Delhi:** Neelam Nath, B5/2, Safdarjung Enclave, New Delhi 110 029; tel. (11) 26180758; fax (11) 26180743.

# Karnataka

The State of Karnataka lies in southern India, a rough crescent resting on the shores of the Arabian Sea, on the west coast, extending its arms inland. At the northern end of Karnataka's seashore lies the small state of Goa. From there the border extends north-eastwards, with Maharashtra beyond it, until it reaches Andhra Pradesh, which lies to the east, and turns south. Tamil Nadu lies to the south-east and Kerala to the south-west. An expanded State of Mysore was created in 1956, as a union of the Kannada-speaking districts, and was renamed Karnataka in 1973. It occupies 191,791 sq km (74,079 sq miles), making it the seventh largest state in India.

The bulk of Karnataka spreads behind the coastal plains and the Western Ghats. The coast itself extends for about 330 km (205 miles), defining the western edge of a narrow strip of estuarine and marine plains varying between 50 km and 80 km wide (wider in the south than in the north). The land rises abruptly to the crest of the Western Ghats and into the heights known as the Malnad—some 650 km from north to south, with elevations normally between 450 m (1,477 ft) and 600 m in the north and between 900 m and 1,500 m in the south. Inland in the south the Malnad swells into the Bababudangiri Hills, with the highest point in the state being at Mullayana Giri (1,925 m). East and south of these highlands extend the plateau lands of the Mysore plains, drained by the Kaveri (often still known as the Cauvery in Karnataka) river system. To the north and east the state stretches down into the central Deccan, that part of the Karnataka plateau (Maidan) directly behind the coastal region being drained by the Tungabhadra, and the even lower, more northern plateau (which is largely constituted by the Deccan Trap) being drained by the Krishna and other rivers. Flat land below 300 m above sea level is only to be found in the coastal belt, so most of the state lies on the Deccan plateau, an undulating landscape traversed by deep ravines and scattered hill country, but which generally slopes towards the east. Thus, most of the great rivers spring in the Western Ghats and empty into the sea on the other side of the peninsula. Rainfall varies dramatically in the two main parts of the state, the coast and sea-facing mountain flanks being extremely wet between June and September (about 1,500 mm—59 inches—in June and July alone), but levels of precipitation drop rapidly beyond the Malnad. The monsoon rains moderate the temperatures, but humidity is extreme on the coast and noticeable inland. Altitude helps give the southern plateau, notably around Bangalore (the state capital—from 1 November 2006 the official English spelling was changed to Bengaluru, pending approval from the central Government—see below) and Mysore (Mysuru), a pleasant climate all year round, but in the north, before the monsoon, temperatures in April and May can often exceed 40°C (104°F) for sustained periods. Bangalore, at 920 m above sea level, records a mean temperature of 27.1°C (80.8°F) in the warmest month, April, and 20.5°C (68.8°F) in the coolest month, January. The city receives both the south-west and the north-east monsoons, albeit tempered by the surrounding heights; it has an annual average rainfall of 870 mm, much of which falls in October and November.

The population of Karnataka was 52,850,562 at 1 March 2001, according to the census results, giving an average density of 276 persons per sq km. The state is the linguistic home for the Dravidian Kannada tongue (Kannarese), which was spoken by 66.2% of the population (1991 census figures). The next most widely spoken are Urdu (10.0%), an Indo-European language related to Hindi (essentially, the language of India's Muslims), and another Dravidian tongue, Telugu (7.4%). Tamil, Marathi, Malayalam and English are also spoken, and there are still tribal peoples with their own speech—such as the nomadic Lambani of the north-west, or the 'honey gatherers', the Kurmuba, on the border with Kerala. In terms of caste, the dominant group (jati) in the north is that of the Lingayats, who have a reputation as reformers, while in the south it is the Vokkaligas, with a conservative, agriculturalist tradition. The overwhelming majority of the population are Hindu (83.9% in 2001), but there are some substantial minority groups. Muslims still accounted for 12.2% of the population (2001 figure), and Christians 1.9%. Historically, Jains were important in the history and culture of Karnataka, and a fundamental influence on the development of Kannada literature, but they now only constitute 0.8% of the population. Another native religion to have declined is Buddhism (0.7%), which is now represented in the state mainly as a result of the settlement of Tibetan refugees in the second half of the 20th century. In 2001 the Scheduled Castes accounted for 16.2% of the population, the Scheduled Tribes for 6.6%.

The urban population had reached 34.0% of the total by 2001. The main centres are Bangalore (India's fourth largest city, with 4.30m. inhabitants in 2001), in south-east Karnataka, Mysore (755,379), which gave the state its old name and is also in the south, the joined cities of Hubli (to be known as Huballi upon central Government approval) and Dharwad (with a combined population of 786,195) in the north of the Western Ghats, Belgaum (Belgavi) just to the north-west of them, and Mangalore (Mangaluru), on the southernmost part of the Karnataka coast. The state is divided into 27 districts, which are grouped into four divisions, centred on Bangalore, Mysore, Belgaum and, in the north-east, Gulbarga (Kalburgi).

## HISTORY

Karnataka provides archaeological evidence for some of the earliest settlements in peninsular India, as well as the oldest agricultural communities (in northern Karnataka) from about 3000 BC. The discovery of iron seems to pre-date its use in the north, weapons from about 1200 BC having been discovered in the northern Malnad. A proto-Dravidian culture had appeared throughout southern India by the middle of the first millennium BC and a distinct Kannada language emerged within about 1,000 years of that—there are Kannada inscriptions dating from the fifth and sixth centuries AD and the earliest known classic of an already established literary tradition is attributed to the ninth century. Early writings in Kannada, as in Telugu (the tongue of the Andhras to the east), owed much to the Jains. Meanwhile, it is a Jain connection that gives the region its first recorded contact with the rest of India. Although it was probably on the fringes of Mauryan power, it was not far from Bangalore, to Sravanabelogala in the south of modern Karnataka, that the first emperor of that dynasty, Chandragupta, is said to have retired at the beginning of the third century BC, to end his life in contemplation. A Jain settlement has been here ever since. Thereafter, a feature of the Karnataka region was its position on the fluctuating border between north and south, which has added richness to its culture and architecture, as well as complexity to its political fortunes. Thus, after the Mauryan hegemony had decayed and disappeared, the Andhran kingdom of the Satavahanas (based at Prathinistapura, Paithan, in modern Maharashtra) dominated much of northern Karnataka (as well as over one-quarter of modern India), while from the south and east there was increasing pressure from the Tamil kingdom of the Pallavas. It was the local struggle against the Pallavas that brought about the rise of the first two powerful dynasties native to Karnataka, the Kadambas in the north and the Gangas in the south. Both established themselves in the mid-fourth century AD and resisted the direct encroachment of the Guptas into south-west India.

In the mid-sixth century Pulakesin I Chalukya overthrew the authority of his overlords, the Kadambas, and laid the foundation for his dynasty's Deccan empire, for the first time bringing the area of modern Karnataka into a single realm. His Chalukyas (sometimes known as the Western Chalukyas) were based at Badami, in central Karnataka, and first extended their authority beyond the River Narmada in the north and to the shores of the Bay of Bengal in the east under Pulakesin II (*c.* 609–42). He was eventually defeated by the resurgent Pallava kingdom based in Tamil Nadu, and this rivalry between the two powers, with fluctuating results, was to weaken both fatally. However, a succession of powerful Chalukya rajahs, such as Vikramaditya I (*c.* 654–68), Vijayaditya (*c.* 696–733) and Vikramaditya II (*c.* 733–44), dominated the west-central Deccan and regularly made incursions as far as the Pallava capital. A more visible legacy is the wealth of temples concentrated around Badami, Aihole and Pattadakal, which blend the architectural traditions of north and south India. However, the continual struggles with the empire to their south meant that the Chalukya kings neglected the north and permitted local feudatories to consolidate their own power. Eventually, in the mid-eighth century, Dantidurga, a dynastic rashtrakuta (head of a region, or governor) from what is now Maharashtra, displaced the Chalukyas. The Rashtrakuta dynasty, based in Ellora (Maharashtra), soon occupied Badami and then forced the submission of the Gangas of the Mysore region, as well as extending its authority over the surviving Chalukya dynasty in the east, in Vengi (in modern Andhra Pradesh). It was then to turn its attention north and to be the first southern dynasty to enter the power play of the *arya varta* and contend for the imperial city of Kanauj (now in Uttar Pradesh).

In 973 the Rashtrakutas were overthrown by a revived Chalukya dynasty, known as the Later Western Chalukyas, or the Kalyana Chalukyas after their new capital in the far north-east of modern Karnataka. The return of this dynasty also saw a return of the rivalry between the Karnatakan plateau and the Tamil lowlands to the south-east. The dominant power there, and the pre-eminent kingdom of southern India for two centuries, was that of the Cholas (who, in 999, finally ended the Ganga dynasty of southern Karnataka). The two dynasties fought to varying conclusions, captured the other's capital and also took on alternative enemies, as the occasion suited. The Chalukya rival to the north was the kingdom of the Paramaras. The greatest kings among the Later Chalukyas were: Someshwara I (1043–68), who built the capital at Kalyana; Vikramaditya VI (1076–1127), celebrated in verse, successful in battle and under whom the standard work on Hindu law, *Mitakshara*, was written (by the great Vijnaneshwara); and his son, Someshwara III (1127–39), himself a scholar and poet. It was under the Later Chalukyas that a mixed poetry and prose form for Kannada literature was developed by the great writers, Pampa, Ponna and Ranna. By the reign of Someshwara III, Chalukya power was in decline and challenged (and, eventually, to be displaced) by two former vassals, both claiming to be of Yadava descent.

In the north, mainly in Maharashtra, but capturing Kalyana in 1186, the Sevunas (sometimes simply known as the Yadavas) under Bhillama V (1173–92) established a powerful kingdom, which, under Singhana II (1199–1247), was to reach as far south as the River Tungabhadra. The main Karnatakan dynasty to succeed the Chalukyas, however, was based in the south around Belur and Dorasamudra (now Halebid—mid-way between Bangalore and Mangalore). There the Hoysalas continued a great temple-building tradition, freed the old Ganga domain from the Cholas (under Vishnuvardhana, who reigned from 1108 to 1141) and then successfully renounced Chalukyan overlordship under Ballala II (1173–1220). Ballala II defeated Someshwara IV Chalukya in 1187, as well as Bhillama V Sevuna, at Soraturu in 1190. He went on to protect the erstwhile threat to the kingdoms of Karnataka, the Cholas, from Pandya attack (for a time), while his son, Narasimha II (1220–35) actually extended Hoysala territory into modern Tamil Nadu. This hegemony over most of the Kannada-speaking regions of the central peninsula was mainly achieved by the canny exploitation of the rivalries of others. At the same time, a feature of even modern politics was being established with the rise of the Lingayats, reformist followers of a Hindu saint, Basavanna, who founded Virosivism at the end of the 12th century. Both the 'Yadava' kingdoms were soon to succumb to a new threat from the north, however, with the arrival in peninsular India of armed Islam. The forces of the Delhi Sultanate repeatedly defeated the Sevunas, in 1296, 1307 and, terminally, in 1318, and were barely held at bay by the last great Hoysala rajah, Ballala III (1291–1343), who both resisted and, if necessary, co-operated with them, only eventually to succumb to the Pandyas of Madurai (Tamil Nadu). Meanwhile, two of Ballala III's commanders, Harihara and Raghavanka, brothers of the house of Sangama, had founded the basis of a Hindu empire that was to hold southern India against the Muslims for over two hundred years.

At the end of the 13th century and beginning of the 14th century the Delhi Sultanate effectively disrupted the four powers of peninsular India (the Sevunas, the Hoysalas, the Pandyas, and the Kakatiyas of Andhra Pradesh) without providing an alternative sovereignty. Muslim raiders, initially motivated by the traditional quest for plunder, made the Deccan a battleground of opportunity, in an environment where religion was not imposed by bloodshed nor even discouraged by punitive taxation. However, the battle lines between an advancing Islam and a resistant Hinduism were, seemingly, to be drawn up by two new monarchies, both of which employed adherents of either religion, whether to wage their wars, to build their monuments and places of worship, or to decorate the arts of their courts. In about 1336 the Sangama brothers established their 'city of victory', Vijayanagar (now Hampi), in central Karnataka, in a naturally defended position on the south bank of the Tungabhadra (acquiring the rest of the Hoysala lands to the south in 1346, upon the death of Virupaksha Ballala). In the following decade an Afghan adventurer by the name of Hasan founded the Bahmani Sultanate, based in the very north-east of modern Karnataka, first at Gulbarga, then, from 1424, at Bidar. Both these empires were to extend their authority across the peninsula, but the main issue at contention was not religion but the rich land between the Tungabhadra and the Krishna rivers, the so-called Raichur Doab. This territorial dispute was settled by treaty in the 1440s, only for the time of peace to be riven by dynastic upheaval in Vijayanagar.

The last effective ruler of the Sangama dynasty, Deva Raya II, died in 1446 and the eastern and south-eastern parts of the empire broke away, eventually to be reclaimed by Narasimha, a general who became the only king of the Saluva dynasty. Moreover, between 1466 and 1481 the Bahmani sultans were able to hold much of Karnataka to the west of Vijayanagar, and also seize Goa. After Narasimha Saluva's death in 1491 the struggle for the succession secured the monarchy for the Taluva dynasty, initially under another Narasimha, then under his brother, Krishna Deva Raya (1509–29). Meanwhile, from the 1490s, the Bahmanid imperium had begun to disintegrate and Krishna Deva Raya was able to occupy the Raichur Doab, threaten the new Deccan sultanates (occupying Bidar in 1512 and Bijapur in 1523), acquire new territory on the Andhran coast and even win victories against the kings of Orissa (1518). Vijayanagar flourished on the booty, the city was considered one of the greatest in India and the arts blossomed (although the kings favoured the Telugu language rather more than Kannada). However, although the semi-feudal organization of Vijayanagar lent the empire military success, it also contained the seeds of its destruction, as the military governors or nayaks gained more entrenched local authority of their own. In addition, the Portuguese added a new ingredient to Indian politics (and possibly interfered with the commercial wealth of the empire), while in the northern Deccan Vijayanagar no longer faced a single complacent sultanate, but a number of fractious, ambitious ones. Moreover, dynastic feuding among the Taluva royalty weakened the monarchy, but also involved the northern sultans in the succession. Intrigue by Aravidu Rama

Raya continued after he finally gained the throne in 1542, eventually provoking the northern sultanates (Bijapur and the small Bidar on Karnatakan soil, and Golconda in Andhra Pradesh to the east) into finally allying against Vijayanagar in 1564. Rama Raya summoned his nayaks, most of who responded, but the imperial forces were routed at the battle of Talikota (Rallasathangadi) in January 1565 and the last lord of Vijayanagar was beheaded. The great capital was simply abandoned by the nayaks, who preferred to defend their own domains, and emptied of its wealth by the departing feudatories and then by the victorious sultans. The empire in the territory of modern Karnataka was to be divided between Bijapur (which was also to annexe the Sultanate of Bidar in 1619) and the southern nayaks. Ultimately, it was the Mughals who would benefit most in southern India.

By the beginning of the 18th century northern Karnataka had existed under Muslim rule for over one century and, during the reign of Aurangzeb (1666–1707), the entire Kannada-speaking region had acknowledged the suzerainty of the Great Mughal. In practical terms, the conflict with Aurangzeb meant that the Marathas ruled much of northern Karnataka, while the nayak families of the south still held their traditional territories. One of the latter, the Hindu Wodeyars of Mysore, had extended their authority east to the region of Bangalore (the city was taken by the Mughals from the Sultan of Bijapur in 1687, and leased, then sold, to the Wodeyars), only to be displaced by their Muslim general, Haidar Ali Khan in 1761. He and his son, Tipu Sultan (who succeeded in 1782), were to doom their experiment in a proto-national state capable of challenging the European powers (increasingly involved in India) by siding with the French rather than the British. The failure of aid against the Marathas (who held most of northern and coastal Karnataka), promised by the British in 1769, ensured Haidar Ali's enmity against the East India Company, and he had the British on the defensive when war resumed in 1780, notably with the great victory at Polilur (near Kanchipuram, Tamil Nadu). In 1786 Tipu Sultan proclaimed Khuda-Dad a state independent of the Mughals and himself emperor. Mysore, however, although wealthy and rapidly modernizing under Tipu Sultan, was, in turn, failed by France (which was about to experience the turbulence of revolution) and was the object of local rivalry and British personal ambitions. Finally, the kingdom was overwhelmed in an assault on Tipu Sultan's summer palace on the island fortress of Shrirangapattana (Srirangapattnam), the king dying in the fighting. The Company restored the Wodeyars to a Mysore they could at least recognize in its original extent. The British retained the Karnataka coast and received more territory once belonging to Tipu Sultan from the Nizam of Hyderabad (Andhra Pradesh) in 1800 (the administration of this ceded territory was headquartered in Penukonda). By 1818 the Marathas had been defeated and Company influence extended into northern Karnataka too (where local rulers, such as the rajah of Shorapur, in the north-east, had supervising political agents appointed—Venkatappa Nayak of Shorapur was one of the few southern princes to join the revolt against the British in 1857). The new order in southern India was British.

The Wodeyars (who moved their capital to Bangalore in 1804) were supervised by a Resident until 1881 (except when a Commissioner held authority between 1831 and 1843), when the Rendition restored power to only the second maharajah since the restoration. A cadet branch of the Wodeyar dynasty fared less well; although their realm of Kodagu (Coorg) had been restored to them in 1788, after eight years of occupation by Mysore. However, the succession of increasingly erratic and often bloody sovereigns was finally ended by the British in 1834, and the territory (in the south-west, between Mysore and Mangalore) was put under a chief commissioner answerable to the authorities in Madras (now Chennai, Tamil Nadu). Kodagu became a 'Part C' state under the 1950 Constitution, but was merged into the larger Mysore in 1956. The 1956 changes came about as the result of the decision to establish language-based federal units, and Mysore (in the south-east of the modern state) was to be the core of the Kannada creation. Princely Mysore had conditionally acceded to the Union upon independence in 1947, fully on 28 June 1949, with its last Maharajah, Jayachamaraja Wodeyar, becoming the first Rajpramukh (a governor of what in 1950 was designated a 'Part B' state). When the new, extended Mysore was created on 1 November 1956 (by the addition of coastal, central and northern territories), Wodeyar became Governor of the whole state, which was renamed Karnataka in 1973. The state experienced central President's Rule twice in the 1970s, once in 1989 and, for one week, in October 1990. Generally it is caste rivalries that complicate party politics in Karnataka, and even the Congress administration of 1999–2004, with a strong majority represented in the state legislature, was at times in danger of succumbing to such factionalism. Congress had displaced the Janata Dal (under J. H. Patel) as the largest party in 1999. Congress eventually chose Somanahalli Malliam Krishna as its legislative leader and he consequently became the 17th person to be Chief Minister since independence. At April 2002 Congress also had 17 of the state's 28 seats in the Lok Sabha, the lower house of the national Parliament, and seven of the 12 in the upper house.

Although Congress won a by-election to the Assembly in February 2003, the party was under pressure, from both the state opposition and the national leadership, after two issues that provoked anti-Tamil sentiment in Karnataka. One was the ongoing dispute with Tamil Nadu over the release of water from the Cauvery (Kaveri) reservoirs, the other the activities of the Tamil forest brigand, Veerappan (notably the kidnapping of the local Janata Dal—United leader, H. Nagappa, who was found dead in December). The bandit was hunted remorselessly into 2004, and was killed in Tamil Nadu in October, during an attempt to apprehend him.

With Karnataka in control of most of the headwaters of the Cauvery, since the first building of reservoirs in the highlands under the British the release of waters to competing areas, be it the Tamil lowlands or the farming districts around Mysore, has been a source of controversy. The Cauvery dispute was first referred to arbitration in 1910, and since independence there have been several attempts to resolve the matter. Negotiations failed in 1974 and in 1989, the latter process continuing to the Supreme Court, which ordered the federal Government to establish a tribunal. This body made an interim award in 1991 of water to be released annually to Tamil Nadu, but the implementation of this award was the focus of disagreement thereafter. Negotiations between the two principal states (Kerala and Puducherry—Pondicherry—are also involved) collapsed in January 1997, with Karnataka threatening a boycott of the tribunal. The dispute again went to the Supreme Court and the federal Government, and it was decided to establish a Cauvery River Authority (CRA), which itself became the subject of passionate argument, at one point even threatening the federal coalition in 1998. Agreement on the CRA was finally reached in August, but disputes resumed in the following year, with Karnataka, facing state elections, reluctant to release more water to Tamil Nadu, claiming that there was no agreement over the timing of when a shortfall in the quota should be released. The dispute was only relieved by the advent of the rains in October. The operations of the CRA, as well as new Governments in both Karnataka and Tamil Nadu, did not prevent the Cauvery dispute re-emerging in June 2002, owing to a delayed monsoon. Again the disputants resorted to the courts, at the beginning of September, with the subsequent CRA ruling being challenged legally by Tamil Nadu and physically by angry farmers (led by G. Made Gowda) in Karnataka, who seized control of the main dam. Chief Minister Krishna secured all-party support in then defying the Supreme Court and refusing to release any waters pending a CRA meeting. Widespread protests resulted in a popular boycott of the prominent Tamil film industry and some violence. Rains in October eased the tension somewhat, but the Government remained in defiance of the judicial authorities and the object of increasing suspicion by the opposition (which accused Krishna of exploiting the dispute for political gain by currying favour with the farmers). Only at the end of the month did Karnataka apologize to the Supreme Court and begin the release of the waters. At no point was a long-term solution reached, although the dispute did not resurface seriously in 2003. However, the persistence of drought in Karnataka prompted the Government to refuse Tamil Nadu's request for a release of waters in January 2004. After the elections a few months later, in July the new Congress state premier acceded to the request of the new Congress Prime Minister and ordered the release of some waters for Tamil Nadu, with rains having relieved some of the pressure on the scarce resources. The Centre again proposed negotiations to reach a long-term solution, but the matter was soon back in the courts, although in September the Supreme Court dismissed a petition by a Karnatakan group for the reconstitution of the disputes panel (Tamil Nadu accused the state of trying to delay the panel from reaching a decision). The tribunal finally published its decision on 5 February 2007, awarding an annual 270,000m. cu ft (7,560m. cu m) of the Cauvery waters to Karnataka, but 419,000m. cu ft to Tamil Nadu (which, however, would only require Karnataka to release 192,000m. cu ft to the other state each year), as well as 30,000m. cu ft to Kerala and 7,000m. cu ft to Puducherry. The tribunal also published a schedule for the release of waters, but urged flexibility and negotiation on the state Governments. Karnataka immediately objected to the settlement (as did the other parties, in time), which provoked unrest across the state and even prompted the resignation of a Union minister from the national cabinet and from the Lok Sabha. The state Governments of Karnataka and Tamil Nadu were urged to negotiate, which the former declared itself willing to do in March, but the tribunal did not seem to have resolved the politically charged dispute over a resource that was too scarce to satisfy any party to the dispute. Protests re-emerged, sometimes violently, in March 2008, over Tamil Nadu's proposal to build a water plant on the Cauvery.

It was apparent fairly early in 2004 that the Government would probably favour early state elections simultaneous with the expected general election. However, the ruling Congress in February suffered the defection of the former Chief Minister, S. Bangarappa (1990–92), and his film-actor son, to the Bharatiya Janata Party (BJP—although the son returned to Congress within weeks and, in March 2005, the father left the BJP and joined the Samajwadi Party). In

March the BJP and the Janata Dal (United), the latter now merged with the Samata Party, finalized an electoral alliance. Meanwhile, the verdict on Krishna was being influenced not so much by the drought as by the perceived corruption and inefficiency in dispensing aid, which was left in the hands of local Assembly deputies. Thus, in state elections, Congress representation in the directly elected lower house, the Legislative Assembly, was reduced from 134 seats to 65, and the BJP emerged as the largest single party, with 79 seats. However, it was a three-way contest in Karnataka, and the Janata Dal—Secular (JDS), the largest successor of the Janata Dal that had once ruled in the state, gained 58 seats. Once the JDS decided to remain true to its secular principles, it was inevitable that the BJP be denied power. Congress, though still the larger of the two parties, had been severely punished by the electorate of Karnataka (the party only won eight Lok Sabha seats in the April–May general election, to the BJP's 18, and two for the JDS), so Chief Minister Krishna accepted responsibility and resigned. His anointed successor, once the JDS had conceded the premiership to Congress, was N. Dharam Singh, a lawyer and, unusually for the state, a Rajput. Singh, who had been in the Assembly since 1972 and almost been premier in 1999, now headed Karnataka's first coalition Government. The JDS legislative leader, K. Siddaramaiah (himself a previous contender for the premiership), was Deputy Chief Minister, but Congress had to concede the sharing of portfolios (an arrangement referred to as the 'Maharashtra model').

Congress won an Assembly by-election in October 2004, but in June 2005 lost the old Assembly seat of former premier Krishna (who had been appointed Governor of Maharashtra, although it was widely rumoured that he might return to state politics) to the JDS and was soundly defeated when Bangarappa retained his Lok Sabha seat on his new Samajwadi ticket. The JDS, however, suffered from the increasingly poor relations between its leader in the legislature, Siddaramaiah, and the veteran party leader, H. Deve Gowda. In early August the Deve Gowda faction summoned a meeting of the JDS deputies, who replaced Siddaramaiah as their leader in the Assembly. Chief Minister Singh then complied with the JDS request that he dismiss his deputy and two other ministers. The new JDS Assembly leader, M. P. Prakash, who was already a minister, duly became Deputy Chief Minister on 6 August. However, the JDS remained critical of its coalition partner, even accusing senior Congress leaders of corruption, while Congress co-operation with Siddaramaiah supporters (he had formed the All-India Progressive Janata Dal) at village elections further alienated the JDS. Even the attack at the Indian Institute of Science in Bangalore on 28 December, in which five people were shot, one fatally, did not interrupt the disintegration of the coalition. The attack, which was attributed to Islamist militants (Lashkar-e-Taiba was soon the main group to be suspected), shocked many out of the complacent assumption that southern India would not be targeted by such terrorist groups, despite some official warnings. (Some Islamist militants were arrested in Mysore in November 2006, an alleged terrorist attack was foiled in January 2007 and one of the participants in an attempted strike against a British airport in July was reported to come from a Bangalore family.) Another shibboleth about to be challenged was that the BJP would never gain power in southern India, because in January 2006 the ruling coalition finally broke apart.

The dissatisfaction of the JDS leadership with Congress was restrained by the refusal to entertain the idea of an alliance with the BJP. However, many of the JDS assembly members were reported to be considering challenging the coalition; on 18 January 2006 a meeting of the legislators unexpectedly went against the policy of Deve Gowda and the national leadership by declaring that they would co-operate with the BJP to oust Congress. The group, which consisted of more than 40 of the 58 JDS deputies, was led by the third son of Deve Gowda, H. D. Kumaraswamy. The BJP acknowledged its support for him as a candidate for the premiership, resulting in fierce criticism of the JDS rebels by Deve Gowda. Chief Minister Singh was given until 27 January to prove his majority. On the day, however, there was considerable tumult in the Assembly, with Congress members citing anti-defection regulations and protesting at Kumaraswamy's recognition as the JDS leader in the legislature, and Singh failed to move the confidence motion. The Governor refused to allow more time to the Government and Singh resigned on 28 January; Kumaraswamy, with the support of 41 JDS deputies, the 79 BJP ones, five from the Janata Dal (United) and five independents, was invited to form a Government. Meanwhile, Deve Gowda, having failed to prevent the alliance with the BJP, resigned the JDS leadership and instituted proceedings that led to the suspension of his son and 39 other legislators from the party. Deve Gowda later withdrew his resignation and acknowledged Kumaraswamy's leadership of the JDS in the Karnataka legislature; likewise in the interests of not splitting the party, the Deve Gowda loyalists supported the new coalition in the Assembly. Kumaraswamy was sworn in as Chief Minister on 3 February, with the BJP leader, B. S. Yediyurappa, as his deputy, and their Government received the support of 138 votes in the Assembly five days later (66 against). The resulting coalition was considered no more robust than the previous one, with a senior BJP figure even accusing Kumaraswamy of corruption, but no party was keen to have early elections. Congress went into opposition, and in July Siddaramaiah resigned his assembly seat, preparatory to his formal joining of Congress (he regained his seat after a hard-fought by-election). The Government courted popularity with a number of pro-Kannada issues, as well as reiterating support for implementation of the 1967 Mahajan Commission report on adjustment of the border with Maharashtra (the Assembly sat in Belgaum, outside Bangalore for the first time, in October in support of northern development and of the border issue) and continuing the Cauvery waters dispute in 2007 (see above). Proposals to close down many of the state's schools teaching in English in September 2006 were moderated in the following month, after much protest. The Government maintained its insistence that schools registered as teaching through the medium of Kannada should not be instructing in English, but English was to become a compulsory subject, as was Kannada in English-medium schools. On 1 November, on the occasion of the 50th anniversary of the state, the Government announced changes to the official English names of Bangalore (Bengaluru) and 10 other cities (pending approval from the central Government), so as to accord more closely with the name in Kannada. By August 2008 the name changes had been approved by the Centre, except that for Belgaum, because it was the subject of a territorial dispute with Maharashtra—this was likely to delay the full implementation of all the name changes. However, such changes were not necessarily popular with all groups, and in January 2007 a Muslim state minister had resigned over the neglect of minorities.

By mid-2007 the ruling coalition was looking increasingly unstable, and there were widespread doubts about whether the JDS would be prepared to hand over power to the BJP on 3 October, as agreed. The Chief Minister claimed that he was ready, but gradually shifted the decision towards being a party one. There were rumours of an alliance with Congress being sought. In September the JDS sought to retain the premiership by offering to join the BJP's national alliance, but the offer was refused. Then criticism of the Chief Minister by the BJP tourism minister was used as a justification for not transferring power, but the minister resigned. At the beginning of October the JDS finally refused to relinquish office; the BJP ministers resigned, on schedule. Congress had rebuffed JDS attempts to form a new coalition and was pressing for early elections. Kumaraswamy originally envisaged more than two weeks before he had to prove a government majority in the Assembly, but in less than a week, after tough discussions with the Governor and further rumours of the BJP gaining power, the Chief Minister resigned. The next day, on 9 October, the Governor invoked President's Rule and the Assembly was suspended. The Governor, Rameshwar Thakur, who had been in office less than two months, had originally favoured dissolution of the Assembly, because any Government was clearly going to be unstable, but suspension left the chance for the politicians to work out something. Over the next few weeks the JDS suffered some dissension, as a prominent Assembly member, M. P. Prakash, and his supporters held themselves distant from the JDS scramble to negotiate with Congress and then with the BJP again. Finally, the original alliance was resurrected, with B. S. Yeddyurappa (the spelling was changed from Yediyurappa following astrological advice) as the candidate for the premiership. The Centre then delayed, provoking accusations of Congress trying to manipulate the crisis for its own advantage, but on 8 November President's Rule was revoked and Yeddyurappa invited to form an administration. The BJP leader was sworn in as Chief Minister on 12 November, the first BJP head of government in a southern state. However, the drama was far from over, as the JDS decided to postpone its ministers being sworn in until after the vote of confidence. The JDS was suffering from some internal tension, as another son of Deve Gowda, H. D. Revanna, held back from welcoming the coalition, which was also disapproved of by Prakash. The JDS imposed a further set of conditions on its participation in Government just before the trust vote on 19 November. The party then voted against the Government and, condemning the betrayal, Yeddyurappa resigned. This time the Governor not only advised President's Rule (20 November) but also dissolution of the Assembly (29 November), although not before last-minute efforts by the JDS to seek support from Congress (perhaps for a post-election scenario).

With elections inevitable, even if the timing was uncertain, the JDS suffered some fractures (Prakash left the JDS, joining Congress in March 2008), as well the illness of Kumaraswamy, who had heart surgery in December 2007. The legislative elections were finally held in May 2008, in three phases, and the BJP won an overwhelming victory, just short of an absolute majority with 110 of the 224 elected seats. Congress increased its tally to 80 seats, while JDS representation, unsurprisingly, was reduced dramatically, to 28 seats. From the remaining six seats, the BJP found three independents to support it in Government (in July four other deputies defected to the BJP, two each from Congress and the JDS; in August two more JDS members and another Congress member defected). On 30 May, Yeddyurappa was again sworn in as Chief Minister. The Government did not have long to enjoy its historic victory before the responsibilities of office were pressing on it. There was the ongoing Cauvery dispute and, in late July, the co-ordinated terrorist bomb blasts in Bangalore, which killed one person and injured many more. One year earlier the links of Islamist activists to the city and elsewhere in Karnataka had been emphasized during an international police investigation of terrorist incidents in the United Kingdom.

## ECONOMY

Karnataka is an agricultural state as far as most people's livelihoods are concerned, but it is also rich in minerals, has a strong and long-established industrial sector and, in Bangalore, has India's premier centre for computer software and information technology. Karnataka was the poorest of the southern states until it edged ahead of Andhra Pradesh in the financial year ending in March 2005. The net state domestic product in 2004/05 put net domestic product, in current prices, at Rs 1,321,980m. or Rs 23,945 per head. Infrastructure in Karnataka is well developed, with road length almost doubling in less than 30 years, to reach 163,000 km in 1998/99, with only 103 of 27,066 inhabited villages unconnected by road by March 1999. There is almost 2,000 km of national highway and over 65% of the road length is surfaced. At the same time there were 2,639 km of broad-gauge railway, as well as some metre-gauge (631 km) and narrow-gauge (102 km) railway length. In 2006 a five-year project to build an urban railway system or metro in Bangalore was approved. There are major domestic airports, with some international links, at Bangalore, Belgaum, Mangalore and Hubli, and a number of other, smaller fields throughout the state. At Mangalore Karnataka has India's ninth largest cargo-handling port, shipping three-quarters of the country's coffee exports and most of its cashew-nut exports (owing to the city's proximity to Kerala), and importing materials such as wood for furniture manufacturing (owing to restrictions on the harvesting of native teak). The state authorities have invested considerable resources into irrigation projects, particularly in the Krishna basin, and into power development. By 2000 installed electrical capacity in the state sector consisted of 67.0% hydroelectric and 32.9% thermal and diesel, as well as a negligible 2.03 MW of wind power. The state was the site of India's first major hydroelectric project (which opened in 1902, on the Cauvery—Kaveri) and the total hydroelectric potential is put at 7,750 MW. In 2006 installed capacity totalled 7,785 MW (71% in the state sector, 16% private and 13% central). Only 294 villages remained to be connected to the power supply at March 2004, while 42% of rural households had electricity. Karnataka also has a respected educational infrastructure, the state's historical strengths in engineering and the sciences contributing to Bangalore's pre-eminence in the software market, and general literacy in the state rose considerably between the national censuses of 1991 and 2001, from 56.0% to 67.0%.

Agriculture, forestry and fishing account for nearly 65% of the working population's economic activities; the primary sector contributed an estimated 30.7% of state income in 1999/2000 (two years later agriculture alone contributed 24.4% of gross domestic product). Of the total land area of Karnataka, 54.7% is cultivable land, used to grow rice, maize, ragi and other millets, cotton (mainly on the northern plateau, especially around Raichur, in the historic Doab), groundnuts (peanuts), spices, fruit (especially around Bangalore), coconuts, coffee (mainly in the south-west), tea and tobacco. In 1999/2000 agricultural activity was affected by poor weather conditions, but production still reached, for example, 9.0m. metric tons of cereals, 1.2m. tons of oilseeds, 37.6m. tons of sugar cane, 848,700 tons of pulses and 664,500 tons of cotton. In the following year record harvests of food grains (11.1m. tons—3.8m. tons of cereals, 1.0m. tons of pulses) and sugar cane (42.9m. tons), as well as 1.5m. tons of oilseeds and 0.9m. tons of cotton. In 2001/02 production had declined, at 8.8m. tons of food grains (54% coarse grains, 36% rice, 9% pulses), 1.1m. tons of oilseeds, 33.8m. tons of sugar cane and 721,100 tons of cotton. The total foodgrain harvest fell even further, to 6.8m. tons in 2002/03 and to an anticipated 6.7m. tons in 2003/04. By the latter year the cotton harvest had declined to 496,000 tons and sugar cane to 26.8m. tons—production in the state was continuing to suffer considerably from drought. Karnataka usually produces almost two-thirds of India's coffee, most of it on and to the south of the Bababudangiri Hills, where it was first grown in the subcontinent in 1670. By 2000 horticulture covered 1.85m. ha (compared to 1.45m. ha in 1990), growing over 13.4m. tons of produce. Mulberry covered some 140,000 ha (see below for details of sericulture). The total livestock and poultry population at the 1997 agricultural census was 47m., and the state provides free veterinary services (in an attempt to combat diseases such as rinderpest, from which Karnataka has been free since the mid-1990s, and foot and mouth) and breeding centres for cattle, sheep, pigs and rabbits. Livestock products were not at record levels by the end of the 1990s, but rose steadily during the early 2000s (5.1m. tons of milk, 2,130m. eggs and 6,482 tons of wool by 2002/03). The area around Virarajendrapet (Virajpet), in Kodagu, is one of the largest producers of honey in Asia.

In 1999 just over 20% of Karnataka was classed as forest, but only just over one-half of that (11% of the total land area) is actually well wooded. There is a planting programme, which attempts to offset shortages of fuelwood and timber (brought about by the pressure of growing human and animal populations), as well as developing the state's famous sandalwood reserves, its teak and eucalyptus plantations, and urban tree areas. Most of the world's sandalwood is produced in Karnataka, Mysore being famous for sandalwood oil and soap. The state also possesses rich fisheries, with 2003/04 production expected to reach a total of 320,000 metric tons (of which 140,000 tons came from inland fishing). The fishing community on inland waters comprised 564,000 people. Marine fishing is based at ports such as Mangalore and Malpe and involves some 200,000 people. Total fishing exports of 8,788 tons earned Rs 627m. in 2003/04.

The secondary sector (mining, manufacturing and power) provided 25.4% of state income in 1999/2000, three-fifths of that from manufacturing. Mining was an expanding sector at the end of the 1990s. Karnataka is the only source in India of felsite, produces most of the country's gold and also possesses important reserves of iron ore (especially in the coffee-growing Bababudangiris), chromite, magnesite, copper, mica and china clay. In 2002/03 production had reached 24.0m. metric tons of iron ore (for 346,600 tons of iron and steel), 26,300 tons of aluminium (not quite four-fifths of the previous year's total), 2,640.5 kg of gold and 252.6 kg of silver. Employment in mining was put at almost 360,000 in 2001/02 and the value of all minerals produced in the following year at Rs 10,580.4m. Manufacturing was also responsible for 1.4m. tons of sugar, 484,600 tons of fertilizer, 5.9 tons of sandalwood oil and 188,700 tons of silk fabric (only just over 70% of production in the previous year). Karnataka has a major silk industry, first developed by Tipu Sultan in Mysore in the late 18th century. Although silk-fabric production was down by almost one-third in 1999/2000 and had halved again four years later, sericulture remains an important activity. In 1998/99 the industry produced 74,600 tons of cocoons, of which 51,000 were marketed, earning foreign exchange worth Rs 2,705.9m. (26.1% of the value of total Indian cocoon exports). Karnataka also manufactures other textiles (an expanding sector), a variety of rail, road and air vehicles and parts, electronic equipment, machine tools, glass, ceramics, cement and cigarettes (including the cheap, local alternative, ganesh bidis, especially at Mangalore). In terms of foreign exports from Karnataka, 55% of earnings came from electronics and software in 2002/03. The state has one of the most impressive industrial growth rates in India during the second half of the 20th century, a record that the Government seeks to perpetuate—it began encouraging information technologies in the state from the mid-1990s, and has policies favouring agro-processing and automobile-parts manufacturing. In 1998/99 there were 1,436 joint-stock companies registered in the state, and 13,422 registered small-scale industrial units (giving employment to 69,579 people, with investment of Rs 5,975.2m.). However, in 2002/03 there were 12,029 registered small-scale units, employing only 30,533, and with investment of Rs 4,083.6m.

The services sector contributed 43.9% to the net domestic product of Karnataka in 1999/2000 (compared to 37.3% in 1993/94). Much of this is owing to the strong showing of the state, particularly Bangalore, in what is sometimes described as India's only globally competitive industry, the software and information-technology sector. In 2001 over 60 such companies were based in Bangalore, and the sector in India survived the global contraction from the last quarter of the year strongly. The state was the first to develop a co-ordinated government policy towards the sector. The banking sector is also strong, relative to many other states, and Karnataka has a flourishing tourist industry, although it is only the seventh most popular domestic tourist destination, accounting for 3.2% of domestic tourist visits in 2002. The state has varied scenery and wildlife, the latter especially in the western Mysore plateau (arguably the richest concentration in southern India) and the Malnad (including elephants, spotted deer, gaur, samba, wild pig, sloth bear, and occasionally tigers and other big cats). Other natural phenomena include Jog Falls, one of the highest waterfalls in the world, where, in the north-west, the Sharavati hurls itself out of the Ghats towards the coast. Pilgrimage sites include the great 10th-century Gommateshwara statue, sacred to Jains, at Sravanabeloga, and a number of sites associated with great Hindu, and Muslim, saints. There are also the Hoysala ruins in the south or, especially, the remains of great Vijayanagar at Hampi, in central Karnataka. Further north are the Chalukya temples or the medieval Muslim capitals, the latter including Bijapur, which contains the world's second largest dome unsupported by pillars, on the Gol Gumbaz. Back in the south is the 'Garden City' of Bangalore or the old capitals of Mysore, in the city of Mysore or the ancient island-fortress of Shrirangapattana, adorned by Tipu Sultan's palaces.

### DIRECTORY

**Governor:** RAMESHWAR THAKUR, Office of the Governor, Raj Bhavan, Raj Bhavan Road, Bangalore 560 001; tel. (80) 2254102; fax (80) 2258150; e-mail rbblr@vsnl.com.

**Chief Minister:** B. S. YEDYURAPPA (Bharatiya Janata Party), Office of the Chief Minister, Vidhana Soudha, 3rd Floor (Room 323), Bangalore 560 001; tel. (80) 2253414; fax (80) 2281021; e-mail smkrisna@bangaloreit.com.

**Speaker of the Legislative Assembly:** JAGADISH SHETTAR, Office of the Karnataka Legislative Assembly, Vidhana Soudha, Bangalore 560 001; tel. (80) 2258171; fax (80) 2092320; the lower house of the bicameral legislature, the Legislative Assembly, has 224 elected mems and one nominated mem.: Bharatiya Janata Party 114; Congress 75; Janata Dal (Secular) 22; independents 6; vacant 7.

**Chairman (Speaker) of the Legislative Council:** Prof. B. K. CHANDRASHEKAR, Office of the Speaker of the Karnataka Legislative Council, Vidhana Soudha, 1st Floor, Bangalore 560 001; tel. (80) 2258575; fax (80) 2252068; the upper chamber of the Karnataka legislature, the Legislative Council, has 75 indirectly elected mems (2 seats vacant at July 2004): Congress 45; Janata Dal (Secular) 12; Bharatiya Janata Party 10; Janata Dal (United) 3; independents 3.

**State Resident Commissioner in New Delhi:** SUDHAKAR RAO, Karnataka Bhavan, Kautilya Marg, Chanakyapuri, New Delhi 110 021; tel. (11) 26889814; fax (11) 26889030; e-mail srao2001@hotmail.com.

## Kerala

The State of Kerala lies in southern India, on the western shores of the tip of the peninsula. Karnataka lies to the north-east and Tamil Nadu to the east. Just south of Kannur (Cannanore) is a small enclave of the Union Territory of Puducherry (Pondicherry), around the small port of Mahe, while another territory, Lakshadweep, is off shore. Kerala, the 'land of the Cheras', was formed as the home of the Malayalam language on 1 November 1956, by uniting most of Travancore-Cochin with the Malabar Coast District and the Kasaragod Taluk of South Cannara District. The state has an area of 38,863 sq km (15,010 sq miles).

Kerala has an historic unity and identity as the coastal lands rising up to the protective heights of the Western Ghats—the 'mountain coast' of Malabar. Physically, the state consists of three regions: the coastal belt, some 590 km (366 miles) in length; the undulating plains of red laterite; and, between 35 km and 120 km inland, the bordering hills and valleys of the Western Ghats, which rise to the highest peak in south India at Anai Mudi (2,695 m or 8,842 ft). The network of rivers, lagoons and manmade waterways that occupies the alluvial hinterland of the coast between Kochi (Cochin) and Kollam (Quilon) is referred to as the backwaters; the northern part, near Kochi, is known as the Kuttanad. It supports a unique ecology dependent upon the alternating floods of sea water and cleansing, perennial rivers. In the mountains, at the restricted Silent Valley National Park, is India's only remaining significant area of tropical evergreen rainforest. The mountains march south from the Karnatakan highlands, the coastal plain widening below, until they rise into the heights of the Nilgiri Hills, inland from Kozhikode (Calicut). The Western Ghats then fall into the Palakkad Gap, the main pass into the interior of the peninsula, before rising up to the Anaimalai and Palni Hills. From the Gap empties the River Ponnani, while further south is the flood-prone Perivar. The climate is tropical and wet, without a distinct dry season, only higher average rainfall between June and September. Where and when it rains can be erratic, but the normal annual level of precipitation is 3,107 mm (122 inches). Kerala is exposed to both the south-west and the north-east monsoons, which can make it humid, but average temperatures rarely exceed 32°C (90°F) and never fall below 20°C (68°F) on the coast.

Although Kerala covers 1.2% of the total area of India, it is home to 3.1% of the national population. Growth rates fell considerably in the last decades of the 20th century and, according to the results of the national census of 1 March 2001, Kerala had reached a total population of 31,841,374 (growth of only 9.4% since 1991—the lowest rate of any state or territory). This gave the state a population density of 819 per sq km. Kerala is an ideal fulfilment of a linguistic state, with 96.6% of the population speaking Malayalam in 1991, the highest proportion speaking one language in any state or territory of India. Malayalam emerged as a distinct language before the ninth century, the Sanskrit of Aryanizing brahmins replacing Tamil as the main influence on the local Dravidian tongue. The population enjoys the best educational, health and social advantages in India, having achieved 100% literacy in many areas and with a culture that traditionally encourages the high social status of women, but there are also extremely primitive tribes in the mountains and a large, regular exodus of workers seeking economic opportunity elsewhere in India or abroad (remittances are an important contributor to the state economy). A 1,000-year-old matrilineal system of inheritance was accompanied by an oppressive and rigid caste structure, reaction to which spurred the evolution of modern education and social reform, in the benefits of which women shared. Keralan society was particularly open to the education-enhancing influence of 19th- and 20th-century missionaries, owing to the long, native presence of different religions on this trading coast. Christianity is meant to have arrived within decades of Jesus Christ's death, and certainly enjoys an ancient tradition, while Islam too was brought fairly promptly by Arab traders in the seventh century. The Jewish community, mainly in Kochi, although now depleted by emigration to Israel, claimed even more venerable representation in Kerala (see below). According to the 2001 census, Hindus constituted 56.2% of the population, Muslims 24.7% and Christians 19.0%. There is no tradition of communal violence in Kerala (apart from isolated incidents, such as between Muslims and Hindus in Marad, a fishing village near Kozhikode, in 2002 and 2003) and both the imported religions have deep local traditions and adaptations. The 2001 census numbered 9.8% of the population among the Scheduled Castes and 1.1% among the Scheduled Tribes.

At the 2001 census 26.0% of the population were urbanized. The largest cities are the three ancient ports of: Thiruvananthapuram (Trivandrum—744,983 inhabitants, according to the census results of 2001), the state capital, in the very south; Kochi (596,473), about one-third of the way up the coast; and Kozhikode (436,556), roughly as far north again. Other important towns on the coast include Badagara and Kannur, going north of Kozhikode, also Ernakulam, the twin city of Kochi, and, south of there, Alappuzha (Allepey) and Kollam. The state is divided into 14 districts.

### HISTORY

The legendary origins of Kerala involve it being reclaimed from the sea by the axe throw of Parasurama, the sixth incarnation of Vishnu. The tale goes on to explain the origins of the country's caste system and unique matrilineal inheritance regime. However, the evidence for the origin of the matriarchy seems to place it in the 10th century, when the wars with the Cholas resulted in a shortage of menfolk and a threat to familial inheritance. By then the great dynasty of Kerala, the Cheras, had ceased to use Tamil as their court language (probably in the seventh century) and had become a Malayalam-speaking native house that had established a second Chera empire. The first Chera dynasty, first established in the Kuttanad, near Alappuzha, had ancient roots and has long provided the most probable origin for the name of the state—a decree of Ashoka Maurya mentions Keralaputra, the 'land of the sons of Cheras', and the Tamils referred to the region as Sera Nadu, which, like Kerala, also means 'land of the Cheras'. This early Chera period shares its history as part of the Tamil world and enjoyed rich trading relations with the Roman world. The Chera capital was at Vanchi, inland, while one of the main ports was at Muziri (Muciri), now Kodungallur (Cranagore). The wealthy coastal principalities of the 'Pepper Coast' attracted settlers and evangelists of several religions—Jews, Christians and Muslims, as well as Aryanizing brahmins who were to transform native 'Hinduism' and provide the basis for the second Chera era. These various, often-powerful groups remained fundamental to the society and history of Kerala.

The original 'black' Jewish community of Kochi (Cochin) claimed to have arrived in Kerala in 587 BC, although some pushed this back to the reign of the biblical king, Solomon, just before the start of the first millennium. The earliest physical evidence dates from the fourth century of the Christian era, but that a small trading community might have been established much earlier is not unlikely. Certainly the local community enjoyed traditional links with the Babylonian Jews (in what is now Iraq), while it also had strong connections with the trade to China. The Jewish community flourished and gained influence and privileges from the local rulers, as when Joseph Rabban was the Jewish leader around AD 1000. Under the Dutch and British, the 'white' Jews increased their number, but both groups have declined considerably since the 1940s, owing to emigration to Israel.

Christianity may well have followed the route of Jewish trading links to the entrepôt coast of south-west India. St Thomas ('Doubting' Thomas), one of the disciples of the Christian messiah, is said to have landed in Kerala, at Kottapuram, near Kodungallur, in 52 and evangelized along the coast and in China before being martyred (in Tamil Nadu) upon his return to India in 72. The strong presence of the 'Thomas Christians' in Kerala probably owes more to the sixth-century missionary work of the Syrian Church (a Nestorian denomination, believing in the dual nature of Christ). The arrival of the Portuguese in the early modern era heralded an overlay of European ecclesiastical tradition on an ancient native one, so Kerala now has a Christian community consisting of an independent Syrian denomination, a Roman Catholic presence including both users of the 'Latin' and of the Syrian rites, and Protestant churches (some of which also inherited the traditions of the Thomas Christians). By the time of the arrival of the Portuguese, the local Christians had adapted to the caste system and local politics, and their merchant princes, such as Mar Sapir Iso of Kollam (Quilon), being unlikely challengers for power in their own right, were often co-opted into the princely struggles.

Meanwhile, another religious community had become established in Kerala, and adapted to local conditions. The Arabs had long dominated the trade routes to Kerala, so it is no surprise that Islam soon arrived among their communities in the major ports of the Malabar Coast, possibly as early as the seventh century, although large-scale evangelization probably only began under an Arab Muslim, Sulaiman, who is meant to have arrived in Kerala in 852, and his colleague, Bavar. Like Christianity, Islam also first reached India at Kodungallur, near which Malik-ibn-Dinar built what is meant to be the first mosque in the country. The Muslims of Kerala, both local people and those of mixed-race descent, came to be known as Moplahs. Their integration into society is attested by the apparent conversion of the last Peruman to Islam (see below), by the presence of a Muslim branch of the royal family of North Kolathiri at Kannur (Cannanore), although this was the only Muslim ruling house in Kerala, and even by the widespread presence of Moplahs among the rural poor.

If an explanation of the presence of the religious minorities is important in the history of Kerala, so too is the 'Aryanization' of the local religion into what became a more recognizable form of Hinduism. The process was well under way by the eighth century, when the great saint, Shankaracharya, was born at Kalady (45 km from Kochi). He is the best known exponent of the Advaita Vedanta school of philosophy, and is still highly revered. The rigidity of the caste system as it was to evolve in Kerala, however, was a much later development—despite the social progressiveness evident in the relatively high status of women, the inherent inequity of the whole system was fundamental in provoking a popular reaction that led to the course of modern politics in the state. The settlement of brahmins in the northern and central parts of Kerala evolved into a local government of hereditary notables, all members of a brahminical caste known as the Nambudiri (who only spread into the far south later, as it came more into the orbit of the other Malayalam realms rather than the Tamil world). The devastation of the ruling and traditional warrior castes from the time of the 10th-century Chola wars, however, helped the rise in status of the Nairs. By the 16th century the Nairs had established themselves as the executors of Nambudiri authority throughout the principalities of Kerala. The consequent disparities between the ruling and the lower castes steadily widened, fuelling an increasing stratification and subdivision of groupings, and leading to an oppressive system, which, at times, virtually institutionalized forms of social and economic slavery. A number of later reform movements, especially in the 19th century, under the influence of Christian missionaries and Western education, helped radicalize the population and enlighten local rulers (in religious terms, culminating in the Temple Entry Proclamation of 1936, admitting the lower castes to equal worshipping rights). This led to the dispossession of the Nairs from dominance and laid the foundations for the 20th-century, left-wing political movements in Kerala.

However, an early consequence of the socio-political dominance of the brahmins was that they provided a foundation for the second Chera dynasty to rule Kerala. The old capital of Vanchi had been sacked by the Pandyas and the apparatus of the kingdom had found refuge in the port of Muziri. Here a new capital was built, called Makotai or Mahodayapura, and its lord was the Chera high king, the Cheraman Perumal, or overlord of Kerala (Keraladhinatha), who presided over a realm divided into great districts (nadu), each ruled by a governor, who usually gained office by inheritance. The highest nobles, therefore, were the princely governors of the main hereditary fiefs: Kolathunad (in the far north—brought under Chera rule by conquest towards the end of the ninth century); Purakizhanad; Kurumpanad; Eranad; Valluvanad; Kizhamalanad; Vempalanad; and, in the very south and created from forcibly seized territories of the ancient Vels and the Ay kings, Venad (it long remained a border territory, without the original Nambudiri settlements and looking as much to the Tamil lands of the Pandyas as to the north; it soon gained immensely in wealth). The second ruling Chera dynasty was known as the Kulasekhara, and the first known lord of Makotai, Varman, was crowned in about 800. He is also known as Kulasekhara Alwar, and is a famous Vaishnavite saint. His successor, Rajasekhara Varman (820–44), is a Saivite saint, under whose reign the Malayalam or Kollam era (Kollavarsham) was introduced in 825. The council convened to determine this era was summoned to the site of a city founded that same year under the authority of the lord of Venad, Udaya Marthanda Varma. Kollam was soon to attract great wealth to Venad, notably under its Christian merchants. The successors to the overlordship and to Venad are both famous—the next Perumal was Sthanu Ravi Kulasekhara (844–85), and the next lord of Venad was Ayyan Adigal Thuruvatikal (the later-deified Ayyan, the Muslim evangelist, Bavan, and another contemporary, the Christian priest and hero, Kadamattathu Kathanar, are still commemorated at a multi-faith shrine at Sabarimala).

Chera power persisted through the devastating Chola wars that began towards the end of the 10th century. The legendary end of the Chera hegemony, and the basis for any legitimacy claimed in the future by the principalities of Kerala, is attributed to the last high king, Cheraman Perumal Nayana, who is reported to have divided his kingdom, converted to Islam and left India for Arabia. The author of what is known as the partition of Kerala is sometimes conflated with the great, early Kulasekhara monarchs, Rajasekhara Varman or Sthanu Ravi, but the historical 'last emperor' is Rama Varma Kulasekhara, who ascended the throne in 1089. The exigencies of the Chola wars had by now brought about the rise of the warrior Nairs (and their chaver suicide squads) and the matrilineal system of inheritance, symptoms of social and economic stress in the country. Rama Varma faced the enmity of the Chola king, Kulothunga I, who sacked Makotai and captured Kollam in 1096. With the help of the chavers, the Chera forces drove back the Chola and regained Kollam in 1102—the city thereafter became the last Kulasekhara capital (Ten Vanchi, the Vanchi of the South), giving Venad a claim to be the most important of the Chera successor principalities, although the later rajahs of Kochi also claimed pre-eminence. Claims of Kulasekhara descent and grants of land came to be a necessity with the disappearance of Rama Varma in 1124. In the succeeding centuries three of some 30 local principalities were to rise to prominence: Venad, Kochi and Kozhikode.

Venad, later known as Thiruvidamkodu or Tiruvankur (Travancore), although it was to be the institutional core of the modern state of Kerala, was peripheral to much of the post-Chera history of the Malabar Coast. In 1125 Rajah Kodai Kerala Varman conquered the district around mainland India's southernmost point, Kanniyakumari (Cape Comorin), which is now in Tamil Nadu (as it had a Tamil-speaking majority in 1956, and despite including the palace of Padmanabhapuram, the capital of Travancore between 1590 and 1750). Also, another conquering ruler, Ravi Varna Kulasekhara (1299–1314), triumphed mainly against the Pandyas. However, the kingdom was very much an inheritor of the Cheras and the culture of Kerala. For instance, in 1678–84 it gained its first woman ruler, Umayamma Rani. In the 18th century it had another two gifted rulers, the first of which (Marthanda Varma 'the Conqueror', 1729–58) expanded the territory of Travancore and moved the capital to Thiruvananthapuram (Trivandrum—when the kingdom was dedicated to Vishnu), while the second (Kartika Tirunal Rama Varma or the Dharma Rajah, 1758–98) consolidated his territories, held out against Mysore (now part of Karnataka) and preserved the princely state as an entity in the transition to a new order of British supremacy.

The history of Kochi languishes in relative obscurity until the advent of the Europeans. Its branch of the royal house, the Perumpadappu Swarupam, provided one of the most senior Keralan ruling princes and held power in the heartland of Nambudiri orthodoxy. Originally, the dynasty was in possession of the rich and ancient port of Kodungallur, but this was destroyed by a catastrophic flood of the Perivar in 1340, to be replaced by nearby Kochi, which, meanwhile, lost place to its new, northern rival at Kozhikode—moreover, Kochi did not favour the dominant Arab traders in the same way.

The hereditary governors of Eranad had conquered coastal Polonad at the end of the 12th century and then built a port at Kozhikode, moving their capital from inland Nediyiruppu. By the 14th century, Kozhikode had become a wealthy trading centre—here the Eradis soon adopted the title of Zamorin (Samutiri—Lord of the Sea), by which they are best known to history, a title earned by the wealth of their port, which commanded the favour of the Arab merchants. Policies of religious toleration no doubt encouraged this alliance, which favoured the Zamorin of Kozhikode against the rajahs of Kochi in their rivalry throughout the 13th–15th centuries. Open conflict had begun when the domain of Kozhikode had expanded far enough south to come into contact with the domains of Kochi and to claim pre-eminence among the heirs of the Chera; the struggle involved all of Kerala in the machinations of the various princes and the split in the brahminical caste (the Panniyur faction supported the Zamorin, while the Cokiram supported Kochi). In the latter part of this period Kozhikode and much of Kerala acknowledged the suzerainty of Vijayanagar (now Hampi, Karnataka).

On 21 May 1498 the Portuguese navigator Vasco da Gama reached Kozhikode and Europeans began to enter the power intrigues of the Malabar Coast, a development that was eventually to bring Kerala within a pan-Indian empire for the first time. The Portuguese would not tolerate the rivalry of the Arab merchants, despite the Zamorin insisting that Kozhikode (or Calicut, as it was known to the Europeans) had always been a free port. In 1503 the first Portuguese forts were established at Kannur, to the north, and, significantly, at Kochi, to the south, as the Rajah of Kochi sought to exploit the enmity of the new players against his traditional rivals in Kozhikode. However, the Zamorin, possibly the wealthiest of Indian princes, invested in improving his navy, which was effectively reorganized under the hereditary admiral, the Kunhali Marakkar. Attacks on Kochi failed, although the loss of 19,000 men in a fruitless land attack on the Portuguese in 1504 was partly counterbalanced by the victory at sea, at Chaul, by the combined forces of the Zamorin, Gujarat and the Arabs of Egypt in 1508. Kunhali II was the greatest of the admirals and Kunhali III, who enjoyed all the privileges of Nair rank, although he was a Muslim, was permitted to build a fortress at modern Kottakkal, some 45 km north of Kozhikode. However, the most successful period of struggle against the Portuguese was over, with serious defeats in 1528 and 1538. In 1540 the Zamorin was forced to make peace with the Portuguese (entrenched in a base to the north, Goa, since 1510) and grant them a monopoly on trade with Kozhikode, although conflict resumed in 1571–88. The resulting peace was opposed by many, including Kunhali IV, who also proclaimed himself the prince of the local Muslims or Moplahs, earning the enmity of the threatened Zamorin, who allied with the Portuguese to occupy Kottakkal and execute the Kunhali Marakkar in 1600.

The arrival of the Dutch in the region was soon to disrupt Portuguese ascendancy. Both the rajahs of Malabar (the Zamorin) and of Kochi used Dutch support against the Portuguese, while the Dutch themselves increasingly interfered in local politics to further their fight against the Portuguese. In 1663 the Dutch seized the Kochi station from the Portuguese and their ascendancy on the Malabar Coast was complete. Although their treaties with the local princes were less acquisitive than those of the Portuguese, the Dutch 'Commanders of the Malabar Coast' earned enmity in Kochi by dominating the rajahs to such an extent that they could even interfere in the succession (as in 1663), and they soon became the object of opposition among many of the rulers. Meanwhile, the arrival of the English (British) East India Company, first at Tellicherry (Thalassery) in 1682, provided another partner in intrigue. Eventually, the Company was persuaded to lend aid to local allies, particularly against the Dutch, helping the Zamorin in 1715–17 and, later, Travancore, which defeated the Dutch at Kulachel in August 1741, breaking their influence. Later, owing to war in Europe, the British occupied the Dutch base in Kochi in October 1795, and the final Indian possessions of the Netherlands were formally ceded in 1818. There had been some local threat to the British Company from the French during the 18th century, when they seized Mahe (still today part of the separate Union Territory of Puducherry) in 1725, but the French impact in Kerala was indirect, through their allies in Mysore.

The attention of Haidar Ali of Mysore was attracted to the coast of Kerala by the rajah of Palghat, who had lost territory to Kozhikode in the 1750s, during the Zamorin's renewed attacks on Kochi (which merely brought Travancore into the war on the side of Kochi, helping to recover its lost territories in 1761–62 and forcing the Zamorin to conclude peace). Kozhikode could not withstand the threats of Mysore, but was unable to pay a war indemnity, prompting the invasion of Haidar Ali in 1766. He was assisted by the forces of Kannur and local Moplahs, and Mysore had one of the best armies in the subcontinent—the then Zamorin could not face the defeat and blew up himself, as well as the last of Kozhikode's pre-eminence, in his palace. Haidar Ali initially installed a governor in the city, but, in an attempt to defuse the Nair revolts, in 1776 restored a new Zamorin to power in return for an annual tribute. In 1778 the forces of Mysore again invaded, demanding the tribute. Kozhikode was occupied and the Zamorin fled to Travancore. Haidar Ali's son, Tipu Sultan, was in command of the troops fighting the Nair resistance until 1782, when he returned to his home territories to secure his succession upon the death of his father. However, in 1788 Tipu Sultan returned to Kerala, the rajahs of which were being supported by his arch-enemy, the British, and again occupied Kozhikode. An attack on Travancore in the following year was thwarted by the flooding of the Perivar, while the continued pressure of local opposition and British arms drove Mysore from northern Malabar by 1790. Two years later Tipu Sultan was forced to conclude a peace with the British and ceded control of central Malabar, the territories once dominated by the Zamorin, to the East India Company. The final defeat of Mysore in 1799 brought the rest of what is now northern Kerala formally under the Company, while the following year, on 21 May, the Zamorin conceded direct administration in Malabar, in return for a pension (the new territories were soon transferred from the jurisdiction of the British presidency in Bombay—now Mumbai, in Maharashtra—to that of Madras—now Chennai, in Tamil Nadu). Meanwhile, the Rajah of Kochi (Rama Varma IX, Saktan Tampuran, 1790–1805) had concluded a subsidiary alliance with the British in 1791, while Travancore was steadily reduced to dependence by being forced to pay for the war against Mysore—the costs of the 1795 treaty provoked popular unrest and consequent Company concerns, pressing Travancore further from independence. In January 1805 a new treaty with the southern Rajah (Bala Rama Varma I, 1798–1810) sealed the kingdom's status as a princely state of what was fast becoming British India. This process could not be reversed by the revolt of the Dalava of Travancore, Velu Thampi, who vainly raised the banner of revolt with his Kundara Declaration of 1807, just as it could not by the Pazhassi Rajah in the north earlier in the decade. The British eventually imposed about one century of peace (except for the various episodes of agrarian unrest by the Moplahs, 1836–56), during which time the Malayalam-speaking peoples were variously exposed to social and economic reform, education programmes and sustained engagement with the rest of India.

Some of the major social changes started under the British have been mentioned above, but there are a few other political landmarks in the decades before independence. The Malabar Coast District was under direct British administration, so it experienced the upheavals of the national freedom struggle, from which Travancore and Kochi were partly insulated. In 1888 the first legislature of any Indian state had been formed when the Legislative Council of Travancore first met, but the campaign for responsible government did not really get under way in the two princely states until the 1930s. In Kochi (or Cochin, as it was generally known in this period) the regime steadily made concessions, including a diarchical form of government (government including some democratically answerable ministers) in 1938, but, on the eve of national independence, a popular ministry took power under Panampally Govinda Menon and the 16th rajah since British overlordship, Keralavarma VII (who only acceded in 1946), formally lost his kingdom. Meanwhile, the premier (dewan) of Travancore, C. P. Ramaswamy Iyer, was more determined to retain power, agitation against him being led by the Travancore State Congress (it was this campaign, and the more left-wing sympathies prevalent throughout Kerala, that resulted in the split in the local Congress and the formation of the Communist Party, confirmed by national developments during the Second World War). Unrest culminated in the 1946 Punnapra-Vayalar Communist uprising, which was harshly suppressed. However, the Dewan's suggestion that his rule would be maintained by Travancore obtaining separate independence from the rest of India united opposition and he eventually conceded reform and accepted exile. In August 1947 Travancore entered an independent Indian Union under the popular ministry of Pattom A. Thanu Pillai, but with the role of rajpramukh or governor filled by the fourth and last reigning Maharajah (the rajahs had been granted the title in 1866), Sir Bala Rama Varma III (1924–47).

The campaign for a single Malayalam state, the reunion of the land of the Cheras, had already begun. The campaign for a united (*aikya*) Kerala gained formal expression in the 1920s, but only gained momentum after independence. On 1 July 1949 the two former princely states united into Travancore-Cochin (designated a 'Part B' state under the 1950 Constitution), with Sir Bala Rama Varma as Rajpramukh and T. K. Narayana Pillai as the first elected premier. The reorganization of the states on a linguistic basis took on a certain logic in southern India following pro-Tamil disturbances in the southernmost part of old Travancore. Thus, on 1 November 1956 (with the original Travancore-Cochin state under President's Rule) the southern tip of India, four taluks of the Kanniyakumari District, was transferred to Madras, while the Malabar Coast District and one taluk of South Cannara District in the north were merged into the new State of Kerala. The princely Rajpramukh was replaced with a civilian Governor.

The first state elections in Kerala, in March 1957, produced the first elected communist Government in the world. However, the administration was dissolved in 1959, after a widespread opposition movement sometimes called the Liberation. Party politics was to continue this turbulent course, governments more usually dominated by Congress, but showing the influence of the left. The Legislative Assembly elected in 1970 was the first to live out its full term (and, indeed, had that term extended to 1977). In 1980 a leftist victory was marred by infighting, which resulted in President's Rule being imposed in Kerala for the eighth time, although the 1982–87 ministry went to its full term. The Left Democratic Front (LDF) coalition lost the 1991 election, but in 1995 the ruling United Democratic Front (UDF) lost its veteran Congress premier, K. Karunakaran. His successor was A. K. Antony, who had briefly served as Chief Minister before, in 1977–78, and who supported Prohibition (of the sale of alcohol) in the 1996 state elections, but was defeated by the LDF. Kerala's 10th ministry was formed under E. K. Nayanar (who died in May 2004) and lasted its full term. On 10 May 2001, however, the UDF conclusively returned to power, with Antony forming a Government supported by 99 of the 140 deputies. The state also has nine seats in the upper house of the all-Indian legislature and 20 in the lower house.

Antony, a native Christian of Kerala, was considered a loyal supporter of the national Congress leadership under Sonia Gandhi and an asset to the state party, but rivalry with the faction led by the former premier, Karunakaran, undermined Congress support. A schism in the party was avoided in April–May 2003, when Karunakaran incurred Gandhi's displeasure by supporting a rival, but defeated, candidate to the official Congress one in an election to choose a Rajya Sabha member. Antony interceded for the veteran politician, fearing that disciplining him would provoke a split. However, the left was also troubled by divisions, while the third traditional political force of the state, the Muslim League, a member of the ruling state coalition, was beginning to question too close an association with Congress. Meanwhile, a petition to the Supreme Court by a Christian priest from Kerala provoked a national debate in mid-2003 about the introduction of a uniform civil code for the country, as indicated by the 1950 Constitution. The priest had objected to the 'discriminatory' nature of laws applying to Christians, unreformed since the British period, but elsewhere in India the introduction of such a code, particularly by a nationalist Government, provoked fears among minority groups.

Rivalries in Congress again appeared in the open in November 2003, when Karunakaran led an attempt to oust Antony. The central leadership tried to mediate between the factions, but in January 2004 the former premier announced his resignation from Congress. However, Antony seemed anxious to appease the veteran leader, and gave Karunakaran's son a post in the Government (but he failed to be elected to the Assembly in a by-election held at the same time as the general election). This deal disillusioned many of Karunakaran's supporters, and the infighting discredited Congress generally. Thus, at the national parliamentary elections in May, Congress failed to win a single seat in the Lok Sabha from Kerala, for the first time ever. Its ally, the Muslim League, only retained one seat, with another one won by the Indian Federal Democratic Party (an ally of the Bharatiya Janata Party, which continued to be without representation in Kerala) in the Christian heartlands. All the 18 other seats were won by the LDF. The central Congress leadership soon took steps to reinforce the party organization, with Karunakaran finding himself and his family excluded from many of the Congress power structures in July. At the end of August, taking responsibility for the general election fiasco, Antony resigned, to be replaced by his close Congress ally, Oomen Chandy.

The new Chief Minister, Chandy, was less in favour than Antony of placating Karunakaran and, by early 2005, had lost patience with the veteran leader. Karunakaran, with his son, K. Muraleedharan, had formed an Indira (I) faction within Congress, which seemed to institutionalize the split that had cost the party so dear at the general election. In March the party leadership decided on a firmer approach and a ban on separate groups within Congress. Despite one last attempt by Antony to broker a compromise, Muraleedharan was expelled from Congress in April. By the end of the month his father had resigned his seat in the Rajya Sabha (to be replaced by Antony) and on 1 May announced that he would form a new party, called National Congress (Indira), with Muraleedharan as its president. The party was eventually named the Democratic Indira Congress (Karunakaran). In early July nine Congress deputies resigned from the state legislature in support of the new party, although this did not threaten the ruling coalition's majority. Meanwhile, in June the opposition had convincingly held two Assembly seats at by-elections, emphasizing the need for Congress to end factionalism before the state elections due in 2006. Nevertheless, even though Chandy organized a more cohesive party, the LDF won a significant victory in local elections in September 2005, strongly supported by Karunakaran's party. By early 2006, however, the left's discomfort with Karunakaran's past as premier meant that the new party was without allies—in the end, after much disagreement reminiscent of the old faction fighting, the Democratic Indira Congress (Karunakaran) reached an electoral accommodation with Congress, but still won only one seat in the new legislature. Meanwhile, the Communist Party of India (Marxist), or CPI—M, the dominant party in the LDF, suffered from its own faction fighting. The modernizing wing, under party secretary Pinarayi Vijayan, had come to dominate the state organization during 2005, to the discomfiture of the veteran leader, V. S. Achuthanandan, but went too far in early 2006 when Achuthanandan was refused a party nomination for the election. The party eventually relented and he went on to lead the LDF to an overwhelming victory in the April–May polls. The LDF gained 98 of the 140 assembly seats (the CPI—M alone 61), leaving only 42 for the UDF (Congress retained only 24 seats and the Muslim League seven). Achuthanandan was eventually confirmed as the CPI—M's candidate for the post of premier. He was sworn in as Chief Minister on 18 May, although the Vijayan faction was strongly represented in the party's ministry list. However, the leadership rivalry continued, with Achuthanandan and Vijayan exchanging criticisms through the media in May 2007; the national leadership of the CPI—M moved to quell the indiscipline by suspending the two politicians from the party's politburo, although they both remained in office in Kerala. The two were again reprimanded in August, but readmitted to the politburo in October. Meanwhile, in December 2006, the Nationalist Congress Party was expelled from its association with the ruling LDF after incorporating Karunakaran's party the previous month. Karunakaran himself rejoined Congress, with the blessing of Sonia Gandhi and the state leadership, in December 2007. The Government became embroiled in controversy with the three major religious communities: the authorities across India were concerned about Pakistan-backed Muslim militancy, and there were allegations that some accused terrorists had links with Kerala; a June 2007 incident that provoked interest in the rules forbidding entry of non-Hindus to some temples prompted the Government into considering legislation to allow entry for all; and Christians protested in July about moves to secularize education. Other events to evoke political interest included: the deadly outbreak of chikungunya (a viral, mosquito-borne disease) in late 2006, which exposed the years of underinvestment in the once model public healthcare system; and the controversies over water, with a dispute over the safety of the Mullaperiyar dam (in Kerala, but operated by Tamil Nadu) from the end of 2006 and the 2007 final ruling of the committee investigating the sharing of the waters of the Kaveri (Cauvery—mainly involving Karnataka and Tamil Nadu). In September the public works minister, from the Kerala Congress (Joseph), resigned from the state Government because of an investigation into a dubious land deal involving his family. Religion soon returned to the political scene, with controversy over the proposed Sethusamudram shipping lane project in Tamil Nadu. The issue provoked rivalries and outbreaks of violence, particularly between secular supporters of the CPI (M), and Hindu activists and BJP supporters. In March there were renewed clashes in Kannur, in Thalassery and even in Delhi.

## ECONOMY

Although Kerala is a state rich in natural and in human resources (Kerala leads India in literacy and mortality rates, its well educated population enjoying the best health indicators in the country), the economy has stagnated for some years. Many of Kerala's workers leave the state, or even the country, to seek employment (more than one-half of the 3.6m. Indians working in the countries of the Arabian peninsula are from Kerala, for instance), which means that remittances are an important source of state income. However, growing instability and risk for foreigners in the Middle East during 2003–04 adversely affected this, with many returning to Kerala, leading to a drop in remittance income and further pressure on already high unemployment figures. Figures from before this period, for net domestic product, estimated that Kerala's state income at current prices had reached Rs 696,020m. in 2001/02. This was Rs 21,310 per head, which edged the state ahead of Tamil Nadu for the first time and made Kerala the wealthiest of the four southern states. By 2004/05 current net domestic product had reached Rs 894,520m. or Rs 27,048 per head. In 1999 there were 219,805 km of roads, of which 1,011 km were national highway. Railways totalled 1,050 km in length, most of it broad gauge, except for 117 km of narrow gauge. There are three major airports, Thiruvananthapuram, Kochi and Kozhikode, with the international links of the last mainly being confined to the countries of the Arabian peninsula, where many of Kerala's work-force seek employment. An airport is also to be built at Kannur. One of the country's 16 major international seaports is in Kochi, which handled 12.8m. metric tons of cargo and 121,649 standard containers in 1999/2000, but the state also has three medium-sized ports and 13 minor ones. Kerala was expected to reach self-sufficiency in energy in 2002, having already achieved an electricity connection for all of its villages (42% of rural households had electricity in 2005). The state is rich in hydroelectric potential, some of which has been developed, but efforts in the 1990s and early 2000s concentrated on installing thermal generation, in order to satisfy demand sooner. At the end of May 2006 the total installed capacity of Kerala was 3,496 MW, of which 60% came from the state sector, 35% from the central sector and the rest from the private sector. Communications infrastructure is also well developed, but a lack of an entrepreneurial climate means that the state has not yet taken advantage of its potential in exploiting new technologies and the internet economy. The educational and social achievements of Kerala are without equal in India, with the literacy rate at 90.9% in 2001 (it was already 89.8% in 1991), although this has not yet translated into comparable success with economic indicators.

The primary sector contributed 25.4% of net state domestic product in 1999/2000 (agriculture alone 21.5%). Agriculture accounted for 18.9% of gross state domestic product in 2001/02. About one-half of the population are dependent upon agriculture economically, although the state is unusual in the predominance of cash crops and is not a major producer of food grains. With plantation crops being grown by smallholders, the sector is particularly vulnerable to fluctuations in international commodity prices (it has also been affected by the lifting of trade barriers against imports), but the state still leads India in the production of many items. Over the last two decades of the 20th century there was a shift from high-volume, low-value crops (like the staple food crop, rice, production of which has fallen from a peak of 1.4m. metric tons in the 1970s to 0.8m. tons in 1999/2000 and to 0.7m. tons by 2001/02 and 2002/03) to low-volume, high-value crops (such as pepper, of which Kerala accounted for some 97% of total Indian production, with 56,400 tons in 1999/2000). Thus, the state no longer produces the most coconuts in India, although the fruit is still one of Kerala's major cash crops, accounting for 40% of the national total and providing a turn-of-the-century annual harvest of 5,167m. nuts—the state continues to lead in the provision of milling copra (dried husks). Also in 1999/2000 Kerala provided 11% of India's total cashew-nut production (cashews, introduced by the Portuguese in the 16th century, are produced both as a food crop and for industry—used in paints and varnishes or for caulking), 94% of rubber production (85% of the area under rubber trees), 21% of coffee production, 11% of tea production and, in a dramatic increase, 70% of cardamom production. Other important crops include areca nut, ginger, cacao, tapioca (introduced in the 1920s and popular because it flourishes rather better than rice on the state's red, laterite soils) and tree spices, such as cinnamon, cloves and some nutmeg. Major fruit crops include banana, pineapple, mango and jackfruit, although horticulture is not developed in the state. In 2001/02 total foodgrain production was only 729,300 tons and sugar-cane production 275,600 tons. In 2002/03 production of coconuts was 5,709m. and of tapioca 2.4m. tons, rice 688,859 tons, rubber 594,917 tons, sugar cane 312,830 tons, areca nuts 107,279 tons, pepper 67,358 tons, cashew nuts 66,087 tons, coffee 63,322 tons, ginger (cured) 32,412 tons, tamarinds 29,514 tons, garlic 10,472 tons, cardamom (processed) 8,680 tons, turmeric (cured) 6,938 tons, tea 5,348 tons and nutmeg 2,086 tons. It has been reckoned that 58% of Kerala's households keep livestock to supplement their incomes. According to the 1997 agricultural census, Kerala was home to 3.4m. head of cattle, 1.7m. buffaloes, 1.9m. goats, 143,000 pigs, 25.6m. poultry (9.0% of India's total) and 1.2m. ducks. As with food crops, Kerala does not satisfy its own demand, except in milk (2.4m. tons in 2000). Milk production rose in the early 2000s, but fell back to 2.4m. tons in 2002/03, although it was expected to recover further in the following year. The state produced just over 171m. dozen eggs (41% of requirement) and 155,080 tons of meat (51%) in 2000. Egg production declined thereafter, to just over 112m. dozen in 2002/03, before beginning to recover. Kerala, as the home of traditional, ayurvedic medicine, also has considerable potential to develop markets for medicinal plants, as well as expertise.

Fisheries are also an important source of export revenue—marine products earned Rs 8,165.5m. in foreign exchange in 1998/99, compared with Rs 7,478.5m. for coffee, Rs 7,449.5m. for cashew kernels, Rs 6,230.9m. for tea and Rs 3,116.7m. for pepper. Kerala possesses both a rich continental shelf (for which the state authorities have had to introduce conservation measures) and an extensive network of inland waterways, supporting 222 marine fishing villages and 113 inland fishing villages. In 1999/2000 there were an estimated 1.1m. people engaged in fishing (77% marine) in Kerala and total fish production was 668,000 metric tons (89% marine). The catch has risen steadily since the 569,000 tons of 1997/98 and has only been exceeded by production of over 710,000 tons in 1990/91 and in 1996/97. Forestry is not a major economic sector, although Kerala has extensive woodland in the Western Ghats, rich in biodiversity—mainly tropical forest (44% moist deciduous, 37% wet evergreen and 1% dry deciduous), but also, in places, some mountain subtropical forest (2%) and a significant amount of farmed plantation (16%). The official figure of some 29% of the total land area as recorded forested territory in Kerala obscures the fact that only about 84% of that total (9,400 sq km of 11,126 sq km) is effectively wooded forest area.

Extractive industries exist in the state, but many of Kerala's mineral resources are not yet being fully exploited. It is reputed to have the finest china clay (kaolin) in the country, while the beach sands of Kollam are rich in heavy minerals (monozite, ilmenite, rutile, zircon and silimanite). Estimated reserves include some 80m. metric tons of china clay and 12m. tons of inferior fire clay, 79m. tons of iron ore, 35m. tons of ilmenite, 11m. tons of bauxite, 3m. tons of rutile and about 1m. tons each of monozite and borophite. Mining and quarrying employed almost 263,000 people in 2001/02 and produced minerals worth Rs 1,603.8m. in 2002/03.

Manufacturing, construction and electricity and other utilities provided 20.7% of net domestic product in 1999/2000, with manufacturing alone accounting for 10.2% (just over one-half registered) and construction for 9.5%. Traditional industries dominate the secondary sector of the economy, led by the coir industry (based in Alappuzha), processing coconut production, and employing 383,000 people (85% women) alone. The whole sector provides employment for over 1m. people, the major activities, apart from coir, being handlooms (employing 200,000 people, directly and indirectly) and handicrafts, and other agro-processing such as of cashews, rubber (based in Kottayam) and tea. Other manufactures include ceramics, electronic goods, telephone cable, chemicals and pharmaceuticals, cigarettes, etc., oils (e.g. lemongrass oil), paints, papers, engineering and precision instruments, glass and petroleum products. The state has begun to encourage information-technology and computer-software companies. At 31 March 1998 there were 180,000 small-scale industrial units in Kerala, employing 909,859 people. At the same point of the following year there were 511 medium and large-scale manufacturing industrial enterprises, of which 19 were central-government concerns and 62 state-government concerns, 29 joint ventures, 16 co-operative endeavours and 385 in the private sector. By 2003 there were over 270,000 small-scale industrial units and some 18,600 working factories.

By 1999/2000 services accounted for 54.0% of net domestic product, with trade, hotels and restaurants alone providing 24.9% (almost as much as the primary sector and more than industry). The next most important services were transport, storage and communications (6.8% of net domestic product), property (4.8%), banking and insurance (4.8%) and, finally, public administration (4.6%). Tourism has recently been developed extensively, as Kerala is blessed with lush scenery, beautiful beaches, an ancient and varied historical legacy, and a rich, cosmopolitan blend of cultures. Nature provides mountain wildlife reserves or the 'backwaters' inland waterways, while three great religions and a myriad of local dynasties and foreign powers have left a profusion of temples, churches and mosques, and of palaces and fortresses. In 2004 foreign and domestic tourists together were expected to exceed 10m. for the first time. In August of that year Kerala's various advantages put it second in the *India Today* ranking of the best large states in the country in which to live (after the Punjab).

### DIRECTORY

**Governor:** RAMKRISHNAN SURYABHAN GAVAI, Office of the Governor, Thiruvananthapuram; tel. (471) 2721100; fax (471) 2720226.

**Chief Minister:** VELIKKAKATHU SANKARAN ACHUTHANANDAN (Communist (CPI—M), Cliff House, Nanthencode, Office of the Chief Minister, Government of Kerala, Secretariat, Thiruvananthapuram 695 003; tel. (471) 2333812; fax (471) 2333489; e-mail chiefminister@kerala.gov.in.

**Speaker of the Legislative Assembly (Niyamasabha):** K. RADHAKRISHNAN, Neethi, Vikas Bhavan PO, Thiruvananthapuram 695 033; tel. (471) 2513007; fax (471) 2308990 (Legislature Secretariat); e-mail speaker@niyamasabha.org; internet www.niyamasabha.org; the unicameral Legislative Assembly has 140 elected mems and one nominated: Communist Party of India—Marxist 62, Congress 24, CPI 17, Muslim League 7, Kerala Congress (M) 7, Janata Dal—Secular 5, Kerala Congress 4, Revolutionary Socialist Party 3, Kerala Congress (Balakrishna Pillai) 1, Janathipathya Samrakshana Samiti 1, Congress (Secular) 1, Kerala Congress (Secular) 1, independents and others 8.

**Resident Commissioner in New Delhi:** INDER JIT SINGH, Kerala House, 3 Jantar Mantar Rd, New Delhi 110 001; tel. (11) 23368581; fax (11) 23368934.

## Madhya Pradesh

The State of Madhya Pradesh lies in central India, as its name suggests, a 'central land' linking the Gangetic plains and the peninsula. Essentially formed from the former princely states of Madhya Bharat (Central India) and the old British Central Provinces and Berar in 1956 (without Berar, which was included in Maharashtra), the state was the largest in India until November 2000, when the eastern region of Chhattisgarh became a separate state. Chhattisgarh lies to the south-east of the 'rump' Madhya Pradesh. The heavily indented northern border is marked by a roughly mushroom-shaped extension of the state to include Gwalior and its environs, with Uttar Pradesh to the east and north-east of this and Rajasthan to the west and north-west. There is a short western border with Gujarat, and Maharashtra lies to the south. Once the largest state in India, since the bifurcation of its old territories Madhya Pradesh has had an area of 308,245 sq km (119,059 sq miles), making it the second largest state (after Rajasthan) and only slightly larger than Maharashtra.

Madhya Pradesh consists largely of dry plateau lands, alleviated by lowlands and low mountain ranges. The Narmada valley, which heads out of the state in the south-west, has the Vindhyan Range to the north, bisecting the state and reaching up along the north-western border, and the higher land of the Mahadeo Hills in the south-west. The Maikala Range defines the eastern border with the new state of Chhattisgarh. North of Gwalior the state reaches into the great northern plains of India, a border along the Chambal stopping Madhya Pradesh territory short of the Yamuna. Apart from the Narmada (Reva), one of India's holy rivers, and the Chambal, the Tapi (Tapti) and the Son are important rivers flowing through the state. Although there are black volcanic soils in places, elsewhere the land is stony and arid. Most rainfall is between June and September, with an annual average of about 1,000 mm (39 inches) in the west, increasing towards the east. The hottest months are before the monsoon, while the winter after it is dry and with a relatively mild heat.

At the census of 2001 Madhya Pradesh had a population of 60,348,023, an increase of almost one-quarter on 1991, making it the seventh most populous state in India, with a population density of 196 per sq km. Much of the region was dominated by two Maratha principalities before the ascendancy of the British, but the state's population overwhelmingly uses Hindi dialects (western variants such as Malvi and Bundelkhandi, and eastern variants such as Bagheli), although there are some Marathi speakers. Otherwise the main minority languages are tribal, notably Gondi or Bhili, which have origins distinct from the Indo-Aryan and Dravidian tongues. Other tribes, such as the Baiga, the Bharia or the Saharia, are less integrated and receive special development assistance. About one-fifth of the population in the post-2000 state were included among the Scheduled Tribes and a further 15% among the Scheduled Castes. However, most of the population practice some form of Hinduism (in 2001, in the divided state, 91.2% were Hindu and 6.2% Muslim, and there were small communities of Jains, Buddhists, Christians and Sikhs).

Just over one-quarter (26.5%) of the population was classified as urban in the 2001 census, according to which Madhya Pradesh had three cities among India's largest: Indore (the 14th largest city in the country), with 1.47m., in the south-west; Bhopal, the capital (India's 15th largest city), with 1.44m., located more towards the centre of the state; and Jabalpur (Jubbulpore), with 932,484 inhabitants, in the east. Gwalior, in the north, is also an important city (827,026). For administrative purposes Madhya Pradesh is divided into 45 districts.

## HISTORY

Madhya Pradesh has not hosted the seat of any of the great pan-Indian empires, but it has featured prominently in the history of the subcontinent. Its highlands rise above the northern heartland of the *arya varta*, and enclose the Narmada, the traditional boundary between north India and the peninsula. The ancient *Daksinapatha* or Southern Route of early Aryanization and trade lies through western Madhya Pradesh, where the ancient realm of Avanti or Malwa flourished in the country around the headwaters of the Betwa (which descends to the Gangetic plains), across the watershed and down to the valley of the Narmada (which flows westwards to the sea). The great city of Ujjain was the traditional capital of Malwa and first famed as the gubernatorial city of Ashoka, who was entrusted with the administration of this, one of the five great provinces of the Mauryan empire. Although the future emperor's time here, according to Buddhist legend, was spent in idle dalliance, emphasizing his change of character upon 'conversion', it was certainly around this time that Sanchi, near the second city of Malwa, Vidisha, first developed as a great Buddhist pilgrimage and temple site, which it was from the third century BC until its abandonment in the 14th century AD. Ujjain itself, a place of mythic significance, remains one of Hinduism's seven holy places, and shares with three other cities the rotating honour of holding the Kumbh Mela (Festival of the Pot, which is what Hindus call Aquarius). After the fall of the Mauryas Malwa was strongly contested by the surrounding successor states, with Ujjain later becoming a major entrepôt at the time the Satavahanas developed trade from the north and centre of India to the west coast. The territory was, therefore, the coveted objective of the Kshatrapas, who eventually secured Malwa, only to lose it to Chandra-Gupta II by the beginning of the fifth century AD. The decay of Gupta power was resisted for longer in Malwa, which became a junior Gupta kingdom, outlasting imperial Magadha. Yashodharman of Malwa ensured this by defeating the scourge of the Guptas, the 'White' Huns, in around 528. Thereafter, it again became the subject of rivalry between northern and Deccan powers, such as Harsha of Thanesar (Haryana) or the Chalukyas of Badami (Karnataka).

The rivalry between the Rashtrakutas of the Deccan and a Gurjara royal clan, the Pratiharas, from the eighth century involved more of western Madhya Pradesh than merely Malwa. The Gurjaras, relatives or precursors of the Rajputs, were powerful throughout the north-west of modern India, the Pratiharas under Vatsaraja having gained sufficient strength from territories in Rajasthan and Malwa to contest the rulers of Bengal for control of the imperial city of Kannauj (Uttar Pradesh). Although the Gurjara-Pratiharas lost Malwa to the Rashtrakutas, who turned their attention northwards in 786, the great fortress of Gwalior, looming above the hills separating the plains and the highlands of Madhya Pradesh, remained their great stronghold at the centre of their fluctuating domains. The final decline of the Gurjara-Pratihara realm can be dated to around 950, when they lost Gwalior to their erstwhile feudatories, the Chandelas. Indeed, throughout northern and western Madhya Pradesh Rajput clans once subject to the Pratiharas came to local prominence from this time. The Chandelas were based in old Jajhauti, Bundelkhand, from about the 10th to the 12th centuries, building the great temples of Khajurajo, which were only abandoned as the centre of Chandela power was forced eastwards. Neighbours to the Chandelas, in eastern Madhya Pradesh, were the Kalachuris, who fought the Later Western Chalukyas so ferociously and who seized Jabalpur (Jubbulpore) as their capital from the Gonds about the end of the 12th century, keeping it as their own seat until their defeat by the Marathas. (Another Gond kingdom, based on Mandla, retained its independence until conquest by the Mughals in the 16th century.) The Rajput clan to gain Malwa, however, was that of the Paramaras. They took Dhar, an upland centre more easily defended than ancient Ujjain, as their capital. The most famous Paramara king was the literary Bhoj, who reigned from about 1010 until the 1050s, making Dhar a centre of learning and poetry. His dynasty held Malwa into the 13th century, although in 1261 Jayavaram, the rajah, was forced to move the capital from Dhar to a still-more defensible site at Mandu. This did not prevent the fall of most of Malwa to the Muslims in 1293, though Mandu itself remained Hindu until 1305.

As one of the main routes into the Deccan, Malwa and other parts of Madhya Pradesh acquired Muslim as well as Rajput and other Hindu rulers, although the generally acknowledged sovereignty of Delhi came with the Mughals rather than the earlier sultans. Mandu, renamed Shadiabad (City of Joy), became the seat of an independent sultanate, until it fell under Mughal rule (when the city was slowly abandoned). Aurangzeb gained the allegiance of most of the princes of central India, although his Afghan supporters sometimes supplanted less willing lords, as they had in Gwalior and did in Bhopal (which allegedly gained its name from Bhoj Paramara). With the decline of Mughal power after Aurangzeb, Bhopal became a distinct Muslim-ruled state in 1723, eventually noted for its consistent loyalty to the British. Further to the south, originally based on Aurangabad (Maharashtra), later in Hyderabad (Andhra Pradesh), Nizam-ul-Mulk was turning his Deccan province into the basis of another independent domain. The main feature of the period, however, was the rise of the Marathas, who rapidly gained land rights throughout the region and made it a bastion of their power. Although the pre-eminent Maratha princes were based in Maharashtra, two powerful dynasties became established in Madhya Pradesh. Of the five great houses of the emerging Maratha confederation, the Peshwas were based in Pune (Maharashtra), the Gaekwads in Vadodara (Gujarat) and the Bhonslas in Berar (now Maharashtra, but until 1956 part of Madhya Pradesh). In Malwa the main leaders were Malhar Rao Holkar (who, in the late 1720s, was awarded territory there, including the new city of Indore in 1733, which became the royal city of the Holkars) and Ranoji Scindia (who was awarded ancient Ujjain—his house gained extensive power throughout north-western Madhya Pradesh, and in Rajasthan and Gujarat, but made its eventual capital at Gwalior in 1766).

Although increasingly independent and intent on expanding their own territories and revenue rights, the Holkars and the Scindias dutifully supported the Peshwa's expedition against the Afghan forces threatening Delhi in 1760. The Marathas were defeated conclusively in the January of the following year, undermining central authority and, indeed, exposing the office of peshwa to the same dynastic manipulations to which the Marathas had subjected the Mughal emperors. The main Maratha power in northern and central India became Mahadji Scindia, who was the ruling prince of Gwalior for some 30 years, until his death in 1794. He gained huge territories with his (expensive) professional army, and resumed Maratha 'protection' of the Mughal emperor, although he and the Holkars also moved to support the court of the peshwas at the end of the 1770s, when the British intervened in the Maratha succession. However, reinforcements from Bengal aborted the nascent concert of princes, even if they did not deliver a victory to the British. In 1780 the Scindia maharajah was surprised in his own great fortress of Gwalior, and he moved to become the peacemaker between the British and the Marathas, securing over two decades of peace in central India. Meanwhile, the territories of Indore flourished under the benevolent and enlightened rule of Rani Ahalyabhai Holkar, the daughter-in-law of Malhar Rao Holkar, who himself had long depended on her guidance before his death in 1766. (This sustained experience of female rule was to be repeated in the next century in the small, nearby princely state of Bhopal, where two Muslim women, Qudsia Begum and her daughter, Sikander Begum, were in power from 1857 until 1926.) However, the death of Ahalyabhai in 1795 left her Holkar successor to intrigue against the new Scindia prince for supremacy among the Marathas, descending to open conflict after the death of the Pune regent, Nana Phadnavis, in 1800. This merely sent the Peshwa to seek the help of the British, who, in 1803–04, marched against the Marathas, forcing them into subsidiary alliance with the East India Company, although not without a considerable military challenge. Despite the final British–Maratha conflict in 1817–18, most of the 19th century saw co-operation between the British and their princely clients, whose lands were interspersed by directly administered territories of the Company. The British title for the area was the Central Provinces (Berar was added later in the century) and the headquarters of the Central India Agency was in Indore. At the time of the 1857 Mutiny and the ensuing Great Rebellion, both the Scindia and Holkar maharajahs remained loyal to the British, although the former's capital of Gwalior was seized by rebellious troops and provided a last stand for them and another of Madhya Pradesh's famous women, Lakshmi Bai, the Rani of Jhansi (now part of Uttar Pradesh).

Both Indore and Gwalior benefited from enlightened princely rule at various periods. The Holkars, for instance, were among the first to open temples and public wells, etc., to 'untouchables' in support of Mahatma Gandhi's campaign for harijan rights. At independence, the Maharajah of Gwalior, George Jivaji Rao Scindia, was instrumental in the formation of the Madhya Bharat Union of princely states from the region, which acceded to the Indian Union in 1948, with Scindia as Rajpramukh (i.e. governor of a 'Part B' state under the 1950 Constitution). The original Madhya Pradesh ('central land' or 'central province') was the old British region of the Central Provinces and Berar, with its capital at Nagpur. In 1956, as part of the linguistic reorganization of the states, predominantly Marathi-speaking Berar (including Nagpur) was attached to what became Maharashtra, while the rest of the Central Provinces, the 17 districts of Mahakoshal, were joined with the 16 districts of Madhya Bharat (excluding a small enclave that was included with Rajasthan), the eight districts of Vindhya Pradesh (a 'Part C' state—administered from the Centre), the two districts of the 'Part C' and former princely state of Bhopal and, finally, the Sironj sub-division (hitherto part of Kotah District in Rajasthan). The resulting State of Madhya Pradesh settled upon Bhopal as its capital, a city that gained international notoriety in December 1984, when the gas disaster at the Union Carbide plant caused the loss and blighting of so many lives (an official report in 1990 attributed some 3,800 deaths and many thousands of disabilities to the incident). In 2004 the Supreme Court ordered the national Government to pay the balance of the compensation due to the victims (approving the proposals in October), while earlier in the year a US court reinstated action that sought to force the company (now owned by Dow Chemicals) to clean the site of the old factory (where chemical leaching was feared to be creating another disaster).

Congress long remained the predominant party of the state, helped by the support of many of the still-respected royal families. Thus, the late Madhavrao Scindia was a Congress politician, and from 2002 his son continued the tradition (although he does not yet have the same prestige as his father), while the Chief Minister for a decade from December 1993, Digvijay Singh, was also the scion of a princely house. Singh became the longest serving Chief Minister of Madhya Pradesh, but this merely served to reinforce the anti-incumbency voting in 2003. He had helped bolster the position of his party in the state legislature by restoring responsibility to government finances, maintaining a record for good governance even through the upheavals (and reduced income) consequent upon the separation of Chhattisgarh into a separate state in 2000. He was not considered in favour with the national leadership of Congress, but was too popular to replace, and remained in charge in the immediate aftermath of the 2003 state and the 2004 general elections. However, despite his social engineering in favour of less favoured groups, Singh could not rebut accusations that the basic infrastructure of the state had not improved during his stewardship, nor could he counter the continuing drought. The opposition soon realized that the most effective attacks on the Government involved roads, power and employment, rather than Hindu-chauvinist rhetoric. By contrast, Singh adopted such rhetoric, often more 'saffron' in tone than that of the BJP, but thereby alienated some minority groups.

Congress had always been strongly challenged in the state by the Hindu-nationalist Bharatiya Janata Party (BJP), under Uma Bharti, which performed well in the state at the 1999 general election to the lower house of the Indian Parliament (to which Madhya Pradesh furnishes 29 members; the state also sends 11 members to the Rajya Sabha). The BJP led the national Government, of which the Prime Minister, Atal Bihari Vajpayee, was born in Madhya Pradesh. The advent of legislative elections at the end of 2003 prompted various political manoeuvres in the months before, including a government decision to divert funds to purchase power from other Congress-led states (to counter the unpopular electricity cuts being widely experienced in the state), controversy over communal tensions and the formation of an opposition 'third front'. The last was a concert agreed in March between the parties opposed to both Congress, in government in the state, and the BJP, in government nationally. A pragmatic arrangement between the BJP and the Samajwadi Party, however, helped counter the Congress understanding with the Bahujan Samaj Party, while Bharti enforced her authority within her own party as she faced a fractious and discordant Congress. Moreover, in the middle of the election campaign Bharti dramatically accused the Chief Minister himself of corruption, as well as the failure to achieve progress for Madhya Pradesh. As a result, at the state elections of 1 December, the BJP swept into power, initially with 173 of the 230 seats in the Legislative Assembly, while Congress only retained 38 (a figure subsequently eroded). Although the BJP share of the overall vote did not increase dramatically (up to 42.5%), the Congress vote collapsed. The Samajwadi Party, allied to the BJP, also gained seven seats. Bharti duly became Chief Minister. Then, in May 2004, despite losing power at the Centre, the BJP in Madhya Pradesh held onto their electoral advantage by winning 25 of the 29 Lok Sabha seats and halving Congress representation to four. Meanwhile, Bharti had become Chief Minister, a sanyasin (religious ascetic) challenged with transforming the fortunes of an underdeveloped state. However, the large majority in the state Assembly meant that the BJP was already allowing itself to be distracted by internal rivalries. Certainly by mid-2004 Bharti was being criticized for favouring her relatives and friends in official appointments, at the expense of party veterans.

In late August 2004 Bharti was forced to resign after an arrest warrant was issued against her, charging her with inciting communal violence during riots in Karnataka in 1994. Babulal Gaur was appointed as her successor. Several days after Bharti was sentenced to 14 days' judicial custody, the Government of Karnataka agreed to withdraw all charges against her and she was released. Then, in early November she accepted the post of General Secretary of the BJP, only to criticize the party leadership. She was expelled from the party shortly afterwards. Although Bharti apologized to the senior national leader, L. K. Advani, who she had defied in public, opposition from other elements within the state party leadership prevented her reinstatement, particularly as she claimed credit for the election victory of the BJP. There were signs of reconciliation only in May 2005 and, at the end of that month, Bharti joined the national executive body of the BJP. By October her supporters had created sufficient pressure for the national leadership to reconsider the occupancy of the Chief Minister's office. On 26 November Bharti was offered reinstatement as General Secretary, while Shivraj Singh Chauhan replaced Gaur as state premier. Two days later Chauhan was formally elected to the leadership of the BJP in the state legislature, provoking 17 deputies, including Bharti, to walk out of the meeting. Some of Bharti's supporters rioted, adding to the drama, but Chauhan proceeded to take office while Bharti and her most prominent supporters were suspended from the BJP. Although Bharti made some appeals to the national leadership, she was expelled from the BJP and, by early 2006, was no longer seeking reconciliation with a party that she considered to have strayed from its ideals (as well as one led by a clique of her enemies). On 30 April the formation of the Bhartiya Janshakti Party was announced and Bharti duly resigned from the legislature, soon announcing that the new organization would contest elections in Uttar Pradesh and the Punjab later in the year. However, in Madhya Pradesh her party did not achieve an electoral breakthrough at by-elections to the state or national legislatures. Instead, the BJP and Congress were the main contenders: in October the BJP retained both Assembly seats being contested (barely, in the case of the one vacated by Bharti); in March 2007 the BJP retained an Assembly seat and won a Lok Sabha seat from Congress, but Congress in turn took the other Lok Sabha seat from the BJP; and in June the BJP unexpectedly lost an Assembly seat to Congress (the seat vacated by the BJP member elected to the Lok Sabha in March). One of the issues used by Congress was the August 2006 murder of an Ujjain college professor who had cancelled an irregular student union election, only to suffer a fatal heart attack after being beaten up by activists of the student wing of the BJP. The professor's son and opposition politicians alleged that the BJP-led state authorities were compromised in their investigation and, indeed, even conspiring to protect the suspects. The Supreme Court stayed the trial in July 2007.

State elections were scheduled for September 2008 and, about a year before, it was already apparent that the BJP intended to exploit *Hindutva* rhetoric in its campaign. In October 2007 the state Government had taken advantage of the Ram Sethu controversy, about the shipping canal cutting through Adam's Bridge in Tamil Nadu, to criticize the Congress-led national Government. An affidavit doubting the historical existence of Lord Rama encouraged the Government of Madhya Pradesh to establish a commission to prove the deity's reality, for instance. Nevertheless, the BJP proceeded to lose three by-elections before the end of the year: an Assembly seat to the Samajwadi Party in November and, in a particular shock to the BJP leadership, an Assembly seat and a Lok Sabha seat to Congress in December. In 2008 the Government of Madhya Pradesh stepped up its criticisms of the Centre and its 'step-motherly' attitude to the state. In July the BJP supported a *bandh* (general strike) in Indore to protest against the revocation of a land grant to a Hindu shrine in Jammu and Kashmir, but violence broke out and a curfew had to be imposed in the city.

## ECONOMY

Madhya Pradesh is a relatively poor state, although some mineral wealth and a developed urban population have contributed to the creation of a modest industrial base. The state Government of Digvijay Singh was noted as the first in India to restore discipline, and a fiscal surplus, to state finances. However, this was at the expense of infrastructure development or of real growth sufficient to counter population increases or to match national growth. Moreover, the division of the state in 2000 lost Madhya Pradesh some rich mineral and forestry reserves in Chhattisgarh, as well as a disproportionate share of the power capacity (unless otherwise stated, figures given in this survey apply to the truncated Madhya Pradesh). In current prices, the net state domestic product in 2004/05 was Rs 914,320m. and Rs 14,069 per head. Particularly given that the rail network of Madhya Pradesh is considered insufficient (although the main route connecting north and south India passes through the state), roads are vital infrastructure. However, in terms of length relative to area, the state possesses only some 30% of the national average. Roads maintained by the state public works department totalled 67,740 km in 1999/2000, and in the 2003 state elections the poor quality of that maintenance was an important issue. There are airports at Bhopal, Indore, Gwalior, Jabalpur and Khajurajo. Although the divided Madhya Pradesh was left with about 70% of the land area and 73% of the population, it retained only 64% of the generating capacity for electricity and a greater proportion of consumption. In 1999/2000 the area that the divided state was to consist of consumed more electricity than it produced (the latter being 14,023.7m. units, of which 15% was produced from hydroelectric sources). Electrification of rural villages, however, had reached 97% of the total at March 2000, but further progress was not reported in the next five years and little more than one-third of rural houses had electricity (34% in Madhya Pradesh and Chhattisgarh together). By 2003 the persistent power shortages were fatally undermining Congress chances of success in the November state elections. The new BJP Government promised rapid action on remedying the power situation. At 30 May 2006 the national Ministry of Power reported an installed capacity in Madhya Pradesh of 6,199 MW (3,745 MW in the state sector, 2,403 MW from the Centre and the balance, albeit small, in the private sector). In the census of 2001 the literacy rate showed a great improvement on that in 1991, rising to 64.1% from 44.7%.

The contribution of the primary sector to net domestic product in 2001/02 was 30.7%. Agriculture alone contributed 26.6% to state gross domestic product. Agriculture is the occupation of most people in Madhya Pradesh—of the main workers (36% of the total population), one-half are classed as cultivators and a further 27% as agricultural labour. The state does not produce sufficient to feed itself, not helped by the loss of the fertile Chhattisgarh plains (which produced some 70% of the rice in the undivided state). Rice is mainly grown in the east, and some in the south-west, along with millets, while in the north it is mainly wheat and pulses, as well as some sugar cane. Other crops include fruit, tobacco, betel leaf, cotton, chilli, vegetables, and oilseeds and groundnut (peanut). The main production figures for the divided state in 1999/2000 were: 15.5m. metric tons of food grains (half-polished rice at 1.7m. tons, wheat at 8.4m. tons and jowar or white sorghum at 0.6m. tons, with other grains and millets, and pulses, making up the balance); 203,000 tons of sugar cane (gur); 456,000 bales of cotton; 5.5m. tons of oilseeds; and 4.4m. tons of soybeans. In 2001/02, according to figures from the Reserve Bank of India, total foodgrain production was 13.1m. tons (1.7m. tons of rice, 5.6m. tons of wheat, 2.7m. tons of coarse grain and 3.0m. tons of pulses), oilseeds 4.4m. tons, cotton 390,400 tons and sugar cane 2.1m. tons. Total foodgrain production in 2002/03 fell to only 9.8m. tons. Agriculture is mainly rainfall fed, which has been a problem in the recent years of persistent drought, but the sector also suffers from low productivity and low-value crops. Livestock is important, and in 2002/03 the sector produced 5.3m. tons of milk, 784.4m. eggs and 672,000 kg of wool. In 1999/2000 some 49% of the total area was sown and 31% forested. About two-fifths of the woodland grows economically important species such as teak, sal and bamboo.

Madhya Pradesh still possesses productive mineral reserves, although it only retained about one-half of the mining revenue of the undivided state. However, until the development of new finds in Chhattisgarh, Madhya Pradesh (Panna District) remains India's only source of diamonds—in 1999/2000 production increased by 18% compared with the previous year, to reach 40,666 carats, worth Rs 179.3m. The same year produced 43.0m. metric tons of coal (worth Rs 27,905.5m.), 22.3m. tons of limestone (Rs 2,191.5m.), 326,000 tons of manganese ore (Rs 536.2m.), 248,000 tons of bauxite (Rs 73.5m.), 155,000 tons of rock phosphate (Rs 118.6m.), 103,000 tons of dolomite (Rs 8.9m.), 92,000 tons of iron ore (Rs 5.3m.), and 74,000 tons of copper ore (Rs 1,037.8m.), as well as fire clay and china clay, laterite and ochre. The contribution of mining and quarrying to the economy rose from 2.8% in 1993/94 to 3.5% in 1999/2000. Mining employed almost 200,000 people (191,131 in 2001/02), while the total value of minerals produced in 2002/03 was Rs 38,554.3m., the fifth largest amount of any state.

The secondary sector contributed 19.9% to net domestic product in 1999/2000, a share that had declined slightly over the previous several years as a result of problems in industrial growth, but in 2001/02 the figure was 26.0%. By August 2000 the number of registered factories had reached 8,420. In 1999/2000 cement (production of 11.2m. metric tons) and newsprint (58,400 tons) had performed well, but textiles had languished. Other industries include those based on agricultural and mineral processing, automobile industries near Indore, the manufacture of electrical and electronic equipment, optical cables and the famous handicraft activities and handloom cloths produced at Chanderi and Maheswar. Recurrent power shortages in the early 2000s did not help industrial production.

The tertiary sector accounted for 43.3% of net domestic product in 2001/02, having edged past the primary sector as the principal contributor to the economy in the late 1990s. Manufacturing for the electronics and telecommunications industries has helped the development of an information-technology sector, but the main services in Madhya Pradesh are government, transport and trade. Tourism is also an important activity, with the state boasting nine national parks and 25 wildlife sanctuaries, including the last known habitat of the swamp deer and the home of the albinotic (white) tigers of Rewa. History has provided a rich monumental, cultural and religious legacy, which attracts visitors.

### DIRECTORY

**Governor:** Dr Balram Jakhar, Office of the Governor, Raj Bhavan, Bhopal 462 003; tel. (755) 2551946; fax (755) 2554711; e-mail rajyapal@mp.nic.in.

**Chief Minister:** Shivraj Singh Chauhan (Bharatiya Janata Party), Office of the Chief Minister, Ballabh Bhavan, Mantralaya, Bhopal 462 004; tel. (755) 2441581; fax (755) 2441781; e-mail cm@vallabh.mp.nic.in; internet www.mpgovt.nic.in.

**Speaker of the Legislative Assembly:** Ishwardas Rohani, Assembly Secretariat, New Vidhan Sabha, Bhopal 462 004; tel. (755) 2440200; fax (755) 2440400; e-mail nicnet@vidhan.mp.nic.in; the unicameral Legislative Assembly has 230 mems (incl. one appointed mem.): Bharatiya Janata Party 176; Congress 34; Samajwadi Party 7; Gondwana Gantantra Party 3; Bahujan Samaj Party 2; Rashtriya Samata Dal 2; independents and others 6.

**State Resident Commissioner in New Delhi:** Loveleen Kakker, Madhya Pradesh Bhavan, 2 Gopinath Bardoloi Marg, Chanakyapuri, New Delhi 110 021; tel. (11) 23019899; fax (11) 23019461; e-mail mpbhawan@bol.net.in.

## Maharashtra

The State of Maharashtra lies in the north-west of peninsular India, tapering inland, then widening slightly. It has borders with seven other constituent parts of the Union. To the south, also on the Arabian Sea coast, is Goa, from where the Maharashtra border reaches into the heart of India in a north-easterly direction; south of this border lie Karnataka and Andhra Pradesh. Maharashtra is hooked over the northern tip of Andhra Pradesh and ends with an eastern border with Chhattisgarh (part of Madhya Pradesh until 2000). To the north lies Madhya Pradesh and, in the north-west, Gujarat. As it nears the coast again, the border with Gujarat is complicated by the presence of Nagar Haveli, an enclave of the inland Union Territory of Dadra and Nagar Haveli. On 1 May 1960 Maharashtra and Gujarat states were formed from the State of Bombay (which itself had been organized into a bilingual state for Marathi and Gujarati speakers only in 1956, having some Marathi-speaking districts added to the old province from what is now Madhya Pradesh and from Hyderabad—now part of Andhra Pradesh). Maharashtra, which retained multilingual Bombay (renamed Mumbai in 1996) as its capital, has an area of 307,713 sq km (118,854 sq miles), making it the third largest state in India (Rajasthan is the largest, while Madhya Pradesh is now only a little bigger than Maharashtra).

The Konkan Coast, which includes the littoral of Maharashtra, is here a broken lowland of low plateaux and narrow, steep-sided river valleys, seldom even 50 km (31 miles) wide. Inland the Western Ghats rise steeply as the flat-topped Sahyadri Range, which, eastwards, falls in steps (ghats) through the Mawal hill country to the dominating plateau land of the interior. There are natural mountain limits to the state in the north (Satpuda Range) and in the rolling granite hills of the east, while the great Maharashtra Desh (plateau) generally falls towards the south-east and east. Much of the Desh, except in the far eastern Vidarbha region and in a small part of the south-west, is largely coterminous with the Deccan Traps, giving it its distinctive black soils. This volcanic geology and weathering has given the interior of Maharashtra its flattened skyline of mesas, further broken by river action. The interior plateau, therefore, actually consists of flat and generally dry interfluves, alternating with open river valleys, the broadest of which result from the systems of the Godavari and its tributaries, the Wardha and the Wainganga, of the Bhima, a tributary of the Krishna, which also rises in the southern parts of the state, and of the westward flowing Tapi-Purna. In the northernmost part of the state, a short border lies along a stretch of the Narmada. Many of these rivers are prone to flooding, owing to the monsoon climate, but Maharashtra suffers more from a scarcity of water resources. Although the Konkan Coast enjoys plentiful precipitation (an annual average of about 2,000 mm—78 inches—more in the south and less in the north), reaching over 4,000 mm per year on the crests of the Sahyadri, the interior is semi-arid. The western plateau can receive only 500 mm in one year, although the eastern regions receive about double that average, later in the season than those areas nearer the coast (where the monsoon from early June brings heavy rains, lasting until September). Temperatures are tropical, summer heat building up from March usually to reach its height in May, and the coast is humid.

Maharashtra is a large state, stretching 900 km into the interior from a 500-km coastline, and it is the most populous state in India after Uttar Pradesh, with 96,878,627 people at the 2001 census, giving it an average population density of 315 per sq km. The natural population growth rate is now lower than the all-India average, but inward migration remains high (accounting for some 23% of the increase in population between 1991 and 2001, based on official estimates). It was estimated that the population surpassed 100m. in September 2002. Maharashtra is home to a variety of indigenous tribal peoples, and to different ethnic and religious groups, most famously in Mumbai, but the *lingua franca* tends to be Marathi (the first tongue of 73.3% of the population in 1991, and spoken by many more). The Marathi-speaking peoples are supposed to have originated in a migration from the north, but they also manifestly included Dravidian and aboriginal tribal elements. The language is a descendant of Maharastri, a Prakrit corruption of Sanskrit, in use in around the third century BC, since modified by other local languages and, most recently, by the Persian in use as the official language of many Muslim courts. The name of the state, therefore, has numerous possible derivations, possibly meaning the land of the Mahars and Rattas, or derived from the word for chariot driver (*rathi*) and, hence, a fighting force, or from a corruption of *maha kantara* (great forest), which is a synonym for Dandakaranya, a name once used for the region. Although most of the outlying areas of the old Bombay presidency where Telugu or Kannada were mostly spoken were awarded to Andhra Pradesh and Karnataka, respectively, when the states were reorganized, these languages are still spoken by significant minorities. History has also left English widely spoken, in urban areas particularly. However, the other main languages after Marathi are Hindi (7.8% of the population at the 1991 census), Urdu (7.3%) and Gujarati (2.6%). Konkani is an important regional language on the coast and Gondi in the north. Ethnically, the Bhil, Warli, Gond, Korku and Gowari tribal groups of the western and northern hill country, are Australoid aboriginals (Scheduled Tribes accounted for 8.9% of the total population of the state in 2001), but the Marathi-speaking Kunbi Marathas are the predominant clans of the state. The Parsis, most of the remainder of whom now live in Mumbai, arrived on the west coast of India from Persia (now Iran) in the eighth century AD, and are now mainly distinguished from the rest of the population by their observance of the ancient Zoroastrian faith. However, the overwhelming majority in the state are adherents of the 'Great Tradition' of Hinduism (80.4% in 2001). There is still a relatively large Muslim population (10.6%). The next largest religious affiliation is to Buddhism (6.0%), but this is not a long-enduring local tradition, as the originally native faith had lost adherence throughout most of India by the 12th century, but rather the result of an acquisition of recent converts from among the lower castes. There are also communities of Jains (1.3%), Christians (1.1%) and Sikhs (0.2%), as well as some Jews (mainly in Mumbai).

According to the results of the 2001 census, 42.4% of the population were urban, the highest percentage among all the states after Goa, Mizoram and Tamil Nadu. There are a number of populous cities in the state, but Mumbai is the largest city in India—the urban agglomeration of Greater Mumbai had a population of 16.4m. (1.6% of the total population of India and 17.0% of the population of Maharashtra), some 12.0m. of these in the city proper. Pune, an old Maratha capital, east beyond the Ghats from Mumbai, is India's ninth largest city (2.5m. in 2001) and Nagpur, in the east of the state and once the capital of Madhya Bharat (most of which is now part of Madhya Pradesh), the 12th largest city (2.1m.). Other important cities are Nashik in the north-west (1.1m.), on the inland slopes of the Western Ghats and one of the four cities to share the site of the triennial Kumbh Mela (most recently held here in 2003), Aurangabad (873,311) further east and, in the south-west, Kolhapur (493,167). Maharashtra is divided into 35 districts.

## HISTORY

Mauryan hegemony followed the so-called Southern Route of Aryanization from the north, through Malwa (based on Ujjain, in modern Madhya Pradesh) to the Deccan (itself a term derived from the Southern Route, *Daksinapatha*). The heartland of modern Maharashtra is where this great north–south conduit is crossed by the ways leading to the narrow passes down to the western coast. The first great realm to be based in the region was that of the Satavahanas, an Andhran dynasty founded by Simukha (271–48 BC), who moved the capital to Prathinistapura (Paithan). The sixth ruler of the dynasty, Satarkani II (184–28 BC), extended Satavahana rule into Malwa and beyond, onto the Gangetic plains. Satavahana success mainly depended on the wealth of the trade they encouraged, with commerce from the north and from the Deccan heading down to the great ports of the Konkan Coast, from Broach (Bharuch, Gujarat) in the north to Sopara and Chaul, nearer modern Mumbai. Trade across the Arabian Sea, notably with the Roman Empire, flourished until around AD 170, when recession had a noticeable archaeological effect on Satavahana society. Satavahana policy had favoured settlement along the trade routes and at their termini, so, while the dynasty itself faithfully observed the Vedic sacrifices and sponsored brahminical settlement, it also supported Buddhism, a philosophy then more favourable to the development of trade. Thus, the great trading and artisanal guilds are prominent in the dedications of the Buddhist monuments and cave temples of the era.

Politically, the Satavahanas are noted for ending the residual authority of the last of the Kanvas of Magadha in 28 BC, under Pulumavi I. Towards the end of the first century AD, however, the Deccan had to suffer Shaka (Scythian) incursions and it took the great Gautamiputra Satarkani (AD 62–86) to drive them out of Malwa, although it was not long before the Kshatrapas challenged them again, particularly along the Konkan Coast and by regaining Malwa. The last years of Pulumavi II (86–114) witnessed the beginning of the Satavahanas' final decline, military defeats and loss of territory confirmed by a contraction in the basis of their wealth. The Satavahana–Kshatrapa rivalry was not just political but also a struggle to control the lucrative Arabian Sea trade. However, this trade was not only divided in the late second century, but in decline. The last monarch of an extensive domain was Yajnasri Satarkani (128–57), who was regularly defeated by the 'Great Satrap', Rudradaman Kshatrapa, and the Satavahanas were soon lost to history thereafter. In the next century the Satavahana hegemony in Maharashtra was gradually replaced by the kingdom of the Vakatakas, whose capital was in Ajanta, and it was this dynasty that obstructed Gupta supremacy in the Deccan. However, the Guptas were engaged in conflict with the Kshatrapas, the enemy of both regimes, so the Vakatakas entered into a matrimonial alliance, with Rudrasena II Vakataka marrying Prabhavati Gupta, a daughter of Chandra-Gupta II. Rudrasena II died in 390 and his queen became regent for 20 years, by which time the Vakatakas were firmly entrenched as allies of the Guptas.

Control of the western Deccan after the Gupta era was contested by a number of dynasties. By the seventh century the Chalukyas of Badami (Karnataka), otherwise known as the Western Chalukyas, had extended their authority not only into Maharashtra but north of the Narmada, as well as east to the Bay of Bengal, but they were mainly concerned with their rivalry with the Tamil south. The Chalukyas were, therefore, supplanted by the Rashtrakutas, who, under Dantidurga (a rashtrakuta or governor of a Chalukya district in Maharashtra from about 733) had been permitted to accumulate considerable territory in Berar, around modern Nagpur. After the death of Vikramaditya II Chalukya in 747, Dantidurga had campaigned as far afield as Madhya Pradesh and southern Gujarat, adopting Ellora as his capital and assuming the title of Consort of the Earth (Prithvi Vallabha—hence, the later Rashtrakutas were known to the Muslims as 'the Balhara'). He successfully held off the Chalukyas once they became aware of his ambitions, but it was left to his uncle and successor, Krishna I (who reigned about 756–73), to destroy their armies and to conquer Badami in about 760. The Rashtrakutas then added most of Karnataka to their domains, later securing control of the Konkan Coast, the submission of the Gangas of south-eastern Karnataka, and the defeat of and subsequent matrimonial alliance with the Eastern Chalukyas of Vengi (in Andhra Pradesh). Krishna I was succeeded by his son, Govinda II, whose uncertain reign did not threaten Rashtrakuta control of the Deccan only because the kingdom's potential rivals were in the far south of India or north in the Gangetic plains. In about 780 he was usurped by his brother, Dhruva. The new king first disciplined his southern and eastern neighbours, before crossing the Narmada some six years after his accession to conquer Malwa, then descending to the Gangetic plains. Although he defeated the two competing powers of the north, which had made of Kannauj (Uttar Pradesh) an imperial city to be fought over, Dhruva himself did not take the capital. Instead he headed back south of the Vindhyan hills laden with booty, in the traditional manner of a Deccan raider. However, this foray was actually to mark the start of an imperial adventure for the Rashtrakutas, the first Deccan dynasty to make a serious bid for power in the north.

Malwa and Rajasthan constituted the realm of Vatsaraja Pratihara, the leader of a Gurjara (possibly related to, or were themselves, early Rajputs) clan, who had amassed sufficient power to threaten Pala control of Kannauj. The Palas themselves were new to power, having become the rulers of Bengal under Gopala in *circa* 750. Gopala's son, Dharmapala (770–810), extended Pala conquests up the course of the Ganga (Ganges), only to join Vatsaraja in defeat by Dhruva. However, the Rashtrakutan incursion had mainly come through Gurjara-Pratihara territory, and, in the aftermath, the Palas were able to seize Kannauj and install their own candidate as king. The Palas clung to supremacy under Dharmapala and his equally long-reigning son, Devapala (810–50), before giving way to about one century of Gurjara-Pratihara dominance. The Rashtrakutas, however, made repeated interventions in northern affairs, first seizing Kannauj itself under Govinda III (793–814), Dhruva's son and successor, but also later under Indra III (914–28), the great-grandson of Govinda III. They were also constantly re-establishing their power vis-à-vis their neighbours in Vengi, southern Karnataka or the Tamil lands. The Rashtrakutas relied on the personal dominance of a king, and so upon the qualities of the reigning individual and, indeed, of his contemporary monarchs. It has been argued that the Rashtrakutan interventions in the *arya varta* were not so much about conquest as about staking a claim to 'relocate' the sacred geography to the Deccan, and many of their magnificent monuments echo such ambitions. Certainly, the Rashtrakutas were a recognizably Hindu dynasty, and their lands a major conduit of *bhakti* Hindu revivalism from the south to the north. (Buddhism effectively seems to have been extinct in the main body of India by the 12th century, and in the peninsula long before.) The reign of Krishna III, between about 939 and 967, was the last chapter in the history of a still-great, but ailing, empire, assailed on many sides. Krishna III died without issue, and the domains of the Rashtrakutas were rent by succession struggles and the competing armies of the Ganga and revived Chalukya (Later Western Chalukya) dynasties of Karnataka. The latter, with their capital at Kalyana (Karnataka), eventually prevailed, and the last, hapless Rashtrakuta was displaced in about 973.

The Later Western Chalukyas dominated the western Deccan for almost two centuries, although they suffered from Paramara and Kalachuri pressure in the north and the Chola rivalry in the south. By the 12th century two increasingly powerful Chalukya feudatories had gained sufficient weight to threaten the rulers of Kalyana, whose weakness was apparent from the middle decades of the century. Both dynasties claimed to be descended from the Yadavas, although the name is applied mainly to the northern dynasty, which was also the first to use Marathi as a court language. In the south the Hoysalas gained control of Karnataka, but in the north the Sevunas (or Yadavas) ruled much of Maharashtra.

Bhillama V Sevuna, who came to the throne in about 1173, confirmed Yadava rule in the north by taking the Chalukyan capital of Kalyana in about 1186, although his advance southwards was halted by the Hoysala king two years before his death in 1192. Under Singhana II (1199–1247), however, the Yadava realm extended as far as the Tungabhadra in southern Karnataka. Generally, its territory roughly corresponded to modern Maharashtra, and the dynasty had to fight to maintain its borders against a number of aggressive neighbours, not least the Delhi Sultanate, which became established in northern India in the 13th century. In such warlike times, it is no surprise to find that the Yadava capital was at Deogiri or Devagiri (later Daulatabad, now Deogarh), guarded by one of the most impregnable fortresses in western India. It was here that Ramachandra Sevuna was surprised in a daring raid by a young Muslim prince, Ala-ud-din Khalji, whose family had recently seized the throne of Delhi. Ramachandra's son and army were campaigning in the south, while the great fortress was low on provisions, so the Yadava king arranged a matrimonial alliance and paid a ransom to Ala-ud-din, who was soon to become sultan, aided by his new wealth and reputation. The Sevuna heir, Sangama, however, was less keen on the new alliance, the tribute was heavy and soon fell into arrears, and the Muslim threat to Hindu kingdoms made more real after 1299, when Devagiri provided a refuge for the exiled rajah of conquered Gujarat. In 1307 the Sultan ordered a military enforcement of his alliance with Ramachandra—the Muslim forces defeated the Yadava army, forced Sangama to flee and again sacked the capital. Ramachandra was taken to Delhi, but reinstated by Ala-ud-din, who thereby gained a helpful ally in transporting his armies south against the peninsular kingdoms. In 1318, during the turbulent years before the Tughluqs seized the throne of Delhi, the Sevunas were finally dispossessed and Devagiri taken as a fortress of the sultanate (briefly to serve as the new capital of Muhammed bin Tughluq in *circa* 1330). Despite the pressure from and ultimate conquest by the Muslims, however, this period is noted for the activity of a number of saintly poets, including Jnanesvara (whose short life was in the last years of Sevuna sovereignty, from about 1271 to 1296), who wrote in Marathi. Possibly the most famous of his contemporaries was Namdev, a tailor as well as a writer, who was born in about 1270 and died in 1350. Such men established a tradition that continued despite Muslim rule, culminating with the 17th-century works of a poet such as Tukaram (1598–1650) or the ascetic and politically active Ramdas (1608–81), who provided Shivaji (see below) with a philosophical inspiration.

Muslim rule by the tolerant Bahmanids, who succeeded to power in the western Deccan with the decline of Delhi's authority in the 14th century, was not onerous, and this continued in the successor sultanates that emerged at the end of the 15th century. The main one on Maharashtran territory was based on the city of Ahmadnagar and ruled by the Nizamshahis. By this time, however, the Mughals had established an empire in northern India and were extending their control into Malwa and Berar. Against them the Deccan sultanates not only deployed their Muslim subjects, but their Hindu ones—Ahmadnagar increasingly depended on the mobile cavalry units supplied by the Maratha warrior aristocracy. Thus, one such nobleman, Maloji Bhonsla, was in 1595 rewarded for his service to Bahadur Nizam II with a princely title, a fort and the estate of Pune (Poona). The sultanate was though weakened by its rivalry with Bijapur (Karnataka) and its capital fell to the Mughals in 1600. Nevertheless, the Ahmadnagar kingdom continued and was, indeed, restored under the leadership of Malik Ambar, who harassed the Mughals and the forces of Bijapur, often using guerrilla tactics, but defeating them conclusively in open battle in 1624. Malik Ambar, a great administrator and general, died in 1626 and the sultanate he had sought to defend was finally incorporated into the Mughal dominions in the 1630s, but he had set an example for the Maratha lords he had so ably employed.

Maloji Bhonsla of Pune was succeeded by his son, Shahji, whose own son (and that of a princess claiming descent from the Sevunas), Shivaji, was born in 1627. From the age of 16 years Chhatrapati Shivaji seems to have been intent on power and on freedom from Muslim rule, extending his tiny kingdom in the 1640s and attacking the powerful state of Bijapur in 1657. Soon he had captured some 40 forts in the Western Ghats and along the coast, defeating Bijapur's best general, Afzal Khan, in 1659, by the stratagem of killing him during negotiations. He then seized more of the Konkan Coast and began to build a navy. However, Bijapur had ceded extensive territories to the Great Mughal in 1657, including the Maratha homeland Shivaji had created, and in 1660 Aurangzeb sent an army south to secure his new domains. Pune and many of the Maratha forts fell, but Shivaji maintained his freedom and his prestige (which attracted Hindu and Muslim followers alike—Shivaji distinguished between *Swarajya* or homeland and foreign-ruled *Mughlai*, but was not oppressive of Muslims) with a number of daring exploits, combining generalship and cunning. By 1665 overwhelming Mughal arms forced Shivaji into negotiations. He conceded Mughal sovereignty, but was left in possession of about one-half of his forts and still commanded a wide-ranging and proficient light cavalry force, which the Mughals were keen to use in their struggle against Bijapur. In 1666 Shivaji was summoned to the presence of the emperor in Delhi, but took insult and made his escape in another much-acclaimed escapade, which eventually led to war in 1670. Shivaji's offensive included a second sack of Surat (Gujarat), the recapture of Pune and the coast, and raids throughout the Mughal Deccan. In 1674 Shivaji began the organization of his personal fiefs and alliances into a Maratha state, now including most of western Maharashtra, by formally assuming kingship. His last campaign established the nucleus of more Maratha territory deep into the south, in the Tamil south-east, but he died of dysentery in 1680.

The 'great kingdom' was then sorely pressed as the Great Mughal brought his court and his armies south and the Marathas were weakened by succession disputes. However, the roving cavalry bands were not defeated by the loss of forts and cities; a parallel Maratha 'administration' was being introduced throughout the Deccan, exacting 'taxes' for protection; even great Mughal cities such as Hyderabad or the lands north of the Narmada were not free from raids, and the Mughals were to lose the initiative with the death of Aurangzeb in 1707. Centralization over the great Maratha warlords, meanwhile, benefited from the rise of Balaji Vishvanath. In 1714 he gained the title of Peshwa, chancellor or first minister of the realm, for securing the support of Kanhoji Angria, the admiral of the Maratha navy. He led the Marathas to intervene in the complicated and bloody politics of the Mughal court in 1718, thus extending Maratha influence into north India. Upon his death in 1721 the office of peshwa became hereditary in his family, with the accession of the talented Baji Rao I. He held together what his father had essentially ensured would be a sort of confederacy by the distribution of revenue rights among the great captains of the Maratha armies. The descendents of Shivaji were not among these new great houses, being confined to the minor principalities of Kolhapur and Satara, while the peshwas reigned from Pune. The Marathas reached Delhi by 1737 and Bengal and Orissa three years later, the mobile and unorthodox nature of their rule proving wide-ranging and difficult to counter. However, although the territory and prestige of the Maratha princes were unmatched in the mid-century, the auguries of their decline had been read. In 1757 the Maratha navy was destroyed, removing the main threat to the rising power of the British in India, and in 1761 the confederate army was defeated by Ahmad Shah Abdali of Afghanistan at Panipat (Haryana). Panipat shattered the credibility of the chancellorship, particularly when compounded by the death of the incumbent peshwa, Balaji Baji Rao, in the immediate aftermath. Succession disputes also compromised the office and allowed the intervention of the British, who had bested the French at around the same time.

The British had long been neighbours of the Marathas, but remained on the coast, founding the city of Bombay (now Mumbai) and moving the East India Company headquarters there in 1672. From there they would join the intrigues of the Maratha court in the late 18th century, provoking assistance from other parts of British India and leading to a series of wars that would end the Maratha challenge to the rise of a new empire. The only other part of modern Maharashtra not to be under Maratha rule by then was in the vestiges of the Mughal province of the Deccan. This was originally based in Aurangabad, but Nizam-ul-Mulk moved his capital to Hyderabad (now in Andhra Pradesh) to escape the constant Maratha threat. In eastern Maharashtra, grants to a branch of the Bhonslas in

Berar provided the foundation for the great Maratha principality based at Nagpur.

The administration in Bombay, wishing to consolidate its possessions, unwisely joined the disputes over the Maratha succession in the 1770s, despite the opposition of the new paramount British authority in Calcutta (now Kolkata, West Bengal). Although the Peshwa from 1774 was a child, Madhavrao Narayan, the Regency Council in Pune was led by the able Nana Phadnavis (Farnavis). His authority was helped by the conclusive defeat of a British expedition against Pune in 1779, and again in 1781, enabling him to command the support of the great Maratha houses of Holkar (based in Indore, now Madhya Pradesh) and Scindia (based in Gwalior, also in modern Madhya Pradesh). After this first war with the British the Maratha kingdoms enjoyed a period of peace and stability, although many of the great leaders died in the 1790s. In 1796 the enforced minority of Peshwa Madhavrao ended in suicide, but Nana Phadnavis maintained his stabilizing power and supervised the succession of the young son of the previous pretender as Baji Rao II. With the death of Nana Phadnavis in 1800 disaster happened to the central Maratha kingdom, with the forces of Holkar and Scindia battling for control of Pune and the young Peshwa fleeing to the British. They duly installed him on his throne, but the price of his independence from Maratha rivals was a subsidiary alliance with the Company, according to the terms of the Treaty of Bassein of 1803. Baji Rao II was restored to Pune, but over the following year the British took vast territories from the other Maratha princes, as well as assuming the 'protection' of the Mughal emperor. Moreover, British reluctance to commit to the administration of central India and Rajasthan and the weakening of the Marathas, who often now resorted to plundering, left a spreading unrest of lawlessness, fuelled by the growth of bandit, or Pindari, bands. By 1817 action had become necessary and the British began preparations for a massive military operation against the Pindaris, obliging the Maratha rajahs to give support. Suspicious of British preparedness to distinguish between Pindari raiders and Maratha forces, the princes were further alarmed at the terms of a new treaty forced on the Peshwa, whereby he renounced any claim to pre-eminence amongst the Maratha leaders. This was resented by many, but most of all by Baji Rao II, who marshalled his forces only to turn them on the British at Pune. He was, however, defeated and, in 1818, captured, deposed and exiled to Kanpur (Cawnpore, now in Uttar Pradesh). His lands were annexed to the Bombay presidency, while the Bhonsla ruler of Nagpur, who had risen in the Peshwa's support, was replaced by a minor and the truncated realm placed in subsidiary alliance with the British, who now dominated India. The story of the peshwas has one footnote to add: Baji Rao died in 1851, but his adopted son, known as Nana Sahib, was caught up in the revolt of 1857–58, to become a final focus of resistance.

Bombay was, by this time, already the largest port in western India, helped by easy access to Europe through the Suez Canal (Egypt) and the presence of a strong, local commercial tradition. Although in the midst of Maratha lands, the city was a cosmopolitan centre for both Marathi- and Gujarati-speaking people, augmented by Goans and many other Indians seeking work in its harbours and industries. Muslims, Parsis and, of course, the immigrant British were prominent in its business and administrative circles. The city soon became the commercial capital of India. A thriving urban middle class, educated according to British norms and at the centre of an imperial web connected to other, differently treated, parts of the Empire, was able to argue the wrongs of the system on the same terms as the rulers. Bombay, although its territories had largely remained loyal in the 1850s, was a source of strength and support to the Indian National Congress, which was founded here in 1885, and was destined to lead the struggle for independence. The emergence of this struggle also witnessed some precursors of modern Maharashtran politics, with the Bombay intelligentsia adopting a more accommodating tone than the radicals, who favoured more widely based, confrontational tactics and wooed the Marathi-speaking population. Thus, Bal Gangadhar Tilak popularized mass actions through his editorship of a Marathi-language newspaper, based in Pune. Indeed, he was one of the earliest proponents of the linguistic state as the basic unit of a future Indian federation. To this argument, 'regionalists' would add the search for historical and cultural identities, which speakers of Marathi easily saw in the struggles of the Maratha princes against Muslim or British rule. Moreover, particularly among a huge population easily incited to a resentment of minorities dominating the wealth and government of Bombay, this could easily take on the trappings of a militant, and nationalist, Hinduism (a form of which had certainly inspired Shivaji). Thus, as predominant Congress control ebbed after independence, a social pressure group in Bombay known as the Army of Shiv (referring either to the deity, Shiva, or to Shivaji), Shiv Sena, transformed itself into a political movement. Shiv Sena soon gained control of the metropolis and, later, of the state. The influence of this movement has certainly consolidated the solid identity of a Maharashtra state, which has finally sought to include the great metropolis of Bombay in a common Maratha heritage—notably by changing the name of the state capital to Mumbai in the 1990s.

The formation of the modern state, the integrity of which may yet be threatened by future bifurcations of a huge territory (notably to create a Vidarbha state in the east—in mid-2003 two veteran Congress politicians, N. K. P. Salve and Vasant Sathe, threatened to form a separate party in support of this), was begun by the States Reorganization Commission. In 1956 a single state was formed as the home for the speakers of two languages, Marathi and Gujarati, with its multilingual capital of Bombay also providing it with a name. The old Bombay presidency in western Maharashtra (essentially, the Konkan Coast and its hinterland between Daman and Goa), had the territories that now constitute Gujarat added, together with five districts of the former domains of the Nizam of Hyderabad, eight districts of the old Central Provinces (Berar, the lands around Nagpur) and some former princely states. Some southern districts were ceded to the new Mysore (later Karnataka) state. The logic of linguistic reorganization was completed on 1 May 1960, when Bombay state was split into Gujarat and Maharashtra, the latter retaining Bombay as its capital. Maharashtra has a directly elected Legislative Assembly, currently with 288 members, an indirectly elected or appointed upper chamber with limited powers, and sends 67 members to the national Parliament (including 48 to the Lok Sabha).

In 1995 the state gained an anti-secular, nationalist administration, formed from a coalition between the national Bharatiya Janata Party (BJP) and the Hindu-Maratha chauvinist party, Shiv Sena (a coalition in existence in the state since 1985). The leader of Shiv Sena, the controversial former political cartoonist Balashaheb (Bal) Thackeray, became Chief Minister. By the late 1990s, however, Congress was in the ascendant again, and it regained power after the 1999 state elections. The balance of power between the two principal blocs (Congress and the Nationalist Congress Party—NCP, in opposition to the BJP and Shiv Sena) was held by a number of other parties, most of which are secular and more inclined to oppose the avowedly Hindu parties. The ruling Congress coalition, under Vilasrao Deshmukh, was constantly considered to be under threat from the slightest fracture to its support in the Assembly. In June 2002 the Government narrowly survived the sudden withdrawal of support by the small Peasants' and Workers' Party (PWP), which had a dispute with the NCP. However, the five PWP legislators did not vote against the administration, when the Governor required a confidence vote to test the coalition's support in the legislature. In addition, the Speaker disqualified seven rebel deputies (the nominated member, one Janata Dal—Secular member and five NCP members) from the Assembly. This left the Democratic Front ruling coalition with support from 144 members, against the opposition's 133.

Continued instability in Congress and in the ruling coalition prompted the national Congress leadership to force the resignation of Deshmukh in January 2003. He was replaced by Sushilkumar Shinde, a dalit, who had first been a candidate for the state premiership in the early 1980s and then, most recently, in 1999. His caste and his friendly relations with the NCP were considered assets, although Congress continued to suffer some internal dissension in 2003, notably with the threatened defections of Sathe and Salve over Vidarbha (they were both taken into hospital in December after going on hunger strikes in support of their demands instead), and that of Abdul Rahman Antulay, the only Muslim ever to be premier of Maharashtra (1980–82), who threatened to join Shiv Sena. Meanwhile, the opposition continued to demand firm action over a series of bomb outrages in the state, which it attributed to Islamist terrorists. The terrorist attacks culminated in an explosion at the Gate of India, in central Mumbai, in late August, which killed at least 45 people and was the worst bombing since 1993. The loss of life was compounded only a few days later, when a stampede at the Kumbh Mela festival being held in Nashik killed another 35 people. Politically, the Government was more concerned towards the end of 2003 and into 2004 with the ramifications of an India-wide fraud scandal, which eventually extended to a senior Mumbai police officer, as well as to the deputy premier, an NCP member. This did not encourage the NCP leader, Sharad Pawar, as he debated whether to remain in coalition with Congress, although by the end of January 2004 the association seemed assured, at least for the general election of April–May. Despite such problems, and the Vidarbha issue, which was pitting western Maharashtra against the east (Congress was reluctant to decide on an issue that could help Shiv Sena, which was strongly opposed to state bifurcation, in state elections due before the end of the year), Congress won four Lok Sabha seats, taking its total to 13 (the NCP won nine, and another ally, Ramdas Athavale, of his own Republican Party of India faction, was also elected). The BJP too won 13 seats, but Shiv Sena lost three (including some prominent politicians, notably in Mumbai), to end up with 12. However, the overall share of the vote for the BJP and Shiv Sena increased slightly. The opposition bloc in July resolved that they had lost support for straying from their ideological *Hindutva* roots. The main losers in Maharashtra from the polarization of politics were the parties of the so-called 'third force' (many leftist and secular, and allied to Congress at the Centre).

Elections to the state legislature were held on 13 October 2004. The contest was closely fought, but the ruling coalition performed rather better than the general election results had indicated. Unexpectedly, however, the NCP had become the larger of the two parties, winning 71 seats to the Congress tally of 69 (a further seat was won by the Republican Party of India for the Democratic Front coalition). Shiv Sena had 62 seats, the BJP 54 and an ally another seat. Many of the 19 independents were rebels of the main parties, leaving only 11 seats for five other parties. The Democratic Front soon garnered enough additional support to be secure in forming a Government, but its actual formation was delayed while the partners discussed which party would provide the premier. Two weeks later, bolstered by leadership of the Centre, Congress had ensured that its nominee would be Chief Minister, although the NCP gained extra cabinet places and provided the deputy premier (who was R. R. Patil). Another surprising development was the return of Vilasrao Deshmukh as Chief Minister. Apart from some tensions between the main two partners in the government coalition, the most political coverage it received in the first half of 2005 originated from a ban on 'dance bars' from April (which did not initially apply to Mumbai and became the subject of court challenges, which continued into 2006) and the corruption investigations that claimed the posts of four ministers before the middle of the year. More news resulted from the tribulations of the opposition, with Shiv Sena suffering a number of defections to the NCP and to Congress. The most important loss was that of the party's leader in the legislature, Narayan Rane. At the beginning of July he expressed dissatisfaction at the executive leadership of Bal Thackeray's son, Uddhav, and announced that he would step down as a Shiv Sena leader. He was promptly sacked from the party and then entered a dispute over whether he would resign as leader of the opposition in the Assembly. Eventually, backed by only 10 other Shiv Sena deputies, he resigned, although his defection deprived Shiv Sena of enough seats to lead the opposition. Gopinath Mund of the BJP was duly appointed to the post. Meanwhile, the final act in the drama, with Rane due formally to join Congress at the end of the month, was overtaken by the advent of torrential rain in Mumbai. Record rainfall for India (944 mm of rain fell in a single day) contributed to extensive flooding in the city and along the Maharashtran coast, even severing most of Mumbai's communication links at one point. The final death toll was put at 1,493, and there was some criticism of the Government's response to the crisis.

Politics in the last months of 2005 were dominated by continued problems in the ranks of Shiv Sena. Raj Thackeray, a nephew of the party leader and a former confidante of Rane, expressed reservations about the dominance of Uddhav. An open split occurred in November, after three more Shiv Sena deputies followed Rane to Congress, while Rane himself, standing for re-election to the legislature as a Congress candidate, trounced Shiv Sena into losing its deposit. Raj complained to Bal Thackeray about Uddhav's leadership and, in December, resigned his party posts. Despite attempts to conciliate the cousins, Raj Thackeray left Shiv Sena in December, but did not follow Rane into Congress, instead founding the Maharashtra Navnirman Sena (MNS) in March 2006. Meanwhile, in January Shiv Sena had seen two more legislators follow the Rane route, while by-elections for three previous defectors were also won by Congress, finally making it the largest party in the Assembly (with 72). In February Congress won only one of the two by-elections, while a new candidate retained one of the seats for Shiv Sena, after other parties were prompted by their dislike of Rane to intervene. However, such political dramas, the February–March struggle against 'bird flu', the murder of a senior BJP leader, Pramod Mahajan, by his brother (as well as the subsequent drug scandal involving Pramod's son and the defection to Congress of another brother) and signs of tension in the ruling coalition were cast into shadow by the terrorist bombs of 11 July. A series of blasts on crowded commuter trains in Mumbai killed about 200 people and injured thousands of others. Militant Islamist groups, eventually linked to Kashmir (Lashkar-e-Taiba was certainly named), were suspected and, although Pakistan condemned the attacks, many in India suspected the country's secret service of having sponsored the perpetrators, which led to the suspension of dialogue between the two countries. In the following months the police accused Pakistan of being behind the attacks, which were allegedly carried out by members of Lashkar-e-Taiba and the Students of the Islamic Movement of India, the latter also being accused of involvement in the September bombings in Malegaon, in north-central Maharashtra. The communal tensions that eventually gained the headlines, however, were those involving dalits in the state. The brutal multiple murder of a dalit family in Kairlanji village in November, exacerbated by the failure of the established media to report the incident for some time, led to protests and outbreaks of violence across the state, but particularly around Nashik. The December desecration of a statue of Dr B. R. Ambedkar (when the 50th anniversary of his death was being commemorated) in Kanpur, Uttar Pradesh, fuelled widespread dalit protests in Maharashtra—Ambedkar, responsible for drawing up the Constitution, was a Maharashtran dalit who had converted to Buddhism. (Buddhist activity had led to publicizing of the Kairlanji killings and the religion remained a popular refuge for dalits protesting against Hindu prejudice, such as at the May 2007 mass conversion by a reported 50,000 dalits at a ceremony in Mumbai.) Congress was concerned by the alienation of the dalits, because it traditionally drew on the support of the lower castes and of Muslims, despite its leadership and that of the NCP being dominated by high-caste Marathas.

The perceived electoral punishment of the ruling parties at the civic polls in 10 municipalities on 1 February 2007 had more to do with their failure to agree an alliance in nine of the cities. The Shiv Sena-BJP alliance was also boosted by Raj Thackeray's MNS party only winning significant representation in Nashik. However, the 'saffron' alliance was under strain, as evidenced by an argument over which candidate to field in a Vidarbha by-election in October 2006; in June 2007 the BJP were enraged when Shiv Sena voted in favour of Pratibha Patil, the candidate of the Congress-led national Government, as President of India. Further tension in the opposition alliance came about in 2008, following the BJP victory in Gujarat elections and, particularly, during the political uproar occasioned by Raj Thackeray. The MNS leader provoked a crisis in the state, as well as national controversy, from early February with some dismissive remarks about people from north India. His context was the issue of immigrant labour, particularly Biharis, and he went on to advocate preference in awarding jobs for those born in Maharashtra—'sons of the soil'. The major parties, including the BJP, all condemned discrimination against fellow Indians and many also, consequently, attacked the ideology of Shiv Sena, the parent party. The opposition, however, accused the Government of a weak response to Raj Thackeray and accused Congress and the NCP of being in collusion with the MNS to split Shiv Sena support. Almost two weeks after his remarks, Raj Thackeray was arrested for incitement, but released on bail; his supporters reacted violently and there was an increase in the number of attacks on people from north India. Nashik, an MNS stronghold, saw the worst of the violence, as well as some 7,000 north Indians fleeing the area. Migrant workers were certainly unpopular in parts of the state and, in March, Bal Thackeray seemed to be trying to reclaim the initiative for Shiv Sena when he, too, criticized Biharis. Raj Thackeray also made further allegedly inflammatory speeches in May. The state Government was accused of again treating the MNS leniently and, worse, attempting to take advantage of the 'sons of the soil' controversy by introducing arguably chauvinistic new regulations requiring all commercial signs to be in Marathi. The main features of coalition politics, however, were speculation about the future of Deshmukh and his troubles with Narayan Rane. Rane criticized Deshmukh in December 2007 and again in August 2008, but the Congress leadership at the Centre did not back another candidate for the premiership. That attitude was probably helped by Pawar of the NCP, who had no fondness for Rane, continuing to support Deshmukh. Rane threatened to resign from the Government in August.

## ECONOMY

Maharashtra, despite being the second most populous state in India, is one of its wealthiest—it has the largest economy of any state in the country, while state income per head is the highest after Goa, Chandigarh, Delhi and Haryana (Maharashtra was overtaken by Haryana in the early 2000s, but then displaced the Punjab in the rankings). Maharashtra has the dynamic financial and film capital of India, Mumbai, as its own capital, as well as a diverse industrial sector and a rich agricultural sector. According to official figures, state income at current prices in 2004/05 was Rs 3,284,510m. or Rs 32,170 per head. The Government prepared for future expansion by investment in infrastructure, notably for information technology and in roads. At March 2003 the total road length in Maharashtra was 224,940 km, including 3,710 km of national highway, 33,705 km of state highway and 92,375 km of district road. At the same time there were 5,450 km of railway length, over three-quarters of it broad gauge (8% metre gauge and 14% narrow gauge). Mumbai (then called Bombay) port gained an advantage over Kolkata (Calcutta—West Bengal) after the opening of the Suez Canal (Egypt) in 1870 and became the commercial centre of the Arabian Sea; it remains India's main seaport. There are also 48 notified minor ports on the Maharashtra coast, as well as another major port at Nhava-Sheva. The main international airport is at Mumbai, which also has two domestic terminals, and there are 21 other airfields throughout the state, although three are restricted to military use and the 17 state-government facilities are not used for commercial passenger flights. In 2002/03 total electricity generation amounted to 64,740m. kWh—consumption totalled 49,945m. kWh, of which industry typically consumed some 40%, and agricultural and domestic consumption each used between one-fifth and one-quarter. In the second half of the 1990s Maharashtra accounted for about 17% of India's total electricity consumption, but for only about 13% of generation. At the end of May 2006 total installed capacity by the state was 10,189 MW, by the private sector 3,649 MW and the state's share of central projects 2,318 MW. In 2006 58% of installed capacity in the state and private sector in Maharashtra was thermally generated and 23% hydroelectricity. All but 61 infeasible villages were electrified by 2005, and 58% of rural households had a supply. The literacy rate in the state improved from 64.9% in 1991 to 74.9% in 2001, giving it the highest rate of all the major states after Kerala.

The primary sector accounted for 15.8% of state income in 2002/03 (compared with 34.4% in 1960/61), although about 55% of workers depended on agriculture and allied activities. However, soil, topography and climate do not favour agriculture in Maharashtra, which is less productive than the Indian average. The state is a major producer of oilseeds (still mainly groundnut, but increasingly soybean and sunflower) and important cash crops include cotton, sugar cane, turmeric and vegetables. The main cereal crops are rice, wheat and millet (especially jowar, otherwise known as great millet or white sorghum, of which Maharashtra habitually produces almost one-half of India's total). In 1999/2000 the jowar crop was 4.6m. metric tons (less than the normal levels during the 1990s), rice 2.6m. tons, bajra (pearl millet) 1.7m. tons and wheat 1.4m. tons (together with 2.2m. tons of pulses, total food grains were 12.7m. tons—but only 10.1m. tons in 2000/01). The same year the state produced 2.7m. tons of oilseeds, 53.1m. tons of sugar cane and 3.1m. tons of cotton, but in 2000/01 2.1m. tons, 49.6m. tons and only 1.8m. tons, respectively. Maharashtra is one of the leading cotton-producing regions of India. In 2001/02 total foodgrain production was 11.2m. tons (of which coarse grains accounted for 5.6m. tons, 16% of the all-India total, rice 2.7m. tons, wheat 1.1m. tons and pulses 1.9m. tons), 2.2m. tons of oilseeds (11% of the all-India total), 45.1m. tons of sugar cane (15%) and 2.7m. tons of cotton (27%). Total foodgrain production was 10.8m. tons in 2002/03 and fell even further, to 10.5m. tons, in 2003/04 (according to preliminary figures), while oilseeds remained at around 2.2m. tons, then rose to 2.7m. tons, in the respective years. Adverse climatic conditions restrained crop yields at the end of the 1990s and into the 2000s, while considerable investment in irrigation has not significantly increased the relatively low proportion of irrigated land. Sugar cane production was severely affected by a pest in 2003 and 2004. There is also a large horticultural sector, producing fruits and vegetables (the area under horticulture, which has a greater yield than for foodgrains, rose from 0.2m. ha in 1990/91 to 1.0m. ha by the end of 2003). Banana production peaked at 4.3m. tons in 2001/02, falling back to 3.6m. tons in the following year, but generally production in this sector increased. In 2002/03 orange production reached 0.9m. tons, grapes 0.8m. tons, mangoes 0.6m. tons and cashews 0.1m. tons, for instance. Livestock products—milk, eggs and meat—all increased slightly in 2001/02 and 2002/03 and again, according to official estimates, in 2003/04. The total livestock population in 1997 was 36.4m. head and poultry 47.3m.

Of the other primary sectors, forest industries are not an important part of the state economy—in 2003 the total forestry area was around 61,900 sq km, about one-fifth of the state's area. Fishing has more potential in Maharashtra, although inland fishing declined at the beginning of the 2000s. The total catch in 2002/03 was 514,000 metric tons (with a gross value of about Rs 13,970m.), of which the marine catch constituted some 75%. The most important extractive industry is coal mining, with coal accounting for about 92% of the value of all minerals extracted in the state in 2002/03 (a total of Rs 28,507m.). That year 31.4m. tons of coal were extracted, in addition to 1.0m. tons of bauxite, 397,000 tons of manganese ore and 8.9m. tons of limestone. Employment in the sector was recorded at 817,305 in the previous year.

The secondary sector of the economy accounted for 30.2% of state income in 1999/2000, but for 24.8% in 2002/03 (compared with 25.7% in 1960/61). Industrial growth was not a strong feature of the state economy in 1999 and the early 2000s, and the sector has a number of poorly performing state-owned enterprises, but, traditionally, industry is an important activity in Mumbai and many other parts of Maharashtra. As the chief city of British India's north-west, and the entrepreneurial and commercial capital of the Empire in the subcontinent, Mumbai developed a strong industrial base (30,000 were employed in the cotton and engineering industries alone in the 1880s), originally concentrated around the ports and railways. The sector is now more diversified, in activity and in location, with the number of registered working factories by 1999 standing at 28,678. Major areas of manufacturing activity include textiles, food products, breweries and beverages, cigarettes and tobacco, paper, printing and publishing, chemicals, petrochemicals and pharmaceuticals, machinery and electrical machinery, and light engineering generally, transport equipment, and jewellery and gems. In 2002/03 Maharashtra was responsible for 19% of India's industrial output.

The tertiary sector accounted for 59.3% of state income in 2002/03 (compared with 39.9% in 1960/61). Maharashtra generated about 15% of the whole country's services output in that year. Mumbai has been India's commercial and financial capital since the 19th century, driven by British merchants (notably after the abolition of the East India Company's monopoly on trade in 1813), local Parsis and Sephardic Jews, as well as the Hindu bania business caste. Both the national stock exchange and the central bank are based in Mumbai, which is also the headquarters of many major companies. More glamorously, the city is also the capital of the country's film industry, the 'Hollywood of India' (or 'Bollywood'), and makes some 200 films per year, making it the world's second largest producer after Hong Kong (a Special Administrative Region of the People's Republic of China). Services, such as among the newer industries involved with the rise of the internet, are also important elsewhere in the state. One of the most widespread growth sectors of service activities is tourism. Apart from Mumbai, the state is rich in historical, scenic and religious sites and could arguably warrant more than its 3.6% share of domestic tourist visits (in 2002, ranking the state fifth in India). Generally, the tertiary sector contributes powerfully to one of India's more prosperous states. Although Maharashtra's economy has a number of structural problems, a testament to its dynamism and strength is that the state still accounted for 17% of foreign direct investment in India in the 10 years since liberalization (August 1991), it sends about 35% of the country's total exports abroad, receives some 60% of its customs duties and one-third of total national income tax.

### DIRECTORY

**Governor:** S. C. Jamir, Office of the Governor, Raj Bhavan, Malabar Hills, Mumbai 400 035; tel. (22) 23632660; fax (22) 23633272; e-mail rajbhavan@maharashtra.gov.in.

**Chief Minister:** Vilasrao Deshmukh (Congress), Office of the Chief Minister, Government of Maharashtra, Mantralaya, Mumbai 400 032; tel. (22) 22025151; fax (22) 22029214; e-mail chiefminister@maharashtra.gov.in.

**Speaker of the Legislative Assembly (Vidhan Sabha):** Babesaheb Kupekar, Legislature Secretariat, Vidhan Bhavan, Mumbai 400 032; tel. (22) 22023101; fax (22) 22024524; the lower house of the bicameral legislature is the Legislative Assembly, which has 287 elected mems (and one nominated mem.): Congress 73; Nationalist Congress Party 71; Shiv Sena 58; Bharatiya Janata Party 54; Communist (CPI—M) 2; independents and others 29.

**Chairman of the Legislative Council (Vidhan Parishad):** Shivajirao Deshmukh, Legislature Secretariat, Vidhan Bhavan, Mumbai 400 032; tel. (22) 22027373; fax (22) 22024524; the upper house of the bicameral legislature is the Legislative Council, which has 78 mems.

**State Special Commissioner and Principal Secretary in New Delhi:** B. S. Meena, Maharashtra Sadan, nr Mandi House, Copernicus Marg, New Delhi 100 001; tel. (11) 23388075; fax (11) 23782804; e-mail maharashtrasadan@vsnl.com; internet www.maharashtrasadan.com.

## Manipur

The State of Manipur, the 'jewelled land', is part of India's north-eastern region. It lies astride a mountainous extension of the Himalayas, with the Naga Hills curving in from the north-east and the Letha range in upper Myanmar (formerly Burma) continuing south. The international frontier with Myanmar lies to the east and to the south of the state, while the neighbouring Indian states are Mizoram to the south-west, Assam to the west and Nagaland in the north-west and north. A princely state until its incorporation into India on 15 October 1949, Manipur was designated a territory before becoming a full state of the Union on 21 January 1972. It has an area of 22,327 sq km (13,865 sq miles).

The broad, alluvial, low-lying basin of central Manipur is cupped by surrounding highlands, which are higher in the north and east. In the south-west, the land falls away to the Cachar plain of Assam, while beyond the eastern hills of the Manipur plateau are the lowlands of Myanmar's Chindwin valley. A Chindwin tributary, the Manipur, drains southwards from the Logtak lake (one of the largest freshwater lakes in India, which varies seasonally in extent from 60 sq km to 260 sq km). Apart from the Barak, which rises in the state and skirts its north-western and western borders, the other main rivers are the Imphal, the Iril, the Thoubal, the Irnag and the Nambol. The state capital, Imphal, lies in the Manipur valley at an altitude of 785 m (2,576 ft), while the surrounding hills average about 2,000 m, but can rise to over 2,590 m in the Siroi Hills. The terrain is less rugged than in many of the mountain states of the north-east, which is why Manipur was a favoured route for invasions from South-East Asia into India (most recently in the Second World War), but it is clad in often thick jungle. The rich and varied flora includes the unique 'paradise flower', the terrestrial Siroi lily (*lilium Macklinae*). Rainfall averages between 2,600 mm (98 inches) and 3,350 mm, and the climate is mild.

The national census of 1 March 2001 put the population of Manipur at 2,166,788 (excluding three sub-divisions of Senapati District), giving a population density of 97 per sq km. For 1991 the total figure was 1,837,149, which gives the state a rate of population growth over the decade rather higher than the national average. The population of Manipur is primarily of southern Mongoloid stock, but is divided between the 10 clans (together known as the salai) of the majority Meitei tribe, who generally live in the Manipur valley, and the main hill tribes of Naga (about 25% of the population) and Kuki (some 15%) peoples. The official language of the state is Manipuri (evolved from Meitei Lon, which has its own script), which was also recognized as one of the official languages of India in 1992, the only Tibeto-Burmese tongue spoken in the country to achieve such a distinction. The Meitei are a Hindu people, and in 1991, of the total population of the state, 57.7% so declared their adherence. At the 2001 census, however, only 46.0% declared themselves Hindu, although the separate classification of belief systems formerly included with Hinduism may have overemphasized the decline (for example, Sanamahism is a local synthesis of Hindu and older Meitei beliefs). With many among the hill tribes having been converted to Christianity from the 19th century onwards, this remained the second largest religion in Manipur (34.0% in 2001—almost exactly the same percentage as in 1991). There is also a Muslim community (8.8%) and small numbers of Buddhists, Sikhs and Jains, with other religions claiming a high 10.9% (see above, on Hindus). Only 2.8% of the 2001 population were from the Scheduled Castes, but 34.2% were of the Scheduled Tribes (among which the Meitei are not counted).

The population is mainly rural, but 26.6% were classed as urban in 2001. Moreover, although the valley area constitutes only about 12% of the total land area, some 75% of the population are reckoned to live here in the heart of Manipur. Imphal, the capital and main town, is situated in the centre of the state, in the Manipur valley. Other major towns are Bishnupur, Moirang, Thoubal, Nambol, Ukhrul and the border trading town of Moreh. The state is divided into nine districts, four in the valley and five, larger, hill districts. Manipur also has six autonomous district councils.

## HISTORY

Manipur is sometimes identified with the land of the Gandharvas, the Mekholy of Vedic literature, but its history is clearer from AD 33, when a freebooting Indian prince, Pakhangba, ascended the throne of one of the seven realms and united the Metei under the Ningthouja clan. The venerable tale of the Manipuri dynasty is recorded in the oral histories, the *Cheitharol Kumbaba*, of the royal house. The kingdom was frequently independent and stable, and sometimes powerful (notably under Ningthou Hanba, Khagemba, 1597–1652), over nearly 2,000 years, but tended to be prone to incursions from Burma (now Myanmar) rather than India, despite the Aryanization of its religion (completed by the 18th century). Indeed, it was to counter a threat from Burma that Manipur first invoked the aid of the British in India, in 1762. With Assam falling increasingly under the sway of the Bengal presidency from its cession in 1826, Manipur's independence was fatally compromised. British intervention in a succession dispute and the crushing of the Meitei resistance, led by Maj.-Gen. Paona Brajabashi, at the battle of Khongjam in 1891, meant that Manipur was declared a protectorate of the Indian Empire in that year. A social upheaval led by women occurred in 1939, while the Japanese, invading from Burma during the Second World War, largely occupied the princely state in 1944. Indeed, it was at Moriang that the anti-British 'Indian National Army' raised its standard in the same year, only for the last great land battle between the Japanese and the Allied forces shortly thereafter, also in Manipur, ended hopes of such an adventure achieving independence.

When Indian independence did come, in August 1947, the sovereignty of princely states such as Manipur was doomed. The Maharajah, Bodh Chandra Singh, signed the Instruments of Accession to India at that time, only then to sign away his throne in the Merger Agreement of 21 September 1949. Manipur became a dependent territory of the Indian Union (a so-called 'Part C' state under the 1950 Constitution) on 15 October 1949, with an administration responsible to the Governor of Assam. An advisory form of government was introduced in 1950–51. In 1957 Manipur became the direct responsibility of the Centre—it was now styled a Union Territory, with a largely elected Territorial Council. In 1963 a Legislative Assembly was established. The administrator, the Chief Commissioner, was styled a Lieutenant-Governor in 1969, and Manipur gained statehood and full membership of the federation on 21 January 1972. This was achieved against a background of considerable unrest and in a bid to placate separatist sentiments. However, often-violent ambitions for independence continued to be demonstrated, and the state also experienced a rising degree of inter-communal disturbance.

Manipur was also the victim of a fractured and fractious party political system. Shifting personal allegiances among the state's politicians, punctuated by periods of central President's Rule, meant that there were 24 chief ministerships and seven Legislative Assemblies between 1972 and 2001. The dissolution of the system after the state elections of January 1998 was a case in point. E. Nipamacha Singh headed a Manipur State Congress Party (MSCP) administration from then until three years later. The desertion of 10 deputies under Thounaojam Chaoba to join the Samata Party (itself in a national coalition supporting the federal ruling party, the Bharatiya Janata Party—BJP), followed by further defections, forced Nipamacha to resign in February 2001. He initially formed a coalition with Radhabinod Koijam of Samata as Chief Minister, only for the new premier to abandon Nipamacha's Congress faction (which later formed the Manipur People's Conference, upon Chaoba's faction gaining recognition as the MSCP) in favour of the support of a People's Front of six parties. The new administration prioritized corruption, law and order, the economy and the state's crumbling finances, with a Government of 33 ministers. By March the People's Front was disintegrating, with the state BJP defying the federal party's instruction to keep supporting the Government. There was even a dispute over the most suitable candidate to be the next premier. On 2 June President's Rule was imposed. The Assembly was finally dissolved in September and new elections announced for the following February. Particularly given the unrest earlier in the year (see below), it was not surprising that many of the established politicians were defeated at the polls; no party won an overall majority. The state branch of the national Congress became the largest single party (initially with 20 seats), electing as its leader in the legislature Okram Ibobi Singh, who became Chief Minister at the beginning of March 2002. He led a coalition Government of the Secular Progressive Front, which not only included Congress, but also the MSCP, the Communist Party of India (CPI) and the Nationalist Congress Party (NCP), with support from the Manipur National Conference member (the latter was treated as an independent, because his party had not yet been officially recognized). Congress was strengthened by the realignment of a number of legislators into the ruling party, while the MSCP suffered from fractures that sent one faction (including Chaoba) into the BJP towards the end of 2002.

That such manoeuvres had been unpopular, as well as irrelevant to the main concern of the Meitei majority, was dramatically demonstrated in the civil strife of 2001. At a meeting in March in Bangkok (Thailand) between representatives of the central Government and a faction of Nagaland's 'underground' armed-resistance group, the National Socialist Council of Nagalim (NSCN), it had been agreed to extend a cease-fire in force in Nagaland since 1997 to Naga areas in other states. People in Manipur and Assam, particularly, perceived this as a threat to the territorial integrity of their own states, despite assurances to the contrary by the federal Government. As local politicians argued about the spoils of office, popular opposition to the so-called Bangkok Agreement gathered strength, culminating in riots in Imphal on 18 June 2001. The Assembly buildings, the Chief Minister's offices and the Speaker's house were all set alight, and other politicians' homes were attacked. The state deputies threatened the national Government with a mass resignation and, amid continuing unrest throughout the north-eastern region, the proposal of a cease-fire extension was retracted. Trouble continued after the state elections, with the ongoing negotiations between the Centre and the NSCN remaining a constant source of anxiety in Manipur. Any ambivalence in assurances by the authorities that Manipur would not suffer any territorial loss caused popular and political reactions in the state. There was also increasing anxiety about the levels of violence engendered by such concerns, with the Chief Minister himself barely escaping with his life in July 2003, after being ambushed by militants some 35 km outside Imphal (two security personnel were killed).

The widespread opposition to the Bangkok Agreement marked a new deterioration in Meitei–Naga relations within Manipur. The closely concentrated majority population of the valley feared the territorial claims of the low-density populations of the hill districts. The Nagas claimed to be in a local majority in almost 70% of Manipur and that they had never acknowledged the maharajahs, let alone the sovereignty of India. The rejection of the cease-fire extension, therefore, provoked unrest among the Nagas, especially in their stronghold in the northern Senapati District, and condemnation both by the NSCN and by Manipur's own Naga umbrella group, the United Naga Council. Moreover, it complicated the sympathies of the Meitei insurgency groups (which had united in a Manipur People's Liberation Front in 1999), who had been engaged in armed action in favour of independence for many years. The earliest militant separatist group had been the United National Liberation Front, founded in 1964. This had been followed by a People's Revolutionary Party of Kangleipak and the People's Liberation Army in the late 1970s, for instance. In 1980 a Kangleipak Communist Party took up arms. Then, the formation of the Kuki National Front in 1988 and the Kuki National Army in 1991 (the latter being the armed wing of the Kuki National Organization—KNO, founded in the previous year) witnessed the late arrival of armed militancy to the third largest ethnic group in the state. Indeed, this last factor contributed to the peak of Naga–Kuki inter-communal violence in 1993. Further violence against the Kuki, allegedly perpetrated by the NSCN, recurred in

1996, making this tribe particularly nervous in the early 2000s over proposals for a 'Greater Nagaland' that would include Kuki territory (such fears probably impelled the KNO to seek parallel negotiations with the Centre in May 2003). Whatever their persuasion, however, the various terrorist groups seemed to be as fractured as the parties of the democratic politicians. Other banned groups included the Kanglei Yawol Kann Lup and the Revolutionary People's Front.

The state Legislative Assembly has 60 seats in total, 19 reserved for the Scheduled Tribes and one for the Scheduled Castes. There was a threat to the cohesion of Congress, which led the Government, in late 2003, with three ministers being dismissed for disloyalty, but Ibobi remained Chief Minister into 2004. He was supported by 35 Assembly members. Congress won one of the two Lok Sabha seats for Manipur in the May general election (leaving the BJP leader and sitting member, Chaoba, in fourth place), but both Congress and the BJP had operated under threat from various militant groups. The influence of these militants even provoked Chaoba (formerly an MSCP and a Samata member) to beg forgiveness from the group threatening him in February. It was unclear whether the militant threat or personal or party unpopularity contributed more to Chaoba's electoral defeat. (The Congress candidate in Outer Manipur had been disqualified before the election, and the constituency anyway was won by an independent.) Such uncertain conditions in the state had given the armed forces considerable authority in parts of Manipur, and it was the alleged abuses and excesses of the military, notably the Assam Rifles, that was increasingly the focus of controversy. The special powers of the military were an issue in the general election campaign, but also provoked widespread unrest, including some violent civil demonstrations in the capital, in July. A number of mysterious deaths in custody had caused protests since February, but the catalyst for violence was the arrest of a woman alleged to be a member of the banned People's Liberation Army, Thangjam Manorama Devi. Some hours later her abused body was found in a nearby village. Women's groups were prominent in the ensuing disturbances (which included a 'naked protest'), but disquiet at the provisions of emergency legislation was expressed by many different political opinions.

Opposition to the Armed Forces (Special Powers) Act 1958, which had been in force in Manipur from 1980, escalated throughout the rest of July 2004 and into August, resulting in some violent protests and a number of *bandhs* or strikes. Although the state Government suspended the provisions of the legislation in the seven Assembly segments of the Imphal municipal area on 12 August, demands for the complete repeal of the Act by the federal authorities continued. The death of a student leader after his attempted self-immolation in protest at the Act increased the resolve of the agitators. Government action against the Apunba Lup 'umbrella' group of 32 protesting civil organizations failed to hinder a general strike and further protests. The alleged failure of the Assam Rifles to co-operate with an investigation into the Manorama Devi case further fuelled popular demonstrations. The Chief Minister continued to condemn the unrest, but at the end of August conceded that his Government also favoured the full repeal of the emergency legislation. The Centre, which had appointed a new governor at the beginning of the month and suggested that the Assam Rifles might be removed from the state (but subsequently contradicted the offer), now announced that the Union Minister of Home Affairs would visit Manipur in the following week. Failure to calm the situation in September and October obliged the Union Government to intervene. Finally, after meetings in New Delhi in early November, the Government conceded that a review of the legislation should be conducted, although both the central and state authorities continued to point out that insurgencies and violent criminality persisted, maintaining the conditions that required a special security regime in Manipur and elsewhere in the north-east.

On 20 November 2004 the Prime Minister, Manmohan Singh, arrived on a visit to Manipur. He emphasized the review of the emergency legislation that had been agreed at meetings in the national capital earlier in the month, confirming that a more 'humane' law should be introduced instead. The Prime Minister invited insurgent groups to conduct peaceful negotiations with the Government. Only in the next month, however, the validity of government anxieties was demonstrated by the abduction of two academics and the ambush and murder of some policemen, both incidents the acts of insurgent groups. Such actions, as well as civil disobedience or strikes in favour of militant demands (sometimes enforced by the threat of violence), are compounded by protests against the Government's failure to protect against militant violence.

Further complications come from Naga activism in favour of union with Nagaland. Public fears regarding the partition of the state to satisfy Naga demands undoubtedly added tension to the protests over the emergency legislation. In June 2005 Naga militants imposed an economic blockade on Manipur that lasted into August. Physical damage to transport infrastructure by insurgents consolidated the state's isolation. There was soon a fuel shortage and, although the army was deployed to allow some traffic into Imphal, renewed criticism of the central Government's inactivity in the north-east, as well as concern about rebel demands in peace negotiations for the union of all Naga areas into one political entity (in July a former premier of Manipur, Rishang Keishing, was revealed to have written to the Prime Minister in support of this). With seven major, active insurgent groups, however, the prospect of any straightforward settlement between the factions, let alone with the state or national authorities, seemed distant. In October the Centre suspended military operations against eight, mostly minor, groups that had expressed support for a peace process, but violence continued sporadically.

At the national level Manipur is also represented by one member of the upper house of Parliament, the Rajya Sabha. With only two Lok Sabha members, and an insurgency that does not threaten foreign involvement, this may contribute towards Manipur's failure to attract much attention from the centre, although the prospect of state elections prompted the Prime Minister in December 2006 to promise investment and to repeat promises of reform of emergency legislation along the lines recommended by the 2005 committee under Justice B. P. Jeevan Reddy. The Chief Minister then granted Muslims in the state a 4% job quota and pledged to review the controversial case of the Tipaimukh dam. However, with continuing insurgent activity and high levels of violent crime (including attacks on the homes of the Chief Minister, the Speaker and the agriculture minister between September 2006 and January 2007), the Government felt unable to match opposition parties' rhetoric against the Armed Forces (Special Powers) Act. Yet Chief Minister Ibobi was the first state premier of Manipur to survive an entire term in power and this promised stability to the electors, which was particularly appealing against a background of bloody unrest (over 400 incidents since the previous state elections), the high number of strikes, demonstrations and blockades during Congress's latest tenure in office and the perceived threat to the very integrity of the state borders posed by Naga claims. In support of those claims, a body called the United Naga Council urged candidates in Naga-dominated constituencies not to stand for political parties, but as independents favouring the union of Naga territories. A number of legislature members from Naga constituencies resigned their seats in advance of the official dissolution of the Assembly, led by two deputies from the Federal Party of Manipur, then the two BJP members and even a Congress deputy. This contributed to the high number of independents elected in the February 2007 elections (10). The main beneficiary of the poll, held in three phases, was Congress, which won in 30 constituencies. With the support of the four members elected for the CPI (led by Ph. Parjint Singh) and the three for the Rashtriya Janata Dal (led by Helaludin Khan), Okram Ibobi Singh returned as Chief Minister. The Government remained a coalition even after Congress won two by-elections in June, retaining one seat and gaining another from the NCP. The latter party thus had its representation in the Assembly reduced from five seats to four, making the Manipur People's Party, with five deputies, the main legislative opposition; the National People's Party had three seats. Congress won the seats despite the Government's May extension of emergency provisions in affected areas for a further six months. Nevertheless, the state continued to be afflicted by insurgency violence, with the Deputy Speaker escaping an attempt on his life in November and a fatality-free attack on the Assembly compound itself in March 2008, followed by the murder of 14 Hindi-speakers in Imphal within two days, for example.

## ECONOMY

Manipur is not a wealthy state, and is in a poor fiscal position, but, despite political and tribal unrest, made some progress in developing irrigation projects and industrialization in the last two decades of the 20th century. Between 1981 and 1997 the net domestic product grew at an annual compound rate of 4.7%, in real terms, although these figures conceal a deterioration relative to the rest of India from about 1990. Real growth in 1997/98 was 9.5%, followed by 5.9% in the succeeding year and 5.6% in both 1999/2000 and 2000/01. By 2004/05, in current prices, net domestic product had reached a total of Rs 36,800m. or Rs 14,901 per head (making it the poorest of the hill states of the north-east, but better off than Assam). What industry Manipur has developed is largely based in the valley, particularly in and around Imphal. Infrastructure is relatively poorly developed, but the road system includes an important link with Myanmar (at Moreh), which ultimately leads back to the transport hub of Dimapur (Nagaland). At March 1999 there were 7,367 km of roads, including only 434 km of national highway, and 1,232 km of state highway and 1,946 km of district roads. Since 1990 Manipur has been linked to the national railway network, through the railhead at Jiribam, near the Assam border. The only airport is a domestic one near Imphal. At the end of May 2006 the installed electricity capacity totalled 157.9 MW (68% from a share in central projects, the rest in the state sector). One year earlier the programme of rural electrification had achieved a connection rate of over 94% of villages (42% of rural households received electricity). The state possessed important hydroelectric potential, some of which had been developed. The literacy rate in Manipur improved from 59.9% in 1991 to 68.9% in 2001.

With agriculture providing the livelihood of most of the rural population (three-quarters of all workers), as well as the underpinnings of the state economy, the progress achieved in the implementation of irrigation projects since the mid-1980s and the ongoing training of skilled personnel was significant. Just under 10% of the state's area is cultivated, with just over one-half of that confined to the central valley, where most of the population live. Wet cultivation had long been usual in the valley area, but the hill peoples still tend to rely on traditional, shifting cultivation methods that involve clearing jungle for planting every few years (*jhum*). The main crops were rice and other foods, while cash crops being encouraged were tea, coffee, rubber, fruits, tree nuts and spices. In 2001/02 Manipur recorded a harvest of 400,500 metric tons of food grains (98% of which was rice), second only to record production of 488,700 tons in 1994/95. Sericulture also received state support. Animal husbandry is important locally, and the state produced 69,000 tons of milk and 73.5m. eggs in 2002/03. The state has large forested areas (78.6% in 1996), which are important not only for timber but also for the profusion of orchids and a number of rare lilies. Agriculture contributed 32.5% of the total value of the net domestic product in 1996/97, with forestry at 3.1% and fishing at 2.6%. Agriculture's share in gross state domestic product was 20.9% in 2001/02.

The growth of industry has been helped by a basis in agricultural processing and the development of hydroelectric power. Mineral resources are few, with 700 or so workers mainly involved in the extraction of limestone for the construction industry—producing minerals worth Rs 2.4m. in 2002/03. The state has a relatively high proportion of the working population in industry (8.1% in 1991), with the greater number based at home. Crafts and handicrafts (notably weaving) are an important manufacturing activity, although government initiatives have also encouraged the growth of small-scale electronics enterprises, to complement a larger, state-owned business. In addition, the federal authorities have based the Centre for Electronics Design and Technology and the Central Institute of Plastics Engineering and Technology in Imphal to help the development of these fields in the state. There are spinning mills, a cement plant, pharmaceuticals, agro-processing and forest-related industries, bricks and bicycle manufacturing, and steel re-rolling active in Manipur. The total contribution of industry (notably construction, which accounts for the variability in the size of the secondary sector) to net domestic product was 10.2% in 1996/97, but would have been greater but for the deficit in utilities.

In 1991 over 21% of the working population were engaged in services. In 1996/97 tertiary activities contributed 51.6% of the net domestic product of the state. Transport, storage and trading activities were important, particularly owing to the easy access to Myanmar—transport, storage, communications, and trade, restaurants and hotels provided 8.0% of the overall total (border trade has been officially encouraged since the 1995 agreement between India and Myanmar). However, both property and business services, and government services provided just over 14% each of net domestic product, which was not a particularly healthy indicator. Tourism has some potential, although civil unrest has been unhelpful and visitors still need permits. Of the 104,000 tourist visits in 2000/01, only 409 were foreigners, but the numbers were increasing. The arts and culture of this formerly princely state are rich, with Manipur famed for its textiles, its dances, and its martial arts and games (the state claims that modern polo was derived from its own horseback game of sagol kangjei, which uses a goat carcass instead of a ball). The natural environment provides a number of attractions to visitors, particularly the world's only 'floating' national park, at Keibul Lamjao on Loktak, where floating 'islands' of vegetation (*phumdi*) feed the sangai, the 'dancing', brow-antlered Elds' deer (the most endangered cervid in the world).

### DIRECTORY

**Governor:** Gurbachan Jagat, Raj Bhavan, Imphal 795 001; tel. (385) 2221444; fax (385) 2221333; e-mail govmani@hub.nic.in.

**Chief Minister:** Okram Ibobi Singh (Congress), Office of the Chief Minister, Government of Manipur, Chief Minister's Secretariat, Imphal 795 001; tel. (385) 2220137; fax (385) 2221398; e-mail cmmani@hub.nic.in.

**Speaker of the Legislative Assembly:** Dr Maniruddin Shaikh (Congress), Assembly Secretariat, Imphal 795 001; tel. (385) 2220239; fax (385) 2220650; e-mail man_speaker@hub.nic.in; internet www.manipurassembly.nic.in; the unicameral Legislative Assembly has 60 mems: Congress 30; Manipur People's Party 5; Nationalist Congress Party 5; Communist Party of India 4; National People's Party 3; Rashtriya Janata Dal 3, independents 10.

**Special Resident Commissioner in New Delhi:** C. R. Chhibber, Manipur Bhavan, 2 Sardar Patel Marg, New Delhi 110 021; tel. (11) 26873009; fax (11) 26111803; e-mail rescm-mn@hub.nic.in; internet www.manipurbhavan.nic.in.

# Meghalaya

The State of Meghalaya occupies the Shillong plateau in the north-eastern region of India. The 'abode of the clouds' rises steeply from the international border with Bangladesh, which runs along the state's southern length. Bangladesh also lies to the west, but there begins the long border with Assam (Asom), above the Brahmaputra lowlands to the north and the Barak valley and Cachar (Kachari) Hills to the east. Meghalaya was formed as an autonomous state within Assam on 2 April 1970, but became a separate state of the Union on 21 January 1972. It has an area of 22,429 sq km (8,660 sq miles).

Lofty Meghalaya comprises the Garo Hills in the west, the central Khasi Hills and the Jaintia Hills, which bulge the state out towards the south-east. The compact, isolated plateau, which defines Meghalaya, is formed of the same ancient granites found in peninsular India. The rolling hills rise to their highest point at Shillong Peak (1,963 m—6,443 ft), although the town itself is at some 1,500 m above sea level. The elevation gives the state a cool and wet climate, while the landscape, with its pine-clad hills, its caverns, waterfalls and lakes has attracted Meghalaya the sobriquet of the 'Scotland of the East'. However, it is prone to severe earthquakes and is actually one of the wettest places on the planet, as the warm monsoon winds between May and September are forced over the plateau. The southern towns of Mawsynram and Cherrapunji (Sohra), in the Khasi Hills, vie for the title of the wettest place in the world: the latter once recorded rainfall of 23,000 mm (906 inches) in one year (a record recently exceeded in Mawsynram), while its average annual rainfall over a 74-year period is 11,430 mm. The average annual rainfall in Shillong, only some 80 km from Cherrapunji, is modest by comparison, at some 2,340 mm. This volume of precipitation, drained into the surrounding lowlands by rivers such as the Umiam, the Jadukata, the Khri, the Simsang, the Kynshi and the Kupli, falls onto a still well forested countryside, rich in wildlife (according to the elephant census of 1993, the state boasts the highest population density of pachyderms per square kilometre in India, counting 2,872 elephants in that year). In general, the climate is mild, with mean temperatures in Shillong in August at 21.1°C (70.0°F) and in January at 9.5°C (49.1°F).

At the census of 1 March 2001 the total population of Meghalaya was 2,318,822, giving a population density of 103 per sq km. The state had experienced a growth rate noticeably higher than the national average since the previous census in 1991, when the total population was 1,774,778. Most of the people belong to the three tribes for whom the hill state was created: the Mongoloid Garo (Achiks), an animist, Bodo people originally from Tibet; the supposedly Austro-Asiatic Khasi; and the Mongoloid Jaintia, who are related to the Shan of Myanmar (Burma). All have distinct cultures and histories, though they share some customs, such as matrilineal succession. In 2001 85.9% of the population were counted among the Scheduled Tribes. The main languages are Khasi and Garo, which are joined by Jaintia and English as official languages of the state. Christianity has been widespread among the hill peoples since the advent of missionaries in the 19th century (indeed, the 2001 census records 70% of the population as Christian), but, traditionally, they are animists worshipping elemental deities. There is a small Muslim community (4%) and 13% of the population were recorded as Hindus at the 2001 census, although others adhere to related traditions.

Most of the population live in rural villages. The urban population was put at 19.6% of the total in 2001, with Shillong, the state capital, as the only town of any size (until the division of the state in 1972, Shillong was the capital of Assam). The main town in the west, in the Garo Hills, is Tura, while the Jaintia headquarters is in Jowai. Near the border with Bangladesh is the old Khasi capital of Cherrapunji. Meghalaya is now divided into seven districts.

### HISTORY

The Garo, Jaintia and Khasi peoples have been largely undisturbed from their hilltop fastnesses for many centuries. Although variously influenced or nominally subject to surrounding powers in Bengal and Assam, the lack of penetration by Hinduism or Islam attests to the hill tribes' usual independence. The relatively widespread adoption of Christianity from the 19th century coincides with formal annexation by the British in India. Until the imperial authorities moved to consolidate their hold on Assam and the north-east region generally, the independence of the Garo, Khasi and Jaintia kings had been tolerated. The Ahoms had brought the Jaintia into the kingdom of Assam at the beginning of the 18th century, but the decay of royal power meant this sovereignty was short-lived. In 1824 the threat of Burmese invasion prompted the king of the Jaintia to seek British protection and other chiefs permitted the passage of British troops through the Khasi Hills. During the establishment of British authority in Assam between 1826 and 1838, a permanent road (completed in 1829) was considered necessary through Khasi lands, while the Jaintia Hills were also annexed as part of Assam in 1835 (itself under the Bengal presidency). The Garo kingdom became a district of Assam in 1869, while in 1874, when Assam was formally separated from the jurisdiction of Bengal, Shillong, in the Khasi Hills, actually became the provincial capital (it remained the capital of Assam until the division of the state in 1972). In 1905 Assam was merged into East Bengal. That experiment ended in 1912, but Assam (then the entire modern north-eastern region of India) remained part of a reunited Bengal until 1919, when it again received provincial status. Eastern Bengal and neighbouring Muslim enclaves became part of Pakistan (East Pakistan—renamed Bangladesh upon its own subsequent achievement of independence) in 1947, while the hill districts of the Garo, Khasi and Jaintia were part of the new India. This final process of partition left some border questions unresolved, although friendly relations between Bangladesh and India did not normally mean this was a problem for Meghalaya (on the southern fringe of which was a debatable 6.5-km stretch of frontier). However, in April 2001 Bangladeshi troops occupied a border post and some of the disputed territory in a clash that left 19 soldiers dead. By June the two national Governments were meeting to resolve the dispute and to discuss the exchange of a number of anomalous enclaves. Meanwhile, in 2004 about 195 km of the 423-km border with Bangladesh were fenced, although this left a considerable stretch permeable to infiltration by insurgents. Particularly with many militants being driven from Bhutan from late 2003, the Indian Government was anxious to stop them re-establishing bases to the south (the militants were also using the Garo Hills as a transit point). Bangladesh denied that its territory was being used for bases of the armed activists, usually operating against targets in Tripura and Assam, but also in Meghalaya (in November 2005 the Indian Border Security Force claimed that there were 192 militant bases in Bangladesh, which was slightly down). With more than 10,000 Bangladeshi nationals discovered in Meghalaya illegally during 1995–2005, the authorities were eager to erect a fence along the frontier, which was to be completed before the end of the decade.

After independence, the hill districts of modern Meghalaya received some autonomy within the state of Assam, but the people remained dissatisfied. Discontent was particularly provoked by the introduction of Assamese as the state language, and the Garo, Jaintia and Khasi were united in their demands upon the federal authorities. In 1970 the hill districts were combined into an autonomous state, Meghalaya, within Assam, and this entity achieved full statehood in January 1972. There were, however, continuing political and insurgent demands for other arrangements in Meghalaya, such as for a 'greater Garoland' (urged by the militant Achik National Volunteers' Council, for example) or for separate Garo and Khasi-Pnar states (as suggested in 2006 by two political parties, the Garo National Council and the Hill State People's Democratic Party—HSPDP, the latter a member of the ruling coalition).

Government of the state usually depends on a coalition of parties in the Legislative Assembly, with no single party ever having a majority. There are 29 members elected from the Khasi Hills districts, 24 from the Garo Hills and seven from the Jaintia Hills. In November–December 2001 Flinder Anderson Khonglam displaced E. K. Mawlong as Chief Minister, making him the sixth person to hold the post since the legislative elections in 1997. Khonglam also earned the distinction of becoming the first independent member of a state legislature in the country to become a chief minister. Moreover, it was claimed that 59 of the 60 members of the Legislative Assembly were former ministers. The fragmented nature of the state legislature was in marked contrast to Meghalaya's consistent (from 1980) election of Congress representatives to the national Parliament, one to the upper house and two to the lower house, although the veteran Congress member, P. A. Sangma (first elected in 1977 and Speaker of the Lok Sabha in 1996–98), was one of the founder members of the Nationalist Congress Party (NCP), for which he retained his seat in 1999. The Rajya Sabha member also joined the NCP.

State elections were held at the end of February 2003, and the Congress-led Meghalaya Democratic Alliance formed a Government at the beginning of March. The Congress leader, D. Dethwelson Lapang, whose party had gained 22 of the 60 seats, became Chief Minister with the support of the United Democratic Party (UDP)'s nine legislators, the Meghalaya Democratic Party's four, the Khun Hynniewtrep National Awakening Movement (KHNAM)'s two and three independents. The former premier, Khonglam, now leader of the HSPDP, which had retained two seats, also offered his support. Stability was the main inducement offered by all the parties, but that Congress was most convincing in its claims was demonstrated by it being the only party to increase its number of seats. The main opposition party was the NCP, with 14 seats, supported by the Bharatiya Janata Party with two. Then, towards the end of 2003, the NCP began to fracture. In December six NCP legislators formed the Meghalaya Nationalist Congress Party and joined the coalition in power (bringing Government support to 49 of the 60 deputies), and also indicated that they would merge with the ruling Congress group. Sangma, who had already indicated that the NCP leadership nationally was split, was resolved to remain opposed to Congress, but was denied the use of the NCP symbols in the April 2004 general election. Just before the poll, therefore, he joined Mamata Banerjee's Trinamool Congress, which was strong in West Bengal, but had no presence traditionally in the north-east. This probably cost Sangma some support, but he was nevertheless re-elected to the Lok Sabha, representing the Nationalist (officially still All India) Trinamool Congress. The national Congress that formed the new Government retained the other seat in Meghalaya. In the Assembly the 'rump' NCP remained under the influence of Sangma; he formally rejoined the party in December 2005, resigning his seat and duly regaining it at a by-election in February 2006 as an NCP candidate.

A Congress Government at the Centre was a help to the state administration. However, in June 2005 there was a concerted and self-imposed attempt to limit media coverage of Chief Minister Lapang and his home affairs minister, following government action against, and alleged harassment of, journalists reporting on some communal tensions. More seriously, Lapang began to lose the confidence of his colleagues. In early June 2006 J. D. Rymbai, the legislative affairs minister, led a boycott by 17 deputies of a meeting of the Congress group in the Assembly, leaving the Chief Minister with the support of only 11 deputies. The dissidents contacted the national party and demanded a change in leadership in the state. Lapang resigned and, on 15 June, Rymbai replaced him as premier of the state Government, still with the support of the coalition partners. Nevertheless, Lapang and his loyalists continued to lobby the central leadership for his reinstatement. Finally, in January the national Congress leadership ordered a secret ballot of the Meghalaya legislators in order to help decide between Rymbai and Lapang. The results of the ballot were never published, but at the end of February Rymbai was asked to resign as Chief Minister. He refused, demanding confirmation from Sonia Gandhi herself, which was duly given in the first week of March. Rymbai continued to claim the support of 15 of the 29 Congress deputies and was emboldened to continue his defiance by the support of the coalition partners. However, the national leadership insisted on its authority and Rymbai resigned on 10 March. Lapang returned as Chief Minister

The disgruntled Congress veteran, Rymbai, joined the UDP, closely followed by two deputies from another Congress ally, the Meghalaya Democratic Party. The UDP and the remaining coalition allies of Congress, as well as the opposition, were not happy with the six power projects agreed by the state Government with private companies. Congress was punished for this neglect of its allies in the aftermath of the state elections on 3 March 2008. Although the ruling party was returned with an increased number of seats (25) and remained the largest single party in the Assembly, the assumption that it would continue in power with the support of its coalition partners was dramatically overturned when an alternative coalition was negotiated by P. A. Sangma of the NCP. By offering the UDP the first half of the legislative term in the premiership, as well as the Speaker's chair, the NCP secured the support of the erstwhile Congress ally. The NCP had won 14 seats (later gaining another seat) and the UDP 11, their claim to forming a Government being cemented by the support of the two HSPDP deputies, each of the KHNAM and BJP ones, and two independents (giving a total of 31). The Governor, however, inducted Lapang back into the premiership on 10 March, given that he was the leader of the largest party and that the new Meghalaya Progressive Alliance had not been a pre-election pact, but gave him only 10 days to prove his majority in the legislature. Only able to muster 28 Assembly members prepared to vote for a Congress administration, Lapang resigned on 19 March and the UDP leader, Dr Donkupar Roy, was sworn in as Chief Minister later that day. Roy, a state legislator since 1987 (first elected as an independent, joining the UDP just before the 1998 elections), had been a deputy premier in the previous administration. He and the NCP leader, Sangma, were to share the premiership for the duration of the eighth Assembly of Meghalaya. P. A. Sangma resigned his Lok Sabha seat in order to sit in the Assembly, where he joined two of his sons, who had also been elected as NCP deputies. His daughter, Agatha, was duly elected to replace him in the national Parliament in May. Congress, meanwhile, was riven by disputes as rival politicians sought to place the blame for alienating the party's allies.

## ECONOMY

Meghalaya is an agricultural state, with its forestry resources providing most state revenues and other potential natural resources as yet largely unexploited. The net domestic product of Meghalaya, in current prices, was Rs 47,540m. in 2004/05, or Rs 19,572 per head. There are no real industrial centres and infrastructure is limited. There are only 456.6 km of national highway in the state, running from western Assam into Bangladesh through the Garo Hills, and from Guwahati (Assam) through the eastern Khasi Hills to Shillong, then south to Sylhet in Bangladesh and south-east to Karminganj (Assam). By March 2003 there were 7,633 km of roads in Meghalaya, of which 48% were tarmacked and the rest gravelled. There are no railways (although there are plans for a rail link with Guwahati) and only one airport, at Umroi, near Shillong, which provides domestic air links. In 2005 there was an installed generational electricity capacity of 286 MW in the state (66% in the state sector, the rest from the Centre) and 69% of villages were electrified (although only 16% of rural households had electricity). The literacy rate increased from 49.1% in 1991 to 63.3% in 2001.

About four-fifths of the population depend on agriculture and the terrain does not permit much expansion of cultivable land, although production was increasing owing to a shift from traditional, *jhum* methods of rotating 'slash and burn'. Foodgrain production increased particularly from the late 1990s, reaching a record harvest of 217,800 metric tons in 2001/02, of which 180,100 tons were rice. The climate offered potential for the development of horticultural cash crops. Meghalaya is already famed for its citrus fruits (Khasi mandarins), but was encouraging the cultivation of non-traditional crops such as medicinal plants, commercial flowers, orchids, mushrooms and oilseeds. Fruits, spices, jute and betelvine are more usually grown, as well as the main food crops, rice and maize. Between 2004 and 2007 Meghalaya had become India's third strawberry producer (after Maharashtra and Haryana). Livestock products in 2003/04 included 682,500 tons of milk and 93.2m. eggs, but imported meat was still needed to supply 28% of meat requirements. The limit on agricultural land is compensated for by extensive tree cover, with some 70% of the land area being covered by woodlands, although only 38% is officially classed as forest. Timber production is essential to the economic health of the state. Inland fisheries provided about one-fifth of requirements in 2003/04, when the total catch was 5,147 tons. There are also important mineral resources, mostly unexploited, although the silimanite (a source of high-grade ceramic clay) deposits are considered the best in the world and Meghalaya accounts for almost all of India's output. There are reserves of coal (estimated at 562m. tons) and limestone (4,500m. tons) yet to be tapped, and other minerals include dolomite, feldspar, kaolin, mica and quartz. Proposals to begin mining uranium in the Khasi Hills provoked some controversy in 2007—reserves were estimated at 9,500 tons of uranium oxide in 9.22m. tons of ore near Domiaset. In June 2008 an important deposit near a remote village even provoked a border dispute with Assam. There were 870 workers in the sector in 2001/02; in that year 5,149 tons of coal and 585 tons of limestone were produced and, in the following year, mineral production was worth Rs 2,820.6m. (the highest in the north-east after Assam). In all, the primary sector contributed 23% of state gross domestic product (GDP) in 2004/05, according to official estimates announced in the 2005 budget speech.

There are no heavy industries, but the processing of natural resources provides some medium-scale activity, notably some cement production (mainly at the Cherrapunji plant, which reached production of 165,000 metric tons per year by the end of the 1990s) and a plywood factory. In 2003/04 there were 4,905 small-scale industrial units, creating jobs for 28,398 people. There is also some manufacturing of beverages and electronic components. In 2004/05 the secondary sector provided 24% of GDP (up from 14% four years previously, with most of the expansion at the expense of the primary sector).

The tertiary sector provided 53% of GDP during 2004/05, the latter dominated by public administration and government expenditure in general. Other services activity is limited, although tourism has potential—the scenery is beautiful, the flora and fauna rich and the cultures unique. In 2001 there were 181,087 tourist visits to the state, of which 2,390 were by foreigners.

### DIRECTORY

**Governor:** Ranjit Shekhar Mooshahary, Raj Bhavan, Shillong 793 001; tel. (364) 2223001; fax (364) 2223338.

**Chief Minister:** Donkupar Roy (United Democratic Party), Office of the Chief Minister, Government of Meghalaya, Shillong 793 001; tel. (364) 2224282; fax (364) 2227913; e-mail cmoffice@shillong.meg.nic.in.

**Speaker of the Legislative Assembly:** Bindo Mathew Lanong, Assembly House, Shillong 793 001; tel. (364) 2224267; fax (364) 2221057; e-mail mmdango@shillong.meg.nic.in; the unicameral Legislative Assembly has 60 mems: Congress 25, Nationalist Congress Party 15, United Democratic Party 11, Hill State People's Democratic Party 2, independents and others 7.

**State Resident Commissioner in New Delhi:** Sailendra Mendiratta, Meghalaya House, 9 Aurangzeb Rd, New Delhi; tel. (11) 23015503; fax (11) 23014471; e-mail rescm-mg@hub1.nic.in.

## Mizoram

The State of Mizoram, formerly the Lushai Hills District at the tip of the southern extension of Assam, is in the north-eastern region of India. It juts southwards, out of India, into an angle between the countries of Bangladesh (to the west) and Myanmar (formerly Burma, to the east). In the north, this 'land of the highlanders' has inter-state boundaries with the former princely states of Tripura to the west and Manipur to the north-east. Directly to the north lies Assam (of which Mizoram formed a part until 1972, when it became a Union Territory under its present name, achieving full statehood on 20 February 1987). Mizoram has an area of 21,081 sq km (8,139 sq miles).

The Mizo (formerly Lushai) Hills from which the state takes its name probably have the most variegated topography of any highlands in the region. A simplified description would be of some half-dozen parallel ranges of hills, running from the north to the south and tending to taper at the ends. The eastern ridges, as they rise towards the Rongklang range in Myanmar, tend to be higher, with the highest point in the state being near the south-eastern border at Blue Mountain (Phawngpui), which reaches 2,164 m (7,102 ft). An average height for Mizoram is some 900 m, with the capital, Aizawl, itself situated at over 1,000 m above sea level. The steep hills are densely forested with bamboo and wild banana, and flank deep gorges hiding rapid rivers like the Dhaleswari or Katakhal (locally known as the Tlawang), the Sonai (Tuirial) and the Tuivawl, draining north, and, in the south, the Kaladan or Kolodine (Chhimtuipui), and the Karnaphuli (Khawthlang tuipui) and its tributaries, such as the Tuilianpui. Flow is very dependent upon the monsoon rains. Mizoram is bisected by the Tropic of Cancer, giving the hill state a mild climate, with an average maximum temperature of 29°C (84°F) in August and an average minimum temperature of 11°C (52°F) in January. The rainy season is in May–September, with Aizawl receiving average annual rainfall of 2,080 mm (81 inches).

The total population grew at a higher than average rate between national censuses, rising from 689,756 in 1991 to 888,573 by March 2001. The population density remained relatively low, however, at 42 per sq km in 2001. According to the 2001 census, Mizoram was the most tribal of all the states in India, in that 94.5% of the population were listed among the Scheduled Tribes (a proportion only matched by Lakshadweep territory). The Mizo tribes are of Mongoloid stock and include the Lushai (after whom all the Mizo peoples were named for much of the past two centuries), the Pawi, the Ralte, the Pang, the Himar or Hmar and the Kuki. They are united not only by kinship, but by common traditions and history—thus, ethically, for instance, they share the Christianity to which many of them converted in the 19th century, as well as more traditional concepts such as *tlawmngaihna*, which is a sort of imperative of welfare, kindness and hospitality. The missionaries also gave the Mizo tongue the Roman script, as well as bringing the people English, which is the state's other official language. Originally animists, according to the 2001 census 87.0% of the population were Christian (mainly Protestant); the next largest religious affiliations recorded were Buddhist (7.9%) and Hindu (3.6%), with small communities of Muslims (1.1%) and others. However, as so often in the borderlands of conflicting faiths or when traditional beliefs have relatively recently been displaced, exact creeds are often vague or even bizarre. The largely nomadic Chakmas of the western borders combine Hinduism, Buddhism and animism, while the surprising presence of Judaism (the small Bne Menashe sect, sometimes called the 'Manipur Jews') dates from 1951. That year a local chieftain, Tchalah, claimed that by divine revelation he had been instructed to lead the people of Mizoram and Manipur (whose identity as descendents of one the lost tribes of Israel, Manesseh, had been suppressed by the Christian missionaries) back to their Jewish roots and, indeed, to Israel.

Although primarily agriculturalists, the 2001 census records that 49.6% of the population of Mizoram were 'urbanized', apart (barely) from Goa, the highest proportion of any state in India. By far the biggest town was the capital, Aizawl, in the north, but other important towns were Lunglei and, even further south, Saiha, and Champhai on the Myanmar border. The state is divided into eight districts. There are three autonomous district councils.

### HISTORY

The Mizo peoples probably originated in north-west China some time in the first millennium of the Christian era, gradually migrating southwards and through Burma (now Myanmar) and into India by the 17th century. They conquered and assimilated other Mongoloid tribes in the Lushai Hills during the 18th century. The first Mizo peoples to move into the highlands were called the Kuki, and the final group were the Lushai themselves. The Mizo developed an autocratic political system based on 300 hereditary chieftainships. With Assam increasingly falling under the East India Company's rule from 1826, Mizo raids on the plantations to the north, particularly from the late 1830s, became a problem for the British authorities. Punitive military expeditions and increasing contact with imperial officials had brought the area under control by the 1870s. More importantly, visiting restrictions not applying to missionaries, the conversion of many Mizo to Christianity helped the process and spread education. In the 1890s the Lushai kingdom was formally annexed to the British Empire, the northern hills falling under the jurisdiction of Assam and the southern hills Bengal. The district was united as the Lushai Hills, and awarded to Assam, in 1898.

The consolidation of administration in the district meant that in 1919 Lushai Hills was declared a 'backward area' (it remains a notified backward area in Indian government parlance) and it became an excluded area in 1935. After the Second World War a political organization that became the Mizo Union began to campaign for a single administration for all Mizo areas, uniting them with Lushai Hills, although other activists wanted all to join Burma upon independence. Autonomy for Lushai Hills was granted in 1952, although that did not satisfy local aspirations, but the introduction of new institutions allowed for the beginning of the abolition of chieftainships. The district suffered the ravages of the so-called Mautam famine in 1959 (caused by the flowering of bamboo encouraging an explosion in a depredatory rat population, which proceeded to eat all available foodstuffs). A local famine committee formed from a cultural society founded by Laldenga evolved into a nationalist movement, the Mizo National Front (MNF). The MNF moved on to support armed action and was proscribed in 1967.

Demands for a separate hill state continued even after Mizoram was separated from Assam, when it gained territorial status in January 1972. Activists continued to campaign, sometimes violently, but the MNF entered negotiations with the federal Government in 1976. Agreement was not reached until a new Prime Minister, Rajiv Gandhi, added fresh impetus to the process, securing an historic compact with the MNF and the state authorities in June 1986. As a result, the MNF disarmed and, on 20 February 1987, Mizoram entered the Union as the 23rd state. Nationalist demands now focus on bringing contiguous Mizo areas into Mizoram.

Since statehood three parties have dominated local politics: Congress; the MNF; and the Mizo People's Conference (MPC). Into the 21st century, Congress is still led by Lal Thanhawla, who has been Chief Minister for three terms, in 1984–86 and 1989–98 (the latter period extended by victory in the 1993 state elections). In the 1998 election the Mizoram Pradesh Congress Committee won only six seats and lost power. Thanhawla was succeeded in the state premiership by Zoramthanga, whose MNF had won 21 of the 40 seats in the Legislative Assembly. Zoramthanga had become leader of the MNF in 1991, upon the death of Laldenga. Laldenga had been Chief Minister in a coalition with Congress during the period leading up to statehood, but the MNF had won 24 seats in the first state elections in 1987 and so ruled alone thereafter. Laldenga lost power to a brief period of President's Rule (federal direct administration), which was followed by a significant loss of seats for the MNF in ensuing electoral contests, despite its continuing to win a large proportion of the votes in the 1998 state elections. The MPC, which was founded by Brig. T. Sailo in 1978 (and won the elections of that year—Sailo headed the territorial Government in 1978 and again in 1979–84), entered an electoral alliance with the MNF for the 1998 state legislative poll, winning 12 seats. The MPC's new leader, Lalmingthangwa, became the Deputy Chief Minister in a coalition administration, until the alliance ended in December 1999.

Elections to the Assembly were held on 1 December 2003. Unlike most of the other states holding elections at this time, Mizoram increased its support for Congress, which won double the number of seats in the previous legislature, gaining 12. However, the winner of the contest was the ruling MNF, which secured a simple majority of 21 seats, confirming the former insurgent, Zoramthanga, as Chief Minister. The main casualty of the poll was the alliance of the MPC and the Zoram Nationalist Party, which between them won only four seats, after conducting an uncompromising nationalist campaign. The all-India Bharatiya Janata Party (BJP), in power at the Centre at the time, again failed to win any representation in the mainly Christian state. Mizoram also sends one member to each of the houses of the national Parliament. The MNF retained the Lok Sabha seat at the May 2004 general election. The state remains disturbed by unrest, with insurgent groups hiding in the often inaccessible hill country and plaguing both the Indian authorities and those in Myanmar. Infiltration across the Bangladesh border prompted the national Government to announce an increase in the border guards in December 2005. In September 2006 the Government announced that the border with Myanmar was to be fenced, following an increase in drugs trafficking. Moreover, stability was also threatened from late 2005 and through 2006 by the impending repetition of the Mautam famine, when the flowering of bamboo encouraged a rodent infestation—rats feasted on the bamboo seeds, increased their population and then threatened food crops. By October 2007 this last stage had been reached, but it was hoped that alternative crops and government action would mitigate the effect of the rodent depredations.

Elections in the first decade of the 21st century were orderly and under threat only from insurgent groups rather than rival political factions. Politically, with a Congress-led Government at the Centre, the MNF administration experienced additional pressure from the opposition, which in June 2005, for instance, accused the ruling party of having unsuitable links with insurgent groups, contributing to its ineffectiveness in countering insurgency. Such concerns led to an opposition confidence motion (which had no chance of passing) in March 2007, followed by a demonstration in Aizawl, protesting that relative peace had been bought by the toleration of insurgent groups, the flourishing of gun and drugs running and the inevitable decay of law and order. There were allegations that the MNF had supplied guns to one group in January; soon after, an incident resulting in the death of some Hmar rebels also undermined the Government's record. The MNF, however, could counter with the end of the Reang insurgency in the previous October: nine years earlier clashes between the Bru, a Reang people, and Mizo tribesmen had forced the displacement of much of the Bru population, which took refuge in Tripura (over 40,000 had fled at one point). In October 2006 over 800 members of the Bru Liberation Front of Mizoram had laid down their arms, seeking accommodation with the Government. The ruling MNF also sought to bolster its standing by ending its association with the BJP-led national opposition alliance in March 2007. It maintained its equidistance from the two main blocs in the national Parliament in July 2008 over the nuclear deal with the USA. With state elections scheduled for September, Congress had been bolstering its support (being rejoined by the Mizoram Congress Party in May). Three other opposition parties united in a 'third front' in August: the MPC, the Zoram Nationalist Party and a civic organization, the Zoram Kuthnathawktu Pawl, allied as the United Democratic Alliance.

## ECONOMY

Mizoram is a poor state, although central subsidies enhance wealth indicators, such as figures for net state domestic product. In 2002/03 the official net domestic product of Mizoram was put at Rs 20,270m. or Rs 22,207 per head. Of all the states in India, only Sikkim had a smaller economy than Mizoram, but in per caput terms the state was the wealthiest in the north-east (helped by central support). There is little industry and infrastructure is limited. One main road heads south from Silchar in Assam, linking Aizawl with Lunglei and now reaching as far as the southernmost town of Tuipang. In 1999 there were 4,787 km of road in the state, over one-half of which was surfaced, but only 270 km consisted of national highway. There were no railways in Mizoram until 1990, when a railhead at Bairabi opened in the north, linking the state to the main line at Silchar. There is an airstrip at Aizawl and another one opened at Lunglei in 1998. The state had 37,718 telephone connections in 2000/01. The state generated 14.07m. units of power in 1999, with the development of electricity resources receiving central government assistance, notably for a hydroelectric project at Tuirual. By 2005 the installed capacity of Mizoram consisted of 60.1 MW in the state sector and 49.1 MW in the central sector (the private sector contributed only 0.2 MW), with only three villages left to be connected to the electricity supply (35% of rural households had electricity). However, in 2000/01 electricity generation within the state only accounted for 9% of total consumption, with the balance having to be imported. All villages had a water supply. Mizoram's educational tradition means that the literacy rate is the second highest for any state or territory in India, at 88.5% in 2001 (rising from 82.3% in 1991).

The primary sector provided 26.6% of the net state domestic product in 2000/01, with agriculture alone accounting for 24.6%, the rest by fishing, forestry and mining. About three-quarters of the population depend upon agriculture, with the 2001 census recording 53% of the population as agricultural workers, mainly cultivators (down from over 60% in 2001). The *jhum* system is seeing declining yields, as a shorter cycle of rotation was the result of growing population, although the Government is encouraging more terracing and other irrigation projects. About one-third of the total cropped area is under *jhum*. The state produced 126,300 metric tons of food grains in 2001/02, of which 84% was rice (*jhum* accounted for three-quarters of the rice cropped area, but only two-thirds of production). Mizoram is famous for fibreless ginger (25,337 metric tons of ginger were produced in 2000/01), but rice, mustard, sugar cane, sesame and potatoes are the main crops. Roses and other blooms (for the cut-flower market), medicinal plants and tea are increasingly encouraged, while traditional horticulture includes citrus, especially kagzi limes, and other fruit. Sericulture involved 3,332 farmers in 2000/01 and produced 2,065 kg of raw silk. The livestock sector, which included 163,000 pigs and 33,000 cattle at the 1997 agricultural census, produced just over 8,300 tons of meat in 2000/01 and 15,000 tons of milk and 30.4m. eggs in 2002/03. Attempts to develop woodland resources have led to an increase in forest cover, with 18% of the state under dense forest cover and 69% under open forest (38% of the state's area consists of reserved forest). The value of forest produce was put at over Rs 12.6m. in 1999/2000. Inland waters provide a locally important fishing industry, with production of 2,900 tons (in 2000/01), employing 4,700 families of marginal or small-scale fish farmers. There is some scope for the extraction of mineral resources, with small reserves of lignite (brown coal), sandstone and pyrites, but current activity hardly amounts to an economic sector, with the total value of minerals produced in 2002/03 put at only Rs 922,000.

The contribution of the secondary sector to state income remained fairly constant throughout the 1990s, and in 2000/01 it accounted for 11.0% of the total. Construction alone provided 10.9% of the total. Manufacturing, therefore, most of it unregistered, is of little significance. The need to import power also limits the contribution of the secondary sector to the state economy. Officially, Mizoram is a non-industrial area, but a new industrial policy announced in 1989 sought to encourage the development of agricultural and forestry processing, handicrafts and other cottage industries such as weaving, and the manufacture of electronic components. Small-scale sericulture (see above), sawmills, furniture manufacture, grain milling, ginger processing (notably at Sairang), fruit-juice concentration and even some oil refining were the main economic concerns in this sector at the beginning of the 2000s. There are no large-scale enterprises. At March 2001 there were some 4,600 small-scale industrial units registered in the state, providing employment for 25,974. A further 5,772 khadi and village industries were also registered

Services, meanwhile, are dominated by government activity. The tertiary sector accounted for 62.4% of the net state domestic product in 2000/01, with public administration alone accounting for 18.7% of the total—only agriculture contributes more. Other important services include property or real estate (14.6%) and trade, hotels and restaurants (10.4%). Transport and storage are relatively undeveloped. There has also been an effort to expand the tourist industry, based on the state's scenery and culture.

### DIRECTORY

**Governor:** Lt-Gen. (retd) M. M. LAKHERA, Raj Bhavan, Aizawl 796 001; tel. (389) 2322262; fax (389) 2323344.

**Chief Minister:** ZORAMTHANGA (Mizo National Front), Office of the Chief Minister, Government of Mizoram, Aizawl 796 001; tel. (389) 2322517; fax (389) 2322245.

**Speaker of the Legislative Assembly:** R. LALCHAMLIANA, Assembly House, Aizawl 796 001; tel. (389) 2326250; fax (389) 2323207; e-mail spkmzmla@alpha.nic.in; the unicameral Legislative Assembly has 40 mems: Mizo National Front 21; Congress 12; Mizo People's Conference 3; Zoram Nationalist Party 1; Mara Democratic Front 1; others 1.

**State Resident Commissioner in New Delhi:** ANINDO MAJUMDAR, Mizoram House, Circular Rd (Pt. Uma Shankar Dixit Marg), Chanakyapuri, New Delhi 110 021; tel. (11) 23016408; fax (11) 23012331; e-mail rescm-miz@hub.nic.in.

## Nagaland

The State of Nagaland is in north-eastern India, on the mountainous border with Myanmar (formerly Burma), which lies to the east. The land of the Naga tribes (the name is said to be derived from a Burmese word, *naka*, meaning those with pierced ears) is one of India's smaller states, until 1957 part of Assam, which lies along the state's long north-western border. There is a short border in the north-east with another Indian state, Arunachal Pradesh, and beyond the ragged southern border lies Manipur state. Nagaland, which became India's 16th state in December 1963, covers an area of 16,579 sq km (6,399 sq miles).

The state lies on the western flanks of the mountain ranges curving south-westwards from the Himalayas, before heading south into the Rongklangs of Myanmar. The crest of the Naga Hills generally serves as the international frontier, so the highest point is on the border, at Saramati, which is 3,826 m (12,557 ft) in height. The thickly wooded highlands include valleys and gorges cut deeply by rivers such as the Dhansiri, the Dayang, the Dikho and the Zungki or Tuzu. Nagaland has a moist, monsoon climate, with average annual rainfall of between 2,000 mm (79 inches) and 2,500 mm. Altitude also affects the temperatures, but the mean summer (June–September) maximum is 31°C (88°F) and the mean winter (October–February) minimum 4°C (39°F).

Nagaland's population was put at 1,990,036 in the census of March 2001, meaning the state had the highest rate of growth of any state or territory in India since the previous decennial census, when it totalled 1,209,546. The population density in 2001 was 120 per sq km. In the same census 89.1% of the population were registered among the Scheduled Tribes, the highest proportion for any state or territory in India after Mizoram. Most of the population of the state are Nagas, an Indo-Mongoloid people, who are usually divided into 16 tribes or groups. The largest tribe is the Konyak, followed by the Ao, the Tangkhul, the Sema and the Angami. The others are the Chakhesang (Chokri), the Chang, the Khiamngan, the Lotha, the Phom, the Pochury, the Rengma, the Sangtam, the Yimchunger and the Zeliang (actually a group of sub-tribes). Another tribe, the Kuki, is often considered not to be a Naga people. There are other Naga tribes outside the borders of the state, in Arunachal Pradesh, Assam and Manipur, and in Myanmar (Kachin state and Sagaing administrative division), with nationalists claiming that the areas they inhabit should be united in a 'Greater' Nagaland (Nagalim). The Naga languages are all of the Tibeto-Burman type, but inter-communication is mainly in English, an official language of the state, and in a pidgin known as Nagalese. Traditionally, the Nagas were animists, but with a conception of a supreme being, which meant that they adapted easily to Christianity, which was adhered to by 90.0% of the population in 2001 (the highest proportion of Christians in any state in India). Hindus are the next largest group represented in the state (7.7%), followed by Muslims (1.8%), and there are small communities of Jains, Buddhists and Sikhs.

Most of the population lives in rural villages (the rate of urbanization in 2001 was 17.2%) and there are only two towns of any size. Kohima, famed as where the Japanese advance was stopped during the Second World War, is the capital, and is located in the far southern highlands of Nagaland, at an altitude of almost 1,500 m. The original Angami settlement of Kohima (Bara basti) claims to be the largest village in Asia. Some 70 km (44 miles) to the north-west is the main town, Dimapur, on the border with Assam, down on the fringes of the plains, and only 195 m above sea level. The only other towns of any size are Mokokchung, Tuensang and Wokha. The state is now divided into eight districts, Dimapur having been made a separate unit.

### HISTORY

The origins of the Naga people are obscure, but they seem to have settled in the Naga Hills (on either side of the India–Myanmar border) by about the 10th century. Legend sometimes ascribes a seafaring origin on Sumatra (Indonesia), but it seems more likely that they followed the traditional migration routes out of China and Mongolia. Tribes of similar stock had been in the area from Vedic times. From the beginning of the 13th century AD the original Kachari (Cachar) realm was based on what is now Naga territory, at Dimapur (Hidimbapur), and it successfully resisted rising Ahom power in the area until the capital was sacked in 1536 and the king soon moved to the Cachar Hills (now in Assam). The Ahoms had clashed with the Nagas during their migration from Burma (now Myanmar) in the 13th century, but otherwise the new rulers of what was coming to be called Assam seldom even claimed more than a tentative sovereignty over the Nagas. It was only when the British added Assam to their Indian empire, from 1826, that the Nagas began to be drawn into surrounding affairs. The British sent a military expedition into the Naga Hills in 1832 and annexed the Angami kingdom (around modern Kohima) in 1866, but did not formally annexe the rest of the territory until 1881, as part of continuing efforts to halt Naga raids. The Naga Hills was the name of two districts under the Viceroy of India, one in Assam and one in Burma. The Kuki kingdom was formally annexed and added to the Assamese district in 1917. The outlawry of traditional practices such as headhunting in the 1890s and the arrival of Christian missionaries (especially Baptists) soon made an impact on the previously isolated Naga tribes. During the Second World War, this isolation was further interrupted by Japanese invasion through Manipur from Burma; Kohima became well known as the place where that advance was halted, in April 1944.

The Nagas had petitioned the imperial authorities to unite their tribes under one administrative unit even before the War, an effort led by the Naga Club. This organization evolved into the Naga National Council (NNC) in 1947, not long before India became independent, without any change of borders in the Naga region. The NNC formed a 'Federal Republic of Nagaland' in 1956, led by A. Z. Phizo, which led both political campaigning and armed action against the federal and local authorities. In 1957 Dr Imkongliba Ao founded a Naga People's Convention, in favour of Nagaland's future within India. That year the central Government also conceded that the Naga Hills District of Assam should be united with a frontier division of what became Arunachal Pradesh. Thus, the territory of the modern state was formed as the Naga Hills and Tuensang Area (NHTA); although no longer part of Assam, that state's governor administered the NHTA for the federal authorities. Agitation continued, however, until the central Government announced in 1960 that the NHTA (renamed Nagaland in 1961) would be granted statehood, which status was achieved on 1 December 1963. The Governor of Assam, initially based in Shillong (now in Meghalaya), was also Governor of Nagaland, until a separate individual was appointed to the post in 1989. Part of the '16-Point Agreement' between the authorities and the Naga People's Convention that led to statehood was an amendment to the Indian Constitution, protecting the primacy of customary law within tribal communities.

Negotiations between the federal and state authorities, and the armed opposition (usually known as the 'underground') represented by the NNC, finally resulted in the signing of the so-called Shillong Accord, which effected a cease-fire. However, there were those in the NNC who demanded that Phizo reject the Accord and, when he did not do so, in 1980 formed a National Socialist Council of Nagaland, later of Nagalim (NSCN), which resumed armed activism. Incidents included several attacks on the prominent Congress politician and five-times Chief Minister, S. C. Jamir, who barely survived two assassination attempts, in 1990 and 1992. However, the majority faction of the NSCN (led by Issak Chisi Swu and Th. Muivah—the main minority faction is led by S. S. Khaplang) also entered negotiations with the authorities and, in August 1997, a cease-fire was declared, which was renewed into 2001, although not all anti-government militancy ended. Such activism has been complicated by splits and rivalries within the underground, as well as by inter-tribal conflicts (as between the Kuki and the Zeliang in 1992–94). A 2001 proposal to extend the cease-fire into other Naga areas, in India, but outside the state, was abandoned by the federal Government after other states in the north-eastern region objected to what they saw as the threat of the practical realization of a Greater Nagaland (Nagalim). Nevertheless, Centre-NSCN contacts continued, with negotiations mainly being conducted in Bangkok, Thailand, but also including a visit to Delhi towards the end of 2002 by a delegation of the NSCN (Issak-Muivah, IM). The NSCN (IM) cease-fire was renewed for another year from June 2003, and discussions between the Centre, local politicians, the tribal 'umbrella' body (Naga Hoho) and the insurgents were ongoing, although the Prime Minister, Atal Bihari Vajpayee, warned in October that there was no consensus favouring a change in borders. Following the general election of 2004, it was considered likely that the new Congress Government at the Centre would heed the advice of Nagaland Congress leader Jamir, but he was unpopular with the NSCN (IM) leadership and, furthermore, was appointed to the governorship of Goa in July. Meanwhile, both the main insurgent groups agreed to meet government representatives for negotiations.

Unrest in the state has punctuated democratic government with periods of centrally administered President's Rule (1975–77, 1988–89, 1992–93 and January–March 2008). Congress, led by Jamir (formally a member of the Naga People's Convention until he founded a state committee for Congress in 1979), held power from the legislative elections of January 1989, retaining state government at two polls thereafter (1993 and 1998). Jamir had first been Chief Minister, in an interim capacity, in 1980, resuming office in 1982–86. He had won the state premiership back in 1989, only to be seriously wounded in an assassination attempt in May 1990—K. L. Chishi acted as Chief Minister until June, then Vamuzo until April 1992, when direct rule was instituted for the interim period until the state elections of the following February. Jamir was returned to office after that election, and again in 1998, but the opposition boycotted the latter election, leaving the overwhelming majority of seats to Congress. In the approach to the next state elections, the first to be held during a cease-fire, the democratic opposition was more organized, and bolstered by splits within Congress, as dissatisfaction with Jamir's leadership spread. A former state premier, the veteran Hokise Sema, formed a local branch of the Bharatiya Janata Party (BJP). A Congress minister, Neiphiu Rio, resigned from the state Government in order to join the opposition Nagaland People's Front (NPF), of which he promptly became leader. Although Congress remained the largest single party in the immediate aftermath of the elections, held at the end of February 2003 (winning 22 seats), an anti-Congress coalition known as the Democratic Alliance of Nagaland pledged to remove Jamir from office. The largest parties in the Alliance were the NPF, which won 19 seats, and the BJP, with eight, supported by the two seats of Janata Dal (United), one of the Samata Party, four independents and, later, the four seats of the National Democratic Movement. The longest-serving Congress Chief Minister in India, therefore, resigned; Neiphiu Rio was sworn in in his place on 6 March. The strength of the coalition Government was improved by subsequent changes in allegiance by some state legislators.

Nagaland also sends two representatives to the Indian legislature, one to the lower house and one to the upper. At the general election of 2004 the NPF conclusively defeated Congress for the Lok Sabha seat, although it was Congress that formed the new Union Government and was, therefore, to be influential in the peace process. With dissension troubling the ranks of the government coalition, Congress mounted a determined effort to win the elections scheduled for early 2008. There were rumours of bringing back veteran leader Jamir, who was declared banned from the state in October 2007 by the insurgent NSCN (IM) and escaped an attempt on his life in November. In December Congress, under its state leader, I. Imphong, proposed a confidence vote in the Assembly, having secured the support of nine deputies who had defected from the NPF. The Government survived the motion on 13 December, with 23 votes against the 19 of Congress, but only after the Speaker had declared the votes of the nine defectors invalid and had barred three independents. Although state elections were imminent, the Centre imposed President's Rule on 3 January 2008. Congress, itself afflicted by dissension, as accommodation of the defectors disadvantaged established party members, failed to win the March state legislative elections. It increased its seat tally to 24, but was displaced as the largest party by the NPF, which secured 26 seats. The BJP, which had not fought the election in an electoral alliance, had two seats, as did the Nationalist Congress Party, so the Democratic Alliance of Nagaland reassembled the coalition, with the support of five independents, and returned to office under Rio of the NPF as Chief Minister.

At the end of July 2004 the NSCN (IM) and the Centre had agreed the extension of the cease-fire for another year, while still edging towards direct negotiations. Despite some incidents, including some lethal explosions in Dimapur in October (with which it seemed the NSCN factions were uninvolved), Swu and Muivah arrived in Delhi on 5 December for meetings with not only the Chief Minister, but also Indian national leaders. There had been a delay in their arrival from the Netherlands, provoked by allegations that the federal Government was treating with, and even supplying arms to, their rivals, including the NSCN (K). The NSCN (IM) was engaged in a sometimes-violent rivalry with the NSCN (K), and confrontations in December were only ended by the latter's declaration of a truce for Christmas and New Year. The NSCN (K) was at a disadvantage, having been weakened since 2003, when army units in Myanmar had overrun its bases, including its headquarters. The NSCN (K) later, in April 2005, agreed with the Union Government that it would extend its cease-fire for another year.

Meanwhile, in December 2004 the NSCN (IM) leaders arrived in Dimapur after almost three decades of exile. They engaged in three weeks of meetings with their supporters, representatives of the churches and of non-governmental organizations and others in civil society. There seemed to be an emerging consensus in favour of a peaceful resolution of the conflict, and substantive negotiations with the Centre, at ministerial level, began at the end of January 2005. Over the following months it became clear that the major sticking point in the negotiations was the issue of uniting the Naga territories into a single unit, an issue that provoked strong feelings in the surrounding states, but also in the underground. The added piquancy was that, of the NSCN leadership, Muivah was born a Tangkhul of northern Manipur (the NSCN-IM is dominated by Tangkhuls, with Swu, a Sema, important in broadening the appeal of the group), while his rival, Khaplang, was born in Myanmar. A number of mainstream politicians, including a former chief minister of Manipur, also supported the union of Naga districts. In early July Muivah returned to the Netherlands (where subsequent negotiations commenced at the end of the month—Swu had departed earlier, for medical reasons). Meanwhile, Muivah had admitted the involvement of Pakistan's secret services in backing for the Naga insurgency, but declared this minimal by comparison with the Indian Government's allegations. General NSCN (IM) satisfaction with the progress of negotiations was not reassuring to neighbouring states that feared dismemberment. Relations between the states and tribes of the north-east of India were not helped by the blockade of Manipur organized by Naga activists in June–August. Moreover, the NSCN (IM) only extended the cease-fire for six months from 1 August, instead of for the usual year. Negotiations between the Centre and the insurgent group resumed in October in Bangkok and, about the cease-fire, in January 2006. The NSCN (IM) continued to allege army violations of the agreement, in support of the Khaplang faction, but extended the cease-fire for a further six months. In July, in Bangkok, a one-year extension was resumed, following promising discussions in the Netherlands the previous month. While the Centre was only prepared to discuss matters within a constitutional framework (i.e. not sovereignty), the flexibility of the Constitution in satisfying Naga aspirations was mooted. However, to the relief of surrounding states, no substantive progress had been achieved in the realization of a Nagalim. The centre and the NSCN (IM) met in October in the Netherlands, while Swu and Muivah arrived in Nagaland for another visit in January 2007, despite threats from the NSCN (K), which had again become involved in clashes with NSCN (IM) supporters in recent months. The main faction once more met with a central delegation in March, followed by discussions on the cease-fire in July, amid signs that the NSCN (IM) leadership was hardening its stance on achievement of unification and 'sovereignty'. However, although negotiations continued, the politics of the underground became more dominated by the increasingly bloody conflict between factions. In September there were clashes between the NSCN and the Manipur-based Kuki Liberation Army, for example, while into 2008 the focus was on dissent within the NSCN movement. A new faction, known as NSCN—Unification, split from the NSCN (IM) around the beginning of the year and, by March, armed clashes between the two groups had killed some 40 people. At the same time there was renewed conflict between the NSCN (IM) and the NSCN (K), claiming about 50 lives by June. In that month the NSCN (K) rejected proffered negotiations with the NSCN (IM) unless the negotiations with the Centre (from which the minority faction was excluded) were suspended. The NSCN (K) objected to 'eastern Nagalim' (i.e. Naga-inhabited districts in Myanmar) being neglected in the agenda for the negotiations.

## ECONOMY

Unrest in Nagaland has hindered development and consumed significant resources without economic benefit. However, although still primarily agricultural, the state possesses some potential in natural resources. During the 1990s Nagaland experienced fairly strong growth until the 1998/99 financial year, when the net state domestic product contracted, in real terms. State income stabilized in the following year, although in per-head terms the contraction continued, but some strong growth thereafter took the current net state domestic product to Rs 44,580m., or Rs 20,746 per head by 2002/03. The only industrial centre is Dimapur, on the Assam plain, which also gives Nagaland access to the North-Eastern Frontier Railway mainline as it passes through, to the national highway network and to air links with Guwahati (Assam), Kolkata (Calcutta, West Bengal) and Delhi. A national highway connects Dimapur to Kohima (and then goes south to Imphal in Manipur). Another road link with Assam is to Amguri, further north, from Mokokchung. The state's main form of transportation, therefore, is by means of the road network, which totalled 9,351 km (5,807 miles) at the end of the 1990s. More than one-half of Nagaland's electrical energy is generated in Assam, the balance being provided by diesel generators and, increasingly, hydroelectric power (a 24-MW plant was under construction at Likimro). Installed capacity in 2006 amounted to 102.7 MW, of which only 30% was in the state sector (of which over four-fifths was hydroelectric), the rest a share in central projects. However, all of the state's villages had been connected to the electricity supply, while 47% of rural households had electricity in 2005. The education system has had to struggle to keep pace with the burgeoning population, but the literacy rate did rise between 1991 and 2001, from 62% to 67%.

Most of the population remains in rural villages, traditionally stockaded and perched on the ridges. Agriculture is the principal economic activity for 84% of the population (1991 figure), who still mainly practise shifting *jhum* 'slash-and-burn' methods. The *jhum* yield fell severely at the end of the 20th century and into the 2000s, as soil fertility deteriorated and erosion increased, because the normal cycle of land lying fallow for 10–15 years declined to two or three years under the pressure of population growth. Terraced cultivation is encouraged as an alternative, but in the late 1990s it still only matched two-fifths of the acreage under *jhum*. Nevertheless, production figures for the state increased throughout the 1990s, the total foodgrain harvest reaching a record 355,400 metric tons in 2001/02. The main food grain is rice (237,300 tons in 2001/02), but maize is also grown. There is no commercial animal husbandry, with 90% of livestock for meat imported into the state, although the state did produce 59,000 tons of milk and 55.9m. eggs in 2002/03. Forestry is the most important source of income, mainly the timber industry, and cover is put at about 17% of the state's land area. A low-grade coal is the only resource mined at present, although Nagaland is considered likely to have some important mineral reserves (chromium, nickel, cobalt, iron ore and limestone have been identified). Moreover, boreholes west of Wokha and natural seepage in the Dikho valley, also near Assam, have suggested the potential for exploitable petroleum reserves. Developing infrastructure to support such exploitation remains the main impediment, while the lack of natural resources to process has blighted the growth of industry. Mining employed about 2,400 people and, in 2002/03, only produced minerals worth Rs 775,000, the lowest amount for any state in India.

Although industrialization has been a priority since the 1970s, there is no heavy industry and few enterprises of any size. Again, transport and power infrastructure, as well as a lack of natural resources and investment income, has hindered progress. Dimapur has a sugar mill (with an installed capacity of 1,000 metric tons per day), a distillery, a brick factory and a television-assembly plant. Elsewhere in Nagaland, there is a pulp-and-paper plant at Tuli, a plywood factory at Tizit, a mini-cement plant at Wazeho, some cabinet and furniture manufacturers, rice mills and fruit-canning plants, and a khandsari (molasses) mill. Cottage industries and handicrafts, notably traditional handloom weaving (particularly shawls in tribal patterns and colours), have been encouraged with the establishment of co-operatives.

Services, even government services, make little contribution to the local economy. Dimapur is the only trading and commercial centre of any significance, while Kohima is the centre of government activity and also on the main route to Imphal. Dimapur and Kohima are the only centres to have much attraction for tourists, although the scenery and tribal culture can be marketed.

## DIRECTORY

**Governor:** K. SANKARANARAYANAN, Raj Bhavan, Kohima 797 001; tel. (370) 2242917; fax (370) 2242898; e-mail rajbhavankohima@nic.in.

**Chief Minister:** NEIPHIU RIO, Office of the Chief Minister, Government of Nagaland, Civil Secretariat, Kohima 797 001; tel. (370) 2240569; fax (370) 2222908; e-mail cmngl@hub.nic.in.

**Speaker of the Legislative Assembly:** KIYAHILIE PESEYIE, Assembly House, Kohima 797 001; tel. (370) 2222963; fax (370) 2221401; the unicameral Legislative Assembly has 60 mems: Nagaland People's Front 26; Congress 24; Bharatiya Janata Party 2; Nationalist Congress Party 2; independents 6.

**State Resident Commissioner in New Delhi:** C. J. PONRAJ, Nagaland House, 29 Aurangzeb Rd, New Delhi 110 021; tel. (11) 23012296; fax (11) 23794240.

# Orissa

The State of Orissa lies on the north-eastern shores of peninsular India, on the Bay of Bengal, with West Bengal to the north-east, Jharkhand (part of Bihar until 2000) to the north and Chhattisgarh (part of Madhya Pradesh until 2000) to the north-west and west. Andhra Pradesh lies to the south or, rather, to the south-east, where it stretches up the coast beneath an inland tail of Orissa that extends south-westwards along the highlands. Orissa, the 'land of the Oriyas', has enjoyed a distinct identity, if a varying extent, for many centuries, a fertile, coastal territory dominating its wooded, hilly hinterland that otherwise bears more resemblance to the predominantly tribal areas of Jharkhand and, to a lesser degree, Chhattisgarh. Long ruled from Bengal, like Bihar, Orissa became a separate province on 1 April 1936, was merged with its princely states in 1949 and became a 'Part A' state under the 1950 Constitution. It was unaffected by the federal reorganization of 1956, as it already constituted a linguistic state. Orissa has an area of 155,707 sq km (60,103 sq miles), making it the seventh largest state of India.

Orissa consists of fertile, coastal, alluvial plains, stretching south-westwards from the mighty Ganga–Brahmaputra delta of old Bengal, and ending where coastal Andhra begins, beyond the narrowing of the plains caused by a seaward thrust of the Eastern Ghats. These heights rise to the peak of Mahendragiri (1,501 m—4,926 ft), to the south of the Mahanadi delta. Beyond Mahendragiri the border includes some of the Kondhan Hills, before crossing the Ghats and reaching further south-westwards, along a tributary of the Godavari. The highlands, the second main geographical area of Orissa, occupy the west of the state. The north consists of plateau land, rising above the Hingir basin, in the north-west, to the loftiness of Garhjat, before falling towards the border with the delta lands of Bengal. Sundering the highlands and dissecting the state is the Mahanadi, dammed into the Hirakud Reservoir from the western border to the head of the central river valley, which forms the fourth geographical area of Orissa, and eventually losing itself in a delta on the plains. North of the Mahanadi, but flowing out of Jharkhand, is the second river of Orissa, the Brahmani. The flat plains are mostly planted with paddy and the hilly interior tends to be heavily forested and sparsely populated, although rich mineral reserves have created a north-western industrial belt. There is a coastline of 482 km (299 miles), distinguished by the gentle bulge of the deltas and, to the south, the near-inlet of Lake Chilika, which is actually separated from the sea by a line of sand dunes. Chilika, at 64 km in length and 16–20 km in width, with an area of some 1,100 sq km, is, therefore, a brackish water and the largest inland lake in Asia. Further inland the mighty Hirakud Reservoir is a man-made lake of 746 sq km behind one of the largest mainstream dams in the world (21 km in length—completed in 1957) and provides both hydroelectricity and water for irrigation. The dam successfully contained the previously regular flooding for many years—that it is not an absolute guarantee was demonstrated by the devastating floods of 2001, occasioned by extremely heavy rains, which hit a state still recovering from the catastrophic cyclone of 1999. The state is exposed to cyclones in October and November, after the main monsoon, which falls heavily on this part of the coast. The average annual rainfall in Orissa is some 1,500 mm (59 inches), but the winter (December–February) is dry. Even in winter temperatures rarely fall below 11°C (52°F), although they are more often near this in the highlands. In the hottest months, normally May, temperatures in Bhubaneswar, the state capital in the Mahanadi delta, can exceed a very hot 42°C (108°F).

At 1 March 2001 the total population of Orissa was officially enumerated at 36,804,660, an average of 236 people per sq km. The main language is Oriya (Odia), which was the first language of 82.8% of the population at the time of the 1991 census, with Hindi at 2.4% and Telugu at 1.6%. Of the other official languages of India, Urdu and Bengali were the next most widely spoken (English is also in general use), but this does not take account of the tribal languages. In 2001 Scheduled Tribes, of which there were 62 in Orissa, accounted for 22.1% of the population. In 1991 the most numerous were the Khonds, but there are also a lot of Santals (who are among the largest tribal groups in India and the dominant one in neighbouring Jharkhand). The Gond and the Oraon are among the other major tribal peoples of the state, while exclusive to the state are the Koya, the Bathudi, the Bonda, the Gbhuyan or Bhuyan, the Juang and

Saora. There are three main language families represented among the tribes: Dravidian; Austric or Munda; and Indo-Aryan. Gondi and Kuvi (the language of the Khond) are Dravidian, and examples of Austric tongues include Santali (one of the oldest languages of India), Bondari (despite the Tibeto-Burmese ethnic origins of the 'naked people') and, of course, Mundari, while the Bathudi and the Gbhuyan speak Indo-Aryan languages. In addition to the Scheduled Tribes, 16.5% of the 2001 population were from the Scheduled Castes and scheduled areas covered about 45% of the state. Despite the continuation of some animist beliefs and practices among the tribes, most have been 'Aryanized' and follow some form of Hinduism, which is the dominating faith of the state—94.4% professed it in 2001. The missionary activity of Christians, who formed 2.4% of the 2001 population, particularly among the lower castes and tribal communities, has attracted sometimes-violent reactions in Orissa since the 1990s. Muslims, never a significant community in Orissa numerically, constituted a further 2.1% of the population, and there were also small groups of Sikhs, Buddhists and Jains (the latter two groups were both once dominant in Orissa in historical times).

The urban population constituted only 15.0% of the total in 2001, and none of India's largest cities are in Orissa. The largest cities of the central plains are: Cuttack (534,654 inhabitants in 2001), the old capital on the main course of the Mahanadi; Bhubaneswar (648,032), the current capital just to the south and further into the delta; and, even further south, on the coast, Puri, one of the four holy abodes of the Hindus and one of the main pilgrimage sites in the country. In the north-west the main city is the industrial centre of Raurkela, while to its south-west, below the Hirakud Reservoir, is Sambalpur. The only other city of comparable size to these centres is Brahmapur, on the plains near the border with Andhra Pradesh. Orissa is divided into 30 districts.

## HISTORY

The ancient kingdom of Kalinga was based on the Orissan coast, its capital in the Mahanadi delta near modern Bhubaneswar, at Dhaulagiri. Kalinga had fallen under the suzerainty of the northern power of Magadha, led by the Nandas and then by the Mauryas, but its control was tenuous. In an age of personal monarchy much of the power of the state depended on the personal prestige, longevity and ability of the individual ruler, much of an empire having to be reasserted upon each succession. The third of the Mauryan emperors, Ashoka Piyadassi (reigned *circa* 271–33 BC), had to proceed against Kalinga about 10 years after his accession, crushing the state bloodily at Dhaulagiri. It is the only specific campaign of any Mauryan emperor that is known, and that is because it provoked a change of heart in Ashoka, who regretted the bloodshed and determined to build an empire grown and maintained on good conduct or *dhamma* rather than force of arms (although he nowhere on his famous rock inscriptions specifically abjures warfare, just as he does not formally 'convert' to Buddhism). By the end of the century Magadhan power was in decline and Orissa drifted into independence under the Chedi kings, the most famous of whom was the third, Kharavela, who probably came to the throne in the middle of the first century BC, but dating him is uncertain. Kharavela, who favoured Jainism rather than the Buddhism of Ashoka, was a military king, whose conquests (mainly known from his own inscriptions) extended widely into north India and on the peninsula.

Although Kalinga and the other kingdoms of Orissa mainly feature in historical accounts as the alleged victims of another rajah's glory, the area was not an automatic fief of ambitious 'world rulers', with various native dynasties flourishing and waxing and waning even when under an imperial suzerain. Thus, there were kingdoms such as Utkal in the north and Toshali in the centre of the modern state, as well as realms that clung to the name of Kalinga. There were myriad dynasties, such as the Mathars of Parlakhemundi, the Sailodbhava and the Eastern Gangas, and overlords from the Satavahanas, to Nagas, the Kushana, the Guptas of a reborn Magadha and Harsha Vardhana. Gautamiputra Satakarni (AD 62–86) conquered Orissa, which remained under the Satavahanas for about one century, before their power decayed. Another period of stability was experienced after the conquest by Samudra-Gupta (335–75), allowing the rise of the Mathars, who helped re-establish brahmanism and prospered with the trade across the Bay of Bengal (the 'Sea of Kalinga'). The fall of the Guptas in the early sixth century coincided with the rise of the coastal dynasty of the Sailodbhava, as well as with the establishment of the Eastern Gangas (although the latter's pre-eminence in Orissa would await the 11th century). The Sailodbhavas, whose greatest king was Sailendra, were a maritime power and spread the name of Kalinga by trading throughout South-East Asia (there are parts of Indonesia where the word for 'Indians' is still 'Klings') and had military adventures in Myanmar. In 736 the Sailodbhava kingdom was occupied by the Bhaumas under Unmattasimha (Sivakar Deva). The Bhaumas, who were Buddhists, had several notable female monarchs (such as Tribhuvana Mahadevi and Dandi Mahadevi) and favoured the name of Utkal for their kingdom. Their sovereignty in Orissa was not absolute and permitted other principalities of varying degrees of independence known as mandalas. In this period the great Orissan tradition of temple building began, notably under the orthodox Kesaris, who, for instance, founded a city at Cuttack under Nrupat Kesari (920–35).

The next paramount dynasty of Orissa was from South Kosala (Chhattisgarh), the Soma or Somavamsi. The Soma kings reigned from the region of Bhubaneswar from about the 930s, increasing their power under Mahasivagupta I Yayati (*c.* 970–1000) and reaching their height in the reign of Chandihara Mahasivagupta III Yayati (1025–55), who ruled over Kalinga, Utkal, Kangoda and Kosala. The main local rival of the Somas was the house of Ganga, based to the south. The Gangas increased their power in the 11th century, seizing the advantage in the turmoil throughout south India that was brought about by the great Chola expedition up the east coast to Bengal in the first half of the century. By the end of the century the Soma forces were being regularly bested by the Gangas and, eventually, their great rajah, Anantavarman Chodaganga (who had acceded as a minor in 1078), invaded Utkal in 1112, supplanting the last Soma within six years. Chodaganga died in 1147, to be followed by 14 more Ganga rajahs of Orissa. They presided over a prosperous trading kingdom from which Buddhism had largely disappeared and that could afford to build further remarkable temple monuments, in defiance of the encroaching threat of Islam in the north and west of the subcontinent. Among the more noteworthy monarchs are: Anangabhima II (1216–38), who established Cuttack as the Ganga capital; his successor, Narasimha I (died around 1264), who invaded the now Muslim-ruled Bengal in 1264; and Langula Narasimha II (1279–1306), who ordered the construction of the great Sun Temple at Konark (Konarak), which provided both a testament of the Hindu faith of the Orissans and a beacon for their sailors. In 1361, however, the Delhi Sultanate finally moved against the usually peaceful Gangas and seized Cuttack. The Gangas, although not dispossessed, were required to send tribute to Delhi and, in their weakness, they were soon displaced by the Gajapati dynasty, the Suryas or Suryavamshas.

The first Gajapati ruler was Kapilendra, who held the throne in about 1434–67 and vigorously fought both Muslim invaders and the Hindu empire of Vijayanagar (based in Karnataka): in 1444 Kapilendra defeated the Sharqui sultan of Jaunpur (now in Uttar Pradesh), the latter having invaded out of the north; in 1456 he fought the encroachments of Vijayanagar to the south; and in 1459 Kapilendra won against the forces of the Deccan sultanate of Bijapur (Karnataka) to the west. The rivalry with Vijayanagar continued on the borders, but the general security of the realm encouraged a religious and literary blooming in the land of the Oriyas. This is particularly noticeable under Kapilendra's grandson, Prataprudra, who succeeded his father in 1497 and reigned for some 40 years. He also concluded the war with Vijayanagar in 1519, determining on the River Krishna as the boundary between the two powers and marrying his daughter to the great emperor, Krishna Deva Raya Taluva. However, the succession was disputed after the death of Prataprudra and the Gajapatis were displaced, briefly, by the Chalukyas of the Andhran coast in the late 1550s, only themselves to lose Orissa to conquest by a Muslim out of Bengal, Bayazid Karrani, in 1568. However, the region was now caught up in the final Mughal effort to break the power of the Afghan dynasts, such as those in Bengal (and Orissa). In 1592 the Afghans were routed by a Rajput general of the Great Mughal, Rajah Manasingh, who incorporated the region into the empire, dividing it into five districts or sarkars, subject to Bengal until 1607, when Orissa was united into a separate province (with Cuttack as capital). The Mughal peace, although it brought some occasional damage to the great temple legacy, benefited the trade of the Oriya-speaking merchants, attracting the attention of the new European presence in India (British posts were established in Orissa in 1633, for instance).

Although some Orissan dynasties survived with a precarious and intermittent independence, the history of the region was now to be one of dependence. Even when Mughal power decayed, the coast at least remained dominated by 'governors' in Bengal or the Deccan. In 1728 the Nizam of Hyderabad (now in Andhra Pradesh) occupied the southern Orissan lands, while in 1751 the Marathas (mainly to the benefit of Raghuji Bhonsla of Nagpur—now in Maharashtra) were ceded the rest by Bengal. Under the Marathas, as elsewhere, the administration was widely considered avaricious and lawless, but religion was patronized and Oriya literature flourished. However, it was under British rule that the Oriya language would benefit most, with the introduction of printing and also of the influence of (and reaction to) Christian missionary activity. The East India Company first acquired territory in Orissa in 1765, but dominated the whole region by 1803—again it was ruled from Bengal. Ill-advised land policies provoked the Paik Revolt of 1817, and in the 1830s there were efforts to subdue the Khonds (in two wars) and the local rajah in southern Orissa, but generally the touch of British rule was initially light in Orissa. Nevertheless, missionaries arrived from the 1820s, Oriya replaced Persian as the official language in 1839 (Persian was the language of the Mughal court, of which the East India Company was still a nominal functionary) and disturbances at the time of the

1857 Sepoy Mutiny were limited. However, this virtual administrative neglect, compounded by poor communications and, maybe, indifference, transformed the failure of the rains in 1866 into the great famine of 1867, in which perhaps one-third of the population, about 1m. people, perished. This disaster pushed the rising middle class, fostered by both English-language education and the growth of printed Oriya literature, towards regional consciousness and, eventually, the independence struggle. A mass meeting in 1903 resolved to press for a separate Orissa province, although the 1905 reforms (in which the district of Sambalpur was added to the Orissa division, from the Central Provinces) merely left the region attached to West Bengal. When the controversial partition of Bengal was reversed in 1912, Bihar and Orissa became a separate province. Finally, under legislation of 1935, Orissa became a province in its own right on 1 April 1936. It elected a Congress ministry in 1937, but independence agitation increased (marred by the so-called Elam massacre) and, upon its achievement, reform was extended by the incorporation of the local princely states into Orissa (almost doubling it in size), effected on 19 August 1949.

The great temple city of Bhubaneswar replaced the medieval and British capital of Cuttack as the headquarters of the state, and it was from here that the local Congress ruled Orissa. However, by the 1970s Congress was fracturing, its standing not helped by the 'Emergency' of Indira Gandhi, the national Prime Minister. Thus, in 1977 a former Congress premier, Bijayananda ('Biju') Patnaik, led the Janata Party to victory in the state elections, although he himself did not head the ministry that held office until 1980. Congress was then returned to power in the elections to the eighth Assembly since independence, forming the 14th ministry, under Janaki Ballav Patnaik, who did not leave office until 1989. Congress was again undermined by in-fighting, the state premier until the 1990 elections, Henananda Biswal, losing to the popular Biju Patnaik and what had become the Janata Dal. Biju Patnaik was Chief Minister until 1995, when Congress could again form a ministry under Janaki Ballav Patnaik. Congress again succumbed to factionalism, with three chief ministers between 1999 and the 2000 state elections, Patnaik being replaced by Giridhar Gomango (who gained an international reputation in the field of tribal music after his humiliating ousting) and Biswal, who returned to the premiership for a few months.

The 2000 state elections were won by Naveen Patnaik, the son of Biju Patnaik, who had entered the national Parliament for the first time only in March 1997, after the death of his father. In December he had founded the Biju Janata Dal (BJD), a regional party, although he is noted for being unfamiliar with Oriya, the state's official language. Allied to the Bharatiya Janata Party (BJP—in office at the Centre), the BJD won an overwhelming victory in the state elections of 2000 and Naveen Patnaik duly became Chief Minister in March. He has a reputation for integrity, but suffered accusations of indecisiveness managing the relief work after the great 1999 cyclone. Later in his term of office the state premier came into conflict with an elder statesman of the party, Dilip Ray, who was elected to the Rajya Sabha as an independent, but with the support of some BJD deputies, provoking further disputes with the ruling party's uneasy BJP allies. Moreover, the BJP at the Centre was not sympathetic to the Orissan Government's representations about the reincorporation of the former princely states of Saraikela and Kharasuan (from late 2000 included in the new state of Jharkhand), although the BJP also suffered from a riot by Hindu militants in March 2002, in which the Assembly building was attacked. It appeared unlikely that Naveen Patnaik would be able to preserve his premiership from a fatal split in his own party or in his coalition with the BJP. The Dilip Ray dispute escalated in late 2002 and into 2003, resulting in a split in the parliamentary party at the national level, but Patnaik remained in control of the main party. Eventually, in February 2004, Ray and his splinter group in Orissa formally joined Congress, which was being reinvigorated by the restored leadership of J. B. Patnaik, a three-times former state premier. The current premier, Naveen Patnaik, however, was bolstered by his reputation for not being corrupt, helped by the view of many voters that the old Congress leadership remained discredited.

Orissa sends 21 deputies to sit in the lower house of Parliament, the Lok Sabha, and has 10 representatives in the upper house, the Rajya Sabha. At the 2004 general election the ruling BJD won 11 Lok Sabha seats, although its allies, the BJP, lost two seats to secure only seven. Congress retained its two seats (its ally, the Jharkhand Mukti Morcha, won the other). In the state elections (which had not been due until 2005, but were instead conducted simultaneously with the national contest), however, Congress improved its representation in the Legislative Assembly to 38 of the 147 members. The ruling coalition lost some seats, but retained a clear majority, thus keeping Naveen Patnaik in power. However, the political atmosphere remained fraught (the Chief Minister was inadvertently injured during a scuffle in the Assembly in November 2004), and the Government was challenged by the state's poverty, which fuels Naxalite and sectarian violence. Thus, in January 2006 there was a serious incident involving tribal protesters against an industrial project in Kalinga Nagar, when a policeman was killed and his colleagues opened fire, fatally hitting 13 villagers. The incident, which provoked an economic blockade of the area (barring of a main highway only ended in March 2007) and was taken up by opposition parties in neighbouring Jharkhand and Chhattisgarh as well, illustrated the problems of rural poverty and the failure to compensate for development. As in West Bengal, an ability to attract investment to the state was not balanced by government handling of the land issues required in effecting the development. A perceived neglect of public health issues (as, for example, with the outbreak of cholera in some districts in August 2007) reinforced allegations that the state Government was not doing much for the mass of the population, although the Congress state leadership seemed unable to capitalize on the situation. Nevertheless, Rahul Gandhi of the national Congress leadership seemed to sense an opportunity to woo the tribal and youth votes in visits to Orissa in March and May 2008. However, the main political drama in March 2008 was the allegation of sexual harassment made against the Speaker of the Assembly by a female security officer. He denied the charges, but resigned his post at the end of the month, while they were investigated (the human rights commission abandoned proceedings and declared a lack of evidence in August, but said a police investigation might continue). In June, with the backing of the Congress opposition, the Government announced that it would seek to correct the official spelling of the state name and language in the national Constitution: from Orissa (Udisa in Hindi) and Oriya (Udiya), respectively, to Odisha and Odia.

There were also increasing incidents of Naxalite violence, which had contributed to the Government's decision to ban the Communist Party of India—Maoist in the state in June 2006. By 2007 it was apparent that Naxalite influence seemed to be spreading faster in Orissa than in any other state or territory of India. A twist to the prevalent tension with the Christian minority in the state followed an outbreak of communal violence in Kandhamal in December. Although the Government declared that conversions were not the cause of the riots, which the church leaders claimed showed signs of having been organized, Hindu activists alleged that Christian groups were linked to the Naxalites. There was certainly evidence for rural poverty and social exclusion of the low-caste and tribal populations fuelling recruitment to both Maoists and Christians, but counter-insurgency policies discounted a direct link. Such policies had to be reviewed in mid-July 2008, following two devastating attacks on the police within three weeks. At the end of June insurgents attacked a police launch returning across a reservoir from an operation against the Naxalites in Andhra Pradesh, killing 33 (five remained missing a fortnight later). Later, a land mine killed 17 policemen. These two incidents followed an attack on a police armoury in Nayagarh in February, when 15 police officers and a civilian were killed. The Government, which declared itself ready to negotiate with Naxalites who gave up their arms, did not allege any links with Pakistan or Bangladesh (although it toughened its policy on Bangladeshi migrants in March), but a tentative link with Nepali Maoists had been made by July.

## ECONOMY

Orissa is a relatively poor state, although the exploitation of its water and mineral resources and the declining rate of growth of its population are allowing a slow improvement. In 2004/05 net state domestic product was Rs 522,400m., at current prices, or Rs 13,601 per head, the latter figure only being lower in Bihar, Jharkhand and Uttar Pradesh. The rail network is inadequate, so roads are important, totalling 232,970 km in length at March 2000, including 2,782 km of national and express highway and 4,816 km of state highway. At the same time the length of railway was only 2,173 km (all broad gauge but for 144 km of narrow gauge); only 14.2% was electrified. Paradwip is one of the 11 major ports of the country, in 1999/2000 exporting 8.9m. metric tons of goods and importing 4.8m. tons; the next most important ports are Gopalpur and Bahabalpur. There are 17 airstrips and 16 helipads, but not all are all-weather fields; the main airport, providing links to cities throughout India, is at Bhubaneswar. The great dam on the Mahanadi in western Orissa, begun soon after independence, is another example of important infrastructure. The dam stopped the regular occurrence of the devastating delta floods and provided power and irrigation water, from the Hirakud Reservoir, which drains an area twice the size of Sri Lanka. However, there were record floods in 2001, after heavy rains left the rivers swollen and the lake too full to retain all the water. Installed capacity in 2006 was 3,476 MW (down from 5,427 MW in the previous year); most usually came from Orissa's share in the production of central stations, but at 1,131 MW the Centre was providing only 36% of the figure for the previous year; the state contributed 2,345 MW, with less than 1 MW from the private sector. Of the state's installed capacity in 2006, 82% was hydro-electric. Four-fifths of villages had access to an electricity supply by March 2005, but only 17.5% of rural households were reckoned to have electricity. Although the population growth rate has slowed, the education system is still struggling to catch up—the literacy rate rose from 49.1% in 1991 to 63.6% in 2001.

Agriculture and animal husbandry contributed almost 29% of the net domestic product of Orissa in 1997/98, and about a similar amount in 1998/99, but this had fallen slightly by 2003/04, standing at some 26%. In 2001/02 the contribution to gross domestic product was 25.4%, which was actually an increase from the 22.8% of the previous year. In 2001 some 65% of all employment, directly or indirectly, depended on the sector. Cultivation is, however, mainly rain fed, not irrigated, resulting in low productivity and a dependence on the weather; the state is exposed to cyclones, suffering from a particularly strong one in 1999. Even before that disaster, the harvests of 1998/99 were low; total foodgrain production was less than normal, at 5.79m. metric tons (owing to population growth and to productivity not keeping pace, foodgrain production per head in the 1990s was less than in the 1950s). The main cereal crop is rice, which covers 74% of the gross cropped area under principal crops, with pulses on 12% and oilseeds on 6%. Paddy generally provides about four-fifths of food grains (95% in 2001/02). In 2001/02 the total foodgrain harvest, at 7.29m. tons, was second in size only to the record one of 1989/90 (7.97m. tons), and rice alone provided 7.15m. tons (8% of the all-India total). However, in the following year the foodgrain harvest, owing to severe drought, was dramatically lower, at 3.56m. tons, but recovered to 7.15m. tons in 2003/04 (with rice accounting for 6.73m. tons). The livestock sector, according to the 1995 agricultural census, was responsible for 14.8m. head of cattle, 1.7m. buffaloes, 5.4m. goats, 1.9m. sheep and 0.6m. pigs. In 1998/99 milk production rose to 833,000 tons, while meat production fell to 35,000 tons (from 48,000 tons the year before). In 2002/03, according to provisional figures, production of milk reached 991,000 tons and of eggs 878m., with both predicted to record further rises in the next year. Sericulture is another traditional activity. The fishing industry has potential in Orissa, particularly marine fishing, and the total catch in 1998/99 was 284,000 tons (representing a substantial increase from 159,000 tons at the beginning of the decade). Of this, 51.0% came from inland fisheries, 43.7% from the sea and 5.2% from brackish fisheries (i.e. Lake Chilika—this last sector was in decline, with the loss of an estimated 40% of fish species from Chilika since the beginning of the 1950s). By 2003/04 total fish production had reached 306,950 tons, with a value of Rs 13,746m. Forests covered 37.3% of the total area of Orissa in 1998/99 (accounting for about 8% of national woodland). Tree cover is not increasing (unlike the area of land registered as forest), but forest produce is bringing in increased revenue (Rs 868.1m. in 1998/99).

In terms of natural resources, Orissa has plentiful supplies of water, while mineral reserves are good. The most important reserves are of coal, iron (some 24% of all-India resources) and manganese ores, bauxite (26%) and chromite (70%). Limestone, nickel, quartz, china clay, copper, vanadium and precious and semi-precious stones are also exploited, but the sector has not yet developed its full potential. In 1998/99 total mineral production was 6.34m. metric tons, valued at Rs 23,655.6m.—barely 2% of production was exported abroad, earning Rs 2,585.8m. In 2002/03 total mineral production was valued at Rs 33,560.9m. In the previous year the sector employed almost 100,000 people, making Orissan mining of high value per worker.

Minerals provide the basis for much of the heavy industry in the state, such as the chrome works, an aluminium plant and steel works, as well as coal-powered thermal power-stations. The nearby presence of both iron ore and coal mines led to the 1955 foundation of the steel plant at Raurkela (started production in 1958), for instance, beginning the transformation of the previously undeveloped, tribal north-west. Processing of agricultural produce and foods is also an important activity. By March 1999 Orissa had 334 large and medium-sized enterprises (with an employment potential of 81,188 people) and 58,079 small-scale industrial units (with an employment potential of 399,000 people). In addition, 50,607 cottage industries (e.g. textile weaving, silver filigree, carving, brass items, terracotta, horn carving and patta painting) provided employment for 92,822 people. Manufacturing contributed 12.1% of net domestic product in 1997/98.

The tertiary sector is important, but somewhat too dependent on government expenditure. The strength of transport activities is an indication of the weak infrastructure in the state. Tourism has considerable potential but is relatively undeveloped, although there is a long-established religious tourist sector catering for the pilgrims to the great sanctuary of Jagannath at holy Puri. Orissa's temple patrimony is second to none in India, notably at Puri, Bhubaneswar and Konark, but as yet attracts few of the profitable foreign tourists. Between 1990 and 1998 tourist numbers grew by over 20%, but foreign tourists by barely 3%. By 1998 1.50m. tourists had visited Orissa in that year, of which only 2.2% were foreign; the industry earned Rs 5,289m., of which 7.4% came from foreigners. There is also the attraction of the beaches and the natural and tribal environment of the interior—for instance, the Simlipal National Park is rich in wildlife, containing one of the earliest tiger reserves, and also sheltering elephants, wolves, chital, deer, gaur, flying squirrels and peacocks.

### DIRECTORY

**Governor:** Murlidhar Chandrakant Bhandare, Office of the Governor, Raj Bhavan, Bhubaneswar 751 008; tel. (674) 2536111; fax (674) 2536582; e-mail govsec@ori.nic.in.

**Chief Minister:** Naveen Patnaik (Biju Janata Dal), Office of the Chief Minister, Government of Orissa, Secretariat, Bhubaneswar 751 001; tel. (674) 2531100; fax (674) 2535100; e-mail cmo@ori.nic.in.

**Speaker of the Legislative Assembly:** (vacant), Assembly Secretariat, Bhubaneswar 751 001; tel. (674) 2536655; fax (674) 2536826; the unicameral Legislative Assembly has 147 mems: Biju Janata Dal 61; Congress 38; Bharatiya Janata Party 32; Jharkhand Mukti Morcha 4; Orissa Gana Parishad 2; Communist (CPI) 1; Communist (CPI—M) 1; Janata Dal (Secular) 1; independents and others 8.

**Resident Commissioner in New Delhi:** I. Srinivas, 4 Bordoloi Marg, Chanakyapuri, New Delhi 110 021; tel. (11) 23019771; fax (11) 23010839; e-mail rescm-or@nic.in.

# The Punjab

The State of the Punjab lies in north-western India, a fragment of the historic Punjab, 'the land of five rivers', which is now partitioned between India (Punjab state itself, Haryana and parts of Himachal Pradesh) and Pakistan. The state forms a rough triangle, set on a southern base, the international frontier on the west, rising towards an apex truncated by a short northern border with Jammu and Kashmir. Himachal Pradesh lies to the north-east. In the south-west is Rajasthan, the rest of the southern border being with Haryana (a part of the greater Punjab state until 1966), a border which undulates in a rough crescent, ultimately curving into a border running northward to meet Himachal Pradesh. Here the separate Union Territory of Chandigarh abuts into Punjab from the east. A single Punjab state had been formed in 1956. Then, on 1 November 1966, the south-eastern end was made into Haryana, while some hill territories in the north-west were added to Himachal Pradesh and the new state capital of Chandigarh was also constituted as a separate unit, administered by the Centre, but continuing to serve as the headquarters of both the Punjab and Haryana. Since that date the territory of the State of the Punjab has remained unchanged, with an area of 50,362 sq km (19,440 sq miles).

The Punjab consists of fertile plains, gently sloping southwards from a line of undulating hills, the Katar Dhar or Shivaliks, which help define the north-eastern border and beyond which rise the Himalayas. The plains are less than 275 m (903 ft) above sea level, falling to below 200 m in the south-west around Abohar, while the Shivaliks reach above 800 m. Apart from a semi-arid area which edges the Rajasthan desert in the south-east, the state is well watered by a number of the principal tributaries of the Indus system, notably the Ravi, the Beas and the Sutlej, as well as by the Ghaggar, a river that dries up before reaching the sea. There is also an extensive canal system, contributing to the maintenance of the largely agricultural landscape. Most rainfall is in the monsoon season (July–September), with the rest of the year divided between cold (October–March) and hot (April–June) seasons, when temperatures vary from as low as 4°C (40°F) up to 43°C (110°F). The average annual rainfall is some 794 mm (31 inches), ranging from 960 mm in the sub-mountainous region to 580 mm in the central plains.

According to the census of March 2001, the total population of the Punjab was 24,358,999, giving an average population density of 483 per sq km. The overwhelming majority use Punjabi, with 92.2% claiming it as their first tongue in the 1991 census (the highest proportion for a single language after Malayalam in Kerala), with most of the rest speaking Hindi (Urdu was spoken by 0.1% of the population). The language can be written in Hindi script, but Punjabi is most commonly written by Sikhs in Gurmukhi (Guru Angad developed this from the established Landa script) and by Muslim speakers in the Perso-Arabic script (sometimes known in this context as Shahmukhi). Punjabi is a western Hindi dialect, largely recognized as a separate language for political expedience in the 1960s, so that Sikh separatism could be satisfied without breaking the constitutional ban on a religion-based state. Punjabi in India is mainly spoken by Sikhs, who made up 59.9% of the state population in 2001, with Hindus comprising 36.9% and Muslims 1.8% (most of the last group having departed or died in the chaos of Partition in 1947), followed by Christians (1.2%), Buddhists and Jains. In the same year 28.9% of the population were recorded among the Scheduled Castes (the highest proportion of any state or territory in India), but there are no officially registered tribal groups.

In 2001, as one of the more urbanized states of India, 33.9% of the population lived in cities and towns of the Punjab. The state capital,

Chandigarh, is not part of the Punjab, and its population is less than that of the largest city, Ludhiana, in central Punjab (which had a population of 1.40m. in 2001, making it the 16th largest city in India). The Sikh holy city of Amritsar, in the north and near the border with Pakistan, is the next largest city (966,862 in 2001), followed by Jalandhar (706,043) and Hoshiarpur, to the north of Ludhiana. There are 17 districts.

## HISTORY

The ancient Punjab, of which the modern state is but a fragment, lies at the heart of Indian history. The Harappans flourished here, and then the Aryans, the latter making of it a heartland from which they extended the *arya varta* eastwards into the Ganga–Yamuna Doab and the length of the Gangetic plains. The literary and geographical roots of Hinduism are in the Punjab, with the Vedas, the world's oldest scriptures, composed here and many of the events of the *Mahabharata* set here. Even the *Ramayana*, while it describes later events centred much further to the east, was probably composed in the Punjab. It was the land of the ancient Kura and Madra clans, but also, habitually, the territory first to experience later incursions from the west and north-west. The Persian (Iranian) emperor, Darius I, first added parts of the Punjab to his realm, under the antecedent of the name of India, in time to be followed by the adventurous conqueror of the Persian Empire, Alexander III ('the Great') of Macedon, who famously contested a Punjabi rajah, Porus (Paurava). Mainly under the peaceful rule of the great Maurya dynasty Buddhism had extended its influence into the Punjab, from the east, to last until the fatal devastations of the Huns (Hiung-nu) at the beginning of the sixth century. For the more destructive invasions of the region came from the north and west, although usually the kingdoms established there were often soon adopting Indian norms and, indeed, pantheons. A more significant arrival, in retrospect, was the arrival of Muslim Arabs, who established kingdoms in Sindh and the Punjabi city of Multan (both now in Pakistan) at the beginning of the eighth century, although most of these early Muslim rulers were more interested in the neighbouring parts of India for raiding rather than conquest. Furthermore, as so often on the borderlands between such separate cultural worlds, healthy hybrids could grow and the Punjab saw the flourishing of Sufism, a more mystical Islam than the orthodox faith prescribed, and of Punjabi, a Multani-Hindi dialect. For instance, Khwaja Moinuddin Chist, a great Sufi saint, arrived in Lahore (the former capital of the Punjab, now in the Pakistani province of that name, just across the international border from Amritsar) in 1190, while at about the same time a Sufi poet, Farid-ud-Din Ganj-i-Shakar (who lived from 1173 to 1265), was the first to write extensively in Punjabi.

By this time more aggressive Muslim invaders were attempting to penetrate to the riches of India through the Punjab. The last Hindu dynasty to rule the region was that of the Shahis, who were originally based in Kabul (now in Afghanistan), but were gradually driven back to the Punjab, their last capital in Kangra (now in Himachal Pradesh). This redoubtable dynasty were a staunch bastion against the incursions of men such as Mahmud of Ghazni (Afghanistan), three generations vainly struggling to stem the Muslim advance, with the last, Trilochanapala Shahi, eventually seeking refuge in Kashmir in the 1010s. The Punjab then fell under a variety of Muslim rulers for the next seven centuries, what is now Indian Punjab (including Haryana and parts of Himachal Pradesh) being most regularly ruled from Delhi, depending on the varying strength of the Sultans or the Mughals, although Hindu princes also continued to retain power locally. Again, a cultural blending was to bring about another strong religious movement.

By the 15th century the Delhi Sultanate was in decay and the Punjab was war torn and troubled. On what is now the Pakistani side of the border, in the village of Sheikhupura, Nanak Dev was born in 1469. He travelled extensively in the Punjab, as well as to Mecca (Saudi Arabia) and, reputedly, to Rome (Italy), and by the time of his death in 1539 had founded a powerful socio-religious movement that sought to purge Hindus and Muslims alike of subjection to caste, dogma, superstition and ritualism. Nanak Dev, the first Guru (master or leader) of the Sikhs (derived from a Sanskrit word for disciples), had founded a panth (brotherhood) that, under persecution by its more orthodox neighbours, evolved from essentially Hindu roots into a humanistic and monotheistic faith, which could properly be called a religion upon the foundation of the Khalsa (the community of the 'pure') on 15 April 1699 by the 10th and last Guru. Of the intervening masters, the first in significance is Guru Arjan (who in 1581 had succeeded Ram Das, who himself had followed his father-in-law, Amar Das, seven years previously; Guru Amar Das was the heir, in 1552, of Guru Nanak's own successor, Guru Angad). Guru Arjan compiled his own compositions, and those of his predecessors and other, non-Sikh writers, into a scripture known as the Adi (Original) Granth. However, the Sikhs fell foul of a Mughal succession crisis and Guru Arjan was executed and succeeded by his young son, Hargobind, in 1606 (he died in 1644). A similar circumstance arose in 1658, when the Sikhs showed hospitality to the pretender to the throne of Aurangzeb, and Guru Har Rai and his young son, Har Krishnan (who is considered to be the eighth guru), were summoned to the imperial court and inducted into the Mughal hierarchy (the father died in 1661, the son in 1664). The Sikhs did not find this acceptable and took another son of Hargobind, Har Rai's brother, Tegh Bahadur, as their ninth guru. Already suspicious of Sikh 'unorthodoxy', the pious Aurangzeb was further angered by Tegh Bahadur's widespread preaching and conversion of Muslims as well as Hindus. By executing Tegh Bahadur, however, Aurangzeb transformed the myriad and hitherto largely pacific Sikh communities into enemies and himself laid the foundations for the Khalsa of warrior-saints founded by Tegh Bahadur's son, Gobind Rai (Gobind Singh from 1699). Under Guru Gobind Singh the Sikhs armed themselves in the foothills of the Himalayas, the hill country of the Punjab (now largely in Himachal Pradesh), and began to change from a force for religious and social reform into a military and political movement. When Gobind Singh was assassinated in 1708, the succession of masters was replaced by the authority of scripture, the Adi Granth (with the addition of Tegh Bahadur's hymns and one couplet by Gobind Singh, the compiler, himself) becoming the Guru Granth.

Politically, Sikh claims, and their militancy against Mughal oppression or opposition, were given precedent by the movement of Banda Bahadur between 1709 and his defeat in 1715. Helped by rural discontent in a normally prosperous Punjab, he led the Sikhs and lower-caste Hindus against the Muslim towns of the eastern Punjab, assuming a royal title and minting the first Sikh coinage. Although Banda Bahadur was defeated, gradually the Sikhs, in a confederation of misals or autonomous 'republics', prevailed in the Punjab. Particularly with the loss of Maratha pre-eminence from 1756, these misals could eventually be welded into the Punjab Raj of Ranjit Singh. Ranjit Singh earned his reputation against the Afghan raiders of the late 18th century, but in 1799 he forcibly became rajah of Lahore. With the conquest of the holy city of Amritsar in 1805 he could begin transforming his dominance of the Punjab into a Sikh empire. However, he was aware of the variegated nature of his subjects, as well as of the rising power of the British (who were by now in occupation of Delhi), and the state he founded, although dominated by Sikhs, was secular in aim and cosmopolitan in nature. Not only did he emulate some of the successful features of the British organization in India, but also he was determined to avoid a confrontation. This feeling was mutual and Ranjit Singh and the East India Company settled on non-aggression and peaceful relations by the 1809 Treaty of Amritsar. To secure this peace Ranjit Singh sacrificed much of the eastern Punjab, settling on the Sutlej rather than the Yamuna as the frontier of his influence (the so-called 'Cis-Sutlej' states in the east of modern Punjab state, and in Haryana, therefore, were left to become princely clients of the British, surviving to independence—some, like Nabha and Patiala, were ruled by Sikh dynasties). Ranjit Singh was left free to consolidate his rule as the Maharajah of the Punjab and to extend his empire as far as Peshawar (Pakistan) and into Kashmir and Ladakh (both in Jammu and Kashmir). Towards the end of his reign he even entertained a joint action with the British against Afghanistan, although the disaster that befell this 'Army of the Indus' (and the contemporary defeat of his Dogra general who had invaded Tibet—now part of the People's Republic of China—in 1840) occurred after his death in 1839.

The Sikh state proved unable to survive the death of its great founder. In 1843 the second maharajah since Ranjit Singh was assassinated and the court intrigues in Lahore descended into bloodshed. Whether the British were already implicated in the succession struggles or not was rendered irrelevant by the massing of troops along the Sutlej frontier, and the approach of yet another British army provoked the Sikh-based armed forces of the Punjab into moving across the Sutlej themselves in late 1845. The army of the Punjab almost prevailed, but were greatly hindered by the treachery of courtier-commanders aiding the British. Two fierce battles near Firozpur (Ferozepore) were followed by bloody contests at Aliwal and Sobraon in early 1846, in the latter of which the British lost only some 2,500 to about 10,000 of their opponents. Nevertheless, the British realized it would be risking too much to try and take Lahore itself and began the traditional methods of reducing the state in size and independence. The frontier shifted from the Sutlej to the Beas, Kashmir was ceded (and promptly sold to the Rajah of Jammu, hitherto a feudatory of the ruler of the Punjab) and a British Resident installed in Lahore to supervise the Regency Council of the young Maharajah, Dhalip Singh. The new regime was given little chance to establish itself, however, falling victim not to court intrigue but to imperial ambition. In 1848 a mutiny in Multan involved the death of two visiting Englishmen, but the British authorities in India resolved to ignore the escalation of the revolt in order to have time to prepare for outright annexation. East India Company forces duly crossed the Sutlej at Firozpur, and then proceeded across the Ravi and the Chenab too. On the Jhelum, at Chillianwala (now in Pakistan), early in 1849 the predominantly Sikh army inflicted on the British one of their worst defeats in the subcontinent. However, this did not prevent the final victory of the British at Gujrat. On

29 March 1849, in the Treaty of Lahore, Maharajah Dhalip Singh was obliged to sign the instruments of annexation, surrendering his sovereignty—and the great Koh-i-noor diamond (which still remains a possession of the British monarchy).

Under British rule the Sikhs continued their martial traditions in the service of the Indian army and remained loyal even during the uprisings following the Sepoy Mutiny of 1857. Although a powerful military and commercial class, however, the Sikhs were greatly involved in the struggle for independence, initially in a pro-reformist capacity (such as with the Namdhari sect). Generally, the Punjab was pro-British, which meant that any sign of trouble was heavily policed by the British authorities, and this was the case during the civil disobedience actions of 1919. On 13 April Brig.-Gen. Reginald Dyer, who had recently arrived in Amritsar with troop reinforcements after some disturbances and forbidden all public meetings (although martial law had not yet been declared), encountered a large gathering in a city square, the Jallianwala Bagh. Many were probably Sikh villagers visiting the holy city for the feast day of Baisakhi; there was certainly no demonstration under way. Dyer sought out no such explanations, initiated no consultations nor issued any warnings, but ordered his troops to fire on the crowd, penned in by buildings. The official inquiry later concluded that over 1,200 men, women and children had been seriously wounded and that 379 died (unofficial reports put the number of fatalities at 530). Dyer was relieved of his command, but never punished, while apart from the act itself, which undermined the moral pretensions of British rule in India, his unrepentant attitude and, indeed, support from some sectors of the British public, alienated moderate opinion in the Punjab and throughout India.

The movement for independence began to acquire irresistible momentum (Punjabi émigrés lent important support and a prominent local leader was Lala Lajpat Rai) and by the end of the Second World War the British had conceded the principle. Tragedy was not over for the Punjab, however, its cultural mix on the borders between the solidly Muslim north-west of the Empire and the *arya varta* leaving it a case of contention between the proposed successor states of Pakistan and the Dominion of India. The Sikhs even demanded a third state, although they were eventually reassured sufficiently by Congress to side with the Hindu-dominated creation. With Congress determined to achieve independence as early as possible, despite the vicious outbreaks of communal violence throughout the Empire, and the Muslim League determined on a separate Pakistan, the British authorities finally conceded Partition (basically of Bengal and the Punjab) in June 1947. Even then the final border was not settled until after the independence celebrations, when a Congress-League commission headed by Sir Cyril Radcliffe, a judge, handed over its report on the 'Line of Partition'. Most of West Punjab had a Muslim majority and most of East Punjab a Hindu-Sikh one, but there was a middle stretch of territory (including Lahore and Amritsar, both of which the Sikhs claimed should be included in India for cultural and historical reasons) where no group had a majority. Nevertheless, demography was the main deciding factor for the Line of Partition and Lahore was included in Muslim Pakistan, although the holy city of Amritsar became part of India. By the time the new boundary was announced communal tensions had already led to forcible expulsions of Hindus and Sikhs from the western Punjab and, by Sikhs anticipating the arrival of refugee co-religionists, of Muslims from the east. The Radcliffe announcement merely escalated the pace, which became increasingly violent as tales of massacres, rapes and other atrocities bred more of the same. The great railway junction at Amritsar was a particular scene of bloodshed, as some 13m. people moved from west to east or east to west in one of the most intense migrations in world history. This was accompanied, between August and October, by anywhere between a conservative 200,000 and a despairing 1m. deaths.

East Punjab became part of the new India, but the territory was not organized in a single unit and still included the hill country that now forms part of Himachal Pradesh. The traditional capital of Lahore was lost to Pakistan, so it was determined that a new centre would be built at Chandigarh (Shimla, or Simla, the old imperial summer capital and now the state capital of Himachal Pradesh, served as an interim headquarters and it was here that the new bicameral Punjab legislature met in April 1952). Meanwhile, the eight princely states of the plains merged into Patiala and the East Punjab States Union (PEPSU), based in Patiala. On the eve of the linguistic reorganization of the states of India, PEPSU (a 'Part B' state) merged into the original, 'Part A' Punjab state, creating a single state with its capital at Chandigarh. Sikh agitation for a separate state could not be satisfied under the country's secular Constitution, nor did it interest the Hindu communities, so Punjabi (mainly spoken by Sikhs) was distinguished from the related Hindi dialects to become an official language upon which a final division of the Punjab could be effected. On 1 November 1966 the south-eastern part of the state became Haryana (a separate, Hindu-dominated member of the Union), the state capital of Chandigarh became a centrally administered Union Territory and a shared capital, while the hill territories of the north-east were added to Himachal Pradesh.

Apart from the abolition of the upper house of the legislature, the Vidhan Parishad (Legislative Council), in January 1970 the institutional and territorial establishment of the modern Punjab state was now complete. Political stability, however, was far from achieved and the Punjab has experienced a number of periods of President's Rule by the Centre. Particularly during the 1980s, when many Sikhs were agitating for outright independence ('Khalistan'), the state was disturbed by trouble. In June 1984 federal troops were ordered to storm the sacred Golden Temple of Amritsar, Sikhism's holiest shrine, in order to dispossess the militant Sant Jarnail Singh Bhindranwale (who died in the fighting—he was not declared a martyr until June 2003). Only months later the Prime Minister responsible for the order, Indira Gandhi, was murdered by two of her Sikh bodyguards, provoking bloody anti-Sikh violence (notably in Delhi). Since then there has eventually been a calmer atmosphere in the politics of the Punjab, which has experienced a typical pattern of alternating Congress and regional-party rule, complicated by the tendency of the Sikh nationalist Akali Dal, particularly, to factionalize and by their alliance with another religious-chauvinist group, the Bharatiya Janata Party (BJP—not otherwise a major party in the Punjab). The Akali Dal and the BJP overwhelmingly won the February 1997 state elections, but were defeated at those held in March 2002. The victory was achieved by Congress because Amarinder Singh, the current Chief Minister (a former army captain and the son of the last Maharajah of Patiala), had led his Shiromani Akali Dal (Panthik) faction into Congress in September 1997, to become the state Congress leader in the following year. This union was able to displace the ruling Shiromani Akali Dal under Parkash Singh Badal in 2002, when the BJP also performed very poorly electorally (the latter probably a local comment on the conduct of national politics).

At the Centre, the Punjab is represented by 13 seats in the Lok Sabha of Parliament and seven in the Rajya Sabha. When the BJP was in power at the Centre, the Government of the Punjab accused it of using its power to advance the cause of its own party and allies locally. However, the opposition in the Punjab, in turn, claimed that allegations of corruption brought against former premier Badal were politically motivated. In 2003 Congress claimed to be maintaining its popularity, its favoured candidates having performed well in local polls (which were not officially conducted on a party basis), but Amarinder Singh was not considered to be as popular locally as he was with the national leadership. Moreover, in June the Shiromani Akali Dal improved its position, when two of the opposition party's main factions were reunited after four years, with the reconciliation of Gurcharan Singh Tohra and Badal. The latter became leader (Tohra died in April 2004). In the 2004 general election (voting for which took place in May in the Punjab) Congress was trounced. The Shiromani Akali Dal won eight Lok Sabha seats and its ally, the BJP, three. Congress retained only two (having won eight in 1999). The ruling party in the Punjab had not been helped by factionalism, the most serious split being resolved only in January, when a dissident against Singh's supposedly autocratic style of leadership, Rajinder Kaur Bhattal (herself a former Chief Minister), was appointed deputy premier. The humiliation in the general election helped strengthen Chief Minister Singh's resolve in the water-sharing dispute of later in the year (see below), even against a new national Government at the Centre led by his own party, Congress. There was further criticism of the Chief Minister's style of leadership from within Congress in May 2006, voiced by Jagmit Singh Brar. Such splits undoubtedly contributed to Congress's defeat in the February 2007 state elections, together with pronounced rises in the prices of basic commodities. The Shiromani Akali Dal, meanwhile, ensured that for this contest its vote would not be so weakened, although, in the event, the main gain in seats was for its BJP ally. The Shiromani Akali Dal won 49 (including one seat for which voting was postponed until March) of the 117 seats, while the BJP increased its tally dramatically to 19. Congress retained 44, suffering severe reverses in its traditional urban strongholds; the remaining five seats were won by minor parties or independents, four of which supported the formation of a Government under Badal. Parkash Singh Badal thus became Chief Minister for a record fourth time, despite the lodging of corruption charges against him (from his earlier premiership in 1997–2002) at the same time. However, court proceedings against senior political figures were not uncommon and sometimes politically motivated. Corruption charges against the outgoing Chief Minister were soon forthcoming, while just before the election a senior BJP politician, the former cricketer Najvot Singh Sidhu, had managed to stay a sentence of culpable homicide against him.

Another situation that became mired in legal manoeuvring involved the leader of the Dera Sacha Sauda. In May 2007 civil peace in the state was disturbed by communal tensions between Sikhs and the followers of a heterodox sect based in Sirsa, in neighbouring Haryana. The Sacha Sauda leader, Gurmeet Ram Rahim Singh, had offended Sikhs by appearing dressed as the 10th Guru of their religion. Violence was scarcely abated by the leader's equivocal apologies, which were rejected by the Sikh high priests. Political implications were complicated, as Rahim Singh had instructed his followers to support Congress in the recent elections, but at the same time Sikh opponents of Chief Minister Badal sought to embarrass his Government by rejecting compromise. The worst violence was confined to mid-May, but intermittent clashes occurred, as well as peaceful protests across several states. By the end of June the arrest of the sect leader was being sought for offending the religious sensibilities of the Sikhs, although at the beginning of August more serious charges of murder and rape were laid against him. Released on bail in November, he continued to be a focus for clashes between his followers and Sikh protesters, sometimes deadly and sometimes provoking larger protests, such as in mid-2008.

In mid-2004 a dispute between the Punjab and Haryana escalated into a constitutional crisis. Haryana had been pressuring for the Sutlej–Yamuna Link (SYL) canal to be completed, but the Punjab Government was reluctant, given the anxieties of its own farmers about resulting water shortages. Haryana and Rajasthan would both benefit from the planned sharing of the resources of the Ravi and the Beas. However, on 12 July 2004 the Punjab Assembly unanimously passed the Termination of Agreements Act (hoping thereby to avoid a Supreme Court instruction of June to give responsibility for construction of the SYL to the Centre). The Punjab legislative move caught the Centre by surprise. The President, however, referred the matter back to the Supreme Court later in the month and, in August, the tribunal ordered six states (not only the Punjab and Haryana, but also Delhi, Jammu and Kashmir, Himachal Pradesh and Rajasthan) to prepare their submissions by mid-September. However, legal moves faltered thereafter, while in February 2005 the Court enquired of the Union Government as to its stand on the legal competence of the Punjabi legislation. Politically, relations between the Punjab and Haryana were not improved on the SYL issue by the election of a Congress Government in the latter state. Likewise, a change of ruling party in the Punjab in 2007 boded little change in water policy, with the ruling Shiromani Akali Dal irking its BJP ally by refusing water releases for Rajasthan. With droughts frequently affecting the north-west, particularly Haryana and Rajasthan, the dispute over water resources did not seem to have any easy solution. Another resource to provoke tension between the ruling party and its BJP ally was energy. A rise in power prices was condemned by the BJP in October 2007, which claimed not to have been consulted. Despite that and other incidents, the coalition claimed to be secure, with Congress failing to exploit any disharmony.

The dialogue between India and Pakistan had visible effects in the Punjab. A 'peace bus' between Lahore (Pakistan) and Amritsar was one of the confidence-building measures that was inaugurated in January 2006, with a further service launched in March, this one between Amritsar and the birthplace of Guru Nanak, Nankana Sahib in Pakistan. However, in July Pakistan was also accused of being the training ground for Sikh 'Khalistan' separatists, who were suspected of trying to revive militancy in the Punjab with bomb attacks in Delhi and Chandigarh during 2005 and in Jalandhar in early 2006. Fears of a resurgence of violent Sikh militants were also raised by a bomb attack on a Ludhiana cinema in October 2007, leaving six dead.

## ECONOMY

The Punjab is known as the 'grain basket' of India, and is the single largest contributor of wheat and rice to central reserves, but also has flourishing secondary and tertiary sectors. Historically, the Punjab has long been the richest state in India, relative to its population, although from the 1990s Maharashtra challenged this position, overtaking in 2002/03, as did Haryana. Otherwise, only Goa, Chandigarh, Delhi and Puducherry (Pondicherry) are wealthier. By 2004/05 the current figures had reached Rs 30,701 per head, or Rs 790,100m. in total. The Punjab claims to have the best infrastructure in the country, with all villages electrified and virtually all connected by metalled roads. The total length of the road network at March 1999 was 42,757 km, of which 1,198 km were national highway. In addition there are over 3,725 km of railway, including the rail link with Pakistan through Amritsar, and eight civilian aviation landing sites, including the airport at Chandigarh and the international airport at Ludhiana. Installed electrical capacity directly owned by the state at the end of March 1997 was 2,256.45 MW (of which 26% was hydroelectric), to which can be added a further 1,266.97 MW, provided by the Punjab's share of common pool projects, and 1,014.13 MW from central projects (4,537.55 MW in all). By 2006 total installed capacity was 6,266 MW, of which 75% was from the state sector (directly owned and the share in the common pool—52% hydroelectric), with most of the rest from the Centre (except for 34 MW from the private sector). All villages have been electrified since 1974, and 77% of rural households have electricity. The state, however, has the highest per head electricity consumption in the country, with seasonal deficits met by imports at times of peak agricultural activity. The literacy rate rose from 58.5% in 1991 to 70.0% in 2001. The strength of the state's physical, fiscal and educational infrastructure, of its agricultural sector, of its investment attractiveness and of its consumer markets put the Punjab first out of India's large states in the 2004 *India Today* survey of the best states in which to live.

In 1996/97 the primary sector (almost entirely agriculture and animal husbandry) accounted for 42.0% of the state's gross domestic product (GDP); agriculture (with animal husbandry) accounted 38.7% in 2001/02. The sector is dominated by the production of food grains, with the Punjab (1.6% of the total land area of the country, 2.4% of the population) harvesting 20% of India's wheat and 9% of its rice, as well as 14% of the cotton (1999 figures—2%, 1% and 2% of world harvests, respectively). In 2001/02 the total foodgrain harvest was 24.89m. metric tons (11.7% of the all-India total), with 15.50m. tons of that being wheat (22%) and 8.82m. tons rice (9%). In 2002/03 total foodgrain production fell to 23.49m. tons (13.5% of the all-India total), but the Punjab remained by far the largest producer after Uttar Pradesh. The provisional foodgrain total for 2003/04 was 24.72m. tons. At the time of independence, however, the state was a foodgrain-deficit area and the current prosperity is a product of the 'Green Revolution' of the late 1960s. In 1951 agriculture contributed 54.4% of GDP and total foodgrain production was 1.99m. tons, over one-half of which was wheat, the rest rice, coarse grains and pulses. Although the figures look similar for the beginning of the 1960s, by then the foundations of future development were being laid—the construction of the Bhakra-Nangal dam project was proceeding (following the Indus Waters Treaty of 1960 with Pakistan), bringing the Punjab plentiful irrigation water (and hydroelectricity), the utilization of which demanded the mandatory consolidation of agricultural holdings. Total foodgrain production had reached 3.16m. tons by 1960/61, but it was in the second half of the decade that new crop varieties (especially wheat), and the increased use of fertilizers, tractors and tube wells, truly revolutionized the sector. In 1970/71 total foodgrain production was 7.30m. tons, just over 70% of which was wheat (although the area under wheat was only just over 40% of the total). The rice 'revolution' of the 1970s further reinforced the sector, although by now equally flourishing secondary and tertiary sectors were forcing down the share of GDP. By the early 1990s the total primary sector accounted for 46.8% of GDP, with food grains covering 76.9% of the total cropped area (wheat alone 43.7%, rice 28.6%—coarse grains and pulses had declined, with oilseeds and cotton retaining a fluctuating share over the years) and reaching total production of 21.58m. tons (wheat 13.34m. tons, rice 7.65m. tons—all 1993/94 figures). The intensity of farmland use had probably reached the highest it could, with some 84% of the land area of the Punjab given over to cultivation, while the levels of mechanization and of the use of fertilizers and pesticides were unmatched in India. By the end of 1998, for instance, the Punjab had some 365,000 tractors, about one-third of the total in all India.

In 1997/98 the Punjab produced 1.49m. bales of cotton (lint), although this was the worst harvest of the decade. The cotton harvest deteriorated from 0.9m. metric tons in that year to only 0.6m. tons in the following year, although it recovered thereafter, to reach 1.3m. tons in 2001/02 (still below the levels usual in most of the 1990s, and far from the record 2.5m. tons of 1989/90). Continuing high levels of government assistance (technical, financial and educational) aim to diversify the sector, and horticulture is being encouraged. The state is already the largest grower of mushrooms in India and of oranges (kinnows)—production of the latter, the Punjab's main fruit crop, was 260,000 metric tons in 1997/98. Pears, mangoes, grapes, peaches, lychees and lemons are also grown, while the main vegetable is potato (the Punjab achieves the best yields of potatoes, and of grapes, in India). Livestock numbers in 1996 (prior to the last agricultural census) were estimated at a total of 9.7m. head, with 15.3m. poultry. Milk production was encouraged from the late 1960s (obviously leading to what could be called a 'white revolution' in the 1970s), and the Punjab now produces the highest per caput amounts of milk and of eggs in the country. In 1997/98 the state produced 7.16m. tons of milk and 2,850m. eggs; five years later these totals had reached 8.7m. tons of milk and 3,468m. eggs, respectively the second and third highest levels in India. Extensive inland waterways enable the Punjab to have an efficient, if relatively small, fishing industry, but the intensity of agricultural land use means that woodland is limited (only 6.1% of the area was designated as forested in 2002). There is some mining activity, with the industry employing a surprising amount of workers (some 270,300 in 2001/02) for production of minerals valued at a relatively modest level (Rs 144m. in 2002/03).

In 1996/97 the secondary sector contributed 24.6% of GDP, and industry has remained the fastest growing economic activity since then. Figures for 2003/04 put the share of GDP at a similar level, however. The main industries include leather goods, hosiery and textiles generally, metal working, light engineering, electronics, the manufacture of hand tools, bicycles and sports goods, pharmaceuticals and the processing of food and other agricultural products. Most producers are small-scale, the number of such units for 1995/96 being put at 191,100 (employing 799,000 people, with production worth Rs 95,000m.), compared with 526 medium-sized and large enterprises (206,000 people, Rs 180,000m.). Exports from the sector were worth Rs 42,000m. in 1998, while the number of industrial concerns in 1998/99 had reached 197,000 small units and 653 medium-sized and large ones. By 2003/04 a fairly stable figure of some 203,000 small units had been reached, while the number of medium-sized and large units, which had dipped, rose again to 645. Industrial activity is spread throughout the state, although some cities have infrastructural advantages (such as the transport node of Amritsar) and others are noted for specializations (such as the steel city of Gobindgarh or the hosiery and textiles centre of Ludhiana, the 'Manchester of India').

In 1996/97 services accounted for 33.4% of GDP, but this had reached 37.3% by 2003/04. The tertiary sector is not as dominated by the expenditure on public administration as in some parts of India, with trade and transport well established economic activities. Although the Partition of the Punjab in 1947 and the recurring tensions with Pakistan ever since have disrupted much of the traditional east–west activity, the state retains a strong transport sector—many 'truckers', drivers of large freight-transport road vehicles, are, anecdotally, from the Punjab. Tourism relies on the Punjab's wealth of historical and religious sites, perhaps the most famous being the Sikhs' Golden Temple in Amritsar. However, local troubles as well as international tensions have prevented the sector from realizing its maximum potential.

### DIRECTORY

**Governor:** Gen. (retd) S. F. Rodrigues (Administrator of Chandigarh *ex officio*), Office of the Governor of Punjab, Raj Bhavan, Vigyan Path, Chandigarh 760 001; tel. (172) 2740740; fax (172) 2741058; e-mail governor@punjabmail.gov.in.

**Chief Minister:** Parkash Singh Badal (Shiromani Akali Dal), Office of the Chief Minister, Government of Punjab, 45, Sector 2, Chandigarh; tel. (172) 2740325; fax (172) 2742821; e-mail cm@punjabmail.gov.in.

**Speaker of the Legislative Assembly (Vidhan Sabha):** Dr Kewal Krishan, Assembly Secretariat, Punjab Vidhan Sabha, Chandigarh; tel. (172) 2740372; fax (172) 2740473; e-mail sppvs@punjabmail.gov.in; the unicameral Legislative Assembly has 117 mems: Shiromani Akali Dal 49; Congress 44; Bharatiya Janata Party 19; independents 5.

**State Principal Resident Commissioner in New Delhi:** J. S. Mani, Punjab House, Copernicus Marg, New Delhi 110 001; tel. (11) 23383804; fax (11) 23782448.

## Rajasthan

The State of Rajasthan lies in north-western India, a landlocked, rough-hewn square of territory along the international border with Pakistan, which lies to the north-west. Southwards, Pakistan abuts slightly into India, so that it also lies, for a lesser distance, beyond the south-western border of Rajasthan. The rest of the south-western border is with another Indian state, Gujarat, while Madhya Pradesh is to the south-east and the north-eastern border is shared with Uttar Pradesh (beyond the eastern corner of the state), Haryana and the Punjab (a very short border in the north of Rajasthan). Rajasthan, the 'land of kings', was once known as Rajputana, or the land of the Rajputs, the 'sons of kings', and the modern state was formed from 19 princely states and three chieftainships between 1948 and 1956. Since eastern Madhya Pradesh was made into the separate state of Chhattisgarh in 2000 Rajasthan has been the largest state in India, at 342,239 sq km (132,190 sq miles) almost the size of Germany.

Rajasthan is a largely arid state, its north-west consisting of India's only true desert, the Great Indian or Thar Desert, stretching the length of the 1,070-km India–Pakistan border. The land rises slowly from the Indus valley to the north-west, falling in the south-west towards Sindh (Pakistan) and the Rann of Kachchh (Gujarat). In the north-east the plateau lands give way to the Yamuna drainage basin, but the main topographical feature of the state is the spine formed by the Aravalli Range, which bisects the state. The Aravalli Range runs roughly parallel to the general line of the south-eastern border, from Mount Abu (potent in the myths of Rajput origins and presided over by the state's highest peak, Guru Shikhar, at 1,720 m—5,645 ft) in the south-west to head north-eastwards and end in the Rewari Hills of southern Haryana. Lying on the Tropic of Cancer, the climate is hot, and the monsoon rains do not always reach Rajasthan. The Aravalli hills and the south-west receive more rain, the former area also being cooler while the latter can be humid, but the rest of the state has average temperatures of 38°C (100°F) in May–August, with summer maximums sometimes reaching 46°C (115°F). In winter, maximum daily temperatures in most areas are between 22°C and 28°C (72°–82°F), with minimums sometimes dipping to 8°C (46°F). More than three-quarters of what rainfall there is tends to fall between July and September.

At the time of the 2001 census there were 56,507,188 people in Rajasthan, making it the eighth most populous state of India, and giving it a population of only several million fewer than that of the United Kingdom. The population density was only 165 per sq km. A higher than average growth rate was recorded since the previous census, although this had not prevented a remarkable growth in the literacy of the population. Most people speak Rajasthani, a Hindi language (89.6% in 1991—the main dialects are Marwari in the west, Jaipuri in the east, Malwi in the south-east and Mewati in the north-east), with the tribal Bhil tongue being the next most widely used (5.0%), followed by Urdu (2.2%), and some Punjabi and Sindhi. The old castes remain an important birthright in Rajasthan, pre-eminent among them, obviously, the Rajputs, the princely and warrior kshatriya caste (the head of all the Rajput clans is acknowledged to be the Maharana of Udaipur), also the priestly brahmins, the merchant vaishyas and several agricultural castes, known here as Jats, Gurjars or Gujjas, Malis and Kalvis. In 2001 17.2% of the population were counted among the Scheduled Castes and 12.6% among the Scheduled Tribes. The most populous tribes are those of the Bhil, who account for about two-fifths of the tribal population, and the Mina or Meena, the most widely spread, but there are other important ones, such as the Garasia, the Sansi, the Kanja, the jungle-dwelling Sahariya, the nomadic blacksmith people, the Gaduliya Lohar, and the Sidhi, a people believed to be descended from Africans arriving in India in the 13th century. Most people are Hindus (accounting for 88.8% of the 2001 population), but there are relatively large Muslim (8.5%), Sikh (1.4%) and Jain (1.2%) communities, as well as some Christians and a few Buddhists.

The proportion of the population living in urban centres was 23.4% in 2001. The state capital is Jaipur (1.87m. inhabitants in 2001, making it the 13th most populous city in India and by far the largest in Rajasthan). Jaipur is located in the north-east of central Rajasthan. The west is dominated by Jodhpur (851,051), the second city of Rajasthan, and the desert centre of Bikaner to its north. The beautiful city of Udaipur is in the south and Kota (694,316) in the south-east. Ajmer (485,575), to the south-west of the capital and on the way to Jodhpur, is famed as a Muslim holy city. Rajasthan is divided into 32 districts.

### HISTORY

The region has long been inhabited, particularly as it has not always been such a dry area. Harappan and post-Harappan cultures flourished here and it experienced the hegemony of the Mauryas (third century BC) and the Guptas (fourth–sixth centuries AD). Between such imperial eras the region was obviously open to the many invaders that would sweep down into the subcontinent from the north-west, out of Persia (Iran) or Bactria (Afghanistan) and Central Asia. Thus, the Bactrian Greeks (Yavanas) were dominant in the second century BC, the Sakas (Scythians) in the second–fourth centuries AD and the Huns (Hiung-nu) in the sixth century. Subsequently, although they were probably largely descended from the Scythian and Hun tribes, the people of what became Rajasthan served as a bulwark against further invasion and consciously thought of themselves as defenders of the Hindu homeland.

The emergence of Rajput dynasties took place between the seventh and 11th centuries, by which time (and for a further century) they controlled much of north India. Given the Hindu loyalties and the martial strength of the Rajputs, it is perhaps no surprise to find the brahmins anxious to discover royal lineages for these warrior princes, who liked to emphasize their ksatriya status, born of the great fire sacrifice of the gods on Mount Abu. Such origins link them to the Gurjaras, and that they share an equally uncertain but probably similar past is indicated by the fact that most of the great Rajput clans of the 10th century onwards had emerged from the disintegration of the imperial order of the Gurjara-Pratiharas of Kannauj (now in Uttar Pradesh). Whatever the origins of the Rajputs, as they naturalized and 'Aryanized', they focused on the martial virtues of their caste status, as well as operating the sort of feudal system that reinforced both the clan and the military structures. The system of land tenure encouraged the surplus wealth of the self-sufficient villages into the hands of the clan prince, who could build palaces and forts, while the geography of their heartland of 'Rajputana' also encouraged the smaller urban settlements that could survive in a dry land, huddled in or around fortified high places that kept them independent. Rajput dynasties were spread throughout north India, but their greatest geographical concentration, and the increasing refinement of the definition of 'Rajput' (not least under the generally admiring British), steadily contracted their territory to modern Rajasthan. The history of the state, therefore, is a mixed one of many principalities, and it is possible only to give a general overview and seize on a few important examples.

The Gurjara clan of the Pratiharas ruled a large part of Rajasthan in the eighth century, when they moved into the imperial politics of Kannauj, and they held sway until the 10th century. The main Rajput clan of the region, which gradually supplanted Gurjara-Pratihara overlordship, however, was that of the Chahamanas (Chauhans) of Ajmer. They extended their rule as far as Delhi in the mid-12th century and it was their 'fort of king Prithviraj' that was transformed into the site of a new imperial capital by the Delhi Sultans. Prithviraj III, who ascended the throne of Ajmer in 1177, himself ruled an empire that included western Rajasthan, the eastern Punjab as far as the foothills of the Himalayas and part of the Ganga–Yamuna Doab, and led a Rajput confederacy, which together effectively blocked the Muslim advance into the rest of India. The Rajput forces successfully drove off the invading army of Muhammed of Ghor (now in Afghanistan) at the first battle at Tarain (Haryana) in 1191. The Muslim forces returned in greater numbers the following year, however, and, in perhaps one of the most decisive battles of Indian history, again fought at Tarain, the Rajput army was routed, Prithviraj III captured and later executed, and the road to Delhi and the *arya varta* opened. Ajmer itself was occupied, but Ghorid control of Rajasthan remained tenuous, as cities were taken and lost regularly before final possession was decided, and many Muslim commanders were more interested in plundering raids and the extortion of tribute rather than the settlement of an empire. For Ajmer itself, its future was largely determined by the arrival in 1192, in the wake of the second battle at Tarain, of Khwaja Moinuddin Chist, a Muslim Sufi saint, who died here in 1235. Although it was ruled, in turn, by the Rajput houses of Mewar (later based in Udaipur), Malwa (a Rajput dynasty of the ancient kingdom in Madhya Pradesh) and Jodhpur, Ajmer became an object of Muslim ambition and was conquered by Akbar, the Mughal emperor, in 1556, who made it a place of pilgrimage. In the palace he built here, Jahangir, Akbar's successor, received the first embassy of the British (from King James I of England and VI of Scotland), and this was to be the only part of modern Rajasthan under the direct administration of British India after 1818 (after the Mughal decline Jodhpur had regained control until losing the area to the Marathas).

The foremost Rajput state, at least in honour, was that of Mewar, which from the 12th century was based on the fort at Chittaurgarh (Chittor), one of the oldest cities in the state (officially founded in the eighth century, but with evidence of much longer habitation). The dynasty of the Ranas of Mewar ruled from here from the 14th century, but moved to the new capital of Udaipur, founded by Maharana Udai Singh, in 1568. Mewar prided itself on its long history of independence, but this entailed constant warfare, resulting in constant poverty, and it was the determined opposition of the house of Sesodia to the Mughals that had caused Akbar to besiege and, eventually, bloodily win Chittaurgarh fort and force the rajah (who had taken refuge in the hills) to found a new city. Mewar was only forced into accommodation of the Mughals by Shah Jahan (emperor in 1627–58)—although the Rana, Amar Singh, avoided making personal submission to the Great Mughal. In fact, the boast of Mewar was that no reigning prince ever made such submission, even in 1680, when Udaipur was sacked by a Mughal army of Aurangzeb, after the Sesodias had backed the insurgency provoked by the emperor's intervention in the succession of Marwar.

Marwar, the dominant state of western Rajasthan, became the realm of the Rathore Rajputs in 1211, after they moved west from a defeat at Kannauj by the invading Muslims. Their capital was at Mandore until 1459, when they were forced to move a little south to Jodhpur, a strategic site on the edge of the desert, from where they could rule vast tracts of Rajasthan and regularly threaten the wealth of Gujarat to the south. The ruler was honoured with a royal title by Akbar, as part of his successful policy of co-opting the great Rajput warrior princes, and the second rajah, Sawai Rajah Sur Singh (who reigned in 1581–95), conquered Gujarat and part of the Deccan for the Great Mughal. Relations with the Mughals were not always happy, however, notably when Aurangzeb undermined the system of incorporating Hindu nobles into the Mughal hierarchy. In Marwar a not unreasonable imperial intervention during a hiatus in the succession was exacerbated into insurrection by the iconoclasm of the occupying forces—the guardians of the young heir, Ajit Singh, sought the help of other Rajput houses after fleeing Delhi in 1678 and so began a struggle that would resume after the death of Aurangzeb and proceed, with varying success, during the decay of Mughal power. Thus, Marwar drove the Mughals from Ajmer and captured Ahmedabad (Gujarat) in the first half of the 18th century. Like most of the other Rajput princes, the house of Jodhpur then experienced the threat of Maratha expansionism and relatively happily entered treaty relations with the British at the time of their victory over the Marathas in 1818. The Rajput princes were greatly honoured in the hierarchy of the new Empire, and more recently a reward for their loyalty during the Great Rebellion of 1857–58 (following the Sepoy Mutiny). The principality of Bikaner was founded in 1488 by a scion of the house of Jodhpur, and its rulers came to have a progressive reputation while under British rule.

The Kachhawaha Rajputs were based in Amer (Amber) from 1037 until Sawai Maharajah Jai Singh II (1699–1744) founded a new capital at Jaipur (now the state capital of Rajasthan) in 1727. The Kachhawahas were among the first Rajputs to lend their services to the Mughals and their reward laid the foundations for a lasting pan-Indian empire that accommodated Hindus as well as the co-religionists of the ruling dynasty. In 1562 Akbar married a daughter of the Kachhawaha house and inducted its nobles into the Mughal hierarchy. This proved to be a successful and continuing way of tying the Rajputs into the imperial order. The Kachhawahas can also be noted for their contribution to the Taj Mahal, the famous monument in Uttar Pradesh, providing the site and much of the marble used in its construction. Like the other rajahs and rulers of the region, the Kachhawahas submitted to British suzerainty in 1818.

The history of British rule in Rajasthan, Rajputana, starts badly, as the defeat of the Marathas at the beginning of the 19th century and the East India Company's subsequent refusal to fill the power vacuum made the region notorious for lawlessness and unrest. Most of the Rajput princes and the few Muslim rulers of the region (such as Tonk) were, therefore, brought into the nascent, new imperial system when the situation began to be rectified in 1818, with the final defeat of the Marathas. Thereafter, political developments largely continued as the responsibility of the princes, although wider developments in British India influenced the states, such as reforming campaigns and the struggle for independence. In terms of representative democracy (seldom involving popular participation in government), for instance, the Maharajah of Bikaner introduced a House of Representatives in 1913, while Jaipur gained a disappointing Vidhan Samiti in 1923 and the Maharana of Udaipur was being forced towards constitutional concessions by the 1940s. Most developments came about as a result of the move towards independence for India (the democratic successor state to the Empire in which the princes of Rajputana would find themselves) and as a result of the formation of the modern state over the following eight years.

On 18 March 1948 Alwar, Bharatpur, Dholpur and Karauli formed the Matsya Union, the first step towards a single state in Rajputana. One week later Banswara, Bundi, Dungerpur, Jhalawar, Kishangarh, Kota, Pratapgarh, Shahpura and Tonk formed another group, known as the Rajasthan Union (Kota, which had become a separate state from Bundi in 1681, became the capital). Only three days later these arrangements were disrupted by the decision of Udaipur to join the latter Union, and the United State of Rajasthan was effected on 18 April 1948. The inclusion of the Sesodia principality encouraged the larger states to join the process of unification, and the United State became Greater Rajasthan on 30 March 1949, with the accession of Bikaner, Jaipur, Jaisalmer and Jodhpur. Six weeks later, on 15 May, the Matsya Union and Greater Rajasthan merged into the United State of Greater Rajasthan (USGR). The rest of the process of creating the modern state was effected under national legislation. Under the Constitution of 26 January 1950 a United Rajasthan added most of the Sirohi principality to the 18 former states in the USGR, creating a single 'Part B' state, while the old Ajmer-Merwara province directly administered by the Centre became a 'Part C' state known simply as Ajmer. Finally, under the State Reorganization Act that took effect on 1 November 1956, modern Rajasthan was formed by the merging of United Rajasthan and Ajmer. The only other territorial adjustments were the additional inclusion in the new state of the Abu Road taluka (formerly part of Sirohi, but then included in Bombay—now Gujarat and Maharashtra—for a time) and Sunel Tappa (hitherto an enclave of Madhya Bharat—now part of Madhya Pradesh), while the Sirohi subdivision of the district of Kota went to Madhya Pradesh. The princes were steadily bereft of power but still retain great respect.

Rajasthan currently sends 25 deputies to the national Lok Sabha and contributes 10 members of the Rajya Sabha in the Parliament of India. National representation is split between Congress, which dominated the state until the end of the 1980s, and the Bharatiya Janata Party (BJP). In 1989 Congress lost the state elections and the BJP retained power until January 1999, when the Assembly elected at the end of the previous year convened with an overwhelming Congress majority. Ashok Gehlot, therefore, succeeded Bhairon Singh Shekhawat as Chief Minister. However, the Congress Government suffered the ramifications of the communal tensions in neighbouring Gujarat, and it was humiliated at by-elections to three Assembly seats towards the end of 2002. The BJP, meanwhile, also tried to exploit traditional caste reverences by appointing a royal Rajput, Vasundhara Raje Scindia, as head of the party in Rajasthan; although she remained a Union minister, in mid-2003 she was confirmed as the party's candidate for the state premiership, despite some negative reaction. Such internal dissensions, as well the perception by some that Hindu chauvinism may have been pushed too far, gave some renewed hopes to Gehlot. However, he did not counter Scindia's appeal to women and Jat voters, and the persistence of drought damaged the popularity of the incumbent Government. Thus, on 1 December 2003 Congress was routed in the state elections, retaining only 56 seats (having held 153 previously). The BJP won convincingly, securing 120 seats (up from 33), and Scindia became Rajasthan's first woman Chief Minister. (With the legislature's Speaker and, from November 2004, a new Governor, all three of the state's chief officials were women—the Governor, Pratibha Patil, resigned in June 2007 and was elected India's first woman President in the following month.) The ascendancy of the BJP was confirmed in May 2004, at the general election, when the party won 21 of the state's 25 Lok Sabha seats (up from 16), while Congress retained only four. In January 2005 a by-election victory against

Congress increased the BJP's representation in the state legislature to 121.

Later in 2005 international attention was drawn to Rajasthan over concerns about the dramatic and hitherto unacknowledged decline in the Indian tiger population. The domestic political ramifications of this issue were considered negligible, but the authorities were nevertheless embarrassed to admit that every tiger in the Sariska reserve, in the north of the state, had disappeared, while numbers had fallen significantly in Ranthambore. The state Government referred the matter for criminal investigation of poachers and their collaborators, while the Union Government was prompted to order a simultaneous, nation-wide census of tigers, to take place in October of that year. Controversy continued into 2007, with the High Court of Rajasthan forced to issue conservation guidelines to officials in May.

Civil order and BJP internal harmony were severely disrupted from mid-2007 by caste tensions in Rajasthan. When seeking election in 2003, Scindia had promised to support the kshatriya and pastoralist Gurjars in their attempts to seek Scheduled Tribe status (they were then counted among the Other Backward Classes—however, Jat agitation to be included in that category in 2000 had diminished the perceived benefits for the Gurjars). Failure of the BJP Government to follow up on this pledge prompted violent protests in September 2006 and, more significantly, in late May 2007. Centred on Dausa, in eastern Rajasthan, Gurjar violence, in support of which category to be reserved to, erupted on 29 May. Two days later the Minas were provoked into violent protests against Gurjar inclusion in the reservation diluting the value of Scheduled Tribe status. With Gurjar demonstrations and *bandhs* spreading to neighbouring states and to Delhi and Uttar Pradesh, the Government of Rajasthan invoked emergency measures for its affected districts on 2 June. Two days later the main Gurjar spokesman, Col Kirori Singh Bainsla, met Chief Minister Scindia and agreed that the agitations should cease while a three-man committee under a judge would investigate the Gurjar claim in preparation for a recommendation to the Centre. Although the unrest subsided, many Gurjars considered the agreement unsatisfactory. However, Bainsla regained the sympathy of many when included among those charged with murder and incitement during the unrest (26 had died). Meanwhile, the BJP was troubled by the contrary allegiances of ministers and deputies during the crisis, with attempts to reimpose discipline decried as unfair by some.

Chief Minister Scindia was anxious to distance the Government from caste and quota politics, with state elections looming in 2008—Gurjars were usually considered an important bank of votes, but the Minas were more numerous. However, the issue continued to reappear, notably in December 2007. The resignation of several Mina legislators emphasized their opposition to Scheduled Tribe status for the Gurjars and, more importantly, the official inquiry recommended other measures, but not inclusion in the Scheduled Tribe category, to help the Gurjar community. The Government of Rajasthan referred the issue to the Centre, in an attempt to distance itself from the controversy. Nevertheless, in mid-May Gurjar protests escalated, following the deaths of 31 people under police guns, at two incidents in as many days. Government and Gurjar representatives inched their way towards negotiations as unrest continued, spreading to Delhi and other states and disrupting rail traffic particularly. At the beginning of June the federal law ministry opined that the issue of reservations was one for the state authorities. Negotiations were agreed and, about a month after the agitation began, the two sides agreed a 5% reservation for the Gurjars in a 'special, separate backward class' (not affecting the existing reservations for the Minas and others). With state elections due in September, the Scindia Government also announced a 14% reservation for the 'poor among upper castes'. The settlement was enacted unanimously by the Assembly in July. Meanwhile, the state had also experienced two significant terrorist attacks, possibly perpetrated by Islamist groups (usually linked by the authorities with Bangladesh) seeking to increase communal tensions and chasten non-orthodox Muslims. In October 2007 a bomb at a Sufi shrine in Ajmer killed three and, more seriously, in May the toll of fatalities from a number of co-ordinated blasts in Jaipur reached 68.

## ECONOMY

Rajasthan is a poor state, its dominant agricultural and pastoral economy, precarious on the edge of the desert, unable to enrich a growing population despite good mineral resources and a thriving tourist industry. Following weak growth since the late 1990s and severe contraction in 2002, the economy began to expand more strongly from 2003. The net state domestic product in 2004/05 was Rs 985,730m., or Rs 16,212 per head. There were 85,008 km of roads in 1998/99, of which some 3,000 km were national highway. There are relatively good rail connections between the main centres of Rajasthan. Jaipur, Jodhpur and Udaipur enjoy good aviation links with the rest of India, and there are a number of other airstrips. In 1998/99 the state generated 10,038.7m. units of electrical power, but was obliged to purchase a further 10,940.0m. units from outside the state. Installed capacity in 2006 consisted of 3,776 MW in the state sector, 1,587 MW from central projects and only 90 MW from the private sector. In March 2005 fewer than 2% of villages had yet to be connected to the electricity supply, although only 22% of rural households actually had electricity. In terms of social infrastructure, the state achieved a dramatic improvement in its literacy rate between the 1991 and 2001 censuses, increasing it from only 38.6% to 61.0%.

Agriculture and animal husbandry is the dominant economic sector, although only 75.1% of the state's area was cultivable in 1998/99 (about one-third dependent on irrigation). Most of the population, therefore, find their fortunes prone to the vagaries of the weather, the failure of the monsoons soon reducing them to being in peril of famine, as happened at the end of the 1990s and in the early 2000s. The sector contributed 28% of gross state domestic product in 2001/02. Record foodgrain production of 14.05m. metric tons was recorded in 1997/98, but output then fell, before rising to 13.98m. tons in 2001/02. In the latter year the oilseeds harvest amounted to 3.13m. tons, sugar cane to only 0.43m. tons (having declined steadily from peak production of 1.41m. tons in 1995/96) and cotton to a mere 280,800 tons (compared with 1.36m. tons in 1996/97). A catastrophic harvest in 2002/03 reduced total foodgrain production by almost one-half, to 7.57m. tons. The main crops are wheat, maize, barley, millets, pulses and other food grains, cotton and tobacco, with the cultivation of vegetables and citrus fruits expanding in the 1990s. Spices such as red chillies, mustard and cumin are also grown. In 1997 total livestock numbers were put at 54.35m. and, traditionally, this agricultural activity is considered more stable than arable farming in such a dry state. Rajasthan is India's leading producer of wool, with production of 19,384 metric tons in 2002/03 (37% of the all-India total). In the same year the state produced 7.8m. tons of milk (more than any other state except Uttar Pradesh and the Punjab) and 636m. eggs. Forestry accounted for only 9.5% of the land area in 2001.

The most important metallic mineral reserves are copper, lead, zinc and silver, tungsten, manganese and iron ore, while other resources include limestone and dolomite, lignite (brown coal), barites, clays, calcite, gypsum, feldspar, fluorite, potash, rock phosphate, silica sand, emeralds and other precious and semi-precious stones, soapstone, marble and granite. The sector employed about 175,600 people in 2001/02 and the following year the total value of minerals amounted to some Rs 24,052m. The extractive sector has also provided a basis for some heavy industry, such as a zinc smelter and a copper plant. Other major industrial activities, apart from the processing of metallic and non-metallic minerals, include textiles and woollens, sugar, chemicals and pharmaceuticals, railway wagons, precision instruments, television sets, etc. There were 10,244 registered factories in 1997. In 1998/99 small-scale industrial units numbered some 199,000, with an employment potential of 778,000 people.

Trade, transport and public administration obviously make important contributions to the tertiary sector, but the state also possesses a strong tourist industry. The many ancient cities and forts of the region, its princely heritage and religious sites are a valuable asset, and the unique desert environment also provides an attraction. Rajasthan is on the traditional tour itinerary of foreign visitors to northern India, but, among the states, is only eighth in importance for domestic tourist visitors (attracting 3.1% of such visits in 2002).

## DIRECTORY

**Governor:** SHILENDRA KUMAR SINGH, Office of the Governor, Raj Bhavan, Civil Lines, Jaipur; tel. (141) 2382737; fax (141) 2382492.

**Chief Minister:** VASUNDHARA RAJE SCINDIA (Bharatiya Janata Party), Office of the Chief Minister, Government of Rajasthan, 8 Civil Lines, Jaipur; tel. (141) 2227351; fax (141) 2381687.

**Speaker of the Legislative Assembly:** SUMITRA SINGH, 11 Civil Lines, Jaipur; tel. (141) 2744321; fax (141) 2744333; e-mail rajassem@raj.nic.in; the unicameral Legislative Assembly has 200 mems: Bharatiya Janata Party 121; Congress 55; Indian National Lok Dal 4; Janata Dal (United) 2; Bahujan Samaj Party 2; Communist (CPI—M) 1; independents and others 15.

**State Principal Resident Commissioner in New Delhi:** J. P. SINGH, Bikaner House, Pandara Rd, New Delhi 110 003; tel. (11) 23073747; fax (11) 23381802.

# Sikkim

The State of Sikkim is in northern India, in the mountains above the Bengal plains. It juts northwards into Tibet (Xizang), part of the People's Republic of China (with which there are international borders to the north and east), and separates Nepal (to the west) from Bhutan (with which there is a short border in the south-east of the state). Sikkim's only border with the rest of India is in the south, with West Bengal. The former principality's name probably derives from a Tsong word (*sukhim*) meaning 'new home' or 'happy home'. Once a much larger realm, Sikkim's decline forced it into dependence on British protection from the 19th century; India, as a successor state to the Empire, formalized Sikkim's status as its own protectorate by treaty in 1950. Democratic politics and Indian intervention in the administration in 1974 led, the following year, to a referendum, the abolition of the monarchy and the accession of Sikkim as the 22nd state of the Indian Union on 15 May 1975. Sikkim became the smallest state in India (until Goa achieved statehood 12 years later), with an area of 7,096 sq km (2,739 sq miles).

The state lies in the eastern Himalayas, traversed by the Great Himalaya and some of its southern spurs. The topography is dominated by the deep valley of the River Tista (Teesta) and, to its west, the rising mass of Kangchenjunga (Kanchendzonga—'House of Five Treasures'), which, at 8,586 m (28,179 ft), is the highest mountain in India, the third highest in the world and the presiding deity of the surrounding country. Only 40 km (25 miles) from the peak of Kangchenjunga, however, is Sikkim's lowest point, at 221 m, in the southern foothills. This indicates the variety and extremity of the altitudinal changes in the landscape, affecting the climate and the flora. About one-third of Sikkim is covered with dense, often inaccessible, forests of sal, sambal and bamboo. The mountainous terrain is slashed by deep ravines and green valleys watered by rivers fed with both snow and rain. The main river, the perennial Tista, flows from north to south, steeply down the east and centre of the state, ultimately flowing into the Brahmaputra (until the great floods of 1787 altered the course of the Ganga—Ganges—the Tista had been a tributary of the latter river). It has sources in the Tista Zhangse and the great Zemu glaciers, in the bleaker, colder north-east of Sikkim, where the more desert-like terrain is barely softened by the two main tributary river valleys, of Lachen and Lachung. The main river system flowing through the south-west of the state is that of the Rangit (Ranjit). The climate can range from tropical in the southern foothills, through temperate, to arctic in the very north and north-east or on the mountain heights. Sikkim generally experiences a considerable amount of rainfall, ranging from 1,260 mm (50 inches) to 5,100 mm per year, varying considerably according to altitude or how far north the place is. Gangtok, the hill-top capital, receives the maximum annual average of rainfall (3,494 mm), while Thanggu, high in the north-west, has the minimum (82 mm). Most rain falls between June and September, when the monsoons penetrate deep into the Himalayas up the valleys of the Tista and the Rangit. Fog is also common throughout the state at this time of year. Average January temperatures in Gangtok, the state capital, range from 4°C to 14°C (39°F–57°F), while by May the lowest average equals the winter month's highest, ranging up to 22°C (72°F).

In terms of population, Sikkim is still the smallest state in India (three territories also have higher populations), with 540,851 people, according to the 2001 census. The rate of increase in population since 1991 was considerably higher than the national average, the total having increased by almost one-third from 406,457. The population density in 2001 was 76 per sq km, although this is misleading, as, owing to the mountainous nature of Sikkim, only about 20% of its territory is habitable. The most populous area is the south-east, while the north is sparsely populated. The latter is also the region reserved to the indigenous Lepchas, who barely account for 10% of the population. An Indo-Mongoloid people, who may be related to the Nagas of north-east India and probably entered Sikkim from Assam or Tibet before the eighth century, they are also known as the Rongpa or Kongpa, 'people of the ravines'. The Bhutias or Bhotias ('of Bhot' or 'of Tibet') arrived in Sikkim from the 14th century, particularly in the 16th century, as aristocratic refugees from strife in Tibet, and are now traders and farmers, noted as hardy pastoralists of the high mountains. There is also a small community of the Magar, who have been present for not much less time. Officially registered Scheduled Tribes, of whom the Lepchas and Bhutias are the largest groups, constitute 20.6% of the total population (2001 figures). The Lepchas alone constituted only 8.7%, and in the mid-2000s there were moves to seek additional protection for this aboriginal population. By far the largest ethnic group, however, is Nepali; these people began to arrive with the Gurkha invasions from the 18th century, mainly the Newars and other clans such as the Chettris or Sherpas. They now form the majority population of Sikkim, but most are not officially scheduled (in 2005 it was agreed that the small Limbu and Tamang groups of Nepali descent should be included among the Scheduled Tribes). As a result, Nepali is the most widely spoken language, in one form or another, although Lepcha and Bhutia are also spoken, while Hindi is the official language and English the working language of government. The Nepali majority also means that Hinduism is the major religion (60.9% of the population in 2001). Mahayana Buddhism, heavily influenced by the animist Bon religion native to the Lepcha (and, indeed, to the Tibetans), claimed the adherence of 28.1% of the population, according to the 2001 census. Historically, Sikkim is a stronghold of the Nyingma pa, the 'old' sect or 'Red Hats' of Tibetan Lamaism, although in 1959 the principality gave refuge to the 16th reincarnation of the Gyalwa Karmapa (who died in 1981) when he fled the Chinese occupation of Tibet. Rumtek monastery, 24 km (15 miles) south-west of Gangtok, is now, therefore, the headquarters of the Kagyu or 'Black Hat' sect. There are 70 monasteries in Sikkim. In 2001 there was a small but growing community of Christians (6.7% in that year, up from 3.3% in 1991), as well as some adherents of Islam (1.4%) and of other religions.

According to the census of 2001, only 11.1% of the population was urbanized, the largest town, the state capital, Gangtok, in the south-east, having a population of barely 30,000. The next largest towns, both also in southern Sikkim and on the main road from Gangtok into West Bengal, are Singtam and Rongphu. Southern Sikkim is split into three of the state's four districts, the south-west being the West District, the south-east the East District, and the narrow strip of land between being the South District—the last with its chief town (Namchi) also near the border and transport links of West Bengal. Mangan is the main town of the North, which district covers almost 60% of the state's territory but contains only 7.7% of the population (1991 figure). The official headquarters of West District is Gyalshing (Gezing), with the ancient capital and religious centre of Yuksam not far to the north. The East District around Gangtok is the most populous, with 43.9% of the total in 1991.

## HISTORY

Sikkim, once known as Basyul, the 'hidden land', was originally inhabited by Naong, Chang and Mon tribes, but these were subsumed into the Lepcha people who had moved onto the southern flanks of the Himalayas from Assam or eastern Tibet in about the eighth century. They were only united under a king or punu in about 1400, when Tur Ve Pa No was crowned. Three more kings succeeded him, until the Lepchas resorted to a looser association of the clans. Meanwhile, Tibetan exiles (the first ancestors of the Bhutias) had began to arrive in the region of Sikkim from the 13th century, although the major influx was not until several hundred years later, during the religious strife between the 'Red Hat' Buddhists and the reformist 'Yellow Hats'. Although Buddhism was probably already present in Sikkim (the great eighth-century Guru Rimpoche, Padmasambhava, is said to have passed through the country on his way to the first conversion of Tibet), the arrival of these 'Red Hat' or Nyingma pa Bhutias certainly ensured that it would become a Buddhist state under the Namgyal dynasty.

The Bhutia family that was to rule Sikkim for over 330 years, until its incorporation into India, first arrived in the region in the 13th century. They were descendants of the legendary prince who had founded the eastern Tibetan kingdom of Minyang in the ninth century. A Guru Tashi led his people south from the Kham region, his eldest son helping a Sakya king and winning himself both the name of Khye Bumsa and a princess in marriage. They settled in the Chumbi valley (where the People's Republic of China now juts down between Bhutan and north-east Sikkim) and established friendly relations with the Lepcha prince of Gangtok, Thekong Tek—not only a chieftain, but also a religious leader. He and Khye Bumsa established a blood-brotherhood treaty at Kabi Lungstok, and the Bhutia dynasty came to hold increasing sway in both the Chumbi and Tista valleys thereafter, particularly after the demise of Thekong Tek and the Lepcha chieftainship. Khye Bumsa was succeeded by his third son, Mipon Rab, who himself had four sons (from whom the four principal clans of Sikkim are said to be descended), the youngest of who, another Guru Tashi, succeeded his father. He moved the capital to Gangtok and ruled over both Lepchas and Bhutias, becoming the first ruler of Sikkim as such. His great grandson, Phuntsok or Penchu, a son of the third ruler to follow Guru Tashi, was to become the first consecrated chogyal ('heavenly king'—both the ruler or gyalpo and the religious head of Sikkim) and first adopted the name of Namgyal for his dynasty.

In 1641, during the time when Lamaist Buddhism was being consolidated in Sikkim, three sages entered the country from different directions and met at Yuksam, in the west. During their debate on establishing a united temporal and spiritual leadership for Sikkim (Tibet had been bestowed upon the Dalai Lama by the Mongol rulers in the previous year), one of these lamas, the evangelizing Lhatsun Chenpo, cited a prophecy of Padmasambhava to silence the competing claims of the clerics. Thus, it was a 38-year-old scion of the ruling house, Phuntsok, who was found to satisfy the prophecy; he was consecrated as the first Chogyal at Yuksam (which became his capital) in 1642, taking one of Lhatsun Chenpo's names as the name of the ruling family. Legitimacy was sought, and gained, through recognition by the Dalai Lama, and Sikkim (then extending much further in all directions from its present borders—including the Chumbi valley, now in Tibet, and Darjiling, West Bengal) thereafter enjoyed Tibetan support.

In 1670 Tensung Namgyal succeeded his father and moved the capital to Rabdentse. Dynastic rivalries after his death in about 1700 then involved an invasion by Bhutan, while the infant king, Chador Namgyal, was taken to refuge in Lhasa, the seat of the Dalai Lama. Tibetan help eventually enabled the recapture of Rabdentse and most of the kingdom. However, Sikkim continued to lose territory to

Bhutan, while the dynastic uncertainty of the next two reigns exacerbated ethnic pretensions and saw the loss of much of the Limbu (Limboo) and the Magar territories. Chador (who in 1716 fell victim to the same half-sister, Pedi, who had fomented the earlier invasion by Bhutan) was succeeded by his infant son, Gyurmed. This Chogyal then died at the age of 26 years, in 1734, without legitimate issue, but claiming a nun was pregnant by him. The male child was named Phuntsok, in a bid to add lustre to his claim, but, not surprisingly, many disputed the authenticity of the succession, particularly among the Bhutia aristocracy. Chandzod Tarwang, a minister and friend of Gyurmed, declared himself the ruler or rajah of Sikkim. However, as the then majority Lepcha population favoured a continuation of Namgyal rule, Tarwang was driven from power in 1737 and the reign of Phuntsok II was then assured by Tibetan support.

Although invasions from Bhutan eventually subsided under the new Chogyal, Sikkim was increasingly under threat from the Gurkhas of Nepal. Seventeen Gurkha incursions were repulsed, until a peace treaty in 1775. Trouble with Nepal continued, however, exacerbated by the accession of another junior to the throne in 1780. Phuntsok II's son, Tenzing, was also to die young, in 1793, but in exile in Lhasa, owing to further Nepalese invasion. However, that the Gurkhas then pressed on into Tibetan territory provoked the anger of China, which also obliged Nepal to vacate some of its conquered territories and permit the restoration of the monarchy in Sikkim. Tenzing's infant son, Tsudphud, was despatched from Lhasa in 1793 to assume his throne. With the loss of territory in the west, Rabdentse was demonstrably too vulnerable and the Chogyal moved the capital to Tumlong. During the long reign of Tsudphud, Sikkim's need for support against the Gurkhas was to reduce it progressively to dependence upon the British. Nepal, denied its expansionist ambitions in Tibet by China, continued to harry Sikkim and the Indian empire of the British. In 1814 war broke out between the British and Nepal, resulting in the 1816 Treaty of Sugauli, after the defeat of the Gurkhas. This led to the 1817 Treaty of Titalia between Sikkim and its new protector, whereby the kingdom regained some of its lost territories. However, with the threat from Nepal settled, Sikkim came to be dominated by relations with its southern neighbour. In 1835 Chogyal Tsudphud was pressured into ceding the district of Darjiling (Darjeeling) to the British, who favoured it as a hill resort and were meant to pay a subsidy to Sikkim for the concession. Disputes over this subsidy caused a deterioration in relations and even resulted in the temporary imprisonment of the Superintendent of Darjeeling by the Sikkimese in 1849. This, in turn, provoked the British expedition of February 1850, which provided for the annexation of Darjiling to India's Bengal Presidency, but left the Sikkimese dissatisfied and willing to raid British lands. An imperial expeditionary force was defeated in 1860, but a larger one occupied Tumlong in 1861 and imposed a new treaty. The chogyals were meant to be placated with the title of maharajah, which indicated their subjection to the Indian empire, and, later, an enhanced subsidy.

Tsudphud, the seventh Chogyal but first Maharajah, died in 1863, to be succeeded by two of his sons, Sidekeong I and then, in 1874, Thutob (Thobden—later Sir Thutob). The latter became more pro-Tibetan after the British favoured the influx of Nepalis into Sikkim, but Tibet itself was beginning to feel the pressure of British expansionism as the Empire sought to build roads into Sikkim and establish trade links through the Himalayas. There were skirmishes with Tibetan forces in the 1880s, but British pressure continued to mount, with a political officer installed in Sikkim in 1889 and a military force being sent into Tibet in 1904. Meanwhile, China had recognized the British protectorate of Sikkim in 1890 and the now largely powerless Chogyal moved the capital to its present site of Gangtok. Sidekeong II succeeded his father in 1914, but did not survive the year and was himself succeeded by his half-brother, Tashi (later Sir Tashi), who, following the restoration of full powers of government to the monarchy in 1918, instituted many reforms. However, he was unwilling to concede many democratic institutions or accession to an independent India. The Chogyal negotiated for the new Indian successor state to assume the protection of Sikkim from the old Empire, and this arrangement was ratified by treaty on 5 December 1950. India assumed responsibility for defence, foreign affairs and strategic communications, and the position of the monarchy was confirmed, although the treaty also provided for increased popular participation in government. India's responsibilities and tensions along the Chinese border meant that by 1961 access to Sikkim was greatly restricted, and this was maintained after the 1962 incidents along the length of the Indian frontier with the People's Republic of China.

The main political parties, notably those with their support among the majority Hindu (Nepali) population, had opposed protectorate status and favoured closer association with India. The royal court had increasing difficulty in ignoring their views given the results of successive general elections, the first in 1952 and the fifth (and the last for independent Sikkim) in 1974. About 20 years after the signing of the Sikkim-India treaty there were beginning to be explicit demonstrations of discontent by the populace, not helped by the opposition to reform and the flamboyant lifestyle of the new Chogyal. Gyalsay Palden Thondup Namgyal had succeeded his father in December 1963, becoming the 12th Chogyal and the sixth and last Maharajah of Sikkim (in the same year the leader of the Chogyal's administration was restyled the Chief Administrative Officer, instead of Chief Minister). Kazi Lhendup Dorji and Krishna Chandra Pradhan, who were eventually to unite their rival parties in the Sikkim Congress, led opposition to the monarchy.

Protests against royal government escalated to such an extent in 1973 that the administration of the country collapsed and the Chogyal was forced to appeal to India for assistance. On 9 April the Indian Government appointed B. S. Das as Chief Administrative Officer of Sikkim. He supervised the introduction of a new constitutional document for the country, which retained a limited monarchy, but exchanged the status of a protectorate for that of an associate state of India. The National Assembly approved the new Constitution in 1974, and Das yielded his position to Kazi Lhendup Dorji, the leader of the Sikkim Congress, who became Prime Minister on 23 July. The Sikkim Congress overwhelmingly won the September general election, giving it the authority to arrange a referendum on the future of the state. The Chogyal continued to oppose the introduction of greater political liberties and the persistent interventions of India. Nevertheless, on 10 April 1975 a reported 97% of the electorate supported the accession of Sikkim to the Indian Union. The Chogyal was effectively deposed as a ruling monarch (he died in 1982, his son, Wangchuk Namgyal, becoming the 13th Chogyal, a post now shorn of executive power or official privileges) and, upon the announcement of the official results on 14 April, was replaced as Chief Executive (later Governor) by Bipen Bihari Lal. The Indian Parliament duly passed the 38th amendment to its basic law on 26 April and Sikkim became the 22nd state of the Union on 16 May.

In 1979 Nar Bahadur Bhandari, of the Sikkim Samgram Parishad (SSP), become the new Chief Minister, which post he was to hold until June 1994 (apart from the brief 'caretaker' premiership of B. B. Gurung in the mid-1980s), conclusively winning the state elections of 1984 and 1989. Bhandari was subsequently charged with corruption while in office. Another caretaker Government, under S. Limboo, held power until the elections of 12 December 1994, when Pawan Kumar Chamling of the Sikkim Democratic Front (SDF) won power. Chamling, a poet as well as a politician, retained power at the next election, as the Front won 23 of the 32 seats in the Legislative Assembly on 3 October 1999. The Front subsequently gained the support of another eight deputies, mainly owing to defections, eroding the ranks of the opposition SSP, which eventually merged with Congress. By 2003 the opposition commanded the support of only one deputy, the veteran Bhandari. The state also sends one member to each of the houses of the national legislature, both of which are held by the SDF, which supported the ruling national coalition. This coalition was ousted in 2004, but in Sikkim, where the legislative elections were held at the same time as voting in the general election (on 10 May), popular sentiment remained loyal to the SDF. Chamling stayed on as premier, supported by 31 of the 32 deputies and with his party retaining the Lok Sabha seat. Bhandari failed to win a seat and the lone Congress voice in the Assembly was, therefore, Tshering Lama. In May 2007 Bhandari was convicted and sentenced to one month's imprisonment for having assets disproportionate to his known sources of income, at the conclusion of a trial that had lasted 13 years (the original case was first registered 10 years before that). In 2008 many of the main political parties in Sikkim declared their support for a new state of 'Gorkhaland', to be created in Darjiling and other, surrounding parts of West Bengal. In June the SDF and Congress appealed to activists in favour of the new state to limit the economic effect on Sikkim of their blockades and disruption to traffic links.

The Chinese border has been closed since 1962. However, in 2003 the federal Government held discussions with the People's Republic of China (which maintained its objections to the incorporation of Sikkim into the Indian Union) and secured some agreement over various outstanding border issues. One of the measures agreed in June, pending further negotiations to improve bilateral relations, was the reopening of a Sikkimese pass, Nathu La, between the two countries. By early 2005 there were expectations that the opening of the pass was imminent, although it was early July 2006 before the pass was opened. However, disputes remained over the border and, towards the end of 2007, the Chinese authorities questioned the status of a strip of territory in northern Sikkim known as the 'finger area' and objected to the Indian construction of stone cairns for shelter there. Occasional incursions by Chinese troops into the area after the winter of 2007/08 provoked protests by India, but did not interrupt the negotiating process.

## ECONOMY

The economy of Sikkim is primarily agricultural, but in a countryside that yields so little suitable land for farmers, it is no surprise to find that it is not a wealthy state. Moreover, not only is Sikkim the smallest state in population, it also has the smallest economy—the net domestic product for the state, in current prices, was some Rs 13,750m. in 2004/05, according to official figures. This gave an income per head (at current prices) of Rs 24,115 (slightly above the all-India average). Sikkim had experienced strong rates of real growth in the second half of the 1990s and into the early 2000s. In the budget speech for 2005/06, the Chief Minister reported that Sikkim was one of the top 10 strongest growing economies in India, with a growth rate of some 8%. Infrastructure is patchily developed, but, with roads being the main arteries of communication in the state, there was a dramatic expansion of the network during the 1990s. At March 1997 there were 2,376 km of roads in the state, of which 40 km were national highway and 678 km state highway; of the total, about 61% of roads were surfaced. Access to remoter locations is also augmented by ropeways. Other forms of transport are only accessible from neighbouring West Bengal, the nearest railhead being at Shiliguri (114 km—71 miles—from Gangtok) and the nearest airport at Bagdogra (124 km from Gangtok). In 2003 it was announced that central grants were to be provided for upgrading the road network and building an airport in the state (at Pakyong). The state Government also hoped to benefit from increased international trade through a reopened border with the People's Republic of China, and was improving road links to Nathu La on the frontier (the pass opened in 2006). It was also hoped that the official inclusion of Sikkim among the grouping of north-eastern states would enable further development. At the end of May 2006, following a significant increase in state provision and a massive increase in central provision, installed electrical capacity was 114.2 MW (60% from the Centre, the rest from state resources), but the state has considerable hydroelectric potential, with some important projects in northern Sikkim, such as those at Kalez and Lachung (in 2006, of the state capacity, 69% was hydroelectric). In early 2005 there were 42 forest villages reckoned to be without an electricity supply, while 57% of rural households did have a supply, although in the same year the Governor, in his budget address, claimed coverage of villages to be 100% for electricity supply and 95% for water. Literacy levels in the state improved over the 1990s, between the two censuses, rising from a rate of 56.9% in 1991 to 69.7% in 2001.

Agriculture is the principal economic sector of the economy of Sikkim, employing some two-thirds of the population. The absolute amount of land available to farmers is limited by topography. Despite this, the amount of land available to agriculture increased dramatically in the 1980s and, to a lesser extent, in the 1990s, although in 2005 the Government identified a decline in the net cropped area as a reason for the decline in agriculture's contribution to net state domestic product (23% in that year, compared with 45% in 1990/91). Attempts at development have focused on productivity, encouragement of organic farming and selecting more valuable crops. The last policy is not without precedent in Sikkim, as the state has long enjoyed a reputation for its large cardamoms. The area planted with cardamom, most of it in the North District, is the largest of any state in India (24,020 ha, or 59,353 acres, at the end of March 1997) and production is also the largest (3,600 metric tons in 1997). Harvests of this important cash crop have remained at a similar level for many years, however, whereas other major crops all nearly doubled their yields over the 1980s (remaining stable during the 1990s). The principal staple crop is maize (39,900 ha planted in 1997), followed by rice (15,950 ha), which is mostly grown in southern Sikkim, as are all the main crops except cardamom. In 1995/96 maize production totalled 56,561 metric tons, rice production 21,876 tons and wheat 15,304 tons. In 2001/02 total foodgrain production amounted to 98,700 tons (including almost 61,000 tons of maize, 22,300 tons of rice, 9,800 tons of wheat and 5,600 tons of pulses), and 6,900 tons of oilseeds were also harvested. Potatoes, ginger, oranges and off-season vegetables are other important cash crops, while the local tea (from the Temi estate) is highly valued, if not a large earner by volume (116,000 kg of tea were harvested in 1997/98). Animal husbandry is an important activity, particularly in the less hospitable parts of the state. According to the 1998 agricultural census, there were 183,385 head of cattle (mainly in the sub-tropical, humid belt of southern Sikkim), 31,207 pigs, 256,840 poultry and, mainly in the North District, 109,143 sheep and goats. There were smaller numbers of yak (again, mainly in the North), buffalo and equines. Provisional figures for 2002/03 put milk production in the state at 38,000 metric tons, egg production at 9m. and wool at 9,000 kg.

The rest of the primary sector of the economy has more potential than is realized. Indeed, much of the potential is not even easily realizable, owing to the terrain. In 1997 Sikkim possessed 545,239 ha (5,452 sq km—more than three-quarters of the total land area of the state) of reserved forestland. These reserves include peaks, etc., under permanent snow, however, so the tree-covered area was more like 265,000 ha (37% of Sikkim's land area), while the total extent of sanctuary areas, including village forests, was 652,076 ha. Extractive activity is not very developed, although the state possesses resources of copper, lead, zinc, coal, graphite and limestone. In 2002/03 there were only two reporting mines, the value of minerals produced being Rs 5.9m.

Sikkim has been officially declared industrially backward. Government development plans from 1996 have especially emphasized the encouragement of entrepreneurs and of small industry and handicraft training. In 1997 the state authorities recorded 1,778 industries registered in Sikkim, over one-half of them in East District and almost one-quarter in South District. Handicrafts for which the state is known include knotted woollen carpets (bearing the dragon emblem), woodcarvings, religious scroll paintings (thanka) and jewellery. Larger scale activities mainly involve the processing of the state's predominant agricultural sector, such as the manufacture of jams and juices, and production from bakeries and the local brewery. There are also concerns manufacturing or assembling plastic goods, leather goods, wristwatches and precision jewel bearings for watches, etc. An industrial development corporation seeks to execute government policy, but attempts to parallel the policy of other Indian states in encouraging 'new technologies', call centres or internet industries are limited by the available infrastructure (there were only 6,102 telephones in use in 1997, mainly in East District).

By 2004 services were reckoned to contribute one-half of the gross state domestic product. The tertiary sector is underpinned by government services, but tourism remains a growth industry in Sikkim, despite some continuing travel restrictions. The number of domestic visitors has risen steadily, the number of foreign visitors more dramatically, the former reaching 107,169 in 1996 and the latter 8,639. In the first six months alone of 1997 there were 67,225 domestic and 5,601 foreign visitors. Sikkim, as a stronghold of the ancient 'red-hatted' Nyingma sect (headquartered at the monastery of Pemayangtse, West District), has long been a centre of pilgrimage for Lamaist Buddhists and of Tibetology, but also now hosts the head of the Kagyu order at Rumtek. Handicrafts and dances illustrate the richness and age of local cultures, while there are more static sites of historical interest at Gangtok and Yuksam. Moreover, the country has a varied climate supporting a wealth of vegetation and a selection of what to visitors are unusual fauna, such as yak, musk and 'barking' (muntjac) deer, the red panda and blue sheep, and even, maybe, the yeti or 'abominable snowman' of legend. On and around Kangchenjunga Sikkim boasts one of the highest national parks in the world.

Sikkim, which enjoys some special tax and other privileges, not least because of its sensitivity so close to the border with the People's Republic of China, receives central government support. For instance, the Union authorities contributed Rs 4,305m. to the development activities of the state annual plan for 2005/06 (state resources provided a further Rs 695m.). In the same financial year the state was to have a total budgeted expenditure of Rs 37,139m. Of the budgeted receipts, only 30% came from state revenues (mainly non-tax revenue).

### DIRECTORY

**Governor:** BALMIKI PRASAD SINGH, Raj Bhavan, Gangtok 737 103; tel. (3592) 222400; fax (3592) 222742; internet www.rajbhavansikkim.gov.in.

**Chief Minister:** PAWAN KUMAR CHAMLING (Sikkim Democratic Front), Office of the Chief Minister, Government of Sikkim, Secretariat, Tashiling, Gangtok 737 101; tel. (3592) 222263; fax (3592) 222245.

**Speaker of the Legislative Assembly:** DAWU NORBA THAKARPA, Assembly House, Nam Nam, Gangtok 737 101; tel. (3592) 223652; fax (3592) 222181; the unicameral Legislative Assembly has 32 mems: Sikkim Democratic Front 31; Congress 1.

**State Resident Commissioner in New Delhi:** ALOK K. SHRIVASTAVA, Sikkim House, 12 Panchsheel Marg, Chanakyapuri, New Delhi 110 021; tel. (11) 26113747; fax (11) 26110679.

# Tamil Nadu

The State of Tamil Nadu extends up the eastern coast of India from the southernmost point of the peninsula, with its southern region facing Sri Lanka across the Gulf of Mannar and the Palk Strait. The other three Dravidian-language states provide Tamil Nadu's external land borders: Kerala lies to the west (stretching north of the southern Kanniyakumari District); Karnataka to the north-west; and Andhra Pradesh to the north. Midway up the eastern coast are enclaves of the Union Territory of Puducherry (Pondicherry), the compact coastal region of Karaikal on the Kaveri (Cauvery) delta and the mosaic of enclaves constituting the region of Puducherry itself further north, just beyond the Ponnaivar. In the north, also on the coast, is the capital city, Chennai, which, under its previous name of Madras, was the capital of a much larger entity (originally one of the three presidencies of British India) until the reorganization of the states along linguistic lines in 1956. In that year the state was dismembered, losing a number of districts and, to a lesser extent, gaining others, re-forming Madras as a state for Tamil-speakers. It was this 'rump' Madras state that was renamed the 'Tamil land' on 14 January 1969. Tamil Nadu has an area of 130,058 sq km (50,202 sq miles).

The Western and Eastern Ghats meet in Tamil Nadu, the former reaching their height in the state in the Nilgiri Hills, where Dodabetta (2,638 m or 8,658 ft), the second highest peak in south India, presides over Tamil Nadu's western extension. South of the Palakkad Gap, which leads through to the Malabar Coast and in the broad eastern entrance to which stands the city of Coimbatore, the Ghats continue the border with Kerala as the Anaimalai and Palni Hills, eventually petering out towards the tip of the peninsula, where lies the other point of communication between the Tamil-speaking heartland and the Malayalam lands of the Chera (Kerala). Tamil Kanniyakumari was part of Travancore (the core of today's Kerala) until 1956, but now gives Tamil Nadu a short south-westward-facing coastline onto the Arabian Sea. Rounding mainland India's southernmost point at Cape Comorin (Kanniyakumari), the eastern coastline is facing the great island of Sri Lanka (formerly Ceylon). The littoral as far north as Point Calimere, the easternmost part of Tamil Nadu (hooked over the north end of Sri Lanka), is known as the Fisheries Coast. It is dissected near Ramanathapuram by an eastward-extending finger of land, continued by Pamban Island and a sunken land bridge to Sri Lanka, dividing the Gulf of Mannar to the south from Palk Bay (the feature is known as Adam's Bridge, from a legend of the region's Muslims, or as Rama's Bridge—Ramar Palam or Ram Sethu—in the Hindu tradition). North of Point Calimere, as far as the mouth of the Krishna in Andhra Pradesh, is the Coromandel Coast, bordering the Bay of Bengal (Lake Pulicat marks the northern end of Tamil Nadu). Behind these shores are broad, fertile plains, reaching back to the hills supporting peninsular India's dominating, central plateau. The main thrust of the lower, dryer Eastern Ghats is north-eastwards from the Nilgiri Hills, dividing the Tamil lowlands from the Deccan proper. The traditional division of Tamil Nadu distinguishes between the highland areas (the Kurinji or mountainous region and the forested or Mullai region) and the lowland areas (the Marudham or fertile plains and the coastal Neidhal), and a small, fifth region of arid, desert-like Palai, north of Kanniyakumari. The Kaveri is the perennial river of the state; it waters the rich and ancient farmlands of the delta, split mainly between Thanjavur and Nagapattinam districts. The climate is tropical, rainfall being brought by the north-east monsoons between October and December, contributing most of the normal annual average of precipitation (977.5 mm or 38 inches). The hottest months are April and May, when it is also humid on the coast, but the hills generally have a more equable climate and winter (November–February) nights there can be distinctly cool. The average maximum temperature on the plains is 44.4°C (111.9°F), while the hill stations record an average maximum of 25.5°C (77.9°F) and an average minimum of 4.4°C (39.9°F).

Tamil Nadu's total population was 62,405,679 at 1 March 2001, recording the lowest growth rate (11.2% in 1991–2001) of any state or territory in India, except Kerala. This gave the state an average population density of 479 per sq km. According to the 1991 census, 86.7% of the population spoke Tamil, India's oldest living language, with a rich literary tradition dating back over 2,000 years. There are a number of Telugu speakers (7.1% in 1991), mainly in the north, as well as speakers of Kannada (2.2%), Urdu (1.9%) and Malayalam (1.2%). English is widely spoken. There are a number of tribal groups in the state, as many as 18 in the Nilgiri Hills, their main redoubt, the largest being the agriculturalist Badagas of the upper plateau, who are rapidly being assimilated into mainstream society, followed by the Irulas of the lower slopes. Other groups include the Kotas, an artisan tribe of the upper plateau, the Kurumbas, noted for burying their dead in a sitting position and, previously, for 'black magic', and the few remaining Todas, whose lifestyle and religion are centred on long-horned buffalo. However, officially, Scheduled Tribes only accounted for some 1.0% of the total population at the time of the 2001 census. Scheduled Castes accounted for 19.0%. The overwhelming majority of people in Tamil Nadu admit an affiliation to the Hindu faith (88.1% of the population in 2001), but there are significant minorities of Christians (6.1%) and Muslims (5.6%), and communities of Jains, Sikhs, Parsis and Buddhists.

In the 2001 census 44.0% of the population of Tamil Nadu were classed as urban (apart from the rather smaller Goa and Mizoram, the highest percentage of any state), and in its capital, Chennai (Madras until 1996), the state houses India's fourth largest urban agglomeration. In 2001 the metropolitan area of Chennai, which covers 174 sq km, had a population of 6.56m. (slightly over one-half of the population of Delhi, the third largest such agglomeration). The population of the city proper at the census contained 4.34m. (fourth largest in India). Chennai is on the coast, in the far north of the state, with the main city of the west being Coimbatore (India's 34th largest city in 2001—930,882 inhabitants) and of the south Madurai (35th—928,869). Like Chennai, both these cities have considerable connected populations outside the city boundaries, the ranking of the urban agglomerations rising to the 19th and 25th largest in India, respectively. There are 29 districts in the state.

## HISTORY

The Dravidians seem to be the original inhabitants of India, at least since about the fourth millennium before the Christian era, even before the rise of the Harappan culture of the Indus basin. Recent discoveries off the coast of Tamil Nadu may hint at an older civilization, evidence of which is claimed to have drowned in the rising waters at the end of the last ice age, but the history of the Tamil people begins in the last half of the first millennium BC. A distinct and recognizable Tamil language emerged long before the other Dravidian tongues (Telugu and Kannada were clearly recognizable before the end of the first millennium AD, while Malayalam only escaped the shadow of its Tamil parent by the 13th century), encouraged by the literary flourishing of the three poetic sangam (assembly or academy) eras. One of the earliest great figures of Tamil literature, writing at some time between the first century BC and the second century AD, was Thiruvalluvar, who wrote the *Thirukkural*. After this period Tamil writers and religious thinkers were instrumental in the transformation of the worship of Krishna into a more passionate devotion (*bhakti*). By the end of the first millennium AD a 'Tamil Veda' had accumulated, a collection of hymns of praise, while the ninth-century *Bhagavata Purana* includes some of Vaishnavite Hinduism's greatest works.

Much of the patronage for these literary and religious accomplishments came from the enduring Tamil dynasties of south India: the Cholas, the Pandyas and the Cheras (all three of which were known to the great northern emperor, Ashoka Maurya), and also, from about the fourth century AD, the Pallavas. The Cholas were based around Thanjavur, on the southernmost part of what would become known as the Coromandel Coast and inland to the head of the Kaveri (Cauvery) delta. The Pandyas lay to the south, around Madurai and into what is now southern Kerala, while the Cheras, still a Tamil dynasty and originally ruling from west of Tiruchchirappalli, ruled most of the rest of that south-western coast beyond the mountains, a region to which they were to give their name. The exact extent of their domains varied, as the relative influences of the dynasties waxed and waned, and historical record is scant. The sangam collections make reference to the warring kings of south India, while the Buddhist histories of Sri Lanka provide some cross reference, so historians can glean some facts, such as the conquest of Sri Lanka by a Chola prince, Elara, in the second century BC. Also, archaeological evidence of flourishing trading ports reinforces the credibility of reports on south India from ancient Europe and China. Thus, the spread of Buddhism and the Jains, or even of Christianity (St Thomas the Apostle, 'Doubting Thomas', is reputed to have died near modern Chennai in AD 72, having evangelized in south India and China), is more understandable in a region reliant on the wealth of busy international commerce. However, a clearer record only emerges with the Pallavas, a dynasty with dubious claims to a northern, Parthian ancestry. Moreover, from this time the remarkably consistent patterns of Tamil history have been established: the long-lasting dynasties; the settled centres of power (Madurai in the south, Thanjavur in the central, Kaveri-delta region and, in the north, Kanchipuram, then Arcot and, finally, Madras—now Chennai); and the recurrent power struggles between the dominant power of the lowlands with a Deccan, often Karnatakan, rival.

Kanchipuram, south-west of Chennai, is one of Hinduism's seven holy places (with the Kaveri, Tamil Nadu also has one of the seven holy rivers), but initially thrived under Buddhism, which reached the area in the third century BC. By the fourth century AD it was home to the Pallava dynasty, as the recorded exploits of a northern emperor, the great Samudra-Gupta, include the defeat and capture of Vishnugopa, the Pallava rajah of Kanchipuram. The Gupta empire of Magadha had reached down the Andhran coast and towards the Kaveri, subjugating the Pallava heartland—it maybe that this experience reinforced the local dynasty sufficiently to assert its supremacy in the south when Gupta power declined. Even before their rise to dominance in the Tamil lands after about 550, the Pallava kings were already enriching Kanchipuram, their literary and administrative capital for over 150 years, with temples and monuments. However, their artistic achievement and political power were to reach their heights only in the seventh and eighth centuries. At this time the port of Mamallapuram (Mahabalipuram) was at the centre of numerous long-distance trading routes to the east and the origin of diplomatic missions to as far away as China or of raids on Sri Lanka or the South-East Asian mainland and islands. While not monopolizing the trade routes or by any means the only Indic influence on the latter region, the Pallavas were a fundamental inspiration in many fields—very obvious, for instance, in the emerging Khmer kingdom of Cambodia (e.g. in temple architecture or the ending of royal names with 'Varman').

Pallava strength waxed with the accession of Simha-Vishnu in the early 550s. He was followed by the successful Mahendra-Varman I in about 590, but it was the next monarch, Narasimha-Varman I ('the Great Wrestler', for whom Mamallapuram is named, and who reigned *circa* 630–88), who really established the reputation of the Pallavas. Although initially bested by the great Chalukyan king,

Pulakesin II, Narasimha-Varman I routed him at Polilur and then captured Badami (now in Karnataka) itself in 642. The Chalukyas recovered in the second half of the century, however, and Kanchipuram was, in turn, taken. The Pallavas had also to contend with a junior (though longer lasting) branch of the Chalukyas established by Pulakesin II in what became Vengi (based on the Krishna delta, in modern Andhra Pradesh). This dynasty, known as the Eastern Chalukyas, became the natural ally of the Pandyas (and, later, of the Cholas), enemies of the Pallavas. Likewise, the Pallavas usually received the support of the Pandyas' traditional enemy, the Cheras. Nevertheless, the seventh century was not yet over before a Pallava resurgence under Parameshvara-Varman I (*c.* 670–700) took the fight back into Chalukyan territory. He left his anointed successor, Narasimha-Varman II (also known as Rajasimha, who acquired over 250 titles during his reign, c. 695–728), to deal with the reactions of the Chalukyas under Vijayaditya—although it can be questioned quite how ruinous these dynastic rivalries were when both monarchs were reaching a peak of monumental temple building, the Chalukya most famously at Pattadakal (Karnataka) and the Pallava at Mamallapuram and, with the Kailasanatha temple, at Kanchipuram. Thereafter, Pallava power declined, with the next Chalukya, Vikramaditya II (c. 733–44), despite his short reign, claiming to have sacked Kanchipuram three times. The Pallava succession struggled on under Parameshvara-Varman II and Nanda-Varman (c. 731–96), but the kingdom was no match for the new Deccan power, the Rashtrakutas, who were mainly concerned with their imperial pretensions in the north, but sometimes had occasion to secure their southern flank by intimidating their neighbours, as the Pallavas experienced in the 780s. By 869 the kingdom had virtually collapsed and before the end of the ninth century, using the opportunity presented by a Pallavan succession crisis, the resilient Cholas had wiped out the dynasty and occupied the heartland of the Pallavas.

The Cholas had begun to restore their sovereignty under Vijayalaya (*c.* 846–71), famous for the conquest of Thanjavur (Tanjore), which was to replace Uraiyur as the dynasty's main capital. His successor, Aditya I, extended his rule into the old Pallava territory to the north and, in about 897, fought a great battle, which established Chola pre-eminence; he also fought off a Pandyan invasion. However, the south Indian dynasty could not yet resist the intervention of a Deccan great power, and Aditya I's son, Parantaka I (*c.* 907–953), was defeated by the last great Rashtrakuta, Krishna III, in 949, leaving the kingdom vulnerable for some decades. The great conqueror and builder, Rajaraja I, who came to the throne in 985, conclusively established Chola power. He reduced the Pandyas and Cheras to subjugation, invaded and plundered Sri Lanka, and acquired island territories in what are now Lakshadweep and the Maldives. The classic struggle between the Tamil south-east and the Deccan north-west resumed as Rajaraja I encountered more resistance from the dynasty that had replaced the Rashtrakutas in Karnataka, a line that claimed descent from the Chalukyas (known as the Later Western Chalukyas or the Chalukyas of Kalyana). The Eastern Chalukyas of Vengi, by contrast, whom Rajaraja I had championed against their *arriviste* cousins, were loyal feudatories and, eventually, very much the same family.

The Chola kingdom seems to have been a more centralized structure than was usual in the history of south India, a temple economy helping to bind disparate areas together in support of particular institutions, and maybe further reinforced by a policy of brahminical settlement (a loyal ruling class, in possession of useful knowledge of irrigation techniques, etc.). The habits of war seemed largely unchanged, with many of the campaigns seeming to be about the acquisition of booty rather than for political, economic or even religious reasons. There may have been a greater degree of brutality involved in some campaigns, enough to account for the implacability of the new Chalukya–Chola rivalry. Early responsibility for this seems to rest with Rajaraja I's son and general, the man who became king as Rajendra I in about 1013. As king, he not only repeated the sack of Sri Lanka and the intimidation of the south, but also sent naval expeditions to the Nicobar Islands and beyond, to raid the Malay Peninsula. This secured Chola supremacy on the trade routes to modern Indonesia and to China, as well as obtaining wealth to finance the traditional temple-building programme. Most famously, Rajendra I's armies went further up the east coast from Andhra, penetrating as far as the mouths of the Ganges (Ganga) in Bengal. Certainly he was aware of the historic reversal of the normal geography of Indian power politics, and to commemorate the event built a new capital—Gangakondaicholapuram, the 'city of the Chola who conquered the Ganga', although it never really replaced Thanjavur and Chidambaram (the former at the head of the Kaveri delta, the latter just to the north, near the coast) as the main centres of Chola power.

The first of Rajendra I's sons to hold power after his death in 1044, Rajadhiraja I, continued successful campaigns against the Chalukyas, even taking their capital of Kalyana, but by the time the next generation gained the throne, in around 1070 (in the person of Rajendra III, also known as Kulotungga I, who reigned until 1122), Chola territorial sway was in decline. In the latter year, or thereabouts, the Cholas lost Sri Lanka, while the Pandyas to the south began to reassert themselves, and there was the constant struggle with the Chalukyas. Nevertheless, the prestige and international standing of the Cholas was unaffected for some time. The last king of note, who went down in defeat before the resurgent Pandyas, was Kulotungga III (1178–1216), but the dynasty struggled on into the century, until it was crushed in the 1250s by the great Sundara Pandya, who ensured the rule of Madurai over the Tamil lands. Others put the final date of Chola power at 1267, but certainly by the time the old Chola capitals and so many other temple cities in the south-east were sacked by Muslim invaders in 1310, the three main dynasties of south India were the Hoysalas of Karnataka, the Kakatiyas of Warangal (near modern Hyderabad, Andhra Pradesh—replacing Vengi as the dominant power to the north of the Tamils) and the Pandyas of Madurai.

The Pandyas, who were the last of the great Tamil dynasties, had an ancient history. Madurai was supposedly founded by the first Pandyan king, Kulasekara, in the sixth century BC and later was the site of the last of the three great sangams, sponsored by the Pandyan court. Located in the far south of the Indian peninsula, the Pandyas had resisted the Pallava rise to pre-eminence and held out against the Rashtrakutas, although they were defeated by Govinda III, who had also sacked Kanchipuram and humiliated the Pallavas in about 805, before turning his attentions to the north again. Later in the ninth century, however, they had to contend with the rise of the Cholas, just to their north, and eventually acknowledged their suzerainty in the 10th century. Some two centuries later, however, the Pandyas could lay claim to being the most powerful Tamil dynasty, although this was to last for little more than another century. By the beginning of the 14th century south India was exposed to the depredations of Muslim raiders from the north, and even Madurai was destroyed in 1310, by Malik Kafur, briefly becoming the seat of a sultanate thereafter. The era of the great Tamil dynasties was over, and the Hindu defence of south India fell to the empire of Vijayanagar (Hampi, Karnataka), which assumed control of the old Pandyan capital of Madurai in 1364. For the next 200 years local nayaks or governors under the emperors of Vijayanagar ruled the Tamil lands, gradually consolidating their authority from ancient capitals such as Madurai and Thanjavur, until the 1565 disintegration of central authority exposed them to the sultanates of the Deccan and, later, the incursions of the Mughals.

By the 17th century southern Tamil Nadu remained largely under the authority of the ruling nayaks, while the north was the domain of the nawabs (again, former governors) of Arcot—their realm came to be known as the Carnatic, a corruption of Karnataka, a term the Deccan sultans had applied to all the lands of south India acquired from Vijayanagar. By this time the Europeans, as well as the Mughals, were making their influence felt in the region. The Portuguese had added Tuticorin to their establishments on the western coast of India, gaining a presence there in 1540, at the same time as they went into Sri Lanka. The Dutch, who had a governor for their posts on the Coromandel Coast from 1608, acquired Tuticorin in 1658, but were to lose all their Indian possessions to the British as a result of war in Europe (the Coromandel Coast territories were occupied by the British in 1780–84 and 1795–1818, then ceded to them permanently in 1825). The Danish too had a presence on the Bay of Bengal, gaining permission from Raghunath, Nayak of Thanjavur, in 1620 to build a fort at Tharangampadi, so creating their base of Tranquebar (administered by a Danish East India Company until 1779). From here, like the Cholas, the Danes made an attempt to move into the Nicobar Islands, but can be better noted for setting up the first printing press for Tamil script (which they adjusted for the purpose of printing). Tranquebar was occupied by the British in 1808–15 and annexed in 1845. The only European presence to present a significant challenge to the British in south India, though late to arrive, was the French. The old French bases in the Tamil country, headquartered in Puducherry, still persist as separate enclaves of a union territory within the modern state. The French began to accumulate territory around Puducherry in 1674, eventually establishing particularly good relations with the nawabs of Arcot, in whose lands lay the main British base.

In 1639 a British trader, Francis Day, was granted land at Madraspatnam (later contracted to Madras) for a factory. The building was completed on St George's Day 1640 and the fortifications of Fort St George were completed in 1654. The expanding settlement soon included the village of Chennaipatnam, named for the father of the local nayak who made the original grant and from which the modern name of the current city is derived. Although it was to lose out in the competition for primacy between the great cities of British India, Madras was the capital of one of the three presidencies and among the most settled parts of the Indian empire—it contains the oldest Anglican church in India (1680), it was the first municipality to receive a royal charter (1688) and sired the Madras Regiment, the oldest in the Indian army (1758). It was some time before it became apparent that it was centre of a growing territorial domain, however, and it was global rivalry of the British and the French that spurred an accumulation of territory and an increase in the sponsorship of local rulers. Madras itself was blockaded by a general of Aurangzeb in 1702 and attacked by Marathas (who had acquired holdings in what is now Tamil Nadu as part of their campaign against the Muslim nawabs of the region) in 1741. The French themselves occupied the city twice, and the soldiers of Mysore flouted British authority on the very outskirts of Madras, but it was to remain permanently under British control from 1758 until independence. By the beginning of this period the British had established their supremacy over the French in India, with Robert Clive occupying Arcot in 1751 and these victories confirmed the general triumph of British imperialism recognized by the 1763 Peace of Paris (concluded in the French capital). French intrigues continued, notably with help to the expanding state of Mysore, which was harassing the nayaks of Madurai from the 1740s, for instance, and coming into increasing conflict with the British thereafter. Mysore's success under Haidar Ali and Tipu Sultan throughout south India (notably at Polilur in 1780, one of the worst military defeats experienced by the British in India) brought about a response on a similar scale from the more and more openly expansionist forces of the East India Company. The final defeat of Mysore, as well as the earlier taming of Hyderabad, removed any rivals to British power in the region, and a reorganization of recent conquests in 1801 therefore brought most of south India under the authority of Madras, which gave its name successively to the presidency, a province and a state, before the linguistic reorganization of states in 1956 confined it to the Tamil heartland. The state was renamed Tamil Nadu in 1969 and the city Chennai in 1996.

Tamil revivalism emerged in the last stages of the national campaign for independence, partly as a response to what was perceived as the high-caste and northern domination of Congress. In 1944 E. V. Ramasami Naicker ('Periyar') founded a secular, anti-brahminical and almost socialist popular movement called the Dravida Kazhagam. However, his atheism and the advocacy of secession alienated many, as well as the scandal of his late marriage to a much younger woman, and it was C. N. Annadurai ('Anna') who split the movement in 1949 and transformed the greater part, the Dravida Munnetra Kazhagam (DMK), into a mainstream, reformist political party, committed to the primacy of Tamil regional culture. Annadurai's decision to take the movement into politics came with the 1956 reorganization of Madras as a Tamil state (a move much criticized by Ramasami, who thought this would distract from the mission of radical social reform), but it was another language issue that propelled the DMK into power. When Hindi replaced English as the official language of India in 1965, there were riots in Madras, where a neutral tongue was preferred to the linguistic domination of the north. Although English remained in use, de facto, at the 1967 state elections Congress was evicted from office and the DMK (which had not advocated an independent state since 1962) installed. Since then, government in Tamil Nadu has been dominated by the DMK and the party that split from it after Annadurai's death, the All-India Anna DMK (AIADMK)—at times both have made political accommodations with Congress and with their ideological enemies from the brahminical Bharatiya Janata Party (BJP), whether locally or nationally.

Upon Annadurai's death in 1969, Muthuvel Karunanidhi became Chief Minister and led the DMK Government until 1976. Allegations of corruption and the opposition of AIADMK, under the charismatic film actor, M. G. Ramachandran ('MGR'), removed Karunanidhi from power and, at one point, he was imprisoned, although it was claimed that the charges were politically motivated. Ramachandran died in 1987, prompting a bitter succession battle within the AIADMK, eventually won by the controversial C. Jayaram Jayalalitha—she too was a film actor, emphasizing the importance of cinema in the reassertion of Tamil language and culture (Annadurai and Karunanidhi were both screenwriters). The publicity surrounding the accession of Jayalalitha was exploited by both Congress, which attempted an ultimately unsuccessful revival in the state, and the DMK, which returned to power with the state elections in 1989. The AIADMK again formed a Government in 1991, after the Centre ousted Karunanidhi (he had been prominent in support of the national coalition that displaced Congress at the end of 1989). Jayalalitha was Chief Minister until Karunanidhi and the DMK returned to power in 1996—the DMK was also involved in the coalition politics at the national level, complicated by the enmity of Congress, which accused the party of complicity in the Tamil separatist movement in Sri Lanka. The new state Government ordered the arrest of Jayalalitha, on charges of abusing her office—after having been confined to prison, she dramatically protested her innocence and promised revenge. She fulfilled this pledge after her party won the May 2001 state elections—Karunanidhi was duly imprisoned. This election victory had been presaged in 1998, when the AIADMK had formed a short-lived alliance 'of convenience' with the BJP, sufficient for the secular Tamil party to win 30 of the 39 state seats in the Lok Sabha, the lower house of the national Parliament (the state also has 18 seats in the upper house, the Rajya Sabha).

In 2001 Jayalalitha, again amid some controversy and despite legal moves against her, regained the premiership of Tamil Nadu and formed an AIADMK Government. She remained in power into 2002 and claimed to have made her peace with Karunanidhi, although the latter alleged that the AIADMK Government was, for instance, behind the various police encounters of his politician sons in 2003—in April one of them, M. K. Stalin, the head of the youth wing of the DMK, was accused of political violence, and in May the other, M. K. Azhagiri, also a DMK leader (although not seen as being aligned with his father and brother), was arrested for the murder of a former DMK minister, T. Kiruttinan. (The murder charges against M. K. Azhagiri were finally abandoned in May 2008.) Jayalalitha also courted controversy with her support for Hindu-nationalist causes (such as the anti-conversions law introduced at the end of 2002, which lower-caste and minority-religions groups claimed could be used discriminatorily), with her proposals to build a new secretariat complex in Chennai and in her stand over the continuing Kaveri waters dispute with Karnataka. In July 2003 the Government dismissed 176,000 government employees, including teachers and civil servants, when they went on strike against the curtailment of various benefits, although a court decision gave rise to a compromise and they were reinstated a few weeks later. However, the dispute was reignited in November, when some of the leaders of the strike were dismissed. In the same month Jayalalitha courted further controversy by instigating more defamation cases against various media organs, as well as by invoking anti-terrorist legislation against a Union minister, a member of the Marumalarchi DMK (MDMK). The leader of the MDMK, Vaiko (V. Gopalaswamy), had likewise been detained under the controversial Prevention of Terrorism Act after allegedly expressing support for a banned Sri Lankan Tamil group in June 2002. Meanwhile, in the middle of 2002 there had been reports that the locally pre-eminent Tamil Maanila Congress was to rejoin the nationally pre-eminent Congress, and the two duly united into a single Congress in August 2003. With the withdrawal of the DMK and then the MDMK from the BJP-led national coalition in December, the way was open for a secular and anti-AIADMK electoral alliance for the general election to be formed between the DMK and Congress. The MDMK also joined and Vaiko, famous for his incarceration, proved to be one of the most popular attractions on the campaign trail in 2004. This alliance prompted the AIADMK and the BJP in Tamil Nadu to confirm that they would contest the general election together. Finally, in January the Pattali Makkal Katchi (PMK) withdrew from the national Government and joined the DMK-led Democratic Progressive Alliance. When voting took place in May 2004 the opposition Alliance won all 39 Lok Sabha seats in Tamil Nadu (16 for the DMK, 10 for Congress and four for its Communist allies, five for the PMK and four for the MDMK), as well as the Puducherry seat.

The complete loss of representation in the lower house of the national Parliament prompted the AIADMK Government to begin repealing some of its more controversial measures later in May 2004: the anti-conversion legislation was abandoned; the defamation suits against newspapers and politicians were discontinued; the government workers dismissed in November were reinstated (the ban on government employees striking was abandoned in 2005); and various cases brought under the anti-terrorist laws were abandoned, for instance. The reintroduction of free power for farmers and concessions for schoolchildren would be costly for the Government and left its economic and financial reforms in some disarray. However, the state Government's handling of the relief efforts after the devastation of the 26 December tsunami (from which the official death toll had reached over 6,200 in Tamil Nadu and Puducherry by the end of the month) was generally perceived to be competent. Against all expectations, the ruling AIADMK retained two Assembly seats at by-elections in May 2005, although there were local sympathy factors at play. The Government may also have benefited from the resolution of the long-running attempt to hunt down a notorious bandit, Veerappan, who was killed by special forces in October 2004. Furthermore, in February 2005 criticisms by a Congress Union minister of the leader of the DMK, the leading party in their alliance in Tamil Nadu, revealed some tensions within the opposition. The DMK was sufficiently dominant, as well as important to the ruling coalition at the Centre, to extract an apology and to deny that Congress would necessarily be included in any administration formed after the Assembly elections scheduled for May 2006 (which the DMK and its allies were still widely expected to win). However, there was some public disquiet about the succession issue within the DMK, with Karunanidhi, already 82 years of age, not expected to serve an entire term as Chief Minister, if elected. Moreover, in March 2006 Vaiko and the MDMK left the alliance with the DMK and aligned with the AIADMK, although remaining supporters of the Government at the Centre. Nevertheless, on 8 May the DMK-led parties secured a conclusive victory in the state elections—the DMK had won 96 of the 234 seats, and its allies another 67 (Congress 34, PMK 18 and the two Communist parties 15). Of the victorious partners, only the PMK secured fewer seats than at the previous election. AIADMK retained only 61 seats, the MDMK had six and the Viduthalai Chiruthaigal

Katchi joined the legislature with two. The remaining two seats were won by an independent and by the Desija Morpokku Dravidar Kazhagam, the latter being a party founded by a famous Tamil actor, Vijayakanth, the previous September. On 13 May Karunanidhi was sworn in as Chief Minister of Tamil Nadu's first coalition Government; later that month his Government announced that it intended to revive an upper chamber for the legislature (the Legislative Council was abolished in 1986), while September saw the first disbursement of free colour television sets to the poor, in fulfilment of campaign promises.

Local elections and a by-election in October 2006 confirmed the ascendancy of the DMK and its allies, although the party of Vijayakanth, considered more 'saffron' in its orientation than the two main parties of the state, made significant progress. Domestic politics into 2007 remained typified by sparring between the Government and AIADMK and between Karunanidhi's sons M. K. Azhagiri and M. K. Stalin. Water politics featured strongly in the debate, as Tamil Nadu was disputing with Kerala over the safety of a dam (ongoing since late 2006) and with Karnataka over the waters of the Kaveri (Cauvery). The latter dispute was supposed to be solved by the final decision, on 5 February, of a 16-year-old tribunal, but populist rhetoric and general dissatisfaction prevented political acceptance of the ruling, even in Tamil Nadu, which was considered to have benefited from the panel's adjudication. Violence erupted again in Karnataka in March 2008, against plans of the Tamil Nadu Government to build a water plant at the Hoggenakkal falls on the Kaveri. With civil disturbances in Tamil Nadu as well, Chief Minister Karunanidhi announced that the Hoggenakkal project would not proceed until after the imminent state elections in Karnataka, but work resumed later in the year. Meanwhile, in March 2007 Vaiko withdrew the support of the MDMK, which had suffered a split in December 2006, from the ruling national coalition. There was continued bad news for the opposition in June, when Congress gained an extra seat in the Assembly, at the expense of AIADMK. Jayalalitha's criticisms of the DMK-led Government into 2008 included accusations of sympathy for separatist Sri Lankan Tamil insurgents. Within the ruling coalition, the main tension remained between the DMK and its junior partner, the PMK. Disputes intensified in March, when the PMK protested over the DMK's refusal to award a Rajya Sabha seat to the smaller party, and in June, when the DMK expelled the PMK from the coalition over an inflammatory speech made by a PMK leader against the Government. Both parties continued to support the Congress-led national Government over the deal with the USA over nuclear energy, but an eventual PMK electoral accommodation with AIADMK appeared more likely, although the DMK did not rule out a rapprochement.

An ongoing complication in state politics, and in relations with the federal authorities, has been the civil war in Sri Lanka. The ruling parties of the state tend to sympathize with the Tamil separatists on the island. Ramachandran was born in Sri Lanka and had links with the leader of the main insurgent group, while the DMK was also suspected of such links. While the Indian Government was reluctant to condone the achievement of a separate Tamil state in Sri Lanka, mainly for domestic reasons, the influence of politicians in Tamil Nadu made the country a useful arbiter and Indian troops helped supervise a cease-fire in 1987–90. However, on 21 May 1991, between the rounds of a general election that would return Congress to power, Rajiv Gandhi, the party leader and former Prime Minister (responsible for sending the troops into Sri Lanka) was assassinated by a Sri Lankan Tamil faction at Sriperumbudur. The civil war on the island continues to send refugees into Tamil Nadu (estimated at about 200,000 in mid-2003), where local politicians remain more ambivalent about their secessionist cousins than the centralist national Government. In 2003 security concerns led the Government of Tamil Nadu to oppose the construction of a bridge across the Palk Strait, connecting India and Sri Lanka, an idea that had been revived by the national premiers in the previous year. During 2007 there was tension over a number of clashes, some fatal, between Indian fishermen and the Sri Lankan navy, which was attempting to stop arms and ammunition reaching the ethnic Tamil rebels in renewed fighting on the island. The Indian navy increased its patrols in the Palk Straits in May. In domestic politics, the Sethusamudram proposal to construct a shipping canal through the shallows of Adam's Bridge (Ram Sethu) ignited fierce passions. The BJP argued that the national Government's proposals would desecrate a Hindu site, while a government affidavit to the Supreme Court in September 2007 said that there was no evidence for the historic existence of Lord Rama (the affidavit was subsequently withdrawn). The leftist parties accused the Government of mishandling the situation and playing into the BJP's hands with such language, although the state Government backed the Centre's proposals. Chief Minister Karunanidhi himself attracted controversy by saying that the tale of Lord Rama and his bridge was a myth. He subsequently incurred the ire of the Supreme Court over demonstrations in favour of the project proceeding. Meanwhile, the national Government proceeded to point out that, in the legend, Lord Rama had destroyed his bridge and, upon serious consideration, that the feature did not qualify as a national monument. However, by mid-2008 alternatives to the dredging of a channel through Adam's Bridge were being considered by the authorities.

## ECONOMY

Tamil Nadu was the wealthiest of the four southern states of India, in per caput terms, until 2002 (when Kerala exceeded it), and had the largest economy after Andhra Pradesh. Tamil Nadu is one of the leading destinations for investment in the whole country. Although accounting for only 4.1% of the area of the country and 6.2% of the estimated population (1997/98 figures), Tamil Nadu contributed 7.4% of national net domestic product and, in the industrial sector, accounted for 10.1% of the value of output. The overall size of the economy ranked fifth of all the states in India (sixth per head). According to official figures, in 2004/05 net domestic product, in current prices, had reached Rs 1,671,830m., or Rs 25,965 per head. There is long established and developed infrastructure in the state, with Tamil Nadu accounting for 8.8% of the total national road length in 1996. Of the state total of public roads in 1999, 151,244 km, 3,773 km were national highway and 56,391 km state highway. Provisional figures for 2002/03 put the total of surfaced roads in the state at almost 136,925 km and of unsurfaced at 41,621 km. In the following year there were 6,093 km of railway-track length, of which 63.8% was broad gauge and the rest metre gauge, serving 528 railway stations. Only 214 km of metre-gauge track were electrified, but 56% of broad-gauge track was. The two major seaports are Chennai (formerly Madras—including the main Ennore port, which deals with fuel tankers) and Tuticorin, although there are also 10 lesser ports. In July 2005, despite the opposition of fishermen and environmentalists, construction work began on the Sethusamudram canal project, linking the Gulf of Mannar with the Bay of Bengal and allowing ships travelling between the east and west coasts of India to avoid sailing around Sri Lanka. The first traffic was expected in November 2008, following expenditure of Rs 24,270m. The international airport at Chennai is augmented by three other domestic terminals elsewhere in the state. Communications infrastructure is well developed, particularly around Chennai, with some 3.4m. telephones in use by 2001. The state electricity board provided an installed capacity of 6,617 MW at May 2006 (an increase of just over one-fifth on the previous year), with a further 2,912 MW from projects operated by the Centre and 2,802 MW from the private sector. The state is fully electrified, and 44% of rural households have electricity. The Government was encouraging private investment and alternative power sources, such as wind and solar energy, particularly as most hydroelectric potential had been used (almost 23% of state-based generation came from hydroelectric sources in 2006). As to the population, health indicators are among the best in the country (although exceeded by neighbouring Kerala), while the literacy rate at the time of the 2001 census (73.5%) showed a remarkable improvement on the previous census (62.7%, in 1991).

Agriculture is still the main activity of most of the population of Tamil Nadu, but the sector's contribution to the economy is no longer dominant. In 1960/61 the share of primary activities in the state economy was 43.5%, but by 1997/98 it was only 20.2%. Official advance estimates for 1999/2000 put the contribution of the primary sector (including mining and quarrying) to the net domestic product of the state at 21.3%, of which agriculture alone provided 18.3% (forestry and logging 0.9% and fishing 1.8%). In 2001/02 agriculture contributed only 15.2% to gross state domestic product, with only Goa and, narrowly, Maharashtra, of all the states, recording a lower proportion. The principal food crop is rice, with paddy accounting for 26% of the total area under cultivation in 2003/04 (down from 34% in 1999), followed by millets and other cereals at 17% (28% in 1999). The Kaveri (Cauvery) delta, farmed and irrigated for thousands of years, is one of the most important 'rice bowls' in India. In 2001/02 rice accounted for 6.9m. metric tons (7.4% of the all-India rice harvest) of total foodgrain production of 8.5m. tons. The total foodgrain harvest fell by about one-10th in the following year. Other important crops include groundnuts (peanuts—11% of cultivated land in 1999) and castor (7%), pulses (10%), sugar cane (4%) and cotton (2%). In 1997/98 Tamil Nadu provided 18% of all-Indian groundnut production, 11% of sugar cane and 8% of cotton. Figures for the low production of 2003/04 put the sugar-cane (gur) harvest at 1.7m. tons, groundnuts at 591,696 tons and cotton at 122,587 tons. Yields, as well as production, increased significantly during the late 1990s, after desilting projects in the Kaveri delta, some reclamation of waste land and the introduction of new crop varieties, but drought was a major problem in the early 2000s. There are large numbers of livestock in Tamil Nadu, with productivity increased by artificial-insemination programmes. However, owing to population increases, milk production, for instance, continues to fall short of local demand (a dip in production meant 4.6m. metric tons for 2001/02, but recovery thereafter was quick). According to the provisional results of the 1997 agricultural census, there were 9.05m. head of cattle and 2.74m. buffaloes, 6.41m. head of goats and 5.26m. sheep, and 18.55m. poultry in the state. The latter produced 4,224m. tons of eggs in

2001/02 (there was a drop to 3,621m. tons in the next year, followed by a recovery), the highest level in India after Andhra Pradesh. Similarly, there was a peak in wool production in 2001/02 (640,000 kg), falling to 613,000 kg thereafter.

Forestry is limited, mainly owing to the lack of woodland cover in the state—21,482 sq km under forest in 2000 (according to a satellite survey), this being 16.5% of the total geographical area, which is lower than the national average of 22.8% and considerably less than the recommended one-third. The area under forest has increased, however, and the state authorities aimed to achieve the nationally mandated one-third of cover by 2012. However, the 17.5% achieved in 2002/03 represented a slight decline compared with the 17.6% of the previous year. Locally, forest products are still important (e.g. sandalwood in Kanniyakumari). By contrast, with 1,076 km of coastline, stretching along a variety of marine environments, the opportunity for fishing is extensive—marine fish production in 2003/04 totalled 381,148 metric tons. Moreover, although there are few perennial rivers in the state, lakes, tanks and other inland waters furnished a further 77,304 tons. The shallow waters and islands off the south-east coast of Tamil Nadu are a good environment for pearl-bearing oysters, and a pearl-fishing industry is centred on Tuticorin, awaiting official declaration of a fishing season (every five–nine years usually). There are important mineral reserves of iron ore, lignite (brown coal), limestone, graphite, clay, gypsum, granite and feldspar, and smaller amounts of gold, copper, magnesite, kaolin and bauxite. Moreover, with 0.93m. people employed (2001/02 figure), Tamil Nadu has more people in mining than any other state in India, although it is only 12th in terms of the value of production—Rs 18,322m. (2002/03).

Industry was originally based on the processing of primary products, particularly developed in a thriving textile industry, which remains important, along with agricultural and fisheries processing. Tamil Nadu provides about two-fifths of India's leather exports (the industry is centred in the northern Palar valley) and accounts for about one-quarter of the country's cotton textiles, for instance. Engineering, petrochemicals and the manufacture of motor vehicles, railway rolling stock and precision tools are other examples of heavy industry. Chennai is the main industrial centre and the centre for three major international automobile manufacturers (Hyundai of the Republic of Korea, Mitsubishi of Japan and Ford Motors of the USA), earning it the sobriquet of the 'Detroit of India'. There are numerous light industries, and information technology has also been encouraged since the late 1990s. Tiruchchirappalli is the largest centre for the production of artificial diamonds in the country, India having superseded Switzerland and Myanmar in this field since the Second World War. There were 32,658 small-scale industrial units in 2000/01, providing employment for 240,332, and 22,939 working factories registered in 1999. By 2002 there were 24,796 working factories, employing an estimated 1.2m. people. The secondary sector expanded from 20.3% of the gross domestic product of Tamil Nadu (then called Madras) in 1960/61 to 34.5% in 1990/91, only to be overtaken by the expansion of services, to settle at 30.1% in 1997/98. In 1999/2000 the sector contributed 27.4% of the net domestic product (manufacturing 19.1%, utilities 1.9%, construction 6.4%).

At the beginning of the 1960s services already provided well over one-third of the state gross domestic product (36.2%), and this contribution reached 43.4% at the beginning of the 1990s. By the end of the 20th century the tertiary sector accounted for over one-half of the state economy (49.8% of gross domestic product in 1997/98 and 51.3% of net domestic product in 1999/2000). Finance, insurance, property and business services (overwhelmingly accounted for by banking and insurance—9.9% of the total net domestic product) was the most important sector by the beginning of the 2000s (15.4% in total), closely followed by community, social and personal services (15.1%—especially public administration at 5.0%) and then trade, hotels and restaurants (14.4%). Chennai is the main financial and business centre, at the node of an extensive transport network for much of the southern and central peninsula—just over 13% of all trade in India goes through the air and sea ports of Tamil Nadu (exports worth Rs 187,712.8m. and imports worth Rs 234,829.0m. in 1998/99). Transport, storage and communications provided 6.5% of net domestic product in 1999/2000. The financial services of Chennai remain fundamental to this sector, but the state is also an important visitor destination, for pilgrims and tourists. Tamil Nadu is a popular destination for foreign tourists, and has the third largest share of domestic tourist visits (14.7% in 2002), following Uttar Pradesh and Andhra Pradesh. In 2004 there were 31.1m. tourist arrivals in Tamil Nadu, of which 1.1m. were foreign (in the previous year the latter accounted for 11.2% of the all-India total). Destinations range from the urban expanse of the state capital to the cool resorts of the hill stations, or from the beaches of the coast to the temple-rich legacy of an ancient and varied history. Wildlife still shelters in the high hills, while the nature sanctuary around Point Calimere (most of it the tidal Great Vedaranayam Salt Swamp) hosts, among other bird life, one of the largest flamingo colonies in Asia.

### DIRECTORY

**Governor:** SURJIT SINGH BARNALA, Governor's Secretariat, Raj Bhavan, Chennai 600 022; tel. (44) 25670099; fax (44) 22350570; e-mail governor@tn.nic.in.

**Chief Minister:** KALAIGNAR M. KARUNANIDHI (Dravida Munnetra Kazhagam), Office of the Chief Minister, Government of Tamil Nadu, Secretariat, Fort St George, Chennai 600 009; tel. (44) 25672345; fax (44) 24670242; e-mail cmcell@sec.tn.nic.in; internet www.tn.gov.in.

**Speaker of the Legislative Assembly:** R. AVUDAIAPPAN KALIMUTHU, Legislative Assembly Secretariat, Fort St George, Chennai 600 009; tel. (44) 25672708; fax (44) 5368956 (Prin. Sec.); e-mail tnasmbly@tn.nic.in (Secretariat); the unicameral Legislative Assembly has 234 elected mems and one nominated (Anglo-Indian) mem.: Dravida Munnetra Kazhagam 96; All-India Anna Dravida Munnetra Kazhagam 61; Congress 34; Pattali Makkal Katchi 18; Communist (CPI—M) 9; Communist (CPI) 6; Marumalarchi Dravida Munnetra Kazhagam 6; Viduthalai Chiruthaigal Katch 2; independents and others 3.

**State Special Resident Commissioner in New Delhi:** PAVAN RAINA, Tamil Nadu House, 6 Kautilya Marg, Chanakyapuri, New Delhi 110 021; tel. (11) 23011087; fax (11) 23016822; e-mail tamilnaduhouse@vsnl.com.

# Tripura

The State of Tripura is one of the 'Seven Sisters', the states of the north-eastern region of India. Formerly a Hindu princely state, Tripura abuts into the predominantly Muslim country of Bangladesh, which surrounds it, except in the north-east, where a neck of territory has short eastern borders (totalling 160 km—99 miles, or 16% of Tripura's total frontier length) with the other Indian states of Assam and Mizoram. Southern Tripura is separated from the bulk of Mizoram to the west by an up-thrusting spur of Bangladesh. Tripura's name is variously ascribed to a locally prominent deity or to an original name of Tuipra ('land adjoining water'—the kings of Tripura sometimes held sway over more territory than that constituting the modern state, which, as it is, lies only some 50 km from the open sea). A protectorate of British India, its last ruler opted to accede to independent India upon the partition of the old Empire in the subcontinent. Tripura officially became part of the Indian Union on 15 October 1949, and a full state in the federation on 21 January 1972. It was the smallest state of India until the accession of Sikkim in 1975, and became the third smallest when Goa became a state in 1987—Tripura has an area of 10,486 sq km (4,048 sq miles).

Tripura fronts the eastern banks of the Ganges (Ganga)-Brahmaputra delta, rising onto the hilly fringe of the great flood plain of eastern Bengal (Bangladesh). The more open, and still extensively forested, plains land of the west and south of Tripura rises from just 15 m (50 ft) above sea level to rolling hill country that dominates the state and reaches a maximum height of 938 m. These hills separate the four northern valleys. The fertile countryside is drained by a number of rivers draining into the delta, notably the Bibiyana and the Fenny, while the landscape is also dotted by lakes (sometimes man-made) such as those at Dumboor, Kamalasagar and Neermahal. The climate is tropical and humid, with the monsoon bringing much of the rainfall, which averages some 2,100 mm (83 inches) per year, although some parts of the state can get over 4,000 mm. Temperatures range from an average minimum of 10°C (50°F) in January to an average maximum of 35°C (95°F) in August.

The state had a total population of 3,199,203 in 2001, according to the results of the March census. With a relatively low rate of population growth over the previous 10 years (the population in 1991 was 2,757,205), the population density had only increased slightly, to 305 per sq km. The most densely populated areas are the low-lying south and west, exposed to the plains of Bangladesh—this helps explain the predominant Bengali population. There are also 19 Scheduled Tribes in Tripura (accounting for 31.1% of the population in 2001—the corresponding figure was 95% at the 1931 census), mainly living in the hills. The largest tribal group in the state is that of the Tripuri, originally a Mongoloid people related to the Bodo, who constitute about one-half of the registered tribal population. Most of them now live in the plains and have long enjoyed the cultural influence of neighbouring Bengal (notably because of royal patronage from the late 19th century and, most famously, because of the close association of the great poet, Rabindrath Tagore, with Tripura). The related Reang tribe (noted for traditionally wearing black and red, apparently as a sign of incurring royal displeasure) are the next largest. Others include the Chakma, the Halum (Kuki peoples who accepted the authority of the Tripuri rajahs; originally grouped into 12 *dafas*, now 16), the Garo, a few of the Lushai (Mizo) in the high hills and the Mog. Most of the population speak Bengali, while the other official language of the state is Kakborak or Tripuri (using the royal Debbara dialect), a Tibeto-Burmese language. Manipuri, Hindi and English are also spoken. At the 2001 census, which recorded that 17.4% of the population were of the Scheduled Castes, 85.6% of the population confessed the Hindu religion, the traditional adherence of this former princely state, while the largest minority faith was that of Islam (9.3%), followed by Christianity (3.2%—there are claims that anywhere between one-10th and one-half of the tribal population is Christian, and at the 1991 census the official figure was only 1.7%) and Buddhism (3.1%). Most Hindus are of the Vaishnavu tradition, although there is some Shakti worship—for instance, among the Malsum, a *dafa* of the Halum. The Chakma and the Mog are Buddhist.

Of the total population in 2001, 17.1% were urban, with Agartala both the state capital and the largest town. Other important towns include Kumarghat, Dharmanagar, Khowai and Udaipur. The state is divided into four districts; there is also one autonomous council for the hill areas.

## HISTORY

There are references to kings in Tripura in Vedic literature and there are claims that the kingdom has existed for some 1,300 years. However, historical evidence of Tripura and its long-lasting Manikya dynasty starts in the 14th century, mainly through the *Rajmala*, the chronicle of the Manikya kings. There is other evidence of the rulers of Bengal extending assistance to Tripura's rajah at this time. The early Manikyas achieved considerable military success, extending their realm at times into Bengal, Assam and Burma (now Myanmar), and from the Garo Hills in the north to the shores of the Bay of Bengal in the south. Tripura was a Hindu kingdom, and its rivalry with the rulers of Bengal brought it into conflict with Muslim princes, governors and nawabs, and, at times, the power of the Manikyas was eclipsed. Mughal sovereignty became a fact at the beginning of the 17th century, but declining central power soon restored the primacy of regional rivalry. Indeed, it was this contest with Bengal that first prompted Tripura to seek aid from the British, established near the coast in Calcutta (now Kolkata, West Bengal). In 1761 Tripura succumbed to British power, with the princely protectorate separated from its more tenuous claims over outlying hill tribes of the region. However, no political agent was installed until 1871, and the Manikyas continued to rule in Tripura before and after that date. Maharajah Krishna Manikya moved the capital to Agartala in the 19th century.

In 1870 Birchandra Kishore Manikya Bahadur ascended the throne of Tripura. Politically, he brought in a number of reforms and modelled his administration after the British system, but he was also an admirer of Bengali culture. Bengali became the language of the court, while the rajah himself developed a friendship with the great Bengali poet and Nobel laureate, Rabindrath Tagore, who was to base some of his works on the legends of the Manikyas. Between 1905 and 1912 the princely state, known as Hill Tippura, became attached to the short-lived province of East Bengal and Assam. The last ruling maharajah, Bir Bikram Kishore Manikya, assumed the throne in 1923. Before his death in May 1947 he decided to opt for coming under the jurisdiction of the new, predominantly Hindu, Dominion of India, which was being formed from the partition of the British Empire in the subcontinent. The neighbouring part of Bengal, East Bengal, became part of Muslim Pakistan (later seceding as Bangladesh), rupturing the princely state's traditional links. Thus, it was the Regent Maharani (for the minor, Kirit Bikram Kishore Dev Karma) who signed the decisive Merger Agreement on 9 September 1949, and the Manikya dynasty finally lost power with the accession of Tripura to the Indian Union on 15 October.

As a territory, or so-called 'Part C' state under the terminology of the 1950 Constitution (altered in the 1956 reorganization of the federal structure), Tripura was initially the responsibility of the Governor of Assam, but it became a centrally administered territory in the latter part of 1956. The Union Territory initially had no legislature, but a popular ministry first took office in July 1963. Tripura became a constituent state of the Union on 21 January 1972. However, tribal and separatist aspirations were not completely satisfied, Bengali immigration continued to provoke discontent, and unrest increased. Another feature of state politics was the influence of the Communists and, indeed, the first Left Front administration took office in 1978 (holding office until 1988 under Nripen Chakraborty), the same year as the separatist insurgency group, the Tripura National Volunteers, was formed. Placatory moves by the central authorities in the mid-1980s secured the disarmament of the Volunteers in 1988, upon agreement to restore alienated tribal lands.

In 1989 the National Liberation Front of Tripura (NLFT) was formed, by Dhanjoy Reang, and it thereafter became prominent in the politically motivated murders and kidnappings that beleaguered the democratic process in the state. From 1993 the NLFT and the All-Tripura Tigers' Front (ATTF) began a programme of targeting the non-tribal (mainly Bengali-speaking) residents of the hill country particularly, and this campaign of death and violence continued into the 21st century. The NLFT is the larger and better organized of the two armed groups, but adds a Christian agenda to its separatist ambitions—it claims that one-half of tribals are Christian and are sympathetic to the NLFT (it is unclear whether the non-Christian tribal peoples sympathize out of sentiment or fear). The NLFT and the ATTF both maintain bases across the border, in Bangladesh, and the Indian Government, which has banned both organizations, claims that they receive active assistance there, albeit usually illicitly. Since the terrorist attacks in the USA in September 2001 there have also been allegations of involvement by Muslim extremists, although this may seem unlikely given the Christian motivation of the NLFT. The two separatist groups have also had armed clashes with each other. Most of the state exists under the provisions of the Disturbed Areas Act, and also has to deal with Reang refugees from Mizoram.

In 2001 the NLFT was responsible for the killing of a great number of politicians of the state's ruling Communist Party of India—Marxist (CPI—M), which was also facing a more conventional, democratic, challenge from the Indigenous Peoples' Front of Tripura. In May 2000 the Indigenous Peoples' Front won 18 of the 30 seats on the Tripura Tribal Areas Autonomous District Council, displacing the CPI (M)-led Left Front, which only retained 10 seats (the Governor nominates two). Many attributed this success of the Peoples' Front to the backing of the NLFT (the ATTF boycotted the elections), a connection denied by the democratic party, but which discredited it from a wider base of support and eventually forced the main tribal party to re-form as the Indigenous Nationalist Party of Tripura (INPT). The CPI (M) had become the 'establishment' party for many of the dissident elements within Tripura, having formed a third Left Front Government in 1993, upon ousting Congress, and been re-elected with an absolute majority in 1998. At that last election Manik Sarkar had become Chief Minister. However, despite the widespread antipathy to an incumbent party seen in many parts of India in different elections, the CPI (M), so often a direct victim, gained some benefits from the terrorist violence. In the February 2003 state elections the Left Front under Sarkar was again returned to power, winning over two-thirds of the Assembly seats, with the opposition alleging that the CPI (M) had emphasized the anti-Bengali nature of the INPT, as well as its supposed links with the NLFT, which had worked to the disadvantage of the tribals' Congress allies. Both before and after the elections there was an escalation in the violence of the NLFT and the ATTF, although supporters of the Left Front were also accused of retaliatory aggression and of violence in the aftermath of the polls. With Bhutan and Myanmar conducting military operations against anti-Indian insurgents camped in their border areas towards the end of 2003, there was increased pressure on Bangladesh to do likewise, although early in 2004 its Government denied that militants, or 'ultras', used its territory as a refuge. Such controversies encouraged the Government of India in its determination to fence the entire border with Bangladesh. Meanwhile, border incidents continued, with two people attempting to cross into India being shot in August 2005, for instance. In February 2006, after the first major militant action of the year, the Indian authorities claimed that the attack was part of a plan to disrupt village elections due later in the month and followed a meeting between various insurgent groups and officials from the secret services of Pakistan and Bangladesh (the two countries denied the allegations). Security along the border was also enhanced in the approach to the 2008 Assembly elections.

The CPI (M), as expected, won both parliamentary seats in the April–May 2004 general election (Tripura voted on 22 April, the only state to do so), and there was a 60% turn-out, despite the boycott urged by the ATTF. The scale of the Left Front victories indicated that the INPT and the insurgents were enjoying less support even in the tribal areas. Furthermore, with the decline in violence, development issues came to the fore and more investment seemed likely. Certainly this perception rewarded the CPI (M) at the 2008 state elections. Despite a breach in the ruling Left Front coalition in January, when the Forward Bloc left the electoral alliance upon being refused the chance to stand for more seats, the Sarkar Government was returned to office with an increased majority. The CPI (M) alone secured 46 of the 60 Assembly seats, with its remaining two Left Front allies winning three seats between them. Congress gained only 10 seats, while its ally, the INPT, secured only one seat.

## ECONOMY

Tripura possesses potentially important resources of natural gas, but is in any case among the better off of the north-eastern states of India, although the proportion of those living in poverty is higher than in the others. State wealth is in spite of the 20th-century disruption to Tripura's historic infrastructural links with what is now Bangladesh and of the more recent insurgency problems. There were also allegations about the centre's lack of investment in Tripura's infrastructure and its links with the rest of the country and internationally, as lamented by the Chief Minister in November 2006, on a visit to Delhi. The state's net domestic product, which stagnated in the middle and late 1990s, but generally grew strongly through the decade, sustained its growth into the 21st century. The net domestic product was put at Rs 67,280m. or Rs 20,357 per head in 2003/04 (at current prices). Agartala was the main industrial centre, such as it was, but other major plains towns accounted for some significant activity, while the original railhead being at Dharmanagar encouraged industry in the north-east. While the length of railway track in Tripura amounted to only 44 km in 1998 (entering from Assam), a link was being extended to Agartala and it was hoped that the state might regain its links with Bangladesh's rail network. Roads totalled 12,547 km in 1998 (of which 454 km were major district roads and 1,463 km other district roads) and remained relatively undeveloped within the state. In September 2003 a bus service between Agartala and Dhaka, the capital of Bangladesh, was inaugurated, raising hopes for the future. By contrast with the railway, air links, while only domestic, are long established in the state, the airport at Agartala having been established by the king in the 1930s. There are three other airfields in Tripura, although they are not in regular use at present. Power generated in the state reached 343.3m. units in 1997/98, by which time Tripura had achieved a power surplus, mainly owing to the use of its natural-gas reserves. In 1999 and in 2002, for instance, power and infrastructure development projects were overwhelmingly the most important in the state, often fuelled by central government aid. Installed capacity at the end of May 2006 comprised 148.4 MW in the state sector and 95.0 MW in the central sector. The private sector contributed only 1.1 MW. In the year before it was reckoned that 96% of villages had been electrified, although only 29% of rural households had electricity. Population growth lower than the national average between 1991 and 2001 meant that educational facilities could keep pace and improve Tripura's literacy rate, from 60.4% to 73.7%, one of the highest in India (there are 17 daily newspapers in the state, all in Bengali except for two in English).

In 1996/97 agriculture contributed 43.3% of net domestic product, while in 1991, according to the census, 63.8% of workers were engaged in the sector (three-fifths of the total in cultivation, over one-third in agricultural labour). In 2001/02 the sector accounted for only 18.2% of gross state domestic product, which was the sixth lowest proportion for any state or territory in India. Rice, sugar cane and jute are the main crops. In 2001/02 the rice harvest totalled 608,800 metric tons (accounting for 96% of all food grains grown in the state), sugar cane 52,200 tons and jute (and mesta) 25,000 tons. With a drive to exceed 40,000 ha (98,840 acres) under rubber by the end of 2002, Tripura is already second to Kerala for this crop in India. Another plantation crop, tea, produced some 6,000 tons per year in the late 1990s, from 57 tea gardens. Horticulture is also an important economic motor, particularly as the lack of use of chemicals means that the sector can market itself with an 'organic' price premium. Fruit production in 1999/2000 reached 36,460 tons of pineapples, 26,620 tons of lychees, 25,240 tons of oranges and 22,000 tons of jackfruit. In the same year 4,190 tons of areca nuts and 1,900 tons of cashew nuts were harvested. Forest (57.8% of the total land area in 1995/96) resources are also being developed for exploitation, but the main other primary economic activity of importance to Tripura is the extraction of natural gas. Although most gas was just used for power projects into the early 2000s, the large reserves of high-quality natural gas should soon prove lucrative for the state, particularly if transport links into and across Bangladesh can be established. Tripura also possesses fire clay, quartz and silica sand. Mining employed 7,839 people in 2001/02, while in the following year the value of minerals produced amounted to Rs 818.5m.

Industry only provided 6.6% of net domestic product in 1996/97, and 6.4% of employment (including construction), but this was relatively significant compared with the other poorer states of the north-east. Power (including natural gas) and infrastructure provide the basis of much recent activity in the industrial sector, which the state authorities have been trying to encourage since the 1980s. However, small-scale enterprises and agricultural processing remain the dominant feature, with notable establishments including tea, sugar, tinned-fruit and fruit-juice producers. The larger enterprises in the state are a jute mill, a spinning mill, a steel mill, a plywood factory and a pharmaceuticals plant. Most manufacturing activity is home-based, with handicrafts (especially handloom weaving) traditionally the main sub-sector. Thus, the state is famous throughout India for its cane and bamboo furniture, etc., and its basketwork. Newer initiatives include the encouraging of the assembly of electronic components.

The tertiary sector contributed 50.1% of net domestic product in 1996/97, although public administration accounted for the single largest sub-sector (at 13.8% of the total). Transport was also important, but the strengthening of this sector probably depended on increased cross-border trade with Bangladesh and the development of transit trade. The traditional links of Tripura with Bengal were disrupted by partition and independence, war and civil war. Cross-border trade with Bangladesh only officially resumed from 1994. Since then Tripura has sought to gain access to that country's rail network and to Chittagong port, nearby to the south, but also to develop a link with the rest of India across Bangladesh, to the Indian state of West Bengal. Tourism also has greater potential if the international frontiers become more permeable, although internal strife in the state makes such more problematic. Attractions include two wildlife reserves (featuring the spectacled monkey and the bison—in 2005 there were even reports that tigers had returned to the north-east), Buddhist pilgrimage sites, Hindu temples (notably the famous Mata Tripureswara of Tripura Sundari, in Udaipur, the ancient capital), tribal cultures and royal palaces.

### DIRECTORY

**Governor:** Dinesh Nandan Sahaya, Raj Bhavan, Pushpavant Palace, Agartala 799 001; tel. (381) 2224091; fax (381) 2224350; e-mail govtrp@trp.nic.in.

**Chief Minister:** Manik Sarkar (CPI—M), Office of the Chief Minister, Government of Tripura, Agartala 799 001; tel. (381) 2324000; fax (381) 2223201; e-mail cmo-trp@hub.nic.in.

**Speaker of the Legislative Assembly:** Ramendra Chandra Debnath, Assembly Secretariat, Ujjayanta Palace, Agartala 799 006; tel. (381) 2223446; fax (381) 2224095; the unicameral Legislative Assembly has 60 mems: Communist (CPI—M) 46; Congress 10; Revolutionary Socialist Party 2; others 2.

**State Resident Commissioner in New Delhi:** Ajeer Vidya, Tripura Bhavan, Kautilya Marg, Chanakyapuri, New Delhi 110 021; tel. (11) 23012693; fax (11) 23793827.

# Uttar Pradesh

The State of Uttar Pradesh lies in northern India, on the Gangetic plain (its mountainous north-west became the separate state of Uttaranchal on 9 November 2000; Uttaranchal was renamed Uttarakhand in 2006). Formerly known as the United Provinces, it acquired its current name, meaning 'northern land' or 'northern province', in 1950. Most of its northern border is an international frontier with Nepal; the rest is with Uttarakhand, which lies to the north of its eastern end. In the north-west the Ganga-Yamuna Doab stretches up an extension the tip of which touches a corner of Himachal Pradesh. To the west is Haryana, except where the National Capital Territory of Delhi has been carved out on both banks of the River Yamuna. Rajasthan also lies to the west, before a southern border continues with Madhya Pradesh, distorted by a tentacle of land that extends a corridor southwards around the town of Jhansi to include Lalitpur. There are other, minor convolutions. In the south-east there are short borders with Chhattisgarh (part of Madhya Pradesh until 2000) and Jharkhand (part of Bihar until 2000), while Bihar lies to the east. Until the bifurcation of the state, Uttar Pradesh was the fourth largest state of the Union, but it is now fifth in ranking by size, having an area of 240,928 sq km (93,058 sq miles—some official sources prefer to give the area as 236,286 sq km), although it remains by far the most populous. It retains 82% of the territory of the undivided state.

The north-western tip has the highest ground, reaching over 600 m (1,960 ft), a patch of sub-Himalayan hill country. Otherwise the landscape is dominated by the flat, fertile plains, sloping slightly some 600 km (373 miles) towards the east, and watered by the mighty Ganga (Ganges) and its tributaries, notably the Yamuna, which helps define the western border, and, further downstream, the Ghaghara. The land between the Yamuna and the Ganga is known as the Doab. The plains are largely agricultural, with few forests remaining. The southern borders are defined by the straggling edges of the peninsular plateau lands, the southern tendril of territory around Lalitpur encompassing higher ground and then, eastwards, the Bundelkhand uplands merging into the lower flanks of the Vindhyan Range. The plains receive monsoon rains between June and September, which alleviate the temperature, but increase humidity. In April–June temperatures can reach as high as 50°C (122°F), untempered by a drying wind that can blow from the west known as the loo. Winter nights are cold, but the days remain warm.

Uttar Pradesh has the largest population of any state in India, some 70m. more than Maharashtra. At 1 March 2001 the 'rump' Uttar Pradesh had a total population of 166,197,921 or 690 per sq km, making it the fourth most densely populated state. Scheduled Castes accounted for 21.1% of the population. More detailed demographic figures for the post-2000 Uttar Pradesh are not yet available, but the main thrust of the 1991 figures remains unaltered by the division of the state, particularly as it barely lost 5% of its population to Uttarakhand (formerly Uttaranchal). In 1991 the most widely spoken language in the undivided Uttar Pradesh was Hindi (90.1%), followed by the related Urdu (9.0%), while the next language was Punjabi (only 0.5%). Likewise, the predominant religion, here in the heart of the *arya varta*, crossed by the sacred Ganga and Yamuna and dotted with holy cities (Varanasi or Kasi, Ayodhya, Mathura and Allahabad or Prayag), remains Hinduism. In 2001 80.6% of the population were Hindu, 18.5% Muslim and only 0.4% Sikh. Most Muslims reside in the so-called 'Muslim belt' between Aligarh (just north of Agra) to Faizabad (just east of Lucknow).

The rate of urbanization was only 20.8% in 2001, the vast numbers of rural millions surrounding a number of great cities. The largest city is Kanpur (Cawnpore), India's eighth largest, with a population of 2.55m. in 2001. Kanpur is in central Uttar Pradesh, on the Ganga just to the south-west of the state capital, Lucknow, which is the 11th largest city in India, with a population of 2.19m. Western Uttar Pradesh is dominated by Agra (1.28m.), downstream on the Yamuna from Delhi, and Meerut (Mirat—1.07m.), just to the north-east of the National Capital Territory. Allahabad (975,393), at the confluence of the Yamuna and the Ganga, is towards the south-east of the state, with Varanasi (Benares—1.09m.) further down the Ganga, as it approaches the borders of Bihar. The other main city of eastern Uttar Pradesh is Gorakhpur (622,701), to the north of the Ghaghara. The state is divided into 70 districts.

## HISTORY

The history of Uttar Pradesh is an ancient one and intimately connected with the very progress of India itself. The ancient tales of the Hindu epics, the *Mahabharata* and the *Ramayana*, and other Vedic legends are based here. Uttar Pradesh lies at the heart of the *arya varta*, the land of the Aryans, and was a necessary possession of any empire with pan-Indian aspirations. However, this means that much of its history has been imposed from without, be it Maurya or Gupta hegemony from Magadha (now Bihar), the alien empire of the Kushana (who established a secondary capital at Mathura), Harsha Vardhana of Thanesar (Haryana) in the seventh century or the much later Sultans and Mughals of Delhi (whose tale is better dealt with in the chapter on the National Capital Territory). Even after Harsha, when his capital of Kannauj (upstream on the Ganga from Kanpur) became an object for imperial contention from the ninth century, the struggling powers were a Gurjara clan (Pratiharas) from the west, the Rashtrakutas from the south and the Palas from Bengal. Moreover, the history of Kannauj ends ignominiously with its rajah, Jai Chand, being the Rajput prince who first invited Muhammed of Ghor, a Muslim Afghan dynast, to invade India in the 12th century—ultimately forcing the flight of the Rathore Rajputs to Rajasthan. Once the Rajput hosts were broken in 1192 and Delhi taken, the sacred lands of the Doab and further down the Gangetic plains were exposed to Muslim raids and, later, settlement. The Buddhist remnants in the east were crushed, finally ending the long tradition of a Buddhist (and Jain) presence in the lands of its foundation, and the Hindu temples of the entire region suffered. Generally, however, the raiders were usually more interested in plunder than merely the desecration of pagan shrines.

With the Sultans of Delhi just across the Yamuna, much of Uttar Pradesh remained dominated by Muslim rulers from the 13th century onwards, although their loyalty to the court varied. Western Uttar Pradesh generally remained subject to the sultans, who first established another seat at Agra at the beginning of the 16th century, but Jaunpur in the east, for instance, could become the capital of the Sharqui sultanate, independent between 1398 and 1479. This pattern repeated itself under the Mughals, although their grip was firmer and lasted longer, but they also patronized the capital at Agra (Akbar built another city at Fatehpur Sikri as well) and incorporated the Hindu rajahs into the imperial order. It was only with the decay of Mughal power from the early 18th century that the local princes and governors could assert their independence. Late Mughal Uttar Pradesh essentially consisted of the imperial domain of Agra, Rohilkhand, Awadh (Oudh), Bundelkhand in the south, Allahabad and Varanasi. There were also some foreign concessions, such as the British post in Agra from 1618. The most important of these territories in the history of the region is probably Awadh. In 1720 a Persian courtier, Nawab Muhammed Sadat Khan Burhan ul-Mulk, established a dynasty here. One of his successors, Asaf ud-Daulah (1775–97), who was obliged formally to cede suzerainty over Varanasi and Allahabad to the British at the beginning of his reign, moved the capital from Faizabad to Lucknow at the same time. By this time the power of the Nawabs had been broken. The erstwhile protectors and allies of the Mughal emperors had been routed by the forces of the East India Company in 1765, leaving the imperial court to become dependent on the Marathas, who were encroaching from the south and west. The British encroached from the east, advancing up the Ganga and the Yamuna as they dealt with the Marathas, reaching Delhi in 1803 and occupying all of Uttar Pradesh by 1805. Meanwhile, the Nawabs of Awadh became loyal servants of the British, and their lands were a valuable recruiting ground for the Company armies. Thus, in 1856 when the Governor-General, Sir James Ramsay, Lord Dalhousie, decided to annex Awadh, dispossessing Wajid Ali in the cause of 'better administration', he provoked a sense of betrayal and outrage throughout what the British called Oudh and prepared the way for the Great Rebellion begun by the Sepoy Mutiny at Meerut (Mirat) the following year. It did not take long for most of Uttar Pradesh to rise in support of the insurgents, soon legitimized by the hapless last Mughal and, later, by Nana Sahib, the heir of the last Maratha peshwa.

The various sieges, reliefs and massacres attributed to both sides during the war did not alter the incorporation of Awadh into the United Provinces of Oudh and Agra thereafter, although the Mutiny won other concessions, as well as the replacement of the Company with the British Crown. Delhi had been included in the North-Western Province in 1832 (at the time of a proposal to make Agra the seat of a fourth British presidency), but as political reform developed and direct rule from Calcutta (now Kolkata, in West Bengal) became less practical, modern Uttar Pradesh began to take shape as the North-Western Province was increasingly grouped with the United Provinces (as the name was officially changed to in 1935) and the headquarters of British administration moved from Allahabad to Lucknow. The province was active in the struggle for independence, and since has produced eight of India's Prime Ministers, including the Nehru-Gandhi dynasty, and a number of Presidents. Uttar Pradesh remains crucial in modern Indian politics, not least because it sends 80 members to the Lok Sabha and 31 to the Rajya Sabha. The results of the 2002 state elections were seen as important to the survival of the Bharatiya Janata Party (BJP) in government at the Centre, for instance, but although its performance was poor the consequences were obscured by the fractious nature of state politics.

Until the 1970s Congress dominated the institutions of Uttar Pradesh, but the political emergence of lower-caste groups favoured alternative parties such as the Janata Party or the Bahujan Samaj Party (BSP). The rise of the BJP completed the disarray of Congress, as the revivalist-nationalist party exploited the dispute over the site of a mosque in Ayodhya (eventually, on 6 December 1992, demolished by Hindu extremists who had long claimed it to have been built over a temple commemorating the place of Rama's birth), an ongoing dispute with national repercussions that provoked massive communal violence at the time—and continued to do so more than a decade later, as witnessed in the 2002 troubles in Gujarat. The late 1990s saw the BJP in power in Uttar Pradesh, but they added internal dissension to an already fractured political scene, which was only complicated by the decision to form a separate hill state of Uttarakhand. Indecisive state elections in March 2002 left Uttar Pradesh under President's Rule until a new coalition was finally agreed, and Mayawati of the BSP, supported by the BJP and the Rashtriya Lok Dal, on 3 May became Chief Minister, a post she had held twice before. Disputes continued, but the state elections in Uttar Pradesh certainly seemed to harden the policies of the BJP-led federal Government. This added to the increasing tensions over the Ayodhya case during 2003, as court cases and conflicting 'expert' reports fuelled the controversy. However, it was the scandal of the Taj Heritage Corridor project (the unauthorized commercial development by the world-famous World Heritage Site, the Taj Mahal) that eventually caused the downfall of the Mayawati administration and, later, allegations of corruption were brought against the former Chief Minister. Even towards the end of 2002 the opposition was alleging that the Government had lost its majority in the state Assembly, but the fracturing of the coalition only began formally at the end of May 2003, when the Rashtriya Lok Dal withdrew from the BSP-led ruling alliance. Mayawati's fate was ensured by the loss of BJP support at the end of August. Moreover, before the end of the year the courts had ordered an investigation into the wealth and business dealings of Mayawati and her family during her tenure as Chief Minister (while what were widely seen as politically motivated corruption cases against her successor in the premiership were abandoned). Towards the end of 2006, in the approach to the state elections, Mayawati was again threatened with prosecution over the 'Taj Corridor', but the case was dropped when she returned to office in 2007.

Mulayam Singh Yadav, the veteran, left-wing, secular leader of the Samajwadi Party, was appointed to form a new Government. On 8 September 2003 he formally gained the confidence of the Assembly, supported by 37 of the 111 BSP deputies (a rebel faction that had just formed the Lok Tantrik BSP or Lok Tantrik Bahujan Dal—there were reports that other legislators were also in dispute with the old BSP leadership), while Congress lent its support from outside the coalition. Yadav had notoriously poor relations with Congress, particularly under Sonia Gandhi, but he had been allied to the party in the past and was eager to secure its participation in the new administration. Yadav had been premier of Uttar Pradesh twice previously, in 1989–91 and in 1994–95, as well as Minister of Defence at the Centre thereafter; he had formed the Samajwadi (Hindi for 'socialist') Party in 1992 and remained its undisputed leader. His secularist principles and popularity with the Muslim community in the state added an interesting dimension to relations with the BJP-led Union Government, particularly over the issue of Ayodhya. However, at the general election of April–May 2004 the BJP was removed from power at the Centre (in Uttar Pradesh losing 15 of the 25 Lok Sabha seats it had won at the 1999 national poll). Congress retained nine seats, to one of which was elected the newest member of the Nehru-Gandhi dynasty to enter national politics, Rahul Gandhi (son of the former Prime Minister, Rajiv Gandhi, and of the current Congress leader, Sonia Gandhi). Uttar Pradesh's ruling Samajwadi Party increased its representation in the national Lok Sabha to 35 seats (its Lok Tantrik BSP ally won three), although its main rival, the BSP, also gained seats, up to a total of 19.

In keeping with his avowedly secular credentials, Yadav committed his party to support of a Congress Government in New Delhi, but this did not prevent relations between the two parties being poor. In June 2004 Rahul Gandhi criticized the law-and-order situation in Uttar Pradesh and cited the Samajwadi Government (although it depended on Congress support) as an obstacle to social and economic progress in the state. Congress had been brought to power by rural dissatisfaction, and was anxious to secure its position in the country's largest state (where the BJP governor was replaced). Congress and the Samajwadi Party in Uttar Pradesh were uneasy allies. Moreover, although reluctant to dismiss a secularist administration in the state, Congress was ready to impose President's Rule should Yadav lose his majority. That majority was threatened during 2006 when at the end of February a court reversed an earlier judicial decision that refused to challenge the old Speaker's ruling allowing the 1993 BSP dissidents to join the Samajwadi Party, thereby questioning their status. The Government created considerable controversy by holding a vote of confidence in anticipation of the judgment (with 207 out of 404 deputies—the opposition walked out). However, in March the Supreme Court ruled that the rebel legislators could stay as a separate group within the Assembly pending a final decision. The matter was complicated further by the decision of five members to return to the BSP, which prompted the Speaker to threaten them with disqualification under the anti-defection laws (in May the courts permitted the Speaker to proceed and he disqualified the five in June). The 37 members of the Lok Tantrik BSP continued to support the Samajwadi Party, despite further legal manoeuvres. Meanwhile, the Gandhi siblings campaigned to improve Congress support in Uttar Pradesh; they were prominent in the campaign to re-elect their mother, Sonia, to the Lok Sabha from Rae Barelli in May 2006. Congress criticized the Samajwadi Government, which, in turn, questioned whether it would continue to support the coalition at the Centre.

Sectarian tensions remained over Ayodhya, particularly following the failed assault on the site by Islamist militants in July 2005. These tensions were heightened by disputes over the ownership of the Taj Mahal. Sporadic outbreaks of communal disputes and violence continued into 2006, while bombs in Varanasi in March raised fears that local militants were receiving support not just from Kashmiri and Pakistan-based groups, but also from connections in Bangladesh. However, any attempt to address such issues or the extent of caste and communal divisions in Uttar Pradesh soon descended into political manoeuvring, particularly given the approach of state polls. Even after the polls, tensions were not eased by bomb blasts in November 2007. Simultaneous explosions at court compounds in three cities—Lucknow, Varanasi and Faizabad—killed 15 and were attributed to Islamist militants. Another example of terrorist violence was an attack on a police training camp in January 2008, which killed eight.

Although the 2007 state elections were not considered to be that violent, the approach to them had been marred by communal tension and sporadic unrest. The Government sought to woo the Muslim vote with minority quotas (a new system was enacted in December 2006), while the BJP tended towards its *Hindutva* rhetoric and Mayawati courted the upper castes in order to broaden her dalit base. Although Yadav had been Chief Minister for more time than any other Uttar Pradesh state premier (albeit over three terms), that his regime was in trouble was indicated by the civic polls of November 2006, when Samajwadi candidates won only one of 12 contested mayoralties, with eight going to the BJP and even three to Congress. Early in 2007 the Rashtriya Lok Dal left the coalition, soon followed by Congress, which cited as its reason the delays to the investigation of a sensational serial killing case in Nithari village, in western Uttar Pradesh, near Delhi. Various attempts were made to undermine the Government's majority in the Assembly, and Yadav accused the Governor of seeking President's Rule, but the administration survived until the state elections, which were held in seven rounds between 7 April and 8 May. The BSP gained an absolute majority, winning 206 (from 99 in 2002) of the 404 seats and putting Mayawati firmly back into the premiership for the fourth time. The Samajwadi Party retained only 97 seats, while the BJP won 50 (and one for its Janata Dal—United ally); Congress kept 22 and the Rashtriya Lok Dal 10.

Mayawati's dominance of Uttar Pradesh politics was demonstrated a year into her Government at by-elections in April 2008. The BSP won all five seats being contested—two in the Lok Sabha and three in the Vidhan Sabha—while Congress and the BJP notably failed to record any progress in their attempts to rebuild their own power bases in the state. Mayawati had been nervous of the Congress policy of targeting dalit votes, with Rahul Gandhi championing farmers' concerns, particularly in the drought-stricken Bundelkhand region. In fact, Gandhi had announced Congress support for a separate state in the region, on either side of the Uttar Pradesh and Madhya Pradesh border (Congress feared never being able to regain power in Uttar Pradesh as a whole). Mayawati, however, also announced that she favoured splitting Uttar Pradesh—with new states in Bundelkhand, Poorvanchal and in the western districts—accusing the Centre of failing to provide development funds. The Chief Minister also attempted to woo the Muslim vote away from Congress, which would make her an invaluable ally for the BJP, together with her influence among dalits in Uttar Pradesh and a number of other states. With relations between Mayawati and Sonia Gandhi deteriorating by early 2008, and Mayawati open in her ambition to become the national Prime Minister, a realignment of political forces in Uttar Pradesh seemed increasingly likely. In June the BSP formally withdrew its support for the federal Government, over the controversial issue of the nuclear energy deal with the USA. The Samajwadi Party supported the Centre, despite some defections as a result. The basis for an electoral alliance between the Samajwadi Party, Congress and, perhaps, the RJD, on the one hand, and the BSP and the BJP, on the other, had begun to emerge.

## ECONOMY

Uttar Pradesh is one of the poorest states of the Union, the sheer size of its population overwhelming what wealth it has, although it should also be noted that there are significant regional disparities within the state (in general, the west tends to perform better economically than the east). Even by 2007 some official measurements of the economy had yet fully to take into account the separation of Uttarakhand (the new state was known as Uttaranchal in 2000–06) from the rest of the Uttar Pradesh. However, the overall size of the economy remained the largest of any state in India, apart from Maharashtra, while the sheer extent of Uttar Pradesh's population contributed further to its significance to the national economy and made it vital to, for example, consumer industries. In 2004/05 the total net domestic product of the state was put at Rs 2,052,490m. or Rs 11,477 per head, the latter figure indicating that only Bihar was poorer. Many of the other figures in this survey apply to the undivided state, notably those for infrastructure—although, except for hydroelectric installations, only relatively small proportions were located in Uttarakhand. In March 1999 the road network totalled 121,761 km, of which 4,036 km was national highway and 9,637 km was state highway. Lucknow is the centre of an extensive rail network, while most of the major cities have airports. There is also considerable traffic on the rivers. In 1997/98 the total installed capacity of electricity was 6,158.75 MW. In Uttar Pradesh after bifurcation, at the end of May 2005 installed capacity was 8,167.7 MW (57% state resources and the rest, apart from 1% from the private sector, a share of central capacity). About 60% of villages were connected to the electricity supply in March 2005; only 11% of the rural households of Uttar Pradesh and Uttarakhand together had electricity. The literacy rate in the divided state, the 'rump' Uttar Pradesh, at the time of the 2001 census, was only 57.4%, although this had risen from 40.7% one decade earlier.

Agriculture is the main occupation of almost four-fifths of the population, and accounts for about one-third of the economy (33.2% of gross state domestic product in 2001/02). Some other figures for the post-2000 state are available. The great plains of the divided Uttar Pradesh grew 43.2m. metric tons of food grains in 2001/02 (one-fifth of the all-India total), of which 58% were wheat, 29% rice and 6% pulses. Sugar-cane production was 116.2m. tons. Oilseeds (1.0m. tons) and some horticultural crops are grown, the main fruits being mango and guava. Uttar Pradesh is no longer a significant producer of cotton. In 2002/03 total foodgrain production was only 36.3m. tons, although Uttar Pradesh remained the largest state producer, still accounting for one-fifth of the national harvest. Livestock is widely kept and fishing takes place in the numerous inland waters, but forestry is limited. Livestock products were an expanding sector in the early 2000s. Uttar Pradesh is the largest milk producer in India, providing 15.3m. tons in 2002/03 (about 18% of the national total). The divided state also produced 842m. eggs and 1,939 tons of wool in that year.

Limestone, magnesite and silica-sand are among the mineral resources of the state, the value of production being Rs 23,594m. in 2002/03, while in the previous year the sector had employed almost 402,000 people. There are cement works and glass factories in Uttar Pradesh, but most processing of primary products is sourced from the agricultural sector. Industrial activities, therefore, include sugar production, cotton yarn, jute, vegetable oils, textiles and carpets, as well as automobiles, small manufactures and light engineering, brassware and bangles. At the end of March 1998, in the undivided state, however, there were 2,281 large and medium-sized industrial enterprises (almost all based on the plains), with employment potential for 723,000 people. There were also 342,000 small-scale units, with employment potential of 1.42m. people. Kanpur is the state's main industrial centre, based on cotton from 1869, but now including aviation, textiles and chemicals.

The tertiary sector obviously had activity created by the sheer number of businesses and of people, with trade and transport prominent. Uttar Pradesh, despite its general poverty compared with other states, is one of the most important consumer markets in India, and not merely because of the great size of the market. Tourism is also a lucrative source of revenue, the state being a centre for religious pilgrimage (most dramatically, the 12m. or so who congregate for the Maha Kumbh Mela, a festival, at Allahabad every 12 years—last held in 2001) and endowed with a wealth of monuments. The state accounts for over one-quarter of domestic tourist visits (27% in 2002).

### DIRECTORY

**Governor:** T. V. RAJESHWAR, Office of the Governor, Raj Bhavan, Lucknow 226 001; tel. (522) 2220494; fax (522) 2225995; e-mail hgovup@up.nic.in.

**Chief Minister:** KUMARI MAYAWATI (Bahujan Samaj Party), Office of the Chief Minister, Government of Uttar Pradesh, Secretariat, Lucknow 226 001; tel. (522) 2239296; fax (522) 2230002; e-mail cmup@up.nic.in.

**Speaker of the Legislative Assembly (Vidhan Sabha):** SUKHDEV RAJBHAR (Bahujan Samaj Party), Assembly Secretariat, Vidhan Bhavan, Lucknow 226 001; tel. (522) 2238174; fax (522) 2239394; e-mail upvs@up.nic.in (Secretariat); the bicameral legislature has a directly elected lower chamber, the Legislative Assembly, with 404 mems: Bahujan Samaj Party (BSP) 206; Samajwadi Party 97; Bharatiya Janata Party 50; Congress 22; Rashtriya Lok Dal 10; Rashtriya Parivartan Dal 2, Akhil Bhartiya Loktantrik Congress 1, Bharatiya Jan Shakti 1, Jan Morcha 1, Janata Dal—United 1, Rashtriya Swabhimaan Party 1, Uttar Pradesh United Democratic Front 1; independents 9; nominated 1; vacant 1.

**Chairman of the Legislative Council (Vidhan Parishad):** SUKHRAM YADAV, Council Secretariat, Vidhan Bhavan, Lucknow 226 001; tel. (522) 2238046; fax (522) 2238232; the Legislative Council has 108 mems.

**State Resident Commissioner in New Delhi:** AJIT K. SETH, 3 Gopinath Bordoloi Marg, Chankyapuri, New Delhi 110 021; tel. (11) 23014263; fax (11) 23715604.

# Uttarakhand

The State of Uttarakhand, the mountainous part of Uttar Pradesh until 9 November 2000, lies in northern India, in the Himalayan Mountains. Uttarakhand was known as Uttaranchal until the end of 2006. The 'north country' has international frontiers with Nepal to the south-east and, with the border lying beyond the crest of the Great Himalaya, Tibet (Xizang—as it is known in the People's Republic of China, of which it forms a part) to the north-east. Another Indian hill state, Himachal Pradesh, is to the north-west, rising above the Punjab plains as Uttarakhand rises above the plains of Uttar Pradesh, the latter being to the west and south. The new state acquired 18% of the territory of the undivided Uttar Pradesh and, therefore, has an area of 53,483 sq km (20,658 sq miles), making it only slightly smaller than Himachal Pradesh, with which it shares many similarities.

Uttarakhand lies along the Himalayas and its subsidiary ranges that lower themselves towards the Gangetic plains. Here the mountains run roughly from the north-west to the south-east, descending from the Great Himalaya (which rises to peaks such as those of holy Badrinath in the north or the heights of Nanda Devi further south—the highest point on the latter, at 7,816 m or 25,643 ft, is the second highest point in territory under the control of the Republic of India) to the Shivaliks and their foothills. The ranges are complicated by south-westward thrusting spurs separated by deeply carved valleys guiding rivers towards the plains. The region is the source of both the Ganga (Ganges) and the Yamuna, sacred rivers of the Hindus. The upper reaches of the Ganga are here known as the Bhagirathi, and one of its principal tributaries (which originates further south in the mountains from where the great river exits onto the plains) is the Alaknanda. The terrain is rugged and wooded, flora varying hugely with altitude. The climate is influenced by the monsoon, when most of the annual average rainfall of over 1,500 mm (59 inches) falls—less in the high mountains—and it is generally mild year-round in the foothills.

At the census of March 2001 the population total for Uttarakhand was 8,489,349 (i.e. about 5% of the combined populations of Uttar Pradesh and Uttarakhand, which had been one state just short of four months previously). This gave a population density of 159 per sq km. Its difference from other hill states, indicating its long integration into the Aryan and Hindu mainstream, is revealed by 2001 figures for the Scheduled Tribes population, putting them at only 3.0% of the total, while Scheduled Castes constituted 17.9%. Few more detailed figures for the census are as yet available, limiting exact data for the new federal unit. The region is also known as Uttarakhand and traditionally consists of the old area of Garhwal and of Kumaon in the south. Other names, such as Devbhumi (home of the gods) or Kedarkhand (abode of Siva), hint at the importance of the sacred geography of the area. There are holy sites all along the course of the Ganga as it rises up towards the mountains, starting on the edge of the foothills with Haridwar, one of the seven holy places of Hinduism, and culminating with Badrinath, one of the four holy abodes. Legends and heroic myths abound. Hinduism is the main religion of a huge majority of the population (85.0% in 2001), just as Hindi (usually Pahari hill dialects) is the main language. Only a few speak any tribal languages, Urdu is confined to some small, urban, Muslim communities (who comprised 14.0% of the population), and the third tongue of the state could well be Punjabi, owing to a pocket of Sikh settlement (fleeing the Punjab in 1947) just to the south-west of Nainital, in Udhamsingh Nagar (2.5% Sikhs in 2001). There are also some Christians, Buddhists and Jains in the state.

The urban population constituted 25.7% of the total in 2001, the main centres being at the provisional state capital of Dehradun, in the north-west, and Haridwar to its south. Further into the mountains from these cities are the old royal capitals of Garhwal, Srinagar and Tehri. In the south the main town is Nainital, a proposed capital and currently the seat of the High Court, with the industrial town of Haldwani to the south and the old centre of Kumaon, Almora, to the north. In the centre of the state, where the Alaknanda valley clefts the mountains upstream from Srinagar, are the towns of Joshimath and, approaching the Chinese border, Badrinath. The state is divided into 13 districts.

### HISTORY

The history of Uttarakhand emerges from the myth smoke of the Vedic era, an uncertain tale of various tribes and peoples, such as the Khasars displaced by Rajputs and brahmins from the plains. Many, of course, were attracted by the pilgrimage centres and the importance of the area in Hindu legend, although Buddhism was more important for almost 1,000 years, until the brahminical revival from the ninth century. The usual political pattern, irrelevant of religious adherence, was of several principalities competing for pre-eminence or submitting to plains powers. Thus, one of the earliest hill states was based at Joshimath (Jyotirdham), while the Katyuris dominated between the sixth and 12th centuries.

In the 12th century the long-established Chand clan gained the ascendancy in the southern and south-western parts of the modern state, an area known as Kumaon, while in Garhwal to the north the Pals (later known as the Sahs) united the chiefs in the 14th century. The various rajahs fought petty wars with each other or neighbouring plains principalities, but peace and growing prosperity in the 17th and 18th centuries again attracted more determined attention from the hegemonic plains powers, this time the Muslim rulers of Delhi or central Uttar Pradesh. The most serious threat, however, came in the 18th century, with Gurkha incursions at the beginning and at the end. Kumaon was particularly overrun, but in reaching towards Kangra (now in Himachal Pradesh) and in descending towards the plains from Kumaon in the latter invasion, the Nepalese attracted the ire of the British, who were now in control of the Gangetic plains. Moreover, the hill princes sought British help in the early 19th century and, in 1815, an expedition was sent to drive out the Gurkhas. By a treaty of 1816 Nepal ceded the hill territories to the East India Company, which then restored the Maharajah to Tehri Garhwal, but retained a directly administered British Garhwal. This combination of direct and princely rule only ended after independence (Tehri acceded to Uttar Pradesh on 18 May 1949), when the hill territories were consolidated into Uttar Pradesh. The hill peoples, however, although they had remained loyal to the British during the disturbances of 1857–58, had been stirred by the struggle for independence and continued the tradition of peaceful protest afterwards in their own, local Chipko movement against logging. The tradition re-emerged in the 1990s with popular campaigning for a separate state.

The Bharatiya Janata Party (BJP), with a majority of the deputies representing the area, was the first to support the campaign for a separate Uttaranchal (Uttarakhand) state. The argument for a state was based on the variation of Pahari dialects from the Hindi spoken on the plains, although otherwise the region was considered so integrated that it had not maintained a particularly distinct identity. However, there was a widespread perception that the hill territories were, inevitably, neglected by the plains with their teeming populations. Eventually, with a BJP federal Government in office and the opposition Congress co-operating to achieve another new state, the Uttar Pradesh Reorganization Act 2000 was passed and, on 9 November, Uttaranchal came into being. Its birth was accompanied by some controversy—for instance, over the site of the capital or in its having three premiers within 18 months of its existence. Nityanand Swamy of the BJP managed to survive as the first Chief Minister for almost one year, until the end of October 2001, when he was replaced (at the insistence of the national party) by the local party president, Bhagat

Singh Koshiyari. However, unexpectedly, and ironically for BJP hopes of having created a 'safe' state, Congress won the 2002 state elections to a new, 70-member, unicameral Assembly (replacing the provisional legislature of 30 members, who had originally been elected to the old Uttar Pradesh house). Congress itself caused some controversy, when the national leadership appointed Narain Dutt Tiwari (a former premier of undivided Uttar Pradesh, but who had opposed the creation of a separate Uttaranchal) to head Congress in the new Vidhan Sabha. Nevertheless, he was duly asked to form a Government, and he became Chief Minister in March.

Tiwari had not been popular with the national leadership since failing to deny ambitions for the Union premiership, but in Uttaranchal he continued in office despite ill health in December 2002 and in early 2003. In mid-2003 the revenue minister was obliged to resign following allegations that he was the father of the child of an unwed mother (rape charges were later brought against him), although in 2004 the accusations receded, culminating in the woman withdrawing the charges. The former minister, Harak Singh Rawat, claimed the scandal was concocted to discredit him by rival political factions. Divisions within the ruling Congress were exacerbated by the contraction of the ministry in July (obliged by a new constitutional amendment), when Tiwari mainly chose to demote supporters of a rival. Tiwari was also under pressure for not having improved the Congress tally of seats in the national Parliament at the May general election. In October he announced his willingness to obey the national leadership if it wished him to make way for a new premier; however, Tiwari remained Chief Minister. Uttarakhand sends five members to the Lok Sabha and three to the Rajya Sabha, which are based in the National Capital Territory. In 2004 Congress retained one of the five lower-house seats, while the BJP lost one of its four, but to the Samajwadi Party. In March 2006 Tiwari's failure to attend a Congress leadership summit in southern India prompted further speculation about his future, with Rawat again urging his replacement—on top of earlier criticism of what was considered the excessive distribution of state posts, despite the strictures of the Centre. With state elections due in 2007, it remained uncertain whether Congress would risk the change, but Tiwari seemed increasingly reluctant to remain in office. In October he stated that he did not want to seek re-election to the Assembly, provoking further infighting in the Congress leadership. The two main contenders for the succession were Tiwari loyalist and information minister, Indira Hridayesh, and Rawat. Meanwhile, the Assembly backed the government proposal to rename the state Uttarakhand, which was the name associated with the campaign for separation, despite BJP objections—the Uttaranchal (Alteration of Name) Act 2006 became law upon presidential assent in December and was gazetted to take effect on 1 January 2007. The Lok Sabha had passed the law despite Samajwadi Party members disrupting the process by agitating for the return of the sacred city of Haridwar to Uttar Pradesh.

Opposition parties alleged that the timing of the name change to Uttarakhand was down to the forthcoming elections, but, if so, a divided Congress leadership, struggling over who was to succeed Tiwari, failed to follow up on that advantage. At the elections to the state legislature, held on 21 February 2007, Congress was ousted from power. The BJP gained 34 seats in the 70-seat legislature, and obtained the support of the three deputies elected for the main regional party, the Uttarakhand Kranti Dal (UKD), and from among the three independents. Congress retained 21 seats, and the Bahujan Samaj Party secured a strong eight. Maj.-Gen. (retd) B. C. Khanduri, a former Union minister, became the BJP's Chief Minister, against the strong contention of Koshiyari. Khanduri formed a Government with the support of the independents and the issue-based support of the UKD (which was particularly interested in pursuing the relocation of the state capital to Gairsain). The new administration soon provoked the ire of the secular opposition, in July, when it introduced a bill against cow slaughter. However, in September Khanduri was easily elected to an Assembly seat, which had been vacated for him by a defector to the BJP from Congress—finally giving the party an absolute majority in the legislature.

## ECONOMY

Uttarakhand is rich in natural resources, but they are difficult to exploit and, as a result, some 70% of the population lives below the officially determined level of measuring poverty (the all-India average is 46%). More accurate comparable data must await the production of statistics specific to the new state, as most of what is available applies to the undivided Uttar Pradesh (see above), which was already one of the poorer states of the Union. Official figures for 2004/05 put total net state domestic product for Uttarakhand (then known as Uttaranchal) at Rs 177,070m., or Rs 19,652 per head. For a mountain state, owing to its long integration into Uttar Pradesh and its importance as a pilgrimage site, Uttarakhand has some fairly well developed infrastructure, including a relatively good road and bridge network, some rail links and two domestic airports, near Dehradun and below Nainital at Pantnagar. There is limited installed power capacity in the state, despite the potential for hydroelectricity generation—it has been estimated that Uttarakhand could generate some 40,000 MW of power. In 2005 the state's installed capacity was 975 MW, with an additional 332 MW of capacity from a share in the Centre's projects. Almost 90% of villages were connected to the electricity supply, but the level of household connections remained low (11% in Uttarakhand and Uttar Pradesh combined). Fulfilling the potential of the state would make Uttarakhand a net exporter of power, but the terrain is difficult and attracting investment to power projects in India, despite the country's need, is considered difficult. Human potential is also being developed, with the literacy rate increasing to 72.3% in 2001, from 57.8% in 1991.

Agriculture is the main economic sector for most people, but this is of limited help to the state economy, as subsistence agriculture is what occupies about three-quarters of the population. Some 71% of land holdings are less than one ha (about 2.47 acres) in size, making the sector inefficient. The main food grains are wheat and, in the north-west, rice—total foodgrain production in 2001/02 amounted to 1.7m. metric tons, of which 0.7m. tons were wheat and 0.6m. tons rice. Total foodgrain production in 2002/03 was 1.6m. tons, reflecting the lower harvests experienced throughout India. Sugar cane is grown nearer the plains, the state producing 2.5% of the all-India total in 2001/02 (7.6m. tons). Horticulture and floriculture is being encouraged, although the state already has a modest reputation for fruits such as apples and mangoes or the famous strawberries of Udhamsingh Nagar. One primary activity that it is hoped will be of increasing importance is forestry and forestry products—Uttarakhand acquired 96% of the forests of the old Uttar Pradesh, and this potential is as yet unexplored, with hopes for products such as medicinal plants. The livestock product sector is also a healthy one, with milk production in 2003/04 provisionally put at 1.1m. tons, egg production at 94.2m. and wool at 446,000 kg.

Mineral resources include limestone, graphite, gypsum, iron ore and copper. Although the mining sector employed 28,704 people in 2001/02, the value of minerals produced was only Rs 68.5m. in 2002/03. It is hoped that the extractive industry, like agriculture, might provide the basis for more value-added endeavours, such as the small cement plant at Nainital or sugar mills. Any major hydroelectric projects should help any industrial development. Small-scale units are already important, particularly for textiles, weaving, handicrafts and some light manufactures.

Services are relatively well developed, with transport and trade encouraged by a long-established tourist industry (which suffered from the access restrictions imposed on the area for the first time between 1960 and 1975, when there was tension along the Chinese border). Religious attractions are numerous, contributing strongly to Uttarakhand being the fourth most visited state by domestic tourists in 2002 (accounting for 4.4% of all visits). There are also some historical remains—the hill resorts of Nainital and Mussoorie, for instance—and large areas of national park, rich in scenery and wildlife. Trekking is recovering, skiing and adventure sports are being encouraged, and pilgrims remain numerous. In mid-2005 a helicopter service to the main pilgrimage sites was announced, as well as other projects, including an eco-tourism development. At that time the tourism department accounted for over one-quarter of the state's income. Another important source of income in such a poor state is the central government; this is visible not so much in the subsidizing of public administration as in the high level of recruitment to the armed forces, as young men seek to escape the poverty of the Uttarakhand valleys.

## DIRECTORY

**Governor:** B. L. Joshi, Office of the Governor, Raj Bhavan, Dehradun 248 001; tel. (135) 2757400; fax (135) 2750014.

**Chief Minister:** Bhuvan Chandra Khanduri (Bharatiya Janata Party), Office of the Chief Minister, Government of Uttarakhand, Civil Secretariat, Dehradun 248 001; tel. (135) 2665090; fax (135) 2665722.

**Speaker of the Legislative Assembly (Vidhan Sabha):** Harbans Kapoor, Office of the Speaker, Assembly Secretariat, Vidhan Sabha, Dehradun 248 001; tel. (135) 2665885; fax (135) 2666788; e-mail info@uttaranchalassembly.org; the unicameral Legislative Assembly has 70 mems: Bharatiya Janata Party 36; Congress 20; Bahujan Samaj Party 8; Uttarakhand Kranti Dal 3; independents 3.

**Principal Resident Commissioner in New Delhi:** Vinita Kumar, 104 Indra Prakash Bldg, 21 Barakhamba Rd, New Delhi 100 001; tel. (11) 23738498; fax (11) 23327713; e-mail rescm-ua@hub.nic.in.

# West Bengal

The State of West Bengal lies in north-eastern India, at the head of the Bay of Bengal. Ancient Bengal (Bangla) consisted of the flat, fertile plains of the mighty Ganga-Brahmaputra delta and it developed a distinct regional identity, strengthened under foreign rule, when Calcutta (now Kolkata) was the capital of all of British India between 1773 and 1911. However, the legacy of Muslim rule and a still numerous Hindu population led to the final Partition of Bengal at independence, when the last Empire of India gave way to modern India, which retained West Bengal, and Pakistan, in which East Bengal became East Pakistan (later, upon achieving its own independence in 1971, Bangladesh). West Bengal consists of a large block of territory on the coast, connected by a corridor of varying narrowness to a northern block of territory beneath the Himalayas. The international frontier with Bangladesh therefore runs the length of West Bengal's eastern border, which curls over the northern end of that country. This northernmost part of West Bengal has the kingdom of Bhutan to the north-east and that of Nepal to the west, but it also connects the bulk of the Republic of India to its north-eastern states, through Assam to the east, and to Sikkim, to the north. To the west of the north–south corridor is Bihar (upstream on the Ganga—Ganges), and, further south, Jharkhand, into which a horn of the main block of West Bengal abuts. Orissa lies down the coast to the south-west. The total area of the state is 88,752 sq km (34,258 sq miles), making it slightly larger than the island of Ireland.

West Bengal, which occupies the western delta of the Ganga and stretches up to the foothills of the Himalayas, is a very flat state, dominated by the cultivation of rice, with villages clinging to any piece of higher ground that might lend protection from not infrequent flooding. The main river of Bengal, the Ganga, is highly mobile over such a flat terrain, easily carving out new courses for itself through the alluvial mud and marshland, and its main course has moved steadily eastwards over recent centuries, leaving the old principal channel to the sea, the Hugli (Hooghly), as a relatively minor waterway. Thus, the main channel of the Ganga crosses the state only at the narrow north point of the main block of West Bengal, before heading into Bangladesh. The southern part of the state is also watered by numerous streams flowing from the Jharkhand hills, such as the Damodar. In the south-east the mangrove swamps of the Sunderbans, which continue into Bangladesh, are the only remnants of the dense woodland that once covered the delta. The area remains a refuge of the tiger population. North-east of the Ganga the state widens into a small block of territory dominated by the cities of Ingraz Bazar (English Bazaar) and Raiganj, then the narrow corridor continues to the north of the state, into Darjiling (Darjeeling—acquired from Sikkim in the mid-19th century) and eastwards and a little south onto the northern side of the Brahmaputra valley and Koch Bihar (Cooch Behar). The northern highlands, consisting of the Eastern Shivaliks and the Darjiling Hills, rise to the highest point at Sandakphu (3,630 m or 11,914 ft), which is on the border with Nepal, and the main river here is the Tista, a tributary of the Brahmaputra, which flows to the south-east of the state. The alpine or, rather, Himalayan landscape and the more temperate climate is in marked contrast to the plains, and different too to the only other hilly territory, in the southern part of the state. The Puruliya highlands in the far west, and the more northerly Rajmahal Hills, are an extension of the ancient rocks of peninsular India, the gently rising edges of the Chotanagpur plateau, decreasingly clad with ancient forest. Such elevations moderate the climate, particularly in the sub-Himalayan north, which can be cold in the mountains and where the average annual rainfall can be anywhere between 3,800 mm and 5,300 mm (148–207 inches), while on the plains it is more usually between 1,140 mm and 1,900 mm. Most rainfall is during the south-west monsoons of June–September, although heavy rain can also accompany fierce electrical storms in late March and April. Between October and February the weather is cooler, clearer and dryer.

The total population of West Bengal in 2001 was put at 80,176,197, making it the fourth most populous state in India. It was, however, the most densely populated state (903 per sq km), having a population approaching that of Germany in less than one-quarter of that country's area. The majority of the people speak Bengali (86.0% in 1991), an eastern Indo-Aryan language most closely related to Assamese, but having common roots with Hindi (spoken by 6.6%) and Urdu (2.1%). The next most widely spoken languages are Nepali (1.3%) and the tribal tongues—there are also some Oriya speakers in the south-west—but English remains the main language of business and government, and is widely spoken. Tribal peoples account for less than one-10th of the population, mainly Santals, Oraons and Mundas in the western plains and hill country, with Bhutias, Lepchas and some Bodos in the north (in 2001 the Scheduled Tribes amounted to 5.5% of the total population). Religion was the basis for the Partition of Bengal, and in 2001 72.5% of the population of West Bengal were Hindu, but there remained a substantial Muslim minority of 25.2%. As for the lesser represented religions, only 0.6% were Christian and 0.3% Buddhist, to name the more numerous. In 2001 23.0% of the population were counted among the Scheduled Castes.

In 2001 the provisional census results put the urban population of West Bengal at 28.0% of the total, including 13.21m. people in the urban agglomeration centred on the state capital, Kolkata (renamed from Calcutta on 24 August 1999, the 309th anniversary of its traditional foundation—the city proper was home to some 4.34m.). Kolkata is the second largest conurbation in India; to its north-west is West Bengal's second largest city, Asansol, with 1.07m. people in its urban agglomeration. The main cities of the far north are Shiliguri and Koch Bihar. The state is divided into 18 districts, fewer than in some smaller and less populous states.

## HISTORY

The history of Bengal is late in starting compared with many parts of the rest of India, but rich and cohesive thereafter. The region's slow development at the eastern end of the *arya varta* was because it was a heavily forested swamp for many centuries, although a Vedic kingdom of Anga (Vanga) was based in the western regions and its conquest by Magadha (based in modern Bihar to the west) opened the Gangetic interior to the sea. It was only after the second conquest of Bengal by Magadha, under Samudra-Gupta in the mid-fourth century of the Christian era, that the marshy, forested wilderness began to be tamed during the Gupta peace. Moreover, the maritime trade, reaching even as far as the Roman Empire, had flourished until the second century and recovered steadily under the Guptas. Hitherto, the main area of Aryanization had been in the west (Vanga) and along the coast (Samatata). Hindu and Buddhist principalities began to appear in Bengal, with permanent settlement gradually penetrating the delta from the north. Thus, by the end of the Gupta era Gauda (Gaur—not far from modern Ingraz Bazar) at the head of the delta had become a major capital, most famously for Sasanka, the great enemy of Harsha Vardhana (of Thanesar, in Haryana, and imperial Kannauj, in Uttar Pradesh) in the seventh century. (Gaur was to be a capital of the succeeding Buddhist Palas, then the Hindu Senas, before succumbing to Muslim sacking and, finally, a catastrophic plague in 1575.) Sasanka, despite his unheroic depiction in tales idolizing Harsha, seems to have been a talented enough ruler to hold off the massed might of the Vardhana Gangetic empire and its ally in Kamrupa (modern Assam), and it was only after his death in the 620s that the rajahs of Bengal submitted to Harsha's domain. Harsha's empire disintegrated rapidly upon his death, although he left Kannauj a legacy of imperial pretensions, and by the end of the eighth century a Bengali dynasty was competing for its possession and rule of north India.

The Palas seem to have been a dynasty from north Bengal, with a minor king, Gopala I, being elected to lead all of Vanga (most of which lay in modern Bangladesh) in about 750. He soon extended his control over the rest of Bengal and into Bihar, this united region becoming the heartland of the Palas—and of the religion they espoused, Buddhism. The Palas were the last major Indian dynasty to sponsor Buddhism, which, as a result, survived longer in Bengal and Bihar against brahminical reaction. Gopala I's son and heir, Dharmapala, ascended the throne in about 770 (or soon after) and continued to expand his power. In the 780s he challenged Vatsaraja Pratihara, the Gurjara high king, for control of Kannauj, but only for both to be defeated in 786 by a Rashtrakutan sally from the south. However, the Gurjaras had suffered a greater threat to their territory and Dharmapala was able to seize Kannauj in the aftermath of the three-way conflict, installing his own candidate as a client rajah in the imperial city. Dharmapala was succeeded in about 810 by an equally long-reigning son, Devapala, retaining Pala supremacy and gaining the homage of kings in Kamrupa, Orissa and elsewhere, although there were constant challenges from the Gurjara-Pratiharas and the Rashtrakutas. Eventually, a succession of weak kings (maybe enervated by pacificism and religiosity) led to the decay of Pala power and, for most of the 10th century certainly, they suffered from the attacks of their rivals. Mahipala I (998–1038) reasserted Pala strength at the beginning of the 11th century, despite a defeat by the unexpected arrival of a Chola raiding army in about 1020, but the dynasty (and the religion it sponsored) suffered a further decline and was eventually supplanted as the paramount house of Bengal by the Hindu Senas. Madanapala, the last Pala, was succeeded in around 1161 by Ballalasena. The Senas did not long enjoy their power, as in the far north-west of the subcontinent the Rajput armies were defeated at Tarain (Haryana) in 1192 by invading Muslims. The gates of India were open, an imperial Sultanate was established in Delhi and freebooting Afghan clans extended Muslim rule into the east and centre of India (although not always in complete loyalty to Delhi). Indeed, the Sena rajah, Lakhsmanasena, was taken at lunch in a daring raid on Nadia by Muhammed Bakhtiyar, the leader of the Khiljis, and 18 other men. The Khiljis had already ransacked several Buddhist universities and desecrated a number of Hindu temples, and proceeded to the conquest of the other Sena capital at Lakhnauti (Gauda), which became their base for assaults on Bhutan and Assam. A Sena succession continued up to the middle of the 13th century, but the power was gone.

The Khiljis had a contested succession after Bakhtiyar's death in 1205, which occasionally prompted one candidate or another to seek the support of the Sultanate, but it was only the invasions of Sultan Iltumish in 1225 and 1229 that compelled obedience. After his death the Khiljis regained their independence and actually installed themselves as the ruling dynasty in Delhi towards the end of the century. This did not mean that the authority of Delhi was better recognized in Bengal (although an attempt to restore control was made in the 1320s), but, effectively, from about 1338 until 1538 the region was to enjoy independence, much of the time under its own sultans. The fractious Ilya dynasty (1282–1486), interrupted by the three Ganesas (1415–36), was succeeded by the four Habshis (1486–94) and then by the Husainis until the Mughal conquest. During this time Bengali trade and culture prospered, and, although ruled by Muslims, it was with the co-operation of many of the Hindu nobility. Indeed, in 1415 a Hindu actually became sultan, although this soon proved unacceptable, even for Bengal; his son, who had adopted Islam, replaced him. Bengali literature and scholarship were encouraged, even under an orthodox, Arab sultan, such as Ala-ud-Din Husain Shah (1493–1519), who is also respected for honouring Hindu spiritual leaders. However, the independence of Bengal was eventually ended by the arrival of a newer and more powerful imperial Muslim dynasty in Delhi, the Mughals. By the end of the 16th century the Great Mughal, Akbar, had finally reduced Bengal to proper obedience, after the imperial challenge of the Afghan Surs and the more local Kararanis. It was only with the decay of Mughal power, despite the occasional intervention of revolt or struggle over the succession, that the rulers of Bengal could again choose whether to exercise their independence.

In 1701 a Deccan-born Brahmin, who had been converted to Islam, taken into imperial service and eventually exercised the *diwani* or chancellorship of Hyderabad (now in Andhra Pradesh), arrived in Bengal as the new Mughal chancellor. His reform of the revenues of the province, including making most of the richer parts of Bengal (i.e. West Bengal and Bangladesh) pay their tax directly to the emperor (through the diwan), earned him a new name from the grateful Aurangzeb—Murshid Quli Khan (or Murshid Quli Jafar Khan), the name by which he is usually known to history. Murshid Quli Khan effectively supplanted the governor, with the emperor's backing, and became the first nawab in all but name, with a new capital at Murshidabad, although he continued loyally to remit the accumulated revenues (some Rs 10m. per year) of Bengal to the Mughal court until his death in 1727. His son-in-law, Shoja ud-Din, was confirmed in succession and died in 1739. The following year Safaraz Khan was usurped in the nawabate by Alivardi Khan, who held power until his death in 1756, to be succeeded by his grandson, the lamentable Siraj-ud-Daula. By this time, the dominant feature of Bengali politics was not the Mughals (by the 1740s revenues were no longer regularly sent to Delhi), but the British, who had first established permanent factories (fortified warehouse bases) in Bengal in 1634. This had followed the efforts of a British surgeon, Gabriel Boughton, to save the life of the daughter of the then Great Mughal, Shah Jahan. Initially outposts of the East India Company presidency based in Madras (now Chennai, Tamil Nadu), but intermittently forming an independent agency in the 1680s and 1690s, Bengal became the seat of a separate British presidency in 1700 owing to the success of the settlement of Calcutta (now Kolkata). The modern city was founded in 1690 around the villages of Kalikata, Sutanuti and Govindpur by Job Charnock (although in May 2003 a court in West Bengal declared in favour of contentions that there was a developing settlement in existence before this date and ordered the state Government to remove official references to Charnock as the founder of Calcutta). The first Fort St William was completed in 1707, and a defensive moat against possible Maratha incursions, the 'Maratha ditch', was dug in 1742 (the Nawab, meanwhile, secured his own domains in Bengal and Bihar by ceding Orissa to the Company in 1751). By this time Calcutta was the busiest port-city in Bengal, and the East India Company, which since 1716 had been in possession of an imperial *firman* (licence to operate commercially within the Mughal Empire), was coveted by the nawabate and feared as a potential rival in the imperial order. Unfortunately for an independent Bengal, however, the Nawab to move against the British was Siraj-ud-Daula, who had already alienated his own ministers and nobility, as well as the representatives of the other European trading nations established in Bengal.

The new, 20-year-old Nawab took Calcutta from the British in 1756 and imprisoned some 70 or more British residents overnight in a small detention cell, the so-called 'Black Hole', from which only 23 emerged alive. What seems to have been an accident nevertheless impaired what feeble attempts Siraj might have made to restore relations with the British and justified the East India Company's military commander, Robert Clive, in his retaliation. Clive retook the city in 1757 and then proceeded against the French in Chandernagore (the Seven Years' War had just begun and was to secure the final British ascendancy over the other Europeans in India), before insisting on continuing the war against the Nawab. He advanced on Murshidabad, and his 3,000 troops met an army of some 50,000 at Plashi (Plassey), where the treachery of the Nawab's commander-in-chief and relative, Mir Jafar, and other courtiers gave the victory to Clive. Mir Jafar was installed as the new Nawab (and recognized by the emperor in Delhi) and obliged to make crippling financial concessions to the British, becoming particularly indebted when Company help was needed to repel Mughal incursions in 1759 and 1760. His failure to honour his new debts resulted in his deposition, in favour of his son-in-law, Mir Qasim, who rewarded the East India Company with lower Bengal, but also instituted reforms designed to strengthen him against further British threats. The British had no compunction, therefore, in restoring the ageing Mir Jafar in 1763 (he died in 1765, to be succeeded by Najm-ud-Daulah and then, in 1766, Saif-ud-Daulah). Mir Qasim enlisted the help of the Mughal emperor, Shah Alam II, and his powerful ally and protector, the autonomous Nawab of Awadh (Oudh), and they invaded Bihar in 1764. Perhaps the most decisive battle of British imperial history in India was fought here at Baksar (Buxar), between the 7,500 disciplined, largely sepoy troops under Maj. Hector Munro and the combined but disorganized Mughal forces of some 40,000. The East India Company triumphed and, the following year, the Mughal granted it the *diwani* of Bengal. Within five years the nawabate was defunct, its treasury removed from Murshidabad to Calcutta and, under the 1773 Regulating Act, on 20 October 1774 the Governor of Bengal, one Warren Hastings, became Governor-General of all three British presidencies in India. Calcutta became an imperial capital after the Great Rebellion (the Bengal army remained loyal to the British), when, in November 1758, the British Crown assumed direct control over the Company's holdings and the Governor-General, therefore, became a Viceroy (the British Queen was proclaimed Empress of India in 1877).

Bengal prospered under the long peace of British rule, while both Hinduism and Islam enjoyed revivals and Bengali culture flourished. This informed later political activity, with figures such as the great Bengali poet and Nobel laureate, Rabindranath Tagore, adding a moral authority to the growing clamour for political independence for India, as well as movements for social and religious reform. It was probably the first Partition of Bengal that catalysed political activism in the presidency—in 1905 West Bengal, with Bihar and Orissa (Hindu), was separated from East Bengal (Muslim) with Assam. The British sought to regularize the administration of the largest province in India, as well as one of the more troublesome sources of criticism, but failed to consult local sentiment and provoked rather than pre-empted communal Hindu–Muslim tensions. Protests in Calcutta and throughout the two provinces eventually prompted the British to reunite Bengal from 1912 (although Assam, and Bihar and Orissa became two separate provinces), but Bengali Muslims were not entirely happy with this decision and few on any side were pleased with the simultaneous relocation of the imperial capital to Delhi. Despite official hopes, the activists of Calcutta remained influential—the city was, after all, still the largest in British India. Bengal produced many prominent figures in the campaign in favour of independence, such as: Tagore; Aurobindo Ghose, the social and religious reformer (see Puducherry—Pondicherry); Bipin Chandra Pal, the radical politician and journalist; and Subhas Chandra Bose (known as Netaji), the leftist Bengali nationalist and Congress leader in the late 1930s (who was obliged to flee British jurisdiction and, under Japanese protection during the Second World War, formed an 'Indian National Army', proclaiming 'Azad Hind'—Free India—in 1943).

Meanwhile, political reforms under legislation of 1935 provided for electoral participation in provincial government throughout British India. In 1937 Congress won every assembly except those of Punjab (also later partitioned) and Bengal, where a narrow Muslim majority was returned. It seemed that the hitherto-dominant, English-speaking Hindus of Calcutta, the Bhadralok, might regret the Partition they had opposed so strongly after all. Certainly it contributed towards the final decision to end the Empire with two successor states, one Hindu dominated and one Muslim, and to partition Bengal, although this would leave East Bengal without the rich metropolis of Calcutta. Before this, in 1943, the privations of wartime and the incompetence of government contributed to the devastations of a severe famine in lower Bengal—a catastrophic 2m.–4m. people are estimated to have died—which also exacerbated communal tensions. With the imminence of independence and the issue of a Muslim state and partition as yet unresolved, an outbreak of communal violence in Calcutta, in which some 4,000 Muslims, Hindus and Sikhs died in August 1946, spread to other parts of the province and beyond in October. Mahatma Gandhi rushed to the region and his efforts probably eased the eventual Partition of Bengal (which had been prefigured anyway in 1905–12), but did not prevent a massive demographic and economic dislocation involving the migration of 5m. people. After independence West Bengal became a 'Part A' state under the 1950 Constitution, and at various points incorporated the local princely states and the French enclave of Chandernagore (the latter annexation was formalized by treaty in 1951) into its territory, finally acquiring its current status and boundaries in 1956, when a transfer of some territory from Bihar ensured that all parts of the state were linked. Links with eastern Bengal, which became East Pakistan and, from the end of 1971, the independent country known as Bangladesh, were disrupted by the historic territory's Partition between two states. Uneasy political relations, complicated by the presence of a still sizeable Muslim minority in West Bengal, had a catastrophic effect on economic interaction. Early 2008 exemplified the various influences on relations between West Bengal and Bangladesh: in January shooting incidents on the border resulted in the death of a youth; in April the first train service in 43 years between Kolkata and Dhaka, the capital of Bangladesh, resumed; and there was ongoing controversy about the status of the Bengali writer Taslima Nasreen. Nasreen was from Bangladesh, but some of her work had provoked condemnation from her own Muslim community, so she had taken refuge in India. The importance of the local Muslim vote to the ruling party in West Bengal prompted criticism of the state Government when it seemed less than eager to offer Nasreen permanent sanctuary in Kolkata.

The only threats to the integrity of West Bengal have been suggestions of a 'Greater Jharkhand', to include some of the tribal areas in the western hills, and demands for a Gurkha (Gorkha) homeland in the north. Most claims for 'Gorkhaland' were calmed by the 1988 creation of the Darjiling Gorkha Hill Council, although discussion of the issue occasionally revives, perhaps mainly for electoral purposes. However, in mid-2008 extra police were sent to Shiliguri, following clashes involving supporters of the Gorkha Janamukti Morcha (GJM), who were agitating for a separate state. The West Bengal Government was not in favour of bifurcation of the state, but conceded the principle of tripartite talks with the GJM and the Centre in early July. In 2005, meanwhile, a movement for the creation of a state based on Koch Bihar (the former princely state of Cooch Behar, which signed a treaty of accession to the Union in 1949) added its voice to the separatist chorus.

Domestic politics have been dominated by the rivalry between Congress and the Communists since the 1960s. In June 1977 Congress was finally ousted by a Left Front coalition headed by the Communist Party of India—Marxist (CPI—M), which has also formed six successive governments since, the seventh and most recent administration in May 2006. Although Congress has not returned to power in the state, it has generally performed better at the level of national elections—West Bengal has 42 seats in the lower house of the national Parliament and 16 in the upper house. The CPI (M) lost urban votes, particularly in Calcutta, at the 1996 state elections, although it made an unexpected revival in 2001. Much of the credit for this went to Buddhadev Bhattacharya, who succeeded the veteran Jyoti Basu as Chief Minister in November 2000, upon the latter's retirement, and began to win back the support of the urban middle classes. The main Congress faction in opposition since the late 1990s had been the Nationalist Trinamool Congress, led by Mamata Banerjee, which received support locally from its Union coalition partner, the Bharatiya Janata Party (BJP). The Trinamool Congress refused to contest a large number of the seats in the local elections of May 2003, however, leaving the ruling Left Front to consolidate its position in the state following the resurgence in its support. Then, in 2004, at the May general election, the Left Front increased its tally from 29 to 35 seats in the lower house of the Indian Parliament, while the Trinamool Congress (recently merged with a Nationalist Congress Party faction from the north-east) lost all but its leader's seat—it had held eight in the previous Lok Sabha—and its BJP ally lost both its seats. The main national Congress party doubled its number of deputies to six and seemed likely to replace the Trinamool faction as the principal anti-Left Front opposition party. When Banerjee declared her continuing loyalty to the BJP-led alliance, some of her colleagues urged a realignment with the majority Congress (ironically, it seems to have been Banerjee's previous unreliability with her allies, her so-called 'flip-flop politics', that had eroded her support base since 2000).

Meanwhile, nationally, the Left Front supported Congress efforts to form a secularist Government and, while refusing to participate, in June 2004 accepted the post of Speaker of the Lok Sabha for its senior parliamentarian, Somnath Chatterjee. However, that alignment at the Centre reinforced Banerjee's refusal to ally with Congress. In April 2005 this led to the first split in the Trinamool faction, when its senior leader in Kolkata took his supporters into an alliance with Congress. However, Congress lacked a charismatic local leader in West Bengal, and the importance of Banerjee to any opposition was reinforced by the results of the civic elections to the Kolkata Municipal Corporation on 19 June. The Trinamool Congress was displaced from office after five years, retaining 42 of the 141 seats (its BJP allies won three), but the Left Front barely gained a majority, despite its recent strong showing in the polls and the split in the opposition. The Congress grouping failed to convince, only gaining 15 seats. A strong showing by the opposition in the Assembly elections seemed to depend on an effective coalition being formed, although this would require several groupings to ignore their alliances at the Centre. However, Congress, mindful of the national coalition, refused to join with Banerjee while her Trinamool Congress remained in alliance with the BJP. Moreover, a reform of the electoral process (which included scrutiny of the roll of voters and polls in five phases), of which the opposition had great hopes, proved unable to counteract their own disunity and the unparalleled grass-roots organization of the CPI (M). When the results of the state elections were declared in May 2006, the Left Front had increased the number of its seats to 233 (out of a total of 294, although one seat was not contested): the CPI (M) had 176, the All India Forward Bloc 23, the Revolutionary Socialist Party (RSP) 20, the CPI eight, the West Bengal Socialist Party four and two other parties one each. The Trinamool alliance had retained only 29 seats and the Jharkhand Party (Naren) one; Congress had 21 and its Gorkha National Liberation Front ally three, with independents and others taking the six remaining elective seats. On 15 May Bhattacharya was asked to form another Government.

During the year following the state elections, there was a change in political fortunes in West Bengal, with government attempts to encourage industry to return to the state exposing Chief Minister Bhattacharya to charges of being the enemy of the peasant farmers. The Trinamool Congress was prominent in orchestrating popular agitation as well as political opposition, even with scuffles in the chamber of the legislature at the end of November 2006. The acquisition of rich agricultural land for the development of a Tata Motors factory in Singur (not far south of Kolkata) led to allegations of the forcible dispossession of farmers; the Government was also accused of preventing opposition politicians from travelling to the area. Attacks on supporters of the CPI (M) and of the industrial development, and the rape and murder of a girl in December, exacerbated tensions on both sides, while Trinamool leader Banerjee reinforced her opposition with a fast that was endangering her health by the end of the month. By January 2007 Banerjee had been persuaded to end her fast and the Government had released a report purporting to show that land had not been forcibly acquired. However, although disturbances were to recur periodically in Singur, attention was shifting to trouble in Nandigram, a village in the south-west of the state. There the Government was interested in creating a special economic zone, for investment by the Salim industrial group of Indonesia, but had not even gone so far as to decide on what land would be needed before local farmers were protesting. In February a policeman was killed and in the following month the Government accused the Trinamool Congress of fomenting unrest in Nandigram and Singur. However, government attempts to re-establish control of Nandigram in mid-March inflamed the situation after gunfire from policemen facing demonstrators resulted in a number of civilian deaths. The CPI (M) found itself unhappy with its national ally, Congress, when a central criminal investigation was initiated, while its state allies, led by the RSP, began to question the Left Front coalition. By the end of the month the Government had abandoned the Nandigram project and apologized for any mishandling of the civil order situation. Sporadic unrest continued in Nandigram, but all-party talks were agreed in mid-May, only for violence to re-emerge in Singur, provoking government recriminations about Trinamool involvement. Certainly the main opposition party felt that it had benefited from the recent controversies, enough to revive talk of a 'grand alliance' against the Left Front (which would involve Congress having to tolerate the involvement of the BJP).

The Trinamool Congress gained a significant victory in East Midnapur at the panchayat elections in May 2008. Violence in Nandigram, which is in the East Midnapur district, had continued, escalating in November 2007 when the state Government had attempted to regain control. A report by various human rights bodies in January 2008 had criticized the Government for failing to control the activities of its local cadres against the peasant demonstrators' Bhumi Ucched Pratirodh Committee. Despite the presence of additional police officers, sent in by the federal authorities, violence flared again during the approach to the local polls in May, with allegations of voter intimidation compounding the strife. However, the Trinamool Congress won control of its first district zilla parishad at the elections, and members of the CPI (M) leadership accepted that the ruling party had not done well electorally, blaming the unpopularity of corruption by some local politicians. Nandigram had also alienated the RSP from its alliance with the CPI (M), although in mid-2008 most of the left-wing parties nationally had found themselves united against the Congress-led central Government's deal on nuclear energy with the USA.

## ECONOMY

West Bengal is the most prosperous state in eastern India, although the relative poverty of its teeming rural millions somewhat counteracts the wealth of its industry and trade, much of which is based in and around Kolkata (Calcutta). The total net domestic product of the state is the highest after Maharashtra and Uttar Pradesh, reaching Rs 1,894,890m. in 2004/05, at current prices, or Rs 22,497 per head (12th among the states—a deterioration on previous years). Infrastructure is well developed, with roads and railways augmented by inland waterways. The total length of roads at March 1996 was 74,459 km, including 1,710 km of national highway and 3,388 km of state highway. Just over one-half of the road length is unsurfaced. There is an extensive rail network, totalling 3,785 km at March 1998. Kolkata is the most important port, historically the main port of eastern India, and is also the site of an international airport. The second seaport is Haldia, and there are numerous airports throughout the state. Total electricity generation in the state amounted to

14,746m. units of power in 1997/98, but demand is high and extra capacity is needed. Nevertheless, during the 1990s West Bengal had become the first state to generate an electricity surplus from its own resources, and in the 2000s it was India's main centre for the development of renewable sources of energy (67 MW by 2006, although 93% of installed capacity remained thermal). The reliability of the state's power supply was certainly one of the attractions for business to return to Kolkata and its environs. Installed capacity at the end of March 2006 amounted to 5,411 MW (67% in the state sector, 20% in the private sector and an atypically low 13% from a share in the Centre's schemes). Over four-fifths of villages were in receipt of an electricity supply, although barely 18% of rural households had electricity. Extensive irrigation projects improve agricultural productivity, but also serve towards taming the floods to which the plains can easily become victim. Other infrastructure projects aim to improve the urban environment of the 'mega-city' of Kolkata, which, together with a stable political environment (the state Government is now much more friendly to business and more discouraging of strike action) and its traditional strengths from engineering to arts, was enjoying something of a revival by the early 2000s. There were some fears that political controversy in late 2006 and into 2007 would deter the return of business to the city. The literacy rate reached 69.2% in 2001 (from 57.7% in 1991).

About one-half of the population is engaged in agriculture, or up to three-quarters if indirectly employed people are included. In 2001/02 agriculture contributed 22.6% of gross state domestic product. West Bengal is the largest producer in India of jute (usually two-thirds of national production—three-quarters of jute and mesta in 2001/02) and of rice (about one-sixth), and accounts for about one-fifth of tea production, mainly in the Darjiling Hills. In 2002/03 total foodgrain production was 15.5m. metric tons, accounting for 8.9% of the national total, but maintaining West Bengal's position as the third largest producer in the country (after Uttar Pradesh and the Punjab). In the previous year total production had been 16.5m. tons, of which rice accounted for 15.3m. tons (wheat 1.0m. tons and pulses 0.2m. tons). Also in 2002/03 667,000 tons of jute were produced, and 493,400 tons of oilseeds. Potatoes are another important crop (5.6m. tons in 1997/98). Betelvine and tobacco are among further crops grown. The livestock sector is not as significant (except for poultry), although in 2002/03 the state produced 3.6m. tons of milk, 2,750m. eggs and 645,000 kg of wool, with continuing increases in production anticipated for the following year. The sector was hit by an outbreak of avian influenza in January 2008, provoking a culling of poultry stocks in much of the state, as well as anthrax among some cattle in February.

Agriculture and mineral resources have provided the basis for industry in the state. Originally, jute was fundamental to the textiles industry of Kolkata and other towns, but food processing and beverages are also important, while local coal and lignite provided the fuel for other manufactures. Mineral fuels are found throughout the state, as is limestone, while the north also has dolomite, copper, iron, lead, silver and zinc reserves, and the south quartz, fire clay, kaolin, silica, some gold and manganese. The value of minerals produced in 2002/03 amounted to Rs 23,932.6m., while the number of people employed in the sector was almost 456,000 in 2001/02. Steel plants, ore-processing units, automobile manufacture, machine building, light engineering and chemicals are among the principal industrial activities, mainly centred in Kolkata and its environs, on the coast, to the west in Kharagpur, to the north-west in Asansol especially and in Durgapur, and in the north at Shiliguri. Government policies to attract industry back to the state met with some success, such as the 2006 reopening of the former Dunlop tyre factory (closed since the late 1990s) by P. K. Ruia or the siting of a Tata Motors plant at Singur (due to begin production in 2008). However, the political and civil unrest provoked by the acquisition of agricultural land for the latter enterprise (see History above) was injurious to the attempts to counter West Bengal's reputation for radicalized labour and a political environment hostile to industry.

West Bengal has a thriving tertiary sector, built on the long-established commercial strength of Kolkata (although Mumbai—Bombay—surpassed it about one century ago) and the network of transport services across the state connecting Assam and the north-east with the rest of India and the Gangetic plains with the coast. There is a large local market for retail trade, and the state is a centre for trade generally. The growing presence of software companies in Kolkata has meant a thriving information technology sector, although how the 2006 formation of India's first trade union in the sector would affect perceived competitiveness remained to be seen. Business services and finance are also important, and tourism is strong. Tourists, apart from those on business, in transit or visiting family, are attracted by the historical sites, such as the landmarks of British Calcutta, the temple city of Bishnupur, Buddhist remains and the old medieval Muslim capitals, as well as the tribal lands of the west or the tea plantations and hill resorts of Darjiling. Natural attractions include the wildlife of the Himalayan foothills, notably rhinoceroses, or of the swampy Sunderbans, notably tigers, but also some of the rare river dolphins of the Ganga. In 2002 West Bengal was the sixth most popular state for domestic tourist visits (although it accounted for only 3.2% of the total).

### DIRECTORY

**Governor:** GOPALKRISHNA GANDHI, Office of the Governor, Raj Bhavan, Kolkata 700 001; tel. (33) 22001641; fax (33) 22002444.

**Chief Minister:** BUDDHADEV BHATTACHARYA (CPI—M), Office of the Chief Minister, Government of West Bengal, Writers' Buildings, Kolkata 700 001; tel. (33) 22145555; fax (33) 22145480; e-mail cm@wb.gov.in.

**Speaker of the Legislative Assembly:** HASIM ABDUL HALIM AMDANGAR, Assembly House, Kolkata 700 001; tel. (33) 22488069; fax (33) 22488160; the unicameral Legislative Assembly has 294 mems: Communist (CPI—M) 176; All India Trinamool Congress 30; All India Forward Bloc 23; Congress 21; Revolutionary Socialist Party (RSP) 20; Communist (CPI) 8; West Bengal Socialist Party 4; Gorkha National Liberation Front 3; independents and others 9.

**State Resident Commissioner in New Delhi:** P. VANAMALI, A-2 State Emporia Bldg, Baba Kharak Singh Marg, New Delhi 110 001; tel. (11) 23344269; fax (11) 23747203.

# National Capital and Union Territories

## Andaman and Nicobar Islands

The Union Territory of the Andaman and Nicobar Islands lies in the Bay of Bengal, along an arc stretching from the Irrawaddy (Ayeyarwady) delta in the north-east to the island of Sumatra in the south-east. The territory's nearest international neighbours, therefore, are, respectively, Myanmar (formerly Burma) and Indonesia. Eastwards, across the Andaman Sea, is the Malay Peninsula, here divided between Myanmar and Thailand. While the northernmost Andaman Islands lie only 193 km (120 miles) from Cape Negrais, the tip of mainland Myanmar, and Great Nicobar is about two-thirds of that distance from Achin Head (Cape Pedro) on the Sumatran coast of Indonesia, the island chain is more significantly separated from the rest of India. Chennai (Madras) in Tamil Nadu is 1,190 km by sea to the west of Port Blair, the territorial capital, in the Andaman Islands, while the coast of West Bengal is some 30 km further, but to the north-west (a little inland, Kolkata, formerly Calcutta, is 2,255 km away). The islands were grouped as a single administrative territory by the imperial Government of India in 1869, restored to British sovereignty in 1945 (after a Japanese occupation since 1942) and transferred to the jurisdiction of independent India in 1947. The Andaman and Nicobar Islands formally became an integral part of India, as the only 'Part D' state, in 1950, to be redesignated (like the former 'Part C' states) a Union Territory in 1956. The islands together cover a land area of 8,249 sq km (3,185 sq miles), of which the Andamans constitute 77.7%, making the Andaman and Nicobar Islands the largest of India's union territories and, indeed, larger than two of its states.

The island chain is grouped into the northern, and more numerous, Andaman Islands and the southern, and slightly more easterly, Nicobar Islands, separated by a deep strait, the Ten Degree Channel (which runs along latitude 10°N). A submerged mountain range has formed almost 300 islands (if islets and reef outcroppings are included, a debatably exact figure of 572 can be arrived at), extending for some 730 km from Landfall Island in the north to Indira Point (Pygmalion Point) on Great Nicobar in the south-east. The Andaman Islands run north–south, consisting of up to 204 distinct islands (26 of which are inhabited) stretched over 467 km, of which the largest is Middle Andaman (1,536 sq km) and the smallest Ross Island (0.8 sq km). Middle Andaman is closely flanked by North Andaman and

South Andaman, all surrounded by a scattering of smaller islands (notably Ritchie's Archipelago), with a tail of them pointing southwards to the more separated Little Andaman. To the east lie Narcondam and Barren Islands. Continuing the crescent chain more towards the south-east are the Nicobars, which thus run off a north–south alignment. This group consists of 19 proper islands, of which 12 are inhabited, with the largest being Great Nicobar (1,045 sq km) and the smallest Pilomillow Island (1.3 sq km—less since the tsunami of 2004). The northernmost is isolated Car Nicobar, then a scattered group of smaller islands, such as Camorta and Nancoury, and finally, beyond the Sombrero Channel, the broken bulk of Little Nicobar and Great Nicobar. Largely covered in heavy rainforest, the islands reach their height at Saddle Peak (North Andaman), which rises to 732 m (267 ft), and in the Nicobar Islands (Great Nicobar), at Mt Thullier (642 m). However, following the earthquake off the coast of Indonesia that triggered the devastating tsunami of 26 December 2004, in 2005 it was reported that the Andaman and Nicobar Islands had tilted, with the northern regions around Diglipur having risen by between 0.5 m and 0.8 m and the southernmost Indira Point having sunk by up to 1.5 m. Moreover, the effects of the earthquake and the tsunami have almost submerged two islands (including Pilomillow) and destroyed infrastructure to the extent that many evacuated people have not yet returned. The climate is tropical, with no extremes, except for the variety offered by the arrival of the monsoons (seasons that usually fall in May–September and November–December) and the possibility of tropical storms at the end of the first monsoon season. The mean annual rainfall for Port Blair is 3,180 mm (125 inches), although actual rainfall in 2002 was only 1,617 mm. The mean minimum temperature in Port Blair during 2002 was 23.5°C (74.3°F), the mean maximum temperature 30.5°C (86.9°F).

The total population of the Andaman and Nicobar Islands, according to the census of March 2001, was 356,152. This was an increase of over one-quarter on the 1991 census result (280,661) and was more than three times the 1971 figure (115,133). The rate of natural growth remains slightly above the national average, but showed some decline in the late 1990s. The population density of the territory in 2001, therefore, was 43 per sq mile, the lowest of any union territory; in all India, only the states of Arunachal Pradesh and, barely, of Mizoram had lower population densities. Most of the population are now of Indian, Burmese or Malay descent, more recently supplemented by refugees from Bangladesh and Myanmar, Indian émigrés from Guyana and Tamils from Sri Lanka. As a result, most of the population are Hindus (69.2% at the 2001 census), with a fairly large Christian community (21.7%) and some Muslims (8.2%), as well small communities of Sikhs and Buddhists. English is used, particularly in government, but the most widely spoken languages are Bengali (23.1% in 1991), then Tamil (19.1%), Hindi (17.6%), Telugu and Malayalam. In 2001 none of the population was counted among the Scheduled Castes, but 8.3% consisted of Scheduled Tribes.

One of the indigenous peoples of the Nicobar Islands, the Nicobarese, a Mongoloid race, is completely assimilated into modern society, but there are five other autochthonous tribal groups, protected by the authorities (together accounting for some 15% of the total population, most of them in the Nicobar Islands). The Great Andamanese, like the other tribal Andaman islanders, a Negrito people, are now living on Strait Island, but were originally the most numerous of the tribes, with some 10,000 in 1789. They have suffered most from contact with the rest of the world. By 1901 there were only 625 and numbers continued to decline, reaching a nadir of 19 in 1969, but rising again to 41 by 1999. Their primitive society was noted, among other things, for not having the use of fire and a unique language with only two number concepts ('one' and 'greater than one'). The Onges of Little Andaman, traditionally foragers, are now dependent on government assistance and confined to two small reservations. The Jarawas of South Andaman and Little Andaman were first contacted by government anthropologists in 1974 and have been considered friendly only since 1998. The people of North Sentinel Island, probably numbering about 400, on 60 sq km, continue to refuse communication, among the few Palaeolithic survivors in the modern world to do so. They are related to the Onges and Jarawas, but have long been isolated. The remaining tribe of the Nicobar Islands, the Shompens, are a Mongoloid people, like their neighbours, the Nicobarese. They are struggling against disease brought by recent contacts and are divided into two groups. The less numerous Mawa Shompens live along the coasts and river valleys of Great Nicobar, while the more hostile majority are found in the Alexandra and Galathia river valleys and on the east coast of the same island. The full impact of the 2004 tsunami on the more isolated tribal peoples remained uncertain for some time. The distribution of the general population among the islands has also been distorted by the tsunami, with some islands completely evacuated and others where the surviving population is awaiting reconstruction before returning—particularly in the Nicobars.

At the 2001 census, 32.6% of the population were classed as urban, by far the largest town being the territorial capital, Port Blair, on South Andaman, which had 100,186 inhabitants (estimated at over 106,000 in 2004). In 2005 the population of Port Blair was boosted by the large number of refugees (more than 13,000) evacuated there after the catastrophic 2004 tsunami. The other main towns include the district capital of the Nicobars on Car Nicobar (which was completely devastated by the tsunami), as well as Rangat and Mayabunder on Middle Andaman, and Diglipur on North Andaman. The territory is divided into two districts.

## HISTORY

Although the indigenous populations have long been isolated from the rest of the world, the two groups of islands lie on the main trade routes between Burma (now Myanmar) and India, and are recorded by the Greek cartographer, Ptolemy, of the second century BC and by the Chinese traveller, Xuan Zang (Hsuan Tsang), of the seventh century AD. Arab merchants from the ninth century also reported the existence of the islands, particularly the Nicobars, which lay on the route to Sumatra (now in Indonesia). Thus, in the 11th century there was an attempt by the Cholas of modern Tamil Nadu, under Rajendra I, to annex the islands. Then, as now, many of the myriad islands were devoid of the savage, native 'head hunters' (as reported by the first recorded Western visitor, in the 13th century, the Venetian, Marco Polo) and proved a tempting base for piratical ventures on the nearby, lucrative trading routes. Indeed, Malay pirates may have partly earned the reputation of ferocity attributed to the locals. In this tradition, the Marathas established a privateer base in the islands in the late 17th century. The famous Maratha admiral, Kanhoji Angre, led this operation in the early 18th century, plaguing European shipping and eluding the British-Portuguese naval task force sent to deal with him. He died, undefeated, in 1729. Dutch pirates and Jesuit missionaries also frequented the islands, while the Danish East India Company claimed the Nicobar Islands (Frederik Ørne Islands), which it also attempted to evangelize, between 1756 and 1848. Modern India's claim to the island chain began in 1788, when the British Governor-General dispatched an army lieutenant (for whom Port Blair is named) to occupy part of the Andaman Islands. Some convicts were sent there in 1794, but the settlement was soon abandoned. It was only after the mainland disturbances of 1857 that the British persevered with their original effort to establish a penal colony in the Andamans.

In 1858 the first Chief Commissioner of the Andaman Islands, Dr James Petition Walker, founded a prison at Port Blair, starting a tradition that earned the colony the name Kalapani ('black blood', referring to the blood shed by the nationalists) in India. It was only after the completion of the Cellular Gaol in 1906 that large numbers of prisoners were sent here, and only thereafter did it become notorious as the destination for those who revolted against the United Kingdom's presence in South and South-East Asia. It was, therefore, an irony that it was the Andaman and Nicobar Islands that formed the 'Azad Hind' (Free India) proclaimed in 1943 by a nationalist who had escaped imprisonment here—Subhas Chandra Bose was its head of state, and the commander-in-chief of the 'Indian National Army', in the only piece of Indian territory then occupied by the Japanese.

The Nicobar Islands (the name is derived from a Tamil word, *nakkavaram*, which means 'land of the naked') were annexed by the Indian authorities on 16 October 1868, and in 1872, during the commission of Maj. (later Gen. Sir) Donald Martin Stewart, were united as an administrative unit with the Andamans. The islands were favoured as a penal colony by the British, particularly in the first half of the 20th century, apart from during the Japanese occupation of 1942–45, when the Chief Commissioner, C. E. Waterfall, was himself a prisoner. However, the Japanese were expelled in 1945 and a new Chief Commissioner, N. K. Patterson, assumed office in Port Blair. In 1947 the first Indian Chief Commissioner, I. Majid, became head of the administration, on behalf of an independent Indian Government, which no longer sought to imprison its political opponents here. The last Chief Commissioner was S. L. Sharma, who, on 12 November 1982, was replaced by a Lieutenant-Governor, M. L. Kampani, who held office until 1985. In the late 1990s the strategic significance of the islands again came to be appreciated, particularly with a Chinese presence on Coco Islands, leased from Myanmar (just north of the Andamans). The national Government established the Far East Naval Command near Port Blair, and in 2001 announced the US $2,000m., five-year development of naval and military facilities in the territory.

In January 2004 a new Lt-Governor, Prof. Ramchandra Ganesh Kapse, assumed power in the territory. Prof. Kapse was a scholar of Marathi literature before pursuing a political career in the Bharatiya Janata Party (BJP), which led the national Government until the general election of April 2004. Ill health prompted the resignation of Kapse in June 2006 and, after an interim period when the Lt-Governor of Pondicherry (now Puducherry) acted for the territory, Lt-Gen. (retd) Bhopinder Singh was appointed to replace him in December. The BJP, which had held the single seat representing the Andaman and Nicobar Islands in the Indian Parliament since 1999, was displaced by Congress in the 2004 general election. The veteran politician, Manoranjan Bhakta, who had held the seat between 1977 and 1999, was returned as the territorial deputy in the Lok Sabha, the lower house, with 56% of the votes cast.

On the morning of 26 December 2004 a massive earthquake off the coast of the Indonesian island of Sumatra propelled a tsunami, or massive wave, of such power that countries all around the Indian Ocean were affected. The Andaman and Nicobar Islands, being relatively so near to the earthquake's epicentre, were devastated by the flooding, with much of the more southerly Nicobar Islands inundated particularly destructively. The physical damage was compounded by the loss of life, with over 3,700 dead, of whom many could not be identified and even more never found. In the first 10 days after the disaster, despite the relief effort being hampered by the physical destruction and by the distance of the islands from the mainland, almost 14,000 people were evacuated to Port Blair and 5,700 to Chennai (Tamil Nadu). By mid-year and the arrival of the monsoon rains, temporary accommodation had been provided for over 10,000 families, although its quality was criticized; permanent reconstruction was expected to take up to two years. A demoralized population remained alarmed by frequent, if minor, earthquakes that continued to trouble the region—in 2005, for instance, and June 2007, June 2008, then three in rapid succession in July. However, in September 2005 the territory was able to conduct local elections, as scheduled, in which Congress performed slightly better than the BJP.

### ECONOMY

The islands have considerable economic potential, notably in forestry, fishing and tourism, but development has not kept pace with a rapidly rising population. Moreover, the infrastructure and economy of the territory were severely damaged by the tsunami of 26 December 2004. Net domestic product increased, in real terms, by 6.8% on the previous year, to Rs 8,130.4m., in 1997/98, a figure subsidized by central government spending (in 2001/02, for instance, revenue receipts from the territory totalled Rs 880.8m., with expenditure at Rs 6,985.0m.). The following year the economy contracted, as it did again in 2000/01, but, after minimal real growth, in 2001/02 the net domestic product, according to estimated figures in current prices, was Rs 9,350m., with net income per head at Rs 25,982. In 2002/03 the respective figures were Rs 10,0400m. and Rs 28,340. Some infrastructural development has created the 333-km (207-mile) Andaman Trunk Road, which already connects Port Blair, in the south of South Andaman, with Rangat, on Middle Andaman, by means of highway and ferry services. In all, at the beginning of 2003, there were 1,169 km of black-topped road and 28 km of other roads. There are regular ferry services connecting 11 of the islands in the Union Territory and regular shipping and air links with the mainland, almost entirely through Port Blair. Car Nicobar too has an airfield. There is a highly subsidized helicopter service, which was augmented in 2003. The 2004 tsunami damaged most port facilities and destroyed many jetties completely, complicating not only relief efforts, but also economic recovery during 2005. Infrastructure in the Nicobars was almost completely destroyed. Power generation depends mainly on imported fuels; installed electricity capacity in 2005 amounting to 45.3 MW (state sector—and a further 20.1 MW in the private sector), and 54% of rural households were reckoned to have electricity. The electricity grid was greatly damaged by the earthquake and tsunami at the end of 2004, although 40% coverage was restored during January 2005. The literacy rate is quite high, at least outside the scheduled population, at 81.2% in 2001 (compared with 73.0% at the previous census in 1991).

The primary sector is the most important part of the economy for the bulk of the population, be it commercial and traditional fishing, the hunting and foraging of many of the tribal population, the subsistence or small-scale agriculture common throughout India, or the forestry activities that hold great potential for the territory. Agriculture accounted for 23.1% of the territory's gross domestic product in 2001/02. The main food and cash crop of the Andaman Islands is paddy rice (total territorial paddy production of 43,788 metric tons in 2005, or 29,192 tons of rice, which was slightly down on the previous year), while the main cash crops of the Nicobars are coconut and areca nut. Tropical fruits are easily grown in the hills, while other field crops include pulses, vegetables, oilseeds and spices. Rubber, red oil, palm oil and some cashews are also increasingly important agricultural products. Many food requirements are shipped to the islands. The total cropped area, according to the agricultural census of 1990/91, was only 20,319 ha. Livestock is important, particularly for the production of eggs (57.8m. anticipated for 2003/04), but also of milk (23,000 tons). During 2005 the Government was attempting to assist in the provision of animals to replace those lost in the 2004 tsunami. With forest covering 86.9% (2003) of the Union Territory's land area, much of it luxuriant rainforest rich in tropical hardwoods, logging and timber processing is fundamental to economic advancement of the islands. The topography creates a variety of available forest, including evergreen and deciduous or hilltop and swamp—the two most valuable timbers, padauk and gurjan, are found only on the Andamans, not on the Nicobar Islands. The Government has divided the forestlands into Primitive Tribal Reserves (41% of the total), accessible only by Indian citizens with permits, with the rest designated Protected Areas, available for the exploitation of their timber resources. A Swedish company owns extensive logging rights. Teak and rosewood have been the most commercially in demand for some years, although small rubber and mahogany plantations have also been justified. Plywood, hardwood and matchwood are exported. According to official statistics, in 2001/02 timber extracted amounted to 4,712 cu m. Fishing is another rich resource being developed, and at the beginning of the 21st century it was the largest industry, although many fishing families lost members in the tsunami and the damage to vessels and fishing industry facilities was severe. However, the industry recovered quickly. At January 2005 official statistics put the number of fishermen at 4,157; 26,940 metric tons of marine fish were landed in that year (and 117 tons of fish from inland waters), with an estimated value of Rs 862.5m. (inland, Rs 5.9m.).

Timber processing is an important part of the industrial sector in the Andaman and Nicobar Islands. This includes the Chatham Saw Mill, one of the oldest and largest in Asia. There are, however, few other even medium-sized industrial units in the islands. At the beginning of 2005 there were five large and medium-sized industrial units in the territory and 1,706 small-scale ones. These figures were up from three and 1,479, respectively, two years earlier, at which 48 of the units were registered factories, employing 5,032 people daily. The main industrial products are plastic bags, conduit pipes and fittings, paints and varnishes, and fibreglass. There are manufacturers of steel furniture, aluminium doors and windows, and beverages, as well as units for agricultural processing, such as rice milling, seed crushing or even small flourmills and bakeries. Most activities are small scale, such as fish processing and handicrafts, but an increasing number are export orientated. With considerable amounts of reconstruction aid coming in, the construction industry performed strongly in 2005 and into 2006 and 2007.

According to official statistics, at 1 January 2003 there were 1,425 shops and commercial establishments and 270 establishments listed under theatres or restaurants (the latter employing 1,200). Tourism is the most important growth area of the services sector, although public administration remains the principal contributor. The tourist industry was the second biggest industry after fishing in the islands, but in the early 2000s only provided 5,000 jobs, on an annual turnover worth some US $0.5m. There are 52 government guest houses and tourist developments in various locations, although Ritchie's Archipelago is the main centre. In 2006 the Government announced plans to develop mass tourism on the islands, while protecting their appeal. The beaches, coral reefs and water-sport facilities are the main attractions of the 'Emerald Isles', augmented by jungle interiors, 'mud' volcanoes, tribal cultures and the old penal colony historical sites. In 1998 there were 79,647 tourist visitors, of whom 4,915 were foreigners. Although total visitor numbers had risen to 95,730 by 2003 (provisional figure), only 5,101 were foreigners. The December 2004 tsunami reduced tourism by 91%, despite the main infrastructure being in the Andaman Islands, which were not so severely affected. In 2005 tourist arrivals totalled 109,582, of whom 4,578 were foreign.

### DIRECTORY

**Lieutenant-Governor:** Lt-Gen. (retd) Bhopinder Singh, Office of the Lieutenant-Governor, Administration of the Andaman and Nicobar Islands, Raj Nivas, Port Blair 744 101; tel. (3192) 233333; fax (3192) 230372; e-mail lg@and.nic.in.

**Chief Secretary:** Chhering Targay, Office of the Chief Secretary, Administration of the Andaman and Nicobar Islands, Secretariat, Port Blair 744 101; tel. (3192) 233110; fax (3192) 232656; e-mail cs@sec.and.nic.in.

**Member of Parliament (in New Delhi) for the Andaman and Nicobar Islands:** Manoranjan Bhakta (Congress), Constituency Office in the Andaman and Nicobar Islands, Port Blair 744 101.

**Resident Commissioner in New Delhi:** Naresh Kumar, 12 Chanakyapuri, New Delhi 110 021; tel. (11) 26119590; fax (11) 26882116; e-mail rcandaman@hotmail.com.

# Chandigarh

The Union Territory of Chandigarh lies in northern India, on the Punjab plains, beneath the foothills of the Himalayas. Built as the capital of the Indian Punjab, after the Partition at independence in 1947, Chandigarh ('fortress of the Goddess of Power', Chandi being a manifestation of Shakti) was constituted as a distinct territory under the authority of the President of India in 1966, to serve as the capital of both the present-day states of Haryana and the Punjab, into which the original state was split in the same year. It is, therefore, enclosed by these two states, the Punjab to the west and north, and Haryana to the east. Chandigarh's hinterland extends too into Himachal Pradesh, which also received territory from the old Punjab state in 1966, and the borders of which lie only a few kilometres beyond the city, to the north. Chandigarh covers a total area of 114 sq km (44 sq miles), making it the third smallest of all the union territories of India.

In March 1948 the Governments of the State of the Punjab and of India approved a plot of land covering 114.59 sq km at the foot of the Shivalik Hills, in Ropar District, as the site of the new state capital. The flat, gently sloping, fertile agricultural land varied in height only between 305 m and 366 m (111–133 ft) above sea level. Three seasonal rivers crossed the chosen tract, with the Patiali Rao now marking the west of the planned city and the Sukhna Choe the east. The mountains to the north of the territory provide a deliberate backdrop to the city and its monumental buildings, the strict grid plan of which is alleviated by linear parkland. The mountains also influence the climate, which is tropical and monsoonal. Most rainfall is in May–August, the wettest month generally being July (which in 2000 received 433 mm—17.0 inches—of rain), the hottest May and the coolest January. In 2000 the mean maximum temperature in May was 37.9°C (100.2°F) and the mean minimum temperature in January was 7.3°C (45.1°F), although extremes ranged from 3°C to 43°C (37°–109°F).

Chandigarh has experienced considerable population growth since its foundation. This has barely been alleviated by the development of satellite towns within the 10 km (just over six miles) forbidden to urbanization by the original planners—thus, Panchkula in Haryana and Sahibzada Ajit Singh Nagar (known as 'S. A. S. Nagar' or by its original name of Mohali) in the Punjab have also grown dramatically, but thereby taken some of the pressure off Chandigarh itself. According to the national census of March 2001, the total population of the Union Territory was 900,635, meaning an increase of 40.3% over 10 years. With most of the area occupied by city, this results in a population density of 7,900 per sq km, a figure only exceeded by that for the National Capital Territory of Delhi. In 2001 17.5% of the population were of the Scheduled Castes. The residents overwhelmingly speak Hindi or Punjabi. According to the 1991 census, 61.1% spoke Hindi and 34.7% Punjabi. However, it is worth noting that at the same time Hindus accounted for 75.8% of the population (78.6% in 2001). The Indian Punjab was divided in 1966 because of Sikh pressure for a separate state—the Sikhs used the creation of linguistic states to press their cause by arguing the distinctness of Punjabi (mainly spoken by Sikhs) from Hindi, but the census figures indicate that, although it served a purpose at the time, equating language and religion generally is unreliable. Although a greater proportion of the population spoke Punjabi in 1991, in terms of religious adherence Sikhs accounted for 20.3% of the total (but only 16.1% by 2001). There are also small Muslim (4.0% in 2001), Christian (0.9%), Jain (0.3%) and Buddhist (0.2%) communities.

The city proper is surrounded by an agricultural 'green belt', but urban areas account for 68% of Chandigarh's total territory, meaning that 89.8% of the population were classed as urbanized in the 2001 census (barely higher than in 1991, when only Delhi achieved a slightly higher rate). The Union Territory consists of the municipal corporation of Chandigarh itself, and 17 panchayat villages.

## HISTORY

The historic Punjab region is the heart of the Aryan homeland, although it was the location of city-based civilizations long before. Chandigarh, at the centre of the Indian Punjab, lies on the plains marking the divide between the Indus and Ganga (Ganges) river systems, which have proved a crucial area over India's long history. The original village of Chandigarh, however, does not figure in this tale until its name was adopted for the city built here during the 1950s. The Partition of the old British-era province of the Punjab upon the dissolution of the Indian Empire in 1947 had deprived independent India of the old Punjabi capital of Lahore (now in Pakistan). A new city was decided upon and the site marked out in 1948. The first planners chosen were from the USA, Albert Mayer and Matthew Nowicki, but the death of Nowicki in February 1950 caused this team to withdraw from the project. The next person chosen to head the project was the noted Swiss architect and city planner, Charles Edouard Jeanneret, more usually known by his professional pseudonym, Le Corbusier.

Le Corbusier retained some features of the original concept, drawn up by Mayer, such as the 'neighbourhood' unit as the main module, the basic framework of the city, including the linear parkland, and many of the chief components (the Capitol complex, the City Centre, etc.). However, he imposed a more severe grid pattern on the layout and incorporated his own ideals and philosophies into what he saw as a single, cohesive monumental composition. His vision is expounded in the so-called Statute of the Land, the Edict of Chandigarh, which includes a commitment to the 'human scale' of the city, an exhaustive classification of roads and a ban on personal statues. Some of these dictates have since been set aside (such as the ban on other urban developments around the city—a 'green belt' originally established by the Periphery Control Act of 1952), sometimes as a result of the divided administrations and sometimes adaptive. One of the main incentives for adaptation was the growth in population, as Le Corbusier envisaged a city containing no more than 500,000 (a total exceeded in the late 1980s). The foundation stone was laid in 1951 and the main buildings soon built, incorporating art as well as architecture (the Open Hand sculpture, for instance, now serves as the city's symbol). The city was a special district of the Punjab, administered by a Chief Commissioner.

The most important political development for Chandigarh came in 1966 as the result of the reorganization of the State of the Punjab. In an attempt to placate Sikh aspirations, the state was divided into the 'rump' Punjab in the north-west and Haryana in the south-east. Some territory was incorporated into the northern, mountain territory (now state) of Himachal Pradesh. The city of Chandigarh was to continue as the capital of both the Punjab and Haryana. The Secretariat, the High Court and the Assembly building (the bicameral legislature of the old state was replaced by two unicameral legislatures, to occupy the two chambers available) are now shared by the new states. To avoid conflict, and pending a final settlement of the city's status, Chandigarh was made a Union Territory, the responsibility of the Union Ministry of Home Affairs, on 1 November 1966. The Chief Commissioner was redesignated the Administrator until 1984. Then, on 1 June of that year the Governor of the Punjab was made the nominal head of the territorial executive— *ex officio*, the Administrator of Chandigarh. The actual head of the Administration, the chief commissioner, continued functioning under the title of Adviser to the Administrator. This arrangement was introduced for a transitional period of two months, but a final decision on the status of Chandigarh was avoided, and the situation has continued indefinitely. The Adviser (currently, Pradip Mehra, the 11th to hold the post since 1984) exercises delegated powers, including all financial powers, and supervises an Administration headed by six secretaries. The Union Territory has no legislature, but elects one member of the Indian Parliament, to the Lok Sabha or lower house. That seat is currently held by P. K. Bansal, a member of the party heading the national Government since May 2004, Congress. Bansal, who served in the Rajya Sabha for the Punjab until being elected the Lok Sabha member for Chandigarh in 1991, regained the seat for a second term in the 1999 general election, and then retained it in 2004. In September 2005 the city experienced a terrorist incident, when a bomb was detonated at the bus station, injuring seven people. The person arrested was connected to Sikh militants and was alleged to have been trained inside Pakistan.

## ECONOMY

Chandigarh is a prosperous city, the capital of two of the country's wealthier states, although its economy is not merely dependent on the government services for which it was built. Economic growth rates in the Union Territory had been sufficient to offset and, indeed, exceed the massive rate of population growth (see above) so, although income per head had reached Rs 42,893, in current prices, by 1999/2000, in real terms this was one-half as much again as in 1993/94. Chandigarh's net domestic product was bigger than that of six states by 2005. In 2004/05 official figures put the total size of the economy at Rs 68,790m. and income per head at Rs 67,370. This latter figure, for net domestic product per head, was the highest for any state or territory in India (having surpassed the figure for Goa in 2003/04), at almost 12 times that for Bihar, the poorest state in the Union. Chandigarh being a small area, and planned from the start, infrastructure is very well developed, and the city also enjoys good links with Delhi and the neighbouring states (there is a railway station and an airport). At March 2001 there were 64 km (40 miles) of national highway in the Union Territory, 139 km of city roads and 73 km of rural or link roads. The total road length, all highways and byways, was given as 1,489 km, which figure remained the same two years later. The city and all the villages not only have access to an electricity supply, but also have public lighting, although power is almost entirely imported (Chandigarh possesses a 3.5% share of the total generation of the Bhakra hydroelectric project on the Punjab–Himachal Pradesh border). In 2005 62 MW of installed capacity came from Chandigarh's share of central projects, while 2 MW alone were territorial. Of rural households, 65% received electricity in that year. There is also a well-developed communications infrastructure, with telephone connections doubling in 10 years, to 181,814 by 2000/01. Together with the high literacy rate (81.8% in 2001, compared with 77.8% in 1991), this puts Chandigarh in a good position to exploit the 'new' or internet economy.

Agriculture contributes even less to the economy of Chandigarh (1.1% of gross domestic product in 2001/02) than it does to that of Delhi. About one-fifth of Chandigarh's land area is cultivable, and most of that is irrigated, so agriculture is able to make a small economic contribution to the territory, as well as providing a protective 'green belt' around the city. The main crop is wheat (3,375 metric tons in 2000/01 and the next year, rather less than in previous years, and 3,215 tons in 2002/03), traditionally followed by maize (500 tons in 2000/01, but only 300 tons in 2002/03) and, increasingly, paddy rice

(350 tons in 2000/01, but 450 tons in 2002/03). Sugar cane also used to be grown, but now fruits and vegetables are being encouraged. Animal husbandry is relatively important in supplying the city. According to official estimates, livestock numbers in the territory have fallen (to 33,000 head by 2000/01, from some 46,000 one decade earlier), although milk production has increased, reaching 44,000 tons annually by 2004. Egg production increased dramatically to 21.8m. in 2002/03, although it was expected to fall back to 19.4m. in the following year. About 28% of the territory was woodland (none of it very dense) in 2003, all of it reserved or otherwise publicly owned. The area given over to fisheries was put at 268 ha in 2002/03, when accrued fish production was 83 metric tons.

Chandigarh was never designed to be an industrial city, although the planners did eventually include an Industrial Area of 597 ha (1,475 acres), realizing that it could contribute and add variety to the local economy. At the end of 2000 there were 528 factories registered in the city, slightly down on the previous year, all but 15 (for example, hosiery and knitting-machine needles, electric meters, antibiotics) of which were small-scale. In 1998/99 this sector had produced net income worth Rs 1,428.7m., from 531 factories, but this was compared with Rs 1,500.7m. in the previous year. That year the factories had employed 25,340 people. By March 2003 there were 492 factories. Food products are an important component of industrial activity in Chandigarh, but the city is also strong in light engineering, and produces electronic equipment, machine tools, pharmaceuticals, plastic goods and leather goods, among other things. However, the small-scale industrial units are dominated by the tractor industry of the surrounding regions, some 40% of them being ancillary to this activity. There were 1,688 registered, working small-scale industrial units in February 2003, employing 15,665 people. A further 834 village or khadi industries in 2002/03 provided industrial production worth Rs 59.8m.

Services dominate the economy of Chandigarh, government activity (the original purpose of the city) still being important. According to a census of government employees by the Administration of Chandigarh in 2001, the city employed 21,816 (which included information such as that, of the total, 64% were Hindus and 34% Sikhs), which was a considerable saving on the 28,834 employed at the peak in 1993. Numbers rose slightly the following year, but were put at 22,101 in 2003. However, as the capital city of two states, and an important centre for a third, it is also a commercial and financial hub, serving as the headquarters of a number of companies, banks and other organizations, as well as a transport node. Tourism is encouraged by the local Administration, its efforts to market the city as a useful centre for foreign tourists witnessed by the significant increase in the average length of stay for such visitors in 2000. However, the number of tourists remains relatively small, with most domestic visitors present for business purposes (42% in 1993) and foreign tourists to sightsee (55%). In 2000 the steadily rising number of visitors reached 486,355 from within India and 14,612 from abroad, having risen from 251,932 and 6,147, respectively, over 10 years. Over the next two years total visitor arrivals increased by about 13%, to 568,720 in 2002 (13,706 international tourist arrivals). The city is a unique example of the urban vision of the Swiss architect, Le Corbusier, but is also readily accessible to the other sites in the historic region of the Punjab.

### DIRECTORY

**Administrator:** Gen. (retd) S.F. Rodrigues (Governor of the Punjab *ex officio*), Office of the Governor of the Punjab (Administrator of Chandigarh), Raj Bhavan, Vigyan Path, Chandigarh 760 001; tel. (172) 2740608; fax (172) 2741058.

**Adviser to the Administrator:** Pradip Mehra, Office of the Adviser, Administration of Chandigarh, Chandigarh 760 001; tel. (172) 2742001.

**Member of Parliament (in New Delhi) for Chandigarh:** Pawan Kumar Bansal (Congress), Constituency Office, 64, Sector 28A, Chandigarh 160 002; tel. (172) 2657565; fax (172) 2641418; e-mail pkbansal@sansad.nic.in.

**Resident Officer in New Delhi:** K. N. Nijhawan, 21-B, Telegraph Lane, K. G. Marg, New Delhi 110 001; tel. (11) 23353359; fax (11) 23736017.

Note: The administrations of Haryana and the Punjab are also based in Chandigarh.

## Dadra and Nagar Haveli

The Union Territory of Dadra and Nagar Haveli consists of two enclaves near the west coast, in the north of the great Indian peninsula. Formerly part of Portuguese India and administered from the nearby coastal town of Daman (Daman and Diu), the much smaller enclave of Dadra is entirely surrounded by Gujarat state, while Nagar Haveli, just south of Dadra, straddles the border between Gujarat and Maharashtra to the south. Nagar Haveli, in turn, houses a small enclave of Gujarat, in the north-west, just south of Silvassa, the territorial capital. Acquired by India in 1954 and formally annexed as a Union Territory in 1961, in advance of the occupation of the rest of Portuguese India, Dadra and Nagar Haveli occupies an area of 491 sq km (190 sq miles), making it the third largest territory in India—much smaller than the Andaman and Nicobar Islands and Delhi, but slightly larger than Puducherry (Pondicherry).

Dadra and Nagar Haveli lies on the edge of the coastal plain, where the land rises towards the lower slopes of the Western Ghats, a lush, forested and well watered land. The territory lies about 30 km (19 miles) inland from the coast, where the main river through Nagar Haveli, the Damanganga, debouches into the sea at Daman. Dadra and Nagar Haveli is subject to the influence of the south-west monsoons, so annual rainfall can often exceed 1,500 mm (60 inches), though most of it falls between June and October. The climate generally is tropical, but moderated by the proximity of the sea.

Between the national censuses of 1991 and 2001, Dadra and Nagar Haveli recorded the second largest rate of increase in population of any state or territory in India, the total rising from 138,477 to 220,490. The population density in 2001 was 449 per sq km. Most of the population is registered as tribal (89% in 1991, although immigration reduced this to 62.2% by 2001). The largest groups are the Konkani peoples (who speak languages of an Indo-Aryan—Southern classification), notably the Koknas, but also Konkans and Katkars, and the Bhil peoples (Bhils and an offshoot, the Dhodias or Dublis, who speak an Indo-Aryan—Central tongue). A smaller tribe represented in the territory is the Warli or Varli, who speak another Indo-Aryan (Southern) language. Bhili or Bhilodi was spoken by 55.0% of the population in 1991, according to the census, Gujarati by 21.9% and Konkani by 12.3%. Hindi and English are also spoken. The overwhelming majority of the population are Hindus (93.5% in 2001—making it one of the most Hindu regions in India), but there are small Muslim (3.0%), Christian (2.9%) and other communities, including almost 900 Jains and 500 Buddhists, as well as more than 120 Sikhs. In 2001 1.9% of the population were in the Scheduled Castes.

Dadra and Nagar Haveli was the least urbanized (8.5% in 1991) of any state or territory in India, but by 2001 was not (22.9%). Silvassa (taken from the Portuguese for forest, *selva*), which has a population over 14,000, is the largest town and the capital of the territory. It is located in the north-west of Nagar Haveli. A few kilometres to the north, through a short stretch of Gujarat, lies the town of Dadra, which, with its immediate environs, constitutes about 2% of the territory's area. Traditionally, the territory consists of 72 villages, but one, Kothar, is submerged, and four others are partly submerged, owing to the construction of the irrigation project on the Damanganga.

### HISTORY

The region in which Dadra and Nagar Haveli lies, being south of the Narmada, has a history more connected to that of central and southern India, particularly Maharashtra, although it has long been exposed to influences from Gujarat. However, the territory itself has figured little in the ebb and flow of events when under the influence of the Mauryas, the Satavahanas, the Vakatakas and Guptas, or the Chalukyas of Gujarat. Its fate has long been linked to that of nearby Daman (now the capital of the Union Territory of Daman and Diu) and it enters modern history as a possession of the Marathas from the 18th century. However, European influences were already being felt in Mughal India, with the English (British) and Dutch in Surat (now in Gujarat) to the north and the English soon to be established in Bombay (now Mumbai, Maharashtra) to the south. Meanwhile, the Portuguese had added Daman to their Indian possessions in 1588. By the middle of the 18th century the Portuguese were coming into occasional conflict with the Marathas, but the latter resolved to try to secure their friendship (as the Marathas preferred to concentrate their efforts against the British) by settling the aggregated revenue of Rs 12,000 from a group of villages (now Dadra and Nagar Haveli) onto the Portuguese. This award was made on 17 December 1779, when Federico Guilherme de Souza was Governor of Portuguese India. Although the Portuguese enclaves were soon to be surrounded by British territory, the authorities in Daman continued to administer the inland pockets of Dadra and of Nagar Haveli into the 20th century and past the independence of the rest of India in 1947.

The incorporation of Dadra and Nagar Haveli into independent India preceded that of the rest of the Portuguese domain. Nationalist volunteers, both from within the territory and from without, combined to 'liberate' the villages in 1954. The authority of the Portuguese Governor-General, Paulo Bénard-Guedes, was rejected in Dadra on 24 July, while a similar insurrection in the larger part of the territory saw a pro-Indian administration installed in Nagar Haveli on 2 August. The Indian Parliament regularized this de facto occupation by the 10th Amendment to the Constitution, which incorporated Dadra and Nagar Haveli into the country as a Union Territory on 11 August 1961. The Portuguese Governor-General, Manuel António Vassalo e Silva, in Goa, as well as the metropolitan Government, protested this action, but soon had to deal with the Indian occupation of the rest of Portuguese India later that very year. Goa, Daman and Diu were themselves formally annexed in March 1962, but Dadra and Nagar Haveli remained a distinct territory, although practical considerations meant that its administration was again linked to that of the others (particularly Daman). Portugal's objections to the annexation were maintained by the International Court of Justice (which is based in the Hague, Netherlands), but the country recognized the loss of its former possessions in 1974.

The first Administrator of the new Union Territory, Tumkur Sivasankar, was appointed to his post in 1962. The 13th incumbent of the post, O. P. Kelkar, held office from 1999 to 2002; he, like his predecessors, was also the Administrator of Daman and Diu (which became a separate territory upon Goa gaining statehood in 1987), and was based in Daman. His successor was Arun Mathur. The territory is represented in the national Parliament by its elected member of the Lok Sabha, currently Mohanbhai Delkar. Delkar was formerly a member of Congress, and first elected to the federal legislature in 1989. He subsequently sat as an independent, but contested the 2004 general election (at which he won his sixth consecutive term, from the highest turn-out in India) as head of his own Bharatiya Navshakti Party. This grouping, previously known as Parivartan Manch, was formed in 2002 to contest local elections in southern Gujarat. It won no seats, but had an impact on the tribal vote, to the detriment of Congress. Delkar is a dominant figure in Dadra and Nagar Haveli, with some opponents alleging intimidation and a few industries claiming his conduct of union negotiations amounted to extortion. In August 1989 it was announced that a Pradesh Council would replace the advisory Varishtha Panchayat; there is also elected local government. A new Adminstrator, R. K. Verma, took office in mid-2006, to be succeeded by S. Gopal in January 2008.

### ECONOMY

Dadra and Nagar Haveli remains largely undeveloped, its population predominantly tribal and its economy agricultural. The Administration does not prepare estimates of domestic product and no recent figures are available. Development projects often take place in conjunction with other administrations, such as industrial development and housing schemes together with Daman and Diu or the Damanganga irrigation project with Daman and Diu and with Gujarat. The total road length in the territory is only about 534 km (332 miles), although 87% of that is surfaced (1998 figures)—68 villages are connected by all-weather roads. The nearest railhead is at Vapi (Gujarat), 17 km north-west of the territorial capital, on the line from Mumbai (formerly Bombay), in Maharashtra, to Ahmedabad, Gujarat. While there is an airstrip at Daman (Daman and Diu), almost 30 km to the north-west, the nearest domestic airport of any size is at Surat (Gujarat), about 120 km from Silvassa, and the nearest international airport at Mumbai, 180 km away. All the villages in Dadra and Nagar Haveli are electrified, but all power is imported (purchased from the Gujarat State Electricity Board). The literacy rate had risen to 60.0% in 2001 (from only 40.7% in 1991), although this also reflects the level of immigration from more developed parts of India, rather than just a dramatic improvement in the education of the local tribal population.

Agriculture is the principal economic activity of most of the population. About 230 sq km of land is under cultivation and production has been aided by the introduction of irrigation schemes since the 1960s (the most recent being the major project on the Damanganga river, involving the Madhuban Dam near Dudhni). The main food crop is paddy (*kharif*, or summer-grown), and pulses, ragi, nagli and other hill-millets are grown as well, as are wheat, sugar cane and vegetables. Fruit production includes mangoes, chikus, lychees and bananas. With forests covering almost another 200 sq km, there is potential for further primary economic activity, and the tribes that depend heavily on this resource have been granted exclusive rights to collect minor forest products free of charge. Livestock produce is important, and the territory produced 9,000 metric tons of milk and 7.0m. eggs in 2002/03.

There is little industry in the Union Territory, although there is some small-scale development of it, helped by government support and tax concessions. Only traditional craftsmen operated in the territory up to 1965, until a small co-operative industrial estate was then established. Since then, the authorities have developed three small estates, at Silvassa, Masat and Khadoli. At March 1998 industry employed 18,414 people. There were 285 medium-sized industrial enterprises, in, for example, textiles, automobile parts, plastics, electronics, chemicals and pharmaceuticals, and soaps and detergents. Cottage, village and other small industries numbered 716, mainly of handicrafts, increasingly aimed at the tourist trade.

Although long dependent on government aid, the territory, with its climate and extensive forest reserves, has been expanding its tourist industry. The natural environment is enhanced by a number of garden attractions, such as the Island Garden on Lake Vanganga, the Hirwa Van on the road from Silvassa to Dadra or the riverside park in Silvassa itself. The capital also has a tribal museum and a small zoological garden, while other places usually visited include Khanvel (Van Vihar) and Dudhni. The overall number of tourists still remains low, but the industry is an important contributor to the tertiary sector, as even government activity is limited, transportation small and services such as banking very undeveloped, particularly outside Silvassa. A few major projects occasionally contribute to construction activity.

### DIRECTORY

**Administrator:** SATYA GOPAL (Administrator of Daman and Diu *ex officio*), Office of the Administration of Dadra and Nagar Haveli, Administrator's Bungalow, Moti Daman, Daman 396 210; tel. (260) 2462777; fax (260) 2642702.

**Member of Parliament (in New Delhi) for Dadra and Nagar Haveli:** MOHANBHAI DELKAR (Bharatiya Navshakti Party), Constituency Office, opp. Cottage Hospital, Samjibhai Delkar Road, Silvassa; tel. (2638) 242796.

**Liaison Officer in New Delhi (for Dadra and Nagar Haveli, and for Daman and Diu):** V. B. SHARMA, F-308, Curzon Road Hostel, K. G. Marg, New Delhi 110 001; tel. (11) 23385369; fax (11) 23781086.

## Daman and Diu

The Union Territory of Daman and Diu consists of two enclaves on the north-western coast of India, flanking the mouth of Gujarat's Gulf of Khambhat (Cambay). Both districts of the territory are bordered by Gujarat state and lie on the Arabian Sea. Daman and Diu, together with Goa, together constituted a Union Territory formed after the annexation of Portuguese India in 1961. Goa became a separate state of the Indian Union on 30 May 1987, when Daman and Diu remained as a territory administered by the central authorities. Daman (formerly Damão), on the east side of the Gulf of Khambhat, is the larger district, having an area of 72 sq km (28 sq miles). Some 786 km (488 miles) to the west, and a little north, is the island district of Diu, covering 40 sq km. The total territorial area of 112 sq km, therefore, is slightly smaller than that of urban Chandigarh, with only Lakshadweep, of all India's territories, smaller than Daman and Diu.

Daman lies on peninsular India's western coast, in the north, not far inside Gujarat's border with Maharashtra. Inland, where the coastal plains begin to rise towards the Western Ghats, is the Union Territory of Dadra and Nagar Haveli, which was administered from Daman as part of Portuguese India until 1954—the territories again share many links. Both the district and the town of Daman are severed by the Damanganga river, which flows from the south-east and the direction of Nagar Haveli. Thus, the smaller part of Daman district lies to the south and west of the river (its southern border defined by the River Kalai), although the old fortified town of Moti, or Greater, Daman is also on the southern bank. It is connected across the river by a bridge with Lesser or Nani Daman. The northern border is along the Kolak river. Daman lies on fertile plains and rises to only about 12 m (39 ft) above sea level. The island of Diu and its two tiny mainland enclaves around Ghoghla and Simbor (the latter just over 20 km eastwards down the coast), lie on the south-facing coast of Gujarat, in Saurashtra, the island lying off the southern tip of the Kathiawar peninsula, at the mouth of the River Chasi. The channel separating Diu from the mainland gives way to the tidal marshes and saltpans of the northern part of the island, which is about 13 km long (west–east) and 3 km wide, rising to 29 m, with a southern coastline of limestone cliffs, rocky coves and a number of beaches. The island is pitted with old quarries and is barren and arid, although there is some wooded land, featuring the branching hoka palms (introduced from Africa) and coconut trees. The island is connected to the mainland by two bridges, the main one at the eastern end, just outside Diu Town, which ends in a foothold of the territory mainly occupied by Ghoghla village (known as Ahmedpur Mandvi on the other side of the Gujarat border). Both Daman and Diu have tropical climates, tempered by their coastal locations, with minimum temperatures at any time of year averaging about 20°C (68°F) and average maximums ranging between 26°C (79°F) and 36°C (97°F). Both districts are subject to the south-west monsoons, and annual rainfall can often exceed 1,500 mm (60 inches). Most of it falls between June and October, with Daman receiving rather more (up to 1,900 mm) than the more northerly Diu.

In 2001, according to the results of the census, the population of Daman and Diu was 158,204. This was an increase of more than one-half as much again as in 1991 (when the total was 101,586), the third highest rate of growth in India, pushing the average population density up significantly, to 1,412 per sq km by 2001. Daman and Diu had the lowest sex ratio (females per 1,000 males) of any state or territory in India in 2001, at 710 (compared to a national average of 933). About three-fifths of the territorial population live in and around Daman (61% in 1991), the rest in Diu. The people essentially share the language, culture and religion of the neighbouring parts of Gujarat, although there is still some sign of the long association with Portugal. In 1991 91.1% of the population of the two enclaves spoke Gujarati, but Portuguese, English, Hindi and Marathi are also used. In 2001 89.7% confessed the Hindu faith, although long periods of rule by infidels have left a legacy of Muslims (7.8%) and Christians (2.1%—almost entirely Roman Catholics). Other religious communities are also represented (among them Jains, Sikhs and Buddhists), and Diu enjoys the distinction of being where the Parsis first arrived in India. In 2001 3.1% of the population were counted among the Scheduled Castes and 8.8% the Scheduled Tribes.

The population of Daman and Diu was defined as 36.2% urban at the March 2001 census (down from 46.8% in 1991), Diu being more urbanized than Daman. The territorial capital is Daman, in the larger and more populous district of the same name, but the larger town in the territory is Diu. There are only the two districts.

## HISTORY

The advent of Portuguese rule in the 16th century was increasingly to insulate Daman and Diu from the historical developments shared by the rest of India for some 450 years. Prior to that, the two towns shared the fates of those areas of Gujarat in which they lay, with Diu claiming the more venerable history. Daman, now the capital of the territory, was a name that appeared in the first century of the Christian era, as applied to the Damanganga river. The area around Daman originally formed the heartland of the county of Lata, variously falling under the influence of dynasties based to the north, in modern Gujarat, or to the south, in Maharashtra. In 1262 a Rajput prince, Ramsingh, established his dynasty in the locality, his successors siting their capital at Ramnagar, inland, at the foot of the Western Ghats in the next century. By the 16th century the area was tributary to Gujarat, which was to cede the town that had grown up at the mouth of the Damanganga and its hinterland to the Portuguese. Diu had fallen under the Portuguese earlier in the century, but had been the object of local power struggles long before that. There is mention of the island in the *Mahabharata*, where it is called Mani Nagar, a Yadava territory, and it served briefly to shelter the exiled Pandavas. In Hindu mythology Diu was known as Jallandharkshetra, after its demon-king, Jallandhar, who harassed and was killed by Lord Vishnu. There is still a famous temple of Jallandhar in the south of the island. In more historical terms, Diu was an important trading post in the time of the Mauryas and a valued possession of the Kshatrapas (Shaka, or Scythian, dynasts known as the 'Western Satraps'), who also held, more tenuously, Daman in the early first millennium of the common or Christian era. Later regional dynasties to hold Diu were to include the Chavdas and their later overlords, the Chalukyas. Still later, Diu was coveted by the Sultanate of Delhi and, as a cause of conflict, was certainly fortified by this time, and the Rajput princes of Gujarat did not succumb until the beginning of the 14th century. The island was then only to leave Muslim rule to lie under a Roman Catholic sovereignty, in the 16th century.

The decay of the Sultanate allowed the ascendancy of powerful marcher lords, who maintained the vigour of Islam's expansion in the subcontinent, and Gujarat was among a number of independent sultanates established at the beginning of the 15th century. Another such proto-state was Kandesh, a narrow strip of land to the south of Gujarat, which briefly encompassed Daman, but soon succumbed to its more powerful northern neighbour. One of the most illustrious sultans of Gujarat, Mahmud Shah or Mahmud 'Bergarha' ('Two Forts' or 'the Beard', 1459–1511) secured the union of Saurashtra, wherein lies Diu, with his mainland patrimony. Ascendancy over another sultanate, Malwa, to the east, was secured soon after Mahmud Berghara's reign, when religious dissension involved the forces of Gujarat, which seized Malwa's capital, Mandu, in 1518 and 1531. However, this rivalry permitted the Government of Gujarat to yield to Portuguese distractions. This was even more the case from later in the 1530s, when Gujarat faced the threat of a new hegemony based in Delhi, the recently installed Mughals.

The Portuguese established their first base at Cochin (Kochi in Kerala) in 1503 and acquired Goa in 1510, the core of their 'State of India'. The European advent to the Indian Ocean trade, hitherto dominated by Arab and other Muslim traders, was to signal a fundamental threat to the traditional, land-based kingdoms. Having started in southern India, at the expense of the Deccan sultanates and Vijayanagar, the Portuguese then began eyeing the lucrative trade of Gujarat, which enjoyed strong links with Mameluke Egypt. Gujarat sustained several Portuguese attacks from 1518. Diu and Daman, at the mouth of the prosperous Gulf of Cambay (Khambhat), soon became particular objects of covetousness. Daman attracted Portuguese interest in 1523, and then Diu was attacked in 1529, and ravaged. The island's defenders abandoned it in advance of another attack in 1531, although another assault in 1533 was repulsed. Their appetite whetted, the Portuguese began to have ambitions to establish Diu as their northern station. Gujarat, under Ahmed Shah, was beginning to feel the threat of the Mughals and, on 5 October 1535, entered into a treaty with the Governor of the 'State of India', who by 1541 had built on Diu what was to become one of the Portuguese empire's most important forts in India. On 10 November 1546 the Portuguese finally seized Diu for their own. Although also already established at Bassein, near what is now Mumbai (Maharashtra), the Portuguese felt the need for another base to face Diu across the Gulf of Cambay. By the 1550s they had determined on Daman, a prosperous trading town. Eventually, a regency council agreed to cede the territory to the Portuguese, in return for a share of the receipts from Diu, but the Government lacked the authority to enforce much against the wishes of the powerful local commanders of the decaying Gujarati sultanate. Daman, with a garrison of 3,000, was captained by an Abyssinian (Ethiopian) Muslim, contemptuous of the concessions made for a king in his minority, and the Portuguese were given leave to help themselves. Early in 1559 the Governor in Goa, Constantino de Braganza, assembled a fleet and sailed into Daman, claiming it easily for the Portuguese Crown against disheartened and faction-ridden opposition. Portugal also gained Simbor, a fort down the coast from Diu, in 1722, and Dadra and Nagar Haveli, in 1779. The latter was settled on the Portuguese by the Marathas, who wished to concentrate their contentions against the rising power of the British. However, the amount of territory and influence falling to the East India Company was steadily curtailing the commerce of Daman and Diu. Finally, the British moved against the lucrative opium trade to Africa that went through Portugal's Indian territories.

Although the wealth of Daman and Diu was long gone by the mid-20th century and the partition and independence of the surrounding territories of British India, Portugal was reluctant to negotiate away its own Indian possessions. In 1954 local agitators and nationalists from India itself wrested control of Dadra and Nagar Haveli from the Portuguese—these enclaves still remain a distinct territory within India, although once again connected with Daman in the practical terms of administration. Finally, the central Government having lost patience with the negotiations, Indian troops moved into Daman and Diu, and Goa, on 18–19 December 1961. A military Governor, Kenneth Candeth (who died in 2003), was installed, holding office until June 1962 (Goa, Daman and Diu became a Union Territory a few months earlier, in March, under legislation that formalized the status retroactively to 20 December 1961). The Portuguese 'State of India', one of the longest lasting of the polities incorporated into modern, independent India, thus came to an end (the annexation was recognized by Portugal in 1974). When Goa became a full state of the Union on 30 May 1987, the 'rump' of the old territory became a separate entity as the current Union Territory of Daman and Diu.

The present Administrator of Daman and Diu (the sixth since 1987), Arun Mathur, has held office since 2002. He is also the Administrator of Dadra and Nagar Haveli, but resides in Daman. The Union Territory's chief elected representative is its Congress member of the national Parliament, Dhaya Bhai Vallabhbhai Patel, although there is also a Pradesh Council as well as elected local government. Patel was first elected in 1999, winning almost one-half of the votes cast, and defeating the incumbent Bharatiya Janata Party (BJP) member, Devji Bhai J. Tandel. He had opposed Tandel as an independent in the previous general election, later being adopted by the Indian National Congress for the 1999 ballot (Congress had only managed to displace the BJP member in the 1996–97 Parliament, hitherto the only interruption to Tandel's tenure since he was first elected in 1989). Patel was elected for a second term at the 2004 general election, narrowly defeating Tandel. Daman had experienced some civil unrest in 2003, in reaction to the official response to the deadly collapse of a bridge across the Damanganga in August. The bridge was reopened in June 2004, but a span collapsed only 45 days later and was due to be opened again in July 2006 (although the contractors then delayed the completion date for a couple of months). A new Adminstrator, R. K. Verma, took office in mid-2006, to be succeeded by S. Gopal in January 2008.

## ECONOMY

Particularly compared with past centuries of trading pre-eminence, Daman and Diu is not a prosperous territory, being dependent on fishing and, increasingly, tourism. The estimated gross domestic product in 2004 was some Rs 9,400m., in current prices. The territory's centrally administered status does mean that it has access to government development funds and that it is an attractive place to visit for those from 'dry' Gujarat wishing for an alcoholic drink (i.e. it has not banned the sale of alcohol). Although neither part of the territory is on the main rail and road networks, both Daman and Diu are easily accessible from them. The main road up the western coast from Mumbai (formerly Bombay), in Maharashtra, to Ahmedabad, in

Gujarat, lies only 14 km (just under nine miles) from Daman, and the nearest railhead is at Vapi (Gujarat), 13 km to the east. Diu lies just 8 km from the highway system, inland at Una (Gujarat) and a similar distance from the nearest railhead, at the port of Delwada (Gujarat) to the east (metre gauge). The total length of surfaced road in Daman is 191 km and in Diu is 70 km. Both Daman (just north-east of Nani Daman) and Diu (near Nagoa) have small airports. All the villages of the Union Territory have access to an electricity supply, mainly from central-government power stations, with Daman having three sub-stations and Diu one. The literacy rate in 2001 was 81.1% (up from 71.2% in 1991).

Agriculture is not a major activity of the territory, with only 1,121 ha (2,770 acres) under cultivation, almost three-quarters of that in the district around Daman. Field and garden crops are grown, including rice and other grains, coconut, sugar cane, vegetables and fruits. Most livestock is kept domestically, but in 2002/03 milk production of 1,000 metric tons was recorded, as well as 3.9m. eggs (the lowest figures for any state or territory in the Union). There are no forests of any significance in Daman and Diu, but, as established ports, both towns support fishing industries.

Industrial development is limited. In 1998 there were 1,334 small-scale industrial enterprises based in Daman and Diu, most of them in Daman. The Omnibus Industrial Development Corporation, established by the Government for the benefit of Daman and Diu and of Dadra and Nagar Haveli, has set up two industrial areas in Daman, in addition to the units based at Dabhel, Bhimpore and Kadaiya. Handicrafts and some processing of agricultural and fisheries products are the main activities, although there are attempts to generate businesses based on new technologies.

Traditionally, both Daman and Diu had economies based on trade, although the last days of significant wealth and power were in the first part of the 19th century. Although neither town is now a major port, services are still an important sector of the economy. There is some tourist trade generated by visitors interested in the Portuguese heritage (the great forts of Moti Daman or Diu and Panikot, for instance, and the churches and older buildings generally), the beaches or, for further example, the Jallandhar temple on Diu. However, the main generator of visitor numbers is the state law in Gujarat forbidding the sale of alcoholic beverages—Daman and Diu do not fall under this regulation and both are attractive to those in neighbouring areas wishing to evade the restrictions. Restaurants and bars are, therefore, numerous and flourishing. In 1997/98 tourist arrivals in Daman numbered 438,340 and in Diu 150,000.

### DIRECTORY

**Administrator:** SATYA GOPAL (also Administrator of Dadra and Nagar Haveli), Office of the Administration of Daman and Diu, Administrator's Bungalow, Moti Daman, Daman 396 210; tel. (260) 2230770; fax (260) 2230775.

**Member of Parliament (in New Delhi) for Daman and Diu:** DAHYABHAI V. PATEL (Congress), Constituency Office, 40A Ghalwad Falia, Dabhel, Nani Daman, Daman 396 210; tel. (236) 2253444; fax (236) 2253355; e-mail dahyabhai@sansad.nic.in.

**Liaison Officer in New Delhi (for Daman and Diu, and for Dadra and Nagar Haveli):** V. B. SHARMA, F-308, Curzon Road Hostel, K. G. Marg, New Delhi 110 001; tel. (11) 23385369; fax (11) 23781086.

## Delhi (National Capital Territory)

The National Capital Territory of Delhi is located in northern India, at the western end of the great Gangetic plain, where the land rises towards the watershed of the Ganga (Ganges) and the Indus and the historic province of the ancient Punjab. The National Capital Territory (NCT) is almost entirely surrounded by Haryana state, except on the east, where it faces across, or edges over, the River Yamuna towards Uttar Pradesh. The NCT was constituted by law in 1991, when the old Union Territory of Delhi (styled a 'Part C' state between 1950 and 1956) received enhanced status and a legislature. However, the city has been the capital of India since soon after the British announced it as such in 1911, actually inaugurating the 'New' Delhi in 1931. The NCT has an area of 1,483 sq km (572 sq miles).

Delhi lies on the west bank of the Yamuna, although the NCT includes territory on the other side of the river. The city's historic importance stems from its strategic location on the main route from the north-west into the Gangetic heartland of northern India, at the narrowest point between the Aravalli Hills (which reach up from the south-west, in Rajasthan) and the wall of the Himalayas to the north. The Delhi Ridge and the Yamuna both descend from the north. The main city-building area lies between them, where the river swings east (and the Ridge slightly south-westwards) and then south again, before South Delhi spreads into the broadening area caused by a south-eastward course of the Yamuna. The capital area of New Delhi is centred on Vijay Chowk (Raisina Hill), dissected by the east–west Rajpath (King's Way), which descends from the Rashtrapati Bhavan, lying on the flanks of the South Ridge, eastwards to the great memorial of India Gate. North of the Rajpath is Rajiv Chowk (Connaught Place), the commercial heart of Delhi, mid-way between the Rashtrapi Bhavan the Lal Qila (Red Fort) to the north-east. Between India Gate and the Yamuna are the old settlements of ancient Indraprasta and the Purana Qila (Old Fort). Southwards, beyond the railway lines, extend the burgeoning, newer suburbs dotted (from west to east) with the remnants of Lal Kot (the so-called first city, confusingly also meaning 'red fort'), Qutb Minar (which marked the 12th-century Muslim conquest of Delhi), Jahanpanah and Siri (the fourth and second cities), and, a lowering citadel on a rocky outcrop of the Ridge, Tughlaqabad (third city). To the north and east of New Delhi lies Shah Jahanabad ('Old' Delhi, the seventh city), dominated by the Lal Qila (Red Fort) and the mighty Jama Masjid (Friday Mosque). Across the river, the barren flood plain of the Yamuna now houses newer suburbs and industrial estates stretching eastwards towards the Hindan river and Ghaziabad (Uttar Pradesh). The city proper, therefore, is located in the south-eastern third of the NCT, while in the south-west the territory extends towards Gurgaon (Haryana) and the north consists of farmland and dormitory settlements. The NCT has an average altitude of 239 m (784 ft) above sea level and, lying in the centre of the landmass of northern India, an extreme climate. Tropical conditions are moderate in the winter months (November–February), while the summer is hot, humid and, in August–September, deluged by monsoon rains. The mean minimum temperature is 4°C (39°F), but daytime temperatures in winter tend to range between 21°C and 30°C (70°–86°F), while the mean maximum temperature reaches 46°C (115°F) in May. Rainfall is heaviest in July (over 200 mm or 8 inches) and, slightly less, in August and then September.

The population of the NCT in 2001 was 13,850,507, a considerable increase on the 9,420,644 of 1991. This decadal rate of growth was over twice the national average and greater than that of any of the states except Nagaland. Among the territories, only Dadra and Nagar Haveli and Daman and Diu exceeded this rate of growth, while Chandigarh almost matched it. The population density, the highest in India, was 9,340 per sq km in 2001. Originally a Muslim, Urdu-speaking city, upon Partition Delhi became a predominantly Hindu city full of refugees from the old Punjab. Hindi is now the main language of the overwhelming majority (81.6%, according to the 1991 census), although Punjabi (7.9%) and Urdu (5.4%) are still relatively important. English, as a language of government and of commerce, is obviously still very widely spoken in the national capital. Hinduism is acknowledged as the religion of 82.0% of the population (2001), Islam 11.7% and Sikhism 4.0%. There are also small communities of Jains and Christians, as well as Buddhists and Bahá'ís (the Lotus Temple of the last looms dramatically over South Delhi). Officially recognized minorities in the territory are Muslims, Christians, Punjabis and, from June 2008, Jains. In 2001 16.9% of the population were counted among the Scheduled Castes.

Delhi is the most urbanized of all the states and territories of India (93.2% of the 2001 population classed as urban), although this special municipality includes a fairly wide rural hinterland of just over one-half of the NCT's area. The capital of the territory, as of the nation, is New Delhi, but this is not a densely populated city centre. Delhi (the city proper, with 10.18m. inhabitants in 2001, is the second largest in India) is a major commercial and industrial centre and draws many of its workers from towns and cities in the surrounding areas of Haryana and Uttar Pradesh.

### HISTORY

Delhi is an ancient city, the seat of many empires, and now the national capital of the Republic of India. Long before it became the capital of Muslim emperors or of British India, it was a site powerful in Hindu legend. By the beginning of the first millennium BC the Aryans had moved eastwards from the Punjab and into the Yamuna-Ganga Doab, on the brink of spreading their *arya varta* heartland the length of the Ganga (Ganges). There is archaeological evidence for the Aryan advance into this area, but no detail to substantiate Vedic tradition. The Doab formed the base of the Kura kingdom, the theatre for the great war described in the epic *Mahabharata*, and it was on the edge of this territory that the Pandavas were to found their new capital of Indraprasta, on the right bank of the Yamuna. Whatever the historicity of this tale, the site has proved attractive ever since.

The ascertainable history of Delhi begins in AD 736, when a Rajput clan of modern Haryana, the Tomaras, founded a city here. This 'first city' was later named for the 'red fort' of Lal Kot, originally built in 1052 by Anangpal Tomara, in what was still a relatively unimportant town in northern India. In the mid-12th century another Rajput dynasty, the Chahamanas (Chauhans) of Ajmer (now in Rajasthan), under Vigraha-raja, conquered Delhi and the land north to the Himalayas. Thus, when Prithviraj III ascended the throne of Ajmer in about 1177 he commanded the only significant Hindu bulwark against Muslim advance from the west. The potentate facing him across a partitioned Punjab was Muhammed of Ghor, who realized that only Prithviraj's Rajput confederacy stood between the armies of Islam and their advance into the rich lands of the Gangetic plain and beyond. Refortified Delhi, its citadel now known as Qila Rai Pithaura (after the king), was the gateway to the rest of India. In 1191 it was Prithviraj III's vassal in Delhi, Govinda-raja, who was reputedly most prominent in the first battle of Tarain (near Thanesar, in Haryana, about 150 km—93 miles—north of Delhi), when the Ghorid advance was halted. However, the second battle of Tarain in the following year witnessed the rout of the Rajputs and secured the fall of Delhi to Ghor's Turkish general, Qutb-ud-din Aibak. By the end of the century Muslim armies were about to move into Bihar and Bengal. Meanwhile, Aibak renamed the 'fort of king Prithviraj' Lal Kot and, just to the south, began the construction of the Qutb Minar complex, notably the great minaret itself and also India's oldest surviving mosque. With the death of his master of Ghor in 1206, Aibak founded what was to be known as the Slave Dynasty (to 1290) and an independent sultanate, based in Delhi.

Under the second dynasty of the Delhi Sultanate, the Khiljis, a new capital was founded by Ala-ud-din (1296–1313), to the north-west of Lal Kot, at Siri (near Hauz Khas). Under the longest lasting of the Sultanate's dynasties, the Tughluqs (1320–1414), three more centres would be built: Tughluqabad, a mighty citadel well to the east of the other settlements, but which only served as the capital in the 1320s; Jahanpanah, sited between Lal Kot and Siri; and the 'fifth city', the first to move back towards Indraprasta and the Yamuna in the north-east, Ferozabad (the citadel, Feroz Shah Kotla, is just south of Old Delhi). Tughluqabad was built by the first of the dynasty, Ghiyas ud-din Tughluq, whose murder was allegedly arranged by his son and successor, Jauna Muhammed bin Tughluq. The latter is a controversial monarch, sometimes known as Muhammed Khuni or Bloody Muhammed, who almost took the Delhi Sultanate to a pan-Indian empire and was also known for his education, erudition and patronage of the arts. However, the consequences of his expensive policies brought ruin to the state. One of these enterprises, in the early years of the reign, was the attempted removal of the capital to the craggy fort of Deogiri, some 13 km to the north-west of Aurangabad (in Maharashtra). This new centre, Daulatabad, was better placed strategically to subdue the more fractious parts of the empire, but such a move may also have been designed to disrupt the influence of the civil and religious establishment of Delhi (dominated by Turks, Persians and Afghans, who were already alienated by Muhammed's promotion of Indians and even non-Muslims). However, despite generous compensation and relocation incentives, in the end the Sultan had to resort to force to move the capital's population. Indeed, he seems to have succeeded in emptying Delhi, obliging its population at least to begin the 1,400-km trek southwards. This seems to have happened around 1330, although the city was soon repopulated by settlement from other provinces and by returning natives. Thus, Tughluqabad and the settlement of Adilabad (built just to the south by Muhammed) lost their status and, when the court returned to Delhi, it was to the 'fourth city', Jahanpanah, also built by Muhammed. In 1351 he was succeeded by his cousin, Feroz Shah, whose capital was largely reused for the building of later cities.

Meanwhile, just 10 years after the death of Feroz Shah, the Mongols under Taimur 'the Lame' (Tamerlane or Tamburlaine) sacked Delhi, in 1398, slaughtering its Hindu inhabitants and looting it of its riches. The Delhi Sultanate limped on, the Saiyyids barely exercising their authority further than the town of Palam (now the site of the city's domestic airport), and the final, Lodi, dynasty (from 1445) achieving only a little more. Although the Sultanate failed to establish a lasting empire, it was succeeded by a number of powerful, Muslim-ruled but better-integrated polities throughout northern India and the Deccan, and it was also to provide an imperial capital to its more successful successors, the Mughals.

Sikander, the second and most successful of the three Lodi Sultans of Delhi, restored some of his state's power to the south, his main rival being the rajah of Gwalior (now in northern Madhya Pradesh). To celebrate his successes, in 1501 he founded a new seat at Agra (Uttar Pradesh), hitherto a small town just over 200 km downriver from Delhi, but which was to rival the old capital for over 150 years. His neglect of the north-west frontier, however, meant that India attracted the attention of the new Mongol ruler of Kabul (now in Afghanistan), Zahir-ud-din Muhammed or Babur ('the Tiger'), whose territories neighboured the nominally Lodi province of the Punjab. Six exploratory incursions from 1505 and increasing dissension among the Lodis themselves resulted in a full-scale invasion by Babur in 1526. At the first of the great battles of Panipat (a town, now in Uttar Pradesh, which lies some 80 km due north of Delhi and just to the east of the Yamuna), Babur's army, crucially in possession of firearms and artillery, routed the numerically superior Lodi forces and killed Sultan Ibrahim. Babur occupied Delhi, while his son and heir, Humayun, took possession of the capital, Agra, and the Lodi treasury. Babur laid the foundations for a Muslim, Mongol (Mughal) empire in India, and was the first of the so-called Great Mughals. Humayun succeeded him in 1530, with Agra still as his main capital, but in 1534 he began the 'sixth city' of Delhi, Dinpanah, with the massive walls of what is now called the Purana Qila (Old Fort). The 15-year displacement of the Mughals by the Afghan Sur clan, led by Sher Khan (subsequently Sher Shah), who drove Humayun into exile in 1540, meant that Dinpanah was razed and replaced with a city named for the new ruler. Shergarh too disappeared, when Humayun regained the throne in 1555. Humayun died in Delhi in the following year and the city was seized by remnants of the Sur, led by a Hindu, Hemu ('Rajah Vikramaditya'), reinforced by a massive force of elephants. This army met the Mughal regent at the fateful field of Panipat and, eventually, was routed, allowing the new emperor (Padshah) to enter a Delhi that would then remain firmly Mughal for almost two centuries.

Although Humayun's successor, Akbar, buried his father in Delhi, he did not return the capital here, but soon moved from Agra to his new city of Fatehpur Sikri (some 40 km west of Agra, also in Uttar Pradesh, but near the border with Rajasthan), to Lahore (now in Pakistan) and then back to Agra. The next Great Mughal, Jahangir (1605–27), remained in Agra until 1618, when the court moved to Kashmir, and his son, Shah Jahan, was the last emperor to be primarily based in Agra. In 1638 he founded a new city to the north of the others, Shahjahanabad, now called Old Delhi, which is dominated by his great mosque and the Red Fort (Lal Qila) enclosing a lavish palace and durbar halls. Although he built the famed Taj Mahal in Agra, and returned to that city in 1650 for the remainder of his life (which ended in 1666—initially confined there by illness and then by his son), it was Shah Jahan who ensured that from the reign of his successor, Aurangzeb (Alamgir I), onwards, Delhi would be identified as the imperial capital of the Mughals.

The great days of the Mughals, however, were already ending. Particularly after the death of Aurangzeb in 1707, the Mughal Empire was to experience decline and humiliation. The most spectacular sign of this was in 1739, when Delhi was sacked by the invading forces of Nadir Shah of Persia (now Iran), who took away enough booty (including the lavish Peacock Throne) to relieve his own subjects of taxation for three years. The city had already been raided by the Marathas in 1737 (who had first become actively involved in Mughal dynastic struggles in 1719, a year of five emperors), and suffered from the depredations of Ahmad Shah Abdali, an Afghan, from 1748 (the end of the surprisingly long reign of Muhammed Shah) onwards. Earlier, in what was to have a more sinister and more long-term impact, at the very end of 1716 the British had been granted a *firman* or imperial directive of privilege and standing within the Mughal Empire. This was secured by the East India Company, which had sent a lavish embassy to Delhi, and the *firman* later justified its interventions and participation in imperial politics. In 1765, after being defeated by the British in the previous year, Shah Alam II (1759–1806) granted the Company the *diwan* or chancellorship of Bengal, effectively a grant of sovereignty under the Mughal order.

The Marathas had again intervened in the imperial succession in Delhi in 1751–52 and their continued presence on that political stage was inevitable after they moved into the Punjab in the wake of Shah Abdali's 1756 sack of Delhi. However, the Maratha confederacy again retook Delhi at the beginning of 1761 and moved to confront the Afghan forces at Panipat, only to be disastrously defeated. The emperor was left a dependent of the Nawab of Awadh (Oudh—now part of Uttar Pradesh), both of them soon to be humbled by the British. Delhi and its Mughal court (still presided over by Shah Alam, despite an attempted usurpation in 1788) then fell to the 'protection' of the great Maratha prince, Mahadji Scindia, who died in 1794. Maratha might began to disintegrate and finally succumbed to the British in the Second Maratha War of 1803–04. In 1803 a British commander, Gen. Gerard Lake, occupied Delhi, with its ageing occupant, Shah Alam II. Under the next two successors to the imperial titles, Shah Akbar II (1806–37) and Bahadur Shah II (1837–58), however, the Mughals were acknowledged merely as 'Kings of Delhi', English replaced Persian as the official language of empire in 1835 and, under Sir James Ramsay, Earl of Dalhousie (Governor-General in 1848–56), it was suggested that the Mughal be recognized only as a prince and that his seat in the Red Fort be handed over to the British (the city was included in the North-Western Provinces from 1832). Such insecurities for even the most eminent of ruling houses under British patronage, as well as religious fears and a resentment of recent administrative and military reforms, provoked the Great Mutiny of 1857 and the ensuing 'First War of Independence'. The Mutiny started at Meerut (Mirat, Uttar Pradesh), about 62 km north of Delhi, and the character of this civil war in northern India was to be transformed by the mutineers hastening to the old capital and placing the ineffectual Bahadur Shah Zafar at their head. British forces soon occupied the Ridge to the north of Delhi and exchanged fire with those holding the city itself, which finally fell to bloodshed and violence in September. Several of the Mughal royal family were murdered and the 82-year-old imperial figurehead was deposed, tried and exiled to the Burmese city of Rangoon (now Yangon, Myanmar), to die in obscurity in 1862.

In 1858, as part of the settlement to pacify India, a royal proclamation declared a decision of the British Parliament whereby all rights and privileges previously enjoyed by the Honourable East India Company were to be resumed by the Crown. Queen Victoria, therefore, became Queen of India and her governor-general a viceroy (this took effect on 1 November). A new order incorporating directly administered territories (now including Delhi, part of the Punjab since 1858) and princely vassals was confirmed in 1876, when Victoria announced that British India was to be an Empire and she an Empress (Kaiser-i-Hind). In January of the following year this was solemnized at a durbar or assemblage to the north of the city, reportedly attended by 84,000, including 63 ruling princes and 300 titular rulers and local nobility. Another two such grand durbars were held here, in 1903, in honour of the coronation of a new King-Emperor, Edward VII (1901–10), and in 1911, for George V (1910–36), who attended in person. At the last, on 12 December, in an attempt to institutionalize the durbar tradition linking the Mughal to the British imperial successions, George V announced that the capital of India would be moved from Calcutta (now Kolkata, West Bengal) back to Delhi. A New Delhi was to be built and, once the transfer was formalized in the following year (when Delhi became a separate province), the apparatus of government began to move up the Ganga. To mark the relocation, the Viceroy, Charles Hardinge, Baron of Penshurst, made a ceremonial entry to Delhi on 23 December 1912, only to have a bomb thrown into his howdah by a nationalist protester. Lord and Lady Hardinge survived, as did the elephant bearing them. Otherwise, there was little drama to accompany the transfer (although rather less satisfaction in Bengal) and the duly constructed New Delhi was inaugurated on 9 February 1931. Until then, the administration functioned largely from the Delhi Cantonment, the Civil Lines, just to the north of Shah Jahan's 'Old' Delhi.

The original site proposed for New Delhi, where George V laid the foundation stone in 1911, was also to the north of the old city, but this was soon deemed unsuitable. In 1913 the foundation stone was removed to Raisina Hill (now Vijay Chowk), where the new capital could fill the space between Old Delhi and the even older Delhis to the south with widely spaced streets and the panoply of empire. The leading architect was Edwin Lutyens, who was to plan the city and to design the great, domed Viceroy's House (now the Rashtrapati Bhavan, the presidential palace), assisted by his friend, Herbert Baker, who was to be responsible for the Secretariat buildings and, after a representative assembly was introduced in 1919, a hastily incorporated chamber for the legislature (now known as Sansad Bhavan or Parliament House). Although both men favoured Western classical forms, there was considerable popular, political and even royal pressure to incorporate at least some Indian architectural features, and the results have variously been described as a true 'synthesis' of styles or as basically classical structures decorated with Indian motifs. As imperial rule approached its end, government had been firmly entrenched again in Delhi, in a city the British effectively built for a successor state—but it was from the Red Fort in Old Delhi that Jawaharlal Nehru was to hail Independence in 1947. The accompanying Partition of the old Empire, however, was to transform Delhi from a predominantly Muslim city into a larger, mainly Hindu one, amid the exchanges of populations and the bloody inter-communal violence sweeping the neighbouring Punjab. The city was to experience an echo of such violence again, in 1984, following the assassination of Indira Gandhi, but this time directed against Sikhs. It was also, particularly in the 1990s, to experience another dramatic growth in population.

Initially a province, then a 'Part C' state from 1950 (with a chief minister from 1952), upon the reorganization of India's federal system in 1956, Delhi and its environs became a Union Territory (without a representative government) on 1 November. There has been some pressure within Delhi for the territory to achieve full statehood, but this is not popular in the rest of India. As a concession, in 1991 Parliament passed the National Capital Territory Act (which took effect on 1 February 1992), the 69th Amendment to the Constitution of India, which gave Delhi special status and a Legislative Assembly. Under the new order, territorial elections were held and in 1993 Madan Lal Khurana of the rightist, Hindu-nationalist Bharatiya Janata Party (BJP) became the first Chief Minister of the newly named National Capital Territory (NCT). Following a scandal, in early 1996 he was succeeded by his party colleague, Sahib Singh Verma, who, in turn, was displaced in October 1998, just weeks before the elections, by the first woman premier, Sushma Swaraj. However, she was not able to salvage the territorial elections for the BJP and, on 3 November, Congress gained control of the city's administration, when another woman, Sheila Dixit, became Chief Minister. This reverse has not prevented the Delhi BJP steadily increasing its representation in the lower house of the national Parliament, the Lok Sabha. In the 1999 general election all seven seats fell to the BJP, although the three Delhi seats in the upper house, the Rajya Sabha (members of which are indirectly elected, by the local assemblies), are from Congress. Delhi and Puducherry (Pondicherry) are the only two territories to send representation to the upper house or to elect legislatures and a government.

The next legislative elections were scheduled for late 2003, and the BJP prepared to challenge Congress rule: in July 2002 Khurana was brought back at the head of the territorial branch of the party; in early 2003 negotiations with the 'pro-poor' Bahujan Samaj Party, then ruling in neighbouring Uttar Pradesh with BJP support, began, in an attempt to bring the party into the territory and challenge Congress for the dalit vote; and in August the federal Cabinet approved legislative proposals to make Delhi a state (despite the doubts of the territorial Government, which objected to anomalies such as the Centre retaining control of law and order in the capital). Dixit's advocacy of popular participation in government, of safety for women and of 'greening' the city were more popular, particularly among women voters, and on 1 December Congress won a convincing victory, securing 47 of the 70 seats in the Assembly. The rejection of the BJP, the leadership of which Khurana had resigned after the territorial poll, was confirmed at the general election of May 2004, when all but one of the NCT's Lok Sabha seats also fell to Congress. Congress won two by-elections in October. In April 2005, however, some dissidents in the local party distressed the Chief Minister with their criticism of her style of leadership. Within a week the national leadership had resolved the dispute—Dixit was too popular a leader to lose. However, rivalry between Dixit and, particularly, local Congress head (since 2004) Rambubu Sharma continued to bedevil the party, prompting the national leadership to reprimand both politicians in September 2006. In August 2007 a land scandal involving officers of the territory was seized on not only by the BJP to criticize Dixit, but also by one of her ministers, Ashok Walia, and his supporters, although the national leadership again seemed determined to maintain party harmony. Meanwhile, Khurana had been found guilty of defaming Dixit in 2003, with allegations of corruption, and in July was criticized by the national leadership of the BJP after demanding the resignation of the party chief, L. K. Advani. In early September Advani's supporters expelled Khurana from the BJP, but he apologized and was reinstated after the intervention of the former Prime Minister, Atal Bihari Vajpayee.

By the second half of 2006 the BJP was concentrating on criticizing Congress, given the approach of municipal elections in 2007 and with the controversial progress of the sealing and demolition drives in the conurbation. The Supreme Court had been warning the municipal authorities about illegal commercial establishments in residential areas since 2005 and, in February 2006, ordered violations of the 2001 Delhi Master Plan to be dealt with. By May the city authorities had sealed 13,000 commercial establishments and protests by the traders were becoming increasingly agitated. Many illegally built developments were demolished. The courts remained adamant, despite appeals by the Centre, which was seeking to introduce an updated plan by January 2007. Violence in September, in which three people lost their lives, helped persuade the courts to delay further sealing during Diwali and until the end of October, but between 8 November and the end of the month more than 2,300 establishments were sealed, as the authorities resumed the drive. The Government sought to mitigate some of the effects, but was powerless against the court until a new plan was introduced, despite appeals from all sides of the political spectrum, including Chief Minister Dixit (who distanced herself from the sealing drives, declaring them in the jurisdiction of the Congress political chief, Sharma). Although the new Delhi Master Plan 2021 was officially notified in the first week of February 2007 and a populist move to regularize thousands of traders and settlements endorsed by the Government, Congress was punished in the elections to the Municipal Corporation of Delhi—the BJP won 164 of the 272 seats, with only 69 for Congress. Dixit blamed Sharma, who blamed the sealings drive, which the new authorities were still obliged to continue, albeit under the new regulations. The central authorities were only able to suspend the sealing and demolition programme in February 2008, declaring that no further actions would be taken for the rest of the year. The timing may have had something to do with the territorial legislative elections being scheduled for September. Congress was still strong in the city, but was not opposed by the BJP alone. The rising star of Mayawati and her Bahujan Samaj Party (BSP) had become a palpable threat to Congress by the beginning of 2008, the dalit Chief Minister of Uttar Pradesh having demonstrated in her home state the BSP's ability to co-opt the traditional Congress vote banks.

## ECONOMY

The National Capital Territory (NCT) of Delhi is one of the richest of the territories and states of India, with a varied economy still obviously strong in government services, but leavened by financial, commercial and industrial activities. In August 2004 its various advantages put it second in the *India Today* ranking of the best small states and territories in the country (after Puducherry—then known as Pondicherry). Between 1991 and 1998 alone the territorial economy had grown, in real terms, by some 21%, and high rates of growth continued (8.2% in 2000/01, for instance, or 9.3% in 2002/03), helping to keep pace with the growth in population. In 2004/05 net domestic product, in current prices, was Rs 830,850m. (Delhi accounted for 3.3% of the national economy). Current income per head was Rs 53,976. The NCT's economy was bigger than that of any other territory or of 18 states, while in per caput terms only Goa, Chandigarh and (since 2002/03) Puducherry were richer. Always strategically located, the NCT enjoys a central location on the country's road and rail networks, and has three airports, three railway stations and three bus stations. The total length of roads in the NCT was 28,508 km. The first line of the Delhi Metro, an urban railway, was begun in 1988 and opened in three stages, most recently in July 2005 (work was continuing on a third line, to open in December, with the first phase of the whole project due to be completed by March 2006). With a massive growth in population, traffic and pollution were increasing problems in the city, however, throughout the 1990s and into the 2000s (1.2m. vehicles were registered in the NCT at the end of March 2003). Problems remain into the 2000s, but, since 1998, after judicial and government intervention, falls in levels of pollution were recorded, although some indicators began to increase again from 2001, and Delhi remains one of the most polluted cities in the world (in terms of suspended particulate matter). One contribution to improving air quality has been the enforced conversion of buses, taxis and auto-rickshaws to consume compressed natural gas rather than diesel, although there were problems in supply. The NCT generates less than one-half of the electricity it needs (all from thermal plants), but, although demand is increasing, the city can afford to import the rest from central-government plants and neighbouring states. Installed capacity amounted to 3,513 MW in May 2006, of which only 27% came from the territory's own resources and the rest from its share from the Centre's sector (and barely 0.1 MW from private sources). The NCT is fully electrified and 60% of rural households had electricity in 2005. The literacy rate in Delhi rose from 75.3% of the population in 1991 to 81.8% in 2001.

State estimates put the contribution of the primary sector to the net domestic product of the territory at only 1.5% in 2001/02. Agriculture is not an important contributor to the economy of the NCT. The net area sown in 2002/03 was 29,116 ha. Although wheat is still the major food crop (137,940 metric tons in 2002/03), vegetables and fruits, and dairy and poultry farming are now encouraged as more commercial, given the nearness of a major urban centre to supply. Likewise, 5,016 ha were devoted to floriculture at the end of March 2003. At the livestock census of 1997 there were 0.2m. head of buffaloes, 0.1m. cows and 25,358 goats. Livestock products in 2003/04 (anticipated production) included 296,000 tons of milk and 24.1m. eggs. In 2001 there were 111 sq km of forest and a further 40 sq km described as having tree cover, which are areas mainly used for recreational use, although there are protected areas.

The secondary sector of the economy accounted for an estimated 21.6% of net domestic product in 2001/02. Delhi is the largest centre in India for small industries (19,672 registered at the end of March 2003), but also has larger concerns. In 2003 there was a total of over 129,000 industrial units registered in the NCT, employing 1.4m. people. At the same time registered factories numbered 7,188. Since the late 1990s the city authorities had been favouring 'high technology' industries in electronics, computer software and the communications sectors. These depended on skilled work-forces and were less polluting. Moreover, in the post-1998 drive against pollution, many thousands of small, but illegal, industrial units were closed down by government order. Products currently made in the NCT include audiovisual equipment, razor blades, light-engineering manufactures and automobile parts, sports goods, textiles and leather working, and chemicals and pharmaceuticals.

In 2001/02 it was estimated that services, the tertiary sector of the territorial economy, provided an overwhelming 77.0% of net domestic product. In 2003/04 the tertiary contribution to gross domestic product was 78%; banking and insurance alone accounted for 22% and trade, restaurants and hotels for 21%. The city is the largest commercial centre in northern India, its status as the national capital not only attracting government expenditure on the central administration but activity from companies and financial institutions siting headquarters or main offices there. Delhi is also a major transport node, both of goods and of people. Many visitors are tourists, often high-spending foreign tourists, who start trips to India in the city or wish to visit local or nearby sights from its imperial legacies.

### DIRECTORY

**Lieutenant-Governor:** Tejendra Khanna, Secretariat, Raj Niwas, Delhi 110 054; tel. (11) 23975022; fax (11) 23937099.

**Chief Minister:** Sheila Dixit (Congress), AB-17, Mathura Road, New Delhi 110 001; tel. (11) 23392020; fax (11) 23392111; e-mail cmdelhi@ren02.nic.in.

**Speaker of the Legislative Assembly:** Ch. Prem Singh, F-301, Lado Sarai, Mehrauli, New Delhi; tel. (11) 23890140; fax (11) 23890375; the unicameral Legislative Assembly has 70 mems: Congress 47; Bharatiya Janata Party 20; Janata Dal (Secular) 1; Nationalist Congress Party 1; independent 1.

## Lakshadweep

The Union Territory of Lakshadweep, until 1973 known as the Laccadive, Minicoy and Amindivi Islands, lies in the Arabian Sea off the west coast of southern India, stretched across similar latitudes to the State of Kerala. Closer still, south of a maritime international border and the Eight Degrees Channel, is the Maldive Islands. The territory consists not of the '100,000 islands' suggested by the name (and, historically, probably also referred to the Maldives), but of 12 atolls, three reefs and five submerged banks. Another suggested origin of the name is that the islands were a landmark target (*laksh*) for ancient navigators across the Arabian Sea. Lakshadweep achieved its present, centrally administered status in 1956, when it was separated from the State of Madras (now Tamil Nadu). It is the smallest of all India's territories or states, with a land area of only 32 sq km (12.4 sq miles), although this somehow manages to enclose 4,200 sq km of lagoon waters (including open reefs, etc.) and to be strewn across 20,000 sq km of territorial waters. The largest of the 10 permanently inhabited islands is Minicoy (Maliku—4.4 sq km), followed by Kavaratti (3.6 sq km) and Kadmat (3.1 sq km). Androth, at 2.8 sq km, is the next largest inhabited island, although when bracketed with surrounding atolls into one of the nine units in Lakshadweep used, for instance, in the provisional census results of 2001, the Androth group had the largest land area, at 4.8 sq km. As single islands, Agatti (2.7 sq km) and Amini (2.6 sq km) follow in the size ranking among the inhabited islands, while the smallest one is Bitra (0.1 sq km), which can often disappear from separate enumeration (usually included with its neighbour to the east, the next smallest inhabited island, Chetlat).

The territory contains India's only coral atolls. It consists of the Laccadive Islands and of Minicoy, the latter one of the largest islands, but isolated south of the Nine Degree Channel, roughly on the latitude of the Keralan capital of Thiruvananthapuram. The Laccadives are themselves grouped into: the southern, Cannanore Islands, which are roughly on a latitude with Kochi (Cochin), a port of Kerala; a central group around the island of Kavaratti (containing the capital); and the northern Amindivi Islands, facing Kozhikode or Calicut (Kerala). A few more reefs and banks straggle northwards. Minicoy is 183 km south (and slightly west) of Kalpeni, in the Cannanores and its nearest neighbour, and 259 km south (and slightly east) of Kavaratti. Minicoy and Kavaratti are each just over 400 km from Kochi, while Kavaratti is only 346 km from Kozhikode. Coral atolls emerging above the ocean from their reef platforms and fertilized by guano (bird droppings) do not rise to a great height above sea level—nowhere above 4 m (13 ft)—and the territory is, therefore, vulnerable to the ongoing climatic changes produced by 'global warming'. The interiors of most of the atolls are thickly forested with coconut trees. The climate is tropical and generally humid, with rainfall usually over 1,600 mm (63 inches) per year, mainly falling during the south-west monsoons and slightly heavier in the south. Annual rainfall was below average in 2001 and even lower in 2002 (1,060 mm in Amini and 1,155 mm in Minicoy). March–May are the hottest months of the year, until the monsoons get under way; the average temperatures on Amini in 2002 ranged between a minimum of 25.2°C (77.4°F) and a maximum of 31.7°C (89.1°F), with Minicoy, as usual, recording a slightly lower average maximum.

The smallest territory of India in terms of population, as well as area, Lakshadweep had 60,650 people at the time of the March 2001 national census. According to the provisional results (60,595), the most populous island groupings were those of Androth (10,720), Kavaratti (10,113) and Minicoy (9,495), and the least populated, Chetlat (2,553). At the previous census, in terms of population, Bitra was the smallest single island, with 225 people; separate figures from the most recent count are not yet available. Bangaram has been developed for tourist use and, so, has a seasonal population working there (61 in 1991). The rate of population growth in Lakshadweep over the decade up to 2001 had fallen to below the national average, to 17.2% (compared to 28.5% in 1981–91). The population density was 1,895 per sq km (2001), owing to the scarcity of land. The most densely populated island in 2001 was Amini (2,834 per sq km), followed by Kavaratti (2,396 per sq km), while the least so was Kalpeni (1,548 per sq km). Ethnically, the people are related to the people of Kerala, and most speak a Malayalam dialect (84.5% in 1991). The exception is Minicoy, which is more closely influenced by the Maldives and where the people speak a Maldivean dialect sometimes called Mahl (written in the Dhivehi script of the Maldives), which shares common roots with Sinhalese. All the indigenous inhabitants are classed in the Scheduled Tribes (they constituted 94.5% of the total population in 2001). There are no Scheduled Castes on the islands, although three Hindu castes survive (landowners, farmers and sailors) despite the population's long adherence to Islam. According to the 2001 census, 95.5% of the population were Muslim (mostly of the Sunnite Shafi school, although there are also some Wahhabis, in Bada, on Minicoy), only 3.7% Hindu and 0.8% Christian. Another long-standing cultural trait of Lakshadweep is the high social status of women, a result of the matrilineal, Marumakkathayam system of inheritance (as in much of Kerala) and the economic independence bestowed by an inalienable share in the family's ancestral property (tharwad). In most of the Laccadives this property is managed by the eldest male member of the family, known as the karanavan, but in Minicoy the pre-eminence of women goes a stage further, preserved, maybe, as a result of the long tradition of seafaring on the island, with the men often away for long periods. On Minicoy, a man marries into the woman's family and adopts her name, while the village (ava or athiri) administrations have an important role for women, including a distinct chief (boduthatha).

According to the 2001 census, of the total population 44.5% were classified as urban (compared to 56.3% in 1991). The main settlements are on Kavaratti, the territorial capital, and on Androth, Amini and Minicoy. Lakshadweep constitutes only one district, but each of the 10 inhabited islands is meant to be seat to a panchayat village assembly. For administrative purposes the territory is divided into four tahsils (each under a tahsildar, except Minicoy, which has had a deputy collector since 1978).

## HISTORY

Local tradition and archaeological and anthropological evidence sometimes seem to conflict, but both are useful in looking at the early history of Lakshadweep. Certainly the islands receive their first written historical mention in records from the first century, after storms enabled a Greek sailor to find a direct route from the Arabian coast to southern India—he mentions the islands as a source for tortoiseshell. By the time of Chola claims to have subjected numerous islands (presumed to be the Maldives and at least part of Lakshadweep) early in the 11th century, the islands had probably become Muslim and were already under the influence of the nearby kingdoms of Kerala. Buddhist remains in Minicoy confirm links with the Maldives (Buddhist until the 12th century), while the people of the Laccadives bear many similarities to the Moplahs (Keralan Muslims). Early Muslim remains on the islands would seem to indicate some substance to the local legend purporting an early conversion to Islam, although some claim that this only happened around the 13th or 14th centuries. Other legends attribute settlement to the time of the last Chera high king, Cheraman Perumal Nayana (early 12th century), who abdicated his throne and set out for the Muslim holy city of Mecca (now in Saudi Arabia). Searchers for him were wrecked on Bangaram, thence making their way to Agatti, and they saw other islands on their way back to the mainland. Soldiers and sailors from the mainland were sent to settle the islands—initially, Androth, Kalpeni and Kavaratti, while another group settled on Amini. These people, in turn, later settled Agatti, Chetlat, Kadmat and Kiltan. They were Hindus and the modern society of Lakshadweep still consists of three castes, but it seems likely that their arrival in the islands predates the time of the great Keralan king. Certainly, in the tale of the Muslim saint and evangelizer, Hazrat Ubaidullah, there was an existing population, and that was in the seventh century (41 AH). Ubaidullah was also shipwrecked, on Amini, but then proceeded to preach the revelation of his Prophet, marrying a local girl and, despite at first being driven from Amini, going on to convert Androth and then the rest of the islands.

These local traditions and cultural remains at least confirm the existence of an island society exposed to outside influences, located, as it was, on the flourishing trade routes of the Indian Ocean. Thus, the seafaring traditions of the menfolk of Minicoy might already have become established by the 13th century, when the Venetian (Italian) traveller, Marco Polo, described its society as the 'female island'. It would not be unreasonable to assume an early exposure to Islam, from the Arab traders who dominated the sea-lanes. Cheras, Pandyas and Cholas all claimed the islands at some point, but by the time of Polo the Laccadives were administered in the name of mainland rulers. This also applied to Minicoy, which the records of the sultans of the Maldives indicate had fallen from their dominion by about 1500. In the 16th century it was to the Hindu rajahs of North Kolathiri, in their palace of Chirakkal near Kannur (Cannanore), in Kerala, that the islanders appealed for help against the depredations of the Portuguese. Europeans valued the coir fibre and the Portuguese raided the islanders for it, even occupying Amini for a time (the invaders were, apparently, defeated by poisoning). Responsibility for the Muslim islands was soon transferred to the head of the Moplah community in Kannur, the Ali Rajah, whose dynastic inheritance was received matrilineally through the Beebi (queen) of the Arrakal line (this branch of the ruling family was Kerala's only Muslim royal house). Arrakal rule, which was unpopular in Lakshadweep, survived longer on the so-called Malabar Coast of modern Kerala than that of the senior, Chirakkal kings, whose independence succumbed to the overlordship of Mysore (southern Karnataka) in the mid-18th century.

In 1743 the Dutch first made mention of 'Lekker-Diva', a name they used thereafter for Lakshadweep, and from which the English 'Laccadives' is derived. Meanwhile, the islanders were still looking to the native rulers on the mainland for help, with the people of Amini sending to the court of Mysore in 1783 for relief from Arrakal rule. In 1787 Tipu Sultan of Mysore, who was a friend of the Beebi of Arrakal, as well as a fellow Muslim, was able to grant the request of the northern islanders. The five Amindivi Islands (Amini, Kadmat, Kiltan, Chetlat and Bitra) were duly attached to his fief of Chirakkal and he appointed what few administrative officers the territory obtained. However, Tipu Sultan was the object of determined hostility from the British, and in 1791 they occupied Kannur and the possessions of the Beebi, so the southern islands were the first to fall under the nominal authority of the East India Company. Then, in 1799 Tipu Sultan's final defeat at Shrirangapattana (Srirangapattnam—now in Karnataka) meant that Chirakkal and the Amindivis were also awarded to the East India Company. In 1800 the new territories were transferred from the jurisdiction of the Bombay (now Mumbai, in Maharashtra) presidency to that of Madras (now Chennai, in Tamil Nadu), and grouped with other former territories of Mysore ceded to the British by the Nizam of Hyderabad (Andhra Pradesh). In effect, the northern islands also continued to be administered from Kannur.

An extremely severe cyclone in 1847 caused such damage in Lakshadweep that the East India Company, represented by Sir William Robinson, offered the rajah a loan to help cover the cost of restoration work in the islands. This was not an unusual arrangement and often served to expand the direct domains of the British in India—when loan payments fell behind, the rest of Lakshadweep fell to the East India Company in 1854, although they continued to be administered through the estate of the Beebi until 1875, when they were attached to the Malabar District. It was only in 1905 that the Laccadive Islands (including the Amindivi Islands) and Minicoy were formally annexed to British India. Some regularization of the administration and legal system was begun, notably under the 1912 Laccadives and Minicoy Regulation, when the first measures of a protective restriction on travel to the islands were also introduced. After independence, in 1956 the archipelago was transferred from the jurisdiction of Madras, when Malabar became part of the new state of Kerala. A referendum had favoured the solution of 1956, but there was some civil unrest on the islands thereafter, particularly in Minicoy, owing to the restriction of links with the Maldives (traditional visits and exchanges could be viewed as smuggling or illegal immigration). Moreover, legal reforms, such as those dealing with property ('land' ownership had been determined by a number of coconut trees rather than territorial area until 1959), provoked some disquiet among traditionalists. The Union Territory of the Laccadive, Minicoy and Amindivi Islands was the responsibility of the federal authorities, although its administrative headquarters remained on the mainland, in the Keralan city of Calicut (Kozhikode), until March 1964, when it was localized on Kavaratti. This accelerated the process of incorporating the territory into the framework of the Indian state. One year later what is now called the Lakshadweep (Laws) Regulation was introduced to govern the territory, which formally adopted its current name in 1973.

The territory's elected representatives sit in local government, but also include one member of the Lok Sabha, the lower house of the national Parliament. From 1967 (the first year the member was elected rather than nominated) until 2004 the national representative of Lakshadweep was P. M. Sayeed, a member of the Indian National Congress and a Deputy Speaker of the Lok Sabha in the 1999–2004 Parliament. However, in May 2004 Lakshadweep voted for Dr P. Pookunhikoya of the Janata Dal (United), who defeated Sayeed by only 71 votes (the smallest margin in the general election). Sayeed was, nevertheless, appointed a cabinet minister in the new Congress-led Government at the Centre, only to die in December 2005. A new administrator for Lakshadweep also took office in mid-2004, and another in August 2006, three months after the inauguration of the 50th anniversary celebrations of Lakshadweep becoming a Union Territory. However, Rajendra Kumar only held office until the appointment of a new Administrator, B. V. Selvaraj, in December.

## ECONOMY

The Union Territory of Lakshadweep has an economy based on commercial as well as subsistence agriculture and fishing, although remittances from locals working abroad (e.g. sailors serving on international shipping lines) and, increasingly, tourism are important contributors to the money economy. This remains relatively small and many financial statistics, such as net domestic product, are not regularly produced for the territory. Other statistics reveal small, but significant, numbers. Thus, although in 1998/99 there were roads totalling 253 km (124 km surfaced or concreted) in length, the more important shipping figures reveal a thorough network of inter-island and mainland links. An airport on Agatti also provides links to the mainland and a centre for inter-island helicopter services. There were 10 telephone exchanges, giving 8,679 connections (143 telephones per 1,000 of estimated population, at March 2003). There was an installed electrical capacity of 9,965 kW in May 2005 (most of it thermally generated, but there are also solar and wave-power schemes, all government owned), while all the inhabited islands, including the seasonally occupied resort island of Bangaram, were electrified (51% of rural households had a supply). The literacy rate is good, at 87.5% in 2001, one of the highest rates in India. On Minicoy the rate was just over 93.0%, while even in Kiltan, which had the lowest literacy rate in Lakshadweep, it was 83.7%.

Coral atolls are not favourable places for extensive agriculture, but the thin, guano-fertilized soil layer supports sufficient vegetables and fruit trees to supplement an islander's fish diet. In 2002/03 the total cropped area on the islands was 2,575 ha, although this included the parts forested by coconut trees. The main agricultural commodity of Lakshadweep is coconut, with 53.1m. harvested in 2002/03. The main products are coir (fibre from the husks) and copra (the dried kernel, from which coconut oil can be extracted). In the same year 98 metric tons of fruits and 42 tons of vegetables were produced (from 72 ha). The agricultural census of 1997 also revealed livestock to be of increasing importance to the local population, with numbers having reached 78,579 poultry, 31,857 goats and 3,339 cattle by then. In 2003/04 anticipated egg production had risen to 7.6m. for the year (still below the 7.9m. of three years earlier, but steadily rising from the 6.7m. of 2001/02). Milk production was developed in the 2000s, and was expected to reach 8,000 tons in 2003/04.

Lakshadweep's environment and extensive waters are rich in marine life and fishing has long been important to the islanders' welfare. The development of a fishing fleet and more mechanized exploitation of the deeps has swelled the importance of the catch in a modern economy. From a catch of just some 600 metric tons in 1960, by 1998/99 the amount of fish landed totalled 14,626 tons. This was a record catch, up from the around 10,000 tons landed per year for much of the previous decade (that mark was exceeded for the first time in 1996). In 2001/02 the total catch was 12,800 tons, but it was only 9,141 tons the next year. The numbers of fishermen had risen to 8,060 and of boats to 640 in 2002/03; Agatti and Kavaratti are the main centres, then Androth, then Minicoy. Overwhelmingly the most important part of the catch (73% in 2002/03) was tuna (tunny fish), the 'chicken of the sea', although shark was also widely fished.

Industry is limited and of recent origin on the islands, what there is being largely based on the processing of agricultural (coconut) and fishing products. Government figures for 1998/99 recorded 17 working factories, employing an average of 287 workers daily. In 2002/03 there were 93 permanently registered and 102 provisionally registered small-scale private industrial units, as well as, in the government sector, seven coir-fibre factories (with production of 248 metric tons), six coir production centres (34 tons), one hosiery unit (5,879 items) and a handicraft centre (171 items). There are industrial co-operative societies and an industrial training institute. By the end of the 1990s the two boat yards, on Kavaratti and on Chetlat, were the only remnants of a proud boat-building tradition in the islands, although the importance of the sea in the local economy is still attested by the flourishing tuna-canning factory on Minicoy. Otherwise, the main manufacturing activity is confined to the handicraft centres (especially on Kavaratti) and to the textile and coir plants that operate on several islands.

Government investment and activity remain important to the territory's economy. The most important development in the tertiary sector, however, has been the tourist industry. Its growth is limited by a need to conserve the environment, which is the territory's appeal, and was initially slow because of transport problems. Tourist numbers are erratic, and can vary widely, but have shown a general increase since the mid-1980s and particularly from the end of that decade. Domestic tourists reached 3,841 in 1991/92, but usually numbered above or near the 3,000 mark thereafter. Foreign tourist numbers peaked in the year before domestic tourist numbers reached their record, at 2,764 in 1990/91, remaining above 1,000 throughout the 1990s, except for the 408 of 1993/94. Numbers visiting from abroad declined in the late 1990s and into the 2000s, so that the domestic market came to be of increasing importance. By 2002/03 there were 4,151 domestic tourists and 580 foreign tourists, to give a total of 4,731 (from 3,798 in the previous year). The beauty of the islands is augmented by water-sports facilities and interesting local cultures, as well as a few sights, such as some of the 52 mosques of Kavaratti or the lighthouse on Minicoy.

### DIRECTORY

**Administrator:** B. V. SELVARAJ, Central Secretariat, Kavaratti 682 555; tel. (4896) 262255; fax (4896) 262184; e-mail lk-admin@ hub.nic .in.

**Member of Parliament (in New Delhi) for Lakshadweep:** Dr PALLICHAPURA POOKUNHIKOYA (Janata Dal—United), Parliament House, New Delhi 110 001; Constituency Office: Amini.

**Liaison Officer in New Delhi:** ASARPAL SINGH, F-301, Curzon Road Hostel, K. G. Marg, New Delhi 110 001; tel. (11) 23386807; fax (11) 23782246.

## Puducherry

The Union Territory of Puducherry (formerly known as Pondicherry) consists of four groups of enclaves dotted around the coast of southern India. The enclaves comprised French India, headquartered in the 'new village' of Puducherry, until 1954, when they were transferred to Indian administration, formally becoming integral parts of the country in 1963, when Puducherry adopted its current status. Puducherry, itself a patchwork of enclaves, and Karaikal are on the eastern coast, surrounded by Tamil Nadu, while much further north Yanam is strung along a riverbank in the Godavari delta of Andhra Pradesh and, on the west coast of India, surrounded by Kerala, is Mahe. The total area of the territory is 480 sq km (185 sq miles), of which Karaikal contributes 160 sq km, Mahe only 9 sq km and Yanam 30 sq km.

All of the Union Territory's regions are on flat, coastal land, although Mahe town is sited on a low hill. Puducherry, the territorial capital, is on the Coromandel Coast, north of the Ponnaivar river, presiding over a collection of blocks and pockets of territory mingled with enclaves of surrounding Tamil Nadu state. The town of Puducherry is 162 km (101 miles) south of Chennai (formerly Madras), the capital of Tamil Nadu, and 22 km north of another Tamil Nadu city, Cuddalore. Further south, also on the Bay of Bengal, 132 km from the territorial capital, is the more compact region of Karaikal, on the Kaveri delta. To the north and east, 870 km from Puducherry, lies its enclave of Yanam, surrounded by Andhra Pradesh. The town and a few attached villages are some 14 km inland from the mouths of the mighty Godavari, where the Koringa (Atreya) branch separates from the Gauthami. On the other side of the Indian peninsula (westwards, 653 km overland from Puducherry), on the Malabar Coast, is the smallest enclave of the territory, Mahe (formerly Mahé). It comprises Mahe town on the south bank of the eponymous river, which flows into the Arabian Sea from the south-east, Kallayi on the north bank and, beyond the main coastal road, stretching further north to the Ponniyar (Moolakadavu) river, Naluthara. The climate of the territory is tropical, the east coast settlements getting most of their rain between October and December and temperatures usually ranging between 21°C (70°F) and 42°C (108°F). Mahe shares the more tempered climate of Kerala, which does not have a totally dry season (its highest rainfall is between June and September) and where maximum temperatures seldom exceed 32°C (90°F).

The results of the 2001 census put the total population of the Union Territory of Puducherry at 974,345, giving an average population density of 2,030 per sq km. In 1991 the total had been 807,785, including 145,703 people in Karaikal, 33,447 in Mahe and 20,297 in Yanam. The people are characteristic of the areas their enclaves neighbour, with Tamil being the main language (89.2% of the population in 1991), but Malayalam being spoken more widely in Mahe (by 4.8% of the territorial population in 1991) and Telugu particularly in Yanam (4.3%). Hindi, French and English are also spoken. Most people are Hindu (86.8% in 2001), but there are significant Christian (7.0%) and Muslim (6.1%) minorities, as well as almost 1,000 Jains and some Sikhs and Buddhists. In 2001 there were no registered tribal peoples, but 16.2% of the population were of the Scheduled Castes.

Puducherry has a very urban population, with 66.6% of the total classed as such in 2001. The main towns are Puducherry, Karaikal, Mahe and Yanam, which also provide the headquarters for the four main regions into which the territory is divided.

### HISTORY

The Union Territory of Puducherry is a legacy of the remnants of the French empire in India, what was left to them of their trading stations after their defeat by the British in the 18th century. However, there is also evidence of older links with Europe—6 km from Puducherry town, at the site of Arikamedu, a port that hosted a thriving first-century trade with the Roman Empire (the site of another such port, Kaveripatnam, is not far from Karaikal). Before that, Puducherry has been identified as Vedapuri, a centre of Vedic learning, and as Podhigai, the home of a famous savant, Agastya Muni, around 1500 BC. Some 3,000 years later, having continued to flourish under the Cholas and Vijayanagar (from the beginning of the 16th century AD under the nayaks of Thanjavur), Puducherry itself finally fell under Muslim rule from Bijapur. This was succeeded by nominal Mughal overlordship in the 17th century and, later, Puducherry attracted the attention of the French, late come among Europeans to the subcontinent.

In 1673 the French established their oldest station at Chandernagore (now in West Bengal) and, one year later, what was to be their capital at Puducherry, acquired from local rulers nominally subordinate to the Mughals. Although the British were to be their main rivals, initially the French and British East India Companies tended to avoid following their countries into war and it was the Dutch who proved most troublesome on the Coromandel Coast in the 17th century. The Dutch seized Puducherry in 1693, but returned the fort, augmented by its immediate surroundings, under the Treaty of Ryswick in 1699. The first of three great governors, François Martin, then resumed office (until December 1706—in all, he was administrator for 33 years) and consolidated French rule in the area, adding the village of Kalapet (originally in order to gain access to timber needed for building work) from the local Mughal nawab, Dawood Khan, in 1703. This piecemeal addition of neighbouring villages and estates continued in the 18th century, contributing to the fragmented nature of Puducherry. The Puducherry region acquired more villages from the nawab in 1706, while Sardar Ali of Arcot (Tamil Nadu), gifted another group in September 1740, when Pierre-Benoît Dumas was Governor (1734–41) and gave refuge from Maratha assailants to the court of Arcot. French India was to be more ambitious, however, under Dumas' successor, Joseph François Dupleix (1742–54), and his able general, Charles de Bussy, when the simmering rivalry with the British broke out into open conflict. Indeed, in 1746 the French seized Madras (now Chennai, the capital of Tamil Nadu), although it was restored to the British two years later, after peace had been concluded in Europe. Henceforth, however, the two powers would continue their conflicts through the medium of local magnates, notably during the wars of succession for Hyderabad (Andhra Pradesh) and its subsidiary nawab of Arcot (whose lands, known as the Carnatic, surrounded Puducherry and Madras). Although the British candidate gained Arcot, it was the French protégé, Muzaffar Jang, who became Nizam of Hyderabad and, in 1750, he granted to Puducherry the inland enclave of Villianur and a number of other villages which took the borders up to the Ponnaivar.

Meanwhile, the other enclaves had also been added to French jurisdiction. In the north, on the Andhran coast ruled from Hyderabad, the French had a 'factory' at Machilipatnam, and in 1723 this operation established a warehouse in what they called Yanam. It was abandoned in 1727, seized back in 1731 and properly re-established in 1742. Various grants and concessions were made by local rulers, but the 1750 grant of Muzaffar Jang, with sovereignty two years later, was probably definitive and the town then acquired importance during French rule of the Andhran coast of the so-called North Circars (and, thereafter, remained a centre of intrigue for local rajahs disaffected with the British). Certainly the French ultimately retained Yanam alone on this stretch of coast. In 1725 Mahé de Labourdonnais captured a town on the Malabar Coast of modern Kerala for France, and it and the river that emptied into the sea there were named for him. Finally, Karaikal was acquired in 1739, although Governor Martin had previously tried to establish a post in Thanjavur not long after the whole area had gained a Maratha ruler in 1675. Then, in 1738 the Subha of Thanjavur agreed to sell Karaikal, the fortress of Karakalachcheri and five villages to the French, only to renege on the deal before they could take possession. The French candidate for the throne of Arcot thereupon occupied the region and it was formally handed over to the French governor on St Valentine's Day, 1739. Intrigues and negotiations continued into the following year, adding to the villages dependent upon Karaikal, and a Mughal grant confirmed French possession in 1741. In 1750, despite often strained relations with the Thanjavur court, a final settlement of territory in Karaikal was made, and it was this territory that was surrendered to the British in 1761. This is not insignificant, as it was what the French had possessed after the settlement of 1763 that was restored to them when a final peace in Europe was concluded after the series of Revolutionary and Napoleonic Wars. The British had occupied all the territories that now constitute Puducherry in 1761, 1778 (restored in 1785) and 1793. The peace agreement of 1814 agreed to restore Puducherry and its dependencies to France, and this was effected in 1816.

In the 19th century trade was no longer as lucrative for Puducherry, but the territory integrated into the local economies and, from 1826, the French authorities successfully encouraged the development of industry (textiles). An echo of the days of imperial struggle 'by proxy' and of Indians utilizing the Franco–British rivalry was later heard when nationalists could find sanctuary in Puducherry from the Raj authorities. Most famously, the Bengali social and religious reformer, Aurobindo Ghose, was to take refuge here in 1910 (after a 1908 conviction for condoning terrorism). A pacifist, with a concept of 'Mother India' that united religion and nationalism, Ghose founded an ashram in Puducherry that became a centre for his Indian and internationalist ideals. His companion and chief disciple from 1920 until his death in 1950 (before French India was reunited with the rest of the country) was a Frenchwoman, Mirra Alfassa ('the Mother'), who was a prominent figure in Puducherry until her own death in 1973. She organized the foundation of nearby Auroville (actually in Tamil Nadu), a city that seeks to further Aurobindo's community ethics and hopes, in 1968. Other nationalist refugees in Puducherry included the poet, Subramania Bharathi, and V. V. C. Iyer. In 1918 the French authorities refused a request from British India to extradite Ghose and other nationalists. Mahatma Gandhi visited Puducherry in 1934, Jawaharlal Nehru in 1939.

French imperial rule in India was to outlast that of the British, although not by long. The Bengali settlement of Chandernagore, virtually a northern suburb of Calcutta (now Kolkata, West Bengal), was to join the Indian Union separately. Almost two years after independence, in June 1949 a referendum in Chandernagore favoured merging with India, and France agreed two months later. Effectively this happened in May 1950, although the treaty formalizing the transfer was only signed on 2 February 1951. Generally, the French authorities seem to have accepted the inevitability of the union with India (in 1948 France and India had agreed to present a popular choice to the people of the territories, while the governor was redesignated a commissioner). Certainly, there was no great popular agitation after a number of civil disturbances by nationalists in the late 1940s, although in 1950 a French naval vessel was obliged to intervene in Mahé—now Mahe—after local crowds replaced the French with the Indian tricolour on the government building. Pressure increased in 1954, as the date for a democratic decision by the people of French India approached. In March two enclaves of the Puducherry region were 'liberated' and in May a 'French India Liberation Government' was proclaimed. However, on 18 October 170 out of 178 elected representatives voted in a secret ballot for merger with India. On 1 November an Indian High Commissioner, Kewal Singh, took over the administration of the territory from the last French governor (Commissioner), André Ménard. France formally ceded sovereignty on 16 August 1962, when the Instruments of Ratification were finally exchanged.

The *de jure* incorporation of Puducherry and its dependencies formalized, India could proceed with integrating the territory and enacting its treaty obligations to the people of former French India. In 1963 the Union Territory of Pondicherry legally became an integral part of the Republic of India, while the national Parliament had passed the Government of Union Territories Act, providing for representative territorial legislatures and democratic government. Until the implementation of the National Capital Territory Act of 1991, Puducherry was the only territory to have a Legislative Assembly and a Chief Minister (the first, Edouard Goubert, took office on 1 July 1963) and to send a representative to the upper house of Parliament, as well as to the lower house. A member of the Dravida Munnetra Kazhagam (DMK) occupied the Rajya Sabhya seat from 1997, when the DMK dominated the Legislative Assembly (which elects the upper house member), while the party allegiance of the Lok Sabha member reflected the more recent electoral successes of Congress in Puducherry. Displaced from power in May 1996 by the DMK (a Tamil party favouring less power for the centre), under R. V. Janakaviraman, Congress returned to power in 2000, even before the next territorial election. The Tamil Maanila Congress (TMC) left the DMK-led coalition in March 2000, so Congress formed an administration under a compromise candidate, who was not a member of the Legislative Assembly at the time, P. Shanmugam (his cabinet included the first Mahe representative in the cabinet in 38 years).

In the territorial elections of 10 May 2001 Congress emerged as the largest single party (11 seats) and, with its TMC electoral allies, commanded 13 seats to the DMK-led alliance's 12 seats (the DMK with seven, the Puducheri Makkal Congress with four and the Bharatiya Janata Party with its first seat in the territory). There were subsequently some alterations in the balance of party allegiances among the deputies, but Congress was able to continue in government. However, Shanmugam had not contested the election and no Congress deputy could be persuaded to resign a seat in favour of the premier, so, under the Constitution, he could not hold office for more than six months. In October he resigned and N. Rangaswamy was elected to replace Shanmugam as Congress leader; he duly became the ninth Chief Minister of Puducherry later in the month, although at the beginning of 2003 there were reports that he was not popular with the national leadership of his party. However, his administration was perceived to be competent, so his office was secure. Moreover, mainly as a result of wider developments in Tamil Nadu and nationally, Congress support was consolidated by its merger with the TMC in August 2003 and its alliance with the DMK, which had left the ruling coalition. Towards the end of the year a secular alliance was established, opposed to Tamil Nadu's ruling All-India Anna DMK (AIADMK) and its Bharatiya Janata Party (BJP) partner. This opposition grouping was completed in January 2004 by the withdrawal of the Pattali Makkal Katchi (PMK) from association with the AIADMK-BJP coalition. It was the PMK that was allotted the candidacy for the Puducherry seat in the DMK-led alliance, despite local Congress discontent, particularly when it was ruling the territory. Congress, however, had held the territory's Rajya Sabha seat since October 2003. The PMK candidate was duly elected to the Lok Sabha in May 2004, as part of the massive surge of support for the secular parties in Tamil Nadu, although in Puducherry it was mainly local issues (notably law and order) that were the subject of campaigning. At the territorial elections of May 2006 the balance of power in the Assembly remained unaltered, with Congress having 10 seats and the DMK its seven, but reinforced by two for the PMK and one for the Communist Party of India (CPI). AIADMK and its partners retained seven seats (AIADMK kept its three and Puducheri Makkal Congress representation fell to three as well, while the Marumalarchi DMK gained a seat), but the BJP lost its seat. Rangaswamy remained Chief Minister, but formed a coalition Government. Also, later in May, the Union Government agreed to introduce legislation implementing the territorial administration's desire to change the territory's name to Puducherry. This proposal became law in September and officially took effect on 1 October. By 2008 a Congress group opposed to Rangaswamy had gained allies. In August the political crisis became overt when five ministers refused to continue in office under his premiership, although he was initially supported by the national Congress leadership.

## ECONOMY

The Union Territory of Puducherry enjoys a similar level of prosperity to its neighbours, the states of southern India (higher than Andhra Pradesh and Kerala, but slightly lower than Tamil Nadu). In August 2004 its various advantages put it first in the *India Today* ranking of the best small states and territories in the country in which to work and live. Owing to the extent of government support for a small territory, official figures for the size of the economy can distort the picture of economic realities—since the mid-1990s Puducherry has been the richest territorial unit in India after Goa, Chandigarh and Delhi, but overtook Delhi in 2002/03. Strong real growth had persisted into the 2000s, and the territory recorded a net domestic product in 2004/05, in current prices, of Rs 58,390m., while income per head was estimated at Rs 56,034. Infrastructure, at least in the Puducherry and Karaikal regions, is relatively good, with many road connections and a total territorial network of 2,251 km (1,398 miles). In 1998 there were 24.7 km of national highway, 68.8 km of state highways, 225.4 km of district and other roads and 257.7 km of rural roads. Since 1869 Puducherry town and Villianur have been connected by a metre-gauge railway line to Villupuram (Tamil Nadu), 40 km from Puducherry, from where there is a broad-gauge connection to Chennai (formerly Madras, Tamil Nadu). The Karaikal branch line, opened in 1898, has an unreliable service, frequently cancelled, while Mahe and Yanam do not have their own stations (the nearest station to Mahe is some 10 km to the north, at Thalassery in Kerala, and the nearest to Yanam is 26 km, also to the north, at Kakinada in Andhra Pradesh). The main international airport serving Puducherry is in Chennai, although Hyderabad (Andhra Pradesh) is also accessible for Yanam, while Kozhikode (Kerala) is 64 km from Mahe. There is a domestic airport at Puducherry, but the other regions do not have their own, although each is near to a facility in a neighbouring state. The installed electricity capacity in the territory is provided mainly by the Centre (142.0 MW in 2005), but there is also some private provision (32.5 MW). Of rural households, 51% had electricity. Literacy in the territory increased from 74.7% of the total population in 1991 to 81.5% in 2001. The territory suffered from the tsunami of 26 December 2004, which killed 107 in Puducherry and 492 in Karaikal, as well as causing considerable damage and leaving 30,000 people homeless.

About 45% of the territorial population is engaged in agriculture and allied pursuits (1997 figure). However, the primary sector is not a major contributor to the overall economy—in 2003/04, according to official estimates made in the 2005 budget speech, the sector contributed only 5.1% of the territory's net domestic product. Agriculture and animal husbandry accounted for 3.0% of the total, and fisheries for 1.8%. Agriculture is a particularly important activity in Karaikal, in terms of both employment and output. All the regions benefit from rich, coastal alluvial soil (except for Mahe, where the red laterite soil is unsuitable for growing the paddy rice staple) and good water supplies (Karaikal used to depend on the flooding of the Kaveri, but now on canals; however, Yanam has limited irrigation, being dependent on the old French Kalva, a canal—its available land area makes significant investment in irrigation unlikely). Rice is the main crop of the regions on the east coast, but the soil is also suitable for pulses and groundnuts, with chillies, spices, sunflowers, cotton, coconuts and vegetables also being grown. Rice and fish are the main exports of Yanam, rice of Karaikal and fish of Mahe. All three regions benefit from rich estuarine fishing grounds, the industry in Mahe being helped by a fish-curing plant built in 1961. The Puducherry region also has an important primary sector, but its economy is more varied and its population more urbanized, so the sector does not carry the same weight here. Crops from this region not only include paddy rice and groundnuts, but also sugar cane and cotton. Livestock in the territory as a whole is important locally, with production including 38,000 metric tons of milk in 2002/03 and 9.6m. eggs. Fishing families were the most severely affected by the tsunami of December 2004, not only in terms of loss of lives and homes, but also because some 6,700 craft were damaged; 792 ha of agricultural land were also affected. There is little forestry in the territory, while the extractive sector is minimal, such activity as there is being confined to some building materials.

The French developed some industrial activity in Puducherry, mainly textiles, but the sector only employed some 8,000 by the time the administration was assumed by India. Total investment of some Rs 12,560m. over the rest of the century meant that this figure had risen to 71,955 as of the end of March 1999. Most of this activity, which had broadened beyond textiles, was concentrated in the Puducherry region, although there was some based in Karaikal, and Yanam produces cement pipes. There is agro-processing and the production of alcoholic beverages, while other products include automobile parts, chemicals, washing machines, computer components and plastic items. The sector suffered from the introduction of the uniform sales tax and, potentially more so, from the entry tax included in the March 2002 Tamil Nadu state budget, which was considered likely to be most serious in its consequences for the manufacturers of paper and of ceramics and tiles. The secondary sector remained the largest contributor to territorial income, accounting for 49.2% of net domestic product in 2003/04.

Services provided 45.8% of net domestic product in 2003/04. Tourism is an important activity in Puducherry, which receives a large proportion of the country's foreign visitors. The territory receives about 0.5m. tourist visits per year, with some 25,000 being foreigners, as well as many short visits. Again, most of the tourist industry is based in the Puducherry region, although it is also important for Mahe. People are attracted by the French cultural and historical legacy, the beaches and the presence of nearby Auroville. The tsunami of December 2004 not only killed around 600 people in the territory, but also damaged tourist facilities and, more importantly, adversely affected booking numbers.

## DIRECTORY

**Lieutenant-Governor:** GOVIND SINGH GURJAR, Raj Nivas (Government House), Puducherry 605 001; tel. (413) 2334051; fax (413) 2334025; e-mail lg@pondy.pon.nic.in.

**Regional Administrator (District Collector) (Karaikal):** SUDIR KUMAR, Regional Executive Office (UT Government), Karaikal 609 602; tel. (4368) 222444; fax (4368) 222025; e-mail reo@kkl.pon.nic.in.

**Regional Administrator (Mahe):** KRISHNA KUMAR SINGH, Regional Executive Office (UT Government), Mahe (Puducherry UT); tel. (490) 2332720; fax (490) 2332906; e-mail reo@mahe.pon.nic.in.

**Regional Administrator (Yanam):** Y. LAKSHMI NARAYANA REDDY, Regional Executive Office (UT Government), Yanam (Puducherry UT); tel. (884) 2321223; fax (884) 2321843; e-mail reo@kkl.pon.nic.in.

**Chief Minister:** V. VAITHILINGAM (Congress), Chief Minister's Secretariat, Goubert Salai (Beach Rd), Puducherry 605 001; tel. (413) 2333399; fax (413) 2333135; e-mail cm@pondy.pon.nic.in.

**Speaker of the Legislative Assembly:** R. RADHAKRISHNAN, Legislative Assembly Building, Puducherry 605 001; tel. (413) 2338373; fax (413) 2332397; e-mail secretary@satyam.net.in; the unicameral Legislative Assembly has 30 mems: Congress 10; Dravida Munnetra Kazhagam 7; All-India Anna Dravida Munnetra Kazhagam 3; Puduchcheri Makkal Congress 3; Pattali Makkal Katchi 2; Communist (CPI) 1; Marumalarchi Dravida 1; and 3 independents.

**Resident Commissioner in New Delhi:** N. SATYAVATHY, Puducherry House, 3 S. P. Marg, Chanakyapuri, New Delhi 110 021; tel. (11) 26118174; fax (11) 26118195.

# Bibliography


**General**

Acharya, S. *Can India Grow Without Bharat?*. New Delhi, Academic Foundation, 2007.

Allchin, F. R., and Allchin, B. *The Rise of Civilisation in India and Pakistan*. Cambridge, Cambridge University Press, 1983.

Allen, Charles. *The Buddha and the Sahibs*. London, John Murray, 2002.

Ayres, Alyssa, and Oldenburg, Philip K. (Eds). *India Briefing: Takeoff at Last?* Armonk, NY, M. E. Sharpe, 2005.

Bagga, R. K., Keniston, Kenneth, and Mathur, Rohit Raj (Eds). *The State, IT and Development*. London, Sage Publications, 2005.

Basham, A. L. *The Wonder that was India*. New York, Hawthorn, 1963.

*A Cultural History of India*. Oxford, Clarendon Press, 1957.

Butalia, Urvashi (Ed.). *Speaking Peace: Women's Voices from Kashmir*. New Delhi, Kali for Women, 2002.

Chopra, Radhika, and Jeffery, Patricia (Eds). *Educational Regimes in Contemporary India*. London, Sage Publications, 2005.

Crawley, W., and Page, David. *Satellites over South Asia: Broadcasting Culture and the Public Interest*. London, Sage Publications, 2001.

Crossette, Barbara. *India: Facing the Twenty-First Century*. Bloomington, IN, Indiana University Press, 1993.

De Bary, W. Theodore (Ed.). *Sources of Indian Tradition*. 2 vols. New York and London, Columbia University Press, 1958.

Deol, Harnik. *Religion and Nationalism in India: The Case of Punjab*. London, Routledge, 2000.

Europa Publications. *The Territories and States of India*. London, Europa Publications, 2002.

Frey, Karsten. *India's Nuclear Bomb and National Security*. Abingdon, Routledge, 2006.

Fuller, Dorian. *The Emergence of Agriculture in South India*. London, UCL Press, 2005.

Ganesh, Kamala, and Thakkar, Usha (Eds). *Culture and the Making of Identity in Contemporary India*. New Delhi, Sage Publications, 2005.

George, Abraham. *India Untouched: The Forgotten Face of Rural Poverty*. Cranston, RI, Writers' Collective, 2005.

Gopal, Kusum. 'Mythical Rights and Land Rights in Northern India', in Abrahamson, A., and Theodosopolous, D. (Eds), *Land, Law and Environment*. London, Pluto Press, 2000.

Gosling, David L. *Science and the Indian Tradition: When Einstein Met Tagore*. Abingdon, Routledge, 2007.

Henige, David P. *Princely States of India: A Guide to Chronology and Rulers*. Bangkok, Orchid Press, 2005.

Hollander, Julia. *Indian Folk Theatres*. Abingdon, Routledge, 2007.

Joshi, A. P., Srinivas, M. D., and Bajaj, J. K. *Religious Demography of India*. Chennai, Centre for Policy Studies, 2003.

Khilnani, Sunil. *The Idea of India*. London, Hamish Hamilton, 1997.

Kundu, Amitabh. *A Handbook of Urbanization in India*. New Delhi, Oxford University Press India, 2005.

Lal, Deepak. *The Hindu Equilibrium, Vol. I: Cultural Stability and Economic Stagnation in India (1500 BC–AD 1980); Vol. II: Aspects of Indian Labour*. Oxford University Press, 1989.

Lewis, Norman. *A Goddess in the Stones: Travels in India*. London, Jonathan Cape, 1991.

Michelutti, Lucia. *The Vernacularisation of Democracy: Politics, Caste and Religion in India*. New Delhi, Routledge India, 2008.

Mittal, Sushil, and Thursby, Gene. *Studying Hinduism: Key Concepts and Methods*. Abingdon, Routledge, 2007.

Naipaul, V. S. *India: A Wounded Civilization*. London, André Deutsch, 1977.

*India: A Million Mutinies Now*. London, Heinemann, 1990.

Pandey, Gyanendra (Ed.). *Hindus and Others: The Question of Identity in India Today*. New Delhi, Viking Penguin, 1993.

Robinson, Francis (Ed.). *Cambridge Encyclopedia of India*. Cambridge University Press, 1989.

Raju, P. T. *The Philosophical Traditions of India*. Abingdon, Routledge, 2008.

Sen, Amartya. *The Argumentative Indian: Writings on Indian History, Culture and Identity*. London, Allen Lane, 2005.

Sen, Mala. *Death by Fire: Sati, Dowry Death and Female Infanticide in Modern India*. London, Weidenfeld and Nicolson, 2001.

Shokoohy, Mehrdad. *Muslim Architecture of South India*. London, RoutledgeCurzon, 2003.

Singh, R. L. (Ed.). *India: Regional Studies*. Kolkata, for 21st International Geog. Congress by Indian Nat. Cttee for Geography, 1968.

Sinha, Arun. *Against the Few: Struggles of India's Rural Poor*. London, Zed Books, 1992.

Tully, Mark. *No Full Stops in India*. London, Viking, 1991.

Tully, Mark, and Wright, Gillian. *India in Slow Motion*. London, Viking, 2002.

Varma, Pavan K. *Being Indian: Inside the Real India*. London, Arrow, 2006.

Westwood, J. N. *Railways of India*. 1974.

Wolpert, Stanley. *India*. Berkeley, CA, University of California Press, 1993.

**History and Politics**

Adeney, Katharine, and Sáez, Lawrence (Eds). *Coalition Politics and Hindu Nationalism*. Abingdon, Routledge, 2005.

Ahmad, Aziz. *Islamic Modernization in India and Pakistan 1857–1964*. London and New York, Oxford University Press, 1966.

Akbar, M. J. *Nehru: The Making of India*. London, Viking, 1989.

*India: The Siege Within*. London, Penguin, 1985.

*Riot after Riot: Reports on Caste and Communal Violence in India*. New Delhi, Penguin Books India Ltd, 1988.

Andersen, Walter, and Damle, S. *The Brotherhood in Saffron*. Boulder, CO, Westview Press, 1987.

Appadorai, A. (Ed.). *Documents on Political Thought in Modern India*. Oxford, Oxford University Press, 1977.

Avari, Burjor. *India: The Ancient Past—A History of the Indian Sub-Continent from c. 7000 BC to AD 1200*. Abingdon, Routledge, 2007.

Ayoob, Mohammed. *India, Pakistan and Bangladesh: Search for a New Relationship*. New Delhi, Indian Council of World Affairs, 1975.

Azad, Abul Kalam. *India Wins Freedom*. Hyderabad, Orient Longman Ltd, 1989.

Baker, C. J., and Washbrook, D. A. *South India, Political Institutions and Political Change 1880–1920*. Delhi, Macmillan, 1975.

Banik, Dan. *Starvation and India's Democracy*. Abingdon, Routledge, 2007.

Baruah, Sanjib. *A Durable Disorder? Understanding the Politics of Northeast India*. New Delhi, Oxford University Press, 2005.

Basrur, Rajesh. *Minimum Deterrence and India's Nuclear Security*. Palo Alto, CA, Stanford University Press, 2005.

Bayly, C. A. *The Local Roots of Indian Politics, Allahabad 1880–1920*. Oxford, Clarendon Press, 1975.

*Indian Society and the Making of the British Empire*. Cambridge University Press, 1988.

Bayly, Susan. *Caste, Society and Politics in India from the 18th Century to the Modern Day*. Cambridge University Press, 1999.

Bhargava, Rajeev (Ed.). *Secularism and its Critics*. New Delhi, Oxford University Press, 1998.

Bhattacharjea, Ajit. *Jayaprakash Narayan: A Political Biography*. New Delhi, Vihas Publishing House, 1975.

Bose, Sugata, and Jalal, Ayesha (Eds). *Nationalism, Democracy and Development: State and Politics in India*. New Delhi, Oxford University Press, 1997.

Bose, Sumantra. *Kashmir: Roots of Conflict, Paths to Peace*. Cambridge, MA, Harvard University Press, 2003.

Bradnock, R. W. *India's Foreign Policy since 1971*. London, Pinter, 1990.

Brass, Paul R. *Language, Religion and Politics in North India*. London, Cambridge University Press, 1975.

*The Politics of India since Independence*. Cambridge University Press, 1990.

Brown, Judith M. *Gandhi and Civil Disobedience: The Mahatma in Indian Politics, 1928–1934*. Cambridge University Press, 1977.

*Gandhi: Prisoner of Hope*. New Haven, CT, Yale University Press, 1989.

*Modern India: The Origins of an Asian Democracy*. New Delhi, Oxford University Press, 2nd edn, 1994.

*Nehru: A Political Life*. New Haven, CT, Yale University Press, 2003.

Chadha, Vivek. *Low Intensity Conflicts in India: An Historical Analysis*. New Delhi, Sage Publications, 2004.

Chakrabarty, Bidyut. *Indian Politics and Society since Independence: Events, Processes and Ideology*. Abingdon, Routledge, 2008.

Chandra, Bipan, *et al. India's Struggle for Independence*. Harmondsworth, Penguin, 1989.

Chatterjee, Partha (Ed.). *State and Politics in India*. New Delhi, Oxford University Press, 1997.

Chellaney, Brahma. *Nuclear Proliferation: The US-Indian Conflict*. London, Sangam Books, 1993.

Chitkara, M. G. *Indo-Pak Relations: Challenge Before New Millennium*. New Delhi, APH Publishing, 2001.

Cohen, Stephen Philip. *India: Emerging Power*. Washington, DC, The Brookings Institution, 2001.

Collins, L., and Lapierre, D. *Freedom at Midnight*. London, Collins, 1975.

Copland, Ian. *The Princes of India in the Endgame of Empire, 1917–1947*. Cambridge, Cambridge University Press, 1997.

Dalrymple, William. *White Mughals: Love and Betrayal in Eighteenth Century India*. London, HarperCollins, 2002.

Dasgupta, C. *War and Diplomacy in Kashmir 1947–48*. London, Sage Publications, 2002.

Derrett, J. Duncan M. *Religion, Law and the State in India*. London, Faber and Faber, 1968.

Desai, Manali. *State Formation and Radical Democracy in India*. Abingdon, Routledge, 2006.

Dewey, Clive, and Hopkins, A. G. (Eds). *The Imperial Impact*. London, Athlone Press, 1977.

Donaldson, R. H. *Soviet Policy towards India: Ideology and Strategy*. 1974.

Edwardes, Michael. *British India 1772–1947*. London, Sidgwick & Jackson, 1967.

*The Myth of the Mahatma*. London, Constable, 1987.

Engineer, Asgharali. *Communal Riots after Independence: A Comprehensive Account*. Delhi, Shipra, 2004.

Epstein, T. S. *South India: Yesterday, Today and Tomorrow*. London, Macmillan, 1973.

Fairservis, Walter A., Jr. *The Roots of Ancient India*. Chicago, IL, and London, University of Chicago, 2nd edn, 1975.

Farwell, Byron. *Armies of the Raj*. London, Viking, 1990.

Fay, Peter Ward. *The Forgotten Army: India's Armed Struggle for Independence, 1942–45*. University of Michigan, 1994.

Findly, Ellison Banks. *Nur Jahan: Empress of Mughal India*. New York and Oxford, Oxford University Press, 1993.

Fischer, Louis. *The Life of Mahatma Gandhi*. London, HarperCollins, 1997.

Frank, Katherine. *The Life of Indira Nehru Gandhi*. London, HarperCollins, 2nd edn, 2002.

Frankel, Francine R. *India's Green Revolution: Political Costs of Economic Growth*. 1971.

*India's Political Economy, 1947–77: The Gradual Revolution*. Princeton, NJ, Princeton University Press, 1979.

Frankel, Francine R., and Rao, M. S. A. (Eds). *Dominance and State Power in Modern India*. 2 vols. New Delhi, Oxford University Press, 1989 and 1990.

Franklin, Michael (Ed.). *Representing India—Indian Culture and Imperial Control in Eighteenth Century British Orientalist Discourse*. London, Routledge, 2000.

French, Patrick. *Liberty or Death: India's Journey to Independence and Division*. London, HarperCollins, 1998.

Fuchs, Stephen. *The Aboriginal Tribes of India*. Macmillan, 1973.

Galanter, Marc. *Competing Equalities*. Berkeley, CA, University of California Press, 1984.

Gandhi, Sonia (Ed.). *Freedom's Daughter: Letters between Indira and Jawaharlal Nehru, 1922–39*. London, Hodder and Stoughton Ltd, 1989.

*Rajiv*. New Delhi, Viking, 1992.

(Ed.). *Two Alone, Two Together: Letters between Indira Gandhi and Jawaharlal Nehru, 1940–64*. London, Hodder and Stoughton Ltd, 1992.

Ganguly, Sumit. *Conflict Unending: India-Pakistan Tensions since 1947*. Oxford, Oxford University Press, 2002.

Gommans, Jos. *Mughal Warfare: Indian Frontiers and Highroads to Empire 1500–1700*. London, Routledge, 2002.

Gopal, Sarvepalli. *Jawaharlal Nehru*. 3 vols. London, Cape, 1975–84.

Gordon, Leonard A. *Brothers Against the Raj: A Biography of Indian Nationalists Sarat and Subhas Chandra Bose*. New York, Columbia University Press, 1992.

Gould, Harold A., and Ganguly, Sumit. (Eds). *The Hope and the Reality: US-Indian Relations from Roosevelt to Reagan*. Boulder, CO, Westview Press, 1993.

Grahi, Pani. *India's Partition: The Story of Imperialism in Retreat*. London, Routledge, 2004.

Griffith, Kenneth. *The Discovery of Nehru: An Experience of India*. London, Michael Joseph, 1990.

Guha, Ramachandra. *Savaging the Civilized: Verrier Elwin, His Tribals, and India*. Chicago, IL, University of Chicago Press, 1999.

Guha, Ramachandra. *India After Gandhi: The History of the World's Largest Democracy*. London, Macmillan, 2007.

Habibullah, A. B. M. *The Foundation of Muslim Rule in India*. Allahabad, 2nd edn, 1961.

Hansen, Thomas, and Jaffrelot, Christophe (Eds). *The BJP and the Compulsions of Politics in India*. New Delhi, Oxford University Press, 1998.

Hardy, Peter. *The Muslims of British India*. Cambridge University Press, 1972.

Harrison, Selig S., and Kemp, Geoffrey. *India and America after the Cold War*. Washington, DC, 1993.

Hasan, Mushirul. *Nationalism and Communal Politics in India, 1885–1930*. New Delhi, Manohar, 1991.

(Ed.). *India's Partition: Process, Strategy and Mobilization*. Oxford University Press, 1993.

*Legacy of a Divided Nation: India's Muslims since Independence*. London, C. Hurst & Co (Publishers) Ltd, 1997.

Hasan, Mushirul, and Roy, Asim (Eds). *Living Together Separately: Cultural India in History and Politics*. New Delhi, Oxford University Press, 2005.

Hazarika, Sanjoy. *Strangers of the Mist: Tales of War and Peace from India's Northeast*. New Delhi, Viking Press, 1995.

Healy, Kathleen. *Rajiv Gandhi: The Years of Power*. New Delhi, Vikas Publishing House, 1989.

Heehs, Peter. *The Bomb in Bengal: The Rise of Revolutionary Terrorism in India*. New Delhi, Oxford University Press, 2005.

Hewitt, Vernon. *Political Mobilisation and Democracy in India: States of Emergency*. Abingdon, Routledge, 2007.

Irani, Cushrow. *Ayodhya: Demolishing a Dream*. New Delhi, UBSPD, 2004

Israel, Milton. *Propaganda and the Press in the Indian Nationalist Struggle, 1920–1947*, South Asian Studies 56. Cambridge University Press, 1994.

Jaffrelot, Christophe. *India's Silent Revolution: The Rise of the Lower Castes in Northern India*. New York, Columbia University Press, 2002.

Jalal, Ayesha. *Democracy and Authoritarianism in South Asia*. Cambridge University Press, 1995.

Jalan, Bilan. *The Future of India: Economics, Politics and Governance*. New Delhi, Penguin, 2005.

James, Lawrence. *Raj: The Making and Unmaking of British India*. London, Little, Brown & Co, 1997.

Jeffrey, Robin (Ed.). *People, Princes and Paramount Power: Society and Politics in the Indian Princely States*. Oxford University Press, 1979.

*What's Happening to India?* London, Macmillan, 1988.

Jenkins, Laura Dudley. *Identity and Identification in India: Defining the Disadvantaged*. London, RoutledgeCurzon, 2002.

Jha, Prem Shankar. *In the Eye of the Cyclone: The Crisis in Indian Democracy*. New Delhi, Viking Penguin, 1993.

*Kashmir 1947: Rival Versions of History*. New Delhi, Oxford University Press, 1995.

Johnson, G. *Provincial Politics and Indian Nationalism. Bombay and the Indian National Congress 1880–1915*. Cambridge University Press, 1974.

Joshi, G. N. *Constitution of India*. 6th edn, 1975.

Joshi, Sanjay. *Fractured Modernity: The Making of a Middle Class in Colonial North India*. New Delhi, Oxford University Press, 2005.

Kapur, Ashok. *India's Nuclear Option: Atomic Diplomacy and Decision Making*. New York, Praeger, 1976.

*India: From Regional to World Power*. Abingdon, Routledge, 2007.

Kapur, Rajiv A. *Sikh Separatism: The Politics of Faith*. London, Allen and Unwin, 1986.

Katzenstein, Mary Fainsod. *Social Movements in India: Poverty, Power, and Politics*. Lanham, MD, Rowman and Littlefield Publrs, 2005.

Keay, John. *The Honourable Company: A History of the English East India Company*. London, HarperCollins, 1992.

*India: A History*. London, HarperCollins, 2000.

Khalidi, Omar. *Khaki and the Ethnic Violence in India*. New Delhi, Three Essays Press, 2003.

Khurshid, Salman. *Beyond Terrorism—New Hope for Kashmir*. New Delhi, UBSPD, 1994.

King, Robert D. *Nehru and the Language Politics of India*. New Delhi, Oxford University Press, 1997.

Kinnvall, Catarina. *Globalization and Religious Nationalism in India: The Search for Ontological Security*. Abingdon, Routledge, 2006.

Kishwar, Madhu Purnima. *Deepening Democracy: Challenges of Governance and Globalization in India*. New Delhi, Oxford University Press, 2005.

Kohli, Atul. *Democracy and Disorder*. Cambridge University Press, 1990.

Kohli, Atul (Ed.). *The Success of India's Democracy*. Cambridge University Press, 2001.

Kopf, D. A. *British Orientalism and the Bengal Renaissance*. Berkeley and Los Angeles, CA, University of California, 1969.

Kothari, Rajani. *State against Democracy: In Search of Humane Governance*. New Delhi, Ajanta, 1988.

(Ed.). *Caste in Indian Politics*. New Delhi, Orient Longmans, 1970.

Kulke, Hermann, and Rothermund, Dietmar. *A History of India*. 3rd edn, London, Routledge, 1997.

Lamb, Alastair. *Crisis in Kashmir, 1947–1966*. London, Routledge and Kegan Paul, 1966.

Ludden, David (Ed.). *Making India Hindu: Religion, Community, and the Politics of Democracy in India*. Oxford, Oxford University Press, 2nd Edn, 2005.

Lumby, E. W. R. *The Transfer of Power in India*. London, Allen and Unwin, 1954.

Malhotra, Inder. *Indira Gandhi: A Personal and Political Biography*. London, Hodder and Stoughton, 1990.

Manor, James (Ed.). *Nehru to the Nineties: The Changing Office of the Prime Minister of India*. New Delhi, Viking Press, 1994.

Mansergh, Nicholas, Lumby, E. W., and Moon, Penderel (Eds). *India: The Transfer of Power, 1942–47*. 12 vols. London, HMSO, 1970–83.

Mansingh, Surjit. *India's Search for Power: Mrs Gandhi's Foreign Policy 1966–82*. London, Sage Publications, 1984.

Marshall, P. J. (Ed.). *Problems of Empire, Britain and India 1757–1813*. London, Allen and Unwin, 1968.

*Bengal: The British Bridgehead*. Cambridge University Press, 1988.

Masani, Zareer. *Indira Gandhi: A Biography*. London, 1974.

*Indian Tales of the Raj*. London, BBC Books, 1988.

Masselos, J. (Ed.). *Struggling and Ruling*. New Delhi, Sterling Publishers Pvt Ltd, 1987.

Mehrotra, S. R. *India and the Commonwealth 1885–1929*. London, Allen and Unwin, 1965.

Mehta, Ved. *Mahatma Gandhi and his Apostles*. London, André Deutsch, 1977.

*Rajiv Gandhi and Rama's Kingdom*. New Haven, CT, Yale University Press, 1995.

Mehta, J. L. *Advanced Study in the History of Modern India: 1707–1813*. New Delhi, New Dawn Press, 2005.

Menon, V. P. *The Integration of the Indian States*. Mumbai, Orient Longmans, 1956.

*The Transfer of Power in India*. Mumbai, Orient Longmans, 1957.

Mernissi, Fatima. *The Forgotten Queens of Islam*. London, Polity Press, 1993.

Mitra, Ashok. *Calcutta Diary*. 1977.

*Hoodlum Years*. Mumbai, Orient Longmans, 1978.

Mitra, Subrata K. *The Puzzle of India's Governance: Culture, Context and Comparative Theory*. Abingdon, Routledge, 2005.

Moon, Sir Penderel. *The British Conquest and Dominion of India*. London, Gerald Duckworth and Co Ltd, 1989.

*Strangers in India*. London, Faber and Faber, 1944.

Moore, R. J. *Liberalism and Indian Politics 1872–1922*. London, Edward Arnold, 1966.

*The Crisis of Indian Unity*. Oxford, Clarendon Press, 1975.

Nanda, B. R. (Ed.). *Indian Foreign Policy: The Nehru Years*. Delhi and Mumbai, Vikas Publishing House, 1976.

*Socialism in India*. Delhi, 1972.

Nandy, Ashis. *The Romance of the State and the Fate of Dissent in the Tropics*. New Delhi, Oxford University Press, 2003.

Nehru, Jawaharlal. *An Autobiography: Jawaharlal Nehru*. New Delhi, Penguin Books, 2004.

Nossiter, T. J. *Communism in Kerala: A Study in Political Adaptation*. London, Hurst, for Royal Institute of International Affairs, 1980.

*Marxist State Governments in India*. London, Pinter, 1988.

Nugent, Nicholas. *Rajiv Gandhi—Son of a Dynasty*. London, BBC Books, 1990.

Padgaonkar, Dileep. *When Bombay Burned*. Delhi, UBSPD, 1994.

Pandey, Gyanendra. *The Construction of Communalism in Colonial North India*. New Delhi, Oxford University Press, 1993.

Pant, Harsh. *Indian Foreign Policy in a Unipolar World*. New Delhi, Routledge India, 2008.

Parkes, Fanny. *Begums, Thugs and White Mughals*. New Delhi, Penguin Books, 2003.

Pearson, M. N. *The Portuguese in India*. Cambridge University Press, 1988.

Perkovich, George. *India's Nuclear Bomb: The Impact on Global Proliferation*. Berkeley, CA, University of California Press, 2000.

Philips, C. H., and Wainwright, Mary (Eds). *Indian Society and the Beginnings of Modernization*. London, SOAS, 1976.

Prasad, Bimla. *The Origins of Indian Foreign Policy*. Kolkata, Bookland, 1960.

Ramunny, Murkot. *The World of Nagas*. New Delhi, Northern Book Centre, 1988.

Read, Anthony, and Fisher, David. *The Proudest Day: India's Long Road to Independence*. London, Jonathan Cape, 1998.

Robb, P. G. *The Government of India and Reform*. Oxford University Press, 1976.

Robinson, F. C. R. *Separatism among Indian Muslims. The Politics of the United Provinces' Muslims 1860–1923*. Cambridge University Press, 1974.

Rudolph, L. I., and S. H. *The Modernity of Tradition*. Chicago, IL, 1967.

*In Pursuit of Lakshmi: The Political Economy of the Indian State*. University of Chicago Press, 1987.

Rushby, Kevin. *Children of Kali: Through India in Search of Bandits, the Thug Cult and the British Raj*. London, Constable, 2002.

Sahgal, Nayantara. *Indira Gandhi: Emergence and Style*. Vikas Publications, 1978.

Sarila, Narendra Singh. *The Shadow of the Great Game*. London, Constable and Robinson, 2006.

Sarkar, Sumit. *Modern India 1885–1947*. New Delhi, Macmillan, 1983.

Sathyamurthy, T. V. (Ed.). *Class Formation and Political Transformation in Post-Colonial India*. New Delhi, Oxford University Press, 1998.

(Ed.). *Region, Religion, Caste, Gender and Culture in Contemporary India*. New Delhi, Oxford University Press, 1998.

Schofield, Victoria. *Kashmir in Conflict: India, Pakistan and the Unending War*. London, I. B. Tauris, 2003.

Schwartzberg, J. E. (Ed.). *An Historical Atlas of South Asia*. London and Chicago, IL, University of Chicago Press, 1978.

Seal, Anil. *The Emergence of Indian Nationalism*. Cambridge University Press, 1967.

Sen, Amartya, and Dreze, Jean. *India: Development and Participation*. Oxford, Oxford University Press, 2002.

Sen, Mala. *India's Bandit Queen: The True Story of Phoolan Devi*. London, HarperCollins, 1992.

Sen Gupta, B. *Soviet-Asian Relations in the 1970s and Beyond: Interpretational Study*. 1976.

Sharma, Jyotirmaya. *Hindutva: Exploring the Idea of Hindu Nationalism*. New Delhi, Viking, 2003.

Shukla, Satyendra R. *Sikkim. The Story of Integration*. New Delhi, S. Chand and Co (Pvt) Ltd, 1976.

Singh, Amarinder. *A Ridge Too Far: War in the Kargil Heights 1999*. Bharat Rakshak, 2001

Singh, B. P., and Varma, K. Pavan (Eds). *The Millennium Book on New Delhi*. New York, Oxford University Press, 2001.

Singh, Khushwant. *A History of the Sikhs*. 2 vols. 1964–66.

Singh, Patwant. *The Second Partition: Fault Lines in India's Democracy*. New Delhi, Hay House Publications (India) Pvt Ltd, 2007.

Singh, Prakash. *Kohima to Kashmir: On the Terrorist Trail*. New Delhi, Rupa & Co, 2001.

Singh, Tavleen. *Kashmir: A Tragedy of Errors*. New Delhi, Viking Press, 1995.

Singh, V. B., and Bose, Shankar. *Data Handbook on Lok Sabha Elections 1952–80*. London, Sage Publications, 1985.

Sisson, Richard, and Rose, Leo E. *War and Secession: Pakistan, India and the Creation of Bangladesh*. Berkeley, CA, University of California Press, 1990.

Sisson, Richard, and Wolpert, Stanley (Eds). *Congress and Indian Nationalism*. Berkeley and Los Angeles, CA, University of California Press, 1988.

Smith, D. E. *India as a Secular State*. Princeton, NJ, Princeton University Press, 1963.

Spear, Percival. *A History of India, Vol. II*. Harmondsworth, Penguin Books, 1965.

Srivastava, C. P. *Lal Bahadur Shastri, Prime Minister of India 1964–66: A Life of Truth in Politics*. Oxford University Press, 1994.

Stern, Robert W. *Changing India*. Cambridge University Press, 1993.

Stokes, Eric. *The Peasant and the Raj*. Cambridge University Press, 1978.

Subedi, Surya P. *Dynamics of Foreign Policy and Law: A Study of Indo-Nepal Relations*. New Delhi, Oxford University Press, 2005.

Suntharalingam, R. *Indian Nationalism. An Historical Analysis*. New Delhi, Vikas, 1983.

Tandon, Prakash. *Punjabi Century 1857–1957*. University of California, 1968.

Tellis, Ashley. *India's Emerging Nuclear Posture*. Oxford, Oxford University Press, 2001.

Thakur, Ramesh. *The Government and Politics of India*. London, Macmillan, 1995.

Thapar, R. A. *History of India, Vol. I*. Harmondsworth, Penguin Books, 1966.

*Asoka and the Decline of the Mauryas*.

*The Penguin History of Early India*. Harmondsworth, Penguin Books, 2003.

*Early India: From the Origins to* AD *1300*. Harmondsworth, Penguin Books, 2003.

Tharoor, Shashi. *Nehru: The Invention of India*. New Delhi, Penguin Books, 2003.

Tinker, Hugh. *Experiment with Freedom: India and Pakistan, 1947*. London, Oxford University Press, 1967.

*India and Pakistan: A Political Analysis*. London, Pall Mall Press, 2nd edn, 1967.

Tomlinson, B. R. *The Indian National Congress and the Raj 1929–1942*. London, Macmillan, 1976.

Tully, Mark, and Jacob, Satish. *Amritsar: Mrs Gandhi's Last Battle*. London, Cape, 1985.

Tully, Mark, and Masani, Zareer. *From Raj to Rajiv*. London, BBC Books, 1988.

Tully, Mark. *India's Unending Journey: Finding Balance in a Time of Change*. London, Rider & Co, 2007.

Vanaik, Achin. *The Painful Transition: Bourgeois Democracy in India*. London, Verso, 1990.

*The Furies of Indian Communalism: Religion, Modernity and Secularisation*. London, Verso, 1997.

Varshney, Ashutosh. *Ethnic Conflict and Civic Life: Hindus and Muslims in India*. New Haven, CT, Yale University Press, 2002.

Washbrook, David. *The Cambridge History of India: South India 1750–1850*. Cambridge, Cambridge University Press, 2005.

Wavell, Lord (Ed. Moon, P.). *The Viceroy's Journal*. 1973.

Weigold, Auriol. *Churchill, Roosevelt and India: Propaganda During World War II*. Abingdon, Routledge, 2008.

Weiner, Myron (Ed.). *State Politics in India*. London, Oxford University Press.

*Party Politics in India: The Development of a Multi-Party System*. Princeton, NJ, Princeton University Press, 1957.

*The Child and the State in India: Child Labour and Education Policy in Perspective*. Princeton, NJ, Princeton University Press, 1991.

Weiner, Myron, and Katzenstein, Mary. *India's Preferential Policies*. Chicago, IL, University of Chicago Press, 1981.

Wolpert, Stanley. *A New History of India*. New York, Oxford University Press, 1976.

*Gandhi's Passion: The Life and Legacy of Mahatma Gandhi*. New York, Oxford University Press, 2001.

Zachariah, Benjamin. *Ideas of Developing India: An Intellectual and Social History*. New Delhi, Oxford University Press, 2005.

**Economy**

Ahluwalia, Isher, and Little, I. M. D. *India's Economic Reforms and Development: Essays for Manmohan Singh*. New Delhi, Oxford University Press, 1997.

Bagchi, A. K. *Private Investment in India, 1900–1939*. Cambridge University Press, 1972.

*Change and Choice in Indian Industry*. Kolkata, K. P. Bagchi and Co, 1980.

Balachandran, G. (Ed.). *India and the World Economy 1850–1950*. Oxford, Oxford University Press, 2005.

Balasubramanyam, V. N. *The Economy of India*. London, Weidenfeld and Nicolson, 1986.

Bardhan, Pranab. *The Political Economy of Development in India*. Oxford University Press, 1984.

Bardhan, Pranab, Dhatta-Chaudhuri, M., and Krishnan, T. N. (Eds). *Development and Change: Essays in Honour of Professor K. N. Raj*. New Delhi, Oxford University Press, 1993.

Baru, Rama V. *Private Health Care in India*. New Delhi, Sage Publications, 1999.

Baru, Sanjaya. *Strategic Consequences of India's Economic Performance*. New Delhi, Academic Foundation, 2006.

*The Political Economy of Indian Sugar: State Intervention and Structural Change*. New Delhi, Oxford University Press, 1989.

Baru, Sanjaya, and Chaudhuri, Saumitra. *Mid-Year Review of the Indian Economy, 1997–98*. New Delhi, Konark Publishers, 1998.

Basu, S. K. *Studies in Economic Problems*. Mumbai, Asia Publishing House, 1965.

Bauer, P. T. *Indian Economic Policy and Development*. London, Allen and Unwin, and New York, Praeger, 1961.

Bhaduri, A., and Nayyar, D. *An Intelligent Person's Guide to Economic Liberalisation in India*. Delhi, Penguin Books India (Pvt) Ltd, 1996.

Bhagwati, Jagdish. *India in Transition. Freeing the Economy*. Oxford, Clarendon Press, 1993.

Bhagwati, J., and Desai, P. *India: Planning for Industrialisation*. Oxford University Press, 1974.

Bhalla, G. S. (Ed.). *Economic Liberalisation and Indian Agriculture*. Delhi, Institute for Studies in Industrial Development, 1994.

Bhatt, Ela R. *We Are Poor But So Many: The Story of Self-Employed Women in India*. New York, Oxford University Press, 2005.

Bhatt, V. V. *Aspects of Economic Change and Policy in India, 1800–1960*. Mumbai, Allied Publishers, 1962.

*A Decade of Performance of Industrial Development Bank of India*. World Bank Paper.

Blyn, G. *Agricultural Trends in India, 1891–1941: Output, Availability and Productivity*. Philadelphia, PA, 1966.

Brahmananda, P. R., and Panchamukhi, V. R. *Development Process of the Indian Economy*. Mumbai, Himalaya Publishing House, 1987.

Byres, Terence J. *State and Development Planning in India*. New Delhi, Oxford University Press, 1994.

*The Indian Economy: Major Debates Since Independence*. New Delhi, Oxford University Press, 1998.

*Selected Economic Writings*. New Delhi, Oxford University Press, 1993.

Chandavarkar, Rajnarayan. *The Origins of Industrial Capitalism in India*. Cambridge, Cambridge University Press, 1995.

Chandok, H. L., and the Policy Group. *India Database: The Economy*. 2 vols. Delhi, Living Media India Ltd, 1990.

Chelliah, Raja J. *Essays in Fiscal and Financial Sector Reforms in India*. New Delhi, Oxford University Press, 1999.

Choudhury, R. A., Gamkhar, S., and Ghose, A. *The Indian Economy and its Performance since Independence*. New Delhi, Oxford University Press, 1990.

Dahlman, Carl, and Utz, Anuja. *India and the Knowledge Economy: Leveraging Strengths and Opportunities*. Washington, DC, World Bank, 2005.

Das, Gurcharan. *India Unbound*. Knopf, 2nd edn, 2001.

Dasgupta, Biplab. *The Oil Industry in India; Some Economic Aspects*. 1971.

*Agrarian Changes and the New Technology in India*. Geneva, UNRISD, 1977.

*Globalization: India's Adjustment Experience*. London, Sage Publications, 2005.

Datta, Amlan. *An Introduction to India's Economic Development since the Nineteenth Century*. Mumbai, Popular Prakashan (Pvt) Ltd, 1989.

D'Costa, Anthony P. *The Long March to Capitalism: Embourgeoisment, Internationalization and Industrial Transformation in India*. Basingstoke, Palgrave Macmillan, 2005.

Desai, Meghnad, *et al. Agrarian Power and Agrarian Productivity in South Asia*. Berkeley, CA, University of California Press, 1984.

Drèze, Jean, and Sen, Amartya. *India: Economic Development and Social Opportunity*. New Delhi, Oxford University Press, 1995.

*Indian Development: Selected Regional Perspectives*. New Delhi, Oxford University Press, 1999.

Dutt, R. C. *Economic History of India*. Delhi, Publications Division, 1960.

Dyson, Tim, Cassen, Robert, and Visaria, Leela. *Twenty-First Century India: Population, Economy, Human Development, and the Environment*. Oxford, Oxford University Press, 2005.

Economist Intelligence Unit. *India to 1990: How Far Will Reform Go?* London, The Economist Publications, 1986.

Epstein, T. A. *Economic Development and Social Change in South India*. Mumbai, Oxford University Press, 1962.

Etienne, Gilbert (translation by Mothersole, Megan). *Studies in Indian Agriculture: The Art of the Possible*. Berkeley, CA, University of California Press, 1968.

Farmer, B. H. *Agricultural Colonization in India since Independence*. Oxford University Press, 1974.

(Ed.). *Green Revolution? Technology and Changes in Rice Growing Areas of Tamil Nadu and Sri Lanka*. London, Macmillan, 1977.

Federation of Indian Chambers of Commerce and Industry (FICCI). *Footprints of Enterprise: Indian Business Through the Ages*. New Delhi, Oxford University Press, 1998.

Fonseca, A. J. *Wage Issues in a Developing Economy: The Indian Experience*. Bombay, 1975, and Delhi, Kolkata and Chennai, 1976; Oxford University Press.

Frankel, Francine R., Hasan, Zoya, Bhargava, Rajeev, and Arora, Balveer. *Transforming India: Social and Political Dynamics of Democracy*. Oxford University Press, 2000.

Friedman, Edward, and Gilley, Bruce (Eds). *Asia's Giants: Comparing China and India*. Basingstoke, Palgrave Macmillan, 2005.

Goldsmith, R. W. *The Financial Development of India, 1860–1977*. New Haven, CT, Yale University Press, 1984.

Guha, Ashok (Ed.). *Economic Liberalisation, Industrial Structure and Growth in India*. Oxford University Press, 1989.

Gupta, Dipankar. *Mistaken Modernity: India Between Worlds*. HarperCollins, 2001.

Gupta, S. P. *Mid Year Review of the Indian Economy, 1995–96*. Delhi, Konark Publishers, 1996.

Gurumurthi, S. *Fiscal Federalism in India*. New Delhi, Vikas Publishing House, 1994.

Gyan, Chand. *The Socialist Transformation of the Indian Economy*. London, Allen and Unwin, 1965.

Hanson, A. H. *The Process of Planning: A Study of India's Five-Year Plans 1950–1964*. London, Oxford University Press, 1966.

Harriss-White, Barbara, and Subramaniam, S. *Illfare in India, Essays on India's Social Sector*. New Delhi, Sage Publications, 1999.

Henderson, P. D. *India: The Energy Sector*. Delhi and London, Oxford University Press for the World Bank, 1975.

Herring, Ronald. *Land to the Tiller*. New Haven, CT, Yale University Press, 1983.

Jalan, Bimal. *India's Economic Crisis: The Way Ahead*. New Delhi, Oxford University Press, 1991.

(Ed.). *Indian Economy: Problems and Prospects*. New Delhi, Viking, 1992.

Jenkins, Rob. *Democratic Politics and Economic Reform In India*. Cambridge, Cambridge University Press, 1999.

Jha, Prem Shankar. *The Economy of India*. New Delhi, Oxford University Press, 1979.

Joshi, Vijay, and Little, I. M. D. *India: Macroeconomics and Political Economy, 1964–1991*. New Delhi, Oxford University Press, 1994.

*India's Economic Reforms, 1991–2001*. New Delhi, Oxford University Press, 1996.

Karlekar, Hiranmay (Ed.). *Independent India: The First Fifty Years*. Oxford, Oxford University Press, 1999.

Kelkar, Vijay, and Rao, V. V. Bhanoji. *India: Development Policy Imperatives*. Delhi, Tata McGraw-Hill Publishing Co Ltd, 1996.

Khusro, A. M. *Unfinished Agenda, India and the World Economy*. New Delhi, Wiley Eastern Ltd, 1994.

Lal, Deepak. *Unfinished Business: India in the World Economy*. Oxford University Press, 1999.

Lala, R. M. *Beyond the Last Blue Mountain: A Life of J. R. D. Tata*. New Delhi, Penguin Books, 1992.

Lucas, R. E. B., and Papanek, G. F. *The Indian Economy, Recent Developments and Future Prospects*. Boulder, CO, Westview Press, 1988.

Maddison, A. *Class Structure and Economic Growth: India and Pakistan since the Moguls*. 1971.

Maira, Arun. *Remaking India: One Country, One Destiny*. New Delhi, Sage Publications, 2005.

Malyarov, O. V. *The Role of the State in the Socio-Economic Structure of India*. New Delhi, Vikas Publishing House, 1983.

Mazumdar, Dipak, Sarkar, Sandip. *Globalization, Labour Markets and Inequality in India*. Abingdon, Routledge, 2008.

Mehrotra, Santosh, and Srivastava, Ranjana and Ravi. *Uncaging the 'Tiger' Economy: Financing Elementary Education in India*. Oxford, Oxford University Press, 2005.

Mehta, B. *India and the World Oil Crisis*. 1974.

Mellor, John W. *The New Economics of Growth: A Strategy for India and the Developing World*. Ithaca, NY, and London, Cornell University Press, 1976.

Mohan, T. T. Ram. *Privatisation in India*. Abingdon, Routledge, 2005.

Mongia, J. N. (Ed.). *Readings in Indian Labour and Social Welfare*. Delhi, Atma Ram, 1976.

Mooij, Jos (Ed.). *The Politics of Economic Reforms in India*. New Delhi, Sage Publications, 2005.

Mookherjee, Dilip (Ed.). *Indian Industry, Policies and Performance*. New Delhi, Oxford University Press, 1994.

Moore, Tomoe. *India's Emerging Financial Market: A Flow of Funds Model*. Abingdon, Routledge, 2007.

Mukherjee, Sadhan. *India's Economic Relations with the USA and the USSR*. New Delhi, Sterling Publishers Pvt Ltd, 1978.

Nair, K. *Three Bowls of Rice: India and Japan, A Century of Effort*. East Lansing, MI, Michigan State University Press, 1973.

Narayanamoorthy, A., and Deshpande, R. S. *Where Water Seeps!: Towards a New Phase in India's Irrigation Reforms*. New Delhi, Academic Foundation, 2005.

Nayak, Satyendra S. *Globalization and the Indian Economy: Roadmap to a Convertible Rupee*. Abingdon, Routledge, 2007.

Nayar, B. R. *India's Mixed Economy*. Mumbai, Popular Prakashan Ltd, 1989.

Nayyar, Deepak (Ed.). *Industrial Growth and Stagnation*. New Delhi, Oxford University Press, 1994.

Nayyar, Deepak, and Badhuri, Amit. *An Intelligent Person's Guide to Economic Liberalisation in India*. New Delhi, Penguin, 1991.

Papola, T. S., and Rodgers, G. (Eds). *Labour Institutions and Economic Development in India*. London, International Labour Office, 1993.

Parikh, Kirit (Ed.). *Mid Year Review of the Indian Economy, 1994–95*. Delhi, Konark Publishers, 1995.

(Ed.). *India Development Report, 1997*. New Delhi, Oxford University Press, 1997.

Patel, I. G. *Glimpses of Indian Economic Policy*. Oxford, Oxford University Press, 2002.

Raj, K. N. *Organisational Issues in Indian Agriculture*. Oxford, Oxford University Press, 1990.

Rajghatta, Chidanand. *The Horse that Flew: How India's Silicon Gurus Spread their Wings*. New Delhi, HarperCollins, 2002.

Rangarajan, C. *Indian Economy: Essays on Money and Finance*. New Delhi, UBS Publishers and Distributors, 1998.

Rao, Hanumnantha. *Agriculture, Food Security, Poverty and Environment: Essays on Post Reform India*. New Delhi, Oxford University Press, 2005.

Rao, M. Govinda, and Singh, Nirvikar. *Political Economy of Federalism in India*. New Delhi, Oxford University Press, 2005.

Rao, V. K. R. V., and Narain, Dharm. *Foreign Aid and India's Economic Development*. London, Asia Publishing House, 1964.

*India's National Income 1950–1980*. London, Sage Publications, 1983.

Reddy, Y. Venugopal. *Monetary and Financial Sector Reforms in India*. New Delhi, UBS Publishers and Distributors, 2000.

Rosen, G. *Democracy and Economic Change in India*. Cambridge University Press for University of California Press, 2nd edn, 1967.

Roy, Tirthankar. *Rethinking Economic Change in India: Labour and Livelihood*. Abingdon, Routledge, 2005.

Sachs, Jeffrey D., Varshney, Ashutosh, and Bajpai, Nirupam. *India in the Era of Economic Reforms*. Oxford University Press, 1999.

Sáez, Lawrence. *Banking Reform in India and China*. New York, Macmillan, 2004.

Sainath, P. *Everbody Loves a Good Drought: Life in India's Poorest Districts*. Delhi, Penguin Books India (Pvt) Ltd, 1997.

Saith, Ashwani, and Vijayabhaskar, M. (Eds). *ICTs and Indian Economic Development: Economy, Work, Regulation*. London, Sage Publications, 2005.

Sandesara, J. C. *Industrial Policy and Planning—1947 to 1991: Tendencies, Interpretations and Issues*. New Delhi, Sage Publications, 1992.

Satyamurthy, T. V. (Ed.). *Industry and Agriculture in India since Independence*. New Delhi, Oxford University Press, 1995.

Sharma, Shalendra D. *Development and Democracy in India*. Boulder, CO, Lynne Rienner, 1999.

Singh, Charan. *India's Economic Policy: The Gandhian Blueprint*. New Delhi, Vikas Publishing House, 1978.

Singh, Pritam. *Federalism, Nationalism and Development: India and the Punjab Economy*. Abingdon, Routledge, 2008.

Srinivasan, T. N. *India's Economic Reforms*. Oxford, Oxford University Press, 2000.

Streeten, P., and Lipton, M. (Eds). *The Crisis of Indian Planning*. London, Oxford University Press, 1968.

Swamy, S. *Economic Growth in China and India 1952–1970*. 1973.

Tripathi, D. (Ed.). *Business and Politics in India: A Historical Perspective*. Delhi, Manohar Publications, 1991.

*The Oxford History of Indian Business*. New Delhi, Oxford University Press India, 2004.

Turner, R. (Ed.). *India's Urban Future*. Berkeley and Los Angeles, CA, University of California Press, and London, Cambridge University Press, 1962.

Varshney, A. *Democracy, Development and the Countryside*. Cambridge, Cambridge University Press, 1995.

Vedavalli, R. *Private Foreign Investment and Economic Development: A Case Study of Petroleum in India*. London, Cambridge University Press, 1976.

Wadhva, C. D. *Some Problems of India's Economic Policy*. 1973.

Zinkin, Maurice, and Ward, Barbara. *Why Help India?* London, Pergamon Press, 1963.

# THE MALDIVES

## Physical and Social Geography

B. H. FARMER

With additions by the editorial staff

The Republic of Maldives (commonly referred to as 'the Maldives') comprises a chain of 1,192 small coral islands in the Indian Ocean, lying about 675 km south-west of Sri Lanka, and extending from just north of the Equator to about 8° N. Of these islands, which cover a land area of 298 sq km (115 sq miles), 197 are inhabited. According to revised results of the census held in March 2006, the population totalled 298,968 (males 151,459, females 147,509), giving an average density of 1,003 per sq km. According to census figures, an estimated 103,693 people resided in the capital, Malé.

The Maldives rests on a submarine ridge, which may be volcanic in origin. The islands are grouped into 26 natural atolls (rings of coral islands, each ring encircling a lagoon: the word *atoll* is itself, in fact, Maldivian), but are divided, for administrative purposes, into 20 atolls. All of the islands consist entirely of coral, coral sand and other coral detritus, and none exceeds a land area of 13 sq km. The average daily temperature ranges from 25°C to 31°C. The average annual rainfall is 2,143 mm. Most of the islands are covered with coconut palms.

The lack of suitable land for construction purposes and attendant population pressures have become major problems, particularly on Malé, where, until the 1990s, buildings were traditionally restricted to one storey. The Malé land-reclamation project was begun in 1979 and completed in 1986. As a result of this US $6m. project, about 600,000 sq m of land was reclaimed, adding around 50% to the total land area of the capital. Another land-creation programme, involving the addition of an island extending to 4 sq km in area, was completed in 2002. The new, artificially constructed, island of Hulhumalé was projected to accommodate 154,000 people. The first group of people moved to the island in early 2004.

The Maldivians are thought to be of mixed descent, deriving from South Indians (Dravidians), Sinhalese and Arabs. The Maldivians' language, Dhivehi, is related to Sinhala. Islam is the state religion, and the Maldivians are Sunni Muslims.

## History

Updated for this edition by Peter Lehr

The people of the Maldives adopted the Islamic faith in the 12th century. The earliest known description of conditions in the islands was recorded by Ibn Batutah, an Arab traveller and historian, in the 14th century. The ruler was then a sultan of the Somavansa dynasty, one of the six great dynasties that, for the most part, ruled the country following its conversion to Islam. The Portuguese, in their rapid and widespread colonization during the 16th century, established themselves on the islands in 1558, but were driven out in 1573. In the 17th century the islands came under the protection of the Dutch rulers of Ceylon (now Sri Lanka). When the British took possession of Ceylon in 1795–96, they extended their protection to the Maldive Islands, and this was formally recorded in an agreement in 1887. The sultanate was made elective in 1932, and the islands remained a British crown protectorate until January 1953, when a Republic was inaugurated. In February 1954, however, the sultanate was restored under a new Constitution.

In 1948, when Ceylon became independent, a new agreement between the United Kingdom and the Maldive Islands provided that the United Kingdom should control the foreign affairs of the islands but should not interfere internally. The Sultan undertook to provide necessary facilities to British forces for the defence of the islands.

In 1956 the Maldivian and British Governments agreed to the establishment of a British air force staging post on Gan, an island in the southernmost atoll, Addu. The Maldivian Government accorded free and unrestricted use by the British Government of Gan Island and of 44.5 ha of Hittadu Island, for radio facilities. Another agreement was signed in 1960, under which the Maldivian Government permitted the continued use by the United Kingdom of Gan and the demarcated area on Hittadu, together with the Addu atoll and the adjacent territorial waters, for a term of 30 years. This period was to be extendable by agreement.

### INDEPENDENCE

The Maldive Islands achieved full independence on 26 July 1965, becoming a full sovereign state with all rights to conduct its own defence and external relations. The British Government, however, retained those facilities in Addu atoll that had been accorded to it in 1960 for purposes of Commonwealth defence. It also undertook to pay the Maldivian Government £100,000, with a further £750,000 spread over five years or more, for economic development. In 1975, however, the United Kingdom decided to close the air force base. With the evacuation of Gan by the British forces completed in March 1976, the 30-year agreement was terminated, creating a large commercial and military vacuum.

In October 1977 the Maldives Government rejected a US $1m. offer from the USSR to lease the former base on Gan, on the grounds that it did not want to lease the island for military purposes, nor to a superpower. In 1981 plans were announced for the establishment of an industrial zone on Gan. By 1990 there were two factories (producing ready-made garments) operating on Gan. The airport on Gan is now fully operational as a civilian airport. It links the capital, Malé, with the south, and, following construction work carried out in the first half of the 2000s, had been upgraded to international standards by 2007 in preparation for international flights, with the opening of tourist resorts in the area.

The Maldives seeks to maintain and develop strong and varied foreign relations in order to obtain more aid and to ensure a peaceful Indian Ocean area. The country participates in numerous international organizations; it has been a member of the Colombo Plan since 1963 and of the UN since 1965. It joined the IMF, the World Bank and the Asian Development Bank (ADB) in 1978, and has been a full member of the Commonwealth since 1985. The Maldives is also a founder member of the South Asian Association for Regional Co-operation (SAARC), which was formally constituted in December 1985. The Maldives' international standing was enhanced in November 1990 and again in May 1997, when it successfully hosted the fifth and ninth SAARC summit meetings, respectively, which were held in Malé. The Maldives' international profile was further heightened in February 1997, when it hosted the Asia-Pacific Ministers' Conference on Tourism and Environment. In January 2000 the Maldives hosted the fourth SAARC Economic Co-operation Conference. In December 2002 the Maldives had diplomatic relations with 135 countries. In November 2004 the Maldives opened its fourth resident diplomatic mission (in addition to those in Sri Lanka, at the UN headquarters in New York, USA, and in London, United Kingdom) in New Delhi, India.

## POLITICAL DEVELOPMENTS

In a national referendum in March 1968, over 80% of voters approved a proposal to establish a republic in place of the sultanate. The Republic of the Maldive Islands was proclaimed on 11 November 1968. Amir Ibrahim Nasir, who had been Prime Minister since 1957, was elected President. The country was renamed the Republic of Maldives in April 1969.

A new Constitution, promulgated in 1968, vested considerable powers in the President, including the right to appoint and dismiss the Prime Minister and the Cabinet of Ministers. In March 1975, following rumours of a coup conspiracy, President Nasir invoked emergency powers and dismissed the Prime Minister, Ahmed Zaki, who was banished to a remote atoll, and the office of Prime Minister was abolished. In June 1978 Nasir announced that, for health reasons, he would not seek re-election at the end of his second five-year term, and in November, following a national referendum, Maumoon Abdul Gayoom, the erstwhile Minister of Transport in Nasir's Cabinet and a former permanent representative of the Maldives to the UN, succeeded Nasir as President. Nasir subsequently left the Maldives to take up residence in Singapore.

Gayoom's Government made the development of poor rural regions a priority, and claimed to have restored freedom to the Republic, such as freedom of the press. It also pursued investigations into the activities of former government officials, notably Nasir's Minister of Public Safety, Amir Abdul Hannan, who had been accused of human rights violations. Nasir himself, who was reputed to have amassed a substantial fortune while in office, was to face trial for misuse of government funds if he returned to the Maldives, and in November 1980 it was announced that the Government intended to try him *in absentia* on a number of charges.

In April 1980 President Gayoom confirmed the discovery of an attempted coup against the Government, and implicated Nasir in the alleged plot. In April 1981 Ahmed Naseem, former Deputy Minister of Fisheries and brother-in-law of Nasir, was sentenced to life imprisonment for plotting to overthrow President Gayoom. Nasir himself vigorously denied any involvement in the plot, and attempts to extradite him from Singapore were unsuccessful. (In July 1990, however, President Gayoom officially pardoned Nasir *in absentia* in recognition of the role that he had played in winning national independence.) In 1983 another unsuccessful plot against President Gayoom was reported. In September he was re-elected as President, for a further five years, by a national referendum in which he obtained 95.6% of the popular vote. In September 1988 Gayoom was again re-elected, unopposed, for a third five-year term, obtaining a record 96.4% of the popular vote.

A third, and more serious, attempt to depose President Gayoom took place in November 1988, when a force of seaborne mercenary troops, numbering about 80 men, landed in Malé and attempted to seize control of important government installations. A number of senior officials, including the Minister of Transport and Shipping, were captured, but the President, who went into hiding, successfully appealed for help to the Indian Government, which dispatched an emergency contingent of 1,600 troops. Although the insurrection was suppressed within a matter of hours, 19 people were reported to have died in the fighting. In their flight from the Indian forces, the mercenaries took a number of hostages, several of whom were subsequently killed. Most of the mercenary force was reported to have been captured as it attempted to escape by sea. The mercenaries were stated to be Sri Lankan members of the Tamil separatist group, the People's Liberation Organization of Tamil Eelam (PLOTE), allegedly recruited by a disaffected Maldivian businessman, Abdullah Luthufi, who was believed to have been acting in concert with the leader of PLOTE, Kadirkamam Uma Maheswaran. The Sri Lankan Government, however, was in no way implicated in the affair. In September 1989 the President commuted to life imprisonment the death sentences imposed on 12 Sri Lankans and four Maldivians who took part in the aborted coup. The Indian Government withdrew its remaining 160 troops from the Maldives in early November.

In February 1990, despite alleged opposition from powerful members of the privileged élite, President Gayoom announced that, as part of proposals for a broad new policy of liberalization and democratic reform, he was planning to introduce legislation, in the near future, enabling him to distribute powers, currently enjoyed by the President alone, amongst other official bodies. A further sign of growing democratization in the Maldives was the holding of discussions by the President's Consultative Council, in early 1990, concerning freedom of speech (particularly in the local press). In April, however, it became apparent that some Maldivians opposed political change, when three pro-reform members of the Majlis (legislature) received anonymous death threats. A few months later, following the emergence of several politically outspoken magazines, including *Sangu* (The Conchshell), there was an abrupt reversal of the Government's policy regarding the liberalization of the press. All publications not sanctioned by the Government were banned, and a number of leading writers and publishers were arrested.

As part of a major cabinet reorganization in late May 1990, President Gayoom dismissed the Minister of State for Defence and National Security, Ilyas Ibrahim (who also held the trade and industries portfolio and headed the State Trading Corporation), from his post, following the latter's abrupt and unannounced departure from the country. The Government later disclosed that Ibrahim (Gayoom's brother-in-law) was to have appeared before a presidential special commission investigating alleged embezzlement and misappropriation of government funds. On his return to the Maldives in August, Ibrahim was placed under house arrest. In March 1991, however, the special commission concluded that there was no evidence of involvement, either direct or indirect, by Ibrahim in the alleged financial misdeeds; in the same month the President appointed Ibrahim as Minister of Atolls Administration. In April Gayoom established an anti-corruption board, which was to investigate allegations of corruption, bribery, fraud, misappropriation of government funds and property, and misuse of government office.

In early August 1993, a few weeks before the Majlis vote on the presidential candidate, Gayoom was informed that Ibrahim, whose position as Minister of Atolls Administration had afforded him the opportunity to build a political base outside Malé (where he already enjoyed considerable popularity), was seeking the presidency and attempting to influence members of the Majlis (at that time, the legislature nominated and elected by secret ballot a single candidate, who was presented to the country in a referendum). In the Majlis vote, held in late August, the incumbent President, who had previously been unanimously nominated for the presidency by the legislature, obtained 28 votes, against 18 for his brother-in-law. For his allegedly unconstitutional behaviour, Ibrahim was charged with attempting to 'influence the members of the Majlis' and he promptly left the country. Ibrahim was subsequently tried *in absentia* and sentenced to 15 years' imprisonment. In addition, his brother, Abbas Ibrahim, was removed from his post as Minister of Fisheries and Agriculture. (Ilyas Ibrahim returned to the Maldives in 1996, when he was placed under house arrest; this restriction was lifted in 1997.) In October 1993 Gayoom's re-election as President for a further five years was endorsed by a national referendum, in which he obtained 92.8% of the popular vote.

In November 1994, at an official ceremony marking Republic Day, President Gayoom outlined various measures intended to strengthen the political system and to advance the process of democratization. These included the granting of greater autonomy and responsibilities to members of the Cabinet of Ministers, the introduction of regulations governing the conduct of civil servants (in order to increase their accountability), the introduction of democratic elections to island development committees and atoll committees, and the establishment of a Law Commission to carry out reforms to the judicial system.

In November 1996 President Gayoom effected an extensive cabinet reshuffle and a reorganization of government bodies, including the establishment of a Supreme Council for Islamic Affairs, which was to be under direct presidential control and was to advise the Government on matters relating to Islam. In early 1997 Gayoom announced that the Citizens' Special Majlis (which was established in 1980 with the specific task of amending the Constitution) had resolved to complete the revision of the Constitution during that year and to implement the amended version by 1 January 1998. The Citizens' Special Majlis finished its 17-year-long task in early November 1997. The revised Constitution was ratified by the President on 27 November and came into effect, as planned, on 1 January 1998. Under the new 156-article Constitution, a formal, multi-candidate contest was permitted for the legislature's nomination for the presidency; no restriction was placed on the number of terms a president might serve; for administrative purposes, the number of atolls was increased from 19 to 20; the Majlis, which was henceforth known as the People's Majlis, was enlarged from 48 to 50 seats; the Citizens' Special Majlis was renamed the People's Special Majlis; the rights of the people were expanded; parliamentary immunity was introduced; the office of auditor-general was created; the post of commissioner of elections was constitutionalized; ministers were afforded greater power; public officers were made more accountable; parliamentary questions were allowed; and judges and magistrates were obliged to take special oaths of loyalty.

In September 1998 five individuals declared their candidacy for the presidency; the People's Majlis unanimously voted by secret ballot for the incumbent President to go forward to the national referendum. In the referendum, which was held in mid-October, Gayoom was re-elected as President for a fifth term in office, obtaining 90.9% of the popular vote. Following his re-election, the President carried out an extensive cabinet reorganization. In an unexpected move, Ilyas Ibrahim was appointed to hold the new portfolio of transport and civil aviation.

In November 1999 elections for 42 members of the 50-seat People's Majlis were conducted (on a non-partisan basis). As part of a government initiative to promote the advancement of women in public life, President Gayoom appointed a woman as the new Island Chief of Himmafushi in June 2001. In December a woman was appointed as Atoll Chief of Vaavu (the first woman to be assigned a senior executive position of an atoll).

Meanwhile, in early 2001 an attempt by 42 prominent Maldivians, including members of the People's Majlis, former cabinet ministers and businessmen, to register the newly formed Maldivian Democratic Party (MDP) was blocked by the People's Majlis on the grounds that the existence of political parties would encourage divisions among the public and, therefore, be counter-productive. It was believed by some, however, that President Gayoom had enforced the decision and, in doing so, had acted unconstitutionally.

In July 2002 three journalists were sentenced to life imprisonment (and their assistant to a term of 10 years), on charges of defamation and inciting violence, after writing articles criticizing the President and the Government. In early 2003 international activists demanded the release of the detainees, claiming that the journalists had not advocated violent opposition to President Gayoom or the Government, and that they had only been exercising their right to freedom of speech. In July a businessman, who had published via the internet an article urging that the Government be overthrown, received a sentence of life imprisonment. At the end of that month Amnesty International issued a report citing frequent incidents of arbitrary detentions, unfair trials and long-term imprisonment and torture of political opponents in the Maldives. The human rights organization urged the authorities to release political prisoners, investigate allegations of torture and reform the criminal justice system. The Maldivian Government strongly denied the allegations.

In late September 2003 the death of a detainee at the prison in Malé provoked rioting, which was violently suppressed by security forces (resulting in the death of a further inmate and a number of severe casualties). Unrest subsequently erupted at a nearby hospital, after injured prisoners were finally taken there, and escalated into widespread anti-Government protests in the capital (the first ever during Gayoom's tenure). A number of public buildings were attacked, including the elections office, high court and police station, before the rioters were dispersed. The security forces (the country's feared National Security Service—NSS) subsequently began to arrest large numbers of alleged demonstrators. Gayoom announced an investigation into the deaths of the prisoners (the number of fatalities increased to four after two died in hospital), and a total of 11 members of the NSS were arrested for their involvement. The Deputy Chief of the NSS and Police Commissioner, Brig. Adam Zahir, was removed (but appointed to a post in the Ministry of Information, Arts and Culture until his reinstatement as Police Commissioner in mid-February 2004 after the inquiry cleared him of any misconduct). Amnesty International reiterated demands for an end to political repression in the Maldives and reform of the judicial system.

On 25 September 2003, nevertheless, Gayoom was re-elected unanimously in the People's Majlis for a sixth presidential term, defeating three other candidates. His re-election was ratified at a national referendum on 17 October, where he secured 90.3% of the votes cast. One day after his new term began, President Gayoom carried out a cabinet reorganization, in which Dr Mohamed Munavvar, the Attorney-General, and Ibrahim Hussain Zaki, the Minister of Planning and National Development, were dismissed. Gayoom gave no reason for the changes, although it was alleged that the two had been removed for supporting reformers attempting to register a political party. Gayoom also announced that the judicial system, executive and legislature would be reformed over the next five years (without specifying what the changes would be) and that a human rights commission would be established in Malé. In the same month political activists decided to establish the MDP (which had been prevented from registering as a political party in the Maldives in 2001—see above) in exile in Sri Lanka, in response to the rise in discontent with the Maldivian Government. In mid-February 2004 members of the MDP claimed that more than 15 of its supporters had been arrested in Malé in an alleged attempt to disrupt a planned protest march; however, the Government asserted that the raids were aimed at criminal offenders and that only eight people had been detained.

In December 2003 a Human Rights Commission was established. At the end of that month a report by the Presidential Commission investigating the death of four prisoners in September 2003 (see above) was submitted to President Gayoom. In his speech to the People's Majlis in January 2004 on the findings of the Commission, Gayoom stated that the security personnel involved in the prisoners' deaths had acted illegally and would be prosecuted. The President also announced that a programme of penal reform was under way. However, Mohamed Latheef, the exiled leader of the MDP, criticized the report, claiming that the names of those responsible for the deaths had been omitted from it, and demanded the President's resignation.

In May 2004 the election, by universal suffrage, of a People's Special Majlis took place. Voters chose 42 members out of 121 independent candidates. The President appointed another eight people to serve on the council; the People's Special Majlis also included members of the People's Majlis and the Council of Ministers. The People's Special Majlis was empowered to amend the Constitution. At the same time Gayoom invited members of the public to send him proposals for constitutional reform; any suggestions submitted by the end of June would be forwarded to the People's Special Majlis. In early June Gayoom himself proposed a number of far-reaching constitutional reforms. He suggested that a President's tenure should be limited to two five-year terms and that women should be allowed to stand for the presidency. According to the reforms, the President would also lose the right to appoint eight members of the People's Majlis. The People's Majlis would become independent of the executive and the post of Prime

Minister would be created. The judiciary would be restructured: a Supreme Court would be created as the highest court of appeal, which the President would appoint on the advice of the People's Majlis. Furthermore, the formation and functioning of political parties would be allowed. The People's Special Majlis, which was sworn in on 15 June, convened in July to discuss the proposals.

In mid-August 2004 President Gayoom declared an indefinite state of emergency after a pro-democracy protest in the capital became violent. A vigil outside the NSS headquarters for the release of political prisoners turned into a demonstration of about 3,000 people. Four police officers were reportedly stabbed and about 185 people were arrested during the protests. The Government called the demonstration a coup attempt, a charge denied by the opposition MDP. The exiled opposition leader Latheef accused the Government of 'ruthlessly suppressing dissent'. The Government invited a European Union (EU) fact-finding team to Malé. The EU envoys, however, were denied access to the detainees and expressed concern about the continuing detention without charge of the alleged protesters and the ongoing state of emergency. By early September 122 people had been released, while about 60 people remained in detention, including the former Attorney-General, Dr Mohamed Munavvar, and members of the People's Special Majlis. On 1 September, meanwhile, Gayoom relinquished the defence and finance portfolios, as part of a cabinet reorganization, in a step towards government reform. Ismail Shafeeu and Mohamed Jaleel were appointed as the new Ministers of Defence and National Security and of Finance and Treasury, respectively. On the same day the police force was relocated as a civil authority under the Ministry of Home Affairs and Environment. Gayoom's announcement was made amid international criticism of the Government's suppression of the August demonstration.

In October 2004 the state of emergency that had been declared in August was revoked. While a curfew was still in place, the lifting of the state of emergency meant that the opposition members indefinitely detained following the August pro-democracy protest would either have to be charged or released from prison. In December four of the detained opposition members were charged with treason. However, later that month President Gayoom announced that all charges of treason and public order offences against those taken into custody following the August protest were to be suspended.

Meanwhile, on 26 December 2004 a tsunami, generated by a massive earthquake in the Indian Ocean, off the coast of Indonesia, devastated many of the low-lying Maldive islands. While the resultant death toll was not as high as might have been expected, several of the islands were rendered uninhabitable and an estimated 15,000 people were left homeless by the disaster. It was feared that the economic consequences of the catastrophe on the Maldives would be profound, owing in large part to the significant contribution made by the tourism industry to the economy.

On 22 January 2005 149 independent candidates contested elections to the People's Majlis. The elections had been postponed from the previous month because of the December tsunami. Candidates supported by the opposition MDP reportedly succeeded in winning 18 of the 42 available legislative seats. However, the Government stated that only 12 opposition candidates had done so, claiming that the results were a sign of widespread popular support for its reform policies. President Gayoom insisted after the election that he intended to establish a multi-party democracy in the Maldives within one year.

In May 2005 Fathimath Nisreen, who had been sentenced to 10 years' imprisonment in July 2002 for allegedly having participated in subversive activities, was freed, having received a presidential pardon. In June 2005 the People's Majlis unanimously approved a constitutional amendment permitting the registration of political parties in the Maldives, reversing its 2001 decision opposing the establishment of a multi-party democracy. The MDP was subsequently officially registered in the Maldives as a political party, together with several others, including the Dhivehi Rayyithunge Party (DRP) established by President Gayoom. In mid-July 2005 Gayoom instigated a major reorganization of his Cabinet in which, most notably, the long-serving Minister of Foreign Affairs, Fathulla Jameel, was dismissed and replaced by Dr Ahmed Shaheed. Jameel later resigned from his seat in the People's Majlis. In the following month Qasim Ibrahim was sworn in as Minister of Finance and Treasury, replacing Mohamed Jaleel.

In August 2005 a protest took place in Malé calling for the release of all political prisoners. Shortly afterwards the Chairman of the MDP, Mohamed Nasheed, was arrested, provoking several days of unrest in the capital and on various other atolls. Nasheed was subsequently charged with terrorism and sedition; his trial began in October. Also in October Jennifer Latheef, daughter of the exiled Mohamed Latheef, was convicted of having incited a riot in Malé in September 2003 (see above) and was sentenced to a 10-year prison term. Amnesty International condemned the trial, describing Jennifer Latheef as a 'prisoner of conscience'. In February 2006 two dissidents who had been sentenced to lengthy prison terms in 2002 were released, having received presidential pardons. From June 2006 representatives of the Government and the MDP engaged in a series of informal talks under the auspices of the British High Commission in Colombo, Sri Lanka, resulting in what subsequently came to be known as the Westminster House Agreement. The Government reportedly agreed, among other points, to release a number of detainees and to hasten constitutional reform, in return for the MDP's assurance that it would curb public demonstrations and renounce violent protest. In July the Government dropped charges against several detainees, and in August 11 prisoners, who had been charged with fuelling civil unrest, were released. Jennifer Latheef, who had been under house arrest since December 2005, was also pardoned and released. Mohamed Nasheed, whose trial had been resumed in May 2006, was released in September, although the charges against him were not withdrawn.

In November 2006 more than 100 members of the MDP were arrested in the run-up to a planned demonstration to demand the swifter implementation of reforms; the rally was subsequently cancelled by the MDP amid fears for the welfare of protesters. Government officials alleged that the MDP had organized the rally as an attempt to overthrow the Government, and that, if it had been held, it would have posed a threat to public safety. In a subsequent report Amnesty International expressed concern at reports of 'repressive measures' being used by government officials. These allegations were vehemently denied by the Government, but they prompted widespread demands for the urgent introduction of a reform programme to prevent the arbitrary detention, mistreatment and torture of dissidents. In December the trial of the acting President of the MDP, Ibrahim Hussain Zaki, recommenced; the initial charge of high treason, arising from a speech that Zaki had made on Dhidhoo island in defence of the right of fishermen to protest, had been amended to a charge of 'enmity, contempt and disharmony'. The issue of press freedom came to the fore again in January 2007, with the commencement of the trial of Nazim Sattar, the Deputy Editor of the independent daily newspaper *Minivan News*. Sattar was charged with 'disobedience to order' for an article published in August 2005 that had quoted criticism of the Star Force unit of the Maldivian police force, resulting in the alleged persecution of the unit by the public.

Meanwhile, in early 2006 meetings of the People's Special Majlis, which had been convened in order that it could begin work upon amending the Constitution, were obstructed by President Gayoom's refusal to permit the removal of presidential appointees from the body. The opposition MDP condemned the continued presence of representatives who had not been elected, stressing that they should be withdrawn in advance of the redrafting of the Constitution, and also proposed that the President's power to assent to the Constitution should be removed. Tensions were heightened in late February when the Speaker of the People's Special Majlis, Abbas Ibrahim, removed a scheduled debate on the matter from the legislative agenda. The MDP boycotted the opening of the People's Majlis in that month in protest at what it alleged to be the President's obstruction of the constitutional amendment process. In March, however, the Government published a 'Roadmap for the Reform Agenda', which projected the passing of a draft constitution by the People's Special Majlis by 31 May 2007 and its ratification within a month of that date; the document also forecast that multi-party elections would be held by 2008. Among the other stated aims of the agenda were judicial and electoral reforms, greater media freedom, the establishment of a Police Integrity Commission and greater autonomy for the atoll and island administrations.

A Police Integrity Commission was established in August 2006, and in November the Human Rights Commission was reconstituted as legally autonomous; however, the introduction of new regulations on press freedom and access to information was delayed indefinitely by the Government in January 2007. A referendum to determine whether to adopt a presidential or parliamentary system of government, which was scheduled to be held in September 2006, was postponed owing to disagreements between the Government and the opposition.

In mid-January 2007 the founder of the MDP, Mohamed Latheef, ended three years of voluntary exile in Sri Lanka with his return to the Maldives. In February the Deputy Chairman of the MDP's parliamentary group, Ibrahim Shareef, defected to the DRP, citing his disapproval of alleged militant elements within his former party. Later in the month a demonstration organized by the MDP in protest at alleged police violence against civilians reportedly attracted an estimated 1,000 participants. In mid-April the discovery in Malé harbour of the corpse of a man who was alleged by some to have died in police custody prompted further demonstrations and numerous arrests; however, according to the subsequent autopsy, which was carried out in Sri Lanka, the man had not been tortured prior to his death. Meanwhile, in the same month the Minister of Higher Education, Employment and Social Security, Abdullah Yameen, resigned amid rumours of discord within the Cabinet. Yameen also stood down as a member of the DRP, and was reported to be planning the creation of a new political party. In early May Qasim Ibrahim was elected Speaker of the People's Special Majlis, succeeding Abbas Ibrahim, who had resigned in the previous month.

In June 2007 it appeared that progress was being made regarding the reform process when the People's Special Majlis announced a new deadline of 30 November 2007 for the drawing up of constitutional amendments. It was also reported that the long-awaited referendum on the system of government was imminent, the Special Majlis having agreed to a poll deadline of August 2007. Meanwhile, the death of an inmate of Maafushi prison in unclear circumstances during a prison revolt (it was initially claimed that he had died of a drug overdose, but it later emerged that no actual cause of death had been discovered) precipitated a hunger strike by hundreds of the deceased's fellow prisoners and public outrage at the regulation and conditions of the prison. Speculation arose in some quarters that the subsequent cabinet reshuffle, in which Minister of Home Affairs Ahmed Thasmeen Ali was transferred to the position of Minister of Atolls Development and the home affairs portfolio assigned to Abdullah Kamaaludheen, was related to the crisis. Further changes to the Cabinet of Ministers took place in August, when Minister of Justice Mohamed Jameel Ahmed and Attorney-General Hassan Saeed resigned, reportedly over impediments and delays to the programme of democratic reforms. Dr Ahmed Shaheed resigned later in the month, and was replaced by Abdullah Shahid; Mohamed Muiz Adnan was appointed Minister of Justice.

A referendum was finally held on 18 August 2007. Results showed that more than 60% of voters supported the presidential form of government as opposed to a parliamentary system. Turn-out was about 70% of the 193,000 eligible voters. The MDP reportedly filed 148 complaints about voting irregularities, such as the alleged inclusion of 10,000 names of deceased voters on the electoral roll, along with more than 15,000 citizens resident abroad. The DRP, in turn, complained that the opposition had engaged in intimidation, violence and illegal campaigning.

The November 2007 deadline for finalizing the draft constitutional amendments was not met by the People's Special Majlis, and discussions on constitutional reform, including proposals with regard to new regulations on freedom of information, were continuing in early 2008. Meanwhile, a press freedom bill was approved by the People's Majlis in August 2007, despite criticisms by Article 19, an international campaign group for freedom of expression, that it fell short of international standards.

In September 2007 the DRP blamed the introduction of a multi-party system and greater media freedom for an increase in social disturbances, a view that was vehemently rejected by journalists. On 29 September 12 tourists were injured when a bomb exploded in a park in the capital, Malé. The explosion—the first recorded terrorist attack to take place in the Maldives—was widely believed to have been perpetrated by Islamist extremists. In December three Maldivian men were each sentenced to 15 years in prison for their part in the incident, which they confessed to having planned as a deliberate attack on the country's vital tourism industry. In an attempt to combat the perceived threat of growing Islamist fundamentalism and to protect the lucrative tourism sector, the Government introduced a number of measures, including arresting suspected extremists, banning the wearing of the full veil in public, advocating the promotion of moderate Islamic views in schools and colleges, forbidding the convention of unlicensed Muslim prayer groups, and banning foreign Islamic clerics from visiting the islands unless they had been explicitly invited by the authorities. While visiting an atoll in the far north of the island chain in January 2008, President Gayoom himself escaped unhurt after an attempted knife attack by a 20-year-old Maldivian man. The Government claimed that the President's political rivals were the most likely organizers of the apparent assassination attempt, rather than Islamist extremists, as some early reports had suggested.

In late June 2008 the People's Special Majlis approved final amendments to the draft Constitution, which was then passed to the Cabinet of Ministers and the President in turn. The new Constitution was ratified by the President on 7 August; major points included the direct election of the President and the restriction of presidential terms of office to two; the election, rather than presidential appointment, of the Speaker and Deputy Speaker of the People's Majlis; the establishment of a Supreme Court as the highest judicial authority; and the granting to citizens the right to hold peaceful demonstrations. The People's Special Majlis and Judicial Advisory Council were duly dissolved, while the Speaker of the People's Majlis, Ahmed Zahir, was replaced by the elected Mohamed Shihab. Meanwhile, the Cabinet of Ministers was in a state of flux as numerous ministers resigned for constitutional and other reasons.

In November 1989 the Maldives hosted an international conference, with delegates from other small island nations, to discuss the threat posed to low-lying island countries by the predicted rise in sea level caused by heating of the earth's atmosphere as a result of pollution (the 'greenhouse effect'). In June 1990 an Environmental Research Unit, which was to operate under the Ministry of the Environment, was established in the Maldives. The Maldives again expressed its serious concern with regard to problems of world-wide environmental pollution when it hosted the 13th conference of the UN's Intergovernmental Panel on Climate Change in September 1997. In September 1999 a special session of the UN General Assembly was convened in New York, USA, to address the specific problems faced by the 43-member Alliance of Small Island States (including the Maldives), notably climate change, rising sea levels and globalization. At the UN Millennium Summit meeting in September 2000 the President of the Maldives again took the opportunity to urge leaders to address environmental issues. The Government expressed its grave disappointment and concern at the USA's decision in April 2001 to reject the Kyoto Protocol to the UN's Framework Convention on Climate Change. The rest of the international community adopted the Protocol in July after many of the targets had been reduced. The USA proposed an alternative in February 2002; however, most nations dismissed it as ineffective. In early March the Maldives, Kiribati and Tuvalu announced their decision to take legal action against the USA for refusing to sign the Kyoto Protocol, thus contributing to the global warming that has produced the rising sea levels that threaten to submerge the islands. At the World Summit on Sustainable Development, held in September in Johannesburg, South Africa, President Gayoom warned the international community that low-lying islands were at greater risk than ever before. He called for urgent action, including the universal ratification and implementation of the Kyoto Protocol, to prevent a global environmental catastrophe. On his return to the Maldives, the President stated that some progress had been made in certain areas, although the decisions were not as far-reaching as desired by small island nations. The President urged the international community to enforce the Kyoto Protocol during a television interview in August 2004, and in a speech at the Non-Aligned Movement Conference in Havana, Cuba, in September 2006, again appealed for international action on climate change and environmental degradation. In November 2007 the island states held a conference on the human dimensions of climate change and adopted a resolution calling for immediate and effective action to protect them from the increasing threats of climate change. In July 2008 a meeting of experts and environment ministers from SAARC member countries finalized a five-year plan of action, with funding expected to be provided by development partners, for management of the adverse effect of climate change in the region. The ministers issued a joint plan to combat the effects of global warming; the plan aimed for regional co-operation and South-South support in terms of technology and knowledge transfer. The ministers also demanded that developed countries establish a special fund dedicated to saving the affected countries from the effects of climate change. In September 2000, meanwhile, the Comprehensive Nuclear Test Ban Treaty was ratified by the Maldives.

# Economy

Revised by the editorial staff

The population is dispersed over 197 coral islands, with individual islands' populations ranging from 100 to more than 5,000 (the population of the capital, Malé, however, totalled an estimated 103,693 at the 2006 census). Tourism, fishing, agriculture and transport services provide the main income in the atolls. Arable land is minimal and, while small amounts of coconuts, millet, sorghum, maize and yams are grown, virtually all the main food staples, such as rice, wheat flour and sugar, have to be imported. A large proportion of the coconut crop is regularly destroyed by rats: eradication programmes are carried out every few years. During the 1970s the growth rate of the Maldivian economy failed to keep pace with the increase in the country's population, which averaged 3% annually. In 1979, according to estimates by the World Bank, the Maldives' gross national income (GNI) per head was US $220 (at average 1978–80 prices), having declined by 0.7% per year, in real terms, since 1970. However, despite the constraints imposed by geography, sparse agricultural resources and a narrowly based economy, the Maldives achieved average annual economic growth of 9.5% between 1978 and 1982. During 1990–99, it was estimated, GNI per head increased, in real terms, at an average annual rate of 3.8%. GNI per head increased by an average of 1.3% per year in 1999–2001. The Maldives' overall gross domestic product (GDP) increased, in real terms, by an average of 7.6% per year in 1996–2006. Although the economy fared well in the first eight months of 2001, the repercussions of the terrorist attacks on the mainland USA in September and the subsequent US-led military action in Afghanistan led to a decline in tourism and a deceleration in economic growth. The trade and financial sectors were also adversely affected by security fears and a global economic slowdown. The fisheries sector, however, fared better and in 2002–04 it continued to expand. The tourism sector made a strong recovery in 2003 and 2004, contributing to the high GDP growth in those years (a respective 8.4% and 8.8%, according to the Asian Development Bank—ADB). However, it was feared that the devastation caused by the Indian Ocean tsunami of 26 December 2004 would have profound economic consequences for the Maldives, in particular with regard to its impact on the tourism and fisheries sectors. Housing and infrastructure were also severely affected by the disaster, which virtually destroyed 14 of the country's inhabited islands and rendered an estimated 5% of the population homeless. GDP decreased by 4.1% in 2005. However, in response to substantial capital investment in the depleted tourism and fishing sectors, a strong economic recovery was recorded in 2006, when GDP grew by an estimated 18.7%. The World Bank estimated the country's GNI for 2006 to be $902m. (at average 2004–06 prices), equivalent to about $2,680 per head. According to the ADB, real GDP increased by 6.6% in 2007 and growth of around 8.0% was forecast for 2008. According to the World Bank, during 1996–2006 the population increased at an average annual rate of 2.7%. The working population at the 2006 census was 110,231 (36.9% of the total population) and, according to the census figures, 14.4% of the total labour force was unemployed at that time. Less than 8% of the work-force were farmers in 1990, producing less than 10% of the GDP. The Government has successfully diversified the economy by developing the shipping and tourist industries.

## FISHING

The fishing industry remains a vital sector of the Maldivian economy, although its contribution to GDP has declined in recent years. It is still the principal source of livelihood for the majority of the population, providing direct employment for almost 10,000 people. The catch consists mainly of tuna, 90% of which was traditionally exported to Sri Lanka in a dried form known as 'Maldive fish'. However, from 1972 the Sri Lankan Government gradually reduced its quota, and by 1978 had ceased importing 'Maldive fish'. This led to a change in the fisheries sector from dried fish to wet fish production, and in 1978, through an agreement with the Marubeni Corporation of Japan, the Maldive Nippon Corporation was formed and the first factory outside Malé for canning and processing fresh fish opened in the Faadhippolhu atoll. Although Sri Lanka resumed imports of 'Maldive fish' in 1979, it imported much less than before, and in the same year the Government announced the formation of the Maldives Fisheries Corporation, 'to exploit the fisheries resources in the most profitable manner for the benefit of the country'. Raw and fresh fish (whether frozen or canned) now constitute the bulk of fish exports.

There are several thousand fishing boats built in the country out of coconut wood, each boat taking about a dozen fishermen. In 1991 the fishing fleet comprised 1,258 pole and line fishing boats (*masdhoani*) and 352 trawling boats (*vadhudhoani*). Since 1974, when the Government introduced a major modernization programme, with the help of a 50-year loan of US $3.2m. from the International Development Association, about 90% of the fishing fleet has been mechanized, diesel engines replacing sails, and more maintenance and repair centres have been built. In 2003 the number of mechanized *masdhoani* totalled approximately 1,100. Although a long-term investment, this has had the unfortunate effect of increasing the cost of fuel imports, but it also helped to increase the output of the fishing industry by more than 100% between 1982 and 1985. The total catch of fish increased from 56,992 metric tons in 1987 to 133,000 tons in 1999. The Second Fisheries Development Project, which was carried out during the 1980s and early 1990s at an estimated total cost of $12.6m., with the help of the World Bank and other international organizations, aimed to improve productivity in the fishing industry. Substantial progress was made. Earnings from the export of canned fish from Felivaru increased from $230,000 in 1983 to $1.6m. in 1985. In 1986 the State Trading Organization invested 60m. rufiyaa in the extension and upgrading of the harbour and refrigeration facilities at the Felivaru Fish Canning Factory in the Faadhippolhu atoll. As a result of improvements to the factory, the Maldives' production of canned fish increased by 400% and the export market expanded. In 1993 two new refrigeration plants (with a total cold storage capacity of 1,000 tons) were constructed, with Japanese and Kuwaiti aid, on Maamendhoo Island in the Laamu atoll, and a new refrigeration plant was later built in the Gaafu Alif atoll. The Third Fisheries Development Project was completed in February 1999, at an estimated cost of $30.5m., with the official opening of the Kooddoo Fisheries Complex in the South Huvadhu atoll. The plan incorporated the construction of a refrigeration complex with a capacity of 1,900 tons, a quay for collector vessels (four of which were purchased as part of the Project) and an ice plant.

In 1985 the Government issued fishing licences to foreign countries, principally France and Spain, enabling them to catch up to 40,000 metric tons of tuna per year within the Maldives' exclusive economic zone (with a range of about 120 km), in return for a 10% royalty on the total catch, based on US landing prices. In 1992 the fishing industry employed about 22.4% of the labour force and provided around 15% of total GDP. In the same year fishing was the Maldives' second largest source of foreign exchange, after tourism. The GDP of the fisheries sector grew by 15% in 1994, compared with 1993. However, poor fish catches in the early part of 1995, combined with large stock levels in the frozen fish export market, resulted in depressed fisheries activity in 1995. In mid-1997 the Minister of Fisheries and Agriculture stated that, partly owing to the Government's successful efforts in improving the quality of Maldivian fish exports, the price of fish from the Maldives on the world market had become markedly stronger. In January 2001 the fresh fish export market was opened to the private sector and in that year the Maldives Industrial Fisheries Company (MIFCO) recorded a 13% increase in sales. In 2003 earnings from fish exports increased by about 37%. In that year revenue from exports of marine products reached 978.8m. rufiyaa, thus accounting for 67.7% of total export earnings. In 2004 exports from fish increased by a further 18%, compared with the previous year.

It was initially feared that the fisheries sector would be adversely affected as a result of the tsunami of December 2004. Approximately 8% of the country's fishing fleet was destroyed in the disaster. However, in 2005 the fishing sector contributed 7.2% of total GDP, and real growth in the sector was estimated at 16.8%, compared with the previous year. The total catch of fish increased to 186,000 metric tons in 2005; the total haul of skipjack tuna rose by 20.5% to 132,100 tons, while the yellowfin tuna catch declined marginally, from 24,800 tons in 2004 to 20,700 tons in 2005. According to ADB figures, exports of fresh tuna increased in 2005 and 2006 by 22.6% and 31.9%, respectively. These improvements in the fishing sector were mostly attributed to MIFCO, which had stimulated development in the sector by providing loans to privately owned vessels, thereby increasing overall capacity. However, in March 2006 the Government announced plans to sell 49% of its shares in MIFCO, following industrial action by fishermen who had been unable to sell a large portion of their catch to the state-run company. In 2006 the total catch of fish decreased slightly, to 184,200 metric tons, and in the following year revenue from exports of marine products totalled US $106m., thus accounting for 98% of total export earnings.

## SHIPPING

Another important commercial sector is the shipping industry, which was established in 1958; two ships were then in operation. By reinvesting the profits, the country was able to develop a sizeable fleet of ships, and in 1980 the profits of the state-owned Maldives Shipping Ltd (later renamed Maldives National Ship Management Ltd and, again, Maldives National Shipping Ltd), with 40 ships, provided 9% of government revenue. The Government tried to develop the shipping industry as much as possible by the training of technical personnel, to replace the foreigners engaged in this activity, and by increasing the total displacement of the fleet. In June 1981 the ADB approved a loan of US $1m. to the Maldives to assist in providing the country's first reliable scheduled shipping services between Malé and the atolls. During the 1980s, however, the shipping sector, which is dependent on third-country trade for more than 90% of its cargo earnings, suffered from the world-wide shipping recession as well as from the effects of the Iran–Iraq war; moreover, the UN Conference on Trade and Development (UNCTAD) code of conduct (effective from 1983), limiting third-country carriers to 20% of international sea freight, curtailed the lucrative trade of Maldivian vessels from Colombo, Sri Lanka. Because of the heavy losses incurred during 1982–84, the Maldivian shipping industry was reorganized, and both its fleet size and its level of operations were substantially reduced. The Maldives' international shipping sector, however, made a small profit in 1987 and 1988. In the early years of the first decade of the 2000s Maldives National Shipping Ltd operated a fleet of seven general cargo vessels and three container vessels. In December 2005 the merchant shipping fleet of the Maldives numbered 70 vessels, with a combined displacement of 87,402 grt (by the end of 2007 the displacement of the fleet had risen to 125,500 grt).

## TOURISM

The Maldives, with its white sandy beaches, clear water and multi-coloured coral formations, offers an ideal setting for the development of a thriving tourist industry. Following the decline of the shipping industry in the 1980s, tourism rapidly gained in importance as an economic sector, and by 1989 it had overtaken the fishing industry as the Maldives' largest source of foreign exchange. Since 1972 tourist facilities have been developed by local private enterprises. In an effort to boost tourism, the Government also introduced ways to improve the infrastructure. Telephones were installed on several resort islands for the first time in 1977, and a Tourist Advisory Board was established in 1981 to expand the industry yet further. Tourism was, initially, seriously affected by the civil disturbances in Sri Lanka, the usual embarkation point for the Maldives. However, the inauguration of direct charter flights carrying tourists from Europe to Malé, as well as the establishment of three new domestic airports (in 1986, 1990 and 1993), increased the Maldives' share of the market and ensured that revenue from tourism was sustained. According to the Second Tourism Master Plan, which was approved by the Government in May 1996, the number of tourist beds was to be increased by 10,000 over the following 10 years, and tourism was to be introduced in new areas, based on the existing transport and communications facilities. Bidding for the 14 islands to be developed for tourism under the Master Plan opened in June 1997. In 1996 the Government declared 1997 'Visit Maldives Year' and launched an intensive promotional campaign. By early 2004 a total of 87 island resorts had been developed for tourists, with 16,800 hotel beds (compared with 11,400 in 1996). It was announced in March of that year that another 11 islands would be converted into resorts and that nine atolls were to be opened up for tourism. There is no tourist accommodation on Malé, on the grounds that it would interfere with the traditional Islamic way of life pursued by the island's inhabitants.

The number of tourists visiting the Maldives rose from 3,789 in 1972/73 to 467,154 in 2000 (the majority of whom were from Europe). This figure decreased in 2001 to 460,984, despite promotional campaigns conducted in the previous year, largely because of concerns over travel safety and stability in the South Asian region after the terrorist attacks on the USA in September. By the end of 2002, however, tourist arrivals had recovered to a total of 484,680. The figure rose again in 2003, to 563,593, and receipts from tourism in that year increased to an estimated 896m. rufiyaa (compared with 883m. rufiyaa in 2002). In 2003 the tourism sector provided 31.5% of GDP. In 2004 tourist arrivals rose to 616,716 and receipts totalled 921.6m. rufiyaa. However, the tourism sector was seriously affected by the tsunami of December 2004. One-quarter of all tourist resorts in the Maldives were forced to close temporarily as a result of the disaster. In addition, the resultant adverse publicity discouraged prospective visitors to the Maldives in the succeeding months. In June 2005 the Ministry of Tourism estimated the cost of rebuilding at US $100m., in addition to a loss of revenue of $200m. Tourist arrivals amounted to just 395,320 in 2005, but receipts remained strong, at 909.3m. rufiyaa, and all the affected resorts had reopened by the end of that year. However, the contribution of the tourism sector to GDP was just 21.8% in 2005, and the sector's GDP declined, in real terms, by 33.1% in that year. Nevertheless, as predicted, tourism figures returned to pre-tsunami levels in 2006, following the reopening of affected resorts and hotels in late 2005. In 2006 tourist arrivals rose to 601,923, representing an increase of 52.3% on the previous year, and tourism receipts showed very strong recovery, reaching an impressive $434m. (just $37.2m. less than in 2004). The phenomenal resurgence of the tourism sector underpinned much of the Maldives' robust economic growth in 2006. Tourism figures for 2007 (675,889 arrivals and receipts of $493.6m.) illustrated continuing healthy recovery in the sector and, moreover, indicated that tourism remained the most dynamic subdivision of the economy. A total of 35 new resorts were opened in the Maldives during that year (a further 50 were scheduled to be opened during 2010–12) and the expansion of the international airport at Malé (where a second runway was to be constructed) and the domestic airport on Gan Island in the southern archipelago—which was due to begin handling international flights in 2008—was expected further to increase tourist arrivals.

## FINANCE

In 1981 the country's first central bank, the Maldives Monetary Authority (MMA), was established, and the currency was changed from rupees to rufiyaa. In 1982 the first commercial bank, the Bank of Maldives Ltd, was opened as a joint venture between the Government and the International Finance Investment Co Ltd of Bangladesh (now the International Finance Investment and Commerce Bank Ltd). Import controls, obliging foreign business executives to use banking facilities in the Maldives, were also announced in 1982. In 1985, aiming to reduce the deficit on the balance-of-payments current account and to remedy a serious shortage of foreign exchange, the Government imposed controls on the supply of bank credit, restricted capital expenditure on development projects, and 'pegged' the exchange rate of the rufiyaa to the currencies of the Maldives' principal trading partners. In 1986 it introduced an import-licensing system, which successfully curtailed expenditure on imports, but this was revoked in March 1987, when the rufiyaa was devalued by 30% and allowed to 'float'.

In September 1992 the MMA introduced a range of restrictive measures, including an increase in bank reserve requirements to 35%, a rise in the ceiling on bank loan rates, the imposition of a minimum deposit rate of 5%, and an increase in bank capital requirements.

In 1993 the Government sold 15% of its shares in the Bank of Maldives Ltd to public companies and 25% to private individuals. The MMA periodically reviews quantitative credit limits for commercial banks and imposes new limits in an attempt to maintain the level of domestic credit expansion. The rate of domestic credit expansion decreased from more than 50% in 1993 to 8.8% in 1997, reflecting a sharp reduction in credit to the Government and to public non-financial bodies.

Following the adverse effects of the international recession in the early 1980s, the fishing and tourism industries made a rapid recovery, and helped to reduce the country's economic deficits. In the first half of the 1990s the visible trade deficit steadily increased, as fish exports declined and imports grew. The decrease in fish exports reflected the slump in global demand, more intense competition from foreign producers and falling prices in the principal European markets. At the same time, imports were boosted by import liberalization measures and by expansionary monetary and fiscal policies. Despite the relative strength of the fisheries sector and buoyant tourist receipts in the latter half of the 1990s, the current-account deficit persisted (rising from 6.8% of GDP in 1998 to 11.1% in 1999) and the visible trade deficit continued to grow (largely owing to a surge in imports associated with development investment in the tourism sector). However, in 2000 the visible trade deficit decreased to US $233.3m. (compared with $262.5m. in 1999), as exports increased and imports declined. The current-account deficit decreased to $51.5m. in 2000 (compared with $81.7m. in the previous year). In 2001 the visible trade deficit and current-account deficit rose to $236.1m. and $58.8m., respectively. In 2002, however, total exports increased significantly, mainly owing to a recovery in international fish prices and stimulus provided by the delayed effects of currency devaluation in 2001. With total imports declining slightly, the visible trade deficit decreased to about $212.4m. in 2002. The current-account deficit was reduced to $35.7m. in that year. In 2003 the trade deficit increased to $262.3m., while the current-account deficit was reduced slightly, to $31.3m. In the following year, according to the IMF, the visible trade deficit reached $383.8m., while the current-account deficit also rose, to an estimated $122.3m., owing to a combination of increased imports and high global prices for petroleum. As a result of the catastrophic effects of the December 2004 tsunami, official sources estimated that the visible trade deficit had risen to $493.8m. in 2005 and the current-account deficit had increased to $269.7m. (compared with the $105.3m. predicted before the disaster). The trade balance deteriorated further in 2006 when, according to the IMF, a deficit of $599.5m. was recorded, together with a $378.6m. deficit on the current account of the balance of payments. Because of the dearth of manufacturing industries, the Maldives has to import most essential consumer and capital goods. In 2007 the principal source of imports was Singapore (accounting for 22.5% of the total); other major sources were the United Arab Emirates, India and Malaysia. In the same year the principal market for exports was Thailand (accounting for 40.9% of the total); other major purchasers were Sri Lanka, France and the United Kingdom. The principal exports in 2007 were marine products (tuna being the largest export commodity). The principal imports were machinery and mechanical appliances and electrical equipment, mineral products, and wood and metal manufactures.

Reflecting an improvement in the country's general economic condition (aided by the fact that the Maldives was not significantly affected by the Asian financial crisis that began in mid-1997), the overall budgetary deficit, including grants, was reduced from 10.6% of GDP in 1995 to about 5.1% in 1998. In 2003 the overall fiscal deficit declined to 4.1% of GDP from 4.9% in the previous year and, in 2004, the deficit was only 2.8% of GDP. The principal contributory factor to a rise in expenditure in the early years of the first decade of the 2000s was the Hulhumalé project, a large-scale infrastructural development programme to create a new town on an island near Malé. The deficit was mainly financed by higher levels of external borrowing on commercial terms. In 2003, however, strong revenue reduced the fiscal deficit, despite a continued expansion of current expenditure. Domestic credit continued to expand significantly in 2003, largely owing to increased credit to the private sector. According to the ADB, broad money increased by 14.6% in that year (compared with a rise of 19.3% in 2002).

Foreign grant aid in 2000 totalled an estimated US $17.7m.; Japan has traditionally been the Maldives' largest aid donor (disbursing $11.9m. in 1997). In the aftermath of the December 2004 tsunami, the Maldives received a significant amount of international aid, in the form of both grants and concessional loans, principally from the UN, the ADB, the World Bank and Japan. A total of $88m. had been pledged in assistance by the end of April 2005, of which $75m. was to be in the form of grants. In June 2006 the Japanese Government announced a $23m. loan to aid reconstruction. The Maldives' total external debt was an estimated $368.2m. at the end of 2005, of which $307.0m. was long-term public debt. In that year the cost of debt-servicing was equivalent to 6.9% of revenue from exports of goods and services. According to the IMF, during 1995–2005 the average annual rate of inflation was 2.8%; consumer prices increased by 3.3% in 2005, by 3.7% in 2006 and were predicted to show a sharp rise, of 7.0%, in 2007. A report published by the IMF in August 2007 warned that the Government's budget for that year made provisions for an unrealistic capital outlay in the tourism sector. While increasing revenues from this sector had facilitated strong economic growth in 2006, there were concerns that the cost of financing resort developments could lead to a serious depletion in the country's international reserves. The post-tsunami reconstruction projects widened the budget deficit considerably. In 2006, in terms of central government finance, there was an estimated fiscal deficit of 845.7m. rufiyaa (equivalent to 7.1% of GDP). The deficit for 2007 was projected to be 3,704.1m. rufiyaa At the end of 2006 external debt remained high, at some 57.2% of GDP. The IMF had previously advised that the Government should increase domestic revenues by broadening its system of taxation, with greater corporate coverage and an *ad valorem* tourism tax.

## OTHER ECONOMIC ACTIVITIES

The harvesting of coconuts forms another significant commercial activity in the Maldives. Coir yarn weaving, in which only women are engaged, is also a major occupation. In spite of several centuries of continued production of this commodity, the methods in use have not undergone much change; the women do the work in their own homes.

Collecting cowries is another occupation in which only women take part. Cowries and other varieties of shells are a natural product meant solely for export, and not generally used for any domestic purpose. Many varieties of shells in demand by collectors are found in the Maldives, including some of the rarest in the world.

Other small-scale cottage industries include mat-weaving, mostly in the three southernmost atolls of the archipelago, and applying lacquer designs on vases and containers. The highly coloured mats have some commercial value abroad. Cadjan weaving is also common on the islands, and cadjan is much in demand because of its value for roofing: the heat of the tropical sun is considerably reduced by its use.

Although these small-scale activities employ nearly one-quarter of the total labour force, there has been little scope for expansion, owing to the limited size of the domestic market. In the late 1980s and 1990s, however, there was a substantial increase in demand for traditional handicrafts, such as lacquer work and shell craft, as a result of the expansion of the tourist market. There are only a small number of 'modern' industries in the Maldives, including fish-canning, garment-making (in early 1998 there were eight garment factories operating in the Maldives) and soft-drink bottling. In 1998 the Foreign Investment Services Bureau announced that seven new garment factories were to be built over the next two years (creating about 7,000 new jobs). In mid-1999 the opening of a cement-packing factory on Thilafushi Island in Malé atoll was expected to bring considerable economic benefits to the Maldives. In an attempt to improve and diversify the domestic socio-economy, particularly in the less advanced outlying atolls, the Government has, since the late 1970s, begun to establish a more modern infrastructure (including better communications systems, sanitation and water supply). One of the major infrastructural projects was the Malé land-reclamation project, completed in 1986. In 1987 the ADB granted a loan of US $6.1m. for the construction of a 4,000-kW power plant, which commenced operations in 1991, on an area of this reclaimed land. Also in that year the Government announced plans to provide telephone facilities and postal services to all the inhabited islands over the next few years. By 1993 postal services were available to all the inhabited islands, telephone facilities were provided in the major islands of seven of the southern atolls and three of the northern atolls and facsimile (fax) services were available to some islands. By mid-1999 the Maldives telecommunications company, Dhivehi Raajjeyge Gulhun Ltd (DHIRAAGU), had provided telephone facilities to all of the inhabited islands. In mid-1999 DHIRAAGU signed a contract worth 47m. rufiyaa with a French telecommunications company for the supply and implementation of a mobile cellular telephone system for the Maldives. By mid-2004 mobile telephone coverage had reached 73% of the population and by March 2007 262,615 inhabitants had subscribed to mobile cellular telephones. In mid-2000 DHIRAAGU launched its 'Instant Internet Access'; by 2004 there were 1,260 internet subscribers. In early 1996, in an effort to combat deforestation, the Government instituted a three-year afforestation programme, which aimed to plant 1m. trees (the target was later increased to 2m. trees, owing to the rapid success of the programme). The numerous development projects undertaken during the 1980s and 1990s resulted in a shortage of labour, which was partly alleviated by employing workers from abroad and by the establishment of vocational training courses. In 2003 about 33,779 expatriate workers (mainly from India, Sri Lanka and Bangladesh) were employed in the Maldives, and it was estimated that in 1999 almost 20% of the country's GDP went to non-Maldivians.

In February 1989 the Government and the Anglo-Dutch company, Royal Dutch Shell, signed a contract permitting exploration for petroleum in the Maldives. Despite the drilling of an offshore test well in 1991, no reserves of petroleum or natural gas have, as yet, been discovered in Maldivian waters. Owing to a surge in commercial activities and a significant increase in construction projects in Malé, demand for electricity in the capital grew rapidly in the late 1980s and early 1990s. Accordingly, plans were formulated in late 1991 to augment the generating capacity of the power station in Malé and to improve the distribution network. By 2004 21 inhabited islands had been provided with electricity. In 2001 the third phase of the Malé power project, further to increase the capital's power supply, was under way. In December the ADB agreed to provide a loan to improve the supply of electricity to some 40 outer islands. In 2006 the ADB supplied another loan, of US $8m., to enable the electrification of those outer islands not included in the first project.

## PROBLEMS AND PROSPECTS

Overall economic performance in the late 1990s was favourable, with greater private-sector participation in the economy, a rise in foreign investment (assisted by the recently established Foreign Investment Promotion Advisory Board), a considerable increase in exports (aided by the expansion of the garment industry), and continued expansion in the tourism sector. Three notable areas of investment in the late 1990s were commercial seaweed farming, pearl cultivation and horticulture (in an attempt to reduce reliance on expensive imports of fruit and vegetables). The Maldives was still, however, confronted with the problem of serious macro-economic imbalances, which have resulted in rising debt, low levels of foreign-exchange reserves and an overvalued nominal exchange rate. In April 2000 Air Maldives, a joint venture between the Government and a Malaysian company, permanently ceased operating international flights, as a result of estimated losses of US $50m.–$70m. This outcome adversely affected the tourist industry and business confidence in 2000. Furthermore, allegations of mismanagement and corruption at the airline were made public. Development in the private sector has been constrained by the dominant role still played by the highly regulated public sector in economic activity. In early 2001, however, the Government opened up the export of fresh and canned fish to the private sector, which subsequently proved successful in increasing export earnings and the industry's contribution to GDP.

According to UN projections, the Maldives' population was expected to double between 1995 and 2025. The high average annual rate of population growth (estimated at 2.5% in 1990–2003), which has placed a heavy burden on the economy in general, is effectively being addressed (according to the results of the March 2000 census, the rate of increase had fallen to 1.96% in 1995–2000, with a further decline, as indicated by the March 2006 census). From 1997, in an attempt to solve the problem of overcrowding in Malé, an artificially constructed island was being developed nearby with the establishment of a new town to relieve congestion in the capital (the Hulhumalé project). In 2005, according to the UN Development Programme (UNDP), the Maldives continued to be classified within the Medium Human Development Category, ranking 100th (just behind Sri Lanka) on a list of 177 countries. In February 2002 the ADB endorsed a three-year country strategy and programme for the Maldives, designed to assist the Maldives in improving living conditions, the education system and access to social infrastructure in the remote islands. In March the Maldives and the ADB signed a poverty reduction partnership agreement, with the joint intentions of reducing the incidence of absolute poverty from 43% in 1998 to 25% by 2015 and promoting involvement of local communities in public-sector decision-making. In December 2003 the ADB approved a loan to boost jobs in the country through improved skills training. In August 2004 the ADB agreed to a US $12m. lending programme over 2005–06 to encourage greater economic development in the outer atolls. The ADB's 2004–06 country strategy and programme for the Maldives also included projects to expand the country's social infrastructure and transport links.

Following the adverse impact of the September 2001 terrorist attacks in the USA (see above), the economy underwent a partial recovery in 2002, which was generated by the revival in tourism and expansion in the fisheries sector. The economy achieved a nearly full recovery in 2003, thanks to an increase in tourism and a significant rise in fish exports, and experienced further positive growth in 2004. However, as a direct result of the December 2004 tsunami, the IMF estimated that GDP in 2005 registered a contraction of 3.6% (at constant prices), whereas growth of 6.5% had been forecast before the disaster. The budgetary cost of reconstruction was projected to reach as much as 13% of total GDP in that year. The tsunami disaster highlighted the vulnerability of the economy to external events and the fact that the long-term prosperity of the Maldives required sustained growth and diversification of activities.

The first group of people moved to the new island of Hulhumalé in 2004. By the end of December around 1,500 people had already moved to the island. The Government hoped to move about 45,000 people to Hulhumalé by 2020. The demand for local construction and transport generated by this project and other regional development programmes has proved beneficial to the economy. This and other regional development programmes, together with the extensive reconstruction work necessary in the aftermath of the tsunami, were expected to stimulate demand for local construction and transport, creating a favourable outlook for the economy in the long-term, despite the short-term set-backs. As part of its long-term development strategy for the low-lying Maldive islands, the Government promulgated a policy of encouraging voluntary population relocation to less vulnerable islands, proposing a plan whereby 'safe islands' would be created, both to increase the efficiency and economy of public-service provision and to guard against further tsunamis and rising sea levels. Continued positive performance of exports was likely, but remained dependent on the international price of tuna. The Government had commenced the introduction of necessary reforms for the development of the financial market and opening up of the public sector to private investment. The Government had also created several committees to develop plans on how to diversify the industrial base and to export products and markets. The implementation of measures to restrain external borrowing, however, remained necessary.

# Statistical Survey

Source (unless otherwise stated): Ministry of Planning and National Development, Ghaazee Bldg, 4th Floor, Ameer Ahmed Magu, Malé 20-05; tel. 3322919; fax 3327351; internet www.planning.gov.mv.

## AREA AND POPULATION

**Area:** 298 sq km (115 sq miles).

**Population:** 270,101 at census of 31 March–7 April 2000; 298,968 (males 151,459, females 147,509) at census of 21–28 March 2006. *Mid-2007* (official estimate): 304,869.

**Density** (official estimate, mid-2007): 1,023 per sq km.

**Administrative Divisions** (population, 2006 census): *Capital City*: Malé 103,693. *Atolls*: North Thiladhunmathi 13,495; South Thiladhunmathi 16,237; North Miladhunmadulu 11,940; South Miladhunmadulu 10,015; North Maalhosmadulu 14,756; South Maalhosmadulu 9,578; Faadhippolhu 9,190; Malé 15,441; North Ari 5,776; South Ari 8,379; Felidhe 1,606; Mulakatholhu 4,710; North Nilandhe 3,765; South Nilandhe 4,967; Kolhumadulu 8,493; Hadhdhunmathi 11,990; North Huvadhu 8,262; South Huvadhu 11,013; Gnaviyani 7,636; Addu 18,026.

**Births, Marriages and Deaths** (2006): Registered live births 5,827 (birth rate 20 per 1,000); Marriages 5,556; Registered deaths 1,084 (death rate 4 per 1,000).

**Expectation of Life** (years at birth, WHO estimates): 72.3 (males 71.5; females 73.2) in 2006. Source: WHO, *World Health Statistics*.

**Economically Active Population** (persons aged 12 years and over, census of March 2006): Agriculture, hunting and forestry 4,236; Fishing 8,388; Mining and quarrying 339; Manufacturing 19,259; Electricity, gas and water 1,229; Construction 5,930; Wholesale and retail trade and repairs 11,711; Restaurants and hotels 12,090; Transport, storage and communications 7,098; Financing, insurance, real estate and business services 1,738; Public administration and defence 15,949; Education 9,872; Health and social work 4,182; Other community, social and personal service activities 3,248; Extra-territorial organizations and bodies 216; Activities not adequately defined 4,746; *Total employed* 110,231 (males 69,701, females 40,530); Unemployed 18,605; *Total labour force* 128,836.

## HEALTH AND WELFARE

### Key Indicators

**Total Fertility Rate** (children per woman, 2005): 2.6.

**Under-5 Mortality Rate** (per 1,000 live births, 2006): 30.0.

**HIV/AIDS** (% of persons aged 15–49, 2001): 0.06.

**Physicians** (per 1,000 head, 2004): 0.92.

**Hospital Beds** (per 1,000 head, 2003): 2.26.

**Health Expenditure** (2005): US $ per head (PPP): 878.

**Health Expenditure** (2005): % of GDP: 12.4.

**Health Expenditure** (2005): public (% of total): 85.6.

**Access to Water** (% of persons, 2004): 83.

**Access to Sanitation** (% of persons, 2004): 59.

**Human Development Index** (2005): ranking: 98.

**Human Development Index** (2005): value: 0.739.

For sources and definitions, see explanatory note on p. vi.

## AGRICULTURE, ETC.

**Principal Crops** (production in long-term leased islands*, metric tons, 2006): Coconuts 78.6; Tender coconut 77.6; Aubergine 41.5; Cucumbers 30.8; Pumpkins 52.9; Bitter gourds 4.4; Ridged peppers 32.9; Papaya 478.4; Watermelons 378.1; Bananas 332.7.

* Comprising the atolls of North Thiladhunmathi, South Thiladhunmathi, North Miladhunmadulu, South Ari, Mulakatholhu, North Nilandhe, Kolhumadulu and Hadhdhunmathi.

**Coconuts** (number): 40.6m. in 2004; 52.4m. in 2005; 64.1m. in 2006.

**Sea Fishing** ('000 metric tons, 2006): Total catch 184.2 (Skipjack tuna—Oceanic skipjack 138.5; Yellowfin tuna 21.8; Sharks, rays, skates, etc. 0.9). Source: FAO.

## INDUSTRY

**Selected Products** (metric tons, 2003): Frozen tuna 47,546; Salted, dried or smoked fish 9.2; Canned fish 7,094. Source: FAO.

**Electric Energy** (million kWh): 177.0 in 2004; 204.1 in 2005; 233.3 in 2006.

## FINANCE

**Currency and Exchange Rates:** 100 laari (larees) = 1 rufiyaa (Maldivian rupee). *Sterling, Dollar and Euro Equivalents* (30 May 2008): £1 sterling = 25.261 rufiyaa; US $1 = 12.800 rufiyaa; €1 = 19.850 rufiyaa; 1,000 rufiyaa = £39.59 = $78.13 = €50.38. *Exchange Rate* (rufiyaa per US dollar): since July 2001 the mid-point rate of exchange has been fixed at US $1 = 12.80 rufiyaa.

**Budget** (central government finance, million rufiyaa, 2007, estimates): *Revenue*: Tax revenue 3,193.9 (Import duty 2,424.1); Other current revenue 3,912.3 (Resort lease rents 1,792.1); Capital revenue 32.4; Grants 958.9; Total 8,097.5. *Expenditure*: General administration of public services 1,892.6; Defence 480.2; Public order and internal security 662.2; Environmental protection 139.3; Education

1,257.1; Health 890.0; Social security and welfare 599.3; Community programmes 3,349.3; Economic services 2,300.1 (Agriculture and fishing 152.4, Trade and industry 149.4, Electricity, gas and water 328.6, Transport and communications 1,405.0, Tourism 111.9); Interest on public debt 305.6; Net lending –74.1; Total 11,801.6 (Current 6,797.2, Capital and net lending 5,004.4).

**International Reserves** (US $ million at 31 December 2007): IMF special drawing rights 0.57; Reserve position in IMF 2.46; Foreign exchange 305.32; Total 308.35. Source: IMF, *International Financial Statistics*.

**Money Supply** (million rufiyaa at 31 December 2007): Currency outside banks 1,141.60; Demand deposits at commercial banks 3,221.37; Total money (incl. others) 4,404.73. Source: IMF, *International Financial Statistics*.

**Cost of Living** (Consumer Price Index; base: 2005 = 100): All items 103 in 2006; 111 in 2007. Source: IMF, *International Financial Statistics*.

**Gross Value Added in Basic Prices** (million rufiyaa at constant 1995 prices, 2007, estimates): Agriculture 205.1; Fishing and fisheries 460.1; Mining (coral and sand) 53.6; Manufacturing 707.4; Electricity and water supply 446.5; Construction 618.0; Wholesale and retail trade 386.4; Transport and communications 1,892.9; Finance, real estate and business services 1,150.3; Tourism 2,799.8; Public administration 1,591.7; Other services 154.5; *Sub-total* 10,466.3; Financial intermediation services indirectly measured –401.6; *Gross value added in basic prices* 10,064.7.

**Balance of Payments** (US $ million, 2006): Exports of goods f.o.b. 215.9; Imports of goods f.o.b. –815.3; *Trade balance* –599.5; Exports of services 473.1; Imports of services –233.1; *Balance on goods and services* –359.5; Other income received 15.0; Other income paid –56.3; *Balance on goods, services and income* –400.8; Current transfers received 105.3; Current transfers paid –83.2; *Current balance* –378.6; Direct investment from abroad 13.9; Other investment assets 113.0; Other investment liabilities 163.7; Net errors and omissions 133.1; *Overall balance* 45.0. Source: IMF, *International Financial Statistics*.

### EXTERNAL TRADE

**Principal Commodities** (US $ million, 2007): *Imports c.i.f.:* Consumer goods 368.2 (Food items 175.0, Tobacco products 7.2, Pharmaceuticals 7.5, Other consumer goods 178.4); Petroleum products 202.9 (Motor spirit—gasoline 20.5, Diesel oil 166.5, Aviation fuel 7.2, Other petroleum products 8.7); Intermediate and capital goods 525.2 (Construction materials 172.3; Paper and paper products 2.9; Medical and surgical supplies 4.8; Computer equipment and supplies 15.3; Machinery and mechanical appliances 22.5; Textiles 8.4; Chemicals and chemical products 7.2; Transport equipment and parts 78.8); Total 1,096.3. *Exports*: Marine products 105.6 (Fresh, chilled or frozen tuna 79.5, *of which* Skipjack 42.0; Yellowfin 35.4; Dried fish 9.2; Canned fish 10.8); Other products (mostly clothing and waste and scrap of alloy steel) 2.1; Total 107.8. *Re-exports:* 120.2.

**Principal Trading Partners** (US $ million, 2006): *Imports*: Australia 25.5; China, People's Republic 24.5; France 11.8; Germany 23.8; India 125.9; Japan 20.7; Malaysia 93.4; Singapore 247.0; Sri Lanka 76.0; Thailand 53.0; United Arab Emirates 209.7; United Kingdom 16.1; USA 22.3; Total (incl. others) 1,096.3. *Exports:* France 7.9; Germany 1.7; Japan 4.9; Singapore 0.8; Sri Lanka 16.1; Thailand 44.1; United Kingdom 12.3; Total (incl. others) 107.8. *Re-exports:* 120.2.

### TRANSPORT

**Road Traffic** (registered motor vehicles, 2006): Passenger cars 2,372; Buses, pick-ups and vans 1,811; Lorries and tractors 675; Motorcycles and mopeds 22,107; Total (incl. others) 28,081.

**Merchant Shipping Fleet** (displacement, '000 gross registered tons at 31 December): 87.4 in 2005; 99.9 in 2006; 125.5 in 2007. Source: Lloyd's Register-Fairplay, *World Fleet Statistics*.

**International Shipping** (freight traffic, '000 metric tons, 1990): Goods loaded 27; Goods unloaded 78. Source: UN, *Monthly Bulletin of Statistics*.

**Civil Aviation** (traffic at Malé International Airport, 2006): *International Flights:* Arrivals 734,733; Departures 723,758. *Domestic Flights:* Arrivals 355,015; Departures 361,191.

### TOURISM

**Tourist Arrivals:** 395,320 in 2005; 601,923 in 2006; 675,889 in 2007.

**Foreign Visitors by Country of Nationality** (2007): Austria 13,673; China, People's Republic 35,976; France 45,301; Germany 72,269; India 17,327; Italy 117,246; Japan 41,121; Russia 31,845; Switzerland 26,183; United Kingdom 125,158; Total (incl. others) 675,889.

**Tourism Receipts** (US $ million): 286.6 in 2005; 433.7 in 2006; 493.6 in 2007.

### COMMUNICATIONS MEDIA

**Radio Receivers** (July 2000): 29,724 registered.

**Television Receivers** (July 2000): 10,701 registered.

**Telephones** (main lines in use): 28,651 in 2002; 30,056 in 2003; 31,503 in 2004.

**Mobile Cellular Telephones:** 41,899 in 2002; 66,466 in 2003; 113,246 in 2004.

**Personal Computers** (2004): 36,000 in use.

**Internet Users** (registered): 1,067 in 2002; 1,155 in 2003; 1,260 in 2004.

**2007:** 32,513 main line telephones in use; 262,615 mobile cellular telephones; 1,326 registered internet users.

Sources: Telecommunications Authority of Maldives, Malé; International Telecommunication Union.

### EDUCATION

**Schools** (2006): 349. Source: Ministry of Education.

**Teachers** (2006): Pre-primary 611; Primary 3,337; Lower secondary 2,565; Upper secondary 185. Source: Ministry of Education.

**Pupils** (2006): Pre-primary 14,330; Primary 54,770; Lower secondary 29,084; Upper secondary 2,214; Special needs 97. Source: Ministry of Education.

**Maldives College of Higher Education** (2003): Academic staff 138; Students 6,898. Source: Maldives College of Higher Education.

**Adult Literacy Rate** (UNESCO estimates): 97.0% (males 97.0%; females 97.1%) in 2007. Source: UNESCO Institute for Statistics.

# Directory

## The Constitution

On 7 August 2008 the President ratified a new 301-article Constitution. The main provisions are summarized below:

### STATE, SOVEREIGNTY AND CITIZENS

The Maldives is a sovereign, independent, democratic republic based on the principles of Islam, and is a unitary State, to be known as the Republic of Maldives. In this Constitution, the Republic of Maldives shall hereinafter be referred to as 'the Maldives'.

The powers of the State of the Maldives shall be vested in the citizens. Legislative power is vested in the People's Majlis (People's Council), executive power is vested in the President and judicial power is vested in the courts of the Maldives.

The religion of the State of the Maldives is Islam. The national language of the Maldives shall be Dhivehi.

### FUNDAMENTAL RIGHTS AND FREEDOMS

Maldivian citizens are equal before and under the law and are entitled to the equal protection and equal benefit of the law. The State has a duty to protect the natural environment, and undertakes to ensure citizens' rights to adequate nourishment, clothing, housing, healthcare and sewerage and electricity systems, and access to communications, transportation and natural resources.

The following are guaranteed: the right to privacy; the right to vote and run for public office; freedom of expression and the media; freedom of assembly and association; protection of the young, the elderly and the disadvantaged; the right to education, to work and to strike; the right to acquire and hold property; freedom of movement. No person shall be arrested or detained, except as provided by law.

Every citizen must respect the Constitution, the rule of law and the rights and freedoms of others.

### THE PEOPLE'S MAJLIS

Legislative authority is vested in the People's Majlis. The People's Majlis shall consist of members elected from Malé and the 20 administrative atolls. The duration of the People's Majlis shall be five years from the first sitting. The Speaker and Deputy Speaker shall be elected from and by the members of the People's Majlis.

There shall be at least three regular sessions of the People's Majlis every year. Unless otherwise provided in the Constitution, matters proposed for passage in the People's Majlis shall be passed by a simple majority.

Prior to the commencement of each financial year, the Minister of Finance shall submit the proposed state budget for approval by the People's Majlis.

A bill passed by the People's Majlis shall become law and enter into force upon being assented to by the President.

Only under certain circumstances may the People's Majlis remove the President or Vice-President. A motion expressing want of confidence in a member of the Cabinet of Ministers may be moved in the People's Majlis.

### THE PRESIDENT

Executive power is vested in the President. The President shall be the Head of State, Head of Government and the Commander-in-Chief of the Armed Forces. The term of office is five years, and no President shall serve for more than two terms.

The President shall be elected directly by the people, with more than 50% of the votes. Each presidential candidate must declare his or her proposed vice-president.

In addition to the powers and functions expressly conferred on or assigned to the President by the Constitution and law, the President shall have the following powers and duties: to preside over the Cabinet of Ministers and to appoint, dismiss or accept the resignations of cabinet members; to appoint or remove members of diplomatic missions of the Maldives; to hold public referendums on major issues; to declare states of emergency, and war and peace.

In the event that the presidency becomes vacant for any reason, the Vice-President shall become President.

### THE CABINET OF MINISTERS

There shall be a Cabinet of Ministers appointed by the President. The Cabinet of Ministers shall consist of the Vice-President, Ministers charged with responsibility for Ministries and the Attorney-General. All appointments to the Cabinet, except that of the Vice-President, must be approved by the People's Majlis.

The Cabinet of Ministers shall discharge the functions assigned to it by the President. The following shall be included in the said functions: to advise and recommend draft bills and proposals to the President, to be prepared for submission to the People's Majlis; to assist the President in formulating government policy on important national and international matters and issues; and to direct, review and co-ordinate the political, economic and social development of the Maldives;

The Attorney-General shall advise the Government on all legal matters affecting the State.

The President may, at his discretion, remove any member of the Cabinet from office, but does not have the discretion to remove the Vice-President from office.

### THE JUDICIARY

Judicial power is vested in the Supreme Court, the High Court and such Trial Courts as established by law. The Supreme Court shall be the highest authority for the administration of justice, and the Chief Justice shall be the highest authority on the Supreme Court.

The Supreme Court shall consist of the Chief Justice and such number of judges as provided by law. The Chief Justice and judges are appointed by the President following consultation with the Judicial Service Commission and approval by a majority in the People's Majlis.

### INDEPENDENT COMMISSIONS AND OFFICES

The following independent and impartial institutions shall exist: the Judicial Service Commission, the Elections Commission, the Civil Service Commission, the Human Rights Commission and the Anti-Corruption Commission. There shall also be an independent and impartial Auditor-General and Prosecutor-General

### PROCLAMATION OF EMERGENCY

In the event of natural disaster, dangerous epidemic disease, war, threat to national security or threatened foreign aggression, the President shall have the right to declare a state of emergency for a period not exceeding 30 days. The declaration must be submitted to the People's Majlis for approval; the People's Majlis has the right to approve, extend or revoke the declaration. Should the President wish to extend the declaration, the approval of the People's Majlis must be obtained.

### GENERAL PROVISIONS

Other provisions made by the Constitution cover the areas of decentralized administration, security services, property, liabilities and legal actions of the State, amendment of the Constitution and transitional matters.

# The Government

### HEAD OF STATE

**President:** MAUMOON ABDUL GAYOOM (took office 11 November 1978; re-elected 30 September 1983, 26 September 1988, 1 October 1993, 16 October 1998 and 17 October 2003).

### THE CABINET OF MINISTERS

(September 2008)

**Senior Ministers:** ABDULLA HAMEED, Dr MOHAMED ZAHIR HUSSAIN, FATHULLA JAMEEL, ALI UMAR MANIKU, UMAR ZAHIR.

**Minister of Defence and National Security:** ISMAIL SHAFEEU.

**Minister of Finance and Treasury:** ABDULLA JIHAD.

**Minister of Environment, Energy and Water:** (vacant).

**Minister of Fisheries, Agriculture and Marine Resources:** (vacant).

**Minister of Foreign Affairs:** ABDULLAH SHAHID.

**Minister of Gender and Family:** AISHATH MOHAMED DIDI.

**Minister of Education:** ZAHIYA ZAREER.

**Minister of Higher Education, Employment and Social Security:** Dr IBRAHIM HASSAN.

**Minister of Justice:** (vacant).

**Minister of Construction and Public Infrastructure:** MOHAMED MAUROOF JAMEEL.

**Minister of Health:** ILYAS IBRAHIM.

**Minister of Tourism and Civil Aviation:** Dr ABDULLA MAUSOOM.

**Minister of Transport and Communication:** MOHAMED SAEED.

**Minister of Planning and National Development:** HAMDOON HAMEED.

**Minister of Home Affairs:** ABDULLAH KAMAALUDHEEN.

**Minister of Atolls Development:** AHMED THASMEEN ALI.

**Minister of Youth and Sports:** Dr AISHATH SHIHAM.

**Minister of Legal Reform, Information and Arts:** MOHAMED NASHEED.

**Minister of Economic Development and Trade:** (vacant).

**Minister of Housing and Urban Development:** Dr ALI HAIDHAR AHMED.

**Attorney-General:** AISHATH AZIMA SHAKOOR.

### MINISTRIES

**President's Office:** Boduthakurufaanu Magu, Malé 20-05; tel. 3320701; fax 3325500; e-mail info@presidencymaldives.gov.mv; internet www.presidencymaldives.gov.mv.

**Attorney-General's Office:** Huravee Bldg, 3rd Floor, Ameer Ahmed Magu, Malé 20-05; tel. 3323809; fax 3314109; e-mail ashraf@agoffice.gov.mv.

**Ministry of Atolls Development:** Faashana Bldg, Boduthakurufaanu Magu, Malé 20-05; tel. 3323070; fax 3327750; e-mail info@atolls.gov.mv; internet www.atolls.gov.mv.

**Ministry of Construction and Public Infrastructure:** Izzuddeenu Magu, Malé 20-01; tel. 3323234; fax 3328300; e-mail admin@construction.gov.mv; internet www.construction.gov.mv.

**Ministry of Defence and National Security:** Ameer Ahmed Magu, Malé 20126; tel. 3322607; fax 3332689; e-mail admin@defence.gov.mv; internet www.defence.gov.mv.

**Ministry of Economic Development and Trade:** Ghaazee Bldg, Ameer Ahmed Magu, Malé 20-05; tel. 3323668; fax 3323840; e-mail contact@trademin.gov.mv; internet www.trademin.gov.mv.

**Ministry of Education:** Ghaazee Bldg, 2nd Floor, Ameer Ahmed Magu, Malé 20-05; tel. 3323262; fax 3321201; e-mail foreign@moe.gov.mv; internet www.moe.gov.mv.

**Ministry of Environment, Energy and Water:** Huravee Bldg, Ameer Ahmed Magu, Malé 20-05; tel. 3324861; fax 3322286; e-mail env@environment.gov.mv; internet www.environment.gov.mv.

**Ministry of Finance and Treasury:** Block 379, Ameenee Magu, Malé 20-379; tel. 3349200; fax 3324432; e-mail admin@finance.gov.mv; internet www.finance.gov.mv.

**Ministry of Fisheries, Agriculture and Marine Resources:** Ghaazee Bldg, 1st Floor, Ameer Ahmed Magu, Malé 20-05; tel.

3322625; fax 3326558; e-mail it@fishagri.gov.mv; internet www.fishagri.gov.mv.

**Ministry of Foreign Affairs:** Boduthakurufaanu Magu, Malé 20-077; tel. 3323400; fax 3323841; e-mail admin@foreign.gov.mv; internet www.foreign.gov.mv.

**Ministry of Gender and Family:** FEN Bldg, 2nd Floor, Ameene Magu, Malé 20156; tel. 3328179; fax 3316237; e-mail admin@mgf.gov.mv; internet www.mgf.gov.mv.

**Ministry of Health:** Ameenee Magu, Malé 20-379; tel. 3328887; fax 3328889; e-mail moh@health.gov.mv; internet www.health.gov.mv.

**Ministry of Higher Education, Employment and Social Security:** Haveeree Hingun, Malé 20-125; tel. 3317172; fax 3331578; e-mail admin@employment.gov.mv; internet www.employment.gov.mv.

**Ministry of Home Affairs:** Huravee Bldg, 3rd Floor, Ameer Ahmed Magu, Malé 20-05; tel. 3323820; fax 3324739; e-mail minhah@dhivenhinet.net.mv; internet www.homeaffairs.gov.mv.

**Ministry of Housing and Urban Development:** MTCC Tower, 7th Floor, Boduthakurufaanu Magu, Malé 20-05; tel. 3321960; fax 3328999; e-mail admin@mhud.gov.mv; internet www.mhud.gov.mv.

**Department of Justice:** Justice Bldg, Orchid Magu, Malé 20-212; tel. 3322303; fax 3325447; e-mail admin@justice.gov.mv; internet www.justice.gov.mv.

**Ministry of Legal Reform, Information and Arts:** Buruzu Magu, Malé 20-04; tel. 3334333; fax 3334334; e-mail informat@dhivehinet.net.mv; internet www.maldivesinfo.gov.mv.

**Ministry of Planning and National Development:** Ghaazee Bldg, 3rd Floor, Ameer Ahmed Magu, Malé 20-125; tel. 3348383; fax 3325371; e-mail info@planning.gov.mv; internet www.planning.gov.mv.

**Ministry of Tourism and Civil Aviation:** Ghazee Bldg, 1st Floor, Ameer Ahmed Magu, Malé 20-05; tel. 3323224; fax 3322512; e-mail info@maldivestourism.gov.mv; internet www.maldivestourism.gov.mv.

**Ministry of Transport and Communication:** Huravee Bldg, Ameer Ahmed Magu, Malé 20-125; tel. 3343433; fax 3343434; e-mail admin@transport.gov.mv; internet www.transport.gov.mv.

**Ministry of Youth and Sports:** PA Complex, 5th Floor, Hilaalee Magu, Malé 20-307; tel. 3326986; fax 3327162; e-mail info@youthsports.gov.mv; internet www.youthsports.gov.mv.

# Legislature

### PEOPLE'S MAJLIS

The People's Majlis (People's Council) comprises members elected by the people of Malé and each of the 20 atolls (for a five-year term). The most recent election was held on 22 January 2005.

**Speaker:** MOHAMED SHIHAB.

**Deputy Speaker:** ANEESA AHMED.

# Election Commission

**Election Commission of Maldives:** PA Complex, 3rd Floor, Hilaalee Magu, Malé; tel. 3324426; fax 3323997; e-mail info@elections.gov.mv; internet www.elections.gov.mv; f. 1998; independent; appointed by the President; Commr of Elections K. D. AHMED MANIK.

# Political Organizations

In June 2005 legislation was approved permitting the establishment of political parties in the Maldives for the first time since 1952.

**Adhaalath Party** (Justice Party): Malé; f. 2005; Leader Sheikh HUSSAIN RASHEED AHMED.

**Dhivehi Rayyithunge Party (DRP)** (Maldivian People's Party): Sinamalé 3 Galolhu, Malé; tel. 3320456; fax 3344774; e-mail info@drp.org.mv; internet www.drp.org.mv; f. 2005; Leader MAUMOON ABDUL GAYOOM.

**Islamic Democratic Party:** Malé; tel. 3326962; fax 3327385; e-mail info@idp.org.mv; internet www.idp.org.mv; f. 2005; Pres. UMAR NASEER.

**Maldivian Democratic Party (MDP):** H. Sharaashaa, 1st Floor, Sosun Magu, Malé 20059; tel. 3340044; fax 3322960; e-mail secretariat@mdp.org.mv; internet www.mdp.org.mv; f. 2001; fmrly based in Colombo, Sri Lanka; official registration in Maldives permitted June 2005; Chair. MARIA AHMED DIDI; Pres. (vacant); Sec.-Gen. HAMID ABDUL GHAFOOR.

**Maldivian National Congress (MNC):** G. Blue Lagoon, 1st Floor, Faashanakilege Magu, Malé; tel. 3316944; fax 3348988; e-mail secretariat@mnc.org.mv; internet www.mnc.org.mv; f. 2007; Founder and Leader MOHAMED MONAZA NAEEM.

**Maldivian Social Democratic Party:** Malé; f. 2006; Leader IBRAHIM ('REEKO') MANIK.

**People's Alliance:** Malé; f. 2008; Founder and Leader ABDULLAH YAMEEN.

**Social Liberal Party (SLP):** Malé; f. 2006; Chair. IBRAHIM ISMAIL ('Ibra') (acting).

# Diplomatic Representation

### HIGH COMMISSIONS IN THE MALDIVES

**Bangladesh:** M. Kurinbee Lodge, 5th Floor, Izzudheen Magu, Malé; tel. 3315541; fax 3315543; e-mail bdootmal@dhivehinet.net.mv; High Commissioner Prof. SELINA MOHSIN (designate).

**India:** H. Athireege-Aage, Ameeru Ahmed Magu, Malé; tel. 3323015; fax 3324778; e-mail hcmale@hicomindia.com.mv; High Commissioner A. K. PANDEY.

**Pakistan:** G. Helengely, Lily Magu, Malé; tel. 3323005; fax 3321832; e-mail pahicmale@hotmail.com; High Commissioner MUHAMMAD ANWAR CHOHAN.

**Sri Lanka:** H. Sakeena Manzil, Medhuziyaaraiyh Magu, Malé 20-05; tel. 3322845; fax 3321652; e-mail highcom@dhivehinet.net.mv; High Commissioner MOHAMED ALI FAROOK.

# Judicial System

The administration of justice is undertaken in accordance with Islamic (*Shari'a*) law. In 1980 the Maldives High Court was established. There are four courts in Malé, and one island court in every inhabited island.

In January 1999 the Government declared that the island court of each atoll capital would thenceforth oversee the administration of justice in that atoll. At the same time it was announced that arrangements were being made to appoint a senior magistrate in each atoll capital.

According to the provisions of the new Constitution, which was enacted in August 2008, a Supreme Court—the highest authority for the administration of justice in the Maldives—was to be formed.

### HIGH COURT

**Chief Justice:** Sheikh MOHAMED RASHEED IBRAHIM.

**Judges:** ABDUL GHANEE MOHAMED, AHMED HAMEED FAHMY, ALI HAMEED MOHAMED, ABDULLA HAMEED.

# Religion

Islam is the state religion, and the Maldivians are Sunni Muslims. In mid-1991 there were 724 mosques and 266 women's mosques throughout the country.

In late 1996 a Supreme Council for Islamic Affairs was established, under the authority of the President's Office. The new body was to authorize state policies with regard to Islam and to advise the Government on Islamic affairs.

**Musthashaaru of the Supreme Council for Islamic Affairs:** (vacant).

**President of the Supreme Council for Islamic Affairs:** MOHAMED RASHEED IBRAHIM.

**Deputy President of the Supreme Council for Islamic Affairs:** MOHAMED GUBAADH ABOOBAKURU.

# The Press

In 1993 the Government established a National Press Council to review, monitor and further develop journalism in the Maldives.

### DAILIES

**Aafathis Daily News:** Feeroaz Magu, Maafannu, Malé 20-02; tel. 3318609; fax 3312425; e-mail aafathis@dhivehinet.net.mv; internet www.aafathisnews.com.mv; f. 1979; daily; Dhivehi and English; Editor AHMED ZAHIR; circ. 3,000.

**Haama Daily:** Ma. Night Rose, Dhilbahaaru Magu, POB 20232, Malé; tel. 3340077; fax 3343726; e-mail haama@haamadaily.com;

internet www.haamadaily.com; Dhivehi and English; Chair. Qasim Ibrahim.

**Hamaroalhi Daily News:** Malé; tel. 3343699; fax 3343697; e-mail editor@hamaroalhi.com.mv; internet www.hamaroalhi.com.mv; f. 2005 as weekly; daily edn commenced 2007; Dhivehi and English; organ of the Dhivehi Rayyithunge Party; politics.

**Haveeru Daily:** Ameenee Magu, POB 20103, Malé; tel. 3325671; fax 3323103; e-mail haveeru@haveeru.com.mv; internet www.haveeru.com.mv; f. 1979; Dhivehi and English; Chair. Mohamed Zahir Hussain; Editor Ali Rafeeq; circ. 4,500.

**Jazeera Daily:** M. Zenthuram, Izzudheen Magu, Malé; tel. 3343738; fax 3343736; e-mail info@jazeera.com.mv; internet www.jazeera.com.mv.

**Miadhu News:** G. Mascot, Koimalaa Hingun, Malé 20-02; tel. 3320700; fax 3320500; e-mail miadhu@dhivehinet.net.mv; internet www.miadhu.com.mv; Propr Ibrahim Rasheed Moosa; Chair. Ahmed Abdulla.

**Minivan News:** Malé; tel. 3334888; e-mail minivan.news@gmail.com; internet www.minivannews.com; f. 2005; independent; predominantly Dhivehi, with English section; Editor Aminath Najeeb.

**Raajje Daily:** Malé; f. 2008; independent; predominantly Dhivehi with English section; Editor Hassan Saeed.

**Sangu Daily:** G. Aabin, Dhonadharaadhahigun, Malé; tel. 3300065; fax 3300064; e-mail sangu@sangudaily.com; internet www.sangudaily.com; Editor Ikram Abdul Latheef.

### PERIODICALS

**Adduvas:** Malé; f. 2000; weekly; news, entertainment, health issues and social affairs; Editor Aishath Velezinee.

**Dheenuge Magu** (The Path of Religion): The President's Office, Boduthakurufaanu Magu, Malé 20-05; tel. 3323701; fax 3325500; e-mail info@presidencymaldives.gov.mv; f. 1986; weekly; Dhivehi; religious; publ. by the President's Office; Editor President Maumoon Abdul Gayoom; Dep. Editor Sheikh Mohamed Rasheed Ibrahim; circ. 7,500.

**Dhivehingetharika** (Maldivian Heritage): National Centre for Linguistic and Historical Research, Soasun Magu, Malé 20-05; tel. 3323206; fax 3326796; e-mail nclhr@dhivehinet.net.mv; internet www.qaumiyyath.gov.mv; f. 1998; Dhivehi; Maldivian archaeology, history and language.

**The Evening Weekly:** Ameenee Magu, POB 20103, Malé; tel. 3325671; fax 3323103; e-mail info@eveningweekly.com.mv; internet www.haveeru.com.mv; weekly; English; owned by the Haveeru news group; Chair. Mohamed Zahir Hussain.

**Faiythoora:** National Centre for Linguistic and Historical Research, Soasun Magu, Malé 20-05; tel. 3323206; fax 3326796; e-mail nclhr@dhivehinet.net.mv; internet www.qaumiyyath.gov.mv; f. 1979; monthly magazine; Dhivehi; Maldivian history, culture and language; Editor Uz Abdulla Hameed; circ. 800.

**Furadhaana:** Ministry of Legal Reform, Information and Arts, Buruzu Magu, Malé 20-04; tel. 3321749; fax 3326211; e-mail informat@dhivehinet.net.mv; internet www.maldivesinfo.com; f. 1990; monthly; Dhivehi; Editor Ibrahim Manik; circ. 1,000.

**Huvaas Magazine:** Ameenee Magu, POB 20103, Malé; tel. 3325671; fax 3323103; e-mail huvaas@haveeru.com.mv; internet www.haveeru.com.mv/huvaas; f. 2001; fortnightly; Chair. Dr Mohamed Zahir Hussain.

**Jamaathuge Khabaru** (Community News): Centre for Continuing Education, Salahudeen Bldg, Malé 20-04; tel. 3328772; fax 3322223; monthly; Dhivehi; Editor Ahmed Zahir; circ. 1,500.

**Maldives News Bulletin:** Maldives News Bureau, Ministry of Legal Reform, Information and Arts, Buruzu Magu, Malé 20-04; tel. 3323838; fax 3326211; e-mail informat@dhivehinet.net.mv; internet www.maldivesinfo.com; f. 1980; weekly; English; Editor Ali Shareef; circ. 350.

**Marine Research Centre Bulletin:** Marine Research Centre, Ministry of Fisheries, Agriculture and Marine Resources, H. White Waves, Malé 20-06; tel. 3322242; fax 3322509; e-mail info@mrc.gov.mv; f. 1984; biannual; fisheries and marine research; Exec. Dir Dr Mohamed Shiham Adam.

**Monday Times:** H. Neel Villa, Boduthakunufaanu Magu, Malé; tel. and fax 3315084; f. 2000; banned 2002; relaunched 2004; weekly.

**Our Environment:** Forum of Writers on the Environment, c/o Ministry of Planning and National Development, Ghaazee Bldg, Ameer Ahmed Magu, Malé 20-05; tel. 3324861; fax 3327351; f. 1990; monthly; Dhivehi; Editor Farouq Ahmed.

**Rasain:** Ministry of Fisheries, Agriculture and Marine Resources, Ghaazee Bldg, Ameer Ahmed Magu, Malé 20-05; tel. 3322625; fax 3326558; e-mail fishagri@dhivehinet.net.mv; f. 1980; annual; fisheries devt.

**Samugaa:** Malé; f. 1995; publ. by the Government Employees' Club.

### NEWS AGENCIES

**Haveeru News Service (HNS):** POB 20103, Malé; tel. 3313825; fax 3323103; e-mail haveeru@haveeru.com.mv; internet www.haveeru.com.mv; f. 1979; Chair. Mohamed Zahir Hussain; Man. Editor Ahmed Zahir.

**Maldives News Bureau (MNB):** Ministry of Legal Reform, Information and Arts, Buruzu Magu, Malé 20-04; tel. 3323836; fax 3326211; e-mail informat@dhivehinet.net.mv; internet www.maldivesinfo.com.

## Publishers

**Corona Press:** Feeroaz Magu, Maafannu, Malé; tel. 3310052; fax 3314741.

**Cyprea Printers:** 25 Boduthakurufaanu Magu, Malé; tel. 3333883; fax 3323523; e-mail cyprea@dhivehinet.net.mv; f. 1984 as Cyprea Printers; Man. Dir Abdulla Saeed.

**Loamaafaanu Print:** Alkariyya Bldg, Ground Floor, Ameenee Magu, Malé 20-354; tel. 3317209; fax 3313815; e-mail haveeru@netlink.net.mv.

**Novelty Printers and Publishers:** M. Vaarey Villa, Izzudhdheen Magu, Malé 20-317; tel. 3318844; fax 3327039; e-mail novelty@dhivehinet.net.mv; general and reference books; Man. Dir Asad Ali.

**Ummeedhee Press:** M. Aasthaanaa Javaahirumagu, Malé 20-02; tel. 3325110; fax 3326412; e-mail ummpress@dhivehinet.net.mv; f. 1986; printing and publishing; Principal Officers Abdul Shakoor Ali, Mohamed Shakoor.

## Broadcasting and Communications

### TELECOMMUNICATIONS

In March 2007 a privately owned submarine fibre-optic cable link between the Maldives and India was inaugurated in an effort to provide more affordable, reliable telecommunications access to islanders and to enhance international connectivity.

**Telecommunications Authority of Maldives:** Telecom Bldg, Husnuheena Magu, Malé 20-04; tel. 3323344; fax 3320000; e-mail secretariat@tam.gov.mv; internet www.tam.gov.mv; f. 2003; regulatory authority; Chair. Dr Hassan Hameed; Dir-Gen. Abdullah Rasheed.

**Dhivehi Raajjeyge Gulhun Ltd (Dhiraagu):** 19 Medhuziyaaraiy Magu, POB 2082, Malé 20-03; tel. 3322802; fax 3322800; e-mail 123@dhiraagu.com.mv; internet www.dhiraagu.com.mv; f. 1988; jtly owned by the Maldivian Govt (55%) and by Cable and Wireless PLC of the United Kingdom (45%); operates all nat. and int. telecommunications services in the Maldives (incl. internet service–Dhivehinet); Chair. Ibrahim Shafiu; CEO Ismail Waheed.

**Wataniya Telecom Maldives Pvt Ltd:** 2nd Floor, Urban Development Bldg, Hulhumalé; tel. 9621111; fax 3350519; internet www.wataniya.mv; f. 2005; provides advanced cellular mobile telephone services throughout the Maldives; Chair. Solah Fahud Sultan; CEO Abraham Smith.

**WARF Telecom International (Pvt) Ltd:** Hulhumalé; f. 2005 by jt venture of Wataniya Telecom Maldives, Reliance Communications (India), and Focus Infocomm to lay fibre-optic cable between Hulhumalé and mainland India; owned by Wataniya Telecom Maldives (65%), Reliance Communications Ltd (20%) and Focus Infocomm (15%); awarded 15-year operating licence in March 2007; CEO Ahmad Haleem.

### RADIO

The Maldives Government was to permit private broadcasting by 3 May 2007 (World Press Freedom Day) under its 'Roadmap for the Reform Agenda' programme, although licences were not awarded until 21 May. Five national radio stations and a number of small local operators secured terrestrial broadcasting rights. The first private radio station commenced broadcasting operations in July.

**Capital Radio:** Malé; tel. 3300956; fax 3334948; e-mail info@capital956.fm; internet www.capital956.fm; f. 2007; operated by Asna Maldives Pte Ltd; broadcasts BBC news bulletins, music, current affairs and analysis programmes; Man. Dir Mohamed Nasheed.

**DhiFM 95.2:** Malé; e-mail admin@dhifm.com; internet dhifm.com; f. 2007; operated by Maldives Media Co Pvt; broadcasts news, music and general interest programmes in Dhivehi and English; operates 24-hour nationwide service; Chief Exec. Dir Ibrahim Khaleel; Editorial Dir Masood Ali.

**HFM 92.6:** Ma. Thimarafusheege, 8th Floor, Dhilbahaaru Magu, POB 20231, Malé; tel. 3301171; fax 3301170; e-mail info@hfm.com

.mv; internet www.hfm.com.mv; f. 2008; operated by Haveeru Media Group; broadcasts 24 hrs daily.

**Radio Eke:** Malé.

**Voice of Islam:** Malé.

**Voice of Maldives (VOM)** (Dhivehi Raajjeyge Adu): Voice of Maldives Bldg, Maafaanu, Malé; tel. 3322840; fax 3317273; e-mail badru@vom.gov.mv; internet www.vom.gov.mv; radio broadcasting began in 1962 under name of Malé Radio; name changed as above in 1980; two channels; home service in Dhivehi and English; Rajje FM in Dhivehi; began broadcasting 24 hrs daily from Jan. 2005; Dir-Gen. Badru Naseer.

### TELEVISION

Under the Maldivian Government's 'Roadmap for the Reform Agenda', licences for the establishment of national television stations were made available to bidders in May 2007. The development represented significant progress towards the liberalization of this previously state-dominated sector.

**Atoll Television:** Majeediyya Alimas Ufaa, Boduthakurufaanu Magu, Henveiru, Malé; tel. 326638; fax 327143; e-mail atoll@airatoll.com; internet www.airatoll.com; f. 2007; operated by Atoll Investment Pvt Ltd.

**DhiTV:** Malé; f. 2008; pvt cable television channel; Founder Champa Mohamed Moosa.

**Future Television:** Malé; f. 2008; broadcasts for 12 hrs daily in Dhivehi; Man. Dir Mohamed Fayaz.

**Television Maldives:** Buruzu Magu, Malé 20-144; tel. 3342200; fax 3325083; e-mail comments@tvm.gov.mv; internet www.tvm.gov.mv; television broadcasting began in 1978; two channels: TVM broadcasts for an average of 18 hrs daily and TVM Plus (f. 1994) broadcasts for 10 hrs daily; covers a 40-km radius around Malé; Exec. Dir Hussain Mohamed; CEO Ali Khalid.

## Finance

(cap. = capital; res = reserves; dep. = deposits; m. = million; brs = branches; amounts in US dollars unless otherwise stated)

### BANKING

#### Central Bank

**Maldives Monetary Authority (MMA):** Umar Shopping Arcade, 3rd Floor, Chandhanee Magu, Maafannu, Malé 20-156; tel. 3323783; fax 3323862; e-mail mail@mma.gov.mv; internet www.mma.gov.mv; f. 1981; bank of issue; supervises and regulates commercial bank and foreign-exchange dealings and advises the Govt on banking and monetary matters; authorized cap. 4m. rufiyaa, res 86.3m. rufiyaa, dep. 2,254.4m. rufiyaa (Dec. 2005); Gov. (vacant); Man. Dir Khadeeja Hassan.

#### Commercial Bank

**Bank of Maldives PLC:** 11 Boduthakurufaanu Magu, Malé 20-094; tel. 3330100; fax 3328233; e-mail bmlho@dhivehinet.net.mv; internet www.bankofmaldives.com.mv; f. 1982; 75% state-owned; cap. 36.5m., res 597.0m., dep. 4,393.9m. (Dec. 2006); Chair. Abdul Hameed Mohamed; Gen. Man. and CEO Serene Ho Oi Khuen; 24 brs.

### DEVELOPMENT FINANCE ORGANIZATION

**Housing Development Finance Corpn:** H. Fulidhooge, 5th Floor, Kalaafaanu Hingun, Malé; tel. 3338810; fax 3315138; f. 2004 to provide public housing loans; 100% state-owned; Chair. Ibrahim Naeem.

### INSURANCE

**Allied Insurance Co of the Maldives (Pte) Ltd:** 04–06 STO Trade Centre, Orchid Magu, Malé 20-02; tel. 3324612; fax 3325035; internet www.alliedmaldives.com; f. 1985; all classes of non-life insurance; operated by State Trading Organization (see below); Chief Exec. Mohamed Maniku; Man. Dir Ismail Riza.

## Trade and Industry

### GOVERNMENT AGENCY

**Foreign Investment Services Bureau (FISB):** Ministry of Economic Development and Trade, Ghazee Bldg, 1st Floor, Ameer Ahmed Magu, Malé; tel. 3323890; fax 3323756; e-mail info@investmaldives.org; internet www.investmaldives.org; under administration of Ministry of Economic Development and Trade; Dir-Gen. Ahmed Naseem.

### CHAMBER OF COMMERCE AND INDUSTRY

**Maldives National Chamber of Commerce and Industry (MNCCI):** G. Viyafaari Hiya, Ameenee Magu, Malé 20-04; tel. 3326634; fax 3310233; e-mail mncci@dhivehinet.net.mv; internet www.mncci.com.mv; f. 1978; merged with the Maldivian Traders' Asscn in 2000; Pres. Ahmed Mujuthaba; Sec.-Gen. Abdullah Faiz.

### INDUSTRIAL AND TRADE ASSOCIATIONS

**Maldives Association of Construction Industry (MACI):** PA Complex, Ground Floor, Hilaalee Magu, Malé; tel. 3318660; fax 3318796; e-mail maci@dhivehinet.net.mv; internet www.maci.org.mv; f. 2001; Pres. Abdul Mohamed; Treas. Ahmed Abdulla.

**Sri Lanka Trade Centre:** Girithereyege Bldg, 3rd Floor, Hithaffinivaa Magu, Malé; tel. 3315183; fax 3315184; e-mail dirsltc@avasmail.com.mv; f. 1993 to facilitate and promote trade, tourism, investment and services between Sri Lanka and the Maldives; Dir M. I. Sufiyan.

**State Trading Organization PLC (STO):** STO Bldg, Boduthakurufaanu Magu, Maafanau, Malé 20-345; tel. 3344333; fax 3344334; e-mail info@stomaldives.net; internet www.stomaldives.com; f. 1964 as Athirimaafannuge Trading Account, renamed as above in 1976; became public limited company in 2001; state-controlled commercial org.; under administration of independent Board of Directors; imports and distributes staple foods, fuels, pharmaceuticals and general consumer items; acts as purchaser for govt requirements; undertakes long-term devt projects; Chair. Ali Mohamed; CEO Ahmed Mohamed.

### UTILITIES

#### Electricity

**Maldives Energy Authority:** Malé; internet www.meew.gov.mv/mea; f. 2006 to replace Maldives Electricity Bureau; under administration of Ministry of Environment, Energy and Water; regulatory authority.

**State Electric Co (STELCO) Ltd:** Ameenee Magu, Malé; tel. 320982; fax 327036; e-mail admin@stelco.com.mv; internet www.stelco.com.mv; f. 1997 to replace Maldives Electricity Board; under administration of Ministry of Economic Development and Trade; provides electricity, consultancy services, electrical spare parts service, etc.; operates 22 power stations; installed capacity 32,921 kW (Dec. 2000); Chair. Ahmed Ali Manik; Man. Dir (vacant); 650 employees (2006).

#### Gas

**Maldive Gas Pvt Ltd:** STO Trade Centre, 1st Floor, Orchid Magu, Malé; tel. 3335614; fax 3335615; e-mail info@maldivegas.com; internet www.maldivegas.com; f. 1999 as a jt venture between State Trading Organization and Champa Gas and Oil Co; Chair. Mohamed Manik.

#### Water

**Maldives Water and Sanitation Authority (MWSA):** Ameenee Magu, Malé; tel. 3317563; fax 3317569; e-mail shaheedha@mwsa.gov.mv; internet www.mwsa.gov.mv; f. 1973; Dir-Gen. Dr Mohamed Ali.

**Malé Water and Sewerage Co Pvt Ltd:** Ameenee Magu, Machangolhi, POB 2148, Malé 20375; tel. 3323209; fax 3324306; e-mail mwsc@dhivehinet.net.mv; internet www.mwsc.com.mv; f. 1995; 76% govt-owned; produces approximately 8,500 metric tons of fresh, desalinated water daily, using seven plants; provides water and sewerage services to the islands of Malé, Hulhumalé and Villingili; provides water services to the island of Maafushi; Chair. Dr Abdulla Naseer; Man.Dir Mohamed Ahmed Didi.

### MAJOR COMPANIES

**Donad Garments Industries:** M. Feeroaz Lodge, Muranga Magu, Malé; tel. 3328292; fax 3321615; f. 1987; manufacture of ready-made garments; CEO Dhon Adam Fulhu; 85 employees.

**E-Biz Maldives (Pvt) Ltd:** 02–04 STO Trade Centre, Malé; tel. 3334858; fax 3334859; e-mail info@ebizmaldives.com; internet www.ebizmaldives.com; f. 2000; provides computer services, software and training.

**Falim Group Pvt Ltd:** H. Hiyaleege, 2nd Floor, Violet Magu, Malé; tel. 3337792; fax 3324216; e-mail info@falim.com.mv; internet www.falim.com.mv; f. 1996; consultancy and management services, software and computing services, travel agency operations; Exec. Chair. Mohamed Ali; Man. Dir Ahmed Ali.

**Fuel Supplies Maldives Pvt Ltd:** Block A, 4th Floor, STO Aifaanu Bldg, Boduthakurufaanu Magu, Malé; tel. 3336655; fax 3313881; e-mail info@fuelmaldives.com; internet www.fuelmaldives.com; f. 2001; supplies diesel and petroleum to Malé and neighbouring atolls.

**Horizon Fisheries (Pvt) Ltd:** 3rd Floor, 12 Boduthakurufaanu Magu, Malé; tel. 3328855; fax 3324455; e-mail info@horizonfisheries.com; internet www.horizonfisheries.com; f. 2003; purchasing, processing and export of skipjack tuna; Chair. AHMED NASHID; Man. Dir ADNAN ALI.

**Lafarge Maldives Cement Pvt Ltd:** 01-01 STO Trade Centre, Orchid Magu, Malé 20-02; tel. 3315313; fax 3315316; e-mail mimcgm@dhivehinet.net.mv; subsidiary of State Trading Org Plc.

**Maldives Electronics Services Co Pvt Ltd:** 02-12/13 STO Trade Centre, Orchid Magu, Malé; tel. 3323536; e-mail admin@mesco.com.mv; internet www.mesco.com.mv; sells and repairs communications equipment; networking solutions; cable products.

**Maldives Industrial Fisheries Co Ltd (MIFCO):** Block 389, Hilaalee Magu, Maafaanu, Malé; tel. 323932; fax 323955; e-mail info@mifco.com.mv; internet www.mifco.com.mv; f. 1993 to replace the Fisheries Projects Implementation Department (f. 1984); 80% owned by Govt, 20% owned by State Trading Organization; under administration of Ministry of Fisheries, Agriculture and Marine Resources; commercial enterprise engaged in fish purchasing, processing, canning and export; operates Felivaru Tuna Processing Plant; Chair. (vacant); Man. Dir MOHAMED ADIL SALEEM.

**Felivaru Tuna Processing Plant:** Felivaru, Lhaviyani Atoll; tel. 6230376; fax 6230375; e-mail iwaseem@felivaru.com.mv; f. 1978; capacity to produce 50 metric tons of canned fish per day; Gen. Man. IBRAHIM WASEEM; Dir (Operations) ADIL SALEEM.

**MIFCO Boatyard Ltd:** Malé; f. 1997; builds and repairs all types of small craft and vessels in wood and fibreglass, especially fishing boats.

**Maldives National Oil Co Ltd (MNOC):** Boduthakurufaanu Magu, Maafannu, Malé 20345; tel. 325635; fax 315337; e-mail info@mnoc.com.mv; internet www.mnoc.com.mv; subsidiary of State Trading Org Plc; Chair. MOHAMED MANIKU.

**Maldives Structural Products Pvt Ltd (MSP):** Alikilegefaanu Magu, Malé; tel. 3337720; fax 3337721; jt venture of State Trading Org PLC and Rainbow Enterprises Pvt Ltd; steel roofing products.

**Malé Aerated Water Co (Pvt) Ltd:** 70 Boduthakurufaanu Magu, POB 20168, Malé; tel. 3326701; fax 3326703; f. 1987; production of soft drinks; bottlers for Coca-Cola in the Maldives; Man. HASSAN HABEEB.

**Multifarm (Pvt) Ltd:** Kaafu Atoll Kuda, Kuda Villingili; tel. 3322365; f. 1985; poultry; CEO Dr AHMED DIDI.

**Multilinx (Maldives) Pvt Ltd:** 2 Fadiyaru Magu, POB 20123, Malé 20-02; tel. 3323113; fax 3323006; e-mail multlnx@dhivehinet.net.mv; internet www.multilinx.com.mv; f. 1983; manufacture of detergents, wood glue, plastic bottles and containers, corrugated boards and cartons, and candles; exports marine products; Chair. and Man. Dir MOHAMED ZAHIR.

**The Silver Company (Pvt) Ltd (SILCO):** Gan'dhakoalhi Magu, Malé 20-02; tel. 327814; fax 327808; e-mail silco@dhivehinet.net.mv; internet www.silco.com.mv; f. 1993; shipping, aviation, yacht handling, cargo packing and forwarding, and customs clearance and delivery services; Man. Dir ABDUL BARI RUSHDI.

# Transport

**Maldives Transport and Contracting Co Ltd (MTCC):** MTCC Bldg, 5th Floor, Boduthakurufaanu Magu, POB 263, Malé 20-181; tel. 3326822; fax 3323221; e-mail info@mtcc.com.mv; internet www.mtcc.com.mv; f. 1980; 60% state-owned, 40% privately owned; marine transport, civil and technical contracting, harbour devt, shipping agents for general cargo, passenger liners and oil tankers; Man. Dir IBRAHIM ATHIF SHAKOOR; Chair. Dr FAATHIN HAMEED.

### SHIPPING

Vessels operate from the Maldives to Sri Lanka and Singapore at frequent intervals, also calling at points in India, Pakistan, Myanmar (formerly Burma), Malaysia, Bangladesh, Thailand, Indonesia and the Middle East. In December 2005 the merchant shipping fleet of the Maldives numbered 70 vessels, with a combined aggregate displacement of 87,402 grt. Smaller vessels provide services between the islands on an irregular basis. Malé is the only port handling international traffic. In 1986 a new commercial harbour was opened in Malé. The Malé Harbour Development Project was implemented during 1991–97, and improved and increased the capacity and efficiency of Malé Port. In July 2003 a new harbour was opened in Fuvah Mulah, on Gnaviyani atoll. Ambitious government-led plans for the construction of 60 new harbours and a transhipment port in the north of the country were under development in 2006–08.

**Maldives Ports Authority (MPA):** Boduthakurufaanu Magu, Maafaanu, Malé 20-250; tel. 3329339; fax 3325293; e-mail info@maldport.com.mv; internet www.maldport.com.mv; f. 1986; owned by govt-owned Maldives Ports Ltd; Man. Dir MAHUDY IMAD; Harbour Master AHMED RASHEED.

**Island Enterprises Pvt Ltd:** Maaram, 1st Floor, Ameeru Ahmed Magu, Henveiru, POB 20169, Malé 20-05; tel. 3323531; fax 3325645; e-mail info@ielmaldives.com; internet www.ielmaldives.com; f. 1978; fleet of eight vessels; exporters of frozen fish, owners of processing plant, shipping agents, chandlers, cruising agents, surveyors and repairs; Man. Dir MAIZAN OMAR MANIK.

**Precision Marine Pvt Ltd:** H. Orchidmaage, Ground Floor, Ameeru Ahmed Magu, POB 20169, Malé 20-05; tel. 3315663; fax 3315107; e-mail info@pmlboatyard.com.mv; internet www.pmlboatyard.com.mv; subsidiary of Island Enterprises Pvt Ltd; mfrs and repairers of fibreglass boats, launches, yachts, marine sports equipment, etc.; Dir OMAR MANIK.

**Maldives National Shipping Ltd:** Ship Plaza, 2nd Floor, 1/6 Orchid Magu, POB 2022, Malé 20-02; tel. 3323871; fax 3324323; e-mail male@maldiveshipping.com.mv; f. 1965; 100% state-owned; fleet of three container vessels; br. in Singapore; Gen. Man. AIMON JAMEEL.

**Matrana Enterprises (Pvt) Ltd:** 79 Majeedhee Magu, Malé; tel. 3331166; fax 3322832; e-mail webmaster@matrana.org; internet www.matrana.org; Sr Exec. MOHAMED ABDULLA.

**Villa Shipping and Trading Co (Pvt) Ltd:** Villa Bldg, POB 2073, Malé 20-02; tel. 3325195; fax 3325177; e-mail info@villa.com.mv; operates five tourist resorts and owns a trading operation supported by a fleet of eight cargo vessels and tankers; Man. Dir QASIM IBRAHIM.

### CIVIL AVIATION

The existing airport on Hululé Island near Malé, which was first opened in 1966, was expanded and improved to international standard with financial assistance from abroad and, as Malé International Airport, was officially opened in 1981. Charter flights from Europe subsequently began. Further expansion was completed in 2006, including the construction of the world's largest water aerodrome. Proposals have been put forward for the construction of a second runway.

In addition, there are four domestic airports covering different regions of the country. These are located on Gan Island, Addu atoll, on Kadhdhoo Island, Hadhdhummathi atoll, on Hanimaadhoo Island, South Thiladhummathi atoll, and on Kaadedhdhoo Island, South Huvadhu atoll; there are plans to build a further airport on Maamigili Island, Alif Dhaal atoll. The airport on Gan Island was to begin servicing international flights in 2008. In early 1995 there were 10 helipads in use in the Maldives.

**Maldives Airport Co Ltd (MACL):** Malé International Airport, Hululé 22-000; tel. 3338800; fax 3331515; e-mail info@maclnet.net; internet www.airports.com.mv; f. 2000; 100% govt-owned; under administration of Ministry of Tourism and Civil Aviation; serviced by 13 charter airlines and 12 scheduled carriers; CEO MOHAMED AMIR.

**Island Aviation Services Ltd:** 1st Floor, STO Aifaanu Bldg, Boduthakurufaanu Magu, Henveiru, Malé; tel. 3335544; fax 3315661; e-mail info@island.com.mv; internet www.island.com.mv; f. 2000; 100% govt-owned; operates domestic flights; commenced regional flights in Jan. 2008; Chair. MOHAMED UMAR MANIK; Man. Dir BANDHU IBRAHIM SALEEM.

**Maldivian Air Taxi:** Kaafu Hulhulé, POB 2023, Malé; tel. 3315201; fax 3315203; e-mail mat@mat.com.mv; f. 1993; seaplane services between Malé and outer islands; operates 15 aircraft; Chair. LARS ERIK NIELSEN; Gen. Man. AUM FAWZY.

**Trans Maldivian Airways (Pvt) Ltd:** Malé International Airport, POB 2079, Malé; tel. 3312444; fax 3323161; e-mail mail@tma.com.mv; internet www.transmaldavian.com; f. 1989 as Hummingbird Island Airways Pvt Ltd; name changed as above in 2000; operates 15 floatplanes; Man. Dir BRAM STELLER.

# Tourism

The tourism industry brings considerable foreign exchange to the Maldives. The islands' attractions include white sandy beaches, excellent diving conditions and multi-coloured coral formations. At the end of 2004 there were 87 island resorts in operation, and some 16,858 hotel beds were available; a further 8,000 beds were to supplement capacity in 2007 when 35 new resorts were scheduled to commence operations. An additional 50 resorts were forecast to open between 2010 and 2012. The annual total of foreign visitors increased from only 29,325 in 1978 to 616,716 in 2004. Revenue from tourism amounted to 921.5m. rufiyaa in the latter year. It was feared that the devastating effect on the Maldives of the tsunami in the Indian Ocean in December 2004 would severely affect the country's tourism industry. By the end of 2005 all the resorts affected by the tsunami had reopened. However, tourist arrivals in that year totalled only 395,320, a decline of 35.9% compared with the previous year. The number of arrivals had almost completely recovered, to a reported 601,923, by the end of 2006 and estimated receipts from tourism in that year increased by an impressive 85.4%, compared with 2005, to reach 1,685.9m. rufiyaa. In 2007 a record number of visitor arrivals was achieved, at 675,889, and receipts from tourism (in US dollar terms) rose by 13.8%, compared with the previous year, to reach US $493.6m.

**Maldives Association of Tourism Industry (MATI):** Gadhamoo Bldg, 3rd Floor, Boduthakurufaanu Magu, POB 2056, Malé; tel. 3326640; fax 3326641; e-mail mati@dhivehinet.net.mv; internet www.mati.com.mv; f. 1984; promotes and develops tourism; Chair. MOHAMED UMAR MANIKU; Sec.-Gen. SIM I. MOHAMED.

**Maldives Tourism Promotion Board:** H. Aage, 3rd Floor, 12 Boduthakurufaanu Magu, Malé 20-05; tel. 3323228; fax 3323229; e-mail mtpb@visitmaldives.com; internet www.visitmaldives.com; f. 1998; Dir Dr ABDULLA MAUSOOM.

**Air Maldives Travel Bureau/Tourist Information:** Aifaan Bldg, Boduthakurufaanu Magu, Malé; tel. 3310917; fax 3318757; e-mail airmldvs@dhivehinet.net.mv; f. 1997.

# Defence

There is no army, navy or air force. A voluntary National Security Service, which was founded in 1892 and renamed the Maldives National Defence Force in April 2006, undertakes paramilitary security duties (including coast-guard duties) and is comprised of some 2,000 members. The first female recruits were sworn into the former National Security Service in February 1989.

**Defence Budget:** Projected at 480.2m. rufiyaa (4.1% of total expenditure) in 2007.

**Commander-in-Chief of the Maldives National Defence Force:** President MAUMOON ABDUL GAYOOM.

**Deputy Commander-in-Chief of the Maldives National Defence Force:** ISMAIL SHAFEEU.

**Chief of Staff of the Maldives National Defence Force:** Maj.-Gen. MOHAMED ZAHIR.

# Education

Until the late 1970s, education was centred largely on the capital, Malé. In 1976 the 16 schools in existence were all in Malé and catered mainly for children of primary school age. In 1977 the Government established a teacher-training institute (which had produced more than 400 qualified teachers by the end of 1986). UNICEF, in particular, has contributed to provincial development, and in 1978 the first primary school outside Malé opened, on Baa atoll. The construction of the first secondary school outside Malé was completed, on Addu atoll, in 1992. By early 2005 there were 22 schools in Malé and 312 schools in the rest of the Maldives.

Education is not compulsory. There are three types of formal education: traditional Koranic schools (*Makthab*), Dhivehi-medium primary schools (*Madhrasa*) and English-medium primary and secondary schools. Primary education begins at six years of age and lasts for five years. Secondary education, beginning at the age of 11, lasts for up to seven years, comprising a first cycle of five years and a second of two years. In 2003/04 the total enrolment at primary and secondary schools was equivalent to 91.5% of the school-age population. In 2004/05 enrolment at primary schools included 79.3% of children in the relevant age-group; the ratio for secondary enrolment of pupils in the relevant age-group was an estimated 62.6% in the same year.

In January 1989 the Government established a National Council on Education, under the chairmanship of the President, to oversee the development of education in the Maldives. The Maldives' higher education establishments include a College of Higher Education (which was opened in October 1998 and which incorporates an Institute of Shari'a and Law), a full-time vocational training centre, a teacher-training institute, an Institute of Hotel and Catering Services, an Institute of Management and Administration, a Science Education Centre, an Institute of Health Sciences, an Institute for Islamic Studies, and a Non-formal Education Centre (renamed as the Centre for Continuing Education in October 2002). The Maldives Centre for Social Education was constructed in 1991 with US $8.5m. of grant aid from Japan. The Maldives Institute of Technical Education, which was completed in late 1996, was expected to alleviate the problem of the lack of local skilled labour.

Projected budgetary expenditure on education by the central Government in 2007 was 1,257.1m. rufiyaa, representing 10.7% of total spending.

# Bibliography


Adeney, M., and Carr, W. K. 'The Maldives Republic', in *The Politics of the Western Indian Ocean Islands*. London, Praeger Publishers, 1975.

Agassiz, A. 'The Coral Reefs of the Maldives', in *Memoirs of the Museum of Comparative Zoology at Harvard College*. Cambridge, MA, 1903.

Asian Development Bank. *Social Sector Profile, Maldives: Social Development Issues for the 21st Century*. Metro Manila, 2001.

Bell, H. C. P. *The Maldive Islands: An Account of the Physical Features, Climate, History, Inhabitants, Production and Trade*. Colombo, Government Printer, 1883.

Butany, W. T. *Report on Agricultural Survey and Crop Production*. Rome, UN Development Programme, 1974.

Gayoom, Maumoon Abdul. *The Maldives: A Nation in Peril*. Malé, Ministry of Planning and National Development, 1998.

Government Printer. *The Maldive Islands: Monograph on the History, Archaeology and Epigraphy*. Colombo, 1940.

Grover, V. *Maldives: Government and Politics*. Oxford, Deep & Deep Publications, 2002.

Heyerdahl, Thor. *The Maldive Mystery*. London, George Allen and Unwin, 1986.

Hockly, T. W. *The Two Thousand Isles: A Short Account of the People, History and Customs of the Maldive Archipelago*. Ottawa, ON, Laurier Books, 2003.

Lateef, K. *An Introductory Economic Report*. Washington, DC, World Bank, 1980.

Maloney, C. 'The Maldives: New Stresses in an Old Nation', in *Asian Survey*. Berkeley, CA, University of California Press, 1976.

*People of the Maldive Islands*. New Delhi, Orient Longman, 1980.

Maniku, Hassan Ahmed. *The Maldives: A Profile*. Malé, Department of Information and Broadcasting, 1977.

*Changes in the Topography of the Maldives*. Maldives, Forum of Writers on the Environment, 1990.

Munch-Peterson, N. F. *Background Paper for Population Needs Mission*. Rome, UN Development Programme, 1981.

Reynolds, C. H. B. *The Maldive Islands*. London, Royal Central Asian Society, 1974.

*Linguistic Strands in the Maldives*. London, School of Oriental and African Studies, 1978.

Smallwood, C. *A Visit to the Maldive Islands*. London, Royal Central Asian Society, 1961.

Webb, Paul A. *Maldives: People and Environment*. Malé, Department of Information and Broadcasting, 1989.

Young, I. A., and Christopher, W. *Memoir on the Inhabitants of the Maldive Islands*. Mumbai, Bombay Geographical Society, 1844.

# NEPAL

## Physical and Social Geography

B. H. FARMER

Nepal is situated between the high Himalayas and the Ganges plains, between India and Tibet (the Xizang Autonomous Region) in the People's Republic of China. It occupies an area of 147,181 sq km (56,827 sq miles) and extends from 26° 20′ to 30° 10′ N, and from 80° 15′ to 88° 15′ E.

### PHYSICAL FEATURES

Nepal's southernmost physical region is the Terai which, like the similar region in India, is a belt of low-lying plain, highly liable to flooding during the monsoon. To the north rises the Himalaya system, the world's greatest mountain range. With the associated Karakoram, Hindu Kush and Pamir ranges, the Himalaya system contains all but two of the 86 mountains over 7,500 m above sea-level. The world's highest peak, Mt Everest (known as Sagarmatha to the Nepalese), rises to 8,848 m and lies on Nepal's frontier with Tibet. A series of transverse or more complex valleys breaks up the simple pattern of parallel ranges, and one of these, the Valley of Nepal, contains the capital, Kathmandu.

### CLIMATE

It is difficult to be at all precise about the climate in the absence of accurate data. It would seem, however, that it exemplifies two main tendencies. In the first place, temperatures, for obvious reasons, decrease as one moves from the Terai through the foothills and internal valleys to higher Himalayan ranges. At Kathmandu, 1,337 m above sea-level, monthly temperatures average 10°C in January and 23°C in May. In January the average daily maximum is 18°C and the average minimum 2°C. In the highest Himalaya, air temperatures are always below freezing point. In the second place, rainfall tends to decrease from east to west, as it does in the Indian plains below. Eastern Nepal receives about 2,500 mm per year; Kathmandu 1,420 mm; and western Nepal about 1,000 mm.

### SOILS AND NATURAL RESOURCES

There is little reliable scientific information on soils. As in corresponding parts of the Indian Himalayas, soils are likely to be skeletal, thin and poor on steep slopes (except where improved artificially under terraced cultivation); and better soils are probably confined to valley bottoms and interior basins, and to the Terai.

There has been a great deal of clearing for cultivation in the Terai, in interior valleys like the Valley of Nepal, and on lower hillsides. Yet in some areas textbook examples of altitudinal zonation may be seen: tropical moist deciduous forests to some 1,200 m; moist hill pine forests from 1,200 to some 2,600 m; coniferous forests at 2,600–3,350 m; and alpine vegetation beginning thereafter.

The only mineral so far discovered in significant quantities is mica, mined east of Kathmandu. There are local workings of lignite in the outermost range of mountains, and small deposits of copper, cobalt and iron ore. Raw materials exist for cement manufacture. In 1986 an agreement was signed allowing two foreign oil companies to explore for petroleum in the area adjoining the borders with India.

### POPULATION AND ETHNIC GROUPS

According to the results of the census of June 2001, Nepal had a total population of 23,151,423. The population is unevenly distributed (average density at mid-2001 was 157.3 per sq km), with fairly dense clusters and ribbons along the valleys and in the Terai, a scatter of isolated upland settlements, and great empty spaces at high altitude.

Nepal is populated by a mixture of Indo-Aryan peoples, who originally migrated from India, and a range of Mongoloid tribes, including the Gurungs, Magars, Rais and Limbus, who speak Tibeto-Burman languages. The Kathmandu valley is the home of the Newar community, while small communities of indigenous peoples and Muslim immigrants are found in the Terai. Large-scale migration from Bangladesh has resulted in a notable demographic transformation in Nepal, with the Muslim population increasing from around 4% of the total in the early 1990s to about 10% by the end of the decade.

## History

LOK RAJ BARAL

Revised by T. LOUISE BROWN, JOHN MCGUIRE and MICHAEL GILLAN, and updated for this edition by CLEMENS SPIESS

Nepal's history has been dictated by its position, located in the Himalayas on the north-east frontier of India, and forming the only practicable gateway to the Indo-Gangetic plains from Tibet (the Xizang Autonomous Region) in the People's Republic of China.

The word 'Nepal', which appeared for the first time in AD 879, means 'the beginning of a new era'. Although ancient Nepalese history is still only partially documented, it is assumed that from about the year 700 BC the Kirantis ruled. Mentioned in Vedic literature and the *Mahabharata*, they are the ancestors of ancient Nepalese groups including the Newars, Rais, Limbus, Tamangs and Sunwars. Probably in the sixth century BC, during the rule of the Kirantis, the founder of Buddhism (Gautama Siddhartha) was born in the small town of Lumbini in the Terai, now near the Indian border. It remains a centre of pilgrimage for Buddhists from all over the world. Between the ninth and the 14th centuries AD, the Valley of Nepal, then, as now, the most important part of the country, was invaded from India until Jaya Sthithi Malla, a southern Indian, began the Malla dynasty. Jaksha Malla, the most able of the Malla kings, extended his power far beyond the Valley. He divided his kingdom among his four heirs in 1488; Kathmandu, Bhatgaon, Patan and Banepa remained intact until the Gurkha conquest. The Gurkhas were originally a warlike tribe of Rajput Kshatriyas who were expelled from India in 1303 by the Sultan of Delhi, Ala-ud-din. They escaped into the hills of central Nepal and gradually spread out into the region of Gorakhnath, where they settled in about 1559. At this time the country was divided into small principalities and was thus later vulnerable to the adventurous and energetic Gurkha, Prithvinarayan Shah.

### THE GURKHAS

Prithvinarayan Shah, the acknowledged founder of modern Nepal, conceived the idea of creating a viable kingdom in the Himalayas by conquering neighbouring territories and assimilating them in socio-political terms. His plan was to conquer the Valley of Nepal and from there to expand in all directions. By a series of campaigns ending in 1767, he gained control of the territories that today constitute Nepal. Just before his death in 1775, he was planning to annex Sikkim (now part of India) in order to establish a continuous boundary with Bhutan.

In addition to providing Nepal with a territorial identity, Prithvinarayan Shah preserved it in its earliest days from foreign intrusion. He was excessively anti-foreign; he wanted to encourage local enterprise and he advised his countrymen to support native industries. Opposing British efforts to open up trade with Tibet and China, he prohibited the entry of certain British traders to Kathmandu and advised the authorities in Lhasa not to be tempted by a British offer of establishing new relations between Bengal and Tibet. During the years 1786–94 the armies of his successor, Bahadur Shah, occupied states of the Baisis and Chaubisis, and Kumaon and Garhwal in the west and Sikkim in the east. A portion of Tibetan Kachhar was also captured. His policy was even more vigorously pursued when his nephew, Rana Bahadur, then aged only 20, assumed power in 1796. He outraged public sentiment by marrying a Brahmin, and subsequently the country split between two warring families, the Pandes and Thapas. A revolt on the part of the Brahmins and hostile courtiers forced Rana Bahadur to abdicate. When he regained the throne in 1804, he dismissed his Prime Minister, Damodar Pande, who had signed a treaty with the East India Co allowing it the right to appoint a British Resident in Nepal.

The next Prime Minister, Bhim Sen Thapa, continued an expansionist policy, which was largely aimed at consolidating his position by keeping his rivals occupied in warfare rather than in manoeuvring for power at court. This policy brought him into conflict with British India, and led to the Anglo-Nepalese War of 1814–16. Bhim Sen Thapa sued for peace in March 1816. The Treaty of Segauli (4 March 1816) gave the British the right to appoint a Resident and to occupy the hills of Kumaon, Garhwal, Nainital Simla, and a great portion of the Terai. In return, the British agreed to withdraw from Sikkim.

### THE RANA SYSTEM

Bhim Sen Thapa's authority remained virtually unchallenged until the young King Rajendra Vikram Shah came of age and decided to take control himself. The Prime Minister was dismissed and imprisoned in 1837; he committed suicide two years later. From the confusion, massacres and intrigues that followed, another powerful figure emerged—Jung Bahadur Rana. He proclaimed himself Prime Minister and Commander-in-Chief of the army, assumed the family name of Rana and, independently of the ruling monarchy, distributed power among his own relations and made his own and their positions hereditary. The Rana family thus attained a complete monopoly of power in every department of Nepalese life: from birth a kinsman could be appointed to high military rank.

Jung Bahadur Rana also reversed the policy of his predecessors by allying himself with the United Kingdom and offering support in its war against the Sikhs. The British encouraged the Ranas to pursue an isolationist policy. Nepal became a recruiting ground for the British armies, in which Gurkha regiments became famous for their toughness and loyalty. At the outbreak of the First World War, the British Government received permission for the free recruitment of Gurkha soldiers. The Rana Chandra Shamsher (who ruled from 1901 to 1929) had his reward in 1923 when the Treaty of Segauli was revised. The Nepalese sought an unequivocal declaration of their independence, but the British Government insisted on retaining those clauses that limited Nepal's external relations to those with the United Kingdom. An annual contribution of 1m. rupees was arranged to be remitted by the Indian exchequer to the Nepalese ruler.

A treaty of 1792 had placed Nepal in an undefined position of vassalage to China, and, until 1900, the Nepalese had sent a goodwill mission to Beijing every 12th year. In 1911, when the revolution in China created confusion in the area's relations, the time came for the next mission; on the advice of the British authorities, however, Chandra Shamsher refused to send a mission. By implication, Nepal thus unilaterally repudiated the 1792 treaty. Chandra Shamsher allowed a lessening of Nepal's isolation in terms of social ideas, and in 1926, under external pressure, he abolished slavery, freeing some 60,000 people at a cost of 3.7m. rupees.

As long as British rulers remained in India, the Ranas felt secure. However, the new ideas which swept across India in the 1930s, and which were realized in 1947 with the coming of Indian independence, influenced the 3m. Nepalese residing in the frontier provinces of Bengal, Bihar and Uttar Pradesh, and, in turn, spread into the Valley of Nepal.

In 1950 the Nepali National Congress was merged with the Nepali Democratic Congress, which had a similar programme, to form the Nepali Congress Party (NCP). With covert encouragement from the monarch, King Tribhuvan, the NCP proceeded with its plans to overthrow the Rana regime, and an armed struggle was organized under the direction of the President of the NCP, Matrika Prasad (M. P.) Koirala.

The Chinese occupation of Tibet in October 1950 undoubtedly influenced the timing of King Tribhuvan's dramatic challenge to the position of the Ranas; in November he refused to sign death warrants of alleged plotters against the Rana regime and sought political asylum in the Indian diplomatic mission. The Indian Government sent aircraft to transport him to Delhi. Along the border the insurgents attacked, captured Nepal's second largest town, Birganj, and proclaimed a rival Government.

The Nepalese army remained loyal to the Rana regime, but the Prime Minister of India, Jawaharlal Nehru, and his colleagues stood firm in their support for the King, and the Nepalese Government finally accepted India's proposals on 7 January 1951. They provided for the King's reinstatement, an amnesty for the insurgents if they surrendered their weapons, elections by 1952, and the formation of an interim government of 14 ministers on the basis of parity between the Ranas and popular representatives. The royal family and the NCP leaders made a triumphal return to Kathmandu on 15 February 1951. Mohun Shumshere Jung Bahadur Rana became the Prime Minister, while Bisweswor Prasad (B. P.) Koirala (half-brother of M. P. Koirala) was appointed to the vital Ministry of Home Affairs. The formation of the new Government represented the end of Rana domination, and the beginning of an experiment in democracy.

### PARLIAMENTARY GOVERNMENT

The experiment soon ran into difficulty. The Ranas were not reconciled to the loss of their century-old absolute power. Personal and ideological differences caused factionalism to emerge within the leadership of the NCP. King Tribhuvan declared a state of emergency in the country in January 1952 and armed the Prime Minister with emergency powers. Parties of the right and left (the Rashtravadi Gorkha Parishad and the Communist Party of Nepal—CPN—respectively) were declared illegal and political meetings banned indefinitely. The King made two attempts to establish an advisory assembly, in July 1952 and May 1954, but internal rivalries and corruption prevented the success of either. The communists, working in 'front' organizations since their party was illegal, made considerable headway, especially among the younger generation of disillusioned intellectuals in Kathmandu.

King Tribhuvan died in March 1955. His heir, Mahendra Bir Bikram Shah Dev, was resolute, immensely hard-working and pragmatic. He made no pretence of believing in parliamentary democracy. Nevertheless, in December 1957 he announced that elections would be held in February 1959. They were held a week after the King had given Nepal its first Constitution providing for a Mahasabha (senate), consisting of 36 members, of whom 18 would be elected by the Pratinidhi Sabha (lower house) and 18 nominated by the King. The lower house would consist of 109 members elected from single-member territorial constituencies. In a country where 96% of the population were illiterate, the elections were held with surprising success. Most candidates gave priority to the abolition of the *birta* system, by which landlords, mostly Ranas, held land tax-free; to the nationalization of the *zamindari* system; to irrigation; to co-operative farming; to cottage industries; and to government-supported medium-sized industries. Most parties subscribed to this programme, though the NCP seemed the most likely to carry it out, if elected; the party's top echelons had subscribed to socialist ideas for many years.

The NCP won 38% of the total votes cast, securing 74 seats out of the 109 in the lower house. The right-wing Gorkha Parishad won 19 seats, or 17.1% of the votes cast, while communist supporters secured four seats, or 7.4%. When the King appointed B. P. Koirala as Prime Minister and the first popularly elected legislature was opened in July 1959, it seemed as if the long road towards democracy was firmly established. Yet the Constitution providing for a parliamentary government and civil rights left sovereignty in fact, not only in form, with the King. He could, for example, force the Prime Minister to resign; he could suspend the Government and rule directly or with newly appointed ministers; he could prorogue the legislature or call for a special sitting; and he had a veto over all legislation and constitutional amendments. This fundamental limitation of the democratic process was a source of frustration for B. P. Koirala. Nevertheless, his electoral majority allowed him to proceed with his schemes for land reform. He gave greater security to tenants and redistributed some of the large estates owned by the Ranas. The Ranas maintained their campaign of obstruction, which Koirala could still have defeated but for a growing tension between himself and the young King. This clash of personalities came to a head on 15 December 1960, when King Mahendra staged a coup, and imprisoned B. P. Koirala and most of the senior leadership of the NCP. He suspended rights guaranteed by the Constitution and dissolved Parliament, substituting his own hand-picked Council of Ministers. Political parties were banned by royal decree in January 1961. The royal *coup d'état* demonstrated the loyalty of the army to the King.

## THE PANCHAYAT SYSTEM

King Mahendra, who profoundly distrusted party politics and politicians, sought to create a 'non-party Panchayat (village council) democracy'. This Panchayat system, proclaimed in 1961 and promulgated under a new Constitution in the following year, comprised a four-tier administrative structure. At its head was the King, who appointed the Prime Minister. This office was filled successively by Dr Tulsi Giri (1962–65), Surya Bahadur Thapa (1965–69) and Kirti Nidhi Bista (1969–70). The King himself was also Prime Minister from April 1970 to April 1971, when Bista was reappointed. Bista resigned in July 1973 and was succeeded as Prime Minister by Nagendra Prasad Rijal.

In September 1967 the Rashtriya Panchayat (National Assembly) adopted a far-reaching programme based on a 'Back to the Village' campaign, and a detailed scheme for Panchayat administration. The decision of NCP leaders in May 1968 to co-operate with the King in the Panchayat system led to the release of B. P. Koirala and his colleagues in October; they subsequently went into self-exile in India. The King and his Council of Ministers introduced well-known royalist supporters into the Government and reiterated the ban on political activity outside the Panchayat system.

King Mahendra died in January 1972, and was succeeded by his son, Birendra Bir Bikram Shah Dev, whose coronation eventually took place in February 1975. King Birendra had been educated in the United Kingdom and the USA, and there were short-lived hopes that he might relax the late King's somewhat autocratic style of government.

In December 1975 Dr Tulsi Giri was again appointed Prime Minister. During 1976 Giri nominated supporters of the banned NCP and ex-communists as members of the Rashtriya Panchayat and there was renewed demand for political change. Numerous amendments to the Constitution were adopted, which allowed for a widening of the franchise and more frequent elections to the Rashtriya Panchayat, but the King's powers were not eroded.

In December 1976 B. P. Koirala returned to Nepal from exile in India, but was immediately arrested and charged with treason. However, six months later, under pressure from India, he was released and left the country. In September 1977 Giri resigned as Prime Minister, primarily because of differences with the King over Koirala's detention. Kirti Nidhi Bista was reappointed Prime Minister. By late 1977 Koirala had been acquitted of five charges of treason and in March 1978 he returned to Nepal to spearhead a renewed campaign for political change. He claimed to have the support of other banned opposition groups, including the CPN. He also had the open sympathy of certain elements in the Rashtriya Panchayat, which resulted in its purge by the King and a strengthening of the Raj Sabha (State Council), the King's personal advisory body.

In April–May 1979 Koirala was put under house arrest, numerous other NCP members were detained, and demonstrations were suppressed with considerable violence by the police: five people were reported to have been killed. In April Bista submitted his resignation as Prime Minister, and King Birendra announced, at the end of May, that a national referendum would be held to choose between the Panchayat system and a multi-party system. In June a new Government was formed by the liberal former Prime Minister, Surya Bahadur Thapa. In the subsequent poll held in May 1980, 54.8% of voters supported the Panchayat system, with reforms, whereas 45.2% favoured a multi-party system.

On 15 December 1980 King Birendra issued a decree under which amendments to the Constitution were made, including the proviso that the appointment of the Prime Minister by the King would henceforth be on the recommendation of the Rashtriya Panchayat. Under the new provisions, legislative elections were held on 9 May 1981, the first of their kind since 1959, although still on a non-party basis. Despite calls by Koirala to boycott the polling on the grounds that it was 'inadequate and undemocratic', 1,096 candidates contested the 112 elective seats in the Rashtriya Panchayat. Only 35 of the 93 pro-Government candidates obtained seats, while newcomers, who pledged to eliminate corruption, improve the economy and reduce unemployment, won a majority. Surya Bahadur Thapa was unanimously re-elected by the Rashtriya Panchayat as Prime Minister on 14 June 1981 and the King installed a 28-member Council of Ministers (on the recommendation of the Prime Minister).

Koirala died in July 1982, leaving a political void in the unofficial opposition. In October there was an extensive ministerial reshuffle to combat growing criticism of bad economic management and corruption. A late monsoon led to droughts and severe food shortages, and the economic situation worsened. Mounting criticism of the Government continued, and Thapa's ministry fell to a vote of no confidence on 11 July 1983, as he had lost the King's support. This was the first time in the 23-year history of the Panchayat system that an incumbent Prime Minister had been removed. His successor as Prime Minister, Lokendra Bahadur Chand, a former Speaker of the Rashtriya Panchayat and effective leader of the opposition, formed a new Council of Ministers.

In March 1985 the NCP held a convention in Kathmandu, and in May embarked upon a campaign of civil disobedience aimed at restoring a multi-party political system and parliamentary rule under a constitutional monarchy. This was followed in June by a series of bomb explosions, resulting in loss of life and apparently orchestrated by two newly formed groups: the Janawadi Morcha—Democratic Front—and the Samyukta Mukti Bahini—United Liberation Torchbearers. These bombings united an otherwise seriously divided Parliament against the extremists and forced the predominantly moderate opposition to abandon its campaign of civil disobedience.

In January 1986 the Government announced that a general election would be held in May. The banned NCP stated that it would take part in the election if the Government would release all political prisoners and abolish the rule requiring all candidates to be members of one of the six Panchayat class organizations. The King announced in the following month that the electoral laws would not be changed, and, consequently, the NCP decided to boycott the election. The NCP planned a new campaign of passive resistance against the Panchayat system for 1987, but the party later announced that it would contest the local elections that were scheduled to be held in March of that year. (The party was to present candidates as members of class organizations.) The Marxist-Leninist faction of the CPN declared that it would also contest the elections. Pro-Government candidates won 65% of the votes in the local elections.

## THE TRANSITION TO DEMOCRACY AND THE FIRST DEMOCRATIC GOVERNMENT, 1991–94

By 1989 the Panchayat system was approaching a crisis. Political instability was exacerbated by a deteriorating economic situation. Indo-Nepalese relations were severely strained and, owing to the failure to renegotiate the vital Trade and Transit Treaty (see below), trade between the two countries was greatly restricted. Thirteen of the usual 15 transit points on the border were closed. As the Nepalese economy was so heavily dependent upon India, these closures had a serious impact, particularly in urban areas where there were shortages of basic commodities. Against this background political tensions mounted and opposition political forces manoeuvred to take advantage of the regime's economic difficulties and to capitalize on the Panchayat system's internal weaknesses.

In early January 1990 six factions of the CPN, together with a labour group, founded the United Left Front (ULF), with Sahana Pradhan as its President. The aim of the alliance was to work for the restoration of democracy. At the end of the month the NCP and the ULF formed a co-ordination committee to conduct the Jana Andolan (People's Movement), and in mid-February the pro-democracy forces launched their campaign. Demonstrations and *bandhs* (general strikes) were held throughout February and March. The Government responded by censoring the media and suppressing the movement through the arrest of leaders of the opposition parties and political activists.

Initially, the Jana Andolan drew much of its support from the professional middle class, but towards the end of March 1990 the complexion of the movement changed as it began to attract mass support. In response to the rapidly expanding challenge to his regime, King Birendra dismissed Marich Man Singh Shrestha's Government (which had taken office in May 1986) on 6 April and appointed the more moderate Chand as Prime Minister. This minor concession, however, served only to incense the participants in the movement and incited them to greater radicalism. On the same day, more than 100,000 people marched towards the royal palace in Kathmandu. The police dispersed the demonstrators with tear gas and baton charges and then opened fire upon them, killing around 50 people. A curfew was subsequently imposed upon the capital. During the curfew, negotiations began between the palace and sections of the Jana Andolan, and on 8 April the King announced that the 30-year ban on political parties was to be ended. At the same time, the leadership of the movement suspended its campaign. However, for many of the political activists, the cessation of the campaign was a betrayal, since, although political parties had been legalized, the formal structures of the Panchayat system remained in place. As a result, the agitation continued, and a week later the King agreed to dissolve all Panchayat organs, including the Rashtriya Panchayat, to dismiss the Chand Government and to appoint an interim government. On 19 April an 11-member coalition Council of Ministers was appointed under the premiership of the President of the NCP, Krishna Prasad (K. P.) Bhattarai. The members of the Government comprised four representatives of the NCP, three from the ULF, two independents and two nominees of the King.

The new Prime Minister announced that a general election would be held, on a multi-party basis, within a year. The principal task of the interim Government was to prepare a new constitution in accordance with the spirit of multi-party democracy and constitutional monarchy. King Birendra stated that he was committed to transforming his role into that of a constitutional monarch and, following further violent clashes in Kathmandu between anti-royalists and police, he ordered the army and the police to comply with the orders of the interim Government in order to facilitate a smooth transition to democracy.

The new Constitution proved a subject of great controversy. The palace manoeuvred in order to preserve as much of the King's power as possible, but the Constitution that was finally promulgated on 9 November 1990 was, in general, a democratic one. The King was reduced to the role of a constitutional monarch, and sovereignty was vested not in the monarchy but in the people. King Birendra did, however, retain some significant authority. For instance, he retained emergency powers so that in the event of an unspecified national crisis he could suspend articles of the Constitution relating to civil liberties and then assume executive authority. Nevertheless, such powers had to be approved after a period of three months by a majority of the House of Representatives, whereupon they could be granted for another three months.

The 1990 Constitution made provision for the election, by universal adult suffrage, of a 205-seat House of Representatives (Pratinidhi Sabha) for a five-year term. The Prime Minister was to be drawn from the party that won a majority in the legislature, and the King was to act on the advice and only with the consent of the Prime Minister and his Council of Ministers. In addition, the Constitution made provision for the establishment of a 60-seat National Assembly (Rashtriya Sabha), which was to be elected by members of the House of Representatives on the basis of proportional representation for a six-year term.

A large number of political parties emerged in the aftermath of the Jana Andolan. The two most important parties were the NCP and the CPN (Unified Marxist-Leninist), the latter more commonly known as the UML. The UML had developed from the ULF, which began to disintegrate following the success of the Jana Andolan. In December 1990 four of the seven constituent parts of the ULF broke away from the front, and in January 1991 the two principal communist factions, the CPN (Marxist) and the CPN (Marxist-Leninist), had merged to form the UML. The extreme left was represented by the United People's Front (UPF), which was an amalgam of radical, Maoist groups.

The general election, which was held on 12 May 1991, was not only peaceful, but was also characterized by a good turn-out (65.2% of the electorate). Of the 20 contending parties, 12 did not win a single seat in the House of Representatives and lost their deposits. The NCP won a comfortable majority (110 seats), but it was soundly defeated by the UML in the eastern hill districts and in some parts of the Terai. In Kathmandu, supposedly an NCP stronghold, the party lost all of the seats but one. By winning 69 seats, the UML established itself as the second largest party in the House of Representatives, followed by the UPF, with nine seats. The acting Prime Minister, K. P. Bhattarai, lost his seat in the capital, and was replaced in the premiership by Girija Prasad (G. P.) Koirala, the General Secretary of the NCP and brother of the late B. P. Koirala.

The aftermath of the May 1991 general election was marked by a clarification of the political positions of the various parties that had emerged after the demise of the Panchayat system. On the right of the political spectrum, the two wings of the former Panchayat politicians, the Rashtriya Prajatantra Party (Chand) and the Rashtriya Prajatantra Party (Thapa), which had contested the general election separately, merged in February 1992 to form the Rashtriya Prajatantra Party (RPP). Within the communist camp, the UML moderated its ideological position in favour of a mixed economy, under the twin influences of the collapse of the USSR and the prospect of eventually gaining power through electoral means. Under the leadership of G. P. Koirala, the centrist NCP Government shifted to the right. The public image of the monarchy and leading members of the former Panchayat regime were rehabilitated with government support. No efforts were made to reform the hierarchy of the armed forces or police, and the secluded staff of the palace secretariat remained largely unchanged. No charges were brought against leading officials of the former Panchayat administration for corruption or human rights violations, and no action was taken in response to the Mallick Commission Report into contraventions of human rights committed during the pro-democracy movement. Replicating the patronage system of the Panchayat regime, the NCP rapidly began to dominate the public administration system and subsequent electoral victories in local government elections were marred by widespread reports of vote-purchasing and ballot-rigging, features that had apparently been absent from the 1991 general election.

In 1992 and 1993 there was continued and increasing rivalry within the senior leadership of the NCP, with the ageing party leader, Ganesh Man Singh, emerging as a radical challenge to the authority of the conservative Prime Minister, G. P. Koirala. In addition to opposition from the leadership of his own party, G. P. Koirala was confronted by growing criticism from the opposition, which focused on a December 1991 agreement made by Koirala in New Delhi, granting the Indian Government access to water from the Tanakpur barrage on the Mahakali River. The terms of this agreement were only subsequently revealed to the Nepalese House of Representatives, which led to calls for the resignation of Koirala for unconstitutional behaviour.

In late 1992 two distinct factions emerged within the UML. One of these, advocating 'multi-party people's democracy' recognized the need to jettison much of the party's Marxist dogma, while the faction advocating 'new people's democracy' adhered to a Leninist concept of the role of the communist party. In 1993 the national UML congress adopted the former policy line, tacitly acknowledging a commitment to working within a democratic multi-party system. In May 1993, Madhav Kumar Nepal replaced Madan Bhandari as the General Secretary of the UML (after the latter's death in a mysterious road accident) and the party launched a rolling programme of protests demanding an end to the 'congressization' of public life and the resignation of G. P. Koirala over the Tanakpur controversy. The agitation was suspended, however, when 2,000 people died in flash floods in 21 of the country's 75 districts, with thousands more left without access to shelter and vital supplies.

The Koirala–Ganesh Man Singh split in the ruling party widened further during 1994. There was doubt over G. P. Koirala's ability to retain the support of NCP parliamentary members when 36 members threatened to withdraw their support for the Government if the Prime Minister failed to institute radical changes. On 10 July the dissidents abstained from an official motion of thanks on the Royal Address, resulting in a vote of 74 for and 86 against the motion, thereby stripping Koirala of his majority. The Prime Minister consequently tendered his resignation, and on the following day King Birendra dissolved the House of Representatives. Koirala was then appointed as interim Prime Minister pending elections, which were hastily brought forward from mid-1996 to 15 November 1994.

## FACTIONAL POLITICS, 1994–98

The elections did not produce a clear majority. The UML emerged as the largest party, winning 88 of the 205 seats in the House of Representatives. As a result of continued feuding within the party, the NCP did not contest the elections as a united body. Consequently, it performed relatively badly, and its legislative representation was reduced from 110 seats in 1991 to 83 seats in 1994. In a dramatic reversal of fortune, the RPP, which was founded by supporters of the former, discredited Panchayat regime, won 20 seats. It thus held the balance of power in the House of Representatives. Following unsuccessful attempts to establish a coalition administration, the UML formed a minority Government headed by the party President, Man Mohan Adhikari. The realities of holding power forced the party to abandon many of its more radical election pledges. In order to calm the Nepalese business élites and anxious aid donors, the UML committed itself to a mixed economy and the Government's programme appeared to approximate that of a socialist rather than a communist party. Yet, at the same time, communist cadres were insisting that the party follow a radical agenda. This situation created severe tensions within the party as the Government sought to reconcile its communist tradition with the pragmatic considerations of power.

In December 1994 the Government launched an ambitious supplementary budget. The centrepiece of this was the 'Build Your Village Yourself' campaign, which aimed to decentralize the development process by granting villages substantial funds so that the community could finance its own development programmes.

A commission was established in January 1995 to investigate the land reform issue. Like its NCP predecessor, the UML Government was censured for assigning the majority of posts to its own supporters and replicating the NCP Government's monopolization of public life. It was also damaged by an unverified corruption scandal over the import of sugar and by the World Bank's decision to withdraw support for the Arun III hydroelectric project.

The consensus between the political parties began to break down when it was widely related that the communists were preparing for a general election and that the UML would increase its electoral support as a result of implementing populist policies. The NCP established an informal alliance with conservative parties and tabled a vote of no confidence in the Government. The UML responded by attempting to dissolve Parliament, to force fresh elections; however, on 28 August 1995 the Supreme Court ruled that the dissolution was unconstitutional. Consequently, the House of Representatives was reconvened, elections were postponed and the UML Government was defeated in a vote of no confidence. On 12 September a coalition Government led by the NCP and headed by the party's parliamentary leader, Sher Bahadur Deuba, was formed.

After the fall of the UML Government there was a sustained period of political instability as coalition governments were formed and were then split by internal factional rivalries within the parties and between coalition partners. G. P. Koirala began to re-establish his authority in the NCP when he was elected as President of the party in May 1996, an appointment that led to ongoing factional tension with Deuba and his supporters. The RPP also remained seriously divided between the Chand and Thapa factions.

Within the UML there was an ongoing power struggle between the 'majority' faction, which advocated less radical policies, and the 'minority' faction, which supported a more dogmatic interpretation of communism. In 1998 these tensions culminated in a split in the parliamentary party, with about one-half (40) of the party's parliamentary deputies forming a breakaway faction entitled the CPN (Marxist-Leninist—ML).

Moreover, in February 1996 a leftist splinter group, the Communist Party of Nepal (Maoist)—CPN (M)—launched a 'people's revolutionary war' in the hills of Nepal, demanding the abolition of the constitutional monarchy and the establishment of a republic. Although this campaign was initially small in scale and did not pose an immediate threat to the political system, it nevertheless disturbed the UML, which was reminded that its position as Nepal's leading revolutionary party was not guaranteed.

In the context of interminable division and intrigue within the major parties and the forging of opportunistic alliances with rival parties, patronage was not sufficient to hold coalitions together, and a series of governments formed and collapsed. In March 1997 the Deuba coalition Government lost a confidence vote and Chand of the RPP was appointed Prime Minister, by forming a Government with the support of the UML and several small parties. In October this Government lost a parliamentary vote of no confidence and King Birendra appointed Surya Bahadur Thapa, the President of the RPP, to replace Chand as Prime Minister. Thapa's Government, however, was wracked by the same instability as its predecessors.

Under an agreement reached when Thapa assumed power, the Prime Minister was to transfer the leadership of the coalition Government to the NCP within an agreed time-frame. By early April 1998, however, Thapa appeared reluctant to relinquish his post and the NCP threatened to withdraw support for the Government unless the Prime Minister resigned immediately. Thapa tendered his resignation on 10 April and the President of the NCP, G. P. Koirala, was appointed Prime Minister. Koirala stated that among the top priorities of the one-party minority Government would be tackling the escalating Maoist insurgency.

Koirala promised to hold general elections in April–May 1999 and, in an attempt to buttress his own precarious administration, in August 1998 the Prime Minister invited the ML to ally itself with the NCP and to create a coalition government. A new coalition administration was consequently formed on 26 August, giving Prime Minister Koirala a comfortable parliamentary majority.

## GOVERNMENT AND THE INCREASING IMPACT OF THE MAOISTS

Meanwhile, the 'people's war' waged by the Maoist activists in the hills of Nepal continued to gather momentum. In May 1998 the Government launched a major police operation in an attempt to curb the guerrilla violence, and in July the Minister of Home Affairs claimed that a total of 257 people had died as a result of the insurgency.

In early December 1998 the ML withdrew from the coalition Government, alleging that its ruling partner, the NCP, had failed to implement a number of agreements drawn up between the two parties. In late December Prime Minister G. P. Koirala tendered his resignation, but was asked to head a new coalition Council of Ministers, which was to govern in an acting capacity pending the holding of a general election. The NCP won an outright majority in the general election, which was held over two rounds on 3 and 17 May 1999, securing 110 of the 205 legislative seats; the UML obtained 68 seats and the RPP (Thapa) took 11 seats, while the ML and the RPP (Chand) both failed to win a single seat.

A new Government, headed by the veteran NCP leader, K. P. Bhattarai, was appointed, but there were signs of severe internal party conflict in December 1999 when about 80 pro-Koirala NCP legislators launched an attempt to oust (by means of a petition) the Prime Minister from his position as the party's parliamentary leader. The political unrest culminated in the presentation of a vote of no confidence against the Prime Minister in mid-February 2000 and, subsequently, the resignation of 11 government ministers. K. P. Bhattarai resigned on 16 March and was replaced by G. P. Koirala six days later.

The new Prime Minister pledged to defeat the Maoist insurgency, curb corruption and improve the performance of the bureaucracy. At the beginning of April 2000 G. P. Koirala instructed the former NCP Prime Minister, Sher Bahadur Deuba, to resume negotiations with the CPN (M) insurgents. In November 1999 the CPN (M) had stated that it required the withdrawal of arrest warrants issued against its leaders, an official investigation into alleged extra-judicial killings of suspected militants by the police and the release of imprisoned activists before it entered into serious peace negotiations. The Government responded in late 1999 and 2000 by releasing a number of Maoist leaders. However, despite some indication of willingness on the part of the Maoist leadership to enter into dialogue, there was a shared absence of trust and, indeed, little evidence that the Government regarded the insurgency as a political problem, rather than as a security problem to be countered by ever harsher action by armed police.

The CPN (M) continued to wage a 'people's war' against the State, a process through which it hoped to replace the constitutional monarchy with a communist state. As part of an overall strategy, militants targeted village and district police stations outside Kathmandu. In the latter half of 2000 the situation worsened when G. P. Koirala sought the support of the Indian Government to suppress the activities of the rebels in locations based in India, particularly in the state of Bihar, a move that provoked the militants to widen their attacks. In September hundreds of Maoist insurgents were reported to have attacked a police station in Dunai, the district headquarters of Dolpa, and a police post in Lamjung, killing 24 police officers and injuring 44. The Royal Nepal Army was criticized for failing to intervene to protect the police from the insurgents. It was, in fact, awaiting permission from the King, who, according to the 1990 Constitution, was required to endorse any action decided by the National Defence Council. Although the Government was keen to use the army to establish a paramilitary force that could control the rebels, the King was reluctant to sanction a decision that could lead to civil war. As the army refused to take orders from anyone but the monarch, the Government was placed in a position of considerable weakness. The Minister of Home Affairs, Govinda Raj Joshi, resigned after admitting his failure to 'maintain law and order in the country'.

This event was yet another example of the Government's inability to assert its authority in the context of the prevailing political system. To complicate issues further, left-wing parties urged the Government to engage in dialogue rather than use the army, suggesting that the latter move could lead to civil war. The first direct unofficial negotiations between the Government and the CPN (M) began at the end of October 2000; however, they were short-lived, and the violent campaign soon resumed.

Tension remained high at the end of 2000 when 56 of the ruling NCP's 113 legislators registered a no confidence motion against the Prime Minister. In early January 2001 the no confidence motion was defeated, but Deuba and his factional supporters began a nation-wide campaign to remove the Prime Minister from the NCP leadership. Although Koirala subsequently attempted to unite the feuding party, he failed to resolve the underlying differences and the Deuba faction continued to refuse to join the Council of Ministers. During the struggle to maintain control of the legislature, the Government was suspected of corruption following a controversial agreement to lease an Austrian aircraft to the Royal Nepal Airlines Corporation, without putting the contract out to a competitive tender. In early February leading opposition parties issued a memorandum to the Prime Minister, demanding his resignation over the aircraft deal and also the worsening security situation. Koirala strongly denied his involvement in the leasing of the Austrian aircraft and the receipt of a large payment. In May the Prime Minister was exonerated of involvement in the case; however, the anti-corruption commission filed cases against 10 other officials.

The Maoist insurgency continued to grow. In the first week of April 2001 alone, militants reportedly killed more than 60 police officers. By this time the insurgency had spread to 73 of the 75 districts of Nepal. Finally, in mid-April, the Prime Minister requested King Birendra to permit the mobilization of the army, suggesting that the country was in a state of emergency. The King appeared reluctant to support such a development.

In April–May 2001 the situation remained tense: the Maoist insurgents maintained their attacks on police stations; strikes closed down businesses and educational institutions across the country; opposition parties continued to criticize the Government; and the ruling party remained beset by internecine divisions. It was clear, therefore, that the prevailing political atmosphere in Nepal was highly unstable. However, what was to follow was completely unanticipated and was to become a watershed in Nepal's history.

## A NEW KING

On the evening of 1 June 2001 King Birendra, Queen Aishwarya and six other members of the royal family were shot dead. The youngest brother of the King was also shot and died later in hospital. The heir to the throne, Crown Prince Dipendra, was gravely wounded. Initial reports suggested that Prince Dipendra had shot members of his family before shooting himself, following a dispute between himself and his mother, regarding his plans to marry Devyani Rani (the daughter of a leading Nepalese politician), of whom the Queen disapproved. An official statement by the King's brother, Prince Gyanendra, claimed that the deaths were the result of an accidental discharge from an automatic weapon. Immediately after the incident the seriously ill Prince Dipendra was pronounced King, and Prince Gyanendra was appointed regent. However, on 4 June King Dipendra died and was succeeded by Gyanendra. In the mean time, rumours about the incident began to spread. Questions were asked as to why the Commander of the Nepalese armed forces did not attend the funeral of the royal family, why there was a delay in an official statement, and why the Prime Minister had not been immediately informed of the deaths. There were rumours that

Gyanendra, who was not present and whose immediate family emerged unharmed from the event, had plotted a conspiracy against the late King Birendra. Some suggested that the deaths were the result of actions by Maoists, while others claimed that India was the perpetrator. These events caused unrest in Kathmandu, and a curfew was imposed. However, it failed to suppress the protests. Shortly after the incident, three journalists of Nepal's largest daily newspaper, *Kantipur*, were arrested on charges of sedition for publishing an article, written by a Maoist leader, supporting the conspiracy theory and calling on the army to overthrow the Government. Following his accession, King Gyanendra established a two-member commission to investigate the killings. The commission, comprising Chief Justice K. P. Upadhaya and the Speaker of the House of Representatives, T. Ranabhat, published its report in mid-June. It confirmed that Prince Dipendra was responsible for the killings and that at the time he had been under the influence of drugs and alcohol.

Meanwhile, concerns continued to mount as the CPN (M) refused to engage in dialogue. Maoist leaders appeared to be taking advantage of the discontent in Nepal by intensifying the insurgency. In mid-July 2001 the Deputy Prime Minister, Ram Chandra Poudel, resigned in protest at the Prime Minister's failure to deal with the discontent and to end the country's political paralysis. Nearly one week later G. P. Koirala resigned, largely because of the opposition's increasing criticism of his approach towards the Maoist insurgency and of his handling of the royal family killings, and also because of long-standing corruption allegations. Thus, 16 months after he had returned to power, G. P. Koirala was forced to relinquish his control to Deuba.

Maoist leaders declared a cease-fire immediately after the appointment of Deuba as Prime Minister in mid-July 2001, but it was not long before the 'temporary truce' collapsed. After three rounds of talks in August, September and November 2001, in which the Maoists sought substantial changes in Nepal's political system, the Maoists ended negotiations. In late November the insurgents resumed their violent campaign: army barracks and other locations throughout Nepal were attacked. The Government responded by declaring a state of emergency and gaining King Gyanendra's authorization to mobilize the army.

Significantly, for the first time since 1996, the army appeared committed to confronting the Maoist insurgents. An ongoing struggle between the security forces (the army and police) and the Maoists ensued, during which the detention of some teachers and journalists and others known to have Maoist connections quickly brought the question of civil rights into public discussion. Furthermore, human rights organizations claimed that the Government had exceeded its authority in suspending Article 23 of the Constitution, thereby allowing it to refuse people the right to judicial representation. The promulgation of an anti-terrorist ordinance, whereby people engaged in what were perceived to be 'terrorist' acts by making political statements could be detained without charge for 90 days was also heavily criticized. Concerns were raised that the police and the army were firing at villages indiscriminately in a supposed attempt to suppress the Maoists. At the same time the Maoists' contravention of human rights caused alarm. The insurgents were accused of killing innocent victims, torturing those who refused to obey their instructions and recruiting children into their fighting units.

Despite government statements that the Maoists were on the retreat, the hostilities intensified. In mid-February 2002 the Maoists attacked and overthrew the Mangalsen army barracks, in Achham district, killing more than 100 soldiers, police officers and civilians. This major victory drew attention to several aspects of the political crisis beleaguering Nepal. First, there was the issue of the emergency, and whether it should be extended and for how long. Second, the relationship between the new King and the army, in other words, the relationship in terms of the Constitution and to what extent it marginalized the Government, was questioned. Finally, there was the issue of the army itself and whether it had the capacity to subdue the Maoist uprising without international assistance. What had previously been a domestic question, therefore, was now rapidly becoming an international one, and in 2002 and 2003 the Nepalese Government was successful in securing pledges from India, the United Kingdom and the USA to provide advisers and military equipment to fight the Maoist insurgency.

## REASSERTION OF ROYAL POWER

In mid-May 2002 Deuba tabled a parliamentary motion proposing a six-month extension of the emergency. However, there was strong political opposition to this proposal and, after the Central Working Party of the governing NCP directed Deuba not to extend the emergency, he recommended that King Gyanendra dissolve the House of Representatives. This took place on 22 May, with a general election scheduled for November; the King then issued a royal ordinance to extend the emergency by three months.

These events led to concerns that the Constitution was being undermined and fears that Deuba's close links to the army and the palace were part of an attempt to subvert parliamentary democracy in favour of the monarchy. Deuba's actions had already caused a rift in the governing NCP, which officially split at the party's general convention in mid-June 2002. The split resulted in several months of political and legal argument as to whether the Deuba or Koirala faction could lay claim to be the 'official' NCP, a dispute that was resolved in mid-September when the Election Commission recognized Koirala's faction as retaining this status.

In early October 2002 Deuba requested that King Gyanendra postpone the national elections, in view of the worsening security situation. On 4 October the King responded by ignoring Deuba's request, dismissing the interim Government, and claiming all executive powers for himself. At the same time he suspended the general election and proposed to create a new, non-elected interim Council of Ministers. These actions highlighted the problematic nature of the 1990 Constitution. By invoking Article 127 of the Constitution, the King intended to claim greater powers than those to which he was entitled. By doing so, he underlined the ongoing tensions that had prevailed between the monarchy and parliamentary parties since the early 1990s. None the less, although there was strong opposition to his move, especially from the NCP and the UML, he skilfully managed the situation. Among other actions, he sought to divide and rule the parties, through offering various incentives. Again, he created a weak interim Council of Ministers, and appointed former premier Lokendra Bahadur Chand of the RPP as Prime Minister, but with a very limited range of powers.

It also seemed that the King had been involved in secret negotiations with the Maoists, who on 29 January 2003 announced a cease-fire. In their public statement, the Maoists demanded the establishment of a conference and an elected constituent assembly. However, they recognized the strength of the palace by not rejecting, in principle, the idea of a constitutional monarchy, a position that represented a distinct change from their earlier demands for a republic. In return, the interim Government lifted the ban on the Maoists. Compelling this situation was the dramatic rise in the number of deaths as a direct result of the armed conflict. Of the 7,500 who had been killed since the beginning of the insurgency, nearly two-thirds died between mid-2002 and mid-2003.

The political parties joined together in May 2003 to establish a movement aiming to mobilize the people in favour of a return to parliamentary democracy. Led by the five major parties, this protest movement brought some pressure to bear on the King, who responded by asking the political parties to submit a name as a replacement for Chand as Prime Minister. However, after Chand stood down from the position in late May, the King appointed Surya Bahadur Thapa as his replacement. In so doing, he ignored the preferred 'compromise' candidate suggested by the political parties: M. K. Nepal, a key figure in the UML.

In late August 2003 the Maoists announced that their official cease-fire with government forces had ended. While the intentions and motivation driving the opposing forces to forge the cease-fire agreement were unclear, the limited duration of the cease-fire suggested that both parties were more committed to a tactical withdrawal than to the pursuit of genuine dialogue.

Indeed, the intensity of the conflict between the army and the Maoists in the months after the cease-fire ended indicated that both parties remained committed to the notion that it was possible to use military force to dictate terms to the other. The costs of renewed conflict were severe, with human rights activists reporting a sharp increase in rights violations and estimating that more than 1,000 people had died in the fighting in the six-month period subsequent to the end of the cease-fire. In March 2004 heavy fighting took place between the Maoists and the army at Beni Bazar and Bhojpur, with both sides claiming that they had inflicted heavy casualties on the other. The Government's preference for a military solution to the Maoist question, in part, related to increased financial and military support (including the supply of assault rifles and transport and combat helicopters) from foreign nations such as the USA, the United Kingdom and India. The Maoists also suffered a major set-back with the arrest of several of their high-ranking leaders in India in early 2004. While the army and the palace reassured foreign supporters that they had achieved advances and greatly reduced the military reach of the insurgents, the Maoists were also able to demonstrate that they had retained the capacity to execute high-profile strikes. In particular, in November 2003 the Maoists ambushed and killed an army Brigadier-General, hitherto the highest-ranking casualty of the conflict. In February 2004 the Maoists marked the eighth anniversary of the launch of their insurgency by detonating bombs in several urban areas. They were able to project themselves in urban politics by organizing several general strikes that were relatively successful in disrupting and suspending daily life in Kathmandu and regional urban centres. The broader political agenda for the Maoists following the collapse of the cease-fire centred upon a demand for all forces, including the parliamentary opposition parties marginalized after the King's assertion of royal prerogative, to unite in order to sideline the monarchy and work towards the establishment of a republic.

While the 'mainstream' parliamentary parties rejected the notion of a direct alliance with the Maoists and the open embrace of the republican cause, in the face of the political impasse between the parties and the King, the broad trend of political life was moving towards a more radical and anti-monarchical orientation. Indeed, a concern for royalist supporters and some foreign observers was that the parties and the Maoists would inevitably look towards an alliance in order to end the political stalemate. In November 2003 these concerns increased after the senior UML leader, M. K. Nepal, reportedly met with key Maoist leaders Prachanda and Baburam Bhattarai in Lucknow, India. The meeting placed tremendous stress on Thapa, who reputedly faced calls from within his own party to resign as Prime Minister in order to release political pressure and to block the trend towards dialogue between the Maoists and the opposition parties. At the same time, the Government faced mounting criticism from international donors, in particular from European nations, over its human rights record and the failure to restore multi-party democracy. These pressures intensified during a series of major pro-democracy demonstrations in Kathmandu, organized by a historic alliance of the five major opposition parties to demand the restoration of multi-party democracy and/or the formation of a more inclusive government. In January 2004 these demonstrations became increasingly strident and radical as student activists became involved and began to clash with police on the streets. G. P. Koirala voiced sympathy for aspects of student and republican demands, pointedly blaming the intransigence of the King and the Government for driving political discourse in this direction. For its part, the UML devised a 'road map to peace' which envisaged a role for the King as a constitutional monarch, yet was also founded on his withdrawal from a strong interventionist role in political affairs. The plan also supported the formation of an all-party government that would initiate dialogue with the CPN (M) and announce fresh elections to be held under the auspices of the UN, and sought amendment of the Constitution in order to ensure the continuity of a multi-party democratic framework. The Maoists soon responded with their own 'road map', which demanded a staged process that would lead to the election of a constituent assembly and the eventual demobilization of the military.

In April 2004, despite reassurances from King Gyanendra that elections would be held within 12 months, the pro-democracy demonstrations in Kathmandu reached a new level of intensity as party and student activists were joined by thousands of concerned, primarily middle-class, citizens who were not formally affiliated to any organization. The strength and breadth of these demonstrations again created stress within the ranks of the Government and reinforced the position of the parliamentary parties within the political arena. The Government and the police force then attempted to restrict the protests, justifying their repressive approach by claiming that Maoist-affiliated revolutionaries had infiltrated the pro-democracy movement. Meanwhile, press reports indicated that the King was unhappy with the established parties, at their inability to contain the protests and open criticism of his rule, including public comment on royal expenditures on civic receptions and luxury vehicles. In response, the King attempted to project a more positive aspect of the role of the monarchy by announcing spending programmes for under-developed regions of the country and by offering to initiate negotiations with the parties in the pro-democracy movement.

In May 2004 Thapa finally relented to the accumulated political pressure and resigned as Prime Minister and, in early June, the King appointed Sher Bahadur Deuba as Prime Minister. Ironically, while the King's decision to dismiss the Deuba Government in 2002 had prompted the pro-democracy protests, his reappointment was obviously an attempt to dissolve the movement and fracture the internal unity of the multi-party pro-democracy alliance. In an immediate sense, this strategy appeared to be successful: the UML agreed to participate in the new Government with the proviso that the King would refrain from a direct and interventionist role in government business. However, given the established rivalry between Deuba and the faction of the NCP led by G. P. Koirala, the appointment also meant that Nepal's other major political party was bitterly opposed to the new Government. Indeed, Koirala responded to these developments in dramatic fashion by refusing to join the Government and by publicly embracing certain aspects of the Maoist's political demands. In particular, Koirala announced that his faction of the NCP would support, in principle, the formation of a constituent assembly that, in turn, might facilitate a referendum on the nation's political system, arguing that this position could lead to a negotiated truce or settlement with the Maoists. In effect, by allowing for common ground with the Maoists and the possibility that the constitutional monarchy could be removed in favour of a republican system, Koirala raised the stakes for both the palace and his mainstream political rivals.

In August 2004 the Maoists instigated a blockade of Kathmandu by threatening supply trucks, and issued threats against several foreign corporations and businesses linked to the King in support of their demand that imprisoned party members should be released. Several bombs exploded in the capital during the blockade action, with blasts at a police post and a government building in the centre of the city. Despite the absence of any physical barriers on supply roads, the blockade tactic was highly effective and clearly designed as a practical demonstration of the increased sway of the Maoists over the capital and their ability to apply pressure to the Government. The Maoists called off the blockade after one week, seemingly aware of the dangers of alienating public opinion because of tightening supplies and rising prices.

On 1 September 2004, one week after the end of the blockade, Kathmandu was again confronted with crisis when communal violence directed at the Muslim minority population affected the city. The riot occurred after media reports were received from Iraq, where US-led forces had occupied the country following their overthrow of the regime of Saddam Hussain in early 2003, stating that 12 Nepalese workers, taken hostage by an extremist group for their supposed collaboration with foreign occupying forces, had been executed in a cruel and gruesome manner. The executions led to criticism of the Deuba Government for its failure to secure the release of the hostages and to concerns for the safety of thousands of Nepalese workers in Iraq. In Kathmandu, violent mobs launched attacks on the city's main mosque and on Muslim-owned small businesses and the offices of Arab airlines, the Egyptian embassy, and employment agencies. A curfew was imposed on the city and two individuals were reportedly killed in confrontations with police. While order was restored, the incidents represented a serious fissure in a local tradition of relative communal amity.

In late August 2004 the Government announced the formation of a peace committee, headed by Prime Minister Deuba, which it was hoped would begin peace talks with the Maoist rebels. However, in the following month the leaders of the CPN (M) rejected all proposals that the party enter into peace negotiations with the Government. In December the Deuba Government set 13 January as the deadline for the Maoists to join talks towards a negotiated solution. However, rather than achieving any forward movement towards peace, the final six weeks of 2004 were characterized by a notable upsurge in combatant casualties in fighting between the army and Maoist rebels in Western Nepal.

## A ROYAL COUP

On 1 February 2005 King Gyanendra moved decisively against the existing Constitution, multi-party democracy and established civil liberties by staging a carefully planned and efficiently executed military-backed coup in order to declare a state of emergency and restore the virtually unconstrained power of the monarchy. Almost all senior political leaders, including Prime Minister Deuba, were arrested and detained, as were hundreds of student and party activists thought capable of mounting immediate protests against the coup. Armed patrols, blockades, the closure of communication networks and the imposition of strict censorship of newspapers, television and FM radio stations ensured the limitation of public dissent. King Gyanendra, in a nationally televised address, justified the emergency by claiming that it would empower a new palace-backed administration and the army to develop an effective response to the Maoist rebellion, and that the action had been made necessary because of the evident failings and ineffective governance of the political parties. While promising to re-establish 'effective democracy' once stability and order were restored to Nepal, the King announced the formation of a small Council of Ministers to govern the nation under his undisputed leadership.

By highlighting the need for decisive action to stabilize and protect the nation from what was represented as a 'terrorist' threat, the King perhaps assumed that popular support could be gained in sufficient measure and that interested foreign powers would eventually be reconciled to the emergency action. In doing so, however, the palace had thereby staked a great deal on its ability to deliver a decisive military victory or to compel the Maoists to accept a negotiated solution on favourable terms, an outcome that few domestic or international observers considered likely. There was also speculation that the palace might have underestimated the strength of international reaction, as the imposition of the emergency and the suspension of basic rights were condemned forthrightly by foreign allies such as the United Kingdom, the USA, and India. More significantly, India and the United Kingdom, reportedly furious at the unforeseen action by the King, announced the immediate suspension of military supplies and assistance, while the USA signalled that its aid was under review.

The political implications of the emergency were manifold. For the Maoists, the declaration of the state of emergency and the suspension of democratic freedoms allowed for an opportunity to propagandize their existing position—that the monarchy was fundamentally autocratic and that a reformist republican state, founded through the formation of an all-party constituent assembly, was the only viable means of breaking the political impasse. More particularly, the Maoists, and their leader Prachanda, almost certainly regarded the emergency as a means of intensifying resentment and widening the political divide between the major parliamentary parties and the palace, while, at the same time, strengthening their own ties to the parties by calling for a 'united front' against the monarchy, the development of a common minimum programme, and the formation of an inclusive democratic constituent assembly. Indeed, it was almost inevitable that the King's action would lead to a relatively polarized political climate and this was reflected in the reported strength of republican sentiment among rank-and-file members across the major parliamentary parties.

A significant aspect of the royal coup was the supporting role that the Royal Nepal Army played and, consequently, there was increased interest on the part of observers as to the Army's future place within state institutions and within Nepalese society. The significance of the Army was already evident given the rapid increase in its size over the preceding four years, to a total of more than 80,000 military personnel. The reported close links between senior ranks and the palace and their strong support for the coup further added to speculation as to the Army's present and future role in Nepalese politics and society. In early 2005 the Army was also drawn into controversy regarding its alleged role in facilitating the creation of village militias and anti-Maoist 'retaliation committees' in certain districts. In particular, from February 2004 there were several reports of the establishment of anti-Maoist village militias, led by local landlords and royalists, in the district of Kapilvastu. These groups were reported to have attacked and killed a number of suspected 'Maoist sympathizers' in the district and to have burned hundreds of houses in the village area of Hallanagar. There were allegations that the latter attack had been instigated by landlords with an interest in driving away landless migrants squatting in the area. While both the Royal Nepal Army and the new Government denied arming and organizing the militia groups, stating that these were a spontaneous effort to resist the abuses of the Maoist rebels, subsequent reports in June 2005 claimed that direct links between the Army and the emerging village militias were increasingly evident in Kapilvastu and neighbouring districts. All of these developments, alongside continuing concerns regarding reported Maoist tactics of abductions and executions in remote village areas, intensified the warnings of international agencies and human rights groups of the severe humanitarian and human rights 'crisis' in Nepal.

In March 2005 the Maoists called for a national general strike in April against the ongoing state of emergency and renewed their call for an alliance with the parliamentary parties. Although typically limited in terms of numbers of participants, in March and April sporadic protest actions were staged in the capital. The palace, however, tried to gain some political leverage by attempting to focus public attention on the alleged past misdeeds and poor governance of the parties and political leaders. In particular, a Royal Commission for Corruption Control (RCCC) investigated and later arrested former Prime Minister Deuba and other former ministers for the possible misuse of public funds.

On 30 April 2005, in the context of local dissent and international pressure, the King announced the official end of emergency rule. The substance of this declaration, however, remained in question: bans and restrictions on protests appeared to remain in force, while there was continuing uncertainty as to future policy liberalization on detained dissidents and media freedoms and the practical implementation of measures to restore multi-party democratic governance. However, the official 'end' of the emergency was effective in softening the position of the Indian Government, which announced within a matter of weeks a resumption of limited military aid, while the USA and the United Kingdom also welcomed the announcement and signalled that the issue of aid transfers would be reviewed.

While the announcement of the end of the emergency was considered, at least in the short term, to have effectively bolstered the King and his administration, in May 2005 Nepal's seven leading political parties met and agreed to work together to oppose the King's 'outdated tyranny' and demand restoration of the parliament and the formation of an all-party government. Thousands of party workers demonstrated in support of the proposed common programme and the palace was angered by official indications that the agenda for the restoration of multi-party democracy had been warmly welcomed by both India and the United Kingdom.

## THE STRUGGLE FOR DEMOCRACY AND CONSTITUTIONAL REFORM

In July 2005 Prachanda proposed co-operation between the seven-party alliance and the CPN (M), calling for the parties to form a team of senior leaders to commence negotiations to forge an understanding. Again, however, the parties responded with caution, emphasizing the need for the Maoists to renounce violence and, in the view of the UML leader, M. K. Nepal, for clarifications and clear commitments to establish 'mutual trust'. As a result, the general environment of opposition politics appeared to be characterized by the gulf between the reluctance of all of the parties to adopt a uniform republican demand and the inability or unwillingness of the Maoists to demonstrate the commitment necessary to forge a common political front.

Between August and November 2005, however, there was a decisive shift in favour of forging such an alliance. A plenary meeting of the CPN (M) leadership was reported to have debated the future direction of the 'people's war' and concluded that a negotiated political settlement was preferable to prolonging the armed conflict. As a result, the Maoist leadership communicated this preference to the parties and its commitment to a future political system based on peaceful multi-party electoral competition. A condition for the Maoists to make this transition, was the creation of a formal alliance with the parties to confront the authoritarian rule of the King. In November 2005 the Maoists met the leaders of all of the major parliamentary parties in New Delhi to negotiate this agreement. That all major parties were present at these discussions and that the negotiations were held in New Delhi with, seemingly, the tacit approval of the Government of India, was a testament to the extent to which the King's repressive tactics had allowed bitter political opponents to find common ground and caused external former supporters to consider alternative strategies towards securing their interests.

The talks resulted in the announcement of a 12-point agreement between the Maoists and the parliamentary parties, with all pledging to work together to launch a mass political movement to end the King's control over state and politics and, after achieving this goal, to explore democratic mechanisms for ushering in a new constitution. Significantly, however, there were differences of opinion between the parties and the Maoists, with the former reported to favour the reconstitution of parliament as the most suitable means of pursuing constitutional reform, while the latter supported internationally supervised elections to create a constituent assembly. None the less, the Maoists were prepared to provide the necessary signals and concessions to make the alliance viable. The agreement indicated that all sides would seek to guarantee positive relationships with neighbouring powers such as India and China, a clear attempt to assuage India's long-standing concerns as to the implications of the rise of the Maoists in Nepal for its own insurgent groups. Senior Maoist leaders such as Prachanda also suggested that a future role for the King as a (ceremonial) head of state would be determined later by the people and the constituent assembly, and repeated earlier assurances on the importance of respecting multi-party political competition. Moreover, the Maoist leadership indicated that success in implementing the agreed political process would be linked to its disarmament as a military force and, as a sign of good faith, it announced a unilateral cease-fire in the armed struggle. Despite the failure of the King and his Government to match this offer, the Maoist leadership was able to demonstrate control over its cadres by upholding a relatively effective cease-fire, with the average daily number of deaths from the conflict falling sharply. In early January 2006, apparently frustrated by the continued refusal of the King to stand down as Supreme Commander-in-Chief of the Army, the Maoists announced the end of their unilateral cease-fire by bombing government buildings in three regional towns.

By early 2006 the King and his Government were evidently under intense international and domestic pressure to advance a reform process, given the formation of the alliance between the Maoists and the parties. Their response was to signal that municipal elections would be held in February as a precursor to full national elections in 2007. The elections proved to be yet another strategic miscalculation: the parties and the Maoists united to call for a total electoral boycott and their success in achieving this goal was evident in reports of less than 10% voter participation and incomplete candidate lists across the nation. While the palace sought to blame the electoral fiasco on voter fear of reprisals from the Maoists, the result was widely interpreted as another indication of the eroding authority of the Government and the political potency of the Maoist/political party alliance.

The Maoists and the parties were now in a position to organize a sustained campaign to depose the King and his Government and in April 2006, in order to coincide with the 16th anniversary of the introduction of multi-party democracy in Nepal, a mass movement of protest and an 'indefinite' general strike across the nation were launched. The protests were immediately successful in bringing out thousands of students and activists onto the streets in major urban areas across the country and there was a gradually broadening popular base to the movement as middle-class professionals and workers joined the protests. The King and his Government responded to the protests in predictable fashion by issuing public ordinances banning political assembly, ordering the police physically to confront protesters on the streets (which soon resulted in several deaths), censoring public broadcasts, detaining hundreds, and imposing curfews in urban centres such as Kathmandu, Pokhara and Bharatpur. The inability of the Government to quell the protests was exposed on 21 April when an estimated 100,000 protesters gathered on Kathmandu's ring road in response to a police 'lock-down' in the centre of the city.

In a final effort to salvage his political authority, the King issued a public invitation to the parties to nominate a preferred prime ministerial candidate to lead a new coalition government. The parties, no doubt mindful of maintaining their political alliance with the Maoists, prevailing popular sentiment and the missed opportunities of the past to guarantee lasting reform, rejected the King's offer and continued to demand that Parliament be reinstated as a means of devolving the powers of the monarchy and taking the first steps towards an inclusive process of constitutional reform. On 24 April 2006, the eve of what was expected to be the most significant single day of national popular protest, the King conceded to these demands by reinstating Parliament. Within days Parliament had convened and G. P. Koirala was sworn in as Prime Minister at the head of a multi-party Government. At the same time, the Maoists lifted a blockade of major highways and announced another unilateral cease-fire in the armed struggle. None the less, the Maoist leadership was also vigilant in monitoring the political process and continued to demand immediate interim constitutional reform and the establishment of a timetable for the dissolution of Parliament and the creation of an inclusive constituent assembly.

The decline of the King's authority continued when, on 18 May 2006, the Nepalese Parliament voted to divest him of his role as Commander-in-Chief of the Army and of all authority to make military appointments. Moreover, the Government and Parliament assumed control over all expenses related to the monarchy, as well as the power to appoint successors to the throne, and moved to rescind the monarchy's claims to divine status from the institutional and ideological architecture of governance by announcing that Nepal would henceforth be a secular state. In June, following a unanimous parliamentary vote, King Gyanendra's right to veto was removed, and in the following month he was divested of the power to appoint judges.

Meanwhile, in mid-June 2006 Prachanda attended a highly publicized 'summit' meeting in Kathmandu with G. P. Koirala, which resulted in an announcement that Parliament was to be dissolved and that an interim government and constitution were to be formed with the full participation of the Maoists. A number of difficult issues, however, remained to be resolved: the demobilization of the army and the disarmament of the Maoist cadres, an agreed timetable and electoral process to form a constituent assembly capable of introducing an effective and stable constitutional foundation; and, finally, a decision over the future role (if any) of the monarch within a reconstituted state.

## THE PEACE PROCESS AND TRANSITION FROM MONARCHY TO REPUBLIC

By August 2006 there were concerns that the delicate negotiations between the multi-party interim Government and the Maoists were in danger of collapsing under the weight of disagreement on a fair and feasible procedure for demobilizing and disarming combatants and on the future role of the monarchy. These differing positions were eventually resolved, however, and in November a binding peace process agreement was announced. With the signing of the Comprehensive Peace Agreement (CPA) between the Government of Nepal and the CPN (M) in November 2006 the 11-year armed conflict between the Army and the Maoists, which had resulted in at least 13,000 deaths, was officially over. The terms of the peace agreement included the voluntary confinement of the Maoist forces into seven camps throughout the country, with both the camps and the collection and storage of arms supervised and monitored by the UN. One of the major goals of the process was the gradual dissolution of the Maoist People's Liberation Army (PLA) with, in the long term, some sections subsumed into a reformed and smaller national army. The agreement was also premised on the Maoists accepting and participating in governance and electoral politics. As a consequence, the interim Parliament was reconstituted in January 2007 to allow the formation of a block of seats for each party to the agreement, with the Maoists allocated 83 of the 330 seats.

The agreement also confirmed a commitment to hold national elections in 2007 to create a constituent assembly that would have the legitimate authority to draw up and approve a new constitution. In December 2006 there were some preliminary efforts towards the reform of politics and governance when the seven-party alliance and the Maoists approved a draft interim Constitution. In April 2007 the Maoists gained formal recognition as a political party capable of contesting elections, finalizing its party symbols and name—the Communist Party of Nepal (Maoist) or the CPN (M). More notably, in the same month the CPN (M) consolidated the peace process by agreeing to join the multi-party interim Government, with five of its senior leaders appointed to ministerial positions. While the Chairman of the party, Prachanda, did not take up a ministerial post, the CPN (M) assumed control of important ministries such as information and communications and local development.

Such progress towards peace and constitutional reform, however, was not sufficient to disguise the trauma generated by more than a decade of conflict and the urgent need for effective rehabilitation. In particular, there was the problem of the resettlement of displaced peoples (estimated to number more than 40,000) and the demobilization and settlement of soldiers in the PLA and the Nepalese army. There was also an evident need to implement an effective and comprehensive mine clearance programme to limit ongoing civilian casualties from land-mines planted by the Nepalese army and from improvised explosive devices utilized by the Maoist forces. The peace agreement also brought greater attention to the investigation of abuses that had reportedly occurred during the conflict. In particular, the Nepalese army continued its internal investigations into thousands of allegations regarding the detention and 'disappearances' of people suspected of links with the Maoists, while Nepal's Supreme Court found that state security forces were linked directly to the disappearance of some 83 people.

There was also evidence of the resurgence of old, and unresolved, conflicts and grievances. A key question came to the foreground: what would be the place of 'minority' (politically marginalized) ethnic, caste, and language groups in a reconstituted state? The issue became especially prominent after the 'Madhesi' community (people descended from migrants of Indian origin) of the Terai plains regions of southern Nepal launched a vigorous agitation movement in early 2007 demanding enhanced political representation and regional autonomy. Led by a political action group, the Madhesi People's Rights Forum (MPRF), a series of violent public protests and strikes was sustained throughout the first four months of 2007. In March the agitation resulted in tens of injuries and deaths and the interim Government issued official bans on the holding of protests and public rallies in several districts. The CPN (M) and a number of other parties in the interim Government linked the unrest in the Terai to alleged interference from the King and his royalist supporters, and there were also suggestions that Hindu 'fundamentalist' organizations in both Nepal and India were fuelling the conflict in a deliberate attempt to destabilize the peace process. Denying accusations that its position failed to recognize the legitimate grievances of minority groups and their neglected interests, the CPN (M) claimed that its support for a federal state structure would actually empower the regions and ethnic minorities and urged action groups to pursue their goals through constitutional means.

A similar demand for greater ethnic inclusiveness and the introduction of a federal system was brought forward in widespread protests by the Nepal Federation of Indigenous Nationalities (NEFIN), which claimed to represent 59 of Nepal's different ethnic groups. Eventually, after the Government had offered talks to all groups involved, leading to two amendments of the interim Constitution (including commitments to federalism, an increase in the number of constituencies in the Terai region, and the introduction of proportional representation for different ethnic groups as well as women within the administration and for more than one-third of the constituent assembly seats to be elected), agreements were reached with both the MPRF and NEFIN by August 2007. The two organizations thereupon withdrew demands for the introduction of a voting system of full proportional representation for the elections to the Constituent Assembly.

Concern within the interim Government and the CPN (M) leadership over the unrest in southern Nepal was intensified by reports that Maoist factions and front organizations in the region were acting with relative autonomy and were involved in clashes with Madhesi and other rival political organizations. In particular, there was controversy over the activities of the Young Communist League (YCL), the Maoist's youth organization. For example, in June 2007 the YCL organized a strike and protests in Kapilvastu district in southern Nepal, the scene of serious abuses carried out during the King's rule, in order to pressurize troops based at a Nepalese army camp into withdrawing from the area. The YCL ended its agitation following firm intervention from the CPN (M) central leadership, but such incidents were seized on by domestic and external critics of the CPN (M) as evidence that the party was unable to renounce 'violence' and 'intimidation' in its political tactics.

With the installation of a new and inclusive interim Government, ongoing efforts to reduce royal influence over state institutions continued to gather momentum. The Government announced plans to remove the King's image from all banknotes, review and reclaim royal properties and revenues, and instigate voluntary retirement or redeployment schemes for palace and other royal staff. A judicial commission, led by a former chief justice, had been established to investigate allegations of violence and human rights abuses inflicted on dissidents during the pro-democracy 'people's movement' of 2006. While the commission ultimately recommended action against more than 200 security officials and ministers in the King's Government, the full report was not released until early August 2007, and there was no serious attempt to lay any charges against the King himself for any of the actions taken in 2006.

In May 2006 the King was removed from the position of Commander-in-Chief of the armed forces and the 'Royal' designation discontinued in all army titles and symbols. None the less, stripping away all vestiges of royal influence on the army was a contentious and incomplete process—with suspicions continuing to be held by the parties and the Maoists that sections of the armed forces and their senior leadership retained sympathy for the King and that another coup to attempt to restore the pre-eminence of the monarchy was a real danger. These concerns led to an amendment to the interim Constitution which allowed for the possibility that the interim Parliament might declare a republic if a two-thirds' majority vote in the house was achieved and on the basis of clear evidence that the King and his supporters had engaged in deliberate attempts to destabilize the peace process and forthcoming elections. For its part, the CPN (M) continued to promote a strong political message that there was no place for the monarchy in its vision of governance. By contrast, the interim Prime Minister, G. P. Koirala, appeared to vacillate on the question of the future of the monarchy. On the one hand, Koirala presided over efforts to remove the influence of the King and palace officials over public life and publicly accepted that a republic was the most likely outcome of impending elections. On the other hand, he refused to consider an immediate end to the monarchy and, in June 2007, publicly floated (and then later denied his support for) a proposal that the King might abdicate in favour of his five-year-old grandson to 'save' a ceremonial role for the monarchy in Nepal.

Speculation and political contestation over the monarchy and governance was prolonged and intensified by the inability of the Government and electoral authorities to proceed with national elections which had originally been scheduled to take place in mid-2007. As stipulated by the peace agreement, these elections would allow for the formation of a constituent assembly which would decide the future role (or abolition) of the monarchy and the final form of the constitution. The postponement was deemed necessary as a result of the political instability in the Terai region in the first half of 2007 and due to the limited time and resources available to election organizers to ensure a fair and efficient electoral process. While all parties agreed to the new scheduled deadline of 22 November for the national elections, the CPN (M) announced that it would not accept any further delay and that such an event would lead to its withdrawal from the Government and the launch of another mass political movement. Soon thereafter, the CPN (M) Central Committee decided to make the party's participation in the November elections conditional on the prior transition of the country from monarchy to republic and the adoption of an electoral system of full proportional representation instead of the prevailing mix of a 'first-past-the-post' and proportional representation voting system. In September, as the scheduled deadline for the constituent assembly elections was nearing and the other parties made no signs of accepting the CPN (M)'s conditions, the Maoists pulled out of the interim Government, putting at risk the fragile process of constitutional reform. In view of this deadlock, the elections were postponed again and protracted inter- and intra-party negotiations were set in motion. Eventually and rather unexpectedly, in late December 2008 an agreement was reached to declare Nepal a 'federal democratic republic' to be formally implemented in the first session of the constituent assembly, and to change the electoral system for the constituent assembly elections by enlarging the assembly to 601 seats, with 335 elected on the basis of proportional representation, 240 elected using the first-past-the-post system and 26 nominated by the Prime Minister. The peace process and constituent assembly elections were thus back on track.

In early 2008, however, soon after 10 April had been announced as the election date for the constituent assembly, the peace process and progress on constitutional reforms were again placed under threat. The Madhesi community of the Terai region launched another wave of protest, once more demanding greater political representation in the constituent assembly elections and regional autonomy in a federal system. Throughout January and February the United Democratic Madhesi Front (UDMF), a loose alliance of several Madhesi parties, staged protests and called a *bandh* covering the Terai region. After some of these demonstrations turned violent and in view of the possibility of another postponement of the constituent assembly elections, last-minute negotiations were instigated. The talks resulted in an agreement between the Government and the UDMF, with vague concessions to the Madhesi community in terms of greater regional autonomy and political representation that halted the unrest in the region. When a similar agreement was reached with a coalition of hill and Terai ethnic groups threatening to disrupt the voting, the elections once again appeared feasible.

Eventually, after frantic and curtailed party campaigning, the elections to the Constituent Assembly took place on 10 April 2008 and produced an unexpectedly high turn-out of approximately 60%. There were reported incidences of disruption, fraud and intimidation, but overall, under the prevailing circumstances and given the tense atmosphere, the elections were remarkably free and fair according to the many international observers on site. The results were intriguing: while the CPN (M) secured 220 seats, short of an absolute majority, it emerged as the strongest party, far ahead of mainstream parties such as the NCP and UML, which were punished and relegated to second and third rank respectively. The Madhesi parties, which were able to file their nominations after the agreement with the Government and because of a deadline extension by the Election Commission, achieved positive results; the MPRF secured 52 seats, making it a powerful fourth party. As expected, the royalist parties suffered a crushing defeat, but many smaller and regional parties were able to enter the Constituent Assembly because of the newly introduced element of proportional representation. The composition of the Constituent Assembly, owing partly to the Election Act's recommendation to guarantee inclusiveness when nominating candidates and to the minority and women quota for the seats elected on the basis of proportional representation, was remarkable for its ethnic inclusiveness and low-caste as well as female participation.

The newly created Constituent Assembly, in its first session on 28 May 2008, formally declared Nepal a federal democratic republic, thus transforming King Gyanendra and his family into ordinary citizens and making room for a largely ceremonial president as the new head of state. Nepal's transition from monarchy to republic was complete. However, there was no guarantee of momentum for the process of constitutional reform. While the King accepted his dismissal with relative ease, the surprise victory of the CPN (M) was met with bitterness and intransigence by the other parties, especially the NCP and the UML, despite pre-election commitments to cross-party unity. Their unwillingness to join a Maoist-led consensus government led to several postponements of constituent assembly meetings to discuss contentious constitutional issues. The main argument of the NCP and the UML as to why they were reluctant to accept the election results and new balance of power by joining such a government or offering co-operation concerned the dissolution or disciplining of the Maoists' semi-military youth wing, the YCL, which continued to exert parallel policing functions, and the dissolution or integration of the PLA into the Nepalese army. The post-election squabbling over the formation of a government and the election of a president thus unveiled the existing potential for political deadlock and showed that a consensus-based approach to the process of writing a new constitution would be difficult to implement. However, the Constituent Assembly convened several times after its historic first sitting and passed five constitutional amendments, one of which paved the way for the constitution (and dissolution) of a new government by simple majority and stipulated the procedure for the election of the president.

The Constituent Assembly elected Ram Baran Yadav, the candidate of the NCP, the UML and MPRF, as the first President of the new republic in a second round of voting on 21 July 2008; neither Yadav nor the CPN (M) candidate, Ramraja Prasad Singh, had obtained enough votes to win the first round. Yadav, Prasad Singh and Paramananda Jha, the newly elected Vice-President, were all ethnic Madhesis. The CPN (M) expressed discontent at the defeat of its candidate and initially conveyed a reluctance to form a government, but in mid-August Prachanda was elected Prime Minister by the Constituent Assembly, defeating Sher Bahadur Deuba of the NCP. Shortly after, a new Council of Ministers was sworn in, comprising members of the CPN (M) and the MPRF; the UML belatedly withdrew from the coalition owing to a dispute about ministerial ranking. Among the CPN (M) appointees, the senior party member Baburam Bhattarai was allocated the finance portfolio, while Ram Bahadur Thapa Badal became Minister of Defence. Among the MPRF appointees, the key portfolio of foreign affairs was allocated to Upendra Yadav.

## FOREIGN RELATIONS

Nepal's relations with India have traditionally been very close. At least geographically, Nepal is a South Asian nation, and the Nepalese Terai is an extension of India's Gangetic plains. The long, open, porous border between the two countries has ensured that the Nepalese economy has become almost an adjunct to the much larger Indian economy. This has had a profound effect upon relations between the two countries, and Nepal has continually struggled to emphasize both its political and economic independence from its huge southern neighbour. Indeed, although the nations share many religious, linguistic, political and general cultural features, the vast difference in size and international power occasionally and inevitably casts India into the role of an oppressive authority. In 1978 the old Trade and Transit Treaty between the two countries was replaced by two treaties (renewed in the mid-1980s), one concerning bilateral trade between India and Nepal, the other allowing Nepal to develop trade with other countries via India. In March 1989 India decided not to renew the two treaties determining trade and transit, insisting that a common treaty covering both issues be negotiated. Nepal refused, stressing the importance of keeping the treaties separate, on the grounds that trade issues are negotiable, whereas the right of transit is a recognized right of land-locked countries. India responded by closing 13 of the 15 transit points through which most of Nepal's trade is conducted. Severe shortages of food and fuel ensued and the prices of basic products increased significantly. It was widely believed that a major issue aggravating the dispute was Nepal's acquisition (in 1988) of Chinese-made military equipment (including anti-aircraft guns) which, according to India, violated the Treaty of Peace and Friendship concluded by India and Nepal in 1950, by the terms of which successive Indian Governments have traditionally considered the entire region south of the Himalayas as belonging to the Indian security system. In June 1990 trade relations were restored after assurances that in future there would be mutual consultations on matters of security. Separate trade and transit treaties (valid for five and seven years, respectively) were signed during a visit by Prime Minister G. P. Koirala to India in December 1991; although, on the vital issue of water resources, Koirala's signing of the Tanakpur Agreement with India became a matter of great domestic political controversy in 1992. Indo-Nepalese relations were further strained by the election of the minority UML Government in November 1994; however, because of political expediency, the UML soon moved to temper its traditionally hostile political rhetoric towards India.

Indo-Nepalese relations improved considerably after 1995. In January 1996 the Indian Minister of External Affairs made an official visit to Nepal, during which he signed a treaty for the Integrated Development of the Mahakali River, which made provision for the joint exploitation of water resources and effectively superseded the Tanakpur Agreement. In 1997 India granted Nepal access to Bangladeshi ports through a new transit facility across Indian territory via the Karkavita–Phulbari road. In early August 2000, less than four months after his accession to the premiership, G. P. Koirala embarked on a 'goodwill visit and confidence-building mission' to India. Koirala's visit helped dispel lingering discontent caused by the hijacking of an Indian Airlines aircraft flying from Kathmandu in 1999, with agreements to co-operate in controlling terrorism, reducing trade barriers, and developing dams and irrigation.

In June 2001 India, like the rest of the world, turned its attention to the killings within the royal family. In view of the growing fear that the Maoist militants would expand their base following this incident, the Indian Government dispatched paramilitary forces to patrol the Indian side of the Nepalese–Indian border. At the same time, the forces joined the Nepalese army, which had been patrolling the Nepalese side of the border since March, in an effort to contain the illegal import and export of arms and drugs. By early 2002 Nepal viewed India as a necessary ally in addressing the Maoist insurgency, especially as close links existed between the Maoists in Nepal and those in Bihar and other parts of north-east India. Support from India was apparent in 2003 and 2004, not only through the provision of military and technical assistance to the army, but also through intelligence work that resulted in the capture of several senior Maoist leaders on the Indian side of the border. While the ongoing political crisis and pro-democracy protests in Nepal caused real concern, in the short term Indian policy-makers appeared to be reconciled to the central role of the King and the suspension of multi-party democracy, evidently viewing the monarchy and a strengthened Nepalese army as a bulwark against the Maoists capturing or causing the state to collapse. Following the victory of the Congress Party-led United Progressive Alliance (UPA) in the 2004 Lok Sabha (parliamentary) elections, India's new Minister of External Affairs, K. Natwar Singh, broadly reaffirmed former government policy by indicating that New Delhi would continue to provide military, political and economic assistance to Nepal in its 'shared commitment' to dealing with the 'internal threat' posed by Maoist groups.

In 2005, however, King Gyanendra appeared to misjudge the strength of India's opposition to his declaration of a state of emergency and suspension of democracy, thereby attracting unusually pointed public criticism and the suspension of military assistance. India's overall attitude towards the 2006 democracy movement initially lacked coherence; it lent full support to the seven-party alliance only after it was clear that the King was fighting a lost battle. After the official end of the emergency in late April, India restored its commitment to military aid. However, the Indian Government, aware of domestic and external criticism of the King and his administration, suggested that this assistance would be reviewed on an ongoing basis. In June 2006 Prachanda stated that India had played an important (but unofficial) part in encouraging the Maoists to engage in talks with the Nepalese political parties. The Communist Party of India (Marxist), India's major leftist party, was instrumental in promoting the peace process and encouraging the CPN (M) to enter open politics. Once convinced of the irreversibility of the political transition, India fully endorsed the peace and constitutional reform process. Although there was no doubt about the Indian Government's preference for the NCP to emerge on top in the constituent assembly elections in April 2008, India's public response to the CPN (M)'s electoral victory was measured and supportive of the election results—despite the CPN (M)'s intention to renegotiate the 1950 Treaty of Peace and Friendship which many conceived as favouring India, and despite the close identification of the Maoist insurgents (Naxalites) in various parts of India with their successful namesakes in Nepal.

Ties with Bangladesh are also important, particularly with regard to the utilization of joint water resources. Nepal and Pakistan have attempted to facilitate trade and tourism through a joint economic commission and a regular air link. However, of the other countries in the region, Bhutan has occupied the most attention. In late 1991 thousands of Bhutanese of Nepalese origin began to flee to east Nepal, following the outbreak of political and ethnic violence in Bhutan. By the end of July 1994 more than 85,000 refugees were living in seven camps (later increased to eight) in the districts of Jhapa and Morang; by early 1996 the total number of refugees had risen to about 100,000. The Bhutanese refugee problem remained unresolved despite numerous rounds of talks between Nepal and Bhutan, although in December 2000 there was agreement on a 'verification' process for determining nationality. This verification process resulted in an official report in 2003, but ultimately did little to address the needs of the Bhutanese refugees, with only a small proportion of the refugees officially allowed to return to Bhutan.

China has contributed a considerable amount to the Nepalese economy, and in the mid-1980s a joint Sino-Nepalese committee on economic co-operation led to an agreement from China to increase its imports from Nepal in order to minimize trade imbalances. Relations between Nepal and China improved further in November 1989, when the Chinese premier, Li Peng, paid an official three-day visit to Kathmandu. In March 1992 the Nepalese Prime Minister, G. P. Koirala, paid an official goodwill visit to Beijing, as did Prime Minister Deuba in April 1996. Although Deuba did not succeed in gaining any major new concessions during his visit, he reiterated Nepal's continuing support of the 'One China' policy. Sino-Nepalese relations were further strengthened in December 1996 by a state visit by the Chinese President, Jiang Zemin, to Nepal.

In 1985 it was agreed that Nepal's border with Tibet (the Xizang Autonomous Region) should be opened. However, the border was closed indefinitely following the outbreak of ethnic violence in Tibet in March 1989. In February 1991 the interim Government of Nepal cancelled a visit by the Dalai Lama, the Tibetan leader in exile, on 'technical grounds'. The cancellation followed Chinese protests made to the Nepalese Government against the proposed visit. The Nepalese authorities have been consistent in their efforts to repatriate refugees fleeing from Tibet and banned a proposed peace march by Tibetans through Nepalese territory in 1995.

For its part, China made no criticism of the Nepalese monarchy, nor gave any support to communist groups in Nepal. At the end of 2000 Nepal and China concluded initial negotiations with regard to proposals to abolish dual tariffs and to promote trade. In 2001 relations were further improved when Nepal's Minister of Foreign Affairs assured the Chinese Minister of National Defence of his full support in suppressing anti-Chinese activities among Tibetans in Nepal and the Chinese Government issued what had become a regular invitation to the King and Queen of Nepal to visit China. Having previously visited China nine times, King Birendra was a strong advocate of close relations between the two countries.

In 2002 China agreed to make the Chinese yuan convertible with the Nepalese rupee in order to facilitate trade between the two countries and to increase the number of Chinese tourists visiting Nepal. In July of that year the Chinese Government hosted a visit by King Gyanendra, which endorsed his position within Nepalese society. However, while the Chinese Government supported the Nepalese authorities in their struggle against the Maoists, unlike India it made no attempt to become involved further, preferring to observe the unfolding of events from a distance. In late May 2003 the interim Government in Nepal forced 18 Tibetan refugees residing in Nepal to return to China. In 2004 this careful nurturing of the relationship with China appeared to lead to significant gains. In particular, Nepal's Chief of Army Staff, after a consultative visit to China in mid-2004, announced that the Chinese Government was willing to boost security co-operation with Nepal in order to improve the army's capacity to deal with internal dissent.

Following the declaration of a state of emergency in February 2005, the King and his administration were beset by criticism from the USA, India and the United Kingdom, which announced that aid and military assistance were either suspended or under review. In this context, the palace made some public overtures to other potential backers within the region such as Pakistan and China. These signals, however, were widely interpreted as a tactical ploy to place pressure on the Indian Government to restore support. Moreover, while the Chinese Minister of Foreign Affairs later visited Nepal and met with the King, the invitation for closer relations was received without any apparent strong enthusiasm from China, which remained focused on the strategic priority of maintaining and improving diplomatic relations with India.

After the CPN (M) committed itself to the peace process and joined the interim Parliament and Government, the party was careful to signal to India and China that it would seek to have 'balanced' and constructive relations with both regional powers. There were also indications that China was beginning to reposition itself in regard to the CPN (M) and its leadership. The Chinese Government sent several diplomatic delegations to establish relations with the interim Government of Nepal and Chinese officials no longer avoided the use of the term 'Maoist' to describe the CPN (M). Following the April 2008 elections and the CPN (M)'s steadfast commitment to Beijing in the face of Tibetan protests in Lhasa and Kathmandu, China intensified engagement with the CPN (M), culminating in the visit of a CPN (M) spokesperson to Beijing in the first week of June.

In 2006–07 the European Union (EU) and the United Kingdom announced multi-million dollar aid programmes to facilitate the peace process, new development projects, debt relief, and resettlement programmes. In contrast, the USA appeared to be somewhat marginalized by its refusal to move away from hardline condemnation of the CPN (M) as a 'terrorist' organization that it depicted as defined by its use of 'violence, extortion and intimidation'. CPN (M) leaders, none the less, expressed a willingness to open up diplomatic relations with the USA, but were united in demanding the removal of all reference to their party as a 'terrorist' organization. Former US President Jimmy Carter, who had visited Nepal and met a wide spectrum of political leaders in the interim Government in June 2007, also headed an international election observation delegation to Nepal's constituent assembly elections in April 2008, welcoming the political transition and criticizing the slow shift in official US policy and the lack of public engagement with the CPN (M). However, after the elections, the USA took some initiatives to reorientate its policy, as evident from the positive reception of the elections and the declaration of the formation of a republic, and a couple of official meetings with the CPN (M) leadership.

The United Nations Mission in Nepal (UNMIN), which was established in August 2006 upon request by the seven-party alliance and the CPN (M) to assist in providing a free and fair atmosphere for the election of the constituent assembly and the peace process, attended the political transition from January 2007 onwards. While UNMIN lent technical assistance during the election process, facilitated dialogue and co-ordinated international support, its role came under criticism. Apart from references to the fact that it was overstaffed and ineffective, its efforts in monitoring disarmament and the integration of the PLA into the regular army did not yield substantial results. UNMIN's mandate was extended until January 2009.

Nepal (with six other countries) is a founder-member of the South Asian Association for Regional Co-operation (SAARC), formally established in 1985: the Association's permanent secretariat was officially inaugurated in Kathmandu in January 1987. Since that time, it has met regularly in this forum to discuss questions relating to development and joint projects that could be funded with support from the UN and other agencies. Among others, it has established monitoring desks for terrorist and drugs offences. It has also facilitated trade agreements between participating countries; Nepal is a co-signatory to the South Asia Free Trade Agreement (SAFTA), drawn up in January 2006 with the aim of reducing tariffs for intra-regional trade among the SAARC members (SAFTA, however, was not due to achieve zero customs duty on the trade of practically all products until 2016). In January 2002 the 11th SAARC summit meeting was held in Kathmandu, where the main topic for discussion was regional co-operation in terms of principal economic and social issues, including the alleviation of poverty. In December of the same year some of these questions were addressed in a follow-up seminar in Kathmandu. Overall, while progress has been slow, the group (which has since 2006 also included Afghanistan) has managed to survive, despite ongoing tensions, especially between India and Pakistan.

# Economy

MARIKA VICZIANY

Revised by CLEMENS SPIESS

The political transition in 2006, which culminated in the election of a Constituent Assembly in April 2008 and the proclamation of Nepal as a republic shortly thereafter, opened a new chapter in the history of Nepal which may prove to be the beginning of a new economic life for the country. As yet, however, Nepal's aspirations for social and economic transformation have not been met, owing to the complexities of the political transition and recurring political unrest. More than two years after King Gyanendra renounced absolute power and parliamentary government was restored in April 2006, political decision-making, including economic policy, is still being hampered by the laborious task of finding a widely-accepted governance formula and drawing up a new constitution. While the peace process was back on track by mid-2008—after the elections to the Constituent Assembly had been postponed twice leading to a temporary abandonment of the interim Government by the Maoists in September 2007 and after tensions had erupted again in the southern Terai region in early 2008, when the Madhesi community staged further protests demanding greater political representation and regional autonomy—the main parties had yet to agree on the formation of a new government and complex issues regarding the future structure of the State had still to be resolved. The April 2008 elections to the Constituent Assembly, overwhelmingly endorsed by international observers as remarkably free and fair, saw the emergence of the Communist Party of Nepal (Maoist)—CPN (M), the party representing the former underground insurgent group whose 'People's War' had destabilized the country for more than a decade, as the strongest party and held the promise of lasting peace and economic recovery. However, the challenge ahead, fuelled by the CPN (M)'s ambitious manifesto pledges and constitutional vision, requires not only the achievement of a *modus vivendi* with other parties, but also the ability to work successfully with a bureaucracy that is unlikely to be keen on implementing Maoist policies.

Prior to the the signing of the Comprehensive Peace Agreement (CPA) between the Government of Nepal and the CPN (M) in November 2006, which officially ended the 11-year armed conflict between the King's army and the Maoists, Nepal had stood at the edge of the abyss and had gradually been abandoned by all but the most determined aid donors. From the outbreak of the Maoist revolt in 1996 until the dramatic events of April 2006 and the cease-fire declaration, at least 13,000 people died and as many as 200,000 were displaced. The political breakthrough and the improved security conditions in the wake of the cease-fire are expected, in time, to lead to a more favourable environment for economic recovery, but the situation remains uncertain owing to persistent ideological differences between the political parties and the Maoists.

The surprise victory of the CPN (M) in April 2008 in the elections to the Constituent Assembly, capturing more than one-third of the seats, was a resounding expression of the voters' desire for change and their frustration with the mainstream parties, especially the Nepali Congress Party (NCP) and the Communist Party of Nepal (Unified Marxist-Leninist—UML), as well as a vindication of the CPN (M)'s strategy of 'peaceful revolution'. The composition of the new Constituent Assembly is also noteworthy owing to its ethnic inclusiveness, the strong representation of regional parties and the inclusion of considerable numbers of low-caste as well as female members. However, the mainstream parties' initial unwillingness to participate in a Maoist-led government, despite pre-election commitments to cross-party unity, and the post-election squabbling over government formation revealed the potential for political stalemate and indicated that a consensus-based approach to the constitutional process and to economic restructuring would be difficult to implement. In addition, the CPN (M) will have to exert greater discipline over its youth wing, the Young Communist League (YCL), which continues to carry out parallel policing functions, and will also have to engineer the proposed integration of the former Maoist combatants' People's Liberation Army (PLA) into the regular Nepalese armed forces—at mid-2008 both the YCL and the PLA remained outside any meaningful democratic control.

Despite the continuing differences between the Maoists and other parties over the future political and economic trajectory of the country, the tension of the last few years has receded. The King has accepted his exclusion from the evolving politics of the country, the royalists have abandoned any hope of continuing to play a major role within the new republican framework, and the military, which before April 2006 had unprecedented power as a result of the emergency powers given to it in early 2005, has retreated to the barracks. It is the Maoists in their new parliamentary avatar, taking over the reins of power, who are now the force to be reckoned with. Any economic reconstruction will, therefore, depend on their policy goals, economic ideology and capacity to deliver results. Prior to the truce of May 2006, the Maoists demanded the establishment of a multi-party constituent assembly and, economically, a policy of self-reliance and independence. While the first demand has been met, there is no sign that the other essential demand has changed drastically. It remains to be seen whether the pragmatism of the CPN (M) revealed during the process leading to the establishment of the Constituent Assembly will be matched by a similar pragmatism when it comes to initiating a process of economic recovery. Ideological quarrels between the Maoists and other parties over the future economic trajectory of Nepal still hold the potential to derail the volatile and fragile process of consolidating governance in the country.

While the leaders of the CPN (M) have told worried investors that the country's economy will be safe in their hands and that the party is committed to capitalism, their economic agenda is not fully clear at this stage. Historically, the Maoists have propagated that theirs is a struggle for those who live in poverty and deprivation—in particular Dalits ('Untouchables'), bonded labourers, poor and landless peasants, women, intellectuals, youth, exploited industrial workers and the seriously disabled, and they have promised land distribution and the abolishment of 'feudal aristocracy'. Their election manifesto for the 2008 Constituent Assembly elections, however, read otherwise. It referred to a 'transitional economic policy' that would focus on public–private partnership and thus create a favourable environment for private-sector investment (both domestic and foreign), for increased productivity and employment generation, and for an improvement in labour relations. Furthermore, they promised that the broad thrust of the Three-Year Interim Development Plan devised in mid-2007, especially its emphasis on agriculture and infrastructure investment, would continue to guide the developmental trajectory of the country. These assurances notwithstanding, structural reforms have to be tackled and the new Maoist-led Government has to demonstrate its capacity to handle immediate challenges such as rising food and fuel prices and power shortages, without endangering fiscal austerity or the environment conducive to investment and higher rates of growth.

## FOREIGN AID

Nepal has been an aid-dependent economy for a long time. In 2003 net foreign economic aid to Nepal totalled US $467m., with the leading five bilateral aid donors being Japan, Germany, the United Kingdom, the USA and Denmark (accounting for $87m., $49m., $45m., $35m. and $33m., respectively). In the fiscal year 2004/05 some 76% of the development budget of Nepal was based on foreign aid: $450m. of a total of $590m. Aid itself represented about 29% of the total Nepalese budget of some $1,550m. By the fiscal year 2005/06, however, foreign aid commitments from bilateral and multilateral donors had begun to fall drastically: compared with 2004/05, in the first eight months of 2005/06 total aid commitments fell by about 54%. This decline reflected the apprehensions of many donors, who began to withdraw or suspend their operations in Nepal. During the first eight months of 2006/07, however, in the wake of the cease-fire agreement of May 2006, foreign aid commitments increased by 61%, compared with the same period in the previous year. Multi-million dollar aid programmes, new development projects, debt relief and resettlement programmes were announced (with considerable input from the European Union and the United Kingdom) in support of the peace process. Several European donors also agreed to co-fund a national Peace Fund, which was designed to assist the financing of the implementation of the CPA in areas such as the rehabilitation of Maoist combatants, the preparation of elections to the Constituent Assembly and general measures to strengthen peace and security. In 2006/07 aid represented about 28% of a total budget of some $2,262m. In 2007/08, as a consequence of a host of new pledges by various bilateral and multilateral donors in the period following the elections in April 2008, foreign aid commitments totalled $851m, an increase of 54%, compared with the previous fiscal year. The main multilateral donors were the Asian Development Bank (ADB) and the World Bank, and the leading bilateral aid donors were Japan, Germany and India (accounting for 21.9%, 22.9%, 8%, 6.5% and 6.2% of net foreign aid to Nepal in 2007/08, respectively).

The long-standing donating agencies, which had drastically reduced aid flows to Nepal during the political crisis, included the Swiss Agency for Development and Cooperation (SDC), Norway, Denmark, Germany and the Netherlands. Japan, Nepal's oldest and largest foreign donor, persisted throughout the worst years, but demanded special protection for its aid workers. Since the 1970s Japan has given Nepal approximately 290,000m. yen of development assistance, trained about 3,600 Nepalese personnel, and supplied some 1,500 Japanese experts to manage aid projects. However, Nepalese analysts have been critical of Japan's assumed preoccupation with technical assistance projects, claiming that these are focused mainly in 'profit-making infrastructure' areas rather than on projects that could have a more immediate impact on mass poverty. This assessment applies more to the first two decades of assistance, when Japan stepped in to help Nepal at a time when the colonial legacy was very weak in terms of infrastructure developments. Since 1970, Japan's aid programme has been much more diversified, and indeed since 1980 has provided Nepal with food aid, health and medical training. In 2006 Japan also responded positively to suggestions from Nepal that it should help with promoting the export of 22 commodities to generate more jobs and long-term training, and in July 2008 it granted US $26m. for the improvement of the Kathmandu-Bhaktapur road. Furthermore, Japan's assessment in 2003 of the driving forces behind the Maoist insurgency correctly stressed poverty, regional disparities, the marginalization of the poor and weak governance. Japanese aid has sought to contribute to poverty alleviation as a means of addressing the Maoist critics.

Japan has no obvious strategic concerns in South Asia. China and India, by contrast, have strong geopolitical interests in all the Himalayan states, including Nepal. In the interests of regional stability, both China and India have long supported the Nepalese Government and rejected any association with the Maoists. However, as pragmatic regimes, both China and India should have no difficulty in adjusting to the current scenario of a Maoist-led Government. Both countries have predictably provided both military and non-military aid to Nepal. India, however, has been less consistent in its policies. Occasionally it has protected Maoist and opposition politicians, for example in December 2005 at the height of the pro-democracy movement. In April 2006, when the demise of the King's authority appeared inevitable, India hesitated between supporting the democracy movement and giving verbal assurances to the King. These inconsistencies can be explained by the strong Maoist insurgency that has re-emerged in eastern India in the last five years: one of the fears of the Indian Government was that the Indian and Nepalese Maoists would join forces establishing a 'red corridor' stretching from Nepal to the south-eastern Indian state of Andhra Pradesh.

Exceeding any Chinese or Indian support, however, has been US involvement in Nepal since the visit of the then Secretary of State, Colin Powell, in January 2002. Military aid to the King was generous, and the US placed the CPN (M) on its list of international terrorist organizations in 2004. US military aid to Nepal between 1994 and 2003 was valued at US $8.3m. in weapons and services. US support in 2003–05 reached approximately $4.5m. US military hardware has been exported to Nepal, including, reportedly, M-16 rifles, grenade launchers, and M-4 carbines to outfit a new ranger battalion. Another estimate cited by a US congressional report notes that total US military aid for the Government's counter-insurgency response was $22m. for light weapons, and that for 2005/06 military support was expected to increase from $1.5m. to $4m., plus some $650,000 for training the armed forces. Increasingly sophisticated equipment was also being provided as part of this aid, including night-vision goggles. Despite this data, it is difficult to obtain a true picture of the total amount of military support from various countries because this kind of aid is divided into so many segments and packages that an aggregated estimate is hard to reach. Moreover, other types of aid include components that promote military assistance—this is especially true of infrastructure programmes, which account for no less than 15% of economic aid to Nepal. The extent of military assistance to Nepal during the 11-year armed conflict between the King's army and the Maoists has compelled think tanks such as Nepal's Policy Institute (NPI) to talk of the 'militarization of foreign aid'. According to a report by Gopal Siwakoti Chintan and Neeru Shrestha of the NPI, the USA's interest was not only in placing a footprint directly into the Himalayan region, but also preventing a communist regime from coming to power by revolutionary means. Whatever the motives, military aid has been an unmitigated disaster for Nepal: it has not saved the monarchy, it has destroyed much of the country's infrastructure, and it has resulted in extensive human rights abuses. Given the dramatic turn of events since April 2006, the extent of military support to the Nepalese state can indeed be regarded as a measure of not only wasted resources but also wasted economic opportunities. Despite the strength of Nepal's armed forces, which faced a Maoist 'people's army' of some 20,000 poorly equipped men, women and children, the King's power proved unsupportable. In the period that culminated in the Nepalese King's effective surrender of power in early 2006, US projections estimated that the domestic security situation needed more than 200,000 armed troops. In dramatic contrast to the US approach, the European Union has provided a total of $24m. in aid for promoting the process of peace and conflict resolution.

The multilateral agencies in Nepal have had a much better record of appropriate development assistance to Nepal than most bilateral aid programmes. During the height of the civil war, the UN persisted with its engagement in Nepal, including programmes in some 1,000 villages under Maoist control. In order to remain effective, the UN Development Programme (UNDP) removed all signs and symbols that associated its work with the Nepalese Government. Multilateral agencies have also been successful in increasing their proportion of total aid commitments to Nepal from about 25% to 80% between 1998 and 2005. Commitments are less reliable, however, than data on actual foreign aid disbursements, which show that multilateral agencies have always accounted for the bulk of assistance to Nepal: between 60% and 75% from the late 1990s to 2005. But whether the aid comes from bilateral or multilateral donors, a generic problem has been the uneven distribution of aid and accusations of corruption.

According to one report, some '82% (of the aid) is spent by the upper-class people'. In the chaos leading up to the dramatic events of April 2006, the polarization of the countryside also allowed the army to appropriate an increasing share of development assistance for its own purposes. Although this appeared to be legitimate under the Integrated Security and Development Programme, the requisitioning of national resources in support of the monarchy's desperate struggle for survival worked against the long-term interests of Nepal's development. One of Nepal's leading economists, Bishwambher Pyakuryal, has also been vocal in criticizing aid donors to Nepal for imposing conditions that no longer apply even to extremely poor African states that are suffering from serious political instability. International donors to Nepal have been preoccupied by the economic fundamentals of Nepal when perhaps they should have focused more on the political fundamentals. However, recent developments in foreign aid inflows and orientation indicate that there is a new confidence in Nepal's return to democracy and peace and that the political dimension of foreign aid is now receiving more attention. This is not only reflected in the rise in foreign aid commitments following the popular uprising of April 2006, but also in the general realization that funding political reconstruction may be as important as economic recovery. This new approach was also evident at the ADB-sponsored Nepal Donor Consultation Meeting held in Kathmandu in February 2008, which attempted to resume the co-ordination of foreign aid policy, which, until 2004, had been done through the Nepal Development Forum.

## KEY ECONOMIC TRENDS

The fact that Nepal has been affected by more than a decade of civil war with an escalating death toll compels the question of whether the national economy has experienced any growth at all. The surprising thing about the country's economic trends is that Nepal continues to experience small rates of economic growth, although given the extent to which civilian government has been disturbed one needs to ask questions about the accuracy of the data on which these estimates are based. However, in an attempt to update and improve its national accounts data, the Central Bureau of Statistics (CBS) has reworked its data processing from the fiscal year 2006/07 onwards and has introduced 2000/01 as the new bench-mark year. In 2004/05 the Nepalese economy showed clear signs of serious economic trouble: for example, the economy did grow but growth rates of gross domestic product (GDP) fell below those of population increase. Moreover, economic growth rates have now fallen to a level that was typical three decades ago. According to the new bench-mark year, the Ministry of Finance confirmed that GDP grew by 3.1% in 2004/05, by 2.8% in 2005/06 and by an estimated 2.5% in 2006/07 (in producer prices). These rates are less than one-half of what was targeted and below earlier growth rates of about 5% achieved during the first half of the 1990s. Agricultural output, excluding fishing and related activities, increased by 3.5% in 2004/05, before slowing to 0.9% in 2005/06 and further to 0.7% in 2006/07 (there was, however, an optimistic forecast of an agricultural output growth rate of 5.2% for 2007/08, which was mainly owing to a recovery in paddy production); manufacturing growth was no more impressive, at 2.6%, 2.0% and 2.2% respectively, with a forecast for 2007/08 expecting only marginal improvement to a 2.5% growth rate. Despite the peace process and political transition, the optimistic forecasts for GDP growth in 2006/07 of 4.5% were not realized, although growth in 2007/08 was projected to rise above the 2.8% average annual performance recorded over the preceding three years and to reach 4.5%. The modest growth rates achieved in 2005/06 and 2006/07 were counterbalanced by much higher rates of inflation than in recent years—about 8.0% and 6.4% respectively (the inflation level in 2004/05 was a more modest 4.0%). The rate of inflation was expected to stay at the same level in 2007/08 as recorded in the previous year owing to the fact that the Government did not raise fuel prices in spite of increasing petroleum prices on the world market. The continuing high rate of inflation is likely to be detrimental to the living standards of ordinary Nepalese, especially if the current surge in food prices worldwide continues. The civil war has certainly taken its toll. In 2005 the Asian Development Bank (ADB) estimated that Nepal will have lost no less than an estimated 60% of the growth that it could have achieved had there not been a civil war. The US Agency for International Development (USAID) has reported that the total value of destroyed property and potential growth has already cost Nepal some US $1,500m. The same report notes that the economic losses are even greater than this if one factors in the 45% increase in defence expenditure between 1997 and 2005. These downward trends are unusual in South Asia.

It is remarkable that the Nepalese economy has managed to achieve any growth, however stunted, under these circumstances. The ADB's explanation remains convincing. Despite the negative impact of the civil war and the massive decline in manufacturing exports after the long-standing Multi-Fibre Agreement governing textile export quotas came to an end in December 2004, the Nepalese economy is so close to subsistence level, with such a dependency on agriculture, that the economic shocks have been less severe. The fact that manufacturing accounts for only some 10% of GDP has also 'shielded' the economy. The key factors that have held the economy together have been foreign aid and remittances (see below). A recent World Bank report on Nepalese poverty highlights the same paradoxes noted by the ADB: despite the conflict the country has been 'resilient'. This resilience, however, seems to be a fragile one, especially if we consider the pending health crisis in Nepal due to the rise of new diseases—in particular the high incidence of HIV infection. After India, Nepal has the highest incidence in South Asia, with Kathmandu contributing disproportionately to the national problem. The data for prevalence rates are unreliable except for those concerning the capital city: a recent survey by Monash University indicated that in Kathmandu among intravenous drug users, 68% are infected, compared with 17% of female sex workers, as many as 10% of migrant workers, and about 5% of men who participate in same-sex sexual activities. Unfortunately, the very things that have saved the Nepalese economy from imploding—in particular the outward migration of its work-force—are strongly linked to imports of not only remittances but also of HIV infection. This, coupled with poverty, ensures that co-infection with tuberculosis (which is typical in South Asia) is also common in Nepal. The failing domestic economy has not only driven workers to seek employment in global markets, but has also created considerable internal displacement, which further contributes to the risk of spreading HIV infection.

An estimated 200,000 or more people have been displaced by the civil war and have added to the ongoing burden of the population who live below the poverty line. Domestic mobility is considerable, even without the civil conflict. According to the World Food Programme (WFP), 75% of low-income migrants in one study reported that they had left their ancestral homes in search of jobs rather than for any reason related to the conflict.

Until the early 1990s Nepal's economy depended on foreign aid. Since then remittances by Nepalese workers in foreign countries have become a major factor in Nepal's economy. In the fiscal year 2007/08 remittances were equivalent to almost double the value of Nepal's earnings from exports of goods. Nepal increasingly looks like an economic satellite of whichever country will take its labour force. By 2003 an estimated 10%–15% of Nepal's labour force were employed abroad and between 1996 and 2007 remittances as a proportion of GDP more than trebled, from 4.5% to 14.2%. One-half of the remittances in 2004 were private transfers. The official remittance business could potentially be even larger if a more effective means of transferring savings into Nepal, especially to the more remote parts of the country, could be devised. As the World Bank report notes, it can take up to two weeks for foreign remittances to reach their destination, and the transaction costs are high. This export trade dates back to the first Anglo–Gurkha War of 1814–16. In early 2000 Nepalese citizens were still serving in foreign armies: an estimated 48,000 in the Indian army and another 3,400 in the British army. Nepal also has an estimated 26,000 British army pensioners and 105,000 retired Nepalese Indian servicemen. In addition to the earnings of currently employed soldiers, the pensions themselves bring in large amounts of foreign currency. Nepalese workers in India alone send NRs 40,000m. each year back to Nepal. According to the 2001 census, 762,181 Nepalese people were working in foreign countries, of whom about 600,000 were in India. The next largest employer of Nepalese labour was Saudi Arabia, with some 123,285 workers. However, these figures are probably underestimates. Nepal's overseas diplomatic missions have played an important role in encouraging overseas employment and have negotiated with some 17 countries for the easier passage of Nepalese contract workers. The net effect of all this movement of people was that by 2001 remittances had reached an estimated US $400m., equivalent to the total official foreign aid received by Nepal. In 2002/03 remittances exceeded total commodity exports to become the chief source of foreign earnings. Compared with the previous year, the value of remittances had also doubled, to $855m., helping to ensure that Nepal's foreign reserves remain at a reasonable level. The level of remittances now outstrips all aid to Nepal (except the extra military aid provided by the USA since late 2001) and is greater than the total net earnings from trade. Indeed, remittances in recent years have been one of the few areas of economic growth. They are such a source of national and personal prosperity that, as part of the Government's fight against Maoist insurgents, some 100,000 young people from the regions most affected by the insurgency were expected to be sent abroad to find work in 2002/03. Estimates by the Economist Intelligence Unit suggested that as many as 15% of Nepal's work-force were living and working abroad in mid-2003, and that remittances were four times greater than foreign aid.

The latest estimates suggested that some 1.2m. Nepalese now work abroad, in about 40 countries. In 2004 total remittances exceeded US $1,000m., making it the most critical sector for the Nepalese economy (this is small, however, compared with India's $23,000m. of remittances). This represented a persistent annual increase of approximately 20% over the preceding decade. In 2006 remittances reached $1,300m., an increase of almost 50% compared with the previous year, and in 2007 there was a further increase to $1,400m. Overseas labourers earn almost the equivalent of about 15% of Nepal's GDP (up from 10% in 2000). New labour agreements with Gulf and Asian countries (including the Republic of Korea, Malaysia and Qatar) in 2007 were expected to help to sustain employment numbers abroad. The net effect of these developments has been that the persistent outflow of Nepalese to foreign countries has not stopped: during the first nine months of 2007/08 there was a massive 23% increase in the total number of Nepalese (167,785 workers) who left for overseas jobs, compared with the number recorded over the same period a year earlier.

Remittances have been identified as a major source of poverty alleviation, enabling otherwise poor families to buy more and better food, housing and education. On the other hand, remittances cannot make a fundamental difference to Nepal's faltering economy and underscore the limited job creation in the country. The sociologist Ganesh Gurung, of the Nepal Institute for Development Studies, commented 'I have not heard of a single business venture funded by remittances'. Remittances can bolster Nepal's balance-of-payments figures, but they cannot serve as the basis of a strategy for economic development. Even their role in the balance-of-payments situation may not be sustainable. As the ADB notes, remittances are prone to decline whenever foreign banks offer attractive interest rates. Nepal could make remittances more attractive by establishing pension plans as Mexico and the Philippines have done.

## POVERTY AND SOCIO-ECONOMIC UNDERDEVELOPMENT

In July 2007 the World Bank ranked Nepal as the 12th poorest country in the world, with an annual per caput income of only US $320 (as of 2006). Even when the income is considered in purchasing-power parity terms, Nepal remains the 28th poorest nation in the world. The UNDP, in its *Human Development Report 2007/2008*, classified Nepal as a 'medium human development' country in 2005, ranking 142nd out of 177 countries. It was less developed than Bangladesh (140th) and Pakistan (136th). The World Bank's World Development Indicators database confirms that the per caput gross national income (GNI) of Nepal is low compared with other countries in South Asia: $320 in 2006, compared with $800 in Pakistan, $1,310 in Sri Lanka, $820 in India, $1,430 in Bhutan and $450 in Bangladesh. Despite these dismal rankings, the latest assessments of changes in poverty between 1996 and 2004 are much more optimistic. The World Bank estimated that poverty levels (headcount poverty rate) fell from 42% to 31% over this period, a decline attributed largely to the great increase in remittances. Citing a study of 72 districts, the World Bank team estimated that, had remittances stagnated between 1996 and 2004, the decline in poverty would have been less than one-half of what actually occurred. If the estimates are accurate, the report will revise earlier views that insisted that poverty levels have remained the same or even risen in Nepal since 1990. All along, the Nepalese Government has refused to resile from its claim that the incidence of poverty had fallen from 42% to 38% of the population. Official estimates, however, have little credibility in Nepal these days. The World Bank survey is too close to official estimates, and hence judgement must be reserved until the emergence of a thorough assessment of these optimistic conclusions. In addition, the survey covers only developments up to 2004, with reliable data for more recent periods so far not available. In the mean time, regional comparisons show that Nepal has the highest proportion of people living below the poverty line in South Asia.

The regional spread of poverty in Nepal has been distinctive: 56% of people living in the Himalayas are very poor, as well as 42% living in the Terai and 41% living in the Hill regions. An average 44% of rural and 23% of urban people are very poor. Moreover, the Kathmandu valley appears to have benefited disproportionately from development, with only 4% living below the poverty line, compared with more than one-third in urban regions beyond the valley. Thus, it is not surprising that the Maoists focused their initial insurgency campaign on rural areas of Nepal and at a distance from Kathmandu. The poorest 20% of households have received less than 8% of total income, whilst the richest 20% have received about 45%. The Gini index (a measurement of the extent to which the distribution of income among individuals or households deviates from an equal distribution) for Nepal was 47.2 in 2003–04. Chronic seasonal food deficits affected 50% of the population in the 1990s, and there was little improvement in major health indicators.

This brief summary of the recent poverty profiles of Nepal needs revision if the recent World Bank report is to be accepted. Poverty has declined largely in response to the increase in aggregate foreign remittances. This in turn has been driven by labour markets well beyond India; overseas labour demand has attracted workers from many poor rural areas. The result is that the rural eastern hill region of Nepal has experienced 'a fourfold increase in the number of households receiving remittances from abroad'. Families in central and eastern Nepal are also the beneficiaries of the largest volume of domestic remittances. The average size of remittances also doubled in these years, to NRs 6,000. Remittances might also have contributed to an increase in wages by an average of 25%; rural wages too grew by 25% between 1996 and 2004. A final driving factor to take into account is the annual 6.7% increase in road building, especially in rural areas. Improved rural transport would have facilitated the out-migration of labour and the in-migration of remittances. The impression one has of the Nepalese economy during the height of the conflict between monarchists and Maoists is that the whole system was shaken up, with workers becoming more mobile and more independent of the patronage of local employers. All of this could well have contributed to increasing the bargaining power of labour. In other words, aggregate poverty, in addition to rural poverty, may well have declined, as the World Bank report suggests. On the other hand, regional disparities have not been affected. The further west one goes, the higher the incidence of poverty: the average in the western region is 27% but in the furthest western regions it rises to 45%. Western Nepal remains the stronghold of the Maoist movement.

Poverty also remains stratified by social status, with the Dalits, tribals and low-caste people suffering a high incidence, and middle and high castes rapidly moving into the middle-class economic categories. The Newars remain the most prosperous social group and the 'underprivileged' untouchable castes the poorest. The incidence of poverty among the latter is around 70%, and is closely followed by poverty among indigenous people—up to 60%. Vast regional disparities accentuate the uneven nature of development in Nepal: the human development indicators for Kathmandu, for instance, are four times higher than those for the most underdeveloped district of Mugu. One significant index of Nepal's economic backwardness is to be found in demographic data. Nepal's population of about 27m. is growing at an average annual rate of 2.1% and, like other less-developed countries, the population is very young: some 39% are 14 years or younger and a total of 60% are under 25 years. The high population growth rate is likely to persist, since mortality remains very high and consequently couples have more babies, in the belief that most will not survive. According to the ADB, in 2004 life expectancy at birth was only 61.6 years for males and 62.4 years for women, while infant mortality in 2005 was about 61 per 1,000 live births. Despite modest immunization campaigns (about one-half of all children were vaccinated in 2000), the death rate remains unacceptably high and driven, in part, by poor nutrition. According to the former Chief Economist of the World Bank, Nicholas Stern, in 2001 about one-half of children under the age of five years suffered arrested growth, about the same proportion were underweight and another 10% suffered from muscle wasting. About 23% of the children born in 1997 will not survive to the age of 40 years and about 14% will not survive to the age of 15 years. Other factors causing ill health include the lack of household facilities: about 30% of families do not have clean drinking water and about 50% do not have toilets.

Despite this, between 1980 and 2000 life expectancy increased by a total of about 14 years. As the rate of mortality declined, attention was increasingly focused on morbidity in Nepal. About one-half of the population suffered from iodine deficiency, which causes goitre, and about one-half of the population under 14 years of age had tuberculosis or leprosy. The World Bank attempted to summarize the inter-relationship between death and morbidity in a new Disability Adjusted Life Years (DALYs) indicator. This index shows that DALYs lost per 1,000 population in Nepal (366) is higher than in China (117) and India (344), but lower than sub-Saharan Africa (574). According to an IMF review of recent economic developments in Nepal, social expenditure as a percentage of Nepal's GDP increased from 3.5% to about 6% between 1985 and 2000, with an average annual of 5.3% being recorded for the period 2000–05, but the allocation was still insufficient to lift people out of poverty. The health infrastructure of Nepal was damaged during the mid-1990s by the closure of 25% of the country's hospitals as part of an attempt to save money. Nepal had about 90 hospitals in 2003, but rural health services continue to depend on village-level clinics or traditional medical practitioners. The Maoist insurgency has had a devastating impact on modern rural health services: facilities have been damaged, doctors refuse to travel to villages, and the links between village services and urban health expertise have been broken. The insurgency has been far more damaging than the lack of government investment in rural health and the problem of urban bias, which is common throughout Asia.

Socio-economic differences are driven by Nepal's dependence on agriculture. The expansion of land under cultivation is limited by the fact that much of Nepal's land is too hilly. The Himalayan region covers 79% of the land mass, and the Terai, which is an extension of the Gangetic plain, comprises 21%. The small area of the Terai accounts for the greater part of agricultural output. It also supports the largest proportion of the Nepal population—about 47.7%, having increased by almost 4% since the early 1980s. Agricultural production needs to move in the direction of intensive technologies, but this is hampered by the lack of many modern inputs. For example, in 2000 the Government continued its attempts to reform the fertilizer industry, but farmers remained reluctant to use fertilizers while they did not have guaranteed access to irrigation water.

Across the border in India, the information technology 'revolution' is generating enormous opportunities for employment, export earnings and joint ventures with foreign companies. Nepal's capacity to respond to similar opportunities, by contrast, is severely hindered by the lack of educational infrastructure. India shares Nepal's problems of illiteracy, but its universities and institutes of technology annually produce vast numbers of highly trained and skilled labour. By 2004 Nepal's literacy rate had increased to 48.6%; however, only 34.9% of females were literate, compared with 62.7% of males. The average length of schooling among adults was 3.3 years in 2000. The next generation of adults might not be at a greater advantage, in view of the fact that, by 2000, compulsory education had been implemented in only seven of Nepal's 75 districts. According to the UN Children's Fund (UNICEF), about 48% of school children left the education system before reaching Grade Five. These figures do not match recent claims by the World Bank that the participation of six- to 15-year-olds had increased from 63% to 73% between 1996 and 2004. Again, time is needed to assess the accuracy of the World Bank's revised estimates. If school retention rates improved during the height of the insurgency, the causes need to be explored. A report by the ADB as late as December 2004 showed that Nepal continued to suffer from high rates of teacher absenteeism: 40% in the case of primary schools, 30% and 20% respectively for lower and higher secondary schools. The quality of teachers is also troubling, given that many teaching positions are sold to the highest bidder: prices for jobs range from between NRs 5,000 and NRs 40,000. Unqualified temporary teachers also enter the system by becoming tenured lecturers after a certain time, regardless of the level of their training.

The situation may now be changing, but the legacy of poor schooling is still reflected in Nepal's unemployment and under-employment problems. Nepal's adult work-force reached some 12m., of which about 5% were unemployed, in the late 1990s. At that time about 50% of the population were underemployed, working for fewer than 40 hours a week. The basic point is that unemployment in desperately poor countries is unlikely because the poor must work regardless of what type of work they can find and how much they get paid. Hence, the low level of unemployment in Nepal is itself an indicator of poverty. A better measure of deprivation would be to look at the nature of employment and terms and conditions. Between 1995 and 2000 real wages in both industry and agriculture declined, forcing the Nepalese Government to declare a minimum agricultural wage of NRs 70 (US $1) per day in the Kathmandu valley. A minimum industrial wage of NRs 74 was also declared, to little avail. One reason for its failure was that it could only be applied to the formal work-force, which constitutes a mere 2% of the Nepal labour force. Implementation of minimum wages in other parts of South Asia has been extraordinarily difficult, owing to a lack of political will or any mechanism for enforcement. It is likely that Nepal will record a similar failure. Perhaps surprisingly, the aforementioned World Bank report on poverty insists that all previous accounts about wages and underemployment have been inaccurate. Instead, the report claimed that between 1996 and 2004 real per caput income and expenditure grew by 4.5% p.a. and real per caput incomes increased by over 40% in the same period. Moreover, the World Bank maintains that real rural wages also increased by about 25%, which is 5% more than the increase in non-agricultural unskilled wages. This, together with the increased remittances into rural Nepal, suggests that despite the civil war total income to rural families was rising from the mid-1990s onwards. Any final judgement on this must, however, await a closer analysis of the database and relevant methodologies applied.

Rural living standards may have risen in the last decade, but not enough to eliminate child labour. Indeed, the rising rural wages that have been referred to above have compelled landless and farming families to substitute cheap child labour for the labour of adults. This appears to have put pressure on boys in particular—the proportion of boys who attend school only and do not work actually declined from 60.4% to 50.9% between 1996 and 2004. Earlier estimates by the International Labour Organization (ILO) showed that almost one-third of Nepal's children between the ages of five and 14 years work, and that this child labour accounts for about 16% (2m. children) of the 12m. in Nepal's labour force. The latest estimates by the World Bank show that about 1.3m. children do not attend school: about one-half of these are under 10 years of age and the other half between 11 and 15. One of the main reasons for this non-attendance is that the costs of education cannot be borne by their families. Many of the young children who do not attend school are also not working, as pressure to work rises with age. For those that do work, the average number of hours per week is about 22. Most of these are unpaid, but about 100,000 under-14-year-olds working in agriculture, construction and manufacturing are paid. In addition, the Australian aid agency AusAID reports that the number of Nepalese children unable to attend school, owing to work obligations, is 5m.

Women carry the bulk of the burdens of poverty: they have few rights, poor access to assets or loans, fewer employment and educational opportunities than men, and less mobility in general. For example, only 11% of women have any land, compared with almost 80% of landowning households. According to the UNDP's *Human Development Report 2007/2008*, Nepal was ranked 127th out of 177 countries in the gender-related development index. Gender disadvantages are reflected in all indicators, especially maternal mortality, with some 415 deaths per 100,000 live births reported in 2001. Discrimination first becomes evident in the enrolment rates at school: in primary schools the enrolment rate for girls is 13% less than for boys; in secondary schools there is a 6% difference. International donors have reported great difficulties in making gender-based programmes work successfully in Nepal. The gender bias is said to be so acute that externally funded projects are able to make little difference. Women have traditionally enjoyed limited participation in the decision-making process at the highest level; for example, until recently only 6% of parliamentary seats were held by women. However, with the incorporation of Maoists into parliamentary politics in 2006–07 the percentage increased to 17.3%, and owing to the recent introduction of quota measures, the representation of women in the Constituent Assembly that was elected in April 2008 was equivalent to one-third of total representatives. None the less, many development projects have increased the social and economic burden on women; dam construction has been particularly onerous. The extent of gender bias varies from community to community. Indo-Aryan women, for example, have greater opportunities to assume entrepreneurial roles than the Tibeto-Burmese. Nepalese women are also the victims of people-trafficking, especially across the border into India. It has been estimated that about 250,000 Nepalese girls work in Indian brothels. Labour mobility is not, however, universally adverse. The World Bank has reported that when men migrate away from their households, the relative freedom of women increases, especially in the area of economic decision-making. However, in extended households where women live with their mothers-in-law, the absence of husbands can further reduce their freedom; this is especially the case if the husband's parents are charged with the role of looking after the family.

## AGRICULTURE AND FORESTRY

Whereas in 2006/07 production of key agricultural crops in Nepal declined by an estimated 2.5%, largely as a result of falling output in the main crop of rice paddy, which was affected by drought, floods and a protracted winter, 2007/08 saw an increase in agricultural production owing to favourable monsoon rains resulting in a strong growth in paddy output. Despite modest diversification, Nepal's economy remains primarily one of subsistence, even though only 36% of GDP is generated by agriculture, fishing and forestry. Nepal is one of the least urbanized countries in Asia: only 17% of the population of 27m. live in towns. The remainder live in villages, depend on agriculture for survival and only intermittently find employment in the services sector. Given the mountainous nature of Nepal, population density is high, at about 570 persons per sq km of cultivated land. The villages depend on about 28% of the land surface that is given over to agriculture: about 40% is under forest cover and the remainder is urban and industrial land. The population dependent on rural employment has fallen from 81% to 66% in the last decade, but economic diversification in rural Nepal remains limited. This persistent dependency on the land has placed intense pressure on natural resources. Limited urbanization and technological stagnation have led to the subdivision and fragmentation of landholdings, reducing 50% of Nepal's farms to under 0.5 ha in size. The pressure of population would be a less serious problem if Nepal could expand agricultural production in the direction of intensive technologies. However, technological innovation has been stagnant and the country's vast water resources have not been harnessed. Only one-third of the land is irrigated, and the incentives to production remain hindered by primitive land tenure arrangements. These structural constraints on agricultural output are more important reasons for the limited success of Nepalese agriculture than population pressure and the fragmentation of landholdings. Between 1981 and 1991 the number of farms of less than 0.5 ha in size increased by 81% and farms between 0.5 and 1 ha grew by 89%.

Agricultural stagnation has been so serious that Nepal remains a food-deficit country, with about one-half of the country's 75 districts routinely facing food shortages. Long-term trends also show that the Nepalese economy has been moving towards the commercialization of agriculture. Taking 1984/85 as the base year, the index of agricultural production in 1999/2000 was 208 for cash crops, 152 for food grains, 186 for other crops, 155 for livestock and 162 overall. In the long term, the increase in cereal crops in particular has been unimpressive: about 2.2% per year for more than 25 years. This has occurred alongside the commercialization of agriculture, a dual trend that might be regarded as a positive indicator for change. However, considering the isolated nature of much of Nepal's population and its continued dependence on agriculture, the relative stagnation of food production is not necessarily a sign of progress. Moreover, agricultural production has only just managed to keep up with population growth. Commercialization could contribute towards the development of agri-industries; however, for this to occur, the rate of crop production must be greatly accelerated. One promising development has been the cultivation and export of coffee. USAID has formed a production consortium of private firms and the Nepalese Government to grow and export arabica coffee, of which Nepal has an excellent variety. The US-based Holland Coffee Group signed a contract in 2004 to buy all the coffee produced by the alliance over the next five years. Coffee production is a welcome diversification owing to its labour-intensive nature. The Holland Coffee Group each year sells about 50,000 metric tons of coffee, of which the Nepalese contribution is only 40 tons. Yet, this small experiment gives rare encouragement in an otherwise dismal situation. Tea production and export is another area of potential growth, partly because Nepal's chief competitor, India, faces declining market demand as a result of the lower quality of tea produced by old trees. In mid-2004 about 40,000 workers were employed in tea production in some 136 plantations, which had doubled their total yield since 1997. Already, the number of jobs in the tea sector has almost reached the levels of employment in garments and also carpets, with the potential for growth being far greater.

To promote agriculture, the Government introduced the Agricultural Perspective Plan, which, with the support of the ADB, aims to rationalize inputs into agriculture. The distribution of fertilizers has been rationalized, with the abolition of subsidies and import liberalization. In other ways, trade in fertilizers has been totally deregulated and privatized, giving rise to serious problems with adulteration. Questions need to be raised about the appropriateness of the ADB's strategy for Nepalese agriculture. The final report on the loan programme in December 2004 reported that, with deregulation, fertilizer usage, even among poor farmers, had increased greatly. At the same time, this needs to be evaluated against Nepal's greatly increased dependency on Indian fertilizer imports. The ADB has encouraged the Nepalese Government to stop the distribution of subsidized food grains, arguing that food can be readily imported from India and that the cost of the foodgrain buffer is too high. However, the costs of these subsidies to the poor should be reassessed now that stability is likely to return to the countryside.

One index of Nepal's dependence on agriculture is the economic instability caused by the failure of the monsoon. Years of accelerated economic growth typically reflect good and timely rains, whilst declines in economic growth rates are usually caused by inclement weather, flooding, poor timing or the lack of rain, as in 1990/91, 1994/95, 1996/97, 1997/98, 2005/06 and 2006/07. However, despite the constraints, Nepal possesses much agricultural potential. The climate and topography are suitable for growing tea and jute, but, unlike its neighbours, Nepal produces neither in large volume. Nepal used to produce jute in abundance, and research in Bangladesh has suggested that modern processing of jute can again turn this fibre into a commodity of great importance to the world economy. Instead, Nepal's agriculture has been concentrated on a narrow range of food and cash crops. The contrast with neighbouring India is dramatic, considering the latter's revolution in dairy produce and a wide range of horticultural goods. Food grains accounted for about 67% of agricultural output in Nepal in 1998/99. The principal crops are rice, maize, wheat, millet and barley. Cash crops constituted about one-third of agricultural production, and consisted of sugar cane, potato, oilseeds, jute and tobacco, in descending order of importance. Jute, once a major crop, accounted for 0.4% of cash crop production in 2001/02. Since 1975 foodgrain production has expanded very slowly, at an average annual rate of about 2.2%. Growth in cash-crop production has been much better—about 6.5% per year during the same period—but unremarkable, in view of the new agricultural technologies that have become available in South Asia. The share of food crops and cash crops in total agricultural production for 2006/07 was estimated at 47.7% and 52.3% respectively. Most damaging of all, per caput output of Nepalese agriculture has hardly changed during the last 30 years.

The principal problem of Nepalese agriculture in terms of production has been low yields. This is a relatively new problem. During the 1960s Nepal had the highest yields in South Asia and met its own food requirements. By 2000 its productivity was between 10% and 30% below that of other South Asian countries. This clearly reflects the lack of investment in agriculture. As a result, since 1980 Nepal has been a food-importing country, in a region largely characterized by food self-sufficiency. In late 2001 the NCP introduced new legislation that promised to address the problem of rural inequality, long recognized as the most basic constraint to agricultural productivity. The limits imposed on landholdings, however, undermined popular support for the programme. In the Terai, for example, the limit was a generous 6.9 ha, compared with the Maoist demand of 2.7 ha. No attempt had been made to implement the new, generous land limits.

Despite the constraints noted above, a recent inventory by the ADB of Nepal's biodiversity shows that no other country in the world can claim to have such a variety of plant and animal species in such a small area of land. To a considerable degree this richness is the product of great topographical and climatic variation within the country, giving rise to almost 6,000 species of flowering plants, including 30 species of rhododendron. Yet despite this abundance, Nepal has not benefited from its bountiful nature, except perhaps in the area of tourism. The possibility of forestry contributing to rural prosperity is constrained by the fact that one-half of Nepal's forest reserves were depleted between 1950 and 1980. Areas of forestation continued to shrink between 1986 and 1994, from 37.4% of the land surface to 29%. Since 1994 an increase, back up to 37.4%, has been recorded, but the statistical bases for these estimates remain unreliable. Certainly the statistical data do not agree with other evidence, all of which points to a contraction of forest lands. Scrub lands have also fluctuated between 5% and 10% of land cover and are currently estimated at about 8.7%. More generally, the biodiversity of Nepal's forests and scrubs has declined severely. Poverty itself has caused deforestation, as wood and its residues are the primary source of fuel for the poor. Deforestation in turn increases poverty, as the time taken to forage grows with the depletion of natural resources. Fuel wood collection, taking as much as 4.7 hours per headload in some parts of Nepal, is arduous work performed by women and children. The poorest families do not collect or use fuel wood; instead they forage for residues left on the ground. The result is a reduction of the amount of humus, leading to poor soil quality. At the upper end of the economic scale, families grow their own fuel wood or substitute fuel wood with alternatives such as kerosene.

Wood shortages have been exacerbated by the growing number of livestock and the smuggling of forest resources into India and China. The most important factor behind the degradation of land and forest resources, however, is the naturally occurring landslides that Nepal is subjected to, largely as a consequence of the mountainous topography. Lesser causes for natural degradation are floods, glacial lake bursts, the clearing of forests and scrubs on the slopes of mountains, soil erosion, desertification and chemical waste products from modern farming and factory production.

The Forest Act of 1993 was introduced to encourage people to own and use their own forest rather than national or state-owned forests. In 1995 the Forest Regulation Act fixed the prices of timber, fruits and other produce and introduced a cess on animals grazing on forest lands. The 1993 Act encouraged the establishment of Forest User Groups to manage 3.5m. ha of community forest. However, the exclusion of the poorest families from these groups and new prices and cesses on forest products hindered environmental protection and gave rise to community discord and resentment. By mid-2003 a total of 1.3m. ha of forest was being managed by more than 12,000 community groups. Some degraded land had also been returned to local communities. The principle behind these developments was that people with local knowledge are better able to look after the forests than even professional groups; however, given the pervasive poverty of forest-dwellers, it is difficult to see how the former has the capacity to invest in restoring degraded land. The cultivation of herbs in forest areas was also actively encouraged in an attempt to develop non-timber products and mixed forestry. However, these initiatives have not had a significant impact, owing to poor implementation and the lack of involvement of local people, who are heavily dependent upon forests for the supply of energy, honey, medicinal herbs and fodder. It remains to be seen whether the National Agro-Biodiversity Policy formulated by the Government in 2007 to address some of the problems mentioned above by integrating agricultural biodiversity concerns with production ones will seriously alter the structural deficits that continue to hamper agricultural productivity and to further environmental degradation.

## INDUSTRY

In 2006/07 industrial production grew at a modest rate of about 2.2%, reflecting, among other things, the international increase in petroleum prices, the shortage of petroleum products and disruptions arising from power cuts. During the 1990s manufacturing growth was unremarkable, and since then has remained weak in response to a significant downturn in global demand for Nepalese products. By early 2002 this unimpressive record had been confirmed by an estimated 30% to 50% decline in the value of total manufactures. One-third of Nepal's industrial output was produced by the garments and woollen carpet industries. The carpet industry remains far more important to the Nepalese economy than the garments industry, because it provides employment for more than 2m. people, compared with the 50,000 employed in the garments sector.

Nepalese industry is limited by many factors. Production is concentrated in a few areas and takes place mainly in small factories. Small-scale cottage industries, which produce baskets, textiles and edible oils, account for around 60% of total industrial output. The remaining 40% of industrial production is derived from modern industries, but at the lower level of the technological scale: brick and tile manufacturing, cement and other construction materials, paper, carpet making, foodgrain processing, vegetable-oil extraction, sugar refining and breweries. Labour-intensive industries, such as carpet and garment production, also have serious underlying difficulties for European buyers, who are under intense consumer pressure not to purchase goods made by child labour. However, the potential for large-scale, heavy industry is greatly constrained by the lack of mineral resources and modern entrepreneurship, together with the strong competition from Indian industries across the border. The lack of venture capital, the escalating insurgency and the non-performing loans given to private companies were additional factors preventing industrial growth. In June 2004 the central bank of Nepal (Nepal Rastra Bank) lowered interest rates for rescheduled loans to financially non-viable firms by 0.5% to 1.5%. The bank also created a special fund of NRs 1,000m. for this purpose. The logic behind such a move is questionable, for it is impossible to see how cheap money by itself can make loss-making enterprises more efficient. In accordance with a ministerial decision taken in February 2007, the Government has invalidated passports of blacklisted loan defaulters and annulled the passports of 80 blacklisted loan defaulters associated with 27 leading business groups. However, the Government appears to be oblivious to its failure effectively to implement past financial allocations to the country's ailing industry. It has been estimated that of the total NRs 2,300m. allocated to helping bankrupt companies, by August 2004 no more than 27% had been allotted to some 150 firms, mainly hotels, in the three years since the scheme began. In the first nine months of 2006/07 only about 15.5% of the industries refinancing programme involving NRs 2,000m. for that fiscal year had been utilized. Labour agitation, infrastructure bottlenecks and power shortages also hindered industrial output in key sectors and slowed down economic recovery following the end of the conflict in 2006. Industrial growth was forecast to improve only marginally in 2007/08, largely in the area of construction and utilities owing to investments in the Middle Marsyangdi Hydropower Project, which aimed to generate 70 MW by late 2008, and to various infrastructure projects financed through foreign aid.

## TOURISM

During the early 1990s the Nepalese Government developed a strategy for promoting development and exports through its tourist sector. Nepal was then overtaken by the insurgency movement that demonstrated the deep divisions within society and dissatisfaction with the monarchical system of government. On 25 December 1999 an Indian Airlines flight from Kathmandu to Afghanistan was hijacked, drawing international attention to the lack of security in Nepal. Although the hijacking was unrelated to the Maoist insurgency, by focusing the spotlight on Nepal it emphasized the extent of domestic instability. As Nepal has emerged from the instability of the last decade or so into a period of peace and (modest) political stability, the tourist trade is slowly recovering. In 2005 less than 300,000 tourists visited Nepal, compared with almost double that number in 1999. The reviving tourist industry is under great pressure owing to supply bottlenecks in transportation and hotel accommodation. Foreign tourist arrivals in August 2006 were more than 12% short of the figures for August 2005. However, tourist arrivals increased by 4.9% during the one-year period from mid-December 2005 to mid-December 2006. Various reports stress that Nepal may not recover as quickly as hoped, partly because of the lack of available seats on flights into Nepal. Thai Airways, Qatar Airways and Gulf Air typically carry European tourists to Nepal, owing to the lack of direct flights from European cities. According to some observers, Nepal needs to give foreign airlines greater access to Nepal instead of protecting its national carrier, Royal Nepal Airlines. To make the revival of tourism a reality, the number of flights into Nepal needs to double, and in 2007 four new international airlines started operating in Nepal; in addition, the existing air service agreements with China, Malaysia, and Thailand have recently been renewed. The Government also predicted that there would be supply constraints in other areas; consequently, in May 2006 it opened the tourist industry to foreign investment as a way of promoting a more rapid revival. The local industry has responded positively to the peace process, with the reopening of hotels, including the five-star Yak & Yeti, which had been closed for some eight months owing to a dispute between management and trade unions. Nepal's trade unions have been closely associated with the Maoists and have absorbed the latter's demands for better working conditions and wages. In the first six months of 2007 tourist arrivals increased by 37.5%, compared with the same period in the previous year, which appeared to indicate a significant recovery in the tourism sector, at least in the short-term. Concerns over possible security threats related to the holding of elections in April 2008 and the closure of Tibet resulted in a short-term decline in the number of tourist arrivals; foreign arrivals in the first six months of 2008, however, totalled 177,163, a 6% rise compared with the number registered during the same period of the previous year.

The trekking industry in particular has been targeted for recovery. Among other things, some of the fees for trekking have been reduced. The Hotel Association Nepal has, however, been disgruntled because the 2006/07 budget did not set aside any government assistance for the hotel sector. Yet such complaints appear to be unreasonable given that the hotel industry in Nepal is dominated by affluent, middle-class families. The 2007/08 budget provided concessions on customs duties for the hotel industry and set aside NRs 170,000m. for the tourism sector, a mere 0.6% of the budget share for an industry that generates around US $170m. every year. The Maoists themselves have taken a positive attitude towards the revitalization of the tourist industry, with Prachanda, the leader of the CPN (M), declaring in July 2006, shortly after the cease-fire declaration, that 'tourism . . . could be a pertinent tool to uplift the living standards of Nepalis'. Baburam Bhattarai agreed, emphasizing that the Maoists had no intention of nationalizing the tourist sector. Despite these commitments, the Maoists had been accused by tour operators of hindering the emerging tourist industry by extortion—making unreasonable financial demands on hotels and other tour operators. This has been denied, and accusations of that kind have abated since the Maoists emerged as the main political and parliamentary power of the country. The politically volatile atmosphere of the transitional period, rising fuel prices, poor infrastructure and the many *bandhs* (strikes), however, have seriously hampered a speedy revival of the tourism sector.

As Nepal moves into recovery mode, the basic factors that used to hinder the development of tourism as a dynamic growth factor in the national economy have re-emerged. In 1999 the average tourist spent US $470. Can this figure be increased? The countries of origin of tourists have also been static for a long time, as indicated by the tourist figures for 2006: about 6.1% of tourists came from the USA and Canada and 28.3% from Europe. These are the tourists who spend the most during their time in Nepal. The number of tourists from India in 2006 represented about 25.7% of the total, but they were less wealthy than the Europeans and also spent less. All tourists had a habit of purchasing goods which had a high import content, thereby making Nepal's net earnings from tourism much lower than the numbers suggested. The low earnings from tourism might also have reflected the Government's tourist promotion policy, which was too narrowly focused on the Kathmandu valley to the detriment of more remote but even more interesting destinations. There is also the question of the competitiveness of Nepal's tourist industry. In early 2001 the tourist industry faced a new problem when workers organized strikes, insisting that hotel bills include a 10% service charge to be paid to employees instead of tipping, which is a far less reliable way of augmenting personal income. The Government and Supreme Court declared that these strikes were illegal and a threat to the country's competitiveness. As a result, the trade-union movement became more supportive of the Maoists, who have been demanding better wages. Since 2001 workers in Nepal have become more rather than less radicalized. It is hard to imagine them retreating from these earlier demands. But does this threaten the revival of the industry? It seems unlikely; there is by now a huge demand among tourists to visit Nepal, and it remains a favourite global destination for walking, trekking, rafting and climbing. However, it would be in the interests of the tourist industry to comply with better wages and conditions, especially in more remote regions. Concern about the future of tourism in Nepal might instead focus on the environmental degradation that threatens some of the country's key national parks, including the Sagarmatha National Park, which has the highest mountains in the world, including Everest.

## ENERGY

The lack of economic diversification in Nepal is reflected in its consumption of energy: 85.5% of energy consumed is 'traditional', meaning biomass in the form of wood, animal waste, straw and other agricultural wastes. Commercial energy use in 2006 accounted for only 13.5% of total consumption, which represented a small increase, of around 6%, in the 12 years since 1994. Given Nepal's large reserves of water and the mountainous terrain, the potential to generate hydropower and export it to the energy-deficit nations to the north (China) and south (India) is enormous. The latest estimates by the ADB suggest that Nepal could generate about 83,000 MW of power, of which about half could be exploited now, given existing technologies. Up to the present day, however, only about 1% of Nepal's energy needs are supplied by hydropower and little is produced for export. Current hydropower generation also represents less than 1% of potential output. One reason for the lack of development in the energy sector is that the cost of hydropower in Nepal is much higher than competitor countries. Energy production has also been privatized, but the successes of this are largely driven by high purchasing costs paid by the Nepalese Government—in effect, these amount to generous subsidies. The record for hydropower production is very disappointing given that the first power plant was established before the First World War. Yet the lack of development has shielded Nepal from possible catastrophes. The continental plates south of the Himalayas continue to collide with the mountains, causing the height of the Himalayas to increase by about 1 cm per year. This movement creates great geophysical instability and is probably the cause of landslides, glacial floods and massive erosion. Building large dams in a landscape of this kind holds many risks which global engineering is unable to manage at this point in time. Of course, not all hydropower projects need to be on a huge scale; small to medium dams could make a difference to Nepalese agriculture and the energy shortages. The micro-hydropower projects that began in the 1970s continue to hold good prospects for generating electricity at the village level, especially for lighting. Unfortunately, maintaining these plants requires skilled labour, which is difficult to find in remote regions, thereby rendering many of them inoperable.

Nepal's water reserves are also controversial when, as with the Mahakali river, they form the western boundary between Nepal and India. India constructed a barrage on the Mahakali under a treaty signed in June 1997. This barrage has been strongly disputed by the Nepalese, who argue that the treaty was misinterpreted by the Indian Government to put India at an advantage. Nepal's capacity to generate hydropower from the Mahakali river must therefore await resolution of this dispute, a situation that has become less likely since the CPN (M) campaigned for the renegotiation of 'unfair' treaties with India in the run-up to the elections to the Constituent Assembly in April 2008.

Recognition of the export potential of Nepal by the Government led to the 2001 Hydropower Development Policy and the 1993 Nepal Electricity Act, which opened the power sector to private investment, including foreign capital. This Act was supported by the Power Trade Agreement between Nepal and India, and the Nepalese Government's decision to prioritize 15 projects for foreign investment. There were also indications that China was considering ways of handling the energy shortage in its western, border provinces by importing energy from neighbouring countries. Nepal could be involved in any such future arrangements. Foreign aid was also vital in developing Nepal's hydroelectricity, but growing concerns by international environmental groups about ecological damage rendered this an uncertain source of support. In 1995, for example, the World Bank withdrew its support from the controversial 402-MW Arun III project. Small dams are less risky and USAID has been encouraging the construction of small 1 MW–10 MW hydroelectric plants such as the one at Piluwakhola. This 3-MW facility was developed by a new private company funded by shareholders, local banks and financiers. The Nepalese Government has acted as a guaranteed buyer of the energy that will be distributed to about 5,000 families in the western region.

Another constraint on energy exports has been the price of Nepalese electricity. The Indian state electricity boards have serious financial problems, yet India has agreed to import 50 MW per year from the Mahakali facility once it commences operation. Despite this, Indian resistance continues, largely because Nepalese hydropower is more expensive than the power that India's large-scale producers can offer.

Nepal has sought to address the high costs of its hydroelectricity by privatizing the domestic industry. In July 2000 the first privately owned generator began production; however, by April 2001 power failures had begun to recur. This is due to the fact that most hydroelectricity in Nepal is generated by 'run-off' river projects that depend on good rainfall or melting snow. Dry weather is a constant threat to production, affecting both private and state facilities. Privatization of the state-controlled power plants has also been proceeding slowly. In March 2002 the Government decided to privatize the Butwal Power Company. The privatization process was, however, interrupted by the Maoist insurgency when attacks were mounted against the Jhimruk power station. Eventually, privatization of the company was finalized in January 2003. In mid-2007, with the peace process gaining momentum and following a four-year interlude when there were no major investments in hydropower, the interim Government took the initiative in licensing numerous new hydropower projects, especially to Indian contractors. In early 2008 memoranda of understanding between the Government and Satluj Jal Vidyut Nigam Ltd of India and the Indian GMR-ITD Consortium were signed to construct the 402-MW Arun III Hydropower Project and the 300-MW Upper Karnali Hydropower Project, respectively. At the same time, the Nepal Electricity Authority also issued power bonds to finance the finalization of the construction of the 70-MW Middle Marsyagandi Hydropower Project and the construction of the 30-MW Chameliya and 14-MW Kulekhani III hydropower projects and invited bids for the construction of the 309-MW Upper Tamakoshi Hydroelectric Project.

## TRANSPORT, COMMUNICATIONS AND TRADE TREATIES

Nepal is a land-locked country, which shares 1,236 km of its border with China and 1,690 km with India. Nepal's location has produced many obstacles to the development of its international trade, much of which depends on the goodwill of neighbouring countries. The topography of Nepal has exacerbated the problems of communication, both on the international and domestic front. All reports on the potential of Nepal point to the need for better transport. The World Bank noted that, by halving the time taken to travel between villages and markets, access to fertilizers and other inputs would improve, thereby greatly increasing productivity of agriculture. Given the difficult terrain, Nepal needs more roads to compensate for the problems of building railways and the lack of navigable rivers. However, according to the World Bank's 'normalized roads index', which measures the actual road mileage compared with what one would expect to find given a country's socio-economic variables, Nepal is ranked low among the poorer countries: 70th out of 119 nations in the late 1990s. Moreover, Nepal's roads are in poor condition and hard to reach. By mid-March 2007 Nepal had 17,609 km of roads, of which only 29.7% had permanent surfaces, 26.9% were gravel and 43.3% were dirt roads that were regularly washed away by floods. However, a more serious problem than the quality of the roads was the complete lack of roads in many parts of rural Nepal. In 2001 vehicles could not access 10 districts owing to the lack of roads. The average walking time to a dirt road that would allow a vehicle to pass was over three hours in 1999. The average walking time to a paved road was well over five hours. These limitations need to be compared with the continuous growth of country or dirt roads. Although impermanent, it is always better to have some roads rather than no roads. Between 1995/96 and 2005/06 the length of dirt roads increased by more than 60% and the development of an improved rural road network figured prominently in both the February 2008 Nepal Donor Consultation Meeting as well as in the current budget. The World Bank report *Nepal Resilience Amidst Conflict* (June 2005) insisted that the growth of even poor-quality roads had helped to facilitate the flow of goods, people and remittances. The report also showed how the access of most social groups, including minorities, to schools, health centres and markets had improved during the preceding decade. The odd exception was access to paved roads—in the majority of cases, access to paved roads had declined rather than increased.

Two new major roads to link Nepal more effectively to China were being constructed in Nepal, funded by Chinese aid. Nepal has even fewer railways, and those that are being constructed are aid-dependent. India has focused on completing the railway between Nepal's container terminal at Birgunj and the Indian railway network. Construction was finished in early 2002 and in July 2004 the first train arrived from Kolkata (Calcutta) in India. Apart from this new railway, the only other Nepalese railway is that built by the British in 1936 linking Nepal to the northern Indian state of Bihar. Despite having 47 airports, Nepal has only one international airport and only five airports with tarred runways. Six airports have been destroyed in recent years by insurgents, further reducing the capacity of Nepal to benefit from tourism. In mid-2007 only 33 airports were in operation. Flights to Nepal are dominated by private carriers, owing to the inefficiency of the state-owned Royal Nepal Airlines Corporation. The Government has been unable to take advantage of the large volume of migrant workers travelling to and from Nepal and foreign labour markets. Meanwhile, privatization of airline services began in the early 1990s. Telephone and telegraphic communications are also poor. In 2007 there were around 1.7m. telephone lines in use (landline and mobile). In early 2002 India agreed to fund the construction of a fibre-optic cable system in Nepal worth US $175m. Investment of this kind is urgently needed, considering that almost 50% of Nepal's villages have no telephone connections. Given Nepal's mountainous terrain, mobile cellular phones would play less of a role in development unless there is massive investment in the construction of relay stations. The lack of modern communications in Nepal has not, however, hindered traditional trade and transport links. The effectiveness of these are reflected in Nepal's important role as a conduit for the global opium trade.

Since the 1973 Non-aligned Summit in Algiers, Algeria, Nepal has considered itself a neutral buffer between India and China. Despite this, Nepal's foreign relations and trade have tended to be dominated by India, beginning in the 1950s with the Treaty of Trade and Commerce and the Citizenship Act. The former established Nepal's right to import and export through Indian territory without customs being imposed on the goods in transit, and the latter allowed Indians to migrate to the Nepalese Terai and become Nepalese citizens. In July 2004 the opening of the railway connecting Kolkata and Nepal's new inland container dock was expected to reduce transit costs by almost 50% and thereby increase Nepal's global competitiveness. Nepal has also developed stronger relations on its northern borders with China. In 1989 Nepal decided to buy weapons from China, and China decided to build a road linking the two countries. These developments displeased India, which immediately retaliated by suspending trade with Nepal. The restoration of democracy in Nepal from the early 1990s again improved relations with India. However, the relationship with China continued to grow in importance, especially given China's decision to prioritize the development of Great Western China, which lies adjacent to Nepal. In addition to transit trade, China is exploring ways of encouraging more bilateral trade. The recent acceleration of infrastructure development in Tibet, Qinghai and Xinjiang by China promises to boost demand for Nepalese products, especially energy. Moreover, a considerable domestic trade has developed between eastern and north-western Nepal via a transit trade that takes Nepal's goods along a Chinese highway running parallel to the Nepal–China border on the Tibetan side. By 2000 four border crossings were open at Yari, Timureghadi, Tatopanii and Olangchunggola, and another 200 could be brought into operation. These border crossings are rapidly proving an important economic addition to the main Kodari highway from Kathmandu to Lhasa (Tibet), a link that was built in 1960 and which is at present the only operational trading point between Nepal and China. Plans to build a 'superhighway' between Lhasa and Shanghai, on the Chinese coast, also open up the possibility of exporting commodities via a new sea outlet in China rather than through India, although the long distances suggest that the freight costs will be prohibitive. New agreements were reached in 1999 for direct flights between Kathmandu and Lhasa and Kathmandu and Shanghai. In 2000 China and Nepal celebrated 45 years of bilateral relations with mutual visits by ministers to discuss, among other issues, common interests in the development of tourism in Tibet and Nepal. In 2002/03 Nepal and China signed two bilateral agreements to encourage tourism between the two countries. China has encouraged these developments in many ways, including the provision of aid. It has also emerged as one of the largest foreign investors in Nepal, especially in the tourism sector. This relationship was affirmed and extended in March 2006 when China agreed to allow Nepal to export some 1,500 articles of trade into China, free of any customs duties. As a consequence, Nepal has recently displayed steadfast commitment and loyalty to Beijing, even in the face of the 2008 Tibetan protests staged in Lhasa and Kathmandu.

Despite the improvement in Nepal-China relations, India remains Nepal's primary partner, as demonstrated by the frequent amendments to the Trade and Transit Treaty, first signed in 1960. Following amendments in 1971, the Treaty provided road transport facilities, warehouse space and port facilities in Calcutta (now known as Kolkata). In 1976 the Treaty was extended, and then replaced in 1978 by two separate treaties, one dealing with bilateral Indo-Nepalese trade and the other allowing Nepal to expand its trade with other countries. In March 1989 India decided not to extend these treaties in response to Nepal's weapons deal with China, and closed 13 of the 15 transit points through which most of Nepal's foreign trade was conducted. In April Nepal announced a new customs tariff system, whereby imports from India no longer received privileged treatment. Uniform import duties were imposed on all imports, regardless of country of origin. In the short term, Nepal's foreign trade deteriorated until trade relations with India were normalized in June 1990 and the transit points reopened. In January 1996 the Trade and Transit Treaty was replaced by two separate agreements: the Nepal-India Trade Agreement and the Nepal-India Transit Agreement. With few exceptions, the trade agreement gave Nepal preferential access to the Indian market by allowing imports of all manufactures without incurring Indian duty. The Nepal-India Transit Agreement, automatically renewed after seven years, made it easier for Nepal to access Indian ports. Prior to reaching this agreement in June 1997, the Indian Government extended a further courtesy to Nepal by providing a new transit route to Bangladesh through Indian territory (see History). As a result of the agreement, bilateral trade between Nepal and India grew significantly. The trade links between India and Nepal were further increased after the dry port at Birgunj became operational in July 2004. Construction of this dry port was completed in December 2000, but it was slow to begin functioning, owing to ongoing disagreements between Nepal and India on a range of issues, including the Customs Tariff Agreement. Expenses incurred by transactions in cross-border trade are expected to reduce by about 40%, owing to the new dry-port facility. In April 2006 the Nepal-India Transit Treaty was again renewed.

A more recent factor that has brought Nepal closer to India has been the Maoist insurgency, common to Nepal and north-eastern India. In March 2002 Nepal and India agreed to collaborate in controlling cross-border militant activity and to begin joint initiatives in trade facilitation and flood control. At the same time, the preferential trade treaty of December 1996 was renegotiated, but to the detriment of Nepal, owing to the imposition of quotas on Nepalese exports to India. In the same month the 1996 trade treaties between Nepal and India were reconfirmed and extended for a further five years, but with some revisions, including the imposition of tariffs on Nepalese exports made from non-Nepalese inputs, and quotas on ghee (clarified butter), yarn, copper wire and zinc oxide. The treaty was renewed in March 2007 for a further five years and allowed the majority of Nepalese manufactured goods as well as agricultural exports unlimited duty-free market access to India on a non-reciprocal basis. However, the renewed treaty did not address the non-tariff barriers that Nepal faced and was not expected to result in an immediate boost to exports. It remains to be seen how the Maoists' intention to renegotiate the various Indo-Nepalese treaties, which many in Nepal perceive as unfairly favouring India, will affect the two countries' trade relations now that the CPN (M) is in power.

In many other ways, Nepal increasingly resembles an extension of the Indian economy. For example, people living near the border with India find it more convenient to subscribe to Indian telecommunication companies than to Nepalese firms. This lack of patriotism, determined by convenience, is unlikely to please the Maoists. Nepal's participation in the South Asian Association for Regional Co-operation (SAARC), the regional headquarters of which is located in Kathmandu, demonstrates the country's stronger links with South Asia, rather than China. Although SAARC was not particularly active in the first decade or so after its establishment in 1983, from the mid-1990s it emerged as a regional economic grouping of growing importance. That growth, however, remains thwarted by hostility between India and Pakistan. As a result, SAARC did not meet for three years from 1999 to January 2002. At the SAARC meeting in Kathmandu in January 2004, the leaders agreed to create the South Asia Free Trade Agreement (SAFTA), which came into force on 1 January 2006. Nepal, together with the other poorer South Asian nations, agreed to abide by the lower tariffs and other provisions by 2015. The long-term outcome of SAARC continues to depend on peace talks between India and Pakistan, but in the short term Nepal is probably going to benefit from the opportunity in this forum to persuade neighbouring states to help it improve cross-border trade, access to world markets and investment in domestic infrastructure and factories. At the 14th summit meeting of SAARC, which was held in New Delhi in April 2007, India declared that it would introduce a zero customs rate by the end of that year to provide entry into its market to the four least developed countries of the SAARC region. This could potentially be of great benefit to Nepal, with India remaining the key regional partner, as symbolized by the fact that Nepal's currency has been pegged to the Indian rupee since 1993.

In 2004 Nepal joined a new regional trade group called the Bay of Bengal Initiative for Multi-Sectoral Technical and Economic Cooperation (BIMSTEC). Originally established in 1997 by India, Bangladesh, Sri Lanka and Thailand, BIMSTEC has been broadened to include Myanmar and Bhutan. Many regard it as an alternative to SAARC; in diplomatic circles it is well known that it was set up as a way of avoiding the delays within SAARC owing to the routine inability of India and Pakistan to agree on issues. Today BIMSTEC still lacks any formal organization, and with the rapprochement between India and Pakistan it may well be overlooked as an alternative bloc, despite its value as a conduit for developing trade and communication links between South Asia and South-East Asia.

## FOREIGN TRADE

Nepal's international exports have generally been in recovery mode since 2001/02: in 2004/05 exports exceeded those of 2001/02 by some 25%. The financial year 2005/06 saw total exports rising by about 2.9% during the first 11 months. However, in the same period of the financial year 2006/07 exports fell by 1.6%, mainly owing to political unrest in the Terai, where the 'Madhesi' community were demanding greater inclusiveness and power-sharing following the promulgation of the interim Constitution. Blockades, protests and bandhs (strikes) disrupted trade and transport across the country, since the Terai region is the primary channel for Nepal's external trade. Since the first two months of 2008 were also marked by political unrest in the Terai, total exports rose only marginally, by 0.4%, in the first 11 months of 2007/08 (exports to India, which had accelerated in the first half of 2007, partly reflecting the impact of the concessions granted to Nepal under the renewed trade treaty between India and Nepal in March 2007, fell by 8.1%). Nepal's imports grew continuously, by about 40%, between 2001/02 and 2004/05, and by about 16.6% in the first 11 months of 2005/06; in the same period of the financial year 2006/07, however, the rate of growth of imports decreased to about 4%, before rising again, to 16.5%, over the same period of 2007/08. As noted elsewhere, Nepal continues to have a balance-of-trade deficit, which grew by about 50% between the early 2000s and 2006, with an additional increase of another 2% during the first eight months of 2006/07. The deficit remained large in 2007/08, at 17.3% of GDP.

Since the early 1990s Nepal's trade pattern has become less and less diversified, with India emerging as the dominant trade partner. A decade ago Nepal's trade with India represented one-third of all Nepal's imports and exports; by 2004/05 this had doubled to 60% and in mid-2008 stood at 64.1%. The commodity composition of trade also lacks diversification. Exports are dominated in equal proportion by garments, woollen carpets and ghee; more minor are the other two principal exports of jute goods and toothpaste. Nepal's imports are dominated by petroleum, followed by (in order of importance) crude palm oil, vehicles and spare parts, and machinery and textiles. In April 2007 a new product exchange regime on petroleum trade between Nepal and India came into effect, allowing Nepal to import processed petroleum products from third countries, thus reducing its dependency on India. During 1996–2006 the Maoist insurgency had a negative impact on the total volume of trade, partly because of the trade blockades imposed by the communists. However, the Maoists cannot be blamed for the lack of trade diversity. On the other hand, because the Nepalese Government was so distracted by the insurgency it experienced enormous difficulty producing an appropriate policy response to the end of the Multi-Fibre Agreement (MFA) in December 2004. The result was that in 2004/05 exports of garments to Europe and the USA declined by a massive 36%, after a previous decline in 2003/04 of about 20%. In the first eight months of 2006/07 the rate of decline appeared to have slowed slightly, to 13.2%. By contrast, in 2005/06 exports of pashminas and carpets recovered (51% and 1.6% respectively), but in 2006/07 declined again, by 35.8% and 7.5% respectively. As the ADB noted, throughout South Asia (notably Bangladesh) exports of garments have increased greatly in response to the end of the MFA in December 2004. In contrast, Nepal has not benefited. Lacking the capacity to plan ahead has put the Nepalese economy into a situation where the development strategies of the 1990s are starting to falter.

These recent policy failures stand in stark contrast to the earlier success which Nepal had in shifting exports away from commodities to manufactures. During the early 1980s agricultural products, such as rice, timber, maize and jute, accounted for some 75% of total exports. By 1990 this had changed dramatically, with manufactured goods and handicrafts, such as garments and carpets, together accounting for 75% of exports. Both industries remain important employers of labour: carpet and pashmina production each employ some 50,000 workers. Since 1990, garments and carpets have declined in their relative importance and ghee has emerged as an equally significant export item. By the early 2000s, hopes of a boom in the pashmina industry had ended as China, Pakistan and India began to produce pashminas, frequently of lower quality but highly price-competitive. In 2001/02 alone, exports of the once-fashionable pashmina decreased by a huge 70%. Garments, by contrast, did well but must now confront the full force of a more competitive international environment. China in particular is now emerging as the world's largest producer of ready-made clothing, controlling about 44% of the global market by the end of 2005. Until the events of April 2006, the garments-textile industry in Nepal had also suffered attacks by Maoists, who, for example, in August 2005 bombed the Jyoti Spinning Mills, some 90 km south of the capital. Garment production and exports peaked in about 2000 and have been in decline since then, and the US market has been a major factor in this. In July 2006 the Garment Association of Nepal reported that exports to the USA had fallen by a further 17%, compared with the previous year. However, as the Indian export market has increased in importance, US influence in the region has declined. In 2004/05, for example, garment exports accounted for only 10% of all exports. Although they were the single biggest item, they were closely followed by exports of carpets to Europe (10% of total shipments) and vegetable ghee to India (8% of total shipments).

## ECONOMIC REFORM AND FOREIGN DIRECT INVESTMENT

Foreign direct investment (FDI) in Nepal has been disappointing because of its low levels and lack of diversity in terms of the industry sectors involved and the countries of origin of investors. The key bottleneck has been the slow pace of deregulation. In 2003/04 78 industries were opened to foreign investment, followed by a further 64 in 2004/05. The financial year 2005/06 saw the Government adopt a more vigorous approach to deregulation by opening a further 1,063 industries to foreign investors. In March 2008 there were 1,336 ongoing foreign investment projects in Nepal. As a result of these efforts, more than 100,000 jobs have been generated. Efforts have also been made to attract investments from non-resident Nepalese by giving them and their families special 10-year visas. The service industries have taken up the bulk of foreign involvement in Nepal—almost 30% of foreign projects are invested in this sector. In addition to this, up to about 25% of projects are involved in the hotel/tourism sector. Manufacturing has represented between 30% and 40% of projects funded by foreign investment, but investment in infrastructure has been virtually non-existent. Around one-half of Nepal's foreign investment has come from two countries: India and China, with the former being by far the most important foreign investor. The way forward will depend critically on the further liberalization of the Nepalese economy, supported by more privatization of the domestic economy, which remains dominated by public-sector enterprises in a number of critical areas. In both private and public sectors, however, there are common needs, including transparency, better and more timely audits and more efficient leadership.

During the 1990s domestic private-sector investment equalled about 17% of GDP, double the proportion reached in the 1980s. In 2004 it accounted for the bulk of investment in Nepal (75%). Yet, the level of investment remains low and deters foreign investment. According to the Heritage Foundation Index, Nepal receives less FDI than any of the other very poor countries, including Uganda, Cambodia and Madagascar. Apart from the slow pace of reform, the Maoist insurgency has until now also dampened foreign interest in Nepal. With the new political situation that has emerged since April 2006, if foreign investment remains sluggish it will reflect the many institutional bottlenecks that put off foreign investors, including the delays in obtaining approvals for projects.

The aggregate potential for investment and employment could be substantially increased if the Government were to develop an export-orientated strategy for Nepal's small and medium-sized enterprises (SMEs), along the lines recently followed by the Indonesian furniture export sector. In the early 2000s, however, the Nepalese Government's restrictions on foreign investment into cottage industries virtually matched those imposed by India a decade ago. Moreover, there is no special SME policy, despite the fact that SMEs provide 95% of all employment outside agriculture. Domestic investment is not able to give much encouragement to the foreign investor because the savings rate is so low (about 7.9% and an estimated 9.1% in 2006 and 2007 respectively) and Nepal has only a very small entrepreneurial class. Nor are there sufficient institutional structures to encourage the pooling of capital. The establishment of the Securities Exchange Board of Nepal (SEBO) and the Nepal Stock Exchange Ltd (NEPSE) in the early 1990s only partially addressed this. These institutions replaced the highly inadequate Securities Exchange Centre Ltd, which dated from 1976. The market capitalization to GDP ratio in Nepal has traditionally been low, but rising, from between 5% and 8% in the early 1990s to 9% in 2004, to 21.4% in 2007, and to 39.5% in mid-June 2008. There has also been a slow growth in the number of companies listed and traded on the NEPSE: 62 and 23, respectively, in February 1994, and only 90 and 47 in December 1996. In June 2001 the number of listed companies peaked at 115, but a year later decreased to 96. During 2004–06 there was a recovery in the number of listed companies: 114 in 2004, 125 in 2005 and 135 in 2006. In mid-2007 there were 131 listed companies, owing to a delisting of 12 combined with an additional listing of eight new companies. In June 2008 148 companies were listed at the NEPSE. Despite this growth and an improvement in the NEPSE index in 2006/07 relative to previous years (the lowest point was reached in 2002/03), the total number of transactions and their value on the stock exchange decreased by about 14% and 52% respectively in the first nine months of 2005/06. However, the number of transactions increased by about 27% in the same period of 2006/07. A longer perspective from the vantage point of 2006/07 shows an upturn in the NEPSE, with the paid-up value of all shares almost tripling since 2000/01 and the value of turnover recovering after 2002/03. Despite this uneven record, the establishment of the NEPSE signified an important departure from the past pattern of dependency on public-sector investment. Further growth of the NEPSE will depend on creating a more diversified portfolio of companies: among the currently listed companies, 113 are bank and financial institutions and production and processing industries, hotels, business entities and hydropower companies account for 21, four, five and three, respectively.

An important part of economic and industrial reform has been the reorganization of Nepal's financial sector. The banking sector of Nepal has been open to foreign investment since the 1980s. In 1987 Grindlays Bank established a joint venture with Standard Chartered (a US bank, which subsequently bought Grindlays), the Nepal Bank and the Nepalese public. Foreign investment in banking, however, will be restrained unless the reform of the domestic banking sector can be accelerated. Change here has depended on creating a new culture and performance standard inside the three key banks: the Nepal Rashtra Bank, which is the state-owned central bank, and the two dominant commercial banks, the Nepal Bank Ltd (NBL) and the Rastriya Banijya Bank (RBB). The Nepal Rashtra Bank has sought to become more efficient by encouraging voluntary retirement of over 550 staff and introducing more efficient accounting methods and new IT systems under the watchful eye of the World Bank. The reforms of the commercial banks began in 2002 when public alarm drew attention to the large size of non-performing loans. Non-performing loans had unwittingly converted the NBL and RBB into Nepal's largest owners of real estate, the main source of investment by Nepalese entrepreneurs. To make matters worse, new loans appeared to have been no more sound than old ones. In 2002 the management of both the NBL and RRB was transferred to the ICC Bank of Ireland, with the understanding that the proportion of non-performing loans would be reduced from 61% to 46% and then to 10% by July 2004. The achievements so far fall short of these targets. The original contract with the ICC Bank has been renewed, in both cases a couple of times since 2002. The problem of non-performing loans continues, even though the size of these has been greatly reduced. By mid-April 2007 the non-performing assets as a percentage of total assets for the NBL and RBB had fallen to about 14.8% and 31.8% respectively. This is still high, but other economic indicators suggest that the reform process is heading in the right direction: instead of losses of billions of rupees, both banks have started to return modest profits. The improvement in financial management reflects better auditing processes that have been introduced by the Irish bank. In the past these commercial banks were unable to generate timely reports, so it was easy for non-performing loans to escalate out of control. Beyond these three banks, the financial sector needs greater diversification. By mid-April 2007 Nepal had 19 commercial banks, 37 development banks, 11 micro-finance institutions including private rural banks, one postal savings bank, 73 finance companies, 17 financial co-operatives, 21 insurance companies and 47 financial NGOs. In the following seven months 29 new financial institutions were created, including three new commercial banks. This growth was important but insufficient to create a competitive environment capable of meeting Nepal's needs. It also underlines the need to enhance the financial system's regulatory framework, especially the supervision powers of the Nepal Rashtra Bank.

Another aspect of the Government's reform programme has been the introduction of market mechanisms into the production and retailing system. Subsidies have been slowly abolished and the prices of essential commodities increased to more realistic levels that reflect market prices. During the late 1990s all fertilizer subsidies were removed and the prices of petroleum, kerosene, diesel and electricity increased. These reversals in government policy gave rise to popular protests and a parliamentary inquiry. However, the policy has remained in place, and there is some evidence to show that the reforms are working, albeit very slowly. During the first half of 2003 petroleum prices were revised upwards again to reflect price increases in India. The rise in kerosene prices in April was highly unpopular and prompted student protests. However, as the World Bank Country Director for Nepal has argued, bringing prices into line with real market rates is an essential stage in establishing the long-term viability of the Nepal Oil Corporation. Moreover, kerosene is a fuel used by the Nepalese rich, not the poor, therefore the negative social impact is minimal. Telecommunication prices, by contrast, have been reduced, largely in response to price reductions and competition from United Telecom (UT), a joint-venture company formed by three Indian telecommunication providers and Nepal Venture (Private) Ltd.

Over time, especially during the last three years, the momentum of economic reform has been difficult to maintain as the focus of government energy shifted first to containing the Maoist insurgency and then, after April 2006, to sustaining the peace process, establishing the interim Government and preparing for the constituent assembly elections. One notable exception was the partial deregulation of oil prices in February 2006. The Government's Nepal Oil Corporation (NOC) retains a monopoly of all oil imports and distribution within Nepal at prices which are fixed but now reflect differential transport costs. The push in this direction has been forced on the Government by the massive losses generated by the NOC. These losses are equivalent to about 1% of GDP and financed through the banking system, which in turn is doubly exposed to the risk of supporting the monopoly. Retail prices, on the other hand, have been fully deregulated. This rationalization, however, is likely to increase the economic burden on the more isolated parts of Nepal. Given the huge increase in oil prices in 2005–06, this was a major pressure point for the Nepalese economy, with prices escalating by up to 25%. In January 2008 the Government reversed fuel price rises of up to 20% in response to violent protests. This contributed to continuing NOC losses and persisting fuel shortages because there simply were no funds available to pay for imports or to settle debts with the NOC's sole supplier, the Indian Oil Corporation.

Privatization has been another element in the reform programme. The need for privatization is amply demonstrated by the outcome of massive government investments into 38 public companies in 2001/02: less than half of these made a profit and the rest became a burden on the public revenues. In 1991–2001 18 out of the 65 state-owned enterprises in Nepal were privatized. The present situation is one where the State still owns fully or partly some 36 enterprises (public enterprises—PEs), of which 42% are operating at a loss. Even those making a profit are not performing at a high level. As with India, it is reasonable to suggest that public enterprises in Nepal are 'sick industries'. Except for the three public utilities, the other PEs are spread fairly evenly between the industry, banking, business and services sectors. The NOC is one of the public sector firms that has been running at spectacular losses, as already noted. But there are many others, all of which appear to have major problems in monitoring their finances. Around 28% of the PEs have only recently completed their audits for 2004/05, two additional PEs have audits only up to 2003/04, the NOC audit process is up to 2002/03; the Nepal Airlines Corporation audit as well as one other are completed only for the period up to 2001/02, and a further PE has had no audit report since the late 1990s. If there was ever a clearer argument for privatization it is surely this lack of financial control. The lack of financial transparency is also a powerful indicator of the degree to which the routine organs of government have been distracted by responses to the Maoist insurgency.

The privatization process in Nepal has been running for more than a decade but, predictably, private investors will not purchase loss-making enterprises. At the same time not all the loss-making enterprises can be liquidated—the impact on society could be too severe. By July 2007 a total of 29 PEs had been privatized, were in the process of being privatized or had been declared bankrupt: of these, 34% were liquidated and the remainder transferred into private ownership by various means. The enterprises that remain in public hands need ongoing reform, especially those with earnings that are just above the break-even point; the risks of these firms faltering are considerable given the weak institutional basis for public enterprises in Nepal.

The privatization policy also needs to encourage entrepreneurs to establish new industries, especially in the power sector, a process that has recently been set into motion. In the past, it was difficult to expand the private sector base for the Nepalese economy beyond the business of hotels, real estate and tourism, but the end of the Maoist insurgency and the return to political stability should make this possible as confidence in the economy returns.

## GOVERNMENT REVENUE AND FINANCE

Historically, like the rest of South Asia, the Nepalese Government has faced a persistent fiscal crisis caused by the growth of total government expenditure beyond the increase in government revenues. During the last few years, however, the disruptions caused by the civil war have contained the fiscal deficit because the apparatus of the State was unable to function efficiently and disburse targeted funding. Under-expenditure on capital development projects was extensive because infrastructure had become a prime target for terrorist attacks. Between 1998/99 and 2004/05 capital expenditure fell by about 23%. In the same period total revenue collection increased by some 20%. More recently, revenue collection has increased, as has capital expenditure to a lesser extent. Despite the limits to capital expenditure, the fiscal deficit has persisted even though it has fallen. This was caused by the slow but continuous rise of recurring government expenditures (although 2007/08 saw a reversal of this trend). In the first seven months of 2007/08 about one-third of the fiscal deficit was covered by foreign loans, the remainder by domestic borrowing.

The Maoist insurgency had a direct impact on Nepal's fiscal burdens by compelling the King to set aside a large portion of his budget for 'defence': defence expenditure in 2004/05 was the second largest item after social services—about 14% compared with 38%. Defence spending had increased by about 30% in a single year. Moreover, the formal figures on defence spending grossly underestimate the real situation, in which funds allocated to other sectors were procured by force by the Nepalese army from district authorities which had no mechanisms of denial or defence. The shrinking fiscal deficit noted above reflects the modest reforms undertaken by the Nepalese Government in recent years, in particular greater efficiency in the collection of value-added tax (VAT), which was introduced in 1997. In recent years income from VAT has been growing annually by about 18%. With the new political circumstances prevailing since April 2006, the capacity of the Nepalese Government to undertake more vigorous capital expenditure activities has accelerated. This means that the nominal revenue surplus will disappear and the burden of foreign and domestic debt will again begin to increase. Rising debt is a normal condition of developing countries. However, during 2005–06 the foreign debt of Nepal fell by about 6% a year. This was partially counterbalanced by an increase of about 8% in the stock of domestic debt. In 2006/07 foreign debt rose by 6.9%, while domestic loans increased by 10.2%. In the first 11 months of 2007/08 foreign debt rose by a further 17.8%.

The major change that can be expected in the Nepalese economy in the coming years is an increase in the ratio of the fiscal deficit relative to GDP. As the peace becomes more stable, government expenditure can be expected to rise more quickly than revenue collection. In contrast to this expectation, since 1998/99 the fiscal deficit has fallen each year, from more than 5% up to 2001/02 to just over 3% in 2004/05. In 2005/06, however, the fiscal deficit as a proportion of GDP increased again, by 0.7%, to reach 3.8%. In the first seven months of 2007/08 the deficit amounted to 1.0% of GDP. A more permanent solution to the fiscal crisis would be to raise taxes on rich rural and urban landlords. By contrast, domestic and foreign firms need production incentives, so increased taxes, levies and customs duties on inputs into the production process will not provide an answer. Like other South Asian administrations, the Nepalese Government has vigorously resisted the idea of introducing income taxes on landlords. Whether the presence of Maoists in the Nepalese Council of Ministers can reverse this reluctance remains to be seen, but it will certainly not be one of the first reforms by the new Government. Traditionally, the landed élites have supported the King, and radical tax reform will make it harder to win them over to the new coalitions that will rule Kathmandu. However, slow fiscal reform can be counterbalanced by other means: once the peace has facilitated the dismantlement of the vast army that has been built up in recent years and the energy and funds of local government redirected towards economic development and social security projects. There were indications of this direction being taken in the 2007/08 and 2008/09 budgets. In both cases, considerable revenue savings could be possible.

### PROSPECTS

The peace process and the resumption of democratic politics in Nepal since April 2006 have created a positive outlook for the first time in more than a decade and have renewed hopes of economic revival. The Maoists, now at the helm of political power, are participating fully in the process of democratization and public announcements by Maoist leaders provide further indications of their determination to play a decisive role in the revival of economic growth and social stability. Throughout Nepal there has been excitement about the country's prospects and domestic optimism has been reflected in international reassessments of Nepal's future. The revival of the tourism industry confirms that international assessments of Nepal are moving in a positive direction. Certainly the recovery of tourist earnings will help to expand the foundations of Nepal's development beyond aid and remittances. How events will actually turn out does depend, however, on the successful early formation of a government and on continuing co-operation between the Maoists and the other parties. However, the Maoists are not likely to relinquish their key objectives, one of which is to work towards a more egalitarian society. The squabbling over government formation and persisting ideological differences add a powerful sting to revivalist optimism: the key question for Nepal now is whether the workable rapprochement between the Maoists and the democratic parties will continue. In addition, the recurring political unrest in the Terai and the protests by *janjati* (indigenous) groups over the perceived exclusive and unjust character of the political system and society underline the fragility of the political transition. With the peace process and democratization in progress, the potential for development has increased considerably and the country has the opportunity to accelerate economic recovery and make improvements with regard to poverty reduction. However, underlying the persisting grievances and demands of the Maoists are the economic fundamentals of poverty. The incidence of poverty may well have fallen in the last decade, but it none the less remains at an unacceptably high level and is distinguished by great regional and social inequalities.

# Statistical Survey

Sources (unless otherwise stated): National Planning Commission Secretariat, Singha Durbar, POB 1284, Kathmandu; tel. (1) 4225879; fax (1) 4226500; e-mail npcs@wlink.com.np; internet www.npc.gov.np; Federation of Nepalese Chambers of Commerce and Industry (FNCCI), Pachali Shahid Shukra FNCCI Milan Marg, Teku, POB 269, Kathmandu; tel. (1) 4262061; fax (1) 4261022; e-mail fncci@mos.com.np; internet www.fncci.org.

## Area and Population

### AREA, POPULATION AND DENSITY

| | |
|---|---|
| Area (sq km) | 147,181* |
| Population (census results) | |
| 22 June 1991 | 18,491,097 |
| 22 June 2001†‡ | |
| Males | 11,563,921 |
| Females | 11,587,502 |
| Total | 23,151,423 |
| Population (estimates at mid-year)§ | |
| 2006 | 27,641,000 |
| 2007 | 28,196,000 |
| 2008 | 28,757,000 |
| Density (per sq km) at mid-2008 | 195.4 |

* 56,827 sq miles.

† Population is *de jure*.

‡ Includes estimates for certain areas in 12 districts where the census could not be conducted, owing to violence and disruption.

§ Source: UN, *World Population Prospects: The 2006 Revision*.

### PRINCIPAL TOWNS
(population at 2001 census)

| | | | |
|---|---|---|---|
| Kathmandu* | 671,846 | Mahendranagar | 80,839 |
| Biratnagar | 166,674 | Butawal | 75,384 |
| Lalitpur | 162,991 | Janakpur | 74,192 |
| Pokhara | 156,312 | Bhaktapur | 72,543 |
| Birgunj | 112,484 | Hetaunda | 68,482 |
| Dharan | 95,332 | Dhangadhi | 67,447 |
| Bharatpur | 89,323 | | |

* Total for urban agglomeration 1,081,845.

**Mid-2007** (incl. suburbs, UN estimate): Kathmandu 895,000 (Source: UN, *World Urbanization Prospects: The 2007 Revision*).

### BIRTHS AND DEATHS
(annual averages, UN estimates)

| | 1990–95 | 1995–2000 | 2000–05 |
|---|---|---|---|
| Birth rate (per 1,000) | 38.1 | 34.5 | 30.2 |
| Death rate (per 1,000) | 12.0 | 9.8 | 8.7 |

Source: UN, *World Population Prospects: The 2006 Revision*.

**2001** (estimates): Birth rate 33.1 per 1,000; Death rate 9.6 per 1,000.

**Expectation of life** (years at birth, WHO estimates): 62.4 (males 61.8; females 62.8) in 2006 (Source: WHO, *World Health Statistics*).

### ECONOMICALLY ACTIVE POPULATION
(1999 labour force survey, '000 persons aged 15 years and over)

| | |
|---|---|
| Agriculture, hunting and forestry | 7,190 |
| Fishing | 13 |
| Mining and quarrying | 8 |
| Manufacturing | 553 |
| Electricity, gas and water | 26 |
| Construction | 344 |
| Wholesale and retail trade | 408 |
| Hotels and restaurants | 114 |
| Transport, storage and communications | 135 |
| Financial intermediation | 19 |
| Real estate, renting and business activities | 32 |
| Public administration and defence | 70 |
| Education | 164 |
| Health and social work | 34 |
| Other community, social and personal services | 57 |
| Private households with employed persons | 289 |
| Extra-territorial organizations and bodies | 8 |
| **Total employed** | 9,463 |

Source: Central Bureau of Statistics, Kathmandu.

**Mid-2005** (official estimates in '000): Agriculture, etc. 12,078; Total labour force 12,998 (Source: FAO).

# Health and Welfare

### KEY INDICATORS

| | |
|---|---|
| Total fertility rate (children per woman, 2006) | 3.4 |
| Under-5 mortality rate (per 1,000 live births, 2006) | 59 |
| HIV/AIDS (% of persons aged 15–49, 2005) | 0.5 |
| Physicians (per 1,000 head, 2004) | 0.21 |
| Hospital beds (per 1,000 head, 2001) | 0.2 |
| Health expenditure (2005): US $ per head (PPP) | 76 |
| Health expenditure (2005): % of GDP | 5.8 |
| Health expenditure (2005): public (% of total) | 28.1 |
| Access to water (% of persons, 2004) | 90 |
| Access to sanitation (% of persons, 2004) | 35 |
| Human Development Index (2005): ranking | 142 |
| Human Development Index (2005): value | 0.534 |

For sources and definitions, see explanatory note on p. vi.

# Agriculture

### PRINCIPAL CROPS

('000 metric tons)

| | 2004 | 2005 | 2006 |
|---|---|---|---|
| Wheat | 1,387 | 1,442 | 1,394 |
| Rice (paddy) | 4,456 | 4,290 | 4,209 |
| Barley | 31 | 29 | 28 |
| Maize | 1,590 | 1,716 | 1,734 |
| Millet | 283 | 290 | 291 |
| Potatoes | 1,643 | 1,739 | 1,975 |
| Sugar cane | 2,305 | 2,376 | 2,463 |
| Beans, dry* | 30 | 30 | 30 |
| Pigeon peas | 19 | 18 | 19 |
| Lentils | 159 | 161 | 158 |
| Mustard seed | 133 | 142 | 139 |
| Garlic | 28 | 29 | 29 |
| Oranges | 34 | 35 | 36 |
| Apples | 34 | 35 | 33 |
| Ginger | 152 | 154 | 154 |
| Jute and jute-like fibres | 17 | 16 | 17 |
| Tobacco (leaves) | 3 | 3 | 3 |

* FAO estimate(s).

**Aggregate production** ('000 metric tons, may include official, semi-official or estimated data): Total cereals 7,747 in 2004, 7,767 in 2005, 7,657 in 2006; Total roots and tubers 1,753 in 2004, 1,849 in 2005, 2,085 in 2006; Total vegetables (incl. melons) 1,930 in 2004, 2,106 in 2005, 2,233 in 2006; Total fruits (excl. melons) 511 in 2004, 519 in 2005, 536 in 2006.

Source: FAO.

### LIVESTOCK

('000 head, year ending September)

| | 2004 | 2005 | 2006 |
|---|---|---|---|
| Cattle | 6,966 | 6,994 | 7,003 |
| Buffaloes | 3,953 | 4,081 | 4,203 |
| Pigs | 935 | 948 | 961 |
| Sheep | 824 | 817 | 812 |
| Goats | 6,980 | 7,154 | 7,422 |
| Chickens | 23,024 | 22,790 | 23,221 |

Source: FAO.

### LIVESTOCK PRODUCTS

('000 metric tons)

| | 2004 | 2005 | 2006 |
|---|---|---|---|
| Cattle meat* | 48.5 | 48.9 | 48.9 |
| Buffalo meat | 133.6 | 139.0 | 142.0 |
| Sheep meat | 2.8 | 2.7 | 2.7 |
| Goat meat | 40.5 | 41.7 | 42.8 |
| Pig meat | 15.4 | 15.7 | 15.8 |
| Chicken meat | 16.1 | 15.5 | 15.6 |
| Cows' milk | 368.5 | 380.0 | 385.3 |
| Buffaloes' milk | 863.3 | 894.6 | 926.9 |
| Goats' milk* | 65.0 | 65.0 | 65.0 |
| Ghee* | 20.2 | n.a. | n.a. |
| Hen eggs* | 26.2 | 26.0 | 26.0 |

* FAO estimates.

Source: FAO.

# Forestry

### ROUNDWOOD REMOVALS

('000 cubic metres, excl. bark, FAO estimates)

| | 2004 | 2005 | 2006 |
|---|---|---|---|
| Sawlogs, veneer logs and logs for sleepers | 1,260 | 1,260 | 1,260 |
| Fuel wood | 12,702 | 12,692 | 12,595 |
| **Total** | 13,962 | 13,952 | 13,855 |

Source: FAO.

### SAWNWOOD PRODUCTION

('000 cubic metres, incl. railway sleepers)

| | 1999 | 2000 | 2001 |
|---|---|---|---|
| Coniferous (softwood)* | 20 | 20 | 20 |
| Broadleaved (hardwood) | 610 | 610 | 610 |
| **Total** | 630 | 630 | 630 |

* FAO estimates.

**2002–06:** Production as in 2001 (FAO estimates).

Source: FAO.

# Fishing

('000 metric tons, live weight)

| | 2004 | 2005 | 2006 |
|---|---|---|---|
| Capture | 19.9 | 20.0 | 20.0 |
| Aquaculture | 20.0 | 22.5 | 25.4 |
| Common carp | 4.1 | 4.6 | 5.2 |
| Bighead carp | 3.0 | 3.4 | 3.9 |
| Silver carp | 6.0 | 6.8 | 7.7 |
| **Total catch** | 39.9 | 42.5 | 45.4 |

Source: FAO.

# Industry

**SELECTED PRODUCTS**

('000 metric tons unless otherwise indicated, year ending 15 July)

| | 2004/05 | 2005/06 | 2006/07 |
|---|---|---|---|
| Cement | 610.0 | 613.6 | 644.3 |
| Iron rods | 166.5 | n.a. | n.a. |
| Jute goods | 32.8 | n.a. | n.a. |
| Raw sugar | 97.7 | 98.5 | 103.4 |
| Tea | 11.5 | 11.6 | 12.2 |
| Vegetable ghee | 199.6 | 179.2 | 188.2 |
| Beer and liquor (million litres) | 39.6 | n.a. | n.a. |
| Soft drinks (million litres) | 46.3 | n.a. | n.a. |
| Paper | 29.0 | 29.9 | 31.4 |
| Cigarettes ('000 million) | 9.4 | 9.5 | 10.0 |
| Cotton clothing (million metres) | 1.5 | n.a. | n.a. |
| Synthetic clothing (million metres) | 11.8 | n.a. | n.a. |
| Soap | 44.3 | 44.8 | 47.1 |

# Finance

**CURRENCY AND EXCHANGE RATES**

**Monetary Units**

100 paisa (pice) = 1 Nepalese rupee (NR).

**Sterling, Dollar and Euro Equivalents** (30 May 2008)

£1 sterling = NRs 135.76;
US $1 = NRs 68.79;
€1 = NRs 106.68;
1,000 Nepalese rupees = £7.37 = $14.54 = €9.37.

**Average Exchange Rate** (rupees per US $)

2005 71.368
2006 72.756
2007 66.415

**BUDGET**

(NRs million, year ending 15 July)*

| Revenue† | 2001/02 | 2002/03 | 2003/04 |
|---|---|---|---|
| Taxation | 39,331 | 42,587 | 48,173 |
| Taxes on income and profits | 8,920 | 8,132 | 9,515 |
| Taxes on property | 1,134 | 1,414 | 1,698 |
| Domestic taxes on goods and services | 16,618 | 18,804 | 21,406 |
| Taxes on international trade and transactions | 12,659 | 14,236 | 15,555 |
| Other revenue | 9,226 | 12,103 | 12,307 |
| Charges, fees, fines, etc. | 1,987 | 2,368 | 3,377 |
| Sales of goods and services | 1,143 | 1,274 | 1,322 |
| Dividends | 2,513 | 2,498 | 2,661 |
| Interest receipts | 1,220 | 925 | 1,657 |
| **Total** | 48,556 | 54,690 | 60,480 |

| Expenditure | 2001/02 | 2002/03 | 2003/04 |
|---|---|---|---|
| Regular expenditure‡ | 42,155 | 45,414 | 47,657 |
| General administration | 7,283 | 7,283 | 7,283 |
| Defence | 5,860 | 7,381 | 8,520 |
| Social services | 13,070 | 13,459 | 14,038 |
| Education | 10,258 | 10,440 | 10,921 |
| Health | 1,980 | 2,032 | 2,121 |
| Economic services | 2,948 | 3,097 | 3,238 |
| Agriculture-related | 508 | 678 | 679 |
| Infrastructure | 1,121 | 1,127 | 1,118 |
| Interest payments | 5,770 | 6,622 | 6,544 |
| Other purposes | 7,224 | 5,806 | 6,235 |
| Development expenditure§ | 29,495 | 27,493 | 29,140 |
| Social services | 9,410 | 10,501 | 11,507 |
| Education | 2,755 | 2,730 | 3,396 |
| Health | 1,877 | 1,620 | 1,847 |
| Provision of drinking water | 1,904 | 2,139 | 2,569 |
| Economic services | 20,085 | 16,992 | 17,633 |
| Agriculture-related | 6,132 | 4,188 | 4,352 |
| Infrastructure | 9,338 | 9,446 | 9,413 |
| **Total** | 71,650 | 72,907 | 76,797 |

* Figures refer to the regular and development budgets of the central Government.

† Excluding grants received (NRs million, estimates): 5,800 in 2001/02; 9,600 in 2002/03; 11,300 in 2003/04.

‡ Excluding amortization payments on domestic and foreign loans.

§ Including net lending and excluding principal repayment from corporations.

Source: IMF, *Nepal: Selected Issues and Statistical Appendix* (February 2006).

**2004/05** (NRs million): *Revenue:* Tax 54,105; Total (incl. others) 70,123. *Expenditure:* Recurrent 61,686; Capital 27,341; Total (incl. others) 102,560 (Source: Federation of Nepalese Chambers of Commerce and Industry, Kathmandu).

**2005/06** (NRs million, estimates): *Revenue:* Tax 57,427; Total (incl. others) 73,500. *Expenditure:* Recurrent 69,067; Capital 28,802; Total (incl. others) 112,075 (Source: Federation of Nepalese Chambers of Commerce and Industry, Kathmandu).

**2006/07** (NRs million, estimates): *Revenue:* Tax 70,046; Total (incl. others) 85,376. *Expenditure:* Recurrent 83,768; Capital 44,976; Total (incl. others) 143,912 (Source: Federation of Nepalese Chambers of Commerce and Industry, Kathmandu).

**2007/08** (NRs million, estimates): *Revenue:* Tax 80,962; Total (incl. others) 103,667. *Expenditure:* Recurrent 98,172; Capital 55,262; Total (incl. others) 168,996 (Source: Federation of Nepalese Chambers of Commerce and Industry, Kathmandu).

**INTERNATIONAL RESERVES**

(US $ million at mid-December)

| | 2003 | 2004 | 2005 |
|---|---|---|---|
| Gold* | 6.5 | 6.5 | 5.4 |
| IMF special drawing rights | 0.8 | 9.7 | 8.8 |
| Reserve position in IMF | 8.6 | — | — |
| Foreign exchange | 1,213.1 | 1,452.5 | 1,490.2 |
| **Total** | 1,229.0 | 1,468.7 | 1,504.4 |

* Valued at US $42.5 per troy ounce in 2003 and 2004, and at $41.9 in 2005.

**2006** (US $ million at mid-December): IMF special drawing rights 9.0.

**2007** (US $ million at mid-December): IMF special drawing rights 9.1.

Source: IMF, *International Financial Statistics*.

**MONEY SUPPLY**
(NRs million at mid-December)*

| | 1998 | 1999 | 2000 |
|---|---|---|---|
| Currency outside banks | 32,244 | 36,929 | 44,526 |
| Private sector deposits with monetary authorities | 2,287 | 4,346 | 3,160 |
| Demand deposits at commercial banks | 10,979 | 13,832 | 15,343 |
| **Total money** | 45,509 | 55,107 | 63,028 |

**2001:** Currency outside banks 51,699; Private sector deposits 3,570; Total money (incl. others) 72,161.

**2002:** Currency outside banks 56,022; Private sector deposits 2,350; Total money (incl. others) 76,589.

**2003:** Currency outside banks 58,076; Private sector deposits 2,557; Total money (incl. others) 81,238.

**2004:** Currency outside banks 65,767; Private sector deposits 3,315; Total money (incl. others) 92,989.

**2005:** Currency outside banks 71,525; Private sector deposits 3,603; Total money (incl. others) 102,233.

**2006:** Currency outside banks 79,016; Private sector deposits 5,356; Total money (incl. others) 116,162.

* Excluding Indian currency in circulation.

Source: IMF, *International Financial Statistics*.

**COST OF LIVING**
(Consumer Price Index; base: 2000 = 100)

| | 2002 | 2003 | 2004 |
|---|---|---|---|
| Food (incl. beverages) | 104.4 | 110.1 | 112.9 |
| Fuel and light | 106.3 | 122.8 | 130.0 |
| Clothing (excl. footwear) | 104.4 | 106.3 | 108.4 |
| Rent | 110.9 | 116.4 | 120.9 |
| **All items** (incl. others) | 105.9 | 112.0 | 115.2 |

Source: ILO.

**All items** (Consumer Price Index; base: 2000 = 100): 122.9 in 2005; 132.2 in 2006; 140.2 in 2007 (Source: IMF, *International Financial Statistics*).

**NATIONAL ACCOUNTS**
(NRs million at current prices, year ending 15 July)

**Expenditure on the Gross Domestic Product**

| | 2003/04 | 2004/05* | 2005/06† |
|---|---|---|---|
| Government final consumption expenditure | 50,381 | 54,426 | 59,245 |
| Private final consumption expenditure | 383,978 | 412,776 | 458,991 |
| Increase in stocks | 35,869 | 53,038 | 68,859 |
| Gross fixed capital formation | 95,124 | 101,094 | 107,624 |
| **Total domestic expenditure** | 565,352 | 621,334 | 694,719 |
| Exports of goods and services | 89,543 | 85,957 | 108,142 |
| *Less* Imports of goods and services | 158,150 | 173,753 | 219,914 |
| **GDP in purchasers' values** | 496,745 | 533,538 | 582,948 |
| **GDP at constant 1994/95 prices** | 312,267 | 320,729 | 326,743 |

* Revised estimates.
† Preliminary estimates.

**Gross Domestic Product by Economic Activity**

| | 2003/04 | 2004/05* | 2005/06† |
|---|---|---|---|
| Agriculture, forestry and fishing | 183,117 | 194,363 | 212,827 |
| Mining and quarrying | 2,377 | 2,530 | 2,669 |
| Manufacturing | 36,634 | 39,286 | 41,768 |
| Electricity, gas and water | 11,355 | 11,892 | 12,508 |
| Construction | 49,029 | 52,922 | 56,558 |
| Trade, restaurants and hotels | 49,718 | 50,168 | 56,139 |
| Transport, storage and communications | 43,668 | 48,724 | 55,919 |
| Finance and real estate | 51,940 | 58,335 | 64,937 |
| Community and social services | 47,081 | 50,431 | 54,544 |
| **Sub-total** | 474,919 | 508,651 | 557,869 |
| *Less* Imputed bank service charges | 15,135 | 17,027 | 18,764 |
| **Gross value added in basic prices** | 459,784 | 491,624 | 539,105 |
| Indirect taxes, *less* subsidies | 36,961 | 41,914 | 43,842 |
| **GDP in market prices** | 496,745 | 533,538 | 582,948 |

* Revised estimates.
† Preliminary estimates.

**BALANCE OF PAYMENTS**
(US $ million )

| | 2004 | 2005 | 2006 |
|---|---|---|---|
| Exports of goods f.o.b. | 773.1 | 902.9 | 848.8 |
| Imports of goods f.o.b. | –1,908.0 | –2,276.5 | –2,441.0 |
| **Trade balance** | –1,134.9 | –1,373.6 | –1,592.2 |
| Exports of services | 460.9 | 380.3 | 385.7 |
| Imports of services | –385.0 | –434.7 | –492.8 |
| **Balance on goods and services** | –1,059.1 | –1,428.0 | –1,699.4 |
| Other income received | 63.0 | 139.9 | 158.2 |
| Other income paid | –78.0 | –91.6 | –96.1 |
| **Balance on goods, services and income** | –1,074.1 | –1,379.7 | –1,637.3 |
| Current transfers received | 1,091.8 | 1,441.3 | 1,695.7 |
| Current transfers paid | –62.8 | –60.5 | –68.9 |
| **Current balance** | –45.0 | 1.1 | –10.4 |
| Capital account (net) | 15.7 | 40.3 | 46.3 |
| Direct investment from abroad | –0.4 | 2.5 | –6.6 |
| Other investment assets | –348.0 | –242.4 | –250.9 |
| Investment liabilities | –140.0 | –36.5 | 260.3 |
| Net errors and omissions | 415.9 | 139.0 | 108.5 |
| **Overall balance** | –101.9 | –96.1 | 147.2 |

Source: IMF, *International Financial Statistics*.

# External Trade

**PRINCIPAL COMMODITIES**
(NRs million, year ending 15 July)

**Imports from India**

| Imports | 2004/05 | 2005/06 | 2006/07* |
|---|---|---|---|
| Rice | 437.1 | 2,309.8 | 1,505.0 |
| Cotton textiles | 1,607.5 | 1,273.0 | 902.1 |
| Synthetic thread | 404.2 | 1,536.4 | 2,190.9 |
| Medicines | 3,691.6 | 4,389.0 | 4,442.4 |
| Chemicals | 3,401.9 | 3,281.4 | 2,567.5 |
| Coal | 803.1 | 1,193.5 | 940.8 |
| Cement | 1,410.2 | 1,933.6 | 2,327.9 |
| Diesel | 10,243.3 | 12,843.3 | 12,635.0 |
| Kerosene | 7,677.2 | 11,995.8 | 10,275.5 |
| Transport vehicles and parts | 5,133.1 | 5,213.7 | 9,794.5 |
| Other machine equipment and parts | 3,010.8 | 3,509.4 | 3,530.5 |
| Motor spirit (petrol) | 4,723.7 | 5,813.6 | 6,675.8 |
| Liquefied petroleum gas | 3,557.7 | 2,351.1 | 2,989.2 |
| Electrical equipment and goods | 1,129.5 | 1,570.9 | 2,360.1 |
| Agricultural equipment and parts | 527.4 | 671.6 | 1,073.1 |
| **Total** (incl. others) | 88,675.5 | 107,143.1 | 117,740.4 |

**IMPORTS FROM OTHER COUNTRIES**

| Imports | 2004/05 | 2005/06 | 2006/07* |
|---|---|---|---|
| Crude palm oil | 2,085.5 | 4,051.1 | 7,121.5 |
| Betel nut | 638.7 | 806.7 | 1,418.3 |
| Crude soybean oil | 834.6 | 1,572.9 | 1,924.2 |
| Textile dyes | 380.9 | 2,095.9 | 2,344.6 |
| Medicines | 701.2 | 1,108.1 | 1,536.9 |
| Gold | 4.9 | 2.9 | 3,519.9 |
| Zinc ingot | 1,266.3 | 2,327.1 | 2,372.5 |
| Copper wire rod, scrapes and sheet | 1,387.2 | 2,089.1 | 1,878.6 |
| Polyethylene granules | 1,972.7 | 3,696.7 | 2,959.7 |
| Electrical equipment and goods | 1,326.4 | 2,872.7 | 2,693.7 |
| Computers and parts | 1,227.0 | 1,353.8 | 2,662.5 |
| Transport vehicles and parts | 1,751.5 | 2,155.7 | 2,660.7 |
| Other machine equipment and parts | 2,695.9 | 2,830.7 | 2,007.4 |
| Telecommunications equipment and parts | 1,860.7 | 1,720.5 | 2,531.0 |
| Aircraft and parts | 980.5 | 1,071.3 | 1,462.8 |
| **Total** (incl. others) | 149,473.6 | 173,780.3 | 191,708.8 |

**EXPORTS TO INDIA**

| Exports | 2004/05 | 2005/06 | 2006/07* |
|---|---|---|---|
| Banaspati ghee | 4,635.9 | 3,861.7 | 4,136.5 |
| Juice | 1,091.3 | 1,139.6 | 1,591.3 |
| Cardamom | 607.0 | 608.1 | 848.1 |
| Polyester yarn | 1,896.3 | 3,476.3 | 2,240.4 |
| Twines | 1,051.2 | 906.9 | 973.1 |
| Other threads | 2,213.7 | 1,898.3 | 4,055.9 |
| Textiles (cotton, synthetic and others) | 2,996.6 | 2,154.6 | 3,056.9 |
| Ready-made garments | 365.9 | 1,137.3 | 765.0 |
| Sacks | 1,456.2 | 1,265.4 | 1,408.6 |
| Chemicals | 1,407.5 | 1,057.5 | 911.5 |
| Toothpaste | 256.6 | 346.5 | 577.4 |
| Galvanized iron sheet | 3,070.3 | 2,345.2 | 1,967.3 |
| Copper wire and rods | 530.1 | 305.8 | 206.0 |
| Other wire | 1,221.4 | 1,504.1 | 1,610.7 |
| Steel pipes | 316.6 | 105.7 | 761.9 |
| **Total** (incl. others) | 38,916.9 | 40,714.7 | 41,874.8 |

**EXPORTS TO OTHER COUNTRIES**

| | 2004/05 | 2005/06 | 2006/07* |
|---|---|---|---|
| Pulses | 106.5 | 191.7 | 488.1 |
| Cardamom | 205.3 | 109.2 | 129.6 |
| Tea | 106.7 | 107.6 | 114.7 |
| Herbs | 54.7 | 19.0 | 39.5 |
| Perfume oil | 48.3 | 8.2 | 21.4 |
| Niger seeds | — | 7.0 | 8.8 |
| Hide and skins | 235.8 | 310.4 | 275.5 |
| Ready-made leather goods | 30.2 | 14.4 | 111.1 |
| Woollen carpet | 5,868.7 | 5,838.7 | 5,600.2 |
| Ready-made garments | 6,124.6 | 6,204.1 | 5,205.5 |
| Pashmina goods | 1,049.8 | 1,577.8 | 931.0 |
| Nepalese paper and paper products | 239.8 | 257.0 | 190.6 |
| Wooden handicraft goods | 124.1 | 173.1 | 65.3 |
| Metal handicraft goods | 520.1 | 257.8 | 130.8 |
| Gold and silver ornaments | 363.2 | 282.4 | 325.4 |
| **Total** (incl. others) | 19,788.8 | 19,519.4 | 18,921.0 |

* Provisional figures.

**PRINCIPAL TRADING PARTNERS**
(NRs million, year ending 15 July)

| Imports | 2004/05 | 2005/06 | 2006/07 |
|---|---|---|---|
| Australia | 1,521.1 | 1,415.3 | 1,854.7 |
| China, People's Republic | 12,859.2 | 12,083.5 | 16,678.6 |
| Germany | 1,570.9 | 2,761.8 | 2,432.7 |
| Hong Kong | 1,286.4 | 930.9 | 1,029.5 |
| India | 88,675.5 | 107,143.1 | 117,740.4 |
| Indonesia | 5,222.7 | 5,647.8 | 11,172.1 |
| Japan | 2,565.2 | 1,935.1 | 3,229.0 |
| Korea, Republic | 2,784.6 | 1,788.9 | 2,380.5 |
| Malaysia | 2,820.9 | 2,474.7 | 2,794.6 |
| New Zealand | 1,229.7 | 1,018.8 | 841.1 |
| Saudi Arabia | 3,138.5 | 2,329.7 | 2,592.7 |
| Singapore | 7,746.8 | 3,375.3 | 5,496.9 |
| Taiwan | 825.7 | 567.9 | 796.0 |
| Thailand | 3,117.5 | 2,602.1 | 3,459.5 |
| United Kingdom | 1,452.2 | 961.4 | 1,727.1 |
| USA | 1,763.8 | 1,677.5 | 4,260.0 |
| **Total** (incl. others) | 149,473.6 | 173,780.3 | 191,708.8 |

| Exports | 2004/05 | 2005/06 | 2006/07 |
|---|---|---|---|
| China, People's Republic | 1,888.5 | 892.6 | 378.0 |
| France | 617.8 | 1,297.5 | 904.0 |
| Germany | 3,121.7 | 2,843.8 | 2,573.7 |
| India | 38,916.9 | 40,714.7 | 41,874.8 |
| Italy | 582.8 | 712.3 | 684.3 |
| United Kingdom | 1,050.0 | 1,184.1 | 998.7 |
| USA | 7,570.7 | 6,993.4 | 5,571.3 |
| **Total** (incl. others) | 58,705.7 | 60,234.1 | 60,795.8 |

# Transport

**ROAD TRAFFIC**
(vehicles registered)

| | 2000/01 | 2001/02 | 2002/03 |
|---|---|---|---|
| Cars, jeeps and vans | 5,152 | 4,374 | 2,906 |
| Buses and minibuses | 1,453 | 1,343 | 730 |
| Tractors | 3,519 | 3,189 | 2,485 |
| Other agro-industrial vehicles | 1,271 | 1,798 | 1,212 |
| Motorcycles | 29,291 | 38,522 | 29,404 |
| **Total** (incl. others) | 40,995 | 49,560 | 37,610 |

Source: Department of Transport Management, Kathmandu.

**CIVIL AVIATION**

**Royal Nepal Airlines Corporation**
(traffic on scheduled services)

| | 2001 | 2002 | 2003 |
|---|---|---|---|
| Kilometres flown (million) | 9 | 10 | 8 |
| Passengers carried ('000) | 641 | 681 | 356 |
| Passenger-km (million) | 1,153 | 1,211 | 663 |
| Total ton-km (million) | 119 | 127 | 64 |

Source: UN, *Statistical Yearbook*.

## Tourism

**FOREIGN TOURIST ARRIVALS**

| Country of residence | 2004 | 2005 | 2006 |
|---|---|---|---|
| Australia | 9,839 | 7,093 | 8,204 |
| Bangladesh | 14,640 | 19,206 | 16,623 |
| China, People's Republic | 12,733 | 21,092 | 15,777 |
| France | 18,992 | 14,108 | 14,293 |
| Germany | 16,031 | 14,345 | 13,686 |
| India | 89,861 | 95,685 | 88,857 |
| Italy | 12,121 | 8,785 | 7,472 |
| Japan | 24,196 | 18,239 | 21,664 |
| Korea, Republic | 10,654 | 10,121 | 12,413 |
| Netherlands | 11,064 | 8,890 | 6,848 |
| Sri Lanka | 16,045 | 18,686 | 27,382 |
| Thailand | 14,680 | 13,614 | 14,332 |
| United Kingdom | 24,644 | 24,950 | 21,180 |
| USA | 20,584 | 18,476 | 19,039 |
| **Total** (incl. others) | 385,297 | 375,398 | 383,926 |

**Tourism receipts** (US $ million, incl. passenger transport): 233 in 2003; 260 in 2004; 160 in 2005.

Source: World Tourism Organization.

## Communications Media

| | 2004 | 2005 | 2006 |
|---|---|---|---|
| Telephones ('000 main lines in use) | 417.9 | 484.6 | 595.8 |
| Mobile cellular telephones ('000 subscribers) | 116.8 | 227.3 | 1,041.8 |
| Personal computers ('000 in use) | 116 | 116 | n.a. |
| Internet users ('000) | 120 | 225 | 249.4 |

**2003:** Daily newspapers 251 titles; Non-daily newspapers 3,490 titles.

**Facsimile machines** ('000 in use, year ending 15 July): 8 in 1999.

**Radio receivers** ('000 in use): 840 in 1997.

**Television receivers** ('000 in use): 170 in 2000; 193 in 2001.

Sources: UNESCO, *Statistical Yearbook*; International Telecommunication Union.

## Education

(2004)

| | Institutions* | Teachers | Students |
|---|---|---|---|
| Primary | 24,746 | 101,483 | 4,030,045 |
| Lower Secondary | 7,436 | 25,962 | 1,444,997 |
| Secondary | 4,547 | 20,232 | 543,764 |

* Including duplication, since many schools offer education at more than one level. The total number of primary, lower secondary and secondary institutions was 26,277.

**Pre-primary:** 1,471 institutions, 257,121 students in 2003.

Source: Ministry of Education and Sports, Kathmandu.

**Adult literacy rate** (UNESCO estimates): 56.5% (males 70.3%; females 43.6%) in 2007 (Source: UNESCO Institute for Statistics).

# Directory

## Interim Constitution

In May 2006, prior to the convening of a Constituent Assembly, the House of Representatives approved a provisional proclamation significantly curtailing the powers of the King. All existing constitutional provisions that contradicted the proclamation were to be nullified. The most significant declarations of the proclamation were: that Nepal would henceforth be designated a secular state; that all legislative powers in the country would be exercised by the House of Representatives; that all executive authority in Nepal would reside with the Council of Ministers; that the Council of State (Raj Parishad) would be abolished; that the 'Royal Nepal Army' would be renamed the 'Nepal Army'; that the monarch would no longer hold the position of Supreme Commander-in-Chief of the Royal Nepal Army; that the monarch would no longer possess the authority to enact laws concerning the royal succession; that the monarch's acts could henceforth be challenged by both the House of Representatives and the courts; and that henceforth sessions of the House of Representatives would no longer be convened by the monarch, but by the Speaker, on the advice of the Prime Minister. In addition, in June, following a unanimous parliamentary vote, King Gyanendra was stripped of his right to veto laws, and in July his mandate to appoint judges was also taken away. The proclamation of May 2006 effectively overrode the Constitution promulgated by the King on 9 November 1990.

Following extensive negotiations between members of the seven-party alliance (a political coalition demanding an end to autocratic governance in Nepal), the Communist Party of Nepal (Maoist) and a UN peace delegation to Nepal, an Interim Constitution was presented in December 2006 and subsequently endorsed on 15 January 2007. (Maoist inclusion in the interim legislature was agreed according to the conditions of a Comprehensive Peace Agreement, which was signed on 21 November 2006 and which promised the disarmament of the Maoist militant groups and the containment of insurgent military personnel in government-supervised camps.) The enactment of the Interim Constitution effected the dissolution of the National Assembly and the House of Representatives and instituted a 330-member Interim Parliament, or 'Legislature-Parliament', which was mandated to formulate a model for the election of a Constituent Assembly, which would draft a permanent Constitution. All constitutional powers of governance formerly commanded by King Gyanendra were transferred to Prime Minister Girija Prasad Koirala, who was nominated Head of State. Executive power was conferred upon the Council of Ministers.

Further requested amendments to the Interim Constitution were confirmed in February 2007, particularly with respect to proportional and comprehensive representation of the Madhesi people and federal governance structure; following the submission of concerns from international observers in the USA, the process of judicial appointments and the administration of justice were also highlighted as issues for revision. A two-thirds' majority parliamentary vote was required to initiate all constitutional amendments. In December the Interim Parliament endorsed a constitutional amendment providing for the abolition of the monarchy; however, the change was to come into effect only upon the approval of the Constituent Assembly. At the same time, the membership of the Constituent Assembly was increased, with a significant number to be elected under the system of proportional representation. Following a legislative election on 10 April 2008, the Constituent Assembly voted to abolish the monarchy and declare Nepal a republic at its first session in May. The Interim Parliament's term was to end following the inaugural meeting of the Constituent Assembly.

The preamble to the Interim Constitution of Nepal, 2063 (2007), envisages the guarantee of the fundamental and human rights of every citizen and the protection of his civil liberty; the rights of the Nepalese people to structure their own Constitution and to engage in the unrestricted, impartial election of a Constituent Assembly; the resolution of class, caste, gender and regional tensions through systematic state restructure; universal adult suffrage and the multi-party system; complete freedom of press; and the provision of an independent judicial system. Democracy, peace, prosperity, economic and social progress, integrity and independence are national priorities. Sovereignty and state governance reside in the Nepalese people. The Constitution is the fundamental law of the land and nullifies any other extraneous laws that it may be attempted to introduce.

Nepal is a multi-ethnic, multi-lingual, religiously multi-denominational, independent, indivisible, sovereign, secular and inclusive democratic state. Nepali is recognized as the national language; Nepali in the Devnagari representation is the official language.

### CITIZENSHIP AND FUNDAMENTAL RIGHTS

At the effective implementation of the Constitution, persons domiciled in Nepal who are eligible to apply for or have acquired citizenship are regarded as Nepali citizens. Honorary or naturalized citizenship may be endowed by the Government in accordance with legal provisions, and shall not be acquired or revoked unless dictated by law. Part Three of the Constitution provides for the fundamental rights of the citizen: all citizens are equal before the law and shall be awarded equal protection from the law; no discrimination is to be practised on the basis of religion, race, sex, caste, tribe, origin, language or ideology; acts of racial discrimination or untouchability shall be punishable by law and the victim eligible for compensation; no person can be deprived of his liberty except in accordance with the law; capital punishment remains abolished; freedom of expression and opinion, freedom to assemble peaceably and without arms, freedom to form political parties or organizations, freedom to form trade unions and associations, freedom of profession, and freedom of movement are also guaranteed. Similarly, pre-censorship of publications and impediment to communication media is prohibited and, thus, the right to press and publications is ensured. In the sphere of criminal justice, the following rights are specified in the Constitution: no person is to be regarded as an offender unless proven so by law, nor punished unless made punishable by law; any indicted person is entitled to confidential legal counsel at the time of arrest and may be represented by their chosen legal practitioner; those persons with insufficient financial means are to be entitled to free legal aid; no person may be tried more than once for the same offence; no one is compelled to testify against himself; no one is to be given punishment greater than that which the law at the time of the offence has prescribed; torture of detainees is prohibited; no person is to be detained without having first been informed about the grounds for such an action; and the detainee must appear before the judicial authorities within 24 hours of his arrest. In addition, provision has also been made to compensate any person who is wrongfully detained. Every citizen is entitled to a clean living environment and state-funded basic health care. A person's right to property and compensation for land reclaimed by the State under national programmes is ensured, and the right to protect and promote one's own language, script and culture have been safeguarded. The right to state-funded education up to secondary level (provided in the child's mother tongue up to primary level) is similarly ensured, while all persons are guaranteed the right to employment, and social security is to benefit all social groups. Exploitation and exile are guarded against. The rights of women to inheritance, protection from violence and sexual discrimination are assured, as are those of children to protection, nurture and state privileges in the case of disadvantaged birth. Additionally, social justice is guaranteed for women and tribal, oppressed and deprived social groups, and all citizens are to be permitted access to information pertaining to themselves or matters of national importance. The right to practise religion and to manage and protect religious places and trusts has been granted to the country's various religious groups. The right to secrecy and inviolability of the person, residence, property, documents, letters and other information is also guaranteed. The right to constitutional resolution secures the enforcement of all other rights designated by the Constitution.

### GOVERNMENT AND LEGISLATURE

The executive powers of the country are vested in the Council of Ministers. The direction, supervision and conduct of the general administration of Nepal are the responsibility of the Council of Ministers. The Prime Minister and Council of Ministers are appointed according to political consensus. The Constituent Assembly comprises 601 members, of whom 575 are elected under the mixed electoral system and 26 are nominated. The Constituent Assembly is responsible for drafting a new Constitution; the tenure of office of its members is two years.

### GOVERNANCE

Part Four of the Constitution details the responsibilities, policies and regulatory tenets of the State, particularly citing the objectives of electoral reform to provide for free and impartial election of the Constituent Assembly, the institution of a multi-party democratic and inclusive political system adherent to citizens' fundamental and human rights, the restructuring of the State to eliminate discrimination against or marginalization of any social group and actively promote full social and economic integration, the promotion of a national socio-economic development programme and prohibition of assets procurement by corrupt means, provision for the relief and rehabilitation of victims of the conflict, including the institution of an investigatory Truth and Reconciliation Commission, and prevention of further violence and conflict through institutionalized peace. In addition, the promotion of national economic independence and growth, enhancement of the people's basic quality of life and state infrastructure, and the adoption of a co-operative and equality driven foreign policy are ensured. No legal challenge may be submitted as to the implementation or otherwise of any such policies.

Part 17 of the Constitution makes provision for local self governance through the institution of district, municipal and village interim organizations. The State, through national and local government, is empowered to marshal revenue and resources in the interests of fulfilling such state policies.

### THE JUDICIARY

The judicial system has three tiers: the Supreme Court, the Appellate Courts and the District Courts. The Supreme Court is the principal court and is also a Court of Record. The Supreme Court consists of a Chief Justice and a maximum of 14 other judges. The Chief Justice is appointed by the Prime Minister on the recommendation of the Constitutional Council; other Supreme Court, Appellate Court and District Court judges are nominated by the Chief Justice on the recommendation of the Judicial Council. A Constituent Assembly Court was established in February 2008 to address election issues.

### OTHER INSTITUTIONS

The Interim Constitution also makes provisions for the establishment of a Constitutional Council, Public Service Commission, Election Commission, National Human Rights Commission, Commission for the Investigation of Abuse of Authority, Auditor General and Attorney-General.

### POLITICAL PARTIES

Political parties are required to register with the Election Commission, and must be non-discriminatory, have democratic aims, and produce the signatures of at least 10,000 voters in support of their application. It has been specifically provided that no law that bans, or imposes restrictions on, political parties may be enacted. Parties whose aims run 'contrary' to the Preamble of the Interim Constitution will be disqualified from registering.

### DEFENCE

The Commander-in-Chief of the Nepal Army is appointed by the Council of Ministers. The Council of Ministers shall work towards the democratization and human rights awareness of the Nepal Army. The Nepal Army is administered and deployed by the Council of Ministers on the recommendation of the National Defence Council, which consists of the Prime Minister, the Minister of Defence, three other ministerial nominees and the Commander-in-Chief. The Council of Ministers shall establish a committee to oversee the assimilation and rehabilitation of Maoist combatants. Certain other procedures are governed by agreements between the (former) Government of Nepal and the Communist Party of Nepal (Maoist).

## The Government

### HEAD OF STATE

**President:** Dr RAM BARAN YADAV (assumed office 23 July 2008).

**Vice-President:** PARAMANANDA JHA.

### COUNCIL OF MINISTERS

(September 2008)

Following the constituent assembly elections on 10 April 2008, a coalition Government was formed, comprising members of the Communist Party of Nepal (Maoist) (CPN—M), the Communist Party of Nepal (Unified Marxist-Leninist—UML), the Madhesi Jana Adhikar Forum Nepal (Madhesi People's Rights Forum Nepal—MPRF), the Sadbhavana Party, the People's Front Nepal (Janamorcha Nepal) and the Communist Party of Nepal (United) (CPN—U).

**Prime Minister:** PUSHPA KAMAL DAHAL ('PRACHANDA') (CPN—M).

**Deputy Prime Minister and Minister of Home Affairs:** BAMDEV GAUTAM (UML).

**Minister of Finance:** BABURAM BHATTARAI (CPN—M).

**Minister of Defence:** RAM BAHADUR THAPA BADAL (CPN—M).

**Minister of Foreign Affairs:** UPENDRA YADAV (MPRF).

**Minister of Peace and Reconstruction:** JANARDAN SHARMA (CPN—M).

**Minister of Law, Justice and Parliamentary Affairs:** DEV GURUNG (CPN—M).

**Minister of Environment, Science and Technology:** GANESH SAH (CPN—U).

**Minister of Culture and State Restructuring:** GOPAL KIRATI (CPN—M).

**Minister of Commerce and Supplies:** RAJENDRA MAHATO (Sadbhavana Party).

**Minister of Agriculture and Co-operatives:** JAYPRAKASH GUPTA (MPRF).

**Minister of Forests and Soil Conservation:** KIRAN GURUNG (UML).

**Minister of Land Reforms and Management:** MATRIKA YADAV (CPN—M).

**Minister of Physical Planning and Construction:** BIJAY GACHHADAR (MPRF).

**Minister of Local Development:** RAMCHANDRA JHA (UML).

**Minister of Tourism and Civil Aviation:** HISILA YAMI (CPN—M).

**Minister of Education:** RENU YADAV (MPRF).

**Minister of Industry:** ASTHA LAXMI SHAKYA (UML).

**Minister of Information and Communications:** KRISHNA BAHADUR MAHARA (CPN—M).

**Minister of Health and Population:** GIRIRAJMANI POKHAREL (People's Front Nepal).

**Minister of Labour and Transport Management:** LEKHRAJ BHATTA (CPN—M).

**Minister of Water Resources:** BISHNU POUDEL (UML).

**Minister of Youth and Sports:** GOPAL SHAKYA (UML).

**Minister of General Administration:** PAMPHA BHUSAL (CPN—M).

### MINISTRIES

In 2008 certain ministries were in the process of being reorganized.

**Prime Minister's Office:** Singha Durbar, POB 43312, Kathmandu; tel. (1) 421000; e-mail info@opmcm.gov.np; internet www.opmcm.gov.np.

**Ministry of Agriculture and Co-operatives:** Singha Durbar, Kathmandu; tel. (1) 4228371; fax (1) 4229139; e-mail memoac@moac.gov.np; internet www.moac.gov.np.

**Ministry of Culture, Tourism and Civil Aviation:** Bhrikutimandap, Kathmandu; tel. (1) 4256217; fax (1) 4227281; e-mail info@tourism.gov.np; internet www.tourism.gov.np.

**Ministry of Defence:** Singha Durbar, Kathmandu; tel. (1) 4211290; fax (1) 4211294.

**Ministry of Education and Sports:** Keshar Mahal, Kantipath, Kathmandu; tel. (1) 4418784; fax (1) 412199; e-mail infomoe@most.gov.np; internet www.moe.gov.np.

**Ministry of Environment, Science and Technology:** Singha Durbar, Kathmandu; tel. (1) 4244609; fax (1) 4225474; e-mail info@most.gov.np; internet www.most.gov.np.

**Ministry of Finance:** Singha Durbar, Kathmandu; tel. (1) 4211809; fax (1) 4211831; e-mail admindivision@mof.gov.np; internet www.mof.gov.np.

**Ministry of Foreign Affairs:** Shital Niwas, Maharajganj, Kathmandu; tel. (1) 4416011; fax (1) 4416016; e-mail adm@mofa.gov.np; internet www.mofa.gov.np.

**Ministry of Forests and Soil Conservation:** Singha Durbar, Kathmandu; tel. (1) 4220067; fax (1) 4223868; e-mail info@mosc.gov.np; internet www.mofsc.gov.np.

**Ministry of General Administration:** Singha Durbar, Kathmandu; tel. (1) 4245367; fax (1) 4242138; e-mail moga@most.gov.np; internet www.moga.gov.np.

**Ministry of Health and Population:** Singha Durbar Plaza, Ramshah Path, Kathmandu; tel. (1) 4262862; fax (1) 4262896; e-mail info@moh.gov.np; internet www.moh.gov.np.

**Ministry of Home Affairs:** Singha Durbar, Kathmandu; tel. (1) 4211224; e-mail moha@wlink.com.np; internet www.moha.gov.np.

**Ministry of Industry, Commerce and Supplies:** Singha Durbar, Kathmandu; tel. (1) 4211967; fax (1) 4211619; e-mail info@moics.gov.np; internet www.moics.gov.np.

**Ministry of Information and Communications:** Singha Durbar, Kathmandu; tel. (1) 4211556; fax (1) 4221729; e-mail moicppme@ntc.net.np; internet www.moic.gov.np.

**Ministry of Labour and Transport Management:** Singha Durbar, Kathmandu; tel. (1) 4247842; fax (1) 4256877; e-mail info@moltm.gov.np; internet www.moltm.gov.np.

**Ministry of Land Reform and Management:** Singha Durbar, Kathmandu; tel. (1) 4225366; fax (1) 4220108; e-mail lrm@most.gov.np; internet www.molrm.gov.np.

**Ministry of Law, Justice and Parliamentary Affairs:** Singha Durbar, Kathmandu; tel. (1) 4223727; fax (1) 4220684; e-mail info@moljpa.gov.np; internet www.moljpa.gov.np.

**Ministry of Local Development:** Sri Mahal, Pulchowk, Lalitpur; tel. (1) 5521727; fax (1) 5522045; e-mail info@mld.gov.np; internet www.mld.gov.np.

**Ministry of Physical Planning and Works:** Singha Durbar, Kathmandu; tel. (1) 4228285; fax (1) 4228420; e-mail info@moppw.gov.np; internet www.moppw.gov.np.

**Ministry of Water Resources:** Singha Durbar, Kathmandu; tel. (1) 4211511; e-mail mowr@most.gov.np; internet www.mowr.gov.np.

**Ministry of Women, Children and Social Welfare:** Singha Durbar, Kathmandu; tel. (1) 4241728; fax (1) 4241516; internet www.mowcsw.gov.np.

## Legislature

### CONSTITUENT ASSEMBLY

The Constituent Assembly, which is responsible for drafting a new Constitution, comprises 601 members, of whom 575 were elected (using the mixed electoral system) and 26 nominated by the incumbent Interim Parliament. The term of office of its members is two years.

**Chairman:** SUBAS CHANDRA NEMBANG.

**Election, 10 April 2008**

| Party | Seats* |
|---|---|
| Communist Party of Nepal (Maoist—M) | 220 |
| Nepali Congress Party (NCP) | 110 |
| Communist Party of Nepal (Unified Marxist-Leninist—UML) | 103 |
| Madhesi People's Rights Forum Nepal | 52 |
| Terai Madhes Loktantrik Party | 20 |
| Sadbhavana Party | 9 |
| Communist Party of Nepal (Marxist-Leninist) | 8 |
| Rashtriya Prajatantra Party (RPP) | 8 |
| Janamorcha Nepal | 7 |
| Communist Party of Nepal (United) | 5 |
| Nepal Workers' and Peasants' Party | 4 |
| Rashtriya Prajatantra Party Nepal | 4 |
| Rastriya Janamorcha | 4 |
| Rashtriya Janashakti Party | 3 |
| Communist Party of Nepal (Unified) | 2 |
| Nepali Janata Dal | 2 |
| Nepali Sadbhavana Party (Anandi Devi) | 2 |
| Rastriya Janamukti Party | 2 |
| Sanghiya Loktantrik Rastriya Manch | 2 |
| Churevawar Rastriya Ekata Party Nepal | 1 |
| Dalit Janajati Party | 1 |
| Nepal Loktantrik Samajbadi Dal | 1 |
| Nepal Pariwar Dal | 1 |
| Nepal Rastriya Party | 1 |
| Samajwadi Prajatantrik Janata Party Nepal | 1 |
| Independents | 2 |
| Nominated | 26 |
| **Total** | 601 |

* Includes seats determined by proportional representation and 'first past the post' systems.

## Election Commission

**Election Commission of Nepal:** Bahadur Bhawan, Kantipath, Kathmandu; tel. (1) 4228663; fax (1) 4229227; e-mail info@election.gov.np; internet www.election.gov.np; independent; appointed by the Prime Minister, on recommendation of a Constitutional Council, for a six-year term; Chief Election Commr BHOJ RAJ POKHAREL.

## Political Organizations

According to the Interim Constitution (which was formally endorsed in January 2007), political parties are required to register with the Election Commission, and must be non-discriminatory, have democratic aims, and produce the signatures of at least 10,000 voters supporting them. No law that bans or imposes restrictions on political parties may be enacted. Parties whose aims run 'contrary' to the Preamble of the Interim Constitution will not be permitted to register. By mid-2007 11 major political parties of the interim Parliament had been registered as official national parties with the Election Commission and confirmed as eligible to contest the forthcoming constituent assembly elections, which were held in April 2008.

**Communist Party of Nepal (Maoist) (CPN—M):** internet www.cpnm.org; f. 1990 as Communist Party of Nepal (Unity Centre), renamed as above in 1995; fmr underground political movement, represented in Interim Parliament in 2007; orchestrated 'people's war' in hills of west Nepal (1996–2006); advocates abolition of constitutional monarchy and establishment of people's republic; merged with Communist Party of Nepal (Unified Marxist-Leninist-Maoist) Sept. 2007; merged with Communist Party of Nepal (Marxist) in Feb. 2008; Leader PUSHPA KAMAL DAHAL ('Prachanda').

**Communist Party of Nepal (Unified):** Kathmandu; f. 2007; Gen. Sec. RAJ SINGH SHRIS.

**Communist Party of Nepal (United):** Kathmandu; f. 2007 following a split in the Communist Party of Nepal (United Marxist); Gen. Sec. GANESH SHAH.

**Green Nepal Party:** Kalikasthan, POB 890, Kathmandu; tel. and fax (1) 4438402; fax (1) 4416547; e-mail greennepal96@wlink.com.np; internet www.nepalgreenparty.com; f. 1996; Chair. KUBER SHARMA; Pres. M. K. RIMAL.

**Madhesi Jana Adhikar Forum Nepal** (Madhesi People's Rights Forum Nepal): f. 2006; Chair. UPENDRA YADAV.

**Nepali Janata Dal:** Tripureshwor, Kathmandu; tel. (1) 4212389; f. 1990; advocates the consolidation of the multi-party democratic system and supports the campaign against corruption; Leader KESHAR JUNG RAYAMAJHI.

**Rashtriya Janashakti Party** (National People's Power Party): Ramalphokhari, Kathmandu; tel. (1) 4437063; fax (1) 4437064; e-mail rjpnepal@info.com.np; f. 2005; Leader SURYA BAHADUR THAPA.

**Rashtriya Prajatantra Party (RPP)** (National Democratic Party—NDP): Charumati Bahal, Chabahil, Kathmandu; tel. (1) 4471071; fax (1) 4423384; e-mail info@rppnepal.com; internet www.rppnepal.org; liberal democratic party; Pres. PASHUPATI SHUMSHERE J. B. RANA; Sec.-Gen. DEEPAK BOHARA.

**Rashtriya Prajatantra Party Nepal:** Kathmandu; tel. (1) 4375455; f. 2008; Pres. RABINDRA NATH SHARMA; Chair. KAMAL THAPA.

**Rastriya Janamorcha:** Kathmandu; tel. (1) 4420226; Pres. CHITRA BAHADUR K. C.

**Rastriya Janamukti Party:** Maha Laxmisthan, Lagan Khel, POB 5569, Kathmandu; tel. (1) 5542212; fax (1) 5525531; e-mail zhedi43@yahoo.com; internet www.janamuktiparty.com; f. 1990; Pres. MALBAR SINGH THAPA.

**Sadbhavana Party:** Kathmandu; Chair. RAJENDRA MAHATO.

**Sanghiya Loktantrik Rastriya Manch:** Kathmandu; Pres. KAMAL CHARAHANG.

**Terai Madhes Loktantrik Party** (Terai Madhes Democratic Party): Kathmandu; tel. (1) 4462398; Pres. MAHANTHA THAKUR.

**Seven-party alliance (SPA):** coalition of left-wing parties.

**Communist Party of Nepal (Unified Marxist-Leninist) (UML):** Madan Nagar, Balkhu, POB 5471, Kathmandu; tel. (1) 4278081; fax (1) 4278084; e-mail uml@ntc.net.np; internet www.cpnuml.org; f. 1991 when two major factions of the Communist Party of Nepal (CPN; f. 1949; banned 1960; legalized 1990)—the Marxist and Marxist-Leninist factions—merged; the Communist Party of Nepal (Marxist-Leninist—ML) seceded in 1998 and rejoined the UML in 2002; the Communist Party of Nepal (Verma) merged with the UML in 2001; Gen. Sec. JHALA NATH KHANAL.

**Nepali Congress Party (NCP):** B. P. Smriti Bhawan, B. P. Nagar, Sanepa, Lalitpur; tel. (1) 5555263; fax (1) 5555188; e-mail ncparty@wlink.com.np; internet www.nepalicongress.org; f. 1947; banned 1960; legalized 1990; Nepali Congress Party—Democratic formed as breakaway faction in 2002, rejoined Sept. 2007; Pres. GIRIJA PRASAD KOIRALA; Gen. Secs K. B. GURUNG, BIMALENDRA NIDHI, Dr RAM BARAN YADAV; 101,000 active members, 500,000 ordinary members.

**Nepali Sadbhavana Party (NSP)** (Nepal Goodwill Party): Shantinagar, New Baneshwor, Kathmandu; tel. (1) 4488068; fax (1) 4470797; f. 1990; promotes the rights of the Madhesiya community, who are of Indian origin and reside in the Terai; demands that the Government recognize Hindi as an official language, that constituencies in the Terai be allocated on the basis of population, and that the Government grant citizenship to those who settled in Nepal before April 1990; in 2003 the party split into two factions, one led by Badri Prasad Mandal, known as the Mandal Group, and the other led by Anandi Devi Singh, known as the Anandi Devi group (the NSP member of the SPA).

**Nepal Workers' and Peasants' Party:** Golmadhi Tole-7, Bhaktapur, Kathmandu; tel. (1) 6610974; fax (1) 6613207; e-mail nwpp@ntc.net.np; Chair. NARAYAN MAN BIJUKCHHEN (Comrade Rohit).

**People's Front Nepal** (Janamorcha Nepal): Kathmandu; f. 2002 following merger of Rashtriya Jana Morcha (National People's Front) and United People's Front; split into three factions in Dec. 2006; Pres. AMIK SHERCHAN; Vice-Chair. LILAMANI POKHAREL.

**United Left Front:** coalition of Nepali communist parties; f. 2002.

**Communist Party of Nepal (Marxist-Leninist) (CPN—ML):** Kathmandu; f. 2002 following the reunification of the Communist Party of Nepal (Marxist-Leninist) with the Communist Party of Nepal (Unified Marxist–Leninist); C. P. Mainali, co-founder of the original CPN(ML) as a break-away faction of the CPN(UML) in 1998, had opposed the merger and formed a separate party under the CPN(ML) title; Leader C. P. MAINALI.

Other parties elected to the Constituent Assembly in April 2008 were Churevawar Rastriya Ekata Party Nepal, Dalit Janajati Party, Nepal Loktantrik Samajbadi Dal, Nepal Pariwar Dal, Nepal Rastriya Party, and Samajwadi Prajatantrik Janata Party Nepal.

## Diplomatic Representation

### EMBASSIES IN NEPAL

**Australia:** Suraj Niwas, Bansbari, POB 879, Kathmandu; tel. (1) 4371678; fax (1) 4371533; internet www.nepal.embassy.gov.au; Ambassador GRAEME LADE.

**Bangladesh:** Maharajgunj Ring Rd, POB 789, Kathmandu; tel. (1) 4372843; fax (1) 4373265; e-mail bdootktm@wlink.com.np; Ambassador IMTIAZ AHMED.

**China, People's Republic:** Baluwatar, POB 4234, Kathmandu; tel. (1) 4419053; fax (1) 4414045; e-mail chinaemb_np@mfa.gov.cn; internet www.fmprc.gov.cn/ce/cenp; Ambassador ZHENG XIANGLIN.

**Denmark:** 761 Neel Saraswati Marg, Lazimpat, POB 6332, Kathmandu; tel. (1) 4413010; fax (1) 4411409; e-mail ktmamb@um.dk; internet www.ambkathmandu.um.dk; Ambassador FINN THILSTED.

**Egypt:** Pulchowk, Lalitpur, POB 792, Kathmandu; tel. (1) 5524812; fax (1) 5522975; Ambassador ABDUL HAMEED MAHMOUD SOLIMAN.

**Finland:** Bishalnagar, POB 2126, Kathmandu; tel. (1) 4416636; fax (1) 4416703; e-mail sanomat.kat@formin.fi; internet www.finland.org.np; Chargé d'affaires a.i. PIRKKO-LIISA KYÖSTILÄ.

**France:** Lazimpat, POB 452, Kathmandu; tel. (1) 4412332; fax (1) 4419968; e-mail consulat@ambafrance-np.org; internet www.ambafrance-np.org; Ambassador GILLES-HENRY GARAULT.

**Germany:** Gyaneshwar, POB 226, Kathmandu; tel. (1) 4412786; fax (1) 4416899; e-mail info@kathmandu.diplo.de; internet www.kathmandu.diplo.de; Ambassador FRANZ RING.

**India:** 336 Kapurdhara Marg, POB 292, Kathmandu; tel. (1) 4410900; fax (1) 4428279; e-mail pic@eoiktm.org; internet www.south-asia.com/embassy-India; Ambassador RAKESH SOOD.

**Israel:** Bishramalaya House, Lazimpat, POB 371, Kathmandu; tel. (1) 4411811; fax (1) 4413920; e-mail info@kathmandu.mfa.gov.il; internet kathmandu.mfa.gov.il; Ambassador DAN STAV.

**Japan:** Panipokhari, POB 264, Kathmandu; tel. (1) 4426680; fax (1) 4414101; e-mail comjpn@mos.com.np; internet www.np.emb-japan.go.jp; Ambassador TATSUO MIZUNO.

**Korea, Democratic People's Republic:** Jhamsikhel, Lalitpur, Kathmandu; tel. (1) 5521855; fax (1) 5525394; Ambassador JANG YONG CHOL.

**Korea, Republic:** Red Cross Marg, Tahachal, POB 1058, Kathmandu; tel. (1) 4270172; fax (1) 4272041; e-mail koreaemb@mos.com.np; Ambassador NAM SANG-JUNG.

**Malaysia:** Block B, 2nd Floor, Karmachari Sanchaya Kosh Bldg, Pulchowk, POB 24372, Lalitpur, Kathmandu; tel. (1) 5010004; fax (1) 5010492; e-mail malkatmandu@kln.gov.my; internet www.kln.gov

.my/perwakilan/kathmandu; Ambassador Dato' ILANKOVAN KOLANDAVELU.

**Myanmar:** Chakupath, Patan Gate, Lalitpur, POB 2437, Kathmandu; tel. (1) 5521788; fax (1) 5523402; Ambassador U AUNG KHIN SOE.

**Norway:** Surya Court, Pulchowk, Lalitpur, POB 20765, Kathmandu; tel. (1) 5545307; fax (1) 5545226; e-mail emb.kathmandu@mfa.no; internet www.norway.org.np; Ambassador TORE TORENG.

**Pakistan:** Pushpanjali, Maharajgunj, Chakrapath, POB 202, Kathmandu; tel. (1) 4374024; fax (1) 4374012; e-mail parepktm@wlink.com.np; Ambassador SOHAIL AMIN.

**Russia:** Baluwatar, POB 123, Kathmandu; tel. (1) 4412155; fax (1) 4416571; e-mail ruspos@info.com.np; internet www.nepal.mid.ru; Ambassador ANDREI LEONIDOVICH TROFIMOV.

**Sri Lanka:** 'Shah Villa', Chundevi Rd, Maharajgunj, POB 8802, Kathmandu; tel. (1) 4720623; fax (1) 4720128; e-mail embassy@srilanka.info.com.np; Ambassador SUMITH NAKANDALA.

**Thailand:** 167/4 Ward No. 3, Maharajgunj-Bansbari Rd, POB 3333, Kathmandu; tel. (1) 4371410; fax (1) 4371409; e-mail thaiemb@wlink.com.np; internet www.thaiembassy.org/kathmandu; Ambassador VANVISA THAMRONGNAVASAWAT.

**United Kingdom:** Lainchaur, POB 106, Kathmandu; tel. (1) 4410583; fax (1) 4411789; e-mail britemb@wlink.com.np; internet www.britishembassy.gov.uk/nepal; Ambassador Dr ANDREW HALL.

**USA:** Panipokhari, POB 295, Kathmandu; tel. (1) 4411179; fax (1) 4419963; e-mail usembktm@state.gov; internet nepal.usembassy.gov; Ambassador NANCY J. POWELL.

# Judicial System

According to the Interim Constitution (which was officially endorsed in January 2007), the judicial system has three tiers: the Supreme Court (which is also a Court of Record), the Appellate Courts and the District Courts. The Supreme Court consists of a Chief Justice and a maximum of 14 other judges. The Chief Justice is appointed by the Prime Minister on the recommendation of the Constitutional Council; other Supreme Court, Appellate Court and District Court judges are nominated by the Chief Justice on the recommendation of the Judicial Council. A Constituent Assembly Court was established in February 2008 to deal with election matters.

**Supreme Court:** Ramashah Path, Kathmandue-mail info@supremecourt.gov.np; internet www.supremecourt.gov.np.

**Chief Justice:** KEDAR PRASAD GIRI.

**Judges of the Supreme Court:** MIN BAHADUR RAYAMAJHEE, ANUP RAJ SHARMA, RAM PRASAD SHRESTHA, KHIL RAJ REGMI, SHARDA SHRESTHA, BALA RAM K. C., TAP BAHADUR MAGAR, DAMODAR PRASAD SHARMA, RAM KUMAR PRASAD SHAH, KALYAN SHRESTHA, GAURI DHAKAL, TAHIR ALI ANSARI, RAJENDRA KOIRALA.

**Registrar:** Dr RAM KRISHNA TIMALSENA.

**Attorney-General:** YAGYAMURTI BANJADE.

# Religion

At the 2001 census, an estimated 80.6% of the population professed Hinduism (the religion of the royal family), while 10.7% were Buddhists and 4.2% Muslims. The actual number of Muslims in the country was considered to be much higher, owing to immigration from Bangladesh. There were an estimated 101,976 Christians in Nepal in 2001.

### BUDDHISM

**All Nepal Bhikkhu Association:** Vishwa Shanti Vihara (World Peace Temple), 465 Ekadantamarga, Minbhawan, New Baneshwar, POB 8973 NPC-327, Kathmandu; tel. (1) 4482984; fax (1) 4482250; e-mail vishwa@ntc.net.np; Treas. BHIKSHU BODHIJNANA.

**Nepal Buddhist Council:** Nahtole, Lalitpur 20; tel. (1) 5534277; e-mail nepal_bp@hotmail.com; Contact MAHISWOR RAJ BAJRACHARYA.

**United Trungram Buddhist Foundation:** Hattigauda, Bansbari, POB 3157, Kathmandu; tel. (1) 4370089; fax (1) 4370292; e-mail utbfnp@hotmail.com; Information Officer GANGJA SINGH GURUNG.

### CHRISTIANITY

#### Protestant Church

**Presbyterian Church of the Kingdom of Nepal:** POB 3237, Kathmandu; tel. and fax (1) 4524450.

#### The Roman Catholic Church

The Church is represented in Nepal by a single apostolic prefecture. At 31 December 2006 there were an estimated 6,942 adherents in the country.

**Apostolic Vicariate:** Church of the Assumption, Everest Postal Care P. Ltd, POB 8975 EPC-343, Kathmandu; tel. (1) 5542802; fax (1) 5521710; e-mail anath@wlink.com.np; f. 1983 as Catholic Mission; Vicar Apostolic Bishop ANTHONY FRANCIS SHARMA.

# The Press

### PRINCIPAL DAILIES

**The Commoner:** Naradevi, POB 203, Kathmandu; tel. (1) 4228236; f. 1956; English; Publr and Chief Editor GOPAL DASS SHRESTHA; circ. 7,000.

**Daily News:** Bhimsensthan, POB 171, Kathmandu; tel. (1) 4279147; fax (1) 4279544; e-mail manju_sakya@hotmail.com; f. 1983; Nepali and English; Chief Editor MANJU RATNA SAKYA; Publr SUBHA LAXMI SAKYA; circ. 20,000.

**Dainik Nirnaya:** Bhairawa; tel. (71) 520117; Nepali; Editor P. K. BHATTACHAN.

**Gorkhapatra:** Dharma Path, POB 23, Kathmandu; tel. (1) 4221478; fax (1) 4222921; internet www.gorkhapatra.org.np/gopa.php; f. 1901; Nepali; govt-owned; Chair. TEJ PRAKASH PANDIT; Editor-in-Chief SHIVA PRASAD BHATTARAI; circ. 75,000.

**The Himalayan Times:** International Media Network Nepal (Pvt) Ltd, APCA House, Baidya Khana Rd, Anam Nagar, POB 11651, Kathmandu; tel. (1) 4771489; fax (1) 4770701; e-mail editorial@thehimalayantimes.com; internet www.thehimalayantimes.com; f. 2001; English; Editor AJAYA BHADRA KHANAL.

**Janadoot:** Ga 2-549, Kamal Pokhari (in front of the Police Station), Kathmandu; tel. (1) 4412501; f. 1970; Nepali; Editor GOVINDA BIYOGI; circ. 6,500.

**Kantipur:** Kantipur Complex, Subhidhanagar, POB 8559, Kathmandu; tel. (1) 4480100; fax (1) 4470178; e-mail narayan@kantipur.com.np; internet www.kantipuronline.com; f. 1993; Nepali; Chief Exec. HEM RAJ GYAWALI; Editor NARAYAN WAGLE; circ. 210,000.

**Kathmandu Post:** Kantipur Complex, Subhidhanagar, POB 8559, Kathmandu; tel. (1) 4480100; fax (1) 4466320; e-mail kpost@kantipur.com.np; internet www.kantipuronline.com; f. 1993; English; Editor PRATEEK PRAHAN; circ. 40,000.

**Motherland:** POB 1184, Kathmandu; English; Editor MANINDRA RAJ SHRESTHA; circ. 5,000.

**Nepal Samacharpatra:** Sagarmatha Press, Ramshah Path, Kathmandu; e-mail sadhana@mail.com.np; internet newsofnepal.com; f. 1945; Nepali; Editor NARENDRA BILAS PANDEY; circ. 1,000.

**Nepali Hindi Daily:** 72 Kalinchok Marg, Maitidevi, POB 49, Kathmandu; tel. (1) 4436374; fax (1) 4435931; e-mail das@ntc.net.np; f. 1954; evening; Hindi; Publr UMA KANT DAS; Chief Editor VIJOY KUMAR DAS; circ. 100,000.

**Rajdhani:** Kathmandu; internet www.rajdhani.com.np; Editor KAPIL KAFLE; circ. 50,000.

**Rising Nepal:** Dharma Path, POB 1623, Kathmandu; tel. (1) 4222279; fax (1) 4224381; e-mail trn@gorkhapatra.org.np; internet www.gorkhapatra.org.np/trn.php; f. 1965; English; Editor-in-Chief AJAY SHUMSHER RANA; circ. 20,000.

**Samaj:** National Printing Press, Dillibazar, Kathmandu; f. 1954; Nepali; Editor MANI RAJ UPADHYAYA; circ. 5,000.

**Samaya:** Kamal Press, Ramshah Path, Kathmandu; f. 1954; Nepali; Editor MANIK LALL SHRESTHA; circ. 18,000.

**Space Time Dainik:** Iceberg Bldg, 3rd Floor, Putali Sadak, Kathmandu; tel. (1) 4419133; fax (1) 4419504; e-mail info@spacetimenetwork.com; internet www.spacetimenetwork.com; f. 2000; Nepali; Man. Dir JAMIM SHAH; circ. 60,000.

**Swatantra Samachar:** Kathmandu; tel. (1) 4419285; f. 1957; Editor MADAN DEV SHARMA; circ. 2,000.

### SELECTED PERIODICALS

**Agricultural Credit:** Agricultural Training and Research Institute, Agricultural Development Bank, Head Office, Ramshah Path, Panchayat Plaza, Kathmandu; tel. (1) 4220756; fax (1) 4225329; 2 a year; publ. by the Agricultural Development Bank; Chair. Dr NARAYAN N. KHATRI; Editor RUDRA PD DAHAL.

**Arpan:** Bhimsensthan, POB 285, Kathmandu; tel. (1) 4244450; fax (1) 4279544; e-mail manju_sakya@hotmail.com; internet www.nepalnews.com.arpan.php; f. 1964; weekly; Nepali; Publr and Chief Editor MANJU RATNA SAKYA; circ. 18,000.

**Awake Weekly Chronicle:** Kathmandu; English.

**Commerce:** Bhimsensthan, POB 171, Kathmandu; tel. (1) 4279636; fax (1) 4279544; e-mail manju_sakya@hotmail.com; f. 1971; monthly; English; Publr and Chief Editor MANJU RATNA SAKYA; Editor SUBHA LAXMI SAKYA; circ. 12,000.

**Current:** Gautam Marg, Kamalpokhari, Kathmandu; tel. (1) 4419484; fax (1) 4445406; e-mail current@namche.com; internet www.current.com.np; f. 1982; weekly; Nepali; publ. by private limited co; Man. Editor KIRAN GAUTAM; Chief Editor DEVENDRA GAUTAM; circ. 10,000.

**Cyber Post:** Kathmandu; fortnightly; computers, electronics.

**Foreign Affairs Journal:** 5/287 Lagon, Kathmandu; f. 1976; 3 a year; articles on Nepalese foreign relations and diary of main news events; Publr and Editor BHOLA BIKRUM RANA; circ. 5,000.

**Himal Southasian:** POB 24393, Kathmandu; tel. (1) 5547279; fax (1) 5552141; e-mail info@himalmag.com; internet www.himalmag.com; f. 1987; monthly; political, business, social and environmental issues throughout South Asia; Editor-in-Chief KANAK MANI DIXIT; Marketing Man. KOMAL MORE.

**The Independent:** Shankher Deep Bldg, Khichhapokhari, POB 3543, Kathmandu; tel. (1) 4249256; fax (1) 4226293; e-mail independ@mos.com.np; internet www.nepalnews.com/independent.htm; f. 1991; weekly; English; Editor SUBARNA B. CHHETRI.

**Janadharana** (People's Opinion): Kathmandu; e-mail janadharana@gmail.com; internet www.nepalnews.com.np/janadharana; weekly; independent; Editor NIMKANT PANDEY.

**Janmabhumi:** Janmabhumi Press, Tahachal, Kathmandu; tel. (1) 4280979; fax (1) 4274795; e-mail sirishnp@hotmail.com; f. 1970; weekly; Nepali; Publr and Editor SHIRISH BALLABH PRADHAN.

**Koseli:** Kathmandu; weekly; Nepali.

**Madhuparka:** Dharmapath, POB 23, Kathmandu; tel. (1) 4222278; f. 1986; monthly; Nepali; literary; Editor-in-Chief KRISHNA BHAKTA SHRESTHA; circ. 20,000.

**Matribhoomi** (Nepali Weekly): Ga 2-549, Kamal Pokhari (in front of the Police Station), Kathmandu; tel. (1) 4412501; weekly; Nepali; Editor GOVINDA BIYOGI.

**Mulyankan:** Kathmandu; monthly, left-wing; Editor SHYAM SHRESTHA.

**Nepal:** Kantipur Complex, Subhidhanagar, POB 8559, Kathmandu; tel. (1) 4480100; fax (1) 4470178; e-mail feedback@kantipuronline.com; internet www.kantipuronline.com/Nepal; f. 2000; fortnightly; Nepali; Editor KISHORE NEPAL.

**Nepal Chronicle:** Maruhiti; weekly; English; Publr and Editor CHANDRA LAL JHA.

**Nepal Overseas Trade Statistics:** Trade and Export Promotion Centre, Pulchowk, Lalitpur, POB 825, Kathmandu; tel. (1) 5525348; fax (1) 5525464; e-mail info@tepc.gov.np; internet www.tepc.gov.np; annual; English.

**Nepal Trade and Export Bulletin:** Trade and Export Promotion Centre, Pulchowk, Lalitpur, POB 825, Kathmandu; tel. (1) 5532642; fax (1) 5525464; e-mail info@tepc.gov.np; internet www.tepc.gov.np; 3 a year; English; Editor BADRI ADHIKARY.

**Nepali Times:** Himalmedia Pvt Ltd, POB 7251, Kathmandu; tel. (1) 5250333; fax (1) 5251013; e-mail editors@nepalitimes.com; internet www.nepalitimes.com; f. 2000; weekly; English; publ. by Himal Media Pvt Ltd; Publr and Chief Editor KUNDA DIXIT; circ. 15,000.

**People's Review:** Pipalbot, Dillibazar, POB 3052, Kathmandu; tel. (1) 4417352; fax (1) 4438797; e-mail preview@ntc.net.np; internet www.peoplesreview.com.np; weekly; English; Editor-in-Chief PUSHPA RAJ PRADHAN; circ. 15,000.

**Rastrabani:** Kathmandu; tel. (1) 4410339; weekly; Nepali; Chief Editor HARI LAMSAL.

**Sanghu Weekly:** Kathmandu; weekly; Editor GOPAL BUDHATHOKI.

**Sanibariya:** Kathmandu; weekly.

**Saptahik Weekly:** Kantipur Complex, Subhidhanagar, POB 8559, Kathmandu; tel. (1) 4480100; fax (1) 4470178; internet www.kantipuronline.com/saptahic_html/saptahik; f. 1997; weekly; Nepali; news and entertainment; Editor SUBASH DHAKAL.

**Spotlight:** POB 7256, Kathmandu; tel. (1) 4410772; e-mail spotlight@mos.com.np; f. 1991; weekly; English; Editor MADHAV KUMAR RIMAL.

**Swatantra Manch Weekly:** POB 49, Kathmandu; tel. (1) 4436374; fax (1) 4435931; e-mail das@ntc.net.np; f. 1985; independent; weekly; Nepali; Publr and Chief Editor VIJOY KUMAR DAS; circ. 30,000.

**The Telegraph:** Ghattekulo, Dillibazar, POB 4063, Kathmandu; tel. (1) 4419370; e-mail tgw@ntc.net.np; weekly; English; Chief Editor NARENDRA P. UPADHYAYA.

**Vashudha:** Makhan, Kathmandu; monthly; English; social, political and economic affairs; Publr and Editor T. L. SHRESTHA.

### NEWS AGENCY

**Rastriya Samachar Samiti (RSS):** Singa Darbar Plaza, Kathmandu; tel. (1) 4262724; fax (1) 4262744; e-mail info@rss.com.np; internet www.rss.com.np; f. 1962; state-operated; Gen. Man. JAYA SHANKAR MAHATO; Chair. MITHARAM BISWOKARMA DUKHI.

### PRESS ASSOCIATIONS

**Federation of Nepalese Journalists (FNJ):** Media Village, Sinamangal, Kathmandu; tel. (1) 4490063; fax (1) 4490085; e-mail fnjnepal@mail.com.np; internet www.fnjnepal.org; f. 1956; Pres. DHARMENDRA JHA; Gen. Sec. K. C. POSHAN.

**Nepal Journalists' Association (NJA):** Maitighar, POB 285, Kathmandu; tel. (1) 4262426; fax (1) 4279544; e-mail manju_sakya@hotmail.com; internet www.nja.org.np; 5,400 mems; Pres. MANJU RATNA SAKYA; Gen. Sec. NIRMAL KUMAR ARYAL.

**Press Council:** Sanchargram, Tilganga, POB 3077, Kathmandu; tel. (1) 4469799; fax (1) 4469894; e-mail prescoun_mdf@wlink.com.np; internet www.presscouncilnepal.org; f. 1970; Chair. RAJENDRA DAHAL; Sec. MUKUNDA PRASAD ACHARYA.

## Publishers

**Educational Enterprise (Pvt) Ltd:** Mahankalsthan, POB 1124, Kathmandu; tel. (1) 4223749; e-mail ishwarbshrestha@yahoo.com; f. 1962; educational and technical; Dir MOHAN SHRESTHA.

**Himal Books:** Himal Association, Patan Dhoka, POB 166, Lalitpur, Kathmandu; tel. (1) 5542544; fax (1) 5541196; e-mail books@himalassociation.org; internet www.himalassociation.org/himalbooks; f. 1992; subsidiary operation of Himal Association; general interest and academic publications in English and Nepali; Exec. Dir BASANTA THAPA.

**International Standards Books and Periodicals (Pvt) Ltd:** Bhotahity Bazaar, Chowk Bhitra, POB 3000, Kathmandu 44601; tel. (1) 4262815; fax (1) 4264179; e-mail u2@ccsl.com.np; f. 1991; Chief Man. Dir YOGYNDRA LALL CHHIPA; Chief Exec. and Man. Dir GANESH LALL SINGH CHHIPA.

**Lakoul Press:** Palpa-Tansen, Kathmandu; educational and physical sciences.

**Mahabir Singh Chiniya Main:** Makhan Tola, Kathmandu.

**Mandass Memorials Publications:** Kathmandu; Man. BASANT RAJ TULADHAR.

**Pilgrims Book House:** Thamel, POB 3872, Kathmandu; tel. (1) 4700942; fax (1) 4700943; e-mail pilgrims@wlink.com.np; internet www.pilgrimsbooks.com; f. 1986; Asian studies, religion and travel; Propr PUSHPA TIWARI.

**Pilgrims Publishing Nepal (Pvt) Ltd:** Goldhunga 4, POB 21646, Kathmandu; tel. (1) 4356764; fax (1) 4700544; e-mail johnsasia@gmail.com; internet www.pilgrimsbooks.com; f. 2000; Exec. Dir JOHN SNYDER; Man. Dir BISHOW BHATTA.

**Ratna Pustak Bhandar:** 71 'Ga' Bank Marg, POB 98, Kathmandu; tel. (1) 4223026; fax (1) 4248421; e-mail rpb@wlink.com.np; f. 1945; textbooks, general, non-fiction and fiction; Propr GOVINDA PRASAD SHRESTHA.

**Royal Nepal Academy:** Kamaladi, Kathmandu; tel. (1) 4221241; fax (1) 4221175; f. 1957; languages, literature, social sciences, art and philosophy; Dep. Admin. Chief T. D. BHANDARI.

**Sajha Prakashan:** Pulchowk, Lalitpur, POB 20259, Kathmandu; tel. (1) 5521118; fax (1) 5544236; e-mail sajhap@wlink.com.np; internet www.sajha.org.np; f. 1964; educational, literary and general; Chair. BISHNU PRASAD GHIMIRE; Gen. Man. Dr DHRUBA CHANDRA GAUTAM.

**Trans Asian Media Pvt Ltd:** Thapathali Crossing, POB 5320, Kathmandu; tel. (1) 4242895; fax (1) 4223889; Man. Editor SHYAM GOENKA.

### GOVERNMENT PUBLISHING HOUSE

**Department of Information:** Ministry of Information and Communications, Singha Durbar, Kathmandu; tel. (1) 4220150; fax (1) 4221729; internet www.moic.gov.np/Departments/Printing.

## Broadcasting and Communications

### TELECOMMUNICATIONS

**Nepal Telecommunications Authority:** 768/12 Thir Bam Sadhak, POB 9754, Baluwatar, Kathmandu; tel. (1) 4446001; fax (1) 4446006; e-mail info@nta.gov.np; internet www.nta.gov.np; telecommunications regulatory body; f. 1998; Chair. DINESH KUMAR SHARMA.

**Nepal Telecom** (Nepal Doorsanchar Co Ltd): Bhadrakali Plaza, POB 11803, Kathmandu; tel. (1) 4210202; fax (1) 4222424; e-mail rkt@ntc.net.np; internet www.ntc.com.np; f. 1975; operates landline and mobile services; 85% state-owned, 10% owned by Nepalese public, 5% owned by Nepal Telecom employees; Man. Dir SUGAT RATNA KANSAKAR.

**Spice Nepal (Pvt) Ltd (SNPL):** Krishna Tower, Buddhanagar, New Baneshwor, Kathmandu; tel. (1) 5554444; fax (1) 5554538; e-mail info@spicenepal.com; internet www.spicenepal.com; f. 2002; jt venture between Kazakhstan-based Group VISOR (75%), Raj Group (20%) and India-based Spice Cell (5%); operates GSM mobile network; Chair. RAJ BAHADUR SINGH; CEO DMITRY ZAIKA.

**STM Telecom Sanchar:** 768/47 Thirbam Sadak, Baluwatar, Kathmandu; tel. (1) 4445981; fax (1) 44419366; e-mail marketing@stmnetworks.com; internet www.stmi.com; f. 2003 as jt venture between the USA, Thailand and Nepal; awarded World Bank-funded project to provide rural telecommunication services to eastern region of Nepal; CEO ABHINAV PURI.

**United Telecom:** Ground Floor, Triveni Complex, Putali Sadak, Kathmandu; tel. (1) 2000050; fax (1) 2499999; e-mail info@utlnepal.com; internet www.utlnepal.com; f. 2003; jt venture between Indian-owned Mahanagar Telephone Nigam Ltd, Videsh Sanchar Nigam Ltd, Telecom Consultants India, and Nepal Venture (Pvt) Ltd; Chair. Shri S. K. GUPTA.

### BROADCASTING

#### Radio

In July 2005 there were 47 commercial and community radio stations in Nepal. A media ordinance adopted by the King in October of that year banned private radio stations in the country from broadcasting news or information-related programmes. Following the April 2006 uprising and revocation of the King's direct rule, the seven-party alliance Government resumed issuing licences to independent broadcasters; by February 2008 licences had been granted to 254 FM operators.

**Radio Nepal:** Radio Broadcasting Service, Government of Nepal, Singha Durbar, POB 634, Kathmandu; tel. (1) 4211910; fax (1) 4211952; e-mail radio@rne.wlink.com.np; internet www.radionepal.org; f. 1951; broadcasts on short wave, medium wave and FM frequencies in 20 regional languages, incl. Nepali and English, for 18 hours daily (incl. two hours of regional broadcasting in the morning and evening); short-wave station at Khumaltar and medium-wave stations at Bhainsepati, Pokhara, Surkhet, Dipayal, Bardibas and Dharan; FM stations at Kathmandu, Kanchanpur, Rupandhi, Chitwan, Makawanpur, Bara, Jumla, Mustang, Ilam, Simikot and Humla; Exec. Dir R. S. KARKI.

**Himalaya Broadcasting Co** (Radio HBC 94 FM): POB 8974, CPC 94, Kathmandu; tel. (1) 4489618; fax (1) 4499788; e-mail hbc94fm@hbc.com.np; internet www.hbc.com.np; f. 1999.

**Hits FM:** POB 21912, Baneshwor, Kathmandu; tel. (1) 4780534; fax (1) 4780543; e-mail info@hitsfm.com.np; internet www.hitsfm.com.np; f. 1996; broadcasts 24 hrs daily; Exec. Dir JEEVAN SHRESTHA.

**Image FM** (Kath FM): POB 5566, Kathmandu; tel. (1) 4230368; fax (1) 4241260; e-mail kath979@wlink.com.np; internet www.imagechannels.com; f. 1999; Station Man. BHARAT SHAKYA.

**Kantipur FM:** Kantipur Complex, Subhidhanagar, POB 8559, Kathmandu; tel. (1) 4480100; fax (1) 4470178; e-mail kfm@kanti.mos.com.np; f. 1998; broadcasts 24 hrs daily; Man. Dir BINOD RAJ GYAWALI; Station Man. PRABHAT RIMAL.

**Radio Lumbini:** Aanandabane VDC, Ward No. 3, Manigram, Rupandehi, Lumbini; tel. (71) 561003; fax (71) 561545; e-mail lumbinifm@mos.com.np; internet www.radiolumbini.org; f. 2000; Station Man. MOHAN CHAPAGAIN.

**Radio Sagarmatha:** Bakhundol, Lalitpur, GPOB 6958, Kathmandu; tel. (1) 5528091; fax (1) 5530227; e-mail stationmanager@radiosagarmatha.org; internet www.radiosagarmatha.org; f. 1997; independent; Chair. LAXMAN UPRETI; Station Man. MOHAN BISTA.

**Times FM:** GPOB 8975, EPC 906, Jawalakhel, Lalitpur, Kathmandu; tel. and fax (1) 5539171; e-mail timesfm@hotnepal.com; Man. Dir R. K. SHRESTHA.

#### Television

In 1986 Nepal's first television station began broadcasting within the Kathmandu valley.

**Nepal Television Corpn:** Singha Durbar, POB 3826, Kathmandu; tel. (1) 4220348; fax (1) 4228312; internet neptv.com.np; f. 1985; operates NTV and NTV2; programmes in Nepali (50%), English (25%) and Hindi/Urdu (25%); regional station at Kohalpur; Chair. and Gen. Man. Dr RISHI RAJ BARAL.

**Avenues TV:** 11 Avenues Plaza, Teku Rd, Ganeshman Marga, Kathmandu; tel. (1) 4227222; fax (1) 4248811; e-mail atv@avenues.tv; f. 2003; news service.

**Image Channel:** 369 Narayan Gopal Sadak, POB 9581, Lazimpat, Kathmandu; tel. (1) 4433141; fax (1) 4432707; e-mail ichannel@wlink.com.np; internet www.imagechannels.com; f. 2003; privately owned; Chair. R. K. MANANDHAR.

**Kantipur Television Network (KTV):** Kantipur Complex, Subhidhanagar, POB 8559, Kathmandu; tel. (1) 4480100; fax (1) 4470178; f. 2003; Chair. HEM RAJ GYAWALI; Man. Dir JEEWA LAMICHHANE.

## Finance

(auth. = authorized; cap. = capital; m. = million; dep. = deposits; res = reserves; brs = branches; amounts in Nepalese rupees)

### BANKING

#### Central Bank

**Nepal Rastra Bank:** Central Office, Baluwatar, POB 73, Kathmandu; tel. (1) 4411834; fax (1) 4414955; e-mail gsd@nrb.org.np; internet www.nrb.org.np; f. 1956; bank of issue; 100% state-owned; cap. 3,000.0m., res 29,191.1m., dep. 27,745.7m. (July 2004); Gov. KRISHNA BAHADUR MANANDHAR (acting); 9 brs.

#### Domestic Commercial Banks

**Kumari Bank Ltd:** Putalisadak, POB 21128, Kathmandu; tel. (1) 4232112; fax (1) 4231960; e-mail info@kbl.com.np; internet www.kumaribank.com; f. 2001; auth. cap. 625m., res 218.6m., dep. 8,020.4m. (July 2006); Chair. NOOR PRATAP RANA.

**Nepal Bank Ltd:** Nepal Bank Bldg, Dharmapath, New Rd, POB 36, Kathmandu; tel. (1) 4222397; fax (1) 4220414; e-mail craigmca@nepalbank.com.np; internet www.nepalbank.com.np; f. 1937; 40% state-owned, 60% owned by Nepalese public; CEO CRAIG MCALLISTER; 96 brs.

**Nepal Industrial and Commercial Bank Ltd (NIC Bank):** Kamaladi, Ganeshthan, POB 7367, Kathmandu; tel. (1) 4222336; fax (1) 4241865; e-mail kamaladi@nicbank.com.np; internet www.nicbank.com.np; f. 1998; privately owned; cap. 600.0m., res 141.5m., dep. 9,515.2m. (July 2006); Chair. JAGDISH PRASAD AGRAWAL; CEO SASHIN JOSHI; 10 brs.

**Rastriya Banijya Bank** (National Commercial Bank): POB 8368, Singha Durbar Plaza, Kathmandu; tel. (1) 4252595; fax (1) 4252931; e-mail secretary@rbb.com.np; internet www.rbb.com.np; f. 1966; 100% state-owned; Chair. Dr BHOLA NATH CHALISE; CEO JANARDAN ACHARYA; 114 brs, 4 regional offices.

#### Joint-venture Banks

**Bank of Kathmandu Ltd:** Kamal Pokhari, POB 9044, Kathmandu; tel. (1) 4414541; fax (1) 4418990; e-mail info@bok.com.np; internet www.bok.com.np; f. 1993; 58% owned by Nepalese public, 42% by local promoters; cap. 463.6m., res 376.2m., dep. 10,485.4m. (July 2006); Chair. SANJAY B. SHAH; Man. Dir RADHESH PANT.

**Everest Bank Ltd:** POB 13384, EBL House, Lazimpat, Kathmandu; tel. (1) 4443377; fax (1) 4443160; e-mail ebl@mos.com.np; internet www.everestbankltd.com; f. 1994; 50% owned by directors, 20% by Punjab National Bank (India) and 30% by the Nepalese public; cap. 518.0m., res 336.2m., dep. 14,118.3m. (July 2006); Chair. BISHNU KRISHNA SHRESTHA; Exec. Dir JASPAL SINGH JASS; 22 brs.

**Global Bank Ltd:** Adarshanagar, Birgunj 13, POB 45, Parsa; tel. (1) 530337; fax (1) 530339; internet www.globalbanknepal.com; f. 2006; Chair. CHANDRA PRASAD DHAKAL; CEO SUMAN NEUPANE.

**Himalayan Bank Ltd:** Karmachari Sanchaya Kosh Bldg, Tridevi Marg, Thamel, POB 20590, Kathmandu; tel. (1) 4227749; fax (1) 4222800; e-mail hbl@hbl.com.np; internet www.himalayanbank.com; f. 1993; 20% owned by Habib Bank Ltd (Pakistan); cap. 772.2m., res 837.4m., dep. 26,924.4m. (July 2006); Chair. MANOJ BAHADUR SHRESTHA; CEO ASOKE S. J. B. RANA; 8 brs.

**Laxmi Bank Ltd:** Hattisar, POB 19593, Kathmandu; tel. (51) 530394; fax (51) 530393; e-mail info@laxmibank.com; internet www.laxmibank.com; f. 2001; cap. 609.9m., res 15.7m., dep. 4,449.1m. (July 2006); Chair. MOHAN GOPAL KHETAN; CEO SUMAN JOSHI.

**Nabil Bank Ltd (Nabil):** Nabil House, Kamaladi, POB 3729, Kathmandu; tel. (1) 4429546; fax (1) 4429548; e-mail nabil@nabilbank.com; internet www.nabilbank.com; f. 1984 as Nepal Arab Bank Ltd, name changed as above Jan. 2000; 50% owned by National Bank of Bangladesh, 30% by the Nepalese public and 20% by Nepalese govt financial institutions; cap. 491.7m., res 2,068.7m., dep. 23,342.3m. (July 2007); Chair. SATYENDRA PYARA SHRESTHA; Chief. Exec. ANIL SHAH; 27 brs.

**Nepal Bangladesh Bank Ltd:** Bijuli Bazar, New Baneshwor, POB 9062, Kathmandu; tel. (1) 4783976; fax (1) 4780316; e-mail nbblho@nbbl.com.np; internet www.nbbl.com.np; f. 1994; 50% owned by

International Finance Investment and Commerce Bank Ltd (Bangladesh), 20% by Nepalese promoters and 30% public issue; cap. 359.9m., res 324.0m., dep. 10,580.7m. (July 2003); CEO SHOVAN DEV PANT; Chair. JEET BAHADUR SHRESTHA; 15 brs.

**Nepal Credit and Commerce Bank Ltd:** NB Bldg, Bagh Bazar, Kathmandu; tel. (1) 4246991; fax (1) 4244610; e-mail nccb@nccbank.com.np; internet www.nccbank.com.np; f. as Nepal Bank of Ceylon, reconstituted as above in Sept. 2002 after Bank of Ceylon (Sri Lanka) sold its shares to NB Group (Nepal); Chair. PRITHIVI RAJ LIGAL; CEO RATNA RAJ BAJRACHARYA; 17 brs.

**Nepal Investment Bank Ltd:** Durbar Marg, POB 3412, Kathmandu; tel. (1) 4228229; fax (1) 4226349; e-mail info@nibl.com.np; internet www.nibl.com.np; f. 1986 as Nepal Indosuez Bank Ltd, name changed as above in June 2002; 50% owned by a consortium of Nepalese investors, 20% by general public, 15% by Rastriya Banijya Bank and 15% by Rastriya Beema Sansthan; cap. 590.6m., res 778.9m., dep. 19,496.1m. (July 2006); Chair. and Chief Exec. PRITHIVI BAHADUR PANDE; 12 brs.

**Nepal SBI Bank Ltd:** Corporate Office, Hattisar, POB 6049, Kathmandu; tel. (1) 4435516; fax (1) 4435612; e-mail nsblco@nsbl.com.np; internet www.nsbl.com.np; f. 1993; 50% owned by State Bank of India, 30% by Nepalese public, 15% by Employees' Provident Fund (Nepal) and 5% by Agricultural Development Bank (Nepal); Chair. B. K. SHRESTHA; Man. Dir V. P. DANI.

**Nepal Sri Lanka Merchant Bank Ltd:** NSLMB Bldg, Kalamadi, POB 12248, Kathmandu; tel. (1) 4440300; fax (1) 4441034; e-mail nslmb@info.com.np; Exec. Dir VED MAN SINGH MALLA.

**Standard Chartered Bank Nepal Ltd:** Grindlays Bhavan, Naya Baneshwor, POB 3990, Kathmandu; tel. (1) 4246753; fax (1) 4226762; internet www.standardchartered.com/np; f. 1986 as Nepal Grindlays Bank; name changed in July 2001; 75% owned by Standard Chartered Bank (United Kingdom) and 25% by the Nepalese public; cap. 374.6m., res 1,008.9m., dep. 23,061m. (July 2006); Chair. CHRISTOPHER LOW; CEO SUJIT MUNDUL; 7 brs.

#### Banking Organization

**Nepal Bankers' Association (NBA):** Heritage Plaza, C and D Block, 2nd Floor, Kamaladi, Kathmandu; e-mail info@nepalbankers.com; internet www.nepalbankers.com; Pres. RADHESH PANT.

#### Development Finance Organizations

**Agricultural Development Bank:** Ramshah Path, Kathmandu; tel. (1) 4262885; fax (1) 4262616; e-mail info@adbn.gov.np; internet www.adbn.gov.np; f. 1968; 93.6% state-owned, 2.1% owned by the Nepal Rastra Bank, and 4.3% by co-operatives and private individuals; specialized agricultural credit institution providing credit for agricultural development to co-operatives, individuals and asscns; receives deposits from individuals, co-operatives and other asscns to generate savings in the agricultural sector; acts as Government's implementing agency for small farmers' group development project, assisted by the Asian Development Bank and financed by the UN Development Programme; operational networks include 14 zonal offices, 37 brs, 92 sub-brs, 52 depots and 160 small farmers' development projects, three Zonal Training Centres, two Appropriate Technology Units; Chair. MUKUNDA PRASAD ARJYAL; Gen. Man. YOGESWOR PANT.

**Nepal Development Bank:** Heritage Plaza, POB 11017, Kamaladi, Kathmandu; tel. (1) 4254639; fax (1) 4245753; e-mail ndevbank@ndbl.com.np; internet www.ndevbank.com; f. 1998; Chair. AMAR GURUNG; CEO SUNANDA B. SHRESTHA.

**Nepal Housing Development Finance Co Ltd:** New Baneswor, POB 5624, Kathmandu; tel. (1) 4780259; fax (1) 4792753; e-mail info@nepalhousing.com; internet www.nepalhousing.com; Chair. BINOD KUMAR GURAGAI; Gen. Man. ACHUT RAJ SAPKOTA.

**Nepal Industrial Development Corpn (NIDC):** NIDC Bldg, Durbar Marg, POB 10, Kathmandu; tel. (1) 4228322; fax (1) 4227428; e-mail nidc@wlink.com.np; internet www.nidc.org.np; f. 1959; state-owned; holds investments of 5,609.9m. in 1,125 industrial enterprises (2000/01); offers financial and technical assistance to private-sector industries; in 2000/01 approved a total of 9.41m. in loans and working capital, and disbursed 8.17m.; Gen. Man. UTTAM NARAYAN SHRESTHA.

### STOCK EXCHANGE

**Nepal Stock Exchange Ltd (NEPSE):** Singha Durbar Plaza, POB 1550, Kathmandu; tel. (1) 4250735; fax (1) 4262538; e-mail info@nepalstock.com; internet www.nepalstock.com; f. 1976; reorg. 1984; converted in 1993 from Securities Exchange Centre Ltd to Nepal Stock Exchange Ltd; 147 listed cos, 139 scripts; Chair. BIMAL PRADAD WAGLE; Gen. Man. REWAT BAHADUR KARKI.

### INSURANCE

**Alliance Insurance Co Ltd:** Durbar Marg, POB 10811, Kathmandu; tel. (1) 4222836; fax (1) 4241411; e-mail sk@aic.wlink.com.np.

**Everest Insurance Co Ltd:** Hattisar, POB 10675, Kathmandu; tel. (1) 4444717; fax (1) 4444366; e-mail eveinsco@mos.com.np; internet www.everestinsurance.com; Chair. RAJENDRA K. KHETAN.

**Himalayan General Insurance Co Ltd:** Durbar Marg, POB 148, Kathmandu; tel. (1) 4231581; fax (1) 4223906; e-mail info@thamel.com; internet www.thamel.com/hgi; f. 1993; CEO MAHENDRA KRISHNA SHRESTHA.

**National Insurance Co Ltd:** Tripureswor, POB 376, Kathmandu; tel. (1) 4250710; fax (1) 4261289; e-mail natinsur@ccsl.com.np; Man. A. S. KOHLI.

**National Life and General Insurance Co Ltd:** Lazimpat, POB 4332, Kathmandu; tel. (1) 4412625; fax (1) 4416427; e-mail nlgi@mail.com.np; Chief Exec. S. K. SINGH; Pres. OM SINGH.

**Neco Insurance Ltd:** Hattisar, POB 12271, Lal Durbar, Kathmandu; tel. (1) 4427354; fax (1) 4418761; e-mail info@necoins.com.np; f. 1994; Chair. JANARDAN AACHARYA; CEO ANIL SHARMA.

**Nepal Insurance Co Ltd:** NIC Bldg, Kamaladi, POB 3623, Kathmandu; tel. (1) 4221353; fax (1) 4225446; e-mail info@nepalinsurance.com; internet www.nepalinsurance.com; Chair. BHARAT KARKI; Man. Dir NIRMAL KUMAR BARAL.

**The Oriental Insurance Co Ltd:** Jyoti Bhavan, POB 165, Kathmandu; tel. (1) 4221448; fax (1) 4223419; e-mail oriental@wlink.com.np; CEO Dr MADHUSUDAN KUMAR.

**Premier Insurance Co (Nepal) Ltd:** Tripureswor Plaza, Tripureswor, POB 9183, Kathmandu; tel. (1) 4259567; fax (1) 4249708; e-mail premier@picl.com.np; internet www.premier-insurance.com.np; f. 1994; Pres. RADHE SHYAM GORKHALI.

**Rastriya Beema Sansthan** (National Insurance Corpn): RBS Bldg, Ramshah Path, POB 527, Kathmandu; tel. (1) 4213882; fax (1) 4262610; e-mail beema@wlink.com.np; internet www.beema.com.np; f. 1967; Gen. Man. BIR BIKRAM RAXAMAJHI.

**Sagarmatha Insurance Co Ltd:** Kathmandu Plaza, Block Y, 4th Floor, Kamaladi, POB 12211, Kathmandu; tel. (1) 4240896; fax (1) 4247947; e-mail sagarmatha@insurance.wlink.com.np; Exec. Dir K. B. BASNYAT.

**United Insurance Co (Nepal) Ltd:** I. J. Plaza, Durbar Marg, POB 9075, Kathmandu; tel. (1) 4246686; fax (1) 4246687; e-mail uic@mail.com.np; internet www.unitedinsurance.com.np; Chair. RAVI BHAKTA SHRESTHA; Gen. Man. RABI MAN JOSHI.

## Trade and Industry

### GOVERNMENT AGENCY

**National Planning Commission (NPC):** Singha Durbar, POB 1284, Kathmandu; tel. (1) 4225879; fax (1) 4226500; e-mail npcs@npcnepal.gov.np; internet www.npc.gov.np; Vice-Chair. JAGADISH CHANDRA POKHAREL.

### DEVELOPMENT ORGANIZATIONS

**National Productivity and Economic Development Centre:** Balaju Industrial District, POB 1318, Kathmandu; tel. (1) 4350566; fax (1) 4350530; e-mail npedc@wlink.com.np; internet www.npedc-nepal.org; functions as secretariat of National Productivity Council; provides services for industrial promotion and productivity improvement through planning research, consultancy, training, seminars and information services; Gen. Man. SHAMBHU NATH PANT (acting).

**National Tea and Coffee Development Board (NTCDB):** New Baneshwor, POB 9683, Kathmandu; tel. (1) 4495792; fax (1) 4497941; e-mail ntcdb@hons.com.np; internet teacoffee.gov.np; f. 1992 to promote and expand the Nepalese tea industry; Vice-Chair. SURAJ VAIDYA.

**National Trading Ltd:** Teku, POB 128, Kathmandu; tel. (1) 4225799; fax (1) 4225151; e-mail info@nationaltrading.com.np; internet www.nationaltrading.com.np; f. 1962; govt-owned; imports and distributes construction materials and raw materials for industry; also machinery, vehicles and consumer goods; operates bonded warehouse, duty-free shop and related activities; brs in all major towns; Chair. L. P. AGRAWAL.

**Nepal Foreign Trade Association:** Bagmati Chamber, 1st Floor, Milan Marg, Teku, POB 541, Kathmandu; tel. (1) 4223784; fax (1) 4247159; e-mail nfta@mos.com.np; f. 1972; Pres. AKHIL KUMAR CHAPAGAIN; Vice-Pres. SATISH KUMAR MORE; 431 mems.

**Nepal Tea Development Corpn Ltd:** Triveni Complex, Putali Sadak, Kathmandu; tel. (1) 4224074; fax (1) 4266133; e-mail ntdc@trivenionline.com; internet www.ntdcltd.com; f. 1966; privatized in early 2000s; commercial production of tea; Contact SUBHASH C. SHANGHAI.

**Trade and Export Promotion Centre (TPC):** Na Tole, Pulchowk, Lalitpur, POB 825, Kathmandu; tel. (1) 5525898; fax (1) 5525464; e-mail info@tepc.gov.np; internet www.tepc.gov.np; f. 1971; govt-owned; Chair. PURSHOTTAM OJHA.

### CHAMBERS OF COMMERCE

**Federation of Nepalese Chambers of Commerce and Industry (FNCCI):** Pachali Shahid Shukra FNCCI Milan Marg, Teku, POB 269, Kathmandu; tel. (1) 4262061; fax (1) 4261022; e-mail fncci@mos.com.np; internet www.fncci.org; f. 1965; comprises 91 District Municipality Chambers (DCCIs), 66 Commodity Associations, 376 leading industrial and commercial undertakings in both the public and private sector, and 10 Bi-national Chambers; publishes annual *Nepal and the World: A Statistical Profile* and directory of members every three years; Pres. KUSH KUMAR JOSHI; Dir-Gen. NEGH NATH NEUPANE.

**Birganj Chamber of Commerce and Industries:** Hospital Rd, Birganj; tel. (51) 522290; fax (51) 526049; e-mail bicci@atcnet.com.np; 605 mems; Pres. VIJAY KUMAR SARAWAGI.

**Lalitpur Chamber of Commerce and Industry:** Mangal Bazar, Patan Durbar Sq., POB 26, Lalitpur; tel. (1) 5521740; fax (1) 5530661; e-mail lcci@mos.com.np; f. 1967; Pres. UMESH LAL AMATYA; Sec.-Gen. NARESH KUMAR SHRESTHA.

**Nepal Chamber of Commerce:** Chamber Bhavan, Kantipath, POB 198, Kathmandu; tel. (1) 4230947; fax (1) 4229998; e-mail chamber@wlink.com.np; internet www.nepalchamber.org; f. 1952; non-profit org. promoting industrial and commercial development; 8,000 regd cos and 1,600 ordinary mems; Pres. SURENDRA BIR MALAKAR; Sec.-Gen. BHAKTA BAHADUR MALLA.

### INDUSTRIAL AND TRADE ASSOCIATIONS

**Association of Craft Producers:** Ravi Bhawan Mode, POB 3701, Kathmandu; tel. (1) 4275108; fax (1) 4272676; e-mail craftacp@mos.com.np; internet acp.org.np; f. 1984; local non-profit org. providing technical, marketing and management services for craft producers; manufacturer, exporter and retailer of handicraft goods; Exec. Dir MEERA BHATTARAI; Programme Dir REVITA SHRESTHA.

**Association of Forest-based Industries and Trade:** Thapathali, POB 2798, Kathmandu; tel. (1) 4216020.

**Association of Nepalese Rice, Oil and Pulses Industries:** POB 20782, Radha Bhawvan, Tripureswor, Kathmandu; tel. (1) 4215676; e-mail nfma@mcmail.com.np; Pres. TOLA RAM DUGAR; Gen. Sec. CHANDRA KRISHNA KARMACHARYA.

**Association of Pharmaceutical Producers of Nepal:** Babar Mahal, POB 21721, Maitighar, Kathmandu; tel. and fax (1) 4231871; e-mail appon@wlink.com.np; Pres. PRADEEP MAN VAIDYA; Sec.-Gen. UMESH LAL SHRESTHA.

**Cargo Agents Association of Nepal:** Thamel, POB 5355, Kathmandu; tel. (1) 4419019; fax (1) 4419858.

**Central Carpet Industries Association of Nepal:** Maitighar, Babar Mahal, POB 2419, Kathmandu; tel. (1) 4259400; fax (1) 4262458; e-mail ccia@enet.com.np; internet www.nepalcarpet.org; Pres. A. G. SHERPA; Gen. Sec. KAPIL PRASAD BAZGAIN.

**Computer Association of Nepal:** 453 Maitidevi, Kathmandu; tel. (1) 4432700; fax (1) 4441998; e-mail info@can.org.np; internet www.can.org.np; f. 1992; asscn of the IT Businessmen's Organization; Pres. BIPLAV MAN SINGH.

**Federation of Handicrafts Associations of Nepal:** Upma Marg, Thapathali, POB 784, Kathmandu; tel. (1) 4244231; fax (1) 4222940; e-mail han@wlink.com.np; internet www.nepalhandicraft.org.np; f. 1972; Pres. PUSKAR MAN SHAKYA.

**Federation of Nepal Cottage and Small Industries (FNCSI):** Chabahil, POB 6530, Kathmandu; tel. (1) 4491528; fax (1) 4468337; e-mail fncsi@ntc.net.np; internet www.fncsi.org.np; business networks in 70 districts; represents interests and promotes development of nation's micro, cottage and small industries; 30,000 general mems (2007); Pres. ANG DENDI SHERPA.

**Garment Association of Nepal:** Shankhamul Rd, New Baneshwor, POB 21332, Kathmandu; tel. (1) 4780691; fax (1) 4780173; e-mail gan@ntc.net.np; internet www.ganasso.org; Pres. KIRAN P. SAAKHA.

**Himalayan Orthodox Tea Producers' Association of Nepal:** Kathmandu; f. 1998; non-profit making org.; represents and promotes the Himalayan tea sector; Chair. SURAJ VAIDYA.

**Leather Footwear and Goods Manufacturers' Association of Nepal:** Bag Bazar, POB 19732, Kathmandu; tel. (1) 4219349; e-mail lfgman@ntc.net.np; Pres. RAM KRISHNA PRASAI.

**Nepal Association of Tour and Travel Agents:** Gairidhara Rd, Goma Ganesh, Naxal, POB 362, Kathmandu; tel. (1) 4419409; fax (1) 4418684; e-mail nata@mail.com.np; internet www.nata.org.np; f. 1966; 280 mems; Pres. RAM KAJI KONEY.

**Nepal Forest Industries Association:** Naxal, Nag Pokhari, POB 5623, Kathmandu; tel. (1) 4411865; fax (1) 4413838; e-mail padmasri@ccsl.com.np; Pres. HARI PRASAD GIRI; Sec.-Gen. ROHINI THAPALIYA.

**Nepal Leather Industries Association:** POB 9944, Anamnagar, Kathmandu; tel. (1) 4265248; fax (1) 4228978; e-mail giris@atcnet.com.np; Pres. SANJAY GIRI; Sec.-Gen. RAMESH RAJ POKHAREL.

**Nepal Plastic Manufacturers' Association:** Kandevsthan, Kupandol, POB 2350, Lalitpur; tel. and fax (1) 5528185; Pres. SHAILENDRA LAL PRADHAN; Sec.-Gen. RAJESWOR LAL JOSHI.

**Nepal Tea Planters' Association:** Bhadrapur-4, Jhapa; tel. (23) 520059; fax (23) 420679; Pres. CHANDI PRASAD PARAJULI; Sec.-Gen. MAL CHAND GOYAL.

**Nepal Textile Industries Association:** Krishna Galli, Lalitpur; tel. (1) 5529290; fax (1) 5520291; Pres. GOPAL P. KSHATRIYA; Sec.-Gen. RAM K. MAHARJAN.

**Nepal Trans-Himalayan Trade Association:** Jyoti Bhawan, Kantipath, POB 133, Kathmandu; tel. (1) 4225490; fax (1) 4254048; e-mail syamukapu@unilever.wlink.com.np; Pres. TRIBHUWAN D. TULADHAR; Gen. Sec. MAHESH TULADHAR.

### UTILITIES

#### Electricity

**Butwal Power Co Ltd:** 313 Ganga Devi Marga, Buddha Nagar, POB 11728, Kathmandu; tel. (1) 4781776; fax (1) 4780994; e-mail service@bpc.com.np; internet www.bpc.com.np; f. 1966; partially privatized in 2003; principal shareholders: 68.95% owned by Shangri-La Energy Ltd, 9.09% by Ministry of Water Resources and 6.05% by Interkraft Norway; 5.91% divided between Nepalese energy orgs and employees; public sector retains 10% ownership; owns and operates Jhimruk and Andhi Khola Hydropower Plants; supplies electricity to the national grid; 326 employees; Chair. GYANENDRA LAL PRADHAN.

**Chilime Hydropower Co Ltd:** Kalikasthan, POB 25210, Kathmandu; tel. (1) 4443077; fax (1) 4443076; e-mail chpcl@wlink.com.np; 51% owned by Nepal Electricity Authority; Dir DAMBER BAHADUR NEPALI.

**Department of Electricity Development:** 576 Bhakti Thapa Sadak-4, POB 2507, Anamnagar, Kathmandu; tel. (1) 4479507; fax (1) 4480257; e-mail info@doed.gov.np; internet www.doed.gov.np; f. 1993; fmrly Electricity Development Centre; name changed as above 1999; under Ministry of Water Resources; Dir-Gen. SRIRANJAN LACOUL.

**Nepal Electricity Authority:** Durbar Marga, Kathmandu; tel. (1) 4252835; fax (1) 4256091; e-mail sapkota.pawan@gmail.com; internet www.nea.org.np; f. 1985 following merger; govt-owned; Chair. GYANENDRA BAHADUR KARKI; Man. Dir and CEO ARJUN KUMAR KARKI.

#### Water

**Nepal Water Supply Corpn:** Tripureswor Marg, POB 5349, Kathmandu; tel. (1) 4262202; fax (1) 4262229; e-mail info@nwsc.com.np; internet www.nwsc.gov.np; f. 1990; govt-owned; Gen. Man. GAUTAM BAHADUR AMATYA.

### MAJOR COMPANIES

#### Breweries and Distilleries

**Gorkha Brewery Pvt Ltd:** POB 4140, Hattisar, Kathmandu; tel. (1) 4444445; fax (1) 4444443; e-mail info@gorkhabrewery.com; internet www.gorkhabrewery.com; f. 1989 as jt venture between Carlsberg Breweries (Denmark) and Khetan Group; diversified from brewing activities to become beverage co in 2006; Chair. RAJENDRA KHETAN; CEO CHANDRA PRAKASH KHETAN.

**Himalayan Brewery Ltd:** POB 1148, Dilli Bazar, Kathmandu; tel. (1) 4375312; fax (1) 4372880; Chair. ROHIT SHRESTHA; Man. Dir REKHA SHRESTHA.

**Jawalakhel Distillery Pvt Ltd:** Jawalakhel, POB 423, Lalitpur; tel. (1) 4523875; fax (1) 4538236; e-mail jd@hdpl.mos.com.np; Chair. VIJAYA KUMAR SHAH.

**Mount Everest Brewery (Pvt) Ltd:** 1213 Bina Chambers, Exhibition Rd, POB 1480, Kathmandu; tel. (1) 4225912; fax (1) 4225785; e-mail aegroup@wlink.com.np; Chief Exec. PIYUSH BAHADUR AMATYA.

**Nepal Distilleries (Pvt) Ltd:** Balaju, POB 45, Kathmandu; tel. (1) 4350725; e-mail anant@nepaldistilleries.com; internet www.khukrirum.com; brands incl. Khukri Rum, Khukri Special, John Bull, Napoleon, Gaule and Old Reserve Whiskey; CEO AMIT GOSWAMI; Man. Dir ADITYA KANOI.

**Shree Distillery (Pvt) Ltd:** Naxal, Chardhunge, Kathmandu; tel. (1) 4416330; fax (1) 4419617; e-mail shreeo@mos.com.np; mfrs Gorkhali Rum; Chief Exec. MATHURA PRASAD MASKEY.

**Sumy Distillery Pvt Ltd:** POB 8975, EPC 5407, Shangrila Complex, Maharajgunj, Chakrapath, Kathmandu; tel. (1) 4720818; fax (1) 4720819; e-mail sumy@mos.com.np; internet www.sumy.com.np; f. 1999; Man. Dir KARMA GHALE.

### Carpets

**Abhijit Carpet Industries (Pvt) Ltd:** Kathmandu Plaza, Kamaladi, POB 3263, Kathmandu; tel. (1) 4245319; fax (1) 4269268; e-mail ashish@aexpgrp.com; Chief Exec. ASHIS K. SEN GUPTA; Man. Dir SHYAM SUNDER.

**Creation Exports Nepal (Pvt) Ltd:** Mitra Park, POB 1244, Kathmandu; tel. (1) 4493860; fax (1) 4486475; e-mail admin@creationexports.com; internet creationexports.com; f. 1988; mfr and export of handmade carpets and rugs; Chair. RAMESH ADHIKARI.

**Shambala Carpet Industries (Pvt) Ltd:** POB 5256, Kathmandu; tel. and fax (1) 4471502; fax (1) 4471758; e-mail gyanratna@wlink.com.np; Chair. TENZIN THAPAL; Man. Dir PEM TEN LAMA.

**Sher Nepal Crafts:** POB 5468, Kathmandu; tel. (1) 4494169; fax (1) 4494320; e-mail bhim107@ntc.net.np; internet www.carpetnepal.com; f. 1985; mfrs and exporters of hand-knotted carpets, pashmina products and knitwear; Chief Exec. BHIM PRASAD SHERCHAN; 210 employees.

**Snowlion Carpets (Pvt) Ltd:** Adwait Marg, Bagh Bazar, POB 596, Kathmandu; tel. (1) 4227130; fax (1) 4225487; e-mail snowlion@ccsl.com.np; Chair. BIJAYA BAHADUR SHRESTHA; Man. Dir NAMGYAL SHRESTHA.

**Srijana Carpet Industry:** POB 939, Kathmandu; tel. (1) 4212080; fax (1) 4220267; Chief Exec. SITA RAM PRASAI.

**Tara Thimi Carpets:** Bhaktapur, Pithu Thimi, Ward No. 1, Kathmandu; tel. (1) 4224412; Chief Exec. NAMGYAL SHRESTHA.

**Timilsina Industries:** 486/10 Maijubahal Marg, Chabahal 7, POB 5618, Kathmandu; tel. (1) 4471119; e-mail timilsinacarpet@hotmail.com; internet www.tci.com.np; mfrs and exports Tibetan rugs and Pashmina products.

### Cement

**Hetauda Cement Industries Ltd:** Hetauda, POB 24, Makawanpur; tel. (57) 520352; fax (57) 521023; e-mail hcilhtd@vianet.com.np; f. 1976; sales NRs 434m. (2001); Chair. INDRA BAHADUR SHRESTHA; Gen. Man. T. K. JHA; 984 employees.

**Udayapur Cement Industries Ltd:** Jaljhale, Udayapur; tel. (35) 521105; fax (35) 521403; Exec. Chair. ASHOK PRASHAD MALLA.

**Vijnars Cement (P) Ltd:** 'Narshing Kunj', POB 4206, Kathmandu; tel. 4420756; fax 4422707; e-mail org@innani.com; Chair. BRIJ GOPAL INNANI.

### Food and Food Products

**Annapurna Vegetable Products (Pvt) Ltd:** Indra Chowk, POB 772, Kathmandu; tel. (1) 4224074; fax (1) 4240780; Chair. B. K. SHANGHAI.

**CG Foods (Nepal) Pvt Ltd:** Chaudhary House, Sanepa, Kathmandu; tel. (1) 5525039; fax (1) 5523818; e-mail info@chaudharygroup.com; internet www.chaudharygroup.com; part of Chaudhary Group; food, beverages and tobacco; Group Pres. and Man. Dir BINOD K. CHAUDHARY.

**Dugar Food and Beverage (Pvt) Ltd:** 'Dugar Niswas', Kantipath, POB 485, Kathmandu; tel. (1) 4244352; fax (1) 4248695; e-mail tmdugar@info.com.np; internet www.tmdugargroup.com; subsidiary co of local T. M. Dugar Group; Group CEO TOLARAM DUGAR.

**General Food Industries (Pvt) Ltd:** P. M. Bhavan, Kupondole, Lalitpur; tel. (1) 5526907; fax (1) 5523501; mfr of noodles and cereal preparations; Chief Exec. RAJENDRA LAL SHRESTHA.

**Gyan Food Products:** K. L. Dugar Group. Kantipath, POB 1991, Kathmandu; tel. (1) 4221602; fax (1) 4225099; e-mail dugarnp@mos.com.np; processor of pulses and related foodstuffs; Man. Dir KUMUD KUMAR DUGAR; Gen. Man. PRADEEP KUMAR CHHAJER.

**Nebico Pvt Ltd:** Balaju Industrial Dist., Balaju, POB 261, Kathmandu; tel. (1) 4350130; fax (1) 4351527; e-mail nebico@bisc.wlink.com.np; f. 1964; mfr of biscuits and confectionery; Chair. MAHANTA LAL SHRESTHA; Man. Dir RABINDRA SHRESTHA.

**Nepal Vegetable Ghee Industries Ltd:** Kalimati, POB 483, Kathmandu; tel. (1) 4271270; fax (1) 4271704; e-mail noonkath@mos.com.np; Chair. RAJENDRA MAN SERCHAN; Gen. Man. SATYA N. SHAH.

**Salt Trading Corpn Ltd:** Kalimati, POB 483, Kathmandu; tel. (1) 4271418; fax (1) 4271704; e-mail info@stcnepal.com; internet www.stcnepal.com; f. 1963 as a jt venture of the public (30%) and private sectors (70%) to manage the import and distribution of salt; also deals in sugar, edible oils, cereals, pulses, spices, wheat flour, tyres, cement, coal and fertilizers; deals in the export of tyres, inner tubes and spinning yarn; Chair. LAXMI DAS MANANDHAR; Gen. Man. URMILA SHRESTHA; 400 employees.

**Shiva Shakti Ghee Udyog (Pvt) Ltd:** Bagmati Chambers, 3rd Floor, Milan Marg, Teku, Kathmandu; tel. (1) 4224762; fax (1) 4225406; e-mail ssgu@gadia.com.np; f. 1988; importers, mfrs and exporters of edible oils; Chair. PARAMA DEVI AGARWAL; Man. Dir SANDEEP K. AGRAWAL.

**Shree Ganesh Biscuit Udyog (Pvt) Ltd:** Kamal Pokhari, POB 1906, Kathmandu; tel. (1) 4410003; fax (1) 4418653; e-mail mabacos@mos.com.np; mfr of biscuits; Chief Exec. BHAMA RAJKARNIKAR; Gen. Man. AMAR RAJKARNIKAR.

**Shree Mahalaxmi Sugar Ltd:** POB 1073, Kathmandu; tel. (1) 5525039; fax (1) 5523818; e-mail ghonp@mos.com.np; Chair. LUNKARAN DAS CHAUDHARY; Man. Dir BIRENDRA KONADIA; 135 employees.

### Footwear

**Birat Shoe Co Ltd:** POB 1887, Kathmandu; tel. (1) 4371632; fax (1) 4372150; e-mail birat@industries.wlink.com.np; Chair. BIR BAHADUR THAPA; Man. Dir BIRAT THAPA; 152 employees.

**Naveen Footwear (Pvt) Ltd:** POB 4045, Kathmandu; tel. (1) 4222258; fax (1) 4225249; Chief Exec. NAVEEN KUMAR PODDAR.

**Pashupati Footwear Industries (Pvt) Ltd:** Main Rd, POB 34, Biratnagar; tel. (21) 526271; fax (21) 5224461; Chief Exec. DAMODAR PRASAD AGRAWAL.

**Relaxo Footwear Industries (Pvt) Ltd:** Shanker Deep Bldg, Khichapokhari, POB 1275, Kathmandu; tel. (1) 4250066; fax (1) 4249105; e-mail lg@wlink.com.np; Chief Exec. MAHESH KUMAR AGRAWAL.

**Universal Footwear Products:** POB 497, Kathmandu; tel. (1) 4225414; fax (1) 4225974; e-mail unigroup@nepalnetwork.com; internet www.unigroup.com.np; Chief Exec. NOOR PRATAP J. B. RANA.

### Metals

**Agrani Aluminium (Pvt) Ltd:** Simra, Bara; tel. and fax (53) 520070; e-mail agrani@mail.com.np; f. 1992; Chair. HULUS CHAND GOLCHHA.

**Bhagawati Steel Industries (Pvt) Ltd:** Jhhonche Tole, Layakusal, POB 556, Kathmandu; Chief Exec. SHASHI KANTA AGRAWAL.

**Everest Iron and Steel (Pvt) Ltd:** Dhakhwa Bldg, Dharmapath, POB 386, Kathmandu; tel. (1) 4220870; Chief Exec. RAVI BHAKTA SHRESTHA.

**Hetaunda Iron and Steel (Pvt) Ltd:** Tripureswor, POB 2544, Kathmandu; tel. (1) 4226058; fax (1) 4229124; e-mail group@sharda.wlink.com.np; Chief Exec. SHIVA RATAN SHARDA; Man. Dir SRI NIVAS; 100 employees.

**Panchakanya Steel (Pvt) Ltd:** POB 2743, Kathmandu; tel. (1) 5526551; fax (1) 5526529; e-mail steel@panchakanya.com.np; internet www.panchakanya.com.np; part of Panchakanya Group; production and marketing of round steel bars; Group Chair. PREM BAHADUR SHRESTHA; Man. Dir PRADEEP KUMAR SHRESTHA.

### Plastics

**Jayant Plastics:** POB 1275, Kathmandu; tel. (1) 4228539; fax (1) 4222105; Chief Exec. KAMLESH KUMAR AGRAWAL.

**Laxmi Plastics (Pvt) Ltd:** GPOB 650, Kathmandu; tel. (1) 5535473; fax (1) 5526837; e-mail npgroup@mos.com.np; f. 1984; production of pipes and fittings; Chief Exec. LAXMI SHRESTHA.

**Narayani Plastics Udyog (Pvt) Ltd:** Bagbazar, POB 1978, Kathmandu; tel. (1) 4224460; Chief Exec. JAGADISH PRASAD CHAUDHARY.

**Nepal Plastics (Pvt) Ltd:** Kupondole, POB 650, Kathmandu; tel. (1) 5535473; fax (1) 5526837; e-mail npgroup@mos.com.np; f. 1977; production of pipes and fittings; Dir KRISHNA GOPAL SHRESTHA; 260 employees.

**Nepal Polythene and Plastic Industries (Pvt) Ltd:** Tripureswor, POB 1015, Kathmandu; tel. (1) 4261749; fax (1) 4261828; Man. Dir ARUN KUMAR KHANAL.

**Pioneer Plastics Industries (Pvt) Ltd:** POB 5009, Kathmandu; tel. (1) 4279791; fax (1) 4279877; Chair. RAM PRASHAD SHRESTHA; Man. Dir NARAYAN PRASAD SHRESTHA.

**Sanghai Plastic Industries (Pvt) Ltd:** POB 1850, Indrachowk, Kathmandu; tel. (1) 4221236; fax (1) 4221003; e-mail ns@col.com.np; Chair. RATAN LAL SANGHAI; Man. Dir PAWAN KUMAR SANGHAI.

### Tea

**Bansal Tea Estate (Pvt) Ltd:** Bhadrapur, Jhapa; tel. (23) 520210; Chief Exec. BANSIDHAR BANSAL.

**Chandragadhi Tea Estate (Pvt) Ltd:** Chandragadhi 2; tel. (23) 20119; Chief Exec. Visnu Raj Pokharel.

**Guranse Tea Estate (Pvt) Ltd:** Voith Tinkune Complex, Sinamangal, Tinkune, POB 233, Kathmandu; tel. (1) 4478301; fax (1) 4471195; e-mail business@voith.com.np; internet www.guransetea.com.np; f. 1990; Pres. Suraj Vaidya; 250 employees.

**Haldibari Tea Industries (Pvt) Ltd:** Haldibari 2, Jhapa, Mechi Zone; tel. (23) 520092; Chief Exec. Baburam Parajuli; 113 employees.

**Mittal Tea Estate (Pvt) Ltd:** Bhadrapur, Jhapa; tel. (23) 520072; Chief Exec. Mohan Lal Agrawal.

### Textiles and Garments

**Ami Apparels (Pvt) Ltd:** 2nd Floor, Y Block, Suite 380/381, Kamaladi, Kathmandu; tel. (1) 4241437; fax (1) 4249392; e-mail aapl@wlink.com.np; internet www.amiapparels.com; Man. Dir Prasant Pokharel; Chair. Madhu Sengupta; 1,000 employees.

**Annapurna Textile Ltd:** 6/31 New Rd, POB 2515, Kathmandu; tel. (1) 4221536; fax (1) 4221403; Chief Exec. A. K. Jatia.

**Arun Textile (Pvt) Ltd:** POB 4297, Kathmandu; tel. (1) 4228992; Chief Exec. Suresh Kumar Sthapit.

**Ashok Textile Industries (Pvt) Ltd:** Mills Area, Rani, Biratnagar; tel. (21) 521951; fax (21) 530221; e-mail atibrt@ecomail.com.np; Chair. Pawan Kumar Lohia; Gen. Man. Sajjan K. Dalmia; 450 employees.

**Cotton Comfort Pvt Ltd:** Sinamangal, POB 3594, Kathmandu; tel. (1) 4473825; fax (1) 4473544; e-mail comfort@mos.com.np; Man. Dir Subrat Dhital.

**Eastern Textile Industries Ltd:** 8/324 Pyukha Tole, Kathmandu; tel. (1) 4222729; fax (1) 4221295; Chief Exec. Sitaram Lohiya.

**Gangadharam Cotton and Terry Fabrics (P) Ltd:** GD Bldg, Suite 100, Jhamsikhel, POB 5953, Lalitpur; tel. (1) 55967; fax (1) 55510; e-mail gctf@yahoo.com; Chief Exec. Toya Nath Lamichhane.

**Gaylord Garments Industries (Pvt) Ltd:** POB 1329, KHA 1/626, Dharam Path, Kathmandu; tel. (1) 4224703; fax (1) 4248112; e-mail makharia@wlink.com.np; Chief Exec. Ramesh Kumar Agrawal.

**Girja Garment Industries:** POB 6258, Kathmandu; tel. (1) 4224185; fax (1) 4421258; Chief Exec. Savitri Devi Innani.

**Global Garments (Pvt) Ltd:** Gyaneswor, POB 1036, Kathmandu; tel. (1) 4417001; fax (1) 4416496; Chief Exec. B. L. Agrawal.

**Global Trading Concern Ltd:** House 59, POB 3127, Seto Dhoka Marg, Jamal, Kathmandu; tel. (1) 4242855; fax (1) 4247088; e-mail globaltc@wlink.com.np; Chief Exec. Anil Kumar Agrawal.

**Imperial Garments Udyog:** POB 40, Kathmandu; tel. (1) 4226870; fax (1) 4226134; Chief Exec. Sanjaya Agrawal.

**Interknit Industries (Pvt) Ltd:** POB 9175, Hattiban, Kathmandu; tel. (1) 5524563; fax (1) 5524338; e-mail info@ansknits.com; internet www.interknitnepal.com; mfr of knitted outerwear; Chair. Gopi Krishna Agrawal; Man. Dir Raj Kumar Todi; 700 employees.

**KTM Quality Fashion Industries (Pvt) Ltd:** Ga-2/205 Old Baneshwor, Kathmandu; tel. (1) 4470423; fax (1) 4474727; Chief Exec. Ananda Bhadari.

**Mahalaxmi Garment Industries Group:** V. Narsing Kunj, New Plaza, Putali Sadak, POB 4206, Kathmandu; tel. (1) 4421048; fax (1) 4421258; e-mail mgigroup@innani.com; f. 1980; mfr and exporter of ready-made garments; Pres. Brij Gopal Innani; Man. Dir V. Narsing Innani; 2,500 employees.

**Momento Apparels (Pvt) Ltd:** Baneshwor-10, POB 4772, Kathmandu; tel. (1) 4950206; fax (1) 4473652; e-mail momento@apparel.wlink.com.np; Chair. Chandi Raj Dhakal; Man. Dir Tika R. Dhakal; 3,000 employees.

**Pragati Textiles Industries (Pvt) Ltd:** Ga-1-684 Gyaneshwor, POB 4482, Kathmandu; tel. (1) 4418378; fax (1) 4418332; e-mail pragati@wlink.com.np; Chief Exec. Bhagwan Das Lohia.

**Rara Apparels Pvt Ltd:** Baneshwor, POB 4232, Kathmandu; tel. (1) 4487577; fax (1) 4474512; e-mail rara@mos.com.np; f. 2001; Man. Dir Harsh Garg.

**Reliance Spinning Mills Ltd:** Shiva Arcade, 3rd Floor, Basantpur, Kathmandu; tel. (1) 4241853; fax (1) 4224461; e-mail reliancektm@wlink.com.np; internet www.relitex.com; mfr of yarns; Chair. and Man. Dir P. K. Golyan; 1,600 employees.

**Shree Gopi Textile Industries (Pvt) Ltd:** 10/268 Indrachowk, Kathmandu; tel. (1) 4221081; Chief Exec. Radhe Shyam Agrawal.

**Shree Textiles Pvt Ltd:** Patan Industrial Estate, Lagankhel, Lalitpur; tel. (1) 5522313; fax (1) 5527912; e-mail shreetex@enet.com.np; internet www.textile.com.np; Chair. Mahesh Lal Pradhan; Man. Dir Narayan Lal Joshi.

**Surya Silks (Pvt) Ltd:** POB 159, Lalitpur; tel. (1) 5521341; fax (1) 5525136; Chief Exec. Maggie Shah.

**Swastic Textile Products (Pvt) Ltd:** Koteshwor, POB 584, Kathmandu; tel. (1) 4473234; Chief Exec. Murali Dhar Agrawal.

**Vishakha Garments (Pvt) Ltd:** POB 1962, Kathmandu; tel. (1) 4526831; fax (1) 4527015; Chief Exec. Madan Prashad Sarawagi.

**Vishal Garments Industries:** Jorpati, Narayantar, opp. Apang Hospital, POB 2740, Kathmandu; tel. (1) 4489270; fax (1) 4489562; e-mail contitex@wlink.com.np; f. 1984; Man. Dir Sajjan Khetan; Exec. Dir Shyam Khetan.

### Wood and Wood Products

**Decor Doors and Wood Products (Pvt) Ltd:** Bhosiko Tole, Kathmandu; tel. (1) 4221412; Chief Exec. Ashok Kumar Agrawal.

**Everest Paper Mills (Pvt) Ltd:** Janakpurdham, Dhanusha; fax (41) 520317; e-mail epm@ntc.net.np; internet everestgroup.com.np; f. 1981; CEO Deepak Saraff; 400 employees.

**Pumori Agro Forestry Industries (Pvt) Ltd:** Mercantile Bldg, Durbar Marg, Kathmandu; tel. (1) 4220773; fax (1) 4225407; mem. of Mercantile Group; Chair. Gopal Raj Bhandari.

**Shree Padma Furniture Factory (Pvt) Ltd:** House No. 147, Narayan Chour Marg, Nag Pokhari, Kathmandu; tel. (1) 4411900; fax (1) 4413838; e-mail padmasri@ccsl.com.np; internet www.padmashreegroup.com; part of Shree Padma Group; Group Exec. Dir Rohini Thapaliya.

**Sundar Furniture Industries (Pvt) Ltd:** Alakhiya Rd, POB 20, Birgunj; tel. (51) 521418; fax (51) 522086; e-mail kedia@atcnet.com.np; internet www.kediaorganisation.com; f. 1974; mfr of office, domestic and hospital furniture; Man. Dir Shankar Lal Kedia.

### Miscellaneous

**Aarti Soap and Chemical Industries (Pvt) Ltd:** Naxal, Nagpokhari, POB 5161, Kathmandu; tel. (1) 4430997; fax (1) 4431211; e-mail aarti@mos.com.np; Chief Exec. Shyam Kumar Lohiya; Chair. Mahesh Kumar Lohia; 132 employees.

**Arihant Multifibers Ltd:** Golchha House, Biratnagar; tel. (21) 525627; fax (21) 524395; e-mail arihant@bcn.com.np; mfr of varieties of jute; Pres. G. N. Pareek; Man. Dir Diwakar Golchha; 4,000 employees.

**Exotic Oriental Crafts (Pvt) Ltd:** Sainbhu, Bhainsepati, Lalitpur, POB 4228, Kathmandu; tel. (1) 5590631; fax (1) 5590816; e-mail exotic@info.com.np; Chief Exec. K. N. Thakur.

**Gorakhkali Rubber Udyog Ltd:** Kalimati, POB 1700, Kathmandu; tel. (1) 4271102; fax (1) 4270367; e-mail grul@wlink.com.np; Chief Exec. R. S. P. Chaurasia.

**Himalaya Auto Industries (Pvt) Ltd:** Tankisinwari, POB 42, Biratnagar; tel. (21) 527654; Chief Exec. Shyam Sundhar Rathi.

**Jai Nepal Auto Industries (Pvt) Ltd:** Balaju Industrial District, Balaju, POB 2350, Kathmandu; tel. (1) 4412634; fax (1) 4419137; Chief Exec. Gauri Lal Shrestha.

**Janakpur Cigarette Factory Ltd:** POB 5, Janakpurdham; tel. (41) 520127; fax (41) 521004; Chief Exec. Padma Prashad Sharma.

**Mahashakti Soap and Chemical Industries (Pvt) Ltd:** Exhibition Rd, POB 534, Kathmandu; tel. (1) 4226638; fax (1) 4225178; e-mail puja@msci.wlink.com.np; Chair. Ashok Kumar Lohia; Man. Dir Rohit Lohia.

**Nepal Battery Co Ltd:** BID, Ring Rd, Balaju, POB 3194, Kathmandu; tel. (1) 4350954; fax (1) 4350913; e-mail eveready@mos.com.np; cap. and res NRs 48.5m., sales NRs 95m. (1999); Chair. A. Roy; 105 employees.

**Nepal Ekarat Engineering Co (Pvt) Ltd:** Tripureswor, Teku Rd, POB 1939, Kathmandu; tel. (1) 4243436; fax (1) 4253612; e-mail neek@wlink.com.np; Chief Exec. Kush Kumar Joshi.

**Nepal Film Development Co:** Balaju Industrial Estate, Balaju, POB 549, Kathmandu; tel. (1) 4350947; fax (1) 4350511; e-mail info@nfdc.com.np; internet www.nfdc.com.np; 51% state-owned, 49% privately owned; Chair. Udhav Poudel.

**Nepal Jute Industries (Pvt) Ltd:** Teenpaini, POB 86, Biratnagar 2; tel. (21) 527657; fax (21) 521434; mfr of jute and hessian bags, twines and yarns; Chief Exec. G. P. Rijal; Man. Dir S. Rijal; 500 employees.

**Nepal Lube Oil Ltd:** Thapathali, POB 1916, Kathmandu; tel. (1) 4241917; fax (1) 4244736; e-mail cggulf@mos.com.np; sales NRs 107.4m. (1999); privatized in 1994; Chief Exec. Sambhu Saran Pd Kayastha.

**Nepal Oil Corpn Ltd:** POB 1140, Babar Mahal, Kathmandu; tel. (1) 4263481; fax (1) 4263499; e-mail info@nepaloil.com.np; internet www.nepaloil.com; govt-owned; Pres. Bd of Dirs Purushotam Ojha.

**Premier Electrical Industries (Pvt) Ltd:** POB 5226, Kathmandu; tel. (1) 4419087; fax (1) 4417784; Chief Exec. Madan K. Shrestha.

**Surya Nepal (Pvt) Ltd:** Shree Bal Sadan Gha 2-513, Kantipath, POB 1864, Kathmandu; tel. (1) 4248260; fax (1) 4227585; e-mail corporate@snpl.com.np; internet www.snpl.com.np; f. 1986; fmrly Surya Tobacco Co; subsidiary of ITC Ltd; Man. Dir HARSH MADHAV DAR; 400 employees.

**Xian Electrical (Nepal) (Pvt) Ltd:** Kamalpokhari, Lal Durbar, POB 6450, Kathmandu; tel. (1) 4417939; fax (1) 4414882; Chief Exec. DEEPMANI RAJBHANDARI.

### TRADE UNIONS

Trade unions were banned in Nepal in 1961, but were legalized again in 1990, following the success of the pro-democracy movement and the collapse of the Panchayat system.

**Nepal Trade Union Congress—I (NTUC—I):** POB 5507, Kathmandu; tel. (1) 5527443; fax (1) 5527469; e-mail ntuc@mos.com.np; internet www.ntuc.org.np; f. 1947 as the Nepal Trade Union Congress; 28 affiliated unions; affiliated to ICFTU; operates in association with Nepali Congress Party; merged with Democratic Confederation of Nepalese Trade Unions in March 2008 and name changed to the above; Co-Pres LAXMAN BASNET, KHILA NATH DAHAL; 192,000 mems.

**General Federation of Nepalese Trade Unions (GEFONT):** Man Mohan Labour Bldg, GEFONT Plaza, Putali Sadak, POB 10652, Kathmandu; tel. (1) 4248072; fax (1) 4248073; e-mail dfa@gefont.org; internet www.gefont.org; f. 1989; 19 affiliated unions; Chair. MUKUNDA NEUPANE.

## Transport

**Ministry of Labour and Transport Management:** Singha Durbar, Kathmandu; tel. (1) 4247842; fax (1) 4256877; e-mail info@moltm.gov.np; internet www.moltm.gov.np; Sec. SHYAM PRASAD MAINALI.

**Interstate Multi-Modal Transport (Pvt) Ltd:** Shiva Sabitri Sadan, 240 Red Cross Marg, Kalimati, Kathmandu; tel. (1) 4271473; fax (1) 4271570; e-mail rauniar@mos.com.np; f. 1975; provides freight forwarding, transport contracting, customs clearance, warehousing and shipping services, transport consultancy, terminal operations, logistics solutions; Gen. Man. ANAND S. RAUNIAR.

### RAILWAYS

**Nepal Railways Corpn Ltd (NRC):** Khajuri, Janakpur; tel. (41) 52082; HQ Jayanagar, India; f. 1937 as Janakpur-Jayanagar Railways; name changed as above June 2004; 53 km open, linking Jayanagar with Janakpur and Bijalpura; narrow gauge; 11 steam engines, 25 coaches and vans, and 20 wagons; Gen. Man. MADAN SINGH MAHAT.

**Nepal Government Railway:** Birganj; f. 1927; 7 steam engines, 12 coaches and 82 wagons; Man. D. SINGH (acting).

### ROADS

In 2007 there were 17,609 km of roads, of which 5,222 km were black-topped and 4,738 km gravel-covered. Around Kathmandu there are short sections of roads suitable for motor vehicles, and there is a 28-km ring road round the valley. A 190-km mountain road, Tribhuwana Rajpath, links the capital with the Indian railhead at Raxaul. The Siddhartha Highway, constructed with Indian assistance, connects the Pokhara valley, in mid-west Nepal, with Sonauli, on the Indian border in Uttar Pradesh. The 114-km Arniko Highway, constructed with Chinese help, connects Kathmandu with Kodari, on the Chinese border. In the early 1990s the final section of the 1,030-km East–West Highway was under construction. A number of north–south roads were also being constructed to connect the district headquarters with the East–West Highway.

A fleet of container trucks operates between Kolkata and Raxaul in India and other points in Nepal for transporting exports to, and imports from, third countries. Trolley buses provide a passenger service over the 13 km between Kathmandu and Bhaktapur.

### ROPEWAY

A 42-km ropeway links Hetauda and Kathmandu and can carry 22 metric tons of freight per hour throughout the year. Food grains, construction goods and heavy goods on this route are transported by the ropeway.

### CIVIL AVIATION

Tribhuvan International Airport is situated about 6 km from Kathmandu. In 2007 Nepal had 47 airports, of various standards; in mid-2007, however, only 33 of these airports were in operation.

**Nepal Airlines Corpn (NAC):** RNAC Bldg, Kantipath, POB 401, Kathmandu 711000; tel. (1) 4220757; fax (1) 4225348; e-mail info@nac.com.np; internet www.royalnepal-airlines.com; f. 1958; fmrly Royal Nepal Airlines Corpn (RNAC); 100% state-owned (scheduled for transfer to private ownership); scheduled services to 30 domestic airfields, international scheduled flights to 10 destinations in Europe, the Middle East and the Far East, charter flights; Chair. MADHAV GHIMERE; Man. Dir GAUTAM DAS SHRESTHA.

The monopoly of the RNAC in domestic air services came to an end in 1992. By 2007 there were about 16 private airlines in Nepal providing domestic cargo and passenger services. (The Government of Nepal announced in August 2007 that foreign airlines operating services to Nepal would be permitted to increase flight frequencies during the height of the tourist season that year—between September and December—in order to ease pressure on existing services and those provided by the national NAC.)

**Buddha Air:** Jawalakhal, Lalitpur, POB 2167, Kathmandu; tel. (1) 5521015; fax (1) 5537726; e-mail buddhaair@buddhaair.com; internet www.buddhaair.com; f. 1997; domestic passenger services; Man. Dir BIRENDRA B. BASNET; Chair. SURENDRA B. BASNET.

**Cosmic Air:** Kalimatidole, Sinamangal, POB 3488, Kathmandu; tel. (1) 4490146; fax (1) 4497569; e-mail soi@wlink.com.np; internet www.cosmicair.com; f. 1997; operates domestic cargo, passenger and mountain flights; began operating flights to a limited no. of Indian destinations in 2004; Exec. Chair. SANJAYA PRADHAM; Man. Dir M. B. MATHEMA.

**Gorkha Airlines:** Maharajgunj, POB 9451, Kathmandu; tel. (1) 4435122; fax (1) 4444525; e-mail gorkha@mos.com.np; internet www.gorkhaairlines.com; f. 1996; scheduled and charter passenger and cargo flights to domestic destinations; Gen. Man. RABINDRA SILWAL.

**Yeti Airlines:** Tilganga, POB 20011, Kathmandu; tel. (1) 4465888; fax (1) 4464977; e-mail yetiair@wlink.com.np; internet www.yetiairlines.com; f. 1998; operates scheduled and chartered domestic flights; Chair. LHAKPA SONAM SHERPA; Man. Dir ANG TSHERING SHERPA.

## Tourism

Tourism is being developed through the construction of new tourist centres in the Kathmandu valley, Pokhara valley and Chitwan. Regular air services link Kathmandu with Pokhara and Chitwan. Major tourist attractions include Lumbini, the birthplace of Buddha, the lake city of Pokhara and the Himalaya mountain range, including Mt Everest, the world's highest peak. In 1989, in an effort to increase tourism, the Government abolished travel restrictions in 18 areas of north-western Nepal that had previously been inaccessible to foreigners. Following the restoration of parliamentary democracy in 1990, tourist arrivals in Nepal rose considerably. Further travel restrictions in the remote areas of the country were abolished in 1991, and efforts were made to attract foreign investment in the Nepalese tourism industry, but the insurgency in the west hindered development in the early 2000s. Hotel bed capacity increased from 32,214 in 1999 to an estimated 36,163 in 2001. Nepal received an estimated 463,646 tourists in 2000. The number of visitor arrivals declined to 361,237 in 2001 and to 275,468 in 2002. In 2003 the number of arrivals rose again, to 338,132, and in 2004 arrivals increased further, to 385,297. However, a deterioration in the domestic security situation in 2005 resulted in a decline in arrivals to 375,398. Tourism receipts declined from US $191m. in 2001 to $135m. in 2002, but increased to $233m. in 2003 and to $260m. in 2004 before falling significantly in 2005, to $160m. The cessation of Maoist hostilities in 2006 and the subsequent peace agreement between the former insurgents and the political parties' alliance appeared to have aided recovery in the tourism sector as visitor arrivals in that year totalled 383,926. Tourism industry reports for 2007 indicated significant growth in arrivals, particularly from Bangladesh, the People's Republic of China and the Republic of Korea, which was attributed to the introduction of additional airline services between Nepal and these countries. Since 2005 access has been granted to a further 175 mountains, raising the total number of mountains open to climbers to 326, in an effort further to promote tourism.

**Nepal Tourism Board:** Tourist Service Centre, Bhrikuti Mandap, POB 11018, Kathmandu; tel. (1) 4256909; fax (1) 4256910; e-mail info@ntb.org.np; internet www.welcomenepal.com; f. 1998; Chair. LEELA MANI POUDEL; CEO PRACHANDA MAN SHRESTHA.

**Hotel Association Nepal (HAN):** Subarna Shamsher Marg, Gairidhara, POB 2151, Kathmandu; tel. (1) 4412705; fax (1) 4424914; e-mail info@hotelassociation.org.np; internet www.hotelassociation.org.np; f. 1966; Pres. NARENDRA BAJRACHARYA.

**Nepal Association of Tour and Travel Agents (NATTA):** Gairidhara Rd, Goma Ganesh, Naxal, POB 362, Kathmandu; tel. (1) 4419409; fax (1) 4418661; e-mail natta@mail.com.np; internet www.natta.org.np; f. 1966 to promote and regulate development in the tourism industry; non-governmental org.; 360 mems; CEO Dr HARI SARMAH.

**Tourist Guide Association of Nepal (TURGAN):** POB 5344, Kamaladi, Kathmandu; tel. (1) 4225102; fax (1) 4423939.

**Trekking Agents Association of Nepal:** Maligaun Ganesthan, POB 3612, Kathmandu; tel. (1) 4427473; fax (1) 4419245; e-mail info@taan.org.np; internet www.taan.org.np; Pres. B. C. NARENDRA; Sec.-Gen. SITA RAM SAPKOTA.

## Defence

As assessed at November 2007, Nepal's total armed forces numbered 69,000 men. Paramilitary forces numbered 62,000 men. Military service is voluntary. An Armed Police Force was formed in 2001 to counteract the Maoist insurgency and numbered an estimated 15,000 in November 2007.

**Defence Budget:** NRs 10,900m. in 2007 (equivalent to approximately 6.4% of total government expenditure).

**Chief of Army Staff:** Lt-Gen. RUKMANGAD KATUWAL.

## Education

Primary education, beginning at six years of age and lasting for five years, is officially compulsory and is provided free of charge in government schools. Secondary education, beginning at the age of 11, lasts for a further five years, comprising a first cycle of three years (lower secondary) and a second of two years (secondary). In 2005/06 the total enrolment at primary and secondary schools was equivalent to an estimated 79% of the school-age population. In 2003/04 enrolment at primary schools included an estimated 79% of children in the relevant age-group (boys 84%; girls 74%), while the ratio for secondary enrolment in 2005/06 was equivalent to an estimated 43% of pupils in the relevant age-group (boys 46%; girls 40%). Some 8,000 pupils attended the country's 321 primary schools in 1950; in 2004 there were an estimated 24,746 primary schools, with a total of 4,030,045 pupils. The number of secondary schools rose from two in 1950 to 11,983 in 2004. In that year there were an estimated 1,988,761 pupils enrolled at secondary schools.

In 1975 the Government began to provide free primary education for five years and to use Nepali as the medium of instruction. Vernacular schools give secular education to villagers in local dialects, while, in addition to Buddhist and Hindu religious establishments, there are a number of Basic schools, on the pattern set in India, which concentrate on handicrafts and agriculture.

The Ministry of Education and Sports supervises the finance, administration, staffing and inspection of government schools, and makes inspection of private schools receiving government subsidies. In other respects, private schools are autonomous. The National Educational Planning Commission recommends educational curricula, and in some cases these have been adopted by the private schools.

The oldest of the colleges of higher education in Nepal is Tri Chandra School in Kathmandu, founded in 1918, which provides four-year arts courses. The only other advanced college in existence before the 1951 Revolution was the Sanskrit College in Kathmandu, founded in 1948. A single college of education was established in 1956 for the training of secondary school teachers and other educational personnel. There are also nine primary teacher-training centres. The first 300-bed teaching hospital for 500 pupils, built with Japanese government assistance, was opened in 1984. There are four state universities and one privately funded university. The Tribhuvan University in Kathmandu had 115,608 students in 2001/02. The second state university, the Mahendra Sanskrit Viswavidyalaya in Beljhundi, Dang, was founded in 1986. In 2000/01 the university had an enrolment of 3,252 students. The Purbanchal University, which was opened in 1995, had 2,840 students in 2001/02, and the Pokhara University, which was opened in 1997, had 2,946 students. In addition, there is one private university—the Kathmandu University in Banepa, Kavrepalanchok, which was opened in 1992. In 2001/02 the university had an enrolment of 1,783 students.

Proposed expenditure on education by the central Government in the 2007/08 budget was NRs 28,072m. (16.6% of total spending). The Eighth Five-Year Plan (1992–97) included proposals to introduce free compulsory secondary education in phases over the next 10 years. By 2000, however, compulsory education had been implemented in only seven of Nepal's 75 districts. According to the UN Development Programme, literacy among the adult population of Nepal was only 49% in 2006; it was hoped that 70% literacy would have been achieved by the conclusion of the 12th Five-Year Plan in 2017.

# Bibliography


Agrawal, H. N. *Administrative System of Nepal: From Tradition to Modernity*. New Delhi, Vikas Publishing House, 1976.

Baral, L. R. *Oppositional Politics in Nepal*. New Delhi, Abhinav, 1977.

Bauer, Kenneth M. *High Frontiers: Himalayan Pastoralists in a Changing World*. New York, Columbia University Press, 2004.

Bhooshan, B. S. *The Development Experience of Nepal*. Delhi, Concept Publishing, 1979.

Bista, Dor Bahadur. *Fatalism and Development in Nepal*. Kolkata, Orient Longman, 1991.

Blaikie, Piers, *et al*. *Nepal in Crisis*. Delhi, Oxford University Press, 1980.

Blaikie, Piers, and Seddon, D. *Peasants and Workers in Nepal*. New Delhi, Viking Publishing House, 1979.

Brown, T. Louise. *The Challenge to Democracy in Nepal: A Political History*. London, Routledge, 1995.

Caplan, Lionel. *Land and Social Change in East Nepal*. London, Routledge and Kegan Paul, 1970.

*Administration and Politics in a Nepalese Town*. London, Oxford University Press, 1971.

*Warrior Gentlemen: Gurkhas in the Western Imagination*. Berghahn Books, 1995.

Chattopadhyay, K. P. *An Essay on the History of Newar Culture*. Kathmandu, Educational Enterprise, 1980.

Chauhan, R. S. *Political Development in Nepal*. Delhi, Associated Publishing House, 1970.

Connell, Monica. *Against a Peacock Sky*. London and New York, Viking, 1991.

Dharamdasani, M. D. *Nepal's Foreign Policy*. New Delhi, Anmol Publications, 2006.

Ferrari, Aurora, with Jaffrin, Guillemette, and Shrestha, Sabin Raj. *Access to Financial Services in Nepal*. World Bank, 2007.

Fisher, James F. *Trans-Himalayan Traders: Economy, Society and Culture in Northwest Nepal*. New Delhi, Motilal Banarsidass Publishers Ltd, 1987.

*Living Martyrs: Individuals and Revolution in Nepal*. Delhi, Oxford University Press, 1997.

Gaige, Frederick H. *Regionalism and National Unity in Nepal*. Berkeley, CA, University of California Press, 1975.

Gould, Tony. *Imperial Warriors*. London, Granta Books, 2000.

Gray, John. *Domestic Mandala: Architecture of Lifeworlds in Nepal*. London, Ashgate, 2006.

Gregson, Jonathan. *Blood Against the Snows*. London, Fourth Estate, 2002

Gupta, Anirudha. *Politics in Nepal*. Mumbai, Allied Publishers, 1964.

Hagen, Toni, Wahlen, F. T., and Corti, W. R. *Nepal: The Kingdom in the Himalayas*. Berne, Kummerly & Frey, 1961.

Haimendorf, C. von F. (Ed.). *Caste and Kin in Nepal, India and Ceylon*. London, East-West Publications, 1966.

*Himalayan Traders*. London, Murray, 1975.

Hamilton, F. *An Account of the Kingdom of Nepal*. Edinburgh, Constable, 1819.

Hofer, A. *The Caste Hierarchy and the State in Nepal: A Study of the Muluki Ain of 1854*. Innsbruck, Universitätsverlag, Wagner, 1979.

Hoftun, M., and Raeper, W. (Eds). *Spring Awakening: An Account of the 1990 Revolution in Nepal*. New Delhi, Penguin Books India, 1992.

Husain, Asad. *British India's Relations with the Kingdom of Nepal*. London, George Allen and Unwin, 1970.

Hutt, Michael J. *Nepali: A National Language and its Literature*. New Delhi, Sterling Publishers Ltd, 1988.

*Nepal in the Nineties: Versions of the Past, Visions of the Future*. New Delhi, Oxford University Press, 1994.

Hutt, Michael J. (Ed.). *Himalayan 'People's War': Nepal's Maoist Rebellion*. London, C. Hurst and Co, 2004.

Ives, J. D., and Messerli, B. *The Himalayan Dilemma: Reconciling Development and Conservation*. London, Routledge, 1989.

Jha, Sunil Kumar. *Nepal: Customs and Etiquette*. London, Kuperard, 2006.

Joshi, B. L., and Rose, L. E. *Democratic Innovations in Nepal: A Study of Political Acculturation*. Berkeley, CA, University of California Press, 1986.

Justice, J. *Politics, Plans and People: Culture and Health Development in Nepal*. Berkeley, CA, University of California Press, 1986.

Karan, Pradyumna P. *Nepal: A Cultural and Physical Geography*. Lexington, KY, University of Kentucky Press, 1960.

Karan, Pradyumna P., and Ishii, Hiroshi. *Nepal: A Himalayan Kingdom in Transition*. New York and London, United Nations University Press, 1996.

Karan, Pradyumna P., and Jenkins, W. M. *The Himalayan Kingdoms: Bhutan, Sikkim and Nepal*. Princeton, NJ, Van Nostrand, 1963.

Khadka, Narayan. *Foreign Aid, Poverty and Stagnation in Nepal*. New Delhi, Vikas Publishing House, 1991.

Kumar, Satish. *Rana Polity in Nepal: Origin and Growth*. Asia Publishing House for the Indian School of International Studies, 1968.

Kyloh, Robert. *From Conflict to Cooperation: Labour Market Reforms that Can Work in Nepal*. Geneva, International Labour Office, 2008.

Landon, Percival. *Nepal*. London, Constable, 1928.

Lawoti, Mahendra. *Towards a Democratic Nepal: Inclusive Political Institutions for a Multicultural Society*. London, Sage Publications, 2005.

LeVine, Sarah. *Rebuilding Buddhism: The Theravada Movement in Twentieth-Century Nepal*. Cambridge, MA, Harvard University Press, 2005.

Macfarlane, A. *Resources and Population: A Study of the Gurungs of Nepal*. Cambridge, Cambridge University Press, 1976.

Malla, Kamal P. (Ed.). *Nepal: Perspectives on Continuity and Change*. Kathmandu, Centre for Nepal and Asian Studies, 1989.

Maslak, Mary Ann. *Daughters of Tharu: Gender, Ethnicity, Religion, and the Education of Nepali Girls*. London, RoutledgeFalmer, 2003.

Messerschmidt, D. A. *The Gurungs of Nepal: Conflict and Change in a Village Society*. Warminster, Aris and Philips, 1976.

Metz, J. J. 'A Reassessment of the Causes and Severity of Nepal's Environmental Crisis', in *World Development*, Vol. 19, No. 7, pp. 805–820, 1991.

Mihaly, Eugene Bramer. *Foreign Aid and Politics in Nepal*. London, Oxford University Press for Royal Institute of International Affairs, 1965.

Mojumdar, Kanchanmoy. *Political Relations between India and Nepal*. New Delhi, Munshiram Manoharlal Publishers Ltd, 1973.

Muni, S. D. *Foreign Policy of Nepal*. Delhi, National Publishing House, 1973.

Nickson, R. A. *Foreign Aid and Foreign Policy: The Case of British Aid to Nepal*. Birmingham, University of Birmingham, Development Administration Group, Papers in the Administration of Development No. 48, 1992.

Observer Research Foundation. *India-Nepal Relations: The Challenge Ahead*. New Delhi, Rupa and Co., 2007.

Panday, Devendra Raj (Ed.). *Foreign Aid and Development in Nepal: Proceedings of a Seminar*. Kathmandu, Integrated Development Systems, 1983.

Pant, Y. P. *Development of Nepal*. Allahabad, Kitab Mahal, 1968.

Parajulee, R. P. *Democratic Transition in Nepal*. Lanham, MD, University Press of America, 2000.

Petech, Luciano. *Medieval History of Nepal*. Rome, Istituto Italiano per il Medio ed Estremo Oriente, 1984.

Pradhan, B. B. *Rural Development in Nepal—Problems and Prospects*. Kathmandu, 1982.

Pradhan, Kumar. *The Gorkha Conquests*. Kolkata, Oxford University Press, 1991.

Pye-Smith, C. *Travels in Nepal*. London, Penguin Books, 1988.

Raeper, William, and Hoftun, Martin (Eds). *Spring Awakening: An Account of the 1990 Revolution in Nepal*. New Delhi, Penguin Books India, 1992.

Ramakant. *Nepal, China and India*. Delhi, Abhinar, 1976.

Ramakant and Upreti, B. C. (Eds). *Indo-Nepal Relations*. New Delhi, South Asian Publishers, 1992.

Rana, Pashupati Shumshere J. B. *Kathmandu: A Living Heritage*. Perennial Press, 1989.

Regmi, D. R. *Ancient Nepal*. Kolkata, Mukhopadhyay, 1960.

*Modern Nepal: Rise and Growth in the Eighteenth Century*. Kolkata, Mukhopadhyay, 1961.

Regmi, M. C. *Land Ownership in Nepal*. Berkeley, CA, University of California Press, 1976.

*Land Tenure and Taxation System in Nepal*. Kathmandu, Ratna Pustak Bhandar, 1978.

Rehnstrom, J. *Development Co-operation in Practice: The United Nations Volunteers in Nepal*. Washington, DC, Brookings Institution, 2000.

Riaz, Ali, and Basu, Subho. *Paradise Lost? State Failure in Nepal*. Lanham, MD, Lexington Books, 2007.

Roberts, Patricia, and Kelly, Thomas L. *Kathmandu: City on the Edge of the World*. London, Weidenfeld & Nicolson, 1990.

Rose, Leo E. *Nepal: Strategy for Survival*. Berkeley, CA, University of California Press, 1971.

Rose, Leo E., and Scholz, J. T. *Nepal: Profile of a Himalayan Kingdom*. Boulder, CO, Westview Press, 1980.

Seddon, D. *Nepal—A State of Poverty*. New Delhi, Vikas Publishing House, 1987.

Shaha, Rishikesh. *Nepali Politics: Retrospect and Prospect*. Oxford, Oxford University Press, 1977.

*Modern Nepal: A Political History, 1769–1955*. 2 vols. New Delhi, Manohar Publications, 1990.

*Politics in Nepal, 1980–1990*. New Delhi, Manohar Publications, 1990.

*Ancient and Medieval Nepal*. New Delhi, Manohar Publications, 1992.

Sharma, Gunanidhi. *Nepal: Missing Elements in the Development Thinking*. New Delhi, Nirala, 2000.

Sharma, Pitamber. *Urbanization in Nepal*. Honolulu, HI, East-West Center, 1989.

Shrestha, N. R. *Landlessness and Migration in Nepal*. Boulder, CO, Westview Press, 1990.

*Historical Dictionary of Nepal*. Lanham, MD, Scarecrow Press, 2003.

Sill, M., and Kirkby, J. *Atlas of Nepal in the Modern World*. London, Earthscan, 1991.

Sitwell, Sacheverell. *Great Temples of the East*. New York, Oblensky, 1962.

Snellgrove, D. *Himalayan Pilgrimage*. Oxford, Bruno Cassirer, 1961.

Stewart, Frank, Upadhyay, Samrat, and Thapa, Manjushree (Eds). *Secret Places*. Honolulu, HI, University of Hawaii Press, 2002.

Subedi, Surya P. *The Dynamics of Foreign Policy Law: A Study in Indo-Nepal Relations*. New Delhi, Oxford University Press, 2005.

Thapa, Deepak, and Sijapati, Bandita. *A Kingdom under Siege: Nepal's Maoist Insurgency, 1996 to 2004*. London, Zed Books, 2004.

Thapa, Manjushree. *Forget Kathmandu: An Elegy for Democracy*. New Delhi, Penguin Books India, 2005.

Tucker, Francis. *Gorkha: The Story of the Gurkhas of Nepal*. London, Constable, 1957.

Tuladhar-Douglas, Will. *Remaking Buddhism for Medieval Nepal: The Fifteenth-Century Reformation of Newar Buddhism*. Abingdon, Routledge, 2006.

Upreti, Bishnu Raj. *Management of Social and Natural Resource Conflict in Nepal: Realities and Alternatives*. New Delhi, Adroit Publishers, 2002.

*Armed Conflict and Peace Process in Nepal: The Maoist Insurgency and Past Negotiations*. New Delhi, Adroit Publishers, 2007.

Uprety, Prem. *Political Awakening in Nepal*. New Delhi, Commonwealth Publishers, 1992.

Waterhouse, David. *The Origins of Himalayan Studies: Brian Houghton Hodgson in Nepal and Darjeeling*. London, Routledge, 2004.

Watkins, Joanne. *Spirited Women: Gender, Religion and Cultural Identity in the Nepal Himalayas*. New York, Columbia University Press, 1996.

Whelpton, John. *Nepal: World Bibliographical Series*. Oxford, Clio Press, 1990.

*Kings, Soldiers and Priests: Nepalese Politics, 1830–57*. New Delhi, Manohar Publications, 1992.

*A History of Nepal*. Cambridge, Cambridge University Press, 2005.

Willesee, Amy, and Whittaker, Mark. *Love and Death in Kathmandu: A Strange Tale of Royal Murder*. New York, St Martin's Press, 2004.

World Bank. *Financial Accountability in Nepal: A Country Assessment*. World Bank, 2003.

Yadav, Satya Bhan. *Institutional Credit and Agricultural Development in Nepal*. New Delhi, Kalinga Publications, 2002.

Zivetz, L. *Private Enterprise and the State in Modern Nepal*. Chennai, Oxford University Press, 1992.

# PAKISTAN

## Physical and Social Geography

B. H. FARMER

The Islamic Republic of Pakistan covers an area of 796,095 sq km (307,374 sq miles), excluding Jammu and Kashmir (the sovereignty of which is disputed with India). The territory of Pakistan extends from 23° 45′ to 36° 50′ N and between 60° 55′ and 75° 30′ E, and is bounded to the west, north-west and north by Iran and Afghanistan (a narrow panhandle in the high Pamirs separates it from direct contact with Tajikistan), to the north-east by the People's Republic of China, to the east and south-east by India and by Jammu and Kashmir, and to the south by the Arabian Sea. Pakistan, like the Republic of India, became independent on 15 August 1947, and inherited, generally speaking, those contiguous districts of the former Indian empire that had a Muslim majority. Its former eastern wing became the independent People's Republic of Bangladesh after the Indo-Pakistan war of December 1971. The capital is Islamabad.

### PHYSICAL FEATURES

Much of Pakistan is mountainous or, at any rate, highland. Its northernmost territories consist of the tangled mountains among which the western Himalayas run into the high Karakoram and Pamir ranges. From these the mighty River Indus breaks out through wild gorges to the plains. West of the Indus lies Chitral, a territory of hill ranges, deep gorges and high plateaux. South of this, on the Afghan border, structures are simpler, consisting essentially of a series of mountain arcs such as the Safed Koh, Sulaiman and Kirthar ranges, less complex in geological structure and lower in height than the Himalayas, Pamirs or Karakoram, breached by famous passes such as the Khaibar and Bolan, and enclosing belts of plateau country. Balochistan, the westernmost part of Pakistan's territory, is essentially a region of plateaux and ranges which run over the border into Iran.

Contrasting strongly with all this high and often mountainous terrain is the plain country to the south-east. Part of the great Indo-Gangetic plain, this consists for the most part of the alluvium brought down by the Indus and its tributaries, of which by far the most important are the five rivers of the Punjab, the Jhelum, Chenab, Ravi, Beas and Sutlej (part of whose course lies, however, in Indian or Kashmiri territory). The southern part of the border with India runs through the waterless wastes of the Thar Desert.

### CLIMATE

The Pakistan plains, like those of northern India, have an annual cycle of three seasons. The 'cool season' (December to February) has relatively low average temperatures (Lahore, 12°C January) but warm days. Karachi, farther south and on the coast, is rather warmer (18°C January average). This season is dry, apart from rain brought by north-westerly disturbances. The 'hot season' (March to May) builds up to very high temperatures (Lahore, 31.5°C May average, but up to 48.5°C by day, and even hotter in that notorious hot-spot, Jacobabad; but rather less hot, 29.5°C May average, in Karachi); this season is dry. From June to September the south-west monsoon brings more wind, lower temperatures, and rains that are everywhere relatively light (3,430 mm in four months at Lahore) and that fall off to little or nothing westward into Balochistan and southward into Sindh and the Thar Desert. Much of Pakistan would, in fact, be agriculturally unproductive in the absence of irrigation. The mountains of Pakistan have a climatic regime modified by altitude and with a winter maximum of rainfall (such as it is) in the north-west, but, again, widely characterized by aridity.

### VEGETATION AND NATURAL RESOURCES

There is very little 'natural' vegetation left, except for poor, semi-desert scrub in uncultivated portions of the plains of Pakistan (such as part of the Thal, between the Indus and Jhelum) and in Balochistan, and montane forests in parts of the western and northern hills (notably the Sulaimans). Even this surviving vegetation has been degraded by man: for instance, by the practice of pastoralism in Balochistan and elsewhere in the western hills and plateaux. Not surprisingly, Pakistan is desperately short of timber, and has actually planted irrigated forests, especially of shisham (*Dalbergia sissoo*), in the Thal and elsewhere.

The soils of the plains of Pakistan, like those in similar physiographic circumstances in India, exhibit considerable variety. Those of the Thar Desert tend to be poor and sandy, and there is a good deal of natural salinity in the more arid tracts, especially in Sindh. More fertile alluvium follows the main rivers and also spreads more widely in the Punjab, but there is, again as in India, the danger of man-induced salinity and alkalinity with the spread of irrigation, and consequent rise in the water-table and capillary ascent of salts to the surface. Indeed, large areas of land have gone out of cultivation for just this reason. The hill areas of Pakistan tend to have poor, skeletal mountain soils, though better conditions prevail in some innermost valleys.

Most of the mineral wealth is concentrated in the mountainous regions of Pakistan. Twenty types of mineral had been identified at the time of partition, but only coal (sub-bituminous and non-coking), rock salt, chromite, gypsum and limestone were mined. Fireclay, silica sand, celestite, ochres and iron ore are now also commercially exploited, and there may be commercial deposits of copper, manganese, bauxite and phosphates. Pakistan's most important energy resource is undoubtedly natural gas, found at Sui and other locations in the Indus plain and piped thence to Lahore, Karachi and other towns. Exploration has also revealed a number of oilfields, and there are hopes of self-sufficiency in petroleum.

### POPULATION

According to the latest census, the population on 2 March 1998 was 132,352,279. The average annual rate of increase between 1990 and 1998 was 2.8%. The estimated population at 1 January 2007 was 158,700,000, giving an average density of 199.3 inhabitants per sq km. Pakistan has densities of more than 300 per sq km in well-watered districts such as Lyallpur. Pakistan also has sizeable conurbations in Karachi (population 9,339,023 at the 1998 census) and Lahore (population 5,143,495 in 1998). In mid-2007, according to UN estimates, the population of Karachi had increased to 12,130,000 and that of Lahore to 6,577,000.

There is considerable ethnic diversity within Pakistan. Tall, relatively fair and blue-eyed Pathans of the western hills contrast with darker, brown-eyed (though also often tall 'plainsmen'—itself a heterogeneous category.

Although the population of Pakistan is overwhelmingl Muslim (about 95% at the 1981 census), it is divided, no only by race but also by linguistic and tribal differences Punjabi, Balochi and Pashto (the language of the Pathans are spoken; the official languages are Urdu and English. Th Punjabi are the principal ethnic group, comprising about tw thirds of the total population; other major groups are th Sindhi, Pashtun, Urdu and Balochi. Tribal divisions a most noticeable in the western hills, but also affect the plai where there are Janglis (once lawless nomads, now large cultivators), Thiringiuzars (camel-herders) and other group

# History*

## KENNETH MCPHERSON

On 15 August 1947 Pakistan gained independence under the leadership of Mohammed Ali Jinnah. The new state was carved out of British India as a homeland for Muslims and, in the process, millions of Muslims, Hindus and Sikhs were displaced in a massive and bloody movement of people.

### THE INHERITANCE OF PARTITION

From its foundation, Pakistan was faced with monumental problems. Some of these were very immediate and resulted from the exodus of millions of Hindus and Sikhs who had dominated both bureaucracy and commerce in the provinces of British India that became Pakistan. The division of the former imperial bureaucracy and armed forces added to the chaos, and Pakistan gained independence with fewer experienced administrators than India and with a much depleted bureaucratic and commercial middle class.

Independence witnessed the creation of two disparate sections. Bengali-speaking East Pakistan, the eastern half of the old province of Bengal, whilst comprising only one-seventh of the area of the new state, contained four-sevenths of the population. Across Indian territory, 1,600 km to the west, was Urdu-speaking West Pakistan (comprising the divided province of Punjab and the old provinces of Sindh, the North-West Frontier Province—NWFP—and Balochistan). The division of Bengal and Punjab created immediate problems for both wings of Pakistan. East Pakistan lost both its capital and the chief port Calcutta (now known as Kolkata), as well as access to the jute-spinning mills of Howrah (Haora), upon which its economy depended. Punjab lost control of its irrigation water headworks for the Indus basin to India, potentially endangering vast tracts of its agricultural land. Within a remarkably short time, however, the new state established a working bureaucratic structure and national defence force, as well as resettling millions of refugees in Punjab and Sindh. In Sindh these refugees, known as *mohajirs*, settled in such large numbers that they challenged the domination of Sindhis in many parts of the province, especially in Pakistan's largest city and main port, Karachi.

However, Pakistan also faced longer-term problems that gave particular shape to its national ethos, political life and foreign policy. These long-term problems have proved much more intractable. Essentially they fall into two categories. First, those relating to unresolved issues in the wake of Partition—principally the status of the Muslim-majority princely state of Kashmir, whose Hindu ruler opted for union with India, border demarcation problems, and the question of the equitable distribution of the waters of the rivers feeding into the Indus basin, but which rise in India-controlled territory. Second, problems arising from the unresolved nature of the state of Pakistan. It originated as a result of agitation within British India for a separate Muslim homeland. However, the debates and agitation that led to the foundation of Pakistan singularly failed to address the issue of the nature of this state. Was it to be an Islamic state? Was it to be governed according to traditional Islamic law? What was the position of non-Muslims within this state? An associated problem was that while India inherited a political system based on well-organized political parties with sophisticated organizational structures, Pakistan gained independence under the leadership of Jinnah and the Muslim League, which was in many ways a 'national front' comprising diverse regionally and class-defined groups temporarily united in their desire for a Muslim homeland that was separate from what they perceived to be a Hindu-dominated India.

### THE ISSUES OF KASHMIR, BORDERS AND WATER

The Kashmir issue has shaped Pakistan's relations with India and its broader foreign policy since 1947. The first Indo-Pakistan military conflict over Kashmir took place in 1947–48, followed by a second war in 1965, a third war in 1971 that led to the establishment of Bangladesh from the ruins of the former East Pakistan, and bouts of terrorist activity in Kashmir that have been almost continuous since the 1980s. Closely associated with the Kashmir issue have been border disputes that have led to armed clashes, such as that over the potentially oil- and gas-rich Rann of Kutch, but in reality they have been a continuation of the ill will between the two countries generated by the traumas of Partition and the ongoing problem of Kashmir.

Initially, the water issue threatened to prove as disruptive as that of Kashmir. In 1964, however, an agreement between the two countries was reached. Yet, in the early 21st century the issue was revived, with the environmental phenomenon of global warming affecting upstream flows and both India and Pakistan positioning themselves for a new round of negotiations over a vital but finite resource.

### POLITICS AND THE NATURE OF THE STATE

Jinnah became the first Governor-General of Pakistan, but his sudden death in September 1948 left the nation without a charismatic leader. The assassination of his successor, Liaquat Ali Khan, in 1951 further undermined the development of a stable political system. In the succeeding decades there were various attempts at constitution-making, all of which were interrupted by periods of military and executive rule. One of the central issues that complicated attempts to develop a working constitution was the debate concerning the role of Islam: was Pakistan simply a refuge for Muslims or was it an Islamic state? In addition there was, and has continued to be, constant debate concerning the nature of executive powers, which usually manifested themselves in the form of alternate bouts of strong executive government interspersed with periods of military intervention and a few much shorter periods in which power resided with democratically elected legislatures at the provincial and central levels.

However, apart from these rather cerebral debates, there have been background debates based on the distinct provincial (and ethnic and linguistic) differences that divide the country. Provincial loyalties and interests have had to contend with loyalties to the centre and with the idea of a unitary Pakistan, and it is this battle that has run parallel to, and intertwined with, other conflicts concerning the structure of the state, constitutionalism and the role of the armed forces and of Islam.

The question of loyalties has been further exacerbated by the unreformed nature of much of traditional Pakistani society and the ever-present influence of the military. Comparisons can be odious but, compared with India, Pakistan did not undertake massive land reform and in the process remove the superstructure of a relatively few wealthy landowning families who commanded the loyalties of the masses. Political leadership in Punjab and Sindh has come mainly from such families—for example, those of Nawaz Sharif and Benazir Bhutto. Nor has the Pakistan army remained a loyal servant of the State; rather, it has regularly intervened to destroy civilian administrations and in the process has gained control of approximately one-third of Pakistan's heavy industry and an overweening influence on foreign policy, even in periods of civilian rule, through the Inter-Services Intelligence Agency (ISI). In addition, the old tribal structure dominated by all-powerful and conservative *khans* (tribal rulers) has survived in the NWFP and Balochistan, where resistance to modernization and the powers of the central State has been fiercest.

#### The Drafting of a Constitution

The first attempt to draft a constitution incorporating the principles of Islam was difficult and revealed the fragile nature of Pakistani politics. Personal antipathy led to squabbles among Jinnah's successors, and it was not until 1955 that a new Constituent Assembly was elected by the various provin-

*Since 1947 (for the pre-1947 history, see the chapter on India).

cial legislatures, which prepared a republican constitution for the country.

## 1956–71: CONSTITUTIONS, A REPUBLIC, PARTIES AND BANGLADESH

The Constitution adopted in March 1956 established a federal republic comprising two provinces (East and West Pakistan), with equal representation in a single legislature and with considerable devolution of powers to the provincial governments. An attempt was made to define the new state's links with Islam: the Head of State was to be a Muslim, but Islam was not declared the state religion. However, no law was to be promulgated that conflicted with Islamic teachings and it was vaguely stated that existing laws were to be brought into conformity with Islam, although the personal laws of non-Muslims were to be respected. In addition, Urdu and Bengali were both recognized as state languages, though English was retained for official purposes.

In practice, the new system was weakened by its failure to develop a strong political party system. Political parties were weak and disorganized and invariably formed around strong individuals rather than ideologies, the major exceptions being, in terms of ideological content, Islamist and leftist parties.

Initially, the Muslim League (founded in 1906 as the All India Muslim League) was the dominant political party in Pakistan, and it was known after 1947 as the Pakistan Muslim League (PML). Under the leadership of Jinnah in the years before Partition, it had become a nationalist coalition representing diverse interests among Muslims. However, once independence had been achieved, the diverse elements within the party began to squabble. Former members of the League founded new parties, but their programmes were no different from those of the League and they were little more than coteries gathered around charismatic individuals. In addition, from the late 1950s religious parties such as Maulana Maududi's political organization of Islamic scholars, *Jamaat-e-Islami Pakistan* (JIP), and later Air Marshal Asghar Khan's *Tehrik-i-Istiqlal* (TI) and two other organizations of Muslim religious scholars (active by 1970)—*Jamiat-e-Ulema-e-Islam* (JUI) and *Jamiat-e-Ulema-e-Pakistan* (JUP) emerged. All of these religious parties advocated an Islamic constitution and the revival of Islamic values. The JIP and similar parties were small and generally lacked a national base, but the bickering within the PML and its tendency to splinter into rival factions and parties enabled Islamist parties such as the JIP to begin to exert undue influence as intermediaries courted by any faction eager to increase its numbers in the legislatures. A precedent was being established that was to shape political life in Pakistan into the 21st century.

A more immediate problem, however, than the fractionalizing of political life in Pakistan in the 1960s was the rise of a vigorous political provincialism in East Bengal (Mujibur Rahman's Awami League—AL—and the National Awami Party—NAP) and in West Pakistan, where Zulfikar Ali Bhutto formed the socialist-leaning Pakistan People's Party (PPP), based primarily on the support his wealthy landowning family drew from Sindh. None of these parties had a broad democratic base and regular membership did not exist. Most parties, except the badly divided PML, and to an extent the NAP, were in effect regional, provincial or sectarian parties. Ironically, the sectarian parties were in many ways the best organized: through the *masjids* (mosques) and *madrassas* (traditional schools teaching Arabic and the Islamic holy text, the Koran) they had what were in effect branch organizations, which provided them with crowds of believers for protests and demonstrations. In terms of voting power the sectarian parties remained a minority, but in a factionalized political system they were able to trade their support with larger political parties and ensure that the question of the relationship between Islam and the state remained a central political issue.

Ghulam Muhammad's successor as President, Iskandar Mirza, epitomized the problem that was to bedevil Pakistani politics to the present day. He had no faith in parliamentary democracy or political parties, and in October 1958 he abrogated the Constitution, in the process abolishing the provincial and central legislatures and banning political parties. Martial law was promulgated under Gen. Ayub Khan, the Commander-in-Chief, who in 1958 removed Mirza from office and declared himself President. Martial law continued until a new Constitution was promulgated in June 1962. This Constitution laid the basis for a military dictatorship that lasted until 1970 when, after several years of increasingly corrupt and inefficient rule, Ayub Khan was overthrown by his Commander-in-Chief, Field Marshal Agha Muhammad Yahya Khan. Martial law was once again proclaimed, and the whole constitutional question was reopened. The President decided to revive the old system of parliamentary government. However, the question of the nature of the state's relationship with Islam was left to be determined by a new National Assembly.

### The Elections in 1970

At Pakistan's first general elections, held in December 1970, two parties were dominant: the AL in East Pakistan and Bhutto's PPP in the two most populous provinces of West Pakistan, Punjab and Sindh. The AL achieved an absolute majority in the central legislature and demanded provincial autonomy and the decentralization of authority. The League swept to victory on the basis of East Bengal's sense of neglect and exploitation by West Pakistan, and on the issue of language, following a long and bloody agitation to preserve the status of Bengali in the face of pressure from West Pakistan to proclaim Urdu the sole national language. Other issues temporarily overwhelmed that of Islam, which had been such a potent force in determining East Bengal's accession to Pakistan in 1947. The AL's victory appalled West Pakistani politicians, and it was their failure to accommodate the League, together with the brutal repression of its supporters in East Pakistan by the Pakistani military, that led to war with India, defeat for Pakistan and the establishment of Bangladesh. The secession of Bangladesh led to Yahya Khan's downfall, and in December 1971 Zulfikar Ali Bhutto, founder and Chairman of the PPP, took over as President.

## THE 1973 CONSTITUTION AND THE RISE AND FALL OF ZULFIKAR ALI BHUTTO

The National Assembly was convened, and in October 1972 agreed upon a federal parliamentary system of government, with four provinces and two legislative houses. The Prime Minister, answerable to the lower house, was to be the Chief Executive, while the President, elected by both houses voting together, was purely a constitutional head. In April 1973 Pakistan acquired a democratic Constitution. In August, President Bhutto became the Prime Minister of Pakistan.

The new Constitution initially seemed to have the support of all parties. In early 1973, however, opposition right- and left-wing parties formed the United Democratic Front (UDF), in order to demand further amendments that would create 'a truly Islamic, democratic and federal Constitution'. Their fears that the Constitution would award too much power to the Prime Minister and the central Government were intensified by events in Balochistan, where tribal fighting was followed, in February 1973, by the imposition of direct presidential rule, the invocation of emergency powers and the banning of the NAP. In February 1975, although boycotted by the opposition parties, the National Assembly adopted a Constitution Bill empowering the Government to extend the state of emergency beyond six months without parliamentary approval. Mean-while, a new party, the National Democratic Party (NDP), was launched in November 1975 from the ruins of the UDF claiming to be the successor to the NAP, the leaders of whic Bhutto had recently jailed.

In advance of national elections scheduled for 7 March 197 a variety of parties formed a broadly based opposition front, th Pakistan National Alliance (PNA). The PML and the recent formed NDP had, in effect, vanished from the political scene-the PML only temporarily owing to one of its regular intern crises, and the NDP permanently—and the main contest w between the PNA and the ruling PPP, led by Bhutto. At t elections, the PPP secured an overwhelming victory in t National Assembly, but the country descended into chaos violence mounted while Bhutto's opponents challenged t legality of the electoral process. The country seemed to be on the verge of civil war.

## MILITARY RULE: THE DICTATORSHIP OF GEN. ZIA, 1977–88

On 5 July 1977, the armed forces took over the administration of the country. They placed the leaders of the PPP and the PNA in 'temporary protective custody' and imposed martial law. The federal legislative chambers were disbanded and the federal and provincial cabinets dismissed, but the Constitution was not abrogated, although some of its clauses were put in abeyance. The incumbent President remained as Head of State, but provincial governors were replaced. Gen. Mohammad Zia ul-Haq, Chief of Army Staff, became martial law administrator, and a four-member military council was constituted. Political activity was banned for a month, although elections were promised for October.

However, on 1 October 1977 Gen. Zia postponed elections indefinitely and charges were brought against Bhutto and a number of his ministers. Bhutto was convicted of two counts of murder and was executed on 4 April 1979. The Government ordered the release of thousands of political detainees who had been imprisoned during the Bhutto regime, including the NAP leaders (in detention since 1975), and a general amnesty was declared in Balochistan in an attempt to conciliate the province. Although the official ban on political activity was perpetuated, some limited activity was allowed.

By the end of 1978 Zia had become President, with a Cabinet comprising five army generals and 10 civilians. Zia pursued the policy of bringing the country's laws into conformity with Islamic law (*Shari'a*) more zealously than any previous ruler. In February 1979 he announced the enforcement of Islamic penal laws with immediate effect, and the introduction of *zakat* (poor tax) from July of that year, and of *ushr* (tax on agricultural produce), together with other measures in line with Islamic economic practice. Interest-free banking was introduced in 1981. A federal *Shari'a* court, replacing the *Shari'a* benches of the high courts, was established in May 1980. The Council of Islamic Ideology was expanded and reconstituted, and ordered to draft an Islamic system of government in Pakistan.

The political parties proved incapable of opposing Zia. In October 1979 he finally announced the indefinite postponement of elections, the dissolution of all political parties, and the reinforcement of martial law. By July 1983 the Zia regime had survived six years without any major challenge to its authority. However, in late 1984 Zia announced that a national referendum would take place in December, in order that he could seek popular approval for his policies and ensure the process of Islamization, as well as secure a five-year term for himself as President. Campaigning in the name of Islam, Zia was able to muster widespread support, especially in the rural areas. Official results claimed a turn-out of 64% of voters, and a 97.7% 'yes' vote.

By the beginning of 1986 there was limited political freedom in Pakistan. Martial law (in force since 1969) was lifted in December 1985, and there was a revival in party political life. In April Benazir Bhutto, the acting PPP Chairwoman, returned to Pakistan, where she received a tumultuous welcome and immediately launched an attack on the regime.

The sudden death of Zia in August 1988 threw the military regime into chaos. The Chairman of the Senate, Ghulam Ishaq Khan, was appointed acting President, and an emergency National Council took charge of government. A state of emergency was declared.

## THE GOVERNMENT OF BENAZIR BHUTTO, 1988–90

)n 16 November 1988 there was a general election for a new ational Assembly. The PPP failed to win an absolute majory, but it was the only party to secure seats in each of the four rovinces and was able to form a working alliance with the *ohajir* party, the *Mohajir* (later *Muttahida*) *Qaumi Moveent* (MQM). Benazir Bhutto was appointed Prime Minister. he *mohajirs* felt neglected by both the Punjabi and Sindhi litical élites and, in their stronghold of Karachi, developed a political platform to agitate for a share of the benefits of the new state.

Although the PPP did well at the federal election, it performed less convincingly at the provincial elections. The PPP established coalition governments in Sindh and the NWFP, while Mohammad Nawaz Sharif, who was Benazir Bhutto's main rival and head of an alliance comprising a faction of the PML and right-wing and Islamist parties known as the Islamic Democratic Alliance (IDA), was elected as Punjab's Chief Minister.

The euphoria of December 1988 evaporated quickly; the law and order situation had worsened; internecine party warfare mounted; no significant legislation was undertaken; and the burden of taxation and the rate of inflation had both greatly increased. The adverse situation was compounded by widespread charges of corruption against high-ranking officials.

On 6 August 1990 President Ghulam Ishaq Khan dissolved the National Assembly, dismissed Prime Minister Benazir Bhutto, declared a state of emergency and announced fresh elections for October. At the end of August the former Prime Minister's husband, Asif Ali Zardari, was charged with possessing illegal arms. Other former ministers were also detained on various charges, and in early September Benazir Bhutto herself was charged with corruption and misuse of power. In early October Zardari was arrested in Karachi on corruption charges.

## THE FIRST GOVERNMENT OF MOHAMMAD NAWAZ SHARIF, 1990–93

At the general election held on 24 October 1990 the IDA succeeded in obtaining 106 seats. The PPP, which had formed the Pakistan Democratic Alliance (PDA) with several small parties, won 45 seats, and the MQM took 15.

On 6 November 1990 Mohammad Nawaz Sharif became Prime Minister. From its inception his Government was faced with a plethora of problems and controversial issues, both political and economic. Despite the Prime Minister's call for reconciliation, Benazir Bhutto opted for a policy of confrontation, while the PDA threatened resignations en masse and frequently boycotted both the federal and Sindh legislative assemblies.

Pakistani involvement in the Gulf War, which began in January 1991, as a result of Iraq's invasion and annexation of Kuwait in the previous year, created the Sharif Government's first crisis. The dispatch of 11,000 Pakistani troops to assist in the UN-authorized military operation, which was being led by the USA, polarized both the Government and popular opinion. Several parties (including the PPP) exploited the wave of anti-US feeling, fuelled by the recent suspension of US aid to Pakistan, to organize pro-Iraqi protests and rallies. The Government, however, succeeded in surviving the popular outcry.

One of the administrative failures of Benazir Bhutto's regime had been its inability to regulate relations between the central and provincial governments. Nawaz Sharif, in contrast, reached settlements with provincial governments on a number of issues and also—as promised to his alliance partners—addressed the issue of Islam and the Constitution. A bill officially to adopt the Islamic legal code became law in May and a series of 'Islamic reforms' were subsequently adopted. These included: the Constitution Amendment Bill, declaring *Shari'a* to be the law of the land; legislation providing for the Islamization of the educational, judicial and economic systems; the promotion of Islamic values through the mass media; and the eradication of corruption, obscenity and other social evils.

However, the Sharif Government failed to resolve Pakistan's chronic law and order problem. Increasing violence throughout the country in 1991 led the National Assembly to give the Prime Minister the authority to establish impromptu trial courts covering terrorism, kidnappings and armed robbery. Despite the establishment of these courts, the law and order situation did not improve in Sindh. The MQM split when more moderate *mohajirs* formed the MQM (A) in protest against extremists within the organization participating in violence against political opponents. In addition to this problem, a constant barrage of criticism from opposition parties confronted the Government. Apart from accusations of nepotism and corruption, the opposition was concerned about official support for Islamist 'fundamentalism', an issue that was, in addition, contributing to increasing factionalism within the IDA.

As a result of the increasing friction between Sharif and the President in April 1993, the President dissolved the National Assembly and dismissed the Prime Minister, accusing him of 'maladministration, nepotism and corruption'. Political chaos resulted, and in May the Supreme Court ordered that the National Assembly, the Prime Minister and the Cabinet be restored to power immediately. However, Sharif's new Government was soon embroiled in a controversy over intervention in the Punjab and NWFP provincial assemblies. The army was called in to help restore order and negotiate a settlement and in July both Ghulam Ishaq Khan and Nawaz Sharif resigned and the federal legislature and provincial assemblies were dissolved. It was announced that a general election was to be held in October. In the turmoil the IDA alliance collapsed and Sharif formed a new party, the PML (Nawaz) (PML—N).

## THE SECOND GOVERNMENT OF BENAZIR BHUTTO, 1993–97

Following the general election, held on 6 and 9 October 1993, Benazir Bhutto formed a coalition Government. However, from its inception the fortunes of the Bhutto Government were complicated by escalating violence, particularly in Sindh, exacerbated by militant MQM members and the supporters of Nawaz Sharif. The second half of 1994 witnessed a further intensification in the confrontation between the Government and the main opposition party, the PML (N), and, from 1995, opposition also came from fundamentalist groups such as the *Tehreek-i-Nifaz-i-Shariat-i-Mohammadi* (TNSM), who were followers of Maulana Sufi Mohammad. Supported by NWFP tribesmen, the TNSM mounted a campaign for the complete replacement of civil law by *Shari'a*. The Government's response, with its combination of forbearance and harshness, including the arrest of Maulana Sufi Mohammad, defused the tension somewhat, although the root causes of poverty and underdevelopment in the tribal regions remained. Indeed, the leading *khans* bitterly opposed any attempts at modernization, which they perceived as threatening their authority.

In contrast, in Sindh the Government was faced with escalating violence. Karachi was riven by wars between rival drug mafias, at times allegedly supported by the Pakistan military intelligence agency, by clashes between the rival factions of the MQM and by sectarian violence between Sunni and Shi'a Muslims. In March 1995 two US consular officials were murdered in an ambush, and it was not until June that concerted action by the security forces, involving extra-judicial means, restored some semblance of order.

The deteriorating law and order situation throughout most of 1995 and the death sentences imposed on two Christians for blasphemy under the terms of Pakistan's Islamic penal code compromised the Government's efforts to encourage large-scale foreign investment in Pakistan. The sentences were later overruled by the High Court in Lahore, but the incident served to highlight the parlous position of religious minorities in Pakistan. In addition, there was increasing lawlessness involving Sunni and Shi'a factions in Punjab.

Meanwhile, to compound the Government's woes, Pakistan was faced with a deteriorating economic situation by the end of 1995. A tough and unpopular mini-budget was introduced in October which, although it averted an economic collapse, led to a rise in the rate of inflation to around 11%.

Despite all the threats to the Bhutto Government, the opposition parties failed to take advantage of the situation. However, the regime soon found itself in the midst of a dispute with the judiciary and attempts by the Government to pressurize the Supreme Court to accommodate its ambitions inflicted immense damage on the image of the Bhutto administration and led to a deterioration in the relationship between Bhutto and President Sardar Farooq Ahmad Khan Leghari (elected in November 1993). By mid-1996 the Bhutto administration was confronted by the ongoing deterioration in Pakistan's law and order situation, as well as a rallying of opposition forces. In November 1996 the President dismissed the Bhutto Government and appointed an interim administration.

## NAWAZ SHARIF'S RETURN TO POWER, 1997–99

In February 1997, following a general election, Nawaz Sharif returned to power. He immediately embarked on a series of populist measures designed to tackle corruption, the foreign-exchange crisis and environmental degradation. In addition, he attempted to normalize relations with India in order to increase bilateral trade. He also sponsored a bill—that received bipartisan political support—which removed the President's power to dismiss the Prime Minister and to dissolve the National Assembly. However, various problems remained. The economic crisis, fuelled by a trade deficit of US $3,000m. in 1995/96, was far from over, while Kashmir still stood in the way of a much-needed normalization of relations with India.

Domestically, political and sectarian violence continued. Also, it appeared as if Saudi Arabia and Iran were fighting a proxy war in Pakistan, as Pakistan's relations with Iran deteriorated over their rivalry in Afghanistan and Central Asia. Several major issues were prominent in the latter half of 1997: first, accusations of financial impropriety against Benazir Bhutto; second, a clash between the judiciary and Prime Minister Nawaz Sharif, which culminated in the resignation of President Farooq Leghari and the dismissal of the Sindhi head of the Supreme Court; third, increasing sectarian and ethnic violence in Punjab and Sindh; and fourth, the increasing alienation of the NWFP, Sindh and Balochistan that had arisen as a result of the 'Punjabization' of the country.

Against a backdrop of a demoralized opposition, the battle between Sharif and the judiciary continued throughout the rest of the year. The conflict centred on the Supreme Court's disapproval of the parallel justice system of summary trial courts introduced in August 1997 under the controversial Anti-Terrorist Law and resulted in the weakening of the judiciary. Although Sharif undermined the power and independence of the judiciary, he proved unable to resolve more immediate and real issues: the widespread sectarian violence throughout the country, ethnic violence in Punjab and Sindh, the influx of weapons from Afghanistan, and the growing influence of the Afghan Taliban movement in the NWFP. Adding to Sharif's problems, relations between Punjab and the other provinces further deteriorated when the Government pressed ahead with plans to construct the Kalabagh dam, which was bitterly opposed by the governments of both Sindh and the NWFP.

In terms of constitutional government, the increasing reliance of the Sharif administration on the army to carry out routine administrative tasks was seen as undermining normal constitutional processes. Not only did intervention by the army undermine the bureaucracy, but it led to increasing popular resentment that the Government was determined to 'Punjabize' the country, to the detriment of all the other provinces.

In economic terms Sharif's Government was a disappointment. The Pakistani economy remained in recession, and the Government's attempts to introduce fiscal reform along lines suggested by the IMF served only to alienate farmers, traders and factions within the PML (N). Luckily for Sharif, the absence of a strong and united opposition to channel the unrest arising from increasing inflation and unemployment staved off the Government's collapse.

Despite the temporary public euphoria that had resulted from the conduct of nuclear tests in May 1998, the repercussions left Pakistan in dire financial crisis. Rather than address these pressing economic issues, Sharif looked to his own political survival and introduced a Constitutional Amendment Bill in August 1998 to align the country's legal code with *Shari'a* law.

Both more liberal Pakistanis and foreign observers were increasingly worried by developments in Pakistan under Sharif. Endemic corruption, the 'Punjabization' of the country, the disputed fairness of accountability processes, attacks on the judiciary, the introduction of *Shari'a* law, the increasing intrusion of the army into public life and attempts to curb the independent press were viewed with growing concern domestically and internationally.

In April 1999 the long-running investigation into the alleged financial irregularities perpetrated by Benazir Bhutto and her husband, Asif Ali Zardari, culminated in each being sentenced to five years' imprisonment. In addition, their property was confiscated, they were jointly fined US $8.6m., and they were automatically disqualified from membership of the federal legislature. Ironically, however, later in that month corruption cases against 30 incumbent and former PML (N) legislators were finalized and allegations were made regarding financial corruption within Nawaz Sharif's family.

Sharif's response to these developments was to turn to Pakistan's traditional diplomatic ruse of improving relations with Russia and the People's Republic of China in order to prove the strategic importance of Pakistan to the USA and to deflect concerns away from the country's internal problems. While such diplomatic activity was indirectly aimed at the USA, more overtly it was part of Pakistan's campaign against India, which was shaped by the Kashmir dispute. India, as always, remained the centre around which Pakistan's foreign policy pivoted. The first half of 1999 was one of the most dramatic periods in the tortured history of Indo-Pakistani relations (see below).

In May 1998 it had been reported that between 600 and 900 well-armed Islamist militants had crossed the Line of Control (LoC) into the Indian-held sector of Kashmir. The militants' initial success in seizing strategic positions was successfully countered by the use of Indian strike aircraft and the Indian Army provoking sporadic exchanges of fire between troops on both sides of the LoC in the Kargil area. The fighting in Kashmir raised the spectre that a nuclear 'umbrella' could also encourage adventurism that would lead to full-scale conventional conflict.

Pakistan was almost universally condemned for encouraging the intrusion. This diplomatic isolation, together with the fear of the withdrawal of IMF financial assistance and the realization that India might widen the conflict with potentially disastrous consequences, apparently prompted Nawaz Sharif's unexpected visit to Washington, DC, for talks with US President Bill Clinton in July 1998. The US visit resulted in the issuing of the Washington Declaration, which prepared the way for the withdrawal of Islamist forces from Indian-held Kashmir. The Declaration represented a moral defeat for Sharif, as it exposed official Pakistani involvement in the infiltration, and the Government's opponents in Pakistan declared it to be a national 'betrayal'.

Throughout 1998 and 1999 Sharif had become increasingly dependent upon the army. Not only was it co-opted to undertake bureaucratic functions, but an upsurge in sectarian and ethnic violence in Karachi encouraged Sharif to devolve further power to the military in November 1998, with the establishment of military courts in Sindh to try 'terrorist' cases. In January 1999 Sharif proposed the establishment of military courts throughout the country, but in February the Supreme Court ruled against the establishment of a parallel judicial system, effectively barring the establishment of military courts.

Sharif's increasingly authoritarian approach to politics, particularly in Karachi and Sindh, led to a rapprochement between the PPP and the MQM (A), based on their opposition to his authoritarianism and Punjabization policies. At the same time the PPP had edged closer to one of its erstwhile foes, the Awami National Party (ANP—a coalition of four small leftist parties formed in 1986). The ANP had severed its ties with the PML (N) earlier that year over its 'broken promise' to rename the NWFP 'Pakhtoonkhwa', and the PPP offered the bait of the levolution of powers to the provincial governments. The ANP had also been alienated by Nawaz Sharif's decision, in the wake of the nuclear test explosions, to announce approval for the construction of the controversial Kalabagh dam. In response to the threat of centralization, including the Government's curtailment of the powers of the Senate owing to the latter's delay in implementing the constitutional amendment imposing *Shari'a* law, opposition groups in the smaller provinces, led by the ANP, formed the Pakistan Oppressed Nations Movement (PONM) in late 1998 and found a supporter for its anti-Punjab stance in the PPP. In mid-September 1999 Nawaz Sharif's position appeared increasingly precarious following the formation of a Grand Democratic Alliance (GDA) by 19 conservative and centrist opposition parties, including the PPP, the MQM (A) and the ANP, which demanded the immediate resignation of the Prime Minister. The various Islamist parties, including the JIP, also intensified their anti-Government protests and rallies throughout the country. The opposition was weakened to some extent, however, by the fact that Benazir Bhutto was unwilling to return to Pakistan for fear of being arrested on charges of corruption.

## THE COUP OF OCTOBER 1999 AND BEYOND

On 12 October 1999 events took an unexpected turn when the Sharif Government was overthrown in a bloodless coup by the Chief of Army Staff and Chairman of the Joint Chiefs of Staff Committee, Gen. Pervez Musharraf. The deposed Prime Minister was subsequently placed under house arrest.

The fourth military coup since 1947 thus brought to an end 11 years of competitive party politics. On 15 October 1999 Musharraf took up the position of Chief Executive, declared a state of emergency, and suspended the Constitution, the National Assembly, the Senate, and the four provincial legislatures. The President and judiciary were, however, left intact, and a relatively free press was permitted to operate. Partisan activity was, unsurprisingly, limited. Musharraf ensured, by means of a Provisional Constitution Order, that his actions could not be challenged by any court of law, thus imposing virtual martial law.

The alliance of political parties that had been built up against Sharif failed to challenge Musharraf. Years of corruption, incompetence and futile rivalry had undermined mass support for the traditional political parties. Many saw the army alone as the only state agency untainted by corruption and, as such, its move to seize power met with little domestic opposition. In international terms, reaction to the coup was relatively subdued. There was some criticism, but such condemnations were not very forceful and were largely pronounced on principle.

Musharraf's immediate concern was to restore both law and order and the economy. He consciously created a 'non-political', technocratic Government that would command both domestic and international support and, presumably, also pave the way for the reconstruction of Pakistani institutional, economic and political life. He replaced all the provincial governors (three of them with military figures), who now acted as provincial Chief Ministers, and announced a two-tier structure to head his administration: a National Security Council (NSC) and a civilian Cabinet. In addition, provincial cabinets were appointed. In the federal Cabinet, the key position of Minister of Foreign Affairs was given to Abdul Sattar, a retired career Foreign Service officer who had served as acting Minister of Foreign Affairs in 1993; the Minister of Finance was Shaukat Aziz, an internationally respected banker. At the beginning of November 1999, meanwhile, as evidence of the military Government's serious determination to confront official corruption, a National Accountability Bureau (NAB) was established. In August the NSC was reconstituted and redefined as the supreme executive body, to represent more closely the military and technocratic mix that Musharraf sought to promote for his Government. The NSC comprised the three chiefs of armed forces and the Ministers of Foreign Affairs, the Interior, Finance and Commerce.

In mid-January 2000 Musharraf moved to silence his most vocal political critics, formally charging Nawaz Sharif and six other PML (N) senior officials (who were later acquitted) with various offences. In early April Sharif was convicted of having attempted to hijack Gen. Musharraf at the time of the coup and of terrorism; he was acquitted on all other charges. Sharif was sentenced to two terms of life imprisonment, heavily fined, and his property was confiscated. The remaining six defendants were acquitted of all charges. In July Sharif was convicted of corruption by a 'National Accountability Court', sentenced to a further 14 years' rigorous imprisonment and disqualified from holding office for 21 years. The international community was critical of both the trials and the severity of the sentences.

Sharif's conviction split the PML (N), particularly as he was now legally disqualified from holding office. Musharraf resolved the question of Sharif's status in the country—possibly as a martyr figure—by unexpectedly releasing him from prison in December 2000 and sending him into exile in Saudi Arabia. In return, Sharif supposedly surrendered his personal and business assets, pledged not to return to Pakistan for 10 years, and agreed not to participate in Pakistani politics for 21 years.

In late 2000 former leaders Nawaz Sharif and Benazir Bhutto, now both in exile, together with 16 other smaller political parties, agreed to form the Alliance for the Restoration of Democracy (ARD), in an effort to end military rule and accelerate a return to democracy in Pakistan. The new alliance superseded the PPP-led GDA.

Although Bhutto's conviction was set aside by the Supreme Court in April 2001, following the emergence of evidence that Nawaz Sharif's Government had forced the judge to convict Bhutto and her husband, both faced further charges of corruption. In June 2001 Bhutto was sentenced *in absentia* (she remained in Dubai) to three years' imprisonment for not appearing in court to answer charges of corruption. Thus, within two months Musharraf had effectively removed his two major political opponents, although he had yet to deal with the ever-present Islamist parties, which had remained on the sidelines during his struggle with Sharif and Bhutto.

Like his military predecessors, Musharraf promised an eventual return to civilian rule and announced wide-ranging measures to address the country's problems. He also stressed, again like his military predecessors, that Pakistan wished to maintain good relations with both the USA and China. Although the Government avoided the subject of the restoration of democracy, it was extremely sensitive to the issue of its own legitimacy. In May 2000 the pro-Government Supreme Court unanimously endorsed the coup's legitimacy, citing 'necessity' in the supreme interest of the public. Despite thus providing legal sanction for the coup, it ordered the Government to achieve its declared objectives and restore civil rule by democratic elections to federal and provincial authorities within three years. However, the Supreme Court gave the Chief Executive the powers to perform all legislative measures and even amend the Constitution under the same doctrine of 'state necessity'.

In terms of policy objectives, the Musharraf Government was long on rhetoric and short on action. A building-boom-inspired revival of the economy did take place, but the long-standing social problems of Pakistan—an imploding public education system, widespread drug addiction, the rapid decline of the public health system, the inflow of millions of refugees from war-torn Afghanistan, and the disadvantages suffered by women and ethnic and sectarian minorities—were only marginally addressed.

The Government also singularly failed to address the education system. *Madrassas*, as centres of traditional Islamic learning and the teaching of Arabic, had existed for centuries and from the 19th century had competed with secular public schools. However, by the late 20th century there had been a resurgence in the number and popularity of *madrassas*, many of which received financial support from orthodox Sunni countries such as Saudi Arabia. In some instances *madrassas* were transformed from day schools to boarding schools where, in addition to the old curriculum, students were exposed to more radical ideas concerning Islam and the role of Muslims in the modern world. Although the *madrassas* fail to offer a modern education, the deficiencies of the public education system are such that many believe that there is little to differentiate the two systems in terms of producing literate and employable graduates. At least the *madrassas* provide a moral education for the children of the poorer classes.

The Government's attitude towards the Islamist political organizations was ambiguous, as were its actions in curbing religious extremism. In April 2000 the Minister of the Interior declared the Government's intention to adopt a firm stance on the issue of sectarianism and, if necessary, to ban sectarian parties and groups. In June, following pressure from the USA and its allies, the Government outlined a plan to suppress networks of militant groups operating in Pakistan and Afghanistan, but in July a decree was issued to revive the Islamic provisions of the suspended Constitution and to incorporate them in the provisional constitutional order, thereby supporting a ban on the passing of any law that conflicted with Islamic principles.

Under increasing domestic and international pressure, President Musharraf announced in August 2001 that federal and provincial elections would be held in early October 2002, in order that Pakistan would be returned to civilian rule before the deadline imposed by the Supreme Court. He also stated his intention to relax the ban on political activity by giving parties time to prepare for the elections. However, the terrorist attacks of 11 September 2001 in New York and Washington, USA, changed all of these plans.

As a result of the events of 11 September, Musharraf's international standing suddenly and dramatically improved. From being on the sidelines of international diplomacy and constantly under pressure to respond to foreign criticisms of his regime, Musharraf now found himself a courted ally in the US 'war on terror'. Foreign criticism of his regime continued, but the reality was that as long as Pakistan adhered to the policy imperatives of the USA—namely conciliation with India, restraint on nuclear proliferation and support for US policies in the Middle East and Afghanistan—there was unlikely to be another humiliation of the magnitude of the Washington Declaration.

The events of 11 September also relieved the pressure on Musharraf regarding the restoration of democracy in Pakistan and the need to seek some sort of political deal with either the PPP or the PML (N), and theoretically left him free to deal with Islamist extremist groups as he wished. In addition, Musharraf took advantage of the new relationship with the USA to strengthen his own position as President. In early April 2002 the Government approved a plan to hold a national referendum seeking endorsement for Musharraf's term of office as President to be extended by five years, and approval of the Government's political and economic programme. The referendum was held at the end of April and, according to official figures, resulted in about 98% of those participating giving their support to the proposal.

Meanwhile, with regard to Islamist groups, Musharraf had to contend with the fact that senior elements within the army sympathized with a number of these groups, and he carefully differentiated between militant and moderate religious organizations as a means of deflecting US concern over this development.

By mid-2002 President Musharraf had considerably strengthened his domestic position by apparently isolating the militants, marginalizing his most dangerous opponents, and assuming the presidency for a period of five years, which ensured that he would later be in a position to strengthen constitutionally the role of the army in Pakistan's political system. Indeed, in July 2002 he introduced a set of reforms, including a range of proposed amendments to the Constitution designed to transform Pakistan's prime ministerial system into a presidential one.

There was immediate opposition to Musharraf's proposed constitutional reforms, and to his suggestion of a National Security Council, in which the armed forces would be given ultimate power over matters relating to national security. Meanwhile, the main opposition parties attempted to prepare for the elections. Benazir Bhutto was re-elected as leader of the PPP, but, given the decree banning parties from contesting an election if any of its office holders had been convicted of an offence, the PPP formed a new party, the Pakistan People's Party Parliamentarians (PPPP), under a new leader, to present a challenge at the forthcoming elections.

Meanwhile, the brother of Nawaz Sharif, Shahbaz Sharif the former Chief Minister of Punjab, was named leader of the PML (N). Nawaz Sharif officially withdrew his candidacy i September 2002, reportedly in solidarity with Bhutto. Th PPPP and PML (N), both under new leadership, were thu permitted to take part in the elections. In response to criti cisms, the President promised to restore democracy an transfer power to an elected government.

In order to safeguard himself against gains by the oppositio parties in the forthcoming elections, Musharraf unilaterall endorsed 29 amendments (as proposed in July) to the Const tution through a Legal Framework Order on 21 August 200

These gave him the power to dissolve the elected National Assembly, extend his term in office and appoint Supreme Court judges. Tellingly, the military was awarded a formal role in governing the country.

## The October 2002 Elections

At the October 2002 elections the PML (Quaid-e-Azam—Q), a pro-Musharraf faction of the PML, won the largest number of directly elected seats (77 out of 272). While there were accusations of poll-rigging, the party did not secure an outright majority and had insufficient seats to form a government in its own right. It was closely followed by the PPPP (with 63 seats) and the Muttahida Majlis-e-Amal (MMA), an alliance of six Islamist parties, (with 45 seats). The Punjab-based PML (N) only won 14 seats. The result indicated that a coalition Government would be formed, in which the religious parties would exert a significant degree of influence.

In the provincial elections the clear victory of the MMA in the NWFP reinforced its bargaining power in the National Assembly. The PML (Q) performed well in Punjab, while the PPP fared better in Sindh than it had nationally. Such an outcome appeared to limit Musharraf's capacity to take unilateral action in foreign affairs, but it placed him in a position in which he could act unilaterally on domestic matters, without attracting external criticism, on the grounds that he had to deal with an unworkable parliamentary system.

In the weeks prior to the opening of the new parliament, the constraints facing Musharraf became more apparent, as the various parties and groupings canvassed a variety of coalitions that might enable them to assume some control over whatever form of government emerged.

Pakistan's relations with the USA further complicated issues. The ARD, for example, supported the alliance with the USA and the 'war on terror'. On the other hand, the MMA was motivated by strong anti-US sentiment and voiced its opposition to the intervention of US forces in Afghanistan and their presence in Pakistan. Posed against these inter-party divisions was the attempt by Musharraf and the army to ensure that a government, formed by consensus, was created around the newly amended Constitution.

Musharraf's attempts to form a working government were driven by his desire to demonstrate to the world that he was instrumental in reforming a corrupt system of governance. Domestically, his opponents accused him of undermining constitutional government with his amendments to the Constitution, which gave him the power, as President, to dismiss the Prime Minister, Cabinet and National Assembly, as well as the right to appoint and dismiss members of the judiciary. In response, Musharraf revived the 1973 Constitution—although in a form that contained his controversial amendments—and, by splitting the MMA, secured enough votes in the National Assembly to be sworn in for a further five-year term as President with a narrow working majority. A very fragile coalition Government, led by the PML (Q) and including dissident members of the MMA, was established.

The new Government faced a number of immediate problems. There was continuing opposition to Musharraf's constitutional arrangements. The President claimed that they represented significant political reforms and encouraged stability. Internationally, the USA supported his arguments, while the European Union (EU) was more critical of his logic. The other major set of difficulties stemmed from his relationship with the USA. There was widespread domestic resentment at changes to the USA's immigration policy (according to which Pakistani nationals should be singled out, along with a number of other nationalities, for greater surveillance). In addition, the US-led action to depose Saddam Hussain in Iraq from March 2003 aroused widespread protest throughout the country, from both the political left and right.

The National Assembly reconvened on 28 June 2003 and by the end of 2003 it appeared that Musharraf was in control of the political situation. Yet his control was contingent upon the behaviour of the MMA. Given its strong position in the state assemblies of the NWFP and Balochistan, and its relatively strong position in the National Assembly, it was unlikely in the short term that the MMA would be prepared to support a move by the PPPP to dissolve the federal legislature. In the longer term, however, there was a possibility that it might review the situation, especially if anti-US sentiment continued to grow.

Throughout 2003 and 2004, however, Musharraf's control over domestic events was seriously challenged. There was a disturbing increase in incidents of violence directed against Pakistan's Shi'a religious minority by militant Sunnis keen to provoke sectarian violence and challenge the alliance between the USA and Pakistan. The serious nature of the challenge posed by militant groups was underlined in December 2003, when President Musharraf twice narrowly escaped death in assassination attempts in Rawalpindi. Other sources of the militants' anger—shared by a cross-section of Pakistani society—were recent shifts in foreign policy concerning relations with India and a resolution of the Kashmir dispute. From the standpoint of the militants this was a blatant betrayal of Pakistan's national interests, while for others the unilateral overtures made by Musharraf to India were seen as further evidence of his authoritarian and anti-constitutional policies. However, Musharraf had challenged domestic constraints on his ability to conduct an independent foreign policy, and, despite widespread criticism, the opposition was divided between Islamist militants and those who, although opposed to Musharraf on many issues, shared his desire to neutralize the militants.

In early 2004, the intense controversy that surrounded the implication of Abdul Qadeer Khan, a founding figure within Pakistan's nuclear programme, along with several associates, in the sale of nuclear materials and technology to nations such as the Democratic People's Republic of Korea (North Korea), Libya and Iran highlighted the complexity of reactions to the USA within Pakistan. Following a public confession by Khan, Musharraf—under pressure from the MMA and several opposition politicians—issued a conditional pardon to Khan on the basis of his heroic popular standing and record of national service. While both Khan and the Government insisted that he had operated unilaterally, the suspicion remained that the military had been involved and that he was little more than a scapegoat. Inevitably, the debate contributed to mounting criticism of the Government and its ally, the USA.

From late 2003, Musharraf strengthened his hold over the state, despite the onslaught of criticism resulting from the nuclear proliferation scandal and concern over his increasingly authoritarian rule. In December, in exchange for promises that he submit to a vote of confidence on his presidency and that he resign from his military post by December 2004, the MMA agreed to allow an altered version of the constitutional amendments to pass through the National Assembly. The amendments were approved on the final day of 2003, and Musharraf won a subsequent vote of confidence on his rule. Consequently, his presidential term was extended to 2007, and all actions taken by the President subsequent to the coup of October 1999 were granted retrospective validation.

The role of the military in government was entrenched further in April 2004, when the National Assembly, in the face of strong protests from many opposition members, approved a bill legitimizing the creation of the NSC as a 'consultative' organization to advise the Government on security and defence matters. The NSC was structured in such a manner as virtually to guarantee presidential control of its proceedings and decisions. Moreover, following this consolidation of centralized power, Musharraf reneged on his promise to relinquish his post as Chief of Army Staff at the end of 2004. The opposition denounced his decision and Musharraf later conceded the point, as in reality it was of little practical significance.

These developments, combined with the selective detention of opponents of the Government, such as the arrest and imprisonment of Javed Hashmi, a leader of the PML (N), led to criticism from opposition forces that the Government was becoming ever more authoritarian. Moreover, in July 2004, when Prime Minister Jamali unexpectedly resigned (reportedly as a result of a critical reference to the role of the military in politics), Chaudhry Shujaat Hussain, leader of the military-aligned PML (Q), was appointed as his interim successor. Musharraf then announced that, once he had been elected as a member of the National Assembly, Shaukat Aziz, Minister of Finance and Revenue and former international corporate banking executive, would be appointed Prime Minister. In August Shaukat Aziz was sworn in as the new Prime Minister and, soon afterwards, indicated his intention to retain control over the Ministry of Finance and Revenue. However, opposition politicians boycotted his election as Prime Minister, on the grounds that they were being asked to 'rubber stamp' a decision by President Musharraf.

In 2005 Musharraf made a surprise move to improve relations with India. His actions were unilateral and, given the support that they received from the USA, immediately provoked resistance from most political parties in Pakistan. Musharraf tackled the core issue that had divided India and Pakistan since 1947—Kashmir. In a populist move, bus links between India and Pakistan were restored, the President visited India to attend a cricket match between India and Pakistan and, coincidentally, in private discussions with the Indian Government made concessions concerning Kashmir that, in effect, removed it from the agenda as the primary issue that had to be resolved between the two countries before other issues could be addressed. In part, this move was due to US pressure, and was motivated by Musharraf's need to gain greater legitimacy within Pakistan. However, Kashmir continued to constitute something of a 'double-edged sword' within Pakistan, where even liberal elements were suspicious of the unilateral nature of Musharraf's proposals and demanded equivalent concessions from India. More extremist groups within the Pakistan body politic, such as the MMA, were equally suspicious of the President's policies, which they perceived as being driven by his overt reliance upon the goodwill of the USA.

While Musharraf won the support of the USA—to the extent that it agreed to sell him 25 F-16 fighter aircraft, much to the annoyance of India, which was subsequently placated by a similar arms deal—Pakistan's domestic politics remained convoluted and contentious. A major problem concerned Musharraf's relationship with the country's extremist groups. The MMA campaigned successfully to force the Government to abandon badly needed measures to reform the *madrassa* educational system, the judiciary remained under the constant threat of political intervention, sectarian strife was widespread and generally unchecked, and the police attacked peaceful marches by human rights organizations.

In the mean time, the Pakistani Government, in an attempt to bolster its domestic legitimacy, was disregarding the activities of extremist Muslim and anti-democratic groups. In the Federally Administered Tribal Areas (FATA) and Northern Areas, the Government took advantage of the regions' anomalous constitutional status and allowed them to be turned into sanctuaries for sectarian and international violence and centres of the arms and drugs trade. Elsewhere, the Government conceded power to tribal leaders (e.g. in Balochistan) and, across rural Pakistan, permitted conservative and extra-legal *jirgas* or *panchayats* to wield enormous power. It also singularly failed to reform a rapidly collapsing public education system and a corrupt police force.

As part of its ongoing attempts to defuse internal political unrest, the Musharraf Government became involved in a number of domestic political dialogues with both ends of the political spectrum in Pakistan: with Islamic conservative parties such as the MMA, and with the PML (N) and the PPPP (both leaders of which remained in exile). The MMA, from its stronghold in the NWFP, singularly failed to respond to Musharraf's overtures.

The stance of the MMA was strengthened by the failure of both the PML (N) and the PPPP to respond to Musharraf's overtures. Both parties attempted to negotiate a common charter of democracy, which essentially demanded the restoration of the 1973 Constitution as it was before the 1999 military coup. Both were critical of Musharraf's overtures to India, ironically also an issue for the MMA. The problem for the PPPP and the PML (N) was that, although critical of the manner of Musharraf's dealings with India, they essentially supported the alliance with the USA and were opposed to the MMA. For them and for Musharraf the most pressing domestic problem continued to be the MMA, which had a 'grass roots' organization unrivalled by any other political party. However, in July 2005 when—under pressure from the British Prime Minister, Tony Blair, following the bombings in London in that month—Musharraf arrested 300 militants in Pakistan, the call of the MMA for nation-wide protests was largely ignored, indicating that its appeal might be on the wane.

Despite the government crackdown on Islamist militants following the London bombings, there was a resurgence in acts of violence attributed to Islamist extremists in the succeeding 12 months. Violence was directed not only at the central Government and the USA, but also resulted from mounting sectarian tensions between Shi'a and Sunni Muslims, and tribal-based violence in the NWFP and Balochistan against the central Government and between rival tribal leaders. Fighting in Balochistan showed signs of escalating into full-scale warfare, with government repression forcing an alliance between conservative tribal leaders and enlightened Balochi nationalists.

In the MMA-controlled NWFP the provincial government moved to impose Taliban-inspired public morality laws, while there was an increase in sectarian violence, with a number of fatal attacks on Shi'as by Sunnis, and internecine warfare between rival tribal leaders. Shi'a and Sunni Muslims also clashed in Sindh. There was a general nation-wide deterioration in Sunni–Shi'a relations, as well as continuing sporadic attacks on Christians. In Balochistan violence continued, with attacks on public installations and the murder of three Chinese workers associated with the central Government's plans to develop the Balochi port of Gwadar as a gateway to Afghanistan and Central Asia. In August 2006 Nawab Akbar Bugti, a prominent tribal leader and activist, was killed in a clash with government forces in Balochistan, leading to strikes and civil unrest. In the tribal areas on the Afghan border, such as the North and South Waziristan Agencies, the Pakistan army was regularly involved in clashes with pro-Taliban militants. However, in September the Government signed an agreement with militants in North Waziristan, included in which was a government pledge to reduce its military presence in the area in exchange for an end to cross-border movement and attacks on government forces. At this time, Pakistan had 80,000 troops deployed in the NWFP and Balochistan to suppress internal rebellion and to root out pro-Taliban and Taliban militants using the region as a base for their operations.

While the Government disavowed Islamist terrorism under pressure from the USA and other Western allies, it continued to walk a fine line in its relationship with domestic Islamist militant groups. Although Musharraf took measures to deal with the controversial issue of the existence of al-Qa'ida and foreign Taliban groups in Pakistan and measures were adopted to ban militant groups, illicit groups such as *Lashkar-e-Taiba* and *Jaish-e-Mohammed* continued to operate under new names and with their infrastructure intact.

The state education system remained in shambles, encouraging the trend among the poorer classes to send their sons to *madrassas* where they receive a conservative and basic education and are fed and clothed. Government claims to have reformed the curriculum of *madrassas* and to have severed the schools' links with Islamist militant groups were highly debatable.

Nationally the judiciary remained muzzled and underfunded while, in the area of women's issues, attacks on women, tribal and village council-sanctioned rapes and forced marriages continued. In broader civil society NGO activity was not encouraged by the Government outside strictly defined parameters: for example, in their response to the catastrophic earthquake of October 2005, where more than 73,000 people were killed and millions left homeless, the Government wa considered to have marginalized civil society relief organiza-tions, instead opting for army-led relief.

From the end of 2006 levels of violence and discord mounte across Pakistan and by mid-2007 the problems facing th regime were legion. Balochistan remained in open revol Conservative pressure on, and harassment of, women i government and the legislature continued. In 2006–07 possib as many as 1,000 women and girls were killed in so-calle 'honour killings' (the murder of a person, almost invariably woman, who has been perceived as having brought dishono to their family) despite some attempts by the regime to provi legislative protection for women.

Islamic sectarianism mounted in the Federally Administered Northern Areas (Gilgit and Baltistan), where the Government's failure to provide meaningful autonomy and basic political rights increased the appeal of sectarian radicals. In the Federally Administered Tribal Areas (FATA), which stretch from South Waziristan to Bajaur along the Afghanistan-Pakistan border, the federal Government drew up peace agreements with pro-Taliban tribal elders according to which the latter confirmed that they would not provide refuge to foreign militants (mainly supporters or members of al-Qa'ida), while the Government, for its part, was obliged either to downgrade its military presence or to consult the elders before launching operations in the region. Not only did these agreements outrage the Afghan Government, but they brought the wrath of the USA down on Musharraf, who later reversed this policy. However, Musharraf's approach to the Taliban and campaign against al-Qa'ida unleashed forces that threatened the regime. Across Pakistan there was an increase in suicide bombings, attacks on rival groups and open defiance of the Government, culminating in the army laying siege to the Red Mosque in Islamabad in July 2007, during which approximately 100 militants, hostages and army officers lost their lives. The regime's problems had been compounded by the emergence of a coalition of opposition groups leading a nationwide protest against the President's dismissal of the Chief Justice, Iftikhar Mohammad Chaudhry, in March 2007 and related unrest in Karachi; this reached a new intensity in May with large-scale rioting and clashes between government supporters and the opposition resulting in more than 41 fatalities. In July Chaudhry's suspension was ruled as unconstitutional and he was reinstated as Chief Justice. The Government's rather crude attempts to suppress the media were also the subject of much debate.

By the second half of 2007, with presidential and legislative elections imminent, the military regime appeared to have lost the support of the majority of political and religious groups in Pakistan, and was facing the spread of an Iraq-like insurgency. Musharraf's response was to sack senior judicial officials and place them under house arrest. In addition he adopted a 'carrot and stick' approach in terms of measures to check the growing influence of Islamist extremists. In the face of growing internal unrest Musharraf declared a state of emergency in November 2007. There was considerable international criticism of this move and Pakistan was expelled from the Commonwealth.

The assassination of Benazir Bhutto on 27 December 2007 was a turning point for Musharraf. He was driven to hold free elections on 18 February 2008, at which his supporters were routed. The PPP, with Asif Ali Zardari and Bilawal Bhutto Zardari as joint Chairmen, won the largest number of seats, followed by Nawaz Sharif's PML (N)—although Sharif could not stand for election due to his standing criminal conviction. In the wake of the election Zardari and Sharif reached an agreement to form a coalition government with Yousaf Raza Gillani from the PPP as Prime Minister. The imprisoned judges were freed and negotiations were begun with Taliban and other Islamist groups in the FATA to reduce the violence being generated from the region.

However, within two months the coalition was in trouble. Sharif withdrew his ministers from the government over the issue of the reinstatement of the dismissed judges. Ostensibly the PPP wanted to move cautiously on the issue, while Sharif argued for their immediate reinstatement. Given the poor record of both the PPP and Sharif with respect to the freedom of the judiciary it seemed most likely that the issue of the judges was a cover for major differences between the two parties with respect to the future of Musharraf. In August 2008, matters came to a head when the PPP and the PML (N) announced that impeachment proceedings against Musharraf were being sought. In a televised address on 18 August, Musharraf announced his resignation as President. Although he denied charges of violation of the Constitution and gross misconduct, Musharraf acknowledged that impeachment proceedings could have provoked further instability in the country. The Chairman of the Senate, Mohammad Mian Soomro, was appointed President in an acting capacity, pending the parliamentary election of a successor. A week later the PML (N) announced its withdrawal from the coalition Government, citing the continuing dispute over the reinstatement of judges. While the PPP had put Zardari forward as its presidential candidate, the PML (N) nominated a former Chief Justice of the Supreme Court, Saeeduzzaman Siddiqui.

## FOREIGN RELATIONS

### Relations with India

Indo-Pakistani relations have generally conditioned the foreign policy of Pakistan. The bitterness engendered by Partition, and the Kashmir dispute, hampered relations between the two states. The result has been that there have been occasions when the two countries have fought local wars, as in Kashmir (1947–48) and the Rann of Kutch (1965), as well as two full-scale wars, in 1965 and 1971.

#### *1971–80*

During these years there was the beginning of a *rapprochement* with India. An agreement was reached at Shimla in July 1972 that provided for the withdrawal of Indian and Pakistani troops from occupied territories. Bilateral relations, however, deteriorated again after India's conduct of a nuclear test in May 1974. An exchange of ambassadors was thus delayed for a further two years. Contacts between the respective governments in February 1978 resulted in further normalization, and paved the way for a new accord on the distribution of Indus waters in April 1978.

In 1974 Pakistan recognized Bangladesh, but relations between the two countries improved only after the collapse of the Mujib regime in August 1975. Pakistan persuaded the West Asian Muslim countries to extend aid to Bangladesh and there evolved a continuing identity of views of the two countries on most international issues that not only strengthened relations between the two states, but caused some concern in India.

#### *The 1980s*

When she returned to power in January 1980 Indian Prime Minister Indira Gandhi proved unsympathetic to some of Pakistan's concerns. Given India's relationship with the USSR, she refused to condemn Soviet intervention in Afghanistan (see below), on the grounds that it was not a threat to Pakistan's security. In addition, New Delhi was annoyed by a US offer of military aid to Pakistan, designed to bolster the country's defences in view of the Soviet threat. Also, while opposed to Pakistan's nuclear programme for peaceful purposes, India officially affirmed its right to produce nuclear weapons, and successfully launched a four-stage rocket, of its own design, to place a satellite into orbit.

Throughout the 1980s mutual suspicions centred on their rival nuclear programmes, large weapons purchases and naval build-ups, and Indian concerns that Pakistan was meddling in the affairs of strife-torn Punjab undermined attempts at confidence building.

#### *The 1990s*

Relations between Pakistan and India reached a crisis in late 1989, when India sent troops into Jammu and Kashmir and placed the Srinagar valley under indefinite curfew. The Indians were responding to an intensification of militant activity led by the outlawed Jammu and Kashmir Liberation Front (JKLF). The JKLF demanded either an independent Kashmir or unification with Pakistan and received verbal support from the President of Pakistani-controlled Azad (Free) Kashmir, Abdul Qayyum Khan. India claimed that militants were trained and armed in Pakistan and had largely organized the violent uprising. Pakistan rejected these claims and India's call for bilateral negotiations and reiterated its commitment to a settlement of the Kashmir problem in accordance with earlier UN resolutions (i.e. proposals to hold a plebiscite under the auspices of the UN in the two parts of the state).

There was a continuous exchange of bellicose statements between Pakistan and India. However, in January 1991 (encouraged by the USA), Pakistan and India agreed to exchange instruments of ratification regarding the December 1988 agreement not to attack each other's nuclear facilities. In April 1991 they agreed that both sides would provide mutual advance notification of troop movements and military exercises, and that aircraft would be allowed to fly over the other's territory through specified air corridors. A timetable was drawn up for further talks on other controversial issues, notably the delimitation of borders in the Siachen area and the decision by India, which caused great concern in Pakistan, to construct a barrage on the River Jhelum, in violation of the 1960 Indus Water Treaty.

Nevertheless, skirmishes along the border in Kashmir increased, and despite Sharif's attempts to improve the strained relations between the two countries, the relationship deteriorated even further in 1993, when India accused Pakistan of involvement in bomb explosions in Mumbai (Bombay), which killed more than 300 people. Pakistan closed its consulate in Mumbai in March 1994 and in June the Pakistani Prime Minister, Benazir Bhutto, described India's test firing of its surface-to-surface missile, *Prithvi*, as 'provocative' and warned of a missile race in the region.

However, in February 1997 the relationship showed signs of possible improvement when, shortly after forming his second ministry, Nawaz Sharif declared that 'we have to learn how to live as good neighbours, now is the time for serious dialogue'. In March talks resumed between the two countries, and in April the Ministers of Foreign Affairs met in Delhi at the end of the Non-aligned Foreign Ministers' Conference. However, relations deteriorated once more in June when there were reports that Indian medium-range *Prithvi* missiles had been moved to a site near the border with Pakistan. A further deterioration of relations occurred later in that year, when there was an upsurge in violence on the LoC, with both sides shelling each other's positions, leading to civilian fatalities.

### *Nuclear Tests*

Clashes between Indian troops and militants continued through 1998 in Kashmir, and yet a further deterioration in Indo-Pakistani relations occurred in April, when Pakistan test-fired a long-range missile capable of hitting any target in India. The missile was named 'Ghauri', after the 12th-century Turkish Muslim invader of India, and was certainly not calculated to encourage warmer relations with the right-wing Bharatiya Janata Party (BJP)-led coalition Government that had come to power in India in March.

In mid-May 1998 India shocked the world by conducting five nuclear weapons tests. The USA immediately imposed sanctions, under the 1994 non-proliferation law, which would cost India as much as US $20,000m. in lost aid. Japan responded similarly, but other members of the G-8 group, while vocal in their criticism of India's actions, advised caution. The USA advised that Pakistan exercise restraint, but Pakistan conducted six nuclear explosions, which immediately subjected it to sanctions that had a major impact on its already fragile economy. In July, in an attempt to defuse the situation, the USA removed some of the sanctions imposed on the two countries.

Throughout 1999 continuing violence in Kashmir further heightened bilateral tensions and, in January 2000, Indian Prime Minister Vajpayee stated that India would 'work towards getting Pakistan declared a terrorist state'. However, following the October 1999 coup in Pakistan, which brought Gen. Pervez Musharraf to power, Pakistan's repeated offers to take part in peace negotiations prevented any further escalation in the hostility between the two countries.

In January 2001 relations between the two states began to improve. Pakistan's assistance to India following a devastating earthquake in Gujarat, together with pressure from the USA, caused India to soften its stance towards Pakistan. In May the Indian Government ended its cease-fire with an invitation to Pakistan to enter negotiations, which Musharraf accepted. The summit meeting was held in mid-July, in the Indian city of Agra. However, the seventh Indo-Pakistani summit in 50 years was, like its predecessors, a failure, because neither side could afford to be seen to retreat from the entrenched principles that had shaped their country's foreign policy since 1947. Relations deteriorated further in December, following an attack by Islamist militants on the Indian Union parliament building in New Delhi. India was not mollified by Musharraf's strong condemnation of the attack and his arrest of the perpetrators, and it sought to use the situation to isolate Pakistan. President Musharraf used his national address in mid-January 2002, delivered in both Urdu and English, skilfully to appease both his domestic constituency and the international community. Although Musharraf was intent on curbing the activities of militant groups, he was constrained by a number of factors, in particular the problematic nature of his own position within Pakistan's domestic political system, and the rise in militant attacks within Pakistan itself. In his efforts to meet the demands of the USA, Musharraf risked alienating major religious groups and political parties, and as a result his capacity to take action was increasingly limited.

However, the events of 11 September 2001 in New York and Washington were to alter radically the nature of Indo-Pakistani relations, although well into 2002 Islamabad and New Delhi seemed still to be entrenched in their traditional positions. Bellicose rhetoric on both sides appeared to bring closer the prospect of a nuclear confrontation. However, behind the scenes the USA was working on both sides to forge a compromise. The USA wanted to be allied with both India and Pakistan in its 'war on terror', and was prepared to make considerable concessions to both if relations improved.

### *The Possibility of a Rapprochement*

In October 2003 India proposed a number of confidence-building measures intended to improve both nuclear security and relations with Pakistan, including the resumption of transport links and improved communication protocols. India expected that this conciliatory move would gain the approval of the USA and the wider international community, while simultaneously putting pressure on Pakistan to reciprocate. In November the Pakistani Prime Minister, Jamali, responded by announcing a unilateral cease-fire along the LoC in Kashmir. From December 2003 and throughout 2004 relations between the two countries steadily, if warily, improved. There were agreements on restoring aircraft overflight and landing rights, and a railway service was inaugurated between Lahore and New Delhi, as well as a bus link across the LoC in Kashmir. However, most significantly, President Musharraf indicated that the until-now sacrosanct Pakistani demand for the implementation of UN resolutions on Kashmir on securing a plebiscite to determine the future of the region could possibly be 'left aside' in favour of alternative solutions that were acceptable to all parties.

Shortly thereafter, India partially reciprocated the concessions by publicly acknowledging that the rate of militant cross-border incursions into Jammu and Kashmir had declined considerably in late 2003. This mellowing on the part of India was followed by a series of meetings between Indian and Pakistani leaders at an unusually productive meeting of the South Asian Association of Regional Co-operation (SAARC—see below), held in Islamabad in January 2004. A joint declaration was issued stating that the two countries would initiate a 'composite dialogue' to settle all outstanding bilateral issues and that this would proceed through a series of regularly scheduled dialogue meetings relating to various issues, including an agreement to discuss Kashmir.

In 2005 there was a major shift in the relationship between Pakistan and India, following the visit of Gen. Musharraf to India and his shifting of the Kashmir issue to the sidelines of future bilateral relations. Undoubtedly, the USA applied pressure on both sides to continue and expand their dialogue and the Musharraf Government made major concessions on the Kashmir issue that indicated its desire to remove this main obstacle to better relations between the two countries. Musharraf argued that settlement of the Kashmir dispute was no longer a precondition to improved relations and, while the Indian reaction to this statement was cautious, there was an expansion of bilateral contacts at the highest levels of government on both sides—and between Pakistan and spokesmen from India's opposition party, the BJP—as they tested th possibilities for expanding the dialogue. The situation i Kashmir remained unsettled but, for the first time, high-leve discussions took place on other issues, most notably th proposed gas pipeline between Iran, Pakistan and India an the distribution of irrigation water. For both India and Pak stan, the energy question was vital and talks continued on th proposal despite opposition from the USA concerning their links with Iran.

In June 2005 India and the USA concluded what was, in effect, a defence alliance, which included a considerable number of bonuses for India relating to investment, technology transfer and possible co-operation in the area of the peaceful use of nuclear energy. The message for Pakistan was quite clear—India had now become the focal point of US attention in South Asia and the USA anticipated a resolution of the major unresolved differences between the two countries. However, if Pakistan continued to co-operate with the USA, and with India, it too would be rewarded with assistance in developing its economy and technological base.

Indo-Pakistani relations in 2005–06 were remarkably stable. The border of divided Kashmir was opened to bus services and civilian traffic in 2005 and the establishment of trans-border truck links has been proposed. The Mumbai bombings in July 2006 (see India) proved to be only a temporary set-back in bilateral relations, and in September President Musharraf and Prime Minister Manmohan Singh held private talks during the Non-Aligned Movement Summit in Havana, Cuba. Islamist terrorism continues in Indian-occupied Kashmir although the Pakistani Government has disavowed links with the groups involved. However, there has been little substantive improvement in Indo-Pakistani relations with regard to Kashmir despite the positive rhetoric on both sides. The problem appears to be different perceptions of how to proceed with the peacemaking process: Pakistan wants the issue of Kashmir put to one side and attention paid to improving other aspects of the bilateral relationship; India, on the other hand, still seems to be fixated on focusing on Kashmir as the core problem to be resolved before all else. At a practical level Pakistan has moved to improve trade between the two countries by removing the tariff on tea and encouraging discussions between business groups in both countries. In addition Pakistan has continued enthusiastically to support the proposed Iran–Pakistan–India gas pipeline as vital to the economic future of all three countries.

Despite the easing tension between India and Pakistan both are concerned to maintain the balance of military power. Both sides have notified each other about the testing of surface-to-surface missiles and they have agreed to form a 'joint mechanism' to combat terrorism, but Pakistan will continue to build nuclear warheads as long as India does likewise, and it has reportedly begun work on a number of nuclear reactors. In addition, both sides continue 'tit-for-tat' testing of conventional and nuclear-capable missiles.

In May 2008 India and Pakistan resumed peace talks, despite the decision of the Pakistani Government to ease restrictions on proscribed Islamic organizations as it sought internal stability. The danger to peace talks exists on several fronts: the new Government has not shown the commitment to peace talks that Musharraf did; in Kashmir indications are that Kashmiris want freedom from both India and Pakistan; and India, facing elections in 2009, shows no inclination to make big concessions. Relations between the two countries cooled considerably in July 2008 when India and the USA reached a nuclear power agreement, much to the chagrin of Pakistan. The bombing of the Indian embassy in Kabul in July led to a further decline in Indo-Pakistani relations, when media reports claimed that the ISI was involved in the bomb attack.

Part of the problem in terms of new Pakistani initiatives is the role of the army and the ISI in national life. A significant share of the national economy is dominated by the army. The ISI appears to have retained a shadowy role in the frayed relationships between Pakistan, India and Afghanistan. Undoubtedly the overwhelming presence of the armed forces and their various agencies in all aspects of Pakistani life and at the highest levels of decision-making complicates any dialogue between the current Government in Pakistan—as it did under Musharraf's Government–and democratic states, amongst whom must be counted India with its deeply rooted suspicions of the ISI and of the inherent instability of Pakistan's serial military and democratic regimes.

### *Relations with Afghanistan*

Afghanistan has been a problem for Pakistan since 1947. The core issue has been Afghanistan's support of agitation among some Pathans in the NWFP for an independent homeland, 'Pakhtoonistan' or 'Pashtunistan'. Lt-Gen. Daud, who overthrew King Zahir Shah in 1973, temporarily revived the dormant Afghan claims to the Pakhtoon areas in Pakistan before bilateral talks between the two countries in 1975–77 briefly improved relations. Following the April 1978 coup in Afghanistan, the Taraki regime in Kabul revived the 'Pakhtoonistan' question, and the internal revolt in Afghanistan inaugurated a stream of refugees into the NWFP and Balochistan that was to prove a drain on Afghanistan for the next 20 years.

The Soviet intervention in Afghanistan in late December 1979 posed an enormous problem for Pakistan. Pakistan was prominent internationally in leading the condemnation of the Soviet invasion and persuaded the Islamic Foreign Ministers' Conference in January 1980 to declare complete solidarity with the Afghan *mujahidin*. Moscow and Kabul repeatedly accused Pakistan of providing military training to Afghan *mujahidin* and refugees. However, Pakistan consistently denied this charge—although there is evidence that such training did take place with covert US support—and justified the assistance provided to the refugees on humanitarian grounds. By 1985 Pakistan had taken in more than 3m. Afghan refugees.

Between 1982 and 1988 negotiations regarding the Afghan crisis were held, under UN auspices, in Geneva, Switzerland. An agreement on a complete Soviet withdrawal was signed in April 1988. The withdrawal of Soviet troops commenced on 15 May and, as scheduled, was completed by 15 February 1989. Neither the *mujahidin* nor Iran played any part in the formulation of the Geneva accords, and, despite initial protests by Pakistan, no agreement was incorporated regarding the composition of an interim coalition government in Afghanistan. Equally importantly, no consensus was reached on the cessation of Soviet aid to the Kabul Government or US aid to the *mujahidin*, with the result that, following the Soviet departure, the supply of weapons to both sides continued and the violent conflict revived.

The overthrow of the Afghan regime by the *mujahidin* in April 1992 was welcomed by Pakistan, and it supported the appointment of an interim coalition Government. Relations between Pakistan and Afghanistan deteriorated, however, in 1994. The turbulence and increasing anti-Pakistan feeling in Afghanistan threatened to extend to the Pakhtoon areas of the NWFP, and also to obstruct the trade with the Central Asian republics of the former USSR and Pakistani hopes of accessing Central Asian oil via an overland pipeline.

The rise of the Islamist Taliban militia led to a worsening of relations between the two countries. Afghanistan accused Pakistan of supporting the Taliban and, following the ransacking of the Pakistani embassy by an anti-Taliban mob, the Afghan ambassador to Pakistan was expelled from the country. Following the capture of Kabul by Taliban troops in September 1996, the Pakistani Government recognized the Taliban regime as the new Afghan Government. At the same time, the Pakistani President stated that his country's stance regarding its neighbour's crisis was that an immediate ceasefire was needed, together with multilateral dialogue regarding demilitarization. The success of the Taliban was seen as a mixed blessing by some Pakistani commentators, despite the increased trade prospects it brought. There was a fear that armed Islamist militants within Pakistan would draw encouragement from the Taliban, and that Afghanistan might fragment along ethnic lines, thereby inviting the intervention of Iran and the development of a linkage between Pathans on both sides of the border.

Until the terrorist attacks on the USA on 11 September 2001, Pakistan's policies towards Afghanistan were ambiguous. At one level it took measures to curb the activities of the Taliban in Pakistan: for example, it acceded to Western demands by closing down a number of Afghan banking operations in Pakistan, and in May 2000 the Afghan Minister of the Interior held talks with his Pakistani counterpart in Islamabad concerning transit trade, narcotics control and the repatriation of Afghan refugees. However, as Gen. Musharraf repeatedly and strongly denied giving military assistance to the Taliban, allegations regarding the involvement of Pakistan's special forces grew. As late as January 2001, with an estimated 1.2m. Afghan refugees in Pakistan, the Pakistani Government continued to offer financial and diplomatic support to the Taliban.

However, also in January 2001 the Pakistani Government agreed to implement the UN sanctions imposed on Afghanistan in that month, but announced that it would attempt to mitigate the effect of the restrictions, warning of a steep increase in refugee numbers and a worsening of the civil war. In mid-April the military Government strongly denied allegations by the Afghan opposition that it was disregarding sanctions, although it was conducting bilateral negotiations with the Taliban regime. In February Musharraf urged the international community to accept and integrate the Taliban, and to assist Afghanistan with its humanitarian crisis.

The events of 11 September 2001 redefined Pakistan's relations with Taliban Afghanistan. The US attack on the Taliban regime enabled Musharraf to revive his flagging relationship with the USA and, once more, Pakistan assumed the mantle of a front-line state. Since then, although India has become the centrepiece of US strategy in South Asia, Pakistan has been able to exert some leverage on the USA, given its strategic geo-political situation and its importance in the continuing war on Islamist militants. Problems remain with Afghanistan. The Pathans of the NWFP relate closely to their kin across the border, and the border itself remains dangerously porous and is a massive conduit for the continuing passage of arms and narcotics.

By 2005/06 relations between Kabul and Islamabad had become increasingly strained. Kabul remained convinced that Pakistan harboured Taliban terrorists, and during George W. Bush's visit to Pakistan in March 2006 the Afghan President joined with senior US officials in Kabul in accusing Pakistan of allowing the al-Qa'ida leadership and operatives to hide in Pakistani border areas, drawing a furious response from Islamabad. In September President Musharraf warned that the Afghan Government was not taking sufficient action against militants operating on the Pakistan–Afghanistan border. According to some commentators, Pakistan was growing increasingly concerned that the USA was downgrading its significance in the 'war on terror' in favour of India and Afghanistan.

Relations between the two countries continued to deteriorate into 2007. To an extent, part of the tension was due to the Indo–Pakistani rivalry being conducted in Kabul, where Indian aid worth US $750m. overshadowed Pakistan's contribution of $150m., and both Indian and US diplomats noted with concern Pakistan's alleged resurgent support for the Taliban. In May 2007 border fighting broke out between Afghan and Pakistani forces and, under international pressure, Pakistan moved to seal its border with Afghanistan as part of a clampdown on Taliban activity in border tribal areas and the infiltration of terrorists into Afghanistan from Pakistan. The role of the ISI in relations between the two countries remained obscure; there were indications that the agency's influence in tribal areas had declined but its activities still elicited suspicions in Kabul and New Delhi.

In 2008 relations deteriorated even further. Afghanistan was concerned that Taliban militants had been launching attacks from Pakistan's tribal areas, and believed that the Pakistani Government had done nothing to restrain them. Consequently, the Afghan Government threatened to launch raids into Pakistan to destroy Taliban bases. In August 2008 the Indian and Afghan Governments announced that, in response to the upsurge in militant activity in border areas and the bombing of the Indian embassy, they were working on a new defence agreement.

### *Pakistan, SAARC and the other South Asian States*

In the late 1970s, following the assassination of the founder president of Bangladesh, Mujibur Rahman, there was a dramatic improvement in relations between Pakistan and Bangladesh. In part this was due to Pakistan's willingness to use its good offices to link Bangladesh to the oil-rich states of the Middle East, and in part it was due to Pakistan's desire to move Bangladesh away from its dependence upon India. Both reasons were attractive for Bangladesh, which welcomed contact with the Islamic heartland, and saw the new relationship with Pakistan as a means of balancing the influence India had wielded over Bangladesh since 1971. In the following decades Pakistan became the conduit through which links with other parts of the Islamic world were developed and through which filtered ideas that shaped a new and more militant Islam in Bangladesh.

For its part Pakistan made few concessions to Bangladesh and consistently refused to repatriate the Urdu-speaking Biharis of Bangladesh, who had been held in camps since the war of independence. The disingenuous Pakistani excuse was that these people originated in Bihar, conveniently overlooking the movement of Muslims from most provinces of northern India (including from Bihar) to what was then West Pakistan in the period 1947–48. The Biharis had the misfortune to opt for East rather than West Pakistan and from 1971 were a refugee population rejected by both Pakistan and Bangladesh.

Pakistan's relationship with Sri Lanka, Nepal and the Maldives has been cordial but distant. None of these countries was of strategic or economic interest to Pakistan and relations with them were essentially mediated through SAARC, which was established as an initiative of Bangladesh in the 1970s. SAARC has its headquarters in Kathmandu, Nepal, holds annual summit meetings of regional heads of states and has initiated myriad committees and ideas about regional co-operation. Unfortunately, SAARC's progress was curbed by the continuing hostility between Pakistan and India, its two most powerful members. Both theoretically supported the ideal of regional co-operation but in reality it was superseded by their own disputes and ambitions. In the last few years, however, with a decline in the overt hostility between India and Pakistan there have been signs that SAARC may slowly be beginning to work. SAFTA came into effect in January 2006 but has yet to be generally implemented. Pakistan has taken the initiative in SAFTA agreements with both Sri Lanka and Bangladesh, and it may be that one of the beneficiaries of the current Indo-Pakistani rapprochement will be SAARC, and in particular SAFTA, as both Pakistan and India have indicated a growing desire to expand and consolidate their trade links with one another (although to date the only concrete moves made in this direction have been by Pakistan).

In April 2007, at the annual meeting of SAARC Ministers of Foreign Affairs, which was held in New Delhi, there were many fulsome statements made by both India and Pakistan regarding regional co-operation, but as yet there has been little new action beyond their plan for the construction of a gas pipeline linking them to Iran.

## Relations Beyond the Subcontinent

### *Relations with the USA*

The state of its relationship with India has had a significant effect upon Pakistan's relations with other nations. In respect of the two major power blocs, Pakistan was inclined towards the West for some years and tried to move closer to the USA, particularly in the 1950s. A mutual defence assistance agreement was concluded in 1954, and in the same year Pakistan became a member of the Southeast Asia Treaty Organization (SEATO). In 1955 it joined the Baghdad Pact (later known as the Central Treaty Organization—CENTO) with the United Kingdom, Turkey, Iraq and Iran. To reinforce CENTO, a further bilateral agreement was concluded with the USA in 1959.

Following India's annexation of Goa in 1961 and the massive military aid that India received from the West in 1962, Pakistan turned its focus away from the USA and onto the development of closer relations with the People's Republic of China and, to a more limited extent, with the USSR. Consequentially economic and military aid from the USA declined sharply, and during the Indo-Pakistan wars of 1965 and 1971, China, along with certain Islamic powers, proved to be Pakistan's only supporters.

In January 1972 Pakistan withdrew from the Commonwealth, in retaliation for the United Kingdom's role in supporting Bangladesh's fight for independence. Attempts to rejoin in the late 1970s were thwarted by India but, following the restoration of democracy, Pakistan was formally invited to rejoin the Commonwealth, which it did on 1 October 1989.

Relations with the USA fluctuated throughout the 1970s, but essentially the trend was one of deterioration. The main problem was US suspicions concerning Pakistan's nuclear programme. These suspicions, and Islamabad's attempts to purchase a reprocessing plant from France, led the USA to cut its arms sales and then suspend all economic aid to Pakistan in 1978–79.

Following the revolution in Iran in early 1979, US-Pakistani relations deteriorated further when reports appeared in the US press later in that year of alleged US government plans to destroy Pakistani nuclear installations through commando action. Relations were worsened by the burning down of the US embassy in Islamabad and an information centre in Lahore in November by a mob protesting against the rumoured sacrilege of the Holy Ka'ba in Mecca. However, the Soviet intervention in Afghanistan in late December, which posed a common threat to the national interests of both Pakistan and the USA, helped to overcome mutual acrimony. Pakistan was now a front-line state in the confrontation between East and West, and attempted to evolve a common policy with the USA and its allies to curb Soviet expansionism.

In the 1980s the USA displayed a new and growing concern for Pakistan's security, with the result that the latter was given supporting funds of US $3,000m. under a five-year programme of economic support, development assistance, and loans for foreign military sales. In addition, the USA agreed to sell 40 F-16 aircraft to assist Pakistan in improving its air defence capabilities. In April 1986, in spite of opposition by India, representatives of Pakistan and the USA concluded a new accord, stipulating that the USA would provide a six-year credit of $4,020m. for economic assistance and purchases of military equipment, to support Pakistan's development priorities and its defence modernization programme. The release of the first instalment of this aid was postponed for several months, however, owing to the US Government's suspicion that Pakistan's nuclear development programme was not being used for peaceful purposes but rather for military ends. Pakistan, like India, continued to resist US pressure to sign the Nuclear Weapons Non-Proliferation Treaty, declaring that it would accede to the treaty only after India had done so.

During her official visit to the USA in June 1989, Benazir Bhutto assured President George Bush and the US Central Intelligence Agency (CIA) that Pakistan had no intention of constructing a nuclear missile. As a result, it was agreed that Pakistan could purchase a further 60 F-16 aircraft at a cost of US $1,400m. However, in October 1990 the USA announced that it was withholding $564m. in economic and military aid, including the proposed sale of the F-16 aircraft, and was abandoning a planned bilateral consultative defence committee (under the terms of the Pressler Amendment), following President Bush's failure to sign a certificate assuring Congress that Pakistan did not possess nuclear weapons. Pakistan, in turn, denied any wrongdoing but US-Pakistani relations deteriorated sharply. Pakistan's relationship with the USA was downgraded further following the Soviet withdrawal from Afghanistan in the late 1980s and the subsequent improvement in US-Soviet relations. Pakistan was no longer considered a front-line state, and a Pakistani delegation to Washington in June 1991 made no progress in securing the resumption of aid. In 1992, in an attempt to improve relations, the Pakistani Government admitted for the first time that it had nuclear weapons capability, but that it had 'frozen' its nuclear programme at the level of October 1989, when it was still some way from producing a nuclear device.

In the first half of 1993 Pakistan was particularly concerned that the USA had included Pakistan on its 'watch-list' of countries of which the governments were suspected of directly sponsoring terrorism. In part this was no doubt due to intensive international lobbying by India, which had long accused Pakistan of abetting the Sikh and Kashmiri separatists. However, in part it was also a legacy of the anti-Soviet uprising in Afghanistan. During this conflict between the Soviet-backed Afghan Government and the *mujahidin* in the 1980s, Islamist militants from around the world, with the support of the USA and Saudi Arabia, had established representative offices in and around Peshawar in the NWFP, which served as conduits for volunteers and weapons to fight the Soviet and government forces in Afghanistan. After the withdrawal of the Soviet troops from Afghanistan in 1988–89, however, these trained fundamentalist fighters were an embarrassment to both the USA and Pakistan, but it was Pakistan that was required to appease US policy in the area. The Pakistani Government attempted to defuse the issue by ordering foreigners without regular visas to leave Pakistan by mid-January 1993, and imprisoning or deporting those who remained. Nawaz Sharif's Government offered to open suspected terrorist training areas for inspection, and in late April dismissed Brig. Imtiaz, the army intelligence chief, who was allegedly linked with some suspected terrorist groups. Consequently, Pakistan was finally removed from the US 'watch-list' in July and avoided being blacklisted as a terrorist country.

In January 1995 the bilateral defence consultative committee (abandoned in 1990) was revived, indicating an improvement in relations. The assassination of two US consulate employees in Karachi in March did little to inspire US confidence in the stability of Pakistan. However, Pakistan's participation in UN peace-keeping operations in Somalia, in Haiti and in Bosnia and Herzegovina, and the continuing extradition of drugs-traffickers and terrorists, created a more favourable view of the country in the USA, which eased Benazir Bhutto's path when she visited Washington in April.

In Washington the content of the US-Pakistani dialogue broadened. The nuclear issue and the continued sanctions under the terms of the 1990 Pressler Amendment remained high on the agenda, but both sides were now also interested in economic issues, with Pakistan particularly keen to attract US investment. The USA had taken the lead in this shift in emphasis during the visit to Pakistan of the US Secretary of Energy in October 1994. Following the Pakistani Prime Minister's visit, in September the US Senate approved the Brown Amendment, which permitted a limited resumption of defence supplies to Pakistan (in the form of US $368m. worth of equipment) but did not allow Pakistan to take delivery of the F-16 aircraft. The Brown Amendment (which was ratified by President Clinton in January 1996) also deleted the Pressler Amendment requirements for economic sanctions, thus clearing the way for the resumption of US economic aid to Pakistan. However, in February 1996 the nuclear issue once more threatened to sour the relationship. The US Government considering delaying the delivery of the military equipment to Pakistan because of the latter's suspected purchase of sensitive nuclear weapons-related equipment from China. These allegations were denied by both Pakistan and China. In August 1996, after a six-year delay, the first consignment of US military equipment arrived in Pakistan.

US-Pakistani relations suffered a set-back in November 1997, following the killing of four US oil executives in Karachi by unidentified gunmen, but the USA once more needed Pakistan as a front-line state, this time in its campaign against Osama bin Laden. US air-strikes against bin Laden in Afghanistan in August 1998 entailed the use of Pakistani airspace and led to a modification of Washington's attitude towards Islamabad. In December Prime Minister Nawaz Sharif held talks with President Clinton in the USA in an attempt to gain support for Pakistan's ailing economy and to persuade the USA to ease the sanctions imposed on Pakistan following its nuclear tests. The US Government, now eager to bolster Pakistan's economic and defence infrastructure, agreed to return the entire payment made by Pakistan for the 28 F-16 fighter aircraft, the delivery of which had been suspended since 1990.

However, the true extent of the new US goodwill was made apparent in March 2000. In that month President Clinton paid a harmonious five-day visit to India, while spending only a few hours in Pakistan. During his brief stopover, the US President publicly warned Pakistan that it faced international ostracism if it continued to adopt a belligerent stance towards Kashmir. In the course of his short meeting with Gen. Musharraf, Clinton urged him to reopen dialogue with India, to take action against terrorist groups operating in and from Pakistan, to sign the CTBT and to expedite the reintroduction of democratic rule. What had become clear was that Pakistan was no longer of prime strategic significance to the USA: this position in South Asia had been usurped by India.

Following the events of 11 September 2001, Washington's assessment of its need to support the forces of moderation in Pakistan against any rise in Islamist militancy to an extent improved Musharraf's standing as an ally of the USA. While, by 2005, Pakistan was not central to US policy in South Asia, its role in the 'war on terror', its possession of nuclear capabilities, its occasional flirtations with China, and the need to contain Islamist militants ensured that the USA continued to support the Musharraf Government. Weapons sales were permitted to Pakistan and increasing pressure was placed on both the Indian and Pakistani Governments to join the international nuclear regime and to limit their ability to develop further nuclear weapons and missiles, as well as to seek some resolution of the problems that had divided them so bitterly since 1947.

In March 2006 the US President visited Pakistan, having first gone to India. During the visit US dissatisfaction with Pakistan's measures to curb domestic Islamist militants and the failure of Musharraf's regime to spread democracy was made clear, although Bush did indicate that he would waive sanctions against companies involved in the gas line project with Iran, despite mounting opposition to such a move on the part of many politicians in the USA. At the end of his visit Bush pronounced himself satisfied with Islamabad's efforts against terrorism.

In June 2006 the USA put pressure on Pakistan to allow UN inspectors to question the disgraced nuclear scientist, Dr Abdul Qadeer Khan, who was believed to hold vital information regarding Iran's nuclear enrichment programme. President Musharraf, however, would not permit access to the scientist, prompting frustration among certain politicians in the USA. This hard-line stand by Musharraf mirrored his concern that he was viewed by some observers as 'George Bush's poodle', a position that he bitterly denied in May in an attempt to counter domestic criticism and unpopularity for his perceived pro-US policies.

During 2006 Islamist militants organized nation-wide protests against the USA, following the publication in January of cartoons in Denmark depicting the Prophet Muhammad, a US air-strike in the same month on a village in the Bajaur region near the border with Afghanistan that killed 18 people, and widespread popular resentment that equated all the perceived evils and anti-Muslim actions and sentiment of the West with the USA.

In February 2007 the US Vice-President, Dick (Richard) Cheney, visited Pakistan, holding uncompromising talks with President Musharraf, reportedly regarding the latter's relationship with Taliban groups in the NWFP, his failure to curb the rise of Islamic extremist groups within Pakistan, and the increasingly undemocratic behaviour of the regime. It was widely believed that the provision of US aid to Pakistan could possibly be at risk (since 2001 Pakistan had received US $10,000m. in aid, with a further $1,000m. due in 2007). In addition, amicable relations between the USA and Pakistan were seen by the latter as vital since US support provided the regime with a degree of international acceptance that would otherwise not be forthcoming.

In January 2008 reported US air-strikes in the tribal areas caused widespread outrage in Pakistan. Following the election in February, the USA became increasingly concerned about the new Government's attempts to reach agreement with militants in the FATA and the Swat valley. The USA appeared to continue to support the presence of Musharraf in the political arena, believing that he was central to the 'war on terrorism' in the region. However, the new Government was in a difficult position, as it had to balance the need to resolve the escalating domestic violence as well as the needs of the USA, whose support of Musharraf and the army continued to rouse anger from most sections of Pakistani society.

In the early months of 2008 relations with the USA deteriorated further. The policy of the new Government of accommodating internal dissent by reaching agreements with militant groups in the Swat valley, in an attempt to prevent suicide bombings and attacks on government buildings and foreign embassies, and the mistaken killing of 11 Pakistani paramilitaries in a US air-strike on a tribal area did little to improve relations. In July 2008 the CIA allegedly accused the ISI of deepening its ties with militants based in the frontier areas, who were held responsible for an upsurge in violence in Afghanistan, reportedly lead by al-Qa'ida operatives, that culminated in the bombing of the Indian embassy in Kabul. The accusation was seized upon by Congressional opponents of President Bush, who sought to block his attempts to upgrade Pakistan's F-16 fighter jets at the expense of US funds allocated to aid Pakistan's counter-terrorism programmes. Ironically Congressional opposition to Bush's plans for Pakistan matched those of many opponents of American activity in the border tribal areas where unilateral American air-strikes not only killed innocent civilians but also infringed the sovereignty of Pakistan.

### *Relations with China*

The Sino-Pakistani relationship has been shaped and defined by the relationships of both countries with India and the USA. Until recently there was limited economic substance to the relationship, which was driven by the needs of both countries to outwit diplomatically either India or the USA or both, and mutually to profit from the sale of arms and nuclear technology—primarily from China to Pakistan.

In September 1986 China and Pakistan signed an agreement in Beijing for co-operation regarding the peaceful use of nuclear energy. In November 1989 the Chinese Prime Minister, Li Peng, made an official visit to Pakistan, during which he announced that China would provide Pakistan with a 300,000-kW nuclear plant. Relations with China remained strong. China officially disapproved of Pakistan's nuclear test explosions in 1998, but there was doubtless more than a little satisfaction in Beijing at the discomfort caused by the explosions in New Delhi and Washington. In July 2000 China was accused of aiding the development of Pakistan's long-range missile programme. China denied the accusation, but in August the Pakistani Minister of Foreign Affairs declared that any co-operation between the two countries in the field of missile technology was consistent with China's obligations under the Missile Technology Control Regime.

In return for diplomatic support at the international level and defence and technology co-operation Pakistan supported China's policies, including the 'One China' policy (of not recognizing the Government of Taiwan). Economic co-operation remained important. By 2000 trade and investment had become an increasingly important facet of the Sino-Pakistani relationship. In August China decided to invest funds into Pakistan's telecommunications facilities and was also considering co-operation in terms of information technology, agriculture and infrastructure. This new economic interest was prompted by the efforts of the USA to isolate China and forge ties with India, and the US allegation that China was exporting missiles to Pakistan.

After the events of 11 September 2001, however, and as the USA shifted its focus to Afghanistan, the concomitant improvement in the US-Pakistani relationship and the increasing supply of military material and aid had the tangible result of decreasing Islamabad's dependence upon China as a supplier of military hardware and investment. Given the strengthening of ties between the USA and India, and between the USA and Pakistan, China has been increasingly concerned about the dangers of containment. In 2005 it launched a major diplomatic campaign, culminating in a tour of South Asia by the Chinese Prime Minister Wen Jiabao, to bolster bilatera relationships—specifically with Pakistan, to co-operate ir curbing Muslim separatism in Xinjiang—and to counter th spread of US influence in the region.

China continues to be a major source of foreign investmen and expertise for Pakistan, whose unstable domestic situatio has discouraged much-needed investment from North Amer ica, Europe and South-East Asia. Chinese experts are involve in a variety of projects associated with the upgrading of Po Gwadar and the development of nuclear power facilities f civilian use. However, continuing unrest in Balochista throughout 2006–07 has curbed Chinese economic activity the area, although Chinese economic interest remains hi elsewhere in Pakistan. There is some international concern that the Chinese are involved in Pakistan's renewed interest in developing its domestic nuclear capabilities.

### *Turkey, Central Asia and the Middle East*

In early 1992 the Economic Co-operation Organization (ECO), comprising Pakistan, Iran and Turkey, was reactivated, and by the end of the year had been expanded to include Afghanistan and the six Central Asian, mainly Muslim, republics of the former USSR; the 'Turkish Republic of Northern Cyprus' joined the ECO in April 1993. Trade delegations from Turkey and the new republics visited Pakistan, and an agreement for the restoration and construction of highways in Afghanistan to link Pakistan with these republics was signed. In order to meet the maritime trade requirements of the Muslim republics, the cargo facilities at Karachi Port were being modernized and expanded. In March 1995 Pakistan, China, Kazakhstan and Kyrgyzstan signed a transit trade agreement, restoring Pakistan's overland trade route with Central Asia, through China.

In 2004–05 Pakistan moved closer to Iran, with the improvement in the relationship driven by the pragmatic issue of its desperate need to secure regular low-cost supplies of energy. Despite opposition from the USA, Pakistan has joined with India and Iran to explore the construction of an overland gas pipeline.

By mid-2006 Dubai was poised to overtake China as the biggest foreign investor in Pakistan, with more than US $30,000m. planned to be invested in property development, financial services, infrastructure and the Port Gwadar project. Dubai Ports was reported to be interested in acquiring management of Port Gwadar, given its potential as a major trading link with Central Asia. In 2005 the Dubai telecommunications company Etisalat purchased a 26% stake in Pakistan Telecom.

### The Rest of the World

Although Pakistan forms part of the international coalition to fight the Taliban and global terrorism, its relations with the USA, Europe and South-East Asia have little substance beyond the military alliance and trade based primarily on the export of cotton textiles.

The low international ranking of Pakistan's business environment combined with domestic insecurity has been the major reason for the low level of foreign direct investment in Pakistan, with the notable exceptions of China and the Middle East. Arms dealers in Europe and the USA continue, along with China, to supply Pakistan, but the only other area of potentially significant foreign investment could be in the area of civilian nuclear energy co-operation. In February 2006 France signed a declaration of co-operation and support for Pakistan and India to be treated on a par with developed nations in this field. In general,the international community—apart from the USA and China—continues to have reservations about the sustainability of the current regime in Islamabad and its ability to reconcile the growing number of divergent domestic pressure groups.

### The Taliban, Terrorism and the Judiciary

From 2001 the improvement of Pakistan's international reputation was largely affected by the global fear of terrorism. As shown above, until then Pakistan's relationship with the Taliban regime in Afghanistan was ambiguous, but the dilemma faced by Pakistan regarding Afghanistan became much more serious after 11 September 2001. The USA announced that the militant Osama bin Laden, reportedly hiding in Afghanistan, was its prime suspect and informed Pakistan that it expected the country's full support in its efforts to identify and punish the perpetrators of the attacks on the mainland.

Although the Taliban expressed regret for the events, they at first refused to surrender bin Laden without detailed proof of his alleged role. Pakistan was placed in an extremely difficult situation. The Government was fully aware that a refusal to assist the USA would lead to its identification as being both an enemy and sympathetic to terrorism, and would risk, at the very least, severe economic penalties and, at the worst, possible invasion. It was also clear that if Pakistan supported the USA, the Government risked domestic violence and upheaval with possible intervention by outside Islamist militant groups. The Government sent a secret delegation to Afghanistan days after the attack in an attempt to work out a compromise; however, this failed, and President Musharraf subsequently declared Pakistan's support for the US-led anti-terrorism coalition.

Pakistan agreed to give the USA access to Pakistan's ISI files on bin Laden and the Taliban, and to close the border with Afghanistan and halt the supply of fuel to the Taliban. It also granted permission for the USA to use Pakistani airspace in the event of military strikes and to base troops at airfields near the Afghan border. In return, the USA announced the lifting of economic sanctions on Pakistan, which had been imposed following the latter's nuclear tests in 1998, and agreed to reschedule the country's debt. In November 2001 Pakistan severed all diplomatic relations with the Taliban. While the two main political parties, the PPPP and the PML (N), supported the official position, anti-US protests took place throughout Pakistan. Religious party leaders and spiritual leaders warned of chaos and anarchy should Pakistan assist US retaliation, and Islamist militants called for *jihad* (holy war) against the USA.

In October 2001 President Musharraf replaced the Chief of the ISI, Lt-Gen. Mahmood Ahmad, who was closely linked with the Taliban, with the more moderate Lt-Gen. Ehsanul Haq. A reorganization of the top ranks of the army command structure also took place, strengthening President Musharraf's power base and enabling him better to control the domestic political crisis.

Once bin Laden and his al-Qa'ida network were held principally responsible for the attacks on the USA, President Musharraf was forced to support the USA and its 'coalition against terror'. British pressure encouraged Musharraf to reverse Pakistan's policy towards the Taliban by ceasing political support and economic aid. In doing so, Musharraf was also compelled to accept the United National Islamic Front for the Salvation of Afghanistan (commonly known as the United Front or Northern Alliance) as a possible US choice as the next government of Afghanistan. Protests against these actions spread throughout Pakistan, especially in the towns bordering Afghanistan, and it was against this background that different elements of Pakistani society voiced their support for the Taliban and opposed the Government's official position.

In the face of strident domestic criticism President Musharraf was strongly supported by the US-led coalition, with the US Secretaries of both State and Defense visiting Pakistan in October and November 2001, respectively. However, these visits were as much intended to remind Musharraf of his obligations to the USA, as they were to endorse his position within Pakistan. In the third week of October US ground troops entered Afghanistan. By the end of the year the Taliban had been effectively overthrown and an interim Government installed.

By the beginning of 2002 President Musharraf was faced by an upsurge of terrorist attacks within Pakistan; a suicide bombing in Karachi in May that killed 14 people, mostly French engineers, was the most notable. In response, he appeared to have assumed a stronger stance against the activities of militant Islamists, and in a speech in mid-January he condemned the extremist organizations based in Pakistan and announced the introduction of measures to combat terrorist activity and religious zealotry. However, his task was made all the more difficult by continuing instability in Afghanistan and incidents such as the US bombing of a wedding party in Afghanistan by mistake, killing at least 30 guests and injuring many others.

Public scepticism in Pakistan with respect to US intentions was heightened by the failure of the USA and its allies to provide the aid that they had pledged for the reconstruction of Afghanistan. By the end of 2002 less than one-quarter of the promised aid had actually been disbursed. The outrage was also exacerbated by the USA's efforts to ensure that the Loya Jirga (Grand National Council) elected Hamid Karzai, rather than the Pashtun former King Zahir Shah, as the President of the Afghan Transitional Administration (which was responsible for administering the country until democratic elections were held in 2004).

## PAKISTAN

Despite these concerns, Pakistan remained publicly supportive of the USA's 'war on terror', and sought to control the movement of militants across the border with Afghanistan by engaging in joint military exercises with the USA to arrest and interrogate suspected Islamist fundamentalists. At the same time, in late December 2002 the Pakistani Government and the Governments of Afghanistan, China, Iran, Tajikistan, Turkmenistan and Uzbekistan signed the Kabul Declaration on Good Neighbourly Relations, in which they acknowledged the sovereignty of Afghanistan and reaffirmed their commitment to help the Transitional Administration effect the changes necessary for peace and stability in the region.

In the period that followed, however, Pakistan's freedom of manoeuvre remained hampered by domestic considerations. Pakistani political parties were divided in their response to Musharraf's policies, and the failure of the USA to bring peace to Afghanistan and the ongoing turbulence in the country has fuelled the anti-US and anti-Musharraf sentiments of Islamist militants and political groupings in Pakistan. The links between elements of the Pakistan military and secret service with Islamist militant groups and terrorists remained suspect, and these added yet another element to the complexity of the domestic issues that President Musharraf had to contend with as he attempted to balance his support for the USA with moves to legitimize his regime nationally and internationally. A rapprochement with India would serve him well, in that it would permit a reduction in the number of Pakistani armed forces on the border with India and increase the number available to police and control the dangerously porous western border, where regional military commanders and the Taliban still operated under a variety of alliances.

In 2004 and 2005 the Pakistani military, aided by technical and intelligence assistance from the USA, intensified its operations against the al-Qa'ida organization and the remnants of the Taliban along the Afghan border. In March 2004 their efforts gained the praise of the US Secretary of State, Gen. Colin Powell, when he visited Pakistan during a South Asian tour. At the same time, he was relatively understated in his comments relating to the proliferation scandal that had recently engulfed Pakistan's nuclear programme. President Musharraf and his Government were also rewarded with a significant symbolic recognition of this alliance when Powell announced that the USA would designate Pakistan a 'major non-North Atlantic Treaty Organization (NATO) ally' an acknowledgement of its role in the 'war on terror', a status that would release further funds and enhance the legitimacy of Musharraf and his Government. None the less, such praise and rewards were not welcomed by Islamist militants and political parties such as the MMA, who saw them simply as evidence of their claim that Musharraf was a lackey of the USA and an enemy of Islam.

In reaction to such domestic complaints President Musharraf adopted a maverick policy of compromise and co-operation with the Taliban and pro-Taliban groups in tribal areas during 2006/07 (as well as a *laissez-faire* approach to the problem of the role of *madrassas* in consolidating Islamic extremism) as a means of both improving his credentials amongst the religious political parties on whom he counted for support and of suppressing al-Qa'ida as part of his contribution to the US-led 'war on terror'. Unfortunately for the Pakistani President, this policy not only outraged the Afghan Government, but it was also not well received by the US Administration, and Musharraf was forced to carry out a humiliating withdrawal of his policy in tribal areas.

By 2007 it was apparent that, while Musharraf's Government was committed to its US partner internationally, domestically the war against terrorism was beset by internal constraints and problems. Despite claims to the contrary, the sources of terrorism—the *madrassas*—remained unreformed, frontier areas continued to be centres of illegal weapons- and drugs-trafficking, and sectarian terrorism continued unchecked. The domestic credibility of Musharraf's Government was sorely tested but the alternatives to Musharraf or any other military leader in Pakistan were not clear, and internationally the US Administration appeared content to admonish but not undermine the regime.

In 2008 the electoral defeat of Musharraf began significantly to alter the relationship between the Pakistani Government and the US-driven war on terrorism (see above). Moves made by the new Government to reach an agreement with militants to defuse domestic terrorism caused considerable concern in the USA.

Internally the question of reinstating the judges removed by Musharraf was still causing considerable discontent, and there was widespread concern that Zardari and Sharif, not known for their respect for the judiciary in previous years, were attempting to create a 'tame' judiciary of their own making rather than simply reinstating the judges removed by Musharraf.

The armed services, if not the ISI, appeared to be maintaining neutrality. Government moves to come to terms with militancy and to control the situation in Swat were popular with the army, just as the heavy hand of the USA was not. Meanwhile, the PPP Government was forced to back down on the issue of the control of the ISI in the face of opposition from the military establishment. Just who was in control of policy-making in the country was far from clear in the latest attempt to establish democratic government in Pakistan.

# Economy

Revised by MATTHEW McCARTNEY

Based on an earlier essay by MARIKA VICZIANY and A. R. KEMAL

### INTRODUCTION

Pakistan's economy has faced various challenges in recent years, including sustaining the high growth rates of gross domestic product (GDP); problems that have plagued Pakistan since independence, such as low tax revenues; the deterioration of law and order; the possibility of more economic instability, in view of rising fiscal and balance of payments deficits; a sharp increase in money supply and consequently high inflation rate; and the failure of growth to improve the lives of the average citizen. In the four years to 2006/07 Pakistan achieved an average annual growth rate of 7.0%, thus making it one of the fastest growing economies in the world. This growth was buttressed by other economic indicators that made many commentators optimistic about its sustainability. Such favourable indicators included foreign private investment inflows, foreign exchange reserves, debt to GDP ratio and rising investment levels. This growth showed some signs of being translated into improved general welfare. The Government claimed in the 2007/08 budget that 12.7m. persons had been pulled out of poverty, and that there had been a sharp reduction in the unemployment rate. The Government of Pakistan entered 2007 with a spirit of optimism. The Economic Survey of 2006/07 states that 'based on the performance of a half a decade of strong, stable, resilient and broad-based economic growth, it appears that Pakistan's economy will continue to be a high mean, low variance economy over the medium term'.

Despite such optimism, there are nagging doubts about the ultimate viability of Pakistan's mini boom. Standard and Poor's has downgraded the country's ratings, while political developments in recent months have left the Government vulnerable and prospects of growth uncertain. Some of these developments include the invalidation of the Pakistan Steel privatization deal, which has cast doubt on the privatization process as a whole; the rising fiscal and trade deficits, creating instability in the system; the assassination of Benazir Bhutto in December 2007 and confrontation between the presidency and a potentially unstable coalition Government; the siege by the army of the Lal Masjid (Red Mosque) in Islamabad; the continued military confrontations in the North-West Frontier Province (NWFP) and Balochistan; and the decision of the USA to make the provision of aid conditional on Pakistan's commitment to the US-led 'war on terror'. Historically Pakistan has been dependent on foreign aid to sustain growth. The stringent political conditions placed on aid by the USA may easily contradict the domestic political realities within Pakistan confronting the political authorities with uncomfortable choices between economic growth and political legitimacy. While there has been some reduction in the poverty levels and unemployment rates, and improvements made in the education and health sectors, these improvement are from a strikingly poor base and huge social problems remain. Pakistan has made significant progress in recovering from the October 2005 earthquake that killed an estimated 75,000 people and left 3.5m. homeless in northern Pakistan. Some 6,400 km of roads were washed away by landslides. Rehabilitation efforts were supported by worldwide assistance led by US $1,000m. from the Asian Development Bank (ADB). Military confrontations continued in Waziristan throughout 2008, including offensives launched by the Pakistani army and missiles being fired by US Predator drones targeted at al-Qa'ida facilities and individuals. The origins of this conflict lie some four years ago with the Government initiating military operations in areas dominated by the Mehsud tribe in an attempt to force tribal militants to submit to state authorities and to expel foreign militants. Some 240 Pakistani soldiers were captured by militants in late 2007.

## STRONG MACROECONOMIC GROWTH

GDP grew at a rate of 7.0% in 2006/07 despite a contraction in the manufacturing sector. Over the same fiscal period agriculture increased by 5.0%, manufacturing by 8.4% (large-scale manufacturing by 8.8%) and the services sector by 8.0%. The industrial sector (especially manufacturing) grew rapidly, although at a rate slower than the Government's target over the three years to 2006/07, but it failed to generate productive employment. Much of the manufacturing growth since 2003/04 has been in the large-scale sectors that tend to be capital intensive rather than labour intensive. Slower rates of improvement in agriculture and labour-intensive sectors such as textiles have reduced the employment-generating effects of economic growth and consequently the impact of development on poverty. Continued growth in the service sector has absorbed labour and contributed to falling rates of unemployment.

Officials insist that the growth rate of around 7.0% is sustainable largely because the ratio of domestic investment to GDP has risen to 23.0%. The private sector has experienced healthy growth since 2001: private-sector investment has increased from 10.2% of GDP to 16.0% of GDP, thus increasing its share in fixed capital formation from 64.5% to 75.7%. There has been rising confidence in Pakistan's economy, reflected in the continued growth in foreign private investment and workers' remittances. Foreign private investment increased to US $6,945m. in 2006/07, compared with $3,873m. in the previous year, and workers' remittances rose to $5,490m. in 2006/07, from $4,600m. the previous year. In 2006/07 foreign exchange reserves exceeded $15,700m. However, the inflation rate continues to be high and even in 2006/07 it was 7.8%, slightly less than the inflation rate of 7.9% in the preceding year. The Sensitive Price Indicator, which accurately measures inflation for the poor, was 10.8% and food inflation reached double digits. On the other hand, core inflation (i.e. Consumer Price Index adjusted for food and fuel inflation) stood at around 5%. This lower rate has mainly been the result of supply bottlenecks, although with the high growth of money supply in 2006/07, there is a danger that both core inflation as well as headline inflation may rise. Similarly, the fiscal deficit increased to 4.3% of GDP in 2006/07 and was the major contributing factor behind the increase in money supply. The trade deficit widened to $13,528m. and the balance-of-payments deficit to $7,000m. The Government remained optimistic, despite these emerging problems, and targeted 7% growth for 2007/08. By the time the 2008/09 budget was announced in June 2008, however, optimism was beginning to flag and GDP growth of 5.8%, manufacturing growth of 5.4% and agricultural growth of 1.5% were forecast. The slowdown in the rates of growth was occurring amid a deterioration in key macroeconomic variables. Inflation, according to budget figures, had accelerated to 11% in 2008. The Government responded with a restrictive monetary policy. Interest rates rose by 3.5 percentage points in the 11 months following July 2007 to 13% in May 2008, the highest level since July 2001. A higher cost of credit, rising energy prices, and continued political and security concerns were also key factors in the economic slowdown.

## POVERTY IN PAKISTAN

Following consistent declines in the level of poverty after independence, particularly with the Green Revolution in agriculture in the 1960s and the migration of many impoverished individuals to seek employment in the Persian (Arabian) Gulf in the 1970s and 1980s, poverty began to re-emerge as an issue in the 1990s. This was caused partly by the gradual decline in GDP growth throughout the decade to below 5% per year, by the worsening measures of inequality and by reductions in government spending. For example, development expenditure fell from 7.6% of GDP in 1991/92 to 3.4% in 1998/99. More recently, however, there has been renewed optimism about the progress of poverty reduction.

On the basis of the Social and Living Standards Measurement Survey (PLSM) for 2004/05, the Government reported a decline in poverty levels from 33.46% in 2000/01 to 23.94% in 2004/05. Over the same period consumption inequality increased from 0.275 to 0.298, measured by the Gini coefficient. The Government's figures are endorsed by the United Nations Development Programme (UNDP) and the World Bank; many others would disagree. Claims of a decline in poverty have been contested by various policy think-tanks and by economists within and outside the country. For example, the reported unprecedented fall in the poverty levels is difficult to reconcile with the sharp increase in income inequality and various pieces of qualitative data. The PLSM collects data on individuals' perceptions of their material well-being. The 2004/05 PLSM found that 50% of the population believed their economic situation to have deteriorated over the preceding three years and another 25% believed that there had been no change in their living standards. The scepticism about poverty estimates was been compounded by the reluctance of the Government to release the PLSM data. Nevertheless, some decline in poverty was expected both because 2000/01 was a poor year for agricultural growth as a result of drought, while 2004/05 was an exceptionally good year for agricultural production—it is still the case that the bulk of the poor in Pakistan are dependent on agriculture, either directly or indirectly, for their livelihoods. Supporting its optimistic claims about declining poverty, the Government stated that 6m. jobs had been created between 2001/02 and 2004/05. However, most of the jobs created were for unpaid family helpers; the creation of jobs in the form of paid employees and self-employed has been minimal.

Despite the claims of a favourable trend in poverty, absolute levels of poverty remain high in both rural and urban areas. Poverty remains significantly more acute for women. There is also a widespread perception that central government policies have failed to ensure balanced regional development. The insurgency movements in Balochistan, Sindh and the NWFP are often blamed on regional imbalances in economic growth. In 1993–99 the incidence of poverty in Pakistan according to government estimates increased from 26% to 32% at a time when poverty within India was reported to be declining rapidly. Of these, 1.6% were extremely poor, 10.4% chronically poor and 20.1% were classified as the transitory poor. Above the poverty line (defined as a monthly consumption expenditure of Rs 748.56 at 1998/99 prices) there were another 20.4% who were classified as being vulnerable to poverty. Such figures remain controversial and poverty estimates should be debated. Over the same period (1993–99) the World Bank estimates that the percentage of Pakistan's poor living on US $1 a day declined sharply to 14%, significantly lower than poverty levels in any other South Asian country, with the exception of Sri Lanka. A recent study by Devarajan and Nabi for the World Bank (June 2006), shows that Pakistan is the only South Asian country in which the incidence of poverty grew between 1990 and 2006. The data for the other South Asian nations can be contested, but in that case the debate is about the extent of the decline rather than the extent of the increase in mass poverty. The report also illustrates the relationship between regional levels of poverty and education: even within the relatively prosperous province of Punjab there are significant regional disparities: in the north the incidence of poverty is 29.8%, in central Punjab the incidence of poverty is 31.8%, while in the southern districts the incidence of poverty is much higher at more than 40%.

Corresponding to estimates that poverty levels had decreased to 23.9% in 2004/05, it was estimated that the extreme poor accounted for 1.0%, compared with 1.1% in 2000/01, the ultra poor for 6.5%, compared with 10.8% in 2000/01, and the poor for 16.4%, compared with 22.5% in 2000/01. However, consumption inequality increased and the data on income inequality was not released because the definition of income of the respective two years was different.

The 2008/09 budget contained a number of measures targeted at the poorest, including plans to provide 1m. housing units for low-income groups and government employees, to extend the reach of micro-credit to an additional 3m. people, to provide more banking credit for self-employment generation, and to provide further tax incentives for the establishment of businesses in backward areas. The budget also promised generous above-inflation wage increases, stating that the minimum wage would be increased by 25% and that all federal employees would receive a 20% wage increase. Civilian and military pensioners were likewise promised a 20% increase in their pensions. It was unclear whether such promises could actually be afforded, however, given that the Government's budget deficit had ballooned.

### Poverty and Agriculture

The rate of poverty remains high in rural Pakistan, despite an officially recorded sharp decline in poverty in rural areas from 39.26% in 2000/01 to 28.13% in 2004/05. Moreover, there has been an increase in socio-economic inequality. The consumption inequality in rural areas rose from 0.237 in 2000/01 to 0.252 in 2004/05. The data on poverty and income inequality across provinces contain many errors and should be used with caution. Nevertheless, the figures do indicate an increase in the incidence of poverty in all the provinces during the 1990s and up to 2000/01. The highest incidence of poverty in 2000/01 occurred in the NWFP (45% in rural areas and 31.2% in urban areas) and the lowest incidence in Balochistan (24.6% in rural areas and 28.4% in urban areas), although this may be reflective of data errors as a result of the small sample for Balochistan. Rural poverty was also very high in Sindh (29.2% in rural areas but significantly lower in urban areas, at 19%). Within the provinces, the impact of poverty was also uneven. Northern Punjab, which had a greater number of agricultural industries, had much less poverty than southern Punjab, which had a more productive agricultural sector but limited non-farm employment. On average, 32.4% of Punjabi farmers and 26.5% of urban residents were poor in 2000/01.

### Poverty and Women

Another poorly understood factor in Pakistan's poverty profile is how the low status and literacy levels of women affect family welfare. Households with illiterate women are twice as likely to be poor as literate households and experience infant mortality rates that are twice as high. Pakistan also has a highly unfavourable gender ratio (108 men for every 100 women) and female labour force participation rates are very low in relation to those of males: 13% compared with 70%. National averages hide the very striking regional and urban/rural inequalities. For example, while 47% of girls in urban Sindh are enrolled in middle school, the figure is only 9% for rural Sindhi girls.

### Poverty and Life Expectancy

Economic underdevelopment is reflected in the low expectation of life for both sexes. In 2004, according to World Health Organization (WHO) estimates, male life expectancy was 62.2 years and female 63.6 years. The human development indicators also underscore regional inequalities, although surprisingly the indicators for Sindh are generally better than those for Punjab; for example, Sindh has the highest literacy rate (55.3%), followed by Punjab (53.3%), NWFP (43%) and Balochistan (36%). Similarly, infant mortality in Pakistan is lowest in Sindh, at 73 per 1,000 live births, followed by NWFP (78), Punjab (80) and Balochistan (88). In other words, despite the apparent relative economic success of the Punjab, this has not always been translated into corresponding improvements in social indicators.

## PAKISTAN'S RURAL SECTOR

### Agricultural Growth

Long-term structural changes have seen a decline in the proportion of national income generated by agriculture, from 50.0% to 20.9% between 1950 and 2007. Despite this, some 43.4% of the workforce continues to depend on agricultural jobs and another 25.8% on non-agricultural jobs in rural areas. The textile industry employs almost 40% of the labour force in the manufacturing sector, which, in turn, depends on the efficiency of cotton production in the villages of Pakistan. The state of agriculture, therefore, determines the living standards of the majority of Pakistanis. Pakistan is one of the most arid countries in the world, and the long history of canal irrigation has not reversed this natural disadvantage. Agricultural output has not been stagnant, but the rate of growth has been well below half that of industry: since 2001 the growth rate has fluctuated between below zero and a maximum of 5%. Arable agriculture in Pakistan is based on the output of four main crops—wheat, cotton, sugar cane and rice. While low output in 2005/06 was driven by the disappointing yields of the first three crops, high growth rates in 2006/07 were due to strong production of wheat and sugar cane. Pakistan is finding itself increasingly deficient in wheat. The Government announced in 2008 that it would have to import 2.5m. metric tons of wheat at double the domestic price. Higher prices of key inputs such as petroleum and fertilizer have undermined local production. Fertilizer prices were reported to have increased by 45% during 2007/08.

Cotton production has likewise suffered, declining from 14.3m. bales in 2004/05 to 11.5m. bales in 2007/08. It is difficult solely to blame weather for this decline; over the same period India increased production by 25% to 31m. bales. India now exports 6m. bales of cotton and Pakistan imports 4m. bales per year. The sharp fall in output in 2008 was atrributed to pest attack, though many were critical that the relevant ministries and agricultural extension services were unable to tackle the problem. The declining cotton crop has had numerous knock-on effects. Cotton is almost exclusively picked by women. Reduced cotton output led to a fall in the availability of cottonseed oil, thus necessitating greater imports of vegetable ghee oil from Malaysia and Indonesia. Cottonseed cake is also used as a feed for livestock. Cotton-based textiles contribute 60% of total exports and 46% of total manufacturing employment. Textile exports correspondingly decreased in 2007/08 (see Trade).

Beyond these commodities, livestock is the most important agrarian sector, accounting for around one-half of the output of the agricultural sector. In 2005/06 it was the 7.5% growth in livestock production that enabled aggregate agricultural output to register a positive growth rate. Although in 2006/07 the rate of growth of livestock declined to 4.3%, it was sufficiently high nevertheless to enable the overall agricultural sector to grow by 5.0%.

The 2008/09 budget promised to increase the support price of wheat, to provide an extra Rs 75,000m. for improvement to water resources (dams, irrigation, etc.), to double the subsidy on fertilizers, to increase credit allocation to farmers, and to reduce excise taxes and import tariffs on certain imports (equipment for grain handling, rice seeds, etc.). Again, a with other budget promises, it was unclear whether the Government would be able to afford to meet these promises.

### Agriculture: The 'White Revolution'

Pakistan succeeded in promoting a 'Green Revolution' in agriculture in the mid-1960s. Between 1965 and 1970 agricultural output increased by an average rate of 6.5% per year. Between 1960 and 1970 overall wheat production increased by 91% and rice production by 141%. These increases were driven by the application of high-yield variety seeds, chemical fertilizers and pesticides. The use of tractors and tubewells also grew rapidly. More recently attention has turned to the so-called 'white revolution' (milk and milk products). Pakistan is a good example of the 'white revolution' that has taken off in South Asia: milk is the most important product of the livestock sector and exceeds the value of any other agricultural commodity. Pakistan is the world's fifth largest producer of milk and, although exceeded by India and the People's Republic of China, produces more milk than Germany, where milk and milk products are a traditional food. Moreover, the volume of output of milk is growing. The downside, however, is that growth is driven by the increasing number of livestock rather than by productivity and, given the aridity of Pakistan, maintaining a huge number of low-yielding livestock exacerbates the fragility of the environment. While only exceeding German annual production by a small amount, Pakistan has three times more milk-yielding animals. Ecological fragility, however, is partially compensated by the ability of even landless rural households to maintain livestock. The 2003 study by the Pro Poor Livestock Policy Initiative organization showed that even if a landless household consumes 70% of the yield of any buffalo it owns, the remaining 30% can be sold to local dairies. The 'white revolution', in other words, has improved the nutrition of the poor and has also increased their monetary income. The viability of even small-scale producers of milk could be further improved by state-sponsored programmes of animal vaccinations and productivity enhancement, and by co-operative milk farming.

### Agriculture and the Army

The role of the military in agriculture in Pakistan is often overlooked. As the country's largest landlord, the army has particular abilities in utilizing its coercive power to assert its control over rural assets and expand these at will. The recent violent conflicts between farmers and the Pakistani army in Okara, Punjab, has served to emphasize these tensions. The international organization Human Rights Watch reported that, following violent clashes between troops and farmers in 2003, children had been tortured in Okara in early 2004 as a means of forcing their parents to sign documents transferring their land rights to the military. The conflict occurred between the Pakistani Rangers (the country's most prestigious paramilitary force) and sharecroppers, who are the tenants of land owned by the Pakistani State. Since the settlement of these canal colonies during British times, shareholders had traditionally paid their rent in kind to the landlord. When the army began to demand cash payments, these rural households were exposed to enormous economic, social and security uncertainty. Both historically and up to the present day, Punjab has supplied the Pakistani military with the bulk of its recruits. Despite this social nexus, the farmers were not protected from the army's brutal intervention to protect its own estate.

Rural desperation can readily escalate into inter-regional conflict, as illustrated by the dispute surrounding the development of the Kalabagh dam. Sindh has protested against Punjab allegedly diverting too much water in the upper reaches of the Indus River. Contrary to the poverty estimates published by various agencies, including the World Bank, the Sindhis claim to be not only amongst the poorest Pakistanis today, but also to have a disproportionate share of the country's poor: namely one-half of those living below the poverty line. The petition presented to the ADB, requesting that it abandon financial support to the dam project, served as an indictment of Gen. Pervez Musharraf's military regime. It stated that 'Due to their total control of the Pakistan military, the northern provinces are in the driving seat and make all the decisions concerning joint resources of Pakistan. . .Sindh has not even been adequately informed on most of these decisions, let alone consulted'. The petitioners praised the British Raj for being the standard-bearer for fairness: widespread consultations about decisions affecting the distribution of the Indus waters were typical in colonial times, and the views of people living on the lower banks of the Indus were not ignored. As the renowned Pakistani journalist Irfan Husain noted, the failure of the Musharraf Government to encourage public debate about the dam transformed the Kalabagh development into another symbol of Punjabi dominance: 'the Government has been unable to rally any major Sindhi, Baloch or Pashtun politician or party to its cause'. Voting against the dam has become a vote against Punjab and a vote for all the other, less populated provinces. Musharraf was also unwise in his language about the dam, claiming that it would prevent water being wasted by flowing into the sea, a perspective that ignored the needs and productivity of the Pakistanis who live on the Indus estuary. The Muttahida Qaumi Movement (MQM) in Sindh again raised the cry of Punjabi imperialism over Sindh.

### Agriculture and Land Ownership

Underlying all of Pakistan's agricultural problems is the pattern of land ownership and the feudal class relations that define the rural areas. Land ownership favours a small number of more wealthy families. At the time of independence owners of 100+ acres comprised 0.5% and 1.0% of owners in the Punjab and Sindh but controlled 25% and 30% of the total land area. The Agricultural Census of 2000 showed that 14.4% of the country's landowners controlled 56.6%, and 5.6% of the landowners had 37.5%, of the total cultivable land area. The Census also revealed that Pakistan had about 6.6m. farms, of which roughly 2.6m. were 'fragmented' or scattered between other farms, thereby making economies of scale at the individual farm level difficult to achieve. Moreover, the average number of fragments per 'farm' was just under four. Since the early 1970s the average farm size has fallen from 5.3 ha to 3.1 ha and the number of farms with less than 2 ha has trebled from about 1m. to almost 4m., or about 60%. Thus 60% of Pakistan's farms accounted for a mere 15% of the total cultivated area. This level of concentration greatly exceeds that in India, where small farms of less than 2 ha account for about 80% of all farms but 36% of cultivated land.

Land reforms based on maximum ceilings were attempted in Pakistan in the late 1950s and again in the 1970s. On both occasions such reforms had only a minimal impact on the pattern of ownership. Politically influential landlords were able to manipulate the implementation of reforms to their own benefit, often through fictitious transfers of ownership to family members and dependents. Of greater influence in shrinking the average size of farms has been the division of ownership at the point of inheritance.

In June 2002 the World Bank Country Assistance Strategy reported on the powerful connections between land ownership and poverty. There is compelling evidence to show that throughout Asia the poorest people are landless. In Pakistan around one-half of the rural population is very poor and this poverty is clearly correlated with landlessness. Viewed from a different perspective, about 75% of the landless as a whole are poor and the landless poor represent some 70% of the rural poor. Land concentration in Pakistan, as elsewhere, has another more indirect link with poverty. Lack of land prevents small farmers from accessing credit through utilizing land as collateral for loans. Even if marginal farmers are keen on land improvement, they cannot access the required resources, although microfinance has somewhat improved the situation.

Patterns of land ownership and use also systematically marginalize women. In Pakistan the role of women in agriculture is restricted to the rearing of animals and menial labouring jobs. Multilateral aid agencies are seeking to rectify this by demanding that irrigation projects involve more women. However, implementing such policies is virtually impossible without powerful incentives, legal reforms and higher literacy rates to give women some control over rural assets. Attempts to establish more microcredit institutions are similarly hampered by the inability of rural women to play a major role in decision-making within the family and, more generally, in society.

PAKISTAN

### Agriculture and the Environment

The extent of environmental damage in some areas has been widespread and interventions by individual farmers can make little difference. Soil erosion, water-logging, salination and deforestation all require wider interventions. The degradation of Pakistan's soil and water resources is so serious that about one-half of Punjab's 550,000 tube wells are recycling water that is so salty it cannot be used for agricultural purposes and is converting soil to *kala kallar* (black alkali soil). The privatization of Pakistan's canal irrigation systems is unlikely to provide any solution to these difficulties. If anything, the privatization of irrigation will strengthen the rural rich at the expense of the rural poor. Irrigation accounts for about 12% of the Public Sector Development Programme's funds. Although absolutely necessary for improving the productivity of the agriculture sector, irrigation tends to benefit mainly the large landlords considering the current structure of land relations in Pakistan. Moreover, the very location of irrigation canals favours the lands of large-scale rather than of small-scale or marginal farmers.

In 1998 a massive grasshopper outbreak occurred in upper Sindh and Balochistan and devastated rice and canola (rapeseed) production. In 2002/03 grasshoppers attacked the cotton crop in upper Sindh. Aridity has intensified the grasshopper attacks on commercial and food crops, owing to the lack of alternative grasses for feeding.

### Agriculture and Corporate Farming

Over the last few years the Government has been considering the proposal of corporate farming, especially for the livestock sector, hoping to boost the prospects of agriculture by encouraging foreign investment with a package of special incentives. Such a policy, however, would be contradictory to Pakistan's anti-poverty programmes owing to the fact that corporate farming world-wide is based on capital-intensive and labour-displacing technologies. Unless matched with new rural strategies for increasing local employment, the 'corporatization' of Pakistani agriculture is likely to exacerbate rather than alleviate rural unemployment.

The 2008/09 budget promised 'large tracts of land will be made available to foreign investors to induct capital and technology in our local farming sector'. The Pakistani Prime Minister was reported to have held lengthy meetings with the Saudi Agriculture Minister during the World Economic Forum in May 2008. It appeared that Saudi investment in agriculture was being actively sought to help cater for lack of domestic investment and also for the food deficit in the Middle East. The UAE was also reported to have acquired some agricultural land in Pakistan recently.

## LONG-TERM GROWTH

### The Legacy of Independence

The 'canal colonies' established prior to the partition of British India were very prosperous and constituted the largest tract of irrigated land anywhere in the world. Pakistan benefited by inheriting some of the expertise and productivity that defined the production of commercial crops, especially wheat and cotton, in Punjab. In contrast to India, Pakistan did not inherit any industrial infrastructure and some of its most successful merchants fled to Bombay (now known as Mumbai) and other parts of India. Industry comprised double the share of GDP in India (12%) as in Pakistan (6%) at the time of independence. The challenge of economic development in Pakistan was complicated by the fact that East Pakistan or East Bengal, now Bangladesh, was located on the other, eastern side of the Indian subcontinent. The prosperity of the jute industries in East Pakistan did not last, however, as jute was displaced by other fibres and eventually by the transport of international trade in containers (which reduced the usage of jute sacking). Hostile relations with neighbours and border disputes with China, India and Afghanistan have given Pakistan a 'siege mentality' and continuously diverted resources from the civilian to the military economy. The economic impact of this perception has been devastating—a huge proportion of the state budget (sometimes amounting to 7% of Pakistan's GDP, although it has steadily decreased to around 3% of GDP) has been devoted to military expenditure. Mutual hostility between India and Pakistan also caused lengthy delays to important bilateral agreements, such as the 1960 Indus Waters Treaty. Since 2003, however, there has been a retreat from this traditional scenario of mutual hostility. Various high-level dialogues, official visits and people-to-people exchanges have occurred. Pakistani popular singers have visited India, joint cricket matches have been played and flights between Delhi and Lahore have recommenced. Since the Congress-led Government came to power in mid-2004 in India the tone of belligerence has abated and Hindu fundamentalism has been somewhat calmed. Many of the institutions of government had to be created from scratch after independence. There were very few Muslims in either the British civil service or army; both institutions had to be re-created. India by contrast largely inherited the British structure and personnel of governance. The political leadership of Pakistan (the Muslim League) were mainly migrants from India and had little political base inside Pakistan. While India's first Prime Minister, Jawaharlal Nehru, stayed in office for 17 years (1947–64), providing an important sense of continuity, the two most prominent political leaders of Pakistan died soon after independence—Jinnah (1948) and Liaquat Ali Khan (1950). Pakistan's early years of independence prior to the coup in 1958 were marked by political chaos and by rapidly changing prime ministers.

Despite these early handicaps and the very pessimistic view of Pakistan's development since independence, we can draw some positives. Pakistan has not merely survived for 60 years (which many contemporaries would have considered impossible in 1947); it has also experienced average annual GDP growth of 5% plus and has transformed the structure of its economy. In 1949/50 manufacturing contributed less than 8% of West Pakistan's GDP and agriculture 53%. In 1947 primary commodities contributed 99.2% of exports. By the late 1990s 25% of GDP originated from manufacturing and only 24% from agriculture, and 75% of exports consisted of manufactured goods.

### Growth and Ethnic, Regional and Linguistic Divisions

In a 1997 paper written by Easterly and Levine a clear correlation was drawn between the extent of ethno-linguistic diversity and long-term economic growth. Pakistan could be considered an important example of a high-diversity society, even though it has experienced reasonable economic growth. Pakistan has been unable to bridge the regional, linguistic and ethnic differences that have persisted since independence. From the outset of independence East Pakistan (Bangladesh) complained that it was being discriminated against. Bengali was not made a national language at independence despite being numerically the most widely spoken language in Pakistan. In the 1960s this turned to complaints of economic exploitation. It was argued that revenues from East Pakistani jute exports were being used to fund industrialization in West Pakistan. These divisions culminated in war in 1970/71 and the attainment of independence by Bangladesh. The period since has various domestic conflicts within Pakistan. Intense rivalry has characterized relations between Punjab province, which is widely perceived to dominate the Government and the economy, and the more rural province of Sindh, which regards itself as economically backward and politically disadvantaged. The tribal province of Balochistan is extremely arid, and its residents widely believe that revenues from their large mineral deposits are being siphoned off to the central Government rather than benefiting the local inhaitants. Karachi, the commercial capital of Pakistan, has still not resolved the ethnic conflict between the original inhabitants of the area and the Muslim immigrants who arrived from India more than 50 years ago and who form the core support group of the MQM. Street violence and bombings became common in Karachi in the 1990s when it emerged as one of the most violent cities on earth. In recent years the situation had improved, but 200 saw renewed violence following the removal from office of the Chief Justice. In addition, Pakistan has witnessed conflic between Muslims and non-Muslims and also between the tw major branches of Islam, Sunni and Shi'a. The lack of inte regional consensus and social cohesion has impeded important economic projects, notably those involving the sharing of irrigation water between Punjab in the north and Sindh in the south.

**Gen. Ayub Khan (1958–68)**

The military coup of Gen. Ayub Khan in 1958 and the imposition of martial law led to a temporary cessation of conflict within Pakistan. Support for the Western non-communist alliance through treaty alliances such as CENTO and SEATO as well as a modern progressive image ensured early and enthusiastic support from the USA that was manifest in military supplies and large amounts of foreign aid. Ayub's Government promoted a profit-investment led pattern of industrialization based on large firms. State-owned development banks directed large loans towards these companies. Special incentives and access to foreign exchange were granted to exporters who diversified away from raw materials to manufactured (mainly textile) goods. Industrial growth generated a new manufacturing sector largely based on textiles. From a virtually non-existent base, large-scale manufacturing grew at double-digit rates and GDP growth reached 7% per year. The period 1958 to 1968 is known by many as 'The Decade of Development'. During the 1950s and 1960s Pakistan was regarded as one of the world's 'miracle' economies and Pakistani economic growth rates were higher than those of any other South Asian country. Long before export-orientated growth strategies had become popular, Pakistan as early as 1965 was exporting more than the aggregated exports of Thailand, Indonesia, Malaysia, the Philippines and Turkey.

The economy had become heavily dependent on foreign aid to fund investment in infrastructure and industry. After war with India in 1965 the USA suspended aid and economic growth slowed sharply. Although many of the very poorest in Pakistan benefited from rapid growth in agriculture and the opening up of employment possibilities abroad, much of the growth had occurred in West Pakistan, where per capita incomes increased from 32% to 61% of the level in East Pakistan. There was also resentment against a small number of well-connected families, mainly migrants from India at the time of independence who controlled the emerging industrial sector. The Government of Ayub Khan was undermined by a ferocious mobilization against his regime focusing on ideas of exclusion and exploitation—from West Pakistan by Zulfikar Ali Bhutto, a charismatic socialist, and from East Pakistan by Sheikh Mujibur Rahman, a Bengali nationalist. Both leaders emerged in the 1970s as the leaders of Pakistan and Bangladesh respectively.

**Zulfikar Ali Bhutto (1971–77)**

Zulfikar Ali Bhutto formed the Pakistan People's Party (PPP) in the 1960s to mobilize opposition against Gen. Ayub. Bhutto assumed power in 1970 with a mandate for fundamental social and economic change. The 'commanding heights' of the economy, previously under private control were nationalized; these included large-scale manufacturing, especially in the capital goods sector, and banks, vegetable oil and rice milling. Land reforms that were drawn up 'to abolish feudalism' were implemented in a lax manner that failed to weaken the power of feudal landlords. In some cases, however, rural landlords did lose land; for example, the holding of the family of former federal minister Ghulam Murtaza Jatoi was reduced by three-quarters.In this case, nevertheless, Jatoi's remaining assets were large enough to make him a local lord and to fund his own political party. Membership of the PPP shifted from radical social reformers to conservative landlords as membership widened in response to its electoral successes. The combined impact of nationalization and the entrenchment of feudal power in Pakistan not only encouraged disproportionate development in favour of the élite, but also made the nationalized assets of Pakistan prone to misappropriation through an increasingly corrupt bureaucracy. During the 1970s, however, the main problem was a decelerating growth rate (to less than 5% per year, from about 7% per year during the 1960s) and economic instability. A beneficial long-term impact of Bhutto's Government was the large increase in public investment in irrigation, manufacturing and infrastructure. Less beneficial was the near total collapse in private investment. The period was also marked by a succession of 'bad-luck' factors, such as the surge in international petroeum prices in 1973, a failure of the cotton crop in 1974/75 and catastrophic floods in 1976/77. In 1977 Zulfikar Ali Bhutto's civilian Government was replaced by a military regime under Gen. Zia ul-Haq, a political transition marked by an extreme brutality that saw, among other things, the hanging of Zulfikar Ali Bhutto on 4 April 1977.

**Gen. Zia ul-Haq (1977–88)**

Zia's regime witnessed a 10-year period of economic growth. GDP growth averaged 6.5% per year, but it was a prosperity built on unsustainable foundations. A critical factor was the large amounts of US aid the Zia Government received in return for Pakistan's unqualified support for the US policies of containing and repelling the Soviet troops in Afghanistan. Aid averaged US $1,450m. per year between 1978 and 1983. During the 1980s Pakistan became the conduit for US aid to anti-communist groups in Afghanistan, namely the *mujahidin* ('holy warriors'), some of whom later formed the Taliban (see the chapter on Afghanistan). After the eventual withdrawal of Soviet troops in early 1989, a prolonged period of factional fighting took place, as a result of which the Taliban grew in strength and established an alternative government of Afghanistan. At this stage, the USA's long-term concerns for the domestic stability of Pakistan and Afghanistan did not extend beyond its need to contain communism, with the result that it failed to foresee how Soviet domination might be replaced by more moralistic regimes based on Islamist fundamentalist principles. Pakistan under Zia experienced considerable economic growth. Long-term constraints on growth such as low rates of saving were not tackled. Public-sector deficit financing became an established feature of economic management under Zia, sustained only by large inflows of foreign remittances from Pakistani workers who had taken up contract work in the Gulf states. Such remittances averaged $2,300m. per year between 1983 and 1988. Private-sector investment revived as Zia eschewed the socialist policies of his predecessor, but his Government failed to support this with long-term public investment.

**Benazir Bhutto (1988–90, 1993–96)**

When Zia died in a mysterious aeroplane crash in 1988, Bhutto's daughter Benazir heralded for many a radical redirection of social and economic policy. In practice she proved a more adept opposition leader, someone more able to mobilize spirited opposition against a military dictator than to manage the complex coalition building and compromises necessary to reform a polity as complex and divisive as Pakistan. Benazir was given little freedom of manoeuvre in office, being constrained by a hostile and powerful military and presidency. The acceptance of a stringent IMF programme negotiated by the preceding caretaker Government was conditional on her assuming power. The most disappointing characteristics of Benazir Bhutto's Government in 1988–90 were the Prime Minister's willingness to exploit Islamist fundamentalism. None of Zia policies of Islamization, which in the eyes of many downgraded the status of women, were repealed. Her regime also became associated with levels of corruption that were unprecedented in Pakistani history. In August 2003 Swiss courts found Benazir Bhutto and her husband Asif Ali Zardari guilty of accepting bribes and of money laundering in 1997–98. The courts ordered the two to repay almost $12m. (the value of the bribes that they had accepted) to the Government of Pakistan. The Swiss courts upheld the earlier judgment of a Pakistani court in 1999, even though in Pakistan the original decision was overturned on appeal. Much of Benazir's attention was taken up with bitter political conflict with Nawaz Sharif. Nawaz Sharif and his party, the Pakistan Muslim League, won the provincial elections in the Punjab. The size and influence of the Punjab in Pakistan led to him forming what in practice became a parallel national government. Throughout the 1990s growth of GDP, manufacturing, exports and private investment experienced a long-term slowdown.

**Nawaz Sharif (1990–93, 1996–99)**

It eventually fell to Nawaz Sharif to undertake fundamental economic reforms. Nawaz was a more experienced politician, having risen to power as a protégé of Gen. Zia. He had a secure power base in the Punjab and close links with the military and ultimately proved more adept than Benazir in promoting reform. Nawaz Sharif came to power in the 1990 general election with a mandate to 'clean up' the country's institutions and to go well beyond the IMF's recommendations of structural adjustment. Foreign direct investment (FDI) into Pakistan was encouraged, private banking was again made possible, and more than one-half of the country's public-sector manufacturing units and one commercial bank were privatized. Import tariffs were substantially reduced, key industries privatized, and pricing and investment decisions were liberalized.

Economic reform was resumed after the elections of 1997, which brought Nawaz Sharif back to power. Such reform dramatically changed the nature of the Pakistani economy but failed to revive growth. Nawaz, as had his predecessors, struggled to mobilize savings and tax revenue, thus leaving the economy vulnerable to the accumulation of domestic and foreign debt. Public investment went on expensive prestige projects that contributed little to economic growth. For example, the Lahore-Islamabad Highway cost US $1,200m., but is only currently used at 10% of capacity. With attacks on the presidency, judiciary and military, Nawaz was accused of attempting to create an 'elective dictatorship'. Eventually, a bloodless military coup, led by Gen. Pervez Musharraf, replaced the civilian Government of Nawaz Sharif in October 1999.

### Gen. Pervez Musharraf (1999–2008)

There are two views about the military dictatorship of Gen. Pervez Musharraf. The first is that he finally provided the strong leadership necessary to push through tough economic reforms. The second is that massive 'debt forgiveness' following the terrorist attacks in the USA in September 2001, when Pakistan sided with the USA in the consequent 'war on terror', has rather been responsible for economic success. Certainly there are indicators that the economy recovered from the disappointing performance of the 1990s. Growth accelerated to more than 8% per year, inflation declined to the lowest level in 15 years, the fiscal deficit to the lowest in 20 years, remittances and the stock market reached their highest ever level, and exports crossed the $10,000m. and later the $20,000 level. The reforms that were used to effect such improvements were similar to those pursued in the 1990s, but they were applied with more conviction and purpose. The reforms included fiscal consolidation, market-orientated structural reforms in the fiscal, banking and corporate sectors, privatization, greater transparency, and significant improvements in the business environment. Unlike the 1990s, many argue that Musharraf took politically unpopular decisions. For example, a tax survey and documentation drive in 1999/2000 unearthed an extra 134,000 new income tax payers and 30,000 new sales tax payers. Throughout the 1990s up to one-third of the Government's budget deficit could be attributed to the losses incurred by public corporations. Tough reforms to state enterprises, reductions in employment and subsidies and charging more realistic, if unpopular, prices for outputs reduced losses considerably. Even enterprises such as Pakistan Steel Mills and Pakistan International Airlines (PIA) started generating profits. Other efforts went into recovering bank loans from politically influential defaulters. Large numbers of senior officials, politicians and business executives were imprisoned, received heavy fines and/or were disqualified from holding office. By 2001/02 a total of $500m. had been recovered from the forced repayment of loans. A key indicator of this success was an increase in private national savings; between 2001 and 2003 this was the key contributor in the turnaround of the external current account. National savings increased from 17% to 22% of GDP over this period and the current-account deficit of 2% of GDP in 2000/01 turned into a surplus, of 5% of GDP, in 2002/03. The Minister of Finance and Revenue (and Prime Minister after August 2004), Shaukat Aziz, who was renowned for his banking experience, devised an economic revival programme in line with the IMF Structural Adjustment and Stabilization Programme. By late 2004 it was clear that Aziz's strategy had started to work when the international economic ratings agency, Standard and Poor's, improved its sovereign credit rating for Pakistan's economy to 'B+', citing better revenue management as one reason for its decision.

Other commentators emphasize Musharraf's luck more than the successful reforms of a strong technocratic government. By the end of the 1990s 56% of government budgetary revenues were being used to service the stock of public debt. Annual debt servicing on the foreign portion of this debt reached US $6,000m.–7,000m. per year, absorbing two-thirds of export revenue. After the controversial nuclear tests in 1998 and the military coup in 1999, Pakistan was excluded from donor aid and lending from the World Bank and IMF. This all changed dramatically in late 2001, however, when Pakistan declared its support for the USA's 'war on terror'. In December 2001 Pakistan was granted relief on $12,500m. of foreign debt; longer repayment terms at lower interest rates were granted, thus saving $1,000m. in annual debt-servicing costs. Pakistan also utilized concessional assistance of up to $3,000m. from the IMF, World Bank and ADB to assist in repaying $4,500m. in private, commercial and short-term debt and to begin augmenting foreign exchange reserves. The ratio of short-term external debt to foreign reserves declined from 207 in 1999 to 42 by June 2002. This dramatic financial windfall, argue some, allowed higher levels of savings, consumption and investment, so generating a domestic boom and also increasing the confidence of foreign investors, in turn boosting portfolio investment, FDI, and workers' remittances.

By the end of 2004 the fiscal crisis had abated and Pakistan had accumulated sufficiently large foreign exchange reserves to withdraw from the IMF's Poverty Reduction and Growth Facility (PRGF), which it had entered three years earlier. The Minister of Finance and Revenue declared that, despite its entitlements, Pakistan would not draw on the IMF for further financial support and would instead raise development funds on the international markets and through more conventional aid from multilateral and bilateral donors. In the words of IMF Director Mohsin Khan, at the Pakistan Development Forum held in April 2005, 'it is extremely rare that a country moves directly from concessional IMF support to international capital market financing. Pakistan's re-entry in the international capital markets, with placements of a Eurobond and an Islamically structured bond (*Sukuk*) on very favourable terms, is a strong indicator of the country's impressive economic rebound'.

It is noticeable that Musharraf sought to establish a regime that combined civilian and military aspects: he did not declare martial law but preferred to style himself as a 'Chief Executive', while simultaneously dismissing the federal legislature. Musharraf had to steer Pakistan through some of its most difficult years and he did this with an astonishing willingness to divert policy away from the route of the past into a new, pragmatic direction. Widely regarded as responsible for the Kargil conflict with India in 1999, he quickly reversed direction and became the USA's most dependable ally in the 'war on terror'. At the same time, one should not underestimate the longer-term impact of Musharraf's earlier policies, in particular his financial support for the Taliban in Afghanistan.

Fiscal reform has addressed some problems in tax structures by assigning various tax heads such as tariffs, sales taxes, excise duties and income taxes to specific objectives, but has failed to increase the tax-to-GDP ratio. In terms of expenditure, deeply ingrained problems remain, in particular Pakistan's traditional neglect of education, health and other human resource development activities. Illiteracy in Pakistan remains very high; it not only acted as a major constraint on development and poverty alleviation but also undermined the chances of Pakistan's democratic experiment succeeding by pushing a growing number of parents in the direction of religious schools or *madrassas* to impart literacy to their children by means of a curriculum that essentially opposes modernization. The impact of illiteracy is devastating for Pakistan in other ways. The high rates of unemployment and low levels of productivity are due to poor and inadequate training, although data indicates that unemployment is actually higher amongst the literate.

### Social Development

William Easterly in 2001 called Pakistan a country that had experienced 'growth without development'. Reasonably rapid rates of economic growth and diversification of the economy from agriculture to industry have not since independence been clearly translated into significant improvements in social indicators. Compared to developing countries with a similar level of national income, Pakistan has 36% fewer births attended by trained personnel, 42% lower health spending per capita, 40% fewer elementary school-age girls who attend primary school, and spends 3.3% more of GDP on defence. Over the last 60 years or so GDP growth in Pakistan has averaged more than 5.5% per year, making Pakistan 39th in the world, according to average income levels. The lack of comparable social development is striking; by the 1990s Pakistan ranked only 120th in the world in terms of human and social development.

### Population and Employment

As of 1 January 2006 Pakistan had a population of 155.36m., with an annual growth rate of around 1.8%. Approximately 67.5% of the population lives in villages and 32.5% in towns. Unlike the rest of South Asia, employment for both rural and urban labour has grown sharply: urban employment increased by 5.7% during 2001–06 and rural employment by 3.9% over the same period. The unemployment rate declined from 7.8% in 2001 to 6.2% in 2006. However, the employment generation has mostly been restricted to unpaid family helpers and there has been very little growth in paid employees or the self-employed. The unemployment rate is higher in urban areas, where it stood at 8.04% in 2006, compared with 5.35% in rural areas. Higher employment generation, however, is no guarantee for poverty reduction. Indeed, most of the poor in Pakistan are working poor and many poor families are compelled to put their children to work in 'sweatshops' to earn sufficient family income for subsistence: there are about 3.3m. child workers in Pakistan, equivalent to approximately 8% of all children under 14. Pakistan's poverty-reduction strategies have sought to generate rural employment through the Khushal Pakistan Programme and Khushhal Pakistan Fund, which target public works development programmes in accordance with local needs. The programme is implemented through members of parliament, who are allocated a sum of Rs 10m. each. They can utilize these funds for various schemes and projects through the provincial ministry of local government and rural development for their constituencies. The Government claims that the programme has created around 1m. temporary jobs. However, like most aspects of Pakistan's development strategy, the outcome of the programme has not been the subject of independent academic analysis. Hence it is impossible to measure its efficacy.

The overwhelming majority of Pakistan's population is Muslim, making Pakistan the second largest Muslim country in the world after Indonesia. Population growth rates have declined from more than 3% annually in the early 1970s to just under 2% in 2006. While these figures show a decline in the population growth rate, the decline has been quite slow. The family-planning programme remains constrained by the combined impact of rural poverty and low female literacy. Infant mortality rates declined between the early 1970s and 2004, from about 110 to 70 deaths per 1,000 live births; however, in rural areas the rate remained high. The total number of live births per woman (the fertility rate) also decreased during this period—from 7.0 to about 3.8. The under-five mortality rate fell from 128 per 1,000 in 1990 to 101 per 1,000 in 2004. One reason for the high level of infant mortality was that infant immunization rates remained low, at about 54%. The pattern of change has, in other words, been mixed. There have been some important achievements, but Pakistan has much further to go along the path of demographic transition. The lack of public investment in education has emerged as a major obstacle. Expenditure has declined from levels already regarded as low: from 2.2% of GDP in the early 1970s to 1.8% in 2000–02 and to less than 1% in the 2002/03 budget. The budget for 2004/05 started to reverse this trend, with an increase in investment in higher education of 84%.

### Education

In the 2005/06 budget the allocation for education was again increased, by 50%, and the allocation for health by 72%; by 2006/07 expenditure had increased to 2.4% of GDP. The minimum wage has also been raised, from Rs 2,500 to Rs 3,000 in 2004/05, Rs 4,000 in 2005/06 and further to Rs 4,600 in 2006/07, and it is to apply to the private sector as much as the public sector. Of course, minimum wages are virtually unenforceable in the informal sector, where most of the poor are employed, so this may not have much impact upon poverty. Nor do budgetary increases automatically improve the welfare of the poorest. Plans to build a Cardiology Centre and Burns Unit in Multan, for example, may not be the most appropriate response to rural health issues in Punjab, although such advanced technology may sound and look impressive to an ill-informed electorate. The Pakistani Government's focus on college and university education has also been controversial. While this directly addresses the country's skilled labour shortages, basic literacy is arguably a higher priority, especially when college education is one area of investment that can be left to the private sector. Basic literacy, by contrast, remains a government responsibility throughout the world. Although Pakistan's official literacy rate increased from 45% in 2001/02 to 54% in 2005/06, it is still significantly lower than India, where it is 70%, and female literacy is critically low. Female literacy in Pakistan today stands at less than 42%, compared with male literacy of 65%. Female literacy varies from 41% in urban Sindh to 3% in the rural NWFP. Rural literacy is much lower than urban: 42% compared with 70%. The new national literacy campaign seeks to raise total literacy to 60% over the next two years. There are a few encouraging signs in the education sector. The enrolment of girls in primary schools in Pakistan has increased greatly during the last decade, thereby improving the ratio of male to female students from 100:51 to 100:75 between 1990 and 2005 (according to the Economist Survey of Pakistan). According to the Pakistan Social and Living Standards Measurement Survey (PSLM) data the gross enrolments at primary level increased from 72% in 2000/01 to 87% in 2004/05 and the net enrolment (school-age children enrolled in primary schools) from 42% to 52% over the same period. Gross enrolment for girls rose from 61% to 80% and net enrolment from 38% to 48% between 2000/01 and 2004/05.

Government schools continue to dominate education in Pakistan, increasing in importance the higher up one goes in the educational system: 58% of primary schools are government-run, and 63%, 70% and 64% respectively of middle, secondary and upper-secondary schools. The characteristics of government schools in Pakistan give the Government special responsibility for what happens to functional literacy and the values of the country's youth generation. Nevertheless *madrassas* are also important. Enrolment estimates at these religious schools vary, the best being 3% of total enrolments at primary school level. The Government is making an effort to change the syllabuses of these schools where extremist thinking is encouraged alongside traditional religious teachings.

### Defence Expenditure

A major constraint on social welfare expenditure is the cost of the Pakistani military. Pakistan has retained a huge army of 550,000 men, a navy of 24,000 personnel, some 2,500 tanks and eight frigates. India's army and naval personnel total roughly double the number in Pakistan, and India has approximately 50% more tanks and frigates. Relative to land size and population, Pakistan clearly spends far more on defence than India does. Defence expenditure continues to use up a vast volume of the State's limited fiscal resources. In the early years of independence the military absorbed some 50%–70% of government revenue. In 2005/06 defence expenditure (totalling Rs 241,063m., excluding pensions) was the second largest government expenditure item after interest payments (Rs 260,021m.). Expenditure heads in total current expenditure during 2005/06 included: interest payments at 18.5%; defence at 17.2%; and public-sector development expenditure at 26.2% In 2004 defence expenditure in India was equivalent to 55% of that country's health and education spending, 40% in Sri Lanka, 38% in Bangladesh and a massive 178% in Pakistan. By the late 1990s Pakistan had nine soldiers for every doctor. The share of defence expenditure as a proportion of total current expenditure, however, declined from 18.3% in 2000/01 to 17.2% in 2005/06. The 2008/09 budget announced by the new civilian Government in mid-2008 promised disclosure of the defence budget for the first time in Pakistan's history so that 'all the relevant details of the defence expenditure will be available for the review and debate of Parliament'.

### Economic Development in South Asia

Secondary-school enrolment levels in Pakistan (45%) are comparable to those in India (48%), but are much lower than elsewhere in Asia, such as Thailand (85%) and China (70%). Other indicators for modern communications are also low in Pakistan: for example, there were only 27 telephone lines per 1,000 population in 2003, compared with 46 in India, 105 in Thailand and 209 in China. However, in recent years there has been a sharp increase in 'teledensity' in Pakistan: in 2006/07 there were 33 fixed lines, 358 mobiles and 11 wireless telephone lines per 1,000 people. Citing the work of Sanjaya Lall, an ADB study also shows the relationship between low levels of education and export performance. In the case of Pakistan, exports are less diversified because the technology intensity of manufactures is high only in low-technology products and is very low in resource-based manufactures and medium- to high-technology goods. Until the 1980s, within South Asia, Pakistan's development was marginally ahead of India's: per caput gross national income (GNI) was US $360, compared with $340 in India, and fewer people remained employed in agriculture than in India (55%, compared with 70%). According to estimates by the World Bank, in 2001 Pakistan's GNI, measured at average 1999–2001 prices, had increased only marginally, to $420 per head. Pakistan's economy was also more export-orientated than all the other countries of South Asia, except for Sri Lanka: foreign trade as a percentage of GDP was 32% in 1988, compared with 13%, 22% and 52% for India, Bangladesh and Sri Lanka, respectively. Despite these positive indicators, even before the 1990s there were good reasons to be concerned about Pakistan's development. Only 36% of the population was literate, compared with 53% in India and 88% in Sri Lanka.

## INDUSTRY

### Industrial Growth Rates since Independence

In 1948 (united) Pakistan produced 75% of the world's jute but had no jute mills, and it produced an annual yield of 1.5m. bales of cotton but had only a tiny number of cotton mills. Exporters were reliant on cotton mills in Ahmedadab and Bombay (now Mumbai) and jute mills in Calcutta (now Kolkata). Between 1949 and 1958 industrial growth was very rapid, although from a negligible base, with large-scale manufacturing expanding by more than an average annual rate of 20%. Much of this growth was based on replacing imports of relatively simple goods such as cement and cigarettes.

Pakistani manufacturing achieved reasonable growth rates during the first four decades of independence; in the 1950s the average annual growth rate was 13.3%, declining in the 1960s to 9.9% (although this was still quite high). The average annual growth rate declined further in the 1970s, to 5.5%, but in the 1980s it once again increased, to 8.2%. Manufacturing growth peaked in 1987/88 at 10.0% and steadily declined thereafter, reaching 3.8% by the late 1990s. By 2003/04 industrial growth had recovered to about 14.0% and it increased further to 15.5% in 2004/05, but declined in the subsequent two years to 10.0% and 8.4%, respectively.

From the beginning, it has been large-scale production that has driven the manufacturing sector, with average annual growth rates of 13% and 8% in the 1960s and 1980s. The large-scale manufacturing sector registered growth rates of 18.1%, 19.9%, 10.7% and 8.8% over the four years to 2006/07. Large-scale manufacturing has dominated the industrial sector, accounting for about 70% of all industrial growth for most of those years. Since 2000 the products that have led growth trends have not been traditional textiles but rather automobiles, electrical goods, pharmaceuticals and leather products. In 2005/06, for example, the respective growth rates for these sectors were: 29.8%, 11.8%, 14.8% and 10.9%. Textiles and apparel, by contrast, registered just under 4% growth in 2005/06, but when this is disaggregated, the data shows that the growth was due largely to cotton yarn (11.6%), while cotton cloth rates showed only negligible change (0.07%).

The growth in the industrial sector could be attributed largely to the demand stimulus from increased consumer borrowing and the rise in exports. Pakistan's automobile industry consists of a growing number and range of foreign assembly plants. The cement industry has become export-orientated, with cement exports directed particularly to Afghanistan and Iraq following the events of 11 September 2001 and the subsequent 'war on terror'.

### Textiles

The textile industry has been the foundation of industrial development in Pakistan since the 1950s. Today, it still accounts for 8.5% of the country's GDP, employs 38% of Pakistan's manufacturing labour force and accounts for a little over 60% of total foreign-exchange earnings. Its growth relative to other modern manufacturing can mainly be attributed to the government policies that raised profitability in the industry. The USA and EU are the largest customers for Pakistan's textiles, buying 25% and 20% respectively of total exports. Since the implementation of the final stage of the international Agreement on Textiles and Clothing on 31 December 2004, Pakistan, along with the key Asian producers of textiles, has managed to hold its own against rising Chinese competition. For example, China's market share by value of US clothing imports increased from about 8% in 2001 to 22% in 2005. This suggests strong competition, but Pakistan's share nevertheless remained relatively stable, at between 1.65% and 1.83%, over the same period. Similarly, Pakistani clothing exports to the EU stayed relatively stable, at about 3% of market share measured by value, while China's market share doubled to about 30%. Pakistan sustained double-digit growth rates in textile exports in the decade to 2005; however, growth slowed to only 6% in 2006/07 and turned negative in 2007/08. This negative growth was offset by higher unit prices which sustained total export revenue. The downturn has been blamed on temporary factors, in particular pests affecting the cotton crop and higher energy prices. The pattern may, however, reflect the competitive threat from China and mark the beginning of serious problems for textile production in Pakistan. Right now, however, Pakistan remains one of the world's top six producers of textiles and clothing: its trade in yarn accounts for 30% of the global yarn trade, and its trade in cotton accounts for 8% of the global cotton trade. Pakistan's textile exports are dominated by three major items: in 2005/06, of textile shipments worth US $8,600m., the leading groups were fabrics (22%), made-up goods including bedclothes (20%) and knitwear (17%). There are various textiles mills in Pakistan producing quality products for export. These companies have 'state of the art' machinery in all the sub-processes of textile manufacturing, although there are technological disparities across textile firms.

A defining characteristic of Pakistan's textile sector has been the long-term dominance of private ownership. State encouragement to new technologies such as jet weaving has been helpful in increasing private investment, which has exceeded government targets. Between 1999 and 2006 total investment in textiles amounted to US $6,000m., the bulk of which went to spinning (47%) and weaving (26%). The Government recently allowed tax-free imports of all textile-related machinery, which is expected to help further improve technology. FDI in the textile industry has also been growing, but given the strength of the domestic firms, foreign investment has been very small. Most FDI has gone into transport, communications, the financial sector and mining. The 2008/09 budget promised a number of measures targeted to help the textiles sector, including a reduction in import duties on sewing machines and on relevant raw materials and chemicals.

### Electricity

A major obstacle to continued growth and competitiveness is poor infrastructure, especially the unreliable electricity supply. As in India, Pakistani manufacturers have resorted to building their own mini power plants to ensure continuous production cycles. Pakistan's power supply is largely controlled by the State, the inefficiencies of which have become a major constraint on industrial expansion. Two of the most dramatic examples of public-sector failure can be found in the Water and Power Development Authority (WAPDA) and the Karachi Electric Supply Company (KESC), which was recently privatized. These two companies, along with two nuclear power plants in the public sector and 21 private operators, generate Pakistan's electricity. The WAPDA and KESC generate, transmit and distribute electricity, but the private companies are only permitted to generate electricity. The main problems in the power sector include poor management; erratic billing practices that fail to reflect the actual usage of electricity; theft by the users; a chronically unreliable supply; and large subsidies. Theft from the grid is aided by the public-sector distribution workers, as the systems of surveillance are weak or non-existent. Public operators routinely collude with influential users of energy. In June 2004 one of the directors of WAPDA was shot dead by an engineer who had become deeply disgruntled by the type of work he had been allocated, an incident that dramatically exemplified the problems endemic in WAPDA. In mid-2004 WAPDA fell short of its targeted electricity output owing to water shortages, despite the growth in production over the previous five years. However, the Government of Pakistan remains determined to switch the balance between hydro and thermal power generation, largely because the former is so much cheaper. The objective is to raise hydropower generation from its present level of 29% to 39% over a six-year period. To this end, more hydropower projects have been initiated, including the highly controversial Ghazi Barotha Project, which is now fully operational. Apart from the needs of agriculture and industry, increased demand from households has put the energy sector under pressure: the total number of consumers has doubled in the last 10 years, to 15m. In that time the percentage of power lost by WAPDA in transmission and distribution has not changed—it remains about 25%, and in the case of KESC it is as high as 35% or more.

## PRIVATIZATION, FINANCE AND REFORM

### Privatization

Since the 1990s the Government has reverted to the pre-1970 strategy of encouraging private-sector activity in industry, banking and other sectors; given the apparent failings of the public sector, this has been an important policy shift. This marks a distinct difference from the situation India where privatization has been extremely slow and more often based on the sale of minority holdings. As the Governor of the State Bank of Pakistan noted in April 2005, the losses of state-owned enterprises generated about one-third of the country's fiscal deficits. To begin with, in 1992 the Muslim Commercial Bank was privatized. By 2001 a total of 108 industrial units had been privatized: 19 in ghee production, 15 roti plants, 14 chemical/fertilizer plants, 11 cement plants, six state-owned banks, seven engineering plants and five energy units. A total of Rs 61m. was raised, 50% of which was obtained from the privatization of Pakistan Telecommunications Ltd. The privatization of the banking sector has been at the forefront of economic reform, with all but one public-sector bank having been privatized. In 2005/06 the privatization programme expanded into new areas, including the sale of the following: Pakistan Telecommunications Ltd (26% of shares sold to Etisalat of the UAE); Carrier Telephone Industries Ltd (sold to Siemens Pakistan); Karachi Electric Supply Corporation Ltd (government shares sold to a consortium consisting of Hassan Associates, Al-Jomiah Holding Co and Premier Mercantile Services); and Pak-Arab Fertilizers (to Pakistan American Fertilizer Ltd). One especially important strategic sale was 75% of the Government's control of Pakistan Steel Mills Corporation Ltd (PSM). By 2007 a total of 163 unit shares (12 unit shares since June 2005) and the privatization proceeds had brought in Rs 421,200m. (Rs 242,500m. since June 2005).

Despite this list of achievements, the privatization policy has come under considerable criticism. Serious questions have been raised about the process of privatization, rising corruption and whether the sale of so many assets has realised important government objectives, namely enhancing efficiency levels and reducing the fiscal deficit. Matters came to a head in late June 2006 when the Supreme Court of Pakistan declared that the sale of 75% of PSM shares to an international consortium was invalid. The consortium consisted of Arif Habib Securities (Pakistan), Al-Tuwairqi (Saudi Arabia) and the Magnitogorsk Iron and Steel Works Open JSC (Russia). As Pakistan's only integrated steel producer, questions were raised regarding whether shifting a monopoly from the state to private sector would generate any pressure for efficiency gains. The sale of PSM has been closely scrutinized by parliamentarians and the public. The decision of the Privatization Commission aroused suspicion when the Commission reviewed the final contract with the international consortium within a mere 48-hour period. Concerns were raised about the sale of a national asset which, since the reforms of 1998, had started to yield considerable profits: between 2002 and 2004 profits increased from Rs 4m. to Rs 10,192m. A third concern was the lack of transparency and the sudden replacement of two of the original private contractors with a new interest group that had strong links to Mauritius (a country with a long-standing reputation as a global centre for money laundering). There were also suspicions that the new buyers were just front men and that the actual buyers were interested Pakistanis or some outsiders who did not want to disclose their identity. The associated sale of parcels of land belonging to the mill in Karachi (land prices had soared in the city) was another issue that emerged when the final sale price of the privatization deal was scrutinized by the Supreme Court. The case in the Supreme Court was filed by two groups of petitioners: the Pakistan Steel Mill Workers' Union and the Wattan Party. The decision of the Supreme Court of Pakistan to nullify the sale of PSM provided a stinging indictment of the process by which the contract had been drawn up and finalized. The decision noted in particular how the Cabinet Committee ignored a recommendation from the Board of the Privatization Commission to include the valuation of net assets and made no attempt to justify why shares sold to the consortium had been undervalued relative to their current market price. Detailed questions were asked about the process by which the sale was negotiated, whether the winning bid was the best available offer and whether the identity of the final consortium partners was acceptable given that the 'bidders are different from the purchasers'. In particular the judgment noted the 'indecent haste' with which the sale had been pushed through. The court's decision raised concerns about the privatization sales that had occurred before the controversy about the steel mills. The court also ruled that the privatization was carried out without the approval of the Council of Common Interests (CCI), which had not even been established by that time. Since then the CCI has been set up, but it is now feared that all transactions where the CCI was to be consulted but was not might now be challenged and the entire future privatization process delayed. In the mean time, the Minister for Privatization announced the Government's determination to reassess the full value of PSM and to again float a sale as soon as possible. The whole matter has now become intensely politicized, with most of the parties including the Pakistan People's Party and the Muslim parties opposing it—for example, the Muttahida Majlis-e-Amal (MMA) in the NWFP has informed the Government of its determination to oppose all privatization of profitable public-sector companies. Some critics have pointed out that Pakistan should study the privatization policies of India and China, where the sale of public assets has been far more constrained and where the old-fashioned commitment to a degree of state control over what Lenin called 'the commanding heights of the economy' continues.

In June 2008 the Minister of Privatisation and Investment announced the privatization programme for 2008/09. The assets to be sold by the Privatization Commission included those of the Heavy Electrical Complex, Pakistan Machine Tool Factory, Lakhra Coal Development Corporation and Pakistan Steel Mills (again). Pressure from the leader of the PPP, Asif Zardari, forced the Commission to abandon the proposed sale of Pakistan State Oil, Pakistan Steel Mills and Pakistan Gas. At mid-2008 there was particular concern about the proposed sale of SME Bank Ltd, since this body was the only one specialized in the financing of small and medium-sized enterprises. There was concern that, once in the private sector, the bank would concentrate on more profitable large loans to large enterprises and so deprive the small sector of credit.

### The Karachi Stock Exchange (KSE)

Economic growth, privatization, rising foreign portfolio investment and the recent political rapprochement between Pakistan and India have made the Karachi Stock Exchange (KSE) into one of the fastest growing and most profitable exchanges in the world. Despite the decision of Supreme Court to invalidate the privatization of PSM, the débâcle surrounding the Chief Justice, the Lal Masjid incident and the general law and order situation in the country, the stock exchange markets of Pakistan have continued to grow rapidly. Those benefiting most from this growth have been the Mutual Funds, including the National Investment Trust (NIT), Pakistan's largest public-sector mutual trust. The total value of the mutual funds increased from Rs 25,000m. in June 2002 to Rs 215,000m. in March 2007. The NIT is a major investor in the KSE, in particular in fuel and energy, financial assets, chemicals and pharmaceuticals. The KSE has performed impressively since 2002: in 2002/03 the index increased by 75%; in 2003/04 by 55%; by another 47% in 2004/05, by 34.1% in 2005/06 and by another 29.8% in the first nine months of 2006/07. Even more impressive has been the growth of the stock exchange itself, which in 2005 had some 1.5m. investors, compared with a mere 70,000 in 2003. Stock market capitalization increased from US $6,500m. in 1999/00 to $75,000m. in 2007/08. Evidence has continued to mount showing that the strength of the KSE is based on both domestic and foreign investors; the portfolio investment in 2006/07 reached US $1,823,000m. However, the stock exchange market has been very volatile; for example, in February 2005 share prices increased by 22.4% while there was a decline in the share prices by 13.4% in May 2006. This volatility is typical of the Asian share markets over the last few years. By March 2007 a total of 655 companies were listed on the KSE. The breakdown of 651 companies listed by the end of the 2005/06 fiscal year indicate that the majority of companies (212) were listed in the cotton and other related textiles, followed by banks and financial institutions (162). The other major groups included sugar and allied (37), pharmaceuticals (35), fuel and energy (28), automobiles and allied (25) and cement (21). There has been an ongoing process of deregistration, which is more significant than new registrations; there were as many as 711 registered companies in 2002, falling to 661 in 2005 and to 651 in 2006. There are two other stock exchanges—in Lahore and Islamabad.

In 2006 the financial calculations of Pakistan's investors became more sophisticated with the launch of the KSE 30 Index. It was argued that the KSE 100 Index exaggerated the strengths of the share market by being based on market capitalization figures. These showed that the KSE had grown by 60% per annum during the previous five years. A more discerning investor market saw the introduction in late August 2006 of the KSE 30 Index based on more realistic criteria. Despite the growth in the size of the stock market and indices of trading, the focus of the KSE remains on secondary trading. Banking still meets the bulk of industrial financing requirements.

### Banking

In 2003–05 the implementation of wide-ranging banking reforms improved the credibility of the Pakistani economy both domestically and internationally. Specifically in banking, new prudential laws were introduced, special banking facilities were made available to small and medium-sized enterprises (SMEs), and the wiring-up of the banking system's automated teller machines (ATMs) was also made more efficient. Efficiency and transparency have improved as a result of mergers and new procedures to improve governance. By 2007 more than 20 mergers had occurred between previously non-viable small banking firms. Transparency has improved, with new rules imposed on bank management and auditing processes. The result is that there are no longer problematic banks due to substantial overhauls. Technological changes in the banking industry in the initial stages was slow. However, although by May 2005 Pakistan still only had 800 ATMs, by December 2006 that number had increased to 1,948. Similarly, the number of online branches increased from 2,897 in June 2005 to 3,947 by December 2006, and the number of credit card holders is growing rapidly.

By late 2004 four major state-sector banks had been privatized during the previous four years: the Muslim Commercial Bank, the Allied Bank of Pakistan, United Bank and the Habib Bank. This brought the total share of government-owned banking assets down to only 22.4%. Despite this, the National Bank of Pakistan is still the country's largest bank and accounts for 19.3% of banking assets, 17.5% of the advances and around 20% of the deposit base. However, it too has sold about one-quarter of its shares to the public. Consumerism has increased in Pakistan, supported by the increased lending to private households. Personal loans now account for about 16.6% of all loans in Pakistan. In the short term this does involve new risks for the banks that have little experience in lending to consumers or SMEs. However, these are not the main reason for Non-Performing Loans (NPLs). Most NPLs have been incurred by large debtors, rather than small-scale borrowers. As a result of new regulations concerning NPLs, there has been a consistent decline in the NPLs of the banking sector, from Rs 181,400m. in 2001 to Rs 141,500m. in 2006, and the ratio of net NPLs to net loans fell from 10.3% in 2001 to only 1.4% in 2006. The high numbers of NPLs in the past reflected the undue personal pressure on the banking sector exerted by the policy makers. In 2006 the most influential firms or individuals, some 0.6% of all banking customers, held some 68.8% of all banking loans in Pakistan, and 1.0% of all customers held 73.5%. Most loans are taken out by textile firms. By March 2008 the capital-adequacy rate in Pakistan's banking system had reached 13.1%, which was more than sufficient to comply with international norms.

Pakistan is an 'Islamic Republic' and it introduced Islamic banking in 1985. Since then the banks in Pakistan have operated on a profit and loss basis. However, their operations are believed to be not much different from those of conventional banks. In recent years the Islamic banks have operated separately from conventional banks and have grown at a rapid rate compared with the conventional banks, although the total deposits and the proportion of deposits held by the Islamic banks remain low. While at the end of 2004 deposits held by the Islamic banks were equivalent to a mere 1% of total banking assets, they had increased to 1.6% by June 2005 and to around 2% by June 2006. This indicates a growth rate of almost 50%, compared with growth of 16% in conventional banks over the same period. Nevertheless, the Government continues to identify itself with western banking traditions as part of its strategy of growth via links with the international economy, although the Supreme Court has recently ruled that the Government itself must adopt Islamic banking practices in the not too distant future.

In the mean time the Government is seeking to curb Pakistan's role as a conduit for international money-laundering. Pakistan is a member of the Asia/Pacific Group on Money Laundering (APG) that was established after 11 September 2001. According to the State Bank of Pakistan, the country has followed all the recommendations made by the APG. New procedures to ensure compliance and surveillance of suspicious transactions have been introduced and are monitored by the central bank. Another important curb on illegal transfers of international funds has been the enactment of new legislation closing down the large number of foreign currency dealers and money-changers. By June 2004 these had been replaced by proper exchange companies or continue business as franchises of other companies. As reported by the IMF in June 2004, the State Bank of Pakistan is observing 'most of the good transparency practices in the area of banking supervision'. Pakistan now has a specific law addressing the problem of money-laundering.

Low levels of savings have been a feature of the Pakistani economy since independence. The savings rate averaged a little over 11% in the 1970s and increased to only 14% in the 1990s. This was far below the levels of savings recorded in India (25%) and China (40%) in the 1990s. With investment rates reaching up to 20%, this situation has implied a constant need to rely on external capital inflows. Private investment increased from just 10.9% of GDP in 2003/04 to 16.2% in 2006/07. The major factor behind the turnaround in private-sector investment has been the massive capital inflows, which accounted for almost 7% of GDP. Domestic and national savings grew to 17.6% and 20.8% of GDP in 2002/03, but have declined since then to 18.0% and 16.1%.

### Corruption

An important component of Pakistan's attempts to re-establish the viability of the private sector and civil institutions in general was the anti-corruption drive. Since September 2001 this has become a non-negotiable part of the new Pakistani-US relationship, owing to the close links between corruption, money-laundering and terrorism. After the attacks on the USA in September 2001 a new law was passed banning politicians with criminal records from contesting elections. At about this time the National Accountability Bureau (NAB) was also established to monitor, investigate and implement the anti-corruption laws. Whilst this was clearly designed to prevent opposition leaders such as Benazir Bhutto and Nawaz Sharif from re-emerging as political leaders, it was, nevertheless, an important step in the reform process. However, some of the bank accounts of Benazir Bhutto that had been 'frozen' have now been restored and the efforts of the NAB have been progressively downgraded. The 2008/09 budget annouced that the NAB was being wound up and would experience an immediate 30% reduction in its budget for 2008/09.

According to Transparency International's Corruption Index, Pakistan was ranked 132 out of 145 countries in 2006. Whereas anecdotal evidence suggests that the illegal economy is probably 300% or 400% larger than the official economy in Pakistan, estimates prepared by the Pakistan Institute of Development Economics indicate that it may be around 34% to 50% of the official economy, which is comparable to India's black market economy, which is reckoned to constitute about 44% of its official economy. The illegal economy's prominence is largely aided by porous borders, the legacy of the Afghanistan war, the history of drugs and arms trading, and the weakness of civil society. The much wider illegal activity of concern in Pakistan is the old practice of *Benami*, whereby assets are held in the name of someone other than the real owner. This practice has now been banned, but the law cannot be enforced. Traditionally, this has allowed unscrupulous and usually large-scale operators to conceal their real financial worth and thus avoid paying taxes and other obligations.

In spite of the bans and prohibitions, perceptions of corruption in Pakistan have not improved—indeed they have worsened. In 2006 Transparency International reported that government corruption had doubled in the four years since 2002: the 'corruption ratio' had risen from 32.7% to 67.3%. Corruption was highest amongst the police, power bureaucracy, judiciary and land administration. Historical comparisons have suggested that current levels of corruption exceed those experienced under Benazir Bhutto (48%) and Nawaz Sharif (34%). Perceptions of corruption have been heightened in particular by the PSM case and the widespread belief that high-ranking officials were involved. It also seriously tarnished, if not destroyed, the reputation of Pakistan's former Prime Minister, Shaukat Aziz. In addition, the steel mill case led to the second 'no-confidence' motion ever to be mooted in the Pakistan Parliament (the first was against Benazir Bhutto in 1989). The 18-page motion was presented to Parliament on 24 August 2006. It had the support of all the opposition parties, Islamist and secular: namely the Alliance for the Restoration of Democracy (ARD) and the MMA. A total of 136 opposition members supported the motion; this amounted to 40% of Pakistan's total of 342 parliamentarians. The Prime Minister was not ultimately censured, but a major political debate had been engendered, accompanied by a charge list of more than 300 pages.

## ENERGY, INFRASTRUCTURE AND INSURGENCY

Energy problems, especially load shedding, have become a constraint on the growth of industry and agriculture. Disputes about energy have also become the basis for the Balochi insurgency movement. Balochi militancy has been focused on the Sui gas fields, which currently fuel an annually growing demand (by 10% or more) for gas and electricity in Pakistan. Located south of Sui is Pakistan's most important city, Karachi, which is heavily dependent on Balochi gas. Attacking gas facilities has proven to be an especially effective strategy against a background of increasing domestic and international petroleum prices, which in 2005/06 reached US $70–$75 per barrel and had risen to more than $150 per barrel by 2008. The Sui fields provide Pakistan with about one-fifth of its total gas requirements. Insurgency also serves as a means of discouraging foreign investment, given that the second most important area of FDI into Pakistan is in the energy sector (worth US $312.7m. in 2005/06). If the Balochi people are not provided with a larger share of the gas revenues, they are determined to reduce foreign investor confidence in Pakistan—an outcome which would have implications for the whole country. Demands for greater control of resource revenues dominated dialogue between the Government and Balochistan's political parties throughout 2004.

State responses to the insurgency have been tough, and on 27 August 2006 the leader of the Balochi insurgency, Nawab Akbar Bugti, was killed in a confrontation between government forces and insurgents. Bugti was no hot-headed, youthful terrorist, but rather a 79-year-old former parliamentarian, a graduate of the elite Aitchison College of Lahore, and widely admired by Balochis and non-Balochis alike. Insurgents, using explosives, rockets and land-mines, have inflicted extensive damage on the province's infrastructure. The attacks on Sui in May and August 2006 also targeted railways. These incidents are not occasional or isolated (although they have become less frequent in recent months), and have compelled the Government to offer armed protection to the gas companies operating in the area. More seriously, as the commentator Ahmad Rashid has argued, no effort was made by the Musharraf regime to engage in dialogue with Balochi leaders. Instead, the regime resorted to military means (often from the air), with no positive outcomes. In August 2008 Musharraf blamed foreign elements for the insurgency, proving again that his Government would not accept that the Balochis might have real grievances that merited a political solution.

The Balochistan insurgency has enormous implications for Pakistan, given that Pakistan is an energy deficit nation where gas accounted for one-half of energy production in 2005/06, followed by oil (28.4%), hydropower (12.7%), coal (7.0%), nuclear power (1.0%) and liquefied petroleum gas (LPG—0.4%). Annual consumption of energy has increased by an average of about 5% in all cases, except for that of petroleum, which has grown by only one-half of that amount. Over time, Pakistan has become increasingly dependent on its gas reserves as a way of conserving national resources and reducing petroleum imports. This policy has recently involved massive US investment in gas exploration.

Despite large gas reserves, Pakistan is not self-sufficient in gas, so importing gas via the construction of various gas lines has been a national priority for the last decade. These pipelines link Pakistan and India to gas supplies in central Asia and Iran. As the analyst Shahram Akbarzadeh argues, the Pakistani Government had three objectives in this strategy: to gain access to energy resources; to increase its regional influence by offering Central Asian republics access to the sea; and to improve its position *vis-à-vis* India in negotiations on Kashmir. International agencies and foreign firms have taken a great interest in the development of these pipelines. The ADB is committed to the Turkmenistan-Afghanistan-Pakistan gas pipeline and is now negotiating to extend the plans for the line into India. The Turkmenistan option will not, however, solve Pakistan's great demand for gas. Consequently two other pipelines are under consideration: an undersea line from the gas fields of Qatar and a second, much more ambitious line from Iran's southern gas fields. The latter is almost in the final stages of negotiation, although it has become increasingly controversial as the USA has taken a tougher stand against Iran's determination to build nuclear weapons capacity, while at the same time signing a nuclear treaty with India. However, Pakistan remains strongly committed to developing its own gas fields as well as transporting its supplies through the various gas pipelines. The Pakistan Government is encouraging conversions of vehicles to compressed natural gas (CNG). Each year about 1m. vehicles convert to CNG, making Pakistan the world's third largest user of CNG after Brazil and

Argentina. The benefits of this include clean air and job creation in a new industry.

Pakistan has developed a 25-year energy security plan, which focuses on the development of coal and alternative renewable energy sources. In the past the emphasis has been on oil and gas exploration and drilling industries dominated by the private sector. Pakistan has good prospects for increasing domestic energy supply. According to the Ministry of Petroleum and Natural Resources, the chances of striking a commercially viable gas field are one in three, compared with the world average of one in 10. About 30% of Pakistan's gas is produced by Pakistan Petroleum Ltd, a state company that is due to sell up to 51% of its equity to private interests. The recent scandal surrounding the case of PSM will no doubt delay this process. Pakistan's proven crude oil reserves total 28,800m. barrels, and British, Italian, Australian, Russian and Malaysian oil companies are involved in drilling. Driven by escalating oil prices, in 2005/06 the Pakistani Government decided to place new importance on exploiting its coal supplies by expanding coal-based energy supplies to meet up to 18% of the country's energy requirements over the next 10 years (up from the current 7%). Pakistan's coal reserves are in the world's top six richest fields. German, US and Chinese firms have been encouraged to invest in the expanded coal sector, especially in the Thar desert region of Sindh. The bulk of Pakistan's cement industry has already shifted its energy requirements away from petroleum to coal. Despite this strategy, petroleum remains the key input for the transport and power sectors. Electricity for industry and household consumption is provided by WAPDA, which has been plagued by serious management issues, as already noted (see Industry above). Since 2006 there has also been an acute problem caused by load shedding.

The 2008/09 budget claimed that Pakistan was suffering a peak demand-supply gap in energy of 4,500 MW. This was compounded by a sharp increase in the petroleum import bill, from US $7,300m. in 2006/07 to $11,400m. in 2007/08. The Government sought to benefit from these higher prices; in 2008 it increased sales tax on almost all petroleum products. Higher petroleum prices also boosted profits considerably throughout 2008 in oil-related state enterprises such as the National Refinery Limited and the Pakistan State Oil Company. There were encouraging signs of a long-term solution to the energy crisis being led by the private sector. In August 2008 Hubco purchased a 75% stake in Laraib Energy and is currently constructing Pakistan's first private-sector hydropower project. The initial development was expected to supply 84 MW of power. Another, and more controversial, solution is the development of nuclear power. In July 2008 the Pakistani Prime Minister told a gathering of international investors in Washington, USA, that Pakistan needed further to develop its nuclear energy resources to tackle the country's acute energy shortage. The Prime Minister argued that Pakistan should seek a deal similar to that recently reached between the USA and India, which gave the latter the opportunity to purchase nuclear reactors. However, the involvement of Pakistani scientists in nuclear proliferation programmes remains a thorny problem.

## TRADE AND THE BALANCE OF PAYMENTS

### Trade

Given the pressures to become globally competitive, the value of a country's international trade relative to GDP is increasingly being seen as a key measure of economic development. According to this indicator, Pakistan has been performing well. Total trade as a proportion of GDP rose from 26% in 2001/02 to 35% in 2005/06. Export growth has contributed to this, averaging about 16% during 2002/03–2005/06; the growth rate fell, however, to just over 3% in 2006/07. Despite increasing diversification, textiles continue to dominate exports, bringing in about 60% of foreign exchange. Even though there has been a shift to higher valued exports of textiles, the quality and standardization of these goods remains suspect. Similarly, though manufactures dominate exports there is little diversification. In 1990/91 manufactures accounted for 57% of exports; by 2006/07 that proportion had increased to 79%. Exports of primary products and semi-manufactures have declined in importance and the former currently accounts for 11% and the latter 10% of export earnings. Imports have also continued to grow and in recent years the growth of imports has been more than double the growth rate of exports. In absolute and percentage terms imports have outstripped exports: the 32.1% growth in imports recorded in 2004/05 was double the growth in exports of 16.7%; in 2005/06 Pakistan's imports grew by 38.8%, compared with an export growth rate of 14.4%; and in 2006/07 imports grew by 6.9%, compared with an export growth rate of 3.4%. The sharp increase in imports in 2005/06 was largely driven by a 64.5% increase in petroleum shipments, followed by a 36% increase in raw materials and a 36% increase in foods. In 2006/07 imports of petroleum products increased by 10%, machinery by 8.8% and textiles and related products by 21.3%. Most of Pakistan's imports are needed for basic economic growth. Food and consumer durable imports have grown rapidly but from a very small base that hardly changes the role of energy and machinery imports into Pakistan. The net result was that Pakistan's classic trade gap, which dates from the earliest years of independence, continued to be a defining and growing feature of the economy. In 2004/05 this deficit was sufficiently powerful to compel Pakistan's balance of payments to move into deficit for the first time since September 2001. In 2005/06 the trade deficit continued to 'surge', reaching $12,112m. Imports exceeded exports by 75%. In 2006/07 the trade gap was $13,528m., 11.5% higher than the previous year. Despite this sharp increase in the trade deficit the Government is continuing with its liberalization policy and has taken various measures to improve the competitiveness of Pakistani products. Pakistan will have to find a niche export market, such as India was able to do in IT customized software. At the same time Pakistan may have to control the oil import bill, as it has sought to do, by shifting domestic consumption to gas and coal. Another strategy adopted by the Pakistani Government has been to negotiate bilateral trade treaties. Pakistan has signed free-trade agreements with Sri Lanka and China, early harvest programmes with Malaysia and Bangladesh, and is in the process of signing such agreements with a number of other countries. With an escalating trade deficit, Pakistan's current account was in poor shape for the third year in a row in 2006/07, reversing the positive balances of the period 2000/01–2002/03. The persistent deficit has left Pakistan extremely dependent on capital inflows from the rest of the world. This has caused a structural tendency towards the growth of debt and dependency on aid donors, in particular the IMF and the USA.

A major long-term constraint on Pakistan's balance of payments has been the lack of export diversification and import dependence on oil and energy. Pakistan's exports remain too focused on a limited range of markets and products. During the last 10 years or so, cotton textiles have continued to dominate. Although the proportion of textiles in total exports has declined somewhat, textiles still account for 60% of total exports. Over time, the USA has become an even more important export market: between 1990 and 2006 exports almost doubled, from about 14% to 27% of the total. After the USA, the next most important markets in 2005/06 were the United Kingdom (accounting for 6% of exports), Dubai (5%), Germany (5%) and Hong Kong (4%). The German and Japanese markets have been declining since the early 1990s, when the former represented 9% and the latter 8% of exports. Now Japan accounts for less than 1% of Pakistan's shipments. The most interesting trend in 2005/06 was the rising importance of Dubai as an export destination: during that year, Dubai overtook Saudi Arabia's level of purchase of Pakistani goods (only 2.3% of total Pakistani exports). All in all, seven countries account for about one-half of Pakistan's shipments.

Pakistan's imports are similarly under-diversified, and not much change has occurred since 1990. The following commodities dominate imports today: machinery and equipment, petroleum and chemicals, edible oils and tea, iron and steel, and fertilizer. The countries from which imports are sourced are also highly concentrated, with Saudi Arabia dominating, owing to the importance of petroleum.

Foreign exchange reserves declined from US $15,700m. in July 2007 to $10,700m. in July 2008, and the rupee depreciated by 18% over the same period. The root of the problem lay with import growth and the resulting increase in the current-account deficit in 2007/08. Of the $9,400m. increase in the import bill, petroleum products accounted for $4,000m., wheat $800m., edible oils $760m., raw cotton $645m. and fertilizers $440m. Export earnings grew by only $2,300m. over the same period; the value of textile exports declined by 2.3% in 2007/08. The current-account deficit increased from $7,400m. in 2006/07 to $14,000m. in 2007/08. Latest indications are that the deficit could soon exceed $20,000m. without corrective measures. Capital inflows have traditionally funded deficits, but in recent years foreign investment and privatization proceeds have contributed considerably. Portfolio investment declined from $8,400m. in 2006/07 to $4,000m. in 2007/08; the difference was covered by drawing from reserves.

Pakistan's food import bill was expected to exceed US $2,500m. in 2007/08, partly owing to the disappointing performance of domestic agriculture. It was also due to increased consumer demand after years of growth of 8% or more, and the fact that specialized imports of dairy products, vegetables, fruits had increased from diverse suppliers such as China, Turkey, the Netherlands, Germany, Australia and Denmark. The 2008/09 budget promised to increase import tariffs on a number of luxury items, including perfumes, ceramics, cigars, chocolates, domestic appliances, cellular telephones and automobiles. Edible oil imports were forecast to increase further, to $1,200m. per year. In response, the Government announced an import substitution programme and provided substantial incentives for increased domestic production.

### Foreign Direct Investment (FDI) and Remittances

In the aftermath of the terrorist attacks in the USA in September 2001, Pakistani residents withdrew large amounts of capital from Western banks and transferred it to developing countries, including Pakistan. This was combined with a surge in workers' remittances as employment opportunities in Gulf countries increased in the wake of surging revenues from oil exports. Overseas remittances reached more than 5% of GDP or US $5,490m. in 2006/07. Remittances were equal to a little less than one-third of the total value of exports of goods. The source of these savings was equally shared by the USA, the United Arab Emirates and Europe, namely one-third each.

Even more impressive than the growth in remittances has been the massive surge in FDI, which increased in 2005/06 by about 131% to reach US $3,521m., and by a further 45.5% to $5,124m. in 2006/07. Measured against GDP, foreign capital was equal to about 7% in 2006/07. This was the largest inflow of foreign investment recorded in the history of Pakistan and revealed enormous international confidence in the country despite the domestic political and social turmoil. Most of the FDI has been invested in Pakistan's telecommunication, oil and gas and financial sectors, while the manufacturing sector has received less (FDI in manufacturing tends to be spent in the automobile industries). About one-third of FDI originates from the USA. The activities of the US-Pakistan Business Council in Washington, DC, provide a good measure of the renewed interest of US companies in Pakistan. In April 2006 the idea of a Bilateral Investment Treaty was proposed as a way of cementing the relationship between the two countries. Within Pakistan, the American Business Council of Pakistan has some 61 members, most of them representing the USA's top companies. US investment in Pakistan is mainly in heavy industry, textiles, IT, financial services and healthcare. In 2002 the Council reported favourably in a survey of its members' attitudes towards doing business in Pakistan: according to the survey, the level of bureaucracy had diminished, government policies were more predictable and sympathetic to the foreign sector, and the majority of companies reported pre-tax profits and the desire to plan further investment in Pakistan. Business executives, it seems, had set aside fears of terrorism and domestic insurgency in favour of taking advantage of the increased demand for investment in Pakistan.

### Tourism

Pakistan's balance of payments has suffered from the country's limited capacity to generate earnings from service exports. The tourism industry, in particular, has failed significantly, despite the many important archaeological sites within Pakistan's boundaries—especially the sites of the Indus Valley civilization. As a result, Pakistan remains one of the most isolated countries in the world and the situation following the September 2001 terrorist attacks on the USA has not helped this. In the mid- to late 1980s the number of foreign tourist arrivals reached an annual average of 440,000. Since then, wars and domestic politics have had an immediate adverse effect on tourism: in 1990, for example, the Gulf War caused tourist arrivals in Pakistan to decline by 50%. As the law and order situation in Pakistan worsened, resulting in the murder and kidnapping of foreign journalists and businessmen, tourist arrivals hardly exceeded the level reached in the 1980s, despite the surge in international tourism before September 2001. In 1997, for example, Pakistan received 375,000 tourists, compared with India's 2.4m. and the People's Republic of China's 23m. In 2001 Pakistan hosted about 500,000 tourists, compared with more than 2.5m. in India and 33m. in China. Pakistan has a 9% share in the South Asian tourist market (where the tourist market includes Iran) in terms of number of arrivals. Pakistan's market share of South Asian tourist earnings, however, was only 1.8% (US $84m.) in 2001. In 2003 and 2004 tourists began to arrive in numbers closer to those of 2001. In 2003 tourist arrivals exceeded 500,000 for the first time since 1950 and increased further, to 648,000, in 2004, bringing in foreign exchange revenues worth $763m. Despite the revival of tourism since 2001, the trend in more recent years is difficult to estimate given the lack of government data immediately available. Although official tourism statistics remain badly out of date, the Government has declared 2007 to be the 'Visit Pakistan Year'. Not much credibility can be attached to this given the unstable domestic situation. Sources indicate that the primary origin of foreign tourists visiting Pakistan is the United Kingdom, which accounted for 31.1% in 2005, followed by 15.2% from the USA, 9.7% from Afghanistan, 7.1% from India, 3.7% from the People's Republic of China and 2.9% from Canada.

## TAXES, BUDGETS AND NATIONAL DEBT

### Debts and Deficits

Historically Pakistan has failed to mobilize the savings and tax revenue required to fund its relatively high investment levels. During the Ayub Khan era in the 1960s for example nearly one-half of total investment was funded from abroad. Pakistan has done well when aid flows have been good and donor sentiment favourable, for example, in the 1980s during the Afghan war and after the terrorist attacks in the USA in September 2001. Conversely, growth has tended to collapse when donor sentiment has turned unfavourable, such as following the end of the Afghan war and especially with the imposition of sanctions after India and Pakistan tested nuclear weapons in 1998.

During the 1990s the Pakistani economy carried a considerable fiscal deficit, which oscillated between 5% and 9% of GDP. A heavy requirement for borrowing had a dramatic effect on the real economy when interest rates were liberalized as part of the general programme of liberalization. Real interest shot upwards, raising the cost of capital and so undermining private investment. By 1998/99 more than 70% of total government revenue was required to fund the interest payments on accumulated public debt. The fiscal deficit declined to 2.4% in 2003/04 due to various factors, including prudent fiscal management that contained expenditure. This marked a distinct break with the recent past. Throughout the 1990s Pakistan had repeatedly failed to meet IMF targets for revenue collection and deficit reduction. Total expenditure remained stuck at around 26% of GDP and total revenue declined from 18.4% of GDP in 1987/88 to 16.5% in 1990/91. The tax-to-GDP ratio had failed to rise despite administrative change. These changes included most importantly the reorganization of the tax department in a manner that enabled it to collect and monitor information more effectively about particular groups of tax payers. Reforms in the customs system have also commenced, in order to collect dues more effectively, especially in Karachi, which processes about one-third of Pakistan's foreign trade. At the same time, like the rest of South Asia, Pakistan has failed to expand the tax base by introducing income taxes for wealthy farmers. Throughout the region this has been one of the most sensitive political issues and none of the parties, not even the Pakistani military, has been willing to take on the power of the landlords. The goods and services tax (GST) can only partially compensate for the loss of revenues resulting from the failure to tax those who can afford it in the countryside.

In May 2008 it was reported that the Ministry of Food, Agriculture and Livestock was conducting a survey of incomes of large and small-scale farmers and reconsidering the imposition of a tax on agricultural incomes. Given that agricultural taxation is really a provincial rather than a federal subject, there would be added difficulties in effecting such a tax reform.

As a result of the more forceful domestic reforms introduced after 1999, public debt fell from about 87.9% of GDP in 1999/2000 to 57.8% in 2005/06, of which external debt accounted for a little less than one-half. The decline in the level of external debts and liabilities was especially dramatic: as a percentage of GDP it decreased to almost 28.1% in 2005/06 from more than 46.3% in 1999/2000. However, despite these reductions the economic pressure exerted by the public debt continues because the interest payments alone take about 28.6% of Pakistan's tax income. The actual debt servicing costs are high, at about US $3,110m. in 2005/06, but still represent a major reduction from the $6,300m. figure recorded in 2001/02.

The tax to GDP ratio continued to decline, from 10.7% in 2001/02 to 10.2% in 2006/07. Efforts to mobilize tax revenue have shown distinct improvements in recent years. In 2007/08 there was a 23% rise in tax collection. This was assisted by administrative reform efforts finally having an effect; in 2007/08 an extra 51,000 tax returns were filed. The 2008/09 budget set a target of an increase in revenue collection of 25%. Pakistan still has only 2.2m. income tax payers of a total population of some 160m. The 2008/09 budget also promised to withdraw 35 income tax exemptions and to launch an amnesty scheme, whereby tax payers can declare past business, capital formation and assets acquired, pay 2% of their market value and not have further risk of investigation. Extra taxes include those to be imposed on electricity consumers, property income, and land development schemes. Other measures proposed in the 2008/09 budget to 'restore fiscal discipline' include promises to 'freeze non-development, non-salary expenditure', phase out subsidies (which are currently estimated at some Rs 400,000m.), and ban the purchase of air-conditioners, motor cars and office equipment by public- sector offices.

Despite some successes, most recently in mobilizing tax revenue, the budget deficit was forecast to rise to up to 10% of GDP in 2008/09. The extent of the deterioration is striking. As recently as November 2006, in consultation with the IMF, Pakistan was targeting a fiscal deficit of 4% and below. The Fiscal Responsibility and Debt Limitation Act (2005) required the Government to eliminate the revenue deficit by June 2008. There is a real risk of undermining the progress made in reducing the stock of public debt with this spate of new borrowing. In May 2008, owing to its concern over the growing domestic and trade deficits, Standard and Poor downgraded Pakistan's credit rating from a B+ to a B on long-term foreign currency debt.

### Foreign Aid and Foreign Capital Inflows

Pakistan benefited from US $58,000m. of foreign development assistance (in 1995 US dollar prices) over the period 1960 to 1998, including 22 adjustments loans from the IMF and World Bank. Over this period it was the third largest recipient of official development assistance in the world after India and Egypt. Between 1966 and 2007 Pakistan received $12,300m. from the ADB, including $2,000m. in 2007 alone. These huge levels of aid have, however, not translated into improved social development. A notorious example is the Social Action Programme (SAP) from the 1990s. The SAP cost $8,000m. between 1993 and 1998, 25% of which was paid for by donors. The aims of the programme were to improve health, education, family planning, rural water supply and sanitation. The SAP was a striking failure—net total primary school enrolment fell during the 1990s, infant mortality declined only slowly, and immunization coverage of under-five-year-olds achieved little more than half its targets.

Following the terrorist attacks in the USA in September 2001, foreign aid to Pakistan has also resumed. In 2000/01 foreign aid decreased to $880m., but by 2005/06 it had recovered to reach more than $3,000m. Much of this aid has been used to retire high-cost foreign debt. After deducting the costs of servicing the foreign debt from gross foreign aid receipts, the net transfers of foreign aid to Pakistan have been a fraction of the intended amount. In the early 1990s the net transfer of aid as a percentage of gross aid disbursed to Pakistan was more than 30%; it then began to decline and since 2000/01 has fluctuated. Provisional estimates for 2005/06 suggest a downturn, with net transfers equating to only 17% of gross transfers. External aid to Pakistan originates largely from the countries that were part of the Aid Consortium to Pakistan and which now participate in the Pakistan Development Forum, which in 2004/05 provided just over three-quarters of all foreign aid to Pakistan; in 2005/06 its share fell to 41%, largely because it was dwarfed by special aid for earthquake relief (54% of total aid).

Pakistan has received a succession of financial 'packages' since 2000: a stand-by IMF credit agreement worth US $596m. was granted in November 2000; then in early December 2001 a three-year financial package valued at $1,322m. was approved by the IMF; followed by assistance in rescheduling debts totalling $12,500m.; and finally three soft loan disbursements valued at $400m. were arranged. The USA also agreed to cancel Pakistani debts totalling some $1,000m. and to reimburse Pakistan for the additional military costs associated with the 'war on terror' in Afghanistan and Iraq. In August 2006 USAID pledged to provide Pakistan with a number of additional aid grants: $1,500m. over the following five years, plus an additional $510m. for further support to the areas destroyed by the 2005 earthquake; $22m. for governance; $41m. for health; and $13.7m. for microcredit. The result is that Pakistan has accumulated large reserves of foreign exchange, which by mid-2002 already totalled some $7,000m. Foreign-exchange reserves exceeded $10,000m. in early March 2003 for the first time in Pakistan's history, sufficient to support 11 months of imports. By the end of April 2004 reserves had increased further, to $12,500m., equivalent to one year of imports. They remained at that level in August 2006, down from a peak of almost $13,000m. in April 2006, but rose again in mid-2007 to reach a record high of more than $15,700m. (these have since declined). On the other hand, by 2003/04 the growth of Pakistan's economy was sufficiently vigorous to enable the Government to retire before schedule $1,170m. of high-interest loans from the ADB. The retirement of this debt included repayments not due for another 15 years. At the same time the Government was able to raise more international capital through the issuing of Eurobonds in February 2004. This was hailed in the Economic Survey of Pakistan as a 'successful return to the international capital markets after a gap of over half a decade'. The Government sought to find $500m. of bonds for five years and found that the issue was four times oversubscribed. These early successes compelled the Government to raise a second issue of Eurobonds in March 2006, worth a total of $800m. for two sets of bonds for 10 and 30 years. Again the issues were oversubscribed by some 250%. The Government has congratulated itself on this success, especially because the long lead time in the case of the 30-year bonds is a measure of investor confidence in Pakistan's future. In 2006/07 Pakistan successfully launched a $1,000m. bond, which was oversubscribed by seven times.

Another important dimension of the Eurobond issue was the ability of Pakistan to persuade the Standard Chartered Bank to negotiate a swap of Pakistan's bonds from high to low interest rates. This was an historic occasion for Pakistan, not because it was the first time such an event had occurred in Pakistan's history, but because it demonstrated the Government's sophistication in managing its foreign debt and developing competencies to compare global money market trends. In addition to Eurobonds, in January 2005 Pakistan raised money in the Middle Eastern markets by floating Islamic leasing bonds (*Sukuk al-Ijara*) worth US $600m. It is only the fourth country in the world to develop these Islamic bonds, which have also contributed to the declining size of Pakistan's international debts since 2000.

### THE FUTURE

The Pakistani economy appeared for a while to be continuing along its optimistic growth path despite the signs of underlying instability. The earthquake of 8 October 2005 did not adversely affect the economy, as the relief supplies poured in almost immediately. Relief work carried out by religious groups has subsequently led to the increasing popularity of fundamentalist Islamist movements. Widespread public frustration with the Musharraf regime (which came to an end in August 2008 on Musharraf's resignation) was based on the perception that, while economic growth indicators had improved, all other indicators had not—there was no serious reduction in poverty, no major investment in educationand no major infrastructure development in remote regions. The emerging consensus is that the growth of Pakistan has benefited only a few and has done so within a system of expanding corruption. The helplessness of people in the face of the 2005 earthquake is a symbol of the deeper problems that, amongst other things, compel poor parents to send their children to one of the 10,000 *madrassas* to receive not only some kind of basic education but also food. The same *madrassas*, however, are seen as educating a new generation of young people with militant views about the direction of Pakistan's future.

More recently growth has slowed sharply, and domestic budget and current-account deficits have increased rapidly, leading to fears that Pakistan has again plunged into a debt crisis. Opinions differ about the longer term impact of the current slowdown in economic growth. The 2008/09 federal budget revealed an essentially optimistic view of Pakistan's economy in the near future. It projected steady, if slower, annual growth of 5.5%, inflation to remain moderate at 12%, investment to remain at 25%, improvements in the fiscal deficit to 4.7% of GDP, in the current-account deficit to 6% of GDP, and foreign exchange reserves to rise to US $12,000m. The Economist Intelligence Unit was, however, more pessimistic. It forecast that real GDP would grow by only 3.6% in 2008/09, recovering to 5.0%–5.5% over the next four years. It also projected that current-account balance would remain high, at 9%–10% of GDP and that the rate of inflation would fall below 6% only by 2012. Such predictions of sustained high levels of debt accumulation see Pakistan returning to its traditional debt-led-growth model and one inevitably featuring periodic crises.

Whether Pakistan should be classified as a flawed or failed state has been widely debated in the international arena, with more recent assessments tending towards the latter. Despite his weaknesses, however, President Musharraf presided over the emergence of a financially more competent Government, the first such administration following many decades of misrule. Moreover, as Prof. Stephen Cohen notes, he was one of the few Pakistani leaders who explicitly associated himself with Mohammed Ali Jinnah's vision of a modern secular Pakistan. This vision, matched with Musharraf's willingness to remind Pakistanis that their country required economic development rather than cross-border conflict, was worthy of international support. However, Professor Cohen's view that Pakistan is not likely to become a failed state is not widely shared. According to a ranking of 146 countries by the US Foreign Policy Journal and the US Fund for Peace think-tank, Pakistan's vulnerabilities shifted it from 34th position in 2005 to ninth position in 2006. Pakistan was, in other words, the ninth most unstable country out of the 146 that were examined, and was ranked even lower than Afghanistan, which was 10th. The 2000 National Intelligence Council (NIC) report *Global Trends 2015* appeared to be equally concerned about the emerging situation in Pakistan. Despite economic growth, the NIC report concluded that 'Pakistan … will not recover easily from decades of political and economic mismanagement, divisive politics, lawlessness, corruption and ethnic friction'. It predicted that a likely future scenario was one in which central government control would shrink to cover only Punjab and the city of Karachi. What the NIC report failed to address, however, was how the prospects of economic growth could make a difference, provided serious efforts were made to distribute the gains to the disaffected regions and to those who continue to live in poverty.

Prospects for economic collaboration with India also exist, but it will require enormous political will to achieve mutually beneficial bilateral collaboration in promoting South Asian textiles. These more optimistic scenarios are not unrealistic: the unexpected visit of L. K. Advani to Pakistan in May–June 2005 was a reminder of what could be done if a leader was determined to make a difference. As one of the architects of *Hindutva* or Hindu fundamentalist politics in India during the last 20 years, Advani's visit demonstrated that dramatic change was possible.

# Statistical Survey

Sources (unless otherwise stated): Federal Bureau of Statistics, 5-SLIC Building, F-6/4, Blue Area, Islamabad; fax (51) 9203233; e-mail statpak@isb.paknet.com.pk; internet www.statpak.gov.pk/depts/index.html; State Bank of Pakistan, Karachi; internet www.sbp.org.pk.

## Area and Population

**AREA, POPULATION AND DENSITY***

| | |
|---|---|
| Area (sq km) | 796,095† |
| Population (census results) | |
| 1 March 1981 | 84,253,644 |
| 2 March 1998 | |
| Males | 68,873,686 |
| Females | 63,478,593 |
| Total | 132,352,279 |
| Population (official estimates at 1 January) | |
| 2005 | 151,550,000 |
| 2006 | 155,360,000 |
| 2007 | 158,700,000 |
| Density (per sq km) at 1 January 2007 | 199.3 |

* Excluding data for the disputed territory of Jammu and Kashmir. The Pakistani-held parts of this region are known as Azad ('Free') Kashmir, with an area of 11,639 sq km (4,494 sq miles) and a population of 1,980,000 in 1981, and Northern Areas (including Gilgit and Baltistan), with an area of 72,520 sq km (28,000 sq miles) and a population of 562,000 in 1981. Also excluded are Junagardh and Manavadar. The population figures exclude refugees from Afghanistan (estimated to number 900,000 in late 2007).

† 307,374 sq miles.

**ADMINISTRATIVE DIVISIONS**
(population at 1998 census)

| | Area (sq km) | Population | Density (per sq km) |
|---|---|---|---|
| *Provinces:* | | | |
| Balochistan | 347,188 | 6,565,885 | 18.9 |
| North-West Frontier Province | 74,522 | 17,743,645 | 238.1 |
| Punjab | 205,345 | 73,621,290 | 358.5 |
| Sindh | 140,913 | 30,439,893 | 216.0 |
| *Federally Administered Tribal Areas* | 27,221 | 3,176,331 | 116.7 |
| *Federal Capital Territory:* | | | |
| Islamabad | 906 | 805,235 | 888.8 |
| **Total** | 796,095 | 132,352,279 | 166.3 |

### PRINCIPAL TOWNS
(population at 1998 census)

| | | | |
|---|---|---|---|
| Karachi | 9,339,023 | Bahawalpur | 408,395 |
| Lahore | 5,143,495 | Sukkur | 335,551 |
| Faisalabad (Lyallpur) | 2,008,861 | Jhang Maghiana (Jhang Sadar) | 293,366 |
| Rawalpindi | 1,409,768 | Shekhupura | 280,263 |
| Multan | 1,197,384 | Larkana | 270,283 |
| Hyderabad | 1,166,894 | Gujrat | 251,792 |
| Gujranwala | 1,132,509 | Mardan | 245,926 |
| Peshawar | 982,816 | Kasur | 245,321 |
| Quetta | 565,137 | Rahimyar Khan | 233,537 |
| Islamabad (capital) | 529,180 | Sahiwal | 208,778 |
| Sargodha | 458,440 | Okara | 201,815 |
| Sialkot | 421,502 | | |

**Mid-2007** ('000, incl. suburbs, UN estimates): Karachi 12,130; Lahore 6,577; Faisalabad (Lyallpur) 2,617; Rawalpindi 1,858; Multan 1,522; Gujranwala 1,513; Hyderabad 1,459; Peshawar 1,303; Islamabad 780; Quetta 768 (Source: UN, *World Urbanization Prospects: The 2007 Revision*).

### BIRTHS AND DEATHS
(annual averages, UN estimates)

| | 1990–95 | 1995–2000 | 2000–05 |
|---|---|---|---|
| Birth rate (per 1,000) | 38.7 | 33.3 | 27.5 |
| Death rate (per 1,000) | 9.8 | 8.8 | 7.7 |

Source: UN, *World Population Prospects: The 2006 Revision*.

**2006** (preliminary): Crude birth rate 26.1 per 1,000; crude death rate 7.1 per 1,000 (Source: Ministry of Finance, *Economic Survey, 2006/07*).

**Expectation of life** (years at birth, WHO estimates): 62.7 (males 61.9; females 63.5) in 2006 (Source: WHO, *World Health Statistics*).

### ECONOMICALLY ACTIVE POPULATION
('000 persons aged 10 years and over, excl. armed forces, at 30 June)

| | 2004 | 2005 | 2006 |
|---|---|---|---|
| Agriculture, hunting, forestry and fishing | 18,084 | 18,431 | 20,364 |
| Mining and quarrying | 28 | 29 | 43 |
| Manufacturing | 5,770 | 5,881 | 6,499 |
| Electricity, gas and water | 282 | 287 | 308 |
| Construction | 2,449 | 2,496 | 2,880 |
| Wholesale and retail trade, and restaurants and hotels | 6,216 | 6,336 | 6,886 |
| Transport, storage and communication | 2,409 | 2,455 | 2,697 |
| Financing, insurance, real estate and business services | 444 | 453 | 518 |
| Community, social and personal services | 6,306 | 6,427 | 6,739 |
| Activities not adequately defined | 21 | 21 | 18 |
| **Total employed** | 42,009 | 42,816 | 46,952 |
| Unemployed | 3,499 | 3,566 | 3,103 |
| **Total labour force** | 45,508 | 46,382 | 50,055 |
| Males | 37,364 | 38,081 | 39,974 |
| Females | 8,144 | 8,301 | 10,081 |

Source: ILO.

## Health and Welfare

### KEY INDICATORS

| | |
|---|---|
| Total fertility rate (children per woman, 2006) | 3.6 |
| Under-5 mortality rate (per 1,000 live births, 2006) | 97 |
| HIV/AIDS (% of persons aged 15–49, 2005) | 0.1 |
| Physicians (per 1,000 head, 2005) | 0.80 |
| Hospital beds (per 1,000 head, 2005) | 0.12 |
| Health expenditure (2005): US $ per head (PPP) | 49 |
| Health expenditure (2005): % of GDP | 2.1 |
| Health expenditure (2005): public (% of total) | 17.5 |
| Access to water (% of persons, 2004) | 91 |
| Access to sanitation (% of persons, 2004) | 59 |
| Human Development Index (2005): ranking | 136 |
| Human Development Index (2005): value | 0.551 |

For sources and definitions, see explanatory note on p. vi.

## Agriculture

### PRINCIPAL CROPS
('000 metric tons)

| | 2004 | 2005 | 2006 |
|---|---|---|---|
| Wheat | 19,500 | 21,612 | 21,277 |
| Rice (paddy) | 7,537 | 8,321 | 8,137 |
| Barley | 98 | 92 | 88 |
| Maize | 2,797 | 3,110 | 2,971 |
| Millet | 193 | 221 | 212 |
| Sorghum | 186 | 153 | 155 |
| Potatoes | 1,938 | 2,025 | 1,568 |
| Sugar cane | 53,419 | 47,244 | 44,666 |
| Sugar beet | 250 | 121 | 93 |
| Dry beans | 148 | 130 | 154 |
| Chick-peas | 611 | 868 | 480 |
| Groundnuts (in shell) | 76 | 69 | 59 |
| Sunflower seed | 359 | 328 | 348 |
| Rapeseed | 401 | 347 | 350 |
| Cottonseed | 4,853 | 4,123 | 4,065 |
| Tomatoes | 413 | 432 | 468 |
| Cauliflower and broccoli | 205 | 206 | 209 |
| Pumpkins, squash and gourds | 244 | 247 | 254 |
| Dry onions | 1,449 | 1,765 | 2,056 |
| Carrots and turnips | 232 | 242 | 244 |
| Okra | 107 | 109 | 112 |
| Watermelons | 386 | 353 | 393 |
| Cantaloupes and other melons | 258 | 236 | 263 |
| Bananas | 148 | 164 | 155 |
| Oranges | 1,232 | 1,361 | 1,721 |
| Tangerines, mandarins, clementines and satsumas | 458 | 505 | 639 |
| Lemons and limes | 78 | 78 | 98 |
| Apples | 352 | 351 | 350 |
| Apricots | 215 | 197 | 190 |
| Peaches and nectarines | 70 | 70 | 72 |
| Plums and sloes | 61 | 60 | 61 |
| Guavas, mangoes and mangosteens | 1,566 | 1,606 | 2,243 |
| Dates | 622 | 497 | 507 |
| Pimento and allspice | 90 | 123 | 62 |
| Cotton (lint) | 2,427 | 2,214 | 2,187 |
| Tobacco (leaves) | 86 | 101 | 113 |

**Aggregate production** ('000 metric tons, may include official, semi-official or estimated data): Total cereals 30,311 in 2004, 33,508 in 2005, 32,839 in 2006; Total roots and tubers 2,403 in 2004, 2,493 in 2005, 2,048 in 2006; Total vegetables (incl. melons) 4,751 in 2004, 5,032 in 2005, 5,449 in 2006; Total fruits (excl. melons) 5,161 in 2004, 5,236 in 2005, 6,379 in 2006.

Source: FAO.

**LIVESTOCK**
('000 head, year ending September)

| | 2004 | 2005 | 2006 |
|---|---|---|---|
| Cattle | 23,800 | 24,200 | 25,500 |
| Buffaloes | 25,500 | 26,300 | 28,400 |
| Sheep | 24,700 | 24,900 | 25,400 |
| Goats | 54,700 | 56,700 | 61,900 |
| Horses | 315 | 313 | 339 |
| Asses, mules or hinnies | 4,353 | 4,450 | 4,580 |
| Camels | 743 | 736 | 738 |
| Chickens* | n.a. | n.a. | 162,000 |
| Ducks* | 3,500 | n.a. | 3,500 |

* FAO estimates.

Source: FAO.

**LIVESTOCK PRODUCTS**
('000 metric tons)

| | 2004 | 2005 | 2006 |
|---|---|---|---|
| Cattle meat | 455 | 465 | 486 |
| Buffalo meat | 524 | 540 | 571 |
| Sheep meat | 161 | 162 | 172 |
| Goat meat | 357 | 370 | 392 |
| Chicken meat | 378 | 384 | 463 |
| Cows' milk | 8,840 | 9,082 | 9,404 |
| Buffaloes' milk | 19,240 | 19,884 | 21,136 |
| Sheep's milk | 32 | 31 | 31 |
| Goats' milk | 675 | 675 | 676 |
| Ghee* | 560.8 | n.a. | n.a. |
| Hen eggs | 381.0† | 400.0† | 425.7* |
| Other poultry eggs* | 7.2 | 7.2 | 7.2 |
| Wool: greasy | 40.0 | 40.7 | 41.0 |

* FAO estimate(s).
† Unofficial figure.

Source: FAO.

# Forestry

**ROUNDWOOD REMOVALS**
('000 cubic metres, excl. bark, FAO estimates)

| | 2004 | 2005 | 2006 |
|---|---|---|---|
| Sawlogs, veneer logs and logs for sleepers | 1,900 | 1,950 | 1,961 |
| Other industrial wood | 780 | 820 | 859 |
| Fuel wood | 26,000 | 26,500 | 26,124 |
| **Total** | 28,680 | 29,270 | 28,944 |

Source: FAO.

**SAWNWOOD PRODUCTION**
('000 cubic metres, incl. railway sleepers)

| | 2004 | 2005 | 2006 |
|---|---|---|---|
| Coniferous (softwood) | 420 | 432 | 432 |
| Broadleaved (hardwood) | 840 | 856 | 881 |
| **Total** | 1,260 | 1,288 | 1,313 |

Source: FAO.

# Fishing

('000 metric tons, live weight)

| | 2004 | 2005 | 2006 |
|---|---|---|---|
| Capture | 479.8 | 434.5 | 489.4 |
| Freshwater fishes | 93.7 | 94.6 | 140.0 |
| Sea catfishes | 30.4 | 26.3 | 28.7 |
| Croakers and drums | 16.9 | 15.9 | 14.7 |
| Largehead hairtail | 25.6 | 23.2 | 23.5 |
| Indian oil sardine | 34.3 | 31.5 | 31.0 |
| Other clupeoids | 19.5 | 16.4 | 16.9 |
| Jacks and crevalles | 6.0 | 3.3 | 4.9 |
| Requiem sharks | 18.9 | 12.3 | 10.7 |
| Skates, rays and mantas | 11.1 | 9.9 | 8.9 |
| Aquaculture | 76.7* | 80.6 | 121.8 |
| **Total catch** | 556.4* | 515.1 | 611.2 |

* FAO estimate.

Source: FAO.

# Mining

('000 metric tons, unless otherwise indicated)

| | 2004/05 | 2005/06 | 2006/07 |
|---|---|---|---|
| Barite (metric tons) | 42,087 | 49,221 | n.a. |
| Chromite (metric tons) | 46,359 | 64,552 | 104,141 |
| Limestone | 14,857 | 18,390 | 24,245 |
| Gypsum | 552 | 601 | 624 |
| Fireclay (metric tons) | 253,501 | 332,528 | n.a. |
| Rock salt | 1,648 | 1,859 | 1,873 |
| Coal | 3,367 | 3,834 | 3,571 |
| Crude petroleum ('000 barrels)* | 24,119 | 23,935 | 24,612 |
| Natural gas (million cu ft)* | 1,344,953 | 1,400,030 | 1,400,000 |

* Estimated production.

# Industry

**SELECTED PRODUCTS**
('000 metric tons, unless otherwise indicated, year ending 30 June)

| | 2004/05 | 2005/06 | 2006/07 |
|---|---|---|---|
| Cotton cloth (million sq m) | 924.7 | 903.8 | 977.8 |
| Cotton yarn | 2,280.6 | 2,546.5 | 2,845.2 |
| Refined sugar | 3,115.8 | 2,959.8 | 3,526.0 |
| Vegetable ghee | 1,048.3 | 1,151.7 | 1,176.6 |
| Cement | 16,353 | 18,564 | 22,739 |
| Urea | 4,606.4 | 4,806.4 | 4,732.5 |
| Superphosphate | 163.1 | 160.8 | 148.9 |
| Sulphuric acid | 91.3 | 94.4 | 96.6 |
| Soda ash | 297.3 | 318.7 | 330.6 |
| Caustic soda | 206.7 | 219.3 | 242.2 |
| Chlorine gas | 19.1 | 18.3 | 17.2 |
| Cigarettes ('000 million) | 61.1 | 64.1 | 66.0 |
| Ammonium nitrate | 329.9 | 327.9 | 330.8 |
| Nitrophosphate | 338.9 | 356.6 | 325.8 |
| Pig-iron | 1,137.2 | 768.0 | 1,008.8 |
| Paper | 163.7 | 167.8 | 161.7 |
| Paperboard | 236.5 | 286.1 | 280.4 |
| Tractors ('000) | 43.7 | 49.4 | 54.6 |
| Bicycles ('000) | 587.9 | 589.6 | 486.4 |
| Motor tyres and tubes ('000) | 11,614 | 13,106 | 17,304 |
| Bicycle tyres and tubes ('000) | 14,512 | 15,491 | 15,602 |
| Electric energy (million kWh) | 86,321 | 94,030 | 97,753 |

# Finance

## CURRENCY AND EXCHANGE RATES

**Monetary Units**
100 paisa = 1 Pakistani rupee.

**Sterling, Dollar and Euro Equivalents** (30 May 2008)
£1 sterling = 132.41 rupees;
US $1 = 67.10 rupees;
€1 = 104.05 rupees;
1,000 Pakistani rupees = £7.55 = $14.90 = €9.61.

**Average Exchange Rate** (Pakistani rupees per US $)
2005 59.515
2006 60.271
2007 60.739

## CENTRAL GOVERNMENT BUDGET
(million rupees, year ending 30 June)

| Revenue | 2005/06 | 2006/07* | 2007/08† |
|---|---|---|---|
| Tax revenue | 715,712 | 839,598 | 1,030,547 |
| Income and corporate taxes‡ | 215,500 | 305,000 | 388,000 |
| Other direct taxes | 9,500 | 15,619 | 20,250 |
| Excise duty | 56,500 | 72,000 | 91,000 |
| Sales tax‡ | 286,500 | 311,000 | 375,000 |
| Taxes on international trade | 136,000 | 134,000 | 154,000 |
| Other taxes revenue | 11,712 | 1,979 | 2,297 |
| Non-tax revenue (incl. surcharges) | 306,992 | 374,445 | 337,592 |
| **Total** | 1,022,704 | 1,214,043 | 1,368,139 |

| Expenditure | 2005/06 | 2006/07* | 2007/08† |
|---|---|---|---|
| Current expenditure | 918,789 | 1,033,532 | 1,056,349 |
| General public service | 563,673 | 634,761 | 881,657 |
| Defence‡ | 241,062 | 252,631 | 275,000 |
| Economic affairs | 67,572 | 91,222 | 78,941 |
| Development expenditure | 153,434 | 200,616 | 297,311 |
| Capital expenditure | 124,140 | 130,334 | 155,373 |
| **Total** | 1,196,364 | 1,364,482 | 1,509,032 |

* Revised estimates.
† Budget estimates.
‡ Exclusively federal.

## INTERNATIONAL RESERVES
(US $ million, last Thursday of the year)

| | 2005 | 2006 | 2007 |
|---|---|---|---|
| Gold* | 915 | 1,273 | 1,645 |
| IMF special drawing rights | 216 | 216 | 215 |
| Foreign exchange | 9,817 | 11,328 | 13,829 |
| **Total** | 10,948 | 12,817 | 15,689 |

* Revalued annually, in June, on the basis of London market prices.

Source: IMF, *International Financial Statistics*.

## MONEY SUPPLY
(million rupees, last Thursday of the year)

| | 2005 | 2006 | 2007 |
|---|---|---|---|
| Currency outside banks | 732,011 | 874,597 | 1,008,186 |
| Demand deposits at scheduled banks | 1,571,500 | 1,821,017 | 2,216,451 |
| **Total money*** | 2,306,838 | 2,700,412 | 3,229,783 |

* Including also private-sector deposits at the State Bank.

Source: IMF, *International Financial Statistics*.

## COST OF LIVING
(Consumer Price Index; base: 2000/01 = 100; year ending 30 June)

| | 2004/05 | 2005/06 | 2006/07 |
|---|---|---|---|
| Food, beverages and tobacco | 125.7 | 134.4 | 148.2 |
| Clothing and footwear | 113.0 | 117.6 | 123.7 |
| Rent | 120.4 | 132.4 | 141.2 |
| Fuel and lighting | 128.5 | 147.2 | 156.7 |
| **All items** (incl. others) | 122.0 | 131.6 | 141.9 |

Source: Ministry of Finance, *Economic Survey 2007/08*.

## NATIONAL ACCOUNTS
(million rupees at current prices, year ending 30 June)

**Expenditure on the Gross Domestic Product**

| | 2005/06 | 2006/07 | 2007/08* |
|---|---|---|---|
| Government final consumption expenditure | 824,300 | 796,204 | 926,101 |
| Private final consumption expenditure | 5,720,225 | 6,549,875 | 8,346,206 |
| Increase in stocks | 121,971 | 139,571 | 167,651 |
| Gross fixed capital formation | 1,565,838 | 1,857,628 | 2,090,540 |
| **Total domestic expenditure** | 8,232,334 | 9,343,278 | 11,530,498 |
| Exports of goods and services | 1,161,257 | 1,231,025 | 1,267,078 |
| *Less* Imports of goods and services | 1,770,386 | 1,851,088 | 2,319,382 |
| **Gross domestic product (GDP) in market prices** | 7,623,205 | 8,723,215 | 10,478,194 |
| **GDP at constant 1999/2000 prices** | 5183,371 | 5,495,127 | 5,822,128 |

* Provisional figures.

**Gross Domestic Product by Economic Activity**

| | 2005/06 | 2006/07 | 2007/08* |
|---|---|---|---|
| Agriculture, forestry and fishing | 1,457,222 | 1,698,000 | 2,016,950 |
| Mining and quarrying | 219,682 | 251,725 | 306,696 |
| Manufacturing | 1,370,793 | 1,566,123 | 1,892,778 |
| Electricity and gas distribution | 153,338 | 165,154 | 158,617 |
| Construction | 179,885 | 213,655 | 277,141 |
| Wholesale and retail trade | 1,262,001 | 1,433,337 | 1,760,491 |
| Transport, storage and communications | 908,409 | 1,029,582 | 1,174,090 |
| Banking and insurance | 364,320 | 451,573 | 582,620 |
| Ownership of dwellings | 184,812 | 206,166 | 235,838 |
| Public administration and defence | 404,628 | 475,871 | 577,554 |
| Community, social and personal services | 653,437 | 766,208 | 923,324 |
| **GDP at factor cost** | 7,158,527 | 8,257,394 | 9,906,099 |
| Indirect taxes | 569,077 | 617,104 | 718,667 |
| *Less* Subsidies | 104,399 | 151,283 | 146,572 |
| **GDP in market prices** | 7,623,205 | 8,723,215 | 10,478,194 |

* Provisional figures.

Source: Ministry of Finance, *Economic Survey 2007/08*.

**BALANCE OF PAYMENTS**
(US $ million)

| | 2005 | 2006 | 2007 |
|---|---|---|---|
| Exports of goods f.o.b. | 15,432 | 17,049 | 18,121 |
| Imports of goods f.o.b. | −21,773 | −26,696 | −28,761 |
| **Trade balance** | −6,341 | −9,647 | −10,640 |
| Exports of services | 3,678 | 3,506 | 3,758 |
| Imports of services | −7,508 | −8,418 | −8,764 |
| **Balance on goods and services** | −10,171 | −14,559 | −15,646 |
| Other income received | 658 | 864 | 1,355 |
| Other income paid | −3,172 | −3,995 | −5,048 |
| **Balance on goods, services and income** | −12,685 | −17,691 | −19,339 |
| Current transfers received | 9,169 | 11,030 | 11,215 |
| Current transfers paid | −90 | −89 | −129 |
| **Current balance** | −3,606 | −6,750 | −8,253 |
| Capital account (net) | 202 | 345 | 175 |
| Direct investment abroad | −44 | −109 | −98 |
| Direct investment from abroad | 2,201 | 4,273 | 5,331 |
| Portfolio investment assets | 19 | −4 | 5 |
| Portfolio investment liabilities | 906 | 1,973 | 2,083 |
| Other investment assets | 126 | −242 | −107 |
| Other investment liabilities | 871 | 1,545 | 2,889 |
| Net errors and omissions | −200 | 520 | 102 |
| **Overall balance** | 475 | 1,551 | 2,127 |

Source: IMF, *International Financial Statistics*.

# External Trade

Note: Data exclude trade in military goods.

**PRINCIPAL COMMODITIES**
(million rupees, year ending 30 June)

| Imports c.i.f. (excl. re-imports) | 2004/05 | 2005/06 | 2006/07 |
|---|---|---|---|
| Food and live animals | 64,540.2 | 103,890.2 | 82,331.1 |
| Mineral fuels, lubricants, etc. | 255,009.8 | 414,113.7 | 469,508.4 |
| Animal and vegetable oils, fats and waxes | 51,009.7 | 50,332.0 | 63,857.3 |
| Chemicals and related products | 213,948.9 | 250,349.8 | 266,954.2 |
| Basic manufactures | 134,011.6 | 200,619.4 | 206,482.0 |
| Machinery and transport equipment | 351,553.7 | 498,388.5 | 546,735.5 |
| **Total** (incl. others) | 1,223,080.0 | 1,711,158.4 | 1,851,805.9 |

| Exports f.o.b. (excl. re-exports) | 2004/05 | 2005/06 | 2006/07 |
|---|---|---|---|
| Rice | 55,392.3 | 69,325.1 | 68,285.9 |
| Raw cotton | 6,549.3 | 4,079.7 | 3,047.8 |
| Leather, leather manufactures and dressed furskins | 18,013.0 | 17,504.5 | 19,474.5 |
| Carpets and rugs | 16,499.1 | 15,398.3 | 13,923.9 |
| Cotton fabrics, cotton yarn and thread | 173,384.4 | 209,008.2 | 209,532.9 |
| Petroleum and related products | 28,281.0 | 49,438.4 | n.a. |
| Garments and hosiery | 182,943.7 | 226,837.0 | 239,882.5 |
| Synthetic textiles | 17,812.2 | 11,990.6 | n.a. |
| Sports goods | 18,236.1 | 20,560.1 | 17,482.8 |
| **Total** (incl. others) | 854,087.7 | 984,840.6 | 1,029,311.7 |

**PRINCIPAL TRADING PARTNERS**
(million rupees, year ending 30 June)

| Imports c.i.f. (excl. re-imports) | 2004/05 | 2005/06 | 2006/07 |
|---|---|---|---|
| Australia | 33,269.7 | 14,611.0 | 17,983.6 |
| Belgium | 10,511.4 | 21,136.9 | 13,617.2 |
| Canada | 11,671.8 | 19,242.1 | 29,982.5 |
| China, People's Republic | 109,390.7 | 161,990.7 | 214,275.2 |
| France | 12,324.3 | 20,380.4 | 25,399.0 |
| Germany | 53,266.5 | 70,423.9 | 73,073.0 |
| Hong Kong | 5,618.9 | 9,799.6 | 11,714.1 |
| India | 32,487.7 | 48,071.6 | 74,938.0 |
| Indonesia | 34,131.1 | 45,379.1 | 51,332.8 |
| Iran | 14,374.7 | 26,942.1 | 24,595.7 |
| Italy | 21,597.6 | 31,353.2 | 32,976.6 |
| Japan | 86,045.9 | 110,175.4 | 105,483.8 |
| Korea, Republic | 32,935.2 | 36,914.6 | 40,699.3 |
| Kuwait | 55,810.4 | 101,934.9 | 104,849.5 |
| Malaysia | 40,265.7 | 42,405.4 | 57,319.4 |
| Netherlands | 8,717.6 | 14,939.5 | 14,894.1 |
| Saudi Arabia | 147,166.5 | 179,258.4 | 211,751.0 |
| Singapore | 22,172.0 | 27,735.4 | 29,224.8 |
| Switzerland | 25,123.4 | 28,230.6 | 19,487.8 |
| Thailand | 24,578.7 | 38,924.1 | 36,201.3 |
| Turkey | 6,108.5 | 11,302.2 | 9,283.4 |
| United Arab Emirates | 101,053.7 | 203,923.2 | 167,906.6 |
| United Kingdom | 31,601.7 | 48,194.1 | 42,382.5 |
| USA | 92,813.5 | 99,219.8 | 139,453.4 |
| **Total** (incl. others) | 1,223,079.1 | 1,711,158.4 | 1,851,805.9 |

| Exports f.o.b. (excl. re-exports) | 2004/05 | 2005/06 | 2006/07 |
|---|---|---|---|
| Afghanistan | 44,393.3 | 63,671.4 | 45,685.8 |
| Australia | 6,600.2 | 7,362.1 | 7,462.4 |
| Bangladesh | 12,226.3 | 16,074.5 | 15,884.3 |
| Belgium | 18,566.8 | 19,265.8 | 21,833.3 |
| Canada | 11,511.1 | 12,510.4 | 12,221.8 |
| China, People's Republic | 21,026.9 | 27,773.1 | 34,927.3 |
| France | 21,809.3 | 20,155.4 | 20,987.7 |
| Germany | 40,862.2 | 41,141.6 | 42,526.5 |
| Hong Kong | 33,120.6 | 40,659.8 | 39,644.8 |
| Italy | 34,920.3 | 35,045.2 | 38,793.9 |
| Japan | 9,757.9 | 7,668.0 | 7,523.8 |
| Korea, Republic | 10,992.8 | 11,446.9 | 10,555.6 |
| Netherlands | 20,477.2 | 23,889.4 | 26,799.1 |
| Saudi Arabia | 20,937.2 | 19,709.7 | 17,350.4 |
| Spain | 20,232.4 | 24,875.6 | 28,230.8 |
| Turkey | 15,339.6 | 18,227.5 | 23,645.5 |
| United Arab Emirates | 65,054.0 | 78,586.5 | 83,990.1 |
| United Kingdom | 52,992.9 | 53,529.8 | 57,609.8 |
| USA | 204,425.5 | 250,989.8 | 253,584.2 |
| **Total** (incl. others) | 854,087.7 | 984,840.6 | 1,029,311.7 |

# Transport

**RAILWAYS**
(year ending 30 June)

| | 2004/05 | 2005/06 | 2006/07 |
|---|---|---|---|
| Passenger journeys ('000) | 78,180 | 81,430 | 83,890 |
| Passenger-km (million) | 24,238 | 25,621 | 26,446 |
| Freight ('000 metric tons) | 6,410 | 6,030 | 6,420 |
| Net freight ton-km (million) | 5,532 | 5,916 | 5,453 |

Source: Ministry of Finance, *Economic Survey, 2007/08*.

**ROAD TRAFFIC**
('000 vehicles in use, year ending 30 June)

| | 2004/05 | 2005/06 | 2006/07 |
|---|---|---|---|
| Motorcycles and scooters | 3,063.0 | 3,791.0 | 4,463.8 |
| Passenger cars | 1,264.7 | 1,999.2 | 1,682.2 |
| Jeeps | 51.8 | 65.7 | 85.4 |
| Station wagons | 140.5 | 140.8 | 169.1 |
| Road tractors | 778.1 | 822.3 | 877.8 |
| Buses | 102.4 | 103.6 | 108.4 |
| Taxicabs | 120.3 | 122.1 | 119.1 |
| Rickshaws | 81.3 | 77.8 | 79.0 |
| Delivery vans and pick-ups | 209.5 | 236.8 | 253.4 |
| Trucks and tankers | 160.4 | 160.4 | 182.0 |

Source: Ministry of Finance, *Economic Survey, 2007/08*.

**SHIPPING**

**Merchant Fleet**
(displacement at 31 December)

| | 2005 | 2006 | 2007 |
|---|---|---|---|
| Number of vessels | 53 | 53 | 53 |
| Total displacement ('000 grt) | 397.6 | 414.6 | 349.0 |

Source: Lloyd's Register-Fairplay, *World Fleet Statistics*.

**International Sea-borne Shipping**
(port of Karachi, year ending 30 June)

| | 2004/05 | 2005/06 | 2006/07 |
|---|---|---|---|
| Goods ('000 long tons): | | | |
| loaded | 6,515 | 6,697 | 7,517 |
| unloaded | 22,100 | 25,573 | 23,329 |

Source: Ministry of Finance, *Economic Survey, 2007/08*.

**CIVIL AVIATION**
(PIA only, domestic and international flights, '000, year ending 30 June)

| | 2004/05 | 2005/06 | 2006/07 |
|---|---|---|---|
| Kilometres flown | 80,699 | 87,273 | 80,302 |
| Passengers carried | 5,132 | 5,828 | 5,732 |
| Passenger-km ('000) | 13,634 | 15,260 | 15,124 |

Source: Ministry of Finance, *Economic Survey, 2007/08*.

# Tourism

**FOREIGN TOURIST ARRIVALS**
('000)

| Country of nationality | 2004 | 2005 | 2006 |
|---|---|---|---|
| Afghanistan | 117.6 | 77.6 | 84.9 |
| Canada | 15.0 | 23.0 | 30.8 |
| China, People's Republic | 17.2 | 29.6 | 36.4 |
| Germany | 18.9 | 24.7 | 27.3 |
| India | 119.7 | 59.6 | 70.2 |
| Japan | 13.4 | 14.1 | 14.4 |
| United Kingdom | 196.3 | 248.6 | 275.1 |
| USA | 87.3 | 121.6 | 126.2 |
| **Total** (incl. others) | 648.0 | 798.3 | 850.6 |

**Receipts from tourism** (US $ million, incl. passenger transport): 620 in 2003; 765 in 2004; 827 in 2005.

Source: partly World Tourism Organization.

# Communications Media

| | 2004 | 2005 | 2006 |
|---|---|---|---|
| Television receivers (number in use)* | 3,833,237 | 7,047,308 | 7,971,882 |
| Telephones ('000 main lines in use) | 4,502.2 | 5,227.8 | 5,240.0 |
| Mobile cellular telephones ('000 subscribers) | 5,022.9 | 12,771.2 | 34,506.6 |
| Internet users ('000) | 10,000 | 10,500 | 12,000 |
| Broadband subscribers ('000) | 22.3 | 44.6 | 56.6 |
| Daily newspapers: | | | |
| number | 291 | 438 | 370 |
| average circulation | 7,817,958 | 7,889,639 | 8,208,874 |
| Other newspapers and periodicals: | | | |
| number | 988 | 1,559 | 1,094 |
| average circulation | 2,166,062 | 2,196,295 | 2,438,008 |

**Radio receivers** ('000 in use): 13,500 in 1997.

**Facsimile machines** ('000 in use): 268 in 1998.

* Estimates as at 30 June; includes Azad Kashmir and Northern Areas.

Sources: partly UNESCO, *Statistical Yearbook*; International Telecommunication Union.

# Education

(2006/07, estimates, unless otherwise indicated)

| | Institutions | Teachers | Students |
|---|---|---|---|
| Primary* | 158,378 | 447,900 | 17,043, 000 |
| Middle | 42,918 | 334,600 | 5,576,000 |
| Secondary | 25,177 | 390,600 | 2,244,000 |
| of which secondary vocational institutes | 3,059† | 17,364 | 284,000 |
| Higher: | | | |
| arts and science colleges | 3,332 | 73,273 | 908,000 |
| professional | 1,371 | 23,676 | 324,988 |
| universities/degree-awarding institutes | 120 | 37,536 | 424,271 |

* Including mosque schools.

† 2005/06 figure.

Source: Ministry of Finance, *Economic Survey 2007/08*.

**Adult literacy rate** (UNESCO estimates): 54.9% (males 68.7%; females 40.2%) in 2007 (Source: UNESCO Institute for Statistics).

# Directory

## The Constitution

The Constitution was promulgated on 10 April 1973, and amended on a number of subsequent occasions (see Amendments, below). Several provisions were suspended following the imposition of martial law in 1977. The (amended) Constitution was restored on 30 December 1985. The Constitution was placed in abeyance on 15 October 1999 following the overthrow of the Government in a military coup. The Constitution, incorporating a Legal Framework Order, was revived on 15 November 2002.

### GENERAL PROVISIONS

The Preamble upholds the principles of democracy, freedom, equality, tolerance and social justice as enunciated by Islam. The rights of religious and other minorities are guaranteed.

The Islamic Republic of Pakistan consists of four provinces—Balochistan, North-West Frontier Province, Punjab and Sindh—and the tribal areas under federal administration. The provinces are autonomous units.

Fundamental rights are guaranteed and include equality of status (women have equal rights with men), freedom of thought, speech, worship and the press and freedom of assembly and association. No law providing for preventive detention shall be made except to deal with persons acting against the integrity, security or defence of Pakistan. No such law shall authorize the detention of a person for more than one month.

### PRESIDENT

The President is Head of State and acts on the advice of the Prime Minister. He is elected by an electoral college, comprising the two chambers of the Federal Legislature and the four Provincial Assemblies, to serve for a term of five years. He must be a Muslim. The President may be impeached for violating the Constitution or gross misconduct.

### FEDERAL LEGISLATURE

The Federal Legislature consists of the President, a lower and an upper house. The lower house, called the National Assembly, has 272 members elected directly for a term of five years, on the basis of universal suffrage (for adults over the age of 21 years), plus 60 female members and 10 members representing minorities. The upper house, called the Senate, has 87 members who serve for six years, with one-half retiring every three years. Each Provincial Assembly is to elect 19 Senators. The tribal areas are to return eight members and the remaining three are to be elected from the Federal Capital Territory by members of the Provincial Assemblies.

There shall be two sessions of the National Assembly and Senate each year, with not more than 120 days between the last sitting of a session and the first sitting of the next session.

The role of the Senate in an overwhelming majority of the subjects shall be merely advisory. Disagreeing with any legislation of the National Assembly, it shall have the right to send it back only once for reconsideration. In case of disagreement in other subjects, the Senate and National Assembly shall sit in a joint session to decide the matter by a simple majority.

### GOVERNMENT

The Constitution provides that bills may originate in either house, except money bills. The latter must originate in the National Assembly and cannot go to the Senate. A bill must be passed by both houses and then approved by the President, who may return the bill and suggest amendments. In this case, after the bill has been reconsidered and passed, with or without amendment, the President must give his assent to it.

### PROVINCIAL GOVERNMENT

In the matter of relations between Federation and Provinces, the Federal Legislature shall have the power to make laws, including laws bearing on extra-territorial affairs, for the whole or any part of Pakistan, while a Provincial Assembly shall be empowered to make laws for that Province or any part of it. Matters in the Federal Legislative List shall be subject to the exclusive authority of the Federal Legislature, while the Federal Legislature and a Provincial Assembly shall have power to legislate with regard to matters referred to in the Concurrent Legislative List. Any matter not referred to in either list may be subject to laws made by a Provincial Assembly alone, and not by the Federal Legislature, although the latter shall have exclusive power to legislate with regard to matters not referred to in either list for those areas in the Federation not included in any Province.

Four provisions seek to ensure the stability of the parliamentary system. First, the Prime Minister shall be elected by the National Assembly and he and the other Ministers shall be responsible to it. Secondly, any resolution calling for the removal of a Prime Minister shall have to name his successor in the same resolution, which shall be adopted by not less than two-thirds of the total number of members of the lower house. The requirement of a two-thirds' majority is to remain in force for 15 years or three electoral terms, whichever is more. Thirdly, the Prime Minister shall have the right to seek dissolution of the legislature at any time even during the pendency of a no-confidence motion. Fourthly, if a no-confidence motion is defeated, such a motion shall not come up before the house for the next six months.

All these provisions for stability shall apply *mutatis mutandis* to the Provincial Assemblies also.

A National Economic Council, to include the Prime Minister and a representative from each province, shall advise the Provincial and Federal Governments.

There shall be a Governor for each Province, appointed by the President, and a Council of Ministers to aid and advise him, with a Chief Minister appointed by the Governor. Each Province has a provincial legislature consisting of the Governor and Provincial Assembly.

The executive authorities of every Province shall be required to ensure that their actions are in compliance with the Federal laws which apply in that Province. The Federation shall be required to consider the interests of each Province in the exercise of its authority in that Province. The Federation shall further be required to afford every Province protection from external aggression and internal disturbance, and to ensure that every Province is governed in accordance with the provisions of the Constitution.

To further safeguard the rights of the smaller provinces, a Council of Common Interests has been created. Comprising the Chief Ministers of the four provinces and four Central Ministers to decide upon specified matters of common interest, the Council is responsible to the Federal Legislature. The constitutional formula gives the net proceeds of excise duty and royalty on gas to the province concerned. The profits on hydroelectric power generated in each province shall go to that province.

### OTHER PROVISIONS

Other provisions include the procedure for elections, the setting up of an Advisory Council of Islamic Ideology and an Islamic Research Institute, and the administration of tribal areas.

### AMENDMENTS

Amendments to the Constitution shall require a two-thirds' majority in the National Assembly and the Senate.

In 1975 the Constitution (Third Amendment) Bill abolished the provision that a State of Emergency may not be extended beyond six months without the approval of the National Assembly and empowered the Government to detain a person for three months instead of one month.

In July 1977, following the imposition of martial law, several provisions, including all fundamental rights provided for in the Constitution, were suspended.

An amendment of September 1978 provided for separate electoral registers to be drawn up for Muslims and non-Muslims.

In October 1979 a martial law order inserted a clause in the Constitution establishing the supremacy of military courts in trying all offences, criminal and otherwise.

On 26 May 1980 the President issued a Constitution Amendment Order, which amended Article 199, debarring High Courts from making any order relating to the validity of effect of any judgment or sentence passed by a military court or tribunal granting an injunction; from making an order or entering any proceedings in respect of matters under the jurisdiction or cognizance of a military court or tribunal, and from initiating proceedings against the Chief Martial Law Administrator or a Martial Law Administrator.

By another amendment of the Constitution, the Federal Shari'a Court was to replace the Shari'a Benches of the High Courts. The Shari'a Court, on the petition of a citizen or the Government, may decide whether any law or provision of law is contrary to the injunction of Islam as laid down in the Holy Koran and the Sunnah of the Holy Prophet.

In March 1981 the Government promulgated Provisional Constitution Order 1981, whereby provision is made for the appointment of one or more Vice-Presidents, to be appointed by the Chief Martial Law Administrator, and a Federal Advisory Council (*Majlis-i-Shura*) consisting of persons nominated by the President. All political parties not registered with the Election Commission on 13 September 1979 were to be dissolved and their properties made forfeit to the Federal Council. Any party working against the ideology, sovereignty or security of Pakistan may be dissolved by the President.

## PAKISTAN

The proclamation of July 1977, imposing martial law, and subsequent orders amending the Constitution and further martial law regulations shall not be questioned by any court on any grounds.

All Chief Justices and Judges shall take a new oath of office. New High Court benches for the interior of the provinces shall be set up and retired judges are debarred from holding office in Pakistan for two years. The powers of the High Courts shall be limited for suspending the operation of an order for the detention of any person under any law providing for preventative detention, or release of any person on bail, arrested under the same law.

The Advisory Council of Islamic Ideology, which was asked by the Government to suggest procedures for the election and further Islamization of the Constitution, recommended non-party elections, separate electorates, Islamic qualifications for candidates and a federal structure with greater devolution of power by changing the present divisions into provinces.

Under the Wafaqi Mohtasib Order 1982, the President appointed a Wafaqi Mohtasib (Federal Ombudsman) to redress injustice committed by any government agency.

In March 1985 the President, Gen. Zia ul-Haq, promulgated the Revival of the 1973 Constitution Order, which increased the power of the President by amendments such as those establishing a National Security Council, powers to dismiss the Prime Minister, the Cabinet and provincial Chief Ministers, to appoint judicial and military chiefs, and to call elections, and indemnity clauses to ensure the power of the President. The Constitution was then revived with the exception of 28 key provisions relating to treason, subversion, fundamental rights and jurisdiction of the Supreme Court. In October 1985 the Constitution (Eighth Amendment) Bill became law, incorporating most of the provisions of the Revival of the 1973 Constitution Order and indemnifying all actions of the military regime. In December the enactment of the Political Parties (Amendment) Bill allowed political parties to function under stringent conditions (these conditions were eased in 1988). In December Gen. Zia lifted martial law and restored the remainder of the Constitution.

In March 1987 the Constitution (Tenth Amendment) Bill reduced the minimum number of working days of the National Assembly from 160 days to 130 days.

In April 1997 the Constitution (Thirteenth Amendment) Bill repealed the main components of the Eighth Constitutional Amendment, thus divesting the President of the power to appoint and dismiss the Prime Minister and Cabinet, to dissolve the legislature, to order a national referendum, and to appoint provincial Governors, the Chairman of the Joint Chiefs of Staff and the three armed forces chiefs (these functions and appointments were, in future, to be carried out subject to a mandatory advice from the Prime Minister).

In October 1998 the Constitution (Fifteenth Amendment) Bill replaced the country's existing legal code with full *Shari'a*; the bill remained to be ratified by the Senate.

Following the overthrow of the Government in a military coup on 12 October 1999, the Constitution was placed in abeyance on 15 October. On the same day a Provisional Constitution Order was promulgated, according to which executive power was transferred to a National Security Council, under the leadership of a Chief Executive. A federal Cabinet, which was to aid and advise the Chief Executive in the exercise of his functions, was to be appointed by the President on the advice of the Chief Executive. The President was to act on, and in accordance with, the advice of the Chief Executive. The National Assembly, Senate and the Provincial Assemblies were suspended and the Chairman and Deputy Chairman of the Senate ceased to hold office.

In July 2000 the Chief Executive issued a decree to revive the Islamic principles of the suspended Constitution and to incorporate them in the Provisional Constitution Order.

On 20 June 2001 the Proclamation of Emergency (Amendment) Order 2001 was promulgated, according to which the Chief Executive assumed the office of President of Pakistan. The National Assembly, Senate and Provincial Assemblies were dissolved with immediate effect. The Speaker and Deputy Speaker of the National Assembly and Provincial Assemblies ceased to hold office with immediate effect. The President later announced that elections to federal and provincial legislatures would be held on 10 October 2002 (see Recent History).

On 21 August 2002 the Legal Framework Order 2002 was promulgated, which sanctioned the President's 29 amendments to the Constitution, including the restoration of Article 58 (2-B), which authorized the President to dissolve the National Assembly (the article was also amended to allow the President to appoint provincial governors in consultation with the Prime Minister), the restoration of Article 243, which gave the President power to appoint the Chairman of the Joint Chiefs of Staff Committee and the three armed forces chiefs and the power to establish the National Security Council to provide consultation to the elected government on strategic matters. Other amendments included the extension of the President's term in office and role as Chief of Army Staff for five years from the date of the election (10 October 2002). The terms of the National Assembly and Senate were to be decreased to four and five years, respectively, and the number of seats in each house to be increased to 342 and 100, respectively. Part III of the Legal Framework Order sanctioned an amendment to Article 71: a Mediation Committee would be established in instances where the Senate disagrees with legislation of the National Assembly, or vice versa. The Mediation Committee would formulate an agreed item of legislation and place it separately before each house for consideration. According to the amendments, the Prime Minister would continue to have the right to seek dissolution of the legislature at any time, but not during the pendency of a no-confidence motion. Ten Orders endorsed by Musharraf since the establishment of military rule were placed in 'Schedule Six', and therefore could not be altered, repealed or amended without the approval of the President. Constitutional protection was thereby awarded to the offices of the National Accountability Bureau and the Governor of the State Bank of Pakistan. Other provisions granted constitutional protection included the lowering of the voting age from 21 to 18 years, the Political Parties' Order, the Local Government Ordinances and the autonomy of the Election Commission. The 1973 Constitution, incorporating the Legal Framework Order, was revived on 15 November 2002.

In late December 2003 the legislature passed the Constitution (Seventeenth Amendment) Bill, comprising several amendments to the 2002 Legal Framework Order (in passing this Bill the legislature also endorsed for the first time the validity of the Legal Framework Order). The Bill allowed the President to remain as Chief of Army Staff until 31 December 2004, when he would have to relinquish his military role. The President also retained the right to dissolve the legislature (on the recommendation of the Prime Minister); the matter would then have to be referred to the Supreme Court within 15 days. The Bill endorsed the lowering of the minimum national voting age to 18 years, and accepted the revised composition of the Senate, National Assembly and provincial assemblies, and clauses relating to political parties.

In April 2004 the legislature approved the National Security Council Bill. This enabled the formation, under the protection of the Constitution, of the National Security Council, a 13-member council chaired by the President and composed of nine civilian politicians and four members of the military. The Council was to serve as a forum for consultation with the Government on matters of national security. Critics protested that the Bill institutionalized the role of the military in national government.

# The Government

### HEAD OF STATE

**President:** MOHAMMAD MIAN SOOMRO (acting).

### CABINET
(August 2008)

Following the general election held on 18 February 2008, a coalition Government was formed, comprising members of the Pakistan People's Party (PPP), the Pakistan Muslim League—Nawaz (PML—N), the Awami National Party (ANP) and the Jamiat-e-Ulema-e-Islam—Fazl (JUI—F), along with one independent member of the National Assembly from the Federally Administered Tribal Areas. In May the PML (N) withdrew its ministers from the Cabinet, and in August the party pulled out of the coalition.

**Prime Minister:** YOUSAF RAZA GILLANI.

**Minister of Defence, with additional charge of Commerce and Textile Industry:** CHAUDHRY AHMED MUKHTAR (PPP).

**Minister of the Environment:** HAMEEDULLAH JAN AFRIDI.

**Minister of Foreign Affairs, with additional charge of Petroleum and Natural Resources:** SHAH MEHMUD QURESHI (PPP).

**Minister of Housing and Works:** REHMATULLAH KAKAR (JUI—F).

**Minister of Information and Broadcasting, with additional charge of Health, Women Development and Culture:** SHERRY REHMAN (PPP).

**Minister of Kashmir Affairs and Northern Areas (KANA), with additional charge of Information Technology and Ports and Shipping:** QAMAR ZAMAN KAIRA (PPP).

**Minister of Labour, Manpower and Overseas Pakistanis and of Religious Affairs, Zakat and Ushr:** SYED KHURSHEED AHMED SHAH (PPP).

**Minister of Law and Justice, with additional charge of Parliamentary Affairs and Human Rights:** FAROOQ H. NAIK (PPP).

**Minister of Local Government and Rural Development:** Haji GHULAM AHMAD BILOUR (ANP).

**Minister of Narcotics Control, with additional charge of Food, Agriculture and Livestock:** NAZAR MUHAMMAD GONDAL (PPP).

**Minister of Population Welfare:** HUMAYUN AZIZ KURD (PPP).

**Minister of Privatization and Investment, with additional charge of Finance, Revenue, Economic Affairs and Statistics:** SYED NAVEED QAMAR (PPP).

**Minister of Social Welfare and Special Education:** Nawabzada KHAWAJA MUHAMMAD KHAN HOTI (ANP).

**Minister of States and Frontier Regions, with additional charge of Sports:** NAJMUDDIN KHAN (PPP).

**Minister of Water and Power, with additional charge of Tourism:** RAJA PERVAIZ ASHRAF (PPP).

### MINISTRIES

**Office of the President:** Aiwan-e-Sadr, Islamabad; tel. (51) 9206060; fax (51) 9208046; internet www.presidentofpakistan.gov.pk.

**Office of the Prime Minister's Secretariat:** Cabinet Secretariat, Cabinet Division, Islamabad; tel. (51) 925190512; e-mail contact@cabinet.gov.pk; internet www.cabinet.gov.pk.

**Ministry of Commerce:** Block A, Pakistan Secretariat, Islamabad; tel. (51) 9201816; fax (51) 9205241; e-mail naveed@commerce.gov.pk; internet www.commerce.gov.pk.

**Ministry of Culture, Minorities, Sports and Youth Affairs:** NFCH, 12th Floor, Green Tower, Blue Area, F-6/3, Islamabad; tel. (51) 9206127; fax (51) 9224697; internet www.heritage.gov.pk.

**Ministry of Defence:** Pakistan Secretariat, No. II, Rawalpindi 46000; tel. (51) 9271107; fax (51) 9271113; e-mail tahir@mod.gov.pk.

**Ministry of Education:** Block D, Pakistan Secretariat, Islamabad; tel. (51) 9212020; fax (51) 9202851; e-mail pak@yahoo.com; internet www.moe.gov.pk.

**Ministry of Environment, Local Government and Rural Development:** Block 4, Old Naval Headquarters, Civic Centre, G-6, Melody, Islamabad; tel. (51) 9224291; fax (51) 9202211; e-mail minister@moenv.gov.pk; internet www.moenv.gov.pk.

**Ministry of Finance:** Block Q, Pakistan Secretariat, Islamabad; tel. (51) 9201941; fax (51) 9202640; e-mail webmaster@finance.gov.pk; internet www.finance.gov.pk.

**Ministry of Food, Agriculture and Livestock:** Block B, Pakistan Secretariat, Islamabad; tel. (51) 9203307; fax (51) 9210616.

**Ministry of Foreign Affairs:** Constitution Ave, Islamabad; tel. (51) 9210335; fax (51) 9207600; e-mail sadiq@mofa.gov.pk; internet www.mofa.gov.pk.

**Ministry of Health:** Block C, Pakistan Secretariat, Islamabad; tel. (51) 9213933; fax (51) 9203944; e-mail minister@health.gov.pk; internet www.health.gov.pk.

**Ministry of Housing and Works:** Block B, Pakistan Secretariat, Islamabad; tel. (51) 9214121; fax (51) 9209125; e-mail minister@housing.gov.pk; internet www.pha.gov.pk.

**Ministry of Industries, Production and Special Initiatives:** Block A, Pakistan Secretariat, Islamabad; tel. (51) 9212164; fax (51) 9205130; e-mail info@moip.gov.pk; internet www.moip.gov.pk.

**Ministry of Information and Broadcasting:** Cyber Wing, 4th Floor, Cabinet Block, Pakistan Secretariat, Islamabad; tel. (51) 9206176; fax (51) 9201350; e-mail webmaster@infopak.gov.pk; internet www.infopak.gov.pk.

**Ministry of Information Technology and Telecommunications:** 4th Floor, Evacuee Trust Bldg, Aga Khan Rd, F-5/1, Islamabad; tel. (51) 9201990; fax (51) 9205233; e-mail minister@moitt.gov.pk; internet www.moitt.gov.pk.

**Ministry of the Interior:** Block R, Room 404, Pakistan Secretariat, Islamabad; tel. (51) 9212026; fax (51) 9202624; e-mail info@interior.gov.pk; internet www.interior.gov.pk.

**Ministry of Kashmir Affairs, Northern Areas and States and Frontier Regions (SAFRON):** Block R, Pakistan Secretariat, Islamabad; tel. (51) 9208442; fax (51) 9207084; e-mail minister@moka.gov.pk; internet www.moka.gov.pk.

**Ministry of Labour, Manpower and Overseas Pakistanis:** Block B, Pakistan Secretariat, Islamabad; tel. (51) 9210077; fax (51) 9203462.

**Ministry of Law, Justice and Human Rights:** Block R, Pakistan Secretariat, Islamabad; tel. and fax (51) 9211278.

**Ministry of Local Government and Rural Development:** Pakistan Secretariat, Islamabad; tel. (51) 9202080; fax (51) 9201165; e-mail minister@lgrd.gov.pk; internet www.lgrd.gov.pk.

**Ministry of Petroleum and Natural Resources:** 3rd Floor, Block A, Pakistan Secretariat, Islamabad; tel. (51) 9210220; fax (51) 9213180; e-mail minister@mpnr.gov.pk; internet www.mpnr.gov.pk.

**Ministry of Planning and Development:** Block P, Pakistan Secretariat, Islamabad; tel. (51) 9204926; fax (51) 9202704; internet www.mopd.gov.pk.

**Ministry of Population Welfare:** Jamil Mohsin Mansion, Civic Centre, G-6, Islamabad 44000; tel. (51) 9207383; fax (51) 9201408; e-mail minister@mopw.gov.pk; internet www.mopw.gov.pk.

**Ministry of Privatisation and Investment:** 5-A, EAC Bldg, Constitution Ave, Islamabad 44000; tel. (51) 9205146; fax (51) 9203076; e-mail info@privatisation.gov.pk; internet www.privatisation.gov.pk.

**Ministry of Railways:** Block D, Pakistan Secretariat, Islamabad; tel. (51) 9218515; fax (51) 9210247; e-mail minister@railways.gov.pk; internet www.railways.gov.pk.

**Ministry of Religious Affairs, Zakat and Ushr:** G-6, Civic Centre, Islamabad; tel. (51) 9214856; fax (51) 9205833; e-mail minister@mra.gov.pk; internet www.mra.gov.pk.

**Ministry of Scientific and Technological Research:** 4th Floor, Evacuee Trust Complex, Aga Khan Rd, F-5/1, Islamabad; tel. (51) 9208026; fax (51) 9204541; e-mail minister@most.gov.pk; internet www.most.gov.pk.

**Ministry of the Textiles Industry:** 2nd Floor, FBC Bldg, Attaturk Ave, G-5/2, Islamabad; tel. (51) 9212799; fax (51) 9214015; e-mail minister@textile.gov.pk; internet www.textile.gov.pk.

**Ministry of Tourism:** Green Trust Towers, 7th Floor, Jinnah Ave, Blue Area, Islamabad 44000; tel. (51) 9203772; fax (51) 9207427; e-mail secretary@tourism.gov.pk; internet www.tourism.gov.pk.

**Ministry of Water and Power:** Block A, 15th Floor, Shaheed-e-Millat, Pakistan Secretariat, Islamabad; tel. (51) 9212442; fax (51) 9224825; e-mail fminister@mowp.gov.pk; internet www.mowp.gov.pk.

**Ministry of Women's Development, Social Welfare and Special Education:** State Life Bldg, 1st Floor, No. 5, Blue Area, China Chowk, F-6/4, Islamabad; tel. (51) 9206328; fax (51) 9201083; e-mail secretary@moya.gov.pk.

## Federal Legislature

### SENATE

The Legal Framework Order, promulgated by the President in August 2002, increased the number of seats in the Senate from 87 to 100. Eighty-eight of the members are elected by the four provincial legislatures; eight are chosen by representatives of the Federally Administered Tribal Areas; and four by the federal capital. Its term of office is six years, but one-half of the membership is renewed after three years. The most recent election was held on 6 March 2006.

**Chairman:** MOHAMMAD MIAN SOOMRO.

**Deputy Chairman:** JAN MOHAMMAD KHAN JAMALI.

**Distribution of Seats, March 2006**

| | Seats |
|---|---|
| Pakistan Muslim League (Quaid-e-Azam Group) | 38 |
| Muttahida Majlis-e-Amal* | 17 |
| Pakistan People's Party Parliamentarians | 9 |
| Muttahida Qaumi Movement | 6 |
| Pakistan Muslim League (Nawaz Group) | 4 |
| Pakistan People's Party (Sherpao Group) | 3 |
| Pakhtoonkhwa Milli Awami Party | 3 |
| Awami National Party | 2 |
| Balochistan National Party (Awami) | 1 |
| Balochistan National Party (Maingal) | 1 |
| Jamhuri Watan Party | 1 |
| Jamiat-e-Ulema-e-Islam (F) | 1 |
| National Alliance† | 1 |
| Pakistan Muslim League (Functional Pir Pagara Group) | 1 |
| Independents | 12 |
| **Total** | 100 |

* Coalition comprising Jamaat-e-Islami Pakistan, Jamiat-e-Ulema-e-Pakistan, Jamiat-e-Ulema-e-Islam (S), Jamiat-e-Ulema-e-Islam (F), Islami Tehreek Pakistan and Jamiat Ahl-e-Hadith.

† Coalition comprising the National People's Party, the Millat Party, the Sindh National Front, the Sindh Democratic Alliance and the National Awami Party.

### NATIONAL ASSEMBLY

In accordance with the Legal Framework Order (LFO), which was promulgated by the President in August 2002, the number of seats in the National Assembly increased from 217 to 342, with 60 seats reserved for women and 10 for non-Muslims. Also incorporated in the

LFO was a reduction in the National Assembly's term of office by one year to four.

**Speaker:** Dr Fehmida Mirza.

**Deputy Speaker:** Faisal Karim Kundi.

**General Election, 18 February 2008**

| | Seats |
|---|---|
| Pakistan People's Party Parliamentarians | 87 |
| Pakistan Muslim League (Nawaz Group) | 67 |
| Pakistan Muslim League | 42 |
| Muttahida Qaumi Movement | 19 |
| Awami National Party | 10 |
| Muttahida Majlis-e-Amal | 5 |
| Pakistan Muslim League (Functional Group) | 4 |
| Balochistan National Party (Awami) | 1 |
| National People's Party | 1 |
| Pakistan People's Party (Sherpao Group) | 1 |
| Independents and others | 29 |
| Reserved | 70 |
| Vacant | 6 |
| **Total** | 342 |

# Provincial Governments

(August 2008)

Pakistan comprises the four provinces of Sindh, Balochistan, Punjab and the North-West Frontier Province, plus the federal capital and Federally Administered Tribal Areas.

### BALOCHISTAN

(Capital—Quetta)

**Governor:** Nawab Zulfiqar Ali Magsi.

**Chief Minister:** Nawab Mohammad Aslam Raisani.

**Legislative Assembly:** 65 seats (Pakistan Muslim League—Quaid-e-Azam Group 20, Pakistan People's Party Parliamentarians 11, Muttahida Majlis-e-Amal 10, Balochistan National Party—Awami 7, Awami National Party 4, National Party 1, independents 10, vacant 2).

### NORTH-WEST FRONTIER PROVINCE

(Capital—Peshawar)

**Governor:** Owais Ahmed Ghani.

**Chief Minister:** Amir Haider Khan Hoti.

**Legislative Assembly:** 124 seats (Awami National Party 46, Pakistan People's Party Parliamentarians 30, Muttahida Majlis-e-Amal 14, Pakistan Muslim League—Nawaz 9, Pakistan People's Party—Sherpao 7, Pakistan Muslim League—Quaid-e-Azam Group 6, independents 9, vacant 3).

### PUNJAB

(Capital—Lahore)

**Governor:** Salman Taseer.

**Chief Minister:** Muhammad Shahbaz Sharif.

**Legislative Assembly:** 371 seats (Pakistan Muslim League—Nawaz 165, Pakistan People's Party Parliamentarians 106, Pakistan Muslim League—Quaid-e-Azam Group 86, Pakistan Muslim League—Functional 4, Muttahida Majlis-e-Amal 2, independents 2, vacant or withheld 6).

### SINDH

(Capital—Karachi)

**Governor:** Dr Ishratul Ebad Khan.

**Chief Minister:** Syed Qaim Ali Shah.

**Legislative Assembly:** 168 seats (Pakistan People's Party Parliamentarians 90, Muttahida Qaumi Movement 51, Pakistan Muslim League—Quaid-e-Azam Group 10, Pakistan Muslim League—Functional 9, Awami National Party 2, National People's Party 2, vacant, withheld and others 4).

# Election Commission

**Election Commission of Pakistan:** Secretariat, Election House, Constitution Ave, G-5/2, Islamabad; e-mail info@ecp.gov.pk; internet www.ecp.gov.pk; independent; Chief Election Commr Justice (retd) Qazi Muhammad Farooq.

# Political Organizations

Some 49 parties, issued with election symbols by the Election Commission, contested the general election on 18 February 2008.

**All Jammu and Kashmir Muslim Conference:** f. 1948; advocates the holding of a free plebiscite in the whole of Kashmir; Leader Sardar Attiq Ahmed Khan.

**Awami National Party (ANP)** (People's National Party): Bacha Khan Markaz, Pajagi Rd, Peshawar; tel. (91) 2246851-3; fax (91) 2252406; e-mail info@awaminationalparty.org; internet www.awaminationalparty.org; f. 1986 by the merger of the National Democratic Party, the Awami Tehrik (People's Movement) and the Mazdoor Kissan (Labourers' and Peasants' Party); federalist and nationalist; the Pakhtoonkhawa Qaumi Party merged with the ANP in February 2006, followed by the National Awami Party Pakistan in June of the same year; Pres. Asfandyar Wali Khan.

**Awami Qiyadat Party** (People's Leadership Party): 88 Race Course Rd, St 3, Rawalpindi Cantt; f. 1995; Chair. Gen. (retd) Mirza Aslam Beg.

**Balochistan National Party (BNP)—Awami:** Quetta; Leader Syed Ehsan Shah; Pres. Israrullah Zehri.

**Balochistan National Party (BNP)—Maingal:** Quetta; e-mail bnpwebadmin@balochistan.net; Leader Sardar Mohammad Akhtar Maingal.

**Jamaat-e-Islami Pakistan (JIP):** Mansoorah, Multan Rd, Lahore 54570; tel. (42) 5419520; fax (42) 5419505; e-mail uroubah@gmail.com; internet www.jamaat.org; f. 1941; seeks the establishment of Islamic order through adherence to teaching of Maulana Maududi, founder of the party; revivalist; right-wing; mem. of Muttahida Majlis-e-Amal (United Action Front); Chair. Amir Qazi Hussain Ahmad; Sec.-Gen. Syed Munawar Hasan; c. 5m. mems (2005).

**Jamhuri Watan Party (Bugti) Balochistan:** Bugti House, Dera Bugti; Pres. Nawab Talal Akbar Khan Bugti.

**Jamiat-e-Ulema-e-Islam (JUI):** Jamia al-Maarf, al-Sharia, Dera Ismail Khan; f. 1950; mem. Muttahida Majlis-e-Amal alliance; advocates adoption of a constitution in accordance with (Sunni) Islamic teachings; split into factions led by Maulana Fazlur Rehman (JUI—F) and Sami ul-Haq (JUI—S).

**Jamiat-e-Ulema-e-Pakistan (JUP):** Burns Rd, Karachi; f. 1948; mem. Muttahida Majlis-e-Amal alliance; advocates progressive (Sunni) Islamic principles and enforcement of Islamic laws in Pakistan; Pres. Dr Abul Khair Mohammad Zubair (acting); Gen. Sec. Qari Zawwar Bahadur.

**Millat Party:** 21-E/3, Gulberg III, Lahore; tel. (42) 5757805; fax (42) 5756718; e-mail millat@lhr.comsats.net.pk; advocates 'true federalism'; Chair. Farooq Ahmad Khan Leghari.

**Muttahida Qaumi Movement (MQM):** 494/8 Azizabad, Federal Area B, Karachi; tel. (21) 6313690; fax (21) 6329955; e-mail mqm@mqm.org; internet www.mqm.org; f. 1984 as Mohajir Qaumi Movement; name changed to Muttahida Qaumi Movement in 1997; associated with the All Pakistan Muttahida Students' Organization (f. 1978 as the All Pakistan Mohajir Students' Organization; name changed July 2006); represents the interests of Muslim, Urdu-speaking immigrants (from India) in Pakistan; seeks the designation of Mohajir as fifth nationality (after Sindhi, Punjabi, Pathan and Balochi); aims to abolish the prevailing feudal political system and to establish democracy; Founder and Leader Altaf Hussain; Pres. Aftab Sheikh.

**National Party:** Faiz Arbab Saryab Rd, Quetta; f. 2003 following merger of Balochistan National Movement and Balochistan National Democratic Party; Chair. Dr Abdul Hayai Baloch.

**National People's Party (NPP):** 18 Khayaban-e-Shamsheer, Defence Housing Authority, Phase V, Karachi; tel. (21) 5854522; fax (21) 5873753; f. 1986; centre left-wing party advocating a just, democratic welfare state for Pakistan; breakaway faction from PPP; Chair. Ghulam Mustafa Jatoi; Parl. Leader Dr Ibrahim Khan.

**Pakhtoonkhwa Milli Awami Party:** Leader Mehmood Khan Achakzai.

**Pakistan Awami Tehreek (PAT):** 365-M Model Town, Lahore; tel. (42) 5169111; fax (42) 5169114; e-mail info@pat.com.pk; internet www.pat.com.pk; Pres. Sahibzada Miskeen Faiz ur Rehman Khan Durani; Sec.-Gen. Dr Anwaar Akhtar.

**Pakistan Democratic Party (PDP):** f. 1969; advocates democratic and Islamic values; Pres. Nawabzada Mansoor Ahmed Khan.

**Pakistan Muslim League (PML):** PML House, F-7/3, Islamabad; internet www.pakistanmuslimleague.info; f. 2004 following merger of PML Quaid-e-Azam Group, PML (Junejo), PML (Functional), PML (Zia-ul-Haq Shaheed), PML (Jinnah) and the Sindh Democratic Alliance; PML (Functional) subsequently split from party; Pres. Chaudhry Shujaat Hussain; Sec.-Gen. Sen. Mushahid Hussain Syed.

**Pakistan Muslim League—Functional (PML—F):** Islamabad; merged with PML Quaid-e-Azam Group, PML (Junejo), PML (Zia-ul-Haq Shaheed), PML (Jinnah) and the Sindh Democratic Alliance in 2004 but subsequently split from party; Leader PIR PAGARA.

**Pakistan Muslim League—Nawaz (PML—N):** House No. 20-H, St 10, F-8/3, Islamabad; tel. (51) 2852662; e-mail pmlisb@hotmail.com; internet www.pmln.org.pk; f. 1993 as faction of Pakistan Muslim League (Junejo); Leader NAWAZ SHARIF; Pres. SHAHBAZ SHARIF; Chair RAJA ZAFARUL HAQ.

**Pakistan People's Party (PPP):** 8, St 19, F-8/2, Islamabad; tel. (51) 2255264; fax (51) 2282741; e-mail ppp@comsats.net.pk; internet www.ppp.org.pk; formed Pakistan People's Party Parliamentarians (PPPP) 2002 in order to meet electoral requirements; advocates Islamic socialism, democracy and a non-aligned foreign policy; Leaders BILAWAL BHUTTO ZARDARI, ASIF ALI ZARDARI.

**Pakistan People's Party (Shaheed Bhutto Group):** 71 Clifton, Karachi; f. 1995 as a breakaway faction of the PPP; Chair. GHINWA BHUTTO; Sec.-Gen. Dr MUBASHIR HASAN.

**Punjabi Pakhtoon Ittehad (PPI):** f. 1987 to represent the interests of Punjabis and Pakhtoons in Karachi; Pres. MALIK MIR HAZAR KHAN.

**Sindh National Front (SNF):** Pres. MUMTAZ BHUTTO.

**Sindh Taraqi Passand Party (STPP):** Leader Dr QADIR MAGSI.

**Tehreek-e-Insaf** (Movement for Justice): Central Secretariat, H-07, Parliament Lodges, Islamabad; tel. (51) 2270744; fax (51) 2873893; e-mail info@insaf.org.pk; internet www.insaf.org.pk; f. 1996; Leader IMRAN KHAN; Sec.-Gen. A. M. SHAHID ZULFIQAR.

# Diplomatic Representation

## EMBASSIES AND HIGH COMMISSIONS IN PAKISTAN

**Afghanistan:** 8, St 90, G-6/3, Islamabad 44000; tel. (51) 2824505; fax (51) 2824504; e-mail contact@islamabad.mfa.gov.af; internet www.islamabad.mfa.gov.af; Ambassador MOHAMMAD ANWAR ANWARZAI.

**Algeria:** 107, St 9, E-7, POB 1038, Islamabad; tel. (51) 2653793; fax (51) 2820912; Ambassador NADIR LARBAOUI.

**Argentina:** 20, Hill Rd, Shalimar F-6/3, POB 1015, Islamabad; tel. (51) 2821242; fax (51) 2825564; e-mail epaki@mrecic.gov.ar; Ambassador RODOLFO MARTIN SARAVIA.

**Australia:** Diplomatic Enclave 1, Constitution Ave and Isphani Rd, G-5/4, POB 1046, Islamabad; tel. (51) 2824345; fax (51) 2820112; e-mail consular.islm@dfat.gov.au; internet www.pakistan.embassy.gov.au; High Commissioner ZORICA MCCARTHY.

**Austria:** 13, St 1, F-6/3, POB 1018, Islamabad 44000; tel. (51) 2209710; fax (51) 2828306; e-mail islamabad-ob@bmeia.gv.at; Ambassador Dr MICHAEL STIGELBAUER.

**Azerbaijan:** House 14, St 87, G-6/3, Atatürk Ave, Islamabad; tel. (51) 2829345; fax (51) 2820898; e-mail azeremb@isb.paknet.com.pk; internet www.azembassy.com.pk; Ambassador Dr EYNULLA YADALLA OGLU MADATLI.

**Bahrain:** House 5, St 83, G-6/4, Islamabad; tel. (51) 2831114; fax (51) 2206732; Ambassador MOHAMMED EBRAHIM MOHAMMED ABD AL-QADIR.

**Bangladesh:** 1, St 5, F-6/3, Islamabad; tel. (51) 2279267; fax (51) 2279266; e-mail bdhcisb@dsl.net.pk; internet www.bdhcpk.org; High Commissioner YASMEEN MURSHED.

**Belgium:** 14, St 17, F-7/2, Islamabad; tel. (51) 2652635; fax (51) 2652631; e-mail islamabad@diplobel.org; internet www.diplomatie.be/islamabad; Ambassador MICHEL GOFFIN.

**Bosnia and Herzegovina:** House No. 1, Kaghan Rd, F-8/3, Islamabad; tel. (51) 2261003; fax (51) 2261004; e-mail ambassador@bosnianembassypakistan.org; internet www.bosnianembassypakistan.org; Ambassador DAMIR DZANKO.

**Brazil:** 50, Atatürk Ave, G-6/3, POB 1053, Islamabad; tel. (51) 2279690; fax (51) 2823034; e-mail brasembp@isb.compol.com; Ambassador CARLOS EDUARDO SETTE CAMARA DA FONSECA COSTA.

**Brunei:** House 5, St 6, F-6/3, Islamabad; tel. (51) 2879636; fax (51) 2823688; e-mail islamabad.pakistan@mfa.gov.bn; High Commissioner Pehin Dato' Haji Panglima Col (retd) Haji ABDUL JALIL BIN Haji AHMAD.

**Bulgaria:** Plot No. 6-11, Diplomatic Enclave, Ramna 5, POB 1483, Islamabad; tel. (51) 2279196; fax (51) 2279195; e-mail bul@isd.wol.net.pk; Ambassador GEORGI GRANCHAROV.

**Canada:** Diplomatic Enclave, Sector G-5, POB 1042, Islamabad; tel. (51) 2086000; fax (51) 2279110; e-mail isbad@international.gc.ca; internet www.international.gc.ca/missions/pakistan; High Commissioner DAVID B. COLLINS.

**China, People's Republic:** Ramna 4, Diplomatic Enclave, Islamabad; tel. (51) 2877279; fax (51) 2279600; e-mail chinaemb_pk@mfa.gov.cn; internet pk.china-embassy.org; Ambassador LUO ZHAOHUI.

**Cuba:** House 37, School Rd, F-6/2, Islamabad; tel. (51) 2824077; fax (51) 2824076; e-mail embacubapakistan@yahoo.com; Ambassador GUSTAVO MACHÍN GÓMEZ.

**Czech Republic:** 49, St 27, Shalimar F-6/2, POB 1335, Islamabad; tel. (51) 2274304; fax (51) 2825327; e-mail islamabad@embassy.mzv.cz; internet www.mzv.cz/islamabad; Ambassador ALEXANDR LANGER.

**Denmark:** House No. 16, Street 21, F-6/2, POB 1118, Islamabad; tel. (51) 2824078; fax (51) 2824076; e-mail isbamb@um.dk; internet www.ambislamabad.um.dk; Ambassador (vacant).

**Egypt:** 38–51, UN Blvd, Diplomatic Enclave, Ramna 5/4, POB 2088, Islamabad; tel. (51) 2209072; fax (51) 2279552; Ambassador HUSSEIN KAMEL HARIDY.

**Finland:** House No. 24, St 89, G-6/3, Islamabad; tel. (51) 2828426; fax (51) 2828427; e-mail finnemb@isd.wol.net.pk; Ambassador PIRJO IRMELI MUSTONEN.

**France:** Constitution Ave, G-5, Diplomatic Enclave 1, POB 1068, Islamabad; tel. (51) 2278730; fax (51) 2822538; e-mail ambafra@isb.comsats.net.pk; internet www.ambafra-pk.org; Ambassador RÉGIS DE BELENET.

**Germany:** Ramna 5, Diplomatic Enclave, POB 1027, Islamabad 44000; tel. (51) 2007100; fax (51) 2279436; e-mail info@isla.diplo.de; internet www.islamabad.diplo.de; Ambassador Dr MICHAEL KOCH.

**Greece:** 33A, School Rd, F-6/2, Islamabad; tel. (51) 2822558; fax (51) 8358985; e-mail gremb.isl@mfa.gr; internet www.grembpak.mfa.gr; Ambassador PETROS MAVROIDIS.

**Holy See:** Apostolic Nunciature, St 5, G-5, Diplomatic Enclave 1, POB 1106, Islamabad 44000; tel. (51) 2278218; fax (51) 2820847; e-mail vatipak@dsl.net.pk; Apostolic Nuncio Most Rev. ADOLFO TITO YLLANA (Titular Archbishop of Montecorvino).

**Hungary:** 12, Margalla Rd, F-6/3, POB 1103, Islamabad; tel. (51) 2823352; fax (51) 2825256; e-mail hungemb@comsats.net.pk; internet www.mfa.gov.hu/emb/islamabad; Ambassador BELA FAZEKAS.

**India:** G-5, Diplomatic Enclave, Islamabad; tel. (51) 2206950; fax (51) 2823386; e-mail hicomind@isb.compol.com; High Commissioner SATYABRATA PAL.

**Indonesia:** St 5, G-5/4, Diplomatic Enclave 1, POB 1019, Islamabad; tel. (51) 2832017; fax (51) 2832013; e-mail unitkom@kbri-islamabad.go.id; internet www.kbri-islamabad.go.id; Ambassador ANWAR SANTOSO.

**Iran:** Plot No. 222, 238, St 2, F-5/1, Islamabad; tel. (51) 2276270; fax (51) 2824839; Ambassador MASHALLAH SHAKERI.

**Iraq:** 57, St 48, F-8/4, Islamabad; tel. (51) 2253734; fax (51) 2253688; e-mail iraqiya@sat.net.pk; Ambassador KAIS SUBHI AL-YACOUBI.

**Italy:** 54 Margalla Rd, F-6/3, POB 1008, Islamabad; tel. (51) 2828982; fax (51) 2829026; e-mail segreteria.ambislamabad@esteri.it; internet www.italian-embassy.org.ae/Ambasciata_Islamabad; Ambassador VINCENZO PRATI.

**Japan:** Plot No. 53-70, Ramna 5/4, Diplomatic Enclave 1, Islamabad 44000; tel. (51) 2279320; fax (51) 2279340; e-mail japanemb@comsats.net.pk; internet www.pk.emb-japan.go.jp; Ambassador SEIJI KOJIMA.

**Jordan:** 99, Main Double Rd, F-10/1, Islamabad; tel. (51) 2297383; fax (51) 2211630; e-mail islamabad@fm.gov.jo; Ambassador SALEH JAWARNEH.

**Kazakhstan:** House 11, St 45, F-8/1, Islamabad; tel. (51) 2262926; fax (51) 2262806; e-mail embkaz@isb.comsats.net.pk; Ambassador VAKYTBEK S. SHABARBAYEV.

**Kenya:** 8A, Embassy Rd, F-6/4, POB 2097, Islamabad; tel. (51) 2876024; fax (51) 2876027; e-mail kenreppk@apollo.net.pk; High Commissioner MISHI MASIKA MWATSAHU.

**Korea, Democratic People's Republic:** House 16 A-B, Park Rd, F-B/2, Islamabad; tel. and fax (51) 2252756; Ambassador RI YONG HWAN.

**Korea, Republic:** Block 13, St 29, G-5/4, Diplomatic Enclave 2, POB 1087, Islamabad; tel. (51) 2279380; fax (51) 2279391; e-mail emb-pk@mofat.go.kr; internet pak-islamabad.mofat.go.kr/eng/index.jsp; Ambassador SHIN UN.

**Kuwait:** Plot Nos 1, 2 and 24, University Rd, G-5, Diplomatic Enclave, POB 1030, Islamabad; tel. (51) 2279413; fax (51) 2829487; Ambassador AZIZ RAHIUM ALEDHANI.

**Kyrgyzstan:** House 163, Street 36, F-10/1, Islamabad; tel. (51) 2212196; fax (51) 2212169; e-mail kyrgyzembassy@dsl.net.pk; Ambassador NURLAN T. AITMURZAYEV.

**Lebanon:** House 6, Street 27, F-6/2, Islamabad; tel. (51) 2278338; fax (51) 2826410; e-mail lebemb@comsats.net.pk; Ambassador WAFIC MUHAMMAD REHAIME.

**Libya:** House 736, Margalla Rd, F-10/2, Islamabad; tel. (51) 2214378; fax (51) 2290093; Ambassador IBRAHIM AL-ABID MUKHTAR.

**Malaysia:** House 34, St 56, F-7/4, Islamabad; tel. (51) 2279570; fax (51) 2824761; e-mail malislamb@kln.gov.my; internet www.kln.gov.my/perwakilan/islamabad; High Commissioner AHMAD SHAHIZAN ABD SAMAD.

**Maldives:** Islamabad; High Commissioner ADAM HASSAN.

**Mauritius:** House 13, St 26, F-6/2, POB 1084, Islamabad; tel. (51) 2824657; fax (51) 2824656; e-mail mauripak@dsl.net.pk; High Commissioner ABDOOL RASCHID MEERUN.

**Morocco:** 6, Gomal Rd, E-7, POB 1179, Islamabad; tel. (51) 2829656; fax (51) 2822745; e-mail sifamapak@morocco-embassy.com.pk; internet www.morocco-embassy.com.pk; Ambassador MOHAMMAD RIDA EL FASSI.

**Myanmar:** 43, St 26, F-6/2, Islamabad; tel. (51) 2879612; fax (51) 2879616; e-mail embassy_myanmar@yahoo.com; Ambassador U MAUNG NYO.

**Nepal:** 2, St 8, F-8/3, Islamabad; tel. (51) 2854696; fax (51) 2854722; e-mail nepem@isb.comsats.net.pk; Ambassador BAL BAHADUR KUNWAR.

**Netherlands:** House No. 28, Margalla Rd, F-7/3, POB 1065, Islamabad; tel. (51) 2004444; fax (51) 2279512; e-mail isl@minbuza.nl; internet www.mfa.nl/isl-en; Ambassador CORNELIS WILHELMUS ANDREAE.

**Nigeria:** 132–135, Diplomatic Enclave 1, Isphani Rd, G-5/4, POB 1075, Islamabad; tel. (51) 2823542; fax (51) 2824104; e-mail nigeria@isb.comsats.net.pk; High Commissioner UMAR EL-GASH MAINA.

**Norway:** 25, St 19, F-6/2, Islamabad; tel. (51) 2279720; fax (51) 2279729; e-mail emb.islamabad@mfa.no; internet www.norway.org.pk; Ambassador AUD MARIT WIIG.

**Oman:** 53, St 48, F-8/4, POB 1194, Islamabad; tel. (51) 2254869; fax (51) 2255074; Ambassador MOHAMMAD BIN SAID BIN MOHAMMAD AL-LAWATI.

**Philippines:** POB 1052, Islamabad; tel. (51) 2824933; fax (51) 2653665; e-mail isdpe@isb.comsats.net.pk; Ambassador JAIME J. YAMBAO.

**Poland:** St 24, G-5/4, Diplomatic Enclave 2, POB 1032, Islamabad; tel. (51) 2600844; fax (51) 2600852; e-mail polemb@dsl.net.pk; internet www.islamabad.polemb.net; Ambassador Dr KRZYSTOF DEBNICKI.

**Portugal:** 66, Main Margalla Rd, F-7/2, Islamabad; tel. (51) 2652491; fax (51) 2652492; e-mail portugal@isb.paknet.com.pk; Ambassador Dr ANTONIO JOSÉ DA CAMARARA ROMALHO ORTIGÃO.

**Qatar:** 20, University Rd, Diplomatic Enclave, G-5/4, Islamabad; tel. (51) 2270833; fax (51) 2270207; e-mail islamabad@mofa.gov.qa; Ambassador HAMAD ALI AL-HENZAB.

**Romania:** 13, St 88, G-6/3, Islamabad; tel. (51) 2826514; fax (51) 2826515; e-mail romania@isb.comsats.net.pk; Chargé d'affaires a.i. BOGDAN TRIFU.

**Russia:** Khayaban-e-Suhrawardy, Diplomatic Enclave, Ramna 4, Islamabad; tel. (51) 2278670; fax (51) 2826552; e-mail russia2@comsats.net.pk; internet www.pakistan.mid.ru; Ambassador SERGEY N. PESKOV.

**Saudi Arabia:** 14, Hill Rd, F-6/3, Islamabad; tel. (51) 2820156; fax (51) 2278816; Ambassador ALI S. AWADH ASSERI.

**Somalia:** 17, St 60, F-8/4, Islamabad; tel. (51) 2854733; fax (51) 2854733; Ambassador ABDISALAAM Haji AHMAD LIBAN.

**South Africa:** House No. 48, Margalla Rd, Khayaban-e-Iqbal, F-8/2, Islamabad; tel. (51) 2262354; fax (51) 2250114; e-mail xhosa@isb.comsats.net.pk; internet www.southafrica.org.pk; High Commissioner DANIEL JABULANI MAVIMBELA.

**Spain:** St 6, G-5, Diplomatic Enclave 1, POB 1144, Islamabad; tel. (51) 2088777; fax (51) 2088774; e-mail embspain@dsl.net.pk; Ambassador JOSÉ MARÍA ROBLES FRAGA.

**Sri Lanka:** 2C, St 55, F-6/4, Islamabad; tel. (51) 2828723; fax (51) 2828751; e-mail srilanka@dsl.net.pk; High Commissioner Dr WIJERATNE BANDARA DORAKUMBURE.

**Sudan:** 1A, St 32, F-8/1, Islamabad; tel. (51) 2263926; fax (51) 2264404; e-mail sudanipk@isb.compol.com; Ambassador DAFAA ALLAH EL-HAJ ALI.

**Sweden:** 4, St 5, F-6/3, Islamabad; tel. (51) 2828712; fax (51) 2825284; e-mail ambassaden.islamabad@foreign.ministry.se; internet www.swedenabroad.se/Start____28997.aspx; Ambassador ANNA KARIN ENESTRÖM.

**Switzerland:** St 6, G-5/4, Diplomatic Enclave, POB 1073, Islamabad; tel. (51) 2279291; fax (51) 2279286; e-mail isl.vertretung@eda.admin.ch; internet www.eda.admin.ch/islamabad; Ambassador MARKUS PETER.

**Syria:** 30 Hill Rd, F-6/3, Islamabad; tel. (51) 2279470; fax (51) 2279472; Ambassador Dr RIAD ISMAT.

**Tajikistan:** House 90, Main Double Rd, F-10/1, Islamabad; tel. (51) 2293462; fax (51) 2299710; e-mail tajemb_islamabad@inbox.ru; Ambassador SAIDBEK B. SIADOV.

**Thailand:** 23, St 25, F-8/2, Islamabad; tel. (51) 5838245; fax (51) 5837422; e-mail thaiemb@dslplus.net.pk; internet www.mfa.go.th/web/1330.php?depid=231; Ambassador SUKHO PIROMNAM.

**Tunisia:** 221, St 21, E-7, Islamabad; tel. (51) 2827869; fax (51) 2653564; Ambassador ZOUHEIR DHAOUADI.

**Turkey:** St 1, Diplomatic Enclave 1, Islamabad; tel. (51) 8319800; fax (51) 2278752; e-mail turkemb@dsl.net.pk; internet www.turkishembassy.org.pk; Ambassador RAUF ENGIN SOYSAL.

**Turkmenistan:** House 22A, Nazim-Ud-Din Rd, F-7/1, Islamabad; tel. (51) 2274913; fax (51) 2278790; e-mail turkmen@comsats.net.pk; Ambassador SAPOR BERDINIYAZOV.

**Ukraine:** 20, St 18, F-6/2, Islamabad; tel. (51) 2274732; fax (51) 2274643; e-mail emb_pk@mfa.gov.ua; Ambassador Dr IHOR PASKO.

**United Arab Emirates:** Plot No. 1-22, Quaid-e-Azam University Rd, Diplomatic Enclave, POB 1111, Islamabad; tel. (51) 2279052; fax (51) 2279063; e-mail uaeempk@isb.paknet.pk; Ambassador ALI MOHAMMED ASH-SHAMSI.

**United Kingdom:** Diplomatic Enclave, Ramna 5, POB 1122, Islamabad; tel. (51) 2012000; fax (51) 2823439; e-mail bhcmedia@isb.comsats.net.pk; internet www.britainonline.org.pk; High Commissioner ROBERT BRINKLEY.

**USA:** Diplomatic Enclave, Ramna 5, POB 1048, Islamabad; tel. (51) 2080000; fax (51) 2276427; e-mail webmasterisb@state.gov; internet islamabad.usembassy.gov; Ambassador ANNE WOODS PATTERSON.

**Uzbekistan:** 2, St 2, F-8/3, Kohistan Rd, Islamabad; tel. (51) 2264746; fax (51) 2261739; e-mail uzbekemb@isb.comsats.net.pk; internet www.pakistan.mfa.uz; Ambassador OYBEK A. USMANOV.

**Vietnam:** House 10A, Street 31, F-6/1, Islamabad; tel. (51) 2850581; fax (51) 2850582; Chargé d'affaires a.i. NGUYEN QUANG THUC.

**Yemen:** 220, St 21, E-7, POB 1523, Islamabad 44000; tel. (51) 2653612; fax (51) 2653615; e-mail yemen22@isb.apollo.net.pk; Ambassador ABDUL ELAH MOHAMED HAJAR.

# Judicial System

A constitutional amendment bill was passed in the National Assembly in October 1998 replacing the country's existing legal code with full Islamic *Shari'a*. The bill remained to be approved, however, by the Senate.

### SUPREME COURT

**Chief Justice:** ABDUL HAMEED DOGAR.

**Attorney-General:** MALIK MUHAMMAD QAYYUM.

### Federal Shari'a Court

**Chief Justice:** HAZIQ-UL-KHAIRI.

**Federal Ombudsman:** Justice JAVED SADIQ MALIK.

**Federal Tax Ombudsman:** Justice MUNIR A. SHEIKH.

# Religion

### ISLAM

Islam is the state religion. The majority of the population are Sunni Muslims, while estimates of the Shi'a sect vary between 5% and 20% of the population. Only about 0.001% are of the Ahmadi sect.

### CHRISTIANITY

About 3% of the population are Christians.

**National Council of Churches in Pakistan:** 32-B, Shahrah-e-Fatima Jinnah, POB 357, Lahore 54000; tel. (42) 7592167; fax (42) 7569782; e-mail nccp@lhr.comsats.net.pk; internet nccpakistan.org; f. 1949; four mem. bodies, 14 assoc. mems; Gen. Sec. VICTOR AZARIAH.

### The Roman Catholic Church

For ecclesiastical purposes, Pakistan comprises two archdioceses, four dioceses and one apostolic prefecture. At 31 December 2006 there were an estimated 1,043,508 adherents in the country.

**Bishops' Conference:** Pakistan Catholic Bishops' Conference, St 55, F-8/4, Kaghan Rd, Islamabad 44000; tel. (42) 6366137; fax (42) 6368336; e-mail cbcp2000@isb.comsats.net.pk; internet www.pcbcsite.org; f. 1976; Pres. Most Rev. LAWRENCE J. SALDANHA (Archbishop of Lahore); Sec.-Gen. Rt Rev. ANTHONY LOBO (Bishop of Islamabad-Rawalpindi).

**Archbishop of Karachi:** Most Rev. EVARIST PINTO, St Patrick's Cathedral, Shahrah-e-Iraq, Karachi 74400; tel. (21) 7781533; fax (21) 7781532.

**Archbishop of Lahore:** Most Rev. LAWRENCE J. SALDANHA, Sacred Heart Cathedral, 1 Mian Mohammad Shafi Rd, POB 909, Lahore 54000; tel. (42) 6366137; fax (42) 6368336; e-mail abishop@lhr.comsats.net.pk; internet www.rcarchdioceselahore.org.pk.

### Protestant Churches

**Church of Pakistan:** Moderator Rt Rev. Dr ALEXANDER JOHN MALIK (Bishop of Lahore), Bishopsbourne, Cathedral Close, The Mall, Lahore 54000; tel. (42) 7233560; fax (42) 7221270; e-mail bishop_lahore@hotmail.com; f. 1970 by union of the fmr Anglican Church in Pakistan, the United Methodist Church in Pakistan, the United Church in Pakistan (Scots Presbyterians) and the Pakistani Lutheran Church; eight dioceses; c. 700,000 mems (1993); Gen. Sec. HUMPHREY PETERS.

**Presbyterian Church of Pakistan:** Gujranwala Theological Seminary, Civil Lines, POB 13, Gujranwala; tel. (431) 259512; fax (431) 258314; e-mail kamil65@gjr.paknet.com.pk; f. 1961; c. 340,000 mems (1989); Moderator Rev. Dr ARTHUR JAMES; Sec. Rev. Dr MAGSOOD KAMIL.

Other denominations active in the country include the Associated Reformed Presbyterian Church and the Pakistan Salvation Army.

### HINDUISM

Hindus comprise about 1.8% of the population.

### BAHÁ'Í FAITH

**National Spiritual Assembly:** 56, H-8/4, Islamabad; tel. (51) 4444699; fax (51) 4444691; e-mail nsapakistan@cyber.net.pk; internet www.bahai.org; f. 1956; Gen. Sec. Prof. MEHRDAD YOSUF.

## The Press

The Urdu press comprises almost 800 newspapers, with *Daily Jang, Daily Khabrain, Nawa-i-Waqt* and *Jasarat* among the most influential. The daily newspaper with the largest circulation is *Daily Jang*. Although the English-language press reaches only a small percentage of the population, it is influential in political, academic and professional circles. The four main press groups in Pakistan are Jang Publications (the *Daily Jang, The News*, the *Daily News* and the weekly *Akhbar-e-Jehan*), the Dawn or Herald Group (the *Dawn*, and the monthly *Herald* and *Spider*), the Khabrain Group (the *Daily Khabrain* and the English language daily *The Post*) and the Nawa-i-Waqt Group (the *Nawa-i-Waqt, The Nation* and the weekly *Family*).

### PRINCIPAL DAILIES

#### Islamabad

**Al-Akhbar:** 44, St 2, I-10/3, Islamabad; tel. (51) 4438862; fax (51) 4438860; e-mail alakabar@dsl.net.pk; Urdu; also publ. in Muzaffarabad; Editor GHULAM AKBAR.

**Daily Khabrain:** 12 Lawrence Rd, Lahore; tel. (42) 111-55-88-55; fax (42) 6314658; e-mail editor1@khabrain.com; internet www.khabrain.com; Urdu; Editor and Proprietor ZIA SHAHID.

**The Nation:** Nawa-i-Waqt House, Zero Point, Islamabad; fax (51) 2202648; e-mail editor@nation.com.pk; internet www.nation.com.pk; English; Editor ARIF NIZAMI; circ. 15,000.

**Pakistan Observer:** Al-Akbar House, Markaz G-8, Islamabad 44870; tel. (51) 2852027; fax (51) 2262258; e-mail observer@comsats.net.pk; internet www.pakobserver.net; f. 1988; English; independent; Editor-in-Chief ZAHID MALIK.

#### Karachi

**Aghaz:** 11 Japan Mansion, Preedy St, Sadar, Karachi 74400; tel. (21) 2720228; fax (21) 2722125; e-mail ex101@hotmail.com; internet www.aghaz.com; f. 1962; evening; Urdu; Chief Editor MOHAMMAD ANWAR FAROOQI; circ. 65,000.

**Amn:** Deen Muhammad Wafai Rd, opposite NED City Campus, Karachi; tel. (21) 2634451; fax (21) 2634454; e-mail amn@cyber.net.pk; Urdu; Editor AJMAL DEHLVI.

**Awami Awaz:** 2nd Floor, New Central Block No. 2, Hockey Stadium, Liaquat Barracks, off Shahrah-e-Faisal, Karachi; tel. (21) 5672949; fax (21) 5672946; e-mail awamiawaz@hotmail.com; Man. Editor Dr KHAIR MUHAMMAD JUNO.

**Barsat:** 246/D-6, PECHS, Karachi; tel. (21) 4535228; fax (21) 4535227; Editor MUHAMMAD SALEEM DAUDPOTA.

**Beopar:** 205 Alfalah Court, I. I. Chundrigar Rd, Karachi; tel. (21) 2636442; fax (21) 2630784; e-mail beopar@yahoo.com.

**Business Daily:** 13th Floor, Chapal Plaze, Hasrat Mohani Rd, Karachi; tel. (21) 2429445; fax (2!) 2429450; Editor TAUQIR MOHAJIR.

**Business Recorder:** Recorder House, 53 Business Recorder Rd, Karachi 74550; tel. (21) 2250071; fax (21) 2222866; e-mail ed.khi@br-mail.com; internet www.brecorder.com; f. 1965; English; Editor WAMIQ A. ZUBERI; Editor-in-Chief M. A. ZUBERI.

**Daily Awam:** Printing House, I. I. Chundrigar Rd, POB 52, Karachi; tel. (21) 2637111; fax (21) 2636066; e-mail awam@awam.com.pk; f. 1994; evening; Urdu; Editor-in-Chief Mir SHAKIL-UR-RAHMAN.

**Daily Beopar:** 205 Alfalah Court, I. I. Chundrigar Rd, Karachi; tel. (21) 2636442; fax (21) 2630784; Urdu; Man. Editor YOUNUS RIAZ.

**Daily Express:** 5 Expressway, off Korangi Rd, Karachi; tel. (21) 5800051-6; fax (21) 58000510; Urdu; Editor TAHIR NAJMI.

**Daily Intekhab:** Liaison Office, 3rd Floor, Mashhoor Mahal Bldg, Kucha Haji Usman, off I. I. Chundrigar Rd, Karachi; tel. (21) 2634518; fax (21) 2631092; e-mail intekhab@comsats.net.pk; internet www.dailyintekhab.com; Urdu; also publ. from Hub (Balochistan) and Quetta; Man. Editor NARGIS BALOCH; Publr and Exec. Editor ANWAR SAJIDI.

**Daily Jang:** HQ Printing House, I. I. Chundrigar Rd, POB 52, Karachi; tel. (21) 2637111; fax (21) 2634395; e-mail jangkarachi@janggroup.com.pk; internet www.jang.com.pk; f. 1940; morning; Urdu; also publ. in Quetta, Rawalpindi, Lahore and London; Editor-in-Chief Mir SHAKIL-UR-RAHMAN; combined circ. 750,000.

**Daily Khabar:** A-8 Sheraton Centre, F. B. Area, Karachi; tel. (21) 210059; Urdu; Exec. Editor FAROOQ PARACHA; Editor and Publr SAEED ALI HAMEED.

**Daily Mohasaba:** Imperial Hotel, M. T. Khan Rd, Karachi; tel. (21) 519448; Urdu; Editor TALIB TURABI.

**Daily Naya Akhbar:** Zia Shahid Printer and Publisher, Muzammil Press, 1301, Mehmoodabad No. 6, Masjid-e-Awais Qarni, Block 7, Karachi; tel. (21) 111-55-88-55; fax (21) 5382271; CEO ZIA SHAHID; Editor AMTNAN SHAHID.

**Daily News:** Al-Rahman Bldg, I. I. Chundrigar Rd, Karachi; tel. (21) 2637111; fax (21) 2634395; e-mail dailynews@janggroup.com.pk; f. 1962; evening; English; Editor S. M. FAZAL; circ. 50,000.

**Daily Public:** Falak Printing Press, 191 Altaf Hussain Rd, New Challi, Karachi; tel. (21) 5687522; Man. Editor INQUILAB MATRI; Editor ANWAR SANROY.

**Daily Sindh Sujag:** Suite 414, 6th Floor, Amber Medical Centre, M. A. Jinnah Rd, Karachi; tel. (21) 2700252; fax (21) 2700249; e-mail sindhsujag786@yahoo.com; Sindhi; political; Editor NASIR DAD BALOCH.

**Daily Special:** Ahbab Printers, Beauty House, nr Regal Chowk, Abdullah Haroon Rd, Sadar, Karachi; tel. (21) 7771655; fax (21) 7722776; Urdu; Editor MOHAMMAD AT-TAYYAB.

**Daily Times:** Plot No. SR 5/12/1, 2nd Floor, Nelson Chamber, I. I. Chundrigar Rd, Karachi; tel. (21) 2213822; fax (21) 2213874; e-mail sarfaraz@dailytimes.com.pk; internet www.dailytimes.com.pk; Editor NAJAM SETHI.

**Dawn:** Haroon House, Dr Ziauddin Ahmed Rd, POB 3740, Karachi 74200; tel. (21) 111444777; fax (21) 5683801; e-mail editor@dawn.com; internet www.dawn.com; f. 1947; English; also publ. from Islamabad, Rawalpindi and Lahore; Chief Exec. HAMEED HAROON; Editor ABBAS NASIR; circ. 110,000 (weekdays), 125,000 (Sundays).

**Deyanet:** 4th Floor, Al Warid Centre, off I. I. Chundrigar Rd, Karachi; tel. (21) 2631556; fax (21) 2631888; Urdu; also publ. in Sukkur and Islamabad; Editor NAJMUDDIN SHAIKH.

**The Finance:** 903–905 Uni Towers, I. I. Chundrigar Rd, Karachi; tel. (21) 2411665; fax (21) 2422560; e-mail tfinance@super.net.pk; English; Chief Editor S. H. SHAH.

**Financial Daily:** 11-C, Jami Commercial St No. 11, Phase VII, DHA, Karachi; tel. (21) 5311893-5; publ. by Data Research & Communications.

**Financial Post:** Bldg No. 106/C, 11 Commercial St, Phase II, Extension, Defence Housing Authority, Karachi; tel. (21) 5381626; fax (21) 5802760; e-mail fpost@gerrys.net; internet www.dailyfpost.com; f. 1994; English; Chief Editor and CEO QUDSIA K. KHAN; Publr WAJID JAWAD.

**Hilal-e-Pakistan:** Court View Bldg, 2nd Floor, M. A. Jinnah Rd, POB 3737, Karachi 74200; tel. (21) 2624997; fax (21) 2624996; Sindhi; Editor MOHAMMAD IQBAL DAL.

**Jago:** Karachi; tel. (21) 2635544; fax (21) 2628137; f. 1990; Sindhi; political; Editor AGHA SALEEM.

**Janbaz:** 9th Floor, Uni Tower, I. I. Chundrigar Rd, Karachi; tel. (21) 2411665; fax (21) 2422560; Editor ALI AKHBAR RIZVI.

**Jasarat:** 3rd Floor, Syed House, I. I. Chundrigar Rd, Karachi 74200; tel. (21) 2630391; fax (21) 2629344; e-mail jasarat@cyber.net.pk; f. 1970; Urdu; Editor ATHAR HASHMI; circ. 50,000.

PAKISTAN

**Jurat:** Jurat House, off I. I. Chundrigar Rd, Karachi; tel. (21) 2637641-4; fax (21) 2637640; Editor MUKHTAR AAQIL.

**The Leader:** Block 5, 609, Clifton Centre, Clifton, Karachi 75600; tel. (21) 5820801; fax (21) 5872206; e-mail info@theleader.com.pk; f. 1958; English; independent; Man. Editor MUNIR M. LADHA; circ. 7,000.

**Mazdur:** Spencer Bldg, I. I. Chundrigar Rd, Karachi 2; f. 1984; Urdu; Editor MOHAMMAD ANWAR BIN ABBAS.

**Millat:** 3rd Floor, Saify Market, Shahrah-e-Liaquat, New Challi, Karachi; tel. (21) 2219022; fax (21) 2211764; internet www.millat.com; f. 1946; Gujarati; independent; Editor INQUILAB MATRI; circ. 22,550.

**Mohasib:** Karachi; fax (21) 2632763; Urdu; also publ. from Abbotabad; Chief Editor ZAFAR MAJAZI; Editor NAEEM AHMAD.

**The Nation:** Block-I, Hockey Stadium, off Khayaban-e-Shamsher, Phase V, Defence Housing Authority, Karachi; tel. (21) 5846622; fax (21) 5848892; e-mail editor@nation.com.pk; internet www.nation.com.pk; English; Editor ARIF NIZAMI.

**The News International:** Al-Rahman Bldg, I. I. Chundrigar Rd, POB 52, Karachi; tel. (21) 2630611; fax (21) 2418343; e-mail thenewskarachi@thenews.com.pk; f. 1990; English; also publ. from Lahore and Rawalpindi/Islamabad; Editor-in-Chief Mir SHAKIL-UR-RAHMAN; Editor TALAT ASLAM.

**Qaum (Nation):** Karachi; Urdu; Editor and Publr MUSHTAQUE SOHAIL; Man. Editor MAMNOONUR REHMAN.

**Qaumi Akhbar:** 14 Ramzan Mansion, Dr Bilmoria St, off I. I. Chundrigar Rd, Karachi; tel. (21) 2633381; fax (21) 2635774; f. 1988; Urdu; offices in Islamabad; Editor ILYAS SHAKIR.

**Roznama Special:** Falak Printing Press, 191 Altaf Hussain Rd, Karachi; tel. (21) 5687522; fax (21) 5687579; Publr and Man. Editor INQUILAB MATRI; Editor ANWAR SEN ROY.

**Savera:** 108 Adam Arcade, Shaheed-e-Millat Rd, Karachi; tel. (21) 419616; Urdu; Editor RUKHSANA SAHAM MIRZA.

**Sindh Tribune:** No. 246-D/6, PECHS, Karachi; tel. (21) 4535227; fax (21) 4332680; English; political; Editor YOUSUF SHAHEEN.

**The Times of Karachi:** Al-Falah Chambers, 9th Floor, Abdullah Haroon Rd, Karachi; tel. (21) 7727740; e-mail iqbalmir@yahoo.com; evening; English; independent; city news; Editor Mir IQBAL AZIZ.

**Ummat:** Room Nos 1–3, VIP Block IV, Hockey Club of Pakistan Stadium, Liaquat Barracks, Karachi; tel. (21) 5655270; fax (21) 5655275; Editor NASEER HASHMI.

### Lahore

**Daily Asas:** 15/26, Davis Rd, Lahore; tel. (42) 6302823; fax (42) 6317096; e-mail info@dailyasas.com.pk; internet www.dailyasas.com.pk.

**Daily Pakistan:** 41 Jail Rd, Lahore; tel. (42) 7576301; fax (42) 7586251; internet www.daily-pakistan.com; f. 1990; Urdu; Chief Editor MUJIBUR RAHMAN SHAMI.

**Daily Times:** Media Times (Pvt) Ltd, 41-N, Industrial Area, Gulberg II, Lahore; tel. (42) 5878614; fax (42) 5878620; e-mail editor@dailytimes.com.pk; Editor NAJAM SETHI.

**Daily Wifaq:** 6A Warris Rd, Lahore; tel. (42) 6367467; e-mail wifaqtimes@yahoo.com; Urdu; also publ. in Rawalpindi, Sargodha and Rahimyar Khan; Editor MUTAHHIR WAQAR; circ. 50,000.

**Mahgribi Pakistan:** Lahore; tel. (42) 53490; Urdu; also publ. in Bahawalpur and Sukkur; Editor M. SHAFAAT.

**The Nation:** NIPCO House, 4 Sharah-e-Fatima Jinnah, POB 1815, Lahore 54000; tel. (42) 6367580; fax (42) 6367005; e-mail editor@nation.com; internet www.nation.com.pk; f. 1986; English; Chair. MAJEED NIZAMI; Editor ARIF NIZAMI; circ. 52,000.

**Nawa-i-Waqt (Voice of the Time):** 4 Sharah-e-Fatima Jinnah, Lahore 54000; tel. (42) 6367551; fax (42) 6367583; internet www.nawaiwaqt.com.pk; f. 1940; English, Urdu; also publ. edns in Karachi, Islamabad and Multan; Editor MAJID NIZAMI; combined circ. 560,000.

**The Sun International:** 15-L, Gulberg III, Ferozepur Rd, Lahore; tel. (42) 5883540; fax (42) 5839951; Editor MAHMOOD SADIQ.

**Tijarat:** 14 Abbot Rd, opp. Nishat Cinema, Lahore; tel. (42) 6312462; fax (42) 6362767; Urdu; Editor JAMIL ATHAR.

### Rawalpindi

**Daily Jang:** Murree Rd, Rawalpindi; internet www.jang.com.pk; f. 1940; also publ. in Quetta, Karachi, Lahore and London; Urdu; independent; Editor Mir JAVED REHMAN; circ. (Rawalpindi) 65,000.

**Daily Wifaq:** Mohallah Waris Khan 604, Murree Rd, Rawalpindi; tel. (51) 553979; e-mail dailywifaq@hotmail.com; f. 1959; also publ. in Lahore, Sargodha and Rahimyar Khan; Urdu; Editor MUSTAFA SADIQ.

**The News:** Al-Rehman Bldg, Murree Rd, Rawalpindi; tel. (51) 5962444; fax (51) 5962269; e-mail thenews@isb.comsats.net.pk; internet www.jang-group.com; f. 1991; also publ. in Lahore and Karachi; English; independent; Chief Editor Mir SHAKIL-UR-RAHMAN.

### Other Towns

**Aftab:** Opposite WASA Office, Bagh Langay Khan Rd, Multan; tel. (61) 4546080; fax (61) 4786083; e-mail aftabmultan@aftabdaily.com; Sindhi; Editor ASAD MUMTAZ SEYAL.

**Al Falah:** Al Falah House, Al Falah Bazar, nr State Life Bldg, Mall Rd, Peshawar; tel. (91) 5853694; f. 1939; Urdu and Pashtu; Editor SYED BADRUDDIN SHAH.

**Al-Jamiat-e-Sarhad:** Kocha Gilania Chakagali, Karimpura Bazar, Peshawar; tel. (91) 2567757; e-mail sagha@brain.net.pk; f. 1941; Urdu and Pashtu; Propr and Chief Editor S. M. HASSAN GILANI.

**Balochistan Times:** Jinnah Rd, Quetta; Editor SYED FASIH IQBAL.

**Basharat:** Peshawar; Urdu; general; also publ. in Islamabad; Chief Editor ANWAR-UL-HAQ; Editor KHALID ATHER.

**Daily Awaz:** Peshawar; political; Man. Editor ALI RAZA MALIK.

**Daily Business Report:** Railway Rd, Faisalabad; tel. (41) 2642131; fax (41) 2621207; f. 1948; Editor ABDUL RASHID GHAZI; circ. 26,000.

**Daily Hewad:** 32 Stadium Rd, Peshawar; tel. (521) 270501; Pashtu; Editor-in-Chief REHMAN SHAH AFRIDI.

**Daily Ibrat Hyderabad:** Ibrat Building, Gadi Khata, Hyderabad; e-mail ibrat@yahoo.com; internet www.dailyibrat.com; Sindhi; Man. Editor Qazi ASAD ABID.

**Daily Khadim-e-Waten:** B-2, Civil Lines, Hyderabad; Editor MUSHATAQ AHMAD.

**Daily Rehber:** 17-B East Trust Colony, Bahawalpur; tel. (621) 884664; fax (621) 874032; e-mail rehberbwp@yahoo.co.uk; f. 1951; Urdu; Chief Editor AKHTER HUSSAIN ANJUM; circ. 250,000.

**Daily Sarwan:** 11-EGOR Colony, Hyderabad; tel. (221) 781382; Sindhi; Chief Editor GHULAM HUSSAIN.

**Daily Shabaz:** Peshawar; tel. (521) 220188; fax (521) 216483; Urdu; organ of the Awami National Party; Chief Editor Begum NASEEM WALI KHAN.

**Frontier Post:** 32 Stadium Rd, Peshawar; tel. (521) 79174; fax (521) 76575; e-mail editor@frontierpost.com.pk; internet www.frontierpost.com.pk; f. 1985; English; left-wing; also publ. in Lahore; closed down temporarily in January 2001, reopened in June; Editor-in-Chief REHMAT SHAH AFRIDI; Editor MUZAFFAR SHAH AFRIDI.

**Jihad:** 15A Islamia Club Bldg, Khyber Bazar, Peshawar; tel. (521) 210522; e-mail jehad@pes.comsats.net.pk; also publ. in Karachi, Rawalpindi, Islamabad and Lahore; Editor SHARIF FAROOQ.

**Kaleem:** Shahi Bazar, Thalla, POB 88, Sukkur; tel. (71) 5622086; fax (71) 5622087; e-mail kaleemsukkur@yahoo.com; Urdu; Editor SHAHID MEHR SHAMSI.

**Kavish:** Sindh Printing and Publishing House, Civil Lines, POB 43, Hyderabad; Chief Editor MUHAMMAD AYUB QAZI; Publr/Editor ASLAM A. QAZI.

**Mashriq:** Quetta; Chief Editor AZIZ MAZHAR.

**Nawai Asma'n:** Mubarak Ali Shah Rd, Hyderabad; tel. and fax (221) 21925; Urdu, Sindhi and Pashtu; Chief Editor DOST MUHAMMAD.

**The News:** Qaumi Printing Press, Peshawar; English; Editor KHURSHID AHMAD.

**Punjab News:** Iftikhar Heights, Aminpur Bazar, POB 419, Faisalabad; tel. (41) 633102; fax (41) 615731; e-mail imranlateef1@hotmail.com; internet www.punjabnews.com.pk; f. 1968; Chief Editor and Publr Sheikh Sultan MAHMOOD; circ. 10,000.

**Sarhad:** New Gate, Peshawar.

**Sindh Guardian:** Tulsi Das Rd, POB 300, Hyderabad; tel. and fax (221) 21926; English; Chief Editor DOST MUHAMMAD.

**Sindh News:** Garikhata, Hyderabad; tel. (221) 20793; fax (221) 781867; Editor Kazi SAEED AKBER.

**Sindh Observer:** POB 43, Garikhata, Hyderabad; tel. (221) 27302; English; Editor ASLAM AKBER KAZI.

**Sindhu:** Popular Printers, Ibrat Bldg, Garhhi Khata, Hyderabad; tel. (221) 783571; fax (221) 783570; Sindhi; political.

**Watan:** 10 Nazar Bagh Flat, Peshawar.

**Zamana:** Jinnah Rd, Quetta; tel. (81) 71217; Urdu; Editor SYED FASIH IQBAL; circ. 5,000.

### SELECTED WEEKLIES

**Akhbar-e-Jehan:** Printing House, off I. I. Chundrigar Rd, Karachi; tel. (21) 2634368; fax (21) 2635693; e-mail editor-in-chief@akhbar-e-jehan.com; internet www.akhbar-e-jehan.com; f. 1967; Urdu; independent; illustrated family magazine; Editor-in-Chief Mir JAVED RAHMAN; circ. 285,000.

**Amal:** Shah Qabool Colony, POB 185, Peshawar; tel. (91) 5704673; e-mail maab_kaifi@hotmail.com; f. 1958; Urdu, Pashtu and English; Chief Editor F. M. Zafar Kaifi; Publr Munazima Maab Kaifi.

**Badban:** Nai Zindagi Publications, Rana Chambers, Old Anarkali, Lahore; Editor Mujibur Rehman Shami.

**Chatan:** Chatan Bldg, 88 McLeod Rd, Lahore; tel. (42) 6311336; fax (42) 6374690; f. 1948; Urdu; Editor Masud Shorish.

**Family Magazine:** 4 Shara-i-Fatima Jinnah, Lahore 54000; tel. (42) 6367551; fax (42) 6367583; circ. 100,000.

**The Friday Times:** 72-F. C. C. Gulberg IV, Lahore; tel. (42) 5673510; fax (42) 5751025; e-mail tft@lhr.comsats.net.pk; internet www.thefridaytimes.com; independent; Editor/Owner Najam Sethi.

**Hilal:** Hilal Rd, Rawalpindi 46000; tel. (51) 56134605; fax (51) 565017; f. 1951; Friday; Urdu; illustrated armed forces; Editor Mumtaz Iqbal Malik; circ. 90,000.

**Insaf:** P/929, Banni, Rawalpindi 46000; tel. and fax (51) 5550903; e-mail insafrwp@isb.paknet.com.pk; f. 1955; Editor Mir Waqar Aziz.

**Lahore:** Galaxy Law Chambers, 1st Floor, Room 1, Turner Rd, Lahore 5; f. 1952; Editor Saqib Zeervi; circ. 8,500.

**Mahwar:** D23, Block H, North Nazimabad, Karachi; Editor Shahida Nafis Siddiqi.

**Memaar-i-Nao:** 39 KMC Bldg, Leamarket, Karachi; Urdu; labour magazine; Editor M. M. Mubasir.

**The Muslim World:** 49-B, Block 8, Gulshan-e-Iqbal, Karachi 75300; POB 5030, Karachi 74000; tel. (21) 4960738; fax (21) 466878; English; current affairs.

**Nairang Khayal:** 8 Mohammadi Market, Rawalpindi; f. 1924; Urdu; Chief Editor Sultan Rashk.

**Nida-i-Millat:** 4 Sharah-e-Fatima Jinnah, Lahore 54000.

**Noor Jehan Weekly:** 32A National Auto Plaza, POB 8833, Karachi 74400; tel. and fax (21) 7723946; f. 1948; Urdu; film journal; Editor Khalid Chawla.

**Pak Kashmir:** Pak Kashmir Office, Soikarno Chowk, Liaquat Rd, Rawalpindi; tel. (51) 74845; f. 1951; Urdu; Editor Muhammed Fayyaz Abbazi.

**Pakistan and Gulf Economist:** 1st Floor, 20-C, Sunset Lane 9, Phase 2 Extension, D. H. A., Karachi 75500; tel. (21) 5883967; fax (21) 5883295; e-mail information@pakistaneconomist.com; internet www.pakistaneconomist.com; f. 1960; English; Editor Ali Haider Gokal; circ. 30,000.

**Parsi Sansar and Loke Sevak:** 8 Mehrabad, 5 McNeil Rd, Karachi 75530; tel. and fax (21) 5656217; e-mail organ@cyber.net.pk; f. 1909; English and Gujarati; Editor Meherji P. Dastur.

**Parwaz:** Madina Office, Bahawalpur; Urdu; Editor Mustaq Ahmed.

**Qallandar:** Peshawar; f. 1950; Urdu; Editor M. A. K. Sherwani.

**Quetta Times:** Albert Press, Jinnah Rd, Quetta; f. 1924; English; Editor S. Rustomji; circ. 4,000.

**Shahab-e-Saqib:** Shahab Saqib Rd, Maulana St, Peshawar; f. 1950; Urdu; Editor S. M. Rizvi.

**Takbeer:** A-1, 3rd Floor, 'Namco Centre', Campbell St, Karachi 74200; tel. (21) 2626613; fax (21) 2627742; e-mail irfanfaruqi@usa.com; f. 1984; Urdu; Sr. Exec. Irfan Kalim Farooq; circ. 70,000.

**Tarjaman-i-Sarhad:** Peshawar; Urdu and Pashtu; Editor Mohammad Shafi Sabir.

**Times of Kashmir:** P/929, Banni, Rawalpindi 46000; tel. (51) 5550903; fax (51) 4411348; e-mail insafrwp@isb.paknet.com.pk; f. 1982; English; Editor Mir Iqbal Aziz.

**Ufaq:** 44H, Block No. 2, PECHS, Karachi; tel. (21) 437992; f. 1978; Editor Wahajuddin Chishti; circ. 2,000.

## SELECTED PERIODICALS

**Aadab Arz:** 190 N. Ghazali Rd, Saman Abad, Lahore 54500; tel. (42) 7582449; monthly; Editor Khalid bin Hamid.

**Aalami Digest:** B-1, Momin Sq., Rashid Minhas Rd, Gulshan-e-Iqbal, Karachi; monthly; Urdu; Editor Zaheda Hina.

**Akhbar-e-Watan:** 68-C, 13th Commercial St, Phase-II, Extension Defence, Karachi; tel. (21) 5886071; fax (21) 5890179; e-mail akhbarewatan@hotmail.com; f. 1977; monthly; Urdu; cricket; Man. Editor Munir Hussain; circ. 63,000.

**Albalagh Darul Uloom:** Korangi Rd, Karachi; monthly; Editor Mohammed Taqi Usmani.

**Al-Ma'arif:** Institute of Islamic Culture, Club Rd, Lahore 54000; tel. (42) 6363127; f. 1950; quarterly; Urdu; Dir and Editor-in-Chief Dr Rashid Ahmad Jallandhri.

**Anchal:** 24 Saeed Mansion, I. I. Chundrigar Rd, Karachi; monthly.

**Archi Times:** B-34, Block 15, Gulshan-e-Iqbal, Karachi; tel. (21) 4977652; fax (21) 4967656; e-mail archtime@cyberaccess.com.pk; internet www.archpresspk.com; f. 1986; monthly; English; architecture; Editor Mujtaba Hussain.

**Architecture and Interiors:** B-34, Block 15, Gulshan-e-Iqbal, Karachi; tel. (21) 4977652; fax (21) 4967656; e-mail aplusi@cyberaccess.com.pk; internet www.archpresspk.com; f. 2001; quarterly; English; Editor Mutjuba Hussain; Man. Editor Murtuza Shikoh.

**Asia Travel News:** 101 Muhammadi House, I. I. Chundrigar Rd, Karachi 74000; tel. (21) 2424837; fax (21) 2420797; fortnightly; travel trade, tourism and hospitality industry; Editor Javed Mushtaq.

**Auto Times:** 5 S. J. Kayani Shaheed Rd, off Garden Rd, Karachi; tel. (21) 713595; fortnightly; English; Editor Muhammad Shahzad.

**Bachoon Ka Risala:** 108–110 Adam Arcade, Shaheed-e-Millat Rd, Karachi; tel. (21) 419616; monthly; Urdu; Editor Rukhsana Seham Mirza.

**Bagh:** 777/18 Federal B Area, POB 485, Karachi; tel. (21) 449662; monthly; Urdu; Editor Rahil Iqbal.

**Bayyenat:** Jamia Uloom-e-Islamia, Binnori Town, Karachi 74800; tel. (21) 4927233; f. 1962; monthly; Urdu; religious and social issues.

**Beauty:** Plot No. 4-C, 14th Commercial St, Defence Housing Authority, Phase II Extension, Karachi; tel. (21) 5805391; fax (21) 5896269; e-mail rmansuri@fascom.com; f. 2000; bi-monthly; English; Chief Editor Riaz Ahmed Mansuri.

**Beemakar** (Insurer): 58 Press Chambers, I. I. Chundrigar Rd, Karachi; e-mail tahakn@cyber.net.pk; f. 1990; monthly; Urdu; Man. Editor Shamshad Ahmad; Editor Ayaz Khan.

**Chand:** 190 N. Ghazali Rd, Saman Abad, Lahore 54500; tel. (42) 7582449; monthly; Editor Masood Hamid.

**The Cricketer:** Plot No. 4-C, 14th Commercial St, Defence Housing Authority, Phase II Extension, Karachi; tel. (21) 5805391; fax (21) 5896269; e-mail rmansuri@fascom.com; f. 1972; monthly; English/Urdu; Chief Editor Riaz Ahmed Mansuri.

**Dastarkhuan:** Plot No. 4-C, 14th Commercial St, Defence Housing Authority, Phase II Extension, Karachi; tel. (21) 5805391; fax (21) 5896269; e-mail rmansuri@fascom.com; f. 1998; bi-monthly; Urdu; Chief Editor Riaz Ahmed Mansuri.

**Defence Journal:** 16B, 7th Central St, Defence Housing Authority, POB 12234, Karachi 75500; tel. (21) 5894074; fax (21) 571710; f. 1975; monthly; English; Editor-in-Chief Ikram Sehgal; circ. 10,000.

**Dentist:** 70/7, Nazimabad No. 3, Karachi 18; f. 1984; monthly; English and Urdu; Editor Naeemullah Husain.

**Dosheeza:** 108–110 Adam Arcade, Shaheed-e-Millat Rd, Karachi; tel. (21) 4930470; fax (21) 4934369; monthly; Urdu; Editor Rukhsana Seham Mirza.

**Duniya-e-Tibb:** Eveready Chambers, 2nd Floor, Mohd Bin Qasim Rd, off I. I. Chundrigar Rd, POB 1385, Karachi 1; tel. (21) 2630985; fax (21) 2637624; e-mail mcm@digicom.net.pk; f. 1986; monthly; Urdu; modern and Asian medicine; Editor Qutubuddin; circ. 12,000.

**Economic Review:** Al-Masiha, 3rd Floor, 47 Abdullah Haroon Rd, POB 7843, Karachi 74400; tel. (21) 7728963; fax (21) 7728957; f. 1969; monthly; economic, industrial and investment research; Editor Ahmad Muhammad Khan.

**Engineering Horizons:** 13-J, Markaz F-7, Islamabad 44000; tel. (51) 2650174; fax (51) 2650943; e-mail asad@imtiaz-faiz.com; internet www.engghorizons.com; f. 1988; monthly; English; Chief Editor Imtiaz Sheikh.

**Engineering Review:** 305 Spotlit Chambers, Dr Billimoria St, off I. I. Chundrigar Rd, POB 807, Karachi 74200; tel. (21) 2632567; fax (21) 2639378; e-mail engineeringreview@yahoo.com; internet www.engineeringreview.com.pk; f. 1975; fortnightly; English; circ. 5,000.

**Film Asia:** 68-C, 13th Commercial St, Phase-II, Extension Defence, Karachi; tel. (21) 5886071; fax (21) 5890179; e-mail akhbarewatan@hotmail.com; f. 1973; monthly; film, television, fashion, art and culture; Man. Editor Munir Hussain; circ. 38,000.

**Good Food:** Plot No. 4-C, 14th Commercial St, Defence Housing Authority, Phase II Extension, Karachi; tel. (21) 5805391; fax (21) 5896269; e-mail rmansuri@fascom.com; f. 1997; bi-monthly; English; Chief Editor Riaz Ahmed Mansuri.

**Hamdard-i-Sehat:** Institute of Health and Tibbi Research, Hamdard Foundation Pakistan, Nazimabad, Karachi 74600; tel. (21) 6616001; fax (21) 6611755; e-mail hamdardfoundation@hamdard.com.pk; f. 1933; monthly; Urdu; Editor-in-Chief Sadia Rashid; circ. 13,000.

**Hamdard Islamicus:** Hamdard Foundation Pakistan, Nazimabad, Karachi 74600; tel. (21) 6620949-54; fax (21) 6611755; e-mail hamdardfoundation@hamdard.com.pk; internet hamdardfoundation.org; f. 1978; quarterly; English; Editor-in-Chief Sadia Rashid; Dir-Gen. Furqan Ahmad Shamsi; circ. 750.

**Hamdard Medicus:** Hamdard Foundation Pakistan, Nazimabad, Karachi 74600; tel. (21) 6620949-54; fax (21) 6611755; e-mail hamdardfoundation@hamdard.com.pk; internet hamdardfoundation.org; f. 1957; quarterly; English; Editor-in-Chief Sadia Rashid; Dir-Gen. Furqan Ahmad Shamsi; circ. 1,000.

**Hamdard Naunehal:** Hamdard Foundation Pakistan, Nazimabad, Karachi 74600; tel. (21) 6620949-54; fax (21) 6611755; e-mail hamdardfoundation@hamdard.com.pk; internet hamdardfoundation.org; f. 1952; monthly; Urdu; Editor MASOOD AHMAD BARAKATI; Dir-Gen. FURQAN AHMAD SHAMSI; circ. 34,000.

**The Herald:** Haroon House, Dr Ziauddin Ahmed Rd, Karachi 74200; tel. (21) 5670001; fax (21) 5687221; e-mail saquib.herald@dawn.com; f. 1970; monthly; English; Editor SAQUIB HANIF; circ. 38,000.

**Hikayat:** 26 Patiala Ground, Link McLeod Rd, Lahore; monthly; Editor SHAHID JAMIL; circ. 25,000.

**Honhar-e-Pakistan:** 56 Aurangzeb Market, Karachi; monthly; Editor MAZHAR YUSAFZAI.

**Hoor:** Hoor St, Lahore; monthly; Editor KHULA RABIA.

**Islami Jumhuria:** Laj Rd, Old Anarkali, Lahore; monthly; Editor NAZIR TARIQ.

**Islamic Studies:** Islamic Research Institute, Faisal Masjid Campus, POB 1035, Islamabad 44000; tel. (51) 850751; fax (51) 250821; e-mail amzia555@apollo.net.pk; f. 1962; quarterly; English, Urdu (Fikro-Nazar) and Arabic (Al Dirasat al-Islamiyyah) edns; Islamic literature, religion, history, geography, language and the arts; Editor Dr ZAFAR ISHAQ ANSARI (acting); circ. 3,000.

**Jamal:** Institute of Islamic Culture, 2 Club Rd, Lahore 54000; tel. (42) 6363127; f. 1950; annual; English; Dir and Editor-in-Chief Dr JULUNDHRI RASHEED.

**Journal of the Pakistan Historical Society:** Bait al-Hikmah, Hamdard University, Muhammad Bin Qasim Ave, Karachi, 74700; tel. (21) 6616001; fax (21) 6611755; e-mail phs@hamdard.edu.pk; f. 1953; quarterly; English; Editor Dr ANSAR ZAHID KHAN; circ. 700.

**Khel-Ke-Duniya:** 6/13 Alyusaf Chamber, POB 340, Karachi; tel. (21) 216888.

**Khwateen Digest:** Urdu Bazar, M. A. Jinnah Rd, Karachi; monthly; Urdu; Editor MAHMUD RIAZ.

**Kiran:** 37 Urdu Bazar, M. A. Jinnah Rd, Karachi; tel. (21) 216606; Editor MAHMUD BABAR FAISAL.

**Leather News:** Iftikhar Chambers, opp. UNI Plaza, Altaf Hussain Rd, POB 4323, Karachi 74000; fax (21) 2631545; f. 1989; Editor ABDUL RAFAY SIDDIQI.

**Ma'arif Feature:** D-35, Block 5, Federal 'B' Area, Karachi 75950; tel. (21) 6349840; fax (21) 6361040; e-mail irak63@gmail.com; f. 1999; journal of the Islamic Research Acad; fortnightly; Urdu; Editor SYED SHAHID HASHMI.

**Medical Variety:** 108–110 Adam Arcade, Shaheed-e-Millat Rd, Karachi; tel. (21) 419616; monthly; English; Editor RUKHSANA SEHAM MIRZA.

**Muslim World Business:** 20 Sasi Arcade, 4th Floor, Main Clifton Rd, POB 10417, Karachi 6; tel. (21) 534870; f. 1989; monthly; English; political and business; Editor-in-Chief MUZAFFAR HASSAN.

**Naey-Ufaq:** 24 Saeed Mansion, I. I. Chundrigar Rd, Karachi; fortnightly.

**NGM Communication:** POB 3540, Post Mall, Gulberg, Lahore 54660; tel. (42) 5879524; e-mail anjeeam@yahoo.com; internet www.geocities.com/anjeeam; f. 1980; owned by Nizam Nizami; English; lists newly released Pakistani publications on the internet; updated weekly; Editor GHUFRAN NIZAMI.

**Pakistan Journal of Applied Economics:** Applied Economics Research Centre, University of Karachi, POB 8403, Karachi 75270; tel. (21) 9243168; fax (21) 4829730; e-mail pjae@aerc.edu.pk; internet www.aerc.edu.pk; twice a year; Editor Prof. Dr SHAHIDA WIZARAT.

**Pakistan Journal of Scientific and Industrial Research:** Pakistan Council of Scientific and Industrial Research, Scientific Information Centre, PCSIR Laboratories Campus, off University Rd, Karachi 75280; tel. (21) 4651740; fax (21) 4651738; e-mail pcsir@cyber.net.pk; f. 1958; bi-monthly; English; Exec. Editor Dr KANIZ FIZZA AZHAR; circ. 1,000.

**Pakistan Management Review:** Pakistan Institute of Management, Management House, Shahrah Iran, Clifton, Karachi 75600; tel. (21) 9251711; e-mail pimkhi@pim.com.pk; internet www.pim.com.pk; f. 1960; quarterly; English; Editor IQBAL A. QAZI.

**Pasban:** Faiz Modh Rd, Quetta; fortnightly; Urdu; Editor MOLVI MOHD ABDULLAH.

**Phool:** 4 Sharah-e-Fatima Jinnah, Lahore 54000; tel. (42) 6314099; fax (42) 6367616; e-mail editor@phool.com.pk; internet www.phool.com.pk; f. 1989; monthly; children's; Chief Editor MAJID NIZAMI; Editor MUHAMMAD SHOAIB MIRZA; circ. 50,000.

**Progress:** 4th Floor, PIDC House, Dr Ziauddin Ahmed Rd, Karachi 75530; tel. (21) 111-568-568; fax (21) 5680005; e-mail h_saquib@ppl.com.pk; f. 1956; monthly; publ. by Pakistan Petroleum Ltd; Editor and Publr NUSRAT NASARULLAH; Chief Exec./Man. Dir S. MUNSIF RAZA.

**Qaumi Digest:** 50 Lower Mall, Lahore; tel. (42) 7225143; fax (42) 7233261; monthly; Editor MUJIBUR REHMAN SHAMI.

**Sabrang Digest:** 47–48 Press Chambers, I. I. Chundrigar Rd, Karachi 1; tel. (21) 211961; f. 1970; monthly; Urdu; Editor SHAKEEL ADIL ZADAH; circ. 150,000.

**Sach-Chee Kahaniyan:** 108–110 Adam Arcade, Shaheed-e-Millat Rd, Karachi; tel. (21) 4930470; fax (21) 4934369; monthly; Urdu; Editor RUKHSANA SEHAM MIRZA.

**Sayyarah:** Aiwan-e-Adab, Urdu Bazar, Lahore 54000; tel. (42) 7321842; f. 1962; monthly; Urdu; literary; Man. Editor HAFEEZ-UR-RAHMAN AHSAN.

**Sayyarah Digest:** 244, Main Market Riwaz Garden, Lahore 54000; tel. (42) 7245412; fax (42) 7325080; e-mail sayyaradigest@brain.com.pk; f. 1963; monthly; Urdu; Chief Editor AMJAD RAUF KHAN; Editor KAMRAN AMJAD KHAN; circ. 40,000.

**Science Magazine:** Science Book Foundation, Haji Bldg, Hassan Ali Efendi Rd, Karachi; tel. (21) 2625647; monthly; Urdu; Editor QASIM MAHMOOD.

**Seep:** Alam Market, Block No. 16, Federal B Area, Karachi; quarterly; Editor NASIM DURRANI.

**Show Business:** 108–110 Adam Arcade, Shaheed-e-Millat Rd, POB 12540, Karachi; tel. (21) 419616; monthly; Urdu; Editor RUKHSANA SEHAM MIRZA.

**Sindh Quarterly:** 36D Karachi Administrative Co-operative Housing Society, off Shaheed-e-Millat Rd, Karachi 75350; tel. (21) 4531988; f. 1973; Editor SAYID GHULAM MUSTAFA SHAH.

**Smash:** Plot No. 4-C, 14th Commercial St, Defence Housing Authority, Phase II Extension, Karachi; tel. (21) 5805391; fax (21) 5896269; e-mail mansuri@fascom.com; f. 2000; monthly; English; Chief Editor RIAZ AHMED MANSURI.

**Spider:** Haroon House, Dr Ziauddin Ahmed Rd, Karachi 74200; tel. (21) 111-444-777; fax (21) 5681544; e-mail spider@spider.tm; internet www.spider.tm; f. 1998; internet monthly; Editor ALI AHSAN HALAI; CEO HAMEED HAROON.

**Sports International:** Arshi Market, Firdaus Colony, Nazimabad, Karachi 74600; tel. (21) 6602171; fax (21) 6683768; e-mail ibp-khi@cyber.net.pk; f. 1972; fortnightly; Urdu and English; Chief Editor KANWAR ABDUL MAJEED; Editor RAHEEL MAJEED.

**Taj:** Jamia Tajia, St 13, Sector 14/B, Buffer Zone, Karachi 75850; monthly; Editor BABA M. ATIF SHAH ANWARI ZAHEENI TAJI.

**Talimo Tarbiat:** Ferozsons (Pvt) Ltd, 60 Shahrah-e-Quaid-e-Azam, Lahore 54000; tel. (42) 6301196; fax (42) 6369204; f. 1941; children's monthly; Urdu; Chief Editor A. SALAM; circ. 50,000.

**Textile Times:** Arshi Market, Firdaus Colony, Nazimabad, Karachi 74600; tel. (21) 6683768; e-mail ibp-khi@cyber.net.pk; f. 1993; monthly; English; Chief Editor KANWAR ABDUL MAJEED; Exec. Editor RAHEEL MAJEED KHAN.

**Trade Chronicle:** Iftikhar Chambers, Altaf Hussain Rd, POB 5257, Karachi 74000; tel. (21) 2631587; fax (21) 2635007; e-mail arsidiqi@fascom.com; f. 1953; monthly; English; trade, politics, finance and economics; Editor ABDUL RAB SIDDIQI; circ. 6,000.

**Trade Link International:** Zahoor Mansion, Tariq Rd, Karachi; monthly; English; Man. Editor M. IMRAN BAIG; Editor IKRAMULLAH QUREISHI.

**TV Times:** Plot No. 4-C, 14th Commercial St, Defence Housing Authority, Phase II Extension, Karachi; tel. (21) 5805391; fax (21) 5896269; e-mail rmansuri@fascom.com; f. 1987; monthly; English; Chief Editor RIAZ AHMED MANSURI.

**UNESCO Payami:** 30 UNESCO House, Sector H-8/1, Islamabad; tel. (51) 434196; fax (51) 431815; monthly; Urdu; publ. by Pakistan National Commission for UNESCO; Editor Dr MUNIR A. ABRO.

**Urdu Digest:** 21-Acre Scheme, Samanabad, Lahore 54500; tel. (42) 7589957; fax (42) 7563646; e-mail urdudigest42@hotmail.com; monthly; Urdu; Editor ALTAF HASAN QURESHEE.

**Voice of Islam:** Jamiatul Falah Bldg, Akbar Rd, Saddar, POB 7141, Karachi 74400; tel. (21) 7721394; f. 1952; monthly; Islamic Cultural Centre magazine; English; Editor Prof. ABDUL QADEER SALEEM; Man. Editor Prof. WAQAR ZUBAIRI.

**Wings:** 101 Muhammadi House, I. I. Chundrigar Rd, Karachi 74000; tel. (21) 2412591; fax (21) 2420797; monthly; aviation and defence; English; Editor and Publr JAVED MUSHTAQ.

**Women's Own:** Plot No. 4-C, 14th Commercial St, Defence Housing Authority, Phase II Extension, Karachi; tel. (21) 5805391; fax (21) 5896269; e-mail rmansuri@fascom.com; f. 1987; monthly; English; Chief Editor RIAZ AHMED MANSURI.

**Yaqeen International:** Darut Tasnif (Pvt) Ltd, Main Hub River Rd, Mujahidabad, Karachi 75760; tel. (21) 2814432; fax (21) 2811304; e-mail daruttasnif@yaqeendtl.com; internet www.yaqeendtl.com; f. 1952; English and Arabic; Islamic organ; Editor Dr HAFIZ MUHAMMAD ADIL.

**Yaran-e-Watan:** Overseas Pakistanis Foundation, Shahrah-e-Jamhuriate, G-5/2, POB 1470, Islamabad 44000; tel. (51) 9224518; fax

(51) 9211613; e-mail yw@opf.org.pk; f. 1982; monthly; Urdu; publ. by the Overseas Pakistanis Foundation; Editor TANVIR HUSSAIN.

**Youth World International:** 104/C Central C/A, Tariq Rd, Karachi; tel. (21) 442211; f. 1987; monthly; English; Editor SYED ADIL EBRAHIM.

### NEWS AGENCIES

**Associated Press of Pakistan (APP):** 18 Mauve Area, Zero Point, G-7/1, POB 1258, Islamabad; tel. (51) 2203073; fax (51) 2203074; e-mail news@app.com.pk; internet app.com.pk; f. 1948; Man. Dir GHULAM HAZOOR BAJWA.

**National News Agency (NNA):** 491-C, Margalla Town, Islamabad 45510; tel. (51) 2840896; fax (51) 2841746; e-mail nnaisb@yahoo.com; f. 1990; Chief Editor SUHAIL ILYAS.

**News Network International:** 2nd Floor, Redco Plaza, Islamabad 44000; tel. (51) 2874344; fax (51) 2826289; e-mail nni2005@isb.paknet.com.pk; internet www.nni-news.com; f. 1992; independent international news agency; news in Arabic, Urdu and English; provides services to 435 newspapers and radio and television channels in South Asia, Europe, the Middle East, the Far East and the USA; Editor-in-Chief QAISAR JAVED; Editor MUHAMMAD TAHIR KHAN.

**Pakistan—International Press Agency (PPA):** 6, St 39, G-6/2, Islamabad 44000; tel. (51) 2279830; fax (51) 2272405; e-mail ppapublications@gawab.com; f. 1991; Urdu; Chief Editor KHALID ATHAR.

**Pakistan Press International (PPI):** Press Centre, Shahrah Kamal Atatürk, POB 541, Karachi; tel. (21) 2623215; fax (21) 2217069; e-mail ppi@ppinewsagency.com; f. 1956; pvt ltd co; Chair. OWAIS ASLAM ALI.

**United Press of Pakistan (Pvt) Ltd (UPP):** 1 Victoria Chambers, Haji Abdullah Haroon Rd, Karachi 74400; tel. (21) 2822738; fax (21) 5682694; e-mail pnrupp2000@yahoo.com; f. 1949; Man. Editor MAHMUDUL AZIZ; 5 brs.

### PRESS ASSOCIATIONS

**All Pakistan Newspaper Employees Confederation:** Karachi Press Club, M. R. Kayani Rd, Karachi; f. 1976; confed. of all press industry trade unions; Pres. MAZHAR ABBAS; Sec.-Gen. PERVAIZ SHAUKAT.

**All Pakistan Newspapers Society:** 32 Farid Chambers, Abdullah Haroon Rd, POB 74400, Karachi 3; tel. (21) 5671256; fax (21) 5671310; e-mail theapns@gmail.com; internet www.apns.com.pk; f. 1949; Pres. HAMEED HAROON; Sec.-Gen. MUHAMMAD ASLAM KAZI.

**Council of Pakistan Newspaper Editors:** c/o United Press of Pakistan, 1 Victoria Chambers, Haji Abdullah Haroon Rd, Karachi 74400; tel. and fax (21) 5682694; Pres. SYED FASEIH IQBAL; Sec.-Gen. WAMIQ A. ZUBERI.

**Pakistan Press Foundation:** Press Centre, Shahrah Kamal Ataturk, Karachi 74200; tel. (21) 2633215; fax (21) 2217069; e-mail ppf@pakistanpressfoundation.org; internet www.pakistanpressfoundation.org; f. 1967; independent media research and training centre for promotion of press freedom; Sec.-Gen. OWAIS ASLAM ALI.

## Publishers

**Alhamra Publishing:** Al-Babar Centre, Office 6, 1st Floor, F-8 Markaz, Islamabad 44000; tel. (51) 2818033; fax (51) 2818076; e-mail contact@alhamra.com; internet www.alhamra.com; f. 2000; publs broad range of subjects incl. fiction, literary criticism, languages, history, education and religion in Urdu and English translations; Man. Dir SHAFIQ NAZ.

**Anjuman Taraqq-e-Urdu Pakistan:** D-159, Block 7, Gulshan-e-Iqbal, Karachi 75300; tel. (21) 461406; f. 1903; literature, religion, textbooks, Urdu dictionaries, literary and critical texts; Pres. AFTAB AHMED KHAN; Hon. Sec. JAMIL UDDIN AALI.

**Camran Publishers:** Jalaluddin Hospital Bldg, Circular Rd, Lahore; f. 1964; general, technical, textbooks; Propr ABDUL HAMID.

**Chronicle Publications:** Iftikhar Chambers, Altaf Hussain Rd, POB 5257, Karachi 74000; tel. (21) 2631587; fax (21) 2635007; e-mail arsidiqi@fascom.com; f. 1953; reference, directories, religious books; Dir ABDUL RAUF SIDDIQI.

**Dasnavi Book House:** Book St, G-6, Mazang Rd, Lahore; tel. (42) 2231518; e-mail bookhome@hotmail.com.

**Economic and Industrial Publications:** Al-Masiha, 3rd Floor, 47 Abdullah Haroon Rd, POB 7843, Karachi 74400; tel. (21) 7728963; fax (21) 7728434; f. 1965; industrial, economic and investment research.

**Elite Publishers Ltd:** D-118, SITE, Karachi 75700; tel. (21) 2573435; fax (21) 2564720; e-mail elite@elite.com.pk; internet www.elite.com.pk; f. 1951; general commercial printing and packaging; Chair. AHMED MIRZA JAMIL; Chief Exec. KHALID JAMIL.

**Ferozsons (Pvt) Ltd:** 60 Shahrah-e-Quaid-e-Azam, Lahore; tel. (42) 111-626-262; fax (42) 6369204; e-mail support@ferozsons.com.pk; internet www.ferozsons.com.pk; f. 1894; general books, school books, periodicals, maps, atlases, stationery products; Man. Dir ZAHEER SALAM; Dir (Business Development) MUQEET SALAM.

**Fiction House:** 18, Mozang House, Lahore; publs quarterly social science journal Tareekh.

**Frontier Publishing Co:** 12-13, Bank Sq. Market, Model Town, Lahore; tel. (42) 5884713; fax (42) 7247323; e-mail asim@fpcpk.com; internet www.fpcpk.com; f. 1951; academic and general; Dirs ASIM MUHAMMAD, ARIF MUHAMMAD.

**Sh. Ghulam Ali and Sons (Pvt) Ltd:** 199 Circular Rd, Lahore 54000; tel. (42) 7352908; fax (42) 6315478; e-mail niazasad@hotmail.com; internet www.ghulamali.com.pk; f. 1887; general, religion, technical, textbooks; Dirs NIAZ AHMAD, ASAD NIAZ.

**Harf Academy:** G/307, Amena Plaza, Peshawar Rd, Rawalpindi.

**Idara Taraqqi-i-Urdu:** S-1/363 Saudabad, Karachi 27; f. 1949; general literature, technical and professional books and magazines; Propr IKRAM AHMED.

**Ilmi Kitab Khana:** Kabeer St, Urdu Bazar, Lahore; tel. (42) 62833; f. 1948; technical, professional, historical and law; Propr Haji SARDAR MOHAMMAD.

**INAYAT Sons:** YMCA Bldg, 16 The Mall, Lahore 54000; tel. (42) 8401335; fax (42) 7231896; e-mail general@inayatsons.com; internet www.inayatsons.com; f. 1971; Propr S. PERVEZ.

**Indus Publications:** 25 Fared Chambers, Abdullah Haroon Rd, Karachi; tel. (21) 5660242; e-mail muzaffar_indus@hotmail.com; f. 1959; printers, publishers and importers of books; Dir AATIF SAFDAR.

**Islamic Book Centre:** 25B Masson Rd, POB 1625, Lahore 54000; tel. (42) 6361803; fax (42) 6360955; e-mail lsaeed@paknetl.ptc.pk; religion in Arabic, Urdu and English; Islamic history, textbooks, dictionaries and reprints; Propr and Man. Dir SUMBLEYNA SAJID SAEED.

**Islamic Publications (Pvt) Ltd:** 3 Court St, Lower Mall, Lahore 54000; tel. (42) 7248676; fax (42) 7214974; e-mail islamicpak@hotmail.com; internet www.islamicpak.com.pk; f. 1959; Islamic literature in Urdu and English; Man. Dir Prof. MUHAMMAD AMIN JAVED; Gen. Man. AMANAT ALI.

**Jamiatul Falah Publications:** Jamiatul Falah Bldg, Akbar Rd, Saddar, POB 7141, Karachi 74400; tel. (21) 7721394; f. 1952; Islamic history and culture; Pres. MUZAFFAR AHMED HASHMI; Sec. Prof. SHAHZADUL HASAN CHISHTI.

**Kazi Publications:** 121 Zulqarnain Chambers, Ganpat Rd, POB 1845, Lahore; tel. (42) 7311359; fax (42) 7350805; e-mail kazipublications@hotmail.com; internet www.brain.net.pk/~kazip; f. 1978; Islamic literature, religion, law, biographies; Propr/Man. MUHAMMAD IKRAM SIDDIQI; Chief Editor MUHAMMAD ASIM BILAL.

**Lark Publishers:** Urdu Bazar, Karachi 1; f. 1955; general literature, magazines; Propr MAHMOOD RIAZ.

**Liberty Books (Pvt) Ltd:** 3 Rafiq Plaza, M. R. Kayani Rd, Saddar, Karachi; tel. (21) 5683026; fax (21) 5684319; e-mail libooks@cyber.net.pk; internet www.libertybooks.com; f. 1980.

**Lion Art Press (Pvt) Ltd:** 112 Shahrah-e-Quaid-e-Azam, Lahore 54000; tel. (42) 6304444; fax (42) 6367728; e-mail lionart786@hotmail.com; f. 1919; general publs in English and Urdu; Chief Exec. KHALID A. SHEIKH; Dir ASMA KHALID.

**Maktaba Darut Tasnif:** Main Hub River Rd, Mujahidabad, Karachi 75760; tel. (21) 2814432; fax (21) 2811307; e-mail daruttasnif@yaqeendtl.com; internet www.yaqeendtl.com; f. 1951; Koran Majeed and Islamic literature; Dir ABDUL BAQI FAROOQI.

**Malik Sirajuddin & Sons:** 48-C, Lower Mall, Lahore 54000; tel. (42) 7225809; fax (42) 7225806; e-mail sirajco@brain.net.pk; f. 1905; general, religion, law, textbooks; Man. MALIK ABDUL ROUF.

**Malik Sons:** Karkhana Bazar, Faisalabad.

**Medina Publishing Co:** M. A. Jinnah Rd, Karachi 1; f. 1960; general literature, textbooks; Propr HAKIM MOHAMMAD TAQI.

**Mehtab Co:** Ghazni St, Urdu Bazar, Lahore; tel. (42) 7120071; fax (42) 7353489; e-mail shashraf@brain.net.pk; f. 1978; Islamic literature; Propr SHAHZAD RIAZ SHEIKH.

**Mohammad Hussain and Sons:** 17 Urdu Bazar, Lahore 2; tel. (42) 7244114; f. 1941; religion, textbooks; Partners MOHAMMAD HUSSAIN, AZHAR ALI SHEIKH, PERVEZ ALI SHEIKH.

**Sh. Muhammad Ashraf:** 7 Aibak Rd, New Anarkali, Lahore 7; tel. (42) 7353171; fax (42) 7353489; e-mail shashraf@brain.net.pk; f. 1923; books in English on all aspects of Islam; Man. Dir SHAHZAD RIAZ SHEIKH.

**National Book Service:** 22 Urdu Bazar, Lahore; tel. (42) 7247310; fax (42) 7247323; e-mail fpc_pak@hotmail.com; internet www.fpcpk.com; f. 1950; academic and primary, secondary and ELT school books; Execs MUHAMMAD ARIF, MUHAMMAD AMIR, MUHAMMAD ASIM.

**Oxford University Press:** Plot No. 38, Sector 15, Korangi Industrial Area, Karachi; tel. (21) 111-693-673; fax (21) 5055071; e-mail oup.pk@oup.com; internet www.oup.com.pk; academic, educational and general; Man. Dir AMEENA SAIYID.

**Pakistan Law House:** Pakistan Chowk, POB 90, Karachi 1; tel. (21) 2212455; fax (21) 2627549; e-mail plh_law_house@hotmail.com; f. 1950; importers and exporters of legal books and reference books; Man. K. NOORANI.

**Pakistan Publishing House:** Victoria Chambers 2, A. Haroon Rd, Karachi 75400; tel. (21) 5681457; fax (21) 5682036; e-mail danyalbooks@hotmail.com; f. 1959; Propr HOORI NOORANI; Gen. Man. AAMIR HUSSEIN.

**Paramount Books:** 152/0, Block 2, PECHS, Karachi 75400; tel. (21) 4310030; e-mail paramount@cyber.net.pk.

**Pioneer Book House:** 1 Avan Lodge, Bunder Rd, POB 37, Karachi; periodicals, gazettes, maps and reference works in English, Urdu and other regional languages.

**Premier Bookhouse:** Shahin Market, Room 2, Anarkali, POB 1888, Lahore; tel. (42) 7321174; Islamic and law.

**Publishers United (Pvt) Ltd:** c/o Gulam Ali Medicine Market, Chowk Lohari Gate, POB 1689, Lahore 54000; tel. (42) 6361306; fax (42) 6316015; e-mail smalipub2@hotmail.com; f. 1950; Islamic studies, history, art, archaeology, literature, Oriental studies, genealogy, scientific, medical, humanities and social sciences; Man. Dir ASAD NIAZ.

**Punjab Religious Books Society:** Anarkali, Lahore 2; tel. (42) 54416; educational, religious, law and general; Gen. Man. A. R. IRSHAD; Sec. NAEEM SHAKIR.

**Reprints Ltd:** 16 Bahadur Shah Market, M. A. Jinnah Rd, Karachi; f. 1983; Pakistani edns of foreign works; Chair. A. D. KHALID; Man. Dir AZIZ KHALID.

**Royal Book Co:** BG-5, Rex Centre, Basement, Fatima Jinnah Rd, Karachi 75530; tel. (21) 5653418; e-mail royalbook@hotmail.com.

**Sang-e-Meel Publications:** 25 Lower Mall, Lahore 54000; tel. (42) 7220100; fax (42) 7245101; e-mail smp@sang-e-meel.com; internet www.sang-e-meel.com; f. 1962; Marketing and Sales Exec. ALI KAMRAN.

**Say Publishing (Pvt) Ltd:** SAI-3, Shahnawaz Arcade, Shahid-e-Millat Rd, Karachi; tel. (21) 4129552; e-mail saybooks@gerry.net.

**Sindhi Adabi Board** (Sindhi Literary and Publishing Organization): Hyderabad; tel. (221) 771276; e-mail sindhiab@yahoo.com; f. 1951; history, literature, culture of Sindh; in Sindhi, Urdu, English, Persian and Arabic; translations into Sindhi, especially of literature and history; chaired by Minister of Education and Literacy, Sindh; Sec. INAM SHEIKH.

**Taj Co Ltd:** Manghopir Rd, POB 530, Karachi; tel. (21) 294221; f. 1929; religious books; Man. Dir A. H. KHOKHAR.

**The Times Press (Pvt) Ltd:** C-18, Al-Hilal Society, off University Rd, Karachi 74800; tel. (21) 4932931; fax (21) 4935602; e-mail timekhi@cyber.net.pk; internet www.timespress.8m.com; f. 1948; printers, publishers and stationery manufacturers, incl. security printing (postal stationery and stamps); registered publishers of Koran, school textbooks, etc.; Dir S. M. MINHAJUDDIN.

**Tooba Publishers:** 85 Sikandar Block, Allama Iqbal Town, Lahore; tel. (42) 5410185; e-mail haroonkallem@hotmail.com; f. 1983; poetry; Man. HAROON KALEEM USMANI.

**Urdu Academy Sind:** Main Urdu Bazar, M. A. Jinnah Rd, Karachi; tel. (21) 2628655; fax (21) 2625992; e-mail urduacademy@cyber.net.pk; f. 1947; brs in Hyderabad and Lahore; academic, reference, general and textbooks; Man. Dir AZIZ KHALID.

**Vanguard Books (Pvt) Ltd:** 72-FCC, Gulberg IV, Lahore; tel. (42) 5763510; fax (42) 5751025; e-mail vbl@brain.net.pk; Chief Exec. NAJAM SETHI.

**West-Pak Publishing Co (Pvt) Ltd:** 17 Urdu Bazar, Lahore; tel. (42) 7230555; fax (42) 7120077; e-mail pakcompany@hotmail.com; f. 1932; textbooks and religious books; Chief Exec. SYED AHSAN MAHMUD.

### GOVERNMENT PUBLISHING HOUSE

**Government Publications:** Office of the Deputy Controller, Stationery and Forms, nr Old Sabzi Mandi, University Rd, Karachi 74800; tel. (21) 9231989; publ. Gazette of Pakistan; Dep. Controller MUHAMMAD AMIN BUTT.

### PUBLISHERS' ASSOCIATION

**Pakistan Publishers' and Booksellers' Association:** YMCA Bldg, Shahrah-e-Quaid-e-Azam, Lahore; Chair. SYED AHSAN MAHMUD; Sec. ZUBAIR SAEED.

## Broadcasting and Communications

### TELECOMMUNICATIONS

Since 2000 the mobile cellular telephone industry has made significant progress in Pakistan. In January 2004 the Government approved legislation providing for enhanced competition in the industry. In 2006 there were 34.5m. mobile cellular telephone subscribers nation-wide.

**Pakistan Telecommunication Authority (PTA):** F-5/1, Islamabad 44000; tel. (51) 2878143; fax (51) 2878155; e-mail administration@pta.gov.pk; internet www.pta.gov.pk; f. 1997; regulatory authority; Chair. Dr MOHAMMAD YASEEN; Dir-Gen. CH. MOHAMMAD DIN.

**Burraq Telecom (Pvt) Ltd:** Plot 94A, St 7, Sector I-10/3, Islamabad; tel. (51) 111-287-727; fax (51) 2112380; e-mail info@burraqtel.com.pk; internet www.burraqtel.com.pk; f. 2004; CEO SADIQ YOUSAF YALMAZ.

**Carrier Telephone Industries (Pvt) Ltd:** 1-9/2 Industrial Area, POB 1098, Islamabad 44000; tel. (51) 4434981; fax (51) 4449581; e-mail niamatullah.khan.ext@siemens.com; internet www.ctipak.com.pk; f. 1969; Man. Dir MALIK MOHAMMAD AMIN.

**Callmate Telips Telecom Ltd:** 99-CF, 1/5 Clifton, Karachi; tel. (21) 5867696; fax (21) 5833006; e-mail info@cttelecom.net; internet www.cttelecom.net; f. 2003; telecommunications services.

**CMPak Ltd:** 68E, Jinnah Ave, Blue Area, Islamabad 44000; tel. (51) 2271105; fax (51) 2271111; private mobile telephone co; acquired from Millicom, Luxembourg, by China Mobile Communications Corpn in Feb. 2007; co name changed from Paktel Ltd to CMPak Ltd in May 2007; CEO GUO YONG HONG.

**Instaphone:** 75 East, Fazal-ul-Haq Rd, Blue Area, POB 1681, Islamabad; tel. (51) 2277400; fax (51) 111-501501; internet www.instaphone.com; private mobile telephone co; CEO SHAHID FEROZ.

**Megatech Communications (Pvt) Ltd:** 47 Banglore Town, off Tipu Sultan Rd, Karachi 75350; tel. (21) 4528954; fax (21) 4533768; e-mail info@megatech.com.pk; internet www.megatech.com.pk; f. 1992; supplier of new digital telephone systems integrated with ISDN/BRI.

**Mobilink:** 42 Kulsum Plaza, 1st Floor, Blue Area, Islamabad; tel. (21) 2273984-9; fax (21) 2826999; e-mail customercare@mobilink.net; internet www.mobilinkgsm.com; subsidiary of Orascom Telecom; Pres. and CEO ZOUHAIR ABDUL KHALIQ.

**National Telecommunication Corporation:** NTC Building, F-5/1, Islamabad; tel. (51) 9206450; e-mail infolhr@ntc.net.pk; internet www.ntc.net.pk; f. 1996 by government; Chair. NOOR-UD-DIN BAQAI.

**Pakistan Telecommunications (Pvt) Ltd (PTCL):** Block E, G-8/4, Islamabad 44000; tel. (51) 4844463; fax (51) 4843991; e-mail info@ptcl.net.pk; internet www.ptcl.com.pk; f. 1990; 74% state-owned; 26% owned by Etisalat (United Arab Emirates); Chair. HIFZ-UR-REHMAN; Pres. and CEO WALID IRSHAID.

**TeleCard Ltd:** 7th Floor, World Trade Centre, 10 Khayaban-e-Roomi, Block 5, Clifton, Karachi 75600; tel. (21) 111-222-124; e-mail customerservices@telecard.com.pk; internet www.telecard.com.pk; Chief Exec. SHAHID FIROZ.

**Telenor:** 13-K, Moaiz Centre, F-7 Markaz, Islamabad; tel. (51) 111-345-700; fax (51) 2651923; internet www.telenor.com.pk; f. 2004; private mobile telephone co; Pres. and CEO TORE JOHNSEN.

**Telephone Industries of Pakistan (TIP):** Khanpur Rd, Haripur 22630, NWFP; tel. (995) 611469; fax (995) 610490; e-mail mdtip@tip.org.pk; internet www.tip.org.pk; f. 1952; mfrs of telecommunications equipment.

**Ufone:** 13-B, F-7 Markaz, Jinnah Super Market, Islamabad; fax (51) 111-333-100; e-mail customercare@ufonegsm.net; internet www.ufone.com; f. 2001; subsidiary of Pakistan Telecommunications (Pvt) Ltd; private mobile telephone co; Pres. and Chief Exec. ABDUL AZIZ.

**Warid Telecom (Pvt) Ltd:** 9th Floor, EFU Bldg, Jail Rd, Lahore; e-mail customerservice@waridtel.com; internet www.waridtel.com; owned by Abu Dhabi Group; CEO MARWAN ZAWAYDEH.

**Wateen Telecom (Pvt) Ltd:** POB 3527, Lahore; fax (21) 4324096; e-mail info@wateen.com; internet www.wateen.com; subsidiary of the Abu Dhabi Group, UAE; mobile and fixed line telephone services; internet, television and multimedia provider; CEO TARIQ MALIK.

### RADIO

**Pakistan Broadcasting Corporation:** National Broadcasting House, Constitution Ave, Islamabad 4400; tel. (51) 9208306; fax (51) 9223827; e-mail info@radio.gov.pk; internet www.radio.gov.pk; f. 1947 as Radio Pakistan; national broadcasting network of 33 stations; home service 24 hrs daily in 17 languages and dialects; external services 11 hrs daily in 15 languages; world service 11.49 hrs daily in two languages; 80 news bulletins daily; Dir-Gen. ASHFAQ GONDAL; Programme Dir NAYYAR MEHMOOD.

**Pakistan Broadcasting Foundation:** Planning and Development, Headquarters, Constitution Ave, Islamabad; tel. (51) 9216942; fax (51) 9204363.

**Azad Kashmir Radio:** Muzaffarabad; state-owned; Station Dir MASUD KASHFI; Dep. Controller (Eng.) SYED AHMED.

**Capital FM:** Islamabad; f. 1995; privately owned; broadcasts music and audience participation shows 24 hrs daily.

**CityFM89:** Penthouse, Anum Empire, Block 7 & 8, KCHS, Karachi; tel. (21) 4390155; fax (21) 4390160; e-mail info@cityFM89.com; internet cityfm89.com; f. 2004; owned by Kohinoor Airwaves (Pvt) Ltd; broadcasts in Karachi, Lahore, Islamabad and Faisalabad; Chief Operating Officer NERMEEN CHINOY.

**FM-100:** Karachi; tel. (21) 2630611; fax (21) 2629311; music station; broadcasts in Karachi, Lahore and Islamabad.

### TELEVISION

**Geo TV:** I. I. Chundrigar Rd, Jang Building, Karachi; tel. (21) 2628614; fax (21) 2636937; e-mail distribution@geo.tv; internet www.geo.tv; f. 2003; Pakistan's first private broadcasting network; broadcasts in Urdu; operates four channels; Pres. IMRAN ASLAM.

**Indus TV Network:** 2nd Floor, Shafi Court, Civil Lines, Mereweather Rd, Karachi; tel. (21) 5693801; fax (21) 5693813; internet www.indus.tv; f. 2000; Pakistan's first independent satellite channel; CEO GHAZANFAR ALI.

**I-Plus TV:** 2nd Floor, Shafi Court, Mereweather Rd, Karachi; tel. (21) 5652283; fax (21) 5652285; e-mail im@industvnetwork.com.

**Pakistan Television Corpn Ltd:** Federal TV Complex, Constitution Ave, POB 1221, Islamabad; tel. (51) 9208651; fax (51) 9211184; e-mail md@ptv.com.pk; internet ptv.com.pk; f. 1964; transmits 24 hrs daily; four channels; Chair. SYED ANWAR MEHMOOD; Man. Dir MUHAMMAD ASHRAF AZIM.

**Shalimar Television Network** (Shalimar Recording and Broadcasting Co Ltd): 36, Sector H-9, POB 1246, Islamabad; tel. (51) 9257396; fax (51) 4434830; e-mail contact@stn.com.pk; internet www.stn.com.pk; f. 1989 as People's Television Network; 92.81% state-owned, 7.19% privately owned; 20 terrestrial stations throughout Pakistan; Man. Dir and CEO RASHID CHOUDHRY; Gen. Man. TARIQ MAHMOOD.

**Tele Biz:** Techno City, Altaf Hussain Rd, Karachi 74000; tel. (51) 2273886; fax (51) 2278795; e-mail telebiz@cyber.net.pk; Bureau Chief ZAFAR SIDDIQI.

**WAQT Television:** 4 Sharah Fatimah Jinnah, Lahore; tel. (42) 6278981; fax (42) 6278980.

## Finance

(cap. = capital; auth. = authorized; p.u. = paid up; res = reserves; dep. = deposits; m. = million; brs = branches; amounts in rupees unless otherwise stated)

### BANKING

In January 1974 all domestic banks were nationalized. In December 1990 the Government announced that it intended to transfer the five state-owned commercial banks to private ownership. By late 1991 the majority of shares in the Muslim Commercial Bank Ltd and the Allied Bank of Pakistan Ltd had been transferred to private ownership. In 1991 the Government granted 10 new private commercial bank licences, the first since banks were nationalized in 1974. In June 2002 the Supreme Court reversed its 1999 ruling that ordered the Government to abolish charging interest. Interest charges, known as 'riba', are forbidden under Islamic law. The ruling would have required all financial institutions to adopt the Islamic style of banking. In late 2002 the State Bank of Pakistan gave banks three options for the launching of Islamic banking: to establish an independent Islamic bank; to open subsidiaries of existing commercial banks; and to establish new branches to carry out Islamic banking operations.

#### Central Bank

**State Bank of Pakistan:** Central Directorate, I. I. Chundrigar Rd, POB 4456, Karachi 2; tel. (21) 9212400; fax (21) 9217234; e-mail info@sbp.org.pk; internet www.sbp.org.pk; f. 1948; bank of issue; controls and regulates currency and foreign exchange; cap. 100m., res 76,067m., dep. 392,506m. (June 2005); Gov. Dr SHAMSHAD AKHTAR; 17 brs.

#### Commercial Banks

**Allied Bank Ltd:** Central Office, Main Clifton Rd, Bath Island, Karachi; tel. (21) 5370499; fax (21) 5370500; e-mail aftab.manzoor@abl.com.pk; internet www.abl.com.pk; f. 1942 as Australasia Bank Ltd; name changed as above 2005; cap. 4,404.6m., res 5,336.2m., dep. 161,907.5m. (Dec. 2005); 49% state-owned; Pres. and Chief Exec. MOHAMMAD AFTAB MANZOOR; Exec. Vice-Pres. RASHID MAQSOOD HAMIDI; 741 brs in Pakistan.

**Arif Habib Bank Ltd:** 2A, R. Y. 16, Old Queens Rd, Karachi; tel. (21) 111–124–725; fax (21) 2463553; e-mail kamalkhan@arifhabibbank.com; internet www.arifhabibbank.com; f. 2006; President and CEO KAMAL UDDIN KHAN.

**Askari Bank Ltd:** AWT Plaza, The Mall, POB 1084, Rawalpindi; tel. (51) 9272289; fax (51) 9273180; e-mail president@askaribank.com.pk; internet www.askaribank.com.pk; f. 1992; cap. 1,507.0m., res 5,862.1m., dep. 118,794.7m. (Dec. 2005); Chair. Lt-Gen. WASEEM AHMED ASHRAF; Pres. and Chief Exec. SHAHARYAR AHMAD; 98 brs.

**Atlas Bank Ltd:** 3rd Floor, Federation House, Abdullah Shah Ghazi Rd, Clifton, Karachi; tel. (21) 111–333–225; fax (21) 5877197; e-mail info@atlasbank.com.pk; internet www.atlasbank.com.pk; President and CEO ABDUL AZIZ RAJKOTWALA.

**Bank Al Habib Ltd:** Mackinnons Bldg, I. I. Chundrigar Rd, Karachi; tel. (21) 2412421; fax (21) 2419752; e-mail info@bankalhabib.com; internet www.bankalhabib.com; f. 1991; cap. 2,191.1m., res 2,668.0m., dep. 75,795.9m. (Dec. 2005); Chief Exec. and Man. Dir ABBAS D. HABIB; 103 brs.

**Bank Alfalah Ltd:** BA Bldg, I. I. Chundrigar Rd, POB 6773, Karachi; tel. (21) 2416811; fax (21) 2424901; e-mail figroup@bankalfalah.com; internet www.bankalfalah.com; f. 1992 as Habib Credit and Exchange Ltd; name changed as above 1998; cap. 5,000.0m., res 2,749.5m., dep. 239,509.3m. (Dec. 2006); 61.66% owned by Abu Dhabi Consortium, 20% public, 12.60% non-residents, 5.19% employees and execs, 0.55% dirs; CEO SIRAJUDDIN AZIZ; 231 brs.

**The Bank of Khyber:** 24 The Mall, Peshawar; tel. (521) 111-959-595; fax (915) 278146; e-mail bokforex@psh.paknet.com.pk; internet www.bok.com.pk; f. 1991; cap. 1,231.0m., res 1,288.9m., dep. 17,452.2m. (Dec. 2005); 51% state-owned; 49% public shareholders; the main branch in Peshawar began Islamic banking operations in June 2003; Man. Dir SYED AHMAD IQBAL ASHRAF; 29 brs.

**The Bank of Punjab:** BOP Tower, 10-B, Block-E-II, Main Blvd, Gulberg-III, POB 2254, Lahore; tel. (42) 5783711; fax (42) 5783713; e-mail sajjad.hussain@bop.com.pk; internet www.bop.com.pk; f. 1989; cap. 4,230.4m., res 10,880.1m., dep. 191,968.9m. (Dec. 2007); 51% owned by provincial govt; Chair. JAVED MEHMOOD; Pres. SAJJAD HUSSAIN; 271 brs.

**Crescent Commercial Bank Ltd:** 5th Floor, Sidco Avenue Centre, Maulana Deen Mohammad Wafai Rd, Karachi 74000; tel. (21) 111-999-333; internet www.cresbank.com; f. 2002; Pres. and CEO SHEHZAD NAQVI; Chair. ZAKI ABDULMOHSEN AL-MOUSA; 18 brs.

**Faysal Bank Ltd:** ST-02, Faysal House, 4th Floor, FIG, Main Shahrah-e-Faisal, Karachi; tel. (21) 2795306; fax (21) 2793131; e-mail fbl@faysalbank.com; internet www.faysalbank.com; f. 1995; merged with Al-Faysal Investment Bank Ltd 2002; cap. 5,296.4m., res 9,378.4m., dep. 112,063.3m. (Dec. 2007); Pres. and CEO NAVED A. KHAN; 107 brs.

**Habib Bank Ltd:** 22 Habib Bank Plaza, I. I. Chundrigar Rd, Karachi 75650; tel. (21) 2411530; fax (21) 2411556; e-mail zmahmood@hblpk.com; internet www.habibbankltd.com; f. 1941; cap. 6,900m., res 16,817m., dep. 439,724m. (Dec. 2006); transferred to private sector Feb. 2004; 51% owned by Agha Khan Fund for Economic Development (United Kingdom), 41% by State Bank of Pakistan and 8% by Government and National Bank of Pakistan; Pres. ZAKIR MAHMOOD; 1,437 brs in Pakistan; 39 foreign brs.

**Habib Metropolitan Bank Ltd:** Mezzanine Floor, Spencer's Bldg, I. I. Chundrigar Rd, POB 1289, Karachi; tel. (21) 2638080; fax (21) 2630404; e-mail info@hmb.com.pk; internet www.hmb.com.pk; f. 1992; fmrly Metropolitan Bank; merged with Habib Bank AG Zurich in 2006; cap. 3,005.0m., equity 10,665.0m., dep. 102,493.0m. (Dec. 2006); Pres. and Chief Exec. KASSIM PAREKH; Exec. Dir MOHAMADALI R. HABIB; 82 brs.

**JS Bank Ltd:** 1st Floor, Shaheen Commercial Complex, Dr Ziauddin Ahmed Rd, Karachi 74200; tel. (21) 2635208; fax (21) 2631803; e-mail info@jsbl.com; internet www.jsbl.com; Pres. NAVEED QAZI.

**KASB Bank Ltd:** Business and Finance Centre, I. I. Chundrigar Rd, Karachi 74000; tel. (21) 2446800; fax (21) 9217588; e-mail international@kasb.com; internet www.kasbbank.com; f. 1995 as Platinum Commercial Bank Ltd; name changed as above 2003; cap.

2,292.7m., res 84.3m., dep. 15,409.7m. (March 2006); Pres. and CEO MUNEER KAMAL; 35 brs.

**Khushhali Bank:** 94 West, 4th Floor, Jinnah Ave, Blue Area, POB 3111, Islamabad; fax (51) 9206080; cap. 1,705.0m., res 15,023.4m. (Dec. 2004); Chair. and Man. Dir GHALIB NISHTAR.

**MCB Bank Ltd:** MCB Tower, I. I. Chundrigar Rd, POB 4976, Karachi 74000; tel. (21) 2270075; fax (21) 2270076; e-mail atif.bajwa@mcb.com.pk; internet www.mcb.com.pk; f. 1947; cap. 4,265.3m., res 18,831.8m., dep. 229,345.2m. (Dec. 2005); Chair. Mian MUHAMMAD MANSHA; Pres. and CEO ATIF ASLAM BAJWA; 1,057 brs in Pakistan, 4 brs abroad.

**Mybank Ltd:** 10th Floor, Business & Finance Centre, I. I. Chundrigar Rd, Karachi; tel. (21) 111-692-265; fax (21) 2471951; e-mail president@mybankltd.com; internet mybankltd.com; f. 1991; fmrly Bolan Bank Ltd; cap. 5,063m., res 878m., dep. 30,153m. (Dec. 2007); Chair. IQBAL ALIMOHAMED; Pres. and CEO MUHAMMAD BILAL SHEIKH; 60 brs.

**National Bank of Pakistan (NBP):** NBP Bldg, I. I. Chundrigar Rd, POB 4937, Karachi 2; tel. (21) 9212208; fax (21) 9212774; e-mail nbp@nbp.com.pk; internet www.nbp.com.pk; f. 1949; cap. 4,924.1m., res 28,798.8m., dep. 476,656.5m. (Dec. 2004); 100% state-owned; Pres. SYED ALI RAZA; 1,491 brs in Pakistan and 22 brs abroad.

**NIB Bank Ltd:** Muhammadi House, I. I. Chundrigar Rd, Karachi; tel. (21) 2420333; fax (21) 2472258; e-mail info@nibpk.com; internet www.nibpk.com; f. 2003; Pres. and CEO KHAWAJA IQBAL HASSAN; 27 brs.

**PICIC Commercial Bank Ltd:** Spencer Bldg, I. I. Chundrigar Rd, POB 572, Karachi 74200; tel. (21) 2638817; fax (21) 2639760; e-mail info@picicbank.com.pk; internet www.picicbank.com.pk; f. 1994 as Schön Bank Ltd; name changed to Gulf Commercial Bank Ltd in 1998; 60% shares and full management of bank acquired by PICIC in February 2001, name changed to above in June 2001; controlling 63.36% stake acquired by NIB Bank (subsidiary of Tamasek Holdings, Singapore) in June 2007 in preparation for proposed full merger with NIB later that year; cap. 2,734.9m., res 867.5m., dep. 59,148.3m. (Dec. 2005); Chair. FRANCES A. ROZARIO; Pres. and CEO KHAWAJA IQBAL HASSAN; 129 brs.

**Prime Commercial Bank Ltd:** 77-Y, Phase III, Defence Housing Authority, Lahore 54792; tel. (42) 5728282; fax (42) 5728181; e-mail primebank@primebank.com.pk; internet www.primebank.com.pk; f. 1991; cap. 2,321.5m., res 1,116.5m., dep. 38,876.1m. (Dec. 2005); Pres. SAEED I. CHAUDHRY; Chair. ABDUL ELAH A. MUKRED; 62 brs.

**Royal Bank of Scotland (RBS) Pakistan:** 16 Abdullah Haroon Rd, Karachi; tel. (21) 5683097; fax (21) 5683432; e-mail info@abnamro.com.pk; internet www.abnamro.com.pk/Pakistan; fmrly ABN AMRO Bank Pakistan Ltd; CEO NAVED A. KHAN.

**Saudi Pak Commercial Bank Ltd:** Saudi Pak Bldg, I. I. Chundrigar Rd, Karachi; tel. (21) 2460475; e-mail president@spcb.com.pk; internet www.saudipakbank.com; f. 1994 as Prudential Commercial Bank, acquired by Saudi Pak Industrial and Agricultural Investment Co (Pvt) Ltd in 2001; cap. 3,847.5m., res 819.2m., dep. 42,617.3m. (Dec. 2005); Chair. MUHAMMAD RASHID ZAHIR; Pres. and CEO MANSOOR MASOOD KHAN; 38 brs.

**Soneri Bank Ltd:** 87 Shahrah-e-Quaid-e-Azam, POB 49, Lahore; tel. (42) 6368142; fax (42) 6368138; e-mail main.lahore@soneribank.com; internet www.soneribank.com; f. 1991; cap. 1,653.5m., res 2,563.3m., dep. 55,848.5m. (Dec. 2005); Chair. ALAUDDIN FEERASTA; Pres. and CEO SAFAR ALI K. LAKHANI; 69 brs.

**Standard Chartered Bank (Pakistan) Ltd:** 3rd Floor, Main Br., POB 5556, I. I. Chundrigar Rd, Karachi; tel. (21) 2450288; fax (21) 2414914; e-mail badar.kazmi@pk.standardchartered.com; internet www.standardchartered.com/pk; Pres. and CEO BADAR KAZMI; 144 brs.

**Union Bank Ltd:** New Jubilee Insurance House, I. I. Chundrigar Rd, Karachi 74200; tel. (21) 2412520; fax (21) 2400842; e-mail ubrokhi@digicom.net.pk; internet www.unionbankpk.com; f. 1991; negotiations towards proposed acquisition by Standard Chartered Bank (India) were well advanced by August 2007; cap. 2,819.8m., res 1,599.9m., dep. 105,918.0m. (Dec. 2005); Chair. ABDULLAH M. A. BASODAN; Pres. and Group CEO SHAUKAT TARIN; 27 brs.

**United Bank Ltd:** State Life Bldg, No. 1, I. I. Chundrigar Rd, POB 4306, Karachi 74000; tel. (21) 2417021; fax (21) 2413492; e-mail president@ubl.com.pk; internet www.ubl.com.pk; f. 1959; cap. 5,180.0m., res 9,137.5m., dep. 311,016.8m. (Dec. 2005); privatized in 2002; Pres. and CEO ATIF BOKHARI; 1,040 brs in Pakistan and 15 brs abroad.

### Leasing Banks (*Modarabas*)

The number of leasing banks (*modarabas*), which conform to the strictures placed upon the banking system by *Shari'a* (the Islamic legal code), rose from four in 1988 to about 45 in 2002. The following are among the most important *modarabas* in Pakistan.

**Asian Leasing Corporation Ltd:** 85-B Jail Rd, Gulberg, POB 3176, Lahore; tel. (42) 484417; fax (42) 484418.

**Atlas Lease Ltd:** Ground Floor, Federation House, Shahrah-e-Firdousi, Main Clifton, Karachi 75600; tel. (21) 5866817; fax (21) 5870543; e-mail all@atlasgrouppk.com; Chair. YUSUF H. SHIRAZI.

**B. R. R. International Modaraba:** 3rd Floor, Dean Arcade, Block 8, Kehkeshan, Clifton, Karachi 75600; tel. (21) 5835026; fax (21) 5870324; e-mail brr@cyber.net.pk.

**Dadabhoy Leasing Co Ltd:** 5th Floor, Maqbool Commercial Complex, JCHS Block, Main Shahrah-e-Faisal, Karachi; tel. (21) 4548171; fax (21) 4547301; Man. (Finance) MOHAMMAD AYUB.

**English Leasing Ltd:** M. K. Arcade, Ground Floor, 32 Davis Rd, Lahore; tel. (42) 6303855; fax (41) 6304251; e-mail englease@hotmail.com; Chair. JAVAID MAHMOOD; CEO MANZOOR ELAHI.

**First Habib Bank Modaraba:** 18 Habib Bank Plaza, I. I. Chundrigar Rd, Karachi 75650; tel. (21) 2412294; fax (21) 2411860; e-mail sukhan@hblpk.com; internet www.habibbankltd.com/html/first_habib_modaraba.htm; f. 1991; wholly owned subsidiary of Habib Bank Ltd; Chair. R. ZAKIR MAHMOOD; CEO SAEED UDDIN KHAN.

**Orix Leasing Pakistan Ltd:** Overseas Investors Chamber of Commerce Bldg, Talpur Rd, Karachi 74000; tel. (21) 2425896; fax (21) 2425897; e-mail olp@orixpakistan.com; internet www.orixpakistan.com; f. 1986; cap. US $10m. (June 2004); Chief Exec. HUMAYUN MURAD.

**Pakistan Industrial and Commercial Leasing Ltd:** 504 Park Ave, 24-A, Block 6, PECHS, Shahrah-e-Faisal, Karachi 75210; tel. (21) 4551045; fax (21) 4520655; e-mail picl@super.net.pk; f. 1987; Chief Exec. MINHAJ-UL-HAQ SIDDIQI.

**Standard Chartered Modaraba:** Standard Services of Pakistan (Pvt) Ltd, Standard Bank Bldg, I. I. Chundrigar Rd, POB 5556, Karachi 74000; tel. (21) 223917; fax (21) 2417197; fmrly First Grindlays Modaraba; Man. Dir SHARIQ SALEEM.

### Islamic Banks

**BankIslami Pakistan Ltd:** 11th Floor, Executive Tower One, Dolmen City, Marine Dr., Block 4, Clifton, Karachi; tel. (21) 111-247-111; fax (21) 5378373; e-mail info@bankislami.com.pk; internet www.bankislami.com.pk; CEO HASSAN BILGRAMI.

**Dawood Islamic Bank Ltd:** Trade Centre, I. I. Chundrigar Rd, Karachi; tel. (21) 2272440; fax (21) 2272465; e-mail nicholaus.schwarz@dawoodislamic.com; internet www.dawoodislamic.com; Pres. and CEO NICOLAUS SCHWARZ.

**Dubai Islamic Bank Pakistan Ltd:** Hassan Chambers, Plot DC-7, Block 7, Clifton, Karachi; tel. (21) 5368556; fax (21) 5821071; e-mail saad.zaman@dib.ae; internet www.dibpak.com; CEO SAAD ZAMAN.

**Emirates Global Islamic Bank Ltd:** Shopping Arcade, Karachi Sheraton Hotel and Towers, Club Rd, Karachi; tel. (21) 5633418; fax (21) 5633427; e-mail feedback@egibl.com; internet www.egibl.com; sponsored by Emirates Investment Group LLC, UAE, and Saudi Arabian investors; Pres. and CEO SYED TARIQ HUSSAIN.

**Meezan Bank Ltd:** 2nd Floor, PNSC Bldg, Moulvi Tamizuddin Khan Rd, Karachi 74000; tel. (21) 5610582; fax (21) 5610375; e-mail info@meezanbank.com; internet www.meezanbank.com; f. 1997 as Al-Meezan Investment Bank; became commercial bank 2002 and name changed as above; cap. 2,036.6m., res 988.0m., dep. 26,011.7m. (Dec. 2005); Pres. and CEO IRFAN SIDDIQUI; Gen. Man. NAJMUL HASAN; 37 brs.

### Co-operative Banks

In 1976 all existing co-operative banks were dissolved and given the option of becoming a branch of the appropriate Provincial Co-operative Bank, or of reverting to the status of a credit society.

**Federal Bank for Co-operatives:** State Bank Bldg, G-5/2, POB 1218, Islamabad; tel. (51) 9204518; fax (51) 9204534; f. 1976; owned jtly by the fed. Govt, the prov. govts and the State Bank of Pakistan; provides credit facilities to each of six prov. co-operative banks and regulates their operations; they in turn provide credit facilities through co-operative socs; supervises policy of prov. co-operative banks and of multi-unit co-operative socs; assists fed. and prov. govts in formulating schemes for development and revitalization of co-operative movement; carries out research on rural credit, etc.; Man. Dir M. AFZAL HUSSAIN; four regional offices.

### Investment Banks

**Asset Investment Bank Ltd:** Rm 1-B, 1st Floor, Ali Plaza, Khayaban-e-Quaid-e-Azam, Blue Area, Islamabad; tel. (51) 2270625; fax (51) 2272506; Chief Exec. SYED NAVEED ZAIDI.

**Atlas Investment Bank Ltd:** 3rd Floor, Federation House, Abdullah shah Ghazi Rd, Main Clifton, Karachi; tel. (21) 111-333-225; fax (21) 5870543; e-mail info@atlasbank.com.pk; internet www.atlasbank.com.pk; 15% owned by Bank of Tokyo-Mitsubishi UFJ Ltd; Chair. YUSUF H. SHIRAZI; CEO AZIZ RAJKOTWALA.

**Crescent Standard Investment Bank Ltd:** 4th Floor, Crescent Standard Tower, 10-B, Block E-2, Gulberg III, Lahore; tel. (42) 5763306; fax (42) 5870359; e-mail csibl@csibl.com; internet www.csibl.com; f. 1990 as Al-Towfeek Investment Bank Ltd; became First Standard Investment Bank Ltd 2002; name changed as above 2004; cap. 737.7m., res 212.1m., dep. 2,219.4m. (Dec. 2003); Chair. MANZUR UL HAQ; Chief Exec. MAHMOOD AHMED.

**Escorts Investment Bank Ltd:** Escorts House, 26 Davis Rd, Lahore; tel. (42) 6371931; fax (42) 6375950; e-mail mailmanager@escortsbank.net; internet escortsbank.net; Pres. and CEO RASHID MANSUR.

**ICI Investment Bank Ltd:** 7th Floor, The Forum, Suite 701–703, 4-20, Block 9, Khayaban-e-Jami, Clifton, Karachi; tel. (21) 111-234-234; fax (21) 111-567-567; e-mail fiibl.khi@interbank.com.pk; Man. Dir and CEO SAMIR AHMED.

**Orix Investment Bank Pakistan Ltd:** 2nd Floor, Islamic Chamber of Commerce Bldg, St 2/A, Block 9, Clifton, Karachi 75600; tel. (21) 5861266; fax (21) 5868862; e-mail ihalvi@orixbank.com; internet www.orixbank.com; f. 1995; Chair. KUNWAR IDREES; Gen. Man. INTISAR H. ALVI.

### Development Finance Organizations

**Bankers' Skill Development Centre:** Hamilton Court, 1st Floor, Suite 206/A, G-1, Main Clifton Rd, Block 7, Karachi 75600; tel. (21) 5306244; fax (21) 5306245; e-mail bsdcvalad@hotmail.com; Pres. and CEO Dr AHSAN H. KHAN.

**First MicroFinanceBank Ltd:** President's Secretariat, 62-C, 25th Commercial St, Tauheed Commercial Area, DHA Phase V, Karachi; tel. (21) 5822432; fax (21) 5822434; Pres. and CEO HUSSAIN TEJANY.

**First Women Bank Ltd:** S.T.S.M. Foundation Bldg, CL-10/20/2 Beaumont Rd, Civil Lines, Karachi 75530; tel. (21) 111-676-767; fax (21) 5657756; e-mail info@fwbl.com.pk; internet www.fwbl.com.pk; f. 1989; cap. and res 590m., dep. 8,690m. (Dec. 2004); Pres. ZARINE AZIZ; 38 brs.

**House Building Finance Corpn:** Finance and Trade Centre, 3rd Floor, Shahrah-e-Faisal, Karachi 74400; tel. (21) 9202314; fax (21) 9202360; e-mail info@hbfc.com.pk; internet www.hbfc.com.pk; provides loans for the construction and purchase of housing units; Man. Dir ZAIGHAM MEHMOOD RIZVI.

**Industrial Development Bank of Pakistan:** State Life Bldg No. 2, Wallace Rd, off I. I. Chundrigar Rd, POB 5082, Karachi 74000; tel. (21) 9213601-10; fax (21) 9213644; e-mail idbp@idbp.com.pk; internet www.idbp.com.pk; f. 1961; provides credit facilities for small and medium-sized industrial enterprises in the private sector; 100% state-owned; Chair. and Man. Dir NAEEM IQBAL; 19 brs.

**Investment Corpn of Pakistan:** NBP Bldg, 5th Floor, I. I. Chundrigar Rd, POB 5410, Karachi 74400; tel. (21) 9212360; fax (21) 9212388; e-mail icp@paknet3.ptc.pk; f. 1966 by the Govt to encourage and broaden the base of investments and to develop the capital market; Man. Dir ISTIQBAL MEHDI; 10 brs.

**Khushhali Bank:** 94W, 4th Floor, Jinnah Ave, Blue Area, Islamabad 44000; tel. (51) 111092-092; internet www.khushhalibank.com.pk; f. 2000 by the Govt under the Asian Development Bank's micro-finance sector development programme; provides micro-loans to the poor and finances reforms in the micro-finance sector; cap. 1,705m. (Aug. 2000); Pres. GHALIB NISHTAR.

**National Investment (Unit Trust) Ltd:** NBP Bldg, 6th Floor, I. I. Chundrigar Rd, POB 5671, Karachi; tel. (21) 2419061; fax (21) 2430623; e-mail info@nit.com.pk; internet www.nit.com.pk; f. 1962; an open-ended mutual fund, mobilizes domestic savings to meet the requirements of growing economic development and enables investors to share in the industrial and economic prosperity of the country; 67,000 Unit holders (1999/2000); Man. Dir ISTIQBAL MEHDI.

**Network Microfinance Bank Ltd:** 202 Azayam Plaza, opp. FTC Bldg, SMCHS, Shahrah-e-Faisal, Karachi; fax (21) 4311722; e-mail nmb@networkmicrobank.com; internet www.networkmicrobank.com; Pres. and CEO M. MOAZZAM KHAN.

**Pak Oman Microfinance Bank Ltd:** 2nd Floor, Tower C, Finance and Trade Centre, Shahrah-e-Faisal, Karachi; tel. (21) 5630941; fax (21) 5630999; e-mail info@pomicro.com; internet www.pomicro.com; Pres. and CEO OZAIR A. HANAFI.

**Pakistan Industrial Credit and Investment Corpn Ltd (PICIC):** State Life Bldg No. 1, I. I. Chundrigar Rd, POB 5080, Karachi 74000; tel. (21) 2414220; fax (21) 2419100; internet www.picic.com; f. 1957 as an industrial development bank to provide financial assistance in both local and foreign currencies, for the establishment of new industries in the private sector and balancing modernization, replacement and expansion of existing industries; merchant banking and foreign exchange activities; total assets 33,949m., cap. 2,736m., res 4,188m. (June 2005); held 97.9% and 2.1% by local and foreign investors respectively; Man. Dir MOHAMMAD ALI KHOJA; Chair. ALTAF M. SALEEM; 19 brs.

**Pakistan Kuwait Investment Co (Pvt) Ltd:** Tower 'C', 4th Floor, Finance and Trade Centre, Shahrah-e-Faisal, POB 901, Karachi 74200; tel. (21) 5660750; fax (21) 5683669; jt venture between the Govt and Kuwait to promote investment in industrial and agro-based enterprises; Man. Dir ISTIQBAL MEHDI.

**Pak-Libya Holding Co (Pvt) Ltd:** Finance and Trade Centre, 5th Floor, Tower 'C', Shahrah-e-Faisal, POB 10425, Karachi 74400; tel. (21) 111-111-115; fax (21) 5682389; e-mail paklibya@paklibya.com.pk; jt venture between the Govts of Pakistan and Libya to promote industrial investment in Pakistan; Man. Dir KHALID SHARWANI.

**Regional Development Finance Corpn:** Ghausia Plaza, 20 Blue Area, POB 1893, Islamabad; tel. (51) 2825131; fax (51) 2201179; promotes industrial investment in the less developed areas of Pakistan; CEO MIRZA GHAGANFAR BAIG; 13 brs.

**Saudi Pak Industrial and Agricultural Investment Co (Pvt) Ltd:** Saudi Pak Tower, 61-A Jinnah Ave, Islamabad; tel. (51) 2273514; fax (51) 2273508; e-mail saudipak@saudipak.com; internet www.saudipak.com; f. 1981 jtly by Saudi Arabia and Pakistan to finance industrial and agro-based projects and undertake investment-related activities in Pakistan; cap. 2,000m., res 732m., dep. 5,900m. (March 2001); CEO MUHAMMAD RASHID ZAHIR; Exec. Vice-Pres. ABDUL JALEEL SHAIKH; 1 br.

**SME Bank Ltd:** Jang Plaza, 2nd Floor, 40 Fazal-ul-Haq Rd, Blue Area, POB 1587, Islamabad; tel. (51) 9217000; fax (51) 9217001; e-mail info@smebank.org; internet www.smebank.org; formed through merger of Regional Development Finance Corpn (RDFC) and Small Business Finance Corpn (SBFC); provides loans for small businesses; Pres. and CEO MANSUR KHAN.

**Youth Investment and Promotion Society:** PIA Bldg, 3rd Floor, Blue Area, Islamabad; tel. (51) 815581; Man. Dir ASHRAF M. KHAN.

**Zarai Taraqiati Bank Ltd (ZTBL):** 1 Faisal Ave, POB 1400, Islamabad; tel. (51) 9252727; fax (51) 9252737; e-mail info@ztbl.com.pk; internet www.ztbl.com.pk; f. 1961; provides credit facilities to agriculturists (particularly small-scale farmers) and cottage industrialists in the rural areas and for allied projects; 100% state-owned; Pres. MANSUR KHAN; 24 zonal offices and 342 brs.

### Banking Associations

**Investment Banks Association of Pakistan:** 7th Floor, Shaheen Commercial Complex, Dr Ziauddin Ahmed Rd, POB 1345, Karachi; tel. (21) 2631396; fax (21) 2630678.

**Modaraba Association of Pakistan:** Chair. WAQAR AJMAL CHAUDHRY.

**Pakistan Banks' Association:** National Bank of Pakistan, Head Office Bldg, 2nd Floor, I. I. Chundrigar Rd, POB 4937, Karachi 2; tel. and fax (21) 2416686; e-mail pba@cyber.net.pk; Chair. M. YOUNAS KHAN; Sec. A. GHAFFAR K. HAFIZ.

### Banking Organizations

**Banking Mohtasib Pakistan:** Secretariat, 5th Floor, Shaheen Complex, POB 604, M. R. Kiyani Rd, Karachi; tel. (21) 9217334; fax (21) 9217375; e-mail info@bankingmohtasib.gov.pk; internet www.bankingmohtasib.gov.pk; resolves public grievances against banks and disputes between banking institutions; offices in Quetta, Lahore, Rawalpindi and Peshawar; Banking Ombudsman AZHAR HAMID.

**Pakistan Banking Council:** Habib Bank Plaza, I. I. Chundrigar Rd, Karachi; tel. (21) 227121; fax (21) 222232; f. 1973; acts as a co-ordinating body between the nationalized banks and the Ministry of Finance and Revenue; Chair. MUHAMMAD ZAKI; Sec. Mir WASIF ALI.

**Pakistan Development Banking Institute:** 4th Floor, Sidco Ave Centre, Stratchen Rd, Karachi; tel. (21) 5688049; fax (21) 5688460.

## STOCK EXCHANGES

**Securities and Exchange Commission of Pakistan:** NIC Bldg, 63 Jinnah Ave, Blue Area, Islamabad 44000; tel. (51) 9218585; fax (51) 9204915; e-mail enquiries@secp.gov.pk; internet www.secp.gov.pk; oversees and co-ordinates operations of exchanges and registration of companies; registration offices in Faisalabad (356-A, 1st Floor, Al-Jamil Plaza, People's Colony, Small D Ground, Faisalabad; tel. (41) 713841), Karachi (No. 2, 4th Floor, State Life Building, North Wing, Karachi; tel. (21) 2415855), Lahore (3rd and 4th Floors, Associated House, 7 Egerton Rd, Lahore; tel. (42) 9202044), Multan (61 Abdali Rd, Multan; tel. (61) 542609), Peshawar (Hussain Commercial Bldg, 3 Arbab Rd, Peshawar), Quetta (382/3, IDBP House, Shahrah-e-Hall, Quetta; tel. (81) 844138) and Sukkur (B-30, Sindhi Muslim Housing Society, Airport Rd, Sukkur; tel. (71) 30517); Chair. RAZI-UR-RAHMAN KHAN.

**Islamabad Stock Exchange (Guarantee) Ltd:** 4th Floor, Stock Exchange Bldg, 101E Faz-ul-haq Rd, Blue Area, Islamabad; tel. (51) 2275045; fax (51) 2275044; e-mail ise@ise.com.pk; internet www.ise

.com.pk; f. 1991; 103 mems; Chair. SHAHARYAR AHMAD; Sec. YOUSUF H. MAKHDOOMI.

**Karachi Stock Exchange (Guarantee) Ltd:** Stock Exchange Bldg, Stock Exchange Rd, Karachi 74000; tel. (21) 111-001-122; fax (21) 2410825; e-mail info@kse.com.pk; internet www.kse.com .pk; f. 1947; 200 mems, 654 listed cos (Jan. 2007); Chair. KAMRAN Y. MIRZA; Man. Dir ADNAN AFRIDI.

**Lahore Stock Exchange (Guarantee) Ltd:** Lahore Stock Exchange Bldg, 19 Khayaban-e-Aiwan-e-Iqbal, POB 1315, Lahore 54000; tel. (42) 6368000; fax (42) 6368484; e-mail info@lahorestock .com; internet www.lahorestock.com; f. 1970; 514 listed cos, 151 mems; Pres. ARIF SAEED; Man. Dir/CEO MIAN SHAKEEL ASLAM.

**National Commodity Exchange Ltd:** 9th Floor, PIC Towers, 32-A Lalazar Drive, M. T. Khan Rd, Karachi; tel. (21) 111-623-623; fax (21) 5611263; e-mail info@ncel.com.pk; internet www.ncel.com.pk; f. 2002; online commodity futures exchange; regulated by Securities and Exchange Commission of Pakistan; Chair. SHAUKAT TARIN; Man. Dir ASSIM JANG.

**Central Depository Co:** CDC House, 99-B, Block B, S. M. C. H. Society, Main Shahrah-e-Faisal, Karachi 74400; tel. (21) 2416774; fax (21) 4326016; e-mail info@cdcpak.com; internet www .cdcpakistan.com; f. 1993 to manage and operate Central Depository System of the financial services industry; CEO HANIF JAKHURA.

## INSURANCE

In 1995 legislation came into effect allowing foreign insurance companies to operate in Pakistan.

**Insurance Division:** Securities and Exchange Commission, 4th Floor, NIC Bldg, Jinnah Ave, Islamabad; tel. (51) 9207091; fax (51) 9208955; internet www.secp.gov.pk; under the Ministry of Finance and Revenue; Commissioner of Insurance SHARIF EJAZ GHAURI; Exec. Dir SHAFAAT AHMED.

### Life Insurance

**American Life Insurance Co (Pakistan) Ltd:** 13th Floor (Level 16), Block 4, Scheme 5, Clifton, Karachi 75600; tel. (21) 111-111-711; fax (21) 5290042; e-mail alico@cyber.net.pk; internet www.alico.com .pk; Chair. and CEO ARIF SULTAN MUFTI.

**EFU Life Assurance Ltd:** 37-K, Block 6, PECHS, Karachi; tel. (21) 111-338-111; fax (21)4535079; e-mail info@efulife.com; internet www.efulife.com; f. 1932; Chair. SAIFUDDIN N. ZOOMKAWALA; Man. Dir and CEO TAHER G. SACHAK.

**Metropolitan Life Assurance Co of Pakistan Ltd:** 310 EFU House, M. A. Jinnah Rd, Karachi 74000; tel. (21) 2311662; fax (21) 2311667; e-mail clientservices@metropolitanlifeassurance.com; internet www.metropolitanlifeassurance.com; f. 1992; Chief Exec. and Man. Dir MAHEEN YUNUS.

**Postal Life Insurance Organization:** 2nd and 3rd Floors, Karachi GPO Bldg, I. I. Chundrigar Rd, Karachi; tel. (21) 9211102; e-mail gmplikar@paknet.pk.com; f. 1884; life and group insurance; Gen. Man. SHAHAR YARUDDIN.

**State Life Insurance Corpn of Pakistan:** State Life Bldg No. 9, Dr Ziauddin Ahmed Rd, POB 5725, Karachi 75530; tel. (21) 111-111-888; fax (21) 9202868; e-mail dhasp@statelife.com.pk; internet www .statelife.com.pk; f. 1972; life and group insurance and pension schemes; Chair. SHAHID AZIZ SIDDIQI.

### General Insurance

**ACE Insurance Ltd:** 6th Floor, NIC Bldg, Abbasi Shaheed Rd, off Shahrah-e-Faisal, Karachi; tel. (21) 5681320; fax (21) 5683935; e-mail zehra.naqvi@ace-ina.com; internet www.ace-ina.com; f. 1853; Chief Exec. ZEHRA NAQVI.

**Adamjee Insurance Co Ltd:** Adamjee House, 6th Floor, I. I. Chundrigar Rd, POB 4850, Karachi 74000; tel. (21) 2410145; fax (21) 2412627; e-mail info@adamjeeinsurance.com; internet www .adamjeeinsurance.com; f. 1960; Man. Dir and CEO ARIF IJAZ.

**Agro General Insurance Co Ltd:** Room No. 416–418, 4th Floor, Continental Trade Centre, Block 8, Main Clifton Rd, Karachi; tel. (21) 5302902-06; fax (21) 5302913; e-mail agiho@cyber.net.pk; f. 1987; Man. Dir and CEO M. JALILULLAH.

**AIG Pakistan New Hampshire Insurance Co:** 7th Floor, Dawood Centre, M. T. Khan Rd, Karachi 75530; tel. (21) 111-111-244; fax (21) 5634022; e-mail info-pakistan@aig.com; internet www.aigpakistan .com; f. 1869; Country Man. GOKTUG GUR.

**Alpha Insurance Co Ltd:** State Life Bldg No. 1B–1C, 2nd Floor, off I. I. Chundrigar Rd, POB 4359, Karachi 74000; tel. (21) 2412609; fax (21) 2419968; f. 1952; Chair. IQBAL M. QURESHI; Man. Dir V. C. GONSALVES; 9 brs.

**Amicus Insurance Co Ltd:** F-50, Block 7, Feroze Nana Rd, Bath Island, POB 3971, Karachi; tel. (21) 5831082; fax (21) 5870220; f. 1991; Chair. M. IRSHAD UDDIN.

**Asia Insurance Co Ltd:** 19C and 19D, Block L, Gulberg III, Ferozepur Rd, Lahore; tel. (42) 5858532; fax (42) 5865579; e-mail asiains@nexlinx.net.pk; f. 1979; Chief Exec. ZAFAR IQBAL SHEIKH.

**Askari General Insurance Co Ltd:** 4th Floor, AWT Plaza, The Mall, POB 843, Rawalpindi; tel. (51) 9272425; fax (51) 9272424; e-mail agicoho@agico.com.pk; internet www.agico.com.pk; f. 1995; Pres. and Chief Exec. M. JAMALUDDIN.

**Business and Industrial Insurance Co Ltd:** 65 East Pak Pavilions, 1st Floor, Fazal-e-Haq Rd, Blue Area, Islamabad; tel. (51) 2278757; fax (51) 2271914; e-mail biic.ltd@yahoo.com; f. 1995; Chair. and Chief Exec. Mian MUMTAZ ABDULLAH.

**Capital Insurance Co Ltd:** Muradia Rd, Model Town, Sialkot; tel. (52) 3563771; fax (52) 3552958; e-mail info@capital-insurance.net; internet www.capital-insurance.net; f. 1998; CEO NAVID IQBAL SHEIKH; Sec. M. I. BUTT.

**Central Insurance Co Ltd:** Dawood Centre, 5th Floor, M. T. Khan Rd, POB 3988, Karachi 75530; tel. (21) 5684019; fax (21) 5680218; e-mail cicl@khi.wol.net.pk; internet www.coninsure.com; f. 1960; Chief Exec. VIQUAR SIDDIQI.

**Century Insurance Co Ltd:** 11th Floor, Lakson Square Bldg No. 3, Sarwar Sheheed Rd, POB 4895, Karachi 74200; tel. (21) 5657445; fax (21) 5671665; e-mail cic@cyber.net.pk; f. 1988; Chair. and Chief Exec. IQBALALI LAKHANI; Dir Mir NADIR ALI.

**CGU Inter Insurance PLC:** 74/1-A, Lalazar, M. T. Khan Rd, POB 4895, Karachi 74000; tel. (21) 5611802; fax (21) 5611456; f. 1861; general and life insurance; Gen. Man. ABDUR RAHIM; 3 brs.

**Commerce Insurance Co Ltd:** 11 Shahrah-e-Quaid-e-Azam, POB 1132, Lahore 54000; tel. (42) 7325330; fax (42) 7230828; f. 1992; Chief Exec. SYED MOIN-UD-DIN.

**Co-operative Insurance Society of Pakistan Ltd:** Co-operative Insurance Bldg, Shahrah-e-Quaid-e-Azam, POB 147, Lahore; tel. (42) 7352306; fax (42) 7352794; f. 1949; Chief Exec. and Gen. Man. CH. AKHTAR MAHMOOD.

**Credit Insurance Co Ltd:** Asmat Chambers, 68 Mazang Rd, Lahore; tel. (42) 6316774; fax (42) 6368868; f. 1995; Chief Exec. MUHAMMAD IKHLAQ BUTT.

**Crescent Star Insurance Co Ltd:** Nadir House, I. I. Chundrigar Rd, POB 4616, Karachi 74000; tel. (21) 2415521; fax (21) 2415474; e-mail crescent_star_ins@hotmail.com; f. 1957; Man. Dir MUNIR I. MILLWALA.

**Dadabhoy Insurance Co Ltd:** Maqbool Commercial Complex, JCHS Block, Main Shahrah-e-Faisal, Karachi; tel. (21) 4545704; fax (21) 4548625; f. 1983; Chief Exec. USMAN DADABHOY.

**Delta Insurance Co Ltd:** 101 Baghpatee Bldg, Altaf Hussain Rd, New Challi, Karachi; tel. (21) 2632297; fax (21) 2422942; f. 1991; Man. Dir SYED ASIF ALI.

**East West Insurance Co Ltd:** 410, EFU House, M. A. Jinnah Rd, POB 6693, Karachi 74000; tel. (21) 2313304; fax (21) 2310821; e-mail info@eastwestins.com; f. 1983; Chair. and Chief Exec. NAVED YUNUS.

**EFU General Insurance Ltd:** EFU House, M. A. Jinnah Rd, Karachi 74000; tel. (21) 2313471; fax (21) 2310450; e-mail info@ efuinsurance.com; internet www.efuinsurance.com; f. 1932; Man. Dir and Chief Exec. SAIFUDDIN N. ZOOMKAWALA.

**Excel Insurance Co Ltd:** 38/C-1, Block 6, PECH Society, Shahrah-e-Faisal, Karachi 75400; tel. (21) 111-777-666; fax (21) 4548076; e-mail eicl@cyber.net.pk; f. 1991; Man. Dir GHULAM H. ALI MOHAMMAD.

**Gulf Insurance Co Ltd:** Gulf House, 1-A Link McLeod Rd, Patiala Grounds, Lahore; tel. (42) 7312028; fax (42) 7234987; f. 1988; Chief Exec. S. ARIF SALAM.

**Habib Insurance Co Ltd:** Insurance House, 6 Habib Sq., M. A. Jinnah Rd, POB 5217, Karachi 74000; tel. (21) 2424038; fax (21) 2421600; e-mail hic@cyber.net.pk; f. 1942; Chair. HAMID D. HABIB; Man. Dir and Chief Exec. ALI RAZA D. HABIB.

**IGI Insurance Ltd:** 7th Floor, The Forum, Suite 701–713m G-20, Block 9, Khayaban-e-Jami, Clifton, Karachi; tel. (21) 5301726-8; fax (21) 5301729; e-mail skhalid@gi.com.pk; internet www.igi.com.pk; Chief Operating Officer S. KHALID YUSUF.

**International General Insurance Co of Pakistan Ltd:** Finlay House, 1st Floor, I. I. Chundrigar Rd, POB 4576, Karachi 74000; tel. (21) 2424976; fax (21) 2416710; e-mail igikhi@cubexs.net.pk; internet www.igi.com.pk; f. 1953; Gen. Man. AHMED SALAHUDDIN.

**Ittefaq General Insurance Co Ltd:** H-16 Murree Rd, Rawalpindi; tel. (51) 5771333; f. 1982; Chief Exec. and Man. Dir Dr SYED ISHTIAQ HUSSAIN SHAH.

**Jupiter Insurance Co Ltd:** 4th Floor, Finlay House, I. I. Chundrigar Rd, POB 4655, Karachi 74000; tel. (21) 2426070; fax (21) 2427660; e-mail jicl20@cyber.net.pk; f. 1994; Chief Exec. MAHMUD HASAN.

**Muslim Insurance Co Ltd:** 3 Bank Sq., Shahrah-e-Quaid-e-Azam, POB 1219, Lahore; tel. (42) 7320542; fax (42) 7234742; e-mail fariq

.rohilla@mickhi.atlasgrouppk.com; f. 1935; Chief Exec. S. C. Subjally.

**National General Insurance Co Ltd:** 401-B, Satellite Town, nr Commercial Market, Rawalpindi; tel. (51) 4427818; fax (51) 4427361; f. 1969; Gen. Man. F. A. Jaffery.

**National Insurance Corpn:** NIC Bldg, Abbasi Shaheed Rd, Karachi 74400; tel. (21) 9202741; fax (21) 9202779; e-mail info@nicl.com.pk; internet www.niclpk.com; govt-owned; sole govt insurance co; Man. Dir Abid Javed Akbar.

**New Jubilee Insurance Co Ltd:** 2nd Floor, Jubilee Insurance House, I. I. Chundrigar Rd, POB 4795, Karachi 74000; tel. (21) 2416022; fax (21) 2416728; e-mail nji@cyber.net.pk; internet www.nji.com.pk; f. 1953; Man. Dir Tahir Ahmed.

**North Star Insurance Co Ltd:** 37–38 Basement, Sadiq Plaza, 69 The Mall, Lahore 54000; tel. (42) 6314308; fax (42) 6375366; e-mail northstarins@hotmail.com; f. 1995; Chief Exec./Man. Dir M. Rafiq Chaudhry.

**Orient Insurance Co Ltd:** 2nd Floor, Dean Arcade, Block No. 8, Kahkeshan, Clifton, Karachi; tel. (21) 5865327; fax (21) 5865724; f. 1987; Man. Dir Fazal Rehman.

**Pak Equity Insurance Co Ltd:** M. K. Arcade, 32 Davis Rd, Lahore; tel. (42) 6361536; fax (42) 6365959; f. 1984; Chief Exec. Ch. Athar Zahoor.

**Pakistan General Insurance Co Ltd:** 3 Bank Sq., Shahrah-e-Quaid-e-Azam, POB 1364, Lahore; tel. (42) 7323569; fax (42) 7230634; f. 1948; Chair. Ch. Azfar Manzoor; Pres. and CEO Ch. Zahoor Ahmad.

**Pakistan Guarantee Insurance Co Ltd:** Al-Falah Court, 3rd and 5th Floors, I. I. Chundrigar Rd, POB 5436, Karachi 74000; tel. (21) 2636111; fax (21) 2638740; f. 1965; Chief Exec. Shakil Raza Syed.

**Pakistan Reinsurance Co Ltd:** PRC Towers, 32A Lalazar Dr., M. T. Khan Rd, POB 4777, Karachi 74000; tel. (21) 9202908; fax (21) 9202921; e-mail pic1@pk.netsolir.com; internet www.pakre.org.pk; Chair. Rukhsana Saleem.

**PICIC Insurance Ltd:** 8th Floor, Shaheen Complex, M. R. Kiyani Rd, Karachi; tel. (21) 2219550; fax (21) 2219561; e-mail info@picicinsurance.com; internet www.picicinsurance.com; Man. Dir and CEO Ahmed Salahuddin.

**Premier Insurance Co of Pakistan Ltd:** 2-A State Life Bldg, 5th Floor, Wallace Rd, off I. I. Chundrigar Rd, POB 4140, Karachi 74000; tel. (21) 2416331; fax (21) 2416572; f. 1952; Chair. Zahid Bashir; CEO Fakhir A. Rahman.

**Prime Insurance Co Ltd:** 505–507, Japan Plaza, M. A. Jinnah Rd, POB 1390, Karachi; tel. (21) 7770801; fax (21) 7725427; f. 1989; Chief Exec. Abdul Majeed.

**Progressive Insurance Co Ltd:** 2nd Floor, Sasi Arcade, Block 7, Main Clifton Rd, Clifton, Karachi; tel. (21) 5823560; fax (21) 5823561; f. 1989; Man. Dir and CEO Abdul Majeed.

**Raja Insurance Co Ltd:** Panorama Centre, 5th Floor, 256 Fatimah Jinnah Rd, POB 10422, Karachi 4; tel. (21) 5670619; fax (21) 5681501; f. 1981; Chair. Raja Abdul Rahman; Man. Dir Sheikh Humayun Sayeed.

**Reliance Insurance Co Ltd:** Reliance Insurance House, 181-A, Sindhi Muslim Co-operative Housing Society, POB 13356, Karachi 74400; tel. (21) 4539415; fax (21) 4539412; e-mail reli-ins@cyber.net.pk; Chief Exec. and Man. Dir Abdul Razak Ahmed.

**Royal & SunAlliance Insurance:** 8th Floor, Shaheen Complex, POB 4930, M. R. Kayani Rd, Karachi 74000; tel. (21) 2635141; fax (21) 2631369; e-mail rsa@cyber.net.pk; internet www.royalsunalliance.com; f. 1989; Chief Exec. and Man. Dir Dr Mumtaz A. Hashmi.

**Royal Exchange Assurance:** P&O Plaza, I. I. Chundrigar Rd, POB 315, Karachi 74000; tel. (21) 2635141; fax (21) 2631369; Man. (Pakistan) Dr Mumtaz A. Hashmi.

**Saudi Pak Insurance Co Ltd:** 2nd Floor, State Life Bldg, No. 2A, Wallace Rd, Karachi; tel. (21) 2418430; fax (21) 2417885; e-mail info@saudipakinsurance.com.pk; Man. Dir and CEO Capt. Azhar Ehtesham Ahmed.

**Seafield Insurance Co Ltd:** 86-Q, Block 2, Allama Iqbal Rd, PECHS, Karachi; tel. (21) 4527592; fax (21) 4527593; e-mail sifcpk89@hotmail.com; f. 1989; Man. Dir Adnan Hafeez.

**Security General Insurance Co Ltd:** Nishat House, 53A Lawrence Rd, Lahore; tel. (42) 6279192; fax (42) 6303466; e-mail sgicl@hotmail.com; f. 1996; Man. Dir Syed Jawad Gillani.

**Shaheen Insurance Co Ltd:** 10th Floor, Shaheen Complex, M. R. Kayani Rd, Karachi 74200; tel. (21) 2626870; fax (21) 2626674; e-mail sihifc@cyber.net.pk; internet www.shaheeninsurance.com.pk; f. 1996; Chief Exec. Shehrayar Akbar Raja.

**Silver Star Insurance Co Ltd:** Silver Star House, 2nd Floor, 5 Bank Sq., POB 2533, Lahore 54000; tel. (42) 7324488; fax (42) 7229966; e-mail info@silverstarinsurance.com; internet www.silverstarinsurance.com; f. 1984; Man. Dir and Chief Exec. Zahir Muhammad Sadiq; Chair. Chaudhry Muhammad Sadiq.

**Trakker Direct Insurance Ltd:** 172-B, 2nd Floor, Najeeb Centre, Block 2, P.E.C.H.S., Karachi; tel. (21) 4322555; fax (21) 4322515; e-mail insurance@trakkerdirect.com; internet www.trakkerdirect.com; CEO Ali Jameel.

**UBL Insurers Ltd:** 8th Floor, State Life Bldg, No. 2, Wallace Rd, off I. I. Chundrigar Rd, Karachi; tel. (21) 111-845-111; fax (21) 2463117; e-mail khalid.hamid@ublinsurers.com; internet www.ublinsurers.com; CEO and Man. Dir Khalid Hamid.

**Union Insurance Co of Pakistan Ltd:** Adamjee House, 9th Floor, I. I. Chundrigar Rd, Karachi; tel. (21) 2416171; fax (21) 2420174; e-mail unionins@cyber.net.pk; Pres. Nishat Raffiq.

**United Insurance Co of Pakistan Ltd:** Nizam Chambers, 5th Floor, Shahrah-e-Fatima Jinnah, POB 532, Lahore; tel. (42) 6361471; fax (42) 6375036; f. 1959; Man. Dir and CEO M. A. Shahid.

**Universal Insurance Co Ltd:** Universal Insurance House, 63 Shahrah-e-Quaid-e-Azam, POB 539, Lahore; tel. (42) 7353458; fax (42) 7230326; e-mail tuic@nexlinx.net.pk; internet www.uic.com.pk; f. 1958; Chief Exec. Begum Zeb Gauhar Ayub Khan; Man. Dir Sardar Khan.

### Insurance Associations

**Insurance Association of Pakistan:** 1713–1715, 17th Floor, Saima Trade Tower A, I. I. Chundrigar Rd, POB 4932, Karachi 74000; tel. (21) 2277165; fax (21) 2277170; e-mail iapho@cyber.net.pk; internet www.iap.net.pk; f. 1948; mems comprise 32 non-life insurance cos and 4 life insurance cos; establishes rules for insurance in the country; regional office in Lahore; Chair. Hasanali Abdullah; Sec. N. A. Usmani.

**Pakistan Insurance Institute:** Shafi Court, 2nd Floor, Mereweather Rd, Karachi 4; f. 1951 to encourage insurance education; Chair. Mohammad Choudhry.

## Trade and Industry

### GOVERNMENT AGENCIES

**Alternative Energy Development Board (AEDB):** 344-B, Prime Minister's Secretariat, Constitution Ave, Islamabad; tel. (51) 9223427; fax (51) 9205790; e-mail support@aedb.org; internet www.aedb.org; f. 2003; mandate incl. development of national plans and policies, undertaking promotion and dissemination of activities in field of renewable energy technologies, facilitation of power generation projects using alternative or renewable energy resources; Chair. Air Marshal (retd) Shahid Hamid.

**Board of Investment (BOI):** Government of Pakistan, Atatürk Ave, Sector G-5/1, Islamabad; tel. (51) 9204339; fax (51) 9215554; e-mail secretary@pakboi.gov.pk; internet www.pakboi.gov.pk; operates under the chairmanship of the Prime Minister of Pakistan and viceroy of the Minister for Privatisation and Investment; Exec. Dir-Gen. Talat Rasheed Rashad Miyan; Sec. Mushtaq Malik.

**Central Board of Revenue:** Constitution Ave, G-5, Islamabad; tel. (51) 9207545; fax (51) 9207540; e-mail helpline@cbr.gov.pk; internet www.cbr.gov.pk; tax authority; Chair. M. Abdullah Yusuf.

**Corporate and Industrial Restructuring Corpn:** 13-C-II, M. M. Alam Rd, Gulberg III, Lahore; tel. (42) 5871532; fax (42) 5761650; e-mail info@circ-gov.com.

**Earthquake Reconstruction and Rehabilitation Authority (ERRA):** Prime Minister's Secretariat (Public), Constitution Ave, Islamabad; tel. (51) 9201254; fax (51) 9209525; e-mail chairman@erra.gov.pk; internet www.erra.gov.pk; f. 2005; Chair. Altaf Saleem.

**Electronic Government Directorate:** 10-D, 3rd Floor, Taimur Chambers, Blue Area West, Islamabad; tel. (51) 9205992; fax (51) 9205981; e-mail contact@e-government.gov.pk; internet www.pakistan.gov.pk/e-government-directorate; f. 2002; fmrly the Information Technology Commission; subsidiary department of the Ministry of Information Technology and Communications; Dir-Gen. of Projects Syed Raza Abbas Shah.

**Engineering Development Board:** 5-A, Constitution Ave, SEDC Bldg (STP), Sector F-5/1, Islamabad 44000; tel. (51) 9205595; fax (51) 9203584; e-mail ceo@edb.gov.pk; internet www.engineeringpakistan.com; CEO Imtiaz A. Rastgar.

**Environmental Protection Agency:** Govt of Sindh, EPA Complex, ST-2/1, Sector 23, Korangi Industrial Area, Karachi; tel. (21) 5065950; fax (21) 5065940.

**Export Processing Zones Authority (EPZA):** Landhi Industrial Area Extension, Mehran Highway, Landhi, Karachi 75150; tel. (21) 5082008; fax (21) 5082009; e-mail info@epza.gov.pk; internet www.epza.gov.pk; Chair. Kamran Mirza.

**Family Planning Association of Pakistan** (Rahnuma—FPAP): 3-A Temple Rd, Lahore 54000; tel. (42) 111-223-366; fax (42) 6368692; e-mail info@fpapak.org; internet www.fpapak.org; f. 1953; executes diversified community uplift programmes and activities; Pres. Begum SURAYYA JABEEN; CEO SYED KAMAL SHAH.

**Geological Survey of Pakistan:** Sariab Rd, POB 15, Quetta; tel. (81) 9211032; fax (81) 9211018; e-mail qta@gsp.gov.pk; internet www.gsp.gov.pk; Dir-Gen. MIRZA TALIB HASAN; Asst Dir MOHSIN ANWAR KAZIM.

**Gwadar Port Authority:** GPA Complex, Fish Harbour Rd, Gwadar 92100; tel. (864) 210073; fax (864) 210075; e-mail gwadarport@hotmail.com; internet www.gwadarport.gov.pk.

**Higher Education Commission:** H-9, Islamabad; tel. (51) 9040305; fax (51) 9290120; e-mail info@hec.gov.pk; internet www.hec.gov.pk; Exec. Dir Dr S. SOHAIL H. NAQVI.

**Intellectual Property Organization of Pakistan (IPO-PAKISTAN):** House 23, St 87, Ataturk Ave (West), G-6/3, Islamabad; tel. (51) 9208146; fax (51) 9208157; e-mail info@ipo.gov.pk; internet www.ipo.gov.pk; f. 2005; Dir-Gen. YASIN TAHIR.

**Karachi Export Processing Zone (KEPZ):** Landhi Industrial Area Extension, Mehran Highway, POB 17011, Karachi 75150; tel. (21) 5082010; fax (21) 5082009; e-mail info@epza.gov.pk; internet www.epza.gov.pk.

**National Accountability Bureau:** Atatürk Ave, G-5/2, Islamabad; tel. (51) 111-622-622; fax (51) 9214502; e-mail infonab@nab.gov.pk; internet www.nab.gov.pk.

**National Aliens Registration Authority (NARA):** C-82, Block 2, Clifton, Karachi; tel. (21) 9251083; f. 2001; registers all foreign nationals who wish to work in Pakistan.

**National Commission for Human Development:** 14th Floor, Shaheed-e-Millat Secretariat, Jinnah Ave, Islamabad; tel. (51) 9216200; fax (51) 9216164; e-mail info@nchd.org.pk; internet www.nchd.org.pk; f. 2002.

**National Database and Registration Authority (NADRA):** State Bank of Pakistan Bldg, Shahrah-e-Jamhuriat, G-5/2, Islamabad; tel. (51) 9201120; e-mail info@nadra.gov.pk; internet www.nadra.gov.pk.

**National Economic Council:** supreme economic body; the governors and chief ministers of the four provinces and fed. ministers in charge of economic ministries are its mems; sr fed. and provincial officials in the economic field are also associated; Chair. Prime Minister.

**National Electric Power Regulatory Authority (NEPRA):** (see Utilities).

**National Energy Conservation Centre (ENERCON):** ENERCON Bldg, G-5/2, Islamabad; tel. (51) 9206005; fax (51) 9206004; e-mail ferts@enercon.gov.pk; internet www.enercon.gov.pk; Man. Dir Dr PERVAIZ TAHIR.

**National Highway Authority (NHA):** (see Transport: Roads).

**National Housing Authority:** Prime Minister's Office, Islamabad; tel. (51) 9202279; fax (51) 9217813; Dir-Gen. SALIM IQBAL QURESHI.

**National Tariff Commission:** State Life Bldg, No. 5, Blue Area, Jinnah Ave, POB 1689, Islamabad 44000; tel. (51) 9208790; fax (51) 9221205; e-mail ntc@ntc.gov.pk; internet www.ntc.gov.pk; f. 1990; Chair. M. IKRAM ARIF.

**National Testing Service (NTS):** 10–11, Plaza 2000, 1st Floor, Plot 43, Markaz I-8, Islamabad; tel. (51) 9258478; fax (51) 9258480; e-mail support@nts.org.pk; internet www.nts.org.pk; conducts assessment programs for students at all educational levels; facilitates employment and career development through subject testing.

**Oil and Gas Regulatory Authority:** Tariq Chambers, Civic Centre, G-6, Islamabad; tel. (51) 9221715; fax (51) 9221714; e-mail secretary@ogra.org.pk; internet www.ogra.org.pk; regulates oil and gas sector; Chair. MUNIR AHMAD.

**Pakistan Electronic Media Regulatory Authority:** Islamabad; tel. (51) 9202174; fax (51) 9219634; e-mail info@pemra.gov.pk; internet www.pemra.gov.pk; f. 2002; Chair. IFTIKHAR RASHID; Dir-Gen. RANA ALTAF MAJID.

**Pakistan National Accreditation Council (PNAC):** Ministry of Scientific and Technological Research, 4th Floor, Evacuee Trust Complex, Aga Khan Rd, F-5/1, Islamabad; tel. (51) 9222310; fax (51) 9222312; e-mail ismailgulkhatak@yahoo.com; f. 1998; Dir-Gen. ABDUL RASHID KHAN.

**Pakistan Software Export Board (Guarantee) Ltd:** 2nd Floor, Evacuee Trust Complex, F-5/1, Aga Khan Rd, Islamabad; tel. (51) 9204074; fax (51) 9204075; e-mail info@pseb.org.pk; internet www.pseb.org.pk; Man. Dir YUSUF HUSSAIN.

**Pakistan Standards and Quality Control Authority (PSQCA):** Pakistan Secretariat, Block 77, Karachi 74400; tel. and fax (21) 9206260; fax (21) 9206263; e-mail psqcadg@super.net.pk; internet www.psqca.com.pk; f. 1996; regulates standards in industry; Dir-Gen. ABDUL GHAFFAR SOOMRO.

**Pakistan Stone Development Co:** I. C. C. I. Bldg, 2nd Floor, Mauve Area, G-8/A, Islamabad; tel. (51) 9263465; fax (51) 9263464; f. 2006; promotes devt of marble and granite sector; Chair. IHSANULLAH KHAN.

**Pakistan Telecommunication Authority:** (see Telecommunications).

**Pakistan Tobacco Board:** 46-B Office Enclave, Phase-V, Hayatabad, POB 188, Peshawar; tel. (91) 9217151; fax (91) 9217149; e-mail mail@ptb.gov.pk; internet www.ptb.gov.pk; f. 1968; regulates, controls and promotes the export of tobacco and related products, and fixes grading standards; Chair. Maj. SAHIBZADA MUHAMMAD KHALID; Research and Devt Dir MUHAMMAD TARIQ.

**Privatisation Commission:** Experts Advisory Cell Bldg, 5A Constitution Ave, Islamabad 44000; tel. (51) 9205146; fax (51) 9203076; e-mail info@privatisation.gov.pk; internet www.privatisation.gov.pk; supervised by Ministry of Privatisation and Investment.

**Sindh Katchi Abadis Authority (SKAA):** Maulana Din Muhammad Wafai Rd, Karachi 74200; tel. (21) 9211278; fax (21) 9211272; e-mail skaa@khi.compol.com; internet www.lgdsindh.com.pk/skaa.htm; f. 1987; govt agency established to regulate and improve slums in Pakistan's southern province; Dir-Gen. MIR NASIR ABBAS.

**Sindh Privatisation Commission:** Sindh Secretariat, 4-A, Block 15, Court Rd, Karachi; tel. (21) 9202077; fax (21) 9202071; e-mail spcsecretary@yahoo.com; Sec. SYED ZULFIQAR ALI SHAH.

**Sustainable Development Policy Institute:** St 3, UN Blvd, Diplomatic Enclave 1, Islamabad; tel. (51) 2278134; fax (51) 2278135; e-mail msf@sdpi.org; internet www.sdpi.org; f. 1992; Co-ordinator MOHAMMAD SHAH FARRUKH.

**Trade Development Authority of Pakistan (TDAP):** Finance and Trade Centre, Block A, 5th Floor, POB 1203, Shahrah-e-Faisal, Karachi 75200; tel. (21) 1114441; fax (21) 9206487; e-mail tdap@tdap.gov.pk; internet www.tdap.gov.pk; f. 1963 as Export Promotion Bureau (EPB) affiliated to the Ministry of Commerce; Trade Development Authority was established in Nov. 2006 by an Ordinance of President Musharraf to assume all functions fmrly dispatched by the EPB; Chair. TARIQ IKRAM; Sec. ZAFAR MAHMOOD.

**Trading Corporation of Pakistan:** 4th and 5th Floors, Finance and Trade Centre, Main Shahrah-e-Faisal, Karachi 75530; tel. (21) 9202947-9; fax (21) 9202722; e-mail tcp@tcp.gov.pk; internet www.tcp.gov.pk; f. 1967; Chair. ABDUL MALIK.

**Utility Stores Corporation of Pakistan:** Plot No. 2039, G-7/F-7, POB 1339, Jinnah Ave, Blue Area, Islamabad; tel. (51) 9210976; fax (51) 9210982; e-mail usc_ho@yahoo.com; internet www.usc.com.pk; f. 1971; Man. Dir Brig. (retd) HAFEEZ AHMED.

## DEVELOPMENT ORGANIZATIONS

**Balochistan Development Authority:** Civil Secretariat, Block 7, Quetta; tel. (81) 9202491; created for economic devt of Balochistan; exploration and exploitation of mineral resources; development of infrastructure, water resources, etc.

**Capital Development Authority:** Islamabad; tel. (51) 9201016; fax (51) 9219413; internet www.cda.gov.pk; Chair. KAMRAN LASHARI.

**Center for International Private Enterprise (Pakistan) (CIPE):** Glass Tower, Suite 214–15, 2 Ft 3, adjacent to PSO House, Main Clifton Rd, Karachi 75530; tel. (21) 5656993; e-mail pakistan@cipe.org; internet www.cipe.org; international org.; affiliate of US Chamber of Commerce and key member of National Endowment for Democracy; US Agency for international Development supports programs of CIPE; Country Dir M. MOIN FUDDA.

**Council for Works and Housing Research (CWHR):** F-40, SITE Hub River Rd, Karachi 75730; tel. (21) 2577236; fax (21) 2577235; e-mail cwhr@khi.comsats.net.pk; internet www.cwhr.gov.pk; f. 1964.

**Faisalabad Industrial Estate Development & Management Co (FIEDMC):** Faisalabad; tel. (41) 8523106; fax (41) 8522884; e-mail fiedmc@fiedmc.com.pk; internet www.fiedmc.com.pk; established by the Punjab state government under the Public Private Partnership system to promote devt of industrial estates; Chair. Mian MUHAMMAD LATIF; CEO KHURRAM IFTIKHAR.

**Gwadar Development Authority:** Governor House Rd, Gwadar; tel. and fax (86) 4211775; e-mail info@gda.gov.pk; internet www.gda.gov.pk; Dir-Gen. AHMAD BAKSH LEHRI.

**Lahore Development Authority (LDA):** LDA Plaza, 9th Floor, Egerton Rd, Lahore; tel. (42) 9201510; internet www.lda.gop.pk; f. 1975; Dir of Admin. ABDUL HAMEED CHAUDHRY.

**Lasbella Industrial Estate Development Authority (LIEDA):** Hub Industrial Trading Estate, Lasbella, Balochistan; tel. (853) 303361; fax (853) 302470; e-mail lieda@lieda.gov.pk; est. under section 3 of Government of Balochistan Ordinance IX (1989);

promotes devt of industrial concerns over 1,000 acre coastal Highway region; Man. Dir Col (retd) BASHIR AHMED NADIM.

**Malir Development Authority:** Main Northern By-Pass, Scheme No. 45, Taisar Town, Karachi; Dir-Gen. AMEERZADA KOHATI; Chair. SYED MUSTAFA KAMAL.

**National Commission for Human Development:** Shaheed-e-Millat Secretariat, 14th Floor, Jinnah Ave, Islamabad; tel. (51) 9216200; fax (51) 9216164; e-mail info@nchd.org.pk; internet www.nchd.org.pk; f. 2001 by presidential decree; facilitates programs towards achievement of the UNDP Millennium Development Goals; Chair. Dr NASIM ASHRAF.

**Pakistan Engineering Council:** Ataturk Ave (East), G-5/2, Islamabad; tel. (51) 9206974; fax (51) 2276224; e-mail info@pec.org.pk; internet www.pec.org.pk; f. 1976; Chair. M. AKRAM SHEIKH.

**Pakistan Gems & Jewellery Development Co (PGJDC):** Regent Plaza Hotel and Convention Centre, M-3 Mezzanine Floor, Shahra-e-Faisal, Karachi; tel. (21) 5631394; fax (21) 5631398; e-mail info@pgjdc.org; internet www.pgjdc.org; f. 2006; est. as non-profit org under Ministry of Industries, Production and Special Initiatives; subsidiary of Pakistan Industrial Devt Corpn; promotes devt of Pakistan's gem and jewellery industry; CEO FAWAD KHAN.

**Pakistan Industrial Technical Assistance Centre (PITAC):** 234 Maulana Jalaluddin Roomi Rd (old Ferozepur Rd), Lahore 54600; tel. (42) 9230699; fax (42) 9230589; e-mail info@pitac.gov.pk; internet www.pitac.gov.pk; f. 1962 by the Govt to provide prototype tooling facilities and spare parts to manufacturing industries and advanced training to industrial personnel in the fields of metal trades and tool engineering design and related fields; under Ministry of Industries, Production and Special Initiatives; provides human resource devt programmes; Chair. MANZAR SHAMIM; Gen. Man. Lt-Col (retd) KHAN M. NAZIR.

**Pakistan Poverty Alleviation Fund:** House No. 1, St 20, F-7/2, Islamabad; tel. (51) 111-000-102; fax (51) 2652246; e-mail info@ppaf.org.pk; internet www.ppaf.org.pk; f. 1997 by the Government; funded by the World Bank; works with non-governmental organizations and private-sector institutions to alleviate poverty; 68 partner orgs nationwide; Chief Exec. and Man. Dir KAMAL HAYAT.

**Quetta Development Authority:** Sarai Rd, Quetta; tel. (81) 9211069.

**Sarhad Development Authority (SDA):** PIA Bldg, Arbab Rd, POB 172, Peshawar; tel. (91) 9211608; fax (91) 9211605; e-mail sda.psh@ntc.net.pk; internet www.sda.org.pk; f. 1972; promotes industrial and commercial devt in the North-West Frontier Province; Chair. GHULAM DASTGIR AKHTAR.

**Small and Medium Enterprises Development Authority (SMEDA):** 6th Floor, LDA Plaza, Egerton Rd, Lahore; tel. (42) 111-111-456; fax (42) 6304926; e-mail helpdesk@smeda.org.pk; internet www.smeda.org.pk; f. 1998; four brs; 18 regional business centres; CEO SHAHAB KHAWAJA.

## CHAMBERS OF COMMERCE

**The Federation of Pakistan Chambers of Commerce and Industry:** Federation House, Main Clifton, POB 13875, Karachi 75600; tel. (21) 5873691; fax (21) 5874332; e-mail fpcci@cyber.net.pk; internet www.fpcci.com.pk; f. 1950; 163 mem. bodies; Pres. TANVIR AHMED SHAIKH; Sec.-Gen. and CEO ZAHID HUSSAIN.

**Islamic Chamber of Commerce and Industry:** St 2/A, Block 9, KDA Scheme 5, Clifton, Karachi 75600; tel. (21) 5874756; fax (21) 5870765; e-mail icci@icci-oic.org; internet www.iccionline.net; f. 1979; Pres. Sheikh SALEH BIN ABDULLAH KAMEL; Sec.-Gen. Dr MOSTAFA HODIEB.

**Overseas Investors' Chamber of Commerce and Industry:** Chamber of Commerce Bldg, Talpur Rd, POB 4833, Karachi 74000; tel. (21) 2426076; fax (21) 2427315; e-mail info@oicci.org; internet www.oicci.org; f. 1860 as the Karachi Chamber of Commerce, name changed to above in 1968; 175 mem. bodies; Pres. WAQAR A. MALIK; Sec.-Gen. UNJELA SIDDIQI.

### Principal Affiliated Chambers

**Azad Jammu and Kashmir Chamber of Commerce and Industry:** 9, Sector G/1, Haul Rd, POB 12, Mirpur 10250; tel. (58610) 34760; fax (58610) 34761; e-mail ajkcci@hotmail.com; internet www.ajkcci.com; f. 1980; Sec. CHAUDHRY MUHAMMAD SHAFIQ.

**Bahawalpur Chamber of Commerce and Industry:** 28 C/A, Abbasi Rd, off Shahrah-e-Azia Bhatti Shaheed, Model Town A, Bahawalpur; tel. and fax (621) 883192; e-mail chamber@pakview.com; Pres. Khawaja MOHAMMAD ILYAS.

**Balochistan Chamber of Commerce and Industry:** Zarghoon Rd, POB 117, Quetta 87300; tel. (81) 2835717; fax (81) 2821948; e-mail qcci@hotmail.com; f. 1984; Pres. Sheikh ABDUL AZIZ; Sec. MUHAMMAD AHMAD.

**Chaman Chamber of Commerce and Industry:** Commerce House, Chaman; tel. (826) 613308.

**Dadu Chamber of Commerce and Industry:** 816, 8th Floor, Progressive Plaza, Beaumont Rd, Karachi; tel. (21) 5219026; fax (21) 5650006; e-mail daduchamber@hotmail.com.

**Dera Ghazi Khan Chamber of Commerce and Industry:** Block 34, Khakwani House, Dera Ghazi Khan, Punjab; tel. (641) 62338; fax (641) 64938; Pres. Khawaja MOHAMMAD YUNUS; Sec. MOHAMMAD MUJAHID.

**Dera Ismail Khan Chamber of Commerce and Industry:** Circular Rd, POB 5, D. I. Khan; tel. (961) 811334; fax (961) 811334; e-mail sjbdn@epistemics.net.

**Faisalabad Chamber of Commerce and Industry:** 2nd Floor, National Bank Bldg, Jail Rd, Faisalabad; tel. (41) 616045; fax (41) 615085; e-mail fcci@fsd.paknet.com.pk; Pres. Mian AFTAB AHMAD; Sec. SYED RIAZ HUSSAIN RIZVI.

**Gwadar Chamber of Commerce and Industry:** Main Clifton Rd, Gwadar; tel. (21) 5375071; fax (21) 5876336; e-mail info@gawadarchamber.com; internet gawadarchamber.com; Pres. ASGHAR AZIZ SANJARANI.

**Gujranwala Chamber of Commerce and Industry:** Aiwan-e-Tijarat Rd, Gujranwala; tel. (55) 3256701; fax (55) 3254440; internet www.gcci.org.pk; f. 1978; Pres. RANA SHAHZAD HAFEEZ; Sec. SYED MUJAHID MUMTAZ.

**Gujrat Chamber of Commerce and Industry:** 26-A, G. T. Rd, S.I.E. POB 169, Gujrat; tel. (4331) 523012; fax (4331) 523011; Pres. CH. IFTIKHAR AHMED.

**Haripur Chamber of Commerce and Industry:** Chamber House, GPO Rd, Haripur; tel. (995) 613364; fax (995) 614664; e-mail haripur-chamber@yahoo.com; internet www.hccl.org.pk; Pres. Haji FAKHAR-E-ALAM; Sec.-Gen. FAQIR MUHAMMAD KHAN.

**Hyderabad Chamber of Commerce and Industry:** Aiwan-e-Tijarat Rd, Saddar, POB 99, Hyderabad 71000; tel. (22) 2784972; fax (22) 2784977; e-mail hcci@muchomail.com; internet www.hyderabadchamber.com; f. 1961; Pres. Haji MUHAMMAD YAQOOB; Sec.-Gen. Dr MOHAMAD ALI MIAN.

**Islamabad Chamber of Commerce and Industry:** Aiwan-e-Sana't-o-Tijarat Rd, Mauve Area, Sector G-8/1, Islamabad; tel. (51) 2250526; fax (51) 2252950; e-mail icci@brain.net.pk; internet www.icci.com.pk; f. 1984; Pres. MUHAMMED IJAZ ABBASI; Sec. MAJID SHABBIR.

**Jhelum Chamber of Commerce and Industry:** G. T. Rd, Jhelum; tel. (544) 646532; fax (544) 646229; e-mail jhelumcci@gmail.com; internet www.jlmcci.com; Pres. RAJA MUHAMMAD ANWER; Sec. Capt. (retd) MUHAMMAD ZAMAN.

**Karachi Chamber of Commerce and Industry:** Aiwan-e-Tijarat Rd, off Shahrah-e-Liaquat, POB 4158, Karachi 74000; tel. (21) 5873691; fax (21) 5874332; e-mail info@karachichamber.com; internet www.karachichamber.com; f. 1960; 11,705 mems; Pres. HAROON FARUQI; Sec. M. NAZIR ALI.

**Khairpur Chamber of Commerce and Industry:** Shop 8, Sachal Shopping Centre, Khairpur; tel. (792) 51505.

**Lahore Chamber of Commerce and Industry:** 11 Shahrah-e-Aiwan-e-Tijarat, POB 597, Lahore; tel. (42) 6305538; fax (42) 6368854; e-mail sect@lcci.org.pk; internet www.lcci.org.pk; f. 1923; 8,000 mems; Pres. MOHAMAD ALI MIAN; Sec. M. LATIF CHAUDHRY.

**Larkana Chamber of Commerce and Industry:** 21–23 Kenedy Market, POB 78, Larkana, Sindh; tel. (741) 457136; fax (741) 440709; e-mail president@larkanachamber.com; internet www.larkanachamber.com; Pres. MOHAMMAD ASLAM SHEIKH.

**Mirpurkhas Chamber of Commerce and Industry:** Khan Chamber, New Town, POB 162, Mirpurkhas, Sindh; tel. (233) 872175; fax (233) 872195; Pres. ABDUL KHALIQUE KHAN; Sec. MOHAMMAD BASIT-ULLAH BAIG.

**Multan Chamber of Commerce and Industry:** Shahrah-e-Aiwan-e-Tijarat-o-Sanat, Multan; tel. (61) 4517087; fax (61) 4570463; e-mail mccimultan@hotmail.com; Pres. Mian MUGHIS A. SHEIKH; Sec. G. A. BHATTI.

**Quetta Chamber of Commerce and Industry:** Zarghoon Rd, POB 117, Quetta 87300; tel. (81) 2821943; fax (81) 2821948; e-mail qcci@hotmail.com; Pres. MOHAMMAD SIDDIQUE KAKAR; Sec. MUHAMMAD AHMED.

**Rawalpindi Chamber of Commerce and Industry:** 39 Mayo Rd, Civil Lines, Rawalpindi; tel. (51) 5110514; fax (51) 5111055; e-mail rcci@isd.wol.net.pk; f. 1952; Pres. HUSSAIN AHMED OZGAN; Sec. MUHAMMAD IFTIKHAR-UD-DIN.

**SAARC Chamber of Commerce and Industry:** House No. 397, St No. 64, I-8/3, Islamabad; tel. (51) 2281396; fax (51) 2281390; e-mail eaqav.ahmad@saarcchamber.com; internet www.saarcchamber.com; f. 1993; Dir WAQAV AHMAD.

**Sargodha Chamber of Commerce and Industry:** 80/2-A, Satellite Town, Sargodha 40100; tel. (48) 9230662; fax (48) 9230663; e-mail sgdacci@hotmail.com; f. 1986; Pres. ABID RAFIQUE KHAWAJA; Sec.-Gen. KASHIF MUKHTAR SHEIKH.

**Sarhad Chamber of Commerce and Industry:** Sarhad Chamber House, Family Park, G. T. Rd, Peshawar; tel. (91) 9213314; fax (91) 9213316; e-mail sccip@brain.net.pk; internet www.scci.org.pk; f. 1958; 3,159 mems; Pres. HAJI MUHAMMAD ASAF; Sec. FAQIR MUHAMMAD.

**Sialkot Chamber of Commerce and Industry:** Shahrah-e-Aiwan-e-Sanat-o-Tijarat, POB 1870, Sialkot 51310; tel. (52) 4261881; fax (52) 4268835; e-mail directorrnd@scci.com.pk; internet www.scci.com.pk; f. 1982; 7,500 mems; Pres. Sheikh ABDUL WAHEED SANDAL; Sec. NAWAZ AHMED TOOR.

**Sukkur Chamber of Commerce and Industry:** Sukkur Chamber House, 1st Floor, opp. Mehran View Plaza, Bunder Rd, Sukkur; tel. (71) 23938; fax (71) 23059; Pres. SHAKEEL AHMED MUKHTAR; Sec. MIRZA IQBAL BEG.

**Thatta Chamber of Commerce and Industry:** PO Shaffiabad, Gharo, Thatta; tel. (14) 7726243; fax (14) 7725122; e-mail malodhi@lodhico.khi2.erum.com.pk.

## INDUSTRIAL AND TRADE ASSOCIATIONS

**Air Cargo Agents' Association of Pakistan:** Suite 305, 3rd Floor, Fortune Centre, 45-A, Block 6, PECHS, Shahrah-e-Faisal, Karachi 75400; tel. (21) 4383501; e-mail acaap@pk.netsolier.com; Sec.-Gen. S. MOHAMMAD ABBAS.

**All Pakistan Cement Manufacturers' Association:** 5th Floor, Maqbool Commercial Comp., J.C.H.S., Shahrah-e-Faisal, Karachi; tel. (21) 5758360.

**All Pakistan Cloth Exporters' Association:** 30/7, Civil Lines, Faisalabad; tel. (41) 644750; fax (41) 617985; e-mail apcea@fsd.paknet.com.pk; Chair. AHMAD KAMAL; Sec. AFTAB AHMAD.

**All Pakistan Cloth Merchants' Association:** 4th Floor, Hasan Ali Centre, Hussaini Cloth Market, nr Mereweather Tower, M. A. Jinnah Rd, Karachi; tel. (21) 2444274; fax (21) 2401423; e-mail pcma@cyber.net.pk; Chair. AHMED CHINOY; Sec.-Gen. RAFIQ KHAN.

**All Pakistan Cotton Powerlooms' Association:** P-79/3, Montgomery Bazaar, Faisalabad; tel. (411) 612929; fax (411) 28171; Chair. CHAUDRY JAVAID SADIQ.

**All Pakistan Furniture Exporters' Association:** Karachi; tel. (21) 5861963; Chair. TURHAN BAIG MOHAMMAD.

**All Pakistan Textile Mills' Association (APTMA):** APTMA House, 44A Lalazar, off Moulvi Tamizuddin Khan Rd, POB 5446, Karachi 74000; tel. (21) 111-700-000; fax (21) 5611305; e-mail aptma@cyber.net.pk; internet www.aptma.org.pk; f. 1959; COO MUHAMMAD AZAM; Chair. SHAFQAT ELLAHI SHEIKH.

**Association of Builders and Developers of Pakistan:** Abed House, St 1-1/10, Block 16, Gulistan-e-Jauhar, Karachi 75290; tel. (21) 8136456; fax (21) 8113648.

**Cigarette Manufacturers' Association of Pakistan:** Caesars Towers (opp. Aisha Bawany Academy), Rm 102, 1st Floor, Main Shahrah-e-Faisal, Karachi 75400; tel. and fax (21) 2789555; e-mail cmaofpak@cyber.net.pk; Sec. TARIQ FAROOQ.

**Cotton Board:** Dr Abbasi Clinic Bldg, 76 Strachan Rd, Karachi 74200; tel. (21) 215669; fax (21) 5680422; f. 1950; Dep. Sec. Dr MUHAMMAD USMAN.

**Federal 'B' Area Association of Trade and Industry:** ST-7, Block 22, Federal 'B' Area, Karachi 75950; tel. (21) 6340362; fax (21) 6360203; e-mail info@fbati.com; internet www.fbati.com; Chair. MASROOR AHMAD ALVI.

**Karachi Cotton Association:** The Cotton Exchange, I. I. Chundrigar Rd, Karachi; tel. (21) 2410336; fax (21) 2413035; e-mail kcapak@cyber.net.pk; internet www.kcapak.org; Chair. A. SHAKOOR DADA; Sec. S. A. JAWED.

**Korangi Association of Trade and Industry:** ST-4/2, 1st Floor, Aiwan-e-Sanat, Sector 23, Korangi Industrial Area, Karachi 74900; tel. (21) 5061211; fax (21) 5061215; e-mail kati@cyber.net.pk; Chair. MASOOD NAQI; Sec. NIHAL AKHTAR.

**Management Association of Pakistan:** 36-A/4, Lalazar, opp. Beach Luxury Hotel, Karachi 74000; tel. (21) 5610903; fax (21) 5611683; e-mail info@mappk.org; internet www.mappk.org; f. 1964; Pres. SOHAIL WAJAHAT H. SIDDIQUI; Exec. Dir FAROOQ HASSAN.

**Pakistan Advertising Association:** Rm 318, 3rd Floor, Hotel Metropole, Club Rd, Karachi; tel. (21) 5671567; fax (21) 5671571; e-mail paa1@cyber.net.pk; internet www.paa.com.pk; Sec. S. NAJMUL HASSAN.

**Pakistan Agricultural Machinery and Implements Manufacturers' Association:** Samundari Rd, Faisalabad; tel. (41) 714517; fax (41) 722721; e-mail iqra@fsd.comsats.net.pk.

**Pakistan Arms and Ammunition Merchants' and Manufacturers' Association:** Metropole Cinema Bldg, Rm 7, Abbot Rd, Lahore; tel. (42) 7239973; fax (42) 7230170; e-mail ssalimali@hotmail.com.

**Pakistan Art Silk Fabrics and Garments Exporters' Association:** 60, The Mall, Lahore; tel. (42) 6360919; fax (42) 6361291; e-mail pasfgea@hotmail.com; internet www.pasfgea.org; Chair. JAMIL MEHBOOB MAGOON; Sec.-Gen. IFTIKHAR AHMED KHAN.

**Pakistan Association of Automotive Parts and Accessories Manufacturers:** 894 Circular Rd, nr Nigar Cinema, Lahore; tel. (42) 7312452; fax (42) 7237613; e-mail secypaapam@hotmail.com.

**Pakistan Association of Builders and Developers:** Abad House, St 1/D, Block 16, Gulistan-e-Jauhar, Karachi; tel. (21) 8113645; fax (21) 8113648; e-mail abadhouse@yahoo.com.

**Pakistan Association of Printing and Graphic Arts:** 214, Mashriq Centre, 2nd Floor, Staduim Rd, Karachi; tel. (21) 4920175; fax (21) 4926625; e-mail info@papgai.com.pk; internet www.papgai.com.pk; f. 1959; affiliated with the federation of Pakistan Chambers of Commerce and Industry; promotion and devt of the printing and graphic arts industry; Chair. GHAS AHMED PIRZADA.

**Pakistan Automotive Manufacturers' Association:** 11 Ilaco House, Abdullah Haroon Rd, Karachi; tel. (21) 5662493; fax (21) 5687247; e-mail pamauto@cyber.net.pk.

**Pakistan Bedwear Exporters' Association:** 245-1-V, Block 6, PECHS, Karachi; tel. (21) 4541149; fax (21) 4541192; e-mail bedwear@fascom.com; Chair. SHABIR AHMED; Sec. S. IFTIKHAR HUSSAIN.

**Pakistan Beverage Manufacturers' Association:** C, 1st Floor, Kiran Centre, M-28, Model Town Extension, Lahore; tel. (42) 5167306; fax (42) 5167316.

**Pakistan Canvas and Tents Manufacturers' and Exporters' Association:** 15/63, Shadman Commercial Market, Afridi Mansion, Lahore 3; tel. (42) 7578836; fax (42) 7577572; e-mail pctmea@wol.net.pk; Chair. ABDUL RAZAK CHHAPRA; Sec. IJAZ HUSSAIN.

**Pakistan Carpet Manufacturers' and Exporters' Association:** 401-A, 4th Floor, Panorama Center, Fatima Jinnah Rd, Saddar, Karachi 75530; tel. (21) 5212189; fax (21) 5679649; e-mail pcmeaho@gerrys.net; internet www.pakistanrug.com.pk; Chair. JAVED-UR-RAHMAN; Sec. A. S. HASHMI.

**Pakistan Chemicals and Dyes Merchants' Association:** Chemicals and Dyes House, Rambharti St, Jodia Bazar, Karachi; tel. (21) 2432752; fax (21) 2430117; e-mail pcdma@super.net.pk; Chair. MAHMOOD SALAM; Sec.-Gen. SYED MUSARRAT ALI.

**Pakistan Commercial Exporters of Towels Association:** PCETA House, 7-H, Block 6, PECHS, Karachi; tel. (21) 4535757; fax (21) 4522372; e-mail pceta@cyber.net.pk; Chair. JAMIL MAHBOOB MAGOON.

**Pakistan Cotton Fashion Apparel Manufacturers' and Exporters' Association:** Rm 5, Amber Court, 2nd Floor, Shahrah-e-Faisal, Shaheed-e-Millat Rd, Karachi 75350; tel. (21) 4533936; fax (21) 4546711; e-mail pcfa@cyber.net.pk; f. 1982; 650 mems; Chair. Dr SHAHZAD ARSHAD.

**Pakistan Cotton Ginners' Association:** 1119–1120, 11th Floor, Uni-Plaza, I. I. Chundrigar Rd, Karachi; tel. (21) 2411406; fax (21) 2423181; e-mail pcga@pgca.org; Pres. MOHAMMAD SAEED; Sec. AIJAZUDDIN GHAURI.

**Pakistan Dairy Association:** 11/19-B, Link Shami Rd, Lahore; tel. (42) 6680041; fax (42) 6682042; e-mail pakdairy@yahoo.com.

**Pakistan Electronic Manufacturers' Association:** 1st Floor, Rizvi Chambers, Akbar Rd, Karachi; tel. (21) 7766912; fax (21) 5874546.

**Pakistan Engineering Council:** Atatürk Ave (East), Sector G-5/2, Islamabad; tel. (51) 2276625; fax (51) 2276224; e-mail info@pec.org.pk; internet www.pec.org.pk; f. 1976.

**Pakistan Film Producers' Association:** Regal Cinema Bldg, Shahrah-e-Quaid-e-Azam, Lahore; tel. (42) 7322904; fax (42) 7241264; Chair. Mian AMJAD FARZEND; Sec. SAMI DEHLVI.

**Pakistan Flour Mills' Association:** Taj Complex, Block C-3, 1st Floor, Line Development Area, M. A. Jinnah Rd, Karachi; tel. (21) 5010556; fax (21) 7780137.

**Pakistan Footwear Manufacturers' Association:** 6-F, Rehman Business Centre, 32-B-III, Gulberg III, Lahore 54660; tel. (42) 5750051; fax (42) 5780276; e-mail pfma@pakfootwear.org; internet www.pakfootwear.org; f. 1984; Chair. NASIR ANWAR; Sec. Col (retd) ARSHAD AYYAZ.

**Pakistan Gloves Manufacturers' and Exporters' Association:** PGMEA Bldg, Kashmir Rd, POB 1330, Sialkot; tel. (52) 4272959; fax (52) 4274860; e-mail pgmea@brain.net.pk; internet www.brain.net.pk/~pgmea; f. 1978; Chair. SOHAIL MASOOD; Sec. MUHAMMAD TAYYAB SHAIKH.

**Pakistan Hardware Merchants' Association:** Mandviwala Bldg, Serai Rd, Karachi 74000; tel. (21) 2420610; fax (21) 2432878; e-mail phmasbcircle@hotmail.com; f. 1961; more than 1,500 mems; Chair. BASIT ALAVI; Sec. SYED ZAFRUN NABI.

**Pakistan Hosiery Manufacturers' Association:** Karachi; tel. (21) 4522769; fax (21) 4543774; Chair. IMRAN ALI; Sec. YUNUS BIN AIYOOB.

**Pakistan Iron and Steel Merchants' Association:** Corner House, 2nd Floor, Preedy St, Saddar, Karachi; tel. (21) 5660270; fax (21) 5682724; Pres. MALIK AHMAD HUSSAIN; Gen. Sec. S. S. REHMAN.

**Pakistan Jute Mills' Association:** 8 Sasi Town Houses, Abdullah Haroon Rd, Civil Lines, Karachi 75530; tel. (21) 5676986; fax (21) 5676463; e-mail pjma@cyber.net.pk; Chair. HUMAYUN MAZHAR; Sec. S. A. H. RIZVI.

**Pakistan Knitwear and Sweaters Exporters' Association:** Rms Nos 1014–1016, 10th Floor, Park Ave, Block 6, PECHS, Shahrah-e-Faisal, Karachi 95350; tel. (21) 4522604; fax (21) 4525747; Chair. NASIR HUSSAIN.

**Pakistan Leather Garments Manufacturers' and Exporters' Association:** 60-C, Mezzanine Floor, 11th Commercial St, DHA Phase II (Extension), Karachi; tel. (21) 5387356; fax (21) 5388799; e-mail plgmea@cyber.net.pk; internet www.plgmea.com; f. 2001; Chair. FAWAD IJAZ KHAN.

**Pakistan Paint Manufacturers' Association:** St 6/A, Block 14, Federal 'B' Area, Karachi 38; tel. (21) 6321103; fax (21) 2560468; f. 1953; Chair. WASSIM A. KHAN; Sec. SYED AZHAR ALI.

**Pakistan Petroleum Exploration and Production Companies' Association:** 1 St 49, Sector F-6/4, Islamabad; tel. (51) 2823928; fax (51) 2276084; e-mail ppepca@isb.comsats.net.pk; internet www.ppepca.org; f. 1995; Chair. PHILIP BYRNE.

**Pakistan Pharmaceutical Manufacturers' Association:** 130–131, Hotel Metropole, Karachi; tel. (21) 5211773; fax (21) 5675608.

**Pakistan Plastic Manufacturers' Association:** 410 Mashrique Shopping Centre, St 6/A, Block No. 14, Gulshan-e-Iqbal, Karachi; tel. (21) 4942336; fax (21) 4944222; e-mail pakppma@pk.netsolir.com; Sec. FAYYAZ A. CHAUDHRY; Pres. ZAKARIA USMAN.

**Pakistan Polypropylene Woven Sacks Manufacturers' Association:** Karachi; Chair. SHOUKAT AHMED.

**Pakistan Poultry Association:** 219 Mashriq Centre, Block 14, Sir Shah Muhammad Suleman Rd, Gulshan-e-Iqbal, Karachi; tel. (21) 4940362; fax (21) 4940364; e-mail ppasee@cyber.net.pk.

**Pakistan Pulp, Paper and Board Mills' Association:** 402 Burhani Chambers, Abdullah Haroon Rd, Karachi 74400; tel. (21) 7726150; Chair. KAMRAN KHAN.

**Pakistan Readymade Garments Manufacturers' and Exporters' Association:** Shaheen View Bldg, Mezzanine Floor, Plot No. 18A, Block 6, PECHS, Shahrah-e-Faisal, Karachi; tel. (21) 4547912; fax (21) 4539669; e-mail info@prgmea.org; internet www.prgmea.org; Chair. BILAL MULLA.

**Pakistan Seafood Industries' Association:** A-2, Fish Harbour, West Wharf, Karachi; tel. (21) 2311117; fax (21) 2310939; e-mail psiapk@hotmail.com.

**Pakistan Ship Breakers' Association:** 608, S. S. Chamber, Siemens Chowrangi, S.I.T.E., Karachi; tel. (21) 293958; fax (21) 256533.

**Pakistan Silk and Rayon Mills' Association:** Rms Nos 44–48, Textile Plaza, 5th Floor, M. A. Jinnah Rd, Karachi 2; tel. (21) 2410288; fax (21) 2415261; e-mail ctech@edu.pk; f. 1974; Chair. M. ASHRAF SHEIKH; Sec. M. H. K. BURNEY.

**Pakistan Small Units Powerlooms' Association:** 2nd Floor, Waqas Plaza, Aminpura Bazar, POB 8647, Faisalabad; tel. (411) 627992; fax (411) 633567.

**Pakistan Soap Manufacturers' Association:** 148 Sunny Plaza, Hasrat Mohani Rd, Karachi 74200; tel. (21) 2634648; fax (21) 2563828; e-mail pakistansma@yahoo.com; Chair. YAQOOB KARIM.

**Pakistan Software Houses Association (PASHA):** D-30, Block 9, Clifton, Karachi 75600; tel. (21) 5866595; fax (21) 5869991; e-mail karachi@pasha.org.pk; internet www.pasha.org.pk; f. 1992; Pres. ZAIN I. SYED.

**Pakistan Sports Goods Manufacturers' and Exporters' Association:** Paris Rd, Sialkot 51310; tel. (432) 267962; fax (432) 261774; e-mail psga@brain.net.pk; Chair. Sheikh AHMED HUSSAIN.

**Pakistan Steel Melters' Association:** 30-S, Gulberg Centre, 84-D/1, Main Boulevard, Gulberg-III, Lahore; tel. (42) 5759284; fax (42) 5712028; e-mail steelmelters@angelfire.com; Chair. Mian MUHAMMAD SAEED.

**Pakistan Steel Re-rolling Mills' Association:** Rashid Chambers, 6-Link McLeod Rd, Lahore 54000; tel. (42) 7227136; fax (42) 7231154; e-mail steel_re_rollers@hotmail.com; Chair. Mian MANZOOR AHMAD; Sec. Lt-Col (retd) S. H. A. BUKHARI.

**Pakistan Sugar Mills' Association:** 24D Rashid Plaza Mezzanine Floor, Jinnah Ave, Islamabad; tel. (51) 2270525; fax (51) 2274153; e-mail psma_centre@yahoo.com; Chair. SHUNAID QURESHI; Sec.-Gen. K. ALI QAZILBASH.

**Pakistan Tanners' Association:** Plot No. 46-C, 21st Commercial St, Phase II Extension, Defence Housing Authority, Karachi 75500; tel. (21) 5880180; fax (21) 5880093; e-mail info@pakistantanners.org.

**Pakistan Tea Association:** Suite 307, Business Plaza, Mumtaz Hassan Rd, off I. I. Chundrigar Rd, Karachi; tel. (21) 2422161; fax (21) 2422209; e-mail pta@cyber.net.pk; Chair. HANIF JANOO.

**Pakistan Vanaspati Manufacturers' Association:** No. 5-B, College Rd, F-7/3, Islamabad; tel. (51) 2274358; fax (51) 2272529; Chair. Sheikh ANJAD RASHEED; Sec. Dr GHULAM M. SAMDANI.

**Pakistan Wool and Hair Merchants' Association:** 27 Idris Chambers, Talpur Rd, Karachi; Pres. Mian MOHAMMAD SIDDIQ KHAN; Sec. KHALID LATEEF.

**Pakistan Woollen Mills' Association:** 25A, Davis Rd, Lahore 54000; tel. (42) 6307691; fax (42) 6306881; e-mail pwma@brain.net.pk; internet www.lcci.org.pk; Chair. Mian MUZAFFAR ALI; Sec. MUHAMMAD RAHEEL CHOHAN.

**Pakistan Yarn Merchants' Association:** Rms Nos 802–803, Business Centre, 8th Floor, Dunolly Rd, Karachi 74000; tel. (21) 2410320; fax (21) 2424896; e-mail pyma@cubexs.net.pk; Pres. KHURSHID A. SHEIKH; Sec. MANZOORUL HASAN HASHMI.

**Rice Exports Association of Pakistan:** 4th Floor, Sadiq Plaza, The Mall, Lahore; tel. and fax (42) 6280196; e-mail reaplhr@brain.net.pk; Chair. Haji ABDUL MAJID.

**Towel Manufacturers' Association of Pakistan:** 77-A, Block A, Sindhi Muslim Co-operative Housing Society, Karachi 74400; tel. (21) 111-360-360; fax (21) 4551628; e-mail tma@towelassociation.com; internet www.towelassociation.com; Chair. PERVEZ AHMED.

## EMPLOYERS' ORGANIZATION

**Employers' Federation of Pakistan:** 2nd Floor, State Life Bldg No. 2, Wallace Rd, off I. I. Chundrigar Rd, POB 4338, Karachi 74000; tel. (21) 2411049; fax (21) 2439347; e-mail efpak@cyber.net.pk; internet www.efpak.com; f. 1950; Pres. ASHRAF WALI MOHAMMAD TABANI; Sec.-Gen. Prof. M. MATIN KHAN.

## UTILITIES

**Water and Power Development Authority (WAPDA):** WAPDA House, Shahrah-e-Quaid-e-Azam, Lahore; tel. (42) 6366911; fax (42) 9202454; internet www.wapda.gov.pk; f. 1958 for devt of irrigation, water supply and drainage, building of replacement works under the World Bank-sponsored Indo-Pakistan Indus Basin Treaty; flood-control and watershed management; reclamation of waterlogged and saline lands; inland navigation; generation, transmission and distribution of hydroelectric and thermal power; partial transfer to private ownership carried out in 1996; Chair. MOHAMMAD SHAKEEL DURRANI.

### Electricity

**Kohinoor Energy Ltd:** Near Tablighi Ijtima, PO Kohinoor Energy, Raiwind Bypass, Lahore; tel. (42) 5392317; fax (42) 5393415; e-mail info@kel.com.pk; internet www.kel.com.pk; f. 1994; jt venture of Saigols Group of Cos and Toyota Tsusho Corpn; Chair. M. NASEEM SAIGOL; CEO MUNEKI UDAKA.

**National Electric Power Regulatory Authority (NEPRA):** OPF Bldg, 2nd Floor, Shahrah-e-Jamhuriat, G-5/2, Islamabad 44000; tel. (51) 9207200; fax (51) 9210215; e-mail info@nepra.org.pk; internet www.nepra.org.pk; f. 1997; fixes the power tariff; Chair. Lt-Gen. (retd) SAEED UZ ZAFAR.

**Hub Power Co Ltd (Hubco):** Islamic Chamber Bldg, 3rd Floor, St 2/A, Block No. 9, Clifton, POB 13841, Karachi 75600; tel. (21) 5874677; fax (21) 5870397; e-mail info@hubpower.com; internet www.hubpower.com; f. 1991; supplies electricity; Chair. MOHAMMAD AHMED ZAINAL ALIREZA; Chief Exec. JAVED MAHMOOD.

**Karachi Electric Supply Corpn Ltd (KESC):** Aimai House, Abdullah Haroon Rd, POB 7197, Karachi; tel. (21) 5685492; fax (21) 5682408; internet www.kesc.com.pk; f. 1913; Chair. ABDUL AZIZ HAMEED AL-JOMAIH; CEO Lt-Gen. SYED MOHAMMAD AMJAD.

**Kot Addu Power Co (KAPCO):** Kot Addu Power Complex, Kot Addu, District Muzaffargarh 34060; tel. (66) 2241336; e-mail info@kapco.com.pk; fax (66) 2241817; internet www.kapco.com.pk; f. 1996; 46% owned by Pakistan Water and Power Development Authority; Chair. IMTIAZ ANJUM.

**National Power Construction Corpn (Pvt) Ltd:** 9 Shadman II, Lahore 54000; tel. (42) 7566019; fax (42) 7566022; e-mail npcc@wol.net.pk; internet www.npcc.com.pk; f. 1974; execution of power projects on turnkey basis, e.g. extra high voltage transmission lines, distribution networks, substations, power generation plants, industrial electrification, external lighting of housing complexes, etc.;

Chair. MUHAMMAD ISMAIL QURESHI; Man. Dir MUHAMMAD AJAZ MALIK; project office in Jeddah (Saudi Arabia).

**Pakistan Atomic Energy Commission (PAEC):** POB 1114, Islamabad; tel. (51) 9209032; fax (51) 9204908; responsible for harnessing nuclear energy for devt of nuclear technology as part of the nuclear power programme; operates Karachi Atomic Nuclear Power Plant—KANUPP (POB 3183, nr Paradise Point, Hawksbay Rd, Karachi 75400; tel. (21) 9202222; fax (21) 7737488; e-mail knpc@khi.comsats.net.pk) and Chasma Nuclear Power Plant (CHASNUPP) at Chasma District, Mianwali (tel. (45202) 41481-5; fax (51) 9278524; email chasnupp@fsd.paknet.com.pk); building another nuclear power station at Kundian; two further facilities were under construction near Karachi in March 2007; establishing research centres, incl. Pakistan Institute of Nuclear Science and Technology (PINSTECH); promoting peaceful use of atomic energy in agriculture, medicine, industry and hydrology; searching for indigenous nuclear mineral deposits; training project personnel; Chair. SHAMIM ANWAR KHAN; Gen. Man. (KANUPP) QAMRUL HODA.

**Pakistan Electric Power Co:** Lahore; f. 1998; Man. Dir MUNAWAR BASEER.

**Pakistan Nuclear Regulatory Authority (PNRA):** POB 1912, Islamabad 44000; tel. (51) 9260162; fax (51) 9263007; e-mail officialmail@pnra.org; internet www.pnra.org; f. 2001 by presidential ordinance; Chair. JAMSHED AZIM HASHMI.

**Private Power and Infrastructure Board (PPIB):** 50 Nazimuddin Rd, F-7/4, Islamabad; tel. (51) 9205421; fax (51) 9217735; e-mail ppib@ppib.gov.pk; internet www.ppib.gov.pk; f. 1994; facilitates participation of private sector in national power generation; Man. Dir MOHAMMAD YOUSUF MEMON.

**Quetta Electric Supply Co Ltd (QESCO):** Zarghoon Rd, Quetta Cantt, Balochistan; tel. (81) 9202211; fax (81) 836554; e-mail qesco@qta.infolink.net.pk; f. 1998; CEO Eng. MUHAMMAD KHATTAK.

### Gas

**Hydrocarbon Development Institute of Pakistan:** Plot 18, Street 6, H-9/1, POB 1308, Islamabad; tel. (51) 9258301; fax (51) 9258310; e-mail info@hdip.com.pk; internet www.hdip.com.pk; f. 1975; re-established Jan. 2006 under Ministry of Petroleum and Natural Resources; national petroleum research and devt org.; provides consultancy and laboratory services to petroleum industry; Chair. AMANULLAH KHAN JADOON; Dir-Gen. and Chief Exec. HILAL A. RAZA.

**Mari Gas Co Ltd (MGCL):** 21 Mauve Area, 3rd Rd, Sector G-10/4, POB 1614, Islamabad; tel. (51) 111-410-410; fax (51) 2297686; e-mail info@marigas.com.pk; internet www.marigas.com.pk; 20% govt-owned; Chair. Lt-Gen. (retd) SYED ARIF HASSAN; Resident Gen. Man. Col (retd) AMJAD JAVED.

**Oil and Gas Development Corpn Ltd (OGDCL):** OGDC House, Blue Area, Islamabad; tel. (51) 9209882; fax (51) 9209859; f. 1961; became a publicly limited co in 1997; 95% govt-owned; plans, promotes, organizes and implements programmes for the exploration and devt of petroleum and gas resources, and the production, refining and sale of petroleum and gas; transfer to private ownership pending; Man. Dir ARSHAD NASSAR; 11,624 employees (Aug. 2005).

**Oil and Gas Regulatory Authority:** Tariq Chambers, Main Civic Centre, Islamabad; tel. (51) 9204516; e-mail registrar@ogra.org.pk; internet www.ogra.org.pk; f. 2002; Chair. MUNIR AHMAD; Vice-Chair. JAWAID INAM.

**Pakistan Petroleum Ltd (PPL):** PIDC House, 4th Floor, Dr Ziauddin Ahmed Rd, POB 3942, Karachi 75530, Sindh; tel. (21) 111-568-568; fax (21) 5680005; e-mail info@ppl.com.pk; internet www.ppl.com.pk; 78.4% govt-owned, 15.5% owned by private Pakistani shareholders and 6.1% owned by International Finance Corpn; Pakistan's largest producer of natural gas; cap. and res Rs 18,393m., sales Rs 10,732m. (July–Dec. 2004); Chief Exec./Man. Dir KHALID RAHMAN; 2,520 employees (2006).

**Petroleum Institute of Pakistan (PIP):** Federation House, 1st Floor, Street 28, Block V, Kehkashan, Clifton, Karachi 75600; tel. (21) 5378701; fax (21) 5378704; e-mail pip@cyber.net.pk; internet www.pip.org.pk; f. 1963; represents all sectors of the petroleum industry (incl. exploration, production, refining, marketing and natural gas); promotes and co-ordinates industry activities; mem. of the International Gas Union and World Petroleum Council; 25 Industrial Collective mems, over 860 individual industry mems; Chair. S. MUNSIF RAZA.

**Sui Northern Gas Pipelines Ltd:** Gas House, 21 Kashmir Rd, Lahore; tel. (42) 9201451; fax (42) 9201302; e-mail info@sngpl.com.pk; internet www.sngpl.com.pk; f. 1964; 36% state-owned; transmission and distribution of natural gas in northern Pakistan; sales Rs 107,897.3m. (2005/06); Chair. ALTAF M. SALEEM; Man. Dir ABDUL RASHID LONE.

**Sui Southern Gas Co Ltd:** 4B Sir Shah Suleman Rd, Block 14, Gulshan-e-Iqbal, Karachi 75000; tel. (21) 9231602; fax (21) 9231604; e-mail info@ssgc.com.pk; internet www.ssgc.com.pk; f. 1988; 70% state-owned; Chief Exec. and Man. Dir MUNAWAR BASEER AHMAD.

### Water

**Faisalabad Development Authority (Water and Sanitation Agency):** POB 229, Faisalabad; tel. (411) 767606; fax (411) 782113; e-mail fwasa@fsd.paknet.com.pk; internet www.fda.gov.pk; f. 1978; Man. Dir Lt-Col (retd) SYED GHIAS-UD-DIN.

**Karachi Water and Sewerage Board:** 9th Mile, Karsaz, Shahrah-e-Faisal, Karachi; tel. (21) 9231882; fax (21) 9231814; e-mail mdkwsb@yahoo.co.uk; f. 1983; Man. Dir Brig. IFTIKHAR HAIDER.

**Lahore Development Authority (Water and Sanitation Agency):** 4-A Gulberg V, Jail Rd, Lahore; tel. (42) 5752483; fax (42) 5752960; f. 1967; Dir-Gen. RAJA MUHAMMAD ABBAS.

## MAJOR COMPANIES

The following is a selection of the major companies in Pakistan:

### Automobiles, Motorcycles and Tractors

**Agriauto Industries Ltd:** 5th Floor, House of Habib, 3 JCHS, Block 7-8, Shahrah-e-Faisal, Karachi 75350; tel. (21) 4541540; fax (21) 4549284; e-mail info@agriauto.com.pk; internet www.agriauto.com.pk; manufactures spare parts and two-wheel vehicles; part of House of Habib group; Chair. R. D. MINWALLA; Chief Exec. QAZI EBADULLAH KHAN; 300 employees.

**Al Ghazi Tractors Ltd:** 11th Floor, NIC Bldg, Abbasi Shaheed Rd, Karachi 74400; tel. (21) 5660881; fax (21) 5689387; e-mail agtl@alghazitractors.com; internet www.alghazitractors.com; Chair. COLIN LEITCH; CEO PARVEZ ALI.

**Atlas Group of Companies:** 2nd Floor, Federation House, Shahrah-e-Firdousi, Main Clifton, Karachi; tel. (21) 2417744; fax (21) 5369486; e-mail agc@atlas.com.pk; internet www.atlasgrouppk.com; sales Rs 15,000m. (2001); Chair. YUSUF H. SHIRAZI.

**Atlas Honda Ltd:** 1 Mcleod Rd, Lahore 54000; tel. (42) 7225015; fax (42) 7233518; e-mail ahlkhi@atlashonda.com.pk; internet www.atlashonda.com.pk; f. 1991; cap. and res Rs 1,492.5m., total assets Rs 4,111.9m. (2003/04); mfr of motorcycles; Chair. YUSUF H. SHIRAZI; CEO SAQUIB H. SHIRAZI.

**Dawood Yamaha Ltd:** 40-C, Block 6, PECHS, Karachi 75400; tel. (21) 4541960; fax (21) 454677; e-mail dyl@dawood-companies.com; internet www.dawood-companies.com/yamaha.html; Chair. AMIN DAWOOD; Chief Exec. YUNUS DAWOOD.

**Dewan Farooq Motors Ltd:** Karachi; tel. (21) 5610552; fax (21) 5610326.

**Gandhara Nissan Ltd:** Gandhara House, 109/2 Clifton, POB 3812, Karachi 6; tel. (21) 576051; fax (21) 5830258; mfr of automobiles and taxis; Chair. Gen. (retd) ALI KULI KHAN KHATTAK.

**Hinopak Motors Ltd:** D-2, S.I.T.E., Manghopir Rd, Karachi; tel. (21) 2563510-8; fax (21) 2578449; e-mail marketing@hinopak.com; internet www.hinopak.com; Man. Dir and CEO KEIJI MAEDA.

**Indus Motor Co Ltd:** Plot No. N.W.Z/1/P-1, Port Qasim Authority, Karachi; tel. (21) 4721100; fax (21) 4549662; e-mail customer.relations@toyota-indus.com; internet www.toyota-indus.com; f. 1993; cap. and res sales Rs 9,054.7m. (2000/01); mfrs of Toyota passenger cars and diesel pick-ups; annual production capacity of 20,000 vehicles; Chair. ALI S. HABIB; Chief Exec. PARVEZ GHIAS; 645 employees.

**Millat Tractors Ltd:** 9 Sheikhupura Rd, Shahdara, Lahore 54950; tel. (42) 7911021; fax (42) 7924166; e-mail info@millat.com.pk; internet www.millat.com.pk; Chair. SIKANDAR M. KHAN; Chief Exec. SOHAIL BASHIR RANA; 515 employees.

**Mitsubishi Motors Pakistan Ltd** (Dewan Mushtaq Motor Co (Pvt) Ltd): Finance and Trade Centre, 7th Floor, Block A, Main Shahra-e-Faisal, Karachi 75250; tel. (21) 5204514; fax (21) 5630830; e-mail contact@mitsubishi-motors.com.pk; internet www.mitsubishi-motors.com.pk.

**National Motors Ltd:** Hub Chouki Rd, S.I.T.E., POB 2706, Karachi 75730; tel. (21) 2560083; fax (21) 2564458; manufactures and assembles trucks, buses and light commercial vehicles; Chair. RAZA KULI KHAN KHATTAK.

**Nexus Automotive (Pvt) Ltd:** 48-D, Block 6, PECH Society, Karachi; tel. (21) 8268182; fax (21) 4528104; e-mail nexusauto@cyber.net.pk; manufactures and distributes Chevrolet cars in Pakistan; Chair. M. A. RAZAQ.

**Pak Suzuki Motor Co Ltd:** DSU-13, Pakistan Steel Industrial Estate, Bin Qasim, Karachi 75000; tel. (21) 4750788; fax (21) 4750101; e-mail customercentre@paksuzuki.com.pk; Chair. and Chief Exec. HIROFUMI NAGAO; 575 employees.

**Pakistan Automobile Corpn Ltd (PACO):** 2nd Floor, Finance and Trade Centre, Tower 'B', Shahrah-e-Faisal, POB 4271, Karachi; tel. (21) 525391; fax (21) 525320; f. 1972; Chair. KAMAL ASFAR.

**Raja Autocars Ltd:** 192-A Raja Sq., SMCHS Society, Karachi; tel. (21) 4550035; fax (21) 4553027; assembles/mfrs Vespa scooters and three-wheel auto rickshaws; Sec. HAKIMMUDIN SHEIKH.

**Saif Nadeem Co:** Corporate Office, 7/B, Malani Mahal, Frere Rd, Karachi; tel. (21) 7725762; operates plant in Lahore; assembles Kawasaki vehicles.

**Shahnawaz Ltd:** 19 West Wharf Rd, Karachi; tel. (21) 2313934; fax (21) 2310623; e-mail khi-snl@shahnawazltd.com; internet www.shahnawazltd.com; agents for Mercedes Benz vehicles.

**Sind Engineering (Pvt) Ltd:** 16 Dockyard Rd, West Wharf, Karachi 74000; tel. (21) 2202721; fax (21) 2313552; e-mail info@mazda-sel.com.pk; internet www.mazda-sel.com.pk; f. 1963; assembles Mazda vehicles; sales Rs 736.5m. (2000); Chair. KAMAL AFSAR; 554 employees.

**Suzuki Motorcycles Pakistan Ltd:** F-14, S.I.T.E., Mauripur Link Rd, POB 2708, Karachi; tel. (21) 2573309; fax (21) 2563895; e-mail suzukimc@paknet3.ptc.pk; cap. and res Rs 439.0m., sales Rs 309m. (June 2002); Chair. MIDHAT A. KIDWAI.

**Worldwide Motors (Pvt) Ltd:** Worldwide House, C-17 Korangi Rd, Defence Housing Authority, Phase II (Extension), Karachi 75500; tel. (21) 5389901; fax (21) 5887467; e-mail sheikh.ishaq@wwm.com.pk; internet www.wwm.com.pk; distributors and importers of automotive and machinery products; Man. (Marketing) SHEIKH ISHAQ.

### Cement

**Attock Cement Pakistan Ltd:** 5th Floor, PNSC Bldg, M. T. Khan Rd, Karachi 74000; tel. (21) 5611019; fax (21) 5636680; e-mail acpl@sat.net.pk; internet www.attockcement.com; 95.7% owned by Pharaon Commercial Investment Group (Saudi Arabia); Chair. Dr GHAITH R. PHARAON; Chief Exec. BABAR BASHIR NAWAZ; 580 employees.

**Chakwal Cement:** 7/1, E-3, Main Boulevard, Gulberg III, Lahore; tel. (42) 5757108; fax (42) 5755760; Chair. and CEO KHAWAJA MOHAMMED JAWED.

**Cherat Cement Co Ltd:** Modern Motors House, Beaumont Rd, Karachi 75530; tel. (21) 5683566; fax (21) 5683425; e-mail cherat@cherat.com; internet cheratcement.com; f. 1981; Chair. MOHAMMAD FARUQUE; Chief Exec./Man. Dir ZAHID FARUQUE; 724 employees.

**Dadabhoy Cement Industries Ltd:** 5th Floor, Maqbool Commercial Complex, Blocks 7 and 8, Jinnah Co-operative Housing Society, Shahrah-e-Faisal, Karachi 75350; tel. (21) 4545704; fax (21) 4548625; e-mail mhdadabhoye@cyber.net.pk; internet www.mhdadabhoy.com/cement.asp; f. 1979; Chair. MOHAMMAD HUSSAIN DADABHOY; 600 employees.

**Envicrete Ltd:** CL 6/5, Abdullah Haroon Rd (adjacent to Frere Hall), Karachi 75530; tel. (21) 5210015; fax (21) 5213044; e-mail info@envicrete.com.pk; internet www.envicrete.com; mfr of concrete block products.

**Fecto Cement Ltd:** 35 Darul-Aman-Housin Society, Blocks 7–8, Shahrah-e-Faisal, Karachi 75350; tel. (21) 4530120; fax (21) 4530123; e-mail cement@cyber.net.pk; internet www.fecto.com.pk/fecto_cement.htm; Chair. MOHAMMAD YASIN FECTO; 594 employees.

**Gharibwal Cement Ltd:** 34 Main Gulberg, POB 1285, Lahore; tel. (42) 111-210-310; fax (42) 5871059; e-mail info@gharibwalcement.com; internet www.gharibwalcement.com; f. 1960; Chair. and Chief Exec. MOHAMMAD TOUSIF PERACHA.

**Javedan Cement Ltd:** 2nd Floor, Pardesi House, Survey No. 2/1, R. Y. 16, Old Queens Rd, Karachi; tel. (21) 111-111-224; fax (21) 2470090; e-mail info@jcl.com.pk; internet www.jcl.com.pk; 89% state-owned; Chair. NASIM BEG; Man. Dir ASIM GANI.

**Kohat Cement Co Ltd:** 37-P, Gulberg II, Lahore; tel. (42) 11-111-5225; fax (42) 5754084; e-mail info@kohatcement.com; internet www.kohatcement.com; cap. and res Rs 1,081.7m., sales Rs 1,715.4m. (2005); Chair. KHAWAR SULTANA; Chief Exec. AIZAZ MANSOOR SHEIKH.

**Maple Leaf Cement Factory Ltd:** 42 Lawrence Rd, Lahore; tel. (42) 6278904; fax (42) 6363184; e-mail mlcfl@kmlg.com; internet www.kmlg.com; f. 1956; cap. and res Rs 3,427m., sales Rs 4,967m. (2003/04); Chair. TARIQ SAYEED SAIGOL; 680 employees.

**Mustehkam Cement Ltd:** 345 Bazar Rd, Westbridge, POB 174, Rawalpindi.

**Pakland Cement Ltd:** Trade Centre, A-14, Block 7–8, KCHS, Shahrah-e-Faisal, Karachi 75350; tel. (21) 4559171; fax (21) 4546992; f. 1985; Chair. TARIQ MOHSIN SIDDIQUI; Gen. Man. N. H. MISTRY.

**State Cement Corpn of Pakistan (Pvt) Ltd:** PEC Bldg, 97-A/B-D Gulberg III, Lahore; tel. (42) 870341; f. 1973; operates public-sector cement plants; distributes cement; Chair. MALIK AMJAD ALI.

**Thatta Cement Co Ltd:** 601, 6th Floor, Business Plaza, Mumtaz Hassan Rd, off I. I. Chundrigar Rd, Karachi 74000; tel. (21) 2423295; fax (21) 2400989; e-mail info@thattacement.com; internet www.thattacement.com.

### Chemicals and Pharmaceuticals

**Bayer Pakistan (Pvt) Ltd:** 4th Floor, Bahria Complex II, M. T. Khan Rd, POB 4641, Karachi; tel. (21) 5611637; fax (21) 5611759; e-mail bayerinfo@cyber.net.pk; Man. Dir B. HANS VENINGA.

**BOC Pakistan Ltd:** West Wharf, Dockyard Rd, POB 4845, Karachi 74000; tel. (21) 2313361; fax (21) 2312968; e-mail info@bocpakistan.com; internet www.bocpakistan.com; f. 1949; fmrly Pakistan Oxygen Ltd; part of the Linde Group; mfr of industrial, medical and speciality gases, gas equipment and welding products; Chair. MUNNAWAR HAMID; Chief Exec. SYED AYAZ BOKHARI; 474 employees.

**Engro Chemical Pakistan Ltd:** PNSC Bldg, 8th Floor, POB 5736, 24 M. T. Khan Rd, Karachi 74000; tel. (21) 5511060; fax (21) 5610688; e-mail info@engro.com; internet www.engro.com; PVC resin plant at Port Qasim; cap. and res Rs 5,218.6m., sales Rs 8,393.9m. (2000); Chair. HUSSAIN DAWOOD; Pres. and CEO ASAD UMAR; 730 employees.

**ICI (Pakistan) Ltd:** ICI House, 5 West Wharf, POB 4731, Karachi 74000; tel. (21) 2313717; fax (21) 2311739; e-mail iciccpa@fascom.com; internet www.icipakistan.com; f. 1952; mfrs of soda ash, sodium bicarbonate, polyester staple fibre, pharmaceuticals, paints and chemicals; markets seeds and imported pharmaceuticals and animal health products; cap. Rs 1,388m., sales Rs 22,156.2m. (2003); Chief Exec. WAQAR A. MALIK; 1,300 employees.

**Ittehad Chemicals Ltd:** 39 Empress Rd, POB 1414, Lahore 54000; tel. (42) 6306586; fax (42) 6365697; e-mail ittehad@pol.com.pk; internet www.ittehadchemicals.com; f. 1962; mfrs of hydrochloric and sulphuric acid, caustic soda and liquid chlorine; Chair. and CEO MUHAMMAD SIDDIQUE KHATRI.

**Ittehad Pesticides:** Kala Shah Kaku, Sheikhupura, POB 886, Lahore; tel. (42) 700128; fax (42) 700134; mfrs of BHC Technical and DDT Technical; Man. Dir CHAUDHRY G. S. MUSHTAQ.

**National Fibres Ltd Pakistan:** Schon Centre, I. I. Chundrigar Rd, Karachi 74200; tel. (21) 219551; fax (21) 2636325.

**Novartis Pharma (Pakistan) Ltd:** 15 West Wharf Rd, Karachi 74000; tel. (21) 2313386-90; fax (21) 2311009; e-mail farid.khan@pharma.novartis.com; internet www.pk.pharma.novartis.com; mfr of pharmaceuticals; fmrly Ciba-Geigy (Pakistan) Ltd; subsidiary of Novartis AG, Switzerland; CEO FARID KHAN.

**Nowshera PVC Co Ltd:** Amangarh, POB 31, Nowshera 24100; tel. (21) 438044; fax (21) 438596; mfrs of PVC Cordrain pipes, alum and of liquid and powder insecticides; Man. Dir A. QADEEM JAN.

**Pak Chemicals Ltd:** Hakimsons Bldg, West Wharf Rd, POB 4739, Karachi 74000; tel. (21) 2313508; fax (21) 2314260; f. 1950; mfrs of sulphuric acid, hydrochloric acid, aluminium sulphate, magnesium sulphate, alum and sodium sulphate; Man. Dir S. M. KHALID; Man. (Marketing) S. H. ANSARI.

**Pakdyes and Chemicals Ltd:** Iskanderabad (Daudkhel) Distt. Mianwali; tel. (459) 2434; a project of Federal Chemicals and Ceramics Corpn (Pvt) Ltd; mfrs of all types of direct and acid dyestuffs for cotton, wool and leather.

**Pakistan Agro Chemicals (Pvt) Ltd:** 38-C/IV, Block 6, PECHS, Karachi 75400; tel. (21) 4534870; fax (21) 4548232.

**Pakistan PVC Ltd:** Al-Haroon, 4th Floor, Garden Rd, Karachi; CEO REYAZ SHAFFI.

**Pharmacia & Upjohn (Pvt) Ltd:** Industrial Triangle, Kahuta Rd, POB 40, Rawalpindi; tel. (51) 8471237; fax (51) 422439; f. 1951; mfrs of pharmaceuticals; Pres. RAUL O. MONTEFUSCO.

**Rhône-Poulenc Rorer Pakistan (Pvt) Ltd:** G. T. Rd, Wah Cantt; tel. (51) 519359; fax (596) 3164; f. 1977; cap. Rs 30m.; mfrs of human pharmaceuticals; Chair. SAADAT HUSSAIN KHAN; Pakistan Rep. TARIQ MOHAMED AMIN.

**Sandoz (Pakistan) Ltd:** 5th and 6th Floors, Bahria Complex, 24 M. T. Khan Rd, Karachi; tel. (21) 5611405; fax (21) 5611062; Chair. Dr MARTIN SYZ.

**Sanofi-aventis Pakistan Ltd:** Plot No. 23, Sector 22, Korangi Industrial Area, Karachi 74900; tel. (21) 5060221; internet www.sanofi-aventis.com.pk; mfr of pharmaceuticals.

**Silchem International (Pvt) Ltd:** Office 107, 1st Floor, Fortune Centre, 45-A, Block 6, PECHS, Shahrah Faisal, Karachi; e-mail silchem@khi.compol.com; Man. Dir JAMAL KHAN.

**Sindh Alkalis Ltd:** 1A, State Life Bldg, 3rd Floor, I. I. Chundrigar Rd, POB 4200, Karachi 74000; tel. (21) 2426783; fax (21) 2425710; Chair. SAIF-UR-RAHMAN.

**Sitara Chemical Industries Ltd:** POB 442, Faisalabad; tel. (41) 4689141; fax (41) 4689147; e-mail scil@sitara.com.pk; internet www.sitara.com.pk; cap. and res Rs 1,658m., sales Rs 3,812m. (2006); Chair. Haji BASHIR AHMED.

### Engineering

**Allied Engineering & Services Ltd:** 21/3 Sector 22, Korangi Industrial Area, Karachi; tel. (21) 5066901; fax (21) 5066921; e-mail admin@aesl.com.pk; internet www.aesl.com.pk; supplier of construction equipment, power generation equipment and lift trucks; Man. Dir SYED FEISAL ALI.

**Climax Engineering Co Ltd:** Climaxabad, G. T. Rd, Gujranwala; tel. (431) 253612; fax (431) 254222; e-mail info@climaxengineering.com; internet www.climaxengineering.com; f. 1940; mfr of transformers, electric motors, meters and air conditioning equipment; Chair. A. G. FAIZI; CEO M. A. QAYYUM.

**Descon Engineering Ltd:** 18 Km, Ferozepur Rd, Lahore 53000; tel. (42) 5805134; fax (42) 5811005; e-mail ahmalik@descon.com.pk; internet www.descon.com.pk; f. 1977; Man. Dir SHAIKH AZHAR ALI.

**Heavy Mechanical Complex:** Taxila 47050; tel. (51) 9270562; fax (51) 9270560; e-mail hmcengg@isb.paknet.pk; internet www.hmc.com.pk; f. 1971; mfr and supplier of sugar, cement, chemical and petrochemical, fertilizer and oil and gas processing plants, boilers, road-rollers, steel structures, steel and iron castings, pressure vessels, machinery and equipment for thermal and hydroelectric power plants, heavy and sophisticated steel structures, and steel and iron heavy castings and forgings; Man. Dir S. ALI ENSER.

**Ittefaq Foundries (Pvt) Ltd:** 32 Empress Rd, Lahore; tel. (42) 306961; fax (42) 305681; f. 1940; Chair. Mian MOHAMMAD SHARIF; Dir (Technical) Mian ILYAS MIRAJ.

**National Engineering Services Pakistan (Pvt) Ltd (NESPAK):** NESPAK House, 1-C, Block N, Model Town Extension Scheme, POB 1351, Lahore 54700; tel. (42) 9090000; fax (42) 9231950; e-mail nespak@wol.net.pk; internet www.nespak.com.pk; f. 1973; multidisciplinary consulting co for engineering projects, including irrigation, dams, bridges, transmission lines, heating, ventilation and air-conditioning, power stations, roads, town planning, etc.; operates both in Pakistan and abroad; Pres. and Man. Dir KARAMAT ULLAH CHAUDRY; Gen. Man. (Business Development) SYED SHAHID HUSSAIN.

**Nowshera Engineering Co Ltd:** P. O. Ferozsons Laboratory, Amangarh, Nowshera, Peshawar; f. 1959; Prin. Officer SYED PHOOL BADSHAH.

**Pakistan Engineering Co Ltd:** 6/7 Ganga Ram Trust Bldg, Shahrah-e-Quaid-e-Azam, Lahore 54000; tel. (42) 7320225; fax (42) 7323108; e-mail peco@lhr.paknet.com.pk; f. 1950; fmrly Batala Engineering Co Ltd; name changed following nationalization; cap. Rs 56.9m, res Rs 10.0m., sales Rs 834.7m. (2005/06); mfrs of pumps, motors, concrete mixers, steel safes, transmission line towers, steel structures and telecommunication towers, etc.; Chair. MIAN SUHAIL ASLAM; Chief Exec. M. IMTIAZ UR-RAHEEM; 500 employees.

**Siemens Pakistan Engineering Co Ltd:** B-72 Estate Ave, SITE, POB 7158, Karachi 75700; tel. (21) 2574910; fax (21) 2563563; e-mail zia.zuberi@siemens.com; internet www.siemens.com.pk; sales Rs 7,110m. (2004); Chair. S. BABAR ALI; 1,284 employees (2004).

**Sind Engineering (Pvt) Ltd:** 16 Dockyard Rd, West Wharf, Karachi 74000; tel. (21) 2202721; fax (21) 2313552; e-mail info@mazda-sel.com.pk; internet www.mazda-sel.com.pk; sales Rs 736.5m. (2000); Chair. KAMAL AFSAR; 554 employees.

**State Engineering Corpn (Pvt) Ltd:** 2nd Floor, Saeed Plaza, Jinnah Ave, Blue Area, Islamabad; tel. (51) 9204391; fax (51) 9220467; e-mail statc@isb.paknet.com.pk; f. 1979; Chair. Mian SUHAIL ASLAM; 5,400 employees.

### Fertilizers

**Dawood Hercules Chemicals Ltd:** 35A Shahrah-e-Abdul Hameed Bin Baadees, POB 1294, Lahore 54000; tel. (42) 6301601; fax (42) 6360343; e-mail dhcl@dawoodhercules.com.pk; internet www.dawoodhercules.com.pk; Chair. HUSSAIN DAWOOD; Exec. Dir A. G. GOHAR.

**Engro Chemical Pakistan Ltd:** 8th Floor, PNSC Bldg, Maulvi Tamizuddin Khan Rd, POB 5736, Karachi 74000; tel. (21) 5611060; fax (21) 5610688; e-mail info@engro.com; internet www.engro.com; cap. and res Rs 5,219m., sales Rs 8,394m. (2000); mfr of urea fertilizer; Chair. HUSSAIN DAWOOD; Pres. and CEO ASAD UMAR.

**Fauji Fertilizer Co:** 93 Harley St, POB 253, Rawalpindi; tel. (51) 9272307; fax (51) 9272316; e-mail ffcrwp@ffc.com.pk; internet www.ffc.com.pk; Pakistan's largest private-sector producer of urea fertilizer; Chair. Lt-Gen. (retd) SYED ARIF HASAN; Chief Exec. and Man. Dir Lt-Gen. (retd) MUNIR HAFIEZ; 1,774 employees.

**FFC Bin Qasim Ltd:** 73 Harley St, Rawalpindi; tel. (51) 565401; fax (51) 582851; plant at Port Qasim, nr Karachi; Chair. L. G. M. ARIF BANGASH; Man. Dir Lt-Gen. (retd) IMTIAZ WARAICH.

**Hazara Phosphate Fertilizers (Pvt) Ltd:** Haripur Hazara, Hattar Rd, Haripur District, North-West Frontier Province; subsidiary of National Fertilizer Corpn of Pakistan (Pvt) Ltd (NFC).

**Lyallpur Chemicals and Fertilizers Ltd:** Jaranwala Rd, POB 13, Faisalabad; tel. (411) 42371; fax (468) 2628; f. 1953; also in Jaranwala; produces superphosphate fertilizer; subsidiary of NFC; Man. Dir A. MANNAN; Gen. Mans MUHAMMAD YOUNAS (Faisalabad), MUNIR AHMED (Jaranwala).

**National Fertilizer Corpn of Pakistan (Pvt) Ltd:** Al-Falah Bldg, 1st Floor, Shahrah-e-Quaid-e-Azam, POB 1730, Lahore; tel. (42) 6302904; fax (42) 6302918; 3 fertilizer plants; Chair. Maj.-Gen. (retd) ZAFAR ABBAS; Gen. Man. (Technical) T. I. CHUGHTAI.

**Pak-American Fertilizer Ltd:** Iskandarabad, Mianwali Dist.; tel. (459) 392346; fax (459) 392715; f. 1956; urea fertilizer production; subsidiary of Azgard Nine Ltd; CEO AHMAD JAUDAT BILAL.

**Pak-Arab Fertilizers (Pvt) Ltd:** P.O. Fertilizer Project, Khanewal Rd, Multan; tel. (61) 9220022; fax (61) 9220021; e-mail pakarab78@hotmail.com; f. 1979; subsidiary of NFC; Man. Dir TANVIR AHMAD.

**PakChina Fertilizers Ltd:** House No. 56, St 88, G-6/3, Embassy Rd, Islamabad; tel. (51) 820667; fax (51) 272882; Man. Dir KHALID MUMTAZ.

**Pak-Saudi Fertilizer (Pvt) Ltd:** Mirpur Mathelo, Ghotki Dist 65050; tel. (71) 613001; fax (71) 612634; f. 1975; subsidiary of NFC; Man. Dir MUHAMMAD YOUNUS; Gen. Man. MEHMOOD AKHTAR; 900 employees.

### Food and Food Products

**Al Abbas Sugar Mills Ltd:** Pardesi House, Survey No. 1/2, R. Y. 16, Old Queens Rd, Karachi 74000; tel. (21) 111-111-224; fax (21) 2470090; e-mail sugar@cyber.net.pk; internet www.alabbassugar.com; mfr and exporter of sugar; Chair. MOHAMMAD IQBAL USMAN; CEO SHUNAID QURESHI.

**Nestlé Milkpak Ltd:** 308 Upper Mall, Lahore; tel. (42) 5757082; fax (42) 5711820; e-mail shahid.siddiqi@pk.nestle.com; sales Rs 7,900m. (2001); mfr and distributor of food, beverages and milk products; Man. Dir FRIEDRICH G. MAHLER.

**Punjab Seed Corpn:** 4 Lytton Rd, Lahore; tel. (42) 9212561; seed trade, crop seed production and marketing; Man. Dir AMANULLAH KHAN NIAZI.

**Rafhan Maize Products Co Ltd:** Rakh Canal East Rd, POB 62, Faisalabad 38060; tel. (41) 8540121; fax (41) 8711016; e-mail corporate@rafhanmaize.com; internet www.rafhanmaize.com; f. 1953; cap. and res Rs 1,560.7m., sales Rs 3,464.8m. (2002); agribased industry processing corn; Chair. JEFFREY B. HEBBLE; Chief Exec./Man. Dir RASHID ALI; 686 employees (2002).

**Rice Export Corpn of Pakistan:** 4th Floor, Block A, Finance and Trade Centre, Shahrah-e-Faisal, POB 457, Karachi; tel. (21) 517021; fax (21) 9202996; f. 1974; procures, mills, cleans, stores, packs and markets standard quality rice for export on monopoly basis; Chair. M. YOUNUS KHAN.

**Sindh Sugar Corpn Ltd:** Shaikh Sultan Trust Bldg, 6th Floor, Beaumont Rd, Karachi 3; Chair. ZAHEER SAJJAD.

### Leather

**Bata Pakistan Ltd:** Batapur, G. T. Rd, Lahore 53400; tel. (42) 6581178; fax (42) 6581176; e-mail bata@brain.net.pk; internet www.batapk.com; mfr of footwear, rubber and plastic products; Chair. M. OLDROYD.

**Din Leather Ltd:** Din House, 35-A/1, Lalazar Area, opp. Beach Luxury Hotel, POB 4696, Karachi 74000; tel. (21) 5610001; fax (21) 5610009; e-mail dingroup@cyber.net.pk; Chief Exec. S. M. MUNEER.

**EPCT Pvt Ltd:** 45–50 Industrial Area, Gulberg III, Lahore; tel. (42) 5756192; fax (42) 5656194; e-mail epct@brain.net.pk; fmrly East Pakistan Chrome Tannery Ltd.

**Eastern Leather Co Pvt Ltd:** 10/A, Block L, Ferozepur Rd, Gulberg III, Lahore 54660; tel. (42) 5885171; fax (42) 5839572; e-mail eastern@brain.net.pk; internet www.easterngroup-pk.com.

**Elegant (Pvt) Ltd:** 7-8/A Justice Sardar Iqbal Rd, Gulberg V, Lahore; tel. (42) 5775611; fax (42) 5775613; e-mail elegant@quettagroup.com; internet www.elegantfootwear.com; mfrs of leather footwear and cotton sports socks; CEO NASIR ANWER SHEIKH.

**HUB Leather (Pvt) Ltd:** Plot 74, Sector 7A, Korangi Industrial Area, Karachi 74900; tel. (21) 5072511; fax (21) 5072535; e-mail email@hubleather.com; internet www.hubleather.com; f. 1983; mfr and exporter of leather garments and accessories; Gen. Man HAIDER M. TAMBAWALA; Man. (Sales) FARUKH TANVEER.

**Khawaja Tanneries (Pvt) Ltd:** Mehr Manzil, Lahari Gate, POB 28, Multan; tel. (61) 511158; fax (61) 511262; e-mail ktm@brain.net.pk; CEO KHAWAJA MOHAMMAD YOUSUF.

**Leather Connections (Pvt) Ltd:** Alam-Porvair City, Bhoptian Chowk, Km 9, Main Raiwind Rd, Rohi Nala, Lahore 53700; tel. (42) 5321401; fax (42) 5321407; e-mail info@leatherconnections.com; internet www.leatherconnections.com; manufactures belt leather and belts; CEO KHURSHID ALAM.

**Leather Field (Pvt) Ltd:** Cheema Sq., Capital Rd, Sialkot; tel. (432) 556272; fax (432) 551942; e-mail info@leatherfield.com; internet www.leatherfield.com; mfr of leather apparel; Chair. and CEO AJMAL CHEEMA.

**Leather Master Pvt Ltd:** Sublime Chowk, Wazirabad Rd, POB 16, Sialkot; tel. and fax (432) 553592; e-mail info@leathermaster.com.pk; internet www.leather.com.pk.

**Mir Yousuf Leatherwear (Pvt) Ltd:** POB 461, Sialkot; tel. (432) 552835; e-mail miryousuf@brain.net.pk.

**Mohamed Ismail Mohamed Aslam (MIMA):** Plot Nos 4-5, Sector 17, Korangi Industrial Area, Karachi 74900; tel. (21) 5060771; fax (21) 5060572; e-mail mima@fascom.com; Sr Asst Man. (Marketing and Sales) MANZOOR HASSAN MODAK.

**Muhammad Shafi Tanneries (Pvt) Ltd:** Shafi House, 35-A/3, M. T. Khan Rd, opp. Beach Luxury Hotel, Karachi 74000; tel. (21) 2579041-4; fax (21) 2564391; e-mail mst@fascom.com; internet www.shafi.com; CEO AMJAD HAFEEZ; Sales Man. YAQOOB ALI.

**Royal Leather Industries Ltd:** 26-B Sundar Das Rd, Zaman Park, Lahore; tel. (42) 636140; fax (42) 6361714; e-mail royal@brain.net.pk.

**Service Industries Ltd:** Service House, 38 Empress Rd, 2 Main Gulberg, Lahore; tel. (42) 571190; fax (42) 5711827; mfr of leather products, footwear, clothes and textiles, rubber products and cars; Chair. SHAHID HUSSAIN; 500 employees.

**Siddiq Leather Works (Pvt) Ltd:** 51 G. T. Rd, Hide Market, POB 1676, Lahore 54900; tel. (42) 795039; e-mail sales@siddiqleather.com; internet www.siddiqleather.com; subsidiary of Shafi Group of Pakistan since 1974; produces various types of finished leather for shoes and garments, mfrs of leather goods and upholstery.

**Universal Leather and Footwear Industries Ltd:** Cavish Court, A-35, KCHSU, Blocks 7 & 8, Shahrah-e-Faisal, POB 5218, Karachi; tel. (21) 4531525; fax (21) 4535208; e-mail ulf@mimagrp.com; Chair. S. M. SALEEM; CEO S. M. SHAKIL.

**Zahur Sancho (Pvt) Ltd:** Plot No. 46, Sector 7-A, Korangi Industrial Area, Karachi 74900; tel. (21) 5061786; fax (21) 5060343.

### Metals

**Ados Pakistan Ltd:** No. 88 Khayaban-e-Iqbal, Sector F-8/2, Islamabad; tel. (51) 2264308; fax (51) 2281978; e-mail ados@akbarassociates.com; iron and steel production; CEO ZIA AKBAR ANSARI.

**Crescent Steel and Allied Products Ltd:** 9th Floor, SIDCO Avenue Centre, 264 R. A. Lines, Karachi 74200; tel. (21) 5674881; fax (21) 5680478; e-mail nazir.kazmi@crescent.com.pk; internet www.crescent.com.pk; Chair. MAZHAR KARIM; CEO AHSAN M. SALEEM.

**Fazal Steel Ltd:** Plot No. 418–421, Industrial Area, I-9, Islamabad; tel. (51) 4434813-4; fax (51) 4433597; e-mail info@fazalsteel.com; internet www.fazalsteel.com; f. 1988; steel rolling; Chair. JAHANGIR AZIZ MALIK.

**Mughal Steel Mills (Pvt) Ltd:** 41 Peco Rd, Badami Bagh, Lahore; tel. (42) 111-000-007; fax (42) 7610160; e-mail info@mughalsteel.com; internet www.mughalsteel.com; steel mfrs, including stainless steel and carbon steel; re-rolling and steel aligning; Chair. JAVED IQBAL MUGHAL; Man. Dir TARIQ IQBAL MUGHAL.

**National Steel Re-rolling Mills (Pvt) Ltd):** 6 Feroze Centre, Fazal-e-Haq Rd, Blue Area, Islamabad; tel. (51) 2272096; fax (51) 2828883.

**New Shalimar Steel Industries (Pvt) Ltd:** 45 Peco Rd, Badami Bagh, Lahore; tel. (42) 7280419; fax (42) 7281181; e-mail info@newshalimar.com; internet www.newshalimar.com; f. 1969; fmrly New Shalimar Steel Re-rolling Mills.

**Pakistan Steel Fabricating Co (Pvt) Ltd:** PSF Administrative Bldg No. 1, POB 9006, Bin Qasim, Karachi 50; tel. (21) 4750910; fax (21) 4750937; e-mail psfcl@psfcl.com; internet www.psfcl.com; f. 1982; Chief Exec. SHAHID ASGHAR.

**Pakistan Steel Mills Corpn (Pvt) Ltd:** Bin Qasim, POB 5429, Karachi 75000; tel. (21) 4750271; fax (21) 4750156; e-mail chairman@paksteel.com.pk; internet www.paksteel.com.pk; f. 1973; iron and steel mfrs; mfrs of coke, coal tar, ammonium sulphate, granulated slag; operates steel mill at Bin Qasim near Karachi, which started production in 1985; annual capacity 1.1m. metric tons; Chair. MOEEN AFTAB; Sec. KHALID M. AKHTAR; 13,180 employees.

**Peoples Steel Mills Ltd:** Javedan Nagar, Manghopir Rd, Karachi 75890; tel. (21) 6979159; fax (21) 6946929; e-mail psm@psmltd.com; internet www.psmltd.com; steel production.

**Razaque Steel Ltd:** B-30, Estate Ave, Shershah, SITE, Karachi 75700; tel. (21) 2561106; fax (21) 2563595; e-mail razaque@cyber.net.pk.

**Saindak Metals (Pvt) Ltd:** Ramswamy Rd, off M. A. Jinnah Rd, Quetta; tel. (81) 65403; fax (81) 65387; state-owned; under Ministry of Petroleum and Natural Resources; technical and financial assistance from Chinese Metallurgical Corpn; Pakistan's largest copper and gold project; production commenced in 1996; ore to be sent to People's Republic of China for refinement; Man. Dir Maj.-Gen. (retd) MASOOD BURKI.

**Zamsun Steel Industries:** E-13/A, SITE, Mauripur Rd, Karachi; tel. (21) 2561168; fax (21) 2582177.

### Oil and Petroleum

**Attock Refinery Ltd:** PO Refinery, Morgah, Rawalpindi 46000; tel. (51) 5487041; fax (51) 5487254; e-mail info@arl.com.pk; internet www.arl.com.pk; f. 1922; 52.5% owned by Attock Oil Co Ltd, 35% owned by Govt; sales US $354m. (2000/01); refining of indigenous crude petroleum; production capacity of 37,500 b/d; produces LPG, gasoline, kerosene, diesel, jet fuel, furnace oil and asphalt; Chair. TARIQ IQBAL KHAN; CEO M. ADIL KHATTAK; 695 employees.

**Bosicor Pakistan Ltd:** 2nd Floor, Business Plaza, Mumtaz Husan Rd, Karachi; tel. (21) 2410099; fax (21) 2410722; internet www.bosicor.com.pk; refinery at Mousa Kund, near Hub, Balochistan; Chair. AMIR ABBASSCIY.

**Caltex Oil (Pakistan) Ltd:** State Life Bldg No. 11, Abdullah Haroon Rd, Karachi; tel. (21) 5681371; fax (21) 5685014.

**National Refinery Ltd:** 7-B, Korangi Industrial Zone, Karachi 74900; tel. (21) 5064135; fax (21) 5054663; internet www.nrlpak.com; Man. Dir M. QAISER JAMAL.

**Pak-Arab Refinery Ltd:** Korangi Creek Rd, POB 12243, Karachi 75190; tel. (21) 5090100; fax (21) 5090929; e-mail info@parco.com.pk; Man. Dir SHAHID K. HAQ; Chair. ZAFAR IQBAL.

**Pak Hy Oils Ltd:** 7B/7C, Korangi Industrial Area, Karachi 74900; tel. (21) 5060106; fax (21) 5054687; e-mail pholplant@cyber.net.pk; internet www.pakhyoils.com; Dir Factory Operations ABDUL MATEEN FAROOQI.

**Pakistan Oilfields Ltd (POL):** POL House, PO Refinery, Morgah, Rawalpindi; tel. (51) 5487589; fax (51) 5487598; e-mail cs@pakoil.com.pk; internet www.pakoil.com.pk; f. 1950; sales Rs 5,539.7m. (2000/01); exploration, drilling and production; Attock Oil Co owns 53.8%, the Govt 34.7%, investment cos 6.1% and the public 5.4%; Chair. Dr GHAITH R. PHARAON; Chief Exec. SAJID NAWAZ; 1,137 employees.

**Pakistan Petroleum Ltd (PPL):** PIDC House, 4th Floor, Dr Ziauddin Ahmed Rd, Karachi 75530; tel. (21) 111-568-568; fax (21) 5680005; e-mail info@ppl.com.pk; internet www.ppl.com.pk; 93.4% govt-owned, 6.1% owned by International Finance Corpn; cap. and res Rs 10,805.7m., sales Rs 12,181.3m. (2002/03); oil and gas exploration and production; 175 wells drilled, nine gasfields and three oilfields discovered; four fields in production: Sui gasfield produced, on average, 687m. cu ft per day and Kandhkot gasfield produced 114m. cu ft per day (2002/03); in 2002/03 Adhi gas-condensate field produced, on average, 1,014 barrels of crude oil, 826 barrels per day of NGL, 31 metric tons per day of LPG and 10m. cu ft per day of gas; in 2002/03 Block-22 (Shikarpur) produced, on average, 19m. cu ft per day of gas; Chair. M. A. K. ALIZAI; Chief Exec./Man. Dir SYED MUNSIF RAZA; 1,818 employees.

**Pakistan Refinery Ltd:** Korangi Creek Rd, POB 4612, Karachi; tel. (21) 5091771; fax (21) 5091780; e-mail info@prl.com.pk; internet www.prl.com.pk; cap. and res Rs 1,360.1m., sales Rs 28,286m. (June 2004); Chief Exec. ZAFAR HALEEM.

**Pakistan State Oil Co Ltd:** PSO House, Khayaban-e-Iqbal, Clifton, POB 3983, Karachi 75600; tel. (21) 9203866; fax (21) 9203835; e-mail psomd@cyber.net.pk; internet www.psocl.com; f. 1976; 25.5% state-owned; sales Rs 158,300m. (2001/02); import, export, storage, distribution, marketing and blending of all kinds of petroleum products, lubricants, LPG/CNG and petrochemicals; Man. Dir JALEES AHMED SIDDIQI; Co Sec. JALIL TARIN.

**Shell Pakistan Ltd:** Shell House, 6 Chaudhry Khaliq-us-Zaman Rd, Karachi 75530; tel. (21) 5689525; fax (21) 5682169; f. 1949; sales Rs 63,633m. (2000/01); Chair. and Man. Dir ZAIVIJI ISMAIL BIN ABDULLAH.

**State Petroleum, Refining and Petrochemical Corpn (Pvt) Ltd (PERAC):** 2nd Floor, PIDC House, Dr Ziauddin Ahmed Rd, Karachi 75530; tel. (21) 5685071; fax (21) 5680615; e-mail perac@digicom.net.pk; f. 1974; Chair. AINUDDIN SIDDIQI.

**Total Atlas Lubricants Pakistan (Pvt) Ltd:** 3rd Floor, Bharia Complex II, M. T. Khan Rd, Karachi; tel. (21) 5610623; fax (21) 5610078; e-mail talpkhi@atlasgrouppk.com; internet www.atlasgrouppk.com/talp.htm.

### Electrical and Computing

**2B Technologies (Pvt) Ltd:** TBT (Pvt) Ltd, Suite 1310 & 1311, 13th Floor, National I.T. Park, Caesar's Tower, Shahrah-e-Faisal, Karachi; e-mail info@2bt.com.pk; internet www.2bt.com.pk; CEO OAMBER ALI HAIDRY.

**AGN Computers:** Unit WH-41, 6th Floor, Technocity, Altaf Hussain Rd, Karachi; tel. (21) 111-111-246; fax (21) 2417962; e-mail info@agncomputers.com; internet www.agncomputers.com; f. 1990; Chief Exec. NAVEED EBRAHIM.

**CC Technologies (Pvt) Ltd:** 6th Floor, Park Ave Bldg, Sharah-e-Faisal, Karachi 75400; tel. (21) 4539010; fax (21) 4539015; e-mail info@cctpak.com; internet www.cctpak.com.

**Clipsal Pakistan (Pvt) Ltd:** 101–102, Sector 15, Korangi Industrial Area, Karachi; tel. (21) 5067278; fax (21) 5063369; e-mail info@clipsal.com.pk; internet www.clipsal.com.pk; f. 1997; mfr of electrical warring accessories, data communications cabling products, low-voltage switchgear etc.; Chief Exec. PERVEZ H. MADRASWALA.

**Commerce Aids and Equipment (Pvt) Ltd:** A-5, Hassan Homes, Kehkashan 5, behind Clifton Centre, Clifton, Karachi; tel. (21) 5878464; fax (21) 5831588; e-mail comaidrs@cyber.net.pk; internet www.cae.com.pk; f. 1982; Chief Exec. M. A. SARWAR.

**Crescent Solutions:** Suite No 408, Block 6, Business Ave, 96-A, Main Shahrah-e-Faisal, Karachi; tel. (21) 4532909; fax (21) 2416942.

**CyberSoft Technologies (Pvt) Ltd:** 123-A Babar Block, New Garden Town, Lahore; tel. (42) 111-600-222; fax (42) 583-3277; e-mail info@cybersoft-tech.com; internet www.cybersoft-tech.com; Chair. ZAHID HALEEM; Pres. and CEO AZFAR MANZOOR.

**Diyatech Pakistan (Pvt) Ltd:** Block 14, F-6, Islamabad; tel. (51) 2877803; fax (51) 2825155; e-mail info@diyatech.com; internet www.diyatech.com.

**Electro Sales and Services:** 104 Progressive Sq., 11-A, Block 6, PECHS, Shahrah-e-Faisal, Karachi; tel. (21) 4310456; fax (21) 4383708; e-mail sales@electro.com.pk; internet www.electro.com.pk; f. 1987; Chief Exec. AMIN MUSTAFA.

**Fascom Systems:** 39-A, Block 6, PECHS, Karachi; tel. (21) 4551001; fax (21) 4556701; e-mail sales@fascom.com.

**Gem Net Internet Services (Pvt) Ltd:** 310–311, Anum Estate, Main Shahrah-e-Faisal, Karachi; e-mail info@gem.net.pk; internet www.gem.net.pk.

**Innovative (Pvt) Ltd:** 4-A Old FCC, Ferozepur Rd, Lahore 54600; tel. (42) 111-000-911; fax (42) 5710376; e-mail lahore@innovative-pk.com; internet www.innovative-pk.com; CEO AMIR W. WAIN.

**Intel Pakistan Corpn:** Suite 222, The Forum, G-20, Block 9, Khayaban-e-Jami, Karachi 75400; tel. (21) 5375203; Country Man. KAZIM HUSSAIN.

**iWays (Pvt) Ltd:** Rm 214, Anum Estate, Plot 49, DECHS, Shahrah-e-Faisal, Karachi; tel. (21) 4390424; e-mail info@iways.net; internet www.iways.net; f. 1998; CEO NADEEM MALIK.

**Kalsoft (Pvt) Ltd:** Mezzanine Floor, 15-C, Rahat Commercial Lane 3, Khayaban-e-Rahat, DHA Phase VI, Karachi; tel. (21) 111-403-020; fax (21) 5849780; e-mail info@kalsoft.com.pk; internet www.kalsoft.com.pk.

**Mahenti Corpn:** G-1/2, opp. P.N.S. Headquarters, Main Gizri, Karachi; tel. (21) 5876547; fax (21) 5866470; e-mail info@mahenti.com; internet www.mahenti.com; f. 1997; computer accessories, furniture, real estate; Chief Exec. MOHAMMED ZIKER MAHENTI.

**Millennium Software (Pvt) Ltd:** 86-C, Khayaban-e-Ittehad, Phase II Ext., Karachi 75500; tel. (21) 5897621; fax (21) 5887324; e-mail millsoft@cyber.net.pk; internet www.millsoft.com.pk; Man. Dir and CEO AHMED ALAUDDIN.

**Netsol Technologies Inc:** Netsol IT Village, Netsol Ave, Ghazi Rd, Lahore 54792; tel. (42) 5727096; fax (42) 5726740; e-mail info@netsolpk.com; internet www.netsolpk.com; CEO SALIM GHAURI.

**Philips Electrical Industries of Pakistan:** Islamic Chamber of Commerce, St.-2A, Block 9, KDA Scheme 5, Clifton, Karachi; tel. (21) 5874641; fax (21) 5874546; e-mail daniyal@hotmail.com; mfr of domestic electrical appliances; Chair. JAVED IQBAL.

**Saltec Powerlink:** 18-C/3, 2nd Floor, Khayaban-e-Tanzeem, D.H.A. Phase 5, Karachi; tel. (21) 5864852; fax (21) 5867144; e-mail info@saltec-powerlink.com; internet www.saltec-powerlink.com; f. 1990; Chief Exec. SALMAN QUADRI.

**Systek (Pvt) Ltd:** 10-L, Block 6, PECHS, Karachi; tel. (21) 4540242; fax (21) 4520215; e-mail marketing@systek-pk.com; internet www.systek-pk.com; f. 1992; Chief Exec. NAVID ANSARI.

**Techlogix Pakistan (Pvt) Ltd:** 50/A, FCC, Zahoor Elahi Rd, Gulberg IV, Lahore; tel. (42) 5763205; fax (42) 5876016; e-mail lahore@techlogix.com; CEO KEWAN QADRE KHAWAJA.

### Textiles, Yarns and Fibres

**Abbasi Textile Mills Ltd:** 17 Abdullah Haroon Rd, Karachi 75530; tel. (21) 5681576; fax (21) 5681575; 47,480 spindles and 205 looms; Chief Exec. SYED WAJID ALI.

**Al Abid Silk Mills Ltd:** A/39 51-B SITE, Manghopir Rd, Karachi 75700; tel. (21) 2560040; fax (21) 2564718; e-mail mail@alabid.com; internet www.alabid.com; mfr of silk and silk products; Chair., CEO and Man. Dir NASEEM A. SATTAR.

**Al Ameen Denim Mills:** A/4 S.I.T.E., Karachi 75700; tel. (21) 2578871; fax (21) 2562450; e-mail info@alameenmills.com; internet www.alameenmills.com.

**Al-Karam Textile Mills (Pvt) Ltd:** 3rd Floor, Karachi Dock Labour Board Bldg, 58 West Wharf Rd, Karachi; tel. (21) 2313031; fax (21) 2310625; e-mail headoffice@alkaram.com; internet www.alkaram.com; 80,616 spindles, 280 conventional looms and 324 shuttle-less looms; Chief Exec. ANWAR Haji KARIM.

**Azam Textile Mills Ltd:** 6 Egerton Rd, Lahore; tel. (42) 6306131; fax (42) 6368699; e-mail azam@saigols.com; internet www.saigols.com; f. 1987; mfr of blended yarn; CEO M. NASEEM SAIGOL; 500 employees.

**Burewala Textile Mills Ltd:** Dawood Centre, M. T. Khan Rd, Karachi 75530; tel. (21) 56860001; fax (21) 5693416; e-mail info.textiles@dawoodgroup.com; internet www.burewala.com; f. 1954; 42,912 spindles and 312 looms; Chair. AHMED DAWOOD; c. 1,400 employees (2000).

**Central Cotton Mills Ltd:** 5th Floor, State Life Bldg, 2, Wallace Rd, Karachi; tel. (21) 5838612; fax (21) 5683051; 53,832 spindles; Chief Exec. MUNIR AHMED.

**Chenab Ltd:** Nishatabad, Faisalabad; tel. (41) 8754472; fax (41) 8752400; e-mail info@chenabgroup.com; internet www.chenabgroup.com; sales Rs 3,650m. (2003); Chief Executive Mian MUHAMMAD LATIF; 8,000 employees (2003).

**Crescent Textile Mills Ltd:** Sargodha Rd, Faisalabad; tel. (41) 111-105-105; fax (41) 111-103-104; e-mail crestex@ctm.com.pk; internet www.ctm.com.pk; cap. and res Rs 1,592.3m., sales Rs 5,470.5m. (2000/01); 113,500 spindles and 1,000 rotors; 187 looms; complete processing unit; Chief Exec. MOHAMMAD ANWAR; 4,800 employees.

**Dawood Lawrencepur Ltd:** Dawood Centre, Moulvi Tamizuddin Khan Rd, POB 3952, Karachi 75530; tel. (21) 5686001; fax (21) 5684108; e-mail deshi@dawoodgroup.com; f. 1951; fmrly Dawood Cotton Mills Ltd; 96,636 spindles and 409 looms; mills at Landhi, Karachi, Lawrencepur and Burewala; Chief Exec. MUHAMMAD SALEEM FAROOQI; Sec. YOUSUF A. DESHI.

**Dewan Salman Fibre Ltd:** Dewan Centre, 3-A Lalazar, Beach Luxury Hotel Rd, Karachi 74000; tel. (21) 5611098; fax (21) 5622341; internet www.dewansalmanfibre.com; plant located at Hattar Industrial Estate, NWFP; produces fabrics, yarns and synthetic fibres; Chair. AKIRA YAMAMURA.

**Dewan Textile Mills Ltd:** H26, S.I.T.E., Kotri, Dist. Dadu, Sindh; tel. (221) 870159; fax (221) 870960; internet www.dewangroup.com.pk; 50,616 spindles; Chief Exec. DEWAN M. ZIA-UR-REHMAN FAROOQUI.

**Fateh Textile Mills Ltd:** POB 69, Hali Rd, S.I.T.E., Hyderabad; tel. (21) 880463; fax (21) 880514; e-mail fatehmills@aol.com; internet www.fatehmills.com; sales Rs 7,091.9m. (2002/03); Chief Exec. ASAD ULLAH BARKAT.

**Fazal Cloth Mills Ltd:** 630, 6th Floor, Stock Exchange, I. I. Chundrigar Rd, Karachi; tel. (21) 226098; 30,600 spindles; Chief Exec. SH. MUBARAK AHMAD.

**Gatron (Industries) Ltd:** 8th Floor, Textile Plaza, M. A. Jinnah Rd, Karachi 74000; tel. (21) 2417172; fax (21) 2416532; e-mail headoffice@gatron-novatex.com; internet www.gatronova.com; f. 1980; cap. and res Rs 1,942m., sales Rs 5,190m. (2004/05); mfr and exporter of polyester filament yarn and polyester chips (textile and bottle grade); Chair. PEER MOHAMMAD DIWAN; Dir A. RAZAK DIWAN; 1,800 employees.

**Gul Ahmed Textile Mills Ltd:** HT 4/B Landhi Industrial Area, Landhi, Karachi 75120; tel. (21) 5020050; fax (21) 5080071; e-mail gulahmed@gulahmed.com; internet www.gulahmed.com; sales Rs 7,000m. (2004); 110,000 spindles; full spinning, weaving, processing, stitching vertical unit; Chief Exec. BASHIR ALI MOHAMMAD.

**Hafiz Textile Mills Ltd:** 97 Alliance Bldg, Moolji St, opp. Mereweather Tower, Karachi 2; tel. (21) 228815; 32,016 spindles and 136 looms; Chief Exec. FAKHRUDDIN USMANI.

**Husein Industries Ltd:** H.T.8, Landhi Industrial & Trading Estate, Landhi, Karachi 75120; tel. (21) 5018536-8; fax (21) 5018545; e-mail husein@digicom.net.pk; internet www.husein.com; 72,040 spindles, 210 shuttle-less looms and 350 automatic looms; dyeing, bleaching, printing and finishing unit; garment, bedlinen and curtains division (with 1,500 sewing machines); Chief Exec. AZIZ L. JAMAL.

**Indus Dyeing and Manufacturing Co Ltd:** Karachi Dock Labour Board Bldg, 58 West Wharf Rd, Karachi; tel. (21) 2310751; fax (21) 2313814; e-mail info@indus-group.com; internet www.indus-group.com; 37,368 spindles; CEO SHAHZAD AHMED.

**Khyber Textile Mills Ltd:** 8th Floor, State Life Bldg No. 2, Wallace Rd, Karachi; tel. (21) 225885; fax (21) 2417138; 38,676 spindles and 160 looms; Chief Exec. FARID M. JADOON.

**Kohinoor Industries Ltd:** 6 Egerton Rd, Lahore; tel. (21) 6368940; fax (42) 6305904; e-mail azamtex@paknet4.ptc.pk; sales Rs 1,936.8m. (2001); 91,320 spindles, 654 looms and 15 shuttle-less looms; exporter and mfr of fine quality 100% cotton yarn; Chief

Exec. Mian M. NASEEM SAIGOL; Man. Dir AZAM SAIGOL; 3,500 employees.

**Kohinoor Textiles Mills Ltd:** Peshawar Rd, Rawalpindi; tel. (51) 5477264; fax (51) 5473083; e-mail taufiquesaigol@hotmail.com; internet www.kmlg.com; f. 1948; sales Rs 7,000m. (2005/06); 140,000 spindles and 220 looms; producer of bed linen and home textiles; Chair. TARIQ S. SAIGOL; Chief Exec. TAUFIQUE S. SAIGOL.

**Lyallpur Cotton Mills:** Factory Area, POB 17, Faisalabad 30870; tel. (411) 610012; fax (411) 619684; a project of Bin Bak Industries (Pvt) Ltd; complete cloth-processing unit; 53,000 spindles; Chair. Haji ABDUL AZIZ AL-RAEE; Chief Exec. Haji ABDUL REHMAN AL-RAEE.

**Mahmood Textile Mills Ltd:** Mehr Manzil, Lohari Gate, Multan; tel. (61) 511158; fax (61) 511262; e-mail mtmltd@brain.net.pk; Chair. Khawaja MUHAMMAD MASOOD; 3,000 employees (1999).

**Masood Textile Mills Ltd:** 16/3 A, Eden Homes, Main Gulberg, Lahore; tel. (42) 5753760; fax (42) 5753629; internet www.masoodtextile.com; 43,200 spindles; Chief Exec. MUHAMMAD NAZIR AHMAD; 11,000 employees.

**Mohammed Farooq Textile Mills:** Plot 6 & 7, Sector 21, Korangi Industrial Area, Karachi 75180; tel. (21) 5011571; fax (21) 5011607; e-mail marketing@mohammadfarooq.com; internet www.mohammadfarooq.com; mfr and export of textiles; CEO FAROOQ SUMAR.

**Mohib Textile Mills Ltd:** 6 FB Awani Complex, Usman Block, New Garden Town, Lahore; tel. (42) 5869800; fax (42) 5830756; 36,312 spindles; Chief Exec. M. ASIF SAIGOL.

**Nagina Cotton Mills Ltd:** 2nd Floor, Shaikh Sultan Trust Bldg No. 2, 26 Civil Lines, Beaumont Rd, Karachi 75530; tel. (21) 5686263; fax (21) 5683215; e-mail info@nagina.com; internet www.nagina.com; sales 3,315.5m. (2000/01); 47,040 spindles; Chair. SHAIKH ENAM ELLAHI; Chief Exec. SHAUKAT ELLAHI SHAIKH; 1,970 employees.

**Nishat Mills Ltd:** P.O., Nishatabad, Faisalabad; tel. (41) 754809; fax (41) 753105; e-mail nishat@fsd.comsats.net.pk; internet www.nishatmillsltd.com; f. 1951; cap. and res Rs 6,120m., sales Rs 13,210m. (2002/03); 181,384 spindles and 564 looms; Chair. NAZ MANSHA; Exec. Sec. MUHAMMAD AZAM; 12,677 employees.

**Quetta Textile Mills Ltd:** Ground Floor, Nadir House, I. I. Chundrigar Rd, Karachi 74000; tel. (21) 2414334; fax (21) 2419593; e-mail accounts@quettagroup.com; internet www.quettagroup.com; 67,000 spindles; Chief Exec. SHAIKH KHALID IQBAL.

**Ravi Rayon Ltd:** 130 Allama Iqbal Rd, Lahore; tel. (42) 6306754; fax (42) 6306753; mills at Kala Shah Kaku, Dist. Sheikhupura; Man. Dir Dr FAYYAZ A. MIAN.

**Rupali Polyester Ltd:** 4th Floor, IEP Bldg, 97-B/D-1, Gulberg III, Lahore; tel. (42) 5713101; fax (42) 5713095; e-mail rupali@nexlinx.net.pk; cap. and res Rs 1,776.3m., sales Rs 2,584.9m. (2002/03); mfrs of polyester filament yarn and staple fibre; Chair. JAFFERALI M. FEERASTA; 1,348 employees.

**Sapphire Textile Mills Ltd:** 149 Cotton Exchange Bldg, I. I. Chundrigar Rd, Karachi 2; tel. (21) 2417500; fax (21) 2416705; e-mail karachi.office@sapphire.com.pk; internet www.sapphire.com.pk; sales Rs 5,356.8m. (2000/01); 55,412 spindles and 1,152 rotors; CEO MUHAMMAD ABDULLAH; 10,000 employees.

**Sargodha Textile Mills Ltd:** Sultanabad, Faisalabad Rd, Sargodha Cantt; tel. 720084; fax 710767; 42,240 spindles and 336 looms; dyeing and finishing; Chief Exec. Mian SAJJAD ASLAM; 2,000 employees.

**Schon Textile Mills Ltd:** Schon Centre, I. I. Chundrigar Rd, Karachi 74200; tel. (21) 2636000; fax (21) 2636325.

**Shaffa International:** 160 Y-C/A, Defence Society, Lahore 54792; tel. (42) 5892232; fax (42) 5731073; e-mail sales@shaffa.com; internet www.shaffa.com; mfrs and exporters of cotton and leather working gloves.

**Sunshine Cotton Mills Ltd:** 71-B/C-2, Gulberg III, Lahore II; tel. (42) 870297; 58,088 spindles; Chief Exec. Mian AFTAB A. SHEIKH.

### Tobacco

**Lakson Tobacco Co Ltd:** Lakson Sq., Bldg No. 2, Sarwar Shaheed Rd, Karachi 74200; tel. (21) 5689080; fax (21) 5683410; e-mail info@lakson.com.pk; internet www.ltc.com.pk; sales Rs 15,457.3m. (2000/01); Chair. IQBAL ALI LAKHANI; 2,520 employees.

**Pakistan Tobacco Co Ltd:** Saudi Pak Tower, 61/A Jinnah Ave Blue Area, Islamabad; tel. (51) 2278370; fax (51) 2278377; e-mail paktobac@best.net.pk; cap. and res Rs 2,217.9m., sales Rs 15,907.0m. (2000); Chair. GOTTFRIED THOMAS; 3,019 employees.

### Miscellaneous

**Associated Industries Ltd:** Amangarh Industrial Area, Nowshera; tel. (923) 610863; fax (923) 610830; f. 1972; privatized in 1992; sales Rs 2,003m. (1999/2000); mfr and sale of edible oils and household chemicals; Chair. and CEO SH. AMJAD RASHID.

**Gemstone Corpn of Pakistan Ltd:** 15/C Railway Rd, University Town, Peshawar; tel. (521) 42062; fax (521) 841990; f. 1979; gem exploration, mining, cutting and polishing, jewellery manufacturing and marketing; Man. Dir Dr NASIR ALI BHATTI; Sec. PERVEZ ELAHI MALIK.

**National Logistic Cell:** Marketing Cell South Zone, POB 7020, Karachi; tel. (21) 2850398; fax (21) 2851316; transportation of bulk dry and liquid cargo (e.g. wheat, rice, machinery, oils, fertilizer, cement, etc.).

**OCS Pakistan (Pvt) Ltd:** Worldwide House, C-17, Korangi Rd, Defence House Authority, Phase II (Extension), Karachi 75500; tel. (21) 5803201; fax (21) 5880606; e-mail ocspak@cyber.net.pk; internet www.shipocs.com; domestic and international couriers.

**Packages Ltd:** Main Clifton Rd, Khayaban-e-Iqbal, Karachi 75600; tel. (21) 5874047; fax (42) 5811195; e-mail kyfm@packages.com.pk; sales Rs 5,495.0m. (2001); mfr and convertor of paper, board and plastic films; Chair. SAYED WAJI ALI.

**Pakistan Industrial Development Corpn (PIDC):** PIDC House, 2nd Floor, Dr Ziauddin Ahmad Rd, Karachi; tel. (21) 5685041; fax (21) 5685506; f. 1962; parastatal body; mfrs of woollen and cotton textiles, carpets, sugar; gas distributors; Chair. JAHANGIR KHAN TAREEN; CEO ABDUL BARI KHAN.

**Trading Corpn of Pakistan (Pvt) Ltd:** 4th and 5th Floors, Finance and Trade Centre, Shahrah-e-Faisal, Karachi 74400; tel. (21) 9202947; fax (21) 9202722; e-mail TCP@TCP.gov.pk; internet tcp.gov.pk; f. 1967; public-sector trading house handling bulk import requirements, such as edible oil and other essential food items; deals in exports of Pakistani products, such as textiles, wheat, leather, rice, etc.; Chair. ABDUL MALIK.

**Unilever Pakistan Ltd:** POB 220, Karachi 74200; tel. (21) 519349; fax (21) 5680914; f. 1996; by merger; mfr of consumer goods.

**Utility Store Corporation of Pakistan:** Plot No. 2039, Jinnah Ave, Blue Area, Islamabad; tel. (51) 9210985; fax (51) 9210982; e-mail USC_ho@yahoo.com; internet www.usc.com.pk; f. 1971; supplies household articles at concessional rates; Chief Officers Brig. (retd) HAFEEZ AHMED, Dr ATTA M. PANHWAR.

### TRADE UNIONS

**National Trade Union Federation Pakistan:** Bharocha Bldg, 2-B/6, Commercial Area, Nazimabad No. 2, Karachi 74600; tel. (21) 628339; fax (21) 6622529; e-mail ntuf@super.net.pk; f. 1999; 50 affiliated unions; covers following fields: steel, agriculture, textiles, garments, leather, automobiles, pharmaceuticals, chemicals, transport, printing, food, shipbuilding, engineering and power; Pres. MUHAMMAD RAFIQUE; Gen. Sec. SALEEM RAZA.

**Pakistan Workers Federation (PWF):** Bakhtiar Labour Hall, 28 Nisbet Rd, Lahore; tel. (42) 7229192; fax (42) 7239529; e-mail cpr@pwf.org.pk; internet www.pwf.org.pk; f. 2005 following the merger of the All Pakistan Federation of Trade Unions, Pakistan National Federation of Trade Unions and All Pakistan Federation of Labour; affiliated with the International Confederation of Free Trade Unions; 10 regional offices; Pres. CH. TALIB NAWAZ; Chair. MUHAMMAD AHMED; Gen. Sec. KHURSHID AHMED.

The principal affiliated federations are:

**Muttahida Labour Federation:** 24, Circular Bldg, Risala Rd, Hyderabad; c. 120,000 mems; Pres. KHAMASH GUL KHATTAK; Sec.-Gen. NABI AHMED.

**National Labour Federation (NLF):** 28, Circular Rd, Hyderabad; Pres. RANA MAHMOOD ALI KHAN.

**Pakistan Central Federation of Trade Unions:** 220 Al-Noor Chambers, M. A. Jinnah Rd, Karachi; tel. (21) 728891.

**Pakistan Railway Employees' Union (PREM):** City Railway Station, Karachi; tel. (21) 2415721; Divisional Sec. BASHIRUDDIN SIDDIQUI.

**Pakistan Trade Union Federation:** Khamosh Colony, Karachi; Pres. KANIZ FATIMA; Gen. Sec. SALEEM RAZA.

**Pakistan Transport Workers' Federation:** 110 McLeod Rd, Lahore; 17 unions; 92,512 mems; Pres. MEHBOOB-UL-HAQ; Gen. Sec. CH. UMAR DIN.

Other affiliated federations include: Pakistan Bank Employees' Federation, Pakistan Insurance Employees' Federation, Automobile, Engineering and Metal Workers' Federation, Pakistan Teachers Organizations' Council, Sarhad WAPDA Employees' Federation, and Balochistan Ittehad Trade Union Federation.

## Transport

### RAILWAYS

**Pakistan Railways:** Empress Rd, Lahore; tel. (42) 9201776; fax (42) 9201783; e-mail gmopr@pakrail.com; internet www.pakrail.com;

state-owned; 11,515 km of track and 7,791 route km; seven divisions (Karachi, Lahore, Multan, Quetta, Rawalpindi, Peshawar and Sukkur); Chair. MOHAMMAD KASHIF MURTAZA; Gen. Man. SALEEMUR RAHMAN KHAN.

### ROADS

The total length of roads was 254,410 km (motorways 339 km, main 6,587 km, secondary 211,846 km, other roads 35,638 km) in 1999. By June 2004 the total length of roads had increased to 258,340 km, 64.7% of which were paved, including 9,031 km of highways and motorways.

Government assistance comes from the Road Fund, financed from a share of the excise and customs duty on sales of petrol and from development loans.

**National Highways Authority:** 27 Mauve Area, G-9/1, Islamabad; tel. (51) 9260350; fax (51) 9261075; e-mail info@nha.gov.pk; internet www.nha.gov.pk; f. 1991; jt venture between Govt and private sector; Chair. Maj.-Gen. IMTIAZ AHMED; Dir-Gen. Brig. SOHAIL MASOOD ALVI.

**Punjab Road Transport Board:** Department of Transport, Pension Cell, 11A Egerton Rd, Lahore.

### SHIPPING

In 1974 maritime shipping companies were placed under government control. The chief port is Karachi. A second port, Port Qasim, started partial operation in 1980. A third port, Port Gwadar, has been developed as a deep-water seaport; construction was completed in March 2005 and the port opened in March 2007. Another port, Port Pasni, which is situated on the Balochistan coast, was completed in 1988. In 1991 the Government amended the 1974 Pakistan Maritime Shipping Act to allow private companies to operate.

**Mercantile Marine Dept:** 70/4, Timber Pond, N. M. Reclamation, Keamari, Karachi 74000; tel. (21) 9263014; fax (21) 9263018; e-mail info@mercantilemarine.gov.pk; internet www.mercantilemarine.gov.pk; f. 1930; ensures safety of life and property at sea and prevention of marine pollution through implementation of national legislation and international conventions; Prin. Officer TARIQ SARDAR.

**Ports and Shipping:** Government of Pakistan, Plot No. 12, Misc. Area, Mai Kolachi Bypass, Karachi 74200; tel. (21) 9204191; e-mail contact@mops.gov.pk; internet www.mops.gov.pk; Dir-Gen. HASSAN ZAIDI.

**Al-Hamd International Container Terminal (Pvt) Ltd:** Plot No. 28, O & L Trans Lyari Quarters, Hawkesbay Rd, New Truck Stand, Karachi; tel. (21) 2352660; fax (21) 2351556; e-mail info@aictpk.com; internet www.aictpakistan.com; Gen. Man. JANAKA GUNAWARDENA.

**Engro Vopak Terminal Ltd:** 1st Floor, Bahrai Complex 1, 24 M. T. Khan Rd, POB 5736, Karachi 74000; tel. (21) 5610954; fax (21) 5611394; e-mail evtl@engro.com; internet www.engro.com.

**Karachi International Container Terminal (KICT):** Administration Bldg, Berths 28–30, Dockyard Rd, West Wharf, Karachi 74000; tel. (21) 2316401; fax (21) 2313816; e-mail info@kictl.com; internet www.kictl.com; f. 1996; Chief Exec. ROGER L. HAWKE.

**Karachi Port Trust (KPT):** Eduljee Dinshaw Rd, Karachi 74000; tel. (21) 9214312; fax (21) 9214329; e-mail chairman@kpt.gov.pk; internet www.kpt.gov.pk; Chair. NASRIN HAQ; Gen. Operations Man. Rear-Adm. AGHA DANISH; Sec. KHALID MOBIN ARSHAD.

**Karachi Shipyard and Engineering Works Ltd:** POB 4419, West Wharf, Dockyard Rd, Karachi 74000; tel. (21) 9214045; fax (21) 9214020; e-mail contact@karachishipyard.com.pk; internet www.karachishipyard.com.pk; f. 1953; building and repairing ships; general engineering; Man. Dir Vice-Adm. IFTIKHAR AHMED RAO.

**Korangi Fisheries Harbour Authority:** Ghashma Goth, Landhi, POB 15804, Karachi 75160; tel. (21) 5013315; fax (21) 5015096; e-mail kfha@sat.net.pk.

**National Tanker Co (Pvt) Ltd (Pak):** 15th Floor, PNSC Bldg, M. T. Khan Rd, Karachi 74000; tel. (21) 5611843; fax (21) 5610780; f. 1981 by the Pakistan National Shipping Corpn and the State Petroleum Refining and Petrochemical Corpn Ltd; aims to make Pakistan self-reliant in the transport of crude petroleum and petroleum products; Chief Exec. Vice-Adm. A. U. KHAN; Dep. Chief Exec. TURAB ALI KHAN.

**Pakistan International Container Terminal Ltd:** 2nd Floor, Business Plaza, Mumtaz Hussain Rd, Karachi 74000; tel. (21) 9203974; fax (21) 2400281; e-mail info@pict.com.pk; internet www.pict.com.pk; Chair. Capt. HALEEM A. SIDDIQI; CEO SHARIQ SIDDIQI.

**Pakistan National Shipping Corpn:** PNSC Bldg, M. T. Khan Rd, POB 5350, Karachi 74000; tel. (21) 9203980; fax (21) 9203974; e-mail communication@pnsc.com.pk; f. 1979 by merger; state-owned; national flag carrier; undertakes global shipping operations; Chair. Vice-Adm. S. T. H. NAQVI; Sec. ZAINAB SULEMAN.

**Port Qasim Authority (PQA):** Bin Qasim, Karachi 75020; tel. (21) 9204211; fax (21) 4730108; e-mail webmaster@portqasim.org.pk; internet www.portqasim.org.pk; f. 1973; Chair. Rear Adm. SYED AFZAL; Sec. AFSAR DIN TALPUR.

**Qasim International Container Terminal:** Berths 5–7, Marginal Wharfs, POB 6425, Port Mohammad Bin Qasim, Karachi 75020; tel. (21) 4739100; fax (21) 4730021; e-mail info@qict.net; internet www.qict.net; f. 1994; CEO CHANGEZ NIAZI; Gen. Man. DARAYUS DIVECHA.

#### Associations

**All Pakistan Shipping Association:** 01-E, 1st Floor, Sattar Chambers, West Wharf Rd, Karachi; tel. (21) 2200742; fax (21) 2200743; e-mail apsa-pak@cyber.net.pk; Chair. MUHAMMAD F. QAISER.

**Pakistan Ship Agents' Association:** GSA House, 19 Timber Pound, Keamari, Karachi 75620; tel. (21) 2850837; fax (21) 2851528; e-mail psaa@cyber.net.pk; internet www.shipezee.com/psaa; f. 1976; Chair. FAROUQ H. RAHIMTOOLA.

**Terminal Association of Pakistan:** 8th Floor, Adamjee House, I. I. Chundrigar Rd, Karachi 74000; tel. (21) 2417131; fax (21) 2416477; e-mail terasspak@cyber.net.pk; Chair. MOHAMMED KASIM HASHAM; Sec. AKHTAR SULTAN.

### CIVIL AVIATION

Karachi, Lahore, Rawalpindi, Peshawar and Quetta have international airports. In April 2007 the first phase of construction for the development of a new international airport at Islamabad commenced following a series of postponements; the project was to cost an estimated Rs 35,000m. and would handle 6.5m. passengers annually upon completion.

In 1992 the Government ended the air monopoly held by the Pakistan International Airlines Corpn, and opened all domestic air routes to any Pakistan-based company.

**Civil Aviation Authority:** Terminal 1 Bldg, Karachi Airport, Karachi; tel. (21) 9248778; fax (21) 9248121; e-mail chr@caapakistan.com.pk; internet www.caapakistan.com.pk; controls all the civil airports; Chair. KAMRAN RASOOL; Sec. KHURSHID ANWAR.

**Air Blue Ltd:** Ground Floor, Saudi Pak Bldg, Jinnah Ave, Islamabad; tel. (51) 111-247-258; e-mail writetous@airblue.com; internet www.airblue.com; f. 2004; CEO SHAHID KHAQAN ABBASI.

**Pakistan International Airlines Corpn (PIA):** Jinnah International Airport, Karachi 75200; tel. (21) 4572011; fax (21) 4570419; e-mail info@piac.com.pk; internet www.piac.com.pk; f. 1954; merged with Orient Airways in 1955; 57.7% govt-owned; operates domestic services to 35 destinations and international services to 40 destinations in 31 countries; reduced number of weekly flights to Europe and the USA from 42 to 24 in March 2007 in response to proscriptive new European Union safety regulations; Chair. CHAUDHRY AHMED MUKHTAR; Man. Dir Capt. MOHAMMAD AIJAZ HAROON.

**Shaheen Air International:** 157B Clifton Rd, Clifton, Karachi 75600; tel. (21) 9251921; fax (21) 9251935; e-mail info@shaheenair.com; internet www.shaheenair.com; f. 1993; operates scheduled domestic services and international services to the Gulf region; Chair. KHALID M. SEHBAI; CEO Air Vice-Marshal (retd) AAMER ALI SHARIEFF.

## Tourism

The Himalayan hill stations of Pakistan provide magnificent scenery, a fine climate and excellent opportunities for field sports, mountaineering, trekking and winter sports. The archaeological remains and historical buildings are also impressive.

In 2006 Pakistan received some 850,600 foreign visitors; receipts from tourism amounted to around US $827m. in 2005.

**Pakistan Tourism Development Corpn:** 22A Saeed Plaza, Jinnah Ave, Blue Area, Islamabad 44000; tel. (51) 9203772; fax (51) 9207427; e-mail info@tourism.gov.pk; internet www.tourism.gov.pk; f. 1970; Chair. HASHIM KHAN; Man. Dir SALMAN JAVED.

## Defence

As assessed at November 2007, the total strength of the armed forces was 619,000: army 550,000, navy 24,000, air force 45,000. There was also a paramilitary force of as many as 304,000 (including a National Guard of 185,000). Military service is voluntary.

**Defence Expenditure:** The projected defence budget for 2007 was Rs 275,000m. at the federal level.

**Chairman of Joint Chiefs of Staff Cttee:** Gen. TARIQ MAJEED.

**Chief of Army Staff:** Gen. ASHFAQ PERVEZ KIYANI.

**Chief of Air Staff:** Air Marshal TANVIR MEHMOOD AHMED.

**Chief of Naval Staff:** Adm. MOHAMMAD AFZAL TAHIR.

**Vice Chief of Army Staff:** (vacant).

## Education

At independence in 1947 Pakistan retained the education system that had been designed by the colonial British administration in India. Efforts to introduce educational reforms and to expand educational facilities were hampered by lack of finances. However, in 1972 the Pakistan Government formulated a new Education Policy which envisaged the enforcement of elementary education and an adult literacy programme, and emphasized the study of Islamiat—the ideological basis for the existence of Pakistan—and the introduction of an agro-technical bias in school education. All institutions, except missions, were nationalized and most colleges and universities became co-educational, although there are still colleges that admit only females.

The Education Policy provided a 10-year course in Islamiat, which includes study of the Koran, the life of Muhammad and the general code for a Muslim. Children of the Sunni and the Shi'a sects follow the same course for the first eight years, then dividing to study separately the rituals of the two sects. Agro-technical subjects are introduced in the seventh and eighth years of schooling.

Development expenditure on science and technology and education and training in 2001/02 was projected at Rs 4,343.3m. (only 3.3% of total development spending). A memorandum of understanding between the Federal Education Directorate and the United Nations Educational, Scientific and Cultural Organisation (UNESCO) was signed in March 2007 under which US $3.4m. would be provided to fund a three-year teachers' development programme in Pakistan. Further provisional assistance of $60m. was pledged by the USA towards the expansion of educational opportunities during 2007.

### PRIMARY AND SECONDARY EDUCATION

Universal and free primary education is a constitutional right, but education is not compulsory. Primary education begins at five years of age and lasts for five years. Secondary education, beginning at the age of 10, is divided into two stages, of three and four years respectively. In 2006/07 there were an estimated 158,378 primary schools (including mosque schools), and total enrolment at those institutions amounted to approximately 17,043,000. With the assistance of the World Bank, a Primary Education Project has been launched to increase educational facilities and improve the quality of instruction.

There were an estimated 42,918 middle schools and 25,177 secondary schools in 2006/07. Enrolment in that year was estimated at about 5.6m. in middle schools and 2.2m. in secondary schools. The secondary education sector includes secondary vocational institutes (an estimated 3,059 schools and 284,000 enrolled pupils in 2006/07).

In 2004/05 67% of children in the relevant age-group (76% of males; 58% of females) were enrolled at primary schools, while enrolment at secondary level included an estimated 20% of pupils of the relevant age (23% of males; 17% of females).

### HIGHER EDUCATION

In 2006/07, according to estimates, there were 3,332 arts and science colleges and 1,371 professional colleges (including educational colleges); enrolment totalled 908,000 and 324,988 respectively. There were 53 public sector universities (including nine degree-awarding institutes) and 325,993 enrolments in 2005/06. The Open University has been established with the technical support of the British Open University.

With the assistance of the Asian Development Bank, 11 polytechnic institutes and a national teacher-training college are being established by the federal Government. Training is to be provided for teachers at polytechnic, commercial and vocational institutes.

# RELATED TERRITORIES

The status of Jammu and Kashmir has remained unresolved since the 1949 cease-fire agreement, whereby the area was divided into sectors administered by India and Pakistan separately. Pakistan administers Azad (Free) Kashmir and the Northern Areas as *de facto* dependencies, being responsible for foreign affairs, defence, coinage, currency and the implementation of UN resolutions concerning Kashmir.

# AZAD KASHMIR

**Area:** 11,639 sq km (4,494 sq miles).

**Population:** 1,980,000 (1981 census).

**Administration:** Government is based on the Azad Jammu and Kashmir Interim Constitution Act of 1974. There are seven administrative districts: Bagh, Bhimber, Kotli, Mirpur, Muzaffarabad, Poonch and Sudhnuti.

**Legislative Assembly:** consists of 48 members: 40 directly elected and eight indirectly elected, including five women.

**Azad Jammu and Kashmir Council:** consists of the President of Pakistan as Chairman, the President of Azad Kashmir as Vice-Chairman, five members nominated by the President of Pakistan, six members by the Legislative Assembly, and, *ex officio*, the Pakistan Minister of Kashmir Affairs and Northern Areas.

**President of Azad Kashmir:** Raja Zulqarnain Khan.

**Prime Minister:** Sardar Attiq Ahmed Khan.

# NORTHERN AREAS

**Area:** 72,520 sq km (28,000 sq miles).

**Population:** 562,000 (1981 census).

**Administration:** There are five administrative districts: Gilgit, Skardu, Diamir, Ghizer and Ghanche. The Northern Areas Council consists of 26 members (24 members are elected in a party-based election and two seats are reserved for women), headed by the federal Minister of Kashmir Affairs and Northern Areas.

# Bibliography

**General**

Abbas, Hassan. *Pakistan's Drift into Extremism: Allah, the Army, and America's War on Terror.* Armonk, NY, M. E. Sharpe, 2004.

Ahmad, Kazi S. A. *Geography of Pakistan.* London, Oxford University Press, 1972.

Ahmed, Akbar S. *Jinnah, Pakistan and Islamic Identity—The Search for Saladin.* London, Routledge, 1997.

Ahtisaari, Martti (Ed.). *Pakistan: Madrasas, Extremism and the Military.* Portland, OR, DIANE Publishing Company, 2003.

Allan, N. (Ed.). *Karakorum Conquered.* Hampshire, Palgrave Publishers, 2002.

Aziz, K. K. *The Making of Pakistan.* Karachi, National Book Foundation, 1976.

Bhutta, Zulfiqar Ahmed (Ed.). *Maternal and Child Health in Pakistan: Challenges and Opportunities.* Karachi, Oxford University Press, 2005.

Bolitho, Hector. *Jinnah: Creator of Pakistan.* London, John Murray, 1954.

Gustafson, Eric (Ed.). *Pakistan and Bangladesh: Bibliographic Essays in Social Science.* Islamabad, University of Islamabad Press, 1976.

Haeri, Shahla. *No Shame for the Sun: Lives of Professional Pakistani Women.* Syracuse, Syracuse University Press, 2002.

Iqbal, Javid. *Ideology of Pakistan.* Lahore, Sang-e-Meel Publications, 2005.

Jalal, Hamid, *et al* (Eds). *Pakistan Past and Present.* London, Stacey International, 1977.

Jinnah, Fatima (Ed. Mujahid, Sharif Al). *My Brother.* Karachi, Quaid-i-Azam Academy, 1987.

Kapur, Ashok. *Pakistan's Nuclear Development.* London, Croom Helm Publishers, 1987.

Khan, Imran. *Indus Journey.* London, Chatto and Windus, 1990.

Khurshid, Anis. *Quaid-i-Azam Mohammad Ali Jinnah: An Annotated Bibliography; Vol. I, Western Languages; Vol. II, Eastern Languages.* Karachi, Quaid-i-Azam Academy, 1978–79.

Klein, Heinz Günther, and Nestvogel, Remote. *Women in Pakistan.* Lahore, Vanguard Books, 1992.

Mai, Mukhtar. *In the Name of Honour.* London, Virago, 2007.

Malik, Hafeez (Ed.). *Iqbal: Poet-Philosopher of Pakistan.* New York, Columbia University Press, 1975.

*Muslim Nationalism in India and Pakistan.* Washington, DC, Public Affairs Press, 1964.

Mir, Amir. *The True Face of Jehadis: Inside Pakistan's Network of Terror.* New Delhi, Roli Books, 2006.

Mohammad Ali, Chaudhri. *The Emergence of Pakistan.* New York, Columbia University Press, 1967.

Mujahid, Sharif Al (Ed.). *Ideological Orientation of Pakistan.* Karachi, National Book Foundation, 1976.

*Quaid-i-Azam Jinnah: Studies in Interpretation.* Karachi, Quaid-i-Azam Academy, 1981.

Mumtaz, Kamil Khan. *Architecture in Pakistan.* Singapore, Mirmar Books, 1986.

Mumtaz, Khawar, and Shaheed, Farida. *Women of Pakistan.* London, Zed Books Ltd, 1988.

Mumtaz, S., Anwar Ali, I., and Racine, J.-L. (Eds). *Pakistan: The Contours of State and Society.* New York, Oxford University Press, 2003.

Naim, C. M. (Ed.). *Iqbal, Jinnah and Pakistan: The Vision and the Reality.* Syracuse, NY, Maxwell Graduate School of Citizenship and Public Affairs, 1979.

Noman, Omar, and Weiner, M. *The Child and the State in India and Pakistan.* Oxford University Press, 1994.

Patel, Rashida. *Islamisation of Laws in Pakistan.* Karachi, Faiza Publishers, 1986.

*Men Versus Women: Gender Inequality in Pakistan.* Karachi, Oxford University Press, 2003.

Qadeer, Mohammad. *Pakistan—Social and Cultural Transformations in a Muslim Nation.* Abingdon, Routledge, 2006.

Qureshi, Ishtiaq Husain. *The Muslim Community of the Indo-Pakistan Subcontinent.* Karachi, Ma'aref, 2nd edn, 1977.

Rahman, Tariq. *Denizens of Alien Worlds: A Study of Education, Inequality and Polarization in Pakistan.* Karachi, Oxford University Press, 2005.

Retallick, John, and Farah, Iffat (Eds). *Transforming Schools in Pakistan: Towards the Learning Community.* Karachi, Oxford University Press, 2005.

Sadullah, Mujahid, *et al* (Eds). *Partition of the Punjab: A Compilation of Documents.* Lahore, National Documentation Centre, 1984.

Sardar Ali, Shaheen, and Rehman, Javaid. *Indigenous Peoples and Ethnic Minorities of Pakistan: Constitutional and Legal Perspectives.* London: Routledge, 2001.

Sayeed, Khalid bin. *Pakistan, the Formative Phase.* Karachi, Pakistan Publishing House, 1960.

Shah, Justice Nasim Hasan. *Judgements on the Constitution, Rule of Law and Martial Law in Pakistan.* Karachi, Oxford University Press, 1993.

Verkaaik, Oskar. *Migrants and Militants: Fun and Urban Violence in Pakistan.* Princeton, NJ, Princeton University Press, 2004.

Weaver, M. A. *Pakistan: In the Shadow of Jihad and Afghanistan.* New York, Farrar, Straus and Giroux, 2003.

Weiss, Anita M. (Ed.). *Islamic Reassertion in Pakistan: The Application of Islamic Laws in a Modern State.* Lahore, Vanguard Books Ltd, 1985.

*Culture, Class and Development in Pakistan.* Lahore, Vanguard Books, 1991.

Wolpert, Stanley. *Jinnah of Pakistan: A Life.* New York, Oxford University Press, 1984.

Yasin, Mohammad, and Banuri, Tariq (Eds). *Dispensation of Justice in Pakistan.* Karachi, Oxford University Press, 2003.

Yusuf, Kaniz F., *et al* (Eds). *Pakistan Resolution Revisited.* Islamabad, National Institute of Historical and Cultural Research, 1990.

Zingel, Wolfgang Peter, and Lallemant, Stephanie (Eds). *Pakistan in the 80s: Ideology, Regionalism, Economy and Foreign Policy.* Lahore, Vanguard Books Ltd, 1985.

**History and Politics**

Afzal, M. Rafique. *Pakistan: History and Politics, 1947–71.* Oxford, Oxford University Press, 2002.

Afzal, R. *Political Parties in Pakistan: Vol. I, 1947–58; Vol. II, 1958–69.* Islamabad, National Commission on Historical and Cultural Research, 1976 and 1986.

Ahmad, Aziz. *Islamic Modernism in India and Pakistan (1857–1964).* London, Oxford University Press for Chatham House, 1967.

Ahmed, Akbar S. *Resistance and Control in Pakistan.* London, Routledge, 2004.

Ahsan, Aitzaz. *The Indus Saga and the Making of Pakistan.* Karachi, Oxford University Press, 1996.

Aijazuddin, F. S. *Historical Images of Pakistan.* Lahore, Ferozensons, 1992.

Ansari, Sarah. *Life after Partition: Migration, Community and Strife in Sindh 1947–1962.* Karachi, Oxford University Press, 2005.

Ayub Khan, Mohammad. *Friends not Masters: A Political Autobiography.* London, Oxford University Press, 1967.

Banerjee, Mukulika. *The Pathan Unarmed: Opposition and Memory in the North West Frontier.* Oxford, James Currey Publishers, 2000.

Baxter, Craig. *Pakistan on the Brink: Politics, Economics and Society.* Lanham, MD, Rowman and Littlefield, 2004.

Baxter, Craig (Ed.). *Zia's Pakistan: Politics and Stability in a Frontline State.* Lahore, Vanguard Books Ltd, 1985.

Baxter, Craig, and Wasti, Syed Razi. *Pakistan: Authoritarianism in the 1980s.* Lahore, Vanguard Books, 1991.

Bennett Jones, Owen. *Pakistan: The Eye of the Storm.* New Haven, CT, Yale University Press, 2002.

Bhutto, Benazir. *Daughter of the East.* London, Hamish Hamilton, 1988.

Binder, Leonard. *Religion and Politics in Pakistan.* Berkeley, CA, University of California Press, 1961.

Braibanti, Ralph. *Research on the Bureaucracy of Pakistan.* Durham, NC, Duke University Press, 1966.

Burki, Shahed Javed. *Pakistan Under Bhutto.* London, Macmillan, 1980.

*Pakistan: The Continuing Search for Nationhood.* Lahore, Pak Book Corporation, 1992.

*Historical Dictionary of Pakistan.* New Delhi, Vision Books, 2005.

Burki, Shahed Javed, and Baxter, Craig (Eds). *Pakistan under the Military: Eleven Years of Zia ul-Haq.* Boulder, CO, Westview Press, 1991.

Callard, Keith. *Pakistan, A Political Study*. London, Allen and Unwin, 1957; Mystic, CT, Lawrence Verry, 1965.

Choudhury, G. W. *Constitutional Development in Pakistan*. Lahore and London, Longmans, 1959; New York, Institute of Pacific Relations, 1959.

*The Last Days of United Pakistan*. Bloomington, IN, Indiana University Press, 1974.

*Pakistan: Transition from Military to Civilian Rule*. London, Scorpion Publishing Ltd, 1988.

Cohen, Stephen Philip. *The Idea of Pakistan*. Washington, DC, The Brookings Institution, 2004.

Datta, S. K. *Pakistan: From Jinnah to Jihad*. New Delhi, UBS Publishers' Distributors, 2002.

Docherty, Paddy. *The Khyber Pass: A History of Empire and Invasion*. London, Faber and Faber, 2007.

Feldman, Herbert A. *Revolution in Pakistan: A Study of the Martial Law Administration*. London and New York, Oxford University Press, 1967.

*From Crisis to Crisis: Pakistan 1962–1969*. London and Karachi, Oxford University Press, 1972.

*The End and the Beginning: Pakistan 1969–1971*. London and Karachi, Oxford University Press, 1976.

Ganguly, Sumit. *The Kashmir Question: Retrospect and Prospect*. London, Frank Cass, 2003.

Goodson, Larry. *The Talibanization of Pakistan*. New York and Basingstoke, Palgrave Macmillan, 2002.

Grare, F. *Pakistan and the Afghan Conflict 1979–1985*. New York, Oxford University Press, 2003.

Halliday, Fred, and Alavi, Hamza. *State and Ideology in the Middle East and Pakistan*. London, Macmillan Education, 1988.

Haqqani, Husain. *Pakistan: Between Mosque and Military*. Washington, DC, Carnegie Endowment for International Peace, 2005.

Hussain, Asif. *Elite Politics in an Ideological State: The Case of Pakistan*. Folkestone, Dawson, 1979.

Hussain, Zahid. *Frontline Pakistan: The Struggle with Militant Islam*. New York, Columbia University Press, 2007.

Hyman, Anthony, Ghayur, Muhammad and Kaushik, Naresh. *Pakistan: Zia and After*. London, Asia Publishing House, 1988.

Jaffrelot, Christophe (Ed.). *Pakistan, Nationalism Without a Nation*. London, Zed Books, 2nd edn, 2002.

*A History of Pakistan and its Origins*. London, Anthem Press, 2002.

Jalal, Ayesha. *The State of Martial Rule: The Origins of Pakistan's Political Economy of Defence*. Cambridge, Cambridge University Press, 1990.

*Democracy and Authoritarianism in South Asia*. Cambridge, Cambridge University Press, 1995.

Jalalzai, Musa Khan. *The Crisis of Governance in Pakistan: Kashmir, Afghanistan, Sectarian Violence and Economic Crisis*. Lahore, Sang-e-Meel Publications, 2003.

Jan, Tarik. *Issues in Pakistani Politics*. Islamabad, Institute of Policy Studies, 1992.

Jawed, Nasim Ahmad. *Islam's Political Culture: Religion and Politics in Predivided Pakistan*. Austin, TX, University of Texas Press, 1999.

M. R. Kazimi (Ed.). *M. A. Jinnah: Views and Reviews*. Oxford, Oxford University Press, 2006.

Kazimi, Muhammad Reza. *Liaquat Ali Khan: His Life and Work*. Karachi, Oxford University Press, 2004.

Kennedy, Charles H. *Bureaucracy in Pakistan*. Karachi, Oxford University Press, 1987.

Khan, Adeel. *Politics of Identity: Ethnic Nationalism and the State in Pakistan*. London, Sage Publications, 2004.

Khan, Asghar (Ed.). *Islam, Politics and the State: The Pakistan Experience*. London, Zed Books, 1985.

Khan, Lt-Gen. Gul Hassan. *Memoirs of Lt-Gen. Gul Hassan Khan*. Karachi, Oxford University Press, 1993.

Khan, Hamid. *Constitutional and Political History of Pakistan*. New York, Oxford University Press, 2001.

Khan, Yasmin. *The Great Partition: The Making of India and Pakistan*. New Haven, CT, Yale University Press, 2007.

Kothari, Smitu, and Mian, Zia (Eds). *Out of the Nuclear Shadow*. London, Zed Books, 2001.

Kras, Sarah Louise, and Schlesinger, Arthur (Eds). *Pervez Musharraf: President of Pakistan (Major World Leaders)*. London, Chelsea House Publishers, 2004.

Kukreja, V. *Contemporary Pakistan: Political Processes, Conflicts and Crises*. London, Sage Publications, 2002.

Lamb, A. *Kashmir—Origins of the Dispute*. Hertford, Roxford Books, 1994.

Lamb, Christina. *Waiting for Allah: Pakistan's Struggle for Democracy*. London, Hamish Hamilton, 1991.

Laporte, R., Jr. *Power and Privilege: Influence and Decision Making in Pakistan*. Los Angeles, CA, University of California Press, 1976.

Lari, S. Z. *A History of Sind*. Karachi, Oxford University Press, 1994.

Low, D. A. (Ed.). *The Political Inheritance of Pakistan*. Basingstoke, Macmillan, 1991.

Mahmood, Safdar. *Pakistan: Political Roots and Development 1947–99*. Oxford University Press, 2000 and 2003.

Malik, I. H. *State and Civil Society in Pakistan: Politics of Authority, Ideology and Ethnicity*. Basingstoke, Macmillan Press Ltd, 1997.

*Islam, Nationalism and the West: Issues of Identity in Pakistan*. Basingstoke, Macmillan Press Ltd, 1999.

Malik, Muhammad Aslam. *The Making of the Pakistan Resolution*. Oxford University Press, 2001.

Manzooruddin, Ahmed (Ed.). *Contemporary Pakistan: Politics, Economy and Society*. Karachi, Royal Book Co, 1982.

Mazari, Sherbaz Khan. *A Journey to Disillusionment*. Karachi, Oxford University Press, 2000.

Mirza, H. *From Plassey to Pakistan: The Family History of Iskander Mirza, the First President of Pakistan*. Lanham, MD, Rowman and Littlefield, 2002.

Musharraf, Pervez. *In the Line of Fire: A Memoir*. London, Simon & Schuster, 2006.

Al Mujahid, Sharif (Ed.). *Muslim League Documents 1900–1947, Vol. I, 1900–1908*. Karachi, Quaid-i-Azam Academy, 1990.

Nanda, Lt-Gen. K. K. *Conquering Kashmir—A Pakistani Obsession*. New Delhi, Lancer Books, 1994.

Naseem, S. M., and Nadvi, K. (Eds). *The Post-Colonial State and Social Transformation in India and Pakistan*. New York, Oxford University Press, 2002.

Nasr, Seyyed Vali Reza. *The Vanguard of the Islamic Revolution: The Jama'at-i Islami of Pakistan*. Berkeley, CA, University of California Press, 1996.

*The Islam Leviathan: Islam and the Making of State Power (Religion and Global Politics)*. New York, Oxford University Press, 2001.

Nayak, Dr Pandav. *Pakistan: Political Economy of a Developing State*. New Delhi, Patriot Publishers, 1988.

Noman, Omar. *Pakistan: Political and Economic History since 1947*. London, Kegan Paul International Ltd, 1991.

Rahman, Maitur. *Second Thoughts on Bangladesh*. London, News and Media, 1979.

Rizvi, Hasan Askari. *Internal Strife and External Intervention: India's Role in the Civil War in East Pakistan*. Lahore, Progressive Publishers, 1981.

*The Military and Politics in Pakistan*. Lahore, Progressive Publishers, 1987.

*Pakistan and the Geostrategic Environment: A Study of Foreign Policy*. London, St Martin's Press, 1993.

Robson, Brian. *Crisis on the Frontier: The Third Afghan War and the Campaign in Waziristan 1919–20*. London, Spellmount Publishers, 2004.

Samad, Yunas. *A Nation in Turmoil: Nationalism and Ethnicity in Pakistan, 1937–1958*. New Delhi, Sage Publications, 1995.

Sareen, Sushant. *The Jihad Factory: Pakistan's Islamic Revolution in the Making*. New Dehli, Hindustan Publishing Corpn, 2005.

Sayeed, Khalid Bin. *The Political System of Pakistan*. London, Allen and Unwin, 1967.

Schofield, Victoria. *Kashmir in Conflict: India, Pakistan and the Unfinished War*. I. B. Tauris, 2000.

Shah, Syed Waqar Ali. *Ethnicity, Islam and Nationalism: Muslim Politics in the North-West Frontier Province 1937–47*. Karachi, Oxford University Press, 2000.

Sharma, R. (Ed.). *The Pakistan Trap*. London, Sangam Books, 2001.

Sherwani, L. A. (Ed.). *Pakistan Resolution to Pakistan*. Karachi, National Publishing House Ltd, 1969.

Siddiqi, Abdul Rehman. *East Pakistan: The Endgame—An Onlooker's Journal 1969–1971*. Karachi, Oxford University Press, 2004.

Sisson, Richard, and Rose, Leo E. *War and Secession: Pakistan, India and the Creation of Bangladesh*. Berkeley, University of California Press, 1990.

Stewart, Jules. *The Khyber Rifles: From the British Raj to Al Qaeda*. Stroud, Sutton Publishing, 2004.

Talbot, Ian. *Provincial Politics and the Pakistan Movement: The Growth of the Muslim League in North-West and North-East India 1937–47*. Karachi, Oxford University Press, 1988.

*Freedom's Cry: The Popular Dimension in the Pakistan Movement and the Partition Experience in North-West India*. Karachi, Oxford University Press, 1996.

*Pakistan: A Modern History*. London, Hurst, 1999.

Talbot, Ian, and Singh, G. (Eds). *Region and Partition: Bengal, Punjab and the Partition of the Subcontinent*. Karachi, Oxford University Press, 1999.

Taylor, David. *Pakistan (World Bibliographical Series, No. 10)*. Oxford, Clio Press, 1990.

Von Vorys, K. *Political Development in Pakistan*. New Jersey, Princeton University Press, 1965.

Wilcox, W. A. *Pakistan: Consolidation of a State*. New York, Columbia University Press, 1964.

Wolpert, Stanley. *Zulfi Bhutto of Pakistan: His Life and Times*. New York, Oxford University Press, 1993.

Wriggins, H. (Ed.). *Pakistan in Transition*. Islamabad, University of Islamabad, 1975.

Zaidi, S. Akbar. *Regional Imbalances and National Questions in Pakistan*. Lahore, Vanguard Books, 1991.

Ziring, Lawrence. *The Ayub Khan Era: Politics in Pakistan 1958–69*. New York, Syracuse University Press, 1971.

*Pakistan: The Enigma of Political Development*. 1980.

*Pakistan in the Twentieth Century: A Political History*. Karachi, Oxford University Press, 1997.

*Pakistan: At the Crosscurrent of History*. Oxford, Oneworld Publications, 2003.

Ziring, Lawrence, Braibanti, Ralph, and Wriggins, H. (Eds). *Pakistan: The Long View*. Durham, NC, Duke University Center for Commonwealth and Comparative Studies, 1977.

**Foreign Relations**

Amin, S. M. *Pakistan's Foreign Policy: A Reappraisal*. New York, Oxford University Press, 2002.

Barnds, W. J. *India, Pakistan and the Great Powers*. New York, Praeger, for the Council on Foreign Relations, 1972.

Brines, R. *The Indo-Pakistan Conflicts*. New York, Pall Mall Press, 1968.

Burke, S. M. *Pakistan's Foreign Policy: An Historical Analysis*. London, Oxford University Press, 1973.

*Main Springs of Indian and Pakistani Foreign Policies*. Oxford University Press, 1975.

Cheema, Pervaiz Iqbal. *Pakistan's Defence Policy, 1947–58*. London, Macmillan Press, 1990.

Choudhury, G. W. *Pakistan's Relations With India*. New York, Praeger, 1968.

*India, Pakistan, Bangladesh and the Major Powers*. New York, The Free Press, and London, Collier Macmillan, 1975.

Dixit, J. N. *India-Pakistan in War and Peace*. London, Routledge, 2002.

Fair, Christine. *The Counterterror Coalitions: Cooperation with Pakistan and India*. Santa Monica, CA, RAND, 2004.

Faruqui, A. *Rethinking the National Security of Pakistan: The Price of Strategic Myopia*. New York, Ashgate Publishing Company, 2003.

Ganguly, Sumit, and Hagerty, Devin T. *Fearful Symmetry: India–Pakistan Crises in the Shadow of Nuclear Weapons*. Seattle, WA, University of Washington Press, 2005.

Hussain, Rizwan. *Pakistan and the Emergence of Islamic Militancy in Afghanistan*. Aldershot, Ashgate, 2005.

Khan, M. Asghar. *Indo-Pakistan War: The First Round*. London, Islamic Information Service, 1979.

Khan, Rais Ahmad. *Forty Years of Pakistan–United States Relations*. Karachi, Royal Book Co, 1992.

Khan, Air Chief Marshal Zulfikar Ali. *Pakistan's Security: The Challenge and the Response*. Lahore, Progressive Publishers, 1987.

Kux, Dennis. *Pakistan: Flawed not Failed State*. Washington, DC, Foreign Policy Association, 2001.

*The United States and Pakistan, 1947–2000: Disenchanted Allies (The Adst-Dacor Diplomats and Diplomacy Series)*. Woodrow Wilson Center Press, 2001.

Lamb, A. *Asian Frontiers: Studies in a Continuing Problem*. London, Pall Mall Press, 1968.

Malik, Hafeez (Ed.). *Soviet-American Relations with Pakistan, Iran and Afghanistan*. New York, St Martin's Press, 1987.

Razvi, M. *The Frontiers of Pakistan: A Study of Frontier Problems in Pakistan's Foreign Policy*. Karachi, National Publishing House, 1971.

Rizvi, Hasan Askari. *Pakistan and the Geostrategic Environment: A Study of Foreign Policy*. London, St Martin's Press, 1993.

Rose, Leo E., and Husain, Noor A. (Eds). *United States—Pakistan Forum: Relations with the Major Powers*. Lahore, Vanguard Books Ltd, 1985.

Singh, S. *Politics of Regionalism in Pakistan*. New Delhi, Kalinga Publications, 2003.

Sridharan, E. *The India-Pakistan Nuclear Relationship: Theories of Deterrence and International Relations*. New Delhi, Routledge India, 2007.

Syed, Anwar Husain. *China and Pakistan: Diplomacy of Entente Cordiale*. London, University of Massachusetts Press, 1975.

Ziring, Lawrence (Ed.). *The Subcontinent in World Politics*. New York, Praeger, 1982.

**Economy**

Addleton, Jonathan. *Undermining the Centre: The Gulf Migration and Pakistan*. Karachi, Oxford University Press, 1992.

Ahmad, V., and Amjad, R. *The Management of Pakistan's Economy: 1947–82*. Karachi, Oxford University Press, 1984.

Amjad, Rashid. *Private Industrial Investment in Pakistan, 1960–1980*. Cambridge, 1982.

Ansari, Javed A. *Financial Management in Pakistan*. Karachi, Oxford University Press, 2005.

Asian Development Bank. *Pakistan 2010: Realizing Pakistan's Full Potential*. Metro Manila, 2003.

Bengali, K., Masood Ahmed, Q., and Jamal, H. *Social Development in Pakistan: Annual Review 2001, Growth, Inequality and Poverty*. New York, Oxford University Press, 2003.

Bhatia, B. M. *Pakistan's Economic Development*. Lahore, Vanguard Books, 1990.

Byerlee, Derek, and Husain, Tariq. *Farming Systems in Pakistan*. Lahore, Vanguard Books, 1992.

Central Statistical Office. *25 Years of Pakistan In Statistics: 1947–1972*. Karachi, Economic Affairs Division, Government of Pakistan, 1972.

Davidson, Andrew, and Ahmad, Munir. *Privatization and the Crisis of Agricultural Extension: The Case of Pakistan*. Aldershot, Ashgate, 2003.

Haq, Mahbubul, *et al*. *Employment Distribution and Basic Needs in Pakistan*. Lahore, Progressive Publishers, 1991.

*Human Development in South Asia*. Karachi, Oxford University Press, 1997.

Hasan, Parvez. *Pakistan's Economy at the Crossroads*. Karachi, Oxford University Press, 1998.

Husain, Ishrat. *Pakistan: The Economy of an Elitist State*. Karachi, Oxford University Press, 1999.

*Economic Management in Pakistan 1999–2002*. Karachi, Oxford University Press, 2004.

Hussain, Akmal. *Pakistan—National Human Development Report: Poverty, Growth and Governance*. Karachi, Oxford University Press, 2004.

James, W. E., and Roy, S. (Eds). *Foundations of Pakistan's Political Economy*. Oxford University Press, 1993.

Kardar, Shahid. *Political Economy of Pakistan*. Lahore, Progressive Publishers, 1991.

Khan, Abdul Jabbar. *Non-Interest Banking in Pakistan: Concept, Practice and Evaluation*. Karachi, Royal Book Co, 1991.

Khan, Shahrukh Rafi. *Fifty Years of Pakistan's Economy: Traditional Topics and Contemporary Concerns*. Karachi, Oxford University Press, 1999.

Kibria, Ghulam. *A Shattered Dream: Understanding Pakistan's Underdevelopment*. Karachi, Oxford University Press, 1999.

Lefèvre, Alain. *Kinship, Honour and Money in Rural Pakistan*. Richmond, Curzon, 1999.

Michel, A. A. *The Indus Rivers: A Study of the Effect of Partition*. New Haven, CT, Yale University Press, 1967.

Nabi, Ijaz (Ed.). *The Quality of Life in Pakistan: Studies in Social Sector Economics*. Lahore, Vanguard Books, 1986.

Nasim, Anjum (Ed.). *Financing Pakistan's Development in the 1990s*. Karachi, Oxford University Press, 1992.

Noman, Omar. *Economic and Social Progress in Asia: Why Pakistan Did Not Become a Tiger*. Karachi, Oxford University Press, 1997.

Pal, Izzud-Din. *Islam and the Economy of Pakistan: A Critical Analysis of Traditional Interpretation.* Karachi, Oxford University Press Pakistan, 2006.

Papanek, Gustav F. *Pakistan's Development: Social Goals and Private Incentives.* Cambridge, MA, Harvard University Press, and London, Oxford University Press, 1967.

Qureshi, Ejaz Aslam (Ed.). *Development Planning in Pakistan.* Lahore, Ferozsons, 1991.

Rajeev, P. V. *Resource Mobilization in India and Pakistan.* New Delhi, Deep and Deep Publications, 1991.

Rehmatullah, S. *Social Welfare in Pakistan.* New York, Oxford University Press, 2003.

Siddiqa, Ayesha. *Military Inc.: Inside Pakistan's Military Economy.* London, Pluto Press, 2007.

Siddiqi, Akhtar Husain. *Pakistan: Its Resources and Development.* Hong Kong, Asian Research Service, 1984.

Social Policy and Development Centre. *Social Development in Pakistan: Annual Review.* Karachi, Oxford University Press, 1999.

State Bank of Pakistan. *Development of the State Bank of Pakistan.* Karachi, 1994.

World Bank Independent Evaluation Group. *Pakistan: An Evaluation of the World Bank's Assistance.* World Bank, 2006.

Zaidi, Syed Akbar. *Regional Imbalances and the National Question in Pakistan.* Lahore, Vanguard Books, 1992.

*Issues in Pakistan's Economy.* Oxford, Oxford University Press, 1999.

# SRI LANKA

## Physical and Social Geography

B. H. FARMER

Revised by G. H. PEIRIS

The Democratic Socialist Republic of Sri Lanka (formerly known as Ceylon) comprises one large island and several islets, lying east of the southern tip of the Indian subcontinent. The maximum north–south length of the island, which (including adjacent small islands) covers an area of 65,525 sq km (25,299 sq miles), is 435 km, and its greatest width is 225 km. The Bay of Bengal lies to its north and east, and the Arabian Sea to its west. Sri Lanka is separated from India by the Gulf of Mannar and the Palk Strait, between which there lies, in very shallow water, a chain of small islands linking Sri Lanka and India. Sri Lanka extends from 5° 55′ to 9° 50′ N and from 79° 42′ to 81° 53′ E.

### PHYSICAL FEATURES

Sri Lanka consists almost entirely of hard ancient crystalline rocks (although recent work has cast doubt on the age of some of them). Unaltered sedimentary rocks are largely confined to the Jaffna peninsula in the north and a strip down the north-west coast.

The highest land in Sri Lanka occupies the south-centre, the 'up-country', and rises to more than 1,500 m above sea-level. The highest point is Piduruthalagala (2,524 m). From the up-country, the land falls by steps to a rolling coastal plain, narrow in the west and south-west, broadest in the north (though even there, isolated hills rise above the general level). The rivers, apart from the longest, the Mahaweli Ganga (which has a complicated course), are generally short and run radially outwards from the up-country.

### CLIMATE

Sri Lanka has temperatures appropriate to its near-equatorial position, modified by altitude up-country. In Colombo, at sea-level, mean monthly temperatures fluctuate only between 25°C in January and 28°C in May. At Nuwara Eliya, at 1,889 m, temperatures range between 14°C in January and 16°C in May.

A fundamental division in Sri Lanka, so far as rainfall and therefore agriculture are concerned, is that between the wet and dry zones. The former occupies the south-western quadrant of the island, and normally receives rain from both the south-west and north-east monsoons. Colombo, for example, has a mean annual rainfall of 2,365 mm: it receives 69 mm in February, the driest month, and 371 mm in May, the wettest. The dry zone, covering the lowlands of the north and east and extending in modified form into the eastern up-country, has a period of severe drought in the south-west monsoon and most of its rain from the north-east. Trincomalee, for example, with a mean annual rainfall of 1,648 mm, receives on average only 69 mm, 28 mm and 51 mm in May, June and July respectively (and mean *expectation* is less than the mean rainfall). However, it receives over 356 mm in both November and December. Commercial crops such as tea and rubber are almost entirely confined to the wet zone.

### SOILS AND NATURAL RESOURCES

The contrast between the wet zone and the dry zone extends into other environmental diversities such as those of soil and vegetation. For example, the 'red-yellow podzolic soils', which are confined to the wet zone, comprise a leached lateritic soil susceptible to rapid degradation when exposed through removal of vegetation to processes of weathering and erosion. The 'reddish-brown earths' are found extensively in those parts of the dry zone with a sub-surface of crystalline rocks; this non-lateritic loamy soil has a potential for sustained high productivity under conditions of sound management. Among the other more important edaphic formations found in Sri Lanka are the 'latosolic soils', which cover the limestone rock strata of the northern and north-western littoral, the 'alluvials' found in association with riverine terrain, and the 'regosols' (sandy soils), which extend over much of the coastal fringe.

The zonal differences in vegetation are reflected in the remnants of natural forests—'wet evergreen forest' (modified by elevation in the highlands to 'sub-montane' and 'montane' types) of the wet zone, and 'dry mixed evergreen forests' (modified in areas of lowest rainfall into shrub and thorn forest) of the dry zone. Rapid deforestation has reduced the aggregate extent of natural forest cover to no more than about 15% of the country. The fertility of the soil, and the biotic characteristics of the forests, now reflect in abundance the impact of ecological disruptions caused by many centuries of intensive use of the land for agriculture and human settlements. Accordingly, both conservation of the soil as well as the preservation of the fauna and flora have become matters of major concern to Sri Lanka.

Gemstones (including high-value varieties such as sapphire, ruby, chrysoberyl, spinel, beryl and topaz), graphite, ilmenite, quartz, mica, industrial clays, limestone and salt are the more important economically useful minerals found in Sri Lanka. The resource base in metallurgical minerals is considered poor, the only commercially exploitable metals known hitherto being titanium, monazite and zircon contained in the beach sands over certain stretches of the sea coast. Of fossil fuels, the only known resource is the low-grade peat found along the swamps adjacent to the west coast. In the absence of both coal and petroleum, biomass (extracted from forests, and by-products of agriculture) and river water harnessed for hydropower are significant as locally available sources of commercial energy.

### POPULATION AND ETHNIC GROUPS

According to the provisional results of the census of July 2001, Sri Lanka had a population of 16,864,544 in 18 out of 25 districts where enumeration was carried out completely. Enumeration was only partially conducted in Mannar, Vavuniya, Batticaloa and Trincomalee districts, owing to security concerns; data from these districts brought the total enumerated population to approximately 17,560,000. The census was not conducted in the districts of Jaffna, Mullaitivu and Kilinochchi, also owing to security concerns. The total estimated population for the entire country at July 2001 was 18,732,255. At mid-2007 this had risen to an estimated 20,010,000. The crude birth rate fell from 37 per 1,000 in 1960 to 22.4 per 1,000 in 1986, and to an estimated 19.0 per 1,000 in 2007. The average population density at mid-2007 was 305.4 per sq km, although the population is very unevenly distributed. The wet zone and most of the up-country have a dense rural population and also contain the principal conurbation, Colombo (estimated population 642,020 at the 2001 census), and a number of other towns, e.g. Kandy (estimated population of 110,049 at the 2001 census). Some of the dry zone remains sparsely peopled, despite considerable colonization since the 1930s.

Sri Lanka has a plural society. The majority group, the Sinhalese, speak a distinctive language (Sinhala) related to the Indo-Aryan tongues of north India, and are mainly Buddhist. There are two groups of Tamils: 'Sri Lankan Tamils', the descendants of Tamil-speaking groups who migrated from

South India many years ago, and 'Indian Tamils', comparatively recent immigrants (who came to Sri Lanka to work on plantations) and their descendants: both are predominantly Hindu. There are also groups of Muslims (comprising 'Moors' and 'Malays') and Christians (drawn from the Sinhalese, Tamil and other communities).

# History

KINGSLEY M. DE SILVA

## ANCIENT SRI LANKA

The island of Sri Lanka was known in ancient times by a variety of names suggestive of wealth, riches and prosperity—the 'Land without Sorrow' to the Chinese and the 'Isle of Gems' to the Tamils of South India; the 'Isle of Delight' to the merchants of Arabia; to the Sinhalese themselves it was Lankadipa, 'the Resplendent Isle'; and Lanka was the name by which the island was known in the great Indian epic, the *Ramayana*. The earliest European account of Sri Lanka, written about 20 years after the death of Alexander the Great, came from Megasthenes, a Seleucid envoy to India, who spoke from hearsay about its elephants, gold and jewels. Pliny is believed to have personally interviewed the Sinhalese envoys to Rome during the reign of Claudius, and Ptolemy's *Geographia* contained a sketch of Sri Lanka, and even identified its capital city, Anuradhapura. Fa Xian, the Chinese scholar monk who visited the island in the fifth century AD, described it as a land where 'the (climate) is temperate and attractive, without any difference of summer and winter. The vegetation is always luxuriant. Cultivation proceeds whenever men think fit: there are no fixed seasons for it'.

Proximity to India brought Sri Lanka within easy range of a diversity of influences from the subcontinent. The narrow stretch of sea that separates it from the subcontinent was adequate, however, to ensure that the civilization that evolved in Sri Lanka developed characteristics which made it more than merely a variant of an Indian prototype, or hybrid, and rather something distinctive or autonomous, although the Indian element was never totally obliterated.

For the study of the island's early history there is a unique source of historical information, the *Mahavamsa* (compiled possibly about the sixth century AD but probably later) and its continuation, the *Culavamsa*, composed by *bhikkhus* (members of the Buddhist order). Permeated naturally enough by a strong religious bias, and encrusted with miracle and invention, these chronicles nevertheless contain a surprisingly full and accurate account of the island's early history. They compare well with chronicles written about the same time in France and England, and have no rival in India.

Both legend and linguistic evidence indicate that the Sinhalese were a people of Indo-Aryan origin who came to the island from Northern India in about 500 BC. The exact location of their original home in India cannot be determined with any degree of certainty. The founding of the Sinhalese state and people are treated in elaborate detail in the *Mahavamsa*, with great emphasis placed upon the arrival of Vijaya (the legendary founding father of the Sinhalese) and his band on the island. Their advent is made to coincide with the *parinibbana* (the passing away of the Buddha), in a deliberate attempt to emphasize the historic role of the island as a bulwark of Buddhist civilization.

It was in the dry zone in north-central Sri Lanka that the early settlements arose. These were riverine in character, and rice was the staple crop. The earliest colonists were dependent on the north-east monsoon to cultivate a single, annual crop of rice. The climate was rigorous if not harsh, the rains seasonal but not reliable. With the expansion of the settlements, the greatest problem was to provide insurance against the not infrequent droughts. As a solution to this problem the ancient Sinhalese developed a highly sophisticated irrigation system, which demonstrated technological skills of an extraordinary nature.

Large-scale irrigation works were first constructed by the beginning of the first century AD using the waters of the Mahaweli Ganga and other rivers whose sources lay in the wet zone. Increasing sophistication in irrigation technology over the next five centuries saw an extension of these activities to cover the water resources of the dry zone, and the development of two major complexes of irrigation works, one based on the Mahaweli Ganga and its tributaries and others drawing on the waters of the Malvatu and Kala oyas. These complexes were developed and elaborated further in subsequent centuries and, by the end of the eighth century, irrigation facilities were adequate, not merely for the opening of extensive tracts of land for cultivation, but also for a more intensive cultivation of land.

Two important cores of Sinhalese civilization developed, and control over these gave the Sinhalese rulers the resources to extend their sway over the whole island. The two cities of Anuradhapura and Polonnaruwa were located in these cores; they became in time, and in succession, the capitals of the whole Sinhalese kingdom. There was a third core in the dry zone of the south, the present area of Magampattu, where the climate was more severe and the rainfall much less reliable. This region—called Ruhuna—was settled by the ancient Sinhalese nearly as early as Anuradhapura itself, and a well developed irrigation system was established there. Ruhuna periodically asserted its independence from the main centres of Sinhalese power in the north-central regions of the island, or served as a refuge for defeated Sinhalese kings or rival claimants to the throne, but it was as frequently controlled from Anuradhapura and seems never to have rivalled it in economic power or population resources.

The introduction of Buddhism to the island influenced and moulded every aspect of the life of the people. Its impact was quite as decisive in its own way as the development of irrigation technology was in economic activity. According to the *Mahavamsa*, the introduction of Buddhism to Sri Lanka occurred during the reign of Devanampiya Tissa (307–267 BC), a contemporary of the great Indian Emperor Ashoka, whose emissary Mahinda (Ashoka's son according to some authorities and brother according to others) converted Devanampiya Tissa to the new faith. However, it is possible that traces of some form of Buddhism might well have existed in the island before the time of Devanampiya Tissa, and that the *Mahavamsa* dramatized the conversion of the former to suit the requirements of its author in his reconstruction of the historical evolution of the island in accordance with the framework he had in mind. Nevertheless, it was from the time of Devanampiya Tissa that Buddhism became the bedrock of the culture and civilization of the island and that Anuradhapura itself became a great centre of Buddhist civilization.

During the reign of Devanampiya Tissa a branch of the sacred bo tree (*ficus religiosa*) at Buddhgaya, under which the Buddha attained enlightenment, was brought to Sri Lanka by Sangamitta, a Buddhist nun believed to be a daughter of Ashoka, and planted at Anuradhapura. This tree still survives—indeed it is the oldest historical tree in the world—and is the object of veneration. In 300 BC Devanampiya Tissa built the elegant Thuparama *dagaba*, or *stupa*, to house two relics of the Buddha, his right collar bone and his alms bowl, both of which he is said to have obtained from Ashoka.

In time the Thuparama came to be overshadowed, in size at least, by four other major *stupas* at Anurudhapura: the Ruvanvalisaya, or the *Maha Stupa*, built by Dutthagamani; the Mirisavatiya, also from the time of Dutthagamani; the Abhayagiri *stupa*, built by Vattagamini Abhaya (87–76 BC) and enlarged by Gajabahu I in the second century AD (the Abhayagiri surpassed even the Ruvanvalisaya in size); and the Jetavanaramaya, built by Mahasen (275–301 BC), which was comparable in size to the third Pyramid of Gizeh.

The Mahavihara monastery (which had the Ruvanvalisaya for its *dagaba)*, established upon the introduction of Buddhism in the reign of Devanampiya Tissa, was the historic centre of Theravada Buddhism in Sri Lanka. During the reign of Vattgamani Abhaya, one of the great events in the annals of Buddhism and in the religious history of the world took place at Aluvihara, near Matale in the present Central Province, when the *Tripitaka*, the teachings of the Buddha—which until this time had been transmitted orally—were committed to writing for the first time. This became the orthodox version of Theravada Buddhism, and added greatly to Sri Lanka's prestige in the Buddhist world. It was to make copies of certain of these scriptures that Fa Xian, the Chinese pilgrim monk, came to the island in AD 411 and stayed for two years. Ironically, it was Vattagamani Abhaya who endowed the Abhayagiri Vihara, which eventually became the centre of a sect with strong Mahayanist leanings, and bitterly opposed to the orthodox Mahavihara.

By the time the *Mahavamsa* came to be written, Buddhism was very much the main influence in shaping the outlook of the masses of the people. It was not merely an ethic or a philosophy but a way of life, a design for living. Equally important, Buddhism—as the state 'religion'—became the indispensable bond between the ruler and the people whom he governed. This connection between religion, culture, language and national identity has continued to exert a powerful influence on the Sinhalese. In the early years of the island's history centrifugal tendencies held sway, with the main centres of agricultural settlement under the control of semi-independent rulers. However, with the expansion of population, an aspiration to all-island sovereignty emerged and Anuradhapura developed into the capital of the kingdom. There were two distinct features in these trends: an increase in the power of the King, the ruler at Anuradhapura; and the problem of control over the outer provinces from the capital, which was just as intractable in a small island like Sri Lanka as it was in the vast Indian subcontinent.

In theory the king was an absolute ruler, but custom and tradition acted as formidable constraints on his absolutism. From the earliest times the ruler was entitled to a share of the land revenues, and to call upon his subjects to render gratuitous service on public works. Part of the agricultural surplus at his disposal was used to pay the officials of the realm, who were allocated grants of land and land revenue. Similarly, grants of land were given to Buddhist monasteries, some of which came to control extensive landholdings. Thus the system of land control, in its own way, acted as a restraint on the ruler's absolutism. While the ruler of the realm exercised certain rights over land, private individuals and institutions—such as monasteries—could purchase and alienate land. The Sinhalese kingdom was not a highly centralized, autocratic structure, but one in which the balance of political forces incorporated a tolerance of centrifugalism characteristic of feudal polities. Land and the rights to land were shared by a wide number of individuals and institutions and held under a wide variety of tenurial obligations. This pattern of land ownership and royal revenue changed little throughout the centuries of Sinhalese kingship.

Although powerful rulers succeeded in unifying the country, such periods of effective central control over the island were rare, and no ruler succeeded in devising an institutional structure capable of surviving when royal power at Anuradhapura was weakened, especially at times—not infrequent—of disputed succession. Nor could it be said that the administrative resources available to the king were adequate to ensure permanent control over the outer provinces—the control of Ruhuna from Anuradhapura was always a formidable problem given the nature of the island's topography.

While central control of the provinces was weak, it had the advantage that instability at the centre did not necessarily extend to the outer provinces. The administrative infrastructure, especially at the village and district level, appears to have been strong and resilient enough to cope with periods of turmoil during power struggles in the upper reaches of the administrative structure at the capital, or during foreign invasions. These were, in a sense, more enduring than the central government institutions. It is this that explains one of the paradoxes of the history of Sri Lanka in ancient times: that so brittle and unstable a political structure could have led to the development of the magnificent irrigation system that was the glory of Sinhalese civilization. No doubt the maintenance of this system in good repair, quite apart from its expansion, required a sophisticated machinery of administration under central control. However, it was the permanent institutions rooted amongst the people at village level that ensured the survival of the system during ancient Sri Lanka's regular periods of turmoil. Thus, Sri Lanka in ancient times was a hydraulic society, without the rigorous, authoritarian and heavily bureaucratic structures which Karl Wittfogel, the theorist of hydraulic civilizations, regarded as the key features of such a polity.

One other important feature of Sri Lanka's social structure needs mention at this point. While Sinhalese society shared with European feudalism the obligation to service as a condition of holding land, whether from secular or religious authorities, there was one vital difference. In Sri Lanka the nature of that obligation was also determined by a person's position in the caste hierarchy. Caste was the basis of social stratification in Sinhalese society. As with regard to practically everything else, caste was an Indian transplant which developed its own peculiar characteristics in Sri Lanka (the irony of a Buddhist civilization absorbing a caste system being perhaps the most significant of these). It is doubtful, however, whether Sinhalese society was ever actually organized on the basis of the conventional four-fold caste hierarchy of Indian society—Brahman, Kshatriya, Vaisya and Sudra. From the beginning there were castes in Sinhalese society that did not resemble Indian castes or sub-castes.

As under the Indian system, most castes had a service or occupational role as their primary distinguishing function. However, in the Sinhalese system—in contrast to the Indian prototype—there was no religious sanction for caste. Caste groups were included within a system of services in which hereditary status was the determinant of role and function. Caste services, however, were not always attached to land. The lower castes could be paid in cash or kind for their services. Thus, the system of caste duties afforded an institutional framework through which members of different castes were brought into relationships with each other.

There is no firm evidence concerning the dates of the first Tamil settlements in the island. Tamil and other literary sources, however, point to substantial urban and trading centres in South India in the third century BC. It is possible that there were trade relations between these centres and Sri Lanka at this time, and that the island's trade with the west may have been through these South Indian ports. As early as 237 BC two Tamil adventurers usurped the principal Sinhalese throne and ruled there for 22 years, while 10 years later came a Cola general, Elara, who ruled at Anuradhapura for 44 years, earning a great reputation for justice and impartial administration.

The long—15-year—campaign waged by Dutthagamini, a Sinhalese prince, which culminated in the defeat of Elara is dramatized as the central theme of the later chapters of the *Mahavamsa* and is developed there into a major confrontation between the Sinhalese and Tamils. However, the evidence suggests that there were large reserves of support for Elara among the Sinhalese, and that Dutthagamini, as a prelude to his final and decisive encounter with Elara, had to face the resistance of other Sinhalese rivals who appear to have been deeply suspicious of his political ambitions. His eventual triumph over Elara was not a victory of a self-conscious Sinhalese proto-nationalism over Dravidian imperialism so much as the first significant success of centripetalism over centrifugalism in Sri Lanka's history. With his victory, Anuradhapura became the capital of the island in a real sense, and remained so till AD 1017.

In the fifth and sixth centuries AD a new factor of instability was introduced into the politics of Sri Lanka, with the rise of three Hindu states in South India, the Pandyas, Pallavas and Colas. The flourishing but very vulnerable irrigation civilization of Sri Lanka's northern plains proved a tempting target for invasion from South India. There was a special quality of hostility in the threat from this quarter. This emerged from the fact that these Dravidian states of South India were militantly Hindu, and that Buddhism, which had maintained its hold in that region up to this time, disappeared in the face of this aggressive Hinduism. This development was not without its effects on the Tamils in Sri Lanka, who became more conscious of their ethnicity, which they sought to identify in terms of culture, language and religion—Dravidian, Tamil and Hindu. The Tamil settlements in the island became sources of support for the South Indian invaders.

In the seventh century AD a Sinhalese prince, Manavamma, seized the throne with Pallava assistance, and the dynasty he established continued to rule for almost three centuries. In the early stages the Pallava influence left its stamp, not merely on the island's politics, but also on the culture of the people, being especially noticeable in architecture and sculpture. But association, if not alliance, with the Pallavas brought political perils in its train.

The fluctuating fortunes of the various South Indian kingdoms were not without effect upon the Sinhalese, who were drawn into these conflicts—voluntarily or involuntarily—as a necessary condition of their geopolitical position in South Asia. The fact is that the Sinhalese kingdom was rather weaker than the neighbouring kingdoms of South India and while, from time to time, it came completely under the influence, if not control, of one or other of them it could still maintain its identity by trying, often with success, to play one of them off against the other or others. Sri Lanka had begun to play a vital part in the power politics of peninsular India.

By the middle of the ninth century the Sinhalese kingdom was drawn into the vortex of South Indian politics in the wake of the Pandyans. The ascendancy of the Pandyans in South Indian politics had immediate consequences for Sri Lanka in the shape of a Pandyan invasion, the inevitable sack of Anuradhapura, and the imposition of a substantial indemnity as the price of Pandyan withdrawal. This was the beginning of a Sinhalese involvement in Pandyan affairs which was to have disastrous consequences for both parties. Within a short while of the Pandyan withdrawal, the Sinhalese invaded Pandya in support of a rebel Pandyan prince, and during their campaign sacked the ancient city of Madurai. In the 10th century the Sinhalese again sent an invading army to the mainland, but on this occasion in support of Pandya against the rising Cola power. The Pandyans were defeated and their ruler fled to Sri Lanka carrying with him the Pandya insignia. The Sinhalese had now to face the wrath of the victors, for whom a desire to capture the Pandya insignia was an added impetus to a retaliatory invasion of Sri Lanka.

Under Rajaraja the Great (985–1018) the Colas, having conquered all South India, extended their control to Sri Lanka, attaching the *rajarata*, the heartland of the Sinhalese kingdom, to the Cola empire. Anuradhapura was sacked once more. Mahinda V, who ascended the throne in 982, was the last of the Sinhalese kings to rule at Anuradhapura. He was taken prisoner by the invading Colas in 1017, and he died in captivity in South India. Under Rajaraja's son, Rajendra (1018–35), Cola power extended beyond the South Asian mainland, and posed a threat to the Sri Vijaya empire in modern Malaya and Sumatra. For 75 years Sri Lanka was ruled as a province of South India, the only such episode in its long history.

With the destruction of Anuradhapura, the Colas established their capital at Polonnaruwa, in the north-east of the dry zone and nearer the Mahaweli Ganga. For the Colas the shift of the capital to Polonnaruwa was determined by considerations of security. The river itself afforded some protection to the city, and it was in a good position to guard against invasion from Ruhuna—the refuge of any potential Sinhalese liberation force—since it lay near the main crossing place on the Mahaweli, which any army from Ruhuna must force.

The Sinhalese rulers never re-established Anuradhapura as the capital. They remembered how Anuradhapura had been sacked again and again in the past, and how dangerously exposed it was to invasion from India. For them, Polonnaruwa had the virtue of offering greater protection against the peril.

Hinduism established itself as the religion of the Tamils; trade links with the Indian Ocean states brought Islam to the island through small groups of Moorish traders who settled in the island from around the eighth century. The Sinhalese kingdom of Sri Lanka's northern plain became, in time, an integral part of the power politics of southern India. It was highly vulnerable to invasion from that quarter, and such incursions were frequent. A Tamil kingdom, which survived for over two centuries, was established in the north of the island in the 13th century.

## WESTERN INFLUENCE AND WESTERN RULE

Western influence began with the Portuguese intrusion into the affairs of the littoral. By 1600 the Portuguese were well established there, despite prolonged resistance from the Sinhalese; within 60 years they were displaced by the Dutch, with the active support of the Sinhalese, and the Dutch, in their turn, by the British in 1795–96. Throughout this period much of the interior of the island remained independent under the Kandyan kings. The Kandyan kingdom maintained its independence until 1815–18, when it was absorbed into the British colony of Ceylon and, for the first time in several centuries, one power controlled all of Sri Lanka. One notable feature of European rule was the introduction of Christianity in all its sectarian variety. None of the Protestant groups, however, developed any strong roots in the island, unlike Roman Catholicism. Under British rule, the economy was transformed through the development of plantation agriculture, with coffee the dominant crop in the earlier stages, to be replaced later on by tea, rubber and coconut. Immigrant Indian workers on the plantations settled in the island in large numbers in the last quarter of the 19th century.

The first phase in the emergence of nationalism in Sri Lanka occurred in the last quarter of the 19th century; this incipient nationalism was primarily religious, Buddhist in outlook and content. It developed a more positive political content and ideology in the early 20th century. In the first two decades of the 20th century the British successfully withstood pressure from sections of the Sri Lanka élite for a share in the administration in the country. The keynotes of the Sri Lankan reform movement were restraint and moderation. The formation of the Ceylon National Congress in 1919 was evidence of the strength of these attitudes rather than any radical departure from them.

The 1920s brought bolder political initiatives, and also a significant heightening of working-class activity and trade union agitation. Foreseeing the eventual transfer of a substantial portion of power to the Sri Lankan political leadership, minority groups, led by the Tamils, were engaged in a determined effort to secure protection of their interests as the price of their support for this process. Constitutional reforms, introduced in 1931, amounted to the first really significant step towards self-government. Equally important was the introduction in that year of universal suffrage. Sri Lanka was the first of the United Kingdom's Asian colonies to secure this right, and few events in Sri Lanka's recent history have had so profound an impact on its politics and society as this.

The final phase in the transfer of power began under the leadership of Stephen Senanayake, the country's first Prime Minister, who was guided by a strong belief in ordered constitutional evolution to dominion status on the analogy of constitutional development in the white dominions. In response to the agitation in Sri Lanka, the British Government appointed the Soulbury Commission in 1944 to examine the island's constitutional problem. The Constitution that emerged from their deliberations was based substantially on one drafted for Senanayake in 1944 by his advisers. It gave the island internal self-government while retaining some imperial safeguards in defence and external affairs, but Sri Lanka's leaders pressed, successfully, for the removal of these restrictions, and the island was granted independence, with dominion status, on 4 February 1948. The transfer of power was smooth and peaceful, a reflection of the moderate tone of the dominant strand of the country's nationalist movement. In general, the situation in the country seemed to provide an impressive basis for a solid start in nation-building and national regeneration.

## INDEPENDENCE AND BEYOND, 1948–70

Stephen Senanayake's policies for the transfer of power in the early years of independence were based on his acceptance of the reality of a plural society. He sought the reconciliation of the legitimate interests of the majority and minority ethnic and religious groups within the context of an all-island polity. This held out the prospect of peace and stability in the vital first phase of independence. It was expected that the new Government would be threatened from the left, but the Marxist parties were too divided to pose an effective challenge. Within a year of the granting of independence, Stephen Senanayake's United National Party (UNP) had entrenched its position in the country and strengthened its hold on Parliament.

The first major challenge to the UNP-dominated Government emerged with Solomon Bandaranaike's formation of the Sri Lanka Freedom Party (SLFP) in September 1951, two months after he had crossed over to the opposition. The SLFP's populist programme sought to attract the large protest vote that went to the Marxist parties for want of a democratic alternative to the UNP, and looked for support in the rural areas which formed the basis of the UNP's hold on political power in the country.

Stephen Senanayake's death in March 1952, far from upsetting the political equilibrium that he had established, actually helped to stabilize it. When, two months later, his son and successor as Prime Minister, Dudley Senanayake, won a massive electoral victory, the verdict of the electorate was in many ways an endorsement of his father's life's work. Nevertheless, by the mid-1950s the UNP's position in the country was being undermined, even though its hold on Parliament appeared to be as strong as ever. The economy was faltering, after a period of prosperity, and an attempt to reduce the budgetary allocation for food subsidies provoked violent opposition, organized by the left-wing parties, in August 1953. Moreover, religious, cultural and linguistic issues were gathering momentum and developing into a force too powerful for the existing social and political establishment to accommodate or absorb. Neither the Government nor its left-wing critics showed much understanding of the sense of outrage and indignation of the Buddhists at what they regarded as the historic injustices suffered by their religion under European rule.

Solomon Bandaranaike successfully channelled this discontent into a massive campaign which swept the UNP out of office in 1956. His decisive victory was a significant point in Sri Lanka's history, for it represented the rejection of the concept of a Sri Lanka nationalism, based on plurality, which Stephen Senanayake had striven to nurture, and the substitution of a more democratic and populist nationalism, which was at the same time fundamentally divisive in its impact on the country because it was unabashedly Sinhalese and Buddhist in content. Against the background of the world-wide celebration in 1956 of the 2,500th anniversary of the death of the Buddha, an intense religious fervour became the catalyst of a populist nationalism, the explosive effect of which was derived from its interconnection with language. Language became the basis of nationalism and Sinhala nationalism was consciously or unconsciously treated as being identical with Sri Lanka nationalism, and this the minorities, especially the Tamils, rejected. As a result, in 1956 there began almost a decade of ethnic and linguistic tensions, erupting occasionally into race riots and religious confrontation.

With the emergence of this linguistic nationalism there was increased pressure for the close association of the State with Buddhism, and a corresponding decline of Christian influence. On the whole, Bandaranaike's Government was much more cautious in handling matters relating to the Christian minority than it was on the language issue. The language struggle took precedence over all else, and there was no desire to add to the problems of the Government by taking on an issue which was just as combustible.

At the time of his assassination in September 1959, the culmination of a bitter struggle for power within his own party, Bandaranaike's hold on the electorate was not as strong as it had been in 1956–57. However, his assassination dramatically changed the political situation and, after a few months of drift and regrouping, the SLFP emerged, under the leadership of his widow, Sirimavo Bandaranaike, more powerful than ever before. Unlike her husband, Sirimavo Bandaranaike was not reluctant to address two inflammable issues simultaneously. As well as pursuing her husband's policy on language, she made a determined bid to bring schools under state control and to secularize education, thus antagonizing the Roman Catholics as decisively as her language policy alienated the Tamils.

A wide variety of economic enterprises, foreign and local, were nationalized. Socialism was viewed as a means of redressing the balance in favour of the Sinhalese Buddhists and Sri Lankan nationals in a situation in which the island's trade was largely dominated by foreign capitalists and the minorities were disproportionately influential within the indigenous capitalist class. This extension of state control over trade and industry was justified on the grounds that it helped to curtail the influence of foreign interests and the minorities.

Two significant events in 1964 were the Bandaranaike-Shastri pact, which laid the basis for an equitable settlement of Sri Lanka's Indian problem, and the establishment of a coalition Government between the SLFP and the Trotskyist Lanka Sama Samaja Party (LSSP). This shift to the left by the SLFP was designed to stabilize the Government after the political turmoil of the early years of Sirimavo Bandaranaike's regime, which saw extended periods of rule under emergency powers in the wake of ethnic and religious confrontations, and an abortive plot by high-ranking police, military and naval officers to overthrow the Government. While the dominance of the SLFP in national politics had resulted in a corresponding decline in the electoral fortunes of the Marxist groups, the *apertura a sinistra* was regarded as a necessity for keeping the UNP out of power. In joining the SLFP in a coalition, the LSSP came to accept the SLFP's stand on religion and did so in order to protect its mass base. However, far from stabilizing the Government, the SLFP's shift to the left had the immediate effect of causing a rift, which precipitated its fall in December 1964 and contributed to its subsequent defeat in the general election of March 1965.

Dudley Senanayake's UNP-dominated coalition enjoyed a five-year term of office (1965–70). A resolute endeavour was made to maximize agricultural productivity, with self-sufficiency in food as the prime objective. The very considerable success achieved in this field gave the whole economy a boost. Yet, while its agricultural policies achieved substantial success, the Government's popularity was eroded by inflation and its conspicuous failure to solve the problem of educated unemployment. The rising expectations of an increasingly educated population had created an almost unmanageable problem for the Government. Sri Lanka, by now, was very much a prime example of population explosion undermining a country's political stability.

Dudley Senanayake made ethnic and religious reconciliation the keynote of his policy. Yet his Government was placed on the defensive from the moment the Federal Party opted to join it in coalition. By a virulent campaign of ethnic hostility directed against Senanayake's policy of ethnic and religious reconciliation, the opposition prevented the Prime Minister from implementing some of the key legislative and administrative measures that would have made his policy effective. The limits of that policy were thus clearly demonstrated.

It was evident that the two Bandaranaikes between them had established a new equilibrium of forces within the country, and that their supporters and associates, such as the Marxist groups, as well as their opponents, such as the UNP, had to accommodate themselves to this. The primary feature of the new balance of forces was the acceptance of the predominance of the Sinhalese Buddhists within the Sri Lanka polity, and a sharp decline in the status of the ethnic and religious minorities.

## THE UNITED FRONT, 1970–77

In their election campaign and their manifesto of 1970, the parties of Sirimavo Bandaranaike's United Front (UF)—the SLFP, the LSSP and the Communist Party of Sri Lanka—held out the distinct assurance of purposeful, systematic and fundamental changes in every sphere of life. However, within a few weeks of their victory, they were confronted by precisely the combination of factors that had brought down their predecessor—unemployment, rising prices and scarcities of food items—and the UF Government floundered just as badly as Dudley Senanayake's administration. More significantly, there was growing opposition from a section of its erstwhile supporters. By mid-March 1971 the Government was faced with a very serious threat from the Janatha Vimukthi Peramuna (JVP, or People's Liberation Front), a radical left-wing organization dominated by educated youths, unemployed or disadvantageously employed. The JVP insurrection that broke out in April, although suppressed with considerable ruthlessness, had a marked influence on future developments. It undoubtedly hastened the proceedings begun under the UF in 1970 for an autochthonous constitution for Sri Lanka; and it gave a tremendous impetus to the adoption of a series of radical economic and social changes, the most far-reaching of which were the Land Reform Law of 1972 and the nationalization of the plantations in 1975. Over the period 1970–75 state control in trade and industry was accelerated and expanded to the point where the State had established a dominance of the commanding heights of the economy.

However, the economic situation deteriorated rapidly. The serious balance-of-payments problem, inherited by the UF Government, was aggravated to a grave crisis partly through the operation of external forces beyond its control. The crux of the problem was that the prices of the country's principal imports, particularly its food, rose to unprecedented levels, especially in 1973–74, while there was no corresponding rise in the price of its exports. The Government was compelled to reduce food subsidies, which were absorbing too much foreign exchange, and cuts in welfare expenditure, begun in 1971, continued through 1973. With inflationary pressures never greater and the problem of unemployment as serious as ever, the Government lost public support, as was evident from its dismal record in by-elections to Parliament. By the middle of 1972 the UNP had recovered from its débâcle at the 1970 polls and re-emerged as a viable democratic alternative to the UF regime.

To save itself from further embarrassment, the Government became increasingly authoritarian. A new republican and indigenous Constitution was adopted in May 1972, under which the state power of the Republic was vested in the National State Assembly (a unicameral legislature). Thus, one of its distinctive features was the absence of meaningful institutional or constitutional checks on executive power. While the new Constitution was a notable landmark in the island's recent history, opposition parties were antagonized by two issues stemming from its adoption. First, the ruling coalition gave itself an extended term of two years (to May 1977) beyond the five years for which it was elected in May 1970. Second, the adoption of the Constitution gave rise to a new phase of communal antagonism in the island, especially as regards relations between the Sinhalese and the indigenous Tamils, and prompted the gradual conversion of a large section of the Tamils of the north to the idea of a separate Tamil state.

In 1974 Sirimavo Bandaranaike negotiated the settlement of the vexed question of the status of the Indians in Sri Lanka. Nearly half a million of them would eventually be integrated into the Sri Lankan polity, and Sri Lankan citizenship would confer on them the political legitimacy which, as an ethnic group, they had not had since 1948. However, the Government's relations with the leadership of the Ceylon Workers' Congress (CWC), the most powerful trade union-dominated political party of the Indians in Sri Lanka, were as unfriendly as those with the leadership of the indigenous Tamils.

By 1975 sharp differences of opinion over the mechanics of the nationalization of foreign-owned plantations on the island led to acrimonious bickering between the SLFP and the LSSP, the two major components of the UF, which culminated in October 1975 in the expulsion of the LSSP from the Government. The political consequences were not immediately evident. On the contrary, the Government sought to stabilize its position by exploiting any political advantage to be gained from staging the non-aligned nations' conference in Colombo in August 1976. The coalition was disintegrating rapidly, however. By the end of February 1977 the UF coalition had been dissolved and what remained was a dispirited and demoralized SLFP Government confronting Sri Lanka's worst wave of strikes for 20 years, which had been engineered by its erstwhile coalition partners. For the first time since March 1960 there was no electoral pact against the UNP.

## RETURN OF THE UNP

In the general election of July 1977 the UNP, under the leadership of Junius Richard Jayewardene, won 140 out of 168 seats in the National State Assembly. Jayewardene had twice rebuilt the UNP—once, following defeat in 1956, and again after he took control of it in 1973. The SLFP won only nine seats (compared with 90 in 1970), while every candidate of the Marxist left was defeated, many of them quite decisively. As a result of the peculiar demographic profile of the island, with a concentration of the Tamils in the north and, to a lesser extent, in the east of the island, the Tamil United Liberation Front (TULF)—with the equivalent of only about one-fifth of the popular vote secured by the SLFP—had more than double the number of seats won by the SLFP and emerged as the main parliamentary opposition party. For the first time since independence a Tamil, Appapillai Amirthalingam, became leader of the opposition.

High on the Government's list of priorities was a reassessment of Sri Lanka's constitutional framework. In late September 1977 the National State Assembly adopted a constitutional amendment establishing a presidential form of government, and the Prime Minister, J. R. Jayewardene, became the first executive President of Sri Lanka on 4 February 1978. The new Constitution, promulgated in September 1978, was a blend of some of the functional aspects of Sri Lanka's previous Constitutions and features of the US, French and British systems of government. One important innovation incorporated into the new Constitution was the introduction of proportional representation on the list system in place of the 'first-past-the-post' principle of representation, which had been based on the British model. Article 19 of the Constitution declared that Sinhala and Tamil were to be the national languages of Sri Lanka (with Sinhala remaining the sole official language), a major departure from the language policy established since the mid-1950s. Equally important was the abolition of the distinction between citizens by descent and citizens by registration, such as the Indian Tamils, thus removing the stigma of second-class citizenship attached to the latter. Combined with the lifting, in December 1977, of the bar on plantation workers resident on estates voting in local government elections, which had been in force since the 1930s, this ensured that citizens of Indian origin, in the main plantation workers, were treated on a par with Sri Lankan citizens by descent. The position of the Indians resident in Sri Lanka was further improved by affording to stateless persons the same civil rights guaranteed by the Constitution to citizens of the country. No previous Constitution, not even that of 1946–48, had offered the minorities a more secure position within the Sri Lankan polity.

The Indian Tamils responded more positively to these conciliatory gestures than the TULF. When S. Thondaman, leader of the CWC, the main political party-cum-trade union of the Indian plantation workers, entered the Cabinet following the introduction of the new Constitution in September 1978, it marked a major breakthrough in Sri Lanka's politics, for it brought the Indian Tamils within Sri Lanka's 'political nation' for the first time since the 1930s.

The Jayewardene Government inherited a stagnant economy, in which, with the nationalization of the plantations, the state sector was in a position of overwhelming dominance. Unemployment was high and inflation a serious problem. The Government's budgetary policy was far removed from that of its predecessors, and aimed at creating a free-market economy after almost 20 years of controls and restrictions. The rate of economic growth improved quite dramatically from 1977 and was sustained at a uniformly high level, explaining, to a large extent, the Government's success in the management of the 'political market', in retaining the initiative in politics, and in keeping its rivals at bay.

From the beginning of its term of office in 1977, the Jayewardene Government benefited greatly from the disarray in the ranks of its opponents. The SLFP, the main opposition party, was unable to implement an effective political challenge to the Government; the party was torn apart by a leadership crisis, aggravated by Sirimavo Bandaranaike's expulsion from Parliament (the National State Assembly having been renamed thus in August 1978) in October 1980 after a presidential commission of inquiry found her guilty on charges of abuse of power. The decline of the 'old' left, particularly the LSSP, was a notable factor in Sri Lanka's politics at this time. The 'new' left, with the factionalized JVP in the vanguard, was as hostile to the 'traditional' left and the SLFP as it was to the Government.

The TULF, now very much a party of the indigenous Tamils, adopted a somewhat ambiguous attitude to the UNP Government. It began, in August 1977, as an opposition party, and an advocate of a separate state for the Tamils. The commitment to separatism was later put aside, however, after negotiations with the Government. Yet the leaders of the TULF were conscious of the challenge from their youth wing, and especially extreme terrorist groups, who combined an adherence to various forms of Marxism with a passionate commitment to separatism. While the TULF leadership sought to maintain a discreet distance from these terrorist groups, ties between them were never completely abandoned.

Despite a creditable record of innovative and imaginative attempts to accommodate the minorities, the Jayewardene Government's term of office was punctuated by ethnic conflict between the Sinhalese majority and the Tamil minority, in particular the Sri Lankan Tamils. One of the major points of controversy between successive Sri Lankan Governments and the Tamils has been the question of the devolution of authority to regional units of administration. Jayewardene's Government took the initiative in providing for a scheme of decentralized administration through district development councils. In August 1980 Parliament approved legislation establishing 24 of these councils, for which elections were held in the following year. The establishment of the councils failed, however, to result in any lasting peace. The country was faced with the problem of a Tamil separatist movement (including a number of guerrilla groups) operating in the north and east of the island. The threat that this movement posed to the Sri Lankan polity was compounded by the existence of a great deal of Tamil separatist sympathy and a strong sense of Tamil ethnic identity in the southern Indian state of Tamil Nadu.

If the results of the 1977 general election appeared to herald a major change of direction in Sri Lankan politics, the presidential election in October 1982 provided confirmation of this. By winning that election, Junius Jayewardene became the first Sri Lankan Head of Government to win two consecutive terms of office. Jayewardene followed this with a deft legal and constitutional, but nevertheless controversial, move—the holding of a referendum on 22 December to ask for a mandate to extend the life of the Parliament, elected in 1977, by a period of six years from August 1983. Although the electorate endorsed this by a large majority, thus effectively guaranteeing the UNP its huge majority in Parliament until 1989, the referendum was widely viewed as a retrograde and undemocratic measure. The opposition had hardly recovered from the referendum when, early in 1983, it was announced that by-elections would be held for 18 seats in which the Government had fared badly at the presidential election and the referendum. These by-elections were held on 18 May, and the UNP won 14 of them. This was accompanied by the ruling party's notable success in the local government elections held on the same date and on 20 May. The UNP won all but five of the local bodies in the Sinhalese areas, with the SLFP winning one and independents four. Neither the JVP nor the 'traditional' left made any significant impact at these elections. As in 1979, only the TULF, which won control of the local bodies in the Tamil areas, stood between the UNP and a clean sweep. However, violence organized by terrorist groups marred the local government elections in the Jaffna peninsula. The TULF won these elections in a very low poll, but in other parts of the northern and eastern regions it won comfortably in a normal poll.

## A TIME OF TROUBLES: 1983–88

The unusually prolonged period of electioneering raised political tension to dangerous levels, and, in recognition of this, a state of emergency was declared in May 1983. This proved to be wholly ineffective in confronting the pressures that were released by an eruption of ethnic violence, directed against the Tamils, in July, the worst such outbreak since 1958. These riots were very widespread, but the most severely affected area was the city of Colombo and its suburbs. The Government needed nearly a week to re-establish its authority and quell the violence.

In early August 1983 a ban on the advocacy of separatism was imposed through the sixth amendment to the Constitution. One immediate result of this was that all TULF members opted to resign from their seats in Parliament. Anura Bandaranaike, the son of Sirimavo Bandaranaike, took over as leader of the parliamentary opposition from Appapillai Amirthalingam. In 1986, when Sirimavo Bandaranaike's civic and political rights were restored as a result of a presidential pardon, she surprised many political observers by her decision to remain outside Parliament as the head of the SLFP while her son continued as leader of the opposition in Parliament.

Another immediate consequence of the political tension of May–July 1983 was pressure from India on behalf of the Tamils, with Indira Gandhi's Government assuming the role of mediator in the conflict between the Sri Lankan Government and Tamil groups. A conference, in which most Sri Lankan political groups (with the exception of the SLFP) and also representatives of religious organizations participated, began in January 1984 and continued throughout the year. As a result of these deliberations, a consensus appeared to have been reached on the crucially important issue of the devolution of power to regional bodies, and much progress had been achieved in regard to other matters, including language policy. By the end of the year, however, this consensus had evaporated amid political controversy. The TULF eventually rejected the proposals as inadequate, while representatives of Buddhist opinion opposed them because they were perceived to be conceding too much to the Tamils. The Government withdrew its own support for the proposals in December 1984. Within a few months, the collapse of the conference led to more formal diplomatic negotiations between the Governments of Sri Lanka and India, and eventually to a meeting between Jayewardene and the Indian Prime Minister, Rajiv Gandhi, in June 1985. A three-month cease-fire was established, and talks were held, under Indian auspices, in Bhutan in July and August 1985 between representatives of the Sri Lankan Government and representatives of the various Tamil separatist groups, including the TULF. Although these talks failed, negotiations continued in New Delhi and eventually yielded a set of proposals for devolution of power in Sri Lanka on the basis of provincial councils. This was the essence of the Delhi Accord of August 1985. The Accord was initialled by the Sri Lankan and Indian Governments, but the Tamil groups that had been consulted during the negotiations refused to sign it. Nevertheless, the principal features of the 1985 Delhi Accord became the basis of future negotiations between the two Governments and Sri Lanka's Tamil groups.

The TULF and some of the Tamil separatist groups continued to press for a single regional unit, encompassing the northern and eastern provinces, as a Tamil ethno-region. Both the Government and the SLFP were strongly opposed to a merger of these two provinces, as were the Muslims resident there. (The Tamils constituted only 40% of the population of the eastern province at the Census of 1981. Their numbers have declined to 33% today.) The main Tamil separatist group, the Liberation Tigers of Tamil Eelam (LTTE), however, would accept nothing short of a separate Tamil state. In a sustained effort to break this deadlock, Indian negotiators made various proposals throughout the second half of 1986, some of which formed part of the 19 December 1986 formula, which the Indian Government proposed as the basis for further negotiations between the Sri Lankan Government and the Tamils. The LTTE, however, rejected this formula as totally unacceptable.

These negotiations took place against the background of regular outbursts of ethnic violence, especially in the north and east of the island, and conflicts between the security forces and

Tamil guerrillas and terrorist groups. In addition, there was fierce internecine fighting among these Tamil separatist groups, in the course of which the LTTE prevailed over their main rivals. The Tamil guerrillas and terrorist groups had the advantage of training facilities and bases in Tamil Nadu and in other parts of India. The existence of the terrorist bases in Tamil Nadu, as well as the refusal of the Indian Government officially to acknowledge their existence (much less to close them down), remained a constant irritant in Indo-Sri Lankan relations. The guerrillas were also helped by a decision of the Sri Lankan Government, taken in mid-1985, to keep its forces in the north of the island within their barracks or camps, as part of an understanding that was reached with the Government of India on the mediatory process. The result of this decision was to give the armed separatist groups effective control over the Jaffna peninsula, which they used to consolidate their position there. From mid-1984, attacks by guerrillas and terrorists increased, but those directed against the security forces were generally repulsed. When, however, the terrorist attacks were directed against unarmed Sinhalese civilians in the eastern and northern central parts of the island, the death toll was heavy. The most serious of such attacks occurred on 14 May 1985, when a heavily-armed group of terrorists made a surprise raid on Anuradhapura, killing nearly 150 civilians. The killings continued during 1986–87, two of the worst such incidents being the bus massacre of more than 120 people near Habarana, in the eastern province, and the bomb explosion (killing more than 100 people) in the main bus station in Colombo, both of which took place in April 1987.

In early 1987 attempts by the LTTE to make a unilateral declaration of independence in the north of the island were treated by the Sri Lankan authorities as gravely provocative. In February government security forces moved into the eastern and northern provinces and cleared them (with the exception of the crowded Jaffna peninsula) of the LTTE and other separatist groups.

Faced with the prospect of a serious erosion of political support as a result of the terrorist outrages in April 1987 (see above), the Government decided to make an attempt to regain control of the Jaffna peninsula. The most important aspect of the subsequent 'Operation Liberation' was to take control of the strategically important Vadamarachchi division of the north-eastern part of the peninsula, to prevent the hitherto easy movement of men and materials from Tamil Nadu. By the end of May the Sri Lankan forces had gained control of this area by means of a remarkably effective military operation. Tamil Nadu responded with a well-publicized monetary grant of US $3.2m. to the LTTE and their allies. The Indian central Government, far from condemning this act of interference in Sri Lankan affairs, also gave its support by making an offer of food aid and petroleum supplies to Jaffna, to be shipped there in Indian vessels. When the first shipment was turned back by the Sri Lankan navy on 3 June, the Indian air force blatantly violated Sri Lankan airspace to drop food parcels and medical supplies in Jaffna on the following day. This constituted an unmistakable demonstration of Indian support for the Tamil separatist movement in Sri Lanka. The Indian supply of food to Jaffna continued over the next few weeks by sea. While this second phase of Indian aid had the formal, but clearly reluctant, approval of the Sri Lankan Government, it was, none the less, as unwelcome as the earlier air-drop of food. The result was that, by the end of June, Indo-Sri Lankan relations were dominated by mutual recrimination and deep suspicion.

By mid-July 1987, however, there were signs of an unforeseen change in attitude and the emergence of a breakthrough in negotiations on a settlement of Sri Lanka's ethnic conflict. By the end of July the Indian and Sri Lankan Governments had reached agreement on the basis of an accord, and, on 29 July, the Indian Prime Minister, Rajiv Gandhi, arrived in Colombo to sign the accord with Jayewardene. The main points of the accord were: the provision of Indian military assistance to help with its implementation (more than 7,000 Indian troops were drafted into Sri Lanka in August); a complete cessation of hostilities, and the surrender of all weapons held by the Tamil militants within 72 hours of the implementation of the accord; the establishment of a system of provincial councils in the island, based on the island's nine provincial units; the linking of the northern and eastern provinces into one administrative unit with an elected provincial council (to be elected within three months); the holding of a referendum in the eastern province, at a date set by the Sri Lankan President, to determine whether the mixed population of Tamils, Sinhalese and Muslims supported this official merger with the northern province into a single Tamil-dominated province; a general amnesty for all Tamil militants after they had surrendered their arms; the repatriation of about 100,000 Tamil refugees in India to Sri Lanka; the resumption of the repatriation of Indian citizens from Sri Lanka, under the terms of agreements reached between the Governments of Sri Lanka and India in 1964 and 1974; the prevention of the use of Indian territory by Tamil militants for military or propaganda purposes; the prevention of the military use of Sri Lankan ports, Trincomalee in particular, by any country in a manner prejudicial to Indian interests; and the provision that Tamil have equal status with Sinhala as an official language. The signing of the accord led to violent protests and widespread civil unrest among the Sinhalese majority in and around Colombo and in the south-west of the country. These demonstrations had the support of the SLFP, of sections of the *sangha* (the Buddhist order), and of a revived JVP.

The early indications of a successful implementation of the accord were encouraging. Sri Lankan security forces in the northern and eastern provinces returned to their barracks and the paramilitary forces were disarmed, as part of the Sri Lankan Government's obligations under the terms of the accord. Tamil separatist groups, including the LTTE and the Eelam Revolutionary Organization of Students, began to surrender their weapons. In September 1987, however, the surrender of arms by the Tamil militant groups became more sporadic, and the implementation of the peace accord was impeded by further bitter factional fighting among the Tamil militias (involving the LTTE in particular), which, in mid-September, necessitated direct intervention by the Indian peace-keeping troops. By early October the surrender of arms had virtually ceased and Tamil guerrillas had launched a series of terrorist attacks on Sinhalese citizens in the eastern province. The destabilization of the eastern province, a region which had, hitherto, been relatively secure under the protection of the Sri Lankan forces, soon reached a point that compelled the Sri Lankan Government to insist on firm action by the Indian Peace-Keeping Force (IPKF) to prevent any further deterioration of the situation. Accordingly, troops of the IPKF were now dispatched to disarm the LTTE and, when faced with resistance, launched a major attack on the guerrilla strongholds in the Jaffna peninsula in the second week of October. Despite obstinate opposition from the LTTE (necessitating the deployment of thousands of reinforcements), the militants' control over the peninsula was eventually ended. The LTTE then withdrew to the forests of the northern province, whence, from the beginning of 1988, they continued the struggle. In the mean time, the size of the IPKF increased from 7,000 in the early months of its presence on the island, to between 75,000 and 100,000 by mid-1988. These numbers were gradually reduced, but in early 1989 the IPKF still had at least 45,000 men in the north and east of the island.

Legislation to give effect to some of the major provisions of the peace accord was approved by the Sri Lankan Parliament in the latter half of 1987. Of these, the most important and controversial was the 13th amendment to the Constitution, establishing a system of provincial councils. The SLFP opposed this legislation, as did the JVP. The latter, which had been officially banned in August 1983 and which was based mainly in the south of the island, initiated a campaign of sporadic violence directed at person and property. The JVP was widely believed to have been involved in an assassination attempt on President Jayewardene in Parliament on 18 August 1987, in which one district minister was killed and several cabinet ministers and members of Parliament were seriously wounded. Another district minister was assassinated in May 1988. It was estimated that, altogether, more than 1,000 members of the UNP, including the party's Chairman and General Secretary, had been killed by the JVP by July 1988. The JVP was also believed to have instigated the murder of the leader of the left-wing Sri Lanka Mahajana Party (SLMP), Vijaya Kumaratunga, who supported the accord. As soon as the Government had definitely decided to hold provincial council elections, the SLFP joined the JVP in organizing a boycott of the elections. The JVP's violence increased in a campaign of intimidation, which was directed at all parties supporting the accord and at candidates for election to the provincial councils.

In February 1988 a new opposition force emerged, when an alliance, named the United Socialist Alliance (USA), was formed by the SLMP, the LSSP, the Communist Party of Sri Lanka, the Nava Sama Samaja Party and, most notably, the Tamil rights group entitled the Eelam People's Revolutionary Liberation Front (EPRLF). Although the USA group, led by Chandrika Bandaranaike Kumaratunga (a daughter of Sirimavo Bandaranaike and the widow of the SLMP's assassinated leader), comprised opposition parties, it expressed full support for the peace accord.

At the elections to seven of the new provincial councils (elections in the northern and eastern provinces were postponed indefinitely), which were held in April and June 1988 (in defiance of the JVP's threats and violence), the UNP won a majority and effective control in all of them, while the USA emerged as the main opposition group. A 'surprise' peace agreement, which was purportedly signed by government officials and alleged representatives of the JVP in May, proved to be a hoax; Rohana Wijeweera, the leader of the JVP, denied that anyone had been authorized to negotiate on behalf of his party. The Government, however, decided to proceed with its decision to rescind the ban on the JVP.

In September 1988, following President Jayewardene's decision not to seek a third term of office, the Prime Minister, Ranasinghe Premadasa, was nominated as the candidate of the ruling UNP for the presidential election, which was due to be held on 19 December. Sirimavo Bandaranaike emerged as the main opposition candidate, with support from an alliance of eight opposition parties, collectively called the Democratic People's Alliance, including the SLFP, the JVP and other minor political groups. In September the President officially authorized the merger of the northern and eastern provinces into a single north-eastern province, prior to the provincial council elections. The JVP reacted violently, and was widely believed to have been responsible for the murder of the Minister of Rehabilitation and Reconstruction, Lionel Jayatilleke, at the end of the month. On 9 October President Jayewardene vested the leadership of the UNP in the Prime Minister. In protest against the proposed election in the new north-eastern province, the JVP organized a series of disruptive strikes, systematic acts of sabotage, prison riots and violent demonstrations in the central, western and southern provinces of the island in October. In an attempt to arrest the escalating violence, the Government invoked emergency regulations, imposed strict curfews in the troubled areas, and deployed armed riot police. In November, however, the JVP intensified its campaign of violence and protest; it demanded a boycott of the presidential election by the SLFP, the dissolution of Parliament, the establishment of a caretaker government, and the holding of a fresh general election. In mid-November the moderate and pro-accord Tamil groups, the EPRLF and the Eelam National Democratic Liberation Front (ENDLF), together with the Sri Lanka Muslim Congress (SLMC), emerged strongly from the elections to the new provincial council of the north-eastern province, while the UNP won only one seat. The poll was boycotted, however, by the LTTE, the TULF and the Sinhalese population in the eastern province. In late November the EPRLF nominated a regional cabinet to administer the new province. In early December Parliament unanimously approved a Constitution Amendment Bill to make Tamil one of the country's two official languages (with Sinhala), thus fulfilling one of the major commitments envisaged in the peace accord.

## THE PRESIDENCY OF RANASINGHE PREMADASA

On 19 December 1988 the presidential election took place, in an environment of unprecedented disruption, and was boycotted by the LTTE and the JVP. None the less, it was estimated that about 55% of the total electorate voted. The UNP's candidate, Prime Minister Ranasinghe Premadasa, won by a narrow margin, with 50.4% of the total votes, while Sirimavo Bandaranaike, the President of the SLFP, received 44.9%. On the following day Parliament was dissolved in preparation for the general election, which was to be held in February 1989 (six months before schedule). In early January Premadasa was sworn in as Sri Lanka's new President, and an interim Cabinet was appointed. In the same month, in a conciliatory gesture to the JVP and the LTTE alike, the Government decided to repeal the state of emergency, which had been in force since May 1983, and to abolish the Ministry of National Security. Shortly after his inauguration, Premadasa offered to negotiate with the extremists and invited all groups to take part in the electoral process. The JVP and the LTTE, however, intensified their campaigns of violence, in protest at the forthcoming general election. In early February the moderate, pro-accord Tamil groups, the EPRLF, the ENDLF and the Tamil Eelam Liberation Organization (TELO), formed a loose alliance, under the leadership of the TULF, to contest the general election. In the election, which was held on 15 February and which was, like the presidential poll, characterized by widespread violence, the UNP won 125 of the 225 contested seats. The new system of proportional representation, which was introduced at this election, was especially advantageous to the SLFP, which became the major opposition force in Parliament, with 67 seats. The comparatively low level of participation (64% of the electorate) confirmed, again, that intimidatory tactics, employed by the LTTE and the JVP, had had an effect on the voters. A few days later, President Premadasa appointed a new Cabinet and in early March he named the Minister of Finance, Dingiri Banda Wijetunga, as the country's new Prime Minister. Although both the LTTE and the JVP rejected a conciliatory offer made by the President in April, in a surprising development, representatives of the LTTE began discussions with government officials in Colombo in the following month.

Negotiations also commenced between Sri Lankan and Indian officials, regarding the withdrawal of the IPKF. Between January and April 1989 five battalions of the IPKF left Sri Lanka, and in early June the Sri Lankan Government announced, in an apparent effort to appease the LTTE and the JVP, that it wanted all Indian troops to have left by the end of July (two years after the arrival of the first troops). With the exception of the EPRLF, which administered the north-eastern province, all other Sri Lankan political groups welcomed this call for a speedy Indian withdrawal. India itself responded cautiously to Premadasa's demand, which had been made without warning or consultation, saying only that it would withdraw at an 'early date'. Rajiv Gandhi stressed that the timetable for a complete withdrawal of troops would have to be decided mutually, and that, before the Indian forces left, he wanted to ensure the security of the Tamils and the devolution of genuine power to the elected local government in the north-eastern province, so that it would resist any post-withdrawal destabilization.

The resultant deadlock in Indo-Sri Lankan relations provoked a wave of anti-Indian feeling in Sri Lanka, and demonstrations and strikes were organized by the JVP to protest against the continued presence of the IPKF in the country. The JVP's renewed campaign of violence reached a peak in June–July 1989, and compelled the Government to reimpose a state of emergency on 20 June, granting the army virtually unlimited powers of arrest and detention.

In the mean time, the LTTE decided to transform their temporary cease-fire agreement with the Sri Lankan army into a general cessation of hostilities against the Government. In response, the Government announced that it would henceforth collaborate with the LTTE to secure the withdrawal of the IPKF from Sri Lanka. This agreement was reached despite the Government's suspicions about the LTTE's involvement in the murder of several prominent Tamil leaders, including the Secretary-General of the TULF, Appapillai Amirthalingam, and the leader of the People's Liberation Organization of Tamil Eelam (PLOTE), Kadirkamam Uma Maheswaran. Although it initially denied any connection with the killings, the LTTE subsequently assumed responsibility for them.

On 13 September 1989 Premadasa convened an All-Party Conference (APC) to discuss the country's ethnic crisis. Some 70 delegates from 21 parties, including the LTTE and the moderate Tamil groups (but excluding the JVP), attended the conference. On 18 September the Governments of Sri Lanka and India signed an agreement in Colombo, whereby India promised to make 'all efforts' to withdraw its remaining 45,000 troops from Sri Lanka by the end of the year and the IPKF was to declare an immediate unilateral cease-fire. In return, the Sri Lankan Government pledged immediately to establish a peace committee for the north-eastern province in an effort to reconcile the various Tamil groups and to incorporate members of the LTTE into the peaceful administration of the province. A co-ordination committee for the withdrawal of the IPKF was established in mid-October.

The JVP suffered a very serious set-back when its leader, Rohana Wijeweera, and his principal deputy, Upatissa Garmanayake, were shot dead by the security forces in November 1989. In the following month the leader of the military wing of the JVP, Saman Piyasiri Fernando, was killed in an exchange of gunfire in Colombo. Between September 1989 and the end of January 1990 the Sri Lankan security forces effectively destroyed the JVP as a political force, thus substantially transforming the country's political scene. All but one member of the JVP's political bureau and most leaders at district level had been killed. It was estimated, however, that the number of people killed in the lengthy struggle between the JVP and the Government might have been as high as 25,000–50,000.

As the Indian troops increased the speed of their withdrawal from Sri Lanka in the latter half of 1989, the LTTE initiated a campaign of violence against their arch-rivals, the more moderate Indian-supported EPRLF, which was mustering a so-called Tamil National Army, with Indian help, in the north-eastern province, to resist the LTTE. The LTTE accused the EPRLF and its allies of forcibly conscripting thousands of Tamil youths into the Tamil army. Following months of peace talks with the Government, however, the political wing of the LTTE was recognized as a political party by the commissioner of elections in December. The LTTE leaders then proclaimed that the newly recognized party would take part in the democratic process (it demanded immediate fresh elections in the north-eastern province) under the new name of the People's Front of the Liberation Tigers (PFLT). By the end of 1989 the inexperienced and undisciplined Tamil National Army had been virtually destroyed by the LTTE, who now appeared to have the tacit support of the central Government and had taken control of much of the territory in the north-eastern province being progressively evacuated by the IPKF.

Following further talks between the Governments of Sri Lanka and India, the completion date for the withdrawal of the IPKF was postponed until the end of March 1990. In early February President Premadasa reconvened the APC in a fresh attempt to end the continuing violence. In early March the EPRLF-dominated north-eastern provincial council, under the leadership of Annamalai Varadharajah Perumal, renamed itself the 'National Assembly of the Free and Sovereign Democratic Republic of Eelam' and gave the central Government a one-year ultimatum to fulfil a 19-point charter of demands. Two weeks later, however, Perumal was reported to have fled to Madras (now known as Chennai) in southern India. The last remaining IPKF troops left Sri Lanka on 24 March, a week ahead of schedule. Their departure was welcomed by both the Government and the LTTE. In the next month the Government eased emergency regulations (including the ban on political rallies) in an effort to restore a degree of normality to the country after years of violence. At the same time, Sri Lanka's security forces, encouraged by the relative lull in violence, halted all military operations against the now much-weakened JVP and the Tamil militant groups.

Thus, a fragile peace was maintained while talks (mainly concerning the proposed dissolution of the north-eastern provincial council and the holding of fresh elections there) continued between the Government and the LTTE until early June 1990, when quite unexpectedly the LTTE attacked and captured about 20 police stations in the Batticaloa and Trincomalee districts, abducting more than 600 Sinhalese and Muslim policemen and subsequently massacring a large number of them. Later in the month an LTTE execution squad, operating in Tamil Nadu in India, raided a block of apartments in Madras in which Annamalai Varadharajah Perumal and other leaders of the EPRLF were living as refugees (see above), killing 13 of them. In mid-June the Government dissolved the north-eastern provincial council (despite protests by the EPRLF), and the holding of fresh elections in the province was postponed indefinitely pending the agreement of the LTTE to participate in them (as earlier promised). By the end of June up to 1,000 people had been killed in the renewed fighting, and many thousands had been made homeless. Attempts to establish a cease-fire foundered, and the Sri Lankan security forces launched a counter-attack. By the end of July, after fierce fighting, the security forces had established control over most parts of the north-eastern province (including Batticaloa, Trincomalee and Amparai), outside the densely populated Jaffna peninsula. Several fortified LTTE camps in the jungles in the north-east were targeted for attack, and, by the end of the year, many of them had fallen to the security forces. The LTTE, however, continued to control a number of fortified jungle hide-outs, from which they launched occasional raids.

In August 1990 the LTTE intensified their campaign of violence in the eastern province against the Muslim population; the renewed strife between the country's two largest minority groups resulted in more than 400 deaths. At the end of August the Government launched an all-out offensive against the Tamil strongholds in the Jaffna peninsula, and, by mid-September, had succeeded in relieving the three-month siege by the LTTE of the old army fort (the fort was later abandoned by the security forces). In October the LTTE launched an attack on the Muslim settlements in the Mannar district of the northern province, and succeeded in expelling the Muslim population from there. The Muslims fled to various parts of the north-central and north-western provinces, where they took up residence as refugees. Although the army later re-established control in the Mannar region and repulsed the LTTE, most of the Muslims were reluctant to return to their homes. In January 1991 the LTTE suffered an apparent set-back when the Indian central Government dismissed the state government in Tamil Nadu, on account of the latter's alleged support for the Tamil militants in Sri Lanka. In early March it was widely suspected that the LTTE were responsible for the assassination of a senior Sri Lankan cabinet member, the Minister of Plantation Industries and Minister of State for Defence, Ranjan Wijeratne. Wijeratne had been in charge of both the government forces' successful offensive against the JVP, several years earlier, and the ongoing offensive against the LTTE. The LTTE presence in the jungles of the north and east continued, while the army strengthened its hold on the towns and main roads there. In July the LTTE made a concerted effort to capture the army camp at Elephant Pass, which guards the entrance to the Jaffna peninsula. They suffered heavy losses when the security forces successfully repulsed the attack. Thereafter, the LTTE strongholds in the Jaffna peninsula came under regular attack by the Sri Lankan forces, which maintained a limited but conspicuous presence there—at the port of Kankesanthurai, the airport at Palaly, and at the naval base of Karainagar.

Throughout 1991 a considerably weakened, but by no means defeated, LTTE made occasional offers of further talks with the Government, but the latter responded by laying down conditions, which were unacceptable to the militant group. Suspected LTTE bomb squads carried out a number of successful missions in Colombo: the assassination of Ranjan Wijeratne (see above) and a bomb attack on an armed-forces building in a residential part of Colombo in late June. More significantly for its regional implications, the LTTE were widely believed to have been responsible for the assassination of the former Indian Prime Minister Rajiv Gandhi (whose party, Congress (I), had reportedly put pressure on the Indian Government to dismiss the administration in Tamil Nadu earlier that year), on 21 May near Madras. In early 1992 the Indian Government proscribed the LTTE in India and banned its activities on Indian soil. LTTE access to bases and other resources in Tamil Nadu was sharply curtailed, while rigorous patrolling of the seas by the Indian navy cut off their traditional sources of arms supplies.

President Premadasa, for his part, consolidated his position within the country, by treating the local government elections in May 1991 as a national 'referendum' on his period in office. Premadasa took a calculated risk in doing so, but the decisive victory of the UNP provided him with the clear mandate that had eluded him in the presidential election of 1988 and the parliamentary election of 1989, owing to the relatively low turn-out on those occasions and the pervasive violence. In early September 1992 the Supreme Court, following a lengthy hearing spanning two-and-a-half years, rejected Sirimavo Bandaranaike's election petition against Premadasa, thus confirming the validity of his election.

In August–September 1991 opposition groups, supported by a dissident section of the UNP, began proceedings for the impeachment of President Premadasa. The impeachment motion listed 24 items of alleged abuses of power, including illegal land deals and failure to consult the Cabinet (thus violating the Constitution). The UNP group that supported the motion included two cabinet members, the Minister of Education, Lalith Athulathmudali, and the Minister of Labour and Vocational Training, G. M. Premachandra, and one former cabinet member, Gamini Dissanayake, all of whom protested against the President's alleged autocratic behaviour. These initiatives heralded the beginning of a significant challenge to the authority of President Premadasa. Although the impeachment motion was rejected by the Speaker of Parliament in early October, and the rebel group was expelled from the party, these events provided evidence of a major split in the UNP. The subsequent establishment of the Democratic United National Front (DUNF) by the dissident UNP group in December appeared to signify a very important change in Sri Lanka's political system: the emergence of a third party with wide political support. This was especially so because the SLFP continued to suffer the debilitating effects of a prolonged and bitter leadership struggle, and remained in a state of unresolved crisis over the succession to Sirimavo Bandaranaike, who had been the head of the party since 1960.

The campaign against the LTTE suffered a serious set-back in early August 1992, when 10 senior officers were killed in a mine explosion near Jaffna. The new leadership of the security services, however, recommenced the stalled efforts to re-establish government control over the areas hitherto dominated by the LTTE—i.e. parts of the northern province and the Jaffna peninsula. Tension between the Muslim and Tamil populations in the north-eastern district of Polonnaruwa drastically increased following the massacre of more than 170 Muslim villagers by suspected LTTE guerrillas in October. In the next month the LTTE were also widely believed to have been responsible for the murder of the naval commander, Vice-Admiral Clancy Fernando, in Colombo. The LTTE themselves lost one of their most senior leaders when Commander Sathasivam Krishnakumar, Velupillai Prabhakaran's chief deputy, was killed at sea in January 1993.

Once the elections for the provincial councils were announced for 17 May 1993 there was a sharp increase in political activity, since the outcome of the poll was expected to affect the results of the presidential election scheduled to be held in October/November 1994. The campaign itself was relatively peaceful until 23 April 1993, when the leader of the DUNF, Lalith Athulathmudali, was assassinated. This precipitated a dangerous political crisis, since, at first, it was widely believed that persons close to the Government were involved in the murder, if indeed they had not planned it. In fact, it subsequently appeared that the assassination was the work of the LTTE. The Athulathmudali killing overshadowed all other issues in the run-up to the provincial council elections, until the assassination, in a suicide bomb attack, of President Premadasa on 1 May, which also killed 23 others. The assassination raised fears about a long period of instability in the country. President Premadasa was the most prominent victim of the LTTE so far, and the manner of the killing had many parallels with the assassination of the former Indian Prime Minister, Rajiv Gandhi. However, in a remarkably smooth transition, the incumbent Prime Minister, Dingiri Banda Wijetunga, was first sworn in as acting President, and subsequently unanimously elected President by Parliament in accordance with the terms of the Constitution. President Wijetunga appointed Ranil Wickremasinghe, who had been Leader of the House since 1989, to replace him as premier. The incoming President quickly established a hold on the political system, and introduced a new style of government which was more open and more democratic than that of his predecessor.

The results of the provincial council elections held in May 1993 proved a set-back for the UNP. While the ruling party won control of four of the seven councils (no polling was carried out in the area covered by the now defunct north-eastern province), the three others went to a combination of the SLFP, the 'traditional' left and the DUNF. Although the UNP received 47% of the votes, as against 36% for the SLFP and the 'traditional' left, it was the first time since 1977 that its percentage of total votes had fallen below 50%, evidence of an erosion of its support base which became more pronounced in the early part of 1994.

The Sri Lankan armed forces achieved considerable success in their fight against ethnic violence in the eastern province in 1993, but were forced to abandon a massive military offensive in the Jaffna peninsula in October owing to the ferocity of the LTTE resistance. In the following month both sides suffered heavy casualties in the course of the battle over the military base at Pooneryn on the Jaffna lagoon. As a result of this military débâcle, in which, according to official figures, more than 600 army and naval personnel were either killed or captured, the Government established a new combined security forces command for the Jaffna and Kilinochchi districts to counter the LTTE threat.

## THE PEOPLE'S ALLIANCE IN POWER

In late 1993 and early 1994 the SLFP seemed hopelessly divided; Anura Bandaranaike's decision to defect to the UNP appeared to provide further evidence of this. Despite the continuing violence, local government elections were held in the eastern province and in the northern town of Vavuniya in early March 1994; the UNP secured the greatest number of seats, while independent Tamil groups also performed well. The LTTE and the TULF boycotted the poll. The ruling party suffered its first major electoral reverse in 17 years at the end of the month, however, when an opposition grouping known as the People's Alliance (PA), of which the main constituents were the SLFP and the traditional Marxist left and which was headed by the former leader of the USA group, Chandrika Kumaratunga, won a clear majority in elections to the southern provincial council. In early May, however, Wijetunga's Government defeated a parliamentary motion of no confidence by 111 votes to 71. On 24 June, in an apparent attempt to catch the opposition by surprise and to enhance his prospects in the forthcoming presidential election, the President dissolved Parliament and announced that early legislative elections were to be held on 16 August, ahead of the presidential election. Wijetunga's ploy failed, however: the PA obtained 48.9% of the votes, thus securing a narrow victory over the UNP, which received 44%. Under the prevailing system of proportional representation, this translated to 105 seats for the PA and 94 for the UNP in the 225-seat Parliament. The 17-year rule of the UNP had thus come to an end. On 18 August President Wijetunga abandoned hope of forming a UNP minority Government and appointed Kumaratunga as Prime Minister, the PA having secured the support of the SLMC, the TULF, the Democratic People's Liberation Front and a small, regional independent group. A new SLFP-dominated Cabinet was appointed on the following day. In line with her electoral pledge to abolish the executive presidency and to establish a parliamentary system in its place, the Prime Minister removed the finance portfolio from the President and assumed responsibility for it herself. Although Wijetunga retained the title of Minister of Defence, actual control of the ministry was expected to be exercised by the Deputy Minister of Defence. The Prime Minister's mother, Sirimavo Bandaranaike, was appointed as Minister without Portfolio. With regard to the Tamil question, overtures were made between the new Government and the LTTE concerning unconditional peace talks (these commenced in mid-October) and at the end of August, as a gesture of goodwill, the Government partially lifted the economic blockade on LTTE-occupied territory. In addition, the Prime Minister created a new Ministry of Ethnic Affairs and National Integration and assumed the portfolio herself, thus revealing her determination to seek an early solution to the civil strife.

In early September 1994 Chandrika Kumaratunga was unanimously elected by the PA as its candidate for the forthcoming presidential polls, while Gamini Dissanayake, the leader of the opposition (who had left the DUNF and returned to the UNP in 1993), was chosen as the UNP's candidate. The election campaign was thrown into turmoil, however, on 24 October 1994, when Dissanayake was assassinated by a suspected LTTE suicide bomber in a suburb of Colombo; more than 50 other people, including the General Secretary of the UNP, Gamini Wijesekara, and the leader of the SLMP, Ossie Abeyagoonasekera, were killed in the blast. The Government declared a state of emergency and suspended the ongoing peace talks with the LTTE. Dissanayake had been an outspoken critic of these talks and had been one of the architects of the 1987 Indo-Sri Lankan accord. In a surprising move, his widow, Srima Dissanayake, was chosen by the UNP to replace him as the party's presidential candidate. The state of emergency was revoked on 7 November (with the exception of the troubled areas in the north and east) to facilitate the fair and proper conduct of the presidential election, which was held on 9 November. Kumaratunga won the election, with 62.3% of the votes, while Srima Dissanayake obtained 35.9%. The Government viewed the victory as a clear mandate for the peace process initiated earlier that year. Sirimavo Bandaranaike was subsequently appointed Prime Minister, for the third time. The new President pledged to abolish the executive presidency before mid-July 1995, on the grounds that she believed that the post vested too much power in one individual, and promised to initiate a programme of social, economic and constitutional change.

The Government and the LTTE resumed peace talks in early January 1995, which resulted in the drawing up of a preliminary agreement on the cessation of hostilities as a prelude to political negotiations. This important development constituted the first formal truce since fighting was renewed in the north-east in June 1990. As an inducement to ending the violence, the Government offered to implement a US $816m. rehabilitation and development programme in the war-torn northern region. A further incentive was the Government's decision to employ foreign observers to monitor the cease-fire. Towards the end of the month, the LTTE modified their central demand and indicated that they would be willing to accept some form of devolution under a federal system, rather than full independence. In April 1995, however, following several rounds of deadlocked negotiations, with both sides accusing each other of making unreasonable demands and proposals, the LTTE unilaterally ended the truce, withdrew from the peace talks and resumed hostilities against the government forces. (As feared, the LTTE had apparently used the 14-week truce period to fortify and consolidate their strategic positions, notably in the eastern province.) In response, the Government cancelled all the concessions made to the guerrillas during the peace negotiations and placed the security forces on alert. A disturbing escalation in the violence was demonstrated at the end of the month by the LTTE deployment, for the first time, of surface-to-air missiles.

With so much of its political energy invested in the peace process, the resurgence of violence in April 1995 constituted a major set-back for the Government. At this point, Kumaratunga's administration adopted a different, 'hearts and minds' approach, namely the preparation of a range of constitutional proposals, including a more comprehensive devolution of power to the provinces than the system prevailing. Details of these proposals were announced at various stages, and in early August an official statement was issued explaining that the proposed new structure was, in essence, a federal system in which the units were named regions rather than provinces. Meanwhile, in July 1995 the Government candidly admitted that one of its principal election proposals, the abolition of the executive presidency, could not be effected by 15 July as earlier promised. In the same month the Government launched another major offensive in the Jaffna peninsula. 'Operation Leap Forward', as it was named, made some initial gains but appeared to have stalled by the end of the month, in part owing to a deliberate decision by the Government to allow it to do so, and in part owing to LTTE counter-attacks. Outside the Jaffna peninsula, LTTE suicide attacks on army positions at Weli-Oya in the eastern province resulted in the most significant reversal that the LTTE had suffered at the hands of the Sri Lankan army since 1992; more than 300 LTTE militants were killed for the loss of just two defenders. Although 'Operation Leap Forward' was initially an anti-climax both for the Government and the armed forces alike, the victory at Weli-Oya was very much a morale booster.

As the Government's offensive against the Jaffna peninsula was intensified in mid-October 1995, under the code name 'Operation Riviresa' ('Operation Sunshine'), tens of thousands of civilians were compelled by the LTTE to flee the area. In retaliation against the army's attack, rather than actively confronting the troops, the LTTE activated explosives on the country's two largest petroleum storage facilities near Colombo, which received virtually all of Sri Lanka's imported petroleum. As a result, about 20% of the island's petroleum supply was destroyed. In mid-November two LTTE suicide bombers caused 18 deaths and more than 50 injuries in Colombo. In early December, however, the Sri Lankan army achieved a major victory in capturing the city of Jaffna and subsequently much of the Jaffna peninsula. Although the military strength and morale of the LTTE were undermined, the rebels, as expected, reverted to guerrilla warfare and further terrorist activity.

The Government's two-pronged approach to the Tamil problem (i.e. military and political), which was adopted in 1995, was continued throughout the second half of the 1990s. Thus, in 1996 the Government's devolution proposals went through the normal political and constitutional processes. The political processes included discussions within a parliamentary select committee, in which the Government needed to convince the opposition UNP that the proposals merited the support of all parties. In the event of their approval by the select committee, the proposals would need to secure a two-thirds' parliamentary majority if they were to become law. Once that stage had been reached, the proposals would then have to be approved by a simple majority in a national referendum. In mid-January a draft legal document of devolution proposals was introduced to facilitate discussion on this controversial subject, while the army launched a fresh offensive in the Jaffna peninsula, code-named 'Operation Rivikirana', to consolidate the gains made in that area. The LTTE retaliated by exploding a truck-bomb at the Central Bank building in Colombo, which resulted in more than 100 deaths. The army resumed its offensive in the Jaffna peninsula in April through 'Operation Riviresa II', and once more met with very little resistance. With 'Operation Riviresa III', which was launched in mid-May, the army completed a successful campaign to bring the whole of the Jaffna peninsula under its control for the first time since 1984–85. When the army offensive in the Jaffna peninsula was at its peak at the end of 1995, the LTTE had forced the population of the areas potentially under attack by the army to move out of the peninsula to the Kilinochchi and Mullaitivu districts. Thousands of people had followed these instructions. After the completion of 'Operation Riviresa III', however, these people moved back to their homes, which constituted a considerable embarrassment for the LTTE.

Although the army had secured control over the whole of the Jaffna peninsula by mid-1996, the LTTE maintained a presence there, and engaged in occasional guerrilla attacks on the troops. In mid-July the LTTE demonstrated their capacity for surprise attacks on army positions, when the isolated military base at Mullaitivu on the north-eastern coast of Sri Lanka was overrun by the LTTE, inflicting very heavy casualties on the army (according to the LTTE, at least 1,200 government soldiers were killed; according to official figures, the army death toll was about 300) and a defeat on the scale of the Pooneryn incident of November 1993. The LTTE also again demonstrated their capacity to launch bomb attacks in the city of Colombo; a bomb in a crowded suburban train left more than 70 people dead on 24 July 1996. In late September the army seized control of the northern town of Kilinochchi, which had served as the new LTTE headquarters since April. In October

Velupillai Prabhakaran and nine other militants were charged with more than 700 criminal acts of terrorism, including the bombing of the Central Bank in January. This constituted the first occasion that the Government had initiated legal action against the LTTE leader. Fierce fighting between the Tamil militants and government troops continued into 1997, both in the north and east of the country; in early March it was estimated that more than 50,000 people had died as a result of the 14-year civil war.

By the beginning of 1997 the Government's political initiative on devolution had clearly stalled. While discussions in the parliamentary select committee continued, there were few signs of any consensus being reached between the Government and the UNP on these reforms. The election promise to abolish the executive presidency, which had originally been scheduled for mid-July 1995, was once again shelved. The long-postponed local government elections were, however, held on 21 March 1997 (voting did not take place in the troubled northern and eastern provinces). Although the Government secured control over a majority of the local bodies, its share of the total popular vote fell to 48%, compared with the 62% it achieved in the presidential election of November 1994. The UNP obtained nearly 42% of the poll. The Government's victory was tarnished, however, by allegations of widespread electoral malpractice. In April 1997 British officials brokered an agreement between the PA Government and the opposition UNP, aimed at creating a bipartisan approach to ending the civil conflict. In an exchange of letters, Kumaratunga agreed to brief Wickremasinghe on any significant developments in the war, while the opposition pledged not to undermine the Government's attempts to negotiate peace with the LTTE.

In May 1997 the Government resumed its offensive against the LTTE: 'Operation Jayasikuru' ('Operation Certain Victory') was launched with the objective of gaining control of 75 km of the main road (the A9) between Vavuniya and Elephant Pass, which is the point of entry to the Jaffna peninsula. The northern highway, if opened, would provide the military with a vital land route to the Jaffna peninsula (hitherto during the civil war, all government troops and supplies had had to be transported by sea or air). This campaign, which was the largest military operation undertaken by the PA Government since the capture of the Jaffna peninsula, had some early successes. The section of the road between Vavuniya and Mankulam was brought under military control, but, owing to the stiff resistance mounted by the LTTE, the campaign made rather slow progress thereafter. In June 1998 the Government imposed an indefinite 'total ban' on news coverage (both local and foreign) of the ongoing civil war. By recapturing Kilinochchi in September, which it had lost to the army nearly two years earlier, the LTTE compelled the government forces to reconsider the rationale behind their campaign. By October 'Operation Jayasikuru', which was estimated to have cost the lives of more than 3,000 government troops, had been abandoned, despite the army's seizure in the previous month of Mankulam, the last major town held by the guerrillas on the vital northern highway. (The operation was officially cancelled by the Government in December.) In November Sri Lankan intelligence reports indicated that the LTTE were in the process of acquiring helicopters and military aircraft. By late 1998 there were also signs that the army had a serious manpower problem (it needed to recruit 20,000 fresh troops), caused partly by desertions and growing numbers of casualties.

Meanwhile, in late August 1997 the Government announced that it would submit its devolution proposals for parliamentary debate in October. In mid-October, however, 18 people were killed and more than 100 injured (including about 35 foreigners) when a truck-bomb exploded in the car park of a Colombo hotel, leading to several hours of shooting between troops and suspected LTTE terrorists in the city's business district. It was widely believed that the LTTE deliberately targeted foreigners in this attack, following the US Government's decision a few days earlier to place the organization on its official list of proscribed international terrorist groups. At the end of the month, despite protests from the UNP, the draft of the proposed constitutional amendments was presented to Parliament. The prospect of peace, however, appeared increasingly remote in late January 1998, when 16 people were killed in a suspected LTTE suicide bombing in Kandy at Sri Lanka's most sacred Buddhist temple, the Dalada Maligawa ('Temple of the Tooth'). This attack was particularly provocative because, aside from the loss of life, the temple itself, one of the most important religious sites in the Buddhist world, suffered severe damage. The following day the Government retaliated by formally outlawing the LTTE, thus apparently ruling out the prospect of further peace negotiations in the near future and focusing instead on a military solution. The Government suffered another set-back in late January when the UNP effectively rejected the proposed devolution programme. The UNP disagreed with the Government's proposal to devolve wide-ranging powers to regional councils—including a Tamil-administered area—and favoured the concept of power-sharing at the centre. Also at the end of January, polls were conducted in Jaffna for the first time in 15 years. The local authority elections, which were monitored by tens of thousands of troops, were contested by a number of moderate Tamil political parties but were, not surprisingly, boycotted by the LTTE. The largest number of seats was won by the Eelam People's Democratic Party, but the turn-out was a mere 28%, owing to LTTE threats to disrupt the voting.

In late January 1998 a special court in Chennai sentenced 10 Indians and 16 Sri Lankans to death for their involvement in the assassination of the former Indian Prime Minister, Rajiv Gandhi, in 1991. (In May 1999, however, the Supreme Court in New Delhi acquitted 19 defendants and commuted the sentences of three others.)

In February and March 1998 47 people were killed and hundreds injured in Colombo as a result of two suicide bombings. In mid-May the recently elected mayor of Jaffna (the first person to hold that position in 14 years), Sarojini Yogeswaran, who was a member of the moderate TULF, was assassinated by two suspected LTTE gunmen after refusing demands by Tamil militants to resign. In September Yogeswaran's replacement, Ponnuthurai Sivapalan, who was also a leading member of the TULF, was killed, along with 19 others, in a suspected LTTE bomb explosion in Jaffna city hall.

The Government's political calculations, in the wake of the attack on the 'Temple of the Tooth', were determined by the need to deal with elections to five provincial councils, which were scheduled to be held in August 1998. Claiming that the security situation would make it virtually impossible to ensure a peaceful election campaign, the Government sought the support of the UNP to introduce a constitutional amendment to postpone the elections. Following the UNP's refusal to support such a move, except on its own terms, the Government was faced with the difficult choice of either proceeding with the holding of the elections or postponing them through a resort to the declaration of a state of emergency. In the mean time the electoral process was initiated, nominations of candidates were received and processed, and the Commissioner of Elections declared 28 August as the date for the elections. On 4 August, however, the Government declared a nation-wide state of emergency. A presidential regulation under the emergency was issued on the following day, formally postponing indefinitely the holding of the provincial elections. The opposition claimed that the Government had deliberately engineered the postponement of the important polls since it was concerned about performing badly in them. At the beginning of 1999 an election was called for the north-western provincial council, which was not among the five where elections had been postponed. The campaign culminated on 25 January in the most violent and corrupt election in the island's history. The systematic 'ballot-stuffing' and booth-capturing organized by the ruling PA was on an unprecedented scale. Civil rights groups and religious leaders joined the opposition UNP in forthright condemnation of the Government for these blatant infringements of electoral laws. The Commissioner of Elections rejected as many as 50,000 votes as clearly fraudulent. Although the PA wrested control of the council from the UNP, the legality of the whole election was challenged before the courts.

The Government's reputation, already badly tarnished by the manner in which the election to the north-western provincial council was conducted, suffered another severe blow when, on the day after polling, the Supreme Court in Colombo overruled President Kumaratunga's order, made in August 1998, postponing elections to five other provincial councils. The Court stated that the presidency had no constitutional right to postpone the elections through the declaration of a state of emergency and asked the election commission to hold the polls within the next three months and to hold all five of them on a single day. The provincial elections, which were eventually held on 6 April 1999, gave the Government no cause for satisfaction. The difference in the percentage of votes gained by the PA and the UNP was reduced to a mere 1%. The Government secured a majority in three councils, but in the two principal councils, the western and central, the PA was forced to head a minority administration. An election to the southern province, which was held in May, also resulted in a PA-led minority administration. One notable feature of this series of provincial elections was the recovery of the JVP as a credible political force (it won around 8% of the vote in total in all of the contested provincial councils, and, specifically, as much as 20% in the Hambantota district of the southern province).

Meanwhile, the LTTE leader presented a carefully worded peace offer in December 1998, which included a demand for third-party mediation. The Government responded by insisting that certain conditions be met before peace talks could commence. Once the north-east monsoon rains had subsided, the army launched another offensive in early March 1999 in the areas controlled by the LTTE in the Mullaitivu district of the northern province. This offensive, which was code-named 'Operation Ranagosa' ('Operation The Sound of War') and the objective of which was to reduce the area under the effective control of the LTTE, was waged intermittently during 1999, along with other minor operations in parts of the northern province. In mid-June, in an unprecedented order, the President temporarily dissolved the powerful National Security Council and stripped the Chief of Defence Staff of sweeping powers. In the same month Kumaratunga promoted 15 PA members to the position of deputy minister, in a move that was widely viewed as an attempt to ensure that politicians remained loyal to the alliance prior to and during the forthcoming general election. The move was heavily criticized by opposition members as financially profligate.

Sri Lanka's fourth presidential election, which was called in October 1999, was held on 21 December, about 11 months ahead of schedule. For the second time in succession the results of a Sri Lankan presidential election were affected by the actions of the LTTE. On this occasion, this phenomenon happened initially with the LTTE inflicting a series of defeats on the Sri Lankan army in the north of the country in October and November, during a brief and very successful campaign, as a result of which the government forces lost control of large areas of territory that they had secured between 1995 and 1997. These demoralizing defeats (amidst reports of large-scale desertions and mutiny in the army ranks) embarrassed the Government of President Kumaratunga and gave the prospects of her principal opponent, Ranil Wickremasinghe of the UNP, an unexpected boost. As a result, the latter's electoral campaign gained in credibility, and by the end of November he seemed a potential victor in the contest. Wickremasinghe sustained this favourable position until a failed assassination attempt by an LTTE suicide bomber on 18 December, the last day of campaigning, left the terrorists' target, Chandrika Kumaratunga, slightly injured and helped to reverse the emerging pro-UNP trend in the election process. The shock of the failed assassination attempt (which killed more than 20 people) was cleverly exploited by the Government through the use of the state-controlled electronic media, particularly television broadcasts, and through hastily organized, small public meetings held throughout virtually the whole country, in direct violation of the ban imposed by electoral laws on any form of electioneering for two days immediately prior to the holding of the election. The principal theme of the Government's last-minute campaign was that the LTTE had planned the assassination to help Wickremasinghe's cause. The margin of Kumaratunga's victory, by 51% of the total votes compared with 43% for Wickremasinghe, was substantially below that of 1994. The JVP candidate's relatively poor performance in the election (which was contested by 13 candidates and attracted a 73% turn-out of the electorate) benefited the incumbent President. Had the JVP garnered more support, Kumaratunga's margin of victory would have been even lower. With allegations made by neutral observers, as well as by the defeated UNP candidate, of widespread electoral violence, blatant malpractices and vote-rigging, the flawed presidential election cost the Government heavily in terms of integrity. In addition, the Government was faced with a serious legal challenge to the validity of the election. In early January 2000, despite tightened security in the capital, another suspected LTTE suicide bomber killed herself and 12 other people outside the office of Prime Minister Bandaranaike in Colombo in what police described as a failed assassination attempt. In June a suicide bomber killed at least 20 people, including the Minister of Industrial Development, Clement V. Gunaratna, at a parade in the capital marking the country's first 'War Heroes' Day'.

Once the President had recovered sufficiently from the trauma of the pre-election attempt on her life (in which she had sustained wounds to her right eye), Kumaratunga applied herself once more to the process of constitutional reform, and by mid-February 2000 she had succeeded in persuading Wickremasinghe and the UNP to send a delegation to participate in the preparation of a new constitution (based on the proposals regarding devolution presented by the Government in 1997). The first such meeting took place in March. Meanwhile, in mid-February the Norwegian Minister of Foreign Affairs, Knut Vollebæk, during a visit to Colombo announced that the Norwegian Government had accepted a request from the Sri Lankan President and the LTTE to serve as a mediator to bring the two parties together for discussions—for a year or so Norway had been posited as a potential facilitator. The Norwegian initiative had little effect in checking the LTTE military operations, which had continued throughout November and December 1999. It was clear that the successes achieved by the LTTE in the last weeks of 1999 were a prelude to a determined bid to capture the large army base at Elephant Pass, on the strategically important isthmus that links the Jaffna peninsula to the rest of the island. The garrison (which had been under government control since the IPKF's withdrawal in 1990) was seized by the LTTE in late April 2000, the group's most spectacular military victory in recent times. In response, a panic-stricken Sri Lankan Government appealed for assistance both from regional powers and from elsewhere to deal with the rapidly advancing LTTE. Adopting a more circumspect policy than its predecessor had done in the 1980s, the Indian central Government decided that it would not interfere directly in the Sri Lankan conflict. All requests for military assistance in the form of weaponry from the Sri Lankan Government were turned down. All that was on offer from India was humanitarian assistance, a pronouncement interpreted in Colombo as including the transfer of Sri Lankan troops out of the Jaffna peninsula presumably by Indian ships, should the need for such an evacuation arise. India also announced, however, that it was extending its ban on the outlawed LTTE for a further two years. A more fruitful initiative by the Sri Lankan authorities was the restoration of diplomatic ties with Israel and successful negotiations with that country for the supply of sophisticated weaponry and military aircraft. Other countries too responded with the supply of arms: namely, Pakistan, China and Russia. On 3 May President Kumaratunga put Sri Lanka on a war footing by invoking the Public Security Ordinance; this constituted the first use of the measure, which gave the police extensive powers of arrest and confiscation, since the country became independent in 1949. At the same time, the President imposed a ban on strikes and political rallies, and stricter censorship on all forms of media reporting.

The resurgence of the LTTE in 1999–2000 had a noticeable effect on Tamil Nadu politicians, in the form of a revival in pro-LTTE sentiment, which had largely been dormant since the assassination of Rajiv Gandhi in 1991. In early June 2000 the Chief Minister of Tamil Nadu, Muthuvel Karunanidhi, called for a partition of Sri Lanka, on the model of the former Czechoslovakia, into two states, one of which would be a Tamil state. There was immediate opposition to this proposal, both within Tamil Nadu and in other parts of India. Karunanidhi's proposition and the outpouring of pro-LTTE sentiment among other Indian politicians belonging to parties of the current governing coalition in New Delhi were acutely embarrassing to the Indian Government. The administration of Atal Bihari Vajpayee indicated clearly enough, and repeatedly, that it would not countenance the establishment of a separate Tamil state in Sri Lanka, and indicated, rather, a preference for the allocation of greater autonomy to the Tamil areas of the island.

Meanwhile, in response to the escalating military crisis, the Sri Lankan Government imposed draconian security measures, banning all activities perceived as a threat to national security and giving sweeping powers to the armed forces and police, and renewed press censorship on the foreign media. By early May 2000 LTTE forces, buoyed up by their recent military gains, were close enough to Jaffna town to suggest that they were poised to drive the Sri Lankan army away from Jaffna and the Jaffna peninsula and to compel the government forces to abandon the airport at Palali and the naval base of Karainagar, which the LTTE had never been able to control previously. Within a month, however, the LTTE advance had lost its early momentum. Whether this was because of a change of leadership in the Sri Lankan army in the Jaffna peninsula, with two experienced generals with exemplary records as field commanders being posted there, whether it was the recent provision of high-tech weaponry, which the army had lacked at the time of the fall of Elephant Pass, that enabled the Sri Lankan security forces to regain the initiative, or whether it was a combination of the two was difficult to assess. The fact remains, however, that by mid-June the threat poised by the LTTE to the Government's control over Jaffna town and the Jaffna peninsula had clearly receded. By early September the army was making efforts to compel the LTTE to move out of some of the towns in the vicinity of Jaffna. Despite early setbacks, these attempts began to prove successful by mid-September. In mid-2000 it was estimated that since the instigation of the civil conflict in 1983 65,000 people had been killed in Sri Lanka as a result of the violence, 1m. had been internally displaced and 600,000 had fled overseas.

In any event, the successful holding operation by the army in Jaffna gave the Government the opportunity to return to its preparation of a new constitution through discussions with the UNP. The Government's avowed objective was to have a new constitution presented to and approved by Parliament in July or August 2000, always bearing in mind the fact that the national legislature's term of office expired on 24 August (unless it was dissolved earlier). The discussions with the UNP leadership on the draft of the new constitution proceeded smoothly enough until early July, when complications arose in the form of sharp disagreements over the role of the current President in a new parliamentary system. While the Government insisted that Kumaratunga should have a dual role, as the new Prime Minister after parliamentary elections, should the elections be won by the PA, and as executive President until the expiry of her current six-year term, the UNP argued that her tenure of the presidency should come to an end within a short time of the promulgation of any new constitution. Approval of the new constitution required a two-thirds' parliamentary majority, which was not possible, however, once the UNP leadership had declared its opposition to the draft constitution; the Tamil parliamentary parties—the EPDP, the Democratic People's Liberation Front and the TULF—also rejected the proposals as giving inadequate autonomy to the Tamil regions of the country. The Government sought to overcome this by attempting to persuade UNP deputies to support the new constitution in Parliament; in the event, a number of UNP MPs did cross over to the opposition during the debate on the constitution in early August. However, the members who did so fell far short of the Government's targeted number. When this situation became clear, the draft constitution was not presented for a vote (voting on the controversial bill was postponed indefinitely). Instead, after an inconclusive and acrimonious debate, amidst large and vociferous crowds expressing their opposition to the draft constitution, Parliament was dissolved on 18 August, and new parliamentary elections were scheduled for October.

Meanwhile, on 10 August 2000 Sirimavo Bandaranaike resigned as Prime Minister and retired from political life at the age of 84; the veteran politician was replaced in the premiership by the erstwhile Minister of Public Administration, Home Affairs and Plantation Industries, Ratnasiri Wickremanayake, who was regarded as a Sinhalese hardliner close to the Buddhist clergy. In mid-September the Minister of Shipping and Shipping Development and President of the SLMC, Mohamed H. M. Ashraff, was killed in a helicopter crash in Kegalle district; a high-level investigation into the incident was immediately ordered amidst speculation that the aircraft had been shot down by LTTE guerrillas.

The results of the parliamentary election of 10 October 2000 were a disappointment to both the PA and the UNP. The election, which according to official figures attracted a turn-out of 75%, was marred by widespread electoral malpractice and systematic violence and intimidation (particularly on the part of the incumbent PA). The PA secured only 45% of the votes cast, and the UNP received 40%. The JVP gained 10 seats (6% of the vote), and from the beginning considered itself a possible balancing force in a Parliament in which neither the PA nor the UNP had won an absolute majority (with 107 and 89 of the 225 seats, respectively). After much bargaining by the two main parties, the PA, having gained the support of the EPDP, National Unity Alliance (NUA) and SLMC, was able to form a coalition with a very narrow majority. It was evident that the Government would be vulnerable to shifts of opinion within Parliament, and throughout the country.

The death of Sirimavo Bandaranaike, on the day of the election, deprived the SLFP of its leader for 40 years, as well as a respected stabilizing influence. The election of Anura Bandaranaike, a member of the UNP and the President's estranged brother, as parliamentary Speaker by a unanimous vote of Parliament was seen, in the early stages at least, as heralding the beginning of a period of greater co-operation between the PA and the UNP. However, in fact, the establishment of a 44-member cabinet, with 38 Deputy Ministers, underlined the inherent instability of the Government, and its potential vulnerability in the face of a challenge by the UNP. Every group in the coalition was represented in the Cabinet, including the SLMC and its affiliate, the NUA. It was evident very soon that President Kumaratunga's principal concern was to ensure the survival of the Government in a situation where, under the terms of the Constitution, Parliament could not be dissolved for at least one year after the previous election, in this instance until 10 October 2001.

The priority for the new Government was established by the LTTE, who declared a unilateral cease-fire to begin on 24 December 2000 as a prelude to talks with the Government, which, they proposed, would be facilitated in the early stages by a Norwegian representative. Although the Government readily accepted the principle of a Norwegian facilitator, it refused to accept the LTTE offer. The Government also refused to lift the proscription on the Tamil group. Instead, it insisted on a set of conditions as a prelude to accepting a unilateral cessation of hostilities. The LTTE, nevertheless, implemented a cease-fire, and regularly renewed it until the end of April 2001, ignoring the conditions set by the Government. The Government evidently suspected the LTTE of seeking a period of time during which it could rebuild its forces and its equipment. The low-intensity conflict continued in the north and east.

By June 2001, however, the Government's priorities had shifted more emphatically to its political survival, as a result of a serious miscalculation on the part of the President. Kumaratunga dismissed the leader of the SLMC, Rauf Hakeem, from his position as Minister of Internal and International Trade, Commerce, Muslim Religious Affairs and Shipping Development, in the belief that his party would not stand by him. However, as a result, six other members of the SLMC withdrew their support from the PA, thereby reducing the coalition Government to a minority in Parliament. The UNP was able to claim, subsequently, that the anti-PA coalition had a parliamentary majority, with 115 of the 225 seats, and challenged the Government with a parliamentary motion of 'no confidence'. A debate in Parliament was proposed to take place in mid-July. As the census was scheduled to take place at this time, the Government suggested mid-August as an appropriate time.

However, in early July 2001 the President unexpectedly prorogued Parliament for two months to forestall an attempt to overthrow the Government and ordered a referendum on 21 August to seek a mandate for a new constitution. The former decision breached a settled principle of democratic government: that Parliament must not be prorogued when the government faces a vote of no confidence, especially when it has lost its majority. The second ruling was unconstitutional: the special provisions in the Constitution that dictate the procedures for constitutional reform had been deliberately ignored.

President Kumaratunga's decisions, which had been taken without prior consultation with the Cabinet, plunged the country into a constitutional crisis. The UNP-led opposition embarked on a campaign of peaceful popular resistance, marred by occasional violent protests, demanding a revocation of the prorogation of Parliament. There was also opposition within the Cabinet, especially to the referendum. As a result, in early August the President considered it expedient to postpone the referendum to mid-October. The announcement was made two weeks after the LTTE attack on Colombo's international airport, and adjacent air base, at the end of July. This raid demonstrated serious flaws in the air force and airport's security system. It also resulted in severe damage to the country's economy and tourist industry. Violence between the Tamil guerrillas and Government escalated following the attack. Earlier that month the President had circumvented Parliament and reimposed state of emergency legislation under anti-terrorism laws. The President also passed an order to reimpose the ban on the LTTE. Unsurprisingly, recent events led to the further erosion of the Government's political credibility.

In an attempt to resolve the crisis, the Prime Minister and some senior cabinet members conducted negotiations with the UNP on a possible coalition Government. Although the UNP showed some interest in this, it eventually decided to join opposition parties to form a UNP-led coalition. The President objected to a UNP government or a UNP-led opposition coalition, and began negotiations with the radical, left-wing JVP. The JVP agreed to support the Government and, in early September, a Memorandum of Understanding (MOU) was signed binding the two parties for one year to a PA-led minority Government, sustained by JVP votes. The left-wing party set 28 conditions in the memorandum, one of which was a reduction of the Cabinet to 20 members. A 22-member cabinet was subsequently sworn in, but three senior Cabinet members had refused to join, an indication of the instability of the Government. According to the JVP's demands, the President also cancelled the referendum on constitutional reform and ordered Parliament to reconvene a day earlier. In addition, the JVP insisted that there should be no negotiations with the LTTE during the one-year period.

In October 2001 the SLFP removed its General Secretary, S. B. Dissanayake, as the Government faced a vote of no confidence, which was to be held on 11 October. It had become clear that the Government would face defeat in the parliamentary vote after 13 members of the coalition, including several ministers, defected to the opposition. President Kumaratunga, therefore, dissolved Parliament one day before the scheduled vote and announced that a general election would be held in early December. The dissolution was condemned by the opposition, which was prevented from proving its majority. However, the decision was constitutional, as the President had waited until one year after the previous election had passed before she dissolved the legislature. Meanwhile, violence between the LTTE and Government continued and showed no signs of abating.

## POLITICS AND POLITICAL CHANGE, 2001–04

The general election of 5 December 2001, like that of October 2000, was marred by electoral malpractices, the blatant exploitation of state resources and vote-rigging (often crude and sometimes adroit) on the part of the outgoing PA. In addition, during both elections the state's print and electronic media were fully and almost exclusively reserved for the election campaign of government candidates. Furthermore, both elections were blighted by systematic violence directed against opposition members under the alleged instruction of senior government officials. The December 2001 parliamentary elections were reported to be the more violent of the two; however, on this occasion the electorate turned against the outgoing Government and the vote-rigging failed decisively.

The UNP-led coalition won a comprehensive victory, securing most of the polling divisions and all but one of the polling districts outside of the northern province. The UNP won 109 of the 225 seats (45.6% of the vote) and the PA obtained 77 seats (37.2%). The JVP secured 16 seats (9.1%) and the Tamil National Alliance (TNA) won 15 seats (3.9%). Political analysts considered that the margin of victory for the UNP and its allies would have been much wider had the election been free and fair. In order to ensure a majority in Parliament, and in recognition of the support received from and through coalition partners, the UNP leader, Ranil Wickremasinghe, formed a United National Front (UNF) Government with the SLMC, TNA and several members of the former PA administration who had defected to the UNP after the election.

The new Government consolidated its position at the local government elections in March 2002. Apart from a few incidents of election violence—well below the levels witnessed in 1999, 2000 and 2001 in terms of intensity or geographical range—the elections were free and fair, in a deliberate and permanent return to the practices of the early 1990s. The PA was overwhelmingly defeated, managing to secure only four out of 247 councils, compared with the UNP's victory in 240 municipal legislatures. The UNP won almost 57% of the total vote, while the PA secured 31% and the JVP nearly 6%.

The political cohabitation between the PA President and the UNF Government proved to be uncomfortable. Sri Lanka was not accustomed to the Prime Minister and President representing two opposing parties (the last time this had occurred was in 1984) and the conventions and practices that would reduce friction between the two parties had not yet developed. One essential factor was the right of the President to dissolve Parliament after one year from the date of the last election. Confronted with the prospect of an election called at the President's convenience after 5 December 2002, the UNF Government proposed that future elections be called on the basis of a parliamentary resolution and that the President's right to dissolve Parliament should not operate while the government had a majority in Parliament. However, the relevant constitutional amendment was not introduced for debate in Parliament, with the result that the President was able to dissolve Parliament in February 2004, although the UNF had a majority in the legislature.

One of the principal political developments that followed the UNF's accession to power was a strengthening of the peace process. An informal cease-fire took effect in December 2001. On 22 February 2002 the Prime Minister and the LTTE leader, Velupillai Prabhakaran, signed an MOU agreeing to an internationally monitored indefinite cease-fire, with the Norwegian Government serving as facilitator. The MOU committed the two sides to specified courses of action and stipulated the conditions for implementation prior to the commencement of peace talks. A Sri Lanka Monitoring Mission (SLMM), operated by several Scandinavian countries and led by Norwegians, conducted the supervision of the implementation of the MOU.

The assumption was that the two parties would maintain the cease-fire and commence peace talks on or before 2 August 2002. This latter deadline was missed but the cessation of hostilities was upheld. On 4 September the Government removed the official ban on the LTTE, a condition that the LTTE insisted upon as a prelude to negotiations. The three-day peace talks began nearly two weeks later in Thailand. During the negotiations the LTTE unexpectedly abandoned their long-standing demand for independence and instead agreed to regional autonomy and self-government. The successful talks ended with both sides agreeing to establish a committee to deal with the return of more than 800,000 internally displaced people to high-security zones operated by the Sri Lankan military; to form a joint task force for humanitarian and reconstruction activities; and to appeal to international donors to support the humanitarian efforts. These talks in Thailand were continued in October–November 2002 and again in January 2003. Talks were also held in Norway in December 2002, Germany in February 2003 and Japan in March 2003. However, the LTTE abruptly withdrew from the talks in April 2003 and did not participate in any further peace negotiations. While the governing coalition elected in February 2004 seemed anxious to continue with the talks, the LTTE did not reciprocate.

In February 2004 the SLFP reached an agreement with the JVP concerning an electoral pact for future elections and the formation of a coalition government with an agreed programme. This new alliance, the United People's Freedom Alliance (UPFA), defeated the UNF at the parliamentary elections held on 2 April 2004. The coalition secured 45.60% of the vote, while the UNP share of the vote declined to 37.83%. The coalition won 105 seats in Parliament, falling short of a majority by eight seats. All subsequent efforts to secure a majority with the support of some opposition parties failed. A key element in Parliament was the Jathika Hela Urumaya (JHU), which held nine seats. This party of *bhikkhus* won nearly 6% of the total vote.

Mahinda Rajapakse, a senior member of the UPFA and former fisheries minister, became the Prime Minister of this rather unstable minority Government. The new coalition won all six provincial councils at the election held on 10 July 2004, but its share of the total vote was very low—reaching around 50% compared with 76% at the parliamentary election.

## THE QUESTION OF THE PRESIDENTIAL ELECTION, 2004–05

The Government established on the basis of the parliamentary elections of April 2004 was expected to bring about a decisive shift in the politics of Sri Lanka, as it was moving towards being a left-wing coalition, with the JVP having assumed a position of great influence in the making of policy and in policy implementation. The JVP also took over the left-wing leadership of the trade unions (with the exception of the plantations). In its early stages the Government seemed intent on radicalizing government affairs, if necessary with a new constitution, or, alternatively, an amended Constitution. All it lacked was a majority in the legislature, or rather the two-thirds' majority needed for constitutional reform. In consequence, the Government initiated a policy of persuading the UNP's allies to 'cross the floor' in the legislature. It succeeded in this objective to some extent, but its failure to secure a majority in the legislature, much less the coveted two-thirds' majority, continued. The UNP was greatly weakened by these defections, especially because the courts ruled in favour of those who did defect.

Despite the initial success of the Government, it soon proved to be no more than a quarrelsome, unstable coalition, which lasted for just over a year after its establishment. The crux of the problem was that the JVP proved to be an unreliable coalition partner, anxious to radicalize government policies but averse to sharing the blame that inevitably resulted from exaggerated expectations of change. Two problems persisted—high and rising prices and high levels of unemployment. The economy had shown signs of improvement under the previous UNP-led coalition. However, by mid-2004, very early in the term of the new Government, it became clear that it had no viable policies to cope with a deteriorating economy.

The electoral pendulum, which had swung so decisively in favour of the UPFA coalition during the 2004 election, thus began its inevitable swing away from it. The Government's problems multiplied when the devastating Asian tsunami struck Sri Lanka in the last week of December 2004. Historically, Sri Lanka has been an island free of tsunamis, volcanoes and earthquakes, affected only by occasional floods. However, on this occasion, one-third of the coastline was severely affected by the huge waves. More than 30,000 lives were lost, and over one-fifth of the population either lost their homes or livelihoods, or suffered substantial losses of income. After some early success in helping people to cope with the devastation, government rehabilitation policies proved to be inadequate and lacking in focus. The tsunami left an unpopular Government even more out of favour and facing a severe crisis of confidence.

The December 2004 tsunami was the worst natural disaster to hit Sri Lanka for centuries. In the Sinhalese areas the densely populated south, and not so densely populated south-east, suffered severely, but the north-east was even more badly affected—whether it was the east coast, with its large Muslim population, or the south-east, which is home to Muslims, Tamils and some Sinhalese, all of whom suffered loss of lives, livelihoods and income. In a grim parallel with the island's ethnic tensions, the Government faced severe criticism from people in the south and south-east who had voted for the coalition in large numbers. The people of the north-east had not voted for the Government, but their criticisms were no less vociferous. Rehabilitation funds were sufficient, but the mechanisms for transfer of funds and supervision of rehabilitation work were either non-existent or utterly inadequate. The Government's perceived ineptitude in the face of the tsunami added greatly to its unpopularity.

Fortunately for Sri Lanka, the tsunami did not affect the most productive parts of the country—the south-west coast was not severely damaged and the plantations were in the hills of the centre of the country. However, the tourism industry was badly affected, as were the coastal fisheries.

Coalition building with the JVP proved to be exceedingly difficult. Apart from its left-of-centre radicalism, the JVP was inflexibly opposed to the LTTE and, throughout the entire period of its association with the administration, it undermined every government effort to reach a policy of accommodation with the LTTE as part of the existing peace process. Faced with the severity of the task of reconstruction in the wake of the tsunami, the Government devised a proposal for an administrative device that could bring the Government and the LTTE together in the reconstruction of areas damaged by the tsunami—and, indeed, in all the affected areas. The device was restricted in its scope to the north and east of the island and to a narrow 2-km strip along the coast. From the outset this mechanism, better known as the Post-Tsunami Operations Management Structure (P-TOMS), became a controversial issue within both the Government and the country as a whole. Nationalists objected to the principle of including the LTTE in the reconstruction process and expressed fears about the P-TOMS becoming the basis of a separate state.

The LTTE agreed to work within the new structure. The UNP, for its part, supported the Government's new device but insisted on its amendment; however, the JVP condemned the P-TOMS and threatened to resign from the coalition if the Government signed the draft agreement. By the end of June 2005 the draft had been signed, and the JVP consequently left the coalition. The Government was thus left with a minority in the legislature and was forced to depend on the various groups within the legislature for support of its political agenda.

Under normal circumstances the UNP would have insisted on the formation of a new government. However, the problem was that the President's term of office was coming to an end, either at the end of 2005 (as the UNP insisted on the basis of the requirements of the Constitution), or by November 2006 (as President Kumaratunga insisted, based on the fact that, although she had come to power in 1999, she had had a later inauguration ceremony, in 2000). Either way, this 'lame duck' presidency complicated calculations with regard to the Government and the legislature. After several attempts to accommodate the President's wishes had failed, the SLFP decided to put forward a proposal to nominate a successor to the President for an election. The party nominated the Prime Minister, Mahinda Rajapakse, as its presidential candidate, with Anura Bandaranaike to serve as Prime Minister.

Under the terms of the Constitution the date for the next presidential election must be determined by the Elections Commissioner. In late August 2005 the Supreme Court ruled that, constitutionally, a presidential election should be held by November 2005, rather than 2006. It was subsequently announced that the poll would take place on 17 November 2005.

In early August 2005 the ongoing peace process with the LTTE suffered a significant set-back after its militants were suspected of involvement in the assassination of the Minister of

Foreign Affairs, Lakshman Kadirgamar, at his home in Colombo. Kadirgamar's death prompted the declaration of a state of emergency in the country. Anura Bandaranaike was later appointed to succeed Kadirgamar as Minister of Foreign Affairs, relinquishing his industry and investment promotion portfolios to the Minister of Finance and Planning, Saratha Amunugama. Later in that month the LTTE agreed to hold their first high-level talks with the Government since 2003 on the issue of the ongoing cease-fire. However, disputes arose over a satisfactory venue for the talks, with the Government insisting that they take place in Sri Lanka, while the LTTE demanded that they be held either in the Tamil-dominated north of the country or at a neutral venue abroad.

In September 2005 Prime Minister Rajapakse concluded an agreement with the JVP whereby, in return for its support in the forthcoming presidential election, he would abandon both the P-TOMS and the Government's commitment to work towards a power-sharing arrangement with the Tamils and would review the existing cease-fire arrangement. It was feared that, in the event of his election, Rajapakse could thus return Sri Lanka to a state of civil war. Meanwhile, the presidential candidate for the UNP, Ranil Wickremasinghe, stressed his commitment to reviving the stalled peace process.

On 17 November 2005 14 candidates contested the presidential election. Mahinda Rajapakse secured a narrow victory over his closest rival, Ranil Wickremasinghe, winning 50.3% of the vote, compared with 48.4% for Wickremasinghe. The election was notable for the low turn-out amongst the country's Tamil population, particularly in the LTTE-controlled northern and eastern areas; this was thought to have played a significant part in Wickremasinghe's defeat, as he had stressed his commitment to the ongoing cease-fire agreement during the electoral campaign. While the LTTE had stated that they would not prevent people from voting, there was widespread evidence that they had done so. Rajapakse subsequently nominated Minister of Agriculture, Public Security, Law and Order and of Buddha Sasana, Ratnasiri Wickremanayake, as Prime Minister. Neither the JVP nor the JHU were awarded any cabinet portfolios. In June 2006 Rajapakse was appointed as Chairman of the SLFP.

### CEASE-FIRE AGREEMENT UNDER PRESSURE

By the end of 2005 Sri Lanka had entered a new phase in the 'cold war' between the Government and the LTTE. The governing coalition did not have a majority in the legislature, leaving it vulnerable to pressure from the JVP, which used its links with the Government to urge an end to the Cease-Fire Agreement (CFA) and to embark on all-out war with the LTTE. The Government adhered to its policy of maintaining the peace, despite the deaths of servicemen and policemen in attacks by the LTTE in various parts of the north-east of the island. The UNP, for its part, backed the Government in its policy of peace. Thus there was no danger of the Government weakening under pressure from the opposition. The result was that the stalemate between the Government and the LTTE continued into 2006, as did the pressure on the Government by the JVP, with its tactics of advocating war as the alternative to the current phase of peace at all costs.

Both the Government and the LTTE showed themselves ready to continue with peace talks, which took place in Geneva in February 2006. It soon became clear, however, that they were not a succession to previous talks that had been held between the UNP Government and the LTTE. The LTTE repeatedly highlighted the need for a clear look at the CFA and put forward two demands. First, it urged that the areas in Jaffna and other parts of the northern province held by the army—the so-called High Security Zone—should be reduced in size so that the legitimate owners of these lands could return and reoccupy them. Second, the Government was asked to disarm the so-called paramilitaries, by which the LTTE meant the Karuna dissidents. The LTTE had originally described the issue of the Karuna dissidents as an internal LTTE matter, but by the time the peace talks were held in early 2006 the LTTE insisted that it was the Government's responsibility to disarm the Karuna faction. This suggested LTTE discomfort with its own inability to do so. The Government agreed; however, its subsequent failure to disarm the paramilitaries, and the Karuna faction in particular, was to cause difficulties in its negotiations with the LTTE.

When the preliminary talks between the Government and the LTTE ended in another stalemate, the LTTE went back on its offer of holding a further set of peace negotiations. The group then suffered a diplomatic reverse when, in May 2006, the European Union (EU) included the LTTE on a list of proscribed organizations deemed to be involved, in or linked to, acts of terrorism. This entailed, *inter alia*, a 'freeze' on the LTTE's financial assets in all 25 EU member states, and a ban on fund-raising within the EU, while LTTE representatives would be prevented from visiting countries of the EU. In July 2006, following LTTE demands in response to this ban, Finland, Denmark and Sweden chose to withdraw their cease-fire monitors from Sri Lanka.

In the mean time the LTTE continued with its policy of official commitment to the CFA and to peace, but engaged nevertheless in episodes of violence. On 15 June 2006 an explosion killed more than 60 persons—men, women and children—who were travelling on a bus at Kebithigollewa, a small town near Anuradhapura, in what could only be described as the worst massacre of civilians since the signing of the CFA in 2002. The question was asked whether this marked a direct confrontation between the Government and the LTTE and whether it heralded the beginning of another Eelam war. After the victims of the massacre were buried in a mass grave, however, the stalemate continued—a stalemate of 'no war and no peace'. The LTTE's denial of any involvement in the attack was received with much scepticism. There was widespread international condemnation of the massacre from India, the USA, Switzerland and France, among numerous other countries. The Indian Government dispatched its Foreign Secretary, Shyam Saran, to Colombo on 3–4 August to urge the Government and the LTTE to resume peace talks.

In mid-July 2006 an even more serious breach of the peace occurred when the LTTE blocked the passage of water at Maavil-Aru, a minor irrigation project in the eastern province. Since the livelihoods of 1,500 or more families—Sinhalese, Tamils and Muslims—were at stake, the Government eventually used force to open the channel. Some viewed the LTTE action as an attempt to compel Sinhalese and Muslims to leave the area served by the waters of the Maavil-Aru channel (i.e. an attempt at 'ethnic cleansing'). Soon after, the LTTE launched an attack on Muttur, a Muslim port-town in the eastern province. Although the attack was repulsed, there was widespread destruction of property, as well as the killing of large numbers of Muslims. The events at Maavil-Aru and at Muttur represented serious set-backs for the LTTE, although the 'no war' pledge appeared to be in force. The Government justified its resorting to armed force as purely defensive action against aggression and as part of a humanitarian attempt to provide water to the paddy lands in the region.

The LTTE had barely recovered from the set-backs at Maavil-Aru and Muttur when it began another attempt to capture Jaffna town and bring it under its control. Hundreds of people were reported to have been killed in the ensuing violence and tens of thousands fled the area. As the battle for Jaffna continued in October 2006 it was difficult to assess what impact the renewed conflict would have on the CFA and the peace process. Although the parties involved in the fighting declared themselves to be committed to peace, there was no consensus on how peace was to be managed or on the constitutional framework required for Sri Lanka to move towards peace on a long-term basis.

In October 2006 the Supreme Court, in a landmark decision, declared that the amalgamation of the northern and eastern provinces, which had taken place in 1988 (see above) under pressure from the Indian Government, had been unconstitutional. Tamil parties protested the move, but the Government accepted the ruling and appointed a separate governor for the eastern province (following the merger there had been one governor for the north-eastern province as a whole); local government polls were also declared for this province.

In 2007 the Government strengthened its position in relation to opposition parties in Parliament. As part of its drive to obtain an overall majority, the Government was able to secure the support of a faction within the UNP, resulting in 19 defections and a major cabinet reshuffle in January; appointments to the new Cabinet included Karu Jayasuriya, the former Deputy Leader of the UNP, as Minister of Public Administration and Home Affairs, and Rohitha Bogollagama as Minister of Foreign Affairs. In October 2006 the UNP had signed an MOU with the Government, in which both parties agreed to pursue a peace policy and adopt other measures to stabilize the country. Following the UNP defections, however, this MOU reportedly became non-functional. The net effect of the crossing over was a diminution in the UNP's position in Parliament rather than an actual strengthening of the Government to any significant extent. The JVP failed to become the principal opposition party despite the decrease in number of UNP parliamentary seats.

Meanwhile, the LTTE finally decided to join peace talks in Geneva, which were held in October 2006. In doing so, the LTTE insisted that the discussions be confined to the 2002 CFA; the Government accepted this stipulation and sent its negotiators to Geneva with the hope that the CFA could be amended. In the ultimate analysis, however, little was achieved, although both sides agreed to uphold the terms of the CFA.

Under pressure from the international community, the LTTE agreed to a second round of peace talks, but by the end of August 2007 no such negotiations had been held. The LTTE's acceptance of further peace talks was apparently designed to keep the Government guessing as to whether regular and successive breaches of the peace process would lead to the resumption of an all-out war policy. As it was, the Government and the LTTE both claimed to be upholding the official 'no war' policy while, in reality, a policy of 'undeclared war' was being conducted by both sides.

For the LTTE, undeclared war amounted to a concerted attempt to cause unrest in the eastern province. Its principal target was the Muslim community, the largest group in that province. Thereafter the Sinhalese settlements in the region were targeted. The Government responded to this LTTE undeclared war with its own version of undeclared war, in which the LTTE's strongholds came under military attack: one after another, LTTE positions succumbed to the Sri Lankan army. One early target was the strategic centre of Sampur, which the LTTE had used as a base for attacking Trincomalee. After Sampur the government forces besieged a number of smaller strongholds and in early May 2007 the military targeted the forests of Toppigala. By mid-July the LTTE had lost control of its jungle bases in Toppigala, and with that the army had captured virtually the whole of the eastern province from the LTTE.

In March and April 2007 the LTTE carried out its first air raids, against military targets around Colombo and elsewhere. During a span of eight to 10 years the LTTE had reportedly created a rudimentary air force of five aircraft, allegedly manufactured in the Czech Republic, along with attendant infrastructure. The LTTE air force was said to be capable of bombing selected targets, but no more than that. Some observers viewed its creation as an act of desperation rather than an actual escalation of the war, while for others it represented a worrying new dimension in the conflict.

The bravado of the LTTE bombing targets close to Colombo, however, could not undermine the Sri Lankan army's successful campaign in the eastern province. One result of the undeclared war was the creation of a refugee situation estimated at between 200,000 and 400,000 people—the majority being Muslims, in addition to Tamils and some Sinhalese. Resettlement and reconstruction efforts commenced, but their immediate impact on the refugee problem in the eastern province was expected to be limited.

## DEVOLUTION PACKAGE

The proposals for a devolution package submitted by the SLFP in May 2007 envisaged the district as the core unit of the devolution exercise, and not the province, as had been the practice since 1987. According to the SLFP's proposals, the district would be the widest extent of power-sharing. When the SLFP recommendations were severely criticized, the party's response was that the proposals represented a basis for future discussions and not a final package. The SLFP stated that a final version of the devolution package would be drawn up, incorporating any necessary amendments in response to the criticisms and objections. However, the proposals were rejected by the majority of the other parties, including the UNP. Nor was the SLFP's insistence on the retention of a unitary state acceptable to the majority, all of whom preferred the drawing up of some form of federal constitution. The SLFP proposals made provision for the amalgamation of contiguous regions (this clause had been incorporated into the package prior to the Supreme Court's rejection of the amalgamation of the northern and eastern provinces); even so, the re-amalgamation of the two provinces was difficult to envisage given the need for a favourable majority in each province. There was no probability of such a majority in the eastern province, in light of the strong opposition of the Muslims and Sinhalese to such a merger. Nevertheless the clause for possible amalgamation was expected to prove useful for the purposes of compromise regarding the constitutional proposals.

## SIGNIFICANT DEVELOPMENTS

The early months of 2008 witnessed two major developments: first, there was the Government's abrogation of the CFA and second, there was the election of members to the eastern provincial council.

By the early part of 2008 the LTTE had lost control of the eastern region, and was reduced to controlling only parts of the northern province, in particular, the district of Mullaitivu. In January the Government had revoked the CFA and embarked on a policy of war against the LTTE. The army won several encounters with the LTTE and Commander Lt-Gen. Sarath Fonseka made the claim that the LTTE had lost the capability of fighting as a conventional army. The LTTE's forces went on to conduct a sharp defensive campaign against the army and continued with guerrilla warfare, resorting to terrorist strikes in many parts of the country.

More significantly, the LTTE lost much of its foreign support. In addition to the EU's ban on its fund-raising operations, it was included on the list of terrorist organizations compiled by the US Federal Bureau of Investigation, and in Canada—which is the home of a large Tamil diaspora—the World Tamil Movement, allegedly an LTTE front organization, was banned. The LTTE was increasingly dependent on its home base for financial assistance, but that support was perhaps adequate to ensure its survival.

At mid-2008 the peace process was at a virtual standstill, with the Government insisting that the LTTE must disarm before peace talks could be renewed and the LTTE showing no signs of accepting that position. The LTTE demonstrated its staying power both by fierce resistance of the army advances in the northern province, and by terrorist attacks in various parts of the country in which the victims were more often the civil population travelling in buses and trains than the police and the security forces. The LTTE made effective use of its supporters among Tamils resident in the suburbs of Colombo and elsewhere for this purpose. In early April the Minister of Highways and Road Development, Jeyaraj Fernandopulle, (together with at least 14 other people) was killed in a suspected LTTE suicide bombing carried out near Colombo. The police and the security forces were unable to trace the LTTE operatives engaging in terrorist strikes. Thus, the weakened LTTE remained a potent force unwilling to disarm to resume peace talks or to surrender.

The creation of a provincial council for the eastern province was crucially important for the separation of the northern and eastern provinces. The election itself, held in May 2008, was won by the SLFP-led coalition, which included the Karuna faction—Tamileela Makkal Viduthalai Pulikal, or TMVP—led by Sivanesathurai Chandrakanthan, better known by his adopted name of Pillayan. The TMVP contested as an armed militia and at least some of the electoral abuses that figured so largely in the ballot stemmed from its activities. After some discussion Pillayan was appointed Chief Minister of the eastern provincial council. Pillayan's elevation was evidence of the relative decline of the LTTE, which always claimed to be the sole representative of the Tamil minority.

Politically, the weakened UNP remained the Government's main opponent in the country and in Parliament. In December 2007 the SLMC withdrew its support for the governing coalition, but this was offset by divisions in the ranks of the UNP and, more so, the partition of the JVP into two factions, one of which was inclined to support the Government, while the main group continued on a dual policy of opposing the Government, especially by organizing trade union action, and yet remaining supportive of the Government within the legislature. The result was that the Government could survive within the legislature by manipulating legislators to present a majority vote on crucial issues. This appeared to be a viable political policy over the remainder of Rajapakse's tenure as President. The next presidential election was due in 2010 and the President was unlikely to test the possibility of a legislative election at a time when there was widespread labour unrest and discontent within the general population about the increases in the price of food. Unemployment remained another problem. It was better, therefore, for the Government to persist with a wafer-thin majority than to risk everything at a legislative election. As a substitute for an election, the Government resorted to elections for some of the provincial councils—in particular the councils for Sabaragamuwa and north central provinces—in both of which the Government had lost its majority. In late August 2008 the Government regained control of the two provinces, winning 25 of the 44 seats in the Sabaragamuwa provincial council and 20 of the 33 seats in the north central council. President Rajapakse considered his party's victory to be an endorsement by voters of the Government's military policy against the LTTE.

In the meantime, the Government hosted the 15th South Asian Association for Regional Co-operation (SAARC) conference. In its efforts to provide security for the visiting delegates, the Government did not hesitate to demolish houses and shops in Colombo and its suburbs, wherever these were regarded as security risks. President Rajapakse regarded the chairmanship of SAARC as a political bonus, even if the costs of the meeting and leadership of SAARC placed additional demands on an economically challenged Government.

Externally there was pressure from India for a revival of the peace process with the LTTE, while the EU in particular expressed concern about the Government's perceived infringements of human rights, about which it was also criticized by non-governmental organizations operating in the country. The opposition parties were less vocal on the issue of human rights than with regard to attacks on journalists, especially on those who were critical of the Government's conduct of the war against the LTTE. In particular these criticisms were directed against exaggerated claims made by the Government on victories in battles against the LTTE. The judiciary and, in particular, the higher judiciary, played a key role in defending human rights and free speech, subjecting government decisions that appeared to contravene them to severe criticism, and often reversing them, despite the consequent embarrassment caused to the Government.

# Economy

S. W. R. DE A. SAMARASINGHE

With a population of 20.2m. at mid-2008, Sri Lanka has been hailed as a model of social welfare for a relatively poor country with a per caput income of US $1,600 (Rs 256,000). It has a literacy rate of 93% and a life expectancy of 72 years for males and 77 years for females. However, it is also viewed as a developing country that has squandered its very considerable economic development potential on account of a bloody internal war that has continued for over 25 years. In the past few years annual economic growth has averaged about 6%, but a considerable proportion of this is related to war spending that does not help long-term sustainable development. The economy displays many of the features that are associated with one that is struggling to break out of its low-income and low-productivity model against the heavy restraints imposed by war.

At least one-quarter of the population live below the poverty line. In a labour force of about 7.5m., one-third of those who are gainfully employed are engaged in agriculture, one-fourth in industry and the remainder, 40%, in services. The relative economic importance of the three leading primary products (tea, rubber and coconut) has sharply declined over the last two decades. In 2007 the three products together accounted for only 2.7% of gross domestic product (GDP) and for about 16% of total visible export earnings. Industrial exports, which constituted a mere 13% of total visible exports in 1980, had climbed to 77% by 2007. Of this 56% came from garments and textiles. The country's manufacturing industry has contributed, on average, about 16% per year to GDP over the past two decades or so. The inability of the economy to raise the share of manufactures above this level, despite relative success in industrial exports, has been one of the more disappointing features of recent economic performance. Against a backdrop of an increase in the population from 7.5m. to more than 20.2m. between independence in 1948 and 2008, maintaining a high economic growth rate to create productive job opportunities with adequate pay for a rapidly increasing labour force and the alleviation of poverty have become two of the most pressing socio-economic priorities.

Sri Lanka's economic development has been impaired by two major events: the 2004 Asian tsunami disaster—after which the international community provided relief and reconstruction assistance—and the resumption of serious military confrontations between the Government and the Liberation Tigers of Tamil Eelam (LTTE) in July 2006, followed by the collapse of the 2002 cease-fire agreement in January 2008, which has jeopardized a large proportion of the US $4,500m. in aid that the country was promised in 2003. Recently the USA removed Sri Lanka from eligibility for Millennium Challenge Corporation assistance that would have brought in several hundred million dollars in aid.

Using gross national income (GNI) per head as the criterion, the World Bank classified Sri Lanka, with a figure of US $1,310 in 2006, as 144th among 209 large and small nations; this means that it is among the poorest one-third of nations. If Sri Lanka's national output is measured in US dollars on an internationally comparable purchasing-power parity (PPP) basis, GNI per caput in 2006 was about $3,730. The ranking remained virtually unchanged at 143. GNI, however, may not be an adequate measure of the country's development. The Human Development Index (HDI) for 2005, calculated by the UN Development Programme (UNDP), using life expectancy at birth, adult literacy and school gross enrolment at primary, secondary and tertiary levels, and GDP per caput on a PPP basis as indices, ranked Sri Lanka 99th on a list of 177 countries. Between 1975 and 2005 Sri Lanka's HDI value rose by about 20%, from 0.619 to 0.743. During that 30-year period the country's per caput income had almost trebled from about $320 to $1,241. In the 1970s and 1980s Sri Lanka enjoyed an HDI value rank far above the level normally associated with its modest per caput income level. Sri Lanka was consistently placed in the top 50% of countries in the ranking. However, recently two changes have occurred: first, the country's HDI ranking is no longer exceptionally high relative to its income level; second, it has slipped down in its HDI ranking. In 1990 it was ranked 76th among 169 countries, placing it in the top 50%, whereas the 2005 rank of 99th placed it in the bottom 50%.

In 1977 Sri Lanka was one of the first developing countries to adopt a programme of economic liberalization-cum-structural adjustment, abandoning a two-decade-old *dirigiste* economic policy. The international donor community, led by the World Bank and the IMF, supported the new policy with substantial aid. The reform programme adopted then included the liberalization of imports, reductions in exchange controls, price controls and rationing, the abolition of the state's monopoly in the import of certain key goods, the establishment of a unified (and pegged floating) exchange rate, the transfer to private sector ownership of selected state enterprises, and the lowering of corporate and personal taxes. Despite political difficulties such as the ethnic war, these reforms have been sustained over three decades and further strengthened in the last 10 years with an accelerated programme of privatization, reform of the public service and further liberalization of current and capital account transactions in the balance of payments. What is even more remarkable is that there is now bipartisan support for a market economy, although the left-of-centre Mahinda Rajapakse administration in power since November 2005 is more nationalistic in its economic philosophy. In 2006 the Government abandoned the reform of several key public enterprises, most notably the Ceylon Electricity Board, which was incurring substantial losses. Ideologically the Government's preference is to secure a greater role for the State in the economy, particularly with regard to the regulation of prices and the subsidization of goods and services, policies that remain popular with the electorate. For example, in early 2008 rapid increases in the price of rice prompted the Government to impose a ceiling on the retail price. However, fiscal constraints limit the Government's capacity to implement further such policies. Moreover, the country's heavy dependence on a narrow range of exports, tourism, remittances from Sri Lankans working abroad, donor assistance and foreign direct investment, ensures that Sri Lanka's economic survival relies on an economic strategy that is not too distant from the forces of globalization.

## GROSS DOMESTIC PRODUCT

According to the Central Bank of Sri Lanka, GDP for 2007, at current factor cost, totalled Rs 3,578,000m. (US $32,000m.). The composition of real GDP has undergone a considerable change following the introduction of economic liberalization in 1977, with the share of value added by agriculture declining from 34.6% of GDP in 1975–77 to 11.5% in 2006–07. The contribution of mining and quarrying has remained virtually unchanged, at just below 2% of GDP, throughout this period. The contribution of construction increased from 3.7% to 7.4%, that of financial services, business services and real estate from 1.4% to 9.1%, that of transport, storage and communications from 8.0% to 11.8%, and that of trade from 18.9% to 22.2%. In the past 20 years there has been modest structural change in the economy in favour of manufacturing. The share of manufacturing in GDP was about 11.7% in the late 1980s; in 2006–07 this figure was 18.8%. The share of public administration and defence increased significantly, from 3.3% in 1975–77 to 9.1% in 2006–07. This was partly due to the expansion of the military during that period. Overall what these numbers portray is an economy that has structurally shifted away from agriculture and towards a variety of services and, to a lesser extent, manufacturing. Over the 10-year period 1996–2006 the share of the employed labour force in services fluctuated between 40% and 45%. Among the services, tourism and information technology stand out as activities with substantial future potential.

In the seven-year period 1970–77, when the economy was relatively closed and highly regulated by the State, the annual real GDP growth rate averaged 2.9%. Economic liberalization after 1977 raised the average rate to more than 4.5%. However, it varied widely from year to year, depending mainly on internal political stability and, to a lesser extent, on global economic conditions. Thus, between 1978 and 1984 the average annual growth rate was a robust 6.1%. In the second half of the 1980s the growth rate decreased to about 3.0%, owing to a decline in investment caused largely by political instability and war. In the 1990s it averaged around 5% per year. During the past seven years the growth rate has varied from a negative 1.5% in 2001 to a high of 7.7% in 2006. As long as the war continues, creating political uncertainty that adversely affects the investment climate and key industries such as tourism, the growth rate remains prone to fluctuations.

## AGRICULTURE

The Sri Lankan economy is dominated by agriculture, especially as an avenue of employment. In early 2008, of a 7.6m.-strong labour force (excluding the northern and eastern provinces), about 2.3m. (32%) were employed in that sector. Sri Lanka's agriculture consists of export-orientated commercial crops and part-subsistence and part-market food crops. The agricultural labour force divides itself roughly equally between the two sectors. The commercial crops are cultivated both in large plantations with hired labour as well as in owner-operated smallholdings. About 1.7m. ha (26%) of the nation's total land area is under cultivation. Of this amount, about 735,000 ha (43% of cultivated land) are under tea, rubber, and coconut, the three principal export crops, and the remainder under food crops (chiefly rice). Smallholders produce the bulk of the coconut crop, 60% of the tea output and a significant proportion of the rubber. Rice and other food crops are almost entirely in the hands of small farmers. Over the past three decades the small-scale farming sector growing food crops has become increasingly commercialized.

### Export Crops

All three principal export crops are grown largely in the south-west quadrant (wet zone) of the island, which receives a well-distributed and reliable rainfall of over 1,900 mm per year. Tea is grown in elevations ranging from a few hundred metres above sea-level to above 2,000 m; teas with the best flavours are usually found at elevations above 1,200 m. Rubber is grown mostly on slopes lying lower than 600 m above sea-level, and coconut is concentrated on the western and southern lowlands. In addition to these three staples, Sri Lanka also cultivates a number of minor export crops such as cocoa, pepper, cloves, nutmeg, cardamom, cinnamon and citronella. In 2007 about 222,000 ha were cultivated with tea and 120,000 ha with rubber. Around 395,000 ha were under coconut. The minor export crops together accounted for a further 76,000 ha in 2007.

In 1972 and 1975, under the land reform, a large proportion of the estates owned by foreign and local private individuals and all estates owned by public companies were nationalized with compensation. The Government became the owner of about 60% of the tea land, 30% of the rubber, and 10% of the coconut. However, the state-owned companies that managed the plantations faced chronic losses in their operations. Thus, in 1992 the Government handed over the management of state-owned plantations to private companies for a five-year period. In 1995 a programme was initiated to extend these leases for a further 50 years, with the companies purchasing 51% of the shares. This, in effect, reversed the 1972 Land Reform Act and moved the plantations back into private ownership. Only a few thousand hectares of marginal tea and rubber remain under public management at present.

There is also continuing fragmentation of some of the larger estates into smaller units, caused partly by the pressure of population on land, partly by the division of large estates into smaller units when selling, and partly by a government policy of land redistribution. As a result, more than 65% of the tea crop is now produced by smallholders who cultivate units smaller than eight ha. In the case of rubber, smallholders account for about one-third of the total output.

State-aided schemes have been in operation since the 1950s to replant tea and rubber land with high-yielding varieties. This effort has been very successful in rubber, where, by the end of 1989, the total area had been replanted. In 1990 the programme completed its first 20-year cycle and entered the second. By contrast, in tea, where the tea bush has a much longer useful lifespan, about 36% of the area had been replanted by the end of 2007. Under a state-sponsored crop diversification programme, an effort is also being made to put uneconomical tea and rubber lands to more profitable agricultural uses. In the case of coconut, some of the land in the more urban areas (especially in the western province) is being lost to urban construction. The Government is considering legislation to restrict the conversion of coconut land for property development. This would not guarantee an increase in coconut production, but would almost certainly lead to a slowdown in the construction industry and a rise in urban property prices and rents.

### Food Crops

According to the 2001 census, only an estimated 15% of Sri Lanka's population lived in urban areas and about 85% lived in rural areas (including tea and rubber plantations). The former figure is probably a substantial underestimate, considering that the urban population at the 1981 census was an estimated 21.5%. The decline in the intervening period was caused by a change in classification of a large number of 'town council' areas, from urban in 1981 to rural in 2001. If this adjustment and actual urban growth during 1981–2002 were taken into account, a well-informed estimate of the urban population would be about 30%–35%. That would still render Sri Lanka a predominantly rural country, where agriculture plays an important role in the economy.

Paddy rice, which is the staple food in Sri Lanka, is the preeminent crop in peasant agriculture, having about 700,000 ha—a little more than 40% of all cultivated land—under asweddumized conditions, spread throughout the island. However, when adequate irrigation is available, the dry zone (i.e. the drier parts of the country outside the southwest quadrant) is considered to be better suited to paddy.

Only about 25% of Sri Lanka's paddy land consists of units of two ha or more. About one-third consists of units of one ha or less. The small size of the typical paddy unit reflects the severe pressure on existing land. The settlement of farming families on undeveloped state-owned land in the dry zone (land colonization) has been the Government's answer to this problem. This programme, which began in the late 1920s, received a major boost under the massive Accelerated Mahaweli Diversion Programme (AMDP) that commenced in 1978 and lasted 20 years. The programme brought about 90,000 ha of new land under paddy cultivation with the help of new irrigation facilities. In addition, a further 84,000 ha of land already under cultivation was provided with additional water from the AMDP. The programme has been the single largest development project ever undertaken in Sri Lanka. Apart from the utility the scheme has provided to the agricultural sector, two other main benefits of the AMDP have been hydroelectric power (HEP) generation and flood control. The total investment in the project has exceeded US $1,500m.

In a few districts, especially in the east and south-east of the island, that have reliable irrigation and enjoy relatively high rice yields small cultivators informally lease their state-allocated land to commercial farmers who cultivate on a larger scale. In contrast, in the rain-fed south-west, which is more urbanized and where non-agricultural employment is readily available, rice cultivation is declining and land is being converted to alternative uses.

Since the early 1950s, paddy cultivation has shown one of the most impressive growth records in the Sri Lankan economy. The annual output of paddy rice increased more than six-fold, from about 450,000 metric tons in the early 1950s to a record 3.34m. tons in 2006. This was the result of both an expansion in the area under cultivation and a rise in land productivity under the impact of the 'Green Revolution'. This has drastically reduced rice imports in the last 10 years, and has given the country greater food security. However, critics point out that it is misleading to assert, as the Government does, that the country has achieved 'self-sufficiency' in rice. They note that wheat accounts for about one-third of cereal consumption and that annual wheat consumption per caput rose by around 50%, from about 30 kg in the late 1980s to about 40 kg in the mid-2000s. Moreover, Sri Lanka is a high-cost producer of rice and is unable to sell the surplus, if any, abroad without incurring a loss.

## MINERAL AND POWER RESOURCES

No comprehensive assessment has been made of Sri Lanka's mineral resources. However, the country has a variety of economically useful minerals such as gemstones, graphite, ilmenite, limestone, quartz, mica, industrial clays, salt, titanium, monazite and zircon. There are no known deposits of coal. The Government has invited petroleum companies to explore for offshore oil.

A few local industries, such as ceramics, cement, glass, salt and bricks, are based on extraction of minerals. Graphite, gemstones and ilmenite are the only three minerals that are extracted in commercially significant quantities for export. In 2007 Sri Lanka exported graphite valued at Rs 420m. (0.5% of the total value of visible exports). Sri Lanka is one of the world's leading suppliers of gemstones. Although no production figures are available, the value of exports of precious and semi-precious stones totalled US $94m. in 2007. Jewellery exports earned an additional $20m. The USA, Europe, Japan and Thailand provide the principal markets for Sri Lankan gems. Sri Lanka is also developing a diamond-cutting and polishing industry. The value of the re-export of diamonds reached $349m. in 2007.

In 2005 Sri Lanka's total commercial energy consumption per head, in terms of kg of petroleum equivalent, was 477 kg. This was equivalent to only about 9% of average consumption in high-income countries. An estimated 47% of energy requirements in the country are met by 'non-commercial' biomass sources, such as fuel wood and agricultural residues. Petroleum, which is the principal source of commercial energy, accounts for about 47% of total energy consumption and hydroelectricity accounts for around 8%. At the end of 2007 Sri Lanka's installed capacity for electricity generation was 2,443 MW (1,323 MW HEP, 1,115 MW thermal power and 3 MW wind power). The AMDP has made a major contribution to the country's HEP capacity; close to one-half of total electricity generated comes from AMDP sources. Private investors in the electricity generation industry accounted for about 27.5% of available capacity and around one-third of the electricity generated. A major concern is the high cost of energy in the country; the average cost of electricity per kWh in Sri Lanka in 2002 was 7.5 US cents, which was one of the highest rates in South Asia. On the positive side, in 2005, when measured on a PPP basis, Sri Lanka produced about US $8 of GDP per unit of energy used compared to an average of $3.60 in the lower middle-income group of countries as a whole.

## MANUFACTURING INDUSTRY

At independence in 1948, Sri Lanka, like most other countries that had been under colonial rule, had a very small manufacturing sector in the economy: manufacturing contributed only about 5% of the national output. Also like most other newly independent countries, Sri Lanka entertained hopes of rapidly developing its manufacturing base. The strategy was to encourage import-substitution industries in a protected market, mostly under state investment and ownership. In the 1960s, under an umbrella of high tariffs and quantitative import restrictions, manufacturing output grew by some 6% per year and by the end of the decade contributed about 10% of GDP. In 1977 some of the protective barriers were dismantled and manufacturing was re-orientated towards export markets. Many of the high-cost manufacturers who almost entirely depended on the domestic market did not survive the policy change, but some industries thrived under the more liberal trade regime. Most notably, the apparel industry, with the assistance of the export quotas that Sri Lanka enjoyed under the Multi Fibre Arrangement (MFA), expanded rapidly. By the late 1980s the proportion of GDP that manufactures accounted for had risen to about 16%, and it has remained around that level through the 1990s and into the 21st century.

The output of producer goods is less important than the production of consumer goods in Sri Lanka's manufacturing industry. Until the end of the 1980s almost all the large-scale manufacturing units were run by state industrial corporations, of which there were 26 at the end of 1989. In 1990 the situation began to change following the launching of an ambitious privatization programme. Between 1990 and 2002 35 state-owned industrial enterprises and two state-owned graphite mines were privatized. The Government has found it difficult to find buyers at the prices it expects for the remaining 10 industrial ventures that it wishes to privatize. The present administration under President Mahinda Rajapakse has decided to halt privatization and restructure the enterprises that remain under state control. However, political and other constraints have become obstacles to the restructuring effort.

The 1960s and 1970s can be characterized as the first phase of Sri Lanka's industrialization, which was driven by an import substitution strategy dominated by the state sector. In the 1980s and 1990s the country entered a second phase, with the private sector playing an increasingly dominant role, aided by the liberal economic policies of the Government and the programme of privatization. Traditionally, the private sector covered a wide range of light consumer goods industries and a small number of producer goods industries, such as machine tools and building materials. Now, having taken over state-owned factories, it is also involved in industries such as steel, fertilizers, tyres, gas, hardware and cement.

The Board of Investment of Sri Lanka (BOISL), which was established in 1978 under the name of the Greater Colombo Economic Commission, acts as a 'one stop' centre for approval of industries throughout the country. Its task is to promote investment, especially foreign private investment, in export-orientated industry in Investment Promotion Zones (IPZs), IT Techno Parks and elsewhere. The BOISL has statutory powers to grant a wide range of concessions to investors, including tax 'holidays' of seven–10 years. Foreign investors are encouraged to invest under 'Build, Operate and Own' (BOO) or 'Build, Operate and Transfer' (BOT) arrangements. By the end of 2007 2,598 firms, with 451,934 employees, were involved in commercial production under BOISL sponsorship. The Government is also providing special incentives to private investors to start industries outside the Colombo metropolitan area, where most of the country's manufacturing activity currently takes place.

## FOREIGN TRADE AND BALANCE OF PAYMENTS

In 2007 the USA was the largest purchaser of Sri Lanka's exports, accounting for about 25.5% of the total value, followed by the United Kingdom (13.2%), India (6.7%), Germany (5.7%) and Belgium and Luxembourg (5.2%). Traditionally, exports to India and other South Asian countries have been limited. However, in recent years, partly aided by a free-trade agreement, the volume and value of exports to this region, especially to India, have risen. During the 1990s imports from India to Sri Lanka rose steadily. In 2007 India contributed 23.1% of Sri Lanka's total imports. The market share of some of Sri Lanka's traditional suppliers, such as Japan (3.7%) and the United Kingdom (2.0%), has declined in recent years. In contrast, the newly industrializing South-East and East Asian countries, notably Singapore (9.9%), Hong Kong (6.4%), and the People's Republic of China (8.2%), have become important suppliers of goods to Sri Lanka. The USA supplied only 3.6% of Sri Lanka's imports in 2007, thus creating a substantial trade balance in favour of the latter. This large trade gap has been one of the barriers that has prevented much progress being made on a Sri Lanka–USA free trade agreement, which Sri Lanka is anxious to reach.

### Balance of Payments

Sri Lanka has suffered from a chronic deficit in the balance of trade and of payments since the late 1950s. The combined impact of import liberalization coupled with increased economic activity, periodic adverse movements in the terms of trade, and either stagnant or fluctuating output in the three major commodity exports worsened this situation after 1977.

Textiles and clothing exports account for about one-half of gross merchandise export earnings. In 2007 textile and garment exports reached a record US $3,342m., which was almost three times the value in 1996. Total merchandise exports in 2007 stood at $7,740m. and total imports at $11,301m. The resultant trade deficit of $3,561m. was equivalent to 10.8% of GDP. In the preceding decade the trade deficit had never fallen below 6.9% of GDP. A figure above 10% is normally considered to be unsustainable. In 2007 the services account recorded a surplus of $239m. Receipts from services amounted to $1,711m., with travel contributing $750m. Interest payments on the foreign debt, which has been growing in recent years, totalled $193m. in 2007.

The goods and services account produced a deficit of US $3,321m. in 2007. Substantial net private transfers, totalling $2,598m., with about 55% of this figure coming from remittances sent by more than 300,000 Sri Lankan workers in West Asia, helped to meet part of this deficit. The overall deficit on the current account balance in 2007 was $1,369m., a figure some 9% smaller than in the previous year.

Since 1977 Sri Lanka has received substantial sums in foreign aid, mainly from Western sources. In 2007 the Government received US $276m. as grants. In addition the Government borrowed $1,051m. from foreign sources for budgetary financing. Of this amount, $270m. came from commercial sources.

Since 1977 Sri Lanka has focused upon foreign direct investment (FDI) as a major resource for development. As part of this strategy the Colombo stock market was liberalized and opened to foreign investors. After an initial bout of success in the early 1980s in attracting investors, the strategy faltered, largely because of the civil war and political instability. Total net FDI was $451m. in 2006 and $548m. in 2007. This 2006 amount was about 2% of the total FDI that entered South Asia and 0.03% of global FDI of $1,352,000m. Net portfolio investment in 2007 was only $101m.

At the end of 2007 the country's external reserves stood at US $4,956m., an amount which would have financed about five months of imports of goods and services. By normal international standards this was a fairly comfortable financial position to be in. Since 2001 the Central Bank of Sri Lanka has decided to allow the Sri Lankan rupee to float independently to determine the rupee exchange rate. During 2006 the Sri Lankan rupee depreciated by 5.2% against the US dollar, by 15% against the euro and by 7% against the Indian rupee. In 2007 the value of the Sri Lankan rupee dropped by about 1% against the US dollar, and by about 12% against the other two currencies.

## FINANCE

### Banking and Investment Finance

The Central Bank of Sri Lanka, the sole bank of issue, also acts as a financial adviser to the Government and administers monetary policy. Over the last five decades it has played an increasingly important role in helping to develop credit facilities for special groups such as peasant farmers, small businesses and the self-employed, who normally do not enjoy access to established lending institutions. It has also created special credit schemes for industrialists and exporters.

In 2007 the number of commercial banks operating in Sri Lanka remained unchanged at 23; 11 of these were local and 12 were branches of foreign banks. At the end of 2007 foreign banks had a total of 42 bank offices, with few, if any, outside Colombo. In contrast, domestic banks had a branch network of 1,253 main offices and 493 minor outlets. The system is dominated by the two state-owned banks, the Bank of Ceylon and the People's Bank, which together accounted for the vast majority of the branch offices and for more than 60% of total bank deposits. By the end of 2007 there was a commercial bank office for every 11,250 of Sri Lanka's inhabitants. Until 1984 the trend was for the bank branch network to increase rapidly. In the second half of the 1980s banks, and the two state-owned banks in particular, slowed down the expansion of the branch office network, partly in order to rationalize and consolidate existing operations. In the 1990s expansion resumed, but at a more measured pace; between 2000 and 2007 the number of branch offices, including minor outlets, increased by 698 (64%).

Over the past two decades or so Sri Lanka's financial system has undergone considerable change. Private banks and allied institutions play a larger role than ever in the provision of credit and collection of private savings. For example, private finance companies that play a key role in the financing of consumer durables and transportation equipment are a significant presence in the market. The Government and the Central Bank have encouraged several innovative steps, including the establishment of an offshore banking facility, merchant banking, unit trusts, leasing companies, primary dealers, and venture capital suppliers. The authorities have also encouraged specialized savings and lending institutions, including six Regional Development Banks, a Housing Finance Institution and a National Savings Bank. In addition, the Government created a National Development Trust Fund (later renamed Lanka Putra Bank) as an apex institution to disburse micro finance. The state-owned Employees Provident Fund (EPF) and the Employees Trust Fund (ETF) have been permitted to invest in the share market. The Central Bank has also made a bid to develop a secondary market for government bills and bonds. In addition, the Colombo stock market has been liberalized, permitting foreign investors to invest. At the same time, the regulatory framework governing market activity has been strengthened.

### Public Finance

In 2007 total central government expenditure (including net lending) amounted to an estimated Rs 841,000m., and total revenue to Rs 565,000m. (23.5% and 15.8% of GDP, respectively). The budget deficit of Rs 277,000m. amounted to 7.7% of GDP. About 42% of this deficit was financed with foreign loans, 11% with foreign grants, and 47% with local loans.

The principal sources of government tax revenue in Sri Lanka in 2007 were sales and excise taxes (31%), value-added taxes (37%), and import duties (11%). Corporate taxes and personal income taxes in Sri Lanka have a narrow base and yielded only 21% of total tax revenue. Although national income rose faster after 1977 than in any previous period, the growth of tax revenue has not increased commensurately.

## ECONOMIC DEVELOPMENT

### Performance

In the modern world a nation's development success is judged by its ability to improve the material living standards of its citizens on a sustained basis, with equity, in an atmosphere of freedom and within an environment-friendly context. Judged by such exacting and comprehensive standards Sri Lanka's achievements, at best, are quite mixed.

On the positive side, state-funded education and health have been part of a bipartisan policy of Sri Lankan governments throughout the period of 1948–2008. This policy, which was inherited from the British administration, has produced some very positive human development figures during this period. Infant mortality has steadily declined from 82 per 1,000 live births to 12; life expectancy at birth has steadily increased from about 55 years to 73 years; and adult illiteracy has fallen from about 35% to around 7%. In international comparative terms these are commendable achievements for a country that in 1950 had a per caput GDP of US $106 and in 2007 $1,617. Comparisons with countries such as Malaysia and Thailand, however, show that Sri Lanka has not fared that well with respect to economic growth, and has almost certainly failed to realize its full potential.

In broad terms, the period between 1948 and 1977 was one of missed economic opportunities compounded by generally poor economic policy. The country failed to diversify its economy by utilizing the substantial foreign exchange reserves that it had accumulated during the Second World War (1939–45). It also neglected to exploit the steady and rapid post-war growth of world markets and world trade. Instead, Sri Lanka continued to rely heavily on its three traditional export crops and attempted to build an industrial sector that largely catered to a small domestic market protected by high tariffs and quantitative import restrictions. The 'socialist' economic ideology that guided this programme between 1956 and 1977 demanded extensive nationalization and state control. It stifled entrepreneurship, discouraged foreign investment, and created a set of mainly inefficient and loss-making state enterprises. Economic growth at best was sluggish and averaged about 3.7% per year. This rate, set off against an average annual population growth rate of about 2.3%, suggests that the growth in per capita income was very modest. Income survey data indicate that the mean income of a household (spending unit) increased at the rate of about one US dollar per year, from US $35 in 1953 to $59 in 1978/79 over a 25-year period. Unemployment data is not available for the 1950s, but the rapid growth of population after 1945 combined with slow economic growth in the 1950s suggest that unemployment would have risen during the decade. In 1963 unemployment was reported to be 16.6% and by 1975 it was 19.7%. The above data taken together support the view that in the first three decades after independence, consumption and material living standards of the average Sri Lankan would not have risen a great deal.

The economy reached a crisis point by the mid-1970s. It could no longer fiscally support the social welfare system that had produced the commendable results in human development as described above. It was this crisis that precipitated a radical change in economic policy in late 1977 from an inward-looking socialist model to an outward-looking liberal market model.

The post-1977 export-orientated and liberal economic strategy has led to a higher level of economic activity and a more diversified and dynamic economy. Between the late 1970s and the mid-1980s total investment expenditure more than doubled in real terms. Rough estimates suggest that, during the same period, about 1.7m. new jobs were created, making a substantial impact on the level of unemployment, which fell from 20% of the labour force to 15%. The agricultural sector registered an annual overall real growth rate of 3% during the period 1978–86, and output of paddy rice alone increased by 55% between 1977 and 1986.

Economic growth decelerated in the second half of the 1980s, partly owing to the uncertain economic climate created by widespread political unrest and the ethnic civil war. Economic growth accelerated after 1990, when political stability was restored in the southern part of the country. For example, manufacturing output doubled in real terms, from Rs 69,000m. in 1990 to Rs 149,000m. in 2000. During the same period industrial exports increased from US $1,031m. to $4,302m.

The economic structure underwent two important structural transformations under the liberal market economy. First, the share of the labour force in agriculture decreased from about 45% in the early 1980s to about 30% in early 2008. Second, in exports, the three primary commodities in 1980—tea, rubber and coconut products—accounted for about 60% of exports and industrial products for about 33%. In 2000 the shares were 17% and 78%, respectively.

These positive results in growth were achieved while sacrificing price stability to some degree. For example, between 1967 and 1977, in the 10 years prior to liberalization, the annual rate of inflation averaged about 6%. Between 1977 and 1990 it averaged about 13% and between 1991 and 2000 about 10%.

In poverty and equity, Sri Lanka's record is mixed. The percentage of the population living below the poverty line is estimated at 25%. This is about the same as India but significantly lower than the other populous South Asian countries, Pakistan, Bangladesh and Nepal. If the percentage of the population living on less than US $2 per day is used to measure poverty, only about 40% of the Sri Lankan population fall into that category. In the other South Asian countries it is 66% or more, with India recording a rate of 80%. State assistance by way of food stamps, poverty-alleviation grants and free health care and education are some of the reasons for the lower poverty rate in Sri Lanka. It is estimated, however, that, despite such programmes, at least one-third, if not more, of children under five years of age suffer from malnutrition.

The distribution of income in the country is only marginally more equitable than that of its South Asian neighbours. Throughout the past 50 years, with the exception of the mid-1970s, the Gini Index (a measurement of the extent to which the distribution of income among individuals or households deviates from an equal distribution) has remained steady at around 0.45. This is a value that in international comparative terms places the country somewhere in the middle, between, at one end, some countries that have relatively high inequity (above 0.55) and those that have relatively low inequity (less than 0.30).

In terms of gender equity, Sri Lanka performs reasonably well in international comparative terms. For example, according to UNDP, in 2004 Sri Lanka was ranked 68th out of 177 countries in its Gender-related Development Index, 25 rankings above its position in the HDI. Unemployment estimates reveal that the female unemployment rate, which stood at around 24% in the mid-1990s, decreased to about 8% in the first quarter of 2008. During the same period the male unemployment rate declined from about 11% to 3.3%. Sri Lanka's total fertility rate has declined, from 3.5 live births per 1,000 women of child-bearing age in 1980 to 1.9 per 1,000 in 2006, one of the lowest rates in the developing world. This is indicative of expanded opportunities for female education and employment as well as changing social attitudes.

The environmental sustainability of Sri Lanka's development effort is becoming an increasingly important theme in public discourse. Between 1980 and 1990 about 300 sq km of land was annually deforested. Encouragingly, this average annual rate of deforestation fell to about 200 sq km during 1990–95. The total forest cover is estimated to have fallen from over 40% in the late 1940s to about 20% in 2007. Soil erosion on slopes in the hill areas of the country has become a significant environmental concern. Industrial pollution, urban solid waste disposal, and damage to the sea coast caused by construction are some of the other key environmental problems confronting the country.

### Problems, Challenges and Prospects

In the past two and a half decades, despite the civil war, Sri Lanka has achieved positive economic growth every year with the exception of 2001: a considerable achievement in economic management. In 2001 the economy contracted by 1.5%. That was an exception attributable to a combination of external and internal forces. Many observers have been intrigued by the fact that, the protracted violent conflict notwithstanding, Sri Lanka has managed to maintain a reasonable growth rate. For example, in the past five years the lowest recorded growth rate was 5.4% (in 2004); in 2003 it was 5.9% and in the other three years it was above 6.0%. This can be partly explained by the fact that the economy in the area of conflict in the north and east is now largely cut off from the rest of the country, with the result that adverse economic conditions in that part of the country have little impact on the rest of the economy. Moreover, defence expenditure actually stimulates economic growth in the south, especially in creating jobs for rural youth. In the short term, the war accrues negative economic effect only when there is a serious security threat in the south that disrupts the more vulnerable industries such as tourism.

However, the long-term impact of the war on the economy is definitely negative. The continuing conflict prevents Sri Lanka from realizing its full economic potential. There are various estimates of the total economic cost of the war over the past 25 years. The specific numbers are debatable, but it is accepted by all that the loss amounted to thousands of millions of US dollars. The economy in the north contracted during the war. Between 1990 and 1995 the annual output of the northern province declined from US $350m. to $250m., resulting in a negative growth rate of 6.2% per year. The decline might have decelerated or ceased after the Government captured the Jaffna peninsula from the LTTE in 1995; however, there was almost certainly no appreciable economic growth in that region.

The war diverted an increasing level of funds in the government budget from development and social welfare to the military. In 1982, just before the conflict intensified, the Government spent US $54m. (3.1% of the budget) on the security forces. In 1990 the amount was $364m. (12.5%), and in 2000 it had risen to $1,018m. (17%). This increase in expenditure on the military was the single main reason for the Government's fiscal difficulties.

In the five-year period 1997–2001 the overall budget deficit as a percentage of GDP never declined below 7.5%. This trend was considered unsustainable and a serious constraint on investment in the private sector, owing to the drain on budgetary resources and its 'crowding out' effect. In 2001 the original budget projected a deficit of 8.5%, but the actual figure was 10.9%. In the latter months of 2001 the Government, entirely motivated by narrow partisan political considerations in the months preceding the general election, aggravated the fiscal problem by instituting some hasty spending measures, such as substantial salary increases for public-sector employees.

The year 2002 brought new hope for the Sri Lankan economy. The 20-year civil war was suspended and a cease-fire agreement was signed between the Government and the LTTE. Probably the most significant part of the peace process was the plan to rehabilitate and reconstruct the areas in the north and east devastated by the war, and, more generally, the programme of work proposed by the Government to revive the moribund economy. Obtaining substantial donor assistance was an indispensable part of this strategy. With these goals in mind, in early 2003 the Government prepared a document entitled 'Regaining Sri Lanka' that described in detail the main elements of development strategy for a post-conflict Sri Lanka. This document formed the basis for discussions with donors who, at a meeting in June in Tokyo, Japan, committed US $4,500m. over a period of four years to Sri Lanka's reconstruction. The donors were to release the money upon the satisfaction of two key conditions. One was that the Government and the LTTE should agree to a political solution to the conflict that would result in a durable peace. The second was that economic reforms should lead to further liberalization of the economy and increase its efficiency. Unfortunately neither of these goals was fully realized. The peace talks between the Government and the LTTE broke down in 2003. In April 2004 the Ranil Wickremasinghe administration that was committed to the cease-fire and to further liberalization of the economy was replaced by a more left-of-centre Government that saw the cease-fire as a betrayal of the interests of the Sinhalese majority population (see below).

The Asian tsunami disaster of December 2004 had particularly profound socio-economic consequences for Sri Lanka. Approximately 31,000 lives were believed to have been lost in the tragedy and, although the huge waves left the commercial areas in the west of the country unaffected, the fisheries and tourism sectors based along the country's coastline sustained extensive damage, resulting in the loss of many livelihoods. In the initial aftermath of the disaster, there were hopes that at least it might serve to bring the LTTE and the Government closer together, owing to the extensive damage that had occurred in Tamil areas of the country. However, rifts soon developed between the two regarding the distribution of aid to affected regions, adversely affecting the reconstruction effort in the north and east of the country.

In 2005 the Government announced that, in addition to the immediate demands of post-tsunami reconstruction, its economic strategy for that year would focus on the improvement of public sector fiscal management, the delivery of public services and the promotion of rural development and small and medium-sized enterprises. In May, at a development forum on tsunami reconstruction, international donors pledged approximately US $3,000m. in reconstruction aid for Sri Lanka, suggesting at the same time that it would be prudent for the Government to focus some attention on the development of the private sector. The momentum generated by reconstruction, together with the emergency financial support offered by international donors, helped to sustain economic expansion over the course of the year and into 2006–07. Concerns that the tourism sector would be significantly affected by the disaster were assuaged by a recovery in the number of tourist arrivals to the country later in 2005, following a significant decline in the first two months of the year. A good performance from the agriculture sector helped to maintain growth momentum in 2006. The level of apparel exports has also been maintained, although Sri Lanka lost its quotas following the end of the MFA in December 2005.

In November 2005 Mahinda Rajapakse, the candidate of the United People Freedom Alliance (UPFA), with the support of the Marxist-nationalist Janatha Vimukthi Peramuna (JVP) and the Buddhist monk party Jathika Hela Urumaya (JHU), won the presidency, narrowly defeating the right-of-centre Ranil Wickremasinghe of the United National Party (UNP). Rajapakse's *Mahinda Chinthana* manifesto promised, among other things, generous subsidies to farmers and consumers, wage increases to government workers, more jobs in the state sector, a more active role for the state in the economy, and a halt to the privatization of state enterprises.

In office Rajapakse appeared to disregard the terms of the cease-fire agreement of February 2002 and embarked on a campaign to defeat the LTTE militarily, culminating in the collapse of the agreement in January 2008. This strategy is quite popular with the constituency that put him in office, especially given that it has enjoyed some success on the battlefield. The Sri Lankan military has more or less cleared the eastern province of the LTTE in a campaign that commenced in December 2006 and lasted until July 2007. Subsequently the army leaders publicly declared that their next step would be to 'clear' the north. The final military and political outcome of this strategy (if successful) is far from certain. However, the economic consequences are becoming clear.

Government defence spending rose from US $900m. (3.8% of GDP) in 2005 to $1,356m. (4.2%) in 2007. In 2008 the defence budget was projected to exceed $1,500m., 40% more than the 2005 figure. The Government is financing the deficit partly through local borrowing, some of it from the banking system. In 2006–08 the Government increasingly resorted to short-term commercial borrowing from abroad. In 2006 such borrowing totalled $475m. and in 2007 the total was $270m.

Some bilateral donors have scaled down assistance to the country, citing their unhappiness about the resumption of hostilities and also about alleged widespread human rights violations on the part of the LTTE, the LTTE breakaway faction known as the 'Karuna' group (which supports the military in the eastern province), as well as sections of the military itself. Germany has suspended assistance to Sri Lanka and the USA has removed it from the list of countries that are eligible to receive grant aid from the Millennium Challenge Account.

Heavy military spending, deficit financing and high petroleum and food prices in the global market have all contributed to inflationary pressure. In 2006 consumer prices increased by 14% and in 2007 by 18%. In 2008 the rate accelerated to over 25% by June–July.

The Government has embarked on some major infrastructure development projects, including a coal-fired power plant and several motorways to improve road transport between a number of major cities. However, some other infrastructure projects, such as a new state-owned low-budget airline that has made massive losses at the expense of the taxpayer and an international airport in the President's constituency, which is in a sparsely populated area of the country, have come under criticism.

The Government has not only failed to contain inflation but it is also finding that it is not able to deliver on some of its key election promises. For example, the generous fertilizer subsidy that candidate Rajapakse promised has been reduced. In the face of escalating petroleum prices he has also not been able to moderate price increases as promised to consumers. The President is under tremendous pressure from the multilateral lending agencies to reform the state-owned electricity monopoly. However, the radical JVP, which played a key role in Rajapakse's election victory, and its trade unions have so far succeeded in preventing him from doing so. This delay has resulted in the lapse of part of a loan that the Asian Development Bank had promised for the reform programme. More generally, essential deregulatory reforms to ease supply bottlenecks have been severely delayed.

The resumption of hostilities between government security forces and the LTTE has cast a shadow over the economy: in 2007 tourist arrivals fell by 11.7% compared with 2006. In the first half of 2008 the industry reported that it is facing a financial crisis. The current climate is certainly not conducive to foreign investment. Random terrorist bomb attacks in Colombo in the past several months have created a climate of fear among the general public and have caused the Government to tighten security. The war has created over 200,000 new internally displaced people in the north and east. However, the Government claims that it has launched a development programme in the eastern region that is now under its control.

Recent monthly surveys that attempt to measure business confidence suggest that the business climate has deteriorated sharply. Rising petroleum prices, spiralling inflation and high interest rates are some of the main causes of the disaffection. Exporters complain that the increasing cost of production and an unfavourable dollar–rupee exchange rate are making their products uncompetitive in the global market. Wage earners are demanding large pay increases to compensate for the rising cost of living. The Government is resisting the demand because it would further enlarge the budget deficit and also contribute to a wage-price spiral. The EU is threatening to withdraw the Generalised System of Preferences Plus (GSP+) tariff that it granted Sri Lanka's exports in 2005, on the grounds that the country is in violation of human rights (EU rules require that GSP+ beneficiary countries maintain a good record of adherence to human rights). In the light of these developments, together with the waning momentum of tsunami reconstruction, the growth of the Sri Lankan economy in 2008 is expected to be below the rate that it achieved in some of the better years in the recent past.

# Statistical Survey

Source (unless otherwise stated): Department of Census and Statistics, 15/12 Maitland Crescent, POB 563, Colombo 7; tel. (11) 2682176; fax (11) 2697594; e-mail dcensus@lanka.ccom.lk; internet www.statistics.gov.lk.

## Area and Population

**AREA, POPULATION AND DENSITY**

| | |
|---|---|
| Area (sq km) | 65,525* |
| Population (census results) | |
| 17 March 1981 | 14,846,750 |
| 17 July 2001 (provisional)† | |
| Males | 8,343,964 |
| Females | 8,520,580 |
| Total | 16,864,544 |
| Population (official estimates at mid-year) | |
| 2005 | 19,668,000 |
| 2006 | 19,886,000 |
| 2007 | 20,010,000 |
| Density (per sq km) at mid-2007 | 305.4 |

* 25,299 sq miles. This figure includes inland water (3,189 sq km).

† Figures refer to 18 out of 25 districts where enumeration was carried out completely. Enumeration was only partially conducted in Mannar, Vavuniya, Batticaloa and Trincomalee districts, owing to security concerns; data from these districts brought the total enumerated population to approximately 17,560,000. The census was not conducted in the districts of Jaffna, Mullaitivu and Kilinochchi, also owing to security concerns. The total estimated population for the entire country at July 2001 was 18,732,255.

**ETHNIC GROUPS**

(census results)

| | 1981 | 2001*† |
|---|---|---|
| Sinhalese | 10,979,561 | 13,810,664 |
| Sri Lankan Tamil | 1,886,872 | 736,484 |
| Indian Tamil | 818,656 | 855,888 |
| Sri Lankan Moors | 1,046,926 | 1,349,845 |
| Others | 114,735 | 111,663 |
| **Total** | 14,846,750 | 16,864,544 |

* Provisional.

† Figures refer to 18 out of 25 districts.

**DISTRICTS**
(population estimates at mid-2006)

| | Area (sq km, excl. inland water)* | Population ('000) | Density (persons per sq km) |
|---|---|---|---|
| Colombo | 676 | 2,421 | 3,581 |
| Gampaha | 1,341 | 2,125 | 1,585 |
| Kalutara | 1,576 | 1,102 | 699 |
| Kandy | 1,917 | 1,361 | 710 |
| Matale | 1,952 | 471 | 241 |
| Nuwara Eliya | 1,706 | 735 | 431 |
| Galle | 1,617 | 1,040 | 643 |
| Matara | 1,270 | 804 | 633 |
| Hambantota | 2,496 | 547 | 219 |
| Jaffna | 929 | 595 | 640 |
| Mannar | 1,880 | 100 | 53 |
| Vavuniya | 1,861 | 164 | 88 |
| Mullaitivu | 2,415 | 145 | 60 |
| Kilinochchi | 1,205 | 142 | 118 |
| Batticaloa | 2,610 | 556 | 213 |
| Ampara | 4,222 | 627 | 149 |
| Trincomalee | 2,529 | 395 | 156 |
| Kurunegala | 4,624 | 1,511 | 327 |
| Puttalam | 2,882 | 745 | 259 |
| Anuradhapura | 6,664 | 791 | 119 |
| Polonnaruwa | 3,077 | 382 | 124 |
| Badulla | 2,827 | 837 | 296 |
| Moneragala | 5,508 | 420 | 76 |
| Ratnapura | 3,236 | 1,073 | 332 |
| Kegalle | 1,685 | 797 | 473 |
| **Total** | 62,705 | 19,886 | 317 |

* As at 1988; revised total land area is 62,336 sq km.

**PRINCIPAL TOWNS**
(provisional, population at 2001 census)

| | | | |
|---|---|---|---|
| Colombo (Kolamba)* | 642,020 | Sri Jayawardenepura (Kotte)† | 115,826 |
| Dehiwala-Mount Lavinia | 209,787 | Kandy (Maha Nuwara) | 110,049 |
| Moratuwa | 177,190 | Kalmunai (Galmune) | 94,457 |
| Jaffna (Yapanaya) | 145,600‡ | Galle (Galla) | 90,934 |
| Negombo (Migamuwa) | 121,933 | | |

* Commercial capital.

† Administrative capital.

‡ Estimated population at mid-1997 (Source: Provincial Councils, Department of Elections).

Source: Thomas Brinkhoff, *City Population* (internet www.citypopulation.de).

**BIRTHS, MARRIAGES AND DEATHS**
(year of registration, provisional)

| | Registered live births | | Registered marriages | Registered deaths | |
|---|---|---|---|---|---|
| | Number | Rate (per 1,000) | Number | Number | Rate (per 1,000) |
| 2000 | 340,144 | 18.4 | 186,548 | 112,569 | 6.1 |
| 2001 | 354,101 | 18.9 | 186,698 | 111,100 | 5.9 |
| 2002 | 363,549 | 19.1 | 190,832 | 110,637 | 5.8 |
| 2003 | 363,343 | 18.9 | 193,387 | 114,310 | 5.9 |
| 2004 | 360,220 | 18.5 | 191,985 | 112,568 | 5.8 |
| 2005 | 370,424 | 18.8 | 194,352 | 129,822 | 6.6 |
| 2006 | 371,264 | 18.7 | 197,458 | 115,424 | 5.8 |
| 2007 | 380,069 | 19.0 | 195,193 | 116,883 | 5.8 |

**Expectation of life** (years at birth, WHO estimates): 72.4 (males 68.7; females 76.3) in 2006 (Source: WHO, *World Health Statistics*).

**ECONOMICALLY ACTIVE POPULATION**
('000 persons aged 10 years and over, excluding northern and eastern provinces)

| | 2004 | 2005 | 2006 |
|---|---|---|---|
| Agriculture, hunting, forestry and fishing | 2,215.3 | 2,059.3 | 2,287.3 |
| Manufacturing | 1,226.0 | 1,292.9 | 1,363.1 |
| Mining and quarrying; Electricity, gas and water; Construction | 349.7 | 417.2 | 526.9 |
| Wholesale and retail trade, repair of motor vehicles, motorcycles and personal household goods | 818.1 | 817.1 | 955.0 |
| Restaurants and hotels | 114.3 | 115.0 | 129.4 |
| Transport, storage and communications | 379.7 | 448.4 | 430.3 |
| Financing, insurance, real estate and business services | 165.9 | 226.1 | 221.1 |
| Public administration and defence | 477.4 | 465.4 | 400.5 |
| Education | 237.1 | 254.4 | 276.8 |
| Health and social work | 92.7 | 120.9 | 109.7 |
| Other community, social and personal services | 109.7 | 113.0 | 123.9 |
| Private households with employed persons | 67.5 | 48.3 | 80.2 |
| Activities not adequately defined | 450.5 | 410.2 | 201.2 |
| **Total employed** | 6,704.0 | 6,788.1 | 7,105.3 |
| Unemployed | 590.3 | 523.7 | 493.4 |
| **Total labour force** | 7,294.3 | 7,311.8 | 7,598.8 |

**2007:** Total employed 7,041.9; Unemployed 447.0; Total labour force 7,488.9.

# Health and Welfare

**KEY INDICATORS**

| | |
|---|---|
| Total fertility rate (children per woman, 2006) | 1.9 |
| Under-5 mortality rate (per 1,000 live births, 2006) | 13 |
| HIV/AIDS (% of persons aged 15–49, 2005) | <0.1 |
| Physicians (per 1,000 head, 2006) | 0.6 |
| Hospital beds (per 1,000 head, 2000) | 2.9 |
| Health expenditure (2005): US $ per head (PPP) | 189 |
| Health expenditure (2005): % of GDP | 4.1 |
| Health expenditure (2005): public (% of total) | 46.2 |
| Access to water (% of persons, 2004) | 79 |
| Access to sanitation (% of persons, 2004) | 91 |
| Human Development Index (2005): ranking | 99 |
| Human Development Index (2005): value | 0.743 |

For sources and definitions, see explanatory note on p. vi.

# Agriculture

**PRINCIPAL CROPS**
('000 metric tons)

| | 2004 | 2005 | 2006 |
|---|---|---|---|
| Rice (paddy) | 2,628 | 3,246 | 3,342 |
| Maize | 35 | 42 | 48 |
| Potatoes | 81 | 79 | 78 |
| Sweet potatoes | 40 | 41 | 42 |
| Cassava (Manioc) | 221 | 223 | 226 |
| Sugar cane | 990 | 992 | 1,137 |
| Dry beans | 8 | 9 | 8 |
| Dry cow-peas | 9 | 11 | 10 |
| Coconuts | 881 | 890 | 913 |
| Copra* | 60 | 67 | 65 |
| Cabbages | 61 | 64 | 59 |
| Tomatoes | 54 | 57 | 61 |
| Pumpkins, squash and gourds | 74 | 87 | 82 |
| Cucumbers and gherkins | 23 | 27 | 25 |
| Aubergines (Eggplants) | 80 | 84 | 88 |
| Chillies and green peppers | 53 | 67 | 67 |
| Dry onions | 77 | 109 | 134 |
| Green beans | 40 | 41 | 41 |

| —*continued* | 2004 | 2005 | 2006 |
|---|---|---|---|
| Carrots | 34 | 37 | 36 |
| Plantains | 540 | 545 | 504 |
| Lemons and limes | 5 | 5 | 5 |
| Guavas, mangoes and mangosteens | 92 | 93 | 85 |
| Pineapples | 58 | 58 | 57 |
| Coffee (green) | 8 | 7 | 7 |
| Tea (made) | 308 | 317 | 311 |
| Pepper | 19 | 18 | 19 |
| Cinnamon | 13 | 13 | 13 |
| Natural rubber | 95 | 104 | 109 |

* Unofficial figures.

**Aggregate production** ('000 metric tons, may include official, semi-official or estimated data): Total cereals 2,668 in 2004, 3,295 in 2005, 3,396 in 2006; Total roots and tubers 342 in 2004, 344 in 2005, 346 in 2006; Total vegetables (incl. melons) 561 in 2004, 640 in 2005, 660 in 2006; Total fruits (excl. melons) 757 in 2004, 768 in 2005, 718 in 2006.

Source: FAO.

**LIVESTOCK**
('000 head, year ending September)

| | 2004 | 2005 | 2006 |
|---|---|---|---|
| Buffaloes | 302 | 308 | 314 |
| Cattle | 1,161 | 1,185 | 1,125 |
| Sheep | 11 | 10 | 14 |
| Goats | 405 | 395 | 382 |
| Pigs | 79 | 85 | 92 |
| Chickens | 11,042 | 11,636 | 13,313 |

Source: FAO.

**LIVESTOCK PRODUCTS**
('000 metric tons)

| | 2004 | 2005 | 2006 |
|---|---|---|---|
| Cattle meat | 28.2 | 29.3 | 26.3 |
| Buffalo meat* | 3.5 | 4.0 | 4.0 |
| Goat meat | 1.4 | 1.5 | 1.5 |
| Pig meat | 2.1 | 2.2 | 2.3 |
| Chicken meat | 94.7 | 97.3 | 78.8 |
| Cows' milk | 134.9 | 136.7 | 139.3 |
| Buffaloes' milk | 25.8 | 26.1 | 26.7 |
| Goats' milk* | 4.9 | 5.1 | 5.1 |
| Hen eggs | 49.6 | 49.0 | 51.1 |

* FAO estimates.

Source: FAO.

## Forestry

**ROUNDWOOD REMOVALS**
('000 cubic metres, excl. bark, FAO estimates)

| | 2003 | 2004 | 2005 |
|---|---|---|---|
| Sawlogs, veneer logs and logs for sleepers | 117 | 117 | 117 |
| Other industrial wood | 577 | 577 | 577 |
| Fuel wood | 5,710 | 5,646 | 5,584 |
| **Total** | 6,404 | 6,340 | 6,278 |

**2006:** Figures assumed unchanged from 2005 (FAO estimates).

Source: FAO.

**SAWNWOOD PRODUCTION**
('000 cubic metres, incl. railway sleepers)

| | 1999* | 2000 | 2001 |
|---|---|---|---|
| Coniferous (softwood) | — | — | 30 |
| Broadleaved (hardwood) | 5 | 29 | 31 |
| **Total** | 5 | 29 | 61 |

* FAO estimates.

**2002–06:** Production assumed to be unchanged from 2001 (FAO estimates).

Source: FAO.

## Fishing

('000 metric tons, live weight)

| | 2004 | 2005 | 2006 |
|---|---|---|---|
| Capture | 309.2 | 167.7 | 230.6 |
| Tilapias | 22.2 | 21.6 | 19.3 |
| Demersal percomorphs | 17.5 | 10.6 | 11.2 |
| Clupeoids | 54.4 | 24.9 | 56.2 |
| Skipjack tuna | 62.3 | 32.5 | 33.8 |
| Carangids | 13.6 | 6.0 | 9.6 |
| Mackerels | 18.4 | 9.7 | 15.6 |
| Sharks, rays, skates etc. | 23.4 | 5.3 | 5.7 |
| Aquaculture | 2.5 | 1.7 | 3.8 |
| **Total catch** | 311.7 | 169.4 | 234.3 |

Source: FAO.

## Mining

('000 metric tons, unless otherwise indicated, estimates)

| | 2004 | 2005 | 2006 |
|---|---|---|---|
| Natural graphite (metric tons) | 3,400 | 3,000 | 3,200 |
| Salt—unrefined | 79 | 80 | 81 |
| Kaolin | 9 | 9 | 10 |
| Phosphate rock (gross weight) | 42 | 43 | 44 |

**Ilmenite concentrates** ('000 metric tons): 34.1 in 1998.

**Zirconium concentrates** ('000 metric tons): 13 in 1999.

Sources: US Geological Survey; UN, *Industrial Commodity Statistics Yearbook*.

## Industry

**SELECTED PRODUCTS**
('000 barrels, unless otherwise indicated)

| | 2004 | 2005 | 2006 |
|---|---|---|---|
| Raw sugar ('000 metric tons) | 21 | 14 | 19 |
| Cigarettes (million units) | 5,003 | n.a. | n.a. |
| Jet fuel* | 650 | 650 | 700 |
| Motor gasoline—petrol* | 2,100 | 2,200 | 2,200 |
| Kerosene* | 1,500 | 1,500 | 1,500 |
| Distillate fuel oil* | 5,100 | 5,200 | 5,300 |
| Residual fuel oil* | 5,100 | 5,100 | 5,000 |
| Cement ('000 metric tons)* | 1,400 | 1,500 | 1,600 |
| Plywood ('000 cu m)† | 14 | 14 | 14 |
| Electric energy (million kWh) | 8,043 | 8,769 | 9,389 |

* Estimates.
† FAO estimates.

**Naptha** ('000 metric tons): 112 in 2002, 99 in 2003, 103 in 2004.

Sources: US Geological Survey; Asian Development Bank, *Key Indicators of Developing Asian and Pacific Countries*; FAO; UN, *Industrial Commodity Statistics Yearbook*.

# Finance

## CURRENCY AND EXCHANGE RATES

**Monetary Units**

100 cents = 1 Sri Lanka rupee (R).

**Sterling, Dollar and Euro Equivalents** (30 May 2008)

£1 sterling = Rs 212.860;
US $1 = Rs 107.859;
€1 = Rs 167.268;
1,000 Sri Lanka rupees = £4.59 = $9.20 = €6.25.

**Average Exchange Rate** (rupees per US $)

| | |
|---|---|
| 2005 | 100.498 |
| 2006 | 103.914 |
| 2007 | 110.626 |

## BUDGET

(Rs million)

| Revenue | 2006 | 2007* | 2008* |
|---|---|---|---|
| Taxation | 424,899 | 541,849 | 653,109 |
| Taxes on income and profits | 47,389 | 55,044 | 141,291 |
| Taxes on domestic goods and services | 263,728 | 323,464 | 390,352 |
| Value-added tax | 164,277 | 201,643 | 251,770 |
| Excise duty (ordinance) | 20,660 | 24,996 | 27,155 |
| Excise duty (special provisions) | 70,523 | 84,350 | 95,185 |
| Stamp duty | 1,495 | 4,200 | 6,251 |
| Taxes on international trade | 80,497 | 100,206 | 115,914 |
| Import duties | 53,006 | 60,432 | 69,551 |
| Licence taxes and other | 2,967 | 4,355 | 5,552 |
| Non-tax revenue | 66,938 | 82,289 | 93,619 |
| Capital revenue | 14,455 | 11,482 | 11,738 |
| Other | 52,483 | 70,807 | 81,881 |
| Foreign grants | 19,911 | 25,750 | 28,750 |
| **Total** | 511,748 | 649,888 | 775,477 |

| Expenditure by category | 2006 | 2007* | 2008* |
|---|---|---|---|
| Recurrent expenditure | 579,040 | 632,836 | 725,440 |
| Personal emoluments | 121,842 | 156,006 | 168,244 |
| Salaries and wages | 81,250 | 108,816 | 113,109 |
| General public services | 18,234 | 25,851 | 40,955 |
| Transfers | 244,040 | 220,386 | 241,133 |
| Retirement benefits | 58,726 | 68,922 | 73,293 |
| Provincial councils | 63,032 | 74,985 | 82,537 |
| Interest payments | 150,778 | 176,843 | 209,845 |
| Other purposes | 44,147 | 53,751 | 65,264 |
| Capital expenditure | 197,012 | 380,346 | 417,577 |
| Public debt repayments | 295,693 | 339,903 | 373,314 |
| Domestic | 246,843 | 268,969 | 287,499 |
| Foreign | 48,851 | 70,935 | 85,814 |
| **Total expenditure** | 1,071,745 | 1,353,085 | 1,516,330 |

| Expenditure by institution | 2006 | 2007* | 2008* |
|---|---|---|---|
| Special spending units | 7,727 | 7,305 | 9,217 |
| Ministries | 1,064,018 | 1,345,780 | 1,507,113 |
| Finance and planning | 533,129 | 587,539 | 675,056 |
| Defence, public security, law and order | 110,230 | 155,704 | 166,447 |
| Nation building and estate infrastructure development | 38,855 | 50,792 | 54,282 |
| Health care and nutrition | 37,482 | 50,993 | 57,800 |
| Public administration and home affairs | 66,845 | 87,209 | 92,000 |
| Local government and provincial councils | 82,936 | 102,932 | 114,770 |
| **Total expenditure** | 1,071,745 | 1,353,085 | 1,516,330 |

* Estimates.

Source: Ministry of Finance and Planning, Colombo.

## INTERNATIONAL RESERVES

(excluding gold, US $ million at 31 December)

| | 2005 | 2006 | 2007 |
|---|---|---|---|
| IMF special drawing rights | 2 | 3 | 7 |
| Reserve position in IMF | 68 | 72 | 76 |
| Foreign exchange | 2,581 | 2,762 | 3,433 |
| **Total** | 2,651 | 2,837 | 3,516 |

Source: IMF, *International Financial Statistics*.

## MONEY SUPPLY

(Rs million at 31 December)

| | 2004 | 2005 | 2006 |
|---|---|---|---|
| Currency outside banks | 99,669 | 114,070 | 135,020 |
| Demand deposits at commercial banks | 88,777 | 116,620 | 124,657 |
| **Total money** (incl. others) | 189,339 | 231,621 | 261,033 |

Source: IMF, *International Financial Statistics*.

## COST OF LIVING

(Consumer Price Index for Colombo; base: 2000 = 100)

| | 2004 | 2005 | 2006 |
|---|---|---|---|
| Food (incl. beverages) | 145.5 | 163.0 | 184.6 |
| Fuel and light | 157.0 | 178.1 | 228.3 |
| Clothing (excl. footwear) | 112.7 | 117.6 | 122.2 |
| Rent | 100.0 | 100.0 | 100.0 |
| **All items** (incl. others) | 143.0 | 159.7 | 181.5 |

**2007:** Food (incl. beverages) 218.2; All items (incl. others) 213.3.

Source: ILO.

## NATIONAL ACCOUNTS

(Rs million at current prices)

**Expenditure on the Gross Domestic Product**

| | 2005 | 2006 | 2007* |
|---|---|---|---|
| Government final consumption expenditure | 321,037 | 451,438 | 546,545 |
| Private final consumption expenditure | 1,692,765 | 1,988,378 | 2,403,167 |
| Increase in stocks | 84,756 | 91,306 | 112,012 |
| Gross fixed capital formation | 573,263 | 730,910 | 884,688 |
| **Total domestic expenditure** | 2,671,821 | 3,262,032 | 3,946,412 |
| Exports of goods and services | 793,153 | 885,381 | 1,046,075 |
| *Less* Imports of goods and services | 1,012,192 | 1,208,757 | 1,414,100 |
| **GDP at market prices** | 2,452,782 | 2,938,656 | 3,578,386 |
| **GDP at factor cost, at constant 2002 prices** | 1,941,671 | 2,090,548 | 2,232,387 |

* Provisional.

**Gross Domestic Product by Economic Activity**

| | 2005 | 2006 | 2007* |
|---|---|---|---|
| Agriculture, hunting, forestry and fishing | 289,906 | 333,114 | 417,353 |
| Mining and quarrying | 35,932 | 46,202 | 56,645 |
| Manufacturing | 478,611 | 564,987 | 661,983 |
| Construction | 167,999 | 216,833 | 264,104 |
| Electricity, gas and water | 57,908 | 72,457 | 87,951 |
| Transport, storage and communications | 287,491 | 344,909 | 423,820 |
| Wholesale and retail trade | 569,255 | 659,597 | 790,628 |
| Hotels and restaurants | 14,218 | 16,646 | 18,367 |
| Finance, real estate and | 205,322 | 266,972 | 328,158 |
| Ownership of dwellings | 88,759 | 103,201 | 126,212 |
| Public administration | 206,497 | 257,837 | 334,261 |
| Private services | 50,886 | 55,902 | 68,905 |
| **GDP at market prices** | 2,452,782 | 2,938,656 | 3,578,386 |

* Provisional.

**BALANCE OF PAYMENTS**
(US $ million)

| | 2004 | 2005 | 2006 |
|---|---|---|---|
| Exports of goods f.o.b. | 5,757 | 6,347 | 6,883 |
| Imports of goods f.o.b. | –7,200 | –7,977 | –9,228 |
| **Trade balance** | –1,443 | –1,630 | –2,345 |
| Exports of services | 1,527 | 1,540 | 1,625 |
| Imports of services | –1,908 | –2,089 | –2,394 |
| **Balance on goods and services** | –1,824 | –2,179 | –3,114 |
| Other income received | 157 | 76 | 312 |
| Other income paid | –360 | –375 | –700 |
| **Balance on goods, services and income** | –2,027 | –2,478 | –3,502 |
| Current transfers received | 1,564 | 1,968 | 2,326 |
| Current transfers paid | –214 | –233 | –258 |
| **Current balance** | –677 | –743 | –1,434 |
| Capital account (net) | 64 | 250 | 291 |
| Direct investment abroad | –6 | –38 | –29 |
| Direct investment from abroad | 233 | 272 | 480 |
| Portfolio investment assets | 111 | 276 | 355 |
| Portfolio investment liabilities | –100 | –216 | –304 |
| Other investment assets | –354 | –223 | 297 |
| Other investment liabilities | –17 | –4 | –111 |
| Net errors and omissions | –189 | –73 | –261 |
| **Overall balance** | –935 | –498 | –717 |

Source: IMF, *International Financial Statistics*.

# External Trade

**PRINCIPAL COMMODITIES**
(Rs million)

| Imports c.i.f. | 2005 | 2006 | 2007* |
|---|---|---|---|
| **Consumer goods** | 165,221 | 206,141 | 221,371 |
| Wheat | 14,200 | 20,679 | 25,891 |
| Durables | 89,611 | 106,607 | 103,627 |
| **Intermediate goods** | 534,804 | 620,131 | 721,473 |
| Petroleum | 166,562 | 215,168 | 276,775 |
| Textiles | 153,957 | 160,987 | 180,689 |
| **Investment goods** | 188,081 | 233,637 | 297,266 |
| Machinery and transport equipment | 119,310 | 148,781 | 178,325 |
| **Total** (incl. others) | 891,359 | 1,066,689 | 1,251,135 |

| Exports f.o.b. | 2005 | 2006 | 2007* |
|---|---|---|---|
| Agricultural products | 116,045 | 134,481 | 166,945 |
| Tea | 81,482 | 91,667 | 113,565 |
| Petroleum products | 13,169 | 19,580 | 18,693 |
| Rubber based products | 13,169 | 19,580 | 53,318 |
| Diamonds | 26,594 | 32,440 | 38,588 |
| Textiles and garments | 291,087 | 320,829 | 369,696 |
| **Total** (incl. others) | 497,695 | 562,450 | 655,170 |

* Provisional.

Source: Central Bank of Sri Lanka, Colombo.

**PRINCIPAL TRADING PARTNERS**
(US $ million)

| Imports c.i.f. | 2004 | 2005 | 2006 |
|---|---|---|---|
| China, People's Republic | 454.0 | 630.6 | 1,218.2 |
| Hong Kong | 619.4 | 648.2 | 486.7 |
| India | 1,439.2 | 1,835.4 | 2,153.4 |
| Iran | 418.7 | 523.9 | 658.6 |
| Japan | 411.7 | 379.7 | 463.0 |
| Korea, Republic | 245.9 | 210.3 | 246.8 |
| Malaysia | 329.2 | 393.5 | 587.5 |
| Singapore | 698.5 | 736.9 | 1,013.8 |
| United Arab Emirates | 202.7 | 296.3 | 372.5 |
| United Kingdom | 312.1 | 276.5 | 212.2 |
| **Total** (incl. others) | 7,999.8 | 8,863.2 | 11,609.3 |

| Exports f.o.b. | 2004 | 2005 | 2006 |
|---|---|---|---|
| France | 102.3 | 121.4 | 110.6 |
| Germany | 274.1 | 271.8 | 299.8 |
| India | 391.5 | 566.4 | 664.5 |
| Italy | 152.9 | 199.6 | 248.7 |
| Japan | 157.6 | 144.6 | 183.1 |
| Russia | 151.0 | 157.7 | 181.9 |
| United Arab Emirates | 137.8 | 170.3 | 210.2 |
| United Kingdom | 779.2 | 777.3 | 850.3 |
| USA | 1,869.3 | 1,988.1 | 2,074.8 |
| **Total** (incl. others) | 5,757.2 | 6,383.7 | 7,361.7 |

Source: Asian Development Bank, *Key Indicators of Developing Asian and Pacific Countries*.

# Transport

**RAILWAYS**

| | 2004 | 2005 | 2006 |
|---|---|---|---|
| Passengers (million) | 114.9 | 114.4 | 105.4 |
| Freight carried ('000 metric tons)* | 1,602 | 1,502 | 1,551 |

* Excluding livestock.

Source: Sri Lanka Railways.

**ROAD TRAFFIC**
(motor vehicles in use at 31 December)

| | 2000 | 2001 | 2002 |
|---|---|---|---|
| Passenger cars | 233,018 | 241,444 | 253,447 |
| Buses and coaches | 64,963 | 66,273 | 67,702 |
| Lorries and vans | 300,712 | 312,495 | 328,913 |
| Road tractors | 133,092 | 138,879 | 146,043 |
| Motorcycles and mopeds | 834,586 | 868,705 | 923,467 |
| **Total** | 1,566,371 | 1,627,796 | 1,719,572 |

Source: International Road Federation, *World Road Statistics*.

### SHIPPING

**Merchant Fleet**
(registered at 31 December)

| | 2005 | 2006 | 2007 |
|---|---|---|---|
| Number of vessels | 82 | 81 | 85 |
| Displacement ('000 grt) | 177.8 | 174.1 | 163.3 |

Source: Lloyd's Register-Fairplay, *World Fleet Statistics*.

**International Sea-borne Shipping**
(freight traffic, '000 metric tons, Colombo, Trincomalee and Galle only)

| | 2004 | 2005 | 2006 |
|---|---|---|---|
| Goods loaded | 11,893 | 13,155 | 15,622 |
| Goods unloaded | 22,066 | 24,145 | 27,039 |

### CIVIL AVIATION

(traffic on scheduled services)

| | 2001 | 2002 | 2003 |
|---|---|---|---|
| Kilometres flown (million) | 34 | 29 | 34 |
| Passengers carried ('000) | 1,719 | 1,741 | 1,958 |
| Passenger-km (million) | 6,641 | 6,327 | 6,910 |
| Total ton-km (million) | 822 | 778 | 864 |

Source: UN, *Statistical Yearbook*.

## Tourism

### FOREIGN TOURIST ARRIVALS*

| Country of residence | 2004 | 2005 | 2006 |
|---|---|---|---|
| Australia | 24,471 | 25,836 | 21,665 |
| Belgium | 5,718 | 3,891 | 6,373 |
| Canada | 14,974 | 21,335 | 14,863 |
| France | 30,422 | 26,641 | 22,703 |
| Germany | 58,932 | 46,320 | 47,296 |
| India | 104,390 | 113,023 | 128,520 |
| Italy | 17,984 | 10,147 | 12,353 |
| Japan | 19,747 | 17,163 | 16,217 |
| Maldives | 15,201 | 24,396 | 24,505 |
| Netherlands | 21,487 | 15,252 | 19,460 |
| Pakistan | 9,629 | 11,056 | 11,165 |
| Switzerland | 10,687 | 8,339 | 7,729 |
| United Kingdom | 107,042 | 92,929 | 88,531 |
| USA | 15,680 | 25,392 | 20,825 |
| **Total** (incl. others) | 566,202 | 549,308 | 559,603 |

* Excluding Sri Lanka nationals residing abroad.

**Tourism receipts** (US $ million, incl. passenger transport): 709 in 2003; 808 in 2004; 729 in 2005.

Sources: Ceylon Tourist Board; World Tourism Organization.

## Communications Media

| | 1999 | 2000 | 2001 |
|---|---|---|---|
| Television receivers ('000 in use) | 1,900 | 2,100 | 2,200 |
| Telephones ('000 main lines in use) | 669.1 | 767.4 | 822.1 |
| Mobile cellular telephones ('000 subscribers) | 256.7 | 430.2 | 667.7 |
| Personal computers ('000 in use) | 105 | 135 | 175 |
| Internet users ('000) | 65.0 | 121.5 | 150.0 |
| Newspapers | 174 | 180 | 189 |
| Books published: titles | 4,655 | 1,818 | n.a. |
| Books published: copies ('000) | n.a. | 25,459.3 | 7,439.1 |

**Facsimile machines** (number in use, estimate): 11,000 in 1994.

**Radio receivers** ('000 in use): 3,850 in 1997.

**2002** ('000): Telephones (main lines in use) 881.4; Mobile cellular telephones (subscribers) 931.6; Personal computers (number in use) 250; Internet users 200.0.

**2003** ('000): Telephones (main lines in use) 939.0; Mobile cellular telephones (subscribers) 1,393.4; Personal computers (number in use) 325; Internet users 280.0; Broadband subscribers 3.4.

**2004** ('000): Telephones (main lines in use) 993.4; Mobile cellular telephones (subscribers) 2,213.6; Personal computers (number in use) 530; Internet users 280.0; Broadband subscribers 20.4.

**2005** ('000): Telephones (main lines in use) 1,244.0; Mobile cellular telephones (subscribers) 3,361.8; Personal computers (number in use) 530; Internet users 350.0; Broadband subscribers 26.1.

**2006** ('000): Telephones (main lines in use) 1,884.1; Mobile cellular telephones (subscribers) 5,412.5; Internet users 428.0; Broadband subscribers 29.1.

Sources: UN, *Statistical Yearbook*; UNESCO, *Statistical Yearbook*; Telecommunications Regulatory Commission of Sri Lanka and International Telecommunication Union.

## Education

(1995)

| | Institutions | Teachers | Students |
|---|---|---|---|
| Primary | 9,657 | 70,537 | 1,962,498 |
| Secondary | 5,771* | 103,572 | 2,314,054 |
| Universities and equivalent | n.a. | 2,344 | 40,035 |
| Distance learning | n.a. | 206 | 20,601 |

* 1992 figure.

**1996:** Primary: 9,554 institutions, 66,339 teachers, 1,843,848 students.

**1997:** Primary: 60,832 teachers, 1,807,751 students; Secondary: 2,313,511 students.

**1998:** Primary: 1,798,162 students.

**2001:** Universities: 12 institutions, 2,999 teachers, 48,899 students.

**2002:** Universities: 12 institutions, 3,225 teachers (excl. open university), 48,667 students (excl. open university).

**2003** (provisional): Universities: 12 institutions, 3,386 teachers (excl. open university), 59,734 students (excl. open university).

Sources: UNESCO, *Statistical Yearbook*; Ministry of Education, Colombo.

**Adult literacy rate** (UNESCO estimates): 91.5% (males 93.2%; females 89.9%) in 2007 (Source: UNESCO Institute for Statistics).

# Directory

## The Constitution

The Constitution of the Democratic Socialist Republic of Sri Lanka was approved by the National State Assembly (renamed Parliament) on 17 August 1978, and promulgated on 7 September 1978. The following is a summary of its main provisions:

### FUNDAMENTAL RIGHTS

The Constitution guarantees the fundamental rights and freedoms of all citizens, including freedom of thought, conscience and worship and equal entitlement before the law.

### THE PRESIDENT

The President is Head of State, and exercises all executive powers, including defence of the Republic. The President is directly elected by the people for a term of six years, and is eligible for re-election. The President's powers include the right to:

(i) choose to hold any portfolio in the Cabinet;

(ii) appoint or dismiss the Prime Minister or any other minister;

(iii) preside at ceremonial sittings of Parliament;

(iv) dismiss Parliament at will; and

(v) submit to a national referendum any Bill or matter of national importance which has been rejected by Parliament.

### LEGISLATURE

The Parliament is the legislative power of the people. It consists of such number of representatives of the people as a Delimitation Commission shall determine. The members of Parliament are directly elected by a system of modified proportional representation. By-elections are abolished, successors to members of Parliament being appointed by the head of the party which nominated the outgoing member at the previous election. Parliament exercises the judicial power of the people through courts, tribunals and institutions created and established or recognized by the Constitution or established by law. Parliament has control over public finance.

### OTHER PROVISIONS

#### Religion

Buddhism has the foremost place among religions and it is the duty of the State to protect and foster Buddhism, while assuring every citizen the freedom to adopt the religion of their choice.

#### Language

The Constitution recognizes two official languages, Sinhala and Tamil. Either of the national languages may be used by all citizens in transactions with government institutions.

#### Amendments

Amendments to the Constitution require endorsement by a two-thirds' majority in Parliament. In February 1979 the Constitution was amended by allowing members of Parliament who resigned or were expelled from their party to retain their seats, in certain circumstances. In January 1981 Parliament amended the Constitution to increase its membership from 168 to 169. An amendment enabling the President to seek re-election after four years was approved in August 1982. In February 1983 an amendment providing for by-elections to fill vacant seats in Parliament was approved. An amendment banning parties that advocate separatism was approved by Parliament in August 1983. In November 1987 Parliament adopted an amendment providing for the creation of eight provincial councils (the northern and eastern provinces were to be merged as one administrative unit); although the northern and eastern provinces were subsequently merged, the Supreme Court announced the merger to be officially invalid in October 2006. In December 1988 Parliament adopted an amendment affording Tamil the same status as Sinhala, as one of the country's two official languages.

## The Government

### HEAD OF STATE

**President:** MAHINDA RAJAPAKSE (sworn in 19 November 2005).

### THE CABINET
(August 2008)

**Prime Minister and Minister of Internal Administration:** RATNASIRI WICKREMANAYAKE.

**Minister of Foreign Affairs:** ROHITHA BOGOLLAGAMA.

**Minister of Defence, of Public Security, Law and Order, of Religious Affairs, of Finance and Planning, and of Nation Building:** MAHINDA RAJAPAKSE.

**Minister of Tourism:** MILINDA MORAGODA.

**Minister of Posts and Telecommunication, and of Special Projects:** MAHINDA WIJESEKERA.

**Minister of Justice:** AMARASIRI DODANGODA.

**Minister of Healthcare and Nutrition:** NIMAL SIRIPALA DE SILVA.

**Minister of Transport:** DULLAS ALAHAPERUMA.

**Minister of Trade, Marketing Development, Co-operatives and Consumer Affairs:** BANDULA GUNAWARDENA.

**Minister of Agricultural Development and Agrarian Services Development:** MAITHRIPALA SIRISENA.

**Minister of Power and Energy:** JOHN SENEVIRATNA.

**Minister of Child Development and Women's Affairs:** SUMEDHA G. JAYASENA.

**Minister of Mass Media and Information:** ANURA PRIYADARSHANA YAPA.

**Minister of Urban Development and Sacred Area Development:** DINESH GUNAWARDENA.

**Minister of Social Services and Social Welfare:** DOUGLAS DEVANANDA.

**Minister of Public Administration and Home Affairs:** KARU JAYASURIYA.

**Minister of Housing and Common Amenities:** FERIAL ASHRAFF.

**Minister of Education:** SUSIL PREMAJAYANTHA.

**Minister of Labour Relations and Manpower:** ATHAUDA SENEVIRATNE.

**Minister of Rural Industries and Self-Employment Promotion:** R. M. S. B. NAVINNE.

**Minister of Vocational and Technical Training:** PIYASENA GAMAGE.

**Minister of Local Government and Provincial Councils:** JANAKA BANDARA THENAKOON.

**Minister of Fisheries and Aquatic Resources:** FELIX PERERA.

**Minister of Science and Technology:** Prof. TISSA VITHARANA.

**Minister of Enterprise Development and Investment Promotion:** Dr SARATH AMUNUGAMA.

**Minister of Constitutional Affairs and National Integration:** D. E. W. GUNASEKERA.

**Minister of Disaster Management and Human Rights:** MAHINDA SAMARASINGHE.

**Minister of Plantation Industries:** D. M. JAYARATNE.

**Minister of Petroleum and Petroleum Resources Development:** A. H. M. FOWZIE.

**Minister of Highways and Road Development:** T. B. EKANAYAKE (acting).

**Minister of Youth Empowerment and Socio-Economic Development:** ARUMUGAN THONDAMAN.

**Minister of Community Development and Social Inequity Eradication:** P. CHANDRASEKERAN.

**Minister of Water Supply and Drainage:** A. L. M. ATHAULLAH.

**Minister of Resettlement and Disaster Relief Services:** ABDUL RISATH BATHIYUTHEEN.

**Minister of Plan Implementation:** P. DAYARATNE.

**Minister of Supplementary Crops Development:** R. M. DHARMADASA BANDA.

**Minister of Parliamentary Affairs:** M. H. MOHOMED.

**Minister of Export Development and International Trade:** Prof. G. L. PEIRIS.

**Minister of Public Estate Management and Development:** MILROY FERNANDO.

**Minister of Land and Land Development:** JEEWAN KUMARANATUNGA.

**Minister of Youth Affairs:** PAVITHRA WANNIARACHCHI.

**Minister of Indigenous Medicine:** TISSA KARALIYADDE.

**Minister of Sports and Public Recreation:** GAMINI LOKUGE.

**Minister of Construction and Engineering Services:** Rajitha Senaratne.

**Minister of Foreign Employment Promotion and Welfare:** Keheliya Rambukwelle.

**Minister of Livestock Development:** R. M. C. B. Rathnayake.

**Minister of Cultural Affairs:** Mahinda Yapa Abeywardena.

**Minister of Higher Education:** Prof. Wiswa Warnapala.

**Minister of Irrigation and Water Management, and of Ports and Aviation:** Chamal Rajapaksa.

**Minister of Industrial Development:** Kumara Welgama.

**Minister of Environment and Natural Resources:** Champika Ranawaka.

## MINISTRIES

**President's Secretariat:** Republic Sq., Colombo 1; tel. (11) 2324801; fax (11) 2331246; e-mail gosl@presidentsl.org; internet www.presidentsl.org.

**Prime Minister's Office:** 58 Sir Ernest de Silva Mawatha, Colombo 7; tel. (11) 2575317; fax (11) 2575454; internet www.pmoffice.gov.lk.

**Ministry of Agricultural Development and Agrarian Services:** 'Govijana Mandiraya', 80/5 Rajamalwatta Rd, Battaramulla, Colombo; tel. (11) 2869553; fax (11) 2868919; e-mail agmin@sltnet.lk; internet www.mimrd.gov.lk.

**Ministry of Child Development and Women's Empowerment:** 177 Nawala Rd, Narahenpita, Colombo 5; tel. (11) 2505584; fax (11) 2369294; e-mail mwa@sltnet.lk.

**Ministry of Community Development and Social Inequity Eradication:** 35/A Dr N. M. Perera Mawatha, Colombo 8.

**Ministry of Constitutional Affairs and National Integration:** 310 Galle Rd, Colombo 3; tel. (11) 2375178; fax (11) 2375181; e-mail consas@constitution.gov.lk; internet www.constitution.gov.lk.

**Ministry of Construction and Engineering Services:** 'Sethsiripaya', 2nd Floor, Battaramulla, Colombo; internet (11) 2867954.

**Ministry of Cultural Affairs:** 'Sethsiripaya', 8th Floor, Battaramulla, Colombo; tel. (11) 2872001; fax (11) 2872021; e-mail mcasec@sltnet.lk.

**Ministry of Defence, Public Security, Law and Order:** 15/5 Baladaksha Mawatha, POB 572, Colombo 3; tel. (11) 2430860; fax (11) 2446300; e-mail secretary@defence.lk; internet www.defence.lk.

**Ministry of Disaster Management and Human Rights:** 2 Wijerama Mawatha, Colombo 7; tel. (11) 2695013; fax (11) 2681980; e-mail info@dmhr.gov.lk; internet www.dmhr.gov.lk.

**Ministry of Education:** 'Isurupaya', Pelawatte, Battaramulla, Colombo; tel. (11) 2785141; fax (11) 2785162; e-mail minedu@moe.gov.lk; internet www.moe.gov.lk.

**Ministry of Enterprise Development and Investment Promotion:** World Trade Centre, West Tower, 25th Level, Echelon Sq, Colombo 1; tel. (11) 2394951; fax (11) 2424960; e-mail secedip@sltnet.lk.

**Ministry of Environment and Natural Resources:** 82 Sampath Paya, Rajamalwatte Rd, Battaramulla, Colombo; tel. (11) 2882112; fax (11) 2863652; e-mail promotion@menr.lk; internet www.menr.lk.

**Ministry of Export Development and International Trade:** 'Rakshana Mandiraya', 6th Floor, 21 Vauxhall St, Colombo 2; tel. (11) 2435002.

**Ministry of Finance and Planning:** Galle Face Secretariat, Colombo 1; tel. (11) 2484500; fax (11) 2449823; e-mail mfsa@sltnet.lk; internet www.treasury.gov.lk.

**Ministry of Fisheries and Aquatic Resources:** Maligawatta, Colombo 10; tel. (11) 2446183; fax (11) 2541184; e-mail secretary@fisheries.gov.lk; internet www.fisheries.gov.lk.

**Ministry of Foreign Affairs:** Republic Bldg, Colombo 1; tel. (11) 2325371; fax (11) 2446091; e-mail publicity@formin.gov.lk; internet www.slmfa.gov.lk.

**Ministry of Foreign Employment Promotion and Welfare:** Level 33, West Tower, World Trade Centre, Colombo 1; tel. (11) 2438734; fax (11) 2438736; e-mail fep_gov@sltnet.lk; internet www.minfep.gov.lk.

**Ministry of Healthcare and Nutrition:** 'Suwasiripaya', 385 Wimalawansha Himi Mawatha, Colombo 10; tel. (11) 2694033; fax (11) 2692694; e-mail dhi@health.gov.lk; internet www.health.gov.lk.

**Ministry of Higher Education:** 18 Ward Place, Colombo 7; tel. (11) 2694486; fax (11) 2697239; e-mail mioh.hied@sltnet.lk; internet www.mohe.gov.lk.

**Ministry of Highways and Road Development:** Sethsiripaya Office Complex, 'C' Wing, 9th Floor, POB 53, Battaramulla, Colombo; tel. (11) 2871821; fax (11) 2862705; e-mail hiwaysec@sltnet.lk; internet www.mohsl.gov.lk.

**Ministry of Housing and Common Amenities:** 'Sethsiripaya', 2nd Floor, Sri Jayawardanapura Kotte, Battaramulla, Colombo; tel. (11) 2861586; fax (11) 2888151; e-mail ministry@mhc.gov.lk.

**Ministry of Indigenous Medicine:** 80/5 'Govijana Mandiraya', Rajamalwatta Road, Battaramulla, Colombo; tel. (11) 2872093; fax (11) 2885126; e-mail inmed@dialogsl.net.

**Ministry of Industrial Development:** 73/1 Galle Rd, Colombo 3; tel. (11) 2392149; fax (11) 2449402; e-mail misec@sltnet.lk; internet www.industry.gov.lk.

**Ministry of Internal Administration:** 51 Sir Ernest de Silva Mawatha, Colombo 7; tel. (11) 2301235.

**Ministry of Irrigation and Water Management:** 11 Jawatta Rd, Colombo 5; tel. (11) 2554000.

**Ministry of Justice and Law Reforms:** Superior Courts Complex Bldg, Colombo 12; tel. (11) 2323022; fax (11) 2320785; internet www.justiceministry.gov.lk.

**Ministry of Labour Relations and Manpower:** Labour Secretariat, 2nd Floor, Narahenpita, Colombo 5; tel. (11) 2581149; fax (11) 2588950; e-mail slmol@slt.lk.

**Ministry of Land and Land Development:** 'Govijana Mandiraya', 80/5 Rajamalwatta Rd, Battaramulla, Colombo; tel. (11) 2887410; fax (11) 2887404; e-mail nips@sltnet.lk.

**Ministry of Livestock Development:** 45 St Michael's Rd, POB 562, Colombo 3; tel. (11) 2541369; fax (11) 2541377; e-mail geethacb@hotmail.com; internet www.livestock.gov.lk.

**Ministry of Local Government and Provincial Councils:** 330 Union Place, Colombo 2; tel. (11) 2305326; fax (11) 2347529; e-mail secpl@minhaprolo.gov.lk; internet www.minhaprolo.gov.lk.

**Ministry of Mass Media and Information:** 163 Kirulapone Mawatha, Polhengoda, Colombo 5; tel. (11) 2513459; fax (11) 2514053; e-mail mediasecretary@media.gov.lk; internet www.media.gov.lk.

**Ministry of Nation Building and Estate Infrastructure Development:** 177 Galle Rd, Colombo 3; tel. (11) 2390895; fax (11) 2382069; e-mail secmdrrn@sltnet.lk.

**Ministry of National Heritage:** 'Sethsiripaya', 8th Floor, Battaramulla, Colombo 3; tel. (11) 2872001.

**Ministry of Parliamentary Affairs:** 464/B Pannipitiya Rd, Pelewatta, Battaramulla; tel. (11) 2786988; fax (11) 2787895; e-mail mpasl@sltnet.lk.

**Ministry of Petroleum and Petroleum Resources Development:** 80 Sir Ernest De Silva Mawatha, Colombo 7; tel. (11) 2564355.

**Ministry of Plan Implementation:** Central Bank Building, 5th Tower, 12th Floor, 30 Janadhipathi Mawatha, Colombo 1; tel. (11) 2477000; fax (11) 2477959; e-mail bhaila@slt.lk.

**Ministry of Plantation Industries:** 55/75 Vauxhall Lane, Colombo 2; tel. (11) 2320901; fax (11) 2303022; e-mail dpmpi@sltnet.lk; internet www.plantationindustries.gov.lk.

**Ministry of Ports and Aviation:** 19 Chaithiya Rd, Colombo 1; tel. (11) 2439350; fax (11) 2431658; e-mail specd@slpa.lk; internet www.ports-aviation.gov.lk.

**Ministry of Posts and Telecommunication:** World Trade Centre, West Tower, Level 18, Colombo 1; tel. (11) 2422591; fax (11) 2323465; e-mail spostele@sltnet.lk.

**Ministry of Power and Energy:** 493/1 T. B. Jaya Mawatha, Colombo 10; tel. (11) 2687768; fax (11) 2681248; e-mail secrepe@sltnet.lk; internet www.mope.gov.lk.

**Ministry of Public Administration and Home Affairs:** Independence Sq., Colombo 7; tel. (11) 2696211; fax (11) 2697410; e-mail info@pubad.gov.lk; internet www.pubad.gov.lk.

**Ministry of Public Estate Management and Development:** 320 T. B. Jayah Mawatha, Colombo 10; tel. (11) 2672505; fax (11) 2672501; e-mail secpemd@sltnet.lk.

**Ministry of Religious Affairs and Moral Upliftment:** 115 Wijerama Mawatha, Colombo 7; tel. (11) 2690896; fax (11) 2690897; e-mail buddhasasanam@yahoo.com.

**Ministry of Resettlement and Disaster Relief Services:** 146 Galle Rd, Colombo 3; tel. (11) 2395109; fax (11) 2395517; e-mail acmrazik@gmail.com; internet www.resettlementmin.gov.lk.

**Ministry of Rural Industries and Self Employment Promotion:** 780 Maradana Rd, Colombo 10; tel. (11) 2669280; fax (11) 2669281; e-mail secofficerisep@sltnet.lk; internet www.risepmin.gov.lk.

**Ministry of Science and Technology:** 561/3 Etvigala Mawatha, POB 1571, Colombo 5; tel. (11) 2554848; fax (11) 2510565; e-mail mstsasad@sltnet.lk; internet www.most.gov.lk.

**Ministry of Social Services and Social Welfare:** 'Sethsiripaya', 5th Floor, Battaramulla, Colombo; tel. (11) 2887349; fax (11) 2877381; e-mail msssec@sltnet.lk; internet www.socialwelfare.gov.lk.

**Ministry of Sports and Public Recreation:** 420 Bauddhaloka Mawatha, Colombo 7; tel. (11) 2669237; fax (11) 2683569; e-mail info@sportsministry.gov.lk.

**Ministry of Supplementary Plantation Crops Development:** 561/3 Elvitigala Mawatha, Colombo 8; tel. (11) 2150722; fax (11) 2375378.

**Ministry of Tourism:** 64 Galle Rd, Colombo 3; tel. (11) 2385241; fax (11) 2399274; e-mail slmts@sltnet.lk; internet www.slmts.slt.lk.

**Ministry of Trade, Marketing Development, Co-operatives and Consumer Services:** 'Rakshana Mandiraya', 7th Floor, 21 Vauxhall St, Colombo 2; tel. (11) 2300341; fax (11) 2447669; e-mail comsec@commerce.gov.lk; internet www.commerce.gov.lk.

**Ministry of Transport:** 1 D. R. Wijewardene Mawatha, POB 588, Colombo 10; tel. (11) 2687105; fax (11) 2687108; e-mail mintrans@sltnet.lk; internet www.transport.gov.lk.

**Ministry of Urban Development and Sacred Area Development:** 'Sethsiripaya', 3rd Floor, Battaramulla, Colombo 3; tel. and fax (11) 2877002; fax (11) 2871835; e-mail secudws@sltnet.lk.

**Ministry of Vocational and Technical Training:** 'Nipunatha Piyasa', 354/2 Elwitigala Mawatha, Narahenpita, Colombo 5; tel. (11) 2597677; fax (11) 2597691; e-mail sec_sdvte@sltnet.lk; internet www.nipunatha.gov.lk.

**Ministry of Water Supply and Drainage:** 34 Thakahashi Bldg, Narahenpita Rd, Nawala; tel. (11) 2808135.

**Ministry of Youth Affairs:** 420 Bouddhaloka Mawatha, Colombo 7.

**Ministry of Youth Empowerment and Socio-Economic Development:** 43 Jawatta Rd, Colombo 5; tel. (11) 2169507.

# President and Legislature

### PRESIDENT

**Presidential Election, 17 November 2005**

| Candidate | Valid votes | % of votes |
|---|---|---|
| Mahinda Rajapakse (UPFA) | 4,887,152 | 50.29 |
| Ranil Wickremasinghe (UNP) | 4,706,366 | 48.43 |
| **Total** (incl. others) | 9,717,039 | 100.00 |

### PARLIAMENT

**Speaker:** W. J. M. LOKUBANDARA.

**Deputy Speaker:** PRIYANKARA JAYARATNE.

**General Election, 2 April 2004**

| Party | Seats |
|---|---|
| United People's Freedom Alliance (UPFA)* | 105 |
| United National Party (UNP) | 82 |
| Tamil National Alliance (TNA) | 22 |
| Jathika Hela Urumaya (JHU) | 9 |
| Sri Lanka Muslim Congress (SLMC) | 5 |
| Others | 2 |
| **Total** | 225 |

* Coalition comprising the Sri Lanka Freedom Party, Janatha Vimukthi Peramuna, Communist Party of Sri Lanka, Democratic United National Front, Lanka Sama Samaja Party and Sri Lanka Mahajana Party.

Note: Direct elections were held for 196 of the 225 seats on the basis of a proportional representation system involving preferential voting; the remaining 29 were chosen from party lists according to each party's national share of the vote.

# Election Commission

**Department of Elections:** Elections Secretariat, Sarana Mawatha, Rajagiriya, Jayawardenapura; tel. (11) 2868441; fax (11) 2868445; e-mail comelesl@sltnet.lk; internet www.slelections.gov.lk; f. 1947; govt dept; establishment of independent commission pending in 2008; Commr of Elections DAYANANDA DISSANAYAKE.

# Political Organizations

**Akhila Ilankai Tamil United Front (AITUK):** e-mail secretary@tamilunitedfront.com; internet www.tamilunitedfront.com; f. 2006; Tamil; advocates federal solution to ethnic conflict; Gen. Sec. K. VIGNESWARAN.

**Ceylon Workers' Congress (CWC):** 'Savumia Bhavan', 72 Ananda Coomarasamy Mawatha, POB 1294, Colombo 7; tel. (11) 2301359; fax (11) 2301355; e-mail cwconline@sltnet.lk; f. 1939; represents the interests of workers in the mercantile and local government sectors and of workers on tea, rubber and coconut plantations; 250,000 mems; Pres. and Gen. Sec. S. R. ARUMUGAN THONDAMAN.

**Democratic People's Liberation Front (DPLF):** 16 Haig Rd, Bambalapitiya, Colombo 4; tel. (11) 2586289; has operated as a national political party since Sept. 1988; political wing of the People's Liberation Organization of Tamil Eelam (PLOTE); Leader DHARMALINGAM SITHADTHAN.

**Democratic Workers' Congress (DWC)** (Political Wing): 70 Bankshall St, POB 1009, Colombo 11; tel. (11) 2439199; fax (11) 2435961; f. 1978 as political wing of DWC trade union (f. 1939); aims to eliminate discrimination against the Tamil-speaking Sri Lankans of recent Indian origin; 201,382 mems (1994); Pres. and Gen. Sec. MANO GANESHAN.

**Desha Vimukthi Janatha Pakshaya** (National Liberation People's Party): 63/24, Wewewatte, Weliweriya; tel. 338812; has operated as a national political party since Sept. 1988; Sec. P. M. PODIAPPUHAMY.

**Deshapriya Janatha Viyaparaya (DJV)** (Patriotic People's Movement): militant, Sinhalese group; associated with the JVP.

**Eelam National Democratic Liberation Front (ENDLF):** 315 Kandy Rd, Kilinochchi; Tamil; supports 1987 Indo-Sri Lankan peace accord; has operated as a national political party since Sept. 1988; Pres. G. GNANASEKARAN; Dep. Gen. Sec. P. RAJARATNAM.

**Eelam People's Democratic Party (EPDP):** 121 Park Rd, Colombo 5; tel. (11) 2551015; fax (11) 2585255; e-mail epdp@sltnet.lk; internet www.epdpnews.com; Tamil; Sec.-Gen. DOUGLAS DEVANANDA.

**Eksath Lanka Podujana Pakshaya:** 43/5 Galle Rd, Colombo 4; tel. (77) 2313321; Sec. U. LALITH WIJETHUNGA.

**Janatha Vimukthi Peramuna (JVP)** (People's Liberation Front): 198/19 Panchikawattha Rd, Colombo 10; tel. (11) 4400511; fax (11) 2786050; e-mail jvplanka@sltnet.lk; internet www.jvpsrilanka.com; f. 1964; banned following a coup attempt in 1971, regained legal status in 1977, banned again in 1983, but regained legal status in 1994; Marxist; Sinhalese support; Leader SOMAWANSA AMARASINGHE.

**Jathika Hela Urumaya (JHU)** (National Heritage Party): 253/C, 'Ravindu', Vihara Mawatha, Weboda; tel. (11) 2810185; fax (11) 2811504; e-mail helaurumaya@gmail.com; internet www.jathikahelaurumaya.org; f. 2004; Buddhist; Sinhalese nationalist; Asst Sec. G. D. D. GUNATHILAKE.

**Liberal Party:** 88/1 Rosmead Place, Colombo 7; tel. (11) 2691589; fax (11) 2699772; e-mail libparty@sri.lanka.net; internet www.liberalparty-srilanka.org; Pres. SWARNA AMARATUNGA; Sec.-Gen. KAMAL NISSANKA.

**Mahajana Eksath Peramuna (MEP)** (People's United Front): 31/27 Narahenpita Rd, Nawala, Rajagiriya; tel. 872318; f. 1956; Sinhalese and Buddhist support; left-wing; advocates economic self-reliance; Pres. DINESH C. R. GUNAWARDENA.

**Muslim National Unity Alliance (MNUA):** Sama Mandiraya, 53 Vauxhall Lane, Colombo 2; tel. (11) 2424187; affiliate party of the Sri Lanka Muslim Congress; has operated as a national political party since 1986; Leader FARIEL ASHRAFF.

**Muslim United Liberation Front:** 134 Hulftsdorp St, Colombo 12; tel. (11) 2501198; has operated as a national political party since Sept. 1988.

**National Freedom Front (NFF):** 377/4 Ratnarama Rd, Hokandara North; tel. (60) 2071340; e-mail info@nffsrilanka.com; internet www.nffsrilanka.com; f. 2008 as a breakaway faction of the JVP; Chair. WIMAL WEERAWANSA; Gen. Sec. NANDANA GUNATILAKA.

**Nava Sama Samaja Party (NSSP)** (New Equal Society Party): Left Front, 17 Barracks Lane, Colombo 2; tel. (11) 2430621; fax (11) 2305963; e-mail nssp@nssp.info; internet www.nssp.info; f. 1977; Trotskyist; operates under the New Left Front; Gen. Sec. LINUS JAYATILAKE; Presidium Member Dr VICKRAMABAHU KARUNARATHNE.

**New Democratic Party (NDP):** C. C. S. M. Complex, 3rd Floor, S-47, Colombo 11; tel. (71) 4302909; fax (11) 2473757; e-mail info@ndpsl.org; internet www.ndpsl.org; f. 1978 as the Sri Lanka Communist Party; adopted current name in 1991; upholds Marxist-Leninist-Mao Zedong philosophy in anti-imperialist campaigning for social justice; publs monthly party newsletter Puthiya Poomi; Gen. Sec. S. K. SENTHIVEL.

**Singhalaye Nithahas Peramuna** (Sinhalese Freedom Front): Sri Panchananda Charity Bldg, Kelani Railway Station Rd, Colombo; f. 1994; nationalist, Buddhist; Pres. ARYA SENA TERA; Sec. Prof. NALIN DE SILVA.

**Sri Lanka Freedom Party—Mahajana Wing (SLFP—M):** Colombo; f. 2007 as breakaway faction of the Sri Lanka Freedom Party, under the leadership of fmr Minister of Foreign Affairs and fmr Minister of Port Development; advocates constitutional reform, incl. revisions to the Executive President's authority; memorandum of understanding signed with United National Party in July 2007 whereby the two parties pledged to contest future elections as a broad coalition (the 'National Congress'); Founder and Leader MANGALA SAMARAWEERA.

**Sri Lanka Muslim Congress:** Sama Mandiraya, 53 Vauxhall Lane, Colombo 2; tel. (11) 2431711; internet www.slmc.org; Leader RAUF HAKEEM.

**Sri Lanka Progressive Front:** 7, 7th Lane, Pagoda Rd, Nugegoda; tel. 826564; f. 1996 following split from Janatha Vimukthi Peramuna; leftist nationalist party; Sec. ROHAN JAYATUNGA .

**Tamileela Makkal Viduthalai Pulikal (TMVP)** (Tamileela Peoples Liberation Tigers—Karuna Group): Colombo; internet www.tmvp.org; f. 2004; political and paramilitary group, fmrly of LTTE; joint asscn with the Eelam National Democratic Liberation Front (India); Leader V. MURALITHARAN ('COL KARUNA'); Dep. Leader S. CHANDRAKANTHAN ('PILLAYAN'); Sec. K. SUPPAKUMARA ('BHARATHI').

**Tamil National Alliance (TNA):** 3rd Floor, Parliamentary Complex, Sri Jeyawardanapura Kotte, Colombo; e-mail enquiries@tamilalliance.net; internet www.tamilalliance.net; f. 2001; alliance of Tamil parties.

**Eelam People's Revolutionary Liberation Front (EPRLF):** 310 Hospital Rd, Jaffna; tel. (21) 2222022; internet www.eprlf.net; Tamil rights group; the party split into two factions, one led by ANNAMALAI VARADHARAJAH PERUMAL, known as the Varadharajah faction, and the other by SURESH K. PREMACHANDRAN, known as the Premachandran faction; c. 1,000 mems.

**Tamil Eelam Liberation Organization (TELO):** 34 Ammankovil Rd, Pandarikulam, Vavuniya; tel. (24) 2222977; fax (24) 2224457; e-mail teloheadoffice@yahoo.com; internet www.telo.org; supports 1987 Indo-Sri Lankan peace accord; has operated as a national political party since Sept. 1988; pro-LTTE; Leader SELVAM ADAIKALANTHAN.

**Tamil United Liberation Front (TULF):** 30/1B Alwis Place, Colombo 3; tel. (11) 2347721; fax (11) 2347721; e-mail tulf2000@yahoo.com; f. 1976 following merger of All Ceylon Tamil Congress (f. 1945) and Federal Party (f. 1949); Pres. VEERASINGHAM ANANDASANGAREE; Sec.-Gen. R. SAMPANTHAN.

**United National Party (UNP):** 30 Sir Marcus Fernando Mawatha, Colombo 7; tel. (11) 5636551; fax (11) 2682905; e-mail info@unp.lk; internet www.unp.lk; f. 1946; democratic socialist; aims at a non-aligned foreign policy, supports Sinhala and Tamil as the official languages and state aid to denominational schools; Leader RANIL WICKREMASINGHE; Chair. RUKMAN SENANAYAKE; Gen. Sec. TISSA ATTANAYAKE.

**United People's Freedom Alliance (UPFA):** 121 Wijerama Mawatha, Colombo 7; tel. (11) 268047; f. 2004; left wing coalition incl. communists and Trotskyists; Chair. (vacant).

**Communist Party of Sri Lanka (CPSL):** 91 Dr N. M. Perera Mawatha, Colombo 800; tel. (11) 2695328; fax (11) 2691610; e-mail dew128@dialogsl.net; f. 1943; advocates establishment of socialist society; seeks broadening of democratic rights and processes, political solution to ethnic problem, defence of social welfare and presses for social justice; supports national sovereignty, territorial integrity and national unity of the country; Gen. Sec. DEW GUNASEKERA.

**Democratic United National Front (DUNF):** 60 1st Lane, Rawathawatte, Moratuwa; tel. (11) 2645566; f. 1991 by dissident group of UNP politicians; 500,000 mems; Leader ARIYAWANS DISSANAYAKE; Pres. D. M. G. EKANAYAKE; Gen. Sec. ARIYAWANSA DISSANAYAKE.

**Lanka Sama Samaja Party (LSSP)** (Lanka Equal Society Party): 457 Dr Colvin R. de Silva Mawatha, Colombo 2; tel. (11) 2676770; f. 1935; Trotskyist; Gen. Sec. WIMALASIRI DE MEL.

**Sri Lanka Freedom Party (SLFP):** 301 T. B. Jayah Mawatha, Colombo 10; tel. (11) 2679113; fax (11) 2685563; e-mail slfp@srilankafreedomparty.org; internet www.srilankafreedomparty.org; f. 1951; democratic socialist; advocates a non-aligned foreign policy, industrial development in both the state sector and the private sector, rapid modernization in education and in the economy, and safeguards for minorities; Chair. MAHINDA RAJAPAKSE; Gen. Sec. MAITHRIPALA SIRISENA.

**Sri Lanka Mahajana (People's) Party (SLMP):** 196 Kolonnawa Rd, Wellampitiya; f. 1984 by fmr mems of the SLFP; social democrats; Leader SARATH KONGAHAGE; Gen. Sec. PREMASIRI PERERA.

**Upcountry People's Front:** 56, Rosita Housing Scheme, Kotagala; tel. (52) 28286; represents interests of workers (mainly of Indian Tamil origin) on tea plantations; Sec. P. CHANDRASEKARAN.

Tamil separatist groups also include the Liberation Tigers of Tamil Eelam (LTTE; Leader VELUPILLAI PRABHAKARAN), the Tamil Eelam Liberation Front (TELF; Gen. Sec. M. K. EELAVENTHAN), the People's Liberation Organization of Tamil Eelam (PLOTE; Leader DHARMALINGAM SIDDHARTHAN; Vice-Pres. KARUVAI A. SRIKANTHASAMI), the People's Revolutionary Action Group, the Ellalan Force and the Tamil People's Protection Party.

# Diplomatic Representation

## EMBASSIES AND HIGH COMMISSIONS IN SRI LANKA

**Australia:** 21 Gregory's Rd, Colombo 7; tel. (11) 2463200; fax (11) 2686453; e-mail austcom@sltnet.lk; internet www.srilanka.embassy.gov.au; High Commissioner KATHY KLUGMAN.

**Bangladesh:** 85 Dharmapala Mawatha, Colombo 7; tel. (11) 2303943; fax (11) 2303942; e-mail bdootlanka@eureka.lk; High Commissioner MOHAMMED SHAHADAT HOSSAIN.

**Canada:** 6 Gregory's Rd, Cinnamon Gdns, POB 1006, Colombo 7; tel. (11) 5326232; fax (11) 5226299; e-mail clmbo@international.gc.ca; internet www.dfait-maeci.gc.ca/world/embassies/srilanka; High Commissioner ANGELA BOGDAN.

**China, People's Republic:** 381/A Bauddhaloka Mawatha, Colombo 7; tel. (11) 2694491; fax (11) 2693799; e-mail chinaemb_lk@mfa.gov.cn; internet lk.china-embassy.org; Ambassador YE DABO.

**Cuba:** 15/9 Maitland Crescent, Colombo 7; tel. (11) 2677170; fax (11) 2669380; e-mail cubaembalk@sltnet.lk; internet embacuba.cubaminrex.cu/srilankaing; Ambassador ENNA VIANT VALDÉS.

**Egypt:** 39 Dickman's Rd, Colombo 5; tel. (11) 2583621; fax (11) 2585292; e-mail egyptemb@sltnet.lk; Ambassador GIHAN AMIN MOHAMED ALI.

**France:** 89 Rosmead Place, POB 880, Colombo 7; tel. (11) 2698815; fax (11) 2699039; e-mail ambfrclb@sltnet.lk; internet www.ambafrance-lk.org; Ambassador MICHEL LUMMAUX.

**Germany:** 40 Alfred House Ave, POB 658, Colombo 3; tel. (11) 2580431; fax (11) 2580440; e-mail info@colombo.diplo.de; internet www.colombo.diplo.de; Ambassador JÜRGEN WEERTH.

**Holy See:** 220 Bauddhaloka Mawatha, Colombo 7 (Apostolic Nunciature); tel. (11) 2582554; fax (11) 2580906; e-mail nuntius@sltnet.lk; Apostolic Nuncio Most Rev. Dr MARIO ZENARI (Titular Archbishop of Zuglio).

**India:** 36–38 Galle Rd, Colombo 3; tel. (11) 2421605; fax (11) 2446403; e-mail cpic@sltnet.lk; internet www.hcicolombo.org; High Commissioner ALOK PRASAD.

**Indonesia:** 400/50 Sarana Rd, off Bauddhaloka Mawatha, Colombo 7; tel. (11) 2674337; fax (11) 2678668; e-mail pensosbud@kbrilk.org; internet www.kbrilk.org; Chargé d'affaires a.i. SUHARDI CONDROSENTONO.

**Iran:** 17 Bullers Lane, Colombo 7; tel. (11) 2501137; fax (11) 2502691; e-mail emb_colombo@mfa.gov.ir; Ambassador BEHNAM BEHRUZ.

**Italy:** 55 Jawatta Rd, Colombo 5; tel. (11) 2588388; fax (11) 2596344; e-mail ambasciata.colombo@esteri.it; internet www.ambcolombo.esteri.it; Ambassador PIO MARIANI.

**Japan:** 20 Gregory's Rd, POB 822, Colombo 7; tel. (11) 2693831; fax (11) 2698629; e-mail cultujpn@sltnet.lk; internet www.lk.emb-japan.go.jp; Ambassador KIYOSHI ARAKI.

**Korea, Democratic People's Republic:** Colombo; Ambassador HAN CHANG-ON.

**Korea, Republic:** 98 Dharmapala Mawatha, Colombo 7; tel. (11) 2699036; fax (11) 2696699; e-mail kesl@koreanembassy.net; Ambassador CHOI KI-CHUL.

**Kuwait:** 292 Bauddhaloka Mawatha, Colombo 7; tel. (11) 2597958; fax (11) 2597954; e-mail cmb@kuwaitembassysl.org; Ambassador FAHID HAJAR SHAOUF AL-MUTAIRI.

**Libya:** 120 Horton Pl., POB 155, Colombo 7; tel. (11) 2693700; fax (11) 2695671; e-mail libya@eureka.lk; Sec. of the People's Bureau ABD-AL KARIM ALI ABD-AL KARIM.

**Malaysia:** 33 Bagatalle Rd, Colombo 3; tel. (11) 2554681; fax (11) 2554684; e-mail malcolmbo@eureka.lk; internet www.kln.gov.my/perwakilan/colombo; High Commissioner ROSLI ISMAIL.

**Maldives:** 25 Melbourne Ave, Colombo 4; tel. (11) 2587827; fax (11) 2581200; e-mail info@maldiveshighcom.lk; internet www.maldiveshighcom.lk; High Commissioner ALI HUSSAIN DIDI.

**Myanmar:** 4A Rosmead Ave, Rosmead Place, Colombo 7; tel. (11) 2696440; fax (11) 2682052; e-mail mmembcmb@eureka.lk; Ambassador U THAN TUN.

**Nepal:** 153 Kynsey Rd, Colombo 8; tel. (11) 2689657; fax (11) 2689655; e-mail mecolombo@eureka.lk; Ambassador DURGA PRASAD BHATTARAI.

**Netherlands:** 25 Torrington Ave, Colombo 7; tel. (11) 2596914; fax (11) 2502855; e-mail col@minbuza.nl; internet www.hollandinsrilanka.org; Ambassador LEUNI CUELENAERE.

**Norway:** 34 Ward Place, Colombo 7; tel. (11) 2469611; fax (11) 2695009; e-mail emb.colombo@mfa.no; internet www.norway.lk; Ambassador TORE HATTREM.

**Pakistan:** 211 De Saram Place, Colombo 10; tel. (11) 2696301; fax (11) 2695780; e-mail parepcolombo@sltnet.lk; High Commissioner Air Vice-Marshal (retd) SHAHZAD ASLAM CHAUDHRY.

**Qatar:** 11 Rajakeeya Mawatha, Old Race Course Ave, Colombo 7; tel. (11) 2690440; fax (11) 2690443; Ambassador ALI HAMAD MUBARAK AL-MARRI.

**Romania:** 14A Cambridge Terrace, Colombo 7; tel. (11) 2683421; fax (11) 2863422; e-mail romania@sltnet.lk; internet www.romania.lk; Chargé d'affaires a.i. IONEL GOMBOS.

**Russia:** 62 Sir Ernest de Silva Mawatha, Colombo 7; tel. (11) 2573555; fax (11) 2574957; e-mail rusemb@itmin.net; internet www.sri-lanka.mid.ru; Ambassador ALEXEY L. SHEBARSHIN.

**Saudi Arabia:** 39 Sir Ernest de Silva Mawatha, Colombo 7; tel. (11) 2682087; fax (11) 2682088; e-mail lkemb@mofa.gov.sa; Ambassador ABDUL ASIA BIN AL JEMAZ.

**South Africa:** 114 Rosmead Place, Colombo 7; tel. (11) 2689926; fax (11) 2688670; e-mail sahc_info@sltnet.lk; High Commissioner BUYISIWE MAUREEN PHETO.

**Sweden:** 49 Bullers Lane, POB 1072, Colombo 7; tel. (11) 4795400; fax (11) 4795450; e-mail ambassaden.colombo@foreign.ministry.se; internet www.swedenabroad.com/colombo; Chargé d'affaires BÖRJE MATTSSON.

**Switzerland:** 63 Gregory's Rd, POB 342, Colombo 7; tel. (11) 2695117; fax (11) 2695176; e-mail col.vertretung@eda.admin.ch; internet www.eda.admin.ch/colombo; Ambassador RUTH FLINT.

**Thailand:** Greenlanka Towers, 9th Floor, 46/46 Nawam Mawatha, Colombo 2; tel. (11) 2302500; fax (11) 2304511; e-mail thaicmb@sltnet .lk; internet www.thaiembassy.org/colombo; Ambassador THINAKORN KANASUTA.

**United Arab Emirates:** 44 Ernest de Silva Mawatha, Colombo 7; tel. (11) 2565052; fax (11) 2564104; Ambassador M. M. MOHAMOUD AL-MAHMOUD.

**United Kingdom:** 190 Galle Rd, Kollupitiya, POB 1433, Colombo 3; tel. (11) 2437336; fax (11) 2430308; e-mail colombo.general@fco.gov .lk; internet www.britishhighcommission.gov.uk/srilanka; High Commissioner Dr PETER HAYES.

**USA:** 210 Galle Rd, POB 106, Colombo 3; tel. (11) 2441272; fax (11) 2429070; internet srilanka.usembassy.gov; Ambassador ROBERT O. BLAKE.

# Judicial System

The judicial system consists of the Supreme Court, the Court of Appeal, the High Court, District Courts, Magistrates' Courts and Primary Courts. The last four are Courts of the First Instance and appeals lie from them to the Court of Appeal and from there, on questions of law or by special leave, to the Supreme Court. The High Court deals with all criminal cases and the District Courts with civil cases. There are Labour Tribunals to decide labour disputes.

The Judicial Service Commission comprises the Chief Justice and two judges of the Supreme Court, nominated by the President. All judges of the Courts of First Instance (except High Court Judges) and the staff of all courts are appointed and controlled by the Judicial Service Commission. The Supreme Court consists of the Chief Justice and not fewer than six and not more than 10 other judges. The Court of Appeal consists of the President and not fewer than six and not more than 11 other judges.

**Chief Justice of the Supreme Court:** SARATH NANDA SILVA.

**Attorney-General:** C. R. DE SILVA.

# Religion

According to the 2001 census, the distribution of the population by religion in 18 out of 25 districts was: Buddhist 76.7%, Muslim 8.5%, Hindu 7.9%, Roman Catholics 6.1% and other Christians 0.8%. The census results did not cover the Tamil-dominated northern and eastern districts, where a higher proportion of Hindus could be expected.

## BUDDHISM

Theravada Buddhism is the predominant sect. There are an estimated 53,000 Buddhist *Bhikkhus* (monks), living in about 6,000 temples.

**All Ceylon Buddhist Congress:** 380 Bauddhaloka Mawatha, Colombo 7; tel. (11) 2688517; fax (11) 2691695; e-mail acbc@isplanka.lk; internet www.acbc.lk; f. 1919; Pres. JAGATH SUMATHIPALA; Jt Secs Maj.-Gen. (retd) JALIYA NAMMUNI, SUNIL SARATH KURUGAMA.

**Sri Lanka Regional Centre of the World Fellowship of Buddhists:** 380 Bauddhaloka Mawatha, Colombo 7; tel. (11) 2681886; fax (11) 2833362; e-mail nationlanka@sltnet.lk; Pres. D. M. JAYATILAKA DISSANAYAKE; Sec. Prof. JAYANTHA WEERAKOON.

## HINDUISM

The majority of the Tamil population are Hindus. According to the 2001 census the Hindu population in 18 out of 25 districts was 1,329,020.

## CHRISTIANITY

**National Christian Council of Sri Lanka:** 368/6 Bauddhaloka Mawatha, Colombo 7; tel. (11) 2671723; fax (11) 2671721; e-mail sec@nccsl.org; internet www.nccsl.org; f. 1945; 13 mem. bodies; Gen. Sec. Rev. Dr JAYASIRI PEIRIS.

### The Anglican Communion

The Church of Ceylon (Sri Lanka) comprises two Anglican dioceses. In 1985 there were about 78,000 adherents.

**Bishop of Colombo:** Rt Rev. DULEEP KAMIL DE CHICKERA, Bishop's House, 358/2 Bauddhaloka Mawatha, Colombo 7; tel. (11) 2684810; fax (11) 2684811; e-mail bishop@eureka.lk; diocese f. 1845.

**Bishop of Kurunegala:** Rt Rev. KUMARA BANDARA SAMUEL ILLANGASINGHE, Bishop's House, Kandy Rd, Kurunegala; tel. (37) 22191; fax (37) 26806; e-mail bishopkg@sltnet.lk; diocese f. 1950.

### The Roman Catholic Church

For ecclesiastical purposes, Sri Lanka comprises one archdiocese and 10 dioceses. At 31 December 2006 there were an estimated 1, 380,998 adherents in the country.

**Catholic Bishops' Conference in Sri Lanka:** 19 Balcombe Place, Cotta Rd, Borella, Colombo 8; tel. (11) 2697062; fax (11) 2699619; e-mail conferencesl@sltnet.lk; internet www.cbcsl.com; f. 1975; Pres. Most Rev. VIANNEY FERNANDO (Bishop of Kandy); Sec.-Gen. Rt Rev. Dr NORBERT M. ANDRADI.

**Archbishop of Colombo:** Most Rev. Dr OSWALD THOMAS COLMAN GOMIS, Archbishop's House, 976 Gnanartha Pradeepaya Mawatha, Colombo 8; tel. (11) 2695471; fax (11) 2692009; e-mail sunilde@sltnet .lk; internet www.archdioceseofcolombo.com.

### The Church of South India

The Church comprises 21 dioceses, including one, Jaffna, in Sri Lanka. The diocese of Jaffna, with an estimated 18,500 adherents in 1997, was formerly part of the South India United Church (a union of churches of the Congregational and Presbyterian/Reformed traditions), which merged with the Methodist Church in South India and the four southern dioceses of the (Anglican) Church of India to form the Church of South India in 1947.

**Bishop in Jaffna:** Rt Rev. Dr DANIEL S. THIAGARAJAH, 36 5/2, Sinsapa Rd, Colombo 6; tel. (11) 2150795; fax (11) 2505805; e-mail bishop@csijaffnadiocese.com; internet csijaffnadiocese.com.

### Other Christian Churches

**Christian Reformed Church:** General Consistory Office, 363 Galle Rd, Colombo 6; tel. (11) 2360861; fax (11) 2582469; e-mail drc1642@sltnet.lk; f. 1642; Pres. of Gen. Consistory Rev. N. ROSHAN MENDIS; Admin. Mgr GODFREY B. EBENEZER.

**Methodist Church:** Methodist Headquarters, 252 Galle Rd, Colombo 3; tel. (11) 2575630; fax (11) 2436090; e-mail methhq@sltnet.lk; internet www.gbgm-umc.org/methchsrilan; 30,139 mems (2000); Pres. of Conference Rev. W. P. EBENEZER JOSEPH; Sec. of Conference Rev. J. C. S. ROHITHA DE SILVA.

Other denominations active in the country include the Sri Lanka Baptist Sangamaya.

## BAHÁ'Í FAITH

**Spiritual Assembly:** Bahá'í National Centre, 65 Havelock Rd, Colombo 5; tel. and fax (11) 2587360; e-mail nsasrilanka@sltnet.lk.

# The Press

## NEWSPAPERS

Newspapers are published in Sinhala, Tamil and English. There are five main newspaper publishing groups:

**Associated Newspapers of Ceylon Ltd:** Lake House, 35 D. R. Wijewardene Mawatha, POB 248, Colombo 10; tel. (11) 2435641; fax (11) 2449069; e-mail webmgr@sri.lanka.net; internet www.lanka .net/lakehouse; f. 1926; nationalized 1973; publr of *Daily News*,

*Evening Observer*, *Thinakaran*, *Lak Janatha* and *Dinamina* (dailies); three Sunday papers: *Sunday Observer*, *Silumina* and *Thinakaran Vaara Manjari*; and 11 periodicals; Chair. JANADASA PEIRIS; CEO TIKIRI KOBBEKADUWA.

**Express Newspapers (Ceylon) Ltd:** 185 Grandpass Rd, POB 160, Colombo 14; tel. (11) 2323841; fax (11) 2439987; e-mail md@expressnewspapers.lk; internet www.virakesari.lk; f. 1930; publr of *Virakesari Daily*, *Mithran Varamalar*, *Metro News* and *Virakesari Weekly* (Sunday); Chair. HARI SELVANATHAN; Man. Dir KUMAR NADESAN.

**Leader Publications (Pvt) Ltd:** 98 Ward Pl., Colombo 7; tel. (75) 2365892; fax (75) 2365891; e-mail editor@thesundayleader.lk; internet www.thesundayleader.lk; publr of *The Sunday Leader* and *Irida Peramuna*.

**Upali Newspapers Ltd:** 223 Bloemendhal Rd, POB 133, Colombo 13; tel. (11) 2497500; e-mail prabath@unl.upali.lk; f. 1981; publr of *The Island*, *Divaina* (dailies), two Sunday papers, *Sunday Island* and *Sunday Divaina*, four weeklies, *Vidusara*, *Navaliya*, *Bindu* and *The Island International* (for sale abroad only), and one bi-weekly, *Vathmana–News Magazine* ; English and Sinhala; Editor-in-Chief PRABATH SAHABANDU; Chair. LAKMENI WIJAYWARDANA WELGAMA.

**Wijeya Newspapers Ltd:** 8 Hunupitiya Cross Rd, Colombo 2; tel. (11) 2314714; fax (11) 2449504; e-mail wnlgen@wijeya.lk; internet www.wijeya.lk; f. 1979; publr of *Daily Mirror*, *The Sunday Times*, *Lankadeepa*, *Irida Lankadeepa* and *Sirikatha*; Sinhala and English; Chair. RANJIT SUJIVA WIJEWARDENE.

### Dailies

**Daily Mirror:** 8 Hunupitiya Cross Rd, Colombo 2; tel. (11) 2314714; fax (11) 2449504; e-mail mirror@wijeya.lk; internet www.dailymirror.lk; f. 1996; English and Sinhala; Editor CHAMPIKA LIYANAARACHCHI; circ. 30,000.

**Daily News:** Lake House, D. R. Wijewardene Mawatha, POB 248, Colombo 10; tel. (11) 2429429; fax (11) 2429210; e-mail editor@dailynews.lk; internet www.dailynews.lk; f. 1918; morning; English; Editor GEOFF WIJEYESINGHE; circ. 65,000.

**Dinakara:** 95 Maligakanda Rd, Colombo 10; tel. (11) 2595754; f. 1978; morning; Sinhala; publ. by Rekana Publrs; official organ of the Sri Lanka Freedom Party; Editor MULEN PERERA; circ. 12,000.

**Dinamina:** Lake House, D. R. Wijewardene Mawatha, POB 248, Colombo 10; tel. (11) 2221181; internet www.dinamina.lk; f. 1909; morning; Sinhala; Editor G. S. PERERA; circ. 140,000.

**Divaina:** 223 Bloemendhal Rd, POB 133, Colombo 13; tel. (11) 2224001; fax (11) 2448103; e-mail gamini@unl.upali.lk; internet www.divaina.com; f. 1982; morning and Sunday; Chief Editor UPALI TENNAKOON.

**Eelanadu:** Jaffna; tel. (21) 22389; f. 1959; morning; Tamil; Chair. S. RAVEENTHIRANATHAN; Editor M. SIVANANTHAM; circ. 15,000.

**The Island:** 223 Bloemendhal Rd, Colombo 13; tel. (11) 2448102; fax (11) 4609198; e-mail prabath@unl.upali.lk; internet www.island.lk; f. 1981; English; Editor GAMINI WEERAKOON; circ. 80,000.

**Lak Janatha:** Lake House, D. R. Wijewardene Mawatha, Colombo 10; tel. (11) 2421181; f. 2005; evening; Sinhala; Editor SUJEEWA DISSANAYAKE.

**Lankadeepa:** 8 Hunupitiya Cross Rd, Colombo 2; tel. (11) 2448321; fax (11) 2438039; e-mail siri@wijeya.lk; internet www.lankadeepa.lk; f. 1986; Sinhala and English; Editor SIRI RANASINGHE; circ. 160,000.

**Namathu Eelanadu:** Jaffna; f. 2002; Tamil; Editor SIVASUBRAMANIAM RAGURAM.

**Peraliya:** Borella Supermarket Complex, 2nd Floor, Colombo 8; Editor SUJEEWA GAMAGE.

**Thinakaran:** Lake House, D. R. Wijewardene Mawatha, POB 248, Colombo 10; tel. (11) 2221181; f. 1932; morning; Tamil; Editor R. SIVAGURUNATHAN; circ. daily 14,000.

**Thinakkural:** 68 Ellie House Rd, Colombo 15; internet www.thinakkural.com; Tamil; also publ. from Jaffna; Editor A. SIYANESACHELVAN.

**Uthayan:** Jaffna; e-mail editorial@uthayan.com; internet www.uthayan.com; Tamil; Chief Editor M. V. KAANAMYLNATHAN.

**Valampuri:** 3, 2nd Lane, Brown Rd, Jaffna; tel. (21) 2227829; fax (21) 2223378; e-mail valampurii@yahoo.com; f. 1999; Tamil; Chief Editor N. VIJAYASUNTHARAM.

**Virakesari Daily:** 185 Grandpass Rd, POB 160, Colombo 14; tel. (11) 2320881; fax (11) 2439987; e-mail kesari10@virakesari.lk; internet www.virakesari.lk; f. 1931; morning; Tamil; Man. Dir KUMAR NADESAN; Editor R. PRABAGAN; circ. 60,000.

### Sunday Newspapers

**Irida Lankadeepa:** 8 Hunupitiya Cross Rd, Colombo 2; tel. (11) 2448321; fax (11) 2438039; e-mail siri@wijeya.lk; internet www.lankadeepa.lk; Sinhala; Chief Editor SIRI RANSINGHE.

**Janasathiya:** 47 Jayantha Weerasekara Mawatha, Colombo 10; f. 1965; Sinhala; publ. by Suriya Publishers Ltd; Editor SARATH NAWANA; circ. 50,000.

**Mithran Varamalar:** 185 Grandpass Rd, Colombo 14; tel. (11) 2320881; fax (11) 2448205; e-mail kesari25@virasekari.lk; internet www.virakesari.lk; f. 1969; Tamil; Man. Dir KUMAR NADESAN; Editor V. THEVARAJ; circ. 29,000.

**Silumina:** Lake House, 35 D. R. Wijewardene Mawatha, Colombo 10; tel. (11) 2324772; fax (11) 2449069; e-mail editor@silumina.lk; internet www.silumina.lk; f. 1930; Sinhala; Editor NIWAL HORANA; circ. 264,000.

**Sunday Island:** 223 Bloemendhal Rd, POB 133, Colombo 13; tel. (11) 2421599; fax (74) 609198; e-mail manik@unl.upali.lk; f. 1981; English; Editor MANIK DE SILVA; circ. 40,000.

**The Sunday Leader:** Colombo Commercial Bldg, 1st Floor, 121 Sir James Peiris Mawatha, Colombo 2; tel. (75) 2365892; fax (75) 2365891; e-mail editor@thesundayleader.lk; internet www.thesundayleader.lk; English; Editor LASANTHA WICKRAMATUNGA.

**Sunday Observer:** D. R. Wijewardene Mawatha, POB 248, Colombo 10; tel. (11) 2429231; fax (11) 2429230; e-mail editor@sundayobserver.lk; internet www.sundayobserver.lk; f. 1923; English; Editor JAYATILLEKE DE SILVA; circ. 125,000.

**Sunday Thinakkural:** 68 Ellie House Rd, Colombo 15; internet www.thinakkural.com/sundaythinakkural; Tamil; also publ. from Jaffna; Editor A. SIYANESACHELVAN.

**The Sunday Times:** 8 Hunupitiya Cross Rd, Colombo 2; tel. (11) 2326247; fax (11) 2423922; e-mail editor@sundaytimes.wnl.lk; internet www.sundaytimes.lk; f. 1986; English and Sinhala; Editor SINGHA RATNATUNGA; circ. 116,000.

**Thinakaran Vaara Manjari:** Lake House, 35 D. R. Wijewardene Mawatha, Colombo 10; tel. (11) 2221181; f. 1948; Tamil; Editor R. SRIKANTHAN; circ. 35,000.

**Virakesari Weekly:** 185 Grandpass Rd, Colombo 14; tel. (11) 2320881; fax (11) 2448205; e-mail webmaster@virakesari.lk; internet www.virakesari.lk; f. 1931; Tamil and English; Man. Dir KUMAR NADESAN; Editor MURUGESAMPILLAI SUBRAMANIAM; circ. 110,000.

## PERIODICALS

(weekly unless otherwise stated)

**Athavan:** Colombo; Tamil.

**Aththa:** 91 Dr N. M. Perera Mawatha, Colombo 8; tel. (11) 2691450; fax (11) 2691610; e-mail dew128@dialogsl.net; f. 1964; Sinhala; publ. by the Communist Party of Sri Lanka; Editor GUNASENA VITHANA; circ. 28,000.

**Business Lanka:** Trade Information Service, Sri Lanka Export Development Board, Level 7, 42 Navam Mawatha, POB 1872, Colombo 2; tel. (11) 2300677; fax (11) 2300715; e-mail tisinfo@tradenetsl.lk; f. 1981; quarterly; information for visiting business executives, etc.; Editor S. D. ISAAC.

**Ceylon Commerce:** National Chamber of Commerce of Sri Lanka, NCCSL Bldg, 450 D. R. Wijewardene Mawatha, POB 1375, Colombo 10; tel. (11) 2689597; fax (11) 2689596; e-mail nccsl@slt.lk; internet www.nationalchamberlk.org; monthly.

**Ceylon Medical Journal:** 6 Wijerama Mawatha, Colombo 7; tel. (11) 2690212; fax (11) 2698802; e-mail slma@eureka.lk; internet www.medinet.lk/cmj; f. 1887; quarterly; Editors Prof. H. JANAKA DE SILVA, Dr A. ABEYGUNASEKERA.

**The Economic Times:** 130/C/8 Jothikarama Mawatha, Pannipitiya; tel. (11) 2796134; fax (11) 4305787; f. 1970; Editor THIMSY FAHIM.

**The Financial Times:** 323 Union Place, POB 330, Colombo 2; tel. (11) 2226181; quarterly; commercial and economic affairs; Man. Editor CYRIL GARDINER.

**Gnanarthapradeepaya:** Colombo Catholic Press, 2 Gnanarthapradeepaya Mawatha, Borella, Colombo 8; tel. (11) 2695984; fax (11) 2692586; e-mail pradeepaya@sltnet.lk; f. 1866; Sinhala; Roman Catholic; Chief Editor Rev. Fr CYRIL GAMINI FERNANDO; Exec. Dir Rev. Fr ROHAN DE ALWIS; circ. 26,000.

**Irudina:** Lithira Publications (Pvt) Ltd, 98 Ward Place, Colombo 7; tel. (11) 5344202; fax (11) 5344200; e-mail editor@irudina.lk; internet www.irudina.lk; f. 2004; Sinhala; Editor MOHAN LAL PIYADASA.

**Janakavi:** 47 Jayantha Weerasekera Mawatha, Colombo 10; fortnightly; Sinhala; Assoc. Editor KARUNARATNE AMERASINGHE.

**Manasa:** 150 Dutugemunu St, Dehiwala, Colombo; tel. (11) 2553994; f. 1978; Sinhala; monthly; science of the mind; Editor SUMANADASA SAMARASINGHE; circ. 6,000.

**Mihira:** Lake House, 35 D. R. Wijewardene Mawatha, Colombo 10; tel. (11) 2419583; f. 1964; Sinhala children's magazine; Editor M. NEWTON PINTO; circ. 145,000.

**Morning Star:** 39 Fussels Lane, Colombo 6; tel. (11) 2511233; fax (11) 2584836; e-mail jdcsiacm@panlanka.net; f. 1841; English and Tamil; publ. by the Jaffna diocese of the Church of South India.

**Nava Yugaya:** Lake House, 35 D. R. Wijewardene Mawatha, Colombo 10; tel. (11) 2419581; f. 1956; literary fortnightly; Sinhala; Editor S. N. SENANAYAKE; circ. 57,000.

**Navaliya:** 223 Bloemendhal Rd, Colombo 13; tel. (11) 2324001; fax (11) 2448103; internet www.navaliya.com; Sinhala; women's interest; Editor CHANDANI WIJETUNGE; circ. 148,260.

**Pathukavalan:** POB 2, Jaffna; tel. (21) 22300; f. 1876; Tamil; publ. by St Joseph's Catholic Press; Editor Rev. Fr RUBAN MARIAMPILLAI; circ. 7,000.

**Puthiya Ulaham:** 115 4th Cross St, Jaffna; tel. (21) 22627; f. 1976; Tamil; six a year; publ. by Centre for Better Society; Editor Rev. Dr S. J. EMMANUEL; circ. 1,500.

**Ravaya:** Colombo; Sinhala; Editor VICTOR IVAN.

**Samajawadhaya:** 91 Dr N. M. Perera Mawatha, Colombo 8; tel. (11) 2595328; monthly; theoretical; publ. by the Communist Party of Sri Lanka.

**Sarasaviya:** Lake House, 35 D. R. Wijewardene Mawatha, Colombo 10; tel. (11) 2429586; f. 1963; Sinhala; films; Editor GRANVILLE SILVA; circ. 56,000.

**Sinhala Bauddhaya:** Maha Bodhi Mandira, 130 Rev. Hikkaduwe Sri Sumangala Nahimi Mawatha, Colombo 10; tel. (11) 1677626; e-mail mahabodhi@asia.com; f. 1906; publ. by The Maha Bodi Society of Ceylon; Hon. Sec. KIRTHI KALAHE; circ. 25,000.

**Sirikatha:** 8 Hunupitiya Cross Rd, Colombo 2; tel. (11) 2314714; fax (11) 2449504; Sinhala women's magazine; Editor SIRI RANASINGHE.

**Sri Lanka Government Gazette:** Government Press, POB 507, Colombo; tel. (11) 2293611; f. 1802; Sinhala and Tamil; official govt bulletin; circ. 54,000.

**Sri Lanka News:** Lake House, 35 D. R. Wijewardene Mawatha, Colombo 10; tel. (11) 2429429; fax (11) 2449069; f. 1938; digest of news and features; printing temporarily suspended from March 2002; Editor RUWAN GODAGE.

**Sri Lanka Today:** Government Dept of Information, 7 Sir Baron Jayatilaka Mawatha, Colombo 1; tel. (11) 2228376; English; quarterly; Editor MANEL ABHAYARATNE.

**Subasetha:** Lake House, 35 D. R. Wijewardene Mawatha, Colombo 10; tel. (11) 2221181; f. 1967; Sinhala; astrology, the occult and indigenous medicine; Editor Capt. K. CHANDRA SRI KULARATNE; circ. 100,000.

**Tharunee:** Lake House, 35 D. R. Wijewardene Mawatha, Colombo 10; tel. (11) 2429588; fax (11) 2449069; f. 1969; Sinhala; women's journal; Editor SUMANA SAPRAMADU; circ. 95,000.

**Vidusara:** 223 Bloemendhal Rd, Colombo 13; tel. (11) 2324001; fax (11) 2448103; internet www.vidusara.com; Sinhala; Editor ANURA SIRIWARDENA; circ. 103,992.

### NEWS AGENCIES

**Lankapuvath** (National News Agency of Sri Lanka): Transworks House, Lower Chatham St, Colombo 1; tel. (11) 2673483; fax (11) 2673011; f. 1978; Chair. D. E. W. GUNASEKARA; Editor G. L. W. WIJESINHA.

**TamilNet:** e-mail tamilnet@tamilnet.com; internet www.tamilnet.com; f. 1997; reports on Tamil affairs.

### PRESS ASSOCIATIONS

**Foreign Correspondents' Association of Sri Lanka:** 20 1/1 Regent Flats, Sir Chittampalan Gardiner Mawatha, Colombo; tel. (11) 2231224.

**Sri Lanka Press Association:** Colombo; Pres. B. H. S. JAYEWARDENE.

## Publishers

**W. E. Bastian and Co (Pvt) Ltd:** 23 Canal Row, Fort, Colombo 1; tel. (11) 2432752; f. 1904; art, literature, technical; Dirs H. A. MUNIDEVA, K. HEWAGE, N. MUNIDEVA, G. C. BASTIAN.

**Buddhist Publication Society:** 54 Sangharaja Mawatha, POB 61, Kandy; tel. (81) 2237283; fax (81) 2223679; e-mail bps@sltnet.lk; internet www.bps.lk; f. 1958; philosophy, religion and theology; Pres. Bhikkhu BODHI.

**Colombo Catholic Press:** 2 Gnanarthapradeepaya Mawatha, Borella, Colombo 8; tel. (11) 2678106; fax (11) 2692586; e-mail colombocp@sltnet.lk; f. 1865; religious; publrs of *The Messenger*, *Gnanarthapradeepaya*, *The Weekly*; Exec. Dir Rev. Fr ROHAN DE ALWIS.

**M. D. Gunasena and Co Ltd:** 217 Olcott Mawatha, POB 246, Colombo 11; tel. (11) 2323981; fax (11) 2323336; e-mail mdgunasena@mail.ewisl.net; internet www.mdgunasena.com; f. 1913; educational and general; Chair M. D. PERCY GUNASENA; Man. Dir M. D. ANANDA GUNASENA.

**Lake House Printers and Publishers Ltd:** 41 W. A. D. Ramanayake Mawatha, POB 1458, Colombo 2; tel. (11) 2433271; fax (11) 2449504; e-mail wnl@wijeya.lk; f. 1965; Chair. R. S. WIJEWARDENE; Sec. D. P. ANURA NISHANTHA KUMARA.

**Pradeepa Publishers:** 34/34 Lawyers' Office Complex, Colombo 12; tel. and fax (11) 2435074; e-mail kjaytie@slt.lk; academic and fictional; Propr K. JAYATILAKE.

**Saman Publishers Ltd:** 49/16 Iceland Bldg, Colombo 3; tel. (11) 2223058; fax (11) 2447972.

**Sarexpo International Ltd:** Caves Bookshop, 81 Sir Baron Jayatilleke Mawatha, POB 25, Colombo 1; tel. (11) 2422676; fax (11) 2447854; e-mail sarexpo@eureka.lk; f. 1876; history, arts, law, medicine, technical, educational; Man. Dir C. J. S. FERNANDO.

**K. V. G. de Silva and Sons (Colombo) Ltd:** Shop No. 5, Liberty Plaza, Colombo 3; tel. (11) 7455646; fax (11) 7555543; e-mail photowave@sltnet.lk; f. 1898; art, philosophy, scientific, technical, academic, 'Ceyloniana', fiction; Man. FREDERICK JAYARATNAM.

### PUBLISHERS' ASSOCIATION

**Sri Lanka Association of Publishers:** 112 S. Mahinda Mawatha, Maradana, Colombo 10; tel. (11) 2695773; fax (11) 2696653; e-mail dayawansajay@hotmail.com; Pres. DAYAWANSA JAYAKODY; Sec.-Gen. GAMINI WIJESURIYA.

## Broadcasting and Communications

### TELECOMMUNICATIONS

**Lanka Communication Services (Pvt) Ltd:** 65C Dharmapala Mawatha, Colombo 7; tel. (11) 2437545; fax (11) 2537547; e-mail webmaster@lankacom.net; internet www.lankacom.net; f. 1991; subsidiary of Singapore Telecom International; Man. Dir ROHITH UDALAGAMA.

**MTN Networks (Pvt) Ltd:** 528 R. A. De Mel Mawatha, Colombo 3; tel. (11) 2678678; fax (11) 2678692; e-mail dialog@dialog.lk; internet www.dialog.lk; wholly owned subsidiary of Telekom Malaysia; operates Dialog GSM, Sri Lanka's largest mobile phone network; Chief Exec. Dr SHRIDHIR SARIPUTTA HANSA WIJAYASURIYA.

**Sri Lanka Telecom Ltd:** Telecom Headquarters, 7th Floor, Lotus Rd, POB 503, Colombo 1; tel. (11) 2329711; fax (11) 2440000; e-mail pr@slt.lk; internet www.slt.lk; 35% owned by Nippon Telegraph and Telephone Corpn (Japan), 49.5% by Govt of Sri Lanka and 3.5% by employees; Chair. P. ASOKA WEERASINGHE DE SILVA; CEO SHOJI TAKAHASHI.

#### Regulatory Authority

**Telecommunications Regulatory Commission of Sri Lanka:** 276 Elvitigala Mawatha, Manning Town, Colombo 8; tel. (11) 2689345; fax (11) 2689341; e-mail dgtsl@trc.gov.lk; internet www.trc.gov.lk; f. 1996; Chair. LALITH WEERATHUNGA; Dir-Gen. PRIYANTHA KARIYAPPERUMA.

### RADIO

**Sri Lanka Broadcasting Corpn:** Independence Sq., POB 574, Colombo 7; tel. (11) 2697491; fax (11) 2691568; e-mail chmnslbc@sltnet.lk; internet www.slbc.lk; f. 1967; under Ministry of Information and Media; controls all broadcasting in Sri Lanka; regional stations at Anuradhapura, Kandy and Matara; transmitting stations at Ambewela, Amparai, Anuradhapura, Diyagama, Ekala, Galle, Kanthalai, Mahiyangana, Maho, Matara, Puttalam, Ratnapura, Seeduwa, Senkadagala, Weeraketiya; home service in Sinhala, Tamil and English; foreign service also in Tamil, English, Sinhala, Hindi, Kannada, Malayalam, Nepali and Telugu; 893 broadcasting hours per week: 686 on domestic services, 182 on external services and 126 on education; Chair. HUDSON SAMARASINGHE; Dir-Gen. SAMANTHA WELIWERIYA.

**Asura FM:** No. 52, 5th Lane, Colombo 3; tel. (11) 2575000; fax (11) 2301082; internet www.asurafm.com; broadcasts 24 hrs daily in Sinhala; Chair. NIRAJ WICKREMESINGHE.

**Colombo Communications (Pvt) Ltd:** 2/9 2nd Floor, Liberty Plaza, 250 R. A. de Mel Mawatha, Colombo 3; tel. (11) 2577924; fax (11) 2577929; commercial station; three channels broadcast 24 hrs daily in English, Sinhala and Tamil.

**Lite FM:** No. 52, 5th Lane, Colombo 3; tel. (11) 2575000; fax (11) 2301082; e-mail lite892@tnlradio.com; internet www.lite892.com; commercial station; broadcasts 24 hrs daily in English; Chair. NIRAJ WICKREMESINGHE.

**MBC Networks (Pvt) Ltd:** 7 Braybrooke Place, Colombo 2; tel. (11) 5340111; fax (11) 5340124; internet www.maharaja.lk; commercial station comprising four channels; broadcasts 24 hrs daily in English, Sinhala and Tamil.

**TNL Radio:** No. 52, 5th Lane, Colombo 3; tel. (11) 2575000; fax (11) 2301082; e-mail info@tnlradio.com; internet www.tnlradio.com; f. 1993; commercial station; broadcasts 24 hrs daily in English; Chair. NIRAJ WICKREMESINGHE.

**Trans World Radio:** 125/3 3rd Lane, Subadrarama Rd, POB 123, Nugegoda; tel. (5) 559321; fax (11) 2817749; e-mail rkoch@twr.org; internet www.twr.org; f. 1978; religious station; broadcasts two hrs every morning Monday–Friday, three hrs Saturday and Sunday morning, and six and a half hrs each evening to Indian subcontinent; Dir (Finance/Administration) ROGER KOCH; Eng. P. VELMURUGAN.

**Voice of Tigers:** Vanni; internet www.eelam.com/vot; f. 1990 by the LTTE; banned until 2003; broadcasts eight and a half hrs daily in Tamil and Sinhala.

### TELEVISION

**Sri Lanka Rupavahini Corpn (SLRC):** Independence Sq., POB 2204, Colombo 7; tel. (11) 2599506; fax (11) 2580929; e-mail ict@rupavahini.lk; internet www.rupavahini.lk; f. 1982; studio at Colombo; transmitting stations at nine locations; broadcasts 18 hrs daily on Channel I, 15 hrs daily on Channel II; Dir-Gen. NISHANTHA RANATUNGA; Chair. M. M. ZUHAIR.

**Independent Television Network (ITN):** Wickremasinghepura, Battaramulla; tel. (11) 2775494; fax (11) 2774591; e-mail itn@slt.lk; internet www.itn.lk; broadcasts about 19 hrs daily; operates Lakhanda Radio (24 hrs; daily); Chair. ANURA SIRIWARDENA; Gen. Man. W. P. A. M. WIJESINGHE.

**EAP Network (Pvt) Ltd:** 676 Galle Rd, Colombo 3; tel. (11) 2503819; fax (11) 2503788; e-mail eapnet@slt.lk; Chair. SOMA EDIRISINGHE; Man. Dir JEEVAKA EDIRISINGHE.

**MTV Channel (Pvt) Ltd:** Araliya Uyana, Depanama, Pannipitiya; tel. (11) 5340111; e-mail info@media.maharaja.lk; f. 1992; broadcasts on three channels in English, Sinhala and Tamil.

**National Television of Tamil Eelam (NTT):** e-mail ntt_news@yahoo.com; f. 2005; broadcasts for two hrs daily.

**Telshan Network (Pvt) Ltd (TNL):** 9D Tower Bldg, 25 Station Rd, Colombo 4; tel. (11) 2596241; fax (11) 2706125; e-mail tnltvr@slt.lk; Chair. and Man. Dir SHANTILAL NILKANT WICKREMESINGHE.

## Finance

(cap. = capital; res = reserves; dep. = deposits; m. = million; brs = branches; amounts in Sri Lanka rupees, unless otherwise indicated)

### BANKING

#### Central Bank

**Central Bank of Sri Lanka:** 30 Janadhipathi Mawatha, POB 590, Colombo 1; tel. (11) 2477000; fax (11) 2477712; e-mail cbslgen@cbsl.lk; internet www.cbsl.gov.lk; f. 1950; sole bank of issue; cap. 15m., res 83,367m., dep. 126,803m. (Dec. 2005); Gov. and Chair. of the Monetary Board AJITH NIVARD CABRAAL; Dep. Govs Dr RANEE JAYAMAHA, W. A. WIJEWARDENA; 3 regional offices.

#### Commercial Banks

**Bank of Ceylon:** 4 Bank of Ceylon Mawatha, POB 241, Colombo 1; tel. (11) 2446811; fax (11) 2447171; e-mail boc@boc.lk; internet www.boc.lk; f. 1939; 100% state-owned; cap. 4,000m., res 3,614m., dep. 262,676m. (Dec. 2006); Chair. Dr GAMINI WICKRAMASINGHE; Gen. Man. B. A. C. FERNANDO; 303 brs in Sri Lanka, 3 brs abroad.

**Commercial Bank of Ceylon Ltd:** Commercial House, 21 Bristol St, POB 856, Colombo 1; tel. (11) 2430416; fax (11) 2449889; e-mail e-mail@combank.net; internet www.combank.net; f. 1969; 29.77% owned by DFCC Bank, 29.91% by govt corpns and 40.32% by public; cap. 2,428.2m., res 13,414.7m., dep. 171,964.1m. (Dec. 2006); Chair. M. J. C. AMARASURIYA; Man. Dir A. L. GOONERATNE; 136 brs.

**Hatton National Bank Ltd:** 479 T. B. Jayah Mawatha, POB 837, Colombo 10; tel. (11) 2664664; fax (11) 2446523; e-mail moreinfo@hnb.net; internet www.hnb.net; f. 1970; 27.1% owned by individuals, 72.9% by institutions; cap. 1,177.6m., res 10,015.8m., dep. 155,808.8m. (Dec. 2006); Chair. RIENZIE T. WIJETILLEKE; Man. Dir and CEO RAJENDRA THEAGARAJAH; 160 brs.

**Nations Trust Bank Ltd:** 242 Union Place, Colombo 2; tel. (11) 4313131; fax (11) 2307854; e-mail info@nationstrust.com; internet www.nationstrust.com; f. 1999; privately owned; acquired Mercantile Leasing Ltd by merger to form Nations Leasing business; cap. 1,257.9m., res 1,265.2m., dep. 22,308.9m. (Dec. 2006); Chair. AJIT GUNEWARDENE; CEO ZULFIQAR ZAVAHIR.

**Pan Asia Banking Corpn Ltd:** 450 Galle Rd, Colombo 3; tel. (11) 2565556; fax (11) 2565558; e-mail pabc@pabcbank.com; internet www.pabcbank.com; f. 1995; 100% privately-owned (82.9% owned by local shareholders, 17.1% by foreign shareholders); cap. 1,106.4m., res 128.7m., dep. 10,082.5m. (Dec. 2006); Chair. A. G. WEERASINGHE; Man. Dir, Gen. Man. and CEO R. NADARAJAH; 18 brs.

**People's Bank:** 75 Sir Chittampalam A. Gardiner Mawatha, POB 728, Colombo 2; tel. (11) 2327841; fax (11) 2433127; e-mail info@peoplesbank.lk; internet www.peoplesbank.lk; f. 1961; 92% owned by Govt, 8% by co-operatives; cap. 4,202.0m. (incl. special lending rights 4,152.0m. capital pending allotment), res 6,254.4m., dep. 269,947.2m. (Dec. 2006); Chair. W. KARUNAJEEWA; CEO and Gen. Man. ASOKA DE SILVA; 324 brs.

**Sampath Bank Ltd:** Sampath Centre Bldg, 110 Sir James Peiris Mawatha, POB 997, Colombo 2; tel. (11) 2303050; fax (11) 2303085; e-mail info@sampath.lk; internet www.sampath.lk; f. 1987; cap. 688.9m., res 5,936.4m., dep. 86,134.9m. (Dec. 2006); Chair. EDGAR GUNATUNGA; Man. Dir/CEO ANIL AMARASURIYA; 100 brs.

**Seylan Bank Ltd:** Ceylinco Seylan Towers, 90 Galle Rd, POB 400, Colombo 3; tel. (11) 2456789; fax (11) 2456456; e-mail info@seylan.lk; internet www.eseylan.com; f. 1988; cap. 1,705.1m., res 4,648.8m., dep. 104,383.2m. (Dec. 2006); Chair. and Man. Dir J. L. B. KOTELAWALA; Gen. Man., Dir and CEO AJITA PASQUAL; 116 brs.

**Union Bank of Colombo Ltd:** 15A Alfred Place, Colombo 3; tel. (11) 2370870; fax (11) 2370692; e-mail ubc@unionb.com; internet www.unionb.com; f. 1995; cap. 1,060.0m., res 9.8m., dep. 7,807.1m. (Dec. 2006); Chair. AJITA DE ZOYSA; CEO and Dir MAHENDRA FERNANDO.

#### Development Banks

**Agricultural and Industrial Credit Corpn of Ceylon:** POB 20, Colombo 3; tel. (11) 2223783; f. 1943; loan cap. 30m.; Chair. V. P. VITTACHI; Gen. Man. H. S. F. GOONEWARDENA.

**DFCC Bank:** 73/5 Galle Rd, POB 1397, Colombo 3; tel. (11) 2442442; fax (11) 2440376; e-mail info@dfccbank.com; internet www.dfccbank.com; f. 1956 as Development Finance Corpn of Ceylon; name changed as above 1997; provides long- and medium-term credit, investment banking and consultancy services; cap. 856.6m., res 8,628.6m., dep. 13,572.6m. (March 2007); Chair. RAJAN BRITO; Gen. Man. and CEO NIHAL FONSEKA; 3 brs.

**National Development Bank Ltd:** DHPL Bldg, 42 Nawam Mawatha, POB 1825, Colombo 2; tel. (11) 2314640; fax (11) 2314642; e-mail contact@ndbbank.com; internet www.ndbbank.com; f. 1979 by an Act of Parliament as National Development Bank of Sri Lanka; subsequently privatized and name changed as above in June 2005; provides long-term finance for projects, equity financing and merchant banking services; cap. 818.6m., res 7,736.2m., dep. 27,183.1 (Dec. 2006); Chair. P. M. NAGAHAWATTE; CEO NIHAL WELIKALA.

**State Mortgage and Investment Bank:** 269 Galle Road, POB 156, Colombo 3; tel. (11) 2573561; fax (11) 2573346; e-mail agmit@smib.lk; internet www.smib.lk; f. 1979; Chair. CHANDIMA WEERAKKODY; Gen. Man. AJITH WEERASINHE.

#### Merchant Banks

**Merchant Bank of Sri Lanka Ltd:** Bank of Ceylon Merchant Tower, 28 St Michael's Rd, POB 1987, Colombo 3; tel. (11) 4711711; fax (11) 2565666; e-mail mbslbank@mbslbank.com; internet www.mbslbank.com; f. 1982; 53.8% owned by Bank of Ceylon; public ltd liability co; cap. p.u. 2,500m., total assets 2,128m. (2003); Chair. JANAKA RATNAYAKE; CEO GAMINI KARUNATHILEKA; 3 brs.

**People's Merchant Bank Ltd:** Hemas House, Level 4, 75 Braybrooke Place, Colombo 2; tel. (11) 2300191; fax (11) 2300190; e-mail pmbank@sltnet.lk; f. 1984 as a subsidiary of People's Bank; total assets 610m. (1999); Chair. Dr G. FERNANDO.

#### Financial Association

**The Finance Houses' Association of Sri Lanka:** 181/1A Dharmapala Mawatha, Colombo 7; tel. (11) 2665865; fax (11) 2665864; e-mail finass@sltnet.lk; internet www.fha.lk; f. 1958; represents the finance cos registered and licensed by the Central Bank of Sri Lanka; Chair. SHILEY PERERA; Sec.-Gen. DENNIS VISWASAM.

### STOCK EXCHANGES

**Securities and Exchange Commission of Sri Lanka:** 11–01 East Tower, 28th and 29th Floors, World Trade Centre, Echelon Sq., Colombo 1; tel. (11) 2439144; fax (11) 2439149; e-mail mail@sec.gov.lk; internet www.sec.gov.lk; f. 1987; Dir-Gen. CHANNA DE SILVA; Chair. GAMINI WICKRAMASINGHE.

**Colombo Stock Exchange:** 04–01, West Block, World Trade Centre, Echelon Sq., Colombo 1; tel. (11) 2446581; fax (11) 2445279; e-mail cse@cse.lk; internet www.cse.lk; f. 1896; stock market; 21 mem. firms and 234 listed cos; Chair. A. N. FONSEKA; CEO SUREKHA SELLAHEWA.

### INSURANCE

**Ceylinco Insurance Co Ltd:** Ceylinco House, 4th Floor, 69 Janadhipathi Mawatha, Colombo 1; tel. (11) 2485757; fax (11) 2485769; e-mail jagath@lanka.com.lk; internet www.ceylinco-insurance.com; f. 1987; general and life insurance; Chair. and Man. Dir J. L. B. KOTELAWALA.

**Eagle Insurance Co Ltd:** 'Eagle House', 75 Kumaran Ratnam Rd, Colombo 2; tel. (11) 2437090; fax (11) 2447620; e-mail info@eagle.com.lk; internet www.eagle.com.lk; f. 1988 as CTC Eagle Insurance Co Ltd; general and life insurance; mem. of Aviva International Holdings Ltd; Man. Dir DEEPAL SOORIYAARACHCHI.

**Hayleys PLC:** Hayley Bldg, 400 Deans Rd, Colombo 10; tel. (11) 2695729; fax (11) 2699299; internet www.hayleys.com; f. 1952; Chair. N. G. WICKREMERATNE; Dep. Chair. A. M. PANDITHAGE.

**National Insurance Corpn Ltd:** 47 Muttiah Rd, POB 2202, Colombo 2; tel. (11) 2445738; fax (11) 2445733; e-mail nicopl@slt.lk; general; Chair. T. M. S. NANAYAKKARA; Sec. A. C. J. DE ALWIS.

**Sri Lanka Insurance Corporation Ltd:** 'Rakshana Mandiraya', 21 Vauxhall St, POB 1337, Colombo 2; tel. (11) 2357537; fax (11) 2447742; e-mail slic@srilankainsurance.com; internet www.srilankainsurance.com; f. 1961; privatized in 2003; all classes of insurance; Chair. D. H. S. JAYAWARDENE; CEO NALAKA GODAHEWA.

**Union Assurance Ltd:** Union Assurance Centre, 20 St Michael's Rd, Colombo 3; tel. (11) 2428428; fax (11) 2343065; e-mail unionassurance@ualink.lk; internet www.ualink.lk; f. 1987; general and life insurance; Chair. AJIT GUNEWARDENE; CEO MARINA THARMARATNAM.

## Trade and Industry

### GOVERNMENT AGENCIES

**Board of Investment of Sri Lanka:** World Trade Centre, West Tower, 26th Floor, Echelon Sq., Colombo 1; tel. (11) 2435027; fax (11) 2422407; e-mail infoboi@boi.lk; internet www.boi.lk; f. 1978 as the Greater Colombo Economic Commission; promotes foreign direct investment and administers the eight Export Processing Zones at Katunayake, Biyagama, Koggala, Mirigama, Malwatta, Horana, Mawathagama and Polgahawela; also administers industrial township at Watupitiwala and industrial parks at Seetawaka and Kandy; Chair. and Dir-Gen. DHAMMIKA PERERA.

**Public Enterprises Reform Commission (PERC):** World Trade Centre, West Tower, 11th Floor, Colombo 1; tel. (11) 2346831; fax (11) 2326116; e-mail info@perc.gov.lk; internet www.perc.gov.lk; f. 1995 to advise Govt on privatization and restructuring of loss-making state-sector enterprises and to promote national economic development; Chair. W. M. BANDUSENA; Dir-Gen. LEEL WICKREMARACHCHI.

**Sri Lanka Gem and Jewellery Exchange:** World Trade Centre, East Low Block, Levels 4 and 5, Echelon Sq., Colombo 1; e-mail slgje@sltnet.lk; internet www.slgemexchange.com; f. 1990; testing and certification of gems, trading booths; Dir-Gen. M. WIJESEKERA; Sen. Man. (Export Promotion) AJITH PERERA.

**National Gem and Jewellery Authority:** 25 Galle Face Terrace, Colombo 3; tel. and fax (11) 2390650; fax (11) 2329352; e-mail chngja@sltnet.lk; internet www.srilankagemautho.com; f. 1971 as State Gem Corpn; Chair. W. HASITHA TILLEKERATNE; Dir-Gen. S. J. S. CHANDRAGUPTHA.

**Trade Information Service:** Sri Lanka Export Development Board, Level 7, 42 Navam Mawatha, POB 1872, Colombo 2; tel. (11) 2300675; fax (11) 2300676; e-mail tisinfo@edb.tradenetsl.lk; internet www.srilankabusiness.com; f. 1981 to collect and disseminate commercial information and to provide advisory services to trade circles; Dir W. M. D. S. WEERAKOON.

### DEVELOPMENT ORGANIZATIONS

**Coconut Development Authority:** 11 Duke St, POB 386, Colombo 1; tel. (11) 2421027; fax (11) 2447602; e-mail cocoauth@panlanka.net; internet www.cda.lk; f. 1972; state body; promotes the coconut industry through financial assistance for mfrs of coconut products, market information, consultancy services and quality assurance; Chair. H. A. TILLEKERATNE.

**Industrial Development Board of Ceylon (IDB):** 615 Galle Rd, Katubedda, POB 09, Moratuwa; tel. (11) 2605326; fax (11) 2607002; e-mail idb@sltnet.lk; internet www.idb.lk; f. 1969; under Ministry of Rural Industries and Self Employment Promotion; promotes industrial development through provincial network; Chair. GAMINI SENANAYAKE; Gen. Man. G. R. JAYATHILAKE.

**Centre for Entrepreneurship Development and Consultancy Services:** 615 Galle Rd, Katubedda, POB 09, Moratuwa; tel. (11) 2632156; f. 1989; Dir T. M. KULARATHNE (acting).

**Centre for Industrial and Technology Information Services (CITIS):** 615 Galle Rd, Katubedda, POB 09, Moratuwa 10400; tel. (11) 2605372; fax (11) 2607002; e-mail idb@sltnet.lk; internet www.idb.lk; f. 1989; disseminates information to small and medium-sized enterprises; Dir G. J. K. ARIYADASA.

**Information and Communication Technology Association of Sri Lanka (ICTA):** 160/24 Kirimandala Mawatha, Colombo 5; tel. (11) 2369099; fax (11) 2369091; e-mail info@icta.lk; internet www.icta.lk; f. 2003; govt-owned; responsible for development of information communication technology in Sri Lanka; COO RESHAN DEWAPURA.

**Janatha Estates Development Board:** 55/75 Vauxhall St, Colombo 2; tel. (11) 2320901; fax (11) 2446577; f. 1975; manages 18 tea and spice plantations; 10,164 employees; 1 regional office.

**Sri Lanka Export Development Board:** Trade Information Service, Level 7, 42 Navam Mawatha, Colombo 2; tel. (11) 2300705; fax (11) 2300715; e-mail tisinfo@edb.tradenetsl.lk; internet www.tradenetsl.lk/edb; f. 1979; Chair. ROHANTHA ATHUKORALA.

### CHAMBERS OF COMMERCE

**Federation of Chambers of Commerce and Industry of Sri Lanka:** 53 Vauxhall Lane, 3rd Floor, Colombo 2; tel. (11) 2304253; fax (11) 2304255; e-mail fccisl@fccisl.lk; internet www.fccisl.lk; f. 1973; a central org. of 53 chambers of commerce and industry and trade asscns representing 12,500 cos throughout Sri Lanka; Pres. NAWAZ RAJABDEEN; Sec.-Gen. SAMANTHA ABEYWICKRAMA.

**All Ceylon Trade Chamber:** 212/45 1/3 Bodhiraja Mawatha, Colombo 11; tel. (11) 2432428; Pres. MUDLIYAR N. W. J. MUDALIGE; Gen. Sec. Y. P. MUTHUKUMARANA.

**Ceylon Chamber of Commerce:** 50 Navam Mawatha, POB 274, Colombo 2; tel. (11) 2421745; fax (11) 2449352; e-mail info@chamber.lk; internet www.chamber.lk; f. 1839; 517 mems; Chair. MAHENDRA DAYANANDA; Sec.-Gen. and CEO PREMA COORAY.

**Ceylon National Chamber of Industries:** Galle Face Court 2, Rm 20, 1st Floor, POB 1775, Colombo 3; tel. (11) 2423734; fax (11) 2331443; e-mail info@cnci.biz; internet www.cnci.biz; f. 1960; 325 mems; Chair. A. K. RATNARAJAH; Sec.-Gen. and CEO UPALI SAMARASINGHE.

**International Chamber of Commerce Sri Lanka:** 141/7 Vauxhall St, POB 1733, Colombo 2; tel. (11) 2307825; fax (11) 2307841; e-mail iccsl@sltnet.lk; internet www.iccsl.lk; f. 1955; Chair. TARIQ M. RANGOONWALA; CEO GAMINI PEIRIS.

**National Chamber of Commerce of Sri Lanka:** NCCSL Bldg, 450 D. R. Wijewardena Mawatha, POB 1375, Colombo 10; tel. (11) 2689600; fax (11) 2689596; e-mail sg@nccsl.lk; internet www.nccsl.lk; f. 1948; Pres. D. EASSUWEREN; Hon. Sec. SUNIL G. WIJESINHA.

### INDUSTRIAL AND TRADE ASSOCIATIONS

**Association of Computer Training Organizations:** 5 Clifford Ave, Colombo 3; tel. (11) 2565193; fax (11) 2713821; e-mail infotel@sri.lanka.net; f. 1991; 29 mems; Pres. KITHSIRI MANCHANAYAKE.

**Ceylon Coir Fibre Exporters' Association:** c/o Volanka Ltd, 193 Minuwangoda Rd, Kotugoda; tel. (11) 2232475; fax (11) 2232477; e-mail com@volanka.com; internet www.slcfa.lk; Chair. INDRAJITH PIYASENA.

**Ceylon Hardware Merchants' Association:** 159 1/5 Mahavidyalaya Mawatha, Colombo 13; tel. (11) 2433085; fax (11) 2423342; 191 mems; Pres. S. THILLAINATHAN.

**Ceylon Planters' Society:** 40/1 Sri Dhammadara Mawatha, Ratmalana; tel. (11) 2715656; fax (11) 2716758; e-mail plansoty@yahoo.com; f. 1936; 1,133 mems (plantation mans); 25 brs and nine regional organizations; Pres. D. K. BENEDICT; Sec. D. N. R. WIJEWARDENA.

**Coconut Products Traders' Association:** c/o Ceylon Chamber of Commerce, 50 Navam Mawatha, POB 274, Colombo 2; tel. (11) 2421745; fax (11) 2449352; e-mail info@chamber.lk; internet www.chamber.lk; f. 1925; Chair. SANJAY PROROA; Sec. E. P. A. COORAY.

**Colombo Rubber Traders' Association:** c/o Ceylon Chamber of Commerce, 50 Navam Mawatha, POB 274, Colombo 2; tel. (11) 2421745; fax (11) 2449352; e-mail info@chamber.lk; internet www.chamber.lk; f. 1918; Chair. A. L. WEERASINGHE; Sec. E. P. A. COORAY.

**Colombo Tea Traders' Association:** c/o Ceylon Chamber of Commerce, 50 Navam Mawatha, POB 274, Colombo 2; tel. (11) 2421745; fax (11) 2449352; e-mail info@chamber.lk; internet www.chamber.lk; f. 1894; 203 mems; Chair. TYEAB AKBARALLY; Sec. E. P. A. COORAY.

**Free Trade Zone Manufacturers' Association:** Plaza Complex, Unit 6 (Upper Floor), IPZ, Katunayake; tel. (11) 2252813; Chair. AJITH DIAS.

**Joint Apparel Association Forum (JAAF):** 16 De Fonseka Rd, Colombo 5; tel. (11) 4528494; fax (11) 2501753; e-mail info@jaafsl.com; internet www.jaafsl.com; f. 2002; co-ordinates and develops apparel industry; Chair. AJITH DIAS; Sec.-Gen. T. G. ARIYARATNE.

**Sea Food Exporters' Association:** c/o Andriesz & Co Ltd, 39 Nuge Rd, Peliyagoda; tel. 530021.

**Software Exporters' Association:** c/o Ceylon Chamber of Commerce, 50 Navam Mawatha, Colombo 2; tel. (11) 2343702; fax (11) 2449352; e-mail rukshika@chamber.lk; internet www.softwaresrilanka.com; f. 1999; 52 mems; Chair. JAYANTHA DE SILVA.

**Sri Lanka Apparel Exporters' Association:** 45 Rosmead Place, Colombo 7; tel. (11) 2670778; fax (11) 2683118; e-mail srilanka-apparel@eureka.lk; internet www.srilanka-apparel.com; f. 1982; Chair. M. L. NOEL PRIYATILLAKE; Sec. HEMAMALI SIRISENA.

**Sri Lanka Association of Manufacturers and Exporters of Rubber Products (SLAMERP):** 425 Thimbirigasyaya Rd, Colombo 5; tel. (11) 2521200; fax (11) 2521222; e-mail slamerp@panlanka.net; f. 1984; Chair. ANANDA CALDERA; Sec.-Gen. C. DIAS BANDARANAYAKE.

**Sri Lanka Association of Printers:** 290 D. R. Wijewardena Mawatha, Colombo 10; tel. (11) 2472315; fax (11) 2386716; e-mail slap@sltnet.lk; internet www.lankaprint.org; f. 1956; 390 mems; publishes quarterly magazine *Printceylon*; Pres. KOSALA TILLEKERATNE; Sec. SHAMAL JAYATHILLEKE.

**Sri Lanka Chamber of the Pharmaceutical Industry:** 15 Tichbourne Passage, Colombo 10; tel. (11) 2694823; fax (11) 2671877; e-mail nimjay@sltnet.lk; Pres. N. DIAS JAYASINHA; Sec. NAUSHAD ISMAIL.

**Sri Lanka Fruit and Vegetables Producers, Processors and Exporters' Association:** c/o Sri Lanka Export Development Board, 42 Navam Mawatha, Colombo 2; tel. (11) 2300705; fax (11) 2304879; e-mail harz47@edb.tradenetsl.lk; internet www.tradenetsl.lk; Sec. M. A. JUNAID.

**Sri Lanka Importers, Exporters and Manufacturers' Association (SLIEMA):** POB 12, Colombo; tel. (11) 2696321; fax (11) 2684480; e-mail tradelink@slt.lk; f. 1955; Pres. WILLIAM JOHN TERRENCE PERERA.

**Sri Lanka Jewellery Manufacturing Exporters' Association:** Colombo; tel. (11) 2445141; fax (11) 2445105; Pres. IFTHIKHAR AZIZ; Sec. CHANAKA ELLAWELA.

**Sri Lanka Shippers' Council:** c/o Ceylon Chamber of Commerce, 50 Nawam Mawatha, POB 274, Colombo 2; tel. (11) 2422156; internet www.slsc.ws.

**Sri Lanka Tea Board:** 574 Galle Rd, POB 1750, Colombo 3; tel. (11) 2587814; fax (11) 2587341; e-mail promotion@pureceylontea.com; internet www.pureceylontea.com; f. 1976 for development of tea industry through quality control and promotion in Sri Lanka and in world markets; Chair. LALITH HETTIARACHCHI; Dir-Gen. H. D. HEMARATNE.

**Sri Lanka Wooden Furniture and Wood Products Manufacturers' and Exporters' Association:** c/o E. H. Cooray & Sons Ltd, 411 Galle Rd, Colombo 3; tel. (11) 2509227; fax (11) 2575198; Pres. PATRICK AMARASINGHE; Sec. PINSIRI FERNANDO.

**Sugar Importers' Association of Sri Lanka:** c/o C. W. Mackie & Co Ltd, 36 D. R. Wijewardena Mawatha, POB 89, Colombo 10; tel. (11) 2423554; fax (11) 2438069; e-mail nalin@export.cwmackie.com; Pres. M. THAVAYOGARAJAH; Sec. C. KAPUWATTA.

## EMPLOYERS' ORGANIZATION

**Employers' Federation of Ceylon:** 385 J3 Old Kotte Rd, Rajagiriya, Colombo; tel. (11) 2867966; fax (11) 2867942; e-mail efc@empfed.lk; internet www.empfed.lk; f. 1929; mem. of International Organization of Employers and Confederation of Asia Pacific Employers; 510 mems; Chair. H. D. S. AMARASURIYA; Dir-Gen. R. L. P. PEIRIS.

## UTILITIES

### Electricity

**Ceylon Electricity Board:** 50 Sir Chittampalam A. Gardiner Mawatha, POB 540, Colombo 2; tel. (11) 2324471; fax (11) 2323935; e-mail admin@ceb.lk; internet www.ceb.lk; f. 1969; Chair. UDAYASRI KARIYAWASAM.

### Water

**National Water Supply and Drainage Board (NWSDB):** Galle Rd, Ratmalana, Colombo; tel. (11) 2638999; fax (11) 2636449; e-mail gm@waterboard.lk; internet waterboard.lk; f. 1975; govt corpn; Chair. S. C. AMARASINGHE.

## CO-OPERATIVES

In 2000 there were an estimated 11,793 co-operative societies in Sri Lanka, with membership totalling 17,235,000.

## MAJOR COMPANIES

**ACL Cables Ltd:** 21 Norris Canal Rd, Colombo 10; tel. (11) 2697652; fax (11) 2696058; e-mail info@acl.lk; internet www.acl.lk; f. 1962; sales Rs 2,072m. (2004/05); manufacture and marketing of cables and conductors; Chair. and Man. Dir U. G. MADANAYAKE; Exec. Dir H. A. S. MADANAYAKE; 515 employees.

**Aitken Spence and Co Ltd:** Vauxhall Towers, 305 Vauxhall St, POB 5, Colombo 2; tel. (11) 2308308; fax (11) 2445406; e-mail info@aitkenspence.lk; internet www.aitkenspence.com; f. 1868; cap. and res Rs 7,567m., total revenue Rs 9,923m. (2004/05); conglomerate with vested interests in hotels, inbound and outbound travel, cargo logistics services, printing and packaging, plantations, ship agency services, property and infrastructure development, and light engineering; agents for Lloyds of London since 1876 and for various airlines; Chair. D. H. S. JAYAWARDENA; Man. Dir J. M. S. BRITO; 3,967 employees.

**Allied Industries Ltd:** 95 Hyde Park Cnr, Colombo 2; tel. (11) 2687395; fax (11) 2687007; manufactures and exports razor blades, disposable razors and pens; Chair. M. P. S. WIJAYAWARDENA; Man. Dir VAJIRA KALINGA WIJAYAWARDENA.

**Asbestos Cement Industries Ltd:** 175 Sri Sumanatissa Mawatha, POB 1361, Colombo 12; tel. (11) 2448145; fax (11) 2449537; e-mail aciho@sltnet.lk; f. 1955; cap. Rs 257m. (1999), sales US $860.7m. (2002); factory at Ratmalana; asbestos cement roofing, ceiling and moulded products; Chair. SEPALA WIMALADHARMA MOLLIGODA; Man. Dir S. SATHIAMOORTHY; 805 employees.

**Asian Electrical and Mineral Industries Ltd:** 411 Ferguson Rd, POB 1091, Colombo 15; tel. (11) 2522943; fax (11) 2526697; f. 1969; sales US $40.5m. (2002); mfrs of electric light bulbs and tubes; Chair. RAY DE COSTA; Gen. Man. L. S. SENEVIRATNE; 100 employees.

**Associated Battery Manufacturers (Ceylon) Ltd:** 31 Katukurunduwatte Rd, Ratmalana; tel. (11) 2713111; e-mail info@abmlanka.com; f. 1960; sales Rs 575m. (2003/04); mfrs of hard rubber and polypropylene automotive and motor-cycle batteries, battery components and antimonial lead; Gen. Man. R. M. D. BANDARA; 188 employees.

**Associated Motorways Ltd:** 185 Union Place, Colombo 2; tel. (11) 2690099; fax (11) 2323781; e-mail amw@eureka.lk; internet www.amwltd.com; f. 1949; cap. and res 1,459.5m., sales Rs 6,624.1m. (2005/06); tyre rebuilding, rubber goods and rubber compounds; Chair. AJITA DE ZOYSA; Dep. Chair. and Man. Dir DESHABANDU TILAK DE ZOYSA; 1,500 employees.

**BCC Lanka Ltd:** Hulftsdorp Mills, Meeraniya St, POB 281, Colombo 12; tel. (11) 2422111; fax (11) 2447139; e-mail bccl@sltnet.lk; total revenue Rs 234.8m. (2002); mfrs and shippers of coconut oil, household and toilet soaps, detergents, etc.; Chair. ROHAN DE ALWIS; 528 employees.

**Blue Diamond Jewellery Worldwide Ltd:** 49 Ring Road, Phase 1, I. P. Z., Katunayake, Colombo 3; tel. (11) 2252497; e-mail bdjwmarketing@slt.lk; internet www.bluediamondjewellery.com; f. 1990; sales Rs 67.2m. (1999/2000); mfr and exporter of jewellery (particularly gold and diamonds); Chair. J. L. B. KOTELAWALA; Dep. Chair. D. R. SENANAYAKE; 180 employees.

**Bogala Graphite Lanka Ltd:** 20 Tickell Rd, Colombo 8; tel. (11) 2693495; fax (11) 2698708; e-mail bogalag@slt.lk; internet www.gk-graphite.lk; f. 1991; sales Rs 112.5m. (2000); mining, processing and export of graphite; Chair. VIJAYA MALALASEKERA; CEO AMILA JAYASINGHE; 600 employees.

**Browns & Co Ltd:** 481 T. B. Jaya Mawatha, POB 200, Colombo 10; tel. (11) 2683230; fax (11) 2686668; e-mail rajithabtl@sltnet.lk; internet www.brownsgroup.com; f. 1875; sales Rs 3,082.3m. (2000/01); air conditioners, ceiling fans, radiators, marine engines, 2-wheel tractors, agricultural trailers and implements, hardware, plastic goods, veterinary pharmaceuticals, etc.; Chair. R. L. NANAYAKKARA; CEO and Man. Dir N. M. PRAKASH; 1,100 employees (1999).

**Building Materials Corpn Ltd:** 541 Sri Sangaraja Mawatha, Colombo 10; tel. (11) 2326701; fax (11) 2445614; e-mail bmcltd@sltnet.lk; internet www.bmc.lk; f. 1971; cap. and res Rs –133.3m., total revenue Rs 248.2m. (2004); import, supply, distribution and sale of building materials; Chair. and Man. Dir LALITHA P. ANDRAHENADI; 362 employees (2004).

**Carson Cumberbatch & Co Ltd:** 61 Janadhipathi Mawatha, Colombo 1; tel. (11) 4739200; fax (11) 4739300; e-mail carsons@carcumb.com; internet www.carsoncumberbatch.com; f. 1913; sales Rs 5,957m. (2003/04); plantations and export of tea, insurance, financial services, real estate, brewing, hotelier; Chair. TILAK DE ZOYSA; Dep. Chair. HARI SELVANATHAN; over 3,468 employees.

**H. Don Carolis & Sons Ltd:** 65 Station Passage, POB 48, Colombo 2; tel. (11) 2325676; fax (11) 2439600; e-mail dons@doncarolis.com;

internet www.doncarolis.com; f. 1860; sales Rs 325m. (2004/05); manufacturers and exporters of wooden furniture; Chair. RAJIV L. HEWAVITARNE; 350 employees.

**Ceylon Agro-Industries Ltd:** 346 Negombo Rd, Seeduwa; tel. (11) 2253527; fax (11) 2253537; e-mail info.cai@prima.com.lk; f. 1992; sales US $18m. (1999); mfrs and exporters of instant noodles, bakery products and oil; poultry processing; Gen. Man. SHUN TIEN SHING; 1,000 employees.

**Ceylon Biscuits Ltd:** POB 3, High Level Rd, Makumbura, Pannipitiya; tel. (11) 2749749; fax (11) 2855367; e-mail ceybis@muncheelk.com; internet www.muncheelk.com; f. 1968; mfr and exporter of biscuits, confectionery and tea; Chair. M. P. WICKRAMASINGHA; Man. Dir LAKSHMAN DE SILVA.

**Ceylon Cold Stores Ltd:** 1 Justice Akbar Mawatha, POB 220, Colombo 2; tel. (11) 2328221; fax (11) 2447422; e-mail coldstor@keells.com; internet www.srilankagingerbeer.com; f. 1866; cap. and res Rs 1,194.4m., sales Rs 4,500.9m. (2004/05); subsidiary of John Keells Holdings Ltd; mfrs, wholesalers, retailers of food and beverages; exports sea foods, spices, essential oils, fruit juices and processed meats; br. at Trincomalee; Chair. V. LINTOTAWELA; Man. Dir SUMITHRA GUNESEKERA; 2,078 employees.

**Ceylon Fertilizer Co Ltd (CFCL):** 62 Chatham St, POB 841, Colombo 1; tel. (11) 2422431; fax (11) 2343991; cap. and res Rs 740.3m., total revenue Rs 2,792.9m. (2004); amalgamation with subsidiary co Thamankaduwa Agro-Fertilizer Co Ltd (TAFCL) approved in August 2007; Personnel Man. W. N. FERNANDO; 392 employees (2004).

**Ceylon Fisheries Corpn:** Rock House Lane, Mutwal, Colombo 15; tel. (11) 2523227; fax (11) 2523385; e-mail cfcch@sltnet.lk; internet www.fisheriescorporation.gov.lk; f. 1964; sales Rs 338.4m. (2004); jt venture; fisheries harbour at Mutwal; cold storage, freezing and processing facilities, fish trading, ice production and trading, fish filleting, and export/import of fish and fish products; Chair. W. A. J. E. FERNANDO; Gen. Man. S. A. SAHABANDU; 665 employees.

**Ceylon Galvanising Industries Ltd:** Lady Catherine Dr., POB 35, Ratmalana; tel. (63) 636711; fax (63) 435649; f. 1967; cap. p.u. Rs 4.5m., sales Rs 262m.; mfrs of galvanized steel sheets; Man. Dir V. BALASUBRAMANIAM; 50 employees.

**Ceylon Glass Co Ltd:** 148 Maligawa Rd, Borupana, Ratmalana, Colombo; tel. (11) 2635481; fax (11) 2635484; e-mail info@ceylonglass.lk; internet www.ceylonglass.com; f. 1956; cap. and res Rs 750.1m., sales Rs 779.4m. (2001/02); production of glass containers; Chair. VIJAY SHAH; Man. Dir and CEO SANJAY TIWARI; 426 employees.

**Ceylon Grain Elevators Ltd:** 15 Rock House Lane, Colombo 15; tel. (11) 2522556; fax (11) 2524163; e-mail info.cge@prima.com; f. 1982; sales Rs 4,238.2m. (2004); feedmilling and broiler operations; poultry and breeder farming; vaccines and poultry equipment trading; shrimp farming; silo, warehouse and transshipment operations; Gen. Man. CHIN HOW CHEONG; Chair. and CEO CHENG CHIH KWONG; 794 employees.

**Ceylon Heavy Industries & Construction Co Ltd:** Office and Works, Oruwela, Athurugiriya; tel. (11) 4440031; fax (11) 2772213; e-mail chicoltd@slt.lk; f. 1961; as Ceylon Steel Corpn Ltd; steel rolling; mfrs of steel rods for building construction, wire products, steel castings, machine tools; welding electrodes; soldering lead; metallographic work and testing, etc.; Chair. and Man. Dir J. C. CHOI.

**Ceylon Hotels Corpn:** 279 Galle Rd, Bambalapitiya, POB 259, Colombo 4; tel. (11) 2598923; fax (11) 2503558; e-mail info@ceylonhotels.lk; internet www.ceylonhotels.lk; f. 1966; state-owned; sales Rs 118.5m. (2001); CEO ANURA LOKUHETTY; Gen. Man. SAHINDA B. WEGODAPOTA.

**Ceylon Leather Products Ltd:** 141 Church Rd, Mattakkuliya, POB 1488, Colombo 15; tel. (11) 2521778; fax (11) 2521702; e-mail infomail@dileather.com; internet www.dileather.com; f. 1990 as Ceylon Leather Products Corpn; privatized in 1991; sales Rs 410.9m. (2002/03); mfrs and exporters of leather, including footwear, sports and leather goods; Man. Dir and CEO SITENDRA SENARATNE; 378 employees.

**Ceylon Oxygen Ltd:** 50 Sri Pannananda Mawatha, Colombo 15; tel. (11) 2524381; fax (11) 4615272; f. 1936; sales US $6.7m. (2005); production and supply of industrial and medical gases, including liquid and gaseous oxygen, nitrogen and carbon dioxide; Chair. MANJU HATHTHOTUWA; CEO NIRAN PIERIS.

**Ceylon Paint Industries Ltd:** Lady Catherine's Dr., Ratmalana, Colombo; tel. (11) 2632831; fax (11) 2698831; e-mail mbdj@eureka.lk; f. 1934; mfrs of 'Crown' paints of England, Glasso automotive refinishes from Glassurit GmbH (BASF) of Germany, PVA, textile binders, adhesives and alkyd resins; Chair. and Pres. MARSH B. DODANWELA; Man. Dir SRIYA DODANWELA; 64 employees.

**Ceylon Pencil Co Ltd** (Atlas): 96 Parakrama Rd, Peliyagoda; tel. (11) 2912879; fax (11) 2912878; e-mail info@atlas.lk; internet www.atlas.lk; produces ball-point pens, pencils and school stationery; Chair. D. S. MADANAYAKE; CEO N. A. MADANAYAKE; 600 employees.

**Ceylon Petroleum Corpn:** Rotunda Tower, 1st Floor, 109 Galle Rd, Colombo 3; tel. (11) 2473644; fax (11) 2473979; e-mail cpccom@ceypetco.com.lk; internet www.ceypetco.gov.lk; f. 1961; state-owned; cap. and res Rs –4,379m., total revenue Rs 63,333m. (2004); exploration, refining and distribution of petroleum and petroleum products; terminal at Kolonnawa, Colombo; refinery at Sapugaskanda; subsidiary: Lanka Lubricants Ltd; Chair. and Man. Dir ASHANTHA DE MEL; 2,156 employees (2004).

**Ceylon Synthetic Textile Mills Ltd:** 752 Baseline Rd, Colombo 9; tel. (11) 2692255; fax (11) 2698852; synthetic textiles; Gen. Man. V. SIVASUDHAN.

**Ceylon Tea Services Ltd** (Dilmah): 111 Negombo Rd, POB 1630, Peliyagoda; tel. and fax (11) 2933070; fax (11) 2933080; e-mail info@dilmahtea.com; internet www.dilmahtea.com; f. 1981; cap. and res Rs 1,489.4m., sales Rs 1,948.8m. (2001/02); sales Rs 4,000m. (2003); production and export of tea bags, herbal infusions, packeted and bulk tea; CEO HIMENDRA RANAWEERA; Marketing Dir DILHAN C. FERNANDO; 800 employees.

**Ceylon Tobacco Co Ltd:** 178 Srimath Ramanathan Mawatha, Colombo 15; tel. (11) 2434231; fax (11) 2447529; e-mail nalin_wickramaratne@bat.com; f. 1932; sales US $44m. (2002); manufacture and marketing of cigarettes and smoking tobacco, export of cigarettes and leaf tobacco, and financial and consultancy services; Chair. JAYAMPATHI BANDARANAYAKE; Man. Dir P. HILTERMANN; 388 employees.

**Chemical Industries (Colombo) Ltd (CIC):** 199 Kew Rd, Colombo 2; tel. (11) 2359359; fax (11) 2446922; internet www.cic.lk; f. 1964 as Trading House for ICI, United Kingdom; represents ICI and Syngenta (jt venture between agribusinesses of UK and Sweden); sales Rs 7,677.6m. (2002/03); total assets of CIC group of cos Rs 9,199.0m.; manufacture and sale of agro-chemicals, industrial chemicals and plastics, pharmaceuticals, diagnostics and consumer products; Chair. and Man. Dir B. R. L. FERNANDO; Chief Operating Officer S. P. S. RANATUNGA; 225 employees.

**Coca-Cola Beverages Sri Lanka Ltd:** 140A Vauxhall St, Colombo 2; tel. (11) 2324211; fax (11) 2421147; f. 1955; sales Rs 1,405.9m. (1997/98); mfr and bottler of soft drinks; Chair. W. D. M. FERNANDO; Country Man. BASIL GADZIOS.

**Contracts and Supplies (Mfg) Ltd:** POB 487, Colombo; tel. (11) 2598436; f. 1974; sales Rs 36m. (1986/87); govt-approved manufacturing of CEYGMA water pumps; Man. Dir R. CUMARASAMY; Tech. Dir N. FERNANDO; 208 employees.

**Dankotuwa Porcelain Ltd:** Kurunegala Rd, Dankotuwa; tel. (31) 4879700; fax (31) 4879799; e-mail info@dankotuwa.com; internet www.dankotuwa.com; f. 1984; sales Rs 677.2m. (2000); manufacture of porcelain; Chair. and Man. Dir SUNIL G. WIJESINGHE; 976 employees.

**Dipped Products PLC:** Hayley Bldg, 400 Deans Rd, Colombo 10; tel. (11) 2683964; fax (11) 2699018; e-mail sonali@dplgroup.com; internet www.dplgroup.com; f. 1976; issued cap. Rs 599.0m., sales Rs 7,000.0m. (2005/06); manufacture and export of household and industrial gloves from natural and synthetic latex; tea and rubber plantations and plantation management; Chair. N. G. WICKRENERATNE; Man. Dir J. A. G. ANANDARAJAH.

**Distilleries Co of Sri Lanka Ltd:** 110 Norris Canal Rd, Colombo 10; tel. (11) 2695295; fax (11) 2696360; internet www.dcslgroup.com; f. 1989; sales Rs 18,800m. (2004); producer of alcoholic beverages, incl. Arrack (exclusive to Sri Lanka); eight assoc. cos; Chair. and Man. Dir D. H. S. JAYAWARDHENA; 1,283 employees (2000).

**Eastern Merchants Ltd:** 341 Union Place, POB 611, Colombo 2; tel. (11) 2325736; fax (11) 2448474; e-mail chiraath@sltnet.lk; internet www.easternmerchants.net; sales Rs 1,102m. (2003); exporters of rubber, cinnamon, dessicated coconut, tea and fibre.

**James Finlay & Co (Colombo) Ltd:** Finlay House, 186 Vauxhall St, Colombo 2; tel. (11) 2421931; fax (11) 2448216; e-mail info@finlays.lk; internet www.finlays.lk; f. 1893; total revenue Rs 2,583m. (2004); tea blending, tea exporting and warehousing, corporate management services, insurance provision, environmental services, airline, tourism and travel services, marketing of industrial and agrochemicals (under BASF–Finlay (Pvt) Ltd concern—jt venture with BASF Aktiengesellschaft, Germany); cultivates and exports tea; Exec. Chair. C. L. K. P. JAYASURIYA; Exec. Dirs E. R. CROOS MORAES, N. K. H. RATWATTE.

**Formosa's Communication Co:** 67/3B Pradeep Mawatha, Colombo 10; tel. (11) 2672374; fax (11) 2672373; f. 1945; manpower consultants; Propr WILLIAM JOHN TERRENCE PERERA.

**GlaxoSmithKline Pharmaceuticals Ltd:** 121 Galle Rd, Kaldemulla, Moratuwa; tel. (11) 2636341; fax (11) 2635000; f. 1956; sales Rs 618.2m. (2002); manufacture and sale of pharmaceuticals; Chair. S. KALYANASUNDARAM; Man. Dir E. M. ANDREE; 229 employees.

**Hayleys PLC:** 400 Deans Rd, POB 70, Colombo 10; tel. (11) 2696331; fax (11) 2699299; e-mail info@cau.hayleys.com; internet www.hayleys.com; f. 1878; as Chas. P. Hayley and Co; name changed as above 1952; cap. and res Rs 7,108.1m., sales Rs 15,503.5m. (2003/04); 60 subsidiary and 13 assoc. cos involved in manufacture and export of coir fibre, coir yarn and twine and coir brush mats for export; manufacture and export of activated carbon, industrial and household brushes and rubber gloves; formulation of crop protection and household chemicals; courier agents; marketing of industrial chemicals and agricultural machinery, power and energy, photographic products, medicines and miscellaneous products on the local market; consultancy services; shipping, freight forwarding and warehousing; insurance; travel agency; hotels; and plantations; Chair. N. G. WICKREMERATNE; Dep. Chair. A. M. PANDITHAGE; 35,359 employees.

**HDDES Extracts (Pvt) Ltd:** HDDES Group, 309, Jayanatha Weerasekara Mawatha, POB 2063, Colombo 10; tel. (11) 2438739; fax (11) 2440556; e-mail hddes@sltnet.lk; internet www.hddes.com; f. 1934; part of the HDDES Group of cos, incl. H. D. De Silva & Sons (Pvt) Ltd and H. D. Plantations; mfrs and exports spices, essential oils, oleoresin and floral extracts; Man. Dir H. G. K. DE SILVA.

**Hemas Holdings (Pvt) Ltd:** 36 Bristol St, POB 911, Colombo 1; tel. (11) 4731731; fax (11) 2332889; e-mail info@hemas.com; internet www.hemas.com; f. 1949; cap. and res Rs 2,627.9m., sales Rs 6,485.4m. (2003/04); revenue Rs 14,163m., profits Rs 1,150m. (2007/08); holding co with interests in health-care, consumer products, leisure, transportation and strategic investment sectors; Chair. LALITH DE MEL; Dir and CEO HUSEIN ESUFALLY.

**Hirdaramani Industries Ltd:** Level 23, West Tower, World Trade Centre, Echelon Sq., Colombo 1; tel. (11) 4797000; fax (11) 2446135; e-mail info@hirdaramani.com; internet www.hirdaramani.com; mfrs of clothing; Chair. LAL HIRDARAMANI.

**Indo-Ceylon Leather Co Ltd:** 148 Prince St, Colombo 11; tel. (11) 2422906; fax (11) 2437615; tanners.

**Jinasena Group:** 4 Hunupitiya Rd, POB 196, Colombo 2; tel. (11) 2448848; fax (11) 2448849; e-mail jinasena@jinasena.com.lk; internet www.jinasena.com; f. 1905; sales Rs 654.4m. (2001); comprises Jinasena Ltd and several other companies; mfrs of agricultural machinery, water pumps, electric motors, paddy threshers, foundry castings, carbon seals; exports lobsters, ladies' garments and tyres; Chair. and Man Dir NIHAL JINASENA; 3,000 employees.

**John Keells Holdings PLC:** 130 Glennie St, POB 76, Colombo 2; tel. (11) 2306000; fax (11) 2447087; e-mail jkh@keells.com; internet www.keells.com; f. 1979; cap. and res Rs 18,815.8m., sales Rs 23,646.1m. (2004/05); holding co with interests in food and beverages, retailing, restaurants, transport, shipping, freight-forwarding, plantation management, tea production, travel agencies and resort ownership, stockbroking, investment banking, computers and business systems, commercial banking, infrastructure, software development, insurance, printing and management and investment trusts; Chair. SUSANTHA RATNAYAKE; Pres. and Dir SUMITHRA GUNESEKERA; 19,405 employees (2001/02).

**Kelani Tyres Ltd:** 203 Union Place, Colombo 2; tel. (11) 2434183; fax (11) 2911598; f. 1991; sales Rs 471m. (1999/2000); factory at Kelaniya; mfrs of pneumatic tyres and rubber products; Chair. CHANAKA DE SILVA; Man. Dir ROHAN T. FERNANDO; 506 employees (2000).

**Kundanmals Group of Cos:** 110–114 Main St, POB 16, Colombo 11; tel. (11) 2323641; fax (11) 2432718; e-mail kundan@slt.lk; f. 1930; sales US $50m. (1999); mfr and exporter of ready-made garments; Chair. M. KUNDANMAL; Man. Dir (Kundanmals Apparel (Pvt) Ltd) G. U. L. JIWATRAM; 3,000 employees.

**Lanka Canneries Ltd:** 45/75, Nawala Rd, Narahenpita, POB 341, Colombo 5; tel. (11) 2586622; fax (11) 2368480; e-mail md-lankacanneries@eureka.lk; internet www.lankacanneries.com; f. 1981; sales Rs 850m. (2004); canned and bottled products; Chair. M. F. DOSSA; Man. NILHAN EKANAYAKE; 400 employees.

**Lanka Ceramic Ltd:** 696 Galle Rd, Colombo 3; tel. (11) 2582262; fax (11) 2500752; e-mail rajiv@lcl.lk; f. 1991; sales Rs 250m. (2004); four mining and processing facilities; 12 retail outlets; mines and refines kaolin, ball clay, feldspar and quartz and supplies to other industries and subsidiaries; subsidiaries: Lanka Wall Tile Ltd, Balangoda and Meepe, Lanka Tile Ltd, Jaltara, and Lanka Ceradec Ltd, Jaltara; Exec. Dir RAJIV CASIE CHITTY; 375 employees.

**Lanka Milk Foods (CWE) Ltd:** POB 4, Welisara, Ragama; tel. (11) 2956263; fax (11) 2956266; e-mail lakspray@eureka.lk; f. 1981; privatized in 1991; cap. and res Rs 798.0m., sales Rs 2,189.3m. (2003/04); production, import, export and packaging of milk and related products; transferred to the private sector in 2001; Chair. Dr V. P. VITTACHI; Man. Dir D. H. S. JAYAWARDENA; 267 employees.

**Lanka Mineral Sands Ltd:** 341/21 Sarana Mawatha, Rajagiriya; tel. (11) 2393716; fax (11) 2393806; e-mail ilmenite@slt.lk; internet www.lankamineralsands.lk; f. 1957; ilmenite, rutile, zircon and monazite plants at Pulmoddai; Chair. SHASHI WELGAMA; Gen. Man. S. A. NANDADEVA.

**Lanka Plywood Products Ltd:** 420 Bauddhaloka Mawatha, POB 1148, Colombo 7; tel. (11) 2694879; state-owned; Chair. D. K. FERNANDO.

**Lanka Tiles Ltd:** 34/5 W. A. D. Ramanayake Mawatha, Colombo 2; tel. (11) 2430988; fax (11) 2437846; e-mail flotiles@slt.lk; internet www.lankatile.com; cap. and res Rs 458.9m., sales Rs 1,354.2m. (2005/06); mfr of ceramic tiles and other flooring products; Chair. A. A. PAGE; Man. Dir J. A. P. M. JAYASEKERA.

**Lanka Walltile Ltd:** 215 Nawala Rd, Narahenpita, Colombo 5; tel. (11) 4526700; fax (11) 4541613; e-mail info@lankawall.com; internet www.lankawall.com; f. 1975; sales Rs 2,713.0m. (2000/01); mfr and exporter of floor and wall tiles; Chair. B. MAHADEVA; Man. Dir Prof. C. L. V. JAYATILLEKE; 1,256 employees.

**C. W. Mackie & Co Ltd:** 36 D. R. Wijewardena Mawatha, POB 89, Colombo 10; tel. (11) 2423554; fax (11) 2440228; e-mail info@cwmackie.com; internet www.cwmackie.com; f. 1922; cap. and res Rs 602.2m., sales Rs 2,416.2m. (Dec. 2006); manufacture and export of rubber and rubber products, coconut and coconut products, fruit drinks and bottled drinking water; import of sugar, refrigeration and air-conditioning components, industrial products, welding equipment and accessories; Chair. and Chief Exec. W. T. ELLAWALA; 243 employees.

**Macksons Paint Industries Ltd** (Multilac): POB 4, Keselwatte, Panadura; tel. (38) 2234155; fax (38) 4281036; e-mail inquiry@mulitlac.com; internet www.multilac.com; f. 1981; mfr and exporter of paints; Chair. AL-HAJ A. W. M. MAKEEN; Man. Dir MIZVER MAKEEN; 300 employees.

**Maliban Biscuit Manufactories Ltd:** 389 Galle Rd, Ratmalana, Colombo; tel. (11) 2738551; fax (11) 2734556; e-mail maliban@malibanbiscuit.com; internet www.malibanbiscuit.com; f. 1954; sales Rs 3,000m. (1997); Chair. A. G. R. SAMARAWEERA; Gen. Man. S. P. GAMAGE; 1,200 employees.

**The Modern Confectionery Works:** 663 Prince of Wales Ave, Colombo; tel. (11) 2431783; fax (11) 2440325; f. 1945.

**Mona Plastics (Pvt) Ltd** (Mona Lanka): 60, Fifth Lane, Colombo 3; tel. (11) 2565460; fax (11) 2565462; e-mail info@monalanka.com; internet www.monalanka.com; f. 1983; mfrs injection moulded plastic collectible items, wooden and resin toys for Hallmark, USA; Gen. Man. BRIAN MUNAWEERA; over 2,000 employees.

**National Paper Co Ltd:** 356 Union Place, POB 1367, Colombo 2; tel. (11) 2324701; fax (11) 2446381; state-owned; paper boards, printing, pulp; Chair. W. H. S. WIJERATNE; Gen. Man. M. A. JUSTIN; factories at Valaichchenai and Embilipitiya.

**Nestlé Lanka Ltd:** 440 T. B. Jayah Mawatha, POB 189, Colombo 10; tel. (11) 2696304; fax (11) 2699437; e-mail priyasath.saparamadu@lk.nestle.com; f. 1980; sales Rs 6,963.8m. (2001); Chair. and Man. Dir G. TARNERO; 660 employees.

**Newell Garments Lanka (Pvt) Ltd:** 63 Upananda Mawatha, Attidiya, Dehiwala; tel. (11) 2724269; fax (11) 2712802; fmrly Lakstar Garments (Pvt) Ltd; name changed to above in 2007; Dir K. SURANGA KULAWICKRAMA.

**Paranthan Chemicals Co Ltd:** 100/25 Sri Ramanathan Mawatha, Colombo 13; tel. (11) 2437556; fax (11) 2437830; e-mail chemco@sltnet.lk; f. 1957; total revenue Rs 154.0m. (2007); importers and distributors of caustic soda, chlorine and hydrochloric acid; industrial unit at Kalutara; 49 employees (2008).

**Pelwatte Sugar Industries Ltd:** 27 Melbourne Ave, POB 1992, Colombo 4; tel. (11) 2501195; fax (11) 2500674; e-mail psilcity@sltnet.lk; internet www.pelwatte.com; f. 1983; sales Rs 1,802.1m. (1999/2000); cultivation and manufacture of sugar and molasses; Chair. ARIYASEELA WICKRAMANAYAKE.

**Prima Ceylon (Pvt) Ltd:** 50 Sri Jayawardenapura Mawatha, Rajagiriya; tel. (11) 2864580; fax (11) 2863709; e-mail sales.pcl@prima.com.lk; flour milling; Gen. Man. LIN HSIN HUI.

**Reckitt Benckiser (Lanka) Ltd:** 41 Lauries Rd, Colombo 4; tel. (11) 2550900; fax (11) 2550906; e-mail reckitts@sri.lanka.net; f. 1962; fmrly Reckitt & Colman of Ceylon; sales Rs 1,310.3m. (2000); mfrs and distributors of pharmaceuticals, and food and household products; Country Man. NAEL AHMED; 450 employees.

**Richard Pieris and Co Ltd:** 310 High Level Rd, Nawinna, Maharagama; tel. (1) 4310500; fax (1) 431077; e-mail cpu@arpico.com; internet www.arpico.com; f. 1940; cap. and res Rs 3,182.7m., sales Rs 10,168.4m. (2004/05); mfrs and exporters of goods from foam rubber and latex mattresses, rubber mats, polyurethane foam, tyre retreading and plastics; tea and rubber plantations; financial services and real estate developers; Chair., Man. Dir and CEO Dr SENA YADDEHIGE.

**Royal Ceramics Lanka Ltd:** 10 R. A. De Mel Mawatha, Colombo 3; tel. (11) 4799400; fax (11) 4720010; e-mail info@rcl.lk; internet www.rocell.com; f. 1990; sales Rs 1,301.2m. (2003/04); mfr of ceramic products; Chair. A. M. WEERASINGHE; 457 employees.

**Salu Sala Ltd:** 93 Jawatte Rd, Colombo 5; tel. (11) 2581727; fax (11) 2586752; state-owned; manufactures textiles and garments.

**D. Samson Industries Ltd:** 110 Kumaran Ratnam Rd, POB 778, Colombo 2; tel. (11) 2320978; fax (11) 2440890; e-mail info@dsi.lk; internet www.dsi.lk; f. 1962; sales Rs 4,541m. (2003); mfrs and exporters of footwear and rubber goods; Chair. D. SAMSON RAJAPAKSA; Man. Dir D. K. RAJAPAKSA; 5,400 employees (2003).

**Shell Co of Sri Lanka Ltd:** 161 Sri Gnanendra Mawatha, Nawala, Rajagiriya, Colombo; fax (11) 2698139; e-mail lubricants@sdk.simis.com; internet www.shell-srilanka.com; exploration and production of petroleum and gas and distribution of petroleum products.

**Sigiri Garments Ltd:** 216 Second Cross St, Colombo 1; tel. (11) 2329347; fax (11) 2449331; e-mail sigiri@sltnet.lk; manufacture of textiles and clothing.

**Sri Lanka Cement Corpn:** 130 W. A. D. Ramanayake Mawatha, POB 1382, Colombo 2; tel. (11) 2440203; fax (11) 2448866; e-mail slcc@sltnet.lk; state-owned; cap. and res Rs 9,997m., total revenue Rs 89,622m. (2005); produces Kankesan brand cement; sells cement and cement-based products; cement works at Puttalam, Kankesan and Ruhunu; combined capacity of cement works meets about 60% of the country's requirements and provides for export; Chair. S. J. PARANAGAMA; Gen. Man. R. M. JAYATILLAKE; 104 employees (2006).

**Sri Lanka Distilleries Ltd:** Wadduwa; tel. (11) 2232523; fax (11) 2232630; e-mail sldlgarc@sltnet.lk; f. 1945; distillers of coconut spirit and neutral alcohol; Chair. RANIL DE SILVA; Man. Dir D. H. S. JAYAWARDENA; 65 employees.

**State Engineering Corpn:** 130 W. A. D. Ramanayake Mawatha, POB 194, Colombo 2; tel. (11) 2430061; e-mail gmsec@itmin.com; cap. and res Rs 116.0m., total revenue Rs 881.9m. (2004); Chair. SARATH KUMARA DE SILVA; 2,837 employees (2004).

**State Fertilizer Manufacturing Corpn:** Sapugaskanda, Kelaniya; tel. (11) 2911833; f. 1966; Chair. A. A. JUSTIN DIAS.

**State Timber Corpn:** 82 Rajamalwatte Rd, Battaramulla; tel. (11) 2866601; fax (11) 2866600; internet www.timco.lk; f. 1968; cap. and res Rs 1,457.6m., total revenue Rs 1,457.6m. (2004); extraction of timber, saw milling, running of timber sales depots, timber seasoning, preservation, import of timber, manufacture of furniture, and special projects connected with timber industry; Chair. CHANDANA J. HAPUTHANTHRI; 3,057 employees (2004).

**Tea Smallholder Factories Ltd:** 320/1 Union Place, Colombo 2; tel. and fax (11) 2335870; e-mail rpk@keells.com; internet www.keells.com/plantations/tea/tea.htm; f. 1991; cap. Rs 150m., sales Rs 1,091.1m. (2000/01); tea processors; Chair. SUSANTHA CHAMINDA RATNAYAKE; Man. Dir JIT GUNARATNE; 1,228 employees.

**Tri-Star Group of Cos:** 30 Maligawa Rd, Ratmalana, Colombo; tel. (11) 2503256; fax (11) 2508758; e-mail inquiries@tristar.org; internet www.tristar.org; manufactures and exports garments; Chair. KUMAR DEWAPURA; CEO CHANDIMA SILVA.

**Unilever Ceylon Ltd:** 258 M. Vincent Perera Mawatha, Colombo 14; tel. (11) 4700800; fax (11) 2445213; e-mail Rohith.Hettiaratchi@unilever.com; internet www.unileversrilanka.com; f. 1938; soaps, cosmetics, toilet preparations, margarine, oils and fats; Chair. AMAL CABRAAL; 1,300 employees.

**United Motors Lanka Ltd:** 100 Hyde Park Cnr, POB 697, Colombo 2; tel. (11) 2448112; fax (11) 2448113; e-mail umll@itmin.com; internet www.unitedmotors.lk; f. 1945; nationalized 1972 and incorporated 1989; sales Rs 1,178.2m. (2000/01); imports and markets Mitsubishi motor vehicles and spare parts; imports agricultural machinery, reconditioned vehicles and machinery, tyres and batteries; Chair. MAHENDRA AMARASURIYA; CEO CHANAKA YATAWARA; 397 employees.

**Usha Industries Ltd:** Ratmalana; e-mail haylect@sri.lanka.net; f. 1961; mfrs of sewing machines, electric fans, etc.; Chair. S. MENDIS; Dir G. S. DEWARAJA; 70 employees.

**P.P.K. Vellaiappa Nadar (Pvt) Ltd:** 148 Prince St, Pettah, Colombo 11; tel. (11) 2341437; fax (11) 2347970; f. 1919; sales US $1m. (1999); tanners and dealers in shoe materials; Chair. and Man. Dir RAM KANAGARAJAN; 50 employees.

### TRADE UNIONS

At the end of 2000 there were 1,588 trade unions functioning in Sri Lanka.

**All Ceylon Federation of Free Trade Unions (ACFFTU):** 94-1/6 York Bldg, York St, Colombo 1; tel. (11) 2431847; fax (11) 2470874; e-mail nwc@itmin.com; 10 affiliated unions; 84,000 mems; Pres. MARCELL C. RAJAHMONEY; Sec.-Gen. ANTON LODWICK.

**Ceylon Federation of Labour (CFL):** 457 Union Place, Colombo 2; tel. (11) 2694273; f. 1957; 16 affiliated unions; 155,969 mems; Pres. Dr COLVIN R. DE SILVA; Gen. Sec. S. S. SIRIWARDANE.

**Ceylon Mercantile, Industrial and General Workers' Union (CMU):** 3 22nd Lane, Colombo 3; tel. (11) 2328157; fax (11) 2434025; e-mail cgscmu@sltnet.lk; Gen. Sec. BALA TAMPOE.

**Ceylon Trade Union Federation (CTUF):** Colombo; tel. (11) 2220365; f. 1941; 24 affiliated unions; 35,271 mems; Sec.-Gen. L. W. PANDITHA.

**Ceylon Workers' Congress (CWC):** 'Savumia Bhavan', 72 Ananda Coomarasamy Mawatha, POB 1294, Colombo 7; tel. (11) 2301359; fax (11) 2301355; e-mail cwconline@sltnet.lk; f. 1939; political entity; represents mainly plantation workers of recent Indian origin; 50 district offices and seven regional offices; 250,000 mems; Pres. MUTHU SIVALINGAM; Gen. Sec. S. ARUMUGAN THONDAMAN.

**Democratic Workers' Congress (DWC):** 70 Bankshall St, POB 1009, Colombo 11; tel. (11) 2423746; fax (11) 2435961; f. 1939; 201,382 mems (1994); Pres. MANO GANESHAN; Gen. Sec. R. KITNAN.

**Government Workers' Trade Union Federation (GWTUF):** 457 Union Place, Colombo 2; tel. (11) 2295066; 52 affiliated unions; 100,000 mems; Leader P. D. SARANAPALA.

**Jathika Sevaka Sangamaya (JSS)** (National Employees' Union): 416 Kotte Rd, Pitakotte, Colombo; tel. (11) 2565432; f. 1959; 357,000 mems; represents over 70% of unionized manual and clerical workers of Sri Lanka; Pres. W. A. NEVILLE PERERA; Sec. SIRINAL DE MEL.

**Lanka Jathika Estate Workers' Union (LJEWU):** 60 Bandaranayakepura, Sri Jayawardenepura Mawatha, Welikada, POB 1918, Rajagiriya; tel. (11) 2865138; fax (11) 2862262; e-mail ljewusl@gmail.com; f. 1958; 350,000 mems; Pres. RAVINDRA SAMARAWEERA; Gen. Sec. K. VELAYUDAM.

**Public Service Workers' Trade Union Federation (PSWTUF):** 35/5, 19–20 Main St, Colombo 11; tel. (11) 2231125; 100 affiliated unions; 100,000 mems.

**Sri Lanka Nidahas Sewaka Sangamaya** (Sri Lanka Free Workers' Union): 301 T. B. Jayah Mawatha, POB 1241, Colombo 10; tel. and fax (11) 2694074; f. 1960; 478 br. unions; 193,011 mems; Gen. Sec. LESLIE DEVENDRA.

**Trade Union Confederation:** Colombo; f. 2008; 40 affiliated unions; Pres. K. S. WEERASEKERA; Sec. H. M. NAWARATNE BANDARA.

## Transport

### RAILWAYS

**Sri Lanka Railways Authority (SLRA):** Colombo; f. 2003; responsible for running of national railway network; Gen. Man. T. LALITHASIRI GUNARUWAH.

**Sri Lanka Railways (SLR):** Olcott Mawatha, POB 335, Colombo 10; tel. (11) 2431177; fax (11) 2446490; e-mail gmr-slr@sltnet.lk; internet www.railway.gov.lk; f. 1864; under Ministry of Transport; operates 1,447 track-km; there are ten railway lines across the country and 164 stations, with 134 sub-stations (2008); Gen. Man. T. L. GUNARUWAN.

### ROADS

In 1999 there were an estimated 96,695 km of roads in Sri Lanka, of which 11,462 km were main roads, while in 2003 the road network was estimated to have expanded to 97,286 km, of which 81% was paved. In April 2002 a major highway linking the Jaffna peninsula with the rest of the country was opened for the first time in 12 years. Delayed construction of a four-lane Southern Expressway, extending from Colombo to Matara and jointly funded by the Asian Development Bank (ADB) and Japanese Bank for InternationalCo-operation, was in progress in 2006 at a revised cost of US $175.2m. Completion was tentatively scheduled for 2010, although by mid-2008 only some 35% of the highway had been constructed. The ADB agreed a $150m. loan to Sri Lanka for the widening and rehabilitation of 350 km of national highways in December 2006, and the Government allocated Rs 3,720m. in 2008 for improvements to 1,208 km of rural roads.

**Ministry of Transport:** 1 D. R. Wijewardene Mawatha, POB 588, Colombo 10; tel. (11) 2687212; fax (11) 2687284; e-mail transplan@eol.lk; internet www.transport.gov.lk; maintains 11,661 km of national highways and 4,429 bridges through the Road Development Authority.

**Department of Motor Traffic:** 581-341 Elvitigala Mawatha, POB 533, Colombo 5; tel. (11) 2694331; fax (11) 2694338; e-mail dmtsl@sltnet.lk.

**Sri Lanka Transport Board:** 200 Kirula Rd, Narahenpita, POB 1435, Colombo 5; tel. (11) 2581120; fax (11) 2368921; e-mail chairmanctb@sltnet.lk; f. 1958; nationalized organization responsible for road passenger transport services consisting of a central transport board, 11 Cluster Bus Cos and one regional transport board; fleet of 8,900 buses (2001); Chair. TUDER CAYARATNE; Sec. D. P. W. DE LIVERA.

### SHIPPING

Colombo is one of the most important ports in Asia and is situated at the junction of the main trade routes. The other main ports of Sri Lanka are Trincomalee, Galle and Jaffna. Trincomalee is the main port for handling tea exports.

**Ceylon Association of Ships' Agents (CASA):** 56 Ward Place, Colombo 7; tel. (11) 2696227; fax (11) 2698648; e-mail casa@sltnet.lk; internet www.casa.lk; f. 1944; primarily a consultative organization; represents mems in dealings with govt authorities; 120 mems; Chair. Capt. Ajith Peiris; Sec.-Gen. Dhammika Walgampaya.

**Sri Lanka Ports Authority:** 19 Chaithya Rd, POB 595, Colombo 1; tel. (11) 2421201; fax (11) 2440651; e-mail info@slpa.lk; internet www.slpa.lk; f. 1979; responsible for all cargo handling operations and harbour development and maintenance in the ports of Colombo, Galle, Kankasanthurai, Trincomalee, Oluvil, Point Pedro and Hambantota; Chair. Saliya Wickramasuririya; Man. Dir W. G. Samaratunga.

#### Shipping Companies

**Ceylon Ocean Lines Ltd:** 'Sayuru Sevana', 46/12 Nawam Mawatha, Colombo 2; tel. (11) 2434928; fax (11) 2439245; e-mail oceanlines@col.lk; f. 1956; shipping agents, freight forwarders, charterers, container freight station operators and bunkers; Dirs Capt. L. P. Weinman, Capt. A. V. Rajendra.

**Ceylon Shipping Corpn Ltd:** 6 Sir Baron Jayatilaka Mawatha, POB 1718, Colombo 1; tel. (11) 2328772; fax (11) 2447547; e-mail cscemail@sri.lanka.net; f. 1971 as a govt corpn; became govt-owned limited liability co in 1992; operates fully-containerized service to Europe, the Far East, the Mediterranean, USA and Canada (East Coast); Chair. Sundra Jayawardhana; Gen. Man. M. S. P. Gunawardena.

**Ceylon Shipping Lines Ltd:** 450 D. R. Wijewardena Mawatha, POB 891, Colombo 10; tel. (11) 2689500; fax (11) 2689510; shipping agents, travel agents, off dock terminal operators; Chair. E. A. Wirasinha; Man. Dir T. D. V. Gunaratne.

**Ceyoceanic Ltd:** 80 Reclamation Rd, POB 795, Colombo 11; tel. (11) 2236071; Dir M. T. G. Anaam.

**Colombo Dockyard Ltd:** Port of Colombo, Graving Docks, POB 906, Colombo 15; tel. (11) 2429000; fax (11) 2446441; e-mail coldock@cdl.lk; internet www.cdl.lk; f. 1974; 51% owned by Onomichi Dockyard Co Ltd, Japan, and 49% by Sri Lankan public and government institutions; four dry-docks, seven repair berths (1,200 m), repair of ships up to 125,000 dwt, and builders of steel/aluminium vessels of up to 3,000 dwt; Chair. S. Tatebe; Man. Dir and CEO M. P. B. Yapa.

**Mercantile Shipping Co Ltd:** Bohen House, 108 Aluthmawatha Rd, Colombo 15; tel. (11) 2331792; fax (11) 2331799.

**Sri Lanka Shipping Co Ltd:** 46/5 Navam Mawatha, POB 1125, Colombo 2; tel. (11) 2336853; fax (11) 2437420; e-mail lankaship@slsc.lk; internet www.srilankashipping.com; f. 1956.

### INLAND WATERWAYS

There are more than 160 km of canals open for traffic.

### CIVIL AVIATION

Civil aviation is controlled by the Government's Department of Civil Aviation. There are airports at Batticaloa, Colombo (Bandaranaike for external flights and Ratmalana for internal), Gal Oya, Palali, Jaffna and Trincomalee. In April 2002 the Government lifted a six-year ban on domestic flights and permitted commercial airlines to resume services to Jaffna.

**Civil Aviation Authority of Sri Lanka:** Supreme Bldg, 64 Galle Rd, Colombo 3; tel. (11) 2433213; fax (11) 2440231; e-mail slcaa@sltnet.lk; internet www.caa.lk; f. 2002; under the supervision of the Ministry of Ports and Aviation; Chair. Air Vice-Marshal P. H. Mendis; CEO and Dir-Gen. Civil Aviation Parakrama Dissanayake.

**SriLankan Airlines Ltd:** World Trade Centre, East Tower, 22nd Floor, Echelon Sq., Colombo 1; tel. (11) 97335555; fax (11) 97335122; e-mail ulweb@srilankan.aero; internet www.srilankan.aero; f. 1979 as Air Lanka Ltd, name changed as above in 1999; international services to Europe, the Middle East, South Asia and the Far East; Chair. Dr P. B. Jayasundera; CEO Manoj Gunawardena.

**Helitours:** Air Headquarters, POB 594, Colombo 2; tel. (11) 2508927; fax (11) 220541; e-mail slafgops@slk.lk; commercial wing of Sri Lankan Air Force; charter services to major tourist destinations.

**Lionair (Pvt) Ltd:** Asian Aviation Centre, Colombo Airport, Ratmalana, Colombo; tel. (11) 2622622; fax (11) 2611540; e-mail citadeld@sierra.lk; f. 1994; scheduled and charter services to eight domestic destinations; Chair. Chandran Rutnam; Man. Dir Asoka Perera.

**Mihin Lanka:** 4-109, Bandaranaike Memorial International Conference Hall, Bauddhaloka Mawatha, Colombo 7; tel. (11) 2699305; fax (11) 2697525; e-mail info@mihinlanka.com; internet www.mihinlanka.com; f. 2007; govt-owned; international services to India, the Maldives, United Arab Emirates, Thailand and Singapore; Chair. Sajin Vas Gunawardena.

## Tourism

As a stopping place for luxury cruises and by virtue of the spectacle of its Buddhist festivals, ancient monuments and natural scenery, Sri Lanka is one of Asia's most important tourist centres. Good motor roads connect Colombo to the main places of interest.

Owing to the continuing intercommunal violence, tourist arrivals decreased from 403,101 in 1995 to 302,265 in 1996 and tourism receipts fell from US $224m. to $168m. The tourism sector, however, recovered well in the latter half of the 1990s, with tourist arrivals reaching 436,440 in 1999. At the end of 2000 the industry appeared to be improving, although arrivals decreased to 400,414 in that year. However, the LTTE attack on Colombo's international airport in July 2001 caused severe damage to the tourist industry. As a result, the number of tourist arrivals in 2001 decreased to 336,794 and tourist receipts fell from $250.8m. to $211.1m. In 2002 the industry recovered; total arrivals reached 393,171 and tourist receipts increased to stand at an estimated $595.0m. Tourist arrivals rose by 27.3% in 2003 to reach 500,642; in the same year tourist receipts totalled an estimated $709.0m. In 2004 tourist arrivals continued to increase, to 566,202, with tourist receipts amounting to $808.0m. In 2005, however, arrivals declined to 549,308; they recovered slightly to reach a total of 559,603 in 2006. Following a deterioration in the security situation, in 2007, according to figures from the Sri Lanka Tourism Development Authority, tourist arrivals decreased to 494,008 and tourist receipts fell to $385m.

**Sri Lanka Tourism Promotion Bureau:** 80 Galle Rd, Colombo 3; tel. (11) 2437059; fax (11) 2440001; e-mail info@srilanka.travel; internet www.srilanka.travel; f. 1966; Chair. Renton de Alwis; Man. Dir Dileep Mudadeniya.

## Defence

As assessed at November 2007, the total strength of the active armed forces was some 150,900 (including recalled reservists): army 117,900, navy 15,000, air force 18,000; the reserve forces numbered 5,500. There were also paramilitary forces of an estimated 88,600 (including an estimated 15,000 National Guard, 13,000 Home Guard and a 3,000-strong anti-guerrilla Special Task Force). Military service is voluntary.

**Defence Budget:** Estimated at Rs 139,000m. for 2007.

**Chief of Defence Staff:** Air Chief Marshal G. Donald Perera.

**Chief of Staff of Army:** Maj.-Gen. Nissanka Wijesinghe.

**Chief of Staff of Navy:** Rear-Adm. Wasantha Tennakoon.

**Chief of Staff of Air Force:** Air Vice-Marshal P. B. Premachandra.

## Education

The formulation of educational policy is the responsibility of the Ministry of Education and Higher Education. The administration and management of the school system is divided into 15 regions. The 2008 budget allocated Rs 20,358m. to the Ministry of Education and Rs 11,430m. to the Ministry of Higher Education, together representing 4.4% of total recurrent expenditure.

Since 1945 education has been available free of charge. In 1997 about 4.3m. pupils attended schools and teachers numbered an estimated 187,539. The total number of schools (including denominational schools and pirivenas, which are attended by Buddhist clergy and lay students) in 2005 was estimated at 9,723, while 282 schools were reported as temporarily closed.

School attendance is officially compulsory for nine years between five and 14 years of age, and each year about 350,000 new pupils start school. Schools are streamed according to the language medium used, either Sinhala or Tamil. Improving the standard of English, which is a compulsory second language, is one of the policy priorities of the Government. In 1960 almost all denominational schools were brought under state control.

### ELEMENTARY AND SECONDARY EDUCATION

Elementary education lasts five years from the ages of five to 10. Its first phase is organized as kindergarten classes. Secondary schooling, beginning at 10 years of age, lasts for up to eight years, comprising a first cycle of six years and a second of two years. A new system of public examinations, the National Certificate of General Education (NCGE), came into effect in 1975 to replace the British examination system. It places emphasis on practical subjects such as mathematics, science, health and physical education, social studies and pre-vocational studies. The Higher National Certificate of Education (HNCE) is more employment-orientated. The pre-university course is being revised to benefit not merely the 10% who enter university, but also those who seek employment on terminating the course. In 2003/04 the total enrolment at primary and secondary schools was equivalent to 88.1% of the school-age population (boys 88%; girls 90%). Primary enrolment in that year included an estimated 97.1% of children in the relevant age-group, while secondary enrolment was equivalent to an estimated 82.5% of children in the relevant age-group (boys 82%; girls 83%).

### HIGHER EDUCATION

Two-year full-time courses in engineering, industry, commerce and agriculture are available at technical institutes and colleges, and may include a year of job experience. Vocational technical education to develop occupational skills begins after eight years of general education and includes two-year full-time craft or trade courses, some of which may also be part-time.

The University of Sri Lanka was founded in 1972 as a single institution with six campuses. These, however, developed a high degree of autonomy and in 1979 became six independent universities. There are 26 teacher-training colleges and 12 universities. There are also 13 polytechnic institutes, eight junior technical colleges and an open university. In 2003 there were an estimated 59,734 students and 3,386 teachers (excluding visiting staff) at the country's universities. A university grants commission supervises and administers all aspects of higher education.

# Bibliography

### General


Arasaratnam, S. *Ceylon*. Englewood Cliffs, NJ, Prentice-Hall, 1964.

Champion, Stephen. *Lanka 1986–1992*. London, Garnet, 1993.

Cooray, L. J. M. *An Introduction to the Legal System of Ceylon*. Colombo, Lake House Investments Ltd, 1972.

de Silva, Daya, and de Silva, C. R. *Sri Lanka (Ceylon) Since Independence 1948–1976: A Bibliographical Survey of the Literature in the Field of Social Sciences in Sri Lanka*. Hamburg, Institute of Asian Affairs, 1978.

de Silva, K. M. (Ed.). *Sri Lanka, A Survey*. London, C. Hurst & Co, 1977.

Deegalle, Mahinda (Ed.). *Buddhism, Conflict and Violence in Modern Sri Lanka*. Abingdon, Routledge, 2006.

DeVotta, Neil. *Blowback: Linguistic Nationalism, Institutional Decay, and Ethnic Conflict in Sri Lanka*. Palo Alto, CA, Stanford University Press, 2004.

Dharmadasa, K. N. O. *Language, Religion and Ethnic Assertiveness: The Growth of Sinhalese Nationalism in Sri Lanka*. Ann Arbor, University of Michigan Press, 1992.

Farmer, B. H. 'Ceylon', in Spate, O. H. K., and Learmonth, A. T. A., *India and Pakistan*. 3rd edn, London, Methuen, 1967.

Goonatilake, Susantha. *Anthropologizing Sri Lanka: A Eurocentric Misadventure*. Bloomington, IN, Indiana University Press, 2001.

*Recolonisation: Foreign Funded NGOs in Sri Lanka*. London, Sage Publications, 2006.

Gunawardena, C. A. *Encyclopedia of Sri Lanka*. New Delhi, Sterling Publishers, 2003.

Jayasuriya, J. E. *Education in Ceylon Before and After Independence 1939–1968*. Colombo, Associated Educational Publishers, 1969.

Johnson, B. L. C., and Scrivenor, M. le M. *Sri Lanka, Land, People and Economy*. London, Heinemann, 1981.

Ludowyk, E. F. C. *The Story of Ceylon*. London, Faber and Faber, 1962.

Lynch, Caitrin. *Juki Girls, Good Girls: Gender and Cultural Politics in Sri Lanka's Global Garment Industry*. Ithaca, NY, ILR Press, 2007.

Malalgoda, K. *Buddhism in Sinhalese Society, 1750–1900*. Berkeley, CA, University of California Press, 1976.

Mortimer, L. R. (Ed.). *Sri Lanka: A Country Study*. Area Handbook Series, Washington, DC, Library of Congress, 1995.

Nubin, W. (Ed.). *Sri Lanka: Current Issues and Historical Background*. Hauppauge, Nova Science Publishers, 2003.

Paranavitana, S. *Art of the Ancient Sinhalese*. Colombo, Lake House Investments Ltd, 1972.

Peiris, G. H. *Development and Change in Sri Lanka*. New Delhi, Macmillan, 1996.

Pieris, Ralph. *Sinhalese Social Organisation*. Colombo, University of Ceylon Press, 1956.

Qadri, Ismail. *Abiding by Sri Lanka: On Peace, Place, and Postcoloniality*. Minneapolis, MN, University of Minnesota Press, 2005.

Raghavan, M. D. *Tamil Culture in Ceylon*. Colombo, Kalai Nilayam Ltd, 1972.

Rahula, Bhikkhu. *History of Buddhism in Ceylon: The Anuradhapura Period*. Colombo, Gunasena, 1956.

Richardson, John. *Paradise Poisoned: Learning About Conflict, Terrorism and Development from Sri Lanka's Civil Wars*. International Centre for Ethnic Studies, 2005.

Salgado, Minoli. *Writing Sri Lanka: Literature, Resistance and the Politics of Place*. Abingdon, Routledge, 2006.

Wickramasinghe, Nira. *Global Civil Society in Sri Lanka*. London, Sage Publications, 2002.


### History and Politics


Bartholomeusz, T. J. *In Defense of Dharma: Just-War Ideology in Buddhist Sri Lanka*. London, RoutledgeCurzon, 2002.

Bhason, Avtar Singh. *India in Sri Lanka: Between Lions and Tigers*. New Delhi, Manas Publications, 2005.

Bush, K. D. *The Intra-Group Dimensions of Ethnic Conflict in Sri Lanka: Learning to Read Between the Lines*. New York, Palgrave Macmillan, 2003.

Chandraprema, C. A. *Sri Lanka: The Years of Terror—The JVP Insurrection, 1987–89*. Colombo, 1992.

Clarance, William. *Ethnic Warfare in Sri Lanka and the UN Crisis*. London, Pluto Press, 2006.

de Mel, Neloufer. *Women and the Nation's Narrative: Gender and Nationalism in Twentieth Century Sri Lanka*. Oxford, Rowman and Littlefield Publishers, 2002.

de Silva, Colvin R. *Ceylon Under the British Occupation*. Colombo, 2 vols, Colombo Apothecaries Press, 1950.

de Silva, K. M. *History of Sri Lanka*. London, Hurst, 1981.

*Managing Ethnic Tensions in Multi-ethnic Societies: Sri Lanka 1880–1985*. Lanham and New York, 1986.

de Silva, K. M. (Ed.). *The University of Ceylon, History of Ceylon, Vol. 3*. Colombo, University of Ceylon Press, 1973.

*Sri Lanka: Problems of Governance*. New Delhi, Konark Publishers, 1993.

de Silva, K. M., and Wriggins, Howard. *J. R. Jayewardene of Sri Lanka: A Political Biography, Volume One: The First Fifty Years, 1906–1956*. London, Anthony Blond/Quartet, 1988; *Volume Two: 1956–1989*. London, Leo Cooper, 1994.

Dixit, J. N. *Assignment Colombo*. Delhi, Konark Publishers, 1998.

Fernando, T. *Alien Winds Across Paradise: A New Look at Sri Lanka's Foreign Relations Through the Ages*. London, Sangam Books, 2003.

Ghosh, P. S. *Ethnicity Versus Nationalism: The Devolution Discourse in Sri Lanka*. London, Sage Publications, 2003.

Gunaratna, Rohan. *Sri Lanka's Ethnic Crisis and National Security*. Colombo, South Asian Network on Conflict Research, 2000.

Hasbullah, S. H. *Sri Lankan Society in an Era of Globalization: Struggling to Create a New Social Order*. London, Sage Publications, 2004.

Hennayake, Nalani. *Culture, Politics, and Development in Postcolonial Sri Lanka*. Lanham, MD, Lexington Books, 2006.

Ismail, Qadri. *Abiding by Sri Lanka: On Peace, Place, and Postcoloniality*. Minneapolis, MN, University of Minnesota Press, 2005.

Jayawardena, K. *Nobodies to Somebodies: The Rise of the Colonial Bourgeoisie in Sri Lanka*. London, Zed Books, 2002.

Jayaweera, Swarna. *Women in Post-Independence Sri Lanka*. London, Sage Publications, 2001.

Jiggins, J. *Caste and Family in the Politics of the Sinhalese.* Cambridge University Press, 1979.

Jupp, J. *Sri Lanka, Third World Democracy.* London, Frank Cass, 1978.

Kearney, R. N. *Communalism and Language in the Politics of Ceylon.* Durham, NC, Duke University Press, 1967.

*The Politics of Ceylon (Sri Lanka).* Ithaca, NY, and London, Cornell University Press, 1973.

Kemper, S. *The Presence of the Past: Chronicles, Politics and Culture in Sinhala Nationalism.* Ithaca, NY, Cornell University Press, 1992.

Ludowyk, E. F. C. *The Modern History of Ceylon.* London, Weidenfeld and Nicolson, 1966.

McGowan, William. *Only Man is Vile: The Tragedy of Sri Lanka.* London, Picador, and New York, Farrar, Straus and Giroux, 1994.

Mendis, G. C. *Early History of Ceylon.* Colombo, 4th edn, 1946.

Mukarji, Apraim. *The War in Sri Lanka.* Har Anand Publications, 2001.

Narayan Swamy, M. R. *Tigers of Lanka: From Boys to Guerrillas.* Delhi, Konark Publishers, 1994.

*Inside an Elusive Mind: Prabhakaran.* 2003.

Nicholas, C. W., and Paranavitana, S. A. *A Concise History of Ceylon.* Colombo, University of Ceylon Press, 1961.

Paranavitana, S. (Ed.). *The University of Ceylon, History of Ceylon, Vol. 1 (Parts 1 & 2).* Colombo, University of Ceylon Press, 1959–60.

Sabaratnam, Lakshmanan. *Ethnic Attachments: The Deployment of Modern Sinhala and Tamil Ethnicity.* 2001.

Samarasinghe, S. W. R. de A., and Samarasinghe, Vidyamali. *Historical Dictionary of Sri Lanka.* London, The Scarecrow Press, 1998.

Silva, N. (Ed.) *The Hybrid Island: Culture Crossings and the Invention of Identity in Sri Lanka.* London, Zed Books, 2002.

Sivarajah, Ambalavanar. *Politics of Tamil Nationalism in Sri Lanka.* International Academic Publishers, 2000.

Tambiah, S. J. *Sri Lanka: Ethnic Fratricide and the Dismantling of Democracy.* Chicago, 1986.

*Buddhism Betrayed? Religion, Politics and Violence in Sri Lanka.* Chicago, IL, University of Chicago Press, 1992.

Wickramasinghe, Nira. *Sri Lanka: A Modern History.* London, C. Hurst & Co, 2005.

*Sri Lanka in the Modern Age: A History of Contested Identities.* London, C. Hurst & Co, 2005.

Wilson, A. Jeyaratnam. *Politics in Sri Lanka, 1947–1973.* London, Macmillan, 1974.

*Electoral Politics in an Emergent State: The Ceylon General Elections of May 1970.* Cambridge University Press, 1975.

*The Gaullist System in Asia, The Constitution of Sri Lanka, 1978.* London, Macmillan, 1980.

*S. J. V. Chelvanayakam and the Crisis of Tamil Nationalism, 1947–1977.* Honolulu, HI, University of Hawaii Press, 1994.

*Sri Lankan Tamil Nationalism: Its Origins and Development in the 19th and 20th Centuries.* Seattle, WA, University of Washington Press, 2000.

Woodward, C. A. *The Growth of a Party System in Ceylon.* Providence, Rhode Island, Brown University Press, 1969.

Woost, Michael D., and Winslow, Deborah (Eds). *Economy, Culture and Civil War in Sri Lanka.* Bloomington, IN, Indiana University Press, 2004.

Wriggins, W. Howard. *Ceylon: Dilemmas of a New Nation.* Princeton, NJ, Princeton University Press, 1960.

**Economy**

Athukorala, Premachandra, and Rajapatirana, Sarath. *Liberalization and Industrial Transformation in Sri Lanka.* Oxford, Oxford University Press, 2000.

Central Bank of Sri Lanka. *Review of the Economy.* Colombo, Central Bank of Sri Lanka, annual.

*Economic Progress of Independent Sri Lanka.* Colombo, Central Bank of Sri Lanka, 1998.

de Silva, W. Indralal. *Population Projections for Sri Lanka: 1921–2041.* Colombo, Institute of Policy Studies, Human Resource Development Series No. 2, 1997.

Department of Census and Statistics. *Statistical Profile of Sri Lanka: A Statistical Compendium to Commemorate the 50th Anniversary of Independence in Sri Lanka.* Colombo, Department of Census and Statistics, 1998.

Dissanayake, Navaratna. *Industrial Accumulation in Sri Lanka: Impact of Policy Shift.* New Delhi, Gyan Publishing House, 2004.

Dunham, David, and Edwards, Chris. *Rural Poverty and Agrarian Crisis in Sri Lanka, 1985–95: Making Sense of the Picture.* Colombo, Institute of Policy Studies, 1997.

Government of Sri Lanka. *Connecting to Growth: Sri Lanka's Poverty Reduction Strategy.* Colombo, 2002.

*National Framework for Relief, Rehabilitation and Reconciliation.* Colombo, June 2002.

Hanna, Nagy K. *From Envisioning to Designing e-Development: The Experience of Sri Lanka.* World Bank, 2007.

Hettiarachchi, Wimal. *Globalization—Liberalizing the Capital Account in Sri Lanka.* Colombo, Institute of Policy Studies, 1998.

Indraratna, A. D. V. de S. *Fifty Years of Sri Lanka's Independence, A Socio-Economic Review.* Colombo, Sri Lanka Institute of Social and Economic Studies (SLISES), 1998.

Institute of Policy Studies. *Sri Lanka: State of the Economy.* Colombo, annual.

Kelegama, Saman. *Development Under Stress: Sri Lankan Economy in Transition.* London, Sage Publications, 2006.

Kelegama, Saman (Ed.). *Economic Policy in Sri Lanka: Issues and Debates.* London, Sage Publications, 2004.

*Ready-Made Garment Industry in Sri Lanka: Facing the Global Challenge.* Colombo, Institute of Policy Studies of Sri Lanka, 2004.

Kember, Steven. *Buying and Believing.* Chicago, IL, University of Chicago Press, 2002.

Knight-John, Malathy. *Performance Contracting: A Strategy for Public Enterprise Reform in Sri Lanka?* Colombo, Institute of Policy Studies, 1997.

Lakshman, W. D. (Ed.). *Dilemmas of Development—Fifty Years of Economic Change in Sri Lanka.* Colombo, Sri Lanka Association of Economics, 1997.

Lakshman, W. D., and Tisdell, Clement A. *Sri Lanka's Development since Independence—Socio-Economic Perspectives and Analysis.* Nova Science Publishers, 2000.

Pal, Miriam S. *Perceptions of the Poor: Poverty Consultations in Four Districts in Sri Lanka.* Asian Development Bank, 2002.

Peebles, Patrick. *The Plantation Tamils of Ceylon.* Leicester, Continuum Publishing Group (Leicester University Press), 2001

Ranasinghe, Malik. *A Method to Analyze Viability of Private Sector Participation in New Infrastructure Projects in Sri Lanka.* Colombo, Institute of Policy Studies, 1998.

Snodgrass, D. *Ceylon: An Export Economy in Transition.* Homewood, IL, Richard D. Irwin, 1966.

Wenzlhuemer, Roland.*From Coffee to Tea Cultivation in Ceylon, 1880–1900: An Economic and Social History.* Leiden, Brill, 2008.

# PART THREE

# Who's Who of South Asia

# WHO'S WHO OF SOUTH ASIA

**ABDULLA, Ahmed;** Maldivian government official; *Minister of Environment, Energy and Water;* b. 26 Sept. 1949, Malé; m.; one s. three d. *Career:* fmr Minister of Health, of Information, Arts and Culture; Acting Minister of Foreign Affairs 2005; Minister of Environment, Energy and Water 2005–; Owner Miadhu newspaper. *Address:* Ministry of Environment, Energy and Water, Huravee Building, Ameer Ahmed Magu, Malé 20-05; G. Mescot, Lonuziyaarai Magu, Malé, Maldives; tel. 3331695; 3322557; fax 3331694; 3321504; e-mail env@environment.gov.mv; minsbureau@gmail.com; internet www.environment.gov.mv.

**ABDULLAH, Abdul Samad;** Maldivian international civil servant and diplomatist; *High Commissioner to Bangladesh. Career:* has served in Maldives Public Service as well as with WHO, has held several sr positions Maldives public health sector, including Dir-Gen. Health Services, Ministry of Health; first resident High Commr to Bangladesh 2008–. *Address:* High Commission of the Maldives, Dhaka, Bangladesh; Ministry of Foreign Affairs, Boduthakurufaanu Magu, Malé, Maldives; tel. (960) 3323400-7; fax (960)3323841; e-mail info@foreign.gov.mv; internet www.foreign.gov.mv.

**ABDULLAH, Farooq,** MB; Indian politician; b. 21 Oct. 1937, Srinagar, Kashmir; m. Mollie Abdullah 1968; one s. three d. *Career:* Chief Minister, Jammu and Kashmir 1982–84, 1986–90, 1996–2002; Pres. State Cen. Labour Union, Jammu and Kashmir Nat. Conf.; Chair. Jammu and Kashmir Muslim Auquaf Trust, Sher-i-Kashmir Nat. Medical Inst. Trust, Sher-i-Kashmir Inst. of Medical Sciences; mem. Parl. 1980–82; mem. India Int. Centre; Gen. Sec. Indo-Arab Friendship Soc., Nat. Integration Council; Nat. Solidarity Award 1998, Eminent Personality of the Year, Indian Medical Asscn 1999. *Address:* 5 Pritvi Raj Road, New Delhi 110 01, India; e-mail farooq.abdullah@hotmail.com.

**ABDULLAH, Omar Farooq,** BCom; Indian politician; *President, Jammu and Kashmir National Conference;* b. 10 March 1970, Rochford, UK; m. Payal Abdullah; two s. *Education:* Sydenham Coll., Mumbai. *Career:* Pres. Youth Nat. Conf.; elected to 12th Lok Sabha, mem. Parl. for Srinagar Constituency (Nat. Conf. Party) 1998, re-elected to 13th Lok Sabha 1999; mem. Cttee of Transport and Tourism, Consultative Cttee, Ministry of Tourism 1998–99; Minister of State for Commerce and Industry 1999–2001, for External Affairs 2001–02; Pres. Jammu and Kashmir Nat. Conf. (JKNC) 2002–. *Address:* Jammu and Kashmir National Conference, Mujahid Manzil, Srinagar 190 002, India; tel. (194) 271500.

**ABU JAFAR, Mohammad,** ACMA; Bangladeshi business executive. *Career:* fmr Finance Man. Everbest Shipping Agencies Ltd; fmr Chair. Bangladesh Steel and Engineering Corpn. *Address:* c/o Bangladesh Steel and Engineering Corporation, BSEC Bhaban, 102 Kazi Nazrul Islam Avenue, Dhaka 1215, Bangladesh.

**ACHARYA, Madhu Raman;** Nepalese diplomatist; *Permanent Representative, United Nations;* b. 24 Feb. 1957, Udavapur; m.; two c. *Education:* Tribhuvan Univ., Kathmandu. *Career:* Asst Lecturer, Tribhuvan Univ. 1982–83; Section Officer, Ministry of Home Affairs 1983–90; Asst Sec., Ministry of Finance 1990–93, Under-Sec. of Finance 1993–96; Jt Sec., Ministry of Foreign Affairs 1996–97; Deputy Chief of Mission, New Delhi, India 1997–98; Amb. to Bangladesh 1998–2001; Foreign Sec. 2001–05; Perm. Rep. to UN, New York 2005–, Chair. Fourth Cttee (Special Political and Decolonization) for 61st session of Gen. Ass. 2006; participated in several UN missions in Cambodia, S Africa, Liberia in 1990s. *Publications:* several books, including Nepal Culture Shift!: Reinventing Culture in the Himalayan Kingdom 2002. *Address:* Permanent Mission of Nepal to the United Nations, 820 Second Avenue, Suite 17B, New York, NY 10017, USA; tel. (212) 370-3988; fax (212) 953-2038; e-mail nepal@un.int; internet www.un.int/nepal.

**ACHUTHANANDAN, V(elikkakathu) S(ankaran);** Indian politician; *Chief Minister of Kerala;* b. 20 Oct. 1923, Punnapra, Alappuzha, Kerala; m. Smt. K. Vasumathy; one s. one d. *Career:* lost parents at early age, forced to give up studies after 7th standard in school; started working by helping elder brother in village cloth shop, later took up job of meshing coir to make ropes at coir factory; began trade union activities and joined State Congress 1938; mem. Communist Party of India (CPI) 1940; imprisoned for five and a half years during Freedom Struggle period and went underground for a further four and half years; mem. State Secr. of CPI 1957; left CPI Nat. Council to form Communist Party of India (Marxist)—CPI(M) 1964, Sr Leader of CPI(M) in Kerala; active in famous Punnapra-Vayalar uprising; State Sec. Kerala CPI(M) 1980–92, mem. Politburo 1985–2007; elected mem. Kerala Legis. Ass. 1967, 1970, 1991, 2001, 2006; Leader of Opposition, Kerala Legis. Ass. 1992–96, 2001–06; mem. Legis. Ass. for Malampuzha constituency, Palghat Dist 2006–; Chief Minister of Kerala 2006–; popularly known as 'Comrade VS'. *Address:* Room No. 141, Third Floor, North Block, Government Secretariat, Thiruvananthapuram 1, Kerala; Cliff House, Nanthancode, Thiruvananthapuram 3, Kerala, India; tel. (471) 2333812; (471) 2314853; fax (471) 2333489; e-mail chiefminister@keralacm.gov.in; internet www.keralacm.gov.in.

**ADAM, Lt-Gen. Anbaree Abdul Sattar;** Maldivian army officer (retd), politician and diplomatist; *High Commissioner to India. Career:* has served as Dir and Dir-Gen. of Nat. Security, Minister of State for Defence and Nat. Security, Chief of Staff of Nat. Security Services (NSS), and Deputy C-in-C of NSS and of Police since 1967; currently High Commr to India (also accred to Nepal and Bhutan). *Address:* High Commission of the Maldives, E-45, Greater Kailash II, New Delhi 110 048, India; tel. (11) 51435701; fax (11) 51435709; e-mail admin@maldiveshighcom.co.in; internet www.maldiveshighcom.co.in.

**ADVANI, Lal Krishna;** Indian politician and fmr journalist and social worker; *Leader of the Opposition;* b. 8 Nov. 1927, Karachi (now in Pakistan); m. Kamala Jagtiani 1965; one s. one d. *Education:* St Patrick's High School, Karachi, D.G. Nat. Coll., Hyderabad, Sind, Govt Law Coll., Bombay (now Mumbai). *Career:* joined Rashtriya Swayam Sevak Sangh (RSS, social work org.) 1942, Sec. of Karachi br. 1947; joined Bharatiya Jana Sangh (BJS) 1951; party work in Rajasthan –1958, Sec. of Delhi State Jana Sangh 1958–63, Vice-Pres. 1965–67; mem. Cen. Exec. of BJS 1966; Jt Ed. BJS paper Organizer 1960–67; mem. interim Metropolitan Council, Delhi 1966, Leader of Jana Sangh Group 1966; Chair. Metropolitan Council 1967; mem. Rajya Sabha 1970, Head of Jana Sangh Parl. Group 1970; Pres. BJS 1973–77 (incorporated in Janata); detained during emergency 1975–77; Gen. Sec. Janata Party Jan.–May 1977; Minister of Information and Broadcasting 1977–79, of Home Affairs and of Kashmir Affairs 1998–99, of Home Affairs 1999–2004; Deputy Prime Minister of India 2002–04; Gen. Sec. Bharatiya Janata Party 1980–86, Pres. 1986–90, 1993–2005; Leader of Opposition, Lok Sabha 1990–91, 1991–96, 2004–. *Publications:* A Prisoner's Scrap-Book, The People Betrayed. *Address:* 1835/16, Kasturbhai Block, Din Dayal Bhawan, J.P. Chowk, Khanpur, Ahmedabad; 30 Prithviraj Raj Road, New Delhi 110 003, India; tel. (11) 23794124 (New Delhi); fax (11) 23017419 (New Delhi); e-mail advanilk@sansad.nic.in; internet www.bjp.org.

**AFEEF, Hassan;** Maldivian politician; *Leader, Parliamentary Group, Maldivian Democratic Party;* m. Farhath Afeef.

*Career:* MP for Thaa Atoll, Shadow Home Minister and Leader of Maldivian Democratic Party Parl. Group. *Address:* Maldivian Democratic Party, H. Sharaashaa, 1st Floor, Sosun Magu, Malé 20059, Maldives; tel. 3340044; fax 3322960; e-mail secretariat@mdp.org.mv; internet www.mdp.org.mv.

**AHADI, Anwar al-Haq,** MBA, PhD; Afghan banker, politician and professor of political science; *Minister of Finance;* b. 12 Aug. 1951, Jigdalai, Sarobi Dist; m. Fatima Gailani. *Education:* Hibibiya High School, American Univ. of Beirut, Lebanon, Northwestern Univ., Chicago, USA. *Career:* fmr mem. of staff Continental Bank of Chicago; joined Afghan Mellat Party (Afghan Social Democratic Party) 1969, elected to Supreme Council 1987, 1990, Pres. 1995–; Asst Prof. of Political Sciences, Carlton Univ. 1984; Banking Dir, Continental Elona Bank, Chicago 1985–87; Prof. of Political Sciences, Providence Univ. 1987–2002; Gov. Da Afghanistan Bank (Cen. Bank of Afghanistan) 2002–04; Minister of Finance 2004–. *Address:* Ministry of Finance, Pashtunistan Wat, Kabul, Afghanistan; tel. (75) 2004199; fax (20) 2103439; e-mail info@mof.gov.af; internet www.mof.gov.af.

**AHMED, Aneesa;** Maldivian politician; *Minister of the President's Office;* b. 29 Sept. 1949, Malé. *Career:* Under-Sec. Ministry of Foreign Affairs 1980–81; Dir-Gen. Foreign Relations, Pres.'s Office April–Nov. 1998; Deputy Minister of Women's Affairs and Social Security 1998–2002, Minister of Women's Affairs, Family Devt and Social Security 2002–06, of the Pres.'s Office 2006–; Head, Dhivehi Rayyithunge Party (DRP) Parl. Group. *Address:* c/o President's Office, Boduthakurufaanu Magu, Malé 20-05; M Lonuveli, Raiveri Hingun, Malé 20-02, Maldives; tel. 3323701; 3326566; fax 3325500; internet www.presidencymaldives.gov.mv.

**AHMED, Fakhruddin,** BA, MA, PhD; Bangladeshi economist, civil servant and fmr central banker; *Honourable Chief Adviser, in charge of Cabinet Division, of the Ministry of Establishment and the Ministry of Information;* b. 1 May 1940, Munshiganj, British India; m. Neena Ahmed; one s. *Education:* Dhaka Univ., Williams Coll., USA, Princeton Univ., USA. *Career:* began career as Lecturer in Econs, Dhaka Univ.; served in Civil Service of Pakistan and in Govt of Bangladesh –1978, lastly as Jt Sec., Econ. Relations Div., Ministry of Finance; several sr positions at World Bank, Washington, DC, USA 1978–2001; Gov. Bangladesh Bank 2001–05; Chair. Palli Karma-Sahayak Foundation (apex fund) 2005–07; Hon. Chief Adviser of Caretaker Govt of Bangladesh, in charge of Cabinet Div., of Ministry of Establishment, of Ministry of Home Affairs and of Election Comm. Secr. 2007–08, Honourable Chief Adviser, in charge of Cabinet Div., of Ministry of Establishment and Ministry of Information 2008–. *Address:* Honourable Chief Adviser's Office, Old Sangshad Bhaban, Tejgaon, Dhaka, Bangladesh; tel. (2) 8151157; fax (2) 8113244; e-mail info@pmo.gov.bd; internet www.pmo.gov.bd.

**AHMED, Maj. Hafizuddin;** Bangladeshi army officer (retd) and politician. *Career:* fmr Minister of Water Resources, of Commerce; mem. Standing Cttee and Vice-Pres. Bangladesh Jatiyatabadi Dal (Bangladesh Nationalist Party), apptd Sec.-Gen. of faction Oct. 2007–. *Address:* Bangladesh Jatiyatabadi Dal, Banani Office, House 23, Road 13, Dhaka, Bangladesh; tel. (2) 8819525; fax (2) 8813063; e-mail bnpbd@e-fsbd.net; internet www.bnpbd.com.

**AHMED, Iajuddin,** BSc, MS, PhD; Bangladeshi soil scientist, academic, politician and head of state; *President;* b. 1 Feb. 1931, Nayagoan, Munshiganj Dist; m. Anwara Begum; three c. *Education:* Munshiganj Haraganga Coll., Dhaka Univ., Univ. of Wisconsin, USA. *Career:* Asst Prof., Dept of Soil Sciences, Dhaka Univ. 1963, Assoc. Prof. 1964–1973, Prof. 1973, Chair. of Dept 1968–69, 1976–79, Provost, Salimullah Muslim Hall 1975–1983, Dean, Faculty of Biological Sciences 1989–1990, 1990–91; Visiting Prof., Cornell Univ. 1983, German Tech. Univ., Berlin 1984, Gatinzens Univ., Germany 1984; adviser to caretaker govt 1991; Chair. Public Service Comm. 1991–93; Chair. Univ. Grants Comm. 1995–99; fmr Chancellor, State Univ. of Bangladesh; Pres. of Bangladesh 2002–, Chief Adviser (Head of Caretaker Govt), Minister of Foreign Affairs, of Defence, of Home Affairs 2006–07; mem. Bangladesh Jatiyabadi Dal (Bangladesh Nationalist Party); mem. Int. Soil Science Asscn, Indian Soil Science Asscn, Bangladesh Soil Science Asscn, Asiatic Soc.; Ibrahim Memorial Gold Medal 1987–88, Sri Gjyan Atish Dipanker Gold Medal 1990, Ekushey Award for Educ. 1995. *Address:* President's Secretariat, Old Sansad Bhaban, Dhaka, Bangladesh.

**AHMED, Imtiaz,** PhD; Bangladeshi academic and diplomatist; *Ambassador to Nepal. Career:* fmr Asst Prof., Dept of Int. Relations, Univ. of Dhaka; fmr Minister and Deputy Chief of Mission, Washington, DC, currently Amb. to Nepal. *Address:* Embassy of Bangladesh, Maharajgunj Ring Road, Kathmandu, Nepal; tel. (1) 4372843; fax (1) 4373265; e-mail bdootktm@wlink.com.np.

**AHMED, Kamal U.;** Bangladeshi television executive; *Director General, Bangladesh Television. Career:* fmr Ed. BBC Bangla Service, London, UK; currently Jt Sec. of Information and Dir Gen. Bangladesh Television. *Address:* National Broadcasting Authority Bhaban, 121 Kazi Nazrul Islam Avenue, Shahbagh, Dhaka - 1000, Bangladesh; tel. (2) 861-6606; fax (2) 862-4839; e-mail dg@btv.gov.bd; internet www.btv.gov.bd.

**AHMED, Lt-Gen. Moeen U.;** Bangladeshi army officer; *Chief of Army Staff;* m. Begum Naznin Moeen; one s. one d. *Education:* Defence Services Command and Staff Coll., Mirpur, US Army Command and Staff Coll., Harvard Univ., Centre for Security Studies of Hawaii, USA. *Career:* began mil. service 1975, fmr positions include Weapons Training Officer, Platoon Commdr Bangladesh Mil. Acad., Brigade Maj., Infantry Brigade, Grade One Staff Officer, Mil. Operations Directorate, Army HQ, Col Infantry Div., Directing Staff Defence Services Command and Staff Coll., Sr Instructor Army Wing, later Chief Instructor, Commdt School of Infantry and Tactics, Mil. Sec. and Master Gen. of Ordnance, Army HQ, promoted to rank of Lt-Gen. 2005, Chief of Army Staff 2005–; fmr Defence Adviser, High Comm. in Pakistan; served with UN Assistance Mission for Rwanda (UNAMIR); Force Commdr's Commendation, US Forces Commendation. *Address:* Office of the Chief of Army Staff, Army Headquarters, GS Branch, Dhaka, Bangladesh; tel. (2) 8752348; fax (2) 8754455; e-mail itdte@army.mil.bd; internet www.bangladesharmy.org.

**AHMED, Qazi Hussain,** MSc; Pakistani politician; *Chairman, Jamaat-e-Islami Pakistan;* b. 1938, Dist of Nowshera, North-West Frontier Prov. (NWFP); m.; four c. *Education:* Islamic Coll., Peshawar. *Career:* teacher; mem. Jamaat-e-Islami Pakistan (JIP) 1970–, fmr Pres. Peshawar Br., Party Sec., Pres. for NWFP, Sec.-Gen. of JIP 1978–87, Chair. 1987–; mem. Senate of Pakistan 1986–96, resigned in protest against corrupt political system, re-elected 2002–; mem. Muttahida Majlis-e-Amal alliance 2002–, Pres. 2004–. *Address:* Jamaat-e-Islami Pakistan, Mansoorah, Multan Road, Lahore 54570; Ziarat Kaka Sahib, Nowshera District, NWFP, Pakistan; tel. (42) 5419504; fax (42) 5419505; e-mail uroobah@pol.com.pk; internet www.jamaat.org.

**AHMED, Salahuddin,** BSc, MA, LLM; Bangladeshi lawyer and government official; *Attorney-General;* b. 8 Feb. 1948, Dhaka. *Education:* London School of Econs, UK, Dhaka Univ., Colombia Univ., USA. *Career:* Asst Prof., Dept of Econs, Dhaka Univ. 1971–77, Asst Prof., Inst. of Business Admin, Dhaka Univ. 1980–83; began practising law 1980, lawyer at High Court 1982–2008; Assoc. Counsel, Dr Kamal Hossain & Assocs (law firm), Dhaka –2008; Additional Attorney-Gen. 2007–08, Attorney-Gen. 2008–; mem. Supreme Court Bar Asscn, Human Rights Bangladesh, South Asian Asscn for Regional Co-operation in Law, Bangladesh Chapter. *Address:* Office of the Attorney General, Bangladesh Supreme Court, Dhaka 2; c/o Dr Kamal Hossain & Associates, Chamber Building, 2nd Floor, 122-124 Motijheel CA, Dhaka 1000, Bangladesh; tel. (2) 433585; e-mail info@minlaw.gov.bd.

**AHMED, Salehuddin,** MA, PhD; Bangladeshi central banker; *Governor and Chairman, Bangladesh Bank;* m.; two c. *Education:* Dhaka Univ., McMaster Univ., Canada. *Career:* Lecturer in Econs, Dhaka Univ. 1970; joined civil service and served in various admin. capacities, including in Centre on Integrated Rural Devt for Asia and the Pacific, Dhaka; fmr Dir-Gen. Bangladesh Acad. for Rural Devt, Comilla, NGO Affairs Bureau of Office of the Prime Minister; Man. Dir Palli Karma Sahayak Foundation (apex funding agency of macro-credit operations in Bangladesh) 1996–2005; Gov. and Chair. Bangladesh Bank (cen. bank) 2005–; mem. advisory bodies of several govt and non-govt agencies in Bangladesh; Distinguished Alumni Award, McMaster Univ. 2006. *Publications:* more than 60 books, reports and journal articles. *Address:* Bangladesh Bank, Motijheel C/A, PO Box 325, Dhaka 1000, Bangladesh; tel. (2) 7120106; fax (2) 9566212; e-mail governor@bangla.net; internet www.bangladesh-bank.org.

**AHMED, Shahabuddin,** MA; Bangladeshi fmr head of state and judge; b. 1930, Pemai of Kendua, Greater Mymensingh Dist; two s. three d. *Education:* Dhaka Univ., Lahore Civil Service Acad., Univ. of Oxford, UK. *Career:* joined Civil Service of Pakistan 1954 as Sub-Div. Officer, later Additional Deputy Commr; transferred to Judicial Br. 1960; fmr Additional Dist and Sessions Judge, Dhaka and Barisal; fmr Dist and Sessions Judge, Comilla and Chittagong; fmr Registrar High Court of E Pakistan; elevated to High Court Bench 1972; apptd Judge of Appellate Div., Supreme Court of Bangladesh 1980; Chief Justice 1990, 1991–95; Chair. Labour Appellate Tribunal 1973–74, Bangladesh Red Cross Soc. 1978–82, Comm. of Inquiry into police shootings of students 1983, Nat. Pay Comm. 1984; Vice-Pres. League of Red Cross and Red Crescent Soc., Geneva, Switzerland; Acting Pres. of Bangladesh 1990–91, Pres. 1996–2001; Hon. Master Hon. Soc. of Gray's Inn, London. *Address:* House Dal Motia, nr Mohammadpur, Dhaka, Bangladesh.

**AHMED, Air Chief Marshal Tanvir Mehmood,** MSc; Pakistani air force officer; *Chief of Air Staff;* b. 1952; m.; four c. *Education:* Pakistan Air Force (PAF) Public School, Sargodha, PAF Acad., Risalpur, Turkish Air War Coll. and Nat. Defence Coll., Islamabad. *Career:* joined PAF and took fighter and operational conversion courses, qualified flying instructor and combat commdr on fighter aircraft, commanded Fighter Squadron, F-16s Flg Wing, PAF Base, Sargodha and PAF Acad., Risalpur, Deputy Dir in Operations Br., Personal Staff Officer to two Air Chiefs, Dir F-16 project, Sr Air Staff Officer at Northern Air Command, Peshawar and Dir-Gen. Air Weapons Complex, Wah, served as Deputy Chief Air Staff Admin and Operations; served in UAE Air Force as fighter instructor pilot; Vice-Chief of Air Staff 2003–06, Chief of Air Staff 2006–; Sitara-i-Basalat, Sitara-i-Imtiaz (Mil.), Hilal-i-Imtiaz (Mil.). *Address:* Office of the Chief of Air Staff, Ministry of Defence, Pakistan Secretariat, No. II, Rawalpindi 46000, Pakistan; tel. (51) 9271107; fax (51) 9271113.

**AHSAN, Chaudhry Aitzaz;** Pakistani barrister, writer, human rights activist and politician; b. 27 Sept. 1945, Murree, Punjab. *Education:* Aitchison Coll. and Government Coll., Lahore, Univ. of Cambridge, UK. *Career:* called to the Bar, Gray's Inn, London 1967; came first in Cen. Superior Services examination but refused to join govt service during mil. rule of Gen. Ayub Khan; currently Sr Advocate, Supreme Court; Pres. Supreme Court Bar Asscn; fought cases in defence of Benazir Bhutto 2001 and fmr Prime Minister Nawaz Sharif, successfully represented Chief Justice Iftikhar Mohammad Chaudhry in Supreme Court of Pakistan 2007; began political career 1970s; mem. Pakistan People's Party (PPP); elected to Punjab Ass. and inducted into prov. cabinet, given portfolio of Information, Planning and Devt 1977 (resgnd); expelled from PPP; became an active leader of Movt for the Restoration of Democracy (MRD) following coup by Gen. Mohammad Zia-ul-Haq, rejoined PPP during martial law period, jailed several times as a political prisoner without trial for active participation in MRD movt; elected to Nat. Ass. from Lahore as PPP cand. 1988, re-elected 1990, lost seat 1993, elected to Senate 1994, Leader of House and Leader of Opposition 1996–99, re-elected to Nat. Ass. as PPP cand. for his traditional seat in Lahore, as well as from Bahawalnagar in Southern Punjab 2002, mem. Standing Cttee on Interior and Standing Cttee on Public Accounts; Fed. Minister for Law and Justice, Interior, Narcotics Control 1988–90; has been under arrest periodically for his involvement in effort to restore Iftikhar Mohammad Chaudhry as Chief Justice of Pakistan following suspension of constitution and removal of Chief Justice Chaudhry from the bench by Pres. Pervez Musharraf 2007; Founder and Vice-Pres. Human Rights Comm. of Pakistan; Asian Human Rights Defender Award, Asian Human Rights Comm., Hong Kong 2008, Award for Distinction in Int. Law and Affairs, New York State Bar Asscn 2008. *Publications:* The Indus Saga and the Making of Pakistan (also Urdu trans., Sindh Sagar Aur Qyam-e-Pakistan), Divided by Democracy (with Lord Meghnad Desai). *Address:* Supreme Court Bar Association of Pakistan, Supreme Court of Pakistan Building, Constitution Avenue, Islamabad, Pakistan; tel. (51) 9215185; fax (51) 9214862; e-mail info@scbap.org; internet www.scbap.org.

**AKHTAR, Shamshad,** BA, MSc, MA, PhD; Pakistani economist and central banker; *Governor, State Bank of Pakistan;* b. Hyderabad, Sindh Prov. *Education:* Univ. of Punjab, Quaid-e-Azam Univ., Univ. of Sussex and Paisley Coll. of Tech. (now Univ. of Paisley), UK, Harvard Univ., USA. *Career:* briefly worked at planning offices in Pakistan at Fed. and Sindh Govt levels; economist, World Bank mission in Pakistan 1980–90; Sr then Prin. Financial Sector Specialist, Asian Devt Bank (ADB) 1990–98; Man. and Coordinator for APEC Finance Ministers' Group 1998–2001, Dir Govt Finance and Trade Div. for E and Cen. Asia Dept, then Deputy Dir Gen. SE Asia Dept 2001–04, Dir Gen. 2004–05; Gov. (first woman) State Bank of Pakistan 2006–; Visiting Fellow, Harvard Univ. Dept of Econs 1987. *Publications:* numerous papers on econs and finance. *Address:* State Bank of Pakistan, Central Directorate, I. I. Chundrigar Road, PO Box 4456, Karachi 2, Pakistan; tel. (21) 24450298; fax (21) 9212440; e-mail governor.office@sbp.org.pk; shamshad.akhtar@sbp.org.pk; internet www.sbp.org.pk.

**AKRAM, Munir,** LLB, MA; Pakistani diplomatist and lawyer; *Permanent Representative, United Nations. Education:* Univ. of Karachi. *Career:* joined Foreign Service 1967, Section Officer, Ministry of Foreign Affairs 1968–69, Dir (UN) 1973–79, Dir-Gen. (UN, Econ. Co-operation and Policy Planning) 1985–88; Second Sec., Perm. Mission of Pakistan to UN, New York 1969–73, Councillor and Deputy Perm. Rep. to UN, Geneva 1979–82, Amb. and Perm. Rep., Geneva 1995–2002, Perm. Rep., New York 2002–; Minister/Counsellor, Embassy of Pakistan, Tokyo 1982–85; Amb. to EC, Belgium and Luxembourg 1988–92; Additional Foreign Sec. 1992–95; Chair. UN Cttee on Non-Governmental Orgs 1970, Special Group on Most Seriously Affected Countries by the Oil Crisis, UN Gen. Ass. Special Session on Raw Materials and Devt 1974, Group on Political Issues, Int. Women's Conf., Nairobi, Kenya 1985, Workshop on Fissile Materials and Tritium 1995, Trade Policy Review Body, Group of 77, Geneva 1997; Pres. Conf. on Disarmament 1996, UN Econ. and Social Council; mem. UN Sec.-Gen.'s Advisory Bd on Disarmament Matters. *Address:* Permanent Mission of Pakistan to the UN, 8 East 65th Street, New York, NY 10021, USA; tel. (212) 879-8600; fax (212) 744-7348; e-mail pakistan@un.int; internet www.un.int/pakistan.

**ALI, Ahmed Thasmeen;** Maldivian politician; *Minister of Atolls Development. Career:* mem. People's Majlis (Parl.), Deputy Speaker; fmr Deputy Dir Ministry of Trade and Industry; Minister of Home Affairs 2005–07, of Atolls Devt 2007–; Chair. Bd Dirs Dhiraagu 2005–; Regional Rep. CPA. *Address:* Ministry of Atolls Development, Faashana Building, Boduthakurufaanu Magu, Malé 20-05, Maldives; tel. 3323070; fax 3327750; e-mail minister@atolls.gov.mv; internet www.atolls.gov.mv.

**ALI, Anwar,** MSc; Pakistani nuclear physicist and administrator; *Chairman, Pakistan Atomic Energy Commission. Education:* Univ. of Punjab, Govt Coll., Lahore, Univ. of Birmingham, UK. *Career:* worked as Dir at Dr A. Q. Khan Research Laboratories (KRL, fmr Eng Research Lab.); joined

Pakistan Atomic Energy Comm. (PAEC) as Asst Scientific Officer 1967, one of pioneers of PAEC's Uranium Enrichment Project-706, Kahuta Research Labs, played key role in PAEC's Directorate of Tech. Devt, Mem. (Tech.) PAEC 2001–, Chair. PAEC 2006–; played key role in formative years of Nat. Defence Complex in developing guidance and control system for Shaheen-I rocket; mem. team of scientists and engineers who carried out nuclear tests at Ras Koh Hills, Chagai region 1998; Hilal-e-Imtiaz; Special Commendation from Chief of Army Staff and Chair. Jt Chiefs of Staff Cttee, Pres.'s Medal for Pride of Performance. *Address:* Pakistan Atomic Energy Commission, PO Box 1114, Islamabad, Pakistan; tel. (51) 9209032; fax (51) 9204908; e-mail feedback@paec.gov.pk; internet www.paec.gov.pk.

**AMARASINGHE, Somawansa;** Sri Lankan politician; *Leader, Janatha Vimukhti Peramuna. Career:* mem. and Leader of Peope's Liberation Front (Janatha Vimukhti Peramuna—JVP), f. 1964, party banned following coup attempt 1971, regained legal status 1977, banned again 1983, regained legal status 1994, Amarasinghe is only surviving mem. of JVP Political Bureau, fled to London, UK and continued to provide party leadership from abroad, returned 2004. *Address:* Janatha Vimukthi Peramuna, 198/19 Panchikawattha Road, Colombo 10, Sri Lanka; tel. (11) 4400511; fax (11) 2786050; e-mail jvplanka@sltnet.lk; internet www.jvpsrilanka.com.

**AMBANI, Anil D.,** MBA; Indian business executive; *Chairman and CEO, Anil Dhirubhai Ambani Group;* b. 4 June 1959, Mumbai; s. of the late Dhirubhai Hirachand Ambani and of Kokilaben Dhirubhai Ambani, brother of Mukesh Ambani (q.v.); m. Tina Ambani; two s. *Education:* Univ. of Bombay (now Mumbai), Univ. of Pennsylvania, USA. *Career:* apptd Co-CEO Reliance Industries Ltd 1983, currently Vice-Chair., Man. Dir; Dir Reliance Europe Ltd; Dir and Vice-Chair. Indian Petrochemicals Corpn Ltd –2005 (resgnd); Chair. and CEO Anil Dhirubhai Ambani Group (cr. after division of Reliance Industries Ltd and comprising Reliance Energy, Reliance Capital, and Reliance Infocomm) 2005–; mem. Rajya Sabha (upper house of Parl.) 2004–06; Chair. Bd Govs Nat. Safety Council; mem. Bd Govs Indian Inst. of Man., Ahmedabad, Indian Inst. of Tech., Kanpur; Business India Businessman of the Year 1997, Indian Alumni Award, Wharton India Econ. Forum 2001, Bombay Man. Asscn Entrepreneur of the Decade Award 2002. *Address:* Reliance Communications Ltd, I Block, 2nd Floor, Dhirubhai Ambani Knowledge City, Mumbai 400 710, India; tel. (22) 3037-5522; fax (22) 3037-5577; e-mail anil.ambani@relianceada.com; internet www.relianceadagroup.com.

**AMBANI, Mukesh D.,** BChemEng, MBA; Indian business executive; *Chairman and Managing Director, Reliance Industries Limited;* b. 19 April 1957, Mumbai; m. Nita Ambani; three c. *Education:* Univ. of Bombay (now Mumbai), Stanford Univ., USA. *Career:* joined family-owned Reliance Industries Ltd (India's largest pvt. co.) 1981, Man. Dir 1986–, Chair. 2002–, also Dir Reliance Europe Ltd (Reliance Energy, Reliance Capital, and Reliance Infocomm spun off to brother's co. Anil Dhirubhai Ambani Enterprises 2005); Chair. Bd Indian Petrochemicals Corpn Ltd, FLAG Telecom; mem. Prime Minister's Advisory Council on Trade and Industry, Council of Scientific and Industrial Research, Bd Govs Nat. Council of Applied Econ. Research, Advisory Council of the Indian Banks Asscn; Chair. Bd Trustees, Indian Inst. of Software Eng; 'Global Leader for Tomorrow', World Econ. Forum, Switzerland 1994, Business India Businessman of the Year Award 1997, 'Distinguished Alumnus of the Decade', Univ. of Mumbai 1999, Ernst & Young Entrepreneur of the Year Award 2000, rated one of 'India's Most Admired CEOs' in Business Barons-Taylor Nelson Sofres-Mode Survey 2002, Mumbai Man. Asscn Entrepreneur of the Decade Award 2002, Asia Soc. Leadership Award Medal 2004. *Address:* Reliance Industries Ltd, Maker Chambers IV, 222, Nariman Point, Mumbai 400 021, India; tel. (22) 22785000; fax (22) 22870303; e-mail M_Ambani@ril.com; internet www.ril.com.

**AMIN, Sohail;** Pakistani diplomatist; *Ambassador to Nepal. Career:* fmr Dir-Gen. for Europe, Ministry of Foreign Affairs; Amb. to Nepal 2005–. *Address:* Embassy of Pakistan, Pushpanjali, Maharajgunj, Chakrapath, POB 202, Kathmandu, Nepal; tel. (1) 4374024; fax (1) 4374012; e-mail parepktm@wlink.com.np.

**AMUNUGAMA, Sarath,** PhD; Sri Lankan politician; *Minister of Enterprise Development and Investment Promotion;* b. 10 July 1939; m. *Career:* fmr Spokesman for People's Alliance (PA); elected mem. Parl. for Kandy Dist; Minister of Northern Rehabilitation 2000; Minister of Culture 2000; Minister of Finance –2005, of Public Admin and Home Affairs 2005–07, of Enterprise Devt and Investment Promotion 2007–. *Address:* Ministry of Enterprise Development and Investment Promotion, 25th Level, West Tower, World Trade Centre, Echelon Square, Colombo 1, Sri Lanka; tel. (11) 2394951; fax (11) 2424960; e-mail secedip@sltnet.lk; internet www.atned.lk.

**ANANDASANGAREE, Veerasingham;** Sri Lankan politician; *President, Tamil United Liberation Front;* b. 15 June 1933, Point Pedro; m.; four c. *Education:* Sri Somaskanda Coll., Christian Coll. Atchuvely, Hartley Coll., Zahira Coll. *Career:* fmr teacher, Hindu Coll., Jaffna, Poonakri MMV, Kotelawela GTM School, Ratmalana, Christ King Coll., Ja-Ela; lawyer 1967–83; joined All Ceylon Tamil Congress 1966, Youth Front Pres. 1970; Chair. Karaichi Village Council 1965–68, Karaichi Town Council 1968–69; joined Tamil United Front (later Tamil United Liberation Front), Propaganda Sec. Tamil United Liberation Front 1976–1983, mem. Politburo 1983–93, Sr Vice-Pres. 1993–2002, Acting Pres. 1998–2001, Pres. 2002–; UNESCO Madanjeet Singh Prize for the promotion of tolerance and non-violence 2006. *Address:* Tamil United Liberation Front, 30/1B Alwis Place, Colombo 3, Sri Lanka; tel. (11) 2347721; fax (11) 2347721.

**ANSARI, Mohammad Hamid,** MA; Indian diplomatist and government official; *Vice-President;* b. 1 April 1937, Kolkata; m. Salma Ansari. *Education:* St Edward's High School, Shimla, St Xavier's Coll., Kolkata, Aligarh Muslim Univ. *Career:* joined Foreign Service 1961, past positions include High Commr to Australia, Amb. to Saudi Arabia, UAE, Afghanistan, Iran, Perm. Rep. to UN, New York; Vice-Chancellor, Aligarh Muslim Univ. 2000–02; Chair. Nat. Comm. for Minorities 2006–07; currently Visiting Prof., Centre for West Asian and African Studies, Jawaharlal Nehru Univ. and Acad. of Third World Studies, Jamia Millia Islamia; Vice-Pres. of India 2007–; Distinguished Fellow, Observer Research Foundation; Padma Shree 1984. *Publications:* numerous articles on West Asian affairs. *Address:* Vice-President's Office, 6 Maulana Azad Road, New Delhi 110 011, India; tel. (11) 23016344; fax (11) 23018124.

**ANTONY, Arackaparambil Kurian,** BA, BL; Indian politician; *Minister of Defence;* b. 28 Dec. 1940, Cherthala, Alappuzha Dist, Kerala; m. Elizabeth Antony; two s. *Education:* Maharajas Coll., Government Law Coll., Ernakulam. *Career:* mem. Rajya Sabha (Parl.) from Kerala 1985–95, 2005–; fmr Minister of Civil Supplies, Consumer Affairs and Public Distribution; Chief Minister of Kerala 1977–78, 1995–96, 2001–04; Minister of Defence 2006–; Chair. Disciplinary Cttee of All India Congress Cttee. *Address:* Ministry of Defence, South Block, New Delhi 110 011; Anjanam, Easwara Vilasam Road, Thiruvananthapuram 695014, India; tel. (11) 23019030; fax (11) 23015403; e-mail ak.antony@sansad.nic.in; internet www.mod.nic.in.

**ANWARZAI, Mohammad Anwar;** Afghan civil servant and diplomatist; *Ambassador to Pakistan;* b. 1937, Kabul; m. Fauzia Asif Anwarzai; two s. two d. *Education:* Nejat (Amani) High School, Law Faculty, Kabul Univ., Univ. of Oxford, UK. *Career:* began career in civil service 1960; sr diplomat, served in various sections of Ministry of Foreign Affairs, including at Archives Dept, UN and Int. Confs Dept, Econ. Dept, Cultural Relations and at Political Div., first diplomatic assignment abroad as jr mem. in Perm. Mission of Afghanistan to UN, New York, Second Sec. 1964–69, represented Afghanistan on different cttees during 21st–24th Sessions of UN Gen. Ass.,

First Sec., Embassy in Moscow 1973–76, Chargé d'affaires a.i., Embassy in Tripoli 1976–78, forced with his family to become political refugees following Soviet invasion of Afghanistan, spent next 23 years in exile, returned to Afghanistan following Bonn Agreement Feb. 2002, assigned to Ministry of Foreign Affairs as Dir Fourth Political Dept responsible for European countries 2002–04, Minister Counsellor, Perm. Mission to UN, Geneva 2004–05, Amb. to Australia 2005–07, to Pakistan 2007–; Co-founder and fmr mem. Bd of Dirs Global Partnership for Afghanistan, Vice-Pres. and COO –2005. *Address:* Embassy of Afghanistan, 8, Street 90, G-6/3, Islamabad 44000, Pakistan; tel. (51) 2824505; fax (51) 2824504; e-mail contact@islamabad.mfa.gov.af; internet www.islamabad.mfa.gov.af.

**ARSALA, Hedayat Amin,** PhD; Afghan politician and economist; nephew of Pir Gailani. *Education:* high school in Kabul, George Washington Univ., Washington, DC, USA. *Career:* ethnic Pashtun descended from Jabar Khel tribe; foreign language trainer for three consecutive Peace Corps training programmes in USA; started his professional career at World Bank Youth Professional Program 1969, held various econ. and sr operational posts 1969–87; returned to Afghanistan to join Afghan resistance to Soviet occupation 1987–89, served as Sr Adviser and mem. Afghan Mujahideen Unity Council; Minister of Finance, Transitional Govt of Afghanistan 1989–92; Minister of Foreign Affairs 1993–96; Sr mem. Exec. Council of Loya Jirga (traditional council of Afghan tribal leaders) 1998–; played key role in Intra-Afghan Bonn Conf. following fall of the Taliban regime 2001; apptd Vice-Chair. and Minister of Finance of the interim admin 2001; named one of four Vice-Pres, Transitional Islamic State of Afghanistan 2001–04, Chair. Ind. Civil Services Admin Reform Comm., adviser to Cen. Statistics Office and Afghan Econ. Cooperation Cttee; mem. Afghan Nat. Security Council; Minister of Commerce and Sr Presidential Adviser 2004–06, Sr Minister in the Cabinet 2006–. *Address:* c/o Office of the President, Gul Khana Palace, Presidential Palace, Kabul, Afghanistan; e-mail webmaster@afghanistangov.org; internet www.president.gov.af.

**ATIQUR RAHMAN, A. K. M.,** PhD; Bangladeshi economist, diplomatist and academic; *Ambassador to Bhutan. Career:* fought during war of independence in 1971; fmr Assoc. Prof., later Prof. and Chair. Dept of Econs, North South Univ., Dhaka, Head of Inst. of Devt, Environmental and Strategic Studies; fmrly with Centre for Studies in Int. Relations and Devt, Kolkata; joined Ministry of Foreign Affairs 1986; fmr Second Sec., later First Sec., Embassy in Rome; Consul-Gen. Embassy in Hong Kong 2003–04; Dir-Gen. Ministry of Foreign Affairs –2007; Amb. to Bhutan 2007–; Vice-Pres. Mercantile Bank Ltd. *Address:* Embassy of Bangladesh, PO Box 178, Upper Choubachu, Thimphu, Bhutan; tel. (2) 322539; fax (2) 322629; e-mail bdoot@druknet.bt; akmatiq@northsouth.edu.

**AZAD, Ghulam Nabi,** MSc; Indian politician; b. 7 March 1949, Soti village, Doda Dist, Jammu and Kashmir; m. Shrimati Shameem Dev Azad 1980; one s. one d. *Education:* Kashmir Univ. *Career:* mem. Indian Nat. Congress; began his political career in 1973, Block Sec., Congress Cttee, Blessa 1973–75, nominated Pres. Jammu and Kashmir Pradesh Youth Congress 1975–77, Pres. Congress Cttee, Doda Dist 1977, nominated Gen. Sec. All India Youth Congress 1977; Pres. All India Muslim Youth Conf. 1978–81; nominated mem. Congress Working Cttee 1986; Gen. Sec. All India Congress Cttee 1987, re-elected as Gen. Sec. nine times; Union Deputy Minister for Company Affairs and Law 1982, later Minister of State; re-elected as mem. Parl. for Washim Constituency 1985; apptd Minister of State for Home Affairs 1985, later Minister of State for Food and Civil Supplies; mem. Rajya Sabha 1990–91; Cabinet Minister for Parl. Affairs 1991, later Cabinet Minister for Tourism and Civil Aviation; Pres. Jammu and Kashmir Pradesh Congress Cttee; Union Minister for Urban Devt and Law and Parl. Affairs 2002–05; Chief Minister of Jammu and Kashmir 2005–08 (resgnd). *Address:* c/o Directorate of Information, Jammu and Kashmir Government, Old Secretariat, Mubarak Mandi Complex, Jammu, 180 001, India.

**AZAM, Air Vice-Marshal Fakhrul;** Bangladeshi air force officer. *Career:* joined Air Force, promoted to Air Commodore, to Air Vice-Marshal 2002, Chief of Air Staff 2002–07; Pres. Bangladesh Hockey Fed. *Address:* c/o Air Force Headquarters, Dhaka Cantonment, Bangladesh.

**AZIMI, Abdul Salam,** PhD; Afghan judge, politician and academic; *Chief Justice of the Supreme Court (Stera Mahkama). Education:* Kabul Univ. and Univ. of Arizona, USA. *Career:* fmr univ. prof.; experience in law and educ. also in Pakistan, Middle East and USA; Minister of Educ. 2001–03; mem. Constitutional Comm. to draft a new Afghan Constitution (primary drafter) 2002–03, Vice-Chair. Constitutional Review Comm. 2003; Head of Scientific and Research Centre of the Univ. of Neb. in Afghanistan –2006; legal adviser to Pres. Hamid Karzai 2004–06; Chief Justice of the Supreme Court (Stera Mahkama) 2006–. *Address:* Supreme Court of Afghanistan (Stera Mahkama), Kabul, Afghanistan.

**AZIZ, Shaukat,** BSc, MBA; Pakistani politician and banker; b. 6 March 1949, Karachi; m.; three c. *Education:* St Patrick's High School, Karachi, Abbottabad Public School, Abbottabad, Govt Islamia Coll., Kasur, Pakistani Business School Inst. of Business Admin, Karachi, Univ. of Karachi. *Career:* various posts with Citibank including Head of Corp. and Investment Banking, Asia Pacific Region, Head of Corp. and Investment Banking for Cen. and Eastern Europe, Middle East and Africa, Corp. Planning Officer, Citicorp, Man. Dir, Saudi American Bank, Global Head, Pvt. Banking, Vice-Pres. 1969–99; Minister of Finance and Revenue, Econ. Affairs and Statistics and of Planning and Econ. Devt 1999–2004; mem. Senate 2002–04; Prime Minister of Pakistan and Minister of Finance and Revenue, Econ. Affairs and Statistics 2004–07. *Address:* c/o Office of the Prime Minister's Secretariat, Constitution Avenue, F-6/5, Cabinet Division, Cabinet Block, Islamabad, Pakistan; tel. (51) 9206111.

**BABUR, Alamgir;** Pakistani diplomatist; *High Commissioner to Bangladesh. Career:* fmr Deputy Perm. Rep., later Acting Perm. Rep. to UN, New York; Dir-Gen. (Americas), Ministry of Foreign Affairs –2005; High Commr to Bangladesh 2005–. *Address:* High Commission of Pakistan, House NE (C)-2, Road No. 71, Gulshan Avenue, Dhaka 1212, Bangladesh; tel. (2) 8825388; fax (2) 8850673; e-mail parepdka@citech-bd.com.

**BADAL, Parkash Singh,** BA; Indian agriculturist and politician; *Chief Minister of Punjab;* b. 8 Dec. 1927, Abulkhurana, Punjab; m. Surinder Kaur; one s. one d. *Career:* entered politics 1947, first elected to Vidhan Sabha 1957; mem. and fmr Pres. Shiromani Akali Dal party; fmr mem. Shiromani Gurdwara Prabandhak Cttee; elected to Ass. 1957, re-elected 1969; Minister for Community Devt Panchayati Raj, Animal Husbandry, Dairying and Fisheries 1969–70; Chief Minister of Punjab 1970–71, 1977–80, 1997–2002, 2007–; imprisoned during State of Emergency 1975–77; elected to Lok Sabha 1977; Minister for Agric. 1977; Leader of Opposition 1980; imprisoned on corruption charges Dec. 2003; Chair. Punjab Arts Council; mem. Nankana Sahib Educational Trust, Ludhiana. *Address:* VPO Badal, Muktsar District; Office of the Chief Minister, Government of Punjab, 45, Sector 2, Chandigarh, India; tel. (172) 740737; (172) 740325; e-mail pws@punjabmail.gov.in; internet punjabgovt.nic.in.

**BAJAJ, Rahul,** LLB, MBA; Indian motor industry executive; *Chairman, Bajaj Auto Ltd;* b. 10 June 1938, Kolkata; m. Rupa Bajaj 1961; two s. one d. *Education:* St Stephen's Coll., Delhi, Govt Law Coll., Bombay (now Mumbai), Harvard Univ., USA. *Career:* Dir Bajaj Auto Ltd 1956–60, Chair. and Man. Dir 1972–2008, Chair. 2008–; Chair. Maharashtra Scooters Ltd 1975–; Pres. Asscn of Indian Automobile Mfrs 1976–78, Mahratta Chamber of Commerce and Industries 1983–85; Vice-Chair., then Chair. Mukand Group 1994–; Chair. Devt Council for Automobiles and Allied Industries 1975–77, Indian Inst. of Tech., Mumbai 2003–; mem. Exec. Cttee

Confed. of Eng Industry 1978– (Pres. 1979–80), Governing Council, Automotive Research Asscn of India 1972–, Devt Council for Automobiles and Allied Industries 1987–, World Econ. Forum's Advisory Council 1984–; Man of the Year Award, Nat. Inst. of Quality Assurance 1975, Business Man of the Year Award, Business India Magazine 1985, Padma Bhushan 2001. *Address:* Mumbai-Pune Road, Akurdi, Pune 411 035, India; tel. (20) 772851; (20) 82857; fax (20) 773398; e-mail rahulbajaj@bajajauto.co.in.

**BALAKRISHNAN, K(onakuppakatil) G(opinathan),** BSc, LLM; Indian judge; *Chief Justice;* b. 12 May 1945. *Career:* enrolled as advocate of Kerala Bar Council 1968; practised civil and criminal law in Erinakulam; apptd a Munsif in Kerala Judicial Service 1973, later resgnd and resumed practice as advocate in Kerala High Court; judge, Kerala High Court 1985–97, Gujarat High Court 1997–98; Chief Justice of High Court of Gujarat 1998–99, of High Court of Judicature, Madras 1999; Judge, Supreme Court 2000–, Chief Justice of India 2007–. *Address:* Supreme Court of India, Tilak Marg, New Delhi 110 001, India; tel. (11) 23388942; fax (11) 23383792; e-mail supremecourt@nic.in; internet www .supremecourtofindia.nic.in.

**BANERJEE, (Kumari) Mamata,** BEd, LLB, MA; Indian politician; *Leader, All India Trinamool Congress;* b. 5 Jan. 1955, Calcutta (now Kolkata). *Education:* Univ. of Calcutta. *Career:* Gen. Sec. Mahila Congress (I), W Bengal 1970–80; Sec. Dist Congress Cttee, Calcutta S 1978–81; mem. Lok Sabha (House of the People, Parl.) 1984, 1991–; mem. numerous parl. cttees 1985–; Gen. Sec. and mem. Nat. Council, All India Youth Congress (I) Cttee 1985–87; mem. Consultative Cttee, Ministry of Human Resource Devt 1987–93, of Home Affairs 1987–88, 1993–96, 1996–97, 1998–99; mem. Exec. Cttee, Congress Parl. Party 1988–, Pradesh Congress Cttee 1989–; Pres. Youth Congress (W Bengal) 1990; Union Minister of State, Human Resource Devt, Dept of Youth Affairs and Sports, and Women and Child Devt 1991–93, of Railways 1999–2001, Minister without Portfolio 2003–04, of Coal and Mines 2004; Chair. Cttee on Railways 1998–99; mem. Gen. Purposes Cttee 1998–99, 2001–; Sec. W Bengal TUC 1981–87; Leader All India Trinamool Congress Parl. Party 1999–. *Publications include:* Upalabdhi, Janatar Darbare, Maa, Pallabi, Manabik, Struggle for Existence, Motherland, Crocodile Island, Trinamool. *Address:* All India Trinamool Congress, 125-D, Parliament House, New Delhi 110 001; C-4, M.S. Flats, B.K.S. Marg, New Delhi 110 001; 30B Harish Chatterjee Street, Kolkata 700 026, West Bengal, India; tel. (11) 24540881; (11) 23384010; fax (11) 24540880; internet www.trinamoolcongress.com.

**BANERJEE, Milon K.;** Indian lawyer; *Attorney-General. Career:* began legal practice in Kolkata in 1955, designated Sr Advocate 1972; Additional Solicitor-Gen. of India 1979–86, Solicitor-Gen. 1986–89, Attorney-Gen. 1992–96, 2004–; Hon. Bencher, Lincoln's Inn, London 2006. *Address:* Office of the Attorney General, Supreme Court of India, Tilak Marg, New Delhi 110 001, India; tel. (11) 3383254; fax (11) 3782101; internet www.supremecourtofindia.nic.in.

**BANJADE, Yagyamurti;** Nepalese lawyer and government official; *Attorney-General. Career:* more than 25 years of legal experience; Attorney-Gen. of Nepal 2006–; mem. Nepal Bar Asscn. *Address:* Office of the Attorney-General, Singh Darbar, Kathmandu, Nepal; tel. (1) 4246860; (1) 4227197; fax (1) 4227282; e-mail info@attorneygeneral.gov.np; internet attorneygeneral.gov.np.

**BARDHAN, Ardhendu Bhushan,** (Kanu Da), MA, LLB; Indian politician and trade unionist; *General-Secretary, Communist Party of India;* b. 25 Sept. 1925, Sylhet (now in Bangladesh); one s. one d. *Career:* mem. Maharashtra State Legis. Ass. 1957–1962; Gen.-Sec. Communist Party of India 1996–. *Address:* Communist Party of India, Ajoy Bhavan, Kotla Marg, New Delhi 110 002; Ajoy Bhavan, 15 Com. Indrajit Gupta Marg, New Delhi 110 002, India; tel. (11) 23235546; fax (11) 23235543; e-mail cpi@cpofindia.org; internet www.cpindia.org.

**BASU, Jyoti,** BA; Indian politician and lawyer; *Leader, Communist Party of India—Marxist (CPI—M);* b. 1914. *Education:* Loreto Day School, St Xavier's School, St Xavier's Coll. *Career:* went to England to study law, called to Middle Temple Bar 1939; during stay in England actively associated with India League and Fed. of Indian Students in England, Sec. of London Majlis and came in contact with CP of Great Britain; returned to Calcutta 1940; joined undivided CP of India; a leader of fmr Eastern Bengal Railroad Workers' Union; elected to Bengal Legis. Council 1946; after Partition remained a mem. of W Bengal Legis. Ass.; arrested for membership of CP after party was banned 1948, but released on orders of High Court; became Chair. Editorial Bd Swadhinata; mem. W. Bengal Legis. Ass. 1952–72; fmr Sec. Prov. Cttee of CP, mem. Nat. Council, Cen. Exec. Cttee and Nat. Secr. until CP split 1963; subsequently mem. Politbureau, CPI—M, currently Leader; imprisoned 1948, 1949, 1953, 1955, 1963, 1965; Deputy Chief Minister and Minister in charge of Finance in first United Front Govt 1967, Deputy Chief Minister in second United Front Govt; narrowly escaped assassination attempt while campaigning in Bihar 1972; mem. Parl. for Satgachia 1977; subsequently Leader of Left Front Legislature Party; Chief Minister of W Bengal 1977–2000. *Address:* Communist Party of India—Marxist, A.K. Gopalan Bhavan, 27–29 Bhai Vir Singh Marg, New Delhi 110 001, India; tel. (11) 23344918; fax (11) 23747483; e-mail cpim@vsnl.com; internet www.cpim.org.

**BHAI, Aziz Mohammad;** Bangladeshi pharmaceuticals executive. *Career:* Founding Chair. and Man. Dir Ambee Pharmaceuticals Ltd 1976–. *Address:* Ambee Pharmaceuticals Ltd, House No. 1, Road No. 71, Gulshan 2, Dhaka 1212, Bangladesh; tel. (2) 8813991; fax (2) 8827777; e-mail info@ambeepharma.com; internet www.ambeepharma.com.

**BHARDWAJ, H.R.,** LLB, MA; Indian politician and lawyer; *Minister of Law and Justice;* b. 17 May 1937, Garhi village, Rohtak Dist; m. Prafulata Bhardwaj 1960; one s. two d. *Education:* B.M. Coll., Shimla, Agra Univ. and Panjab Univ., Chandigarh. *Career:* mem. Nat. Exec., Indian Youth Congress 1957; Public Prosecutor, Delhi High Court 1972–77; Sr Standing Counsel for Uttar Pradesh, Supreme Court of India 1980–82; mem. Rajya Sabha 1982–, mem. Home Affairs Cttee 1998–2004; Minister of State for Law and Justice 1984–89, 1992–96; Sr Vice-Pres., Inst. of Constitutional and Parl. Studies, New Delhi 1988–90; Minister of State for Planning and Programme Implementation 1991–96; Minister of Law and Justice 2004–; mem. Advisory Council, Delhi Devt Cttee 2000–. *Address:* Ministry of Law and Justice, 'A' Wing, Shastri Bhavan, Dr Rajendra Prasad Road, New Delhi 110 001; E-7/19, Charimili, Bhopal, Madhya Pradesh, India; tel. (11) 23384777; fax (11) 23387259; e-mail lawmin@caselaw .delhi.nic.in; hansrajb@sansad.nic.in; internet www.lawmin .nic.in.

**BHATT, Om P.;** Indian central banker; *Chairman, State Bank of India. Career:* joined State Bank of India (SBI) as probationary office 1972, held several positions including Scheme Coordinator of br. computerization at Cen. Office of SBI, Regional Man. with Jaipur Zone, Gen. Man. with Lucknow Zone and Chief Gen. Man. with North Zone, Man. Dir State Bank of Travancore, Man. Dir and Group Exec. SBI April–Oct. 2006, Chair. 2006–. *Address:* State Bank of India, Corporate Centre, Madame Cama Road, PO Box 10121, Mumbai 400 021, India; tel. (22) 22022799; fax (22) 22851391; e-mail sbiid@boms.vsnl.net.in; internet www .statebankofindia.com; www.sbi.co.in.

**BHATTACHARYA, Buddhadev,** BA; Indian politician; *Chief Minister of West Bengal;* b. 1 March 1944, Kolkata; m.; one d. *Education:* Sailendra Sarkar Vidyalaya and Presidency Coll., Kolkata. *Career:* mem. Communist Party of India—Marxist Secr., Cen. Cttee, mem. of Politburo; Minister-in-Charge, W Bengal Information and Public Relations Dept 1977–1982, Dept of Information and Cultural Affairs 1987–1999, Dept of Local Govt, Dept of Urban Devt and Metropolitan Devt 1987–1991, Dept of Information and Cultural Affairs 1991–93, 1994, 1996, Dept of Urban Devt and Municipal Affairs 1991–93, Dept of Home Affairs and Dept of Information Tech. 1996–99, Deputy Chief Minister of West Bengal 1999–2000, Chief Minister 2000–. *Publication:* collection of poems and plays. *Address:* Office of the Chief Minister, Government of West Bengal, Writers' Buildings, Kolkata 700 001, India; tel. (33) 22145555; fax (33) 22145480; e-mail cm@wb.gov.in; internet www.wbgov.com.

**BHATTARAI, Baburam;** Nepalese politician and fmr guerrilla leader; *Minister of Finance. Education:* Chandigarh Univ. *Career:* Leader, Communist Party of Nepal (Maoist), fmr commdr of rebel army, Sr mem. Standing Cttee of the Politburo; Minister of Finance 2008–. *Address:* Ministry of Finance, Singha Durbar, Kathmandu, Nepal; tel. (1) 4211809; fax (1) 4211831; e-mail admindivision@mof.gov.np; internet www.mof.gov.np.

**BHUTTO ZARDARI, Bilawal;** Pakistani politician; *Co-Chairman, Pakistan People's Party;* b. 21 Sept. 1988, grandson of fmr Prime Minister Zulfiqar Ali Bhutto. *Education:* Karachi Grammar School, Froebels Int. School, Islamabad, Rashid School for Boys, Dubai, Univ. of Oxford, UK. *Career:* has spent most of his life outside Pakistan, travelling with his mother who went into self-imposed exile in 1999, moving between London and Dubai; fmr Vice-Pres. Student Council, Rashid School for Boys, Dubai; Co-Chair. (with his father) Pakistan People's Party following assassination of his mother Benazir Bhutto Dec. 2007–; currently studying history at Christ Church, Univ. of Oxford. *Address:* Pakistan People's Party, 8 Street 19, F-8/2, Islamabad Karachi, Pakistan; tel. (51) 2255264; fax (51) 2282741; e-mail ppp@comsats.net.pk; internet www.ppp.org.pk.

**BIN LADEN, Osama;** Saudi Arabia-born guerrilla leader; b. Jeddah; m. five wives including Najua Ghanem; three c.; Amal al-Sadah; one d.; (divorced from one wife); more than 20 c. *Education:* King Abdul-Aziz Univ., Jeddah. *Career:* funded and joined troops fighting against Soviet Union in Afghanistan 1979; co-f. group to send aid to Afghan resistance and establish recruitment centres mid-1980s; f. org. to support Islamist opposition movts 1988; expelled from Saudi Arabia for anti-govt activities 1991, Saudi Arabian citizenship removed for 'irresponsible activities' 1994; moved to Sudan 1991, expelled following pressure from USA and UN 1996; continued to support Islamist extremist activities from Afghanistan; as head of the al-Qa'ida org. believed to have masterminded attacks on World Trade Center, New York, and Pentagon, Washington, DC on 11 Sept. 2001.

**BIRLA, Basant Kumar;** Indian business executive; *Chairman, Century Textiles and Industries Ltd;* b. 16 Feb. 1921; m.; one s. two d. *Career:* Chair. Century Textiles and Industries Ltd, Century Enka Ltd, Jay Shree Tea & Industries Ltd, Kesoram Industries & Cotton Mills Ltd, Bharat Commerce & Industries Ltd; Gov. Birla Inst. of Tech. *Address:* Century Textiles and Industries Ltd, Century Bhavan, Dr Annie Besant Road, Worli, Mumbai, 400 030, India; tel. (22) 24957000; fax (22) 24309491; e-mail centextho@centurytext .com; internet www.centurytext.com.

**BIRLA, Ganga Prasad,** BSc; Indian industrialist; b. 2 Aug. 1922, Calcutta (now Kolkata); m. Nimala Devi Birla 1952; one s. one d. *Education:* Calcutta Univ. *Career:* Chair. Hindustan Motors Ltd, Orient Paper & Industries Ltd 1957–; Man. Dir Birla Brothers Pvt. Ltd 1982–; Chair. Bd Govs Birla Inst. of Tech., Ranchi, Birla Inst. of Scientific Research; Pres. Bd Govs Calcutta Medical Research Inst., Man. Cttee BM Birla Heart Research Centre, Kolkata; Pres. Indian Paper Mills Asscn, Calcutta 1947–48, 1954–55, 1955–56, Employers' Asscn, Calcutta 1962–63, 1964–65; mem. Red Cross Soc. *Address:* 9/1 RN Mukherjee Road, Kolkata 700 001; Birla House, 8/9 Alipore Road, Kolkata 700 027, India; tel. (33) 22480135; (33) 24791285.

**BIRLA, Krishna Kumar;** Indian business executive; b. 12 Oct. 1918, Pilani; s. of G. D. Birla; m. Manorama Devi 1941; three d. *Education:* Univs of Calcutta, Delhi and Punjab. *Career:* Pres. Indian Sugar Mills Asscn 1946–47, Indian Chambers of Commerce Calcutta 1963–64, Fed. of Indian Chambers of Commerce and Industry 1974–75 (Chair. Indo-Japan and Indo-American Jt Councils and Perm. Invitee Exec. Cttee and Steering Cttee), Marwari Relief Soc., Calcutta 1965–67; Chair. and Man. Dir Texmaco Ltd; Chair. Birla Inst. of Tech. and Science, The Hindustan Times, Zuari Industries Ltd, Chambal Fertilizers and Chemicals Ltd, Sutlej Industries Ltd, India Steam Ship Co Ltd; fmr Dir Cen. Bd of State Bank of India, Industrial Credit and Investment Corpn of India; Sheriff of Calcutta 1961; mem. Nat. Railway Users' Consultative Cttee 1956–57, Cen. Advisory Council of Industries 1959–67, Bd of Trade, Council of Scientific and Industrial Research, Nat. Integration Council, Advisory Cttee on Narcotic Drugs and Psychotropic Substances, Ministry of Finance, Shri Mata Vaishno Devi Shrine Bd, Govt of Jammu and Kashmir, Nat. Cttee for Celebration of 40 Years of India's Independence and Pandit Jawaharlal Nehru's Centenary, Cttee on Finance and Consultative Cttee for Ministry of Finance; elected to Rajya Sabha 1984, 1990, 1996; Hon. DLitt; INC (Rajasthan). *Address:* Birla House, 7, Tees January Marg, New Delhi 110 011; Birla Building, 9/1, R.N. Mukherjee Road, Kolkata, 700 001, India.

**BIRLA, Kumar Mangalam,** MBA; Indian business executive; *Chairman, Aditya Birla Group;* b. 14 June 1967; m. Neerja Birla; three c. *Education:* London Business School, UK. *Career:* Chair. Aditya Birla Group 1997–; apptd mem. Governing Bd Securities and Exchange Bd of India 1998, also served as Chair. Cttees on Corporate Governance and Insider Trading; mem. Bd Tata Iron and Steel Co., Larsen and Toubro, Maruti Udyog Ltd; mem. Bd G. D. Birla Medical Research and Educ. Foundation; mem. Bd Govs Birla Inst. of Tech. and Science, Indian Inst. of Man.; mem. London Business School's Asia Pacific Advisory Bd; has served on various professional and regulatory bds including Prime Minister's Advisory Council on Trade and Industry, Nat. Council of Confed. of Indian Industry, Apex Advisory Council of Associated Chambers of Commerce and Industry of India, Govt of UP's High Powered Investment Task Force; Hon. Fellow, London Business School; Hon. DLitt (Banaras Hindu Univ.); Mumbai Pradesh Youth Congress's Rajiv Gandhi Award for Business Excellence and Contribution to the Country, named as one of World Econ. Forum's Young Global Leaders 2004, Ernst & Young Indian Entrepreneur of the Year 2005, awards from Inst. of Dirs, The Hindustan Times, Giants Int., Amity Business School, Nat. Inst. of Industrial Eng, The Economic Times, Business India. *Address:* Aditya Birla Centre, S. K. Ahire Marg, Worli, Mumbai 400 025, India; tel. (22) 56525000; fax (22) 56525750; e-mail pragnya.ram@ adityabirla.com; internet www.adityabirla.com.

**BIRLA, Sudershan Kumar;** Indian business executive. *Career:* Chair. Mysore Cement Ltd –2007, Birla Eastern Ltd, Birla Metals Ltd; Dir Century Textiles and Industries Ltd –2006, Birla Brothers Pvt. Ltd. *Address:* Birla House, 7, Tees January Marg, New Delhi, 110 011, India.

**BOGOLLAGAMA, Rohitha;** Sri Lankan lawyer and politician; *Minister of Foreign Affairs;* b. 5 Aug. 1954, Nikaweratiya; m.; two c. *Education:* Ananda Coll. and Sri Lanka Law Coll. *Career:* apptd attorney 1976; fmr Chair. Sri Lanka Cement Corpn, Sathosa Printers; fmr Dir Foreign Employment Bureau; Legal and Political Adviser to Voice of America project in Sri Lanka 1991–99; Chair. and Dir-Gen. Bd of Investment of Sri Lanka 1993–2000; mem. Parl. (United National Party—UNP) 2000–, served on Parl. Consultative Cttees on Finance, Foreign Affairs, Defence, Industrial Devt and Investment Promotion and Power and Energy 2000–05, Chair. Cttee on Public Enterprises 2005–07, Minister of Industrial Devt 2001–04, of Enterprise Devt and Investment Promotion 2004–07, of Foreign Affairs 2007–. *Address:* Ministry of Foreign Affairs, Republic Building, Colombo 1, Sri Lanka; tel. (11) 2325371; fax (11) 2446091; e-mail cypher@ formin.gov.lk; internet www.slmfa.gov.lk.

**CABRAAL, Ajith Nivard;** Sri Lankan chartered accountant and central banker; *Governor, Central Bank of Sri Lanka. Career:* est. own man. consultancy before taking up public service 2005; fmr Chair. and/or Dir of several quoted and unquoted public cos; Sec., Ministry of Plan Implementation and Adviser to Pres. on Econ. Affairs –2006, also served as mem. Bd Strategic Enterprises Man. Agency; mem. Govt Team at Geneva Talks with Liberation Tigers of Tamil Eelam Feb. 2006; represented Govt in Millennium Challenge Fund negotiations with US Govt; Gov. Cen. Bank of Sri Lanka 2006–, Chair. Monetary Bd; fmr Eisenhower Fellow; Founder-Chair. Corp. Governance Cttee; fmr Pres. Business Recovery and Insolvency Practitioners Asscn of Sri Lanka; Past Pres. Inst. of Chartered Accountants of Sri Lanka, S Asian Fed. of Accountants, St Peter's Coll. Old Boys Union; fmr mem. Bd Securities and Exchange Comm., Nat. Inst. of Business Man., Postgraduate Inst. of Man., Univ. of Moratuwa. *Publications:* Towards a Sri Lankan Renaissance, Lak Mawata Muthu Potak (A String of Pearls for Mother Lanka, collection of more than 60 short essays submitted to popular nat. newspapers 2003–04). *Address:* Central Bank of Sri Lanka, 30 Janadhipathi Mawatha, PO Box 590, Colombo 1, Sri Lanka; tel. (11) 2477000; fax (11) 2477712; e-mail cbslgen@cbsl.lk; internet www.cbsl.gov.lk.

**CHAKRAVARTY, Pinak Ranjan;** Indian diplomatist; *High Commissioner to Bangladesh;* m. Radha Chakravarty. *Career:* Chief of Protocol, Ministry of Foreign Affairs 2003–05, Jt Sec. 2005; Amb. to the Philippines 2005–06; High Commr to Bangladesh 2007–. *Address:* High Commission of India, House No. 2, Road No. 142, Gulshan-1, Dhaka, Bangladesh; tel. (2) 9889339; fax (2) 8817487; e-mail hc@hcidhaka.org; internet www.hcidhaka.org.

**CHAMLING, Pawan Kumar;** Indian politician, poet and writer; *Chief Minister of Sikkim;* b. 22 Sept. 1950, Yangang Busty, South Sikkim; m. Tika Maya Chamling; four s. four d. *Career:* began career as ind. farmer; entered politics in 1973; Vice-Pres. Dist Youth Congress 1975; Pres. Sikkim Handicapped Persons Welfare Mission 1976–77; Ed. Nava Jyoti 1976–77, Founder Nirman Prakashan 1977, Ed. Nirman (quarterly literary magazine) 1977–; Gen. Sec. and Vice-Pres. Sikkim Prajatantra Congress 1978–84; Pres. of Yangang Gram Panchayat 1982; mem. Sikkim Legis. Ass. 1985–; Minister for Industries, Printing and Information and Public Relations 1989–92; formed Sikkim Democratic Front Party 1993, Leader 1993–; Chief Minister of Sikkim 1994–; Chair. Sikkim Distilleries Ltd 1985–; Hon. PhD (Manipal Univ.) 2003; numerous awards including Chinton Puraskar 1987, Bharat Shiromani 1996, Man of the Year 1998, The Greenest Chief Minister of India 1998, Man of Dedication 1999, Secular India Harmony Award 1998, Manav Sewa Puraskar 1999, Pride of India Gold Award 1999, Best Citizen of India 1999, Poets' Foundation Award 2001, Nat. Citizens of India Award 2002. *Publications include:* Veer koh Parichaya (poem) 1967, Antahin Sapana Meroh Bipana 1985, Perennial Dreams and My Reality, Prarambhek Kabitaharu 1991, Pratiwad 1992, Damthang Heejah ra Aajah 1992, Ma koh Hun 1992, Prarambheek Kabitaharu 1993, Sikkim ra Narikon Maryadha 1994, Crucified Prashna Aur Anya Kabitaye 1996, Sikkim ra Prajatantra 1996, Democracy Redeemed 1997, Prajatantra koh Mirmireymah 1997, Meroh Sapana Ko Sikkim 2002, Perspectives and Vision 2002. *Address:* CM Secretariat, Tashiling, Gangtok, Sikkim 737 101; Ghurpisay, Namchi, South Sikkim 737 126, India; tel. (3592) 222263; (3592) 228200; (3595) 263748; (3592) 222536; fax (3592) 222245; (3592) 224710; e-mail cm-skm@nic.in; internet sikkim.nic.in.

**CHAND, Lokendra Bahadur,** BA, LLB; Nepalese politician; b. 15 Feb. 1940, Kurkuriya Village, Bashulinga Village Devt Cttee, Baitadi; m.; seven c. *Education:* Pithauragarh, India, Tri-Chandra Coll., Kathmandu, DSB Degree Coll., Nainital, India and DAV Post-Grad. Coll., Dehradun, India. *Career:* Founding mem. Shree Basudev High School, Liskita, served voluntarily as teacher 1961–64; practising advocate 1964–68; Vice-Chair. Lisakita Village Panchayat, Baitadi Dist 1968, Chair. Baitadi Dist Panchayat 1970, Pres. Mahakali Zonal Panchayat 1973, Vice-Chair. and Chair. Rastriya Panchayat (Nat. Ass.) 1974; Founder Rastriya Prajatantra Party (RPP), Chair. 1991, Leader and Pres. Parl. Bd after unification of Thapa and Chand Group 1994; elected mem. Parl. (RPP) for both constituencies of Baitadi Dist 1995; Prime Minister of Nepal 1983–85, 1990, 1997, 2002–03; Founding Chair. Mahakali Sewa Samaj 1967; mem. Nepal Red Cross Soc. Cen. Exec. Cttee 1970. *Publications include:* Bahraun Kheladi (Twelfth Player), Visarjan (short stories) (Madan Puruskar Prize), Hiunko Tanna, Indra Dhanush, Aparichit Netako Saathi; also satirical essays, humorous plays and collections of short stories. *Address:* c/o Prime Minister's Office, Singha Durbar, Kathmandu, Nepal.

**CHANDRA, Subhash;** Indian media executive; *Chairman, Zee Entertainment Enterprises;* m.; three c. *Career:* fmr rice packer in Hissar, Haryana; now Chair. Entertainment Enterprises (satellite TV network), Patco, SitiCable; launched TV channel in Marathi language 1999; fmr jt owner (with Rupert Murdoch) of Zee Cinema, Zee TV and Zee India TV/Zee News. *Address:* Zee Entertainment Enterprises, 135 Continental Building, Dr A B Road (Worli), Mumbai 400 018, India; tel. (22) 66971234; fax (22) 24900302; internet www.zeetelevision.com.

**CHATTERJEE, Somnath,** MA; Indian politician, lawyer and trade unionist; *Speaker of Lok Sabha; Leader, Communist Party of India—Marxist;* b. 25 July 1929, Tezpur, Assam; m. Renu Chatterjee; one s. two d. *Education:* Calcutta (now Kolkata) Univ., Univ. of Cambridge and Middle Temple, UK. *Career:* mem. Communist Party of India—Marxist (CPI—M) 1968–, currently Leader; mem. Lok Sabha 1971–, Chair. Cttee on Subordinate Legislation 1977–79, 1991–93, Cttee on Privileges 1990–91, Cttee on Railways 1993–96, Cttee on Communications 1996–97, 1998–99, Leader of CPI—M in Lok Sabha 1991–97, Speaker 2004–; Chair. Bengal Table Tennis Asscn, Life Saving Soc., Kolkata; mem. Cricket Asscn of Bengal, India Int. Centre; Outstanding Parliamentarian Award 1996. *Address:* Speaker's Office, Lok Sabha Secretariat, 17 Parliament House, New Delhi 110 001, India; tel. (11) 23017795; fax (11) 23792927; e-mail speakerloksabha@sansad.nic.in; internet www.speakerloksabha.nic.in.

**CHAUDHRY, Iftikhar Mohammad,** BA, LLB; Pakistani judge; b. 12 Dec. 1948. *Career:* called to Bar 1974; enrolled as Advocate of the High Court 1976, Advocate of the Supreme Court 1985; Advocate Gen., Balochistan 1989–90; Additional Judge, Balochistan High Court 1990–99, also served as Banking Judge, Judge of Special Court for Speedy Trials, Judge of Customs Appellate Courts and Company Judge; Chief Justice High Court of Balochistan 1999–2000; elevated to Supreme Court 2000, Chief Justice of Pakistan 2005–March 2007, reinstated July–Nov. 2007 (suspended for refusing to ratify Pres. Musharraf's emergency rule); Pres. High Court Bar Asscn, Quetta; Chair. Balochistan Local Council Election Authority 1992–, Prov. Review Bd for Balochistan, Enrolment Cttee of Pakistan Bar Council, Supreme Court Bldg Cttee; fmr Chair. Pakistan Red Crescent Soc., Balochistan; mem. Bar Council. *Address:* Supreme Court of Pakistan, Constitution Avenue, Islamabad; 54-B Zarghon Road, Quetta, Pakistan; tel. (51) 9220581; fax (51) 9213452; internet www.supremecourt.gov.pk.

**CHAUDHRY, Air Vice-Marshal Shahzad Aslam,** MSc; Pakistani air force officer (retd) and diplomatist; *High Commissioner to Sri Lanka;* m.; five c. *Education:* Air Command and Staff Coll., USA, Nat. Defence Coll., Islamabad. *Career:* served in various command/staff and instructional roles during air force career including Officer Commanding F-16 Squadron 1987–89, Officer Commanding F-16 Wing 1996–97, Base Commdr, Pakistan Air Force Base, Rafiqui 2000–02, Air Officer Commanding Southern Air Command 2003, Deputy Chief of Air Staff (Operations), Pakistan Air Force 2003–06; Air Attaché, Pakistan High Comm., London 1992–96; High Commr to Sri Lanka 2006–; mem. UN Asscn of Sri Lanka; Hilal-e-Imtiaz (Mil.), Sitara-e-Imtiaz (Mil.), Tamgha-e-Basalat, Professional Efficiency Badge. *Address:* High Commission of Pakistan, No. 211 De Saram Place, Colombo 10, Sri Lanka; tel. (11) 2696301; fax (11) 2695780; e-mail parepcolombo@sltnet.lk; internet www.mfa.gov.pk/Green_Book/Srilanka_GB.htm.

**CHAUTALA, Om Prakash;** Indian politician; *Leader, Indian National Lok Dal;* b. 1 Jan. 1935. *Career:* Chief Minister of Haryana 1989, 1990, 1999, 2000–05; Pres. Haryana Unit, Indian Nat. Lok Dal 1999; Pres. Haryana State Janata Dal; Nat. Gen. Sec. Samajwadi Janata Party; Leader Indian Nat. Lok Dal (later United National Progressive Alliance, after merger with other regional parties). *Address:* Indian National Lok Dal, 18 Janpath, New Delhi 110 001, India; tel. (11) 23793409.

**CHIDAMBARAM, Palaniappan,** BSc, LLB, MBA; Indian politician; *Minister of Finance;* b. 16 Sept. 1956, Kanadukathan, Tamil Nadu; m. Nalini Chidambaram; one c. *Education:* Presidency Coll., Madras Univ., Harvard Business School, USA. *Career:* first elected to Parl. 1984; Deputy Minister, Dept of Commerce and Dept of Personnel 1985; Minister of State, Depts of Personnel and Home Affairs 1986–89; Minister of State, Dept of Commerce 1991–92, 1995–96; Minister of Finance 1996–98, 2004–; Trustee Rajiv Gandhi Foundation, Indian Asscn of Literature. *Address:* Ministry of Finance, North Block, New Delhi 110 001, India; tel. (11) 23094905; fax (11) 23093422; e-mail mprasad@nic.in; internet www.finmin.nic.in.

**CHOEDRA, His Holiness the 70th Je Khenpo Trulku Jigme;** Bhutanese ecclesiastic; *Chairman, Council for Ecclesiastical Affairs. Career:* believed to be reincarnation of Maitreya, as well as the Mahasiddha Saraha, Hungchen Kara, Kheuchung Lotsawa, and His Holiness Pema Tsering; elected 70th Je Khenpo of Bhutan 1996, title given to highest religious official of Bhutan, Leader of Cen. Monk Body, also formally the leader of Drukpa sect of Kagyupa School of Tibetan Buddhism; adviser to the King; Chair. Council for Ecclesiastical Affairs (Dratshang Lhentshog). *Address:* Council for Ecclesiastical Affairs (Dratshang Lhentshog), PO Box 254, Thimphu, Bhutan; tel. (2) 322754; fax 2) 323867; e-mail dratsang@druknet.bt.

**CHOHAN, Muhammad Anwar;** Pakistani diplomatist; *High Commissioner to the Maldives. Education:* Asia-Pacific Center for Security Studies. *Career:* High Commr to the Maldives 2006–. *Address:* High Commission of Pakistan, G. Helengely, Lily Magu, Malé, Maldives; tel. 3323005; fax 3321832; e-mail pahicmale@hotmail.com; internet www.mofa.gov.pk/Green_Book/Maldives_GB.htm.

**CHOUDHURY, Liaquat Ali;** Bangladeshi diplomatist; *High Commissioner to India;* m. Homaira Choudhury; one s. one d. *Education:* Dhaka Univ. and in Paris. *Career:* career diplomat with Bangladesh Foreign Service, served abroad in Perm. Missions to UN, New York and Geneva, Bangladesh High Comm., New Delhi, seconded to S Asian Asscn for Regional Cooperation (SAARC) Secr. as Dir and Head of Poverty Eradication Div., Kathmandu, Nepal 1995–99, Dir-Gen. Multilateral Econ. Affairs, UN, Int. Orgs, S Asia and SAARC Divs, Ministry of Foreign Affairs 2001–03, Amb. to the Netherlands 2003–05, promoted to rank of Sec. and Grade A Amb. 2005, High Commr to India 2005–. *Address:* High Commission of Bangladesh, EP-39 Dr S. Radhakrishnan Marg, Chanakyapuri, New Delhi 110 021, India; tel. (11) 24121389; fax (11) 26878953; e-mail bhcdelhi@mantraonline.com; internet www.bhcdelhi.org.

**CHOUHAN, Shivraj Singh,** MA; Indian politician; *Chief Minister of Madhya Pradesh;* b. 5 March 1959, Jait village, Sehore Dist; m. Smt. Sadhana Singh 1992; two s. *Education:* Barkatullah Univ., Bhopal. *Career:* Pres. Model Higher Secondary School Students Union 1975; participated in underground movt against Emergency 1976–77, imprisoned in Bhopal Jail; joined Rashtriya Swayamsevak Sangh (Nat. Volunteers' Union—Hindu nationalist org.) 1977; Organizing Sec. Akhil Bhartiya Vidyarthi Parishad (ABVP) 1977–78, Jt Sec. ABVP 1978–80, Gen. Sec. 1980–83, mem. Nat. Exec. of ABVP 1982–83; Jt Sec. Bhartiya Janta Yuva Morcha (BJYM) 1984–85, Gen. Sec. BJYM, Madhya Pradesh (MP) 1985–88, Pres. BJYM, MP 1988–91, Gen. Sec. All India BJYM 1992–, Nat. Pres. 2000–03; mem. Bharatiya Janata Party (BJP), fmr Pres. MP state party unit, Gen. Sec. BJP, MP 1992–94, 1997–98, later Nat. Sec. BJP, Pres. BJP, MP 2005–; elected to State Ass. from Budhni Constituency 1990–91; a convener of Akhil Bhartiya Keshariya Vahini 1991–92; five-time MP (Lok Sabha—Lower House of Parl.) 1991–, first representing Vidisha, currently represents Budhni, Sehore Dist, MP in State Ass., mem. Cttee, Ministry of Human Resources Devt 1992–96, mem. Cttee on Labour and Welfare 1993–96, mem. Hindi Salahkar Samiti 1994–1996, mem. Cttee on Urban and Rural Devt, mem. Consultative Cttee, Ministry of Human Resources Devt 1996–97, mem. Cttee on Urban and Rural Devt and its Sub-Cttee on Ministry of Rural Areas and Employment 1998–99, mem. Cttee on Agric. 1999–2000, mem. Cttee on Public Undertakings 1999–2001, Chair. House Cttee (Lok Sabha), mem. Consultative Cttee, Ministry of Communications 2000–04, mem. Cttee on Agric. 2004, mem. Jt Cttee on Offices of Profit 2004, Sec. Parl. Bd 2004, Sec. (Cen. Election Cttee), Chair. Housing Cttee 2004, mem. Cttee on Ethics 2004; Chief Minister of MP 2005–; Gold Medal in Philosophy, Barkatullah Univ. *Address:* Office of the Chief Minister, Bhopal, Madhya Pradesh; 1 Shyamla Hills, Bhopal, Madhya Pradesh, India; tel. (755) 2441581; (755) 2442231; e-mail cm@mp.gov.in; internet www.mp.gov.in.

**CHOWDHURY, A. Q. M. Badruddoza,** FRCPE, FRCP(CLAS), TDD; Bangladeshi surgeon and fmr head of state; b. 1939; m. Hasina Chowdhury; one s. two d. *Education:* St Gregory High School, Dhaka Coll., Dhaka Medical Coll., Univ. of Wales, UK. *Career:* practised as physician specializing in treatment of tuberculosis; Founding Sec.-Gen. Bangladesh Nationalist Party 1978, fmr Deputy Leader; fmr Sr Deputy Prime Minister, Minister of Health and Family Planning, of Foreign Affairs; Pres. of Bangladesh 2001–02; Co-founder and Pres. Liberal Democratic Party 2006–; fmr Pres. Nat. Anti-Tuberculosis Asscn of Bangladesh, Int. Union Against Tuberculosis; led Bangladesh del. to World Health Conf., Geneva 1978, 1979 and many dels to int. confs on tuberculosis and chest diseases; Hon. Fellow, Coll. of Physicians and Surgeons (Bangladesh); Nat. TV Award 1976. *Publications:* many research papers in nat. and int. journals; essays and plays. *Address:* Liberal Democratic Party (LDP), House 19, Road 12, Baridhara, Dhaka 1212; Residence Bari Dhar, near Gulshan, Dhaka, Bangladesh; tel. (2) 8855252; fax (2) 9890978; e-mail info@ldp-bangladesh.org; internet www.ldp-bangladesh.org.

**CHOWDHURY, Iftekhar Ahmed,** BA, MA, PhD; Bangladeshi diplomatist; *Adviser (Minister) for Foreign Affairs and for Expatriates' Welfare and Overseas Employment;* b. 25 Oct. 1946, British India; m. Nicole Chowdhury; one d. *Education:* Dhaka Univ., Australian Nat. Univ., Canberra. *Career:* began diplomatic career 1969; Deputy Sec., Ministry of Shipping and Aviation 1972–74; Deputy Chief of External Resources Div., Planning Comm. 1974–76; Counsellor, Embassy in Bonn, FRG 1983–86; First Counsellor, Perm. Mission to UN, New York 1986–88, Deputy Perm. Rep. 1988–91, Perm. Rep. 2001–07, Vice-Chair. Exec. Bd UNICEF 1998–99, 2005–06, Pres. Conf. on Disarmament 1999, Special Adviser to Sec.-Gen. of UNCTAD 2001, Vice-Pres. 59th UN Gen. Ass., Chair. Comm. for Social Devt 2002–03, Chair. Second Cttee of UN Gen. Ass. (Econ. and Financial) 2003–04, Chair. Comm. on Population and Devt 2005–06; Dir-Gen. Econ. Affairs, Ministry of Foreign Affairs 1991–94; Amb. to Qatar 1994–96; Amb. and Perm. Rep. to UN, Geneva 1996–2000; Adviser (Minister) for Foreign Affairs to Caretaker Govt of Bangladesh, with responsibility for Ministry of Expatriates' Welfare and for Ministry for Chittagong Hill Tracts Affairs 2007–08, for Foreign Affairs and for Expatriates' Welfare and Overseas Employment 2008–; Kt Order of St Gregory the Great (Vatican) 1999; named by New York City Council "one of the world's leading diplomatic leaders" 2003. *Address:* Ministry of Foreign Affairs, Segunbagicha, Dhaka 1000, Bangladesh; tel. (2) 9562862; fax (2) 9555283; e-mail webmaster@mofabd.org; internet www.mofa.gov.bd.

**CHOWDHURY, M. Nurunnabi;** Bangladeshi business executive. *Career:* Chair. Bangladesh Textile Mills Corpn. *Address:* Bangladesh Textile Mills Corporation, Bastra

Bhaban, 7–9 Kawran Bazar, Dhaka, Bangladesh; tel. (2) 911 5051; fax (2) 814600.

**DAHAL, Pushpa Kamal**, (Prachanda); Nepalese politician and fmr guerrilla leader; *Prime Minister. Career:* Gen. Sec. Communist Party of Nepal (Maoist) 1989–2001, Chair. 2001–, leader of Maoist insurgency –2006, negotiated with seven-party alliance, signed comprehensive peace agreement with Govt Nov. 2006, Communist Party of Nepal (Maoist) entered Parl. and Govt 2007; Prime Minister 2008–. *Address:* Prime Minister's Office, Singha Durbar, POB 43312, Kathmandu, Nepal; tel. (1) 421000; e-mail info@opmcm.gov.np; internet www.opmcm.gov.np; www.cpnm.org.

**DAWOOD, Mohammad Hussain;** Pakistani industrialist; *Career:* Chair. Dawood Group of Industries, Chair. and CEO Dawood Hercules Chemicals Ltd, Dawood Cotton Mills and other cos within group; mem. Bd Dirs Dawood Bank Ltd; Hon. Consul of Italy in Punjab 2002. *Address:* Dawood Group of Industries, 35A Shahrah-e-Abdul Hameed Bin Baadees (Empress Road), Lahore 54000, Pakistan; tel. (42) 6301601; fax (42) 6360343; e-mail mhd@dgi.com.pk; internet www.dawoodgroup.com.

**DAYANANDA, Mahendra;** Sri Lankan business executive. *Career:* Exec. Dir 1872 Clipper Tea Co. Ltd, B. P. De Silva Holdings Ltd; Dir Capital Suisse Asia, Risis Ltd, De Silva (Ceylon) Ltd; Chair. Tea Tang Ltd; Vice-Chair., then Chair. Colombo Tea Traders' Asscn; Deputy Chair. Ceylon Chamber of Commerce, currently Chair.; Vice-Pres. Sri Lanka Japan Business Cttee; mem. Nat. Bd of Arbitrators. *Address:* B.P De Silva Investments Ltd., 18, Charles Drive, Colombo 3; Ceylon Chamber of Commerce, 50 Navam Mawatha, PO Box 274, Colombo 2, Sri Lanka; tel. (2) 576757; (1) 380150; fax (2) 576869; (1) 449352; e-mail mahen@chamber.lk; internet www.chamber.lk.

**DE SILVA, C. R.;** Sri Lankan lawyer and government official; *Attorney-General. Education:* Royal Coll. *Career:* joined Attorney-Gen.'s Dept as State Counsel 1976, promoted to Sr State Counsel 1983, Deputy Solicitor-Gen. 1992–96, Additional Solicitor-Gen. 1996–99, took silk 1997, Solicitor-Gen. 1999–2007, Attorney-Gen. 2007–. *Address:* Chamber 48, Attorney-General's Department, Colombo, Sri Lanka; tel. (11) 440239; (11) 323595; fax (11) 329992; e-mail attorneygen@mail.ewisl.net; attorney@sri.lanka.net; counsel@sri.lanka.net; internet www.attorneygeneral.gov.lk.

**DE ZOYSA, Tilak;** Sri Lankan business executive; *Chairman, Carson Cumberbatch & Company Ltd. Career:* Deputy Chair. and Man. Dir Associate Motorways Ltd 1993–; Chair. Carson Cumberbatch & Co. Ltd 2001–; fmr Pres. Nat. Chamber of Commerce; fmr Chair. Ceylon Chamber of Commerce; Dir Bukit Darah Co. Ltd 2004–; Vice-Pres. Sri Lanka–France Business Council 2004–; mem. Monetary Bd of Sri Lanka; mem. Bd Dirs Taj Lanka Hotels Ltd; mem. Tariff Advisory Council; Hon. Consul for Croatia 1999–; Order of the Rising Sun, Gold Rays with Neck Ribbon, Japan. *Address:* Carson Cumberbatch & Co. Ltd, 61 Janadhipathi Mawatha, Colombo 1, Sri Lanka; tel. (11) 4739200; fax (11) 4739300; e-mail carsons@carcumb.com; internet www.carsoncumberbatch.com.

**DEEN, Mohamed Waheed;** Maldivian government official; *Minister of Youth and Sports;* b. 3 March 1947, Malé; m. Aisha Sayed Mohamed; four s. eight d. *Education:* attended coll. in Sri Lanka. *Career:* ; Vice-Pres. Maldives Chamber of Commerce and Industries; mem. Human Rights Comm. of the Maldives; Minister of Atolls Devt 2005–07, of Youth and Sports 2007–; exec. mem. Maldives Tourism Advisory Bd; exec. mem. Maldives Tourism Promotion Bd; exec. mem. Sports Tourism Cttee; Exec. Vice-Pres. Commonwealth Bodybuilding Fed.; Exec. Vice-Pres. Asian Bodybuilding Fed.; founder mem. and Chair. Diabetes and Cancer Soc.; mem. Exec. Bd Maldives Asscn of Tourism Industry; founder Maldives Bodybuilding Fed.; founder and Pres. Maldives Surfing Asscn; Man. Dir Orchid Holdings; Dir Thulhagiri Development, HPL Resorts; CEO Orchid Resorts; Man. Dir Deens Orchid Agency; Presidential Commemoration for Nat. Service in recognition of service rendered to the nation during terrorist attack of November 1988, Nat. Award in recognition of service to the tourism industry 1993, Nat. Award in recognition of service to community devt 1997, Hon. Award from Ministry of Tourism in recognition of 25 years of distinguished service rendered towards sustainable devt of tourism in Maldives. *Address:* Ministry of Youth and Sports, PA Complex, 5th Floor, Hilaalee Magu, Malé 20-307, Maldives; Deens Villa, Mihelli Goathé, Henveinu, Malé, The Maldives; tel. 3326986; 6640088; fax 3327162; e-mail info@youthsports.gov.mv; internet www.youthsports.gov.mv; www.bandos.com.mv.

**DELWAR HOSSAIN, Khandaker;** Bangladeshi politician; *Secretary-General, Bangladesh Jatiyatabadi Dal (Bangladesh Nationalist Party). Career:* Chief Whip of Parl. 1991–96, 2001–06, Chief Whip of the Opposition 1996–2001; mem. Bangladesh Jatiyatabadi Dal (Bangladesh Nationalist Party), mem. Standing Cttee, Sec.-Gen. 2007–. *Address:* Bangladesh Jatiyatabadi Dal (Bangladesh Nationalist Party), Banani Office, House 23, Rd 13, Dhaka, Bangladesh; tel. (2) 8819525; fax (2) 8813063; e-mail bnpbd@e-fsbd.net; internet www.bnpbd.com.

**DESHMUKH, Vilasrao,** BSc; Indian politician; *Chief Minister of Maharashtra;* b. 26 May 1945, Babhalgaon, Latur Dist. *Education:* Pune Univ. *Career:* Pres. Osmanabad Dist Youth Congress 1975–78; Dir Maharashtra State Co-operative Bank 1979–; mem. Maharashtra Legis. Ass. 1980–95; Minister of State responsible for revenue, co-operation, agric., home affairs, industry, educ., transport, tourism and agric. 1982–95; mem. (Congress Party) Latur Ass., Latur Dist 1999–; Leader Congress Legislature Party in Maharashtra 2004–; Chief Minister of Maharashtra 1999–2003, 2004–; f. Manjra Charitable Trust. *Address:* Office of the Chief Minister, Government of Maharashtra, Mantralaya, Mumbai 400 032, India; tel. (22) 2202-5151 ext. 3503; fax (22) 2202-9124; e-mail chiefminister@maharashtra.gov.in; internet www.maharashtra.gov.in.

**DEUBA, Sher Bahadur,** MA; Nepalese politician; b. 12 June 1946, Angra, Dadeldhura Dist; m. Arju Deuba; one s. *Education:* Tribhuvan Univ. *Career:* Chair. Far Western Students Cttee, Kathmandu 1965; served a total of nine years' imprisonment for political activities 1966–85; Founder-mem. Nepal Students' Union 1970; Research Fellow, LSE 1988–90; active in Popular Movt for Restoration of Democracy in Nepal 1991; mem. Parl. 1991–; Minister of Home Affairs; Leader Parl. Party, Nepali Congress 1994; Prime Minister 1995–97, 2001–02, 2004–05; Minister of Foreign Affairs and Defence 2001–02; sentenced to two-year jail term for graft July 2005, released Feb. 2006; fmr Pres. Nepali Congress Party (Democratic) (merged again with Nepali Congress under Girja Prasad Koirala as Nepali Congress 2007). *Address:* Parliament of Nepal, Singha Durbar, Kathmandu, Nepal; tel. (1) 227480; fax (1) 4222923; e-mail nparl@ntc.net.np; internet www.parliament.gov.np.

**DEVE GOWDA, Haradanahalli Dodde Gowda;** Indian politician; *President, Janata Dal (Secular);* b. 18 May 1933, Haradan ahalli; m.; four s. two d. *Education:* Govt polytechnic inst. *Career:* trained as civil engineer; ran contracting business; elected to Karnataka State Legis. in 1960s; imprisoned during state of emergency in 1970s; Minister of Public Works and Irrigation, Karnataka –1980; Chief Minister of Karnataka 1995–96; fmr mem. Lok Sabha; Leader multiparty United Front 1996; Prime Minister, Minister of Home and Agric., Science and Tech., Personnel and Atomic Energy 1996–97; currently President Janata Dal (Secular). *Address:* Janata Dal (Secular), 5 Safdarjung Lane, New Delhi 110 003, India; tel. (11) 23794499.

**DHUMAL, Prem Kumar;** Indian politician and government official; *Chief Minister of Himachal Pradesh;* b. 10 April 1944, Samirpur, Hamirpur; m. Smt. Sheela Devi 1972. *Education:* Punjab Univ., Chandigarh, Guru Nanak Dev Univ., Amritsar. *Career:* lectured at pvt. coll. in Punjab before joining Bhartiya

Janata Yuva Morcha (BJYM) and becoming its Vice-Pres. 1982; associated with many social orgs, including Bharat Vikas Parishad, Vivekanand Memorial Soc. and Himachal Hitkarini Sabha; State Sec. BJYM 1980, Vice-Pres. 1982–85; Gen. Sec. Bharatiya Janata Party (BJP) 1985–93, Pres. BJP 1993–98; contested parl. election 1984, elected MP to Lok Sabha (BJP) for Hamirpur constituency 1989, 1991, 2007, mem. Consultative Cttee Union Ministry of Communications 1989–96, Standing Cttee for Transport and Tourism and Railway Convention Cttee 1991–96, Nat. Council for Teachers' Educ. 1993–96, Alt. Chair. Estimates Cttee of Lok Sabha 1989–91; fmr Indian Rep. in Int. Parl. Union; Leader of Opposition in Himachal Pradesh State Legis. Ass. 2003–07; Chief Minister of Himachal Pradesh 1998–2003, 2007–. *Address:* 301 Himachal Sadan, Sardar Patel Marg, New Delhi; Village and PO Samirpur, Teh. Bhoranj, Hamirpur Dist, 177601, Himachal Pradesh, India; tel. (11) 24108878; (98) 68180104 (mobile); (1972) 275060; internet himachal.gov .in; premkumardhumal.com.

**DIDI, Ali Hussain;** Maldivian civil servant and diplomatist; *High Commissioner to Sri Lanka. Career:* joined civil service 1983, Dir Passport Office 2001–03, Controller of Immigration and Emigration March–Dec. 2003, Dir-Gen. Dept of Penitentiary and Rehabilitation, Ministry of Home Affairs and Environment 2004; Chair. Malé Municipality 2004–07; CEO Maldives Airports Co. 2007–08; High Commr to Sri Lanka 2008–. *Address:* Maldives High Commission, 23 Kaviratne Place, Colombo 6, Sri Lanka; tel. (11) 2365686; (11) 2587827; (11) 5516302; fax (11) 2581200; e-mail info@maldiveshighcom .lk; internet www.maldiveshighcom.lk.

**DIDI, Maria Ahmed;** Maldivian politician and lawyer; *Chairperson, Maldivian Democratic Party. Education:* educated in India, earned law degree in UK. *Career:* first qualified female lawyer in Maldives; fmr state prosecutor and Asst Exec. Dir, Attorney-Gen.'s Office; one of six women mems of People's Majlis (Parl.), nonaligned MP, now mem. Maldivian Democratic Party 2005– (Chair. 2008–), for Kaafu Atol since 2005, one of only two elected women (other four apptd by Pres.); organized first-ever women's rights rally in Maldives in 2006; co-recipient, first Int. Women of Courage Award, US Dept of State 2007. *Address:* Maldivian Democratic Party, 1st Floor, M. Gloryge, Fareedhee Magu, Malé, Maldives; tel. 3340044; fax 3322960; e-mail secretariat@mdp.org.mv; internet www.mdp.org.mv.

**DINDAR, Mohammad Naim,** BS, Dip.Agric.; Afghan banker; *Chief Executive, Banke Millie Afghan;* b. 29 Sept. 1947. *Education:* American Univ. of Beirut, Lebanon. *Career:* Exchange Student, American Field Service 1964–65; Pres. Afghan Students' Asscn 1968–69; fmr Chief of Staff, Ministry of Finance; fmr Pres., Int. Relations, Antinarcotic Comm.; Sr Agriculture Analyst, Office of Agricultural Affairs; Chair. and CEO Banke Millie Afghan 2005–; Vice-Chair. Afghan Banking Asscn; mem. Bd Afghan Telecom, Ariana, Afghan Red Crescent. *Publications:* Afghan Marketing (co–author) 1975; contribs to Journal of Agriculture; several translations. *Address:* Banke Millie Afghan, PO Box 522, Jade Ibne Sina, Kabul, Afghanistan; tel. (20) 2102221; fax (20) 2101801; e-mail info@bma.com.af; internet www.bma.com.af.

**DISSANAYAKE, Dayananda;** Sri Lankan government official. *Career:* currently Commr of Elections; acted as Commonwealth Observer during elections in Guyana Aug. 2006. *Address:* Office of the Commissioner of Elections, Elections Secretariat, Sarana Mawatha, Rajagiriya, Jayawardenapura, Sri Lanka; tel. (11) 2868441; (11) 2776681; fax (11) 2868445; e-mail comelesl@sltnet.lk; internet www.slelections .gov.lk.

**DIXIT, Kamal Mani,** BA; Nepalese business executive; b. 2 Sept. 1929, Kathmandu; m. Aniu Dixit; two s. one d. *Career:* mem. of Bd Salt Trading Corpn 1967–71, Vice-Chair. 1971–95, Chair. 1995–; Chair. Nepal Vegetable Ghee Industries Ltd; acted in Adikabi Shanubhakta Ltd; GDB by King of Nepal 2004. *Publications:* nearly 50 books. *Address:* Salt Trading Corporation Ltd, Kalimati, PO Box 483, Kathmandu, Nepal; tel. (1) 4271418; (1) 5536338; fax (1) 4271704; (1) 5536390; e-mail salt@stcnepal.com; kmldxt@gmail.com; internet www.stcnepal.com.

**DIXIT, Sheila,** MA; Indian politician; *Chief Minister of Delhi;* b. 31 March 1938; m. Vinod Dikshit (deceased); one s. one d. *Education:* Convent of Jesus and Mary School and Delhi Univ. *Career:* mem. Parl. 1984–89; Minister of Parl. Affairs, Minister of State in the Prime Minister's Office 1986–89; Pres. Delhi Pradesh Congress Cttee 1998; Chief Minister, Govt of Nat. Capital Territory of Delhi 1998–; Sec. Indira Gandhi Memorial Trust. *Address:* Office of the Chief Minister, Delhi Secretariat, IP Estate, New Delhi 110002; 3 Motilal Nehru Place, New Delhi, India; tel. (11) 23392020; (11) 23018998; fax (11) 23392111; (11) 23018726; e-mail cmdelhi@nic.in; internet delhigovt.nic.in.

**DODANGODA, Amarasiri;** Sri Lankan politician; *Minister of Justice and Law Reforms. Career:* fmr Minister of Vocational Training and Rural Industries; apptd Minister of Human Resources Devt, Tech. and Vocational Educ. 2001; Minister of Public Admin and Home Affairs 2004–05; Minister of Justice and Law Reforms 2005–. *Address:* Ministry of Justice and Law Reforms, Superior Courts Complex Bldg, Colombo 12, Sri Lanka; tel. (11) 2323022; fax (11) 2320785; e-mail Secmoj@srilanka.net; internet www.justiceministry .gov.lk.

**DOGAR, Hon. Abdul Hameed,** BSc, LLB; Pakistani judge; *Chief Justice of the Supreme Court;* b. 22 March 1944, Gaarhi Mori, Khairpur Dist, Sindh Prov. *Education:* Int. Islamic Univ. Islamabad, Al-Azhar Univ., Cairo, Egypt, Macca and Madina Univ., Saudi Arabia. *Career:* joined judicial service with appointment to High Court 1995, elevated to Supreme Court 2000, Chief Justice of Pakistan 2007– (took oath on Prov. Constitution Order which replaced the Constitution 3 Nov. 2007, later took fresh oath according to Article 178 of the Constitution 15 Nov. 2007); Sec., Dist Bar Asscn, Khairpur 1973–74, Pres. 1987–88, 1989–90, 1991–92, 1993–94, 1994–95; Vice-Chair. Dist Council, Khairpur 1979–83; Jt Sec., High Court Bar Asscn, Sukkur Bench 1984–85; Chair. Bd Govs IBA March–April 2000; mem. Sindh Madresah Bd, Karachi 1980–83, Syndicate, Shah Abdul Latif Univ., Khairpur 1996–2000; mem. Bd Govs, Bd of Intermediate and Secondary Educ., Sukkur 1988–90, Nat. Univ. of Modern Languages, Islamabad 2003; Judge-in-Charge, Supreme Court Employees' Co-operative Housing Soc., Islamabad 2004; Acting Chief Election Commr July–Aug. 2004, Nov.—Dec. 2004, 2005–06; Chair. Supreme Judicial Council, Law and Justice Comm., Fed. Judicial Acad., Nat. Judicial Policy-making Cttee, Governing Body, Access to Justice Devt Fund; Hon. Sec. Dist Red Crescent Soc., Khairpur 1980–85. *Address:* Supreme Court of Pakistan, Constitution Avenue, Islamabad, Pakistan; tel. (51) 9220581; fax (51) 9213452; e-mail info@ supremecourt.gov.pk; internet www.supremecourt.gov.pk.

**DORAKUMBURE, Wijeratne Bandara;** Sri Lankan diplomatist. *Career:* High Commr to Pakistan 2007–. *Address:* High Commission of Sri Lanka, 2c, St 55, F-6/4, Islamabad, Pakistan; tel. (51) 2828723; fax (51) 2828751; e-mail srilanka@isb.comsats.net.pk.

**DORJI, Dasho Karma;** Bhutanese civil servant; *Secretary, Ministry of Trade and Industry; Chairman, State Trading Corporation of Bhutan. Education:* St Joseph's Coll., Darjeeling, India, State Univ. of New York, USA. *Career:* joined Ministry of Foreign Affairs 1974, various posts at missions to UN, USA and India, Amb. to Bangladesh (also accred to Maldives, Thailand and Repub. of Korea) 1989–93; Dir Dept of Power 1993–96, Jt Sec. for Power 1996–2000, Sec. Ministry of Trade, Industry and Power 2000–; currently Chair. State Trading Corpn of Bhutan; Man.-Dir Karma Group Org.; mem. Bd Bank of Bhutan, Bhutan Devt Finance Corpn, Bhutan Board Products Ltd; Pres. Bhutan Table Tennis Fed.; Nyekemship with Red Scarf and Sword of Honour 1998. *Address:* Ministry of Trade and Industry, Tashichhodzong, PO Box 141, Thimphu, Bhutan; tel. (2) 322211; fax (2) 323617; e-mail kdorjee@druknet.bt; internet www.mti.gov.bt.

**DORJI, Lyonpo Kinzang,** BA; Bhutanese politician, government official and central banker; *Chairman, Royal Monetary Authority;* b. 1951, Chali, Mongar Dist. *Education:* Kolkata, India. *Career:* Zonal Admin. for Sarpang, Zhemgang, Trongsa and Bumthang 1989–1991; Dir Gen. Ministry of Agric. 1991–93, Jt Sec. 1993–94, Sec. 1994–98, Deputy Minister 1998, Minister 1998–2003; elected Speaker Nat. Ass. 1997; Prime Minister, Chair. 2002–03; Minister of Works and Human Settlements 2003–07; Interim Prime Minister 2007–08; Chair. Royal Monetary Authority (cen. bank) 2008–, Dept of Planning, Tourism Council of Bhutan 2008–; Coronation Medal 1999. *Address:* Office of the Chairman, Royal Monetary Authority of Bhutan, PO Box 154, Thimphu; Tourism Council of Bhutan, PO Box 126, Thimphu, Bhutan; tel. (2) 323111; (2) 323251; fax (2) 322847; (2) 323695; e-mail rma@rma.org.bt; dot@tourism.gov.bt; internet www.rma.org .bt; www.tourism.gov.bt.

**DORJI, 'Rongthong' Kunley;** Bhutanese politician; *President, Druk National Congress;* b. 7 Jan. 1939, Wangdicholing, Bhumthang. *Career:* fmr businessman; moved to Nepal 1991; Founder-Pres. Nepal-based Druk Nat. Congress 1994–; currently battling extradition case in New Delhi since 1998. *Publications:* Silent Suffering in Bhutan Part I, Silent Suffering in Bhutan Part II, Call of the Drum (booklet), The Main Points Behind The Unhealthy Politics Being Played In The Democractic Process That Is Unfolding In Bhutan (booklet). *Address:* Druk National Congress, B-125, 1st Floor, Dayanand Colony, Lajpat Nagar IV, New Delhi, 110 024, India; tel. (11) 65641453; (11) 26472636; fax (11) 26472636; e-mail dnc@bhutandnc.com; dnc2006@gmail.com; internet www.bhutandnc.com.

**DORJI, Lyonpo Sangye Ngedup,** BA; Bhutanese politician and fmr diplomatist; *Leader, People's Democratic Party;* b. 1953, Nobgang, Punakha Dist; m.; four c. *Education:* Dr Graham's Homes School, Kalimpong, St Stephen's Coll., New Delhi, India. *Career:* joined Bhutanese Foreign Service 1976, served at Perm. Mission to UN, New York 1977, First Sec., New Delhi 1986, Amb. to Kuwait 1986–89; Dir of Trade and Industry, Ministry of Commerce and Industry 1989–92; Jt Sec., Planning Comm. 1991; Sec. of Health 1994–95, of Health and Educ. 1995–98, Deputy Minister of Health and Educ. 1998–99, Minister of Health and Educ. 1999–2003; Chair. Council of Ministers 1999–2000, Prime Minister 2005–06; Minister of Agric. 2001–05; Leader, People's Democratic Party 2007–; Chair. Exec. Cttee WHO 1996–99; mem. Bd of Dirs Global Alliance for Vaccines and Immunization (GAVI); responsible for establishing Health Trust Fund, Nat. Tech. Training Authority, Nat. Employment Bd, Royal Univ. of Bhutan, Inst. for Zorig Chusum, Trashiyangtse, Be Somebody movt, Educ. Staff Welfare Fund, Youth Counselling, Scouts Programme, Land Man. Campaign; Red Scarf 1987, Orange Scarf 1998, Druk Thuksay Medal (Heart Son of Bhutan) 1999, Coronation Medal 1999. *Address:* People's Democratic Party, Drizang Lam, Lower Motithang, Thimphu, Bhutan; tel. (2) 335557; fax (2) 335757; e-mail secretary@pdp.bt; internet www.pdp.bt.

**DORJI, Dasho Tshering;** Bhutanese government official and diplomatist; *Ambassador to Bangladesh. Career:* fmr Sec.-Gen. Bhutan Chamber of Commerce and Industry; fmr Sec., Ministry of Works and Human Settlements; Amb. to Bangladesh 2008–. *Address:* Embassy of Bhutan, House 12, Road 107, Gulshan 2, Dhaka 1212, Bangladesh; tel. (2) 8826863; fax (2) 8823939; e-mail bhtemb@bdmail.net.

**DOSTAM, Gen. Abdul Rashid;** Afghan politician and militant leader; *Chief of Staff to Commander-in-Chief of Armed Forces;* b. 1954, Khowja Dokoh, Juzjan Prov. *Career:* fmr plumber; with Oil and Gas Exploration Enterprise 1979; undertook mil. training in USSR 1980; Commdr pro-Soviet Jozjani Dostum Militia, N Afghanistan 1980–92; Defence Minister in Pres. Najibullah's Govt (1986–92); allied with Gulbuddin Hekmatyar's Pashtun warriors and Shi'a guerrillas following transition of power 1992; est. Itehad Shamal/ Northern Unity org. which controlled most N Afghanistan provs 1993–97; fled to Turkey when Taliban occupied Mazar-i-Sharif 1997; returned to fight with Northern Alliance (NA) against Taliban 2001; Deputy Minister of Defence 2001–04; presidential cand. 2004; Chief of Staff to C-in-C of Armed Forces 2005–; Leader, Junbesh-i Melli-i Islami (Nat. Islamic Movt), Uzbek mil. wing of NA –2005; mem. Jabhe-ye-Motahed-e-Milli (United Nat. Front) 2007–; f. Balkh Air (airline); awarded Hero of the Repub. of Afghanistan Medal by Pres. Najibullah. *Address:* c/o Ministry of Defence, Shash Darak, Kabul, Afghanistan.

**EHSAS, Mohammad Qasim;** Afghan trade union leader; *President of the Central Council, National Union of Afghanistan Employees. Career:* fmr mem. Parcham (leftist party); fmr Deputy Minister of Commerce; cand. in elections 2005; currently Pres. of Cen. Council Nat. Union of Afghanistan Employees; adviser to Workers' Del., 95th Session of ILO Conf., Geneva 2006. *Address:* Central Council of National Union of Afghanistan Employees, Aryana Square in front of Urdu Puplication Department, Shashdarak, PO Box 756, Kabul, Afghanistan; tel. (20) 01959.

**EIDE, Kai,** BA; Norwegian diplomatist; *Special Envoy of the Secretary-General to Afghanistan, United Nations;* b. 28 Feb. 1949, Sarpsborg; m. Gro Holm; two d. *Education:* Univ. of Oslo. *Career:* entered Norwegian Foreign Service 1975, mem. Del. to CSCE Follow-up Meeting in Belgrade 1977–78, Madrid 1980–82, Sec., Embassy in Prague 1977–78, First Sec. 1979–82, First Sec. Del. to Conf. on Disarmament in Europe, Stockholm 1983–84, First Sec. Del. to NATO, Brussels 1984–87; Deputy Dir Pvt. Office of NATO Sec.-Gen. 1987–89; State Sec., Office of the Prime Minister, Oslo 1989–90; Minister Counsellor and Deputy Perm. Rep. to NATO 1991–93, Amb. to Int. Conf. on the Fmr Yugoslavia (ICFY) 1993–95, Amb. and Special Adviser on Balkan Area, Ministry of Foreign Affairs 1996, Special Rep. of UN Sec.-Gen. and Head of UN Mission in Bosnia and Herzegovina, Sarajevo 1997–98, Amb. and Del. to OSCE, Vienna 1998–2002, Chair. OSCE Perm. Council 1999, mem. Mitchell Cttee Staff (Sharm el Sheikh Fact Finding Mission) 2000–01, Perm. Rep. to NATO, Brussels 2002–06, Special Envoy of UN Sec.-Gen. to Kosovo 2005, to Afghanistan 2008–; Political Dir, Ministry of Foreign Affairs 2006–08; Special Adviser, Planning Div., STATOIL 1991. *Publications:* several publs on foreign and security matters. *Address:* United Nations Assistance Mission in Afghanistan (UNAMA), PO Box 5858, Grand Central Station, New York, NY 10163-5858, USA; UNAMA, PO Box 1428, Islamabad, Pakistan; UNAMA, Peace Street, Kabul, Afghanistan; tel. (0831) 246000 (Brindisi, Italy); fax (212) 963-2669 (New York); (0831) 246069 (Brindisi, Italy); e-mail spokesperson-unama@un.org; internet www.unama-afg.org.

**ELAHI, Chaudhry Pervez;** Pakistani politician; *President, Pakistan Muslim League (Q) in Punjab;* b. 1 Nov. 1945. *Education:* Forman Christian Coll., Univ. of London, UK. *Career:* mem. Punjab Prov. Ass. 1985–, Deputy Leader, then Leader of the Opposition 1993–96, Speaker 1997–99; Minister of Local Govt and Rural Devt, Punjab 1985–86, 1988–1990, 1990–93; Chief Minister of Punjab 2002–07; Pres. Pakistan Muslim League (Q) party in Punjab; mem. Nat. Security Council. *Address:* 30C, Ch. Zahur Elahi Road, Gulberg-II, Lahore, Pakistan; e-mail info@pml.org.pk; internet www.pml .org.pk.

**ERSHAD, Lt-Gen. Hossain Mohammad;** Bangladeshi politician and fmr army officer; b. 1 Feb. 1930, Rangpur; m. Raushan Ershad 1956; one s. one adopted d. *Education:* Univ. of Dhaka, Officers' Training School, Kohat, Pakistan. *Career:* first appointment in 2nd E Bengal Regt 1952; several appointments in various units including Adjutant, E Bengal Regt Centre, Chittagong 1960–62; completed staff course, Quetta Staff Coll. 1966; promoted Lt-Col 1969; Commdr 3rd E Bengal Regt 1969–70, 7th E Bengal Regt 1971–72; Adjutant-Gen. Bangladesh Army; promoted Col 1973; attended Nat. Defence Coll., New Delhi, India 1975; promoted Brig. 1975, Maj.-Gen. 1975; Deputy Chief of Army Staff 1975–78, Chief 1978–86; rank of Lt-Gen. 1979; led mil. takeover in Bangladesh March 1982; Chief Martial Law Admin. and Pres. Council of Ministers 24 March 1982, adopted title of Prime

Minister Oct. 1982, of Pres. of Bangladesh Dec. 1983, elected Pres. of Bangladesh Oct. 1986, resigned Dec. 1990; also Minister of Defence 1986–90, of Information 1986–88; fmrly in charge of several ministries including Home Affairs; Chief Adviser Bangladesh Freedom Fighters' Asscn; Chair. Bangladesh Olympic Asscn, Bangladesh Lawn Tennis Fed.; UN Population Award 1987; sentenced to ten years' hard labour on charges of keeping unlicensed firearms, acquitted after appeal 1995; sentenced to a further ten years' imprisonment for illegally amassing money 1992, to seven years' imprisonment for graft 1993, to five years' imprisonment for misappropriation of funds 2000, to six months' imprisonment for attempting to influence the proceedings in a corruption case 2002, to two years' imprisonment for corruption 2006, acquitted of several corruption charges from the previous decade 2006, sentenced to two years' imprisonment on corruption charges 2006, sentence suspended due to time already served 2007.

**ESHAQ, Mohammad;** Afghan radio and television administrator and engineer; *Director-General, Radio-Television Afghanistan. Career:* fmr Man. Dir Afghan News (English-language daily); fmr Man. Dir Payam-e Mojahed (weekly publ. of Jamiat-e Eslami—Islamic Society); fmr Deputy Minister of Aviation and Tourism; fmr rep. of Northern Alliance in Washington, DC; Dir-Gen. Radio-TV Afghanistan 2002–; mem. Bd Int. Acad. of TV Arts and Sciences 2003–. *Address:* Radio-Television Afghanistan, St 10, Lane 2, Wazir Akbar Khan, PO Box 544, Kabul, Afghanistan; tel. (20) 2101086; e-mail rtakabul@hotmail.com; mohammadeshaq@hotmail.com.

**ESMATI, Zabiullah;** Afghan airline executive; *President, Ariana Afghan Airlines. Career:* fmrly lived in Calif., USA; Dir Gen. Ind. Admin of Anti-Bribery and Corruption (GIAAC) –2007, Pres. Ariana Afghan Airlines 2007–. *Address:* Ariana Afghan Airlines, PO Box 76, Ansari Watt, Kabul, Afghanistan; tel. (20) 2100351; fax (873) 762523846; e-mail afghanairlines@yahoo.com; flyariana@mail.com; info@flyariana.com; internet www.flyariana.com.

**ETEBARI, Sher Mohammad;** Afghan politician; *Minister of Refugees and Repatriation. Career:* fmr Head of Int. Relations Bureau, Ministry of Educ.; Minister of Refugees and Repatriation 2007–. *Address:* Ministry of Refugees and Repatriation, Jungaluk, off Darulaman Road, Kabul, Afghanistan; e-mail afgmorr@afgmorr.com.

**FAHIM, Makhdoom Amin;** Pakistani politician; b. Hala Taluka. *Career:* Vice-Chair. Pakistan People's Party (PPP), Leader PPP Parliamentarians faction to contest elections 2002, currently Leader Parl. Group; Acting Chair. Alliance for the Restoration of Democracy 2003, currently Chair. *Address:* Pakistan People's Party (PPP), 8, St 19, F-8/2, Islamabad; 11-A, 2nd Sun Set Street, DHA, Karachi, Pakistan; tel. (51) 2255264; fax (51) 2282741; e-mail csppp@comsats.net.pk; internet www.ppp.org.pk.

**FAHIM KHAN, Marshal Mohammad Qassim;** Afghan politician and fmr guerrilla leader; b. 1957, Omarz Dist, Panjshir Valley; m.; three c. *Education:* Kabul Islamic Inst., Kabul Univ. *Career:* qualified doctor; joined troops fighting USSR occupation forces 1979–89; joined Northern Alliance (NA), led NA forces into Kabul 1992, Head of Intelligence, Chief of Staff, Leader 2001–02; Vice-Pres. and Minister of Defence, Afghan Interim Authority Dec. 2001–June 2002, Afghan Transitional Authority 2002–04; currently mem. Meshrano Jirga (upper house of parl.) and Sr Adviser to Pres. Karzai. *Address:* c/o Office of the President, Gul Khana Palace, Presidential Palace, Kabul, Afghanistan.

**FARHANG, Mohammad Amin,** PhD; Afghan government official and economist; *Minister of Commerce and Industry;* b. 1940, Kabul. *Education:* Esteqlal High School, Kabul Univ., Köln Univ., Germany. *Career:* Prof. of Econs, Kabul Univ. and Dir Nat. Economy Inst. 1974–78; imprisoned because of opposition to Communist regime 1978–82; emigrated to Germany 1982; fmr Prof. Ruhr Univ., Co-ordinator Afghanistan Archive; returned to Afghanistan 2001; Minister of Reconstruction 2001, of Economy 2005–06, of Commerce and Industry 2006–. *Publications:* numerous articles. *Address:* Ministry of Commerce and Industry, Darulaman Wat, Kabul, Afghanistan; tel. (20) 2290090; fax (20) 2500356; e-mail info@commerce.gov.af; internet www.commerce.gov.af.

**FAROOK, M. L. Mohamed Ali;** Sri Lankan diplomatist. *Career:* currently High Commr to the Maldives. *Address:* High Commission of Sri Lanka, H. Sakeena Manzil, Medhuziyaaraiyh Magu, Malé 20-05, The Maldives; tel. 3322845; fax 3321652; e-mail highcom@dhivehinet.net.mv.

**FAROOQ, Qazi Muhammad,** BL; Pakistani judge (retd) and government official; *Chief Election Commissioner;* b. 6 Jan. 1938, Abbottabad. *Education:* Dennys High School, Rawalpindi, Gordon Coll., Rawalpindi, Univ. Law Coll., Lahore, Nat. Inst. of Public Admin, Lahore, Inst. of Shariah and Legal Profession, Islamabad, Islamic Univ., Madina Munawwara. *Career:* lawyer in Abbottabad –1967; joined PCS (Judicial Br.) 1967, worked as Civil Judge in Charsadda, Lakki Marwat, Bannu and as Sr Civil Judge, Mardan 1967–74, promoted as Additional Dist and Session Judge 1974, served at Haripur, Abbottabad and Mansehra 1974–77, promoted as Dist and Session Judge 1977, served at Mansehra, Bannu and Peshawar 1977–82; Prov. Election Commr NW Frontier Prov. 1982–88; Registrar Peshawar High Court 1988–91, Judge of Peshawar High Court 1991–99, Chief Justice Peshawar High Court 1999–2000; Judge, Supreme Court of Pakistan 2000–03; Judge-in-Charge, Fed. Judicial Acad., Islamabad 2000–03; Chief Election Commr 2006–; Chair. Cttee of Admin, Al-Mizan Foundation 2005–; mem. Law Reforms Comm. 2000–03, Law and Justice Comm. of Pakistan 2005–. *Address:* Election Commission of Pakistan Secretariat, Election House, Constitution Avenue G-5/2, Islamabad, Pakistan; tel. (51) 9201915; fax (51) 9205300; e-mail cec@ecp.gov.pk; internet www.ecp.gov.pk.

**FAROOQI, Khaled;** Afghan politician; *Leader, Hizb-i Islami Afghanistan (Islamic Party of Afghanistan). Career:* Leader of Hizb-i Islami (Islamic Party) in Paktika Prov., led breakaway faction that claimed to renounce violence and support US-trained Afghan Nat. Army, higher educ. for women, free elections and moves to disarm pvt. militias 2001, Leader, Hizb-i Islami Afghanistan (Islamic Party of Afghanistan) 2006–; mem. Parl. (Paktika Prov.) 2005–, Chair. Cttee on Communication, Urban Devt, Water, Power and Municipal Affairs 2005–. *Address:* Hizb-i Islami Afghanistan (Islamic Party of Afghanistan), Area A, Khushal Mena, Kabul, Afghanistan; tel. (79) 9421474.

**FARUQUE, Mohammad,** BEng; Pakistani industrialist; *Chairman, Ghulam Faruque Group;* b. 14 Jan. 1930, Magpur, India; one d. two s. *Education:* Univ. of Southern Calif. *Career:* Chair. Ghulam Faruque Group, conglomerate which includes Cherat Cement Co. Ltd, Mirpurkhas Sugar Mills Ltd, Greaves Pakistan (Pvt.) Ltd. *Address:* Ghulam Faruque Group, Modern Motors House, Beaumont Road, Karachi 75530, Pakistan; tel. (21) 5682565; (21) 5888889; fax (21) 5682839; e-mail faruque@fascom.com.

**FERNANDES, George;** Indian trade unionist and politician; *Leader, Janata Dal—United;* b. 3 June 1930, Bangalore, Karnataka; m. Leila Kabir 1971; one s. *Education:* St Peter's Seminary, Bangalore. *Career:* joined Socialist Party of India 1949, mem. Nat. Cttee 1955–77, Treas. 1964, Chair. 1971–77; Ed. Konkani Yuvak (Konkani Youth) monthly in Konkani language 1949, Raithavani weekly in Kannada language 1949, Dockman weekly in English 1952–53, also New Society; fmr Chief Ed. Pratipaksha weekly in Hindi; trade union work in S Kanara 1949, 1950, in Bombay (now Mumbai) and Maharashtra 1950–58; Founding Pres. All-India Radio Broadcasters and Telecasters Guild, Khadi Comm. Karmachari Union, All-India Univ. Employees' Confed.; Pres. All-India Railwaymen's Fed. 1973–77; organized nat. railways strike 1974; Treas. All-India Hind Mazdoor Sabha 1958; formed Hind Mazdoor Panchayat 1958, Gen. Sec. for over 10 years; Convenor, United Council of Trade Unions; fmr mem. Gen.

Council of Public Services Int., Int. Transport Workers' Fed.; Founder-Chair. New India Co-operative Bank Ltd (fmrly Bombay Labour Co-operative Bank Ltd); Gen. Sec. Samyukta Socialist Party of India 1969–70; mem. Bombay Municipal Corpn 1961–68; mem. for Bombay City, Lok Sabha 1967–77; went underground on declaration of emergency 1975; mem. Janata Party 1977, Gen. Sec. 1985–86; mem. for Muzzafarpur, Bihar, Lok Sabha 1977–79, also elected to Lok Sabha 1980, 1989, 1991, 1996, 1998; Minister of Communications March–July 1977, of Industry 1977–79 (resgnd from Govt 1979), for Railways 1989–90, for Kashmir Affairs 1990–91, of Defence 1998–2001, 2001–04; Deputy Leader Lok Dal 1980–; mem. Standing Parl. Cttee on Finance 1993–96, also Consultative Cttee on Home Affairs, mem. Standing Parl. Cttee on External Affairs 1996, also Consultative Cttee on Human Resources Devt; Pres. Samata Party 1994–2000, 2002–04; fmr Pres. Janata Dal—United, currently Sr Leader; Chair. Editorial Bd Pratipaksh (Hindi monthly); Ed. The Other Side (English language monthly); Pres. Hind Mazdoor Kisan Panchayat; Chair. India Devt Group, London 1979, Schumacher Foundation 1979; fmr mem. Press Council of India; mem. Amnesty International, People's Union for Civil Liberties; involved in anti-nuclear and environmental campaigns. *Publications:* What Ails the Socialists: The Kashmir Problem, The Railway Strike of 1974, George Fernandes Speaks. *Address:* Janata Dal—United (People's Party—United), 7 Jantar Mantar Road, New Delhi 110 001; 3 Krishna Menon Marg, New Delhi 110011; 30 Leonard Road, Richmond Town, Bangalore, Karnataka 560025, India; tel. (11) 23368833; (80) 22214143 (Bangalore); (11) 23793397 (New Delhi); (11) 23015403 (New Delhi); fax (11) 23368138.

**FERNANDO, Merrill J.;** Sri Lankan business executive; *Founder and Chairman, Dilmah;* b. May 1930, Negombo; m.; two s. *Career:* began career as insp. with US petroleum co.; selected for training as tea taster, travelled to Mincing Lane, London, UK; worked in UK tea co. before returning to Sri Lanka; joined A. F. Jones & Co. and became its Man. Dir within two years, bought out British shareholders and ran business with another pnr; supplied first ever consignment of Ceylon tea direct to then USSR 1950s; est. Merrill J. Fernando & Co. Ltd, supplied bulk tea to most of world's major tea brands 1960s–70s; lost tea plantation to nationalization 1970s, sold business with intention of emigrating from Sri Lanka, remained in Sri Lanka and est. M. J. F. Exports Ltd 1974; registered trademark DILMAH in face of opposition from bulk tea customers early 1980s; DILMAH Tea launched in Australia 1988, thereafter in NZ and to date in 82 countries world-wide; est. The Merrill J. Fernando Charitable Foundation. *Address:* Dilmah, PO Box 1630, Colombo 10, Sri Lanka; tel. (11) 2933070; fax (11) 2933080; e-mail info@dilmahtea.com; internet www.dilmahtea.com.

**FITRAT, Abdul Qadeer,** BA, MA; Afghan central banker; *Governor and Chairman, Supreme Council (Supervisory Board), Da Afghanistan Bank (Central Bank of Afghanistan). Education:* secondary school, Kabul, Int. Islamic Univ., Islamabad, Pakistan, Wright State Univ., Dayton, Ohio, USA. *Career:* fmr Asst Research Coordinator for USAID-supported project, ESSP, Peshawar, Pakistan; fmr Chair. Bank-e-Millie Afghan, Kabul early 1990s; Consultant Economist, IMF, Washington, DC late 1990s; First Deputy Gov. Da Afghanistan Bank (Cen. Bank of Afghanistan) 1995, Gov. 1996, Gov. and Chair. Supreme Council (Supervisory Bd) 2007–; consumer banker to First Union Nat. Bank, northern Va 2000–01; Advisor to Exec. Dir, World Bank 2004–07. *Address:* Da Afghanistan Bank, Ibne Sina Wat, Kabul, Afghanistan; tel. (20) 2100301; (20) 2102812; fax (20) 2100305; e-mail governor.office@centralbank.gov.af; internet www.centralbank.gov.af.

**GANDHI, Rahul,** BA; Indian politician; *General-Secretary, Indian National Congress;* b. 19 June 1970, brother of Priyanka Gandhi-Vadra. *Education:* St Stephen's Coll., New Delhi, Harvard Univ., USA. *Career:* descendant of Nehru-Gandhi political dynasty; worked in London with strategy consultancy firm Monitor Group; returned to India in 2002 to start software co.; canvassed for Congress Party on behalf of his mother in Amethi constituency, UP 1999; election campaign in parl. elections supervised by his sister Priyanka Gandhi 2004; MP (Lok Sabha) for Amethi constituency 2004–; mem. Indian Nat. Congress, Gen.-Sec. 2007–, mem. Congress Working Cttee 2007–. *Address:* Indian National Congress, 24 Akbar Road, New Delhi 110 011, India; tel. (11) 23019080; fax (11) 23017047; internet www.congress.org.in.

**GANDHI, Sonia;** Indian (b. Italian) politician; *President, Indian National Congress;* b. 9 Dec. 1946, Italy; m. Rajiv Gandhi 1968 (fmr Prime Minister of India) (died 1991); one s. one d. *Education:* Univ. of Cambridge, UK, Nat. Gallery of Modern Art, Delhi. *Career:* Pres. Rajiv Gandhi Foundation; mem. Indian Nat. Congress Cttee, Pres. 1998–2006 (resgnd), reappointed 2007–; mem. Nat. Advisory Council –2006 (resgnd); Leader of Opposition in Parl. (Lok Sabha) –2004; ranked by Forbes magazine amongst 100 Most Powerful Women (third) 2004, (13th) 2006, (sixth) 2007. *Publications:* Rajiv 1992, Rajiv's World 1994. *Address:* Indian National Congress, 24 Akbar Road, New Delhi 110011; Rajiv Gandhi Foundation, Jawahar Bhawan, Dr Rajendra Prasad Road, New Delhi 110001; 10 Janpath, New Delhi 110011, India; tel. (11) 23019080; (11) 23014161; (11) 23755117; fax (11) 23017047; e-mail aicc@congress.org.in; internet www.congress.org.in; www.soniagandhi.org.

**GANGULY, Ashok,** MS, PhD, FRSC; Indian business executive; *Chairman, Firstsource Solutions Limited. Education:* Univ. of Illinois, USA, Mumbai Univ. *Career:* fmr Chair. Hindustan Lever Ltd; fmr Chief Tech. Officer and Dir Unilever; Chair. Imperial Chemical Industries (ICI) India Ltd 1996–2003, ICICI OneSource Ltd (I-OneSource, later Firstsource Solutions Ltd); Dir Cen. Bd Reserve Bank of India; Dir British Airways plc 1996–2005, Wipro Corpn 1999–, ICICI Knowledge Park Ltd, Mahindra & Mahindra Ltd, Tata AIG Life Insurance Co. Ltd; mem. Advisory Bd Microsoft Corpn (I) Pvt. Ltd, Prime Minister's Council on Trade and Industry, Investment Comm., Nat. Knowledge Comm.; Padma Bhushan 1987, Hon. CBE 2006; Business Man of the Year, India 1996, Madhuri and Jagdish N. Sheth Int. Alumni Award for Exceptional Achievement 2003. *Address:* Firstsource Solutions Ltd, 6th Floor Peninsula Chambers, Ganpatrao Kadam Marg, Lower Parel, Mumbai 400 013, India; tel. (22) 6666-0805; fax (22) 6666-0807; internet .

**GAYOOM, Maumoon Abdul,** MA; Maldivian politician and head of state; *President;* b. 29 Dec. 1937, Malé; m. Nasreena Ibrahim 1969; two s. two d. *Education:* Al-Azhar Univ., Cairo, Egypt. *Career:* Research Asst in Islamic History, American Univ. of Cairo 1967–69; Lecturer in Islamic Studies and Philosophy, Abdullahi Bayero Coll., Ahmadu Bello Univ., Nigeria 1969–71; teacher, Aminiya School 1971–72; Man. Govt Shipping Dept 1972–73; writer and trans., Press Office 1972–73, 1974; Under-Sec. Telecommunications Dept 1974; Dir Telephone Dept 1974; Special Under-Sec. Office of the Prime Minister 1974–75; Deputy Amb. to Sri Lanka 1975–76; Under-Sec. Dept of External Affairs 1976; Perm. Rep. to UN 1976–77; Deputy Minister of Transport 1976, Minister 1977–78; Pres. of Repub. of Maldives and C-in-C of the Armed Forces and of the Police 1978–; Gov. Maldives Monetary Authority 1981–2004; Minister of Defence and Nat. Security 1982–2004, of Finance 1989–93, of Finance and Treasury 1993–2004; mem. Constituent Council of Rabitat Al-Alam Al-Islami; Grand Order of Mugunghawa 1984, Hon. GCMG 1997; Hon. DLitt (Aligarh Muslim Univ. of India) 1983, Hon. DrLit (Jamia Millia Islamia Univ., India) 1990, Hon. DLit (Pondicherry Univ.) 1994; Global 500 Honour Roll (UNEP) 1988, Man of the Sea Award (Lega Navale Italiana) 1991, WHO Health-for-All Gold Medal 1998, DRV Int. Environment Award 1998, Al-Azhar Univ. Shield 2002. *Publication:* The Maldives: A Nation in Peril. *Address:* The President's Office, Boduthakurufaanu Magu, Malé; Ma. Ki'nbigasdhoshuge, Malé, 20229; The Presidential Palace (Theemuge), Orchid Magu, Malé, 20208, Maldives (Official Residence); tel. 3323701; fax 3325500; e-mail info@presidencymaldives.gov.mv; internet presidencymaldives.gov.mv.

**GENTILINI, Fernando,** LLB; Italian diplomatist; *Senior Civilian Representative in Afghanistan, NATO;* b. 2 March 1962, Subiaco, Rome. *Education:* Univ. of Rome. *Career:* Second Lt, Italian Army (Artillery) 1987; joined diplomatic service 1990, Second Sec. (Econs and Trade), Embassy in Addis Ababa 1992–95, First Sec. 1995–96; First Sec., Perm. Mission to EU, Brussels 1996–99, Rep. Policy Planning and Early Warning Unit, EU Council Secr. 1999–2000; Head of Unit for Western Balkans, Ministry of Foreign Affairs 2002–04; EU High Rep.'s Personal Rep. to Kosovo 2004; seconded to Policy Unit, Office of Sec.-Gen. and High Rep. for Common Foreign and Security Policy, Brussels 2004–06; Deputy Diplomatic Adviser to Prime Minister 2006–08; Sr Civilian Rep. in Afghanistan, NATO 2008–; Cavaliere Ufficiale dell'Ordine al Merito della Repubblica 2006. *Address:* North Atlantic Treaty Organization (NATO), boulevard Léopold III, 1110 Brussels, Belgium; tel. (02) 707-50-41; fax (02) 707-50-57; e-mail natodoc@hq.nato.int; internet www .nato.int.

**GHANI, Owais Ahmed;** Pakistani engineer and government official; *Governor of North-West Frontier Province. Career:* Kakar Pushtun by tribe; fmr Fed. Minister for Labour in Musharraf-led mil. govt and later Minister for Industries in NW Frontier Prov. –2003; Gov. of Balochistan 2003–08, of North-West Frontier Prov. 2008–; Pres. Pakistan Red Crescent Soc. Balochistan Br.; Chancellor Balochistan Univ. of Information Tech. and Man. Sciences. *Address:* Office of the Governor, Peshwar, North West Frontier Province, Pakistan; e-mail info@nwfp.gov.pk; internet www.nwfp.gov pk.

**GHAZANFAR, Hosna Banu,** BA, MA, PhD; Afghan politician and academic; *Minister of Women's Affairs;* b. 1 Feb. 1957, Balkh. *Education:* Sultan Razia High School, Mazar-e-Sharif, Stawarpool Qafqaaz Univ., St Petersburg Univ., Russia. *Career:* fmr Lecturer of Literature, Kabul Univ., fmr Dean of Faculty of Literature and Language; Minister of Women's Affairs (first female minister in cabinet) 2006–. *Publications include:* The Human Fate, Predations in the 21st Century, The Secrets of Beauty and Attraction, Self Realization. *Address:* Ministry of Women's Affairs, beside Cinema Zainab, Shar-i-Nau, Kabul, Afghanistan; tel. (20) 2201378; fax (20) 2201378; e-mail info@mowa.gov.af; internet www.mowa.gov .af.

**GILLANI, Makhdoom Syed Yousaf Raza,** BA, MA; Pakistani politician; *Prime Minister;* b. 9 June 1952, Karachi; m. Elahi Gilani; four s. one d. *Education:* La Salle High School, Multan, Univ. of the Punjab, Lahore. *Career:* mem. Pakistan People's Party 1988–, Sr Vice-Chair. 1998–; mem. Cen. Leadership Muslim League, Pakistan 1978; cabinet mem. in three-year govt of Prime Minister Muhammad Khan Junejo, Minister of Housing and Works 1985–86, of Railways Jan.–Dec. 1986; Chair. Dist Council, Multan; mem. Nat. Ass. from Multan 1985–, Speaker 1993–97; served in cabinet of fmr Prime Minister, the late Benazir Bhutto, as Minister of Tourism 1989–90, of Housing and Works Jan.–Jan. 1990; tried on charges of abusing his authority by govt anti-corruption agency 1997, accused of putting more than 500 unqualified people from his constituency on govt payroll when he was House Speaker, imprisoned 2001–06; Prime Minister of Pakistan 2008–. *Publication:* Reflections of Yusuf's Well. *Address:* Office the Prime Minister's Secretariat, Constitution Avenue, F-6/5, Cabinet Division, Cabinet Block, Islamabad, Pakistan; tel. (51) 9206111; (51) 925190512; e-mail contact@ cabinet.gov.pk; internet www.cabinet.gov.pk.

**GIRI, Rt Hon. Kedar Prasad;** Nepalese judge; *Chief Justice. Career:* experience with various judicial and quasi-judicial bodies, including Royal Law Reform Comm., Chair. Land Limitation Execution Cttee, Land Reform Ministry and all levels of courts in Nepal, Acting Chief Justice of Nepal Sept.–Oct. 2007, Chief Justice of Nepal Oct. 2007–. *Address:* Supreme Court of Nepal, Ramashah Path, Kathmandu, Nepal; e-mail info@supremecourt.gov.np; internet www .supremecourt.gov.np.

**GODREJ, Adi Burjor,** MS; Indian business executive; *Chairman, Godrej Group;* b. 3 April 1942, Bombay (now Mumbai); m. Parmeshwar Mader 1966; one s. two d. *Education:* St Xavier's High School and Coll., Bombay and Massachusetts Inst. of Tech., USA. *Career:* Chair. The Godrej Group, Godrej Consumer Products Ltd, Godrej Foods Ltd, Godrej Industries Ltd, Godrej Sara Lee Ltd, Godrej Properties Ltd, Godrej Tea Ltd, Keyline Brands UK; Dir Godrej & Boyce Mfg Co. Ltd, Godrej Agrovet Ltd, Godrej Int. Ltd, Godrej Global MidEast FZE; Chair. Bd Trustees Dadabhai Naoroji Memorial Prize Fund; mem. Tau Beta Pi (The Eng Honour Soc.), Confed. of Indian Industries; mem. Governing Bd Indian School of Business; fmr Chair. and Pres. Indian Soap and Toiletries Makers' Asscn, Cen. Org. for Oil Industry and Trade, Solvent Extractors' Asscn of India, Indo-American Soc., Compound Livestock Feeds Mfrs Asscn, Indo-American Soc., Bd Govs Narsee Monjee Inst. of Man. Studies; Rajiv Gandhi Award 2002, Globoil India Legend 2002, Scodet Life Time Achievement Award 2003. *Address:* Godrej Industries Ltd, Pirojshanagar, Eastern Express Highway, Vikhroli, Mumbai 400079; Aashraye Godrej House, 67 H Walkeshwar Road, Mumbai 400006, India; tel. (22) 25188060; (22) 25188010; (22) 23642956; (22) 23642955; fax (22) 25188062; (22) 23645159; e-mail abg@godrej.com; internet www .godrejindia.com.

**GOGOI, Tarun,** LLB; Indian lawyer and politician; *Chief Minister of Assam (Asom);* b. 1 April 1936, Rangajan Tea Estate, Jorhat Dist; m. Dolly Gogoi 1972; one s. one d. *Education:* Gauhati Univ. *Career:* mem. Jorhat Municipal Council 1968–71, Leader Assam Youth Community 1971; elected to Lok Sabha 1971–; Jt Sec. All India Congress Cttee 1976, Gen. Sec. 1985; Pres. Assam Pradesh Congress (I) Cttee 1986–1990, 1996–, Vice Pres. 1991; Minister of Food 1991–93; Minister of State for the Food Processing Industry 1993–95; mem. Assam Legis. Ass. 1996–98; Pres. Assam Pradesh Congress Cttee 1996–2001; Chief Minister of Assam (Asom) 2001–; Chair. Assam Small Industrial Devt Corpn; Dir Vayudoot; mem. Bar Council Assam;. *Address:* Office of the Chief Minister, Government of Assam, Janata Bhavan, Guwahati 781 006, India; tel. (361) 2266188; fax (361) 2262069; e-mail asmgovt@asm.nic.in; internet assamgovt.nic .in.

**GOPAL, Satya;** Indian civil servant and government official; *Administrator of Dadra and Nagar Haveli and of Daman and Diu. Career:* mem. Indian Admin. Service, currently Admin. Union Territories of Dadra and Nagar Haveli and of Daman and Diu. *Address:* Office of the Administrator, Silvassa, Dadra and Nagar Haveli, India; tel. 2642777 (Dadra and Nagar Haveli); 2230700 (Daman and Diu); fax 2642702; e-mail administrator@dnh.nic.in; internet dnh.nic.in; www.daman .nic.in.

**GOPALASAMY, V.,** (Vaiko); Indian politician; *Leader, Marumalarchi Dravida Munnetra Kazhagam. Career:* trained as a lawyer; fmr mem. Dravida Munnetra Kazhagam; Founder-Leader Marumalarchi Dravida Munnetra Kazhagam; jailed on charges of terrorism July 2002, later released. *Address:* Marumalarchi Dravida Munnetra Kazhagam, 'Thayagam', No. 141, Rukmani Lakshmi Pathi Salai, Egmore, Chennai 600008, India.

**GOPALASWAMI, N.,** MSc; Indian government official; *Chief Election Commissioner;* b. 21 April 1944, Needamangalam (then in Thanjavur dist), Tamil Nadu. *Education:* St Joseph's Coll., Tiruchirappalli, Univ. of Delhi, Univ. of London, UK. *Career:* mem. Indian Admin. Service 1966–, served in state of Gujarat in various capacities 1967–92, including Dist Magistrate in dists of Kutch and Kheda, Municipal Commr, Surat, Dir of Relief, Dir Higher Educ. and Jt Sec. (Home Dept) Govt of Gujarat, Man. Dir Gujarat Communication and Electronics Ltd, Vadodara, mem. (Admin and Purchase) Gujarat Electricity Bd, Sec. to Govt (Science and Tech. in Tech. Educ.) and Sec. Dept of Revenue; served Govt of India 1992–2004, worked as Adviser (Educ.) in Planning Comm., Jt Sec., Dept of Electronics, in charge of Software Devt and Industry Promotion Div. and also Head of Software Tech. Park of India Soc.

and SATCOMM India Soc., Sec. Dept of Culture, Sec.-Gen. Nat. Human Rights Comm., Union Home Sec. –2004; Election Commr 2004–06, Chief Election Commr (with rank of Judge of the Supreme Court) 2006–; mem. Delimitation Comm. 2005–; int. observer in USA during presidential election Nov. 2004, gen. elections in Mauritius July 2005; first recipient of Prof. Mitra Gold Medal, Univ. of Delhi 1965. *Address:* 77 Lodhi Estate, New Delhi 110 003; Election Commission of India, Nirvachan Sadan, Ashoka Road, New Delhi 110 001, India; tel. (11) 23713689; (11) 24652424; fax (11) 23711023; e-mail gopalaswamin@eci.gov.in; internet www.eci.gov.in.

**GUNATILAKA, Nandana;** Sri Lankan politician; *General Secretary, National Freedom Front. Career:* Chair. United People's Freedom Alliance (later People's Alliance) 2004–08; Gen. Sec. Nat. Freedom Front 2008–; fmr mem., politburo mem. and presidential cand. Janatha Vimukthi Peramuna party (resgnd 2006). *Address:* National Freedom Front, 377/4 Ratnarama Rd, Hokandara North, Sri Lanka; tel. (60) 2071340; e-mail info@nffsrilanka.com; internet www.nffsrilanka.com.

**GYANENDRA BIR BIKRAM SHAH DEV,** BA; b. 7 July 1974, Kathmandu; brother of the late King Birendra Bir Bikram Shah Dev; m. Komal Rajya Laxmi Devi Shah 1970; one s. one d. *Education:* St Joseph's Coll., Darjeeling, India, Tribhuvan Univ. Kathmandu. *Career:* King of Nepal 2001–08; Supreme Commdr Royal Nepalese Army –2006; has made state visits to India 2002, China 2002; official visits to India 1976, Democratic People's Repub. of Korea 1978, Repub. of Korea 1987; other visits to India, Pakistan, China, Bhutan, Thailand, Myanmar, Singapore, USA, USSR, UK, The Netherlands, Denmark, Germany, France, Italy, Switzerland, Saudi Arabia, Turkey, Yugoslavia, Romania, Hungary, Bulgaria, Czechoslovakia, Australia, New Zealand, Belgium, Spain, UAE, Austria, Canada, Iran; Chair. (currently Patron) Lumbini Devt Trust 1986–1991, King Mahendra Trust for Nature Conservation 1982–2001; Founding mem. 1001-Nature Trust 1986; Patron, Pushupati Area Devt Trust; Chancellor Tribhuvan Univ. and Mahendra Sanskrit Univ.; special interest in conservation and preservation of natural and man-made heritage; declared state of emergency, took over as Chair. of Council of Ministers Feb. 2005, relinquished power April 2006, stripped of most constitutional powers 2006, monarchy abolished May 2008; Hon. mem. Worlwide Fund for Nature; Grand Cross of the House Order of Orange (Netherlands) 1967, Kt Grand Cordon of the Most Exalted Order of the White Elephant (Thailand) 1979, Grand Cross Ordre nat. du Mérite 1983, Kt Grand Cross of the Most Distinguished Order of St Michael and St George 1986, Grand Cross of Order of Isabel la Católica (Spain) 1987, His Holy Majesty, King of the Lands of the Nepalese People and Kt of the Holy and Most Majestic Order of the Rose of Jordan, Sovereign of all Orders of the Kingdom of Nepal.

**HAKEEM, Abdul Rauf;** Sri Lankan politician; *Minister of Posts and Telecommunications. Education:* Royal Coll. Colombo. *Career:* fmr First Sec. Sri Lanka Muslim Congress (SLMC) Working Cttee, Deputy Sec.-Gen., then Sec.-Gen., currently Leader SLMC; Minister of Internal and Int. Trade and Commerce, of Shipping Devt and of Muslim Religious Affairs –2001; Minister of Port Devt and Shipping and of Eastern Devt and Muslim Religious Affairs 2001–04, of Posts and Telecommunications 2007–. *Address:* Ministry of Posts and Telecommunications, Level 18, West Tower, World Trade Centre, Colombo 1; Sri Lanka Muslim Congress, Sama Mandiraya, 53 Vauxhall Lane, Colombo 2, Sri Lanka; tel. (11) 22431711 (SLMC); (11) 2422591; fax (11) 2323465; e-mail spostele@sltnet.lk; internet www.slmc.org; www.priu.gov.lk/Ministries/Min_Posts_Telecommunication.

**HAMIED, Yusuf K.,** PhD; Indian pharmaceuticals industry executive; *Chairman and Managing Director, Cipla Limited;* b. 25 July 1936; m. *Education:* Univ. of Cambridge, UK. *Career:* began career as research officer Cipla Ltd, Man. Dir 1976–, Chair. 1989–; Fellow, Christ's Coll., Cambridge; Nat. Award, Dept of Science and Tech., Padma Bhushan 2005. *Address:* Cipla Ltd, Mumbai Central, 289 J.B.B. Marg, Mumbai 400 008, India; tel. (22) 23095521; fax (22) 23070013; internet www.cipla.com.

**HASHIM PREMJI, Azim,** BS; Indian business executive; *Chairman and Managing Director, Wipro Ltd;* b. 24 July 1945, Mumbai; m. Yasmeen Premji; two s. *Education:* Stanford Univ., USA. *Career:* took over father's Western India Vegetable Products Ltd (WIPRO) vegetable oil business upon his death 1966; Chair., CEO and Man. Dir Wipro Ltd (IT and software co.), Bangalore 1983–; mem. Prime Minister's Cttee for Trade and Industry; f. Azim Premji Foundation 2001; Dr hc Indian Inst. of Tech., Manipal Acad. of Higher Educ. 2000; Sir M. Visvesvaraya Memorial Award 2000, Businessman of the Year 2000, Business India magazine, Business Leader of the Year, Econ. Times 2004, Padma Bhushan 2005, Faraday Medal 2005. *Address:* Wipro Ltd, Doddakannelli, Sarjapur Road, Bangalore, Karnataka 560 035; Bakhtawar, 229, Nariman Point, Mumbai 400021, India; tel. (80) 28440011; (80) 5569991; fax (80) 28440256; e-mail azim.premji@corp.wipro.co.in; internet www.wipro.com; www.azimpremjifoundation.org.

**HASHMI, Makhdoom Javed;** Pakistani politican; b. Multan; m.; two d. *Career:* fmr Fed. Minister for Labour, fmr Minister for Health and Population Welfare; mem. Pakistan Muslim League (Nawaz) apptd Parl. Leader 1999, fmr Acting Pres.; mem. Alliance for the Restoration of Democracy 2003–; arrested Oct. 2003, sentenced April 2004 to 23 years in prison for inciting mutiny in the army, forgery and defamation, released Aug. 2007. *Address:* Pakistan Muslim League (Nawaz), House No. 20–H, Street 10, F-8/3, Islamabad, Pakistan; tel. (51) 2852662; e-mail pmlisb@hotmail.com; internet www.pmln.org.pk.

**HASHWANI, Sadruddin;** Pakistani business executive; *Chairman, Hashoo Group;* m.; two s. three d. *Career:* business ventures in cotton, petroleum, hotel industry, real estate, trading, and property devt 1950–; f. Hashwani Hotels Ltd, Net 21; Founder and Chair. Hashoo Group. *Address:* Hashoo Group, PEC Building Ataturk Avenue G-5/2, PO Box 1670, Islamabad, Pakistan; tel. (51) 2272890; fax (51) 2274812; e-mail info@hashoogroup.com; hashwani@net21pk.com; internet www.hashoogroup.biz.

**HASSAN, M.A.;** Bangladeshi pharmaceuticals executive. *Career:* f. Aristopharma Ltd 1986, currently Chair. and Man. Dir. *Address:* Aristopharma Ltd, 7 Purana Paltan Line, Dhaka 1000, Bangladesh; tel. (2) 93516913; fax (2) 8317005; e-mail aplhc@bangla.net; internet www.aristopharma.com.

**HEKMATYAR, Gulbuddin;** Afghan politician and fmr guerrilla leader; *Leader, Gulbuddin Islamic Party;* b. 1947, Imam Saheb, Kunduz Prov. *Education:* Kabul Univ. *Career:* mem. Muslim Youth 1970; imprisoned 1972–73; fled to Pakistan 1973; Leader Hizb-i Islami Mujahidin Movt against Soviet-backed regime; Prime Minister of Afghanistan 1993–94, 1996–97; returned from exile in Iran 1998; currently Leader Hizb-i Islami Gulbuddin (Gulbuddin Islamic Party).

**HOODA, Bhupinder Singh,** BA, LLB; Indian politician, agriculturist and lawyer; *Chief Minister of Haryana;* b. 15 Sept. 1947, Sanghi, Rohtak Dist; m. Asha Hooda 1976; one s. one d. *Education:* Punjab Univ., Chandigarh, Univ. of Delhi. *Career:* Pres. Block Congress Cttee, Kiloi, Haryana 1972–77; Sr Vice-Pres. Haryana Pradesh Youth Congress 1982–83, Pres. 1982–83; Chair. Panchayat Samiti, Rohtak 1983–87, Panchayat Parishad, Haryana 1984–87; mem. Lok Sabha 1991–, mem. Cttee on Agric. 1996–97, 1998–99, on Subordinate Legislation 1998–99; mem. All India Congress Cttee 1992–; mem. Exec. Congress Parl. Party 1994–; Convenor Haryana Congress Parl. Group 1994–96; Pres. Haryana Pradesh Congress Cttee 1997–2002; mem. Consultative Cttee Ministry of Communication 1998–99, Cttee on Subordinate Legislation; mem. Haryana Vidhan Sabha 2000–, Leader of the Opposition 2002–04; Leader Haryana Legislature Party 2005–; Chief Minister of Haryana 2005–; Pres. All India Young Farmers' Asscn, Haryana; Founder-mem. and Working Pres. All India Freedom Fighters' Successors' Org.; Working Pres. Nat. Fed. of Railway Porters, Vendors and Bearers; Sec. Jat Educ. Soc., Rohtak, Farmers' Parl. Forum 1991–; mem. Man. Cttee, D.A.V. Educational Soc., Hasangarh, Haryana. *Address:* Kothi No. 1, Sector 3, Chandigarh; Matu Ram Bhawan, Model Town, Delhi Road, Rohtak, Haryana, India; tel. (172) 2749394; (1262) 42283; fax (1262) 212030; e-mail cm@hry.nic.in; hoodabhupindersingh@hry.nic.in; internet haryana.nic.in/government/cmbio.

**HOSSAIN, Mohammed Shahadat;** Bangladeshi diplomatist; *High Commissioner to Sri Lanka. Career:* fmr Dir-Gen. Directorate-Gen. of Health Services, Ministry of Health and Family Welfare; High Commr to Sri Lanka 2006–. *Address:* Bangladeshi High Commission, 85 Dharmapala Mawatha, Colombo 7, Sri Lanka; tel. (11) 2303943; fax (11) 2303942; e-mail bdootlanka@eureka.lk.

**HUDA, A. T. M. Shamsul,** BA, MA, MPA, PhD; Bangladeshi civil servant; *Chief Election Commissioner;* b. 10 July 1943. *Education:* East Pakistan Secondary Educ. Bd, Dhaka Univ., Cen. Public Service Comm., Syracuse Univ., USA. *Career:* Asst Commr, Cadre of the Civil Service of Pakistan 1966–68; Sub-Div. Officer, in sub-dist in what is now Bangladesh and Pakistan 1968–71; Deputy Dir (Food), Punjab, West Pakistan 1971; Additional Deputy Commr 1971–72; Deputy Sec., Establishment Div. 1972–75, 1979–82; Research Asst, World Bank, Washington, DC, USA 1978–79, Maxwell School, Syracuse Univ. 1978–79; Deputy Sec., Ministry of Agric. and Forests 1981–82, Jt Sec. 1982–84, Project Coordinator, Bangladesh Jute Seed Project 1982–84, Project Dir, Agricultural Man. Devt Programme 1981–84; mem. Directing Staff, Bangladesh Public Admin Training Centre 1984–88; Jt Sec., Ministry of Irrigation, Water Devt and Flood Control 1988–91, Additional Sec. and Chair. Bangladesh Water Devt Bd 1991–92; Man. Dir Bangladesh Agricultural Devt Bank 1992–94; Sec., Banking Div., Ministry of Finance 1994–96; Sec., Ministry of Water Resources 1996–2000 (retd); Chief Election Commr 2007–. *Publications include:* The Small Farmer and the Problem of Access 1983, Co-ordination in Public Administration in Bangladesh 1987, Sustainability of Projects for Higher Agricultural Education: A Case Study of Bangladesh Agricultural University 1988. *Address:* Election Commission Secretariat, Block-5/6, Sher-e-Bangla Nagar, Dhaka 1207, Bangladesh; tel. (2) 8115212; fax (2) 8117834; e-mail ecs@bol-online.com; internet www.ecs.gov.bd.

**HUQOOQMAL, Mahbuba;** Afghan politician; *Adviser on Women's Affairs;* b. Kabul. *Education:* Malalai High School, Kabul Univ. *Career:* scientific cadre, Faculty of Law and Political Sciences, Kabul Univ. 1965, Lecturer 1965–96; Dir Women Lawyers Asscn 1965–69; mem. Constitutional Comm. –1979; Head of Afghan Women's Rights Asscn 1994; migrated to Peshawar when the Taliban took power in Kabul; Lecturer, Ummahatul Moamenin (Afghan) Univ., Peshawar; Vice-Chair. Special Ind. Comm. for Convening Emergency Loya Jirga 2001; apptd Minister of State for Women's Affairs 2002, currently Adviser on Women's Affairs. *Address:* c/o Ministry of Women's Affairs, Kabul, Afghanistan.

**HUSSAIN, Altaf,** BPharm; Pakistani politician; *Leader, Muttahida Qaumi Movement;* b. 17 Sept. 1953, Karachi; m. *Education:* Karachi Univ. *Career:* Founder and Leader Muttahida Qaumi Movt (MQM); in exile in UK since 1992. *Address:* MQM International Secretariat, 54–58, First Floor, Elizabeth House, High Street, Edgware, Middx, HA8 7EJ, England; tel. (20) 8905-7300; fax (20) 8952-9282; e-mail mqm@mqm.org; internet www.mqm.org.

**HUSSAIN, Chaudhry Shujaat;** Pakistani politician; *President, Pakistan Muslim League;* b. 27 Jan. 1946; m.; two s. one d. *Education:* Forman Christian Coll., Lahore and Univ. of London, UK. *Career:* mem. Majlis-e-Shoora 1982–85; mem. Nat. Ass. 1985–, Leader of Opposition 1988–90; Fed. Minister for Infomationa and Broadcasting 1986, for Industries and Production 1987–88, of the Interior 1990–93, 1997–99, of Narcotics Control 1997–99; Pres. Pakistan Muslim League 2004–; Prime Minister of Pakistan June–Aug. 2004; Hon. Consul-Gen. to Repub. of Korea 1982–; Order of Diplomatic Service Merit Ueung-in-Metal. *Address:* Pakistan Muslim League, PML House, F-7/3, Islamabad, Pakistan; tel. (11) 1001947; e-mail shujaat_hussain@pakistanmuslimleague.info; internet www.pakistanmuslimleague.info.

**IBOBI SINGH, Okram,** BA; Indian politician and social worker; *Chief Minister of Manipur;* b. 19 June 1948, Thoubal Athokpam Makha Leikai; m. Landhoni Devi; one s. two d. *Career:* mem. Manipur Legis. Ass. 1984–; Chair. Khadi and Village Industries Board 1985–88; fmr Minister of Municipal Admin, Housing and Urban Devt and of Industries, Manipur; Chief Minister of Manipur 2002–; Pres. Manipur Pradesh Congress Cttee 1999–; Sec. Congress Legislature Party. *Address:* Chief Minister's Secretariat, Imphal 795 001, Manipur, India; tel. (385) 2225206; e-mail cmmani@hub.nic.in; internet manipur.nic.in.

**IBRAHIM, Mohamed Rasheed;** Maldivian judge. *Career:* Chief Justice, Supreme Court. *Address:* Supreme Court of the Maldives, Malé, Maldives; tel. 3323092; fax 3316471.

**IBRAHIM, Qasim,** (Buruma Qasim); Maldivian politician and business executive; b. 10 Feb. 1952, Malé; m.; four s. four d. *Career:* began career as clerk at Govt Hosp., Malé 1969, accountant 1972–73; Man. M/S Alia Furniture Mart 1973; subsequently worked for Crescent (trading org.) 1973; joined outlet of Maldivian Govt Bodu Store (now known as State Trading Org.) 1974; set up own trading business in 1976, registered business as Villa Shipping and Trading Co. Ltd 1986, Villa Shipping (Singapore) Pte Ltd was incorporated in Singapore 1991, opened offices in Frankfurt, Germany 1996, est. Villa Hotels, Tokyo 2001, Villa Hotels, Hong Kong 2002, currently Chair. and Man. Dir Villa Group of Cos; mem. Parl. 1989; Founding mem. Maldivian Democratic Party 2001; Minister of Finance and Treasury 2005–08; Gov. Maldives Monetary Authority –2008; fmr Pres. People's Special Majlis; Pres. South Asian Asscn for Regional Cooperation Chamber of Commerce and Industry; Founder-mem. and Pres. Maldives Nat. Chamber of Commerce and Industry; Founder-mem., Vice-Pres. and mem. Bd Maldives Asscn of Tourism Industry; mem. Bd Maldives Ports Authority; fmr mem. Bd Bank of Maldives. *Address:* M-Maafannu Villa, Malé, Maldives; e-mail qasim@villa.com.mv; internet www.villahotels.com.

**INNANI, Brij Gopal;** Nepalese business executive; *Group President, Mahalaxmi Garment Industries Group. Career:* Group Pres. Mahalaxmi Garment Industries Group; fmr Pres. Garment Asscn of Nepal; Chair. Asian Textiles and Garments Council 2001–03; Chair. Shri Laxmi Narsingh Dibyadham, Maheswari Soc. of Kathmandu; mem. Fed. of Nepalese Chambers of Commerce and Industry, London Chamber of Commerce and Industry, Nepal-India Chamber of Commerce and Industry, Nepal-Britain Chamber of Commerce and Industry, Red Cross Soc.; King Birendra Coronation Silver Jubilee Gold Medal, Golden Jubilee Gold Medal. *Address:* Mahalaxmi Garment Industries Group, V. Narsing Kunj, New Plaza, Putali Sadak, POB 4206, Kathmandu, Nepal; tel. (1) 4421048; fax (1) 4421258; e-mail mgigroup@inani.com.np.

**ISLAM, A. B. Mirza Azizul,** BA, MA, PhD; Bangladeshi economist and politician; *Adviser (Minister) in charge of Ministry of Finance and Ministry of Planning;* b. 23 Feb. 1941, Sujanagar, Pabna; m. Nilufar Aziz; one s. *Education:* Dhaka Univ., Williams Coll. and Boston Univ., USA. *Career:* Lecturer, Dhaka Univ. 1962–64; joined Civil Service of Pakistan 1964; worked in different capacities in admin. service 1967–82; Econ. Affairs/Sr Econ. Affairs Officer, UN-ESCAP, Bangkok 1982–86, Dir Research and Policy Analysis Div. 1993–2001; Chief of Developing Econs Section, UN Centre on Transnational Corpns, New York 1987–92; consultant to UNCTAD, World Bank and Centre for Policy Dialogue 2002–03; Chair. Bangladesh Securities & Exchange Comm. 2003–06; Chair. Sonali Bank April–Nov. 2006; Hon. Adviser to Caretaker Govt, in charge of Ministry of Finance, of Planning, of Commerce and of Posts and Telecommunications 2007–08, in charge of Ministry of Finance, Ministry of

Planning 2008–. *Address:* Ministry of Finance, Bangladesh Secretariat, Building 7, 3rd Floor, Dhaka 1000, Bangladesh; tel. (2) 7164444; fax (2) 7166200; e-mail hfmoff@bdmail.net; internet www.mof.gov.bd.

**ISLAM, Atharul;** Bangladeshi government official and business executive. *Career:* Additional Sec., Govt of Bangladesh and Chair. Bangladesh Jute Mills Corpn. *Address:* Bangladesh Jute Mills Corporation, Adamjee Court (Annexe-1), 115-120, Motijheel Commercial Area, Dhaka 1000, Bangladesh; tel. (2) 9553364; fax (2) 9564740; e-mail bjmc@bttb.net.bd; info@bjmc.gov.bd; internet www.bjmc.gov.bd.

**JAFFEER, Musthafa Mohamed,** BComm, MA; Sri Lankan diplomatist; *Permanent Representative, United Nations;* m.; two c. *Education:* Univ. of Jaffna, Monash Univ., Australia. *Career:* Asst Dir Econ. Affairs Div., Ministry of Foreign Affairs 1988–90; Third Sec., High Comm. in New Delhi 1990–91; Second Sec., High Comm. in London 1991–94; Deputy Dir, West Div., Ministry of Foreign Affairs 1995–96, Deputy Dir East Div. 1996–97; Minister Councillor, Embassy in Beijing 1997–2001; Dir UN and Multilateral Affairs, Human Rights and Conf. Div., Ministry of Foreign Affairs 2001–02; Amb. to Viet Nam 2003–06; Chief of Protocol, Ministry of Foreign Affairs 2006–08; Perm. Rep. to UN, New York 2008–; Fellow, Monash Univ. 1995–96. *Address:* Permanent Mission of Sri Lanka to the United Nations, 630 Third Avenue, 20th Floor, New York, NY 10017, USA; tel. (212) 986-7040; fax (212) 986-1838; e-mail srilanka@un.int.

**JAHAN, Ismat,** BA, MA; Bangladeshi lawyer and diplomatist; *Permanent Representative, United Nations. Education:* Dhaka Univ., Fletcher School, Tufts Univ., with cross-registered course works at Harvard Univ., USA. *Career:* career diplomat 1982–; fmr Fellow, School of Foreign Service, Georgetown Univ., Washington, DC; served in various capacities at Ministry of Foreign Affairs as well as missions abroad including Perm. Missions to UN in New York and Geneva, and High Comm. in New Delhi; Dir-Gen. Int. Orgs, UN and Multilateral Econ. Affairs, Ministry of Foreign Affairs –2005; Amb. to the Netherlands 2005–07; Amb. and Perm. Rep. to UN, New York 2007–. *Address:* Permanent Mission of Bangladesh, 227 East, 14th Floor, 45th Street, New York, NY 10017, USA; tel. (212) 867-3434; fax (212) 972-4038; e-mail bangladesh@un.int; internet www.un.int/bangladesh.

**JALAL, Masooda;** Afghan paediatrician and fmr government official; b. Kapisa province; m.; three c. *Education:* medical school, Kabul. *Career:* pvt. practice in paediatrics 1988–92; health consultant, UN 1993–2004; presidential cand. in Afghanistan 2004; Minister of Women's Affairs 2004–06. *Address:* c/o Ministry of Women's Affairs, Kabul, Afghanistan.

**JAMALI, Mir Zafarullah Khan,** MA; Pakistani politician; b. 1 Jan. 1944, Rowjhan, Balochistan; m.; four s. one d. *Education:* Murree Royal Coll., Aitchison Coll., Lahore, Punjab Univ. *Career:* tribal elder from SW Prov. of Balochistan; joined Pakistan People's Party1970s; elected mem. Prov. Ass., Balochistan 1977; fmr Minister for Food and Information; Minister for Food and Agric. 1982, for Local Govt, for Water and Power 1985, for Railways 1986; mem. Nat. Ass. 1985–89; Chief Minister for Balochistan 1988–89; Rep. to UN 1991; elected ind. mem. Nat. Ass. 1993–, mem. Cabinet 1997–2004; Senator for Balochistan 1997–2006; Sr mem. Pakistan Muslim League –1999; mem. Pakistan Muslim League—Quaid-e-Azam; Prime Minister of Pakistan 2002–04 (resgnd); fmr mem. Nat. Security Council. *Address:* c/o Office of the Prime Minister, Constitution Avenue, Islamabad, Pakistan.

**JAMEEL, Hon. Fathulla,** BA; Maldivian politician and international organization official; *Senior Minister;* b. 5 Sept. 1942, Malé; m. 1st Aishath Ibrahim (divorced); two s. (one deceased); m. 2nd Fathimath Moosa Didi; one step-d. *Education:* Al-Azhar and Ein Shams Univs, Cairo, Egypt. *Career:* foreign service training, Ministry of Foreign Affairs, Canberra, Australia; teacher, Majeediyya School, Malé 1969–73; Under-Sec., Ministry of External Affairs; Acting Under-Sec., Dept. of Foreign Aid, Office of the Prime Minister 1974; Acting Under-Sec., Ministry of Transport 1975; Deputy Head Dept of External Affairs 1976–77; Perm. Rep. to UN, New York 1977–78; Minister of External (later Foreign) Affairs 1978–2005; Acting Minister of Planning and Devt 1982–83; mem. Parl. (Pres.'s nominee) 1989–; Sr Minister 2008–; mem. Nat. Educ. Council 1989–; Minister of State for Planning and Devt 1990–91; Gov. of Maldives to IMF 1979–83, to Asian Devt Bank 1979–83, to World Bank (IBRD) 1979–, to Islamic Devt Bank 1980–; Chair. Nat. Youth Council 1979–81, DHIRAAGU (Nat. Telecommunication Co.) 1988–, Maldives Fisheries Corpn 1990–91; mem. Fisheries Advisory Bd 1979–, Nat. Planning Council 1981–, Bd of Dirs Maldives Monetary Authority 1981–, Tourism Advisory Bd 1981–, Bd MNSL (Nat. Shipping Co.) 1979–; mem. Supreme Council for Islamic Affairs 1997–; mem. Commonwealth Consultative Group on issues related to small states; recipient of first Commonwealth Award from Oxford Centre for Islamic Studies 1999. *Address:* c/o President's Office, Boduthakurufaanu Magu, Malé, 20–05, Maldives; tel. 3320701; fax 3325500; e-mail info@presidencymaldives.gov.mv; internet www.presidencymaldives.gov.mv.

**JATOI, Ghulam Mustafa;** Pakistani politician and landowner; *Chairman, National People's Party;* b. 14 Aug. 1932, New Jatoi; m. 1st 1951; m. 2nd 1965; five s. three d. *Career:* elected Pres. Nawabshah Dist Council 1954, Sindh Prov.; elected mem. W Pakistan Ass. 1956, Nat. Ass. of Pakistan 1962, 1965, 1970, 1977, 1989, 1990, 1993, 1997; del. to UN Gen. Ass. 1962, 1965, to IPU Conf., Ottawa (elected Vice-Pres. of Conf.) 1965; Fed. Minister for Communications, Political Affairs, Railways and Natural Resources 1971; Special Envoy of Pres. to Indonesia, Malaysia, Japan 1972, of Prime Minister to Turkey 1976; Founder-mem. People's Party; fmr aide to the late Zulfikar Ali Bhutto, Prime Minister of Pakistan; fmr Chief Minister of Sindh; imprisoned for political activities 1977; led Movt for Restoration of Democracy against mil. regime; Founder Nat. People's Party; Leader of Opposition 1988; Leader of Combined Opposition Parties 1989–90, currently Chair.; Leader of Islamic Democratic Alliance for 1990 election; caretaker Prime Minister of Pakistan Aug.–Nov. 1990; Chair. Grand Nat. Alliance for 2002 election. *Address:* National People's Party (NPP), Jatoi House, 18 Khayaban-e-Shamsheer Defence Housing Authority, Phase V, Karachi, Pakistan; tel. (21) 5854522; fax (21) 5873753.

**JAYALALITHA, C. Jayaram;** Indian politician and fmr film actress; *Leader, All-India Anna Dravida Munnetra Kazhagam;* b. 24 Feb. 1948, Mysore City. *Career:* has appeared in over 100 films; joined All-India Anna Dravida Munnetra Kazhagam 1982, Propaganda Sec. 1983, Deputy Leader, currently Leader; elected mem. Rajya Sabha (Parl.) 1984; Chief Minister, Tamil Nadu 1991–96, 2001–06; Kalaimamani Award 1971–72. *Publications:* numerous publs. *Address:* All-India Anna Dravida Munnetra Kazhagam (AIADMK), 226 Avvai Shanmugam Salai, Royapet, Chennai 600 014, India; tel. (44) 28132266; fax (44) 28133510; e-mail aiadmk@vsnl.net.

**JAYASINGHE, Chrysantha Romesh;** Sri Lankan diplomatist; *High Commissioner to India;* b. 1955. *Career:* joined Foreign Service as Asst Dir UN Div. 1981, apptd Amb. to Belgium and EU 2000, High Commr to India 2005–, also accred as Amb. to Bhutan 2006–; Adviser, Sri Lankan Del. to Bd of Govs, Asian Devt Bank 2006. *Address:* Sri Lankan High Commission, 27 Kautilya Marg, Chanakyapuri, New Delhi 110 021, India; tel. (11) 23010201; fax (11) 23793604; e-mail lankacom@del2.vsnl.net.in.

**JAYASUNDERA, P. B.,** BA, MA, PhD; Sri Lankan civil servant, government official and airline industry executive; *Chairman, SriLankan Airlines Ltd. Education:* Univ. of Colombo, Boston Univ. and Williams Coll., USA. *Career:* held several sr positions in Cen. Bank of Sri Lanka –1980; with civil service since 1980, econ. adviser 1990, Dir-Gen. Dept of Fiscal Policy and Econ. Affairs 1995, Deputy Sec. to Treasury 1997–99, Sec.

to Treasury 1999–2008; Chair. SriLankan Airlines Ltd 2008–; fmr Chair. Public Enterprises Reform Comm.; fmr Sr Policy Advisor, Ernst & Young; fmr consultant to IMF and World Bank on country assignments; found guilty by Supreme Court of acting with dishonest intent in sale of Lanka Marine Services Ltd shares and of misleading Bd of Investment, ordered to pay Rs 500,000 compensation July 2008. *Address:* Head Office, SriLankan Airlines Ltd, Level 22, East Tower, World Trade Centre, Echelon Square, Colombo 1, Sri Lanka; tel. (19) 7335555; fax (19) 7335122; e-mail ulweb@srilankan.aero; internet www.srilankan.aero.

**JAYAWARDENA, D. H. S.;** Sri Lankan business executive; *Chairman, Aitken Spence & Company. Career:* Founder-Dir, Man. Dir Stassen Group; Man. Dir Distilleries Co. of Sri Lanka, Lanka Milk Foods (CWE) Ltd; Dir Hatton Nat. Bank; fmr Chair. Air Lanka (now Sri Lankan Airlines); Chair. Sri Lanka Insurance Corpn; Chair. Aitken Spence & Co. 2003–; mem. Bd Dirs Colombo Stock Exchange; Sr Advisor to Pres. on Int. Trade and Investment; Dir Bd of Investment of Sri Lanka. *Address:* Aitken Spence & Company Ltd., Vauxhall Towers, 305 Vauxhall Street, POB 5, Colombo 2, Sri Lanka; tel. (11) 2308308; fax (11) 2445406; e-mail dhsjayawardena@aitkenspence.lk; internet www.aitkenspence.com.

**JHA, Paramananda,** LLM; Nepalese lawyer and politician; *Vice-President;* b. 20 April 1945, Saptari; m. *Education:* Tribhuvan Univ., Xavier Univ., Belgium. *Career:* joined civil service as Section Officer 1972, becoming Jt Sec., Ministry of Justice 1976; Judge, Kathmandu Dist Court, Zonal and Appellate courts, later Acting Justice, Supreme Court –2007 (resgnd); mem. Madhesi Jana Adhikar Forum Nepal (Madhesi People's Rights Forum Nepal); Vice-Pres. of Nepal 2008–. *Address:* Office of the Vice President, Kathmandu, Nepal.

**JIHAD, Abdullah;** Maldivian economist, central banker and politician; *Minister of Finance and Treasury. Career:* held several positions in Ministry of Finance, including Minister of State; Gov. Maldives Monetary Authority (first ind. gov.) 2007–08; Minister of Finance and Treasury 2008–. *Address:* Ministry of Finance and Treasury, Block 379, Ameenee Magu, Malé 20-379, Maldives; tel. 3328790; 3349200; fax 3324432; e-mail admin@finance.gov.mv; internet www.finance.gov.mv.

**JINASENA, Deshamanya T. N.,** BTech (Eng), DIC (Hons), CEng, FIESL; Sri Lankan company director; *Managing Director, Jinasena Group of Companies;* b. 13 July 1940, Colombo. *Education:* Loughborough Univ., UK. *Career:* apptd Chair. Jinasena Group 1965–, Man. Dir 1965–, business ventures in hotel industry, agricultural machinery, tyres, garments, pumps, seafood, tractors; Dr hc (Loughborough); Hon. DTech. *Address:* Jinasena Group, 4 Hunupitiya Road, PO Box 196, Colombo 2; 9 Gampaha Road, Ekala, Ja Ela, Sri Lanka; tel. (1) 2448848; (1) 2232383; fax (1) 2448815; (1) 2232383; e-mail nihal@jinasena.com.lk; tnjhome@eureka.lk; internet www.jinasena.com.

**KALAM, Aavul Pakkiri Jainulabidin Abdul,** PhD; Indian fmr head of state and nuclear scientist; b. 15 Oct. 1931, Dhanushkodi, Rameswaram Dist. *Education:* Madras Inst. of Tech. *Career:* mem. staff Space Dept 1960s and 1970s, later Defence Lab., Hyderabad; launched India's first satellite 1980, masterminded integrated guided missile devt and nuclear programmes, developed Agni, Trishul and Prithvi missiles, responsible for carrying out underground nuclear tests 1998; fmr Cabinet Minister and Prin. Scientific Adviser to Govt 1999–2001; Chair. Tech. Information, Forecasting and Assessment Council; head of an agricultural devt agency; Pres. of India 2002–07; Padma Bhusan 1981, Padma Vibhushan 1990, Bharat Ratna 1997. *Publications include:* Yenudaya Prayana (Tamil poems), Wings of Fire (bestselling autobiog.) 1999, Eternal Quest (children's novel), Ignited Minds: Unleashing the Power Within India 2001. *Address:* c/o President's Office, Rashtrapati Bhavan, New Delhi 110 004; 10 Rajaji Marg, New Delhi, India.

**KAMALUDHEEN, Abdullah,** BSc; Maldivian politician; *Minister of Home Affairs;* b. 12 July 1954; m.; five c. *Education:* Majeediyya School and Almeda Univ., USA. *Career:* clerk, Ministry of Foreign Affairs 1972; Admin. Sec., Office of the Pres. 1972–76; Under-Sec., Port Comm. and Public Works Dept, Ministry of Finance 1976–77, Dir 1977–82; Dir Dept of Tourism and Foreign Investment, Office of the Pres. 1978, Dir Dept of Public Works and Labour 1982–89, Dir Islamic Centre 1984–93; Minister of Public Works and Labour 1989–93; Chair. and Man. Dir Maldives Ports Authority 1990–93; Chair. Bank of Maldives Ltd 1990–93, Maldives Electricity Board 1991–93; Exec. Dir, Maldives National Ship Man. Ltd 1991–93; mem. Parl. 1992–; mem. Constitutional Ass. 1995–; Minister of Human Resources, Employment and Labour 1998–2003, of Fisheries, Agric. and Marine Resources 2003–07, of Home Affairs 2007–. *Address:* Ministry of Home Affairs, Huravee Bldg, 3rd Floor, Ameer Ahmed Magu, Malé 20-05, Maldives; tel. 3321752; fax 3324739; e-mail minhah@dhivenhinet.net.mv; internet www.homeaffairs.gov.mv.

**KAMAT, Digambar V.,** BSc; Indian politician; *Chief Minister of Goa;* b. 8 March 1954, Margao, Goa; m. *Career:* Councillor, Margao Municipal Council 1985–90; mem. Legis. Ass. of State of Goa 1994–, mem. Cttee on Govt Assurances 1995–96, 1996–97, 1997–98, 1999–2000 (fmr Chair.), Select Cttee on Bill No. 29 of Goa Advocates Welfare Fund Bill 1995, Business Advisory Cttee 1996–97, House Cttee to study Model Rent Control Legislation, Panel of Presiding Mems 1997–98, Cttee on Public Undertakings, Chair. Public Accounts Cttee 1999–2000; Minister for Power, Protocol, and Art and Culture 1999; mem. Town and Country Planning Bd; Minister for Power, Urban Devt and Mines 2002; Chief Minister of Goa 2007–; Chair. Produce Market Cttee 1979–91; mem. Southern Planning and Devt Authority 1986–89; mem. Exec. Cttee Nat. Council of State Agricultural Marketing Bd, New Delhi 1992–94; Vice-Chair. COSAMB 1994–96; mem. State Consumer Protection Council 1993–96; Founder-mem. Damodar Educ. Soc.; Sec. Model Educ. Soc.; mem. Advisory Cttee for Parshuram Girijan Samaj; Treas., Margao Cricket Club 1973; Pres. Sparkling Stars Asscn, Margao 1973–74; Founder-Pres. Rotary Club of Margao 1973, Samrat Club; mem. Goa, Daman and Diu State Council of Sports 1976–78; Vice-Pres. Goa Badminton Asscn 1980–83, Pres. 1999–2000; mem. and Trustee, Margao Ambulance Trust; Hon. Sec. Goa Badminton Asscn; COSAMB Award, Nat. Council of State Agricultural Marketing Bd, New Delhi; Bakshi Jivabadada Kerkar State Award, Govt of Goa. *Address:* Goa Legislature Secretariat, Alto-Porvorim, Goa, 403521; Sanrit Apartments, 1st Floor, nr Masjid, Malbhat, Margao, Goa, India; tel. (832) 2224845; (832) 2730432; fax (832) 2411054; e-mail mla-marg.goa@nic.in; internet goavidhansabha.gov.in.

**KAMATH, K. V.,** BSc, MBA; Indian banker; *CEO and Managing Director, Industrial Credit and Investment Corporation of India Ltd (ICICI);* b. 2 Dec. 1947, Mangalore, Karnataka; m.; one s. one d. *Education:* Karnataka Regional Educational College, Indian Inst. of Man. *Career:* mem. of staff, Industrial Credit and Investment Corpn of India Ltd (ICICI) 1971–88, Man. Dir and CEO 1996–; Adviser, Asian Devt Bank, Manila 1988–96; mem. Man. Cttee, Associated Chambers of Commerce and Industry; mem. Nat. Council Confed. of Indian Industry; mem. Governing Bd Indian Inst. of Man., Ahmedabad, Indian School of Business, Nat. Inst. of Bank Man., Manipal Acad. of Higher Educ.; Asian Business Leader of the Year, CNBC 2001, Businessman of the Year, Business India magazine 2005, Outstanding Business Leader of the Year, CNBC-TV18 2006. *Address:* ICICI Bank Limited, ICICI Bank Towers, Bandra-Kurla Complex, Mumbai 400051, India; tel. (22) 26531414; fax (22) 26531167; e-mail info@icicibank.com; internet www.icicibank.com.

**KAPOOR, Gen. Deepak,** MA, MBA; Indian army officer; *Chief of Army Staff;* b. 1948; m. Kirti Kapoor; one s. one d. *Education:* Sainik School, Kunjpara, Defence Services Staff Coll., Wellington, Nat. Defence Coll., New Delhi, Indira Gandhi Nat. Open Univ., New Delhi. *Career:* commissioned into Regt of Artillery 1967, veteran of Indo-Pak War in eastern theatre (Bangladesh) 1971, Chief Operations Officer for UNOSOM II (UN Operation in Somalia – Phase 2)

1994–95, commanded 161 Infantry Brigade in Uri, Jammu and Kashmir, 22nd Mountain Div. (as part of a Strike Corps during Operation Parakram) 2001–02, Chief of Staff of 4 Corps in Tezpur (involved in counter-insurgency operations in Assam), promoted to Lt-Gen., commanded 33 Corps at Siliguri, West Bengal, commanded Army Training Command (ARTRAC) in Shimla, Commdr Northern Army, apptd Hon. ADC to Pres. of India, Sr Col Commdt Regt of Artillery, Vice-Chief of Army –2007, Chief of Army Staff 2007–, Hon. Col of Brigade of the Guards 2008–; Vishisht Seva Medal 1996, Sena Medal 1998, Ati Vishisht Seva Medal 2006, Param Vishisht Seva Medal 2007. *Address:* Additional Directorate General of Public Information B 30, South Block, Integrated HQ of MoD (Army), DHQ PO, New Delhi 110 011, India; tel. (11) 23018531; fax (11) 23015403; e-mail a_l_c@vsnl.com; internet indianarmy.nic.in.

**KARUNANIDHI, Muthuvel**, (Kalaignar); Indian politician and playwright; *Chief Minister of Tamil Nadu; Leader, Dravida Munnetra Kazhagam;* b. 3 June 1924, Thirukkuvalai, Thanjavur; m. Dayalu Karunanidhi; four s. two d. *Education:* Thiruvarur Bd High School. *Career:* Ed.-in-Charge Kudiarasu; journalist and stage and screen playwright in Tamil, acting in his own plays staged to collect party funds; has written over 35 film-plays including the screen version of the Tamil classic Silappadhikaram, stage plays and short stories; started first student wing of the Dravidian movt called Tamilnadu Tamil Manavar Mandram; one of founder-mems of Dravida Munnetra Kazhagam Legis. Party (DMK) 1949, Treas. 1961, Deputy Leader 1962–67, Pres. 1969–; Founder-; mem. Tamil Nadu Legis. Ass. 1957–; led the Kallakkudi Agitation and was imprisoned for six months; State Minister of Public Works 1967–69; Chief Minister of Tamil Nadu (Madras) 1969–76 (presidential rule imposed), 1989–90, 1996–2001, 2006–; arrested on corruption charges 2001, then released; Thamizha Vell (Patron of Tamil), Asscn of Research Scholars in Tamil 1971; Ed. DMK Murasoli (Tamil daily organ), Kudiyarasu; Founder Mutharam (journal), State Govt News Reel, Arau Studio, Tamil Arasu (govt journal); Hon. DLitt (Annamalai Univ., Tamil Nadu) 1971. *Publications include:* Thenpandi Singham (Raja Rajan Award) and over 100 books of prose and poetry; also screenplays. *Address:* Office of the Chief Minister, Government of Tamil Nadu, Secretariat, Fort St George, Chennai 600 009; Dravida Munnetra Kazhagam, Anna Arivalayam, Teynampet, Chennai 600 018; 7A S. Gopalapuram, IV Street, Chennai 600 086, India; tel. (44) 25672345; (44) 28115225; fax (44) 25671441; e-mail cmcell@tn.nic.in; internet www.tn.gov.in.

**KARZAI, Hamid,** MA; Afghan politician and head of state; *President;* b. 24 Dec. 1954, Karz, Qandahar; m. Zeenat Karzai 1999; one s. *Education:* Habibia High School, Simla Univ., India. *Career:* Dir of Information, Nat. Liberation Front 1985–86, Deputy Dir, Political Office 1986–89; Dir Foreign Relations Dept, Office of Interim Pres. 1989–91; fmr official rep. of deposed Afghan king, Zahir Shah; Deputy Foreign Minister 1992–96; went into exile 1996–2001; Chief of Popolzai tribe, S Afghanistan 1999–; served as consultant to Union Oil Co. of Calif. (UNOCAL), USA; mem. Del. to Future of Afghanistan Govt Talks, Bonn Nov. 2001; Chair. Afghan Interim Authority Dec. 2001–June 2002; Pres. of Transitional Authority (elected by Loya Jirga) June 2002–Nov. 2004, elected Pres. of Afghanistan Nov. 2004–; Hon. KCMG 2003; Hon. DLitt (Himachal Univ.) 2003, Hon. DLit (Nebraska Univ.) 2005, Hon. DJur (Georgetown Univ.) 2006; Int. Rescue Cttee Freedom Award 2002, American Bar Asscn Asia Rule of Law Award 2003, Int. Republican Inst. Freedom Award 2003, Philadelphia Liberty Medal 2004, Int. Der Steiger Award 2007. *Address:* Office of the President, Gul Khana Palace, Presidential Palace, Kabul, Afghanistan; e-mail president@afghanistangov.org; internet www.president.gov.af.

**KASURI, Khurshid Mehmoud,** BA, DPhil; Pakistani politician; b. 1941, Lahore. *Education:* Punjab Univ., Univs of Cambridge and Oxford, UK. *Career:* fmr Sec.-Gen. Tehrik-e-Istiqlal; first Sec.-Gen. People's Democratic Alliance 1990–93; Fed. Minister for Parl. Affairs, Interim Govt 1991–93; mem. Pakistan Muslim League 1997–; mem. Nat. Ass. 1997–; Minister of Foreign Affairs 2002–07, also of Law, Justice and Human Rights 2002–04; cand. in parl. elections 2008; mem. Nat. Security Council. *Address:* c/o Ministry of Foreign Affairs, Constitution Avenue, Islamabad, Pakistan; tel. (51) 9210335.

**KATUWAL, Lt-Gen. Rukmangad;** Nepalese army officer; *Chief of Army Staff;* b. 1944, Okahldhunga dist. *Career:* Deputy Chief of Army Staff –Aug. 2006, Acting Chief of Army Staff Aug.–Sept. 2006, Chief of Army Staff (first commoner officer) Sept. 2006–. *Address:* Office of the Chief of Army Staff, Ministry of Defence, Singha Durbar, Kathmandu, Nepal; tel. (1) 4211290; fax (1) 4211294; e-mail mod@mos.com.np.

**KHAIRI, Haziq-ul-,** BA, MA, LLB; Pakistani judge and writer; *Chief Justice, Federal Shari'a Court of Pakistan;* b. 5 Nov. 1931, Delhi, India. *Education:* Anglo-Arabic Higher Secondary School, Darya Ganj Delhi and in Karachi, Univ. of Karachi. *Career:* migrated with family upon partition of India; apptd Judge of Sindh High Court, Prov. Ombudsman (Sindh); fmr mem. Council of Islamic Ideology; currently Chief Justice Fed. Shari'a Court of Pakistan; Chair. Thinker's Forum (Hamdard Shura), Karachi; ex-officio mem. Nat. Judicial Policy Making Cttee, Law and Justice Comm., Advisory Bd Al-Mizan Foundation, Admin Cttee of Al-Mizan Foundation, Bd of Govs, Bd of Trustees, Council of Trustees and Selection Bd Int. Islamic Univ., Islamabad; Chief Patron SAARC Health, Pakistan; mem. Syndicate, Baqai Medical Univ.; Pres., Cen. and West Asian Studies, Univ. of Karachi; mem. Human Rights Comm. of Pakistan; Pres. Anglo-Arabic School and Coll. Old Boys Asscn; Trustee, Transparency International (Pakistan). *Address:* Federal Shari'a Court, Islamabad, Pakistan.

**KHALEEL, Ahmed;** Maldivian diplomatist; *Permanent Representative, United Nations;* b. 17 March 1962; m.; one d. *Career:* Third Sec., High Comm. in Colombo, Sri Lanka 1981–83; Third Sec., Perm. Mission to UN, New York 1984–88; Sr Sec., Dept of External Resources, Ministry of Foreign Affairs 1988–90; Second Sec., Perm. Mission to UN, New York 1990–91; Deputy Dir Protocol Div., Ministry of Foreign Affairs 1992–93; First Sec., Perm. Mission to UN, New York 1994–2002, Counsellor, 2002–06, Deputy Perm. Rep. 2005–06; Minister-Counsellor, Embassy in Tokyo 2006–07; Perm. Rep. to UN, New York 2008–. *Address:* Permanent Mission of the Maldives to the United Nations, 820 Second Avenue, Suite 800c, New York, NY 10017, USA; tel. (212) 599-6195; fax (212) 661-6405; e-mail mdv@undp.org; internet www.un.int/maldives.

**KHALILI, Abdul Karim;** Afghan politician; *Second Vice-President. Career:* Leader Hizb-i Wahadat i Islami (Unity Party), an alliance of anti-Taliban fighters from Hazara ethnic minority, located in Bamian prov.; driven out of Cen. Afghanistan by Taliban 1998; Leader Bamian prov. 2001–; apptd Vice-Pres. Transitional Authority 2002, elected Second Vice-Pres. 2004–. *Address:* c/o Office of the President, Gul Khana Palace, Presidential Palace, Kabul, Afghanistan. internet www.president.gov.af.

**KHAN, Abdul Qadeer,** PhD; Pakistani scientist; b. 1935, Bhopal, India; m.; two d. *Education:* Univ. of Karachi, Catholic Univ. of Leuven, Belgium. *Career:* mem. of staff, Physical Dynamics Research Lab., Amsterdam 1972–76; est. Eng Research Labs (now Dr A. Q. Khan Research Labs), Kahuta 1976, Chair. –2001; Pres.'s Special Science and Tech. Adviser with Ministerial Rank 2001–04; Patron-in-Chief Dr A. Q. Khan Inst. of Tech. and Man.; Hilal-e-Imtiaz 1989, Nishan-e-Imtiaz 1996. *Address:* Dr A. Q. Khan Institute of Technology and Management, ICCTS Plaza 81, F-7/G-7 Markaz, Blue Area, Islamabad, Pakistan; tel. (51) 9268141; fax (51) 9268156; e-mail stcd@comsats.net.pk; internet www.krl.com.pk.

**KHAN, Asfandyar Wali,** BA; Pakistani politician; *President, Awami National Party;* b. 19 Feb. 1949, Charsadda, North-West Frontier Prov.; grandson of Khan Abdul Ghaffar Khan, 'Badshah Khan' (King of Khans, founder of non-violent

Pashtun political movt, Khudai Khidmatgar (Servants of God) in undivided India. *Education:* Aitchison Coll., Lahore, Univ. of Peshawar. *Career:* joined opposition to Ayub Khan as student activist; imprisoned by govt of Zulfiqar Ali Bhutto and convicted as part of Hyderabad tribunal for 15 years 1975, released 1978, stayed away from electoral politics until 1990; Leader of Pakhtun Student Fed. prior to being elected to prov. ass. 1990; elected to Nat. Ass. 1993, re-elected 1997, 2008; Pres. Awami Nat. Party 1999–2002 (resgnd), 2003–; elected to Senate 2003. *Address:* Awami National Party, Bacha Khan Markaz, Pajagi Road, Peshawar, Pakistan; tel. (91) 2246851; fax (91) 2252406; e-mail info@awaminationalparty.org; internet www.awaminationalparty.org.

**KHAN, Sardar Attiq Ahmed,** MA; Pakistani politician and writer; *Prime Minister of Azad Jammu and Kashmir;* b. 1 Jan. 1955, Ghaziabad, Tehsil Dheerkot, Bagh Dist. *Education:* Madina Univ., Saudi Arabia. *Career:* fmr Chair. youth and student wing All Jammu and Kashmir Muslim Conf., later Chief Organizer, All Jammu and Kashmir Muslim Conf., Pres. 2002–06; elected mem. Legis. Ass. three times; Prime Minister of Azad Jammu and Kashmir 2006–. *Address:* Office of the Prime Minister, Muzaffarabad, Azad Jammu and Kashmir; All Jammu and Kashmir Muslim Conference, PO Box 184, Satellite Town, Rawalpindi 46300, Pakistan; tel. (51) 111-456-789 (Rawalpindi); (58710) 42354 (Rawalpindi); e-mail primeminister@ajk.gov.pk; internet www.ajk.gov.pk.

**KHAN, Gen. Besmellah;** Afghan military officer; *Chief of Army Staff. Career:* fought with Northern Alliance against Taliban; fmr Deputy Minister of Defence, Chief of Staff, Ministry of Defence; fmr Chief Commdr Kabul garrison; currently Chief of Gen. Staff, Afghanistan Nat. Army. *Address:* Afghanistan National Army Headquarters, Kabul, Afghanistan.

**KHAN, Rear Adm. Hasan Ali;** Bangladeshi naval officer; b. 11 Feb. 1950, Hat-Lakshmipur, Gaibandha; m. Afsana Khan; two d. *Education:* Defence Service Command and Staff Coll., Nat. Defence Coll., Mirpur. *Career:* Officer Cadet Navy 1969, mem. Exec. Br. 1972, has commanded several ships, fmr positions include Asst Chief of Naval Staff, Naval Sec., Naval Admin. Authority Dhaka –2005, Chief of Naval Staff 2005–07. *Address:* c/o Ministry of Defence, Old High Court Building, Dhaka, Bangladesh; tel. (2) 259082.

**KHAN, Ishratul Ebad;** Pakistani government administrator. *Career:* Gov. of Sindh Prov. 2002–. *Address:* Office of the Governor of Sindh, Karachi, Pakistan; tel. (21) 9201201-3; e-mail governor@governorsindh.gov.pk; internet www.sindh.gov.pk.

**KHAN, Gen. Mohammed Ismail;** Afghan politician; *Minister of Water and Energy;* b. 1954, Herat. *Education:* Kabul Mil. Coll. *Career:* served as officer in Afghan army; fmr Mujahidin Commdr during Soviet occupation; joined Jamiat-i Islami (Islamic Soc.) 1979; led uprising and liberated Herat from Soviet control; Gov. of Herat 1993–97, 2001–04; taken prisoner by Taliban following re-occupation of Herat 1997, escaped in 2000; Mil. Commdr Herat –2003; Minister of Water and Energy 2004–; mem. Northern Alliance. *Address:* Ministry of Water and Energy, Kabul, Afghanistan.

**KHAN, Raja Zulqarnain,** BA; Pakistani politician; *President of Azad Kashmir;* b. 15 March 1936, Gujrat. *Education:* New Delhi Modern High School, Aitcheson Coll., Lahore, Govt Coll., Lahore. *Career:* Co-founder Jammu Kashmir Liberation League 1960; Minister in cabinet of Pres. Maj.-Gen. Abdul Rehman of Azad Jammu Kashmir (AJK) 1969; elected mem. AJK Legis. Ass. from Samani constituency (then in Mirpur Dist, now in Bhimbher Dist) 1975, elected mem. AJK Legis. Ass. from Bhimbher constituency 1985; Minister for Finance, Planning and Devt, Health and Revenue 1985–91, for Finance and Planning and Devt 1991–96; elected mem. Jammu and Kashmir Council 1996–2001; adviser to Chair. AJK Council and to the Prime Minister; cand. of All Jammu Kashmir Muslim Conf. in presidential elections Aug. 2006; Pres. Azad Kashmir 2006–. *Address:* Office of the President, Azad Kashmir Government, Muzaffarabad, Pakistan. internet www.ajk.gov.pk.

**KHAN, Tariq Aziz-ud-din;** Pakistani diplomatist; *Ambassador to Afghanistan;* b. Peshawar. *Career:* fmr Consul Gen., Los Angeles; served twice in Kabul in sr diplomatic positions; Chief of Protocol, Ministry of Foreign Affairs –2005; Amb. to Afghanistan 2005–. *Address:* Embassy of Pakistan, 10 Nijat Watt Rd, Wazir Akbar Khan, Kabul, Afghanistan; tel. (20) 2300911; fax (20) 2300912; e-mail embassy@pakembassykbl.com; internet www.pakembkbl.com.

**KHAN, Zaffar Ahmad;** Pakistani engineer and business executive; *Chairman, Pakistan International Airlines Corporation. Education:* Peshawar Univ., one-year training programme in Japan, Advanced Man. Program, Univ. of Hawaii, short courses at INSEAD, Paris and Harvard Business School, USA. *Career:* joined Esso Pakistan Fertilizer Co. (later known as Exxon Chemical) 1969, was transferred overseas to serve Exxon Chemical in Hong Kong, USA and Singapore 1973–82, Vice-Pres. Marketing and Dir of Exxon Chemical Pakistan Ltd 1982, held various posts in all divs including Marketing, Manufacturing, Finance and Corp. Services 1982–91, played role in the first employee-led buyout in corp. history of Pakistan which resulted in Engro Chemical Pakistan Ltd 1991, Pres. and CEO 1997–2004; Chair. Pakistan Int. Airlines Corpn 2007–; Chair., mem. or fmr mem. various pvt. and public sector bds, including Engro Asahi, Engro Vopak, United Bank, Sui Southern Gas Co., PTML (Ufone), PTCL, Pakistan Steel, Unilever Pakistan, Karachi Stock Exchange, Nat. Commodity Exchange, Pakistan Inst. of Corp. Governance, Acumen Fund, State Bank of Pakistan; Pres. Overseas Chamber of Commerce and Industry; has also served on numerous advisory cttees of Govt of Pakistan, including Econ. Advisory Bd, Pay and Pension Cttee, Cttee that developed Nat. Environment Quality Standards; mem. Pakistan Centre for Philanthropy; Chair. fund-raising cttee of Agha Khan Univ.; Sitara-e-Imtiaz. *Address:* Pakistan International Airlines Corporation, Head Office, Jinnah International Airport, Karachi 75200, Pakistan; tel. 111-786-786; (21) 457-2011; fax (21) 457-2225; (21) 457-0419; e-mail info@piac.com.pk; internet www.piac.com.pk.

**KHAN HOTI, Amir Haider;** Pakistani politician and government official; *Chief Minister of North West Frontier Province;* b. 1971, Mardan; grandson of Khan Abdul Wali Khan, nephew of Asfandiyar Wali Khan, Pres. of Awami Nat. Party, of Begum Naseem Wali Khan, grandson of Amir Muhammad Khan. *Education:* Atchison Coll., Lahore, Working Edwards Coll. *Career:* began political career from platform of Awami Nat. Party; fought his first election in 2002 from PF 23 Mardan 1; Chief Minister North West Frontier Prov. 2008–. *Address:* Office of the Chief Minister, North West Frontier Province, Peshawar, Pakistan; e-mail info@nwfp.gov.pk; internet www.nwfp.gov.pk.

**KHANAL, Jhala Nath;** Nepalese politician; *General Secretary, Communist Party of Nepal (Unified Marxist-Leninist). Education:* Tribhuvan Univ. *Career:* mem. Standing Cttee Communist Party of Nepal (Unified Marxist-Leninist—UML), managed foreign relations wing of party, Gen. Sec. 1980, 2008–; one of ministers during interim govt following restoration of democracy in Nepal 1990; Minister of Information and Communications 1997; participant in first regional political party conf., Bangkok, Thailand 2002. *Address:* Communist Party of Nepal (UML), PO Box No. 5471, Madan Nagar, Balkhu, Kathmandu, Nepal; tel. (1) 278081; fax (1) 278084; e-mail uml@ntc.net.np; internet www.cpnuml.org.

**KHANDU, Dorjee;** Indian politician; *Chief Minister of Arunachal Pradesh;* b. 3 March 1955, Gyangkhar village; m.; four s. two d. *Career:* began career in Intelligence Corps, Indian Army; mem. Arunachal Pradesh State Ass. 1990–; Minister of State for Co-operation 1995–96; State Cabinet Minister of Animal Husbandry and Veterinary and Dairy Devt 1996–98, of Power 1998–2006, of Mines, Relief and Rehabilitation 2002–03, of Relief and Rehabilitation and

Disaster Man. 2003–04; Chief Minister of Arunachal Pradesh 2007–. *Address:* Office of the Chief Minister, Government of Arunachal Pradesh, Naharlagun, 791110, India; tel. (360) 2212173; (360) 2214306; internet arunachalipr.gov.in.

**KHANDURI, Maj.-Gen. Bhuwan Chandra,** BSc, BE, MIE; Indian engineer and army officer (retd), politician and management consultant; *Chief Minister of Uttarakhand;* b. 1 Oct. 1934, Dehradun, Uttaranchal; m. Smt. Aruna Khanduri 1964; one s. one d. *Education:* Allahabad Univ., College of Mil. Eng, Pune, Inst. of Engineers, New Delhi and Inst. of Defence Man., Secunderabad. *Career:* served in Corps of Engineers, Indian Army 1954–1990; mem. Parl. (Garhwal constituency, Uttarakhand) 1991–96, 1998–; mem. Bharatiya Janata Party (BJP), Chief Whip, Parl. Party 1991–96, 1998–99, 2004, mem. Nat. Exec. 1992–97, 2000–, Vice-Pres. Uttar Pradesh State 1996–97; Minister of State (with ind. charge) for Roads, Transport and Highways 2000–03, Minister with Cabinet rank 2003–04; Chief Minister of Uttarakhand 2007–; mem. Cttee on Public Accounts 1998–99, on Rules, Business Advisory 1998–99, 1999–2000, 2004, on Home Affairs 1998–99, 1999–2000 and Convenor of sub-Cttee on Personnel Policy of Cen. Para-Mil. Forces, Consultative Cttee, Ministry of Defence, Cttee on Public Undertakings 1999–2001, on Ethics; Chair. Cttee on Finance 2004; mem. Cttee on Gen. Purposes, Consultative Cttee Ministry of Petroleum and Natural Gas; Patron, Parvatiya Sanskriti Parishad, Dehradun 1990–93, Chandra Ballabh Trust; Founder and Pres. Poorva Sainik Seva Parishad, Uttar Pradesh 1992–2000, Uttarakhand Pradesh Sangarsh Samsiti 1994–96; mem. Wild Life Soc. of India 1990–2000, G.B. Pant Himalaya Environment and Devt Cttee 1998–2000; Ati Vishisht Seva Medal for Distinguished Service in the Indian Army 1982. *Address:* Jai Durga Niwas, 12, Vikas Marg, Pauri Garhwal, 246001; Office of the Chief Minister, Camp Office, Annexe Circuit House, New Cantt Road, Dehradun, 248001, India; tel. (135) 2755100; fax (135) 2755102; e-mail bc.khanduri@nic.in; internet www.uttara.in.

**KHATIWADA, Pradeep;** Nepalese diplomatist; *Ambassador to Bangladesh. Career:* career diplomat, Counsellor and Chargé d'affaires a.i., later Amb. to USA, Washington, DC 1990s, First Sec. and Deputy Chief of Mission, Embassy in New Delhi –2006; Jt Sec., Ministry of Foreign Affairs 2006–07; Amb. to Bangladesh 2007–. *Address:* Embassy of Nepal, United Nations Road, Road 2, Diplomatic Enclave, Baridhara, Dhaka, Bangladesh; tel. (2) 601790; fax (2) 8826401; e-mail rnedhaka@bdmail.net.

**KHATOON, Akram,** MA, DAIBP (Hons); Pakistani banking executive; b. 26 Sept. 1937, Ajmair, India. *Education:* Punjab Univ., Lahore and Inst. of Bankers, Pakistan. *Career:* trainee officer, State Bank of Pakistan; Man. Muslim Commercial Bank All Women Br. 1961, then Regional Man., Deputy Head Personnel Div. –1981, Chief of Training Women's Banking Div. 1981–89, Pres. First Women Bank Ltd 1989–2001; Vice-Pres. Sindh Sr Citizens Council 2000–; Sr Vice-Pres. Pakistan Fed. of Business and Professional Women, Karachi 2004–; Pres. Pakistani Fed. of Univ. Women 2005–; mem. Bd Dirs Inst. of Public Admin, First Micro Finance Bank Pakistan 2002–; mem. Council Inst. of Bankers in Pakistan; mem. Bd Govs Jinnah Women's Univ., Karachi 2007–; Fellow, Inst. of Bankers, Pakistan; Woman of the Year Award 1990, Haznat Khadi Tut Kubna (PBUK) Award 1994, Star Woman of the Year 1997, and approx. 60 other awards from various financial and women's orgs. *Publications include:* numerous articles on banking and finance and women's issues for nat. and int. newspapers and magazines. *Address:* B-34, Block D, North Nazimabad, Karachi, Pakistan; tel. (21) 6637187; (21) 6639667; e-mail akramkhatoon@yahoo.com; haseena@cyber.net.com; haseena@cyber.net.pk.

**KIYANI, Gen. Ashfaq Pervez;** Pakistani army officer; *Chief of Army Staff;* b. April 1952, Jehlum; m.; one s. one d. *Education:* Mil. Coll., Jhelum, Command and Staff Coll., Quetta, Command and Gen. Staff Coll., Fort Leavenworth, USA, Nat. Defence Coll., Islamabad. *Career:* commissioned in Baloch Regt 1971 and participated in war; commanded infantry bn, infantry brigade, infantry div. and corps; Deputy Mil. Sec. for Benazir Bhutto 1988–89; fmr Dir-Gen. of Mil. Operations; Corps Commdr of Rawalpindi 2003–04; Dir-Gen. Inter-Services Intelligence 2004–07; chosen to carry out investigations of two assassination attempts on Gen. Pervaiz Musharraf; Vice-Chief of Army Staff (also promoted to four-star Gen.) Oct.–Nov. 2007, Chief of Army Staff Nov. 2007–; Pres. Pakistan Golf Fed. 2004–. *Address:* Ministry of Defence, Pakistan Secretariat, No. II, Rawalpindi 46000, Pakistan; tel. (51) 9271107; fax (51) 9271113.

**KOIRALA, Girija Prasad;** Nepalese politician; b. 1925; one d. *Career:* Founding mem. and Pres. Nepal Trade Union Congress 1948; Pres. Morang Dist, Nepali Congress 1952–60; imprisoned after 1960 coup 1960–67, exiled in India with sr Nepali Congress Party leaders and workers 1968, returned to Nepal 1975; Gen. Sec. Nepali Congress Party 1975–91; Sr Leader Satyagraha (civil disobedience movt) and put under house arrest for nine months 1987; Sr Leader and Nepali Congress Party Gen. Sec. Jana Andolan (Mass Movt) that restored multi-party system in Nepal 1990; mem. House of Reps and Leader Parl. Party of Nepali Congress Party 1991; Prime Minister of Nepal 1991–94, 1998–99, 2000; Interim Prime Minister 2006–08 (resgnd), also Minister of Defence, of Health and Population and of the Royal Palace; Pres. Nepali Congress Party 2001–. *Address:* Nepali Congress Party, Bhansar Tole, Teku, Kathmandu, Nepal. internet www.nepalicongress.org.

**KRISHNAMOORTHY, V.;** Sri Lankan diplomatist; *High Commissioner to Bangladesh. Career:* fmr First Sec. and Head of Chancery, Perm. Rep. of Sri Lanka to Org. for Prohibition of Chemical Weapons, The Hague, Netherlands; currently High Commr to Bangladesh; Patron Sri Lanka-Bangladesh Chamber of Commerce and Industry. *Address:* High Commission of Sri Lanka, House 4A, Road 113, Gulshan Model Town, Dhaka 1212, Bangladesh; tel. (2) 9896353; fax (2) 8823971; e-mail slhc@citechco.net.

**KUMAR, Naveen;** Indian television administrator. *Career:* mem. Indian Admin. Service 1975–; Dir-Gen. Doordarshan (nat. broadcaster) 2004–06. *Address:* c/o Doordarshan, Mandi House, Doordarshan Bhawan, Copernicus Marg, New Delhi 110 001, India.

**KUMAR, Nitish,** BSc (Eng); Indian engineer and politician; *Chief Minister of Bihar;* b. 1 March 1951, Bakhtiarpur, Patna, Bihar; m. Smt. Manju Kumari Sinha 1973; one s. *Education:* Bihar Coll. of Eng, Patna. *Career:* involved in JP Movt led by Jayaprakash Narayan 1974–77, detained under the Maintenance of Internal Security Act 1974, and also during Emergency 1975; mem. Bihar Legis. Ass. 1985–89, mem. Cttee on Petitions 1986–87, Cttee on Public Undertakings 1987–89; Pres. Yuva Lok Dal 1987–88; elected to Lok Sabha 1989–, mem. Janata Dal (United) party, Sec.-Gen. Janata Dal, Bihar 1989, Gen. Sec. 1991–93, Deputy Leader of Janata Dal in Parl. 1991–93, Leader 2004–, mem. House Cttee 1989–90 ( resgnd), mem. Railway Convention Cttee 1991–96, Chair. Cttee on Agric. 1993–96, mem. Cttee on Estimates 1996, Gen. Purposes Cttee 1996, 2004, Jt Cttee on the Constitution 1996 (Eighty-first Amendment Bill 1996), Cttee on Defence 1998, Cttee on Coal and Steel 2004, Cttee of Privileges 2004, Union Minister of State, Agriculture and Co-operation April–Nov. 1990, Union Minister for Railways and for Surface Transport 1998–99, resgnd following railway accident at Gaisal in NE India Aug. 1999; Union Minister for Surface Transport Oct.–Nov. 1999, for Agric. Nov. 1999–March 2000; Union Minister for Agric. 2000–01, with additional charge of Railways March–July 2001, Union Minister for Railways 2001–04; led Nat. Democratic Alliance to victory in Bihar Ass. elections Nov. 2005; Chief Minister of Bihar 3 March 2000, resgnd seven days later, Chief Minister of Bihar 2005–; Founder-mem. Samata Party Movt. *Address:* Office of the Chief Minister, Patna, Bihar; Vill. Hakikatpur, PO Bakhtiarpur, Distt. Patna 800 001, Bihar, India; tel. (612) 2223886; (98) 68180490 (mobile); (612) 2222079; e-mail cmbihar@nic.in; internet gov.bih.nic.in.

**KUMAR, Rajendra;** Indian government official. *Career:* joined Indian Admin. Service; fmr Dir (Educ.) Govt of Nat. Capital Territory of Delhi; Commr-cum-Sec. (Health/ Finance), Union Territory of Andaman and Nicobar Islands –2006; Admin. of Lakshadweep 2006; Chair. Lakshadweep Devt Corpn, SPORTS (Soc. for Promotion of Recreational Tourism and Sports); ex-officio Insp. Gen. of Police. *Address:* c/o Office of the Administrator, Kavaratti 682555, Lakshadweep, India.

**LAKHANI, Amin Mohammed,** BSc, MBA; Pakistani business executive; *Managing Director, Lakson Group of Companies. Education:* Stanford Univ., Wharton School of Business, Univ. of Pennsylvania, USA. *Career:* currently Man. Dir Lakson Group, conglomerate with interests in computer software, tobacco, cosmetics, insurance, fast food and textiles; CEO McDonald's Pakistan; Founding mem. Pakistan Chapter, Young Press' Org.; Hon. Consul-Gen. of Repub. of Singapore in Pakistan; Public Service Star, Govt of Singapore. *Address:* Lakson Group of Companies, Lakson Square Building No. 2, Sarwar Shaheed Road, Karachi, Pakistan; tel. (21) 5688243; fax (21) 5680093; e-mail amin@cyber.net.pk; internet www.lakson.com.pk.

**LATHEEF, Mohamed;** Maldivian politician; *Spokesperson, Maldivian Democratic Party;* one d. *Career:* fmr mem. Parl.; fmr Vice-Pres. Maldives Nat. Chamber of Commerce; Co-Founder Maldivian Democratic Party (banned opposition group), currently Spokesperson. *Address:* Maldivian Democratic Party (MDP), 1st Floor, M. Gloryge, Fareedhee Magu, Malé, The Maldives; tel. 3340044; fax 3322960; e-mail secretariat@mdp.org.mv; internet www.mdp.org.mv.

**LEGHARI, Farooq Ahmed Khan;** Pakistani politician and fmr head of state; *Chairman, Millat Party;* b. 29 May 1940, Dera Ghazi Khan; m. 1965; two s. two d. *Education:* Punjab Univ. and Univ. of Oxford, UK. *Career:* joined Pakistan People's Party 1973; Chief Baluchi Leghari Tribe; Pakistan Civil Service 1964–73; elected to Senate 1975, to Nat. Ass. 1977; Minister for Production 1977; periods of imprisonment for opposition to Govt 1977–88; Sec.-Gen. Pakistan People's Party and mem. Exec. Cttee 1978; elected mem. Nat. Ass. and Prov. Ass. 1988–, Leader of Opposition, Prov. Ass. 1988; Minister for Water and Power 1988–90; Deputy Leader of Opposition 1990–93; Minister of Finance 1993, of Foreign Affairs Oct.–Nov. 1993; Pres. of Pakistan 1993–97; dismissed Govt of Benazir Bhutto 1996; Organizer and Founder Millat Party 1998, currently Chair. *Address:* Millat Party, 21-E/3, Gulberg, Lahore; Village Choti, District Dera Ghazikhan, Punjab, Pakistan; tel. (42) 5757805; (42) 5756718; e-mail millat@lhr.comsats.net.pk.

**LODIN, Azizullah,** BA, PhD; Afghan politician and government official; *President, Independent Election Commission of Afghanistan;* b. 1939, Herat. *Education:* high school in Kabul, Kabul Univ., Univ. of Köln, Germany. *Career:* Lecturer, Faculty of Econs, Kabul Univ. 1976–78; held as political prisoner and put in Pule-Charkhi for involvement with Anti-Communist activist group in Kabul 1978–80; joined mujahidin movt as political adviser to leadership of Harakat Inqlab Islami Afghanistan, Peshawar, Pakistan 1980; fmr Vice-Chair. Political Dept, Islamic Unity of Afghanistan, mem. Supreme Council 1983–85; worked on Afghan refugee affairs and liaisons with Govt of Pakistan and Int. Orgs; Founder Afghan's Doctor Union outside the country (first Afghan non-governmental org. in Pakistan); Founder Nahid-e-Shahid High School for Afghan refugee girls, Peshawar 1983; Chair. Afghan del. at Tribunal de peuple, Sorbonne, Paris, France 1981; Dir Political Dept, Islamic Revolutionary Party of Afghan mujahidin, Peshawar 1985–89; Econ. and Political Adviser to Pres. of Afghan Interim Govt chaired by Prof. Mujadidy; fmr mem. Bd of Dirs Reconstruction Authority for Afghanistan; fmr Pres. Task Force Cttee for Emergency Assistance Inside Afghanistan; Head of Afghan Consulting GmbH, Herat 1992–95; served as Pres. Afghan Econ. Council, SW Prov.; attached to resistance org. against Taliban in Iran 1995–2001; Founder Cyprus Peace Conf.; fmr Head of Political Affairs, Cyprus Del. to Bonn Conf. and a signing mem. of Bonn Agreement; Adviser to Pres. Karzai in SW Prov., Herat 2003; Pres. Gen. Admin of Anti-Bribery and Corruption, with rank of Minister 2003–04; Gen. Sec. Secr. of Nat. Ass. of Afghanistan 2004–07; Pres. Ind. Election Comm. of Afghanistan 2007–. *Address:* Independent Election Commission, PO Box 979, IEC compound, Jalalabad Road, Paktia Kot, Kabul, Afghanistan; tel. (752) 035203 (mobile); e-mail info@iec.org.af; internet www.iec.org.af.

**LOHIA, Ashok Kumar;** Nepalese business executive. *Career:* f. Mahashakti Soap and Chemical Industries Pvt. Ltd 1970, currently Chair. *Address:* Mahashakti Soap and Chemical Industries Pvt. Ltd, 534 Exhibition Road, Kathmandu, Nepal; tel. (1) 4226638; fax (1) 4225178; e-mail puja@msci.wlink.com.np.

**LOKUBANDARA, W(ijesinghe) J(ayaweera) M(udiyanselage);** Sri Lankan attorney and politician; *Speaker of the Parliament;* b. 5 Aug. 1941; m. *Career:* mem. Parl. (United Nat. Party) for Badulla, currently Speaker of the Parl., mem. Cttee of Selection, House Cttee, Cttee on Standing Orders, Cttee on Parl. Business; fmr Minister for Justice, Law Reform and Nat. Integration and Minister for Buddha Sasana. *Address:* Office of the Speaker, Parliament of Sri Lanka, Sri Jayewardenepura Kotte, Colombo; No. 14, Samagi Mawatha, Gangodawila, Nugegoda, Colombo, Sri Lanka; tel. (11) 2777100; fax (11) 2777564; e-mail webmaster@parliament.lk; internet www.parliament.lk.

**McKIERNAN, Gen. David D.,** MPA; American army officer; *Commander, International Security Assistance Force (ISAF), NATO. Education:* The Coll. of William & Mary, Shippensburg Univ., Pa. *Career:* received ROTC comm., entered US Army 1972, gained experience in the Balkans as a staff officer 1990s, joined Allied Command Europe Rapid Reaction Corps (ARRC) serving as Deputy Chief of Staff G-2/G-3 forward deployed in both Sarajevo, Bosnia-Herzegovina and Rheindahlen (Mönchengladbach), Germany 1996–98, Deputy Chief of Staff, Operations, HQ, US Army, Europe and Seventh Army during period of simultaneous operations in Bosnia, Albania and Kosovo 1998–99, assigned as G-3 (Operations), HQ, Dept of the Army 2001–02, assumed command of Third US Army and US Army Forces Cen. Command (ARCENT) 2002, became Coalition Forces Land Component Commdr for US Cen. Command in preparation for Operation Iraqi Freedom, led all coalition and US conventional ground forces that attacked Iraq March 2003, assigned as Deputy Commdg Gen./Chief of Staff for US Army Forces Command (largest major command in US Army), assumed command of 7th Army/US Army Europe, commands have included: 1st Bn, 35th Armor (Iron Knights), 1st Armored Div. 1988–90, 1st Brigade (Iron Horse), 1st Cavalry Div. 1993–95, 1st Cavalry Div. 1999–2001, 3rd US Army/Combined Forces Land Component Command 2002–04, Commdr CFLCC 2002–04, 7th US Army/US Army Europe 2005–, Commdg Gen. US Army, Europe 2004–08, Commdr Int. Security Assistance Force (ISAF), NATO 2008–; awards and decorations include Ranger Tab, Parachutist Badge, Army Achievement Medal (with Oak Leaf Cluster), Army Commendation Medal (with 3 Oak Leaf Clusters), Meritorious Service Medal (with 3 Oak Leaf Clusters), Defense Meritorious Service Medal, Bronze Star, Legion of Merit (with 2 Oak Leaf Clusters), Defense Superior Service Medal, Army Distinguished Service Medal (with Oak Leaf Cluster), Defense Distinguished Service Medal; hon. doctorate in Public Service (The Coll. of William & Mary). *Address:* International Security Assistance Force (ISAF) Headquarters, Kabul, Afghanistan; Media Operations Center, NATO Headquarters, Blvd Leopold III, 1110 Brussels, Belgium; e-mail moc.web@hq.nato.int; internet www.nato.int/isaf.

**MAGSI, Nawab Zulfikar Ali;** Pakistani politician and government official; *Governor of Balochistan;* b. 14 Feb. 1954, Jhal Magsi, Balochistan. *Education:* Aitchison Coll., Lahore. *Career:* current Nawab (Chief) of Magsi Tribe; first came to politics in 1977, won seat in prov. ass. as ind. cand.; served in numerous prov. ministries, also worked in Home Ministry 1990s; mem. Pakistan People's Party; Chief Minister of Balochistan Prov. in Govt of Benazir Bhutto May–July

1993, Oct. 1993–96; stood as ind. cand. from his native PB-32 Jhal Magsi constituency and won without opposition Feb. 2008; Gov. of Balochistan 2008–. *Address:* Governor House, Quetta, Balochistan, Pakistan; tel. (81) 9202170; fax (81) 9202178; e-mail info@balochistan.gov.pk; internet www .balochistan.gov.pk.

**MAHATO, Rajendra;** Nepalese politician; *Chairman, Sadbhavana Party. Career:* Nepal Sadbhavana Party (NSP) cand. for Sarlahi-2 constituency in parl. election 1994, won seat 1999; broke away from NSP and formed own party, called Sadbhavana Party 2007, Chair. 2007–; Minister for Industry, Commerce and Supply 2007–08; resgnd from interim Parl. Jan. 2008; won Sarlahi-4 seat in Constituent Ass. election April 2008. *Address:* Sadbhavana Party, Kathmandu, Nepal.

**MAHINDRA, Keshub,** BSc, CIMgt; Indian business executive; *Chairman, Mahindra & Mahindra Ltd;* b. 9 Oct. 1923, Simla; m. Sudha Y. Varde 1956; three d. *Education:* Wharton Business School, Univ. of Pennsylvania, USA. *Career:* joined Mahindra and Mahindra Ltd 1947, Chair. 1963–; Chair. Housing and Urban Devt Corpn Ltd 1971–75, Indian Inst. of Man., Ahmedabad 1975–85, India Nominating Cttee "Single Nation Programme", Eisenhower Exchange Fellowships, USA 1998–2005; Pres. Asscn of Indian Automobile Mfrs 1964–65, Bombay Chamber of Commerce and Industry 1966–67, Assoc. Chamber of Commerce and Industry 1969–70, MVIRDC, World Trade Center 1978–95, Employers' Fed. of India 1985–97, Indo-American Soc. 1991–92; mem. Bd Govs Mahindra United World Coll. of India; Dir Bombay Dyeing and Mfg Co. Ltd, Bombay Burmah Trading Corpn Ltd, Tata Iron and Steel Co. Ltd, Tata Chemicals Ltd, Housing Devt Finance Corpn Ltd (now Vice-Chair.), United World Coll. Int. Ltd, UK, Mahindra Ugine Steel Co. Ltd (now Chair.), Infrastructure Leasing & Financial Services Ltd, etc.; mem. Apex Advisory Council of Assoc. Chambers of Commerce and Industry of India, Int. Council Asia Soc. New York, USA 1983–97; Pres. Centre for Research in Rural and Industrial Devt, Chandigarh, Governing Council, Univ. of Pennsylvania Inst. for Advanced Study of India, New Delhi; Pres. Emer., Employers' Fed. of India; Vice-Pres. Nat. Soc. for Clean Cities; Chair. Mahindra Foundation, Bombay First, Health and Environment Cttee, Bd Trustees, Population First; Chair. and Founder Trustee, Bombay City Policy Research Foundation; Chair. and Trustee, K.C. Mahindra Educ. Trust; Founding mem., Indo-Hellenic Friendship League, Governing Council, Integrated Research and Action for Devt (IRADe), New Delhi; mem. Foundation Bd, Int. Man. Inst., Geneva 1984–89, Prime Minister's Council on Trade and Industry, Governing Body of HelpAge India 2000–04, Governing Body/ Bd Govs of Bharat Shiksha Kosh 2002–05, Governing Bd United Way of Mumbai, Bombay First, Int. Advisory Bd Univ. of Pennsylvania Center for Advanced Study of India, Philadelphia; Hon. Fellow, All India Man. Asscn 1990; Hon. mem. Business Advisory Council, IFC, Washington 1986–96, Rotary Club of Bombay; Chevalier Légion d'honneur 1987; Giants Int. Business Leadership Award 1972–82, NIF-Mody Enterprises Man of the Year Award 1980, Madras Man. Asscn Business Leadership Award 1983, Business India Indian Businessman of the Year 1989, Rotary Award for Vocational Excellence 1992, Shiromani Award 1992, Rashtra Bhushan Award, FIE Foundation 1993, Vikas Jyoti Award for Outstanding Services, Contribs and Achievements 1993, Sir Jengahir Ghandy Medal for Industrial Peace, XLRI, Jemshedpur 1994, Rotary Vocational Excellence Award in the Field of Industry 1996, IMC Diamond Jubilee Endowment Trust Award 1998, Motorindia Automan Award 2000, Dadabhai Naoroji Int. Award for Excellence and Lifetime Achievement 2000, All India Man. Asscn Lifetime Achievement Award for Man. 2003, Award from Overdrive for Excellence in Indian Automotive Hall of Pride 2004, Inst of Compnay Secs of India Lifetime Achievement Award for Excellence in corp Governance 2004, Qimpro Platinum Standard – Statesman for Quality – Business Award 2005. *Address:* Mahindra & Mahindra Ltd, Gateway Building, Apollo Bundee, Mumbai 400 001; St Helen's Court, Pedder Road, Mumbai 400 026, India; tel. (22) 22875488; (22) 23514206; fax (22) 22875489; e-mail mahindra.keshub@mahindra.com; internet www .mahindraworld.com.

**MAJEED, Gen. Tariq,** MA; Pakistani army officer; *Chairman, Joint Chiefs of Staff Committee;* b. Aug. 1950, Lahore. *Education:* Command and Staff Coll., Quetta, Malaysian Armed Forces Staff Coll., Kuala Lumpur, Asia-Pacific Center for Security Studies, Honolulu, Hawaii, Nat. Defence Coll., Islamabad. *Career:* commissioned in Pakistan Army (Infantry, Baloch Regt) 1971, has commanded Light Anti-Tank Unit and an Infantry Bn, two Infantry Brigades, Infantry Div., participated in Indo-Pakistan War 1971, took part, as GOC Lahore in absence of Corps Commdr, in counter-coup launched by army high command against then govt of Mian Nawaz Sharif Oct. 1999, also led mil. operation on Jamia Hafsa, Dir Gen. Mil. Intelligence 2001–03, promoted to Lt-Gen. Dec. 2003, Chief of Gen. Staff 2003–06, Commdr 10 Corps, Rawalpindi 2006–07, in charge of armed forces who took down armed militias stationed inside mosque at Lal Masjid Siege 2007, promoted to four-star Gen. Oct. 2007, Chair. Jt Chiefs of Staff Cttee Oct. 2007–; Hilal-e-Imtiaz (Mil.), Nishan-e-Imtiaz (Mil.). *Address:* Joint Chiefs of Staff Committee, Joint Staff Headquarters, Chaklala, Rawalpindi, Pakistan.

**MAJOR, Air Chief Marshal Fali Homi;** Indian air force officer; *Chief of the Air Staff;* b. 29 May 1947, Secunderabad; m. Zareen Major; one s. one d. *Education:* Wesley High School, Secunderabad, Nat. Defence Coll., Army War Coll. *Career:* commissioned in Indian Air Force (IAF) 1967, has flown over 7,000 hours on Sentinel, T-6G, Mi-4, Mi-8 and Mi-17 helicopters, as Wing Commdr, commanded IAF's first Mi-17 Squadron, which operated at Siachen Glacier (world's highest battlefield), as Group Capt., commanded another Mi-17 Squadron, leading it during operations of Indian Peace Keeping Force in Sri Lanka, as Station Commdr of Air Force Station Sarsawa, led rescue of 11 passengers from stranded cable car at resort in Himachal Pradesh, has held several important staff and field appointments, including Jt Dir (Helicopter Operations) and Dir Operations (Transport & Helicopter), Air Officer Commdg Leh (Ladakh) following Kargil conflict 1999, promoted to rank of Air Vice-Marshal 2002, Asst Chief of the Air Staff (Personnel Airmen & Civilians) at Air HQ 2002–04, promoted to rank of Air Marshal 2004, Deputy Chief of Integrated Defence Staff (Operations), HQ Integrated Defence Staff 2004–05, directed relief, rescue and rehabilitation operations of Indian Armed Forces in India and abroad in aftermath of tsunami of Dec. 2004, Air Officer C-in-C Eastern Air Command 2005–07, Chief of the Air Staff 2007–; Vayu Sena Medal (Gallantry), Shaurya Chakra for gallantry, Ati Vishist Seva Medal 2002, Param Vishisht Seva Medal 2006. *Address:* Public Relations Officer, Indian Air Force, Directorate of Public Relations, Ministry of Defence, Room No. 91, South Block, New Delhi, 110 011, India; tel. (11) 23019745; (11) 23010231 (ext. 6903); e-mail pro_iaf2006@yahoo.co.in; internet indianairforce.nic .in.

**MALIK, Iftikhar Ali,** BA; Pakistani business executive; *CEO, Guard Group of Industries;* b. 30 Dec. 1944, Lahore. *Education:* FC Coll., Lahore. *Career:* currently CEO Guard Group (autofilter, brake lining and brake oil mfrs); Chair. Pakistan Automobile Spare Parts Importers and Dealers Asscn 1985–86; mem. Exec. Cttee Lahore Chamber of Commerce and Industry 1980, Pres. 1990; Vice-Pres. and Zonal Chair. Fed. of Pakistan Chambers of Commerce and Industry 1994–97, Pres. and Life Mem. 2001–02; Life Mem. SAARC Chamber of Commerce and Industry (currently Vice-Chair.), Indo–Pak Chamber of Commerce and Industry; Mem. Man. Cttee, ECO Chamber of Commerce and Industry; Chair. Punjab Olympic Asscn; Vice-Chair. Mumtaz Bakhtawar Trust Hosps; Special Lifetime Mem. Confed. of Asia Pacific Chambers of Commerce and Industry; Vice-Chair. Pakistan Olympic Asscn. *Address:* Guard Group of Industries, 80 Badami Bagh, POB 465, Lahore; 57-FCC, Gulberg III, Lahore, Pakistan; tel. (42) 7725616; (42) 5757996; fax (42) 7722627; e-mail guard@brain.net.pk; internet www.mbmt.org.

**MALIK, Shahid,** MA; Pakistani diplomatist; *High Commissioner to India;* m. Ghazala Malik. *Career:* joined Foreign Service Acad. 1972, worked as section officer, Ministry of Foreign Affairs; fmr directing staff mem. Lahore Civil Services Acad.; Deputy High Commr, New Delhi 1992–95, High Commr to India 2006–; served as Political Affairs Counsellor, Washington, DC, also postings to embassies in Tokyo and Rome; Dir-Gen. and Additional Foreign Sec., Ministry of Foreign Affairs 2001–02; High Commr to Canada 2002–06 (also accred to Guyana 2003–06). *Address:* High Commission of Pakistan, 2/50g Shanti Path, Chanakyapuri, New Delhi 110 021, India; tel. (11) 26110601; fax (11) 26872339; e-mail pakhc@nda.vsnl.net.in.

**MANANDHAR, Krishna Bahadur,** MA; Nepalese central banker; *Chairman and Acting Governor, Nepal Rastra Bank (Central Bank). Education:* Tribhuvan Univ., Univ. of Manchester, UK. *Career:* Research Officer, Centre for Econ. Devt and Admin, Kathmandu 1973; Section Officer, Planning Comm. 1973–74; served as Asst Research Officer, Asst Controller, later Deputy Chief Controller at Nepal Rastra Bank (Cen. Bank), Exec. Dir Foreign Exchange Dept *c.* 2003, Deputy Gov. Nepal Rastra Bank –2007, Chair., Acting Gov. and Chair. Man. Cttee 2007–; mem. Bd of Dirs Rastriya Banijya Bank 1998–99, Nepal Arab Bank 1999–; Trustee and mem. Senate, Kathmandu Univ. *Address:* Nepal Rastra Bank, Central Office, Baluwatar, PO Box 73, Kathmandu, Nepal; tel. (1) 4412963; fax (1) 4410159; e-mail gsd@nrb.org.np; internet www.nrb.org.np.

**MANGAL, Mohammad Gulab;** Afghan politician; *Governor, Helmand Province;* b. Paktika Prov. *Career:* fmr UN worker; fmr Loya Jirga (grand council) Del. from Paktia Prov.; Gov. of Paktika Prov. 2004–06, of Laghman Prov. 2006–08, of Helmand Prov. 2008–. *Address:* Office of the Governor, Lashkhar Gah, Helmand Province, Afghanistan.

**MANIK, K. D. Ahmed;** Maldivian government official; *Commissioner of Elections. Career:* Deputy Minister of Environment and Construction –2005; Commr of Elections and Registrar of Political Parties 2005–. *Address:* Office of the Commissioner of Elections, PA Complex, 3rd Floor, Hilaalee Magu, Malé, Maldives; tel. 3324426; fax 3323997; e-mail info@elections.gov.mv; internet www.elections.gov.mv.

**MANIKU, M. U.;** Maldivian business executive. *Career:* Founder-Chair. Universal Enterprises Pvt. Ltd; fmr Special Econ. Adviser to the Pres.; Chair. Maldives Asscn of Tourism Industry. *Address:* Maldives Association of Tourism Industry, Gadhamoo Building, 3rd Floor, Henveyru, Malé, Maldives; tel. 3326640; fax 3326641; e-mail mati@dhivehinet.net.mv.

**MANSHA, Mian Mohammad;** Pakistani industrialist; *Chairman, Nishat Group; Career:* Chair. Nishat Group, conglomerate with interests in banking, insurance, textiles and cement, including Muslim Commercial Bank, Nishat Mills, D. G. Khan Cement. *Address:* Nishat Chunian, 31-Q, Gulberg II, Lahore 54660, Pakistan; tel. (42) 5761730; fax (42) 5878696; e-mail info@nctex.com; internet www.nctex.com.

**MANWANI, Harish,** BA, MA; Indian business executive; *Chairman, Hindustan Unilever Limited;* m.; two d. *Education:* Mumbai Univ., Advanced Man. Program, Harvard Business School, USA. *Career:* joined Hindustan Lever Ltd (HLL) in 1976, Div. Vice-Pres. Marketing, Detergents 1995, mem. Bd as Dir for Personal Products 1995, also held regional responsibility for Cen. Asia and Middle East Business Group, moved to UK as Sr Vice-Pres. (Global Hair Care and Oral Care) and Exec. Vice-Pres. Latin America Business Group 2000–01, Pres. (Home and Personal Care), Latin America Business Group 2001–04, also served as Chair. Unilever's Latin America Advisory Council, Pres. and CEO (Home and Personal Care), N America Business Group 2004–05, joined Unilever Exec. as Pres. Asia and Africa 2005–, also Chair. (non-exec.) HLL 2005–; mem. Exec. Bd Indian School of Business. *Address:* Hindustan Lever Ltd, Hindustan Lever House, 165/166 Backbay Reclamation, Mumbai 400 020, India; tel. (22) 3983-0000; fax (22) 2287-1970; e-mail webmaster@unilever.com; internet www.hll.com.

**MARAPANE, Tilak Janaka;** Sri Lankan politician. *Career:* fmr Attorney-Gen.; Minister of Defence and of Transport, Highways and Aviation 2001–04. *Address:* c/o Ministry of Defence, 15/5 Baladaksha Mawatha, POB 572, Colombo 3, Sri Lanka.

**MASOUD, Ahmad Wali,** MA; Afghan diplomatist and politician; *Leader, Nizat-i Melli-i Afghanistan (National Movement of Afghanistan);* b. 1 Nov. 1964, Kabul; brother of the late Ahmed Shah Masoud, leader of Northern Alliance mil. forces in Afghanistan, and of Ahmad Zia Masoud; m. Beheshta Masoud; three d. *Education:* Muslim Public School, Peshawar, Pakistan, Mid-Cornwall Coll. of Further Educ., Polytechnic of Cen. London and Westminster Univ., UK. *Career:* Foreign News Reporter, Times Newspaper 1989; Ed. Ariana News Bulletin 1989–1992; Rep. Jamiat-i Islami (Islamic Soc.), main political faction in Afghanistan, fighting Russian occupation 1989–92; Second Sec., Embassy of Afghanistan, London 1992, First Sec. and Chargé d'affaires a.i. 1993, Minister Counsellor and Chargé d'affaires a.i. 1993–2003, Amb. to UK 2003–07; currently Leader, Nizat-i Melli-i Afghanistan (Nat. Movt of Afghanistan), Kabul. *Address:* Nizat-i Melli-i Afghanistan, Kabul, Afghanistan.

**MASOUD, Ahmad Zia;** Afghan diplomatist and politician; *First Vice-President;* b. 1 May 1956, brother of the late Ahmad Shah Masoud and Ahmad Wali Masoud. *Education:* Lycée Esteqlal and Kabul Polytechnic Inst. *Career:* mem. Shora-e-Nizar Movt; Amb. to Russian Fed. (non-resident Envoy to Moldova, Armenia, Azerbaijan, Georgia and Belarus), Moscow 2002–04; First Vice-Pres. 2004–. *Address:* c/o Office of the President, Gul Khana Palace, Presidential Palace, Kabul, Afghanistan; e-mail president@afghanistangov.org; internet www.president.gov.af.

**MAYAWATI, Kumari,** BA, BEd, LLB; Indian lawyer and politician; *Chief Minister of Uttar Pradesh and President, Bahujan Samaj Party;* b. 15 Jan. 1956, Badalpur, Gautam Budh Nagar Dist, UP. *Education:* Delhi Univ., Meerut Univ. *Career:* Chief Minister of UP (first Dalit Chief Minister of an Indian state) 1995, 1997, 2002–03, 2007–; Pres. Bahujan Samaj Party 2003–; fmr mem. Legis. Ass. UP 1996–; mem. UP Legis. Council 2007–; fmr mem. Parl. (Lok Sabha); currently mem. Parl. (Rajya Sabha); several honours and awards. *Publications:* Bahujan Samaj Aur Uski Rajniti (Hindi version) 2000, (English version) 2001, Bahujan Movement Ka Safarnama (two vols) 2006. *Address:* Office of the Chief Minister, Government of Uttar Pradesh, Suchna Bhawan, Park Road, Lucknow, 226001; C-57, Indrapuri, New Delhi, 110012; 13A Mall Avenue, Lucknow, 226001, India; tel. (11) 2621122; fax (11) 2239401; e-mail upinformation@gmail.com; internet www.upgov.nic.in.

**MAZUMDAR-SHAW, Kiran,** BSc; Indian business executive; *Chairman and Managing Director, Biocon India Ltd;* b. 23 March 1953, Bangalore; m. John Shaw 1997. *Education:* Bishop Cotton Girls School, Mount Carmel Coll., Bangalore, Bangalore Univ., Ballarat Coll., Melbourne Univ., Australia. *Career:* trainee Brewer, Carlton & United Breweries, Melbourne and trainee Maltster, Barrett Bros & Burston, Australia 1975–77; Brewery Consultant, Jupiter Breweries Ltd, Calcutta (now Kolkata) 1975–76; Tech. Man. Standard Malting Corpn, Baroda 1976; Trainee Man. Biocon Ltd, Cork, Repub. of Ireland 1978; Chair. and Man. Dir Biocon India Ltd 1978–; Dir Pharmacia United Ltd, Bangalore 1987–94; Chair. Syngene Int., Bangalore 1994–; Chair. Clinigene Int., Bangalore 2000–; mem. Bd Bio-Ventures for Global Health; Chair. and Mission Leader Confed. of Indian Industries Nat. Task Force on Biotechnology; Council mem. Basic Chemicals, Pharmaceuticals and Cosmetics Export Promotion Council 1983–; Vice-Pres. Asscn of Women Entrepreneurs of Karnataka (AWAKE) 1983–89, Indo-American Chamber of Commerce, Bangalore 1986–87; mem. Prime Minister's Council on Trade and Industry in India, Confed. of Indian Industries, Greater Mysore Chamber of Industries, Advisory Cttee, Dept of Biotechnology, Young Presidents' Org., Research Council, CFTRI, Bangalore Agenda Task Force, Bd of Science Foundation, Ireland; mem. Bd Govs ndian Inst. of Man. Bangalore; Trustee Karnataka Chitrakala Parishat; Chair. All India Art Exhbn; participated in various int. seminars; Padma Shri 1989, Padma Bhushan 2005; Hon. DSc (Ballarat) 2004; Dr hc (Manipal Acad. of Higher Educ.) 2005; Gold Award for Best Woman Entrepreneur, Inst. of Marketing Man. 1982, AWAKE Outstanding Contrib. Award 1983, Rotary Award for Best Model Employer 1983, Jaycees Outstanding Young Person Award 1987, Int. Women's Asscn (Chennai) Woman of the Year 1998–99, Nat. Award for Best Small Industry, Sir M. Visveswaraya Memorial Award, Fed. of Karnataka Chambers of Commerce and Industry 2002, Rajyotsava Award 2002, Ernst & Young Entrepreneur of the Year Award in Healthcare and Life Sciences Category 2002, Australian Alumni High Achiever Award, IDP Australian Alumni Asscn 2003, Whirlpool GR8 Women Award for Science and Tech. 2004, The Economic Times Business Woman of the Year Award 2004, Indian Chamber of Commerce Lifetime Achievement Award 2005, ranked by Fortune magazine amongst 50 Most Powerful Women in Business outside the US (44th) 2005, (48th) 2006, (50th) 2007. *Publication:* Ale and Arty. *Address:* Biocon India Ltd, 20th K M, Hosur Road, Electronic City, Bangalore, 560100 India; tel. (80) 28082808; fax (80) 28523423; e-mail contact.us@biocon.com; internet www.biocon.com.

**MEHTA, Adm. Sureesh;** Indian naval officer; *Chief of Naval Staff and Chairman, Joint Chiefs of Staff Committee;* b. 18 Aug. 1947; m. Maria Teresa Mehta; two c. *Education:* Nat. Defence Acad., Defence Services Staff Coll., Wellington, Nat. Defence Coll., New Delhi. *Career:* commissioned in Indian Navy 1967, joined Fleet Air Arm and flew Sea Hawk jet fighters from carrier INS Vikrant 1967, carried out instructional duties as Directing Staff in Defence Services Staff Coll., earlier appointments included command of frigate INS Beas and guided missile frigate INS Godavari, also commanded Naval Air Stations, INS Garuda, C-in-C Eastern Naval Command 2005–06, other operational Flag appointments have included Flag Officer Naval Aviation, Fleet Commdr Western Fleet during Kargil Crisis 1999, has held various staff appointments in Flag rank at New Delhi, including Asst Controller Carrier Projects, Asst Chief of Personnel (Human Resources Devt), Controller of Personnel Services, Chief of Personnel, Dir-Gen. Coast Guard, Deputy Chief of Naval Staff, Chief of Naval Staff 2006–, currently Chair. Jt Chiefs of Staff Cttee; Ati Vishist Seva Medal 1995, Param Vishist Seva Medal 2005. *Address:* Office of the Chief of Naval Staff, Integrated Headquarters of Ministry of Defence (Navy), Sena Bhawan, New Delhi, 110 0111, India; e-mail webmasterindiannavy@nic.in; internet indiannavy.nic.in.

**MENON, Raghu;** Indian civil servant, government official and airline executive; *Chairman and Managing Director, Air-India Ltd. Career:* officer of Indian Admin. Service of Assam-Nagaland cadre 1974, served in Ministry of Information and Broadcasting, apptd Jt Sec., Ministry of Civil Aviation 2002, Special Sec. and Financial Advisor –2008, Chair. and Man. Dir Air-India Ltd (state-owned airline merged with Indian airline under Nat. Aviation Co. of India Ltd) 2008–. *Address:* Air-India Ltd, 3rd Floor, Tower-II, Jeevan Bharati 124, Connaught Circus, New Delhi, 110 001, India; tel. (11) 23731225; e-mail info@home.airindia.in; internet home .airindia.in.

**MIRZA, Fehmida,** MB BS; Pakistani politician, physician and business executive; *Speaker, National Assembly;* b. 20 Dec. 1956, Karachi; m. Zulfikar Ali Mirza; two s. two d. *Education:* Liaquat Medical Coll., Jamshoro. *Career:* physician at MCH Centre, then School Health Centre 1983–89; Dir Mirza Sugar Mills 1989–99, CEO 1999–; mem. Nat. Ass. representing Badin 1997–, Speaker 2008–; mem. Pakistan People's Party. *Address:* Office of the Speaker, National Assembly of Pakistan, Parliament House, Islamabad, Pakistan; tel. (51) 9221082; fax (51) 9221106; internet www.na.gov.pk.

**MISTRY, Pallonji;** Indian construction industry executive; *Chairman, Shapoorji Pallonji Group;* b. 1 June 1929; m.; four c. *Career:* fmr Chair. Forbes Gokak –2003, Associated Cement Cos Ltd –2004; currently Chair. Shapoorji Pallonji Group; largest individual shareholder in Tata Sons (holding co.); Hon. Mem. World Zarathushti Chamber of Commerce 2004. *Address:* Shapoorji Pallonji & Co. Ltd, Shapoorji Pallonji Centre, 41/44 Minoo Desai Marg, Colaba, Mumbai 400005, India; tel. (22) 67490263; fax (22) 66338176; internet www .shapoorji.com.

**MITTAL, Som,** BEng; Indian engineer and computer industry executive; *President, National Association of Software and Services Companies;* b. 7 Feb. 1952. *Education:* Indian Inst. of Tech., Kanpur, Indian Inst. of Man., Ahmedabad. *Career:* has worked for Larsen & Toubro, Escorts and Compaq; set up SRF Ltd jt venture; worked for Wipro Infotech, CEO Business Solutions Div. 1993–94; fmr Pres. and CEO Digital Equipment (India) Ltd, Bangalore; Head of Services Business for Asia-Pacific and Japan region, Hewlett-Packard –2007; Vice-Chair. Nat. Asscn of Software and Services Cos (NASSCOM), Chair. 2003–04, Pres. 2008–; mem. Nat. Council and fmr Chair. Confed. of Indian Industry; mem. Exec. Council and past Pres. (South) Mfrs Asscn of Information Tech.; mem. Chief Minister's Task Force (Govt of Karnataka), Governing Council Indian Inst. of Information Tech.; Founder-mem. Bd of Educ. Standards. *Address:* NASSCOM, 607, 5th Floor, Oxford Towers, Airport Road, Kodihalli, Bangalore, 560 008, India; tel. (80) 41151705 (ext. 706); fax (80) 41151707; e-mail president@nasscom.in; internet www.nasscom.in.

**MITTAL, Sunil Bharti;** Indian telecommunications executive; *Chairman and Group Managing Director, Bharti Enterprises;*m.; two s. one d. *Education:* Punjab Univ., Harvard Univ., USA. *Career:* Founder Bharti Enterprises 1976–, Dir 1995–, Chair. and Group Man. Dir 2001–; Chair. Indo-US Jt Business Council; mem. Nat. Council of Confed. of Indian Industry, Fed. of Indian Chambers of Commerce and Industry; Hon. Consul of Seychelles, Hon. Fellow Inst. of Electronics and Telecommunication Engineers of India; Padma Bhushan 2007; Hon. DSc (Govind Ballabh Pant Univ. of Agric. and Tech.); Communication World Telecom Man of the Year 1997, Business India Businessman of the Year 2002, GSM Asscn Chairman's Award 2008. *Address:* Bharti Tele-Ventures Ltd, Qutab Ambience (at Qutab Minar), Mehrauli Road, New Delhi 110 030, India; tel. (11) 41666000; fax (11) 41666011; e-mail corpcomm@bharti.com; internet www.airtel.in.

**MODI, Narendra Damodardas,** MA; Indian politician; *Chief Minister of Gujarat;* b. Sept. 1950, Vadnagar, Mehsana Dist. *Education:* Gujarat Univ. *Career:* mem. Nava Nirman Andolan movt 1972–77; joined Bharatiya Janata Party 1986, Gen. Sec. for Gujarat 1988, elected to Ass. 1995, Nat. Sec., Delhi 1995, re-elected in Gujarat 1998, Gen. Sec. for Himachal Pradesh, the Punjab and Haryana 1998–2001, Nat. Gen. Sec. 1999–; Chief Minister of Gujarat 2001–03, 2003–. *Publications include:* Sangharsha ma Gujarat (Gujarat under Struggle), Setu Bandh, Patra Roop Guruji. *Address:* Office of the Chief Minister, Block No. 1, 5th Floor, New Sachivalaya, Ganghinagar, 382 010, Gujarat, India; tel. (79) 23232611; (79) 23232601; fax (79) 23222101; (79) 23222020; e-mail cm@ gujaratindia.com; internet www.gujaratindia.com.

**MOHAMMAD, Haji Din;** Afghan provincial governor and fmr rebel leader; *Governor of Kabul Province. Career:* fmr mem. Yunus Khalis faction, Hizb-i Islami; fmr Mujahidin commdr; Gov. Nangarhar Prov. 2002–05, Kabul Prov. 2005–. *Address:* Office of the Governor, Kabul, Afghanistan.

**MOHAMMED, Gen. Atta;** Afghan military commander; *Governor of Balkh Province;* b. 1965, Qalander Shah Colony, Mazar e Sharif; m. 1992; six c. *Education:* Bakhter High School and at univ. in Tajikistan. *Career:* fought Soviet occupation in Mazar-i-Sharif as Mujahed mil. officer under the command of Ustad Zabiullah 1980s, following assassination of Ustad Zabiullah was selected as Deputy Commdr of Mujahed forces that belonged to Zabiullah 1987; his forces captured Balkh from forces of communist govt 1993; rank of Lt-Gen. 1993; apptd Chief of Politics and Mil. of Jamiat e Mili Islami (Islamic Soc.) and mem. High Comm. of Islamic Govt of Afghanistan 1993; apptd Commdr 7th Army Corps 1994; led troops to recapture northern provs 2001; promoted to Gen. 2002; Gov. of Balkh Prov. 2004–; Medal of Educ., Ministry of Educ., Shining Star of Educ., Educ. Presidency, title of Man of Peace, Univ. of Mazar e Sharif, honoured by Ministry of Information, Culture and Tourism and by Ministry of Women's Affairs, numerous other honours and awards. *Address:* Office of the Governor, Mazar-i-Sharif, Balkh Province, Afghanistan; tel. (70) 500500 (mobile); fax +873763036469; e-mail The_Balkh_Government@yahoo.com.

**MOHAQQEQ, Haji Mohammad;** Afghan politician and fmr rebel leader; *Founder and Leader, Hizb-i Wahdat-i Islami Mardum-i Afghanistan (People's Islamic Unity Party of Afghanistan);* b. Charkent Dist, Balkh Prov. *Education:* Mazar-e-Sharif. *Career:* Chair. Political Cttee and Admin. of Northern Areas, Hizb-i-Wahdat-i Islami (Islamic Unity Party); fmr Minister of the Interior; led several attacks against Taliban Govt; Minister of Planning, Interim Govt 2001–04; presidential cand. 2004; Founder and Leader Hizb-i Wahdat-i Islami Mardum-i Afghanistan (People's Islamic Unity Party of Afghanistan); Deputy Chair. Jabahai Tafahim Millie (Nat. Understanding Front); mem. Hazara community. *Address:* Hizb-i Wahdat-i Islami Mardum-i Afghanistan, Kabul, Afghanistan.

**MOHSIN, Selina;** Bangladeshi educationalist, academic and diplomatist; *High Commissioner to the Maldives. Education:* various degrees and postgraduate diplomas and sr officer training from univs and int. insts in USA, France and UK. *Career:* joined Educ. Service of the then East Pakistan 1970; Chief Educ. Officer, Commonwealth Secr., London, UK 1990s; Sr Educ. Adviser to Programme Support Unit, Canadian Int. Devt Agency –2008; High Commr to the Maldives 2008–. *Address:* Bangladesh High Commission, M. Kurinbee Lodge, 5th Floor, Izzudheen Magu, Malé, Maldives; tel. 3315541; fax 3315543; e-mail bdootmal@dhivehinet.net.mv.

**MOJADDEDI, Sibghatullah;** Afghan religious leader and politician; *Speaker, Meshrano Jirga; Leader, Jebha-i-Nejat-i-Melli;* b. 1929. *Education:* Al-Azhar Univ., Cairo, Egypt. *Career:* imprisoned for involvement in plot to assassinate Soviet Prime Minister Nikita Krushchev 1959–64; f. Jami'at Ulamai Mohammadi (Org. of Muslim Clergy) 1972; f. Jebha-i-Nejat-i-Melli Afghanistan (Nat. Liberation Front of Afghanistan) 1979, Leader 1979–; acting Pres. Unity Govt 1992; Head Govt of Mujaheddin Council, Kabul 1992–94; currently Speaker, Meshrano Jirga (House of Elders). *Address:* Jebha-i-Nejat-i-Melli (National Liberation Front), Pashtun, Afghanistan.

**MOQBEL, Zarar Ahmad;** Afghan politician; *Minister of Interior Affairs. Career:* Deputy Minister of Interior Affairs –Sept. 2005, Acting Minister of Interior Affairs Sept. 2005–March 2006, Minister of Interior Affairs March 2006–. *Address:* Ministry of Interior Affairs, Shar-i-Nau, Kabul, Afghanistan; tel. (93) 32441.

**MUKERJEA, Pratim (Peter),** MBA; British/Indian broadcasting executive; *Chief Strategy Officer, INX Media Pvt. Ltd;* b. London, England; m. Indrani Mukerjea; two s. one d. *Education:* business studies, Hatfield, Herts. *Career:* began career with Heinz (UK), later with British Store House and advertising agency O&M (UK office); fmr Regional Group Account Dir, DDB Needham Advertising, Hong Kong; fmr Account Dir, Ogilvy & Mather, New Delhi and London; Sales Dir (Hong Kong, later India and Middle East) Star TV 1993–97, Exec. Vice-Pres. 1997–99, CEO Star India 1999–2007; Co-founder, with his wife, and Chief Strategy Officer INX Media Pvt. Ltd 2007–; mem. Bd Dirs ESPN STAR Sports, Hathway, Media Content and Communications Services (India) for Star News. *Address:* INX Media Pvt. Ltd, INX House, Dr Dadasaheb Bhadkamkar Marg, Grant Road (E), Mumbai 400 007, India; tel. (22) 66019999; fax (22) 66019898; e-mail inxmediainfo@inxtv.in; internet www.inxnetwork.in.

**MUKHERJEE, Pranab Kumar,** LLB, MA; Indian politician; *Minister of External Affairs;* b. 11 Dec. 1935, Kirnahar, Birbhum Dist, W Bengal; m.; two s. one d. *Education:* Univ. of Calcutta. *Career:* started career as lecturer; Ed. Palli-O-Panchayat Sambad (Bengali monthly); Founder-Ed. Desher Dak (Bengali weekly) 1967–71; mem. Rajya Sabha 1969–, Leader 1980–88; Deputy Minister of Industrial Devt, Govt of India 1973; Deputy Minister for Shipping and Transport Jan.–Oct. 1974; Minister of State, Ministry of Finance 1974–75; Minister for Revenue and Banking 1975–77; Minister of Commerce 1980–82, of Finance Jan.–Sept. 1982, 1982–85, of Commerce 1993–95, of External Affairs 1995–96, of Defence 2004–06, of External Affairs 2006–; Deputy Chair. Planning Comm. with Cabinet rank; f. Rashtriya Samajwadi Congress 1987–; mem. Exec. Cttee Congress (I) Party 1972–73, All India Congress Cttee 1986; Treas. Congress (I) Party, mem. Working Cttee, Deputy Leader in Rajya Sabha; Pres. W Bengal Pradesh Congress Cttee; Hon. DLitt. *Publications:* Bangla Congress: An Aspect of Constitutional Problems in Bengal 1967, Mid-term Election 1969, Off the Track 1987, Challenges Before the Nation 1992. *Address:* Ministry of External Affairs, South Block, New Delhi 110 011; S-22, Greater Kailash-II, New Delhi 110 048; 13 Talkatora Road, New Delhi 110 001, India; 2-A, 1st Floor, 602/7 Kabi Bharti Sarni (Lake Road), Kolkata 700 029; tel. (11) 23011127 (ministry); (11) 3737623; (11) 6474025; (11) 6435656; fax (11) 23011463 (ministry); e-mail pkm@sansad.nic.in; internet meaindia.nic.in.

**MUKHTAR, Chaudhry Ahmed;** Pakistani politician and business executive; *Minister of Defence, with additional charge of Commerce and Textile Industry. Career:* Owner Service Shoe business and several other cos in Pakistan; sr leader of Pakistan People's Party, Gujrat Dist; fmr Minister of Commerce in Govt of Benazir Bhutto 1993–96; mem. Parl. for Gujrat-II 2008–; Minister of Defence, with additional charge of Commerce and Textile Industry 2008–; Chair. Pakistan International Airlines. *Address:* Ministry of Defence, Pakistan Secretariat, No. II, Rawalpindi 46000, Pakistan; tel. (51) 9271107; fax (51) 9271113; e-mail tahir@mod.gov.pk; internet www.mod.gov.pk.

**MUNAVVAR, Mohamed;** Maldivian lawyer; *President, Maldivian Democratic Party. Career:* fmr Attorney-Gen., Repub. of the Maldives; arrested Aug. 2004, transferred to house arrest Oct.–Dec. 2004 (charges withdrawn); legal advisor to Maldivian Democratic Party –2007, Pres. 2007–. *Address:* Maldivian Democratic Party (MDP), 1st Floor, M. Gloryge, Fareedhee Magu, Malé, Maldives; tel. 3340044; fax 3322960; e-mail secretariat@maldiviandemocraticparty.org; internet www.maldiviandemocraticparty.org.

**MUNJAL, Brijmohan Lall;** Indian business executive; *Chairman and Managing Director, Hero Group;* b. 1923, Kamalia, Pakistan. *Career:* started career making bicycle parts; Chair., Man. Dir Hero Group (bicycle manufacturer), Hero Honda Motors Ltd (Honda partner for making motorcycles); Padma Bhushan; Ernst & Young Entrepreneur of the Year Award, Madras Man. Asscn Business Leadership Award 2002. *Address:* Hero Honda Motors Ltd, 34 Community Centre, Basant Lok, Vasant Vihar, New Delhi 110057, India; tel. (11) 26142451; fax (11) 26143321; internet www.herohonda.com.

**MURSHED, Yasmeen,** BA, MA; Bangladeshi educationalist, business executive and diplomatist; *High Commissioner to Pakistan;* b. 19 May 1945, Calcutta, India; grand-d. of Khawaja Shahabuddin, fmr Prime Minister of Pakistan; m. Syed Tanweer Murshed (died 1988); one s. one d. *Education:* Viqarunnisa Noon School, Dhaka, Univ. of the Punjab, Pakistan. *Career:* began career in educ. as a teacher in various insts, including Karachi Grammar School, Islamabad Model School for Girls, Govt Coll. for Women, Islamabad 1967–71; returned to Bangladesh after Liberation and began teaching small groups of students at home 1971; est.

Scholastica Tutorial 1977 (later known as Scholastica), currently Chair. Bd of Man.; Chair. Etcetera Bangladesh (Pvt.) Ltd, Office and Home Solutions (Pvt.) Ltd, Scholastica Transport Services (Pvt.) Ltd, Printcraft Co. Ltd, Services for Professional Educ. and Enterprise Devt; mem. Bd of Dirs United Insurance Co. Ltd, Chittagong Stock Exchange; undertook role in Centre for Analysis and Choice early 1990s; has represented Bangladesh at several int. confs and meetings, participated in Sixth Int. Conf. of the Asscn for Women in Devt, Washington, DC 1993; Founding mem. and first Pres. Asia/Pacific Women in Politics Network; del. to Muslim Women's Conf., Beijing and Beyond: Implementing the Platform for Action in Muslim Societies, Washington, DC 1996, Asscn for Women in Devt Forum, Washington, DC 1996, NDI Conf. on Consolidating the Third Wave Democracies: Trends and Challenges, Taiwan 1995, Global Best Practices with Cambridge, Delhi 2006 and others; writes column on books and writers for The Daily Star; mem. Ascent Educ. Devt Trust (Founder-mem.), Educ., Science, Tech. and Cultural Devt Trust, Standard Chartered-Financial Express Corp. Social Responsibility Trust, Int. Chamber of Commerce (Bangladesh), Commonwealth Soc. of Bangladesh; mem. Jury Bd The Daily Star and DHL Business Awards 2004, DCCI Business Awards 2005. *Publications:* several textbooks on econs and Islamic studies and articles for journals, newspapers and magazines. *Address:* Bangladesh High Commission, House No. 1, Street No. 5, F-6/3, Islamabad, Pakistan; tel. (51) 2279267; fax (51) 2279266; e-mail bdhcisb@dsl.net.pk; internet www.bdhcpk.org.

**MUSHARRAF, Gen. (retd) Pervez;** Pakistani fmr army officer and fmr head of state; b. 11 Aug. 1943, Delhi, India; m. Sehba Farid 1968; one s. one d. *Education:* St Patrick's High School, Karachi, Forman Christian Coll., Lahore, Command and Staff Coll., Quetta, Nat. Defence Coll., Rawalpindi, Royal Coll. of Defence Studies, UK. *Career:* spent early childhood in Turkey 1949–56; joined Pakistan Mil. Acad. 1961; commd in Artillery Regt 1964; fought in 1965 war with India (Imtiazi Sanad Gallantry Award); spent much of mil. career in Special Services Group; Company Commdr Commando Battalion Indo-Pakistan War 1971; Dir-Gen. Mil. Operations, Gen. HQ 1993–95; apptd C-in-C of Pakistani Army Oct. 1998, Chair. Jt Chiefs of Staff Cttee 1999, led mil. coup 1999, Chief of Staff 1999–2007; Chief Exec. Nat. Security Council of Pakistan 1999–2002; Pres. of Pakistan 2001–08 (resgnd). *Publication:* In the Line of Fire: A Memoir 2006. *Address:* c/o Office of the President, Aiwan-e-Sadr, Islamabad, Pakistan.

**NADAR, Shiv;** Indian business executive and electrical engineer; *Chairman and CEO, HCL Group;* b. 1946; m.; one c. *Career:* systems analyst Cooper Eng; Sr Man. Trainee DCM Ltd 1968; f. HCL Overseas (later HCL Consulting, now HCL Technologies) 1991, currently Chair. and CEO HCL Group. *Address:* HCL Infosystems Ltd, E-4, 5, 6 Sector 11, Noida 201 301, Uttar Pradesh, India; tel. (91) 2526518; fax (91) 2550923; e-mail webhost@hcl.in; internet www.hclinfosystems.com.

**NAEEM, Mohamed Monaza;** Maldivian business executive and politician; *Founder and Leader, Maldivian National Congress. Career:* f. Monaza Contracting Co. Pvt. Ltd 1978; MP for Laamu Atoll, Chair. Business Cttee of Special Majlis 2007–; Founder and Leader of Maldivian Nat. Congress 2007; sr mem. People's Asscn. *Address:* Maldivian National Congress, G. Blue Lagoon, 1st Floor, Faashanakilege Magu, Malé, Maldives; tel. 3316944; fax 3348988; e-mail secretariat@mnc.org.mv; internet www.mnc.org.mv; www.monaza.mv.

**NAEEMI, Abdul Jabbar;** Afghan diplomatist, politician and government official; *Governor, Wardak Province. Career:* served as rep. from Kandahar Prov. to Loya Jirga (Grand Ass.); election agent for Hamid Karzai in Pakistan 2004, campaigned for Karzai and worked on educating local Afghans about the democratic process; Gov. Wardak Prov. 2004–; follower of Pashtun spiritual leader Pir Sayed Ahmed Gailani and mem. Gailani's Nat. Islamic Front party. *Address:* Office of the Governor, Maidan Wardak Province, Meydan Shahr, Afghanistan; tel. (793) 31188 (mobile); (702) 27292 (mobile); fax (20) 2201746; e-mail webmaster@ajnaeemi.com; internet ajnaeemi.com.

**NAKANDALA, Amaralal Sumith;** Sri Lankan diplomatist; *Ambassador to Nepal;* m. Dammika Nakandala. *Education:* Univ. of Peradeniya, Inst. of Social Studies, The Hague, Netherlands. *Career:* spent three years at High Comm. in New Delhi, Deputy High Commr for southern India, Chennai 2001–06, Amb. to Nepal 2006–. *Address:* Embassy of Sri Lanka, Chundevi Marg, Maharajung, Kathmandu, Nepal; tel. (1) 4720623; (1) 4721381; fax (1) 4720128; e-mail embassy@srilanka.info.com.np.

**NASEER, Umar;** Maldivian fmr police officer, business executive and politician; *President, Islamic Democratic Party. Education:* English Prep School, Malé. *Career:* conscripted into Nat. Security Service, later sent to Scotland Yard, London, UK for police training, promoted to Sergeant on return, later transferred to Maldives Water Supply Unit; opened fire safety equipment dealership Alarms Pvt. Ltd; cand. in parl. elections for Malé constituency, failed to secure seat; started tour co. Whale Submarine to promote underwater sightseeing, later sold his share of co. to Qasim Ibrahim; Co-founder and Pres. Islamic Democratic Party 2005–. *Address:* Islamic Democratic Party, Malé, Maldives; tel. 3326962; fax 3327385; e-mail info@idp.org.mv; internet www.idp.org.mv.

**NASHEED, Mohamed,** BSc; Maldivian journalist and political activist; b. 17 May 1967, Malé; m. Laila Ali; two d. *Education:* John Moores Univ., Liverpool, UK. *Career:* fmr journalist for Sangu magazine; Dir Safari Tours Maldives 1994–98; mem. Parl. 1999–2001; Dir Oriental Acad. Centre 2001–; Co-founder and mem. Gen. Council, Maldivian Democratic Party (MDP), fmr Chair., MDP presidential cand. 2008; arrested several times for political reasons, adopted as prisoner of conscience by Amnesty Int. 1996; Hon. mem. Int. PEN. *Publications:* Dhagadu Dhahanan: Internal Feuding and Anglo-Dhivehi Relations 1800–1900 1995, Maldives: Historical Overview of Dhivehi Policy, Hithaa Hithuge Gulhuu. *Address:* Maldivian Democratic Party, H. Sharaashaa, 1st Floor, Sosun Magu, Malé 20059; G. Canaray-ge, Malé, Maldives; tel. 3340044; 3342776; fax 3322960; e-mail secretariat@mdp.org.mv; nasheedm@gmail.com; internet www.mdp.org.mv.

**NASHID, Ahmed;** Maldivian business executive. *Career:* Chair. Horizon Fisheries Pvt. Ltd. *Address:* Horizon Fisheries Private Ltd, 3rd Floor, No. 12, Boduthkurufaanu Magu, Malé, Maldives; tel. 3328855; fax 3324455; e-mail info@horizonfisheries.com; internet www.horizonfisheries.com.

**NATH, Kamal,** BCom; Indian politician; *Minister of Commerce and Industry;* b. Nov. 1946, Kanpur; m.; two s. *Education:* Doon School, Dehra Dun, St Xavier's Coll. *Career:* joined Indian Nat. Congress 1968 as youth worker; first elected to Parl. for Chhindwara 1980, re-elected 1985, 1989, 1991, 1998, 1999, 2004; mem. Del. to UN Gen. Ass. 1982–83; apptd Minister of Environment and Forests 1991, later Minister of Textiles; Minister of Commerce and Industry 2004–; Sec.-Gen. Indian Nat. Congress; mem. Congress Working Cttee; Pres. Bd Govs Inst. of Man. Tech.; Chair. Madhya Pradesh Devt Council. *Address:* Ministry of Commerce and Industry, Udyog Bhavan, New Delhi 110 011; No. 1 Tughlak Road, New Delhi 110 011, India; tel. (11) 23016664; (11) 23792233; fax (11) 23014335; (11) 23793396; e-mail cim@ub.nic.in; knath@knath.com; internet www.commin.nic.in.

**NAWAZ SHARIF, Mohammed;** Pakistani politician and industrialist; *President, Pakistan Muslim League—Nawaz (PML—N);* b. 25 Dec. 1949, Lahore; m. 1971; two s. two d. *Education:* Govt Coll. and Punjab Univ. Law Coll., Lahore. *Career:* started work in Ittefaq faction industrial group 1969; Finance Minister, Govt of the Punjab 1981–85, Chief Minister of Punjab 1985–90; Prime Minister of Pakistan 1990–93 (dismissal ruled unconstitutional), resgnd July 1993, Prime Minister 1997–99 (removed in coup), concurrently Minister of Defence and Finance; sentenced to life imprisonment for terrorism and hijacking April 2000; released from imprisonment, went in exile in Jeddah, Saudi Arabia Dec. 2000, allowed to return to Pakistan Aug. 2007; Pres. Pakistan Muslim League, Punjab 1985, Islami Jamhoori Ittehad 1988; Pres. Pakistan Muslim League—Nawaz (PML—N) 2002–. *Address:* Pakistan Muslim League—Nawaz (PML—N), House No. 20-H, Street 10, Sector F-8/3, Islamabad; 180–181-H, Ittefaq Colony, Model Town, Lahore, Pakistan; tel. (51) 2852661; 856069; fax (51) 2852662; e-mail pmlisb@hotmail .com; internet www.pmln.org.pk.

**NEMBANG, Subas Chandra,** BA, BL; Nepalese barrister and politician; *Chairperson, Constituent Assembly;* b. 11 March 1953; m. *Career:* fmr Minister of Law, Justice and Parl. Affairs; fmr mem. Standing Cttee; Leader of Communist Party of Nepal (Unifed Marxist-Leninist—UML), mem. Cen. Cttee; Sr Most Advocate, Supreme Court of Nepal; Speaker of the Interim Parl. ('Legislature-Parl.') –2008, Chair. Security Special Cttee, House of Reps Proclamation Implementation Special Cttee, Business Man. Advisory Cttee, Chair. Constituent Ass. 2008–. *Address:* Office of the Chairperson, Constituent Assembly of Nepal, Kathmandu; Suntalabari-2, Ilam Constituency No. 2, Nepal; tel. (1) 4228459 (constituency); fax (1) 4222923 (constituency; e-mail nparl@ntc.net.np; parliament@ntc.net.np; internet www.parliament.gov.np.

**NEPAL, Madhav Kumar;** Nepalese politician; b. Rautahat Dist. *Education:* Thakur Ram Campus, Birgunj. *Career:* Deputy Prime Minister 1995; mem. Communist Party of Nepal (Unified Marxist Leninist—UML), Gen. Sec. –2008, Head of Foreign Dept 2008–, mem. Standing Cttee. *Address:* Communist Party of Nepal (UML), PO Box 5471, Madan Nagar, Balkhu, Kathmandu, Nepal; tel. (1) 278081; fax (1) 278084; e-mail uml@ntc.net.np; internet www.cpnuml.org.

**NILEKANI, Nandan M.,** BEng, BTech; Indian business executive; *Co-Chair, Infosys;* b. 2 June 1955. *Education:* Indian Inst. of Tech. *Career:* Co-Founder, Dir Infosys 1981–, later Man. Dir, Pres. and COO, CEO, Pres. and Man. Dir 2002–07, Co-Chair. 2007–; Co-Founder India's Nat. Asscn of Software and Service Cos (NASSCOM), Bangalore Chapter of The IndUS Entrepreneurs (TiE); mem. Asia Pacific Regional Advisory Bd, London Business School, Global Advisory Council, The Conf. Bd; Co-Chair. Business Leaders Dialogue, Initiative for Social Innovation Through Business, Aspen Inst.; Co-Chair. Advisory Bd, IIT Bombay Heritage Fund; Chair. Govt of India's IT for the Power Sector task force, Bangalore Agenda task force; Alumnus Award, Indian Inst. of Tech. 1999, Corporate Citizen of the Year, Fortune Asian Businessman of the Year 2003, Asia Business Leaders Awards 2004. *Address:* Infosys, Plot No. 44&97A, Electronics City, Hosur Road, Bangalore 560 100; 856, 13th Main, III Block, Koramangala, Bangalore 560 034, India; tel. (80) 8520261; (80) 25536150; fax (80) 8520362; (80) 25534654; e-mail nandan_mn@infosys.com; internet www.infosys.com.

**NORBU, Lyonpo Wangdi,** BA; Bhutanese politician and civil servant; *Minister of Finance;* b. 1954, Galing, Trashigang Dist; m. Aum Pem Zangmo; one s. one d. *Education:* Scotch Coll., Australia, Univ. of Western Australia. *Career:* various posts within Ministry of Finance since 1977 including Dir Dept of Budget and Accounts, Auditor Gen. Royal Audit Authority, Finance Sec.; Minister of Finance 2003–07 (resgnd), 2008–; mem. Nat. Ass. from Bartsham-Shongphu constituency, Trashigang; fmr Chair. Royal Monetary Authority. *Address:* Ministry of Finance, Tashichhodzong, PO Box 117, Thimphu, Bhutan; tel. (2) 322223; fax (2) 323154; e-mail yanki@mof.gov.bt.

**OLI, K. P. Sharma;** Nepalese politician; b. 22 Feb. 1952; m. *Career:* mem. CP of Nepal 1970–, mem. Area Cttee 1970, Dist Cttee 1971, Head, Jhapa Movt Organizing Cttee 1972; imprisoned 1973–87; mem. CP Cen. Cttee 1987, head of Lumbini zone –1990; mem. Standing Cttee and Head of Foreign Dept 1992–; Founder and Pres. Nat. Democratic Youth Fed. 1990; Head, Dept of Publicity and Propaganda 1993; Head, Parl. Affairs 1995–, Deputy Leader 1999–2002, Head, Party School 2004–; mem. House of Reps for Jhapa Dist 1991–2002, 2006–; Minister for Home Affairs, 1994–95; Deputy Prime Minister and Minister for Foreign Affairs 2006–07; led comm. investigating Dasdhunga jeep accident 1993; mem. Presidium of Afro-Asian Peoples' Solidarity Org. (AAPSO) in Nepal 1994–2000, Pres. 2000–. *Address:* Parliament of Nepal, Singha Durbar, Kathmandu, Nepal; tel. 4227480; fax 4222923; e-mail nparl@ntc.net.np; internet www.parliament.gov.np.

**OMAR, Mullah Mohammad;** Afghan fmr guerrilla leader and politician; b. 1959, Uruzgan Prov.; m. Guljana Omar 1995; two other wives; five c. (one s. died 2001). *Career:* studied in several Islamic schools; joined jihad (Islamic holy war) against Soviet occupation in 1980s, became a deputy chief commdr Mujahidin guerrilla movt fighting Soviet occupation forces; helped form, recruit for and consolidate the Taliban regime (with Osama bin Laden q.v.) 1994; declared Afghanistan a 'complete' Islamic State (Islamic Emirate of Afghanistan); Leader Taliban-apptd Interim Council of Ministers 1996–2001, given title Emir al-Mo'menein (Commdr of the Faithful); went into hiding during US-led mil. action against Taliban and al-Qa'ida targets in Afghanistan, following suspected al-Qa'ida terrorist attacks in USA Sept. 2001.

**OSMANI, S. R.;** Bangladeshi businessman. *Career:* Dir of Finance Petrobangla, Bangladesh Oil, Gas and Mineral Corpn, Acting Chair., then Chair. 2003–06. *Address:* c/o Petrocenter Bhaban, 3 Kawran Bazar C/A, POB 849, Dhaka, 1215, Bangladesh.

**PAL, Shri Satyabrata;** Indian diplomatist; *High Commissioner to Pakistan;* m. *Career:* Deputy Perm. Rep., UN, New York 1979–93, 1997–2002; Deputy Sec. and Dir, Ministry of External Affairs 1983–88; Deputy High Commr, Dhaka 1988–91; High Commr Gaborone, Botswana 1991–94; Jt Sec. Ministry of External Affairs 1994–97; Deputy High Commr, London 2002–05; High Commr to South Africa 2005–06, to Pakistan 2006–. *Address:* High Commission of India, G-5, Diplomatic Enclave, Islamabad, Pakistan; tel. (51) 2828375; fax (51) 2823102; e-mail hicomind@isb.compol.com.

**PANDEY, A. K.;** Indian diplomatist; *High Commissioner to the Maldives. Career:* Jt Sec., Ministry of Foreign Affairs –2005; High Commr to the Maldives 2005–. *Address:* Indian High Commission, H. Athireege-Aage, Ameeru Ahmed Magu, Malé, Maldives; tel. 3323015; fax 3324778.

**PARAS BIR BIKRAM SHAH DEV;** Nepalese; b. 30 Dec. 1971, Kathmandu; m. Himani Rajya Laxmi Devi Shah 2000; one s. two d. *Education:* St Joseph's Coll., Darjeeling, India, Budhanilkantha School, Schiller Int. Univ., UK. *Career:* proclaimed Crown Prince of Nepal 26 Oct. 2001, heir-apparent to throne of Nepal until monarchy was abolished and replaced by secular fed. repub. May 2008; Chair. Council of Royal Reps during state visits; Coordinator, Zoo Devt Cttee, King Mahendra Trust for Nature Conservation –2001, Chair. King Mahendra Trust for Nature Conservation 2001–; conferred title of Grand Master of all Orders of the Kingdom of Nepal 2006; Shubha Rajyabhisheka Padaka 1975, Gaddi Aarohan Ko Rajat Mahotsav Padaka, 2028–2053 B.S. 1997, Vishista Seva Padaka 1999, Birendra-Aishwarya Seva Padaka 2001, Suprasiddha Prabala Gorkha Dakshina Bahu 2001, Daivi Prakopa Piditoddhara Padaka 2003, Maha Ujjvala Keertimaya Nepal-Shreepada (First Class) 2004, Birendra-Mala 2006, Ati Maha Gauravamaya Supradeepta Birendra Prajatantra Bhaskara 2006.

**PASHTUN, Yousef,** BSc; Afghan politician; *Minister of Urban Development and Housing;* b. 1947, Kandahar. *Education:* American Univ. of Beirut, Lebanon. *Career:* fmr Lecturer, Kabul Univ.; Minister of Urban Affairs 2002–03; Gov. of Qandahar Prov. 2003–04; Minister of Urban Development and Housing 2004–. *Address:* Ministry of Urban Development and Housing, Micro-rayon 3, Kabul, Afghanistan.

**PASWAN, Ram Vilas,** BL, MA; Indian politician; *Minister of Chemicals and Fertilizers and of Steel;* b. 5 July 1946,

Shaharbanni, Bihar; m. Reena Paswan; one s. three d. *Education:* Kosi Coll., Khagaria, Patna Univ. *Career:* mem. Bihar Legis. Ass. 1969; Gen. Sec. Lok Dal, Bihar 1974; mem. Lok Sabha 1977–, Leader of the House 1996; Gen. Sec. Janata Party 1987–88, Janata Dal 1988–90; Sec. Nat. Front 1988–90; Minister of Labour and Welfare 1989–90, of Railways 1996–98, of Communications 1999–2001, of Coal and Mines 2001–02, of Chemicals and Fertilizers and of Steel 2004–; Pres. Lok Jan Shakti Party. *Address:* Ministry of Chemicals and Fertilizers, Shastri Bhavan, New Delhi 110 001, India; tel. (11) 23386519; fax (11) 23015477; internet chemicals.nic .in.

**PATIL, Pratibha Devisingh,** LLB, MA; Indian politician and head of state; *President;* b. 19 Dec. 1934, Jalgaon, Mahar; m. D.R. Shekhawat; one s. one d. *Career:* mem. Mahar Ass. 1962–85, Deputy Minister 1967–72, Cabinet Minister for Social Welfare 1972–74, for Public Health and Social Welfare 1974–75, for Prohibition, Rehabilitation and Cultural Affairs 1975–76, for Educ. 1977–78, for Urban Devt and Housing 1982–83; Deputy Chair. Rajya Sabha (Council of States, Parl.) 1986–88; mem. Lok Sabha 1991; Gov. of Rajasthan 2004–07; Pres. of India 2007–; Vice-Chair. Nat. Fed. for Co-op Urban Banks and Credit Soc.; Chair. Bhartiya Granin Mahila Sangh, Mahar; Organizer Women Home Guards, Jalgaon Dist 1962; mem. Standing Cttee, All India Women's Council; Convener first Women's Conf., Delhi. *Address:* Office of the President, Rashtrapati Bhavan, New Delhi 110 004; 57 New Congress Nagar, Opp. Govt. Milk Scheme, Amravati, Maharashtra, India; tel. (11) 23015321; fax (11) 23017290; e-mail presidentofindia@rb.nic.in; internet www.presidentofindia .nic.in.

**PATIL, Shivraj V.;** Indian politician; *Minister of Home Affairs;* b. 12 Oct. 1935, Chakur, Maharashtra. *Education:* Osmania Univ., Univ. of Bombay (now Mumbai). *Career:* Pres. Latur Municipality 1967–69, 1971–72; mem. Maharashtra Legis. Ass. 1972–79; mem. Lok Sabha 1980, Speaker of 10th Lok Sabha 2004–; Minister of State, including Defence, Commerce, Science and Tech., Space and Tourism portfolios 1980–89; Minister of Home Affairs 2004–. *Address:* Ministry of Home Affairs, North Block, Central Secretariat, New Delhi 110 001, India; tel. (11) 23092011; fax (11) 23093750; e-mail mhaweb@mhant.delhi.nic.in; internet www.mha.nic.in.

**PATNAIK, Naveen,** BA; Indian politician; *Chief Minister of Orissa;* b. 16 Oct. 1946. *Education:* Delhi Univ. *Career:* mem. Lok Sabha 1997–; State Minister of Steel and Mines 1998–99, of Mines and Minerals 1999–2000, of Water Resources, Information and Tech. 2000–02, of Home, Agric. and Admin 2000–, of Works, Parl. Affairs, Housing, Health, Families and Rural Devt 2001–02, of Finance, Planning and Co-ordination 2002–, mem. Library Cttee, Standing Cttee on Commerce, Gen. Purpose Cttee; Chief Minister of Orissa 2000–; Founder and Pres. Pres. Biju Janata Dal; Founding mem. Indian Nat. Trust for Art and Cultural Heritage. *Publications:* A Second Paradise, A Desert Kingdom, The Garden of Life. *Address:* Office of the Chief Minister, Government of Orissa, Bhubaneswar, Orissa; Naveen Nivas, Aerodrome Road, Bhubaneswar, District Khurda, 751001, Orissa, India; tel. (674) 2590299; (674) 2531100; e-mail cmo@ori.nic.in; internet orissagov.nic.in.

**PAWAR, Sharadchandra Govindrao,** BCom; Indian politician; *Minister of Agriculture and of Consumer Affairs, Food and Public Distribution*; *President, Nationalist Congress Party;* b. 12 Dec. 1940, Katychiwadi, Pune; m. Pratibha Pawar 1967; one d. *Career:* Head, State Level Youth Congress; Gen. Sec. Maharashtra Pradesh Congress Cttee; elected to State Legis. 1967, held Portfolios of Home and Publicity and Rehabilitation; Minister of State and Educ. and Youth Welfare, Home, Agric. and Industries and Labour; Chief Minister of Maharashtra 1978–80, 1988–91; Minister of Defence 1991–92; Minister of Agric. and of Consumer Affairs, Food and Public Distribution 2004–; Pres. Nat. Congress (opposition) 1981–86; rejoined Congress (I) 1986; fmr Pres. Congress Forum for Socialistic Action; Sec. Defence Cttee; mem. Lok Sabha 1996–; Leader of Opposition 1998–99; Pres. Nationalist Congress Party 1999–; Pres. Maharashtra Kabbadi Asscn, Maharashtra Olympic Asscn, Agricultural Devt Foundation, Mumbai Cricket Asscn. *Address:* Ministry of Agriculture, Krishi Bhavan, Dr Rajendra Prasad Road, New Delhi 110 001; Nationalist Congress Party, 10 Dr Bishambhar Das Marg, New Delhi 110 001; Ramalayan, 44-A Pedder Road, Mumbai 400026, India; tel. (11) 23383370; (11) 23359218; (22) 23659191; fax (11) 23384129; (11) 23352112.

**PEIRIS, Gamini Lakshman,** DPhil, PhD; Sri Lankan politician and academic; *Minister of Export Development and International Trade;* b. 13 Aug. 1946, Colombo; m. Savitri N. Amarasuriya 1971; one d. *Education:* St Thomas' Coll., Mount Lavinia, Univ. of Ceylon and New Coll., Oxford, UK. *Career:* Prof. of Law, Univ. of Colombo 1979, Dean, Faculty of Law 1982–88; Vice-Chancellor, Univ. of Colombo –1994; Dir Nat. Film Corpn of Sri Lanka 1973–88; Commr Law Comm. of Sri Lanka 1986–; mem. Inc. Soc. of Legal Educ. 1986–; Visiting Fellow, All Souls Coll. Oxford 1980–81; Butterworths Visiting Fellow, Inst. of Advanced Legal Studies, Univ. of London 1984; Distinguished Visiting Fellow, Christ's Coll. Cambridge, UK 1985–86; Smuts Visiting Fellow in Commonwealth Studies, Univ. of Cambridge 1985–86; Chair. Cttee of Vice-Chancellors of the Univs of Sri Lanka; Minister of Justice, Constitutional Affairs, Ethnic Affairs and Nat. Integration and Deputy Minister of Finance 1994–99; Minister of Enterprise Devt, Industrial Policy and Investment Promotion and of Constitutional Affairs 1999–2004, of Export Devt and Int. Trade 2007–; mem. United People's Freedom Alliance (UPFA) 2007–; Vice-Chair. Janasaviya Trust Fund; mem. Securities Council of Sri Lanka 1987–; mem. Pres. Comm. on Youth Unrest 1989; mem. Nat. Educ. Comm., Exec. Cttee of Asscn of Teachers and Researchers in Intellectual Property Law, Bd Govs Inst. of Fundamental Studies; Assoc. mem. Int. Acad. of Comparative Law; Presidential Award 1987. *Publications:* Law of Unjust Enrichment in South Africa and Ceylon 1971, General Principles of Criminal Liability in Ceylon 1972, Offences Under the Penal Code of Sri Lanka 1973, The Law of Evidence in Sri Lanka 1974, Criminal Procedure in Sri Lanka 1975, The Law of Property in Sri Lanka 1976, Landlord and Tenant in Sri Lanka 1977; numerous articles on comparative and admin. law and law of evidence. *Address:* Ministry of Export Development and International Trade, 'Rakshana Mandiraya', 21 Vauxhall Street, Colombo, Sri Lanka; No. 37, Kirula Place, Off Kirula Road, Colombo 05,.

**PENJO, Daw,** MA; Bhutanese diplomatist; *Permanent Representative, United Nations;* b. 7 March 1958; m.; three c. *Education:* Univ. of Delhi, India, Tufts Univ., USA. *Career:* joined Ministry of Foreign Affairs 1980; assigned to Perm. Mission to UN, Geneva 1986–90; Head of Bilateral and Multilateral Div., Ministry of Foreign Affairs 1990–94; First Sec. and Deputy Chief of Mission, Dhaka, Bangldesh 1994–97; Counsellor and Deputy Chief of Mission, New Delhi 1997–2000; Dir of Bilateral Dept 2000–03; Amb. Perm. Rep. to UN, New York 2003–; Amb. (non-resident) to Canada 2003–. *Address:* Permanent Mission of Bhutan, 2 United Nations Plaza, 27th Floor, New York, NY 10017, USA; tel. (212) 826-1919; fax (212) 826-2998; e-mail pmbnewyork@aol .com; internet www.un.org.

**PENJOR, Rinzin,** BCom, LLB, LLM; Bhutanese lawyer and government official; *Attorney-General;* b. Kazhi geog, Wangduephodrang. *Education:* Shri Ram Coll. of Commerce, New Delhi and Delhi Univ., India, Lord Dalhousie Law Coll., Canada. *Career:* began career with High Court 1989, has served as Drangpoen in Tsirang, Sarpang and Punakha Dist Courts; militia officer with Royal Bhutan Army 1990–95; Attorney-Gen. 2008–; Patang. *Address:* Office of the Attorney General, Cabinet Secretariat, Tashichhodzong, Thimphu, Bhutan; tel. (2) 321437; fax (2) 321438; e-mail cabinet@ druknet.bt; internet www.bhutan.gov.bt.

**PERERA, Air Chief Marshal G. Donald;** Sri Lankan air force officer; *Chief of Defence Staff; Education:* Nat. Defence Coll., India, Air Command and Staff Coll., Air Univ., Maxwell Air Force Base, Ala, USA. *Career:* participated in Air

Operations in North and East since 1983, Chief of Staff 1998–2002, Commdr Sri Lanka Air Force 2002–06, Chief of Defence Staff 2006–; Vishista Seva Vibhushanaya, Utthama Seva Padakkama, Repub. of Sri Lanka Armed Services Medal, Sri Lanka Air Force 50th Anniversary Medal, Sri Lanka Armed Services Long Service Medal, Presidential Inauguration Medal, 50th Independence Anniversary Commemoration Medal, North and East Operations Medal, Purna Bhumi Padakkama, Vadamarachchi Operations Medal, Riviresa Campaign Service Medal. *Address:* c/o Group Capt. N. H. V. Gunaratne, Commanding Officer, Sri Lanka Air Force, Colombo, Sri Lanka; tel. (11) 2441044; e-mail info@airforce.lk; internet www.airforce.lk.

**POKHAREL, Bhoj Raj;** Nepalese civil servant. *Career:* currently Chief Election Commr. *Address:* Election Commission, Kantipath, Kathmandu, Nepal; tel. (1) 4228663; fax (1) 4229227; e-mail election@mos.com.np; internet www.election-commission.org.np.

**PRABHAKARAN, Velupillai;** Sri Lankan resistance leader; *Leader, Liberation Tigers of Tamil Eelam;* b. 26 Nov. 1954, Velvettithurai, Jaffna Penninsula; m. Mathy Parabhakaran 1984; two s. one d. *Career:* participated in Tamil protest movt 1970s, Founder and Leader Liberation Tigers of Tamil Eelam (LTTE); accused of involvement in murder of Mayor of Jaffna 1975, Indian Prime Minister Rajiv Gandhi 1991, convicted in absentia 1998; waged civil war against Sri Lankan Govt for 20 years with objective of securing ind. state for Tamil people.

**PRADHAN, Lyonpo Om,** BA; Bhutanese diplomatist, politician and business executive; *Chairperson, Druk Holding and Investments Ltd;* b. 6 Oct. 1946; m.; three c. *Education:* Delhi Univ., India. *Career:* various posts in Ministry of Trade, Industry and Forests 1969–80; Perm. Rep. to the UN 1980–84, 1998–2004; Amb. to India (also accred to Nepal and Maldives) 1984–85, Head of Bhutanese Del. to first and second rounds of boundary talks with China; Deputy Minister, Ministry of Trade and Industry 1985–89, Head of Del. to fifth round of boundary talks with China; Minister for Trade and Industry 1989–98; fmr Chief, Policy Devt and Coordination Monitoring and Reporting Unit, UN Office of High Rep. for the Least Developed Countries, Landlocked Countries and Small Island Developing Sites (UN-OHRLLS); Chair. Druk Holding and Investments Ltd 2007–; mem. Nat. Ass., Council of Ministers; Chair. State Trading Corpn, Chhukha Hydroelectric Project Corpn and Tala Hydroelectric Project Authority; mem. Planning Comm., Nat. Environment Comm. *Address:* Druk Holding and Investments Ltd, PO Box 1127, Motithang, Thimphu, Bhutan; tel. (2) 336257; fax (2) 336259; e-mail info@dhi.bt; internet www.dhi.bt.

**PRASAD, Alok,** BA, MA; Indian diplomatist; *High Commissioner to Sri Lanka;* m. Nandini Prasad; two c. *Education:* Delhi Univ. *Career:* joined Indian Foreign Service 1974, has represented India in various capacities in Germany, UN (New York), the Netherlands, Nepal, Burma and Botswana; also worked in Prime Minister's Office; Jt Sec. for Americas Div., Ministry of External Affairs, New Delhi 1995–2000; Deputy Chief of Mission, Washington, DC 2000–04; High Commr to Singapore 2004–06, to Sri Lanka 2006–; Fellow, Center for Int. Affairs, Harvard Univ., USA. *Address:* High Commission of India, 36–38 Galle Road, Colombo 03, Sri Lanka; tel. (11) 2447285; (11) 2580970; fax (11) 2446403; e-mail hc.colombo@mea.gov.in; internet www.hcicolombo.org.

**PRASAD, Jayant;** Indian diplomatist; *Ambassador to Afghanistan. Education:* Univ. of Delhi, Jawaharlal Nehru Univ., New Delhi. *Career:* taught modern Indian history at St Stephen's Coll., Delhi 1974–76; entered Indian Foreign Service 1976, Rapporteur of UN Comm. on Human Rights, Geneva 1986–87, served as Head of Americas Div., Ministry of External Affairs, New Delhi, as Amb. to Algeria, as Staff Officer for Foreign Sec. and as First Sec., Perm. Mission of India to UN, Geneva, Amb. and Perm. Rep. to Conf. on Disarmament, Geneva 2004–07, mem. UN Sec.-Gen.'s Advisory Bd on Disarmament Matters, Amb. to Afghanistan 2008–; Fellow, Weatherhead Centre for Int. Affairs, Harvard Univ., USA 1998–99. *Address:* Embassy of India, Malalai Wat, Shar-i-Nau, Kabul, Afghanistan; tel. (873) 763095560; fax (873) 763095561; e-mail embassy@indembassy-kabul.com.

**QAMAR, Syed Naveed,** BSc, MS, MBA; Pakistani politician; *Minister of Privatization and Investment, with additional charge of Finance, Revenue, Economic Affairs and Statistics;* b. 22 Sept. 1955, Karachi; m.; one s. three d. *Education:* Univ. of Manchester, UK, Northrop Univ. and California State Univ., USA. *Career:* mem. Computer Science faculty, FAST-NU (then called FAST-ICS) 1988–89; sr mem. Pakistan People's Party, currently mem. Cen. Exec. Cttee; elected mem. Prov. Ass., Sindh 1988–90, mem. Nat. Ass. 1990–93, 1993–96, 1997–99, elected from NA-222 (Tando Muhammad Khan-cum-Hyderabad-cum-Badin) constituency in gen. elections 2008; Prov. Minister (Sindh) for Information 1990; Chair. Privatization Comm. 1993; Fed. Minister for Finance and Privatization 1996; Minister of Privatization and Investment, with additional charge of Finance, Revenue, Econ. Affairs and Statistics 2008–. *Address:* Ministry of Finance, Block Q, Pakistan Secretariat, Islamabad Karachi, Pakistan; tel. (51) 9201941; fax (51) 9202640; e-mail webmaster@finance.gov.pk; naveedqamar@yahoo.com; internet www.finance.gov.pk.

**QANOONI, Younis;** Afghan politician; *Speaker, Wolasi Jirga;* b. 1957, Panjshir Valley. *Education:* Kabul Univ., also studied in India and USA. *Career:* joined mujahidin troops fighting against Soviet occupation forces 1979–89; Jt Minister of Defence 1993; co-f. Defence of the Motherland and United Nat. Islamic Front for the Salvation of Afghanistan (Unifsa–Northern Alliance) 1996; political head of NA's main Jamiat-i Islami party 2001; Leader NA Del. to Future of Afghanistan Govt Talks, Bonn Nov. 2001; Minister of the Interior, Afghan Interim Authority Dec. 2001–June 2002; Minister of Educ. 2002–04 (resgnd); Head of Nizzat-i-Milli Party 2002; presidential cand. 2004; Founder and Leader Hizb-i Afghanistan-i Nawin (New Afghanistan Party) 2005–; Chair. Nat. Understanding Front (opposition coalition) 2005, currently Speaker of Wolasi Jirga (lower house of parl.). *Address:* c/o Hizb-i Afghanistan-i Nawin (New Afghanistan Party), Kabul, Afghanistan.

**QAYYUM, Malik Muhammad;** Pakistani lawyer, judge and government official; *Attorney-General;* b. 18 Dec. 1944. *Career:* Sr Advocate, Supreme Court; began career as legal practitioner 1964; elected Sec., Bar Asscn, Lahore 1970, Pres. Dist Bar Asscn, Lahore 1980; mem. Punjab Bar Council 1984–88; Deputy Attorney-Gen. of Pakistan 1984–88; Judge, Lahore High Court 1988–2001 (resgnd); Attorney-Gen. of Pakistan 2007–; mem. Pakistan Law Comm.; Chief Ed. Pakistan Supreme Court Cases. *Address:* Office of the Attorney General, Supreme Court of Pakistan, Constitution Avenue, Islamabad, Pakistan; tel. (51) 9220581; fax (51) 9213452; e-mail info@supremecourt.gov.pk; internet www.supremecourt.gov.pk.

**QURESHI, Makhdoom Shah Mehmu,** BA, MA; Pakistani politician; *Minister of Foreign Affairs, with additional charge of Petroleum and Natural Resources;* b. 22 June 1966, Murree. *Education:* Aitchison Coll., Lahore, Forman Christian Coll., Lahore, Corpus Christi Coll., Cambridge, UK. *Career:* grew up in Multan; returned to Pakistan following law studies in UK 1983; elected to Prov. Ass. 1985; contested and won local, prov. and nat. elections from his home constituency in Multan; has served as Minister for Planning and Devt Punjab, Minister of Finance, Punjab, and Fed. Minister for Parl. Affairs in Govt of Benazir Bhutto; also served as Chair. Dist Council for Multan and first Dist Nazim under Musharraf admin; represented Pakistan People's Party (PPP) Punjab as their prime ministerial cand. 2002; sr mem. PPP and Pres. PPP Punjab; Minister of Foreign Affairs, with additional charge of Petroleum and Natural Resources 2008–. *Address:* Ministry of Foreign Affairs, Constitution Avenue, Islamabad, Pakistan; tel. (51) 9210335; fax (51) 9207600; e-mail sadiq@mofa.gov.pk; internet www.mofa.gov.pk.

**RABBANI, Burhanuddin;** Afghan politician and academic; *Leader, Jamiat-i-Islami;* b. 1940, Faizabad, Badakhshan Prov. *Education:* Kabul Univ., Al Azhar Univ., Cairo. *Career:* fmr Lecturer in Islamic Law, Kabul Univ.; Pres. United Nat. Islamic Front for the Salvation of Afghanistan (UNIFSA) (also known as Northern Alliance); leader Jamiat-i Islami (Islamic Soc.) 1971–; left Afghanistan 1974; made armed raids against govt of Mohammed Daoud from base in Pakistan; returned to Afghanistan 1992; elected Pres. of Afghanistan by Mujahidin Exec. Council 1992; forced to step down when Taliban occupied Kabul 1996; continued to be recognized as Pres. of Islamic State of Afghanistan by UN –2001; currently Leader Jamiat-i Islami party. *Address:* Jamiat-i-Islami, Karte Parwan, Phase 2, Badaam Bagh, Afghanistan; tel. (70) 278950.

**RAHEEN, Sayed Makhdoom,** MA, PhD; Afghan diplomatist; *Ambassador to India;* b. 1946, Kabul. *Education:* Tehran Univ., Iran. *Career:* apptd Lecturer, Kabul Univ. 1973; fmr Head of Bureau of Afghan Culture and Art, Ministry of Information, Culture and Tourism; fmr mem. Drafting Cttee of Constitution of Afghanistan; mem. Grand Nat. Ass. (Loya Jirga) 1976; put under house arrest following Communist coup d'etat April 1978; moved to Pakistan after Soviet invasion; apptd mem. High Council and Chair. Cttee of Culture and Publicity, Islamic Unity of Afghanistan Mujahedeen 1982; selected as Head of Radio Free Kabul by Mujahidin parties; served as adviser with rank of Minister to Pres. of Afghan Interim Govt; co-f. Nat. Islamic Movt of Afghanistan in Peshawar, Pakistan 1988; abandoned Afghan resistance and left for USA following disagreements with Jihad leaders 1991; Co-founder and first Chair. Asscn for Peace and Democracy for Afghanistan 1996; mem. Exec. Cttee Loya Jirga, Rome 1998; selected as Minister of Information, Culture and Tourism of Interim Admin, Bonn Conf. 2002; Chair. Kabul City Council 2003; Amb. to India 2007–; Medal for serving the freedom of speech and promoting cultural activities, presented by HM Zahir Shah 2004. *Publications:* Tears of Khorasan, The Mourners, reply to Khalili (poetry), Today's Muslims (in Pashto); several books and articles on culture, literature, history and Islamic Sufism, the works of Sayed Jamaludeen Afghani, Daqiqi Nama, research on Amir Khosrow, and the Relations of Afghanistan and the subcontinent; f. and published resistance magazines and papers, in Dari, Pashto, Urdu, Arabic and English. *Address:* Embassy of Afghanistan, Plot No. 5, Block 50-F, Shanti Path, Chanakyapuri, New Delhi 110 021, India; tel. (11) 26883601; fax (11) 26875439; e-mail embassyafghanistan@yahoo.co.in.

**RAHMAN, A. S. F.;** Bangladeshi business executive; *Chairman, Beximco Group. Career:* Chair. Beximco Group, including Beximco Pharmaceutical Ltd, Beximco Holdings Ltd, Beximco Agro-Chemicals Ltd, Beximco Foods Ltd, Beximco Synthetics Ltd, Comtrade Beximco Apparels Ltd, Sonali Ansh., Beximco Infusions Ltd; Dir IPDC; mem. Bd of Govs Bangladesh Enterprise Inst. *Address:* Beximco Pharmaceuticals Ltd, 17 Dhanmondi R/A, Road No. 2, Dhaka 1205, Bangladesh; tel. (2) 9127721; fax (2) 8613470; internet www.beximco.net.

**RAHMAN, M. Saifur;** Bangladeshi chartered accountant and politician; b. March 1932, Maulvibazar, Sylhet Div.; m.; three s. one d. *Education:* Dhaka Univ. *Career:* f. chartered accountancy firm, Rahman Rahman Huq; Minister of Finance, Planning, Commerce and Foreign Trade 1976–1982, of Finance and Planning 2001–06; Chair. of various cabinet cttees 1976–1982, 1991–94; mem. Jatiya Sangsad (Nat. Ass.) 1979–82, 1996–99, 2001; acting Chair. Bangladesh Jatiyatabadi Dal (Bangladesh Nationalist Party); fmr Chair. Bd Govs IMF, World Bank. *Address:* Bangladesh Jatiyatabadi Dal, Banani Office, House 23, Road 13, Dhaka; c/o Rahman Rahman Huq, 9 Mohakhali C/A, 11th floor, Dhaka, 1212 Bangladesh; tel. (2) 8819525; fax (2) 8813063; e-mail bnpbd@e-fsbd.net; internet www.bnpbd.com.

**RAHMAN, Zillur;** Bangladeshi politician; *Acting President, Bangladesh Awami League. Career:* fmr Sec. and mem. Presidium Bangladesh Awami League, Acting Pres. 2008–. *Address:* Bangladesh Awami League, 23 Bangabandhu Avenue, Dhaka, Bangladesh; e-mail info@albd.org; internet www.albd.org.

**RAISANI, Nawab Muhammad Aslam Khan,** MA; Pakistani politician and farmer; *Chief Minister of Balochistan;* b. 5 July 1955, Sarawan, Balochistan. *Education:* Univ. of Balochistan. *Career:* Tumandar of Raisani Tribe; became Chief of Sarawan and Raisani tribe following his father's assassination; fmr Deputy Man., BDA; fmr Purchase Officer, PASCO, Jacobabad; apptd as DSP in Balochistan police force following graduation; Minister for Agric., Cooperative, Labour and Manpower in caretaker Prov. Govt Cabinet 1988; Minister for Food and Fisheries in caretaker Prov. Cabinet; elected mem. Prov. Ass. from PB-27 Mastung; mem. Prov. Ass. of Balochistan 1988, 1990, 1993, 2002; joined Pakistan Nat. Party (PNP) 1989, elected Parl. Leader of PNP in Prov. Ass.; apptd Pres. PNP of Balochistan 1990; Minister for Finance in Prov.; joined Pakistan People's Party 1999, mem. Cen. Exec. Cttee; Chief Minister of Balochistan 2008–; Pres. Chamber of Agric., Balochistan; Founder and fmr Pres. Fed. of Chambers of Agric. Pakistan. *Address:* Office of the Chief Minister, Quetta, Balochistan, Pakistan; e-mail info@balochistan.gov.pk; internet www.balochistan.gov.pk.

**RAJAPAKSE, Mahinda;** Sri Lankan politician, lawyer and head of state; *President, Minister of Defence, Public Security, Law and Order, Religious Affairs, Nation Building and Finance and Planning;* b. 18 Nov. 1945, Hambantota. *Education:* Richmond Coll., Galle, Nalanda and Thurstan Colls, Colombo. *Career:* fmr lawyer, Tangalle; mem. Parl. for Beliatta 1970; fmr Minister of Labour, of Fisheries, of Ports and Shipping; Leader of the Opposition 2002–04; Prime Minister of Sri Lanka 2004–05; Pres. of Sri Lanka Nov. 2005–, Minister of Defence and of Finance and Planning 2005–07, of Defence, Public Security, Law and Order, Religious Affairs, Nation Building and Finance and Planning 2007–; mem. United People's Freedom Alliance; Pres. Sri Lankan Cttee for Solidarity with Palestine; Chair. Sri Lanka Freedom Party 2006–; Sri Rohana Janaranjana 2000. *Address:* President's Secretariat, Republic Square, Colombo 1, Sri Lanka; tel. (11) 2324801; fax (11) 2331246; e-mail gosl@presidentsl.org; internet www.presidentsl.org; www.mahindarajapaksa.com.

**RAJU, B. Ramalinga,** BCom, MBA; Indian business executive; *Chairman, Satyam Computer Services Ltd;* m. Nandini Raju; two s. *Education:* Loyola Coll., Vijayawada, Ohio Univ., USA. *Career:* Co-founder and Chair. Satyam Computer Services Ltd, Satyam Infoway Ltd and VisionCompass, Inc. 1987–, jt ventures include Satyam–GE Software Services Ltd, Satyam Venture Eng Services Pvt. Ltd, Satyam Manufacturing Technologies Ltd, Satyam ideaEdge Technologies Pvt. Ltd, CA Satyam ASP Pvt. Ltd; f. several trusts and charities including Alambana, Naandi and the Byyrajyu Foundation; Chair. Nat. Asscn of Software and Service Cos 2006–07; Dr hc (Andhra Univ.) 2007; Ernst & Young Entrepreneur of the Year Award 2000, 2007, Dataquest IT Man. of the Year Award 2001, Asia Business Leader Award for Corp. Citizen of the Year, Hong Kong 2002. *Address:* Satyam Computer Services Ltd., Bahadurpally Village, Qutubullapur Mandal, RR District, 500 855, India; tel. (40) 30633535; fax (40) 23097515; e-mail abhijit_roy@satyam.com; internet www.satyam.com.

**RAMADORAI, Subramaniam,** BSc, BEng, MSc; Indian business executive; *CEO and Managing Director, Tata Consultancy Services;* b. 6 Oct. 1944. *Education:* Delhi Univ., Indian Inst. of Science, Bangalore, Univ. of Calif. and Massachusetts Inst. of Tech., USA. *Career:* jr engineer, Tata Consultancy Services (TCS) 1972, later set up TCS's operations in New York 1979, CEO and Man. Dir TCS 1996–, Chair. Tata Technologies Ltd; Chair. CMC Ltd; Ind. Dir (non-exec.) Hindustan Lever Ltd 2002–; mem. Bd of Dirs Nicholas Piramal; IT Adviser to Qingdao City and Hangzhou City, People's Repub. of China; Fellow, Inst. of Electrical and Electronics Engineers, Indian Nat. Acad. of Engineers; Vice-Chair. Nat. Asscn of Software Companies (NASSCOM); Asia Business Leader of the Year Award, Hong Kong 2002, Business India Businessman of the Year 2004, UK Trade and Investment Special Recognition

Award 2005, Padma Bhushan 2006. *Address:* Tata Consultancy Services, TCS House, Raveline Street, Mumbai 400001, India; tel. (22) 22080522; fax (22) 67781188; e-mail ceo.office@tcs.com; internet www.tcs.com.

**RAMDOSS, Anbumani,** MD; Indian physician and politician; *Minister of Health and Family Welfare;* b. 9 Oct. 1968, Puducherry; m.Shrimati Sowmiya Anbumani 1991; three d. *Education:* Madras Medical Coll., London School of Economics, UK. *Career:* fmr medical practitioner, Tamil Nadu; mem. Parl. (Pattali Makkal Katchi) from Rajya Sabha 2004–, Minister of Health and Family Welfare 2004–; co-founded Nat. Rural Health Mission 2005; Leader Pattali Makkal Katchi; Pres. Pasumai Thayagam (Green Mother Land). *Address:* Ministry of Health and Family Welfare, Chamber No. 348, Nirman Bhavan, Maulana Azad Road, New Delhi 110 011; 30/34, 4th Cross Street, Kasturibai Nagar, Raja Anamalai Puram, Chennai 600 028, Tamil Nadu, India; tel. (11) 23018863; fax (11) 23014252; e-mail resp-health@hub.nic.in; internet www.mohfw.nic.in.

**RANA, Pashupati S. J. B. R.,** BA; Nepalese politician; *Chairman, Rashtriya Prajatantra Party;* b. 7 May 1941, Laxmi Niwas, Kathmandu; m. Rani Usha Rajya Laxmi Devi Rana (Princess of Gwailor); two d. *Education:* Haileybury, ISC and New Coll., Oxford, UK. *Career:* mem. Parl. 1973–; Minister of Educ., Transport, Civil Aviation and Tourism 1979, Minister of Water Resources 1983–86, 1995–98, Minister of Panchayat and Local Devt 1986–88, Minister of Foreign Affairs, Finance, Water Resources and Communications 1990, Gen. Sec. Rashtriya Prajatantra Party (Nat. Democratic Party) 1991–97, Chair. 2003–; mem. India-Int. Centre, Int. Council Asia Soc.; Pres. Alliance Française. *Address:* Central Secretariat, Rashtriya Prajatantra Party, Charumati Bahal, Chabahil, Kathmandu; Bijaya Bas, POB 271, Maharaj Gunj, Kathmandu, Nepal; tel. (1) 4471071; (1) 4437902; fax (1) 4435173; (1) 4423384; e-mail info@rppnepal.com; p-rana@ntc.net.np; internet www.rppnepal.org.

**RANGASAMY, Thiru N.;** Indian politician; b. 4 Aug. 1950. *Career:* Chief Minister of Union Territory of Puducherry (fmrly Pondicherry) 2001–. *Address:* Office of the Chief Minister, Puducherry Legislative Assembly, Puducherry 605 001; 9 Vinayakar Koil Street, Thilarshpet, Puducherry 605 009, India; tel. 2333399; fax 2333135; e-mail cm@pon.nic.in; cm@pondy.pon.nic.in; internet pondicherry.nic.in.

**RAO, K. Chandrasekhar,** MA.; Indian politician; *President, Telangana Rashtra Samithi;* b. 17 Feb. 1954, Chintamadaka; m. Smt. Kalvakuntla Shobha 1969; one s. one d. *Education:* Osmania Univ., Hyderabad. *Career:* mem. Andhra Pradesh Legis. Ass. 1985–2004, Chair. Cttee on Public Undertakings 1992–93, Deputy Speaker 1999–2001; Minister of State, Govt of Andhra Pradesh 1987–88, Cabinet Minister 1997–99; mem. Lok Sabha from Karimnagar, Andhra Pradesh constituency 2004–06 (resgnd), 2006– (re-elected in bye election); Minister without Portfolio May–Nov. 2004, Minister of Labour and Employment 2004–06; Founder and Pres. Telangana Rashtra Samithi. *Address:* 8-2-220/110/1/3, Road No. 14, Banjara Hills, Hyderabad, Andhra Pradesh; Telangana Rashtra Samithi, Karimnagar, India; tel. (40) 23555798.

**RAO, Nirupama,** MA; Indian diplomatist; *Ambassador to China;* b. 6 Dec. 1950; m. Sudhakar Rao; two s. *Education:* Marathwada Univ. *Career:* joined Foreign Service 1973; First Sec. (Agreement), Mission in Colombo 1981–83; Desk Officer, Southern Africa and Nepal Desks, Ministry of External Affairs, then with East Asia Div. 1984–92; Minister for Press Affairs, Embassy in Washington, DC 1993–95; Amb. to Peru 1995–98; Deputy Chief of Mission, Embassy in Moscow 1998–99; Head of Div. in charge of Multilateral Econ. Relations, Ministry of External Affairs 2000–01, Jt Sec. for External Publicity and Official Spokesperson 2001–02, Additional Sec. Human Resources Div. 2002–04, Foreign Service Inspector 2004; High Commr to Sri Lanka 2004–06; Amb. to China 2006–; fmr Fellow specializing in Asia-Pacific Security, Center for Int. Affairs (now Weatherhead Center), Harvard Univ., USA; Distinguished Int. Exec. in Residence, Univ. of Maryland, USA 1999–2000. *Address:* Embassy of India, 1 Ri Tan Dong Lu, Jian Guo Men Wai, Beijing 100600, The People's Republic of China; tel. (10) 65321908; fax (10) 65324684; internet www.indianembassy.org.cn.

**RASSOUL, Zalmai,** MD; Afghan physician and government official; *National Security Adviser;* b. 1923, Kabul. *Education:* Estiqlal High School, Univ. of Paris, France. *Career:* worked at Research Inst. of Cardiac Diseases, Paris, Mil. Hosp. of Saudi Arabia; served as Chief of Staff of HM King Mohammad Zahir Shah, Rome; worked for Haqiqat e Afghan publ. regarding Jihad in Afghanistan, Paris; Minister of Civil Aviation and Tourism and Nat. Security Adviser, Interim Govt of Afghanistan; currently Nat. Security Adviser, Govt of Afghanistan. *Publications:* 30 medical books and booklets published in Europe and USA. *Address:* Office of the President, Gul Khana Palace, Presidential Palace, Kabul, Afghanistan; e-mail president@afghanistangov.org; internet www.president.gov.af.

**REDDY, K. Anji,** PhD; Indian pharmaceuticals industry executive; *Chairman, Dr Reddy's Laboratories Ltd. Education:* Andhra Christian Coll., Guntur, Univ. of Bombay (now Mumbai), Nat. Chemical Lab., Pune. *Career:* worked for Indian Drugs and Pharmaceuticals Ltd 1969–75; Founder and Man. Dir Uniloids Ltd 1976–80; Man. Dir Standard Organics Ltd 1980–84; Founder and Chair. Dr Reddy's Laboratories Ltd 1984–; Founder Dr Reddy's Research Foundation, Dr Reddy's Foundation for Human and Social Devt; Chair. Bd of Dirs GAIN Foundation, Geneva; mem. Bd of Dirs Diana Hotels Ltd, Biotech India Consortium Ltd, Biomed Ltd, WaterHealth International, Inc. 2005–; mem. Bd of Trade; Sir P.C. Ray Award, Indian Chemical Manufacturers Asscn 1984, 1992, Achiever of the Year Award, Chemtech Foundation 2000, Padmashri Award 2001. *Address:* Dr Reddy's Laboratories Ltd, Corporate Office, 7-1-27 Ameerpet, Hyderabad 500 016, India; tel. (40) 66511532; fax (40) 23739666; internet www.drreddys.com.

**REDDY, Y. S. Rajasekhara,** MBBS; Indian surgeon and politician; *Chief Minister of Andhra Pradesh;* b. 8 July 1949, Pulivendula, Cuddapah Dist; m. Smt. Vijayalakshmi 1971; one s. one d. *Education:* M. R. Coll. of Gulbarga, S. V. Medical Coll., Tirupathy. *Career:* fmr Medical Officer, CSI Campbell Hosp., Jammalamadugu; est. Y.S. Raja Reddy Hosp., Pulivendula 1973; elected to Andhra Pradesh Legis. Ass. (Indian Nat. Congress) 1978, Minister of Rural Devt, Health and Educ. 1980–83, Leader of Opposition 1999–2004; Pres. Andhra Pradesh Congress Cttee 1983–85, 1998–2000; served four terms in Lok Sabha; Chief Minister of Andhra Pradesh 2004–. *Address:* Office of the Chief Minister, Government of Andhra Pradesh, C-Block, 4th Floor, AP Secretariat, Hyderabad; Greenlands Circle, Begumpet, Hyderabad, India; tel. (40) 23456698; (40) 23410333; fax (40) 23452498; e-mail cmap@ap.nic.in; internet www.aponline.gov.in; www.ysr.in.

**REDDY, Y. Venugopal;** Indian central banker and academic; *Governor, Reserve Bank of India. Career:* joined Indian Admin. Service in 1964, has held several key positions including Sec. (Banking), Ministry of Finance, Additional Sec., Ministry of Commerce, Jt Sec., Ministry of Finance, Prin. Sec., Govt of Andhra Pradesh; Deputy Gov. Reserve Bank of India 1996–2002, Gov. 2003–; Exec. Dir for India, Sri Lanka, Bangladesh and Bhutan, IMF 2002–; Visiting Prof., Osmania Univ.; Visiting Faculty in Admin. Staff, Coll. of India; fmr Visiting Fellow, LSE. *Publications include:* numerous publications on finance, planning and public enterprises. *Address:* Reserve Bank of India, Central Office Building, Shahid Bhagat Singh Road, POB 10007, Mumbai, 400 001, India; tel. (22) 22661602; fax (22) 22658269; e-mail helpprd@rbi.org.in; internet www.rbi.org.in.

**REHMAN, Maulana Fazlur;** Pakistani politician; b. 21 Aug. 1953, Abdulkhel Banyala area in Dera Ismail Khan dist, North-West Frontier Prov.. *Education:* Dar-al-Ulum Haqania, Akura, Khatak. *Career:* Sec.-Gen. Jamiat-e-Ulema-e-Islam 1974–2007, now heads own faction of JUI, Jamiat-e-Ulema-e-Islam—Fazl 2007–, also Sec.-Gen. Muttahida Majlis-e-Amal political coalition; mem. Nat. Ass., fmr Leader of the Opposition. *Address:* c/o Jamiat-e-Ulema-e-Islam (JUI), Jamia al-Maarf, al-Sharia, Dera Ismail Khan, Pakistan.

**RIO, Neiphiu;** Indian politician; *Chief Minister of Nagaland;* b. 11 Nov. 1950, Tuophema village, Kohima Dist; m.; one s. five d. *Education:* St Joseph's Coll., Darjeeling and Kohima Arts Coll. *Career:* mem. Nagaland Legis. Ass. 1989–2002, 2004–; State Minister of Sports and School Educ. 1989–91, of Higher and Tech. Educ., Arts and Culture 1991–93, of Works and Housing 1993–98, of Home Affairs 1998–2002; Chair. Nagaland Industrial Devt Corpn (NIDC), Nat. Khadi and Village Industries Bd (NKVIB), Devt Authority of Nagaland; Chief Minister of Nagaland 2003–; Leader Democratic Alliance of Nagaland 2004–; Hon. Vice-Pres. Indian Red Cross Soc.; Lifetime Deputy Gov. (Hon.), Bd Govs American Biographical Inst. Research Asscn 1999–. *Address:* Office of the Chief Minister, Government of Nagaland, Civil Secretariat, Kohima 797 001, India.

**RODRIGUES, Gen. Sunith Francis,** MA; Indian army officer (retd) and government official; *Governor of the Punjab and Administrator of Union Territory of Chandigarh;* b. 19 Sept. 1933, Bombay (now Mumbai); m. Jean Rodrigues; two s. one d. *Education:* St Xavier's High School, Bombay, Defence Services Staff Coll. (DSSC), Royal Coll. of Defence Studies, UK. *Career:* joined Jt Services Wing, Indian Mil. Acad. 1949, commissioned into Regt of Artillery 1952, commanded mountain artillery regt 1970–71, served as Gen. Staff Officer during Indo-Pak War at a Corps HQ 1971, of a div. 1973–75, commanded mountain brigade at high altitude 1975–77, Chief Instructor (Army) at DSSC 1978–81, commanded div. deployed at high altitude on becoming Maj.-Gen. 1981, Chief of Staff of a corps 1983–85, Dir-Gen. Mil. Training and promoted to rank of Lt-Gen. 1985–86, commanded corps in northern sector 1986–89, apptd Hon. ADC to Pres. 1987, served as Vice-Chief of Army Staff 1987–89, GOC-in-C Cen. Command April–Oct. 1989, GOC-in-C Western Command Nov. 1989–June 1990, Chief of Army Staff 1990–93; Dir Int. Centre, Goa 1993–99; served two terms on Nat. Security Advisory Bd; mem. Exec. Council Goa Univ. for seven years, Man. Cttee Goa Chamber of Commerce and Industry; Gov. of Punjab and Admin. of Union Territory of Chandigarh 2004–; mem. Goa Planning Bd, Bd Govs Goa Inst. of Man.; Vishisht Seva Medal (VSM) for distinguished service 1972, Param Vishisht Seva Medal (PVSM) 1988. *Address:* Office of the Governor, Chandigarh, Punjab; Pb. Raj Bhawan, Sector 6, Chandigarh, Punjab, India; tel. (172) 2740740; (172) 2740740; e-mail governor@punjabmail.gov.in; internet punjabgovt.nic .in.

**ROY, Donkupar,** PhD; Indian politician and government official; *Chief Minister of Meghalaya;* b. 10 Nov. 1954. *Education:* North Eastern Hill Univ., Shillong. *Career:* worked as prof. before entering politics; first won Shella Ass. seat in Meghalaya as ind. cand. 1987, re-elected 1993, subsequently re-elected three times; joined United Democratic Party (UDP) 1998, currently Head of UDP; held several portfolios under Chief Minister of Meghalaya, including Health, Educ., Finance and Planning Implementation, before becoming Deputy Chief Minister, formed alliance with handful of other parties to form govt under banner of Meghalaya Progressive Alliance, Chief Minister of Meghalaya 2008–. *Address:* Office of the Chief Minister, Shillong 793 001, Meghalaya, India; tel. (364) 2224282 (ext. 2200); (94) 36104815 (mobile); (364) 2227121; (364) 2226599; fax (364) 2227913; e-mail info@meghalaya.nic.in; internet meghalaya .nic.in.

**ROY, Prannoy,** PhD; Indian broadcasting executive, political analyst and economist; *President, New Delhi Television;* b. 15 Oct. 1949; m. Radhika Roy. *Education:* Doon School, Dehradun, Haileybury School, Queen Mary Coll. and Univ. of London, UK, Delhi School of Econs. *Career:* Chartered Accountant, PriceWaterhouse India 1979–83; Election Analyst 1980–85; Assoc. Prof. Delhi School of Econs 1985–86; Econ. Adviser, Ministry of Finance 1986–87; anchor and Ed.-in-Chief for several TV news, budget and election programmes 1998–; Founder, Pres. New Delhi TV Ltd (NDTV) 1988–; Leverhulme Fellow; Priyadarshini Acad. Bombay Felicitations Award, Dynasty Culture Club Hall of Fame Award for Best Anchor Person 1991, TV and Video Award for Best Anchor Person 1993, B. D. Goenka Award for Excellence in Journalism 1994, 1995, Maharana Mewar Foundation Award for Contrib. to Journalism 1996, Indian Dance Theatre Best Personality of the Year Award 1998, Screen Videocon Award for Lifetime Achievement 1998, Ernst & Young Entrepreneur of the Year Award (Media). *Address:* New Delhi Television Ltd (NDTV), Archana, Greater Kailash Part 1, New Delhi 110 048, India; tel. (11) 26446666; e-mail prannoy@ndtv.com; internet www.ndtv.com.

**ROY SAHARA, Subrata;** Indian business executive; *Managing Worker and Chairman, Sahara India Pariwar;* m. Swapna Roy 1974; two s. *Career:* f. Sahara Group 1978, currently and Man. Worker and Chair. Sahara India Pariwar, cos include Sahara India Financial Corpn Ltd, Sahara Care House, Sahara Infrastructure and Housing; Noble Citizen Award 1986, Baba-E-Rozgar 1992, Karmaveer Samman 1995, Nat. Citizen Award 2001, Businessman of the Year Award 2002, Global Leadership Award 2004, Lifetime Achievement Award 2004, Mother Teresa Millenium Award for Renowned Industrialist 2005, ITA ICON 2007. *Publications:* Shanti Sukh: Santushti, Maan-Samman: Atmasamman. *Address:* Sahara India Pariwar, Sahara Information and Contact Point, PO Box 2, Gomti Nagar, Lucknow 10, India; fax (522) 2303818; e-mail info@saharaindiapariwar.org; internet www .sahara.in; www.sahara.in/saharasri.

**RUHUL AMIN, M. M.,** LLB, MA; Bangladeshi judge; *Chief Justice of Bangladesh;* b. 23 Dec. 1942, Laxmipur. *Education:* Dhaka Univ., Nat. Judicial Coll., USA. *Career:* began career as asst judge in fmr East Pakistan, promoted to dist judge 1984, served courts in Chittagong, Cox's Bazar, Kishoreganj and Jessore, visited several US courts to learn about alternative dispute resolution and court admin 1990, apptd High Court Judge 1994, visited Sri Lanka, India and Nepal to learn about their judicial services and salary structure of judges; Judge, Sr Appellate Div., Supreme Court of Bangladesh 2003–08; Chair. Judicial Service Comm. 2004–08; Chief Justice of Bangladesh 2008–. *Address:* Supreme Court of Bangladesh, Dhaka 2, Bangladesh.

**SABIT, Abdul Jabar;** Afghan lawyer and government official; *Attorney-General. Career:* legal adviser, Ministry of the Interior –2006; Attorney-Gen. 2006–; mem. official del. that visited Afghan prisoners held by US Govt in Guantánamo Bay detainment camp, Cuba 2006. *Address:* Office of the Attorney-General, Ministry of Justice, Pashtunistan Wat, Kabul, Afghanistan; tel. (20) 2101322.

**SAIFULLAH KHAN, Javed,** BA, MBA; Pakistani business executive; *Chairman, Saif Holdings. Education:* Carnegie Mellon Univ., Univ. of Pittsburgh, USA. *Career:* joined Saif Group of Cos 1973, Chair. Saif Holdings 1990–, holding co. of Saif Group consisting of interests in telecommunications, information tech., cement and textiles, including Pakistan Mobile Communications Pvt. Ltd, Saif Telecom Ltd, Transworld Assocs Pvt. Ltd, Saif Textile Mills; Sr Advisor Galen Capital Group LLC, USA; mem. Bd of Dirs Pakistan Int. Airlines Corpn, Pakistan Mobile Communications Ltd, Lok Virsa; mem. Bd of Investment, Govt of Pakistan; mem. Exec. Cttee Pakistan Petroleum Exploration and Production Cos; fmr Chair. Cen. Man. Cttee, All Pakistan Textile Mills Asscn; fmr mem. Task Force, Information Tech. and Telecommunication Advisory Bd, Ministry of Science and Tech.; Sitara I Imtiaz 2007. *Address:* Saif Group, Kulsum Plaza 42, Blue Area, Islamabad, Pakistan; tel. (51) 2823924; fax (51) 2277843; e-mail info@saifgroup.com; internet www.saifgroup .com.

**SAIGOL, Mian Naseem;** Pakistani business executive; *Chairman, Saigol Group of Companies. Career:* Chair. Saigol Group of Cos, conglomerate with interests in automobiles, eng, power, information tech., including Kohinoor Textile Mills; Chair. Pak Elektron Ltd (PEL); Chair. and CEO

Kohinoor Power Co. Ltd; est. Union Bank 1991; mem. Commonwealth Business Council, mem. Bd of Dirs 2006–08;. *Address:* Pak Electron Ltd, 17 Aziz Avenue, Canal Bank, Lahore, Pakistan; tel. (42) 5717364-5; fax (42) 5715105; internet www.pel.com.pk.

**SALEH, Amrullah;** Afghan government official; *Head, National Security Directorate;* b. Panjshir Prov. *Education:* high school educ., Afghanistan. *Career:* served as trans. between CIA officers and Northern Alliance leader Ahmad Shah Massoud 2001, helped remove Taliban from power with support of US-led coalition late 2001; fmr Chief Liaison Officer with foreign mil. and diplomatic corps, Kabul; fmr political officer, spokesman and relief co-ordinator; fmr Deputy Chief of Afghanistan Intelligence, focused on foreign relations; Sr mem. Nat. Security Directorate, Head of Directorate 2004–; Hon. DSc (Cleary Univ., Mich.) 2005. *Address:* National Security Directorate, Kabul, Afghanistan; e-mail ahmad.afg@gmail.com.

**SAMAR, Sima,** DMed; Afghan politician and physician; *Chairperson, Afghanistan Independent Human Rights Commission;* b. Feb. 1957, Jaghoori, Ghazni. *Education:* Kabul Univ. *Career:* exiled in Pakistan following Soviet invasion; Founder and Dir Shuhada Org., f. Shuhada hosp. for Afghan women and children, Quetta, Pakistan 1989, founder of three medical clinics, four hosps and girls' schools in rural Afghanistan (also providing medical training, literacy programmes and food aid), f. school for refugee girls in Quetta, f. Shuhada Org.; mem. Women Living Under Muslim Law; political activist and opponent of women's subjugation under Taliban regime; Vice-Chair. and Minister of Women's Affairs, Afghan Interim Authority 2001–02; currently Chair. Afghanistan Ind. Human Rights Comm.; UN Special Rapporteur for Human Rights in Sudan 2005–; Perdita Huston Human Rights Award, John Humphrey Freedom Award 2001, UN Asscn of the Nat. Capital Area 2003, Jonathan Mann Award for Health and Human Rights 2004, Profile in Courage Award 2004, ranked by Forbes magazine amongst 100 Most Powerful Women (74th) 2004, (28th) 2006, (92nd) 2007. *Address:* Afghanistan Independent Human Rights Commission, Pul-i-Surkh, Karti 3, Kabul; Shuhada Organization, Karte 3, Pule Surkh, Kabul, Afghanistan; tel. (20) 2500676; (20) 2501247; fax (20) 2500677; e-mail aihrc@aihrc.org.af; sima_samar@yahoo.com; internet www.aihrc.org.af.

**SANDAGIRI, Adm. Daya,** MSc; Sri Lankan naval officer; b. Veyangoda. *Education:* St Mary's Coll. Veyangoda, Kegalu Maha Vidyalaya. *Career:* joined Royal Ceylon Navy (now Sri Lanka Navy) 1966, Sub-Lt 1973, Commdr of the Navy 2001–05, promoted to rank of Adm. 2005; Chief of Defence Staff 2004–06; Deputy Sec., Ministry of Defence 2006–, suspended June 2006 accused of engaging in malpractice in arms purchases.

**SARABI, Habiba;** Afghan politician, pharmacist and women's rights activist; *Governor of Bamiyan Province;* b. 5 Dec. 1957, Mazar-e Sharif; m.; three c. *Education:* Aisha Durani High School, Kabul Univ. *Career:* licensed pharmacist; with Nat. Inst. of Medicine, Kabul 1983–87; teacher Intermediate Medical Inst., Kabul 1988–96; exile in Pakistan 1996–2001; Prof. and Gen. Man. Afghanistan Inst. of Learning 1997–2001; medical aid to women and children in refugee camps on Afghanistan–Pakistan border 2001; Dir of Humanitarian Assistance for the Women and Children of Afghanistan, Peshawar 2002; Minister of Women's Affairs 2002–04; Gov. of Bamiyan Prov. (first female gov. in Afghanistan) 2005–; WHO Fellowship Training Programme, All India Inst. of Medical Science 1998; Jason Award, USA 2005, Malalai Maiwand Medal from Pres. Karzai 2005. *Address:* Chawney, Governor's Office, Bamyan, Afghanistan; tel. 799300120; 202400008; e-mail bamyangovernor@yahoo.com.

**SARKAR, Manik;** Indian politician; *Chief Minister of Tripura;* b. 22 Jan. 1949, Radhakishorepur. *Education:* Maharaja Bir Bakram Coll., Calcutta Univ. *Career:* mem. Communist Party of India—Marxist 1968–, mem. State Cttee 1972, State Secr. 1978, mem. Central Cttee 1985, State Sec. 1993, State Left Front Convenor, mem. Politburo 1998; mem. Tripura Legis. Ass. 1980–; Chief Minister of Tripura 1998–. *Address:* Chief Minister's Secretariat, Agartala, Tripura, India; tel. (381) 2324000; fax (381) 2223201; e-mail cmo-trp@hub.nic.in; internet tripura.nic.in.

**SAYEED, Hafiz Mohammad;** Pakistani militant leader. *Career:* fmr Prof. of Eng., Univ. of Tech. and Eng, Lahore; Co-Founder and Leader, Lashkar-e-Taiba (banned militant group), Founder and Leader Jamaat-ud-Dawa; detained, then placed under house arrest 2002, released Nov. 2002. *Address:* Jamaat-ud-Dawa, Bdehai Road, Peshawar, Pakistan; tel. (521) 2262189; fax (521) 2260800; e-mail Jdawa@hotmail.com; internet www.jamaatuddawa.org.

**SCINDIA, Vasundhara Raje,** BA; Indian politician; *Chief Minister of Rajasthan;* b. 8 March 1953, Bombay (now Mumbai); m. Raja Hemant Singh 1972; one s. *Education:* Presentation Convent, Kodaikanal, Sophia Coll., Mumbai Univ. *Career:* MLA for Dholpur 1984–89; Vice-Pres. Bharatiya Janata Party (BJP) Yuva Morcha 1984–89; Vice-Pres. Rajasthan State BJP 1985–89, Pres. 2002–; mem. Lok Sabha 1989–; Jt Sec. BJP Parl. Cttee 1997; Union Minister for Foreign Affairs 1998–99; Minister for Small Scale Industries and Agric. and Rural Industries (Ind. charge) 1999–2003; State Minister for Personnel and Training, Pensions and Welfare, Personnel, Public Grievance and Pension Ministry, Atomic Energy and Space Dept 1999–2003; Chief Minister of Rajasthan 2003–; numerous visits abroad for various social causes; UN Women Together Award 2007. *Address:* Chief Minister's Secretariat, Government of Rajasthan, Jaipur, Rajasthan; Pratap Chowk, Jhalawar 326 001, India; e-mail me@vasundhara-raje.com; internet www.rajasthan.gov.in; www.vasundhara-raje.com.

**SEN, Nirupam;** Indian diplomatist; *Permanent Representative, United Nations. Career:* joined Foreign Service 1969; served in Moscow, Warsaw, Budapest, London; fmr Amb. to Bulgaria, to Norway; fmr Minister for Commerce and Industry; High Commr to Sri Lanka 2002–04; Perm. Rep. to UN, New York 2004–. *Address:* Permanent Representative of India to the United Nations, 235 East 43rd Street, New York, NY 10017, USA; tel. (212) 490-9660; fax (212) 490-9656; e-mail india@un.int; indiaun@prodigy.net; internet www.un.int/india.

**SHAFEEU, Ismail;** Maldivian politician; *Minister of Defence and National Security. Career:* fmr Minister of Educ. 2002–03; Minister of Home Affairs and Environment 2003–04, of Defence and Nat. Security 2004–; Chair. Dhiraagu Ltd. *Address:* Ministry of Defence and National Security, Bandaara Koshi, Ameer Ahmed Magu, Malé 20-05, Maldives; tel. 3322607; fax 3332800; e-mail admin@defence.gov.mv; internet www.defence.gov.mv.

**SHAH, Syed Qaim Ali,** BA, LLB; Pakistani lawyer and politician; *Chief Minister of Sindh;* b. 1935, Khairpur dist; m. 1st (deceased); m. 2nd (deceased); m. 3rd; four s. seven d. from three marriages. *Education:* Univ. of Karachi, SM Law Coll., Karachi. *Career:* elected Chair. Dist Council, Khairpur in Ayub Khan's era; pioneer mem. Pakistan People's Party (PPP) 1967; elected mem. Nat. Ass. 1970; Fed. Minister for Industries and Kashmir Affairs during Zulfikar Ali Bhutto's premiership; Pres. PPP Sindh 1973–77, 1987–97, 2004–; elected mem. Prov. Ass. 1990, later Leader of Sindh Ass., re-elected five times; elected Senator 1997; Chief Minister of Sindh 1988–90, 2008–. *Address:* Chief Minister House, Dr Ziauddin Ahmed Road, Karachi, Sindh; Jilani House, Khairpur, Pakistan; tel. (21) 9202051–4; e-mail info@sindh.gov.pk; internet www.sindh.gov.pk.

**SHAHID, Abdullah;** Maldivian politician; *Minister of Foreign Affairs;* m.; three c. *Education:* Canberra Coll. of Advanced Educ., Australia, Fletcher School of Law and Diplomacy, Tufts Univ., USA. *Career:* began civil service career in Foreign Ministry 1983; mem. Constitutional Ass. 1994; mem. Parl. 1995–; Exec. Sec. to the Pres. 1995–2005; Minister of State for Foreign Affairs 2005–07, Minister of

Foreign Affairs 2007–. *Address:* Ministry of Foreign Affairs, Boduthakurufaanu Magu, Malé 10-307, The Maldives; tel. 3323400; fax 3323841; e-mail ministerbureau@foreign.gov.mv; internet www.foreign.gov.mv.

**SHAHRANI, Nematullah,** PhD; Afghan politician; *Minister of Hajj and Religious Affairs;* b. Jorm Dist, Badakhshan. *Education:* Abu Hanifa School, Kabul Univ., Al-Azhar Univ., Egypt. *Career:* fmr Prof. of Sharia, Kabul Univ.; fmr Ed.-in-Chief, Sharayat magazine; Vice-Pres., Transitional Authority 2002–04; Dir Constitutional Drafting Cttee 2002; Minister of Hajj and Religious Affairs 2004–. *Publications include:* Quran Shenaasy (Knowing the Holy Quran), Feqeh Islami Wa Qanoon e Gharb (Islamic Fiqh and Western Law); numerous articles and books on Sharia law. *Address:* Ministry of Hajj and Religious Affairs, nr District 10, Shir Pur, Shar-i-Nau, Kabul, Afghanistan; tel. (20) 2201338.

**SHAKOOR, Aishath Azima;** Maldivian lawyer, politician and government official; *Attorney-General. Career:* fmr Deputy Minister of Home Affairs; MP apptd by Pres. Maumoon Abdul Gayoom; Pres. Women's Wing of Dhivehi Rayyithunge Party; Attorney-Gen. 2007–. *Address:* Attorney-General's Office, Huravee Building, 3rd Floor, Ameer Ahmed Magu, Malé 20-05, Maldives; tel. 3323809; fax 3314109; e-mail ashraf@agoffice.gov.mv.

**SHAMS, Mohammad Jalil,** PhD; Afghan economist, academic and politician; *Minister of Economy. Education:* Sultan Ghias-ud-din Ghoori High School, Herat, Cairo Univ., Egypt, Bochum Univ., Germany. *Career:* Asst Prof., School of Econs, Kabul Univ. 1964–66; Vice-Pres. Banke Milli-e-Afghan, Hamburg, Germany 1969–71; Man. Dir Afghan Nat. Bank, London, UK 1971–74; Lecturer in Econs, Essen Polytechnic Germany 1973–74; Deputy Minister of Foreign Affairs 1992–94 (resgnd in protest against internal conflict in Afghanistan); Deputy Minister of Energy and Water 2005–06; Minister of Economy 2006–. *Address:* Ministry of Economy, 5th Floor, Malik Asghar Square, Kabul, Afghanistan.

**SHANGHVI, Dilip,** BCom; Indian pharmaceutical industry executive; *Chairman and Managing Director, Sun Pharmaceutical Industries Ltd;* m.; two c. *Education:* Calcutta Univ. *Career:* Founder and Man. Dir Sun Pharmaceutical Industries Ltd 1983–, Chair. 1999–; Chair. Bd of Dirs Caraco Pharmaceutical Labs Ltd 1997–; mem. Advisory Cttee Global Bio Pharma Conf. Group; Ernst and Young Entrepreneur of the Year in Health Care and Life Sciences 2005. *Address:* Sun Pharmaceutical Industries Limited, 17-B, Mahal Industrial Estate, Mahakali; Sun Pharmaceutical Industries Limited, Caves Road, Qudhen East, Mumbai 93, India; tel. (22) 56455645; fax (22) 56455685; e-mail piedadedsouya@sunpharma.com; internet www.sunpharma.com.

**SHANKAR, Uday;** Indian journalist and media executive; *COO, Star India. Education:* Jawaharlal Nehru Univ., New Delhi. *Career:* worked at The Times of India, Sunday Mail, India Today and Sahara (launched news div. of Sahara TV); fmr Ed. and News Dir Aaj Tak, launched Aaj Tak Headlines Today; joined Star News as CEO Media Content and Communications Services, Star Group 2004–07, COO Star India 2007–. *Address:* Star India, 1st Floor, Central Wing, Thapar House, 124 Janpath, New Delhi 110 001, India; tel. (11) 42494900; fax (11) 41049490; e-mail info@star.co.in; internet www.star.co.in; www.indya.com.

**SHARIF, Muhammad Shahbaz;** Pakistani politician; *Chief Minister of Punjab and President, Pakistan Muslim League—Nawaz;* b. 1950, Lahore; brother of Nawaz Sharif, fmr Prime Minister of Pakistan; m. 1st Nusrat Shahbaz 1973; two s. three d.; m. 2nd Aaliya Honey 1993 (divorced); one d.; m. 3rd Tehmina Durrani. *Career:* Chief Minister of Punjab 1997–99 (ousted in mil. coup of Gen. Pervez Musharraf 1999); Pres. Pakistan Muslim League—Nawaz 2002–; lived in exile in Saudi Arabia and London before being allowed to return to Pakistan 2007; Chief Minister of Punjab 2008–. *Address:* Office of the Chief Minister, Government of Punjab, 3rd Floor, 3rd Building, Aiwan-e-Iqbal Egerton Road, Lahore, Punjab; Pakistan Muslim League—Nawaz, House No. 20-H, Street 10, F-8/3, Islamabad, Pakistan; tel. (42) 9203151; (51) 2852662 (Islamabad); fax (42) 9203154; e-mail webmaster@punjab.gov.pk; pmlisb@hotmail.com; internet www.punjab.gov.pk; www.pmln.org.pk.

**SHARMA, Sheel Kant,** MS, PhD; Indian diplomatist and international organization executive; *Secretary-General, South Asian Association for Regional Cooperation (SAARC);* b. 10 Jan. 1950; m. Meenu Sharma. *Education:* Indian Inst. of Tech., Mumbai. *Career:* joined Foreign Service 1973, served as Third Sec., Embassy in Kuwait and Second Sec., Embassy in Saudi Arabia 1976–77, Under-Sec., Middle East Desk, Ministry of External Affairs 1978–81, Fellow, Inst. of Defence Studies and Analysis, New Delhi 1981–82, Deputy Sec. (North), Ministry of External Affairs 1982–83, First Sec. (Disarmament), Perm. Mission to UN, Geneva and Alt. Rep. to UN Conf. on Disarmament 1983–86, Counsellor and Deputy Chief of Mission, Embassy in Algiers 1986–89, Dir (UN Div.) and Disarmament Head, Ministry of External Affairs, New Delhi 1989–91, Jt Sec. (South and Disarmament) in charge of India's relations with ASEAN, Indo-China and South Pacific 1991–94; seconded to IAEA, Vienna, served as sr professional in External Relations and Policy Coordination Div. 1994–2000; Jt Sec. (Disarmament and Int. Security Affairs) 2000–03, Additional Sec. (Int. Orgs), Ministry of External Affairs 2003–04, Amb. to Austria and Perm. Rep. to all Int. Orgs, Vienna 2004–08, Sec.-Gen. South Asian Asscn for Regional Cooperation (SAARC) 2008–; Chair. G-77 Vienna Chapter 2005; mem. India Int. Centre, India Habitat Centre. *Publications:* articles in journals and UN reports. *Address:* South Asian Association for Regional Co-operation (SAARC), PO Box 4222, Tridevi Marg, Kathmandu, Nepal; tel. (1) 4221785; fax (1) 4227033; e-mail saarc@saarc-sec.org; internet www.saarc-sec.org.

**SHEKHAWAT, Bhairon Singh;** Indian politician; b. 23 Oct. 1923; m. Suraj Kanwar; one d. *Career:* mem. Rajasthan Legis. Ass. 1952–72, 1977–2002; mem. Rajya Sabha 1974–77; Chief Minister of Rajasthan 1977–80, 1990–92, 1993–98; Vice-Pres. of India 2002–07 (resgnd); fmr Leader, Janata Dal, Bharatiya Janata Party. *Address:* 31 Aurangazeb Road, New Delhi, India.

**SHERCHAN, Amik;** Nepalese politician. *Career:* Chair. People's Front Nepal (Janamorcha Nepal); Deputy Prime Minister and Minister of Health and Population 2006–07. *Address:* c/o Ministry of Health and Population, Singh Durbar Plaza, Ramshah Path, Kathmandu, Nepal.

**SHERPAO, Aftab Ahmad Khan;** Pakistani politician; b. 20 Aug. 1944. *Career:* f. Pakistan People's Party—PPP (Sherpao Group), breakaway faction, faction rejoined PPP 2002; fmr Chief Minister of North-West Frontier Prov.; fmr Minister of Water and Power, of Inter-Prov. Co-ordination and of Kashmir Affairs, Northern Areas and State and Frontier Regions; Minister of the Interior 2004–07. *Address:* c/o Pakistan People's Party, 8, Street 19, F-8/2, Islamabad, Pakistan; tel. (51) 2255264; fax (51) 2282741; e-mail ppp@comsats.net.pk; internet www.ppp.org.pk.

**SHERZAI, Gul Agha;** Afghan politician; *Governor of Nangarhar. Career:* Gov. of Kandahar prior to Taliban takeover, in exile in Quetta, Pakistan 1994–2001, reinstated as Gov. of Kandahar 2002–04, Gov. of Nangarhar 2004–; Minister of Urban Affairs 2003; fmr Minister of Urban Devt and Housing; Minister of Public Works –2004; fmr ministerial adviser to Pres. Hamid Karzai. *Address:* Office of the Governor, Jalalabad, Nangarhar Province, Afghanistan.

**SHINWARI, Dilbar Jan Arman;** Afghan politician and government official; *Governor, Zabul Province. Career:* fmr anti-Soviet insurgent who fled to Pakistan during Taliban rule of Afghanistan; Gov. Zabul Prov. 2005–; known for close involvement with US Prov. Reconstruction Team based in Qalat. *Address:* Office of the Governor, Qalat, Zabul Province, Afghanistan.

**SHRESTHA, Ambica,** BA; Nepalese business executive; *Managing Director, Kathmandu Travels and Tours;* b. 12 Feb. 1933; two d. *Education:* in India. *Career:* Man. Dir Kathmandu Travels and Tours, Nepal Trek and Natural History Expeditions; Dir Davs Enterprises Pvt. Ltd; Pres. Dwarika's Hotel; mem. Transparency Int. Nepal anti-corruption organisation (Pres. Exec. Cttee 1996–); Pres. Int. Fed. of Business and Professional Women; Hon. Consul of Spain; Pata Heritage Award, Business and Professional Women's Club 1980, Gorkha Dakchin Bahu Award. *Address:* c/o Kathmandu Travels and Tours Ltd, POB 459, Battisputali, Kathmandu, Nepal; tel. (1) 471577; fax (1) 471379; e-mail ktt@mail.com.np; internet www.kttgroup.com.

**SHRESTHA, Indra Bahadur;** Nepalese business executive; *Chairman, Hetauda Cement Industries Ltd. Career:* fmr Pres. CCI Makawanpur; Chair. Hetauda Cement Industries Ltd; Pres. Lalitpur Chamber of Commerce and Industry; mem. Nat. Exec. Cttee, Amnesty Int. Nepal 2004. *Address:* Hetauda Cement Industries Ltd, PO Box 24, Hetauda, Makawanpur; Lalitpur Chamber of Commerce and Industry, Mangal Bazar, PO Box 26, Lalitpur, Nepal; tel. (1) 5521740; fax (1) 5530661; e-mail lcci@mos.com.np.

**SILVA, Hon. Sarath Nanda,** LLM; Sri Lankan judge; *Chief Justice of the Supreme Court. Education:* Univ. of Brussels, Belgium. *Career:* Advocate of the Supreme Court of Sri Lanka 1967; Crown Counsel, Attorney Gen.'s Dept 1968, Sr State Counsel 1975, Deputy Solicitor Gen. 1979; Lecturer, Sri Lanka Law Coll. 1981–87; Judge, Court of Appeal 1987–1994, Pres. 1994; Judge of the Supreme Court 1995–99, Chief Justice 1999–; Lecturer in Civil Law, Sri Lanka Law Coll. 1981–87; Attorney Gen. 1996; Pres.'s Counsel 1996. *Address:* Supreme Court of Sri Lanka, Superior Courts Complex, Colombo 12, Sri Lanka; tel. (1) 328651; fax (1) 435446.

**SILVA, Tilwin;** Sri Lankan politician; *General Secretary, Janatha Vimukthi Peramuna (JVP);* b. 26 Feb. 1956. *Career:* Gen. Sec. Janatha Vimukthi Peramuna (People's Liberation Front) 1995–. *Address:* Janatha Vimukthi Peramuna, 198/19 Panchikawattha Road, Colombo 10, Sri Lanka; tel. (11) 4400511; fax (11) 2786050; e-mail contact@jvpsrilanka.com; internet www.jvpsrilanka.com.

**SINGAY, Lyonpo Jigme,** MBBS, MPH; Bhutanese politician; b. 5 May 1954, Themnangbi, Mongar Dist. *Education:* Delhi Univ., India, San Diego State Univ., USA. *Career:* Deputy Dir Public Health Div., Dept of Health Services 1987–89, Jt Dir, Dept of Health Services 1989–1993, Dir Div. of Health Services 1994–98; Sec. Royal Civil Service Comm. 1998–2003; Minister of Health 2003–07 (resgnd); mem. People's Democratic Party; Red Scarf 1997, Orange Scarf 2003. *Address:* c/o People's Democratic Party, Drizang Lam, Lower Motithang, Thimphu; Tshogdu Chenmo, Secretariat, Gyelyong Tshokhang, POB 139, Thimphu; Themnangbi, Mongar Dzongkhag, Bhutan; tel. (2) 322729; (2) 322136; fax (2) 324210; internet www.nab.gov.bt.

**SINGH, Lt-Gen. (retd) Bhopinder;** Indian army officer (retd) and government official; *Lieutentant-Governor of Andaman and Nicobar Islands and of Puducherry;* b. 20 March 1946, Allahabad, UP; m. Bhawanee Singh. *Education:* Nat. Defence Acad. *Career:* commissioned into Rajput Regt 1965, held several command, staff and instructional appointments, commanded troops in Indo-Pak wars 1965, 1971, led counter-insurgency operations in Jammu and Kashmir, Mizoram and Assam, has been an Instructor at Indian Mil. Acad., held Gen. Staff tenures at Kargil and Kashmir Valley, commanded 17 Rajput Bn, commanded Rajput Regimental Centre, Fategarh, UP; fmr Mil., Naval and Air Attaché in Addis Ababa; as Maj.-Gen. was Additional Dir-Gen. of Org. (AG's Br.), Army HQ; Mil. Sec. to Pres. of India and Col of Pres.'s Bodyguard 1997–; Col, Rajput Regt 2002; Lt-Gov. of Andaman and Nicobar Islands 2006–, of Puducherry 2008–; Param Vishisht Seva Medal (PVSM), Ati Vishisht Seva Medal (AVSM); Army Commdr's Commendation, Ethiopian Govt Commendation Certificate. *Address:* Office of the Governor, Andaman and Nicobar Administration, Port Blair, Andaman and Nicobar Islands, India; tel. 233333; 233300; e-mail lg@and.nic.in; lgandaman@hotmail.com; lgandaman@yahoo.com; internet www.and.nic.in.

**SINGH, Durgesh Man;** Nepalese diplomatist; *Ambassador to India. Education:* student of Prime Minister of India Manmohan Singh. *Career:* fmr Amb. to Belgium, Amb. to India 2008–. *Address:* Embassy of Nepal, Barakhamba Road, New Delhi 110 001, India; tel. (11) 23329218; fax (11) 23326857; e-mail nepembassydelhi@bol.net.in.

**SINGH, Harpal,** BA, BS, MPA; Indian business executive; *Chairman, Ranbaxy Laboratories Limited. Education:* The Doon School, St Stephen's Coll., New Delhi, CSCH, Calif., USA. *Career:* has held sr positions in Tata Admin. Service, Hindustan Motors, Telco, and Bd-level responsibility at Shaw Wallace; Sr Advisor (Corp. Projects), Mahindra and Mahindra; Chair. Fortis Healthcare Ltd, Fortis Financial Services Ltd, Fortis Securities Ltd; Chair. (non-exec.) Ranbaxy Labs Ltd 2007–. *Address:* Ranbaxy Laboratories Ltd, Corporate Office, Plot 90, Sector 32, Gurgaon 122001, Haryana, India; tel. (124) 4135000; fax (124) 4135001; e-mail seema.ahuja@ranbaxy.com; internet www.ranbaxy.com.

**SINGH, Manmohan,** PhD; Indian economist and politician; *Prime Minister and Minister-in-charge of Personnel, Public Grievances and Pensions, of Planning, of Atomic Energy, of Space, of Coal and of the Environment and Forests;* b. 26 Sept. 1932, Gah, Punjab (now Pakistan); m. Gursharan Kaur; three d. *Education:* Univ. of Punjab, Univs of Cambridge and Oxford, UK. *Career:* Lecturer, Univ. of Punjab 1957–69; Prof. Delhi School of Econs 1969–71; econ. adviser, Ministry of Foreign Trade 1971–72; Chief Econ. Adviser, Ministry of Finance 1972–76; Dir Reserve Bank of India 1976–80, Gov. 1982–85; Mem.-Sec. Planning Comm. 1980–82, Deputy Chair. 1985–87; Sec.-Gen., Commr South Comm. 1987–90; econ. adviser to Prime Minister 1990–91; Minister of Finance 1991–96; mem. Rajya Sabha (Parl.) 1991–, Leader of Opposition 1995–2004; Prime Minister of India and Minister-in-charge of Personnel, Public Grievances and Pensions, of Planning, of Atomic Energy, of Space 2004–, also Minister of External Affairs 2005–06, Minister of Coal and of the Environment and Forests 2007–; Dr hc (Univ. of Cambridge) 2006. *Publication:* India's Export Trends and Prospects for Self-Sustained Growth 1964. *Address:* Prime Minister's Office, South Block, New Delhi, 110 011; 7 Safdarjung Lane, New Delhi, 110011, India; tel. (11) 23013040; (11) 3018668; fax (11) 23016857; e-mail manmohan@sansad.nic.in; internet www.pmindia.nic.in.

**SINGH, Rajnath,** MSc; Indian politician and farmer; *President, Bharatiya Janata Party;* b. 10 July 1951, Bhabhora village, Tehsil Chakia of Varanasi dist, UP; m. Savitri Singh; two s. one d. *Education:* Gorakhpur Univ. *Career:* Lecturer in Physics, K.B. Postgraduate Coll., Mirzapur, UP; served in various capacities with Rashtriya Swayamsevak Sangh (Nat. Volunteers' Union—Hindu nationalist org.) since 1964; Org. Sec. Akhil Bharthiya Vidyarthi Parishad (Gorakhpur Div.) 1969–71; apptd Sec. Bharatiya Jana Sangh's Mirzapur Unit 1974; joined JP Movt and was apptd its Dist Convenor; apptd Dist Pres. Jana Sangh 1975; jailed during Emergency 1975, remained in jail until elections 1977; elected as mem. Legis. Ass. from Mirzapur constituency 1977; held several positions in Bharatiya Janata Yuva Morcha (BJYM), UP State Unit as well as in Nat. Exec., BJP Sec. in UP 1983–84, State Pres. BJYM 1984–86, Nat. Gen. Sec. BJYM 1986–88, Nat. Pres. BJYM 1988, Vice-Pres. BJP, UP 1990, Pres. 1997–99, mem. Nat. Exec. BJP, Gen. Sec. Cen. BJP org. 2002–05, Pres. BJP 2005–; mem. UP Legis. Council 1988–94; Minister of Educ. 1991–94; elected to Rajya Sabha 1994, mem. Advisory Cttee on Industry 1994–96, Consultative Cttee for Ministry of Agric., Business Advisory Cttee, House Cttee, Cttee on Human Resource Devt, Chief Whip of BJP in Rajya Sabha; Union Minister for Surface Transport 1999–2000; Chief Minister of UP 2000–02; Union Minister of Agric. 2002. *Publication:* book on the causes of and solutions to unemployment problems. *Address:* BJP Central Office, 11 Ashoka Road,

New Delhi 110 001, India; tel. (11) 23382234; fax (11) 23782163; e-mail bjpco@vsnl.com; internet www.bjp.org.

**SINGH, Raman,** BSc, BAMS; Indian medical practitioner and politician; *Chief Minister of Chhattisgarh;* b. 15 Oct. 1952, Thathapur, Kawardha Dist; m. Smt. Beena Singh; one s. one d. *Education:* Univ. of Ravishankar, Raipur. *Career:* Ayurvedic medical practitioner; MLA 1990–92, 1993–98; mem. Bharatiya Janata Party (BJP) (Pradesh Mantri) 1996–; Pres. BJP Legislature Party 2003–; mem. Lok Lekha Samitti Public Accounts Samitti, Legis. Cttee; mem. Lok Sabha for Rajnandgaon 1990–, later BJP Chief Whip; Union Minister of State for Commerce and Industry 1999–2003; Chief Minister of Chhattisgarh 2003–. *Address:* Government of Chhattisgarh, Mantralaya, Raipur 492 001, Chhattisgarh, India; tel. (771) 2221000; e-mail cmcg@nic.in; internet chhattisgarh.nic.in.

**SIRCAR, Muhammad Jamiruddin;** Bangladeshi barrister and politician; *Speaker of Jatiya Sangsad (Parliament);* b. 1 Dec. 1931. *Career:* mem. Bangladesh Jatiyatabadi Dal (Bangladesh Nationalist Party); MP for Panchagarh-1, Seat-1, currently Speaker of Jatiya Sangsad (Parl.); Acting Pres. of Bangladesh June–Sept. 2002. *Address:* Jatiyo Sangshad Bhaban, Dhaka; 21 Baily Road, Ramna, Dhaka - 1000, Bangladesh; tel. (2) 8111499; (2) 933480; e-mail info@parliament.gov.bd; internet www.parliament.gov.bd; www.parliamentofbangladesh.org.

**SOOD, Rakesh,** PhD; Indian academic and diplomatist; *Ambassador to Nepal. Career:* joined Ministry of External Affairs 1976, has served in Missions in Brussels, Dakar, Geneva and Islamabad, Dir and Jt Sec. for Disarmament and Int. Security Affairs, Ministry of External Affairs 1992–2000, Amb. and Perm. Rep. to UN Conf. on Disarmament, UN Disarmament Comm., Geneva 2000–03; Alt. Rep. of Dept of Atomic Energy at Council of CERN 2001–03; Deputy Chief of Mission, Washington, DC 2003–04, Amb. to Afghanistan 2004–08, to Nepal 2008–; Chair. Meeting of States Parties to the Convention on Prohibitions or Restrictions on the Use of Certain Conventional Weapons Which May be Deemed to be Excessively Injurious or to Have Indiscriminate Effects 2002–03, UN Sec.-Gen.'s Group of Govt Experts to Identify and Trace, in a Timely and Reliable Manner, Illicit Small Arms and Light Weapons, in All its Aspects 2002; fmr mem. UN Sec.-Gen.'s Advisory Bd on Disarmament Matters, UN Sec.-Gen.'s Expert Groups on Conventional Arms and on Verification; has participated in negotiations on Chemical Weapons Convention and Nuclear-Test-Ban Treaty (CTBT) at Conf. on Disarmament; has represented India in UN Disarmament Comm. meetings, First Cttee of UN Gen. Ass., CTBT negotiations, Biological Weapons Convention and Inhumane Weapons Convention Review Confs, Third Special Session of UN Gen. Ass. devoted to Disarmament, Non-Aligned Movt confs and summits, ASEAN Regional Forum meetings, Middle-East Arms Control and Regional Security Working Group, India-Pakistan talks, bilateral talks with USA, UK, France, Russia, Japan, Germany and China on disarmament, nonproliferation, int. security and export control issues. *Publications:* numerous articles on disarmament, nonproliferation and security-related issues. *Address:* Embassy of India, 336 Kapurdhara Marg, POB 292, Kathmandu, Nepal; tel. (1) 4410900; fax (1) 4428279; e-mail pic@eoiktm.org; internet www.south-asia.com/embassy-India.

**SOOMRO, Mohammad Mian,** BSc, MSc; Pakistani banker and politician; *Acting President and Chairman of the Senate;* b. 19 Aug. 1950, Sindh. *Education:* Forman Christian Coll., Lahore, Punjab Univ., Northrop Univ., USA. *Career:* Head of Soomro tribe; mem. Pakistan Muslim League (PML); held various positions in nat. and int. orgs, including Bank of America; fmr Gen. Man. and CEO Int. Bank of Yemen, Faysal Islamic Bank of Bahrain, Muslim Commercial Bank, Agriculture Devt Bank of Pakistan, Fed. Bank of Cooperatives, Nat. Bank of Pakistan; Chair. Pakistan Banks Assn 1997–2000; mem. Governing Council Inst. of Bankers in Pakistan 1997–2000; mem. Bd of Dirs Shell Pakistan Ltd, Pakistan Int. Airlines Corpn, Pakistan Refinery Ltd (Shell Petroleum Jt Venture), Pak Arab Refinery, Pak Arab Fertilizer, Bank Al-Jazira (Jeddah, Saudi Arabia), Nat. Investment Trust, Investment Co-operation of Pakistan, Nat. Discounting Services Ltd, Nat. Exchange Co. (Abu Dhabi), Nat. Bank Modaraba Man. Co. Ltd, First Women Bank Ltd, Consolidated Leasing Co., Nat. Construction Co., Pakistan Tourism Devt Corpn (all 1997–2000); helped establish micro-credit banking in Pakistan; Gov. of Sindh 2000–02; Senator 2003–, Chair. of the Senate 2003–, Chair. Finance Cttee; Acting Pres. 2008–. *Address:* Office of the President, Aiwan-e-Sadr, Islamabad; Senate of Pakistan, Parliament House, Islamabad, Pakistan; tel. (51) 9206060; (51) 9223475; fax (51) 9208046; (51) 9223477; e-mail chairman@senate.gov.pk; internet www.presidentofpakistan.gov.pk; www.senate.gov.pk.

**SOREN, Shibu;** Indian politician; *Chief Minister of Jharkhand; Leader, Jharkhand Mukti Morcha;* b. 11 Jan. 1944, Nemra dist., Bihar; m. Rupi Devi; three s. one d. *Career:* elected to Rajya Sabha 1989, 1991, 1996, 1998; Minister of Coal May–July 2004 (resgnd), reinstated Nov. 2004, resgnd March 2005; Chief Minister of Jharkhand March 2005–06, 2008–; Minister for Coal 2004–06 (resgnd); currently Leader Jharkhand Mukti Morcha; sentenced to life imprisonment on abduction and murder charges 2006. *Address:* c/o Jharkhand Mukti Morcha, Bariatu Road, Ranchi 834 008, India.

**SPANTA, Rangin Dadfar,** PhD; Afghan academic and government official; *Minister of Foreign Affairs;* b. 1954, Herat prov. *Education:* Kabul Univ., Aachen Univ., Germany. *Career:* began living in Germany 1982; Prof., Inst. of Political Science, Tech. Univ. of Aachen –2005, Dir Third World Studies Inst.; returned to Afghanistan to teach at Kabul Univ. 2005; Spokesperson Alliance for Democracy; advisor to Pres. on Int. affairs 2005; Minister of Foreign Affairs 2006–. *Address:* Ministry of Foreign Affairs, Malak Azghar Road, Kabul, Afghanistan; tel. (70) 104024; fax (20) 2100360; e-mail contact@mfa.gov.af; internet www.mfa.gov.af.

**TANIN, Zahir,** MD; Afghan journalist, physician and diplomatist; *Permanent Representative, United Nations;* b. 1 May 1956; m.; two c. *Education:* Kabul Medical Univ., BBC Leadership Programme. *Career:* began career as journalist in Kabul 1980; freelance writer in France 1992–93; fmr Ed.-in-Chief Afkbar-e-Haftah and Sabawoon Magazine; Research Fellow, Int. Relations Dept, LSE, UK 1994–95; Producer, BBC World Service 1995–2000, Sr Producer 2000–01, Ed. Afghanistan and Cen. Asia (Persian Section) 2001–03, Persian/Pashto Section in Afghanistan 2003–06; Perm. Rep. to the UN, New York 2006–. *Radio:* The Oral History of Afghanistan in the 20th Century (29-part series; BBC). *Publications include:* The Communist Regime in Afghanistan (co-author), Afghanistan in the Twentieth Century. *Address:* Permanent Mission of Afghanistan to the United Nations, 360 Lexington Avenue, 11th Floor, New York, NY 10017, USA; tel. (212) 972-1212; fax (212) 972-1216; e-mail afgwatan@aol.com; internet www.mfa.gov.af.

**TARAR, Muhammad Rafiq;** Pakistani politician and lawyer; b. 2 Nov. 1929, Pir Kot, Gujranwala Dist; m.; three s. one d. *Education:* Govt Islamia High School, Gujranwala, Guru Nanak Khalsa Coll., Gujranwala, Punjab Univ. Law Coll. *Career:* legal practice, Gujranwala; Additional Sessions Judge, Gujranwala, Bahawalnagar, Sargodha; mem. Lahore High Court 1974, Chief Justice of Punjab 1989; mem. Electoral Comm. of Pakistan 1980–89; mem. Supreme Court 1991–94; Senator, Pakistan Muslim League March–Dec. 1997; Pres. of Pakistan 1998–2001. *Address:* House 457, G-3, Johar Town, Lahore, Pakistan.

**TASEER, Salmaan;** Pakistani chartered accountant, business executive and politician; *Governor of Punjab; Education:* qualified as chartered accountant (England and Wales). *Career:* began business career by setting up two chartered accountancy and man. consultancy firms, KPMG, United Arab Emirates and Taseer Hadi Khalid & Co., Pakistan; est. First Capital Securities Corpn Ltd 1994; currently Chair. and CEO First Capital and Worldcall Group; actively involved in establishing other cos in financial services sector as well as telecommunications, media, insurance and real estate devt sectors in Pakistan; also owns Daily Times newspaper, Business Plus TV channel, Pace shopping malls and Hyatt hotel range in Pakistan; mem. Bd Export Promotion Bureau of Pakistan, Bd USF (Universal Service Fund) Co. Ltd; began political career as student mem. of Zulfikar Ali Bhutto's Pakistan People's Party (PPP) late 1960s; active in Pakistan Youth politics; ran movt for Zulfikar Bhutto's release and against his arrest and death sentence; mem. Nat. Ass. 1988, 1990, resgnd from exec. membership of PPP; returned to politics when selected as Fed. Minister for Industries, Production and Special Initiatives in caretaker govt of Prime Minister Muhammad Mian Soomro 2007–08; Gov. of Punjab 2008–. *Publications:* political biography of Prime Minister Zulfikar Ali Bhutto. *Address:* Governor House, Government of Punjab, Lahore, Punjab; First Capital/Worldcall Group, 103-C/II Gulberg III, Lahore, Punjab, Pakistan; tel. (42) 9203151 (Govt); (42) 111-947-947; fax (42) 9203154 (Govt); (42) 5757590; e-mail webmaster@punjab.gov.pk; info@worldcall.com.pk; internet www.punjab.gov.pk; www.worldcall.com.pk.

**TATA, Ratan N.,** BSc; Indian business executive; *Chairman, Tata Sons Ltd;* b. 28 Dec. 1937, nephew of J. R. D. Tata. *Education:* Cornell Univ., Harvard Business School, USA. *Career:* joined Tata Group 1962, Chair. Tata Industries 1981–, Chair. Tata Sons Ltd (holding co. comprising 80 cos) 1991–; also Chair. various cos in Tata Group, including Tata Steel, Tata Engineering, Tata Motors, Tata Chemicals and Tata Power, Corus (following acquisition of Corus by Tata Steel in April 2007) 2007–; Chair. Indian Investment Comm.; mem. Indian Prime Minister's Council on Trade and Industry, Nat. Hydrogen Energy Bd, Nat. Mfg Competitiveness Council, Global Business Council on HIV/AIDS; mem. Int. Advisory Council, Singapore Econ. Devt Bd; mem. Int. Investment Council, Repub. of SA; mem. Int. Advisory Bd Mitsubishi Corpn, American Int. Group, JP Morgan Chase; Trustee Rand Corpn, Cornell Univ., Univ. of Southern Calif., Foundation Bd, Ohio State Univ.; Hon. DBA (Ohio State Univ.), Hon. DTech (Asian Inst. of Tech., Bangkok), Hon. DS (Warwick Univ.); Padma Bhushan 2000. *Address:* Tata Sons Ltd., Bombay House, 24 Homi Mody Street, Mumbai 400 001, India; tel. (22) 22049131; fax (22) 22042333; internet www.tata.com.

**THACKERAY, Balashaheb Keshav (Bal);** Indian politician; *President, Shiv Sena;* b. 23 Jan. 1927. *Career:* fmr cartoonist, Free Press Journal Mumbai and int. dailies; est. Marmik cartoon weekly 1960, Daily Saamana newspaper 1989, Dopahar ka Saamana; Founder-Pres. Shiv Sena. *Address:* Shiv Sena, Shiv Sena Bhavan, Ram Ganesh Gadkari Chowk, Dadar, Mumbai, 400 028, India; tel. (22) 24309128; e-mail shivalay@shivsena.org; internet www.shivsena.org.

**THAKUR, Mahantha;** Nepalese politician; *President, Terai Madhes Loktantrik Party. Career:* fmr Nepal Congress leader; Minister for Science and Tech. –2007 (resgnd); Pres. Terai Madhes Loktantrik Party 2007–. *Address:* Terai Madhes Loktantrik Party, Kathmandu, Nepal; tel. (1) 4462398.

**THAPA, Surya Bahadur;** Nepalese politician; *President, Rashtriya Janashakti Party;* b. 20 March 1928, Muga, East Nepal; m. 1953; one s. three d. *Education:* Allahabad Univ., India. *Career:* House Speaker, Advisory Ass. to King of Nepal 1958; mem. Upper House of Parl. 1959; Minister of Forests, Agric., Commerce and Industry 1960, of Finance and Econ. Affairs 1962; Vice-Chair. Council of Ministers, Minister of Finance, Econ. Planning, Law and Justice 1963; Vice-Chair. Council of Ministers, Minister of Finance, Law and Gen. Admin. 1964–65; Chair. Council of Ministers, Minister of Palace Affairs 1965–69; Prime Minister of Nepal and Minister of Palace Affairs 1979–83; Minister of Finance 1979–80, of Defence 1980–81, 1982–83, of Foreign Affairs 1982; Prime Minister of Nepal 1997–98, Prime Minister and Minister of Royal Palace Affairs, of Defence, of Home Affairs, of Foreign Affairs, of Industry, Commerce and Supplies, of Law, Justice and Parl. Affairs, of Agric. and Co-operatives, of Population and the Environment, of Water Resources, of Land Reforms and Man., of Women, Children and Social Welfare, of Forest and Soil Conservation, of Science and Tech., of Labour and Transport Man., of Gen. Admin, of Local Devt and of Health, Interim Govt 2003–04 (resgnd); Pres. Rashtriya Prajatantra Party 1990–2002; Pres. Rashtriya Janashakti Party (split from Rashtriya Prajatantra Party Nov. 2004) 2005–; mem. Royal Advisory Cttee 1969–72; arrested and released 1972, 1975; Hon. DLitt (Kurukshetra Univ.); Tri-Sahkti-Patta 1963, Gorkha Dakshinbahu I 1965, Om Rama Patta 1980; several Nepalese and foreign awards. *Address:* Rashtriya Janashakti Party (National People's Power Party), Ramalphokhari, Kathmandu, Nepal; tel. (1) 4437063; fax (1) 4437064; e-mail rjpnepal@info.com.np.

**THINLEY, Lyonchhen Jigmi Yozer,** MA; Bhutanese politician; *Prime Minister and Chairman;* b. 1952, Bumthang. *Education:* St Stephen's Coll., India, Pennsylvania State Univ., USA. *Career:* mem. civil service 1954–1983, Head, Royal Civil Service Comm. Secr., Dir Educ. Dept; fmr Perm. Rep. to UN, New York; fmr Chair. Council of Ministers; Minister of Foreign Affairs 1998–2003; Prime Minister, Chair. and Minister of Home and Cultural Affairs 2003–04; Minister of Home and Cultural Affairs 2004–07 (resgnd), Prime Minister and Chair. 2008–; Founder and Pres. Druk Phuensum Tshogpa (DPT) party 2007–; Red Scarf 1987, Druk Thuksey and Coronation Medals 1999. *Address:* Cabinet Secretariat, Tashichhodzong, Thimphu; Druk Phuensum Tshogpa (DPT), Thimphu; Druk Phuensum Tshogpa (DPT), Chang Lam, Thimphu, Bhutan; tel. (2) 321437; (2) 336336 (DPT); fax (2) 321438; (2) 335845 (DPT); e-mail cabinet@druknet.bt; dpt@druknet.bt; internet www.dpt.bt.

**THONDAMAN, Arumugam Ramanathan;** Sri Lankan politician; *Minister of Youth Empowerment and Socio-Economic Development;* b. 29 May 1964. *Career:* fmr Minister of Livestock Devt and Estate Infrastructure; Minister of Housing and Plantation Infrastructure –2004; Pres. and Gen. Sec. Ceylon Workers' Congress; Minister of Youth Empowerment and Socio-Economic Development 2007–. *Address:* Ministry of Youth Empowerment and Socio Economic Development, 15a, Flower Terrace, Colombo 7; No. 09 2/2, Rajakeeya Mawatha, Mayfair Flats, Colombo 7, Sri Lanka.

**TOBGYE, Lyonpo Sonam;** Bhutanese judge. *Career:* currently Chief Justice, High Court; Chair. Nat. Judicial Comm. 2003–. *Address:* High Court (Thrimkhang Gongma), Thimphu, Bhutan; tel. 322344; fax 322921; e-mail judiciary@druknet.bt; internet www.judiciary.gov.bt.

**TSHERING, Lyonpo Dago;** Bhutanese diplomatist and politician; *Ambassador to India;* b. (Dago Tshering), 17 July 1941, Paro. *Education:* Univ. of Bombay, Indian Admin. Service Training, Mussoorie and Indian Audit and Accounts Service Training, Simla, India, Univ. of Manchester, UK, Nat. Admin, Tokyo. *Career:* Asst, Ministry of Devt 1961–62; Asst, Office of the Chief Sec. 1962–63; returned to Ministry of Devt 1963, Sec. 1965–71; mem. Nat. Ass. 1968–1990; mem. Royal Advisory Council 1968–70; First Sec., Bhutan Embassy in India 1971–73; Deputy Perm. Rep. to UN 1973–74, Perm. Rep. 1974–80, 1984–85; Amb. to Bangladesh 1980–84; Minister of Home Affairs 1985–98; Amb. to India 1998–; Orange Scarf. *Address:* Embassy of Bhutan, Chandragupta Marg, Chanakyapuri, New Delhi 110 021, India; tel. (11) 26889807; fax (11) 26876710; e-mail bhutan@vsnl.com.

**TSHERING, Dozin (Brig.) Goongloen Wogma Batoo;** Bhutanese army officer; *Chief Operations Officer, Royal Bhutan Army;* b. Nov. 1951, Toebesa, Thimphu. *Education:* Indian Mil. Acad., Dehradun, Defence Services Staff Coll., Wellington, India. *Career:* completed Young Officer's Course, Commando Course, Intelligence Staff Officer's Course, Jr Command Course and Sr Command Course; commissioned into Royal Bhutan Army 1971, has held various command posts, apptd Operations and Training Officer 1976, commanded Wing 4 and Wing 7, apptd Commdt of mil. training centre 1988, Deputy Chief Operations Officer 1991, Commdr Command Centre 1997, promoted to rank of Dozin (Brig.)

1997; Deputy Chief Operations Officer Royal Bhutan Army Feb.–Nov. 2005, Chief Operations Officer Nov. 2005–; Druk Yurgyal Medal, Drakpoi Wangyal Medal, Drakpoi Thugsey Medal, Drakpoi Khorlo Medal. *Address:* Royal Bhutan Army Headquarters, Thimphu, Bhutan.

**TSHERING, Lyonpo Ugyen,** BA; Bhutanese politician and diplomatist; *Minister of Foreign Affairs;* b. 8 Aug. 1954, Thimphu; m. *Education:* Univ. of Calif., Berkeley, USA. *Career:* joined Govt Planning Comm. 1978, apptd Co-ordinator bilateral and multilateral assistance to Govt 1983, Project Co-ordinator, Computer Support Centre 1984, apptd Sec. Computerization Cttee 1983, Dir Planning Comm. 1986–89, now Vice-Chair.; Perm. Rep. to UN, New York 1989–98; apptd Editorial Adviser to Nat. Ass. 1980; fmr Chair. Asian Devt Bank; apptd Chair. World Bank Projects Implementation Cttee 1984; Chair. Tech. Cttee on Rural Devt, SAARC 1988–89; Sec., Ministry of Foreign Affairs 2001–03; Minister of Labour and Human Resources 2003–07 (resgnd); Minister of Foreign Affairs 2008–; Red Scarf 1998. *Address:* Ministry of Foreign Affairs, Convention Centre, POB 103, Thimphu, Bhutan; tel. (2) 321413; internet www.mfa.gov.bt.

**TSHULTIM, Dasho Jigme,** BA; Bhutanese diplomatist and politician; *Speaker of the National Assembly. Education:* St Joseph's Coll., Darjeeling, India, Univ. of Manchester, UK. *Career:* served in Govt as Head of Tourism, Dzongda and Zhung Dronyer (Chief of Protocol); Amb. to Bangladesh (also accred to Pakistan, Maldives, Sri Lanka and S Korea) 2004–07; mem. Bhutan People's Unity Party; mem. Parl. for Radhi-Sakteng constituency, Trashigang 2008–, Speaker of Nat Ass. 2008–. *Address:* Office of the Speaker, National Assembly Secretariat, Gyelyong Tshokhang, PO Box 139, Thimphu, Bhutan; tel. (2) 322729; fax (2) 324210; e-mail jtshultim@nab.gov.bt; internet www.nab.gov.bt.

**VAGHUL, Narayanan,** BCom; Indian banker. *Career:* mem. of staff, State Bank of India 1957–1974; fmr Dir Nat. Inst. of Bank Man.; Exec. Dir Cen. Bank of India 1978–1981; Chair., Man. Dir Bank of India 1981–84; Chair. (non-exec.) Industrial Credit and Investment Corpn of India Ltd (ICICI) 1985–, fmrly also Man. Dir. *Address:* ICICI Bank, PO Box 18712, Andheri East, Mumbai 400 069, India; e-mail info@icicibank .com.

**VAJPAYEE, Atal Bihari,** MA; Indian politician; b. 25 Dec. 1924, Gwalior, MP. *Education:* Victoria (now Laxmibai) Coll., Gwalior, D.A.V. Coll., Kanpur. *Career:* mem. Rashtriya Swayamsewak Sangh 1941, Indian Nat. Congress 1942–46; mem. Lok Sabha 1957–62, 1967–84 (for New Delhi 1977–84), 1991–, Rajya Sabha 1962–67, 1986; Founder-mem. Bharatiya Jana Sangh 1951, Parl. Leader 1957–77; Chair. Cttee on Govt Assurance 1966–67, Public Accounts Cttee, Lok Sabha 1967–70, 1991–93; detained during Emergency 1975–77; Founder-mem. Janata Party 1977, Pres. Bharatiya Janata Party 1980–86, Parl. Leader 1980–84, 1986; Minister of External Affairs 1977–79; Leader of Opposition, Lok Sabha 1993–98, Chair. Standing Cttee on External Affairs 1993–96; Minister of External Affairs 1998; Prime Minister of India 15–28 May 1996, 1998–2004, also Minister of Health and Family Welfare, Atomic Energy and Agric. 1998–2004; Chair. Nat. Security Council 1998–2004; mem. Nat. Integration Council 1961–; fmr Ed. Rastradharma (monthly), Panchjanya (weekly), Swadesh and Veer Arjun (dailies); Dr hc (Kanpur Univ.) 1993; Bharat Ratna Pte Govind Ballabh Pant Award 1994, Padma Vibhushan 1992, Lokmanya Tilak Puruskar. *Publications:* New Dimensions of India's Foreign Policy, Jan Sangh Aur Musalmans, Three Decades in Parliament; collections of poems and numerous articles. *Address:* c/o Bharatiya Janata Party (BJP) (Indian People's Party), 11 Ashok Rd, New Delhi 110 001; 7 Race Course Road, New Delhi 110011, India; tel. (11) 23018939; fax (11) 23019545.

**VENDRELL, Francesc,** LLB, MA; Spanish United Nations official and academic; *EU Special Representative in Afghanistan,*b. 15 June 1940. *Education:* Univ. of Barcelona, Univs of London and Cambridge, UK. *Career:* joined UN 1968; Chief, then Dir for Europe and the Americas Office of Research and Collection of Information, Office of the UN Sec.-Gen. 1987–92; Deputy Personal Rep. of Sec.-Gen. for Cen. American Peace Process 1989–91; rep. Sec.-Gen. during first phase of Guatemala peace negotiations 1990–92; Dir for Special Political Assignments 1992; Sr Political Adviser to Special Envoy in Haiti 1993; Dir E Asia and Pacific Div., Dept of Political Affairs 1993–97; Dir Combined Asia and Pacific Div. 1998–99; Officer-in-Charge, Office of Asst Sec.-Gen. for Political Affairs (Asia, Pacific, the Americas and Europe) 1999–2000; apptd Deputy Personal Rep. of Sec.-Gen. for E Timor (now Timor-Leste) 1999; Special Rep. of Sec.-Gen. and Head of Special Mission to Afghanistan (UNSMA) with rank of Asst Sec.-Gen. 2000–02; EU Special Rep. in Afghanistan 2002–; Visiting Prof., Rutgers Univ. Law School, NJ, USA 1972–74, Yale Univ. Law School, CT 1977, 1979; Dir of Studies, The Hague Acad. of Int. Law, Netherlands 1979. *Address:* Council of the European Union, Rue de la Loi, 175, 1048 Brussels, Belgium; tel. (2) 281-61-11; fax (2) 281-69-34; internet www.consilium .europa.eu.

**VYAS, Sudhir;** Indian diplomatist; *Ambassador to Bhutan;* b. 1953. *Career:* joined the foreign service 1977, has held diplomatic posts in Cairo, Algiers, Nepal, Islamabad, Mission to UN, New York; Deputy Sec. for Bhutan, Ministry of External Affairs 1984–86; Amb. to UAE –2005, to Bhutan 2005–. *Address:* Embassy of India, India House, Jungshina, Thimphu, Bhutan; tel. (2) 322162; fax (2) 323195; e-mail hocbht@druknet.bt.

**WADIA, Nusli;** Indian industrialist; *Chairman, Bombay Dyeing & Manufacturing Company Ltd;* m. Maureen Wadia; two s. *Career:* Chair. Bombay Dyeing & Manufacturing Co. Ltd, Gherzi Eastern Ltd, Bombay Burmah Trading Corpn Ltd, BRT Ltd, NW Exports Ltd, Britannia Industries Ltd, National Peroxide Ltd, Citurgia Biochemicals Ltd, Wadia BSN India Ltd; Chair. and Man. Dir Nowrosjee Wadia & Sons Ltd; Dir Anil Starch Products Ltd, Tata Chemicals Ltd, Atul Products Ltd, Naira Holdings Ltd, Radley Cotton Mills Ltd, ABI Holdings Ltd, Associated Biscuits International Ltd; mem. Bd Oberoi Group. *Address:* Bombay Dyeing, Neville House, J. N. Heredia Marg, Ballard Estate, Mumbai 400 038, India; tel. (22) 22618071; fax (22) 22614520; internet www .bombaydyeing.com.

**WAJED, Sheikh Hasina;** Bangladeshi politician; *President, Awami League;* b. 28 Sept. 1947, Tungipara, Gopalganj Dist, E Pakistan (now Bangladesh); m. M. A. Wazed Miah; one s. one d. *Education:* Univ. of Dhaka. *Career:* active in politics as a student; arrested during civil war 1971; assumed leadership of opposition Awami League from her father, first elected Pres. 1981, fifth time in 2002–; lived in exile 1975–81; arrested and placed under house arrest on several occasions during 1980s; Prime Minister of Bangladesh 1996–2001, also Minister of the Armed Forces Div., of the Cabinet Div., of Special Affairs, of Defence, of Power, Energy and Mineral Resources and of the Establishment; charged with corruption and alleged plundering of state funds while in office Dec. 2001; Leader of official parl. opposition 2001–; arrested on extortion charges July 2007; shared Houphouet-Boigny Peace Prize 1999. *Publications:* several books and numerous articles. *Address:* Bangladesh Awami League (AL), 23 Bangabandhu Avenue, Dhaka, Bangladesh; e-mail president@albd.org; internet www.albd.org.

**WANGCHUCK, HM Dasho Jigme Khesar Namgyal,** (The Druk Gyalpo —'Dragon King'— of Bhutan), MPhil; b. 21 Feb. 1980. *Education:* Cushing Acad. and Wheaton Coll., USA, Magdalen Coll., Oxford, UK. *Career:* proclaimed Crown Prince Oct. 2004; succeeded to throne 14 Dec. 2006, on the abdication of his father; participated in official visits; Chair. Bhutan Trust Fund for Environmental Conservation; Pres. Bhutan-India Friendship Asscn; Chancellor Royal Univ. of Bhutan; Chief Patron Scouts Asscn of Bhutan; Patron Royal Soc. for the Protection of Nature, Bhutan Chamber of Commerce and Industry, India-Bhutan Foundation, European Convention of Bhutan Socs, Oxford Centre for Buddhist Studies, Bhutan Shooting Fed.; Red Scarf 2002. *Address:*

Royal Palace, Thimphu, Bhutan. internet www.bhutan.gov.bt.

**WANGCHUCK, HM Jigme Singye;** Bhutanese fmr ruler; b. 11 Nov. 1955; m.; ten c. (including HM King Dasho Jigme Khesar Namgyal Wangchuck). *Education:* North Point, Darjeeling, Ugyuen Wangchuk Acad., Paro, also in UK. *Career:* Crown Prince March 1972; succeeded to throne 24 July 1972, crowned 2 June 1974, abdicated 14 December 2006; Chair. Planning Comm. of Bhutan 1972–; C-in-C of Armed Forces; Chair. Council of Ministers 1972–98. *Address:* Royal Palace, Thimphu, Bhutan. internet www.bhutan.gov.bt.

**WANGCHUCK, Lyonpo Khandu,** BA; Bhutanese politician; *Minister of Economic Affairs;* b. 24 Nov. 1950. *Education:* St Stephen's Coll., India. *Career:* Asst Sec., Ministry of Trade, Industry and Forests 1974, Deputy Dir 1976, Man. Dir Industrial Devt Corpn 1978, Dir of Trade and Commerce 1980–84; Dir of Agric. 1986, Dir Gen. 1987–89, Sec. 1989–1991; Sec. Royal Civil Service Comm. 1991–94; Prime Minister and Chair. 2001–02, 2006–July 2007 (resgnd); Minister of Trade and Industry 1998–2003, of Foreign Affairs 2003–07 (resgnd), of Econ. Affairs 2008–; mem. Nat. Ass. for Lamgong-Wangchang constituency; mem. Druk Phuensum Tshogpa party; fmr Chair. Bhutan Nat. Bank; Red Scarf 1987, Orange Scarf 1998, Coronation Medal 1999. *Address:* Ministry of Economic Affairs, Tashichhodzong, POB 141, Thimphu; Jangsa, Shari Geog, Paro, Bhutan; tel. (2) 322211; fax (2) 323617; e-mail kdorjee@druknet.bt; internet www.mti.gov.bt.

**WANGCHUK, Dasho Lhatu;** Bhutanese diplomatist, government official and airline industry executive; *Chairman, Druk Air (Royal Bhutan Airlines). Career:* fmr Chief of Protocol and Acting Foreign Sec., Ministry of Foreign Affairs; Amb. to Bangladesh –2004; Dir-Gen. Dept of Tourism 2004–07; Chair. Druk Air (Royal Bhutan Airlines) 2007–. *Address:* Druk Air-Royal Bhutan Airlines, Paro, Bhutan; e-mail info@drukair.com.bt; internet www.drukair.com.bt.

**WANGDI, Dasho Kunzang,** BA, MPA; Bhutanese government official; *Chief Election Commissioner;* b. 17 July 1953; m. Pem Tandi. *Education:* Delhi Univ., India, Pennsylvania State Univ., USA. *Career:* worked in various capacities in govt ministries for more than 28 years; Auditor-Gen. 1999–2005; Chief Election Commr 2006–, in charge of two rounds of trial elections in 2007 and first ever parl. elections in 2008. *Publications:* drafted Royal Charters, Audit Act, Anti-Corruption Act, Election Acts. *Address:* Election Commission of Bhutan, Thimphu, Bhutan; tel. (2) 334762; fax (2) 334763; e-mail kwangdi@druknet.bt; internet www.election-bhutan.org.bt.

**WARDAK, Gen. Abdul Rahim;** Afghan government official and military officer; *Minister of Defence;* b. 1945, Wardak Prov.. *Education:* Habibia High School, Ali Naser Acad. of Cairo, Egypt. *Career:* previous positions include Lecturer Cadet Univ., Asst of Protocol, Ministry of Defence, Mil. Attaché, India, Dir Mil. Officers Soc., Educ. Comm., Disarmament Program; apptd Chief of Army Staff 1992; fmr Deputy Minister of Defence, Minister of Defence 2004–. *Address:* Ministry of Defence, Shash Darak, Kabul, Afghanistan; tel. (20) 2100451; fax (20) 2104172.

**WEERASOORIYA, Gen. C. S.;** Sri Lankan army officer (retd) and diplomatist; m. Dilhani Weerasooriya. *Career:* commanded Operation Jayasikurui to regain the Liberation Tigers of Tamil Eelam-held Wanni and Mullaitivu areas and subsequently to open a land route through Wanni and Kilinochchi dists to link up with Jaffna Peninsula 1997; Commdr of the Army (rank of Lt-Gen.) 1998–2000; High Commr to Pakistan 2001–07; Rana Wickrama Padakkama, Rana Sura Padakkama, Vishista Seva Vibhushanaya, Uttama Seva Padakkama. *Address:* c/o Ministry of Foreign Affairs, Republic Building, Colombo 1, Sri Lanka; tel. (11) 2325371; fax (11) 2446091; e-mail publicity@formin.gov.lk; internet www.slmfa.gov.lk.

**WICKREMANAYAKE, Ratnasiri;** Sri Lankan politician; *Prime Minister and Minister of Internal Administration. Career:* elected mem. Mahajana Eksath Peramuna for Horana 1960; apptd Deputy Minister of Justice 1970; Gen. Sec. Sri Lankan Freedom Party 1977; won Kalutara Dist seat 1994; apptd Minister of Public Admin, Home Affairs and Plantation and Leader of the House 1994; Prime Minister of Sri Lanka 2000–01; Minister of Buddha Sasana and Religious Affairs 2000–02; Chair. United People's Freedom Alliance; Prime Minister and Minister of Internal Admin 2005–; ex-officio Chair. Bd of Govs Cen. Cultural Fund. *Address:* Prime Minister's Office, 58, Sir Ernest de Silva Mawatha, Colombo 7, Sri Lanka; tel. (11) 2575317; fax (11) 2575454; internet www.pmoffice.gov.lk.

**WICKREMASINGHE, Ranil,** LLB; Sri Lankan politician and lawyer; *Leader, United National Party;* b. 24 March 1949, Colombo; m. Maithree Wickremasinghe 1995. *Education:* Royal Coll. of Colombo, Univ. of Colombo and Sri Lanka Law Coll. *Career:* attorney-at-law, Supreme Court; elected mem. Parl. 1977, 1989; Leader of House 1989–93; Deputy Minister of Foreign Affairs 1977–79; Minister of Youth Affairs and Employment 1978–89, of Educ. 1980–89, of Industries 1989–90, of Industries, Science and Tech. 1990–94; Prime Minister of Sri Lanka 1992, 2001–04, also Minister of Policy Devt and Implementation 2001–04; Leader, United Nat. Party 1994–, Leader of the Opposition 1994–2001, 2006–; cand. in presidential elections 1999, 2005. *Address:* United National Party (UNP), 30 Sir Marcu Fernando Mawatha, Colombo 7, Sri Lanka; tel. (11) 5636551; fax (11) 2682905; e-mail info@unp.lk; internet www.unp.lk.

**WIJETUNGA, Dingiri Banda;** Sri Lankan politician and fmr head of state; b. 15 Feb. 1922, Polgahanga, Kandy; m.; one d. *Career:* official in Co-operative Dept 1942–47; joined United Nat. Party 1946; mem. of Parl. for Udunuwara 1965; apptd Minister of Information and Broadcasting 1977, of Power and Highways 1978, of Power and Energy 1979, of Agricultural Devt and Research and of Food 1987; Gov. Northwestern Prov. 1988; Prime Minister of Sri Lanka and Minister of Finance 1989–93; elected Exec. Pres. of Sri Lanka 1993–94. *Address:* c/o Office of the President, Republic Square, Colombo 1, Sri Lanka.

**YADAV, Lalu Prasad;** Indian politician; *Minister of Railways;* b. 1948; m. Rabri Devi. *Career:* elected to Lok Sabha 1977; Chief Minister of Bihar 1990–97; Leader Rashtriya Janata Dal (Nat. People's Party); Minister of Railways 2004–. *Address:* Ministry of Railways, Rail Bhavan, Raisina Road, New Delhi 110 001; Rashtriya Janata Dal, 13, V. P. House, Rafi Marg, New Delhi 110 011, India; tel. (11) 23386645; fax (11) 23382637; e-mail secyrb@rb.railnet.gov.in; internet www.indianrailways.gov.in.

**YADAV, Ram Baran,** MBBS, MD; Nepalese head of state, physician and politician; *President;* b. 4 Feb. 1948, Sapahi, Dhanusa dist. *Education:* Calcutta Medical Coll., Inst. of Medical Educ. and Research, India. *Career:* worked as physician for more than two decades in hospitals in south Nepal's Terai region; joined Nepali Congress Party 1987, Gen. Sec. –2008 (resgnd); elected to House of Reps 1991, 1994; Minister for Health 1991–94; Pres. of Nepal (first elected Pres.) 2008–. *Address:* Office of the President, Kathmandu, Nepal.

**YADAV, Sharad,** BSc, BEE; Indian politician; *President, Janata Dal (United);* b. 1 July 1947, Babai Dist, Hoshangabad, Madhya Pradesh; m. Rekha Yadav; one s. one d. *Education:* Jabalpur Eng Coll. *Career:* active youth leader, took part in several mass movements; detained 1969–70, 1972, 1975; mem. Lok Sabha (Parl.) 1974–; Pres. Yuva Janata 1977, Yuva Lok Dal 1979; mem. Rajya Sabha 1986–87; Minister of Textiles and Food Processing Industries 1989–90, of Civil Aviation 1999–2001, of Labour 2001–02, of Consumer Affairs, Food and Public Distribution 2002–04; Gen. Sec. Janata Dal 1989–97, Acting Pres. 1995–97, Pres. 1997– (party merged with Lok Shakti to form Janata Dal—United 1999). *Address:* Janata Dal (United), 7 Jantar Mantar

Road, New Delhi, 110 001; 7 Tughlak Road, New Delhi, 110 003 India; tel. (11) 23368833; (11) 23792738; fax (11) 23368138; (11) 23017118.

**YADAV, Upendra;** Nepalese politician; *Minister of Foreign Affairs. Career:* joined Maoists and was briefly in dist leadership; Chair. Madhesi Jana Adhikar Forum Nepal (Madhesi People's Rights Forum Nepal) 2006–, has demanded that Terai (also known as Madhesh and Morung) region of Nepal should be considered an ind. state with its own govt; Minister of Foreign Affairs 2008–. *Address:* Ministry of Foreign Affairs, Shital Niwas, Maharajganj, Kathmandu; Madhesi Jana Adhikar Forum Nepal, Kathmandu, Nepal; tel. (1) 4416011; fax (1) 4416016; e-mail adm@mofa.gov.np; internet www.mofa.gov.np.

**YAMEEN, Abdullah;** Maldivian politician; brother of Pres. Maumoon Abdul Gayoom. *Career:* fmr Minister of Trade, Industries and Labour; Chair. State Trading Org., Island Aviation, Electricity Bd; fmr Minister of Higher Educ., Employment and Social Security; left govt's Dhivehi Raiyyithunge Party (Maldivian People's Party) 2007; Founder and Leader People's Alliance party 2008–. *Address:* c/o Ministry of Higher Education, Employment and Social Security, Malé, Maldives.

**YEDDYURAPPA, B(okanakere) S(iddalingappa),** BA; Indian politician and government official; *Chief Minister of Karnataka;* b. ( b. Bokanakere Siddalingappa Yediyurappa), 27 Feb. 1943, Bookanakere village, Mandya Dist, Karnataka; m. Smt. Maithra Devi Yediyurappa 1967 (died 2004); two s. three d. *Career:* mem. Bharatiya Janata Party (BJP); represents Shikaripura in Karnataka Legis. Ass.; first-div. clerk in social welfare dept 1965; clerk, Veerabhadra Shastri's Shankar rice mill, Shikaripur 1965–67; set up hardware shop in Shimoga; Sec. Rashtriya Swayamsevak Sangh's Shikaripur unit 1970–72; Pres. Taluk unit, Jan Sangh 1972–75; Pres. Town Municipality of Shikaripur 1975; imprisoned during Emergency in India 1975–77, lodged in Bellary and Shimoga jails; Pres. Shikaripur Taluk unit of BJP 1980–85, Pres. Shimoga Dist unit of BJP 1985–88, Pres. BJP unit, Karnataka 1988; first elected to Lower House of Karnataka Legislature 1983, has represented Shikaripur constituency five times, mem. Eighth, Ninth, Tenth and Eleventh Legis. Ass (Lower House) of Karnataka, Leader of Opposition, Tenth Ass., lost election 1999, nominated by BJP to become mem. Legis. Council (Upper House) of Karnataka; helped H. D. Kumaraswamy of Janata Dal (Secular) party bring down coalition govt of Dharam Singh, Kumaraswamy formed govt with help of BJP in Karnataka; Deputy Chief Minister and Minister of Finance in Kumaraswamy's Govt 2006–07, Chief Minister of Karnataka (prior to collapse of coalition govt) 12–19 Nov. 2007 (first BJP mem. to become Chief Minister of a South Indian state) 2008–. *Address:* Office of the Chief Minister, Room No. 323, Vidhana Soudha, Bangalore 560 001, Karnataka, India; tel. (80) 22253414; (80) 22253424; e-mail info@karnataka.gov.in; internet www.karnataka.gov.in.

**YUNUS, Muhammad;** Bangladeshi banker and academic; *Managing Director and CEO, Grameen Bank;* m. Afrizi Yunus; one d. *Education:* Vanderbilt Univ., USA. *Career:* Prof. of Econs, Chittagong Univ. 1976; f. Grameen Bank Project, pioneering microcredit loans to those in extreme poverty Dec. 1976, changed to ind. bank, Grameen Bank Sept. 1983, now Man. Dir, CEO; f. Nagorik Shakti political party 2007; Dir UN Foundation; mem. Int. Advisory Group, Fourth World Conf. on Women, Beijing 1993–95, Advisory Council for Sustainable Econ. Devt 1993, UN Expert Group on Women and Finance; Founding Man. Dir German Telephones 1998–; Hon. LLD (Warwick) 1996; Independence Day Award, Pres.'s Award and Cen. Bank Award (all Bangladesh), Ramon Magsaysay Award (Philippines), Aga Khan Award for Architecture, Mohamed Shabdeen Award for Science (Sri Lanka), World Food Prize (USA), Nobel Peace Prize (jtly with Grameen Bank) 2006. *Publications include:* Creating a World Without Poverty: How Social Business Can Transform Our Lives 2008. *Address:* Grameen Bank, Mirpur 1, Dhaka 1216, Bangladesh; tel. (2) 801138; fax (2) 803559; e-mail grameen.bank@grameen.net; internet www.grameen-info.org.

**ZAHIR, Ahmed,** BA; Maldivian politician and journalist; *President (Speaker), People's Majlis;* b. 26 Sept. 1945; m.; one s. two d. *Career:* teacher until 1978; journalist for Reuters and Asia Week –1978; fmr Project Officer (Marubeni), Dept of Tourism and Foreign Investment, Asst Dir Tourism Section, then Dir, Dir-Gen. Dept of Tourism; Deputy Minister Ministry of Tourism, Attorney-Gen.'s Office; fmr Minister of Transport and Shipping, of Transport and Communications, of Justice; mem. People's Majlis (Parl.), Vice-Pres. (Deputy Speaker) –2004, Pres. (Speaker) 2004–, chaired numerous standing cttees; mem. Bd Dirs Maldives Nat. Ship Man. Ltd; mem. Maldives Press Council; fmr Publr and Ed. Hafta weekly newspaper; led three parl. dels including the first Maldivian parl. del. to an int. conf.; Presidential Award for Meritorious Work in Journalism 1980, Golden Pen Award on 50th Anniversary of Maldivan Journalism 1993. *Publication:* A Guide Book on Saudi Arabia. *Address:* People's Majlis Secretariat, Medhuziyaaraiy Magu, Malé 20080, Maldives; tel. 3313214; fax 3315258; e-mail speaker@majlis.gov.mv; internet www.majlis.gov.mv.

**ZAHIR, Maj.-Gen. Mohamed;** Maldivian army officer; *Chief of Staff, Maldives National Defence Force;* m. Fathimath Amira; four s. one d. *Education:* Hendon Police Coll., London, UK, Naval Postgraduate School, Monterey, Calif., USA, Sr Execs in Nat. and Int. Security Program, John F. Kennedy School of Govt, USA. *Career:* joined civil service and worked in various Govt Depts before enlisting in Maldives Nat. Defence Force (MNDF— fmrly Nat. Security Service (NSS)) 1978, promoted to rank of Sergeant and commissioned as officer 1980, undertook various command positions within different units of MNDF, Deputy Chief of Staff, MNDF –1996, also commanded MNDF Defence Inst. for Training and Educ. (fmrly known as NSS Training Unit), promoted to rank of Brig., Chief of Staff, MNDF 1996–, promoted to rank of Maj.-Gen. 2004, Chair. MNDF Advisory Council; Medal for Exceptional Bravery 1988, Presidential Medal, Distinguished Service Medal, Dedicated Service Medal. *Address:* Office of the Chief of Staff, Maldives National Defence Force, Bandaara koshi, Ameer Ahmed Magu, Malé, Maldives; tel. 3322607; fax 3322496; e-mail media@mndf.gov.mv; internet www.mndf.gov.mv.

**ZARDARI, Asif Ali;** Pakistani business executive and politician; *Co-Chairman, Pakistan People's Party;* b. 21 July 1956, Karachi; m. Benazir Bhutto 1987 (died 2007); one s. two d. *Education:* Cadet Coll. Petaro, Karachi. *Career:* imprisoned on blackmail charges 1990–93 (charges dropped); mem. Nat. Ass. for Nawabshah 1993–96, Fed. Minister of the Environment 1993; imprisoned on corruption charges 1996–2004 (charges dropped); mem. Senate 1997–99 (parl. dissolved); Co-Chair. Pakistan People's Party (PPP) (following assassination of Benazir Bhutto) 2007–; Dir M/s Zardari Group (Pvt.) Ltd. *Address:* Pakistan People's Party, 8, Street 19, F-8/2, Islamabad, Pakistan; tel. (51) 2255264; fax (51) 2282741; e-mail ppp@comsats.net.pk; internet www.ppp.org.pk.

**ZAWAHIRI, Ayman az-,** MS, DMed; Egyptian guerrilla leader and physician; b. 19 June 1951, grandson of Rabi'a Zawahiri. *Education:* Cairo Univ. *Career:* paediatrician; mem. The Muslim Brotherhood (arrested for membership 1966); Founder Egyptian Islamic Jihad; imprisoned on firearms charge following Egyptian Pres. Sadat's assassination 1981–84; joined mujahidin troops fighting Soviet occupation forces in Afghanistan 1984; co-f. Int. Front for Fighting Jews and Crusaders (with Osama bin Laden q.v.) 1998; co-f. al Qa'ida; accused of planning bombings of US embassies in E Africa 1998; personal physician and political adviser to Osama bin Laden; fmr Leader Vanguards of Conquest Movt.

**ZIA, Begum Khaleda;** Bangladeshi politician; *Chairman, Bangladesh Jatiyatabadi Dal (Bangladesh Nationalist Party);* b. 15 Aug. 1945; m. Capt. Ziaur Rahman (later Pres. of Bangladesh) 1960 (deceased); two s. *Education:* Surendranath Coll., Dinajpur. *Career:* held captive during Bangladesh's war of independence; Vice-Chair. Bangladesh Jatiyatabadi Dal (Bangladesh Nationalist Party) (BNP) 1982–84, Chair. 1984–; helped to form seven-party alliance leading to ousting of Pres. Ershad from power 1990; Prime Minister of Bangladesh 1991–96, 2001–06, Minister in charge of Armed Forces Div., Cabinet Div., Chittagong Hill Tracts Affairs, Defences, Establishment, Power, Energy and Mineral Resources, Primary and Mass Educ. 2001–06; Chair. SAARC 1993–95, 2005–; ranked by Forbes magazine amongst 100 Most Powerful Women (14th) 2004, (29th) 2005, (33rd) 2006. *Publications:* Together for Better Tomorrow: Speeches of Begum Khaleda Zia 1992, Visions for the Future: Selected Speeches of Begum Khaleda Zia 2002. *Address:* Bangladesh Nationalist Party, Banani Office, House 23, Road 13, Dhaka, Bangladesh; House No. 6, Shaheed Moinul Road, Dhaka Cantonment, Dhaka, Bangladesh; tel. (2) 8819525; (2) 8159897; (2) 8821666; fax (2) 8813063; e-mail bnpbd@e-fsbd.net; internet www.bnpbd.com.

**ZIMBA, Lyonpo Yeshey,** MA (Econs); Bhutanese politician; *Minister of Works and Human Settlements;* b. 10 Oct. 1952, Omladama, Punakha Dist; m. Thuji Zangmo; one s. three d. *Education:* Univ. of Wisconsin. *Career:* joined civil service in the Royal Secr. 1974, planning officer, Ministry of Planning 1977, Jt Sec. 1991; apptd Chair. Royal Monetary Authority (Cen. Bank) 1986; Chair. Bank of Bhutan; Minister of Finance 1998–2003; Prime Minister and Chair. Council of Ministers 2000–01, 2004–05; Minister of Trade and Industry 2003–04, 2005–07 (resgnd), of Works and Human Settlements 2008–; Silver Medal for Scholastic Achievement, Gold Medal for Best All-Round Coll. Student, Red Scarf 1991, Druk Thuksey and Coronation Medals 1999. *Address:* Ministry of Works and Human Settlements, POB 791, Thimphu, Bhutan; tel. (2) 327998; fax (2) 323122; e-mail mowhs@mowhs.gov.bt; internet www.mowhs.gov.bt.

**ZORAMTHANGA,** BA; Indian politician; *Chief Minister of Mizoram;* b. 13 July 1944, Samthang village; m. Roneihsangi Rohlira 1988; one s. one d. *Education:* Champhai Gandhi Memorial High School and Imphal D.M. Coll., Manipur. *Career:* Sec. to Pres. Pu Laldenga, Leader of Mizo Nat. Front 1969–75, exiled with Pu Laldenga to Pakistan 1972–76, Foreign Rep. 1972–76; Minister of Finance and Educ., Mizoram State Govt 1987–90; Pres. Mizo Nat. Front 1990–; Chief Minister of Mizoram 1998–. *Address:* Office of the Chief Minister, Government of Mizoram, Aizawl 796 001, India; tel. (389) 2322150; fax (389) 2322245; internet mizoram.nic.in.

PART FOUR

# Regional Information

# REGIONAL ORGANIZATIONS

## THE UNITED NATIONS

**Address:** United Nations, New York, NY 10017, USA.

**Telephone:** (212) 963-1234; **fax:** (212) 963-4879; **internet:** www.un.org.

The United Nations (UN) was founded on 24 October 1945. The organization, which has 192 member states, aims to maintain international peace and security and to develop international co-operation in addressing economic, social, cultural and humanitarian problems. The principal organs of the UN are the General Assembly, the Security Council, the Economic and Social Council, the International Court of Justice and the Secretariat. The General Assembly, which meets for three months each year, comprises representatives of all UN member states. The Security Council investigates disputes between member countries, and may recommend ways and means of peaceful settlement: it comprises five permanent members (the People's Republic of China, France, Russia, the United Kingdom and the USA) and 10 other members elected by the General Assembly for a two-year period. The Economic and Social Council comprises representatives of 54 member states, elected by the General Assembly for a three-year period: it promotes co-operation on economic, social, cultural and humanitarian matters, acting as a central policy-making body and co-ordinating the activities of the UN's specialized agencies. The International Court of Justice comprises 15 judges of different nationalities, elected for nine-year terms by the General Assembly and the Security Council: it adjudicates in legal disputes between UN member states.

**Secretary-General:** BAN KI-MOON (Republic of Korea) (2007–11).

### MEMBER STATES IN SOUTH ASIA

(with assessment for percentage contributions to UN budget for 2007–09, and year of admission)

| | | |
|---|---|---|
| Afghanistan | 0.001 | 1946 |
| Bangladesh | 0.010 | 1974 |
| Bhutan | 0.001 | 1971 |
| India | 0.450 | 1945 |
| Maldives | 0.001 | 1965 |
| Nepal | 0.003 | 1955 |
| Pakistan | 0.059 | 1947 |
| Sri Lanka | 0.016 | 1955 |

## Diplomatic Representation

### PERMANENT MISSIONS TO THE UNITED NATIONS

(August 2008)

**Afghanistan:** 360 Lexington Ave, 11th Floor, New York, NY 10017; tel. (212) 972-1212; fax (212) 972-1216; e-mail afgwatan@aol.com; Permanent Representative Dr ZAHIR TANIN.

**Bangladesh:** 227 East, 45th Street, 14th Floor, New York, NY 10017; tel. (212) 867-3434; fax (212) 972-4038; e-mail bangladesh@un.int; internet www.un.int/bangladesh; Permanent Representative ISMAT JAHAN.

**Bhutan:** 2 United Nations Plaza, 27th Floor, New York, NY 10017; tel. (212) 826-1919; fax (212) 826-2998; e-mail pmbnewyork@aol.com; Permanent Representative DAW PENJO.

**India:** 235 East 43rd St, New York, NY 10017; tel. (212) 490-9660; fax (212) 490-9656; e-mail india@un.int; internet www.un.int/india; Permanent Representative NIRUPAM SEN.

**Maldives:** 820 Second Ave, Suite 800C, New York, NY 10017; tel. (212) 599-6195; fax (212) 661-6405; e-mail mdv@undp.org; internet www.un.int/maldives; Permanent Representative AHMED KHALEEL.

**Nepal:** 820 Second Ave, Suite 17B, New York, NY 10017; tel. (212) 370-3988; fax (212) 953-2038; e-mail nepal@un.int; internet www.un.int/nepal; Permanent Representative MADHU RAMAN ACHARYA.

**Pakistan:** 8 East 65th St, New York, NY 10021; tel. (212) 879-8600; fax (212) 744-7348; e-mail pakistan@un.int; internet www.un.int/pakistan; Permanent Representative MUNIR AKRAM.

**Sri Lanka:** 630 Third Ave, 20th Floor, New York, NY 10017; tel. (212) 986-7040; fax (212) 986-1838; e-mail srilanka@un.int; Permanent Representative HEWA M. G. S. PALIHAKKARA.

### OBSERVERS

**Asian-African Legal Consultative Organization:** 404 East 66th St, Apt 12C, New York, NY 10021; tel. (212) 734-7608; e-mail aalco@un.int; Permanent Representative K. BHAGWAT-SINGH (India).

**Commonwealth Secretariat:** 800 Second Ave, 4th Floor, New York, NY 10017; tel. (212) 599-6190; fax (212) 808-4975; e-mail comsec@thecommonwealth.org.

**International Committee of the Red Cross:** 801 Second Ave, 18th Floor, New York, NY 10017; tel. (212) 599-6021; fax (212) 599-6009; e-mail log.nyc@icrc.org; Head of Delegation DOMINIQUE BUFF.

**International Criminal Police Organization:** One United Nations Plaza, Rm 2610, New York, NY 10017; tel. (917) 367-3463; fax (917) 367-3476; e-mail m.ragg@interpol.int; Special Representative (vacant).

**IUCN—The World Conservation Union:** 406 West 66th St, New York, NY 10023; tel. and fax (212) 734-7608.

**Organization of the Islamic Conference:** 130 East 40th St, 5th Floor, New York, NY 10016; tel. (212) 883-0140; fax (212) 883-0143; e-mail oicny@un.int; internet www.oicun.org; Permanent Representative ABDUL WAHAB.

Several intergovernmental organizations, including the Economic Co-operation Organization and the Islamic Development Bank, have a standing invitation to participate as observers but do not maintain permanent offices at the UN.

## United Nations Information Centres/Services

**Bangladesh:** POB 3658, Dhaka 1000; tel. (2) 8117868; fax (2) 8112343; e-mail unic.dhaka@undp.org; internet www.unicdhaka.org.

**India:** 55 Lodi Estate, New Delhi 110 003; tel. (11) 24628877; fax (11) 24620293; e-mail unicindia@unicindia.org; internet www.unic.org.in; also covers Bhutan.

**Nepal:** POB 107, UN House, Kathmandu; tel. (1) 524200; fax (1) 523991; e-mail registry.np@undp.org; internet kathmandu.unic.org.

**Pakistan:** POB 1107, House No. 26, 88th St, G-6/3, Islamabad; tel. (51) 2270610; fax (51) 2271856; e-mail unic.islamabad@unic.org; internet www.un.org.pk/unic.

**Sri Lanka:** POB 1505, 202/204 Bauddhaloka Mawatha, Colombo 7; tel. (1) 580691; fax (1) 501396; e-mail unic.lk@undp.org; internet colombo.unic.org.

# Economic and Social Commission for Asia and the Pacific—ESCAP

**Address:** United Nations Bldg, Rajadamnern Nok Ave, Bangkok 10200, Thailand.

**Telephone:** (2) 288-1234; **fax:** (2) 288-1000; **e-mail:** unisbkk.unescap@un.org; **internet:** www.unescap.org.

The Commission was founded in 1947, at first to assist in post-war reconstruction, and subsequently to encourage the economic and social development of Asia and the Far East; it was originally known as the Economic Commission for Asia and the Far East (ECAFE). The title ESCAP, which replaced ECAFE, was adopted after a reorganization in 1974. From 2002 ESCAP's administrative structures and programme activities underwent a process of intensive restructuring.

### MEMBERS

| | | |
|---|---|---|
| Afghanistan | Korea, Democratic People's Republic | Philippines |
| Armenia | Korea, Republic | Russia |
| Australia | Kyrgyzstan | Samoa |
| Azerbaijan | Laos | Singapore |
| Bangladesh | Malaysia | Solomon Islands |
| Bhutan | The Maldives | Sri Lanka |
| Brunei | Marshall Islands | Tajikistan |
| Cambodia | Micronesia, Federated States | Thailand |
| China, People's Republic | Mongolia | Timor-Leste |
| Fiji | Myanmar | Tonga |
| France | Nauru | Turkey |
| Georgia | Nepal | Turkmenistan |
| India | Netherlands | Tuvalu |
| Indonesia | New Zealand | United Kingdom |
| Iran | Pakistan | USA |
| Japan | Palau | Uzbekistan |
| Kazakhstan | Papua New Guinea | Vanuatu |
| Kiribati | | Viet Nam |

### ASSOCIATE MEMBERS

| | | |
|---|---|---|
| American Samoa | Hong Kong | Northern Mariana Islands |
| Cook Islands | Macao | |
| French Polynesia | New Caledonia | |
| Guam | Niue | |

## Organization

(August 2008)

### COMMISSION

The main legislative organ of ESCAP is the Commission, which meets annually at ministerial level to examine the region's problems, to review progress, to establish priorities and to decide upon the recommendations of the Executive Secretary or the subsidiary bodies of the Commission. It reports to the UN Economic and Social Council (ECOSOC). Ministerial and intergovernmental conferences on specific issues may be held on an ad hoc basis with the approval of the Commission, although no more than one ministerial conference and five intergovernmental conferences may be held during one year.

### COMMITTEES AND SPECIAL BODIES

The following Committees advise the Commission and help to oversee the work of the Secretariat. The Committees meet every two years, and their sub-committees meet in the intervening years.

**Committee on Poverty Reduction:** has sub-committees on Poverty Reduction Practices and Statistics.

**Committee on Managing Globalization:** has sub-committees on International Trade and Investment, Transport Infrastructure and Facilitation and Tourism, Environment and Sustainable Development, and Information, Communications and Space Technology.

**Committee on Emerging Social Issues:** has sub-committees on Socially Vulnerable Groups and Health and Development.

**Special Body on Least Developed and Landlocked Developing Countries:** meets every two years.

**Special Body on Pacific Island Developing Countries:** meets every two years.

In addition, an Advisory Committee of permanent representatives and other representatives designated by members of the Commission functions as an advisory body; it generally meets every month.

### SECRETARIAT

The Secretariat operates under the guidance of the Commission and its subsidiary bodies. It consists of the Office of the Executive Secretary and two servicing divisions, covering administration and programme management, in addition to the following substantive divisions: Development of Pacific Island Countries and Territories; Environment and Sustainable Development; Information, Communication and Space Technology; Poverty and Development; Social Development (including Emerging Social Issues); Statistics; Trade and Investment; and Transport and Tourism. The Secretariat also includes a Least Developed Countries Co-ordination Unit, and the UN Information Service/Bangkok.

**Executive Secretary:** NOELEEN HEYZER (Singapore).

### SUB-REGIONAL OFFICE

**ESCAP Pacific Operations Centre (EPOC):** Private Mail Bag, Suva, Fiji; tel. 3319669; fax 3319671; e-mail epoc@un.org; internet www.unescap.org/epoc; f. 1984, relocated to Fiji 2005; responsible for ESCAP's sub-programme on Development of Pacific Island Countries and Territories; assists Pacific island governments in forming and implementing national sustainable development strategies, particularly poverty reduction programmes that create access to services by socially vulnerable groups; conducts research, promotes regional co-operation and knowledge-sharing, and provides advisory services, training and pilot projects.

## Activities

ESCAP acts as a UN regional centre, providing the only intergovernmental forum that includes the whole of Asia and the Pacific, and executing a wide range of development programmes through technical assistance, advisory services to governments, research, training and information. In 1992 ESCAP began to reorganize its programme activities and conference structures in order to reflect and serve the region's evolving development needs. The approach that was adopted focused on regional economic co-operation, poverty alleviation through economic growth and social development, and environmental and sustainable development. In May 2002, having considered the recommendations of an intergovernmental review meeting held in March, ESCAP determined to implement a further restructuring of its conference structures and thematic priorities. Three main thematic programmes were identified: poverty reduction (comprising sub-programmes on poverty and development, and on statistics), managing globalization (with sub-programmes on trade and investment, environment, and space technology); and emerging social issues (with sub-programmes on health and development, gender and development, and population and social integration). In May 2007 the Commission, convened in Almaty, Kazakhstan, commemorated the 60th anniversary of ESCAP and reaffirmed its central role in fostering regional and sub-regional co-operation.

**Emerging Social Issues:** ESCAP's Emerging Social Issues Division comprises three sections: Health and Development, Gender and Development, and Population and Social Integration. The Division's main objective is to assess and respond to regional trends and challenges in social policy and human resources development, with particular emphasis on the planning and delivery of social services and training programmes for disadvantaged groups, including the poor, youths, women, the disabled, and the elderly. It aims to strengthen the capacity of public and non-government institutions to address the problems of marginalized social groups and to foster partnerships between governments, the private sector, community organizations and all other involved bodies. The Health and Development section promotes health for all as a critical condition for economic growth and social stability: it supports the strengthening of human resources, adequate health financing, improved delivery of health services, access to affordable medicines, and health promotion. In 2008 ongoing projects included promotion of sustainable strategies for universal access to health care, particularly in the Greater Mekong sub-region; and strengthening life skills to reduce young people's vulnerability to HIV and AIDS and to substance abuse. The Gender and Development section promotes the advancement of women by helping to improve their access to education, economic resources, information and communication technologies and decision-making; it is also committed to combating violence against women, including trafficking. The Population and Social Integration section provides technical assistance to national population programmes, conducts research and assists the exchange of information; promotes the rights of people with disabilities; supports improvement of access to social services by poor people; and helps governments to form policies that take into account the increasing proportion of older people in the population. The Division implements global and regional mandates, such as the Programme of Action of the World Summit for Social Development and the Jakarta Plan of Action on Human Resources Development. The Biwako Millennium Framework for Action towards an Inclusive, Barrier-free and Rights-based Society for Persons with Disabilities in Asia and the Pacific was adopted by ESCAP as a regional guideline underpinning the Asian and Pacific Decade of Disabled Persons (2003–12). In 1998 ESCAP initiated a programme of assistance in establishing a regional network of Social Development Management Information Systems (SOMIS). ESCAP collaborated with other agencies towards the adoption, in November 2001, of a Regional Platform on Sustainable Development for Asia and the Pacific. The Commission undertook regional preparations for the World Summit on Sustainable Development, which was held in Johannesburg, South Africa, in August–September 2002. In following up the summit ESCAP undertook to develop a bio-diversity park, which was officially inaugurated in Rawalpindi, Pakistan, in January 2005. The Commission also prepares specific publications relating to population and implements the Programme of Action of the International Conference on Population and Development. The Secretariat co-ordinates the Asia-Pacific Population Information Network (POPIN). The fifth Asia and Pacific Population Conference, sponsored by ESCAP, was held in Bangkok, Thailand, in December 2002. In September 2004 ESCAP convened a senior-level intergovernmental meeting on the regional review and implementation of the Beijing Platform for Action (Beijing + 10), relating to gender equality.

**Environment and Sustainable Development:** ESCAP is concerned to strengthen national capabilities to achieve environmentally sound and sustainable development by integrating economic concerns, such as the sustainable management of natural resources, into economic planning and policies. The Environment and Sustainable Development Division comprises sections on Energy Resources, Environment, and Sustainable Development and Water Resources. The Division was responsible for implementation of the Regional Action Programme for Environmentally Sound and Sustainable Development for the period 2001–05. Other activities have included the promotion of integrated water resources development and management, including water quality and conservation and a reduction in water-related natural disasters; strengthening the formulation of policies in the sustainable development of land and mineral resources; and the consideration of energy resource options, such as rural energy supply, energy conservation and the planning of power networks. Through the Division ESCAP prepares a report entitled State of the Environment in Asia and the Pacific which is published at five-yearly intervals, most recently in 2005. Following the massive earthquake and consequent devastating sea movements, or tsunamis, that occurred in late December 2004 in the Indian Ocean, ESCAP assisted other UN and international agencies with an initial emergency response and undertook early reviews of the impact of the event. In January 2005 the Executive Secretary appointed a Task Force on Tsunami Disaster Management to assist countries to address issues relating to natural disaster management, and to raise those issues at a regional level. The chairman of the Task Force was also appointed co-chair of an Inter-Agency Regional Task Force on Tsunami Relief and Rehabilitation that was established at a heads of agency meeting, convened by ESCAP later in that month, with particular responsibility to exchange information relating to rehabilitation and reconstruction in the aftermath of the tsunami disaster and to more general capacity-building on disaster preparedness. At the end of January a ministerial meeting, in Phuket, Thailand, approved the establishment of a regional tsunami early-warning system. ESCAP administers the voluntary, multi-donor Tsunami Regional Trust Fund which was inaugurated in late 2005 to support reconstruction and national and regional efforts to establish the early-warning system. ESCAP helped to organize a ministerial conference on environment and development, which was convened in Seoul, Republic of Korea, in March 2005. Representatives of the 52 countries attending the meeting adopted a Regional Implementation Plan for Sustainable Development in Asia and the Pacific (2006–10) and a Seoul Initiative on Environmentally Sustainable Economic Growth. The Division supports efforts to co-ordinate and monitor implementation of these initiatives. In particular, it received a mandate to work on issues related to climate change caused by global warming: it collates information, conducts regional seminars on adapting to climate change, and provides training in clean technology and guidance on reduction of harmful gas emissions. The inaugural meeting of the Asia-Pacific Regional Platform on Climate Change and Development was organized by ESCAP in March 2008.

**Information, Communication and Space Technology:** ESCAP's Information, Communication and Space Technology Division comprises the following sections: Information and Communication Technology (ICT) Policy, ICT Applications, and Space Technology Applications. The Division aims to strengthen capacity for access to and the application of ICT and space technology, in order to maximize the benefits of globalization. It supports the development of cross-sectoral policies and strategies, and also supports regional co-operation aimed at sharing knowledge between advanced and developing economies and in areas such as cyber-crime and information security. In May 2005 the Commission approved the establishment, in the Republic of Korea, of the Asian and Pacific Training Centre for ICT for Development (APCICT); APCICT was inaugurated in June 2006 (see below). In June 2005 the Division convened a senior-level meeting of experts to consider technical issues relating to disaster management and mitigation in Asia and the Pacific. The Division organized several conferences in preparation for the second phase of the World Summit on the Information Society (WSIS), which took place in November 2005, and co-ordinates regional activities aimed at achieving WSIS targets for the widespread use of ICT by 2015. During 2007 the Division organized projects and workshops in various countries of the region on the provision of ICT for rural communities, in particular for women entrepreneurs. It helps members to include space technology in their development planning, for example the use of satellites in meteorology, disaster prevention, remote sensing and distance learning. In August 2007 the Division hosted an international meeting on the use of space technology to combat avian influenza and other infectious diseases. A meeting of national policy-makers on disaster management was convened in March 2008 to discuss access to satellite information as a means of predicting and managing natural disasters.

**Poverty and Development:** The work of the Poverty and Development Division is undertaken by the following sections: Development Policy, Socio-economic Analysis and Poverty Reduction. The Division aims to increase the understanding of the economic and social development situation in the region, with particular attention given to the attainment of the UN Millennium Development Goals (MDGs), sustainable economic growth, poverty alleviation, the integration of environmental concerns into macroeconomic decisions and policy-making processes, and enhancing the position of the region's disadvantaged economies, including those Central Asian countries undergoing transition from a centrally-planned economy to a market economy. The Division is responsible for the provision of technical assistance, and the production of relevant documents and publications. The 63rd Commission, meeting in Almaty, Kazakhstan, in May 2007, endorsed a regional plan, developed by ESCAP, UNDP and the Asian Development Bank, to support poorer member countries to achieve the MDGs. Assistance was to be provided in the following areas: knowledge and capacity-building; expertise; resources; advocacy; and regional co-operation in delivering public goods (including infrastructure and energy security). The Commission also approved a resolution urging greater investment in health care in all member countries.

**Statistics:** ESCAP's Statistics Division provides training and advice in priority areas, including national accounts statistics, poverty indicators, gender statistics, population censuses and surveys, and the strengthening and management of statistical systems. It supports co-ordination throughout the region of the development, implementation and revision of selected international statistical standards, and, in particular, co-ordinates the International Comparison Programme (ICP) for Asia and the Pacific (part of a global ICP initiative). The Division disseminates comparable socio-economic statistics, with increased use of the electronic media, promotes the use of modern technology in the public sector and trains senior-level officials in the effective management of ICT. Training is provided by the Statistical Institute of Asia and the Pacific (see below).

**Trade and Investment:** ESCAP aims to help members to benefit from globalization by increasing global and regional flows of trade and investment. Its Trade and Investment Division provides technical assistance and advisory services. It aims to enhance institutional capacity-building; gives special emphasis to the needs of least-developed, land-locked and island developing countries, and to Central Asian countries that are in transition to a market economy,in accelerating their industrial and technological advancement, promoting their exports, and furthering their integration into the region's economy; supports the development of electronic commerce and other information technologies in the region; and promotes the intra-regional and inter-subregional exchange of trade, investment and technology through the strengthening of institutional support services such as regional information networks. The Division functions as the secretariat of the Asia-Pacific Trade Agreement (APTA), concluded in 1975 to promote regional trade through mutually agreed concessions by the participating states (in 2008 they comprised Bangladesh, the People's Republic of China, India, Laos and Sri Lanka). Since 2004 the Division has organized an annual Asia-Pacific Business Forum, involving representatives of governments, the private sector and civil society. It operates the Asia-Pacific Trade and Investment Agreements Database, the Trade and Transport Facilitation Online Database and an on-line Directory of Trade and Investment-Related Organizations, and publishes the Asia-Pacific Trade and Investment Review twice a year. The Division acts as the Secretariat of the Asia-Pacific Research and Training Network on Trade (ARTNeT), established in 2004, which aims to enhance the region's research capacity. ESCAP, with the World Trade Organization (WTO), implements a technical assistance programme, helping member states to implement WTO agreements and to participate in ongoing multilateral trade negotiations.

**Transport and Tourism:** ESCAP's Transport and Tourism Division aims to improve the regional movement of goods and people, and to strengthen the role of tourism in economic and social development. The Division has three sections: Transport Infrastructure, Transport Facilitation, and Transport Policy and Tourism. Its principal task is the implementation of the Asian Land Transport Infrastructure Development (ALTID) programme, initiated in 1992. ALTID projects include the development of the Trans-Asian Railway and of the Asian Highway road network. Other activities are aimed at improving the planning process in developing infrastructure facilities and services, in accordance with the Regional Action Programme (Phase II, 2002–06) of the New Delhi Action Plan on Infrastructure Development in Asia and the Pacific, which was adopted at a ministerial conference held in October 1996, and at enhancing private sector involvement in national infrastructure development through financing, management, operations and risk-sharing. The Division aims to reduce the adverse environmental impact of the provision of infrastructure facilities and to promote more equitable and easier access to social amenities. A Ministerial Conference on Infrastructure Development was organized by ESCAP in November 2001. An Intergovernmental Agreement on the Asian Highway Network (adopted in 2003, identifying some 141,000 km of roads in 32 countries) came into effect in July 2005. The first meeting of a working group on the highway, which was to convene twice a year, was held in December. By November 2007 about 10,000 km of the highway network had been upgraded to meet the minimum standards set by the Agreement, and in that month an Asian Highway Investment Forum was convened by ESCAP to finance the improvements still required on a further 12,000 km of the network. In November ESCAP organized an intergovernmental meeting to conclude a draft agreement on the establishment of a Trans-Asian Railway Network, comprising some 80,900 km of rail routes. The intergovernmental accord was adopted in April 2006. In 2004 ESCAP and the UN Economic Commission for Europe (ECE) initiated a project for developing Euro-Asian transport linkages, aiming to identify and overcome the principal obstacles (physical and otherwise) along the main transport routes linking Asia and Europe. In November 2003 ESCAP approved a new initiative, the Asia-Pacific Network for Transport and Logistics Education and Research (ANTLER), to comprise education, training and research centres throughout the region. In November 2006 a Ministerial Conference on Transport was held in Busan, Republic of Korea. The Busan Declaration, adopted by the meeting, outlined a long-term development strategy for regional transport and identified investment priorities. The meeting also adopted a Ministerial Declaration on Road Safety which pledged to implement safety measures to save some 600,000 lives in the region in the period 2007–15. Tourism concerns include the development of human resources, improved policy planning for tourism development, greater investment in the industry, and minimizing the environmental impact of tourism. A Plan of Action for Sustainable Tourism in the Asia and Pacific Region (1999–2005) was adopted in April 1999, and a second phase of the Plan was to cover the period 2006–12. A Network of Asia-Pacific Education and Training Institutes in Tourism, established in 1997, comprised 211 institutes and organizations in 2008. Throughout all its activities the Division devotes particular attention to the needs and concerns of least-developed, land-locked and island developing nations, and economies in transition in the region.

## CO-OPERATION WITH OTHER ORGANIZATIONS

ESCAP works with other UN agencies and non-UN international organizations, non-governmental organizations, academic institutions and the private sector; such co-operation includes joint planning of programmes, preparation of studies and reports, participating in meetings, and sharing information and technical expertise. In July 1993 a memorandum of understanding (MOU) was signed by ESCAP and the Asian Development Bank, outlining priority areas of co-operation between the two organizations. These were: regional and sub-regional co-operation; issues concerning the least-developed, land-locked and island developing member countries; poverty alleviation; women in development; population; human resource development; the environment and natural resource management; statistics and data bases; economic analysis; transport and communications; and industrial restructuring and privatization. The two organizations were to co-operate in organizing workshops, seminars and conferences, in implementing joint projects, and in exchanging information and data on a regular basis. A new MOU between the two organizations was signed in May 2004 with an emphasis on achieving poverty reduction throughout the region. In 2001 ESCAP, with the Bank and UNDP, established a regional partnership to promote the MDGs (see above); a joint regional report on implementation of the goals was prepared by the partnership and published in June 2005 prior to a global review, conducted at the UN General Assembly in September, and a further regional review was published in 2007. In May 2007 ESCAP endorsed a regional plan developed by the partnership with the aim of addressing regional challenges (in particular those faced by poorer countries) to the achievement of the MDGs. The UN Special Programme for the Economies of Central Asia (SPECA), begun in 1998, is implemented jointly by ESCAP and ECE: SPECA helps the participating countries to strengthen regional co-operation, particularly in the areas of water resources, energy and transport, and creates incentives for economic development and integration into the economies of Asia and Europe. In May 2007 ESCAP signed an MOU with ECE and the Eurasian Economic Community to strengthen co-operation in sustainable development, in support of the MDGs. In the following month ESCAP signed an MOU with the International Organization for Migration to provide for greater co-operation and co-ordination on international migration issues.

## REGIONAL INSTITUTIONS

**Asian and Pacific Centre for Agricultural Engineering and Machinery (APCAEM):** A-7/F, China International Science and Technology Convention Centre, 12 Yumin Rd, Chaoyang District, Beijing 100029, People's Republic of China; tel. (10) 8225-3581; fax (10) 8225-3584; e-mail info@unapcaem.org; internet www.unapcaem.org; f. 1977 as Regional Network for Agricultural Engineering and Machinery, elevated to regional centre in 2002; aims to reduce poverty by enhancing environmentally sustainable agriculture and food production, and applying 'green' and modern agro-technology for the well-being of producers and consumers; work programmes comprise agricultural engineering, food chain management, and agro-enterprise development and trade; undertakes research, training, technical assistance and the exchange of information. Active mems: Bangladesh, People's Republic of China, Democratic People's Republic of Korea, Fiji, India, Indonesia, Iran, Mongolia, Nepal, Pakistan, Philippines, Republic of Korea, Sri Lanka, Thailand, Viet Nam; Dir Dr JOONG-WAN CHO; *APCAEM Policy Brief* (quarterly).

**Asian and Pacific Centre for Transfer of Technology:** APCTT Bldg, POB 4575, C-2 Qutab Institutional Area, New Delhi 110 016, India; tel. (11) 26966509; fax (11) 26856274; e-mail postmaster@apctt.org; internet www.apctt.org; f. 1977 to assist countries of the ESCAP region by strengthening their capacity to develop, transfer and adopt technologies relevant to the region, and to identify and promote regional technology development and transfer; operates Business Asia Network (www.business-asia.net) to promote technology-based co-operation, particularly between small and medium-sized enterprises; Dir Dr KRISHNAMURTHY RAMANATHAN; publs *Asia Pacific Tech Monitor*, *VATIS Updates on Biotechnology*, *Food Processing*, *Ozone Layer Protection*, *Non-Conventional Energy*, and *Waste Management* (each every 2 months).

**Asian and Pacific Training Centre for ICT for Development (APCICT):** Bonbudong, 3rd Floor Songdo Techno Park, 7-50 Songdo-dong, Yeonsu-gu, Incheon City, Republic of Korea; tel. 245-1700; fax 245-7712; e-mail staff@unapcict.org; internet www.unescap.org/icstd/applications/apcict.asp; f. 2006 to provide training to ICT policy-makers and professionals, advisory services and analytical studies, to promote best practices in the field of ICT, and to contribute to narrowing the digital divide in the region; Dir HYUEN-SUK RHEE.

**Centre for Alleviation of Poverty through Secondary Crops' Development in Asia and the Pacific (CAPSA):** Jalan Merdeka 145, Bogor 16111, Indonesia; tel. (251) 343277; fax (251) 336290; e-mail capsa@uncapsa.org; internet www.uncapsa.org; f. 1981 as CGPRT Centre, current name adopted April 2004; initiates and promotes socio-economic and policy research, training, dissemination of information and advisory services to enhance the living conditions of rural poor populations reliant on secondary crop agriculture; Dir Dr TACO BOTTEMA (Netherlands); publs *CAPSA Flash* (monthly), *Palawija News* (3 a year), working paper series, monograph series and statistical profiles.

**Statistical Institute for Asia and the Pacific (SIAP):** JETRO-IDE Building, 2–2 Wakaba 3-chome, Mihama-ku, Chiba-shi, Chiba 2618787, Japan; tel. (43) 2999782; fax (43) 2999780; e-mail staff@unsiap.or.jp; internet www.unsiap.or.jp; f. 1970 as Asian Statistical Institute, present name 1977; became a subsidiary body of ESCAP in 1995; trains government statisticians at the Institute and in various co-operating countries in Asia and the Pacific; prepares teaching materials, assists in the development of training on official statistics in national and sub-regional centres; Dir DAVAASUREN CHULTEMJAMTS (Mongolia); *publ. SIAP Newsletter* (annually).

### ASSOCIATED BODIES

**ESCAP/WMO Typhoon Committee:** PAGASA, 4th Floor, Science Garden, Agham Rd, Diliman, Quezon City, Philippines; tel. and fax (632) 4349026; e-mail tcs@philonline.com; internet www.tcsphilippines.org; f. 1968; an intergovernmental body sponsored by ESCAP and the World Meteorological Organization for mitigation of typhoon damage; aims to establish efficient typhoon and flood warning systems through improved meteorological and telecommunication facilities; promotes disaster preparedness, trains personnel and co-ordinates research. The committee's programme is supported from national resources and also by UNDP and other international and bilateral assistance. Mems: Cambodia, People's Republic of China, Hong Kong, Japan, Democratic People's Republic of Korea, Republic of Korea, Laos, Macao, Malaysia, Philippines, Singapore, Thailand, USA, Viet Nam; Co-ordinator Dr ROMAN L. KINTANAR.

**WMO/ESCAP Panel on Tropical Cyclones:** Technical Support Unit (TSU), c/o Pakistan Meteorological Dept, POB 1214, H-8/2, Islamabad, Pakistan; tel. (51) 9257314; fax (51) 4432588; e-mail tsupmd@hotmail.com; internet www.tsuptc-wmo.org; f. 1972 to mitigate damage caused by tropical cyclones in the Bay of Bengal and the Arabian Sea. Mems: Bangladesh, India, the Maldives, Myanmar, Oman, Pakistan, Sri Lanka, Thailand; TSU Co-ordinator Dr QAMAR-UZ-ZAMAN CHAUDHRY.

## Finance

For the two-year period 2006–07 ESCAP's programme budget, an appropriation from the UN budget, was US $71.9m. The regular budget is supplemented annually by funds from various sources for technical assistance.

## Publications

*Annual Report*.
*Asia-Pacific Development Journal* (2 a year).
*Asia-Pacific in Figures* (annually).
*Asia-Pacific Population Journal* (3 a year).
*Asia-Pacific Trade and Investment Review* (2 a year).
*Bulletin on Asia-Pacific Perspectives* (annually).
*Economic and Social Survey of Asia and the Pacific* (annually).
*Environment and Sustainable Development News* (quarterly).
*ESCAP Energy News* (2 a year).
*ESCAP Human Resources Development Newsletter* (2 a year).
*ESCAP Population Data Sheet* (annually).
*ESCAP Tourism Review* (annually).
*Foreign Trade Statistics of Asia and the Pacific* (every 2 years).
*Key Economic Developments and Prospects in the Asia-Pacific Region* (annually).
*Population Headliners* (several a year).
*Poverty Alleviation Initiatives* (quarterly).
*Socio-Economic Policy Brief* (several a year).
*State of the Environment in Asia and the Pacific* (every 5 years).
*Statistical Indicators for Asia and the Pacific* (quarterly).
*Statistical Newsletter* (quarterly).
*Statistical Yearbook for Asia and the Pacific*.
*Technical Co-operation Yearbook*.
*Trade and Investment Information Bulletin* (monthly).
*Transport and Communications Bulletin for Asia and the Pacific* (annually).
*Water Resources Journal* (annually).
Manuals; country and trade profiles; commodity prices; statistics; Atlas of Mineral Resources of the ESCAP Region (country by country)

# United Nations Children's Fund—UNICEF

**Address:** 3 United Nations Plaza, New York, NY 10017, USA.

**Telephone:** (212) 326-7000; **fax:** (212) 887-7465; **e-mail:** info@unicef.org; **internet:** www.unicef.org.

UNICEF was established in 1946 by the UN General Assembly as the UN International Children's Emergency Fund, to meet the emergency needs of children in post-war Europe. In 1950 its mandate was expanded to respond to the needs of children in developing countries. In 1953 the General Assembly decided that UNICEF should become a permanent branch of the UN system, with an emphasis on programmes giving long-term benefits to children everywhere, particularly those in developing countries. In 1965 UNICEF was awarded the Nobel Peace Prize.

## Organization

(August 2008)

### EXECUTIVE BOARD

The Executive Board, as the governing body of UNICEF, comprises 36 member governments from all regions, elected in rotation for a three-year term by ECOSOC. The Board establishes policy, reviews programmes and approves expenditure. It reports to the General Assembly through ECOSOC.

### SECRETARIAT

The Executive Director of UNICEF is appointed by the UN Secretary-General in consultation with the Executive Board. The administration of UNICEF and the appointment and direction of staff are the responsibility of the Executive Director, under policy directives laid down by the Executive Board, and under a broad authority delegated to the Executive Director by the Secretary-General. In January 2007 there were more than 8,000 UNICEF staff positions, of which about 85% were in field offices.

**Executive Director:** ANN M. VENEMAN (USA).

### UNICEF OFFICES

**Regional Office for South Asia:** POB 5815, Leknath Marg, Kathmandu, Nepal; tel. 4419082; fax 4419479; e-mail rosa@unicef.org.

**UNICEF Innocenti Research Centre:** Piazza SS. Annunziata 12, 50122 Florence, Italy; tel. (055) 20330; fax (055) 2033220; e-mail florence@unicef.org; internet www.unicef-irc.org; f. 1988.

**UNICEF Supply Division:** UNICEF Plads, Freeport 2100, Copenhagen, Denmark; tel. 35-27-35-27; fax 35-26-94-21; e-mail supply@unicef.org; internet www.unicef.org/supply.

### NATIONAL COMMITTEES

UNICEF is supported by 37 National Committees, mostly in industrialized countries, whose volunteer members, numbering more than 100,000, raise money through various activities, including the sale of greetings cards. The Committees also undertake advocacy and awareness campaigns on a number of issues and provide an important link with the general public.

## Activities

UNICEF is dedicated to the well-being of children, adolescents and women and works for the realization and protection of their rights within the frameworks of the Convention on the Rights of the Child, which was adopted by the UN General Assembly in 1989 and by 2008 was almost universally ratified, and of the Convention on the Elimination of All Forms of Discrimination Against Women, adopted by the UN General Assembly in 1979. Promoting the full implementation of the Conventions, UNICEF aims to ensure that children world-wide are given the best possible start in life and attain a good level of basic education, and that adolescents are given every opportunity to develop their capabilities and participate successfully in society. The Fund also continues to provide relief and rehabilitation assistance in emergencies. Through its extensive field network in some 156 developing countries and territories, UNICEF undertakes, in co-ordination with governments, local communities and other aid organizations, programmes in health, nutrition, education, water and sanitation, the environment, gender issues and development, and other fields of importance to children. Emphasis is placed on low-cost, community-based programmes. UNICEF programmes are increasingly focused on supporting children and women during critical periods of their life, when intervention can make a lasting difference. UNICEF is actively involved in global-level partnerships for child protection, including the Inter-Agency Co-ordination Panel on Juvenile Justice; the Inter-Agency Working Group on Unaccompanied and Separated Children; the Donors' Working Group on Female Genital Mutilation/Cutting; the Better Care Network; the Study on Violence Against Children; the Inter-Agency Standing Committee (IASC) Task Force on Protection from Sexual Exploitation and Abuse in Humanitarian Crises; and the IASC Task Force on Mental Health and Psychological Support in Emergency Settings. In 2006 UNICEF allocated 11% of its total programme assistance towards policy advocacy and partnerships for children's rights.

Since 2005 young people from the Group of Eight (G8) nations (Canada, France, Germany, Italy, Japan, Russia, the United Kingdom and the USA) have participated in a Junior 8 (J8) summit, organized with support from UNICEF on the fringes of the annual G8 summit. The J8 summits address issues including education, energy, HIV/AIDS, and tolerance. The fourth J8 summit meeting took place in Chitose, Hokkaido, Japan, in July 2008.

The five principal themes of UNICEF's medium-term strategic plan for the period 2006–09 are: young child survival and development; basic education and gender equality, including the Fund's continued leadership of the UN Girls' Education Initiative (UNGEI); HIV/AIDS and children, including participation in the Joint UN Programme on HIV/AIDS (UNAIDS—see below); child protection from violence, exploitation and abuse; and policy advocacy and partnerships for children's rights. These priorities are guided by the relevant UN Millennium Development Goals (MDGs) adopted by world leaders in 2000, and by the 'A World Fit for Children' declaration and plan of action endorsed by the UN General Assembly Special Session on Children in 2002 (see below).

UNICEF served as the substantive secretariat for, and played a leading role in helping governments and other partners prepare for, the UN General Assembly Special Session on Children, which was held in May 2002 to assess the outcome of the World Summit for Children convened in 1990 (which had made commitments to reducing mortality rates for infants and children; reducing the maternal mortality rate; reducing severe malnutrition amongst children under five; ensuring universal access to safe drinking water and to sanitary means of excreta disposal; and ensuring universal access to basic education) and to determine a set of actions and objectives for the next 10 years. At the Session the General Assembly adopted a declaration entitled 'A World Fit for Children', reaffirming its commitment to the agenda of the 1990 summit, and outlining a plan of action that resolved to achieve as yet unmet World Summit goals by 2010 and to work towards the attainment by 2015 of 21 new goals and targets supporting the MDGs in the areas of education, health and the protection of children. The latter included: a reduction of mortality rates for infants and children under five by two-thirds; a reduction of maternal mortality rates by three-quarters; a reduction by one-third in the rate for severe malnutrition among children under the age of five; and enrolment in primary education by 90% of children. In December 2007 a special session of the UN General Assembly reviewed progress attained so far towards 'A World Fit for Children'. UNICEF's annual publication *The State of the World's Children* includes social and economic data relevant to the well-being of children. It was reported in this publication in 2007 that one of the most powerful constraints to realizing children's rights and achieving the MDGs was discrimination against women. In 1995 UNICEF developed its Multiple Indicator Cluster Survey (MICS) method of data collection, which was in the 2000s being used as a main tool in measuring progress towards the achievement of the UN MDGs.

In 2000 UNICEF launched a new initiative, the Global Movement for Children—comprising governments, private- and public-sector bodies, and individuals—which aimed to rally world-wide support to improve the lives of all children and adolescents. In April 2001 a 'Say Yes for Children' campaign was adopted by the Global Movement, identifying 10 critical actions required to further its objectives. These were: eliminating all forms of discrimination and exclusion; putting children first; ensuring a caring environment for every child; fighting HIV/AIDS; eradicating violence against and abuse and exploitation of children; listening to children's views; universal education; protecting children from war; safeguarding the earth for children; and combating poverty. UNICEF hosts the Child Survival Partnership, launched in 2003 by UNICEF, WHO, the World Bank and other partners to act as a forum for the promotion of co-ordinated action in support of efforts to reduce the level of child mortality in 42 targeted developing countries.

UNICEF, in co-operation with other UN agencies, promotes universal access to and completion of basic and good quality education. The Fund, with UNESCO, UNDP, UNFPA and the World Bank, co-sponsored the World Conference on Education for All, held in Thailand in March 1990, and undertook efforts to achieve the objectives formulated by the conference, which included the elimination of disparities in education between boys and girls. UNICEF participated in and fully supports the objectives and framework for action adopted by the World Education Forum in Dakar, Senegal, in April 2000. UNICEF supports education projects in sub-Saharan Africa, South Asia and countries in the Middle East, North Africa, and Latin America and the Caribbean, and leads and acts as the secretariat of the United Nations Girls' Education Initiative (UNGEI), which aims to increase the enrolment of girls in primary schools in more than 100 countries. In 2006 about 115m. school-age children world-wide, of whom more than one-half were girls, remained deprived of basic education. Some 21.3% of the Fund's programme assistance was allocated to basic education and gender equality in 2006.

In 2005 approximately 500,000 girls in Afghanistan were enrolled in schools for the first time, and in March 2007 an UNGEI project (the Afghanistan Girls' Education Initiative—AGEI) was launched in that country.

Major 'back-to-school' campaigns and enrolment drives were launched in countries struck by the December 2004 Indian Ocean tsunamis; within three months of the disaster 90% of affected children had returned to school.

UNICEF works to improve safe water supply, sanitation and hygiene, and thereby reduce the risk of diarrhoea and other water-borne diseases. In partnership with other organizations the Fund supports initiatives to make schools in more than 90 developing countries safer through school-based water, sanitation and hygiene programmes. UNICEF places great emphasis on increasing the testing and protection of drinking water at its source as well as in the home. In 2006 UNICEF and partners established the Global Task Force on Water and Sanitation with the aim of providing all children with access to safe water, and accelerating progress towards MDG targets on safe drinking water and basic sanitation.

UNICEF aims to break the cycle of poverty by advocating for the provision of increased development aid to developing countries, and aims to help poor countries obtain debt relief and to ensure access to basic social services. UNICEF is the leading agency in promoting the 20/20 initiative, which was endorsed at the World Summit for Social Development, held in Copenhagen, Denmark, in March 1995. The initiative encourages the governments of developing and donor countries to allocate at least 20% of their domestic budgets and official development aid respectively, to healthcare, primary education and low-cost safe water and sanitation.

UNICEF estimates that the births of some 50m. children annually are not officially registered, and promotes universal registration in order to prevent the abuse of children without proof of age and nationality, for example through trafficking, forced labour, early marriage and military recruitment. It estimates that some 218m. children were involved in exploitative labour (excluding domestic work) in 2004, and approximately 126m. children aged five–17 were believed to be engaged in hazardous work. It is estimated that, annually, around 1.2m. children world-wide are trafficked. The Fund, which vigorously opposes the exploitation of children as a violation of their basic human rights, works with ILO and other partners to promote an end to exploitative and hazardous child labour, and supports special projects to provide education, counselling and care in developing countries. UNICEF co-sponsored and actively participated in the Second Congress Against Commercial Sexual Exploitation of Children held in Yokohama, Japan, in December 2001. Some 10.2% of the Fund's direct programme assistance was allocated to the improved protection of children in 2006.

In 2006 UNICEF allocated 51% of its programme assistance to young child survival and development. The Fund estimated that around 9.7m. children under five years of age died in 2006 (compared with some 20m. and 13m. child mortalities in, respectively, 1960 and 1990), mainly in developing countries, and the majority from largely preventable causes. UNICEF has worked with WHO and other partners to increase global immunization coverage against the following six diseases: measles, poliomyelitis, tuberculosis, diphtheria, whooping cough and tetanus. In 2003 UNICEF, WHO, the World Bank and other partners established a new Child Survival Partnership, which acts as a forum for the promotion of co-ordinated action in support of efforts to save the children's lives in 42 targeted developing countries. In September 2005 UNICEF, WHO and other partners launched the Partnership for Maternal, Newborn and Child Health, formed to accelerate progress towards MDGs four and five, which aim to reduce child and maternal mortality respectively. In 2000 UNICEF, WHO, the World Bank and a number of public- and private-sector partners launched the Global Alliance for Vaccines and Immunization (GAVI, subsequently renamed the Gavi Alliance), which aims to protect children of all nationalities and socio-economic groups against vaccine-preventable diseases. GAVI's strategy includes improving access to sustainable immunization services, expanding the use of existing vaccines, accelerating the development and introduction of new vaccines and technologies and promoting immunization coverage as a focus of international development efforts.

The results of integrated approaches to child health, such as the Accelerated Child Survival and Development (ACSD) strategy and community-based Integrated Management of Childhood Illnesses (IMCI) programme, have demonstrated new potential to reduce child mortality. The ACSD strategy, implemented by UNICEF since 2002, is an intensive combination of life-saving interventions including the promotion of antenatal care, vaccination and breast-feeding, volunteer health-worker follow-up of newborns and the distribution of insecticide-treated mosquito nets. Focused in 97 high-mortality districts in 11 mainly West African countries, ACSD has reached around 16m. people, including 2.8m. children under the age of five.

In 2006 UNICEF issued a report entitled *Pneumonia: The Forgotten Killer of Children*, which identified pneumonia as the primary medical cause of all deaths of children under five years of age.

At the UN General Assembly Special Session on Children, in 2002, goals were set to reduce measles deaths by 50%. Expanded efforts by UNICEF, WHO and other partners led to a reduction in world-wide measles deaths by around 60% between 1999 and 2005.

UNICEF-assisted programmes for the control of diarrhoeal diseases promote the low-cost manufacture and distribution of prepackaged salts or home-made solutions. The use of 'oral rehydration therapy' has risen significantly in recent years, and is believed to prevent more than 1m. child deaths annually. During 1990–2000 diarrhoea-related deaths were reduced by one-half. UNICEF also promotes the need to improve sanitation and access to safe water supplies in developing nations in order to reduce the risk of diarrhoea and other water-borne diseases (see 20/20 initiative, above). To control acute respiratory infections, another leading cause of death in children under five in developing countries, UNICEF works with WHO in training health workers to diagnose and treat the associated diseases. Around 1m. children die from malaria every year, mainly in sub-Saharan Africa. In October 1998 UNICEF, together with WHO, UNDP and the World Bank, inaugurated a new global campaign, Roll Back Malaria, to fight the disease. UNICEF is actively engaged in developing innovative and effective ways to distribute highly-subsidized insecticide-treated mosquito nets at local level, thereby increasing the proportion of children and pregnant women who use them.

According to UNICEF estimates, around 25% of children under five years of age are underweight, while each year malnutrition contributes to about one-half of the child deaths in that age group and leaves millions of others with physical and mental disabilities. More than 2,000m. people world-wide (mainly women and children in developing countries) are estimated to be deficient in one or more essential vitamins and minerals, such as vitamin A, iodine and iron. UNICEF supports national efforts to reduce malnutrition, for example, fortifying staple foods with micronutrients, widening women's access to education, improving the nutritional status of pregnant women, improving household food security and basic health services, providing food supplies in emergencies, and promoting sound child-care and feeding practices. Since 1991 more than 19,000 hospitals in about 130 countries have been designated 'baby-friendly', having implemented a set of UNICEF and WHO recommendations entitled '10 steps to successful breast-feeding'. In 1996 UNICEF expressed its concern at the impact of international economic embargoes on child health, citing as an example the extensive levels of child malnutrition recorded in Iraq. UNICEF remains actively concerned at the levels of child malnutrition and accompanying diseases in Iraq and in the Democratic People's Republic of Korea, which has also suffered severe food shortages.

UNICEF estimates that more than 500,000 women die every year during pregnancy or childbirth, largely because of inadequate maternal healthcare. For every maternal death, approximately 30 further women suffer permanent injuries or chronic disabilities as a result of complications during pregnancy or childbirth. With its partners in the Safe Motherhood Initiative—UNFPA, WHO, the World Bank, the International Planned Parenthood Federation, the Population Council, and Family Care International—UNICEF promotes measures to reduce maternal mortality and morbidity, including improving access to quality reproductive health services, educating communities about safe motherhood and the rights of women, training midwives, and expanding access to family planning services. Under the Global Partnership for Maternal, Newborn and Child Health, UNICEF works with WHO, UNFPA and other partners in countries with high maternal mortality to improve maternal health and prevent maternal deaths. UNICEF and partners work with governments and policy-makers to ensure that emergency obstetric care is a priority in national health plans. In 200 UNICEF activities in this area included support for obstetric facilities and training in, and advocacy of, women's health issues such as avoiding child marriage, eliminating female genital mutilation/cutting (FGM/C), and preventing malaria and promoting the uptake of tetanus toxoid vaccinations and iron and folic acid supplements among pregnant women.

UNICEF is concerned at the danger posed by HIV/AIDS to the realization of children's rights and in 2006 allocated 5.5% of its programme expenditure to this area. At the end of 2007 it was estimated that 2.1m. children under the age of 15 were living with HIV/AIDS world-wide. During that year some 420,000 children under the age of 15 were estimated to have been newly infected with the HIV virus, while 290,000 died as a result of AIDS and AIDS-related illnesses. It is believed that more than 15m. children world-wide have lost one or both parents to AIDS since the start of the pandemic. UNICEF's priorities in this area include prevention of infection among young people (through, for example, support for education programmes and dissemination of information through the media), reduction in mother-to-child transmission, care and protection of orphans and other vulnerable children, and care and support for children, young people and parents living with HIV/AIDS. UNICEF works closely in this field with governments and co-operates with other UN agencies in the Joint UN Programme on HIV/AIDS (UNAIDS), which became operational on 1 January 1996. In July 2002 UNICEF, UNAIDS and WHO jointly produced a study entitled *Young People and HIV/AIDS: Opportunity in Crisis*, examining young people's sexual behaviour patterns and knowledge of HIV/AIDS. UNICEF advocates Life Skills-Based Education as a means of empowering young people to cope with challenging situations and encouraging them to adopt healthy patterns of behaviour. In July 2004 UNICEF and other partners produced a *Framework for the Protection, Care and Support of Orphans and Vulnerable Children Living in a World with HIV and AIDS*. In October 2005 UNICEF launched Unite for Children, Unite Against AIDS, a campaign that was to provide a platform for child-focused advocacy aimed at reversing the spread of HIV/AIDS amongst children, adolescents and young people; and to provide a child-focused framework for national programmes based on the following four pillars: the prevention of mother-to-child HIV transmission, improved provision of paediatric treatment, prevention of infection among adolescents and young people, and protection and support of children affected by HIV/AIDS. In January 2007 UNICEF issued *Children and AIDS: A stocktaking report* detailing the progress and challenges of the previous year.

UNICEF provides emergency relief assistance to children and young people affected by conflict, natural disasters and food crises. In situations of violence and social disintegration the Fund provides support in the areas of education, health, mine-awareness and psychosocial assistance, and helps to demobilize and rehabilitate child soldiers. In recent years several such operations have been undertaken, including in Afghanistan, Burundi, Democratic Republic of the Congo, Iraq, Liberia, the Palestinian territories, Sierra Leone, Somalia and Sudan. In December 2007 UNICEF appealed for some US $237.4m. through the UN Consolidated Inter-Agency Appeal Process to fund emergency assistance to children and women in emergencies in 2008. In 1999 UNICEF adopted a Peace and Security Agenda to help guide international efforts in this field. Emergency education assistance includes the provision of 'Edukits' in refugee camps and the reconstruction of school buildings. In the area of health the Fund co-operates with WHO to arrange 'days of tranquility' in order to facilitate the immunization of children in conflict zones. Psychosocial assistance activities include special programmes to support traumatized children and help unaccompanied children to be reunited with parents or extended families.

In 2005 the Fund assisted an estimated 1.5m. children and young people who had been displaced from their homes by the devastating December 2004 Indian Ocean tsunamis. UNICEF's relief and recovery efforts included the provision of emergency immunization to prevent an increase in the prevalence of fatal childhood diseases; the provision of basic medicines; supply of safe water and provision of basic sanitation; provision of fortified supplementary food to young children and to pregnant and lactating women; care for traumatized children; identification and protection of the large numbers of orphans and children who had been separated from their families; and the provision of education kits for children whose schooling had been disrupted by the natural disaster and the rehabilitation of schools.

In response to the earthquake that devastated parts of northern Pakistan and bordering areas of Afghanistan and India in October 2005, UNICEF provided emergency supplies of blankets, warm-weather clothing, tents, medicines, infant food, and water purification tablets.

In 2006 UNICEF provided primary health care to some 2.1m. people in Darfur, Sudan, and worked with partners to supply camps with safe water and basic sanitation to the region. During that year UNICEF also conducted a 'Go to School' campaign in Darfur, and 1.2m. children were also immunized against polio and given vitamin A supplements.

In the mid-2000s UNICEF country offices prepared contingency plans for a possible future avian influenza pandemic among humans, with a particular focus on children, as part of the inter-agency response to the threat.

An estimated 250,000 children are involved in armed conflicts as soldiers, porters and forced labourers. UNICEF encourages ratification of the Optional Protocol to the Convention on the Rights of the Child on the involvement of children in armed conflict, which was adopted by the General Assembly in May 2000 and entered into force in February 2002, and bans the compulsory recruitment of combatants below the age of 18. The Fund also urges states to make unequivocal statements endorsing 18 as the minimum age of voluntary recruitment to the armed forces. It is estimated that land-mines kill and maim between 8,000 and 10,000 children every year. The Convention on the Prohibition of the Use, Stockpiling, Production and Transfer of Anti-Personnel Mines and on their Destruction was adopted in December 1997 and entered into force in March 1999. By July 2008 the Convention had been ratified by 156 countries. UNICEF is committed to campaigning for its universal ratification and full implementation, and also supports mine-awareness campaigns.

During 2005 the UN's Inter-Agency Standing Committee (IASC), concerned with co-ordinating the international response to humanitarian disasters, developed a concept of organizing agency assistance to IDPs through the institutionalization of a 'Cluster Approach', currently comprising 11 core areas of activity. UNICEF was designated the lead agency for the clusters on Education (jointly with Save The Children); Emergency Telecommunications (jointly with OCHA and WFP); Nutrition; Protection of IDPs in natural disaster situations and of non-IDP civilians in conflict situations (with UNHCR and OHCHR); and Water, Sanitation and Hygiene.

## Finance

UNICEF is funded by voluntary contributions from governments and non-governmental and private-sector sources. UNICEF's income is divided into contributions for 'regular resources' (used for country programmes of co-operation approved by the Executive Board, programme support, and management and administration costs) and contributions for 'other resources' (for special purposes, including expanding the outreach of country programmes of co-operation and ensuring capacity to deliver critical assistance to women and children, for example during humanitarian crises). UNICEF's total income in 2007 was estimated at US $3,013m. and its total expenditure at US $2,782m.

In 2007 some 52.4% of the Fund's total expenditure was allocated to child survival and development, 20.3% to basic education and gender equality, 10% to child protection, 9.3% to policy advocacy and partnerships, 6.4% to HIV/AIDS prevention and treatment, and 1.1% towards other areas.

## Publications

*Progress for Children* (in English, French and Spanish).

*The State of the World's Children* (annually, in Arabic, English, French, Russian and Spanish and about 30 other national languages).

*UNICEF Annual Report* (in English, French and Spanish).

*UNICEF at a Glance* (in English, French and Spanish).

*Young People in Changing Societies* (annually).

Reports and studies; series on children and women; nutrition; education; children's rights; children in wars and disasters; working children; water, sanitation and the environment; analyses of the situation of children and women in individual developing countries.

# United Nations Development Programme—UNDP

**Address:** One United Nations Plaza, New York, NY 10017, USA.

**Telephone:** (212) 906-5295; **fax:** (212) 906-5364; **e-mail:** hq@undp.org; **internet:** www.undp.org.

The Programme was established in 1965 by the UN General Assembly. Its central mission is to help countries to eradicate poverty and achieve a sustainable level of human development, an approach to economic growth that encompasses individual well-being and choice, equitable distribution of the benefits of development, and conservation of the environment. UNDP advocates for a more inclusive global economy. UNDP is the focus of UN efforts to achieve the Millennium Development Goals.

## Organization

(August 2008)

UNDP is responsible to the UN General Assembly, to which it reports through ECOSOC.

### EXECUTIVE BOARD

The Executive Board is responsible for providing intergovernmental support to, and supervision of, the activities of UNDP and the UN Population Fund (UNFPA). It comprises 36 members: eight from Africa, seven from Asia and the Pacific, four from eastern Europe, five from Latin America and the Caribbean and 12 from western Europe and other countries. Members serve a three-year term.

### SECRETARIAT

Offices and divisions at the Secretariat include: an Operations Support Group; Offices of the United Nations Development Group, the Human Development Report, Development Studies, Audit and Performance Review, Evaluation, and Communications; and Bureaux for Crisis Prevention and Recovery, Resources and Strategic Partnerships, Development Policy, and Management. Five regional bureaux, all headed by an assistant administrator, cover: Africa; Asia and the Pacific; the Arab states; Latin America and the Caribbean; and Europe and the Commonwealth of Independent States.

**Administrator:** Kemal Derviş (Turkey).

**Associate Administrator:** Ad Melkert (Netherlands).

**Assistant Administrator and Director, Regional Bureau for Asia and the Pacific:** David Lockwood (acting).

### COUNTRY OFFICES

In almost every country receiving UNDP assistance there is an office, headed by the UNDP Resident Representative, who usually also serves as UN Resident Co-ordinator, responsible for the co-ordination of all UN technical assistance and operational development activities, advising the Government on formulating the country programme, ensuring that field activities are undertaken, and acting as the leader of the UN team of experts working in the country. The offices function as the primary presence of the UN in most developing countries.

### OFFICES OF UN RESIDENT CO-ORDINATORS IN SOUTH ASIA

**Afghanistan:** Shah Mehmood Ghazi Watt, Kabul; tel. (20) 2101682; e-mail registry.af@undp.org; internet www.undp.org.af; Resident Co-ordinator Bo Asplund.

**Bangladesh:** POB 224, Dhaka 1000; tel. (2) 8118600; fax (2) 8113196; e-mail registry.bd@undp; internet www.undp.org.bd; Resident Co-ordinator Renata Lok Dessallien.

**Bhutan:** UN House, GPO Box 162, Dremton Lam, Thimphu; tel. (2) 322424; fax (2) 322657; e-mail fo.btn@undp.org; internet www.undp.org.bt; Resident Co-ordinator Nicholas Rosellini.

**India:** POB 3059, 55 Lodhi Estate, New Delhi 110003; tel. (11) 46532333; fax (11) 24627612; e-mail webadmin.in@undp.org; internet www.undp.org.in; Resident Co-ordinator Maxine Olson.

**Maldives:** POB 2058, UN Bldg, Buruzu Magu, Radhdebai Higun, Malé; tel. 3324501; fax 3324504; e-mail registry.mv@undp.org; internet www.mv.undp.org; Resident Co-ordinator Patrice Coeur-Bizot.

**Nepal:** UN House, POB 107, Pulchowk, Kathmandu; tel. (1) 5523200; fax (1) 5523991; e-mail registry.np@undp.org; internet www.undp.org.np; Resident Co-ordinator Robert Piper.

**Pakistan:** House 12, St 17, F 7/2, Islamabad; tel. (51) 825-5600; fax (51) 265-5014; e-mail webmaster@undp.un.org.pk; internet www.undp.org.pk; Resident Co-ordinator Fikret Akcura.

**Sri Lanka:** POB 1505, 204 Bauddhaloka Mawatha, Colombo 7; tel. (11) 2580691; fax (11) 2581116; e-mail registry.lk@undp.org; internet www.undp.lk; Resident Co-ordinator Neil Buhne.

## Activities

UNDP provides advisory and support services to governments and UN teams with the aim of advancing sustainable human development and building national development capabilities. Assistance is mostly non-monetary, comprising the provision of experts' services, consultancies, equipment and training for local workers. Developing countries themselves contribute significantly to the total project costs in terms of personnel, facilities, equipment and supplies. UNDP also supports programme countries in attracting aid and utilizing it efficiently. A network of nine Sub-regional Resource Facilities (SURFs) has been established to strengthen and co-ordinate UNDP's role as a global knowledge provider and channel for sharing knowledge and experience.

During the late 1990s UNDP undertook an extensive internal process of reform, 'UNDP 2001', which placed increased emphasis on its activities in the field and on performance and accountability. In 2001 UNDP established a series of Thematic Trust Funds to enable increased support of priority programme activities. In accordance with the more results-oriented approach developed under the 'UNDP 2001' process UNDP introduced a new Multi-Year Funding Framework (MYFF), which outlined the country-driven goals around which funding was to be mobilized, integrating programme objectives, resources, budget and outcomes. The MYFF was to provide the basis for the Administrator's Business Plans for the same duration and enables policy coherence in the implementation of programmes at country, regional and global levels. A Results-Oriented Annual Report (ROAR) was produced for the first time in 2000 from data compiled by country offices and regional programmes. In September 2000 the first ever Ministerial Meeting of ministers of development co-operation and foreign affairs and other senior officials from donor and programme countries, convened in New York, USA, endorsed UNDP's shift to a results-based orientation.

In accordance with the second phase of the MYFF, covering 2004–07, UNDP focused on the following five practice areas: democratic governance; poverty reduction; energy and the environment; crisis prevention and recovery; and combating HIV/AIDS. Other important 'cross-cutting' themes, to be incorporated throughout the programme areas, included gender equality and the empowerment of women, information and communication technologies, and human rights. UNDP's Strategic Plan for the period 2008–11 emphasized UNDP's 'overarching' contribution to achieving sustainable human development through capacity development strategies, to be integrated into all areas of activity. Other objectives identified by the Plan included strengthening national ownership of development projects and promoting and facilitating South-South co-operation.

From the mid-1990s UNDP assumed a more active and integrative role within the UN system-wide development framework. UNDP Resident Representatives—usually also serving as UN Resident Co-ordinators, with responsibility for managing inter-agency co-operation on sustainable human development initiatives at country level—were to play a focal role in implementing this approach. In order to promote its co-ordinating function UNDP allocated increased resources to training and skill-sharing programmes. In 1997 the UNDP Administrator was appointed to chair the UN Development Group (UNDG), which was established as part of a series of structural reform measures initiated by the UN Secretary-General, with the aim of strengthening collaboration between all UN funds, programmes and bodies concerned with development. The UNDG promotes coherent policy at country level through the system of UN Resident Co-ordinators (see above), the Common Country Assessment mechanism (CCA, a country-based process for evaluating national development situations), and the UN Development Assistance Framework (UNDAF, the foundation for planning and co-ordinating development operations at country level, based on the CCA). Within the framework of the Administrator's Business Plans for 2000–03 a new Bureau for Resources and Strategic Partnerships was established to build and strengthen working partnerships with other UN bodies, donor and programme countries, international financial institutions and development banks, civil society organizations and the private sector. The Bureau was also to serve UNDP's regional bureaux and country offices through the exchange of information and promotion of partnership strategies.

## MILLENNIUM DEVELOPMENT GOALS

UNDP, through its leadership of the UNDG and management of the Resident Co-ordinator system, has a co-ordinating function as the focus of UN system-wide efforts to achieve the so-called Millennium Development Goals (MDGs), pledged by 189 governments attending a summit meeting of the UN General Assembly in September 2000. The objectives were to establish a defined agenda to reduce poverty and improve the quality of lives of millions of people and to serve as a framework for measuring development. There are eight MDGs, as follows, for which one or more specific targets have been identified:

i) to eradicate extreme poverty and hunger, with the aim of reducing by 50% the number of people with an income of less than US $1 a day and those suffering from hunger by 2015, and to achieve full and productive employment and decent work for all, including women and young people;

ii) to achieve universal primary education by 2015;

iii) to promote gender equality and empower women, in particular to eliminate gender disparities in primary and secondary education by 2005 and at all levels by 2015;

iv) to reduce child mortality, with a target reduction of two-thirds in the mortality rate among children under five by 2015;

v) to improve maternal health, specifically to reduce by 75% the numbers of women dying in childbirth and to achieve universal access to reproductive health by 2015;

vi) to combat HIV/AIDS, malaria and other diseases, with targets to have halted and begun to reverse the incidence of HIV/AIDS, malaria and other major diseases by 2015 and to achieve universal access to treatment for HIV/AIDS for all those who need it by 2010;

vii) to ensure environmental sustainability, including targets to integrate the principles of sustainable development into country policies and programmes, to reduce by 50% the number of people without access to safe drinking water by 2015, to achieve significant improvement in the lives of at least 100m. slum dwellers by 2020;

viii) to develop a global partnership for development, including efforts to deal with international debt, to address the needs of least developed countries and landlocked and small island developing states, to develop decent and productive youth employment, to provide access to affordable, essential drugs in developing countries, and to make available the benefits of new technologies.

UNDP plays a leading role in efforts to integrate the MDGs into all aspects of UN activities at country level and to ensure the MDGs are incorporated into national development strategies. The Programme supports efforts by countries, as well as regions and sub-regions, to report on progress towards achievement of the goals, and on specific social, economic and environmental indicators, through the formulation of MDG reports. These form the basis of a global report, issued annually by the UN Secretary-General since mid-2002. UNDP also works to raise awareness of the MDGs and to support advocacy efforts at all levels, for example through regional publicity campaigns, target-specific publications and support for the Millennium Campaign to generate support for the goals in developing and developed countries. UNDP provides administrative and technical support to the Millennium Project, an independent advisory body established by the UN Secretary-General in 2002 to develop a practical action plan to achieve the MDGs. Financial support of the Project is channelled through a Millennium Trust Fund, administered by UNDP. In January 2005 the Millennium Project presented its report, based on extensive research conducted by teams of experts, which included recommendations for the international system to support country level development efforts and identified a series of Quick Wins to bring conclusive benefit to millions of people in the short-term. International commitment to achieve the MDGs by 2015 was reiterated at a World Summit, convened in September. In November 2007 the UN, in partnership with two major US companies, launched an online MDG Monitor to track progress and to support organizations working to achieve the goals.

UNDP, ESCAP and the Asian Development Bank established a regional partnership in 2001 to promote the MDGs. In June 2005 the partnership published a joint regional report on the implementation of the goals. A regional road map developed by the partnership with the aim of addressing regional challenges to the achievement of the MDGs was endorsed by regional governments in May 2007. In October 2006 UNDP, ESCAP and the Asian Development Bank sponsored a South Asia Millennium Development Goal Forum, convened in Kathmandu, Nepal, with the aim of developing a specialized sub-regional road map for promoting the MDGs.

## DEMOCRATIC GOVERNANCE

UNDP supports national efforts to ensure efficient and accountable governance, to improve the quality of democratic processes, and to build effective relations between the state, the private sector and civil society, which are essential to achieving sustainable development. As in other practice areas, UNDP assistance includes policy advice and technical support, capacity-building of institutions and individuals, advocacy and public information and communication, the promotion and brokering of dialogue, and knowledge networking and sharing of good practices.

UNDP works to strengthen parliaments and other legislative bodies as institutions of democratic participation. It assists with constitutional reviews and reform, training of parliamentary staff, and capacity-building of political parties and civil organizations as part of this objective. UNDP undertakes missions to help prepare for and ensure the conduct of free and fair elections. Increasingly, UNDP is also focused on building the long-term capacity of electoral institutions and practices within a country, for example voter registration, election observation, the establishment of electoral commissions, and voter and civic education projects.

Within its justice sector programme UNDP undertakes a variety of projects to improve access to justice, in particular for the poor and disadvantaged, and to promote judicial independence, legal reform and understanding of the legal system. UNDP also works to promote access to information, the integration of human rights issues into activities concerned with sustainable human development, as well as support for the international human rights system.

Since 1997 UNDP has been mandated to assist developing countries to fight corruption and improve accountability, transparency and integrity (ATI). It has worked to establish national and international partnerships in support of its anti-corruption efforts and used its role as a broker of knowledge and experience to uphold ATI principles at all levels of public financial management and governance. UNDP publishes case studies of its anti-corruption efforts and assists governments to conduct self-assessments of their public financial management systems.

In March 2002 a UNDP Governance Centre was inaugurated in Oslo, Norway, to enhance the role of UNDP in support of democratic governance and to assist countries to implement democratic reforms in order to achieve the MDGs. The mandate for the work of the Centre during the period 2005–09 incorporated activities in the following areas: governance and poverty eradication; governance and conflict prevention; civil society, empowerment and governance; and learning and capacity development.

In July 2000 a sub-regional conference on urbanization and good governance was held at the SAARC secretariat, in Kathmandu, Nepal, jointly organized by the Nepalese Government and UNDP. The meeting adopted the Kathmandu Declaration, which incorporated a strategic vision on governance in South Asia. In 2008 UNDP was working with the Election Commission in Bangladesh in order to formulate a new voter registration list prior to national elections that were scheduled to be held later in that year. In March UNDP assisted in the conduct of the first multi-party democratic elections to be held in Bhutan.

Within the democratic governance practice area UNDP supports more than 300 projects at international, country and city levels designed to improve conditions for the urban poor, in particular through improvement in urban governance. The Local Initiative Facility for Urban Environment (LIFE) undertakes small-scale projects in low-income communities, in collaboration with local authorities, the private sector and community-based groups, and promotes a participatory approach to local governance. UNDP also works closely with the UN Capital Development Fund to implement projects in support of decentralized governance, which it has recognized as a key element to achieving sustainable development goals.

UNDP aims to ensure that, rather than creating an ever-widening ‘digital divide’, ongoing rapid advancements in information technology are harnessed by poorer countries to accelerate progress in achieving sustainable human development. UNDP advises governments on technology policy, promotes digital entrepreneurship in programme countries and works with private-sector partners to provide reliable and affordable communications networks. The Bureau for Development Policy operates the Information and Communication Technologies for Development Programme, which aims to promote sustainable human development through increased utilization of information and communications technologies globally. The Programme aims to establish technology access centres in developing countries. A Sustainable Development Networking Programme focuses on expanding internet connectivity in poorer countries through building national capacities and supporting local internet sites. UNDP has used mobile internet units to train people even in isolated rural areas. In 1999 UNDP, in collaboration with an international communications company, Cisco Systems, and other partners, launched NetAid, an internet-based forum (accessible at www.netaid.org) for mobilizing and co-ordinating fundraising and other activities aimed at alleviating poverty and promoting sustainable human development in the developing world. With Cisco Systems and other partners, UNDP has worked to establish academies of information technology to support training and capacity-building in developing countries. UNDP and the World Bank jointly host the secretariat of the Digital Opportunity Task Force, a partnership between industrialized and developing countries, business and non-governmental organizations that was established in 2000. UNDP is a partner in the Global Digital Technology Initiative, launched in 2002 to strengthen the role of information and communications technologies in achieving the development goals of developing countries. In January 2004 UNDP and Microsoft Corporation announced an agreement to develop jointly information and communication technology (ICT) projects aimed at assisting developing countries to achieve the MDGs.

## POVERTY REDUCTION

UNDP’s activities to facilitate poverty eradication include support for capacity-building programmes and initiatives to generate sustainable livelihoods, for example by improving access to credit, land and technologies, and the promotion of strategies to improve education and health provision for the poorest elements of populations (with a focus on women and girls). UNDP aims to help governments to reassess their development priorities and to design initiatives for sustainable human development. In 1996, following the World Summit for Social Development, which was held in Copenhagen, Denmark, in March 1995, UNDP launched the Poverty Strategies Initiative (PSI) to strengthen national capacities to assess and monitor the extent of poverty and to combat the problem. All PSI projects were to involve representatives of governments, the private sector, social organizations and research institutions in policy debate and formulation. Following the introduction, in 1999, by the World Bank and IMF of Poverty Reduction Strategy Papers (PRSPs), UNDP has tended to direct its efforts to helping governments draft these documents, and, since 2001, has focused on linking the papers to efforts to achieve and monitor progress towards the MDGs. In early 2004 UNDP inaugurated the International Poverty Centre, in Brasília, Brazil, which aimed to foster the capacity of countries to formulate and implement poverty reduction strategies and to encourage South-South co-operation in all relevant areas of research and decision-making. In particular, the Centre aimed to assist countries to meet Millennium goals and targets through the research and implementation of pro-poor growth policies and social protection and human development strategies, and the monitoring of poverty and inequality.

UNDP country offices support the formulation of national human development reports (NHDRs), which aim to facilitate activities such as policy-making, the allocation of resources and monitoring progress towards poverty eradication and sustainable development. In addition, the preparation of Advisory Notes and Country Co-operation Frameworks by UNDP officials helps to highlight country-specific aspects of poverty eradication and national strategic priorities. In January 1998 the Executive Board adopted eight guiding principles relating to sustainable human development that were to be implemented by all country offices, in order to ensure a focus to UNDP activities. Since 1990 UNDP has published an annual *Human Development Report*, incorporating a Human Development Index, which ranks countries in terms of human development, using three key indicators: life expectancy, adult literacy and basic income required for a decent standard of living. In 1997 a Human Poverty Index and a Gender-related Development Index, which assesses gender equality on the basis of life expectancy, education and income, were introduced into the Report for the first time. Also in 1997 a UNDP scheme to support private-sector and community-based initiatives to generate employment opportunities, MicroStart, became operational.

UNDP is committed to ensuring that the process of economic and financial globalization, including national and global trade, debt and capital flow policies, incorporates human development concerns. It was actively concerned to ensure that the Doha Development Round of World Trade Organization (WTO) negotiations achieve an expansion of trade opportunities and economic growth to less developed countries. With the UN Conference on Trade and Development (UNCTAD), UNDP manages a Global Programme on Globalization, Liberalization and Sustainable Human Development, which aims to support greater integration of developing countries into the global economy. UNDP manages a Trust Fund for the Integrated Framework for trade-related technical assistance to least-developed countries, which was inaugurated in 1997 by UNDP, the IMF, the International Trade Centre, UNCTAD, the World Bank and the WTO, and is the lead agency for its capacity development component.

UNDP’s Asia Pacific Trade and Investment Initiative, based in Colombo, Sri Lanka, produces technical support documents on different aspects of trade and investment to assist regional governments in forming their policies.

In September 2007 UNDP issued an *Afghanistan Human Development Report*.

In 1996 UNDP initiated a process of collaboration between city authorities world-wide to promote implementation of the commitments made at the 1995 Copenhagen summit for social development and to help to combat aspects of poverty and other urban problems, such as poor housing, transport, the management of waste disposal, water supply and sanitation. The so-called World Alliance of Cities Against Poverty was formally launched in October 1997, in the context of the International Decade for the Eradication of Poverty. The first Forum of the Alliance was convened in October 1998, in Lyon, France; it has subsequently been held every two years.

UNDP sponsors the International Day for the Eradication of Poverty, held annually on 17 October.

## ENVIRONMENT AND ENERGY

UNDP plays a role in developing the agenda for international co-operation on environmental and energy issues, focusing on the relationship between energy policies, environmental protection, poverty and development. UNDP promotes the development of national capacities and other strategies that support sustainable development practices, for example through the formulation and implementation of Poverty Reduction Strategies and National Strategies for Sustainable Development.

UNDP recognizes that desertification and land degradation is a major cause of rural poverty and promotes sustainable land management, drought preparedness and reform of land tenure as means of addressing the problem. It also aims to reduce poverty caused by land degradation through implementation of environmental conventions at a national and international level. In 2002 UNDP inaugurated an Integrated Drylands Development Programme which aimed to ensure that the needs of people living in drylands are met and considered at a local and national level. The Drylands Development Centre implements the programme in 19 African, Arab and West Asian countries. UNDP is also concerned with sustainable management of forestries, fisheries and agriculture. Its Biodiversity Global Programme assists developing countries and communities to integrate issues relating to sustainable practices and biodiversity into national and global practices. Since 1992 UNDP has administered a Small Grants Programme, funded by the Global Environment Facility (GEF), to support community-based initiatives concerned with biodiversity conservation, prevention of land degradation and the elimination of persistent organic pollutants. The Equator Initiative was inaugurated in 2002 as a partnership between UNDP, representatives of governments, civil society and businesses, with the aim of reducing poverty in communities along the equatorial belt by fostering local partnerships, harnessing local knowledge and promoting conservation and sustainable practices.

UNDP promotes clean energy technologies (through the Clean Development Mechanism) and aims to extend access to sustainable energy services, including the introduction of renewable alternatives to conventional fuels, as well as access to investment financing for sustainable energy. In December 2005 UNDP launched an MDG Carbon Facility, which aimed to channel increased carbon financing to projects that contribute directly to achieving MDGs in developing countries. The first projects under the MDG Carbon Facility were inaugurated in February 2008, in Uzbekistan, the former Yugoslav republic of Macedonia, Yemen and Rwanda. UNDP supports other efforts to promote international co-operation in the management of chemicals. It was actively involved in the development of a Strategic Approach to International Chemicals Management which was adopted by representatives of 100 governments at an international conference convened in Dubai, UAE, in February 2006.

UNDP works to ensure the effective governance of freshwater and aquatic resources, and promotes co-operation in transboundary water management. It works closely with other agencies to promote safe sanitation, ocean and coastal management, and community water supplies. In 1996 UNDP, with the World Bank and the Swedish International Development Agency, established a Global Water Partnership to promote and implement water resources management. UNDP, with the GEF, supports an extensive range of projects which incorporate development and ecological requirements in the sustainable management of international waters. These include the Global Mercury Project, The Yellow Sea Large Marine Ecosystem project, the Dnipro Basin Environment Programme, and projects in the Gulf of Guinea, Lake Tanganyika, and the Red Sea and Gulf of Aden.

### CRISIS PREVENTION AND RECOVERY

UNDP collaborates with other UN agencies in countries in crisis and with special circumstances to promote relief and development efforts, in order to secure the foundations for sustainable human development and thereby increase national capabilities to prevent or mitigate future crises. In particular, UNDP is concerned to achieve reconciliation, reintegration and reconstruction in affected countries, as well as to support emergency interventions and management and delivery of programme aid. It aims to facilitate the transition from relief to longer-term recovery and rehabilitation. Special development initiatives in post-conflict countries include the demobilization of former combatants and destruction of illicit small armaments, rehabilitation of communities for the sustainable reintegration of returning populations and the restoration and strengthening of democratic institutions. UNDP is seeking to incorporate conflict prevention into its development strategies. UNDP has established a mine action unit within its Bureau for Crisis Prevention and Recovery in order to strengthen national and local demining capabilities including surveying, mapping and clearance of anti-personnel landmines. UNDP also works closely with UNICEF to raise mine awareness and implement risk reduction education programmes, and manages global partnership projects concerned with training, legislation and the socio-economic impact of anti-personnel devices.

UNDP is the focal point within the UN system for strengthening national capacities for natural disaster reduction (prevention, preparedness and mitigation relating to natural, environmental and technological hazards). UNDP's Bureau of Crisis Prevention and Recovery, in conjunction with the Office for the Co-ordination of Humanitarian Affairs and the secretariat of the International Strategy for Disaster Reduction, oversees the system-wide Capacity for Disaster Reduction Initiative (CADRI), which was inaugurated in 2007, superseding the former United Nations Disaster Management Training Programme. In February 2004 UNDP introduced a Disaster Risk Index that enabled vulnerability and risk to be measured and compared between countries and demonstrated the correspondence between human development and death rates following natural disasters. UNDP was actively involved in preparations for the second World Conference on Disaster Reduction, which was held in Kobe, Japan, in January 2005. Following the Kobe Conference UNDP initiated a new Global Risk Identification Programme. During 2005 the Inter-Agency Standing Committee, concerned with co-ordinating the international response to humanitarian disasters, developed a concept of providing assistance through a 'cluster' approach, comprising core areas of activity. UNDP was designated the lead agency for the Early Reconstruction and Recovery cluster, linking the immediate needs following a disaster with medium- and long-term recovery efforts.

In January 2002 UNDP, the World Bank and the Asian Development Bank announced the results of a jointly-prepared preliminary 'needs assessment' report for reconstruction efforts in Afghanistan: it was estimated that US $15,000m. in donor financing would be required over 10 years. In 2003 UNDP implemented a Recovery and Employment Afghanistan Programme (REAP), assisting the Afghan Transitional Authority with the development of a database to track aid donations and supporting civil service reforms. During 2002–06 UNDP mobilized more than $1,300m. in donor financing for Afghanistan. In November 2005, in response to the devastating Indian Ocean tsunami of December 2004, UNDP launched a Regional Programme on Capacity-building for Sustainable Recovery and Risk Reduction. The Programme aims, in co-operation with UNDP country offices and disaster management agencies in India, Indonesia, the Maldives, Sri Lanka and Thailand, to provide technical assistance to tsunami-affected countries and to support the development of early warning systems. UNDP has also undertaken projects to rehabilitate livelihoods in affected areas. In 2007 UNDP provided technical support to the newly-established National Disaster Management Authority in Pakistan. In November UNDP led the early recovery cluster co-ordination group, established following a tropical cyclone in Bangladesh, which undertook an immediate needs assessment and environmental rapid assessment.

### HIV/AIDS

UNDP regards the HIV/AIDS pandemic as a major challenge to development, and advocates for making HIV/AIDS a focus of national planning and national poverty reduction strategies; supports decentralized action against HIV/AIDS at community level; helps to strengthen national capacities at all levels to combat the disease; and aims to link support for prevention activities, education and treatment with broader development planning and responses. UNDP places a particular focus on combating the spread of HIV/AIDS through the promotion of women's rights. UNDP is a co-sponsor, jointly with WHO, the World Bank, UNICEF, UNESCO, UNODC, ILO, UNFPA, WFP and UNHCR, of the Joint UN Programme on HIV/AIDS (UNAIDS), which became operational on 1 January 1996. UNAIDS co-ordinates UNDP's HIV and Development Programme. Since 2003 UNDP has worked in partnership with the Global Fund to Fight HIV/AIDS, TB and Malaria, in particular to support the local principal recipient of grant financing and to help to manage fund projects.

UNDP administers a global programme concerned with intellectual property and access to HIV/AIDS drugs, to promote wider and cheaper access to antiretroviral drugs. In December 2005 the World Trade Organization agreed to amend the agreement on Trade-Related Aspects of Intellectual Property Rights (TRIPS) to allow countries without a pharmaceutical manufacturing capability to import generic copies of patented medicines.

UNDP's Regional HIV and Development Programme for South and North East Asia, the second phase of which was entitled REACH beyond Borders, promotes an integrated approach to containing the spread and impact of HIV/AIDS in the region. It aims to build partnerships and enhanced co-operation between governments and organizations at national and regional levels, and highlights specific issues, for example the vulnerability of mobile populations and reducing discrimination of people affected by HIV/AIDS.

## Finance

UNDP and its various funds and programmes are financed by the voluntary contributions of members of the United Nations and the Programme's participating agencies, as well as through cost-sharing by recipient governments and third-party donors. In 2008–11 total voluntary contributions were projected at US $20,600m., of which $5,300m. constituted regular (core) resources, $5,000m. bilateral donor contributions, $5,500m. contributions from multilateral partners and $4,800m. cost-sharing by programme country governments.

## Publications

*Annual Report of the Administrator*.
*Choices* (quarterly).
*Human Development Report* (annually).
*Poverty Report* (annually).
*Results-Oriented Annual Report*.

## Associated Funds and Programmes

UNDP is the central funding, planning and co-ordinating body for technical co-operation within the UN system. A number of associated funds and programmes, financed separately by means of voluntary contributions, provide specific services through the UNDP network. UNDP manages a trust fund to promote economic and technical co-operation among developing countries.

### CAPACITY 2015

UNDP initiated Capacity 2015, as a successor to its Capacity 21 scheme, at the World Summit for Sustainable Development, which was held in August–September 2002. Capacity 2015 aims to support developing countries in expanding their capabilities to meet the Millennium Development Goals. An information and learning network was to be established to promote and facilitate the participation of civil society and local communities in the sustainable development process.

### GLOBAL ENVIRONMENT FACILITY (GEF)

The GEF, which is managed jointly by UNDP, the World Bank (which hosts its secretariat) and UNEP, began operations in 1991 and was restructured in 1994. Its aim is to support projects concerning climate change, the conservation of biological diversity, the protection of international waters, reducing the depletion of the ozone layer in the atmosphere, and (since October 2002) arresting land degradation and addressing the issue of persistent organic pollutants. The GEF acts as the financial mechanism for the Convention on Biological Diversity and the UN Framework Convention on Climate Change. UNDP is responsible for capacity-building, targeted research, pre-investment activities and technical assistance. UNDP also administers the Small Grants Programme of the GEF, which supports community-based activities by local non-governmental organizations, and the Country Dialogue Workshop Programme, which promotes dialogue on national priorities with regard to the GEF. In August 2006 some 32 donor countries pledged US $3,130m. for the fourth periodic replenishment of GEF funds (GEF-4), covering the period 2007–10. At February 2008 UNDP GEF-funded projects amounted to $7,470m. for 560 initiatives. An additional $479.7m. had been committed under the Small Grants Programme.

**Chair. and CEO:** MONIQUE BARBUT (France).

**Executive Co-ordinator UNDP-GEF Unit:** YANNICK GLEMAREC; 304 East 45th St, 9th Floor, New York, NY 10017, USA; fax (212) 906-6998; e-mail gefinfo@undp.org.

### MONTREAL PROTOCOL

Through its Montreal Protocol Unit UNDP collaborates with public and private partners in developing countries to assist them in eliminating the use of ozone-depleting substances (ODS), in accordance with the Montreal Protocol to the Vienna Convention for the Protection of the Ozone Layer, through the design, monitoring and evaluation of ODS phase-out projects and programmes. In particular, UNDP provides technical assistance and training, national capacity-building and demonstration projects and technology transfer investment projects. By December 2006 the Executive Committee of the Montreal Protocol had approved grants for projects and activities that had resulted in the elimination of an estimated 158,737 metric tons of ODS production.

### UNDP DRYLANDS DEVELOPMENT CENTRE (DDC)

The Centre, based in Nairobi, Kenya, was established in February 2002, superseding the former UN Office to Combat Desertification and Drought (UNSO). (UNSO had been established following the conclusion, in October 1994, of the UN Convention to Combat Desertification in Those Countries Experiencing Serious Drought and/or Desertification, Particularly in Africa; in turn, UNSO had replaced the former UN Sudano-Sahelian Office.) The DDC was to focus on the following areas: ensuring that national development planning takes account of the needs of dryland communities, particularly in poverty reduction strategies; helping countries to cope with the effects of climate variability, especially drought, and to prepare for future climate change; and addressing local issues affecting the utilization of resources.

**Director:** PHILIP DOBIE (United Kingdom); POB 30552, 00100 Nairobi, Kenya; tel. (20) 7624640; fax (20) 7624648; e-mail ddc@undp.org; internet www.undp.org/drylands.

### UNITED NATIONS CAPITAL DEVELOPMENT FUND (UNCDF)

The Fund was established in 1966 and became fully operational in 1974. It invests in poor communities in least-developed countries through local governance projects and microfinance operations, with the aim of increasing such communities' access to essential local infrastructure and services and thereby improving their productive capacities and self-reliance. UNCDF encourages participation by local people and local governments in the planning, implementation and monitoring of projects. The Fund aims to promote the interests of women in community projects and to enhance their earning capacities. A Special Unit for Microfinance (SUM), established in 1997 as a joint UNDP/UNCDF operation, was fully integrated into UNCDF in 1999. UNCDF/SUM helps to develop financial services for poor communities and supports UNDP's MicroStart initiative. UNCDF was a co-sponsor of the International Year of Microcredit in 2005 and hosts the UN high-level Advisors Group on Inclusive Financial Sectors. At mid-2008 UNCDF was supporting programmes and funds in 39 countries. Programme expenditure in 2007 amounted to US $28.7m., of which $20.3m. was allocated to Africa.

**Executive Secretary a.i.:** HENRIETTE KEIJZERS (Netherlands); Two United Nations Plaza, 26th Floor, New York, NY 10017, USA; fax (212) 906-6479; e-mail info@uncdf.org; internet www.uncdf.org.

### UNITED NATIONS DEVELOPMENT FUND FOR WOMEN (UNIFEM)

UNIFEM is the UN's lead agency in addressing the issues relating to women in development and promoting the rights of women worldwide. The Fund provides direct financial and technical support to enable low-income women in developing countries to increase earnings, gain access to labour-saving technologies and otherwise improve the quality of their lives. It also funds activities that include women in decision-making related to mainstream development projects. UNIFEM has supported the preparation of national reports in 30 countries and used the priorities identified in these reports and in other regional initiatives to formulate a Women's Development Agenda for the 21st century. Through these efforts, UNIFEM played an active role in the preparation for the UN Fourth World Conference on Women, which was held in Beijing, People's Republic of China, in September 1995. UNIFEM participated at a special session of the General Assembly convened in June 2000 to review the conference, entitled Women 2000: Gender Equality, Development and Peace for the 21st Century (Beijing + 5). In March 2001 UNIFEM, in collaboration with International Alert, launched a Millennium Peace Prize for Women. UNIFEM maintains that the empowerment of women is a key to combating the HIV/AIDS pandemic, in view of the fact that women and adolescent girls are often culturally, biologically and economically more vulnerable to infection and more likely to bear responsibility for caring for the sick. In March 2002 UNIFEM launched a three-year programme aimed at making the gender and human rights dimensions of the pandemic central to policy-making in 10 countries. A new online resource (www.genderandaid s.org) on the gender dimensions of HIV/AIDS was launched in February 2003. Following the massive earthquake and tsunami that struck parts of the Indian Ocean in late December 2004, UNIFEM undertook to promote the needs and rights of women and girls in all emergency relief and reconstruction efforts, in particular in Indonesia, Sri Lanka and Somalia, and supported capacity-building of grass-roots organizations. UNIFEM was a co-founder of WomenWatch (accessible online at www.un.org/womenwatch), a UN system-wide resource for the advancement of gender equality. UNIFEM manages the UN's Trust Fund in Support of Actions to Eliminate Violence Against Women (established in 1996), which by early 2008 had awarded grants in excess of US $19.0m. in support of more than 263 initiatives in around 115 countries. In November 2007 UNIFEM launched a year-long campaign, 'Say NO to Violence against Women', to raise awareness of the issue and generate world-wide support for efforts to end violence against women. Programme expenditure in 2006 totalled $57.0m.

**Director:** INÉS ALBERDI (Spain); 304 East 45th St, 15th Floor, New York, NY 10017, USA; tel. (212) 906-6400; fax (212) 906-6705; e-mail unifem@undp.org; internet www.unifem.org.

### UNITED NATIONS VOLUNTEERS (UNV)

The United Nations Volunteers is an important source of middle-level skills for the UN development system supplied at modest cost, particularly in the least-developed countries. Volunteers expand the scope of UNDP project activities by supplementing the work of international and host-country experts and by extending the influence of projects to local community levels. UNV also supports technical co-operation within and among the developing countries by encouraging volunteers from the countries themselves and by forming regional exchange teams comprising such volunteers. UNV is involved in areas such as peace-building, elections, human rights, humanitarian relief and community-based environmental programmes, in addition to development activities.

The UN International Short-term Advisory (UNISTAR) Programme, which is the private sector development arm of UNV, has increasingly focused its attention on countries in the process of economic transition. Since 1994 UNV has administered UNDP's Transfer of Knowledge Through Expatriate Nationals (TOKTEN) programme, which was initiated in 1977 to enable specialists and professionals from developing countries to contribute to development efforts in their countries of origin through short-term technical assignments. In March 2000 UNV established an Online Volunteering Service to connect development organizations and volunteers using the internet. As at November 2006 some 9,000 volunteers from 169 countries had been engaged in online collaborations.

At the end of April 2008 5,647 UNVs were serving in 123 countries. At that time the total number of people who had served under the initiative amounted to more than 35,000 in over 140 countries.

**Executive Co-ordinator:** FLAVIA PANSIERI (Italy); POB 260111, 53153 Bonn, Germany; tel. (228) 8152000; fax (228) 8152001; e-mail information@unvolunteers.org; internet www.unv.org.

# United Nations Environment Programme—UNEP

**Address:** POB 30552, Nairobi 00100, Kenya.

**Telephone:** (20) 621234; **fax:** (20) 623927; **e-mail:** info@unep.org; **internet:** www.unep.org.

The United Nations Environment Programme was established in 1972 by the UN General Assembly, following recommendations of the 1972 UN Conference on the Human Environment, in Stockholm, Sweden, to encourage international co-operation in matters relating to the human environment.

## Organization

(August 2008)

### GOVERNING COUNCIL

The main functions of the Governing Council (which meets every two years in ordinary sessions, with special sessions taking place in the alternate years) are to promote international co-operation in the field of the environment and to provide general policy guidance for the direction and co-ordination of environmental programmes within the UN system. It comprises representatives of 58 states, elected by the UN General Assembly, for four-year terms, on a regional basis. The Global Ministerial Environment Forum (first convened in 2000) meets annually as part of the Governing Council's regular and special sessions. The Governing Council is assisted in its work by a Committee of Permanent Representatives.

### SECRETARIAT

Offices and divisions at UNEP headquarters include the Offices of the Executive Director and Deputy Executive Director; the Secretariat for Governing Bodies; Offices for Evaluation and Oversight, Programme Co-ordination and Management, and Resource Mobilization; and divisions of communications and public information, early warning and assessment, policy development and law, policy implementation, technology and industry and economics, regional co-operation and representation, environmental conventions, and Global Environment Facility co-ordination.

**Executive Director:** ACHIM STEINER (Germany).

### REGIONAL OFFICES

**Asia and the Pacific:** United Nations Bldg, 2nd Floor, Rajadamnern Nok Ave, Bangkok 10200, Thailand; tel. (2) 288-1234; fax (2) 280-3829; e-mail uneproap@un.org; internet www.roap.unep.org.

### OTHER OFFICES

**Convention on International Trade in Endangered Species of Wild Fauna and Flora (CITES):** 15 chemin des Anémones, 1219 Châtelaine, Geneva, Switzerland; tel. 229178139; fax 227973417; e-mail info@cites.org; internet www.cites.org; Sec.-Gen. WILLEM WOUTER WIJNSTEKERS (Netherlands).

**Global Programme of Action for the Protection of the Marine Environment from Land-based Activities:** POB 16227, 2500 BE The Hague, Netherlands; tel. (70) 3114460; fax (70) 3456648; e-mail gpa@unep.nl; internet www.gpa.unep.org; Officer-in-Charge ANJAN DATTA (Bangladesh).

**Secretariat of the Basel Convention:** CP 356, 13–15 chemin des Anémones, 1219 Châtelaine, Geneva, Switzerland; tel. 229178218; fax 227973454; e-mail sbc@unep.ch; internet www.basel.int; Exec. Sec. KATHERINA KUMMER PEIRY.

**Secretariat of the Multilateral Fund for the Implementation of the Montreal Protocol:** 1800 McGill College Ave, 27th Floor, Montréal, QC, Canada H3A 3J6; tel. (514) 282-1122; fax (514) 282-0068; e-mail secretariat@unmfs.org; internet www.multilateralfund.org; Chief Officer MARIA NOLAN.

**Secretariat of the UN Framework Convention on Climate Change:** Haus Carstanjen, Martin-Luther-King-Str. 8, 53175 Bonn, Germany; tel. (228) 815-1000; fax (228) 815-1999; e-mail secretariat@unfccc.int; internet www.unfccc.int; Exec. Sec. YVO DE BOER (Netherlands).

**UNEP/CMS (Convention on the Conservation of Migratory Species of Wild Animals) Secretariat:** Hermann-Ehlers-Str. 10, 53113 Bonn, Germany; tel. (228) 8152402; fax (228) 8152449; e-mail secretariat@cms.int; internet www.cms.int; Exec. Sec. ROBERT HEPWORTH.

**UNEP Chemicals:** International Environment House, 11–13 chemin des Anémones, 1219 Châtelaine, Geneva, Switzerland; tel. 229178192; fax 227973460; e-mail chemicals@unep.ch; internet www.chem.unep.ch; Dir Dr MAGED YOUNES.

**UNEP Division of Technology, Industry and Economics:** 15 rue de Milan, 75441 Paris, Cedex 09 France; tel. 1-44-37-14-50; fax 1-44-37-14-74; e-mail unep.tie@unep.fr; internet www.unep.fr; Dir SILVIE LEMMET (France).

**UNEP International Environmental Technology Centre (IETC):** 2–110 Ryokuchi koen, Tsurumi-ku, Osaka 538-0036, Japan; tel. (6) 6915-4581; fax (6) 6915-0304; e-mail ietc@unep.or.jp; internet www.unep.or.jp; Exec. Dir PER MENZONY BAKKEN (Norway).

**UNEP Ozone Secretariat:** POB 30552, Nairobi, Kenya; tel. (20) 762-3850; fax (20) 762-4691; e-mail ozoneinfo@unep.org; internet ozone.unep.org; Exec. Sec. MARCO GONZÁLEZ (Costa Rica).

**UNEP-SCBD (Convention on Biological Diversity—Secretariat):** 413 St Jacques St, Office 800, Montréal, QC, Canada H2Y 1N9; tel. (514) 288-2220; fax (514) 288-6588; e-mail secretariat@cbd.int; internet www.cbd.int; Exec. Sec. AHMED DJOGHLAF (Algeria).

**UNEP Secretariat for the UN Scientific Committee on the Effects of Atomic Radiation:** Vienna International Centre, Wagramerstrasse 5, POB 500, 1400 Vienna, Austria; tel. (1) 26060-4330; fax (1) 26060-5902; e-mail malcolm.crick@unscear.org; internet www.unscear.org; Sec. Dr MALCOLM CRICK.

## Activities

UNEP serves as a focal point for environmental action within the UN system. It aims to maintain a constant watch on the changing state of the environment; to analyse the trends; to assess the problems using a wide range of data and techniques; and to promote projects leading to environmentally sound development. It plays a catalytic and co-ordinating role within and beyond the UN system. Many UNEP projects are implemented in co-operation with other UN agencies, particularly UNDP, the World Bank group, FAO, UNESCO and WHO. About 45 intergovernmental organizations outside the UN system and 60 international non-governmental organizations have official observer status on UNEP's Governing Council, and, through the Environment Liaison Centre in Nairobi, UNEP is linked to more than 6,000 non-governmental bodies concerned with the environment. UNEP also sponsors international conferences, programmes, plans and agreements regarding all aspects of the environment.

In February 1997 the Governing Council, at its 19th session, adopted a ministerial declaration (the Nairobi Declaration) on UNEP's future role and mandate, which recognized the organization as the principal UN body working in the field of the environment and as the leading global environmental authority, setting and overseeing the international environmental agenda. In June a special session of the UN General Assembly, referred to as 'Rio + 5', was convened to review the state of the environment and progress achieved in implementing the objectives of the UN Conference on Environment and Development (UNCED), held in Rio de Janeiro, Brazil, in June 1992. The meeting adopted a Programme for Further Implementation of Agenda 21 (a programme of activities to promote sustainable development, adopted by UNCED) in order to intensify efforts in areas such as energy, freshwater resources and technology transfer. The meeting confirmed UNEP's essential role in advancing the Programme and as a global authority promoting a coherent legal and political approach to the environmental challenges of sustainable development. An extensive process of restructuring and realignment of functions was subsequently initiated by UNEP, and a new organizational structure reflecting the decisions of the Nairobi Declaration was implemented during 1999. UNEP played a leading role in preparing for the World Summit on Sustainable Development (WSSD), held in August–September 2002 in Johannesburg, South Africa, to assess strategies for strengthening the implementation of Agenda 21. Governments participating in the conference adopted the Johannesburg Declaration and WSSD Plan of Implementation, in which they strongly reaffirmed commitment to the principles underlying Agenda 21 and also pledged support to all internationally-agreed development goals, including the UN Millennium Development Goals adopted by governments attending a summit meeting of the UN General Assembly in September 2000. Participating governments made concrete commitments to attaining several specific objectives in the areas of water, energy, health, agriculture and fisheries, and biodiversity. These included a reduction by one-half in the proportion of people world-wide lacking access to clean water or good sanitation by 2015, the restocking of depleted fisheries by 2015, a reduction in the ongoing loss in biodiversity by 2010, and the production and utilization of chemicals without causing harm to human beings and the environment by 2020. Participants determined to increase usage of renewable energy sources and to develop integrated water resources management and water efficiency plans. A large number of partnerships between governments, private-sector interests and civil society groups were announced at the conference.

In May 2000 UNEP's first annual Global Ministerial Environment Forum (GMEF) was held in Malmö, Sweden, attended by environment ministers and other government delegates from more than 130 countries. Participants reviewed policy issues in the field of the environment and addressed issues such as the impact on the environment of population growth, the depletion of earth's natural resources, climate change and the need for fresh water supplies. The Forum issued the Malmö Declaration, which identified the effective implementation of international agreements on environmental matters at national level as the most pressing challenge for policy-makers. The Declaration emphasized the importance of mobilizing domestic and international resources and urged increased co-operation from civil society and the private sector in achieving sustainable development. The GMEF was subsequently convened annually.

### ENVIRONMENTAL ASSESSMENT AND EARLY WARNING

The Nairobi Declaration resolved that the strengthening of UNEP's information, monitoring and assessment capabilities was a crucial element of the organization's restructuring, in order to help establish priorities for international, national and regional action, and to ensure the efficient and accurate dissemination of emerging environmental trends and emergencies.

In 1995 UNEP launched the Global Environment Outlook (GEO) process of environmental assessment. UNEP is assisted in its analysis of the state of the global environment by an extensive network of collaborating centres. The fourth umbrella report on the GEO assessment process (GEO-4) was issued in October 2007, identifying climate change, land degradation and loss of biodiversity as the world's greatest environmental challenges. The following regional and national *GEO* reports have been produced in recent years: *Africa Environment Outlook* (2002), *Brazil Environment Outlook* (2002), *Caucasus Environment Outlook* (2002), *North America's Environment* (2002), *Latin America and the Caribbean Environment Outlook* (2003), *Andean Environment Outlook* (2003), *Pacific Environment Outlook* (2005), *Caribbean Environment Outlook* (2005), *Atlantic and Indian Oceans Environment Outlook* (2005), and *Africa Environment Outlook -2* (2006). UNEP is leading a major Global International Waters Assessment (GIWA) to consider all aspects of the world's water-related issues, in particular problems of shared transboundary waters, and of future sustainable management of water resources. UNEP is also a sponsoring agency of the Joint Group of Experts on the Scientific Aspects of Marine Environmental Pollution and contributes to the preparation of reports on the state of the marine environment and on the impact of land-based activities on that environment. In November 1995 UNEP published a Global Biodiversity Assessment, which was the first comprehensive study of biological resources throughout the world. The UNEP—World Conservation Monitoring Centre (UNEP—WCMC), established in June 2000 in Cambridge, United Kingdom,, manages and interprets data concerning biodiversity and ecosystems, and makes the results available to governments and businesses. In 2007 the Centre undertook the 2010 Biodiversity Indicators Programme, with the aim of supporting decision-making by governments so as to reduce the threat of extinction facing vulnerable species. UNEP is a partner in the International Coral Reef Action Network—ICRAN, which was established in 2000 to manage and protect coral reefs world-wide. In June 2001 UNEP launched the Millennium Ecosystems Assessment, which was completed in March 2005. Other major assessments undertaken included GIWA (see above); the Assessment of Impact and Adaptation to Climate Change; the Solar and Wind Energy Resource Assessment; the Regionally-Based Assessment of Persistent Toxic Substances; the Land Degradation Assessment in Drylands; and the Global Methodology for Mapping Human Impacts on the Biosphere (GLOBIO) project.

UNEP's environmental information network includes the Global Resource Information Database (GRID), which converts collected data into information usable by decision-makers. The UNEP-INFOTERRA programme facilitates the exchange of environmental information through an extensive network of national 'focal points'. By July 2008 177 countries were participating in the network. Through UNEP-INFOTERRA UNEP promotes public access to environmental information, as well as participation in environmental concerns. UNEP aims to establish in every developing region an Environment and Natural Resource Information Network (ENRIN) in order to make available technical advice and manage environmental information and data for improved decision-making and action-planning in countries most in need of assistance. UNEP aims to integrate its information resources in order to improve access to information and to promote its international exchange. This has been pursued through UNEPnet, an internet-based interactive environmental information- and data-sharing facility.

UNEP's information, monitoring and assessment structures also serve to enhance early-warning capabilities and to provide accurate information during an environmental emergency.

### POLICY DEVELOPMENT AND LAW

UNEP aims to promote the development of policy tools and guidelines in order to achieve the sustainable management of the world environment. At a national level it assists governments to develop and implement appropriate environmental instruments and aims to co-ordinate policy initiatives. Training workshops in various aspects of environmental law and its applications are conducted. UNEP supports the development of new legal, economic and other policy instruments to improve the effectiveness of existing environmental agreements.

UNEP was instrumental in the drafting of a Convention on Biological Diversity (CBD) to preserve the immense variety of plant and animal species, in particular those threatened with extinction. The Convention entered into force at the end of 1993; by July 2008 189 states and the European Community were parties to the CBD. The CBD's Cartagena Protocol on Biosafety (so called as it had been addressed at an extraordinary session of parties to the CBD convened in Cartagena, Colombia, in February 1999) was adopted at a meeting of parties to the CBD held in Montréal, Canada, in January 2000, and entered into force in September 2003; by July 2008 the Protocol had been ratified by 146 states parties and the European Community. The Protocol regulates the transboundary movement and use of living modified organisms resulting from biotechnology in order to reduce any potential adverse effects on biodiversity and human health. It establishes an Advanced Informed Agreement procedure to govern the import of such organisms. In January 2002 UNEP launched a major project aimed at supporting developing countries with assessing the potential health and environmental risks and benefits of genetically modified (GM) crops, in preparation for the Protocol's entry into force. In February the parties to the CBD and other partners convened a conference, in Montréal, to address ways in which the traditional knowledge and practices of local communities could be preserved and used to conserve highly threatened species and ecosystems. The sixth conference of parties to the CBD, held in April 2002, adopted detailed voluntary guidelines concerning access to genetic resources and sharing the benefits attained from such resources with the countries and local communities where they originate; a global work programme on forests; and a set of guiding principles for combating alien invasive species. UNEP supports co-operation for biodiversity assessment and management in selected developing regions and for the development of strategies for the conservation and sustainable exploitation of individual threatened species (e.g. the Global Tiger Action Plan). It also provides assistance for the preparation of individual country studies and strategies to strengthen national biodiversity management and research. UNEP administers the Convention on International Trade in Endangered Species of Wild Flora and Fauna (CITES), which entered into force in 1975 and comprised 172 states parties at January 2008.

A new CITES Tiger Enforcement Task Force met for the first time in New Delhi, India, in April 2001; all trade in tigers and tiger parts is prohibited under CITES.

In October 1994 87 countries, meeting under UN auspices, signed a Convention to Combat Desertification (see UNDP Drylands Development Centre), which aimed to provide a legal framework to counter the degradation of drylands. An estimated 75% of all drylands have suffered some land degradation, affecting approximately 1,000m. people in 110 countries. UNEP continues to support the implementation of the Convention, as part of its efforts to protect land resources. UNEP also aims to improve the assessment of dryland degradation and desertification in co-operation with governments and other international bodies, as well as identifying the causes of degradation and measures to overcome these.

UNEP is the lead UN agency for promoting environmentally sustainable water management. It regards the unsustainable use of water as the most urgent environmental and sustainable development issue, and estimates that two-thirds of the world's population will suffer chronic water shortages by 2025, owing to rising demand for drinking water as a result of growing populations, decreasing quality of water because of pollution, and increasing requirements of industries and agriculture. In 2000 UNEP adopted a new water policy and strategy, comprising assessment, management and co-ordination components. The Global International Waters Assessment (see above) is the primary framework for the assessment component. The management component includes the Global Programme of Action (GPA) for the Protection of the Marine Environment from Land-based Activities (adopted in November 1995), and UNEP's freshwater programme and regional seas programme. The GPA for the Protection of the Marine Environment for Land-based Activities focuses on the effects of activities such as pollution on freshwater resources, marine biodiversity and the coastal ecosystems of small-island developing states. UNEP aims to develop a similar global instrument to ensure the integrated management of freshwater resources. It promotes international co-operation in the management of river basins and coastal areas and for the development of tools and guidelines to achieve the sustainable management of freshwater and coastal resources. In 2007 UNEP initiated a South-South Co-operation programme on technology and capacity-building for the management of water resources. UNEP provides scientific, technical and administrative support to facilitate the implementation and co-ordination of 14 regional seas conventions and 13 regional plans of action, and is developing a strategy to strengthen collaboration in their implementation. The new water policy and strategy emphasizes the need for improved co-ordination of existing activities. UNEP aims to play an enhanced role within relevant co-ordination mechanisms, such as the UN open-ended informal consultation process on oceans and the law of the sea.

In 1996 UNEP, in collaboration with FAO, began to work towards promoting and formulating a legally binding international convention on prior informed consent (PIC) for hazardous chemicals and pesticides in international trade, extending a voluntary PIC procedure of information exchange undertaken by more than 100 governments since 1991. The Convention was adopted at a conference held in Rotterdam, Netherlands, in September 1998, and entered into force in February 2004. It aims to reduce risks to human health and the environment by restricting the production, export and use of hazardous substances and enhancing information exchange procedures.

In conjunction with UN-Habitat, UNDP, the World Bank and other organizations and institutions, UNEP promotes environmental concerns in urban planning and management through the Sustainable Cities Programme, as well as regional workshops concerned with urban pollution and the impact of transportation systems. In 1994 UNEP inaugurated an International Environmental Technology Centre (IETC), with offices in Osaka and Shiga, Japan, in order to strengthen the capabilities of developing countries and countries with economies in transition to promote environmentally sound management of cities and freshwater reservoirs through technology co-operation and partnerships.

UNEP has played a key role in global efforts to combat risks to the ozone layer, resultant climatic changes and atmospheric pollution. UNEP worked in collaboration with the World Meteorological Organization to formulate the UN Framework Convention on Climate Change (UNFCCC), with the aim of reducing the emission of gases that have a warming effect on the atmosphere, and has remained an active participant in the ongoing process to review and enforce the implementation of the Convention and of its Kyoto Protocol. UNEP was the lead agency in formulating the 1987 Montreal Protocol to the Vienna Convention for the Protection of the Ozone Layer (1985), which provided for a 50% reduction in the production of chlorofluorocarbons (CFCs) by 2000. An amendment to the Protocol was adopted in 1990, which required complete cessation of the production of CFCs by 2000 in industrialized countries and by 2010 in developing countries. The Copenhagen Amendment, adopted in 1992, stipulated the phasing out of production of hydrochlorofluorocarbons (HCFCs) by 2030 in developed countries and by 2040 in developing nations. In 1997 the ninth Conference of the Parties (COP) to the Vienna Convention adopted a further amendment which aimed to introduce a licensing system for all controlled substances. The 11th COP, meeting in Beijing, People's Republic of China, in November–December 1999, adopted the Beijing Amendment, which imposed tighter controls on the import and export of HCFCs, and on the production and consumption of bromochloromethane (Halon-1011, an industrial solvent and fire extinguisher). The Beijing Amendment entered into force in December 2001. At the 19th COP (also the 20th anniversary meeting of the adoption of the Montreal Protocol), held in September 2007, states parties to the Vienna Convention agreed to advance the deadline for the elimination of HCFCs: production and consumption were to be frozen by 2013, and were to be phased out in developed countries by 2020 and in developing countries by 2030. A Multilateral Fund for the Implementation of the Montreal Protocol was established in June 1990 to promote the use of suitable technologies and the transfer of technologies to developing countries. UNEP, UNDP, the World Bank and UNIDO are the sponsors of the Fund, which by April 2008 had approved financing for about 5,700 projects and activities in 146 developing countries at a cost of around US $2,280m. Commitments of $400.4m. were made to the sixth replenishment of the Fund, covering the three-year period 2006–08. (The total budget for 2006–08 was $470.0m., the remainder deriving from the following sources: $59.6m. to be carried over from the 2003–05 triennium and $10m. to be provided from interest accruing.)

### POLICY IMPLEMENTATION

UNEP's Division of Environmental Policy Implementation incorporates two main functions: technical co-operation and response to environmental emergencies.

With the UN Office for the Co-ordination of Humanitarian Assistance (OCHA), UNEP has established a joint Environment Unit to mobilize and co-ordinate international assistance and expertise for countries facing environmental emergencies and natural disasters. In mid-1999 UNEP and UN-Habitat jointly established a Balkan Task Force (subsequently renamed UNEP Balkans Unit) to assess the environmental impact of NATO's aerial offensive against the then Federal Republic of Yugoslavia. In November 2000 the Unit led a field assessment to evaluate reports of environmental contamination by debris from NATO ammunition containing depleted uranium, concluding that there was no evidence of widespread contamination of the ground surface by depleted uranium, but that considerable scientific uncertainties remained, for example as to the safety of groundwater and the longer-term behaviour of depleted uranium in the environment, and recommending precautionary action. In 2007 UNEP's Post-Conflict Disaster Management Branch was established, replacing earlier initiatives, and in that year it was engaged in rehabilitation programmes in Afghanistan, Indonesia, Lebanon, Liberia, Maldives, Nigeria, the Palestinian territories, Somalia, Sri Lanka and Sudan.

UNEP, together with UNDP and the World Bank, is an implementing agency of the Global Environment Facility (GEF), which was established in 1991 as a mechanism for international co-operation in projects concerned with biological diversity, climate change, international waters and depletion of the ozone layer. UNEP services the Scientific and Technical Advisory Panel, which provides expert advice on GEF programmes and operational strategies.

### TECHNOLOGY, INDUSTRY AND ECONOMICS

The use of inappropriate industrial technologies and the widespread adoption of unsustainable production and consumption patterns have been identified as being inefficient in the use of renewable resources and wasteful, in particular in the use of energy and water. UNEP aims to encourage governments and the private sector to develop and adopt policies and practices that are cleaner and safer, make efficient use of natural resources, incorporate environmental costs, ensure the environmentally sound management of chemicals, and reduce pollution and risks to human health and the environment. In collaboration with other organizations and agencies UNEP works to define and formulate international guidelines and agreements to address these issues. UNEP also promotes the transfer of appropriate technologies and organizes conferences and training workshops to provide sustainable production practices. Relevant information is disseminated through the International Cleaner Production Information Clearing House. UNEP, together with UNIDO, has established 34 National Cleaner Production Centres to promote a preventive approach to industrial pollution control. In October 1998 UNEP adopted an International Declaration on Cleaner Production, with a commitment to implement cleaner and more sustainable production methods and to monitor results. In 1997 UNEP and the Coalition for Environmentally Responsible Economies initiated the Global Reporting Initiative, which, with participation by corporations, business associations and other organizations and stakeholders, develops guidelines for voluntary reporting by companies on their economic, environmental and social performance. In April 2002 UNEP launched the 'Life-Cycle Initiative', which aims to assist governments, businesses and other consumers with adopting environmentally sound policies and practice, in view of the upward trend in global consumption patterns. UNEP Finance Initiatives (FI) is a programme encouraging banks, insurance companies and other financial institutions to invest in an environmentally responsible way: an annual FI Global Roundtable meeting is held, together with regional meetings. In April 2007 UNEP hosted the first Business for Environment meeting, on corporate environmental responsibility, in Singapore, and in October UNEP's 24th annual consultative meeting with representatives of business and industry took place in Sao Paulo, Brazil. During 2007 UNEP's Programme on Sustainable Consumption and Production established an International Panel for Sustainable Resource Management (comprising experts whose initial subjects of study were to be the environmental risks of biofuels and of metal recycling), and initiated forums for businesses and non-governmental organizations in this field.

UNEP provides institutional servicing to the Basel Convention on the Control of Transboundary Movements of Hazardous Wastes and their Disposal, which was adopted in 1989 with the aim of preventing the disposal of wastes from industrialized countries in countries that have no processing facilities. In March 1994 the second meeting of parties to the Convention determined to ban the exportation of hazardous wastes between industrialized and developing countries. The third meeting of parties to the Convention, held in 1995, proposed that the ban should be incorporated into the Convention as an amendment. The resulting so-called Ban Amendment (prohibiting exports of hazardous wastes for final disposal and recycling from states and/or parties also belonging to OECD and, or, the European Union, and from Liechtenstein, to any other state party to the Convention) required ratification by three-quarters of the 62 signatory states present at the time of adoption before it could enter into effect; by July 2008 the Ban Amendment had been ratified by 63 parties. In 1998 the technical working group of the Convention agreed a new procedure for clarifying the classification and characterization of specific hazardous wastes. The fifth full meeting of parties to the Convention, held in December 1999, adopted the Basel Declaration outlining an agenda for the period 2000–10, with a particular focus on minimizing the production of hazardous wastes. At July 2008 the number of parties to the Convention totalled 170. In December 1999 132 states adopted a Protocol to the Convention to address issues relating to liability and compensation for damages from waste exports. The governments also agreed to establish a multilateral fund to finance immediate clean-up operations following any environmental accident.

The UNEP Chemicals office was established to promote the sound management of hazardous substances, central to which has been the International Register of Potentially Toxic Chemicals (IRPTC). UNEP aims to facilitate access to data on chemicals and hazardous wastes, in order to assess and control health and environmental risks, by using the IRPTC as a clearing house facility of relevant information and by publishing information and technical reports on the impact of the use of chemicals.

UNEP's OzonAction Programme works to promote information exchange, training and technological awareness. Its objective is to strengthen the capacity of governments and industry in developing countries to undertake measures towards the cost-effective phasing-out of ozone-depleting substances. UNEP also encourages the development of alternative and renewable sources of energy. To achieve this, UNEP is supporting the establishment of a network of centres to research and exchange information of environmentally sound energy technology resources.

### REGIONAL CO-OPERATION AND REPRESENTATION

UNEP maintains six regional offices. These work to initiate and promote UNEP objectives and to ensure that all programme formulation and delivery meets the specific needs of countries and regions. They also provide a focal point for building national, sub-regional and regional partnership and enhancing local participation in UNEP initiatives. Following UNEP's reorganization a co-ordination office was established at headquarters to promote regional policy integration, to co-ordinate programme planning, and to provide necessary services to the regional offices.

UNEP provides administrative support to several regional conventions, for example the Lusaka Agreement on Co-operative Enforcement Operations Directed at Illegal Trade in Wild Flora and Fauna, which entered into force in December 1996 having been concluded under UNEP auspices in order to strengthen the implementation of the CBD and CITES in Eastern and Central Africa. UNEP also organizes conferences, workshops and seminars at national and regional levels, and may extend advisory services or technical assistance to individual governments.

### CONVENTIONS

UNEP aims to develop and promote international environmental legislation in order to pursue an integrated response to global environmental issues, to enhance collaboration among existing convention secetariats, and to co-ordinate support to implement the work programmes of international instruments.

UNEP has been an active participant in the formulation of several major conventions (see above). The Division of Environmental Conventions is mandated to assist the Division of Policy Development and Law in the formulation of new agreements or protocols to existing conventions. Following the successful adoption of the Rotterdam Convention in September 1998, UNEP played a leading role in formulating a multilateral agreement to reduce and ultimately eliminate the manufacture and use of Persistent Organic Pollutants (POPs), which are considered to be a major global environmental hazard. The agreement on POPs, concluded in December 2000 at a conference sponsored by UNEP in Johannesburg, South Africa, was adopted by 127 countries in May 2001 and entered into force in May 2004.

UNEP has been designated to provide secretariat functions to a number of global and regional environmental conventions (see above for list of offices).

### COMMUNICATIONS AND PUBLIC INFORMATION

UNEP's public education campaigns and outreach programmes promote community involvement in environmental issues. Further communication of environmental concerns is undertaken through the media, an information centre service and special promotional events, including World Environment Day, photography competitions, and the awarding of the Sasakawa Prize (to recognize distinguished service to the environment by individuals and groups) and of the Global 500 Award for Environmental Achievement. In 1996 UNEP initiated a Global Environment Citizenship Programme to promote acknowledgment of the environmental responsibilities of all sectors of society.

## Finance

UNEP derives its finances from the regular budget of the United Nations and from voluntary contributions to the Environment Fund. A budget totalling US $152m. was approved by the Governing Council for 2008–09.

## Publications

*Annual Report*.
*APELL Newsletter* (2 a year).
*Cleaner Production Newsletter* (2 a year).
*Climate Change Bulletin* (quarterly).
*Connect* (UNESCO-UNEP newsletter on environmental degradation, quarterly).
*Earth Views* (quarterly).
*Environment Forum* (quarterly).
*Environmental Law Bulletin* (2 a year).
*Financial Services Initiative* (2 a year).
*GEF News* (quarterly).
*Global Water Review*.
*GPA Newsletter*.
*IETC Insight* (3 a year).
*Industry and Environment Review* (quarterly).
*Leave it to Us* (children's magazine, 2 a year).
*Managing Hazardous Waste* (2 a year).
*Our Planet* (quarterly).
*OzonAction Newsletter* (quarterly).
*Tierramerica* (weekly).
*Tourism Focus* (2 a year).
*UNEP Chemicals Newsletter* (2 a year).
*UNEP Update* (monthly).
*UNEP Year Book* (annually).
*World Atlas of Biodiversity*.
*World Atlas of Coral Reefs*.
*World Atlas of Desertification*.

Studies, reports (including *Atlantic and Indian Oceans Environment Outlook 2005*), legal texts, technical guidelines, etc.

# United Nations High Commissioner for Refugees—UNHCR

**Address:** CP 2500, 1211 Geneva 2 dépôt, Switzerland.

**Telephone:** 227398111; **fax:** 227397312; **e-mail:** unhcr@unhcr.org; **internet:** www.unhcr.org.

The Office of the High Commissioner was established in 1951 to provide international protection for refugees and to seek durable solutions to their problems. In 1981 UNHCR was awarded the Nobel Peace Prize.

## Organization

(August 2008)

### HIGH COMMISSIONER

The High Commissioner is elected by the United Nations General Assembly on the nomination of the Secretary-General, and is responsible to the General Assembly and to the UN Economic and Social Council (ECOSOC).

**High Commissioner:** António Manuel de Oliveira Guterres (Portugal).

**Deputy High Commissioner:** L. Craig Johnstone (USA).

### EXECUTIVE COMMITTEE

The Executive Committee of the High Commissioner's Programme (ExCom), established by ECOSOC, gives the High Commissioner policy directives in respect of material assistance programmes and advice in the field of international protection. In addition, it oversees UNHCR's general policies and use of funds. ExCom, which comprises representatives of 66 states, both members and non-members of the UN, meets once a year.

### ADMINISTRATION

Headquarters include the Executive Office, comprising the offices of the High Commissioner, the Deputy High Commissioner and the Assistant High Commissioner. The Inspector General, the Director of the UNHCR liaison office in New York, and the Director of the Department of International Protection report directly to the High Commissioner. The other principal administrative units are the Division of Financial and Supply Management, the Division of Human Resources Management, the Division of External Relations, the Division of Information Systems and Telecommunications, the Division of International Protection Services, and the Department of Operations, which is responsible for the five regional bureaux covering Africa; Asia and the Pacific; Europe; the Americas and the Caribbean; and Central Asia, South-West Asia, North Africa and the Middle East; and also includes the Division of Operational Services and the Emergency and Security Service. At July 2006 there were 263 UNHCR offices in 116 countries world-wide. At that time UNHCR employed 6,540 people (including short-term staff), of whom more than 80% were working in the field. In that year a Structural and Management Change Process was initiated, with the aim of reviewing and improving UNHCR's processes and structures.

## Activities

The competence of the High Commissioner extends to any person who, owing to well-founded fear of being persecuted for reasons of race, religion, nationality or political opinion, is outside the country of his or her nationality and is unable or, owing to such fear or for reasons other than personal convenience, remains unwilling to accept the protection of that country; or who, not having a nationality and being outside the country of his or her former habitual residence, is unable or, owing to such fear or for reasons other than personal convenience, is unwilling to return to it. This competence may be extended, by resolutions of the UN General Assembly and decisions of ExCom, to cover certain other 'persons of concern', in addition to refugees meeting these criteria. Refugees who are assisted by other UN agencies, or who have the same rights or obligations as nationals of their country of residence, are outside the mandate of UNHCR.

In recent years there has been a significant shift in UNHCR's focus of activities. Increasingly UNHCR has been called upon to support people who have been displaced within their own country (i.e. with similar needs to those of refugees but who have not crossed an international border) or those threatened with displacement as a result of armed conflict. In addition, greater support has been given to refugees who have returned to their country of origin, to assist their reintegration, and UNHCR is working to enable local communities to support the returnees, frequently through the implementation of Quick Impact Projects (QIPs). In 2004 UNHCR led the formulation of a UN system-wide Strategic Plan for internally displaced persons (IDPs). During 2005 the UN's Inter-Agency Standing Committee (IASC), concerned with co-ordinating the international response to humanitarian disasters, developed a concept of organizing agency assistance to IDPs through the institutionalization of a 'Cluster Approach', currently comprising 11 core areas of activity. UNHCR is the lead agency for the clusters on Camp Co-ordination and Management (in conflict situations; IOM leads that cluster in natural disaster situations), Emergency Shelter, and (jointly with OHCHR and UNICEF) Protection.

In the mid-2000s UNHCR widened its scope from its mandate to protect and assist people fleeing persecution and violence in response to the enormous impact of two devastating natural disasters. Following the series of tidal waves (tsunamis), emanating from an earthquake in the Indian Ocean, that devastated coastal regions in 14 countries in South and South-East Asia and East Africa in December 2004, UNHCR requested emergency funding totalling US $77m. in support of a 12-month relief operation to provide shelter, non-food relief supplies and logistical support for survivors in Aceh, Indonesia (close to the epicentre of the earthquake), Sri Lanka and Somalia. This was part of a pan-UN inter-agency appeal for $1,100m. In October 2005 UNHCR provided an immediate response to support survivors of the South Asian earthquake that struck northern Pakistan and bordering areas of India and Afghanistan. In May 2008 UNHCR donated tents to provide shelter for some 55,000 people following a devastating earthquake in Sichuan province, People's Republic of China.

UNHCR has been increasingly concerned with the problem of statelessness, where people have no legal nationality, and promotes new accessions to the 1954 Convention Relating to the Status of Stateless Persons and the 1964 Convention on the Reduction of Statelessness. UNHCR maintains that a significant proportion of the global stateless population has not hitherto been systematically identified. In October 2006 ExCom urged member states to share with UNHCR data on stateless persons and on persons with undetermined nationality.

Addressing the annual meeting of ExCom in October 2007 the High Commissioner, while emphasizing that UNHCR was not mandated to manage migration, urged a concerted international effort to raise awareness and comprehension of the broad patterns (including the scale, complexity, and causes—such as poverty and the pursuit of improved living standards) of global displacement and migration. In order to fulfil UNHCR's mandate to support refugees and others in need of protection within ongoing mass movements of people, he urged better recognition of the mixed nature of many 21st century population flows, often comprising both economic migrants and refugees, asylum-seekers and victims of trafficking who required detection and support. It was also acknowledged that conflict and persecution—the traditional reasons for flight—were being increasingly compounded by factors such as environmental degradation and detrimental effects of climate change.

At December 2007 the total population of concern to UNHCR, based on provisional figures, amounted to 31.7m. At that time the refugee population world-wide totalled 9.7m. UNHCR was also concerned with some 730,640 recently returned refugees, 13.7m. IDPs, 2.1m. returned IDPs, 2.9m. stateless persons, 739,986 asylum-seekers, and 0.7m. others. UNHCR maintains an online statistical population database, accessible at www.unhcr.org/statistics/populationdatabase.

World Refugee Day, sponsored by UNHCR, is held annually on 20 June.

### INTERNATIONAL PROTECTION

As laid down in the Statute of the Office, UNHCR's primary function is to extend international protection to refugees and its second function is to seek durable solutions to their problems. In the exercise of its mandate UNHCR seeks to ensure that refugees and asylum-seekers are protected against *refoulement* (forcible return), that they receive asylum, and that they are treated according to internationally recognized standards. UNHCR pursues these objectives by a variety of means that include promoting the conclusion and ratification by states of international conventions for the protection of refugees. UNHCR promotes the adoption of liberal practices of asylum by states, so that refugees and asylum-seekers are granted admission, at least on a temporary basis.

The most comprehensive instrument concerning refugees that has been elaborated at the international level is the 1951 United Nations Convention relating to the Status of Refugees. This Convention, the scope of which was extended by a Protocol adopted in 1967, defines the rights and duties of refugees and contains provisions dealing with a variety of matters which affect the day-to-day lives of refugees. The application of the Convention and its Protocol is supervised by UNHCR. Important provisions for the treatment of refugees are also contained in a number of instruments adopted at the regional level. These include the 1969 Convention Governing the Specific Aspects of Refugee Problems adopted by the Organization of African Unity (now the African Union—AU) member states in 1969, the European Agreement on the Abolition of Visas for Refugees, and the 1969 American Convention on Human Rights.

UNHCR has actively encouraged states to accede to the 1951 United Nations Refugee Convention and the 1967 Protocol: 147 states had acceded to either or both of these basic refugee instruments by July 2008. An increasing number of states have also adopted domestic legislation and/or administrative measures to implement the international instruments, particularly in the field of procedures for the determination of refugee status. UNHCR has sought to address the specific needs of refugee women and children, and has also attempted to deal with the problem of military attacks on refugee camps, by adopting and encouraging the acceptance of a set of principles to ensure the safety of refugees. In recent years it has formulated a strategy designed to address the fundamental causes of refugee flows. In 2001, in response to widespread concern about perceived high numbers of asylum-seekers and large-scale international economic migration and human trafficking, UNHCR initiated a series of Global Consultations on International Protection with the signatories to the 1951 Convention and 1967 Protocol, and other interested parties, with a view to strengthening both the application and scope of international refugee legislation. A consultation of 156 Governments, convened in Geneva, in December 2001, reaffirmed commitment to the central role played by the Convention and Protocol. The final consultation, held in May 2002, focused on durable solutions and the protection of refugee women and children. Subsequently, based on the findings of the Global Consultations process, UNHCR developed an Agenda on Protection with six main objectives: strengthening the implementation of the 1951 Convention and 1967 Protocol; the protection of refugees within broader migration movements; more equitable sharing of burdens and responsibilities and building of capacities to receive and protect refugees; addressing more effectively security-related concerns; increasing efforts to find durable solutions; and meeting the protection needs of refugee women and children. The Agenda was endorsed by ExCom in October 2002. In September of that year the High Commissioner for Refugees launched the *Convention Plus* initiative, which aimed to address contemporary global asylum issues by developing, on the basis of the Agenda on Protection, international agreements and measures to supplement the 1951 Convention and 1967 Protocol.

UNHCR is one of the 10 co-sponsors of UNAIDS.

## ASSISTANCE ACTIVITIES

The first phase of an assistance operation uses UNHCR's capacity of emergency response. This enables UNHCR to address the immediate needs of refugees at short notice, for example, by employing specially trained emergency teams and maintaining stockpiles of basic equipment, medical aid and materials. A significant proportion of UNHCR expenditure is allocated to the next phase of an operation, providing 'care and maintenance' in stable refugee circumstances. This assistance can take various forms, including the provision of food, shelter, medical care and essential supplies. Also covered in many instances are basic services, including education and counselling.

As far as possible, assistance is geared towards the identification and implementation of durable solutions to refugee problems—this being the second statutory responsibility of UNHCR. Such solutions generally take one of three forms: voluntary repatriation, local integration or resettlement in another country. Where voluntary repatriation, increasingly the preferred solution, is feasible, the Office assists refugees to overcome obstacles preventing their return to their country of origin. This may be done through negotiations with governments involved, or by providing funds either for the physical movement of refugees or for the rehabilitation of returnees once back in their own country. UNHCR supports the implementation of the Guidance Note on Durable Solutions for Displaced Persons, adopted in 2004 by the UN Development Group.

When voluntary repatriation is not an option, efforts are made to assist refugees to integrate locally and to become self-supporting in their countries of asylum. This may be done either by granting loans to refugees, or by assisting them, through vocational training or in other ways, to learn a skill and to establish themselves in gainful occupations. One major form of assistance to help refugees re-establish themselves outside camps is the provision of housing. In cases where resettlement through emigration is the only viable solution to a refugee problem, UNHCR negotiates with governments in an endeavour to obtain suitable resettlement opportunities, to encourage liberalization of admission criteria and to draw up special immigration schemes. During 2006 an estimated 27,700 refugees (as well as 1,860 family reunification cases) were resettled under UNHCR auspices.

In the 1990s UNHCR consolidated efforts to integrate certain priorities into its programme planning and implementation, as a standard discipline in all phases of assistance. The considerations include awareness of specific problems confronting refugee women, the needs of refugee children, the environmental impact of refugee programmes and long-term development objectives. In an effort to improve the effectiveness of its programmes, UNHCR has initiated a process of delegating authority, as well as responsibility for operational budgets, to its regional and field representatives, increasing flexibility and accountability. A Policy Development and Evaluation Service reviews systematically UNHCR's operational effectiveness.

All UNHCR personnel are required to sign, and all interns, contracted staff and staff from partner organizations are required to acknowledge, a Code of Conduct, to which is appended the UN Secretary-General's bulletin on special measures for protection from sexual exploitation and sexual abuse. The post of Senior Adviser to the High Commissioner on Gender Issues, within the Executive Office, was established in 2004.

## SOUTH ASIA

From 1979, as a result of civil strife in Afghanistan, there was a massive movement of refugees from that country into Pakistan and Iran creating the world's largest refugee population, which reached a peak of almost 6.3m. people in 1990. In 1988 UNHCR agreed to provide assistance for the voluntary repatriation of refugees, both in ensuring the rights of the returning population and in providing material assistance such as transport, immunization, and supplies of food and other essentials. In April 1992, following the establishment of a new Government in Afghanistan, refugees began to repatriate in substantial numbers, although, meanwhile, large numbers of people continued to flee into Pakistan as a result of persisting insecurity. From October 1996 an escalation of hostilities in northern and western regions of Afghanistan resulted in further massive population displacement. The total number of returnees from Iran and Pakistan during the decade 1988–98 amounted to more than 4.2m. UNHCR, with other UN agencies, attempted to meet the immediate needs of IDPs and recent returnees in Afghanistan through systematic monitoring and, for example, by initiating small-scale multi-sectoral QIPs to improve shelter, rural water supply and local infrastructure; organizing income-generating and capacity-building activities; and providing food and tools. However, the ongoing civil conflict, as well as successive severe droughts and harsh winter conditions, caused renewed population displacement, precluding a settlement of the refugee situation and entailing immense difficulties in undertaking comprehensive relief efforts. Activities were disrupted by periodic withdrawals of UN international personnel owing to security concerns.

The humanitarian crisis in Afghanistan worsened considerably during 2000. In mid-2001 UNHCR warned that the food insecurity in the country was continuing to deteriorate and that population movements were ongoing. In September, prompted by the threat of impending military action directed by a US-led global coalition against targets in the Taliban-administered areas of Afghanistan, UNHCR launched a US $252m. appeal to finance an emergency relief operation to cope with the potentially large further movement of Afghan refugees and IDPs. Although all surrounding countries imposed 'closed border' policies (with Pakistan reportedly permitting limited entry to Afghans in possession of correct travel documentation), it was envisaged that, were the security situation to deteriorate significantly, large numbers of Afghans might attempt to cross into the surrounding countries (mainly Iran and Pakistan) at unsecured points of entry. UNHCR urged the adoption of more liberal border policies and began substantially to reinforce its presence in Iran and Pakistan. Activities undertaken included the supply of basic relief items, such as tents and health and hygiene kits, and assistance with the provision of community services, such as education for school-age children. The construction and maintenance of new camps near the Pakistan-Afghanistan border was initiated in co-operation with the Pakistan Government and other agencies, and new refugee shelters were to be constructed in Iran. Emergency contingency plans were also formulated for a relief initiative to assist a projected further 500,000 IDPs (in addition to the large numbers of people already displaced) inside

Afghanistan. Large population movements out of cities were reported from the start of the international political crisis. An estimated 6m. Afghans (about one-quarter of the total population) were believed to be extremely vulnerable, requiring urgent food aid and other relief supplies. In mid-September all foreign UN field staff were withdrawn from Afghanistan for security reasons; meanwhile, in order to address the humanitarian situation, a Crisis Group was established by several UN agencies, including UNHCR, and a crisis management structure came into operation at UNHCR headquarters. In October (when air-strikes were initiated against Afghanistan) UNHCR opened a staging camp at a major crossing point on the Afghanistan-Pakistan border, and put in place a system for monitoring new refugee arrivals (implemented by local people rather than by UNHCR personnel). It was estimated that from October 2001–January 2002 about 50,000 Afghan refugees entered Pakistan officially, while about 150,000 crossed into the country at unofficial border points; many reportedly sought refuge with friends and relatives. Much smaller movements into Iran were reported. Spontaneous repatriations also occurred during that period (reportedly partly owing to the poor conditions at many camps in Pakistan), and UNHCR-assisted IDP returns were also undertaken. UNHCR resumed operations within Afghanistan in mid-November 2001, distributing supplies and implementing QIPs, for example the provision of warm winter clothing. From that month some 130,000 Afghan refugees in Pakistan were relocated from inadequate accommodation to new camps. On 1 March 2002, following the adoption in December 2001 by the international community of the Bonn Agreement on provisional arrangements for stabilizing Afghanistan, UNHCR initiated, jointly with the new interim Afghan administration, an assisted repatriation programme. UNHCR also concluded tripartite accords on repatriation with the Afghan authorities and with Iran and Pakistan. In March 2002 UNHCR signed a new agreement with the Iranian Government to grant access to Afghans in detention centres throughout that country and to undertake a screening programme for asylum-seekers, in order to deal with the problem of undocumented refugees. At 31 December 2007 Pakistan was hosting some 1,700 recognized Afghan refugees, 886,700 registered Afghans assisted by UNHCR in refugee villages, and 1.1m. Afghans in 'refugee-like' situations (living outside refugee villages and not in receipt of UNHCR material assistance but benefiting from UNHCR advocacy and return reintegration support). Meanwhile, some 906,971 UNHCR-assisted Afghan refugees remained in Iran (in addition to about 1m. unregistered Afghans, some of whom were to be deported during 2008), and 9,011 Afghan refugees remained in India (all UNHCR-assisted). By early 2008 around 4.7m. refugees had returned from Pakistan and Iran since early 2002; of these, 373,125 returned during 2007 (nearly all with UNHCR assistance). UNHCR provides returning refugees with transport and an initial reintegration package, including a cash grant and food and basic household items, and monitors their situation. Particular focus is placed upon the situation of returnee women and prevention of gender-based violence, and on encouraging the return of professional workers, especially doctors and teachers. The Office also works to improve local infrastructure and water supply facilities, and by the end of 2007 had completed the construction of more than 200,000 shelter units. UNHCR aims to strengthen the capacity of the Afghan Government to manage the return and sustainable reintegration of refugees and IDPs. In early 2006, following the termination in September 2005 of the process determined by the 2001 Bonn Agreement and the adoption by the UN-sponsored London Conference on Afghanistan, convened on 31 January–1 February 2006, of the Afghanistan Compact as a framework for international assistance until end-2010, UNHCR developed an outline strategy for its Afghan operations over 2007–09, during which period it envisaged the voluntary return of a further 1.6m. Afghans.

In September 2005 Afghanistan acceded to the 1951 Convention relating to the Status of Refugees and its 1967 Protocol.

In October 2005 parts of northern Pakistan and bordering areas of India and Afghanistan were struck by a devastating earthquake, killing more than 80,000 people, injuring an estimated 74,000, rendering more than 3m. homeless, destroying local infrastructure and, owing to mountainous terrain and the isolation of many affected communities, causing unprecedented logistical challenges to aid agencies. UNHCR, with capabilities already on the ground as a result of its operations in support of Afghan refugees (see above), provided an immediate response, distributing to survivors tents and blankets from stores within the country. Further shelter materials were then brought in from global stockpiles, and UNHCR also provided stoves and kerosene for heating to help survivors to cope with severe winter conditions at 144 camps in the earthquake zone. In August 2006 UNHCR transferred responsibility for managing the camps to the Pakistan authorities; nevertheless, the Office was to continue to participate in planning and capacity-building activities.

In 1991–92 thousands of people of Nepalese ethnic origin living in Bhutan sought refuge from alleged persecution by fleeing to eastern Nepal. In December 2000 Bhutan and Nepal reached agreement on a joint verification mechanism for the repatriation of the refugees, which had been hitherto the principal issue precluding a resolution of the situation. The first verification of Bhutanese refugees was undertaken in March 2001. By March 2008 there remained around 107,000 Bhutanese refugees residing in seven camps in Nepal, all of whom were receiving UNHCR assistance in the form of food, shelter, medical care and water, and 25,000 of whom were registered for resettlement. At the end of that month UNHCR launched an operation to resettle more than 10,000 of the Nepalese refugees, mainly to the USA. During 2007 the Nepalese Government extended citizenship to some 2.6m. of the 3.5m. stateless people hitherto resident in Nepal.

During 1983–2001 hostilities between the Sri Lankan Government and Tamil separatists resulted in the displacement of more than 1m. Sri Lankan Tamil refugees (who sought shelter in India) and IDPs. Ongoing efforts by UNHCR to repatriate the Sri Lankan refugees were disrupted in late 1995 by an offensive by Sri Lankan government troops against the northern Jaffna peninsula, which caused a massive displacement of the local Tamil population. Increasing insecurity from late 1999 prompted further population movements.However, following the conclusion of a cease-fire agreement between the Sri Lankan Government and Tamil separatists in February 2002, the number of spontaneous returns accelerated. From April 2006 conflict between Tamil separatists and the Sri Lankan Government escalated once again, prompting a new wave of internal displacement and refugee movements to India during 2006–07. In 2006–07 UNHCR provided emergency relief items to most of the estimated 190,000 new Sri Lankan IDPs; monitored the human rights situation and advised the Sri Lankan authorities about the treatment of the displaced population; and established about 60 sites to accommodate the new IDPs. During 2006 UNHCR also supported the relocation of some 900 long-standing Sri Lankan IDP families. At 31 December 2007 there were 459,567 Sri Lankan IDPs of concern to UNHCR and 158,600 recently returned IDPs, as well as an estimated 72,934 Sri Lankan refugees remaining in camps in southern India. At end-December 2007 India's total refugee population of some 161,537 also included 77,200 refugees from the People's Republic of China (mainly Tibetans).

### CO-OPERATION WITH OTHER ORGANIZATIONS

UNHCR works closely with other UN agencies, intergovernmental organizations and non-governmental organizations (NGOs) to increase the scope and effectiveness of its operations. Within the UN system UNHCR co-operates, principally, with the World Food Programme in the distribution of food aid, UNICEF and the World Health Organization in the provision of family welfare and child immunization programmes, OCHA in the delivery of emergency humanitarian relief, UNDP in development-related activities and the preparation of guide-lines for the continuum of emergency assistance to development programmes, and the Office of the UN High Commissioner for Human Rights. UNHCR also has close working relationships with the International Committee of the Red Cross and the International Organization for Migration. In 2005 UNHCR worked with 578 NGOs as 'implementing partners', enabling UNHCR to broaden the use of its resources while maintaining a co-ordinating role in the provision of assistance.

### TRAINING

UNHCR organizes training programmes and workshops to enhance the capabilities of field workers and non-UNHCR staff, in the following areas: the identification and registration of refugees; people-orientated planning; resettlement procedures and policies; emergency response and management; security awareness; stress management; and the dissemination of information through the electronic media.

## Finance

The United Nations' regular budget finances a proportion of UNHCR's administrative expenditure. The majority of UNHCR's programme expenditure (about 98%) is funded by voluntary contributions, mainly from governments. The Private Sector and Public Affairs Service aims to increase funding from non-governmental donor sources, for example by developing partnerships with foundations and corporations. Following approval of the Unified Annual Programme Budget any subsequently identified requirements are managed in the form of Supplementary Programmes, financed by separate appeals. The total Unified Annual Programme Budget for 2007 was projected at US $1,043m.

## Publications

*Global Trends* (annually).

*Refugees* (quarterly, in English, French, German, Italian, Japanese and Spanish).

*Refugee Resettlement: An International Handbook to Guide Reception and Integration.*

*Refugee Survey Quarterly.*

*Refworld* (annually).

*Sexual and Gender-based Violence Against Refugees, Returnees and Displaced Persons: Guide-lines for Prevention and Response.*

*The State of the World's Refugees* (every 2 years).

*Statistical Yearbook* (annually).

*UNHCR Handbook for Emergencies.*

Press releases, reports.

## Statistics

**PERSONS OF CONCERN TO UNHCR IN SOUTH ASIA**
('000 persons, at 31 December 2007*)

| Host country | Refugees† | Asylum-seekers | Returned refugees | Others of concern‡ |
|---|---|---|---|---|
| Afghanistan | 0.0 | 0.0 | 373.9 | 161.7 |
| Bangladesh | 27.6 | 0.1 | — | — |
| India | 161.5 | 2.4 | — | — |
| Nepal | 130.7 | 1.6 | — | 900.1 |
| Pakistan | 2,035.0 | 3.1 | 0.0 | — |
| Sri Lanka | 0.2 | 0.2 | 2.0 | 618.2 |

* Figures are provided mostly by governments, based on their own records and methods of estimations. Countries with fewer than 10,000 persons of concern to UNHCR are not listed.

† Includes persons in refugee-like situations who receive advocacy but not material support from UNHCR.

‡ Mainly internally displaced persons (IDPs), recently-returned IDPs or stateless persons.

# United Nations Peace-keeping

**Address:** Department of Peace-keeping Operations, Room S-3727-B, United Nations, New York, NY 10017, USA.

**Telephone:** (212) 963-8077; **fax:** (212) 963-9222; **internet:** www.un.org/Depts/dpko/.

United Nations peace-keeping operations have been conceived as instruments of conflict control. The UN has used these operations in various conflicts, with the consent of the parties involved, to maintain international peace and security, without prejudice to the positions or claims of parties, in order to facilitate the search for political settlements through peaceful means such as mediation and the good offices of the UN Secretary-General. Each operation is established with a specific mandate, which requires periodic review by the UN Security Council. In 1988 the United Nations Peace-keeping Forces were awarded the Nobel Peace Prize.

United Nations peace-keeping operations fall into two categories: peace-keeping forces and observer missions. Peace-keeping forces are composed of contingents of military and civilian personnel, made available by member states. These forces assist in preventing the recurrence of fighting, restoring and maintaining peace, and promoting a return to normal conditions. To this end, peace-keeping forces are authorized as necessary to undertake negotiations, persuasion, observation and fact-finding. They conduct patrols and interpose physically between the opposing parties. Peace-keeping forces are permitted to use their weapons only in self-defence.

Military observer missions are composed of officers (usually unarmed), who are made available, on the Secretary-General's request, by member states. A mission's function is to observe and report to the Secretary-General (who, in turn, informs the Security Council) on the maintenance of a cease-fire, to investigate violations and to do what it can to improve the situation. Peace-keeping forces and observer missions must at all times maintain complete impartiality and avoid any action that might affect the claims or positions of the parties.

The UN's peace-keeping forces and observer missions are financed in most cases by assessed contributions from member states of the organization. In recent years a significant expansion in the UN's peace-keeping activities has been accompanied by a perpetual financial crisis within the organization, as a result of the increased financial burden and some member states' delaying payment. At 31 May 2008 outstanding assessed contributions to the peace-keeping budget amounted to some US $1,800m.

By August 2008 the UN had deployed a total of 63 peace-keeping operations, of which 13 were authorized in the period 1948–88 and 50 since 1988. At 30 April 2008 118 countries were contributing some 88,202 uniformed personnel to the ongoing operations, of whom 74,429 were peace-keeping troops, 11,236 civilian police and 2,539 military observers.

In 2008 the Department of Peace-keeping Operations was directly supporting three political and peace-building missions (in addition to those maintained by the Department of Political Affairs): the UN Assistance Mission in Afghanistan (established in March 2002), the UN Integrated Office in Sierra Leone (established in January 2006 as a successor to the UN peace-keeping operation in that country), and the UN Integrated Office in Burundi (established in January 2007, again succeeding a UN peace-keeping operation).

## UNITED NATIONS MILITARY OBSERVER GROUP IN INDIA AND PAKISTAN—UNMOGIP

**Address:** Rawalpindi, Pakistan (November–April), Srinagar, India (May–October).

**Head of Mission and Chief Military Observer:** Brig.-Gen. MATS WIGSELIUS (Sweden) (acting).

The Group was established in 1948 by UN Security Council resolutions aiming to restore peace in the region of Jammu and Kashmir, the status of which had become a matter of dispute between the Governments of India and Pakistan. Following a cease-fire which came into effect in January 1949, the military observers of UNMOGIP were deployed to assist in its observance. There is no periodic review of UNMOGIP's mandate. In 1971, following the signature of a new cease-fire agreement, India claimed that UNMOGIP's mandate had lapsed, since it was originally intended to monitor the agreement reached in 1949. Pakistan, however, regarded UNMOGIP's mission as unchanged, and the Group's activities have continued, although they have been somewhat restricted on the Indian side of the 'line of control', which was agreed by India and Pakistan in 1972.

At 31 May 2008 there were 45 military observers deployed on both sides of the 'line of control'; it is supported by 71 international and local civilian personnel. The approved budget for the operation for the period 2008–09 was US $17.0m.

# United Nations Peace-building

**Address:** Department of Political Affairs, United Nations, New York, NY 10017, USA.

**Telephone:** (212) 963-1234; **fax:** (212) 963-4879; **internet:** www.un.org/Depts/dpa/.

The Department of Political Affairs provides support and guidance to UN peace-building operations and political missions working in the field to prevent and resolve conflicts or to promote enduring peace in post-conflict societies. The UN Assistance Mission in Afghanistan, UN Integrated Office in Sierra Leone and UN Integrated Office in Burundi are directed by the Department of Peace-keeping Operations.

The World Summit of UN heads of state held in September 2005 approved recommendations made by the UN Secretary-General in his March 2005 report entitled 'In Larger Freedom: Towards Development, Security and Human Rights for All' for the creation of an intergovernmental advisory Peace-building Commission. In December the UN Security Council and General Assembly authorized the establishment of the Commission; it was inaugurated, as a special subsidiary body of both the Council and Assembly, in June 2006. A multi-year standing peace-building fund, financed by voluntary contributions from member states and mandated to support post-conflict peace-building activities, was established in October 2006. A Peace-building Support Office was established within the UN Secretariat to administer the fund, as well as to support the Commission. At August 2008 the Peace-building Commission was actively concerned with the situation in four African countries: Burundi, Central African Republic, Liberia, and Guinea-Bissau.

In December 2007 a new United Nations Regional Centre for Preventive Diplomacy for Central Asia (UNRCCA) was inaugurated in Ashgabat, Turkmenistan, which was to be administered by the Department of Political Affairs.

## UNITED NATIONS ASSISTANCE MISSION IN AFGHANISTAN—UNAMA

**Address:** POB 5858, Grand Central Station, New York, NY 10163-5858, USA.

**Telephone:** (813) 246000; **fax:** (831) 246069; **e-mail:** spokesperson-unama@un.org; **internet:** www.unama-afg.org.

**Special Representative of the UN Secretary-General:** KAI EIDE (Norway).

The United Nations Assistance Mission in Afghanistan (UNAMA) was established by the UN Security Council in March 2002. UNAMA's mandate has subsequently been renewed annually. The Mission was initially authorized to fulfil tasks assigned to the UN under the December 2001 Bonn Agreement on provisional arrangements for Afghanistan. Following the termination in September 2005 of the process determined by the Bonn Agreement, and the adoption of the Afghanistan Compact by the London Conference on Afghanistan, co-chaired by the UN and Afghanistan from 31 January–1 February 2006, UNAMA is responsible for assisting Afghanistan's Government with the implementation of the Afghanistan Compact. The Compact represents a framework for co-operation between the Afghan authorities, the UN and the international community until end-2010. The Compact identifies three key and interdependent pillars of activity for its term: security; governance, rule of law and human rights; and economic and social development. In addition, the Compact will also focus on the elimination of Afghanistan's narcotics industry. The Mission is also mandated to provide political and strategic advice for the peace process; provide good offices; promote human rights; provide technical assistance; and, in co-operation with the Afghan authorities, to manage all UN humanitarian relief, recovery, reconstruction and development activities. Peace-building tasks that fall under UNAMA's political mandate include the prevention and resolution of conflicts; building confidence and the promotion of national reconciliation; monitoring the political and human rights situation; and investigating human rights violations. As appropriate, UNAMA is charged with recommending corrective actions; maintaining dialogue with Afghan leaders, political parties, civil society groups, institutions and representatives of the central authorities; and undertaking good offices to foster the peace process. The implementation of the Bonn Agreement during the transitional period included the following institutional measures: emergency Loya Jirga (2002); constitutional Loya Jirga (2004); presidential elections (2004); legislative elections (2005). Nineteen UN agencies work together with their Afghan government counterparts and with national and international NGO partners. UNAMA co-ordinates all of the activities of the UN system, whose programme of work is determined by Afghan needs and priorities.

At 31 July 2008 UNAMA comprised 17 military observers, three police officers and 40 UN Volunteers; at 31 May there were, in addition, 222 international civilian and 1,104 local civilian personnel. In time, as part of its pursuit of strong, sustainable Afghan institutions, UNAMA aims to appoint Afghan nationals to posts that have traditionally been occupied by expatriates.

## UNITED NATIONS MISSION IN NEPAL—UNMIN

**Address:** Birendra International Convention Center (BICC) Complex, New Baneshwor, Kathmandu, Nepal.

**Telephone:** (1) 5010036; **fax:** (1) 5010040; **e-mail:** info@unmin.org.np; **internet:** www.unmin.org.np.

**Special Representative of the UN Secretary-General and Head of Office:** IAN MARTIN (United Kingdom).

The United Nations Mission in Nepal (UNMIN), authorized by a resolution of the UN Security Council in January 2007, is mandated to monitor the cease-fire and assist, through technical support and monitoring activities, with the election of a Constituent Assembly as provided for under the Comprehensive Peace Agreement concluded between the Nepalese Government and the Communist Party of Nepal (Maoist) in November 2006. UNMIN also chairs the Joint Monitoring Co-ordinating Committee, comprising members of the Nepalese armed forces and Maoist forces, which is the mechanism for co-ordinating decisions related to monitoring the management of arms and armed personnel. Arms monitors maintain a presence at the main Maoist army cantonment sites and at the main Nepalese army barracks. During 2007 UNMIN arms monitors also completed the verification and registration of Maoist armed personnel. Mine experts advise on the safe storage and destruction of anti-personnel devices. Civil affairs officers are mandated to assist the process of re-establishment of local governance and public security, and encourage local dialogue to promote peace-building. Specialized officers in each region have been appointed to monitor and advise upon child protection and to encourage the inclusion of women and other marginalized groups in the democratic process. UNMIN works closely with the Office of the United Nations High Commissioner for Human Rights (OHCHR) to monitor the human rights situation in the country. The election of a Constituent Assembly was postponed twice in 2007, having first been scheduled to be held in June, and later in November. A new date, of 10 April 2008, was agreed upon by the main political parties in December 2007. UNMIN undertook fully to deploy electoral advisors throughout the regions and to monitor compliance with the cease-fire code of conduct. In early March 2008 10 people were killed when an UNMIN helicopter crashed in eastern Nepal. The general election was conducted in the following month, as scheduled. UNMIN provided technical assistance to the Electoral Commission in all 75 districts of the country and operated mobile civil affairs teams (alongside OHCHR human rights officers) in 45 districts. In addition, arms monitors operated mobile patrols from the mission's five regional headquarters. The inaugural meeting of the country's new Constituent Assembly was convened in late May. In July UNMIN's five regional headquarters were closed and the mission began to scale down its operations. The Head of Office, Ian Martin, affirmed that UNMIN remained committed to supporting the country's transition to democratic governance and to its long-term development.

At 31 July 2008 UNMIN comprised 72 military observers, five police officers and 106 UN Volunteers; at 31 May there were, in addition, 203 international civilian and 337 local civilian personnel. A budget of US $88.8m. was approved for the Mission in 2007.

# World Food Programme—WFP

**Address:** Via Cesare Giulio Viola 68, Parco dei Medici, 00148 Rome, Italy.

**Telephone:** (06) 65131; **fax:** (06) 6513-2840; **e-mail:** wfpinfo@wfp.org; **internet:** www.wfp.org.

WFP, the principal food aid organization of the United Nations, became operational in 1963. It aims to alleviate acute hunger by providing emergency relief following natural or man-made humanitarian disasters, and supplies food aid to people in developing countries to eradicate chronic undernourishment, to support social development and to promote self-reliant communities.

## Organization

(August 2008)

### EXECUTIVE BOARD

The governing body of WFP is the Executive Board, comprising 36 members, 18 of whom are elected by the UN Economic and Social Council (ECOSOC) and 18 by the Council of the Food and Agriculture Organization (FAO). The Board meets four times each year at WFP headquarters.

### SECRETARIAT

WFP's Executive Director is appointed jointly by the UN Secretary-General and the Director-General of FAO and is responsible for the management and administration of the Programme. In 2006 there were 10,587 staff members, of whom nearly 92% were working in the field. WFP administers some 87 country offices, in order to provide operational, financial and management support at a more local level, and maintains six regional bureaux, located in Bangkok, Thailand (for Asia), Cairo, Egypt (for the Middle East, Central Asia and Eastern Europe), Panama City, Panama (for Latin America and the Caribbean), Johannesburg, South Africa (for Southern Africa), Kampala, Uganda (for Central and Eastern Africa), and Dakar, Senegal (for West Africa).

**Executive Director:** JOSETTE SHEERAN (USA).

## Activities

WFP is the only multilateral organization with a mandate to use food aid as a resource. It is the second largest source of assistance in the UN, after the World Bank group, in terms of actual transfers of resources, and the largest source of grant aid in the UN system. WFP handles more than one-third of the world's food aid. WFP is also the largest contributor to South–South trade within the UN system, through the purchase of food and services from developing countries. WFP's mission is to provide food aid to save lives in refugee and other emergency situations, to improve the nutrition and quality of life of vulnerable groups and to help to develop assets and promote the self-reliance of poor families and communities. WFP aims to focus its efforts on the world's poorest countries and to provide at least 90% of its total assistance to those designated as 'low-income food-deficit'. At the World Food Summit, held in November 1996, WFP endorsed the commitment to reduce by 50% the number of undernourished people, no later than 2015. During 2007 WFP food assistance benefited some 86.1m. people (including 53.6m. children) in 80 countries, of whom 23.8m. received aid through development projects, 15.3m. through emergency operations, and 47.0m. through Protracted Relief and Recovery Operations (PRROs). Total food deliveries in 2007 amounted to 3.3m. metric tons. WFP rations comprise basic food items (cereals, oil and pulses), and, where possible, additional complementary items (such as meat or fish, vegetables, fruit, fortified cereal blends, sugar and condiments).

WFP aims to address the causes of chronic malnourishment, which it identifies as poverty and lack of opportunity. It emphasizes the role played by women in combating hunger, and endeavours to address the specific nutritional needs of women, to increase their access to food and development resources, and to promote girls' education. It also focuses resources on supporting the food security of households and communities affected by HIV/AIDS and on promoting food security as a means of mitigating extreme poverty and vulnerability and thereby combating the spread and impact of HIV/AIDS. In February 2003 WFP and the Joint UN Programme on HIV/AIDS (UNAIDS) concluded an agreement to address jointly the relationship between HIV/AIDS, regional food shortages and chronic hunger, with a particular focus on Africa, South-East Asia and the Caribbean. In October of that year WFP became a co-sponsor of UNAIDS. WFP urges the development of new food aid strategies as a means of redressing global inequalities and thereby combating the threat of conflict and international terrorism.

WFP food donations must meet internationally-agreed standards applicable to trade in food products. In May 2003 WFP's Executive Board approved a policy on donations of genetically modified (GM) foods and other foods derived from biotechnology, determining that the Programme would continue to accept donations of GM/biotech food and that, when distributing it, relevant national standards would be respected.

WFP participated in the High-Level Conference on World Food Security and the Challenges of Climate Change and Bioenergy that was convened by FAO in June 2008 to address the impact of soaring levels of food and fuel prices in recent months. At that time WFP determined to allocate some US $1,200m in extra-budgetary funds to alleviate hunger in 62 worst-affected countries. In mid-June WFP's Executive Board approved a four-year strategic plan that aimed to provide a new institutional framework to support vulnerable populations affected by the ongoing global food crisis and by possible future effects of global climate change. The plan emphasised prevention of hunger through early warning systems and analysis, local purchase of food, the use of focused cash and voucher programmes to ensure the accessibility to hungry people of already locally available food, and the maintenance of efficient and effective emergency response systems.

Since the 1990s WFP has developed a range of mechanisms to enhance its preparedness for emergency situations (such as conflict, drought and other natural disasters) and to improve its capacity for responding effectively to crises as they arise. A new programme of emergency response training was inaugurated in 2000, while security concerns for personnel was incorporated as a new element into all general planning and training activities. Through its Vulnerability Analysis and Mapping (VAM) project, WFP aims to identify potentially vulnerable groups by providing information on food security and the capacity of different groups for coping with shortages, and to enhance emergency contingency-planning and long-term assistance objectives. In 2008 VAM field units were operational in more than 50 countries.

Since 2003 WFP has been mandated to provide aviation transport services to the wider humanitarian community. The key elements of WFP's emergency response capacity are its strategic stores of food and logistics equipment, stand-by arrangements to enable the rapid deployment of personnel, communications and other essential equipment, and the Augmented Logistics Intervention Team for Emergencies (ALITE), which undertakes capacity assessments and contingency-planning. During 2000 WFP led efforts, undertaken with other UN humanitarian agencies, for the design and application of local UN Joint Logistics Centre facilities, which aimed to co-ordinate resources in an emergency situation. In 2001 a UN Humanitarian Response Depot was opened in Brindisi, Italy, under the direction of WFP experts, for the storage of essential rapid response equipment. In that year the Programme published a set of guidelines on contingency planning. During 2005 the UN's Inter-Agency Standing Committee (IASC), concerned with co-ordinating the international response to humanitarian disasters, developed a concept of organizing agency assistance to IDPs through the institutionalization of a 'Cluster Approach', currently comprising 11 core areas of activity. WFP was designated the lead agency for the clusters on Emergency Telecommunications (jointly with OCHA and UNICEF) and Logistics. During January 2008–June 2009 WFP was implementing a special operation to improve country-specific communications services in order to enhance country-level cluster capacities.

Through its development activities, WFP aims to alleviate poverty in developing countries by promoting self-reliant families and communities. Food is supplied, for example, as an incentive in development self-help schemes and as part-wages in labour-intensive projects of many kinds. In all its projects WFP aims to assist the most vulnerable groups and to ensure that beneficiaries have an adequate and balanced diet. Activities supported by the Programme include the settlement and resettlement of groups and communities; land reclamation and improvement; irrigation; the development of forestry and dairy farming; road construction; training of hospital staff; community development; and human resources development such as feeding expectant or nursing mothers and school children, and support for education, training and health programmes. No individual country is permitted to receive more than 10% of the Programme's available development resources. During 2001 WFP initiated a new Global School Feeding Campaign to strengthen international co-operation to expand educational opportunities for poor children and to improve the quality of the teaching environment. In 2003 WFP launched a *19-Cents-a-day* campaign to encourage donors to support its school feeding activities (19 US cents being the estimated cost of one school lunch). During 2007 school feeding projects benefited 19.3m. children.

Following a comprehensive evaluation of its activities, WFP is increasingly focused on linking its relief and development activities to provide a continuum between short-term relief and longer-term rehabilitation and development. In order to achieve this objective, WFP aims to integrate elements that strengthen disaster mitigation into development projects, including soil conservation, reafforestation, irrigation infrastructure, and transport construction and rehabilitation; and to promote capacity-building elements within relief operations, e.g. training, income-generating activities and environmental protection measures. In 1999 WFP adopted a new Food Aid and Development policy, which aims to use food assistance both to cover immediate requirements and to create conditions conducive to enhancing the long-term food security of vulnerable populations. During that year WFP began implementing PRROs, where the emphasis is on fostering stability, rehabilitation and long-term development for victims of natural disasters, displaced persons and refugees. PRROs are introduced no later than 18 months after the initial emergency operation and last no more than three years. When undertaken in collaboration with UNHCR and other international agencies, WFP has responsibility for mobilizing basic food commodities and for related transport, handling and storage costs. Some 31 new PRROs were approved in 2007.

In 2007 WFP operational expenditure in Asia amounted to US $484.7m. (18% of total operational expenditure in that year), including $320.5m. for emergency relief operations, $28.1m. for special operations, and $121.6m. for agricultural, rural and human resource development projects.

WFP has been active in Afghanistan, where severe drought and conflict have caused massive food insecurity and population displacement. WFP is currently implementing a PRRO covering the period 1 January 2006–31 December 2008, extending support to an estimated 6.6m. Afghans. The operation aims to provide rations to vulnerable individuals (e.g. IDPs, TB patients and their families, school children, teachers and illiterate people) in food-insecure areas, through food-for-work, food-for-training and food-for-education activities, in partnership with the Afghanistan Government and with other organizations. Capacity-building support to national agencies is incorporated into the PRRO. In January 2008 WFP appealed for US $77m. to finance food assistance which, during March–June, it targeted at some 1.4m. Afghans in rural areas, and 1.1m. inhabitants of urban areas of Afghanistan, who were suffering the effects of soaring global commodity prices. In March 2008 WFP raised the budget of the ongoing PRRO to $450.4m. (from $213.6m.) to cover additional food costs incurred owing to the food price crisis. In response to the devastation to southern Bangladesh caused by Cyclone Sidr in November 2007, WFP was implementing during November 2007–December 2008 a $73.8m. emergency operation to provide food assistance and recovery activities for 2.2m. Bangladeshis. An 18-month PRRO covering the period June 2007–December 2008 targeted 1.3m. post-conflict food-insecure people in Nepal. During October 2007–September 2009 a PRRO was under way to assist 507,000 individuals in food-insecure households in Balochistan and the Federally-Administered Tribal Areas of Pakistan.

Following a massive earthquake in the Indian Ocean in December 2004, which caused a series of tidal waves, or tsunamis, that devastated coastal regions in 14 countries in South and South-East Asia and East Africa, initial WFP emergency operations were funded from the Immediate Response Account (see below). In January 2005 WFP requested emergency funding of US $256m., of which $185m. was to support an initial six-month programme to provide food aid to 2m. people affected by the natural disaster, mainly in Sri Lanka, the Maldives and Indonesia, and $72m. was for three Special Operations, concerned with logistics augmentation, air support and the establishment of a UN Joint Logistics Centre for Inter-Agency Co-ordination, of which WFP was the lead agency. In Indonesia (close to the epicentre of the earthquake) WFP established new field offices and an Emergency Operations Centre in the capital, Jakarta. From mid-2005 WFP focused its activities, increasingly, on recovery and rebuilding communities.

## Finance

The Programme is funded by voluntary contributions from donor countries, intergovernmental bodies such as the European Commission, and the private sector. Contributions are made in the form of commodities, finance and services (particularly shipping). Commitments to the International Emergency Food Reserve (IEFR), from which WFP provides the majority of its food supplies, and to the Immediate Response Account of the IEFR (IRA), are also made on a voluntary basis by donors. WFP's operational expenditures in 2007 amounted to some US $2,753m. Contributions by donors in that year totalled $2,705m.

## Publications

*Annual Report.*
*Food and Nutrition Handbook.*
*School Feeding Handbook.*
*World Hunger Series.*

# Food and Agriculture Organization of the United Nations—FAO

**Address:** Viale delle Terme di Caracalla, 00100 Rome, Italy.

**Telephone:** (06) 5705-1; **fax:** (06) 5705-3152; **e-mail:** fao-hq@fao.org; **internet:** www.fao.org.

FAO, the first specialized agency of the UN to be founded after the Second World War, aims to alleviate malnutrition and hunger, and serves as a co-ordinating agency for development programmes in the whole range of food and agriculture, including forestry and fisheries. It helps developing countries to promote educational and training facilities and to create appropriate institutions.

## Organization

(August 2008)

### CONFERENCE

The governing body is the FAO Conference of member nations. It meets every two years, formulates policy, determines the organization's programme and budget on a biennial basis, and elects new members. It also elects the Director-General of the Secretariat and the Independent Chairman of the Council. Regional conferences are also held each year.

### COUNCIL

The FAO Council is composed of representatives of 49 member nations, elected by the Conference for rotating three-year terms. It is the interim governing body of FAO between sessions of the Conference. There are eight main Governing Committees of the Council: the Finance and Programme Committees, and the Committees on Commodity Problems, Fisheries, Agriculture, Forestry, World Food Security, and Constitutional and Legal Matters.

### SECRETARIAT

There are some 3,600 FAO staff, of whom about one-half are based at headquarters. FAO maintains five regional offices (see below), nine sub-regional offices, five liaison offices (in Yokohama, Japan; Washington, DC, USA, liaison with North America; Geneva, Switzerland and New York, USA, with the UN; and Brussels, Belgium, with the European Union), and some 74 country offices. Work is undertaken by the following departments: Agriculture and Consumer Protection; Economic and Social Development; Fisheries and Aquaculture; Forestry; Human, Financial and Physical Resources; Knowledge and Communication; Natural Resource Management and Environment; and Technical Co-operation.

**Director-General:** JACQUES DIOUF (Senegal).

### REGIONAL OFFICE

**Asia and the Pacific:** Maliwan Mansion, 39 Phra Atit Rd, Bangkok 10200, Thailand; tel. (2) 697-4000; fax (2) 697-4445; e-mail fao-rap@fao.org; internet www.fao.org/world/regional/rap/; Regional Rep. HE CHANGCHUI.

## Activities

FAO aims to raise levels of nutrition and standards of living by improving the production and distribution of food and other commodities derived from farms, fisheries and forests. FAO's ultimate objective is the achievement of world food security, 'Food for All'. The organization provides technical information, advice and assistance by disseminating information; acting as a neutral forum for discussion of food and agricultural issues; advising governments on policy and planning; and developing capacity directly in the field.

In November 1996 FAO hosted the World Food Summit, which was held in Rome and was attended by heads of state and senior government representatives of 186 countries. Participants approved the Rome Declaration on World Food Security and the World Food Summit Plan of Action, with the aim of halving the number of people afflicted by undernutrition, at that time estimated to total 828m. world-wide, by no later than 2015. A review conference to assess progress in achieving the goals of the summit, entitled World Food Summit: Five Years Later, held in June 2002, reaffirmed commitment to this objective, which is also incorporated into the UN Millennium Development Goals (MDGs). During that month FAO announced the formulation of a global 'Anti-Hunger Programme', which aimed to promote investment in the agricultural sector and rural development, with a particular focus on small-scale farmers, and to enhance food access for those most in need, for example through the provision of school meals, schemes to feed pregnant and nursing mothers and food-for-work programmes. FAO hosts the UN System Network on Rural Development and Food Security, comprising some 20 UN bodies, which was established in 1997 as an interagency mechanism to follow-up the World Food Summits.

In November 1999 the FAO Conference approved a long-term Strategic Framework for the period 2000–15, which emphasized national and international co-operation in pursuing the goals of the 1996 World Food Summit. The Framework promoted interdisciplinarity and partnership, and defined three main global objectives: constant access by all people to sufficient, nutritionally adequate and safe food to ensure that levels of undernourishment were reduced by 50% by 2015 (see above); the continued contribution of sustainable agriculture and rural development to economic and social progress and well-being; and the conservation, improvement and sustainable use of natural resources. It identified five corporate strategies (each supported by several strategic objectives), covering the following areas: reducing food insecurity and rural poverty; ensuring enabling policy and regulatory frameworks for food, agriculture, fisheries and forestry; creating sustainable increases in the supply and availability of agricultural, fisheries and forestry products; conserving and enhancing sustainable use of the natural resource base; and generating knowledge. In October 2007 the report of an Independent External Evaluation into the role and functions of FAO recommended that the organization elaborate an immediate action plan for reform to ensure its continued efficiency and effectiveness.

In April 2008 the UN Secretary-General appointed FAO's Director-General as Vice-Chairman of a High Level Task Force (HLTF) on the Global Food Security Crisis, which aimed to address the impact of soaring levels of food and fuel prices in recent months and formulate a comprehensive framework for action.

World Food Day, commemorating the foundation of FAO, is held annually on 16 October.

### AGRICULTURE AND CONSUMER PROTECTION

FAO's overall objective is to lead international efforts to counter hunger and to improve levels of nutrition. Within this context FAO is concerned to improve crop and grassland productivity and to develop sustainable agricultural systems to provide for enhanced food security and economic development. It provides member countries with technical advice for plant improvement, the application of plant biotechnology, the development of integrated production systems and rational grassland management. There are groups concerned with the main field cereal crops, i.e. rice, maize and wheat, which *inter alia* identify means of enhancing production, collect and analyse relevant data and promote collaboration between research institutions, government bodies and other farm management organizations. In 1985 and 1990 FAO's International Rice Commission endorsed the use of hybrid rice, which had been developed in the People's Republic of China, as a means of meeting growing demand for the crop, in particular in the Far East, and has subsequently assisted member countries to acquire the necessary technology and training to develop hybrid rice production. In Africa FAO has collaborated with the West African Rice Development Association to promote and facilitate the use of new rice varieties and crop management practices. FAO is the lead agency for the International Year of the Potato (2008), which aims to highlight the importance of the potato in combating world hunger.

FAO is also concerned with the development and diversification of horticultural and industrial crops, for example oil seeds, fibres and medicinal plants. FAO collects and disseminates data regarding crop trials and new technologies. It has developed an information processing site, Ecocrop, to help farmers identify appropriate crops and environmental requirements. FAO works to protect and support the sustainable development of grasslands and pasture, which contribute to the livelihoods of an estimated 800m. people world-wide.

FAO's plant protection service incorporates a range of programmes concerned with the control of pests and the use of pesticides. In February 2001 FAO warned that some 30% of pesticides sold in developing countries did not meet internationally accepted quality standards. In November 2002 FAO adopted a revised International Code of Conduct on the Distribution and Use of Pesticides (first adopted in 1985) to reduce the inappropriate distribution and use of pesticides and other toxic compounds, particularly in developing countries. In September 1998 a new legally-binding treaty on trade in hazardous chemicals and pesticides was adopted at an international conference held in Rotterdam, Netherlands. The so-called Rotterdam Convention required that hazardous chemicals and pesticides banned or severely restricted in at least two countries should not be exported unless explicitly agreed by the importing country. It also identified certain pesticide formulations as too dangerous to be used by farmers in developing countries, and incorporated an obligation that countries halt national production of those hazardous compounds. The treaty entered into force in February 2004. FAO was co-operating with UNEP to provide an interim secretariat for the Convention. FAO has promoted the use of Integrated Pest Management (IPM) initiatives to encourage the use, at local level, of safer and more effective methods of pest control, such as biological control methods and natural predators.

FAO hosts the secretariat of the International Plant Protection Convention (first adopted in 1951, revised in 1997) which aims to prevent the spread of plant pests and to promote effective control measures. The secretariat helps to define phytosanitary standards, promote the exchange of information and extend technical assistance to contracting parties (169 at May 2008).

FAO is concerned with the conservation and sustainable use of plant and animal genetic resources. It works with regional and international associations to develop seed networks, to encourage the use of improved seed production systems, to elaborate quality control and certification mechanisms and to co-ordinate seed security activities, in particular in areas prone to natural or man-made disasters. FAO has developed a World Information and Early Warning System (WIEWS) to gather and disseminate information concerning plant genetic resources for food and agriculture and to undertake periodic assessments of the state of those resources. FAO is also developing, as part of the WIEWS, a Seed Information Service to extend information to member states on seeds, planting and new technologies. In June 1996 representatives of more than 150 governments convened in Leipzig, Germany, at an International Technical Conference organized by FAO to consider the use and conservation of plant genetic resources as an essential means of enhancing food security. The meeting adopted a Global Plan of Action, which included measures to strengthen the development of plant varieties and to promote the use and availability of local varieties and locally adapted crops to farmers, in particular following a natural disaster, war or civil conflict. In November 2001 the FAO Conference adopted the International Treaty on Plant Genetic Resources for Food and Agriculture, which was to provide a framework to ensure access to plant genetic resources and to related knowledge, technologies and funding. The Treaty entered into force in June 2004, having received the required number of ratifications, and the first meeting of the Treaty's Governing Body was convened in June 2006. At mid-2008 some 54 states had acceded to the Treaty.

FAO's Animal Production and Health Division is concerned with the control and management of major animal diseases, and, in recent years, with safeguarding humans from livestock diseases. Other programmes are concerned with the contribution of livestock to poverty alleviation, the efficient use of natural resources in livestock production, the management of animal genetic resources, promoting the exchange of information and mapping the distribution of livestock around the world. In 2001 FAO established a Pro-Poor Livestock Policy Initiative to support the formulation and implementation of livestock-related policies to improve the livelihood and nutrition of the world's rural poor, with an initial focus on the Andean region, the Horn of Africa, West Africa, South Asia and the Mekong.

The Emergency Prevention System for Transboundary Animal and Plant Pests and Diseases (EMPRES) was established in 1994 to strengthen FAO's activities in the prevention, early warning, control and, where possible, eradication of pests and highly contagious livestock diseases (which the system categorizes as epidemic diseases of strategic importance, such as rinderpest or foot-and-mouth; diseases requiring tactical attention at international or regional level, e.g. Rift Valley fever; and emerging diseases, e.g. bovine spongiform encephalopathy—BSE). EMPRES has a desert locust component, and has published guidelines on all aspects of desert locust monitoring. FAO has assumed responsibility for technical leadership and co-ordination of the Global Rinderpest Eradication Programme (GREP), which has the objective of eliminating the disease by 2010. In November 1997 FAO initiated a Programme Against African Trypanosomiasis, which aimed to counter the disease affecting cattle in almost one-third of Africa. In November 2004 FAO established a specialized Emergency Centre for Transboundary Animal Disease Operations (ECTAD) to enhance FAO's role in assisting member states to combat animal disease outbreaks and in co-ordinating international efforts to research, monitor and control transboundary disease crises. In May 2004 FAO and the World Organisation for Animal Health (OIE) signed an agreement to clarify their respective areas of competence and improve co-operation, in response to an increase in contagious transboundary animal diseases (such as foot-and-mouth disease and avian influenza, see below). The two bodies agreed to establish a global framework on the control of transboundary animal diseases, entailing improved international collaboration and circulation of information. In early 2006 the Global Early Warning and Response System for Major Animal Diseases, including Zoonoses (GLEWS), was established by FAO, OIE and the World Health Organization (WHO) to strengthen their joint capacity to detect, monitor and respond to animal disease threats.

In September 2004 FAO and WHO declared an ongoing epidemic in certain east Asian countries of the H5N1 strain of highly pathogenic avian influenza (HPAI) to be a 'crisis of global importance': the disease was spreading rapidly through bird populations and was also transmitting to human populations through contact with diseased birds (mainly poultry). In that month FAO published *Recommendations for the Prevention, Control and Eradication of Highly Pathogenic Avian Influenza in Asia*. In April 2005 FAO and OIE established an international network of laboratories and scientists (OFFLU) to exchange data and provide expert technical advise on avian influenza. In the following month FAO, with WHO and OIE, launched a global strategy for the progressive control of the disease. In November a conference on Avian Influenza and Human Pandemic Influenza, jointly organized by FAO, WHO and OIE and the World Bank, issued a plan of action identifying a number of responses, including: supporting the development of integrated national plans for H5N1 containment and human pandemic influenza preparedness and response; assisting countries with the aggressive control of H5N1 and with establishing a more detailed understanding of the role of wild birds in virus transmission; nominating rapid response teams of experts to support epidemiological field investigations; expanding national and regional capacity in surveillance, diagnosis, and alert and response systems; expanding the network of influenza laboratories; establishing multi-country networks for the control or prevention of animal transboundary diseases; expanding the global antiviral stockpile; strengthening veterinary infrastructures; and mapping a global strategy and work plan for co-ordinating antiviral and influenza vaccine research and development. In June 2006 FAO and OIE convened a scientific conference on the spread of H5N1 that advocated as a basis for H5N1 management early detection of the disease in wild birds, improved biosecurity and hygiene in the poultry trade, rapid response to disease outbreaks, and the establishment of a global tracking and monitoring facility involving participation by all relevant organizations, as well as by scientific centres, farmers' groupings, bird-watchers and hunters, and wildlife and wild bird habitat conservation bodies. The conference also urged investment in telemetry/satellite technology to improve tracking capabilities. International conference and pledging meetings on the disease have been convened in Beijing, People's Republic of China (PRC), in January 2006, Bamako, Mali, in December and in New Delhi, India, in December 2007. In January 2008 FAO warned that the virus remained a global threat with recent outbreaks confirmed in Bangladesh, Benin, PRC, Egypt, Germany, India, Indonesia, Iran, Israel, Myanmar, Poland, Russia, Ukraine, Turkey and Viet Nam. In August a new strain of HPAI not previously recorded in sub-Saharan Africa was detected in Nigeria.

In December 1992 FAO, with WHO, organized an International Conference on Nutrition, which approved a World Declaration on Nutrition and a Plan of Action, aimed at promoting efforts to combat malnutrition as a development priority. Since the conference, more than 100 countries have formulated national plans of action for nutrition, many of which were based on existing development plans such as comprehensive food security initiatives, national poverty alleviation programmes and action plans to attain the targets set by the World Summit for Children in September 1990. FAO promotes other efforts, at household and community level, to improve nutrition and food security, for example a programme to support home gardens. It aims to assist the identification of food insecure and vulnerable populations, both through its *State of Food Insecurity in the World* reports and taking a lead role in the development of Food Insecurity and Vulnerability Information and Mapping Systems (FIVIMS), a recommendation of the World Food Summit. In 1999 FAO signed a memorandum of understanding with UNAIDS on strengthening co-operation to combat the threat posed by the HIV/AIDS epidemic to food security, nutrition and rural livelihoods. FAO is committed to incorporating HIV/AIDS into food security and livelihood projects, to strengthening community care and to highlighting the importance of nutrition in the care of those living with HIV/AIDS.

FAO is committed to promoting food quality and safety in all different stages of food production and processing. It supports the development of integrated food control systems by member states, which incorporate aspects of food control management, inspection, risk analysis and quality assurance. The joint FAO/WHO Codex Alimentarius Commission, established in 1962, aims to protect the health of consumers, ensure fair trade practices and promote the co-ordination of food standards activities at an international level. In January 2001 a joint team of FAO and WHO experts issued a report concerning the allergenicity of foods derived from biotechnology (i.e. genetically modified—GM—foods). In July the Codex Alimentarius Commission agreed the first global principles for assessing the safety of GM foods, and approved a series of maximum levels of environmental contaminants in food. In June 2004 FAO published guidelines for assessing possible risks posed to plants by living modified organisms (LMOs). In July 2001 the Codex Alimentarius Commission adopted guidelines on organic livestock production, covering organic breeding methods, the elimination of growth hormones and certain chemicals in veterinary medicines, and the use of good quality organic feed with no meat or bone meal content. In January 2003 FAO organized a technical consultation on biological risk management in food and agriculture which recognized the need for a more integrated approach to so-called biosecurity, i.e. the prevention, control and management of risks to animal, human and plant life and health. FAO has subsequently developed a *Toolkit*, which was published in 2007, to help countries to develop and implement national biosecurity systems and to enhance biosecurity capacity. In October 2006 FAO inaugurated a new Crisis Management Centre (CMC) to co-ordinate the organization's response to outbreaks of H5N1 and other major emergencies related to animal or food health.

FAO aims to assist member states to enhance the efficiency, competitiveness and profitability of their agricultural and food enterprises. FAO extends assistance in training, capacity building and the formulation of agribusiness development strategies. It promotes the development of effective 'value chains' connecting primary producers with consumers and supports other linkages within the agribusiness industry. Similarly, FAO aims to strengthen marketing systems, links between producers and retailers and training in agricultural marketing and works to improve the regulatory framework for agricultural marketing. FAO promotes the use of new machinery and technologies to increase agricultural production and extends a range of services to support mechanization, including training, maintenance, testing and the promotion of labour saving technologies. Other programmes are focused on farm management, post-harvest management, food and non-food processing, rural finance, and rural infrastructure. FAO helps reduce immediate post-harvest losses, with the introduction of improved processing methods and storage systems. FAO participates in PhAction, a forum of 12 agencies that was established in 1999 to promote post-harvest research and the development of effective post-harvest services and infrastructure.

FAO's Joint Division with the International Atomic Energy Agency (IAEA) is concerned with the use of nuclear techniques in food and agriculture. It co-ordinates research projects, provides scientific and technical support to technical co-operation projects and administers training courses. A joint laboratory in Seibersdorf, Austria, is concerned with testing biotechnologies and in developing non-toxic fertilizers (especially those that are locally available) and improved strains of food crops (especially from indigenous varieties). In the area of animal production and health, the Joint Division has developed progesterone-measuring and disease diagnostic kits. Other sub-programmes of the Joint Division are concerned with soil and water, plant breeding and nutrition, insect pest control and food and environmental protection.

## NATURAL RESOURCES MANAGEMENT AND ENVIRONMENT

FAO is committed to promoting the responsible and sustainable management of natural resources and other activities to protect the environment. FAO assists member states to mitigate the impact of climate change on agriculture, to adapt and enhance the resilience of agricultural systems to climate change, and to promote practices to reduce the emission of greenhouse gases from the agricultural sector. In recent years FAO has strengthened its work in the area of using natural biomass resources as fuel, both at grassroots level and industrial processing of cash crops. In 2006 FAO established the International Bioenergy Platform to serve as a focal point for research, data collection, capacity-building and strategy formulation by local, regional and international bodies concerned with bioenergy. FAO also serves as the secretariat for the Global Bioenergy Partnership, which was inaugurated in May 2006 to facilitate the collaboration between governments, international agencies and representatives of the private sector and civil society in the sustainable development of bioenergy. In June 2008 FAO hosted a High Level Conference on World Food Security and the Challenges of Climate Change and Bioenergy. The meeting adopted a Declaration on Food Security, urging the international donor community to increase its support to developing countries and countries with economies in transition. The Declaration also noted an urgent need to develop the agricultural sectors and expand food production in such countries and for increased investment in rural development, agriculture and agribusiness.

FAO aims to enhance the sustainability of land and water systems, and as a result to secure agricultural productivity, through the improved tenure, management, development and conservation of those natural resources. The organization promotes equitable access to land and water resources and supports integrated land and water management, including river basin management and improved irrigation systems. FAO has developed AQUASTAT as a global information system concerned with water and agricultural issues, comprising databases, country and regional profiles, surveys and maps.

Within the FAO's Natural Resources Management and Environment Department is a Research and Extension Division, which provides advisory and technical services to support national capacity-building, research, communication and education activities. It maintains several databases which support and facilitate the dissemination of information, for example relating to proven transferable technologies and biotechnologies in use in developing countries. The Division advises countries on communication strategies to strengthen agricultural and rural development, and has actively supported the use of rural radio. FAO is the UN lead agency of an initiative, 'Education for Rural People', which aims to improve the quality of and access to basic education for people living in rural areas and to raise awareness of the issue as an essential element of achieving the MDGs. The Research and Extension Division hosts the secretariat of the Global Forum on Agricultural Research, which was established in October 1996 as a collaboration of research centres, non-governmental and private sector organizations and development agencies. The Forum aims to strengthen research and promote knowledge partnerships concerned with the alleviation of poverty, the increase in food security and the sustainable use of natural resources. The Division also hosts the secretariat of the Science Council of the Consultative Group on International Agricultural Research (CGIAR), which, specifically, aims to enhance and promote the quality, relevance and impact of science within the network of CGIAR research centres and to mobilize global scientific expertise.

## FISHERIES AND AQUACULTURE

FAO aims to facilitate and secure the long-term sustainable development of fisheries and aquaculture, in both inland and marine waters, and to promote its contribution to world food security. In March 1995 a ministerial meeting of fisheries adopted the Rome Consensus on World Fisheries, which identified a need for immediate action to eliminate overfishing and to rebuild and enhance depleting fish stocks. In November the FAO Conference adopted a Code of Conduct for Responsible Fishing, which incorporated many global fisheries and aquaculture issues (including fisheries resource conservation and development, fish catches, seafood and fish processing, commercialization, trade and research) to promote the sustainable development of the sector. In February 1999 the FAO Committee on Fisheries adopted new international measures, within the framework of the Code of Conduct, in order to reduce over-exploitation of the world's fish resources, as well as plans of action for the conservation and management of sharks and the reduction in the incidental catch of seabirds in longline fisheries. The voluntary measures were endorsed at a ministerial meeting, held in March and attended by representatives of some 126 countries, which issued a declaration to promote the implementation of the Code of Conduct and to achieve sustainable management of fisheries and aquaculture. In March 2001 FAO adopted an international plan of action to address the continuing problem of so-called illegal, unreported and unregulated fishing (IUU). In that year FAO estimated that about one-half of major marine fish stocks were fully exploited, one-quarter under-exploited, at least 15% over-exploited, and 10% depleted or recovering from depletion. IUU was estimated to account for up to 30% of total catches in certain fisheries. In October FAO and the Icelandic Government jointly organized the Reykjavik Conference on Responsible Fisheries in the Marine Ecosystem, which adopted a declaration on pursuing responsible and sustainable fishing activities in the context of ecosystem-based fisheries management (EBFM). EBFM involves determining the boundaries of individual marine ecosystems, and maintaining or rebuilding the habitats and biodiversity of each of these so that all species will be supported at levels of maximum production. In March 2005 FAO's Committee of Fisheries adopted voluntary guidelines for the so-called eco-labelling and certification of fish and fish products, i.e. based on information regarding capture management and the sustainable use of resources.

FAO undertakes extensive monitoring, publishing every two years *The State of World Fisheries and Aquaculture*, and collates and maintains relevant databases. It formulates country and regional profiles and has developed a specific information network for the fisheries sector, GLOBEFISH, which gathers and disseminates information regarding market trends, tariffs and other industry issues. FAO aims to extend technical support to member states with regard to the management and conservation of aquatic resources, and other measures to improve the utilization and trade of products, including the reduction of post-harvest losses, preservation marketing and quality assurance. FAO promotes aquaculture (which contributes almost one-third of annual global fish landings) as a valuable source of animal protein and income-generating activity for rural communities. It has undertaken to develop an ecosystem approach to aquaculture (EAA) and works to integrate aquaculture with agricultural and irrigation systems. In February 2000 FAO and the Network of Aquaculture Centres in Asia and the Pacific (NACA) jointly convened a Conference on Aquaculture in the Third Millennium, which was held in Bangkok, Thailand, and attended by participants representing more than 200 governmental and non-governmental organizations. The Conference debated global trends in aquaculture and future policy measures to ensure the sustainable development of the sector. It adopted the Bangkok Declaration and Strategy for Aquaculture Beyond 2000.

## FORESTRY

FAO is committed to the sustainable management of trees, forests and forestry resources. It aims to address the critical balance of ensuring the conservation of forests and forestry resources while maximising their potential to contribute to food security and social and economic development. FAO's Strategic Plan for Forestry was approved in March 1999; its main objectives were to maintain the environmental diversity of forests, to realize the economic potential of forests and trees within a sustainable framework, and to expand access to information on forestry. In March 2007 the Committee on Forestry requested that a consultative process be initiated to develop a new strategic plan, with the intention that it be presented for discussion at the next meeting of the Committee to be held in March 2009. Regional forestry commissions were to consider the strategy at their meetings to be convened throughout 2008.

FAO assists member countries to formulate, implement and monitor national forestry programmes, and encourages the participation of all stakeholders in developing plans for the sustainable management of tree and forest resources. FAO also helps to implement national assessments of those programmes and of other forestry activities. At a global level FAO undertakes surveillance of the state of the world's forests and publishes a report every two years. A separate Forest Resources Assessment is published every five years, the latest (for 2010) was initiated in March 2008. FAO is committed to collecting and disseminating accurate information and data on forests. It maintains the Forestry Information System (FORIS) to make relevant information and forest-related databases widely accessible.

FAO is a member of the Collaborative Partnership on Forests, which was established in April 2004 on the recommendation of the UN's Economic and Social Council. FAO organizes a World Forestry Congress, generally held every six years; the next was to be convened in Buenos Aires, Argentina, in October 2009.

## ECONOMIC AND SOCIAL DEVELOPMENT

FAO provides a focal point for economic research and policy analysis relating to food security and sustainable development. It produces studies and reports on agricultural development, the impact of development programmes and projects, and the world food situation, as well as on commodity prices, trade and medium-term projections. It supports the development of methodologies and guidelines to improve research into food and agriculture and the integration of wider concepts, such as social welfare, environmental factors and nutrition, into research projects. In November 2004 the FAO Council adopted a set of voluntary Right to Food Guidelines, and established a dedicated administrative unit, that aimed to 'support the progressive realization of the right to adequate food in the context of national food security' by providing practical guidance to countries in support of their efforts to achieve the 1996 World Food Summit commitment and UN MDG relating to hunger reduction. FAO's Statistical Division assembles, analyses and disseminates statistical data on world food and agriculture and aims to ensure the consistency, broad coverage and quality of available data. The Division advises member countries on enhancing their statistical capabilities. It maintains FAOSTAT as a core database of statistical information relating to nutrition, fisheries, forestry, food production, land use, population etc. In 2004 FAO developed a new statistical framework to provide for the organization and integration of statistical data and metadata from sources within a particular country. CountrySTAT was piloted in Kenya, Kyrgyzstan and Ghana in 2005 and in 15 more developing countries in 2006/07. FAO's internet-based interactive World Agricultural Information Centre (WAICENT) offers access to agricultural publications, technical documentation, codes of conduct, data, statistics and multimedia resources. FAO compiles and co-ordinates an extensive range of international databases on agriculture, fisheries, forestry, food and statistics, the most important of these being AGRIS (the International Information System for the Agricultural Sciences and Technology) and CARIS (the Current Agricultural Research Information System). In June 2000 FAO organized a high-level Consultation on Agricultural Information Management (COAIM), which aimed to increase access to and use of agricultural information by policy-makers and others. The second COAIM was held in September 2002 and the third meeting was convened in June 2007.

FAO's Global Information and Early Warning System (GIEWS), which become operational in 1975, maintains a database on and monitors the crop and food outlook at global, regional, national and sub-national levels in order to detect emerging food supply difficulties and disasters and to ensure rapid intervention in countries experiencing food supply shortages. It publishes regular reports on the weather conditions and crop prospects in sub-Saharan Africa and in the Sahel region, issues special alerts which describe the situation in countries or sub-regions experiencing food difficulties, and recommends an appropriate international response. FAO has also supported the development and implementation of Food Insecurity and Vulnerability Information and Mapping Systems (FIVIMS) and hosts the secretariat of the inter-agency working group on development of the FIVIMS. In October 2007 FAO inaugurated an online Global Forum on Food Security and Nutrition, to contribute to the compilation and dissemination of information relating to food security and nutrition throughout the world. In August 2008 a regular report of the GIEWS identified 33 countries as being in crisis and requiring external assistance, of which 21 were in Africa, 11 in Asia and the Near East and one in Latin America and the Caribbean. All countries were identified as lacking the resources to deal with critical problems of food insecurity, including many severely affected by the high cost of food and fuel.

In July 2007 GIEWS issued a special report on the food production situation in Nepal.

### TECHNICAL CO-OPERATION

The Technical Co-operation Department has responsibility for FAO's operational activities, including policy development assistance to member countries; the mobilization of resources; investment support; field operations; emergency operations and rehabilitation; and the Technical Co-operation Programme.

FAO provides policy advice to support the formulation, implementation and evaluation of agriculture, rural development and food security strategies in member countries. It administers a project to assist developing countries to strengthen their technical negotiating skills, in respect to agricultural trade issues. FAO also aims to co-ordinate and facilitate the mobilization of extrabudgetary funds from donors and governments for particular projects. It administers a range of trust funds, including a Trust Fund for Food Security and Food Safety, established in 2002 to generate resources for projects to combat hunger, and the Government Co-operative Programme. FAO's Investment Centre, established in 1964, aims to promote greater external investment in agriculture and rural development by assisting member countries to formulate effective and sustainable projects and programmes. The Centre collaborates with international financing institutions and bilateral donors in the preparation of projects, and administers cost-sharing arrangements, with, typically, FAO funding 40% of a project. The Centre is a co-chair (with the German government) of the Global Donor Platform for Rural Development, which was established in 2004, comprising multilateral, donor and international agencies, development banks and research institutions, to improve the co-ordination and effectiveness of rural development assistance.

FAO's Technical Co-operation Programme, which was inaugurated in 1976, provides technical expertise and funding for small-scale projects to address specific issues within a country's agriculture, fisheries or forestry sectors. An Associate Professional Officers programme co-ordinates the sponsorship and placement of young professionals to gain experience working in an aspect of rural or agricultural development.

In 1994 FAO initiated the Special Programme for Food Security (SPFS), designed to assist low-income countries with a food deficit to increase food production and productivity as rapidly as possible, primarily through the widespread adoption by farmers of improved production technologies, with emphasis on areas of high potential. Within the SPFS framework are national and regional food security initiatives, all of which aim towards the MDG objective of reducing the incidence of hunger by 50% by 2015. In 2007 the SPFS was operational in 102 countries, of which 82 were categorized as 'low-income food-deficit'. The Programme promotes South-South co-operation to improve food security and the exchange of knowledge and experience. By 2007 38 bilateral co-operation agreements were in force, for example, between Egypt and Cameroon, and Viet Nam and Benin.

FAO organizes an annual series of fund-raising events, 'TeleFood', some of which are broadcast on television and the internet, in order to raise public awareness of the problems of hunger and malnutrition. Since its inception in 1997 public donations to TeleFood have reached some US $20m., financing more than 2,500 'grass-roots' projects in 130 countries. The projects have provided tools, seeds and other essential supplies directly to small-scale farmers, and have been especially aimed at helping women.

The Technical Co-operation Division co-ordinates FAO's emergency operations, concerned with all aspects of disaster and risk prevention, mitigation, reduction and emergency relief and rehabilitation, with a particular emphasis on food security and rural populations. FAO works with governments to develop and implement disaster prevention policies and practices. It aims to strengthen the capacity of local institutions to manage and mitigate risk and provides technical assistance to improve access to land for displaced populations in countries following conflict or a natural disaster. Other disaster prevention and reduction efforts include dissemination of information from the various early-warning systems and support for adaptation to climate variability and change, for example by the use of drought-resistance crops or the adoption of conservation agriculture techniques. Following an emergency FAO works with governments and other development and humanitarian partners to assess the immediate and longer-term agriculture and food security needs of the affected population. It has developed an Integrated Food Security and Humanitarian Phase Classification Scheme to determine the appropriate response to a disaster situation. Emergency co-ordination units may be established to manage the local response to an emergency and to facilitate and co-ordinate the delivery of inter-agency assistance. In order to rehabilitate agricultural production following a natural or man-made disaster FAO provides emergency seed, tools, other materials and technical and training assistance. During 2005 the UN's Inter-Agency Standing Committee, concerned with co-ordinating the international response to humanitarian disasters, developed a concept of providing assistance through a 'cluster' approach, comprising core areas of activity. FAO was designated the lead agency for the Agriculture cluster. FAO also contributes the agricultural relief and rehabilitation component of the UN's Consolidated Appeals Process, which aims to co-ordinate and enhance the effectiveness of the international community's response to an emergency. In April 2004 FAO established a Special Fund for Emergency and Rehabilitation Activities to enable it to response promptly to a humanitarian crisis before making an emergency appeal for additional resources.

In January 2005, following a massive earthquake in the Indian Ocean in December 2004, which caused a series of tidal waves, or tsunamis, that devastated coastal regions in 14 countries in South and South-East Asia and East Africa, FAO requested emergency funding of US $26m. to support an initial six-month rehabilitation operation to restore the livelihoods of fishermen and farmers affected by the natural disaster. FAO subsequently became the lead UN agency for the rehabilitation of agricultural, fisheries and forestry sectors of tsunami-affected countries. In July 2008 FAO appealed for $33.5m. to continue emergency rehabilitation efforts and help to resume food production and restore the livelihoods of fishermen and farmers in areas of Myanmar affected by tropical cyclone 'Nargis', which devastated large areas of the coastal delta region in May. Following the severe earthquake that struck northern Pakistan and bordering areas of India and Afghanistan in October 2005, FAO appealed for US $25m. to fund a post-earthquake early recovery and short-term rehabilitation programme, focusing on restoring the livelihoods of 200,000 surviving farming households through the provision of agricultural inputs such as seeds, fertilizer, fodder and tools; and through the rehabilitation of damaged rural infrastructure. Since the 1980s FAO has provided consistent support for the agricultural sector in Afghanistan (devastated for many years by conflict and drought). Since December 2001 FAO has supported the food security strategy of the Afghan administration, which has aimed to move emphasis from relief to rehabilitation efforts.

## FAO Statutory Bodies

(based at the Rome headquarters, unless otherwise indicated)

**Animal Production and Health Commission for Asia and the Pacific:** c/o FAO Regional Office, Maliwan Mansion, 39 Phra Atit Rd, Bangkok 10200, Thailand; f. 1975 to support national and regional livestock production and research; 17 member states.

**Asia and Pacific Commission on Agricultural Statistics:** c/o FAO Regional Office, Maliwan Mansion, 39 Phra Atit Rd, Bangkok 10200, Thailand; f. 1962 to review the state of food and agricultural statistics in the region and to advise member countries on the development and standardization of agricultural statistics; 25 member states.

**Asia and Pacific Plant Protection Commission:** c/o FAO Regional Office, Maliwan Mansion, Phra Atit Rd, Bangkok 10200, Thailand; f. 1956 (new title 1983) to strengthen international co-operation in plant protection to prevent the introduction and spread of destructive plant diseases and pests; 25 member states.

**Asia-Pacific Fishery Commission:** c/o FAO Regional Office, Maliwan Mansion, 39 Phra Atit Rd, Bangkok 10200, Thailand; f. 1948 to develop fisheries, encourage and co-ordinate research, disseminate information, recommend projects to governments, propose standards in technique and management measures; 20 member states.

**Asia-Pacific Forestry Commission:** internet www.apfcweb.org; f. 1949 to advise on the formulation of forest policy, and review and co-ordinate its implementation throughout the region; to exchange information and advise on technical problems; 29 member states.

**Codex Alimentarius Commission** (Joint FAO/WHO Food Standards Programme): e-mail codex@fao.org; internet www.codexalimentarius.net; f. 1962 to make proposals for the co-ordination of all international food standards work and to publish a code of international food standards; established Intergovernmental Task Force on Foods Derived from Biotechnology in 1999; Trust Fund to support participation by least-developed countries was inaugurated in 2003; there are numerous specialized Codex committees, e.g. for food labelling, hygiene and additives, pesticide residues, milk and milk products, and processed fruits and vegetables; 165 member states.

**Commission for Controlling the Desert Locust in Southwest Asia:** f. 1964 to carry out all possible measures to control plagues of the desert locust in Afghanistan, India, Iran and Pakistan.

**Indian Ocean Fishery Commission:** f. 1967 to promote national programmes, research and development activities, and to examine management problems; 41 member states.

**International Rice Commission:** internet www.fao.org/ag/AGP/AGPC/doc/field/commrice/welcome.htm; f. 1949 to promote national and international action on production, conservation, distribution and consumption of rice, except matters relating to international trade; supports the International Task Force on Hybrid Rice, the Working Group on Advanced Rice Breeding in Latin America and the Caribbean, the Inter-regional Collaborative Research Network on Rice in the Mediterranean Climate Areas, and the Technical Co-operation Network on Wetland Development and Management/Inland Valley Swamps; 60 member states.

## Finance

FAO's Regular Programme, which is financed by contributions from member governments, covers the cost of FAO's Secretariat, its Technical Co-operation Programme (TCP) and part of the cost of several special action programmes. The budget for the two-year period 2008–09 totalled US $929.8m. Much of FAO's technical assistance programme is funded from extra-budgetary sources, predominantly by trust funds that come mainly from donor countries and international financing institutions.

## Publications

*Commodity Review and Outlook* (annually).

*Ethical Issues in Food and Agriculture*.

*FAO Statistical Yearbook* (annually).

*FAOSTAT Statistical Database* (online).

*Food Crops and Shortages* (6 a year).

*Food Outlook* (5 a year).

*Food Safety and Quality Update* (monthly; electronic bulletin).

*Forest Resources Assessment*.

*The State of Agricultural Commodity Markets* (every 2 years).

*The State of Food and Agriculture* (annually).

*The State of Food Insecurity in the World* (annually).

*The State of World Fisheries and Aquaculture* (every 2 years).

*The State of the World's Forests* (every 2 years).

*Unasylva* (quarterly).

*Yearbook of Fishery Statistics*.

*Yearbook of Forest Products*.

Commodity reviews; studies, manuals. A complete catalogue of publications is available at www.fao.org/icatalog/inter-e.htm.

# International Bank for Reconstruction and Development—IBRD (World Bank)

**Address:** 1818 H St, NW, Washington, DC 20433, USA.

**Telephone:** (202) 473-1000; **fax:** (202) 477-6391; **e-mail:** pic@worldbank.org; **internet:** www.worldbank.org.

The IBRD was established in December 1945. Initially it was concerned with post-war reconstruction in Europe; since then its aim has been to assist the economic development of member nations by making loans where private capital is not available on reasonable terms to finance productive investments. Loans are made either directly to governments, or to private enterprises with the guarantee of their governments. The World Bank, as it is commonly known, comprises the IBRD and the International Development Association (IDA). The affiliated group of institutions, comprising the IBRD, the IDA, the International Finance Corporation (IFC), the Multilateral Investment Guarantee Agency (MIGA) and the International Centre for Settlement of Investment Disputes (ICSID, see below), is referred to as the World Bank Group.

## Organization

(August 2008)

Officers and staff of the IBRD serve concurrently as officers and staff in the IDA. The World Bank has offices in New York, Brussels, Paris (for Europe), Frankfurt, London, Geneva and Tokyo, as well as in more than 100 countries of operation. Country Directors are located in some 30 country offices.

### BOARD OF GOVERNORS

The Board of Governors consists of one Governor appointed by each member nation. Typically, a Governor is the country's finance minister, central bank governor, or a minister or an official of comparable rank. The Board normally meets once a year.

### EXECUTIVE DIRECTORS

The general operations of the Bank are conducted by a Board of 24 Executive Directors. Five Directors are appointed by the five members having the largest number of shares of capital stock, and the rest are elected by the Governors representing the other members. The President of the Bank is Chairman of the Board.

### PRINCIPAL OFFICERS

The principal officers of the Bank are the President of the Bank, three Managing Directors, three Senior Vice-Presidents and 24 Vice-Presidents.

**President and Chairman of Executive Directors:** ROBERT B. ZOELLICK (USA).

**Vice-President, South Asia:** ISABEL GUERRERO (Chile).

## Activities

### FINANCIAL OPERATIONS

IBRD capital is derived from members' subscriptions to capital shares, the calculation of which is based on their quotas in the IMF. At 30 June 2007 the total subscribed capital of the IBRD was US $189,801m., of which the paid-in portion was $11,486m. (6.1%); the remainder is subject to call if required. Most of the IBRD's lendable funds come from its borrowing, on commercial terms, in world capital markets, and also from its retained earnings and the flow of repayments on its loans. IBRD loans carry a variable interest rate, rather than a rate fixed at the time of borrowing.

IBRD loans usually have a 'grace period' of five years and are repayable over 15 years or fewer. Loans are made to governments, or must be guaranteed by the government concerned, and are normally made for projects likely to offer a commercially viable rate of return. In 1980 the World Bank introduced structural adjustment lending, which (instead of financing specific projects) supports programmes and changes necessary to modify the structure of an economy so that it can restore or maintain its growth and viability in its balance of payments over the medium-term.

The IBRD and IDA together made 301 new lending and investment commitments totalling US $24,695.8m. during the year ending 30 June 2007, compared with 279 (amounting to $23,641.2m.) in the previous year. During 2006/07 the IBRD alone approved commitments totalling $12,828.8m. (compared with $14,135.0m. in the previous year). Disbursements by the IBRD in the year ending 30 June 2007 amounted to $11,055m.

IBRD operations are supported by medium- and long-term borrowings in international capital markets. During the year ending 30 June 2007 the IBRD's net income amounted to –US $140m.

The World Bank's primary objectives are the achievement of sustainable economic growth and the reduction of poverty in developing countries. In the context of stimulating economic growth the Bank promotes both private sector development and human resource development and has attempted to respond to the growing demands by developing countries for assistance in these areas. In March 1997 the Board of Executive Directors endorsed a 'Strategic Compact' to increase the effectiveness of the Bank in achieving its central objective of poverty reduction. The reforms included greater decentralization of decision-making, and investment in front-line operations, enhancing the administration of loans, and improving access to information and co-ordination of Bank activities through a knowledge management system comprising four thematic networks: the Human Development Network; the Environmentally and Socially Sustainable Development Network; the Finance, Private Sector and Infrastructure Development Network; and the Poverty Reduction and Economic Management Network. In 2000/01 the Bank adopted a new Strategic Framework which emphasized two essential approaches for Bank support: strengthening the investment climate and prospects for sustainable development in a country, and supporting investment in the poor. In September 2001 the Bank announced that it was to join the UN as a full partner in implementing the so-called Millennium Development Goals (MDGs), and was to make them central to its development agenda. The objectives, which were approved by governments attending a special session of the UN General Assembly in September 2000, represented a new international consensus to achieve determined poverty reduction targets. The Bank was closely involved in preparations for the International Conference on Financing for Development, which was held in Monterrey, Mexico, in March 2002. The meeting adopted the Monterrey Consensus, which outlined measures to support national development efforts and to achieve the MDGs. During 2002/03 the Bank, with the IMF, undertook to develop a monitoring framework to review progress in the MDG agenda. The first *Global Monitoring Report* was issued by the Bank and IMF in April 2004. Other efforts to support a greater emphasis on development results were also undertaken by the Bank during 2003/04 as part of a new strategic action plan, and the Bank has continued closely to monitor its contribution to poverty reduction objectives.

The Bank's efforts to reduce poverty include the compilation of country-specific assessments and the formulation of country assistance strategies (CASs) to review and guide the Bank's country programmes. Since August 1998 the Bank has published CASs, with the approval of the government concerned. A new results-based CAS initiative was piloted in 2003/04. In 1998/99 the Bank's Executive Directors endorsed a Comprehensive Development Framework (CDF) to effect a new approach to development assistance based on partnerships and country responsibility, with an emphasis on the interdependence of the social, structural, human, governmental, economic and environmental elements of development. The Framework, which aimed to enhance the overall effectiveness of development assistance, was formulated after a series of consultative meetings organized by the Bank and attended by representatives of governments, donor agencies, financial institutions, non-governmental organizations, the private sector and academics.

In December 1999 the Bank introduced a new approach to implement the principles of the CDF, as part of its strategy to enhance the debt relief scheme for heavily indebted poor countries (HIPCs, see below). Applicant countries were requested to formulate, in consultation with external partners and other stakeholders, a results-oriented national strategy to reduce poverty, to be presented in the form of a Poverty Reduction Strategy Paper (PRSP). In cases where there might be some delay in issuing a full PRSP, it was permissible for a country to submit a less detailed 'interim' PRSP (I-PRSP) in order to secure the preliminary qualification for debt relief. The approach also requires the publication of annual progress reports. In 2001 the Bank introduced a new Poverty Reduction Support Credit to help low-income countries to implement the policy and institutional reforms outlined in their PRSP. The first credits were approved for Uganda and Viet Nam in May and June respectively. Increasingly, PRSPs have been considered by the international community to be the appropriate country-level framework to assess progress towards achieving the MDGs. A joint review of the poverty reduction strategy approach was undertaken by the Bank and IMF in 2004/05.

In September 1996 the World Bank/IMF Development Committee endorsed a joint initiative to assist HIPCs to reduce their debt burden to a sustainable level, in order to make more resources available for poverty reduction and economic growth. A new Trust Fund was established by the World Bank in November to finance the initiative. The Fund, consisting of an initial allocation of US $500m. from the IBRD surplus and other contributions from multilateral creditors, was to be administered by IDA. In early 1999 the World Bank and IMF initiated a comprehensive review of the HIPC initiative. In June the group of seven industrialized nations and Russia (G8), meeting in Cologne, Germany, agreed to increase contributions to the HIPC Trust Fund and to cancel substantial amounts of outstanding debt, and proposed more flexible terms for eligibility. In September the Bank and IMF reached an agreement on an enhanced HIPC scheme, with further revenue to be generated through the revaluation of a percentage of IMF gold reserves. It was agreed that, in order to qualify for debt relief and additional concessional lending, countries were to formulate a PRSP, and should demonstrate prudent financial management in the implementation of the strategy for at least one year. Those countries still deemed to have an unsustainable level of debt at the pivotal 'decision point' of the process were to qualify for assistance. In the majority of cases a sustainable level of debt was targeted at 150% of the net present value (NPV) of the debt in relation to total annual exports (compared with 200%–250% under the original HIPC scheme). Other countries with a lower debt-to-export ratio were to be eligible for assistance under the initiative, providing that their export earnings were at least 30% of GDP (lowered from 40%) and government revenue at least 15% of GDP (reduced from 20%). In September 2005 the Bank and IMF endorsed a proposal of the G8 to cancel all debt owed by countries that had reached their completion point, under a new Multilateral Debt Relief Initiative. By mid-2008 23 countries had reached completion point and a further 10 had reached decision point of the process, including Afghanistan, approved in July 2007. Debt relief for Afghanistan under the enhanced HIPC scheme was estimated to amount to $571.4m. in NPV terms.

During 2000/01 the World Bank strengthened its efforts to counter the problem of HIV and AIDS in developing countries. In November 2001 the Bank appointed its first Global HIV/AIDS Adviser. In September 2000 a new Multi-Country HIV/AIDS Programme for Africa (MAP) was launched, in collaboration with UNAIDS and other major donor agencies and non-governmental organizations. Some US $500m. was allocated to the initiative and was used to support efforts in seven countries. In February 2002 the Bank approved an additional $500m. for a second phase of MAP, which was envisaged to assist HIV/AIDS schemes in a further 12 countries, as well as regional activities. A MAP initiative for the Caribbean, with a budget of $155m., was launched in 2001. The Bank has undertaken research into the long-term effects of HIV/AIDS, and hosts the Global HIV/AIDS Monitoring and Evaluation Support Team of UNAIDS. In November 2004 the Bank launched an AIDS Media Center to improve access to information regarding HIV/AIDS, in particular to journalists in developing countries.

In March 2007 the Board of Executive Directors approved an action plan to develop further its Clean Energy for Development Investment Framework, which had been formulated in response to a request by the G8 heads of state, meeting in Gleneagles, United Kingdom, in July 2005. The action plan focused on efforts to improve access to clean energy, in particular in sub-Saharan Africa; to accelerate the transition to low carbon-emission development; and to support adaptation to climate change. During 2007 the Bank undertook to develop a strategic framework on climate change and development, which aimed to support the efforts of developing countries to adapt to climate change and to achieve low-carbon energy growth, while working to reduce poverty.

In addition to providing financial services, the Bank also undertakes analytical and advisory services, and supports learning and capacity-building, in particular through the World Bank Institute (see below), the Staff Exchange Programme and knowledge-sharing initiatives. The Bank has supported efforts, such as the Global Development Gateway, to disseminate information on development issues and programmes, and, since 1988, has organized the Annual Bank Conference on Development Economics (ABCDE) to provide a forum for the exchange and discussion of development-related ideas and research. In September 1995 the Bank initiated the Information for Development Programme (InfoDev) with the aim of fostering partnerships between governments, multilateral institutions and private-sector experts in order to promote reform and investment in developing countries through improved access to information technology.

### TECHNICAL ASSISTANCE

The provision of technical assistance to member countries has become a major component of World Bank activities. The economic and sector work (ESW) undertaken by the Bank is the vehicle for considerable technical assistance and often forms the basis of CASs and other strategic or advisory reports. In addition, project loans and credits may include funds earmarked specifically for feasibility studies, resource surveys, management or planning advice, and training. The Economic Development Institute has become one of the most important of the Bank's activities in technical assistance. It provides training in national economic management and project analysis for government officials at the middle and upper levels of responsibility. It also runs overseas courses aiming to build up local training capability, and administers a graduate scholarship programme.

The Bank serves as an executing agency for projects financed by the UN Development Programme (UNDP). It also administers projects financed by various trust funds.

Technical assistance (usually reimbursable) is also extended to countries that do not need Bank financial support, e.g. for training and transfer of technology. The Bank encourages the use of local consultants to assist with projects and stimulate institutional capability.

The Project Preparation Facility (PPF) was established in 1975 to provide cash advances to prepare projects that may be financed by the Bank. In 1992 the Bank established an Institutional Development Fund (IDF), which became operational on 1 July; the purpose of the Fund was to provide rapid, small-scale financial assistance, to a maximum value of US $500,000, for capacity-building proposals. In 2002 the IDF was reoriented to focus on good governance, in particular financial accountability and system reforms.

### ECONOMIC RESEARCH AND STUDIES

In the 1990s the World Bank's research, conducted by its own research staff, was increasingly concerned with providing information to reinforce the Bank's expanding advisory role to developing countries and to improve policy in the Bank's borrowing countries. The principal areas of current research focus on issues such as maintaining sustainable growth while protecting the environment and the poorest sectors of society, encouraging the development of the private sector, and reducing and decentralizing government activities.

The Bank chairs the Consultative Group on International Agricultural Research (CGIAR), which was founded in 1971 to raise financial support for international agricultural research work for improving crops and animal production in developing countries; it supports 15 research centres.

### CO-OPERATION WITH OTHER ORGANIZATIONS

The World Bank co-operates with other international partners with the aim of improving the impact of development efforts. It collaborates with the IMF in implementing the HIPC scheme and the two agencies work closely to achieve a common approach to development initiatives. The Bank has established strong working relationships with many other UN bodies, in particular through a mutual commitment to poverty reduction objectives. In May 2000 the Bank signed a joint statement of co-operation with the OECD. The Bank holds regular consultations with other multilateral development banks and with the European Union with respect to development issues. The Bank-NGO Committee provides an annual forum for discussion with non-governmental organizations (NGOs). Strengthening co-operation with external partners was a fundamental element of the Comprehensive Development Framework, which was adopted in 1998/99 (see above). In 2001/02 a Partnership Approval and Tracking System was implemented to provide information on the Bank's regional and global partnerships.

In 1997 a Partnerships Group was established to strengthen the Bank's work with development institutions, representatives of civil society and the private sector. The Group established a new Development Grant Facility, which became operational in October, to support partnership initiatives and to co-ordinate all of the Bank's grant-making activities. Also in 1997 the Bank, in partnership with the IMF, UNCTAD, UNDP, the World Trade Organization (WTO) and International Trade Commission, established an Integrated Framework for Trade-related Assistance to Least Developed Countries, at the request of the WTO, to assist those countries to integrate into the global trading system and improve basic trading capabilities.

In June 1995 the World Bank joined other international donors (including regional development banks, other UN bodies, Canada, France, the Netherlands and the USA) in establishing a Consultative Group to Assist the Poorest (CGAP), which was to channel funds to the most needy through grass-roots agencies. An initial credit of approximately US $200m. was committed by the donors. The Bank manages the CGAP Secretariat, which is responsible for the administration of external funding and for the evaluation and approval of project financing. The CGAP provides technical assistance, training and strategic advice to microfinance institutions and other relevant bodies. As an implementing agency of the Global Environment Facility (GEF) the Bank assists countries to prepare and supervise GEF projects relating to biological diversity, climate change and other environmental protection measures. It is an example of a partnership in action which addresses a global agenda, complementing Bank country assistance activities. Other funds administered by the Bank include the Global Program to Eradicate Poliomyelitis, launched during the financial year 2002/03, the Least Developed Countries Fund for Climate Change, established in September 2002, an Education for All Fast-Track Initiative Catalytic Trust Fund, established in 2003/04, a Carbon Finance Assistance Trust Fund, established in 2004/05, and a Trust Fund for Anti-Money Laundering and Combating Financing of Terrorism for Asia-Pacific and for Central America and the Caribbean, established in 2005/06. In 2006/07 the Bank established a Global Facility for Disaster Reduction and Recovery. In September 2007 the Bank's Executive Directors approved a Carbon Partnership Facility and a Forest Carbon Partnership Facility to support its climate change activities. In May 2008 the Bank inaugurated the Global Food Response Programme to provide financial support, with resources of some $1,200m., to help meet the immediate needs of countries affected by the escalating cost of food production and by food shortages. Grants and loans were to be allocated on the basis of rapid needs assessments, conducted by the Bank with the FAO, the WFP and IFAD. As part of the facility a Multi-Donor Trust Fund was to be established to facilitate co-ordination among donors and to leverage financial support for the rapid delivery of seeds and fertilizer to small-scale farmers. By August $123m. had been approved under the programme for 14 countries.

In March 1998 the Bank helped to organize the first Asia Development Forum, which convened some 300 representatives of government, the private sector and academia to discuss the region's prospects for economic recovery. A second Forum was held in June 2000, in Singapore, and the third, organized by the Bank with the Asian Development Bank, the ADB Institute, and ESCAP to enhance further development capacity, was convened in June 2001, in Bangkok, Thailand. A fourth Forum was held in Seoul, Republic of Korea, in November 2002, on the theme of trade and poverty.

The Bank is a lead organization in providing reconstruction assistance following natural disasters or conflicts, usually in collaboration with other UN agencies or international organizations, and through special trust funds. In November 2001 the Bank worked with UNDP and the Asian Development Bank to assess the needs of Afghanistan following the removal of the Taliban authorities in that country. At an International Conference on Reconstruction Assistance to Afghanistan, held in Tokyo, Japan, in January 2002, the Bank's President proposed extending US $500m. in assistance over a 30-month period, and providing an immediate amount of $50m.–$70m. in grants. In May an Afghanistan Reconstruction Trust Fund was established to provide a co-ordinated financing mechanism to support the interim administration in that country. The Bank is the Administrator of the Fund, which is managed jointly by the Bank, Asian Development Bank, Islamic Development Bank and the UNDP. By December 2007 contributions to the Trust Fund amounted to $2,400m. pledged by 28 countries. At the end of 2004 the Bank responded immediately to assist countries affected by a massive earthquake and subsequent tsunami which devastated many coastal areas of some 14 countries in the Indian Ocean. Bank staff undertook assessments and other efforts to accelerate recovery planning, mobilize financial support and help to co-ordinate relief and recovery efforts in affected regions. Some $672m. was allocated by the Bank, mainly in grants to be directed to Indonesia, Sri Lanka and the Maldives, for the first phase of reconstruction efforts. By the end of June 2005 the Bank had committed some $837.5m. to tsunami recovery programmes in India, Indonesia, the Maldives and Sri Lanka, in particular to repair damaged services, to assist the reconstruction of housing and to restore livelihoods. In October the Bank, with the Asian Development Bank, undertook a preliminary damage and needs assessment following a massive earthquake in north-west Pakistan. The cost of the disaster was estimated at $5,200m., with initial reconstruction funding requirements of $3,500m. The Bank committed some $475m. to support relief efforts and in December approved a further IDA emergency recovery credit amounting to $400m. An international donors' conference was convened in November.

The Bank has worked with FAO, WHO and the World Organisation of Animal Health (OIE) to develop strategies to monitor, contain and eradicate the spread of highly pathogenic avian influenza. In September 2005 the Bank organized a meeting of leading experts on the issue and in November it co-sponsored, with FAO, WHO and the OIE, an international partners conference, focusing on control of the disease and preparedness planning for any future related influenza pandemic in humans. In January 2006 the Bank's Board of Directors approved the establishment of a funding programme, with resources of up to US $500m., to assist countries to combat the disease. Later in that month the Bank co-sponsored, with the European Commission and the People's Republic of China, an International Ministerial Pledging Conference on Avian and Human Pandemic Influenza, convened in Beijing. Participants pledged some $1,900m. to fund disease control and pandemic preparedness activities at global, regional and country levels.

The Bank conducts co-financing and aid co-ordination projects with official aid agencies, export credit institutions, and commercial banks to leverage additional concessional funds for recipient countries. During the year ending 30 June 2007 130 Bank projects leveraged US $6,300m. in co-financing.

### EVALUATION

The Independent Evaluation Group is an independent unit within the World Bank. It conducts Country Assistance Evaluations to assess the development effectiveness of a Bank country programme, and studies and publishes the results of projects after a loan has been fully disbursed, so as to identify problems and possible improvements in future activities. In addition, the department reviews the Bank's global programmes and produces the *Annual Review of Development Effectiveness*. In 1996 a Quality Assurance Group was established to monitor the effectiveness of the Bank's operations and performance.

In September 1993 the Bank established an independent Inspection Panel, consistent with the Bank's objective of improving project implementation and accountability. The Panel, which became operational in September 1994, was to conduct independent investigations and report on complaints from local people concerning the design, appraisal and implementation of development projects supported by the Bank. By March 2008 the Panel had received 52 formal requests for inspection.

### IBRD INSTITUTIONS

**World Bank Institute (WBI):** founded in March 1999 by merger of the Bank's Learning and Leadership Centre, previously responsible for internal staff training, and the Economic Development Institute (EDI), which had been established in 1955 to train government officials concerned with development programmes and policies. The new Institute aimed to emphasize the Bank's priority areas through the provision of training courses and seminars relating to poverty, crisis response, good governance and anti-corruption strategies. From 2004 the Institute was to place greater emphasis on individual country needs and on long-term institutional capacity-building. During 2006/07 WBI activities reached more than 75,000 participants world-wide. The Institute has continued to support a Global Knowledge Partnership, which was established in 1997 to promote alliances between governments, companies, other agencies and organizations committed to applying information and communication technologies for development purposes. Under the EDI a World Links for Development programme was also initiated to connect schools in developing countries with partner establishments in industrialized nations via the internet. In 1999 the WBI expanded its programmes through distance learning, a Global Development Network, and use of new technologies. A new initiative, Global Development Learning Network (GDLN), aimed to expand access to information and learning opportunities through the internet, videoconferences and organized exchanges. In 2007 there were some 120 GDLN centres, or affiliates. At that time formal partnership arrangements were in place between WBI and almost 200 learning centres and public, private and non-governmental organizations; a further 250 informal partnerships were also in place; Vice-Pres. RAKESH NANGIA (acting); publs *Annual Report*, *Development Outreach* (quarterly), other books, working papers, case studies.

**International Centre for Settlement of Investment Disputes (ICSID):** founded in 1966 under the Convention of the Settlement of Investment Disputes between States and Nationals of Other States. The Convention was designed to encourage the growth of private foreign investment for economic development, by creating the possibility, always subject to the consent of both parties, for a Contracting State and a foreign investor who is a national of another Contracting State to settle any legal dispute that might arise out of such an investment by conciliation and/or arbitration before an impartial, international forum. The governing body of the Centre is its Administrative Council, composed of one representative of each Contracting State, all of whom have equal voting power. The President of the World Bank is (*ex officio* ) the non-voting Chairman of the Administrative Council. By mid-2008 143 countries had signed and ratified the Convention to become ICSID Contracting States. At that time 268 cases had been registered with the Centre, of which 142 had been concluded and 126 were pending consideration; Sec.-Gen. NASSIB G. ZIADÉ (Chile/Lebanon) (acting).

## Publications

*Abstracts of Current Studies: The World Bank Research Program* (annually).
*African Development Indicators* (annually).
*Annual Report on Operations Evaluation*.
*Annual Report on Portfolio Performance*.
*Annual Review of Development Effectiveness*.
*Doing Business* (annually).
*EDI Annual Report*.
*Global Commodity Markets* (quarterly).
*Global Development Finance* (annually).
*Global Economic Prospects* (annually).
*ICSID Annual Report*.
*ICSID Review—Foreign Investment Law Journal* (2 a year).
*Joint BIS-IMF-OECD-World Bank Statistics on External Debt* (quarterly).
*New Products and Outreach* (EDI, annually).
*News from ICSID* (2 a year).
*Poverty Reduction and the World Bank* (annually).
*Poverty Reduction Strategies Newsletter* (quarterly).
*Research News* (quarterly).
*Staff Working Papers*.
*World Bank Annual Report*.
*World Bank Atlas* (annually).
*World Bank Economic Review* (3 a year).
*The World Bank and the Environment* (annually).
*World Bank Research Observer*.
*World Development Indicators* (annually).
*World Development Report* (annually).

## Statistics

**IBRD LOANS APPROVED IN SOUTH ASIA, 1 JULY 2006–30 JUNE 2007**
(US $ million)

| Country | Purpose | Amount |
|---|---|---|
| India | Orissa socio-economic development* | 150.0 |
| | Punjab state road network | 250.0 |
| | Third Andhra Pradesh economic development policy loan* | 150.0 |
| | Tamil Nadu irrigated agriculture modernization and water bodies restoration and management* | 335.0 |
| | Andhra Pradesh community-based tank management* | 94.5 |
| | Himachal Pradesh state roads investment | 220.0 |
| | Strengthening rural credit co-operatives* | 300.0 |
| Pakistan | Second Punjab irrigation sector development policy loan | 100.0 |

* Joint IBRD/IDA project.

Source: *World Bank Annual Report 2007*.

# International Development Association—IDA

**Address:** 1818 H Street, NW, Washington, DC 20433, USA.

**Telephone:** (202) 473-1000; **fax:** (202) 477-6391; **internet:** www.worldbank.org/ida.

The International Development Association began operations in November 1960. Affiliated to the IBRD, IDA advances capital to the poorer developing member countries on more flexible terms than those offered by the IBRD.

## Organization

(August 2008)

Officers and staff of the IBRD serve concurrently as officers and staff of IDA.

**President and Chairman of Executive Directors:** ROBERT B. ZOELLICK (USA).

## Activities

IDA assistance is aimed at the poorer developing countries (i.e. those with an annual GNP per capita of less than US $1,065 were to qualify for assistance in 2007/08) in order to support their poverty reduction strategies. Under IDA lending conditions, credits can be extended to countries whose balance of payments could not sustain the burden of repayment required for IBRD loans. Terms are more favourable than those provided by the IBRD; credits are for a period of 35 or 40 years, with a 'grace period' of 10 years, and carry no interest charges. At mid-2007 80 countries were eligible for IDA assistance, including several small-island economies with a GNP per head greater than $1,065, but which would otherwise have little or no access to Bank funds, and 16 so-called 'blend borrowers' which are entitled to borrow from both the IDA and IBRD.

IDA's total development resources, consisting of members' subscriptions and supplementary resources (additional subscriptions and contributions), are replenished periodically by contributions from the more affluent member countries. An agreement to provide a substantial replenishment of funds, amounting to some US $34,000m. for the period 1 July 2005–30 June 2008, was concluded in February 2005. New contributions pledged by 40 donor countries amounted to $20,700m. of the total replenishment. The agreement incorporated a renewed focus on stimulating economic growth in support of the Millennium Development Goals, with a strengthened monitoring and results-assessment agenda based on poverty reduction objectives. The replenishment programme also placed greater emphasis on the use of grants to address the needs of the poorest countries, in particular those most vulnerable to debt. Negotiations on the 15th replenishment of IDA funds (IDA15) commenced in March 2007, in Paris, France. Participants selected the following 'special themes' for further discussion: the role of IDA in global aid architecture; the effectiveness of IDA assistance at country level; and IDA's role in fragile states. In December an agreement was concluded to replenish IDA resources by some $41,600m., for the period 1 July 2008–30 June 2011, of which $25,100m. was pledged by 45 donor countries.

During the year ending 30 June 2007 new IDA commitments amounted to US $11,867m. for 189 projects, compared with $9,506m. in the previous year. Of total IDA assistance during 2006/07 $5,759.4m. (49%) was for Africa and $4,032.1m. (34%) for South Asia. One-third of lending was for infrastructure projects. An increasing proportion of IDA lending, accounting for some 18% of total financing in 2006/07, is in the form of grants for the poorest or most vulnerable countries.

IDA administers a Trust Fund, which was established in November 1996 as part of a World Bank/IMF initiative to assist heavily indebted poor countries (HIPCs). In September 2005 the World Bank's Development Committee and the International Monetary and Financial Committee of the IMF endorsed a proposal of the Group of Eight (G8) industrialized countries to cancel the remaining multilateral debt owed by HIPCs that had reached their completion point under the scheme (see IBRD). In December IDA convened a meeting of donor countries to discuss funding to uphold its financial capability upon its contribution to the so-called Multilateral Debt Relief Initiative (MDRI). The scheme was approved by the Board of Executive Directors in March 2006 and entered into effect on 1 July. By early 2007 total debt relief provided by IDA since the HIPC initiative commenced was estimated to be US $53,600m., including $36,400m. committed under the MDRI. In July Afghanistan became the 31st country to reach the decision point in the HIPC process. Accordingly it was eligible for interim debt relief under the enhanced initiative, amounting to some $571.4m. in net present value, of which $75.2m. was from IDA resources.

## Publication

*Annual Report*.

## Statistics

**IDA CREDITS APPROVED IN SOUTH ASIA, 1 JULY 2006–30 JUNE 2007**
(US $ million)

| Country | Purpose | Amount |
|---|---|---|
| Afghanistan | Second national solidarity programme investment grant | 120.0 |
| | Avian influenza control and human pandemic preparedness and response | 8.0 |
| | Private sector development support | 25.0 |
| | Emergency irrigation rehabilitation investment grant (additional financing) | 25.0 |
| | Civil service reform | 20.4 |
| | Third programmatic support for institution-building development policy grant | 80.0 |
| | Public financial management reform | 33.4 |
| Bangladesh | Railway reform | 40.0 |
| | Social investment programme (additional financing) | 8.0 |
| | Fourth development support development policy credit | 200.0 |
| | Second poverty alleviation microfinance (additional financing) financial intermediary credit | 15.0 |
| | Avian influenza preparedness and response | 16.0 |
| | Third programmatic education sector development support development policy credit | 100.0 |
| Bhutan | Second rural access specific investment grant | 10.0 |
| | Private sector development | 8.0 |
| | Second development policy grant | 12.0 |
| India | Orissa socio-economic development* | 75.0 |
| | Second reproductive and child health specific investment credit | 360.0 |
| | Second national tuberculosis control specific investment credit | 170.0 |
| | Karnataka health system development and reform | 141.8 |
| | Uttaranchal rural water supply and sanitation | 120.0 |
| | Punjab rural water supply and sanitation | 154.0 |
| | Third Andhra Pradesh economic development policy credit* | 75.0 |
| | Tamil Nadu irrigated agriculture modernization and water bodies restoration and management* | 150.0 |
| | Andhra Pradesh community-based tank management* | 94.5 |
| | Third national HIV/AIDS control specific investment credit | 250.0 |
| | Mizoram state roads (additional financing) specific investment credit | 18.0 |
| | Bihar rural livelihoods specific investment credit | 63.0 |
| | Vocational training improvement | 280.0 |
| | Strengthening rural credit co-operatives* | 300.0 |
| Nepal | Poverty alleviation fund (additional financing) learning and innovation grant | 25.0 |
| | Avian influenza control | 18.2 |
| | Second higher education specific investment grant | 60.0 |
| Pakistan | Punjab land records management and information systems | 45.7 |
| | Second poverty alleviation fund (additional financing) specific investment credit | 138.0 |
| | Second poverty reduction support development policy credit | 350.0 |
| | Second North-West Frontier Province development policy credit | 130.0 |
| | Sindh education development policy credit | 100.0 |
| | Fourth Punjab education development policy credit | 100.0 |
| | Second Partnership for Polio Eradication (additional financing) specific investment credit | 21.1 |
| Sri Lanka | Puttalam housing rehabilitation and land management | 32.0 |
| | Renewable energy for rural economic development (additional financing) | 40.0 |

* Joint IBRD/IDA project.

Source: *World Bank Annual Report 2007*.

# International Finance Corporation—IFC

**Address:** 2121 Pennsylvania Ave, NW, Washington, DC 20433, USA.

**Telephone:** (202) 473-3800; **fax:** (202) 974-4384; **e-mail:** information@ifc.org; **internet:** www.ifc.org.

IFC was founded in 1956 as a member of the World Bank Group to stimulate economic growth in developing countries by financing private-sector investments, mobilizing capital in international financial markets, and providing technical assistance and advice to governments and businesses.

## Organization

(August 2008)

IFC is a separate legal entity in the World Bank Group. Executive Directors of the World Bank also serve as Directors of IFC. The President of the World Bank is *ex officio* Chairman of the IFC Board of Directors, which has appointed him President of IFC. Subject to his overall supervision, the day-to-day operations of IFC are conducted by its staff under the direction of the Executive Vice-President. In 2007 IFC initiated a process of revising and expanding its executive management. The senior management team was to include eight Vice-Presidents responsible for regional and thematic groupings. At the end of June 2007 IFC had 3,134 staff members, of whom 51% were based in field offices.

### PRINCIPAL OFFICERS

**President:** Robert B. Zoellick (USA).

**Executive Vice-President:** Lars Thunell (Sweden).

**Director, South Asia Department:** Paolo Martelli.

### OFFICES IN SOUTH ASIA

**Bangladesh:** Bay's Galleria, 2nd Floor, 57 Gulshan Ave, Gulshan, Dhaka 1212; tel. (2) 988-6568; fax (2) 989-4744; e-mail bangladesh@ifc.org; also covers Bhutan and Nepal; Resident Rep.Country Man. Per Kjellerhaug.

**India (Chennai):** 56 First Avenue, 2nd Floor, Shastri Nagar, Adyar, Chennai 600020, Tamil Nadu; tel. (44) 24462570; fax (44) 24462571; e-mail southasia@ifc.org; Head Prasad Gopalan.

**India (Mumbai):** Godrej Bhavan, 3rd Floor, Murzban Rd, Mumbai 400001; tel. (22) 66652000; fax (22) 66652001; e-mail southasia@ifc.org; Senior Man. Sujoy Bose.

**India (New Delhi):** 50-m, Shanti Path, Gate No. 3, Niti Marg, Panchsheel Marg, Chanakyapuri, New Delhi 110021; tel. (11) 41111000; fax (11) 41111001; e-mail southasia@ifc.org; DirSenior Man. IyadAnita MalasGeorge.

**Sri Lanka:** DHPL Bldg, 15th Floor, Navam Mawatha, Colombo 2; tel. (11) 4740957; fax (11) 47495017; e-mail srilanka@ifc.org; also covers the Maldives; Resident Rep.Country Man. GILLES GALLUDEC.

## Activities

IFC aims to promote economic development in developing member countries by assisting the growth of private enterprise and effective capital markets. It finances private sector projects, through loans, the purchase of equity, quasi-equity products, and risk management services, and assists governments to create conditions that stimulate the flow of domestic and foreign private savings and investment. IFC may provide finance for a project that is partly state-owned, provided that there is participation by the private sector and that the project is operated on a commercial basis. IFC also mobilizes additional resources from other financial institutions, in particular through syndicated loans, thus providing access to international capital markets. IFC provides a range of advisory services to help to improve the investment climate in developing countries and offers technical assistance to private enterprises and governments. Increasingly IFC is focused on extending assistance to 'frontier' markets, i.e. those designated by the World Bank as low-income or high-risk countries or regions. Other strategic priorities in 2006/07 included building long-term relationships with local companies; ensuring environmental and social sustainability; helping the private sector strengthen infrastructure, from ports and roads to schools and hospitals; and developing local financial markets. In November 2004 IFC announced the establishment of a Global Trade Finance Programme, with initial funding of some US $500m., which aimed to support SME importers and exporters in emerging markets, to facilitate South-South trade in goods and services, and to extend technical assistance and training to local financial institutions. (An additional $500m. was approved in January 2007.) By August 2008 some 200 banks were participating in the initiative.

To be eligible for financing projects must be profitable for investors, as well as financially and economically viable; must benefit the economy of the country concerned; and must comply with IFC's environmental and social guidelines. IFC aims to promote best corporate governance and management methods and sustainable business practices, and encourages partnerships between governments, non-governmental organizations and community groups. In 2001/02 IFC developed a Sustainability Framework to help to assess the longer-term economic, environmental and social impact of projects. The first Sustainability Review was published in mid-2002. In 2002/03 IFC assisted 10 international banks to draft a voluntary set of guidelines (the Equator Principles), based on IFC's environmental, social and safeguard monitoring policies, to be applied to their global project finance activities. A revised set of Equator Principles was released in July 2006. (By May 2008 60 financial institutions had signed up to the Equator Principles.)

IFC's authorized capital is US $2,450m. At 30 June 2007 paid-in capital was $2,365m. The World Bank was originally the principal source of borrowed funds, but IFC also borrows from private capital markets. IFC's net income amounted to $2,618m. in 2006/07, compared with $1,278m. in the previous year.

In the year ending 30 June 2007 project financing approved by IFC amounted to US $9,995m. for 299 projects in 69 countries (compared with $8,275m. for 284 projects in the previous year). Of the total approved in 2006/07 $8,220m. was for IFC's own account, while $1,775m. was in the form of loan syndications and underwriting of securities issues and investment funds by more than 100 participant banks and institutional investors. Generally, IFC limits its financing to less than 25% of the total cost of a project, but may take up to a 35% stake in a venture (although never as a majority shareholder). Disbursements for IFC's account amounted to $5,841m. in 2006/07 (compared with $4,428m. in the previous year).

In 2006/07 the largest proportion of investment commitments, for IFC's account, was allocated to Latin America and the Caribbean (21.7%). Sub-Saharan Africa received 16.8%, the Middle East and North Africa 13.6%, Southern Europe and Central Asia 12.8%, South Asia 12.4%, East Asia and the Pacific 10.9%, Central and Eastern Europe 8.1%, and global projects 3.8%. In that year 41.2% of total financing committed was for global financial markets. Other commitments included global manufacturing and services (16.5%), infrastructure (12.1%) and oil, gas and mining (10.9%).

During the year ending 30 June 2007 IFC approved total financing of US $1,073m. for 30 projects in three countries in South Asia—Bangladesh, India and the Maldives. IFC also supported 12 projects in Pakistan (which it classifies under the Middle East and North Africa region). IFC's strategy for South Asia includes supporting regional integration into the global economy, increasing private-sector participation in infrastructure projects, promoting energy efficiency and cleaner production practices, promoting the development of small and medium-sized enterprises (SMEs) and improving access to financial services by enhancing financial institution capacity. IFC's SouthAsia Enterprise Development Facility, inaugurated in 2002, provides technical assistance aimed at strengthening the business environment and expanding financial services for smaller businesses in Bangladesh, Bhutan, Nepal and neighbouring states in northeastern India. SMEs in Afghanistan are supported by the Private Enterprise Partnership for the Middle East, established in October 2004. In March 2007 IFC inaugurated a new fund to support reform of the investment climate in Bangladesh. In March 2008 IFC, with other bilateral and multilateral donors, established an Infrastructure Advisory Facility for South Asia to support countries in the region to develop infrastructure projects, mainly through public-private partnerships. The facility, based in New Delhi, India, was established with an initial US $20m., of which IFC contributed $5m.

IFC's Private Sector Advisory Services (PSAS), jointly managed with the World Bank, advises governments and private enterprises on policy, transaction implementation and foreign direct investment. The Foreign Investment Advisory Service (FIAS), jointly operated and financed with the World Bank and MIGA, provides technical assistance and advice on promoting foreign investment and strengthening the country's investment framework at the request of governments. FIAS completed 83 projects in 2006/07, bringing a total of 760 projects since the Service was established in 1987. Under the Technical Assistance Trust Funds Program (TATF), established in 1988, IFC manages resources contributed by various governments and agencies to provide finance for feasibility studies, project identification studies and other types of technical assistance relating to project preparation. In 2004 a Grassroots Business Initiative was established, with external donor funding, to support businesses that provide economic opportunities for disadvantaged communities in Africa, Latin America, and South and Southeast Asia. Other areas of advisory services include carbon finance, cleaner technologies and sustainable investing.

# SouthAsia Enterprise Development Facility

The SouthAsia Enterprise Development Facility was established in October 2002 to deliver technical assistance and support to small and medium-sized enterprises (SMEs) in Bangladesh, Bhutan, Nepal and neighbouring states in northeastern India and to stimulate the business environment in those areas. In particular, it aimed to improve access to financial and business development services and to develop and strengthen links between SMEs and larger corporations.

**Headquarters:** United House, 10 Gulshan Ave, 4th Floor, Gulshan 1, Dhaka; tel. (2) 986-1711; fax (2) 989-4744; e-mail bangladesh@ifc.org; Gen. Man. ANIL SINHA.

## Publications

*Annual Report*.

*Doing Business* (annually).

*Emerging Stock Markets Factbook* (annually).

*Impact* (quarterly).

*Lessons of Experience* (series).

*Results on the Ground* (series).

*Review of Small Businesses* (annually).

*Sustainability Report* (annually).

Discussion papers and technical documents.

# Multilateral Investment Guarantee Agency—MIGA

**Address:** 1818 H Street, NW, Washington, DC 20433, USA.

**Telephone:** (202) 473-6163; **fax:** (202) 522-2630; **internet:** www.miga.org.

MIGA was founded in 1988 as an affiliate of the World Bank. Its mandate is to encourage the flow of foreign direct investment to, and among, developing member countries, through the provision of political risk insurance and investment marketing services to foreign investors and host governments, respectively.

## Organization

(August 2008)

MIGA is legally and financially separate from the World Bank. It is supervised by a Council of Governors (comprising one Governor and one Alternate of each member country) and an elected Board of Directors (of no less than 12 members).

**President:** ROBERT B. ZOELLICK (USA).

**Executive Vice-President:** JAMES BOND (France) (acting).

## Activities

The convention establishing MIGA took effect in April 1988. Authorized capital was US $1,082m. In April 1998 the Board of Directors approved an increase in MIGA's capital base. A grant of $150m. was transferred from the IBRD as part of the package, while the capital increase (totalling $700m. callable capital and $150m. paid-in capital) was approved by MIGA's Council of Governors in April 1999. A three-year subscription period then commenced, covering the period April 1999–March 2002 (later extended to March 2003). At 30 June 2007 109 countries had subscribed $745.8m. of the new capital increase. At that time total subscriptions to the capital stock amounted to $1,885.6m., of which $359.7m. was paid-in.

MIGA guarantees eligible investments against losses resulting from non-commercial risks, under four main categories:

(i) transfer risk resulting from host government restrictions on currency conversion and transfer;

(ii) risk of loss resulting from legislative or administrative actions of the host government;

(iii) repudiation by the host government of contracts with investors in cases in which the investor has no access to a competent forum;

(iv) the risk of armed conflict and civil unrest.

Before guaranteeing any investment, MIGA must ensure that it is commercially viable, contributes to the development process and is not harmful to the environment. During the fiscal year 1998/99 MIGA and IFC appointed the first Compliance Advisor and Ombudsman to consider the concerns of local communities directly affected by MIGA- or IFC-sponsored projects. In February 1999 the Board of Directors approved an increase in the amount of political risk insurance available for each project, from US $75m. to $200m.

During the year ending 30 June 2007 MIGA issued 45 investment insurance contracts for 29 projects with a value of US $1,400m. Since 1988 the total investment guarantees issued amounted to some $17,400m., through 884 contracts in support of 556 projects.

MIGA works with local insurers, export credit agencies, development finance institutions and other organizations to promote insurance in a country, to ensure a level of consistency among insurers and to support capacity-building within the insurance industry. MIGA also offers investment marketing services to help to promote foreign investment in developing countries and in transitional economies, and to disseminate information on investment opportunities. In early 2007 MIGA's technical assistance services were amalgamated into the Foreign Advisory Investment Service (FIAS, see IFC), of which MIGA became a lead partner, along with IFC and the World Bank.

In October 1995 MIGA established a new network on investment opportunities, which connected investment promotion agencies (IPAs) throughout the world on an electronic information network. The so-called IPA*net* aimed to encourage further investments among developing countries, to provide access to comprehensive information on investment laws and conditions and to strengthen links between governmental, business and financial associations and investors. A new version of IPA*net* was launched in 1997 (and can be accessed at www.ipanet.net). In June 1998 MIGA initiated a new internet-based facility, 'PrivatizationLink', to provide information on investment opportunities resulting from the privatization of industries in developing economies. In October 2000 a specialized facility within the service was established to facilitate investment in Russia (russia.privatizationlink.com). During 2000/01 an office was established in Paris, France, to promote and co-ordinate European investment in developing countries, in particular in Africa and Eastern Europe. In March 2002 MIGA opened a regional office, based in Johannesburg, South Africa. In September a new regional office was inaugurated in Singapore, in order to facilitate foreign investment in Asia.

In April 2002 MIGA launched a new service, 'FDIXchange', to provide potential investors, advisors and financial institutions with up-to-date market analysis and information on foreign direct investment opportunities in emerging economies (accessible at www.fdixchange.com). An FDIXchange Investor Information Development Programme was launched in January 2003. In January 2004 a new FDI Promotion Centre became available on the internet (www.fdipromotion.com) to facilitate information exchange and knowledge-sharing among investment promotion professionals, in particular in developing countries. (A Serbian language version was launched in June 2005.) During 2003/04 MIGA established a new fund, the Invest-in-Development Facility, to enhance the role of foreign investment in attaining the Millennium Development Goals. In 2005/06 MIGA supported for the first time a project aimed at selling carbon credits gained by reducing greenhouse gas emissions; it provided US $2m. in guarantee coverage to the El Salvador-based initiative. A new internet service, relating to political risk management and insurance, was launched during 2006/07 (www.pri-center.com).

In July 2004 an Afghanistan Investment Guarantee Facility, to be administered by MIGA, became operational to provide political risk guarantees for foreign investors in that country.

## Publications

*Annual Report.*

*MIGA News* (online newsletter; every 2 months).

Other guides, brochures and regional briefs.

# International Fund for Agricultural Development—IFAD

**Address:** Via del Serafico 107, 00142 Rome, Italy.

**Telephone:** (06) 54591; **fax:** (06) 5043463; **e-mail:** ifad@ifad.org; **internet:** www.ifad.org.

IFAD was established in 1977, following a decision by the 1974 UN World Food Conference, with a mandate to combat hunger and eradicate poverty on a sustainable basis in the low-income, food-deficit regions of the world. Funding operations began in January 1978.

## Organization

(August 2008)

### GOVERNING COUNCIL

Each member state is represented in the Governing Council (the Fund's highest authority) by a Governor and an Alternate. Sessions are held annually with special sessions as required. The Governing Council elects the President of the Fund (who also chairs the Executive Board) by a two-thirds majority for a four-year term. The President is eligible for re-election.

### EXECUTIVE BOARD

Consists of 18 members and 18 alternates, elected by the Governing Council, who serve for three years. The Executive Board is responsible for the conduct and general operation of IFAD and approves loans and grants for projects; it holds three regular sessions each year. An independent Office of Evaluation reports directly to the Board.

The governance structure of the Fund is based on the classification of members. Membership of the Executive Board is distributed as follows: eight List A countries (i.e. industrialized donor countries), four List B (petroleum-exporting developing donor countries), and six List C (recipient developing countries), divided equally among the three Sub-List C categories (i.e. for Africa, Europe, Asia and the Pacific, and Latin America and the Caribbean).

**President and Chairman of Executive Board:** LENNART BÅGE (Sweden).

**Vice-President:** KANAYO F. F. NWANZE (Nigeria).

## Activities

IFAD provides financing primarily for projects designed to improve food production systems in developing member states and to strengthen related policies, services and institutions. In allocating resources IFAD is guided by: the need to increase food production in the poorest food-deficit countries; the potential for increasing food production in other developing countries; and the importance of improving the nutrition, health and education of the poorest people in developing countries, i.e. small-scale farmers, artisanal fishermen, nomadic pastoralists, indigenous populations, rural women, and the rural landless. All projects emphasize the participation of beneficiaries in development initiatives, both at the local and national level. Issues relating to gender and household food security are incorporated into all aspects of its activities. IFAD is committed to achieving the so-called Millennium Development Goals (MDGs), pledged by governments attending a special session of the UN General Assembly in September 2000, and, in particular, the objective to reduce by 50% the proportion of people living in extreme poverty by 2015. In 2001 the Fund introduced new measures to improve monitoring and impact evaluation, in particular to assess its contribution to achieving the MDGs.

In December 2006 the Executive Board adopted IFAD's Strategic Framework for 2007–10, in which it reiterated its commitment to enabling the rural poor to achieve household food security and to overcome their poverty. Accordingly, the Fund's efforts were to focus on ensuring that poor rural populations have improved and sustainable access to, and sufficiently developed skills to take advantage of: natural resources; better agricultural technologies and production services; a broad range of financial services; transparent competitive agricultural input and produce markets; opportunities for rural off-farm employment and enterprise development; and local and national policy and programming processes. Within this Framework the Fund has also formulated regional strategies for rural poverty reduction, based on a series of regional poverty assessments. In 2003 a new Policy Division was established under the External Affairs Department to co-ordinate policy work at the corporate level. A Policy Forum was launched in 2004, comprising IFAD senior management and staff. During 2007–09 IFAD was implementing a performance-enhancing Action Plan for Improving its Development Effectiveness.

IFAD is a leading repository in the world of knowledge, resources and expertise in the field of rural hunger and poverty alleviation. In 2001 it renewed its commitment to becoming a global knowledge institution for rural poverty-related issues. Through its technical assistance grants, IFAD aims to promote research and capacity-building in the agricultural sector, as well as the development of technologies to increase production and alleviate rural poverty. In recent years IFAD has been increasingly involved in promoting the use of communication technology to facilitate the exchange of information and experience among rural communities, specialized institutions and organizations, and IFAD-sponsored projects. Within the strategic context of knowledge management, IFAD has supported initiatives to establish regional electronic networks, such as Electronic Networking for Rural Asia/Pacific (ENRAP, currently in its third phase), and FIDAMERICA in Latin America and the Caribbean (established in 1995 and currently in its fourth phase), as well as to develop other lines of communication between organizations, local agents and the rural poor.

IFAD participated in the High-Level Conference on World Food Security and the Challenges of Climate Change and Bioenergy, convened by FAO in Rome, Italy, in June 2008. The meeting adopted a Declaration on Food Security, which noted an urgent need to develop the agricultural sectors and expand food production in developing countries and countries with economies in transition, and for increased investment in rural development, agriculture and agribusiness.

IFAD is empowered to make both loans and grants. Loans are available on highly concessionary, intermediate and ordinary terms. Highly concessionary loans carry no interest but have an annual service charge of 0.75% and a repayment period of 40 years, including a 10-year grace period. New Debt Sustainability Framework (DSF) grant financing was introduced in 2007 in place of highly concessional loans for heavily indebted poor countries (HIPCs). Intermediate term loans are subject to a variable interest charge, equivalent to 50% of the interest rate charged on World Bank loans, and are repaid over 20 years. Ordinary loans carry a variable interest charge equal to that charged by the World Bank, and are repaid over 15–18 years. In 2007 highly concessionary loans represented some 73% of total lending in that year, DSF grants 17.6%, intermediate loans 3.2%, and ordinary loans 6.2%. Research and technical assistance grants are awarded to projects focusing on research, training, and project preparation and development. In order to increase the impact of its lending resources on food production, the Fund seeks as much as possible to attract other external donors and beneficiary governments as cofinanciers of its projects. In 2007 external cofinancing accounted for some 33.5% of all project funding, while domestic contributions, i.e. from recipient governments and other local sources, accounted for 22%.

In October 2007 the HIPC Trust Fund, administered by the World Bank, transferred US $104.1m. to IFAD, representing the first instalment of about $282m. which was to offset the impact of IFAD's debt relief commitments to post-decision point HIPC countries on the Fund's available resources for the disbursement of loans and grants. At 31 December 2007 IFAD had fulfilled its debt relief requirements to all of the 30 HIPCs that had met their decision points at that time.

IFAD's development projects usually include a number of components, such as infrastructure (e.g. improvement of water supplies, small-scale irrigation and road construction); input supply (e.g. improved seeds, fertilizers and pesticides); institutional support (e.g. research, training and extension services); and producer incentives (e.g. pricing and marketing improvements). IFAD also attempts to enable the landless to acquire income-generating assets: by increasing the provision of credit for the rural poor, it seeks to free them from dependence on the capital market and to generate productive activities.

In addition to its regular efforts to identify projects and programmes, IFAD organizes special programming missions to certain selected countries to undertake a comprehensive review of the constraints affecting the rural poor, and to help countries to design strategies for the removal of these constraints. In general, projects based on the recommendations of these missions tend to focus on institutional improvements at the national and local level to direct inputs and services to small farmers and the landless rural poor. Monitoring and evaluation missions are also sent to check the progress of projects and to assess the impact of poverty reduction efforts.

The Fund supports projects that are concerned with environmental conservation, in an effort to alleviate poverty that results from the deterioration of natural resources. In addition, it extends environmental assessment grants to review the environmental consequences of projects under preparation. In October 1997 IFAD was appointed to administer the Global Mechanism of the Convention to Combat Desertification in those Countries Experiencing Drought and Desertification, particularly in Africa, which entered into force in December 1996. The Mechanism was envisaged as a means of mobilizing and channelling resources for implementation of the Convention. A series of collaborative institutional arrangements were to be concluded between IFAD, UNDP and the World Bank in order to facilitate the effective functioning of the Mechanism. IFAD is an executing agency of the Global Environmental Facility, specializing in the area of combating rural poverty and environmental degradation.

During 2007 IFAD approved lending for eight operations in Asia and the Pacific, involving loans amounting to US $172.1m. (or 32.1% of the total committed in that year). Under a new Field Presence Pilot Programme, approved by the Executive Board in 2003 in order to strengthen project implementation, policy dialogue, partnership building and knowledge management, IFAD established field offices in the following countries in 2004: the People's Republic of China (also covering the Democratic People's Republic of Korea and Mongolia), India and Viet Nam.

In mid-1998 IFAD inaugurated the Electronic Networking for Rural Asia/Pacific Projects (ENRAP), see above, initially as a pilot project in eight countries in the region to bring the benefits of the internet to rural development projects. A Poverty Alleviation Training Programme for Asia and the Pacific (PATAP) was initiated in 1995.

In February 1998 IFAD inaugurated a new Trust Fund to complement the multilateral debt initiative for heavily indebted poor countries (HIPCs). The Fund was intended to assist IFAD's poorest members deemed to be eligible under the initiative to channel resources from debt repayments to communities in need. In February 2000 the Governing Council approved full participation by IFAD in the enhanced HIPC debt initiative agreed by the World Bank and IMF in September 1999.

During 1998 the Executive Board endorsed a policy framework for the Fund's provision of assistance in post-conflict situations, with the aim of achieving a continuum from emergency relief to a secure basis from which to pursue sustainable development. In July 2001 IFAD and UNAIDS signed a memorandum of understanding on developing a co-operation agreement. A meeting of technical experts from IFAD, FAO, WFP and UNAIDS, held in December, addressed means of mitigating the impact of HIV/AIDS on food security and rural livelihoods in affected regions.

During the late 1990s IFAD established several partnerships within the agribusiness sector, with a view to improving performance at project level, broadening access to capital markets, and encouraging the advancement of new technologies. Since 1996 it has chaired the Support Group of the Global Forum on Agricultural Research (GFAR), which facilitates dialogue between research centres and institutions, farmers' organizations, non-governmental bodies, the private sector and donors. In October 2001 IFAD became a co-sponsor of the Consultative Group on International Agricultural Research (CGIAR). In 2006 IFAD reviewed the work of the International Alliance against Hunger, which was established in 2004 to enhance co-ordination among international agencies and non-governmental organizations concerned with agriculture and rural development, and national alliances against hunger.

## Finance

In accordance with the Articles of Agreement establishing IFAD, the Governing Council periodically undertakes a review of the adequacy of resources available to the Fund and may request members to make additional contributions. The seventh replenishment of IFAD funds, covering the period 2007–09, amounted to US $720m. The provisional budget for administrative expenses for 2008 amounted to $74.1m., while some $5.5m. was budgeted in that year to the Fund's Office of Evaluation.

## Publications

*Annual Report*.
*IFAD Update* (2 a year).
*Rural Poverty Report*.
*Staff Working Papers* (series).

## Statistics

**PROJECTS IN SOUTH ASIA APPROVED IN 2007**

| Country | Purpose | Loan amount (SDR m.*) |
|---|---|---|
| Bangladesh | Finance for enterprise development and employment creation | 23.2 |
| | National agricultural technology project | 12.3 |
| Nepal | Poverty alleviation fund, phase II | 2.5 |
| Pakistan | Increasing sustainable microfinance | 22.9 |

* The average value of the SDR—Special Drawing Right—in 2007 was US $1.58025.

# International Monetary Fund—IMF

**Address:** 700 19th St, NW, Washington, DC 20431, USA.

**Telephone:** (202) 623-7000; **fax:** (202) 623-4661; **e-mail:** publicaffairs@imf.org; **internet:** www.imf.org.

The IMF was established at the same time as the World Bank in December 1945, to promote international monetary co-operation, to facilitate the expansion and balanced growth of international trade and to promote stability in foreign exchange.

## Organization

(August 2008)

**Managing Director:** DOMINIQUE STRAUSS-KAHN (France).

**First Deputy Managing Director:** JOHN LIPSKY (USA).

**Deputy Managing Directors:** TAKATOSHI KATO (Japan), MURILO PORTUGAL (Brazil).

**Director, Asia and Pacific Department:** ANOOP SINGH (India) (designate).

### BOARD OF GOVERNORS

The highest authority of the Fund is exercised by the Board of Governors, on which each member country is represented by a Governor and an Alternate Governor. The Board normally meets annually. The voting power of each country is related to its quota in the Fund. An International Monetary and Financial Committee (IMFC, formerly the Interim Committee) advises and reports to the Board on matters relating to the management and adaptation of the international monetary and financial system, sudden disturbances that might threaten the system and proposals to amend the Articles of Agreement.

### BOARD OF EXECUTIVE DIRECTORS

The 24-member Board of Executive Directors is responsible for the day-to-day operations of the Fund. The USA, United Kingdom, Germany, France and Japan each appoint one Executive Director. There is also one Executive Director from the People's Republic of China, Russia and Saudi Arabia, while the remainder are elected by groups of the remaining countries.

### REGIONAL REPRESENTATION

There is a network of regional offices and Resident Representatives in more than 90 member countries. In addition, special information and liaison offices are located in Tokyo, Japan (for Asia and the Pacific), in New York, USA (for the United Nations), and in Europe (Paris, France; Geneva, Switzerland; Belgium, Brussels; and Warsaw, Poland, for Central Europe and the Baltics).

**Regional Office for Asia and the Pacific:** 21F Fukoku Seimei Bldg, 2-2-2, Uchisaiwai-cho, Chiyodu-ku, Tokyo 100, Japan; tel. (3) 3597-6700; fax (3) 3597-6705; f. 1997; Dir AKIRA ARIYOSHI.

## Activities

The purposes of the IMF, as defined in the Articles of Agreement, are:

(i) To promote international monetary co-operation through a permanent institution which provides the machinery for consultation and collaboration on monetary problems;

(ii) To facilitate the expansion and balanced growth of international trade, and to contribute thereby to the promotion and maintenance of high levels of employment and real income and to the development of members' productive resources;

(iii) To promote exchange stability, to maintain orderly exchange arrangements among members, and to avoid competitive exchange depreciation;

(iv) To assist in the establishment of a multilateral system of payments in respect of current transactions between members and in the elimination of foreign exchange restrictions which hamper the growth of trade;

(v) To give confidence to members by making the general resources of the Fund temporarily available to them, under adequate safeguards, thus providing them with the opportunity to correct maladjustments in their balance of payments, without resorting to measures destructive of national or international prosperity;

(vi) In accordance with the above, to shorten the duration of and lessen the degree of disequilibrium in the international balances of payments of members.

In joining the Fund, each country agrees to co-operate with the above objectives. In accordance with its objective of facilitating the expansion of international trade, the IMF encourages its members to accept the obligations of Article VIII, Sections two, three and four, of the Articles of Agreement. Members that accept Article VIII undertake to refrain from imposing restrictions on the making of payments and transfers for current international transactions and from engaging in discriminatory currency arrangements or multiple currency practices without IMF approval. At the end of 2007 some 90% of members had accepted Article VIII status.

In 2000/01 the Fund established an International Capital Markets Department to improve its understanding of financial markets and a separate Consultative Group on capital markets to serve as a forum for regular dialogue between the Fund and representatives of the private sector. In mid-2006 the International Capital Markets Department was merged with the Monetary and Financial Systems Department to create the Monetary and Capital Markets Department, with the intention of strengthening surveillance of global financial transactions and monetary arrangements. In June 2008 the Managing Director presented a new Work Programme, comprising the following four immediate priorities for the Fund: to enable member countries to deal with the current crises of reduced economic growth and escalating food and fuel prices, including efforts by the Fund to strengthen surveillance activities; to review the Fund's lending instruments; to implement new organizational tools and working practices; and to advance further the Fund's governance agenda.

## QUOTAS

**Membership and Quotas in South Asia**
(million SDR)

| Country | August 2008 |
|---|---|
| Afghanistan | 161.9 |
| Bangladesh | 533.3 |
| Bhutan | 6.3 |
| India | 4,158.2 |
| Maldives | 8.2 |
| Nepal | 71.3 |
| Pakistan | 1,033.7 |
| Sri Lanka | 413.4 |

* The Special Drawing Right (SDR) was introduced in 1970 as a substitute for gold in international payments, and was intended eventually to become the principal reserve asset in the international monetary system. Its value (which was US $1.06560 at 15 August 2008, and averaged $1.58025 in 2007) is based on the currencies of the five largest exporting countries. Each member is assigned a quota related to its national income, monetary reserves, trade balance and other economic indicators; the quota approximately determines a member's voting power and the amount of foreign exchange it may purchase from the Fund. A member's subscription is equal to its quota. Quotas are reviewed at intervals of not more than five years, to take into account the state of the world economy and members' different rates of development. In January 1998 the Board of Governors approved an increase of some 45% of total IMF resources, bringing the total value of quotas to approximately SDR 212,000m. By January 1999 member states having at least 85% of total quotas (as at December 1997) had consented to the new subscriptions enabling the increase to enter into effect. The Twelfth and Thirteenth General Reviews were concluded without an increase in quotas in January 2003 and 2008, respectively. At August 2008 total quotas in the Fund amounted to SDR 217,372.7m.

## RESOURCES

Members' subscriptions form the basic resource of the IMF. They are supplemented by borrowing. Under the General Arrangements to Borrow (GAB), established in 1962, the Group of Ten industrialized nations (G10—Belgium, Canada, France, Germany, Italy, Japan, the Netherlands, Sweden, the United Kingdom and the USA) and Switzerland (which became a member of the IMF in May 1992 but which had been a full participant in the GAB from April 1984) undertake to lend the Fund as much as SDR 17,000m. in their own currencies to assist in fulfilling the balance of payments requirements of any member of the group, or in response to requests to the Fund from countries with balance of payments problems that could threaten the stability of the international monetary system. In 1983 the Fund entered into an agreement with Saudi Arabia, in association with the GAB, making available SDR 1,500m., and other borrowing arrangements were completed in 1984 with the Bank for International Settlements, the Saudi Arabian Monetary Agency, Belgium and Japan, making available a further SDR 6,000m. In 1986 another borrowing arrangement with Japan made available SDR 3,000m. In May 1996 GAB participants concluded an agreement in principle to expand the resources available for borrowing to SDR 34,000m., by securing the support of 25 countries with the financial capacity to support the international monetary system. The so-called New Arrangements to Borrow (NAB) was approved by the Executive Board in January 1997. It was to enter into force, for an initial five-year period, as soon as the five largest potential creditors participating in NAB had approved the initiative and the total credit arrangement of participants endorsing the scheme had reached at least SDR 28,900m. While the GAB credit arrangement was to remain in effect, the NAB was expected to be the first facility to be activated in the event of the Fund's requiring supplementary resources. In July 1998 the GAB was activated for the first time in more than 20 years in order to provide funds of up to US $6,300m. in support of an IMF emergency assistance package for Russia (the first time the GAB had been used for a non-participant). The NAB became effective in November, and was used for the first time as part of an extensive programme of support for Brazil, which was adopted by the IMF in early December. (In March 1999, however, the activation was cancelled.) In November 2002 NAB participants approved Chile's Central Bank as the 26th participant.

## FINANCIAL ASSISTANCE

The Fund makes resources available to eligible members on an essentially short-term and revolving basis to provide members with temporary assistance to contribute to the solution of their payments problems. Before making a purchase, a member must show that its balance of payments or reserve position makes the purchase necessary. Apart from this requirement, reserve tranche purchases (i.e. purchases that do not bring the Fund's holdings of the member's currency to a level above its quota) are permitted unconditionally. Exchange transactions within the Fund take the form of members' purchases (i.e. drawings) from the Fund of the currencies of other members for the equivalent amounts of their own currencies.

With further purchases, however, the Fund's policy of conditionality means that a recipient country must agree to adjust its economic policies, as stipulated by the IMF. All requests other than for use of the reserve tranche are examined by the Executive Board to determine whether the proposed use would be consistent with the Fund's policies, and a member must discuss its proposed adjustment programme (including fiscal, monetary, exchange and trade policies) with IMF staff. (New guidelines on conditionality, which, *inter alia*, aimed to promote national ownership of policy reforms and to introduce specific criteria for the implementation of conditions given different states' circumstances, were approved by the Executive Board in September 2002.) Purchases outside the reserve tranche are made in four credit tranches, each equivalent to 25% of the member's quota; a member must reverse the transaction by repurchasing its own currency (with SDRs or currencies specified by the Fund) within a specified time. A credit tranche purchase is usually made under a 'Stand-by Arrangement' with the Fund, or under the Extended Fund Facility. A Stand-by Arrangement is normally of one or two years' duration, and the amount is made available in instalments, subject to the member's observance of 'performance criteria'; repurchases must be made within three-and-a-quarter to five years. An Extended Arrangement is normally of three years' duration, and the member must submit detailed economic programmes and progress reports for each year; repurchases must be made within four-and-a-half to 10 years. A member whose payments imbalance is large in relation to its quota may make use of temporary facilities established by the Fund using borrowed resources, namely the 'enlarged access policy' established in 1981, which helps to finance Stand-by and Extended Arrangements for such a member, up to a limit of between 90% and 110% of the member's quota annually. Repurchases are made within three-and-a-half to seven years. In October 1994 the Executive Board approved a temporary increase in members' access to IMF resources, on the basis of a recommendation by the then Interim Committee. The annual access limit under IMF regular tranche drawings, Stand-by Arrangements and Extended Fund Facility credits was increased from 68% to 100% of a member's quota, with the cumulative access limit remaining at 300% of quota. The arrangements were extended, on a temporary basis, in November 1997.

In addition, special-purpose arrangements have been introduced, all of which are subject to the member's co-operation with the Fund to find an appropriate solution to its difficulties. The Compensatory Financing Facility (CCF) provides compensation to members whose export earnings are reduced as a result of circumstances beyond their control, or which are affected by excess costs of cereal imports. In December 1997 the Executive Board established a new Supplemental Reserve Facility (SRF) to provide short-term assistance to members experiencing exceptional balance of payments difficulties resulting from a sudden loss of market confidence. The SRF was activated immediately to provide SDR 9,950m. to the Republic of Korea, as part of a Stand-by Arrangement amounting to SDR 15,550m. (at that time the largest amount ever committed by the Fund). In July 1998 SDR 4,000m. was made available to Russia under the SRF and, in December, some SDR 9,100m. was extended to Brazil under the SRF as part of a new Stand-by Arrangement. In January 2001 some SDR 2,100m. in SRF resources were approved for Argentina as part of an SDR 5,187m. Stand-by Arrangement augmentation. (In January 2002 the Executive Board approved an extension of one year for Argentina's SRF repayments.) The SDR 22,821m. Stand-by credit approved for Brazil in September 2002 included some SDR 7,600m. committed under the SRF. In April 1999 an additional facility, the Contingent Credit Lines (CCL), was established to provide short-term financing on similar terms to the SRF in order to prevent more stable economies being affected by adverse international financial developments and to maintain investor confidence. No funds were ever committed under the CCL, however, and in November 2003 the Executive Board resolved to allow the facility to terminate, as scheduled, at the end of that month. The Board requested further consideration of other precautionary arrangements to limit the risk of financial crises. In April 2004 the Board approved a new initiative, the Trade Integration Mechanism, to support countries experiencing short-term balance of payments shortfalls as a result of multilateral trade liberalization. Bangladesh, in July, was the first country to obtain assistance in accordance with the Mechanism (in the form of an augmentation of an existing PRGF arrangement).

In October 1995 the Interim Committee of the Board of Governors endorsed recent decisions of the Executive Board to strengthen IMF financial support to members requiring exceptional assistance. An Emergency Financing Mechanism was established to enable the IMF to respond swiftly to potential or actual financial crises, while additional funds were made available for short-term currency stabilization. (The Mechanism was activated for the first time in July 1997, in response to a request by the Philippines Government to reinforce the country's international reserves, and was subsequently used during that year to assist Thailand, Indonesia and the Republic of Korea, and, in July 1998, Russia.) Emergency assistance was also to be available to countries in a post-conflict situation, extending the existing arrangements for countries having been affected by natural disasters, to facilitate the rehabilitation of their economies and to improve their eligibility for further IMF concessionary arrangements. Assistance, typically, was to be limited to 25% of a member's quota, although up to 50% would be permitted in certain circumstances. In May 2001 the Executive Board decided to provide a subsidized loan rate for post-conflict emergency assistance for PRGF-eligible countries and an account was established to administer contributions from bilateral donors. In January 2005 the Executive Board decided to extend the subsidized rate for natural disasters. During 2006/07 the Fund approved assistance of SDR 50.8m. for Lebanon under the emergency post-conflict assistance facility.

In November 1999 the Fund's existing facility to provide balance of payments assistance on concessionary terms to low-income member countries, the Enhanced Structural Adjustment Facility, was reformulated as the Poverty Reduction and Growth Facility, with greater emphasis on poverty reduction and sustainable development as key elements of growth-orientated economic strategies. Assistance under the PRGF (for which 77 countries were deemed eligible) was to be carefully matched to specific national requirements. Prior to drawing on the facility each recipient country was, in collaboration with representatives of civil society, non-governmental organizations and bilateral and multilateral institutions, to develop a national poverty reduction strategy, which was to be presented in a Poverty Reduction Strategy Paper (PRSP). PRGF loans carry an interest rate of 0.5% per year and are repayable over 10 years, with a five-and-a-half-year grace period; each eligible country is normally permitted to borrow up to 140% of its quota (in exceptional circumstances the maximum access can be raised to 185%). A PRGF Trust replaced the former ESAF Trust. In January 2006 a new Exogenous Shocks Facility was inaugurated to provide concessional assistance on the same terms as those of the PRGF for countries not eligible for funding under the PRGF.

During 2006/07 the IMF approved regular funding commitments for new arrangements amounting to SDR 237.4m. for two new Stand-by Arrangements, compared with a total of SDR 8,336m. in the previous year. Ten new PRGF arrangements, amounting to SDR 401.2m., were approved in 2006/07, together with the augmentation of two existing arrangements (SDR 36.8m.) and the reduction, by SDR 75m., of a further arrangement. During 2006/07 members' purchases from the general resources account amounted to SDR 2,329m., compared with SDR 2,156m. in the previous year. Outstanding IMF credit at 30 April 2007 totalled SDR 11,216m., compared with SDR 23,144m. in the previous year.

During the financial year 2006/07 a new Stand-by Arrangement was approved for Afghanistan, amounting to SDR 81.0m.

The PRGF supports, through long-maturity loans and grants, IMF participation in an initiative to provide exceptional assistance to heavily indebted poor countries (HIPCs), in order to help them to achieve a sustainable level of debt management. In all 41 HIPCs were identified, of which 33 were in sub-Saharan Africa. Resources for the HIPC initiative are channelled through the PRGF Trust. In early 1999 the IMF and World Bank initiated a comprehensive review of the HIPC scheme, in order to consider modifications of the initiative and to strengthen the link between debt relief and poverty reduction. A consensus emerged among the financial institutions and leading industrialized nations to enhance the scheme, in order to make it available to more countries, and to accelerate the process of providing debt relief. In September the IMF Board of Governors expressed its commitment to undertaking an off-market transaction of a percentage of the Fund's gold reserves (i.e. a sale, at market prices, to central banks of member countries with repayment obligations to the Fund, which were then to be made in gold), as part of the funding arrangements of the enhanced HIPC scheme; this was undertaken during the period December 1999–April 2000. Under the enhanced initiative it was agreed that countries seeking debt relief should first formulate, and successfully implement for at least one year, a national poverty reduction strategy (see above). In May 2000 Uganda became the first country to qualify for full debt relief under the enhanced scheme. In September 2005 the IMF and World Bank endorsed a proposal of the Group of Eight (G8) nations to achieve the cancellation by the IMF, IDA and African Development Bank of 100% of debt claims on countries that had reached completion point under the HIPC initiative, in order to help them to achieve their Millennium Development Goals. The debt cancellation was to be undertaken within the framework of a Multilateral Debt Relief Initiative (MDRI). The IMF's Executive Board determined, additionally, to extend MDRI debt relief to all countries with an annual per capita of GDP $380, to be financed by IMF's own resources. Other financing was to be made from existing bilateral contributions to the PRGF Trust Subsidy Account. The initiative became effective in January 2006 once the final consent of the 43 contributors to the PRGF Trust Subsidy Account had been received. By the end of 2007 the IMF had committed some SDR 2,304m. under the MDRI scheme.

## SURVEILLANCE

Under its Articles of Agreement, the Fund is mandated to oversee the effective functioning of the international monetary system. Accordingly, the Fund aims to exercise firm surveillance over the exchange rate policies of member states and to assess whether a country's economic situation and policies are consistent with the objectives of sustainable development and domestic and external stability. The Fund's main tools of surveillance are regular, bilateral consultations with member countries conducted in accordance with Article IV of the Articles of Agreement, which cover fiscal and monetary policies, balance of payments and external debt developments, as well as policies that affect the economic performance of a country, such as the labour market, social and environmental issues and good governance, and aspects of the country's capital accounts, and finance and banking sectors. In April 1997, in an effort to improve the value of surveillance by means of increased transparency, the Executive Board agreed to the voluntary issue of Press Information Notices (PINs) following each member's Article IV consultation with the Board, to those member countries wishing to make public the Fund's views. Other background papers providing information on and analysis of economic developments in individual countries continued to be made available. The Executive Board monitors global economic developments and discusses policy implications from a multilateral perspective, based partly on World Economic Outlook reports and Global Financial Stability Reports. In addition, the IMF studies the regional implications of global developments and policies pursued under regional fiscal arrangements. The Fund's medium-term strategy, initiated in 2006, determined to strengthen its surveillance policies to reflect new challenges of globalization on international financial and macroeconomic stability. In June 2007 the Executive Board approved a Decision on Bilateral Surveillance to update and clarify principles for a member's exchange rate policies and to define best practice for the Fund's bilateral surveillance activities.

In April 1996 the IMF established the Special Data Dissemination Standard (SDDS), which was intended to improve access to reliable economic statistical information for member countries that have, or are seeking, access to international capital markets. In March 1999 the IMF undertook to strengthen the Standard by the introduction of a new reserves data template. By April 2007 64 countries had subscribed to the Standard. The financial crisis in Asia, which became apparent in mid-1997, focused attention on the importance of IMF surveillance of the economies and financial policies of member states and prompted the Fund further to enhance the effectiveness of its surveillance through the development of international standards in order to maintain fiscal transparency. In December 1997 the Executive Board approved a new General Data Dissemination System (GDDS), to encourage all member countries to improve the production and dissemination of core economic data. The operational phase of the GDDS commenced in May 2000. By August 2008 93 countries were participating in the GDDS. The Fund maintains a Dissemination Standards Bulletin Board (accessible at dsbb.imf.org), which aims to ensure that information on SDDS subscribing countries is widely available.

In April 1998 the then Interim Committee adopted a voluntary Code of Good Practices on Fiscal Transparency: Declaration of Principles, which aimed to increase the quality and promptness of official reports on economic indicators, and in September 1999 it adopted a Code of Good Practices on Transparency in Monetary and Financial Policies: Declaration of Principles. The IMF and World Bank jointly established a Financial Sector Assessment Programme (FSAP) in May 1999, initially as a pilot project, which aimed to promote greater global financial security through the preparation of confidential detailed evaluations of the financial sectors of individual countries. It remained under regular review by the Boards of Governors of the Fund and World Bank. During 2006/07 18 FSAP assessments were completed, of which six were updated assessments. As part of the FSAP Fund staff may conclude a Financial System Stability Assessment (FSSA), addressing issues relating to macroeconomic stability and the strength of a country's financial system. A separate component of the FSAP are Reports on the Observance of Standards and Codes (ROSCs), which are compiled after an assessment of a country's implementation and observance of internationally recognized financial standards. By March 2008 540 ROSCs had been published for 136 economies.

In March 2000 the IMF Executive Board adopted a strengthened framework to safeguard the use of IMF resources. All member countries making use of Fund resources were to be required to publish annual central bank statements audited in accordance with internationally accepted standards. It was also agreed that any instance of intentional misreporting of information by a member country should be made public. In the following month the Executive Board approved the establishment of an Independent Evaluation Office (IEO) to conduct objective evaluations of IMF policy and operations. The Office commenced activities in July 2001. In 2006/07 the Office concluded an evaluation on the IMF and Aid to Sub-Saharan Africa.

In April 2001 the Executive Board agreed on measures to enhance international efforts to counter money-laundering, in particular through the Fund's ongoing financial supervision activities and its programme of assessment of offshore financial centres (OFCs). In November the IMFC, in response to the terrorist attacks against targets in the USA, which had occurred in September, resolved, *inter alia*, to strengthen the Fund's focus on surveillance, and, in particular, to extend measures to counter money-laundering to include the funds of terrorist organizations. It determined to accelerate efforts to assess offshore centres and to provide technical support to enable poorer countries to meet international financial standards. In March 2004 the Board of Directors resolved that an anti-money laundering and countering the financing of terrorism (AML/CFT) component be introduced into regular OFC and FSAP assessments conducted by the Fund and the World Bank, following a pilot programme undertaken from November 2002 with the World Bank, the Financial Action Task Force and other regional supervisory bodies. The first phase of the OFC assessment programme was concluded in February 2005, at which time 41 of 44 contacted jurisdictions had been assessed and the reports published.

### TECHNICAL ASSISTANCE

Technical assistance is provided by special missions or resident representatives who advise members on every aspect of economic management, while more specialized assistance is provided by the IMF's various departments. In 2000/01 the IMFC determined that technical assistance should be central to the IMF's work in crisis prevention and management, in capacity-building for low-income countries, and in restoring macroeconomic stability in countries following a financial crisis. Technical assistance activities subsequently underwent a process of review and reorganization to align them more closely with IMF policy priorities and other initiatives.

The IMF Institute, which was established in 1964, trains officials from member countries in macroeconomic management, financial analysis and policy, balance of payments methodology and public finance. The IMF Institute also co-operates with other established regional training centres and institutes in order to refine its delivery of technical assistance and training services. The IMF is a co-sponsor, with UNDP and the Japan administered account, of the Joint Vienna Institute, which was opened in the Austrian capital in October 1992 and which trains officials from former centrally-planned economies in various aspects of economic management and public administration. In May 1998 an IMF—Singapore Regional Training Institute (an affiliate of the IMF Institute) was inaugurated, in collaboration with the Singaporean Government, in order to provide training for officials from the Asia-Pacific region. In January 1999 the IMF, in co-operation with the African Development Bank and the World Bank, announced the establishment of a Joint Africa Institute, in Abidjan, Côte d'Ivoire, which was to offer training to officials from African countries. Also in 1999 a joint Regional Training Programme, administered with the Arab Monetary Fund, was established in the United Arab Emirates. During 2000/01 the Institute established a new training programme with government officials in Liaoning Province, the People's Republic of China. A regional training centre for Latin America became operational in Brasilia, Brazil in 2001. In July 2006 the Joint India-IMF Training Programme was inaugurated in Pune, India.

## Publications

*Annual Report*.
*Balance of Payments Statistics Yearbook*.
*Civil Society Newsletter* (quarterly).
*Direction of Trade Statistics* (quarterly and annually).
*Emerging Markets Financing* (quarterly).
*Finance and Development* (quarterly).
*Financial Statements of the IMF* (quarterly).
*Global Financial Stability Report* (2 a year).
*Global Monitoring Report* (annually, with the World Bank).
*Government Finance Statistics Yearbook*.
*IMF Commodity Prices* (monthly).
*IMF Financial Activities* (weekly, online).
*IMF in Focus* (annually).
*IMF Research Bulletin* (quarterly).
*IMF Survey* (monthly, and online).
*International Financial Statistics* (monthly and annually).
*Joint BIS-IMF-OECD-World Bank Statistics on External Debt* (quarterly).
*Quarterly Report on the Assessments of Standards and Codes*.
*Staff Papers* (quarterly).
*World Economic Outlook* (2 a year).
Other country reports, economic and financial surveys, occasional papers, pamphlets, books.

# United Nations Educational, Scientific and Cultural Organization—UNESCO

**Address:** 7 place de Fontenoy, 75352 Paris 07 SP, France.

**Telephone:** 1-45-68-10-00; **fax:** 1-45-67-16-90; **e-mail:** bpi@unesco.org; **internet:** www.unesco.org.

UNESCO was established in 1946 'for the purpose of advancing, through the educational, scientific and cultural relations of the peoples of the world, the objectives of international peace and the common welfare of mankind'.

## Organization

(August 2008)

### GENERAL CONFERENCE

The supreme governing body of the Organization, the Conference meets in ordinary session once in two years and is composed of representatives of the member states. It determines policies, approves work programmes and budgets and elects members of the Executive Board.

### EXECUTIVE BOARD

The Board, comprising 58 members, prepares the programme to be submitted to the Conference and supervises its execution; it meets two times a year.

### SECRETARIAT

The organization is headed by a Director-General, appointed for a four-year term. There are Assistant Directors-General for the main thematic sectors, i.e education, natural sciences, social and human sciences, culture, and communication and information, as well as for the support sectors of external relations and co-operation and of administration.

**Director-General:** Koïchiro Matsuura (Japan).

### CO-OPERATING BODIES

In accordance with UNESCO's constitution, national Commissions have been set up in most member states. These help to integrate work within the member states and the work of UNESCO. Most member states also have their own permanent delegations to UNESCO. UNESCO aims to develop partnerships with cities and local authorities.

### FIELD CO-ORDINATION

UNESCO maintains a network of offices to support a more decentralized approach to its activities and enhance their implementation at field level. Cluster offices provide the main structure of the field co-ordination network. These cover a group of countries and help to co-ordinate between member states and with other UN and partner agencies operating in the area. In 2008 there were 27 cluster offices covering 143 states. In addition 21 national offices serve a single country, including those in post-conflict situations or economic transition and the nine most highly-populated countries. The regional bureaux (see below) provide specialized support at a national level.

### REGIONAL BUREAUX

**Regional Bureau for Education in Asia and the Pacific:** POB 967, Bangkok 10110, Thailand; tel. (2) 391-0577; fax (2) 391-0866; e-mail bangkok@unescobkk.org; internet www.unescobkk.org; Dir SHELDON SCHAEFFER.

## Activities

In the implementation of all its activities UNESCO aims to contribute to achieving the UN Millennium Development Goal (MDG) of halving levels of extreme poverty by 2015, as well as other MDGs concerned with education and sustainable development. UNESCO is the lead agency for the International Decade for a Culture of Peace and Non-violence for the Children of the World (2001–10). In November 2007 the General Conference approved a medium-term strategy to guide UNESCO during the period 2008–13. UNESCO's central mission as defined under the strategy was to contribute to building peace, the alleviation of poverty, sustainable development and intercultural dialogue through its core programme sectors (Education; Natural Sciences; Social and Human Sciences; Culture; and Communication and Information). The strategy identified five 'overarching objectives' for UNESCO in 2008–13, within this programme framework: Attaining quality education for all; Mobilizing scientific knowledge and science policy for sustainable development; Addressing emerging ethical challenges; Promoting cultural diversity and intercultural dialogue; and Building inclusive knowledge societies through information and communication.

### EDUCATION

UNESCO recognizes education as an essential human right, and an overarching objective for 2008–13 was to attain quality education for all. Through its work programme UNESCO is committed to achieving the MDGs of eliminating gender disparity at all levels of education and attaining universal primary education in all countries by 2015. The focus of many of UNESCO's education initiatives are the nine most highly-populated developing countries (Bangladesh, Brazil, the People's Republic of China, Egypt, India, Indonesia, Mexico, Nigeria and Pakistan), known collectively as the E-9 ('Education-9') countries.

UNESCO leads and co-ordinates global efforts in support of 'Education for All' (EFA), which was adopted as a guiding principle of UNESCO's contribution to development following a world conference, convened in March 1990. In April 2000 several UN agencies, including UNESCO and UNICEF, and other partners sponsored the World Education Forum, held in Dakar, Senegal, to assess international progress in achieving the goal of Education for All and to adopt a strategy for further action (the 'Dakar Framework'), with the aim of ensuring universal basic education by 2015. The Dakar Framework, incorporating six specific goals, emphasized the role of improved access to education in the reduction of poverty and in diminishing inequalities within and between societies. UNESCO was appointed as the lead agency in the implementation of the Framework, focusing on co-ordination, advocacy, mobilization of resources, and information-sharing at international, regional and national levels. It was to oversee national policy reforms, with a particular focus on the integration of EFA objectives into national education plans. An EFA Global Action Plan was formulated in 2006 to reinvigorate efforts to achieve EFA objectives and, in particular, to provide a framework for international co-operation and better definition of the roles of international partners and of UNESCO in leading the initiative. UNESCO's medium-term strategy for 2008–13 committed the organization to strengthening its role in co-ordinating EFA efforts at global and national levels, promoting monitoring and capacity-building activities to support implementation of EFA objectives, and facilitating mobilization of increased resources for EFA programmes and strategies (for example through the EFA-Fast Track Initiative, launched in 2002 to accelerate technical and financial support to low-income countries).

UNESCO advocates 'Literacy for All' as a key component of Education for All, regarding literacy as essential to basic education and to social and human development. UNESCO is the lead agency of the UN Literacy Decade (2003–12), which aims to formulate an international plan of action to raise literacy standards throughout the world and to assist policy-makers to integrate literacy standards and goals into national education programmes. The Literacy Initiative for Empowerment (LIFE) was developed as an element of the Literacy Decade to accelerate efforts in some 35 countries where illiteracy is a critical challenge to development. UNESCO is also the co-ordinating agency for the UN Decade of Education for Sustainable Development (2005–14), through which it aims to establish a global framework for action and strengthen the capacity of education systems to incorporate the concepts of sustainable development into education programmes. The April 2000 World Education Forum recognized the global HIV/AIDS pandemic to be a significant challenge to the attainment of Education for All'. UNESCO, as a co-sponsor of UNAIDS, takes an active role in promoting formal and non-formal preventive health education. Through a Global Initiative on HIV/AIDS and Education (EDUCAIDS) UNESCO aims to develop comprehensive responses to HIV/AIDS rooted in the education sector, with a particular focus on vulnerable children and young people. An initiative covering the 10-year period 2006–15, the Teacher Training Initiative in sub-Saharan Africa, aims to address the shortage of teachers in that region (owing to HIV/AIDS, armed conflict and other causes) and to improve the quality of teaching.

A key priority area of UNESCO's education programme is to foster quality education for all, through formal and non-formal educational opportunities. It assists members to improve the quality of education provision through curricula content, school management and teacher training. UNESCO aims to expand access to education at all levels and to work to achieve gender equality. In particular, UNESCO aims to strengthen capacity-building and education in natural, social and human sciences and promote the use of new technologies in teaching and learning processes.

The Associated Schools Project (ASPnet—comprising some 7,900 institutions in 176 countries in 2008) has, since 1953, promoted the principles of peace, human rights, democracy and international co-operation through education. It provides a forum for dialogue and for promoting best practices. At tertiary level UNESCO chairs a University Twinning and Networking (UNITWIN) initiative, which was established in 1992 to establish links between higher education institutions and to foster research, training and programme development. A complementary initiative, Academics Across Borders, was inaugurated in November 2005 to strengthen communication and the sharing of knowledge and expertise among higher education professionals. In October 2002 UNESCO organized the first Global Forum on International Quality Assurance, Accreditation and the Recognition of Qualifications to establish international standards and promote capacity-building for the sustainable development of higher education systems.

Within the UN system UNESCO is responsible for providing technical assistance and educational services in the context of emergency situations. This includes establishing temporary schools, providing education to refugees and displaced persons, as well as assistance for the rehabilitation of national education systems. In Palestine, UNESCO collaborates with UNRWA to assist with the training of teachers, educational planning and rehabilitation of schools.

### NATURAL SCIENCES

The World Summit on Sustainable Development, held in August–September 2002, recognised the essential role of science (including mathematics, engineering and technology) as a foundation for achieving the MDGs of eradicating extreme poverty and ensuring environmental sustainability. UNESCO aims to promote this function within the UN system and to assist member states to utilise and foster the benefits of scientific and technical knowledge. A key objective for the medium-term strategy 2008–13 was to mobilize science knowledge and policy for sustainable development. Throughout the natural science programme priority was to be placed on Africa, least developed countries and small island developing states. The Local and Indigenous Knowledge System (LINKS) initiative aims to strengthen dialogue among traditional knowledge holders, natural and social scientists and decision-makers to enhance the conservation of biodiversity, in all disciplines, and to secure an active and equitable role for local communities in the governance of resources.

In November 1999 the General Conference endorsed a Declaration on Science and the Use of Scientific Knowledge and an agenda for action, which had been adopted at the World Conference on Science, held in June–July 1999, in Budapest, Hungary. By leveraging scientific knowledge, and global, regional and country level science networks, UNESCO aims to support sustainable development and the sound management of natural resources. It also advises governments on approaches to natural resource management, in particular the collection of scientific data, documenting and disseminating good practices and integrating social and cultural aspects into management structures and policies. UNESCO's Man and the Biosphere Programme supports a world-wide network of biosphere reserves (comprising 531 sites in 105 countries at July 2008), which aim to promote environmental conservation and research, education and training in biodiversity and problems of land use (including the fertility of tropical soils and the cultivation of sacred sites). The third World Congress of Biosphere Reserves was held in Madrid, Spain, in February 2008. UNESCO also supports a Global Network of National Geoparks (57 in 18 countries at July 2008) which was inaugurated in 2004 to promote collaboration among managed areas of geological significance to exchange knowledge and expertise and raise awareness of the benefits of protecting those environments.

UNESCO promotes and supports international scientific partnerships to monitor, assess and report on the state of Earth systems. With the World Meteorological Organization and the International Council of Science, UNESCO sponsors the World Climate Research Programme, which was established in 1980 to determine the predictability of climate and the effect of human activity on climate. UNESCO hosts the secretariat of the World Water Assessment Programme (WWAP), which prepares the periodic *World Water Development Report*. UNESCO is actively involved in the 10-year project, agreed by more than 60 governments in February 2005, to develop a Global Earth Observation System of Systems (GEOSS). The project aims to link existing and planned observation systems in order to provide for greater understanding of the earth's processes and dissemination of detailed data, for example predicting health epidemics or weather phenomena or concerning the management of ecosystems and natural resources. UNESCO's Intergovernmental Oceanographic Commission serves as the Secretariat of the Global Ocean Observing System. The International Geoscience Programme, undertaken jointly with the International Union of Geological Sciences (IUGS), facilitates the exchange of knowledge and methodology among scientists concerned with geological processes and aims to raise awareness of the links between geoscience and sustainable socio-economic development. The IUGS and UNESCO jointly initiated the International Year of Planet Earth (2008).

UNESCO is committed to contributing to international efforts to enhance disaster preparedness and mitigation. Through education UNESCO aims to reduce the vulnerability of poorer communities to disasters and improve disaster management at local and national levels. It also co-ordinates efforts at an international level to establish monitoring networks and early-warning systems to mitigate natural disasters, in particular in developing tsunami early-warning systems in Africa, the Caribbean, the South Pacific, the Mediterranean Sea and the North East Atlantic similar to those already established for the Indian and Pacific oceans. Other regional partnerships and knowledge networks were to be developed to strengthen capacity-building and the dissemination of information and good practices relating to risk awareness and mitigation and disaster management. Disaster education and awareness were to be incorporated as key elements in the UN Decade on Education for Sustainable Development (see above). UNESCO is also the lead agency for the International Flood Initiative, which was inaugurated in January 2005 at the World Conference on Disaster Reduction, held in Kobe, Japan. The Initiative aimed to promote an integrated approach to flood management in order to minimize the damage and loss of life caused by floods, mainly with a focus on research, training, promoting good governance and providing technical assistance

A priority of the natural science programme for 2008–09 was to promote policies and strengthen human and institutional capacities in science, technology and innovation. At all levels of education UNESCO aimed to enhance teaching quality and content in areas of science and technology and, at regional and sub-regional level, to strengthen co-operation mechanisms and policy networks in training and research. With the International Council of Scientific Unions and the Third World Academy of Sciences, UNESCO operates a short-term fellowship programme in the basic sciences and an exchange programme of visiting lecturers.

UNESCO is the lead agency of the New Partnership for Africa's Development (NEPAD) Science and Technology Cluster and the NEPAD Action Plan for the Environment.

## SOCIAL AND HUMAN SCIENCES

UNESCO is mandated to contribute to the world-wide development of the social and human sciences and philosophy, which it regards as of great importance in policy-making and maintaining ethical vigilance. The structure of UNESCO's Social and Human Sciences programme takes into account both an ethical and standard-setting dimension, and research, policy-making, action in the field and future-oriented activities. One of UNESCO's so-called overarching objectives in the period 2008–13 was to address emerging ethical challenges.

A priority area of UNESCO's work programme on Social and Human Sciences for 2008–09 was to promote principles, practices and ethical norms relevant for scientific and technological development. It fosters international co-operation and dialogue on emerging issues, as well as raising awareness and promoting the sharing of knowledge at regional and national levels. UNESCO supports the activities of the International Bioethics Committee (IBC—a group of 36 specialists who meet under UNESCO auspices) and the Intergovernmental Bioethics Committee and hosts the secretariat of the 18-member World Commission on the Ethics of Scientific Knowledge and Technology (COMEST), established in 1999, which aims to serve as a forum for the exchange of information and ideas and to promote dialogue between scientific communities, decision-makers and the public.

The priority Ethics of science and technology element aims to promote intergovernmental discussion and co-operation; to conduct explorative studies on possible UNESCO action on environmental ethics and developing a code of conduct for scientists; to enhance public awareness; to make available teaching expertise and create regional networks of experts; to promote the development of international and national databases on ethical issues; to identify ethical issues related to emerging technologies; to follow up relevant declarations, including the Universal Declaration on the Human Genome and Human Rights (see below); and to support the Global Ethics Observatory, an online world-wide database of information on applied bioethics and other applied science- and technology-related areas (including environmental ethics) that was launched in December 2005 by the IBC.

UNESCO itself provides an interdisciplinary, multicultural and pluralistic forum for reflection on issues relating to the ethical dimension of scientific advances, and promotes the application of international guidelines. In May 1997 the IBC approved a draft version of a Universal Declaration on the Human Genome and Human Rights, in an attempt to provide ethical guide-lines for developments in human genetics. The Declaration, which identified some 100,000 hereditary genes as 'common heritage', was adopted by the UNESCO General Conference in November and committed states to promoting the dissemination of relevant scientific knowledge and co-operating in genome research. In October 2003 the General Conference adopted an International Declaration on Human Genetic Data, establishing standards for scientists working in that field, and in October 2005 the General Conference adopted the Universal Declaration on Bioethics and Human Rights. At all levels UNESCO aims to raise awareness and foster debate about the ethical implications of scientific and technological developments and promote exchange of experiences and knowledge between governments and research bodies.

UNESCO recognizes that globalization has a broad and significant impact on societies. It is committed to countering negative trends of social transformation by strengthening the links between research and policy formulation by national and local authorities, in particular concerning poverty eradication. In that respect, UNESCO promotes the concept that freedom from poverty is a fundamental human right. In 1994 UNESCO initiated an international social science research programme, the Management of Social Transformations (MOST), to promote capacity-building in social planning at all levels of decision-making. In 2003 the Executive Board approved a continuation of the programme but with a revised strategic objective of strengthening links between research, policy and practice. In 2008–13 UNESCO aimed to promote new collaborative social science research programmes and to support capacity-building in developing countries.

UNESCO aims to monitor emerging social or ethical issues and, through its associated offices and institutes, formulate preventative action to ensure they have minimal impact on the attainment of UNESCO's objectives. As a specific challenge UNESCO is committed to promoting the International Convention against Doping in Sport, which entered into force in 2007. UNESCO also focuses on the educational and cultural dimensions of physical education and sport and their capacity to preserve and improve health.

Fundamental to UNESCO's mission is the rejection of all forms of discrimination. It disseminates information aimed at combating racial prejudice, works to improve the status of women and their access to education, promotes equality between men and women, and raises awareness of discrimination against people affected by HIV/AIDS, in particular among young people. In 2004 UNESCO inaugurated an initiative to enable city authorities to share experiences and collaborate in efforts to counter racism, discrimination, xenophobia and exclusion. As well as the International Coalition of Cities against Racism, regional coalitions were to be formed with more defined programmes of action. A Coalition of Cities against Discrimination in Asia and the Pacific (APCaRD) was inaugurated in Bangkok, Thailand, in August 2006. An International Youth Clearing House and Information Service (INFOYOUTH) aims to increase and consolidate the information available on the situation of young people in society, and to heighten awareness of their needs, aspirations and potential among public and private decision-makers. Supporting efforts to facilitate dialogue among different cultures and societies and promoting opportunities for reflection and consideration of philosophy and human rights, for example the celebration of World Philosophy Day, are also among UNESCO's fundamental aims.

## CULTURE

In undertaking efforts to preserve the world's cultural and natural heritage UNESCO has attempted to emphasize the link between culture and development. In December 1992 UNESCO established the World Commission on Culture and Development, to strengthen links between culture and development and to prepare a report on the issue. The first World Conference on Culture and Development was held in June 1999, in Havana, Cuba. In November 2001 the General Conference adopted the UNESCO Universal Declaration on Cultural Diversity, which affirmed the importance of intercultural dialogue in establishing a climate of peace. UNESCO's medium-term strategy for 2008–13 recognized the need for a more integrated approach to cultural heritage as an area requiring conservation and development and one offering prospects for dialogue, social cohesion and shared knowledge.

A priority element of UNESCO's draft work programme on Culture for 2008–09 was promoting cultural diversity through the safeguarding of heritage and enhancement of cultural expressions. In January 2002 UNESCO inaugurated the Global Alliance on Cultural Diversity, to promote partnerships between governments, non-governmental bodies and the private sector with a view to supporting cultural diversity through the strengthening of cultural industries and the prevention of cultural piracy. In October 2005 the General Conference approved an International Convention on the Protection of the Diversity of Cultural Expressions. It entered into force in March 2007 and the first session of the intergovernmental committee servicing the Convention was convened in Ottawa, Canada, in December.

UNESCO's World Heritage Programme, inaugurated in 1978, aims to protect historic sites and natural landmarks of outstanding universal significance, in accordance with the 1972 UNESCO Convention Concerning the Protection of the World Cultural and Natural Heritage, by providing financial aid for restoration, technical assistance, training and management planning. At July 2008 the 'World Heritage List' comprised 878 sites in 145 countries, of which 679 had cultural significance, 174 were natural landmarks, and 25 were of 'mixed' importance. UNESCO also maintains a list of 'World Heritage in Danger'. UNESCO is assisting in the preservation of several sites and monuments in South Asia, including the Taj Mahal (India), the ancient city of Moenjodaro (Pakistan) and the sacred city of Anuradhapura (Sri Lanka). In early 2001 UNESCO condemned an alleged edict by the then fundamentalist Islamist Taliban regime in Afghanistan ordering the destruction of all statues in that country which, owing to their representation of human likenesses, were regarded as non-Islamic. In March UNESCO protested strongly against the reported destruction by order of the Taliban of two ancient monuments of Buddha at Bamiyan. In January 2002, following the overthrow of the Taliban in late 2001, the newly-appointed Afghan Interim Administration requested UNESCO to co-ordinate all international and bilateral activities to protect Afghanistan's cultural heritage; UNESCO subsequently initiated a campaign to assess the situation. In March 2002 a memorandum of understanding was concluded between UNESCO and the Interim Administration providing for UNESCO to manage international efforts towards rehabilitating the national museum in Kabul, where a number of artefacts had been destroyed under Taliban rule. In October UNESCO's Executive Board approved the establishment of an International Co-ordination Committee for the Safeguarding of Afghanistan's Cultural Heritage, to be administered by UNESCO with participation by other agencies and organizations, donor nations and experts. The 12th century minaret and archaeological remains of Jam, and the cultural landscape and archaeological remains of the Bamiyan Valley, were added to the 'World Heritage List in Danger list' in 2002 and 2003, respectively.

UNESCO supports the safeguarding of humanity's non-material 'intangible' heritage, including oral traditions, music, dance and medicine. An Endangered Languages Programme was initiated in 1993. By 2008 the Programme estimated that, of some 6,700 languages spoken world-wide, about one-half were endangered. It works to raise awareness of the issue, for example through publication of the *Atlas of the World's Languages in Danger of Disappearing*, to strengthen local and national capacities to safeguard and document languages and administers a Register of Good Practices in Language Preservation. In October 2003 the UNESCO General Conference adopted a Convention for the Safeguarding of Intangible Cultural Heritage, which provided for the establishment of an intergovernmental committee and for participating states to formulate national inventories of intangible heritage. The Convention entered into force in April 2006 and the intergovernmental committee convened its inaugural session in November. The second session was held in Tokyo, Japan, in September 2007. A List of Intangible Cultural Heritage in Need of Urgent Safeguarding was scheduled to be operational by 2009. In May 2001, November 2003 and November 2005 (i.e. before the Convention entered into effect) UNESCO awarded the title of 'Masterpieces of the Oral and Intangible Heritage of Humanity' to a total of 90 examples of intangible heritage deemed to be of outstanding value. UNESCO's culture programme also aims to safeguard movable cultural heritage and to support and develop museums as a means of preserving heritage and making it accessible to society as a whole.

In November 2001 the General Conference authorized the formulation of a Declaration against the Intentional Destruction of Cultural Heritage. In addition, the Conference adopted the Convention on the Protection of the Underwater Cultural Heritage, covering the protection from commercial exploitation of shipwrecks, submerged historical sites, etc., situated in the territorial waters of signatory states. UNESCO also administers the 1954 Hague Convention on the Protection of Cultural Property in the Event of Armed Conflict and the 1970 Convention on the Means of Prohibiting and Preventing the Illicit Import, Export and Transfer of Ownership of Cultural Property. In 1992 a World Heritage Centre was established to enable rapid mobilization of international technical assistance for the preservation of cultural sites. Through the World Heritage Information Network (WHIN), a world-wide network of more than 800 information providers, UNESCO promotes global awareness and information exchange.

UNESCO aims to support the development of creative industries and or creative expression. Through a variety of projects UNESCO promotes art education, supports the rights of artists, and encourages crafts, design, digital art and performance arts. In October 2004 UNESCO launched a Creative Cities Network to facilitate public and private sector partnerships, international links, and recognition of a city's unique expertise. At July 2008 nine cities were participating in the network. UNESCO is active in preparing and encouraging the enforcement of international legislation on copyright, raising awareness on the need for copyright protection to uphold cultural diversity, and is contributing to the international debate on digital copyright issues and piracy.

Within its ambition of ensuring cultural diversity, UNESCO recognizes the role of culture as a means of promoting peace and dialogue. Several projects have been formulated within a broader concept of Roads of Dialogue. In Central Asia a project on intercultural dialogue follows on from an earlier multi-disciplinary study of the ancient Silk Roads trading routes linking Asia and Europe, which illustrated many examples of common heritage. Other projects include a study of the movement of peoples and cultures during the slave trade, a Mediterranean Programme, the Caucasus Project and the Arabia Plan, which aims to promote world-wide knowledge and understanding of Arab culture. UNESCO has overseen an extensive programme of work to formulate histories of humanity and regions, focused on ideas, civilizations and the evolution of societies and cultures. These have included the *General History of Africa*, *History of Civilizations of Central Asia*, and *History of Humanity*. In 2008–09 UNESCO endeavoured to consider and implement the findings of the Alliance of Civilizations, a high-level group convened by the UN Secretary-General that published a report in November 2006.

## COMMUNICATION AND INFORMATION

UNESCO regards information, communication and knowledge as being at the core of human progress and well-being. The Organization advocates the concept of knowledge societies, based on the principles of freedom of expression, universal access to information and knowledge, promotion of cultural diversity, and equal access to quality education. In 2008–13 it determined to consolidate and implement this concept, in accordance with the Declaration of Principles and Plan of Action adopted by the World Summit on the Information Society (WSIS) in November 2005.

A key strategic objective of building inclusive knowledge societies was to be through enhancing universal access to communication and information. At national and global levels UNESCO promotes the rights of freedom of expression and of access to information. It promotes the free flow and broad diffusion of information, knowledge, data and best practices, through the development of communications infrastructures, the elimination of impediments to freedom of expression, and the development of independent and pluralistic media, including through the provision of advisory services on media legislation, particularly in post-conflict countries and in countries in transition. UNESCO recognizes that the so-called global 'digital divide', in addition to other developmental differences between countries, generates exclusion and marginalization, and that increased participation in the democratic process can be attained through strengthening national communication and information capacities. UNESCO promotes policies and mechanisms that enhance provision for marginalized and disadvantaged groups to benefit from information and community opportunities. Activities at local and national level include developing effective 'infostructures', such as libraries and archives and strengthening low-cost community media and information access points, for example through the establishment of Community Multimedia Centres (CMCs). Many of UNESCO's principles and objectives in this area are pursued through the Information for All Programme, which entered into force in 2001. It is administered by an intergovernmental council, the secretariat of which is provided by UNESCO. UNESCO also established, in 1982, the International Programme for the Development of Communication (IPDC), which aims to promote and develop independent and pluralistic media in developing countries, for example by the establishment or modernization of news agencies and newspapers and training media professionals. the promotion of the right to information, and through efforts to harness informatics for development purposes and strengthen member states' capacities in this field.

UNESCO supports cultural and linguistic diversity in information sources to reinforce the principle of universal access. It aims to raise awareness of the issue of equitable access and diversity, encourage good practices and develop policies to strengthen cultural diversity in all media. In 2002 UNESCO established Initiative B@bel as a multidisciplinary programme to promote linguistic diversity, with the aim of enhancing access of under-represented groups to information sources as well as protecting under-used minority languages. UNESCO's Programme for Creative Content supports the development of and access to diverse content in both the electronic and audiovisual media. The Memory of the World project, established in 1992, aims to preserve in digital form, and thereby to promote wide access to, the world's documentary heritage. By July 2008 158 inscriptions had been included on the project's register, originating from 67 countries, one private foundation and one international organization (the archives of the ICRC's former International Prisoners of War Agency, 1914–1923, submitted by the ICRC in 2007). UNESCO also supports other efforts to preserve and disseminate digital archives and, in 2003, adopted a Charter for the Preservation of Digital Heritage.

UNESCO promotes freedom of expression, of the press and independence of the media as fundamental human rights and the basis of democracy. It aims to assist member states to formulate policies and legal frameworks to uphold independent and pluralistic media and infostructures and to enhance the capacities of public service broadcasting institutions. In regions affected by conflict UNESCO supports efforts to establish and maintain an independent media service and to use it as a means of consolidating peace. UNESCO also aims to develop media and information systems to respond to and mitigate the impact of disaster situations, and to integrate these objectives into wider UN peace-building or reconstruction initiatives. UNESCO is the co-ordinating agency for 'World Press Freedom Day', which is held annually on 3 May. The theme for 2008 was 'Access to information and the empowerment of people'. It also awards an annual World Press Freedom Prize. UNESCO maintains an Observatory on the Information Society, which provides up-to-date information on the development of new ICTs, analyses major trends, and aims to raise awareness of related ethical, legal and societal issues. UNESCO promotes the upholding of human rights in the use of cyberspace. In 1997 it organized the first International Congress on Ethical, Legal and Societal Aspects of Digital Information ('INFOethics').

UNESCO promotes the application of information and communication technology for sustainable development. In particular it supports efforts to improve teaching and learning processes through electronic media and to develop innovative literacy and education initiatives, such as the ICT-Enhanced Learning (ICTEL) project. UNESCO also aims to enhance understanding and use of new technologies and support training and ongoing learning opportunities for librarians, archivists and other information providers.

## Finance

UNESCO's activities are funded through a regular budget provided by contributions from member states and extrabudgetary funds from other sources, particularly UNDP, the World Bank, regional banks and other bilateral Funds-in-Trust arrangements. UNESCO co-operates with many other UN agencies and international non-governmental organizations.

UNESCO's proposed Regular Programme budget for the two years 2008–09 was US $631m.

## Publications

(mostly in English, French and Spanish editions; Arabic, Chinese and Russian versions are also available in many cases)

*Atlas of the World's Languages in Danger of Disappearing* (online).

*Copyright Bulletin* (quarterly).

*Encyclopedia of Life Support Systems* (online).

*International Review of Education* (quarterly).

*International Social Science Journal* (quarterly).

*Museum International* (quarterly).

*Nature and Resources* (quarterly).

*The New Courier* (quarterly).

*Prospects* (quarterly review on education).

*UNESCO Sources* (monthly).

*UNESCO Statistical Yearbook*.

*World Communication Report*.

*World Educational Report* (every 2 years).

*World Heritage Review* (quarterly).

*World Information Report*.

*World Science Report* (every 2 years).

Books, databases, video and radio documentaries, statistics, scientific maps and atlases.

## Specialized Institutes and Centres

**Abdus Salam International Centre for Theoretical Physics:** Strada Costiera 11, 34014 Trieste, Italy; tel. (040) 2240111; fax (040) 224163; e-mail sci_info@ictp.it; internet www.ictp.it; f. 1964; promotes and enables advanced study and research in physics and mathematical sciences; organizes and sponsors training opportunities, in particular for scientists from developing countries; aims to provide an international forum for the exchange of information and ideas; Dir KATEPALLI R. SREENIVASEN (India).

**European Centre for Higher Education (CEPES):** Str. Stirbei Vodă 39, 010102 Bucharest, Romania; tel. (1) 313-0839; fax (1) 312-3567; e-mail info@cepes.ro; internet www.cepes.ro; Dir Dr JAN SADLAK.

**International Bureau of Education (IBE):** POB 199, 1211 Geneva 20, Switzerland; tel. 229177800; fax 229177801; e-mail doc.centre@ibe.unesco.org; internet www.ibe.unesco.org; f. 1925, became an intergovernmental organization in 1929 and was incorporated into UNESCO in 1969; the Council of the IBE is composed of representatives of 28 member states of UNESCO, designated by the General Conference; the Bureau's fundamental mission is to deal with matters concerning educational content, methods, and teaching/learning strategies; an International Conference on Education is held periodically; Dir CLEMENTINA ACEDO (Venezuela); publs *Prospects* (quarterly review), *Educational Innovation* (newsletter), educational practices series, monographs, other reference works.

**UNESCO International Centre for Technical and Vocational Education and Training:** Görrestr. 15, 53113 Bonn, Germany; tel. (228) 243370; fax (228) 2433777; e-mail info@unevoc.unesco.org; internet www.unevoc.unesco.org; f. 2002; promotes high-quality lifelong technical and vocational education in UNESCO's member states, with a particular focus on young people, girls and women, and the disadvantaged; Dir RUPERT MACLEAN.

**UNESCO International Institute for Capacity Building in Africa (UNESCO–IICBA):** ECA Compound, Africa Ave, POB 2305, Addis Ababa, Ethiopia; tel. (11) 5445284; fax (11) 514936; e-mail info@unesco-iicba.org; internet www.unesco-iicba.org; f. 1999 to promote capacity building in the following areas: teacher education, curriculum development; educational policy, planning and management, and distance education; Dir JOSEPH NJIMBIDT NGU (Cameroon).

**UNESCO International Institute for Educational Planning (IIEP):** 7–9 rue Eugène Delacroix, 75116 Paris, France; tel. 1-45-03-77-00; fax 1-40-72-83-66; e-mail information@iiep.unesco.org; internet www.unesco.org/iiep; f. 1963; serves as a world centre for advanced training and research in educational planning; aims to help all member states of UNESCO in their social and economic development efforts, by enlarging the fund of knowledge about educational planning and the supply of competent experts in this field; legally and administratively a part of UNESCO, the Institute is autonomous, and its policies and programme are controlled by its own Governing Board, under special statutes voted by the General Conference of UNESCO; a satellite office of the IIEP was opened in Buenos Aires, Argentina, in June 1998; Dir MARK BRAY (United Kingdom).

**UNESCO International Institute for Higher Education in Latin America and the Caribbean:** Avda Los Chorros con Calle Acueducto, Edif. Asovincar, Altos de Sebucán, Apdo 68394, Caracas 1062-A, Venezuela; tel. (212) 286-0555; fax (212) 286-0527; e-mail prensa@unesco.org.ve; internet www.iesalc.unesco.org.ve; Dir ANA LÚCIA GAZZOLA.

**UNESCO Institute for Information Technologies in Education:** 8 Kedrova St, 117292 Moscow, Russia; tel. (495) 129-29-90; fax (495) 129-12-25; e-mail info@iite.ru; internet www.iite.ru; the Institute aims to formulate policies regarding the development of, and to support and monitor the use of, information and communication technologies in education; it conducts research and organizes training programmes; Dir Dr VLADIMIR KINELEV.

**UNESCO Institute for Life-long Learning:** Feldbrunnenstr. 58, 20148 Hamburg, Germany; tel. (40) 448-0410; fax (40) 410-7723; e-mail uil@unesco.org; internet www.unesco.org/education/uil; f. 1951, as the Institute for Education; a research, training, information, documentation and publishing centre, with a particular focus on adult basic and further education and adult literacy; Dir ADAMA OUANE (Mali).

**UNESCO Institute for Statistics:** CP 6128, Succursale Centre-Ville, Montréal, QC, H3C 3J7, Canada; tel. (514) 343-6880; fax (514) 343-6882; e-mail uis@unesco.org; internet www.uis.unesco.org; f. 2001; collects and analyses national statistics on education, science, technology, culture and communications; Dir HENDRIK VAN DER POL (Netherlands).

**UNESCO Institute for Water Education:** Westvest 7, 2611 AX Delft, Netherlands; tel. (15) 2151-715; fax (15) 2122-921; e-mail info@unesco-ihe.org; internet www.unesco-ihe.org; f. 2003; activities include advisory and policy-making functions; setting international standards for postgraduate education programmes and professional training in the water sector; education, training and research; and co-ordination of a global network of water sector organizations; Dir Prof. RICHARD A. MEGANCK.

# World Health Organization—WHO

**Address:** Ave Appia 20, 1211 Geneva 27, Switzerland.

**Telephone:** 227912111; **fax:** 227913111; **e-mail:** info@who.int; **internet:** www.who.int.

WHO, established in 1948, is the lead agency within the UN system concerned with the protection and improvement of public health.

## Organization

(August 2008)

### WORLD HEALTH ASSEMBLY

The Assembly meets in Geneva, once a year. It is responsible for policy making and the biennial programme and budget; appoints the Director-General; admits new members; and reviews budget contributions.

### EXECUTIVE BOARD

The Board is composed of 32 health experts designated by, but not representing, their governments; they serve for three years, and the World Health Assembly elects 10–12 member states each year to the Board. It meets at least twice a year to review the Director-General's programme, which it forwards to the Assembly with any recommendations that seem necessary. It advises on questions referred to it by the Assembly and is responsible for putting into effect the decisions and policies of the Assembly. It is also empowered to take emergency measures in case of epidemics or disasters.

**Chairman:** NIMAL SIRIPALA DE SILVA (Sri Lanka).

### SECRETARIAT

**Director-General:** Dr MARGARET CHAN (People's Republic of China).

**Deputy Director-General:** Dr ANARFI ASAMOA-BAAH (Ghana).

**Assistant Directors-General:** DENIS AITKEN (United Kingdom) (Representative of the Director-General for Partnership and UN Reform), ALA ALWAN (Iraq) (Non-communicable Diseases and Mental Health), Dr CARISSA F. ETIENNE (Dominica) (Health Systems and Services), TIMOTHY G. EVANS (Canada) (Information, Evidence and Research), Dr DAVID L. HEYMANN (USA) (Health Security and Environment and Representative of the Director-General for Polio Eradication), Dr ERIC LAROCHE (France) (Health Action in Crises), DAISY MAFUBELU (South Africa) (Family and Community Health), HIROKI NAKATANI (Japan) (HIV/AIDS, TB, Malaria and Neglected Tropical Diseases), ANDREY V. PIROGOV (Russia) (Executive Director of the WHO Office at the UN), NAMITA PRADHAM (India) (General Management), SUZANNE WEBER-MOSDORF (Germany) (Executive Director of the WHO Office at the EU).

### PRINCIPAL OFFICES

Each of WHO's six geographical regions has its own organization, consisting of a regional committee representing relevant member states and associate members, and a regional office staffed by experts in various fields of health.

**South-East Asia Office:** World Health House, Indraprastha Estate, Mahatma Gandhi Rd, New Delhi 110002, India; tel. (11) 23370804; fax (11) 23379507; e-mail registry@searo.who.int; internet www.searo.who.int; Dir Dr SAMLEE PLIANBANGCHANG.

**WHO Centre for Health Development:** I. H. D. Centre Bldg, 9th Floor, 5–1, 1-chome, Wakinohama-Kaigandori, Chuo-ku, Kobe, Japan; tel. (78) 230-3100; fax (78) 230-3178; e-mail wkc@who.or.jp; internet www.who.or.jp; f. 1995 to address health development issues; Dir Dr JACOB KUMARESAN (India).

**WHO Lyon Office for National Epidemic Preparedness and Response:** 58 ave Debourg, 69007 Lyon, France; tel. 4-72-71-64-70; fax 4-72-71-64-71; e-mail oms@lyon.who.int; supports global capacity-building for detection of and response to epidemics of infectious diseases; provides bridging role between WHO headquarters, the regional offices and ongoing activities in the field; Dir Dr GUÉNAËL RODIER.

**WHO Mediterranean Centre for Vulnerability Reduction (WMC):** rue du Lac Windermere, BP 40, 1053 Les Berges du Lac, Tunisia; tel. (71) 964-681; fax (71) 764-4558; e-mail info@wmc.who.int; internet wmc.who.int; f. 1997; advocates globally for appropriate health policies; trains health professionals; supports capacity-building for community action at grassroots level; works closely with WHO's regional offices; Dir (vacant).

## Activities

WHO's objective is stated in its constitution as 'the attainment by all peoples of the highest possible level of health'. 'Health' is defined as 'a state of complete physical, mental and social well-being and not merely the absence of disease and infirmity'.

WHO has developed a series of international classifications, including the *International Statistical Classification of Disease and Related Health Problems (ICD)*, providing an etiological framework of health conditions, and currently in its 10th edition; and the complementary *International Classification of Functioning, Disability and Health (ICF)*, which describes how people live with their conditions.

WHO acts as the central authority directing international health work, and establishes relations with professional groups and government health authorities on that basis.

It provides, on request from member states, technical and policy assistance in support of programmes to promote health, prevent and control health problems, control or eradicate disease, train health workers best suited to local needs and strengthen national health systems. Aid is provided in emergencies and natural disasters.

A global programme of collaborative research and exchange of scientific information is carried out in co-operation with about 1,200 national institutions. Particular stress is laid on the widespread communicable diseases of the tropics, and the countries directly concerned are assisted in developing their research capabilities.

It keeps diseases and other health problems under constant surveillance, promotes the exchange of prompt and accurate information and of notification of outbreaks of diseases, and administers the International Health Regulations. It sets standards for the quality control of drugs, vaccines and other substances affecting health. It formulates health regulations for international travel.

It collects and disseminates health data and carries out statistical analyses and comparative studies in such diseases as cancer, heart disease and mental illness.

It receives reports on drugs observed to have shown adverse reactions in any country, and transmits the information to other member states.

It promotes improved environmental conditions, including housing, sanitation and working conditions. All available information on effects on human health of the pollutants in the environment is critically reviewed and published.

Co-operation among scientists and professional groups is encouraged. The organization negotiates and sustains national and global partnerships. It may propose international conventions and agreements, and develops and promotes international norms and standards. The organization promotes the development and testing of new technologies, tools and guidelines. It assists in developing an informed public opinion on matters of health.

WHO's first global strategy for pursuing 'Health for all' was adopted in May 1981 by the 34th World Health Assembly. The objective of 'Health for all' was identified as the attainment by all citizens of the world of a level of health that would permit them to lead a socially and economically productive life, requiring fair distribution of available resources, universal access to essential health care, and the promotion of preventive health care. In May 1998 the 51st World Health Assembly renewed the initiative, adopting a global strategy in support of 'Health for all in the 21st century', to be effected through regional and national health policies. The new approach was to build on the primary health care approach of the initial strategy, but was to strengthen the emphasis on quality of life, equity in health and access to health services. The following have been identified as minimum requirements of 'Health for all':

Safe water in the home or within 15 minutes' walking distance, and adequate sanitary facilities in the home or immediate vicinity;

Immunization against diphtheria, pertussis (whooping cough), tetanus, poliomyelitis, measles and tuberculosis;

Local health care, including availability of essential drugs, within one hour's travel;

Trained personnel to attend childbirth, and to care for pregnant mothers and children up to at least one year old.

In the implementation of all its activities WHO aims to contribute to achieving by 2015 the UN Millennium Development Goals (MDGs) that were agreed by the September 2000 UN Millennium Summit. WHO has particular responsibility for the MDGs of: reducing child mortality, with a target reduction of two-thirds in the mortality rate among children under five; improving maternal health, with a specific goal of reducing by 75% the numbers of women dying in childbirth; and combating HIV/AIDS, malaria and other diseases. In addition, it directly supports the following Millennium 'targets': halving the proportion of people suffering from malnutrition; halving the proportion of people without sustainable access to safe drinking water and basic sanitation; and providing access, in co-operation with pharmaceutical companies, to affordable, essential drugs in developing countries. Furthermore, WHO reports on 17 health-related MDG indicators; co-ordinates, jointly with the World Bank, the High-Level Forum on the Health MDGs, comprising government ministers, senior officials from developing countries, and representatives of bilateral and multilateral agencies, foundations, regional organizations and global partnerships; and undertakes technical and normative work in support of national and regional efforts to reach the MDGs.

The Eleventh General Programme of Work, for the period 2006–15, defined a policy framework for pursuing the principal objectives of building healthy populations and combating ill health. The Programme took into account: increasing understanding of the social, economic, political and cultural factors involved in achieving better health and the role played by better health in poverty reduction; the increasing complexity of health systems; the importance of safeguarding health as a component of humanitarian action; and the need for greater co-ordination among development organizations. It incorporated four interrelated strategic directions: lessening excess mortality, morbidity and disability, especially in poor and marginalized populations; promoting healthy lifestyles and reducing risk factors to human health arising from environmental, economic, social and behavioural causes; developing equitable and financially fair health systems; and establishing an enabling policy and an institutional environment for the health sector and promoting an effective health dimension to social, economic, environmental and development policy. WHO is the sponsoring agency for the Health Workforce Decade (2006–15).

During 2005 the UN's Inter-Agency Standing Committee (IASC), concerned with co-ordinating the international response to humanitarian disasters, developed a concept of organizing agency assistance to IDPs through the institutionalization of a 'Cluster Approach', comprising 11 core areas of activity. WHO was designated the lead agency for the clusters on Health.

### COMMUNICABLE DISEASES

WHO identifies infectious and parasitic communicable diseases as a major obstacle to social and economic progress, particularly in developing countries, where, in addition to disabilities and loss of productivity and household earnings, they cause nearly one-half of all deaths. Emerging and re-emerging diseases, those likely to cause epidemics, increasing incidence of zoonoses (diseases or infections passed from vertebrate animals to humans by means of parasites, viruses, bacteria or unconventional agents), attributable to factors such as environmental changes and changes in farming practices, outbreaks of unknown etiology, and the undermining of some drug therapies by the spread of antimicrobial resistance are main areas of concern. In recent years WHO has noted the global spread of communicable diseases through international travel, voluntary human migration and involuntary population displacement.

WHO's Communicable Diseases group works to reduce the impact of infectious diseases world-wide through surveillance and response; prevention, control and eradication strategies; and research and product development. The group seeks to identify new technologies and tools, and to foster national development through strengthening health services and the better use of existing tools. It aims to strengthen global monitoring of important communicable disease problems. The group advocates a functional approach to disease control. It aims to create consensus and consolidate partnerships around targeted diseases and collaborates with other groups at all stages to provide an integrated response. In 2000 WHO and several partner institutions in epidemic surveillance established a Global Outbreak Alert and Response Network (GOARN). Through the Network WHO aims to maintain constant vigilance regarding outbreaks of disease and to link world-wide expertise to provide an immediate response capability. In March 2005 GOARN responded to an outbreak of Marburg haemorrhagic fever in Angola, which, by July, had killed more than 300 people. From March 2003 WHO, through the Network, was co-ordinating the international investigation into the global spread of Severe Acute Respiratory Syndrome (SARS), a previously unknown atypical pneumonia. From the end of that year WHO was monitoring the spread through several Asian countries of the virus H5N1 (a rapidly mutating strain of zoonotic highly pathogenic avian influenza—HPAI) that was transmitting to human populations through contact with diseased birds, mainly poultry. It was feared that H5N1 would mutate into a form transmissable from human to human. In February 2005 WHO issued guidelines for the global surveillance of the spread of H5N1 infection in human and animal populations. WHO urged all countries to develop influenza pandemic preparedness plans and to stockpile antiviral drugs, and in May, in co-operation with the UN Food and Agriculture Organization (FAO) and the World Organisation for Animal Health (OIE), it launched a Global Strategy for the Progressive Control of Highly Pathogenic Avian Influenza. A conference on Avian Influenza and Human Pandemic Influenza that was jointly organized by WHO, FAO, OIE and the World Bank in November 2005 issued a plan of action identifying a number of responses, including: supporting the development of integrated national plans for H5N1 containment and human pandemic influenza preparedness and response; assisting countries with the aggressive control of H5N1 and with establishing a more detailed understanding of the role of wild birds in virus transmission; nominating rapid response teams of experts to support epidemiological field investigations; expanding national and regional capacity in surveillance, diagnosis, and alert and response systems; expanding the network of influenza laboratories; establishing multi-country networks for the control or prevention of animal trans-boundary diseases; expanding the global antiviral stockpile; strengthening veterinary infrastructures; and mapping a global strategy and work plan for co-ordinating antiviral and influenza vaccine research and development. An International Pledging Conference on Avian and Human Influenza, convened in January 2006 in Beijing, People's Republic of China (PRC), and co-sponsored by the World Bank, European Commission and PRC Government, in co-operation with WHO, FAO and OIE, requested a minimum of US $1,200m. in funding towards combating the spread of the virus. By June 2008 a total of 385 human cases of H5N1 had been laboratory-confirmed, in Azerbaijan, Bangladesh, Cambodia, PRC, Djibouti, Egypt, Indonesia, Iraq, Laos, Nigeria, Pakistan, Thailand, Turkey and Viet Nam, resulting in 243 deaths. Cases in poultry had become endemic in parts of Asia, and recent outbreaks in poultry had been reported in some European and Middle Eastern countries, and in some countries in West, Central and Northeast Africa.

One of WHO's major achievements was the eradication of smallpox. Following a massive international campaign of vaccination and surveillance (begun in 1958 and intensified in 1967), the last case was detected in 1977 and the eradication of the disease was declared in 1980. In May 1996 the World Health Assembly resolved that, pending a final endorsement, all remaining stocks of the smallpox virus were to be destroyed on 30 June 1999, although 500,000 doses of smallpox vaccine were to remain, along with a supply of the smallpox vaccine seed virus, in order to ensure that a further supply of the vaccine could be made available if required. In May 1999, however, the Assembly authorized a temporary retention of stocks of the virus until 2002. In late 2001, in response to fears that illegally-held virus stocks could be used in acts of biological terrorism (see below), WHO reassembled a team of technical experts on smallpox. In January 2002 the Executive Board determined that stocks of the virus should continue to be retained, to enable research into more effective treatments and vaccines.

In 1988 the World Health Assembly launched the Global Polio Eradication Initiative (GPEI), which aimed, initially, to eradicate poliomyelitis by the end of 2000; this target was subsequently advanced to 2005, and most recently to 2008 (see below). National Immunization Days (NIDs, facilitated in conflict zones by the negotiation of so-called 'days of tranquility') have been employed in combating the disease, alongside the strengthening of routine immunization services. Vitamin A has also been administered during NIDS in order to reduce nutritional deficiencies in children and thereby boost their immunity. Since the inauguration of the GPEI WHO has declared the following regions 'polio-free': the Americas (1994); Western Pacific (2000); and Europe (2002). In August 1996 WHO, UNICEF and Rotary International, together with other national and international partners, initiated a campaign to 'Kick Polio out of Africa', with the aim of immunizing more than 100m. children in 46 countries against the disease over a three-year period. In January 2004 ministers of health of affected countries, and global partners, meeting under the auspices of WHO and UNICEF, adopted the Geneva Declaration on the Eradication of Poliomyelitis, in which they made a commitment to accelerate the drive towards eradication of the disease, by improving the scope of vaccination programmes. Significant progress in eradication of the virus was reported in Asia during that year. In sub-Saharan Africa, however, an outbreak originating in northern Nigeria in mid-2003—caused by a temporary cessation of vaccination activities in response to local opposition to the vaccination programme—had spread, by mid-2004, to 10 previously polio-free countries. These included Côte d'Ivoire and Sudan, where ongoing civil unrest and population displacements impeded control efforts. During 2004–05 some 23 African governments, including those of the affected West and Central African countries, organized, with support from the African Union, a number of co-ordinated mass vaccination drives, which resulted in the vaccination of about 100m. children. By mid-2005 this localized epidemic was declared over; it was estimated that nearly 200 children in the region had been paralyzed by the disease since mid-2003. In January 2004 the GPEI adopted a strategic plan for the eradication of polio covering the period 2004–08, which entailed the following key objectives: securing the world-wide interruption of poliovirus transmission (from 2004); achieving certification of global polio eradication (during 2006–08); developing guidelines for the Global Oral Polio Vaccine Cessation Phase (2006–08); and mainstreaming the GPEI (from 2009). Some 1,313 polio cases were confirmed world-wide in 2007, of which 1,208 were in the countries designated at that time as polio-endemic (Afghanistan, India, Nigeria and Pakistan) and 107 in non-endemic countries. (In 1988 35,000 cases had been confirmed in 125 countries, with the actual number of cases estimated at around 350,000.)

WHO is committed to the elimination of leprosy (the reduction of the prevalence of leprosy to less than one case per 10,000 population). The use of a highly effective combination of three drugs (known as multi-drug therapy—MDT) resulted in a reduction in the number of leprosy cases world-wide from 10m.–12m. in 1988 to 259,017 in January 2007. The number of countries having more than one case of leprosy per 10,000 had declined to four by that time (Brazil, Democratic Republic of the Congo, Mozambique and Nepal), compared with 122 in 1985. The country with the highest prevalence of leprosy cases at January 2007 was Brazil (3.21 per 10,000 population) and the country with the highest number of cases was India (139,252). The Global Alliance for the Elimination of Leprosy, launched in November 1999 by WHO, in collaboration with governments of affected countries and several private partners, including a major pharmaceutical company, aims to support the eradication of the disease through the provision until end-2010 of free MDT treatment. In June 2005 WHO adopted a Strategic Plan for Further Reducing the Leprosy Burden and Sustaining Leprosy Control Activities, covering the period 2006–10 and following on from a previous strategic plan for 2000–05. In 1998 WHO launched the Global Buruli Ulcer Initiative, which aimed to co-ordinate control of and research into Buruli ulcer, another mycobacterial disease. In July of that year the Director-General of WHO and representatives of more than 20 countries, meeting in Yamoussoukro, Côte d'Ivoire, signed a declaration on the control of Buruli ulcer. In May 2004 the World Health Assembly adopted a resolution urging improved research into, and detection and treatment of, Buruli ulcer.

The Special Programme for Research and Training in Tropical Diseases, established in 1975 and sponsored jointly by WHO, UNDP and the World Bank, as well as by contributions from donor countries, involves a world-wide network of some 5,000 scientists working on the development and application of vaccines, new drugs, diagnostic kits and preventive measures, and an applied field research on practical community issues affecting the target diseases.

The objective of providing immunization for all children by 1990 was adopted by the World Health Assembly in 1977. Six diseases (measles, whooping cough, tetanus, poliomyelitis, tuberculosis and diphtheria) became the target of the Expanded Programme on Immunization (EPI), in which WHO, UNICEF and many other organizations collaborated. As a result of massive international and national efforts, the global immunization coverage increased from 20% in the early 1980s to the targeted rate of 80% by the end of 1990. In 1992 the Assembly resolved to reach a new target of 90% immunization coverage with the six EPI vaccines; to introduce hepatitis B as a seventh vaccine; and to introduce the yellow fever vaccine in areas where it occurs endemically.

In June 2000 WHO released a report entitled 'Overcoming Antimicrobial Resistance', in which it warned that the misuse of antibiotics could render some common infectious illnesses unresponsive to treatment. At that time WHO issued guidelines which aimed to mitigate the risks associated with the use of antimicrobials in livestock reared for human consumption.

### HIV/AIDS, TB, MALARIA AND NEGLECTED DISEASES

Combating the human immunodeficiency virus/acquired immunodeficiency syndrome (HIV/AIDS), tuberculosis (TB) and malaria are organization-wide priorities and, as such, are supported not only by their own areas of work but also by activities undertaken in other areas. In July 2000 a meeting of the Group of Seven industrialized nations and Russia, convened in Genoa, Italy, announced the formation of a new Global Fund to Fight AIDS, TB and Malaria (as previously proposed by the UN Secretary-General and recommended by the World Health Assembly) (see below).

The HIV/AIDS epidemic represents a major threat to human well-being and socio-economic progress. Some 95% of those known to be infected with HIV/AIDS live in developing countries, and AIDS-related illnesses are the leading cause of death in sub-Saharan Africa. It is estimated that more than 25m. people world-wide died of AIDS during 1981–2007. WHO supports governments in developing effective health-sector responses to the HIV/AIDS epidemic through enhancing their planning and managerial capabilities, implementation capacity, and health systems resources. The Joint UN Programme on HIV/AIDS (UNAIDS) became operational on 1 January 1996, sponsored by WHO and other UN agencies; the UNAIDS secretariat is based at WHO headquarters. Sufferers of HIV/AIDS in developing countries have often failed to receive advanced antiretroviral (ARV) treatments that are widely available in industrialized countries, owing to their high cost. (It was estimated in 2005 that only 15% of HIV/AIDS patients were receiving the optimum treatment.) In May 2000 the World Health Assembly adopted a resolution urging WHO member states to improve access to the prevention and treatment of HIV-related illnesses and to increase the availability and affordability of drugs. A WHO-UNAIDS HIV Vaccine Initiative was launched in that year. In June 2001 governments participating in a special session of the UN General Assembly on HIV/AIDS adopted a Declaration of Commitment on HIV/AIDS. WHO, with UNAIDS, UNICEF, UNFPA, the World Bank, and major pharmaceutical companies, participates in the 'Accelerating Access' initiative, which aims to expand access to care, support and ARVs for people with HIV/AIDS. In March 2002, under its 'Access to Quality HIV/AIDS Drugs and Diagnostics' programme, WHO published a comprehensive list of HIV-related medicines deemed to meet standards recommended by the Organization. In April WHO issued the first treatment guidelines for HIV/AIDS cases in poor communities, and endorsed the inclusion of HIV/AIDS drugs in its *Model List of Essential Medicines* (see below) in order to encourage their wider availability. The secretariat of the International HIV Treatment Access Coalition, founded in December of that year by governments, non-governmental organizations, donors and others to facilitate access to ARVs for people in low- and middle-income countries, is based at WHO headquarters. In 2006 WHO, UNAIDS and partner organizations negotiated a framework approach aimed at achieving universal access to HIV/AIDS prevention, treatment, care and support by 2010. The resulting document was entitled the '2007–10 Strategic Framework for UNAIDS support to countries' efforts to move towards universal access'. WHO supports the following *Three Ones* principles, endorsed in April 2004 by a high-level meeting organized by UNAIDS, the United Kingdom and the USA, with the aim of strengthening national responses to the HIV/AIDS pandemic: for every country there should be one agreed national HIV/AIDS action framework; one national AIDS co-ordinating authority; and one agreed monitoring and evaluation system.

At December 2007 4m. people in South and South-East Asia were reported to have HIV/AIDS, of whom an estimated 340,000 were newly infected during the year. In 2005 an estimated 5.7m. people were living with HIV/AIDS in India, with serious localized epidemics under way in a number of states, including Tamil Nadu, Maharashtra and Andhra Pradesh.

In 1995 WHO established a Global Tuberculosis Programme to address the challenges of the TB epidemic, which had been declared a global emergency by the Organization in 1993. According to WHO estimates, one-third of the world's population carries the TB bacillus. In 2006 this generated 9.2m. new active cases (0.7m. in people co-infected with HIV), and killed 1.7m. people (0.7m. of whom were also HIV-positive). TB is the principal cause of death for people infected with the HIV virus and an estimated one-third of people living with HIV/AIDS globally are co-infected with TB. Some 22 high-burden countries account for four-fifths of global TB cases. The largest concentration of TB cases is in South-East Asia. WHO provides technical support to all member countries, with special attention given to those with high TB prevalence, to establish effective national tuberculosis control programmes. WHO's strategy for TB control includes the use of the expanded DOTS (direct observation treatment, short-course) regime, involving the following five tenets: sustained political commitment to increase human and financial resources and to make TB control in endemic countries a nation-wide activity and an integral part of the national health system; access to quality-assured TB sputum microscopy; standardized short-course chemotherapy for all cases of TB under proper case-management conditions; uninterrupted supply of quality-assured drugs; and maintaining a recording and reporting system to enable outcome assessment. Simultaneously, WHO is encouraging research with the aim of further advancing DOTS, developing new tools for prevention, diagnosis and treatment, and containing new threats (such as the HIV/TB co-epidemic). Inadequate control of DOTS in some areas, leading to partial and inconsistent treatments, has resulted in the development of drug-resistant and, often, incurable strains of TB. The incidence of so-called Multidrug Resistant TB (MDR-TB) strains, that are unresponsive to at least two of the four most commonly used anti-TB drugs, has risen in recent years, and WHO estimates that about four-fifths are 'super strains', resistant to at least three of the main anti-TB drugs; of the 14.4m. prevalent cases of TB in 2006, some 0.5m. were reported to be MDR. WHO has developed DOTS-Plus, a specialized strategy for controlling the spread of MDR-TB in areas of high prevalence.

The 'Stop TB' partnership, launched by WHO in 1999, in partnership with the World Bank, the US Government and a coalition of non-governmental organizations, co-ordinates the Global Plan to Stop TB, which represents a 'roadmap' for TB control. The current phase of the plan, covering the period 2006–15, aims to facilitate the achievement of the MDG of halting and beginning to reverse by 2015 the incidence of TB by means of access to quality diagnosis and treatment for all; to supply ARVs to 3m. TB patients co-infected with HIV; to treat nearly 1m. people for MDR-TB; to develop a new anti-TB drug by 2010 and a new vaccine by 2015; and to develop rapid and inexpensive diagnostic tests at the point of care. The Global TB Drug Facility, launched by 'Stop TB' in 2001, aims to increase access to high-quality anti-TB drugs for sufferers in developing countries.

In September 2006 WHO expressed strong concern at the emergence of strains of Extensive Drug Resistant TB (XDR-TB) that are virtually untreatable with most existing anti-TB drugs. XDR-TB is believed to be most prevalent in Eastern Europe and Asia.

In October 1998 WHO, jointly with UNICEF, the World Bank and UNDP, formally launched the Roll Back Malaria (RBM) programme. The disease acutely affects at least 350m.–500m. people, and kills an estimated 1m. people, every year. Some 90% of all malaria cases occur in sub-Saharan Africa. It is estimated that the disease directly causes 18% of all child deaths in that region. The global RBM Partnership, linking governments, development agencies, and other parties, aims to mobilize resources and support for controlling malaria. The RBM Partnership Global Strategic Plan for the period 2005–15, adopted in November 2005, lists steps required to intensify malaria control interventions with a view to attaining targets set by the Partnership for 2010 and 2015 (the former targets include: ensuring the protection of 80% of people at risk from malaria and the diagnosis and treatment within one day of 80% of malaria patients, and reducing the global malaria burden by one-half compared with 2000 levels; and the latter: achieving a 75% reduction in malaria morbidity and mortality over levels at 2005). WHO recommends a number of guidelines for malaria control, focusing on the need for prompt, effective antimalarial treatment, and the issue of drug resistance; vector control, including the use of insecticide-treated bednets; malaria in pregnancy; malaria epidemics; and monitoring and evaluation activities. WHO, with several private- and public-sector partners, supports the development of more effective anti-malaria drugs and vaccines through the 'Medicines for Malaria' venture.

**Global Fund to Fight AIDS, TB and Malaria:** 6–8 chemin Blandonnet, 1214 Vernier-Geneva, Switzerland; tel. 227911700; fax 227911701; e-mail info@theglobalfund.org; internet www.theglobalfund.org; f. 2000 as a partnership between governments, civil society, private-sector interests, UN bodies (including WHO, UNAIDS, the IBRD and UNDP), and other agencies to raise resources for combating AIDS, TB and malaria; the Fund supports but does not implement assistance programmes; US $9,700m. was pledged by international donors at a conference convened in Sept. 2007 to replenish the Fund during 2008–10; by July 2008 the Fund had approved $10,800m. (of which $5,500m. had been disbursed) in respect of more than 550 grants supporting prevention and treatment programmes in 136 countries; by that time the cumulative allocation of grant funding by region was as follows: Africa (57%), the Middle East and North Africa and South Asia (15%), East Asia and the Pacific (13%), Eastern Europe and Central Asia (8%), and Latin America and the Caribbean (8%); while the approximate distribution by health sector was: HIV/AIDS (61%), malaria (25%), TB (14%) and strengthening of health systems (1%); Exec. Dir Dr MICHEL KAZATCHKINE.

**Joint UN Programme on HIV/AIDS (UNAIDS):** 20 ave Appia, 1211 Geneva 27, Switzerland; tel. 227913666; fax 227914187; e-mail communications@unaids.org; internet www.unaids.org; established in 1996 to lead, strengthen and support an expanded response to the global HIV/AIDS pandemic; activities focus on prevention, care and support, reducing vulnerability to infection, and alleviating the socioeconomic and human effects of HIV/AIDS; launched the Global Coalition on Women and AIDS in Feb. 2004; in June 2005 adopted a policy position paper for intensifying HIV prevention; co-sponsors: WHO, UNICEF, UNDP, UNFPA, UNODC, ILO, UNESCO, the World Bank, WFP, UNHCR; Exec. Dir PETER PIOT (Belgium).

### NON-COMMUNICABLE DISEASES AND MENTAL HEALTH

The Non-communicable Diseases and Mental Health group comprises departments for the surveillance, prevention and management of uninfectious diseases, such as those arising from an unhealthy diet, and departments for health promotion, disability, injury prevention and rehabilitation, mental health and substance abuse. Surveillance, prevention and management of non-communicable diseases, tobacco, and mental health are organization-wide priorities.

Addressing the social and environmental determinants of health is a main priority of WHO. Tobacco use, unhealthy diet and physical inactivity are regarded as common, preventable risk factors for the four most prominent non-communicable diseases: cardiovascular diseases, cancer, chronic respiratory disease and diabetes. WHO aims to monitor the global epidemiological situation of non-communicable diseases, to co-ordinate multinational research activities concerned with prevention and care, and to analyse determining factors such as gender and poverty. In 1998 the organization adopted a resolution on measures to be taken to combat non-communicable diseases; their prevalence was anticipated to increase, particularly in developing countries, owing to rising life expectancy and changes in lifestyles. For example, between 1995 and 2025 the number of adults affected by diabetes world-wide was projected to increase from 135m. to 300m. In 2005 chronic diseases reportedly accounted for nearly 30m. deaths globally.

The sixth Global Conference on Health Promotion, convened jointly by WHO and the Thai Government, in Bangkok, Thailand, in August 2005, adopted the Bangkok Charter for Health Promotion in a Globalized World, which identified current key challenges, actions and commitments.

In February 1999 WHO initiated a new programme, 'Vision 2020: the Right to Sight', which aimed to eliminate avoidable blindness (estimated to be as much as 80% of all cases) by 2020. Blindness was otherwise predicted to increase by as much as twofold, owing to the increased longevity of the global population.

In May 2004 the World Health Assembly endorsed a Global Strategy on Diet, Physical Activity and Health; it was estimated at that time that more than 1,000m. adults world-wide were overweight, and that, of these, some 300,000 were clinically obese. WHO has studied obesity-related issues in co-operation with the International Association for the Study of Obesity (IASO). The International Task Force on Obesity, affiliated to the IASO, aims to encourage the development of new policies for managing obesity. WHO and FAO jointly commissioned an expert report on the relationship of diet, nutrition and physical activity to chronic diseases, which was published in March 2003.

WHO's programmes for diabetes mellitus, chronic rheumatic diseases and asthma assist with the development of national initiatives, based upon goals and targets for the improvement of early detection, care and reduction of long-term complications. WHO's cardiovascular diseases programme aims to prevent and control the major cardiovascular diseases, which are responsible for more than 14m. deaths each year. It is estimated that one-third of these deaths could have been prevented with existing scientific knowledge. The programme on cancer control is concerned with the prevention of cancer, improving its detection and cure, and ensuring care of all cancer patients in need. In May 2004 the World Health Assembly adopted a resolution on cancer prevention and control, recognizing an increase in global cancer cases, particularly in developing countries, and stressing that many cases and related deaths could be prevented. The resolution included a number of recommendations for the improvement of national cancer control programmes. WHO is a co-sponsor of the Global Day Against Pain, which was held for the first time in 2004 and was to take place thereafter annually on 11 October. The Global Day highlights the need for improved pain management and palliative care for sufferers of diseases such as cancer and AIDS, with a particular focus on patients living in low-income countries with minimal access to opioid analgesics, and urges recognition of access to pain relief as a basic human right.

The WHO Human Genetics Programme manages genetic approaches for the prevention and control of common hereditary diseases and of those with a genetic predisposition representing a major health importance. The Programme also concentrates on the further development of genetic approaches suitable for incorporation into health care systems, as well as developing a network of international collaborating programmes.

WHO works to assess the impact of injuries, violence and sensory impairments on health, and formulates guidelines and protocols for the prevention and management of mental problems. The health promotion division promotes decentralized and community-based health programmes and is concerned with developing new approaches to population ageing and encouraging healthy life-styles and self-care. It also seeks to relieve the negative impact of social changes such as urbanization, migration and changes in family structure upon health. WHO advocates a multi-sectoral approach—involving public health, legal and educational systems—to the prevention of injuries, which represent 16% of the global burden of disease. It aims to support governments in developing suitable strategies to prevent and mitigate the consequences of violence, unintentional injury and disability. Several health promotion projects have been undertaken, in collaboration between WHO regional and country offices and other relevant organizations, including: the Global School Health Initiative, to bridge the sectors of health and education and to promote the health of school-age children; the Global Strategy for Occupational Health, to promote the health of the working population and the control of occupational health risks; Community-based Rehabilitation, aimed at providing a more enabling environment for people with disabilities; and a communication strategy to provide training and support for health communications personnel and initiatives. In 2000 WHO, UNESCO, the World Bank and UNICEF adopted the joint Focusing Resources for Effective School Health (FRESH Start) approach to promoting life skills among adolescents.

Mental health problems, which include unipolar and bipolar affective disorders, psychosis, epilepsy, dementia, Parkinson's disease, multiple sclerosis, drug and alcohol dependency, and neuropsychiatric disorders such as post-traumatic stress disorder, obsessive compulsive disorder and panic disorder, have been identified by WHO as significant global health problems. Although, overall, physical health has improved, mental, behavioural and social health problems are increasing, owing to extended life expectancy and improved child mortality rates, and factors such as war and poverty. WHO aims to address mental problems by increasing awareness of mental health issues and promoting improved mental health services and primary care.

The Substance Abuse department is concerned with problems of alcohol, drugs and other substance abuse. Within its Programme on Substance Abuse (PSA), which was established in 1990 in response to the global increase in substance abuse, WHO provides technical support to assist countries in formulating policies with regard to the prevention and reduction of the health and social effects of psychoactive substance abuse. PSA's sphere of activity includes epidemiological surveillance and risk assessment, advocacy and the dissemination of information, strengthening national and regional prevention and health promotion techniques and strategies, the development of cost-effective treatment and rehabilitation approaches, and also encompasses regulatory activities as required under the international drugs-control treaties in force.

The Tobacco or Health Programme aims to reduce the use of tobacco, by educating tobacco-users and preventing young people from adopting the habit. In 1996 WHO published its first report on the tobacco situation world-wide. According to WHO, about one-third of the world's population aged over 15 years smoke tobacco, which causes approximately 3.5m. deaths each year (through lung cancer, heart disease, chronic bronchitis and other effects). In 1998 the 'Tobacco Free Initiative', a major global anti-smoking campaign, was established. In May 1999 the World Health Assembly endorsed the formulation of a Framework Convention on Tobacco Control (FCTC) to help to combat the increase in tobacco use (although a number of tobacco growers expressed concerns about the effect of the convention on their livelihoods). The FCTC entered into force in February 2005. The greatest increase in tobacco use is forecast to occur in developing countries.

### FAMILY AND COMMUNITY HEALTH

WHO's Family and Community Health group addresses the following areas of work: child and adolescent health, research and programme development in reproductive health, making pregnancy safer and men and women's health. Making pregnancy safer is an organization-wide priority. The group's aim is to improve access to sustainable health care for all by strengthening health systems and fostering individual, family and community development. Activities include newborn care; child health, including promoting and protecting the health and development of the child through such approaches as promotion of breast-feeding and use of the mother-baby package, as well as care of the sick child, including diarrhoeal and acute respiratory disease control, and support to women and children in difficult circumstances; the promotion of safe motherhood and maternal health; adolescent health, including the promotion and development of young people and the prevention of specific health problems; women, health and development, including addressing issues of gender, sexual violence, and harmful traditional practices; and human reproduction, including research related to contraceptive technologies and effective methods. In addition, WHO aims to provide technical leadership and co-ordination on reproductive health and to support countries in their efforts to ensure that people: experience healthy sexual development and maturation; have the capacity for healthy, equitable and responsible relationships; can achieve their reproductive intentions safely and healthily; avoid illnesses, diseases and injury related to sexuality and reproduction; and receive appropriate counselling, care and rehabilitation for diseases and conditions related to sexuality and reproduction.

In September 1997 WHO, in collaboration with UNICEF, formally launched a programme advocating the Integrated Management of Childhood Illness (IMCI). IMCI recognizes that pneumonia, diarrhoea, measles, malaria and malnutrition cause some 70% of the approximately 11m. childhood deaths each year, and recommends screening sick children for all five conditions, to obtain a more accurate diagnosis than may be achieved from the results of a single assessment. WHO's Division of Diarrhoeal and Acute Respiratory Disease Control encourages national programmes aimed at reducing childhood deaths as a result of diarrhoea, particularly through the use of oral rehydration therapy and preventive measures. The Division is also seeking to reduce deaths from pneumonia in infants through the use of a simple case-management strategy involving the recognition of danger signs and treatment with an appropriate antibiotic.

### SUSTAINABLE DEVELOPMENT AND HEALTHY ENVIRONMENTS

The Sustainable Development and Healthy Environments group focuses on the following areas of work: health in sustainable development; nutrition; health and environment; food safety; and emergency preparedness and response. Food safety is an organization-wide priority.

WHO promotes recognition of good health status as one of the most important assets of the poor. The Sustainable Development and Healthy Environment group seeks to monitor the advantages and disadvantages for health, nutrition, environment and development arising from the process of globalization (i.e. increased global flows of capital, goods and services, people, and knowledge); to integrate the issue of health into poverty reduction programmes; and to promote human rights and equality. Adequate and safe food and nutrition is a priority programme area. WHO collaborates with FAO, the World Food Programme, UNICEF and other UN agencies in pursuing its objectives relating to nutrition and food safety. An estimated 780m. people world-wide cannot meet basic needs for energy and protein, more than 2,000m. people lack essential vitamins and minerals, and 170m. children are estimated to be malnourished. In December 1992 WHO and FAO hosted an international conference on nutrition, at which a World Declaration and Plan of Action on Nutrition was adopted to make the fight against malnutrition a development priority. Following the conference, WHO promoted the elaboration and implementation of national plans of action on nutrition. WHO aims to support the enhancement of member states' capabilities in dealing with their nutrition situations, and addressing scientific issues related to preventing, managing and monitoring protein-energy malnutrition; micronutrient malnutrition, including iodine deficiency disorders, vitamin A deficiency, and nutritional anaemia; and diet-related conditions and non-communicable diseases such as obesity (increasingly affecting children, adolescents and adults, mainly in industrialized countries), cancer and heart disease. In 1990 the World Health Assembly resolved to eliminate iodine deficiency (believed to cause mental retardation); a strategy of universal salt iodization was launched in 1993. In collaboration with other international agencies, WHO is implementing a comprehensive strategy for promoting appropriate infant, young child and maternal nutrition, and for dealing effectively with nutritional emergencies in large populations. Areas of emphasis include promoting healthcare practices that enhance successful breast-feeding;

appropriate complementary feeding; refining the use and interpretation of body measurements for assessing nutritional status; relevant information, education and training; and action to give effect to the International Code of Marketing of Breast-milk Substitutes. The food safety programme aims to protect human health against risks associated with biological and chemical contaminants and additives in food. With FAO, WHO establishes food standards (through the work of the Codex Alimentarius Commission and its subsidiary committees) and evaluates food additives, pesticide residues and other contaminants and their implications for health. The programme provides expert advice on such issues as food-borne pathogens (e.g. listeria), production methods (e.g. aquaculture) and food biotechnology (e.g. genetic modification). In July 2001 the Codex Alimentarius Commission adopted the first global principles for assessing the safety of genetically modified (GM) foods. In March 2002 an intergovernmental task force established by the Commission finalized 'principles for the risk analysis of foods derived from biotechnology', which were to provide a framework for assessing the safety of GM foods and plants. In the following month WHO and FAO announced a joint review of their food standards operations. In February 2003 the FAO/WHO Project and Fund for Enhanced Participation in Codex was launched to support the participation of poorer countries in the Commission's activities.

WHO's programme area on environmental health undertakes a wide range of initiatives to tackle the increasing threats to health and well-being from a changing environment, especially in relation to air pollution, water quality, sanitation, protection against radiation, management of hazardous waste, chemical safety and housing hygiene. In 2008 it was estimated that some 1,200m. people worldwide had no access to clean drinking water, while a further 2,600m. people are denied suitable sanitation systems. WHO helped launch the Water Supply and Sanitation Council in 1990 and regularly updates its *Guidelines for Drinking Water Quality*. In rural areas the emphasis continues to be on the provision and maintenance of safe and sufficient water supplies and adequate sanitation, the health aspects of rural housing, vector control in water resource management, and the safe use of agrochemicals. In urban areas assistance is provided to identify local environmental health priorities and to improve municipal governments' ability to deal with environmental conditions and health problems in an integrated manner; promotion of the 'Healthy City' approach is a major component of the programme. Other programme activities include environmental health information development and management, human resources development, environmental health planning methods, research and work on problems relating to global environment change, such as UV-radiation. The WHO Global Strategy for Health and Environment, developed in response to the WHO Commission on Health and Environment which reported to the UN Conference on Environment and Development in June 1992, provides the framework for programme activities. In May 2008 the 61st World Health Assembly adopted a resolution urging member states to take action to address the impact of climate change on human health.

Through its International EMF Project WHO is compiling a comprehensive assessment of the potential adverse effects on human health deriving from exposure to electromagnetic fields (EMF). In June 2004 WHO organized a workshop on childhood sensitivity to EMF.

WHO's work in the promotion of chemical safety is undertaken in collaboration with ILO and UNEP through the International Programme on Chemical Safety (IPCS), the Central Unit for which is located in WHO. The Programme provides internationally evaluated scientific information on chemicals, promotes the use of such information in national programmes, assists member states in establishment of their own chemical safety measures and programmes, and helps them strengthen their capabilities in chemical emergency preparedness and response and in chemical risk reduction. In 1995 an Inter-organization Programme for the Social Management of Chemicals was established by UNEP, ILO, FAO, WHO, UNIDO and OECD, in order to strengthen international co-operation in the field of chemical safety. In 1998 WHO led an international assessment of the health risk from bendocine disruptors (chemicals which disrupt hormonal activities).

Since the major terrorist attacks perpetrated against targets in the USA in September 2001, WHO has focused renewed attention on the potential malevolent use of bacteria (such as bacillus anthracis, which causes anthrax), viruses (for example, the variola virus, causing smallpox) or toxins, or of chemical agents, in acts of biological or chemical terrorism. In September 2001 WHO issued draft guidelines entitled 'Health Aspects of Biological and Chemical Weapons'.

Within the UN system, WHO's Department of Emergency and Humanitarian Action co-ordinates the international response to emergencies and natural disasters in the health field, in close co-operation with other agencies and within the framework set out by the UN's Office for the Co-ordination of Humanitarian Affairs. In this context, WHO provides expert advice on epidemiological surveillance, control of communicable diseases, public health information and health emergency training. Its emergency preparedness activities include co-ordination, policy-making and planning, awareness-building, technical advice, training, publication of standards and guidelines, and research. Its emergency relief activities include organizational support, the provision of emergency drugs and supplies and conducting technical emergency assessment missions. The Division's objective is to strengthen the national capacity of member states to reduce the adverse health consequences of disasters. In responding to emergency situations, WHO always tries to develop projects and activities that will assist the national authorities concerned in rebuilding or strengthening their own capacity to handle the impact of such situations. Under the UN's Consolidated Inter-agency Appeal Process (CAP) for 2008, launched in December 2007, WHO appealed for US $93.9m. to fund its emergency humanitarian operations.

In January 2005, following a massive earthquake in the Indian Ocean in December 2004, which caused a series of tidal waves, or tsunamis, that devastated coastal regions in 14 countries in South and South-East Asia and East Africa, WHO requested emergency funding of US $67.1m. to support an initial six-month relief operation. Priorities included the establishment of a local disease surveillance and early warning system; co-ordination of humanitarian health assistance at international and national level; guidance on critical public health matters (such as disease outbreak response, water quality and sanitation, and mental health and pre-existing disease management); ensuring equitable access to essential health care; and ensuring the prompt provision of medical supplies.

### HEALTH TECHNOLOGY AND PHARMACEUTICALS

WHO's Health Technology and Pharmaceuticals group, made up of the departments of essential drugs and other medicines, vaccines and other biologicals, and blood safety and clinical technology, covers the following areas of work: essential medicines—access, quality and rational use; immunization and vaccine development; and worldwide co-operation on blood safety and clinical technology. Blood safety and clinical technology are an organization-wide priority.

In January 1999 the Executive Board adopted a resolution on WHO's Revised Drug Strategy which placed emphasis on the inequalities of access to pharmaceuticals, and also covered specific aspects of drugs policy, quality assurance, drug promotion, drug donation, independent drug information and rational drug use. Plans of action involving co-operation with member states and other international organizations were to be developed to monitor and analyse the pharmaceutical and public health implications of international agreements, including trade agreements. In April 2001 experts from WHO and the World Trade Organization participated in a workshop to address ways of lowering the cost of medicines in less developed countries. In the following month the World Health Assembly adopted a resolution urging member states to promote equitable access to essential drugs, noting that this was denied to about one-third of the world's population. WHO participates with other partners in the 'Accelerating Access' initiative, which aims to expand access to antiretroviral drugs for people with HIV/AIDS (see above).

WHO reports that 2m. children die each year of diseases for which common vaccines exist. In September 1991 the Children's Vaccine Initiative (CVI) was launched, jointly sponsored by the Rockefeller Foundation, UNDP, UNICEF, the World Bank and WHO, to facilitate the development and provision of children's vaccines. The CVI has as its ultimate goal the development of a single oral immunization shortly after birth that will protect against all major childhood diseases. An International Vaccine Institute was established in Seoul, Republic of Korea, as part of the CVI, to provide scientific and technical services for the production of vaccines for developing countries. In September 1996 WHO, jointly with UNICEF, published a comprehensive survey, entitled *State of the World's Vaccines and Immunization*. In 1999 WHO, UNICEF, the World Bank and a number of public- and private-sector partners formed the Global Alliance for Vaccines and Immunization (GAVI), which aimed to expand the provision of existing vaccines and to accelerate the development and introduction of new vaccines and technologies, with the ultimate goal of protecting children of all nations and from all socio-economic backgrounds against vaccine-preventable diseases.

WHO supports states in ensuring access to safe blood, blood products, transfusions, injections, and healthcare technologies.

### INFORMATION, EVIDENCE AND RESEARCH

The Information, Evidence and Research group addresses the following areas of work: evidence for health policy; health information management and dissemination; and research policy and promotion and organization of health systems. Through the generation and dissemination of evidence the Information, Evidence and Research group aims to assist policy-makers assess health needs, choose intervention strategies, design policy and monitor performance, and thereby improve the performance of national health systems.

The group also supports international and national dialogue on health policy.

WHO co-ordinates the Health InterNetwork Access to Research Initiative (HINARI), which was launched in July 2001 to enable relevant authorities in developing countries to access biomedical journals through the internet at no or greatly reduced cost, in order to improve the world-wide circulation of scientific information; by July 2008 more than 3,750 publications were being made available to health institutions in 113 countries.

## Finance

WHO's regular budget is provided by assessment of member states and associate members. An additional fund for specific projects is provided by voluntary contributions from members and other sources, including UNDP and UNFPA.

A regular budget of US $3,745.1m. was proposed for 2008–09, of which some 10.9%, or $407.5m., was provisionally allocated to South-East Asia.

## Publications

*Bulletin of the World Health Organization* (monthly).

*Eastern Mediterranean Health Journal* (annually).

*International Classification of Functioning, Disability and Health—ICF*.

*International Statistical Classification of Disease and Related Health Problems*.

*Model List of Essential Medicines* (every two years).

*Pan-American Journal of Public Health* (annually).

*3 By 5 Progress Report*.

*Toxicological Evaluation of Certain Veterinary Drug Residues in Food* (annually).

*Weekly Epidemiological Record* (in English and French, paper and electronic versions available).

*WHO Drug Information* (quarterly).

*WHO Global Atlas of Traditional, Complementary and Alternative Medicine*.

*WHO Model Formulary*.

*World Health Report* (annually, in English, French and Spanish).

*World Malaria Report (with UNICEF)*.

*Zoonoses and Communicable Diseases Common to Man and Animals*.

Technical report series; catalogues of specific scientific, technical and medical fields available.

# Other UN Organizations Active in the Region

### OFFICE FOR THE CO-ORDINATION OF HUMANITARIAN AFFAIRS—OCHA

**Address:** United Nations Plaza, New York, NY 10017, USA.

**Telephone:** (212) 963-1234; **fax:** (212) 963-1312; **e-mail:** ochany@un.org; **internet:** ochaonline.un.org.

The Office was established in January 1998 as part of the UN Secretariat, with a mandate to co-ordinate international humanitarian assistance and to provide policy and other advice on humanitarian issues. It administers the Humanitarian Early Warning System, as well as Integrated Regional Information Networks (IRIN) to monitor the situation in different countries and a Disaster Response System. A complementary service, Reliefweb, which was launched in 1996, monitors crises and publishes information on the internet.

The IRIN–Central Asia Office, based in Islamabad, Pakistan, covers Afghanistan, Iran, Kazakhstan, Kyrgyzstan, Nepal, Pakistan, Tajikistan, Turkmenistan and Uzbekistan. A sub-office is located in Bishkek, Kyrgyzstan.

**Under-Secretary-General for Humanitarian Affairs and Emergency Relief Co-ordinator:** Sir JOHN HOLMES (United Kingdom).

### UNITED NATIONS OFFICE ON DRUGS AND CRIME—UNODC

**Address:** Vienna International Centre, POB 500, 1400 Vienna, Austria.

**Telephone:** (1) 26060-0; **fax:** (1) 26060-5866; **e-mail:** unodc@unodc.org; **internet:** www.unodc.org.

The Office was established in November 1997 (as the UN Office of Drug Control and Crime Prevention) to strengthen the UN's integrated approach to issues relating to drug control, crime prevention and international terrorism. It comprises two principal components: the United Nations Drug Programme and the Crime Programme.

**Executive Director:** ANTONIO MARIA COSTA (Italy).

### OFFICE OF THE UNITED NATIONS HIGH COMMISSIONER FOR HUMAN RIGHTS—OHCHR

**Address:** Palais Wilson, 52 rue de Paquis, 1201 Geneva, Switzerland.

**Telephone:** 229179290; **fax:** 229179022; **e-mail:** infodesk@ohchr.org; **internet:** www.ohchr.org.

The Office is a body of the UN Secretariat and is the focal point for UN human-rights activities. Since September 1997 it has incorporated the Centre for Human Rights. The High Commissioner is the UN official with principal responsibility for UN human rights activities.

**High Commissioner:** NAVANETHEM PILLAY (South Africa).

### UNITED NATIONS HUMAN SETTLEMENTS PROGRAMME—UN-HABITAT

**Address:** POB 30030, Nairobi, Kenya.

**Telephone:** (20) 621234; **fax:** (20) 624266; **e-mail:** infohabitat@unhabitat.org; **internet:** www.unhabitat.org.

UN-Habitat was established, as the United Nations Centre for Human Settlements, in October 1978 to service the intergovernmental Commission on Human Settlements. It became a full UN programme on 1 January 2002, serving as the focus for human settlements activities in the UN system.

**Executive Director:** ANNA KAJUMULO TIBAIJUKA (Tanzania).

### UNITED NATIONS CONFERENCE ON TRADE AND DEVELOPMENT—UNCTAD

**Address:** Palais des Nations, 1211 Geneva 10, Switzerland.

**Telephone:** 229171234; **fax:** 229070043; **e-mail:** info@unctad.org; **internet:** www.unctad.org.

UNCTAD was established in 1964. It is the principal organ of the UN General Assembly concerned with trade and development, and is the focal point within the UN system for integrated activities relating to trade, finance, technology, investment and sustainable development. It aims to maximize the trade and development opportunities of developing countries, in particular least-developed countries, and to assist them to adapt to the increasing globalization and liberalization of the world economy. UNCTAD undertakes consensus-building activities, research and policy analysis and technical co-operation.

**Secretary-General:** Dr SUPACHAI PANITCHPAKDI (Thailand).

### UNITED NATIONS POPULATION FUND—UNFPA

**Address:** 220 East 42nd St, New York, NY 10017, USA.

**Telephone:** (212) 297-5020; **fax:** (212) 297-4911; **internet:** www.unfpa.org.

Created in 1967 as the Trust Fund for Population Activities, the UN Fund for Population Activities (UNFPA) was established as a Fund of the UN General Assembly in 1972 and was made a subsidiary organ of the UN General Assembly in 1979, with the UNDP Governing Council (now the Executive Board) designated as its governing body. In 1987 UNFPA's name was changed to the United Nations Population Fund (retaining the same acronym).

**Executive Director:** THORAYA A. OBAID (Saudi Arabia).

# UN Specialized Agencies

### INTERNATIONAL ATOMIC ENERGY AGENCY—IAEA

**Address:** POB 100, Wagramerstrasse 5, 1400 Vienna, Austria.

**Telephone:** (1) 26000; **fax:** (1) 26007; **e-mail:** official.mail@iaea.org; **internet:** www.iaea.org.

The Agency was founded in 1957 as an autonomous intergovernmental organization, although it is administratively part of the UN system and reports annually to the UN General Assembly. Its main objectives are to enlarge the contribution of atomic energy to peace, health and prosperity throughout the world, and to ensure that materials and services provided by the Agency are not used to further any military purpose.

**Director-General:** Dr MOHAMMAD EL-BARADEI (Egypt).

### INTERNATIONAL CIVIL AVIATION ORGANIZATION—ICAO

**Address:** 999 University St, Montréal, QC H3C 5H7, Canada.

**Telephone:** (514) 954-8219; **fax:** (514) 954-6077; **e-mail:** icaohq@icao.org; **internet:** www.icao.int.

ICAO was founded in 1947, on the basis of the Convention on International Civil Aviation, signed in Chicago, in 1944, to develop the techniques of international air navigation and to help in the planning and improvement of international air transport.

**Secretary-General:** TAÏEB CHÉRIF (Algeria).

**Regional Office for Asia and the Pacific:** 252/1 Vibhavadi Rangsit Rd, Chatuchak, Bangkok 10900, Thailand; tel. (2) 537-8189; fax (2) 537-8199; e-mail icao_apac@bangkok.icao.int; internet www.bangkok.icao.int/; Dir LALIT B. SHAH.

### INTERNATIONAL LABOUR ORGANIZATION—ILO

**Address:** 4 route des Morillons, 1211 Geneva 22, Switzerland.

**Telephone:** 227996111; **fax:** 227988685; **e-mail:** ilo@ilo.org; **internet:** www.ilo.org.

ILO was founded in 1919 to work for social justice as a basis for lasting peace. It carries out this mandate by promoting decent living standards, satisfactory conditions of work and pay and adequate employment opportunities. Methods of action include the creation of international labour standards; the provision of technical co-operation services; and training, education, research and publishing activities to advance ILO objectives.

**Director-General:** JUAN O. SOMAVÍA (Chile).

**Regional Office for Asia and the Pacific:** POB 2-349, Bangkok 10200, Thailand; tel. (2) 288-1234; fax (2) 288-1735; e-mail bangkok@ilo.org; Dir SACHIKO YAMAMOTO.

### INTERNATIONAL MARITIME ORGANIZATION—IMO

**Address:** 4 Albert Embankment, London, SE1 7SR, United Kingdom.

**Telephone:** (20) 7735-7611; **fax:** (20) 7587-3210; **e-mail:** info@imo.org; **internet:** www.imo.org.

The Inter-Governmental Maritime Consultative Organization (IMCO) began operations in 1959, as a specialized agency of the UN to facilitate co-operation among governments on technical matters affecting international shipping. Its main aims are to improve the safety of international shipping, and to prevent pollution caused by ships. IMCO became IMO in 1982.

**Secretary-General:** EFTHIMIOS MITROPOULOS (Greece).

### INTERNATIONAL TELECOMMUNICATION UNION—ITU

**Address:** Place des Nations, 1211 Geneva 20, Switzerland.

**Telephone:** 227305111; **fax:** 227337256; **e-mail:** itumail@itu.int; **internet:** www.itu.int.

Founded in 1865, ITU became a specialized agency of the UN in 1947. It acts to encourage world co-operation for the improvement and use of telecommunications, to promote technical development, to harmonize national policies in the field, and to promote the extension of telecommunications throughout the world.

**Secretary-General:** HAMADOUN TOURÉ (Mali).

### UNITED NATIONS INDUSTRIAL DEVELOPMENT ORGANIZATION—UNIDO

**Address:** Vienna International Centre, POB 300, 1400 Vienna, Austria.

**Telephone:** (1) 260260; **fax:** (1) 2692669; **e-mail:** unido@unido.org; **internet:** www.unido.org.

UNIDO began operations in 1967 and became a specialized agency in 1985. Its objectives are to promote sustainable and socially equitable industrial development in developing countries and in countries with economies in transition. It aims to assist such countries to integrate fully into global economic system by mobilizing knowledge, skills, information and technology to promote productive employment, competitive economies and sound environment.

**Director-General:** KANDEH YUMKELLA (Sierra Leone).

### UNIVERSAL POSTAL UNION—UPU

**Address:** Weltpoststr., 3000 Bern 15, Switzerland.

**Telephone:** 313503111; **fax:** 313503110; **e-mail:** info@upu.int; **internet:** www.upu.int.

The General Postal Union was founded by the Treaty of Berne (1874), beginning operations in July 1875. Three years later its name was changed to the Universal Postal Union. In 1948 UPU became a specialized agency of the UN. It aims to develop and unify the international postal service, to study problems and to provide training.

**Director-General:** EDOUARD DAYAN (France).

### WORLD INTELLECTUAL PROPERTY ORGANIZATION—WIPO

**Address:** 34 chemin des Colombettes, 1211 Geneva 20, Switzerland.

**Telephone:** 223389111; **fax:** 227335428; **e-mail:** wipo.mail@wipo.int; **internet:** www.wipo.int.

WIPO was established in 1970. It became a specialized agency of the UN in 1974 concerned with the protection of intellectual property (e.g. industrial and technical patents and literary copyrights) throughout the world. WIPO formulates and administers treaties embodying international norms and standards of intellectual property, establishes model laws, and facilitates applications for the protection of inventions, trademarks etc. WIPO provides legal and technical assistance to developing countries and countries with economies in transition and advises countries on obligations under the World Trade Organization's agreement on Trade-Related Aspects of Intellectual Property Rights (TRIPS).

**Director-General:** Dr KAMIL IDRIS (Sudan) (until 30 Sept. 2008), FRANCIS GURRY (Australia) (from 1 Oct. 2008).

### WORLD METEOROLOGICAL ORGANIZATION—WMO

**Address:** 7 bis, ave de la Paix, 1211 Geneva 2, Switzerland.

**Telephone:** 227308111; **fax:** 227308181; **e-mail:** wmo@wmo.int; **internet:** www.wmo.int.

WMO was established in 1950 and was recognized as a Specialized Agency of the UN in 1951, aiming to improve the exchange of information in the fields of meteorology, climatology, operational hydrology and related fields, as well as their applications. WMO jointly implements, with UNEP, the UN Framework Convention on Climate Change.

**Secretary-General:** MICHEL JARRAUD (France).

### WORLD TOURISM ORGANIZATION—UNWTO

**Address:** Capitán Haya 42, 28020 Madrid, Spain.

**Telephone:** (91) 5678100; **fax:** (91) 5713733; **e-mail:** omt@world-tourism.org; **internet:** www.world-tourism.org.

The World Tourism Organization was established in 1975 and was recognized as a Specialized Agency of the UN in December 2003. It works to promote and develop sustainable tourism, in particular in support of socio-economic growth in developing countries.

**Secretary-General:** FRANCESCO FRANGIALLI (France).

# ASIAN DEVELOPMENT BANK—ADB

**Address:** 6 ADB Ave, Mandaluyong City, 0401 Metro Manila, Philippines; POB 789, 0980 Manila, Philippines.

**Telephone:** (2) 6324444; **fax:** (2) 6362444; **e-mail:** information@adb.org; **internet:** www.adb.org.

The ADB commenced operations in December 1966. The Bank's principal functions are to provide loans and equity investments for the economic and social advancement of its developing member countries, to give technical assistance for the preparation and implementation of development projects and programmes and advisory services, to promote investment of public and private capital for development purposes, and to respond to requests from developing member countries for assistance in the co-ordination of their development policies and plans.

### MEMBERS

There are 48 member countries and territories within the ESCAP region and 19 others (see list of subscriptions below).

## Organization

(August 2008)

### BOARD OF GOVERNORS

All powers of the Bank are vested in the Board, which may delegate its powers to the Board of Directors except in such matters as admission of new members, changes in the Bank's authorized capital stock, election of Directors and President, and amendment of the Charter. One Governor and one Alternate Governor are appointed by each member country. The Board meets at least once a year. The 41st Bank Annual Meeting was held in Madrid, Spain in May 2008.

### BOARD OF DIRECTORS

The Board of Directors is responsible for general direction of operations and exercises all powers delegated by the Board of Governors, which elects it. Of the 12 Directors, eight represent constituency groups of member countries within the ESCAP region (with about 65% of the voting power) and four represent the rest of the member countries. Each Director serves for two years and may be re-elected.

Three specialized committees (the Audit Committee, the Budget Review Committee and the Inspection Committee), each comprising six members, assist the Board of Directors in exercising its authority with regard to supervising the Bank's financial statements, approving the administrative budget, and reviewing and approving policy documents and assistance operations.

The President of the Bank, though not a Director, is Chairman of the Board.

**Chairman of Board of Directors and President:** HARUHIKO KURODA (Japan).

**Vice-Presidents:** URSULA SCHÄFER-PREUSS (Germany), ZHAO XIAOYU (People's Republic of China), BINDU LOHANI (Nepal), C. LAWRENCE GREENWOOD, Jr (USA).

### ADMINISTRATION

The Bank had 2,443 staff at 31 December 2007.

Five regional departments cover Central and West Asia, East Asia, the Pacific, South Asia, and Southeast Asia. Other departments and offices include Private Sector Operations, Central Operations Services, Regional and Sustainable Development, Strategy and Policy, Cofinancing Operations, and Economics and Research, as well as other administrative units.

There are Bank Resident Missions in Afghanistan, Azerbaijan, Bangladesh, Cambodia, the People's Republic of China, India, Indonesia, Kazakhstan, Kyrgyzstan, Laos, Mongolia, Nepal, Pakistan, Papua New Guinea, Sri Lanka, Tajikistan, Thailand, Uzbekistan and Viet Nam, all of which report to the head of the regional department. There are Extended Missions in Kerala and Tamil Nadu (India), Sumatra (Indonesia) and the Maldives. In addition, the Bank maintains a country office in the Philippines, a Special Office in Timor-Leste, a Pacific Liaison and Co-ordination Office in Sydney, Australia, and a South Pacific Regional Mission, based in Vanuatu (with a Sub-regional Office in Fiji). Representative Offices are located in Tokyo, Japan, Frankfurt am Main, Germany (for Europe), and Washington, DC, USA (for North America).

**Managing Director-General:** RAJAT M. NAG.

### INSTITUTE

**ADB Institute (ADBI):** Kasumigaseki Bldg, 8th Floor, 2–5 Kasumigaseki 3-chome, Chiyoda-ku, Tokyo 100-6008, Japan; tel. (3) 3593-5500; fax (3) 3593-5571; e-mail info@adbi.org; internet www.adbi.org; f. 1997 as a subsidiary body of the ADB to research and analyse long-term development issues and to disseminate development practices through training and other capacity-building activities; Dean Dr MASAHIRO KAWAI (Japan).

### FINANCIAL STRUCTURE

The Bank's ordinary capital resources (which are used for loans to the more advanced developing member countries) are held and used entirely separately from its Special Funds resources (see below). A fourth General Capital Increase (GCI IV), amounting to US $26,318m. (or 100%), was authorized in May 1994. At the final deadline for subscription to GCI IV, on 30 September 1996, 55 member countries had subscribed shares amounting to $24,675.4m.

At 31 December 2007 the position of subscriptions to the capital stock was as follows: authorized US $55,977.8m.; 'callable' subscribed $52,040.7m.

The Bank also borrows funds from the world capital markets. Total borrowings during 2007 amounted to US $8,854m. (compared with $5,576m. in 2006). At 31 December 2007 total outstanding debt amounted to $31,569m.

In July 1986 the Bank abolished the system of fixed lending rates, under which ordinary operations loans had carried interest rates fixed at the time of loan commitment for the entire life of the loan. Under the new system the lending rate is adjusted every six months, to take into account changing conditions in international financial markets.

## Activities

Loans by the ADB are usually aimed at specific projects. In responding to requests from member governments for loans, the Bank's staff assesses the financial and economic viability of projects and the way in which they fit into the economic framework and priorities of development of the country concerned. In 1985 the Bank decided to expand its assistance to the private sector, hitherto comprising loans to development finance institutions, under government guarantee, for lending to small and medium-sized enterprises; a programme was formulated for direct financial assistance, in the form of equity and loans without government guarantee, to private enterprises. In 1992 a Social Dimensions Unit was established as part of the central administrative structure of the Bank, which contributed to the Bank's increasing awareness of the importance of social aspects of development as essential components of sustainable economic growth. During the early 1990s the Bank also aimed to expand its role as project financier by providing assistance for policy formulation and review and promoting regional co-operation, while placing greater emphasis on individual country requirements. During that period the Bank also introduced a commitment to assess development projects for their impact on the local population and to avoid all involuntary resettlement where possible and established a formal procedure for grievances, under which the Board may authorize an inspection of a project by an independent panel of experts, at the request of the affected community or group.

The currency instability and ensuing financial crises affecting many Asian economies in the second half of 1997 and in 1998 prompted the Bank to reflect on its role in the region. The Bank resolved to strengthen its activities as a broad-based development institution, rather than solely as a project financier, through lending policies, dialogue, co-financing and technical assistance. In mid-1999 the Bank approved a technical assistance grant to establish an internet-based Asian Recovery Information Centre, within a new Regional Monitoring Unit, which aimed to facilitate access to information regarding the economic and social impact of the Asian financial crisis, analyses of economic needs of countries, reform programmes and monitoring of the economic recovery process. (In April 2005 the Unit was replaced by an Office of Regional Economic Integration, which aimed to promote economic co-operation and integration among developing member countries and to contribute to economic growth within the whole region.)

In November 1999 the Board of Directors approved a new overall strategy objective of poverty reduction, which was to be the principal consideration for all future Bank activities. The strategy incorporated key aims of supporting sustainable, grass-roots based economic growth, social development and good governance. During 2000 the Bank began to refocus its country strategies, projects and lending targets to complement the poverty reduction strategy. In addition, it initiated a process of consultation to formulate a long-term strategic framework, based on the target of reducing by 50% the incidence of extreme poverty by 2015, one of the so-called Millennium Development Goals (MDGs) identified by the UN General Assembly. The framework, establishing the operational priorities and principles for reducing poverty, was approved in March 2001. A review of the strategy, initiated at the end of 2003, concluded that more comprehensive, results-oriented monitoring and evaluation be put in place, with reference to both country strategies and programmes and management systems. It also recommended a closer alignment of Bank operations with national poverty reduction strategies. The review determined to include capacity development as a new overall thematic priority for the Bank, in addition to environmental sustainability, gender and development, private sector development and regional co-operation. In mid-2004 the Bank initiated a separate reform agenda to incorporate the strategy approach 'Managing for development results' throughout the organization. In July 2006 the Bank adopted a strategy to promote regional co-operation and integration in order to combat poverty through collective regional and cross-border activities.

In June 2006 the Bank convened a panel of eminent persons to assess the Bank's future role within the region. The report of the panel, submitted in March 2007, prompted further wide-ranging consultations. In April 2008 the Bank published a new long-term strategic framework to cover the period 2008–20 ('Strategy 2020'), replacing the previous 2001–15 strategic framework, in recognition of the unprecedented economic growth of recent years and its associated challenges, including the effect on natural resources, inadequate infrastructure to support economic advances, and widening disparities both within and between developing member countries. The Bank determined to refocus its activities onto three critical agendas: inclusive economic growth; environmentally sustainable growth; and regional integration. It determined to initiate a process of restructuring its operations into five core areas of specialization: infrastructure; environment, including climate change; regional co-operation and integration; financial sector development; and education. Some 80% of Bank lending was to be allocated to these five areas by 2012. Under the strategy the Bank resolved to act as an agent of change, stimulating economic growth and widening development assistance, for example by supporting the private sector with more risk guarantees, investment and other financial instruments, placing greater emphasis on good governance, promoting gender equality and improving accessibility to and distribution of its knowledge services. It also committed to expand its partnerships with other organizations, including with the private sector and other private institutions. The strategy was endorsed at the annual meeting of the Board of Governors, convened in Madrid, Spain, in May.

In 2007 the Bank approved 96 loans for 82 projects amounting to US $10,105.6m. Loans from ordinary capital resources in 2007 totalled $8,212.8m., while loans from the ADF amounted to $1,892.8m. The largest proportion of assistance, amounting to some 39% of total lending, was allocated to the transport and communications sector. The largest borrower was Pakistan, accounting for some 20% of total lending.

In 2007 the Bank approved 39 grants amounting to US $672.7m. financed by Special Funds (see below) and other bilateral and multilateral sources. It also approved 242 technical assistance projects, with funding of $243.3m., five equity investments amounting to $80.0m., and four multitranche financing facilities, totalling some $4,024.0m. The Bank's Operations Evaluation Office prepares reports on completed projects, in order to assess achievements and problems. In April 2000 the Bank announced that, from 2001, some new loans would be denominated in local currencies, in order to ease the repayment burden on recipient economies.

The Bank co-operates with other international organizations active in the region, particularly the World Bank group, the IMF, UNDP and APEC, and participates in meetings of aid donors for developing member countries. In May 2001 the Bank and UNDP signed a memorandum of understanding (MOU) on strategic partnership, in order to strengthen co-operation in the reduction of poverty, for example the preparation of common country assessments and a common database on poverty and other social indicators. Also in 2001 the Bank signed an MOU with the World Bank on administrative arrangements for co-operation, providing a framework for closer co-operation and more efficient use of resources. In May 2004 the Bank signed a revised MOU with ESCAP to enhance co-operation activities to achieve the MDGs. In early 2002 the Bank worked with the World Bank and UNDP to assess the preliminary needs of the interim administration in Afghanistan, in preparation for an International Conference on Reconstruction Assistance to Afghanistan, held in January, in Tokyo. The Bank pledged to work with its member governments to provide highly concessional grants and loans of some US $500m. over two-and-a-half years, with a particular focus on road reconstruction, basic education, and agricultural irrigation rehabilitation. In June 2008, at an international donors' conference held in Paris, France, the Bank pledged up to $1,300m. to finance infrastructure projects in Afghanistan in the coming five years. A new policy concerning co-operation with non-governmental organizations (NGOs) was approved by the Bank in 1998. The Bank administers an NGO Center to provide advice and support to NGOs on involvement in country strategies and development programmes.

In June 2004 the Bank approved a new policy to provide rehabilitation and reconstruction assistance following disasters or other emergencies. The policy also aimed to assist developing member countries with prevention, preparation and mitigation of the impact of future disasters. At the end of December the Bank announced assistance amounting to US $325m. to finance immediate reconstruction and rehabilitation efforts in Indonesia, the Maldives and Sri Lanka, which had been severely damaged by a series of large waves, or tsunamis, that had spread throughout the Indian Ocean as a result of a massive earthquake that had occurred close to the west coast of Sumatra, Indonesia. Of the total amount $150m. was to be drawn as new lending commitments from the Asian Development Fund. Teams of Bank experts undertook to identify priority operations and initiated efforts, in co-operation with governments and other partner organizations, to prepare for more comprehensive reconstruction activities. In accordance with the 2004 policy initiative, an interdepartmental task force was established to co-ordinate the Bank's response to the disaster. In January 2005, at a Special ASEAN Leaders' Meeting, held in Jakarta, Indonesia, the Bank pledged assistance amounting to $500m.; later in that month the Bank announced its intention to establish a $600m. Multi-donor Asian Tsunami Fund to accelerate the provision of reconstruction and technical assistance to countries most affected by the disaster. In March 2006 the Bank hosted a high-level co-ordination meeting on rehabilitation and reconstruction assistance to tsunami-affected countries. In October the Bank, with representatives of the World Bank, undertook an immediate preliminary damage and needs assessment following a massive earthquake in north-west Pakistan, which also affected remote parts of Afghanistan and India. The report identified relief and reconstruction requirements totalling some $5,200m. The Bank made an initial contribution of $80m. to a Special Fund (see below) and also pledged concessional support of up to $1,000m. for rehabilitation and reconstruction efforts in the affected areas.

The Bank has actively supported regional, sub-regional and national initiatives to enhance economic development and promote economic co-operation within the region. The Bank is the main co-ordinator and financier of a Greater Mekong Sub-region (GMS) programme, initiated in 1992 to strengthen co-operation between Cambodia, the People's Republic of China, Laos, Myanmar, Thailand and Viet Nam. Projects undertaken have included transport and other infrastructure links, energy projects and communicable disease control. The first meeting of GMS heads of state was convened in Phnom-Penh, Cambodia, in November 2002. A Core Environment Programme was inaugurated in 2005. Other sub-regional initiatives supported by the Bank include the Central Asian Regional Economic Cooperation (CAREC), South Asia Sub-regional Economic Cooperation (SASEC) initiative, the Indonesia, Malaysia, Thailand Growth Triangle (IMT-GT), and the Brunei, Indonesia, Malaysia, Philippines East ASEAN Growth Area (BIMP-EAGA).

## SPECIAL FUNDS

The Bank is authorized to establish and administer Special Funds. The Asian Development Fund (ADF) was established in 1974 in order to provide a systematic mechanism for mobilizing and administering resources for the Bank to lend on concessionary terms to the least-developed member countries. In 1998 the Bank revised the terms of ADF. Since 1 January 1999 all new project loans are repayable within 32 years, including an eight-year grace period, while quick-disbursing programme loans have a 24-year maturity, also including an eight-year grace period. The previous annual service charge was redesignated as an interest charge, including a portion to cover administrative expenses. The new interest charges on all loans are 1%–1.5% per annum. During 2007 36 ADF loans were approved, amounting to US $1,893m. In May 2008 30 donor countries pledged $4,200m. towards the ninth replenishment of ADF resources (ADF X), which totalled $11,300m. to provide resources for the four-year period 2009–12. The total amount included replenishment of the Technical Assistance Special Fund (see below).

The Bank provides technical assistance grants from its Technical Assistance Special Fund (TASF). By the end of 2007 the Fund's total resources amounted to US $1,361.3m. During 2007 $77.5m. was approved under the TASF project preparation and advisory activities. The Japan Special Fund (JSF) was established in 1988 to provide finance for technical assistance by means of grants, in both the public and private sectors. The JSF aims to help developing member countries restructure their economies, enhance the opportunities for attracting new investment, and recycle funds. The Japanese Government had committed a total of 111,000m. yen (equivalent to some $956.4m.) to the JSF by the end of 2007. During 2007 the Bank approved 55 technical assistance projects for the JSF, amounting to $43.1m., bringing a total of $1,017.2m. approved since 1988. The Bank administers the ADB Institute Special Fund, which was established to finance the ADB Institute's operations. By

31 December 2007 cumulative commitments to the Special Fund amounted to 15,800m. yen (or $133.0m.).

In February 2005 the Bank established the Asian Tsunami Fund, with funds of US $600m., to accelerate the provision of reconstruction and technical assistance to countries most affected by the natural disaster that had affected several countries in the region in December 2004. At the end of 2007 the Fund's uncommitted resources amounted to $40.0m. The Pakistan Earthquake Fund was established in November 2005, with a commitment from the Bank of $80m., to help to deliver emergency grant financing and technical assistance required for immediate rehabilitation and reconstruction efforts following the massive earthquake that had occurred in October. Further contributions, amounting to $51.4m., have been made by Australia, Belgium, Finland and Norway. In February 2007 the Bank established, with an initial $40.0m., the Regional Co-operation and Integration Fund to fund co-operation and integration activities in the region. By the end of 2007 the Fund's total resources amounted to $41.2 million, of which $33.8m. was uncommitted.

### TRUST FUNDS

The Bank also manages and administers several trust funds and other bilateral donor arrangements. The Japanese Government funds the Japan Scholarship Program, under which 2,235 scholarships had been awarded to recipients from 35 member countries between 1988 and 2007. In May 2000 the Japan Fund for Poverty Reduction was established, with an initial contribution of 10,000m. yen (approximately US $92.6m.) by the Japanese Government, to support ADB-financed poverty reduction and social development activities. By the end of 2007 cumulative commitments to the Fund totalled $360.4m. and 103 projects, amounting to $266.3m., had been approved for implementation. A Japan Fund for Information and Communication Technology (ICT) was established in July 2001, for a three-year period (later extended by one year until mid-2005), to promote the advancement and use of ICT in developing member countries. In March 2004 a Japan Fund for Public Policy Training was established, with an initial contribution by the Japanese Government, to enhance capacity-building for public policy management in developing member countries.

The majority of grant funds in support of the Bank's technical assistance activities are provided by bilateral donors under channel financing arrangements (CFAs), the first of which was negotiated in 1980. CFAs may also be processed as a thematic financing tool, for example concerned with renewable energy, water or poverty reduction, enabling more than one donor to contribute. A Co-operation Fund for Regional Trade and Financial Security Initiative was established in July 2004, with contributions by Australia, Japan and the USA, to support efforts to combat money laundering and the financing of terrorism. Other financing partnerships facilities may also be established to mobilize additional financing and investment by development partners. In November 2006 the Bank approved the establishment of an Asia Pacific Carbon Fund (within the framework of a Carbon Market Initiative) to finance clean energy projects in developing member countries. In the following month the Bank established a Water Financing Partnership Facility to help to achieve the objectives of its Water Financing Program. In July 2008 the Bank established a new Future Carbon Fund to stimulate investment in clean energy projects beyond 2012 (when the Kyoto Protocol regulating trade in carbon credits was due to expire).

## Finance

Internal administrative expenses totalled US $325.5m. in 2007 and were budgeted at $357.2m. for 2008.

## Publications

*ADB Business Opportunities* (monthly).

*ADB Institute Newsletter*.

*ADB Review* (monthly).

*Annual Report*.

*Asia Economic Monitor* (2 a year).

*Asian Development Outlook* (annually).

*Asian Development Review* (2 a year).

*Basic Statistics* (annually).

*Development Asia* (2 a year).

*Key Indicators for Asia and the Pacific* (annually).

*Law and Policy Reform Bulletin* (annually).

*Sustainability Report*.

Studies and technical assistance reports, information brochures, guidelines, sample bidding documents, staff papers.

## Statistics

**SUBSCRIPTIONS AND VOTING POWER**
(31 December 2007)

| Country | Voting power (% of total) | Subscribed capital (% of total) |
|---|---|---|
| **Regional:** | | |
| Afghanistan | 0.325 | 0.034 |
| Armenia | 0.537 | 0.298 |
| Australia | 4.917 | 5.773 |
| Azerbaijan | 0.653 | 0.444 |
| Bangladesh | 1.114 | 1.019 |
| Bhutan | 0.303 | 0.006 |
| Brunei | 0.580 | 0.351 |
| Cambodia | 0.338 | 0.049 |
| China, People's Republic | 5.442 | 6.429 |
| Cook Islands | 0.301 | 0.003 |
| Fiji | 0.353 | 0.068 |
| Georgia | 0.571 | 0.341 |
| Hong Kong | 0.733 | 0.543 |
| India | 5.352 | 6.317 |
| Indonesia | 4.646 | 5.434 |
| Japan | 12.756 | 15.571 |
| Kazakhstan | 0.942 | 0.805 |
| Kiribati | 0.302 | 0.004 |
| Korea, Republic | 4.320 | 5.026 |
| Kyrgyzstan | 0.537 | 0.298 |
| Laos | 0.310 | 0.014 |
| Malaysia | 2.472 | 2.717 |
| The Maldives | 0.302 | 0.004 |
| Marshall Islands | 0.301 | 0.003 |
| Micronesia, Federated States | 0.302 | 0.004 |
| Mongolia | 0.310 | 0.015 |
| Myanmar | 0.733 | 0.543 |
| Nauru | 0.302 | 0.004 |
| Nepal | 0.416 | 0.147 |
| New Zealand | 1.524 | 1.532 |
| Pakistan | 2.037 | 2.174 |
| Palau | 0.301 | 0.003 |
| Papua New Guinea | 0.373 | 0.094 |
| Philippines | 2.200 | 2.377 |
| Samoa | 0.301 | 0.003 |
| Singapore | 0.570 | 0.340 |
| Solomon Islands | 0.304 | 0.007 |
| Sri Lanka | 0.761 | 0.579 |
| Taiwan | 1.168 | 1.087 |
| Tajikistan | 0.527 | 0.286 |
| Thailand | 1.385 | 1.358 |
| Timor-Leste | 0.306 | 0.010 |
| Tonga | 0.302 | 0.004 |
| Turkmenistan | 0.501 | 0.253 |
| Tuvalu | 0.300 | 0.001 |
| Uzbekistan | 0.836 | 0.672 |
| Vanuatu | 0.304 | 0.007 |
| Viet Nam | 0.571 | 0.341 |
| **Sub-total** | 65.040 | 63.390 |
| **Non-regional:** | | |
| Austria | 0.570 | 0.340 |
| Belgium | 0.570 | 0.340 |
| Canada | 4.474 | 5.219 |
| Denmark | 0.570 | 0.340 |
| Finland | 0.570 | 0.340 |
| France | 2.156 | 2.322 |
| Germany | 3.752 | 4.316 |
| Ireland | 0.570 | 0.340 |
| Italy | 1.741 | 1.803 |
| Luxembourg | 0.570 | 0.340 |
| Netherlands | 1.117 | 1.023 |
| Norway | 0.570 | 0.340 |
| Portugal | 0.570 | 0.340 |
| Spain | 0.570 | 0.340 |
| Sweden | 0.570 | 0.340 |
| Switzerland | 0.764 | 0.582 |
| Turkey | 0.570 | 0.340 |
| United Kingdom | 1.929 | 2.038 |
| USA | 12.756 | 15.571 |
| **Sub-total** | 34.960 | 36.610 |
| **Total** | 100.000 | 100.000 |

**LENDING ACTIVITIES BY SECTOR**

| Sector | 2007 Amount (US $ million) | 2007 % | 1968–2007 % |
|---|---|---|---|
| Agriculture and natural resources | 146.3 | 1.4 | 12.5 |
| Education | 145.0 | 1.4 | 4.4 |
| Energy | 1,403.7 | 13.9 | 19.6 |
| Finance | 1,158.0 | 11.5 | 12.5 |
| Health, nutrition and social protection | 50.0 | 0.5 | 2.3 |
| Industry and trade | 95.0 | 0.9 | 4.2 |
| Law, economic management and public policy | 1,179.5 | 11.7 | 4.3 |
| Transport and communications | 3,925.8 | 38.8 | 24.3 |
| Water supply, sanitation and waste management | 408.2 | 4.0 | 5.2 |
| Multi-sector | 1,594.1 | 15.8 | 10.6 |
| **Total** | 10,389.3 | 100.00 | 100.00 |

**LENDING ACTIVITIES BY COUNTRY, 2007**
(US $ million)

| Country | Ordinary Capital | ADF | Total |
|---|---|---|---|
| Armenia | — | 66.6 | 66.6 |
| Azerbaijan | 246.0 | 10.0 | 256.0 |
| Bangladesh | 500.0 | 465.7 | 965.7 |
| Cambodia | 8.0 | 27.0 | 35.1 |
| China, People's Republic | 1,306.7 | — | 1,306.7 |
| Georgia | 25.0 | — | 25.0 |
| India | 1,386.4 | — | 1,386.4 |
| Indonesia | 995.0 | 50.0 | 1,045.0 |
| Kazakhstan | 100.0 | — | 100.0 |
| Kyrgyzstan | — | 15.0 | 15.0 |
| Maldives | 4.5 | 5.3 | 9.8 |
| Malaysia | 10.0 | — | 10.0 |
| Mongolia | 10.0 | — | 10.0 |
| Pakistan | 1,565.0 | 454.8 | 2,019.8 |
| Papua New Guinea | 60.0 | 40.0 | 100.0 |
| Philippines | 583.8 | — | 583.8 |
| Samoa | — | 26.6 | 26.6 |
| Sri Lanka | 327.5 | 115.0 | 442.5 |
| Tajikistan | — | 71.7 | 71.7 |
| Uzbekistan | 96.0 | 30.0 | 126.0 |
| Viet Nam | 968.9 | 515.0 | 1,483.9 |
| Sub-regional (Central and West Asia) | 20.0 | — | 20.0 |
| **Total** | 8,212.8 | 1,892.8 | 10,105.6 |

Source: *ADB Annual Report 2007*.

# THE COMMONWEALTH

**Address:** Commonwealth Secretariat, Marlborough House, Pall Mall, London, SW1Y 5HX, United Kingdom.

**Telephone:** (20) 7747-6500; **fax:** (20) 7930-0827; **e-mail:** info@commonwealth.int; **internet:** www.thecommonwealth.org.

The Commonwealth is a voluntary association of 53 independent states (at August 2008), comprising more than one-quarter of the world's population. It includes the United Kingdom and most of its former dependencies, and former dependencies of Australia and New Zealand (themselves Commonwealth countries). All Commonwealth countries accept Queen Elizabeth II as the symbol of the free association of the independent member nations and as such the Head of the Commonwealth.

### MEMBERS IN SOUTH ASIA

| | |
|---|---|
| India | Pakistan* |
| Maldives | Sri Lanka |

* Pakistan withdrew from the Commonwealth in 1972. It rejoined in October 1989. However, it was suspended from participation in meetings during the period October 1999–May 2004 and, once again, during November 2007–May 2008.

## Organization

(August 2008)

The Commonwealth is not a federation: there is no central government nor are there any rigid contractual obligations such as bind members of the United Nations.

The Commonwealth has no written constitution but its members subscribe to the ideals of the Declaration of Commonwealth Principles unanimously approved by a meeting of heads of government in Singapore in 1971. Members also approved the Gleneagles Agreement concerning apartheid in sport (1977); the Lusaka Declaration on Racism and Racial Prejudice (1979); the Melbourne Declaration on relations between developed and developing countries (1981); the New Delhi Statement on Economic Action (1983); the Goa Declaration on International Security (1983); the Nassau Declaration on World Order (1985); the Commonwealth Accord on Southern Africa (1985); the Vancouver Declaration on World Trade (1987); the Okanagan Statement and Programme of Action on Southern Africa (1987); the Langkawi Declaration on the Environment (1989); the Kuala Lumpur Statement on Southern Africa (1989); the Harare Commonwealth Declaration (1991); the Ottawa Declaration on Women and Structural Adjustment (1991); the Limassol Statement on the Uruguay Round of multilateral trade negotiations (1993); the Millbrook Commonwealth Action Programme on the Harare Declaration (1995); the Edinburgh Commonwealth Economic Declaration (1997); the Fancourt Commonwealth Declaration on Globalization and People-centred Development (1999); the Coolum Declaration on the Commonwealth in the 21st Century: Continuity and Renewal (2002); the Aso Rock Commonwealth Declaration and Statement on Multilateral Trade (2003); the Malta Commonwealth Declaration on Networking for Development (2005); and the Munyonyo Statement on Respect and Understanding (2007).

### MEETINGS OF HEADS OF GOVERNMENT

Commonwealth Heads of Government Meetings (CHOGMs) are private and informal and operate not by voting but by consensus. The emphasis is on consultation and exchange of views for co-operation. A communiqué is issued at the end of every meeting. Meetings are normally held every two years in different capitals in the Commonwealth. The 2007 meeting was held in Kampala, Uganda, in November. The next meeting was scheduled to be convened in 2009, in Trinidad and Tobago.

### OTHER CONSULTATIONS

Meetings at ministerial and official level are also held regularly. Since 1959 finance ministers have met in a Commonwealth country in the week prior to the annual meetings of the IMF and the World Bank. Meetings on education, legal, women's and youth affairs are held at ministerial level every three years. Ministers of health hold annual meetings, with major meetings every three years, and ministers of agriculture meet every two years. Ministers of finance, trade, labour and employment, industry, science, tourism and the environment also hold periodic meetings.

Senior officials—cabinet secretaries, permanent secretaries to heads of government and others—meet regularly in the year between meetings of heads of government to provide continuity and to exchange views on various developments.

### COMMONWEALTH SECRETARIAT

The Secretariat, established by Commonwealth heads of government in 1965, operates as an international organization at the service of all Commonwealth countries. It organizes consultations between governments and runs programmes of co-operation. Meetings of heads of government, ministers and senior officials decide these programmes and provide overall direction. A Board of Governors, on which all eligible member governments are represented, meets annually to review the Secretariat's work and approve its budget. The Board is supported by an Executive Committee which convenes four times a year to monitor implementation of the Secretariat's work programme. The Secretariat is headed by a secretary-general, elected by heads of government.

In 2002 the Secretariat was restructured, with a view to strengthening the effectiveness of the organization to meet the priorities determined by the meeting of heads of government held in Coolum, Australia, in March 2002. Under the reorganization the number of deputy secretaries-general was reduced from three to two. Certain work divisions were amalgamated, while new units or sections, concerned with youth affairs, human rights and good offices, were created to strengthen further activities in those fields. Accordingly, the new divisional structure was as follows: Legal and constitutional affairs; Political affairs; Corporate services; Communications and public affairs; Strategic planning and evaluation; Economic affairs; Governance and institutional development; Social transformation programmes; and Special advisory services. In addition there were units responsible for human rights, youth affairs, and project management and referrals, and an Office of the Secretary-General. In 2004 the youth affairs unit acquired divisional status.

The Secretariat's strategic plan for 2008/09–11/12, approved by the Board of Governors in May 2008, set out two main, long-term objectives for the Commonwealth: to support member countries in preventing or resolving conflicts, to strengthen democracy and the rule of law, and to achieve greater respect for human rights; and to support pro-poor policies for economic growth and sustainable development in member countries. Four programmes were to facilitate the pursuit of the first objective, 'Peace and Democracy': Good Offices for Peace; Democracy and Consensus Building; Rule of Law; and Human Rights. The second objective—'Pro-Poor Growth and Sustainable Development'—was to be achieved through the following four programmes: Public Sector Development; Economic Development; Environmentally Sustainable Development; and Human Development.

**Secretary-General:** Kamalesh Sharma (India).

**Deputy Secretaries-General:** Gabaipone Mmasekgoa Masire-Mwamba (Botswana), Ransford Smith (Jamaica).

# Activities

### INTERNATIONAL AFFAIRS

In October 1991 heads of government, meeting in Harare, Zimbabwe, issued the Harare Commonwealth Declaration, in which they reaffirmed their commitment to the Commonwealth Principles declared in 1971, and stressed the need to promote sustainable development and the alleviation of poverty. The Declaration placed emphasis on the promotion of democracy and respect for human rights and resolved to strengthen the Commonwealth's capacity to assist countries in entrenching democratic practices. In November 1995 Commonwealth heads of government, convened in New Zealand, formulated and adopted the Millbrook Commonwealth Action Programme on the Harare Declaration, to promote adherence by member countries to the fundamental principles of democracy and human rights (as proclaimed in the 1991 Declaration). The Programme incorporated a framework of measures to be pursued in support of democratic processes and institutions, and actions to be taken in response to violations of the Harare Declaration principles, in particular the unlawful removal of a democratically-elected government. A Commonwealth Ministerial Action Group on the Harare Declaration (CMAG) was to be established to implement this process and to assist the member country involved to comply with the Harare principles. On the basis of this Programme, the leaders suspended Nigeria from the Commonwealth with immediate effect, following the execution by that country's military Government of nine environmental and human rights protesters and a series of other violations of human rights. The meeting determined to expel Nigeria from the Commonwealth if no 'demonstrable progress' had been made towards the establishment of a democratic authority by the time of the next summit meeting. In addition, the Programme formulated measures to promote sustainable development in member countries, which was considered to be an important element in sustaining democracy, and to facilitate consensus-building within the international community.

In December 1995 CMAG convened for its inaugural meeting in London, United Kingdom. The Group initially comprised the ministers of foreign affairs of Canada, Ghana, Jamaica, Malaysia, New Zealand, South Africa, the United Kingdom and Zimbabwe, and its membership was to be reconstituted periodically (at August 2008 CMAG comprised the ministers of foreign affairs of Canada, Lesotho, Malaysia, Malta, Papua New Guinea, St Lucia, Sri Lanka, Tanzania and the United Kingdom). The inaugural CMAG meeting commenced by considering efforts to restore democratic government in the three Commonwealth countries then under military regimes, i.e. The Gambia, Nigeria and Sierra Leone. At the second meeting of the Group, in April 1996, ministers commended the conduct of presidential and parliamentary elections in Sierra Leone and the announcement by The Gambia's military leaders that there would be a transition to civilian rule. In June a three-member CMAG delegation visited The Gambia to reaffirm Commonwealth support of the transition process in that country and to identify possible areas of further Commonwealth assistance. In August the Gambian authorities issued a decree removing the ban on political activities and parties, although shortly afterwards they prohibited certain parties and candidates involved in political life prior to the military take-over from contesting the elections. CMAG recommended that in such circumstances no Commonwealth observers should be sent to either the presidential or parliamentary elections, which were held in September 1996 and January 1997 respectively. Following the restoration of a civilian Government in early 1997, CMAG requested the Commonwealth Secretary-General to extend technical assistance to The Gambia in order to consolidate the democratic transition process. In April 1996 it was noted that the human rights situation in Nigeria had continued to deteriorate. CMAG, having pursued unsuccessful efforts to initiate dialogue with the Nigerian authorities, outlined a series of punitive and restrictive measures (including visa restrictions on members of the administration, a cessation of sporting contacts and an embargo on the export of armaments) that it would recommend for collective Commonwealth action in order to exert further pressure for reform in Nigeria. Following a meeting of a high-level delegation of the Nigerian Government and CMAG in June, the Group agreed to postpone the implementation of the sanctions, pending progress on the dialogue. (Canada, however, determined, unilaterally, to impose the measures with immediate effect; the United Kingdom did so in accordance with a decision of the European Union to implement limited sanctions against Nigeria.) A proposed CMAG mission to Nigeria was postponed in August, owing to restrictions imposed by the military authorities on access to political detainees and other civilian activists in that country. In September the Group agreed to proceed with the visit (which then took place in November) and to delay further a decision on the implementation of sanction measures. In July 1997 the Group reiterated the Commonwealth Secretary-General's condemnation of a military coup in Sierra Leone in May, and decided that the country's participation in meetings of the Commonwealth should be suspended pending the restoration of a democratic government.

In October 1997 Commonwealth heads of government, meeting in Edinburgh, United Kingdom, endorsed CMAG's recommendation that the imposition of sanctions against Nigeria be held in abeyance pending the scheduled completion of a transition programme towards democracy by October 1998. It was also agreed that CMAG be formally constituted as a permanent organ to investigate abuses of human rights throughout the Commonwealth.

In March 1998 CMAG commended the efforts of the Economic Community of West African States (ECOWAS) in restoring the democratically-elected Government of President Ahmed Tejan Kabbah in Sierra Leone, and agreed to remove all restrictions on Sierra Leone's participation in Commonwealth activities. Later in that month, a representative mission of CMAG visited Sierra Leone to express its support for Kabbah's administration and to consider the country's needs in its process of reconstruction. At the CMAG meeting held in October members agreed that Sierra Leone should no longer be considered under the Group's mandate; however, they urged the Secretary-General to continue to assist that country in the process of national reconciliation and to facilitate negotiations with opposition forces to ensure a lasting cease-fire. A Special Envoy of the Secretary-General was appointed to co-operate with the UN, ECOWAS and the Organization of African Union (OAU, now African Union—AU) in monitoring the implementation of the Sierra Leone peace process, and the Commonwealth has supported the rebuilding of the Sierra Leone police force. In September 2001 CMAG recommended that Sierra Leone be removed from its remit, but that the Secretary-General should continue to monitor developments there.

In April 1998 the Nigerian military leader, Gen. Sani Abacha, announced that a presidential election was to be conducted in August, but indicated that, following an agreement with other political organizations, he was to be the sole candidate. In June, however, Abacha died suddenly. His successor, Gen. Abdulsalam Abubakar, immediately released several prominent political prisoners, and confirmed his intention to abide by the programme for transition to civilian rule. In October CMAG, convened for its 10th formal meeting, acknowledged Abubakar's efforts towards restoring a democratic government and recommended that member states begin to remove sanctions against Nigeria and that it resume participation in certain Commonwealth activities. The Commonwealth Secretary-General subsequently announced a programme of technical assistance to support Nigeria in the planning and conduct of democratic elections. Staff teams from the Commonwealth Secretariat observed local government, and state and governorship elections, held in December and in January 1999, respectively. A Commonwealth Observer Group was also dispatched to Nigeria to monitor preparations and conduct of legislative and presidential elections, held in February. While the Group reported several irregularities in the conduct of the polling, it confirmed that, in general, the conditions had existed for free and fair elections and that the elections were a legitimate basis for the transition of power to a democratic, civilian government. In April CMAG voted to readmit Nigeria to full membership on 29 May, upon the installation of the new civilian administration.

In 1999 the Commonwealth Secretary-General appointed a Special Envoy to broker an agreement in order to end a civil dispute in Honiara, Solomon Islands. An accord was signed in late June, and it was envisaged that the Commonwealth would monitor its implementation. In October a Commonwealth Multinational Police Peace Monitoring Group was stationed in Solomon Islands; this was renamed the Commonwealth Multinational Police Assistance Group in February 2000. Following further internal unrest, however, the Group was disbanded. In June CMAG determined to send a new mission to Solomon Islands in order to facilitate negotiations between the opposing parties, to convey the Commonwealth's concern and to offer assistance. The Commonwealth welcomed the peace accord concluded in Solomon Islands in October, and extended its support to the International Peace Monitoring Team that was established to oversee implementation of the peace accords. CMAG welcomed the conduct of parliamentary elections held in Solomon Islands in December 2001. CMAG removed Solomon Islands from its agenda in December 2003 but was to continue to receive reports from the Secretary-General on future developments.

In mid-October 1999 a special meeting of CMAG was convened to consider the overthrow of the democratically-elected Government in Pakistan in a military coup. The meeting condemned the action as a violation of Commonwealth principles and urged the new authorities to declare a timetable for the return to democratic rule. CMAG also resolved to send a four-member delegation, comprising the ministers of foreign affairs of Barbados, Canada, Ghana and Malaysia, to discuss this future course of action with the military regime. Pakistan was suspended from participation in meetings of the Commonwealth with immediate effect. The suspension, pending the restoration of a democratic government, was endorsed by heads of government, meeting in November, who requested that CMAG keep the situation in Pakistan under review. At the meeting, held in Durban, South Africa, it was agreed that no country would serve for more than two consecutive two-year terms. CMAG was requested to remain actively involved in the post-conflict development and rehabilitation of Sierra Leone and the process of consolidating peace. In addition, it was urged to monitor persistent violations of the Harare Declaration principles in all countries. Heads of government also agreed to establish a new ministerial group on Guyana and to reconvene a ministerial committee on Belize, in order to facilitate dialogue in ongoing territorial disputes with neighbouring countries. The meeting established a 10-member Commonwealth High Level Review Group to evaluate the role and activities of the Commonwealth. In 2000 the Group initiated a programme of consultations to proceed with its mandate and established a working group of experts to consider the Commonwealth's role in supporting information technology capabilities in member countries.

In June 2000, following the overthrow in May of the Fijian Government by a group of armed civilians, and the subsequent illegal detention of members of the elected administration, CMAG suspended Fiji's participation in meetings of the Commonwealth pending the restoration of democratic rule. In September, upon the request of CMAG, the Secretary-General appointed a Special Envoy to support efforts towards political dialogue and a return to democratic rule in Fiji. The Special Envoy undertook his first visit in December. In December 2001, following the staging of democratic legislative elections in August–September, Fiji was readmitted to Commonwealth meetings on the recommendation of CMAG. Fiji was removed from CMAG's agenda in May 2004, although the Group determined to continue to note developments there, as judgments were still pending in the Fiji Supreme Court on unresolved matters concerning the democratic process. In December 2006, following the overthrow of the Fijian Government by the military, an extraordinary meeting of CMAG determined that Fiji should once again be suspended from meetings of the Commonwealth, pending the reinstatement of democratic governance. Political developments in Fiji were considered by CMAG at its next regular meeting, held in New York, USA, in September 2007. The Group urged the Fijian authorities to hold a democratic general election by March 2009 and determined to keep the situation in that country under review. Addressing the situation in Fiji again at its May 2008 meeting, CMAG expressed concern at the pace of election preparations.

In March 2001 CMAG resolved to send a ministerial mission to Zimbabwe, in order to relay to the government the Commonwealth's concerns at the ongoing violence and abuses of human rights in that country, as well as to discuss the conduct of parliamentary elections and extend technical assistance. The mission was rejected by the Zimbabwe Government, which queried the basis for CMAG's intervention in the affairs of an elected administration. In September, under the auspices of a group of Commonwealth foreign ministers partly derived from CMAG, the Zimbabwe Government signed the Abuja Agreement, which provided for the cessation of illegal occupations of white-owned farms and the resumption of the rule of law, in return for financial assistance to support the ongoing process of land reform in that country. In January 2002 CMAG expressed strong concern at the continuing violence and political intimidation in Zimbabwe. The summit of Commonwealth heads of government convened in early March (see below) also expressed concern at the situation in Zimbabwe, and, having decided on the principle that CMAG should be permitted to engage with any member Government deemed to be in breach of the organization's core values, mandated a Commonwealth Chairperson's Committee on Zimbabwe to determine appropriate action should an impending presidential election (scheduled to be held during that month) be found not to have been conducted freely and fairly. Following the publication by a Commonwealth observer team of an unfavourable report on the conduct of the election, the Committee decided to suspend Zimbabwe from meetings of the Commonwealth for one year. In March 2003 the Committee concluded that the suspension should remain in force pending consideration by the next summit of heads of government.

In March 2002, meeting in Coolum, near Brisbane, Australia, Commonwealth heads of government adopted the Coolum Declaration on the Commonwealth in the 21st Century: Continuity and Renewal, which reiterated commitment to the organization's principles and values. Leaders at the meeting condemned all forms of terrorism; welcomed the Millennium Development Goals (MDGs) adopted by the UN General Assembly; called on the Secretary-General to constitute a high-level expert group on implementing the objectives of the Fancourt Declaration; pledged continued support for small states; and urged renewed efforts to combat the spread of HIV/AIDS. The meeting adopted a report on the future of the Commonwealth drafted by the High Level Review Group. The document recommended strengthening the Commonwealth's role in conflict prevention and resolution and support of democratic practices; enhancing the good offices role of the Secretary-General; better promoting member states' economic and development needs; strengthening the organization's role in facilitating member states' access to international assistance; and promoting increased access to modern information and communications technologies. The meeting expanded CMAG's mandate to enable the Group to consider action against serious violations of the Commonwealth's core values perpetrated by elected administrations (such as that in Zimbabwe, see above) as well as by military regimes.

A Commonwealth team of observers dispatched to monitor legislative and provincial elections that were held in Pakistan, in October 2002, found them to have been well-organized and conducted in a largely transparent manner. The team made several recommendations on institutional and procedural issues. CMAG subsequently expressed concern over the promulgation of new legislation in Pakistan following the imposition earlier in the year of a number of extra-constitutional measures. CMAG determined that Pakistan should continue to be suspended from meetings of the Commonwealth, pending a review of the role and functioning of its democratic institutions. Pakistan's progress in establishing democratic institutions was welcomed by a meeting of CMAG in May 2003. In November 2002 a Commonwealth Expert Group on Papua New Guinea, established in the previous month to review the electoral process in that country (in view of unsatisfactory legislative elections that were conducted there in July), made several recommendations aimed at enhancing the future management of the electoral process.

In December 2003 the meeting of heads of government, held in Abuja, Nigeria, resolved to maintain the suspension of Pakistan and Zimbabwe from participation in Commonwealth meetings. President Mugabe of Zimbabwe responded by announcing his country's immediate withdrawal from the Commonwealth and alleging a pro-Western bias within the grouping. Support for Zimbabwe's position was declared by a number of members, including South Africa, Mozambique, Namibia and Zambia. A Commonwealth committee, consisting of six heads of government, was established to monitor the situation in Zimbabwe and only when the committee believed sufficient progress had been made towards consolidating democracy and promoting development within Zimbabwe would the Commonwealth be consulted on readmitting the country.

In concluding the 2003 meeting heads of government issued the Aso Rock Commonwealth Declaration, which emphasized their commitment to strengthening development and democracy, and incorporated clear objectives in support of these goals. Priority areas identified included efforts to eradicate poverty and attain the MDGs, to strengthen democratic institutions, empower women, promote the involvement of civil society, combat corruption and recover assets (for which a working group was to be established), facilitate finance for development, address the spread of HIV/AIDS and other diseases, combat the illicit trafficking in human beings, and promote education. The leaders also adopted a separate statement on multilateral trade, in particular in support of the stalled Doha round of World Trade Organization negotiations.

In response to the earthquake and tsunami that devastated coastal areas of several Indian Ocean countries in late December 2004, the Commonwealth Secretary-General appealed for assistance from Commonwealth Governments for the mobilization of emergency humanitarian relief. In early January 2005 the Secretariat dispatched a Disaster Relief Co-ordinator to the Maldives to assess the needs of that country and to co-ordinate ongoing relief and rehabilitation activities, and later in that month the Secretariat sent emergency medical doctors from other member states to the Maldives. In mid-January, meeting during the fifth Summit of the Alliance of Small Island States, in Port Louis, Mauritius, the Secretaries-General of the Commonwealth, the Caribbean Community and Common Market (CARICOM), the Pacific Islands Forum and the Indian Ocean Commission determined to take collective action to strengthen the disaster-preparedness and response capacities of their member countries in the Caribbean, Pacific and Indian Ocean areas.

In May 2004 Pakistan was readmitted to the Commonwealth. However, CMAG urged the prompt separation of the military and civilian offices held by the President Musharraf, deeming this arrangement to be undemocratic. In February 2005 CMAG expressed serious concern that Musharraf had failed to relinquish the role of chief of army staff. Noting President Musharraf's own undertaking not to continue as chief of army staff beyond 2007, the Group stated its view that the two offices should not be combined in one person beyond the end (in that year) of the current presidential term. CMAG recommended that the Secretary-General should maintain high-level contacts with Pakistan. In September 2005 CMAG urged Pakistan to accelerate its democratic reforms. Meeting in London in early November, following Musharraf's re-election as President of Pakistan in early October, CMAG condemned the recent abrogation of Pakistan's Constitution and the institution there of a non-constitutional state of emergency; expressed grave concern at the recent dismissal of the Chief Justice and several other members of the judiciary and their placement under house arrest, and at other actions taken against lawyers, opposition politicians and civil society leaders, and at the suspension of all private media broadcasts and restrictions on the press; and noted with alarm a recent legislation that retrospectively gave military courts the right to try civilians on charges of 'anti-national activities'. While welcoming an announcement by President Musharraf that parliamentary elections would be staged in early 2008, CMAG maintained that such elections would only be credible if the state of emergency were revoked and constitutional rights restored. CMAG also noted with concern that Musharraf continued to retain the role of chief of army staff. The Group urged the Government of Pakistan to fulfil its obligations in accordance with Commonwealth principles through the implementation of the following measures: immediate repeal of the state of emergency, immediate release of political party leaders, lawyers, journalists and other activists detained under the state of emergency, and full restoration of the Constitution and of the independence of the judiciary; and for President Musharraf to relinquish his role as chief of army staff. Meeting on 22 November CMAG noted that these measures had not been implemented, as a consequence of which Pakistan was once again suspended from the Councils of the Commonwealth 'pending restoration of democracy and rule of law in the country'. President Musharraf relinquished his command of the Pakistan military at the end of November and the state of emergency was lifted in the following month. The Pakistan authorities did not invite the Commonwealth to send an observer mission to monitor the parliamentary elections that were held in that country in February 2008. Meeting in May 2008 CMAG commended the transition to a democratically-elected government in Pakistan, though it urged reform of the electoral system, and welcomed recent positive actions made by the Pakistan regime, including the relaxation of restrictions on the media and the release of political detainees. CMAG concluded that Pakistan should be readmitted to meetings of the Councils of the Commonwealth, and requested the Secretary-General to continue to provide technical assistance to the Pakistan Government towards strengthening the country's democratic institutions and processes.

The 2007 meeting of Commonwealth heads of government, convened in Kampala, Uganda, in November, issued the Munyonyo Statement on Respect and Understanding, which commended the work of the Commonwealth Commission on Respect and Understanding (established in 2005) and endorsed its recently published report entitled *Civil Paths to Peace* aimed at building tolerance and understanding of diversity. In June 2008 the Commonwealth issued the Marlborough House Statement on Reform of International Institutions, declaring that ongoing global financial turbulance and soaring food and fuel prices highlighted the poor responsiveness of some international organizations mandated to promote economic stability, and determining to identify underlying principles and actions required to reform and renew the international system. The Secretary-General was, accordingly, to develop an Action Plan on Reform of International Institutions.

**Political Affairs Division:** assists consultation among member governments on international and Commonwealth matters of common interest. In association with host governments, it organizes the meetings of heads of government and senior officials. The Division services committees and special groups set up by heads of government dealing with political matters. The Secretariat has observer status at the United Nations, and the Division manages a joint office in New York to enable small states, which would otherwise be unable to afford facilities there, to maintain a presence at the United Nations. The Division monitors political developments in the Commonwealth and international progress in such matters as disarmament and the Law of the Sea. It also undertakes research on matters of common interest to member governments, and reports back to them. The Division is involved in diplomatic training and consular co-operation.

In 1990 Commonwealth heads of government mandated the Division to support the promotion of democracy by monitoring the preparations for and conduct of parliamentary, presidential or other elections in member countries at the request of national governments. In 2008 (by August) a Commonwealth observer group had been dispatched to observe parliamentary elections in Belize, in February.

Under the reorganization of the Secretariat in 2002 a Good Offices Section was established within the Division to strengthen and support the activities of the Secretary-General in addressing political conflict in member states and in assisting countries to adhere to the principles of the Harare Declaration. The Secretary-General's good offices may be directed to preventing or resolving conflict and assisting other international efforts to promote political stability. At August 2008 Special Envoys of the Secretary-General were active in six member countries: Cameroon, The Gambia, Guyana, Kenya, the Maldives and Tonga.

**Human Rights Unit:** undertakes activities in support of the Commonwealth's commitment to the promotion and protection of fundamental human rights. It develops programmes, publishes human rights materials, co-operates with other organizations working in the field of human rights, in particular within the UN system, advises the Secretary-General, and organizes seminars and meetings of experts. The Unit aims to integrate human rights standards within all divisions of the Secretariat.

## LAW

**Legal and Constitutional Affairs Division:** promotes and facilitates co-operation and the exchange of information among member governments on legal matters and assists in combating financial and organized crime, in particular transborder criminal activities. It administers, jointly with the Commonwealth of Learning, a distance training programme for legislative draftsmen and assists governments to reform national laws to meet the obligations of international conventions. The Division organizes the triennial meeting of ministers, Attorneys General and senior ministry officials concerned with the legal systems in Commonwealth countries. It has also initiated four Commonwealth schemes for co-operation on extradition, the protection of material cultural heritage, mutual assistance in criminal matters and the transfer of convicted offenders within the Commonwealth. It liaises with the Commonwealth Magistrates' and Judges' Association, the Commonwealth Legal Education Association, the Commonwealth Lawyers' Association (with which it helps to prepare the triennial Commonwealth Law Conference for the practising profession), the Commonwealth Association of Legislative Counsel, and with other international non-governmental organizations. The Division provides in-house legal advice for the Secretariat. The *Commonwealth Law Bulletin*, published four times a year, reports on legal developments in and beyond the Commonwealth. The Division promotes the exchange of information regarding national and international efforts to combat serious commercial crime through its other publications, *Commonwealth Legal Assistance News* and *Crimewatch*.

The heads of government meeting held in Coolum, Australia, in March 2002 endorsed a Plan of Action for combating international terrorism. A Commonwealth Committee on Terrorism, convened at ministerial level, was subsequently established to oversee its implementation.

A new expert group on good governance and the elimination of corruption in economic management convened for its first meeting in May 1998. In November 1999 Commonwealth heads of government endorsed a Framework for Principles for Promoting Good Governance and Combating Corruption, which had been drafted by the group. The conference of heads of government that met in Coolum in March 2002 endorsed a Commonwealth Local Government Good Practice Scheme, to be managed by the Commonwealth Local Government Forum (established in 1995).

## ECONOMIC CO-OPERATION

In October 1997 Commonwealth heads of government, meeting in Edinburgh, United Kingdom, signed an Economic Declaration that focused on issues relating to global trade, investment and development and committed all member countries to free-market economic principles. The Declaration also incorporated a provision for the establishment of a Trade and Investment Access Facility within the Secretariat in order to assist developing member states in the process of international trade liberalization and promote intra-Commonwealth trade.

In May 1998 the Commonwealth Secretary-General appealed to the Group of Eight industrialized nations (G-8) to accelerate and expand the initiative to ease the debt burden of the most heavily indebted poor countries (HIPCs—see World Bank and IMF). In October Commonwealth finance ministers, convened in Ottawa, Canada, reiterated their appeal to international financial institutions to accelerate the HIPC initiative. The meeting also issued a Commonwealth Statement on the global economic crisis and endorsed proposals to help to counter the difficulties experienced by several countries. These measures included a mechanism to enable countries to suspend payments on all short-term financial obligations at a time of emergency without defaulting, assistance to governments to attract private capital and to manage capital market volatility, and the development of international codes of conduct regarding financial and monetary policies and corporate governance. In March 1999 the Commonwealth Secretariat hosted a joint IMF-World Bank conference to review the HIPC scheme and initiate a process of reform. In November Commonwealth heads of government, meeting in South Africa, declared their support for measures undertaken by the World Bank and IMF to enhance the HIPC initiative. At the end of an informal retreat the leaders adopted the Fancourt Commonwealth Declaration on Globalization and People-Centred Development, which emphasized the need for a more equitable spread of wealth generated by the process of globalization, and expressed a renewed commitment to the elimination of all forms of discrimination, the promotion of people-centred development and capacity-building, and efforts to ensure that developing countries benefit from future multilateral trade liberalization measures. In June 2002 the Commonwealth Secretary-General urged more generous funding of the HIPC initiative. Meetings of ministers of finance from Commonwealth member countries participating in the HIPC initiative are convened twice a year, as the Commonwealth HIPC Ministerial Forum. The Secretariat aims to assist HIPCs and other small economies through its Debt Recording and Management System (DRMS), which was first used in 1985 and updated in 2002. In mid-2005 the People's Republic of China became the 55th country (and the 12th non-Commonwealth member) to sign up to the System. The first Pan Commonwealth CS-DRMS User Group meeting was convened in June 2006, at which time there were 56 user countries. In July 2005 the Commonwealth Secretary-General welcomed an initiative of the G-8 to eliminate the debt of those HIPCs that had reached their completion point in the process, in addition to a commitment substantially to increase aid to Africa.

In February 1998 the Commonwealth Secretariat hosted the first Inter-Governmental Organizations Meeting to promote co-operation between small island states and the formulation of a unified policy approach to international fora. A second meeting was convened in March 2001, where discussions focused on the forthcoming WTO ministerial meeting and OECD's Harmful Tax Competition Initiative. In September 2000 Commonwealth finance ministers, meeting in Malta, reviewed the OECD initiative and agreed that the measures, affecting many member countries with offshore financial centres, should not be imposed on governments. The ministers mandated the involvement of the Commonwealth Secretariat in efforts to resolve the dispute; a joint working group was subsequently established by the Secretariat with the OECD. In April 2002 a meeting on international co-operation in the financial services sector, attended by representatives of international and regional organizations, donors and senior officials from Commonwealth countries, was held under Commonwealth auspices in Saint Lucia. In September 2005 Commonwealth finance ministers, meeting in Barbados, considered new guide-lines for Public Financial Management Reform.

The first meeting of governors of central banks from Commonwealth countries was held in June 2001 in London, United Kingdom.

The Commonwealth Secretariat was to participate in the €20m. 'Hub and Spokes' project, launched in October 2004 by the European Commission, with the Agence Intergouvernementale de la Francophonie, as a capacity-building initiative in the areas of trade policy formulation, mainstreaming trade in poverty reduction strategies, and participation in international trade negotiations for the African, Caribbean and Pacific (ACP) group of countries. The Secretariat was to manage the project in 55 of the 78 ACP member states.

In November 2005 Commonwealth heads of government issued the Malta Declaration on Networking the Commonwealth for Development, expressing their commitment to making available to all the benefits of new technologies and to using information technology networks to enhance the effectiveness of the Commonwealth in supporting development. The meeting endorsed a new Commonwealth Action Programme for the Digital Divide and approved the establishment of a special fund to enable implementation of the programme's objectives. Accordingly a Commonwealth Connects programme was established in August 2006 to develop partnerships and help to strengthen the use of and access to information technology in all Commonwealth countries. The 2005 Heads of Government Meeting also issued the Valletta Statement on Multilateral Trade, emphasizing their concerns that the Doha Round of WTO negotiations proceed steadily, on a development-oriented agenda, to a successful conclusion and reiterating their objectives of achieving a rules-based and equitable international trading system. A separate statement drew attention to the specific needs and challenges of small states and urged continued financial and technical support, in particular for those affected by natural disasters.

**Economic Affairs Division:** organizes and services the annual meetings of Commonwealth ministers of finance and the ministerial group on small states and assists in servicing the biennial meetings of heads of government and periodic meetings of environment ministers. It engages in research and analysis on economic issues of interest to member governments and organizes seminars and conferences of government officials and experts. The Division actively supports developing Commonwealth countries to participate in the Doha Round of multilateral trade negotiations and is assisting the ACP group of countries to negotiate economic partnership agreements with the European Union. It continues to help developing countries to strengthen their links with international capital markets and foreign investors. The Division also services groups of experts on economic affairs that have been commissioned by governments to report on, among other things, protectionism; obstacles to the North-South negotiating process; reform of the international financial and trading system; the debt crisis; management of technological change; the impact of change on the development process; environmental issues; women and structural adjustment; and youth unemployment. A separate section within the Division addresses the specific needs of small states and provides technical assistance. The work of the section covers a range of issues including trade, vulnerability, environment, politics and economics. A Secretariat Task Force services a Commonwealth Ministerial Group of Small States which was established in 1993 to provide strategic direction in addressing the concerns of small states and to mobilize support for action and assistance within the international community. The Economic Affairs Division also co-ordinates the Secretariat's environmental work and manages the Iwokrama International Centre for Rainforest Conservation and Development.

The Division played a catalytic role in the establishment of a Commonwealth Equity Fund, initiated in September 1990, to allow developing member countries to improve their access to private institutional investment, and promoted a Caribbean Investment Fund. The Division supported the establishment of a Commonwealth Private Investment Initiative (CPII) to mobilize capital, on a regional basis, for investment in newly-privatized companies and in small and medium-sized businesses in the private sector. The first regional fund under the CPII was launched in July 1996. The Commonwealth Africa Investment Fund (Comafin), was to be managed by the United Kingdom's official development institution, the Commonwealth Development Corporation, to assist businesses in 19 countries in sub-Saharan Africa, with initial resources of US $63.5m. In August 1997 an investment fund for the Pacific Islands was launched, with an initial capital of $15.0m. A successor fund, with financing of some $20m., was launched in October 2005. A $200m. South Asia Regional Fund was established at the heads of government meeting in October 1997. In October 1998 a fund for the Caribbean states was inaugurated, at a meeting of Commonwealth finance ministers. The 2001 summit of Commonwealth heads of government authorized the establishment of a new fund for Africa (Comafin II): this was inaugurated in March 2002, and attracted initial capital in excess of $200m.

## SOCIAL WELFARE

**Social Transformation Programmes Division:** consists of three sections concerned with education, gender and health.

The **Education Section** arranges specialist seminars, workshops and co-operative projects, and commissions studies in areas identified by ministers of education, whose three-yearly meetings it also services. Its present areas of emphasis include improving the quality of and access to basic education; strengthening the culture of science, technology and mathematics education in formal and non-formal areas of education; improving the quality of management in institutions of higher learning and basic education; improving the performance of teachers; strengthening examination assessment systems; and promoting the movement of students between Commonwealth countries. The Section also promotes multi-sectoral strategies to be incorporated in the development of human resources. Emphasis is placed on ensuring a gender balance, the appropriate use of technology, promoting good governance, addressing the problems of scale particular to smaller member countries, and encouraging collaboration between governments, the private sector and other non-governmental organizations.

The **Gender Affairs Section** is responsible for the implementation of the Commonwealth Plan of Action for Gender Equality, covering the period 2005–15, which succeeded the Commonwealth Plan of Action on Gender and Development (adopted in 1995 and updated in 2000). The Plan of Action supports efforts towards achieving the MDGs, and the objectives of gender equality adopted by the 1995 Beijing Declaration and Platform for Action and the follow-up Beijing + 5 review conference held in 2000. Gender equality, poverty eradication, promotion of human rights, and strengthening democracy are recognized as intrinsically inter-related, and the Plan has a particular focus on the advancement of gender mainstreaming in the following areas: democracy, peace and conflict; human rights and law; poverty eradication and economic empowerment; and HIV/AIDS. In February–March 2005 Commonwealth ministers responsible for gender affairs attended the Beijing + 10 review conference.

The **Health Section** organizes ministerial, technical and expert group meetings and workshops, to promote co-operation on health matters, and the exchange of health information and expertise. The Section commissions relevant studies and provides professional and technical advice to member countries and to the Secretariat. It also supports the work of regional health organizations and promotes health for all people in Commonwealth countries.

**Youth Affairs:** A Youth Affairs unit, reporting directly to a Deputy Secretary-General, was established within the Secretariat in 2002. The unit acquired divisional status in 2004.

The Division administers the **Commonwealth Youth Programme (CYP)**, which was initiated in 1973 to promote the involvement of young people in the economic and social development of their countries. The CYP, funded through separate voluntary contributions from governments, was awarded a budget of £2.6m. for 2006/07. The Programme's activities are centred on four key programmes: Youth Enterprise Development; Youth Networks and Governance; Youth Participation; and Youth Work, Education and Training. Regional centres are located in Zambia (for Africa), India (for Asia), Guyana (for the Caribbean), and Solomon Islands (for the Pacific). The Programme administers a Youth Study Fellowship scheme, a Youth Project Fund, a Youth Exchange Programme (in the Caribbean), and a Youth Service Awards Scheme. It also holds conferences and seminars, carries out research and disseminates information. The Commonwealth Youth Credit Initiative, launched in 1995, provides funds, training and advice to young entrepreneurs. A Plan of Action for Youth Empowerment, covering the period 2007–15, was approved by the sixth meeting of Commonwealth ministers responsible for youth affairs, held in Nassau, Bahamas, in May 2006. The first Commonwealth Youth and Sports Congress was scheduled to be held in India, in 2009. The sixth Commonwealth Youth Forum was convened in Entebbe, Uganda, in November 2007.

In March 2002 Commonwealth heads of government approved the Youth for the Future initiative to encourage and use the skills of young people throughout the Commonwealth. It was to comprise four main components: Youth enterprise development; Youth volunteers; Youth mentors; and Youth leadership awards.

### TECHNICAL ASSISTANCE

**Commonwealth Fund for Technical Co-operation (CFTC):** f. 1971 to facilitate the exchange of skills between member countries and to promote economic and social development; it is administered by the Commonwealth Secretariat and financed by voluntary subscriptions from member governments. The CFTC responds to requests from member governments for technical assistance, such as the provision of experts for short- or medium-term projects, advice on economic or legal matters, in particular in the areas of natural resources management and public-sector reform, and training programmes. The CFTC also administers the Langkawi awards for the study of environmental issues, which is funded by the Canadian Government; the proposed CFTC budget for 2006/07 amounted to £25.6m.

CFTC activities are mainly implemented by the following divisions:

**Governance and Institutional Development Division:** strengthens good governance in member countries, through advice, training and other expertise in order to build capacity in national public institutions. The Division administers the Commonwealth Service Abroad Programme (CSAP), which is funded by the CFTC. The Programme extends short-term technical assistance through highly qualified volunteers. The main objectives of the scheme are to provide expertise, training and exposure to new technologies and practices, to promote technology transfers and sharing of experiences and knowledge, and to support community workshops and other grassroots activities.

**Special Advisory Services Division:** advises on economic and legal issues, such as debt and financial management, natural resource development, multilateral trade issues, export marketing, trade facilitation, competitiveness and the development of enterprises.

# Commonwealth Organizations

(in the United Kingdom, unless otherwise stated)

### PRINCIPAL BODIES

**Commonwealth Business Council:** 18 Pall Mall, London, SW1Y 5LU; tel. (20) 7024-8200; fax (20) 7024-8201; e-mail info@cbcglobal.org; internet www.cbcglobal.org; f. 1997 by the Commonwealth Heads of Government Meeting to promote co-operation between governments and the private sector in support of trade, investment and development; the Council aims to identify and promote investment opportunities, in particular in Commonwealth developing countries, to support countries and local businesses to work within the context of globalization, to promote capacity-building and the exchange of skills and knowledge (in particular through its Information Communication Technologies for Development programme), and to encourage co-operation among Commonwealth members; promotes good governance; supports the process of multilateral trade negotiations and other liberalization of trade and services; represents the private sector at government level; Dir-Gen. and CEO Dr MOHAN KAUL.

**Commonwealth Foundation:** Marlborough House, Pall Mall, London, SW1Y 5HY; tel. (20) 7930-3783; fax (20) 7839-8157; e-mail geninfo@commonwealth.int; internet www.commonwealthfoundation.com; f. 1966; intergovernmental body promoting people-to-people interaction, and collaboration within the non-governmental sector of the Commonwealth; supports non-governmental organizations, professional associations and Commonwealth arts and culture; awards an annual Commonwealth Writers' Prize; funds are provided by Commonwealth govts; Chair. Prof. GUIDO DE MARCO (Malta); Dir Dr MARK COLLINS (United Kingdom); publ. *Commonwealth People* (quarterly).

**Commonwealth of Learning (COL):** 1055 West Hastings St, Suite 1200, Vancouver, BC V6E 2E9, Canada; tel. (604) 775-8200; fax (604) 775-8210; e-mail info@col.org; internet www.col.org; f. 1987 by Commonwealth Heads of Government to promote the devt and sharing of distance education and open learning resources, including materials, expertise and technologies, throughout the Commonwealth and in other countries; implements and assists with national and regional educational programmes; acts as consultant to international agencies and national governments; conducts seminars and studies on specific educational needs; core financing for COL is provided by Commonwealth governments on a voluntary basis; in 2006 heads of government endorsed an annual budget for COL of C $12m; Pres. and CEO Sir JOHN DANIEL (Canada/UK); publs *Connections*, *EdTech News*.

The following represents a selection of other Commonwealth organizations:

### AGRICULTURE AND FORESTRY

**Commonwealth Forestry Association:** Crib, Dinchope, Craven Arms, Shropshire, SY7 9JJ; tel. (1588) 672868; fax (870) 0116645; e-mail cfa@cfa-international.org; internet www.cfa-international.org; f. 1921; produces, collects and circulates information relating to world forestry and promotes good management, use and conservation of forests and forest lands throughout the world; mems: 1,200; Pres. DAVID BILLS (Australia/UK); publs *International Forestry Review* (quarterly), *Commonwealth Forestry News* (quarterly), *Commonwealth Forestry Handbook* (irregular).

**Standing Committee on Commonwealth Forestry:** Forestry Commission, 231 Corstorphine Rd, Edinburgh, EH12 7AT; tel. (131) 314-6137; fax (131) 316-4344; e-mail libby.jones@forestry.gsi.gov.uk; f. 1923 to provide continuity between Confs, and to provide a forum for discussion on any forestry matters of common interest to mem. govts which may be brought to the Cttee's notice by any mem. country or organization; 54 mems; 2010 Conference: United Kingdom; Sec. LIBBY JONES; publ. *Newsletter* (quarterly).

### COMMONWEALTH STUDIES

**Institute of Commonwealth Studies:** 28 Russell Sq., London, WC1B 5DS; tel. (20) 7862-8844; fax (20) 7862-8820; e-mail ics@sas.ac.uk; internet commonwealth.sas.ac.uk; f. 1949 to promote advanced study of the Commonwealth; provides a library and meeting place for postgraduate students and academic staff engaged in research in this field; offers postgraduate teaching; Dir Prof. RICHARD CROOK; publs *Annual Report*, *Collected Seminar Papers*, *Newsletter*, *Theses in Progress in Commonwealth Studies*.

### COMMUNICATIONS

**Commonwealth Telecommunications Organization:** 26–28 Hammersmith Grove, London, W6 7BA; tel. (870) 7777697; fax (870) 0345626; e-mail info@cto.int; internet www.cto.int; f. 1967 as an international development partnership between Commonwealth and non-Commonwealth governments, business and civil society organizations; aims to help to bridge the digital divide and to achieve social and economic development by delivering to developing countries knowledge-sharing programmes in the use of information and communication technologies in the specific areas of telecommunications, IT, broadcasting and the internet; CEO Dr EKWOW SPIO-GARBRAH; publs *CTO Update* (quarterly), *Annual Report*, *Research Reports*.

### EDUCATION AND CULTURE

**Association of Commonwealth Universities (ACU):** Woburn House, 20-24 Tavistock Sq., London, WC1H 9HF; tel. (20) 7380-6700; fax (20) 7387-2655; e-mail info@acu.ac.uk; internet www.acu.ac.uk; f. 1913; promotes international co-operation and understanding; provides assistance with staff and student mobility and development programmes; researches and disseminates information about universities and relevant policy issues; organizes major meetings of Commonwealth universities and their representatives; acts as a liaison office and information centre; administers scholarship and fellowship schemes; operates a policy research unit; mems: c. 500 universities in 36 Commonwealth countries or regions; Sec.-Gen. Dr JOHN ROWETT; publs include *Yearly Review*, *Commonwealth Universities Yearbook*, *ACU Bulletin* (quarterly), *Report of the Council of the ACU* (annually), *Who's Who of Executive Heads: Vice-Chancellors, Presidents, Principals and Rectors*, *International Awards*, student information papers (study abroad series).

**Commonwealth Association for Education in Journalism and Communication (CAEJAC):** c/o Faculty of Law, University of Western Ontario, London, ON N6A 3K7, Canada; tel. (519) 661-3348; fax (519) 661-3790; e-mail caejc@julian.uwo.ca; f. 1985; aims to foster high standards of journalism and communication education and research in Commonwealth countries and to promote co-operation among institutions and professions; c. 700 mems in 32 Commonwealth countries; Pres. Prof. SYED ARABI IDID (Malaysia); Sec. Prof. ROBERT MARTIN (Canada); publ. *CAEJAC Journal* (annually).

**Commonwealth Association of Science, Technology and Mathematics Educators (CASTME):** 7 Lion Yard, Tremadoc Rd, London, SW4 7NQ; tel. (20) 7819-3932; fax (20) 7720-5403; e-mail mirkka.juntunen@lect.org.uk; internet www.castme.org; f. 1974; special emphasis is given to the social significance of education in these subjects; organizes an Awards Scheme to promote effective teaching and learning in these subjects, and biennial regional seminars; Hon. Sec. Dr LYN HAINES; publ. *CASTME Journal* (quarterly).

**Commonwealth Council for Educational Administration and Management:** Department of Education, University of Cyprus, POB 20537, 1678 Lefkosia, Cyprus; tel. 22753739; fax 22377950; e-mail edpetros@ucy.ac.cy; internet www.cceam.org; f. 1970; aims to foster quality in professional development and links among educational administrators; holds nat. and regional confs, as well as visits and seminars; mems: 24 affiliated groups representing 3,000 persons; Pres. Dr PETROS PASHIARDIS; publ. *International Studies in Educational Administration* (2 a year).

**Commonwealth Education Trust:** New Zealand House, 80 Haymarket, London, SW1Y 4TQ; tel. (20) 7024-9822; fax (20) 7024-9833; e-mail info@commonwealth-institute.org; internet www.commonwealth-institute.org; f. 2007 as the successor trust to the Commonwealth Institute; funds the Centre of Commonwealth Education, established in 2004 as part of Cambridge University; supports the Lifestyle of Our Kids (LOOK) project initiated in 2005 by the Commonwealth Institute (Australia).

**League for the Exchange of Commonwealth Teachers:** 7 Lion Yard, Tremadoc Rd, London, SW4 7NQ; tel. (870) 7702636; fax (870) 7702637; e-mail info@lect.org.uk; internet www.lect.org.uk; f. 1901; promotes educational exchanges between teachers throughout the Commonwealth; Dir ANNA TOMLINSON; publ. *Annual Review*.

### HEALTH

**Commonwealth Medical Trust (COMMAT):** BMA House, Tavistock Sq., London, WC1H 9JP; tel. (20) 7272-8492; fax (1689) 890609; e-mail office@commat.org; internet www.commat.org; f. 1962 (as the Commonwealth Medical Association) for the exchange of information; provision of tech. co-operation and advice; formulation and maintenance of a code of ethics; promotes the Right to Health; liaison with WHO and other UN agencies on health issues; meetings of its Council are held every three years; mems: medical asscns in Commonwealth countries; Dir MARIANNE HASLEGRAVE.

**Commonwealth Pharmaceutical Association:** 1 Lambeth High St, London, SE1 7JN; tel. (20) 7572-2364; fax (20) 7572-2508; e-mail admin@commonwealthpharmacy.org; internet www.commonwealthpharmacy.org; f. 1970 to promote the interests of pharmaceutical sciences and the profession of pharmacy in the Commonwealth; to maintain high professional standards, encourage links between members and the creation of nat. asscns; and to facilitate the dissemination of information; holds confs (every four years) and regional meetings; mems: pharmaceutical asscns from over 40 Commonwealth countries; Pres. Dr GRACE ALLEN YOUNG; publ. *Quarterly Newsletter*.

**Commonwealth Society for the Deaf** (Sound Seekers): 34 Buckingham Palace Rd, London, SW1W 0RE; tel. (20) 7233-5700; fax (20) 7233-5805; e-mail sound.seekers@btinternet.com; internet www.sound-seekers.org.uk; f. 1959; undertakes initiatives to establish audiology services in developing Commonwealth countries, including mobile clinics to provide outreach services; aims to educate local communities in aural hygiene and the prevention of ear infection and deafness; provides audiological equipment and organizes the training of audiological maintenance technicians; conducts research into the causes and prevention of deafness; Chief Exec. GARY WILLIAMS; publ. *Annual Report*.

**Sightsavers International:** Grosvenor Hall, Bolnore Rd, Haywards Heath, West Sussex, RH16 4BX; tel. (1444) 446600; fax (1444) 446688; e-mail info@sightsavers.org; internet www.sightsavers.org; f. 1950 to prevent blindness and restore sight in developing countries, and to provide education and community-based training for incurably blind people; operates in collaboration with local partners in some 30 developing countries, with high priority given to training local staff; Chair. Lord NIGEL CRISP; Chief Exec. Dr CAROLINE HARPER; publ. *Sight Savers News*.

### INFORMATION AND THE MEDIA

**Commonwealth Broadcasting Association:** 17 Fleet St, London, EC4Y 1AA; tel. (20) 7583-5550; fax (20) 7583-5549; e-mail cba@cba.org.uk; internet www.cba.org.uk; f. 1945; gen. confs are held every two years (2008: Bahamas); mems: c. 100 in more than 50 countries; Pres. ABUBAKAR JIJIWA; Sec.-Gen. ELIZABETH SMITH; publs *Commonwealth Broadcaster* (quarterly), *Commonwealth Broadcaster Directory* (annually).

**Commonwealth Journalists Association:** c/o Canadian Newspaper Association, 890 Yonge St, Suite 200, Toronto, ON M4W 3P4, Canada; tel. (416) 575-5377; fax (416) 923-7206; e-mail bcantley@cna-acj.ca; internet www.cjaweb.com; f. 1978 to promote co-operation between journalists in Commonwealth countries, organize training facilities and confs, and foster understanding among Commonwealth peoples; Exec. Dir BRYAN CANTLEY; publ. *Newsletter* (3 a year).

**Commonwealth Press Union** (Association of Commonwealth Newspapers, News Agencies and Periodicals): 17 Fleet St, London, EC4Y 1AA; tel. (20) 7583-7733; fax (20) 7583-6868; e-mail lindsay@cpu.org.uk; internet www.cpu.org.uk; f. 1950; promotes the welfare of the Commonwealth press; provides training for journalists and organizes biennial confs; mems: c. 750 newspapers, news agencies, periodicals in 49 Commonwealth countries; Exec. Dir LINDSAY ROSS; publ. *Annual Report*.

### LAW

**Commonwealth Lawyers' Association:** c/o Institute of Commonwealth Studies, 28 Russell Sq., London, WC1B 5DS; tel. (20) 7862-8824; fax (20) 7862-8816; e-mail cla@sas.ac.uk; internet www.commonwealthlawyers.com; f. 1983 (fmrly the Commonwealth Legal Bureau); seeks to maintain and promote the rule of law throughout the Commonwealth, by ensuring that the people of the Commonwealth are served by an independent and efficient legal profession; upholds professional standards and promotes the availability of legal services; organizes the biannual Commonwealth Law Conference; Sec-Gen. CLAIRE MARTIN; publs *The Commonwealth Lawyer*, *Clarion*.

**Commonwealth Legal Advisory Service:** c/o British Institute of International and Comparative Law, Charles Clore House, 17 Russell Sq., London, WC1B 5DR; tel. (20) 7862-5151; fax (20) 7862-5152; e-mail info@biicl.org; f. 1962; financed by the British Institute and by contributions from Commonwealth govts; provides research facilities for Commonwealth govts and law reform commissions; Chair. Rt Hon. Lord BROWNE-WILKINSON; publ. *New Memoranda* series.

**Commonwealth Legal Education Association:** c/o Legal and Constitutional Affairs Division, Commonwealth Secretariat, Marlborough House, Pall Mall, London, SW1Y 5HX; tel. (20) 7747-6415; fax (20) 7747-6406; e-mail clea@commonwealth.int; internet www.cleaonline.org; f. 1971 to promote contacts and exchanges and to provide information regarding legal education; Gen. Sec. JOHN HATCHARD; publs *Commonwealth Legal Education Association Newsletter* (3 a year), *Directory of Commonwealth Law Schools* (every 2 years).

**Commonwealth Magistrates' and Judges' Association:** Uganda House, 58–59 Trafalgar Sq., London, WC2N 5DX; tel. (20) 7976-1007; fax (20) 7976-2394; e-mail info@cmja.org; internet www.cmja.org; f. 1970 to advance the administration of the law by promoting the independence of the judiciary, to further education in law and crime prevention and to disseminate information; confs and study tours; corporate membership for asscns of the judiciary or courts of limited jurisdiction; assoc. membership for individuals; Pres. Rt Hon. Justice Tan Sri Dato' Siti NORMA YAAKOB; Exec. Vice-Pres. Lord Justice HENRY BROOKE; publs *Commonwealth Judicial Journal* (2 a year), *CMJA News*.

## PARLIAMENTARY AFFAIRS

**Commonwealth Parliamentary Association:** Westminster House, Suite 700, 7 Millbank, London, SW1P 3JA; tel. (20) 7799-1460; fax (20) 7222-6073; e-mail hq.sec@cpahq.org; internet www.cpahq.org; f. 1911 to promote understanding and co-operation between Commonwealth parliamentarians; organization: Exec. Cttee of 35 MPs responsible to annual Gen. Assembly; 175 brs in national, state, provincial and territorial parliaments and legislatures throughout the Commonwealth; holds annual Commonwealth Parliamentary Confs and seminars; also regional confs and seminars; Sec.-Gen. Dr WILLIAM F. SHIJA; publ. *The Parliamentarian* (quarterly).

## PROFESSIONAL AND INDUSTRIAL RELATIONS

**Commonwealth Association of Architects:** POB 508, Edgware, Middx, HA8 9XZ; tel. (20) 8951-0550; fax (20) 8951-0550; e-mail info@comarchitect.org; internet comarchitect.org; f. 1964; an asscn of 38 socs of architects in various Commonwealth countries; objectives: to facilitate the reciprocal recognition of professional qualifications; to provide a clearing house for information on architectural practice; and to encourage collaboration. Plenary confs every three years; regional confs are also held; Exec. Dir TONY GODWIN; publs *Handbook, Objectives and Procedures: CAA Schools Visiting Boards, Architectural Education in the Commonwealth* (annotated bibliography of research), *CAA Newsnet* (2 a year), a survey and list of schools of architecture.

**Commonwealth Association for Public Administration and Management (CAPAM):** 1075 Bay St, Suite 402, Toronto, ON M5S 2B1, Canada; tel. (416) 920-3337; fax (416) 920-6574; e-mail capam@capam.org; internet www.capam.org; f. 1994; aims to promote sound management of the public sector in Commonwealth countries and to assist those countries undergoing political or financial reforms; an international awards programme to reward innovation within the public sector was introduced in 1997, and is awarded every 2 years; more than 1,200 individual mems and 80 institutional memberships in some 80 countries; Pres. GERALDINE FRASER-MOLEKETI (South Africa); Exec. Dir and CEO DAVID WAUNG.

## SCIENCE AND TECHNOLOGY

**Commonwealth Engineers' Council:** c/o Institution of Civil Engineers, 1 Great George St, London, SW1P 3AA; tel. (20) 7665-2005; fax (20) 7223-1806; e-mail neil.bailey@ice.org.uk; internet www.ice.org.uk/cec; f. 1946; the Council is a virtual organization that links engineering institutions across the Commonwealth, providing them with an opportunity to exchange views on collaboration and mutual support; mems: 46 institutions in 44 countries; Pres. Prof. TONY RIDLEY; Sec.-Gen. TOM FOULKES.

**Commonwealth Geological Surveys Forum:** c/o Commonwealth Science Council, CSC Earth Sciences Programme, Marlborough House, Pall Mall, London, SW1Y 5HX; tel. (20) 7839-3411; fax (20) 7839-6174; e-mail comsci@gn.apc.org; f. 1948 to promote collaboration in geological, geochemical, geophysical and remote sensing techniques and the exchange of information; Geological Programme Officer Dr SIYAN MALOMO.

## SPORT

**Commonwealth Games Federation:** 2nd Floor, 138 Piccadilly, London, W1J 7NR; tel. (20) 7491-8801; fax (20) 7409-7803; e-mail info@thecgf.com; internet www.thecgf.com; the Games were first held in 1930 and are now held every four years; participation is limited to competitors representing the mem. countries of the Commonwealth; 2010 games: New Delhi, India, in October; mems: 72 affiliated bodies; Pres. MICHAEL FENNELL; CEO MICHAEL HOOPER.

## YOUTH

**Commonwealth Youth Exchange Council:** 7 Lion Yard, Tremadoc Rd, London, SW4 7NQ; tel. (20) 7498-6151; fax (20) 7622-4365; e-mail mail@cyec.org.uk; internet www.cyec.org.uk; f. 1970; promotes contact between groups of young people of the United Kingdom and other Commonwealth countries by means of educational exchange visits, provides information for organizers and allocates grants; provides host governments with technical assistance for delivery of the Commonwealth Youth Forum, held every two years (2007: Uganda); 222 mem. orgs; Chief Exec. V. S. G. CRAGGS; publs *Contact* (handbook), *Exchange* (newsletter), *Final Communiqués* (of the Commonwealth Youth Forums), *Safety and Welfare* (guide-lines for Commonwealth Youth Exchange groups).

**Duke of Edinburgh's Award International Association:** Award House, 7–11 St Matthew St, London, SW1P 2JT; tel. (20) 7222-4242; fax (20) 7222-4141; e-mail sect@intaward.org; internet www.intaward.org; f. 1956; a self-development programme for young people, comprising Service, an Adventurous Journey, Physical Recreation, and Skills, in which participants set their own goals and measure their progress against them; more than 6m. young people have participated in the scheme; has a presence in more than 125 countries (not confined to the Commonwealth); Sec.-Gen. GILLIAN SHIRAZI; publs *Award World* (2 a year), *Annual Report*, handbooks and guides.

## MISCELLANEOUS

**Commonwealth Countries League:** 7 The Park, London, NW11 7SS; tel. (20) 8451-6711; e-mail info@ccl-int.org.uk; internet www.ccl-int.org.uk; f. 1925 to secure equal opportunities and status between men and women in the Commonwealth, to act as a link between Commonwealth women's orgs, and to promote and finance secondary education of disadvantaged girls of high ability in their own countries, through the CCL Educational Fund; holds meetings with speakers and an annual conf., organizes the annual Commonwealth Fair for fund-raising; individual mems and affiliated socs in the Commonwealth; Sec. STUART HETHERINGTON-BELL; publs *CCL Newsletter* (3 a year), *Annual Report*.

**Commonwealth War Graves Commission:** 2 Marlow Rd, Maidenhead, Berks, SL6 7DX; tel. (1628) 634221; fax (1628) 771208; internet www.cwgc.org; casualty and cemetery enquiries; e-mail casualty.enq@cwgc.org; f. 1917 (as Imperial War Graves Commission); responsible for the commemoration in perpetuity of the 1.7m. members of the Commonwealth Forces who died during the wars of 1914–18 and 1939–45; provides for the marking and maintenance of war graves and memorials at some 23,000 locations in 150 countries; mems: Australia, Canada, India, New Zealand, South Africa, United Kingdom; Pres. HRH The Duke of KENT; Dir-Gen. RICHARD KELLAWAY.

**Council of Commonwealth Societies:** c/o Royal Commonwealth Society, 25 Northumberland Ave, London, WC2N 5AP; tel. (20) 7766-9200; fax (20) 7930-9705; e-mail ccs@rcsint.org; internet www.rcsint.org/day; f. 1947; provides a forum for the exchange of information regarding activities of mem. orgs which promote understanding among countries of the Commonwealth; co-ordinates the distribution of the Commonwealth Day message by Queen Elizabeth, organizes the observance of and promotes Commonwealth Day, and produces educational materials relating to the occasion; seeks to raise the profile of the Commonwealth; mems: 30 official and unofficial Commonwealth orgs; Chair. Lord ALAN WATSON; Sec. ALICE KAWOWA.

**Royal Commonwealth Ex-Services League:** 48 Pall Mall, London, SW1Y 5JG; tel. (20) 7973-7263; fax (20) 7973-7308; e-mail mgordon-roe@commonwealthveterans.org.uk; internet www.commonwealthveterans.org.uk; links the ex-service orgs in the Commonwealth, assists ex-servicemen of the Crown who are resident abroad; holds triennial confs; 56 mem. orgs in 48 countries; Grand Pres. HRH The Duke of EDINBURGH; publ. *Annual Report*.

**Royal Commonwealth Society:** 25 Northumberland Ave, London, WC2N 5AP; tel. (20) 7930-6733; fax (20) 7930-9705; e-mail info@rcsint.org; internet www.rcsint.org; f. 1868; to promote international understanding of the Commonwealth and its people; organizes meetings and seminars on topical issues, and cultural and social events; library housed by Cambridge University Library; more than 10,000 mems; Chair. Baroness PRASHAR; Dir STUART MOLE; publs *Annual Report, Newsletter* (3 a year), conference reports.

**Royal Over-Seas League:** Over-Seas House, Park Place, St James's St, London, SW1A 1LR; tel. (20) 7408-0214; fax (20) 7499-6738; e-mail info@rosl.org.uk; internet www.rosl.org.uk; f. 1910 to promote friendship and understanding in the Commonwealth; clubhouses in London and Edinburgh; membership is open to all British subjects and Commonwealth citizens; Dir-Gen. ROBERT F. NEWELL; publ. *Overseas* (quarterly).

**Victoria League for Commonwealth Friendship:** 55 Leinster Sq., London, W2 4PW; tel. (20) 7243-2633; fax (20) 7229-2994; e-mail victorialeaguehq@btconnect.com; internet www.victorialeague.co.uk; f. 1901; aims to further personal friendship among Commonwealth peoples and to provide hospitality for visitors; maintains Student House, providing accommodation for students from Commonwealth countries; has brs elsewhere in the UK and abroad; Chair. JOHN KELLY; Gen. Sec. JOHN M. W. ALLAN; publ. *Annual Report*.

# ECONOMIC CO-OPERATION ORGANIZATION—ECO

**Address:** 1 Golbou Alley, Kamranieh St, POB 14155-6176, Tehran, Iran.

**Telephone:** (21) 22831733; **fax:** (21) 22831732; **e-mail:** registry@ecosecretariat.org; **internet:** www.ecosecretariat.org.

The Economic Co-operation Organization (ECO) was established in 1985 as the successor to the Regional Co-operation for Development, founded in 1964.

### MEMBERS

| | | |
|---|---|---|
| Afghanistan | Kyrgyzstan | Turkey |
| Azerbaijan | Pakistan | Turkmenistan |
| Iran | Tajikistan | Uzbekistan |
| Kazakhstan | | |

The 'Turkish Republic of Northern Cyprus' has been granted special guest status.

## Organization

(August 2008)

### SUMMIT MEETING

The first summit meeting of heads of state and of government of member countries was held in Tehran in February 1992. Summit meetings are generally held at least once every two years. The ninth summit meeting was convened in Baku, Azerbaijan, in May 2006. The 10th summit meeting was scheduled to be held in Islamabad, Pakistan, in October 2008.

### COUNCIL OF MINISTERS

The Council of Ministers, comprising ministers of foreign affairs of member states, is the principal policy- and decision-making body of ECO. It meets at least once a year.

### REGIONAL PLANNING COUNCIL

The Council, comprising senior planning officials or other representatives of member states, meets at least once a year. It is responsible for reviewing programmes of activity and evaluating results achieved, and for proposing future plans of action to the Council of Ministers.

### COUNCIL OF PERMANENT REPRESENTATIVES

Permanent representatives or Ambassadors of member countries accredited to Iran meet regularly to formulate policy for consideration by the Council of Ministers and to promote implementation of decisions reached at ministerial or summit level.

### SECRETARIAT

The Secretariat is headed by a Secretary-General, who is supported by two Deputy Secretaries-General. The following Directorates administer and co-ordinate the main areas of ECO activities: Trade and investment; Transport and communications; Energy, minerals and environment; Agriculture, industry and tourism; Project and economic research and statistics; Human resources and sustainable development; and International relations. The Secretariat services regular ministerial meetings held by regional ministers of agriculture; energy and minerals; finance and economy; industry; trade and investment; and transport and communications.

**Secretary-General:** KHURSHID ANWAR (Pakistan).

## Activities

The Regional Co-operation for Development (RCD) was established in 1964 as a tripartite arrangement between Iran, Pakistan and Turkey, which aimed to promote economic co-operation between member states. ECO replaced the RCD in 1985, and seven additional members were admitted to the Organization in November 1992. The main areas of co-operation are transport (including the building of road and rail links, of particular importance as seven member states are landlocked), telecommunications and post, trade and investment, energy (including the interconnection of power grids in the region), minerals, environmental issues, industry, and agriculture. ECO priorities and objectives for each sector are defined in the Quetta Plan of Action and the Istanbul Declaration; an Almaty Outline Plan, which was adopted in 1993, is specifically concerned with the development of regional transport and communication infrastructure. The period 1998–2007 was designated as the ECO Decade of Transport and Communications. Meeting in October 2005, in Astana, Kazakhstan, the ECO Council of Ministers adopted a document entitled *ECO Vision 2015*, detailing basic policy guidelines for the organization's activities during 2006–15, and setting a number of targets to be achieved in the various areas of regional co-operation.

In 1990 an ECO College of Insurance was inaugurated. A joint Chamber of Commerce and Industry was established in 1993. The third ECO summit meeting, held in Islamabad, Pakistan, in March 1995, concluded formal agreements on the establishment of several other regional institutes and agencies: an ECO Trade and Development Bank, in Istanbul, Turkey (with main branches in Tehran, Iran, and Islamabad, Pakistan); a joint shipping company, airline, and an ECO Cultural Institute, all to be based in Iran; and an ECO Reinsurance Company and an ECO Science Foundation, with headquarters in Pakistan. In addition, heads of state and of government endorsed the creation of an ECO eminent persons group and signed the following two agreements in order to enhance and facilitate trade throughout the region: the Transit Trade Agreement (which entered into force in December 1997) and the Agreement on the Simplification of Visa Procedures for Businessmen of ECO Countries (which came into effect in March 1998). The sixth ECO summit meeting, held in June 2000 in Tehran, urged the completion of the necessary formalities for the creation of the planned ECO Trade and Development Bank and ECO Reinsurance Company. The ECO Cultural Institute was inaugurated in that year. The Shipping Company is now also operational. In May 2001 the Council of Ministers agreed to terminate the ECO airline project, owing to its unsustainable cost, and to replace it with a framework agreement on co-operation in the field of air transport. The ECO Trade and Development Bank, headquartered in Istanbul, was inaugurated in late 2006, and commenced operations in 2008; it was expected that branches would subsequently be opened in Iran and Pakistan. In May 2007 the draft articles of agreement for the establishment of the planned ECO Reinsurance Company were finalized.

In September 1996, at an extraordinary meeting of the ECO Council of Ministers, held in Izmir, Turkey, member countries signed a revised Treaty of Izmir, the Organization's founding charter. An extraordinary summit meeting, held in Ashgabat, Turkmenistan, in May 1997, adopted the Ashgabat Declaration, emphasizing the importance of the development of the transport and communications infrastructure and the network of transnational petroleum and gas pipelines through bilateral and regional arrangements in the ECO area. In May 1998, at the fifth summit meeting, held in Almaty, Kazakhstan, ECO heads of state and of government signed a Transit Transport Framework Agreement (TTFA) and a memorandum of understanding to help combat the cross-border trafficking of illegal goods. (The TTFA entered into force in May 2006.) The meeting also agreed to establish an ECO Educational Institute in Ankara, Turkey. In June 2000 the sixth ECO summit encouraged member states to participate in the development of information and communication technologies through the establishment of a database of regional educational and training institutions specializing in that field. ECO heads of state and government also reconfirmed their commitment to the Ashgabat Declaration. In December 2001 ECO organized its first workshop on energy conservation and efficiency in Ankara. The seventh ECO summit, held in Istanbul, Turkey, in October 2002, adopted the Istanbul Declaration, which outlined a strengthened and more proactive economic orientation for the Organization.

Convening in conference for the first time in March 2000, ECO ministers of trade signed a Framework Agreement on ECO Trade Co-operation (ECOFAT), which established a basis for the expansion of intra-regional trade. The Framework Agreement envisaged the eventual adoption of an accord providing for the gradual elimination of regional tariff and non-tariff barriers between member states. The so-called ECO Trade Agreement (ECOTA) was endorsed at the eighth ECO summit meeting, held in Dushanbe, Tajikistan, in September 2004. Heads of state and government urged member states to ratify ECOTA at the earliest opportunity, in order to achieve their vision of an ECO free trade area by 2015. The meeting also requested members to ratify and implement the Transit Transport Framework Agreement (see above), to support economic co-operation throughout the region.

ECO ministers of agriculture, convened in July 2002, in Islamabad, adopted a declaration on co-operation in the agricultural sector, which specified that member states would contribute to agricultural rehabilitation in Afghanistan, and considered instigating a mechanism for the regional exchange of agricultural and cattle products. In December 2004, meeting in Antalya, Turkey, agriculture ministers approved the Antalya Declaration on ECO Co-operation in Agriculture and adopted an ECO plan of action on drought management and mitigation. In March 2007, meeting in Tehran, ECO ministers of agriculture approved the concept of an ECO Permanent Commission for Prevention and Control of Animal Diseases and Control of Animal Origin Food-Borne Diseases (ECO-PCPCAD). In April 2007 an ECO experts' group convened to develop a work plan on biodiversity in the ECO region with the aim of promoting co-operation towards achieving a set of agreed biodiversity targets over the period 2007–15. An ECO Seminar on Ecotourism was held in Kastamonu Province, Turkey, in the following month. In September 2007 the ECO Regional Center for Risk Management of Natural Disasters was inaugurated in Mashhad, Iran; the Center was to promote co-operation in drought monitoring and early warning. An ECO International Conference on Disaster Risk Management was convened in the following month, in Islamabad, Pakistan. In February 2006 a high-level group of experts on health was formed; its first meeting, held in the following month, focused on the spread of avian influenza in the region.

A meeting of ministers of industry, convened in November 2005, approved an ECO plan of action on privatization, envisaging enhanced technical co-operation between member states, and a number of measures for increasing cross-country investments; and adopted a declaration on industrial co-operation. The first meeting of the heads of ECO member states' national statistics offices, convened in January 2008 in Tehran, adopted the ECO Framework of Co-operation in Statistics and a related plan of action. An ECO Trade Fair was staged in Pakistan, in July 2008. The Organization maintains ECO TradeNet, an internet-based repository of regional trade information.

ECO has co-operation agreements with several UN agencies and other international organizations in development-related activities. An ECO-UNODC Project on Drug Control and Co-ordination Unit commenced operations in Tehran in July 1999. In December 2007 the ECO Secretary-General welcomed, as a means of promoting regional peace and security, the inauguration of the UN Regional Centre for Preventive Diplomacy in Central Asia (UNRCCA), based in Ashgabat, Turkmenistan. In that month ECO and the Shanghai Co-operation Organization signed a memorandum of understanding on mutual co-operation in areas including trade and transportation, energy and environment, and tourism. ECO has been granted observer status at the UN, OIC and WTO.

In November 2001 the UN Secretary-General requested ECO to take an active role in efforts to restore stability in Afghanistan and to co-operate closely with his special representative in that country. In June 2002 the ECO Secretary-General participated in a tripartite ministerial conference on co-operation for development in Afghanistan that was convened under the auspices of the UN Development Programme and attended by representatives from Afghanistan, Iran and Pakistan. The ECO summit meeting in October authorized the establishment of a special fund to provide financial assistance for reconstruction activities in Afghanistan. Projects to be implemented by the fund were reviewed during the first mission of the ECO Secretariat to Afghanistan, led by the Secretary-General in June 2005.

## Finance

Member states contribute to a centralized administrative budget.

## Publications

*ECO Annual Economic Report.*
*ECO Bulletin* (quarterly).
*ECO Environment Bulletin.*

# EUROPEAN UNION

### EUROPEAN UNION-SOUTH ASIA RELATIONS

The European Union (EU) was formally established on 1 November 1993 under the Treaty on European Union; prior to that date it was known as the European Community (EC). Bilateral non-preferential co-operation agreements were signed with Bangladesh, India, Pakistan and Sri Lanka between 1973 and 1976. A further agreement with India, extended to include co-operation in trade, industry, energy, science and finance, came into force in December 1981. A third agreement, which entered into effect in August 1994, included commitments to develop co-operation between the two sides and improve market access, as well as on the observance of human rights and democratic principles. The first EU-India summit meeting was held in Lisbon, Portugal, in June 2000. In November 2003 the EU urged India to reciprocate the EU's open market stance towards India by lowering its import tariffs on European products. In November 2004 the EU and India signed a 'strategic partnership' agreement, which was expected significantly to improve their relationship; the agreement—described as a reflection of 'India's growing stature and influence'—meant that India became a special EU partner alongside the USA, Canada, the People's Republic of China (PRC) and Russia. The sixth EU-India summit meeting, held in New Delhi, India, in September 2005, adopted a joint action plan to implement the strategic partnership. It was agreed to establish a dialogue on security issues, disarmament and non-proliferation, to increase co-operation in efforts to combat terrorism, and to create a high-level trade group to examine ways of strengthening economic relations. An agreement on India's participation in the EU's 'Galileo' civil satellite navigation and positioning system was also signed. The eighth EU-India summit meeting was held in New Delhi in November 2007. A joint statement was subsequently issued, in which India and the EU welcomed the signature of a memorandum of understanding on the country strategy paper for 2007–10, which allocated some €260m. in support of the joint action plan for India and the country's millennium development goals. A new and extended agreement with Pakistan on commercial and economic co-operation entered into force in May 1986; in May 1992 an agreement was signed on measures to stimulate private investment in Pakistan. A new accord with Sri Lanka, designed to promote co-operation in areas such as trade, investment and protection of the environment, entered into force in April 1995. A similar agreement with Nepal entered into force in June 1996. (In 2002–06 assistance granted to Nepal in the framework of a national indicative programme totalled an estimated €70m.). In July 1996 EU Governments authorized the European Commission to conclude similar agreements with Bangladesh and Pakistan. A draft co-operation agreement was initialled with Pakistan in April 1998. However, following the military coup in Pakistan in October 1999, the agreement was suspended. Political dialogue with Pakistan recommenced on an ad hoc basis in November 2000, and the co-operation agreement was signed in November 2001; a joint statement was issued on the occasion, in which Pakistan reiterated its firm commitment to return to democratic government. The co-operation agreement with Pakistan entered into force in April 2004. In January 2007 the European Commission proposed an assistance package for Pakistan in 2007–11 that amounted to €200m., compared with €125m. in development co-operation funding granted in 2002–06. Financial assistance until 2011 was to be concentrated on rural development in Pakistan's North West Frontier Province and in Baluchistan; and on the development of education and human resources. In February 2008 the EU deployed an Election Observation Mission to Pakistan, to monitor the conduct of the general election. Meanwhile, the new co-operation accord with Bangladesh (which replaced the 1976 commercial co-operation agreement) was signed in May 2000 and came into force in March 2001. In 2002–06, within the framework of a country strategy paper, assistance granted to Bangladesh totalled €290m., including €60m. for trade and economic co-operation, the largest such allocation made by the EU for that purpose world-wide. In June 2008 the European Commission pledged humanitarian assistance totalling €13m. to support reconstruction efforts in Bangladesh, following a a devastating cyclone in November 2007. The EU had already provided some €20.4m. in humanitarian aid to fund relief work in the immediate aftermath of the cyclone.

The EU pledged assistance for the reconstruction of Afghanistan following the removal of the Taliban regime in late 2001, and in 2002 announced development aid of €1,000m. for the period 2002–06, in addition to humanitarian aid. (By the end of 2006 the total of €1,000m. had been exceeded.) In March 2003 the European Commission hosted, along with the World Bank, the Afghanistan High Level Strategic Forum. The Government of Afghanistan convened the meeting to discuss with its principal partners, donors and multilateral organizations the progress and future vision for state-building in Afghanistan, as well as the long-term funding requirements for reconstruction. In 2004–05 the EU provided substantial support for the election process in Afghanistan, dispatching a Democracy and Election Support Mission to assess the presidential election, which was held in October 2004, and a full Election Observation Mission to monitor legislative and provincial elections, which took place in September 2005. In November the EU and Afghanistan adopted a joint declaration on a new partnership aimed at promoting Afghanistan's political and economic development and strengthening EU-Afghan relations. Increased co-operation was envisaged in areas such as political and economic governance, judicial reform, counter-narcotics measures and human rights, while the declaration also provided for a regular political dialogue, in the form of annual meetings at ministerial level. The EU welcomed the launch by the UN-sponsored London Conference on Afghanistan, held on 31 January–1 February 2006, of the Afghanistan Compact, representing a framework for co-operation between the government of Afghanistan, the UN and the international community for a five-year period terminating at the end of 2010. In January 2007 the European Commission proposed a package of financial support for Afghanistan in 2007–10, totalling some €610m. Reform of Afghanistan's justice system, rural development, in particular the promotion of alternatives to poppy cultivation, and the health sector were identified as the priority areas on which EU assistance should focus. In May 2007 the Council adopted a Joint Action on a proposed EU police mission to Afghanistan; EUPOL, comprising some 160 police officers, was officially launched on 15 June, and aimed to help develop a police force in Afghanistan that would work to respect human rights and operate within the framework of the rule of law, and to address the issue of police reform at central, regional and provincial levels. In addition, a programme of judicial reform was launched.

In September 2001 the EU adopted a new Communication on relations with Asia for the coming decade. Representing an updating of the 1994 strategy, this focused on strengthened partnership, particularly in the areas of politics, security, trade and investment. It aimed to reduce poverty and to promote democracy, good governance and the rule of law throughout the region. Partnerships and alliances on global issues were to be forged. A fundamental aim was to strengthen the EU's presence in Asia, promoting mutual awareness and knowledge on both sides. To this end, the EU increased the number of EU delegation offices in the region.

In late December 2004 ECHO responded immediately to the devastating earthquake and tsunami which struck in the Indian Ocean by providing food, water supplies and shelter to those made homeless. In January 2005 the European Commission President pledged €473m. in assistance for countries affected by the disaster, of which €123m. was for humanitarian support and €350m. for longer-term reconstruction efforts. EU governments pledged a further €1,000m. in aid. An EU Action Plan was concluded at the end of January 2005 to co-ordinate available resources and to meet the immediate needs of the affected regions. In May the Commission published a Tsunami Indicative Programme, detailing plans for reconstruction and aid in Indonesia, Sri Lanka and the Maldives. In October, in response to an earthquake that devastated parts of northern Pakistan and bordering areas of India and Afghanistan, killing more than 80,000 people, injuring an estimated 74,000, rendering more than 3m. homeless, and destroying local infrastructure, the EU provided an assistance package of €98.6m., which was channelled through ECHO and the EU mechanism for civil protection.

In May 1995 ASEAN and EU senior officials endorsed an initiative to convene an Asia-Europe Meeting of heads of government (ASEM). The first ASEM summit was held in March 1996 in Bangkok, Thailand. It was agreed to launch an Asia-Europe Partnership for Greater Growth, in order to expand trade, investment and technology transfer. An Asia-Business Forum was to be formed, as well as an Asia-Europe Foundation in Singapore to promote educational and cultural exchanges. The second ASEM summit, convened in the United Kingdom in April 1998, was dominated by economic and financial concerns, and both sides' declared intention to prevent a return to protectionist trading policies. The meeting established an ASEM Trust Fund, under the auspices of the World Bank, to alleviate the social impact of the financial crisis. Other initiatives adopted by ASEM were an Asia-Europe Co-operation Framework to co-ordinate political, economic and financial co-operation, a Trade Facilitation Action Plan, and an Investment Promotion Action Plan, which incorporated a new Investment Experts Group. The meeting resolved to promote efforts to strengthen relations in all areas, and to establish a series of working bodies to promote specific areas of co-operation. ASEM heads of government convened for the third time in Seoul, Republic of Korea, in October 2000. ASEM III welcomed the ongoing rapprochement between the two Korean nations, declared a commitment to the promotion of human rights, and endorsed several initiatives related to globalization and information technology. The meeting established a new Asia-Europe Co-operation Framework (AECF), identifying ASEM's principles and priorities for the next 10 years. ASEM VI, convened in Helsinki, Finland, in September 2006, addressed the theme '10 Years of ASEM: Global Challenges and Joint Responses'. For the first time, the summit was attended by Bulgaria, India, Mongolia, Pakistan, Romania and the ASEAN Secretariat. The participants adopted a Declaration on Climate Change, aimed at promoting efforts to reach consensus in international climate negotiations, and the Helsinki Declaration on the Future of ASEM, detailing guide-lines and practical recommendations for developing future ASEM co-operation. ASEM VII was to be held in Beijing, the People's Republic of China, in September 2008.

# ISLAMIC DEVELOPMENT BANK

**Address:** POB 5925, Jeddah 21432, Saudi Arabia.

**Telephone:** (2) 6361400; **fax:** (2) 6366871; **e-mail:** idbarchives@isdb.org; **internet:** www.isdb.org.

The Bank was established following a conference of Ministers of Finance of member countries of the Organization of the Islamic Conference (OIC), held in Jeddah in December 1973. Its aim is to encourage the economic development and social progress of member countries and of Muslim communities in non-member countries, in accordance with the principles of the Islamic *Shari'a* (sacred law). The Bank formally opened in October 1975. The Bank and its associated entities—the Islamic Research and Training Institute, the Islamic Corporation for the Development of the Private Sector, the Islamic Corporation for the Insurance of Investment and Export Credit, and the International Islamic Trade Finance Corporation—constitute the Islamic Development Bank Group.

### MEMBERS

There are 56 members.

## Organization

(August 2008)

### BOARD OF GOVERNORS

Each member country is represented by a governor, usually its Minister of Finance, and an alternate. The Board of Governors is the supreme authority of the Bank, and meets annually. The 33rd meeting was convened in Jeddah, Saudi Arabia, in June 2008.

### BOARD OF EXECUTIVE DIRECTORS

The Board consists of 14 members, seven of whom are appointed by the seven largest subscribers to the capital stock of the Bank; the remaining seven are elected by Governors representing the other subscribers. Members of the Board of Executive Directors are elected for three-year terms. The Board is responsible for the direction of the general operations of the Bank.

### ADMINISTRATION

In addition to the President of the Bank, there are three Vice-Presidents, responsible for Operations, Trade and Policy, and Corporate Resources and Services.

**President of the Bank and Chairman of the Board of Executive Directors:** Dr Ahmad Mohamed Ali (Saudi Arabia).

**Vice-President Operations:** Dr Amadou Boubacar Cisse (Niger).

**Vice-President Trade and Policy:** Dr Syed Jaafar Aznan (Malaysia).

**Vice-President Corporate Resources and Services:** Dr Syed Jaafar Aznan (Malaysia) (acting).

### FINANCIAL STRUCTURE

The Bank's unit of account is the Islamic Dinar (ID), which is equivalent to the value of one Special Drawing Right (SDR) of the IMF (average value in 2007 SDR 1 = US $1.58025). In May 2006 the Bank's Board of Governors approved an increase in the authorized capital from ID 15,000m. to ID 30,000m. At January 2008 total committed subscriptions amounted to ID 13,870.01m.

**SUBSCRIPTIONS**
(million Islamic Dinars, as at 9 January 2008)

| | | | |
|---|---|---|---|
| Afghanistan | 9.93 | Maldives | 9.23 |
| Albania | 9.23 | Mali | 18.19 |
| Algeria | 459.22 | Mauritania | 9.77 |
| Azerbaijan | 18.19 | Morocco | 91.69 |
| Bahrain | 25.88 | Mozambique | 9.23 |
| Bangladesh | 182.16 | Niger | 24.63 |
| Benin | 18.19 | Nigeria | 4.65 |
| Brunei | 45.85 | Oman | 50.92 |
| Burkina Faso | 24.63 | Pakistan | 459.22 |
| Cameroon | 45.85 | Palestine | 19.55 |
| Chad | 9.77 | Qatar | 97.73 |
| Comoros | 2.50 | Saudi Arabia | 3,685.13 |
| Côte d'Ivoire | 4.65 | Senegal | 45.89 |
| Djibouti | 4.96 | Sierra Leone | 4.96 |
| Egypt | 1,278.67 | Somalia | 4.96 |
| Gabon | 54.58 | Sudan | 72.77 |
| The Gambia | 9.23 | Suriname | 9.23 |
| Guinea | 45.85 | Syria | 18.49 |
| Guinea-Bissau | 4.96 | Tajikistan | 4.96 |
| Indonesia | 406.48 | Togo | 4.96 |
| Iran | 1,293.34 | Tunisia | 19.55 |
| Iraq | 48.24 | Turkey | 1,165.86 |
| Jordan | 73.50 | Turkmenistan | 4.96 |
| Kazakhstan | 19.29 | Uganda | 24.63 |
| Kuwait | 985.88 | United Arab Emirates | 1,045.96 |
| Kyrgyzstan | 4.96 | Uzbekistan | 2.50 |
| Lebanon | 9.77 | Yemen | 92.38 |
| Libya | 1,478.24 | | |
| Malaysia | 294.01 | | |

## Activities

The Bank adheres to the Islamic principle forbidding usury, and does not grant loans or credits for interest. Instead, its methods of project financing are: provision of interest-free loans, mainly for infrastructural projects which are expected to have a marked impact on long-term socio-economic development; provision of technical assistance (e.g. for feasibility studies); equity participation in industrial and agricultural projects; leasing operations, involving the leasing of equipment such as ships, and instalment sale financing; and profit-sharing operations. Funds not immediately needed for projects are used for foreign trade financing. Under the Import Trade Financing Operations (ITFO) scheme, funds are used for importing commodities for development purposes (i.e. raw materials and intermediate industrial goods, rather than consumer goods), with priority given to the import of goods from other member countries. In AH 1424 the Bank adopted a new group strategic framework, which identified three principal objectives: the promotion of Islamic financial industry and institutions; poverty alleviation; and the promotion of co-operation among member countries. To achieve these objectives, the Bank determined the following as priority areas of activity: human development; agricultural development and food security; infrastructure development; intra-trade among member countries; private sector development; and research and development in Islamic economics, banking and finance. In 2005 the Bank initiated a consultation process, led by a commission of eminent persons, to develop a new long-term strategy for the Bank. A document on the AH 1440 Vision was published in March 2006.

By 9 January 2008 the Bank had approved a total of ID 14,844.8m. (equivalent to some US $20,532.4m.) for project financing and technical assistance since operations began in 1976, ID 21,944.1m. ($29,799.1m.) for foreign trade financing, and ID 501.1m. ($640.8m.) for special assistance operations, excluding amounts for cancelled operations. During the Islamic year 1428 (20 January 2007 to 9 January 2008) the Bank approved a net total of ID 3,573.1m., for 327 operations.

The Bank approved 39 loans in the Islamic Year 1428, amounting to ID 239.2m. These loans supported projects concerned with the education and health sectors, infrastructural improvements, and agricultural developments. During that year the Bank's total disbursements totalled ID 2,307.5m., bringing the total cumulative disbursements since the Bank began operations to ID 26,089.2m. The Bank approved 73 technical assistance operations during that year in the form of grants and loans, amounting to ID 10.9m.

Import trade financing approved during the Islamic year 1428 amounted to ID 1,697.3m. for 67 operations. By the end of that year cumulative import trade financing amounted to ID 17,510.7m. During AH 1427 the Bank's export financing scheme was formally dissolved, although continued to fund projects pending the commencement of operations of the International Islamic Trade Finance Corporation (ITFC, see below). The Bank also finances other trade financing operations, including the Islamic Corporation for the Development of the Private Sector (ICD, see below), the Awqaf Properties Investment Fund and the Treasury Department. In addition, a Trade Co-operation and Promotion Programme supports efforts to enhance trade among OIC member countries. In June 2005 the Board of Governors approved the establishment of the ITFC as an autonomous trade promotion and financing institution within the Bank Group. The inaugural meeting of the ITFC was held in February 2007. In May 2006 the Board of Governors approved a new fund to reduce poverty and support efforts to achieve the UN Millennium Development Goals, in accordance with a proposal of the OIC. It was inaugurated, as the Islamic Solidarity Fund for Development, in May 2007; at that time 28 countries had pledged US $1,600m. to the Fund. The Fund became operational in early 2008.

In AH 1407 (1986–87) the Bank established an Islamic Bank's Portfolio for Investment and Development (IBP) in order to promote the development and diversification of Islamic financial markets and to mobilize the liquidity available to banks and financial institutions. During AH 1427 the IBP approved eight operations amounting to ID 135.8m. During AH 1428 resources and activities of the IBP were transferred to the newly-established ITFC. The Bank's Unit Investment Fund (UIF) became operational in 1990, with the aim of mobilizing additional resources and providing a profitable channel for investments conforming to *Shari'a*. The initial issue of the UIF was US $100m., which has subsequently been increased to $325m. The Fund finances mainly private sector industrial projects in middle-income countries and also finances short-term trade operations. In October 1998 the Bank announced the establishment of a new fund to invest in infrastructure projects in member states. The Bank committed $250m. to the fund, which was to comprise $1,000m. equity capital and a $500m. Islamic financing facility. In November 2001 the Bank signed an agreement with Malaysia, Bahrain, Indonesia and Sudan for the establishment of an Islamic financial market. In April 2002 the Bank, jointly with governors of central banks and the Accounting and Auditing Organization for Islamic Financial Institutions, concluded an agreement, under the auspices of the IMF, for the establishment of an Islamic Financial Services Board. The Board, which was to be located in Kuala Lumpur, Malaysia, was intended to elaborate and harmonize standards for best practices in the regulation and supervision of the Islamic financial services industry. In August 2003 the Bank mobilized some $400m. from the international financial markets through the issue of the International Islamic Sukuk bond.

The Bank's Special Assistance Programme was initiated in AH 1400 to support the economic and social development of Muslim communities in non-member countries, in particular in the education and health sectors. It also aimed to provide emergency aid in times of natural disasters, and to assist Muslim refugees throughout the world. Operations undertaken by the Bank are financed by the Waqf Fund (formerly the Special Assistance Account). By the end of AH 1428 some US $640.8m. had been approved under the Waqf Fund Special Assistance Programme for 1,185 operations, of which 465 were in member countries and 720 were for Muslim organizations and communities in non-member countries. Other assistance activities include scholarship programmes, technical co-operation projects and the sacrificial meat utilization project (see below). In January 2005 the Bank allocated $500m. to assist the survivors of the Indian Ocean earthquake and tsunami which struck coastal areas in 14 countries in late December 2004. The Bank dispatched missions to provide emergency relief to Indonesia, the Maldives and Sri Lanka, and planned to send further teams to assess the requirements for reconstruction. The Bank approved an assistance programme amounting to $501.6m. following a massive earthquake in north-west Pakistan that occurred in October 2005. The funds aimed to support recovery, rehabilitation and reconstruction efforts. The Bank increasingly has worked to assist post-conflict member countries in rehabilitation and reconstruction. It is a member of the management committee of the Afghanistan Reconstruction Trust Fund, which was established in 2001; during 2003 the Bank approved an operation to assist Afghan refugees. In December 2003 the Bank approved a Programme for Reconstruction of Iraq, with funding of ID 365.5m. ($500m.) to be implemented over a five-year period. In October 2002 the Bank's Board of Governors, meeting in Burkina Faso, adopted the Ouagadougou Declaration on the co-operation between the Bank group and Africa, which identified priority areas for Bank activities, for example education and the private sector. The Bank pledged $2,000m. to finance implementation of the Declaration over the five years 2004–08. A new IDB Special Programme for the Development of Africa was endorsed at a summit meeting of the OIC held in March 2008.

In AH 1404 (1983–84) the Bank established a scholarship programme for Muslim communities in non-member countries to provide opportunities for students to pursue further education or other professional training. The programme also assists nine member countries on an exceptional basis. By the end of the Islamic year 1428 5,237 people had graduated and 2,640 were undertaking studies under the scheme, at a cost of ID 50m. The Merit Scholarship Programme, initiated in AH 1412 (1991–92), aims to develop scientific, technological and research capacities in member countries through advanced studies and/or research. A total of 392 scholarships had been awarded, at a cost of ID 11m., by the end of AH 1428. In AH 1419 (1998–99) a Scholarship Programme in Science and Technology for IDB Least Developed Member Countries became operational for students in 20 eligible countries. By the end of AH 1428 205 students had been selected under the programme to study in other Bank member countries, of whom 92 had graduated under the Programme.

The Bank's Programme for Technical Co-operation aims to mobilize technical capabilities among member countries and to promote the exchange of expertise, experience and skills through expert missions, training, seminars and workshops. In December 1999 the Board of Executive Directors approved two technical assistance grants to support a programme for the eradication of illiteracy in the Islamic world, and one for self-sufficiency in human vaccine production. The Bank also undertakes the distribution of meat sacrificed by Muslim pilgrims. The Bank was the principal source of funding of the International Centre for Biosaline Agriculture, which was established in Dubai, UAE, in September 1999.

### BANK GROUP ENTITIES

**International Islamic Trade Finance Corporation:** Jeddah, Saudia Arabia; f. 2007; commenced operations Jan. 2008; aims to promote trade and trade financing in Bank member countries, to facilitate access to public and private capital, and to promote investment opportunities; auth. cap. US $3,000m.; subs. cap. $750m.; CEO Dr WALID AL WOHAIB.

**Islamic Corporation for the Development of the Private Sector (ICD):** POB 54069, Jeddah 21514, Saudi Arabia; tel. (2) 6441644; fax (2) 6444427; e-mail icd@isdb.org; internet www.icd-idb.org; f. 1999; to identify opportunities in the private sector, provide financial products and services compatible with Islamic law, mobilize additional resources for the private sector in member countries, and encourage the development of Islamic financing and capital markets; the Bank's share of the capital is 50%, member countries 30% and public financial institutions of member countries 20%; p.u. cap. US $330.1m. (Jan. 2008); mems: 44 countries, the Bank, and five public financial institutions (a further seven countries have signed the Articles of Agreement and are in the process of ratification); CEO and Gen. Man. KHALID M. AL-ABOODI.

**Islamic Corporation for the Insurance of Investment and Export Credit (ICIEC):** POB 15722, Jeddah 21454, Saudi Arabia; tel. (2) 6445666; fax (2) 6379504; e-mail idb.iciec@isdb.org.sa; internet www.iciec.com; f. 1994; aims to promote trade and the flow of investments among member countries of the OIC through the provision of export credit and investment insurance services; auth. cap. ID 100m., subscribed cap. ID 97.24m. (Jan. 2008); mems: 35 member states and the Islamic Development Bank (which contributes 50% of its capital); Gen. Man. Dr ABDEL RAHMAN A. TAHA.

**Islamic Research and Training Institute:** POB 9201, Jeddah 21413, Saudi Arabia; tel. (2) 6361400; fax (2) 6378927; e-mail irti@isdb.org; internet www.irti.org; f. 1982 to undertake research enabling economic, financial and banking activities to conform to Islamic law, and to provide training for staff involved in development activities in the Bank's member countries; the Institute also organizes seminars and workshops, and holds training courses aimed at furthering the expertise of government and financial officials in Islamic developing countries; Acting Dir BASHIR ALI KHALLAT; publs *Annual Report*, *Islamic Economic Studies* (2 a year), various research studies, monographs, reports.

## Publication

*Annual Report*.

## Statistics

**OPERATIONS APPROVED, ISLAMIC YEAR 1428**
(20 January 2007–9 January 2008)

| Type of operation | Number of operations | Amount (million Islamic Dinars) |
|---|---|---|
| Total project financing | 183 | 1,737.8 |
| Project financing | 110 | 1,726.8 |
| Technical assistance | 73 | 10.9 |
| Trade financing operations* | 82 | 1,818.3 |
| Special assistance operations | 62 | 17.0 |
| **Total**† | 327 | 3,573.1 |

* Including operations by the ICD, the Islamic Bank's Portfolio, the UIF, and the Awqaf Properties Investment Fund.
† Excluding cancelled operations.

**DISTRIBUTION OF PROJECT FINANCING AND TECHNICAL ASSISTANCE BY SECTOR, ISLAMIC YEAR 1428**
(20 January 2007–9 January 2008)

| Sector | Number of operations | Amount (million Islamic Dinars) | % |
|---|---|---|---|
| Agriculture and agro-industry | 6 | 30.2 | |
| Industry and mining | 7 | 89.6 | 12.9 |
| Transport and communications | 21 | 407.1 | 27.1 |
| Public utilities | 24 | 463.2 | 29.1 |
| Social services | 51 | 226.9 | 22.4 |
| Financial services/Other | 38 | 155.3 | 0.8 |
| **Total*** | 147 | 1,372.3 | 100.0 |

* Excluding cancelled operations.

Source: *Islamic Development Bank: Annual Report 1428 H.*

# ORGANIZATION OF THE ISLAMIC CONFERENCE—OIC

**Address:** Kilo 6, Mecca Rd, POB 178, Jeddah 21411, Saudi Arabia.

**Telephone:** (2) 690-0001; **fax:** (2) 275-1953; **e-mail:** info@oic-oic.org; **internet:** www.oic-oci.org.

The Organization was formally established in May 1971, when its Secretariat became operational, following a summit meeting of Muslim heads of state at Rabat, Morocco, in September 1969, and the Islamic Foreign Ministers' Conference in Jeddah in March 1970, and in Karachi, Pakistan, in December 1970.

### MEMBERS

| | | |
|---|---|---|
| Afghanistan | Indonesia | Qatar |
| Albania | Iran | Saudi Arabia |
| Algeria | Iraq | Senegal |
| Azerbaijan | Jordan | Sierra Leone |
| Bahrain | Kazakhstan | Somalia |
| Bangladesh | Kuwait | Sudan |
| Benin | Kyrgyzstan | Suriname |
| Brunei | Lebanon | Syria |
| Burkina Faso | Libya | Tajikistan |
| Cameroon | Malaysia | Togo |
| Chad | The Maldives | Tunisia |
| Comoros | Mali | Turkey |
| Côte d'Ivoire | Mauritania | Turkmenistan |
| Djibouti | Morocco | Uganda |
| Egypt | Mozambique | United Arab Emirates |
| Gabon | Niger | Uzbekistan |
| The Gambia | Nigeria | Yemen |
| Guinea | Oman | |
| Guinea-Bissau | Pakistan | |
| Guyana | Palestine | |

Note: Observer status has been granted to Bosnia and Herzegovina, the Central African Republic, Russia, Thailand, the Muslim community of the 'Turkish Republic of Northern Cyprus', the Moro National Liberation Front (MNLF) of the southern Philippines, the United Nations, the African Union, the Non-Aligned Movement, the League of Arab States, the Economic Co-operation Organization, the Union of the Arab Maghreb and the Co-operation Council for the Arab States of the Gulf. The revised OIC Charter, endorsed in March 2008, made future applications for OIC membership and observer status conditional upon Muslim demographic majority and membership of the UN.

## Organization

(August 2008)

### SUMMIT CONFERENCES

The supreme body of the Organization is the Conference of Heads of State, which met in 1969 at Rabat, Morocco, in 1974 at Lahore, Pakistan, and in January 1981 at Mecca, Saudi Arabia, when it was decided that ordinary summit conferences would normally be held every three years in future. An extraordinary summit conference was convened in Doha, Qatar, in March 2003, to consider the situation in Iraq. A further extraordinary conference, held in December 2005, in Mecca, Saudi Arabia, determined to restructure the OIC. The 11th ordinary Conference was held in Dakar, Senegal, in March 2008. The summit conference troika comprises member countries equally representing OIC's African, Arab and Asian membership.

### CONFERENCE OF MINISTERS OF FOREIGN AFFAIRS

Conferences take place annually, to consider the means for implementing the general policy of the Organization, although they may also be convened for extraordinary sessions. The ministerial conference troika comprises member countries equally representing OIC's African, Arab and Asian membership.

### SECRETARIAT

The executive organ of the organization, headed by a Secretary-General (who is elected by the Conference of Ministers of Foreign Affairs for a five-year term, renewable only once) and four Assistant Secretaries-General (similarly appointed).

**Secretary-General:** Prof. Dr EKMELEDDIN IHSANOGLU (Turkey).

At the summit conference in January 1981 it was decided that an International Islamic Court of Justice should be established to adjudicate in disputes between Muslim countries. Experts met in January 1983 to draw up a constitution for the court; however, by 2008 it was not yet in operation.

### EXECUTIVE COMMITTEE

The third extraordinary conference of the OIC, convened in Mecca, Saudi Arabia, in December 2005, mandated the establishment of the Executive Committee, comprising the summit conference and ministerial conference troikas, the OIC host country, and the OIC Secretariat, as a mechanism for following-up resolutions of the Conference.

### STANDING COMMITTEES

**Al-Quds Committee**: f. 1975 to implement the resolutions of the Islamic Conference on the status of Jerusalem (Al-Quds); it meets at the level of foreign ministers; maintains the Al-Quds Fund; Chair. King MUHAMMAD VI OF MOROCCO.

**Standing Committee for Economic and Commercial Co-operation (COMCEC):** f. 1981; Chair. ABDULLAH GÜL (Pres. of Turkey).

**Standing Committee for Information and Cultural Affairs (COMIAC):** f. 1981; Chair. ABDOULAYE WADE (Pres. of Senegal).

**Standing Committee for Scientific and Technological Co-operation (COMSTECH):** f. 1981; Chair. (vacant).

Other committees comprise the Islamic Peace Committee, the Permanent Finance Committee, the Committee of Islamic Solidarity with the Peoples of the Sahel, the Eight-Member Committee on the Situation of Muslims in the Philippines, the Six-Member Committee on Palestine, the Committee on United Nations reform, and the ad hoc Committee on Afghanistan. In addition, there is an Islamic Commission for Economic, Cultural and Social Affairs, and there are OIC contact groups on Bosnia and Herzegovina, Kosovo, Jammu and Kashmir, Sierra Leone, and Somalia. A Commission of Eminent Persons was inaugurated in 2005.

## Activities

The Organization's aims, as proclaimed in the Charter (adopted in 1972, with revisions endorsed in 1990 and 2008), are:

(i) To promote Islamic solidarity among member states;

(ii) To consolidate co-operation among member states in the economic, social, cultural, scientific and other vital fields, and to arrange consultations among member states belonging to international organizations;

(iii) To endeavour to eliminate racial segregation and discrimination and to eradicate colonialism in all its forms;

(iv) To take necessary measures to support international peace and security founded on justice;

(v) To co-ordinate all efforts for the safeguard of the Holy Places and support of the struggle of the people of Palestine, and help them to regain their rights and liberate their land;

(vi) To strengthen the struggle of all Muslim people with a view to safeguarding their dignity, independence and national rights;

(vii) To create a suitable atmosphere for the promotion of co-operation and understanding among member states and other countries.

The first summit conference of Islamic leaders (representing 24 states) took place in 1969 following the burning of the Al Aqsa Mosque in Jerusalem. At this conference it was decided that Islamic governments should 'consult together with a view to promoting close co-operation and mutual assistance in the economic, scientific, cultural and spiritual fields, inspired by the immortal teachings of Islam'. Thereafter the foreign ministers of the countries concerned met annually, and adopted the Charter of the Organization of the Islamic Conference in 1972.

At the second Islamic summit conference (Lahore, Pakistan, 1974), the Islamic Solidarity Fund was established, together with a committee of representatives which later evolved into the Islamic Commission for Economic, Cultural and Social Affairs. Subsequently, numerous other subsidiary bodies have been set up (see below).

### ECONOMIC CO-OPERATION

A general agreement for economic, technical and commercial co-operation came into force in 1981, providing for the establishment of joint investment projects and trade co-ordination. This was followed by an agreement on promotion, protection and guarantee of investments among member states. A plan of action to strengthen economic co-operation was adopted at the third Islamic summit conference in 1981, aiming to promote collective self-reliance and the development of joint ventures in all sectors. In 1994 the 1981 plan of action was revised; the reformulated plan placed greater emphasis on private-sector participation in its implementation. Although several meetings of experts were subsequently held to discuss some of the 10 priority focus areas of the plan, little progress was achieved in implementing it during the 1990s and early 2000s. In October 2003 a meeting of COMCEC endorsed measures aimed at accelerating the implementation of the plan of action.

The fifth summit conference, held in 1987, approved proposals for joint development of modern technology, and for improving scientific and technical skills in the less developed Islamic countries. The first international Islamic trade fair was held in Jeddah, Saudi Arabia, in March 2001.

In 1991 22 OIC member states signed a Framework Agreement on a Trade Preferential System (TPS-OIC) among the OIC Member States; this entered into force in 2003, following the requisite ratification by more than 10 member states, and was envisaged as representing the first step towards the eventual establishment of an Islamic common market. A Trade Negotiating Committee (TNC) was established following the entry into force of the Framework Agreement. The first round of trade negotiations on the establishment of the TPS-OIC, concerning finalizing tariff-reduction modalities and an implementation schedule for the Agreement, was held during April 2004–April 2005. In November 2006, at the launch of the second round of negotiations, ministers adopted a road-map for establishing the TPS-OIC by 1 January 2009. In June 2007 the TNC adopted rules of origin for the TPS-OIC.

The first OIC Anti-Corruption and Enhancing Integrity Forum was convened in August 2006 in Kuala Lumpur, Malaysia.

## CULTURAL CO-OPERATION

The Organization supports education in Muslim communities throughout the world, and was instrumental in the establishment of Islamic universities in Niger and Uganda. It organizes seminars on various aspects of Islam, and encourages dialogue with the other monotheistic religions. Support is given to publications on Islam both in Muslim and Western countries. The OIC organizes meetings at ministerial level to consider aspects of information policy and new technologies.

## HUMANITARIAN ASSISTANCE

Assistance is given to Muslim communities affected by wars and natural disasters, in co-operation with UN organizations, particularly UNHCR. A resolution on the status of refugees in the Muslim world that was adopted by the 10th OIC summit meeting, held in October 2003, urged all member states to accede to the 1951 UN Convention on the Status of Refugees. In March 2008 a conference of OIC leaders and Islamic non-governmental organizations determined to establish an OIC centre for the analysis of humanitarian requirements in OIC member states. The countries of the Sahel region (Burkina Faso, Cape Verde, Chad, The Gambia, Guinea, Guinea-Bissau, Mali, Mauritania, Niger and Senegal) receive particular attention as victims of drought. OIC member states have provided humanitarian assistance to the Muslim population affected by the conflict in Chechnya, and to Darfur, southern Sudan. In 2008 the OIC and Islamic Development Bank were planning an international conference on the rehabilitation and reconstruction of Darfur. The OIC has established trust funds to assist vulnerable people in Afghanistan, Bosnia and Herzegovina, and Sierra Leone. In March 2008 the OIC launched a humanitarian support operation for Palestinians in Gaza; an initial 'assistance caravan' transported medical supplies and equipment to the area.

## POLITICAL CO-OPERATION

Since its inception the OIC has called for vacation of Arab territories by Israel, recognition of the rights of Palestinians and of the Palestine Liberation Organization (PLO) as their sole legitimate representative, and the restoration of Jerusalem to Arab rule. The 1981 summit conference called for a *jihad* (holy war—though not necessarily in a military sense) 'for the liberation of Jerusalem and the occupied territories'; this was to include an Islamic economic boycott of Israel. In 1982 Islamic ministers of foreign affairs decided to establish Islamic offices for boycotting Israel and for military co-operation with the PLO. The 1984 summit conference agreed to reinstate Egypt (suspended following the peace treaty signed with Israel in 1979) as a member of the OIC, although the resolution was opposed by seven states.

In August 1990 a majority of ministers of foreign affairs condemned Iraq's recent invasion of Kuwait, and demanded the withdrawal of Iraqi forces. In August 1991 the Conference of Ministers of Foreign Affairs obstructed Iraq's attempt to propose a resolution demanding the repeal of economic sanctions against the country. The sixth summit conference, held in Senegal in December, reflected the divisions in the Arab world that resulted from Iraq's invasion of Kuwait and the ensuing war. Twelve heads of state did not attend, reportedly to register protest at the presence of Jordan and the PLO at the conference, both of which had given support to Iraq. Disagreement also arose between the PLO and the majority of other OIC members when a proposal was adopted to cease the OIC's support for the PLO's *jihad* in the Arab territories occupied by Israel, in an attempt to further the Middle East peace negotiations.

In August 1992 the UN General Assembly approved a non-binding resolution, introduced by the OIC, that requested the UN Security Council to take increased action, including the use of force, in order to defend the non-Serbian population of Bosnia and Herzegovina (some 43% of Bosnians being Muslims) from Serbian aggression, and to restore its 'territorial integrity'. The OIC Conference of Ministers of Foreign Affairs, which was held in December, demanded anew that the UN Security Council take all necessary measures against Serbia and Montenegro, including military intervention, in order to protect the Bosnian Muslims.

A report by an OIC fact-finding mission, which in February 1993 visited Azad Kashmir while investigating allegations of repression of the largely Muslim population of the Indian state of Jammu and Kashmir by the Indian armed forces, was presented to the 1993 Conference. The meeting urged member states to take the necessary measures to persuade India to cease the 'massive human rights violations' in Jammu and Kashmir and to allow the Indian Kashmiris to 'exercise their inalienable right to self-determination'. In September 1994 ministers of foreign affairs, meeting in Islamabad, Pakistan, agreed to establish a contact group on Jammu and Kashmir, which was to provide a mechanism for promoting international awareness of the situation in that region and for seeking a peaceful solution to the dispute. In December OIC heads of state approved a resolution condemning reported human rights abuses by Indian security forces in Kashmir.

In July 1994 the OIC Secretary-General visited Afghanistan and proposed the establishment of a preparatory mechanism to promote national reconciliation in that country. In mid-1995 Saudi Arabia, acting as a representative of the OIC, pursued a peace initiative for Afghanistan and issued an invitation for leaders of the different factions to hold negotiations in Jeddah.

A special ministerial meeting on Bosnia and Herzegovina was held in July 1993, at which seven OIC countries committed themselves to making available up to 17,000 troops to serve in the UN Protection Force in the former Yugoslavia (UNPROFOR). The meeting also decided to dispatch immediately a ministerial mission to persuade influential governments to support the OIC's demands for the removal of the arms embargo on Bosnian Muslims and the convening of a restructured international conference to bring about a political solution to the conflict. In December 1994 OIC heads of state, convened in Morocco, proclaimed that the UN arms embargo on Bosnia and Herzegovina could not be applied to the Muslim authorities of that Republic. The Conference also resolved to review economic relations between OIC member states and any country that supported Serbian activities. An aid fund was established, to which member states were requested to contribute between US $500,000 and $5m., in order to provide further humanitarian and economic assistance to Bosnian Muslims. In relation to wider concerns the conference adopted a Code of Conduct for Combating International Terrorism, in an attempt to control Muslim extremist groups. The code commits states to ensuring that militant groups do not use their territory for planning or executing terrorist activity against other states, in addition to states refraining from direct support or participation in acts of terrorism. In a further resolution the OIC supported the decision by Iraq to recognize Kuwait, but advocated that Iraq comply with all UN Security Council decisions.

In July 1995 the OIC contact group on Bosnia and Herzegovina (at that time comprising Egypt, Iran, Malaysia, Morocco, Pakistan, Saudi Arabia, Senegal and Turkey), meeting in Geneva, declared the UN arms embargo against Bosnia and Herzegovina to be 'invalid'. Several Governments subsequently announced their willingness officially to supply weapons and other military assistance to the Bosnian Muslim forces. In September a meeting of all OIC ministers of defence and foreign affairs endorsed the establishment of an 'assistance mobilization group' which was to supply military, economic, legal and other assistance to Bosnia and Herzegovina. In a joint declaration the ministers also demanded the return of all territory seized by Bosnian Serb forces, the continued NATO bombing of Serb military targets, and that the city of Sarajevo be preserved under a Muslim-led Bosnian Government. In November the OIC Secretary-General endorsed the peace accord for the former Yugoslavia, which was concluded, in Dayton, USA, by leaders of all the conflicting factions, and reaffirmed the commitment of Islamic states to participate in efforts to implement the accord. In the following month the OIC Conference of Ministers of Foreign Affairs, convened in Conakry, Guinea, requested the full support of the international community to reconstruct Bosnia and Herzegovina through humanitarian aid as well as economic and technical co-operation. Ministers declared that Palestine and the establishment of fully-autonomous Palestinian control of Jerusalem were issues of central importance for the Muslim world. The Conference urged the removal of all aspects of occupation and the cessation of the construction of Israeli settlements in the occupied territories. In addition, the final statement of the meeting condemned Armenian aggression against Azerbaijan, registered concern at the persisting civil conflict in Afghanistan, demanded the elimination of all weapons of mass destruction and pledged support for Libya (affected by the US trade embargo). Ministers determined that an intergovernmental group of experts should be established in 1996 to address the situation of minority Muslim communities residing in non-OIC states.

In December 1996 OIC ministers of foreign affairs, meeting in Jakarta, Indonesia, urged the international community to apply pressure on Israel in order to ensure its implementation of the terms of the Middle East peace process. The ministers reaffirmed the importance of ensuring that the provisions of the Dayton Peace Agreement for the former Yugoslavia were fully implemented, called for a peaceful settlement of the Kashmir issue, demanded that Iraq fulfil its obligations for the establishment of security, peace and stability in the region and proposed that an international conference on peace and national reconciliation in Somalia be convened. In March 1997, at an extraordinary summit held in Pakistan, OIC heads of state and of government reiterated the organization's objective of increasing international pressure on Israel to ensure the full implementation of the terms of the Middle East peace process. An 'Islamabad Declaration' was also adopted, which pledged to increase co-operation between members of the OIC. In June the OIC condemned the decision by the US House of Representatives to recognize Jerusalem as the Israeli capital. The Secretary-General of the OIC issued a statement rejecting the US decision as counter to the role of the USA as sponsor of the Middle East peace plan.

In early 1998 the OIC appealed for an end to the threat of US-led military action against Iraq arising from a dispute regarding access granted to international weapons inspectors. The crisis was averted by an agreement concluded between the Iraqi authorities and the UN Secretary-General in February. In March OIC ministers of foreign affairs, meeting in Doha, Qatar, requested an end to the international sanctions against Iraq. Additionally, the ministers urged all states to end the process of restoring normal trading and diplomatic relations with Israel pending that country's withdrawal from the occupied territories and acceptance of an independent Palestinian state. In April the OIC, jointly with the UN, sponsored new peace negotiations between the main disputing factions in Afghanistan, which were conducted in Islamabad, Pakistan. In early May, however, the talks collapsed and were postponed indefinitely. In September the Secretaries-General of the OIC and UN agreed to establish a joint mission to counter the deteriorating security situation along the Afghan–Iranian border, following the large-scale deployment of Taliban troops in the region and consequent military manoeuvres by the Iranian authorities. They also reiterated the need to proceed with negotiations to conclude a peaceful settlement in Afghanistan. In December the OIC appealed for a diplomatic solution to the tensions arising from Iraq's withdrawal of co-operation with UN weapons inspectors, and criticized subsequent military airstrikes, led by the USA, as having been conducted without renewed UN authority. An OIC Convention on Combating International Terrorism was adopted in 1998. An OIC committee of experts responsible for formulating a plan of action for safeguarding the rights of Muslim communities and minorities met for the first time in 1998.

In early April 1999 ministers of foreign affairs of the countries comprising OIC's contact group met to consider the crisis in Kosovo. The meeting condemned Serbian atrocities being committed against the local Albanian population and urged the provision of international assistance for the thousands of people displaced by the conflict. The group resolved to establish a committee to co-ordinate relief aid provided by member states. The ministers also expressed their willingness to help to formulate a peaceful settlement and to participate in any subsequent implementation force. In June an OIC Parliamentary Union was inaugurated; its founding conference was convened in Tehran, Iran.

In early March 2000 the OIC mediated contacts between the parties to the conflict in Afghanistan, with a view to reviving peace negotiations. Talks, held under OIC auspices, ensued in May. In November OIC heads of state attended the ninth summit conference, held in Doha, Qatar. In view of the significant deterioration in relations between Israel and the Palestinian (National) Authority (PA) during late 2000, the summit issued a Declaration pledging solidarity with the Palestinian cause and accusing the Israeli authorities of implementing large-scale systematic violations of human rights against Palestinians. The summit also issued the Doha Declaration, which reaffirmed commitment to the OIC Charter and undertook to modernize the organization's organs and mechanisms. Both the elected Government of Afghanistan and the Taliban sent delegations to the Doha conference. The summit determined that Afghanistan's official participation in the OIC, suspended in 1996, should not yet be reinstated. In early 2001 a high-level delegation from the OIC visited Afghanistan in an attempt to prevent further destruction of ancient statues by Taliban supporters.

In May 2001 the OIC convened an emergency meeting, following an escalation of Israeli–Palestinian violence. The meeting resolved to halt all diplomatic and political contacts with the Israeli government, while restrictions remained in force against Palestinian-controlled territories. In June the OIC condemned attacks and ongoing discrimination against the Muslim Community in Myanmar. In the same month the OIC Secretary-General undertook a tour of six African countries—Burkina Faso, The Gambia, Guinea, Mali, Niger and Senegal—to promote co-operation and to consider further OIC support for those states. In August the Secretary-General condemned Israel's seizure of several Palestinian institutions in East Jerusalem and aerial attacks against Palestinian settlements. The OIC initiated high-level diplomatic efforts to convene a meeting of the UN Security Council in order to discuss the situation.

In September 2001 the OIC Secretary-General strongly condemned major terrorist attacks perpetrated against targets in the USA. Soon afterwards the US authorities rejected a proposal by the Taliban regime that an OIC observer mission be deployed to monitor the activities of the Saudi Arabian-born exiled militant Islamist fundamentalist leader Osama bin Laden, who was accused by the US Government of having co-ordinated the attacks from alleged terrorist bases in the Taliban-administered area of Afghanistan. An extraordinary meeting of OIC ministers of foreign affairs, convened in early October, in Doha, Qatar, to consider the implications of the terrorist atrocities, condemned the attacks and declared its support for combating all manifestations of terrorism within the framework of a proposed collective initiative co-ordinated under the auspices of the UN. The meeting, which did not pronounce directly on the recently-initiated US-led military retaliation against targets in Afghanistan, urged that no Arab or Muslim state should be targeted under the pretext of eliminating terrorism. It determined to establish a fund to assist Afghan civilians. In February 2002 the Secretary-General expressed concern at statements of the US administration describing Iran and Iraq (as well as the Democratic People's Republic of Korea) as belonging to an 'axis of evil' involved in international terrorism and the development of weapons of mass destruction. In early April OIC foreign ministers convened an extraordinary session on terrorism, in Kuala Lumpur, Malaysia. The meeting issued the 'Kuala Lumpur Declaration', which reiterated member states' collective resolve to combat terrorism, recalling the organization's 1994 code of conduct and 1998 convention to this effect; condemned attempts to associate terrorist activities with Islamists or any other particular creed, civilization or nationality, and rejected attempts to associate Islamic states or the Palestinian struggle with terrorism; rejected the implementation of international action against any Muslim state on the pretext of combating terrorism; urged the organization of a global conference on international terrorism; and urged an examination of the root causes of international terrorism. In addition, the meeting strongly condemned Israel's ongoing military intervention in areas controlled by the PA. The meeting adopted a plan of action on addressing the issues raised in the declaration. Its implementation was to be co-ordinated by a 13-member committee on international terrorism. Member states were encouraged to sign and ratify the Convention on Combating International Terrorism in order to accelerate its implementation. In June 2002 ministers of foreign affairs, meeting in Khartoum, Sudan, issued a declaration reiterating the OIC call for an international conference to be convened, under UN auspices, in order clearly to define terrorism and to agree on the international procedures and mechanisms for combating terrorism through the UN. The conference also repeated demands for the international community to exert pressure on Israel to withdraw from all Palestinian-controlled territories and for the establishment of an independent Palestinian state. It endorsed the peace plan for the region that had been adopted by the summit meeting of the League of Arab States in March.

In June 2002 the OIC Secretary-General expressed his concern at the escalation of tensions between Pakistan and India regarding Kashmir. He urged both sides to withdraw their troops and to refrain from the use of force. In the following month the OIC pledged its support for Morocco in a territorial dispute with Spain over the small island of Perejil, but called for a negotiated settlement to resolve the issue.

An extraordinary summit conference of Islamic leaders convened in Doha, Qatar, in early March 2003, to consider the ongoing Iraq crisis welcomed the Saddam Hussain regime's acceptance of UN Security Council Resolution 1441 and consequent co-operation with UN weapons inspectors, and emphatically rejected any military strike against Iraq or threat to the security of any other Islamic state. The conference also urged progress towards the elimination of all weapons of mass destruction in the Middle East, including those held by Israel. In May the 30th session of the Conference of Ministers of Foreign Affairs, entitled 'Unity and Dignity', issued the Tehran Declaration, in which it resolved to combat terrorism and to contribute to preserving peace and security in Islamic countries. The Declaration also pledged its full support for the Palestinian cause and rejected the labelling as 'terrorist' of those Muslim states deemed to be resisting foreign aggression and occupation. The 10th OIC summit meeting, held in October, in Putrajaya, Malaysia, issued the Putrajaya Declaration, in which Islamic leaders resolved to enhance Islamic states' role and influence in international affairs. The leaders adopted a plan of action that entailed: reviewing and strengthening OIC positions on international issues; enhancing dialogue among Muslim thinkers and policy-makers through relevant OIC insitutions; promoting constructive dialogue with other cultures and civilizations; completing an ongoing review of the structure and efficacy of the OIC Secretariat; establishing a working group to address means of enhancing the role of Islamic education; promoting among member states the development of science and technology, discussion of ecological issues, and the role of information communication technology in development; improving mechanisms to assist member states in post-conflict situations; and advancing trade and investment through data-sharing and encouraging access to markets for products from poorer member states.

In mid-May 2004 the OIC Secretary-General urged combat forces in Iraq to respect the inviolability of that country's holy places. Shortly afterwards he condemned the ongoing destruction of Palestinian homes by Israeli forces, and consequent population displacement, particularly in Rafah, Gaza. He urged international organizations to condemn Israel's actions and appealed to the UN Security Council to intervene promptly in the situation and to compel Israel to respect international law. In June the Secretary-General welcomed progress achieved by a round of expert-level talks on nuclear confidence-building measures conducted during that month by India and Pakistan. An observer mission dispatched by the OIC to monitor presidential elections held in the Palestinian territories in early January 2005, at the request of the PA, was rejected by Israel. Later in that month the inaugural meeting of an OIC Commission of Eminent Persons was convened in Putrajaya, Malaysia. The Commission was mandated to finalize recommendations in the following areas: the preparation of a strategy and plan of action enabling the Islamic community to meet the challenges of the 21st century; the preparation of a comprehensive plan for promoting enlightened moderation, both within Islamic societies and universally; and the preparation of proposals for the future reform and restructuring of the OIC system. An OIC Digital Solidarity Fund was inaugurated in May 2005. In December the third extraordinary OIC summit, convened in Mecca, Saudi Arabia, adopted a 'Ten-Year Programme of Action to Meet the Challenges Facing the Umma in the 21st Century', a related Mecca Declaration and a report by the Commission of Eminent Persons. The summit determined to restructure the OIC, and mandated the establishment of an Executive Committee, comprising the summit conference and ministerial conference troikas (equally reflecting the African, Arab and Asian member states), the OIC host country, and the OIC Secretariat, as a mechanism for following-up Conference resolutions.

In January 2006 the OIC strongly condemned the publication in a Norwegian newspaper of a series of caricatures of the Prophet Muhammad that had originally appeared in a Danish publication in September 2005 and had caused considerable offence to Islamists. In August 2006 the OIC convened a meeting of humanitarian bodies in Istanbul, Turkey, to address means of collecting donations for and delivering assistance to victims of the ongoing crises in Lebanon and the Palestinian territories. Shortly afterwards a meeting of the newly-formed Executive Committee, held in Kuala Lumpur, Malaysia, agreed to form a Contact Group for Lebanon, to be co-ordinated by Malaysia. In October a meeting of Iraqi Islamic scholars from all denominations issued the Makkah Declaration on the Iraqi situation, in which they urged unity between different Islamic factions in that country. The first OIC Conference on Women was held in the following month, on the theme 'the role of women in the development of OIC member states'.

In December 2007 the OIC organized the first International Conference on Islamaphobia, aimed at addressing concerns that alleged instances of defamation of Islam appeared to be increasing world-wide (particularly in Europe). These were being observed by an Islamic Observatory on Islamophobia, established in September 2006. The 11th OIC heads of state summit meeting, held in Dakar, Senegal, in March 2008, endorsed a revised OIC Charter. The summit welcomed recent contacts between the Israeli and Palestinian leaders. Participation by OIC member states in the OIC Digital Solidarity Fund was promoted, and the meeting also requested each member state to establish a board to monitor national implementation of the Tunis Declaration on the Information Society, adopted by the November 2005 second phase of the World Summit on the Information Society. In view of a reported rise in anti-Islamic attacks in western nations, OIC leaders denounced stereotyping, profiling and discrimination, and urged the promotion of Islam by Islamic states as a 'moderate, peaceful and tolerant religion'.

## Finance

The OIC's activities are financed by mandatory contributions from member states.

## Subsidiary Organs

**Islamic Centre for the Development of Trade:** Complexe Commercial des Habous, ave des FAR, BP 13545, Casablanca, Morocco; tel. (2) 314974; fax (2) 310110; e-mail icdt@icdt.org; internet www.icdt.org; f. 1983 to encourage regular commercial contacts, harmonize policies and promote investments among OIC mems; Dir-Gen. ALLAL RACHDI; publs *Tijaris: International and Inter-Islamic Trade Magazine* (bi-monthly), *Inter-Islamic Trade Report* (annually).

**Islamic Jurisprudence (Fiqh) Academy:** POB 13917, Jeddah, Saudi Arabia; tel. (2) 667-1664; fax (2) 667-0873; internet www.fiqhacademy.org.sa; f. 1982; Sec.-Gen. Sheikh MOHAMED HABIB IBN AL-KHODHA.

**Islamic Solidarity Fund:** c/o OIC Secretariat, POB 178, Jeddah 21411, Saudi Arabia; tel. (2) 680-0800; fax (2) 687-3568; f. 1974 to meet the needs of Islamic communities by providing emergency aid and the finance to build mosques, Islamic centres, hospitals, schools and universities; Chair. Sheikh NASIR ABDULLAH BIN HAMDAN; Exec. Dir ABDULLAH HERSI.

**Islamic University in Uganda:** POB 2555, Mbale, Uganda; tel. (45) 33502; fax (45) 34452; e-mail iuiu@info.com.co.ug; internet www.iuiu-mbale.com; f. 1988 to meet the educational needs of Muslim populations in English-speaking African countries; second campus in Kampala; mainly financed by OIC; Rector Dr AHMAD KAWESA SENGENDO.

**Islamic University of Niger:** BP 11507, Niamey, Niger; tel. 723903; fax 733796; internet www.universite_say.ne/; f. 1984; provides courses of study in *Shari'a* (Islamic law) and Arabic language and literature; also offers courses in pedagogy and teacher training; receives grants from Islamic Solidarity Fund and contributions from OIC member states; Rector Prof. ABDELALI OUDHRIRI.

**Islamic University of Technology (IUT):** Board Bazar, Gazipur 1704, Dhaka, Bangladesh; tel. (2) 980-0960; fax (2) 980-0970; e-mail vc@iut-dhaka.edu; internet www.iutoic-dhaka.edu; f. 1981 as the Islamic Centre for Technical and Vocational Training and Resources, named changed to Islamic Institute of Technology in 1994, current name adopted in June 2001; aims to develop human resources in OIC mem. states, with special reference to engineering, technology, tech. and vocational education and research; 135 staff and 646 students; library of 26,500 vols; Vice-Chancellor Prof. Dr IMTIAZ HOSSAIN; publs *News Bulletin* (annually), *Journal of Engineering and Technology* (2 a year), annual calendar and announcement for admission, reports, human resources development series.

**Research Centre for Islamic History, Art and Culture (IRCICA):** POB 24, Beşiktaş 80692, İstanbul, Turkey; tel. (212) 2591742; fax (212) 2584365; e-mail ircica@ircica.org; internet www.ircica.org; f. 1980; library of 60,000 vols; Dir-Gen. Prof. Dr HALIT EREN; publs *Newsletter* (3 a year), monographical studies.

**Statistical, Economic and Social Research and Training Centre for the Islamic Countries:** Attar Sok 4, GOP 06700, Ankara, Turkey; tel. (312) 4686172; fax (312) 4673458; e-mail oicankara@sesrtcic.org; internet www.sesrtcic.org; f. 1978; Dir-Gen. S. ALPAY; publs *Journal of Economic Co-operation among Islamic Countries* (quarterly), *InfoReport* (quarterly), *Statistical Yearbook* (annually).

## Specialized Institutions

**International Islamic News Agency (IINA):** King Khalid Palace, Madinah Rd, POB 5054, Jeddah 21422, Saudi Arabia; tel. (2) 665-8561; fax (2) 665-9358; e-mail iina@islamicnews.org.sa; internet www.islamicnews.org.sa; f. 1972; distributes news and reports daily on events in the Islamic world, in Arabic, English and French; Dir-Gen. ERDEM KOK.

**Islamic Educational, Scientific and Cultural Organization (ISESCO):** BP 2275 Rabat 10104, Morocco; tel. (37) 772433; fax (37) 772058; e-mail cid@isesco.org.ma; internet www.isesco.org.ma; f. 1982; Dir-Gen. Dr ABDULAZIZ BIN OTHMAN ALTWAIJRI; publs *ISESCO Newsletter* (quarterly), *Islam Today* (2 a year), *ISESCO Triennial*.

**Islamic States Broadcasting Union (ISBU):** POB 6351, Jeddah 21442, Saudi Arabia; tel. (2) 672-1121; fax (2) 672-2600; internet www.isboo.org; f. 1975; Sec.-Gen. HUSSEIN AL-ASKARY.

## Affiliated Institutions

**International Association of Islamic Banks (IAIB):** King Abdulaziz St, Queen's Bldg, 23rd Floor, Al-Balad Dist, POB 9707, Jeddah 21423, Saudi Arabia; tel. (2) 651-6900; fax (2) 651-6552; f. 1977 to link financial institutions operating on Islamic banking principles; activities include training and research; mems: 192 banks and other financial institutions in 34 countries; Sec.-Gen. SAMIR A. SHAIKH.

**Islamic Chamber of Commerce and Industry:** POB 3831, Clifton, Karachi 75600, Pakistan; tel. (21) 5874756; fax (21) 5870765; e-mail icci@icci-oic.org; internet icci-oic.org; f. 1979 to promote trade and industry among member states; comprises nat. chambers or feds of chambers of commerce and industry; Sec.-Gen. AQEEL AHMAD AL-JASSEM.

**Islamic Committee for the International Crescent:** POB 17434, Benghazi, Libya; tel. (61) 95823; fax (61) 95829; f. 1979 to attempt to alleviate the suffering caused by natural disasters and war; Sec.-Gen. Dr AHMAD ABDALLAH CHERIF.

**Islamic Solidarity Sports Federation:** POB 5844, Riyadh 11442, Saudi Arabia; tel. and fax (1) 482-2145; f. 1981; Sec.-Gen. Dr MOHAMMAD SALEH GAZDAR.

**Organization of Islamic Capitals and Cities (OICC):** POB 13621, Jeddah 21414, Saudi Arabia; tel. (2) 698-1953; fax (2) 698-1053; e-mail webmaster@oicc.org; internet www.oicc.org; f. 1980; aims to preserve the identity and the heritage of Islamic capitals and cities; to achieve and enhance sustainable development in member capitals and cities; to establish and develop comprehensive urban norms, systems and plans to serve the growth and prosperity of Islamic capitals and cities and to enhance their cultural, environmental, urban, economic and social conditions; to advance municipal services and facilities in the member capitals and cities; to support member cities' capacity-building programmes; and to consolidate fellowship and co-ordinate the scope of co-operation between members; comprises 147 capitals and cities as active members, eight observer members and 15 associate members, in Asia, Africa, Europe and South America; Sec.-Gen. OMAR KADI.

**Organization of the Islamic Shipowners' Association:** POB 14900, Jeddah 21434, Saudi Arabia; tel. (2) 663-7882; fax (2) 660-4920; e-mail oisa@sbm.net.sa; f. 1981 to promote co-operation among maritime cos in Islamic countries; in 1998 mems approved the establishment of a new commercial venture, the Bakkah Shipping Company, to enhance sea transport in the region; Sec.-Gen. Dr ABDULLATIF A. SULTAN.

**World Federation of Arab-Islamic Schools:** POB 3446, Jeddah, Saudi Arabia; tel. (2) 670-0019; fax (2) 671-0823; f. 1976; supports Arab-Islamic schools world-wide and encourages co-operation between the institutions; promotes the dissemination of the Arabic language and Islamic culture; supports the training of personnel.

# SOUTH ASIAN ASSOCIATION FOR REGIONAL CO-OPERATION—SAARC

**Address:** POB 4222, Tridevi Marg, Kathmandu, Nepal.

**Telephone:** (1) 4221785; **fax:** (1) 4227033; **e-mail:** saarc@saarc-sec.org; **internet:** www.saarc-sec.org.

The South Asian Association for Regional Co-operation (SAARC) was formally established in 1985 in order to strengthen and accelerate regional co-operation, particularly in economic development.

### MEMBERS

| | |
|---|---|
| Afghanistan | Maldives |
| Bangladesh | Nepal |
| Bhutan | Pakistan |
| India | Sri Lanka |

Observers: People's Republic of China, Iran, Japan, Republic of Korea, the European Union.

### TECHNICAL COMMITTEES

SAARC's Integrated Programme of Action is implemented by seven Technical Committees covering: Agriculture and rural development; Energy; Environment, meteorology and forestry; Human resource development; Science and technology; Social development; and Transport and communications. Each committee is headed by a representative of a member state and meets annually.

### SECRETARIAT

The Secretariat was established in 1987 to co-ordinate and oversee SAARC activities. It comprises the Secretary-General and a Director from each member country. The Secretary-General is appointed by the Council of Ministers, after being nominated by a member state, and serves a three-year term of office. The Director is nominated by member states and appointed by the Secretary-General for a term of three years, although this may be increased in special circumstances.

**Secretary-General:** Dr SHEEL KANT SHARMA (India).

## Organization

(August 2008)

### SUMMIT MEETING

Heads of state and of government of member states represent the body's highest authority, and a summit meeting is normally held annually. The 14th summit meeting was convened in New Delhi, India, in April 2007. The 15th summit meeting was held in Colombo, Sri Lanka, in August 2008.

### COUNCIL OF MINISTERS

The Council of Ministers comprises the ministers of foreign affairs of member countries, who meet twice a year. The Council may also meet in extraordinary session at the request of member states. The responsibilities of the Council include formulation of policies, assessing progress and confirming new areas of co-operation.

### STANDING COMMITTEE

The Committee consists of the secretaries of foreign affairs of member states. It has overall responsibility for the monitoring and co-ordination of programmes and financing, and determines priorities, mobilizes resources and identifies areas of co-operation. It usually meets twice a year, and submits its reports to the Council of Ministers. The Committee is supported by an ad hoc Programming Committee made up of senior officials, who meet to examine the budget of the Secretariat, confirm the Calendar of Activities and resolve matters assigned to it by the Standing Committee.

## Activities

The first summit meeting of SAARC heads of state and government, held in Dhaka, Bangladesh, in December 1985, resulted in the signing of the Charter of the South Asian Association for Regional Co-operation (SAARC). In August 1993 ministers of foreign affairs of seven countries, meeting in New Delhi, India, adopted a Declaration on South Asian Regional Co-operation and launched an Integrated Programme of Action (IPA), which identified the main areas for regional co-operation. The ninth summit meeting, held in May 1997, authorized the establishment of a Group of Eminent Persons to review the functioning of the IPA. On the basis of the group's recommendations a reconstituted IPA, to be administered by a more efficient arrangement of Technical Committees, was initiated in June 2000.

SAARC is committed to improving quality of life in the region by accelerating economic growth, social progress and cultural development; promoting self-reliance; encouraging mutual assistance; increasing co-operation with other developing countries; and co-operating with other regional and international organizations. The SAARC Charter stipulates that decisions should be made unanimously, and that 'bilateral and contentious issues' should not be discussed. Regular meetings, at all levels, are held to further co-operation in areas covered by the Technical Committees (see above). A priority objective is the eradication of poverty in the region, and in 1993 SAARC endorsed an Agenda of Action to help achieve this. A framework for exchanging information on poverty eradication has also, since, been established. The 11th SAARC summit meeting, held in Kathmandu, Nepal, in January 2002, adopted a convention on regional arrangements for the promotion of child welfare in South Asia. The 11th summit also determined to reinvigorate regional poverty reduction activities in the context of the UN General Assembly's Millennium Development Goal of halving extreme poverty by 2015, and of other internationally-agreed commitments. The meeting reconstituted the Independent South Asian Commission on Poverty Alleviation—ISACPA, which had been established in 1991. ISACPA reported to the 12th summit meeting of heads of state, held in Islamabad, Pakistan, in January 2004. The 12th summit meeting, held in Islamabad, Pakistan, in January 2004, declared poverty alleviation to be the overarching goal of all SAARC activities and requested ISACPA to continue its work in an advocacy role and to prepare a set of SAARC Development Goals (SDGs) for future consideration. At the meeting heads of state endorsed a Plan of Action on Poverty Alleviation, and also adopted a SAARC Social Charter that had been drafted by with assistance from representatives of civil society, academia, non-governmental organizations and government, under the auspices of an inter-governmental expert group, and incorporated objectives in areas including poverty alleviation, promotion of health and nutrition, food security, water supply and sanitation, children's development and rights, participation by women, and human resources development. The 13th SAARC summit meeting, held in Dhaka, Bangladesh, in November 2005, declared the SAARC Decade of Poverty Alleviation covering the period 2006–15 and determined to replace SAARC's Three-tier Mechanism on Poverty Alleviation (established in 1995) with a Two-tier Mechanism on Poverty Alleviation, comprising ministers and secretaries responsible for poverty alleviation at national level. The 14th summit meeting, held in New Delhi, India, in April 2007, acknowledged ISACPA's efforts in elaborating the SDGs and entrusted the Two-tier Mechanism with monitoring progress towards the achievement of these. SAARC's 15th summit meeting, held in Colombo, Sri Lanka, in August 2008, noted that a mid-term review of the attainment of the SDGs would be completed by 2009.

The 2002 summit urged the development of a regional strategy for preventing and combating HIV/AIDS and other communicable diseases; the SAARC Tuberculosis Centre (see below) was to play a co-ordinating role in this area. In April 2003 SAARC ministers of health convened an emergency meeting to consider the regional implications of the spread of Severe Acute Respiratory Syndrome (SARS), a previously unknown atypical pneumonia. In November of that year SAARC ministers of health determined to establish a regional surveillance and rapid reaction system for managing health crises and natural disasters; the August 2008 summit meeting approved the development of a Natural Disaster Rapid Response Mechanism. An emergency meeting of health and agriculture and livestock ministers was convened in New Delhi, India, in January 2004 to address the spread of Avian Influenza.

In January 1996 the first SAARC Trade Fair was held, in New Delhi, India, to promote intra-SAARC commerce. At the same time SAARC ministers of commerce convened for their first meeting to discuss regional economic co-operation. The sixth trade fair was held in New Delhi, India, in January 2005. A group on customs co-operation was established in 1996 to harmonize trading rules and regulations within the grouping, to simplify trade procedures and to upgrade facilities. In 1999 a regional action plan to harmonize national standards, quality control and measurements came into effect. In August 2001 SAARC commerce ministers met, in New Delhi, to discuss a co-ordinated approach to the World Trade Organization (WTO) negotiations.

A Committee on Economic Co-operation (CEC), comprising senior trade officials of member states, was established in July 1991 to monitor progress concerning trade and economic co-operation issues. In the same year the summit meeting approved the creation of an inter-governmental group to establish a framework for the promotion of specific trade liberalization measures. A SAARC Chamber of Commerce (SCCI) became operational in 1992, with headquarters in Karachi, Pakistan. (The SCCI headquarters were subsequently transferred to Islamabad, Pakistan.) In April 1993 ministers signed a SAARC Preferential Trading Arrangement (SAPTA), which came into effect in December 1995. The 10th summit meeting proposed a series of measures to accelerate progress in the next round of SAPTA trade negotiations, including a reduction in the domestic content requirements of SAPTA's rules of origin, greater tariff concessions on products being actively traded and the removal of certain discriminatory and non-tariff barriers. In December 1995 the Council resolved that the ultimate objective for member states should be the establishment of a South Asian Free Trade Area (SAFTA), superseding SAPTA. An Agreement on SAFTA was signed in January 2004, at the 12th summit, and on 1 January 2006 it entered into force, providing for the phased elimination of tariffs: these were to be reduced to 30% in least developed member countries and to 20% in the others over an initial two-year period, and subsequently to 0–5% over a period of five years. The Agreement established a mechanism for administering SAFTA and for settling disputes at ministerial level.

A SAARC Youth Volunteers Programme (SYVOP) enables young people to work in other member countries in the agriculture and forestry sectors. The Programme is part of a series of initiatives designed to promote intra-regional exchanges and contact. A Youth Awards Scheme to reward outstanding achievements by young people was inaugurated in 1996. Founded in 1987, the SAARC Audio-visual Exchange Programme (SAVE) broadcasts radio and television programmes on social and cultural affairs to all member countries, twice a month, in order to disseminate information about SAARC and its members. SAVE organizes an annual SAARC Telefilm festival. The SAARC Consortium of Open and Distance Learning was established in 2000. A Visa Exemption Scheme, exempting 21 specified categories of person from visa requirements, with the aim of promoting closer regional contact, became operational in March 1992. A SAARC citizens forum promotes interaction among the people of South Asia. In addition, SAARC operates a fellowships, scholarships and chairs scheme and a scheme for the promotion of organized tourism. The 12th SAARC summit meeting designated 2006 as South Asia Tourism Year.

In June 2005 SAARC ministers of the environment met in special session to consider the impact of the devastating earthquake and subsequent massive ocean movements, or tsunamis, that struck in the Indian Ocean at the end of 2004. The meeting reviewed an assessment of the extent of loss and damage in each country, and of the relief and rehabilitation measures being undertaken. Ministers resolved to strengthen early warning and disaster management capabilities in the region, and determined to support the rehabilitation of members' economies, in particular through the promotion of the tourism sector. In July 2008 SAARC ministers of the environment, meeting to discuss climate change, adopted a SAARC Action Plan and Dhaka Declaration on Climate Change, urging close co-operation in developing projects and raising mass awareness on climate change.

From October 2004 SAARC implemented, under supervision from the ADB, a Regional Multimodal Transport Study; this was extended in 2007 to cover Afghanistan. The first South Asia Energy dialogue was convened in March 2007 in New Delhi, India.

At the third SAARC summit, held in Kathmandu in November 1987, member states signed a regional convention on measures to counteract terrorism. The convention, which entered into force in August 1988, commits signatory countries to the extradition or prosecution of alleged terrorists and to the implementation of preventative measures to combat terrorism. Monitoring desks for terrorist and drugs offences have been established to process information relating to those activities. The first SAARC conference on co-operation in police affairs, attended by the heads of the police forces of member states, was held in Colombo in July 1996. The conference discussed the issues of terrorism, organized crime, the extradition of criminals, drugs-trafficking and drug abuse. A convention on narcotic drugs and psychotropic substances was signed during the fifth SAARC summit meeting, held in Malé in 1990. The convention entered into force in September 1993, following its ratification by member states. It is implemented by a co-ordination group of drug law enforcement agencies. At the 11th SAARC summit member states adopted a convention on the prevention of trafficking of women and children for prostitution. The 12th summit adopted an Additional Protocol on Suppression of Terrorism with a view to preventing the financing of terrorist activities.

There is a wide network of SAARC Regional Centres. In 1998 an Agricultural Information Centre was established, in Dhaka, Bangladesh, to serve as a central institution for the dissemination of knowledge and information in the agricultural sector. It maintains a network of centres in each member state, which provide for the efficient exchange of technical information and for strengthening agricultural research. An agreement establishing a Food Security Reserve to meet emergency food requirements was signed in November 1987, and entered into force in August 1988. In 2004 the 12th summit meeting determined to establish a Food Bank incorporating a Food Reserve comprising 241,580 metric tons of wheat and/or rice; the Food Bank was to act as a regional food security reserve during times of normal food shortages as well as during emergencies. The Inter-governmental Agreement establishing the SAARC Food Bank was signed by leaders attending the 14th summit meeting in April 2007. Other regional institutions include the SAARC Tuberculosis Centre in Thimi, Nepal, which opened in July 1992 with the aim of preventing and reducing the prevalence of the disease in the region through the co-ordination of tuberculosis control programmes, research and training; a SAARC Documentation Centre, established in New Delhi in May 1994; and a SAARC Meteorological Research Centre which opened in Dhaka in January 1995. A Human Resources Development Centre was established in Islamabad, Pakistan in 1999. In January 2004 the summit meeting endorsed the establishment of a Cultural Centre, to be based in Sri Lanka, a Coastal Zone Management Centre, in the Maldives, and an Information Centre in Nepal. In July the Council of Ministers approved the establishment of additional regional centres for forestry, to be based in Bhutan, and for energy, to be located in Pakistan. Regional funds include a SAARC-Japan Special

Fund established in September 1993. One-half of the fund's resources, provided by the Japanese Government, was to be used to finance projects identified by Japan, including workshops and cultural events, and one-half was to be used to finance projects identified by SAARC member states. The eighth SAARC summit meeting, held in New Delhi in May 1996, established a South Asian Development Fund, comprising a Fund for Regional Projects, a Regional Fund and a fund for social development and infrastructure building. A meeting of SAARC financial experts, held in September 2005, submitted for further consideration by the Association proposals that the South Asian Development Fund should be replaced by a new SAARC Development Fund (SDF), comprising a Social Window (to finance poverty alleviation projects), an Infrastructure Window (for infrastructure development) and an Economic Window (for non-infrastructure commercial programmes). The meeting also considered the possibility of establishing a South Asian Development Bank. A roadmap for the establishment of the SDF was endorsed by the SAARC Council of Ministers in August 2006, and the first meeting of a newly-constituted SDF Board was convened in February 2007.

SAARC co-operates with other regional and international organizations. In February 1993 SAARC signed a memorandum of understanding with UNCTAD whereby both parties agreed to exchange information on trade control measures, in order to increase transparency and thereby facilitate trade. In February 1994 SAARC signed a framework co-operation agreement with ESCAP to enhance co-operation on development issues through a framework of joint studies, workshops and information exchange. A memorandum of understanding with the European Commission was signed in July 1996. SAARC has also signed co-operation agreements with UNICEF (in 1993), the Asia Pacific Telecommunity (1994), UNDP (1995), UN Drug Progamme (1995), the International Telecommunication Union (1997), the Canadian International Development Agency (1997), WHO (2000), and UNIFEM (2001). An informal dialogue at ministerial level has been conducted with ASEAN and the European Union since 1998. SAARC and WIPO hold regular consultations concerning regional co-operation on intellectual property rights, and regular consultations are convened with the WTO. During 2004 memorandums of understanding were signed with the Joint UN Programme on HIV/AIDS (in April), the UN Population Fund (UNFPA, in June), and with the South Asia Co-operative Environment Programme (SACEP, in July). In September 2005 SAARC hosted the 10th Consultative meeting of executive heads of sub-regional organizations of Asia and the Pacific. SAARC, with ESCAP, was to lead a new joint working group on disaster management.

## Finance

The national budgets of member countries provide the resources to finance SAARC activities. The Secretariat's annual budget is shared among member states according to a specified formula.

## Publications

*SAARC News* (3/4 a year).

Other official documents, regional studies, reports.

## Regional Apex Bodies

**Association of Persons of the Legal Communities of the SAARC Countries (SAARCLAW):** 495 HSIDC, Udyog Vihar Phase V, N. H. 8, Gurgaon 122016, National Capital Region, India; tel. (124) 4040193; fax (124) 4040194; e-mail info@saarclaw.com; internet www.saarclaw.com; f. 1991; recognized as a SAARC regional apex body in July 1994; aims to enhance exchanges and co-operation amongst the legal communities of the sub-region and to promote the development of law; Pres. Dr ABHISHEK M. SINGHVI; Sec.-Gen. TANIA AMIR.

**SAARC Chamber of Commerce and Industry (SCCI):** House 397, St 64, I-8/3, Islamabad, Pakistan; tel. (51) 4860611; fax (51) 4860610; e-mail info@saarcchamber.com; internet www.saarcchamber.com; f. 1992; promotes economic and trade co-operation throughout the sub-region and greater interaction between the business communities of member countries; organizes SAARC Economic Co-operation Conferences and Trade Fairs; Pres. TARIQ SAYEED; Dir WAQAR AHMAD.

**South Asian Federation of Accountants (SAFA):** c/o Institute of Chartered Accountants of India, ICAI Bhavan, POB 7100, Indraprastha Marg, New Delhi 110002, India; tel. (11) 23370195; fax (11) 23379334; e-mail safa@icai.org; internet www.esafa.org; f. 1984; recognized as a SAARC regional apex body in Jan. 2002; aims to develop regional co-ordination for the accountancy profession; Pres. SYED SHABBAR ZAIDI; Sec.-Gen. Dr ASHOK HALDIA.

Other recognized regional bodies include the South Asian Association for Regional Co-operation of Architects, the Association of Management Development Institutions, the SAARC Federation of University Women, the SAARC Association of Town Planners, the SAARC Cardiac Society, the Association of SAARC Speakers and Parliamentarians, the Federation of State Insurance Organizations of SAARC Countries, the Federation of State Insurance Organizations of SAARC Countries, the SAARC Diploma Engineers Forum, the Radiological Society of SAARC Countries, the SAARC Teachers' Federation, the SAARC Surgical Care Society and the Foundation of SAARC Writers and Literature.

# OTHER REGIONAL ORGANIZATIONS

## Agriculture, Food, Forestry and Fisheries

(for organizations concerned with agricultural commodities, see Commodities)

**CAB International (CABI):** Nosworthy Way, Wallingford, Oxon, OX10 8DE, United Kingdom; tel. (1491) 832111; fax (1491) 833508; e-mail corporate@cabi.org; internet www.cabi.org; f. 1929 as the Imperial Agricultural Bureaux (later Commonwealth Agricultural Bureaux), current name adopted in 1985; aims to improve human welfare world-wide through the generation, dissemination and application of scientific knowledge in support of sustainable development; places particular emphasis on sustainable agriculture, forestry, human health and the management of natural resources, with priority given to the needs of developing countries; compiles and publishes extensive information (in a variety of print and electronic forms) on aspects of agriculture, forestry, veterinary medicine, the environment and natural resources, and Third World rural development; maintains regional centres in the People's Republic of China, India, Kenya, Malaysia, Pakistan, Switzerland, Trinidad and Tobago, and the United Kingdom; mems: 45 countries and territories; Chair. Dr JOHN REGAZZI.

**CABI Bioscience:** Bakeham Lane, Egham, Surrey, TW20 9TY, United Kingdom; tel. (1491) 829080; fax (1491) 829100; e-mail bioscience.egham@cabi.org; internet www.cabi-bioscience.org; f. 1998 by integration of the following four CABI scientific institutions: International Institute of Biological Control; International Institute of Entomology; International Institute of Parasitology; International Mycological Institute; undertakes research, consultancy, training, capacity-building and institutional development measures in sustainable pest management, biosystematics and molecular biology, ecological applications and environmental and industrial microbiology; maintains centres in Kenya, Malaysia, Pakistan, Switzerland, Trinidad and Tobago, and the United Kingdom; Dir Dr JOAN KELLEY.

**Indian Ocean Tuna Commission (IOTC):** POB 1011, Victoria, Mahé, Seychelles; tel. 225494; fax 224364; e-mail iotc.secretary@iotc.org; internet www.iotc.org; f. 1996 as a regional fisheries organization with a mandate for the conservation and management of tuna and tuna-like species in the Indian Ocean; mems: Australia, Belize, People's Republic of China, the Comoros, European Union, Eritrea, France, Guinea, India, Indonesia, Iran, Japan, Kenya, Republic of Korea, Madagascar, Malaysia, Mauritius, Oman, Pakistan, Philippines, Seychelles, Sudan, Sri Lanka, Tanzania, Thailand, United Kingdom, Vanuatu; co-operating non-contracting parties: Indonesia, Senegal South Africa; Exec. Sec. ALEJANDRO ANGANUZZI (Argentina).

**International Crops Research Institute for the Semi-Arid Tropics (ICRISAT):** Patancheru, Andhra Pradesh 502 324, India; tel. (40) 30713222; fax (40) 30713072; e-mail icrisat@cgiar.org; internet www.icrisat.org; f. 1972 to promote the genetic improvement of crops and for research on the management of resources in the world's semi-arid tropics, with the aim of reducing poverty and protecting the environment; research covers all physical and socio-economic aspects of improving farming systems on unirrigated land; maintains regional centres in Nairobi, Kenya (for eastern and southern Africa) and in Niamey, Niger (for western and central Africa); Dir-Gen. Dr WILLIAM D. DAR (Philippines); publs *ICRISAT Report* (annually), *Journal of Semi-Arid Tropical Agricultural Research* (2 a year), information and research bulletins.

**International Food Policy Research Institute (IFPRI):** 2033 K St, NW, Washington, DC 20006, USA; tel. (202) 862-5600; fax (202) 467-4439; e-mail ifpri@cgiar.org; internet www.ifpri.org; f. 1975; co-operates with academic and other institutions in further research; develops policies for cutting hunger and malnutrition; committed to increasing public awareness of food policies; Chair. Dr ROSS GARNAUT (Australia); Dir Gen. JOACHIM VON BRAUN (Germany)

**International Service for National Agricultural Research (ISNAR):** IFPRI, ISNAR Division, ILRI, POB 5689, Addis Ababa, Ethiopia; tel. (11) 646-3215; fax (11) 646-2927; e-mail ifpri-addisababa@cgiar.org; fmrly based in The Hague, Netherlands, the ISNAR Program relocated to Addis Ababa in 2004, under the governance of IFPRI; Dir Dr WILBERFORCE KISAMBA-MUGERWA.

**International Rice Research Institute (IRRI):** Los Baños, Laguna, DAPO Box 7777, Metro Manila, Philippines; tel. (2) 5805600; fax (2) 5805699; e-mail irri@cgiar.org; internet www.irri.org; f. 1960; conducts research on rice, with the aim of developing technologies of environmental, social and economic benefit; works to enhance national rice research systems and offers training; operates Riceworld, a museum and learning centre about rice; maintains a library of technical rice literature; organizes international conferences and workshops; Dir-Gen. Dr ROBERT S. ZEIGLER; publs *Rice Literature Update*, *Hotline*, *Facts about IRRI*, *News about Rice and People*, *International Rice Research Notes*.

**International Water Management Institute (IWMI):** 127 Sunil Mawatha, Pelawatte, Battaramulla, Sri Lanka; tel. (11) 2880000; fax (11) 2786854; e-mail iwmi@cgiar.org; internet www.iwmi.org; f. 1984 as International Irrigation Management Institute; aims to improve the management of land and water resources in support of food, livelihoods and nature; addresses water and land management challenges confronting poor communities in developing countries; research agenda organized around four priority themes: basin water management; land, water and livelihoods; agriculture, water and cities; and water management and environment; cross-cutting activities include: assessment of land and water productivity, and their relationship to poverty; identifying interventions that improve productivity and access to/sustainability of natural resources; and assessment of the impacts of interventions; works through collaborative research with partners world-wide and targets policy makers, development agencies, individual farmers and private-sector organizations; Dir-Gen. COLIN CHARTRES (Australia).

**Network of Aquaculture Centres in Asia and the Pacific (NACA):** POB 1040, Kasetsart University Post Office, Bangkok 10903, Thailand; tel. (2) 561-1728; fax (2) 561-1727; e-mail publications@enaca.org; internet www.enaca.org; f. 1990; promotes the development of aquaculture in the Asia and Pacific region through development planning, interdisciplinary research, regional training and information; mems: Australia, Bangladesh, Cambodia, People's Republic of China, Hong Kong, India, Indonesia, Iran, Democratic People's Republic of Korea, Malaysia, Myanmar, Nepal, Pakistan, Philippines, Sri Lanka, Thailand and Viet Nam; Dir-Gen. SENA S. DE SILVA; publs *NACA Newsletter* (quarterly), *Aquaculture Asia* (quarterly).

**WorldFish Center** (International Centre for Living Aquatic Resources Management—ICLARM): Jalan Batu Maung, Batu Maung, 11960 Bayan Lepas, Penang, Malaysia; POB 500, GPO, 10670 Penang; tel. (4) 626-1606; fax (4) 626-5530; e-mail worldfishcenter@cgiar.org; internet www.worldfishcenter.org; f. 1973; became a mem. of the Consultative Group on International Agricultural Research (CGIAR) in 1992; aims to contribute to food security and poverty eradication in developing countries through the sustainable development and use of living aquatic resources; carries out research and promotes partnerships; Dir-Gen. Dr STEPHEN J. HALL; publ. *NAGA* (quarterly newsletter).

**World Organisation of Animal Health:** 12 rue de Prony, 75017 Paris, France; tel. 1-44-15-18-88; fax 1-42-67-09-87; e-mail oie@oie.int; internet www.oie.int; f. 1924 as Office International des Epizooties (OIE); objectives include promoting international transparency of animal diseases; collecting, analysing and disseminating scientific veterinary information; providing expertise and promoting international co-operation in the control of animal diseases; promoting veterinary services; providing new scientific guide-lines on animal production, food safety and animal welfare; launched in May 2005, jointly with FAO and WHO, a Global Strategy for the Progressive Control of Highly Pathogenic Avian Influenza (H5N1), and, in partnership with other organizations, has convened conferences on avian influenza; experts in a network of 156 collaborating centres and reference laboratories; 172 mems; Dir-Gen. BERNARD VALLAT; publs *Disease Information* (weekly), *World Animal Health* (annually), *Scientific and Technical Review* (3 a year), other manuals, codes etc.

## Arts and Culture

**Organization of World Heritage Cities:** 15 rue Saint-Nicolas, Québec, QC G1K 1M8, Canada; tel. (418) 692-0000; fax (418) 692-5558; e-mail secretariat@ovpm.org; internet www.ovpm.org; f. 1993 to assist cities inscribed on the UNESCO World Heritage List to implement the Convention concerning the Protection of the World Cultural and Natural Heritage (1972); promotes co-operation between city authorities, in particular in the management and sustainable development of historic sites; holds an annual General Assembly, comprising the mayors of member cities; mems: 233 cities world-wide; Sec.-Gen. LEE MINAIDIS (interim); publ. *OWHC Newsletter* (2 a year, in English, French and Spanish).

**Royal Asiatic Society of Great Britain and Ireland:** 14 Stephenson Way, London, NW1 2HD, United Kingdom; tel. (20) 7388-4539; fax (20) 7391-9429; e-mail info@royalasiaticsociety.org; internet www.royalasiaticsociety.org; f. 1823 for the study of history and cultures of the East; mems: c. 700, branch societies in Asia; Pres. Prof. ANTHONY STOCKWELL; Dir Dr A. POWELL; publ. *Journal* (3 a year).

## Commodities

**Asian and Pacific Coconut Community (APCC):** 3rd Floor, Lina Bldg, Jalan H. R. Rasuna Said Kav. B7, Kuningan, Jakarta 12920, Indonesia; POB 1343, Jakarta 10013; tel. (21) 5221712; fax (21) 5221714; e-mail apcc@indo.net.id; internet www.apccsec.org; f. 1969 to promote and co-ordinate all activities of the coconut industry, to achieve higher production and better processing, marketing and research; organizes annual Coconut Technical Meeting (COCOTECH); mems: Fiji, India, Indonesia, Kiribati, Malaysia, Marshall Islands, Federated States of Micronesia, Papua New Guinea, Philippines, Samoa, Solomon Islands, Sri Lanka, Thailand, Vanuatu, Viet Nam; Chair. OSCAR GARIN; Exec. Dir ROMULO N. ARANCON, Jr; publs *Cocomunity* (monthly), *CORD* (2 a year), *CocoInfo International* (2 a year), *Coconut Statistical Yearbook*, guide-lines and other ad hoc publications.

**Association of Natural Rubber Producing Countries (ANRPC):** Bangunan Getah Asli, 148 Jalan Ampang, 7th Floor, 50450 Kuala Lumpur, Malaysia; tel. (3) 2611900; fax (3) 2613014; e-mail anrpc@capo.jaring.my; f. 1970 to co-ordinate the production and marketing of natural rubber, to promote technical co-operation amongst members and to bring about fair and stable prices for natural rubber; holds seminars, meetings and training courses on technical and statistical subjects; a joint regional marketing system has been agreed in principle; mems: India, Indonesia, Malaysia, Papua New Guinea, Singapore, Sri Lanka, Thailand, Viet Nam; Sec.-Gen. G. W. S. K. DE SILVA; publs *ANRPC Statistical Bulletin* (quarterly), *ANRPC Newsletter*.

**International Coffee Organization (ICO):** 22 Berners St, London, W1T 3DD, United Kingdom; tel. (20) 7612-0600; fax (20) 7612-0630; e-mail info@ico.org; internet www.ico.org; f. 1963 under the International Coffee Agreement, 1962, which was renegotiated in 1968, 1976, 1983, 1994 (extended in 1999) and 2001; aims to improve international co-operation and provide a forum for intergovernmental consultations on coffee matters; to facilitate international trade in coffee by the collection, analysis and dissemination of statistics; to act as a centre for the collection, exchange and publication of coffee information; to promote studies in the field of coffee; and to encourage an increase in coffee consumption; mems: 45 exporting and 32 importing countries; Chair. of Council MAURO OREFICE (Italy); Exec. Dir NÉSTOR OSORIO (Colombia).

**International Cotton Advisory Committee (ICAC):** 1629 K St, NW, Suite 702, Washington, DC 20006-1636, USA; tel. (202) 463-6660; fax (202) 463-6950; e-mail secretariat@icac.org; internet www.icac.org; f. 1939 to observe developments in world cotton; to collect and disseminate statistics; to suggest measures for the furtherance of international collaboration in maintaining and developing a sound world cotton economy; and to provide a forum for international discussions on cotton prices; mems: 44 countries; Exec. Dir Dr TERRY TOWNSEND (USA); publs *Cotton This Week!* (internet/e-mail only), *Cotton This Month*, *Cotton: Review of the World Situation* (every 2 months), *Cotton: World Statistics* (annually), *The ICAC Recorder*, *World Textile Demand* (annually), other surveys, studies, trade analyses and technical publications.

**International Grains Council (IGC):** 1 Canada Sq., Canary Wharf, London, E14 5AE, United Kingdom; tel. (20) 7513-1122; fax (20) 7513-0630; e-mail igc@igc.org.uk; internet www.igc.org.uk; f. 1949 as International Wheat Council, present name adopted in 1995; responsible for the administration of the International Grains Agreement, 1995, comprising the Grains Trade Convention (GTC) and the Food Aid Convention (FAC, under which donors pledge specified minimum annual amounts of food aid for developing countries in the form of grain and other eligible products); aims to further international co-operation in all aspects of trade in grains, to promote international trade in grains, and to achieve a free flow of this trade, particularly in developing member countries; seeks to contribute to the stability of the international grain market; acts as a forum for consultations between members; provides comprehensive information on the international grain market; mems: 25 countries and the EU; Exec. Dir ETSUO KITAHARA; publs *World Grain Statistics* (annually), *Wheat and Coarse Grain Shipments* (annually), *Report for the Fiscal Year* (annually), *Grain Market Report* (monthly), *IGC Grain Market Indicators* (weekly).

**International Jute Study Group (IJSG):** 145 Monipuriparu, Tejgaon, Dhaka 1215, Bangladesh; POB 6073, Gulshan, Dhaka; tel. (2) 9125581; fax (2) 9125248; e-mail info@jute.org; internet www.jute.org; f. 2002 as successor to International Jute Organization (f. 1984 in accordance with an agreement made by 48 producing and consuming countries in 1982, under the auspices of UNCTAD); aims to improve the jute economy and the quality of jute and jute products through research and development projects and market promotion; Sec.-Gen SUDRIPTA ROY.

**International Organization of Spice Trading Associations (IOSTA):** c/o American Spice Trade Association, 2025 M St, NW, Suite 800, Washington, DC 20036, USA; tel. (202) 367-1127; fax (202) 367-2127; e-mail info@astaspice.org; f. 1999; mems: eight national and regional spice organizations.

**International Pepper Community (IPC):** 4th Floor, Lina Bldg, Jalan H. R. Rasuna Said, Kav. B7, Kuningan, Jakarta 12920, Indonesia; tel. (21) 5224902; fax (21) 5224905; e-mail ipc@indo.net.id; internet www.ipcnet.org; f. 1972 for promoting, co-ordinating and harmonizing all activities relating to the pepper economy; mems: Brazil, India, Indonesia, Malaysia, Federated States of Micronesia, Papua New Guinea, Sri Lanka, Thailand; Exec. Dir ANANDAN ABDULLAH; publs *Pepper Statistical Yearbook*, *International Pepper News Bulletin* (quarterly), *Directory of Pepper Exporters*, *Directory of Pepper Importers*, *Weekly Prices Bulletin*, *Pepper Market Review*.

**International Silk Association:** 34 rue de la Charité, 69002 Lyon, France; tel. 4-78-42-10-79; fax 4-78-37-56-72; e-mail isa-silk.ais-sole@wanadoo.fr; f. 1949 to promote closer collaboration between all branches of the silk industry and trade, develop the consumption of silk, and foster scientific research; collects and disseminates information and statistics relating to the trade and industry; organizes biennial congresses; mems: employers' and technical organizations in 40 countries; Gen. Sec. X. LAVERGNE; publs *ISA Newsletter* (monthly), congress reports, standards, trade rules, etc.

**International Sugar Organization:** 1 Canada Sq., Canary Wharf, London, E14 5AA, United Kingdom; tel. (20) 7513-1144; fax (20) 7513-1146; e-mail exdir@isosugar.org; internet www.isosugar.org; administers the International Sugar Agreement (1992), with the objectives of stimulating co-operation, facilitating trade and encouraging demand; aims to improve conditions in the sugar market through debate, analysis and studies; serves as a forum for discussion; holds annual seminars and workshops; sponsors projects from developing countries; mems: 81 countries producing some 83% of total world sugar; Exec. Dir Dr PETER BARON; publs *Sugar Year Book*, *Monthly Statistical Bulletin*, *Market Report and Press Summary*, *Quarterly Market Outlook*, seminar proceedings.

**International Tea Committee Ltd (ITC):** 1 Carlton House Terrace, London, SW1Y 5DB, United Kingdom; tel. (20) 7839-5090; e-mail inteacom@globalnet.co.uk; internet www.inttea.com; f. 1933 to administer the International Tea Agreement; now serves as a statistical and information centre; in 1979 membership was extended to include consuming countries; producer mems: national tea boards or asscns in Bangladesh, People's Republic of China, India, Indonesia, Kenya, Malawi, Sri Lanka; consumer mems: United Kingdom Tea Asscn, Tea Asscn of the USA Inc., Irish Tea Trade Asscn, Netherland Coffee Roasters and Tea Packers' Asscn, and the Tea Asscn of Canada; assoc. mems: Netherlands and UK ministries of agriculture, and national tea boards/asscns in eight producing countries; Chief Exec. MANUJA PEIRIS; publs *Annual Bulletin of Statistics*, *Monthly Statistical Summary*.

**International Tea Promotion Association (ITPA):** c/o Tea Board of Kenya, POB 20064, City Sq., 00200 Nairobi, Kenya; tel. (20) 572421; fax (20) 562120; e-mail teaboardk@kenyaweb.com; internet www.teaboard.or.ke; f. 1979; mems: eight countries; Chair. NICHOLAS NGANGA; publ. *International Tea Journal* (2 a year).

**International Tobacco Growers' Association (ITGA):** Av. Gen. Humberto Delgado 30-A, 6001-081 Castelo Branco, Portugal; tel. (272) 325901; fax (272) 325906; e-mail itga@tobaccoleaf.org; internet www.tobaccoleaf.org; f. 1984 to provide a forum for the exchange of views and information of interest to tobacco producers; mems: 20 countries producing over 80% of the world's internationally traded tobacco; Chief Exec. ANTÓNIO ABRUNHOSA (Portugal); publs *Tobacco Courier* (quarterly), *Tobacco Briefing*.

**International Tropical Timber Organization (ITTO):** International Organizations Center, 5th Floor, Pacifico-Yokohama, 1-1-1, Minato-Mirai, Nishi-ku, Yokohama 220-0012, Japan; tel. (45) 223-1110; fax (45) 223-1111; e-mail itto@itto.or.jp; internet www.itto.or.jp; f. 1985 under the International Tropical Timber Agreement (1983); a new treaty, ITTA 1994, came into force in 1997; provides a forum for consultation and co-operation between countries that produce and consume tropical timber, and is dedicated to the sustainable development and conservation of tropical forests; facilitates progress towards 'Objective 2000', which aims to move as rapidly as possible towards achieving exports of tropical timber and timber products from sustainably managed resources; encourages, through policy and project work, forest management, conservation and restoration, the further processing of tropical timber in producing countries, and the gathering and analysis of market intelligence and economic information; mems: 33 producing and 26 consuming countries and the EU; Exec. Dir EMMANUEL ZE MEKA (Cameroon); publs *Annual Review and Assessment of the World Timber Situation*, *Tropical Timber Market Information Service* (every 2 weeks), *Tropical Forest Update* (quarterly).

**Organization of the Petroleum Exporting Countries (OPEC):** 1020 Vienna, Obere Donaustrasse 93, Austria; tel. (1) 211-12-279; fax (1) 214-98-27; internet www.opec.org; f. 1960 to unify and co-ordinate members' petroleum policies and to safeguard their interests generally; holds regular conferences of member countries to set reference prices and production levels; conducts research in energy studies, economics and finance; provides data services and news services covering petroleum and energy issues; mems: Algeria, Iran, Iraq, Kuwait, Libya, Nigeria, Qatar, Saudi Arabia, United Arab Emirates, Venezuela; Sec.-Gen. ABDULLA SALEM EL-BADRI (Libya); publs *Annual Report*, *Annual Statistical Bulletin*, *OPEC Bulletin* (monthly), *OPEC Review* (quarterly), *Monthly Oil Market Report*.

**OPEC Fund for International Development:** Postfach 995, 1010 Vienna, Austria; tel. (1) 515-64-0; fax (1) 513-92-38; e-mail info@opecfund.org; internet www.opecfund.org; f. 1976 by mem. countries of OPEC, to provide financial co-operation and assistance for developing countries; in 2004 commitments amounted to US $528.6m; Dir-Gen. SULEIMAN J. AL-HERBISH (Saudi Arabia); publs *Annual Report*, *OPEC Fund Newsletter* (3 a year).

# Development and Economic Co-operation

**Afro-Asian Rural Development Organization (AARDO):** No. 2, State Guest Houses Complex, Chanakyapuri, New Delhi 110 021, India; tel. (11) 24100475; fax (11) 24672045; e-mail aardohq@nde.vsnl.net.in; internet www.aardo.org; f. 1962 to act as a catalyst for the co-operative restructuring of rural life in Africa and Asia and to explore opportunities for the co-ordination of efforts to promote rural welfare and to eradicate hunger, thirst, disease, illiteracy and poverty; carries out collaborative research on development issues; organizes training; encourages the exchange of information; holds international conferences and seminars; awards 150 individual training fellowships at nine institutes in Egypt, India, Japan, the Republic of Korea, Malaysia and Taiwan; mems: 15 African countries, 14 Asian countries, one African associate; Sec.-Gen. ABDALLA YAHIA ADAM (Sudan); publs *Afro-Asian Journal of Rural Development* (2 a year), *Annual Report*, *AARDO Newsletter* (2 a year).

**Asian and Pacific Development Centre:** Pesiaran Duta, POB 12224, 50770 Kuala Lumpur, Malaysia; tel. (3) 6511088; fax (3) 6510316; internet www.apdc.org; f. 1980; undertakes research and training, acts as clearing-house for information on development and offers consultancy services, in co-operation with national institutions; current programme includes assistance regarding the implementation of national development strategies; the Centre aims to promote economic co-operation among developing countries of the region for their mutual benefit; mems: 19 countries and two associate members; CEO Dr FRANKLIN P. KIM; publs *Annual Report*, *Newsletter* (2 a year), *Asia-Pacific Development Monitor* (quarterly), studies, reports, monographs.

**Asia-Pacific Mountain Network (APMN):** c/o International Centre for Integrated Mountain Development, GPO Box 3226, Khumaltar, Lalitpur, Nepal; tel. (1) 5003222; fax (1) 5003299; e-mail apmn@mtnforum.org; internet apmn.icimod.org; f. 1995; forum for the production and dissemination of information on sustainable mountain development, reducing the risk of mountain disasters, economic development, the elimination of poverty, and cultural heritage; mems: about 2,000.

**Association of Development Financing Institutions in Asia and the Pacific (ADFIAP):** Skyland Plaza, 2nd Floor, Sen. Gil J. Puyat Ave, Makati City, Metro Manila, 1200 Philippines; tel. (2) 8161672; fax (2) 8176498; e-mail inquires@adfiap.org; internet www.adfiap.org; f. 1976 to promote the interests and economic development of the respective countries of its member institutions, through development financing; mems: 66 institutions in 32 countries; Chair. ISOA KALOUMAIRA (Fiji); Sec.-Gen. OCTAVIO B. PERALTA; publs *Asian Banking Digest*, *Journal of Development Finance* (2 a year), *ADFIAP Newsletter*, *ADFIAP Accompli*, *DevTrade Finance*.

**Central Asia Regional Economic Co-operation (CAREC):** CAREC Unit, ADB, POB 789, 0980 Manila, Philippines; tel. (2) 6325857; fax (2) 6362387; internet www.adb.org/Carec; f. 1997; a sub-regional alliance supported by several multilateral institutions (Asian Development Bank, European Bank for Reconstruction and Development, International Monetary Fund, Islamic Development Bank, United Nations Development Programme, and World Bank) to promote economic co-operation and development; supports projects in the following priority areas: transport, energy, trade policy, trade facilitation; mems: Afghanistan, Azerbaijan, Kazakhstan, Kyrgyzstan, Mongolia, Tajikistan, Uzbekistan, Xinjiang Uygur Autonomous Region (of the People's Republic of China).

**Colombo Plan:** Bank of Ceylon Merchant Tower, 13th Floor, 28 St Michael's Rd, Colombo 03, Sri Lanka; tel. (11) 2564448; fax (11) 2564531; e-mail info@colombo-plan.org; internet www.colombo-plan.org; f. 1950, as the Colombo Plan for Co-operative Economic and Social Development in Asia and the Pacific, by seven Commonwealth countries, to encourage economic and social development in that region, based on principles of partnership and collective effort; the Plan comprises four training programmes: the Drug Advisory Programme, to enhance the capabilities of officials, in government and non-governmental organizations, involved in drug abuse prevention and control; the Programme for Public Administration, to develop human capital in the public sector; the Programme for Private Sector Development, which implements skill development programmes in the area of small and medium-sized enterprises and related issues; and the Staff College for Technician Education (see below); all training programmes are voluntarily funded, while administrative costs of the organization are shared equally by all member countries; developing countries are encouraged to become donors and to participate in economic and technical co-operation activities; mems: 25 countries; Sec.-Gen. KITTIPAN KANJANAPIPATKUL (Thailand); publs *Annual Report*, *Colombo Plan Focus* (quarterly), *Consultative Committee Proceedings and Conclusions* (every 2 years).

**Colombo Plan Staff College for Technician Education:** POB 7500, Domestic Airport Post Office, NAIA, Pasay City 1300, Philippines; tel. (2) 6310991; fax (2) 6310996; e-mail cpsc@skyinet.net; internet www.cpsc.org.ph; f. 1973 with the support of member governments of the Colombo Plan; aims to enhance the development of technician education systems in developing mem. countries; Dir MAN-GON PARK; publ. *CPSC Quarterly*.

**Developing Eight (D-8):** Müşir Fuad Paşa Yalısı (Eski Tersane), Sakıp Sabancı Cad. 90, Istinye 80860 İstanbul, Turkey; tel. (212) 2775513; fax (212) 2775519; e-mail developing-8@mfa.gov.tr; internet www.mfa.gov.tr/d-8/; inaugurated at a meeting of heads of state in June 1997; aims to foster economic co-operation between member states and to strengthen the role of developing countries in the global economy; project areas include trade and industry, agriculture, human resources, telecommunications, rural development, finance (including banking and privatization), energy, environment, and health; fifth Summit meeting: convened in Bali, Indonesia, May 2006; mems: Bangladesh, Egypt, Indonesia, Iran, Malaysia, Nigeria, Pakistan, Turkey; Exec. Dir AYHAN KAMEL.

**Group of 15 (G15):** G15 Technical Support Facility, 1 route des Morillons, CP 2100, 1218 Grand Saconnex, Geneva, Switzerland; tel. 227916701; fax 227916169; e-mail tsf@g15.org; internet www.g15.org/gftsfcontact.html; f. 1979 by 15 developing nations during the ninth summit of the Non-Aligned Movement; retains its original name although current membership totals 18; convenes biennial summits to address the global economic and political situation and to promote economic development through South-South co-operation and North-South dialogue; mems: Algeria, Argentina, Brazil, Chile, Egypt, India, Indonesia, Iran, Jamaica, Kenya, Malaysia, Mexico, Nigeria, Peru, Senegal, Sri Lanka, Venezuela, Zimbabwe.

**Group of 77 (G77):** c/o UN Headquarters, Rm S-3953, New York, NY 10017, USA; tel. (212) 963-3515; fax (212) 963-1753; e-mail g77off@unmail.org; internet www.g77.org/; f. 1964 by the 77 signatory states of the 'Joint Declaration of the Seventy-Seven Countries' (the G77 retains its original name, owing to its historic significance, although its membership has expanded since inception); first ministerial meeting, held in Algiers, Algeria, in Oct. 1967, adopted the Charter of Algiers as a basis for G77 co-operation; subsequently G77 Chapters were established with liaison offices in Geneva (UNCTAD), Nairobi (UNEP), Paris (UNESCO), Rome (FAO/IFAD), Vienna (UNIDO), and the Group of 24 (G24) in Washington, DC (IMF and World Bank); as the largest intergovernmental organization of developing states in the United Nations the G77 aims to enable developing nations to articulate and promote their collective economic interests and to improve their negotiating capacity with regard to global economic issues within the United Nations system; in Sept. 2006 G77 ministers of foreign affairs, and the People's Republic of China, endorsed the creation the establishment of a new Consortium on Science,

Technology and Innovation for the South (COSTIS); a chairperson, who also acts as spokesperson, co-ordinates the G77's activities in each Chapter; the chairmanship rotates on a regional basis between Africa, Asia, and Latin America and the Caribbean; the supreme decision-making body of the G77 is the South Summit, convened at five-yearly intervals (2005: Doha, Qatar); the annual meeting of G77 ministers of foreign affairs is convened at the start (in September) of the regular session of the UN General Assembly; periodic sectoral ministerial meetings are organized in preparation for UNCTAD sessions and prior to the UNIDO and UNESCO General Conferences, and with the aim of promoting South-South co-operation; special ministerial meetings are also convened from time to time, for example a special meeting was convened in São Paulo, Brazil, in June 2004 to commemorate the G77's 40th anniversary; mems: 131 developing countries.

**Indian Ocean Rim Association for Regional Co-operation (IOR–ARC):** Sorèze House, Wilson Ave, Vacoas, Mauritius; tel. 698-3979; fax 698-5390; e-mail iorarchq@intnet.mu; the first intergovernmental meeting of countries in the region to promote an Indian Ocean Rim initiative was convened in March 1995; charter to establish the Asscn was signed at a ministerial meeting in March 1997; aims to promote the sustained growth and balanced devt of the region and of its mem. states and to create common ground for regional economic co-operation, *inter alia* through trade, investment, infrastructure, tourism, and science and technology; seventh meeting of Council of Ministers held in Tehran, Iran, March 2007; mems: Australia, Bangladesh, India, Indonesia, Iran, Kenya, Madagascar, Malaysia, Mauritius, Mozambique, Oman, Singapore, South Africa, Sri Lanka, Tanzania, Thailand, United Arab Emirates and Yemen. Dialogue Partner countries: People's Republic of China, Egypt, France, Japan, United Kingdom. Observer: Indian Ocean Tourism Org; Chair. LAKSHMAN KADIRGAMAR (Sri Lanka); Exec. Dir TUAN ZAROOK A. SAMSUDEEN (Sri Lanka).

**International Centre for Integrated Mountain Development (ICIMOD):** 4/80 Jawalakhel, Lalitpur, GPO Box 3226, Kathmandu, Nepal; tel. (1) 5525313; fax (1) 5524509; e-mail icimod@icimod.org; internet www.icimod.org; f. 1983; an autonomous organization sponsored by regional member countries and by the governments of Nepal, Germany, Switzerland, Austria, Netherlands and Denmark, to help promote an economically and environmentally sound ecosystem and to improve the living standards of the population in the Hindu Kush-Himalaya; aims to serve as a focal point for multi-disciplinary documentation, training and applied research, and as a consultative centre in scientific and practical matters pertaining to mountain development; participating countries: Afghanistan, Bangladesh, Bhutan, People's Republic of China, India, Myanmar, Nepal, Pakistan; Dir-Gen. ANDREAS SCHILD (Switzerland).

**Partners in Population and Development:** IPH Bldg, 2nd Floor, Mohakhali, Dhaka 1212, Bangladesh; tel. (2) 988-1882; fax (2) 882-9387; e-mail partners@ppdsec.org; internet www.south-south-ppd.org; f. 1994; aims to implement the decisions of the International Conference on Population and Development, held in Cairo, Egypt in 1994, in order to expand and improve South-South collaboration in the fields of family planning and reproductive health; administers a Visionary Leadership Programme, a Global Leadership Programme, and other training and technical advisory services; mems: 21 developing countries; Exec. Dir SANGEET HARRY JOOSEERY.

**World Economic Forum:** 91–93 route de la Capite, 1223 Cologny/Geneva, Switzerland; tel. 228691212; fax 227862744; e-mail contact@weforum.org; internet www.weforum.org; f. 1971; the Forum comprises commercial interests gathered on a non-partisan basis, under the stewardship of the Swiss Government, with the aim of improving society through economic development; convenes an annual meeting in Davos, Switzerland; organizes the following programmes: Technology Pioneers; Women Leaders; and Young Global Leaders; and aims to mobilize the resources of the global business community in the implementation of the following initiatives: the Global Health Initiative; the Disaster Relief Network; the West-Islamic World Dialogue; and the G-20/International Monetary Reform Project; the Forum is governed by a guiding Foundation Board; an advisory International Business Council; and an administrative Managing Board; regular mems: representatives of 1,000 leading commercial companies world-wide; selected mem. companies taking a leading role in the movement's activities are known as 'partners'.

## Economics and Finance

**Asian Clearing Union (ACU):** 207/1 Pasdaran Ave, POB 15875/7177, 16646 Tehran, Iran; tel. (21) 22842076; fax (21) 22847677; e-mail acusecret@cbi.ir; internet www.asianclearingunion.org; f. 1974 to provide clearing arrangements, whereby members settle payments for intra-regional transactions among the participating central banks, on a multilateral basis, in order to economize on the use of foreign exchange and promote the use of domestic currencies in trade transactions among developing countries; part of ESCAP's Asian trade expansion programme; the Central Bank of Iran is the Union's agent; from Jan. 1996 the value of one Asian Monetary Unit (also referred to as an ACU Dollar) was aligned with that of one US dollar; mems: central banks of Bangladesh, Bhutan, India, Iran, Myanmar, Nepal, Pakistan, Sri Lanka; Sec.-Gen. LIDA BORHAN-AZAD; publs *Annual Report*, monthly newsletter.

**Asian Reinsurance Corporation:** 17th Floor, Tower B, Chamnan Phenjati Business Center, 65 Rama 9 Rd, Huaykwang, Bangkok 10320, Thailand; tel. (2) 245-2169; fax (2) 248-1377; e-mail asianre@asianrecorp.com; internet www.asianrecorp.com; f. 1979 by ESCAP with UNCTAD, to operate as a professional reinsurer, giving priority in retrocessions to national insurance and reinsurance markets of member countries, and as a development organization providing technical assistance to countries in the Asia-Pacific region; cap. (auth.) US $15m., (p.u.) $9m.; mems: Afghanistan, Bangladesh, Bhutan, People's Republic of China, India, Iran, Republic of Korea, Philippines, Sri Lanka, Thailand; Gen. Man. S. A. KUMAR.

**Association of Asian Confederations of Credit Unions (AACCU):** 24 Soi 60 Ramkanheang Rd, Bangkapi, Bangkok 10240, Thailand; tel. (2) 374-3170; fax (2) 374-5321; e-mail accu@aaccu.coop; internet www.aaccu.net; links and promotes credit unions and co-operatives in Asia, provides research facilities and training programmes; mems: in credit union leagues and federations in 24 Asian countries; Pres. OH-MAN KWON; CEO RANJITH HETTIARACHCHI (Thailand); publs *ACCU News* (every 3 months), *Annual Report*, *ACCU Directory*.

**Financial Action Task Force (FATF)** (Groupe d'action financière—GAFI): 2 rue André-Pascal, 75775 Paris Cédex 16, France; tel. 1-45-24-79-45; fax 1-44-30-61-37; e-mail contact@fatf-gafi.org; internet www.fatf-gafi.org; f. 1989, on the recommendation of the Group of Seven industrialized nations (G7), to develop and promote policies to combat money laundering and the financing of terrorism; formulated a set of recommendations (40+9) for countries world-wide to implement; established partnerships with regional task forces in the Caribbean, Asia-Pacific, Central Asia, Europe, East and South Africa, the Middle East and North Africa and South America; mems: 34 state jurisdictions, the European Commission, and the Co-operation Council for the Arab States of the Gulf; observer: India, Republic of Korea; Pres. JAMES SASSOON (United Kingdom); Exec. Sec. ALAIN DAMAIS; publs *Annual Report*, *e-Bulletin*.

**Group of 20 (G20):** internet www.g20.org; f. Sept. 1999 as an informal deliberative forum of finance ministers and central bank governors representing both industrialized and 'systemically important' emerging-market nations; aims to strengthen the international financial architecture and to foster sustainable economic growth and development; in 2004 participating countries adopted the G20 Accord for Sustained Growth and stated a commitment to high standards of transparency and fiscal governance; the IMF Managing Director and IBRD President participate in G20 annual meetings (Nov. 2008: São Paulo, Brazil); mems: ministers of finance and central bank governors of Argentina, Australia, Brazil, Canada, People's Republic of China, France, Germany, India, Indonesia, Italy, Japan, Republic of Korea, Mexico, Russia, Saudi Arabia, South Africa, Turkey, United Kingdom, USA and the European Union.

**Insurance Institute for Asia and the Pacific:** Zapote Rd, Alabang, Metro Manila, Philippines; tel. (2) 8420691; fax (2) 8420692; f. 1974 to provide insurance management training and conduct research in subjects connected with the insurance industry; publ. *IIAP Journal* (quarterly).

**Intergovernmental Group of 24 (G24) on International Monetary Affairs and Development:** 700 19th St, NW, Rm 3-600 Washington, DC 20431, USA; tel. (202) 623-6101; fax (202) 623-6000; e-mail G24@G24.org; internet www.g24.org/; f. 1971; aims to co-ordinate the position of developing countries on monetary and development finance issues; operates at the political level of ministers of finance and governors of central banks, and also at the level of government officials; mems (Africa): Algeria, Côte d'Ivoire, DRC, Egypt, Ethiopia, Gabon, Ghana, Nigeria, South Africa; (Latin America and the Caribbean): Argentina, Brazil, Colombia, Guatemala, Mexico, Peru, Trinidad and Tobago and Venezuela; (Asia and the Middle East): India, Iran, Lebanon, Pakistan, Philippines, Sri Lanka and Syrian Arab Republic; the People's Republic of China has the status of special invitee at G24 meetings; G77 participant states may attend G24 meetings as observers.

## Education

**Asian South Pacific Bureau of Adult Education (ASPBAE):** c/o MAAPL, Eucharistic Congress Bldg No. 3, 9th Floor, 5 Convent St,

Colaba, Mumbai 400 039, India; tel. (22) 22021391; fax (22) 22832217; e-mail aspbae@vsnl.com; internet www.aspbae.org; f. 1964 to assist non-formal education and adult literacy; organizes training courses and seminars; provides material and advice relating to adult education; mems in 31 countries and territories; Sec.-Gen. MARIA-LOURDES ALMAZAN-KHAN; publ. *ASPBAE News* (3 a year).

**Asian Confederation of Teachers:** c/o FIT, 55 Abhinav Apt, Mahturas Rd Extn, Kandivli, Mumbai 400 067, India; tel. (22) 8085437; fax (22) 6240578; e-mail vsir@hotmail.com; f. 1990; mems in 10 countries and territories; Pres. MUHAMMAD MUSTAPHA; Sec.-Gen. VINAYAK SIRDESAI.

**Asian Institute of Technology (AIT):** POB 4, Klong Luang, Pathumthani 12120, Thailand; tel. (2) 516-0144; fax (2) 516-2126; e-mail president@ait.ac.th; internet www.ait.ac.th; f. 1959; Master's, Doctor's and Diploma programmes are offered in four schools: Advanced Technologies, Civil Engineering, Environment, Resources and Development, and Management; specialized training is provided by the Center for Library and Information Resources (CLAIR), the Continuing Education Center, the Center for Language and Educational Technology, the Regional Computer Center, the AIT Center in Viet Nam (based in Hanoi) and the Swiss-AIT-Viet Nam Management Development Program (in Ho Chi Minh City); other research and outpost centres are the Asian Center for Engineering Computations and Software, the Asian Center for Research on Remote Sensing, the Regional Environmental Management Center, the Asian Center for Soil Improvement and Geosynthetics and the Urban Environmental Outreach Center; there are four specialized information centres (on ferro-cement, geotechnical engineering, renewable energy resources, environmental sanitation) under CLAIR; the Management of Technology Information Center conducts short-term courses in the management of technology and international business; Pres. Prof. SAID IRANDOUST; publs *AIT Annual Report*, *Annual Report on Research and Activities*, *AIT Review* (3 a year), *Prospectus*, other specialized publs.

**Association of South-East Asian Institutions of Higher Learning (ASAIHL):** Secretariat, Rm 113, Jamjuree 1 Bldg, Chulalongkorn University, Phyathai Rd, Bangkok 10330, Thailand; tel. (2) 251-6966; fax (2) 253-7909; e-mail oninnat@chula.ac.th; internet www.seameo.org/asaihl; f. 1956 to promote the economic, cultural and social welfare of the people of South-East Asia by means of educational co-operation and research programmes; and to cultivate a sense of regional identity and interdependence; collects and disseminates information, organizes discussions; mems: 160 university institutions in 16 countries; Pres. DATO DZULKIFLI ABDUL RAZAK; Sec.-Gen. Dr NINNAT OLANVORAVUTH; publs *Newsletter*, *Handbook* (every 3 years).

## Environmental Conservation

**Consortium for Oceanographic Research and Education (CORE):** 1201 New York Ave, NW, Suite 420, Washington, DC 20005, USA; tel. (202) 332-0063; fax (202) 332-9751; e-mail coml@coreocean.org; internet www.comlsecretariat.org; f. 1999 to launch and host the International Steering Committee and Secretariat for the Census of Marine Life, a 10-year initiative to assess the diversity, distribution and abundance of marine life being implemented by a network of researchers from more than 70 countries; aims to promote, support and advance the science of oceanography; Pres. RICHARD WEST.

**Global Coral Reef Monitoring Network:** POB 772, Townsville MC 4810, Australia; tel. (7) 4729-8452; fax (7) 4729-8449; e-mail c.wilkinson@aims.gov.au; internet www.gcrmn.org; f. 1994, as an operating unit of the International Coral Reef Initiative; aims include improving the management and sustainable conservation of coral reefs, strengthening links between regional organizations and ecological and socioeconomic monitoring networks, and disseminating information to assist the formulation of conservation plans; Global Co-ordinator Dr CLIVE WILKINSON (Australia).

**International Coral Reef Initiative:** internet www.icriforum.org; f. 1994 at the first Conference of the Parties of the Convention on Biological Diversity; a partnership of governments, non-governmental organizations, scientific bodies and the private sector; aims to highlight the degradation of coral reefs and provide a focus for action to ensure the sustainable management and conservation of these and related marine ecosystems; in 1995 issued a Call to Action and a Framework for Action; Co-Chair. (2007–09) ROBERT GUDNEY (Mexico), STEPHANIE CASWELL (USA).

**IUCN—The World Conservation Union:** 28 rue Mauverney, 1196 Gland, Switzerland; tel. 229990000; fax 229990002; e-mail webmaster@iucn.org; internet www.iucn.org; f. 1948, as the International Union for Conservation of Nature and Natural Resources; supports partnerships and practical field activities to promote the conservation of natural resources, to secure the conservation of biological diversity as an essential foundation for the future; to ensure wise use of the earth's natural resources in an equitable and sustainable way; and to guide the development of human communities towards ways of life in enduring harmony with other components of the biosphere, developing programmes to protect and sustain the most important and threatened species and eco-systems and assisting governments to devise and carry out national conservation strategies; incorporates the Species Survival Commission (SSC), a science-based network of volunteer experts aiming to ensure conservation of present levels of biodiversity; compiles annually-updated Red List of Threatened Species, comprising in 2007 some 41,415 species, of which 16,306 were threatened with extinction and 65 only found in captivity or in cultivation; maintains a conservation library and documentation centre and units for monitoring traffic in wildlife; mems: more than 1,000 states, government agencies, non-governmental organizations and affiliates in some 140 countries; Pres. MOHAMMED VALLI MOOSA (South Africa); Dir-Gen. JULIA MARTON-LEFÈVRE (USA); publs *World Conservation Strategy*, *Caring for the Earth*, *Red List of Threatened Plants*, *Red List of Threatened Species*, *United Nations List of National Parks and Protected Areas*, *World Conservation* (quarterly), *IUCN Today*.

**South Asia Co-operative Environment Programme (SACEP):** 10 Anderson Rd, Colombo 05, Sri Lanka; tel. (11) 2589787; fax (11) 2589369; e-mail info@sacep.org; internet www.sacep.org; f. 1982; aims to promote regional co-operation in the protection and management of the environment, in particular in the context of sustainable economic and social development; works closely with governmental and non-governmental national, regional and international institutions in conservation and management efforts; Governing Council meets regularly; working to establish a South Asia Biodiversity Clearing House Mechanism; also actively developing specific projects: the conservation and integrated management of marine turtles and their habitats in the South Asia Seas region; reef-based corals management; accelerated penetration of cost effective renewable energy technologies; the establishment of a Basel Convention Sub-regional Centre for South Asia; protected areas management of world heritage sites and implementation of the Ramsar Strategic Plan at a sub-regional level; mems: Afghanistan, Bangladesh, Bhutan, India, Maldives, Nepal, Pakistan, Sri Lanka; Dir-Gen. Dr A. A. BOAZ; publs *SACEP Newsletter*, *South Asia Environmental and Education Action Plan*, other reports.

**World Ocean Observatory:** c/o Open Space Institute, 1350 Broadway, Rm 201, New York, NY 10018, USA; tel. (212) 356-4295; e-mail info@theW2O.net; internet www.thew2o.net; f. 2004; recommendation of the final report of the Independent World Commission on the Oceans; serves as a focal point for ocean-related information from governments, non-governmental organizations and other networks; aims to enhance public awareness of the importance of oceans and facilitate the dissemination of information; maintains an online radio station and organizes other online events; Dir PETER NEILL; publ. *World Ocean Observer* (monthly).

**WWF International:** 27 ave du Mont-Blanc, 1196 Gland, Switzerland; tel. 223649111; fax 223648836; e-mail info@wwfint.org; internet www.panda.org; f. 1961 (as World Wildlife Fund), name changed to World Wide Fund for Nature in 1986, current nomenclature adopted 2001; aims to stop the degradation of natural environments, conserve bio-diversity, ensure the sustainable use of renewable resources, and promote the reduction of both pollution and wasteful consumption; addresses six priority issues: forests, freshwater, marine, species, climate change, and toxics; has identified, and focuses its activities in, 200 'ecoregions' (the 'Global 200'), believed to contain the best part of the world's remaining biological diversity; actively supports and operates conservation programmes in more than 90 countries; mems: 54 offices, five associate orgs, c. 5m. individual mems world-wide; Pres. Chief EMEKA ANYAOKU (Nigeria); Dir-Gen. JAMES P. LEAPE; publs *Annual Report*, *Living Planet Report*.

## Government and Politics

**Afro-Asian Peoples' Solidarity Organization (AAPSO):** 89 Abdel Aziz Al-Saoud St, POB 11559-61 Manial El-Roda, Cairo, Egypt; tel. (2) 3636081; fax (2) 3637361; e-mail aapso@idsc.net.eg; internet www.aapso.fg2o.org; f. 1958; acts among and for the peoples of Africa and Asia in their struggle for genuine independence, sovereignty, socio-economic development, peace and disarmament; mems: national committees and affiliated organizations in 66 countries and territories, assoc. mems in 15 European countries; Sec.-Gen. NOURI ABDEL RAZZAK HUSSEIN (Iraq); publs *Solidarity Bulletin* (monthly), *Socio-Economic Development* (3 a year).

**Eastern Regional Organization for Public Administration (EROPA):** National College of Public Administration, Univ. of the Philippines, Diliman, Quezon City 1101, Philippines; tel. and fax (2)

9297789; e-mail eropa.secretariat@gmail.com; internet www.eropa.org.ph; f. 1960 to promote regional co-operation in improving knowledge, systems and practices of governmental administration, to help accelerate economic and social development; organizes regional conferences, seminars, special studies, surveys and training programmes; accredited, in 2000, as an online regional centre of the UN Public Administration Network for the Asia and Pacific region; there are three regional centres: Training Centre (New Delhi), Local Government Centre (Tokyo), Development Management Centre (Seoul); mems: 11 countries, 74 groups, 394 individuals; Sec.-Gen. PATRICIA A. STO TOMAS (Philippines); publs *EROPA Bulletin* (quarterly), *Asian Review of Public Administration* (2 a year).

**Global Elders:** POB 49785, London WC2H 7WQ, United Kingdom; e-mail info@theelders.org; internet www.theelders.org; f. 2001; aims to alleviate human suffering world-wide by offering a catalyst for the peaceful resolution of conflicts, seeking new approaches to unresolved global issues, and sharing wisdom; comprises: Kofi Annan (Ghana), Ela Bhatt (India), Lakhdar Brahimi (Algeria), Gro Brundtland (Norway), Jimmy Carter (USA), Fernando H Cardoso (Brazil), Graça Machel (Mozambique), Nelson Mandela (South Africa), Desmond Tutu (South Africa), Mary Robinson (Ireland), Aung San Suu Kyi (Myanmar), Muhammad Yunus (Bangladesh), Li Zhaoxing (People's Republic of China).

**Group of Eight (G8):** an informal meeting of developed nations, then comprising France, Germany, Italy, Japan, the USA and United Kingdom, first convened in Nov. 1975, at Rambouillet, France, at the level of heads of state and government; Canada became a permanent participant in 1976, forming the Group of Seven major industrialized countries—G7; from 1991 Russia was invited to participate in the then G7 summit outside the formal framework of co-operation; from 1994 Russia contributed more fully to the G7 political dialogue and from 1997 Russia became a participant in nearly all of the summit process scheduled meetings, excepting those related to finance and the global economy; from 1998 the name of the co-operation framework was changed to Group of Eight—G8, and since 2003 Russia has participated fully in all scheduled summit meetings, including those on the global economy; the European Union is also represented at G8 meetings, although it may not chair fora; G8 heads of government and the President of the European Commission and President of the European Council convene an annual summit meeting, the chairmanship and venue of which are rotated in the following order: France, USA, United Kingdom, Russia, Germany, Japan, Italy, Canada (2008: Hokkaido Toyako, Japan); G8 summit meetings address and seek consensus, published in a final declaration, on social and economic issues confronting the international community; the following ('+8') nations: Australia, Brazil, People's Republic of China, India, Indonesia, Mexico, Republic of Korea and South Africa were guest participants at the June 2008 G8 summit; G8 sectoral ministerial meetings (covering areas such as energy, environment, finance and foreign affairs) are held on the fringes of the annual summit, and further G8 sectoral ministerial meetings are convened through the year; mems: Canada, France, Germany, Italy, Japan, Russia, the USA and United Kingdom; European Union representation.

**Non-aligned Movement (NAM):** c/o Permanent Representative of Cuba to the UN, 315 Lexington Avenue, New York, NY 10016; tel. (212) 689-7215; fax (212) 779-1697; e-mail cuba@un.int; internet www.canada.cubanoal.cu; f. 1961 by a meeting of 25 Heads of State, with the aim of linking countries that had refused to adhere to the main East/West military and political blocs; co-ordination bureau established in 1973; works for the establishment of a new international economic order, and especially for better terms for countries producing raw materials; maintains special funds for agricultural development, improvement of food production and the financing of buffer stocks; South Commission promotes co-operation between developing countries; seeks changes in the United Nations to give developing countries greater decision-making power; holds summit conference every three years; 14th conference (September 2006): Havana, Cuba; mems: 118 countries.

## Industrial and Professional Relations

**International Trade Union Confederation-Asian Pacific (ITUC-AP):** One Marina Blvd, NTUC Centre, 9th Floor, Singapore 018989; tel. 63273590; fax 63273576; e-mail gs@ituc-ap.org; internet www.ituc-ap.org; f. 2007 by merger of ICFTU-APRO (f. 1951) and Brotherhood of Asian Trade Unionists (f. 1963); mems: 68 affiliate organizations in 29 countries; Pres. G. RAJASEKARAN (Malaysia); Gen. Sec. NORIYUKI SUZUKI (Japan); publs *Asian and Pacific Labour* (monthly), *ICFTU-APRO Labour Flash* (2 a week).

## Law

**Asian-African Legal Consultative Organization (AALCO):** E-66, Vasant Marg, Vasant Vihar, New Delhi 110057, India; tel. (11) 26152251; fax (11) 26152041; e-mail mail@aalco.int; internet www.aalco.int; f. 1956 to consider legal problems referred to it by member countries and to serve as a forum for Afro-Asian co-operation in international law, including international trade law, and economic relations; provides background material for conferences, prepares standard/model contract forms suited to the needs of the region; promotes arbitration as a means of settling international commercial disputes; trains officers of member states; has permanent UN observer status; has established four International Commercial Arbitration Centres in Kuala Lumpur, Malaysia, Cairo, Egypt, Lagos, Nigeria and Tehran, Iran; mems: 47 countries; Pres. BRIGITTE MABANDLA (South Africa); Sec.-Gen. Dr WAFIK ZAHER KAMIL (Egypt).

**Law Association for Asia and the Pacific (LAWASIA):** LAWASIA Secretariat, GPO Box 980, Brisbane, Qld 4001, Australia; tel. (7) 3222-5888; fax (7) 3222-5850; internet www.lawasia.asn.au; f. 1966; provides an international, professional network for lawyers to update, reform and develop law within the region; comprises six Sections and 21 Standing Committees in Business Law and General Practice areas, which organize speciality conferences; also holds a biennial conference (2007: Hong Kong); mems: national orgs in 23 countries; 1,500 mems in 55 countries; Pres. MAH WENG KWAI (Malaysia); publs *Directory* (annually), *Journal* (annually), *LAWASIA Update* (3 times a year: April, Aug., Dec.).

## Medicine and Health

**Asia-Pacific Academy of Ophthalmology (APAO):** c/o Dept of Ophthalmology and Visual Sciences, Chinese University of Hong Kong, 3/F 147 K Argyle St, Kowloon, Hong Kong; tel. 27623171; fax 27159490; e-mail secretariat@apaophth.org; internet www.apaophth.org; f. 1956; holds Congress annually since 2006 (previously every two years); mems: 17 mem. orgs; Pres. YASUO TANO; Sec.-Gen. DENNIS LAM.

**Asia Pacific Dental Federation (APDF):** c/o 242 Tanjong Katong Rd, Singapore 437030; tel. 6345-3125; fax 6344-2116; e-mail droliver@singnet.com.sg; internet www.apdf.info; f. 1955 to establish closer relationships among dental asscns in Asian and Pacific countries and to encourage research on dental health in the region; administers the International College of Continuing Dental Education (ICCDE); holds congress every year; mems: 27 national dental asscns; Pres. Dr ARIF R. ALVI; Sec.-Gen. Dr OLIVER HENNEDIGE.

**ICDDR, B: Centre for Health and Population Research:** GPO Box 128, Dhaka 1212, Bangladesh; tel. (2) 8860523; fax (2) 8823116; e-mail info@icddrb.org; internet www.icddrb.org; f. 1960 as Pakistan-SEATO Cholera Research Laboratory, international health research institute (International Centre for Diarrhoeal Disease Research, Bangladesh—ICDDR, B since 1978; undertakes research, training and information dissemination on diarrhoeal diseases, child health, nutrition, emerging infectious diseases, environmental health, sexually transmitted diseases, HIV/AIDS, poverty and health, vaccine evaluation and case management, with particular reference to developing countries; supported by 55 governments and international orgs; Exec. Dir Prof. DAVID A. SACK; publs *Annual Report*, *Journal of Health, Population and Nutrition* (quarterly), *Glimpse* (quarterly), *Shasthya Sanglap* (3 a year), *Health and Science Bulletin* (quarterly), *SUZY* (newsletter, 2 a year), scientific reports, working papers, monographs, special publications.

**International Association for the Study of Obesity (IASO):** 231 North Gower St, London, NW1 2NR, United Kingdom; e-mail enquiries@iaso.org; internet www.iaso.org; f. 1986; supports research into the prevention and management of obesity throughout the world and disseminates inormation regarding disease and accompanying health and social issues; incorporates the International Obesity Task Force; international congress every four years (2006: Sydney, Australia); Exec. Dir CAROLINE SMALL.

## Posts and Telecommunications

**Asia-Pacific Telecommunity (APT):** No. 12/49, Soi 5, Chaengwattana Rd, Thungsonghong, Bangkok 10210, Thailand; tel. (2) 573-0044; fax (2) 573-7479; e-mail aptmail@apt.org; internet www.apt.org; f. 1979 to cover all matters relating to telecommunications in the region; serves as the focal organization for ICT in the Asia-Pacific region; contributes, through its various programmes and activities, to the growth of the ICT sector in the region and assists members in their preparation for global telecommunications conferences, as well as promoting regional harmonization for such events; mems: Afghanistan, Australia, Bangladesh, Bhutan, Brunei, People's Republic of China, Fiji, India, Indonesia, Iran, Japan, Korea, Democratic Republic of Korea, Republic of Korea, Laos, Malaysia, Maldives, Marshall Islands, Federated States of Micronesia, Mongolia, Myanmar, Nauru, Nepal, New Zealand, Pakistan, Palau, Papua New Guinea, Philippines, Samoa, Singapore, Sri Lanka, Thailand, Tonga, Viet Nam; assoc. mems: Republic of China, Cook Islands, Hong Kong, Macao, Niue; 101 affiliated mems; Exec. Dir AMARENDRA NARAYAN.

**Asian-Pacific Postal Union:** APPU Bureau, POB 1, Laksi Post Office, 111 Chaeng Wattana Rd, Bangkok 10210, Thailand; tel. (2) 573-7282; fax (2) 573-1161; e-mail admin@appu-bureau.org; internet www.appu-bureau.org; f. 1962 to extend, facilitate and improve the postal relations between the member countries and to promote co-operation in the field of postal services; holds Congress every five years; mems: postal administrations in 30 countries; Dir SOMCHAI REOPANICHKUL; publs *Annual Report*, *Exchange Program of Postal Officials*, *APPU Newsletter*.

## Press, Radio and Television

**Asia-Pacific Broadcasting Union (ABU):** POB 1164, 59700 Kuala Lumpur, Malaysia; tel. (3) 22823592; fax (3) 22844382; e-mail info@abu.org.my; internet www.abu.org.my; f. 1964 to foster and co-ordinate the development of broadcasting in the Asia-Pacific area, to develop means of establishing closer collaboration and co-operation among broadcasting orgs, and to serve the professional needs of broadcasters in Asia and the Pacific; holds annual General Assembly; mems: 194 in 54 countries and territories; Pres. ABDUL RAHMAN HAMID (Malaysia) (acting); Sec.-Gen. DAVID ASTLEY (Australia); publs *ABU News* (every 2 months), *ABU Technical Review* (every 2 months).

**Organization of Asia-Pacific News Agencies (OANA):** c/o Bernama News Agency, 38 Jalan 1/65A, 50400 Kuala Lumpur, Malaysia; tel. (3) 26939933; fax (3) 26981102; internet www.oananews.org; f. 1961 to promote co-operation in professional matters and mutual exchange of news, features, etc. among the news agencies of Asia and the Pacific via the Asia-Pacific News Network (ANN); 13th General Assembly: Bangkok, Thailand, 2007; mems: 40 news agencies in 33 countries; Pres. SYED JAMIL JAAFAR (Malaysia); Sec.-Gen. AZMAN UJANG.

**Press Foundation of Asia:** POB 1843, S & L Bldg, 3rd Floor, 1500 Roxas Blvd, Manila, Philippines; tel. (2) 5233223; fax (2) 5224365; e-mail pfa@pressasia.org; f. 1967; an independent, non-profit-making organization governed by its newspaper members; acts as a professional forum for about 200 newspapers in Asia; aims to reduce cost of newspapers to potential readers, to improve editorial and management techniques through research and training programmes and to encourage the growth of the Asian press; operates *Depthnews* feature service; mems: 200 newspapers; Exec. Chair. MAZLAN NORDIN (Malaysia); Chief Exec. MOCHTAR LUBIS (Indonesia); publs *Pressasia* (quarterly), *Asian Women* (quarterly).

## Religion

**Christian Conference of Asia (CCA):** c/o Payap Univ. Muang, Chiang Mai 50000, Thailand; tel. (53) 243906; fax (53) 247303; e-mail cca@cca.org.hk; internet www.cca.org.hk; f. 1957 (present name adopted 1973) to promote co-operation and joint study in matters of common concern among the Churches of the region and to encourage interaction with other regional Conferences and the World Council of Churches; planned relocation to Chiang Mai, Thailand, pending; mems: more than 100 churches and councils of churches from 18 Asian countries; Gen. Sec. Dr PRAWATE KHID-ARN; publ. *CCA News* (quarterly).

**Muslim World League (MWL)** (Rabitat al-Alam al-Islami): POB 537, Makkah, Saudi Arabia; tel. (2) 5600919; fax (2) 5601319; e-mail info@themwl.org; internet www.themwl.org; f. 1962; aims to advance Islamic unity and solidarity, and to promote world peace and respect for human rights; provides financial assistance for education, medical care and relief work; has 45 offices throughout the world; Sec.-Gen. Prof. Dr ABDULLAH BIN ABDUL MOHSIN AL-TURKI; publs *Al-Aalam al Islami* (weekly, Arabic), *Dawat al-Haq* (monthly, Arabic), *Muslim World League Journal* (monthly, English), *Muslim World League Journal* (quarterly, Arabic).

**Theosophical Society:** Adyar, Chennai 600 020, India; tel. (44) 24915552; fax (44) 4902706; e-mail intl.hq@ts-adyar.org; internet www.ts-adyar.org; f. 1875; aims at universal brotherhood, without distinction of race, creed, sex, caste or colour; study of comparative religion, philosophy and science; investigation of unexplained laws of nature and powers latent in man; mems: 32,000 in 70 countries; Pres. RADHA S. BURNIER; Int. Sec. MARY ANDERSON; publs *The Theosophist* (monthly), *Adyar News Letter* (quarterly), *Brahmavidya* (annually).

**World Fellowship of Buddhists:** 616 Benjasiri Pk, Soi Medhinivet off Soi Sukhumvit 24, Bangkok 10110, Thailand; tel. (2) 661-1284; fax (2) 661-0555; e-mail wfb-hq@asianet.co.th; internet www.wfb-hq.org; f. 1950 to promote strict observance and practice of the teachings of the Buddha; holds General Conference every 2 years; 146 regional centres in 37 countries; Pres. PHAN WANNAMETHEE; Hon. Sec.-Gen. PHALLOP THAIARRY; publs *WFB Journal* (6 a year), *WFB Review* (quarterly), *WFB Newsletter* (monthly), documents, booklets.

**World Hindu Federation:** c/o Dr Jogendra Jha, Pashupati Kshetra, Kathmandu, Nepal; tel. (1) 470182; fax (1) 470131; e-mail hem@karki.com.np; f. 1981 to promote and preserve Hindu philosophy and culture and to protect the rights of Hindus, particularly the right to worship; executive board meets annually; mems: in 45 countries and territories; Sec.-Gen. Dr JOGENDRA JHA (Nepal); publ. *Vishwa Hindu* (monthly).

## Science

**Federation of Asian Scientific Academies and Societies (FASAS):** c/o Academy of Sciences Malaysia, 902 Jalan Tun Ismail, 50480 Kuala Lumpur, Malaysia; tel. (3) 26949898; fax (3) 26945858; e-mail admin@akademisains.gov.my; internet www.fasas.com.my; f. 1984 to stimulate regional co-operation and promote national and regional self-reliance in science and technology, by organizing meetings, training and research programmes and encouraging the exchange of scientists and of scientific information; mems: 16 national scientific academies and societies from Afghanistan, Australia, Bangladesh, People's Republic of China, India, Republic of Korea, Malaysia, Nepal, New Zealand, Pakistan, Philippines, Singapore, Sri Lanka, Thailand; Pres. Tan Sri Datuk Dr OMAR ABDUL RAHMAN (Malaysia); Sec. Dato' IR LEE YEE CHEONG (Malaysia).

**International Council for Science (ICSU):** 51 blvd de Montmorency, 75016 Paris, France; tel. 1-45-25-03-29; fax 1-42-88-94-31; e-mail secretariat@icsu.org; internet www.icsu.org; f. 1919 as International Research Council; present name adopted 1931; new statutes adopted 1996; to co-ordinate international co-operation in theoretical and applied sciences and to promote national scientific research through the intermediary of affiliated national organizations; General Assembly of representatives of national and scientific members meets every three years to formulate policy. The following committees have been established: Cttee on Science for Food Security, Scientific Cttee on Antarctic Research, Scientific Cttee on Oceanic Research, Cttee on Space Research, Scientific Cttee on Water Research, Scientific Cttee on Solar-Terrestrial Physics, Cttee on Science and Technology in Developing Countries, Cttee on Data for Science and Technology, Programme on Capacity Building in Science, Scientific Cttee on Problems of the Environment, Steering Cttee on Genetics and Biotechnology and Scientific Cttee on International Geosphere-Biosphere Programme. The following services and Inter-Union Committees and Commissions have been established: Federation of Astronomical and Geophysical Data Analysis Services, Inter-Union Commission on Frequency Allocations for Radio Astronomy and Space Science, Inter-Union Commission on Radio Meteorology, Inter-Union Commission on Spectroscopy, Inter-Union Commission on Lithosphere; national mems: academies or research councils in 98 countries; Scientific mems and assocs: 105 nat. scientific bodies and 29 int. scientific unions; Pres. GOVERDHAN MEHTA; Exec. Sec. THOMAS ROSSWALL; publs *ICSU Yearbook*, *Science International* (quarterly), *Annual Report*.

## Social Sciences

**Eastern Regional Organisation for Planning and Housing:** POB 10867, 50726 Kuala Lumpur, Malaysia; tel. (3) 20925217; fax (3) 20924217; e-mail info@earoph.net; internet www.earoph.net; f. 1958 to promote and co-ordinate the study and practice of housing and regional town and country planning; maintains offices in Japan, India and Indonesia; mems: 57 organizations and 213 individuals in 28 countries; Pres. CANDY BROAD (Australia); Sec.-Gen. KHAIRIAH TALHA; publs *EAROPH News and Notes* (monthly), *Town and Country Planning* (bibliography).

**International Peace Institute:** 777 United Nations Plaza, New York, NY 10017-3521, USA; tel. (212) 687-4300; fax (212) 983-8246; e-mail ipi@ipinst.org; internet www.ipacademy.org; f. 1970 (as the International Peace Academy) to promote the prevention and settlement of armed conflicts between and within states through policy research and development; educates government officials in the procedures needed for conflict resolution, peace-keeping, mediation and negotiation, through international training seminars and publications; off-the-record meetings are also conducted to gain complete understanding of a specific conflict; Chair. RITA E. HAUSER; Pres. TERJE ROD-LARSEN.

**International Union for Oriental and Asian Studies:** Közraktar u. 12A 11/2, 1093 Budapest, Hungary; f. 1951 by the 22nd International Congress of Orientalists (now the International Congress of Asian and North African Studies) under the auspices of UNESCO, to promote contacts between orientalists throughout the world, and to organize congresses, research and publications; mems: in 24 countries; Pres. Prof. GEORG HAZAI; publs *Philologiae Turcicae Fundamenta*, *Materalien zum Sumerischen Lexikon*, *Sanskrit Dictionary*, *Corpus Inscriptionum Iranicarum*, *Linguistic Atlas of Iran*, *Matériels des parlers iraniens*, *Turcology Annual*, *Bibliographieegyptologique*.

## Social Welfare and Human Rights

**Global Humanitarian Forum:** 9 ave de la Paix, 1202 Geneva, Switzerland; tel. 229197500; fax 229197519; e-mail ghf-geneva@ghf-geneva.org; internet www./www.ghf-geneva.org; f. 2007 to support dialogue and encourage partnerships to focus international attention on and generate increased investment towards addressing key humanitarian concerns; also seeks to place international migration issues on the global agenda; CEO WALTER FUST (Switzerland).

**Global Migration Group (GMG):** 2003, as the Geneva Migration Group; renamed as above in 2006; mems: ILO, IOM, UNCTAD, UNDP, United Nations Department of Economic and Social Affairs (UNDESA), UNFPA, OHCHR, UNHCR, UNODC, and the World Bank; holds regular meetings to discuss issues relating to int. migration, chaired by mem. orgs on a six-month rotational basis.

**International Federation of Red Cross and Red Crescent Societies:** 17 chemin des Crêts, Petit-Saconnex, CP 372, 1211 Geneva 19, Switzerland; tel. 227304222; fax 227330395; e-mail secretariat@ifrc.org; internet www.ifrc.org; f. 1919 to prevent and alleviate human suffering and to promote humanitarian activities by national Red Cross and Red Crescent societies; conducts relief operations for refugees and victims of disasters, co-ordinates relief supplies and assists in disaster prevention; Pres. JUAN MANUEL SUÁREZ DEL TORO RIVERO (Spain); Sec.-Gen. MARKKU NISKALA (Finland); publs *Annual Report*, *Red Cross Red Crescent* (quarterly), *Weekly News*, *World Disasters Report*, *Emergency Appeal*.

**International Organization for Migration (IOM):** 17 route des Morillons, CP 71, 1211 Geneva 19, Switzerland; tel. 227179111; fax 227986150; e-mail info@iom.int; internet www.iom.int; f. 1951 as Intergovernmental Committee for Migration; name changed in 1989; a non-political and humanitarian organization, activities include the handling of orderly, planned migration to meet the needs of emigration and immigration countries and the processing and movement of refugees, displaced persons etc. in need of international migration services; mems: 120 states; observer status is held by 20 states and 71 intergovernmental and non-governmental organizations; Dir-Gen. BRUNSON MCKINLEY (USA); publs include *International Migration* (quarterly), *Migration* (quarterly, in English, French and Spanish), *World Migration Report* (every 2 years, in English).

**Médecins sans frontières (MSF):** 78 rue de Lausanne, CP 116, 1211 Geneva 21, Switzerland; tel. 228498400; fax 228498404; internet www.msf.org; f. 1971; independent medical humanitarian org. composed of physicians and other members of the medical profession; aims to provide medical assistance to victims of war and natural disasters; operates longer-term programmes of nutrition, immunization, sanitation, public health, and rehabilitation of hospitals and dispensaries; awarded the Nobel peace prize in 1999; mems: national sections in 21 countries in Europe, Asia and North America; Pres. Dr CHRISTOPHE FOURNIER; publ. *Activity Report* (annually).

**World Social Forum (WSF):** Support Office: Rua General Jardim 660, 7th Floor, São Paulo, Brazil 01223-010; e-mail forumsocialmundial.org.br; internet www.forumsocialmundial.org; f. 2001 as an annual global meeting of civil society bodies; the first WSF was held in Porto Alegre, Brazil, in Jan. 2001; a Charter of Principles was adopted in June 2002; the WSF is a permanent global process which aims to pursue alternatives to neo-liberal policies and commercial globalization; its objectives include the development and promotion of democratic international systems and institutions serving social justice, equality and the sovereignty of peoples, based on respect for the universal human rights of citizens of all nations and for the environment; the sixth (2006) Forum was polycentric, held in Bamako (Mali), Caracas (Venezuela), and Karachi (Pakistan), and the seventh (2007) Forum was convened in Nairobi, Kenya; an International Council, comprising 129 civil society organizations and commissions, guides the Forum and considers general political questions and methodology; the Support Office in São Paulo, Brazil, provides administrative assistance to the Forum process, to the International Council and to the specific organizing committees for each annual event; mems: civil society organizations and movements world-wide.

## Tourism

**Pacific Asia Travel Association (PATA):** Unit B1, 28th Floor, Siam Tower, 989 Rama 1 Rd, Pratumwan, Bangkok 10330, Thailand; tel. (2) 658-2000; fax (2) 658-2010; e-mail patabkk@pata.org; internet www.pata.org; f. 1951; aims to enhance the growth, value and quality of Pacific Asia travel and tourism for the benefit of PATA members; holds annual conference and travel fair; divisional offices in Germany (Frankfurt), Australia (Sydney), USA (Oakland, CA) and the People's Republic of China (Beijing); mems: more than 1,200 governments, carriers, tour operators, travel agents and hotels; Pres.and CEO PETER DE JONG (Netherlands); Sec. and Treas. HIRAN COORAY (Sri Lanka); publs *PATA Compass* (every 2 months), *Statistical Report* (quarterly), *Forecasts Book*, research reports, directories, newsletters.

## Trade and Industry

**Asian Productivity Organization:** Hirakawacho Daiichi Seimei Bldg 2F, 1-2-10 Hirakawa-cho, Chiyoda-ku, Tokyo 102–0093, Japan; tel. (3) 5226-3920; fax (3) 5226-3950; e-mail apo@apo-tokyo.org; internet www.apo-tokyo.org; f. 1961 as non-political, non-profit making, non-discriminatory regional intergovernmental organization with the aim of contributing to the socio-economic development of Asia and the Pacific through productivity promotion; activities cover industry, agriculture and service sectors, with the primary focus on human resources development; five key areas are incorporated into its activities: knowledge management, green productivity, strengthening small and medium enterprises, integrated community development and development of national productivity organizations; serves its members as a think tank, catalyst, regional adviser, institution builder and clearing house; mems: 20 countries; Sec.-Gen. SHIGEO TAKENAKA; publs *APO News* (monthly), *Annual Report*, *APO Asia-Pacific Productivity Data and Analysis*, other books and monographs.

**Confederation of Asia-Pacific Chambers of Commerce and Industry (CACCI):** 13th Floor, 3 Sungshou Rd, Taipei 110, Taiwan; tel. (2) 27255663; fax (2) 27255665; e-mail cacci@ttn.net; internet www.cacci.org.tw; f. 1966; holds biennial conferences to examine regional co-operation, and an annual Council meeting; liaises with governments to promote laws conducive to regional co-operation; serves as a centre for compiling and disseminating trade and business information; encourages contacts between businesses; conducts training and research; mems: 26 national chambers of commerce and industry the region, also affiliate and special mems; Pres. HARVEY CHANG; Dir-Gen. Dr WEBSTER KIANG; publs *CACCI Profile* (monthly), *CACCI Journal of Commerce and Industry* (2 a year).

## Transport

**Association of Asia Pacific Airlines:** Kompleks Antarabangsa, 9th Floor, Jalan Sultan Ismail, 50250 Kuala Lumpur, Malaysia; tel. (3) 21455600; fax (3) 21452500; e-mail aapahdq@aapa.org.my; internet www.aapairlines.org; f. 1966 as Orient Airlines Asscn; present name adopted in 1997; as the trade association of the region's airlines, the AAPA aims to represent their interests and to provide a forum for all members to exchange information and views on matters of common concern; maintains international representation in Brussels, Belgium, and in Washington, DC, USA; mems: 17 scheduled international airlines (carrying approx. one-fifth of global passenger traffic and one-third of global cargo traffic); Dir-Gen. ANDREW J. HERDMAN; publs *Annual Report*, *Annual Statistical Report*, *Monthly International Statistics*, *Orient Aviation* (10 a year).

## Youth and Students

**Asia Students Association:** 353 Shanghai St, 14/F, Kowloon, Hong Kong; tel. 23880515; fax 27825535; e-mail asasec@netvigator.com; f. 1969; aims to promote students' solidarity in struggling for democracy, self-determination, peace, justice and liberation; conducts campaigns, training of activists, and workshops on human rights and other issues of importance; there are Student Commissions for Peace, Education and Human Rights; mems: 40 national or regional student unions in 25 countries and territories; Secretariat LINA CABAERO (Philippines), STEVEN GAN (Malaysia), CHOW WING-HANG (Hong Kong); publs *Movement News* (monthly), *ASA News* (quarterly).

**WFUNA Youth:** c/o WFUNA, 1 United Nations Plaza, Room DC1-1177, New York, NY 10017, USA; tel. (212) 963-5610; fax (212) 963-0447; e-mail coordinating.committee@qmail.com; internet www.wfuna-youth.org; f. 1948 by the World Federation of United Nations Associations (WFUNA) as the International Youth and Student Movement for the United Nations (ISMUN), independent since 1949; an international non-governmental organization of students and young people dedicated especially to supporting the principles embodied in the United Nations Charter and Universal Declaration of Human Rights; encourages constructive action in building economic, social and cultural equality and in working for national independence, social justice and human rights on a world-wide scale; maintains regional offices in Austria, France, Ghana, Panama and the USA; mems: asscns in over 100 mem. states of the UN.

**World Alliance of Young Men's Christian Associations:** 12 Clos. Belmont, 1208 Geneva, Switzerland; tel. 228495100; fax 228495110; e-mail office@ymca.int; internet www.ymca.int; f. 1855; mems: federation of YMCAs in 124 countries with a membership of over 45 m.; Pres. MARTIN MEIßNER (Germany) (2006–10); Sec.-Gen. Dr BARTHOLOMEW SHAHA; publ. *YMCA World* (quarterly).

# MAJOR COMMODITIES OF SOUTH ASIA

Note: For each of the commodities in this section, there is a statistical table relating to recent levels of production. Each production table shows estimates of output for the world and for South Asia. In addition, the table lists the main producing countries of South Asia and, for comparison, the leading producers from outside the region.

## ALUMINIUM AND BAUXITE

Aluminium is the second most abundant metallic element in the earth's crust after silicon, comprising about 8% of the total. However, it is much less widely used than steel, despite having about the same strength and only half the weight. Aluminium has important applications as a metal because of its lightness, ease of fabrication and other desirable properties. Other products of alumina (aluminium oxide trihydrate, into which bauxite, the commonest aluminium ore, is refined) are materials in refractories, abrasives, glass manufacture, other ceramic products, catalysts and absorbers. Alumina hydrates are used for the production of aluminium chemicals, fire retardant in carpet-backing, and industrial fillers in plastics and related products.

The major markets for aluminium are in transportation, building and construction, electrical machinery and equipment, consumer durables and the packaging industry. Transportation was estimated to have accounted for fractionally more than one-third and containers and packaging for about 20% of all US and Canadian aluminium end-use in 2006. Although the production of aluminium is energy-intensive, its light weight results in a net saving, particularly in the transportation industry, where the use of the metal as a substitute for steel, in particular in the manufacture of road motor vehicles and components, is well established. In the early 1990s steel substitution accounted for about 16% of world aluminium consumption, and it has been forecast that aluminium demand by the motor vehicle industry alone could more than double, to exceed 5.7m. metric tons in 2010, compared with around 2.4m. tons in 1990. Aluminium is valued by the aerospace industry for its weight-saving characteristics and for its low cost relative to alternative materials. Aluminium-lithium alloys command considerable potential for use in this sector, although the traditional dominance of aluminium in the aerospace industry has been challenged since the 1990s by 'composites' such as carbonepoxy, a fusion of carbon fibres and hardened resins, the lightness and durability of which can exceed that of many aluminium alloys.

World markets for finished and semi-finished aluminium products were, until the early 2000s, dominated by six Western producers—Alcan (Canada), Alcoa, Reynolds, Kaiser (all USA), Pechiney (France) and algroup (Switzerland). Proposals for a merger between Alcan, algroup and Pechiney, and between Alcoa and Reynolds, were announced in August 1999. However, the proposed terms of the Pechiney-Alcan-algroup merger encountered opposition from the European Commission, on the grounds that the combined grouping could restrict market competition and adversely affect the interests of consumers. The tripartite merger plan was abandoned in April 2000, in favour of a merger between Alcan and algroup, which was effected in October. The amalgamation of Alcoa and Reynolds was approved by the European Commission and the US Government in May 2000. In 2003, having agreed to meet conditions imposed by the European Commission and the US Department of Justice in respect of safeguarding free competition, Alcan was permitted to purchase Pechiney. One of the most significant stipulations regarding Alcan's purchase of Pechiney was a requirement that it divest some of its rolled aluminium products assets. In late 2004, as a consequence of this divestment, a new rolled aluminium products group, Novelis, was emerging. In 2002, after the purchase of Germany's VAW, Norway's Norsk Hydro became the world's third largest integrated aluminium concern. Prior to the mergers detailed above the level of dominance of the six major Western producers had been reduced by a significant geographical shift in the location of alumina and aluminium production to countries where cheap power is available, such as Australia, Brazil, Norway, Canada and Venezuela. The Gulf states of Bahrain and Dubai (United Arab Emirates), with the advantage of low energy costs, also produce primary aluminium. Since the mid-1990s Russia has emerged as a significant force in the world aluminium market (see below), and in 2000 the country's three principal producers, together with a number of plants located in the Commonwealth of Independent States, joined together to form the Russian Aluminium Co (RUSAL). In March 2007 United Company RUSAL was formed by RUSAL's merger with Russia's second largest aluminium producer, Siberian-Urals Aluminium Company (SUAL), and the alumina assets of Switzerland's Glencore International AG. In mid-2008 United Company RUSAL claimed to be the world's largest aluminium company, accounting for almost 12% of world output of primary aluminium and 15% of global alumina production. In late 2007 the multinational mining concern Rio Tinto purchased Canada's Alcan Inc.—like RUSAL Rio Tinto Alcan, as the Rio Tinto division formed by the purchase was named, also claims to be the world's biggest aluminium company. In February 2008 China's principal aluminium producer, Aluminium Corpn of China (Chinalco), and US Alcoa jointly purchased a 12% stake in Rio Tinto in a move that was perceived as intended to obstruct an attempt by the Anglo-Australian mining company BHP Billiton to take over Rio Tinto, although Chinalco and Alcoa indicated that they had no immediate intentions to attempt to take over Rio Tinto themselves. According to observers, a merger of BHP Billiton and Rio Tinto would give the resulting company a high degree of control across a wide range of mineral commodities, including aluminium.

Bauxite is the principal aluminium ore, but nepheline syenite, kaolin, shale, anorthosite and alunite are all potential alternative sources of alumina, although not currently economic to process. Of all bauxite mined, approximately 85% is converted to alumina ($Al_2O_3$) for the production of aluminium metal. The developing countries, in which at least 70% of known bauxite reserves are located, supply some 50% of the ore required. The industry is structured in three stages: bauxite mining, alumina refining and smelting. While the high degree of 'vertical integration' (i.e. the control of successive stages of production) in the industry means that a significant proportion of trade in bauxite and alumina is in the form of intra-company transfers, and the increasing tendency to site alumina refineries near to bauxite deposits has resulted in a shrinking bauxite trade, there is a growing free market in alumina, serving the needs of the increasing number of independent (i.e. non-integrated) smelters.

The alumina is separated from the ore by the Bayer process. After mining, bauxite is fed direct to process if mine-run material is adequate (as in Jamaica), or else it is crushed and beneficiated. Where the ore 'as mined' presents handling problems, or weight-reduction is desirable, it may be dried prior to shipment.

At the alumina plant the ore is slurried with spent-liquor direct, if the soft Caribbean type is used, or, in the case of other types, it is ball-milled to reduce it to a size that will facilitate the extraction of the alumina. The bauxite slurry is then digested with caustic soda to extract the alumina from the ore while leaving the impurities as an insoluble residue. The digest conditions depend on the aluminium minerals in the ore and the impurities. The liquor, with the dissolved alumina, is then separated from the insoluble impurities by combinations of sedimentation, decantation and filtration, and the residue washed to minimize the soda losses. The clarified liquor is concentrated and the alumina precipitated by seeding with hydrate. The precipitated alumina is then filtered, washed and calcined to produce alumina. The ratio of bauxite to alumina is approximately 1.95:1.

The smelting of the aluminium is generally by electrolysis in molten cryolite. Because of the high consumption of electricity by this process, alumina is usually smelted in areas where low-cost electricity is available. However, most of the electricity now used in primary smelting in the Western world is generated by hydroelectricity—a renewable energy source.

The recycling of aluminium is economically (as well as environmentally) desirable, as the process uses only 5% of the electricity required to produce a similar quantity of primary aluminium. Aluminium that has been recycled from scrap currently accounts for approximately 30% of the total annual world output of primary aluminium. With the added impetus of environmental concerns, considerable growth occurred world-wide in the recycling of used beverage cans (UBC) during the 1990s. In the middle of that decade, according to aluminium industry estimates, the recycling rate of UBC amounted to at least 55% world-wide. In the USA in 2004 a UBC recycling rate of 51.2% was reported, while in Brazil in 2006, according to the Associação Brasileira do Alumínio and the Associação Brasileira dos Fabricantes de Latas de Alta Reciclabilidade, 95% of all aluminium cans sold were recycled—a rate equivalent to 139,000 metric tons of metal, or 10,300m. individual cans. The International Aluminium Institute (IAI) stated in 2007 that more than 63% of global aluminium beverage cans were being recycled, making this the world's most recycled container.

In 2007, according to the International Aluminium Institute (IAI), world output of primary aluminium totalled an estimated 37.4m. metric tons, of which Asian producers accounted for about 16.3m. tons. The USA normally accounts for more than one-quarter of total aluminium consumption (excluding communist and former communist countries). The USA was for long the world's principal producing country, but in 2001 US output of primary aluminium was surpassed by that of Russia and the People's Republic of China. In 2002–06 Canadian production, in addition to that of Russia and China, also exceeded that of the USA. In 2007, according to the World Bureau of Metal Statistics (WBMS), production of primary aluminium by China was estimated to have been almost five times that of the USA. Chinese production was also anticipated to expand by a greater rate than that of the USA in 2008.

Aluminium consumption has been advancing significantly in India in recent years. India has the world's fifth largest bauxite reserves, estimated to be at least 770m. metric tons in 2007. Indian bauxite is of high quality (about 90% metallurgical grade), and production has generally increased in recent years. India's estimated output of alumina, however, fell from 2.8m. tons in 2002 to 2.5m. tons in 2003. Production recovered slowly thereafter, reaching 2.6m. tons in 2004, 2.7m. tons in 2005, and 2.8m. tons once again in 2006. About 60% of the country's recoverable bauxite is in the eastern state of Orissa, and this is complemented by large reserves of high-quality ore in Gujarat and Maharashtra. In 2003, according to the US Geological Survey (USGS), five companies were engaged in the production of alumina and aluminium: Bharat Aluminium Co Ltd (BALCO), Hindalco Industries Ltd, Indian Aluminium Co Ltd (INDAL), Madras Aluminium Co Ltd (MALCO) and National Aluminium Co Ltd (NALCO). Hindalco, INDAL and MALCO were all private companies. The combined annual production capacities of all of the above companies for alumina and aluminium in 2003 were, respectively, some 2.5m. tons and 714,000 tons. These have subsequently been boosted by the partial completion of a smelter expansion programme by Hindalco. In 2004 it was reported that Sterlite Industries Ltd planned to invest US $2,000m. in the expansion of its aluminium operations in Orissa state. Following protracted legal proceedings related to the environmental and social impact of its project to mine bauxite at Lanjigarh, in August 2008 Vedanta Resources, of which Sterlite is a subsidiary, announced that the Supreme Court of India had approved the scheme. Vedanta, meanwhile completed the construction of an alumina refinery at Lanjigarh, with eventual production, supplying BALCO and other domestic users, projected to reach 1.4m. tons per year,. A further alumina refinery project in Orissa, that of Utkal Alumina International Ltd, has also been subject to lengthy delay because of concerns regarding the social and environmental impact on the local community. Hindalco became the sole operator of the project in 2007, following the withdrawal of Alcan. In 2007 Vedanta Resources announced plans to expand facilities at the BALCO aluminium plant in the Korba region of Chhattisgarh. The development of a new smelter at this site was expected to increase capacity by around 650,000 tons, thereby making Korba the only plant in the world to supply aluminium in excess of 1m. tons per year. Since the inadequacy of existing electrical power supply had at times hampered aluminium production, Vedanta was to construct a power plant near the site of the new smelter, with a projected output of 540 MW per year. India was reported to have exported more than 2m. tons of metallurgical-grade bauxite in 2002, and was forecast to export as much as 4m. tons in 2004.

**Production of Bauxite**
(crude ore, '000 metric tons)

| | 2006 | 2007* |
|---|---|---|
| **World total** (excl. USA)* | 178,000 | 190,000 |
| South Asia* | 12,700 | 13,000 |
| **Leading regional producer** | | |
| India | 12,700 | 13,000 |
| **Other leading producers** | | |
| Australia | 62,300 | 64,000 |
| Brazil | 21,000 | 24,000 |
| China, People's Repub. | 21,000 | 32,000 |
| Greece | 2,450 | 2,400 |
| Guinea† | 14,500 | 14,000 |
| Guyana† | 1,400 | 2,000 |
| Jamaica† | 14,900 | 14,000 |
| Kazakhstan | 4,800 | 4,900 |
| Russia | 6,600 | 6,000 |
| Suriname | 4,920 | 5,000 |
| Venezuela | 5,500 | 5,500 |

* Estimated production.
† Dried equivalent of crude ore.
Source: US Geological Survey.

On 2 January 2004 the London quotation for primary aluminium closed at US $1,600 per metric ton, the first time the quotation had reached that level since February 2001. On 30 January a closing price of $1,636.5 per ton was recorded. The London quotation strengthened further in February, closing at $1,754 per ton on 18 February, but thereafter declined somewhat to end the month at $1,702 per ton. The London price remained above $1,625 per ton throughout March, ending the month at $1,688.5 per ton. Sharp increases occurred from early April, and on 16 April a closing price greater than $1,800 per ton ($1,802) was recorded. Prices in April rose to their highest levels for more than eight years. By 10 May, however, the quotation had fallen to $1,575 per ton. On 2 June a closing price of $1,703.5 was recorded, rising to $1,721 per ton on 21 June. Stocks of aluminium held by the London Metal Exchange (LME) rose as high as 1,453,125 tons in January. From February until the end of June, however, they declined steadily. At the end of February they totalled 1,393,675 tons, but stocks had fallen to 940,200 tons by the end of June. For the whole of 2004 the average quotation for primary aluminium traded on the LME was $1,717 per ton, 19.9% higher than the average price recorded in 2003. The higher price in 2004 was attributed to a substantial increase in global demand for aluminium, in particular from China, that had outstripped, and led to a heavy fall in, world inventories: the global market was in deficit for the first time since 2000. Growth in demand world-wide from the aerospace and automotive sectors was especially strong in 2004. Aluminium also benefited, in the early part of the year, from even sharper increases in the prices of those metals, such as copper and steel, for which it can be substituted. At the end of 2004 stocks of aluminium held by the LME, at 692,775 tons, were more than 50% lower than at the end of 2003.

In 2005, the average price of aluminium traded on the LME, at US $1,898 per metric ton, was 10.6% higher than in 2004. During the year aluminium traded within a range of $1,675–$2,289 per ton. Stocks of metal held by the Exchange declined steadily during the first half of 2005, from 654,025 tons at the end of January to 535,525 tons at 30 June. By December 2005, however, inventories had recovered to 643,700 tons.

At US $2,567 per metric ton, the average price of aluminium traded on the LME in 2006 was 35.2% higher than that recorded in 2005. During the year the metal traded within a range of $2,267–$3,275 per ton. Generally, stocks of aluminium held by the LME rose in the first half of 2006, reaching 710,075 tons at the end of January and 779,100 tons at the end of March. At the end of June inventories totalled 760,900 tons. In the second half of the year, however, stocks declined steadily in September–November, before rising in December to total 698,425 tons. Key market influences 2006 were increased Chinese consumption and the renewed interest of investment funds in aluminium, in combination with restructuring in European and the US aluminium sectors.

In 2007 the average price of aluminium traded on the LME increased by 2.8%, compared with the previous year, to US $2,639 per metric ton. During 2007 aluminium traded within a range of $2,317–$2,953 per ton. Prices fluctuated throughout the year, but, generally, were lower in the second half than in the first. Chinese consumption of the metal remained a key market influence in 2007. In January–May, according to analysts, Chinese utilization rose by 47%, while consumption world-wide in the same period grew at a substantially lower rate of 10.5%. LME inventories of aluminium rose steadily in January–May, totalling 833,525 tons at the end of that period. In June, however, they declined to 823,625 tons. By the end of September stocks had risen to 937,400 tons, but they fell in October, to 918,250 at the end of that month. At the end of 2007 LME stocks of aluminium totalled 929,450 tons.

In January–May 2008 the average price of aluminium traded on the LME ranged between US $2,446 per metric ton (January) and $3,005 per ton (March). Aluminium traded within a range of $2,359–$3,175 per ton in the first five months of the year. Stocks of the metal held by the LME, meanwhile, had risen to 1,077,175 tons by the end of May, compared with 956,475 tons at the end of January. At mid-2008, according to analysts, while the general trend in the prices of base metals was downward, aluminium prices remained steady, supported by a continued decline in the value of the US dollar and by concern about the possible effects of shortages of electric power affecting the South Africa aluminium sector. However, it was anticipated that prices would decline in the second half of the year as a consequence of weak demand in the West. Growth in demand was expected to continue to derive from China, whose principal aluminium-consuming industries continued to record substantial increases in output. Demand in the USA continued to be characterized as weak, as a consequence of the general economic repercussions of the so-called 'sub-prime' crisis (stemming from low-income borrowers' inability to meet repayment obligations on lending). In Europe and Japan demand was likewise restrained.

The IAI, based in London, is a global forum of producers of aluminium dedicated to the development and wider use of the metal. In 2008 the IAI had 25 member companies, representing every part of the world, including Russia and China, and responsible for more than 80% of global primary aluminium production.

## COAL

Coal is a mineral of organic origin, formed from the remains of vegetation over millions of years. There are several grades: anthracite, the hardest coal with the highest proportion of carbon, which burns smoke-free; bituminous and sub-bituminous coal, used for industrial power: some is made into coke when the volatile matter is driven off by heating; and lignite or brown coal, the lowest grade and nearest to the peat stage. Anthracite and bituminous coal are classed as 'hard' coal. Coal gas is made from brown coal, but is not widely used for energy except in the republics of the former USSR.

Geographically, coal is one of the most evenly distributed of the fossil fuels. Of estimated world proven reserves of 847,488m. metric tons at the end of 2007 (comprising 430,896m. tons of anthracite and bituminous coal and 416,592m. tons of sub-bituminous coal and lignite), about 24% were located in the Far East and Australasia (excluding India and Pakistan), some 30% in North America (including Mexico), around 27% in the republics of the former USSR and 7% in Europe (including Turkey). The reserves of India and Pakistan, which constitute most of those of the South Asia region, accounted for 7.0% of estimated world proven reserves at the end of 2007.

During the period 1981–2005, according to the World Coal Institute, annual world production of hard coal (i.e. excluding sub-bituminous coal and lignite) increased from 2,796m. metric tons to an estimated 4,973m. tons: a rise of more than 77%. High levels of output and demand were maintained during the 1990s, owing to the increasing use of coal world-wide as the primary fuel for electricity generation. In 2007 coal was estimated to have accounted for about 29% of this demand, which is expanding at (approximately) an annual rate of more than 2%. Environmentalists have, however, increasingly criticized the large-scale use of fossil fuels as a prime causative factor in 'acid rain' pollution and the warming of the global atmosphere by accretions of carbon gases. In 2007 coal was estimated to have accounted for about 44.1% of the combined primary energy consumption of Bangladesh, India and Pakistan. In 2003 coal was utilized to generate 69% of India's electricity, one of the highest levels of dependency on coal for that purpose in the world. The combined consumption of coal by Bangladesh, India and Pakistan accounted for 11.2% of total Asian-Pacific consumption and for 6.7% of world consumption in 2007.

As the greater part of coal output is consumed within the producing country, only a relatively small proportion of coal production enters world trade. In 2006 an estimated 570m. metric tons of steam coal (for power generation) was traded internationally, together with about 201m. tons of coking coal (for use in metallurgical industries). About 90% of total world consumption of coal is both mined and used in the same producing countries, mainly the USA and the People's Republic of China. In 2007 China was estimated to have accounted for 39.7% of world coal production, and for 41.3% of world consumption.

**Production of Coal***
(million metric tons)

| | 2006 | 2007 |
|---|---|---|
| **World total** | 6,187.2 | 6,395.5 |
| **Leading regional producer** | | |
| India | 449.2 | 478.2 |
| **Other leading producers** | | |
| Australia | 385.3 | 393.9 |
| China, People's Repub. | 2,373.0 | 2,536.7 |
| Germany | 197.1 | 201.9 |
| Indonesia | 181.1 | 174.8 |
| Kazakhstan | 96.2 | 94.4 |
| Poland | 156.1 | 145.8 |
| Russia | 309.2 | 314.2 |
| South Africa | 256.8 | 269.4 |
| Ukraine | 80.2 | 76.3 |
| USA | 1,054.8 | 1,039.2 |

* Commercial solid fuels only, comprising bituminous coal and anthracite (hard coal), and lignite and brown (sub-bituminous) coal.

Source: BP, *Statistical Review of World Energy 2008*.

India has the fourth largest coal reserves in the world, after the USA, Russia and China, but nevertheless requires some imports of coal to satisfy domestic requirements. The Indian coal industry is, in any case, vulnerable to competition from foreign suppliers of lower-priced, higher quality coal. In particular, India is obliged to import most of the coking coal it requires owing to the generally high ash content and low calorific value of indigenous coal. Coal, of which India is, after China and the USA, the third largest consumer, is the country's prime source of commercial energy. In late 2005 there were reportedly 390 operating mines. With the assistance of foreign technology and a programme of modernization, India significantly increased its coal production during the 1990s. However, as most of India's reserves can only be exploited through underground mining, most further growth in production will depend on the availability of the substantial capital required to develop them, at the expense of productivity. In 2005 the Government was reported to have abandoned attempts undertaken since 2002 to increase private participation in coal mining and production efficiency owing to the opposition of organized labour. The establishment of a regulatory authority for coal has also, reportedly, been considered, with a view to allocating coal mining blocks on the basis of bidders' technical and financial capabilities. Nearly all of the country's mines are under the control of Coal India Ltd (CIL), which is responsible for about 90% of production. CIL's 10th five-year plan, covering the period April 2002–March 2007, projected the development of six new open-cast mines, to be undertaken by CIL subsidiaries. CIL was to invest US $1,290m. in coal production in the plan period. As noted above, India relies heavily on coal for power generation. Heavy industry is the other principal consumer. In 2007 India consumed 208.0m. metric tons (oil equivalent) of coal, compared with 142.8m. tons (oil equivalent) in 1995. It has been forecast that consumption will rise to some 390m. tons by 2010, and to more than 460m. tons by 2020.

Pakistan reportedly possesses huge unexploited reserves of coal that would be sufficient, if developed, to meet national requirements for about 100 years. In 2007, however, production amounted to just 3.6m. metric tons, while consumption in that year totalled 4.6m. tons (oil equivalent). Coal met about 8% of Pakistan's primary energy needs in 2007, and in 2004 was used to generate less than 1% of the country's electricity. However, the discovery of substantial reserves of low ash, low sulphur lignite in Sindh province is expected to increase consumption for power generation. Bangladesh consumed 400,000 tons (oil equivalent) of coal in 2007. In 2004 the discovery of a deposit in Dianpur containing an estimated 50m. tons of coal was reported to have been made. Also in 2004, Asia Energy PLC, in which Australia's Deepgreen Minerals Corpn Ltd has a share of 25.6%, was reported to be conducting a feasibility study on its Phulbari coal project in Bangladesh's north-west. Resources at Phulbari reportedly amounted to some 400m. tons, and work was being undertaken with the aim of producing 9m.–15m. tons annually from 2009 for both domestic consumption and export. Asia Energy PLC was also a potential participant in a project to construct a coal-fired power plant with generating capacity of 2,500 MW up to about 2050. Elsewhere in the region, Sri Lanka was reported in 2004 to be preparing to construct its first coal-fired power plant. Afghanistan also possesses small reserves of coal: the US Geological Survey (USGS) put production at 185,000 tons in 2003.

As noted above, only a relatively small proportion of the total amount of coal produced world-wide enters world trade. In the international market for coking coal Australia accounts for more than one-half of all exports; and in that for thermal coal, for about one-fifth of all exports. Japan is the destination of more than 60% of Australia's coal exports and, as a result, Australian exporters negotiate prices direct with Japanese users. In 2006, unlike those for most other steel-making raw materials, contract prices for Australian premium hard coking coal were reported to have fallen compared with the previous year. The decline was attributed to producers' swift response to increased global demand for the commodity. Contract prices were reported to have been settled at about US $115 per metric ton, compared with $125 per ton in 2005. Contract prices fell by about 17% in 2007, to around $98 per ton, reflecting a marginal easing of demand and increased supplies, in particular from Australia. However, limited capacity at Australian ports subsequently contributed to supply shortages in that year, delaying shipments of coal by as much as three weeks. Severe flooding—which impeded production and forced the closure of a number of mines in Queensland during January–February 2008—was expected to reduce global inventories by up to 5%. The contract price for Australian premium hard coking coal was, therefore, subject to a significant increase, with reports indicating that key purchasers had agreed to pay around $300 per ton in 2008. In early 2006 it was reported that many contract prices for semi-soft metallurgical coals had been concluded at about $55 per ton. However, some major Australian producers, including Rio Tinto and Xstrata Coal, continued to negotiate at that time, asserting that the decline from the benchmark price of $80 in 2005 was unrepresentative of the supply situation pertaining in early 2006. A further, slight decline in contract prices for semi-soft metallurgical coals, to an average of about $54.50 per ton, was forecast for 2007.

According to industry data, annual average import prices (c.i.f.) for both coking and steam coal in the Japanese market declined fairly steadily during the course of the 1990s. In 2000 the average price for coking coal was US $39.69 per metric ton, while the price of imported steam coal averaged $34.58 per ton in that year. In 2001 slightly higher average prices of, respectively, $41.33 per ton and $37.96 per ton, were recorded. In 2002, while the average import price of coking coal (the tight specifications for which limit its availability) rose to $42.01 per ton, that of steam coal fell to $36.90 per ton. The average import price of both coking and steam coal in the Japanese market declined in 2003, to, respectively, $41.75 per ton and $34.74 per ton. In 2004 the average import price of coking coal rose markedly, by about 47%, to $60.96 per ton, while that of steam coal increased by a similarly substantial margin, of about 48%, to $51.34 per ton. Further substantial increases, of, respectively, 47%, to $89.33 per ton, and 23%, to $62.90 per ton, were recorded in the average import prices of coking and steam coal in the Japanese market in 2005. The average price of Japanese coking coal increased marginally in 2006, to $93.46 per ton, before declining to $88.24 per ton in 2007. Japanese steam coal reached an average price of $63.04 per ton in 2006, rising to $69.86 per ton in 2007.

## COCONUT (*Cocos nucifera*)

The coconut palm is a tropical tree, up to 25 m tall, with a slender trunk surmounted by a feathery crown of leaves. The geographical origins of the tree are thought to be in the Asia-Pacific region. Its presence in most coastal areas and on many islands in the tropics is largely due to man, who introduced it to West Africa and the Americas. The tree's fruits first appear after about six years, though the palm may not reach full bearing until it is about 20 years old. It may continue fruiting for a further 60 years. (Hybrid varieties have advanced the time of initial fruiting from the sixth to the fourth year, and the onset of full bearing from the 20th to the 10th year.) The fruits, green at first but turning yellow as they ripen, are often left to fall naturally, but, as many are then over-ripe, harvesting by hand is widely practised.

Coconut, the most important of all cultivated palms, is frequently a smallholder crop, found mainly in small plots around houses and in gardens, although in the Philippines the average coconut farm covers 4–7 ha in area. The plant's fruit, fronds and wood provide many thousands of families with a cash income as well as basic necessities such as food, drink, fuel and shelter. The palms grow with little or no attention where conditions are favourable. More than 80 varieties are known, divided broadly into tall palms, produced by cross-pollination, and dwarf palms, which are self-pollinating. The sap of the coconut palm itself can be evaporated to produce sugar or fermented to make an alcoholic drink called 'toddy'. This may be distilled to produce a spirit called 'arrack'.

**Production of Coconuts**
('000 metric tons)

| | 2006 | 2007 |
|---|---|---|
| **World total** | 55,210 | 54,623 |
| South Asia | 11,918 | 10,354 |
| **Leading regional producers** | | |
| India* | 11,005 | 9,400 |
| Sri Lanka* | 913 | 954 |
| **Other leading producers** | | |
| Brazil | 2,978 | 2,771 |
| Indonesia† | 16,375 | 17,000 |
| Malaysia* | 570 | 568 |
| Mexico | 102 | 102* |
| Papua New Guinea* | 660 | 677 |
| Philippines | 14,958 | 15,580 |
| Thailand | 1,815 | 1,705 |
| Viet Nam | 982 | 962* |

* FAO estimate(s).
† Unofficial figures.

Coconut oil is a rich source of medium-chain triglycerides (MCT), whose applications in medical nutrition include infant milk formulas and foods for persons unable to digest and assimilate fats. Its other food applications include use as a flavouring and also as an ingredient to prolong the shelf life of certain food products.

All parts of the fruit have their uses. Beneath the outer skin is a thick layer of fibrous husk. The fibres can be combed out to produce coir (from the Malay word *kayar*, which means 'cord'), a material used for making ropes, coconut matting, brushes, mattresses and upholstery (see below). Inside the husk is the nut—what people in temperate areas think of as a 'coconut' since the whole fruit is not usually imported. The nut has a hard shell, inside which is a thin white fleshy layer of edible 'meat'. The nut's hollow interior is partially filled with a liquid called 'coconut water' which is gradually absorbed as the fruit ripens. This 'water' is a refreshing and nutritious drink when taken from a young nut (7–8 months), while that from more mature nuts can be prepared as a soft drink and is also used in the production of yeast, alcohol, wine and vinegar. The so-called 'coconut milk' is the white, creamy extract obtained after pressing freshly grated coconut 'meat'. Coconut flour, a by-product of 'coconut milk', is a useful nutritional source of dietary fibre. The shells are mainly utilized as fuel, but small quantities are used to make containers, ornaments, ladles and buttons, and pulverized shells can be used as filler in plastics moulding, plywood and mosquito coil repellants. Raw coconut shell is a more efficient fuel after it has been carbonized into charcoal and, on further processing, can be converted into the still more efficient activated carbon, which finds a market in highly industrialized countries concerned with pollution control.

After harvesting, the fruits are split open, the husk is removed and the nuts are usually broken open. The 'meat' is sometimes eaten directly or used to prepare desiccated coconut, widely used in the bakery and confectionery trades. However, by far the most important economic product of the plant is obtained by drying the 'meat' into copra, either in the sun or in a kiln which may be heated by burning the coconut shells. The dried copra is the source of coconut oil, used mainly in the manufacture of soap, detergent and cosmetics, and also as a cooking oil and in margarine production. As technology advances, more uses for coconut oil are being developed. Experiments have shown that it can be converted into diesel fuel, and a programme of conversion might alleviate the financial burden on countries that are heavily dependent on petroleum imports. The residue left after the extraction of oil from copra is a valuable oilcake for feeding livestock, particularly dairy cattle.

Good copra has an oil content of about 64%. Most extraction is done in the coconut-growing countries, although there is a substantial trade in copra to countries that extract the oil themselves. Although the largest producer of copra, the Philippines was overtaken as the largest exporter in 1992 by Papua New Guinea, whose copra sales represented 15.4% of the world export trade in 2004 and 15.2% in 2005. The eclipse of the Philippines as a copra exporter, however, has been attributable to increased levels of crushings of its copra into crude coconut oil for export. In 2002 Papua New Guinea was overtaken in turn as the largest exporter of copra by Indonesia, whose sales in that year accounted for more than one-third of the world export trade. Indonesia retained the status of leading copra exporter in 2004 and 2005, accounting for almost 39% of foreign sales world-wide in the latter year. Japan was formerly the main importer of copra, but it has been overtaken by Germany, which in the mid-1990s accounted, on average, for about 20%–25% of all imports. That share has declined in more recent years, however. In 2001, albeit exceptionally, Japanese imports again exceeded those of Germany. Germany regained primacy in 2002, but accounted for only about 13% of copra imports world-wide in that year. In 2005, when Japanese imports of copra declined to a negligible level, Germany's imports represented 14.5% of the world total. German imports of copra rose substantially in 2004, accounting for more than 20% of all imports world-wide in that year. Germany's partners within the European Union (EU) also constitute a major market for copra, coconut oil, desiccated coconut and copra meal.

**Production of Copra**
('000 metric tons)

| | 2005 | 2006 |
|---|---|---|
| **World total** | 5,556 | 5,370 |
| South Asia | 817 | 815 |
| **Leading regional producers** | | |
| India* | 750 | 750 |
| Sri Lanka* | 67 | 65 |
| **Other leading producers** | | |
| Indonesia* | 1,460 | 1,310 |
| Malaysia* | 48 | 51 |
| Mexico | 210 | 204 |
| Mozambique† | 48 | 46 |
| Papua New Guinea* | 90 | n.a. |
| Philippines | 2,234 | 2,200* |
| Thailand | 72† | 65* |
| Viet Nam† | 243 | 243 |

* Unofficial figure(s).
† FAO estimate(s).

Coconut oil has encountered competition from the development of more productive annual oilseed crops, such as soybeans and rapeseed in the northern hemisphere, and from oil palm in the tropics. Up to 7 metric tons of oil per ha can be produced from oil palm, compared with a maximum of 3.25 tons from coconuts. The necessity for the production of copra prior to the extraction of oil has further eroded the competitiveness of coconuts in the world market for vegetable oils. In 2005 the Philippines accounted for about 46% of world exports of coconut oil. The USA is the main importer, taking, on average, a little more than one-fifth of total world imports in recent years. In

2007, according to FAO estimates, world production of coconut oil was 3,158,627 tons, including 394,000 tons from South Asia. The major producing countries in that year were the Philippines (an estimated 1,258,000 tons) and Indonesia (an estimated 775,000 tons). By comparison, the output of India, South Asia's leading producer, totalled an estimated 372,000 tons in 2007. Sri Lanka, Bangladesh, Pakistan and the Maldives are all also producers of coconut oil, although on a much smaller scale. In 2007 Sri Lankan output amounted to an estimated 22,000 tons, that of Bangladesh to an estimated 21,800 tons, Pakistan some 8,664 tons and the Maldives about 1,380 tons.

The Philippines is the world's largest exporter of coconut products, and about one-third of its population is directly or indirectly dependent on the coconut sector for a livelihood.

International promotion of biodegradable products during the late 1990s generated a revival of demand for coir products, of which India is the largest producer and exporter, principally to markets in the EU and the USA, which in 2004 were estimated to have accounted for some 87% of world imports of mats, matting and rugs, etc., made from coir. In 2006 Indian production of (brown) coir fibre totalled an estimated 314,000 metric tons, while that of Sri Lanka amounted to an estimated 76,600 tons. India produced an estimated 270,000 tons of coir yarn in 2006. Sri Lanka, however, lacks coir textile production facilities and produced only an estimated 5,500 tons of coir yarn in the same year. Indian exports of coir products totalled some 49,950 tons in 2006, while those of Sri Lanka amounted to about 6,430 tons. Indonesia and the Philippines, each of whose coconut output exceeds that of India, are both deficient in facilities for coir production.

The Asian and Pacific Coconut Community, with headquarters in Jakarta, Indonesia, was established in 1969. Its 15 members account for more than 90% of world coconut output and exports of coconut products.

In January 2002 the index of export prices for copra stood at 49, while that for coconut oil was 52. The import price of Philippine copra in Europe has varied widely in recent years. In 1997 the price at European ports averaged US $433.75 per metric ton, but this declined to $411.03 in 1998. In 1999 the price averaged $462.27 per ton, but this declined steeply in 2000, to only $308.92 per ton. In 2001 the average price fell sharply again, to only $195.55 per ton. During the first quarter of 2002 the average import price of Philippine copra at European ports recovered to $228.29 per ton. The average price rose further, to $245.23 per ton, in April, and again, to $263.26 per ton, in May.

The import price of Philippine coconut oil has also fluctuated considerably. The market for coconut oil was depressed in the first half of 2000, with plentiful supplies of the commodity (and of palm oil) available. In July coconut oil was traded in Europe at only US $380 per metric ton. The average import price of coconut oil of Philippine origin (c.i.f. Rotterdam) was $450.3 per ton in 2000, and fell further in 2001, to only $318.1 per ton. In 2002, however, an average price of $421 per ton was recorded. In December 2003 the import price of coconut oil rose as high as $583 per ton, and for the whole of 2003 an average price of $467.3 per ton was recorded. In 2004 the average Rotterdam quotation rose to $660.8 per ton. According to FAO, prices in the oilcrop complex (in which copra is included) were influenced in the October 2003–September 2004 marketing year by very tight supplies of soybeans and by slower growth in output of palm oil. In 2005 the average price eased somewhat, to $617 per ton. During the first seven months of 2006 the Rotterdam quotation for imported Philippine coconut oil ranged between $569 per ton (January) and $591 per ton (February). In July the average quotation was $583 per ton. The average price for 2006 was $607 per ton. The effects of the 2006 typhoon season in the Philippines, which had inflicted considerable damage on the sector, caused a contraction in the supply of raw coconut, with the result that during the first seven months of 2007 there was an associated increase in the value of coconut oil: the average monthly price fluctuated between $731 per ton in January and $979 per ton in June.

## COTTON (*Gossypium*)

This is the name given to the hairs that grow on the epidermis of the seed of the plant genus *Gossypium*. The initial development of the cotton fibres takes place within a closed pod, called a boll, which, after a period of growth of about 50–75 days (depending upon climatic conditions), opens to reveal the familiar white tufts of cotton hair. After the seed cotton has been picked, the cotton fibre, or lint, has to be separated from the seeds by means of a mechanical process, known as ginning. Depending upon the variety and growing conditions, it takes about three metric tons of seed cotton to produce one ton of raw cotton fibre. After ginning, a fuzz of very short cotton hairs remains on the seed. These are called linters, and may be removed and used in the manufacture of paper, cellulose-based chemicals, explosives, etc.

About one-half of the cotton produced in the world is used in the manufacture of clothing, about one-third is used for household textiles, and the remainder for numerous industrial products (tarpaulins, rubber reinforcement, abrasive backings, filters, high-quality papers, etc.).

The official cotton 'season' (for trade purposes) runs from 1 August to 31 July of the following year, and quantities are measured in both metric tons and bales; for statistical purposes, one bale of cotton is 226.8 kg (500 lb) gross or 217.7 kg (480 lb) net.

The price of a particular type of cotton depends upon its availability relative to demand and upon characteristics related to yarn quality and suitability for processing. These include fibre length, fineness, cleanliness, strength and colour. The most important of these is length. Generally, the length of the fibre determines the quality of the yarn produced from it, with the longer fibres being preferred for the finer, stronger and more expensive yarns.

Cotton is the world's leading textile fibre. However, with the increased use of synthetics, cotton's share in the world's total consumption of fibre declined from 48% in 1988 to only about 40% in 2007. About one-third of the decline in its market share was attributed to increases in the real cost of cotton relative to prices of competing fibres, and the remaining two-thirds to other factors, for example greater use of chemical fibre filament yarn (yarn that is not spun but is extruded in a continuous string) in domestic textiles, such as carpeting. The break-up of the Council for Mutual Economic Assistance (the communist countries' trading bloc) in 1990, and of the USSR in 1991, led to substantial reductions in cotton consumption in those countries and also contributed to cotton's declining share of the world market. Officially enforced limits on the use of cotton in the People's Republic of China (which generally accounted for about 25%–30% of cotton consumption world-wide) also had an impact on the international market. According to data compiled by the International Cotton Advisory Committee (ICAC), consumption of cotton world-wide expanded by 3.8% in 2007, the ninth successive year of expansion, to a record level of 26.9m. metric tons. However, 2007 was also the second successive year in which the rate of growth in consumption declined.

The area devoted to cotton cultivation totalled 31m.–36m. ha between the 1950s and the early 1990s, accounting for about 4% of world cropped area. During the mid-1980s, however, world cotton consumption failed to keep pace with the rate of growth in production, and the resultant surpluses led to a fall in prices—which had serious consequences for those countries that rely on cotton sales for a major portion of their export earnings. In the mid-1990s, despite improvements in world price levels, cotton cultivation came under pressure from food crop needs, and world-wide the harvested areas under cotton declined from more than 35m. ha in 1995/96 to 33m. ha in 1996/97. According to the US Department of Agriculture (USDA), the area under cotton world-wide totalled about 34.7m. ha in 2006/07; it was forecast to decline to about 33.3m. ha in 2007/08, and, again, to some 32.4m. ha, in 2008/09.

Cotton is a major crop in India and Pakistan, the two leading South Asian producers. Exports of yarn, fabric and garments are also an important source of income in the Indian sub-continent. India and Pakistan were generally net exporters of cotton in the 1980s and early 1990s. According to USDA data, Indian cotton production totalled 4.1m. metric tons in 2004/05, while exports amounted to 144,000 tons. In 2005/06 output remained firm at 4.1m. tons, although exports increased significantly, to 751,000 tons, with analysis suggesting that this in large part reflected a surge in exports to China. According to USDA, production increased in 2006/07 to reach 4.7m. tons; foreign sales accounted for 994,000 tons of Indian output during that year. There was a further increase in production in 2007/08, to 5.4m. tons, according to USDA data. This substantial rate of increase was considered to reflect the rising use of genetically modified seeds in India's cotton sector. An accompanying increase in the volume of exported cotton was also recorded, with USDA placing the figure at around 1.6m. tons for 2007/08.

Pakistan's cotton crop totalled about 2.4m. metric tons in 2004/05, falling to 2.2m. tons in 2005/06. Despite greater planting in 2006/07, there was no significant change in output overall. Production of just under 2.2m. tons was reported in that year, with the poor result attributed to heavy flooding in Punjab and Sindh provinces, as well as an outbreak of mealybugs (*Phenacoccus manihoti*). As a consequence, Pakistan recorded a 42% rise in imports of cotton in 2006/07, to 500,000 tons. During the 1990s Pakistan's cotton yield often exceeded the requirements of internal demand, and exports peaked in the 1995/96 marketing year, at 311,000 tons. However, rising consumption linked to Pakistan's burgeoning textile industry placed increasing pressure on domestic supply. Exports fluctuated thereafter, and the country became, for the most part, a net importer of cotton. Pakistan accounted for 9.9% of global demand in 2007/08, according to USDA data. While the Government had planned to increase acreage in 2007/08, a reduced crop was planted in that marketing year, owing to shortages of fertilizer, electricity and high-quality seeds. Furthermore, rising international prices for cereals (particularly rice) prompted many farmers to diversify their activities in favour of more lucrative crops. According to USDA, Pakistan's cotton production declined to 1.9m. tons in 2007/08, while imports rose to 806,000 tons. Elsewhere in South Asia, Bangladesh is one of the world's major importers of cotton (see below).

**Production of Cotton**
('000 metric tons)

| | 2006/07 | 2007/08 |
|---|---|---|
| **World total** | 26,557 | 25,976 |
| South Asia | 6,936 | 7,366 |
| **Leading regional producers** | | |
| India | 4,746 | 5,400 |
| Pakistan | 2,155 | 1,938 |
| **Other leading producers** | | |
| Argentina | 174 | 152 |
| Australia | 294 | 124 |
| Brazil | 1,524 | 1,557 |
| China, People's Repub. | 7,729 | 7,795 |
| Egypt | 212 | 218 |
| Greece | 305 | 288 |
| Syria | 222 | 250 |
| Turkey | 849 | 675 |
| USA | 4,700 | 4,182 |
| Uzbekistan | 1,165 | 1,197 |

Source: USDA.

In 2007/08, according to data compiled by USDA, the leading exporters of cotton were the USA, India, Uzbekistan, Brazil and Australia. Other important exporters in that year were Greece, Turkmenistan and Burkina Faso. In 2007/08 the main cotton-importing countries were China (2.5m. tons), Pakistan (806,000 tons), Turkey (697,000 tons) and Bangladesh (610,000 tons). In 2005/06 USDA estimated that China's imports of cotton more than trebled, compared with the previous year, rising to some 4.2m. tons and thus representing about 43% of world imports of cotton. Chinese cotton consumption has risen sharply in recent years as a consequence of the rapid expansion of the country's textile industry, in particular its export-orientated sectors. In 2006/07, according to USDA, China's consumption of cotton increased to 10.9m. tons, representing 41% of global demand. The expansion of the indigenous cotton sector meant that China was able to meet a greater portion of this demand, and imports decreased accordingly in that year, with USDA reporting a decline of 30%. However, a similar rate of expansion in productive capacity did not follow in 2007/08, while domestic consumption continued to increase. Chinese imports thus rose by 8.6% in the 2007/08 marketing year.

Although co-operation in cotton affairs has a long history, there have been no international agreements governing the cotton trade. Proposals in recent years to link producers and consumers in price-stabilization arrangements have been opposed by the USA (the world's largest cotton exporter), and by Japan and the European Union. The ICAC, an inter-governmental body, established in 1939, with its headquarters in Washington, DC, publishes statistical and economic information and provides a forum for consultation and discussion among its 40 members.

Liverpool, United Kingdom, is the historic centre of cotton-trading activity, and international cotton prices are still collected by organizations located in Liverpool. However, almost no US cotton has been imported through Liverpool in recent years. Consumption in the textile industry in the United Kingdom has fallen to only about 2,000 metric tons in recent years, according to ICAC data, most of which comes from Africa, Greece, Spain and Central Asia. The price for Memphis cotton, from the USA, quoted in international markets is c.i.f. North European ports, of which Bremen, Germany, is the most important.

The average price for Memphis Territory cotton in North Europe (compiled on the basis of daily prices) declined by 18% in 1999/2000, compared with the previous cotton year, to US $1,328 per metric ton, but recovered somewhat, to $1,371 per ton, in 2000/2001. In 2001/02, however, the average Memphis quotation slumped to only $994 per ton, a decline of more than 27% compared with the previous (cotton) year. According to FAO, and based on calendar years, the weighted average of official weekly prices for cotton that comprise the Cotlook 'A' index was $1,394 per ton in 2003, but declined to $1,365 per ton in 2004. In 2005 the weighted average of official weekly cotton prices fell to $1,220 per ton, increasing slightly, to $1,272 per ton, in 2006. In 2007 the average weekly Cotlook 'A' index recovered to $1,320 per ton. In the first four months of 2008 official weekly cotton prices rose markedly, to $1,629 per ton. The index ranged between $1,502 per ton (January) and $1,826 per ton (March). According to FAO, the recovery in cotton prices was a consequence of a reduction in cotton plantings in the USA that had resulted from the diversion of agricultural land to the production of grains for biofuel feedstock.

The principal Liverpool index of cotton import prices in North Europe is based on an average of the cheapest five quotations from a selection of styles of medium-staple fibre. In 1999 the index recorded an average offering price of 53.1 US cents per lb: its lowest annual level since 1986. In 2000 the index recorded an average offering price of 59.1 cents per lb. Slow growth in production and strengthened demand for cotton were the main reasons cited for the recovery in prices. In 2001, however, the decline in prices resumed, and in that year the index recorded an average offering price of only 48 cents per lb. This declined further in 2002, to only 46 cents per lb. In 2003 the index recorded an average offering price of 63 cents per lb, but this declined slightly, to 62 cents per lb, in 2004. The value of cotton declined once again in 2005, in which year the index registered an average price of 55 cents per lb. Prices recovered somewhat in 2006 and 2007, reaching an annual average of 58 cents per lb and 60 cents per lb, respectively. Speculative investment in commodity markets (largely a response to the falling value of the US dollar, as inventories remained high) contributed to higher cotton prices in the first half of 2008. In the first quarter the average price of cotton recorded by the index rose to 76 cents per lb, and it remained at the same level in April–June. The price averaged 74 cents per lb in May, rising to 77 cents per lb in June. However, demand was not expected to keep pace with cotton prices above 70 cents per lb, a factor that was thought likely to moderate further increases, particularly in the longer term.

In March 2003 the World Trade Organization (WTO) established a panel to rule on a claim by Brazil that subsidies and other measures enjoyed by US producers, users and exporters of cotton had harmed its interests. The US Cotton Farm Program had reportedly been represented by Brazil and by some other countries as inconsistent with the USA's obligations in respect of the WTO, and as the most important factor in the fall in world cotton prices from the mid-1990s—to the point at which, in 2001/02, the Cotlook 'A' index was at its lowest level for 30 years. Some analysts, however, contended that the decline in the world price of cotton could not be attributed solely or even mainly to the subsidization of US (and EU and Chinese) output, but that it was instead the consequence of a combination of structural changes, such as competition from synthetics, affecting the production and consumption of cotton; the appreciation of the US dollar, which had depressed nominal prices of cotton; the extent of China's net trade in cotton; and a number of unusual factors that affected world cotton output in 2001/02. Brazil was the sole initiator of a legal process at the WTO, but, as noted above, it was not the only critic of the subsidization of cotton production in the USA and elsewhere. A number of West and Central African countries have argued that they ought to be compensated, within the framework of the international regulation of trade, for financial losses incurred as a result of the subsidization of US, EU and Chinese cotton production. The cost of producing cotton in West and Central Africa is among the lowest in the world, and African producers would be able to compete strongly with their US, EU and Chinese counterparts were it not for subsidies, which, they have argued, aggravated the fall in the world price of cotton detailed above. In a review of studies of the effects of subsidization on the world market for cotton, FAO stated in the early 2000s that current levels of EU output of cotton could be imported at one-third of the cost of production, and that in some years in the USA the cost of subsidies to cotton producers was greater than the total value of world exports of cotton at prevailing prices. In September 2004 the WTO panel that investigated the US–Brazil dispute ruled overwhelmingly in Brazil's favour. In March 2005, following an appeal by the USA, the panel's ruling was upheld in respect of all critical points of the dispute. As a consequence, the USA would be obliged to bring the subsidies found to be at fault into compliance with its WTO obligations.

## JUTE

Jute fibres are obtained from *Corchorus capsularis* (known in the trade as white jute) and *C. olitorius* (known in the trade as tossa jute). Jute-like fibres include a number of jute substitutes, the main ones being kenaf or mesta and roselle (*Hibiscus* spp.) and Congo jute or paka (*Urena lobata*). The genus *Corchorus* includes about 40 species distributed throughout the tropics, with the largest number of species being found in Africa.

Jute flourishes in the hot damp regions of Asia. Commercial fibre varies from yellow to brown in colour and consists of tow (bunches of strands), which is pressed into bales of 181.4 kg (400 lb) after it has been retted (softened).

Jute has a number of uses. The relatively cheap, hard-wearing fibre is used to manufacture sacking for the storage of grains, cocoa, coffee and other food crops, which currently accounts for about 75% of consumption. Much of the remainder of the crop is taken by manufacturers of carpet-backing and other quality users. The finest jute standards are spun into carpet yarn and woven into curtains and wall coverings; in the area of quality goods jute is less under threat from synthetics. Jute is mixed with wool, after treatment with petroleum-derived softening agents (see below), and processed into cheap clothing fabrics or blankets in developing Asian countries. In its traditional market, however, jute has, despite its biodegradability, encountered strong competition from lighter synthetic materials. Its use as packaging is under challenge from wood and plywood, and has been diminishing, in response to the trend towards bulk-handling containerization. The main jute-producing countries, however, have continued to stress the environmental desirability of jute use, and anxieties about the health aspects of petroleum use in the retting process have been overcome by the introduction of castor oil as the softening agent. Prospects exist for an expansion in world demand for jute in the growing market for 'environmentally friendly' jute packaging and products, and for high-quality blended jute fabrics for wall-hangings and furnishings. Investment has additionally been made in the potential for use of jute in so-called 'technical textile' applications, such as geotextiles, used particularly in civil engineering, and, within the agricultural and horticultural sector, agrotextiles. Jute is also being promoted for use as a component in plastics production as a partial substitute for petroleum products.

Bangladesh and India are the principal producers and exporters of raw jute and fabrics. In both countries most of the growers of jute are small farmers whose livelihood depends entirely on their annual crop of the fibre. In 2006/07 about almost 94% of world exports of raw jute were supplied by Bangladesh, which exports some 85%–90% of its jute and jute goods. Bangladesh derived 4.1% of its total export earnings from foreign sales of raw jute and jute goods in that year. In 2006/07 Bangladesh's exports of raw jute rose to 439,300 metric tons, compared with 440,500 tons in the previous year. The jute sector has traditionally employed about 45% of the country's industrial work-force, and accounts, according to Bangladesh's Ministry of Jute, for about 10% of total employment in the economy. About one-half of the annual output is exported as raw fibre, while the remainder is processed in local mills for export as jute goods.

Bangladesh has sought to reduce its high dependence on sales of jute and jute products for foreign earnings. However, there are few alternatives for export, other than fish and tea, and in recent years attention has turned increasingly to the possible diversification of the uses of jute. Some farmers have abandoned the cultivation of jute in favour of rice, for its assured market and better price; during 1985/86–1990/91 the area under jute cultivation was reduced from more than 1m. ha to under 500,000 ha. The area sown to jute recovered to 577,493 ha in 1996/97, but declined to only 407,928 ha in 1998/99. It fell even further in 2003/04, to just 390,526 ha, before recovering slightly, to 410,000 ha, in 2006/07, according to FAO estimates. Bangladesh has attempted, with little success, to strengthen its share of the carpet market by reducing the gap between the country's capacity of 140,000 sq m and the global demand for 3.5m. sq m per year. As the world's dominant exporter of jute and jute goods, Bangladesh is far more vulnerable than India to declining world demand for jute, and to growing competition on the international market and from synthetics. This vulnerability was apparent, in mid-2002, in the Government's announcement of its intention to close the Adamjee jute mill, south of Dhaka, with the loss of 25,000 jobs. The decision to close the mill, the largest in the world, was attributed to a world-wide decline in the jute industry. Adamjee was reported at the time of the Government's announcement to be losing millions of dollars each year. India, meanwhile, consumes virtually all of its raw jute domestically, supplementing its own production with imports of high quality fibre. India has traditionally been the world's largest importer of jute, although imports of raw jute by Pakistan, normally the second largest South Asian market, surpassed those of India in 2001. In 2007, however, Indian imports, totalling an estimated 162,700 metric tons, exceeded those of both Pakistan (110,100 tons) and the People's Republic of China (125,700 tons). In 2006/07 the area under jute in India totalled an estimated 950,000 ha, compared with some 935,000 ha in 2005/06.

In 1993 the Government of Bangladesh responded to its jute industry's financial difficulties by announcing plans to create a fund offering low-interest loans to jute mills and to ban the production of polythene bags and other synthetic products threatening the jute market. Further assistance was sought from the World Bank, which undertook to provide US $250m. to finance a restructuring of the jute industry. The proposals included the closure of loss-making mills, reductions in the labour force and the transfer to private ownership of the majority of the plants operated by the state-owned Bangladesh Jute Mills Corpn. However, delays have occurred in implementing the privatization programme. Heavy floods in September 1998 were reported to have affected more than 70% of the jute-growing areas of Bangladesh. Following initial expectations that the country's substantial reserves of jute would avert any immediate shortfall in domestic or export requirements, the impact of severe drought in early 1999 reduced the crop by about 12%, adversely affecting both domestic mill production and supplies available for export. According to FAO estimates, world production of jute, kenaf and allied fibres increased by about 4% in 2006/07, to 3.2m metric tons. Between 2000/01 and 2006/07 Bangladeshi output declined by about 6.8%, to an estimated 800,000 tons, while that of India increased by some 12.3%, to an estimated 2.1m. tons. Chinese production has also risen, from 60,000 tons in 2000/01 to about 99,000 tons in 2006/07.

Elsewhere in South Asia, Nepal produces jute on a small scale. Nepalese output declined to 16,775 metric tons in 2006/07, compared with 17,100 tons in 2005/06. Pakistan and Bhutan produce jute on a still smaller scale.

The longer-term outlook for the jute industry in Bangladesh, as well as other producing areas, depends, in large part, on the achievement of higher crop yields.

In 2000 the average export price of raw jute at Bangladeshi ports (BWD-grade jute, f.o.b. Mongla) was US $279 per metric ton, and this rose sharply, to $331 per ton, in 2001. In 2002, however, a very sharp decline in the average price, to only $185 per ton, was recorded. The average export price of Bangladeshi BWD-grade jute recovered to $243 per ton in 2003. In 2004 the average export price of BWD-grade jute at Bangladeshi ports was $293 per ton. In 2005 a substantial increase in the average price, to $381 per ton, was recorded. The average export price in 2006 reached $385 per ton, representing a marginal increase of 0.9% on the previous year. In January–May 2008 the average monthly export price of BWD-grade jute ranged between $383 per ton (January) and $460 per ton (May).

FAO and the United Nations Conference on Trade and Development (UNCTAD) provide international forums for the discussion of jute developments. Jute is one of the crops eligible for assistance from the Common Fund for Commodities (CFC, established by an UNCTAD agreement in 1989), which aims to stabilize commodity prices. An international jute (and allied fibres) agreement (IJA) was negotiated in 1982 by 48 producing and consuming countries, but lapsed in 1984, when the requisite number of consumer countries failed to ratify the agreement. A subsequent IJA was negotiated, under the auspices of UNCTAD, in 1989. The International Jute Organization (IJO), which administered the agreement, was based in Dhaka, Bangladesh. It also conducted research and development projects, and promoted the competitiveness of jute in relation to synthetic substitutes. In 1998 the IJO's membership comprised five exporting countries (Bangladesh, the People's Republic of China, India, Nepal and Thailand) and 20 importing countries, together with the European Union (EU). In January 1999, however, India announced its withdrawal from the IJO, which had declined to appoint India's nominee for the post of executive director. Thailand, citing its domestic economic problems, withdrew from the IJO in March. India rejoined the organization in December, but Thailand remained outside. Meanwhile, some EU members believed that the IJO had failed to promote trade in jute, and consequently favoured the organization's disbandment.

Following preparatory meetings at IJO headquarters, the UN Conference on Jute and Jute Products was convened in March 2000, under UNCTAD auspices, in Geneva, Switzerland. However, the EU and its member countries (which together accounted for about 30% of the IJO's financing) declined to attend this meeting or a resumed session in Dhaka in early April. A draft text for an 'International Instrument of Co-operation', to succeed the IJA, was supported by jute-producing countries, but, without the consent of major consumers, no agreement could be concluded. At a subsequent meeting of the IJO's governing council, the EU rejected adoption of the successor 'instrument'. As a result, the IJA expired in April, at the end of its term, and the IJO entered a liquidation process. However, a working group, including representatives of producing countries, was formed to consider future international co-operation on jute affairs. It was hoped that these countries would continue to obtain support for jute projects from the CFC. In March 2001, under UNCTAD auspices, the UN Conference on Jute and Jute Products established the International Jute Study Group (IJSG) as the successor entity to the IJO. *Inter alia*, the objectives of the IJSG are to provide an effective framework for international co-operation among its members with regard to all relevant aspects of the world jute economy; and to promote the expansion of international trade in jute and jute products. Membership of the IJSG, which has its headquarters in Dhaka, is open to all states (and to the EU) with an interest in the production and consumption of, and international trade in, jute and jute products. The terms of reference of the IJSG formally entered into force in April 2002, once a number of states (including the member states of the EU) together accounting for 60% of trade (imports and exports combined) in jute and jute products had given notice of their formal acceptance of the IJSG's terms of reference. Another forum for jute co-operation is FAO's Intergovernmental Group on Jute, Kenaf and Allied Fibres, which normally convenes every two years. The Group convened most recently in January–February 2007.

**Production of Jute, Kenaf and Allied Fibres**
('000 metric tons, FAO estimates)

| | 2006 | 2007 |
|---|---|---|
| **World total** | 3,099 | 3,226 |
| South Asia | 2,845 | 2,958 |
| **Leading regional producers** | | |
| Bangladesh | 800 | 800 |
| India | 2,026 | 2,140 |
| Nepal | 17 | 17 |
| **Other leading producers** | | |
| Brazil | 26 | 27 |
| China, People's Repub. | 87 | 99 |
| Myanmar | 30 | 30 |
| Russia | n.a. | n.a. |
| Thailand | 31 | 31 |
| Uzbekistan | 20 | 20 |
| Viet Nam | 11 | 11 |

### RICE (*Oryza sativa*)

Rice is the staple food in most of the countries of monsoon Asia, and about 90% of the total world area under rice lies within the region. Rice is the main food crop because it is well suited to Asian climatic conditions, producing high yields of a nutritious grain where other cereal crops will not readily grow. Wet rice cultivation is typically associated with the alluvial lowlands of monsoon Asia, but rice will tolerate a wide range of geographic, climatic and ecological conditions, and is even grown under upland cultivation.

There are two cultivated species of rice, *Oryza sativa* and *O. glaberrima*. *O. sativa*, which is native to tropical Asia, is widely grown in tropical and semi-tropical areas, while the cultivation of *O. glaberrima* is limited to the high rainfall zone of West Africa. In Asia and Africa unmilled rice is referred to as 'paddy', but 'rough' rice is the common appellation in the West. After removal of the outer husk, it is called 'brown' rice. After the grain is milled to remove the bran layers, it is described as 'milled' rice. As rice loses 30%–40% of its weight in the milling process it is usually traded in the milled form, to minimize shipping expenses.

Rice is an annual grass belonging to the same family as (and having many similar characteristics to) small grains such as wheat, oats, rye and barley. It is principally the semi-aquatic nature of rice that distinguishes it from other grain species, and this is an important factor in determining its place of origin, its dominant role in monsoon Asia and its extension to other environments. Rice varieties may broadly be classified into two main groups: *indica* and *japonica*. (There is also an intermediate, or *java*, type, cultivated in parts of Indonesia.) However, many rice varieties currently being grown are improved crosses of *indica* and *japonica* rices. The *indica* group, prevalent in South and South-East Asia, and covering a high proportion of the total rice area of Asia, has been associated with low yields and primitive production techniques. The *japonica* types (which predominate in East Asia), while not inherently more productive than the *indica* types, are more responsive to natural and artificial fertilizers and give higher average yields.

**Production of Paddy Rice**
('000 metric tons)

| | 2006 | 2007 |
|---|---|---|
| **World total** | 644,116 | 650,193 |
| South Asia | 202,058 | 203,689 |
| **Leading regional producers** | | |
| Bangladesh* | 43,504 | 43,504 |
| India | 139,137 | 141,134* |
| Nepal | 4,209 | 3,681 |
| Pakistan | 8,137 | 8,300* |
| Sri Lanka | 3,342 | 3,131 |
| **Other leading producers** | | |
| Brazil | 11,527 | 11,080 |
| Cambodia | 6,264 | 5,995† |
| China, People's Repub. | 184,128 | 185,490 |
| Egypt | 6,755 | 6,665 |
| Indonesia | 54,455 | 57,049* |
| Japan | 10,695 | 10,970† |
| Korea, Dem. People's Repub.† | 2,368 | 2,165 |
| Korea, Repub. | 6,324 | 5,960 |
| Malaysia* | 2,154 | 2,231 |
| Myanmar* | 30,600 | 32,610 |
| Nigeria | 4,042 | 4,677 |
| Philippines | 15,327 | 16,000 |
| Thailand | 29,269 | 27,879 |
| USA | 8,788 | 8,956 |
| Viet Nam | 35,827 | 35,567† |

* Unofficial figure(s).
† FAO estimate(s).

Underlying the low average rice yields in South Asia (including India, Bangladesh and Sri Lanka) and also in South-East Asia, compared with those in East Asia (the People's Republic of China, the Koreas, Japan and Taiwan), are the lack of modern varieties which are adapted to local conditions, and the shortage of associated technology, including fertilizers and pesticides, and of adequate and timely supplies of water. Conventional rice varieties respond to increased fertilizer usage by producing more leaf and stalk instead of grain, causing the plant to lodge (fall over), decreasing net yields.

One of the most important roles of the International Rice Research Institute (IRRI), based in the Philippines, is to develop new technologies with the aim of improving the lives of poor rice farmers and consumers. During the 1960s the IRRI developed a series of stiff-stemmed, semi-dwarf varieties, bearing upright leaves, that respond positively to high rates of fertilizer application and other improved cultural practices. These improved varieties may yield as much as 10 metric tons of paddy rice per ha, while old varieties may yield less than 1 ton per ha. Agronomists at the IRRI, and in national programmes, are continually developing varieties that will tolerate drought, flood, deep water and sub-optimum temperatures, and high-yielding varieties (HYVs) which are designed for areas without costly irrigation or where water is scarce. Farmers cultivating these varieties may expect a reduced risk of crop failures, and are more likely to invest in other production inputs. In the late 1990s the IRRI was developing new HYVs that, it believed, could increase harvest yields by 20%–30% by the early 2000s. Hybrid rice technology developed by the IRRI has clearly demonstrated yields that are 1–1.5 tons per ha higher than modern inbred varieties commonly cultivated in such countries as India and Bangladesh. In 2003, according to the IRRI, the area under rice hybrids increased to 280,000 ha in India. Bangladesh was reported to have also begun to commercialize this technology on, initially, some 10,000 ha. The IRRI also reported that cold-tolerance genes were being incorporated into cold-susceptible Bangladeshi rice varieties in order to improve the yield potential for Bangladeshi farmers cultivating rice during the winter (or boro) season. It was forecast by the IRRI in 1997 that annual world rice production would have to advance by 70% by 2025 in order to keep pace with current rates of population growth.

Thailand became the world's leading rice exporter in 1981, and rice has remained the country's principal agricultural export commodity. Owing to the depressed state of the world rice market from the early 1980s and the achievement of self-sufficiency by a number of Asian countries, Thailand increased its exports of rice largely at the expense of the USA. However, the decision by the USA to include rice in its Food Security Act, which came into operation in 1986 (making US-grown rice eligible for subsidized export credits), significantly affected the level of sales from Asian rice producers by undercutting the price of their exports. During the late 1980s, however, Thailand substantially expanded sales of its high quality rice to the European Community (now the European Union—EU), Russia, South Africa, Saudi Arabia and Iran. Thailand's dominance in the world rice market has come under increasing pressure in recent years from India and Viet Nam.

India, whose rice production has increased markedly since the late 1980s, emerged as a major exporter during 1993–95, when the relaxation of government restrictions led to a rise in export sales from 767,660 metric tons in 1993 to 4.9m. tons in 1995. However, the volume of India's exports is subject to the maintenance of rice stocks for domestic use at a statutory minimum level of 10m. tons. In 1998, owing to poor crops in a number of importing countries, India's rice exports again approached 5m. tons. The return of more favourable growing conditions in 1999 had an adverse effect on this trade, particularly with Bangladesh, which is normally a substantial importer of Indian rice. Export sales declined to 1.9m. tons in that year, and again in 2000, to 1.5m. tons, according to FAO. In 2001 India exported 2.2m. tons of rice. The country resumed the role of a major supplier to the international rice market in 2002, unprecedentedly high stocks having exerted pressure on the Government to subsidize foreign sales. Exports totalled 5.1m. tons in that year. In 2003, according to FAO, India's exports of rice totalled 3.5m. tons. Foreign sales remained at a high level in 2004, amounting to 4.8m. tons, but then declined in 2005, when the volume exported was 4.0m. tons. Following concerns relating to diminished rice stocks, the Indian Government imposed a ban on rice exports (with the exception of basmati) in October 2007. The ban was subsequently revoked, following protests by major importing countries. However, the rapid increase in prices for this commodity (see below) prompted, once again, the cessation of non-basmati rice exports in April 2008. Meanwhile, import duties on rice were relaxed as the authorities sought to ease pressure on domestic suppliers.

In Bangladesh, where some two-thirds of the population are engaged in livelihood activities that are related to rice, per caput consumption of rice is greater than in any other country where it is the staple food. Most rice in Bangladesh is grown by smallholders, who cultivate the grain for family consumption and market the marginal surplus. In some recent years Bangladesh has almost achieved self-sufficiency in rice. Output in 2006, at 43.5m. metric tons, was more than double the level achieved in 1980—about 20.8m. tons. Bangladeshi imports of rice rose steeply in each year in the second half of the 1990s, with the exception of 1997, reaching more than 2.2m. tons in 1999. In 2000 and 2001 improved crops reduced the country's need to purchase rice, imports in those years totalling, respectively, about 450,000 tons and 150,000 tons. In 2002, however, imports rose sharply, to about 940,000 tons, and they increased again in 2003, to some 1.3m. tons. In 2005, according to FAO, Bangladesh's imports of rice remained at a high level, totalling some 991,809 tons. It is unclear whether Bangladesh will be able to achieve and sustain self-sufficiency in rice. While imports declined by 37% in 2005, to 622,284 tons, modern cultivation techniques continued to exhibit negative effects, such as loss of rice biodiversity, a decline in soil fertility and groundwater contamination. The liberalization of trade poses another challenge to the sector. Bangladeshi rice farmers receive far fewer subsidies than their Indian counterparts, and cheaper Indian rice finds a ready market in Bangladesh, where it depresses local prices, discouraging Bangladeshi farmers from rice cultivation.

Rice is Pakistan's third most important agricultural export crop, after wheat and cotton, and is grown on some 10% of the country's cultivated land—2.6m. ha in 2006, according to FAO. According to the Rice Exporters Association of Pakistan, rice contributes about 6.7% of all agricultural value added and about 1.6% of the country's gross domestic product. In 1987–88 the rice export sector was opened to private interests, thus ending the monopoly of the Rice Export Corpn of Pakistan. As in India and Bangladesh, rice production has increased substantially since the 1980s. In 1999 a crop of more than 7.7m. metric tons was recorded. Output remained well above 7m. tons in 2000, but declined to about 5.8m. tons in 2001. In 2002 production increased to about 6.7m. tons, and it reached 7.3m. tons in 2003. Output increased again, to some 7.5m. tons, in 2004, and to about 8.3m. tons in 2005. Annual exports of rice by Pakistan averaged about 1.8m. tons in the second half of the 1990s. In 2000 about 2m. tons were exported, and the total rose to more than 2.4m. tons in 2001. The volume of rice exported fluctuated within a range of 2m.–3m. tons in 2002–05. In the 2006/07 financial year revenue from rice exports amounted to 68,285.9m. Pakistani rupees (equivalent to 6.6% of total exports), compared with 69,325.1m. rupees in 2005/06 (7.0%). Recent turmoil on international food markets (see below) was expected to benefit Pakistan's rice exporters in 2007/08, following India's decision to restrict foreign sales of rice. A substantial increase in the volume and value of exports was subsequently projected for that year, and it was widely anticipated that Pakistan would surpass India as principal supplier of the global rice market—at least until such time as India resumed trading at previous levels.

Rice, grown on about 55% (some 1.4m. ha in 2006) of cultivated land in Nepal, dominates the country's agricultural sector, the economy's most important sector. About one-quarter of Nepal's gross domestic product is derived from the rice sector. In recent years there has been a shift to the cultivation of HYVs (see above), and this has led farmers to apply fertilizers to crops, unlike when local varieties are grown. Annual production averaged about 3.7m. metric tons in the second half of the 1990s. In each year in 2000–06 Nepal's production of rice was greater than 4m. tons, although it declined to 3.7m. tons in 2007, according to FAO data. Nepal has little involvement in the trading of rice, importing less than 50,000 tons annually in most recent years, with 2000, when imports approached 200,000 tons, notable among the exceptional years. Concerns relating to the security of the country's food supply prompted Nepal to impose an export ban on rice (in addition to a number of other staple foods) in the first of half of 2008.

As in Nepal, in Sri Lanka, where more than 30% of the total labour force is involved either directly or indirectly in the rice sector, rice is cultivated as a subsistence crop. The country is very largely self-sufficient in production, in theory at least. In the 1990s there were fairly large annual variations in production, and, as a consequence, in the quantity of rice imported annually. Average annual production in 2000–07 was about 3.0m. metric tons, compared with about 2.5m. tons in the 1990s. Import requirements have continued to fluctuate in recent years. In 1999, for instance, more than 200,000 tons was imported. In 2000 the amount was only about 15,000 tons. In 2002 imports rose again, to approach 100,000 tons, but they amounted to only some 34,518 tons in 2003. In 2004 the quantity imported increased very substantially, to more than 240,697 tons. The volume of rice imported more than halved in 2005, however, falling to 51,729 tons. It has been estimated that Sri Lanka needs to stabilize annual production at about 3.1m. tons in order to meet increased demand resulting from population growth, a slight increase in consumption per head and requirements for seed.

The bulk of rice production is consumed in the producing countries, and international trade generally accounts for less than 5% of world output. Governments are the principal (but not exclusive) traders, and five countries dominate the export market in most years: Thailand, Viet Nam, the USA, China and India. Both India and Pakistan export rice to a wide variety of destinations in Asia, the Middle East, Africa and Europe. Under the EU's EBA (Everything but Arms) Regulation, adopted in 2001, whereby least developed countries (including Afghanistan, Bangladesh, Bhutan and Nepal) were granted duty-free access to the EU for all products except arms and ammunition, full liberalization of the import regime for rice was scheduled to enter effect in 2009.

The average export price of Thai milled white rice ('Thai 100% B second grade', f.o.b. Bangkok) in 2000 was US $206.7 per metric ton, but in 2001 the price fell to only $177.4 per ton. While world output of rice advanced in 1999/2000, the volume of trade declined, as many major importing countries, assisted by favourable weather, increased production. In 2002 the average export price of Thai milled white rice recovered to $196.9 per ton, and in 2003 an average price of $200.9 per ton was recorded. In 2004 the average price strengthened again, to $244.5 per ton, and in 2005 it rose by almost 19%, to $290.5 per ton. A further increase, of 7.1%, to $311.2 per ton, was recorded in 2006. At $334.5 per ton, the average export price of Thai milled white rice was 7.5% higher in 2007 than in 2006. In October–December 2007 the average monthly price increased by 11.3%, from $337.5 per ton to $375.7 per ton, and in February 2008 an increase of more than 20% compared with January, to $463 per ton, was recorded. Having risen to $567 per ton in March, in April the average price of Thai milled white rice increased by more than 50%, to $853.3 per ton. In May, at $962.6 per ton, the average price was 150% higher than that recorded in January. In June, however, a decline of 9.6%, to $870.3 per ton, was registered. Market observers placed the unprecedentedly high levels to which international prices of rice rose in the first half of 2008 in the context of a rising trend in the prices of basic food commodities—in particular wheat, soya, maize, rape and palm oil—that had been apparent for two years, prompted to a large extent by the inability, owing to such factors as accelerated urbanization and crop losses attributed to climate change, of supply to keep pace with increasing demand for food that proceeded from a generally higher standard of living in developing countries—especially in Asia. More immediately, the very high price of wheat, which prompted higher demand for rice, and increases in the prices of agricultural inputs (seed, fertilizers, pesticides, etc.) which were themselves the consequence of higher prices for energy, and a high level of speculative investment in agricultural commodities (which had come to be viewed as a refuge from rising inflation and the weakness of the US dollar), were cited as additional factors behind this rising trend. (For a three-month period in the first half of 2008 rice reportedly became the agricultural 'market of choice' for speculative funds.) It was noted that the rise in the price of rice from November 2007 was not driven by shortage of supply: world output reached a record level in 2007, and, as of the second quarter of 2008, FAO forecast that another record crop would be harvested in 2008. Rather, high prices for rice stemmed from export curbs or other restrictions imposed by some major rice-exporting countries—including the People's Republic of China, India, Egypt and Viet Nam—as part of attempts to restrain domestic consumer price inflation. At the end of March 2008, for example, Viet Nam announced that it would reduce its exports by 25% in 2008, after the increase in the price that had already occurred since the beginning of the year had caused consumer prices generally to rise by 20%—a 12-year record. According to FAO, a further aggravating factor was very large tenders for rice issued by the Philippines. where, in response to social unrest caused by high food prices, the Government had initiated a rice-distribution programme. Thailand was also reported to have distributed rice from stocks on its domestic market at a discount of 40% on the prevailing international price. These policies—with some countries reducing exports and others increasing imports—were of particular significance because of the small proportion of world rice production that enters world trade. FAO noted at April 2008 that although the availability of new supplies from the 2007 secondary rice crop in the northern hemisphere and from the 2008 main crop in the southern hemisphere was likely to cause prices to fall in the immediate future, prices were expected to remain 'extremely firm' until at least the beginning of the third quarter of 2008 unless export restrictions were relaxed—especially in the context of the low level of stocks in Thailand and the USA, and in view of probable substantial purchases by Iran, Iraq, Nigeria, Saudi Arabia and Senegal.

## SOYBEANS

The soybean plant (*Glycine max* or *G. soya*) is a legume, a member of the pea family (*fabaceae*). Like other legumes it is able to collect its own nitrogen from the air and release it into the soil. The soybean has accordingly played an important role in the maintenance of soil fertility under traditional crop rotation regimes. Owing to the plant's sensitivity to light, it has been possible to optimize cultivation through the selection of varieties adapted, according to the length of their crop durations, to geographical differences in daylight hours. It is the breeding of such varieties that has allowed successful cultivation to extend from northern, temperate zones, where the soybean originated, to, for example, subtropical and tropical regions of the USA and South America. In North America, the main area of cultivation, soybeans are generally planted in the late spring. The plant flowers in the summer, producing 60–80 pods from which two to four pea-sized beans are harvested in the autumn.

Cultivation of the soybean plant is thought to have originated more than 5,000 years ago in northern China, and to have spread southwards from there to Korea, Japan and throughout south-east Asia. In the regions of its origin and early dissemination the soybean has for centuries been a primary source of protein for human consumption. However, it was not until the mid-20th century that soybeans began to be traded internationally to a significant degree.

During the Second World War, and into the 1950s and 1960s, US soybean production was greatly expanded, with the aim of substituting domestically produced soybean oil for imported oils and fats. Thereafter, the protein-rich meal, which is a by-product of crushing for oil, was used to boost livestock production in the USA. Until recently, the soybean had for long been the most important source of vegetable oil world-wide. Today, however, the oil palm rivals it as the most important source and is likely to supersede it definitively in the near future. Soybean meal, meanwhile, accounts for about 70% of the world's supply of protein-rich animal feedstuffs. The meal (also known as cake), almost all of which is used for livestock feed, is the most valuable product obtained from processing, generally accounting for 50%–75% of total value, depending on the difference in the prices of meal and oil. Furthermore, in addition to the traditional foods derived from soy for human consumption, the plant's derivatives are widely employed in processed foods marketed in Europe and North America. Among many industrial applications, the soybean also provides a raw material for the manufacture of ink, soap, paint and a fuel for diesel engines. It remains uncertain, however, the extent to which demand will increase for soybeans as a biofuel feedstock, since, under production and trading regimes as of mid-2008, especially in the European Union (EU), the economic viability of many other crop-derived feedstocks was superior to that of soybeans.

The USA has dominated world production of soybeans since the 1950s, when its output overtook that of China. In 2006/07, according to the US Department of Agriculture (USDA), US production amounted to some 87m. metric tons, equivalent to about 36.6% of total world output of some 237m. tons. US output in 2005/06 was about 83m. tons—representing some 38% of the global total of about 221m. tons. In 2004/05 US production, at 85m. tons, accounted for around 39.4% of global output totalling about 216m. tons. Despite consistently improving harvests, however, the USA's share of world production has been in decline since the 1970s, when the country was regularly the source of more than two-thirds of global output. Soybeans are also grown in Canada—in 2006/07, with output totalling about 3.5m. tons, Canada ranked as the world's seventh largest producer.

One of the reasons for the decline in the USA's share of world production has been very substantial increases in the output of Latin America and the Caribbean, which since 2002 (with the exception of 2004, when North America—the USA and Canada—regained primacy) has ranked as the world's largest producer region. Brazil is the largest Latin American producer, and the second largest world-wide, with output of 59m. metric tons in 2006/07 and 57m. tons in 2005/06. Production by Argentina, the world's third largest producer, amounted to about 49m. tons in 2006/07, compared with some 41m. tons in the previous crop year. Paraguay, with production of about 6.2m. tons in 2006/07 and 3.6m. tons in 2005/06, is the other major producer among Latin American and Caribbean countries. According to FAO, Bolivian output of soybeans amounted to some 1.7m. tons in 2006.

In South Asia India is the only country that ranks as a major producer of soybeans, its output in 2006/07, according to the USA, having amounted to 7.7m. metric tons, or about 3.2% of global production in that crop year, when India was the fifth largest producer world-wide. In 2005/06, according to the same source, Indian production of soybeans totalled 7m. tons, equivalent, again, to some 3.2% of ouput world-wide.

The People's Republic of China complements the list of major producers of soybean in world terms, its output, according to USDA, having totalled some16m. metric tons in 2006/07—about 7% of global production—compared with some 16.4m. tons in 2005/06 and around 17.4m. tons in 2004/05.

**Production of Soybeans**
('000 metric tons)

| | 2005/06 | 2006/07 |
|---|---|---|
| **World total** | 220,537 | 237,361 |
| **Leading regional producer** | | |
| India | 7,000 | 7,690 |
| **Other major producers** | | |
| Argentina | 40,500 | 48,800 |
| Brazil | 57,000 | 59,000 |
| Canada | 3,161 | 3,460 |
| China, People's Rep. | 16,350 | 15,967 |
| Paraguay | 3,640 | 6,200 |
| USA | 83,368 | 86,770 |

Source: US Department of Agriculture, *Oilseeds: World Markets and Trade* (May 2008).

The pattern of production of soybean meal is similar to that of unprocessed soybeans. The USA is the dominant world producer, its output in 2006/07 amounting to some 39m. metric tons, or 25% of world production in that year, according to USDA. On a regional basis, however, world output is dominated by Latin America—Argentina, Brazil and, to a lesser extent, Mexico—where aggregated production totalled about 53m. tons in 2006/07 (Argentina, 26m. tons; Brazil, 24m. tons; Mexico, 3m. tons). As with soybeans, India is the only significant producer of soybean meal in South Asia, its output having totalled about 5.3m. tons in 2006/07, according to USDA, and about 4.8m. tons in 2005/06. India thus ranked as the world's fifth largest individual producer of soybean meal in both of those crop years—and sixth when the aggregated output of the member states of the EU is taken into consideration.

China complements the list of major producers of soybean meal in world terms—it is the second largest producer after the USA—with output of some 28m. tons in 2006/07.

**Production of Soybean Meal**
('000 metric tons)

| | 2005/06 | 2006/07 |
|---|---|---|
| **World total** | 145,728 | 153,896 |
| **Leading regional producer** | | |
| India | 4,772 | 5,268 |
| **Other major producers** | | |
| Argentina | 25,012 | 26,061 |
| Brazil | 21,892 | 23,800 |
| China, People's Rep. | 27,296 | 28,090 |
| European Union | 10,760 | 11,550 |
| Mexico | 3,030 | 3,158 |
| USA | 37,416 | 39,033 |

Source: US Department of Agriculture, *Oilseeds: World Markets and Trade* (May 2008).

As with soybean meal, the USA is the world's leading individual producer of soybean oil, with output totalling some 9m. metric tons in 2006/07, or about 25% of world production amounting to about 36m. tons in that crop year. On a regional basis, Latin America—again, Argentina, Brazil and Mexico—dominates world output, the region's aggregated production totalling about 12.7m. tons in 2006/07 (Argentina, 6.4m. tons; Brazil, 5.9m. tons; Mexico, 0.7m. tons), equivalent to some 35% of output world-wide in that year. In 2006/07 China ranked—after the USA and Argentina—as the world's third largest producer of soybean oil, with production totalling about 6.3m. tons. The member states of the EU occupied fifth position, with output amounting to about 2.6m. tons.

India is the only significant South Asian producer of soybean oil, with output of about 1.2m. metric tons in 2006/07, according to USDA, and some 1.7m. tons in 2005/06.

**Production of Soybean Oil**
('000 metric tons)

| | 2005/06 | 2006/07 |
|---|---|---|
| **World total** | 34,553 | 36,331 |
| **Leading regional producer** | | |
| India | 1,050 | 1,180 |
| **Other major producers** | | |
| Argentina | 5,998 | 6,424 |
| Brazil | 5,430 | 5,890 |
| China, People's Rep. | 6,149 | 6,340 |
| European Union | 2,460 | 2,640 |
| USA | 9,248 | 9,292 |

Source: US Department of Agriculture, *Oilseeds: World Markets and Trade* (May 2008).

Soybeans are by far the most important oilseed in international trade. In 2006/07, according to USDA, soybean imports, totalling about 69.1m. metric tons, accounted for some 86% of all world oilseed imports (including, additionally, those of copra, cottonseed, palm kernels, groundnuts, rapeseed and sunflowerseed), totalling about 81m. tons, while exports of soybeans, at some 71m. tons, were equivalent to about 85% of world exports of oilseeds amounting to 84m. tons. Rapeseed, which ranks as the second largest oilseed in international trade, accounted for no more than about 9% of all oilseed imports in 2006/07, and for about 8% of all oilseeds exported. On a regional basis, the countries of the Far East and Australia constitute the most important export market for unprocessed soybeans, China alone, the world's main importing country, receiving shipments totalling about 30m. tons, or about 42% of total world imports, in 2006/07, followed by the member states of the EU (22%), Japan (6%) and Mexico (5.6%). The combined imports of China, Japan, the Republic of China (Taiwan), Indonesia, Thailand and the Republic of Korea accounted for some 57% of the world total in 2006/07. The USA is the world's leading exporter of soybeans, with foreign sales totalling some 30m. tons in 2006/07—equivalent to about 42% of world exports. On a regional basis, Latin America ranks as the leading world exporter of soybeans, the aggregated exports of Brazil, Argentina and Paraguay accounting for some 53% of global exports in 2006/07. Brazil ranked as the world's second largest exporter country in 2006/07, with foreign sales totalling some 23m. tons, followed by Argentina, with some 10m. tons, Paraguay (4m. tons) and Canada (about 2m. tons).

Soybean meal is the leading protein meal in international trade, accounting for 79% of all world exports of protein meal in 2006/07, according to USDA. In comparison, exports of palm kernel meal—the second most widely traded protein meal—accounted for only about 6% of total world exports of protein meal in that year. International trade in soybean meal has increased steadily since the 1970s. Latin America is the leading exporting region, accounting for about 74% of world exports totalling 54m. metric tons in 2006/07, according to USDA. Within the region, Argentina overtook Brazil as the leading exporter in the late 1990s. In 2006/07 Argentina and Brazil accounted, respectively, for 47% and 24% of total world exports of soybean meal, while Paraguay accounted, approximately, for an additional 3%. After Argentina and Brazil, the USA ranked as the world's third largest exporter of soybean meal in 2006/07, with foreign sales totalling about 8m. tons—some 15% of total world exports—followed, in fourth position, by India, the only significant South Asian exporter, whose exports contributed a little more than 6% of the world total. In 2006/07 the member states of the EU accounted for by far the largest share—43%—of world imports of soybean meal totalling about 52m. tons. Most other significant importers of soybean meal—Thailand, Indonesia, the Republic of Korea, Viet Nam, Japan, the Philippines and Malaysia—were located in Far East Asia, their aggregated imports accounting for some 24% of the world total. Mexico and Canada are also significant importers of soybean meal, their imports accounting, respectively, for 3.4% and 2.8% of total world imports in 2006/07.

While soybeans dominate international trade in unprocessed oilseeds and soybean meal world trade in protein meals, trade in vegetable oils is dominated by palm oil, which in 2006/07, according to USDA, accounted for about 55% of world exports of vegetable oils (including, additionally, coconut, cottonseed, olive, palm, palm kernel, groundnut, rapeseed (canola), soybean and sunflowerseed oils) totalling about 48m. metric tons, and for some 57% of vegetable oil imports—amounting to about 47m. tons—world-wide. Soybean oil, which costs about one-fifth more than palm oil to produce, ranks second, accounting for 22% of world vegetable oil exports and about 21% of world vegetable oil imports in 2006/07. In that year Argentina ranked as the world's leading exporter of soybean oil, its foreign sales, at about 6m. tons, accounting for about 56% of world exports totalling some 11m. tons. The combined exports of Argentina, Brazil and Paraguay represented more than 82% of world exports of soybean oil in 2006/07, far greater than those of any other region or trading bloc. China was the world's leading importer of soybean oil in 2006/07, accounting for about one-quarter of world imports totalling some 9.7m. tons, followed by India (14.5%) and the member states of the EU (10%). Elsewhere in South Asia, Bangladesh is a noteworthy importer of soybean oil, receiving shipments of about 327,000 tons in 2006/07, according to USDA. According to some forecasts, it is anticipated that demand, supply and trade in vegetable oil may increase by as much as 30% by 2015—and, owing to the complexity of the calculations involved, increasing demand for biofuels has not always been factored into medium-term predictions. Soybean oil has hitherto accounted for only a small proportion—relative to, above all, rapeseed oil and sunflowerseed oil—of vegetable oil-derived biodiesel and, under current production and trading conditions, trails palm oil and rapeseed oil, as well as other crops, such as sugar and cassava, that can be used as biodiesel feedstocks—in terms of economic viability.

As there are relatively few major producers of soybeans worldwide, and as soybeans are the most important oilseed in world trade, US policy has influenced not only the world market for soybeans, but also the markets for the seven major competing oilseeds—rapeseed, sunflowerseed, cottonseed, groundnuts, flaxseed, copra and palm kernels. Moreover, with regard to unprocessed soybeans, US influence has been reinforced by the fact that international trade has historically been comparatively free of tariffs and other restrictions on imports. (Tariffs applied to protect the oilseed-processing industries of importing countries, however, have typically been fixed at about twice the rate applied to the unprocessed commodity.) Since the mid-1970s, however, the USA's dominance of the international soybean market has steadily declined, in spite of growth in both production and export volume. Above all, this has been due to the rapid expansion in production and exports by Argentina and Brazil, whose individual exports of soybean meal and soybean oil have both overtaken those of the USA. Lower-cost production of soybeans in Argentina and Brazil has given those countries a considerable competitive advantage in international markets.

The leading role of the USA in the production and export of soybeans means that US prices are the most accurate and readily available guide to the international market. According to USDA, the US farm price for soybeans averaged US $205 per metric ton in 2005/06 (October–September), rising to $254 per ton in 2006/07. (In 1996/97 the US farm price averaged $274 per ton.) In October 2007–April 2008 the average price rose steeply, to $382 per ton, ranging between $307 per ton in October and an estimated $434 per ton in April.

Fluctuations in prices for soybean products tend to follow variations in the price of unprocessed beans, with an additional vulnerability to market conditions for alternatives, especially in the case of soybean oil. In 2005/06 (October–September) the average US wholesale price for soybean meal (48% protein) was US $192 per metric ton, rising to $226 per ton in 2006/07. In October 2007–April 2008 the average US wholesale price increased to $345 per ton, ranging between $287 per ton in October and $365 per ton in January and March. In 2005/06 the quotation (f.o.b.) for Brazilian soybean meal (45%–46%) protein at Rio Grande was $176 per ton. The representative Brazilian quotation rose to $199 per ton in 2006/07. In October–April 2007/08 an average price of $320 per ton was recorded at Rio Grande, the quotation ranging between $280 per ton (October) and $354 per ton (February). The price of Argentinian soybean meal pellets (f.o.b.) at Buenos Aires averaged $158 per ton in 2005/06, rising to $181 per ton in 2006/07. In October 2007–April 2008 the average representative Argentinian quotation was $282 per ton, soybean meal having traded within a range of $250–$304 per ton in that period. In 2005/06 the average import price (f.o.b., ex-mill) of soybean meal recorded at Hamburg, Germany, was $215 per ton. In 2006/07 the average import price recorded at Hamburg rose to $276 per ton. In October 2007–April 2008 the average import price recorded at Hamburg increased to $459 per ton, having traded between $400 per ton (October) and an estimated $541 per ton (April) in that period.

According to USDA, the average US price of soybean oil (wholesale tank, crude) was US $516 per metric ton in 2005/06 (October–September). In 2006/07 the average US price increased to $684 per ton. In October 2007–April 2008 a substantial increase in the average US price for soybean oil, to $1,091 per ton, was registered. The representative Brazilian quotation (f.o.b. bulk rate) for soybean oil averaged $474 per ton in 2005/06, rising to $673 per ton in 2006/07. In October 2007–April 2008 the average Brazilian quotation rose to $1,165 per ton, having traded between $896 per ton (October) and $1,354 per ton (February) in that period. In 2005/06 the representative quotation (f.o.b.) for soybean oil of Argentine origin averaged $467 per ton, rising to $667 per ton in 2006/07. In October 2007–April 2008 the average Argentine quotation rose to $1,209 per ton, having ranged between $832 per ton (October) and $1,496 per ton (February) in that period. At Rotterdam, Netherlands, an average import price (Dutch f.o.b., ex-mill) of $573 per ton was registered for soybean oil in 2005/06. In 2006/07 the average Rotterdam quotation increased to $771 per ton. In October 2007–April 2008 the average import price at

Rotterdam ranged between $1,012 per ton (October) and $1,476 per ton (March), averaging $1,270 per ton.

At mid-2008 FAO reported that international prices for oilseeds, cakes and vegetable oils continued to be characterized by a rising trend that had begun in 2005/06. In June 2008 the continued strength of prices that had risen to record levels in the first quarter of the year reportedly reflected, on the one hand, the influence of world markets for grains and, on the other, a fall in production of oilseeds world-wide that was causing reduced growth in supplies of oils and fats and a decline in supplies of oilseed meals on a hitherto unseen scale. At the same time, greater demand for vegetable oils and oilseed meal world-wide, that would unavoidably cause a sharp fall in inventories, had combined with uncertain weather conditions and changes to trade policies to propel prices upwards. Additional price volatility was reported to have derived from disturbances—themselves caused by the instability of world prices—to the normal trading patterns of countries such as China and India. FAO forecast that prices of oilseeds and their derivatives might possibly stabilize and weaken as the 2007/08 season progressed, and in 2008/09, in line with anticipated increases in plantings of oilseeds. However, the need to replenish stocks was expected to ensure that prices remained substantially in excess of levels recorded in 2006/07. Any sustained weakening of prices was regarded as unlikely since initial declines would stimulate demand for vegetable oils for use as biofuel feedstock—especially in view of the historically elevated level of the price of petroleum.

## SUGAR

Sugar is a sweet crystalline substance, which may be derived from the juices of various plants. Chemically, the basis of sugar is sucrose, one of a group of soluble carbohydrates which are important sources of energy in the human diet. It can be obtained from trees, including the maple and certain palms, but virtually all manufactured sugar is derived from two plants, sugar beet (*Beta vulgaris*) and sugar cane, a giant perennial grass of the genus *Saccharum*.

**Production of Sugar Cane**
('000 metric tons)

| | 2006 | 2007 |
|---|---|---|
| **World total*** | 1,388,674 | 1,237,032 |
| South Asia* | 340,630 | 105,470 |
| **Leading regional producers** | | |
| India | 281,172 | 355,520 |
| Pakistan | 44,666 | 54,752 |
| **Other leading producers** | | |
| Argentina* | 19,000 | 19,200 |
| Australia | 38,169 | 36,000 |
| Brazil | 457,246 | 514,080 |
| China, People's Repub. | 100,435 | 105,651 |
| Colombia* | 39,000 | 40,000 |
| Cuba | 11,060 | 11,100* |
| Indonesia† | 25,200 | 25,200 |
| Mexico | 50,676 | 50,680 |
| Philippines | 24,345 | 25,300* |
| South Africa | 20,275 | 20,500* |
| Thailand | 47,658 | 64,366 |
| USA | 27,033 | 27,751 |

* FAO estimate(s).
† Unofficial figures.

Sugar cane, found in tropical areas, grows to a height of up to 5 m. The plant is native to Polynesia, but its distribution is now widespread. It is not necessary to plant cane every season as, if the root of the plant is left in the ground, it will grow again in the following year. This practice, known as 'ratooning', may be continued for as long as three years, after which yields begin to decline. Cane is ready for cutting 12–24 months after planting, depending on local conditions. More than half of the world's sugar cane is still cut by hand, but rising costs are hastening the changeover to mechanical harvesting. The cane is cut as close as possible to the ground, and the top leaves, which may be used as cattle fodder, are removed.

After cutting, the cane is loaded by hand or by machine into trucks or trailers and towed directly to a factory for processing. Sugar cane rapidly deteriorates after it has been cut and should be processed as soon as possible. At the factory the cane passes first through shredding knives or crushing rollers, which break up the hard rind and expose the inner fibre, and then to squeezing rollers, where the crushed cane is subjected to high pressure and sprayed with water. The resulting juice is heated, and lime is added for clarification and the removal of impurities. The clean juice is then concentrated in evaporators. This thickened juice is next boiled in steam-heated vacuum pans until a mixture or 'massecuite' of sugar crystals and 'mother syrup' is produced. The massecuite is then spun in centrifugal machines to separate the sugar crystals (raw cane sugar) from the residual syrup (cane molasses).

Production data for sugar cane generally cover all crops harvested, except crops grown explicitly for feed. The second table covers the production of raw sugar by the centrifugal process. In 2006 global output of non-centrifugal sugar (i.e. produced from sugar cane which has not undergone centrifugation) was estimated at about 1,557m. metric tons. The main producer of non-centrifugal sugar is India, with output of 356m. tons in 2007.

**Production of Centrifugal Sugar**
(raw value, '000 metric tons, local marketing year)

| | 2006/07 | 2007/08 |
|---|---|---|
| **World total** | 164,183 | 165,487 |
| South Asia | 34,7782 | 33,488 |
| **Leading regional producers** | | |
| India | 30,780 | 28,930 |
| Pakistan | 3,615 | 4,163 |
| **Other leading producers** | | |
| Australia | 4,822 | 5,031 |
| Brazil | 31,450 | 32,100 |
| China, People's Repub. | 12,855 | 14,500 |
| Colombia | 2,354 | 2,360 |
| Cuba | 1,150 | 900 |
| Germany | 4,456 | n.a. |
| Indonesia | 1,900 | 1,950 |
| Mexico | 5,633 | 5,950 |
| Philippines | 2,232 | 2,275 |
| Poland | 2,175 | n.a. |
| South Africa | 2,235 | 2,273 |
| Thailand | 6,720 | 7,650 |
| Turkey | 1,980 | 1,900 |
| Ukraine | 2,850 | 2,010 |
| USA | 7,663 | 7,614 |

Sources: FAO; US Department of Agriculture (USDA), Foreign Agricultural Service.

Most of the world's output of raw cane sugar is sent to refineries outside the country of origin, unless the sugar is for local consumption. India, Thailand, Brazil and Cuba are among the few cane-producers that export part of their output as refined sugar. The refining process further purifies the sugar crystals and eventually results in finished products of various grades, such as granulated, icing or castor sugar. The ratio of refined to raw sugar is usually about 0.9:1.

As well as providing sugar, quantities of cane are grown in some countries for seed, feed, fresh consumption, the manufacture of alcohol and other uses. Molasses may be used as cattle feed or fermented to produce alcoholic beverages for human consumption, such as rum, a distilled spirit manufactured in Caribbean countries. Sugar cane juice may be used to produce ethyl alcohol (ethanol). This chemical can be utilized, either exclusively or mixed with petroleum derivatives, as a fuel for motor vehicles. The steep rise in the price of petroleum after 1973 made the large-scale conversion of sugar cane into alcohol economically attractive (particularly to developing countries), especially as sugar, unlike petroleum, is a renewable source of energy. Several countries developed alcohol production by this means in order to reduce petroleum imports and to support cane growers. Ethanol-based fuel, a type of biofuel which generates fewer harmful exhaust hydrocarbons than petroleum-based fuel, may be known as 'gasohol', 'alcogas' or 'green petrol'. The pioneer in this field was Brazil, which operates the largest 'gasohol' production programme in the world. From 1975, in the aftermath ofthe first global oil crisis, the Government created an extensive distribution network to transport ethanol-based fuel to filling stations, where its price was kept low by the granting of subsidies to ethanol producers. By the early 1980s almost every new car sold in Brazil was fuelled exclusively by ethanol. In the 1990s, however, a shortage of ethanol, in conjunction with lower world petroleum prices and the Government's withdrawal of ethanol subsidies, resulted in a sharp fall in Brazil's output of these vehicles. Research to improve efficiency in ethanol production continued meanwhile, so that by the time oil prices reached new heights in the mid-2000s the production cost of ethanol had been reduced by two-thirds. Since mid-2005, the popularity of ethanol-fuelled motor vehicles has begun to rise again. A programme is under way in Brazil that aims to establish ethanol as a global export commodity, in the world trade of which Brazil currently accounts for more than 50%. US imports of ethanol were expected to rise substantially in 2006 as domestic refineries phased out the use of the gasoline additive methyl tertiary butyl ether (MTBE). According to FAO, the prospects for the use of ethanol as a fuel world-wide have been boosted by the historically high levels to which petroleum prices rose in 2005–08. Increased concerns over climate change have further strengthened the prospects of ethanol use world-wide, while new energy legislation in the EU and the USA has incorporated the need for a greater use of biofuel. In early 2007 the European Council ruled that biofuels should contribute 10% of fuel use by 2020 (a 20% increase), and in December 2007 the US Congress adopted the Energy Independence and Security Act, which requires an increase in the production of renewable fuels, from 4,000m. gallons (15,160m. litres) to 36,000m. gallons (136,440m. litres) by 2022. Global output of ethanol (including ethanol derived from crops other than sugar, such as maize) increased by 70% in 2000–06, from 30,000m. litres to 51,000m. litres. It has been forecast that ethanol production will reach 54,000m. litres—equivalent to 1% of world petroleum consumption—in 2010. Sugar cane cultivation is expected to expand in line with ethanol production, as it is the most cost-effective feedstock for biofuel production. In the Far East and Australasia unsuccessful attempts to establish 'gasohol' production were made in the Philippines and Papua New Guinea, while plans to initiate a 'gasohol' project in Thailand have been postponed indefinitely. Pakistan produced 36,500 litres of fuel-grade ethanol in 2006, most of which was exported to the US market. In that year the Government of Pakistan initiated a pilot study to test the feasibility of developing a domestic market for locally produced ethanol. The pilot scheme required that three petrol stations—located in Islamabad, Karachi and Lahore—blend Pakistani ethanol into their petroleum at a ratio of 10%. However, there remained considerable doubt as to whether Pakistan would be able to develop sufficient capacity to meet new demand from an internal market: in addition to a lack of capital funding, there was considered to be a lack of significant expertise to implement a large-scale production strategy. The operating costs of the conversion process remained high, since Pakistan processes ethanol from sugar to molasses initially and then converts the molasses into ethanol. Moreover, only four of the country's 21 operational distilleries were producing fuel-grade ethanol.

In recent years the promotion of biofuels has become increasingly controversial. In April 2008 a report compiled by the World Bank argued that the drive for biofuels by the US and European governments had been the most important factor responsible for the rapid increase in the prices of internationally traded food commodities since 2002. In the same month a UN report warned that unchecked expansion of the production of biofuel jeopardized food security in developing countries, not only by raising food prices, but also by making 'substantial demands on the world's land and water resources at a time when demand for both food and forest products is also rising rapidly'. The UN urged governments that regulations to manage the growth of the biofuel industry be put in place.

After the milling of sugar, the cane has dry fibrous remnants known as bagasse, which is usually burned as fuel in sugar mills but can be pulped and used for making fibreboard, particle board and most grades of paper. As the costs of imported wood pulp have risen, cane-growing regions have turned increasingly to the manufacture of paper from bagasse. In view of rising energy costs, some countries are encouraging the use of bagasse as fuel for electricity production to save foreign exchange expended on imports of petroleum. Another by-product, cachaza, has been utilized as an animal feed.

Sugar has in recent years encountered increased competition from other sweeteners, including maize-based products, such as isoglucose (a form of high-fructose corn syrup, or HFCS), and chemical additives, such as saccharine, aspartame (APM) and xylitol. Consumption of HFCS in the USA was equivalent to about 42% of the country's sugar consumption in the late 1980s, while in Japan and the Republic of Korea HFCS accounted for 19% and 25%, respectively, of domestic sweetener use. APM was the most widely used high-intensity artificial sweetener in the early 1990s, although its market dominance was under challenge from sucralose, which is about 600 times as sweet as sugar (compared with 200–300 times for other intense sweeteners) and is more resistant to chemical deterioration than APM. From the late 1980s research was conducted in the USA to formulate means of synthesizing thaumatin, a substance derived from the fruit of the West African katemfe plant, *Thaumatococcus daniellii*, which is about 2,500 times as sweet as sugar. As of 2005, the use of thaumatin had been approved in the European Union (EU), Israel, Japan and—as a flavouring agent—in the USA. In 1998 the US Government approved the domestic marketing of sucralose, the only artificial sweetener made from sugar. Sucralose was stated to avoid many of the taste problems associated with other artificial sweeteners.

The major sugar producers in South Asia are India and Pakistan. Although India is, after Brazil, usually the world's second largest producer of sugar cane and of centrifugal sugar, the quantity it exports (intermittently), owing to a combination of price and quality considerations, is of only marginal significance to the international market. Since the late 1980s India has occasionally had recourse to imports of sugar in order to satisfy domestic requirements. According to India's Ministry of Agriculture, output of sugar cane increased by an average of 1.1% per year between 1999/2000–2006/07, while the total area of farm land dedicated to sugar production increased steadily, reaching a new record of 4.8m. ha in the 2006/07 marketing year. Production of sugar cane was an estimated 355.5m. metric tons in 2006/07, up from 281.2m. tons in 2005/06. Preliminary estimates for 2007/08 showed ouput of 340.6m. tons. Meanwhile, the further increase in farm land dedicated to sugar cane production was largely attributable to increased sugar prices and an associated rise in demand. Improved irrigation (90.7% of farm land in 2003/04) and better pest control also resulted in increased production in 2006/07 and 2007/08. Increased stocks (for which there was no export outlet) and depressed local prices in the early 2000s generated a financial crisis in the sugar sector that necessitated government action. Relief measures included a programme, initiated in nine states in January 2003, to produce ethanol from molasses and sugar cane juice for fuel purposes; and loans, made on concessionary terms, to state governments, to enable them to meet unusually high arrears in cane payments to farmers. (In 2004 the Indian Supreme Court rejected legal action pursued by the Indian sugar industry against state governments, in an attempt to achieve a rationalization of sugar cane pricing policies which, the industry claims, elevate the cost of sugar production to an abnormally high level.) Strong sugar prices were reported to have led to higher prices for sugar cane in 2005/06, and these, in combination with prompt payments to farmers by sugar mills, contributed to the increased availability of sugar cane for sugar production. According to sugar industry sources cited by USDA in early 2006, a considerable improvement in the fiscal situation of the Indian sugar industry was attributable to higher sugar prices. In 2005/06 investment in the Indian sugar industry was reported to have increased by more than 90%, to some 52,000m. Indian rupees. According to USDA, India was a net exporter of centrifugal sugar in 2007/08, when foreign sales were estimated to have reached 3.7m. tons;. India did not import any centrifugal sugar that year. India's Ministry of Petroleum announced plans to distribute ethanol-blended gasoline nation-wide in the 2006/07 sugar marketing year.

In Pakistan, according to official provisional figures published by FAO, 1,029,000 ha were sown to sugar cane in 2006/07, mainly in the province of Punjab. In 2005/06 output of sugar (raw value) was estimated to have fallen to about metric 2.6m. tons, compared with about 2.9m. tons in 2004/05 and some 4m. tons in both 2003/04 and 2002/03. The declines in output in 2004/05 and 2005/06 were attributed to prolonged drought, and in the longer term the area sown to sugar cane is expected to decline as, in order to conserve water resources, Pakistan is believed to need to adopt alternative cultivation patterns which favour crops that are less water-intensive than sugar cane (or rice). Production none the less recovered in 2006/07 and 2007/08, to some 3.6m. tons and 4.2m. tons, respectively. In 2006 experiments with growing sugar beet in Punjab and Sindh provinces were reported to have shown promising results. Like India, Pakistan's involvement in the international trading of sugar is of minimal significance. The country was a net importer in both 2006/07 and 2007/08, with purchases amounting to 200,000 tons and 110,000 tons in each of those years, respectively. USDA forecast that Pakistan's imports would rise to 550,000 tons in 2008/09, as production would once again fail to meet domestic demand.

The first International Sugar Agreement (ISA) was negotiated in 1958, and its economic provisions operated until 1961. A second ISA did not come into operation until 1969. It included quota arrangements and associated provisions for regulating the price of sugar traded on the open market, and established the International Sugar Organization (ISO) to administer the agreement. However, the USA and the six original members of the European Community (EC, now the EU) did not participate in the ISA, and, following its expiry in 1974, it was replaced by a purely administrative interim agreement, which remained operational until the finalization of a third ISA, which took effect in 1978. The new agreement's implementation was supervised by an International Sugar Council (ISC), which was empowered to establish price ranges for sugar-trading and to operate a system of quotas and special sugar stocks. Owing to the reluctance of the USA and EC countries (which were not a party to the agreement) to accept export controls, the ISO ultimately lost most of its power to regulate the market, and since 1984 the activities of the organization have been restricted to compiling statistics and providing a forum for discussion between producers and consumers. Subsequent ISAs, without effective regulatory powers, have been in operation since 1985. The USA withdrew from the ISO at the end of 1992, following a disagreement over the formulation of members' financial contributions.

In tandem with world output of cane and beet sugars, stock levels (of centrifugal sugar) are an important factor in determining the prices at which sugar is traded internationally. These stocks, which were at relatively low levels in the late 1980s, increased significantly in the 1990s, although not, according to USDA data, in each successive trading year (September–August). In the early 1990s rises in stocks were due partly to the disruptive effects of the Gulf War on demand in the Middle East (normally a major sugar-consuming area), and were also a result of considerably increased production in Mexico and the Far East. Another factor was the increased area under sugar cane and beet in the EU and in Australia.

In 2003/04, according to data released by USDA, when world sugar production totalled about 142m. metric tons and consumption some 140m. tons, stocks of sugar held world-wide totalled about 38m. tons. In 2004/05, when the output of sugar world-wide totalled about 141m. tons and consumption rose to about 142m. tons, stocks declined, to some 34m. tons. In 2005/06, when world production of sugar amounted to about 145m. tons and world consumption to some 144m. tons, world sugar stocks fell for a third consecutive year, to about 32m. tons. In 2006/07, when world production of sugar totalled 164m. tons and world consumption 151m. tons, world sugar stocks increased to some 40m. tons. World stocks of sugar increased further, to 45m. tons, in 2007/08, while world production amounted to 165m. tons and consumption to 156m. tons. In 2008/09, on the basis of a projected decline in world production to 163m. tons and an increase in consumption to 160m. tons, USDA forecast that stocks would fall to 41m. tons.

In mid-2005 the European Commission announced proposals radically to reform the EU's sugar regime. In April the World Trade Organization, in response to a complaint by Brazil, Australia and Thailand, had ruled that some of the EU's subsidized exports of sugar originating in African, Caribbean and Pacific countries were illegal. A significant contraction in EU sugar production was expected to result from the reform of the regime, which was implemented from July 2006. Reforms included a substantial reduction in support granted to domestic (EU) sugar producers—the EU's intervention price was to be reduced by 36% over four years—and quota adjustments. This was followed, in September 2007, by an additional array of disincentives and compensatory measures that aimed to encourage producers to renounce 3.8m. tons of sugar quota in addition to the 2.2m. tons they had already relinquished. The European Commission also agreed that compulsory quota cuts would be imposed in 2010, should the desired reduction not have been achieved by then. Under the EU's EBA (Everything but Arms) Regulation, adopted in 2001, whereby least developed countries were granted duty-free access to the EU for all goods except arms and ammunition, full liberalization of the import regime for sugar was scheduled to enter effect in 2009.

In 2001 world sugar prices rose in response to, among other factors, reduced output in Cuba as a consequence of hurricane damage to crops there and reduced sugar beet production in the EU. For the whole of the year the ISA daily price averaged 8.64 US cents per lb. In 2002, however, the average ISA daily price declined to only 6.9 cents per lb. The decline in 2002 was particularly pronounced in the early part of the year as it became clear that there would be a substantial increase in Brazil's output of sugar cane and, consequently, in that country's export potential. The ISA recorded a marginally higher average daily price, of 7.10 cents per lb, in 2003. In 2004, again, a marginally higher daily price, of 7.16 cents per lb, was recorded. On a monthly basis, however, the ISA daily price rose markedly in the final quarter of 2004, averaging 8.41 cents per lb in October, 8.14 cents per lb in November and 8.26 cents per lb in December. In February 2005 the average ISA daily price rose to 9.12 cents per lb, and in November an average daily price of 11.38 cents per lb was recorded. For the whole of 2005 the average ISA daily price was 9.90 cents per lb. The average ISA daily price rose by 49%, to 14.75 cents per lb, in 2006, while displaying a high level of volatility. The highest average monthly price, 18.05 cents per lb, was recorded in February, and the lowest, 11.65 cents per lb, in December. In 2007 the average price declined by 32%, compared with 2006, to 10.07 cents per lb. The lowest average monthly price, 9.38 cents per lb, was recorded in June, and the highest, 11.01 cents per lb, in January. This decline in prices was largely attributed to continued substantial excess of supply, and was exacerbated by the weakness of the US dollar. According to the ISO, prices in real terms were too low to cover production costs. However, the relative weakness of sugar prices, compared with other agricultural commodities, subsequently spurred speculative investment and sugar prices recovered in the first two months of 2008, to an average of 13.37 cents per lb. The average price of the No. 5 sugar contract (refined sugar, f.o.b. Europe, for immediate delivery) traded on the London International Financial Futures Exchange (LIFFE) was 11.29 cents per lb in 2001. Successive declines in the average price, to, respectively, 10.35 cents per lb and 9.74 cents per lb, were recorded in 2002 and 2003. In 2004, however, the average price recovered to 10.87 cents per lb. In 2005 a substantial increase in the average contract price, to 13.19 US cents per lb, was recorded. The average price of white sugar traded on LIFFE increased to $418.19 per ton (18.97 cents per lb) in 2006, but declined to $307.53 per ton (13.95 cents per lb) in 2007.

The Group of Latin American and Caribbean Sugar Exporting Countries (GEPLACEA) complements the activities of the ISO (whose 71 members, on the basis of data for 2002, account for 83% of world sugar production, 65% of world sugar consumption, 92% of world sugar exports and 36% of world sugar imports) as a forum for co-operation and research.

### TEA (*Camellia sinensis*)

Tea is a beverage made by infusing in boiling water the dried young leaves and unopened leaf-buds of the tea plant, an evergreen shrub or small tree. Black and green tea are the most common finished products. The former accounts for the bulk of the world's supply, and is associated with machine manufacture and plantation cultivation, which guarantees an adequate supply of leaf to the factory. The latter, produced mainly in the People's Republic of China and Japan, is grown mostly on smallholdings, and much of it is consumed locally. There are two main varieties of tea, the China and the Assam, although hybrids may be obtained, such as Darjeeling. In this survey, wherever possible, data on production and trade relate to made tea, i.e. dry, manufactured tea. Where figures have been reported in terms of green (unmanufactured) leaf, appropriate allowances have been made to convert the reported amounts to the approximate equivalent weight of made tea.

Total recorded tea exports by producing countries achieved successive records in each of the years 1983–90. World exports (excluding transactions between former Soviet republics) declined in 1991 and 1992, but rose by 13.7% in 1993. However, the total fell by 10.3% in 1994. Export volume increased again in 1995 and 1996, rising further, to 1,203,785 metric tons, in 1997. World tea exports reached a new record of 1,304,896 tons in 1998, but eased to 1,261,399 tons in 1999. In 2000 export volume attained a new record level of 1,328,909 tons, a total exceeded in 2001 when world export volume increased to 1,392,163 tons. Exports of tea world-wide attained a new record level, of 1,441,809 tons, in 2002, but were estimated to have fallen by 3%, to 1,398,295 tons, in 2003. In 2004 foreign sales of tea world-wide increased by 12%, to a new record level of an estimated 1,566,484 tons. World exports rose again, to total an estimated 1,563,378 tons in 2005 and continued to increase in 2006, to a new record level of an estimated 1,585,796 tons. However, foreign sales of tea world-wide were estimated to have contracted in 2007, to 1,565,161 tons. Global production of tea reached an unprecedented level in 1998, with record crops in all of the major producing countries (India, China, Kenya and Sri Lanka). In 1999, however, world output declined (from 3,026,340 tons in 1998) to 2,944,961 tons, although China and Sri Lanka again reported record crops. In 2000 production increased to 2,933,479 tons, spurred, once again, by record crops in China and Sri Lanka. In 2001 world production of tea exceeded 3m. tons for a second time. Record crops in China and Kenya contributed to an increase in global output of 4.4%, to 3,061,283 tons. In 2002 China and Sri Lanka achieved record production, but world output of tea rose only marginally, to 3,086,795 tons. In 2003 production of tea world-wide increased by 4.2%, to an estimated 3,216,760 tons. China was estimated to have achieved record production in 2003, for an eighth successive year. In 2004, for a fourth consecutive year, world production of tea was estimated to have reached a record level, of 3,328,651 tons, China, Kenya and India all having recorded their highest output ever in that year. The advance in world tea output continued both in 2005, when global production rose by 4.2% to an estimated 3,468,288 tons, and in 2006, when it increased by a further 2.4%, to reach another record level, of 3,551,300 tons. In 2006 China and India's joint tea output accounted for 56% of global production—China's output, which exceeded 1m. tons for the first time, represented 29% of production world-wide, while that of India accounted for 27%). Global production of tea advanced by a further 4.9%, to an estimated 3,726,938 tons, in 2007, despite declines in the output of India and Sri Lanka. Chinese output again accounted for some 29% of global production. There was a marked increase, of almost 19%, in Kenyan output in 2007.

India and Sri Lanka have traditionally been the two leading exporters of made tea, with approximately equal sales. The quantity that they jointly supply remained fairly stable in 1977–96 (350,000–425,000 tons per year), but advanced to some 458,000 tons in 1997. Their joint export sales rose to 472,947 tons in 1998, but declined to 452,044 tons in 1999. Indian and Sri Lankan joint export sales increased to 484,486 tons in 2000, but fell to 467,360 tons in 2001. Foreign sales of tea by India and Sri Lanka recovered to 484,072 tons in 2002, but fell by 4.8%, to 460,844 tons, in 2003. In 2004 India and Sri Lanka's joint export sales of tea increased to 484,512 tons. In 2005 joint foreign sales by the two leading South Asian producers increased by 2%, to 493,997. In 2006 their combined foreign sales exceeded 500,000 tons for the first time, having increased by 7.4% to total 530,653 tons. In 2007, however, joint exports by India and Sri Lanka totalled only 450,964, 15% less than in 2006. India's foreign sales of tea fell heavily, by more than 27%, in 2007, while those of Sri Lanka declined by about 7%. During the 1960s India and Sri Lanka together exported more than two-thirds of all the tea sold by producing countries, but their joint foreign sales gradually declined; during the 1970s they came to constitute less than one-half of world exports, and in 2007 the proportion was estimated at 29%. From 1990 until 1995, when it was displaced by Kenya, Sri Lanka ranked as the main exporting country. Exports by Sri Lanka again took primacy in 1997, when Kenya's tea sales declined sharply. Sri Lanka remained the principal tea exporter in 1998, despite a strong revival in Kenyan exports, and again in 1999, although tea sales by both countries declined in the latter year. By 2003 Sri Lanka had apparently re-established itself as the world's leading exporter of tea, its foreign sales having exceeded those of Kenya by, on average, a fairly substantial margin in each year in 2000–03. In 2004 and 2005, however, Kenya again overtook Sri Lanka as the main tea exporting country. In 2004 Kenya's shipments rose sharply, by about 24%, to some 333,802 tons, compared with 2003, and in 2005 the country's foreign sales rose by a further 1.6%, to an estimated 339,134 tons. Kenya's exports in 2005 were equivalent to almost 70% of the combined foreign sales of India and Sri Lanka. In 2006, albeit by a small margin, Sri Lanka regained the rank of principal exporting country, Kenyan sales having declined by 7.5%. Kenya's foreign sales recovered strongly in 2007, however, propelling the country into the first place among tea exporters world-wide. Exports by India have been surpassed by those of China (whose sales include a large proportion of green tea) in every year since 1996; China's exports in 2007 were less than 5,000 tons lower than those of Sri Lanka.

Almost all of Sri Lanka's tea exports, which totalled 294,254 metric tons in 2007 (compared with 314,915 tons in 2006 and 298,769 tons in 2005), are in the form of black tea. After clothing, tea is the country's main source of foreign exchange, accounting for 16.3% of total export earnings in 2006 and for a provisional 17.3% in 2007. The principal buyers of Sri Lankan tea in 2005 were Russia, the United Arab Emirates and Iran. Turkey, Japan and Jordan were other important destinations for tea from Sri Lanka in 2005. Colombo is the largest single auction site for tea in Asia (and, usually, in the world—the volume of tea traded at Mombasa, Kenya, was greater than that traded at Colombo in 2003–05), the Indian auction market being divided between several locations. The volume of tea traded at Colombo increased in each year in 1993–2002, but declined by 2.4% in 2003, and by a further 1.2%, to 269,868 tons, in 2004; there was some recovery in 2005, when the volume traded was 273,055 tons.

Tea is India's principal agricultural export, but its contribution to total export earnings has diminished in recent years, falling from 4.6% in the year ending 31 March 1987 to 1.4% in 1997/98. Exports of tea contributed 1.6% of India's total export earnings in 1998/99, and only an estimated 1.1% in 1999/2000. India's tea exports, which totalled 204,353 metric tons in 2000, declined to only 179,857 tons in 2001. In 2002 foreign sales by India recovered to 198,087 tons, but fell by 14%, to 170,277 tons, in 2003. In 2004 India's foreign sales of tea increased by 13.8%, to 193,908 tons. India's exports of tea increased again, to 195,228 tons in 2005, and by a further 10%, to 215,738 tons, in 2006. In 2007, however, exports of tea declined by 27%, to just 156,710 tons. Since 1985 India has applied an upper limit of 220,000 tons to annual tea exports, regulating the volume of sales in each quarter in order to maximize earnings of foreign exchange. In contrast to coffee and cocoa, a large share of all the tea produced world-wide is consumed in producing countries. India is the world's largest consumer of tea, and the domestic market expanded steadily during the 1990s and in 2000–06. In 2000 prices for Indian tea declined, largely as a consequence of growing international competition: the domestic market had increasingly to contend with cheaper tea imports from Kenya, Viet Nam and Indonesia. As a result, the Government increased import duty on tea from 15% to 35% in May 2000, and in July it announced that restrictions on the foreign ownership of tea companies were to be abolished (thus allowing 100% foreign participation), in an effort to encourage increased investment and productivity. In March 2001 India raised the basic duty applied to imports of tea to 70%. The basic import duty on tea was increased again, to 100%, in November 2002. These measures notwithstanding, the average annual price of tea sold at the country's two principal auction markets—Kolkata (Calcutta) and Guwahati—declined further in each year in 2001–03. The average price of tea traded at Kolkata recovered slightly in 2003–04, but fell again in 2005, when it was 14% lower than in 2000. The average price of tea traded at Guwahati fell by 26.4% between 2000 and 2005.

Elsewhere in the region, Bangladesh is also a producer and exporter of tea, albeit on a far smaller scale than Sri Lanka or India. Bangladeshi production totalled an estimated 57,955 metric tons in 2007, compared with 53,265 tons in 2006 and 60,600 tons in 2005. Foreign sales by Bangladesh declined substantially, by 7.9%, in 1998–2007, although not in each successive year. In 1998 they totalled 22,215 tons, but in 2007 were estimated to have amounted to only 10,555 tons, though that represented a 20% increase on the previous year. Nepal produces tea on a far smaller scale still. However, largely as a result of government efforts to commercialize the agricultural sector, Nepalese tea exports rose substantially in 1998–2007. In 2007 Nepalese output was estimated at 13,700 tons, compared with estimated output of 13,500 tons in 2006 and 13,000 tons in 2005. The increase in Nepal's foreign sales was particularly marked between 2001, when they amounted to only 70 tons, and 2002, when they totalled an estimated 2,090 tons. In the 12 months to July 2007 Nepal's tea exports were estimated at 7,000 tons.

**Production of Made Tea**
('000 metric tons)

| | 2006 | 2007 |
|---|---|---|
| **World total*** | 3,551.3 | 3,726.9 |
| South Asia* | 1,333.5 | 1,321.2 |
| **Regional producers** | | |
| Bangladesh[1] | 53.3 | 58.0 |
| India*[2] | 955.9 | 944.9 |
| Nepal* | 13.5 | 13.7 |
| Sri Lanka[3] | 310.8 | 304.6 |
| **Other leading producers** | | |
| Argentina | 88.0 | 90.0 |
| China, People's Repub.[4] | 1,028.1 | 1,094.0* |
| Indonesia*[5] | 140.0 | 149.5 |
| Iran* | 20.0 | 17.0 |
| Japan[6] | 99.5 | 100.0* |
| Kenya | 310.6 | 369.6 |
| Malawi | 45.0 | 48.1 |
| Turkey* | 142.0 | 178.0 |
| Uganda | 36.7 | 44.9 |
| Viet Nam[7] | 142.5 | 148.3 |

* Provisional.
[1] Including a small quantity of green tea (about 210 tons in 2005).
[2] Including a small quantity of green tea (about 6,000 tons in 2005).
[3] Including a small quantity of green tea (2,418 tons in 2005).
[4] Mainly green tea (691,020 tons in 2005).
[5] Including green tea (about 40,800 tons in 2005).
[6] Almost all green tea (99,300 tons in 2005).
[7] Including green tea (about 39,000 tons in 2005).

Source: International Tea Committee, *Supplement to Annual Bulletin of Statistics 2007*.

For many years the United Kingdom was the largest single importer of tea. However, the country's annual consumption of tea per person, which amounted to 4.55 kg in 1958, has declined in recent years, averaging 2.46 kg in 1994–96 and 1995–97, before recovering marginally, to 2.51 kg, in 1996–98. However, consumption fell back to 2.44 kg in 1997–99, and again, in 1998–2000, to 2.33 kg. In 1999–2001 an average of 2.27 kg per head of tea was consumed in the United Kingdom. Average consumption per head in the United Kingdom declined again in 2000–02, to 2.26 kg; and once more, to 2.24 kg, in 2001–03. In 2002–04 annual average consumption of tea per head in the United Kingdom fell again, to 2.20 kg, and it continued its decline in 2003–05, to an estimated 2.12 kg. A similar trend has been observed in other developed countries, although it is not so clear in the Republic of Ireland, the world's largest consumer of tea per caput, where annual consumption per person advanced from 3.17 kg in 1994–96 to 3.23 kg in 1995–97, before evidencing a slight decline, to 2.95 kg, in 1996–98. Irish annual consumption per person declined again, to 2.78 kg, in 1997–99, and to 2.69 kg in 1998–2000. In 1999–2001, however, average annual Irish consumption per head rose to 2.71 kg, and in 2000–02 a further increase, to 2.75 kg, was recorded. In 2001–03 average annual consumption per person of tea in the Republic of Ireland rose sharply, to 2.96 kg, and it remained at that level in 2002–04. Average annual consumption per person resumed its decline in 2003–05, however. At 2.79 kg, none the less, it remained above the levels recorded in 1996–2002. From the late 1980s consumption and imports expanded significantly in the developing countries (notably Middle Eastern countries) and, particularly, in the USSR, which in 1989 overtook the United Kingdom as the world's principal tea importer. However, internal factors, following the break-up of the USSR in 1991, caused a sharp decline in tea imports by its successor republics; as a result, the United Kingdom regained its position as the leading tea importer in 1992. In 1993 the former Soviet republics (whose own tea production had fallen sharply) once more displaced the United Kingdom as the major importer, but in 1994 the United Kingdom was again the principal importing country. Since 1999, however, imports by the former USSR have exceeded those of the United Kingdom by a substantial and, generally, increasing margin. In 2007 Russia imported an estimated 173,000 metric tons of tea, accounting for 11.8% of the world market, followed by the United Kingdom, with an estimated 131,240 tons (8.9%), the USA (113,651 tons, or 7.8%) and Pakistan (an estimated 110,000 tons, or 7.5%). Other major importers of tea in 2007 were Egypt, Dubai (United Arab Emirates), Morocco and Iran.

Much of the tea traded internationally is sold by auction, principally in the exporting countries. Until declining volumes brought about their termination in June 1998 (Kenya having withdrawn in 1997, and a number of other exporters, including Sri Lanka and Malawi, having established their own auctions), the weekly London auctions had formed the centre of the international tea trade. At the London auctions, five categories of tea were offered for sale: 'low medium' (based on a medium Malawi tea), 'medium' (based on a medium Assam and Kenyan tea), 'good medium' (representing an above-average East African tea), 'good' (referring to teas of above-average standard) and (from April 1994) 'best available'. At the end of June 1998, with the prospect of a record Kenyan crop, the quotation for 'medium' tea at the final London auction was £980 per ton. Based on country of origin, the highest priced tea at London auctions during 1989–94 was that from Rwanda, which realized an average of £1,613 per ton in the latter year. The quantity of tea sold at these auctions declined from 43,658 tons in 1990 to 11,208 tons in 1997.

As noted above, Colombo is the largest single auction site for tea in Asia. In contrast to London, volumes traded at the Colombo auctions moved generally upward during the 1990s and continued to do so in 2000–02. Total annual sales at the Colombo auctions increased from 229,436 metric tons in 1995 to 229,980 tons in 1996. A further increase, to 254,967 tons, was recorded in 1997, and again, to 256,033 tons, in 1998. In 1999 the volume of tea traded rose to 260,448 tons. In 2000 a total of 276,913 tons was traded at Colombo. Further increases, to, respectively, 279,460 tons and 280,024 tons, were recorded in 2001 and 2002. In 2003, however, the volume of tea traded at Colombo declined by 2.4%, compared with the previous year, to 273,234 tons. Sales at Colombo declined again in 2004, by 1.2%, to 269,868 tons, but recovered to 273,055 tons in 2005. Meanwhile, the average price per ton of all tea traded at Colombo rose from 72,220 Sri Lankan rupees (Rs), equivalent to US $1,409, in 1995 to Rs 104,040 ($1,882) in 1996 and to Rs 119,360 ($2,023) in 1997. The average price increased again, to Rs 134,250 ($2,078) per ton in 1998, but declined to Rs 114,960 ($1,633) in 1999. In 2000 the average price of all tea traded at Colombo increased to Rs 135,060 ($1,754) per ton. Further increases in the average price in terms of rupees per ton, to, respectively, Rs 143,540 ($1,606) and Rs 148,660 ($1,554), were recorded in 2001 and 2002. In 2003, however, the average price of tea traded at Colombo declined slightly, to Rs 148,320 ($1,537) per ton. In 2004 a substantial increase, of about 21%, to Rs 180,180 ($1,781) per ton, was recorded. The average price of tea increased further, to Rs 184,420 ($1,808) per ton, in 2005. During the first six months of 2006 the monthly average price of tea traded at Colombo ranged between Rs 180,170 ($1,736) per ton, in June, and Rs 199,160 ($1,971) per ton, in March.

An International Tea Agreement (ITA), signed in 1933 by the governments of India, Ceylon (now Sri Lanka) and the Netherlands East Indies (now Indonesia), established the International Tea Committee (ITC), based in London, as an administrative body. Although ITA operations ceased after 1955, the ITC has continued to function as a statistical and information centre. In 2008 there were seven producer/exporter members (the tea boards or associations of Kenya, Malawi, India, Indonesia, Bangladesh and Sri Lanka, and the China Chamber of Commerce of Import and Export of Foodstuffs, Native Produce and Animal By-products), five consumer members, 13 associate members and 13 corporate members.

In 1969 the FAO Consultative Committee on Tea (renamed Intergovernmental Group on Tea in 1970) was formed, and an exporters' group, meeting under this committee's auspices, set voluntary export quotas in an attempt to avert an overall long-term decline in the real price of tea. This succeeded in raising prices for two years, but collapsed subsequently as (mainly) African countries—Kenya in particular—opposed efforts to restrict their rapidly increasing production. The regulation of tea prices is further complicated by the perishability of tea, which impedes the effective operation of a buffer stock. India, while opposing the revival of a formal ITA to oversee supplies and prices, has advocated greater co-operation between producers in order to regulate the market.

## TOBACCO (*Nicotiana tabacum*)

Tobacco originated in South America and was used in rituals and ceremonials or as a medicine; it was smoked and chewed for centuries before its introduction into Europe, the Middle East, Africa and the Indian sub-continent in the 16th century. The generic name *Nicotiana* denotes the presence of the alkaloid nicotine in its leaves. The most important species in commercial tobacco cultivation is *N. tabacum*. Another species, *N. rustica*, is widely grown, but on a smaller scale, to yield cured leaf for snuff or simple cigarettes and cigars.

In 2007, according to FAO, tobacco was harvested from about 2.5m. ha world-wide. Commercially grown tobacco (from *N. tabacum* ) can be divided into four major types—flue-cured, air-cured (including burley, cigar, light and dark), fire-cured and sun-cured (including oriental)—depending on the procedures used to dry or 'cure' the leaves. Each system imparts specific chemical and smoking characteristics to the cured leaf, although these may also be affected by other factors, such as the type of soil on which the crop is grown, the type and quantity of fertilizer applied to the crop, the cultivar used, the spacing of the crop in the field and the number of leaves left at topping (the removal of the terminal growing point). Each type is used, separately or in combination, in specific products (e.g. flue-cured in Virginia cigarettes). All types are grown in Asia.

As in other major producing areas, local research organizations in Asia have developed new cultivars with specific, desirable chemical characteristics, disease-resistance properties and improved yields. Almost all tobacco production in South Asia is from smallholdings; there is no cultivation of the crop on estates, as is common with tea. Emphasis has been placed on improving yields by the selection of cultivars, by the increased use of fertilizers and by the elimination or reduction of crop loss (through use of crop chemicals) and on reducing requirements for hand labour through the mechanization of land preparation and the use of crop chemicals. Harvesting continues to be entirely a manual operation, as the size of farmers' holdings and the cost of harvesting devices (now commonly used in the USA and Canada) preclude such development in Asia. The flue-curing process requires energy in the form of oil, gas, coal or wood. To ensure that supplies of wood are continuously renewed, the tobacco industry in, for example, Pakistan and Sri Lanka encourages the planting of trees. Following extensive research into the possibility of converting waste materials, such as rice husks, into products generating energy, a waste-pelletizing plant entered operation in Mysore, India.

The principal type of tobacco cultivated by Asian farmers is flue-cured. (Production of dark air-cured tobacco is limited mainly to India, China, Pakistan and Indonesia. Asia is not a significant producer of fire-cured and oriental tobaccos.) Of the countries producing this tobacco in South Asia, the most important is India. In each year in 2000–07, with the exception of 2001 (when its output was outstripped by that of the USA), India ranked as the world's third largest producer, after China and Brazil. A wide variety of tobaccos are grown in 16 Indian states—notably Andhra Pradesh, Gujarat and Karnataka, which accounted for 80% of raw tobacco production in 2005—including the cigarette varieties Virginia, burley and oriental. However, the majority of Indian tobaccos (including *natu*, *bidi*, *hooka* (hookah), chewing, cigar and cheroot tobaccos) are non-cigarette types. Consequently, in spite of its high ranking in terms of world production, India contributed only about 6% of world exports of raw tobacco (by volume) in 2005. Raw leaf accounted for about 90% of the total volume and value of Indian tobacco exports. Flue-cured Virginia, output of which amounted to some 38% of total production in 2005, accounts for the bulk of exports. According to FAO, India's revenues from exports of both raw and manufactured tobacco rose from US $42m. in 1970 to some $270m. in 2005. In the 1990s the most important markets for Indian exports of raw tobacco were those of Europe, notably Russia and Belgium. Saudi Arabia was traditionally the most important importer of Indian hookah paste, while Bahrain, Oman, Singapore and the United Arab Emirates were among the major markets for Indian *bidis*. Exports of tobacco contributed less than 1% of India's total export earnings in 2006/07, but, as a relatively low-cost producer—Indian flue-cured Virginia has been assessed by FAO as being perhaps the cheapest on the world market—the country could substantially increase its export revenue from tobacco and command a greater share of the world tobacco market by redirecting its production from non-cigarette tobacco to flue-cured Virginia and burley varieties.

**Production of Tobacco**
(unmanufactured, farm sales weight, '000 metric tons)

| | 2006 | 2007 |
|---|---|---|
| **World total** | 6,615 | 6,324 |
| South Asia | 703 | 720 |
| **Leading regional producers** | | |
| Bangladesh | 38 | 39* |
| India | 552 | 555* |
| Pakistan | 113 | 126 |
| **Other leading producers** | | |
| Brazil | 900 | 919 |
| China, People's Repub. | 2,746 | 2,395 |
| Greece | 37 | 19 |
| Indonesia | 178 | 180* |
| Italy* | 110 | 100 |
| Korea, Dem. People's Repub.* | 65 | 63 |
| Korea, Repub.* | 34 | 36 |
| Malawi* | 115 | 118 |
| Myanmar* | 35 | 36 |
| Philippines | 38 | 40* |
| Thailand* | 70 | 70 |
| Turkey | 98 | 98* |
| USA | 330 | 353 |
| Viet Nam | 43 | 43* |
| Zimbabwe | 44 | 79 |

* FAO estimate(s).

Tobacco is an important cash crop in Pakistan, where it is cultivated mainly in the North West Frontier and Punjab provinces.

In 2005 flue-cured, dark air-cured, oriental, light air-cured and burley were the varieties cultivated. Of these, flue-cured tobacco contributed about two-thirds of total output in 2005, when the area planted with it increased by 25%, compared to 2004, to occupy one-half of the total area cultivated with tobacco in the country. While both the area planted with and output of the light air-cured variety remained stable in 2005, they decreased for all of the other varieties cultivated. According to estimates by the US Department of Agriculture (USDA), output of flue-cured tobacco amounted to 66,630 metric tons in 2005 and that of light air-cured tobacco to 22,000 tons. In 2007, according to FAO, Pakistan harvested some 126,000 tons of tobacco from about 62,000 ha, about 6% of which was exported, mainly to Egypt, Russia, Ukraine and the USA. Tobacco exports accounted for less than 1% of Pakistan's foreign sales in 2006/07. Of the other tobacco-producing countries in the South Asia region, output in Bangladesh, which entered the export market in 1982, remained fairly static at about 35,000–40,000 tons annually in 1983–2006, of which 24% was exported in 2006. Sri Lanka, also once solely a producer of tobacco for domestic consumption, now exports small quantities of both flue-cured and air-cured tobacco. In 2006 43% of the country's relatively modest output of tobacco (3,700 tons) was exported.

About one-quarter of world tobacco production is traded internationally. Until 1993, when it was overtaken by Brazil, the USA was the world's principal tobacco-exporting country. According to USDA, the average value of US exports of unmanufactured tobacco was US $6,450 per metric ton in 2005. The country's total earnings from such exports were $1,058m. in 2005. Since 1993 Brazil has consolidated its position as the world's leading exporter of tobacco, largely at the expense of the USA and Zimbabwe. Brazil's share of global exports increased in volume from 13% in 1993 to about one-quarter in 2005. Tobacco exports contributed 1.2% of Brazil's total export revenue in 2005. Flue-cured Virginia and Burley account for by far the majority of Brazilian output—respectively 79% and 16% in 2005. In that year in southern Brazil flue-cured Virginia and Burley were sown on 88% of all land cultivated with tobacco. North-east Brazil, meanwhile, specializes in the production of cigar and cigarettes leaves. As a consequence of increased international demand for flue-cured Virginia, the area cultivated with tobacco in southern Brazil increased by 26% in 2003–05, while it decreased by 12% in the north-east.

The International Tobacco Growers' Association (ITGA), with headquarters in Castelo Branco, Portugal, was formed in 1984 by growers' groups in Argentina, Brazil, Canada, Malawi, the USA and Zimbabwe. In 2008 its members numbered 20 countries, including India and Pakistan. ITGA members account for more than 80% of the world's internationally traded tobacco. The Association provides a forum for the exchange of information among tobacco producers, conducts research and publishes studies on tobacco issues.

## WHEAT (*Triticum*)

The most common species of wheat, *T. vulgare*, includes hard, semi-hard and soft varieties which have different milling characteristics but which, in general, are suitable for bread-making. Another species, *T. durum*, is grown mainly in semi-arid areas, including regions bordering the Mediterranean Sea. This wheat is very hard, and is suitable for the manufacture of semolina, the basic ingredient of pasta and couscous. A third species, spelt (*T. spelta*), is also included in production figures for wheat. It is grown in very small quantities in parts of Europe and is used mainly as animal feed.

Although a most adaptable crop, wheat does not thrive in hot and humid climates, and it requires timely applications of water (either through rainfall or irrigation). Wheat is an important crop in most countries in Asia north of the Tropic of Cancer, wherever the terrain is favourable and sufficient water is available. The most concentrated producing areas in the South Asia region are to be found in Pakistan and northern India.

World wheat production declined during the 1990s, albeit only marginally, at an average rate of less than 0.1% a year. The fall was largely due to the sharp decline in agricultural output in the former USSR, excluding which the trend in world production growth has been upward. Wheat production is highly variable from year to year. Part of the variation is attributable to weather conditions, particularly rainfall, in the main producing areas, but national policies on support for producers have also been a major influence. In the 1990s several major wheat-producing countries, including leading exporters, pursued policies of market deregulation, and began to remove the links between producers' support and the financial returns from particular commodities. This encouraged their farmers more readily to switch between crops according to expected relative market returns. After 1996, for example, when wheat was in short supply on world markets, output was stimulated in many growing areas, and a record 613m. metric tons was harvested in 1997. Unfavourable weather, particularly in Russia and the People's Republic of China, reduced output to about 594m. tons in 1998, but, owing to low growth in consumption, exporting countries' stocks remained high, and farmers' returns fell. This discouraged plantings for the 1999 season, when production totalled only about 588m. tons. Production declined further in 2000, to some 586m. tons, but increased to about 590m. tons in 2001. In 2002 wheat production world-wide fell sharply, to only about 575m. tons, partly as a result of substantial declines in Australian and North American output. A further sharp decline occurred in 2003, when estimated output totalled only about 561m. tons. Wheat production recovered to a new record level of 633m. tons in 2004. Output totalled 629m. tons in 2005, and was estimated to have declined again, to 606m. tons, in 2006. (As of May 2008 FAO had revised its assessment of the 2006 crop to 597m. tons.) At May 2008 FAO estimated that production in 2007 totalled about 605m. tons, and forecast that output would rise to a new record level of 658m. tons in 2008. The greater part of the increase forecast was expected to derive from the major wheat-exporting countries. In the northern hemisphere larger harvests were expected in all regions except Asia, where it was anticipated that output would remain, approximately, unchanged relative to the previous year's record production. FAO forecast that aggregate (i.e. spring and winter) output in the USA would amount to 65m. tons in 2008, the biggest crop for 10 years. On the assumption of average yields, it was forecast that Canadian production would total 26m. tons. In the European Union (EU), meanwhile, it was forecast that aggregate output would increase by some 15%, compared with 2007, to about 138m. tons. In the member countries of the Commonwealth of Independent States (CIS) that were located in Europe a bumper crop of 70m. tons was anticipated. Among the key Asian producers, the wheat crops in both Iran and Kazakhstan were forecast to decline slightly, to, respectively, 11m. tons and 14m. tons. In India, however, as of May 2008, record production of some 77m. tons appeared likely. In Australia, assuming rainfall returned to normal levels, output was forecast to recover sharply, to about 26m. tons—double the level recorded in 2007. At May 2008 FAO assessed international trade in wheat at about 113m. tons in 2006. This trade was estimated to have declined to 110m. tons in 2007, and was forecast to rise slightly, to 110.5m. tons, in 2008. Asian imports of wheat in 2008 were forecast to increase by about 4.7m. tons, relative to 2007, to about 49m. tons, boosted by greater demand from, notably, Iran, Iraq and Saudi Arabia. At the same time, a sharp decline in Indian imports was anticipated. Total imports of wheat by African countries were forecast to reach about 29.7m. tons, sustained at close to the record level recorded in 2007 by increased demand from Algeria, Egypt, Libya and Tunisia. Imports by the member states of the EU, however, were forecast to fall sharply as a result of the anticipated recovery in output there. With regard to exports in 2008, FAO noted that those of the USA could decline, despite the strong increase in US output, owing to increased domestic demand for feed wheat and the historically low level of carryover stocks. It was anticipated, however, that most other major exporters—including Australia, Canada and the EU member states—would expand their foreign sales. Among the wheat-exporting countries of the CIS, Ukraine and Russia were regarded as likely to expand their exports.

In South Asia wheat production increased steadily from 1975, when it totalled about 32m. metric tons, to more than 100m. tons in 2000. Growth in output occurred in all of the wheat-producing countries of the region, major and minor. In Bangladesh, for instance, government subsidies, together with the conversion of irrigated land to the cultivation of wheat and increased use of fertilizers, raised output from about 117,000 tons in 1975 to more than 820,000 tons in 1980. By 1999 Bangladeshi production was approaching 2m. tons, although it stabilized at about 1.7m. tons annually in 2000–03. FAO indicated that output fell to about 1.3m. tons in 2004, and more heavily in 2005, to only an estimated 976,000 tons. Output continued to fall in 2006, to 735,000 tons, although preliminary figures for 2007 suggested a marginal increase, to 765,000 tons. In a normal year, according to the US Department of Agriculture (USDA), wheat now accounts for about 10% of all grain consumed as food in Bangladesh. In Nepal output grew steadily from 330,000 tons in 1975 to more than 1m. tons in 1999, and has subsequently stabilized at, on average, about 1.3m. tons annually. It reached 1.5m. tons in 2007.

In India the introduction of high-yielding and high-response varieties, more extensive irrigation and greater use of fertilizers caused production to double, to 54m. metric tons, in the 15 years to 1989. Government support prices have generally maintained interest in wheat-growing, and have encouraged greater use of agricultural inputs. An unbroken succession of favourable monsoons enabled wheat output to advance rapidly in the 1990s, to reach 69m. tons in 1997. In 2000 production rose to more than 76m. tons, but it declined in 2001, to about 70m. tons. Output rose again in 2002, to about 73m. tons, but fell back sharply, to only about 66m. tons, in 2003. In 2004 output rose to just over 72m. tons, but it declined once again in 2005, to nearly 69m. tons. Production remained at around 69m.tons in 2006, but increased to 75m. tons in 2007. Disposal of abundant crops has occasionally proved difficult, and the Indian Government has supported prices by means of sizeable procurements, while authorizing exports in some years. None the less, the margin between output and the steady rise in wheat demand has remained narrow, while relatively minor crop set-backs, as in 1998, necessitate imports to safeguard food security and stabilize retail prices. In 2006/07 India purchased a substantial quantity of wheat (6,708,000 tons) on the international market for the first time in many years, and in August 2007 India again indicated that it would require further imports in order to meet domestic demand and build up stocks in advance of its next harvest.

The other major producer in the region is Pakistan, where, although largely irrigated, production remains vulnerable to hot weather. Incentives offered to growers by the Government have resulted in increased levels of production, although fertilizers have not always been readily accessible and seed availability has been variable. In 2004 USDA reported that domestic consumption continued to expand at an annual rate of 2%–3% as a result of population growth. Pakistan recorded its largest harvest on record in 2007/08: USDA estimated production of 23,300 tons in that year, and forecast output of 21,500 tons in the 2008/09 marketing year.

World consumption, which has, in the long term, been increasing at a similar rate to production, varies much less from year to year. Food use is increasing at about 1.5% per year. Most of the increase is in Far East Asia, including the South Asian sub-region. Of approximately 415m. metric tons of wheat used for direct human food world-wide, Far East Asia accounts for about one-half, and China for one-half of that. Wheat food use has been expanding at the expense of rice: its growth is associated with rising consumer incomes and an increasing number of fast-food outlets. Substantial amounts of wheat are used for feed in Europe and, when prices are favourable, in North America. Substantial quantities were also used for feed in the 1980s in the former USSR, but this volume has decreased sharply in response to the diminution in livestock numbers. In Far East Asia some wheat is used for feed in Japan, while the Republic of Korea imports wheat for feed when prices are low in comparison with those of coarse grains such as sorghum and maize (corn).

Wheat is the principal cereal in international trade. According to USDA data, amounts exported in 2004/05–2007/08 have ranged between 109m.–115m. metric tons annually. The main exporters are the USA, whose share declined from about 30% of the total in the first half of the 1990s to about 24% in 2005/06, and some 22% in 2006/07. USDA forecast, however, that the share of the USA in world exports of wheat would increase to about one-third in 2007/08. Other major exporters are Canada, the member states of the European Union (EU), Australia and Argentina. In 2001/02 and 2002/03 the EU was not only a major exporter of wheat, but also the world's principal importer of the cereal. EU imports declined substantially in 2003/04, however, owing to the introduction of a system of import quotas designed to curb purchases of cheap Ukrainian and Russian wheat. Developed countries were formerly the principal consumers, but the role of developing countries as importers has been steadily increasing and they now regularly account for approximately two-thirds of world imports.

In regional terms, South Asia is a relatively minor importer of wheat, accounting for just 3.6% of total world imports in 2005. India imports wheat occasionally in order to replenish its stockpiles, but is virtually self-sufficient in most years. Imports of wheat by Bangladesh vary according to the size of the country's grain harvest and to the relative prices of wheat and rice on world markets. These imports rose from about 1m. metric tons in 1998 to some 2.4m. tons in 1999, when severe flooding affected rice supplies. Imports rose to 2.4m. tons again in 2001, fell to about 1.6m. tons in 2002, and increased again, to some 2.4m. tons, in 2003. In 2004 Bangladeshi purchases declined somewhat, to about 2.1m. tons a level that was maintained in 2005. Pakistan has traditionally imported wheat from the USA, although Australia has also captured a significant share of the market in recent years. Annual purchases averaged about 2.3m. tons in the 1990s, and in 1999 more than 3m. tons were imported. Since 2000, however, imports have both fallen and varied much more widely from year to year, ranging between about 1m. tons in 2000 and about 1.4m. tons in 2005. According to USDA estimates, Pakistan's imports of wheat declined to 55,000 tons in the 2006/07 marketing year, despite a forecast slight contraction in national output. The decline in imports was attributed to a levy of 10% introduced by the Government in May 2006 in order to encourage local sales at the expense of imports. In 2007/08 wheat imports amounted to 1.7m. tons.

**Production of Wheat**
('000 metric tons, including spelt)

| | 2006 | 2007 |
|---|---|---|
| **World total*** | 598,441 | 607,045 |
| South Asia* | 110,636 | 119,503 |
| **Leading regional producers** | | |
| India | 69,355 | 74,890 |
| Pakistan | 21,277 | 23,520 |
| **Other leading producers** | | |
| Argentina | 14,550 | 14,000 |
| Australia | 10,822 | 13,039 |
| Canada | 25,265 | 20,641 |
| China, People's Repub. | 104,470 | 109,860 |
| France | 35,367 | 33,219 |
| Germany | 22,428 | 21,367 |
| Iran* | 14,500 | 15,000 |
| Russia | 45,006 | 49,390 |
| Turkey | 20,010 | 17,678 |
| Ukraine | 13,947 | 13,800 |
| United Kingdom | 14,747 | 13,362 |
| USA | 49,316 | 53,603 |

* FAO estimates.

A lengthy period of low international wheat prices, and heavily subsidized competition among the major exporting countries, was interrupted in 1995–96 after exporting countries' stocks had fallen to their lowest levels for 20 seasons. Prices rose to record levels, but the resultant stimulus to output led to a rapid accumulation of stocks, and by 1998 prices were again very low as competition intensified between exporting countries. Because direct export subsidies were limited under international trade agreements, much of this competition took the form of offers of credit to importing countries.

The export price (f.o.b. Gulf ports) of US No. 2 Hard Winter, one of the most widely traded wheat varieties, averaged US $119 per metric ton in 2000, rising to $130 per ton in 2001. An average price of $151 per ton was recorded in 2002. In 2003 the average price declined marginally, to $150 per ton. In 2004 an increase of about 7.3%, to $161 per ton, was recorded in the export price of wheat, but in 2005 the average price fell to $158 per ton. In 2006 the average price recovered to $200 per ton, and it continued to rise, substantially, to $264 per ton, in 2007. During the first three months of 2008 the average monthly export price of US No. 2 Hard Winter wheat rose sharply, to reach a record $481 per ton in March. The average monthly price subsequently declined, however, falling to $343 per ton in July, as large increases in plantings were expected to lead to record wheat production in 2008. The USA in particular was expected to release some of the 15m. ha of land from its Conservation Reserve Program for the 2009 crop year. However, the World Bank estimated that as, in 2007/08, stocks of wheat were at their lowest level since at least 1960, any unforecast decline in production would prevent wheat stocks from recovering and would lead quickly to renewed price increases. The decline in stocks was attributed largely to the conversion of land in traditional wheat-exporting countries, such as Argentina, Canada and EU member states, to crops such as rapeseed for the production of biofuel feedstock for the USA and EU.

Since 1949 nearly all world trade in wheat has been conducted under the auspices of successive international agreements, administered by the International Wheat Council (IWC) in London. The early agreements involved regulatory price controls and supply and purchase obligations, but such provisions became inoperable in more competitive market conditions, and were abandoned in 1972. The IWC subsequently concentrated on providing detailed market assessments to its members and encouraging them to confer on matters of mutual concern. A new Grains Trade Convention, which entered into force in July 1995, gave the renamed International Grains Council (IGC) a wider mandate to consider all coarse grains as well as wheat. This facilitates the provision of information to member governments, and enhances their opportunities to hold consultations. In addition, links between governments and industry are strengthened at an annual series of grain conferences sponsored by the IGC. In mid-2007 the IGC had eight individual exporting members (including India), together with the member states of the EU, and 17 importing members (including Pakistan).

Since 1967 a series of Food Aid Conventions (FACs), linked to the successive Wheat and Grains Trade Conventions, have ensured continuity of supplies of food aid in the form of cereals to needy countries. Under the latest FAC, negotiated in 1999, the 22 donor countries (including the member states of the EU) have pledged to supply a minimum of some 5m. metric tons of food aid annually to developing countries, with priority being given to least developed countries and other low-income food-importing countries. Aid is to be provided mostly in the form of cereals, and all aid given to least developed countries is to be in the form of grants. The FAC seeks to improve the effectiveness, and increase the impact, of food aid by improved monitoring and consultative procedures. In mid-2004 FAC members undertook a renegotiation of the 1999 FAC in order 'to strengthen its capacity to meet identified needs when food aid is the appropriate response'. However, it was decided that this renegotiation should await the conclusion of discussions on trade-related food aid issues in agriculture negotiations at the World Trade Organization. In the mean time, it was agreed to extend the FAC, 1999, for two years from July 2005; further, one-year extensions were agreed in mid-2007 and mid-2008.

**ACKNOWLEDGEMENTS**

We gratefully acknowledge the assistance of the following bodies in the preparation of this section: the Centro Internacional de Agricultura Tropical; the United Coconut Association of the Philippines, Inc; the International Monetary Fund; the International Aluminium Institute; the International Rice Research Institute; the International Sugar Organization; the International Tea Committee; the International Tobacco Growers' Association; the Food and Agriculture Organization of the UN (FAO); the US Department of Agriculture (USDA); and the US Geological Survey, US Department of the Interior. Unless otherwise indicated, FAO is the source for all agricultural production tables.

# CALENDARS AND WEIGHTS AND MEASURES

## The Islamic Calendar

The Islamic era dates from 16 July 622, which was the beginning of the Arab year in which the *Hijra* ('flight' or migration) of the prophet Muhammad (the founder of Islam), from Mecca to Medina (in modern Saudi Arabia), took place. The Islamic or *Hijri* Calendar is lunar, each year having 354 or 355 days, the extra day being intercalated 11 times every 30 years. Accordingly, the beginning of the *Hijri* year occurs earlier in the Gregorian Calendar by a few days each year. Dates are reckoned in terms of the *anno Hegirae* (AH) or year of the Hegira (*Hijra*). The Islamic year 1429 AH began on 10 January 2008.

The year is divided into the following months:

| | | | |
|---|---|---|---|
| 1. Muharram | 30 days | 7. Rajab | 30 days |
| 2. Safar | 29 days | 8. Shaaban | 29 days |
| 3. Rabia I | 30 days | 9. Ramadan | 30 days |
| 4. Rabia II | 29 days | 10. Shawwal | 29 days |
| 5. Jumada I | 30 days | 11. Dhu'l-Qa'da | 30 days |
| 6. Jumada II | 29 days | 12. Dhu'l-Hijja | 29 or 30 days |

The *Hijri* Calendar is used for religious purposes throughout the Islamic world, and is the official calendar in Saudi Arabia. In most Arab countries it is used in conjunction with the Gregorian Calendar for official purposes, but in Indonesia, Malaysia and Pakistan the Gregorian Calendar has replaced it. In Afghanistan, however, the Persian Calendar is used for official purposes.

### PRINCIPAL ISLAMIC FESTIVALS

**New Year:** 1st Muharram. The first 10 days of the year are regarded as holy, especially the 10th.

**Ashoura:** 10th Muharram. Celebrates the first meeting of Adam and Eve after leaving Paradise, also the ending of the Flood and the death of Husain, grandson of the prophet Muhammad. The feast is celebrated with fairs and processions.

**Mouloud (Birth of Muhammad):** 12th Rabia I.

**Leilat al-Meiraj (Ascension of Muhammad):** 27th Rajab.

**Ramadan (Month of Fasting)**

**Id al-Fitr or Id al-Saghir or Küçük Bayram (The Small Feast):** Three days beginning 1st Shawwal. This celebration follows the constraint of the Ramadan fast.

**Id al-Adha or Id al-Kabir or Büyük Bayram (The Great Feast, Feast of the Sacrifice):** Four days beginning on 10th Dhu'l-Hijja. The principal Islamic festival, commemorating Abraham's sacrifice and coinciding with the pilgrimage of Muslims to Mecca. Celebrated by the sacrifice of a sheep, by feasting and by donations to the poor.

| Islamic Year | 1428 | 1429 | 1430 |
|---|---|---|---|
| New Year | 20 Jan. 2007 | 10 Jan. 2008 | 29 Dec. 2008 |
| Ashoura | 29 Jan. 2007 | 19 Jan. 2008 | 19 Jan. 2009 |
| Mouloud | 31 March 2007 | 20 March 2008 | 9 March 2009 |
| Leilat al-Meiraj | 10 Aug. 2007 | 30 July 2008 | 20 July 2009 |
| Ramadan begins | 13 Sept. 2007 | 1 Sept. 2008 | 22 Aug. 2009 |
| Id al-Fitr | 13 Oct. 2007 | 1 Oct. 2008 | 20 Sept. 2009 |
| Id al-Adha | 20 Dec. 2007 | 8 Dec. 2008 | 27 Nov. 2009 |

Note: Local determinations may vary by one day from those given here.

## Hindu Calendars

In India there are two principal Hindu calendars, the Vikrama and the Saka.

The Vikrama or Samvat era is dated from a victory of King Vikramaditya in 58 BC. The year 2008 of the Christian era therefore corresponds to 2065 in the Vikrama era. The New Year begins in March or April in eastern India, but in October or November in the western States.

The Saka era, beginning in AD 78, is attributed to the Saka King Kanishka. The year 2008 of the Christian era corresponds with 1930 of the Saka era.

The Official Calendar in India, adopted in 1957, is based on the Saka year, but has been fixed in relation to the Gregorian Calendar so that New Year (Chaitra 1) falls on 22 March except in Leap Years, when it falls on 21 March. This calendar is used for dating official documents, for All India Radio broadcasts, and other official purposes; however, the Gregorian Calendar is still widely used in India.

### FESTIVALS

**Holi:** Spring Festival in honour of Krishna, usually held in March.

**Mahendra Jatra:** Nepalese festival seeking to ensure the monsoon rains; June.

**Dussera:** 10-day festival of Durga; early October.

**Diwali:** Festival of lights, dedicated to Lakshmi; late October or early November.

Numerous local agricultural and commemorative festivals are also observed.

## Buddhist and the South Indian Calendars

The Buddhist era (BE) is attributed to the death of Gautama Buddha, historically dated at about 483 BC. The era in use is dated, in fact, from 544 BC, making the year 2008 of the Christian era equal to 2551 of the Buddhist era. The Jain era, based on the death of Mahavira, starts in 528 BC, making AD 2008 equal to 2535.

In South Asia there is widespread use of a lunar year of 354 days, with months of alternately 29 or 30 days, and with extra (intercalary) months approximately every third year. Under this system, New Year may fall in either April or March.

Sri Lanka adopted the Buddhist calendar as its official and commercial calendar in 1966. Sunday is treated as a normal working day, while the lunar quarter days (Poya days) are public holidays; some of these are two-day holidays. New Year is on 13 or 14 April.

### FESTIVALS

The principal festivals in the Buddhist calendars are the New Year and the spring and autumn equinox, and local festivals connected with important pagodas.

# Weights and Measures

The following tables indicate the values of the principal weights and units of measurement which are in common use as alternatives to the metric and imperial systems

## WEIGHT

| Unit | Country | Metric equivalent | Imperial equivalent |
|---|---|---|---|
| Candy | Sri Lanka | 254 kg | 560 lb |
| | India—Mumbai | 254 kg | 560 lb |
| | India—Chennai | 226.8 kg | 500 lb |
| Charak | Afghanistan | 1.7278 kg | 3.894 lb |
| Chittack | India | 57.5 g | 2.057 oz |
| Kharwar | Afghanistan | 564.528 kg | 1,246.2 lb |
| Khord | Afghanistan | 110.28 g | 3.89 oz |
| Maund | Bangladesh | 37.29 kg | 82.28 lb |
| | India—Mumbai | 12.7 kg | 28 lb |
| | India—Chennai | 11.34 kg | 25 lb |
| | Pakistan | 37.29 kg | 82.28 lb |
| Pa | India | 235 g | 8.288 oz |
| Picul, Pikul, Picol, Taam or Tam | India | 60.48 kg | 133.33 lb |
| Quintal | India | 100 kg | 220.462 lb |
| Seer | Afghanistan | 7.07 kg | 15.58 lb |
| | India—Chennai | 0.28 kg | 0.617 lb |
| | India—Mumbai | 0.33 kg | 0.72 lb |
| | Pakistan | 0.93 kg | 2.057 lb |
| Tola | India and Pakistan | 11.66 g | 180 grains |
| Visham | India | 1.36 kg | 3 lb |

## LENGTH

| Unit | Country | Metric equivalent | Imperial equivalent |
|---|---|---|---|
| Coss | India—West Bengal, Pakistan and Bangladesh | 1,920.2 m | 2,000 yd |
| Danda | India, Pakistan and Bangladesh | 1.83 m | 2 yd |
| Gereh-gaz-sha | Afghanistan | 6.6 cm | 2.6 in |
| Girah | Pakistan | 5.7 cm | 2.25 in |
| Gudge, Gueza, Guz or Ver | India—West Bengal | 91.44 cm | 36 in |
| | India—Mumbai | 68.58 cm | 27 in |
| | India—Chennai | 83.82 cm | 33 in |
| | Pakistan and Bangladesh | 91.44 cm | 36 in |
| Hath | India, Pakistan and Bangladesh | 45.72 cm | 18 in |
| Jareeb | Pakistan—Punjab | 20.117 m | 22 yd |
| Koss | India—West Bengal | 1,828.8 m | 2,000 yd |
| Ungul | India, Pakistan and Bangladesh | 1.9 cm | 0.75 in |

## CAPACITY

| Unit | Country | Metric equivalent | Imperial equivalent |
|---|---|---|---|
| Bottle | Sri Lanka | 0.73 l | 0.16 gall |
| Ser | India | 1 l | 1.76 pints |

## AREA

| Unit | Country | Metric equivalent | Imperial Equivalent |
|---|---|---|---|
| Bigha | India | 0.253 ha | 0.625 acre |
| | Pakistan—Punjab | 1354.5 sq m | 1,620 sq yds |
| | Bangladesh | 1337.8 sq m | 1,600 sq yds |
| Cawny or Cawnie | India—Chennai | 0.534 ha | 1.322 acres |
| Chattak | Bangladesh | 4.18 sq m | 5 sq yds |
| Cottah | Bangladesh | 66.89 sq m | 80 sq yds |
| Marabba | Pakistan | 10.12 ha | 25 acres |
| Morabba | Pakistan—Punjab | 10.12 ha | 25 acres |
| Square | Sri Lanka | 83.61 sq m | 100 sq yds |

## QUANTITY

| Unit | Country | Quantity |
|---|---|---|
| Crore | India, Pakistan, Bangladesh | 10,000,000 (1,00,00,000) |
| Lakh | India, Pakistan, Bangladesh | 100,000 (1,00,000) |

# Metric to Imperial Conversions

| Metric units | Imperial units | To convert metric into imperial units multiply by: | To convert imperial into metric units multiply by: |
|---|---|---|---|
| **Weight:** | | | |
| Gram | Ounce (Avoirdupois) | 0.035274 | 28.3495 |
| Kilogram (kg) | Pound (lb) | 2.204623 | 0.453592 |
| Metric ton ('000 kg) | Short ton (2,000 lb) | 1.102311 | 0.907185 |
| | Long ton (2,240 lb) | 0.984207 | 1.016047 |
| | (The short ton is in general use in the USA, while the long ton is normally used in the UK and the Commonwealth.) | | |
| **Length:** | | | |
| Centimetre (cm) | Inch | 0.3937008 | 2.54 |
| Metre (m) | Yard (= 3 feet) | 1.09361 | 0.9144 |
| Kilometre (km) | Mile | 0.62137 | 1.609344 |
| **Volume:** | | | |
| Cubic metre (cu m) | Cubic foot | 35.315 | 0.028317 |
| | Cubic yard | 1.30795 | 0.764555 |
| **Capacity:** | | | |
| Litre (l) | Gallon (= 8 pints) | 0.219969 | 4.54609 |
| | Gallon (US) | 0.264172 | 3.78541 |
| **Area:** | | | |
| Square metre (sq m) | Square yard | 1.19599 | 0.836127 |
| Hectare (ha) | Acre | 2.47105 | 0.404686 |
| Square kilometre (sq km) | Square mile | 0.386102 | 2.589988 |

# Systems of Measurement

**WEIGHT**

| | |
|---|---|
| Afghanistan | Kharwar = 80 Seer<br>Seer = 4 Charak<br>Charak = 16 Khord |
| India, Pakistan and Bangladesh | Maund = 40 Seer<br>Seer = 16 Chittack<br>Pa = 20 Tola |

**LENGTH**

| | |
|---|---|
| India, Pakistan and Bangladesh | Coss = 1,000 Danda<br>Danda = 2 Gudge<br>Gudge = 2 Hath<br>Hath = 24 Ungul |

**AREA**

| | |
|---|---|
| Pakistan | Bigha = 20 Cottah<br>Cottah = 16 Chattah |

# RESEARCH INSTITUTES

## ASSOCIATIONS AND INSTITUTIONS STUDYING SOUTH ASIA*

### AFGHANISTAN

**Afghanistan Research and Evaluation Unit (AREU):** Charahi Ansari (across from Insaf Hotel), Kabul; e-mail areu@areu.org.pk; internet www.areu.org.pk; conducts and facilitates research in Afghanistan; Dir ANDREW WILDER; publ. *AREU Issues Papers Series*.

**Kabul Center for Strategic Studies:** Chahah Rahi Dehbori, Kabul; tel. (75) 2028458; e-mail info@kabulcenter.org; internet www.kabulcenter.org; f. 2007; Co-founder and CEO WAILIULLAH RAHMANI; Co-founder and Exec. Dir RAHMANI RAHMANI.

### AUSTRALIA

**Asian Economics Centre:** Dept of Economics, University of Melbourne, Vic 3010; tel. (3) 8344-3880; fax (3) 8344-6899; e-mail lcameron@unimelb.edu.au; internet www.ecom.unimelb.edu.au/dept/AEC; fmrly Asian Business Centre; Dir Assoc. Prof. GARY MAGEE (acting); Dep. Dir Assoc. Prof. LISA CAMERON (acting).

**Asian Studies Program, La Trobe University:** Vic 3086; tel. (3) 9479-1315; fax (3) 9479-1880; e-mail asianstudies@latrobe.edu.au; internet www.latrobe.edu.au/www/asianstudies; f. 1994; Assoc. Prof. RAJ PANDEY.

**Australia South Asia Research Centre:** Australian National University, Canberra, ACT 0200; tel. (2) 6125-2683; fax (2) 6125-0443; e-mail asarc@anu.edu.au; internet rspas.anu.edu.au/asarc; f. 1994; research on the economics and politics of development in the South Asian region, particularly India; Exec. Dir Prof. RAGHBENDRA JHA.

**Faculty of Asian Studies, Australian National University:** Canberra, ACT 0200; tel. (2) 6125-0006; fax (2) 6125-0745; e-mail enquiries.asianstudies@anu.edu.au; internet www.anu.edu.au/asianstudies; Dean Prof. KENT ANDERSON.

**Monash Asia Institute:** Monash University, Clayton, Vic 3800; tel. (3) 9905-2124; fax (3) 9905-5370; e-mail marika.vicziany@adm.monash.edu.au; internet www.monash.edu.au/mai; f. 1988; incorporates China Research Centre, National Centre for South Asian Studies, Japanese Studies Centre, Malaysian Studies Centre, Asia Pacific Health and Nutrition Centre and Centre of Southeast Asian Studies; publishes specialist academic publications on Asia, Asian studies and related fields through MAI Press, an imprint of Monash University Press; runs regular series of seminars and occasional major international conferences focusing on issues relating to the Asia-Pacific region; Dir Prof. MARIKA VICZIANY.

**School of Languages and Cultures, University of Sydney:** Brennan Bldg, University of Sydney, NSW 2006; tel. (2) 9351-2869; fax (2) 9351-2319; e-mail slc@arts.usyd.edu.au; internet www.arts.usyd.edu.au/school/slc; f. 1991; includes the depts of Asian Studies, Chinese Studies, Japanese and Korean Studies, Indian Subcontinental Studies, and Southeast Asian Studies; Head Prof. JEFFREY RIEGELS.

### AUSTRIA

**Afro-Asiatisches Institut in Wien** (Afro-Asian Institute in Vienna): 1090 Vienna, Türkenstrasse 3; tel. (1) 3105145-0; fax (1) 3105145-312; e-mail office@aai-wien.at; internet www.aai-wien.at; f. 1959; religious, cultural, economic and scientific exchanges between Austria and African and Asian countries; assistance to students from Africa and Asia; public relations, lectures, seminars.

### BANGLADESH

**Asiatic Society of Bangladesh:** 5 Old Secretariat Rd, Ramna, Dhaka 1000; tel. (2) 7168940; fax (2) 9560500; e-mail assoenpr@bangla.net; Pres. Prof. EMAJUDDIN AHAMED; Gen. Sec. Prof. S. M. MAHFUZUR RAHMAN; publs *Journal of the Asiatic Society of Bangladesh (Humanities)*, *Journal of the Asiatic Society of Bangladesh (Science)*, *Bangladesh Asiatic Society Patrika (Bangla)*.

**Bangladesh Institute of Development Studies:** E-17, Agargaon, Sher-E-Bangla Nagar, GPO Box 3854, Dhaka 1207; tel. (2) 324596; fax (2) 8113023; e-mail info@sdnbd.org; f. 1957; promotes and conducts studies and research in development economics, demography and other social sciences relating to planning for national development and social welfare; library of over 120,000 books, documents, journals, and microfiches; Dir-Gen. Prof. ABU AHMED ABDULLAH; publs include *Research Report*, *Research Monograph*.

**Bangladesh Institute of International and Strategic Studies:** 1/46 Elephant Rd, Dhaka 1000; tel. (2) 406234; fax (2) 832625; internet www.bangla.net/webera/biiss; f. 1978; Dir-Gen. Maj.-Gen. GHULAM QUADER.

**Bureau of Socio-Economic Research and Training (BSERT):** Bangladesh Agricultural University, Mymensingh 2202; tel. (91) 52275; fax (91) 55810; e-mail bsertbau03@yahoo.com; f. 1965; conducts and promotes socio-economic research, particularly on rural problems in Bangladesh; Chair. Prof. M. SERAJUL ISLAM; publs include *Bangladesh Journal of Agricultural Economics* (2 a year).

**Institute of Bangladesh Studies:** University of Rajshahi, Rajshahi 6205; tel. (721) 750064; fax (721) 750064; e-mail ibsru@yahoo.com; Dir Prof. M. ZAINUL ABEDIN; Sec. M. ZAIDUR RAHMAN; publs *Journal of the Institute of Bangladesh Studies* (annually), *IBS Journal* (annually), *Institute of Bangladesh Studies Alumni Associations Journal* (every 2 years).

**Varendra Research Museum:** Rajshahi; f. 1910; conducts research in history, archaeology, anthropology, literature, and art; collects and preserves archaeological and other relics, ancient MSS; library of c. 15,000 vols; 8,250 items in museum, including 4,500 ancient MSS; Dir Dr SAIFUDDIN CHOWDHURY; publ. *Journal* (annually).

### BELGIUM

**Egmont—Institut Royal des Relations Internationales:** 69 rue de Namur, 1000 Brussels; tel. (2) 223-4114; fax (2) 223-4116; e-mail info@egmontinstitute.be; internet www.egmontinstitute.be; f. 1947; research in international relations, economics, law and politics; specialized library containing 700 vols and 200 periodicals; archives; holds lectures and conferences; Pres. Viscount E. DAVIGNON; Dir-Gen. RAF VAN HELLEMONT; publs *Studia Diplomatica* (every 3 months).

**European Institute for Asian Studies (EIAS):** 35 rue des Deux Eglises, 1040 Brussels; tel. (2) 230-8122; fax (2) 230-5402; e-mail eias@eias.org; internet www.eias.org; Chair. Prof. Dr LUDO CUYVEES; Sec.-Gen. DICK GUPWELL; publs *The EurAsia Bulletin* (monthly), *EIAS Briefing Papers*.

**Institut Orientaliste:** Faculté de Philosophie et Lettres, Université Catholique de Louvain, Collège Erasme, 1348 Louvain-la-Neuve; tel. (10) 474958; fax (10) 479169; e-mail ori@glor.ucl.ac.be; internet www.fltr.ucl.ac.be/FLTR/GLOR/ORI; f. 1936; Pres. Prof. RENÉ LEBRUN; publs *Le Muséon* (2 a year), *Bibliothèque du Muséon*, *Publications de l'Institut Orientaliste de Louvain (PIOL)*, *Corpus Scriptorum Christianorum Orientalium (CSCO)*.

### BHUTAN

**The Centre for Bhutan Studies:** POB 1111, Thimpu; tel. 321003; fax 321001; e-mail cbs.bt@undp.org; f. 1999; Head KARMA URA.

### CANADA

**Canadian Council for International Co-operation:** 1 Nicholas St, Suite 300, Ottawa, ON K1N 7B7; tel. (613) 241-7007; fax (613) 241-5302; e-mail info@ccic.ca; internet www.ccic.ca; f. 1968; information and training centre for international development and forum for voluntary agencies; 100 mems; Pres. and CEO GERRY BARR; publs include newsletter and directory of NGOs working overseas.

**Canadian Institute of International Affairs:** 205 Richmond St West, Suite 302, Toronto, ON M5V 1V3; tel. (416) 977-9000; fax (416) 977-7521; e-mail mailbox@ciia.org; internet www.ciia.org; f. 1928; research in international relations; library containing 8,000 vols; Chair. JOHN MACNAUGHTON; Pres. and CEO DOUGLAS GOOLD; publs *Behind the Headlines* (quarterly), *International Journal* (quarterly), *Annual Report*.

**Centre for Developing-Area Studies:** McGill University, 3715 rue Peel, Montréal, QC H3A 1X1; tel. (514) 398-3507; fax (514) 398-8432; e-mail adm.cdas@mcgill.ca; internet www.mcgill.ca/cdas; Dir Dr PHILIP OXHORN; publ. *Discussion Paper Series*.

**Department of Asian Studies, University of British Columbia:** Vancouver, BC V6T 1Z2; tel. (604) 822-0019; fax (604) 822-8937; e-mail astudies@interchange.ubc.ca; internet www.asia.ubc.ca; f. 1961; instruction and research in East, South and South-East Asia; Head Dr PETER NOSCO.

**Institute of Asian Research:** University of British Columbia, C. K. Choi Bldg, 1855 West Mall, Vancouver, BC V6T 1Z2; tel. (604) 822-4688; fax (604) 822-5207; e-mail iar@interchange.ubc.ca; internet

*See also Regional Organizations

www.iar.ubc.ca; f. 1978; Dir PITMAN B. POTTER; publ. *Asia Pacific Report* (2 a year).

**International Development Research Centre:** POB 8500, Ottawa K1G 3H9; tel. (613) 236-6163; fax (613) 563-2476; e-mail info@idrc.ca; internet www.idrc.ca; f. 1970 as a public corpn to support scientific research aimed at helping communities in the developing world find solutions to social, environmental and economic problems; has regional offices in Singapore, India, Uruguay, Egypt, Kenya and Senegal; Pres. MAUREEN O'NEIL; publs *Reports* (online magazine) and books.

## PEOPLE'S REPUBLIC OF CHINA

**China Centre for International Studies (CCIS):** 22 Xianmen Dajie, POB 1744, Beijing 100017; tel. (10) 63097083; fax (10) 63095802; f. 1982; conducts research on international relations and problems; organizes academic exchanges; Dir-Gen. LI LUYE.

**West Asian and African Studies Institute:** Chinese Academy of Social Sciences, 3 Zhangzhizhong Rd, Beijing 100007; e-mail iwaas@public.fhnet.cn.net; f. 1961; Dir-Gen. Prof. YANG GUANG.

## CROATIA

**Institute for International Relations:** 10000 Zagreb, POB 303, ul. Ljudevita Farkaša Vukotinovića 2/II; tel. (1) 4877460; fax (1) 4828361; e-mail ured@irmo.hr; internet www.imo.hr; f. 1963; affiliated to the University of Zagreb and the Ministry of Science and Technology; Dir Prof. Dr MLADEN STANIČIĆ; publs include *Croatian International Relations Review* (quarterly), *Culturelink* (3 a year).

## CZECH REPUBLIC

**Czech Society for Eastern Studies:** c/o Oriental Institute, Academy of Sciences, Pod vodárenskou věží 4, 182 08 Prague 8; tel. (2) 66052483; fax (2) 86581897; e-mail aror@orient.cas.cz; f. 1958; 71 mems; Pres. LŮBICA OBUCHOVÁ.

**Orientální ústav AV ČR** (Oriental Institute of the Academy of Sciences of the Czech Republic): Pod vodárenskou věží 4, 182 08 Prague 8; tel. (2) 66052492; fax (2) 86581897; e-mail orient@orient.cas.cz; internet www.orient.cas.cz; f. 1922; research on languages, social and economic aspects, etc. of Asia and Africa; Chinese library of 66,177 vols, general library of more than 190,000 vols; Dir Dr STANISLAVA VAVROUŠKOVÁ; publs *Archiv orientální* (quarterly), *Nový Orient* (quarterly).

## FINLAND

**Suomen Itämainen Seura** (Finnish Oriental Society): c/o Dept of Asian and African Studies, Unioninkatu 38B, POB 59, University of Helsinki, 00014 Helsinki; tel. (9) 19122224; fax (9) 19122094; e-mail saana.teppo@helsinki.fi; internet www.helsinki.fi/jarj/sis; f. 1917; 187 mems; Pres. Prof. TAPANI HARVIAINEN; Sec. SAANA TEPPO; publ. *Studia Orientalia*.

**World Institute for Development Economics Research of the United Nations University (UNU-WIDER):** Katajanokanlaituri 6B, 00160 Helsinki; tel. (9) 6159911; fax (9) 61599333; e-mail wider@wider.unu.edu; internet www.wider.unu.edu; f. 1984; research and training centre of the UNU (Japan); publs include *WIDER Discussion Papers*, *Policy Briefs*, *Research Papers*, *Annual Lectures*, *WIDER Angle* (Newsletter).

## FRANCE

**Centre des Hautes Etudes sur l'Afrique et l'Asie Modernes:** 13 rue du Four, 75006 Paris; tel. 1-43-26-96-90; fax 1-40-51-03-58; internet www.ccfr.bnf.fr; f. 1936; library of 16,000 vols; Dir J. P. DOUMENGE; publs *La Lettre du Cheaam* (quarterly), *Notes africaines, asiatiques et caraïbes* (irregular).

**Institut National des Langues et Civilisations Orientales:** 2 rue de Lille, 75343 Paris Cedex 07; tel. 1-49-26-42-74; fax 1-49-26-42-99; internet www.inalco.fr; courses in 88 languages; research; information centre; organizes international exchanges; specializes in international relations; Pres. JACQUES LEGRAND; publs research serials, textbooks, translations, etc.

**Musée National des Arts Asiatiques Guimet:** 6 place d'Iéna, 75116 Paris; tel. 1-56-52-53-00; fax 1-56-52-53-54; internet www.museeguimet.fr; f. 1889; library of 100,000 vols; art, archaeology, religions, literature and music of India, Central Asia, Tibet, Pakistan, Viet Nam, China, Korea, Japan, Cambodia, Thailand, Laos, Myanmar (fmrly Burma) and Indonesia; Dir JEAN-FRANÇOIS JARRIGE; Librarian F. MACOUIN; publs *Annales du Musée Guimet*, *Arts Asiatiques*.

**Société Asiatique:** 3 rue Mazarine, 75006 Paris; tel. and fax 1-44-41-43-14; internet www.aibl.fr/fr/asie/present.html; f. 1829; library of 100,000 vols; 750 mems; Pres. DANIEL GIMARET; publs *Journal Asiatique* (2 a year), *Nouveaux Cahiers*.

## GERMANY

**Deutsch-Indische Gesellschaft eV:** 70173 Stuttgart, Charlottenplatz 17; tel. (711) 297078; fax (711) 2991450; e-mail DGesellsch@aol.com; internet www.dig-ev.de.

**Deutsche Gesellschaft für Asienkunde eV** (German Association for Asian Studies): 20148 Hamburg, Rothenbaumchaussee 32; tel. (40) 445891; fax (40) 4107945; e-mail post@asienkunde.de; internet www.asienkunde.de; f. 1967; promotion and co-ordination of contemporary Asian research; 850 mems; Pres. Dr CHRISTIAN P. HAUSWEDELL; Sec. JÖRG JOSWIAK; publs *ASIEN: The German Journal on Contemporary Asia*, *Wirtschaft und Kultur* (quarterly).

**Deutsche Gesellschaft für Auswärtige Politik eV** (German Society for Foreign Affairs): 53113 Bonn, Adenauerallee 131, Postfach 1425; tel. (228) 2675-0; fax (228) 2675-173; e-mail DGAP@compuserve.com; internet www.dgap.org; f. 1955; promotes research on problems of international politics; library of 50,000 vols; 1,600 mems; Pres. Dr WERNER LAMBY; Exec. Vice-Pres. Dr IMMO STABREIT; Dir Research Inst. Prof. Dr KARL KAISER; publs *Internationale Politik* (monthly), *Die Internationale Politik* (annually).

**Deutsche Morgenländische Gesellschaft eV (DMG)** (German Oriental Society): Orientalisches Seminar, Islamwissenschaft/Turkologie, 79085 Freiburg/Brsg., Werthmannplatz 3; tel. (761) 2033159; fax (761) 2033152; e-mail Jens.Peter.Laut@orient.uni-freiburg.de; internet www.dmg-web.de; f. 1845; sponsors research and holds meetings and lectures in the field of Oriental studies; 650 mems; Sec. Prof. Dr JENS PETER LAUT; publs include *Zeitschrift*, *Abhandlungen für die Kunde des Morgenlandes*.

**GIGA Institut für Asien-Studien** (German Institute of Global and Area Studies): 20148 Hamburg, Rothenbaumchaussee 32; tel. (40) 4288740; fax (40) 4107945; e-mail ias@giga-hamburg.de; internet www.giga-hamburg.de/ias; f. 1956; research and documentation into all aspects of contemporary South, South-East and East Asia; Pres. Prof Dr ROBERT KAPPEL; Dir Dr PATRICK KÖLLNER (acting); publs *China aktuell—Journal of Current Chinese Affairs*; *Südostasien aktuell—Journal of Current Southeast Asian Affairs*; *Japan aktuell—Journal of Current Japanese Affairs* (all quarterly).

**Museum für Asiatische Kunst** (Indian Art): Staatliche Museen zu Berlin-Preussischer Kulturbesitz, 14195 Berlin, Takustrasse 40; tel. (30) 8301361; fax (30) 8301502; e-mail mik@smb.spk-berlin.de; formed through merger of Museum für Indische Kunst and Museum für Ostasiatische Kunst; South, South-Eastern, Eastern and Central Asian art; Dir Prof. Dr WILLIBALD VEIT; publs include series *Veröffentlichungen des Museums für Indische Kunst*.

**Museum für Islamische Kunst** (Islamic Art and Antiquities): Staatliche Museen zu Berlin Preussischer Kulturbesitz, 10178 Berlin, Bodestrasse 1–3; tel. (30) 20905400; fax (30) 20905402; e-mail isl@smb.spk-berlin.de; internet www.smb.spk-berlin.de/isl; f. 1904; Dir Prof. Dr CLAUS-PETER HAASE.

**Südasien-Institut der Universität Heidelberg:** 69120 Heidelberg, Im Neuenheimer Feld 330; tel. (6221) 548900; fax (6221) 544998; e-mail info@sai.uni-heidelberg.de; internet www.sai.uni-heidelberg.de; f. 1962; Dir Prof. WILLIAM SAX; Exec. Sec. MANFRED HAKE; publs include *Beiträge zur Südasienforschung* and *South Asian Studies*.

## HUNGARY

**Magyar Tudományos Akadémia Világgazdasági Kutató Intézete** (Institute for World Economics of the Hungarian Academy of Sciences): 1014 Budapest, Országház u. 30; tel. (1) 224-6760; fax (1) 224-6761; e-mail vki@vki.hu; internet www.vki.hu; f. 1967; library of 103,000 vols; Dir ANDRAS INOTAI; publs *Working Papers* (c. 15 a year, in English), *Kihívások* (10–15 a year, in Hungarian), *Muhelytanulmányok* (10–15 a year, in Hungarian).

## INDIA

**Abul Kalam Azad Oriental Research Institute:** Public Gardens, Hyderabad 500 004; tel. (842) 2230805; f. 1959; research in history, philosophy, culture and languages; library of 15,000 vols; Pres. MAHMOOD BIN MUHAMMAD; Hon. Sec.and Dir MIR KAMALUDDIN ALI KHAN.

**All-India Oriental Conference:** Bhandarkar Oriental Research Institute, Pune 411 004; tel. (20) 25656932; e-mail bori1@vsnl.net; f. 1919; 1,200 mems; Pres. Prof. Dr RAJENDER MISHEA; Sec. Prof. SAROJA BHATE; publs *Proceedings of its Sessions*, *Index of Papers* (in 4 vols).

**Anjuman-i-Islam Urdu Research Institute:** 92 Dadabhoy Nowroji Rd, Mumbai 400 001; tel. (22) 22620177; fax (22) 2621610; f. 1947; research in Urdu, Islamic studies, etc; library of rare books; Pres.

SAMI KHATIB; Dir SHAMIM TARIQ; publs include *Nawa-e-Adab* (4 a year).

**Asiatic Society:** 1 Park St, Kolkata 700 016; tel. (33) 22497250; e-mail aslibcal@cal.vsnl.net; internet www.asiaticsocietycal.com; f. 1784; 2,162 mems; Pres. Prof. BISWANATH BANERJEE; Gen. Sec. Prof. RARNAKANTA CHAKRABORTY; publs include *Journal* (quarterly), *Monthly Bulletin*, *Year Book*, *Bibliotheca Indica*, monographs.

**The Asiatic Society of Mumbai:** Town Hall, Shahid Bhagat Singh Rd, Mumbai 400 023; tel. (22) 22660956; fax (22) 22665139; e-mail asbl@bom2.vsnl.net.in; internet www.asiaticsociety.org; f. 1804 as Bombay Literary Society; guides postgraduate students; promotes and publishes research in culture, arts and literature in relation to Asia, and India in particular; offers scholarships and fellowships; established in 1973 Dr P. V. Kane Research Institute for Oriental Studies, later renamed the MM Dr P. V. Kane Institute for Postgraduate Studies and Research; 2,816 mems; 247,022 vols, 2,493 manuscripts, 11,830 coins; Pres. B. G. DESHMUKH; Hon. Sec. HARIDAS K.; publs include *Journal* (annual), monographs and reports.

**Bhandarkar Oriental Research Institute:** Pune 411 004; tel. (20) 5656932; f. 1917; Sec. Dr M. G. DHADPHALE; Curator Dr S. D. LADDU; 1,466 mems; library of 100,782 vols, 31,000 MSS; publs include *Annals of the Bhandarkar Oriental Research Institute* (annually).

**K. R. Cama Oriental Institute and Library:** 136 Mumbai Samachar Marg, Mumbai 400 023; tel. (22) 22843893; fax (22) 22876593; e-mail krcamaoi@vsnl.com; f. 1916; 308 mems; library of 24,055 vols, 2,000 MSS, 161 journals; Pres. MUCHERJI N. M. CAMA; Hon. Secs H. N. MODI, N. B. MODY; Librarians S. V. KODE, S. D. SAHASRABUDDHE; publs incl. *Journal* (annually).

**Centre for Development Studies:** Prasanth Nagar Rd, Ulloor, Trivandrum 695 011; tel. (471) 2448881; fax (471) 2447137; e-mail somannair@cds.ac.in; internet www.cds.edu; f. 1971; promotes interdisciplinary research and academic instruction in disciplines relevant to development issues; library of 124,000 vols; Dir K. N. NAIR; Librarian-in-charge M. CHIDAMBARAM PILLAI.

**Centre for Policy Research:** Dharma Marg, Chanakyapuri, New Delhi 110 021; tel. (11) 26115273; fax (11) 26872746; e-mail cprindia@vsnl.com; internet www.cprindia.org; f. 1973; studies major policy issues in India and suggests alternative options; Pres. and Chief Exec. PRATAP BHANU MEHTA.

**Centre for South, Central, South-East Asian and South-West Pacific Studies:** Jawaharlal Nehru University, New Mehrauli Rd, New Delhi 110 067; tel. (11) 26704350; fax (11) 26741435; e-mail mahendra.lama@vsnl.com; Chair. Prof. MAHENDRA P. LAMA.

**Centre for West Asian and African Studies:** Jawaharlal Nehru University, New Mehrauli Rd, New Delhi 110 067; tel. (11) 26107676, Ext. 2372; fax (11) 26165886; Chair. Dr AJAY DUBEY.

**Indira Gandhi Institute of Development Research (IGIDR):** Gen. A. K. Vaidya Marg, Goregaon (E), Mumbai 400 065; tel. (22) 28400919; fax (22) 28402752; internet www.igidr.ac.in; f. 1986; Dir Dr R. RADHAKRISHNA.

**Rajiv Gandhi Institute for Contemporary Studies:** Jawahar Bhawan, Dr Rajendra Prasad Rd, New Delhi 110 001; tel. (11) 23755117; fax (11) 23755119; e-mail info@rgfindia.com; internet www.rgfindia.com; f. 1991.

**Ganganatha Jha Kendriya Sanskrit Vidyapeetha:** Chandrashekhar Azad Park, Allahabad 211 002; tel. (532) 2460957; f. 1943; fmrly G. N. Jha Research Institute; research into Sanskrit and other branches of Indology; library of 100,000 vols, 80,000 Sanskrit MSS; Prin. Dr GAYA CHARAN TRIPATHI; publs include *Quarterly Research Journal*, critically edited original Sanskrit texts and studies in Indology.

**Gujarat Research Society:** Dr Madhuri Shah Campus, Ramkrishna Mission Marg, Khar (West), Mumbai 400 052; tel. (22) 26462691; fax (22) 26047398; f. 1936 to organize and co-ordinate research in social and cultural activities; library of 10,000 vols; Pres. KALLOLINI P. HAZARAT; publ. *Journal of the Gujarat Research Society* (quarterly).

**Heras Institute of Indian History and Culture:** St Xavier's College Campus, 5 Mahapalika Marg, Mumbai 400 001; tel. (22) 22620665 ext. 320/321; e-mail herasinstitute@hotmail.com; internet herasinstitute.musuem.com; f. 1926 as the Indian Historical Research Institute; Dir Dr AUBREY A. MASCARENHAS; publs include *Indica* (2 a year).

**Indian Council for Cultural Relations:** Azad Bhavan, Indraprastha Estate, New Delhi 110 002; tel. (11) 23319309; fax (11) 23712639; e-mail iccr@giasdL01.vsnl.net.in; f. 1950 to establish and strengthen cultural relations between India and other countries, and to project Indian culture abroad; 12 overseas cultural centres; arranges exhbns, exchange visits, conferences, seminars and lectures; administers J. Nehru Award for International Understanding; library of over 55,000 vols; Dir-Gen. HIMACHAL SOM; publs include *Indian Horizons* (in English, quarterly).

**Indian Council for Research on International Economic Relations (ICRIER):** India Habitat Centre, Core 6A, 4th Floor, Lodi Rd, New Delhi 110 003; tel. (11) 24627447; fax (11) 24620180; e-mail director@icrier.res.in; focuses on trade and investment, WTO-related issues, economic reforms in India, India's external economic policies, foreign policy, regional economic co-operation; Chair. of Bd Dr I. G. PATEL; Dir and Chief Exec. Dr ISHER JUDGE AHLUWALIA.

**Indian Council of World Affairs:** Sapru House, Barakhamba Rd, New Delhi 110 001; tel. (11) 23319055; fax (11) 23310638; e-mail dsicwa@yahoo.com; f. 1943; statutory institution for the study of Indian and international questions; 1,500 mems; library of 128,000 vols, 374 periodicals, 2.5m. press-cuttings, microfilms and microfiches, and UN and EU publs; Pres. BHAIRON SINGH SHEKHAWAT; Dir-Gen. (vacant); publs *India Quarterly* (journal of international affairs), *Foreign Affairs Reports* (monthly).

**Indian Society for Afro-Asian Studies:** 297 Saraswati Kunj, Indraprastha Extension, Mother Dairy Rd, New Delhi 110 092; tel. (11) 22248246; fax (11) 22425698; e-mail isaas@giasdl01; f. 1980; research and promotion of co-operation among African and Asian countries; Pres. LALIT BHASIN; Gen. Sec. Dr DARAMPAL; publs monographs, papers.

**Institute of Economic Growth:** University Enclave, Delhi 110 007; tel. (11) 27667260; fax (11) 27667410; e-mail system@ieg.ernet.in; internet www.iegindia.org; f. 1958; research into the problems of social and economic development of South and South-East Asia; major research themes include: macroeconomic analysis and policy; globalization and trade; industry and development; agriculture and rural development; environmental and natural resource economics; population and human resource development; social change and social structure; health economics and policy; and labour and welfare; library and documentation services; Dir Prof. KANCHAN CHOPRA; publs include *Contributions to Indian Sociology: New Series* (3 a year).

**International Academy of Indian Culture:** J 22 Hauz Khas Enclave, New Delhi 110 016; tel. (11) 26515800; e-mail lokesh.chandra@yahoo.co.in; f. 1935 to study India's artistic and historic relations with other Asian countries; library of 200,000 vols, 40,000 MSS; Hon. Dir Dr LOKESH CHANDRA; publ. *Satapitaka Series* (irregular).

**Islamic Research Association:** c/o Anjuman-i-Islam Islamic Research Institute, opp. V. T. Station, 92 Dadabhoy Nowroji Rd, Mumbai 400 001; tel. (22) 22620177; f. 1933; Pres. Dr M. ISHAQUE JAMKAHANAWALA; Dir Prof. NIZAMUDDIN S. GOREKAR; publs research studies.

**Kuppuswami Sastri Research Institute:** 84 Thiru Vi Ka Rd, Sanskrit College Campus, Mylapore, Chennai 600 004; tel. (44) 24985320; e-mail ksrisans@gmail.com; internet www.ksrisanskrit.in; promotion of oriental learning; 500 mems; library of 50,000 books; 1,000 palm-leaf manuscripts; Dir Dr V. KAMESWARI; Sec. B. MADHAVAN; publs include *Journal of Oriental Research*.

**Maha Bodhi Society:** 4A Bankim Chatterjee St, Kolkata 700 073; tel. (33) 22415214; fax (33) 22412100; f. 1891; 23 brs in other cities and countries; 1,395 mems; Gen. Sec. Ven. M. WIPULASARA MAHA THERA; publs include *Mahabodhi* (English, monthly).

**Namgyal Institute of Tibetology:** Gangtok, Sikkim; e-mail nitsikkim@yahoo.co.in; internet www.tibetology.net; f. 1958; research centre for study of Mahayana (Northern Buddhism) and Himalayan cultures; library of Tibetan literature (canonical of all sects and secular) in MSS and xylographs; museum of icons and art objects; Pres. SUDARSHAN AGARWAL (Gov. of Sikkim); Dir TASHI DENSAPA; publs include *Bulletin of Tibetology* (2 a year) and publications in Tibetan, Sanskrit and English.

**Nava Nalanda Mahavihara** (Nalanda University): PO Nalanda, Bihar 803 111; tel. (6112) 281672; fax (6112) 281505; e-mail nnmdirector@sify.com; f. 1951; under Ministry of Culture; postgraduate studies and research in Pali, Buddhist studies, ancient Indian and Asian history and philosophy, Tibetan, Sanskrit, Chinese and Japanese; library of 50,000 vols; Dir Dr RAVINDRA PANTH; publs include *Nava Nalanda Mahavihara Research* (annually).

**Oriental Institute:** Maharaja Sayajirao University of Baroda, opp. Palace Gate, Palace Rd, Vadodara 390 001, Gujarat; tel. (265) 2425121; f. 1927; library of 49,005 vols on Indology and Sanskrit and 29,189 MSS; 30 mems; Dir Prof. M. L. WADEKAR; publs include *Gaekwad's Oriental Series*, *M.S. University Research Series*, *M.S. University Oriental Series*, *Journal of the Oriental Institute* (English, quarterly), *Svadhaya* (Gujarati, quarterly).

**Research and Information System for Developing Countries:** Zone IV-B, 4th Floor, India Habitat Centre, Lodhi Rd, New Delhi 110 003; tel. (11) 24682176; fax (11) 24682173; e-mail dgoffice@ris.org.in; internet www.newasiaforum.org; trade and development issues; Dir-Gen. Dr NAGESH KUMAR; publs include *South Asia Development and Cooperation Reports* (every 2 years), *World Trade and Development Reports* (every 2 years), *South Asia Economic Journal* (2 a year),

*Asian Biotechnology and Development Review* (3 a year), *New Asia Monitor* (quarterly).

**Socio-Economic Research Institute:** C-19 and C-39, College St Market, Kolkata 700 007; tel. (33) 22410775; fax (33) 22415152; f. 1959; Pres. Prof. TARUN C. DUTT; publs include *Bulletin of the Socio-Economic Research Institute*.

**Sri Venkateswara University Oriental Research Institute:** Tirupati, Chittoor, Andhra Pradesh 517 502; tel. (877) 2249666, Ext. 291; fax (877) 2429101; e-mail orientalresearchinstitute@yahoo.co .in; f. 1939; research in language and literature, philosophy and religion, arts and archaeology, history and Indian heritage; library of 30,405 vols, 20,000 MSS; Dir V. VENKATARAMANA REDDY; publs include *Oriental Journal* (annually), critical editions and monographs.

**Vishveshvaranand Vishva Bandhu Institute of Sanskrit and Indological Studies:** Panjab University, PO Sadhu Ashram, Hoshiarpur 146 021; tel. and fax (1882) 221002; e-mail poojasood@ rediffmail.com; f. 1965; postgraduate teaching, research and study in Indology and Sanskrit, including language, literature and religion; library of 76,440 books and journals, 3,000 MSS; information centre f. 1998; Chair. Prof. G. D. BHARADWAJ; publs *Panjab University Indological Series*, *Vishveshvaranand Indological Journal*.

## IRAN

**Asia Institute:** University of Shiraz, Shiraz; tel. (71) 32111; Dir Dr Y. M. NAVABI; publs *Bulletin*, monographs.

**Institute for Political and International Studies:** Shaheed Bahonar Ave, Shaheed Aghaii St, POB 19395-1793, Tajrish, Tehran; tel. (21) 2571010; fax (21) 270964; f. 1983; research and information on international relations, economics, law and Islamic studies; library of 22,000 vols; publs include *Iranian Journal of International Affairs* (quarterly).

## ISRAEL

**Harry S. Truman Research Institute for the Advancement of Peace:** The Hebrew University of Jerusalem, Mt Scopus, Jerusalem 91905; tel. (2) 5882300; fax (2) 5828076; e-mail truman@savion.huji .ac.il; internet www.truman.huji.ac.il; f. 1965; conducts and sponsors social science and historical research, organizes conferences and publs works on many regions, including Asia; Dir Prof. EYAL BEN ARI.

**Institute of Asian and African Studies:** The Hebrew University of Jerusalem, Mt Scopus, Jerusalem 91905; tel. (2) 5883659; fax (2) 5883658; e-mail AsiaAfrica@h2.hum.cc.huji.ac.il; internet asiafrica .huji.ac.il; f. 1926 as Institute of Oriental Studies; provides degree and postgraduate courses, covering history, social sciences and languages, in Chinese, Japanese, Korean, Tibetan and South Asian studies; Dir Prof. MEIR BAR-ASHER; Sec. YEHUDIT MAGEN.

## ITALY

**The Bologna Center of the Paul H. Nitze School of Advanced International Studies of the Johns Hopkins University:** Via Belmeloro 11, 40126 Bologna; tel. (051) 2917811; fax (051) 228505; e-mail Registrar@jhubc.it; internet www.jhubc.it; f. 1955; graduate studies in international affairs and economics; Dir KENNETH H. KELLER; publs *Bologna Center Catalogue*, *EuroSAIS* (alumni newsletter), occasional papers series.

**Istituto Affari Internazionali (IAI):** Via Angelo Brunetti 9, 00186 Rome; tel. (06) 3224360; fax (06) 3224363; f. 1965; Dir GIANNI BONVICINI; publs include *The International Spectator* (English, quarterly).

**Istituto per gli Studi di Politica Internazionale (ISPI):** Palazzo Clerici, Via Clerici 5, 20121 Milan; tel. (02) 8633131; fax (02) 8692055; e-mail ispi.segreteria@ispionline.it; internet www .ispionline.it; f. 1933 for the promotion of the study and knowledge of all problems concerning international relations; seminars at post-graduate level; library of 100,000 vols; Pres. BORIS BIANCHERI; publs *ISPI Relazioni Internazionali* (quarterly), papers (20 a year).

**Istituto Universitario Orientale** (Oriental University Institute): Dept of Asian Studies, Piazza San Domenico Maggiore 12, 80134 Naples; tel. (081) 5517855; fax (081) 5517852; e-mail bibsa@iuo.it; f. 1732; library of 230,000 vols, 2,000 periodical titles; Dir Prof. ALBERTO VENTURA; publs include four series (*Maior, Minor, Serie Tre* and *Baluchistan Monograph Series*), *Annali* and *Ming Qing Yanjiu*.

## JAPAN

**Nihon Boeki Shinkokiko Ajia Keizai Kenkyusho** (Institute of Developing Economies, Japan External Trade Organization—IDE–JETRO): 3-2-2 Wakaba, Mihama-ku, Chiba-shi, Chiba 261-8545; tel. (43) 299-9500; fax (43) 299-9724; e-mail info@ide.go.jp; internet www .ide.go.jp; Ajia Keizai Kenkyusho est. 1960, merged with JETRO 1998; independent administrative institution; research on economic and related subjects in Asia and other developing areas; aims to promote economic co-operation and to improve trade relations between Japan and the developing countries; 247 mems; Chair. YASUO HAYASHI; library of 576,604 vols; publs include *Ajia Keizai* (Japanese, monthly), *Ajiken Warudo Torendo* (World Trends, Japanese, monthly), *The Developing Economies* (English, quarterly), occasional papers series (English, irregular).

**Nihon-Indogaku-Bukkyogakkai** (Japanese Association of Indian and Buddhist Studies): c/o Dept of Indian Philosophy and Buddhist Studies, Graduate School of Humanities and Sociology, University of Tokyo, 7-3-1 Hongo, Bunkyo-ku, Tokyo 113-0033; tel. (3) 3813-5903; f. 1951; 2,500 mems; Pres. SENGAKU MAYEDA; publ. *Indogaku Bukkyogaku Kenkyu* (Journal of Indian and Buddhist Studies).

**Nihon Kokusai Mondai Kenkyusho** (The Japan Institute of International Affairs): Tokyo; tel. (3) 3503-7261; fax (3) 3595-1755; internet www.jiia.or.jp; f. 1959; Chair. YOSHIZANE IWASA; Pres. NOBUO MATSUNAGA; publs include *Kokusai Mondai* (International Affairs, monthly), *Japan Review of International Affairs* (4 a year), newsletters, books and monographs.

**Research Institute for the Study of Languages and Cultures of Asia and Africa (ILCAA):** Tokyo University of Foreign Studies, Asahicho 3-11-1, Fuchu, Tokyo 183-8534; tel. (42) 330-5600; fax (42) 330-5610; e-mail director@aa.tufs.ac.jp; internet www.aa.tufs.ac.jp; f. 1964; library of 65,445 vols; Dir KOJI MIYAZAKI; publs *Journal of Asian and African Studies* (2 a year), *Newsletter* (3 a year).

**United Nations Centre for Regional Development:** Nagono 1-47-1, Nakamura-ku, Nagoya 450-0001; tel. (52) 561-9377; fax (52) 561-9375; e-mail rep@uncrd.or.jp; internet www.uncrd.or.jp; f. 1971; undertakes training, research, consultation and information exchange on regional development issues affecting developing countries; Dir KAZUNOBU ONOGAWA; publs *Regional Development Dialogue* (2 a year), *Regional Development Studies* (annually).

## MEXICO

**Centro de Estudios de Asia y Africa** (Centre for Asian and African Studies): El Colegio de México, Camino al Ajusco 20, Pedregal de Sta Teresa, México DF 10740; tel. (5) 449-3000; fax (5) 645-0464; e-mail cmondragon@colmex.mx; internet www.colmex.mx/centros/ceaa/ index.htm; f. 1964; part of El Colegio de México; Dir BENJAMÍN PRECIADO SOLÍS; publ. *Estudios de Asia y Africa* (quarterly).

## NEPAL

**Centre for Nepal and Asian Studies:** Tribhuvan University, POB 3757, Kirtipur, Kathmandu; tel. (1) 4331740; fax (1) 4331184; e-mail cnastu@htp.com/np; f. 1972; conducts political and social research both in Nepalese and Asian contexts; Exec. Dir Prof. Dr TIRTHA PRASAD MISHRA; publs include *Contributions to Nepalese Studies* (2 a year), monographs, bibliographies, occasional papers.

**Institute for Integrated Development Studies:** Baneshwor, POB 2254, Kathmandu; tel. (1) 4494519; fax (1) 447831; e-mail iids@wlink.com.np; Chair. Dr MOHAN MAN SAINJU; publs include *Sambad* (quarterly).

**Nepal Council of World Affairs:** NCWA Bldg, Harihar Bhawan, Pulchowk, POB 2588, Lalitpur, Kathmandu; tel. (1) 4526222; f. 1948; Pres. Dr SOORYA LAL AMATYA; publ. *Nepal Council of World Affairs Journal* (annually).

**United Nations Regional Centre for Peace and Disarmament in Asia and the Pacific:** United Nations Office for Disarmament Affairs, UN Bldg, Pulchowk, General Post Office Box 107, Kathmandu; tel. (1) 5010257; fax (1) 5010223; e-mail UNODA-RCPD@un .org; f. 1988; Special Co-ordinator for Peace and Disarmament Programmes in Asia and the Pacific ROMAN HUNGER.

## NETHERLANDS

**International Institute for Asian Studies (IIAS):** POB 9515, 2300 RA Leiden; tel. (71) 5272227; fax (71) 5274162; e-mail iias@let .leidenuniv.nl; internet www.iias.nl; based in Leiden and Amsterdam; post-doctoral research centre; Dir Prof. MAX SPARREBOOM; publ. *IIAS Newsletter*.

## PAKISTAN

**Anjuman Taraqqi-e-Urdu Pakistan:** D-159, Block 7, Gulshan-e-Iqbal, Karachi 75300; tel. (21) 2724023; f. 1903 for promotion of Urdu language and literature; preparing a six-vol. bibliography of Urdu books in collaboration with UNESCO; lending library of 20,000 vols, research library of 26,000 vols, 4,000 MSS; Pres. AFTAB AHMED KHAN; Sec. JAMILUDDIN A'ALI; publs *Urdu* (quarterly), *Qaumi Zaban* (monthly).

**Centre for South Asian Studies:** University of the Punjab, Quaid-i-Azam Campus, Lahore 54590; tel. (42) 9231143; fax (42) 9231173; e-mail centreforsouthasianstudies@yahoo.com; f. 1975; study of socio-economic and political developments in South Asia, particularly of issues relating to Pakistan, India, Bangladesh, Nepal,

Bhutan, Sri Lanka and Maldives; Dir Prof. Dr SADIQ A. GILL; publs include *South Asian Studies* (2 a year).

**Institute of Development Studies:** North-West Frontier Province Agricultural University, Peshawar; tel. (521) 41986; f. 1953; Dir MUHAMMAD AHMAD KHAN; publs include *Journal of Development Studies*.

**Islamic Research Institute:** POB 1035, Islamabad 44000; tel. (51) 850751; fax (51) 853360; f. 1960 to conduct and co-ordinate research in Islamic studies; organizes seminars, conferences etc; library of 75,000 vols, 1,300 microfilms and microfiches, 258 MSS; 170 cassettes; Dir-Gen. Dr ZAFAR ISHAQ ANSARI; publs include *Al-Dirasat al-Islamiyyah* (Arabic, quarterly), *Islamic Studies* (English, quarterly), *Fikr-o-Nazar* (Urdu, quarterly), monographs.

**Mahbub-ul-Haq Human Development Centre (MHHDC):** 42 Embassy Rd, G-6/3, Islamabad; f. 1995 as the Human Development Centre, renamed as above in 1998; organizes professional research, policy studies and seminars in the area of human development, with a special focus on the South Asian region; library of over 2,000 volumes on economic, social and political issues with a special focus on the South Asian region; Pres. KHADIJA HAQ; Dir Dr SARFRAZ K. QURESHI; publs include *Human Development in South Asia* (annual), *Mahbub-ul-Haq Development Review* (biannual).

**Pakistan Economic Research Institute (PERI):** 24 Mianmir Rd, Upper Mall Scheme, Lahore 15; f. 1955 to undertake socio-economic investigations and co-ordinate research in economic problems of Pakistan; to collect, compile and interpret statistical data; to publish the results and findings of investigations; Dir A. AZIZ ANWAR; Sec. A. R. ARSHAD; publs research papers, reports.

**Pakistan Historical Society:** Bait al-Hikmah Library, Hamdard University, Mohd Qasim Ave, Karachi 74700; tel. (21) 6996001; fax (21) 6996002; e-mail phs@hamdard.edu.pk; f. 1950; historical studies and research; particularly history of Islam and of India and Pakistan; library of 7,709 vols; Pres. SADIA RASHID; Gen. Sec. Dr ANSAR ZAHID KHAN; publs *Journal* (quarterly), monographs, research studies.

**Pakistan Institute of Development Economics:** POB 1091, Islamabad 44000; tel. (51) 9206610; fax (51) 9210886; e-mail pide@isb.paknet.com.pk; internet www.pide.org.pk; f. 1957; conducts research on development economics in general and on Pakistan's economic issues in particular, providing a foundation on which economic policy-making can be based; provides in-service training in economic analysis, research methods and project evaluation; offers academic programmes for postgraduate students; library of 33,532 vols, 280 current periodicals, 6,200 microfiches and 21,200 research papers/reports; Sec. MUHAMMAD ASLAM; publs include *Pakistan Development Review* (quarterly), essays, monographs, statistical papers, reprints, bibliographies, research reports.

**Pakistan Institute of International Affairs:** Aiwan-e-Sadar Rd, POB 1447, Karachi 74200; tel. (21) 5682891; fax (21) 5686069; e-mail piia@cyber.net.pk; f. 1947 to promote interest and research in international affairs; library of over 32,400 vols; over 600 mems; Chair. FATEHYAB ALI KHAN; Sec. Dr QAZI SHAKIL AHMAD; publs *Pakistan Horizon* (quarterly), books and monographs.

**Quaid-i-Azam Academy:** 297 M. A. Jinnah Rd, Karachi 74800; tel. (21) 7218184; f. 1976; research on Quaid-i-Azam Mohammad Ali Jinnah, the historical background (incl. cultural, religious, literary, linguistic, social, economic and political aspects) of the Pakistan Movement and various aspects of Pakistan; library of 25,000 vols and 950 microfilms of newspapers; Dir Dr MUHAMMAD ALI SIDDIQUI; publs bibliographies, research studies, monographs and documents (in English, Urdu and other Pakistani languages).

**Research Society of Pakistan:** University of the Punjab, New Campus, Lahore; tel. (42) 9231176; f. 1963; conducts research into the origins of Pakistan and its culture, politics, literature, linguistics, history, topography and archaeology; Pres. Lt-Gen. (retd) ARSHAD MAHMOOD; Dir Dr S. QALB-I-ABID; publs include *Journal of the Research Society of Pakistan* (2 a year).

## POLAND

**Institute of Developing Countries:** University of Warsaw, ul. Karowa 20, 00-324 Warsaw; tel. (22) 55-23-237; fax (22) 55-23-227; e-mail ikr@uw.edu.pl; internet www.ikr.uw.edu.pl; f. 1962; undergraduate and postgraduate studies; interdisciplinary research on developing countries; Dir Prof. MIROSŁAWA CZERNY.

**Institute of Oriental Studies:** 00-927 Warsaw, ul. Krakowskie Przedmieście 26/28; tel. (22) 55-20-349; e-mail dyrekcja@orient.uw.edu.pl; internet www.orient.uw.edu.pl/~pto; f. 1922; Pres. Prof. JOLANTA SIERAKOWSKA-DYNDO; Sec. MARIA KOZŁOWSKA; publ. *Przeglad Wschodni*.

**Komitet Nauk Orientalistycznych PAN** (Committee for Oriental Studies of the Polish Academy of Sciences): 00-927 Warsaw, ul. Krakowskie Przedmieście 26/28; tel. (22) 5520459; internet kno.pan.pl; f. 1952; Asian and African studies, particularly social sciences; Pres. Prof. Dr MAREK MEJOR; publs *Rocznik Orientalistyczny* (2 a year), series *Prace orientalistyczne* (irregular).

## PORTUGAL

**Museu Etnográfico da Sociedade de Geografia de Lisboa** (Ethnographical Museum): Rua Portas de Santo Antão 100, 1100 Lisbon; tel. (1) 3425068; fax (1) 3464553; e-mail soc.geografia.lisboa@clix.pt; f. 1875; native arts, arms, clothing, musical instruments, statues of navigators and historians, relics of voyages of discovery, scientific instruments; Dir Prof. JOÃO PEREIRA NETO; Curator Dr MANUEL CANTINHO.

## RUSSIA

**Centre for Indian Studies:** Russian Academy of Sciences, 103777 Moscow, ul. Rozhdestvenka 12; tel. (095) 923-62-82; fax (095) 975-23-96; f. 1988; part of the Institute of Oriental Studies; Dir Dr A. A. KUTSENKOV; publ. *Azia i Afrika Segodny* (monthly).

**Institute of World Economy and International Relations:** 117859 Moscow, ul. Profsoyuznaya 23; tel. (095) 120-43-32; fax (095) 310-70-27; e-mail ineir@sovam.com; f. 1956; Dir VLADEN A. MARTYNOV; publs include *Otnosheniya* (monthly).

**Moscow State Institute of International Relations:** 119454 Moscow, Vernadskogo pr. 76; tel. (095) 434-91-58; fax (095) 434-90-66; internet www.mgimo.ru; f. 1944; library of 920,000 vols; Rector ANATOLII V. TORKUNOV; publ. *Moscow Journal of International Law*.

## SINGAPORE

**Asia Research Institute (ARI):** Shaw Foundation Bldg, AS7, Level 4, 5 Arts Link, National University of Singapore, Singapore 117570; tel. 65163810; fax 67791428; e-mail arisec@nus.edu.sg; internet www.ari.nus.edu.sg; f. 2001 to provide a focus for multi-disciplinary research on the Asian region; Dir ANTHONY REID.

**Institute of South Asian Studies:** 469A Bukit Timah Rd, #07-01, Tower Block, Singapore 259770; tel. 65164232; fax 63144586; e-mail isasdir@nus.edu.sg; internet www.isas.nus.edu.sg; f. 2004; part of the National University of Singapore; Chair. GOPINATH PILLAI; Dir Prof. TAI YONG TAN.

## SRI LANKA

**Maha Bodhi Society of Sri Lanka:** 130 Rev. Hikkaduwe Sri, Sumangala Na Himi Mawatha, Colombo 10; tel. (11) 2698079; fax (11) 2673472; e-mail mahabodhi@asia.com; f. 1891 for the world propagation of Buddhism; 700 mems; Pres. Ven. BANAGALA UPATISSA NAYAKA THERO; Hon. Sec. M. M. P. SENARATHNE; publ. *Sinhala Bauddhaya* (monthly).

**Marga Institute:** 93/10 Dutugemunu Mawatha, Colombo 6; tel. (11) 2828544; fax (11) 2828597; e-mail marga@sri.lanka.net; internet www.margasrilanka.org; f. 1972; non-profit, multi-disciplinary research organization undertaking study of development issues in Asian region; library of 30,000 books and journals; Chief Exec. BASIL ILANGAKOON; publ. *The Marga Journal*.

**Regional Centre for Strategic Studies:** 2 Elibank Rd, Colombo 5; tel. (11) 2599734; fax (11) 2599993; e-mail rcss@sri.lanka.net; internet www.rcss.org; conducts research into strategic and international issues pertaining to South Asia; Exec. Dir Prof. SRIDHAR K. KHATRI.

**Royal Asiatic Society of Sri Lanka:** 1st Floor, Mahaweli Centre and Royal Asiatic Society Bldg, 96 Ananda Coomaraswamy Mawatha, Colombo 7; tel. and fax (11) 2699249; e-mail rassl@col7.metta.lk; internet www.rassrilanka.org; f. 1845; object of the Society is to institute and promote enquiries into the history, religions, languages, literature, arts, sciences and social conditions of the present and fmr inhabitants of Sri Lanka and connected cultures; library contains one of the largest existing collections of books on Sri Lanka, and others on Indian and Eastern culture in general; Pres. Dr K. D. PARANAVITANA; Hon. Secs Dr K. ARUNASIRI, M. G. SAMARAWEERA; publ. *Journal* (annually).

## SWITZERLAND

**Centre for Asian Studies (CEA):** Graduate Institute of International and Development Studies, 63 rue de Lausanne, CP 36, 1211 Geneva 21; tel. (22) 9085820; fax (22) 7383996; e-mail duc@hei.unige.ch; internet graduateinstitute.ch; f. 1971; Dir Prof. JEAN-LUC MAURER; publs books, research reports, occasional papers, articles and newsletters.

**Institut universitaire d'Etudes du Développement:** 20 rue Rothschild, CP 136, 1211 Geneva 21; tel. (22) 908-4365; fax (22) 908-6273; e-mail iued@iued.unige.ch; internet www.iued.unige.ch; f. 1961; a centre of higher education, training and research into development problems, incl. those of Asia; conducts courses, seminars and practical work; Dir MICHEL CARTON; publs *Cahiers de l'IUED*, *Annuaire suisse de politique de développement*, *Itinéraires*.

**Schweizerische Asiengesellschaft** (Swiss Asia Society): c/o Ostasiatisches Seminar, Universität Zürich, Zürichbergstrasse 4, 8032 Zürich; tel. (1) 634-3181; fax (1) 634-4921; e-mail office@oas.unizh.ch; internet www.sagw.ch/dt/Mitglieder/outer.aspzid=40; f. 1939; 185 mems; Pres. Prof. Dr V RUDOLPH; publs *Asiatische Studien / Etudes Asiatiques* (quarterly), *Schweizer Asiatische Studien / Etudes Asiatiques Suisses* (series).

**Schweizerisches Institut für Auslandforschung** (Swiss Institute of International Studies): Seilergraben 49, 8001 Zürich; tel. (44) 632-6362; fax (44) 632-1947; e-mail siafcd@pw.unizh.ch; internet www.siaf.ch; Dir Prof. DIETER RULOFF; publ. *Sozialwissenschaftliche Studien* (annually).

## THAILAND

**Asian Institute of Technology (AIT):** POB 4, Klong Luang, Pathumthani 12120; tel. (2) 516-0110; fax (2) 516-2126; e-mail jlarmand@ait.ac.th; internet www.ait.ac.th; f. 1959; Pres. Prof. JEAN-LOUIS ARMAND; publs *AIT Annual Report*, *Annual Report on Research and Activities*, *AIT Review* (3 a year), *Prospectus*, other specialized publs.

## UNITED KINGDOM

**Asia Pacific and Africa Collections** (British Library): 96 Euston Rd, London, NW1 2DB; tel. (20) 7412-7873; fax (20) 7412-7641; e-mail apac-enquiries@bl.uk; internet www.bl.uk/collections/asiapacificafrica.html; f. 1801; c. 1,200,000 European and Oriental printed books, 175,000 vols and files of archival records (1600–1948), 70,000 Oriental MSS, European MSS, 14,000 vols and boxes, 15,500 British paintings and drawings relating principally to India and the East, 11,000 Oriental drawings and miniatures, 2,900 prints and over 250,000 photographs; Head GRAHAM W. SHAW; publs *Guides* and catalogues of the collections.

**Asia Research Centre:** London School of Economics and Political Science, Houghton St, London, WC2A 2AE; tel. (20) 7955-7388; fax (20) 7107-5285; e-mail c.s.lee2@lse.ac.uk; internet www.lse.ac.uk/collections/asiaResearchCentre; f. 1995; conducts social science research on Asia; Dir Dr ATHAR HUSSAIN.

**Catholic Institute for International Relations (CIIR):** Unit 3, Canonbury Yard, 190A New North Rd, London, N1 7BJ; tel. (20) 7354-0883; fax (20) 7359-0017; e-mail ciir@ciir.org; internet www.ciir.org; f. 1940; information and research on developing countries; recruits professionals for development projects overseas; Exec. Dir CHRISTINE ALLEN.

**Centre for Asia-Pacific Studies, Nottingham Trent University:** Faculty of Humanities, Nottingham Trent University, Clifton Lane, Nottingham, NG11 8NS; tel. (115) 848-3175; fax (115) 848-6319; e-mail roy.smith@ntu.ac.uk; internet human.ntu.ac.uk/research/caps; Dir Dr ROY SMITH.

**Centre for South Asian Studies, University of Edinburgh:** School of Social and Political Studies, University of Edinburgh, 55 George Sq., Edinburgh, EH8 9LL; tel. (131) 650-3976; e-mail south.asian@ed.ac.uk; internet www.csas.ed.ac.uk; f. 1988; Convenor Prof. ROGER JEFFERY.

**Centre of South Asian Studies, University of Cambridge:** Laundress Lane, Cambridge, CB2 1SD; tel. (1223) 338094; fax (1223) 767094; e-mail webmaster@s-asian.cam.ac.uk; internet www.s-asian.cam.ac.uk; f. 1964; Administrator Dr KEVIN GREENBANK.

**Faculty of Oriental Studies:** University of Oxford, Pusey Lane, Oxford, OX1 2LE; tel. (1865) 278200; fax (1865) 278190; e-mail orient@orinst.ox.ac.uk; internet www.orinst.ox.ac.uk; f. 1960; Sec. CHARLOTTE VINNICOMBE; comprises Oriental Institute and Institute for Chinese Studies.

**Institute of Asia-Pacific Studies, University of Nottingham:** School of Politics, University Park, Nottingham, NG7 2RD; tel. (115) 951-4862; fax (115) 951-4859; e-mail gary.rawnsley@nottingham.ac.uk; internet www.nottingham.ac.uk/iaps; Dir Dr GARY RAWNSLEY.

**Institute of Commonwealth Studies:** 28 Russell Sq., London, WC1B 5DS; tel. (20) 7862-8844; fax (20) 7862-8820; e-mail ics@sas.ac.uk; internet www.commonwealth.sas.ac.uk; f. 1949 to promote advanced study of the Commonwealth; provides a library and meeting place for postgraduate student and academic staff engaged in research on this field; offers postgraduate teaching; Dir RICHARD CROOK; publs *Annual Report*, *Collected Seminar Papers*, *Newsletter*, *Theses in Progress in Commonwealth Studies*.

**Institute of Development Studies at the University of Sussex:** Brighton, Sussex, BN1 9RE; tel. (1273) 606261; fax (1273) 621202; e-mail ids@ids.ac.uk; internet www.ids.ac.uk/ids; f. 1966; research, teaching and communications on international development; Dir KEITH BEZANSON; publs include *IDS Bulletin* (quarterly), *IDS Discussion Papers*, *Annual Report*, *Research Reports*.

**International Institute for Strategic Studies (IISS):** Arundel House, 13–15 Arundel St, Temple Place, London, WC2R 3DX; tel. (20) 7379-7676; fax (20) 7836-3108; internet www.iiss.org; f. 1958; conducts research and analysis, and provides a forum for contacts on military and political developments relevant to the prospects, course and consequences of conflict world-wide; c. 2,500 individual mems and 400 corporate and institutional mems; Chair. Prof. FRANÇOIS HEISBOURG; Dir-Gen. and Chief Exec. Dr JOHN CHIPMAN; publs include *The Military Balance* (annual), *Strategic Survey* (annually), *Strategic Comments* (10 a year), *Survival: Global Politics and Strategy* (every 2 months), *Adelphi Papers* (monograph series).

**Oriental Ceramic Society:** POB 517, Cambridge, CB21 5BE; tel. and fax (1223) 881328; e-mail ocslondon@btinternet.com; internet ocs-london.com; f. 1921 to increase knowledge and appreciation of Eastern ceramic and other arts; Pres. ROSEMARY SCOTT; Sec. MARY PAINTER.

**Overseas Development Institute:** Costain House, 111 Westminster Bridge Rd, London, SE1 7JD; tel. (20) 7922-0300; fax (20) 7922-0399; e-mail odi@odi.org.uk; internet www.odi.org.uk; f. 1960 as a research centre and forum for the discussion of development issues; publishes its research findings in books and working papers; library of over 15,000 vols; Chair. Baroness JAY; Dir SIMON MAXWELL; publs include *Development Policy Review*, *Disasters: The Journal of Disaster Studies and Management*.

**Royal Asiatic Society of Great Britain and Ireland:** 60 Queen's Gardens, London, W2 3AF; tel. (20) 7724-4741; e-mail info@royalasiaticsociety.org; internet www.royalasiaticsociety.org; f. 1823 for the study of the history, sociology, institutions, customs, languages and art of Asia; c. 700 mems; c. 700 subscribing libraries; brs in various Eastern cities; library of 50,000 vols and 1,500 MSS; Curator ALISON OHTA; Librarian KATHY LAZENBATT; publs *Journal* and monographs.

**Royal Commonwealth Society:** 25 Northumberland Ave, London, WC2N 5AP; tel. (20) 7766-9231; fax (20) 7930-9705; e-mail info@rcsint.org; internet www.rcsint.org; f. 1868; est. to promote international understanding of the Commonwealth and its people; organizes meetings and seminars on topical issues, and cultural and social events; library housed by Cambridge University Library; Chair. Baroness PRASHAR; Dir STUART MOLE; publs *Annual Report*, *Newsletter* (3 a year), conference reports.

**Royal Institute of International Affairs:** Chatham House, 10 St James's Sq., London, SW1Y 4LE; tel. (20) 7957-5700; fax (20) 7957-5710; e-mail contact@chathamhouse.org.uk; internet www.chathamhouse.org.uk; f. 1920 to facilitate the scientific study of international questions; c. 3,000 mems; Chair. Dr DEANNE JULIUS; Dir ROBIN NIBLETT; publs include *International Affairs* (6 a year), *The World Today* (monthly), *Chatham House Papers*, *Annual Report*, etc.

**Royal Society for Asian Affairs:** 2 Belgrave Sq., London, SW1X 8PJ; tel. (20) 7235-5122; e-mail info@rsaa.org.uk; internet www.rsaa.org.uk; f. 1901; 1,200 mems; library of c. 6,500 vols; Pres. Lord DENMAN; Chair. Sir HAROLD WALKER; Sec. N. J. M. CAMERON; publ. *Journal* (3 a year).

**St Antony's College Asian Studies Centre:** Oxford, OX2 6JF; tel. and fax (1865) 274559; e-mail asian@sant.ox.ac.uk; internet www.sant.ox.ac.uk/asian; f. 1954; devoted to the comparative study of modern Asia; Dir Dr MARK REBICK.

**School of Development Studies, University of East Anglia:** Norwich, NR4 7TJ; tel. (1603) 592807; fax (1603) 451999; e-mail dev.general@uea.ac.uk; internet www.uea.ac.uk/dev; f. 1970; teaching, research and advisory work; Dean Dr BRUCE LANKFORD.

**School of Oriental and African Studies (SOAS):** University of London, Thornhaugh St, Russell Sq., London, WC1H 0XG; tel. (20) 7898-4034; fax (20) 7898-4039; e-mail study@soas.ac.uk; internet www.soas.ac.uk; f. 1916; centre for the study of Asia, Africa and the Middle East; includes Centre of Chinese Studies, Centre of South Asian Studies, Centre of South East Asian Studies, Centre of Korean Studies, Japan Research Centre, Contemporary China Institute, Centre for the Study of Japanese Religion, Centre for the Study of the Literature of Asia and Africa, Centre of East Asian Law; Dir Prof. PAUL WEBLEY; publs include *The Bulletin*, *China Quarterly*.

**School of Oriental and African Studies Library:** Thornhaugh St, Russell Sq., London, WC1H 0XG; tel. (20) 7898-4163; fax (20) 7898-4159; e-mail libenquiry@soas.ac.uk; internet www.soas.ac.uk/library/index.cfm; f. 1916; c. 1,500,000 vols and pamphlets; 4,700 current periodicals, 54,000 maps, 7,000 microforms, 2,000 DVDs and videos, 2,800 manuscripts and private papers collections, extensive missionary archives; all covering Asian and African languages, literatures, philosophy, religions, history, law, cultural anthropology, art and archaeology, music, film and media studies, gender studies, development studies, economics, politics and finance; Librarian DAVID PERROW (acting).

## UNITED STATES OF AMERICA

**American Oriental Society:** Near East Division, Hatcher Graduate Library, University of Michigan, Ann Arbor, MI 48109-1205; tel. (734) 647-4760; fax (734) 763-6743; e-mail jrodgers@umich.edu; internet www.umich/edu/~aos; f. 1842; 1,400 mems; library of 23,000 vols; Pres. (vacant); Sec.-Treas. JONATHAN RODGERS; publs *Journal of the American Oriental Society* (quarterly), *AOS Monograph Series* (irregular).

**The Asia Foundation:** POB 193223, San Francisco, CA 94119; tel. (415) 982-4640; fax (415) 392-8863; e-mail info@asiafound.org; internet www.asiafoundation.org; br. in Washington, DC, and 17 offices throughout Asia; private, non-profit NGO; f. 1951; library of 3,370 vols; supports programs in Asia that help improve governance, law, and civil society, women's empowerment; economic reform and development, and international relations; collaborates with private and public partners to support leadership and institutional development, exchanges, and policy research; Pres. DOUGLAS BEREUTER; publ *Annual Report*.

**Asian Art Museum of San Francisco/Chong-Moon Lee Center for Asian Art and Culture:** 200 Larkin St, San Francisco, CA 94102; tel. (415) 581-3500; fax (415) 581-4700; e-mail pr@asianart.org; internet www.asianart.org; f. 1966; museum and centre of research and publication on outstanding collections representing the countries and cultures of Asia; holds over 17,000 Asian works of art spanning 6,000 years of history; library of 35,000 vols; Dir JAY XU.

**Asian Cultural Council:** 437 Madison Ave, New York, NY 10022; tel. (212) 812-4300; fax (212) 812-4299; e-mail acc@accny.org; internet www.asianculturalcouncil.org; f. 1980; supports cultural exchanges in the visual and performing arts between the USA and Asia; publicly supported; Dir RALPH SAMUELSON.

**Association for Asian Studies (AAS):** 1021 E. Huron St, Ann Arbor, MI 48104; tel. (734) 665-2490; fax (734) 665-3801; internet www.aasianst.org; f. 1941; Exec. Dir MICHAEL PASCHAL; publs include *Asian Studies Newsletter* (quarterly), *Journal of Asian Studies* (quarterly), *Education About Asia* (3 a year) and monographs.

**The Brookings Institution:** 1775 Massachusetts Ave, NW, Washington, DC 20036-2188; tel. (202) 797-6000; fax (202) 797-6004; e-mail brookinfo@brook.edu; internet www.brook.edu; f. 1916; research, education and publishing in economics, govt, and foreign policy; maintains Social Science Computation Center; education division, Center for Public Policy Education, organizes conferences and seminars; 50 resident scholars; library of c. 85,000 vols; Pres. STROBE TALBOTT; publs *Annual Report*, *The Brookings Review* (quarterly), *Brookings Papers on Economic Activity* (3 a year), *Brookings Papers on Education Policy* (annually), *Brookings/Wharton Papers on Financial Policy* (annually).

**Centers for South and Southeast Asian Studies, University of Michigan:** 1080 South University, Ste 3640, Ann Arbor, MI 48109-1106; tel. (734) 764-0352; fax (734) 936-0996; e-mail csseas@umich.edu; internet www.umich.edu/~iinet/csseas; Dir (South Asia) SUMATHI RAWASWAMY; Dir (Southeast Asia) JUDITH BECKER; Dir (Southeast Asia Business Program, Business School) LINDA LIM (tel. (734) 763-5796); publs *Michigan Papers on South and Southeast Asia*, *Michigan Studies of South and Southeast Asia*, *Michigan Studies in Buddhist Literature* (occasional papers), *Journal of Asian Business* (quarterly).

**Center for South Asia Studies, University of California:** 10 Stephens Hall 2310, University of California, Berkeley, CA 94720-2310; tel. (510) 642-3608; fax (510) 643-5793; e-mail csas@uclink4.berkeley.edu; internet www.ias.berkeley.edu/southasia; Chair. Prof. THOMAS METCALF.

**Cornell University South Asia Program:** 170 Uris Hall, Ithaca, NY 14853; tel. (607) 255-8493; fax (607) 254-5000; e-mail amp18@cornell.edu; internet www.einaudi.cornell.edu/SouthAsia; Dir Prof. ALAKA BASU.

**Council on Foreign Relations, Inc:** 58 East 68th St, New York, NY 10065; tel. (212) 434-9400; fax (212) 434-9800; e-mail communications@cfr.org; internet www.cfr.org; f. 1921; 3,600 mems; Pres. RICHARD N. HAASS; publs include *Foreign Affairs* (every 2 months).

**Council on Regional Studies:** 218 Palmer Hall, Princeton University, Princeton, NJ 08544; tel. (609) 258-4720; f. 1961; Chair. Prof. EZRA N. SULEIMAN.

**East-West Center—Center for Cultural and Technical Interchange between East and West, Inc:** 1601 East-West Rd, Honolulu, HI 96848; tel. (808) 944-7111; fax (808) 944-7970; e-mail ewcinfo@EastWestCenter.org; internet www.eastwestcenter.org; f. 1960 by Congress to promote better relations and understanding among the nations and peoples of Asia, the Pacific and the USA through co-operative study, training and research; conducts multi-disciplinary programmes on environmental policy, population, resources, development, journalism and Pacific Islands development; provides awards and grants to scholars, journalists, graduate students, and managers to participate in the Center's studies; Pres. Dr CHARLES MORRISON.

**Freer Gallery of Art and Arthur M. Sackler Gallery:** 1050 Independence Ave, SW, Washington, DC 20013-7012; tel. (202) 633-4880; e-mail publicaffairsasia@si.edu; internet www.asia.si.edu; f. 1906, opened 1923; conducts research on the major collections of Asian and late 19th and early 20th century American art, gift of the late Charles L. Freer; art collection of 37,000 objects; library of 55,000 vols, 75,000 slides; Dir Dr JULIAN RABY; publs include *Artibus Asiae*, *Ars Orientalis*.

**Henry M. Jackson School of International Studies:** University of Washington, Seattle, WA 98195; tel. (206) 543-4370; fax (206) 685-0668; e-mail jsis@u.washington.edu; internet www.jsis.artsci.washington.edu; Dir ANAND YANG.

**The Jamestown Foundation:** 4516 43rd Street NW, Washington, DC 20016; tel. (202) 483-8888; internet www.jamestown.org; f. 1984; Pres. GLEN E. HOWARD; publs include *Terrorism Monitor*.

**Library of International Relations:** 565 W Adams, Chicago, IL 60661; tel. (312) 906-5600; fax (312) 906-5685; f. 1932; financed by voluntary contributions; stimulates interest and research in international problems; conducts seminars and offers special services to businesses and academic institutions; library of 560,000 items.

**Museum of Fine Arts, Boston:** 465 Huntington Ave, Boston, MA 02115; tel. (617) 369-3222; fax (617) 859-7031; e-mail jearle@mfa.org; internet www.mfa.org; f. 1876; has dept of Asiatic art with major collection of Chinese, Japanese and Indian painting and sculpture, Japanese prints and metalwork, Chinese, Korean and Vietnamese ceramics, the arts of the Islamic world, and a selection of Oceanic and African art; library of 65,000 books, periodicals and pamphlets; Dir Dr MALCOLM A. ROGERS; Chair, Dept of Art of Asia, Oceania and Africa JOE EARLE.

**National Bureau of Asian Research (NBR):** 1215 Fourth Ave, Suite 1600, Seattle, WA 98161; tel. (206) 632-7370; fax (206) 632-7487; e-mail nbr@nbr.org; internet www.nbr.org; conducts research on policy-related issues in East, Central and South Asia and Russia; Pres. RICHARD J. ELLINGS; publs include NBR book series, *NBR Analysis*, *NBR Briefing*, *NBR Bulletin*, *NBR Special Reports*, *Asia Policy*.

**Princeton Institute for International and Regional Studies:** Princeton University, Aaron Burr Hall, Princeton, NJ 08544-1022; tel. (609) 258-4851; fax (609) 258-3988; e-mail pzimmer@princeton.edu; internet www.princeton.edu/~piirs; f. 2003; international and regional studies; Dir KATHERINE S. NEWMAN; publs include *World Politics* (quarterly), monographs.

**St John's University Institute of Asian Studies:** 8000 Utopia Parkway, Jamaica, NY 11439; tel. (718) 990-6582; fax (718) 990-1881; e-mail linj@stjohns.edu; Dir Dr JOHN LIN.

**School of Hawaiian, Asian and Pacific Studies:** University of Hawaii, Moore Hall 309, 1890 East-West Rd, Honolulu, HI 96822; tel. (808) 956-8324; fax (808) 956-6345; e-mail edgara@hawaii.edu; internet www.hawaii.edu/shaps; administers Centers for Chinese, Hawaiian, Japanese, Korean, Pacific Islands, Philippine, South Asian, South-East Asian and Buddhist Studies; Interim Dean EDGAR A. PORTER.

**School of International and Public Affairs:** Columbia University, 420 West 118th St, New York, NY 10027; tel. (212) 854-4604; Dean LISA ANDERSON.

**Walter H. Shorenstein Asia/Pacific Research Center:** Stanford University, Encina Hall, Rm E301, 616 Serra St, Stanford, CA 94305-6055; tel. (650) 723-9741; fax (650) 723-6530; e-mail asia-pacific-research-center@stanford.edu; internet aparc.stanford.edu; Dir Prof. GI-WOOK SHIN.

**Southern Asian Institute:** 1128 International Affairs Bldg, Columbia University, New York, NY 10027; tel. (212) 854-3616; fax (212) 864-4847; Dir JOHN S. HAWLEY.

**University of California Department of South and South-east Asia Studies:** 7233 Dwinelle Hall, Berkeley, CA 94720-2540; tel. (510) 642-4564; fax (510) 643-2959; e-mail rospatt@berkeley.edu; internet ls.berkeley.edu/dept/sseas.

**University of Pennsylvania, Department of South Asia Studies:** 820 Williams Hall, Philadelphia, PA 19104-6305; tel. (215) 898-7475; fax (215) 573-2138; internet www.southasia.upenn.edu; library of 400,000 vols; Chair. MICHAEL MEISTER; Librarian DAVID NELSON.

# SELECT BIBLIOGRAPHY—BOOKS

See also bibliographies at end of relevant chapters in Part Two.


Adams, Richard, Aggrawal, Reena, and Maimbo, Samuel Munzele. *Migrant Labor Remittances in South Asia*. World Bank, 2005.

Agarwal, Bina. *A Field of One's Own: Gender and Land Rights in South Asia*. New York, Cambridge University Press, 1994.

Agrawal, D. P. *Ancient Metal Technology and Archaeology of South Asia: A Pan-Asian Perspective*. New Delhi, Aryan Books International, 2000.

Agrawal, Pradeep, *et al*. *Economic Restructuring in East Asia and India: Perspectives on Policy Reform*. Singapore, Institute of Southeast Asian Studies, 1995.

Agrawal, Pradeep, Gokran, Subir V., Mishira, Veena, Parikh, Kirit S., and Sen, Kunal. *Policy Regimes and Industrial Competitiveness—A Comparative Study of East Asia and India*. Singapore, Institute of Southeast Asian Studies, 2000.

Alagappa, Muthiah (Ed.). *Coercion and Governance: The Declining Political Role of the Military in Asia*. Stanford, CA, Stanford University Press, 2001.

Antlöv, Hans, and Ngo Tak-Wing (Eds). *The Cultural Construction of Politics in Asia*. Richmond, Surrey, Curzon Press, 1999.

Ariff, Mohamed, and Khalid, Ahmed M. *Liberalization, Growth and Transitional Economics in Asia*. Cheltenham, Edward Elgar Publishing, 1999.

Ashraf, Kazi Khaleed, and Belluardo James (Eds). *An Architecture of Independence: The Making of Modern South Asia*. New York, Architectural League of New York, 1998.

Asian Development Bank. *Asian Development Outlook*. Manila, ADB, annually.

*A Continent in Change: Thirty Years of the Asian Development Bank*. Manila, ADB, 1997.

*The Future of Asia in the World Economy*. Manila, ADB, 1998.

*The Global Trading System and Developing Asia*. Manila, ADB, 1997.

*Growth Triangles in Asia—A New Approach to Regional Economic Cooperation*. Manila, ADB, 1998.

Athukorala, Prema-Chandra. *Trade Policy Issues in Asian Development*. London, Routledge, 1998.

Athukorala, Prema-Chandra (Ed.). *The Economic Development of South Asia*. Cheltenham, Edward Elgar Publishing, 2002.

Babu, Suresh, and Gulati, Ashok (Eds). *Economic Reforms and Food Security: The Impact of Trade and Technology in South Asia*. Binghamton, NY, Haworth Press Inc, 2005.

Bales, Kevin. *Disposable People: New Slavery in the Global Economy*. Berkeley, CA, University of California Press, 2000.

Banerjee, Paula, Chaudhury, Sabyasachi Basu Ray, and Das, Samir Kumar (Eds). *Internal Displacement in South Asia: The Relevance of the UN's Guiding Principles*. New Delhi, Sage Publications, 2005.

Barua, Pradeep P. *The State at War in South Asia*. Lincoln, NE, University of Nebraska Press, 2005.

Bates, Crispin. *Subalterns and Raj: South Asia since 1600*. Abingdon, Routledge, 2007.

Baxter, Craig, *et al*. *Government and Politics in South Asia*. Boulder, CO, Westview Press, 1998.

Blair, Sheila S., and Bloom, Jonathan M. (Eds). *Art, Religion and Politics in South Asia*. Leiden, E. J. Brill, 2004.

Bloom, David E., and Godwin, Peter (Eds). *The Economics of HIV and AIDS: The Case of South and South East Asia*. Oxford, Oxford University Press, 1997.

Bose, Sugata. *A Hundred Horizons: The Indian Ocean in the Age of Global Empire*. Cambridge, MA, Harvard University Press, 2006.

Bose, Sugata, and Jalal, Ayesha. *Modern South Asia—History, Culture, Political Economy*. London, Routledge, 2nd edn, 2004.

Bose, Tapan K. *Protection of Refugees in South Asia: Need for Legal Framework*. Kathmandu, South Asia Forum for Human Rights, 2000.

Bracken, Paul. *Fire in the East: The Rise of Asian Military Power and the Second Nuclear Age*. London, HarperCollins, 1999.

Bradnock, Robert W. *Agricultural Change in South Asia*. London, John Murray, 1984.

Breckenridge, Carol A., and van der Veer, Peter. *Orientalism and the Postcolonial Predicament: Perspectives on South Asia*. Philadelphia, PA, University of Pennsylvania Press, 1993.

Brown, Michael E., and Ganguly, Sumit (Eds). *Government Policies and Ethnic Relations in Asia and the Pacific*. Cambridge, MA, Massachusetts Institute of Technology, 1998.

Carr, Brian, and Mahalingam, Indira (Eds). *Companion Encyclopedia of Asian Philosophy*. London, Routledge, 1996.

Cauquelin, Josiane, Lim, Paul, and Mayer-Konig, Birgit (Eds). *Asian Values—Encounter with Diversity*. Richmond, Surrey, Curzon Press, 1998.

Chadda, Maya. *Building Democracy in South Asia: India, Nepal, Pakistan*. Boulder, CO, Lynne Rienner, 2000.

Champa Publishers. *Fifty Years of the State and Human Rights in South Asia*. Delhi, Champa Publishers, 1998.

Chang Ho-Joon. *The Political Economy of Industrial Policy*. Basingstoke, Macmillan Press, 1996.

Chapman, Graham. *The Geopolitics of South Asia: From Early Empires to the Nuclear Age*. Aldershot, Ashgate Publishing, 2nd edn, 2003.

Chari, P. R., Cheema, Pervais Iqbal, and Cohen, Stephen Philip. *Perception, Politics and Security in South Asia*. London, RoutledgeCurzon, 2003.

Chari, P. R., and Gupta, Sonika (Eds). *Human Security in South Asia: Energy, Gender, Migration and Globalisation*. New Delhi, Social Science Press, 2003.

Chari, P. R., Joseph, Mallika, and Chandran, Suba (Eds). *Missing Boundaries: Refugees, Migrants, Stateless and Internally Displaced Persons in South Asia*. New Delhi, Manohar Publishers and Distributors, 2004.

Chatterjee, Indrani. *Unfamiliar Relations: Family and History in South Asia*. Piscataway, NJ, Rutgers University Press, 2004.

Chowdhury, Mahfuzul H. *Democratization in South Asia: Lessons from American Institutions*. Aldershot, Ashgate Publishing, 2003.

Clark, Cal, and Roy, K. C. *Comparing Development Patterns in Asia*. Boulder, CO, Lynne Rienner, 1997.

Claus, Peter, Diamond, Sarah, and Mills, Margaret. *South Asian Folklore: An Encyclopedia*. New York, Routledge, 2003.

Daechsel, Markus. *The Politics of Self-Expression: The Urdu Middle-Class Milieu of Early 20th Century India and Pakistan*. Abingdon, Routledge, 2005.

Desai, Meghnad. *Development and Nationhood: Essays in the Political Economy of South Asia*. New Delhi, Oxford University Press, 2005.

Desai, Meghnad, Rudolph, Susanne Hoeber, and Rudra, Ashok (Eds). *Agrarian Power and Agricultural Productivity in South Asia*. Berkeley, CA, University of California Press, 1984.

Dittmer, Lowell. *South Asia's Nuclear Security Dilemma: India, Pakistan, and China*. Armonk, NY, M. E. Sharpe, 2004.

Dixit, J. N. *India-Pakistan in War and Peace*. London, Routledge, 2002.

Dossani, Rafiq, and Rowen, Henry (Eds). *Prospects for Peace in South Asia*. Stanford, CA, Stanford University Press, 2005.

Dunung, Sanjyot P. *Doing Business in Asia: The Complete Guide*. Singapore, Simon and Schuster, 1995.

Ernst, Carl W., and Lawrence, Bruce B. *Sufi Martyrs of Love: The Chishti Order in South Asia and Beyond*. Basingstoke, Palgrave Macmillan, 2003.

Europa Publications. *A Political and Economic Dictionary of South Asia*. London, Europa Publications, 2004.

Fair, C. Christine. *Urban Battle Fields of South Asia: Lessons Learned from Sri Lanka, India and Pakistan*. Santa Monica, CA, RAND Corpn, 2005.

Farrington, John, and Lewis, David (Eds). *Nongovernmental Organizations and the State in Asia: Rethinking Roles in Sustainable Agricultural Development*. London and New York, Routledge, 1993.

Gaeffke, Peter, and Utz, David A. *Science and Technology in South Asia*. Philadelphia, PA, Department of South Asia Regional Studies, University of Pennsylvania, 1985.

Ganguly, Debjani. *Caste, Colonialism and Counter-Modernity.* Abingdon, Routledge, 2005.

Ganguly, Sumit (Ed.). *The Kashmir Question: Retrospect and Prospect.* London, Frank Cass, 2003

George, Sudhir Jacob (Ed.). *Intra and Inter-State Conflicts in South Asia.* New Delhi, South Asian Publishers, 2001.

Ghosh, Papiya. *Partition and the South Asian Diaspora: Extending the Subcontinent.* Abingdon, Routledge, 2007.

Ghosh, Partha S. *The Politics of Personal Law in South Asia: The Uniform Civil Code, the Identity Issue and the Discourse of Nationalism.* Abingdon, Routledge, 2007.

Gilson, Julie. *Asia Meets Europe.* Cheltenham, Edward Elgar Publishing, 2002.

Gommans, Jos L., and Kolff, Dirk H. A. (Eds). *Warfare and Weaponry in South Asia, 1000–1800.* New Delhi, Oxford University Press, 2000.

Goonesekere, Savitri (Ed.). *Violence, Law, and Women's Rights in South Asia.* London, Sage Publications, 2004.

Gopal, Kusum. 'Poverty, Globalisation and Being Gender Sensitive', *UN Division for the Advancement of Women*, November 2001.

Gosling, David. *Religion and Ecology in India and Southeast Asia.* London, Routledge, 2001.

Hagerty, Devin T. *The Consequences of Nuclear Proliferation: Lessons from South Asia.* Cambridge, MA, MIT Press, 1998.

*South Asia in World Politics.* Lanham, MD, Rowman and Littlefield Publishers, 2005.

Hasan, Mushirul, and Nakazato, Nariaki (Eds). *The Unfinished Agenda: Nation Building in South Asia.* New Delhi, Manohar Publishers and Distributors, 2001.

Horton, Susan. *Women and Industrialization in Asia.* London, Routledge, 1995.

Hossain, Moazzem, Islam, Iyanatul, and Kibria, Reza. *South Asian Economic Development—Transformation, Opportunities and Challenges.* London, Routledge, 1999.

Hutchison, Jane, and Brown, Andrew (Eds). *Organising Labour in Globalising Asia.* London, Routledge, 2001.

Ingco, Merlinda (Ed.). *Agriculture, Trade and the WTO in South Asia: Creating a Trading Environment for Development.* World Bank, 2003.

Jacobsen, Knut A. (Ed.). *South Asians in the Diaspora: Histories and Religious Traditions.* Leiden, E. J. Brill, 2003.

Jalal, Ayesha. *Democracy and Authoritarianism in South Asia—A Comparative and Historical Perspective.* Cambridge, Cambridge University Press, 1995.

Jeffery, Patricia, and Basu, Amrita (Eds). *Appropriating Gender: Women's Activism and Politicized Religion in South Asia.* London, Routledge, 1998.

Jeshurun, Chandran (Ed.). *China, India, Japan and the Security of Southeast Asia.* Singapore, Institute of Southeast Asian Studies, 1993.

Joeck, Neil. *Maintaining Nuclear Stability in South Asia.* Oxford, Oxford University Press for the International Institute for Strategic Studies, 1997.

Johnson, Donald Clay. *Agile Hands and Creative Minds: A Bibliography of Textile Traditions in Afghanistan, Bangladesh, Bhutan, India, Nepal, Pakistan and Sri Lanka.* Bangkok, Orchid Press, 2000.

Kabeer, Naila, Nambissan, Geetha B., and Subrahmanian, Ramya (Eds). *Child Labour and the Right to Education: Needs Versus Rights?* New Delhi, Sage Publications, 2003.

Kapur, Ashok. *Regional Security Structures in Asia.* London, RoutledgeCurzon, 2002.

Kaur, Ravinder (Ed.). *Religion, Violence and Political Mobilisation in South Asia.* London, Sage Publications, 2005.

Khan, Saira. *Nuclear Proliferation Dynamics in Protracted Conflict Regions: A Comparative Study of South Asia and the Middle East.* Aldershot, Ashgate Publishing, 2002.

Khilnani, R. K. *Nuclearisation in South Asia.* New Delhi, Commonwealth Publishers, 2000.

Kinnvall, Catarina, and Jonsson, Kristina. *Globalization and Democratization in Asia—The Construction of Identity.* London, RoutledgeCurzon, 2002.

Krepon, Michael, Jones, Rodney W., and Haider, Zaid (Eds). *Escalation Control and the Nuclear Option in South Asia.* Washington, DC, Henry L. Stimson Center, 2004.

Kumar, Ranjit. *South Asian Union: Problems, Possiblities and Prospects.* New Delhi, Manas Publications, 2005.

Leaman, Oliver (Ed.). *Encyclopedia of Asian Philosophy.* London, Routledge, 2000.

Lee, Chung H. *Financial Liberalization and the Economic Crisis in Asia.* London, RoutledgeCurzon, 2002.

Leifer, Michael. *Asian Nationalism.* London, Routledge, 2000.

Lieten, G.K., Srivastava, Ravi, and Thorat, Sukhadeo. *Small Hands in South Asia: Child Labour in Perspective.* New Delhi, Manohar Publishers and Distributors, 2004.

Lipton, Michael, and Osmani, Siddiqur. *The Quality of Life in Emerging Asia.* Brighton, University of Sussex, 1996.

Ludden, David. *Agricultural Production and South Asian History.* New Delhi, Oxford University Press India, 2005.

*An Agrarian History of South Asia.* Cambridge, Cambridge University Press, 1999.

Maddison, Angus, Rao, Prasada D. S., and Shepherd, William (Eds). *The Asian Economies in the Twentieth Century.* Cheltenham, Edward Elgar Publishing, 2002.

Madsen, Stig Toft (Ed.). *State, Society and Human Rights in South Asia.* New Delhi, Manohar Publications, 1996.

*State, Society and the Environment in South Asia.* Richmond, Surrey, Curzon Press, 1999.

Mahbub-ul-Haq Human Development Centre. *Human Development in South Asia 2001: Globalisation and Human Development.* Karachi, Oxford University Press, 2002.

*Human Development in South Asia 2002: Agriculture and Rural Development.* Karachi, Oxford University Press, 2003.

*Human Development in South Asia 2003: The Employment Challenge.* Karachi, Oxford University Press, 2004.

Mahbubani, Kishore. *Can Asians Think?* Singapore, Times Books International, 1998.

Mahmud, Wahiduddin (Ed.). *Adjustment and Beyond: The Reform Experience in South Asia.* Basingstoke, Macmillan Press, 2000

Majumdar, Boria, and Mangan, J. A. *Sport in South Asian Society: Past and Present.* Abingdon, Routledge, 2005.

Malick, K. *Politics, Technology and Bureaucracy in South Asia.* Leiden, E. J. Brill, 1983.

Malik, Iftikhar. *Jihad, Hindutva and the Taliban: South Asia at the Crossroads.* Karachi, Oxford University Press Pakistan, 2005.

Malik, Jamal. *Madrasas in South Asia: Teaching terror?* Abingdon, Routledge, 2007.

Mallick, Ross. *Development, Ethnicity and Human Rights in South Asia.* New Delhi, Sage Publications, 1998.

Margolis, Eric. *War at the Top of the World—The Struggle for Afghanistan, Kashmir and Tibet.* London, Routledge, 2001.

Mascarenhas, R. C. *Comparative Political Economy of East and South Asia: A Critique of Development Policy and Management.* Basingstoke, Macmillan Press, 1999.

Matinuddin, Kamal. *The Nuclearization of South Asia.* Karachi, Oxford University Press, 2002.

Meyer, Karl E. *The Dust of Empire: The Race for Mastery in the Asian Heartland.* New York, PublicAffairs, 2003.

Mishra, Pramod Kumar. *Women in South Asia: Dowry, Death and Human Rights Violations.* AuthorsPress, 2000

Mitra, Subrata K. *Political Parties in South Asia.* Westport, CT, Praeger, 2004.

Mittal, Sushil, and Thursby, Gene (Eds). *Religions of South Asia: An Introduction.* Abingdon, Routledge, 2006.

Morris, Jan. *Stones of Empire: The Buildings of the Raj.* Oxford, Oxford University Press, 2005.

Mukherjee-Reed, Ananya. *Corporate Capitalism in Contemporary South Asia: Conventional Wisdoms and South Asian Realities.* London, Palgrave Macmillan, 2003.

Najam, Adil. *Environment, Development and Human Security: Perspectives from South Asia.* Lanham, MD, University Press of America, 2003.

Narain, Jai P. (Ed.). *AIDS in Asia: The Challenge Ahead.* Thousand Oaks, CA, Sage Publications, 2004.

Osella, Filippo, and Gardner, Katy (Eds). *Migration, Modernity and Social Transformation in South Asia.* London, Sage Publications, 2004.

Pandey, V. C. (Ed.). *Environment, Security and Tourism Development in South Asia*, 3 vols. Delhi, Isha Books, 2004.

*Sustainable Development in South Asia.* Delhi, Kalpaz Publications, 2003.

Parekh, Bhikhu, Singh, Gurharpal, and Vertovec, Stephen (Eds). *Culture and Economy in the Indian Diaspora.* London, Routledge, 2003.

Paswain, Nawal K. *Agricultural Trade in South Asia: Potential and Policy Options.* New Delhi, APH Publishers, 2003.

Peerenboom, Randall. *Asian Discourses of Rule of Law.* London, Routledge, 2003.

Peters, David H., and Yazbeck, Abdo S. (Eds). *Health Policy Research in South Asia: Building Capacity for Reform.* World Bank, 2003.

Pinches, Michael (Ed.). *Culture and Privilege in Capitalist Asia.* London, Routledge, 1999.

Qureshy, M. N. *Geophysical Framework of India, Bangladesh and Pakistan.* London, CRC Press, 2003.

Rahman, Taiabur. *Parliamentary Control and Government Accountability in South Asia: A comparative analysis of Bangladesh, India and Sri Lanka.* Abingdon, Routledge, 2007.

Raina, Vinod, Chowdhury, Amit, and Chowdhury, Samit. *The Dispossessed: Victims of Development in Asia.* Hong Kong, Arena Press, 1999.

Raman, J. Sri. *Flashpoint: How the US, India, and Pakistan Brought Us to the Brink of Nuclear War.* Monroe, ME, Common Courage Press, 2003.

Ridinger, Robert B. Marks. *The Archaeology of the Indian Subcontinent and Sri Lanka: A Selected Bibliography.* Westport, CT, Greenwood Press, 2001.

Robb, Peter. *The Concept of Race in South Asia.* New Delhi, Oxford University Press India, 1997.

Robin, Jeffrey (Ed.). *Asia: The Winning of Independence: the Philippines, India, Indonesia, Vietnam, Malaya.* London, Macmillan Press, 1981.

Rodrigues, Hillary. *Introducing Hinduism.* Abingdon, Routledge, 2006.

Rutton, Mario. *Rural Capitalists in Asia—A Comparative Analysis on India, Indonesia and Malaysia.* Richmond, Surrey, Curzon Press, 2001.

Sahadevan, P. (Ed.). *Conflict and Peacemaking in South Asia.* New Delhi, Lancer Books, 2001.

Sathasivam, Kanishkan. *Uneasy Neighbours: India, Pakistan and US Foreign Policy.* Aldershot, Ashgate Publishing, 2005.

Schofield, Victoria. *Kashmir in Conflict: India, Pakistan and the Unending War.* London, I. B. Tauris, 2nd edn, 2003.

Sharma, Kishor (Ed.). *Trade Policy, Growth and Poverty in Asian Developing Countries.* London, Routledge, 2003.

Shastri, Amita, and Wilson, A. Jeyaratnam. *The Post-colonial State of South Asia: Political and Constitutional Problems.* Richmond, Surrey, Curzon Press, 2000.

Singh, Khushwant. *The Illustrated History of the Sikhs.* New Delhi, Oxford University Press India, 2006.

Southworth, Franklin. *Linguistic Archaeology of South Asia.* Abingdon, Routledge, 2005.

Srivastava, Sanjay. *Sexual Sites, Seminal Attitudes: Sexualities, Masculinities and Culture in South Asia.* London, Sage Publications, 2004.

Stern, Robert W. *Democracy and Dictatorship in South Asia: Dominant Classes and Political Outcomes in India, Pakistan and Bangladesh.* Westport, CT, Praeger, 2001.

Subrahmanyam, Sanjay (Ed.). *Land, Politics and Trade in South Asia.* New Delhi, Oxford University Press, 2004.

Sugiyama, Shinya, and Grove, Linda. *Commercial Networks in Modern Asia.* Richmond, Surrey, Curzon Press, 2000.

Suryadinata, Leo (Ed.). *Nationalism and Globalization: East and West.* Singapore, Institute of Southeast Asian Studies, 2000.

Synott, Hilary. *The Causes and Consequences of South Asia's Nuclear Tests.* Oxford, Oxford University Press for the International Institute for Strategic Studies, 1999.

Thakur, Ramesh, and Wiggen, Oddny (Eds). *South Asia in the World: Problem Solving Perspectives on Security, Sustainable Development, and Good Governance.* Tokyo, United Nations University Press, 2004.

Timmer, Marcel. *The Dynamics of Asian Manufacturing—A Comparative Perspective in the Late Twentieth Century.* Cheltenham, Edward Elgar Publishing, 2000.

Tinker, Hugh. *South Asia: A Short History.* Honolulu, HI, University of Hawaii Press, 1990.

Toh Thian Ser (Ed.). *Megacities, Labour and Communications.* Singapore, Institute of Southeast Asian Studies, 1998.

Trautmann, Thomas. *The Aryan Debate.* New Delhi, Oxford University Press India, 2005.

Tripathi, Vibha. *The Age of Iron in South Asia.* New Delhi, Aryan Books International, 2001.

Tsing, Anna Lowenhaupt (Ed.). *Nature in the Global South: Environmental Projects in South and Southeast Asia.* Durham, NC, Duke University Press, 2003.

United Nations. *Asian and Pacific Developing Economies and the First WTO Ministerial Conference: Issues of Concern.* New York, 1996.

*Assessing the Potential and Direction of Agricultural Trade within the ESCAP Region.* New York, 1996.

*BISTEC-EC (Bangladesh, India, Sri Lanka, Thailand—Economic Cooperation) Development Programme.* New York, 1998.

*Trade Prospects for the Year 2000 and Beyond for the Asian and Pacific Region.* New York, 1996.

*Women in Asia and the Pacific 1985/93.* New York, 1995.

Van Schendel, Willem. *The Bengal Borderlands: Beyond State and Nation in South Asia.* London, Anthem Press, 2005.

Vanaik, Achin (Ed.). *Globalization and South Asia: Multidimensional Perspectives.* New Delhi, Manohar Publishers and Distributors, 2004.

Vartola, Juha, *et al* (Eds). *Development NGOs Facing the 21st Century: Perspectives from South Asia.* Kathmandu, Institute for Human Development, 2000.

Verma, Anil, Lansbury, Russell, and Kochan, Thomas (Eds). *Employment Relations in Asian Economies.* London, Routledge, 1995.

Weightman, Barbara A. *Dragons and Tigers: A Geography of South, East and Southeast Asia.* Singapore, John Wiley & Sons, 2003.

Wignaraja, Poona, and Sirivardana, Susil (Eds). *Pro-Poor Growth and Governance in South Asia: Decentralization and Participatory Development.* London, Sage Publications, 2004.

Williams, Louise. *Wives, Mistresses and Matriarchs: Asian Women Today.* St Leonards, NSW, Allen & Unwin, 1999.

Yong Tan Tai, and Kudaisya, Gyanesh. *The Aftermath of Partition in South Asia.* London, Routledge, 2000.

# SELECT BIBLIOGRAPHY—PERIODICALS

*Annals of the Bhandarkar Oriental Research Institute:* Bhandarkar Oriental Research Institute, Pune 411 004, India; tel. (20) 25656932; e-mail boril@vsnl.net; f. 1917; Indology and Oriental Studies; annually; Editors M. G. DHADPHALE, S. D. LADDU.

*Archiv orientální:* Journal of African and Asian Studies of the Oriental Institute of the Czech Academy of Sciences, Pod vodárenskou věží 4, 182 08 Prague 8, Czech Republic; tel. (2) 6605-2483; fax (2) 8658-1897; e-mail aror@orient.cas.cz; internet aror.orient.cas.cz; f. 1929; book reviews and notes; contributions in English or French and German; quarterly; Editor Dr STANISLAVA VAVROUŠKOVÁ.

*Artibus Asiae:* Museum Rietberg Zürich, Gablerstr. 15, 8002 Zürich, Switzerland; tel. (1) 2063131; fax (1) 2063132; e-mail artibus.asiae@zuerich.ch; internet www.artibusasiae.com; in co-operation with the Arthur M. Sackler Gallery, Smithsonian Institution, Washington, DC, USA; f. 1925; Asian art and archaeology; illustrated; 2 a year; Editor-in-Chief Dr AMY MCNAIR.

*Arts of Asia:* 803-6 Kowloon Centre, 29–39 Ashley Rd, Kowloon, Hong Kong; tel. 23762228; fax 23763713; e-mail info@artsofasianet.com; internet www.artsofasianet.com; f. 1971; 6 a year; Publr and Editor TUYET NGUYET.

*Arts Asiatiques:* Musée National des Arts Asiatiques Guimet, 6 Place d'Iéna, 75116 Paris, France; tel. 1-55-73-31-77; e-mail arts.asiatiques@efeo.net; internet www.museeguimet.fr; f. 1924; annually.

*Asia and Pacific Review:* World of Information, CEB Ltd, 2 Market St, Saffron Walden, Essex CB10 1HZ, United Kingdom; tel. (1799) 521150; fax (1799) 524805; e-mail info@worldinformation.com; internet www.worldinformation.com.

*Asian Affairs:* Journal of the Royal Society for Asian Affairs, 2 Belgrave Sq., London, SW1X 8PJ, United Kingdom; tel. (20) 7235-5122; fax (20) 7259-6771; e-mail info@rsaa.org.uk; internet www.rsaa.org.uk; covers economic, cultural and political matters relating to the Near and Middle East, Central Asia, South and South-East Asia, and the Far East; 3 a year; Editor BARNEY SMITH.

*Asian Economic Review:* Indian Institute of Economics, Federation House, 11-6-841 Red Hills, Hyderabad 500 004, India; tel. (40) 23393512; fax (40) 23395083; e-mail iieaer@yahoo.com; f. 1958; 3 a year; Editor Dr SUBRAHMANYAM UPPADA.

*Asian Ethnicity:* 4 Park Sq., Milton Park, Abingdon, Oxon, OX14 4RN, United Kingdom; tel. (20) 7017-6000; fax (20) 7017-6336; e-mail journals.orders@tandf.co.uk; internet www.tandf.co.uk/journals; f. 2000; 3 a year; Editor-in-Chief Prof. CHIH-YU SHIH.

*Asian News Digest:* A-126, Niti Bagh, New Delhi 110 049, India; tel. (11) 26565140; fax (11) 26862857; f. 1955; as *Asian Recorder*, renamed 2000; record of Asian events; weekly; Editor A. K. B. MENON.

*Asian Population Studies:* 4 Park Sq., Milton Park, Abingdon, Oxon, OX14 4RN, United Kingdom; tel. (20) 7017-6000; fax (20) 7017-6336; e-mail journals.orders@tandf.co.uk; internet www.tandf.co.uk/journals; f. 2005; 3 a year; Editor Prof. GAVIN JONES.

*Asian Profile:* POB 1211, Metrotown Regional Post Office, Burnaby, BC V5H 4J8, Canada; tel. (604) 8211321; fax (604) 2760813; e-mail info@asianresearchservice.com; internet www.asianresearchservice.com; f. 1973; multi-disciplinary study of Asian affairs; 6 a year; Editor NELSON LEUNG.

*Asian Security:* 4 Park Sq., Milton Park, Abingdon, Oxon, OX14 4RN, United Kingdom; tel. (20) 7017-6000; fax (20) 7017-6336; e-mail journals.orders@tandf.co.uk; internet www.tandf.co.uk/journals; f. 2005; 3 a year; Editor-in-Chief SUMIT GANGULY.

*Asian Studies Review:* Asia Institute, University of Melbourne, Vic 3010, Australia; e-mail asianstudiesreview@gmail.com; internet asaa.asn.au/publications/asr.php; journal of the Asian Studies Association of Australia; 4 a year; Editor Assoc. Prof. MAILA STIVENS.

*Asian Thought and Society: An International Review:* Dept of Political Science, State University of New York, Oneonta, NY 13820, USA; tel. (607) 431-3553; fax (607) 431-2107; f. 1976; analysis of social structures and changes in Pacific and South Asian countries with special reference to social and intellectual development in historical perspective; 3 a year; Editor-in-Chief I. J. H. TS'AO.

*Asiatische Studien / Etudes Asiatiques:* Verlag Peter Lang, Moosstr. 1, Postfach 350, CH-2542 Pieterlen, Switzerland; tel. (32) 376-1717; fax (32) 376-1727; e-mail info@peterlang.com; internet www.peterlang.com; journal of the Swiss Asia Society; Editor R. GASSMANN, Ostasiatisches Seminar der Universität Zürich, Zürichbergstrasse 4, 8032 Zürich, Switzerland; tel. (1) 634-3181; fax (1) 634-4921; e-mail office@oas.unizh.ch; 4 a year.

*ASIEN* (The German Journal on Contemporary Asia): Deutsche Gesellschaft für Asienkunde eV (German Association for Asian Studies), Rothenbaumchaussee 32, 20148 Hamburg, Germany; tel. (40) 445891; fax (40) 4107945; e-mail post@asienkunde.de; internet www.asienkunde.de; f. 1981; quarterly; Editor GÜNTER SCHUCHER.

*Australian Journal of International Affairs:* Journal of the Australian Institute of International Affairs, 32 Thesiger Court, Deakin, ACT 2600, Australia; e-mail william.tow@anu.edu.au; f. 1947; 4 a year; Editor Prof. WILLIAM TOW (e-mail w.tow@anu.edu.au).

*Bangladesh Development Studies:* Journal of the Bangladesh Institute of Development Studies, E-17, Agargaon, Sher-e-Bangla Nagar, GPO Box 3854, Dhaka 1207, Bangladesh; tel. (2) 8129603; fax (2) 8113023; internet www.bids-bd.org; f. 1973; quarterly; Chair. QUAZI SHAHABUDDIN; Exec. Editor SAJJAD ZOHIR.

*Bulletin de l'Ecole Française d'Extrême-Orient (BEFEO):* Ecole Française d'Extrême-Orient, 22 ave du Président Wilson, 75116 Paris, France; tel. 1-53-70-18-37; fax 1-53-70-87-39; internet www.efeo.fr; f. 1901; annually.

*Bulletin of the School of Oriental and African Studies:* School of Oriental and African Studies, University of London, Thornhaugh St, Russell Sq., London, WC1H OXG, United Kingdom; tel. (20) 7898-4064; fax (20) 7898-4849; e-mail bulletin@soas.ac.uk; internet www.soas.ac.uk; publ. by Cambridge University Press for the School of Oriental and African Studies, University of London; f. 1917; 3 a year; Editor Prof. G. R. HAWTING.

*Contemporary South Asia:* 4 Park Sq., Milton Park, Abingdon, Oxon, OX14 4RN, United Kingdom; tel. (20) 7017-6000; fax (20) 7017-6336; e-mail journals.orders@tandf.co.uk; internet www.tandf.co.uk/journals/; 4 a year; Editor APURBA KUNDU.

*Critical Asian Studies:* 4 Park Sq., Milton Park, Abingdon, Oxon, OX14 4RN, United Kingdom; tel. (20) 7017-6000; fax (20) 7017-6336; e-mail journals.orders@tandf.co.uk; internet www.tandf.co.uk/journals; 4 a year; Man. Editor THOMAS P. FENTON.

*The Developing Economies:* Nihon Boeki Shinkokiko Ajia Keizai Kenkyusho (Institute of Developing Economies, Japan External Trade Organization), 3-2-2 Wakaba, Mihama-ku, Chiba-shi, Chiba 261-8545, Japan; fax (43) 299-9726; e-mail journal@ide.go.jp; internet www.ide.go.jp/English/Publish/De; f. 1962; in English; quarterly.

*Development and Socio-Economic Progress:* Afro-Asian People's Solidarity Organization, 89 Abdel Aziz Al-Saoud St, POB 11559, El Malek El Saleh, Cairo, Egypt; tel. (2) 3636081; fax (2) 3637361; e-mail aapso@idsc.net.eg; 3 a year; Exec. Editor E. A. VIDYASKERA; Editor-in-Chief NOURI ABDEL RAZZAK HUSSEIN.

*Eastern Economist:* United Commercial Bank Bldg, Parliament St, New Delhi 110 001, India; f. 1943; economic and financial weekly; Editor V. BALASUBRAMANIAN.

*Economic and Political Weekly:* Hitkari House, 284 Shahid Bhagatsingh Rd, Mumbai 400 001, India; tel. (22) 22696073; fax (22) 22696072; e-mail epw@vsnl.com; internet www.epw.org.in; f. 1966; weekly; Editor C. RAMMANOHAR REDDY.

*Estudios de Asia y Africa:* Centre for Asian and African Studies, El Colegio de México, Camino al Ajusco 20, Pedregal de Sta Teresa, México DF 10740, Mexico; tel. (5) 5449-3000, ext. 3116; fax (5) 5645-0464; e-mail bprecia@colmex.mx; quarterly; Editor BENJAMÍN PRECIADO SOLÍS.

*Far Eastern Economic Review:* GPO Box 160, Hong Kong; tel. 25737121; fax 25031549; e-mail service@feer.com; internet www.feer.com; f. 1946; 10 a year; circ. 20,000; Editor HUGO RESTALL.

*Geographical Review of India:* The Geographical Society of India, 35 Ballygunge Circular Rd, Kolkata 700 019, India; f. 1933; quarterly; Editor Prof. H. R. BETAL.

*History of Development Studies:* Asia Pacific Press, The Australian National University, Canberra, ACT 0200, Australia; tel. (2) 6125-8258; fax (2) 6125-8448; e-mail books@asiapacificpress.com; internet www.asiapacificpress.com; irregular; Managing Editor DEBRA GROGAN.

*India Perspectives:* Ministry of External Affairs, External Publicity Division, 149, A Wing, Shastri Bhavan, New Delhi 110 001, India; tel.

(11) 23389471; fax (11) 23782391; e-mail bharat_b47@yahoo.com; internet meaindia.nic.in/iphome; monthly; Editor BHARAT BHUSHAN.

*India Quarterly:* Indian Council of World Affairs, Sapru House, Barakhamba Rd, New Delhi 110 001, India; tel. (11) 23317249; fax (11) 23311208; f. 1943; in English; quarterly.

*India Review:* Taylor and Francis, Inc, 325 Chestnut St, Suite 800, Philadelphia, PA 19106, USA; tel. (800) 354-1420; fax (215) 625-8914; e-mail editor@indiareview.org; internet www.indiareview.org; f. 2002; quarterly; Editor SUMIT GANGULY.

*India Today:* Living Media India Ltd, 1-A, Hamilton House, Connaught Pl., New Delhi 110 001, India; e-mail itgo@india-today.com; internet www.indiatoday.com; f. 1975; weekly; Editor-in-Chief AROON PURIE; Editor PRABHU CHAWLA.

*Indian Advocate:* Bar Association of India, Chamber No. 93, Supreme Court Bldg, New Delhi 110 001, India; quarterly; Editor R. K. P. SHANKARDASS.

*Indian Economic Review:* Delhi School of Economics, University of Delhi, Delhi 110 007, India; tel. (11) 27666703; fax (11) 27667159; e-mail ier@econdse.org; internet www.ierdse.org; f. 1952; 2 a year; Editors PARTHA SEN, PAMI DUA.

*Indian Economic and Social History Review:* Sage Publications India Pvt Ltd, B-42 Panchsheel Enclave, POB 4109, New Delhi 110 017, India; tel. and fax (11) 26491290; e-mail journalsubs@indiasage.com; internet www.indiasage.com; f. 1963; quarterly; Editors SUNIL KUMAR, SANJAY SUBRAHMANYAM.

*Indian Journal of International Law:* Indian Society of International Law, 9 Bhagwandass Rd, New Delhi 110 001, India; e-mail rpanand@giasd101.vsnl.net.in; f. 1961; quarterly; Editor-in-Chief RAHMATULLAH KHAN.

*Indian Literature:* Sahitya Akademi, National Academy of Letters, Rabindra Bhavan, 35 Ferozeshah Rd, New Delhi 110 001, India; tel. (11) 23386626; fax (11) 23382428; e-mail secy@ndb.vsnl.net.in; internet www.sahitya-akademi.gov.in; in English; bi-monthly; Editor NIRMAL KANTI BHATTACHARJEE.

*Indian Political Science Review:* c/o Dept of Political Science, University of Delhi, Delhi 110 007, India; 2 a year; Editor HARNAM SINGH.

*Indian Studies: Past and Present:* 3 Sambhunath Pandit St, Kolkata 20, India; f. 1959; in English; quarterly; Editor DEBIPRASAD CHATTOPADHYAHYA.

*Indica:* Heras Institute of Indian History and Culture, St Xavier's College, Mahapalika Marg, Mumbai 400 001, India; tel. (22) 22620665; e-mail herasinstitute@hotmail.com; f. 1964; in English; 2 a year; Editor Dr AUBREY A. MASCARENHAS.

*Inter-Asia Cultural Studies:* 4 Park Sq., Milton Park, Abingdon, Oxon, OX14 4RN, United Kingdom; tel. (20) 7017-6000; fax (20) 7017-6336; internet www.informaworld.com/riac; 4 a year; Exec. Editors CHEN KUAN-HSING, CHUA BENG HUAT.

*International Studies:* Sage Publications India Pvt Ltd, B-42 Panchsheel Enclave, POB 4109, New Delhi 110 017, India; tel. and fax (11) 26491290; e-mail journalsubs@indiasage.com; internet www.indiasage.com; journal of the School of International Studies, Jawaharlal Nehru University, New Delhi 110 067, India; in English; quarterly; Editor C. S. R. MURTHY.

*Internationales Asienforum:* Arnold-Bergstraesser-Institut, Windausstr. 16, 79110 Freiburg, Germany; tel. (761) 888780; fax (761) 8887878; e-mail abifr@abi.uni-freiburg.de; internet www.arnold-bergstraesser.de; political and socio-economic developments, Asian studies; 4, or 2 double editions, a year.

*Islamic Culture:* POB 35, Banjara Hills Post Office, Hyderabad 500 034, India; e-mail chamlija@hd1.vsnl.net.in; f. 1927; in English; quarterly; Editor SHAHID ALI ABBASI.

*Islamic Studies:* POB 1035, Islamabad, Pakistan; tel. (51) 850751; fax (51) 853360; f. 1962; all aspects of Islam; in English; quarterly; Editor Dr ZAFAR ISHAQ ANSARI.

*Journal of the American Oriental Society:* American Oriental Society, Hatcher Graduate Library, University of Michigan, Ann Arbor, MI 48109-1205, USA; tel. (734) 647-4760; f. 1842; quarterly; Editor E. GEROW, Reed College, Portland, OR 97202, USA.

*Journal of Asian History:* Harrassowitz Verlag, 65174 Wiesbaden, Germany; tel. (611) 530901; fax (611) 530999; e-mail verlag@harrassowitz.de; internet www.harrassowitz.de; f. 1967; in English, French, German, Russian; 2 a year; Editor DENIS SINOR, Goodbody Hall, Indiana University, Bloomington, IN 47405, USA; tel. (812) 855-0959; fax (812) 855-7500; e-mail sinord@indiana.edu.

*Journal of Asian Studies:* Association for Asian Studies, 1021 E Huron St, Ann Arbor, MI 48104, USA; f. 1941; in English; quarterly; selected articles on history, arts, social sciences, philosophy and contemporary issues; extensive book reviews.

*Journal of the Asiatic Society of Bangladesh (Humanities):* Asiatic Society of Bangladesh, 5 Old Secretariat Rd, Ramna, Dhaka 1000, Bangladesh; tel. (2) 9667586; fax (2) 9560500; e-mail assoenpr@bangla.net; f. 1956; 2 a year; Editor MAHMUD-UL AMEEN.

*Journal of the Asiatic Society of Bangladesh (Science):* Asiatic Society of Bangladesh, 5 Old Secretariat Rd, Ramna, Dhaka 1000, Bangladesh; tel. (2) 9667586; fax (2) 9560500; e-mail assoenpr@bangla.net; f. 1975; 2 a year.

*Journal of Asiatic Studies:* Asiatic Research Center, Korea University, Anam-dong, 5-ga 1, Sungbuk-gu, Seoul, Republic of Korea; tel. (2) 926-1926; fax (2) 924-9123; e-mail syongcho@kuccnx.korea.ac.kr; internet www.asiacenter.or.kr; f. 1958; 2 a year; Editor CHOI SANG-YONG.

*Journal Asiatique:* La Société Asiatique, 3 rue Mazarine, 75006 Paris, France; tel. and fax 1-44-41-43-14; f. 1822; covers all phases of Oriental research; 2 a year; Editor ANNA SCHERRER-SCHAUB.

*Journal of Indian History:* Dept of History, University of Kerala, Karyavattam PO, Trivandrum 695 518, India; f. 1921; 3 a year; Editor K. K. KUSUMAN.

*Journal of the Indian Law Institute:* Bhagwandas Rd, New Delhi 110 001, India; tel. (11) 3386321; e-mail ili@nde.vsnl.net.in; f. 1956; quarterly; Editor Prof. K. N. CHANDRASEKHARAN PILLAI.

*Journal of Indian Philosophy:* Kluwer Academic Publishers, POB 989, 3300 AZ Dordrecht, Netherlands; tel. (78) 6576000; fax (78) 6576254; e-mail services@wkap.nl; internet www.wkap.nl; f. 1970; 6 a year; Editor PHYLLIS GRANOFF.

*Journal of the Institute of Bangladesh Studies:* Institute of Bangladesh Studies, Rajshahi University, 6205 Rajshahi, Bangladesh; tel. (721) 750985; fax (721) 750064; e-mail ibs@rajbd.com; f. 1976; annually; Editor PRITI KUMAR MITRA.

*Journal of the Oriental Institute:* Maharaja Sayajirao University of Baroda, opp. Palace Gate, Palace Rd, Vadodara 390 001, Gujarat, India; f. 1951; quarterly; Editor Prof. M. L. WADEKAR.

*Journal of Oriental Research:* c/o Kuppuswami Sastri Research Institute, 84 Thiru Vi Ka Rd, Mylapore, Chennai 600 004, India; annually; Editor Dr V. KAMESWARI.

*Journal of the Oriental Society of Australia:* Dept of Japanese and Korean Studies, A18, School of Languages and Cultures, University of Sydney, Sydney, NSW 2006, Australia; tel. (2) 9351-2869; fax (2) 9351-2319; e-mail slc@arts.usyd.edu.au; internet www.arts.usyd.edu.au/departs/japanese; f. 1961; annually; Editor LEITH MORTON.

*Journal of the Pakistan Historical Society—Historicus:* Pakistan Historical Society, Bait al-Hikmah, Central Library, Hamdard University, Karachi 74700, Pakistan; tel. (21) 6616001; fax (21) 6611755; e-mail hamdardfoundation@hamdard.com.pk; internet www.hamdardfoundation.org; f. 1953; quarterly; Editor Dr ANSAR ZAHID KHAN; circ. 700.

*Journal of the Royal Asiatic Society of Great Britain and Ireland:* 14–16 Stephenson Way, London, NW1 2HD, United Kingdom; e-mail info@royalasiaticsociety.org; internet www.royalasiaticsociety.org; f. 1834; covers all aspects of oriental research; 3 a year; Editor Dr SARAH ANSARI.

*Journal of the Royal Asiatic Society of Sri Lanka:* Mahaweli Centre and Royal Asiatic Society Bldg, 96 Ananda Coomaraswamy Mawatha, Colombo 7, Sri Lanka; tel. and fax (1) 2699249; f. 1845; annually; Editor PADMA EDIRISINGHA.

*Journal of South Asian Literature:* English Dept, 201 Morrill Hall, Michigan State University, East Lansing, MI 48824-1035, USA; tel. (517) 355-9571; fax (517) 353-3755; 2 a year; Editors CARLO COPPOLA, SURJIT DULAI.

*LAWASIA:* Law Association for Asia & the Pacific, GPOB 980, Brisbane, Qld 4001, Australia; tel. (7) 3222-5888; fax (7) 3222-5850; e-mail lawasia@lawasia.asn.au; internet www.lawasia.asn.au; f. 1966; legal issues related to Asia and the Pacific; annually.

*Al Ma'arif:* Institute of Islamic Culture, Club Rd, Lahore 3, Pakistan; f. 1950; in Urdu; monthly; Editor M. ISHAQ BHATTI; Dir Prof. M. SAEED SHEIKH.

*Marg:* Marg Publications (division of National Centre for the Performing Arts), Army and Navy Bldg, 148 Mahatma Gandhi Rd, Mumbai 400 001, India; tel. (22) 22842520; fax (22) 22047102; e-mail margpub@tata.com; internet www.marg-art.org; f. 1946; quarterly magazine of the arts; General Editor PRATAPADITYA PAL.

*Marga:* Marga Institute, POB 601, 93/10 Dutugemunu Mawatha, Colombo 6, Sri Lanka; tel. (11) 2828544; fax (11) 2828597; quarterly; Man. Editor BASIL ILANGAKOON.

*Modern Asian Studies:* Cambridge University Press, The Edinburgh Bldg, Shaftesbury Rd, Cambridge, CB2 2RU, United Kingdom; tel. (1223) 326070; e-mail journals-subscriptions@cambridge.org; internet www.journals.cambridge.org; f. 1967; quarterly; Editor Dr GORDON JOHNSON.

*Modern Sri Lanka Studies:* University of Peradeniya, Peradeniya, Sri Lanka; social sciences; 2 a year; Editors Prof. RANJITH AMARASINGHE, Prof. W. M. SIRISENA.

*Le Muséon:* Université Catholique de Louvain, Institut Orientaliste, place Blaise-Pascal 1, B-1348 Louvain-la-Neuve, Belgium; tel. (10) 473793; fax (10) 472001; e-mail lemuseon@uclouvain.be; internet www.fltr.ucl.ac.be/FLTR/GLOR/ORI/LeMuseon.htm; f. 1881; oriental studies; 2 double vols a year; Pres. Prof. B. COULIE; Editor Prof. A. SCHMIDT.

*Oriental Art Magazine Ltd:* 90 Park Ave, Suite 1700, New York, NY 10016, USA; 260 Orchard Rd, 10-10 The Heeren, Singapore 238855; tel. (65) 7379931; fax (65) 7373190; e-mail orientalart@orientalartmag.com; f. 1949; quarterly; Editor AILEEN LAU TAN.

*Oriental Geographer:* Bangladesh Geographical Society, Dept of Geography and Environment, University of Dhaka, Dhaka 1000, Bangladesh; tel. (2) 9661900; fax (2) 865583; f. 1957; 2 a year.

*Pakistan Development Review:* Pakistan Institute of Development Economics, POB 1091, Islamabad 44000, Pakistan; tel. (51) 9211857; fax (51) 9210886; e-mail library@pide.org.pk; internet www.pide.org.pk; f. 1957; quarterly; Editor Dr NAUSHIN MAHMOOD.

*Pakistan Economic and Social Review:* Dept of Economics, University of the Punjab, Quaid-i-Azam Campus, Lahore 54590, Pakistan; tel. (42) 5863997; biannually; Editor RAFIQ AHMAD.

*Pakistan Horizon:* Pakistan Institute of International Affairs, Aiwan-e-Sadar Road, POB 1447, Karachi 74200, Pakistan; tel. (21) 5682891; fax (21) 5686069; e-mail piia@cyber.net.pk; f. 1948; in English; quarterly; Editor Dr QAZI SHAKIL AHMAD.

*Perspectives on Global Development and Technology:* Brill, POB 9000, 2300 PA Leiden, Netherlands; tel. (71) 5353500; fax (71) 5317532; e-mail cs@brill.nl; internet www.brill.nl; f. 2002; 4 a year; Editor R. PATTERSON.

*Przegląd Orientalistyczny:* Polskie Towarzystwo Orientalistyczne, Redakcja, 00-927 Warsaw, Krakowskie Przedmieście 26/28, Instytut Orientalistyczny UW, Poland; tel. (22) 55-20-353; quarterly; Editor Prof. Dr hab. DANUTA STASIK.

*Quarterly Review of Historical Studies:* Institute of Historical Studies, 35 Theatre Rd, Kolkata 700017, India; tel. (33) 2475236; f. 1961; quarterly; Editor Prof. BRATINDRA NATH MUKHERJEE.

*Rocznik Orientalistyczny:* Warsaw University Oriental Institute, 00927 Warsaw 64, ul. Krakowskie Przedmieście 26/28, Poland; e-mail mmdziekan@poczta.onet.pl; f. 1915; 2 a year; Editor-in-Chief MAREK M. DZIEKAN.

*South Asia: Journal of South Asian Studies:* School of Historical Studies, Monash University, Melbourne, Vic 3800, Australia; tel. (3) 9905-2201; fax (3) 9905-2210; e-mail ian.copland@arts.monash.edu.au; internet taylorandfrancis.co.uk/journals; f. 1971; owned by South Asian Studies Asscn; 3 a year; Editor Assoc. Prof. IAN COPLAND.

*South Asia Research:* Sage Publications Ltd, 1 Oliver's Yard, 55 City Rd, London EC1Y 1SP, United Kingdom; tel. (20) 7324-8500; fax (20) 7324-8600; e-mail market@sagepub.co.uk; internet www.sagepub.co.uk; f. 1980; 3 a year; Editor WERNER MENSKI.

*South Asian Anthropologist:* S. C. Roy Institute of Anthropological Studies, H1/98 Harmu Housing Colony, Ranchi 834002, Jharkhand, India; tel. (651) 2341456; e-mail pdashsharma@rediffmail.com; f. 1980; owned by S. C. Roy Inst. of Anthropological Studies; biannually; Editor P. DASH SHARMA.

*South Asian Popular Culture:* 4 Park Sq., Milton Park, Abingdon, Oxon, OX14 4RN, United Kingdom; tel. (20) 7017-6000; fax (20) 7017-6336; e-mail journals.orders@tandf.co.uk; internet www.tandf.co.uk/journals; f. 2003; 2 a year; Editors RAJINDER KUMAR DUDRAH, K. MOTI GOKULSING.

*South Asian Survey:* Sage Publications India Pvt Ltd, B-42 Panchsheel Enclave, POB 4109, New Delhi 110 017, India; tel. and fax (11) 26491290; e-mail journalsubs@indiasage.com; internet www.indiasage.com; publication of the Indian Council for South Asian Cooperation; 2 a year; Editor VARUN SAHNI.

*Sri Lanka Journal of the Humanities:* c/o Dept of English, University of Peradeniya, Peradeniya, Sri Lanka; tel. (81) 2392543; fax (81) 2388933; e-mail walter@ids.lk; f. 1975; 2 a year; Editor S. W. PERERA.

*The Statesman:* 4 Chowringhee Sq., Kolkata 700 001, India; tel. (33) 22127070; e-mail thestatesman@vsnl.com; internet www.thestatesman.net; f. 1875; overseas weekly; in English; Editor and Man. Dir RAVINDRA KUMAR.

*Studia Orientalia:* Suomen Itämainen Seura (Finnish Oriental Society), c/o Institute for Asian and African Studies, University of Helsinki, PO Box 59, 00014 Helsinki, Finland; tel. 19122224; fax 19122094; e-mail saana.teppo@helsinki.fi; internet www.helsinki.fi/jarj/sis; f. 1917; Secretary SAANA TEPPO.

*Svadhyaya:* Oriental Institute, Maharaja Sayajirao University of Baroda, opp. Palace Gate, Palace Rd, Vadodara 390 001, Gujarat, India; f. 1962; quarterly; Gujarati; Editor Prof. M. L. WADEKAR.

*Terrorism Monitor:* The Jamestown Foundation, 4516 43rd Street NW, Washington, DC 20016, USA; tel. (202) 483-8888; e-mail pubs@jamestown.org; internet www.jamestown.org; f. 2003; fortnightly; Man. Editor JULIE SIRRS.

*Third World Quarterly:* Dept of Geography, Royal Holloway, University of London, Egham, Surrey, TW20 0EX, United Kingdom; fax (20) 8947-1243; internet www.tandf.co.uk/journals; 8 a year; Editor SHAHID QADIR.

*Viewpoint:* POB 540, Lahore, Pakistan; tel. (42) 301285; f. 1975; weekly; Editor MAZHAR ALI KHAN.

*Wiener Zeitschrift für die Kunde des Morgenlandes:* Institut für Orientalistik der Universität Wien, 1090 Vienna, Spitalgasse 2, Hof 4, Austria; tel. (1) 4277-43401; fax (1) 4277-9434; e-mail wzkmorders.orientalistik@univie.ac.at; internet www.univie.ac.at/orientalistik; f. 1887; annually; Editor GISELA PROCHAZKA-EISL.

*Wiener Zeitschrift für die Kunde Südasiens (WZKS)* (Vienna Journal of South Asian Studies): Dept for South Asian, Tibetan and Buddhist Studies—South Asian Studies, A-1090 Vienna, University Campus, Spitalgasse 2, Yard 2, Austria; tel. (1) 4277-43511; fax (1) 4277-9435; e-mail istb@univie.ac.at; internet www.istb.univie.ac.at; f. 1957; published by the Austrian Academy of Sciences Press; annually; Editors G. OBERHAMMER, K. PREISENDANZ, CH. H. WERBA.

# INDEX OF REGIONAL ORGANIZATIONS

(Main reference only)

160°
120°
80°
40°
0°
ARCTIC OCEAN
Beaufort Sea
Baffin Bay
GREENLAND (DENMARK)
JAN MAYEN (NORWAY)
Denmark Strait
Davis Strait
ICELAND
Reykjavík
Norwegian Sea
FAROE ISLANDS (DENMARK)
Arctic Circle
ALASKA (USA)
Hudson Bay
Gulf of Alaska
CANADA
UNITED KINGDOM
North Sea
Oslo
ISLE OF MAN (UK)
NORTHERN IRELAND
GREAT BRITAIN
IRELAND
Dublin
NETHER-LANDS
Amsterdam
London
BELGIUM
Brussels
CHANNEL ISLANDS (UK)
Paris
LUXEMBOURG
FRANCE
LIECHTENSTEIN
ANDORRA
MONACO
Ottawa
SAINT PIERRE AND MIQUELON (FRANCE)
UNITED STATES OF AMERICA
Washington DC
PORTUGAL
SPAIN
Madrid
Lisbon
GIBRALTAR (UK)
MELILLA (SP)
Algiers
Rabat
CEUTA (SP)
MOROCCO
ALGERIA
TUNISIA
WESTERN SAHARA
NORTH ATLANTIC OCEAN
BERMUDA (UNITED KINGDOM)
Gulf of Mexico
BAHAMAS
Tropic of Cancer
HAWAII (USA)
MEXICO
Havana
CUBA
Mexico City
TURKS AND CAICOS ISLANDS (UK)
DOMINICAN REPUBLIC
PUERTO RICO (USA)
BRITISH VIRGIN ISLANDS (UK)
US VIRGIN ISLANDS (USA)
SAINT-BARTHÉLEMY (FRANCE)
SAINT CHRISTOPHER AND NEVIS
ANTIGUA AND BARBUDA
GUADELOUPE (FRANCE)
MARTINIQUE (FRANCE)
BARBADOS
SAINT VINCENT AND THE GRENADINES
CAYMAN ISLANDS (UK)
HAITI
Santo Domingo
Port-au-Prince
JAMAICA
Kingston
ANGUILLA (UK)
SAINT-MARTIN (FRANCE)
MONTSERRAT (UK)
DOMINICA
SAINT LUCIA
NETHERLANDS ANTILLES (NL)
ARUBA (NL)
GRENADA
TRINIDAD AND TOBAGO
BELIZE
Belmopan
GUATEMALA
Guatemala City
HONDURAS
Tegucigalpa
San Salvador
EL SALVADOR
NICARAGUA
Managua
COSTA RICA
San José
PANAMA
Panamá
Caracas
VENEZUELA
Georgetown
Paramaribo
GUYANA
SURINAME
FRENCH GUIANA (FRANCE)
Bogotá
COLOMBIA
Quito
ECUADOR
PERU
Lima
BRAZIL
Brasília
La Paz
BOLIVIA
Sucre
PARAGUAY
Asunción
CHILE
Santiago
Buenos Aires
URUGUAY
Montevideo
ARGENTINA
MAURITANIA
Nouakchott
MALI
CAPE VERDE
Praia
SENEGAL
Dakar
GAMBIA
Banjul
Bamako
Niamey
GUINEA-BISSAU
Conakry
GUINEA
BURKINA FASO
Ouagadougou
NIGER
Abuja
Freetown
SIERRA LEONE
Monrovia
LIBERIA
CÔTE D'IVOIRE
Yamoussoukro
Abidjan
GHANA
Accra
TOGO
BENIN
Porto-Novo
Lagos
Cotonou
Malabo
EQUATORIAL GUINEA
SÃO TOMÉ AND PRÍNCIPE
São Tomé
ASCENSION (UNITED KINGDOM)
SAINT HELENA (UNITED KINGDOM)
SOUTH ATLANTIC OCEAN
PACIFIC OCEAN
FRENCH POLYNESIA (FRANCE)
COOK ISLANDS (NEW ZEALAND)
Tropic of Capricorn
PITCAIRN ISLANDS (UNITED KINGDOM)
TRISTAN DA CUNHA (UNITED KINGDOM)
FALKLAND ISLANDS (UNITED KINGDOM)
SOUTH GEORGIA AND THE SOUTH SANDWICH ISLANDS (UNITED KINGDOM)
Antarctic Circle
Africa South of the Sahara
Central and South-Eastern Europe
Eastern Europe, Russia and Central Asia
The Far East and Australasia
The Middle East and North Africa
South America, Central America and the Caribbean
South Asia
The USA and Canada
Western Europe
www.europaworld.com